U.S. & WORLD CURRENCY AUCTIONS

Your Notes Deserve World
Worldwide A

Fr. 379b $1000 1890 Treasury Note
PCGS Extremely Fine 40
Realized $3,290,000

DC-19 $500 1911
PMG Very Fine 20
Realized $322,000

China People's Republic 10000 Yuan 1951 Pick 858Aa
PCGS Very Fine 20
Realized $199,750

Bahamas Bahamas Government $100 L. 1965 Pick 25a
PMG Choice About Uncirculated 58
Realized $42,300

Zanzibar Government 10 Rupees 1.2.1928 Pick 3
PCGS Apparent Very Fine 25
Realized $64,625

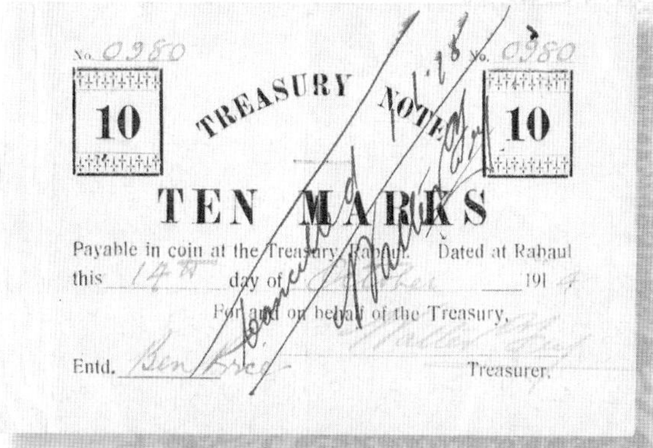

German New Guinea Treasury 10 Marks 14.10.1914 (1.1.1915) Pick 2b
PCGS Extremely Fine 40
Realized $49,937

Contact a Heritage Consignment Director today:
800-872-6467, ext. 1001 or Currency@HA.com

DALLAS | NEW YORK | BEVERLY HILLS | SAN FRANCISCO | CHICAGO | PALM BEACH

Always

THE WORLD'S LARGEST
NUMISMATIC AUCTIONEER

Paul R. Minshull #16591. Paul R. Minshull #LSM0605473; Heritage Auctic
& #LSM0624318BP. K. Guzman #0762165; Heritage Auctions #1364738
BP 17.5%; see HA.com 40305

Alex Perakis Coins & Currency, Inc.

Visit our website to view our inventory of:

- World Banknotes
- Large Type Notes
- Small Type Notes
- Fractional Currency
- National Banknotes
- Obsolete Currency
- MPC's
- And much more!

www.perakiscurrency.com

~ WE ARE ALWAYS BUYING & SELLING WORTHWHILE MATERIAL ~

LAYAWAY PLAN AVAILABLE

Layaway plan available over $250. 25% down, balance up to 60 days. NO interest charge.

We are now accepting MasterCard and VISA on orders over $100.00.

TERMS:
A. 10-day return privilege. Satisfaction a must.
B. Please add $10 for Postage and Handling.
C. Phone orders may be advisable to reserve some notes.
D. All personal checks, from persons not known to me, must clear.
E. PA residents must add 6% sales tax.

Pcda

Recipient of Krause Publications' Customer Service Award for 20 straight years.

WWW.PERAKISCURRENCY.COM

P.O. Box 246
Lima, PA 19037
Phones:
(610) 565-1110
(610) 627-1212

Fax: (610) 891-1466 • PA E-mail: apcc1@msn.com

ALL YOUR COLLECTING SUPPLIES IN ONE PLACE

BROOKLYN GALLERY COINS & STAMPS INC.

8725 – 4TH AVE. BROOKLYN, N.Y. 11209

Phone: (718) 745-5701
Fax: (718) 745-2775
Website: WWW.BROOKLYNGALLERY.COM
Email: INFO@BROOKLYNGALLERY.COM

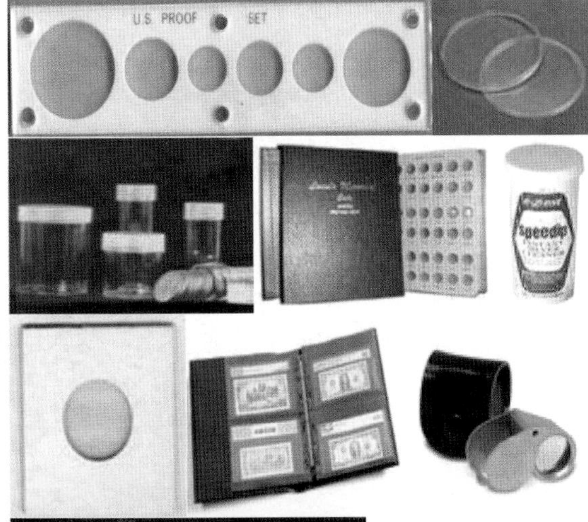

We carry all your collecting supply needs for coins, paper money, stamps, post cards and sports cards at discounts of up to 40%. All major brands of holders, albums and storage options are available for your collecting needs. Also, we have available a large selection of current reference books and price catalogs, including many out of print and hard to find titles.

Visit our website: www.brooklyngallery.com

CALL OR EMAIL FOR OUR FREE 100+ PAGE SUPPLY CATALOG

PMG makes submissions easy for
THE WHOLE WORLD
with 8 convenient locations

No matter where you live, you can easily submit your notes to PMG for expert grading and authentication. PMG grades more notes from more countries than any other grading service, and every note that PMG certifies is backed by its comprehensive guarantee of grade and authenticity—the strongest in the industry.

To learn how to submit your notes to PMG, contact our offices:

NORTH AMERICA
+1 877 764 5570 toll-free
Service@PMGnotes.com

EUROPE
+49 89 255 47 545
Europe@PMGnotes.com

ASIA
+852 2115 3639
Asia@PMGnotes.com

PMGnotes.com | 877-PMG-5570

Official Grading Service of

United States | Germany | Hong Kong | China | South Korea | Singapore | Taiwan | Japan

~ YOUR SOURCE FOR WORLDWIDE BANKNOTE SPECIMENS ~

NOW AVAILABLE!

Our Worldwide Banknote Specimens Catalog 10th Edition
Over 500 new specimens notes added to our list and much more!
Get your copy of our Worldwide Banknote Specimens catalog for free!
Just send us your address or download it from our website.

ALWAYS BUYING & SELLING BANKNOTES!

Make an appointment to our Premiere Showroom we have: United States - State Revenue Stamp Specimens, U.S. Stock Specimens, Worldwide Specimen Bonds & a large selection of Vignettes & Die Proofs all priced and ready to sell!!

SHOP ONLINE AT: WWW.CHAMPIONSTAMP.COM

Banknote Division
432 West 54th St., New York, NY 10019
Tel: (212) 489-8130 ~ Fax: (212) 581-8130
Website: www.championstamp.com
E-Mail: championstamp@aol.com

SCWPMG2014H

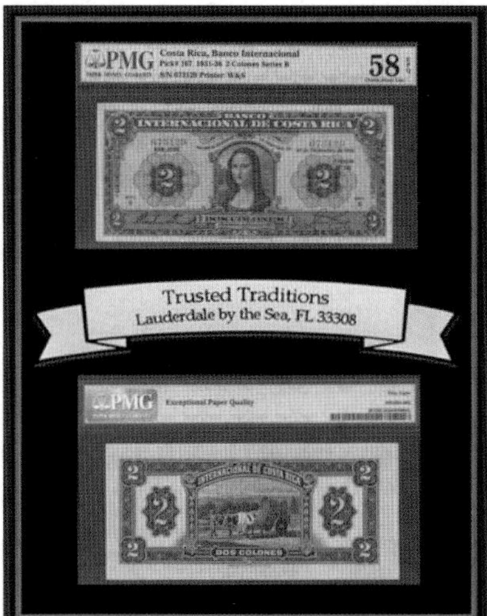

VIETNAM PICK 4A SPECIMEN
PCGS 67 PPQ
"The Old Man At the Temple"

We are always Selling, Desperately needing to BUY Please offer US your notes

TT PK 167 1931-36 COSTA RICA 2 COLONES PMG 58 EPQ MONA LISA!!! FINEST KNOWN!

Trusted Traditions.com • 954-938-9700

275 Commercial Blvd Lauderdale by the Sea, FL 33308
http://www.trustedtraditions.com | sales@trustedtraditions.com

BANKNOTE WORLD

Buying and Selling
World Banknotes, Collectible Coins, & Bullion.

We have the largest
Zimbabwe Banknotes
stock in the World.

We have a large collection
of PMG/PCGS Graded Banknotes.

We sell Banknotes and Coins
in Wholesale.

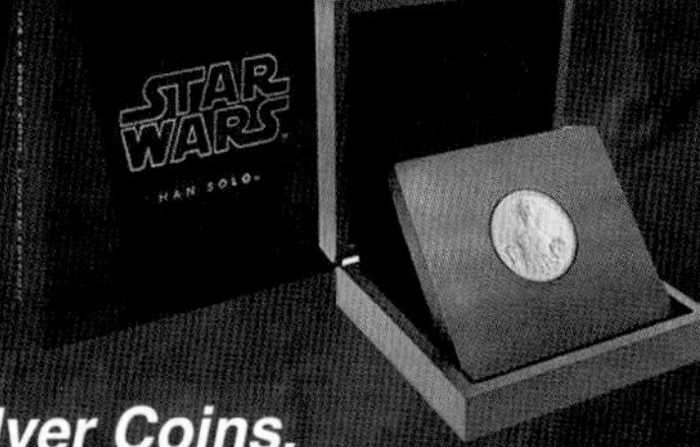

We sell Gold and Silver Coins.

Shop from anywhere in the World!

WWW.BANKNOTEWORLD.COM/SHOP

BNWorld Inc. 1641 Kaiser Ave, Irvine, California 92614 - U.S.A 888-448-9199 8:00 AM to 4:30 PM

SUBSCRIBE TODAY

AND SAVE 56%! ONE FULL YEAR AT A GREAT LOW RATE

1 YEAR
(12 issues) $25.99

Get all the coin information you need in one place! Order ***World Coin News*** now and you'll get 12 issues packed with international coin news, emerging market trends and tips on how you can cash in on them, recaps of coin shows, auctions, events and more!

DON'T WAIT! Log on to subscribe.worldcoinnews.net and subscribe today.

Call 1-866-836-7871. You can also write to us at: PO Box 421751, Palm Coast, FL 32142-1751.
Mention offer code A4BWCA.

In Canada, add $15 (includes GST/HST). Outside the U.S. and Canada, add $30. Outside the U.S., remit payment in U.S. funds with order. Please allow 4-6 weeks for first-issue delivery. Annual newsstand rate $59.88. World Coin News is published 12 times per year which may include an occasional special, combined or expanded issue that may count as two issues.

„For all rare, exotic or unusual coins and banknotes from antiquity to modern age I am your passionate reliable partner to contact!"

Christoph Gärtner

International offer of COINS, PAPER MONEY & MORE: www.auktionen-gaertner.de

WE ARE ALWAYS LOOKING FOR

Coins from antique to modern age

- Ancients and middle ages
- World coins and medals
- German coins and medals before 1871
- German Empire, Weimar republic
- Third Reich
- German coins and GDR
- Euro-coins
- Gold- and silver coins (bullion coins)
- Banknotes, decorations, shares
- Emergency money and Numisbriefe

TAKE ADVANTAGE OF

Free appraisals & high-quality advice

- International public auctions 3 times a year
- Discreet and high-quality advice from our experts
- Prompt and reliable processing
- Free pick-up service at your home for large consignments
- Reasonable consignment fees with no hidden costs *(„flat-fee all inclusive")*
- Internationally distributed auction catalogues
- Huge international customer base *(over 155,000 collectors and dealers)*
- International cooperation partners in: Australia, Austria, Canada, Singapore und the United States

CONSIGNMENT & OUTRIGHT PURCHASE IS ALWAYS POSSIBLE

(Finder´s fee for agents guaranteed)

Steinbeisstr. 6+8 / 74321 Bietigheim-Bissingen, Germany / Tel. +49-(0)7142-789400
Fax. +49-(0)7142-789410 / info@auktionen-gaertner.de / www.auktionen-gaertner.de

Coin world_2017

EXCLUSIVE OFFER *now at* ShopNumismaster.com

ENJOY 10% OFF educational products, resources, projects and more – enter code **NUMISPUB10** at check-out and save 10% off select products.

SAVE 10%
On Your Next Purchase

No minimum order and no end date.

From the same great providers of education, articles and inspiration you experience reading *Numismatic News*, **check out ShopNumismaster.com and save now!**

Promo Code Exclusions Apply: Your special discount/coupon code will allow you to take 10% OFF many (not all) of the items you find at ShopNumismaster.com. Your discount/coupon code is not valid for purchasing gift cards, subscriptions, pre-orders, value packs, VIP memberships, or items that ship directly from manufacturers. Discounts cannot be applied to previous purchases. Valid for one use per customer only. Other exclusions may apply.

3484859
Item # 13411654

769.55
STA

Standard Catalog of® WORLD PAPER MONEY

General Issues • 1368-1960

Edited by Tracy L. Schmidt

16th Edition

285531

The World's Authority on Paper Money

$90 — 6/14/2019

Copyright ©2016 F+W Media, Inc.

All rights reserved. No portion of this publication may be reproduced or transmitted in any form or by any means, electronic or mechanical, including photocopy, recording, or any information storage and retrieval system, without permission in writing from the publisher, except by a reviewer who may quote brief passages in a critical article or review to be printed in a magazine or newspaper, or electronically transmitted on radio, television, or the Internet.

Published by

Krause Publications, a division of F+W Media, Inc.
700 East State Street • Iola, WI 54990-0001
715-445-2214 • 888-457-2873
www.krausebooks.com

To order books or other products call toll-free 1-800-258-0929
or visit us online at www.shopnumismaster.com

ISSN 1538-2001
ISBN-13: 978-1-4402-4707-1
ISBN-10: 1-4402-4707-2

Cover and Interior Design by Sandi Carpenter
Edited by Tracy L. Schmidt

Printed in the United States of America

10 9 8 7 6 5 4 3 2 1

Introduction

Welcome to this 16th edition of the *Standard Catalog of® World Paper Money, General Issues.* For those of you already familiar with this volume, we have continued to enhance our image quality and expand our descriptions. Numerous additions have been made to the variety listings as new information becomes available. Extensive specimen variety listings continue to be added throughout.

This volume presents bank notes issued by governments, national banks or the few regional banks which circulated over a large area. Companion volumes to this edition are the *Standard Catalog of® World Paper Money, Specialized Issues* which covers bank notes issued on a regional and local level in addition to military and foreign exchange issues and the *Standard Catalog of® World Paper Money, Modern Issues – 1961* to present which lists bank notes of a national scope dated since 1961.

Notes of a particular bank are listed in release date order, and then grouped in ascending denomination order. In the cases of countries where more than one issuing authority is in effect at a single time, follow the bank headings in the listings and it will become apparent if that country's content is organized by date or alphabetical by issuing authority. In the cases where a country had changed from a kingdom to a republic all the banknotes of the kingdom's era would be listed before that of the republic. Please use the extensive Bank Note Issuer Index in the introduction area of this book for further assistance or guidance.

An Invitation

Users of this catalog may find a helpful adjunct to be the Bank Note Reporter, the only monthly newspaper devoted exclusively to North American and world paper money. Each issue presents up-to-date news, feature articles and valuable information. All purchasers of this catalog are invited to subscribe to the *Bank Note Reporter.*

To purchase additional Krause Publications titles on banknotes please visit www.shopnumismaster.com. You will find our more specialized catalogs available there for purchase in addition to the rest of the standard catalog series.

A review of modern paper money collecting

Paper money collecting is probably as old as paper money itself. However, this segment of the numismatic hobby did not begin to reach a popularity approaching that of coin collecting until the latter half of the 1970s. While coins and paper money are alike in that both served as legal obligations to facilitate commerce, long-time paper money enthusiasts know the similarity ends there.

Coins were historically guaranteed by the intrinsic value of their metallic content - at least until recent years when virtually all circulating coins have become little more than legal tender tokens, containing little or no precious metal - while paper money possesses a value only when it is accepted for debts or converted into bullion or precious metals. With many note issues, this conversion privilege was limited and ultimately negated by the imposition of redemption cutoff dates.

The development of widespread collector interest in paper money of most nations was inhibited by a near total absence of adequate documentation. No more than four decades ago collectors could refer to only a few catalogs and dealer price lists of limited scope, most of which were difficult to acquire, or they could build their own knowledge through personal collecting pursuits and contact with fellow collectors.

The early catalogs authored by Albert Pick chronicled issues of Europe and the Americas and were assembled as stepping-stones to the ultimate objective, which became reality with publication of the first *Standard Catalog of World Paper Money* in 1975. That work provided collectors with fairly complete listings and up-to-date valuations of all recorded government note issues of the 20th century, incorporating Pick's previously unpublished manuscripts on Africa, Asia and Oceania, plus many earlier issues.

The completely revised and updated 22nd edition of Volume III, *Modern Issues,* along with this companion 16th edition Volume II, *General Issues,* presents a substantial extension of the cataloging effort initiated in 1975 and revised in succeeding editions. As the most comprehensive world paper money references ever assembled, they fully document the many and varied legal tender paper currencies issued and circulated by over 380 past and current government issuing authorities of the world from 1368 to present.

Falling within the scope of the *Specialized Issues* volume are all state, local, municipal and company releases which circulated under auspices of recognized regional governments and their banking agents. These are notes which enjoyed legitimate circulation in their respective countries, sometimes for a broad region or area, sometimes for the entire nation. In compiling this catalog we have excluded those issues which had a seriously limited circle of circulation, such as the vast number of private Notgeld issued by many German and Austrian states and cities particularly in the period during and between the World Wars, as well as similar Chinese local issues and those very limited circulation issues of other nations and time periods.

New To This Edition

In the interest of making the book easier for users, we have added two abbreviations to the listings in book: BC: for back color and PC for paper color. We have expanded our coverage of Bulgaria and continued to revise Ireland listings and images. Replacement note variety listings have been added to the Philippines section and images have been added to Portugal.

There are many improvements throughout the book thanks to our wonderful contributors. It has been a pleasure getting to know and work with each of them.

Tracy L. Schmidt
Editor

Table of Contents

Photo Submissions:

If you would like to submit photos we can accept them for existing listings electronically as JPGs in an email attachment. To be useful, they must be named with the country and the catalog number and be sized at 100% at 300 dpi. For suggested new listing images please name with the country and denomination provide the correct accompanying listing text in the email. My email address is Tracy.Schmidt@fwmedia.com.

Data Submissions:

Making the most accurate information available to users of our catalogs is important. If you have suggested corrections to existing listings please feel free to contact me at Tracy.Schmidt@fwmedia.com and I will review them with you.

Country List

Acknowledgments

The contributions to this catalog have been many and varied, and to recognize them all would be a volume in itself. Accordingly, we wish to acknowledge these collectors, scholars and dealers in the world paper money field, both past and present, for their specific contributions to this work through the submission of notes for illustration, improved descriptive information and market valuations.

Esko Ahlroth
Jan Alexandersson
Walter D. Allan
Carl A. Anderson
Mark B. Anderson
Jorge E. Arbelaez
Donald Arnone
Thomas Augustsson
Keith Austin
Oksana Bandriuska
Adriaan C.F. Beck
Dan Bellan
Milt Blackburn
Joseph E. Boling
Wilfred A. Bracke
William Brandimore
Dwight Brown
Colin R. Bruce II
Mahdi Bseiso
Weldon D. Burson
Lance K. Campbell
Arthur D. Cohen
Scott E. Cordry
Guido Crapanzano
Ray Czahor
Howard A. Daniel III
Michel Dufour
Wilhelm Eglseer
Esko Ekman
W.A. Frick
Lee Gordon
Flemming Lyngbeck Hansen
James A. Haxby
Anton Holt
Armen Hovsepian
Alex Kaglyan
Olaf Kiener
Josef Klaus
Tristan Kolm
Lazare Kovame
Andrei Kraptchev
Michael Lang
Akos Ledai
Stu Lumsden
Ma Tak Wo
Martin MacDaid
Ranko Mandic
Art Matz
Ali Mehilba
Donald Medcalf
Juozas Minikevicius
Arthur H. Morowitz
Jon Morowitz
Richard Murdoch
Tanju Mutlu
Frank Passic
Antonio E. Pedraza
Juan Pena
A.A.C. de Albergaria Pinheiro
Laurence Pope
Rick Ponterio
Miguel A. Pratt-Myans
Yahya J. Qureshi
Kavan Ratnatunga
John Rishel
Alistair Robb
William M. Rosenblum
Raul D. Rosso
Claudio Rotondaro
Alan Sadd
Sergio Sanchez
Wolfgang Schuster
Hartmut Schoenawa
Robert Schwartz
Timothy R.G. Sear
Christian Selvais
Joel Shafer
Ladislav Sin
Evzen Sknovril
Gary Snover
Mauricio Soto
Jeremy Steinberg
Tim Steiner
Zeljko Stojanovic
Alim A. Sumana
Steven Tan
Mehmet Tolga Taner
Reiny Tetting
Frank Tesson
Mark Tomasko
Anthony Tumonis
Michael Vort-Ronald
Ludek Vostal
George Warner
Pam West
Stewart Westdal
Joseph Zaffern
Christof Zellweger

Based on the original work of Albert Pick

Cover note image courtesy of Heritage Auctions

Back cover notes courtesy of Ray Czahor, Andrei Kraptchev, Martin MacDaid and Tanju Mutlu

How To Use This Catalog

Catalog listings consist of all regular and provisional notes attaining wide circulation in their respective countries for the period covered. Notes have been listed under the historical country name. Thus Dahomey is not under Benin, as had been the case in some past catalogs. The listings continue to be grouped by issue range rather than by denomination, andthe listing format should make the bank name, issue dates as well as catalog numbers and denominations easier to locate. These improvements have been made to make the catalog as easy to use as possible for you.

The editors and publisher make no claim to absolute completeness, just as they acknowledge that some errors and pricing inequities will appear. Correspondence is invited with interested persons who have notes previously unlisted or who have information to enhance the presentation of existing listings in succeeding editions of this catalog.

Catalog Format

Listings proceed generally according to the following sequence: country, geographic or political, chronology, bank name and sometimes alphabetically or by date of first note issue. Release within the bank, most often in date order, but sometimes by printer first.

Catalog number — The basic reference number at the beginning of each listing for each note. For this Modern Issues volume the regular listings require no prefix letters except when 'a' or 'b' appear within the catalog number as a suffix or variety letter. (Military and Regional prefixes are explained later in this section.)

Denomination — the value as shown on the note, in western numerals. When denominations are only spelled out, consult the numerics chart.

Date — the actual issue date as printed on the note in day-month-year order. Where more than one date appears on a note, only the latest is used. Where the note has no date, the designation ND is used, followed by a year date in parentheses when it is known. If a note is dated by the law or decree of authorization, the date appears with an L or D.

Descriptions of the note are broken up into one or more items as follows:

Color — the main color(s) of the face, and the underprint are given first. If the colors of the back are different, then they follow the face design description.

Design — The identification and location of the main design elements if known. Back design elements identified if known.

Printer — often a local printer has the name shown in full. Abbreviations are used for the most prolific printers. Refer to the list of printer abbreviations elsewhere in this introduction.

Valuations — are generally given under the grade headings of Good, Fine and Extremely Fine for early notes; and Very Good, Very Fine and Uncirculated for the later issues. Listings that do not follow these two patterns are clearly indicated. UNC followed by a value is used usually for specimens and proofs when lower grade headings are used for a particular series of issued notes.

Catalog suffix letters

A catalog number followed by a capital 'A', 'B' or 'C' indicated the incorporation of a listing as required by type or date it may indicate newly discovered lower or higher denominations to a series which needed to be fit into long standing listings. Listings of notes for regional circulation are distinguished from regular national issues with the prefix letter 'R'; military issues use a 'M' prefix; foreign exchange certificates are assigned a 'FX' prefix. Varieties, specific date or signature listings are shown with small letters 'a' following a number within their respective entries. Some standard variety letters include: 'ct' for color trials, 'p' for proof notes, 'r' for remainder notes, 's' for specimen notes and 'x' for errors.

Denominations

The denomination as indicated on many notes issued by a string of countries stretching from eastern Asia, through western Asia and on across northern Africa, often appears only in unfamiliar non-Western numeral styles. With the listings that follow, denominations are always indicated in Western numerals.

A comprehensive chart keying Western numerals to their non-Western counterparts is included elsewhere in this introduction as an aid to the identification of note types. This compilation features not only the basic numeral systems such as Arabic, Japanese and Indian, but also the more restricted systems such as Burmese, Ethiopian, Siamese, Tibetan, Hebrew, Mongolian and Korean. Additionally, the list includes other localized variations that have been applied to some paper money issues.

In consulting the numeral systems chart to determine the denomination of a note, one should remember that the actual numerals styles employed in any given area, or at a particular time, may vary significantly from these basic representations. Such variations can be deceptive to the untrained eye, just as variations from Western numeral styles can prove deceptive to individuals not acquainted with the particular style employed.

Dates and Date Listing Policy

In previous editions of this work it was the goal to provide a sampling of the many date varieties that were believed to exist. In recent times, as particular dates (and usually signature

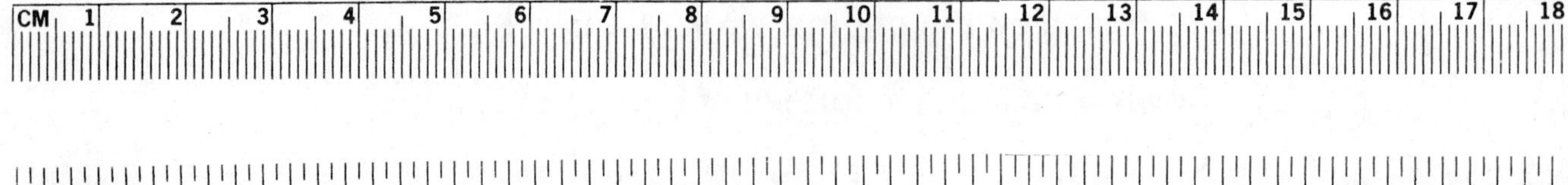

combinations) were known to be scarcer, that particular series was expanded to include listings of individual dates. At times this idea has been fully incorporated, but with some series it is not practicable, especially when just about every day in a given month could have been an issue date for the notes.

Accordingly, where it seems justifiable that date spans can be realistically filled with individual dates, this has been done. In order to accommodate the many new dates, the idea of providing variety letters to break them up into narrower spans of years has been used. If it appears that there are too many dates for a series, with no major differences in value, then a general inclusive date span is used (beginning and ending) and individual dates within this span are not shown.

For those notes showing only a general date span, the only important dates become those that expand the range of years, months or days earlier or later. But even they would have no impact on the values shown.

Because a specific date is not listed does not necessarily mean it is rare. It may be just that it has not been reported. Those date varieties known to be scarcer are cataloged separately. Newly reported dates in a wide variety of listings are constantly being reported. This indicates that research into the whole area is very active, and a steady flow of new dates is fully expected upon publication of this edition.

Valuations

Valuations are given for most notes in three grades. Earlier issues are usually valued in the grade headings of Good, Fine and Extremely Fine; later issues take the grade headings of Very Good, Very Fine and Uncirculated. While it is true that some early notes cannot be valued in Extremely Fine and some later notes have no premium value in Very Good, it is felt that this coverage provides the best uniformity of value data to the collecting community. There are exceptional cases where headings are adjusted for either single notes or a series that really needs special treatment.

Valuations are determined generally from a consensus of individuals submitting prices for evaluation. Some notes have NO values; this does not necessarily mean they are expensive or even rare, but it shows that no pricing information was forthcoming. A number of notes have a 'Rare' designation, and no values. Such notes are generally not available on the market, and when they do appear the price is a matter between buyer and seller. No book can provide guidance in these instances except to indicate rarity.

Valuations used in this book are based on the IBNS grading standards and are stated in U.S. dollars. They serve only as aids in evaluating paper money since actual market conditions throughout the worldwide collector community are constantly changing. In addition, particularly choice examples of many issues listed often bring higher premiums than values listed. Users should remember that a catalog such as this is only a guide to values.

FV (for Face Value) is used as a value designation on new issues as well as older but still redeemable legal tender notes in lower conditions. FV may appear in one or both condition columns before Uncirculated, depending on the relative age and availability of the note in question. Some non-current notes which are still exchangeable carry FV designations.

Collection care

The proper preservation of a collection should be of paramount importance to all in the hobby - dealers, collectors and scholars. Only a person who has housed notes in a manner giving pleasure to him or herself and others will keep alive the pleasure of collecting for future generations. The same applies to the way of housing as to the choice of the collecting specialty: it is chiefly a question of what most pleases the individual collector.

Arrangement and sorting of a collection is most certainly a basic requirement. Storing the notes in safe paper envelopes and filing boxes should, perhaps, be considered only when building a new section of a collection, for accommodating varieties or for reasons of saving space when the collection has grown quickly.

Many paper money collections are probably housed in some form of plastic-pocketed album, which are today manufactured in many different sizes and styles to accommodate many types of world paper money. Because the number of bank note collectors has grown continually over the past thirty-five years, some specialty manufacturers of albums have developed a paper money selection. The notes, housed in clear plastic pockets, individually or in groups, can be viewed and exchanged without difficulty. These albums are not cheap, but the notes displayed in this manner do make a lasting impression on the viewer.

A word of concern: certain types of plastic and all vinyl used for housing notes may cause notes to become brittle over time, or cause an irreversible and harmful transfer of oils from the vinyl onto the bank notes.

The high demand for quality that stamp collectors make on their products cannot be transferred to the paper money collecting fraternity. A postage stamp is intended for a single use, then is relegated to a collection. With paper money, it is nearly impossible to acquire uncirculated specimens from a number of countries because of export laws or internal bank procedures. Bends from excessive counting, or even staple holes, are commonplace. Once acquiring a circulated note, the collector must endeavor to maintain its state of preservation.

The fact that there is a classification and value difference between notes with greater use or even damage is a matter of course. It is part of the opinion and personal taste of the individual collector to decide what is considered worthy of collecting and what to pay for such items.

For the purposed of strengthening and mending torn paper money, under no circumstances should one use plain cellophane tape or a similar material. These tapes warp easily, with sealing marks forming at the edges, and the tape frequently discolors. Only with the greatest of difficulty (and often not at all) can these tapes be removed, and damage to the note or the printing is almost unavoidable. The best material for mending tears is an archival tape recommended for the treatment and repair of documents.

There are collectors who, with great skill, remove unsightly spots, repair badly damaged notes, replace missing pieces and otherwise restore or clean a note. There is a question of morality by tampering with a note to improve its condition, either by repairing, starching, ironing, pressing or other methods to possibly deceive a potential future buyer. Such a question must, in the final analysis, be left to the individual collector.

Issuer and Bank Index

C

D

E

F

G

H

I

J

P

Q

R

S

T

U

V

W

Z

Foreign Exchange

The latest foreign exchange rates below apply to trade with banks in the country of origin. The left column shows the number of units per U.S. dollar at the official rate. The right column shows the number of units per dollar at the free market rate. Rates recorded March 10, 2016.

Country	#/$	#/$
Afghanistan (New Afghani)	.68	–
Albania (Lek)	.123	–
Algeria (Dinar)	.108	–
Andorra uses Euro	0.910	–
Angola (Readjust Kwanza)	.158	–
Anguilla uses E.C. Dollar	2.70	–
Antigua uses E.C. Dollar	2.70	–
Argentina (Peso)	15.4	–
Armenia (Dram)	.491	–
Aruba (Florin)	1.79	–
Australia (Dollar)	1.34	–
Austria (Euro)	0.910	–
Azerbaijan (New Manat)	1.62	–
Bahamas (Dollar)	0.993	–
Bahrain Is. (Dinar)	0.374	–
Bangladesh (Taka)	.77	–
Barbados (Dollar)	2.00	–
Belarus (Ruble)	21,068	–
Belgium (Euro)	0.910	–
Belize (Dollar)	1.95	–
Benin uses CFA Franc West	.519	–
Bermuda (Dollar)	1.00	–
Bhutan (Ngultrum)	.67	–
Bolivia (Boliviano)	6.66	–
Bosnia-Herzegovina (Conv. marka)	1.78	–
Botswana (Pula)	11.0	–
British Virgin Islands uses U.S. Dollar	1.00	–
Brazil (Real)	3.73	–
Brunei (Dollar)	1.36	–
Bulgaria (Lev)	1.77	–
Burkina Faso uses CFA Franc West	.597	–
Burma (Kyat)	1,199	–
Burundi (Franc)	1,540	–
Cambodia (Riel)	3,912	–
Cameroon uses CFA Franc Central	.597	–
Canada (Dollar)	1.34	–
Cape Verde (Escudo)	.100	–
Cayman Islands (Dollar)	0.816	–
Central African Rep.	.597	–
CFA Franc Central	.597	–
CFA Franc West	.597	–
CFP Franc	.109	–
Chad uses CFA Franc Central	.597	–
Chile (Peso)	.669	–
China, P.R. (Renminbi Yuan)	6.52	–
Colombia (Peso)	3,110	–
Comoros (Franc)	.441	–
Congo uses CFA Franc Central	.597	–
Congo-Dem.Rep. (Congolese Franc)	.914	–
Cook Islands (Dollar)	1.48	–
Costa Rica (Colon)	.523	–
Croatia (Kuna)	6.85	–
Cuba (Peso)	.22	27
Cyprus (Euro)	0.910	–
Czech Republic (Koruna)	.24	–
Denmark (Danish Krone)	6.79	–
Djibouti (Franc)	.178	–
Dominica uses E.C. Dollar	2.70	–
Dominican Republic (Peso)	.45	–
East Caribbean (Dollar)	2.70	–
East Timor (U.S. Dollar)	1.00	–
Ecuador (U.S. Dollar)	1.00	–
Egypt (Pound)	7.81	–
El Salvador (U.S. Dollar)	1.00	–
Equatorial Guinea uses CFA Franc Central	.597	–
Eritrea (Nafka)	15.0	–
Estonia (Euro)	0.910	–
Ethiopia (Birr)	.21	–
Euro	0.910	–
Falkland Is. (Pound)	0.704	–
Faroe Islands (Krona)	6.79	–
Fiji Islands (Dollar)	2.08	–
Finland (Euro)	0.910	–
France (Euro)	0.910	–
French Polynesia uses CFP Franc	.108	–
Gabon (CFA Franc)	.597	–
Gambia (Dalasi)	.39	–
Georgia (Lari)	2.45	–
Germany (Euro)	0.910	–
Ghana (New Cedi)	3.84	–
Gibraltar (Pound)	0.704	–
Greece (Euro)	0.910	–
Greenland uses Danish Krone	6.79	–
Grenada uses E.C. Dollar	2.70	–
Guatemala (Quetzal)	7.52	–
Guernsey uses Sterling Pound	0.704	–
Guinea Bissau uses CFA Franc West	.597	–
Guinea Conakry (Franc)	7,571	–
Guyana (Dollar)	.198	–
Haiti (Gourde)	.61	–
Honduras (Lempira)	.22	–
Hong Kong (Dollar)	7.77	–
Hungary (Forint)	.282	–
Iceland (Krona)	.127	–
India (Rupee)	.62	–
Indonesia (Rupiah)	13,123	–
Iran (Rial)	30,195	–
Iraq (Dinar)	1,150	–
Ireland (Euro)	0.910	–
Isle of Man uses Sterling Pound	0.704	–
Israel (New Sheqel)	3.90	–
Italy (Euro)	0.910	–
Ivory Coast uses CFA Franc West	.597	–
Jamaica (Dollar)	.120	–
Japan (Yen)	.113	–
Jersey uses Sterling Pound	0.704	–
Jordan (Dinar)	0.706	–
Kazakhstan (Tenge)	.343	–
Kenya (Shilling)	.100	–
Kiribati uses Australian Dollar	1.34	–
Korea-PDR (Won)	.135	–
Korea-Rep. (Won)	1,211	–
Kuwait (Dinar)	0.300	–
Kyrgyzstan (Som)	.73	–
Laos (Kip)	7,910	–
Latvia (Lats)	0.640	–
Lebanon (Pound)	1,472	–
Lesotho (Maloti)	15.4	–
Liberia (Dollar)	.90	–
Libya (Dinar)	1.36	–
Liechtenstein uses Swiss Franc	0.998	–
Lithuania (Litas)	3.14	–
Luxembourg (Euro)	0.910	–
Macao (Pataca)	7.82	–
Macedonia (New Denar)	.55	–
Madagascar (Ariary)	3,170	–
Malawi (Kwacha)	.715	–
Malaysia (Ringgit)	4.11	–
Maldives (Rufiya)	14.9	–
Mali uses CFA Franc West	.597	–
Malta (Euro)	0.910	–
Marshall Islands uses U.S.Dollar	1.00	–
Mauritania (Ouguiya)	.337	–
Mauritius (Rupee)	.34	–
Mexico (Peso)	17.9	–
Moldova (Leu)	19.7	–
Monaco uses Euro	0.910	–
Mongolia (Tugrik)	2,038	–
Montenegro uses Euro	0.910	–
Montserrat uses E.C. Dollar	2.70	–
Morocco (Dirham)	9.82	–
Mozambique (New Metical)	.49	–
Namibia (Rand)	15.4	–
Nauru uses Australian Dollar	1.34	–
Nepal (Rupee)	.106	–
Netherlands (Euro)	0.910	–
Netherlands Antilles (Gulden)	2.00	–
New Caledonia uses CFP Franc	.109	–
New Zealand (Dollar)	1.48	–
Nicaragua (Cordoba Oro)	.28	–
Niger uses CFA Franc West	.597	–
Nigeria (Naira)	.197	–
Northern Ireland uses Sterling Pound	0.704	–
Norway (Krone)	8.56	–
Oman (Rial)	0.384	–
Pakistan (Rupee)	.103	–
Palau uses U.S.Dollar	1.00	–
Panama (Balboa) uses U.S.Dollar	1.00	–
Papua New Guinea (Kina)	2.98	–
Paraguay (Guarani)	5,591	–
Peru (Nuevo Sol)	3.39	–
Philippines (Peso)	.47	–
Poland (Zloty)	3.93	–
Portugal (Euro)	0.910	–
Qatar (Riyal)	3.64	–
Romania (New Leu)	4.06	–
Russia (Ruble)	.72	–
Rwanda (Franc)	.739	–
St. Helena (Pound)	0.624	–
St. Kitts uses E.C. Dollar	2.70	–
St. Lucia uses E.C. Dollar	2.70	–
St. Vincent uses E.C. Dollar	2.70	–
Samoa (Tala)	2.27	–
San Marino uses Euro	0.910	–
Sao Tome e Principe (Dobra)	22,298	–
Saudi Arabia (Riyal)	3.75	–
Scotland uses Sterling Pound	0.704	–
Senegal uses CFA Franc West	.597	–
Serbia (Dinar)	.112	–
Seychelles (Rupee)	11.8	–
Sierra Leone (Leone)	4,027	–
Singapore (Dollar)	1.38	–
Slovakia (Euro)	0.910	–
Slovenia (Euro)	0.910	–
Solomon Islands (Dollar)	8.10	–
Somalia (Shilling)	.579	–
Somaliland (Somali Shilling)	.579	4,000
South Africa (Rand)	15.4	–
Spain (Euro)	0.910	–
Sri Lanka (Rupee)	.142	–
Sudan (Pound)	6.06	–
Surinam (Dollar)	3.96	–
Swaziland (Lilangeni)	15.4	–
Sweden (Krona)	8.47	–
Switzerland (Franc)	0.998	–
Syria (Pound)	.220	–
Taiwan (NT Dollar)	.33	–
Tajikistan (Somoni)	7.87	–
Tanzania (Shilling)	2,143	–
Thailand (Baht)	.35	–
Togo uses CFA Franc West	.597	–
Tonga (Pa'anga)	2.30	–
Transdniestra (Ruble)	.72	–
Trinidad & Tobago (Dollar)	6.41	–
Tunisia (Dinar)	2.03	–
Turkey (New Lira)	2.91	–
Turkmenistan (Manat)	3.49	–
Turks & Caicos uses U.S. Dollar	1.00	–
Tuvalu uses Australian Dollar	1.34	–
Uganda (Shilling)	3,327	–
Ukraine (Hryvnia)	.26	–
United Arab Emirates (Dirham)	3.67	–
United Kingdom (Sterling Pound)	0.704	–
Uruguay (Peso Uruguayo)	.32	–
Uzbekistan (Sum)	2,846	–
Vanuatu (Vatu)	.111	–
Vatican City uses Euro	0.910	–
Venezuela (New Bolivar)	6.28	35
Vietnam (Dong)	22,003	–
Yemen (Rial)	.215	–
Zambia (Kwacha)	11.3	–
Zimbabwe (Dollar)	.373	–

Standard International Grading Terminology and Abbreviations

U.S. and ENGLISH SPEAKING LANDS	UNCIRCULATED	EXTREMELY FINE	VERY FINE	FINE	VERY GOOD	GOOD	POOR
Abbreviation	UNC	EF or XF	VF	FF	VG	G	PR
BRAZIL	(1) DW	(3) S	(5) MBC	(7) BC	(8)	(9) R	UTGeG
DENMARK	O	01	1+	1	1÷	2	3
FINLAND	0	01	1+	1	1?	2	3
FRANCE	NEUF	SUP	TTB or TB	TB or TB	B	TBC	BC
GERMANY	KFR	II / VZGL	III / SS	IV / S	V / S.g.E.	VI / G.e.	G.e.s.
ITALY	FdS	SPL	BB	MB	B	M	—
JAPAN	未使用	極美品	美品	並品	—	—	—
NETHERLANDS	FDC	Pr.	Z.F.	Fr.	Z.g.	G	—
NORWAY	0	01	1+	1	1÷	2	3
PORTUGAL	Novo	Soberbo	Muito bo	—	—	—	—
SPAIN	Lujo	SC, IC or EBC	MBC	BC	—	RC	MC
SWEDEN	0	01	1+	1	1?	2	—

BRAZIL

FE — Flor de Estampa
S — Soberba
MBC — Muito Bem Conservada
BC — Bem Conservada
R — Regular
UTGeG — Um Tanto Gasto e Gasto

DENMARK

O — Uncirkuleret
01 — Meget Paent Eksemplar
1+ — Paent Eksemplar
1 — Acceptabelt Eksemplar
1 —Noget Slidt Eksemplar
2 — Darlight Eksemplar
3 — Meget Darlight Eskemplar

FINLAND

00 — Kiiltolyönti
0 — Lyöntiveres
01 — Erittäin Hyvä
1+ — Hyvä
1? — Heikko
2 — Huono

FRANCE

NEUF — New
FDC — Fleur De Coin
SPL — Splendide
SUP — Superbe
TTB — Très Très Beau
TB — Très Beau
B — Beau
TBC — Tres Bien Conserve
BC — Bien Conserve

GERMANY

VZGL — Vorzüglich
SS — Sehr schön
S — Schön
S.g.E. — Sehr gut erhalten
G.e. — Gut erhalten
G.e.S. — Gering erhalten Schlecht

ITALY

Fds — Fior di Stampa
SPL — Splendid
BB — Bellissimo
MB — Molto Bello
B — Bello
M — Mediocre

JAPAN

未使用 — Mishiyo
極美品 — Goku Bihin
美品 — Bihin
並品 — Futuhin

NETHERLANDS

Pr. — Prachtig
Z.F. — Zeer Fraai
Fr. — Fraai
Z.g. — Zeer Goed
G — Goed

NORWAY

0 — Usirkuleret eks
01 — Meget pent eks
1+ — Pent eks
1 — Fullgodt eks
1- — Ikke Fullgodt eks
2 — Darlig eks

ROMANIA

NC — Necirculata (UNC)
FF — Foarte Frumoasa (VF)
F — Frumoasa (F)
FBC — Foarte Bine Conservata (VG)
BC — Bine Conservata (G)
M — Mediocru Conservata (POOR)

SPAIN

EBC — Extraordinariamente Bien Conservada
SC — Sin Circular
IC — Incirculante
MBC — Muy Bien Conservada
BC — Bien Conservada
RC — Regular Conservada
MC — Mala Conservada

SWEDEN

0 — Ocirkulerat
01 — Mycket Vackert
1+ — Vackert
1 — Fullgott
1? — Ej Fullgott
2 — Dalight

IBNS Grading Standards for World Paper Money

The following introduction and Grading Guide is the result of work prepared under the guidance of the Grading Committee of the International Bank Note Society (IBNS). It has been adopted as the official grading standards of that society.

Introduction

Grading is the most controversial component of paper money collecting today. Small differences in grade can mean significant differences in value. The process of grading is so subjective and dependent on external influences such as lighting, that even a very experienced individual may well grade the same note differently on separate occasions.

To facilitate communication between sellers and buyers, it is essential that grading terms and their meanings be as standardized and as widely used as possible. This standardization should reflect common usage as much as practicable. One difficulty with grading is that even the actual grades themselves are not used everywhere by everyone. For example, in Europe the grade 'About Uncirculated' (AU) is not in general use, yet in North America it is widespread. The European term 'Good VF' may roughly correspond to what individuals in North America call 'Extremely Fine' (EF).

The grades and definitions as set forth below cannot reconcile all the various systems and grading terminology variants. Rather, the attempt is made here to try and diminish the controversy with some common-sense grades and definitions that aim to give more precise meaning to the grading language of paper money.

How to look at a banknote

In order to ascertain the grade of a note, it is essential to examine it out of a holder and under a good light. Move the note around so that light bounces off of it at different angles. Try holding the note obliquely, so the note is even with your eye as you look up at the light. Hard-to-see folds or slight creases will show up under such examination. Some individuals also lightly feel along the surface of the note to detect creasing.

Cleaning, Washing, Pressing of Banknotes

a) Cleaning, washing or pressing paper money is generally harmful and reduces both the grade and the value of a note. At the very least, a washed or pressed note may lose its original sheen and its surface may become lifeless and dull. The defects a note had, such as folds and creases, may not necessarily be completely eliminated and their telltale marks can be detected under a good light. Carelessly washed notes may also have white streaks where the folds or creases were (or still are).

b) Processing of a note which started out as Extremely Fine will automatically reduce it at least one full grade.

Unnatural Defects

Glue, tape or pencil marks may sometimes be successfuly removed. While such removal will leave a cleaned surface, it will improve the overall appearance of the note without concealing any of its defects. Under such circumstances, the grade of that note may also be improved.

The words "pinholes", "staple holes", "trimmed", "graffiti", "writing on face", "tape marks" etc. should always be added to the description of a note. It is realized that certain countries routinely staple their notes together in groups before issue. In such cases, the description can include a comment such as "usual staple holes" or something similar. After all, not everyone knows that certain notes cannot be found otherwise.

The major point of this section is that one cannot lower the overall grade of a note with defects simply because of the defects. The value will reflect the lowered worth of a defective note, but the description must always include the specific defects.

GRADING

Definitions of Terms

UNCIRCULATED: A perfectly preserved note, never mishandled by the issuing authority, a bank teller, the public or a collector.

Paper is clean and firm, without discoloration. Corners are sharp and square without any evidence of rounding. (Rounded corners are often a tell-tale sign of a cleaned or "doctored" note.)

NOTE: Some note issues are most often available with slight evidence of very light counting folds which do not "break" the paper. Also, French-printed notes usually have a slight ripple in the paper. Many collectors and dealers refer to such notes as AU-UNC.

ABOUT UNCIRCULATED: A virtually perfect note, with some minor handling. May show very slight evidence of bank counting folds at a corner or one light fold through the center, but not both. An AU note canot be creased, a crease being a hard fold which has usually "broken" the surface of the note.

Paper is clean and bright with original sheen. Corners are not rounded.

NOTE: Europeans will refer to an About Uncirculated or AU note as "EF-Unc" or as just "EF". The Extremely Fine note described below will often be referred to as "GVF" or "Good Very Fine".

EXTREMELY FINE: A very attractive note, with light handling. May have a maximum of three light folds or one strong crease.

Paper is clean and firm, without discoloration. Corners are sharp and square without any evidence of rounding. (Rounded corners are often a tell-tale sign of a cleaned or "doctored" note.)

VERY FINE: An attractive note, but with more evidence of handling and wear. May have several folds both vertically and horizontally.

Paper may have minimal dirt, or possible color smudging.

Paper itself is still relatively crisp and not floppy.

There are no tears into the border area, although the edges do show slight wear. Corners also show wear but not full rounding.

FINE: A note that shows consideralble circulation, with many folds, creases and wrinkling.

Paper is not excessively dirty but may have some softness.

Edges may show much handling, with minor tears in the border area. Tears may not extend into the design. There will be no center hole because of excessive folding.

Colors are clear but not very bright. A staple hole or two would would not be considered unusual wear in a Fine note. Overall appearance is still on the desirable side.

VERY GOOD: A well used note, abused but still intact.

Corners may have much wear and rounding, tiny nicks, tears may extend into the design, some discoloration may be present, staining may have occurred, and a small hole may sometimes be seen at center from excessive folding.

Staple and pinholes are usually present, and the note itself is quite limp but NO pieces of the note can be missing. A note in VG condition may still have an overall not unattractive appearance.

GOOD: A well worn and heavily used note. Normal damage from prolonged circulation will include strong multiple folds and creases, stains, pinholes and/or staple holes, dirt, discoloration, edge tears, center hole, rounded corners and an overall unattractive appearance. No large pieces of the note may be missing. Graffiti is commonly seen on notes in G condition.

FAIR: A totally limp, dirty and very well used note. Larger pieces may be half torn off or missing besides the defects mentioned under the Good category. Tears will be larger, obscured portions of the note will be bigger.

POOR: A "rag" with severe damage because of wear, staining, pieces missing, graffiti, larger holes. May have tape holding pieces of the note together. Trimming may have taken place to remove rough edges. A Poor note is desiralble only as a "filler" or when such a note is the only one known of that particular issue.

A word on crimps to otherwise uncirculated notes.

Due to inclusion of wide security foils, crimps appear at the top and bottom edge during production or counting. Thus notes which are uncirculated have a crimp. Examples without these crimps are beginning to command a premium.

International Bank Note Society

The International Bank note Society (IBNS) was formed in 1961 to promote the study and collecting of world paper money. A membership of almost 2,000 in over 90 nations draws on the services of the Society for advancing their knowledge and their collections.

The benefits of the society include the quarterly IBNS Journal, a full color, 80-page magazine featuring learned writings on the notes of the world, their history, artistry and technical background. Additionally each member receives a directory, which lists members by name—with their contact details and collecting interests—as well as by geographic location. The Society conducts auctions in which all members may participate.

One of the greatest strengths of IBNS membership is the facility for correspondence with other members around the world for purposes of exchanging notes, and for obtaining information and assistance with research projects or the identification of notes. Information about the Society can be found at www.theIBNS.org

Application for Membership in the International Bank Note Society

Name: ______________________

Address: ______________________

City: ______________________

Province/State: ______________________

Postal/Zip Code: ______________________

Country: ______________________

Telephone: ______________________

E-mail: ______________________

Website: ______________________

Collecting Interest: ______________________

Do you want your postal address and web site published in the printed Membership Directory? ❑ Yes ❑ No

Do you want your e-mail address published in the printed Membership Directory? ❑ Yes ❑ No

Do you want your postal address and web site published in the PDF version of the Membership Directory? ❑ Yes ❑ No

Do you want your email address published in the PDF version of the Membership Directory? ❑ Yes ❑ No

Do you want your e-mail address to appear on the IBNS web site? ❑ Yes ❑ No

Are you a banknote dealer? ❑ Yes ❑ No

Type of Membership:

Individual	❑ $US33.00	❑ £20.00	❑ $AU37.50
Group	❑ $US33.00	❑ £20.00	❑ $AU37.50
Junior (Under 18)	❑ $US16.50	❑ £10.00	❑ $AU18.75
Family	❑ $US33.00	❑ £20.00	❑ $AU37.50

Mail to: IBNS US Membership Secretary, PO Box 081643, Racine, WI 53408-1643, USA

Or application for membership can be completed on line at: **www.theIBNS.org**

For further information please contact **us-secretary@ibns.biz or general-secretary@ibns.biz**

Bank Note Printers

Printers' names, abbreviations or monograms will usually appear as part of the frame design or below it on face and/or back. In some instances the engraver's name may also appear in a similar location on a note. The following abbreviations identify printers for many of the notes listed in this volume:

ABNC	American Bank Note Company (USA)
BABN(C)	British American Bank Note Co., Ltd. (Canada)
B&S	Bouligny & Schmidt (Mexico)
BDDK	Bunddesdruckerei (Germany)
BEPP	Bureau of Engraving & Printing, Peking (China)
BF	Banque de France (France)
BFL	Barclay & Fry, Ltd. (England)
BWC	Bradbury, Wilkinson & Co. (England)
CABB	Compania Americana de Billetes de Banco (ABNC)
CBC	Columbian Banknote Co. (US)
CBNC	Canadian Bank Note Company (Canada)
CC	Ciccone Calcografica S.A. (Italy)
CCBB	Compania Columbiana de Billetes de Banco (CBC)
CdM-	Casa de Moeda (Brazil)
CdM-	Casa de Moeda (Argentina, Chile, etc.)
CHB	Chung Hua Book Co. (China)
CMN	Casa de Moneda de la Nacion (Argentina)
CMPA	Commercial Press (China)
CNBB	Compania Nacional de billetes de Banco (NBNC)
CONB	Continental Bank Note Company (US)
CPF	Central Printing Factory (China)
CSABB	Compania Sud/Americana de billetes de Banco (Argentina)
CS&E	Charles Skipper & East (England)
DBM-A	Devlet Banknot Matbaas1-Ankara (Turkey)
DLR or (T)DLR	De La Rue (England)
DTB	Dah Tung Book Co., and Ta Tung Printing (China)
E&C	Evans & Cogswell (CSA)
EAW	E.A. Wright (US)
FLBN	Franklin-Lee Bank Note Company (US)
FNMT	Fabrica Nacional de Moneda y Timbre (Spain)
G&D	Giesecke & Devrient (Germany)
HBNC	Hamilton Bank Note Company (USA)
HKB	Hong Kong Banknote (Hong Kong)
HKP	Hong Kong Printing Press (Hong Kong)
H&L	Hoyer & Ludwig, Richmond, Virginia (CSA)
HLBNC	Homer Lee Bank Note Co. (US)
H&S	Harrison & Sons, Ltd. (England)
IBB	Imprenta de Billetes-Bogota (Colombia)
IBSFB	Imprenta de Billetes-Santa Fe de Bogota (Colombia)
IBNC	International Bank Note Company (US)
JBNC	Jeffries Bank Note Company (US)
JEZ	Joh, Enschede en Zonen (Netherlands)
K&B	Keatinge & Ball (CSA)
KBNC	Kendall Bank Note Company, New York (USA)
LN	Litographia Nacional (Colombia)
NAL	Nissen & Arnold (England)
NBNC	National Bank Note Company (US)
OCV	Officina Carte-Valori (Italy)
OBDI	Officina Della Banca D'Italia (Italy)
OFZ	Orell FŸssli, Zurich (Switzerland)
P&B	Perkins & Bacon (England)
PBC	Perkins, Bacon & Co. (England)
PB&P	Perkins, Bacon & Petch (England)
SBNC	Security Banknote Company (US)
TDLR or (T)DLR	Thomas De La Rue (England)
UPC	Union Printing Co., Ltd. (China)
UPP	Union Publishers & Printers Fed. Inc. (China)
USBNC	United States Banknote Corp. (US)
WDBN	Western District Banknote Fed. Inc.
W&S	Waterlow & Sons Ltd. (England)
WPCo	Watson Printing Co. (China)
WWS	W.W. Sprague & Co. Ltd. (England)

Specimen notes

To familiarize private banks, central banks, law enforcement agencies and treasuries around the world with newly issued currency, many nations provide special "Specimen" examples of their notes. Specimens are actual bank notes, complete with dummy or all zero serial numbers and signatures bearing the overprinted and/or perforated word "SPECIMEN" in the language of the country of origin itself or where the notes were printed.

Some countries have made specimen notes available for sale to collectors. These include Cuba, Czechoslovakia, Poland and Slovakia after World War II and a special set of four denominations of Jamaica notes bearing red matched star serial numbers. Also, in 1978, the Franklin Mint made available to collectors specimen notes from 15 nations, bearing matching serial numbers and a Maltese cross device used as a prefix. Several other countries have also participated in making specimen notes available to collectors at times.

Aside from these collectors issues, specimen notes may sometimes comand higher prices than regular issue notes of the same type, even though there are far fewer collectors of specimens. In some cases, notably older issues in high denominations, specimens may be the only form of such notes available to collectors today. Specimen notes are not legal tender or redeemable, thus have no real "face value".

The most unusual forms of specimens were produced by Waterlow and Sons. They printed special off colored notes for salesman's sample books adding the word SPECIMEN and their seal.

Some examples of how the word "SPECIMEN" is represented in other languages or on notes of other countries follow:

AMOSTRA: Brazil
CAMPIONE: Italy
CONTOH: Malaysia
EKSEMPLAAR: South Africa
ESPƒCIME: Portugal and Colonies
ESPECIMEN: Various Spanish-speaking nations
GIAY MAU: Vietnam
MINTA: Hungary
MODELO: Brazil
MODEL: Albania
MUSTER: Austria, Germany
MUESTRA: Various Spanish-speaking nations
NUMUNDEDIR GECMEZ: Turkey
ORNEKTIR GECMEZ: Turkey
ОБРАЗЕЦ or **ОБРАЗЕЦЪ:** Bulgaria, Russia, U.S.S.R.
PARAUGS: Latvia
PROFTRYK: Sweden
UZORAK: Croatia
WZOR: Poland
ЗАГВАР: Mongolia

Dating

Determining the date of issue of a note is a basic consideration of attribution. As the reading of dates is subject not only to the vagaries of numeric styling, but to variations in dating roots caused by the observation of differing religious eras or regal periods from country to country, making this determination can sometimes be quite difficult. Most countries outside the North African and Oriental spheres rely on Western date numerals and the Christian (AD) reckoning, although in a few instances note dating has been tied to the year of a reign or government.

Countries of the Arabic sphere generally date their issues to the Muslim calendar that commenced on July 16, 622 AD when the prophet Mohammed fled from Mecca to Medina. As this calendar is reckoned by the lunar year of 354, it is about three percent (precisely 3.3 percent) shorter than the Christian year. A conversion formula requires you to subtract that percent from the AH date, and then add 621 to gain the AD date.

A degree of confusion arises here because the Muslim calendar is not always based on the lunar year (AH). Afghanistan and Iran (Persia) used a calendar based on a solar year (SH) introduced around 1920. These dates can be converted to AD by simply adding 621. In 1976, Iran implemented a solar calendar based on the founding of the Iranian monarchy in 559 BC. The first year observed on this new system was 2535(MS) which commenced on March 20,1976.

Several different eras of reckoning, including the Christian (AD) and Muslim (AH), have been used to date paper money of the Indian subcontinent. The two basic systems are the Vikrama Samvat (VS) era that dates from October 18, 58 BC,. and the Saka (SE) era, the origin of which is reckoned from March 3, 78 AD.

Dating according to both eras appears on notes of several native states and countries of the area.

Thailand (Siam) has observed three different eras for dating. The most predominant is the Buddhist (BE) era originating in 543 BC. Next is the Bangkok or Ratanakosind-sok (RS) era dating from 1781 AD (and consisting of only 3 numerals), followed by the Chula-Sakarat (CS) era dating from 638 AD, with the latter also observed in Burma.

Other calendars include that of the Ethiopian (EE) era that commenced 7 years, 8 months after AD dating, and that of the Hebrew nation beginning on October 7, 3761 BC. Korea claims a dating from 2333 BC which is acknowledged on some note issues.

The following table indicates the years dating from the various eras that correspond to 2015 by Christian (AD) calendar reckoning. It must be remembered that there are overlaps between the eras in some instances:

Christian Era (AD)	—	2015
Mohammedan era (AH)	—	AH1436
Solar year (SH)	—	SH1394
Monarchic Solar era (MS)	—	MS 2574
Vikrama Samvat era (VS)	—	SE 2072
Saka era (SE)	—	Saka 1937
Buddhist era (BE)	—	BE 2558
Bangkok era (RS)	—	RS 234
Chula-Sakarat era (CS)	—	CS1377
Ethiopian era (EE)	—	EE2007
Jewish era	—	5775
Korean era	—	4348

Paper money of Oriental origin - principally Japan, Korea, China, Turkestan and Tibet - generally date to the year of the government, dynastic, regnal or cyclical eras, with the dates indicated in Oriental characters usually reading from right to left. In recent years some dating has been according to the Christian calendar and in Western numerals reading from left to right.

More detailed guides to the application of the less prevalent dating systems than those described, and others of strictly local nature, along with the numeral designations employed, are presented in conjunction with the appropriate listings.

Some notes carry dating according to both the locally observed and Christian eras. This is particularly true in the Arabic sphere, where the Muslim date may be indicated in Arabic numerals and the Christian date in Western numerals.

In general the date actually shown on a given paper money issue is indicated in some manner. Notes issued by special Law or Decree will have L or D preceding the date. Dates listed within parentheses may differ from the date appearing on the note; they have been documented by other means. Undated notes are listed with ND, followed by a year only when the year of actual issue is known.

Timing differentials between the 354-day Muslim and the 365-day Christian year cause situations whereby notes bearing dates of both eras have two date combinations that may overlap from one or the other calendar system.

China - Republic 9th year, 1st month, 15th day (15.1.1920), read r. to l.

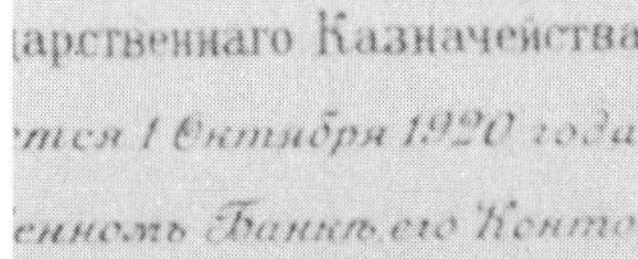

Russia-1 October 1920

Poland - 28 February 1919

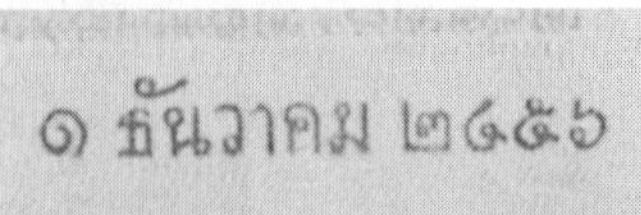

Thailand (Siam) - 1 December 2456

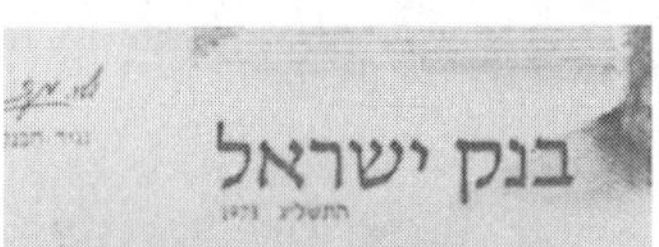

Israel - 1973, 5733

Indonesia - 1 January 1950

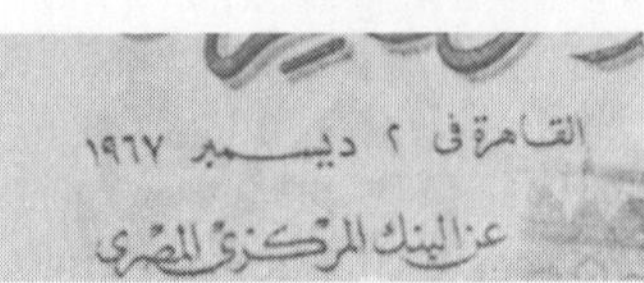

Egypt - 1967 December 2

Korea - 4288 (1955)

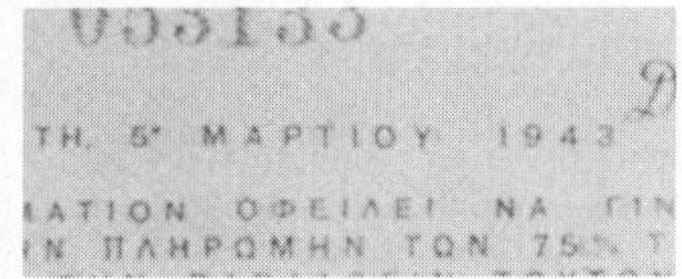

Greece - 5 March 1943

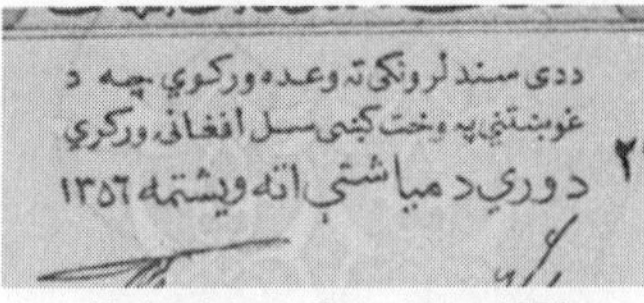
Afghanistan - Solar Year 1356

English	January	February	March	April	May	June	July	August	September	October	November	December
Albanian	Kallnuer	Fruer	Mars	Prill	Maj	Qershuer	Korrik	Gusht	Shtatuer	Tetuer	Nanduer	Dhetuer
Czech	Leden	Únor	Brezen	Duben	Kveten	Cerven	Cervenec	Srpen	Zári	Ríjen	Listopad	Prosinec
Danish	Januar	Februari	Maart	April	Maj	Juni	Juli	August	September	Oktober	November	December
Dutch	Januari	Februari	Maart	April	Mei	Juni	Juli	Augustus	September	Oktober	November	December
Estonian	Jaanuar	Veebruar	Marts	Aprill	Mai	Juuni	Juuli	August	September	Oktoober	November	Detsember
French	Janvier	Fevrier	Mars	Avril	Mai	Juin	Jillet	Août	Septembre	Octobre	Novembre	Decembre
Finnish	Tammikuu	Helmikuu	Maaliskuu	Huhtikuu	Toukokuu	Kesakuu	Heinakuu	Elokuu	Syyskuu	Lokakuu	Marraskuu	Joulukuu
German	Januar	Februar	Marz	April	Mai	Juni	Juli	August	September	Oktober	November	Dezember
Hungarian	Januar	Februar	Marcius	Aprilis	Majus	Junius	Julius	Augusztus	Szeptember	Oktober	November	December
Indonesian	Djanuari	Februari	Maret	April	Mai	Djuni	Djuli	Augustus	September	Oktober	Nopember	Desember
Italian	Gennaio	Fabbraio	Marzo	Aprile	Maggio	Giugno	Luglio	Agosto	Settembre	Ottobre	Novembre	Dicembre
Lithuanian	Sausis	Vasaris	Kovas	Balandis	Geguzis	Birzelis	Liepos	Rugpiutis	Rugsejis	Spalis	Lapkritis	Gruodis
Norwegian	Januar	Februar	Mars	April	Mai	Juni	Juli	August	September	Oktober	November	Desember
Polish	Styczen	Luty	Marzec	Kwiecien	Maj	Cerwiec	Lipiec	Sierpien	Wrzesien	Pazdziernik	Listopad	Grudzien
Portuguese	Janerio	Fevereiro	Marco	Abril	Maio	Junho	Julho	Agosto	Setembro	Outubro	Novembro	Dezembro
Romanian	Ianuarie	Februarie	Martie	Aprilie	Mai	Iunie	Iulie	August	Septembrie	Octombrie	Noiembrie	Decembrie
Croatian	Sijecanj	Veljaca	Ozujak	Travanj	Svibanj	Lipanj	Srpanj	Kolovoz	Rujan	Listopad	Studeni	Prosinac
Spanish	Enero	Febrero	Marzo	Abril	Mayo	Junio	Julio	Agosto	Septiembre	Octubre	Noviembre	Diciembre
Swedish	Januari	Februari	Mars	April	Maj	Juni	Juli	Augusti	September	Oktober	November	December
Turkish	Ocak	Subat	Mart	Nisan	Mayis	Haziran	Temmuz	Agusto	Eylul	Ekim	Kasim	Aralik
Arabic-New (condensed)	يناير	فبراير	مارس	ابريل	مايو	يونيو	يوليو	أغسطس	سبتمبر	أكتوبر	نوفمبر	ديسمبر
(extended)	ينـــاير	فبراير	مارس	ابريل	مايو	يونيه	يوليه	اغسطس	سبتمبر	اكتوبر	نوفمبر	ديسمبر
Persian (Solar)	فروردين	ارديبهشت	خرداد	تير	مرداد	شهريور	مهر	آبان	آذر	دی	بهمن	اسفند
(Lunar)	محرم	صفر	ربيع الاول	ربيع الثانی	جمادی الاول	جمادی الثانی	رجب	شعبان	رمضان	شوال	ذيقعده	ذوالحجه
Chinese	正月	二月	三月	四月	五月	六月	七月	八月	九月	十月	十一月	十二月
Japanese	月一	月二	月三	月四	月五	月六	月七	月八	月九	月十	月一十	月二十
Greek	Ιανοναριοδ	Φεβροναριοδ	Μαρτιοδ	Απιλιοδ	Μαιοδ	Ιουνιοδ	Ιουλιοδ	Αυγουατοδ	Εεπτεμβπιοδ	Οκτωβπιοδ	Νοεμπιοσ	Δεκεμβριος
Russian	ЯНВАРЬ	ФЕВРАЛЬ	МАРТ	АПРЕЛЬ	МАИ	ИЮНЬ	ИЮЛЬ	АВГУСТ	СЕПТЯБРЬ	ОКТЯБРЬ	НОЯБРЬ	ДЕКАБРЬ
Serbian	Јануар	Фебруар	Марг	Април	Мај	Јун	Јул	Август	Септембар	Октобар	Новембар	Децембар
Ukranian	Січень	Лютий	Березень	Квітень	Травень	Червень	Липень	Серпень	Вересень	Жовтень	Листопад	Грудень
Yiddish	יאַנואַר	פעברואַר	מערץ	אַפּריל	מײַ	יוני	יולי	אויגוסט	סעפּטעמבער	אָקטיאַבער	נאָוועמבער	דעצעמבער
Hebrew (Israeli)	ינואר	פברואר	מרץ	אפריל	מאי	יוני	יולי	אוגוסט	ספטמבר	אוקטובר	נובמבר	דצמבר

Note: Word spellings and configurations as represented on actual notes may vary significantly from those shown on this chart.

A Guide To International Numerics

	ENGLISH	CZECH	DANISH	DUTCH	ESPERANTO	FRENCH
1/4	quarter	jedna ctvrina	én kvart	een-kwart	unu-kvar'ono	quart
1/2	half	jedna polovinal	én halv	halve	unu-du'one	demi
1	one	jedna	én	een	unu	un
2	two	dve	to	twee	du	deux
3	three	tri	tre	drie	tri	trois
4	four	ctyri	fire	vier	kvar	quatre
5	five	pet	fem	vijf	kvin	cinq
6	six	sest	seks	zes	ses	six
7	seven	sedm	syv	zeven	sep	sept
8	eight	osm	otte	acht	ok	huit
9	nine	devet	ni	negen	nau	neuf
10	ten	deset	ti	tien	dek	dix
12	twelve	dvanáct	tolv	twaalf	dek du	douze
15	fifteen	patnáct	femten	vijftien	dek kvin	quinze
20	twenty	dvacet	tyve	twintig	du'dek	vingt
24	twenty-four	dvacetctyri	fireogtyve	vierentwintig	du'dek kvar	vingt-quatre
25	twenty-five	dvacetpet	femogtyve	vijfentwintig	du'dek kvin	vingt-cinq
30	thirty	tricet	tredive	dertig	tri'dek	trente
40	forty	ctyricet	fyrre	veertig	kvar'dek	quarante
50	fifty	padesát	halvtreds	vijftig	kvin'dek	cinquante
60	sixty	sedesát	tres	zestig	ses'dek	soixante
70	seventy	sedmdesát	halvfjerds	zeventig	sep'dek	soixante-dix
80	eighty	osemdesát	firs	tachtig	ok'dek	quatre-vingt
90	ninety	devadesát	halvfems	negentig	nau'dek	quatre-vingt-dix
100	one hundred	sto	hundrede	honderd	unu-cento	cent
1000	thousand	tis'c	tusind	duizend	mil	mille

	GERMAN	HUNGARIAN	INDONESIAN	ITALIAN	NORWEGIAN	POLISH
1/4	viertel	egy-negyed	satu per empat	quarto	en-fjeerdedel	jedna czwarta
1/2	halb	fél	satu per dua	mezzo	halv	podowa
1	ein	egy	satu	uno	en	jeden
2	zwei	kettö	dua	due	to	dwa
3	drei	három	tiga	tre	tre	trzy
4	vier	négy	empat	quattro	fire	cztery
5	fünf	öt	lima	cinque	fem	piec'
6	sechs	hat	enam	sei	seks	szes'c'
7	sieben	hét	tujuh	sette	sju	siedem
8	acht	nyolc	delapan	otto	atte	osiem
9	neun	kilenc	sembilan	nove	ni	dziewiec'
10	zehn	t'z	sepuluh	dieci	ti	dziesiec'
12	zwölf	tizenketto	dua belas	dodici	tolv	dwanas' cie
15	fünfzehn	tizenöt	lima belas	quindici	femten	pietnas'cie
20	zwanzig	håsz	dua puluh	venti	tjue or tyve	dwadzies'cia
24	vierundzwanzig	håszonnégy	dua puluh empat	ventiquattro	tjue-fire or tyve-fire	dwadzies'cia-cztery
25	fünfundzwanzig	huszonöt	dua puluh lima	venticinque	tjue-fem or tyve-fem	dwadzies'cia-piec
30	dreissig	harminc	tiga puluh	trenta	tredve	trydzies'ci
40	vierzig	negyven	empat puluh	quaranta	forti	czterdries'ci
50	fünfzig	ötven	lima puluh	cinquanta	femti	piec'dziesiat
60	sechzig	hatvan	enam puluh	sessanta	seksti	szes'c'dziesiat
70	siebzig	hetven	tujuh pulu	settanta	sytti	siedemdziesiat
80	achtzig	nyolcyan	delapan puluh	ottonta	åttio	osiemdziesiat
90	neunzig	kilencven	sembilan puluh	novanta	nitti	dziewiec'dziesiat
100	hundert	száz	seratus	cento	hundre	jeden-sto
1000	tausend	ezer	seribu	mille	tusen	tysiac

	PORTUGUESE	ROMANIAN	SERBO-CROATIAN	SPANISH	SWEDISH	TURKISH
1/4	quarto	un-sfert	jedna ceturlina	carto	en-fjördedel	bir ceyrek
1/2	meio	o-jumatate	jedna polovina	medio	hölft	bir yarim
1	um	un	jedan	uno	en	bir
2	dois	doi	dva	dos	tva	iki
3	trÊs	trei	tri	tres	tre	üc
4	quatro	patru	cetiri	cuatro	fyra	dört
5	cinco	cinci	pet	cinco	fem	bes
6	seis	sase	sest	seis	sex	alti
7	sete	sapte	sedam	siete	sju	yedi
8	oito	opt	osam	ocho	åtta	sekiz
9	nove	noua	devet	nueve	nio	dokuz
10	dez	zece	deset	diez	tio	on
12	doze	doisprezece	dvanaest	doce	tolv	oniki
15	quinze	cincisprezece	petnaest	quince	femton	onbes
20	vinte	douazeci	dvadeset	veinte	tugu	yirmi
24	vinte-quatro	douacei si patru	dvadeset cetiri	veinticuatro	tjugu fyra	jirmidört
25	vinte-cinco	douacei si cinci	dvadeset pet	veinticinco	tjugu fem	yirmibes
30	trinta	treizeci	trideset	treinta	trettio	otuz
40	quarenta	patruzeci	cetrdeset	cuarenta	fyrtio	kirk
50	cinquenta	cincizeci	padeset	cincuenta	femtio	elli
60	sessenta	saizeci	sezdeset	sesenta	sextio	altmis
70	setenta	saptezeci	sedamdeset	setenta	sjuttio	yetmis
80	oitenta	optzeci	osamdeset	ochenta	åttio	seksen
90	noventa	nouazeci	devedeset	noventa	nittio	doksan
100	cem	suta	sto	cien	hundra	yüz
1000	mil	mie	Serbo hiljada	mil	tusen	bin

Standard International Numeral Systems

Prepared especially for the ***Standard Catalog of Paper Money***© 2016 by Krause Publications

Western	0	½	1	2	3	4	5	6	7	8	9	10	50	100	500	1000
Roman			I	II	III	IV	V	VI	VII	VIII	IX	X	L	C	D	M
Arabic-Turkish	٠	١/٢	١	٢	٣	٤	٥	٦	٧	٨	٩	١٠	٥٠	١٠٠	٥٠٠	١٠٠٠
Malay-Persian	۰	۱/۲	۱	۲	۳	۴	۵	٦ or ۶	۷	۸	۹	۱۰	۵۰	۱۰۰	۵۰۰	۱۰۰۰
Eastern Arabic	۰	۱/۲	۱	۲	۳	۴	۵	۶	۷	۸	۹	۱۰	۵۰	۱۰۰	۵۰۰	۱۰۰۰
Hyderabad Arabic	۰	۱/۲	۱	۲	۳	۴	۵	۶	۷	۸	۹	۱۰	۵۰	۱۰۰	۵۰۰	۱۰۰۰
Indian (Sanskrit)	०	१/२	१	२	३	४	५	६	७	८	९	१०	५०	१००	५००	१०००
Assamese	০	১/২	১	২	৩	৪	৫	৬	৭	৮	৯	১০	৫০	১০০	৫০০	১০০০
Bengali	০	১/২	১	২	৩	৪	৫	৬	৭	৮	৯	১০	৫০	১০০	৫০০	১০০০
Gujarati	૦	૧/૨	૧	૨	૩	૪	૫	૬	૭	૮	૯	૧૦	૫૦	૧૦૦	૫૦૦	૧૦૦૦
Kutch	०	१/२	१	२	३	४	५	६	७	८	९	१०	५०	१००	५००	१०००
Devavnagri	०	१/२	१	२	३	४	५	६ or ६	७	८	९ or ९	१०	५०	१००	५००	१०००
Nepalese	०	१/२	१	२	३	४	५	६	७	८	९	१०	५०	१००	५००	१०००
Tibetan	༠	༡/༢	༡	༢	༣	༤	༥	༦	༧	༨	༩	༡༠	༥༠	༡༠༠	༥༠༠	༡༠༠༠
Mongolian	᠐	᠑/᠒	᠑	᠒	᠓	᠔	᠕	᠖	᠗	᠘	᠙	᠑᠐	᠕᠐	᠑᠐᠐	᠕᠐᠐	᠑᠐᠐᠐
Burmese	၀	၁/၂	၁	၂	၃	၄	၅	၆	၇	၈	၉	၁၀	၅၀	၁၀၀	၅၀၀	၁၀၀၀
Thai-Lao	๐	๑/๒	๑	๒	๓	๔	๕	๖	๗	๘	๙	๑๐	๕๐	๑๐๐	๕๐๐	๑๐๐๐
Lao-Laotian	໐		໑	໒	໓	໔	໕	໖	໗	໘	໙	໑໐				
Javanese	꧐		꧑	꧒	꧓	꧔	꧕	꧖	꧗	꧘	꧙	꧑꧐	꧕꧐	꧑꧐꧐	꧕꧐꧐	꧑꧐꧐꧐
Ordinary Chinese Japanese-Korean	零	半	一	二	三	四	五	六	七	八	九	十	十五	百	百五	千
Official Chinese			壹	貳	叁	肆	伍	陸	柒	捌	玖	拾	拾伍	佰	佰伍	仟
Commercial Chinese			〡	〢	〣	〤	〥	〦	〧	〨	〩	十	〥十	〡百	〥百	〡千
Korean		반	일	이	삼	사	오	육	칠	팔	구	십	오십	백	오백	천
Georgian			ა	ბ	გ	დ	ე	ვ	ზ	ჱ	თ	ი	ნ	რ	ფ	ჩ
			11 ია	20 კ	30 ლ	40 მ	60 ჲ	70 ო	80 პ	90 ჟ	200 ს	300 ტ	400 უ	600 ქ	700 ღ	800 ყ
Ethiopian	◆		፩	፪	፫	፬	፭	፮	፯	፰	፱	፲	፶	፻	፭፻	፲፻
				20 ፳	30 ፴	40 ፵	60 ፷	70 ፸	80 ፹	90 ፺						
Hebrew			א	ב	ג	ד	ה	ו	ז	ח	ט	י	נ	ק	תק	
				20 כ	30 ל	40 מ	60 ס	70 ע	80 פ	90 צ	200 ר	300 ש	400 ת	600 תר	700 תש	800 תת
Greek			Α	Β	Γ	Δ	Ε	Τ	Ζ	Η	Θ	Ι	Ν	Ρ	Φ	Α
				20 Κ	30 Λ	40 Μ	60 Ξ	70 Ο	80 Π		200 Σ	300 Τ	400 Υ	600 Χ	700 Ψ	800 Ω

Hejira Date Conversion Chart

HEJIRA (Hijira, Hegira), the name of the Muslim era (A.H. = Anno Hegirae) dates back to the Christian year 622 when Mohammed "fled" from Mecca, escaping to Medina to avoid persecution from the Koreish tribemen. Based on a lunar year the Muslim year is 11 days shorter.

*=Leap Year (Christian Calendar)

AH Hejira	AD Christian Date
1010	1601, July 2
1011	1602, June 21
1012	1603, June 11
1013	1604, May 30*
1014	1605, May 19
1015	1606, May 9
1016	1607, April 28
1017	1608, April 17*
1018	1609, April 6
1019	1610, March 26
1020	1611, March 16
1021	1612, March 4*
1022	1613, February 21
1023	1614, February 11
1024	1615, January 31
1025	1616, January 20*
1026	1617, January 9
1027	1617, December 29
1028	1618, December 19
1029	1619, December 8
1030	1620, November 26*
1031	1621, November 16
1032	1622, November 5
1033	1623, October 25
1034	1624, October 14*
1035	1625, October 3
1036	1626, September 22
1037	1627, September 12
1038	1628, August 31*
1039	1629, August 21
1040	1630, August 10
1041	1631, July 30
1042	1632, July 19*
1043	1633, July 8
1044	1634, June 27
1045	1635, June 17
1046	1636, June 5*
1047	1637, May 26
1048	1638, May 15
1049	1639, May 4
1050	1640, April 23*
1051	1641, April 12
1052	1642, April 1
1053	1643, March 22
1054	1644, March 10*
1055	1645, February 27
1056	1646, February 17
1057	1647, February 6
1058	1648, January 27*
1059	1649, January 15
1060	1650, January 4
1061	1650, December 25
1062	1651, December 14
1063	1652, December 2*
1064	1653, November 22
1065	1654, November 11
1066	1655, October 31
1067	1656, October 20*
1068	1657, October 9
1069	1658, September 29
1070	1659, September 18
1071	1660, September 6*
1072	1661, August 27
1073	1662, August 16
1074	1663, August 5
1075	1664, July 25*
1076	1665, July 14
1077	1666, July 4
1078	1667, June 23
1079	1668, June 11*
1080	1669, June 1
1081	1670, May 21
1082	1671, May 10
1083	1672, April 29*
1084	1673, April 18
1085	1674, April 7
1086	1675, March 28
1087	1676, March 16*
1088	1677, March 6
1089	1678, February 23
1090	1679, February 12
1091	1680, February 2*
1092	1681, January 21
1093	1682, January 10
1094	1682, December 31
1095	1683, December 20
1096	1684, December 8*
1097	1685, November 28
1098	1686, November 17
1099	1687, November 7
1100	1688, October 26*
1101	1689, October 15
1102	1690, October 5
1103	1691, September 24
1104	1692, September 12*
1105	1693, September 2
1106	1694, August 22
1107	1695, August 12
1108	1696, July 31*
1109	1697, July 20
1110	1698, July 10
1111	1699, June 29
1112	1700, June 18
1113	1701, June 8
1114	1702, May 28
1115	1703, May 17
1116	1704, May 6*
1117	1705, April 25
1118	1706, April 15
1119	1707, April 4
1120	1708, March 23*
1121	1709, March 13
1122	1710, March 2
1123	1711, February 19
1124	1712, February 9*
1125	1713, January 28
1126	1714, January 17
1127	1715, January 7
1128	1715, December 27
1129	1716, December 16*
1130	1717, December 5
1131	1718, November 24
1132	1719, November 14
1133	1720, November 2*
1134	1721, October 22
1135	1722, October 12
1136	1723, October 1
1137	1724, September 19
1138	1725, September 9
1139	1726, August 29
1140	1727, August 19
1141	1728, August 7*
1142	1729, July 27
1143	1730, July 17
1144	1731, July 6
1145	1732, June 24*
1146	1733, June 14
1147	1734, June 3
1148	1735, May 24
1149	1736, May 12*
1150	1737, May 1
1151	1738, April 21
1152	1739, April 10
1153	1740, March 29*
1154	1741, March 19
1155	1742, March 8
1156	1743, February 25
1157	1744, February 15*
1158	1745, February 3
1159	1746, January 24
1160	1747, January 13
1161	1748, January 2
1162	1748, December 22*
1163	1749, December 11
1164	1750, November 30
1165	1751, November 20
1166	1752, November 8*
1167	1753, October 29
1168	1754, October 18
1169	1755, October 7
1170	1756, September 26*
1171	1757, September 15
1172	1758, September 4
1173	1759, August 25
1174	1760, August 13*
1175	1761, August 2
1176	1762, July 23
1177	1763, July 12
1178	1764, July 1*
1179	1765, June 20
1180	1766, June 9
1181	1767, May 30
1182	1768, May 18*
1183	1769, May 7
1184	1770, April 27
1185	1771, April 16
1186	1772, April 4*
1187	1773, March 25
1188	1774, March 14
1189	1775, March 4
1190	1776, February 21*
1191	1777, February 1
1192	1778, January 30
1193	1779, January 19
1194	1780, January 8*
1195	1780, December 28*
1196	1781, December 17
1197	1782, December 7
1198	1783, November 26
1199	1784, November 14*
1200	1785, November 4
1201	1786, October 24
1202	1787, October 13
1203	1788, October 2*
1204	1789, September 21
1205	1790, September 10
1206	1791, August 31
1207	1792, August 19*
1208	1793, August 9
1209	1794, July 29
1210	1795, July 18
1211	1796, July 7*
1212	1797, June 26
1213	1798, June 15
1214	1799, June 5
1215	1800, May 25*
1216	1801, May 14
1217	1802, May 4
1218	1803, April 23
1219	1804, April 12*
1220	1805, April 1
1221	1806, March 21
1222	1807, March 11
1223	1808, February 28*
1224	1809, February 16
1225	1810, February 6
1226	1811, January 26
1227	1812, January 16*
1228	1813, January 6
1229	1813, December 24
1230	1814, December 14
1231	1815, December 3
1232	1816, November 21*
1233	1817, November 11
1234	1818, October 31
1235	1819, October 20
1236	1820, October 9*
1237	1821, September 28
1238	1822, September 18
1239	1823, September 8
1240	1824, August 26*
1241	1825, August 16
1242	1826, August 5
1243	1827, July 25
1244	1828, July 14*
1245	1829, July 3
1246	1830, June 22
1247	1831, June 12
1248	1832, May 31*
1249	1833, May 21
1250	1834, May 10
1251	1835, April 29
1252	1836, April 18*
1253	1837, April 7
1254	1838, March 27
1255	1839, March 17
1256	1840, March 5*
1257	1841, February 23
1258	1842, February 12
1259	1843, February 1
1260	1844, January 22*
1261	1845, January 10
1262	1845, December 30
1263	1846, December 20
1264	1847, December 9
1265	1848, November 27*
1266	1849, November 17
1267	1850, November 6
1268	1851, October 27
1269	1852, October 15*
1270	1853, October 4
1271	1854, September 24
1272	1855, September 13
1273	1856, September 1*
1274	1857, August 22
1275	1858, August 11
1276	1859, July 31
1277	1860, July 20*
1278	1861, July 9
1279	1862, June 29
1280	1863, June 18
1281	1864, June 6*
1282	1865, May 27
1283	1866, May 16
1284	1867, May 5
1285	1868, April 24*
1286	1869, April 13
1287	1870, April 3
1288	1871, March 23
1289	1872, March 11*
1290	1873, March 1
1291	1874, February 18
1292	1875, February 7
1293	1876, January 28*
1294	1877, January 16
1295	1878, January 5
1296	1878, December 26
1297	1879, December 15
1298	1880, December 4*
1299	1881, November 23
1300	1882, November 12
1301	1883, November 2
1302	1884, October 21*
1303	1885, October 10
1304	1886, September 30
1305	1887, September 19
1306	1888, September 7*
1307	1889, August 28
1308	1890, August 17
1309	1891, August 7
1310	1892, July 26*
1311	1893, July 15
1312	1894, July 5
1313	1895, June 24
1314	1896, June 12*
1315	1897, June 2
1316	1898, May 22
1317	1899, May 12
1318	1900, May 1
1319	1901, April 20
1320	1902, April 10
1321	1903, March 30
1322	1904, March 18*
1323	1905, March 8
1324	1906, February 25
1325	1907, February 14
1326	1908, February 4*
1327	1909, January 23
1328	1910, January 13
1329	1911, January 2
1330	1911, December 22
1331	1912, December 11
1332	1913, November 30
1333	1914, November 19
1334	1915, November 9
1335	1916, October 28*
1336	1917, October 17
1337	1918, October 7
1338	1919, September 26
1339	1920, September 15*
1340	1921, September 4
1341	1922, August 24
1342	1923, August 14
1343	1924, August 2*
1344	1925, July 22
1345	1926, July 12
1346	1927, July 1
1347	1928, June 20*
1348	1929, June 9
1349	1930, May 29
1350	1931, May 19
1351	1932, May 7*
1352	1933, April 26
1353	1934, April 16
1354	1935, April 5
1355	1936, March 24*
1356	1937, March 14
1357	1938, March 3
1358	1939, February 21
1359	1940, February 10*
1360	1941, January 29
1361	1942, January 19
1362	1943, January 8
1363	1943, December 28
1364	1944, December 17*
1365	1945, December 6
1366	1946, November 25
1367	1947, November 15
1368	1948, November 3*
1369	1949, October 24
1370	1950, October 13
1371	1951, October 2
1372	1952, September 21*
1373	1953, September 10
1374	1954, August 30
1375	1955, August 20
1376	1956, August 8*
1377	1957, July 29
1378	1958, July 18
1379	1959, July 7
1380	1960, June 25*
1381	1961, June 14
1382	1962, June 4
1383	1963, May 25
1384	1964, May 13*
1385	1965, May 2
1386	1966, April 22
1387	1967, April 11
1388	1968, March 31*
1389	1969, March 20
1390	1970, March 9
1391	1971, February 27
1392	1972, February 16*
1393	1973, February 4
1394	1974, January 25
1395	1975, January 14
1396	1976, January 3*
1397	1976, December 23*
1398	1977, December 12
1399	1978, December 2
1400	1979, November 21
1401	1980, November 9*
1402	1981, October 30
1403	1982, October 19
1404	1983, October 6
1405	1984, September 27*
1406	1985, September 16
1407	1986, September 6
1408	1987, August 26
1409	1988, August 14*
1410	1989, August 3
1411	1990, July 24
1412	1991, July 13
1413	1992, July 2*
1414	1993, June 21
1415	1994, June 10
1416	1995, May 31
1417	1996, May 19*
1418	1997, May 9
1419	1998, April 28
1420	1999, April 17
1421	2000, April 6*
1422	2001, March 26
1423	2002, March 15
1424	2003, March 5
1425	2004, February 22*
1426	2005, February 10
1427	2006, January 31
1428	2007, January 20
1429	2008, January 10*
1430	2008, December 29
1431	2009, December 18
1432	2010, December 8
1433	2011, November 27
1434	2012, November 15*
1435	2013, November 5
1436	2014, October 25
1437	2015, October 15
1438	2016, October 3*
1439	2017, September 22
1440	2018, September 12
1441	2019, September 1
1442	2020, August 20*
1443	2021, August 10
1444	2022, July 30
1445	2023, July 19
1446	2024, July 8*
1447	2025, June 27
1448	2026, June 17
1449	2027, June 6
1450	2028, May 25*

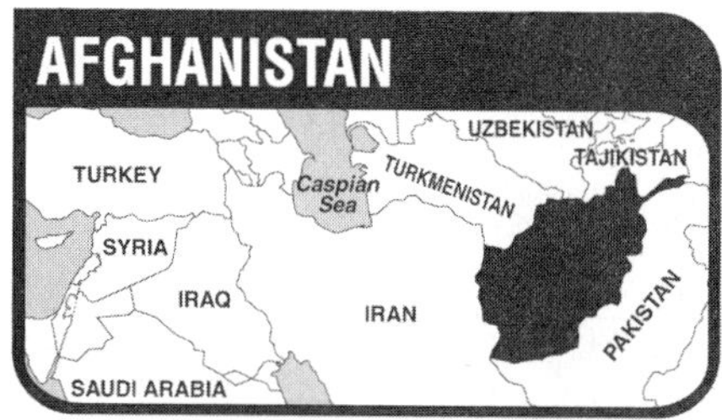

The Islamic Republic of Afghanistan, which occupies a mountainous region of Southwest Asia, has an area of 647,500 sq. km. and a population of 32.74 million. Capital: Kabul. It is bordered by Iran, Pakistan, Tajikistan, Turkmenistan, Uzbekistan and Peoples Republic of China's Sinkiang Province. Agriculture and herding are the principal industries; textile mills and cement factories are additions to the industrial sector. Cotton, wool, fruits, nuts, sheepskin coats and hand-woven carpets are exported but foreign trade has been sporadic since 1979.

Ahmad Shah Durrani unified the Pashtun tribes and founded Afghanistan in 1747. The country served as a buffer between the British and Russian empires until it won independence from national British control in 1919. A brief experiment in democracy ended in a 1973 coup and a 1978 Communist counter-coup. The Soviet Union invaded in 1979 to support the tottering Afghan Communist regime, touching off a long and destructive war. The USSR withdrew in 1989 under relentless pressure by internationally supported anti-Communist mujahedin rebels. A series of subsequent civil wars saw Kabul finally fall in 1996 to the Taliban, a hardline Pakistani-sponsored movement that emerged in 1994 to end the country's civil war and anarchy. Following the 11 September 2001 terrorist attacks in New York City, a US, Allied, and anti-Taliban Northern Alliance military action toppled the Taliban for sheltering Osama Bin Ladin. The UN-sponsored Bonn Conference in 2001 established a process for political reconstruction that included the adoption of a new constitution, a presidential election in 2004, and National Assembly elections in 2005. In December 2004, Hamid Karzai became the first democratically elected president of Afghanistan and the National Assembly was inaugurated the following December. Despite gains toward building a stable central government, a resurgent Taliban and continuing provincial instability - particularly in the south and the east - remain serious challenges for the Afghan Government.

RULERS:

Amanullah, SH1298-1307/1919-1929AD
Habibullah Ghazi (rebel, known as Baccha-i-Saqao) AH1347-1348/1929AD
Muhammad Nadir Shah, SH1308-1312/1929-1933AD
Muhammad Zahir Shah, SH1312-1352/1933-1973AD

MONETARY SYSTEM:

1 Rupee = 100 Paise to 1925
1 Rupees = 10 Afghani, 1925-
1 Afghani = 100 Pul
1 Amani = 20 Afghani

KINGDOM - PRE-REBELLION

Treasury

1919-1920 Issue

1	**1 Rupee**	VG	VF	UNC
	SH1298-99. Green. Arms of King Amanullah at right center. Encountered with and without counterfoil at left. Uniface. Back: Seal.			
	a. SH 1298 (1919). Red serial #.	10.00	35.00	90.00
	b. SH 1299 (1920). Red, black or blue serial #.	5.00	25.00	65.00

1A	**1 Rupee**	Good	Fine	XF
	SH1299 (1920). Brown. Arms of King Amanullah at right center. Without serial #. Back: Without seal. 11x2mm.			
	a. Issued note.	140	500	—
	ct. Color trial. Two known.	—	—	—

Color Abbreviation Guide

New to the *Standard Catalog of ® World Paper Money* are the following abbreviations related to color references:

BC: Back color
PC: Paper color

2	**5 Rupees**	VG	VF	UNC
	SH1298-99. Black on brownish pink underprint. Arms at top center. Date on design at left and right center. Encountered with and without counterfoil at left. Uniface. Back: Seal. BC: Green, purple and tan.			
	a. SH1298 (1919).	10.00	45.00	125
	b. SH1299 (1920).	5.00	22.50	90.00
	c. ND (No date).	—	—	—

Add 20% to market valuations indicated for unissued examples of these notes complete with counterfoil.

4	**50 Rupees**	VG	VF	UNC
	ND, SH1298 (1919). Black on green underprint. Arms at top center. Encountered with and without counterfoil at left. Uniface.	12.50	55.00	175

Add 20% to market valuations indicated for unissued examples of these notes complete with counterfoil.

5	**100 Rupees**	VG	VF	UNC
	SH1299 (1920). Green and gray. Arms at top center. Encountered with and without counterfoil at left. Uniface.	10.00	50.00	140

Add 20% to market valuations indicated for unissued examples of these notes complete with counterfoil.

1926-1928 Issue

6	**5 Afghanis**	VG	VF	UNC
	ND. Light brown and gray on pink and light green underprint. Arms at top center. Back: French text, without handstamps. BC: Greenish gray.	5.00	15.00	75.00

		VG	VF	UNC
7	**5 Afghanis** SH1305 (1926). Dark red. Denomination in upper corners.			
	a. Back green, purple and tan.	27.50	90.00	250
	b. Face green, purple and tan. Back lilac. Toughra at center.	30.00	120	350
	c. Uniface. Back lilac.	15.00	50.00	150
	d. Uniface. Back blue. Rare.	—	—	—

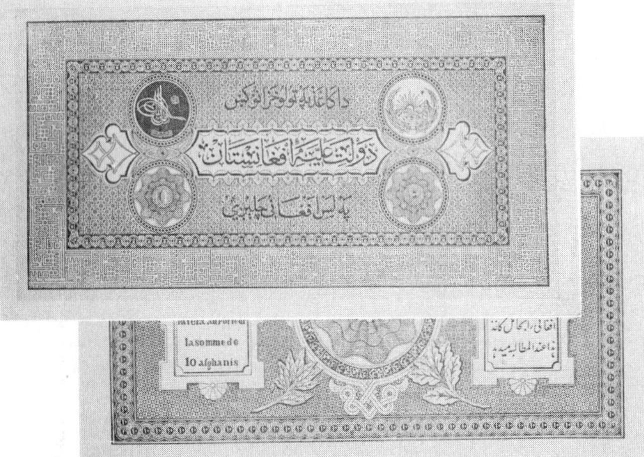

		VG	VF	UNC
8	**10 Afghanis** ND. Brown with tan border. Back: French text at left, without handstamps. BC: Green.	4.00	10.00	45.00

		VG	VF	UNC
9	**10 Afghanis** SH1307 (1928). Black and orange with green border. Back: French text at left without handstamps. With or without serial #. BC: Brown.			
	a. Without watermark.	7.50	25.00	90.00
	b. Watermark: Small squares.	5.00	12.50	55.00

		VG	VF	UNC
10	**50 Afghanis** SH1307 (1928). Green, and red with light brown underprint. Back: French text at left, Persian at right without handstamps. With and without serial #. BC: Green.			
	a. Without watermark.	5.00	15.00	70.00
	b. Watermark: Small squares. Light and dark green varieties.	7.50	40.00	125

1928 REBELLION

Baccha I Saqao

1928 Afghani Issue

		Good	Fine	XF
11	**5 Afghanis** SH1307 (1928). Light brown and gray on pink and light green underprint. National emblem at top center, with one validation handstamp. Back: Three different handstamps, one having the date. Handstamps on #6. BC: Greenish gray.	10.00	30.00	150

		Good	Fine	XF
12	**10 Afghanis** SH1307 (1928). Brown with tan border. Handstamps. One validation handstamp. Back: French text at left, Persian at right. Three different handstamps, one having the date. Handstamps on #8. BC: Green.	7.50	12.50	65.00
13	**50 Afghanis** SH1307 (1928). Green and red with light brown underprint. With and without serial # and handstamps. One validation handstamp. Back: Three different handstamps, one having the date. Light and dark green varieties. Handstamps on #10. BC: Green.	5.00	12.50	65.00

1928 Rupee Issue

		Good	Fine	XF
14	**1 Rupee** ND (1928-1929). Green on yellow underprint. French text at left. Uniface.			
	a. Without additional handstamps.	12.50	55.00	175
	b. With three additional handstamps.	20.00	75.00	300

KINGDOM - POST REBELLION

Ministry of Finance

1936 Issue

		Good	Fine	XF
15	**2 Afghanis** SH1315 (1936). Blue and multicolor. Emblem at top center. In Pashtu language. Block letters and serial #. Back: Independence Monument at center. In Farsi language. Printer: OF-Z.	10.00	20.00	100
16	**5 Afghanis** SH1315 (1936). Lilac and multicolor. Emblem at left, monument a right. In Pashtu language. Block letters and serial #. Back: In Farsi language. Printer: OF-Z.	12.50	50.00	125
16A	**5 Afghanis** SH1315 (1936). Green and multicolor. Emblem at left, monument at right. In Pashtu language. Block letters and serial #. Back: In Farsi language. Printer: OF-Z	12.50	50.00	125
17	**10 Afghanis** SH1315 (1936). Dark brown and multicolor. Arms at left, monument at right. In Pashtu language. Block letters and serial #. Back: In Farsi language. Printer: OF-Z.	20.00	70.00	150

		Good	Fine	XF
18	**20 Afghanis** SH1315 (1936). Red-brown and multicolor. Arms at left, monument at right. In Pashtu language. Block letters and serial #. Back: In Farsi language. Printer: OF-Z.	50.00	120	300

		Good	Fine	XF
19	**50 Afghanis** SH1315 (1936). Blue and multicolor. Arms at left, monument at right. In Pashtu language. Block letters and serial #. Back: In Farsi language. Printer: OF-Z.	60.00	200	550
20	**100 Afghanis** SH1315 (1936). Violet and multicolor. Arms at left, monument at right. In Pashtu language. Block letters and serial #. Back: In Farsi language. Printer: OF-Z.	90.00	275	850

Note: #16-20 w/block letters only. Unc. set $400.00.

ND Issue

		VG	VF	UNC
16B	**5 Afghanis** ND. Lilac and multicolor. Emblem at left, Independence monument at right. In Farsi language. Red serial #. Back: In Pashtu language. Printer: OF-Z	12.50	50.00	125

		VG	VF	UNC
16C	**5 Afghanis** ND. Green and multicolor. Emblem at left, Independence monument at right. Like #16B. In Farsi language. Red serial #. Back: In Pashtu language. Printer: OF-Z	75.00	300	—
17A	**10 Afghanis** ND. Dark brown and multicolor. Arms at left, monument at right. In Farsi language. Red serial #. Back: In Pashtu language. Printer: OF-Z.	12.50	65.00	150
18A	**20 Afghanis** ND. Red-brown and multicolor. Arms at left, monument at right. In Farsi language. Red serial #. Back: In Pashtu language. Printer: OF-Z.	25.00	70.00	250
19A	**50 Afghanis** ND. Blue and multicolor. Arms at left, monument at right. In Farsi language. Red serial #. Back: In Pashtu language. Printer: OF-Z.	30.00	125	350

		VG	VF	UNC
20A	**100 Afghanis** ND. Violet and multicolor. Arms at left, monument at right. In Farsi language. Red serial #. Back: In Pashtu language. Printer: OF-Z.	45.00	250	650

Bank of Afghanistan

1939 Issue

No.	Description	VG	VF	UNC
21	**2 Afghanis** SH1318 (1939). Brown and multicolor. Portrait King Muhammad Zahir (first portrait) at left. Without imprint. Back: Colossal Buddha statue at Bamiyan (destroyed by the Taliban).	1.25	5.00	20.00

No.	Description	VG	VF	UNC
22	**5 Afghanis** SH1318 (1939). Green and multicolor. King Muhammad Zahir (first portrait). Without imprint.	1.25	4.00	15.00
23	**10 Afghanis** SH1318; SH1325. Dark red. King Muhammad Zahir (first portrait). Without imprint.			
	a. SH1318 (1939).	5.00	10.00	25.00
	b. SH1325 (1946).	5.00	10.00	25.00
24	**20 Afghanis** SH1318; SH1325. Violet and multicolor. King Muhammad Zahir (first portrait). Without imprint.			
	a. SH1318 (1939).	225	1,000	—
	b. SH1325 (1946).	225	1,000	—

No.	Description	VG	VF	UNC
25	**50 Afghanis** SH1318; SH1325. Blue and multicolor. King Muhammad Zahir (first portrait). Without imprint. 12x2mm.			
	a. SH1318 (1939).	10.00	20.00	60.00
	b. SH1325 (1946).	10.00	20.00	60.00
26	**100 Afghanis** SH1318; 1325. Dark green and multicolor. King Muhammad Zahir (first portrait). Without imprint.			
	a. SH1318 (1939).	12.50	30.00	75.00
27	**500 Afghanis** SH1318 (1939). Lilac and multicolor. King Muhammad Zahir (first portrait). Without imprint.	90.00	225	950
27A	**1000 Afghanis** SH1318 (1939). Brown, green and multicolor. King Muhammad Zahir (first portrait). Without imprint.	125	500	1,500

1948-1951 Issue

No.	Description	VG	VF	UNC
28	**2 Afghanis** SH1327 (1948). Black, blue and multicolor. King Muhammad Zahir (second portrait). Without imprint. Signature varieties. Back: Fortress. BC: Black.	0.75	2.50	10.00

No.	Description	VG	VF	UNC
29	**5 Afghanis** SH1327 (1948). Green and multicolor. King Muhammad Zahir (second portrait). Without imprint. Signature varieties. BC: Green.	0.75	2.50	10.00
30	**10 Afghanis** SH1327-36. Greenish brown multicolor. King Muhammad Zahir (second portrait). Without imprint. Signature varieties.			
	a. SH1327 (1948).	4.00	12.50	35.00
	b. SH1330 (1951).	2.50	7.50	25.00
	c. SH1333 (1954).	4.00	17.50	55.00
	d. SH1336 (1957).	1.50	5.00	20.00
30A	**10 Afghanis** SH1327 (1948). Brown and multicolor. King Muhammad Zahir (second portrait). Without imprint. Signature varieties.	2.50	7.50	30.00
31	**20 Afghanis** SH1327-36. Blue and multicolor. King Muhammad Zahir (second portrait). Without imprint. Signature varieties.			
	a. SH1327 (1948).	3.00	20.00	55.00
	b. SH1330 (1951).	3.00	25.00	90.00
	c. SH1333 (1954).	3.00	15.00	45.00
	d. SH1336 (1957).	3.00	10.00	35.00
32	**50 Afghanis** SH1327 (1948). Green and multicolor. King Muhammad Zahir (second portrait). Without imprint. Signature varieties.	5.00	15.00	50.00
33	**50 Afghanis** SH 1330-36. Brown and multicolor. King Muhammad Zahir (second portrait). Without imprint. Signature varieties.			
	a. SH1330 (1951).	6.00	17.50	60.00
	b. SH1333 (1954).	7.50	25.00	75.00
	c. SH1336 (1957).	6.00	20.00	50.00

No.	Description	VG	VF	UNC
34	**100 Afghanis** SH1327-36. Purple and multicolor. King Muhammad Zahir (second portrait). Without imprint. Signature varieties. Back: Tomb of King Habibullah in Jalalabad.			
	a. SH1327 (1948).	7.50	25.00	140
	b. SH1330 (1951).	6.00	20.00	110
	c. SH1333 (1954).	10.00	40.00	175
	d. SH1336 (1957).	5.00	15.00	95.00
35	**500 Afghanis** SH1327-1336. Blue and green. King Muhammad Zahir (second portrait). Without imprint. Signature varieties.			
	a. SH1327 (1948).	25.00	90.00	400
	b. SH1333 (1954).	25.00	110	525
	c. SH1336 (1957).	30.00	140	475

No.	Description	VG	VF	UNC
36	**1000 Afghanis** SH1327 (1948). Brown. King Muhammad Zahir (second portrait). Without imprint. Signature varieties.	50.00	140	550

The Republic of Albania, a balkan republic bounded by the Montenegro, Macedonia, Greece and the Adriatic Sea, has an area of 11,100 sq. mi. (28,748 sq. km.) and a population of 3.5 million. Capital: Tirana. The country is mostly agricultural, although recent progress has been made in manufacturing and mining sectors. Petroleum, chrome, iron, copper, cotton textiles, tobacco and wood products are exported.

Since it had been part of the Greek and Roman Empires, little is known of the eary history of Albania. After Roman rule it was overrun by Goths, Bzantines, Venetians and Turks. Skanderbeg, the national hero, resisted the Turks and established an independent Albania in 1443. In 1468 the country again fell to the Turks and remained part of the Ottoman Empire for the next 400 years.

Independence was re-established by revolt in 1912, and the present borders established in 1913 by a conference of European powers which, in 1914, placed Prince William of Wied on the throne - popular discontent forced his abdication within months. In 1920, following World War I and occupancy by several nations, a republic was set up. Ahmet Zogu seized the presidency in 1925, and in 1928, proclaimed him self king with the title Zog I. At the start of World War II, when Albania was invaded by Italy, Zog fled. Victor Emanuel of Italy ruled for a time. Upon the surrender of Italy to the Allies in 1943, German troops occupied the country. They withdrew in 1944, and communist partisans seized power, naming Gen. Enver Hoxha provisional president. IN 1946, following a vicotry by the communist front in 1945 elections, a new constitution modeled on that of the Soviet Union was adopted. In accordance with the 1976 constitution the official name of the country was changes from the Peoples Republic of Albania to the Peoples Socialist Republic of Albania. A general strike by trade unions in 1991 forced the communist government to resign. A new government was elected in March 1992. In 1997 Albania had a major financial crisis which caused civil distrubances and the fall of the administration.

KINGDOM

Banka Kombëtare e Shqipnis

Banca Nazionale d'Albania

1925-1926 Issue

		Good	Fine	XF
1	**5 Lek / 1 Frank AR** ND (1925). Brown and green on multicolor underprint. Eagle on shield at lower center. Printer: Richter & Co, Naples. BC: Brown on multicolor underprint.			
	a. Issued note.	3,000	6,000	12,000
	s. Specimen.	—	Unc	600

		VG	VF	UNC
2	**5 Franka Ari** ND (1926). Dark green on multicolor underprint. Portrait boy's head at right. Back: Vizirs Bridge over river Kiri at center. BC: Purple and multicolor.			
	a. Signature Alberti. Series A-L.	—	—	—
	b. Signature Bianchini. Series M-X.	7.50	35.00	250
	s. Specimen.	—	—	100

		VG	VF	UNC
3	**20 Franka Ari** ND (1926). Dark blue on multicolor underprint. Portrait youth's head at left. Back: Drin Bridge and country landscape near Skutari at center. BC: Red-brown.			
	a. Issued note.	10.00	100	350
	s. Specimen.	—	—	200

		Good	Fine	XF
4	**100 Franka Ari** ND (1926). Lilac on multicolor underprint. Gomsiqe Bridge near Puka at center, portrait King A. Zogu at right. Back: Landscape with river Drin near Skutari. BC: Blue-green and lilac.			
	a. Issued note.	500	1,500	3,000
	s. Specimen.	—	Unc	500

ITALIAN OCCUPATION - 1939-1942

Banka Kombëtare e Shqipnis

Banca Nazionale d'Albania

1939 ND Provisional Issue

		Good	Fine	XF
5	**100 Franka Ari** ND (1939). Lilac on multicolor underprint. Gomisiqe Bridge near Puka at center, portrait King A. Zogu at right. Back: Landscape with river Drin near Skutari. BC: Blue-green and lilac.	200	1,000	1,500

Note: Many of these notes have been chemically washed which has changed the colors.

1939 ND Issue

		VG	VF	UNC
6	**5 Franga** ND (1939). Olive-green and blue. Back: Double headed eagle at left center. BC: Blue on multicolor underprint. Watermark: Victor Emanuel III.			
	a. Issued note.	2.00	15.00	100
	s. Specimen.	—	—	150

#	Description	VG	VF	UNC
7	**20 Franga** ND (1939). Green on olive-green underprint. Seated Roma at bottom center, wolf with Romulus and Remus at right. Back: Double-headed eagle at center. BC: Red-brown and multicolor. Watermark: Victor Emanuel III; Skanderbeg. Printer: ODBI.	3.00	20.00	120

1940 ND Issue

#	Description	VG	VF	UNC
8	**100 Franga** ND (1940). Lilac-brown on multicolor underprint. Peasant woman seated on sheaves with sickle, green double-headed eagle in center. BC: Red-brown and lilac. Printer: ODBI.	10.00	40.00	200
9	**2 Lek** ND (1940). Lilac-blue on orange-brown underprint. Male head at right, crowned arms at left center. Back: Crowned double-headed eagle at left.	4.00	15.00	60.00

#	Description	VG	VF	UNC
10	**5 Lek** ND (1940). Blue and black on yellow underprint. Double-headed eagle at bottom center, crowned arms at left and Italia at right. Back: Crowned arms at left, female bust at right. BC: Dark brown on yellow underprint. Watermark: Italia. Printer: ODBI.	5.00	17.50	75.00

#	Description	VG	VF	UNC
11	**10 Lek** ND (1940). Red and black on brown underprint. Double-headed eagle at bottom center. Back: Crowned arms at left, Italia at right. BC: Dark blue on yellow underprint. Watermark: Victor Emanuel III. Printer: ODBI.	2.00	10.00	40.00

PEOPLES REPUBLIC

Banka e Shtetit Shqiptar

1945 Provisional Issue

Overprint on #10 and 11 exist; however these are currently considered unofficial.

#	Description	Good	Fine	XF
11A	**10 Lek** ND (1945). Red on brown underprint. Overprint on #11. Unofficial fantasy.	—	—	—

#	Description	Good	Fine	XF
12	**20 Franka Ari** ND (1945). Dark blue on multicolor underprint. Portrait youth's head at left. New bank name and double-headed eagle in rectangular overprint on #3. Back: Drin Bridge and country landscape near Skutari at center. BC: Red-brown.			
	a. Prefix A-E.	15.00	85.00	—
	b. Prefix F-J.	8.00	40.00	—

#	Description	Good	Fine	XF
13	**20 Franga** ND (1945). Blue and brown on green underprint. Reclining Roma at bottom center, wolf with Romulus and Remus at right. New bank name and double-headed eagle in rectangular overprint on #7. Back: Double-headed eagle at center. BC: Red-brown and multicolor. Watermark: Victor Emanuel III; Skanderbeg. Printer: ODBI	12.50	65.00	—
14	**100 Franga** ND (1945). Lilac-brown. Peasant woman seated on sheaves with sickle and sheaves at right. New bank name and double-headed eagle in rectangular overprint on #8. BC: Red-brown and lilac. Printer: ODBI	15.00	80.00	—

Note: The note previously listed as #15 could not be confirmed as existing.

1945 Issue

No.	Description	VG	VF	UNC
15	**5 Franga** 1.5.1945. Green, blue and brown on blue underprint. Skanderbeg at left. Back: Arms (eagle) at left. BC: Green on multicolor underprint.	1.50	6.00	20.00

No.	Description	VG	VF	UNC
16	**20 Franga** 1.5.1945. Dark blue and brown on multicolor underprint. Skanderbeg at left. Back: Arms (eagle) at left. BC: Dark blue on multicolor underprint.	2.00	7.50	25.00

No.	Description	VG	VF	UNC
17	**100 Franga** 1.5.1945. Brown and green on multicolor underprint. Skanderbeg at left. Back: Arms (eagle) at left. BC: Brown on multicolor underprint.	3.00	10.00	30.00

No.	Description	VG	VF	UNC
18	**500 Franga** 1.5.1945. Brown and dark blue on multicolor underprint. Skanderbeg at left. Back: Arms (eagle) at left. BC: Brown on multicolor underprint.	25.00	100	400

Note: The note formerly listed as #18A could not be confirmed as existing.

1947 Issue

No.	Description	VG	VF	UNC
19	**10 Lekë** 1947. Brown on multicolor underprint. Arms (eagle) at left, soldier with rifle at right.	1.50	7.50	22.50
20	**50 Lekë** 1947. Dark brown on green underprint. Arms (eagle) at left, soldier with rifle at right.	2.25	12.50	32.50
21	**100 Lekë** 1947. Violet on multicolor underprint. Arms (eagle) at left, soldier with rifle at right.	4.50	25.00	100

No.	Description	VG	VF	UNC
22	**500 Lekë** 1947. Brown on multicolor underprint. Arms (eagle) at left, soldier with rifle at right.	8.00	37.50	125

		VG	VF	UNC
23	**1000 Lekë** 1947. Dark brown on multicolor underprint. Arms (eagle) at left, soldier with rifle at right.	8.00	45.00	300

1949 Issue

		VG	VF	UNC
24	**10 Lekë** 1949. Red and dark blue on green underprint. Arms at center. Back: Arms at right. BC: Red on green underprint.	1.00	5.00	12.50

		VG	VF	UNC
25	**50 Lekë** 1949. Dark blue on green and multicolor underprint. Skanderbeg at right. Back: Soldier's head at right. BC: Dark blue on green underprint.	1.50	5.00	15.00
26	**100 Lekë** 1949. Green on multicolor underprint. Soldier at left, arms at upper center right.	2.50	7.50	22.50

		VG	VF	UNC
27	**500 Lekë** 1949. Brown-violet on multicolor underprint. Hay harvest scene with tractor. Back: Peasant woman with sheaf of wheat at left, arms at right.	3.50	12.50	30.00

		VG	VF	UNC
27A	**1000 Lekë** 1949. Dark brown on multicolor underprint. Portrait Skanderbeg at left, oil well derricks at right. Back: Arms at left, miner with jackhammer at right.	4.50	35.00	300

1957 Issue

		VG	VF	UNC
28	**10 Lekë** 1957. Red, blue and green. Arms at center. Back: Arms at right. Watermark: BSHSH within outlines, repeated.			
	a. Issued note.	0.25	0.75	2.00
	s. Specimen. Red overprint: *MODEL* on face and in reverse on back.	—	—	10.00

		VG	VF	UNC
29	**50 Lekë** 1957. Violet on green underprint. Skanderbeg at right. Back: Arms at center, soldier at right. Watermark: BSHSH within outlines, repeated.			
	a. Issued note.	0.35	1.25	4.00
	s. Specimen. Red overprint: *MODEL* on face and in reverse on back.	—	—	10.00

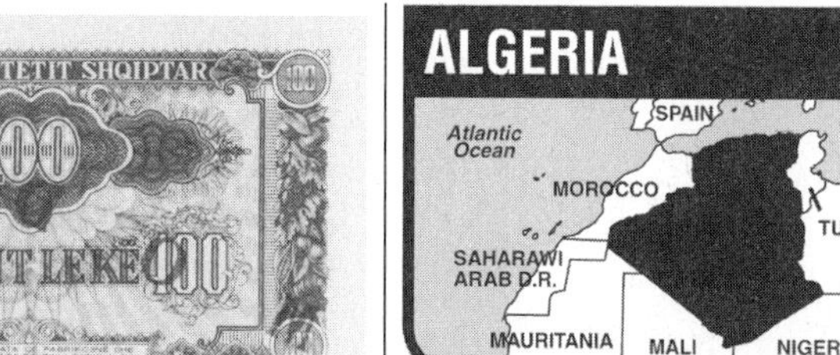

30 100 Lekë

1957. Green. Soldier at left, arms at upper right center. Watermark: BSHSH within outlines, repeated.

	VG	VF	UNC
a. Issued note.	0.50	1.75	5.00
s. Specimen. Red overprint: *MODEL* on face and in reverse on back.	—	—	10.00

31 500 Lekë

1957. Brown-violet. Harvest scene at center, Skanderbeg at right. Back: Peasant woman with sheaf of wheat at left, arms at right. Watermark: BSHSH within outlines, repeated.

	VG	VF	UNC
a. Issued note.	1.00	3.00	10.00
s. Specimen. Red overprint: *MODEL* on face and in reverse on back.	—	—	15.00

32 1000 Lekë

1957. Violet on multicolor underprint. Portrait Skanderbeg at left, oil well derricks at right. Back: Arms at left, miner with jackhammer at right. Watermark: BSHSH within outlines, repeated.

	VG	VF	UNC
a. Issued note.	1.25	4.00	12.50
s. Specimen. Red overprint: *MODEL* on face and in reverse on back.	—	—	15.00

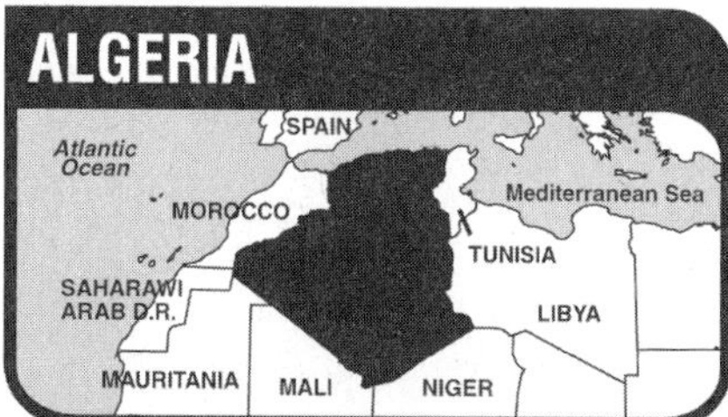

The People's Democratic Republic of Algeria, a North African country fronting on the Mediterranean Sea between Tunisia and Morocco, has an area of 2.382 million sq. km. and a population of 33.77 million. Capital: Algiers. Most of the country's working population is engaged in agriculture although industrial diversification, financed by oil revenues, is making steady progress. Wines, fruits, iron and zinc ores, phosphates, tobacco products, liquified natural gas, and petroleum are exported.

After more than a century of rule by France, Algerians fought through much of the 1950s to achieve independence in 1962. Algeria's primary political party, the National Liberation Front (FLN), has dominated politics ever since. Many Algerians in the subsequent generation were not satisfied, however, and moved to counter the FLN's centrality in Algerian politics. The surprising first round success of the Islamic Salvation Front (FIS) in the December 1991 balloting spurred the Algerian army to intervene and postpone the second round of elections to prevent what the secular elite feared would be an extremist-led government from assuming power. The army began a crackdown on the FIS that spurred FIS supporters to begin attacking government targets. The government later allowed elections featuring pro-government and moderate religious-centered parties, but did not appease the activists who progressively widened their attacks. The fighting escalated into an insurgency, which saw intense fighting between 1992-98 and which resulted in over 100,000 deaths - many attributed to indiscriminate massacres of villagers by extremists. The government gained the upper hand by the late-1990s and FIS's armed wing, the Islamic Salvation Army, disbanded in January 2000. However, small numbers of armed militants persist in confronting government forces and conducting ambushes and occasional attacks on villages. The army placed Abdelaziz Bouteflika in the presidency in 1999 in a fraudulent election but claimed neutrality in his 2004 landslide reelection victory. Longstanding problems continue to face Bouteflika in his second term, including the ethnic minority Berbers' ongoing autonomy campaign, large-scale unemployment, a shortage of housing, unreliable electrical and water supplies, government inefficiencies and corruption, and the continuing activities of extremist militants. The 2006 merger of the Salafist Group for Preaching and Combat (GSPC) with al-Qaida (followed by a name change to al-Qaida in the Lands of the Islamic Maghreb) signaled an increase in bombings, including high-profile, mass-casualty suicide attacks targeted against the Algerian government and Western interests. Algeria must also diversify its petroleum-centered economy, which has yielded a large cash reserve but which has not been used to redress Algeria's many social and infrastructure problems.

RULERS:

French to 1962

MONETARY SYSTEM:

1 Franc = 100 Centimes to 1960
1 Nouveau Franc = 100 Old Francs, 1959-64

FRENCH ADMINISTRATION

Banque de l'Algérie

ALGER (ALGIERS)

1852 Issue

#1-2, 4 not assigned.

#	Note	Good	Fine	XF
3	**100 Francs** ca. 1852-1860. Black. "France" greeting Arab between two reclining women at bottom center. Proof.	—	—	—
5	**500 Francs** ca. 1852-1860. Black. Allegorical male with ship's rudder and mast with sail at left, allegorical male with trident and anchor at right, ancient galleys at upper left and right. "France" greeting Arab between two reclining women at bottom center. Proof.	—	—	—
6	**1000 Francs** 16.10.1870. Blue. Allegorical male with ship's rudder and mast with sail at left, allegorical male with trident and anchor at right, ancient galleys at upper left and right. Medallic caduceus between two reclining women at bottom center. Proof.	—	—	—

1861 Issue

#7-9 not assigned.

#	Note	Good	Fine	XF
10	**100 Francs** ca. 1861-1868. Blue. Allegorical male with ship's rudder and mast with sail at left, allegorical male with trident and anchor at right, caduceus between two cornucopiae at top center. Ancient galley between two reclining women. Proof.	—	—	—
11	**500 Francs** ca. 1861-1868. Blue. Allegorical male with ship's rudder and mast with sail at left, allegorical male with trident and anchor at right, caduceus between two cornucopiae at top center. Frame for date with *ALGER* between two reclining women.			
	a. Issued note without overprint.	—	—	—
	b. Overprint: *Succ. d'Oran.* 26.7.1865.	—	—	—
	c. Overprint: *Succ. de Bone.* 14.4.1868.	—	—	—
	d. Overprint: *Succ. de Constantine.* 4.10.1870; 16.11.1870.	—	—	—

1868-1877 Issue

#12 Not assigned. Note: For 1000 Francs on 100 Francs 1892, overprint: *BANQUE DE L'ALGÉRIE* on remainders of Banque de France type (#65b), see Tunisia #31.

		Good	Fine	XF
13	**5 Francs** 31.5.1873. Blue. Mercury at left, peasant at right.	425	—	—

		Good	Fine	XF
14	**10 Francs** 10.2.1871; 15.5.1871; 20.11.1871. Blue. Head at left and right.	—	—	—

		Good	Fine	XF
15	**20 Francs** 1873; 22.10.1874; 2.8.1877; 24.8.1887; 27.10.1892. Blue. Mercury at left, Hercules at right.	550	1,100	2,500
16	**25 Francs** 15.10.1870; 15.10.1872. Blue. Standing figure at left and right, head at lower center. Rare.	—	—	—

		Good	Fine	XF
17	**50 Francs** 1873; 21.6.1877. Blue. Cherubs at lower left and right, woman's head at bottom center. Back: Four medallic heads on oval band design.	550	1,100	2,500

		Good	Fine	XF
18	**100 Francs** 1874; 1883; 1887; 1892; 1903. Blue. Boy with oar and hammer at left, boy with shovel and sickle at right, woman's head between snakes at bottom center.	550	1,350	3,000
19	**500 Francs** 1874; 1903. Blue. Fortuna at left, Mercury at right. Two boys seated at bottom. Rare.	—	—	—
20	**1000 Francs** 1875; 1903. Blue. Woman with oar at left, blacksmith at right. Two boys with lion at bottom. Rare.	—	—	—

Bone

1868-1877 Issue

#21-24 not assigned.

		Good	Fine	XF
25	**50 Francs** 14.4.1868. Blue. Rare.	—	—	—

		Good	Fine	XF
27	**100 Francs** 9.8.1877. Blue. Boy with oar and hammer at left, boy with shovel and sickle at right, woman's head between snakes at bottom center. Punch hole cancelled.	—	—	—

Color Abbreviation Guide

New to the *Standard Catalog of ® World Paper Money* are the following abbreviations related to color references:

BC: Back color
PC: Paper color

Constantine

1868-1877 Issue

#28-33, 35-37, 39 not assigned.

		Good	Fine	XF
34	**50 Francs** 20.9.1870. Blue. Rare.	—	—	—

		Good	Fine	XF
38	**500 Francs** 4.10.1870; 16.11.1870. Blue. Allegorical male with ship's rudder and mast with sail at left, allegorical male with trident and anchor at right, caduceus between two cornucopiae at top center, frame for date with *ALGER* between two reclining women. Punch hole cancelled.	—	—	—

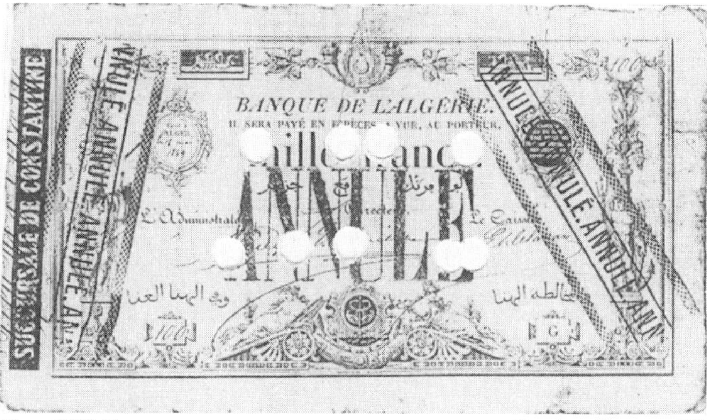

		Good	Fine	XF
40	**1000 Francs** 18.5.1869. Blue.	—	—	—

Oran

1861 Issue

#41-44, 47-48, 50 not assigned.

		Good	Fine	XF
45	**50 Francs** 26.7.1864; 26.10.1864. Blue. Rare.	—	—	—

		Good	Fine	XF
46	**100 Francs** 26.10.1861; 8.4.1864. Black. Allegorical male with ship's rudder and mast with sail at left, allegorical male with trident and anchor at right, caduceus between two cornucopiae at top center, "France" greeting Arab between two reclining women at bottom center. Punch hole cancelled. Rare.	—	—	—

		Good	Fine	XF
49	**1000 Francs** 11.8.1868. Blue. Allegorical male with ship's rudder and mast with sail at left, allegorical male with trident and anchor at right, ancient galleys at upper left and right, medallic caduceus between two reclining women at bottom center. Punch hole cancelled.	—	—	—

W/o Branch

1903-1912 Issue

#50-70 not assigned and being held for Philippeville and Tlemcen branches, from which no notes are currently known. #71-76 like #13, 15, 17-20 but without *ALGER* or any branch name overprint.

		Good	Fine	XF
71	**5 Francs** 1909-1925. Blue. Mercury seated at left, peasant seated at right. Back: Facing lion's head at top, medallic head of Mercury at left and Alexander the Great at right.			
	a. 15.12.1909; 4.7.1911; 12.6.1912; 17.7.1914; 23.11.1914; 2.3.1915.	22.50	90.00	300
	b. 1.8.1916-6.4.1925.	17.50	65.00	250
		VG	**VF**	**UNC**
72	**20 Francs** July 1903; May 1910. Blue. Mercury at left, Hercules at right.	—	—	—

		Good	Fine	XF
73	**50 Francs** 21.3.1903; 2.3.1904; 15-29.4.1910. Blue. Cherubs at lower left and right, woman's head at bottom center. Back: Four medallic heads on oval band design.	115	325	675
74	**100 Francs** 6.3.1907; 18.9.1911; 6.10.1911; 9.10.1911; 26.3.1919. Blue. Boy standing with ornamented rudder and hammer at left, boy standing with shovel and sickle at right, woman's head in wreath between snakes at bottom center.	70.00	200	550

No.	Description	Good	Fine	XF
75	**500 Francs** 1903-1924. Blue. Fortuna at left, Mercury at right, two boys seated at bottom.			
	a. 1903; 15.5.1909.	140	385	1,000
	b. 28.11.1918; 3.12.1918; 24.1.1924; 22.2.1924; 25.2.1924.	80.00	225	750
	s. Specimen. 33.5.3091 (sic).	—	Unc	750

No.	Description	Good	Fine	XF
76	**1000 Francs** 1903-1924. Blue. Woman with oar at left, blacksmith at right, two boys with lion at bottom.			
	a. 1903; 1909.	325	675	1,750
	b. 16.11.1918; 25.11.1918; 28.11.1918; 5.1.1924; 1.2.1924; 8.2.1924; 25.3.1924; 16.4.1924; 7.5.1924.	115	275	725

1913-1926 Issue

No.	Description	VG	VF	UNC
77	**5 Francs** 1924-1941. Red-orange, blue and multicolor. Girl with kerchief at right. 4 signature varieties. Back: Veiled woman with fruit at center right, wharf scene behind. BC: blue and mlticolor. Watermark: Draped head of woman.			
	a. Serial # at upper center 1924-15.1.1941.	0.50	5.00	35.00
	b. Without serial #. 24.1.1941-25.9.1941.	0.25	2.00	25.00
78	**20 Francs** 1914-1942. Dull purple on blue underprint. Portrait young woman at lower right. 4 signature varieties. Back: Two youths with plants. Watermark: Arabic seal top left, draped head of woman bottom right. 166x105mm.			
	a. 9.2.1914-1921.	55.00	300	—
	b. 17.6.1924-31.5.1932.	2.00	35.00	165
	c. 1933-13.3.1942.	1.00	6.00	75.00

No.	Description	Good	Fine	XF
79	**50 Francs** 1.8.1913; 11.9.1913; 17.9.1913; 25.9.1913. Violet. Mosque at right, aerial view of city of Algiers at bottom center. Back: Child picking fruit from tree, woman seated at center. Watermark: Draped head of woman at left, Arabic seal at right.	325	775	—
		VG	**VF**	**UNC**
80	**50 Francs** 28.5.1920-1938. Green. Mosque at right, aerial view of city of Algiers at bottom center. Like #79. 3 signature varieties. Back: Child picking fruit from tree, woman seated at center. Watermark: Draped head of woman at left, Arabic seal at right.			
	a. Issued note.	55.00	115	350
	s. Specimen. 1.2.9124 (sic).	—	—	225

No.	Description	VG	VF	UNC
81	**100 Francs** 1921-1938. Purple and brown on blue underprint. Two boys at left, Arab with camel at right.			
	a. 3.1.1921; 22.9.1921;	60.00	225	—
	b. 1.5.1928-20.10.1938.	30.00	115	275

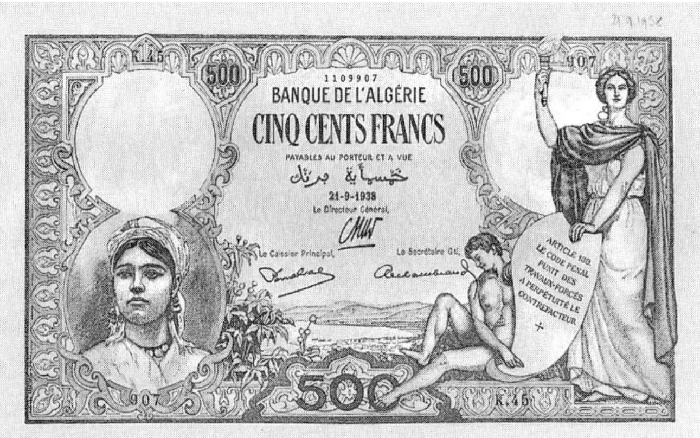

82	**500 Francs**	VG	VF	UNC
	28.6.1926; 2.8.1926; 20.9.1938; 21.9.1938; 22.9.1939; 17.1.1942; 21.1.1942; 25.2.1942. Green and blue-violet on multicolor underprint. Girl's head at left, woman with torch and youth at right. Back: Seated and standing figures with pictures and landscape in background.	40.00	300	—

83	**1000 Francs**	VG	VF	UNC
	28.6.1926-21.9.1939. Brown-violet. Woman with sword and child at left. Algerian woman with child at right. Back: "France" seated with arm on shoulder of seated Arab woman at upper center.			
	a. Issued note.	115	475	—
	s. Specimen. ND.	—	—	700

1938-1939 Issue

84	**50 Francs**	VG	VF	UNC
	2.9.1938-19.8.1942. Multicolor. Veiled woman and man with red fez at right. Back: City with ruins of amphitheatre in background. Watermark: Woman's head.	1.00	10.00	65.00

85	**100 Francs**	VG	VF	UNC
	3.7.1939-5.3.1942. Multicolor. Algerian with turban at left. Back: Plowing with oxen at center. Watermark: Woman's head.	1.50	22.50	100

VICHY GOVERNMENT

Banque de l'Algérie

1941 Issue

86	**1000 Francs**	Good	Fine	XF
	12.11.1941; 12.12.1941; 6.8.1942; 17.8.1942; 7.10.1942; 19.10.1942; 6.11.1942. Multicolor. French colonial family and field work. Watermark: Woman's head.	15.00	80.00	300

Note: For #86 with overprint: *TRÉSOR*, see France #112.

1942 Issue

87	**50 Francs**	VG	VF	UNC
	27.7.1942-3.4.1945. Multicolor. Veiled woman and man with red fez at right. Like #84. Back: City with ruins of amphitheatre in background. Watermark: *BANQUE DE L'ALGÉRIE.*	1.25	12.50	75.00

88	**100 Francs**	VG	VF	UNC
	27.3.1942-23.7.1945. Multicolor. Algerian with turban at left. Like #85. Back: Plowing with oxen at center. Watermark: *BANQUE DE L'ALGÉRIE.*	1.00	15.00	85.00

		Good	Fine	XF
89	**1000 Francs** 6.3.1942; 25.3.1942; 14.4.1942; 17.8.1942; 7.10.1942; 6.11.1942. Multicolor. French colonial family and field work. Like #86. Watermark: *BANQUE DE L'ALGÉRIE.*	15.00	80.00	300

		VG	VF	UNC
90	**5000 Francs** 1942 Blue and pink. Young Algerian woman at left, woman with torch and shield at right. Back: Two women with jugs at center. Watermark: Ornamental design and head.			
	a. 2.1.1942; 23.1.1942; 20.2.1942; 9.4.1942; 18.5.1942; 22.6.1942; 22.7.1942; 17.8.1942; 22.8.1942; 24.8.1942.	225	550	—
	s. Specimen. 9.4.1942; 26.6.1942.	—	—	700

Note: For #90 with overprint: *TRÉSOR,* see France #113.

ALLIED OCCUPATION

Banque de l'Algérie

1942-1943 Issue

		VG	VF	UNC
91	**5 Francs** 16.11.1942. Green. Back: Facing woman at right.	0.25	1.50	6.50

		VG	VF	UNC
92	**20 Francs** 1942-1945. Purple on blue underprint. Portrait young woman at lower right. Similar to #78. Back: Two youths with plants. Watermark: *BANQUE de l'ALGÉRIE.* 122x99mm.			
	a. Signature titles: *L'Inspecteur Général* and *Le Caissier Principal.* 11.11.1942-30.5.1944.	0.50	5.00	35.00
	b. Signature titles: *Le Caissier Principal* and *Le Secrétaire Général.* 29.11.1944; 2.2.1945; 3.4.1945; 7.5.1945.	0.50	6.00	40.00
92A	**20 Francs** 17.3.1943. Specimen perforated *SPECIMEN.* Dark green with red and black text.	—	—	—

		Good	Fine	XF
93	**500 Francs** 29.3.1943-23.12.1943. Blue and green. Two boys at left, Bedouin with camel at right.	10.00	75.00	250

Note: For #93 with overprint: *TRÉSOR* see France #111.

1944-45 Issue

		VG	VF	UNC
94	**5 Francs** 1944 Red, blue and multicolor. Girl with kerchief at right. Similar to #77 but smaller size. Back: Veiled woman with fruit at center right, wharf scene behind.			
	a. Signature titles: *L'Inspecteur Gal.* and *Le Caissier Pal.* 8.2.1944.	0.25	1.00	7.00
	b. Signature titles: *Secret. Gen.* and *Caissier Principal.* 2.10.1944.	0.25	1.00	6.50

#	Note	Good	Fine	XF
95	**500 Francs** 15.9.1944. Violet. Two boys at left, Bedouin with camel at left. Like #93. Watermark: *BANQUE DE L'ALGÉRIE* repeated.	10.00	75.00	250

#	Note	VG	VF	UNC
96	**1000 Francs** 23.3.1945; 23.5.1945; 23.3.1949. Multicolor. Woman at left, sailing ship at right. Back: Farmers at left, woman with Liberty at right.	550	1,750	—

FRENCH ADMINISTRATION - POST WWII

Région Economique d'Algérie

1944 First Issue

Law 31.1.1944

This series was exchangeable until 1.3.1949.

#	Note	VG	VF	UNC
97	**50 Centimes** *L.1944.* Red. Fig trees at center, palm tree at left and right. Back: Eight coat-of-arms in border.			
	a. Series letter: C; C1-C4.	0.35	1.50	7.50
	b. Series letter: F; F1.	0.75	3.00	15.00
98	**1 Franc** *L.1944.* Blue to dark blue. Fig trees at center, palm tree at left and right. Back: Eight coat-of-arms in border.			
	a. Series letter: B; B1-B4.	0.35	1.50	7.50
	b. Series letter: E; E1.	0.75	3.00	15.00

#	Note	VG	VF	UNC
99	**2 Francs** *L.1944.* Dark green to olive-black. Fig trees at center, palm tree at left and right. Back: Eight coat-of-arms in border.			
	a. Series letter: A; A1-A3.	0.50	2.00	10.00
	b. Series letter: D; D1; D2.	1.00	4.00	20.00

1944 Second Issue

#	Note	VG	VF	UNC
100	**50 Centimes** *L.1944.* Orange to red. Fig trees at center, palm tree at left and right. Overprint: *2e T.* at left, series letter at right. Back: Eight coat-of-arms in border.	0.40	1.75	8.50

#	Note	VG	VF	UNC
101	**1 Franc** *L.1944.* Blue to dark blue. Fig trees at center, palm tree at left and right. Overprint: *2e T.* at left, series letter at right. Back: Eight coat-of-arms in border.	0.40	1.75	8.50
102	**2 Francs** *L.1944.* Dark green. Fig trees at center, palm tree at left and right. Overprint: *2e T.* at left, series letter at right. Back: Eight coat-of-arms in border.	0.50	2.25	11.50

Banque de l'Algérie

1946-1948 Issue

#	Note	VG	VF	UNC
103	**20 Francs** 4.6.1948. Green. Ornamental design.	1.00	7.50	50.00
104	**1000 Francs** 9.12.1946; 7.2.1947; 8.5.1947; 18.9.1947; 4.11.1947; 18.11.1947. Brown and yellow. Isis at right.	40.00	175	400
105	**5000 Francs** 4.11.1946; 4.7.1947; 7.10.1949. Multicolor. Pythian Apollo at left.	40.00	165	400

Banque de l'Algérie et de la Tunisie

Note: For 50 FRANCS type of 1946 (3.2.1949) see Tunisia #23. For 100 FRANCS type of 1946 see Tunisia #24. For 500 FRANCS type of 1946 see Tunisia #25. For 1000 FRANCS type of 1950 see Tunisia #29. For 5000 FRANCS type of 1950 see Tunisia #30.

1949-1955 Issue

#	Note	VG	VF	UNC
106	**500 Francs** 3.1.1950-8.8.1956. Green and multicolor. Ram at center, Bacchus at right.			
	a. Issued note.	20.00	100	300
	s. Specimen. Perforated: *SPECIMEN.*	—	—	600

		VG	VF	UNC
107	**1000 Francs**			
	1949-1958. Brown and yellow. Isis at right. Like #104.			
	a. 13.10.1949; 22.11.1949; 8.3.1950; 6.7.1950; 20.9.1950; 14.12.1950.	17.50	100	300
	b. 17.4.1953-24.4.1958.	15.00	85.00	250
	s. Specimen. Perforated: *SPECIMEN*.	—	—	400

		VG	VF	UNC
108	**5000 Francs**			
	25.11.1949; 2.2.1950; 15.5.1951. Multicolor. Pythian Apollo at left, penal code blacked out at bottom center. Like #105.	25.00	120	350

		VG	VF	UNC
109	**5000 Francs**			
	1949-1956. Multicolor. Pythian Apollo at left, penal code shows at bottom center. Like #108.			
	a. 7.10.1949; 8.11.1949; 14.11.1949; 3.5.1950; 25.5.1950; 20.7.1950; 25.7.1950; 31.7.1950; 30.8.1950; 15.5.1951; 3.10.1951; 6.11.1951; 12.11.1951.	25.00	120	350
	b. 11.2.1952; 20.3.1953; 12.5.1953; 22.6.1953; 1.9.1953; 12.5.1955; 21.6.1955; 1.12.1955; 11.12.1955; 4.1.1956.	25.00	100	300

		VG	VF	UNC
110	**10,000 Francs**			
	31.1.1955-9.10.1957. Blue and multicolor. Audouin's gulls with city of Algiers in background.	25.00	140	400

1960 Provisional Issue

		VG	VF	UNC
111	**5 NF on 500 Francs**			
	29.10.1956; 2.11.1956; 13.11.1956. Overprint on #106. Green and multicolor. Ram at center, Bacchus at right.	75.00	275	700
112	**10 NF on 1000 Francs**			
	13.5.1958; 27.5.1958; 22.7.1958; 23.7.1958. Overprint on #107. Brown and yellow. Isis at right.	75.00	275	700

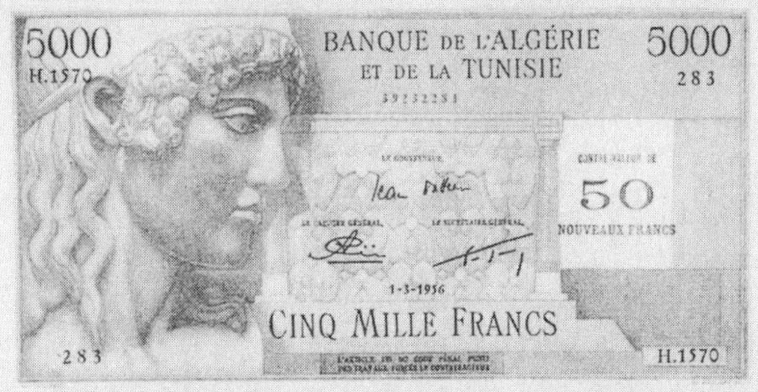

		VG	VF	UNC
113	**50 NF on 5000 Francs**			
	1.3.1956; 27.2.1956. Overprint on #109. Multicolor. Pythian Apollo at left, penal code shows at bottom center.	165	450	—

		VG	VF	UNC
114	**100 NF on 10,000 Francs**			
	22.1.1958-14.3.1958. Overprint on #110. Blue and multicolor. Audouin's gulls with city of Algiers in background.	165	450	—

Banque de l'Algérie

1956-1958 Issue

		VG	VF	UNC
115	**100 Francs**			
	ND. Multicolor. Head at right. Like #116. Back: Bank name in French. (Not issued).	—	—	1,650

		VG	VF	UNC
116	**500 Francs**			
	8.2.1956; 17.5.1956. Multicolor. Head at right. Back: Bank name in Arabic. (Not issued).			
	a. Fully printed note.	—	—	1,650
	s. Specimen.	—	—	—

117	500 Francs	VG	VF	UNC
	2.1.1958-22.4.1958. Blue-green and multicolor. Griffon vulture and Tawny eagle perched on rock. Back: Native objects and sheep.	15.00	85.00	300

117A	1000 Francs	VG	VF	UNC
	ND. Multicolor. Rare.	—	—	—

117B	5000 Francs	VG	VF	UNC
	ND. Multicolor.	—	—	—

1959 Issue

118	5 Nouveaux Francs	VG	VF	UNC
	1959. Green and multicolor. Ram at bottom center, Bacchus at right. Back: Like #106.			
	a. 31.7.1959; 18.12.1959.	12.50	85.00	340
	s. Specimen. 31.7.1959.	—	—	175

119	10 Nouveaux Francs	VG	VF	UNC
	1959-1961. Brown and yellow. Isis at right. Back: Like #104.			
	a. 31.7.1959-2.6.1961.	12.50	100	350
	s. Specimen. 31.7.1959.	—	—	185

120	50 Nouveaux Francs	VG	VF	UNC
	1959. Multicolor. Pythian Apollo at left, penal code shows at bottom center. Back: Like #109.			
	a. 31.7.1959; 18.12.1959.	32.50	175	550
	s. Specimen. 31.7.1959.	—	—	400

121	100 Nouveaux Francs	VG	VF	UNC
	1959-1961. Blue and multicolor. Seagulls with city of Algiers in background. Back: Like #110.			
	a. 31.7.1959; 18.12.1959.	60.00	225	600
	b. 3.6.1960; 25.11.1960; 10.2.1961; 2.6.1961; 29.9.1961.	30.00	115	425
	s. Specimen. 31.7.1959.	—	—	200

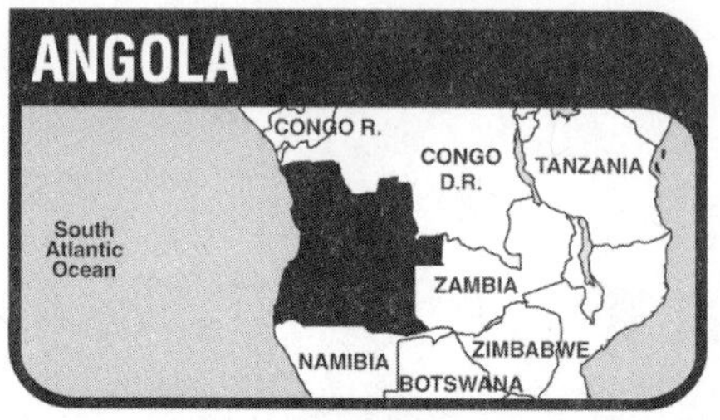

ANDORRA

Bay of Biscay FRANCE SPAIN Mediterranean Sea

Andorra (Principal d' Andorra), previously an autonomous co-principality that became a sovereign nation with a constitution in May 1993. It is situated on the southern slopes of the Pyreness Mountains between France and Spain, has an area of 175 sq. mi. (453 sq. km.) and a population of 80,000. Capital: Andorra la Vella. Tourism is the chief source of income. Timber, cattle and derivatives, and furniture are exported. According to tradition, the independence of Andorra derives from a charter Charlemagne granted the people of Andorra in 806 in recognition of their help in battling the Moors. An agreement between the Court of Foix (France) and the Bishop of Seo de Urgel (Spanish) in 1278 to recognize each other as Co-Princes of Andorra gave the state what has been its politcal form and territoral extent continously to the present day. Over the years, the title on the French side passed to the Kings of Navarre, then to the Kings of France, and is now held by the President of France. In 1806, Napoleon declared Andorra a republic, but today it is referred to as a principality. During the Spanish Civil War, there was an issue of emergency money in the Catalan language.

MONETARY SYSTEM:

1 Pesseta (Catalan) = 100 Centims

1936 SPANISH CIVIL WAR

Consell General de les Valls d'Andorra

Decret No. 112 - 1936 First Issue

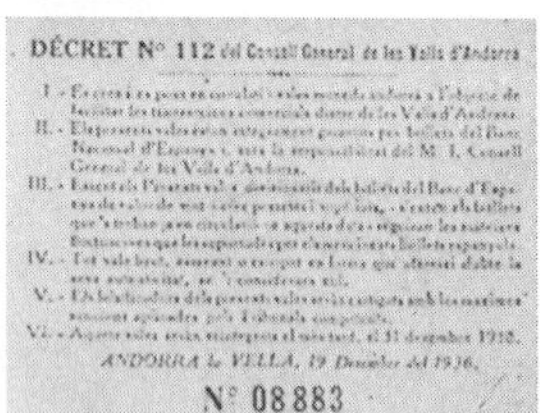

No.	Denomination	VG	VF	UNC
1	**1 Pesseta** 19.12.1936. Blue. Arms at top center.	285	875	2,500
2	**2 Pessetes** 19.12.1936. Blue. Arms at top center.	325	975	2,900
3	**5 Pessetes** 19.12.1936. Blue. Arms at top center.	375	1,250	3,750
4	**10 Pessetes** 19.12.1936. Blue. Arms at top center.	550	1,750	5,500

1936 Second Issue

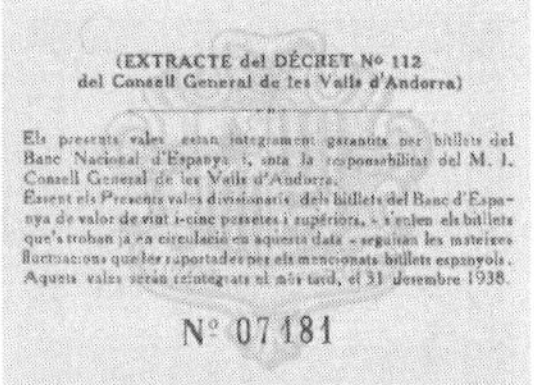

No.	Denomination	VG	VF	UNC
5	**50 Centims** 19.12.1936. Brown on tan underprint. Arms at top center. BC: Blue on tan underprint.	85.00	275	825
6	**1 Pesseta** 19.12.1936. Brown. Arms at top center.	90.00	300	875
7	**2 Pessetes** 19.12.1936. Brown. Arms at top center.	200	650	1,950
8	**5 Pessetes** 19.12.1936. Brown. Arms at top center.	325	1,050	3,000

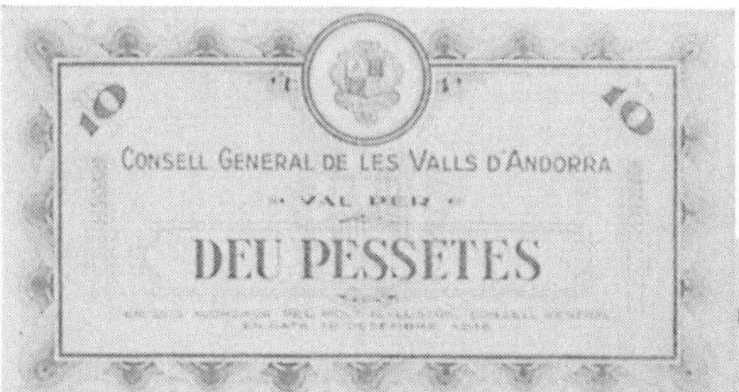

No.	Denomination	VG	VF	UNC
9	**10 Pessetes** 19.12.1936. Brown. Arms at top center.	400	1,450	5,000

ANGOLA

The Peoples Republic of Angola, a country on the west coast of southern Africa bounded by Zaïre, Zambia and Namibia (South-West Africa), has an area of 1.25 million sq. km. and a population of 12.53 million, predominantly Bantu in origin. Capital: Luanda. Most of the people are engaged in subsistence agriculture. However, important oil and mineral deposits make Angola potentially one of the richest countries in Africa. Iron and diamonds are exported.

Angola is rebuilding its country after the end of a 27-year civil war in 2002. Fighting between the Popular Movement for the Liberation of Angola (MPLA), led by Jose Eduardo Dos Santos, and the National Union for the Total Independence of Angola (UNITA), led by Jonas Savimbi, followed independence from Portugal in 1975. Peace seemed imminent in 1992 when Angola held national elections, but UNITA renewed fighting after being beaten by the MPLA at the polls. Up to 1.5 million lives may have been lost - and 4 million people displaced - in the quarter century of fighting. Savimbi's death in 2002 ended UNITA's insurgency and strengthened the MPLA's hold on power. President Dos Santos has announced legislative elections will be held in September 2008, with presidential elections planned for sometime in 2009.

RULERS:

Portuguese to 1975

MONETARY SYSTEM:

1 Milreis = 1000 Reis = 20 Macutas to 1911
100 Centavos - 1 Escudo, 1911
1 Escudo = 1 Milreis
1 Escudo = 100 Centavos, 1954-1977

STEAMSHIP SEALS

Type I
LOANDA

Type II
LISBOA

Type III
C,C,A

C,C,A = Colonias, Commercio, Agricultura.

PORTUGUESE ADMINISTRATION

Junta da Fazenda Publica da Provincia d'Angola

1861 Issue

No.	Denomination	Good	Fine	XF
1	**1000 Reis** 1.7.1861; 13.9.1867. Black. Arms at top center, legend ends: ...*D'ANGOLA*. Various date and signature varieties. 150x120mm.	—	—	—
2	**2000 Reis** 1.7.1861. Red. Arms at top center, legend ends: ...*D'ANGOLA*. Various date and signature varieties. 160x120mm.	—	—	—
3	**5000 Reis** 1861. Black. Arms at top center, legend ends: ...*D'ANGOLA*. Various date and signature varieties. 160x120mm.	—	—	—
4	**20,000 Reis** 1861. Black. Arms at top center, legend ends: ...*D'ANGOLA*. Various date and signature varieties. 160x120mm.	—	—	—

1877-1884 Issue

No.	Denomination	Good	Fine	XF
5	**1000 Reis** 1.10.1884. Black on gray underprint. Arms at top center, legend ends: ...*DE ANGOLA*. Various date and signature varieties. 186x134mm.	—	—	—
6	**2000 Reis** Arms at top center, legend ends: ...*DE ANGOLA*. Various date and signature varieties.	—	—	—
7	**5000 Reis** Black. Arms at top center, legend ends: ...*DE ANGOLA*. Various date and signature varieties.	—	—	—

		Good	Fine	XF
8	**10,000 Reis** Black. Arms at top center, legend ends: ...*DE ANGOLA.* Various date and signature varieties.	—	—	—
9	**20,000 Reis** 1.10.1877. Black on blue underprint. Arms at top center, legend ends: ...*DE ANGOLA.* Various date and signature varieties. 196x137mm.	—	—	—

Banco Nacional Ultramarino

1865 Issue

		Good	Fine	XF
10	**5000 Reis** 1865. Black. Sailing ship at top center. *Succursal* (Branch) *em LOANDA.* Various date and signature varieties. 211x127mm.	—	—	—

		Good	Fine	XF
11	**10,000 Reis** 7.7.1865. Black. Sailing ship at top center. *Succursal* (Branch) *em LOANDA.* Various date and signature varieties. 176x111mm.	—	—	—
12	**20,000 Reis** 1865. Black. Sailing ship at top center. *Succursal* (Branch) *em LOANDA.* Various date and signature varieties. 215x126mm.	—	—	—

1876-1877 Issue

		Good	Fine	XF
13	**1000 Reis** 1876. Black. Sailing ship at top center. Various date and signature varieties.	—	—	—

		Good	Fine	XF
14	**2000 Reis** 1.6.1877. Black. Sailing ship at top center. Various date and signature varieties.	—	—	—
15	**2500 Reis** 1876. Black. Sailing ship at top center. Various date and signature varieties.	—	—	—

1878-1890 Issue

		Good	Fine	XF
16	**1000 Reis** 1878-1890. Black. Sailing ship at top center. Various date and signature varieties. 173x120mm.	—	—	—
17	**2000 Reis** 21.3.1888. Green. Sailing ship at top center. Various date and signature varieties.	—	—	—

		Good	Fine	XF
18	**5000 Reis** 1878-90. Sailing ship at top center. Various date and signature varieties.	Good	Fine	XF
	a. Issued note.	—	—	—
	b. With two oval handstamps: *Cobre 1896.* (-old date 30.6.1880).	—	—	—
19	**10,000 Reis** 1878-1890. Sailing ship at top center. Various date and signature varieties.	—	—	—
20	**20,000 Reis** 28.1.1890. Similar to #14. Gray-green. Sailing ship at top center. Various date and signature varieties. 168x115mm.	—	—	—

1892 Emergency Issue

Issued because of small change shortages. Redeemed in 1905.

		Good	Fine	XF
20A	**100 Reis** 1892; 1893; 1895. Black on red-brown underprint. Crowned arms at upper center.	175	550	—
20B	**200 Reis** 1892; 1893; 1895. Red on green underprint. Crowned arms at upper center.	—	—	—
20C	**500 Reis** 1892; 1893; 1895. Blue on ivory underprint. Crowned arms at upper center.	—	—	—

1897-1905 Issue

		Good	Fine	XF
21	**1000 Reis** 2.1.1897. Green. Man with bow and arrow at left, ship at top center. Various date and signature varieties.	—	—	—

		Good	Fine	XF
22	**2500 Reis** 20.2.1905. Gray-blue. Sailing ship at left, landscape at center. Date and signature varieties. 144x105mm.	—	—	—

		Good	Fine	XF
23	**5000 Reis** 2.1.1897. Purple. Woman seated, sailing ship at center right. Date and signature varieties. 169x124mm.	—	—	—

		Good	Fine	XF
24	**10,000 Reis** 20.2.1905. Lilac. Woman seated at left, sailing ship at center, Mercury at right. Various date and signature varieties. 168x125mm.	—	—	—

1909 Provisional Issue

		Good	Fine	XF
25	**2500 Reis** 1.3.1909. Black on multicolor underprint. Vasco da Gama at left. Steamship seal type I. 147x94mm.	—	—	—
26	**5 Mil Reis** 1.3.1909. 159x100mm.	—	—	—

1909 Regular Issue

		Good	Fine	XF
27	**1000 Reis** 1.3.1909. Green and yellow underprint. Steamship seal Type I. Printer: BWC. 139x81mm.	175	550	—
28	**1000 Reis** 1.3.1909. Green and yellow underprint. Steamship seal Type III. Printer: BWC. 139x81mm.	175	550	—

		Good	Fine	XF
29	**2500 Reis** 1.3.1909. Black on multicolor underprint. Portrait Vasco da Gama at left. Arms at upper center. Sailing ships at right. Steamship seal below. Type I. Back: Seated allegorical woman looking out at ships. Printer: BWC. 147x94mm.	200	650	—
30	**2500 Reis** 1.3.1909. Black on multicolor underprint. Portrait Vasco da Gama at left, arms at upper center. Steamship seal below. Type III. Back: Seated allegorical woman looking out at ships. Printer: BWC. 147x94mm.	225	650	—
31	**5 Mil Reis** 1.3.1909. Black on multicolor underprint. Vasco da Gama at left, arms at upper center. Sailing ships at right. Steamship seal below. Type I. Back: Seated allegorical woman looking out at sailing ships at center. Printer: BWC. 159x100mm.	225	800	—
32	**5 Mil Reis** 1.3.1909. Black on multicolor. Portrait Vasco da Gama at left, arms at upper center. Steamship seal below. Type III. Back: Seated allegorical woman looking out at ships. Printer: BWC. 159x100mm.	225	800	—
33	**10 Mil Reis** 1.3.1909. Black on multicolor underprint. Portrait Vasco da Gama at left, arms at upper center. Sailing ships at right. Steamship seal below. Type I. Back: Seated allegorical woman looking out at ships. Printer: BWC. 177x106mm.	225	900	—
34	**10 Mil Reis** 1.3.1909. Black on multicolor underprint. Portrait Vasco da Gama at left, arms at upper center. Steamship seal below. Type III. Back: Seated allegorical woman looking out at ships. Printer: BWC. 177x106mm.	225	900	—

		Good	Fine	XF
35	**20 Mil Reis** 1.3.1909. Black on multicolor underprint. Portrait Vasco da Gama at left, arms at upper center. Harbor scene at right. Steamship seal below. Type I. Back: Seated allegorical woman looking out at ships. Printer: BWC. 180x115mm.	250	1,100	—
36	**20 Mil Reis** 1.3.1909. Black on multicolor underprint. Portrait Vasco da Gama at left, arms at upper center. Steamship seal below. Type III. Back: Seated allegorical woman looking out at ships. Printer: BWC. 180x115mm.	250	1,100	—
37	**50 Mil Reis** 1.3.1909. Black-green on multicolor underprint. Portrait Vasco da Gama at left, arms at upper center. Harbor scene at right. Steamship seal below. Type I. Back: Seated allegorical woman looking out at ships. Printer: BWC. 201x123mm.	350	1,500	—
38	**50 Mil Reis** 1.3.1909. Black-green on multicolor underprint. Portrait Vasco da Gama at left, arms at upper center. Steamship seal below. Type III. Back: Seated allegorical woman looking out at ships. Printer: BWC. 201x123mm.	350	1,500	—

1914 Issue

		Good	Fine	XF
39	**10 Centavos** 5.11.1914. Purple. Arms at right. Steamship seal Type II. Back: Seated allegorical woman looking out at ships. Printer: BWC. 116x70mm.			
	a. Black overprint: *LOANDA* 28mm long; letters with serifs.	10.00	55.00	200
	b. Green overprint: *LOANDA* 23mm long; sans-serif letters.	7.50	40.00	125

		Good	Fine	XF
40	**10 Centavos** 5.11.1914. Purple. Arms at right. Steamship seal Type III. Back: Seated allegorical woman looking out at ships. Printer: BWC. 116x70mm.	7.00	45.00	115

#41 *Deleted.*

42 **20 Centavos** — Good | Fine | XF

5.11.1914. Blue. Arms at right. Steamship seal Type II. Back: Seated allegorical woman looking out at ships. Printer: BWC. 123x71mm.

	Good	Fine	XF
a. Black overprint: *LOANDA* 28mm long; letters with serifs.	7.50	55.00	185
b. Red overprint: *LOANDA* 23mm long; sans-serif letters.	7.50	45.00	115

		Good	Fine	XF
43	**20 Centavos** 5.11.1914. Blue. Arms at right. Steamship seal Type III. Back: Seated allegorical woman looking out at ships. Printer: BWC. 123x71mm.	5.00	45.00	115

#44 Deleted.

		Good	Fine	XF
45	**50 Centavos** 5.11.1914. Green. Arms at right. Steamship seal Type II. Back: Seated allegorical woman looking out at ships. Printer: BWC. 123x71mm.	7.50	45.00	125
46	**50 Centavos** 5.11.1914. Green. Arms at right. Steamship seal Type III. Back: Seated allegorical woman looking out at ships. Printer: BWC. 123x71mm.			
	a. Blue overprint: *LOANDA* 28mm long; letters with serifs.	10.00	55.00	140
	b. Red overprint: *LOANDA* 23mm long; sans-serif letters.	7.50	45.00	125

1914 Provisional Issues

		Good	Fine	XF
47	**50 Centavos** 5.11.1914. Green. Arms at right. Printer: BWC. 126x71mm.	50.00	450	—
48	**50 Centavos** 5.11.1914. Green. Arms at right. Steamship seal Type II. Printer: BWC. 126x71mm.	65.00	450	—

1918 Issue

		Good	Fine	XF
49	**5 Centavos** 19.4.1918. Gray-green on yellow underprint. Design similar to Steamship seal Type II at right. Back: Seamship seal Type II at center. 98x63mm.	12.50	50.00	200
50	**20 Centavos** 19.4.1918. Brown on yellow-orange underprint. Pillar at left and right, seated woman at right. Back: Steamship seal Type II at center. 98x62mm.	60.00	400	—

1920 Issue

		Good	Fine	XF
51	**10 Centavos** 1.1.1920. Red. Ship at left and right. 108x66mm.	50.00	300	—
52	**20 Centavos** 1.1.1920. Green. Angels at left and right. 108x66mm.	65.00	400	—
53	**50 Centavos** 1.1.1920. Blue. Mercury at left, allegory at right. Back: Ship at center. BC: Brown. 126x77mm.	65.00	400	—
54	**50 Escudos** 1.1.1920. Blue on light green underprint. Arms at upper center. Back: Lake and trees at center. BC: Brown on gold underprint. 126x77mm.	—	—	—

Note: N#54 is known as the "Porto Issue" as the notes were printed there.

1921 Issue

		Good	Fine	XF
55	**1 Escudo** 1.1.1921. Green. Portrait Francisco de Oliveira Chamico at left, arms at bottom center. Steamship seal Type III at right. Back: Seated allegorical woman looking out at ships. Printer: BWC. 130x82mm.	12.50	55.00	200
56	**2.50 Escudos** 1.1.1921. Blue. Portrait Francisco de Oliveira Chamico at left, arms at bottom center. Steamship seal Type III at right. Back: Seated allegorical woman looking out at ships. Printer: TDLR. 135x90mm.	25.00	150	450
57	**5 Escudos** 1.1.1921. Dark green. Portrait Francisco de Oliveira Chamico at left, arms at bottom center. Steamship seal Type III at right. Back: Seated allegorical woman looking out at ships. Printer: BWC. 153x94mm.	25.00	150	450
58	**10 Escudos** 1.1.1921. Brown. Portrait Francisco de Oliveira Chamico at left, arms at bottom center. Steamship seal Type III at right. Back: Seated allegorical woman looking out at ships. Printer: BWC. 160x106mm.	50.00	250	650

		Good	Fine	XF
59	**20 Escudos** 1.1.1921. Blue. Portrait Francisco de Oliveira Chamico at left, arms at bottom center. Steamship seal Type III at right. Back: Seated allegorical woman looking out at ships. Printer: BWC. 174x115mm.	55.00	300	750
60	**50 Escudos** 1.1.1921. Light Brown. Portrait Francisco de Oliveira Chamico at left, arms at bottom center. Steamship seal Type II at right. Back: Seated allegorical woman looking out at ships. Printer: BWC. 185x122mm.	200	750	—
61	**100 Escudos** 1.1.1921. Green. Portrait Francisco de Oliveira Chamico at left, arms at bottom center. Steamship seal Type III at right. Back: Seated allegorical woman looking out at ships. Printer: BWC. 194x126mm.	300	925	—

Republica Portuguesa - Angola

1921 Issue

		VG	VF	UNC
62	**50 Centavos** 1921. Gray on light brown underprint. Woman plowing at left center, arms at lower right. Back: Allegories of Industry at left, Navigation at right, arms at center. 114x77mm.	5.00	45.00	150

1923 Issue

#	Denomination	VG	VF	UNC
63	**50 Centavos**			
	1923. Brown with red text at center. Dock scene at left, woman seated holding wreath at right. Back: Explorers at shoreline. 112x76mm.			
	a. Issued note.	4.00	20.00	125
	s. Specimen.	—	—	500

Provincia de Angola - Junta da Moeda

Decree No. 12.124 of 14.8.1926

#	Denomination	Good	Fine	XF
64	**1 Angolar** *D.1926.* Green. Portrait Diogo Cao at lower left, plants at right. Signature varieties. Back: Waterbuck head at center. Printer: TDLR. 120x70mm.	6.00	45.00	150

#	Denomination	Good	Fine	XF
65	**2 1/2 Angolares** *D.1926.* Purple. Portrait Paulo Dias de Novaes at lower left, palms at right. Signature varieties. Back: Black rhinoceros at center. Printer: TDLR. 130x81mm.	10.00	100	300
66	**5 Angolares** *D.1926.* Red-brown. Portrait Paulo Dias de Novaes at left, palms at right. Signature varieties. Back: Elephant at center. Printer: TDLR. 140x89mm.			
	a. Issued note.	40.00	250	550
	s. Specimen. Punch hole cancelled.	—	Unc	650

#	Denomination	Good	Fine	XF
67	**10 Angolares** *D.1926.* Blue. Two people weaving and spinning at left center, bridge and mountain at right. Back: Lion at center. 150x100mm.	60.00	350	750

Provincia de Angola - Governo Geral de Angola

Decree No. 31.942 of 28.3.1942

#	Denomination	Good	Fine	XF
68	**1 Angolar** *D.1942.* Green. Portrait Diogo Cao at lower left. Like #64. Back: Waterbuck head at center. Printer: TDLR. 120x70mm.	4.00	30.00	125

#	Denomination	Good	Fine	XF
69	**2 1/2 Angolares** *D.1942.* Purple. Portrait Paulo Dias de Novaes at lower left. Like #65. Back: Rhinoceros at center. Printer: TDLR. 130x81mm.	7.50	45.00	150

Commemorative Issue

Decree No. 37.086 of 6.10.1948

300th Anniversary Restoration of Angola to Portuguese Rule 1648-1948

#	Denomination	VG	VF	UNC
70	**1 Angolar** *D.1948.* Green. Landing boat, seamen and sailing ships at left center. Back: Waterbuck head at center. 120x69mm.	15.00	75.00	225

#	Denomination	VG	VF	UNC
71	**2 1/2 Angolares** *D.1948.* Purple. Bombardment of fortress. Back: Rhinoceros at center. 130x78mm.	20.00	100	300

Banco de Angola

1927 Issue

72	**20 Angolares**	Good	Fine	XF
	1.6.1927. Red on blue underprint. Portrait Salvador Correia at center. Jungle river. Signature title varieties. Back: Hippo at center. Printer: TDLR. 150x95mm.	80.00	350	900
73	**20 Angolares**	Good	Fine	XF
	1.6.1927. Dark brown on green underprint. Portrait Salvador Correia at center. Jungle river. Signature title varieties. Like #72. Back: Hippo at center. Printer: TDLR.			
	a. Issued note.	70.00	350	900
	s. Specimen.	—	Unc	950
74	**50 Angolares**	Good	Fine	XF
	1.6.1927. Purple on rose underprint. Portrait Salvador Correia at center. Waterfall. Signature title varieties. Back: Leopard. Printer: TDLR. 166x104mm.	125	625	1,500
74A	**50 Angolares**	Good	Fine	XF
	1.6.1927. Purple on green underprint. Portrait Salvador Correia at center. Waterfall. Signature title varieties. Like #74. Back: Leopard. BC: Brown-violet. Printer: TDLR.	125	625	1,500

75	**100 Angolares**	Good	Fine	XF
	1.6.1927. Green on blue underprint. Portrait Salvador Correia at left. Flamingos. Signature title varieties. Back: Crocodile. Printer: TDLR. 172x109mm.	200	1,250	—

76	**500 Angolares**	Good	Fine	XF
	1.6.1927. Blue on green underprint. Portrait Salvador Correia at left. Shoreline with palm trees. Signature title varieties. Back: Eagle. Printer: TDLR. 180x116mm.			
	a. Issued note.	—	—	—
	s. Specimen.	—	—	2,250

1944-1946 Issue

77	**5 Angolares**	VG	VF	UNC
	1.1.1947. Brown on yellow underprint. Three men at left, portrait Gen. Carmona at right. Back: Two women at left, small monument at right. BC: Green. Printer: W&S. 133x67mm.			
	a. Issued note.	8.00	55.00	225
	s. Specimen. Red overprint: *SPECIMEN* and punch hole cancelled.	—	—	750

78	**10 Angolares**	VG	VF	UNC
	D.14.8.1946 (1.6.1947). Dark blue and dark brown. Portrait Padre A. Barroso at right, children at left. Back: *Treaty of Simalambuco 1885.* BC: Dark blue. 141x75mm.			
	a. Issued note.	12.50	125	350
	s. Specimen. Red overprint *SPECIMEN* and punch hole cancelled.	—	—	750

79	**20 Angolares**	Good	Fine	XF
	1.12.1944. Lilac. Man standing at left, portrait Correia at right, fortress at center. Back: *Reconquest of Luanda 1648.* Printer: TDLR. 148x80mm.			
	a. Issued note.	17.50	125	350
	s. Specimen. Red overprint *SPECIMEN* and punch hole cancelled.	—	Unc	1,000
80	**50 Angolares**	Good	Fine	XF
	1.10.1944. Green. Portrait Pereira at right. Back: *Founding of Benguela 1617.* Printer: TDLR. 156x89mm.			
	a. Issued note.	40.00	250	550
	s. Specimen. Red overprint *SPECIMEN* and punch hole cancelled.	—	Unc	1,000
81	**100 Angolares**	Good	Fine	XF
	2.12.1946. Blue. Portrait Sousa Coutinho at right, arms at lower center. Back: European explorers and Africans. Printer: TDLR. 164x97mm.			
	a. Issued note.	75.00	325	700
	s. Specimen. Red overprint *SPECIMEN* and punch hole cancelled.	—	Unc	1,000
82	**1000 Angolares**	Good	Fine	XF
	1.6.1944. Carmine, blue and multicolor. Portrait Joao II at right. Back: Return of Diogo Cao, 1489. BC: Purple. Printer: TDLR. 179x111mm.			
	a. Issued note.	—	—	—
	s. Specimen. Red overprint *SPECIMEN* and punch hole cancelled.	—	—	—

1951-1952 Issue

83	**20 Angolares**	Good	Fine	XF
	1.3.1951. Lilac. Portrait Correia at right, fortress at center. Like #79. Back: *Reconquest of Luanda 1648.* Printer: TDLR. 148x80mm.	12.50	125	350
84	**50 Angolares**	Good	Fine	XF
	1.3.1951. Green. Portrait Pereira at right. Like #80. Back: *Founding of Benguela 1617.* 156x89mm.	30.00	225	550
85	**100 Angolares**	Good	Fine	XF
	1.3.1951. Red-brown and deep blue. Portrait Sousa Coutinho at right. Like #81. Back: European explorers and Africans. 164x97mm.			
	a. Issued note.	50.00	275	625
	s. Specimen. Red overprint TDLR oval.	—	Unc	750

		Good	Fine	XF
86	**1000 Angolares** 1.3.1952. Carmine. Portrait Joao II at right. Back: *Return of Diogo Cao, 1489.* BC: Purple. Printer: TDLR. 179x111mm.			
	a. Issued note.	—	—	—
	s. Specimen.	—	—	—

1956 Issue

Escudo System

		VG	VF	UNC
87	**20 Escudos** 15.8.1956. Lilac on multicolor. Portrait Porto at right, dock at left. Signature varieties. Back: Gazelle running. BC: Red-brown. Printer: TDLR. 130x62mm.	1.50	4.00	22.50

		VG	VF	UNC
88	**50 Escudos** 15.8.1956. Green on multicolor. Portrait H. de Carvalho at right, airport at left. Signature varieties. Back: Wildebeest herd at waterhole. Printer: TDLR. 136x66mm.			
	a. Issued note.	2.00	10.00	55.00
	s. Specimen.	—	—	—

		VG	VF	UNC
89	**100 Escudos** 15.8.1956. Blue on multicolor underprint. Portrait S. Pinto at right, Salazar Bridge at left. Signature varieties. Back: Elephants at waterhole. BC: Purple. Printer: TDLR. 149x70mm.			
	a. Issued note.	3.00	22.50	175
	s. Specimen.	—	—	—

		VG	VF	UNC
90	**500 Escudos** 15.8.1956. Orange on blue underprint. Portrait R. Ivens at left, Port of Luanda at center. Signature varieties. Back: Two rhinoceros at center. BC: Purple. Printer: TDLR. 154x75mm.	12.50	125	450

		VG	VF	UNC
91	**1000 Escudos** 15.8.1956. Brown on multicolor underprint. Portrait B. Capelo at right, dam at left center. Signature varieties. Back: Sable herd at center. BC: Black. Printer: TDLR. 158x80mm.	22.50	175	600

ARGENTINA

The Argentine Republic, located in South America, has an area of 2.76 million sq. km. and a population of 40.48 million. Capital: Buenos Aires. Its varied topography ranges from the subtropical lowlands of the north to the towering Andean Mountains in the west and the windswept Patagonian steppe in the south. The rolling, fertile pampas of central Argentina are ideal for agriculture and grazing, and support most of the republic's population. Meat packing, flour milling, textiles, sugar refining and dairy products are the principal industries. Oil is found in Patagonia, but most of the mineral requirements must be imported.

In 1816, the United Provinces of the Rio Plata declared their independence from Spain. After Bolivia, Paraguay, and Uruguay went their separate ways, the area that remained became Argentina. The country's population and culture were heavily shaped by immigrants from throughout Europe, but most particularly Italy and Spain, which provided the largest percentage of newcomers from 1860 to 1930. Up until about the mid-20th century, much of Argentina's history was dominated by periods of internal political conflict between Federalists and Unitarians and between civilian and military factions. After World War II, an era of Peronist authoritarian rule and interference in subsequent governments was followed by a military junta that took power in 1976. Democracy returned in 1983, and has persisted despite numerous challenges, the most formidable of which was a severe economic crisis in 2001-02 that led to violent public protests and the resignation of several interim presidents. The economy has recovered strongly since bottoming out in 2002.

MONETARY SYSTEM:

1 Peso (m/n) = 100 Centavos to 1970
1 Peso = 8 Reales = 100 Centavos

REPUBLIC

Banco Nacional

L. 1883 First Issue

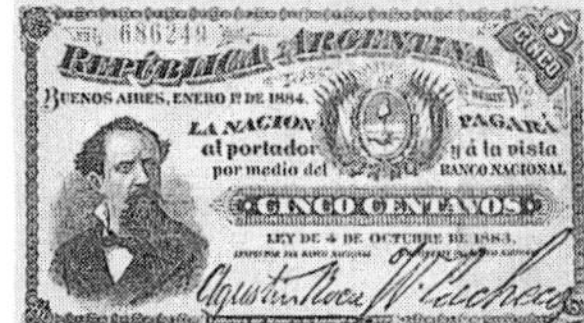

		Good	Fine	XF
1	**5 Centavos** 1.1.1884. Black on gray underprint. Nicolás Avellaneda at left, arms at upper right center. Signature varieties. BC: Green. Printer: R. Lange, Buenos Aires.	7.50	22.50	75.00

		Good	Fine	XF
2	**10 Centavos** 1.1.1884. Black on pink and yellow underprint. Arms at lower left, portrait Domingo Sarmiento at right. Signature varieties. Back: Liberty head at left. BC: Brown. Printer: R. Lange, Buenos Aires.	12.50	37.50	125

		Good	Fine	XF
3	**20 Centavos** 1.1.1884. Black on green underprint. Portrait Bartolomé Mitre at upper center, arms below. Signature varieties. BC: Orange. Printer: R. Lange, Buenos Aires.	3.00	15.00	60.00

3a 20 Centavos — Good / Fine / XF

1.1.1884. Black on blue underprint. Arms at left, Mitre at center. Signature varieties. Back: Arms at center. BC: Blue. Printer: R. Lange, Buenos Aires — 15.00 / 60.00 / 150

4 50 Centavos — Good / Fine / XF

1.1.1884. Black on grayish-brown underprint. Portrait Josto Jose Urquiza at center, arms below. Signature varieties. Back: Woman at center. BC: Brown. Printer: R. Lange, Buenos Aires — 15.00 / 60.00 / 150

L. 1883 Second Issue - Notes dated 1884

5 5 Centavos — Good / Fine / XF

1.1.1884. Black on brown and yellow underprint. Portrait Avellaneda at left, arms at right. 3 signature varieties. Back: Helmeted Athena at center. BC: Brown. Printer: ABNC. — 3.00 / 12.50 / 25.00

6 10 Centavos — Good / Fine / XF

1.1.1884. Black on green underprint. Portrait Sarmiento at left, arms at right. Two serial # varieties. 3 signature varieties. Back: Gaucho on horseback at center. BC: Green. Printer: ABNC. — 3.00 / 12.50 / 25.00

7 20 Centavos — Good / Fine / XF

1.1.1884. Arms at left, portrait Mitre at right. 3 signature varieties. Printer: ABNC.

a. Black on light reddish-brown underprint. 2 serial # varieties. Back brown; steer head at center. — 5.00 / 15.00 / 25 .00

b. Black without underprint. Series P. — — / — / —

8 50 Centavos — Good / Fine / XF

1.1.1884. Black on brown underprint. Arms at lower left, portrait Urquiza at right. 3 signature varieties. Back: Three girls at center. BC: Red-brown. Printer: ABNC. — 10.00 / 25.00 / 75.00

Banco de la Nación Argentina

L. 1890 Issue - Notes dated 1891

Ley No. 2707 del 21 de Agosto de 1890

209 5 Centavos — Good / Fine / XF

1.11.1891. Black on blue underprint. Arms at left, Avellaneda at right. 5 signature varieties. Large and small serial # varieties. Back: Helmeted Athena at center. BC: Gray to blue-green. Printer: CSABB, Buenos Aires. — 3.00 / 10.00 / 20.00

210 10 Centavos — Good / Fine / XF

1.11.1891. Black on brown underprint. Arms at left, portrait Domingo Sarmiento at right. 5 signature varieties. Back: Gaucho on horseback at center. BC: Brown. Printer: CSABB, Buenos Aires. — 3.00 / 10.00 / 22.50

211 20 Centavos — Good / Fine / XF

1.11.1891. Black on green underprint. Portrait Bartolomé Mitre at left, arms at right. Back: Steer head at center. BC: Green. Printer: CSABB, Buenos Aires.

a. Signature titles: *Inspector.../Presidente...* — 10.00 / 25.00 / 75.00

b. Signature titles: *Sindico/Presidente...* 4 signature varieties. — 3.00 / 10.00 / 20.00

212 50 Centavos — Good / Fine / XF

1.1.1891. Light ochre and black. Justo Jose Urquiza at left, arms at right. *CINCUENTA* underprint. Signature titles as 211a. Back: Three girls at center. BC: Brown. Printer: CSABB, Buenos Aires. — 25.00 / 45.00 / 175

212A 50 Centavos — Good / Fine / XF

1.11.1891. Light ochre and black. Urquiza at left, arms at right. Like #212 but *50* in underprint. 3 signature varieties. Signature titles as 211b. Back: Three girls at center. BC: Brown. Printer: CSABB, Buenos Aires. — 5.00 / 25.00 / 60.00

L. 1891 Issue - Notes dated 1892

Ley No. 2822 del 29 Septembre de 1891

		Good	Fine	XF
213	**5 Centavos** 1.5.1892. Black on blue underprint. Arms at left, Avellaneda at right. 3 signature varieties.Similar to #209. Back: Helmeted Athena at center. BC: Gray to blue-green. Printer: CSABB, Buenos Aires.	5.00	25.00	60.00

		Good	Fine	XF
214	**10 Centavos** 1.5.1892. Black on brown underprint. Arms at left, portrait Sarmiento at right. 3 signature varieties. Similar to #210. Back: Gaucho on horseback at center. BC: Brown. Printer: CSABB, Buenos Aires.	5.00	25.00	60.00

		Good	Fine	XF
215	**20 Centavos** 1.5.1892. Black on green underprint. Portrait Mitre at left, arms at right. 3 signature varieties. Similar to #211. Back: Steer head at center. BC: Green. Printer: CSABB, Buenos Aires.	5.00	25.00	60.00

		Good	Fine	XF
216	**50 Centavos** 1.5.1892. Light ochre and black. Urquiza at left, arms at right. *50* in underprint. 3 signature varieties. Similar to #212A. Back: Three girls at center. BC: Brown. Printer: CSABB, Buenos Aires.	7.50	30.00	75.00

1895 First Issue

Ley No. 3062 del 8 de Enero de 1894

		Good	Fine	XF
218	**1 Peso** 1.1.1895. Black on green and brown. Portrait Adm. Brown at left, arms at center, woman with lyre at right. 2 signature varieties. Back: Arms at center. BC: Green. Printer: CSABB, Buenos Aires.			
	a. Issued note.	6.00	20.00	75.00
	r. Remainder perforated: *SIN VALOR.*	—	Unc	75.00

		Good	Fine	XF
219	**2 Pesos** 1.1.1895. Black on light brown and green underprint. Child with flag at left, portrait Alvear at right. Back: Arms of the 14 provinces around large numeral at center. BC: Brown. Printer: CSABB, Buenos Aires.			
	a. Issued note.	100	400	—
	r. Remainder perforated: *SIN VALOR.*	—	Unc	325
	p. Face and back proofs perforated like b.	—	Unc	350

		Good	Fine	XF
220	**5 Pesos** 1.1.1895. Black on pink and green underprint. Dragon at left, arms at upper center, portrait V. Sarsfield at right. 3 signature varieties. Back: Sailing ships at center. BC: Slate blue. Printer: CSABB, Buenos Aires.			
	a. Issued note.	50.00	200	—
	r. Remainder perforated: *SIN VALOR.*	—	Unc	175

		Good	Fine	XF
221	**10 Pesos** 1.1.1895. Black on yellow-brown underprint. Woman and monument at left, arms at upper center, portrait N. Laprida at right. 3 signature varieties. Back: Ornamental design. BC: Brown. Printer: CSABB, Buenos Aires.			
	a. Issued note.	100	400	—
	r. Remainder perforated: *SIN VALOR.*	—	Unc	350

222	20 Pesos	Good	Fine	XF
	1.1.1895. Black on light green and light orange underprint. Seated woman writing at left, arms at upper center, portrait Arenales at right. 2 signature varieties. Back: Liberty with cap at center. BC: Green. Printer: CSABB, Buenos Aires.			
	a. Issued note.	150	650	—
	r. Remainder perforated: *SIN VALOR.*	—	Unc	400

223	50 Pesos	Good	Fine	XF
	1.1.1895. Black on red underprint. Ship at left, portrait Pueyrredon at right, arms at center. 2 signature varieties. Back: Ship at center. Printer: CSABB, Buenos Aires.			
	a. Issued note.	—	—	—
	r. Remainder perforated: *SIN VALOR.*	—	Unc	500

224	100 Pesos	Good	Fine	XF
	1.1.1895. Black on red and celeste underprint. Portrait Moreno and child at left, arms at center. 2 signature varieties. Printer: CSABB, Buenos Aires.			
	a. Issued note.	500	1,000	1,500
	r. Remainder perforated: *SIN VALOR.* Rare.	—	—	—

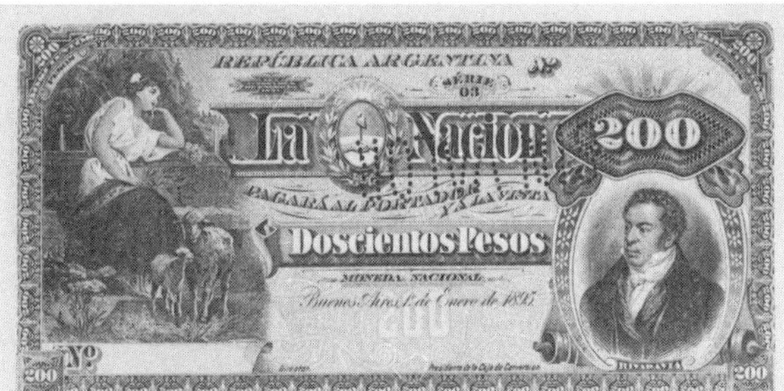

225	200 Pesos	Good	Fine	XF
	1.1.1895. Black on red and celeste underprint. Portrait Rivadavia at right, reclining female with sheep at left, arms at upper center. 2 signature varieties. Back: Allegorical woman on back. Printer: CSABB, Buenos Aires.			
	a. Issued note.	700	1,000	1,500
	r. Remainder perforated: *SIN VALOR.* Rare.	—	—	—

226	500 Pesos	Good	Fine	XF
	1.1.1895. Black on red and celeste underprint. Portrait Belgrano at lower right, female with child at left, arms at top center. 2 signature varieties. Back: Angel with globe at center. Printer: CSABB, Buenos Aires.			
	a. Issued note. Rare.	—	—	—
	r. Remainder perforated: *SIN VALOR.* Rare.	—	—	—

227 1000 Pesos — Good | Fine | XF

1.1.1895. Black on red underprint. Portrait San Martin at right, seated woman and child at left, arms at upper center. 2 signature varieties. Printer: CSABB, Buenos Aires.

	Good	Fine	XF
a. Issued note. Rare.	—	—	—
r. Remainder perforated: *SIN VALOR*. Rare.	—	—	—

1895 Second Issue

Ley No. 2707 del 21 de Agosto de 1890

228 10 Centavos — Good | Fine | XF

19.7.1895. Black on red underprint. Arms at left, portrait Sarmiento at right. Back: Liberty at center. BC: Red. Printer: BWC.

	Good	Fine	XF
a. Issued note.	3.00	12.50	35.00
s. Specimen.	—	Unc	150

229 20 Centavos — Good | Fine | XF

19.7.1895. Black on green underprint. Portrait Mitre at left, arms at right. Back: Helmeted woman at center. BC: Green. Printer: BWC.

	Good	Fine	XF
a. Issued note.	5.00	25.00	50.00
s. Specimen.	—	Unc	175

230 50 Centavos — Good | Fine | XF

19.7.1895. Black on brown underprint. Arms at left, portrait Urquiza at right. 3 signature varieties. Back: Columbus at center. BC: Brown. Printer: BWC.

	Good	Fine	XF
a. Issued note.	5.00	25.00	75.00
p1. Proof. Uniface face.	—	—	—
p2. Proof. Uniface back.	—	—	—
s. Specimen.	—	Unc	250

Caja de Conversion

1899 Issue

Ley de 20 de Septiembre de 1897

WATERMARK VARIETIES		
Wmk. A:	Wmk. B:	Wmk. C:
PE of *PESO*	PE of *PESO*	Pe of *PESO*

231 50 Centavos — Good 40.00 | Fine 125 | XF 300

ND (1899-1900). Gray-blue. Without underprint. Woman seated with torch (Progreso motif) at left, 7 digit red serial #, with specially coded prefix and suffix letters.

232 1 Peso — Good 45.00 | Fine 150 | XF 350

ND (1900). Gray-blue-pink. Without underprint. Woman seated with torch (Progreso motif) at left, 7 digit red serial #, with specially coded prefix and suffix letters.

233 100 Pesos — Good 200 | Fine 600 | XF —

ND (1899). Blue and green. Without underprint. Woman seated with torch (Progreso motif) at left, 7 digit red serial #, with specially coded prefix and suffix letters.

1900-1901 Issue

234 50 Centavos — Good 60.00 | Fine 175 | XF 350

ND (1900). Gray-blue. Liberty (Progreso) with torch at left, 7 digit red serial # with specially coded prefix and suffix letters. Letter A. 130x67mm.

235 1 Peso — Good 60.00 | Fine 175 | XF 350

ND (1900-1903). Gray-blue. Liberty (Progreso) with torch at left, 7 digit red serial # with specially coded prefix and suffix letters. Letter B. 150x77mm.

236 5 Pesos — Good 60.00 | Fine 175 | XF 350

ND (1900-1903). Blue, yellow and pink. Liberty (Progreso) with torch at left, 7 digit red serial # with specially coded prefix and suffix letters. Letter C. 170x87mm.

237 10 Pesos — Good 70.00 | Fine 200 | XF 450

ND (1900-1903). Blue and gray. Liberty (Progreso) with torch at left, 7 digit red serial # with specially coded prefix and suffix letters. Letter D. 190x97mm.

238 50 Pesos — Good 100 | Fine 250 | XF 550

ND (1900-1903). Pinkish-blue and gray. Liberty (Progreso) with torch at left, 7 digit red serial # with specially coded prefix and suffix letters. Letter E. 195x100mm.

239 100 Pesos — Good 200 | Fine 600 | XF —

ND (1900-1903). Liberty (Progreso) with torch at left, 7 digit red serial # with specially coded prefix and suffix letters. Letter H. 200x107mm.

240 500 Pesos — Good — | Fine — | XF —

ND (1900-1901). Blue and yellow. Liberty (Progreso) with torch at left, 7 digit red serial # with specially coded prefix and suffix letters. Letter H. 210x117mm. Rare.

241 1000 Pesos — Good — | Fine — | XF —

ND (1901). Rare. Pinkish-blue and violet. Liberty (Progreso) with torch at left, 7 digit red serial # with specially coded prefix and suffix letters. Letter P. 220x127mm.

1903-1905 Issue

#236A-241A reduced size.

236A 5 Pesos — Good 60.00 | Fine 175 | XF 350

ND (1903-1907). Liberty (Progreso) with torch at left, 7 digit red serial # with specially coded prefix and suffix letters. Letter C. 3 signature varieties. 144x72mm.

237A 10 Pesos — Good 60.00 | Fine 175 | XF 350

ND (1903-1907). Liberty (Progreso) with torch at left, 7 digit red serial # with specially coded prefix and suffix letters. Letter D. 3 signature varieties. 158x77mm.

238A 50 Pesos — Good 70.00 | Fine 200 | XF 450

ND (1903-1906). Liberty (Progreso) with torch at left, 7 digit red serial # with specially coded prefix and suffix letters. Letter E. 3 signature varieties. 173x83mm.

239A 100 Pesos — Good 100 | Fine 250 | XF 550

ND (1903-1906). Liberty (Progreso) with torch at left, 7 digit red serial # with specially coded prefix and suffix letters. Letter H. 2 signature varieties. 180x88mm.

240A 500 Pesos — Good — | Fine — | XF —

ND (1905). Liberty (Progreso) with torch at left, 7 digit red serial # with specially coded prefix and suffix letters. Letter N. 188x93mm. Rare.

241A 1000 Pesos — Good — | Fine — | XF —

ND (1905-1908). Liberty (Progreso) with torch at left, 7 digit red serial # with specially coded prefix and suffix letters. Letter P. 196x98mm. Rare.

1906-1907 Issue

		Good	Fine	XF
235B	**1 Peso** ND (1906-1908). 7 digit serial # with specially coded prefix and suffix letters. Letters A-D. 2 signature varieties. 130x65mm.	50.00	175	350

		Good	Fine	XF
236B	**5 Pesos** ND (1907-1908). 7 digit serial # with specially coded prefix and suffix letters. Letters A-D. 2 signature varieties. 144x71mm.	60.00	175	350

		Good	Fine	XF
237B	**10 Pesos** ND (1907-1908). 7 digit serial # with specially coded prefix and suffix letters. Letters A-C. 2 signature varieties. 158x77mm.	60.00	175	350

1908-1923 Issue

		VG	VF	UNC
242	**50 Centavos** ND (1918-1921). Dark blue on aqua, lilac and lightt green underprint. Liberty (Progreso) with torch. Printed *RA* monogram and *50 CENTAVOS* in light green. 1 signature variety.	1.50	5.00	15.00

		VG	VF	UNC
242A	**50 Centavos** ND (1922-1926). Dark blue on light blue-green underprint. Liberty (Progreso) with torchat left, with RA monogram at upper left. Eight digit serial #. 2 signature varieties. Like #242. Watermark: *RA* monogram and *50 CENTAVOS*.	0.75	2.25	7.50

		VG	VF	UNC
243	**1 Peso** ND (1908-1935). Blue on pink paper. Liberty (Progreso) with torch at left, with RA monogram at upper left. Eight digit serial #. BC: Green. Watermark: *RA* monogram. 130x65mm.			
	a. Watermark: A. ND (1908-1925). Series A-C. 7 signature varieties.	2.00	10.00	40.00
	b. Watermark: B. ND (1925-1932). Series D-E. 3 signature varieties.	1.50	6.00	15.00
	c. Watermark: C. ND (1932-1935). Series F. 2 signature varieties.	1.00	3.00	7.00

		VG	VF	UNC
244	**5 Pesos** ND (1908-1935). Blue. Liberty (Progreso) with torch at left, with RA monogram at upper left. Eight digit serial #. BC: Dark red. 144x71mm.			
	a. Watermark: A. ND (1908-1925). Series A. 7 signature varieties.	5.00	20.00	60.00
	b. Watermark: B. ND (1925-1932). Series B. 3 signature varieties.	5.00	15.00	35.00
	c. Watermark: C. ND (1933-1935). Series C.	2.00	7.50	30.00

		VG	VF	UNC
245	**10 Pesos** ND (1908-1935). Blue. Liberty (Progreso) with torch at left, with RA monogram at upper left. Eight digit serial #. BC: Green. 158x77mm.			
	a. Watermark: A. ND (1908-1925). Series A. 7 signature varieties.	5.00	15.00	35.00
	b. Watermark: B. ND (1925-1932). Series B. 3 signature varieties.	5.00	15.00	35.00
	c. Watermark: C with Gen. San Martin at upper left. ND (1933-1935). Series C. 2 signature varieties.	2.00	5.00	15.00

		VG	VF	UNC
246	**50 Pesos** ND (1908-1935). Blue. Liberty (Progreso) with torch at left, with RA monogram at upper left. Eight digit serial #. 172x83mm.			
	a. Watermark: A. ND (1908-1925). Series A. 7 signature varieties.	20.00	75.00	150
	b. Watermark: B. ND (1925-1932). Series B . 2 signature varieties.	15.00	60.00	140
	c. Watermark: C with Gen. San Martin at upper left. ND (1934-1935). Series C.	15.00	50.00	125

		VG	VF	UNC
247	**100 Pesos** ND (1908-1932). Blue on aqua underprint. Liberty (Progreso) with torch at left, with RA monogram at upper left. Eight digit serial #. BC: Olive. 180x88mm.			
	a. Watermark: A. ND (1908-1925). Series A. 5 signature varieties.	50.00	125	250
	b. Watermark: B. ND (1926-1932). Series B. 2 signature varieties.	15.00	40.00	90.00

		VG	VF	UNC
248	**500 Pesos** ND (1909-1935). Blue. Liberty (Progreso) with torch at left, with RA monogram at upper left. Eight digit serial #. BC: Brownish-purple. 188x93mm. PC: Blue.			
	a. Watermark: A. ND (1909-1924). Series A. 4 signature varieties.	125	300	750
	b. Watermark: B. ND (1929-1930). Series B.	60.00	150	375
	c. Watermark: C with Gen. San Martin at upper left. ND (1935). Series C.	40.00	100	225

		VG	VF	UNC
249	**1000 Pesos** ND (1910-1934). Blue on aqua underprint. Liberty (Progreso) with torch at left, with RA monogram at upper left. Eight digit serial #. BC: Red. 196x98mm.			
	a. Watermark: A. ND (1910-1927). Series A. 3 signature varieties.	125	250	600
	b. Watermark: B. ND (1929). Series B.	125	250	600
	c. Watermark: C. with Gen. San Martin at upper left. ND (1934). Series C.	60.00	125	350

Banco Central de la Republica Argentina

Signature Titles:

A - *GERENTE GENERAL*
B - *SUBGERENTE GENERAL*
C - *GERENTE GENERAL* and *PRESIDENTE*
D - *SUBGERENTE GENERAL* and *VICE-PRESIDENTE*
E - *SUBGERENTE GENERAL* and *PRESIDENTE*
F - *VICE PRESIDENTE* and *PRESIDENTE*
G - *PRESIDENTE B.C.R.A.* and *PRESIDENTE H.C. SENADORES*
H - *PRESIDENTE B.C.R.A.* and *PRESIDENTE H.C. DIPUTADOS*
I - *VICE PRESIDENTE* and *GERENTE GENERAL*

Art. 36 - Ley 12.155 (First Issue)

		VG	VF	UNC
249A	**1 Peso** ND. Deep brown-orange. Head of Republica at center. Uniface face proof without signature, serial # or watermark.	—	—	15.00

		VG	VF	UNC
249B	**5 Pesos** ND. Blue-black. Head of Republica at right. Uniface face proof without signature, serial # or watermark.	—	—	15.00

Art. 36 - Ley 12.155 (Second Issue)

		VG	VF	UNC
250	**50 Centavos** ND (1942-1948). Blue. Liberty (Progreso) with torch at left. Banco Central designation just above signatures at bottom. 4 signature varieties. 2 watermark varieties.	VG	VF	UNC
	a. Signature titles: C in black. Serie C, D.	1.00	3.50	7.50
	b. Signature titles: C in blue. Serie D.	1.50	4.50	12.50
	c. Signature titles: E in blue. Serie D.	1.50	4.50	12.50
251	**1 Peso** ND (1935). Blue. Liberty (Progreso) with torch at left. Banco Central designation just above signatures at bottom. 6 signature varieties. PC: Pink.	VG	VF	UNC
	a. Signature titles: C in blue. Serie I.	0.75	2.25	6.00
	b. *SUB* added in black to signature titles C in blue. Serie I-J.	1.25	3.00	7.50
	c. Signature titles: E in black. Serie J-K.	1.25	3.00	7.50
	d. Signature titles: C in black. Serie G-I.	1.00	3.00	7.50
252	**5 Pesos** ND (1935). Blue. Liberty (Progreso) with torch at left. Banco Central designation just above signatures at bottom. 4 signature varieties.	VG	VF	UNC
	a. Signature titles: C in blue. Serie D.	2.00	5.00	15.00
	b. Signature titles: E in black. Serie D.	3.75	15.00	30.00
	c. Signature titles: C in black. Serie E.	2.00	5.00	15.00

1935 - Ley No. 12.155 de 28 de Marzo de 1935

		VG	VF	UNC
253	**10 Pesos** *L.1935* (1936-1946). Blue. Large heading *El Banco Central.* Liberty (Progreso) with torch at left. Signature titles: C. 2 signature varieties. Serie D. BC: Green. Watermark: San Martin.			
	a. Issued note.	6.00	17.50	50.00
	s. Specimen. Overprint: *MUESTRA.*	—	—	225
254	**50 Pesos** *L.1935* (1936-1943). Blue. Large heading *El Banco Central.* Liberty (Progreso) with torch at left. Signature titles: C. Serie D. Watermark: San Martin.	11.50	35.00	100

		VG	VF	UNC
255	**100 Pesos** *L.1935* (1936-1943). Blue on green underprint. Large heading *El Banco Central.* Liberty (Progreso) with torch at left. Signature titles: C. Serie C. BC: Gray. Watermark: San Martin.	10.00	30.00	80.00

1948 - Ley No. 12.962 del 27 de Marzo de 1947

		VG	VF	UNC
256	**50 Centavos** *L.1947* (1948-1950). Blue. Liberty (Progreso) with torch at left. 2 signature varieties. Serie E. Printer: CMN.	0.35	1.00	3.00

		VG	VF	UNC
257	**1 Peso** *L.1947* (1948-1951). Blue. Liberty (Progreso) with torch at left. 2 signature varieties. Serie L-N. BC: Green. Printer: CMN. PC: Pink.	0.50	1.50	4.00
258	**5 Pesos** *L.1947* (1949-1951). Blue. Liberty (Progreso) with torch at left. Serie F. BC: Light red. Printer: CMN.	0.65	1.85	5.00

1950 - Ley No. 12.962 del 27 de Marzo de 1947

		VG	VF	UNC
259	**50 Centavos** *L.1947* (1950-1951). Brown. Head of Republica at left. Back: Open book of constitution at center. BC: Green.			
	a. *Garrasi* at lower right, letter A. (1950).	0.25	1.00	3.00
	b. Without *Garrasi* at lower right, letter A. (1951).	0.25	1.00	3.00

Note: For 50 centavos type of #259 w/letter B see #261.

1952 Commemorative Issue

#260, Declaration of Economic Independence (#263 regular issue) w/dates: *1816-1947.*

#	Description	VG	VF	UNC
260	**1 Peso** ND (1952-1955). Brown, violet and blue. Justice holding sword and scale at center. Back: Building at center, *"1816-1947"* at top on back.			
	a. Signature Bosio-Gomez Morales. Serie A.	0.50	3.50	10.00
	b. Signature Palarea-Revestido. Serie A-C.	0.25	1.00	3.00

1951 - Leyes Nos. 12.962 y 13.571

#	Description	VG	VF	UNC
261	**50 Centavos** ND (1951-1956). Brown. Head of Republica at left. Letter B. 2 signature varieties. Like #259. Printer: CMN.	0.25	1.00	3.00
262	**1 Peso** ND (1951-1952). Blue. Liberty (Progreso) with torch at left. Serie Ñ. BC: Green. Printer: CMN. PC: Pink	0.35	1.50	4.00

#	Description	VG	VF	UNC
263	**1 Peso** ND (1956). Brown, violet and blue. Justice holding sword and scale at center. 2 signature varieties. Serie C-D. Printer: CMN.			
	a. Watermark: *1* without dark line in upper part.	0.25	1.00	3.00
	b. Watermark: *1* with dark line in upper part.	0.25	1.00	3.00

#	Description	VG	VF	UNC
264	**5 Pesos** ND (1951-1959). Blue. Liberty (Progreso) with torch at left. 6 signature varieties. BC: Light red. Serie G-H. Printer: CMN.			
	a. Watermark: A, red serial #.	0.50	2.00	6.00
	b. Watermark: B, red serial #.	0.50	2.00	6.00
	c. Watermark: C, red serial #.	0.50	2.00	6.00
	d. Watermark: C, black serial #. Serie H.	0.35	1.50	6.00
	x. Error with *Leyes Nos. 19.962 y 13.571.* Serie H.	1.00	4.00	12.50

1943 - Ley No. 12.155 de 28 de Marzo de 1935

#	Description	VG	VF	UNC
265	**10 Pesos** *L.1935* (1942-1954). Red. Portrait Gen. San Martin in uniform at right. 8 signature varieties. Serie A-C. Back: Meeting scene. Watermark: Large or small head of Gen. Belgrano.			
	a. Red signature with signature titles C.	2.50	12.50	40.00
	b. Black signature with signature titles C.	0.60	1.75	5.00
	c. Red signature with signature titles E.	2.00	8.00	25.00

#	Description	VG	VF	UNC
266	**50 Pesos** *L.1935* (1942-1954). Green. Portrait Gen. San Martin in uniform at right. 6 signature varieties. Signature titles: C. Serie A. Back: Army in mountains.			
	a. Green signature	4.00	25.00	60.00
	b. Black signature	1.75	7.00	20.00
	c. Red serial #.	15.00	35.00	70.00

#	Description	VG	VF	UNC
267	**100 Pesos** *L.1935* (1943-1957). Brown. Portrait Gen. San Martin in uniform at right. 7 signature varieties. Serie A. Back: Spanish and Indians.			
	a. Brown signature with signature titles E.	3.50	20.00	50.00
	s. Black signature with signature titles C.	1.75	7.00	20.00

#	Description	VG	VF	UNC
267A	**100 Pesos** *L.1935.* Purple and violet on pale green and orange underprint. Portrait Gen. San Martin in uniform at right. Uniface face proof without signature, serial # or watermark.	—	—	15.00

#	Description	VG	VF	UNC
268	**500 Pesos** *L.1935.* (1944-1954). Blue. Portrait Gen. San Martin in uniform at right. 5 signature varieties. Serie A. Back: Banco Central.			
	a. Blue signature with signature titles E.	12.50	60.00	150
	b. Black signature with signature titles C.	6.25	25.00	60.00
268A	**500 Pesos** *L.1935.* Deep blue on pale green underprint. Portrait Gen. San Martin in uniform at right. Proof without signature, serial # or watermark. Back: Banco Central.	—	—	15.00

		VG	VF	UNC
269	**1000 Pesos**			
	L.1935. (1944-1955). Purple. Portrait Gen. San Martin in uniform at right. 5 signature varieties. Serie A. Back: Sailing ship.			
	a. Purple signature with signature titles E.	12.50	60.00	150
	b. Black signature with signature titles C.	4.50	17.50	55.00

1954-1957 ND Issue - Leyes Nos. 12.962 y 13.571.

		VG	VF	UNC
270	**10 Pesos**			
	ND (1954-1963). Meeting scene on back 10 signature varieties. Serie D-G. Red. Portrait Gen. San Martin in uniform at right.			
	a. Signature titles: C.	0.40	1.25	4.00
	b. Signature titles: D.	0.40	1.25	4.00
	c. Signature titles: E.	0.25	1.00	3.00

		VG	VF	UNC
271	**50 Pesos**			
	ND (1955-1968). Green. Portrait Gen. San Martin in uniform at right. 13 signature varieties in red or black. 3 serial # varieties. Series B-C with gray underprint. Series D without underprint. Back: Army in mountains.			
	a. Signature titles: C.	0.50	2.00	6.00
	b. Signature titles: D.	0.20	1.25	20.00
	c. Signature titles: E.	0.60	2.25	7.00
	d. Litho printing on back. Signature titles: E. Serie C, D.	0.25	1.00	3.00

		VG	VF	UNC
272	**100 Pesos**			
	ND (1957-1967). Brown. Portrait Gen. San Martin in uniform at right. 10 signature varieties. 2 serial # varieties. Serie B-D with gray underprint. Serie D without underprint. Back: Spanish and Indians.			
	a. Signature titles: C.	0.50	2.00	6.00
	b. Signature titles: D.	1.25	5.00	15.00
	c. Signature titles: E.	0.50	2.00	6.00

		VG	VF	UNC
273	**500 Pesos**			
	ND (1955-1965). Purple. Portrait Gen. San Martin in uniform at right. 9 signature varieties. 3 serial # varieties in red or black. Serie B, C. Back: Sailing ship.			
	a. Signature titles: C.	1.25	5.00	15.00
	b. Signature titles: D.	1.25	5.00	15.00
	c. Signature titles: E.	1.00	4.00	12.00

		VG	VF	UNC
274	**1000 Pesos**			
	ND (1954-1964). Blue. Portrait Gen. San Martin in uniform at right. 6 signature varieties. 3 serial # varieties in red or black. Serie B. Back: Banco Central.			
	a. Signature titles: C.	2.50	10.00	30.00
	b. Signature titles: E.	3.25	13.50	40.00

1960-1969 ND Issue

		VG	VF	UNC
275	**5 Pesos**			
	ND (1960-1962). Brown on yellow underprint. General José de San Martin in uniform at right. 3 signature varieties. Serie A. Back: People gathering before building. Printer: CMN.			
	a. Signature titles: D.	0.30	1.50	6.00
	b. Signature titles: C.	0.75	3.00	12.50
	c. Signature titles: E.	0.40	1.75	5.50

The Republic of Armenia is bounded to the north by Georgia, to the east by Azerbaijan and to the south and west by Turkey and Iran. It has an area of 29,743 sq. km and a population of 2.97 million. Capital: Yerevan. Agriculture including cotton, vineyards and orchards, hydroelectricity, chemicals - primarily synthetic rubber and fertilizers, and vast mineral deposits of copper, zinc and aluminum and production of steel and paper are major industries.

Armenia prides itself on being the first nation to formally adopt Christianity (early 4th century). Despite periods of autonomy, over the centuries Armenia came under the sway of various empires including the Roman, Byzantine, Arab, Persian, and Ottoman. During World War I in the western portion of Armenia, Ottoman Turkey instituted a policy of forced resettlement coupled with other harsh practices that resulted in an estimated 1 million Armenian deaths. The eastern area of Armenia was ceded by the Ottomans to Russia in 1828; this portion declared its independence in 1918, but was conquered by the Soviet Red Army in 1920. Armenian leaders remain preoccupied by the long conflict with Muslim Azerbaijan over Nagorno-Karabakh, a primarily Armenian-populated region, assigned to Soviet Azerbaijan in the 1920s by Moscow. Armenia and Azerbaijan began fighting over the area in 1988; the struggle escalated after both countries attained independence from the Soviet Union in 1991. By May 1994, when a cease-fire took hold, Armenian forces held not only Nagorno-Karabakh but also a significant portion of Azerbaijan proper. The economies of both sides have been hurt by their inability to make substantial progress toward a peaceful resolution. Turkey imposed an economic blockade on Armenia and closed the common border because of the Armenian separatists' control of Nagorno-Karabakh and surrounding areas.

MONETARY SYSTEM:

1 Ruble = 100 Kopeks

1 Dram = 100 Lumma

AUTONOMOUS REPUBLIC

ГОСУДАРСТВЕННАГО БАНКА ЭРИВАНСКОЕ ОТДѢЛЕНІЕ

Government Bank, Yerevan Branch

1919 First Issue

		Good	Fine	XF
1	**5 Rubles**	5.00	10.00	40.00
	1919. Black on blue underprint. Many color shades. Without Armenian text at upper left and right. Date of АВГУЧТЬ (August) 1919. Back: Date of 15 НОЯБРЯ (November) 1919.			

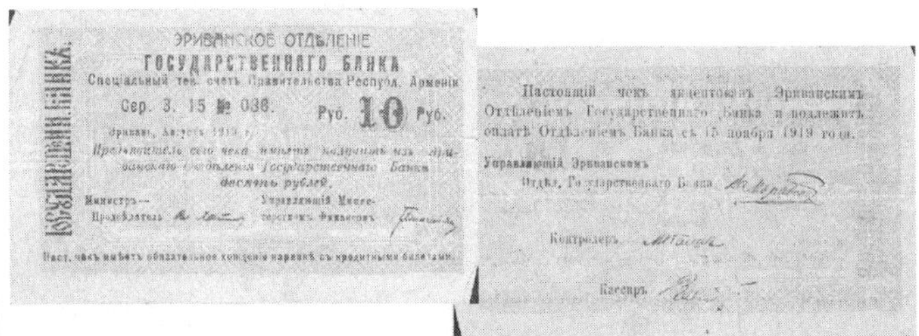

		Good	Fine	XF
2	**10 Rubles**			
	1919. Black on pink underprint. Many color shades. Without Armenian text at upper left and right. Date of АВГУЧТЬ (August) 1919. Back: Date of 15 НОЯБРЯ (November) 1919.			
	a. Issued note.	4.00	10.00	30.00
	x. Misprint with text inverted.	7.00	15.00	45.00

3	**25 Rubles**	Good	Fine	XF
	1919. Dark gray. Many color shades. Value numerals in middle and 4 corners. Without Armenian text at upper left and right. Date of АВГУЧТЬ (August) 1919. Back: Date of 15 НОЯБРЯ (November) 1919.			
	a. Issued note.	10.00	35.00	90.00
	x. Error printed in brown.	30.00	70.00	200

4	**50 Rubles**	Good	Fine	XF
	1919. Green. Many color shades. Value numerals in middle and 4 corners. Without Armenian text at upper left and right. Date of АВГУЧТЬ (August) 1919. Back: Date of 15 НОЯБРЯ (November) 1919.	20.00	55.00	175

5	**100 Rubles**	Good	Fine	XF
	1919. Green. Many color shades. Plain value numerals in black. Without Armenian text at upper left and right. Date of АВГУЧТЬ (August) 1919. Back: Date of 15 НОЯБРЯ (November) 1919.	15.00	45.00	90.00

6	**250 Rubles**	Good	Fine	XF
	1919. Orange. Many color shades. Plain value numerals in black. Without Armenian text at upper left and right. Date of АВГУЧТЬ (August) 1919. Like #5. Back: Date of 15 НОЯБРЯ (November) 1919.	15.00	45.00	90.00

7	**500 Rubles**	Good	Fine	XF
	1919. Blue. Many color shades. Plain value numerals in black. Without Armenian text at upper left and right. Date of АВГУЧТЬ (August) 1919. Like #5. Back: Date of 15 НОЯБРЯ (November) 1919.	15.00	45.00	90.00

8	**1000 Rubles**	Good	Fine	XF
	1919. Lilac. Many color shades. Plain value numerals in black. Without Armenian text at upper left and right. Date of АВГУЧТЬ (August) 1919. Like #5. Back: Date of 15 НОЯБРЯ (November) 1919.	15.00	45.00	90.00

1919 Second Issue

9	**50 Rubles**	Good	Fine	XF
	1919. Green. Many color shades. Ornamental value numerals. Without Armenian text at upper left and right. Date of АВГУЧТЬ (August) 1919. Back: Date of 15 НОЯБРЯ (November) 1919.	15.00	40.00	80.00

10	**100 Rubles**	Good	Fine	XF
	1919. Light green. Many color shades. Ornamental value numerals. Without Armenian text at upper left and right. Date of АВГУЧТЬ (August) 1919. Like #9. Back: Date of 15 НОЯБРЯ (November) 1919.			
	a. Issued note.	15.00	40.00	80.00
	x. Error printed in yellow.	7.00	30.00	80.00

11	**250 Rubles**	Good	Fine	XF
	1919. Light brown. Many color shades. Ornamental value numerals. Without Armenian text at upper left and right. Date of АВГУЧТЬ (August) 1919. Like #9. Back: Date of 15 НОЯБРЯ (November) 1919.	15.00	40.00	80.00

12	**500 Rubles**	Good	Fine	XF
	1919. Blue. Many color shades. Ornamental value numerals. Without Armenian text at upper left and right. Date of АВГУЧТЬ (August) 1919. Like #9. Back: Date of 15 НОЯБРЯ (November) 1919.	20.00	45.00	90.00

13	**1000 Rubles**	Good	Fine	XF
	1919. Lilac. Many color shades. Ornamental value numerals. Without Armenian text at upper left and right. Date of АВГУЧТЬ (August) 1919. Like #9. Back: Date of 15 НОЯБРЯ (November) 1919.	25.00	50.00	100

1920 First Issue

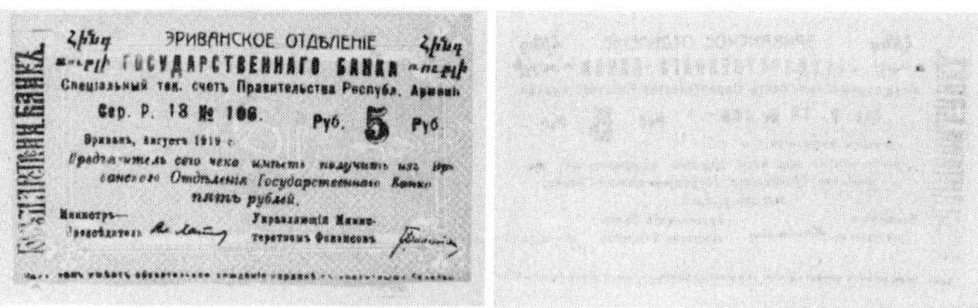

14	**5 Rubles**	Good	Fine	XF
	1919 (1920). Gray-blue. Many color shades. Armenian text at upper left and right. Date of АВГУЧТЬ (August) 1919. Back: Date of 15 НОЯБРЯ (November) 1919.			
	a. Issued note.	10.00	25.00	50.00
	x. Misprint with text: ГОЧУДАРЧТВЕНАГО.	10.00	25.00	50.00
	y. Misprint with text on back.	12.00	30.00	60.00

15	**10 Rubles**	Good	Fine	XF
	1919 (1920). Pink-brown. Many color shades. Armenian text at upper left and right. Date of АВГУЧТЬ (August) 1919. Back: Date of 15 НОЯБРЯ (November) 1919.			
	a. Issued note.	15.00	30.00	60.00
	x. Misprint with text: ГОЧУДАРЧТВЕНАГО.	15.00	30.00	60.00
	y. Misprint with underprint inverted.	15.00	30.00	60.00
	z. Misprint with text: ДЕЕЧЯТЬ.	20.00	35.00	70.00

16	**25 Rubles**	Good	Fine	XF
	1919 (1920). Brown. Many color shades. Armenian text at upper left and right. Date of АВГУЧТЬ (August) 1919. Back: Date of 15 НОЯБРЯ (November) 1919.			
	a. Issued note.	20.00	35.00	70.00
	x. Misprint with text: ГОЧУДАРЧТВЕНАГО.	20.00	35.00	70.00
	y. Misprint with text: ДВАДЦАШЬ.	30.00	45.00	90.00

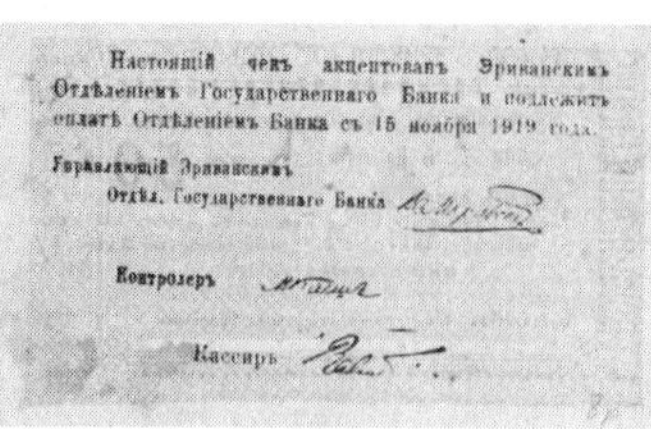

17	**50 Rubles**	Good	Fine	XF
	1919 (1920). Black on turquoise underprint. Many color shades. Armenian text at upper left and right. Date of АВГУЧТЬ (August) 1919. Back: Date of 15 НОЯБРЯ (November) 1919.			
	a. Issued note.	20.00	35.00	70.00
	x. Misprint with text on back.	20.00	35.00	70.00
	y. Misprint with text on back inverted.	20.00	35.00	70.00
	z. Misprint with text: ГОЧУДАРЧТВЕНАГО.	30.00	45.00	90.00

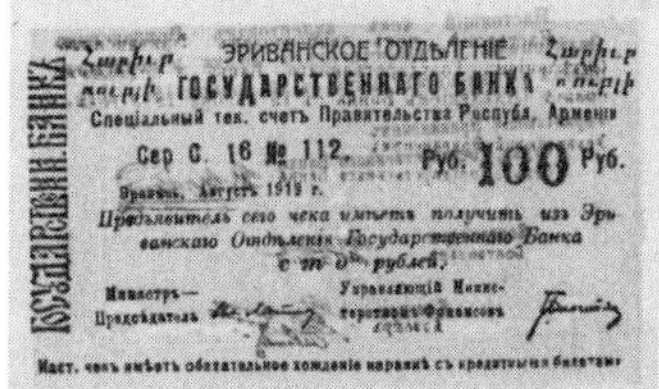

18 100 Rubles

1919 (1920). Black on yellow-green underprint. Many color shades. Armenian text at upper left and right. Date of АВГУЧТЬ (August) 1919. Back: Date of 15 НОЯБРЯ (November) 1919.

	Good	Fine	XF
a. Issued note.	10.00	25.00	50.00
x. Misprint with text on back.	10.00	25.00	50.00
y. Misprint with text on back inverted.	30.00	45.00	90.00
z. Misprint with text: МИНЧТЕРЧТВОМЪ.	30.00	45.00	90.00

1920 Second Issue

19 25 Rubles

1919 (1920). Gray-brown. Many color shades. Date of АВГУЧТЬ (August) 1919. Stamped signature. Back: Date of 15 ЯНВАРЯ (January) 1920.

	Good	Fine	XF
a. Issued note.	15.00	45.00	90.00
x. Misprint with text on back.	15.00	45.00	90.00
y. Misprint with text on back inverted.	40.00	65.00	125

20 25 Rubles

1919 (1920). Brown. Many color shades. Date of АВГУЧТЬ (August) 1919. Signature in facsimile print. Back: Date of 15 ЯНВАРЯ (January) 1920.

	Good	Fine	XF
a. Issued note.	15.00	40.00	80.00
x. Misprint with text on back.	15.00	40.00	80.00
y. Misprint with underprint inverted.	30.00	45.00	90.00

21 50 Rubles

1919 (1920). Green-blue. Many color shades. Date of АВГУЧТЬ (August) 1919. Back: Date of 15 ЯНВАРЯ (January) 1920.

Good	Fine	XF
10.00	45.00	90.00

22 100 Rubles

1919 (1920). Light green. Many color shades. Date of АВГУЧТЬ (August) 1919. Back: Date of 15 ЯНВАРЯ (January) 1920.

Good	Fine	XF
10.00	35.00	70.00

23 250 Rubles

1919 (1920). Pink. Many color shades. Date of АВГУЧТЬ (August) 1919. Stamped signature. Back: Date of 15 ЯНВАРЯ (Jaunuary) 1920.

	Good	Fine	XF
a. Issued note.	15.00	35.00	85.00
x. Misprint with text: ПЯТЬДНЧТЯЪ.	15.00	35.00	85.00
y. Misprint with text on back inverted.	15.00	35.00	85.00

24 250 Rubles

1919 (1920). Yellow-brown. Many color shades. Numerals of value in black. Date of АВГУЧТЬ (August) 1919. Signature in facsimile print. Back: Date of 15 ЯНВАРЯ (Jaunuary) 1920.

Good	Fine	XF
20.00	50.00	100

25 250 Rubles

1919 (1920). Yellow-brown. Many color shades. Like #24 but numerals of value in light blue. Date of АВГУЧТЬ (August) 1919. Signature in facsimile print. Back: Date of 15 ЯНВАРЯ (January) 1920.

Good	Fine	XF
40.00	125	250

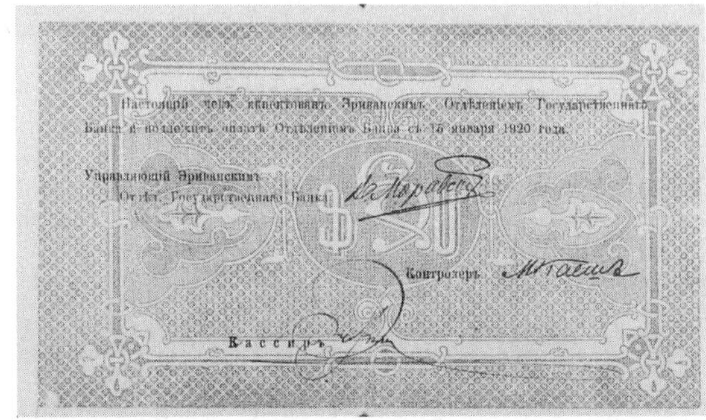

26 500 Rubles

1919 (1920). Light blue to gray-blue. Many color shades. Date of АВГУЧТЬ (August) 1919. Back: Date of 15 ЯНВАРЯ (January) 1920.

	Good	Fine	XF
a. Issued note.	20.00	45.00	90.00
x. Misprint with underprint inverted.	30.00	80.00	125

27 1000 Rubles

1919 (1920). Black. Many color shades. Date of АВГУЧТЬ (August) 1919. Back: Date of 15 ЯНВАРЯ (January) 1920.

	Good	Fine	XF
a. Light violet underprint.	15.00	35.00	70.00
b. Orange-brown underprint.	15.00	35.00	70.00
c. Pink underprint. White paper.	15.00	35.00	70.00
d. Pink underprint. Watermark. Buff paper.	15.00	35.00	70.00
x. Misprint with text on back.	15.00	35.00	70.00
y. Misprint with underprint inverted.	15.00	35.00	70.00

28 5000 Rubles

1919 (1920). Black. Many color shades. Date of АВГУЧТЬ (August) 1919. Back: Date of 15 ЯНВАРЯ (January) 1920.

	Good	Fine	XF
a. Gray underprint.	20.00	60.00	125
b. Light purple underprint. White paper.	20.00	60.00	125
c. Light purple underprint. Watermark. Buff paper.	20.00	60.00	125
x. Misprint with underprint inverted.	40.00	90.00	175

		Good	Fine	XF
29	**10,000 Rubles** 1919 (1920). Green. Many color shades. Date of АВГУЧТЬ (August) 1919. Back: Stamped signature. Date of 15 ЯНВАРЯ (January) 1920.			
	a. Issued note.	15.00	35.00	60.00
	x. Misprint with numerals of value reversed.	20.00	45.00	90.00
	y. Misprint with text on back.	20.00	45.00	90.00
	z. Misprint with margin text from top to bottom at left.	20.00	40.00	80.00

1920 Third Issue

		VG	VF	UNC
30	**50 Rubles** 1919 (1920). Brown on orange underprint. Facing dragons at left and right. Printer: W&S.	20.00	45.00	90.00

		VG	VF	UNC
31	**100 Rubles** 1919 (1920). Green on orange and yellow underprint. Landscape with mountains. Back: Eagle at center. Printer: W&S.	20.00	50.00	100

		VG	VF	UNC
32	**250 Rubles** 1919 (1920). Violet on green and yellow underprint. Back: Woman spinning at left. Printer: W&S.	30.00	75.00	150

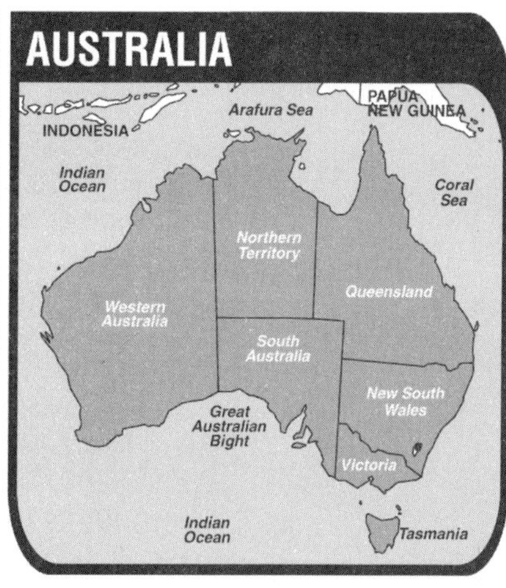

The Commonwealth of Australia, the smallest continent and largest island in the world, is located south of Indonesia between the Indian and Pacific oceans. It has an area of 7.68 million sq. km. and a population of 21 million. Capital: Canberra. Due to its early and sustained isolation, Australia is the habitat of such curious and unique fauna as the kangaroo, koala, platypus, wombat and barking lizard. The continent possesses extensive mineral deposits, the most important of which are gold, coal, silver, nickel, uranium, lead and zinc. Livestock raising, mining and manufacturing are the principal industries. Chief exports are wool, meat, wheat, iron ore, coal and nonferrous metals.

Aboriginal settlers arrived on the continent from Southeast Asia about 40,000 years before the first Europeans began exploration in the 17th century. No formal territorial claims were made until 1770, when Capt. James Cook took possession in the name of Great Britain. Six colonies were created in the late 18th and 19th centuries; they federated and became the Commonwealth of Australia in 1901. The new country took advantage of its natural resources to rapidly develop agricultural and manufacturing industries and to make a major contribution to the British effort in World Wars I and II. In recent decades, Australia has transformed itself into an internationally competitive, advanced market economy. It boasted one of the OECD's fastest growing economies during the 1990s, a performance due in large part to economic reforms adopted in the 1980s. Long-term concerns include climate-change issues such as the depletion of the ozone layer and more frequent droughts, and management and conservation of coastal areas, especially the Great Barrier Reef.

RULERS:

British

MONETARY SYSTEM:

1 Shilling = 12 Pence
1 Pound = 20 Shillings = 2 Dollars
1 Pound = 20 Shillings; to 1966

COMMONWEALTH

Australian Bank of Commerce

1910 Superscribed Issue

		Good	Fine	XF
A72	**1 Pound** ND (1910).	15,000	40,000	110,000
A73	**5 Pounds** ND (1910).	—	—	—
A74	**10 Pounds** ND (1910).	—	—	—
A75	**50 Pounds** ND (1910).	—	—	—

Bank of Adelaide

1910 Superscribed Issue

		Good	Fine	XF
A76	**1 Pound** ND (1910).	10,000	35,000	100,000
A77	**5 Pounds** ND (1910).	17,000	50,000	150,000
A78	**10 Pounds** ND (1910).	—	—	—
A79	**20 Pounds** ND (1910).	—	—	—

No.	Description	Good	Fine	XF
A80	**50 Pounds** ND (1910).	—	—	—
A81	**100 Pounds** ND (1910).			
	a. Adelaide.	—	—	—
	b. Hobart.	15,000	45,000	130,000
	c. Melbourne.	—	—	—
	d. Perth.	10,000	35,000	100,000
	e. Sydney.	10,000	35,000	100,000

Bank of Australasia

1910 Superscribed Issue

No.	Description	Good	Fine	XF
A82	**5 Pounds** ND (1910).			
	a. Hobart.	—	—	—
	b. Perth.	—	—	—
A83	**10 Pounds** ND (1910).			
	a. Adelaide.	—	—	—
	b. Brisbane.	30,000	80,000	175,000
	c. Hobart.	—	—	—
	d. Melbourne.	—	—	—
	e. Perth.	30,000	80,000	175,000
	f. Sydney.	—	—	—
A84	**50 Pounds** ND (1910).			
	a. Adelaide.	—	—	—
	b. Hobart.	—	—	—
	c. Melbourne.	—	—	—
	d. Sydney.	—	—	—
A85	**100 Pounds** ND (1910).			
	a. Melbourne.	—	—	—

Bank of New South Wales

1910 Superscribed Issue

No.	Description	Good	Fine	XF
A86	**1 Pound** ND (1910).			
	a. Melbourne.	18,000	50,000	140,000
	b. Sydney.	15,000	45,000	120,000
	c. No domicile.	—	—	—
A87	**5 Pounds** ND (1910).			
	a. Sydney.	—	—	—
A88	**10 Pounds** ND (1910).			
	a. Adelaide.	—	—	—
	b. Melbourne.	—	—	—
	c. Sydney.	—	—	—
	d. No domicile.	40,000	100,000	190,000
A89	**20 Pounds** ND (1910).			
	a. Adelaide.	—	—	—
	b. Melbourne.	—	—	—
	c. Perth.	—	—	—
	d. Sydney.	—	—	—
A90	**50 Pounds** ND (1910).			
	a. Adelaide.	—	—	—
	b. Melbourne.	—	—	—
	c. Sydney.	—	—	—
A91	**100 Pounds** ND (1910).			
	a. Adelaide.	—	—	—
	b. Melbourne.	—	—	—
	c. Sydney.	—	—	—

Bank of Victoria

1910 Superscribed Issue

No.	Description	Good	Fine	XF
A92	**1 Pound** ND (1910).	10,000	35,000	105,000
A93	**5 Pounds** ND (1910).	—	—	—
A94	**10 Pounds** ND (1910).			
	a. Adelaide.	—	—	—
	b. Melbourne.	35,000	90,000	190,000
	c. Perth.	—	—	—
	d. Sydney.	—	—	—
A95	**20 Pounds** ND (1910).	—	—	—
A96	**50 Pounds** ND (1910).	—	—	—

City Bank of Sydney

1910 Superscribed Issue

No.	Description	Good	Fine	XF
A97	**1 Pound** ND (1910).	20,000	60,000	140,000
A98	**5 Pounds** ND (1910).	—	—	—
A99	**10 Pounds** ND (1910).	—	—	—
A100	**20 Pounds** ND (1910).	—	—	—
A101	**50 Pounds** ND (1910).	—	—	—

Commercial Bank of Australia

1910 Superscribed Issue

No.	Description	Good	Fine	XF
A102	**1 Pound** ND (1910).			
	a. Melbourne.	—	—	—
	b. Perth.	20,000	60,000	160,000
A103	**5 Pounds** ND (1910).			
	a. Hobart.	—	—	—

Commercial Bank of Tasmania

1910 Superscribed Issue

No.	Description	Good	Fine	XF
A104	**1 Pound** ND (1910).			
	a. Hobart.	15,000	50,000	150,000
	b. Launceston.	18,000	55,000	160,000
A105	**5 Pounds** ND (1910).			
	a. Launceston.	—	—	—
A106	**10 Pounds** ND (1910).			
	a. Hobart.	—	—	—
A107	**20 Pounds** ND (1910).	—	—	—

Commercial Banking Company of Sydney
1910 Superscribed Issue

No.	Description	Good	Fine	XF
A108	**1 Pound**			
	ND (1910).	9,000	40,000	125,000
A109	**5 Pounds**			
	ND (1910).	—	—	—
A110	**10 Pounds**			
	ND (1910).	—	—	—

English, Scottish & Australian Bank
1910 Superscribed Issue

No.	Description	Good	Fine	XF
A111	**1 Pound**			
	ND (1910).			
	a. Adelaide.	—	—	—
	b. Melbourne.	15,000	50,000	145,000
	c. Sydney.	—	—	—
A112	**5 Pounds**			
	ND (1910).			
	a. Adelaide.	—	—	—
	b. Melbourne.	—	—	—
	c. Sydney.	—	—	—
A113	**10 Pounds**			
	ND (1910).			
	a. Adelaide.	—	—	—
	b. Melbourne.	—	—	—
A114	**20 Pounds**			
	ND (1910).			
	a. Adelaide.	—	—	—
	b. Melbourne.	—	—	—
A115	**50 Pounds**			
	ND (1910).			
	a. Adelaide.	—	—	—
	b. Melbourne.	—	—	—
	c. Sydney.	—	—	—

Color Abbreviation Guide

New to the *Standard Catalog of® World Paper Money* are the following abbreviations related to color references:

BC: Back color
PC: Paper color

London Bank of Australia
1910 Superscribed Issue

No.	Description	Good	Fine	XF
A116	**1 Pound**			
	ND (1910).			
	a. Adelaide.	—	—	—
	b. Melbourne.	5,000	18,000	50,000
A117	**5 Pounds**			
	ND (1910).	—	—	—
A118	**10 Pounds**			
	ND (1910).			
	a. Adelaide.	—	—	—
	b. Melbourne.	—	—	—
	c. Sydney.	—	—	—
A119	**50 Pounds**			
	ND (1910).			
	a. Adelaide.	—	—	—
	b. Melbourne.	—	—	—
	c. Sydney.	—	—	—
A120	**100 Pounds**			
	ND (1910).			
	a. Adelaide.	—	—	—
	b. Melbourne.	—	—	—
	c. Sydney.	—	—	—

National Bank of Australasia
1910 Superscribed Issue

No.	Description	Good	Fine	XF
A121	**1 Pound**			
	ND (1910).			
	a. Adelaide.	—	—	—
	b. Melbourne.	5,000	15,000	65,000
	c. Perth.	7,000	20,000	75,000
	d. Sydney.	—	—	—
A122	**5 Pounds**			
	ND (1910).			
	a. Adelaide.	—	—	—
	b. Melbourne.	15,000	40,000	110,000
	c. Perth.	—	—	—
	d. Sydney.	—	—	—
A123	**10 Pounds**			
	ND (1910).			
	a. Adelaide.	25,000	75,000	180,000
	b. Melbourne.	—	—	—
	c. Perth.	30,000	80,000	190,000
A124	**20 Pounds**			
	ND (1910).			
	a. Adelaide.	—	—	—
	b. Melbourne.	45,000	125,000	400,000
	c. Perth.	—	—	—
A125	**50 Pounds**			
	ND (1910).			
	a. Adelaide.	—	—	—
	b. Melbourne.	—	—	—
	c. Sydney.	—	—	—

		Good	Fine	XF
A126	**100 Pounds** ND (1910).			
	a. Overprint on Melbourne.	—	—	—
	b. Overprint on Perth.	—	—	—

Queensland Government
1910 Superscribed Issue

		Good	Fine	XF
A127	**1 Pound** ND (1910).	—	—	—
A128	**5 Pounds** ND (1910).	—	—	—

Royal Bank of Australia
1910 Superscribed Issue

		Good	Fine	XF
A129	**1 Pound** ND (1910).			
	a. Melbourne.	20,000	75,000	185,000
	b. Sydney.	15,000	70,000	175,000

Union Bank of Australia
1910 Superscribed Issue

		Good	Fine	XF
A130	**1 Pound** ND (1910).			
	a. Adelaide.	15,000	45,000	150,000
	b. Melbourne.	10,000	35,000	130,000
	c. Perth.	12,500	100,000	150,000
A131	**5 Pounds** ND (1910).			
	a. Adelaide.	—	—	—
	b. Hobart.	—	—	—
	c. Melbourne.	—	—	—
	d. Perth.	—	—	—
	e. Sydney.	—	—	—
A132	**10 Pounds** ND (1910).			
	a. Adelaide.	—	—	—
	b. Hobart.	—	—	—
	c. Perth.	—	—	—
	d. Sydney.	—	—	—
A133	**20 Pounds** ND (1910).			
	a. Adelaide.	—	—	—
	b. Hobart.	—	—	—
	c. Melbourne.	45,000	130,000	420,000
	d. Perth.	—	—	—
	e. Sydney.	—	—	—
A134	**50 Pounds** ND (1910).			
	a. Adelaide.	—	—	—
	b. Melbourne.	—	—	—

Western Australian Bank
1910 Superscribed Issue

		Good	Fine	XF
A135	**1 Pound** ND (1910).	20,000	75,000	185,000
A136	**5 Pounds** ND (1910).	—	—	—
A137	**10 Pounds** ND (1910).	—	—	—

Commonwealth of Australia, Treasury Notes
1913 First Issue

		Good	Fine	XF
1	**5 Shillings** ND (ca. 1916). Black on green underprint. Portrait King George V at left. BC: Green.			
	a. Signature C. J. Cerutty and J. R. Collins. (Not issued).	—	—	125,000
	s1. Specimen without signature	—	—	75,000
	s2. With violet handstamp: *Specimen*. Signature C. J. Cerutty and J. R. Collins. (Not issued).	—	—	85,000

		Good	Fine	XF
1A	**10 Shillings** ND (1913). Dark blue on multicolor underprint. Arms at left. Red serial #. Signature J. R. Collins and G. T. Allen. Back: Goulburn Weir (Victoria) at center.			
	a. Red serial # M 000001.	—	—	1,000,000
	b. Red serial #M 000002 to 000005.	—	—	200,000
	c. Red serial # M 000006 to 000100.	7,500	22,500	100,000
1B	**1 Pound** ND (1914-1915 -old date 1.9.1894). Pale blue and pink. Allegorical woman with anchor standing at left, arms at right. Signature J. R. Collins and G. T. Allen. A reprint of the English, Scottish & Australian Bank Limited superscribed: *AUSTRALIAN NOTE*. Serial # prefix and suffix *A, B*.	10,000	30,000	125,000

Note: Because of the shortage of currency created by WWI, old plates from the English, Scottish and Australian Bank Limited were used for a special printing of 1,300,000 notes.

		Good	Fine	XF
2	**1 Pound** ND (1913-1914). Emergency rainbow pound. Black text on blue, orange and multicolor underprint. *Australian Note* at top. Signature J. R. Collins and G. T. Allen.			
	a. With *No.* by serial #.	7,500	22,500	100,000
	b. Without *No.* by serial #.	7,500	22,500	100,000
2A	**1000 Pounds** ND (1914-1924). Light blue. Arms at bottom center. Flock of Merino sheep (Bungaree, S.A.) at center.			
	a. Signature J. R. Collins and G. T. Allen.	—	200,000	700,000
	b. Signature J. Kell and J. R. Collins.	—	200,000	800,000

Note: #2A was issued primarily for interbank transactions only, but a few were released to the public.

1913 Second Issue

		Good	Fine	XF
3	**10 Shillings** ND (1913-1918). Dark blue on multicolor underprint. Arms at left. Black serial #. Back: Goulburn Weir (Victoria) at center.			
	a. Signature J. R. Collins and G. T. Allen (1914). Five serial # varieties.	3,000	10,000	42,500
	b. Signature C. J. Cerutty and J. R. Collins (1918). 2 serial # varieties.	2,000	7,500	30,000

		Good	Fine	XF
4	**1 Pound** ND (1913-1918). Dark blue on multicolor underprint. Crowned arms at center. Back: Gold mine workers at center.			
	a. Signature J. R. Collins and G. T. Allen (1914). Red serial #.	10,000	20,000	45,000
	b. As a. but blue serial #. Serial # prefix: Q, R, S, T.	500	1,250	—
	c. As a. Three other serial # prefixes.	1,000	3,000	30,000
	d. Signature C. J. Cerutty and J. R. Collins (1918).	250	2,500	25,000

		Good	Fine	XF
4A	**5 Pounds** ND (1913). Dark blue on multicolor underprint. Arms at left. Back: River landscape (Hawkesbury) at center without mosaic underprint of 5s.	10,000	25,000	75,000

		Good	Fine	XF
5	**5 Pounds** ND (1913-1918). Dark blue on multicolor underprint. Arms at left. Back: River landscape (Hawkesbury) at center with mosaic underprint of 5s.			
	a. Signature J. R. Collins and G. T. Three serial # varieties.	1,000	7,500	50,000
	b. Signature C. J. Cerutty and J. R. Allen (1918). Serial # suffix V.	7,000	20,000	100,000
	c. Signature C. J. Cerutty and J. R. Allen (1918). Serial # with prefix and suffix letter.	500	2,500	30,000

		Good	Fine	XF
6	**10 Pounds** ND (1913-1918). Dark blue on multicolor underprint. Arms at bottom center. Back: Horse-drawn wagons loaded with sacks of grain (Narwonah, N.S.W.) at center.			
	a. Signature J. R. Collins and G. T. Allen.	4,000	20,000	75,000
	b. Signature C. J. Cerutty and J. R. Collins (1918). Three serial # varieties.	2,500	12,500	40,000

		Good	Fine	XF
7	**20 Pounds** ND (1914-1918). Dark blue on multicolor underprint. Arms at left. Back: Lumberjacks cutting a tree (Bruny Isle, Tasmania) at center.			
	a. Signature J. R. Collins and G. T. Allen.	7,500	25,000	10,000
	b. Signature C. J. Cerutty and J. R. Collins (1918). Serial # prefix X.	10,000	37,500	125,000
	c. Signature C. J. Cerutty and J. R. Collins (1918). Serial number suffix X.	7,500	22,500	85,000

		Good	Fine	XF
8	**50 Pounds** ND (1914-1918). Blue on multicolor underprint. Arms at top center. Back: Flock of Merino sheep (Bungaree, S. A.) at center.			
	a. Signature J. R. Collins and G. T. Allen.	7,500	27,500	150,000
	b. Signature C. J. Cerutty and J. R. Collins (1918). Small serial # prefix Y.	10,000	40,000	125,000
	c. Signature C. J. Cerutty and J. R. Collins (1918). Serial # suffix Y.	7,500	35,000	100,000
	d. Signature C. J. Cerutty and J. R. Collins (1918). Large serial # preffix Y.	5,000	22,500	75,000

		Good	Fine	XF
9	**100 Pounds** ND (1914-1918). Blue on multicolor underprint. Arms at left. Back: Upper Yarra River (Victoria) at left center, Leura Falls (N.S.W.) at center right.			
	a. Signature J. R. Collins and G. T. Allen.	20,000	32,500	250,000
	b. Signature C. J. Cerutty and J. R. Collins (1918). Serial # suffix Z.	17,500	30,000	150,000
	c. Signature C. J. Cerutty and J. R. Collins (1918). Serial # prefix Z.	15,000	25,000	125,000

Commonwealth Bank of Australia

1923-1925 Issue

10	1/2 Sovereign	VG	VF	UNC
	ND (1923). Dark brown and brown on multicolor underprint. Portrait King George V at right, arms at left with title: *CHAIRMAN OF DIRECTORS NOTE ISSUE DEPT. / COMMONWEALTH BANK OF AUSTRALIA* below lower left signature. Signature D. Miller and J. R. Collins Back: Goulburn Weir (Victoria) at center.	750	1,500	7,000

11	1 Pound	VG	VF	UNC
	ND (1923). Dark olive-green on multicolor underprint. Portrait King George V at right, arms at left with title: *CHAIRMAN OF DIRECTORS NOTE ISSUE DEPT. / COMMONWEALTH BANK OF AUSTRALIA* below lower left signature. Signature D. Miller and J. R. Collins Back: Capt. Cook's Landing at Botany Bay at center. Printer: T. S. Harrison.			
	a. Serial # prefix H; J; K.	7,500	20,000	50,000
	b. Fractional serial # prefix.	400	2,500	15,000

12	1 Pound	VG	VF	UNC
	ND (1923). Dark olive-green on multicolor underprint. Portrait King George V at right, arms at left with title: *CHAIRMAN OF DIRECTORS NOTE ISSUE DEPT. / COMMONWEALTH BANK OF AUSTRALIA* below lower left signature. Signature D. Miller and J. R. Collins Back: Capt. Cook's landing at Botany Bay at center.			
	a. Serial # prefix J; K.	10,000	35,000	150,000
	b. Fractional serial # prefix.	250	7,500	12,500

13	5 Pounds	VG	VF	UNC
	ND (1924-1927). Deep blue on multicolor underprint. Portrait King George V at right, arms at left with title: *CHAIRMAN OF DIRECTORS NOTE ISSUE DEPT. / COMMONWEALTH BANK OF AUSTRALIA* below lower left signature. Back: River landscape (Hawkesbury) at center.			
	a. J. Kell and J. R. Collins (1924).	1,000	4,000	35,000
	b. J. Kell and J. Heathershaw (1927).	925	3,500	25,000
	c. Signature E. C. Riddle and J. Heathershaw (1927).	7,500	20,000	100,000

14	10 Pounds	VG	VF	UNC
	ND (1925). Proof without signature. Deep red on multicolor underprint. Portrait King George V at right, arms at left with title: *CHAIRMAN OF DIRECTORS NOTE ISSUE DEPT. / COMMONWEALTH BANK OF AUSTRALIA* below lower left signature. Back: Horse-drawn wagons loaded with sacks of grain at lower center.	—	—	—

1926-1927 Issue

15	1/2 Sovereign	VG	VF	UNC
	ND (1926-1933). Dark brown and brown on multicolor underprint. Portrait King George V at right, arms at left with title: *GOVERNOR / COMMONWEALTH BANK OF AUSTRALIA* below lower left signature. Like #10. Back: Goulburn Weir (Victoria) at center.			
	a. J. Kell and J. R. Collins (1926).	900	1,400	40,000
	b. J. Kell and J. Heathershaw (1927).	1,200	4,000	45,000
	c. Signature E. C. Riddle and J. Heathershaw (1927).	200	900	25,000
	d. Signature E. C. Riddle and H. J. Sheehan (1933).	500	2,500	30,000

16	1 Pound	VG	VF	UNC
	ND (1926-1932). Dark olive-green on multicolor underprint. Portrait King George V at right, arms at left with title: *GOVERNOR / COMMONWEALTH BANK OF AUSTRALIA* below lower left signature. Like #12. Back: Capt. Cook's landing at Botany Bay at center.			
	a. J. Kell and J. R. Collins (1926).	300	2,200	17,000
	b. J. Kell and J. Heathershaw (1927).	750	1,500	15,000
	c. Signature E. C. Riddle and J. Heathershaw (1927).	200	750	6,000
	d. Signature E. C. Riddle and H. J. Sheehan (1932).	400	2,500	12,500

		VG	VF	UNC
17	**5 Pounds**			
	ND (1927-1932). Deep blue on multicolor underprint. Portrait King George V at right, arms at left with title: *GOVERNOR / COMMONWEALTH BANK OF AUSTRALIA* below lower left signature. Like #13. Back: River landscape (Hawkesbury) at center.			
	a. J. Kell and J. Heathershaw (1927).	2,000	7,500	5,000
	b. Signature E. C. Riddle and J. Heathershaw (1928).	500	1,500	15,000
	c. Signature E. C. Riddle and H. J. Sheehan (1932).	200	6,000	40,000

		VG	VF	UNC
18	**10 Pounds**			
	ND (1925-1933). Deep red on multicolor underprint. Portrait King George V at right, arms at left with title: *GOVERNOR / COMMONWEALTH BANK OF AUSTRALIA* below lower left signature. Like #14. Back: Horse-drawn wagons loaded with sacks of grain (Narwonah, N.S.W.) at center.			
	a. J. Kell and J. R. Collins (1925).	5,000	25,000	75,000
	b. Signature E. C. Riddle and J. Heathershaw (1925).	400	1,500	40,000
	c. Signature E. C. Riddle and H. J. Sheehan (1933).	15,000	40,000	100,000

1933-1934 Issue

		VG	VF	UNC
19	**10 Shillings**	500	2,000	15,000
	ND (1933). Brown on multicolor underprint. Portrait King George V at right. Signature E. C. Riddle and H. J. Sheehan. Back: Allegorical manufacturers at center, large *1/2* at left. Watermark: Edward (VIII), Prince of Wales.			

		VG	VF	UNC
20	**10 Shillings**	350	1,000	7,500
	ND (1934). Brown on multicolor underprint. Portrait King George V at right. Signature E. C. Riddle and H. J. Sheehan. Back: Allegorical manufacturers at center, large *1/2* at left. Watermark: Edward (VIII), Prince of Wales.			

		VG	VF	UNC
21	**10 Shillings**	200	750	7,500
	ND (1936-1939). Reduced size from #19 and #20. Orange on multicolor underprint. Portrait King George V at right. Signature E. C. Riddle and H. J. Sheehan. Back: Allegorical manufacturers at center, large *10/-* at left. Watermark: Edward (VIII), Prince of Wales.			

		VG	VF	UNC
22	**1 Pound**			
	ND (1933-1938). Dark green on multicolor underprint. Portrait King George V at right. Signature E. C. Riddle and H. J. Sheehan. Back: Shepherds with sheep at center, large *L1* at left. Watermark: Edward (VIII), Prince of Wales.			
	a. Issued note.	100	300	3,750
	s. Specimen.	—	—	—

		VG	VF	UNC
23	**5 Pounds**			
	ND (1933-1939). Deep blue on multicolor underprint. Portrait King George V at left. Signature E. C. Riddle and H. J. Sheehan. Back: Dock workers with sacks, bales and barrels at upper left. Watermark: Edward (VIII), Prince of Wales.			
	a. Pink face of King.	1,500	5,000	25,000
	b. White face of King.	1,500	5,000	25,000

		VG	VF	UNC
24	**10 Pounds** ND (1934-1939). Deep red on multicolor underprint. Portrait King George V at center. Signature E. C. Riddle and H. J. Sheehan. Back: Group symbolizing agriculture at upper right. Watermark: Edward (VIII), Prince of Wales.	1,250	3,000	20,000

1938-1940 Issue

		VG	VF	UNC
24A	**5 Shillings** ND (1946). Black on red-brown underprint. Portrait King George VI at center. Signature H. T. Armitage and S. G. McFarlane. Back: Australian crown coin design at center. BC: Red-brown. (Not issued).	—	—	—

		VG	VF	UNC
25	**10 Shillings** ND (1939-1952). Orange on multicolor underprint. Portrait King George VI at right. Like #21. Back: Allegorical manufacturers at center, large *10/* at left. Watermark: Captain Cook.			
	a. Orange signature H. J. Sheehan and S. G. McFarlane (1939).	50.00	350	3,500
	b. Black signature H. T. Armitage and S. G. McFarlane (1942).	30.00	150	1,500
	c. Black signature H. C. Coombs and G. P. N. Watt (1949).	35.00	160	1,600
	d. Black signature H. C. Coombs and R. Wilson (1952).	50.00	275	2,750
	r1. As b. Replacement.	7,500	35,000	100,000
	r2. As c. Replacement.	1,500	6,500	50,000
	r3. As d. Replacement.	2,000	7,500	55,000

		VG	VF	UNC
26	**1 Pound** ND (1938-1952). Dark green on multicolor underprint. Portrait King George VI at right. Like #22. Back: Shepherds with sheep at center. Watermark: Captain Cook.			
	a. Green signature H. J. Sheehan and S. G. McFarlane (1938).	60.00	200	1,750
	b. Black signature H. T. Armitage and S. G. McFarlane (1942).	40.00	100	800
	c. Black signature H. C. Coombs and G. P. N. Watt (1949).	45.00	110	850
	d. Black signature H. C. Coombs and R. Wilson (1952).	45.00	120	1,200
	r1. As b. Replacement.	4,000	20,000	75,000
	r2. As c. Replacement.	1,500	10,000	40,000
	r3. As d. Replacement.	1,750	12,500	50,000

		VG	VF	UNC
27	**5 Pounds** ND (1939-1952). Deep blue on multicolor underprint. Portrait King George VI at left. Like #23. Back: Workers with sacks, bales and barrels at upper left. Watermark: Captain Cook.			
	a. Blue signature H. J. Sheehan and S. G. McFarlane (1939).	275	1,500	15,000
	b. Black signature H. T. Armitage and S. G. McFarlane (1941).	75.00	350	3,250
	c. Black signature H. C. Coombs and G. P. N. Watt (1949).	80.00	400	4,000
	d. Black signature H. C. Coombs and R. Wilson (1952).	85.00	425	4,250

		VG	VF	UNC
28	**10 Pounds** ND (1940-1952). Deep red on multicolor underprint. Portrait King George VI at bottom center. Like #24. Back: Group symbolizing agriculture at upper right. Watermark: Captain Cook.			
	a. Red signature H. J. Sheehan and S. G. McFarlane (1940).	400	2,500	17,500
	b. Black signature H. T. Armitage and S. G. McFarlane (1942).	250	900	9,000
	c. Black signature H. C. Coombs and G. P. N. Watt (1949).	250	900	9,000
	d. Black signature H. C. Coombs and R. Wilson (1952).	350	2,250	15,000

		VG	VF	UNC
28A	**50 Pounds** ND (1939). Specimen. Purple on multicolor underprint. Portrait King George VI. Watermark: Captain Cook.	—	—	—

Note: All but a few examples were destroyed in 1958.

28B	100 Pounds	VG	VF	UNC
	ND (1939). Brown on multicolor underprint. Portrait King George VI. Signature H. J. Sheehan and S. G. McFarlane. Specimen.	—	—	—

Note: All but a few examples were destroyed in 1958.

1953-1954 Issue

29	10 Shillings	VG	VF	UNC
	ND (1954-1960). Dark brown on multicolor underprint. Arms at lower left. Portrait M. Flinders at right. Signature H. C. Coombs and R. Wilson with title *GOVERNOR / COMMONWEALTH BANK OF AUSTRALIA* below lower left signature. Back: Parliament in Canberra at left center. Watermark: Capt. James Cook.			
	a. Issued note.	50.00	100	550
	r. Replacement note.	2,500	12,500	35,000

30	1 Pound	VG	VF	UNC
	ND (1953-1960). Dark green on multicolor underprint. Arms at upper center, medallic portrait Queen Elizabeth II at right. Signature H. C. Coombs and R. Wilson with title *GOVERNOR / COMMONWEALTH BANK OF AUSTRALIA* below lower left signature. Back: Facing medallic portrait C. Sturt and H. Hume. Watermark: Capt. James Cook.			
	a. Issued note.	20.00	40.00	350
	r. Replacement note.	1,500	7,500	22,500

31	5 Pounds	VG	VF	UNC
	ND (1954-1959). Blue on multicolor underprint. Arms at upper left, portrait Sir J. Franklin at right. Signature H. C. Coombs and R. Wilson with title *GOVERNOR / COMMONWEALTH BANK OF AUSTRALIA* below lower left signature. Back: Sheep and agricultural products between bull and cow's head. Watermark: Capt. James Cook.			
	a. Issued note.	50.00	250	1,300
	s. Specimen.	—	—	—

32	10 Pounds	VG	VF	UNC
	ND (1954-1959). Red and black on multicolor underprint. Portrait Gov. Phillip at left, arms at upper center. Signature H. C. Coombs and R. Wilson with title *GOVERNOR / COMMONWEALTH BANK OF AUSTRALIA* below lower left signature. Back: Symbols of science and industry at center, allegorical woman kneeling with compass at right.			
	a. Issued note.	75.00	300	2,500
	s. Specimen.	—	—	—

COMMONWEALTH OF AUSTRALIA

Reserve Bank

1960-1961 ND Issue

35	5 Pounds	VG	VF	UNC
	ND (1960-1965). Black on blue underprint. Arms at upper left, portrait Sir John Franklin at right. Signature H. C. Coombs and R. Wilson with title *GOVERNOR / RESERVE BANK of AUSTRALIA* below lower left signature. Like #31. Back: Cattle, sheep and agricultural products across center. BC: Blue. Watermark: Capt. James Cook.			
	a. Issued note.	35.00	150	500
	r. Serial # suffix *, replacement.	750	5,000	20,000
	s. Specimen.	—	8,000	60,000

36	10 Pounds	VG	VF	UNC
	ND (1960-1965). Black on red underprint. Arms at top center, portrait Gov. Arthur Philip at left. Signature H. C. Coombs and R. Wilson with title *GOVERNOR / RESERVE BANK of AUSTRALIA* below lower left signature. Like #32. Back: Symbols of science and industry. Watermark: Capt. James Cook.			
	a. Issued note.	50.00	300	1,000
	s. Specimen.	—	10,000	75,000

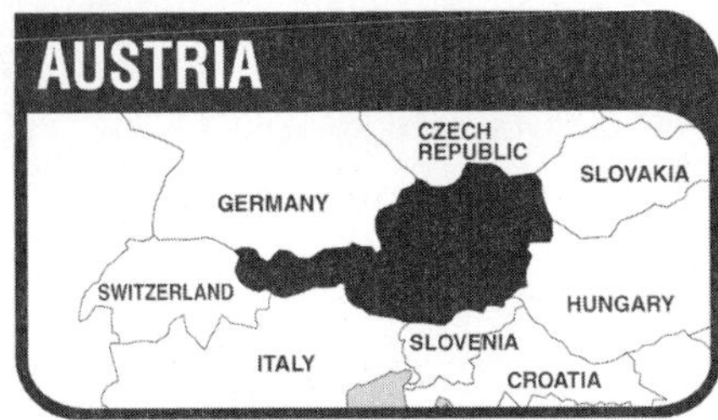

The Republic of Austria (Oesterreich), a parliamentary democracy located in mountainous central Europe, has an area of 83,870 sq. km. and a population of 8.2 million. Capital: Vienna. Austria is primarily an industrial country. Machinery, iron and steel, textiles, yarns and timber are exported.

Once the center of power for the large Austro-Hungarian Empire, Austria was reduced to a small republic after its defeat in World War I. Following annexation by Nazi Germany in 1938 and subsequent occupation by the victorious Allies in 1945, Austria's status remained unclear for a decade. A State Treaty signed in 1955 ended the occupation, recognized Austria's independence, and forbade unification with Germany. A constitutional law that same year declared the country's "perpetual neutrality" as a condition for Soviet military withdrawal. The Soviet Union's collapse in 1991 and Austria's entry into the European Union in 1995 have altered the meaning of this neutrality. A prosperous, democratic country, Austria entered the EU Economic and Monetary Union in 1999.

RULERS:

Maria Theresa, 1740-1780
Joseph II, jointly with his Mother, 1765-1780 alone, 1780-1790
Leopold II, 1790-1792
Franz II (I), 1792-1835 (as Franz II, 1792-1806) (as Franz I, 1806-1835)
Ferdinand I, 1835-1848
Franz Joseph, 1848-1916
Karl I, 1916-1918

MONETARY SYSTEM:

1 Gulden = 60 Kreuzer, 1754-1857
1 Gulden = (Florin) = 100 Kreuzer, 1857-1892
1 Krone = 100 Heller, 1892-1924
1 Schilling = 100 Groschen, 1924-1938, 1945-2002

KINGDOM

Note on "Formulare" examples: Corresponding to the following listings through the 1840s there existed so-called "Formulare" examples, notes without seal, signatures or serial numbers which were destined to be displayed in various banking houses. These notes are included in many collections as they are the only examples available of these early types.

Wiener Stadt Banco

1759 Issue

Zettel = Note.

		Good	Fine	XF
A1	**10 Gulden**			
	1.11.1759. Black. Value in German, Czech and Hungarian languages. Signature Peter Joseph von Rosler. Uniface.			
	a. Issued note. Unique.	—	—	—
	b. "Formulare".	—	—	—
A2	**25 Gulden**	**Good**	**Fine**	**XF**
	1.11.1759. Black. Value in 3 languages. Signature Peter Joseph von Rosler. Uniface.			
	a. Issued note. Unique.	—	—	—
	b. "Formulare".	—	—	—

1762 Issue

		Good	Fine	XF
A3	**5 Gulden**			
	1.7.1762. Black. Printer: Jakub Degen, Wein. 85x170mm.			
	a. Issued Note.	—	—	—
	b. "Formulare".	—	—	550
A4	**10 Gulden**	**Good**	**Fine**	**XF**
	1.7.1762. Black, value red. Printer: Jakub Degen, Wein. 85x196mm.			
	a. Issued note.	—	—	—
	b. "Formulare".	—	—	550
A5	**25 Gulden**	**Good**	**Fine**	**XF**
	1.7.1762. Black, value ochre. Printer: Jakub Degen, Wein. 85x196mm.			
	a. Issued note.	—	—	—
	b. "Formulare".	—	—	550
A6	**50 Gulden**	**Good**	**Fine**	**XF**
	1.7.1762. Black, value green. Printer: Jakub Degen, Wein. 85x196mm.			
	a. Issued note.	—	—	—
	b. "Formulare".	—	—	550
A7	**100 Gulden**	**Good**	**Fine**	**XF**
	1.7.1762. Red, value green. Printer: Jakub Degen, Wein. 85x196mm.			
	a. Issued note.	—	—	—
	b. "Formulare".	—	—	550

1771 Issue

		Good	Fine	XF
A8	**5 Gulden**			
	1.7.1771. Black. Printer: J. S. Degen, Wein. 85x170mm.			
	a. Issued note.	—	—	—
	b. "Formulare".	—	—	625
A9	**10 Gulden**	**Good**	**Fine**	**XF**
	1.7.1771. Black. Printer: J. S. Degen, Wein. 85x170mm.			
	a. Issued note.	—	—	—
	b. "Formulare".	—	—	625
A10	**25 Gulden**	**Good**	**Fine**	**XF**
	1.7.1771. Black. Printer: J. S. Degen, Wein. 85x170mm.			
	a. Issued note.	—	—	—
	b. "Formulare".	—	—	625

		Good	Fine	XF
A11	**50 Gulden**			
	1.7.1771. Black. Printer: J. S. Degen, Wein. 85x170mm.			
	a. Issued note.	—	—	—
	b. "Formulare".	—	—	625
A12	**100 Gulden**	**Good**	**Fine**	**XF**
	1.7.1771. Black. Printer: J. S. Degen, Wein. 85x170mm.			
	a. Issued note.	—	—	—
	b. "Formulare".	—	—	625
A13	**500 Gulden**	**Good**	**Fine**	**XF**
	1.7.1771. Black. Printer: J. S. Degen, Wein. 85x170mm.			
	a. Issued note.	—	—	—
	b. "Formulare".	—	—	625
A14	**1000 Gulden**	**Good**	**Fine**	**XF**
	1.7.1771. Black. Printer: J. S. Degen, Wein. 85x170mm.			
	a. Issued note.	—	—	—
	b. "Formulare".	—	—	625

1784 Issue

		Good	Fine	XF
A15	**5 Gulden**			
	1.11.1784. Black. Watermark: WIENER STADT / BANCO ZETTEL. Printer: J. S. Degen, Wein. 87x190mm.			
	a. Issued note.	1,400	—	—
	b. "Formulare".	—	—	250
A16	**10 Gulden**	**Good**	**Fine**	**XF**
	1.11.1784. Black. Watermark: WIENER STADT / BANCO ZETTEL. Printer: J. S. Degen, Wein. 87x190mm.			
	a. Issued note.	—	—	—
	b. "Formulare".	—	—	250
A17	**25 Gulden**	**Good**	**Fine**	**XF**
	1.11.1784. Black. Watermark: WIENER STADT / BANCO ZETTEL. Printer: J. S. Degen, Wein. 87x190mm.			
	a. Issued note.	—	—	—
	b. "Formulare".	—	—	250
A18	**50 Gulden**	**Good**	**Fine**	**XF**
	1.11.1784. Black. Watermark: WIENER STADT / BANCO ZETTEL. Printer: J. S. Degen, Wein. 87x190mm.			
	a. Issued note.	—	—	—
	b. "Formulare".	—	—	250
A19	**100 Gulden**	**Good**	**Fine**	**XF**
	1.11.1784. Black. Watermark: WIENER STADT / BANCO ZETTEL. Printer: J. S. Degen, Wein. 87x190mm.			
	a. Issued note.	—	—	—
	b. "Formulare".	—	—	250
A20	**500 Gulden**	**Good**	**Fine**	**XF**
	1.11.1784. Black. Watermark: WIENER STADT / BANCO ZETTEL. Printer: J. S. Degen, Wein. 152x138mm.			
	a. Issued note.	—	—	—
	b. "Formulare".	—	—	250
A21	**1000 Gulden**	**Good**	**Fine**	**XF**
	1.11.1784. Black. Watermark: WIENER STADT / BANCO ZETTEL. Printer: J. S. Degen, Wein. 152x138mm.			
	a. Issued note.	—	—	—
	b. "Formulare".	—	—	250

1796 Issue

		Good	Fine	XF
A22	**5 Gulden** 1.8.1796. Black. Watermark: WIENER STADT / BANCO ZETTEL. Printer: J. S. Degen, Wein. 90x200mm.			
	a. Issued note.	115	450	1,700
	s. "Formulare.	45.00	170	685
A23	**10 Gulden** 1.8.1796. Black. Watermark: WIENER STADT / BANCO ZETTEL. Printer: J. S. Degen, Wein. 90x200mm.	145	570	2,250
A24	**25 Gulden** 1.8.1796. Black. Watermark: WIENER STADT / BANCO ZETTEL. Printer: J. S. Degen, Wein. 90x200mm.	—	—	—
A25	**50 Gulden** 1.8.1796. Black. Watermark: WIENER STADT / BANCO ZETTEL. Printer: J. S. Degen, Wein. 90x200mm.	—	—	—
A26	**100 Gulden** 1.8.1796. Black. Watermark: WIENER STADT / BANCO ZETTEL. Printer: J. S. Degen, Wein. 90x200mm.	—	—	—
A27	**500 Gulden** 1.8.1796. Black. Watermark: WIENER STADT / BANCO ZETTEL. Printer: J. S. Degen, Wein. 90x200mm.	—	—	—
A28	**1000 Gulden** 1.8.1796. Black. Watermark: WIENER STADT / BANCO ZETTEL. Printer: J. S. Degen, Wein. 90x200mm.	—	—	—

1800 Issue

A29

A30

		Good	Fine	XF
A29	**1 Gulden** 1.1.1800. Black. Watermark: Value as Arabic and Roman numeral. 73x155mm.	5.50	23.00	90.00
A30	**2 Gulden** 1.1.1800. Black. Watermark: Value as Arabic and Roman numeral. 75x160mm.	5.50	23.00	90.00

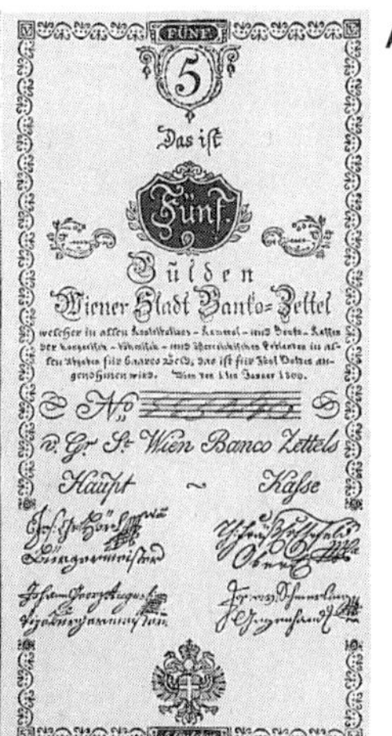

A31

A32

		Good	Fine	XF
A31	**5 Gulden** 1.1.1800. Black. Watermark: Value as Arabic and Roman numeral. 77x160mm.			
	a. Issued note.	7.00	28.50	125
	b. "Formulare".	—	—	135

Exists as forgery printed in France during the reign of Napoleon (often on blue paper). Valued about the same as an original.

		Good	Fine	XF
A32	**10 Gulden** 1.1.1800. Black. Watermark: Value as Arabic and Roman numeral. 78x135mm.			
	a. Issued note.	11.00	50.00	225
	b. "Formulare".	—	—	100

Exists as forgery printed in France during the reign of Napoleon (often on blue paper). Valued about the same as an original.

		Good	Fine	XF
A33	**25 Gulden** 1.1.1800. Black. Watermark: Value as Arabic and Roman numeral. 85x135mm.			
	a. Issued note.	42.00	175	685
	b. "Formulare".	—	—	—

Exists as forgery printed in France during the reign of Napoleon (often on blue paper). Valued about the same as an original.

		Good	Fine	XF
A34	**50 Gulden** 1.1.1800. Black. Watermark: Value as Arabic and Roman numeral.			
	a. Issued note.	—	—	—
	b. "Formulare".	—	—	—

Exists as forgery printed in France during the reign of Napoleon (often on blue paper). Valued about the same as an original.

		Good	Fine	XF
A35	**100 Gulden** 1.1.1800. Black. Watermark: Value as Arabic and Roman numeral. 95x127mm.			
	a. Issued note.	115	450	1,700
	b. "Formulare".	—	—	—

Exists as forgery printed in France during the reign of Napoleon (often on blue paper). Valued about the same as an original.

		Good	Fine	XF
A36	**500 Gulden** 1.1.1800. Black. Watermark: Value as Arabic and Roman numeral. 130x100mm.			
	a. Issued note.	—	—	—
	b. "Formulare".	—	—	100

Exists as forgery printed in France during the reign of Napoleon (often on blue paper). Valued about the same as an original.

		Good	Fine	XF
A37	**1000 Gulden** 1.1.1800. Black. Watermark: Value as Arabic and Roman numeral. 140x92mm.			
	a. Issued note.	—	—	—
	b. "Formulare".	—	—	—

Exists as forgery printed in France during the reign of Napoleon (often on blue paper). Valued about the same as an original.

1806 Issue

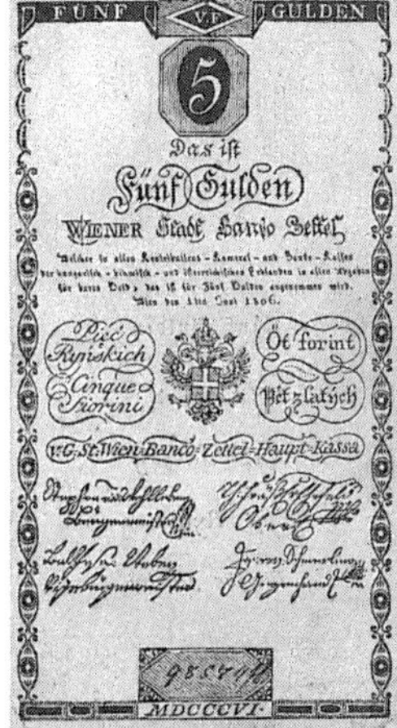

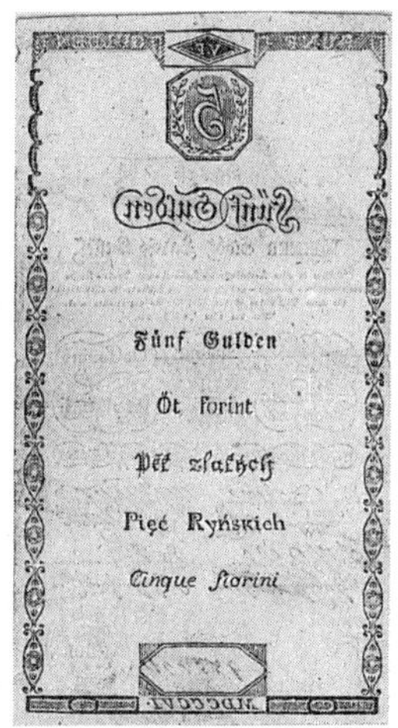

		Good	Fine	XF
A38	**5 Gulden** 1.6.1806. Black. Emblem of city of Wein. Value in 5 languages. Watermark: Value. 78x140mm.			
	a. Issued note.	7.00	28.50	125
	b. "Formulare".	—	—	80.00

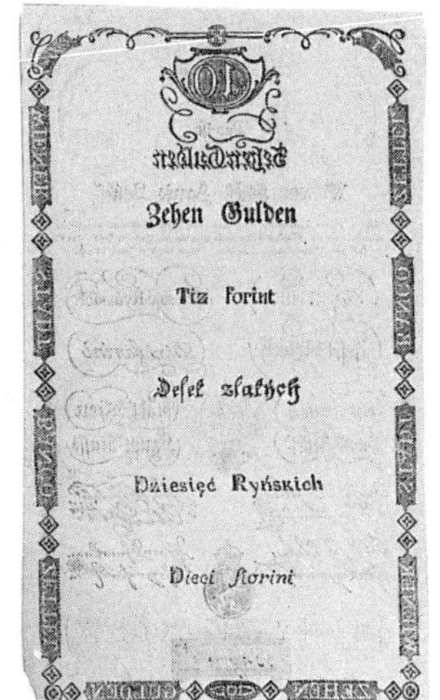

		Good	Fine	XF
A39	**10 Gulden** 1.6.1806. Black. Emblem of Wein and State emblem of Czech Kingdom. Value in 5 languages. Watermark: Value. 87x148mm.			
	a. Issued note.	11.00	50.00	225
	b. "Formulare".	—	—	170

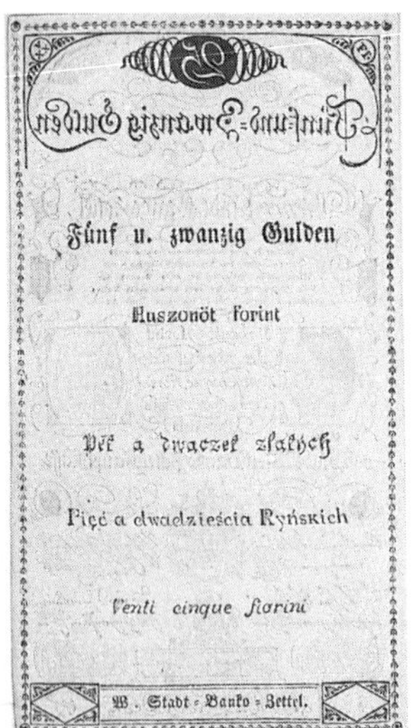

		Good	Fine	XF
A40	**25 Gulden** 1.6.1806. Black. Emblem of the city of Hungary. Watermark: WIENER - STADT / DANCO ZETTEL / VON / 25 GULDEN / 18 06 90x160mm.			
	a. Issued note.	55.00	225	900
	b. "Formulare".	—	—	285

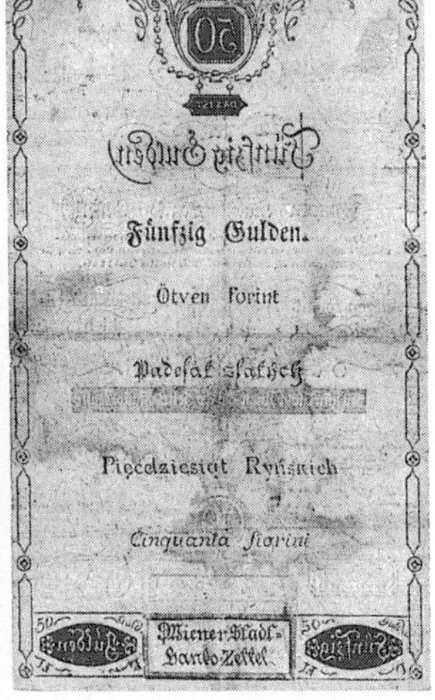

		Good	Fine	XF
A41	**50 Gulden** 1.6.1806. Black and brown. Emblem of the city of Wein. 92x152mm.			
	a. Issued note.	85.00	340	1,700
	b. "Formulare".	—	—	285

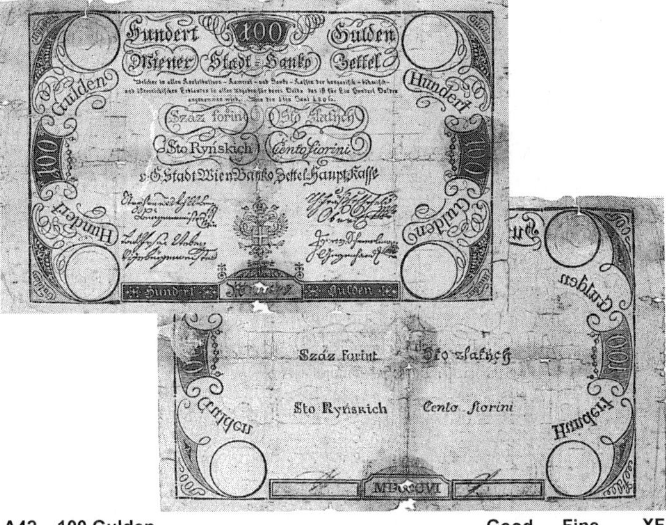

		Good	Fine	XF
A42	**100 Gulden** 1.6.1806. Black and red. Emblem of the city of Wein. 154x94mm.			
	a. Issued note.	115	450	2,250
	b. "Formulare".	—	—	285
A43	**500 Gulden** 1.6.1806. Black and red. Emblem of the city of Wein. 162x100mm.	**Good**	**Fine**	**XF**
	a. Rare. Issued note.	—	—	—
	b. "Formulare".	—	—	170

Privilegirte Vereinigte Einlösungs und Tilgungs Deputation

1811 Issue

Einlösungs - Scheine **= Demand Notes**

		Good	Fine	XF
A44	**1 Gulden** 1.3.1811. Black. Imperial eagle, value in 4 languages. Printer: Dominicaner Gebude, Wein. 86x60mm.			
	a. Issued note.	8.50	40.00	170
	b. "Formulare".	—	—	170
A45	**2 Gulden** 1.3.1811. Black. Imperial eagle, value in 4 languages. Printer: Bominicaner Gebaude, Wein. 88x60mm.	**Good**	**Fine**	**XF**
	a. Issued note.	55.00	250	900
	b. "Formulare".	—	—	170
A46	**5 Gulden** 1.3.1811. Black. Imperial eagle. value in 4 languages. Printer: Dominicaner Gebaude, Wein. 115x79mm.	**Good**	**Fine**	**XF**
	a. Issued note.	425	—	—
	b. "Formulare".	—	—	285

		Good	Fine	XF
A47	**10 Gulden** 1.3.1811. Black. Imperial eagle. Value in 4 languages. Printer: Dominicaner Gebaude, Wein. 133x87mm.			
	a. Issued note.	425	—	—
	b. "Formulare".	—	—	285

		Good	Fine	XF
A48	**20 Gulden**	Good	Fine	XF
	1.3.1811. Black. Imperial eagle. Value in 4 languages. Printer: Dominicaner Gebaude, Wein. 133x87mm.			
	a. Issued note. Rare.	—	—	—
	b. "Formulare".	—	—	285
A49	**100 Gulden**	Good	Fine	XF
	1.3.1811. Black. Imperial eagle. Value in 4 languages. Printer: Dominicaner Gebaude, Wein. 134x90mm.			
	a. Issued note. Rare.	—	—	—
	b. "Formulare".	—	—	285

1813 Issue

Anticipations - Scheine (Anticipation Notes)

		Good	Fine	XF
A50	**2 Gulden**	Good	Fine	XF
	16.4.1813. Black. Value in 4 languages. Uniface. Watermark: ANT SCHEIN. 65x98mm.			
	a. Issued note.	28.00	95.00	395
	b. "Formulare".	—	—	170
A51	**5 Gulden**	Good	Fine	XF
	16.4.1813. Black. Value in 4 languages. Uniface. Watermark: ANT SCHEIN. 78x112mm.			
	a. Issued note.	115	450	—
	b. "Formulare".	—	—	170
A52	**10 Gulden**	Good	Fine	XF
	16.4.1813. Black. Value in 5 languages. Uniface. Watermark: ANT SCHEIN. 125x86mm.			
	a. Issued note. Rare.	425	—	—
	b. "Formulare".	—	—	170
A53	**20 Gulden**	Good	Fine	XF
	16.4.1813. Black. Value in 4 languages. Uniface. Watermark: ANT SCHEIN. 130x85mm.			
	a. Issued note.	—	—	—
	b. "Formulare".	—	—	170

Oesterreichische National Zettel Bank

1816 Issue

		Good	Fine	XF
A54	**5 Gulden**	Good	Fine	XF
	1.7.1816. Black. Printer: Dominikaner-Gebaude, Wein. 178x115mm.			
	a. Issued note.	570	—	—
	b. "Formulare".	—	—	225
A55	**10 Gulden**	Good	Fine	XF
	1.7.1816. Black. Printer: Dominikaner-Gebaude, Wein. 178x115mm.			
	a. Issued note.	—	—	—
	b. "Formulare."	—	—	225
A56	**25 Gulden**	Good	Fine	XF
	1.7.1816. Black. Printer: Dominikaner-Gebaude, Wein. 178x115mm.			
	a. Issued note.	—	—	—
	b. "Formulare".	—	—	225
A57	**50 Gulden**	Good	Fine	XF
	1.7.1816. Black. Printer: Dominikaner-Gebaude, Wein. 178x115mm.			
	a. Issued note.	—	—	—
	b. "Formulare".	—	—	225
A58	**100 Gulden**	Good	Fine	XF
	1.7.1816. Black. Printer: Dominikaner-Gebaude, Wein. 178x115mm.			
	a. Issued note.	—	—	—
	b. "Formulare".	—	—	225
A59	**500 Gulden**	Good	Fine	XF
	1.7.1816. Black. Printer: Dominikaner-Gebaude, Wein. 178x115mm.			
	a. Issued note.	—	—	—
	b. "Formulare".	—	—	225
A60	**1000 Gulden**	Good	Fine	XF
	1.7.1816. Black. Printer: Dominikaner-Gebaude, Wein. 178x115mm.			
	a. Issued note.	—	—	—
	b. "Formulare".	—	—	225

Privilegirte Oesterreichische National-Bank

1825 Issue

		Good	Fine	XF
A61	**5 Gulden**	Good	Fine	XF
	23.6.1825. Black and red. Watermark: Value and ornaments. 125x90mm.			
	a. Issued note.	135	725	—
	b. "Formulare".	—	—	145
A62	**10 Gulden**	Good	Fine	XF
	23.6.1825. Black and red. Watermark: Value and ornaments. 90x140mm.			
	a. Issued note.	250	1,000	—
	b. "Formulare".	—	—	145
A63	**25 Gulden**	Good	Fine	XF
	23.6.1825. Black and red. Watermark: Value and ornaments. 145x100mm.			
	a. Issued note.	—	—	—
	b. "Formulare".	—	—	285
A64	**50 Gulden**	Good	Fine	XF
	23.6.1825. Black and red. Watermark: Value and ornaments. 155x110mm.			
	a. Issued note.	—	—	—
	b. "Formulare".	—	—	285
A65	**100 Gulden**	Good	Fine	XF
	23.6.1825. Black and red. Watermark: Value and ornaments. 160x115mm.			
	a. Issued note.	—	—	—
	b. "Formulare".	—	—	285
A66	**500 Gulden**	Good	Fine	XF
	23.6.1825. Black and red. Watermark: Value and ornaments. 155x105mm.			
	a. Issued note.	—	—	—
	b. "Formulare".	—	—	225
A67	**1000 Gulden**	Good	Fine	XF
	23.6.1825. Black. 176x125mm.			
	a. Issued note.	—	—	—
	b. "Formulare".	—	—	225

1833-1834 Issue

No.	Description	Good	Fine	XF
A68	**5 Gulden** 9.12.1833. Black. Watermark: Bank name and value. 129x91mm.	140	565	—
A69	**10 Gulden** 8.12.1834. Black. Watermark: Bank name and value. 140x110mm.	140	565	—

1841 Issue

No.	Description	Good	Fine	XF
A70	**5 Gulden** 1.1.1841. Black. Profile of Austria at top center, arms between cherubs below. Watermark: PONB and value. 130x105mm.			
	a. Issued note.	85.00	340	—
	b. "Formulare".	—	—	450
A71	**10 Gulden** 1.1.1841. Black. Austria at top center. Watermark: PONB and value. 105x130mm.			
	a. Issued note.	115	565	—
	b. "Formulare".	—	—	450
A72	**50 Gulden** 1.1.1841. Black. Eleven female heads (Pomona) at top center. Watermark: PRIV OST NATIONALBANK / 50 50 188x115mm.			
	a. Issued note.	—	—	—
	b. "Formulare".	—	—	450
A73	**100 Gulden** 1.1.1841. Black. Eleven female heads (Pomona) at top center. Watermark: PRIV OST NATIONALBANK / 50 50. 202x122mm.			
	a. Issued note.	—	—	—
	b. "Formulare".	—	—	450

No.	Description	Good	Fine	XF
A74	**1000 Gulden** 1.1.1841. Black. Eleven female heads (Pomona) at top center, two heads of Austria facing below, allegorical woman standing at left and right. Watermark: PONB and value. 208x125mm.			
	a. Issued note.	—	—	—
	b. "Formulare".	—	—	450

1847 Issue

No.	Description	Good	Fine	XF
A75	**5 Gulden** 1.1.1847. Black. Atlas and Minerva at left, Austria at right. Watermark: Value and ornaments. 133x108mm.	85.00	450	—
A76	**10 Gulden** 1.1.1847. Black. Atlas and Minerva at left, Austria at right. Watermark: Value and ornaments. 110x138mm.	115	510	—

No.	Description	Good	Fine	XF
A77	**100 Gulden** 1.1.1847. Black. Austria at left, Atlas and Minerva at right, crowned shield at top center, arms below. Watermark: Value and ornaments. 210x132mm. Rare.	—	—	—
A78	**1000 Gulden** 1.1.1847. Black. Austria at lower left and right, Atlas and Minerva at left and right. Watermark: Value and ornaments. 210x132mm. Rare.	—	—	—

1848 Issue

No.	Description	Good	Fine	XF
A79	**1 Gulden** 1.5.1848. Black and green. Uniface. 110x83mm.			
	a. Issued note.	22.00	85.00	400
	s. Specimen. Yellowish paper.	20.00	75.00	285
A80	**2 Gulden** 1.5.1848. Black. Uniface. 120x80mm.			
	a. Issued note.	42.00	170	685
	s. Specimen. Yellowish paper.	20.00	75.00	285

1848-1854 Issue

No.	Description	Good	Fine	XF
A81	**1 Gulden** 1.7.1848. Black. Austria at top center, arms below at bottom. Watermark: Value. 73x127mm.	14.00	55.00	205

No.	Description	Good	Fine	XF
A82	**2 Gulden** 1.7.1848. Black. Atlas and Minerva at left, Austria at right, arms at bottom center. Watermark: Value. 130x73mm.	25.00	100	395
A83	**10 Gulden** 1.7.1854. Black. Austria at left, Atlas and Minerva at right. Watermark: Star and value. 145x116mm.	225	850	—

1858 Issue

A84 1 Gulden
1.1.1858. Black and red. Austria at top center, arms at bottom. Watermark: Value. 74x127mm.

Good	Fine	XF
8.50	35.00	170

A85 10 Gulden
1.1.1858. Black and red. Man with genius on pedestal at left and right, Austria with lion below. Watermark: Value. 143x115mm.

Good	Fine	XF
85.00	400	1,700

A86 100 Gulden
1.3.1858. Black and red. Austria at left, arms between two cherubs at top center, god of the river Danube at right. Watermark: Value and ornament. 207x132mm. Rare.

Good	Fine	XF
—	—	—

A87 1000 Gulden
1.3.1858. Black and red. Woman symbolizing power at left, with symbol of abundance. Rare.

Good	Fine	XF
—	—	—

1859-1863 Issue

A88 5 Gulden
1.5.1859. Black and red. Austria at top center, Imperial eagle at bottom. Value in 11 languages. Watermark: OESTER WAEHRUNG and value. 107x130mm.

Good	Fine	XF
30.00	195	550

A89 10 Gulden
15.1.1863. Black and green. Shepherd, miner and peasant. Value in 11 languages. 145x119mm.

Good	Fine	XF
28.50	170	900

A90 100 Gulden
15.1.1863. Black and green. Two cherubs with coins at left, supported arms at bottom center, two cherubs with sword, book and purse at right. Watermark: Value. 210x133mm.

Good	Fine	XF
—	—	—

K.K. Hauptmünzamt

Münzschein (Coin Note)

1849 Issue

A91 6 Kreuzer
1.7.1849. Black on green underprint. Arms at center. 60x44mm.

Good	Fine	XF
2.75	14.00	45.00

A92 10 Kreuzer
1.7.1849. Black. Arms at center. 90x39mm.

	Good	Fine	XF
a. Rose underprint.	4.00	20.00	55.00
b. Light blue underprint.	4.00	20.00	55.00

1860 Issue

A93 10 Kreuzer
1.11.1860. Black on light brown underprint of waves. Hercules, female with wreath and arrows, angels. Value in 10 languages. 56x39mm.

	Good	Fine	XF
a. Plain edges.	1.50	5.50	34.00
b. Serrated edges. White watermark. Paper.	4.50	17.00	55.00

A94 10 Kreuzer
1.11.1860. Black on light brown underprint. Value in 11 languages. Back: *Oest.* at bottom left, *Wahr.* at right. BC: Green. 88x39mm.

Good	Fine	XF
2.75	14.00	45.00

A95 10 Kreuzer
1.11.1860. Black on green underprint. Two boys. Value in 7 languages. *10* at bottom left and right. 86x37mm.

Good	Fine	XF
2.75	14.00	45.00

K.u.K. Staats-Central-Cassa

All "Cassa-Anweisungen" were interest bearing notes except #A96. Most of them exist only as "Formulare" which give general design characteristics.

1848 Issue

No.	Denomination	Good	Fine	XF
A96	**30 Gulden** 1.9.1848.			
	a. Issued note.	—	—	—
	b. "Formulare".	—	—	—
A97	**60 Gulden** 1.9.1848.			
	a. Issued note.	—	—	—
	b. "Formulare".	—	—	—
A98	**90 Gulden** 1.9.1848.			
	a. Issued note.	—	—	—
	b. "Formulare".	—	—	—
A99	**300 Gulden** 1.9.1848.			
	a. Issued note.	—	—	—
	b. "Formulare".	—	—	—
A100	**600 Gulden** 1.9.1848.			
	a. Issued note.	—	—	—
	b. "Formulare".	—	—	—
A101	**900 Gulden** 1.9.1848.			
	a. Issued note.	—	—	—
	b. "Formulare".	—	—	—

1849 First Issue

No.	Denomination	Good	Fine	XF
A102	**10 Gulden** 1.1.1849.			
	a. Issued note.	—	—	—
	b. "Formulare".	—	—	550
A103	**25 Gulden** 1.1.1849.			
	a. Issued note.	—	—	—
	b. "Formulare".	—	—	550
A104	**50 Gulden** 1.1.1849.			
	a. Issued note.	—	—	—
	b. "Formulare".	—	—	550
A105	**100 Gulden** 1.1.1849.			
	a. Issued note.	—	—	—
	b. "Formulare".	—	—	550
A106	**500 Gulden** 1.1.1849.			
	a. Issued note.	—	—	—
	b. "Formulare".	—	—	550
A107	**1000 Gulden** 1.1.1849.			
	a. Issued note.	—	—	—
	b. "Formulare".	—	—	550

1849 Second Issue

No.	Denomination	Good	Fine	XF
A108	**5 Gulden** 1.3.1849.	425	—	—
A109	**10 Gulden** 1.3.1849.	—	—	—
A110	**25 Gulden** 1.3.1849.	—	—	—
A111	**50 Gulden** 1.3.1849.	—	—	—
A112	**100 Gulden** 1.3.1849.	—	—	—
A113	**500 Gulden** 1.3.1849.	—	—	—
A114	**1000 Gulden** 1.3.1849.	—	—	—

1849 Third Issue

No.	Denomination	Good	Fine	XF
A115	**30 Gulden** 1.3.1849.	—	—	—
A116	**60 Gulden** 1.3.1849.	—	—	—
A117	**90 Gulden** 1.3.1849.	—	—	—
A118	**300 Gulden** 1.3.1849.	—	—	—
A119	**600 Gulden** 1.3.1849.	—	—	—
A120	**900 Gulden** 1.3.1849.	—	—	—

1849 Fourth Issue

No.	Denomination	Good	Fine	XF
A121	**5 Gulden** 1.7.1849.	140	565	2,250
A122	**10 Gulden** 1.7.1849.	—	—	—
A123	**25 Gulden** 1.7.1849.	—	—	—
A124	**50 Gulden** 1.7.1849.	—	—	—
A125	**100 Gulden** 1.7.1849.	—	—	—
A126	**500 Gulden** 1.7.1849.	—	—	—
A127	**1000 Gulden** 1.7.1849.	—	—	—

1850 Issue

No.	Denomination	Good	Fine	XF
A128	**50 Gulden** 1.1.1850.	—	—	—
A129	**100 Gulden** 1.1.1850.	—	—	—
A130	**500 Gulden** 1.1.1850.	—	—	—
A131	**1000 Gulden** 1.1.1850.	—	—	—

K.K. Staats-Central-Casse

All "Reichs-Schatzscheine" were 3% interest-bearing notes except #A135-A137.

1850 Issue

No.	Denomination	Good	Fine	XF
A132	**100 Gulden** 1.1.1850. Black. Two women, miner and farmers. Watermark: KKCK and ornament. 186x112mm.			
	a. Issued note.	—	—	—
	b. "Formulare".	—	—	—
A133	**500 Gulden** 1.1.1850. Black. Watermark: KKCK and ornament. 190x118mm.			
	a. Issued note.	—	—	—
	b. "Formulare".	—	—	—
A134	**1000 Gulden** 1.1.1850. Black. Husband and wife with dog, scientist, merchant. Watermark: KKCK and ornament.			
	a. Issued note.	—	—	—
	b. "Formulare".	—	—	—

1851 Issue

No.	Denomination	Good	Fine	XF
A135	**5 Gulden** 1.1.1851. Black. Bearded man with club at left, helmeted woman at right, arms at bottom center. Watermark: KKCK and wreath or ornament. 130x100mm.			
	a. Issued note.	37.00	140	450
	b. "Formulare".	—	—	—
A136	**10 Gulden** 1.1.1851. Black. Floating woman at left, floating warrior at right. Watermark: KKCK and wreath or ornament. 134x104mm.			
	a. Issued note.	225	850	—
	b. "Formulare".	—	—	—

		Good	Fine	XF
A137	**50 Gulden** 1.1.1851. Black. Scene of plowing with Emperor Joseph II, aide and O. Trnka, farmer from Slavikovice (Moravia) at lower center. Watermark: KKCK and wreath or ornament. 198x125mm.			
	a. Issued note.	—	—	—
	b. "Formulare".	—	—	—
A138	**100 Gulden** 1.1.1851. 186x112mm.	—	—	—
A139	**500 Gulden** 1.1.1851.	—	—	—
A140	**1000 Gulden** 1.1.1851.	—	—	—

1852 Issue

		Good	Fine	XF
A141	**100 Gulden** 1.1.1852.	—	—	—
A142	**500 Gulden** 1.1.1852.	—	—	—
A143	**1000 Gulden** 1.1.1852.	—	—	—

1853 First Issue

		Good	Fine	XF
A144	**100 Gulden** 1.1.1853. 186x112mm.			
	a. Issued note.	—	—	—
	b. "Formulare".	—	—	—
A145	**500 Gulden** 1.1.1853. 190x118mm.			
	a. Issued note.	—	—	—
	b. "Formulare".	—	—	—
A146	**1000 Gulden** 1.1.1853. 190x118mm.			
	a. Issued note.	—	—	—
	b. "Formulare".	—	—	—

1853 Second Issue

		Good	Fine	XF
A147	**100 Gulden** 8.10.1853. 186x112mm.			
	a. Issued note.	—	—	—
	b. "Formulare".	—	—	—
A148	**500 Gulden** 8.10.1853. 190x118mm.			
	a. Issued note.	—	—	—
	b. "Formulare".	—	—	—
A149	**1000 Gulden** 8.10.1853. 190x118mm.			
	a. Issued note.	—	—	—
	b. "Formulare".	—	—	—

K.K. Staats-Central-Casse

1866 Issue

		Good	Fine	XF
A150	**1 Gulden** 7.7.1866. Black on green underprint. Woman seated holding gear at lower left, Mercury seated at right. Back: Ten coats-of-arms in border, value in 10 languages. BC: Gray. Watermark: STN. 80x122mm.	4.00	17.00	80.00

		Good	Fine	XF
A151	**5 Gulden** 1866-1867. Black on pink underprint. Woman with lyre at upper left, elderly man seated at upper right. Back: Ten coats-of-arms in wreath around central eagle. BC: Brown. Watermark: STN. 117x70mm.			
	a. 7.7.1866-18.1.1867. Black serial (block) #.	85.00	285	—
	b. Red serial (block) #.	20.00	65.00	395

		Good	Fine	XF
A152	**50 Gulden** 25.8.1866. Black on green-blue underprint. Warrior with lion at left, woman with dragon and book at right. Back: Two men. BC: Olive and brown. Watermark: STAATS NOTE / 50 / GULDEN. 196x130mm.	80.00	450	2,250

K.K. Reichs-Central-Cassa

1881-1884 Issue

		Good	Fine	XF
A153	**1 Gulden** 1.1.1882. Blue on gray-brown underprint. Medallic head of Emperor Franz Joseph at upper center. German text. Back: Hungarian text. 70x120mm.	4.00	15.00	55.00

		Good	Fine	XF
A154	**5 Gulden** 1.1.1881. Green on gray-brown underprint. Medallic head of Emperor Franz Joseph at upper center. Woman with book at left, woman in armor at right. German text. Back: Hungarian text. 140x94mm.	14.00	55.00	285

		Good	Fine	XF
A155	**50 Gulden** 1.1.1884. Blue on gray-brown underprint. Medallic head of Emperor Franz Joseph at upper center. Two boys at left and at right. German text. Back: Hungarian text. 171x111mm.	—	—	—

1888 Issue

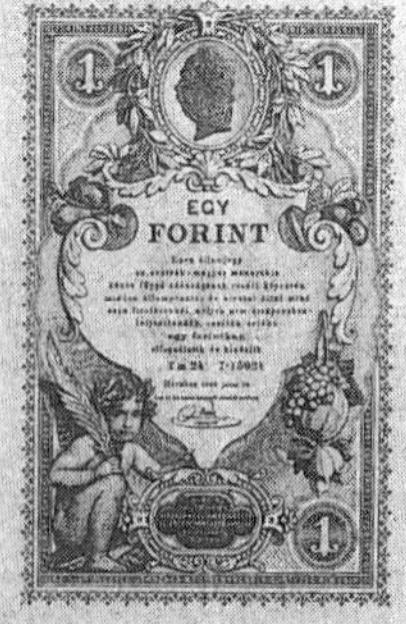

		Good	Fine	XF
A156	**1 Gulden** 1.7.1888. Blue. Medallic portrait Franz Joseph at upper center, kneeling angel at bottom right. German text. Back: Reversed image at top, kneeling angel at bottom left. Hungarian text. 69x105mm.	4.25	17.00	65.00

Oesterreichisch-Ungarische Bank

Austro-Hungarian Bank

1880 Issue

		Good	Fine	XF
1	**10 Gulden** 1.5.1880. Blue and brown. Women at left and right. Back: Hungarian text. 132x90mm.	20.00	85.00	395

As the denomination is only in German and Hungarian, the Czech users often scratched out those printed denominations and hand wrote the value in Czech on the bank note as a protest.

		Good	Fine	XF
2	**100 Gulden** 1.5.1880. Blue and brown. Boy with sheaf and sickle at left, boy with book at right. Back: Hungarian text. 153x107mm.	—	—	—

1900-1902 Issue

		Good	Fine	XF
4	**10 Kronen** 31.3.1900. Lilac and gray. Young angel at left and right. Back: Hungarian text. 122x80mm.	50.00	225	900

		Good	Fine	XF
5	**20 Kronen** 31.3.1900. Red and green underprint. Cherub with Portrait woman over arms at left. Back: Hungarian text. 138x91mm.	35.00	165	680

		Good	Fine	XF
6	**50 Kronen** 2.1.1902. Blue on rose underprint. Seated woman at left and at right, arms at upper center. Back: Hungarian text. 158x102mm.	10.00	40.00	285

		Good	Fine	XF
7	**100 Kronen** 2.1.1902. Green on rose underprint. Seated woman with child at left, blacksmith stands at anvil at right. Back: Hungarian text. 158x102mm.	85.00	350	1,150

		Good	Fine	XF
8	**1000 Kronen** 2.1.1902. Blue. Woman at right. Back: Hungarian text. 194x129mm.			
	a. Gray-green underprint.	1.00	4.50	15.00
	b. Rose underprint. Later issue from Series #1440 onward.	1.00	5.00	17.00

1904-1912 Issue

		Good	Fine	XF
9	**10 Kronen** 2.1.1904. Purple on red, dark blue and dark green underprint. Portrait Princess Rohan at right. 138x81mm.	2.00	8.50	35.00

		Good	Fine	XF
10	**20 Kronen** 2.1.1907. Blue on red-brown and green underprint. Arms at upper left, Austria at upper center, portrait woman at right. 153x91mm.	7.00	28.50	135
11	**100 Kronen** 2.1.1910. Blue. Woman with flowers at right. 164x109mm.	85.00	350	1,140

		Good	Fine	XF
12	**100 Kronen** 2.1.1912. Green on red and blue underprint. Facing portrait woman at right. Back: Profile portrait of woman at upper right.	—	3.00	17.00

1913-1914 Issue

		VG	VF	UNC
13	**20 Kronen** 2.1.1913. Blue on green and red underprint. Portrait woman at upper left, arms at upper right. Back: Arms at upper left, portrait woman at upper right. 152x91mm.	3.00	17.00	75.00
14	**20 Kronen** 2.1.1913. Blue on green and red underprint. Portrait woman at upper left, arms at upper right. Like #13 but with *II AUFLAGE* (2nd issue) at left border. Back: Arms at upper left, portrait woman at upper right. Watermark: XX XX. 152x91mm.	5.00	25.00	85.00
15	**50 Kronen** 2.1.1914. Blue and green. Woman at center. Watermark: Tile pattern. 163x101mm.	2.25	12.00	50.00

1914-1915 Issue

		VG	VF	UNC
17	**2 Kronen** 5.8.1914. Blue on green and red underprint. Portrait girl at upper center. BC: Brown-orange on green underprint. 114x68mm.			
	a. Thin paper, series A or B. 2 serial # varieties.	16.00	60.00	250
	b. Heavier paper, series C.	1.25	5.50	22.00

		VG	VF	UNC
19	**10 Kronen** 2.1.1915. Blue and green. Arms at upper left, portrait boy at bottom center. Back: Arms at upper left, portrait young man at upper right. 150x80mm.	1.25	5.50	25.00

1916-1918 Issue

		VG	VF	UNC
20	**1 Krone** 1.12.1916. Red. Woman's head at upper left and right. Value in 8 languages. Block #1000-1700. Back: Helmeted warrior's bust at center on back. 113x69mm.	—	2.25	9.00

Note: For #20 with block # over 7000 see Hungary #10.

		VG	VF	UNC
21	**2 Kronen** 1.3.1917. Red on gray underprint. Woman at left and right. Block #1000-1600 and Block #A1000-1100. 2 serial # varieties. 125x84mm.	—	2.25	9.00

Note: For #21 with block # over 7000 see Hungary #11.

		VG	VF	UNC
23	**25 Kronen** 27.10.1918. Blue on gray-brown underprint. Girl at left. Up to block #2000. 137x82mm.	20.00	85.00	340

Note: For #23 w/block # over 3000 see Hungary #12 and #13.

		VG	VF	UNC
24	**200 Kronen** 27.10.1918. Green on pink underprint. Girl at left. Series B. 170x100mm.	42.00	155	550

Note: For #24 Series A see Hungary #14-16.

		VG	VF	UNC
25	**10,000 Kronen** 2.11.1918. Purple. Woman at right. 195x130mm.	25.00	140	450

Kriegsdarlehenskasse Kassenschein

War State Loan Bank

1914 Issue

		VG	VF	UNC
26	**250 Kronen** 26.9.1914. Red and green on light red underprint. Arms at left, three allegorical figures standing at right. Back: Black text.	70.00	230	900

		VG	VF	UNC
27	**2000 Kronen** 26.9.1914. Green and brown on light green underprint. Arms at left, three allegorical figures standing at right. Back: Black text.	70.00	230	900

		VG	VF	UNC
28	**10,000 Kronen** 26.9.1914. Lilac and dark blue on light lilac underprint. Arms at left, three allegorical figures standing at right. Back: Black text.	70.00	230	900

REPUBLIC - PRE WWII

Oesterreichisch-Ungarischen Bank Kassenschein

1918-1919 Issue

		Good	Fine	XF
29	**1000 Kronen** 28.10.1918. Green. Uniface.	135	550	2,250
30	**1000 Kronen** 30.10.1918. Green. Uniface. Like #29.	—	—	—
31	**5000 Kronen** 25.10.1918.	—	—	—
32	**5000 Kronen** 5.2.1919. Olive. Back: Printed.	—	—	—
33	**10,000 Kronen** 26.10.1918. Back: Printed.	—	—	—
34	**10,000 Kronen** 4.11.1918. Back: Printed.	—	—	—
35	**100,000 Kronen** 3.10.1918. Violet and brown. Back: Printed.	—	—	—
36	**1,000,000 Kronen** 18.11.1918. Red-brown. Uniface.	—	—	—

1921 Issue

Note: For Treasury notes of various Hungarian branch offices, see Hungary #4-9.

		Good	Fine	XF
37	**1000 Kronen** 23.12.1921. Green.	115	450	1,140

		Good	Fine	XF
38	**5000 Kronen** 23.12.1921. Olive.	—	—	—
39	**10,000 Kronen** 23.12.1921. Blue.	—	—	—
40	**100,000 Kronen** 23.12.1921. Violet.	—	—	—

1920 Issue

		Good	Fine	XF
41	**1 Krone** 4.10.1920. Red. Women's head at upper left and right. Block #1000-1700. Back: Helmeted warrior's bust at center.	8.00	34.00	115
42	**2 Kronen** 4.10.1920. Red on gray underprint. Woman at left and right. Block #1000-1600 and Block #A1000-1100. 2 serial # varieties.			
	a. Overprint on German side.	10.00	40.00	125
	b. Overprint on Hungarian side.	12.00	50.00	150

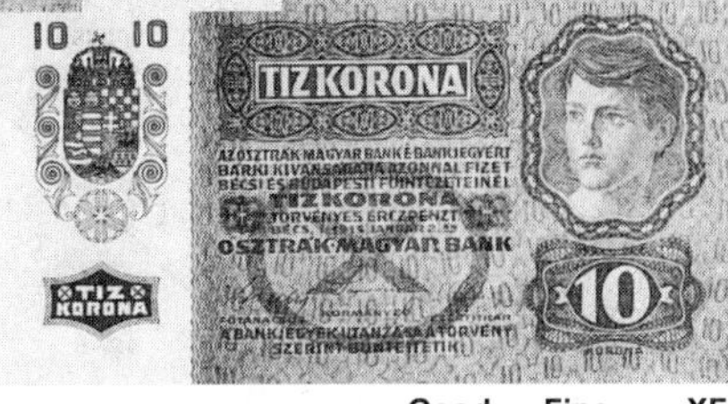

		Good	Fine	XF
43	**10 Kronen** 4.10.1920. Blue and green. Arms at upper left, portrait boy at bottom center. Back: Arms at upper left, portrait young man at upper right.	6.00	25.00	90.00
44	**20 Kronen** 4.10.1920. Blue on green and red underprint. Portrait woman at upper left, arms at upper right. Back: Arms at upper left, portrait woman at upper right.	35.00	140	550
45	**20 Kronen** 4.10.1920. Blue on green and red underprint. Portrait woman at upper left, arms at upper right. With *II AUFLAGE* (2nd issue) at left border. Back: Arms at upper left, portrait woman at upper right. Watermark: XX XX.	6.00	25.00	90.00
46	**50 Kronen** 4.10.1920. Blue and green. Woman at center. Watermark: Tile pattern.	11.00	45.00	190

		Good	Fine	XF
47	**100 Kronen** 4.10.1920. Green on red and blue underprint. Facing portrait woman at right. Back: Profile portrait of woman at upper right.	4.00	17.00	70.00
48	**1000 Kronen** 4.10.1920 (-old date 2.1.1902). Blue. Woman at right.	2.50	11.00	40.00

1919 Issue

		VG	VF	UNC
49	**1 Krone** ND (1919 -old date 1.12.1916). Red. Woman's head at upper left and right. Block #1000-1700. Back: Helmeted warrior's bust at center.	—	0.75	3.50

		VG	VF	UNC
50	**2 Kronen** ND (1919 -old date 1.3.1917). Red on gray underprint. Woman at left and right. Block #1000-1600 and Block #A1000-1100. 2 serial # varieties.	—	0.75	3.50

		VG	VF	UNC
51	**10 Kronen** ND (1919 -old date 2.1.1915). Blue and green. Arms at upper left, portrait boy at bottom center. Back: Arms at upper left, portrait young man at upper right.			
	a. Issued note.	—	1.50	5.50
	b. With handstamp: *NOTE ECHT, STEMPEL FALSCH* (note genuine, overprint forged). Reported not confirmed.	—	—	—

		VG	VF	UNC
52	**20 Kronen** ND (1919 -old date 2.1.1913). Blue on green and red underprint. Portrait woman at upper left, arms at upper right. Back: Arms at upper left, portrait woman at upper right.	0.75	2.50	15.00

		VG	VF	UNC
53	**20 Kronen** ND (1919 -old date 2.1.1913). Blue on green and red underprint. Portrait woman at upper left, arms at upper right. With *II AUFLAGE* (2nd issue) at left border. Back: Arms at upper left, portrait woman at upper right. Watermark: XX XX.			
	a. Issued note.	—	1.25	4.50
	b. With handstamp: *NOTE ECHT, STEMPEL FALSCH* (note genuine, overprint forged.)	10.00	20.00	35.00

		VG	VF	UNC
54	**50 Kronen** ND (1919 -old date 2.1.1914). Blue and green. Woman at center. Watermark: Tile pattern.			
	a. Issued note.	0.50	2.75	11.00
	b. With handstamp: *NOTE ECHT, STEMPEL FALSCH* (note genuine, overprint forged.)	30.00	60.00	200

		VG	VF	UNC
55	**100 Kronen** ND (1919 -old date 2.1.1912). Green on red and blue undrprint. Facing portrait woman at right. Back: Profile portrait of woman at upper right. Hungarian text.			
	a. Issued note.	0.50	2.25	9.00
	b. With handstamp: *NOTE ECHT, STEMPEL FALSCH* (note genuine, overprint forged.)	30.00	60.00	200
	c. With handstamp: *NOTE ECHT, STEMPEL NICHT KONSTATIERBAR* (note genuine, overprint cannot be verified.)	35.00	75.00	250

		VG	VF	UNC
56	**100 Kronen** ND (1919 -old date 2.1.1912). Green on red and blue underprint. Facing portrait woman at right. Back: Profile portrait of woman at upper right. German text.	0.50	2.25	9.00

		VG	VF	UNC
57	**1000 Kronen** ND (1919 -old date 2.1.1902). Blue on rose underprint. Woman at right. Back: Hungarian text.			
	a. Issued note.	—	1.25	5.00
	b. With handstamp: *NOTE ECHT, STEMPEL FALSCH* (note genuine, overprint forged.)	—	—	—
	c. With handstamp: *NOTE ECHT, STEMPEL NICHT KONSTATIERBAR* (note genuine, overprint cannot be verified). Reported not confirmed.	—	—	—

		VG	VF	UNC
58	**1000 Kronen** ND (1919 -old date 2.1.1902). Blue. Woman at right, with additional black overprint: *ECHT / OESTERREICHISCH-UNGARISCHE BANK / HAUPTANSTALT WIEN.*	20.00	50.00	150

		VG	VF	UNC
59	**1000 Kronen** ND (1919 -old date 2.1.1902). Blue. Woman at right. Back: German text. 194x130mm.	1.00	4.50	13.50

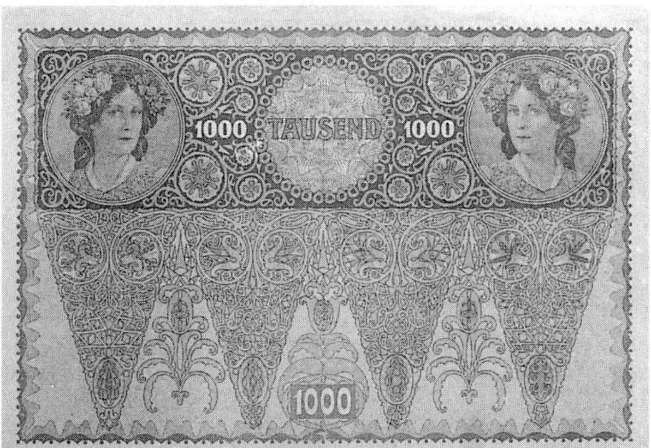

		VG	VF	UNC
60	**1000 Kronen** ND (1919 -old date 2.1.1902). Blue. Woman at right. Back: Ornaments, portrait of woman at upper left and right.	0.50	2.00	10.00

		VG	VF	UNC
61	**1000 Kronen** ND (1919 -old date 2.1.1902). Blue. Woman at right. Like # 60 but with additional red overprint*II AUFLAGE*(2nd issue). Back: Ornaments, portrait of woman at upper left and right.	0.50	2.00	10.00

		VG	VF	UNC
62	**10,000 Kronen** ND (1919 -old date 2.11.1918). Purple. Woman at right. Back: Hungarian text. 192x128mm.			
	a. Issued note.	50.00	150	400
	b. With handstamp *NOTE ECHT, STEMPEL FALSCH* (note genuine, overprint forged).	60.00	200	500

		VG	VF	UNC
63	**10,000 Kronen** ND (1919 -old date 2.11.1918). Purple. Woman at right, with additional black overprint: *ECHT. ÖSTERR - UNGAR. BANK HAUPTANSTALT WIEN.* Back: Hungarian text.	50.00	150	400

		VG	VF	UNC
64	**10,000 Kronen** ND (1919 -old date 2.11.1918). Purple. Woman at right. Like #25 and #62. Back: German text.	2.00	8.00	25.00

		VG	VF	UNC
65	**10,000 Kronen** ND (1919 -old date 2.11.1918). Purple. Woman at right. Like #25 and #62. Back: Ornaments, portrait woman at upper left and right.	2.00	8.00	25.00

		VG	VF	UNC
66	**10,000 Kronen** ND (1919 -old date 2.11.1918). Purple. Woman at right. Like #65, but *II AUFLAGE* (2nd issue) in left margin. Back: Ornaments and portrait woman at upper left and right.	0.50	1.00	10.00

Austrian Government

1922 First Issue

		VG	VF	UNC
73	**1 Krone** 2.1.1922. Red. Uniface. 79x57mm.	—	—	1.00

		VG	VF	UNC
74	**2 Kronen** 2.1.1922. Red. Woman at upper right. Uniface. 83x60mm.	—	—	1.00

		VG	VF	UNC
75	**10 Kronen** 2.1.1922. Blue-violet. Child at right. 94x70mm.	—	—	1.00

		VG	VF	UNC
76	**20 Kronen** 2.1.1922. Purple. Bearded man at right. 100x74mm.	—	—	1.00

		VG	VF	UNC
77	**100 Kronen** 2.1.1922. Green. Princess Rohan at right. 109x79mm.	—	—	2.00

		VG	VF	UNC
78	**1000 Kronen** 2.1.1922. Blue. Woman at right. 115x86mm.	—	1.50	5.00

		VG	VF	UNC
79	**5000 Kronen** 2.1.1922. Green and red-brown. Portrait woman at right. 195x106mm.	2.75	14.00	65.00

		VG	VF	UNC
80	**50,000 Kronen** 2.1.1922. Red-brown and green. Portrait woman at right. 2 serial # varieties. 195x106mm.	8.50	34.00	200

		VG	VF	UNC
81	**100,000 Kronen** 2.1.1922. Blue and green. Portrait woman in floral frame at right. 196x132mm.	17.00	100	650

1922 Second Issue

		VG	VF	UNC
82	**100,000 Kronen** 11.9.1922. Purple.	—	—	—
83	**5,000,000 Kronen** 11.9.1922. Green.	—	—	—

1922 Third Issue

		VG	VF	UNC
84	**500,000 Kronen** 20.9.1922. Brown-lilac. Portrait woman with three children at right. 198x107mm.			
	a. Issued note.	100	450	1,700
	s. Specimen. Perforated *MUNSTER*.	—	—	700

Oesterreichische Nationalbank

Austrian National Bank

1924 First Issue

		VG	VF	UNC
85	**10,000 Kronen** 2.1.1924. Purple and green. Girl at upper right. 127x79mm.	2.50	11.00	45.00
86	**1,000,000 Kronen** 1.7.1924. Woman at right.	—	—	—

1924 Reform Issue

		VG	VF	UNC
87	**1 Schilling on 10,000 Kronen** 2.1.1924. Purple and green. Girl at upper right. 127x79mm.	3.25	15.00	50.00

1925 Issue

		Good	Fine	XF
88	**5 Schillinge** 2.1.1925. Green. Arms at upper left, portrait youth (by painter E. Zwiauer) at upper right. 154x81mm.	12.50	55.00	285
89	**10 Schillinge** 2.1.1925. Brown-violet. Man at right. 166x86mm.	10.00	45.00	250

		Good	Fine	XF
90	**20 Schillinge** 2.1.1925. Green. Arms at upper left, portrait woman at upper right. 179x89mm.	35.00	140	550
91	**100 Schillinge** 2.1.1925. Blue and multicolor. Woman at right. 192x95mm.	150	550	1,900

		Good	Fine	XF
92	**1000 Schillinge** 2.1.1925. Blue on green and red-brown underprint. Portrait woman at right. 205x97mm.	—	—	—

1927-1930 Issue

		Good	Fine	XF
93	**5 Schilling** 1.7.1927. Blue on green underprint. Portrait Prof. Dr. H. Brücke with compasses at left. Back: Terraced iron ore mining near Eisenerz (Steirmark) at top left center. 111x65mm.	5.50	23.00	90.00

		Good	Fine	XF
94	**10 Schilling** 3.1.1927. Blue on green and red underprint. Mercury at top. Back: Allegorical woman (Harvest) and Dürnstein Castle at bottom. 125x70mm.	8.00	34.00	115

		Good	Fine	XF
95	**20 Schilling** 2.1.1928. Green. Girl at left, farmer at right. Back: Farmer in field.	5.50	23.00	90.00

		Good	Fine	XF
96	**50 Schilling** 2.1.1929. Blue on brown-olive. Woman at left, man at right. 158x77mm.	40.00	170	900
97	**100 Schilling** 3.1.1927. Violet and green. Allegorical female (Sciences) at right. Back: Science Academy in Vienna. 170x85mm.	9.00	35.00	135

		Good	Fine	XF
98	**1000 Schilling** 2.1.1930. Blue-violet on green underprint. Woman with statue of Athena at upper right. Back: Salzburg in mountains. Watermark: Woman's head. 193x89mm.			
	a. Issued note.	—	—	—
	s. Specimen.	—	Unc	1,750

1933-1936 Issue

		VG	VF	UNC
99	**10 Schilling** 2.1.1933. Blue. Woman in national costume at top. Back: Arms above Grossglockner Mountain at top. 125x70mm.			
	a. Numerals of value in 4 corners on diagonal lines.	9.00	28.00	135
	b. Numerals of value in 4 corners on diagonal and vertical lines.	9.00	28.00	135

		VG	VF	UNC
100	**50 Schilling** 2.1.1935. Blue-violet on green underprint. Hubert Sterrer as youth at right. Back: Village of Maria Wörth and Lake Wörth *(Wörthersee)*. 157x78mm.	125	550	—

		VG	VF	UNC
101	**100 Schilling** 2.1.1936. Dark green on multicolor underprint. Woman with Edelweiss at right. (Not issued).	—	—	—

Note: During 1938-1945 the following German notes were in circulation: #171, 173, 174, 179-186, 188-190.

ALLIED OCCUPATION - WWII

Alliierte Militärbehörde

Allied Military Authority

1944 Issue

		VG	VF	UNC
102	**50 Groschen** 1944. Red-brown.			
	a. Printer: Forbes Lithograph Corp. Watermark: *MILITARY AUTHORITY* watermark barely visible and without wavy lines.	20.00	65.00	225
	b. Printed in England. Watermark: Wavy lines.	0.75	3.50	11.50

		VG	VF	UNC
103	**1 Schilling** 1944. Blue on green underprint.			
	a. Printer: Forbes Lithograph Corp. Watermark: *MILITARY AUTHORITY* watermark barely visible and without wavy lines.	1.25	6.50	22.00
	b. Printed in England. Watermark: Wavy lines.	0.75	3.50	11.50

		VG	VF	UNC
104	**2 Schilling** 1944. Blue and black.			
	a. Printer: Forbes Lithograph Corp. Watermark: *MILITARY AUTHORITY* watermark barely visible and without wavy lines.	2.25	11.50	45.00
	b. Printed in England. Watermark: Wavy lines.	0.75	3.50	11.50

		VG	VF	UNC
105	**5 Schilling** 1944. Lilac.	0.75	4.00	13.00

		VG	VF	UNC
106	**10 Schilling** 1944. Green.	1.00	4.50	16.00

		VG	VF	UNC
107	**20 Schilling**	VG	VF	UNC
	1944. Blue on violet underprint.	1.00	4.50	16.00
108	**25 Schilling**	VG	VF	UNC
	1944. Brown on lilac underprint.			
	a. Issued note.	28.00	115	450
	r. Replacement with small "x" to right of serial #.	—	—	—

		VG	VF	UNC
109	**50 Schilling**	VG	VF	UNC
	1944. Brown on light orange underprint.	1.25	6.50	22.00

		VG	VF	UNC
110	**100 Schilling**	VG	VF	UNC
	1944. Green on multicolor underprint.			
	a. Serial # prefix fraction without line.	2.75	11.50	34.00
	b. Serial # prefix fraction with line.	2.75	17.00	65.00
111	**1000 Schilling**	VG	VF	UNC
	1944. Blue on green and multicolor underprint.	70.00	285	1,140

RUSSIAN OCCUPATION - WWII

Republik Österreich

1945 Issue

Issued (20.12.1945) during the Russian occupation.

		VG	VF	UNC
112	**50 Reichspfennig**	VG	VF	UNC
	ND. Brown on orange underprint. Specimen stamped and perforated: *MUSTER*.	—	—	—

		VG	VF	UNC
113	**1 Reichsmark**	VG	VF	UNC
	ND. Green.			
	a. Space below *1* at left and *Reichs-/mark* 2mm.	2.75	11.50	45.00
	b. Space below *1* at left and *Reichs-/mark* 3mm.	1.50	5.50	23.00

REPUBLIC

Oesterreichische Nationalbank

Austrian National Bank

1945 Issue

		VG	VF	UNC
114	**10 Schilling**	VG	VF	UNC
	29.5.1945. Blue-violet on brown underprint. Woman in national costume. Similar to #99. 2 serial # varieties. Back: Arms above Grossglockner Mountain at top.	1.50	4.50	17.00

		VG	VF	UNC
115	**10 Schilling**	VG	VF	UNC
	29.5.1945. Blue-violet. Woman in national costume. Like #114, but *ZWEITE AUSGABE* (2nd issue) in lower design. 2 serial # varieties. Back: Arms above Grossglockner Mountain at top.	1.75	7.00	28.50

		VG	VF	UNC
116	**20 Schilling**	VG	VF	UNC
	29.5.1945. Blue-green on brown underprint. Many color variations. Girl at left, farmer at right. Similar to #95. 2 serial # varieties. Back: Farmer in field.	1.75	7.00	30.00

117	**50 Schilling**	VG	VF	UNC
	29.5.1945. Dark green on brown underprint. Many color varieties. Hubert Sterrer as youth at right. Similar to #100. Back: Building and lake scene.	11.50	55.00	225

118	**100 Schilling**	VG	VF	UNC
	29.5.1945. Blue-violet on gray underprint. Many color varieties. Woman (allegory of the sciences) at right. Back: Academy of Sciences in Vienna at center.	3.00	14.00	55.00

119	**100 Schilling**	Good	Fine	XF
	29.5.1945. Blue-violet on gray underprint. Many color varieties. Woman (allegory of the sciences) at right. Like #118, but with *ZWEITE AUSGABE* (2nd issue) vertically at right. Back: Academy of Sciences in Vienna at center.	—	Unc	1,700

120	**1000 Schilling**	Good	Fine	XF
	29.5.1945. Green. Woman with figure of Athena at upper right. Similar to #98. Back: Salzburg in mountains.			
	a. Issued note.	—	Unc	1,700
	s. Specimen.	—	Unc	900

1945-1947 Issue

121	**5 Schilling**	VG	VF	UNC
	4.9.1945. Blue or violet on gray-green underprint. Many color varieties. Portrait Prof. Dr. H. Brücke with compass at left. Similar to #93. Back: Terraced iron mining near Eisenerz (Steirmark) at top left center.	4.50	23.00	90.00

122	**10 Schilling**	VG	VF	UNC
	2.2.1946. Brown and multicolor. Portrait woman at upper right. Back: Mint tower in Solbad Hall (Tirol) at top center.	7.00	28.50	135

123	**20 Schilling**	VG	VF	UNC
	2.2.1946. Brown and multicolor. Woman at center. Back: St. Stephen's church in Vienna at center.	8.50	55.00	340

124 100 Schilling

2.1.1947. Dark green on violet, blue and multicolor underprint. Portrait woman in national costume at right. Back: Mountain scene. BC: Lilac and green.

VG	VF	UNC
11.00	85.00	500

125 1000 Schilling

1.9.1947. Dark brown on gray green underprint. Woman with figure of Athena at upper right, with *ZWEITE AUSGABE* vertically at left (2nd issue). Back: Salzburg in mountains.

VG	VF	UNC
70.00	345	1,700

1949-1954 Issue

126 5 Schilling

1951. Violet on gray-green. Portrait Prof. Dr. H. Brücke with compass at left. Like #121, but with *AUSGABE 1951* in left margin. Back: Terraced iron mining near Eisenerz (Steirmark) at top left center.

VG	VF	UNC
8.50	40.00	170

127 10 Schilling

2.1.1950. Purple. Buildings at lower left center, horseman of the Spanish Royal Riding School at right. Back: Belvedere Castle in Vienna at left center. BC: Brown.

VG	VF	UNC
4.25	22.50	80.00

128 10 Schilling

2.1.1950. Purple. Buildings at lower left center, horseman of the Spanish Royal Riding School at right. Like #127. Back: Belvedere Castle in Vienna at left center. BC: Brown.

VG	VF	UNC
3.50	20.00	70.00

129 20 Schilling

2.1.1950. Brown on red and blue underprint. Portrait Joseph Haydn at right. Back: Tower at left, cherub playing kettledrum at center.

	VG	VF	UNC
a. *OESTERREICHISCHE* in underprint.	14.00	65.00	285
b. Error in bank name *OESTERREICHISCEE* in underprint (Error visible in second or third line at bottom of underprint at bottom).	8.50	43.00	170

130 50 Schilling

2.1.1951. Lilac and violet on multicolor underprint. Portrait J. Prandtauer at right. Back: Woman at left, cloister in town of Melk at center, urn at right.

VG	VF	UNC
8.50	45.00	170

131 100 Schilling

3.1.1949. Dark green on lilac and purple underprint. Cherub at lower left, woman's head at upper right. Back: Mermaid at left center, Vienna in background. BC: Olive green and purple.

VG	VF	UNC
10.00	45.00	200

132 100 Schilling

3.1.1949. Dark green on lilac and purple underprint. Cherub at lower left, woman's head at upper right. Like #131. Back: Mermaid at left center, Vienna in background. BC: Olive green and purple.

VG	VF	UNC
10.50	50.00	200

133	100 Schilling	VG	VF	UNC
	2.1.1954. Green on multicolor underprint. F. Grillparzer at right. Back: Castle Dürnstein.			
	a. Issued note.	9.50	40.00	150
	s. Specimen.	—	—	90.00

134	500 Schilling	VG	VF	UNC
	2.1.1953. Dark brown on blue and red underprint. Prof. Wagner-Jauregg at right. Back: University of Vienna.			
	a. Issued note.	15.00	55.00	285
	s. Specimen.	—	—	170

135	1000 Schilling	VG	VF	UNC
	2.1.1954. Blue on multicolor underprint. A. Bruckner at right. Back: Bruckner organ at St. Florian.			
	a. Issued note.	40.00	170	800
	s. Specimen.	—	—	400

1956-1965 Issues

136	20 Schilling	VG	VF	UNC
	2.7.1956. Brown on red-brown and multicolor underprint. Carl Auer Freiherr von Welsbach at right, arms at left. Back: Village Maria Rain, church and Karawanken mountains.			
	a. Issued note.	2.25	8.50	35.00
	s. Specimen.	—	—	90.00

138	100 Schilling	VG	VF	UNC
	1.7.1960 (1961). Dark green on multicolor underprint. Violin and music at lower left, Johann Strauss at right, arms at left. Back: Schönbrunn Castle.			
	a. Issued note.	2.75	11.00	45.00
	s. Specimen.	—	—	90.00

140	1000 Schilling	VG	VF	UNC
	2.1.1961 (1962). Dark blue on multicolor underprint. Viktor Kaplan at right. Back: Dam and Persenburg Castle, arms at right. 148x75mm.			
	a. Issued note. Rare.	—	—	—
	s. Specimen.	—	—	2,000

Note: #140 was in use for only 11 weeks.

141	1000 Schilling	VG	VF	UNC
	2.1.1961 (1962). Dark blue on multicolor underprint with blue lines up to margin. Viktor Kaplan at right. Back: Dam and Persenburg Castle, arms at right. 158x85mm.			
	a. Issued note.	5.50	40.00	225
	s. Specimen. Overprint and perforated: *Muster.*	—	—	135

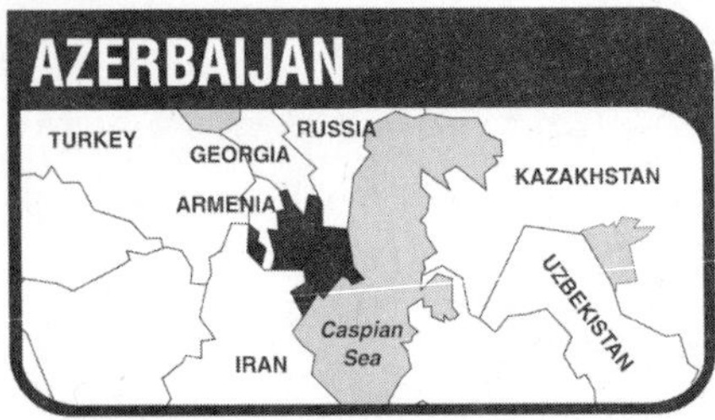

The Republic of Azerbaijan includes the Nakhichevan Autonomous Republic and Nagorno-Karabakh Autonomous Region (which was abolished in 1991). Situated in the eastern area of Transcaucasia, it is bordered in the west by Armenia, in the north by Georgia and the Russian Federation of Dagestan, to the east by the Caspian Sea and to the south by Iran. It has an area of 86,600 sq. km. and a population of 8.18 million. Capital: Baku. The area is rich in mineral deposits of aluminum, copper, iron, lead, salt and zinc, with oil as its leading industry. Agriculture and livestock follow in importance.

Azerbaijan - a nation with a majority-Turkic and majority-Muslim population - was briefly independent from 1918 to 1920; it regained its independence after the collapse of the Soviet Union in 1991. Despite a 1994 cease-fire, Azerbaijan has yet to resolve its conflict with Armenia over the Azerbaijani Nagorno-Karabakh enclave (largely Armenian populated). Azerbaijan has lost 16% of its territory and must support some 600,000 internally displaced persons as a result of the conflict. Corruption is ubiquitous, and the government has been accused of authoritarianism. Although the poverty rate has been reduced in recent years, the promise of widespread wealth from development of Azerbaijan's energy sector remains largely unfulfilled.

MONETARY SYSTEM:

1 Manat = 10 Soviet Rubles, to 1992

1 New Manat = 5,000 Old Manat, 2005-

AUTONOMOUS REPUBLIC

Azerbaijan Republic

АЗЕРБАИДЖАНСКАЯ РЕСІТУБЛИКА

1919 First Issue

		VG	VF	UNC
1	**25 Rubles** 1919. Lilac and brown. Color, paper and serial # varieties exist.	15.00	25.00	75.00

		VG	VF	UNC
2	**50 Rubles** 1919. Blue-green and brown. Color, paper and serial # varieties exist.	20.00	40.00	75.00

1919 Second Issue

		VG	VF	UNC
5	**100 Rubles** 1919. Brown. Persian title. Back: Similar to #9 except different Russian title.	15.00	40.00	75.00

		VG	VF	UNC
6	**250 Rubles** 1919. Lilac, brown and green.			
	a. Issued note.	20.00	40.00	75.00
	p. Green, brown and rose. Proof.	—	—	150

1920 First Issue

		VG	VF	UNC
7	**500 Rubles** 1920. Dark brown and dull gray-green on lilac and multicolor underprint. Series I-LV.	20.00	50.00	100

1920 Second Issue

		VG	VF	UNC
8	**1 Ruble** 1920. Unfinished proof print.	30.00	60.00	175

Azerbaijan Government

АЗЕРБАИДЖАНСКОЕ ПРАВИТЕЛЬСТВО

1919 Issue

		VG	VF	UNC
9	**100 Rubles** 1919. Brown. Russian title. Back: Similar to #5 except different Russian title.			
	a. Without series on back.	20.00	50.00	100
	b. With СЕРІЯ (ВТОРАЯ) series on back.	20.00	50.00	100

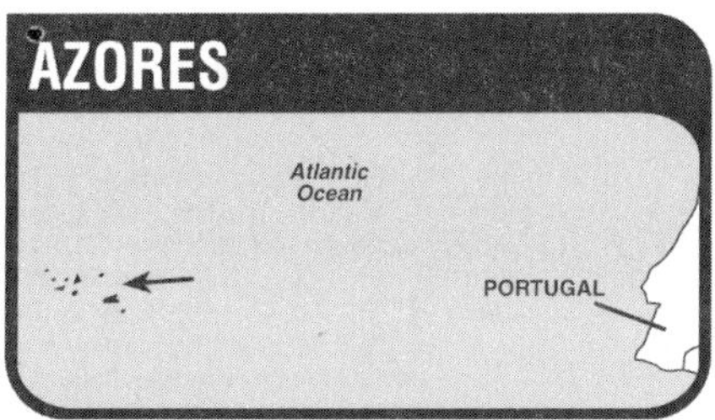

The Azores, an archipelago of nine islands of volcanic origin, are located in the Atlantic Ocean 740 miles (1,190 km.) west of Cape de Roca, Portugal. They are under the administration of Portugal, and have an area of 902 sq. mi. (2,336 sq. km.) and a population of 252,000. Principal city: Ponta Delgada. The natives are mainly of Portuguese descent and earn their livelihood by fishing, wine making, basket weaving, and the growing of fruit, grains and sugar cane. Pineapples are the chief item of export. The climate is particularly temperate, making the islands a favorite winter resort. The Azores were discovered about 1427 by the Portuguese navigator Diago de Silves. Portugal secured the islands in the 15th century and established the first settlement, on Santa Maria, about 1432. From 1580 to 1640 the Azores were subject to Spain. Angra on Terceira Island became the capital of the captaincy-general of the Azores in 1766 and it was here in 1826 that the constitutionalists set up a pro-Pedro government in opposition to King Miguel in Lisbon. The whole Portuguese fleet attacked Terceira Island and was repelled at Praia, after which Azoreans, Brazilians and British mercenaries defeated Miguel in Portugal. Maria de Gloria, Pedro's daughter, was proclaimed queen of Portugal on Terceira Island in 1828. A U.S. naval base was established at Ponta Delgada in 1917. After World War II, the islands acquired a renewed importance as a refueling stop for transatlantic air transport. The United States maintains defense bases in the Azores as part of the collective security program of NATO. Since 1976 the Azores are an Autonomous Region with a regional government and parliament.

RULERS:
Portuguese

MONETARY SYSTEM:
1 Milreis = 1000 Reis to 1910
1 Escudo = 100 Centavos 1910-

PORTUGUESE ADMINISTRATION

Banco de Portugal

1876-1885 Issue

#1-3 overprint: *S. MIGUEL.*

#	Denomination	Good	Fine	XF
1	**5 Mil Reis** 1.12.1885. Blue. Standing figure at left and right, arms at lower center. Back: Arms at center. Hand dated.	—	—	—
2	**10 Mil Reis** 28.1.1878. Blue. Three figures with arms at center. Hand dated. BC: Red. Rare.	—	—	—
3	**20 Mil Reis** 30.8.1876. Blue and brown. Portrait of King with crown above at upper center. Hand dated. BC: Light brown. Rare.	—	—	—

1895 Issue

#4-7 with inscription: *Pagavel nos Agencias dos Acres.*

#	Denomination	Good	Fine	XF
4	**5 Mil Reis** 1.10.1895. Light blue. Allegorical figure of "Patria" at left arms at upper center. With inscription: *Pagavel nos Agencias dos Acôres.* Back: Arms at center.	—	—	—
5	**10 Mil Reis** 1.10.1895. Light brown. Allegorical figure of Agriculture at left, Commerce at right. With inscription: *Pagavel nos Agencias dos Acôres.* Back: Standing figure at left and right. Rare.	—	—	—
6	**20 Mil Reis** 1.10.1895. Orange. Allegorical figure of Industry at left, Commerce at right. With inscription: *Pagavel nos Agencias dos Acôres.* BC: Blue on dark orange underprint. Rare.	—	—	—
7	**50 Mil Reis** 1.10.1895. Red. Allegorical figure of Industry at left, Commerce at right, arms at lower center. With inscription: *Pagavel nos Agencias dos Acôres.* Back: Arms at center. BC: Red and blue. Rare.	—	—	—

1905-1910 Issues

#8-14 overprint: *MOEDA INSULANA*, with or without large *AÇÔRES* diagonally on face in red between bars of *AÇÔRES* one or more times on face and back. Regular issue Portuguese types and designs are used, though colors may vary. Notes payable in silver (prata) or gold (ouro). This issue circulated until 1932.

#	Denomination	Good	Fine	XF
8	**2 1/2 Mil Reis Prata** 30.6.1906; 30.7.1909. Black on orange, blue and olive underprint. Portrait of A. de Albuquerque at right. Back: Mercury at left. On Portugal #107.			
	a. Face without diagonal overprint 2 signature varieties.	300	900	3,000
	b. Face with red diagonal overprint: *AÇÔRES.*	300	900	3,000
9	**5 Mil Reis Prata** 30.1.1905. Black, green and brown. Three figures with arms at center. Back: Arms at center. On Portugal #83.	1,500	3,000	—

#	Denomination	Good	Fine	XF
10	**10 Mil Reis Ouro** 30.1.1905. Like Portugal #81, but different color. Blue on light green underprint. Luis de Camoes at left, two figures and globe at lower center, ships at right. Back: Infante D. Henrique at upper left. Watermark: A. de Albuquerque.	1,750	4,500	—

#	Denomination	Good	Fine	XF
11	**10 Mil Reis Ouro** 30.1.1905. Brown and yellow. Luis de Camoes at left, two figures and globe at lower center, ships at right. Back: Infante D. Henrique at upper left. Watermark: A. de Albuquerque. On Portugal #81.	1,750	4,500	—

Color Abbreviation Guide

New to the *Standard Catalog of ® World Paper Money* are the following abbreviations related to color references:

BC: Back color
PC: Paper color

		Good	Fine	XF
12	**10 Mil Reis Ouro** 30.9.1910. Green on light tan underprint. Five men representing sculpture, painting, reading, music and writing. Back: Allegorical woman at left, helmeted woman at right. On design type of Portugal #108.	1,750	4,500	—

		Good	Fine	XF
13	**20 Mil Reis Ouro** 30.1.1905. Brown and light red. Standing figure at left and right, arms at lower center. On Portugal #82.	1,500	4,000	—

		Good	Fine	XF
14	**50 Mil Reis Ouro** 30.1.1905. Blue on red underprint. Statues of Principe Perfetto and B. Dias at left and right, heads of Pero de Alenquer and Diogo Cao at lower left and right, with anchor and ships, allegorical woman at center right. Back: Arms at left. On design type of Portugal #85.	—	—	—

BAHAMAS

The Commonwealth of The Bahamas is an archipelago of about 3,000 islands, cays and rocks located in the Atlantic Ocean east of Florida and north of Cuba. The total land area of the chain of islands is 10,070 sq. km. They have a population of 307,400. Capital: Nassau. The Bahamas imports most of their food and manufactured products and exports cement, refined oil, pulpwood and lobsters.Lucayan Indians inhabited the islands when Christopher Columbus first set foot in the New World on San Salvador in 1492. British settlement of the islands began in 1647; the islands became a colony in 1783. Since attaining independence from the UK in 1973, The Bahamas have prospered through tourism and international banking and investment management.

RULERS:
British

MONETARY SYSTEM:
1 Shilling = 12 Pence
1 Pound = 20 Shillings to 1966

BRITISH ADMINISTRATION

Bank of Nassau

ND Issue (ca. 1870s)

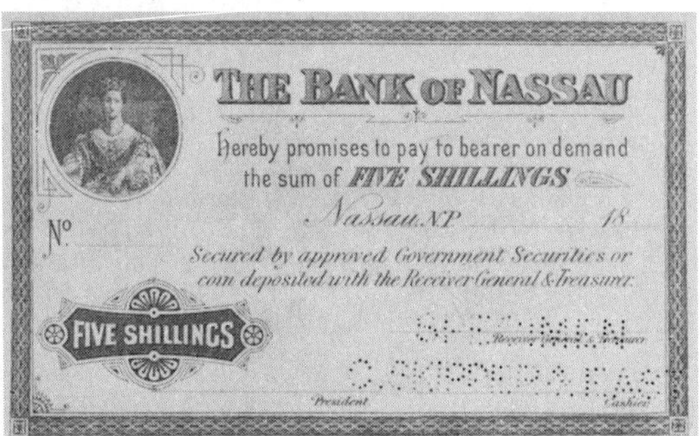

		Good	Fine	XF
A1	**5 Shillings** 18xx. Red. Portrait Queen Victoria at upper left. Printer: CS&E. Specimen.	—	—	750
A2	**10 Shillings** 18xx. Red. Queen Victoria at top center. Printer: CS&E. Specimen.	—	—	750
A3	**10 Shillings** 18xx. Blue. Printer: CS&E. Specimen.	—	—	750
A4	**10 Shillings** 18xx. Brown. Printer: CS&E.	—	—	750
A4A	**1 Pound** 18xx. Light orange. Queen Victoria at center. Printer: CS&E. Specimen.	—	—	750

1897 Issue

		Good	Fine	XF
A4B	**5 Shillings** 18xx. Black. Ship seal at left, portrait of a man at right. Uniface.	—	—	750

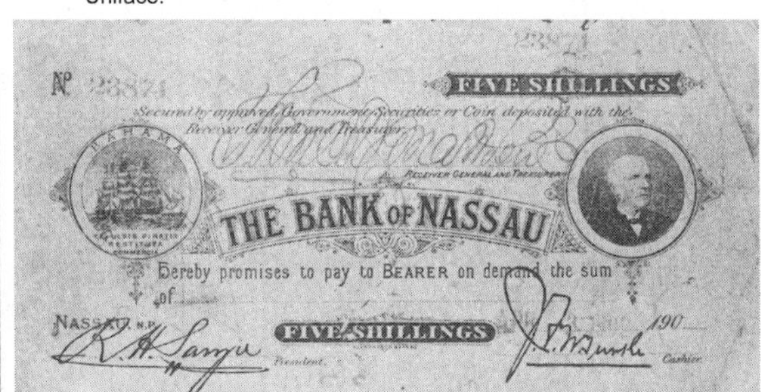

		Good	Fine	XF
A5	**5 Shillings** 28.1.1897; 3.4.1902. Blue. Ship seal at left, portrait of a man at right. Uniface.	500	1,750	—
A7	**1 Pound** 190x. Blue. Ship seal at left, portrait of a man at right. Uniface.	—	—	—

1906 Issue

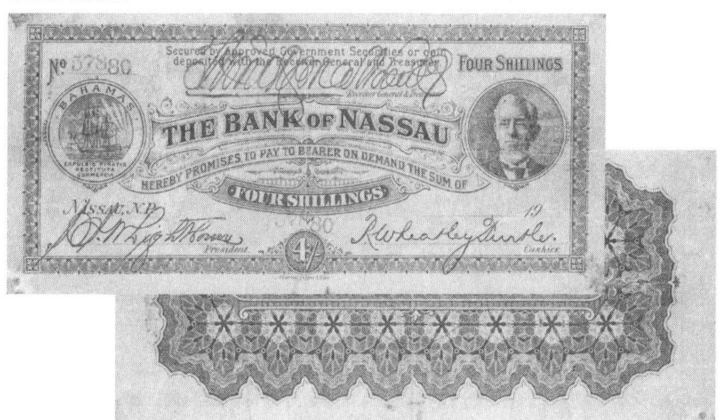

		Good	Fine	XF
A8	**4 Shillings** 11.5.1906; 22.10.1910; 19.3.1913; 16.4.1913; 21.1.1916. Green. Arms at left, portrait of a man at right. BC: Red-brown. Printer: CS&E.	500	1,500	—
A8A	**1 Pound** 190x. Black. Ship seal at left, portrait of a man at right. Unsigned remainder.	—	—	—

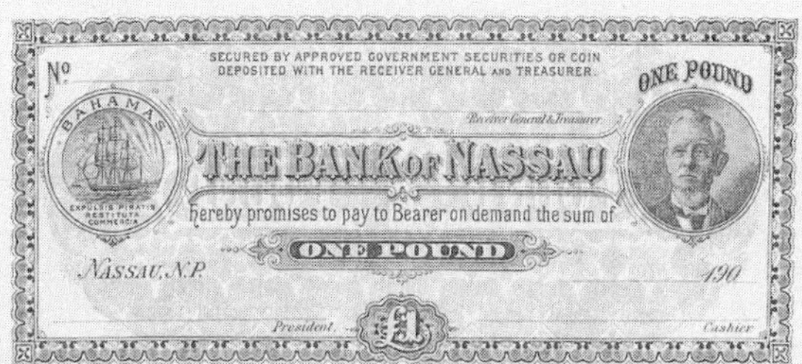

		Good	Fine	XF
A8B	**1 Pound** 190x. Deep green. Ship seal at left, portrait of a man at right. Proof.	—	—	—

Public Treasury, Nassau

Interest paid at least until June 1973.

1868 Issue

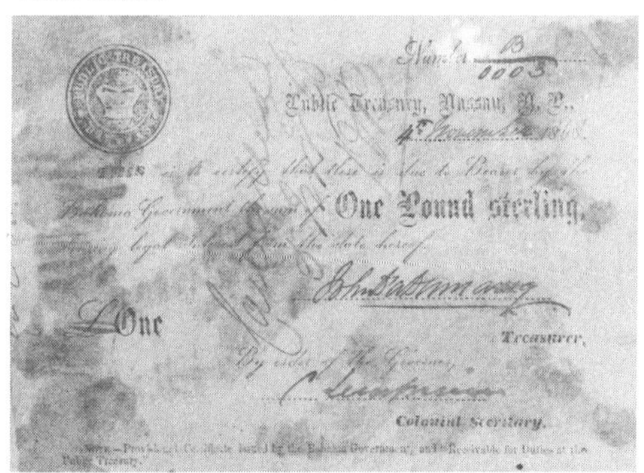

		Good	Fine	XF
A9	**1 Pound** 4.11.1868-1869. Circular Public Treasury seal at upper left. Signature varieties. Handwritten dates. Rare.	—	—	—

Bahamas Government

1869 Issue

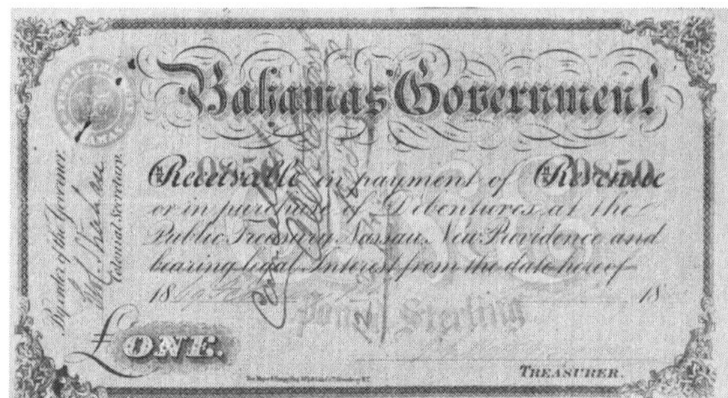

		Good	Fine	XF
A10	**1 Pound** 1.2.1869. Black on light blue underprint. Circular Public Treasury seal at upper left. Printer: Major and Knapp. Rare.	—	—	—

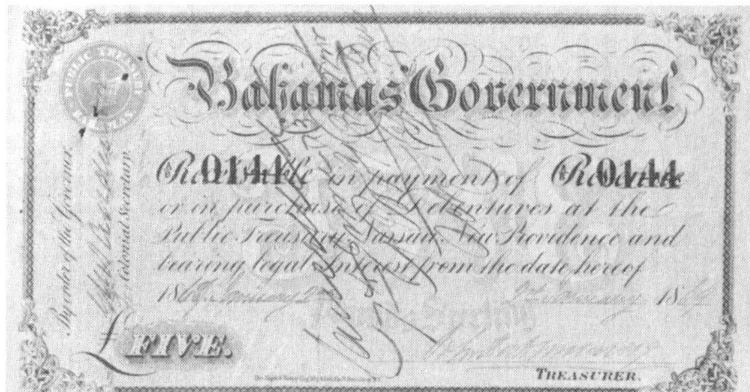

		Good	Fine	XF
A11	**5 Pounds** 2.1.1869; 1.2.1869. Rare. Black on red-violet underprint. Circular Public Treasury seal at upper left. Printer: Major and Knapp.	—	—	—

1919 Currency Note Act

		Good	Fine	XF
1	**4 Shillings** *L.1919.* Ship seal at right. Back: Government building. Rare.	—	—	—

		Good	Fine	XF
2	**4 Shillings** *L.1919.* Black on green underprint. Donkey cart at left, ship seal at center, bushes at right. BC: Green. Printer: CBNC (without imprint).			
	a. No serial # prefix. Signature H. E. W. Grant at left.	150	500	2,000
	b. Serial # prefix *A*. Signature A. C. Burns at left.	125	325	1,250
3	**10 Shillings** *L.1919.* Black on red underprint. Donkey cart at left, ship seal at center, bushes at right. BC: Red. Printer: CBNC (without imprint).	Good	Fine	XF
	a. No serial # prefix. Signature H. E. W. Grant at left.	275	1,250	—
	b. Serial # prefix *A*. Signature A. C. Burns at left.	275	1,250	—
4	**1 Pound** *L.1919.* Black on gray underprint. Donkey cart at left, ship seal at center, bushes at right. BC: Black. Printer: CBNC (without imprint).	Good	Fine	XF
	a. No serial # prefix. Signature H. E. W. Grant at left.	275	1,000	3,500
	b. Serial # prefix *A*. Signature A. C. Burns at left.	275	950	3,250

1919 Currency Note Act (1930)

No.	Denomination	Good	Fine	XF
5	**4 Shillings** *L.1919* (1930). Green. Ship seal at left, King George V at right. Signature varieties. Printer: W&S.	100	275	1,000

No.	Denomination	Good	Fine	XF
6	**10 Shillings** *L.1919* (1930). Red. Ship seal at left, King George V at right. Signature varieties. Printer: W&S.			
	a. Issued note.	500	1,750	—
	ct. Color trial. Purple-Violet.	—	Unc	5,850

No.	Denomination	Good	Fine	XF
7	**1 Pound** *L.1919* (1930). Black. Ship seal at left, King George V at right. Signature varieties. Printer: W&S.	200	600	1,250

1936 Currency Note Act

No.	Denomination	VG	VF	UNC
9	**4 Shillings** *L.1936.* Green. Ship seal at left, King George VI at right. Watermark: Columbus. Printer: TDLR.			
	a. Signature J. H. Jarrett with title: *COLONIAL SECRETARY COMMISSIONER OF CURRENCY* at left.	25.00	100	600
	b. Signature W. L. Heape at left.	20.00	75.00	500
	c. Signature D. G. Stewart at left, Walter K. Moore at right.	25.00	100	550
	d. Signature D. G. Stewart at left, Basil Burnside at right.	25.00	100	550
	e. Signature title: *COMMISSIONER OF CURRENCY* at left.	12.50	50.00	450
	s1. As a. Specimen. Perforated: *SPECIMEN.*	—	—	1,000
	s2. As b. Specimen. Perforated: *CANCELLED.*	—	—	1,000

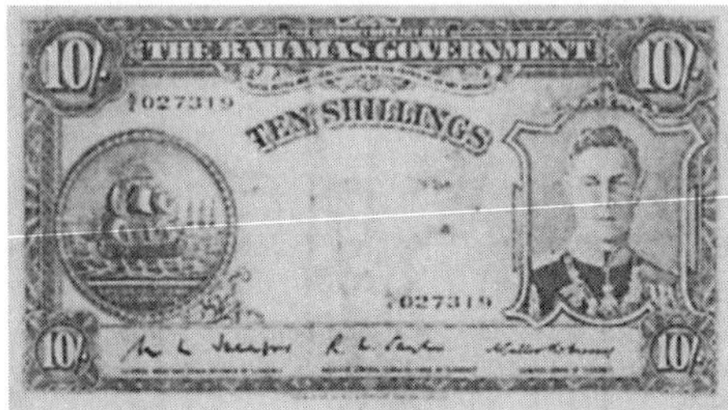

No.	Denomination	VG	VF	UNC
10	**10 Shillings** *L.1936.* Red. Ship seal at left, portrait King George VI at right. Watermark: Columbus. Printer: TDLR.			
	a. Signature J. H. Jarrett with title: *COLONIAL SECRETARY COMMISSIONER OF CURRENCY* at left.	50.00	300	1,000
	b. Signature W. L. Heape at left.	40.00	275	1,000
	c. Signature D. G. Stewart at left, Walter K. Moore at right.	40.00	275	900
	d. Signature title: *COMMISSIONER OF CURRENCY* at left.	25.00	100	800
	s. As d. Specimen. Perforated: *CANCELLED.*	—	—	1,000

No.	Denomination	VG	VF	UNC
11	**1 Pound** *L.1936.* Black. Ship seal at left, King George VI at right. Watermark: Columbus. Printer: TDLR.			
	a. Signature J. H. Jarrett with title: *COLONIAL SECRETARY COMMISSIONER OF CURRENCY* at left.	75.00	300	1,200
	b. Signature W. L. Heape at left.	50.00	250	1,000
	c. Signature D. G. Stewart at left, Walter K. Moore at right.	75.00	275	1,100
	d. Signature D. G. Stewart at left, Basil Burnside at right.	50.00	250	1,000
	e. Signature title: *COMMISSIONER OF CURRENCY* at left.	40.00	200	850
	s. As b. Specimen. Perforated: *CANCELLED.*	—	—	1,000

No.	Denomination	VG	VF	UNC
12	**5 Pounds** *L.1936.* Blue-violet on multicolor underprint. Ship seal at left, King George VI at right. Watermark: Columbus. Printer: TDLR.			
	a. Signature D. J. Stewart with title: *COLONIAL SECRETARY COMMISSIONER OF CURRENCY* at left.	550	1,300	—
	b. Signature title: *COMMISSIONER OF CURRENCY* at left.	100	400	1,100

COMMONWEALTH

Bahamas Government

1953 Issue

		VG	VF	UNC
13	**4 Shillings** ND (1953). Green. Ship seal at left, portrait Queen Elizabeth II at right. Printer: TDLR.			
	a. Center signature H. R. Latreille, Basil Burnside at right.	17.50	90.00	450
	b. Center signature W. H. Sweeting, Basil Burnside at right.	17.50	90.00	450
	c. Center signature W. H. Sweeting, Chas. P. Bethel at right.	17.50	90.00	450
	d. Center signature W. H. Sweeting, George W. K. Roberts at right.	17.50	90.00	450

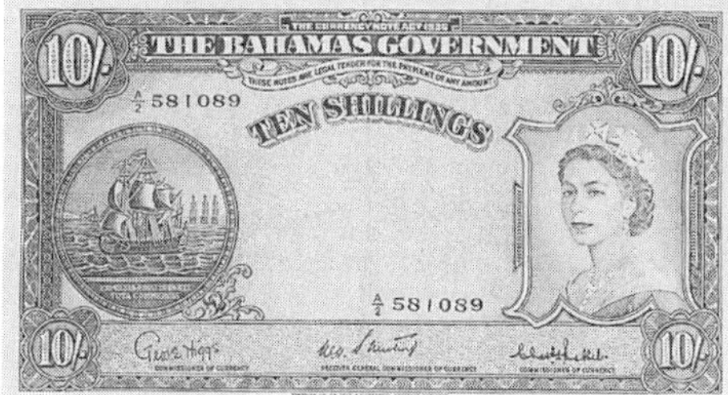

		VG	VF	UNC
14	**10 Shillings** ND (1953). Red. Ship seal at left, portrait Queen Elizabeth II at right. Printer: TDLR.			
	a. Center signature H. R. Latreille, Basil Burnside at right.	40.00	200	1,000
	b. Center signature W. H. Sweeting, Basil Burnside at right.	40.00	200	1,000
	c. Center signature W. H. Sweeting, Chas. P. Bethel at right.	40.00	200	1,000
	d. Center signature W. H. Sweeting, George W. K. Roberts at right.	40.00	200	1,000

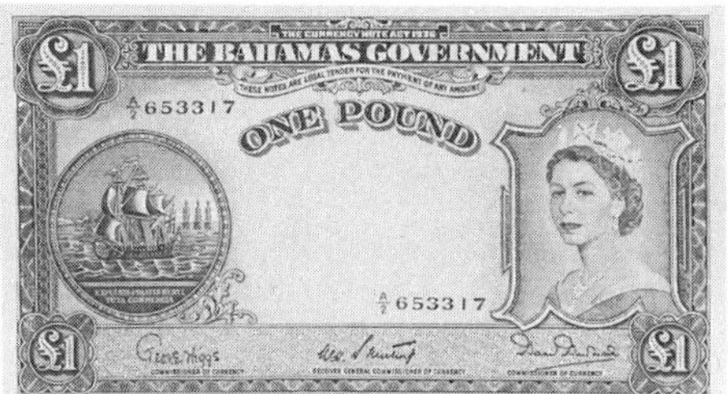

		VG	VF	UNC
15	**1 Pound** ND (1953). Black. Ship seal at left, portrait Queen Elizabeth II at right. Printer: TDLR.			
	a. Center signature H. R. Latreille, Basil Burnside at right.	150	550	1,750
	b. Center signature W. H. Sweeting, Basil Burnside at right.	150	550	1,750
	c. Center signature W. H. Sweeting, Chas. P. Bethel at right.	150	550	1,750
	d. Center signature W. H. Sweeting, George W. K. Roberts at right.	100	450	1,000

		VG	VF	UNC
16	**5 Pounds** ND (1953). Blue. Portrait Queen Elizabeth II at right.			
	a. Center signature H. R. Latreille, Basil Burnside at right. Rare.	—	—	—
	b. Center signature W. H. Sweeting, Basil Burnside at right.	175	800	3,900
	c. Center signature W. H. Sweeting, Chas. P. Bethel at right.	175	800	3,900
	d. Center signature W. H. Sweeting, George W. K. Roberts at right.	175	800	3,900
	s1. As b. Specimen. Perforated: *CANCELLED*.	—	—	2,000
	s2. As c. Specimen. Perforated: *CANCELLED*.	—	—	2,000

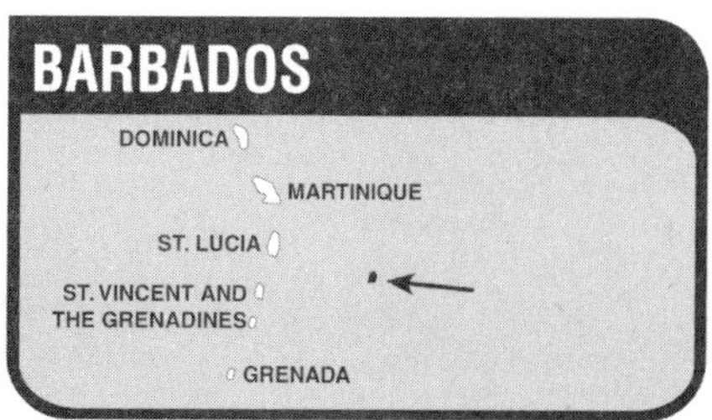

Barbados, an independent state within the British Commonwealth, is located in the Windward Islands of the West Indies east of St. Vincent. The coral island has an area of 431 sq. km and a population of 281,900. Capital: Bridgetown.

The island was uninhabited when first settled by the British in 1627. Slaves worked the sugar plantations established on the island until 1834 when slavery was abolished. The economy remained heavily dependent on sugar, rum, and molasses production through most of the 20th century. The gradual introduction of social and political reforms in the 1940s and 1950s led to complete independence from the UK in 1966. In the 1990s, tourism and manufacturing surpassed the sugar industry in economic importance.

RULERS:

British to 1966

MONETARY SYSTEM:

1 British West Indies Dollar = 4 Shillings - 2 Pence
5 British West Indies Dollars = 1 Pound - 10 Pence
1 Dollar = 100 Cents, 1950-

BRITISH ADMINISTRATION

Government of Barbados

1915 Issue

		Good	Fine	XF
1	**1 Pound** 1915-1917. (28,000 issued).	—	—	—

1938-1943 Issue

		VG	VF	UNC
2	**1 Dollar** 1938-1949. Green, brown-violet and multicolor. Neptune on horse-drawn cart at left, portrait King George VI at right. Date and signature varieties. Watermark: Two horse heads. Printer: BWC.			
	a. 3.1.1938.	25.00	125	750
	b. 1.9.1939; 1.12.1939; 1.6.1943.	20.00	100	650
	c. 1.1.1949.	40.00	150	850

		Good	Fine	XF
3	**2 Dollars** 1938-1949. Brown and green. Neptune on horse-drawn cart at left, portrait King George VI at right. Date and signature varieties. Watermark: Two horse heads. Printer: BWC.			
	a. 3.1.1938.	150	1,500	2,100
	b. 1.9.1939; 1.12.1939; 1.6.1943.	125	1,100	1,850
	c. 1.1.1949.	150	1,500	2,100

		Good	Fine	XF
4	**5 Dollars** 1939-1943. Purple and blue. Neptune on horse-drawn cart at left, portrait King George VI at right. Date and signature varieties. Watermark: Two horse heads. Printer: BWC.			
	a. 1.9.1939; 1.12.1939.	250	600	1,750
	b. 1.6.1943.	125	550	1,100

		Good	Fine	XF
5	**20 Dollars** 1.6.1943. Pink and green. Neptune on horse-drawn cart at left, portrait King George VI at right. Date and signature varieties. Watermark: Two horse heads. Printer: BWC.			
	a. Issued note.	1,000	1,750	—
	s. Specimen.	—	Unc	1,500

		Good	Fine	XF
6	**100 Dollars** 1.6.1943. Brown and black. Neptune on horse-drawn cart at left, portrait King George VI at right. Date and signature varieties. Watermark: Two horse heads. Printer: BWC.			
	a. Issued note. (One verified). Rare.	—	—	—
	s. Specimen.	—	Unc	6,000

BELGIAN CONGO

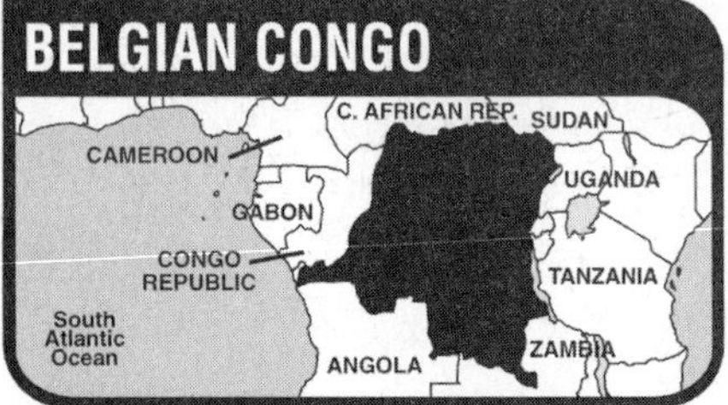

Belgian Congo (now the Congo Democratic Republic), located in the south-central part of Africa, has an area of 905,378 sq. mi. (2,344,920 sq. km.) and a population of 13.6 million. Capital: Kinshasa. The mineral-rich country produces copper, tin, diamonds, gold, zinc, cobalt and uranium. In ancient times the territory comprising the Belgium Congo was occupied by Negrito peoples (Pygmies) pushed into the mountains by Bantu and Nilotic invaders. The interior was first explored by the American correspondent Henry Stanley, who was subsequently commissioned by King Leopold II of Belgium to conclude development treaties with the local chiefs. The Berlin conference of 1885 awarded the area to Leopold, who administered and exploited it as his private property until it was annexed to Belgium in 1907. Belgium received the mandate for the German territories of Ruanda-Urundi as a result of the international treaties after WWI. During WWII Belgian Congolese troops fought on the side of the Allies, notably in Ethiopia. Following the eruption of bloody independence riots in 1959, Belgium granted the Belgian Congo independence as the Republic of the Congo on June 30, 1960.

RULERS:

Leopold II, 1885-1907
Belgium, 1907-1960

MONETARY SYSTEM:

1 Franc = 100 Centimes to 1967

CONGO FREE STATE

Etat Independant du Congo

INDEPENDENT STATE OF THE CONGO

1896 Issue

		Good	Fine	XF
1	**10 Francs** 7.2.1896. Black on yellow and green underprint. Child holding cornucopia at center. Back: Woman's head at left. Printer: W&S.			
	a. Issued note.	1,800	2,500	3,000
	b. As a. Punch hole cancelled.	450	600	1,000
	r1. Remainder. Without date or signature.	—	—	2,000
	r2. Remainder. Without serial #, with signatures.	—	—	2,000

#1 also circulated in Belgium during 1914. Issued in Bruxelles.

		Good	Fine	XF
2	**100 Francs** 7.2.1896. Black on yellow and brown underprint. Woman seated holding caduceus at left center, lion at upper right. Back: Portrait woman at center. Printer: W&S.			
	a. Issued note.	2,500	3,250	4,000
	b. As a. Punch hole cancelled.	750	1,200	1,500
	r. Remainder. Without date or signature	—	—	2,000

#2 also circulated in Belgium during 1914. Issued in Bruxelles.

BELGIAN CONGO

Banque du Congo Belge

BANK OF THE BELGIAN CONGO

1914 Issue

#	Description	Good	Fine	XF
3	**1 Franc** 9.10.1914; 9.1.1920; 2.6.1920. Black on red underprint. Woman seated with sheaf of grain and wheel at left. *ELISABETHVILLE.* Signature varieties. Printer: W&S.	100	275	450

#	Description	Good	Fine	XF
3B	**1 Franc** 15.10.1914; 15.1.1920; 26.6.1920. Black on red underprint. Woman seated with sheaf of grain and wheel at left. *MATADI.* Signature varieties. Printer: W&S.	75.00	200	300

#	Description	Good	Fine	XF
4	**5 Francs** 9.10.1914; 19.3.1919; 2.3.1920; 2.6.1920; 2.4.1921; 2.4.1924. Black on pale blue underprint. Woman seated with child by beehive at left. *ELIZABETHVILLE.* Signature varieties. Back: Elephant and hippo at center. Printer: W&S.	100	250	400
4A	**5 Francs** 26.10.1914; 19.3.1919; 3.3.1920; 3.6.1920; 3.4.1921; 3.4.1924. Black on pale blue underprint. Woman seated with child by beehive at left. *KINSHASA.* Signature varieties. Like #4. Back: Elephant and hippo at center. Printer: W&S.	100	250	400

#	Description	Good	Fine	XF
4B	**5 Francs** 15.10.1914; 26.3.1920; 26.4.1921. Black on pale blue underprint. Woman seated with child by beehive at left. *MATADI.* Signature varieties. Like #4. Back: Elephant and hippo at center. Printer: W&S.	100	250	400
4C	**5 Francs** 30.10.1914; 4.3.1920; 4.4.1921. Black on pale blue underprint. Woman seated with child by beehive at left. *STANLEYVILLE.* Signature varieties. Like #4. Back: Elephant and hippo at center. Printer: W&S.	100	250	400

1912-1937 Issue

#	Description	Good	Fine	XF
8	**5 Francs** 1924-1930. Red, brown and green. Huts, palm trees at left. Back: River steamboat. Watermark: Elephant's head. Printer: BNB (without imprint).			
	a. *ELISABETHVILLE.* 2.12.1924; 2.7.1926.	100	300	500
	b. *LEOPOLDVILLE.* 3.12.1924; 3.7.1926.	100	300	500
	c. *MATADI.* 26.12.1924; 26.7.1926.	100	300	500
	d. *STANLEYVILLE.* 4.12.1924; 4.7.1926.	100	300	500
	e. Without office overprint. 21.1.1929; 4.4.1930.	50.00	150	400

#	Description	Good	Fine	XF
9	**10 Francs** 10.9.1937. Brown. Market scene. Back: Water bucks, trees at center right. Watermark: Elephant's head. Printer: BNB (without imprint).	100	200	500

#	Description	Good	Fine	XF
10	**20 Francs** 1912-1937. Green. Portrait Ceres at upper left, woman kneeling with hammer and anvil, woman reclining with elephant tusk at left. Signature varieties. Back: Waterfront village and canoe. Watermark: Elephant's head. Printer: BNB (without imprint).			
	a. *ELISABETHVILLE.* 10.9.1912; 2.5.1914; 2.3.1920; 2.11.1920; 2.10.1925; 2.7.1926; 2.7.1927.	500	800	1,250
	b. *KINSHASA.* 10.9.1912; 3.5.1914; 3.3.1917; 3.3.1920; 3.11.1920.	500	900	1,500
	c. *LEOPOLDVILLE.* 3.10.1925; 3.7.1926; 3.7.1927.	500	800	1,400
	d. *MATADI.* 10.9.1912; 26.12.1913; 26.4.1914; 26.3.1920; 26.11.1920;26.10.1925; 26.7.1926; 26.6.1927.	500	800	1,400
	e. *STANLEYVILLE.* 10.9.1912; 4.5.1914; 4.3.1920; 4.11.1920; 4.10.1925; 4.7.1926; 4.7.1927.	500	800	1,400
	f. Without office overprint. 1.2.1929; 15.9.1937.	125	300	500

11	**100 Francs**	Good	Fine	XF
	1912-1929. Blue. Woman standing holding portrait Ceres, young boy seated on rock with elephant tusks and produce below at left, woman kneeling with fabric at right. Signature varieties. Back: Woman and child at left, fisherman with canoe paddle and fishing net. Watermark: Elephant's head. Printer: BNB (without imprint).			
	a. *ELISABETHVILLE.* 2.2.1914; 2.3.1920; 2.11.1920; 2.7.1926; 2.7.1927.	500	900	1,750
	b. *KINSHASA.* 10.9.1912; 3.2.1914; 3.3.1917; 3.3.1920; 3.11.1920.	400	1,000	1,750
	c. *LEOPOLDVILLE.* 3.7.1926; 3.7.1927.	400	1,000	1,750
	d. *MATADI.* 10.9.1912; 26.2.1914; 26.3.1917; 26.3.1920; 26.11.1920; 26.7.1926; 26.6.1927.	400	1,000	1,750
	e. *STANLEYVILLE.* 10.9.1912; 4.3.1917; 4.3.1920; 4.11.1920; 4.7.1926; 4.7.1927.	400	1,000	1,750
	f. Without office overprint. 1.2.1929.	200	600	1,000

12	**1000 Francs**	Good	Fine	XF
	1920. Brown. Two men and child at left with head of Ceres. Signature varieties. Back: Seated woman with lyre at left. Watermark: Elephant's head. Printer: BNB (without imprint).			
	a. *ELISABETHVILLE.* 2.11.1920. Reported not confirmed.	—	—	—
	b. *KINSHASA.* 3.11.1920.	1,800	3,000	5,000
	c. *LEOPOLDVILLE.* 1926/27. Reported not confirmed.	—	—	—
	d. *MATADI.* 26.11.1920.	1,800	3,000	5,000
	e. *STANLEYVILLE.* 4.11.1920.	2,000	5,000	8,000

1941-1950 Issue

13	**5 Francs**	Good	Fine	XF
	10.6.1942. Red on green underprint. Woman seated with child by beehive at left. Deuxieme Emission - 1942. Back: Elephant and hippo at center. Printer: W&S.	30.00	125	400

13A	**5 Francs**	Good	Fine	XF
	1943-1947. Blue-gray on orange underprint. Woman seated with child by beehive at left. Like #13. Back: Elephant and hippo at center.			
	a. 10.1.1943. *TROISIEME EMISSION-1943.*	15.00	75.00	150
	b. 10.8.1943. *QUATRIEME EMISSION-1943.*	15.00	75.00	150
	c. 10.3.1944. *CINQUIEME EMISSION-1944.*	15.00	75.00	150
	d. 10.4.1947. *SIXIEME EMISSION-1947.*	15.00	75.00	150

13B	**5 Francs**	Good	Fine	XF
	18.5.1949; 7.9.1951; 15.2.1952. Blue-gray on orange underprint. Woman seated with child by beehive at left. Like #13. Without *EMISSION* overprint. Back: Elephant and hippo at center.	10.00	50.00	100

14	**10 Francs**	Good	Fine	XF
	10.12.1941. Green on blue and pink underprint. Dancing Watusi at left. Without Emission overprint. Back: Soldiers on parade at right. Watermark: Okapi head. Printer: W&S.	75.00	125	300

14A	**10 Francs**	Good	Fine	XF
	10.12.1941. Blue on blue and pink underprint. Without Emission overprint. Like #14.	100	200	500

14B	**10 Francs**	VG	VF	UNC
	10.7.1942. Brown on green and pink underprint. Dancing Watusi at left. Like #14. Back: Soldiers on parade at right. Watermark: Okapi head. Printer: W&S.			
	a. Issued note.	75.00	150	350
	s. Specimen.	—	—	—

14C	**10 Francs**	Good	Fine	XF
	10.2.1943. Violet on pink underprint. Dancing Watusi at left. Like #14. Back: Soldiers on parade at right. Watermark: Okapi head. Printer: W&S.	25.00	125	400

14D	**10 Francs**	Good	Fine	XF
	10.6.1944. Gray-blue on pink underprint. Dancing Watusi at left. Like #14. Back: Soldiers on parade at right. Watermark: Okapi head. Printer: W&S.	15.00	50.00	200

14E	**10 Francs**	Good	Fine	XF
	11.11.1948; 15.8.1949; 14.3.1952; 12.5.1952. Gray-blue on pink underprint. Dancing Watusi at left. Like #14. Without *EMISSION.* overprint. Back: Soldiers on parade at right. Watermark: Okapi head. Printer: W&S.	10.00	50.00	150

		Good	Fine	XF
15	**20 Francs** 10.9.1940. Blue. Longboat (pirogue) with seven oarsmen at left center. Without *EMISSION* overprint. Back: Working elephant at center right. Watermark: Elephant's head. Printer: TDLR.	40.00	200	400
15A	**20 Francs** 10.3.1942. Violet. Longboat (pirogue) with seven oarsmen at left center. Like #15. Back: Working elephant at center right. Watermark: Elephant's head. Printer: TDLR.	40.00	200	400

		Good	Fine	XF
15B	**20 Francs** 10.12.1942. Orange. Longboat (pirogue) with seven oarsmen at left center. Like #15. Back: Working elephant at center right. Watermark: Elephant's head. Printer: TDLR.	40.00	200	400
15C	**20 Francs** 10.3.1943. Orange. Longboat (pirogue) with seven oarsmen at left center. Like #15. Back: Working elephant at center right. Watermark: Elephant's head. Printer: TDLR.	40.00	200	400
15D	**20 Francs** 10.5.1944. Orange. Longboat (pirogue) with seven oarsmen at left center. Like #15. Back: Working elephant at center right. Watermark: Elephant's head. Printer: TDLR.	40.00	200	400

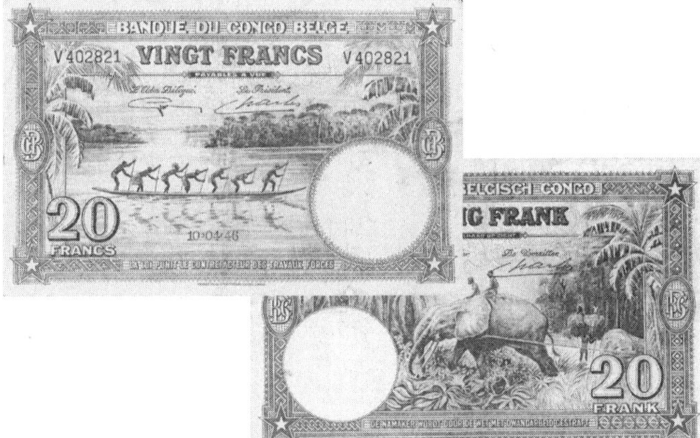

		Good	Fine	XF
15E	**20 Francs** 10.4.1946. Blue. Longboat (pirogue) with seven oarsmen at left center. Without *EMISSION* overprint. Like #15. Back: Working elephant at center right. Watermark: Elephant's head. Printer: TDLR.	20.00	80.00	250
15F	**20 Francs** 10.8.1948. Blue. Longboat (pirogue) with seven oarsmen at left center. Like #15. Back: Working elephant at center right. Watermark: Elephant's head. Printer: TDLR.	15.00	40.00	125
15G	**20 Francs** 18.5.1949. Blue. Longboat (pirogue) with seven oarsmen at left center. Like #15. Back: Working elephant at center right. Watermark: Elephant's head. Printer: TDLR.	15.00	40.00	125
15H	**20 Francs** 11.4.1950. Blue. Longboat (pirogue) with seven oarsmen at left center. Like #15. Back: Working elephant at center right. Watermark: Elephant's head. Printer: TDLR.	15.00	40.00	125

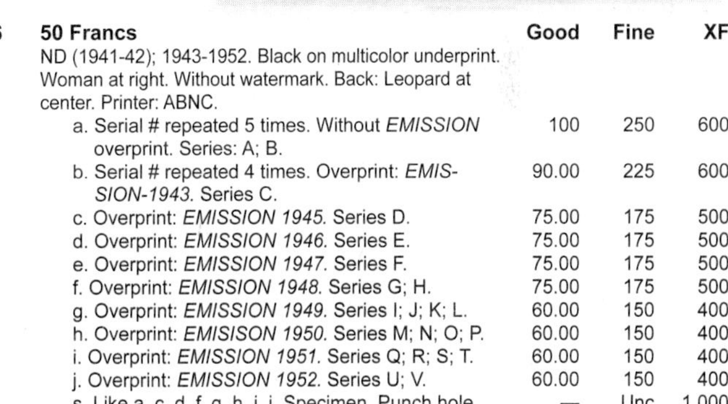

		Good	Fine	XF
16	**50 Francs** ND (1941-42); 1943-1952. Black on multicolor underprint. Woman at right. Without watermark. Back: Leopard at center. Printer: ABNC.			
	a. Serial # repeated 5 times. Without *EMISSION* overprint. Series: A; B.	100	250	600
	b. Serial # repeated 4 times. Overprint: *EMISSION-1943*. Series C.	90.00	225	600
	c. Overprint: *EMISSION 1945*. Series D.	75.00	175	500
	d. Overprint: *EMISSION 1946*. Series E.	75.00	175	500
	e. Overprint: *EMISSION 1947*. Series F.	75.00	175	500
	f. Overprint: *EMISSION 1948*. Series G; H.	75.00	175	500
	g. Overprint: *EMISSION 1949*. Series I; J; K; L.	60.00	150	400
	h. Overprint: *EMISISON 1950*. Series M; N; O; P.	60.00	150	400
	i. Overprint: *EMISSION 1951*. Series Q; R; S; T.	60.00	150	400
	j. Overprint: *EMISSION 1952*. Series U; V.	60.00	150	400
	s. Like a, c, d, f, g, h, i, j. Specimen. Punch hole cancelled.	—	Unc	1,000

		Good	Fine	XF
17	**100 Francs** 1944-1951. Blue and green. Two elephants, palm trees at center. Back: Man, three oxen at center right. Watermark: Zebra's head. Printer: W&S.			
	a. Without *EMISSION* overprint. 10.5.1944.	75.00	200	500
	b. *DEUXIEME EMISSION-1944*. 10.6.1944.	80.00	225	600
	c. Without *EMISSION* overprint. 11.3.1946; 10.4.1947.	50.00	125	400
	d. Without *EMISSION* overprint. 16.7.1949; 14.9.1949; 13.3.1951; 7.9.1951.	50.00	125	400

		Good	Fine	XF
18	**500 Francs** ND (1929). Black on multicolor underprint. Portrait woman at upper center. Without *EMISSION* overprint. Series 1. Serial # repeated 5 times. Back: Elephants bathing at center. Printer: ABNC.			
	a. Issued note.	800	2,000	3,500
	s. Specimen.	—	Unc	800

		VG	VF	UNC
18A	**500 Francs** ND (1941); 1943; 1945. Brown, yellow and blue. Portrait woman at upper center. Like #18. Back: Elephants bathing at center. Printer: ABNC.			
	a. Series 2. Serial # repeated 5 times. Without *EMISSION*, overprint. ND (1941).	—	—	—
	b. Series 3. Overprint: *EMISSION 1943.* Serial # repeated 4 times.	—	—	—
	c. Series 4. *EMISSION 1945.* Serial # repeated 4 times.	—	—	—
	s. As a, b. Specimen. Punch hole cancelled.	—	—	—

		Good	Fine	XF
19	**1000 Francs** 1944-1947. Brown-black, yellow and blue. Three Warega fisherman at left. Back: Two musicians at left and center, portrait youth at right. Watermark: Leopard's head. Printer: W&S.			
	a. 10.5.1944.	1,000	3,000	4,500
	b. 11.2.1946; 10.4.1947.	500	1,250	2,250

		VG	VF	UNC
19A	**5000 Francs** 7.8.1950. Red-brown on multicolor underprint. Portrait of female at left. Back: Three men in canoe at center. Watermark: Lion head. Printer: BWC. (Not issued).			
	s. Specimen. Punch hole cancelled.	—	—	4,500

		Good	Fine	XF
20	**10,000 Francs** 10.3.1942. Black and green. Uniface. Watermark: BCB/BBC and a five pointed star. Printer: W&S. 14x3mm. Specimen only.	—	—	3,000

Note: #20 is believed to have been used for interbank and real estate transactions.

Banque Centrale du Congo Belge et du Ruanda-Urundi

1952 Issue

		VG	VF	UNC
21	**5 Francs** 1.10.1952-15.9.1953. Blue-gray on orange underprint. Woman seated with child by beehive at left. Similar to #13. Without watermark. Back: Elephant and hippo at center. Printer: W&S.	10.00	20.00	85.00

		VG	VF	UNC
22	**10 Francs** 1.7.1952-31.8.1952. Gray-blue on pink underprint. Dancing Watusi at left. Similar to #14. Back: Soldiers on parade at right. Watermark: Giraffe's head. Printer: W&S.	15.00	50.00	225

		VG	VF	UNC
23	**20 Francs** 1.7.1952-1.9.1952. Blue. Pirogue with seven oarsmen at left center. Similar to #15. Back: Working elephant at center right. Watermark: Elephant's head. Printer: TDLR.	30.00	125	450

		VG	VF	UNC
24	**50 Francs** 15.7.1952-15.12.1952. Multicolor. Woman at right. Similar to #16. Without watermark. Back: Leopard at center. Printer: ABNC.			
	a. Issued note.	60.00	250	600
	s. Specimen. Punch hole cancelled.	—	—	—

		VG	VF	UNC
25	**100 Francs** 1952-1954. Blue and green. Two elephants, palm trees at center. Signature varieties. Similar to #17. Back: Native, three oxen at center right. Printer: W&S.			
	a. 1.7.1952-15.11.1953. Watermark: Zebra's head.	30.00	150	450
	b. 15.12.1954. Without watermark.	30.00	150	450

1953 Issue

		VG	VF	UNC
26	**20 Francs** 15.12.1953-15.4.1954. Olive green on yellow underprint. Woman at left, waterfall in background at center. Back: Queen Astrid laboratory in Leopoldville at center, man with spear at right. Watermark: Elephant's head. Printer: TDLR.			
	a. Issued note.	10.00	75.00	300
	s. Specimen. Red overprint: *SPECIMEN* on both sides.	—	—	850

		VG	VF	UNC
27	**50 Francs** 15.11.1953-1.3.1955. Green on multicolor underprint. Portrait woman at left. Back: Two fisherwomen with net at center right. Watermark: Leopard's head. Printer: BWC.			
	a. 15.11.1953-15.4.1954.	40.00	125	500
	b. 1.1.1955-1.3.1955.	40.00	125	500

28 500 Francs

15.3.1953-1.1.1955. Purple on orange underprint. Portrait girl at left. Back: Okapi at center. Watermark: Lion's head. Printer: BWC.

	Good	Fine	XF
a. 15.3.1953; 15.4.1953.	200	500	1,200
b. 1.1.1955.	200	500	1,200

29 1000 Francs

1.8.1953-1.4.1955. Blue. Portrait African male at left, boat along river at bottom center. Back: Waterbuck drinking at center. Watermark: Waterbuck's head. Printer: BWC.

	Good	Fine	XF
a. 1.8.1953-15.9.1953.	200	600	1,200
b. 15.2.1955-1.4.1955.	200	600	1,200

1955-1958 Issue

30 10 Francs

1955-1959. Gray-blue on blue and orange underprint. Soldier at left. Back: Antelope at right. Watermark: Giraffe's head. Printer: W&S.

	VG	VF	UNC
a. Signature titles: *LE PREMIER-DIRECTEUR* and *LE GOUVERNEUR.* 15.1.1955-1.6.1955.	2.00	7.50	35.00
b. Signature titles: *UN DIRECTEUR* and *LE GOUVERNEUR.* 15.7.1956-1.12.1959. Serial # prefix as leter or fraction format.	2.00	7.50	50.00

31 20 Francs

1.12.1956-1.12.1959. Green on multicolor underprint. Young boy at left, reservoir in background at center. Back: River landscape at center, young girl at right. Watermark: Elephant's head. Printer: TDLR.

VG	VF	UNC
3.00	10.00	40.00

32 50 Francs

1.3.1957-1.10.1959. Red on multicolor underprint. Workers at modern weaving machinery at center right. Back: Huts, weaving by hand at left. Watermark: Leopard's head. Printer: BWC (without imprint).

VG	VF	UNC
4.00	15.00	60.00

33 100 Francs

1955-1960. Green on multicolor underprint. Portrait King Leopold II at left. Back: Basket weavers at center. Printer: BNB (without imprint).

	VG	VF	UNC
a. Signature titles: *LE GOUVERNEUR* and *LE PREMIER-DIRECTEUR.* Watermark: Elephant's head. 15.1.1955-1.10.1956.	4.00	15.00	60.00
b. Signature titles: *LE GOUVERNEUR* and *UN DIRECTEUR.* Watermark: Elephant's head. 1.10.1956-1.4.1960.	4.00	15.00	60.00
c. Like b. 1.9.1960. Without watermark.	4.00	15.00	60.00
s. As a. Specimen. Red overprint: *SPECIMEN* on both sides.	—	—	500

		VG	VF	UNC
34	**500 Francs** 1.9.1957-1.7.1959. Brown-violet on multicolor underprint. Ships dockside at Leo-Kinshasa wharf at center. Back: Africans transporting fruit in pirogue at center. Watermark: Lion's head. Printer: TDLR.	20.00	150	450

		VG	VF	UNC
35	**1000 Francs** 15.7.1958-1.9.1959. Deep blue on multicolor underprint. Portrait King Baudouin at left, aerial view of Leopoldville at lower center. Back: Huts at right. Watermark: Waterbuck's head. Printer: BWC (without imprint).	15.00	75.00	350

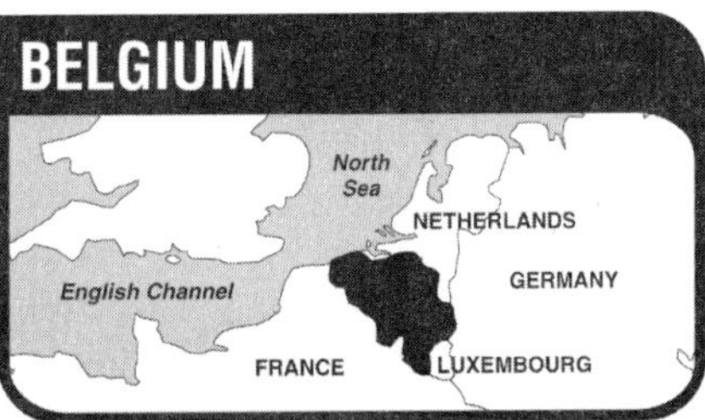

The Kingdom of Belgium, a constitutional monarchy in northwest Europe, has an area of 30,528 sq. km. and a population of 10.40 million, chiefly Dutch-speaking Flemish and French-speaking Walloons. Capital: Brussels. Agriculture, dairy farming, and the processing of raw materials for re-export are the principal industries. "Beurs voor Diamant" in Antwerp is the world's largest diamond trading center. Iron and steel, machinery, motor vehicles, chemicals, textile yarns and fabrics comprise the principal exports.

Belgium became independent from the Netherlands in 1830; it was occupied by Germany during World Wars I and II. The country prospered in the past half century as a modern, technologically advanced European state and member of NATO and the EU. Tensions between the Dutch-speaking Flemings of the north and the French-speaking Walloons of the south have led in recent years to constitutional amendments granting these regions formal recognition and autonomy.

RULERS:

Leopold I, 1831-1865
Leopold II, 1865-1909
Albert I, 1909-34
Leopold III, 1934-51
Baudouin I, 1952-93
Albert II, 1993-

MONETARY SYSTEM:

1 Franc = 100 Centimes to 2001
1 Belga = 5 Francs

KINGDOM - 1810-1914

Société de Commerce de Bruxelles

ca 1810 Issue

#1, 2, 4, 7 are held in reserve.

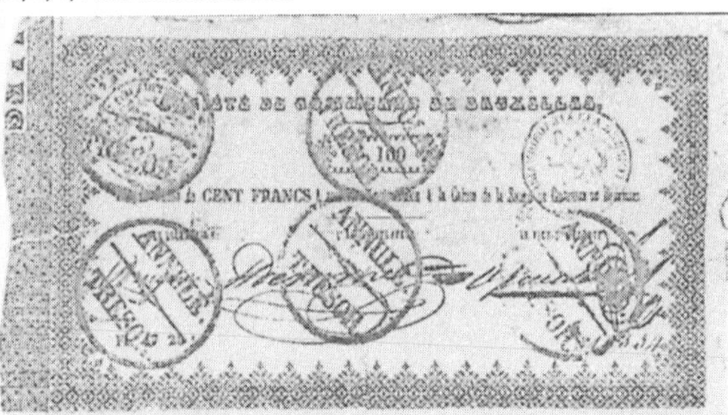

		Good	Fine	XF
3	**100 Francs** ND. Black. Uniface.	—	—	—
5	**1000 Francs** ND. Black. Uniface. Rare.	—	—	—
6	**1000 Francs** ND. Blue. Uniface. Requires confirmation.	—	—	—

Société Générale pour Favoriser l'Industrie Nationale

1822-1826 Issue

Various dates from 1826. Signature varieties exist.

		Good	Fine	XF
8	**1/2 Florin** 1.10.1826. Uniface. Rare.	—	—	—
9	**1 Florin** Requires confirmation.	—	—	—
10	**2 Florins** Requires confirmation.	—	—	—
11	**3 Florins** Rare.	—	—	—
12	**5 Florins** Requires confirmation.	—	—	—
13	**10 Florins** Uniface. Rare.	—	—	—
14	**25 Florins** Rare.	—	—	—

#	Denomination	Good	Fine	XF
15	**50 Florins** Rare.	—	—	—
16	**100 Florins** Rare.	—	—	—
17	**250 Florins** Rare.	—	—	—
18	**500 Florins** Rare.	—	—	—
19	**1000 Florins** 1822-1830. Uniface. Rare.	—	—	—

1837-1848 Issue

#	Denomination	Good	Fine	XF
20	**5 Francs** ND (1848). Uniface.	1,500	2,500	4,000
21	**20 Francs** ND (1848). Uniface. Rare.	—	—	—
22	**50 Francs** 6.2.1837. Uniface.Rare.	—	—	—
23	**100 Francs** 6.2.1837. Uniface. Rare.	—	—	—
24	**500 Francs** 6.2.1837. Uniface. Rare.	—	—	—
25	**1000 Francs** 6.2.1837. Uniface. Rare.	—	—	—

Banque de Belgique

1835 Issue

#	Denomination	Good	Fine	XF
26	**5 Francs** ND (1835). Uniface. Rare.	—	—	—
27	**20 Francs** ND (1835). Uniface. Rare.	—	—	—
28	**50 Francs** ND (1835). Uniface. Rare.	—	—	—
29	**100 Francs** ND (1835). Uniface. Rare.	—	—	—
30	**1000 Francs** ND (1835). Uniface. Rare.	—	—	—

Banque de Flandre

Ghent

1841 Issue

#	Denomination	Good	Fine	XF
32	**100 Francs** ND (1841). Uniface. Rare.	—	—	—

#	Denomination	Good	Fine	XF
33	**250 Francs** ND (1841). Uniface. Rare.	—	—	—

Note: Denominations of 25 and 1000 Francs require confirmation.

Banque Liègeoise et Caisse d'Épargnes

Liège

1835 Issue

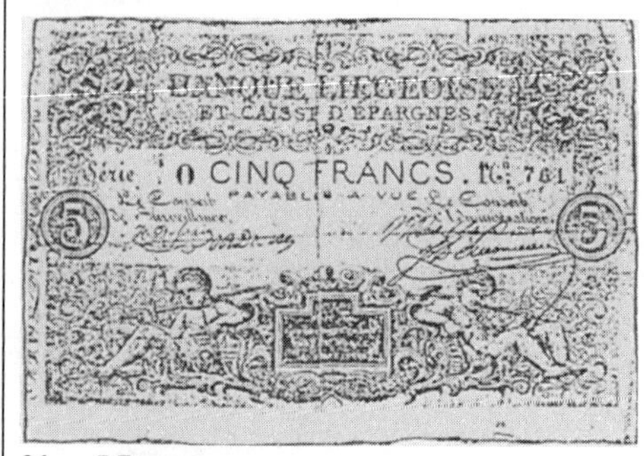

#	Denomination	Good	Fine	XF
34	**5 Francs** ND (1835). Yellow. Rare.	—	—	—
35	**10 Francs** ND (1835). Yellow. Rare.	—	—	—
36	**25 Francs** ND (1835). Green. Rare.	—	—	—
37	**50 Francs** ND (1835). Green. Rare.	—	—	—

Note: Denominations of 100, 200, 500 and 100 Francs require confirmation.
#38-40 not assigned.

Banque Nationale de Belgique

1851-1856 Issue

#	Denomination	Good	Fine	XF
41	**20 Francs** *L.5.5.1850.* Black. Ceres reclining at lower left, Neptune at lower right. 16 signature varieties. Rare.	—	—	—

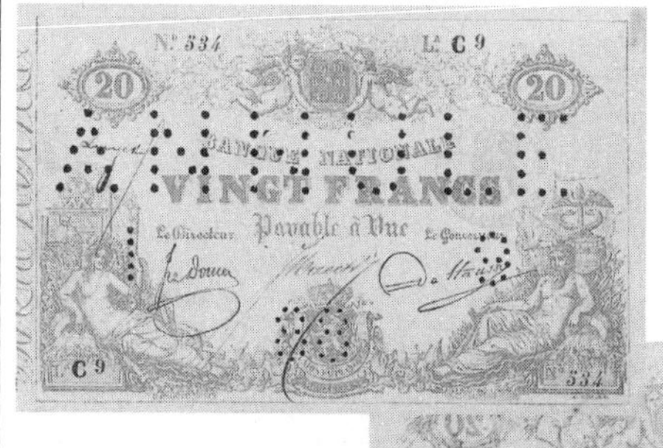

#	Denomination	Good	Fine	XF
42	**20 Francs** *L.5.5.1850.* (ca.1851-62). Blue on green underprint. Ceres reclining at lower left, Neptune at lower right. 7 signature varieites. Rare.	—	—	—
43	**50 Francs** 2.1.1851-4.10.1851. Rose. Cherubs in four corners. 5 signature varieties. BC: Pink.	5,000	8,000	—
44	**50 Francs** 1.6.1852. Blue. Cherubs in four corners. 5 signature varieties. Rare.	—	—	—
45	**50 Francs** ca.1851-2.1.1862. Blue on green underprint. Cherubs in four corners. 5 signature varieties. Rare.	—	—	—
46	**100 Francs** 2.1.1851-1.6.1852. Cherubs in four corners. 2 signature varieties. Rare.	—	—	—
47	**100 Francs** 2.1.1856. Blue. Woman seated with two lions at bottom center. 4 signature varieties. BC: Blue and red. Rare.	—	—	—
48	**500 Francs** 2.1.1851. Blue. Cherubs in four corners.	—	—	—
49	**500 Francs** 1.6.1852. Black. Two allegorical figures at left (Industry and Trade) and at right (Liberty and Justice). 3 signature varieties. Rare.	—	—	—
50	**500 Francs** 1.6.1852. Blue. Two allegorical figures at left (Industry and Trade) and at right (Liberty and Justice). 3 signature varieties. Rare.	—	—	—

		Good	Fine	XF
51	**1000 Francs** 2.1.1851-1.6.1852. Black. Cherubs in four corners. 3 signature varieties. Rare.	—	—	—
52	**1000 Francs** 22.8.1853. Blue. Two allegorical figures left and right (Industry and trade). 4 signature varieties. Rare.	—	—	—

1869-1873 Issue

		Good	Fine	XF
53	**20 Francs** 25.1.1869-29.6.1878. Blue. Two allegorical figures (Helen and Paris). 4 signature varieties.	3,000	5,000	—

		Good	Fine	XF
54	**50 Francs** 3.4.1871-6.7.1871. Blue. Woman and two children at left, child with crown of laurel leaves at right. Back: Children leaning on cornucopia. Rare.	—	—	—
55	**100 Francs** 4.3.1869-14.8.1882. Blue. Seated man at left, woman with sceptre at right. 5 signature varieties. Back: Two allegorical figures (Security) at left, (Progress) at right. Rare.	—	—	—
56	**500 Francs** 9.5.1873-25.9.1886. Blue on pink underprint. Allegorical figures at left (Science) and at right (Art). Rare.	—	—	—
57	**1000 Francs** 31.5.1870-2.2.1884. Blue. Neptune at left, and Amphitrite at right. 4 signature varieties. Rare.	—	—	—

1875 Issue

		Good	Fine	XF
58	**50 Francs** 19.7.1875-30.6.1879. Blue on gray underprint. Woman and two children at left, group of children in background. 2 signature varieties. Red serial #. Back: Children leaning on corcuicopia. Rare.	—	—	—

1879; 1881 Issue

		Good	Fine	XF
59	**20 Francs** 8.8.1879-17.10.1892. Blue on gray underprint. Two allegorical figures (Helen and Paris) without counterfoil. 5 signature varieties.	800	2,000	3,000

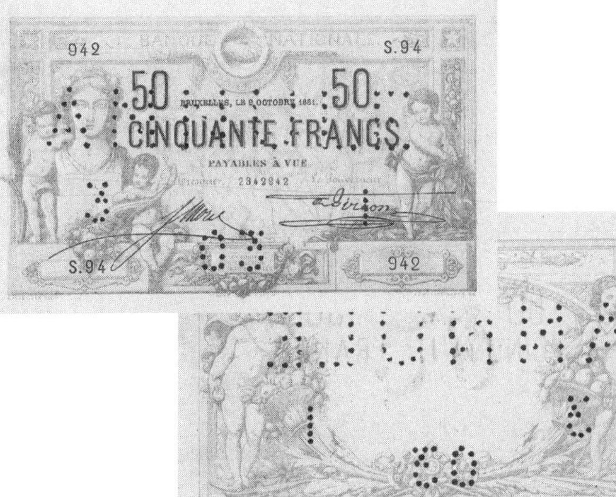

		Good	Fine	XF
60	**50 Francs** 3.1.1881-23.8.1887. Blue. Women and two children at left, modifications in engraving. Without counterfoil. Back: Children leaning on cornucopia.	2,000	3,000	—

1883-1896 Issue

		Good	Fine	XF
61	**20 Francs** 13.12.1892-29.6.1896. Blue on brown underprint. Allegorical figures at left (Agriculture and Trade) and at right (Industry). Back: Allegory of Art seated at center.	800	1,500	2,250

62	20 Francs	Good	Fine	XF
	30.7.1896-30.12.1909. Dark red and green. Minerva with lion at left. 4 signature varieties. Back: Arms of thirty towns. BC: Brown.			
	a. Signatures Van Hoegaerden, Verstraeten.	200	550	800
	b. Signatures Van Hoegaerden, Verstraeten (Director).	200	550	800
	c. Signatures Van Hoegaerden, Tschaggeny (2.3.1905-25.5.1905).	250	600	850
	d. Signatures de Lantsheere, Tschaggeny (1.7.1905-30.12.1909)	90.00	150	400

63	50 Francs	VG	VF	UNC
	26.9.1887-30.12.1908. Blue and black. Medallic female head and children.			
	a. Signatures Jamar, Morel (26.9.1887-014.8.1888). Rare.	—	—	—
	b. Signatures Anspach, Bauffe (19.9.1888-23.2.1890). Rare.	—	—	—
	c. Signatures Van Hoegaerden, Verstraeten.	1,750	3,000	—
	d. Signatures Van Hoegaerden, Verstraeten (Director).	1,750	3,000	—
	e. Signatures Van Hoegaerden, Tschaggeny (7.4.1905-29.4.1905).	2,000	3,500	—
	f. Signatures de Lantsheere, Tschaggeny (27.7.1905-30.12.1908).	1,000	2,000	—

64	100 Francs	VG	VF	UNC
	5.6.1883-31.7.1905. Blue on light brown underprint. Seated man at left, woman with sceptre at right. Modifications in engraving and without counterfoil. 7 signature varieties. Back: Two allegorical figures (Security) at left, (Progress) at right. Watermark: Minerva.			
	a. Signatures Jamar, Morel. (5.6.1883-017.3.1888).	1,600	2,500	—
	b. Signatures Anspach, Bauffe (3.1.1888-13.2.1890).	1,600	2,500	—
	c. Signatures Anspach, Verstraeten (11.11.1890-17.11.1890).	1,600	2,500	—
	d. Signatures Van Hoegaerden, Verstraeten.	1,000	2,000	2,750
	e. Signatures Van Hoegaerden, Verstraeten (Director).	750	1,500	2,250
	f. Signatures Van Hoegaerden, Tschaggeny (1.3.1905-24.4.1905). Rare.	—	—	—
	g. Signatures de Lantsheere, Tschaggeny (5.7.1905-31.7.1905).	2,000	3,250	—

65	500 Francs	VG	VF	UNC
	1.1.1887-11.3.1908. Blue and red on gray underprint. Bank name and denomination in red surrounded by women and small angels.			
	a. Signatures Jamar, Morel (1.1.1887-23.2.1887). Rare.	—	—	—
	b. Signatures Van Hoegaerden, Verstraeten. Rare.	—	—	—
	c. Signatures Van Hoegaerden, Verstraeten (Director).	2,750	3,750	—
	d. Signatures de Lantsheere, Tschaggeny (11.1.1905-11.3.1908).	2,250	3,000	4,500

		VG	VF	UNC
66	**1000 Francs** 3.1.1884-30.4.1908. Blue and multicolor. Like #73 but slight design modifications.			
	a. Signatures Jamar, Morel (3.1.1884-28.3.1888). Rare.	—	—	—
	b. Signatures Anspach, Verstraeten (1.11.1890-6.1.1891). Rare.	—	—	—
	c. Signatures Van Hoegaerden, Verstraeten. Rare.	—	—	—
	d. Signatures Van Hoegaerden, Verstraeten (Director).	5,000	6,500	9,000
	e. Signatures de Lantsheere, Tscheggeny (12.1.1906-30.4.1908).	5,000	6,500	9,000

1905-1910 Issue

		VG	VF	UNC
67	**20 Francs** 3.1.1910-19.7.1920. Red and green. Minerva with lion at left. Black serial #. 3 signature varieties. Back: Arms of thirty towns. BC: Brown.	10.00	60.00	125

		VG	VF	UNC
68	**50 Francs** 1909-1926. Dark green on light green and blue underprint. Seated woman (Agriculture) at left and (Law) at right. Back: Several figures (Intelligence and Industry).			
	a. 1.5.1909-5.2.1914. With embossed arabesque design on border. 2 signature varieties.	125	200	400
	b. 1919-24.5.1923. Signatures Vander Rest, Stacquet. Without embossed arabesque design on border.	40.00	75.00	175
	c. Signatures Hautain, Stacquet (25.5.1923-20.9.1926).	40.00	75.00	175
	d. Signatures Franck, Stacquet (1.10.1926).	800	1,600	—

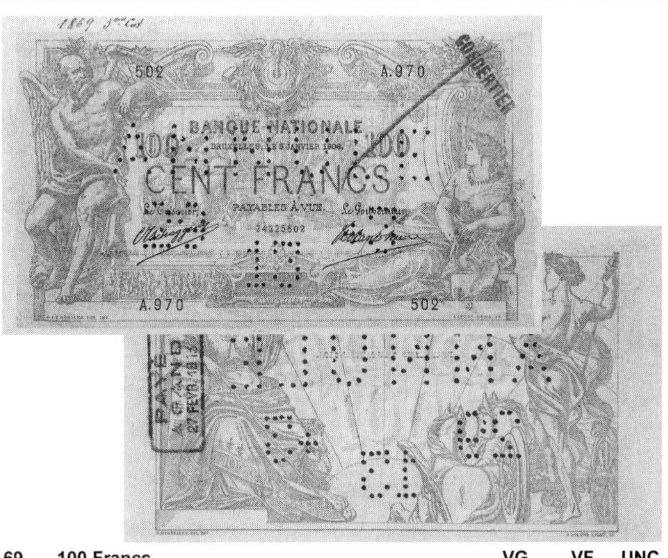

		VG	VF	UNC
69	**100 Francs** 31.7.1905-7.3.1906. Blue and brown. Seated man at left, woman with sceptre at right with brown denomination. Like #64. Back: Two allegorical figures (Security) at left, (Progress) at right.	1,250	—	—

		VG	VF	UNC
70	**100 Francs** 15.3.1906-21.12.1908. Brown and black. Quadriga driven by Ceres at left and Neptune at right. Back: Women (Sowing) at left and (Harvesting) at right. BC: Green.	750	1,750	3,500

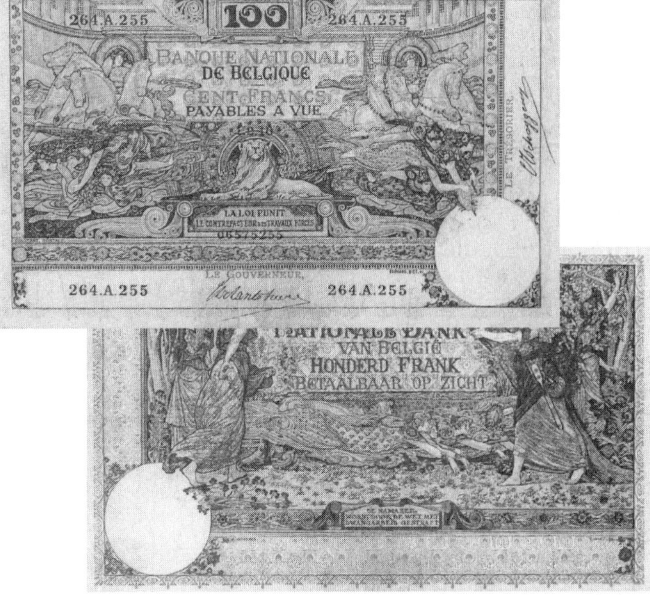

		VG	VF	UNC
71	**100 Francs**			
	12.1.1909-1914. Black and brown on pink and pale green underprint. Quadrigas driven by Ceres at left and Neptune at right. Similar to #70. 2 signature varieties. Back: Women (Sowing) at left and (Harvesting) at right. Medallion and white edges below and right, embossed arabesque. BC: Green. Watermark: Minerva.	50.00	100	225

		VG	VF	UNC
72	**500 Francs**			
	1910-1925. Blue and green on gray underprint. Bank name and denomination (only in Francs) in green surrounded by women and small angels. Similar to #65. 4 signature varieties.			
	a. 13.10.1910-1914. With embossed arabesque design on border. 2 signature varieties.	1,500	2,750	—
	b. 25.1.1919-31.7.1925. Without embossed arabesque design on border. 3 signature varieties.	200	350	750

		VG	VF	UNC
72A	**1000 Francs**			
	13.4.1908. Blue on multicolor underprint. Neptune at left, Aphrodite at right. Circles in corners. BC: Blue and brown. Rare.	—	—	—

		VG	VF	UNC
73	**1000 Francs**			
	3.7.1909-24.1.1921. Green. Nepture at left and Amphitrite at right. 3 signature varieties.	750	1,500	2,500

1914; 1919 Issue

		VG	VF	UNC
74	**5 Francs**			
	1914; 1919. Brown and orange. Allegorical figures at left and right. Back: Three allegorical figures.			
	a. 1.7.1914.	60.00	150	300
	b. 25.1.1919. Watermark: *BNB*.	50.00	125	250
75	**5 Francs**	VG	VF	UNC
	1914-1921. Green and brown. Allegorical figures at left and right. Like #74.			
	a. 1.7.1914.	25.00	75.00	125
	b. 27.12.1918-3.1.1921. Watermark: *BNB*.	20.00	60.00	100

		VG	VF	UNC
76	**20 Francs**			
	1.9.1914. Red and green. Minerva with lion at left. Red serial #, date below. Like #67. Back: Arms of thirty towns. BC: Brown.	1,250	1,750	2,750

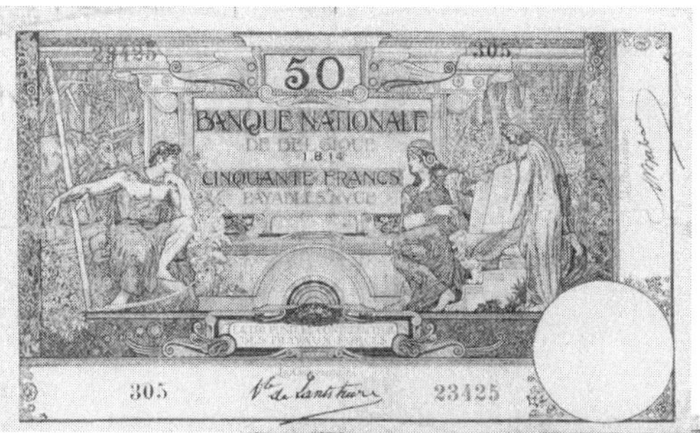

77 **50 Francs** — VG 1,600 · VF 2,500 · UNC 3,500
1.8.1914. Green. Embossed arabesque design on border. Red serial #. Like #68.

78 **100 Francs** — VG 20.00 · VF 60.00 · UNC 125
1914-16.10.1920. Black and brown. Quadrigas driven by Ceres at left and Neptune at right. Like #71 but without embossed arabesque. 2 sign varieties. Back: Women (Sowing) at left and (Harvesting) at right. Medallion and white edges below. BC: Green. Watermark: Minerva.

79 **100 Francs** — VG · VF · UNC
12.9.1914-1.10.1914. Black and brown. Quadrigas driven by Ceres at left and Neptune at right. Like #78 but with red serial #. Back: Women (Sowing) at left and (Harvesting) at right. Medallion and white edges below. BC: Green. Watermark: Minerva.

	VG	VF	UNC
a. Emission Anvers (12.6.1914-28.12.1914). Series 511, 514. Rare.	—	—	—
b. Emission Ostende (1.10.1914). Series 251.	3,500	5,500	—

80 **1000 Francs** — VG 1,000 · VF 1,750 · UNC 3,000
17.1.1919-31.3.1919. Brownish-yellow and black. Like #73 but without edge printing.

1914 Comptes Courants Issue

81 **1 Franc** — VG 50.00 · VF 100 · UNC 150
27.8.1914. Blue on gray underprint.

82 **2 Francs** — VG 75.00 · VF 125 · UNC 250
27.8.1914. Brown on gray underprint.

83 **20 Francs** — VG 1,500 · VF 2,250 · UNC 3,000
27.8.1914. Blue and brown. King Leopold I at left.

84 **100 Francs** — VG — · VF — · UNC —
27.8.1914. Blue on gray underprint. King Leopold I at left. Rare.

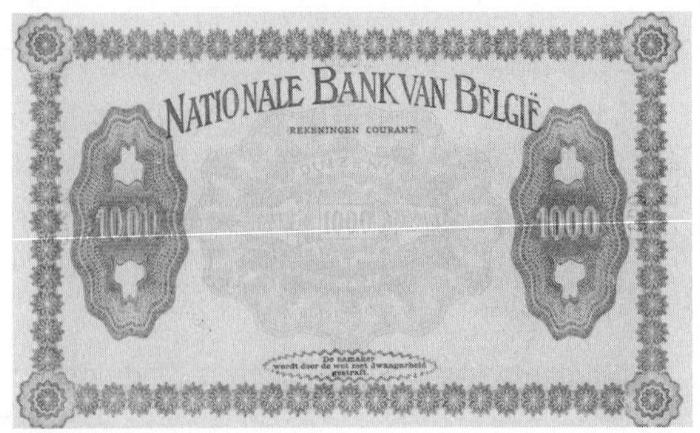

#	Description	VG	VF	UNC
85	**1000 Francs** 27.8.1914. Wine red. King Leopold I at left. Rare.	—	—	—

GERMAN OCCUPATION - WWI

Société Générale de Belgique

1915 Issue

#86-88, 90 Notes issued by the bank during the German occupation and after the war carry various printing dates during 1915-1918.

#	Description	VG	VF	UNC
86	**1 Franc** 1915-1918. Portrait Queen Louise-Marie at left.			
	a. 1.3.1915-31.1.1916. Violet on pink underprint.	15.00	30.00	85.00
	b. 1.2.1916-29.10.1918. Mauve on pink underprint.	15.00	30.00	85.00

#	Description	VG	VF	UNC
87	**2 Francs** 1.4.1915-25.5.1918. Reddish brown on light green underprint. Portrait Queen Louise-Marie at left.	60.00	100	275

#	Description	VG	VF	UNC
88	**5 Francs** 2.1.1915-14.7.1918. Green on gray underprint. Portrait Queen Louise-Marie at left. BC: Blue and green.	250	450	1,000

#	Description	VG	VF	UNC
89	**20 Francs** 1.2.1915-11.10.1918. Blue on pink underprint. Portrait Peter Paul Rubens at left.	1,000	1,750	3,275

#	Description	VG	VF	UNC
90	**100 Francs** 26.12.1914-2.9.1918. Brown and green on pink and green underprint. Portrait Queen Louise-Marie at left.	2,100	3,275	—

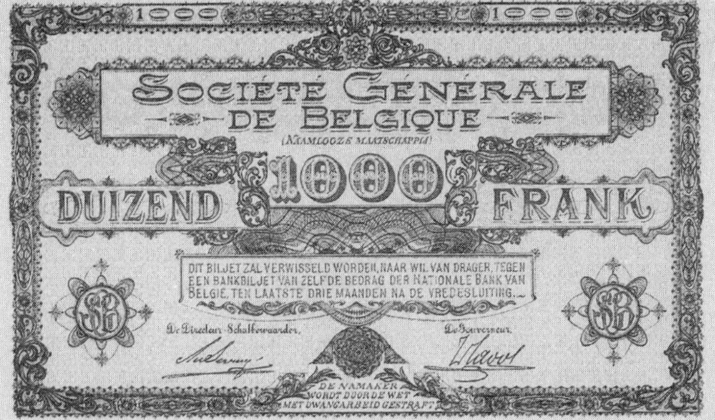

#	Description	VG	VF	UNC
91	**1000 Francs** 18.9.1915-26.10.1918. Brown and green on light green underprint. Portrait Peter Paul Rubens at left.	12,500	22,500	—

KINGDOM - 1920-1944

Banque Nationale de Belgique

1920-1922 Issue

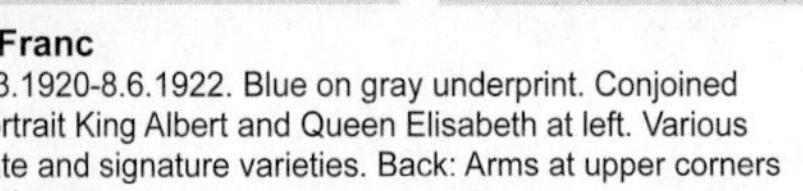

#	Description	VG	VF	UNC
92	**1 Franc** 1.3.1920-8.6.1922. Blue on gray underprint. Conjoined portrait King Albert and Queen Elisabeth at left. Various date and signature varieties. Back: Arms at upper corners and center.	8.00	17.50	30.00

		VG	VF	UNC
93	**5 Francs** 1.4.1922-25.6.1926. Blue on light brown underprint. Conjoined portrait King Albert and Queen Elisabeth at left. 2 signature varieties. Back: Seated man looking at factory scene.	12.50	25.00	40.00

		VG	VF	UNC
94	**20 Francs** 1.6.1921-10.4.1926. Brown on light blue and brown underprint. Conjoined portrait King Albert and Queen Elisabeth at left. 2 signature varieties. Back: City view with large buildings at center right.	90.00	150	275

		VG	VF	UNC
95	**100 Francs** 1.4.1921-2.6.1927. Lilac-brown. Conjoined portrait King Albert and Queen Elisabeth at left. 3 signature varieties. Back: Man with tools at right.	15.00	40.00	75.00
96	**1000 Francs** 15.6.1922-28.10.1927. Blue on pink underprint. Conjoined portrait King Albert and Queen Elisabeth at left. 3 signature varieties.	150	200	350

1926 Issue

		VG	VF	UNC
97	**5 Francs** 14.6.1926-10.5.1931. Blue on light brown underprint. Conjoined portrait King Albert and Queen Elisabeth at left. 2 signature varieties. Back: Seated man looking at factory scene.			
	a. Signatures Hautain, Stacquet (14.6.1926-26.6.1926).	250	400	500
	b. Signatures Franck, Stacquet (4.11.1926-10.5.1931).	12.00	22.00	40.00

		VG	VF	UNC
98	**20 Francs** 14.4.1926-27.1.1940. Brown on light blue and yellow-green underprint. Conjoined portrait King Albert and Queen Elisabeth at left. 3 signature varieties.			
	a. Signatures Hautain, Stacquet (14.4.1926-21.8.1926).	375	450	600
	b. Signatures Franck, Stacquet (27.9.1926-16.1.1932).	15.00	25.00	40.00
	c. Signatures Janssen, Sontag (2.1.1940-27.1.1940).	30.00	70.00	125

1927-1929 Issue

		VG	VF	UNC
99	**50 Francs-10 Belgas** 1.3.1927; 23.3.1927. Green. Seated woman (Agriculture) at left and (Law) at right. 3 signature varieties. Like #68b but without embossed arabesque design on border. Back: Several figures (Intelligence and Industry).	300	500	750
100	**50 Francs-10 Belgas** 1.9.1927-6.1.1928. Brown on yellow underprint. Peasant woman with sheaf and two horses at left center. Back: Allegorical figure holding sailing ship and large cornucopia.	300	600	900
101	**50 Francs-10 Belgas** 1.10.1928-20.4.1935. Green on yellow underprint. Peasant woman with sheaf and two horses at left center. Like #100. Back: Allegorical figure holding sailing ship and large cornucopia.	30.00	45.00	75.00

Note: For #101 with *TRÉSORERIE* overprint see #106.

102	100 Francs-20 Belgas	VG	VF	UNC
	1.7.1927-2.8.1932. Blue-black on ochre and pale blue underprint. Portraits of King Albert and Queen Elizabeth at left. Similar to #95. Back: Man with tools at right. Watermark: King Leopold I.	12.00	20.00	35.00

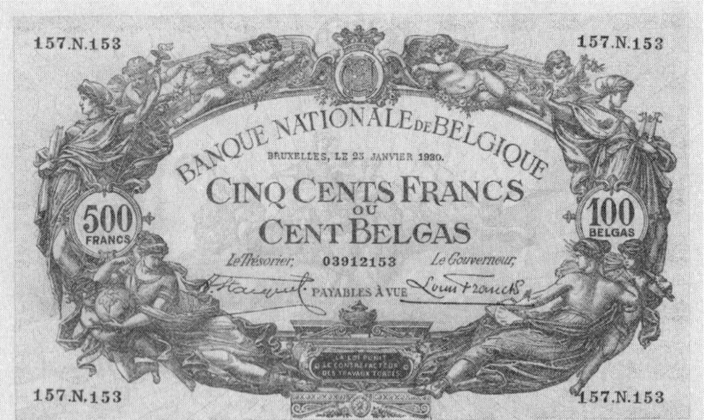

103	500 Francs-100 Belgas	VG	VF	UNC
	3.1.1927-16.11.1936. Blue and green. Bank name and denomination surrounded by women and small angels. Signature on face only. 2 signature varieties.			
	a. Signatures Franck, Stacquet (3.1.1927-29.12.1934).	25.00	50.00	80.00
	b. Signatures Franck, Sontag (2.11.1936-16.11.1936).	125	200	300

104	1000 Francs-200 Belgas	VG	VF	UNC
	2.4.1928-28.11.1939. Green on multicolor underprint. Portrait King Albert and Queen Elisabeth at left. Signature on face only. 3 signature varieties.	20.00	40.00	75.00

105	10,000 Francs-2000 Belgas	VG	VF	UNC
	22.11.1929-28.8.1942. Blue on pink underprint. Quadriga driven by Ceres at left, and Neptune at right, lion at center. 3 signature varieties. Back: Two allegorical figures.	350	550	800

1933; 1935 Issue

		VG	VF	UNC
106	**50 Francs-10 Belgas** 20.4.1935-28.4.1947. Dark green on blackish green on light green and orange underprint. Peasant woman with sheaf and two horses at left center. Like #100 but with overprints. 6 signature varieties. Back: Allegorical figure holding sailing ship and large cornucopia.	8.00	12.50	20.00

		VG	VF	UNC
107	**100 Francs-20 Belgas** 1.5.1933-15.9.1943. Gray on light brown underprint. Portrait Queen Elisabeth at left, woman with crown and fruit at center, portrait King Albert at right. 4 signature varieties. Back: Allegorical figures at center. French text on back. Watermark: King Leopold I.	4.00	9.00	15.00

1938 Issue

		VG	VF	UNC
108	**5 Francs** 1.3.1938-11.5.1938. Blue on light brown underprint. Portrait King Albert and Queen Elisabeth at left. Like #93 but with overprint. 2 signature varieties. Back: Seated man looking at factory scene.			
	a. Issued note.	6.00	12.00	20.00
	x. Error date: 4.5.1988.	12.00	25.00	50.00

		VG	VF	UNC
109	**500 Francs-100 Belgas** 3.2.1938-4.10.1943. Blue and green. Bank name and denomination surrounded by women and small angels. Like # 103 but signatures on both sides. 2 signature varieties.	15.00	25.00	40.00

1939 Issue

		VG	VF	UNC
110	**1000 Francs-200 Belgas** 12.12.1939-26.10.1944. Green. Portrait King Albert and Queen Elisabeth at left. Like #104 but signatures on both sides. 2 signature varieties.	15.00	25.00	40.00

1940 Issue

		VG	VF	UNC
111	**20 Francs** 27.1.1940-13.6.1947. Brown on light blue and brown underprint. Portrait King Albert and Queen Elisabeth at left. Like #94 but with overprint. Date at top center. 4 signature varieties. Back: Bruxelles square at center right.	10.00	18.00	30.00

1941 Issue

		VG	VF	UNC
112	**100 Francs-20 Belgas** 17.1.1941-10.9.1943. Gray on light brown underprint. Portrait Queen Elisabeth at left, woman with crown and fruit at center, portrait King Albert at right. Like #107 but with Flemish text. Back: Allegorical figures at center.	6.00	12.00	20.00

1944 Issue

		VG	VF	UNC
113	**100 Francs-20 Belgas** 20.9.1944-4.11.1944. Orange. Portrait Queen Elisabeth at left, woman with crown and fruit at center, portrait King Albert at right. Like #107 but with French text. Back: Allegorical figures at center.	50.00	120	150
114	**100 Francs-20 Belgas** 20.9.1944-4.11.1944. Orange. Portrait Queen Elisabeth at left, woman with crown and fruit at center, portrait King Albert at right. Like #112 but with Flemish text. Back: Allegorical figures at center.	60.00	150	200
115	**1000 Francs-200 Belgas** 21.4.1944-26.10.1944. Red. Portrait King Albert and Queen Elisabeth at left. Signatures on both sides. Like #110.	1,000	1,500	2,250

1948 Issue

		VG	VF	UNC
116	**20 Francs** 1.9.1948. Brown. Portrait King Albert and Queen Elisabeth at left, wings at top center. Date at top left. 4 signature varieties. Back: Bruxelles square at center right.	12.00	18.00	30.00

GERMAN OCCUPATION - WWII

Banque d'Emission a Bruxelles

ca 1941 Issue

		VG	VF	UNC
117	**50 Francs** ND. Gray-blue on yellow underprint. Requires confirmation.	—	—	—
118	**100 Francs** ND. Green. Requires confirmation.	—	—	—
119	**100 Francs** ND. Brown. Requires confirmation.	—	—	—

		VG	VF	UNC
120	**10,000 Francs** ND. Blue. Farm woman with sickle and plants at center. Back: Five standing allegorical female figures under tree. (Not issued). Rare.	—	—	—

KINGDOM IN EXILE - 1943

Banque Nationale de Belgique

1943-1945 Issue

		VG	VF	UNC
121	**5 Francs-1 Belga** 1.2.1943 (1944). Red on pink and light blue underprint. Printer: TDLR (without imprint).			
	a. Issued note.	3.00	6.00	10.00
	s. As a. Specimen.	—	—	—

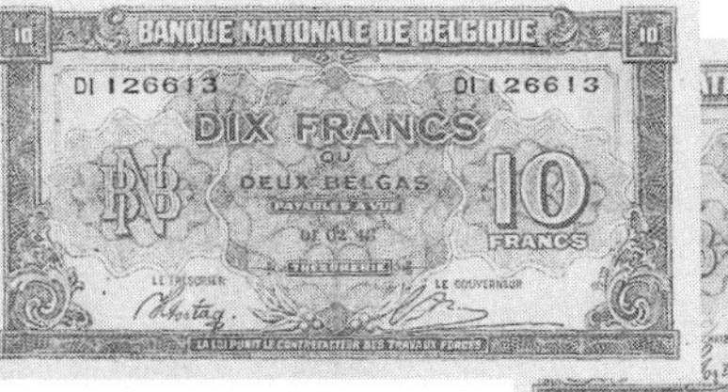

		VG	VF	UNC
122	**10 Francs-2 Belgas** 1.2.1943 (1944). Green on light green and light pink underprint. Printer: TDLR (without imprint).	3.00	6.00	10.00

123	100 Francs-20 Belgas	VG	VF	UNC
	1.2.1943 (1944). Red and green. Queen Elisabeth at left, woman with crown and fruit at center, King Albert at right. Like #107 but smaller size. Back: Allegorical figures at center. Printer: BWC (without imprint).	12.00	25.00	40.00

124	500 Francs-100 Belgas	VG	VF	UNC
	1.2.1943 (1944). Blue, pink and multicolor. Back: Reclining figure. Printer: BWC (without imprint).	90.00	180	250
125	1000 Francs-200 Belgas	VG	VF	UNC
	1.2.1943 (1944). Brown and violet. Back: Reclining figure. Printer: BWC (without imprint).	450	650	1,000

KINGDOM - 1944-PRESENT

Banque Nationale de Belgique

Nationale Bank van Belgie

1944-1945 Issue

126	100 Francs	VG	VF	UNC
	3.11.1945-31.12.1950. Brown, pink and yellow. Portrait Leopold I at left, Justice Palace, Brussels at center. 2 signature varieties. Back: Mounted troops at center right. Watermark: Leopold I	12.50	25.00	50.00

127	500 Francs	VG	VF	UNC
	7.11.1944-1.4.1947. Brown and yellow. Portrait King Leopold II wearing a military cap at left, Antwerp Cathedral at center. Back: Congo landscape and boat.			
	a. Signatures Frére, Sontag (7.11.1944-4.7.1945).	120	200	275
	b. Signatures Frére, Pirsoul (17.3.1947-1.4.1947).	300	450	650

128	1000 Francs	VG	VF	UNC
	16.10.1944-1.7.1948. Blue. Portrait King Albert I wearing steel helmet at left, monument at center. Back: City view of Veurne.			
	a. Signatures Theunis, Sontag (16.1.1944-3.11.1944).	70.00	125	200
	b. Signatures Frére, Sontag (7.11.1944-1.4.1946).	60.00	100	150
	c. Signatures Frére, Pirsoul (17.3.1947-1.7.1948).	150	275	350

1950-1952 Issue

129	100 Francs	VG	VF	UNC
	1952-1959. Black on brown and multicolor underprint. Portrait King Leopold I at left. Back: Building at center, portrait Fr. Orban.			
	a. Signature Frère-Pirsoul. 1.8.1952-4.12.1952.	10.00	20.00	40.00
	b. Signature Frère-Vincent. 10.9.1953-30.6.1957.	10.00	20.00	40.00
	c. Signature Ansiaux-Vincent. 1.7.1957-26.2.1959; 16.03.59.	10.00	20.00	40.00
	s. As a. Specimen.	—	—	—

130	500 Francs	VG	VF	UNC
	1.4.1952-29.5.1958. Brown and yellow. Portrait King Leopold II at left. 3 signature varieties. Back: Four heads (painting by P. P. Rubens).			
	a. Issued note.	75.00	125	150
	s. Specimen.	—	—	—

		VG	VF	UNC
131	**1000 Francs** 2.1.1950-28.7.1958. Blue and multicolor. Portrait King Albert at left. 3 signature varieties. Back: Geeraert and lock scene.			
	a. Issued note.	60.00	100	150
	s. Specimen.	—	—	—

Royaume de Belgique - Trésorerie

Koninkrijk Belgie - Thesaurie

1948; 1950 Issue

		VG	VF	UNC
132	**20 Francs** 1950; 1956. Lilac, violet and blue. Portrait R. de Lassus at center. Back: Portrait P. de Monte at center. Watermark: King Leopold I.			
	a. Signature Van Heurck 1.7.1950.	1.00	3.00	6.00
	b. Signature Williot 3.4.1956.	1.00	3.00	6.00

		VG	VF	UNC
133	**50 Francs** 1948; 1956. Yellow, green, violet and multicolor. Farm woman with fruit at left, man planting a tree at right. Back: Farmer with scythe at left, woman with sheaf at right. Watermark: King Leopold I.			
	a. Signature Van Heurck 1.6.1948.	2.00	4.00	8.00
	b. Signature Williot 3.4.1956.	2.00	4.00	8.00

BERMUDA

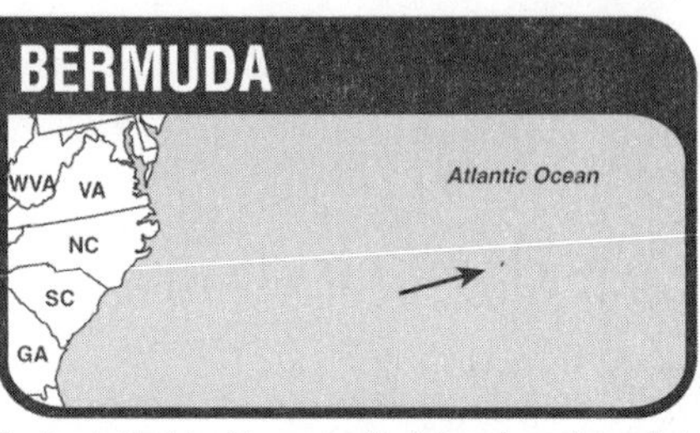

The Parliamentary British Colony of Bermuda, situated in the western Atlantic Ocean 1,062 km. east of North Carolina, has an area of 53.3 sq. km. and a population of 66,500. Capital: Hamilton. Concentrated essences, beauty preparations, and cut flowers are exported.

Bermuda was first settled in 1609 by shipwrecked English colonists headed for Virginia. Tourism to the island to escape North American winters first developed in Victorian times. Tourism continues to be important to the island's economy, although international business has overtaken it in recent years. Bermuda has developed into a highly successful offshore financial center. Although a referendum on independence from the UK was soundly defeated in 1995, the present government has reopened debate on the issue.

RULERS:
British

MONETARY SYSTEM:
1 Shilling = 12 Pence
1 Pound = 20 Shillings, to 1970

BRITISH ADMINISTRATION

Bermuda Government

1914 Issue

		Good	Fine	XF
1	**1 Pound** 2.12.1914. Black on green underprint. Arms at left. BC: Green. Printer: ABNC.	750	2,000	—

1920-1927 Issue

		Good	Fine	XF
2	**2 Shillings 6 Pence** 1.8.1920. Brown. Portrait King George V at center. Back: Sailing ship at center. (Not issued). Rare.	—	—	—

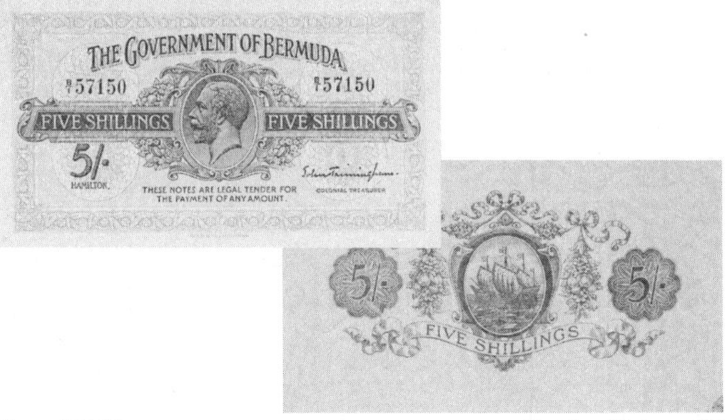

		Good	Fine	XF
3	**5 Shillings** 1920; ND(1935). Brown and green. Portrait King George V at center. Back: Sailing ship at center. BC: Purple. Printer: TDLR.			
	a. Signature title: *RECEIVER GENERAL*. 1.8.1920.	350	850	2,750
	b. Signature title: *COLONIAL TREASURER*. ND (1935).	325	800	2,500

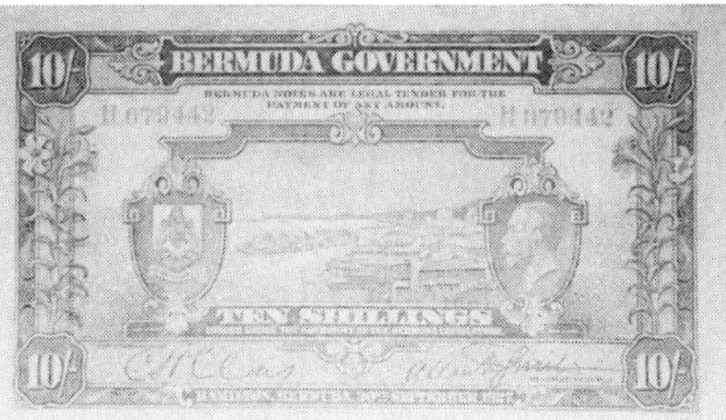

		Good	Fine	XF
4	**10 Shillings** 30.9.1927. Red on multicolor underprint. Arms at left, harbor at St. George at center, portrait King George V at right. Back: Royal crest at center. Printer: W&S.	300	750	2,250

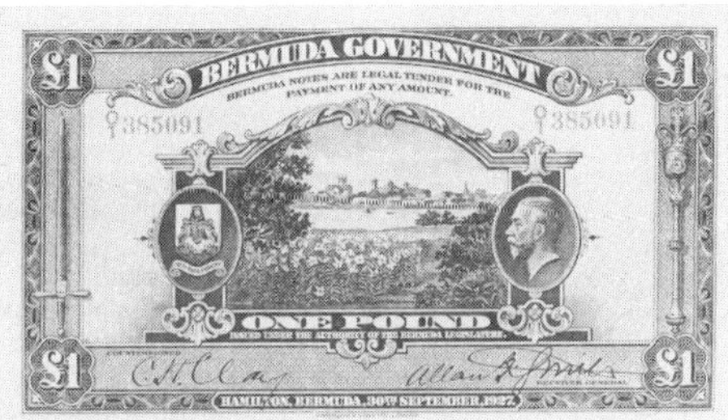

5 **1 Pound**
30.9.1927. Blue on multicolor underprint. Arms at left, view of Hamilton at center, King George V at right. Printer: W&S.

	VG	VF	UNC
a. Leter serial # prefix.	750	2,250	7,500
b. Fractional letter/number serial # prefix.	500	2,000	4,000

1937-1941 Issue

6 **1 Shilling**
1.3.1939. Specimen only. Multicolor. Portrait King George VI at upper center. Back: Royal crest. Printer: BWC.

VG	VF	UNC
—	—	—

7 **2 Shillings 6 Pence**
1.3.1939. Specimen only. Multicolor. Portrait King George VI at upper center. Back: Royal crest. Printer: BWC.

VG	VF	UNC
—	—	—

8 **5 Shillings**
12.5.1937. Brown on multicolor underprint. Portrait King George VI at upper center. Date in bottom center frame under picture of Hamilton harbor. Back: Royal crest. Printer: BWC.

	VG	VF	UNC
a. Single letter prefix.	15.00	90.00	500
b. Fractional format letter-number prefix.	7.50	40.00	325

9 **10 Shillings**
12.5.1937. Green on multicolor underprint. Portrait King George VI at upper center. Date in bottom center frame under picture of Gate's Fort in St. George. Back: Royal crest. Printer: BWC.

VG	VF	UNC
275	850	—

10 **10 Shillings**
12.5.1937. Red on multicolor underprint. Portrait King George VI at upper center. Date in bottom center frame under picture of Gate's Fort in St. George. Like #9. Back: Royal crest. Printer: BWC.

	VG	VF	UNC
a. Single letter prefix.	35.00	225	900
b. Fractional style letter-number prefix.	20.00	150	650

11 **1 Pound**
12.5.1937. Blue on multicolor underprint. Portrait King George VI at right. Bridge at left. Back: Royal crest. Printer: BWC.

	VG	VF	UNC
a. Single letter prefix.	30.00	175	—
b. Fractional format letter-number prefix.	20.00	150	650

12 **5 Pounds**
1.8.1941. Brown on multicolor underprint. Portrait King George VI at right. Ship entering Hamilton harbor at left. Back: Royal crest. BC: Brown, pink and green. Printer: BWC.

VG	VF	UNC
450	1,500	—

13 **5 Pounds**
1.8.1941. Orange on multicolor underprint. Portrait King George VI at right. Ship entering Hamilton harbor at left. Like #12. Back: Royal crest. Printer: BWC.

VG	VF	UNC
350	1,150	—

1943 Issue

13A **10 Shillings**
1.4.1943. Specimen. Portrait King George VI at center. Like #15.

VG	VF	UNC
—	—	—

1947 Issue

14 **5 Shillings**
17.2.1947. Brown on multicolor underprint. Portrait King George VI at upper center, date at left. Similar to #8. Back: Royal crest. Printer: BWC.

VG	VF	UNC
15.00	100	500

15 **10 Shillings**
17.2.1947. Red on multicolor underprint. Portrait King George VI at upper center, date at left. Gate's Fort in St. George at bottom center. Similar to #9. Back: Royal crest Printer: BWC.

VG	VF	UNC
35.00	250	900

16 **1 Pound**
17.2.1947. Blue on multicolor underprint. Portrait King George VI in profile at right, bridge at left, date at center above *ONE POUND.* Similar to #11. Back: Royal crest Printer: BWC.

VG	VF	UNC
30.00	200	850

17 **5 Pounds**
17.2.1947. Light orange on multicolor underprint. Portrait King George VI, facing at right, ship entering Hamilton Harbor at left. Similar to #13. Back: Royal crest. BC: Light orange and green. Printer: BWC.

VG	VF	UNC
750	2,500	7,500

1952 Issue

18 **5 Shillings**
1952; 1957. Brown on multicolor underprint. Portrait Queen Elizabeth II at upper center, Hamilton Harbor in frame at bottom center. Back: Royal crest. Printer: BWC.

	VG	VF	UNC
a. 20.10.1952.	15.00	65.00	225
b. 1.5.1957.	10.00	50.00	150
s. As b. Specimen.	—	—	—

1952-1966 Issue

19	10 Shillings	VG	VF	UNC
	1952-1966. Red on multicolor underprint. Portrait Queen Elizabeth II at upper center, Gate's Fort in St. George in frame at bottom center. Back: Arms at center. Printer: BWC.			
	a. 20.10.1952.	25.00	75.00	425
	b. 1.5.1957.	15.00	40.00	200
	c. 1.10.1966.	20.00	60.00	250
	s. As b. Specimen.	—	—	—

20	1 Pound	VG	VF	UNC
	1952-1966. Blue on multicolor underprint. Queen Elizabeth II at right. Bridge at left. Back: Arms at center. Printer: BWC.			
	a. 20.10.1952.	30.00	100	550
	b. 1.5.1957. Without security strip.	25.00	75.00	400
	c. 1.5.1957. With security strip.	22.50	70.00	350
	d. 1.10.1966.	20.00	60.00	275
	s. As d. Specimen.	—	—	—
	ct. Green on multicolored underprint.	—	—	1,000

21	5 Pounds	VG	VF	UNC
	1952-1966. Orange on multicolor underprint. Portrait Queen Elizabeth II at right, large value at left, ship entering Hamilton Harbor at left. Back: Arms at center. BC: Orange and green. Printer: BWC.			
	a. 20.10.1952.	300	1,250	2,500
	b. 1.5.1957. Without security strip.	300	1,000	2,000
	c. 1.5.1957. With security strip.	300	1,125	2,250
	d. 1.10.1966.	300	1,250	2,500
22	10 Pounds	VG	VF	UNC
	28.7.1964. Purple on multicolor underprint. Portrait Queen Elizabeth II at right. Back: Arms at center. Printer: BWC.	150	600	2,750

BOHEMIA & MORAVIA

GERMANY
POLAND
BOHEMIA
MORAVIA
SLOVAKIA
SOVIET UNION
AUSTRIA
HUNGARY
ROMANIA

Bohemia, a province in northwest Czechoslovakia, was combined with the majority of Moravia in central Czechoslovakia (excluding parts of north and south Moravia which were joined with Silesia in 1938) to form a German protectorate in March 1939. Toward the end of 1945, the protectorate was dissolved and Bohemia and Moravia once again became part of Czechoslovakia.

MONETARY SYSTEM:
1 Koruna = 100 Haleru

GERMAN OCCUPATION - WWII

Protektorat Böhmen und Mähren

Protectorate of Bohemia and Moravia

1939 Provisional Issue

#1, 2 are state notes with circular handstamp (usually blurred printing with large letters) or machine (usually finer printing with small letters) overprint: *Protektorat Böhmen und Mähren, Protektorat Cechy a Morava.*

1	1 Koruna	VG	VF	UNC
	ND (1939). Overprint on Czechoslovakia #27. Blue. Liberty wearing cap at right. Back: Arms at left. BC: Red and blue.			
	a. Handstamp: *Böhmen und Mähren...*	1.50	8.00	35.00
	b. Machine overprint: *Böhmen und Mähren...*	2.00	10.00	40.00
	s1. Hand stamp overprint. Perforated: *SPECIMEN*	20.00	50.00	180

2	5 Korun	VG	VF	UNC
	ND (1939). Overprint on Czechoslovakia #28. Lilac and violet. Portrait J. Jungmann at right. Back: Woman at left. BC: Violet.			
	a. Handstamp: *Böhmen und Mähren...*	10.00	40.00	90.00
	b. Machine overprint: *Böhmen und Mähren...*	25.00	35.00	260
	s. Perforated: *SPECIMEN.*	35.00	120	300

1940 Issue

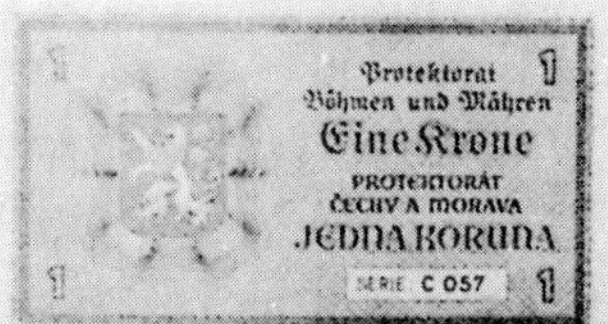

3	1 Koruna	VG	VF	UNC
	ND (1940). Brown on blue underprint. Girl at right. Back: Arms at left. BC: Red and blue.			
	a. Issued note.	0.25	2.50	8.00
	s. Perforated: *SPECIMEN.*	—	1.50	5.00

4	5 Korun	VG	VF	UNC
	ND (1940). Green on blue and brown underprint. Woman at right. Back: Woman at left. BC: Violet.			
	a. Issued note.	0.50	3.00	10.00
	s. Perforated: *SPECIMEN.*	0.25	1.00	4.00

5	**50 Korun**	VG	VF	UNC
	12.9.1940. Dark brown on gray underprint. Woman at right. Back: Arms at left. BC: Green.			
	a. Issued note.	3.00	12.00	75.00
	p. Print proof of woman.	—	—	10.00
	s. Perforated: *SPECIMEN.*	1.00	2.50	10.00

6	**100 Korun**	VG	VF	UNC
	20.8.1940. Blue. View of Castle and Charles Bridge in Prague. BC: Red center with blue and maroon lettering.			
	a. Issued note.	3.00	15.00	90.00
	s. Perforated: *NEPLATNÉ* or *SPECIMEN.*	1.00	2.50	10.00

7	**100 Korun**	VG	VF	UNC
	20.8.1940. Blue. View of Castle and Charles Bridge in Prague. Like #6. Back: *II. AUFLAGE* (2nd issue) at left margin. BC: Blue center with blue lettering.			
	a. Issued note.	2.00	10.00	50.00
	b. Issued note, Series Gb.	10.00	30.00	150
	s. Perforated: *SPECIMEN.*	1.00	2.50	10.00

1942-1944 Issue

8	**10 Korun**	VG	VF	UNC
	8.7.1942. Brown on light orange underprint. Portrait girl at right. 2 serial # varieties. Back: Arms at center right in underprint.			
	a. Issued note.	0.50	4.00	20.00
	b. Issued note, Series Nb.	4.00	18.00	40.00
	s. Perforated: *NEPLATNÉ* or *SPECIMEN.*	0.50	2.00	7.00

9	**20 Korun**	VG	VF	UNC
	24.1.1944. Green on light green underprint. Fruit across center, portrait boy at right. 3 serial # varieties. Back: Arms at center in underprint.			
	a. Issued note.	0.50	3.00	20.00
	s. Perforated: *SPECIMEN.*	—	1.00	4.00

10	**50 Korun**	VG	VF	UNC
	25.9.1944. Brownish gray. Wreath at center portrait woman at right. Back: Arms at center in underprint.			
	a. Issued note.	5.00	20.00	85.00
	s. Perforated: *NEPLATNÉ* or *SPECIMEN.*	0.50	4.00	30.00

Nationalbank für Böhmen und Mähren

National Bank for Bohemia and Moravia

1942-1944 Issue

11	**500 Korun**	VG	VF	UNC
	24.2.1942. Dark brown on multicolor underprint. Portrait P. Brandl at right. BC: Olive and multicolor.			
	a. Issued note.	8.00	25.00	150
	s. Perforated: *SPECIMEN.*	1.00	4.00	10.00

12	**500 Korun**	VG	VF	UNC
	24.2.1942. Dark brown on multicolor underprint. Portrait P. Brandl at right. Back: With *II. AUFLAGE - II. VYDANI.* (2nd issue) at left margin. BC: Olive and multicolor.			
	a. Issued note.	5.00	12.00	40.00
	p. Print proofs of L. Brandl.	—	—	10.00
	s. Perforated: *SPECIMEN.*	1.00	4.00	10.00

13	**1000 Korun**	VG	VF	UNC
	24.10.1942. Dark green on green and brown underprint. Portrait P. Parler at right.			
	a. Issued note.	8.00	25.00	150
	s. Perforated: *SPECIMEN.*	2.00	8.00	25.00

		VG	VF	UNC
14	**1000 Korun** 24.10.1942. Dark green. Portrait P. Parler at right. Like #13. Back: Blue and brown guilloche. With *II AUFLAGE - II VYDANI* (2nd issue) at left margin.			
	a. Issued note.	2.00	7.50	35.00
	s. Perforated: *NEPLATNÉ* or *SPECIMEN.*	1.00	3.00	12.00
15	**1000 Korun** 24.10.1942. Dark green. Portrait P. Parler at right. Like #13. Back: Multicolor guilloche. With *II AUFLAGE-II VYDANI* (2nd issue) at left margin.	**VG**	**VF**	**UNC**
	a. Issued note.	4.00	25.00	100
	p. Print proofs of P. Parler	—	—	10.00
	s. Perforated: *SPECIMEN.*	1.00	3.00	13.00

		VG	VF	UNC
16	**5000 Korun** 25.10.1943 (-old date 6.7.1920). Brown-violet. Perforated: *SPECIMEN.*	5.00	20.00	75.00

		VG	VF	UNC
17	**5000 Korun** 24.2.1944. Gray. Portrait St. Wenceslas at right. BC: Brown and multicolor.			
	a. Issued note.	40.00	200	420
	p. Print proofs of St. Wenceslas.	—	—	20.00
	s. Perforated: *SPECIMEN.*	2.00	6.00	20.00

The Republic of Bolivia, a landlocked country in west central South America, has an area of 1,098,580 sq. km. and a population of 9.25 million. Capitals: La Paz (administrative); Sucre (constitutional). Mining is the principal industry and tin the most important metal. Minerals, petroleum, natural gas, cotton and coffee are exported.

Bolivia, named after independence fighter Simon Bolivar, broke away from Spanish rule in 1825; much of its subsequent history has consisted of a series of nearly 200 coups and countercoups. Democratic civilian rule was established in 1982, but leaders have faced difficult problems of deep-seated poverty, social unrest, and illegal drug production. In December 2005, Bolivians elected Movement Toward Socialism leader Evo Morales president - by the widest margin of any leader since the restoration of civilian rule in 1982 - after he ran on a promise to change the country's traditional political class and empower the nation's poor majority. However, since taking office, his controversial strategies have exacerbated racial and economic tensions between the Amerindian populations of the Andean west and the non-indigenous communities of the eastern lowlands.

MONETARY SYSTEM:

1 Peso Boliviano = 100 Centavos, 1962-1987
1 Boliviano = 100 Centavos, 1987-

SPECIMEN NOTES:

All *SPECIMEN, MUESTRA, MUESTRA SIN VALOR* and *ESPECIMEN* notes always have serial #'s of zero.

REPUBLIC

Tesoreria de la República de Bolivia

1902 Issue

#91-95 Intended for circulation in the northwest during the Acre territory conflict with Brazil. Beware of notes with forged signatures.

		VG	VF	UNC
91	**50 Centavos** 29.11.1902. Black on green underprint. Shield with flags and eagle at center. Series E-J. BC: Green. Printer: ABNC.			
	a. Issued note.	1.50	5.00	25.00
	s. Specimen.	—	—	200

		VG	VF	UNC
92	**1 Boliviano** 29.11.1902. Black on brown and olive underprint. Shield with flags and eagle at left, tropical vegetation at right. Series F-I; K. BC: Brown. Printer: ABNC.			
	a. Issued note.	2.00	5.00	25.00
	s. Specimen.	—	—	200

		Good	Fine	XF
93	**5 Bolivianos** 29.11.1902. Black on pale blue underprint. Shield with flags and eagle at left, tree on hill at right. BC: Dark blue. Printer: ABNC.			
	p. Without series. Proof.	—	—	—
	r. Unsigned remainder.	100	250	500
	s. Specimen.	—	Unc	1,250

		Good	Fine	XF
94	**10 Bolivianos** 29.11.1902. Black on orange underprint. Shield with flags and eagle at left, tropical vegetation at right. Back: Woman's head at center. BC: Orange. Printer: ABNC.			
	p. Without series. Proof.	—	—	—
	r. Unsigned remainder.	100	250	500
	s. Specimen.	—	Unc	1,750

		Good	Fine	XF
95	**20 Bolivianos** 29.11.1902. Black on olive underprint. Tropical trees at. left, man tapping tree at right. Back: Woman's head at center. BC: Olive. Printer: ABNC.			
	p. Without series. Proof.	—	—	—
	r. Unsigned remainder.	150	600	—
	s. Specimen.	—	Unc	2,000

Banco de la Nación Boliviana

ND 1911 Provisional Issue

New bank name overprint in red on earlier issues of the Banco Bolivia y Londres. Old date 1.2.1909.

		Good	Fine	XF
96	**1 Boliviano** ND (1911). Series A. Overprint: *Banco De La Nacion Boliviana* in red.	75.00	400	—
97	**5 Bolivianos** ND (1911). Overprint: *Banco De La Nacion Boliviana* in red.	—	—	—
98	**10 Bolivianos** ND (1911). Overprint: *Banco De La Nacion Boliviana* in red.	—	—	—
99	**20 Bolivianos** ND (1911). Overprint: *Banco De La Nacion Boliviana* in red.	—	—	—
100	**50 Bolivianos** ND (1911). Overprint: *Banco De La Nacion Boliviana* in red.	—	—	—
101	**100 Bolivianos** ND (1911). Overprint: *Banco De La Nacion Boliviana* in red.	—	—	—

1911 Regular Issue

		Good	Fine	XF
102	**1 Boliviano** 11.5.1911. Black with brown, green and purple quilloches at sides. Mercury at center. Signature varieties. Back: Arms at center. BC: Green. Printer: ABNC.			
	a. Black series letters from A-Z and AA-ZZ. (AB-AL have large letters, AM-AZ small letters).	1.00	3.00	10.00
	b. Red series A1-Z2.	1.00	3.00	10.00
	p. Proof.	—	Unc	400
	s. As a or b. Specimen.	—	Unc	125

		Good	Fine	XF
103	**1 Boliviano** 11.5.1911. Black on green and multicolor underprint. Different guilloches at sides. Mercury at center. Red series A1-J1. Similar to #102. Signature varieties. Back: Arms at center. BC: Green. Printer: ABNC.			
	a. Issued note.	1.00	3.00	10.00
	s. Specimen.	—	Unc	125

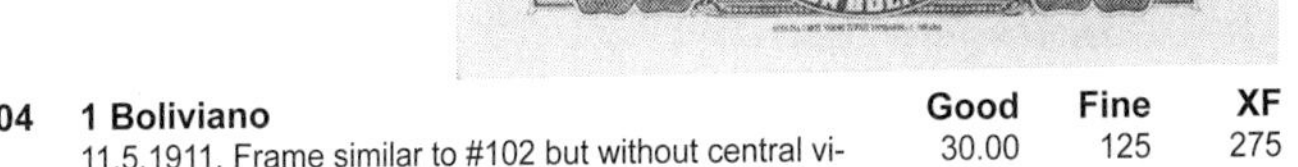

		Good	Fine	XF
104	**1 Boliviano** 11.5.1911. Frame similar to #102 but without central vignette. Series A1-Z1. Watermark: Large head of Mercury at center. BC: Deep green. Printer: CPM.	30.00	125	275

	105 5 Bolivianos	Good	Fine	XF
	11.5.1911. Black with multicolor guilloche. Mercury seated at left. Signature varieties. Back: Arms at center. BC: Blue-gray. Printer: ABNC.			
	a. Black series A-Z, AA-JJ, KK-PP.	1.00	4.00	15.00
	b. Red series QQ-ZZ, A1-D1.	1.00	4.00	15.00
	p. Proof.	—	Unc	400
	s. As a or b. Specimen.	—	Unc	150

	106 5 Bolivianos	Good	Fine	XF
	11.5.1911. Black on tan and blue underprint with different guilloche. Mercury seated at left. Red series A-E. Similar to #105. Signature varieties. Back: Arms at center. BC: Blue-gray. Printer: ABNC.			
	a. Issued note.	1.00	4.00	15.00
	s. Specimen.	—	Unc	150

	107 10 Bolivianos	Good	Fine	XF
	11.5.1911. Black on multicolor guilloches. Mercury seated at right. Signature varieties. Back: Arms at center. BC: Deep brown. Printer: ABNC.			
	a. Black series A-K.	1.00	5.00	15.00
	b. Red series L-P.	1.00	5.00	15.00
	p. Proof.	—	Unc	400
	s. As a or b. Specimen.	—	Unc	150

	108 20 Bolivianos	Good	Fine	XF
	11.5.1911. Black on multicolor guilloches. Mercury seated at center. Error *VEINTE PESOS* as entire border text. Signature varieties. Back: Arms at center. BC: Orange. Printer: ABNC.			
	a. Issued note. Series A.	275	—	—
	p. Back proof.	—	Unc	3,500

	109 20 Bolivianos	Good	Fine	XF
	11.5.1911. Black on multicolor guilloches. Mercury seated at center. Corrected inscription *VEINTE BOLIVIANOS* in frame. Like #108. Signature varieties. Back: Arms at center. BC: Orange. Printer: ABNC.			
	a. Black series A; B.	5.00	20.00	60.00
	b. Red series C; D.	5.00	20.00	60.00
	p. Proof.	—	Unc	500
	s. As a or b. Specimen, punch hole cancelled. Red overprint: SPECIMEN.	—	Unc	200

	109B 20 Bolivianos	Good	Fine	XF
	11.5.1911. Black on multicolor guilloches. Mercury seated at center. Similar to #109 but different guilloches. Corrected inscription *VEINTE BOLIVIANOS* in frame. Red series A. Signature varieties. Back: Arms at center. BC: Orange. Printer: ABNC. 184x89mm.	5.00	20.00	60.00

	110 50 Bolivianos	Good	Fine	XF
	11.5.1911. Black on multicolor guilloches. Mercury seated at left. Black series A. Signature varieties. Back: Arms at center. BC: Olive. Printer: ABNC.			
	a. Issued note.	20.00	70.00	150
	p. Proof.	—	Unc	650
	s. Specimen. Punch hole cancel.	—	Unc	450

	111 100 Bolivianos	Good	Fine	XF
	11.5.1911. Black on multicolor guilloches. Mercury seated at center. Black series A. Signature varieties. Back: Arms at center. Printer: ABNC.			
	a. Issued note.	12.00	40.00	110
	p. Proof.	—	Unc	550
	s. Specimen. Red overprint twice on face. Punch hole cancelled.	—	Unc	350

Banco Central de Bolivia

1929 Provisional Issue

New bank name overprint (1928) on earlier series of El Banco de la Nación Boliviana. Old date 11.5.1911.

		Good	Fine	XF
112	**1 Boliviano** ND (1929). Black on green and multicolor underprint. Mercury at center. Red series from K1-Z4. Back: Arms at center. Overprint: *BANCO CENTRAL DE BOLIVIA* in blue or black on #103.	0.20	1.00	4.00

		Good	Fine	XF
113	**5 Bolivianos** ND (1929). Black on tan and blue underprint. Mercury seated at left. Red series F-U. Back: Arms at center. Overprint: *BANCO CENTRAL DE BOLIVIA* in blue on #106.	1.00	5.00	25.00

		Good	Fine	XF
114	**10 Bolivianos** ND (1929). Black on multicolor guilloches. Mercury seated at right. Red series A-H. Back: Arms at center. BC: Brown-orange. Overprint: *BANCO CENTRAL DE BOLIVIA* in blue on face of #107 but with different gullioche.			
	a. Issued note.	0.60	3.00	15.00
	s. Specimen.	—	Unc	175

		Good	Fine	XF
115	**20 Bolivianos** ND (1929). Black on multicolor guilloches. Mercury seated at center. Red series B-D. Back: Arms at center. BC: Orange. Printer: ABNC. Overprint: *BANCO CENTRAL DE BOLIVIA* in blue on #109.			
	a. Issued note.	4.00	12.00	60.00
	s. Specimen.	—	Unc	225

		Good	Fine	XF
116	**50 Bolivianos** ND (1929). Black. Mercury seated at center. Red series A. Back: Arms at center. BC: Orange. Printer: ABNC. Overprint: *BANCO CENTRAL DE BOLIVIA.* in blue on #110 but with different guilloche.			
	a1. Issued note.	4.00	12.00	60.00
	s. Specimen.	—	Unc	225

		Good	Fine	XF
117	**100 Bolivianos** ND (1929). Black. Mercury seated at center. Red series A. Back: Arms at center. Printer: ABNC. Overprint: *BANCO CENTRAL DE BOLIVIA* in red-violet.			
	a. Issued note.	8.00	20.00	80.00
	s. Specimen.	—	Unc	475

Law of 20.7.1928 First Issue

		VG	VF	UNC
118	**1 Boliviano** *L.1928.* Deep brown on green, orange and rose underprint. Portrait S. Bolívar at left, view of Potosí and mountain at right center. Series A-Z; A1-A6. Many signature varieties. Back: Arms. BC: Deep blue. Printer: ABNC.			
	a. Issued note.	0.20	1.00	5.00
	s. Specimen. Red overprint: *SPECIMEN* twice on face. Without signature. Series J5. Punch hole cancelled.	—	—	125

		VG	VF	UNC
119	**1 Boliviano** *L.1928.* Deep brown. Portrait S. Bolívar at center. Series A-Z1. Back: Arms. BC: Deep blue. Printer: ABNC.			
	a. Issued note.	0.20	1.00	4.00
	s. Specimen. Red overprint: *SPECIMEN* on face twice. Without series; series A.	—	—	125

#	Description	VG	VF	UNC
120	**5 Bolivianos** *L.1928.* Deep green on blue, brown and rose underprint. Portrait S. Bolívar at left, view of Potosí and mountain at right. Series A-Z; A1-Z10. Many signature varieties. Back: Arms. BC: Deep blue. Printer: ABNC.			
	a. Issued note.	0.40	2.00	7.50
	s. Specimen. Red overprint: *SPECIMEN* twice on face. Without signature. Series H7; U3. Punch hole cancelled.	—	—	125

#	Description	VG	VF	UNC
121	**10 Bolivianos** *L.1928.* Deep blue on rose, green and lilac underprint. Portrait S. Bolívar at left, view of Potosí and mountain at right. Series A-V4. Many signature varieties. Back: Arms. BC: Red. Printer: ABNC.			
	a. Issued note.	0.60	3.00	12.50
	s. Specimen. Red overprint: *SPECIMEN* twice on face. Without signature. Series B4. Punch hole cancelled.	—	—	125

#	Description	VG	VF	UNC
122	**20 Bolivianos** *L.1928.* Brown on multicolor underprint. Portrait S. Bolívar at left, view of Potosí and mountain at right. Series A-Z3. Many signature varieties. Back: Arms. BC: Green. Printer: ABNC.			
	a. Issued note.	0.80	4.00	17.50
	s. Specimen. Blue overprint: *SPECIMEN* twice on face. Without signature. Series R. Punch hole cancelled.	—	—	125

#	Description	VG	VF	UNC
123	**50 Bolivianos** *L.1928.* Purple on green, lilac and yellow underprint. Portrait S. Bolívar at left, view of La Paz at center, portrait of A.J. de Sucre at right. Series A-G. Back: Arms. BC: Red. Printer: ABNC.			
	a. Issued note.	3.00	15.00	50.00
	s. Specimen.	—	—	125
124	**50 Bolivianos** *L.1928.* Purple on green, lilac and yellow underprint. Portrait S. Bolívar at left, view of La Paz at center, portrait of A.J. de Sucre at right. Series H-Z. Back: Arms. BC: Orange. Printer: ABNC.	VG	VF	UNC
	a. Issued note.	2.00	10.00	35.00
	s. Specimen.	—	—	125

#	Description	VG	VF	UNC
125	**100 Bolivianos** *L.1928.* Blue-black on rose, ochre and green underprint. Portrait S. Bolívar at left, view of La Paz at center, portrait of A.J. de Sucre at right. Series A-M. Back: Arms. BC: Deep brown. Printer: ABNC.			
	a. Issued note.	1.75	9.00	37.50
	s. Specimen.	—	—	125

Note: The rose underprint on #125 fades easily; no premium for notes without rose underprint.

#	Description	VG	VF	UNC
126	**500 Bolivianos** *L.1928.* Olive-green on multicolor underprint. Portrait S. Bolívar at left, view of La Paz at center, portrait of A.J. de Sucre at right. Back: Arms. BC: Purple. Printer: ABNC.			
	a. Series A. Hand signed.	60.00	200	—
	b. Series A, B. Printed signature.	4.00	20.00	75.00
	s. Specimen.	—	—	125

127 1000 Bolivianos

L.1928. Red on green, orange and lilac underprint. Portrait S. Bolívar at left, view of La Paz at center, portrait A.J. de Sucre at right. Series A. Back: Arms. BC: Deep blue-gray. Printer: ABNC.

	VG	VF	UNC
a. Hand signed.	60.00	200	—
b. Printed signature.	15.00	75.00	175
s. Specimen.	—	—	125

Law of 20.7.1928 Second Issue

128 1 Boliviano

L.1928. Brown. Portrait S. Bolívar at center. Signature varieties. Back: Arms at center. BC: Deep blue. Printer: W&S.

	VG	VF	UNC
a. Without *EMISION* overprint. Series A-D14.	0.10	0.50	1.50
b. *EMISION 1951*. Series E14-Q14.	0.50	3.00	10.00
c. *EMISION 1952*. Series Q14-R16.	0.05	0.25	0.75

129 5 Bolivianos — VG 0.10, VF 0.50, UNC 3.00

L.1928. Grayish green. Portrait S. Bolívar at center. Series A-R6. Signature varieties. Back: Arms at center. BC: Olive. Printer: W&S.

130 10 Bolivianos — VG 0.25, VF 1.25, UNC 6.00

L.1928. Deep blue on green and yellow underprint. Portrait S. Bolívar at center. Series A-T3. Signature varieties. Back: Arms at center. BC: Red. Printer: W&S.

131 20 Bolivianos — VG 0.25, VF 1.50, UNC 7.50

L.1928. Brown on green, lilac and orange underprint. View of Potosí at left center, portrait S. Bolívar at right. Series A-L6. Signature varieties. Back: Arms at center. BC: Deep green. Printer: W&S.

132 50 Bolivianos — VG 0.50, VF 2.00, UNC 15.00

L.1928. Purple on green, lilac and yellow underprint. View of Potosí at left center, portrait S. Bolívar at right. Series A-H3. Signature varieties. Back: Arms at center. BC: Orange. Printer: W&S.

133 100 Bolivianos — VG 2.00, VF 10.00, UNC 30.00

L.1928. Dark gray on orange, lilac and rose underprint. View of Potosí at left center, portrait S. Bolívar at right. Series A-E2. Signature varieties. Back: Arms at center. BC: Deep brown. Printer: W&S.

134 500 Bolivianos — VG 3.00, VF 15.00, UNC 45.00

L.1928. Olive-green on rose and pale yellow-green underprint. View of La Paz at left center. Series A-G. Signature varieties. Back: Arms at center. BC: Purple. Printer: W&S.

135 1000 Bolivianos — VG 5.00, VF 25.00, UNC 75.00

L.1928. Rose on yellow, green and light blue underprint. View of La Paz at left center. Series A-D. Signature varieties. Back: Arms at center. BC: Gray. Printer: W&S.

Decree of 16.3.1942

136 5000 Bolivianos — VG 30.00, VF 85.00, UNC 225

D.1942. Red-brown and multicolor. Miner at center. Series A. Signature varieties. Back: Arms at center. BC: Black on pink, yellow and green underprint. Printer: W&S.

137 10,000 Bolivianos — VG 30.00, VF 85.00, UNC 225

D.1942. Deep blue and multicolor. Puerta del Sol at center. Series A. Signature varieties. Back: Arms at center. BC: Black on pink, yellow and green underprint. Printer: W&S.

Law of 20.12.1945

138 5 Bolivianos	VG	VF	UNC
L.1945. Brown on green and sky blue underprint. Portrait S. Bolívar at right, arms at left. Signature varieties. Back: Arms at center. BC: Brown. Printer: TDLR.			
a. Without *EMISION* overprint. Series A-Q.	0.20	0.40	1.00
b. *EMISION 1951* in 1 or 2 lines. Series C; D.	0.50	2.00	6.00
c. *EMISION 1952.* Series D.	0.25	0.75	2.25
d. Remainder without overprint or signature. Series K; C1.	—	—	1.50

139 10 Bolivianos	VG	VF	UNC
L.1945. Blue on rose, brown and sky blue underprint. Portrait A. J. de Sucre at right, arms at left. Signature varieties. Back: Potosí scene. BC: Dark olive. Printer: TDLR.			
a. *EMISION 1951.* Series A.	1.00	3.00	6.50
b. *EMISION 1952.* Series A; B.	0.20	0.50	1.00
c. Without *EMISION.* overprint. Series C.	0.25	0.75	3.00
d. Remainder without overprint or signature. Series R; V; C1.	—	—	1.50

140 20 Bolivianos	VG	VF	UNC
L.1945. Brown and multicolor. Portrait S. Bolívar at right, arms at left. Series A-Q. Signature varieties. Back: Obverse and reverse of 1862 coin and Potosí Mint. BC: Deep red. Printer: TDLR.			
a. Issued note.	0.20	0.40	1.50
r. Remainder without signature. Series B1.	—	—	—
s. Specimen. TDLR oval stamp at bottom center.	—	—	75.00

141 50 Bolivianos	VG	VF	UNC
L.1945. Purple on green and sky blue underprint. Portrait. A. J. de Sucre at right, arms at left. Series A-Z; A1-K1. Signature varieties. Back: Cows at water hole. BC: Green. Printer: TDLR.	0.25	0.75	2.50

142 100 Bolivianos	VG	VF	UNC
L.1945. Black and multicolor. Portrait S. Bolívar at right, arms at left. Series A-W. Signature varieties. Back: Farmers. BC: Purple. Printer: TDLR.	0.75	3.00	10.00

143 500 Bolivianos	VG	VF	UNC
L.1945. Green on red, lilac and yellow underprint. Portrait A. J. de Sucre at right, arms at left. Series A-C. Signature varieties. Back: Oil well. BC: Orange. Printer: TDLR.	1.25	5.00	15.00

144 1000 Bolivianos	VG	VF	UNC
L.1945. Red on multicolor underprint. Portrait S. Bolívar at right, arms at left. Series A-C. Signature varieties. Back: Miners at center. BC: Black. Printer: TDLR.	1.75	8.50	25.00

145 5000 Bolivianos	VG	VF	UNC
L.1945. Brown and multicolor. Portrait A. J. de Sucre at right, arms at left. Series A. Signature varieties. Back: Puerta del Sol and llama at left. BC: Blue. Printer: TDLR.	5.00	17.50	55.00

146 10,000 Bolivianos	VG	VF	UNC
L.1945. Blue and multicolor. Portrait S. Bolívar at right, arms at left, flags at center. Series A. Signature varieties. Back: Independence proclamation at left center. BC: Green. Printer: TDLR.	6.00	25.00	75.00

Law of 20.12.1945 Second Issue

		VG	VF	UNC
147	**100 Bolivianos**			
	L.1945. Black and multicolor. Portrait G. Villarroel at right, arms at left. Series A-Z; A1-T1. Signature varieties. Back: Oil refinery. BC: Purple. Printer: TDLR.	0.15	0.40	1.50

		VG	VF	UNC
148	**500 Bolivianos**			
	L.1945. Green on red, blue and orange underprint. Portrait Busch at right, arms at left. Series A-Z; A1-D1. Signature varieties. Back: Miners. BC: Orange. Printer: TDLR.	0.50	1.50	7.50

		VG	VF	UNC
149	**1000 Bolivianos**			
	L.1945. Red on green, rose and blue underprint. Portrait Murillo at right, arms at left. Series A-Z; A1-C1. Signature varieties. Back: Man with native horn at center. BC: Black. Printer: TDLR.	0.50	1.50	7.50

		VG	VF	UNC
150	**5000 Bolivianos**			
	L.1945. Brown and multicolor. Portrait A. J. de Sucre at right, arms at left. Series AP.Signature varieties. Back: Puerta del Sol at center. BC: Blue. Printer: TDLR.	2.00	8.50	25.00

		VG	VF	UNC
151	**10,000 Bolivianos**			
	L.1945. Blue and multicolor. Flags at center, portrait S. Bolivar at right, arms at left. Series A-Z; A1-C2. Back: Independence proclamation at center. BC: Green. Printer: TDLR.	2.00	8.50	25.00

The Federative Republic of Brazil, which comprises half the continent of South America, is the only Latin American country deriving its culture and language from Portugal. It has an area of 8,511,965 sq. km. and a population of 196.34 million. Capital: Brasília.Following three centuries under the rule of Portugal, Brazil became an independent nation in 1822 and a republic in 1889. By far the largest and most populous country in South America, Brazil overcame more than half a century of military intervention in the governance of the country when in 1985 the military regime peacefully ceded power to civilian rulers. Brazil continues to pursue industrial and agricultural growth and development of its interior. Exploiting vast natural resources and a large labor pool, it is today South America's leading economic power and a regional leader. Highly unequal income distribution and crime remain pressing problems.

RULERS:

Pedro II, 1831-1889

MONETARY SYSTEM:

1 Milreis = 1000 Reis, 1833-1942
1 Cruzeiro = 100 Centavos, 1942-1967

PORTUGUESE ADMINISTRATION

Administracão Geral dos Diamantes

Royal Diamond Administration

1771-1792 Colonial Issue

Drafts issued by the Administration to pay successful diamond prospectors. Values of the drafts were filled in by hand for amounts of gold paid for the diamonds. Drafts were exchangeable into coins and circulated at full face value as paper currency.

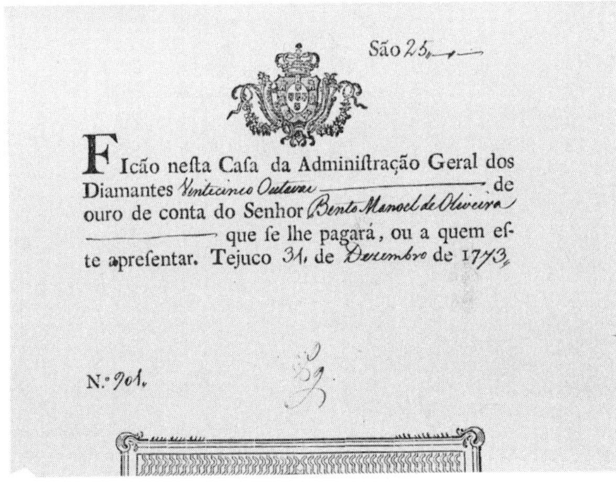

São 25,—

Fícão neſta Caſa da Adminiſtração Geral dos Diamantes Vinte cinco Outavas ——— de ouro de conta do Senhor Bento Manoel de Oliveira ——— que ſe lhe pagará, ou a quem eſte apreſentar. Tejuco 31, de Dezembro de 1773,

N.° 901.

		Good	Fine	XF
A101	**VARIOUS AMOUNTS**			
	1771-1792. Black. Stubs from draft forms printed in Lisbon.	50.00	125	300

IMPERIO DO BRASIL

Trocos de Cobre

Copper Exchange Notes

Lei de 3 de Outobro de 1833

Notes issued throughout all provincial offices in exchange for debased copper coinage. Names of individual provinces were handwritten on each piece issued. All denominations were reportedly issued by all 18 provinces, though some in small amounts. Almost all were issued in Ceará Province. Values shown are for the most available of each denomination. #A151-A157 Printed in Rio de Janeiro. Many notes are found w/ paper damaged by tannic acid in the early ink used for official handwritten signatures.

A151 1 Mil Reis | Good | Fine | XF
ND. Black. Arms at left. Uniface.

	Good	Fine	XF
a. 1 signature.	25.00	50.00	300
b. 2 signature.	25.00	50.00	300

A152 2 Mil Reis | Good | Fine | XF
ND. Black. Arms at left. Uniface.

	Good	Fine	XF
a. 1 signature.	25.00	50.00	300
b. 2 signature.	25.00	50.00	300

A153 5 Mil Reis | Good | Fine | XF
ND. Black. Arms at left. Uniface.

	Good	Fine	XF
a. 1 signature.	25.00	50.00	300
b. 2 signature.	25.00	50.00	300

A154 10 Mil Reis | Good | Fine | XF
ND. Light green. Arms at left. Uniface.

	Good	Fine	XF
a. 1 signature.	25.00	75.00	350
b. 2 signature.	25.00	75.00	350

A155 20 Mil Reis | Good | Fine | XF
ND. Light green. Arms at left. Uniface.

	Good	Fine	XF
a. 1 signature.	25.00	100	400
b. 2 signature.	25.00	75.00	300

A156 50 Mil Reis | Good | Fine | XF
ND. Dark green. Arms at left. Uniface.

	Good	Fine	XF
a. 1 signature.	25.00	100	450
b. 2 signature.	25.00	100	400

A157 100 Mil Reis | Good | Fine | XF
ND. Olive. Arms at left. Uniface.

	Good	Fine	XF
a. 1 signature.	50.00	150	500
b. 2 signature.	50.00	150	500

No Thesouro Nacional

National Treasury

Decreto de 1 Junho de 1833 (1835-1836) Estampa 1

A201 1 Mil Reis | Good | Fine | XF
D. 1833. Black. Arms crowned at left, decreto at right, Agriculture view at upper center. Uniface. Printer: PB&P. | 75.00 | 200 | 500

A202 2 Mil Reis | Good | Fine | XF
D. 1833. Black. Arms crowned at left, decreto at right, The Arts at upper center. Uniface. Printer: PB&P. | 100 | 250 | 750

A203 5 Mil Reis | Good | Fine | XF
D. 1833. Black. Arms crowned at left, decreto at right, Commerce at upper center. Uniface. Printer: PB&P. | 250 | 750 | 1,500

A204 10 Mil Reis | Good | Fine | XF
D. 1833. Black. Arms crowned at left, decreto at right, portrait Dom Pedro II at center. Uniface. Printer: PB&P. | 225 | 750 | 1,500

A205 20 Mil Reis | Good | Fine | XF
D. 1833. Black. Arms crowned at left, decreto at right, two seated figures (Justice) with date of Brazilian Independence at upper center. Uniface. Printer: PB&P. | 300 | 750 | 1,500

A206 50 Mil Reis | Good | Fine | XF
D. 1833. Black. Arms crowned at left, decreto at right, Allegory of the discovery of Brazil at upper center. Uniface. Printer: PB&P. | 300 | 750 | 1,500

A207 100 Mil Reis | Good | Fine | XF
D. 1833. Black. Arms crowned at left, decreto at right, Scene at Recife at upper center. Uniface. Printer: PB&P. | 1,500 | 2,250 | 5,000

A208 200 Mil Reis | Good | Fine | XF
D. 1833. Black. Arms crowned at left, decreto at right, View of Bahia at upper center. Uniface. Printer: PB&P. | 1,500 | 2,250 | 5,000

A209 500 Mil Reis | Good | Fine | XF
D. 1833. Black. Arms crowned at left, decreto at right, View of Rio de Janeiro at upper center. Uniface. Printer: PB&P. | 2,250 | 5,000 | 10,000

Decreto de 1 Junho de 1833 (1830-1844) Estampa 2

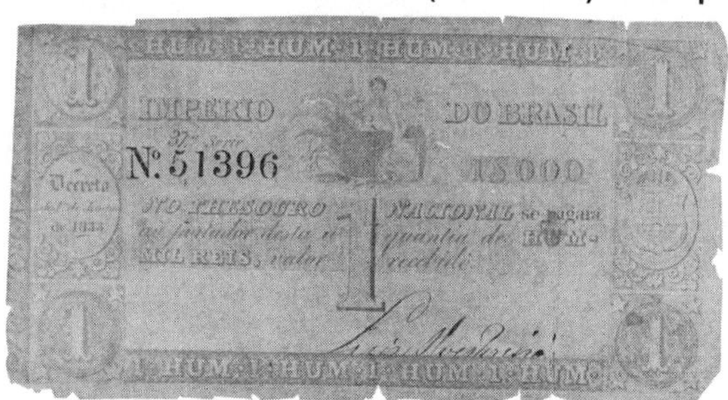

A210 1 Mil Reis | Good | Fine | XF
D. 1833. Orange. Decreto at left, arms at right, Commerce at upper center. Uniface. Like #A203. Printer: PB&P. PC: Yellow. | 250 | 550 | 1,250

A211 2 Mil Reis | Good | Fine | XF
D. 1833. Orange. Decreto at left, arms at right, Agriculture view at upper center. Uniface. Like #A201. Printer: PB&P. | 100 | 250 | 500

A212 5 Mil Reis | Good | Fine | XF
D. 1833. Orange. Decreto at left, arms at right, The arts at upper center. Uniface. Like #A202. Printer: PB&P. | 300 | 750 | 1,500

A213 10 Mil Reis | Good | Fine | XF
D. 1833. Blue and sepia. Decreto at left, arms at right, Allegory of the discovery of Brazil at upper center. Uniface. Like #A206. Printer: PB&P. | 250 | 700 | 1,500

A214 20 Mil Reis | Good | Fine | XF
D. 1833. Blue and sepia. Decreto at left, arms at right, Dom Pedro II at center. Uniface. Like #A204. Printer: PB&P. | 250 | 700 | 1,500

A215 50 Mil Reis | Good | Fine | XF
D. 1833. Blue and sepia. Decreto at left, arms at right, two seated figures (Justice) with date of independence of Brazil at upper center. Uniface. Like #A205. Printer: PB&P. | 250 | 700 | 1,500

A216 100 Mil Reis | Good | Fine | XF
D. 1833. Green. Decreto at left, arms at right, View of Rio de Janeiro at upper center. Uniface. Like #A209. Printer: PB&P. | 1,000 | 2,500 | 5,000

A217 200 Mil Reis | Good | Fine | XF
D. 1833. Green. Decreto at left, arms at right, Scene of Recife at upper center. Uniface. Like #A207. Printer: PB&P. | 2,000 | 4,000 | 7,500

		Good	Fine	XF
A218	**500 Mil Reis** *D. 1833.* Green. Decreto at left, arms at right, View of Bahia at upper center. Uniface. Like #A208. Printer: PB&P.	3,000	6,500	12,500

Decreto de 1 Junho de 1833 (1843-60) Estampa 3

		Good	Fine	XF
A219	**1 Mil Reis** *D. 1833.* Black on blue underprint. Commerce at upper center. Uniface. Printer: PBC.	75.00	225	750

		Good	Fine	XF
A220	**2 Mil Reis** *D. 1833.* Black on green underprint. Agriculture view at upper center. Uniface. Printer: PBC.	75.00	225	750

W/o Decreto ca. 1850

		Good	Fine	XF
A221	**5 Mil Reis** ND. Black. Royal emblem with crown at left, agriculture view at upper center, arms at right. Uniface. Printer: PB&P.	150	400	850
A222	**10 Mil Reis** ND. Orange. Royal crest at left, two seated figures (Justice) with date of independence at upper center, arms at right. Uniface. Printer: PB&P.	300	750	1,500

		Good	Fine	XF
A223	**20 Mil Reis** ND. Blue. Royal crest at left, allegory of the discovery of Brazil at upper center, arms at right. Uniface. Printer: PB&P. PC: Yellow.	250	500	1,000
A224	**50 Mil Reis** ND. Black on red underprint. Royal crest at left, portrait Dom Pedro II at upper center, arms at right. Uniface. Printer: PB&P.			
	a. Issued note.	500	1,500	3,250
	r. Unissued remainder.	—	Unc	2,250
A225	**100 Mil Reis** ND. Black. Arms at left, view of Bahia at upper center, royal crest at right. Uniface. Printer: PB&P.			
	a. Issued note.	2,000	4,500	9,000
	r. Unissued remainder.	—	Unc	2,250
A226	**200 Mil Reis** ND. Black. Arms at left, view of Rio de Janeiro at upper center, royal crest at right. Uniface. Printer: PB&P.	1,500	3,250	6,500
A227	**500 Mil Reis** ND. Black. Arms at left, scene of Recife at upper center, royal crest at right. Uniface. Printer: PB&P. PC: Orange.	3,000	6,000	15,000

Estampa 4, 1852-1867

		Good	Fine	XF
A228	**1 Mil Reis** ND. Black on blue underprint. Portrait Dom Pedro II at left, Justice, Agriculture and Commerce seated at upper center, crowned arms at right. Uniface. Printer: PBC.	75.00	200	450
A229	**2 Mil Reis** ND. Black on green underprint. Justice and Truth at upper center. Uniface. Printer: PBC.	75.00	200	450
A230	**5 Mil Reis** ND. Black. Arms at left, two seated figures (Justice) with date of independence at upper center, royal emblem with crown at right. Uniface. Printer: PB&P.	150	300	750
A231	**10 Mil Reis** ND. Black on brown underprint. Agriculture with Brazilian arms at upper center. Uniface. Printer: PBC.			
	a. Issued note.	150	300	750
	x. Counterfeit.	—	—	100

Note: Most examples seen of #A231 are counterfeits. Underprint wording on these forgeries ends in *REIS* at right instead of *MIL* as on genuine notes. Forgeries have irregular imprint lettering.

		Good	Fine	XF
A232	**20 Mil Reis** ND. Black. Peace, Agriculture and Science at upper center. Uniface. Printer: PB&P.	300	700	1,500
A233	**50 Mil Reis** ND. Black on blue underprint. Agriculture and Commerce at upper center. With or without *ESTAMPA 4a* on note. Uniface. Printer: PBC.			
	a. Issued note.	300	700	1,500

		Good	Fine	XF
A234	**100 Mil Reis** ND. Black on purple underprint. Allegrical figures at left and right, allegory of the discovery of Brazil at upper center. Uniface. Printer: PBC.	500	1,000	3,000

		Good	Fine	XF
A235	**200 Mil Reis** ND. Black on purple underprint. Dom Pedro II at upper left and lower right, arms at lower left and upper right, two seated figures (Justice) with date of independence at upper center and without date on column. Uniface. Printer: PBC.	750	1,500	4,000
A236	**500 Mil Reis** ND. Black on green underprint. Allegorical figures at left and right, Agriculture, Art and Commerce at center. Uniface. Printer: PBC.	1,500	3,500	7,500

Estampa 5, 1860-1868

		Good	Fine	XF
A237	**5 Mil Reis** ND. Black on brown underprint. Arms at left, Justice and Commerce with arms at center, portrait Dom Pedro II at right. Uniface. Printer: PBC.	125	275	600
A238	**10 Mil Reis** ND. Black on purple underprint. Allegorical figures left and right, portrait Dom Pedro II at upper center, arms with cherubs at lower center. Uniface. Printer: PBC.	300	750	1,500

		Good	Fine	XF
A239	**20 Mil Reis** ND. Black on green underprint. Portrait Dom Pedro II at left, Commerce at center, arms at right. Uniface.			
	a. Without *ESTAMPA*. Series 1-8.	150	300	600
	b. With *ESTAMPA 5a*. Series 9-10.	150	300	600

Color Abbreviation Guide

New to the *Standard Catalog of® World Paper Money* are the following abbreviations related to color references:

BC: Back color
PC: Paper color

Estampa 6, 1866-1870

		Good	Fine	XF
A240	**5 Mil Reis** ND. Black on brown underprint. Commerce, Art and Science with medallic portrait of Dom Pedro II at center. Uniface. Printer: PBC.	350	750	1,500

		Good	Fine	XF
A241	**20 Mil Reis** ND. Black on green underprint. Allegorical figures at left and right, Rio de Janeiro harbor at center. Uniface. Printer: PBC.	—	—	900

Estampa 1, 1874

		Good	Fine	XF
A242	**500 Reis** ND (21.12.1874). Black on orange underprint. Arms at left, portrait Dom Pedro II at center, seated woman at right. BC: Orange. Printer: ABNC.	150	300	750

Estampa 2, 1880

		Good	Fine	XF
A243	**500 Reis** ND (1.9.1880). Black on orange-brown underprint. Woman reclining at left, portrait Dom Pedro II at center, woman sitting at right. BC: Orange-brown. Printer: ABNC.			
	a. 1 serial #, 1880.	75.00	150	300
	b. 2 serial #, 1885.	100	200	400

Estampa 5, 1870-1878

		Good	Fine	XF
A244	**1 Mil Reis** ND (1870). Black on blue underprint. Portrait Dom Pedro II at left, boat, tree and steam train at center, arms at right. BC: Blue. Printer: ABNC.	75.00	250	450

		Good	Fine	XF
A245	**2 Mil Reis** ND (1870). Black on green underprint. Portrait Dom Pedro II at left, arms at center, trees at right. BC: Green. Printer: ABNC.	25.00	150	300

		Good	Fine	XF
A246	**50 Mil Reis** ND (1874-1885). Black on light green and brown underprint. Dom Pedro II at left, abundance at center, arms at right. BC: Brown. Printer: ABNC.	50.00	450	850

		Good	Fine	XF
A247	**100 Mil Reis** ND (1877). Black on red and green underprint. Arms at left, Dom Pedro II at center, woman at right. Back: Arms at center. BC: Orange. Printer: ABNC.			
	a. Single serial #.	125	750	1,500
	b. 2 serial #.	125	750	1,500

		Good	Fine	XF
A248	**200 Mil Reis** ND (1874). Black on red and blue underprint. Tree at left, Dom Pedro II at center, arms at right. Back: Seated woman at left and right. BC: Green & black. Printer: ABNC.	250	1,500	3,000

		Good	Fine	XF
A249	**500 Mil Reis** ND (ca.1885). Black on orange and blue underprint. Arms at left, portrait Dom Pedro II at center, woman at right. Back: Portrait Dom Pedro II at left, arms at right. BC: Brown and black. Printer: ABNC.	2,000	4,000	9,000

Estampa 6, 1869-1882

		Good	Fine	XF
A250	**1 Mil Reis** ND (1879). Black on green underprint. Arms at left, portrait Dom Pedro II at center, seated woman at right. BC: Green. Printer: ABNC.			
	a. 1 serial #, 1879.	100	300	700
	b. 2 serial #, 1885.	100	300	700

		Good	Fine	XF
A251	**2 Mil Reis** ND (1882). Black on blue underprint. Cherub with arms at left ("Bachus"), Dom Pedro II at right center. BC: Blue. Printer: ABNC.			
	a. Issued note.	25.00	250	600
	s. Specimen. Red overprint: SPECIMEN on face, punch hole cancelled	—	Unc	300

		Good	Fine	XF
A252	**10 Mil Reis** ND (1869). Black on green underprint. Portrait Dom Pedro II at left, two seated women with arms at center, tree at right. BC: Green. Printer: ABNC.	50.00	400	800

		Good	Fine	XF
A252A	**20 Mil Reis** ND (ca.1868). Black on orange underprint. Allegorical woman with industrial elements at left, portrait Dom Pedro II at center, arms at right. BC: Orange. Printer: ABNC. Proof.	—	—	—

A253 50 Mil Reis — Good / Fine / XF: 75.00 / 750 / 1,750
ND (1889). Black on orange and yellow underprint. Portrait Dom Pedro II at left, allegorical woman at right. Back: Large building at center. BC: Brown and black. Printer: ABNC.

A254 200 Mil Reis — Good / Fine / XF: 1,000 / 2,000 / 5,000
ND (1889). Black on blue and yellow underprint. Shoreline scene at left, Dom Pedro II at center, arms at right. Back: Scene of the first Mass held in Brazil at center. BC: Black and orange. Printer: ABNC.

Estampa 7, 1869-1883

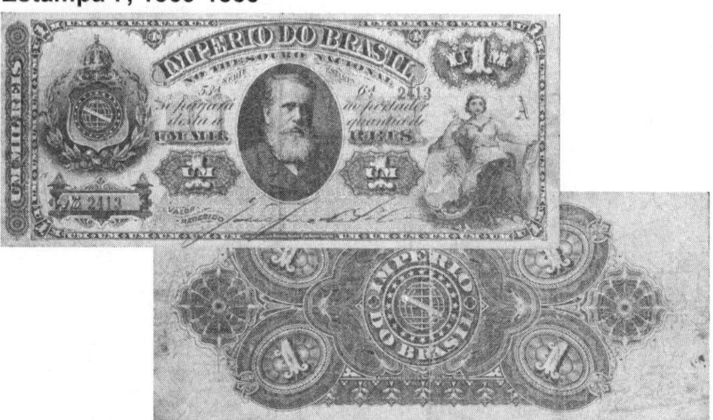

A255 1 Mil Reis — Good / Fine / XF: 25.00 / 250 / 500
ND. Black on green underprint. Building and arms at left, portrait Dom Pedro II at right. Back: Equestrian statue of Dom Pedro I. BC: Black and green. Printer: ABNC.

A256 2 Mil Reis — Good / Fine / XF: 25.00 / 250 / 500
ND. Black on brown underprint. Portrait Dom Pedro II at left, arms at right. Back: Arms at left. BC: Brown. Printer: ABNC.

A257 5 Mil Reis — Good / Fine / XF: 50.00 / 250 / 550
ND (1869). Black on brown underprint. Truth at left, arms at center, portrait Dom Pedro II at right. With or without *ESTAMPA 7* (1874) on note. BC: Brown. Printer: ABNC.

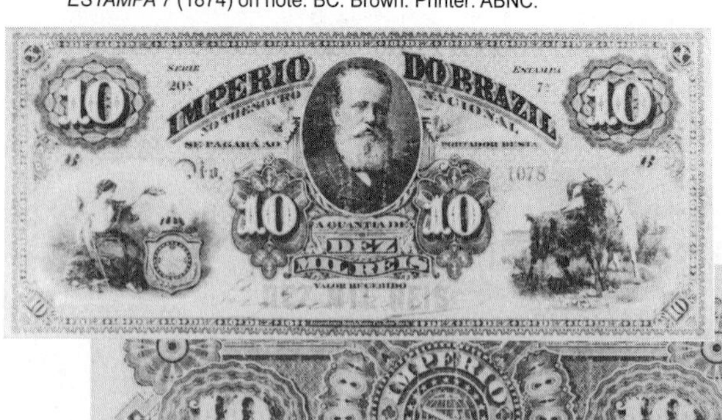

A258 10 Mil Reis
ND (1883). Black on orange and green underprint. Justice with arms at left, portrait Dom Pedro II at center, two rams at right. Back: Arms at center. BC: Green. Printer: ABNC.

	Good	Fine	XF
a. 1 serial #, 1883.	75.00	500	1,200
b. 2 serial #, 1886.	75.00	500	1,200

A259 20 Mil Reis — Good / Fine / XF: 100 / 600 / 1,500
ND. Black on gold and green underprint. Portrait Dom Pedro II at left, woman leaning on column with arms at center, seated woman at right. Back: Arms at center. BC: Brown. Printer: ABNC.

Estampa 8, ca. 1885

A260 2 Mil Reis — Good / Fine / XF: 35.00 / 300 / 900
ND. Black on brown underprint. Portrait Dom Pedro II at left, church at right. Back: Street scene and Rio de Janeiro Post Office. BC: Blue and black. Printer: ABNC.

A261 5 Mil Reis — Good / Fine / XF: 50.00 / 350 / 1,200
ND. Black on purple, orange and blue underprint. Woman with wheat at left, portrait Dom Pedro II at center, man with sheep at right. 1 or 2 serial #. Back: Arms at center. BC: Brown. Printer: ABNC.

		Good	Fine	XF
A262	**10 Mil Reis** ND. Black on green and orange underprint. Portrait Dom Pedro II at left, arms at center, standing woman at right. ("Fortuna"). Back: Arms at center. BC: Green. Printer: ABNC.	75.00	500	1,250

		Good	Fine	XF
A263	**20 Mil Reis** ND. Black on orange and green underprint. Two women with arms in column at left, portrait Dom Pedro II at right. Back: Arms at left. BC: Brown. Printer: ABNC.	75.00	500	1,250

Estampa 9, 1888

		Good	Fine	XF
A264	**5 Mil Reis** ND (6.1888). Black on orange and blue underprint. Portrait Dom Pedro II at left, cherub at center, Art at right. Back: Arms at center. BC: Brown. Printer: ABNC.	35.00	350	900

SECTION IV, 1892-1897

REPUBLIC REGIONAL ISSUES

Republica dos Estados Unidos do Brasil

Thesouro Nacional

1891-1931 Issue

#1-93 Some individual notes are designated by Estampas...(*E* = printings).

		Good	Fine	XF
1	**500 Reis** *E. 3A* (1893). Black on yellow underprint. Woman with sheep at left, woman at right. Printer: ABNC			
	a. 1 handwritten signature. Serie 1-20; 151-160.	15.00	75.00	150
	b. 2 printed signature. Serie 21-150.	15.00	100	300
	s. Specimen.	—	Unc	450

		Good	Fine	XF
2	**500 Reis** Without *Estampa* (1901). Violet on ochre underprint. Liberty at left. Back: Arms at center. BC: Blue-gray. Printer: BWC.	50.00	225	500
3	**1 Mil Reis** *E. 7A* (1891). Black on green underprint. Imperial Museum at left, child holding caduceus at right. BC: Green. Printer: ABNC.			
	a. Back frame 63mm high. 1 handwritten signature with serie letter.	25.00	125	475
	b. Back frame 65mm high. 2 printed signature with serie letter.	25.00	150	600
	c. Back frame 60mm high and horizontal bar at center removed. 1 handwritten signature without serie letter.	25.00	125	475
	s. Specimen.	—	Unc	750

		Good	Fine	XF
4	**1 Mil Reis** Blue on ochre underprint. Liberty at top center. Printer: BWC. Without *Estampa E.8A* (1902).	100	400	1,800

		Good	Fine	XF
5	**1 Mil Reis** *E. 9A* (1917). Black on orange underprint. Imperial Museum at left, child holding caduceus at right. Like #3. BC: Orange. Printer: ABNC.			
	a. Issued note.	35.00	75.00	350
	s. Specimen.	—	Unc	500
6	**1 Mil Reis** *E. 10A* (1919). Blue on multicolor underprint. Padre D. A. Feijo at center. BC: Green. Printer: ABNC.			
	a. Issued note.	40.00	75.00	400
	s. Specimen.	—	Unc	350

		Good	Fine	XF
7	**1 Mil Reis** *E. 11A* (1920). Blue on pink underprint. Portrait D. Campista at center. Printer: CdM (without imprint).	15.00	100	300
8	**1 Mil Reis** *E. 12A* (1921). Blue on olive underprint. Portrait D. Campista at center. Printer: CdM.	10.00	50.00	150
9	**1 Mil Reis** *E. 13A* (1923). Brown on ochre underprint. Portrait D. Campista at center. Printer: CdM.	10.00	50.00	150
10	**2 Mil Reis** *E. 8A* (1890). Black on ochre underprint. Woman seated with child at left, building and church at right. Printer: ABNC.			
	a. Small background lettering at top: *IMPERIO DO BRASIL DOIS MIL REIS.* Series 11-45.	10.00	150	600
	b. Small background lettering at top, only *DOIS MIL REIS.* Series 46-140.	10.00	150	600
	c. Without series letter. Series 28.	10.00	150	600
	s. Specimen.	—	Unc	1,250
11	**2 Mil Reis** *E. 9A* (1900). Black on lilac and violet underprint. Woman at right ("Zella"). Back: Woman with spear at center. Printer: ABNC.			
	a. Issued note.	20.00	225	700
	s. Specimen.	—	Unc	600

		Good	Fine	XF
12	**2 Mil Reis** Green on ochre underprint. Liberty at lower right. Printer: BWC. W/o *Estampa; E.10A* (1902).	30.00	250	700

		Good	Fine	XF
13	**2 Mil Reis** *E. 11A* (1918). Black on red-brown and green underprint. Woman at right ("Zella"). Like #11. Back: Woman with spear at center. BC: Orange. Printer: ABNC.			
	a. Issued note.	15.00	100	400
	s. Specimen.	—	Unc	600
14	**2 Mil Reis** *E. 12A* (1919). Blue on multicolor underprint. Marques de Olinda, P. de Araujo Lima at center. Printer: ABNC.	Good	Fine	XF
	a. Issued note.	20.00	100	400
	s. Specimen.	—	Unc	750
15	**2 Mil Reis** *E. 13A* (1920). Blue on ochre underprint. Portrait J. Murtinho at center. Printer: CdM (without imprint).	Good 20.00	Fine 100	XF 400
16	**2 Mil Reis** *E. 14A* (1921). Blue on olive underprint. Portrait J. Murtinho at left. Printer: CdM (without imprint).	Good 10.00	Fine 50.00	XF 300
17	**2 Mil Reis** *E. 15A* (1923). Brown on yellow underprint. Portrait J. Murtinho at center. Printer: CdM.	Good 10.00	Fine 50.00	XF 300

		Good	Fine	XF
18	**5 Mil Reis** *E. 9A* (1890). Black on pink and blue underprint. Man at left, woman seated at right ("Arts"). Letters A-E. BC: Brown. Printer: ABNC.			
	a. Issued note.	20.00	150	450
	s. Specimen.	—	Unc	1,000
19	**5 Mil Reis** *E. 10A* (1903). Designer: Georges Duval Inv. et del. Brown on ochre underprint. Woman seated with flowers and fruits. Letter A-F.	Good 20.00	Fine 150	XF 450
20	**5 Mil Reis** *E. 11A* (1907). Sepia. Woman seated with flowers and fruits. Like #19 but without designer's name. Printer: CdM.	Good 40.00	Fine 400	XF 1,000
21	**5 Mil Reis** *E. 12A* (1908). Sepia on ochre underprint. Woman seated with flowers and fruits. Like #19 and 20, without designer's name. Printer: George Duval and CdM.	Good 40.00	Fine 400	XF 1,000

		Good	Fine	XF
22	**5 Mil Reis** *E. 13A* (1909). Black on multicolor underprint. Woman seated with laurel wreath and statuette at left. Printer: ABNC.			
	a. Issued note.	25.00	150	500
	s. Specimen.	—	Unc	750
23	**5 Mil Reis** *E. 14A* (1912). Black on multicolor underprint. Woman seated at right. Printer: ABNC.	Good	Fine	XF
	a. Issued note. (Not issued).	175	1,500	3,250
	s. Specimen.	—	Unc	7,500

		Good	Fine	XF
24	**5 Mil Reis** *E. 14A* (1913). Black on multicolor underprint. Portrait B. do rio Branco (foreign minister) at center. Printer: ABNC.			
	a. Issued note.	15.00	100	400
	s. Specimen.	—	Unc	600
25	**5 Mil Reis** *E. 15A* (1918). Black on claret underprint. Watermark at left. BC: Wine red. Printer: CPM.	Good 30.00	Fine 200	XF 500
26	**5 Mil Reis** *E. 16A* (1920). Green on light green. Pres. F. de Paula Rodrigues Alves at center. Printer: CdM.	Good 20.00	Fine 150	XF 450
27	**5 Mil Reis** *E. 17A* (1922). Brown on green underprint. Pres. F. de Paula Rodrigues Alves at center. Like #26. Printer: CdM.	Good 15.00	Fine 150	XF 400
28	**5 Mil Reis** *E. 18A* (1923). Sepia on yellow underprint. Portrait Pres. F. de Paula Rodrigues Alves at center. Printer: CdM.	Good 15.00	Fine 150	XF 400

		Good	Fine	XF
29	**5 Mil Reis** *E. 19A* (1925). Blue on multicolor underprint. Portrait B. do Rio Branco (foreign minister) at center. Back: Three allegorical figures at center. BC: Reddish-brown. Printer: ABNC.			
	a. *BRAZIL*. 1 handwritten signature.	5.00	40.00	250
	b. *BRASIL; Estampa* and serial # together.	5.00	25.00	200
	c. *BRASIL; Estampa* and serial # separated.	5.00	25.00	200
	s. As a or b. Specimen.	—	Unc	400

		Good	Fine	XF
30	**10 Mil Reis** *E. 8A* (1892). Black on multicolor underprint. Girl with distaff at left, woman with wheel at right ("Fortuna"). Letters A-D. BC: Green. Printer: ABNC.	40.00	200	600
31	**10 Mil Reis** *E. 9A* (1903). Carmine on yellow underprint. Woman with boy at right. Letters A-D. Printer: George Duval.	Good 50.00	Fine 600	XF 1,250
32	**10 Mil Reis** *E. 10A* (1907). Brown on ochre underprint. Woman with boy at right. Like #31. Printer: CdM.	Good 50.00	Fine 60.00	XF 1,250
33	**10 Mil Reis** *E. 11A* (1907). Black on red-brown, green and orange underprint. Woman holding law book with lion at left. Back: Caixa de Amortizacao at center. BC: Green. Printer: ABNC.	Good	Fine	XF
	a. Issued note.	40.00	300	900
	s. Specimen.	—	Unc	750
34	**10 Mil Reis** *E. 12A* (1912). Black on multicolor underprint. Woman with eagle at left. BC: Purple. Printer: ABNC.	Good	Fine	XF
	a. Issued note.	40.00	300	900
	s. Specimen.	—	Unc	1,250

35 10 Mil Reis — Good / Fine / XF
E. 13A (1914). Pink and brown underprint. Printer: CPM. — 50.00 / 400 / 1,250

36 10 Mil Reis — Good / Fine / XF
E. 14A (1918). Blue on multicolor underprint. Portrait F. de Campos Salles at center. Printer: ABNC.

	Good	Fine	XF
a. Issued note.	25.00	150	600
s. Specimen.	—	Unc	1,250

37 10 Mil Reis — Good / Fine / XF
E. 15A (1923). Ochre underprint. Woman with plants at center. Printer: CdM. — 25.00 / 350 / 900

38 10 Mil Reis — Good / Fine / XF
E. 16A (1924). Green. S. Alves Barroso Jr. at center. Printer: CdM. — 25.00 / 350 / 900

39 10 Mil Reis — Good / Fine / XF
E. 17A (1925). Blue on multicolor underprint. Portrait Pres. Manuel Ferraz de Campos Salles at center. Printer: ABNC.

	Good	Fine	XF
a. *BRAZIL.* 1 handwritten signature.	5.00	25.00	100
b. *BRAZIL.* 2 printed signature.	7.50	150	300
c. *BRASIL; Estampa* and serial # separated, handwritten signature.	5.00	25.00	100
d. *BRASIL; Estampa* and serial # together, handwritten signature.	5.00	25.00	100
s1. As a, c. Specimen	—	Unc	250
s2. As b. Specimen.	—	Unc	1,000

40 20 Mil Reis — Good / Fine / XF
E. 8A (1892). Black on orange underprint. Two women with cupid at left, women repeating at right. Printer: ABNC. — 50.00 / 350 / 900

41 20 Mil Reis — Good / Fine / XF
Without *Estampa* (1900). Violet on ochre underprint. Woman with boy at left, woman at right. Back: Arms. BC: Pale blue. Printer: BWC.

	Good	Fine	XF
a. With *NOVEMBRE.*	50.00	350	900
b. With *NOVEMBRO.*	40.00	300	750

42 20 Mil Reis — Good / Fine / XF
E. 10A (1905). Brown on ochre underprint. Boy seated at left, and at right, woman in circle at lower left. Back: Arms. BC: Pale blue. Printer: George Duval. — 45.00 / 325 / 850

43 20 Mil Reis — Good / Fine / XF
E. 11A (1907). Brown on ochre underprint. Boy seated at left, and at right, woman in circle at lower left. Like #42. Back: Arms. BC: Pale blue. Printer: CdM and George Duval. — 45.00 / 325 / 850

44 20 Mil Reis — Good / Fine / XF
E. 12A (1909). Black on multicolor underprint. Woman seated with branch at center. Printer: ABNC.

	Good	Fine	XF
a. Issued note.	50.00	350	900
s. Specimen.	—	Unc	900

45 20 Mil Reis — Good / Fine / XF
E. 13A (1912). Black on multicolor underprint. Woman reclining at center. Printer: ABNC.

	Good	Fine	XF
a. Issued note.	15.00	85.00	300
s. Specimen.	—	Unc	700

46 20 Mil Reis — Good / Fine / XF
E. 14A (1919). Blue on multicolor underprint. Firstt Pres. M. Manuel Deodoro do Fonseca at center. Printer: ABNC.

	Good	Fine	XF
a1. Issued note.	12.50	75.00	275
s. Specimen.	—	Unc	600

47 20 Mil Reis — Good / Fine / XF
E. 15A (1923). Brown on yellow underprint. Woman with child at center. Printer: CdM. — 25.00 / 300 / 900

48 20 Mil Reis — Good / Fine / XF
E. 16A (1931). Blue on multicolor underprint. First Pres. Manuel Deodoro do Fonseca at center. Back: Allegorical woman at center. BC: Orange. Printer: ABNC.

	Good	Fine	XF
a. *BRAZIL.* 1 handwritten signature.	3.00	45.00	100
b. *BRAZIL.* 2 printed signature.	3.00	75.00	225
c. *BRASIL; Estampa* and serial # separated, handwritten signature.	3.00	20.00	45.00
d. *BRASIL; Estampa* and serial # together, handwritten signature.	3.00	20.00	115
s1. As a, c. Specimen.	—	Unc	250
s2. As b. Specimen.	—	Unc	500

49 50 Mil Reis — Good / Fine / XF
E. 7A (1893). Yellow underprint. Woman seated with two children at left, woman standing with flag at right. Letters A-D. Back: First Mass in Brazil at center. BC: Brown and black. Printer: ABNC.

	Good	Fine	XF
a. Issued note.	20.00	250	600
s. Specimen.	—	Unc	1,750

50 50 Mil Reis — Good / Fine / XF
Without *Estampa; E.8A.* (1900). Violet on ochre underprint. Woman seated at left, woman at center. Printer: BWC.

	Good	Fine	XF
a. With *NOVEMBRE.*	20.00	250	750
b. With *NOVEMBRO.*	20.00	250	750

51 50 Mil Reis — Good / Fine / XF
E. 9A (1906). Brown on green underprint. Boy at left and at right, woman in circle left of center. Printer: George Duval — 20.00 / 600 / 1,750

52 50 Mil Reis — Good / Fine / XF
E. 10A (1908). Sepia-green and red-brown. Boy at left and at right, woman in circle left of center. Like #51. Printer: CdM and George Duval. — 20.00 / 700 / 1,600

53 50 Mil Reis — Good / Fine / XF
E. 11A (1908). Black on multicolor underprint. Steamboat with sails. Back: City view, river, mountains at center. BC: Olive. Printer: ABNC and George Duval.

	Good	Fine	XF
a. Issued note.	20.00	700	1,300
s. Specimen.	—	Unc	2,500

		Good	Fine	XF
54	**50 Mil Reis** *E. 12A* (1912). Black on multicolor underprint. Youth seated at right. Printer: ABNC.	50.00	300	750

		Good	Fine	XF
55	**50 Mil Reis** *E. 13A* (1915). Black on ochre underprint. Printer: CPM.			
	a. 1 handwritten signature.	30.00	150	500
	b. 2 printed signature.	30.00	150	500
56	**50 Mil Reis** *E. 14A* (1916). Black and multicolor. Woman seated with sword and flag at left, woman with wreath at right. Printer: ABNC.	Good	Fine	XF
	a. Issued note.	30.00	150	500
	s. Specimen.	—	Unc	1,000
57	**50 Mil Reis** *E. 15A* (1923). Blue on yellow-green. Woman seated with scarf at center. Printer: CdM.	150	1,750	3,750

		Good	Fine	XF
58	**50 Mil Reis** *E. 16A* (1925). Blue on multicolor underprint. Pres. A da Silva Bernardes at center. Printer: ABNC.			
	a. Issued note.	20.00	100	400
	s. Specimen.	—	Unc	500
59	**50 Mil Reis** *E. 17A* (1936). Violet. Portrait J. Xavier da Silveira, Jr. at left. Printer: W&S.	15.00	50.00	300
60	**100 Mil Reis** *E. 6A* (1892). Black on multicolor underprint. Street scene with buildings at left, ship at right, woman at center. Letters A-D. Printer: ABNC.	50.00	300	900
61	**100 Mil Reis** *E. 7A* (1897). Black on multicolor underprint. Woman seated with Cupid at right. Printer: ABNC.	45.00	250	750
62	**100 Mil Reis** Blue on ochre underprint. Woman with sickle and Cupid at left. Letters A-D. Printer: BWC. Without *Estampa* (1901).	50.00	350	1,200
62A	**100 Mil Reis** Blue and pink. Liberty with stars at left. Printer: BWC. Without *Estampa E.8A* (1901). PC: Tan. BC: Brown.	75.00	750	1,500

		Good	Fine	XF
63	**100 Mil Reis** *E. 9A* (1904). Blue on yellow underprint. Woman seated with two children reading at center. Printer: George Duval.	60.00	600	1,300
64	**100 Mil Reis** *E. 10A* (1907). Carmine on ochre underprint. Woman in circle at lower left.	50.00	500	1,200
65	**100 Mil Reis** *E. 11A* (1909). Black on multicolor underprint. Woman seated with child at left. Printer: ABNC.	Good	Fine	XF
	a. Issued note.	50.00	500	1,200
	s. Specimen.	—	Unc	2,500
66	**100 Mil Reis** *E. 12A* (1912). Black on multicolor underprint. Woman seated with wreath at left. Printer: ABNC.	Good	Fine	XF
	a. Issued note.	50.00	400	1,000
	s. Specimen.	—	Unc	2,000
67	**100 Mil Reis** *E. 13A* (1915). Green underprint. Printer: CPM.	50.00	300	750

		Good	Fine	XF
68	**100 Mil Reis** *E. 14A* (1919). Blue on multicolor underprint. Portrait A. Augusto Moreira Pena at center. Printer: ABNC.			
	a. Issued note.	50.00	250	700
	s. Specimen.	—	Unc	1,250
69	**100 Mil Reis** *E. 15A* (1924). Sepia on ochre underprint. Portrait R. Barbosa at center. Printer: CdM.	50.00	650	1,400

		Good	Fine	XF
70	**100 Mil Reis** *E. 16A* (1925). Blue on multicolor underprint. Portrait A. Augusto Moreira Pena at center. Printer: ABNC.			
	a. *BRAZIL*. 1 handwritten signature.	15.00	100	350
	b. *BRAZIL*. 2 printed signature.	25.00	200	500
	c. *BRASIL; Estampa* and serial # together, handwritten signature.	12.50	125	400
	d. *BRASIL; Estampa* and serial # separated, handwritten signature.	12.50	125	400
	s1. As a, c, d. Specimen.	—	Unc	750
	s2. As b. Specimen.	—	Unc	1,250

No.	Denomination	Good	Fine	XF
71	**100 Mil Reis**	Good	Fine	XF
	E. 17A (1936). Dark blue on multicolor underprint. Portrait A. Santos Dumont at right. Printer: W&S.	12.50	75.00	350
72	**200 Mil Reis**	Good	Fine	XF
	E. 7A (1892). Black on multicolor underprint. Woman seated at left and at right, helmsman at center. Letters A-C. Printer: ABNC.	75.00	750	1,600
73	**200 Mil Reis**	Good	Fine	XF
	E. 8A (1897). Black on bicolored underprint. Woman with child at right. Letters A-D. Printer: ABNC.			
	a. Issued note.	75.00	750	1,600
	s. Specimen.	—	Unc	3,500
74	**200 Mil Reis**	Good	Fine	XF
	(1901). Violet on ochre underprint. Woman seated with child at left, woman at center. Printer: BWC. Without *Estampa E.9A.*	60.00	750	1,500

No.	Denomination	Good	Fine	XF
75	**200 Mil Reis**	Good	Fine	XF
	E. 10A (1905). Blue on yellow underprint. Ship and coastline at center, flanked by two women. Printer: George Duval and Emile Grosbie.	60.00	750	1,500
76	**200 Mil Reis**	Good	Fine	XF
	E. 11A (1908). Black on multicolor underprint. Woman and child reading at center. Printer: ABNC.			
	a. Issued note.	50.00	500	1,000
	s. Specimen.	—	Unc	2,000
77	**200 Mil Reis**	Good	Fine	XF
	E. 12A (1911). Black on multicolor underprint. Two women seated at right. Printer: ABNC.			
	a. Issued note.	60.00	600	1,200
	s. Specimen.	—	Unc	2,000
78	**200 Mil Reis**	Good	Fine	XF
	E. 13A (1916). Black on ochre underprint. Back: Building. Plate modifications. Printer: CPM			
	a. 1 handwritten signature.	60.00	600	1,200
	b. 2 printed signature.	60.00	600	1,200
79	**200 Mil Reis**	Good	Fine	XF
	E. 14A (1919). Blue on multicolor underprint. Portrait P. Jose de Moraes e Barros at center. Printer: ABNC.			
	a. Issued note.	50.00	325	600
	s. Specimen.	—	Unc	1,100
80	**200 Mil Reis**	Good	Fine	XF
	E. 15A (1922). Sepia on ochre underprint. Woman seated at center. Printer: CdM.	50.00	600	1,450

No.	Denomination	Good	Fine	XF
81	**200 Mil Reis**	Good	Fine	XF
	E. 16A (1925). Blue on multicolor underprint. Portrait P. Jose de Moraes e Barros at center. Back: Building at center. BC: Brown. Printer: ABNC.			
	a. *BRAZIL*. 1 handwritten signature.	15.00	150	400
	b. *BRASIL; Estampa* and serial # together.	10.00	125	350
	c. *BRASIL; Estampa* and serial # separated.	10.00	125	350
	s1. As a. Specimen.	—	Unc	600
	s2. As b, c. Specimen.	—	Unc	800

No.	Denomination	Good	Fine	XF
82	**200 Mil Reis**	Good	Fine	XF
	E. 17A (1936). Red-brown on multicolor underprint. J. Saldanha Marinho at right. Printer: W&S.	10.00	100	250

No.	Denomination	Good	Fine	XF
83	**500 Mil Reis**	Good	Fine	XF
	E. 6A (1897). Black on multicolor underprint. Woman seated at center flanked by women in circles. Letters A-C. Printer: ABNC.			
	a. Issued note.	125	1,250	2,500
	s. Specimen.	—	Unc	6,000
84	**500 Mil Reis**	Good	Fine	XF
	Without *Estampa E.7A* (1901). Green on ochre underprint. Woman with distaff at left, woman at right. Printer: BWC.	125	1,250	2,500
85	**500 Mil Reis**	Good	Fine	XF
	E. 8A (1904). Red. Woman with child at left and right.	125	1,250	2,500
86	**500 Mil Reis**	Good	Fine	XF
	E. 9A (1908). Black on multicolor underprint. Woman with trumpet and sword at left, woman with wreath and palm branch at right. Printer: ABNC.			
	a. Issued note.	125	1,250	2,500
	s. Specimen.	—	Unc	5,500

No.	Denomination	Good	Fine	XF
87	**500 Mil Reis**	Good	Fine	XF
	E. 10A (1911). Black multicolor underprint. Woman with wreath at center flanked by Cupids. Printer: ABNC.			
	a. Issued note.	60.00	275	550
	s. Specimen.	—	Unc	1,250
88	**500 Mil Reis**	Good	Fine	XF
	E. 11A (1917). Black on multicolor underprint. Back: Building. Printer: CPM.	125	1,250	2,500

		Good	Fine	XF
89	**500 Mil Reis**	**Good**	**Fine**	**XF**
	E. 12A (1919). Blue on multicolor underprint. Portrait J. Bonifacio de Andrade e Silva at center. Printer: ABNC.			
	a. Issued note.	60.00	350	1,000
	s. Specimen.	—	Unc	1,500
90	**500 Mil Reis**	**Good**	**Fine**	**XF**
	E. 13A (1924). Red. Man seated at center with train in background. Printer: CdM.	150	1,750	4,000

		Good	Fine	XF
91	**500 Mil Reis**	**Good**	**Fine**	**XF**
	E. 14A (1925). Blue on multicolor underprint. J. Bonifacio de Andrade e Silva at center. Like #89. Printer: ABNC.			
	a. *BRAZIL*. 1 Handwritten signature.	40.00	300	750
	b. *BRAZIL*. 2 Printed signature.	45.00	325	850
	s1. As a. Specimen.	—	Unc	1,250
	s2. As b. Specimen.	—	Unc	2,500

		Good	Fine	XF
92	**500 Mil Reis**	**Good**	**Fine**	**XF**
	E. 15A (1931). Blue on multicolor underprint. M. Peixoto at center. Printer: ABNC.			
	a. *BRAZIL*. 1 handwritten signature.	12.50	60.00	500
	b. *BRAZIL*. 2 printed signature.	12.50	60.00	400
	c. *BRASIL; Estampa* and serial # together. Handwritten signature.	10.00	40.00	350
	d. *BRASIL; Estampa* and serial # separated. Handwritten signature.	10.00	40.00	350
	s1. As a. Specimen.	—	Unc	800
	s2. As b, c. Specimen.	—	Unc	500
93	**1000 Mil Reis**	**Good**	**Fine**	**XF**
	E. 1A (1921). Blue on yellow underprint. Woman seated with sword and Mercury symbol at left. Printer: CdM.	125	1,500	3,250

Caixa de Conversão

Closed down in 1920 and later absorbed by the Caixa de Estabilizacão.

1906, Estampa 1

		Good	Fine	XF
94	**10 Mil Reis**	**Good**	**Fine**	**XF**
	6.12.1906. Brown. Woman with shield at left, portrait A. Pena at center. Back: Bank building at center. Printer: W&S.	10.00	30.00	100

Note: #94 is very often encountered as a lithographic counterfeit.

		Good	Fine	XF
95	**20 Mil Reis**	**Good**	**Fine**	**XF**
	6.12.1906. Blue. Portrait A. Pena at left, bank building at right. Back: Steam train at center. Printer: W&S.	20.00	50.00	150
96	**50 Mil Reis**	**Good**	**Fine**	**XF**
	6.12.1906. Brown and pink. Portrait A. Pena at left, bank building at center. Back: Three allegorical women at center. Printer: W&S.	50.00	200	700
97	**100 Mil Reis**	**Good**	**Fine**	**XF**
	6.12.1906. Green and yellow. Portrait A. Pena at center, bank building at right. Letters A-C. Back: Trees at center. Printer: W&S.	50.00	250	750

		Good	Fine	XF
98	**200 Mil Reis**	**Good**	**Fine**	**XF**
	6.12.1906. Black, yellow and red. Portrait A. Pena at right, bank building at center. Letters A-D. Back: Allegorical women with cows, sheaves and farm implements. Printer: W&S.	75.00	300	1,000

1906, Estampa 1a

		Good	Fine	XF
99	**500 Mil Reis**	**Good**	**Fine**	**XF**
	6.12.1906. Green. Man standing at left, portrait A. Pena at right. Back: Bank at lower center. Printer: JEZ.			
	a. Issued note.	100	450	1,250
	s. Specimen.	—	Unc	1,000
100	**1 Conto De Reis = 1000 Mil Reis**	**Good**	**Fine**	**XF**
	6.12.1906. Brown. Winged allegorical male at left, portrait A. Pena at right. Back: Bank at lower center. Printer: JEZ.	400	1,750	3,500

1910, Estampa 2

No.	Denomination	Good	Fine	XF
101	**10 Mil Reis**	Good	Fine	XF
	31.12.1910. *E. 2.* Blue. Printer: CPM.	35.00	250	750
102	**50 Mil Reis**	Good	Fine	XF
	31.12.1910. *E. 2A.* Brown. Building at center. BC: Purple. Printer: CPM.	40.00	400	800

Provisional Issue

Black *NA CAIXA DE CONVERSAO* on modified plates or overprint on Thesauro Nacional notes.

No.	Denomination	Good	Fine	XF
102A	**10 Mil Reis**	Good	Fine	XF
	E. 1A. L. 1906. Carmine on yellow underprint. Woman with boy at right. Modified plate of #31. New black text of *NA CAIXA DE CONVERSAO.*	40.00	650	1,500
102C	**20 Mil Reis**	Good	Fine	XF
	E. 1A. L. 1906. Brown on ochre underprint. Boy seated at left and at right, woman in circle at lower left. Modified plate of #42. New black text of *NA CAIXA DE CONVERSAO.*	40.00	650	1,500
102E	**100 Mil Reis**	Good	Fine	XF
	E. 10A. L. 1906. Carmine on ochre underprint. Woman in circle at lower left.	40.00	850	1,750
102F	**500 Mil Reis**	Good	Fine	XF
	E. 8A. L. 1906. Red. Woman with child at left and right.	125	1,750	4,000

Caixa de Estabilizacao, Valor Recebido em Ouro

Estampa 1A

No.	Denomination	Good	Fine	XF
103	**10 Mil Reis**	Good	Fine	XF
	18.12.1926. Black on multicolor guilloche. Woman at center. ("Reverie"). 6 signature varieties. Back: Coastal scenery. BC: Dark brown. Printer: ABNC.			
	a. Issued note.	25.00	100	425
	s. Specimen.	—	Unc	500
104	**20 Mil Reis**	Good	Fine	XF
	18.12.1926. Black on multicolor guilloche. Woman at center. ("Reverie"). 6 signature varieties. Back: City and trees at center. BC: Red. Printer: ABNC.			
	a. Issued note.	25.00	125	450
	s. Specimen.	—	Unc	500

No.	Denomination	Good	Fine	XF
105	**50 Mil Reis**	Good	Fine	XF
	18.12.1926. Black on multicolor guilloche. Woman at center. ("Reverie"). 6 signature varieties. Back: Cavalry charge at center. BC: Orange. Printer: ABNC.			
	a. Issued note.	50.00	300	1,000
	s. Specimen.	—	Unc	900
106	**100 Mil Reis**	Good	Fine	XF
	18.12.1926. Black on multicolor guilloche. Woman at center. ("Reverie"). 6 signature varieties. Back: Bank at center. BC: Green. Printer: ABNC.			
	a. Issued note.	50.00	275	900
	s. Specimen.	—	Unc	1,000
107	**200 Mil Reis**	Good	Fine	XF
	18.12.1926. Black on multicolor guilloche. Woman at center. ("Reverie"). 6 signature varieties. Back: Cavalry and infantry battle scene at center. BC: Blue-black. Printer: ABNC.			
	a. Issued note.	60.00	300	950
	s. Specimen.	—	Unc	1,500
108	**500 Mil Reis**	Good	Fine	XF
	18.12.1926. Black on multicolor guilloche. Woman at center. ("Reverie"). 6 signature varieties. Back: Naval battle at center. BC: Blue. Printer: ABNC.			
	a. Issued note.	110	750	2,000
	s. Specimen.	—	Unc	3,500
109	**1 Conto De Reis = 1000 Mil Reis**	Good	Fine	XF
	18.12.1926. Black on multicolor guilloche. Woman at center. ("Reverie"). 6 signature varieties. Back: Mission scene. BC: Purple. Printer: ABNC.			
	a. Issued note.	160	1,000	3,000
	s. Specimen.	—	Unc	5,000

1926 Issue

#109A-109F Black *A CAIXA DE ESTABILISACAO...* overprint within rectangular frame on Thesouro Nacional notes. 2 printed signature at lower part of note.

No.	Denomination	Good	Fine	XF
109A	**10 Mil Reis**	Good	Fine	XF
	E. 17A. Blue on multicolor underprint. Portrait Pres. Manuel Ferraz de Campos Salles at center. Series 10.	10.00	65.00	200
109B	**20 Mil Reis**	Good	Fine	XF
	E. 16A. Blue on multicolor underprint. First Pres. Manuel Deodoro do Fonseca at center. Series 10. Back: Allegorical woman at center. BC:Orange.	10.00	75.00	225

No.	Denomination	Good	Fine	XF
109C	**50 Mil Reis**	Good	Fine	XF
	E. 16A. Blue on multicolor underprint. Pres. A da Silva Bernardes at center. Series 9, 10.	10.00	65.00	200
109D	**100 Mil Reis**	Good	Fine	XF
	E. 16A. Blue on multicolor underprint. Portrait A. Augusto Moreira Pena at center. Series 10.	17.50	125	300
109E	**200 Mil Reis**	Good	Fine	XF
	E. 16A. Blue on multicolor underprint. Portrait P. Jose de Moraes e Barros at center. Series 10. Back: Building at center. BC: Brown.	15.00	100	275
109F	**500 Mil Reis**	Good	Fine	XF
	E. 14A. Blue on multicolor underprint. J. Bonifacio de Andrade e Silva at center. Series 5.	100	1,250	2,250

Banco do Brasil

1923 Provisional Issue

No.	Denomination	Good	Fine	XF
110	**500 Mil Reis**	Good	Fine	XF
	8.1.1923. Blue on yellow underprint. Man seated with train in background. BC: Brown. Printer: CdM. 100	1,700	3,500	
110A	**1000 Mil Reis = 1 Conto de Reis**	Good	Fine	XF
	E. 1A. ND. Carmine. Woman seated with sword and Mercury symbol at left.	100	2,000	4,000

Lei N. 4635 a de 8 de Janeriode 1923

#110B-113, 115, 117 with 1 hand signature. All others with 2 printed signatures.

No.	Denomination	Good	Fine	XF
110B	**1 Mil Reis**	Good	Fine	XF
	L. 1923. E. 1A. Black on green underprint. Portrait C. Salles at center. Series #1-278. 1 hand signature. Back: Arms at center. BC: Green on pink underprint. Printer: ABNC.			
	a. Issued note.	1.00	5.00	12.50
	s. Specimen.	—	Unc	125

Note: #110B with series #279-500 were issued in 1944 as Cruzeiro notes. See #131A.

111	**2 Mil Reis**	Good	Fine	XF
	L. 1923. E. 1A. Black on multicolor underprint. Portrait P. de Moraes at right. 1 hand signature. Back: Arms. Printer: ABNC.			
	a. Issued note.	3.00	10.00	20.00
	s. Specimen.	—	Unc	125

112	**5 Mil Reis**	Good	Fine	XF
	L. 1923. E. 1A. Black on yellow-green underprint. Portrait B. do Rio Branco at left. 1 hand signature. Back: Arms at center. BC: Red and multicolor. Printer: ABNC.			
	a. Issued note.	5.00	40.00	250
	s. Specimen.	—	Unc	125
113	**5 Mil Reis**	Good	Fine	XF
	L. 1923. E. 2A. Black on yellow-green underprint. Portrait B. do Rio Branco at left. Like #112 but with different guilloche. 1 hand signature. Back: Arms. Printer: ABNC.			
	a. Issued note.	5.00	40.00	250
	p1. Proof. Uniface face on card.	—	Unc	—
	p2. Proof. Uniface back on card.	—	Unc	—
	s. Specimen.	—	Unc	150

114	**10 Mil Reis**	Good	Fine	XF
	L. 1923. E. 1A. Black on multicolor underprint. Portrait S. Vidal at center. 2 printed signatures. Back: Building at center. Printer: ABNC.			
	a. Issued note.	5.00	40.00	250
	s. Specimen.	—	Unc	200

115	**10 Mil Reis**	Good	Fine	XF
	L. 1923. E. 2A. Black on multicolor underprint. Portrait R. Alves at center. 1 hand signature. Back: Building at center. Printer: ABNC.			
	a. Issued note.	15.00	100	450
	s. Specimen.	—	Unc	200

116	**20 Mil Reis**	Good	Fine	XF
	L. 1923. E. 1A. Black on multicolor underprint. Portrait A. Bernardes at right. 2 printed signatures. Back: Monroe Palace at center. Printer: ABNC.			
	a. Issued note.	15.00	100	450
	p. Face proof.	—	Unc	125
	s. Specimen.	—	Unc	400
117	**20 Mil Reis**	Good	Fine	XF
	L. 1923. E. 2A. Black on multicolor underprint. Portrait A. Bernardes at right. Like #116. 1 hand signature. Back: Building at center. Printer: ABNC.			
	a. Issued note.	15.00	100	450
	s. Specimen.	—	Unc	450

118	**50 Mil Reis**	Good	Fine	XF
	L. 1923. E. 1A. Black on multicolor underprint. Portrait D. da Fonseca at left. 2 printed signatures. Back: Canal at center. Printer: ABNC.			
	a. Issued note.	25.00	150	450
	s. Specimen.	—	Unc	800

119	**50 Mil Reis**	Good	Fine	XF
	L. 1923. E. 2A. Black on multicolor underprint. Portrait M. de Olinda at left. 2 printed signatures. Back: Canal at center. Printer: ABNC.			
	a. Issued note.	25.00	150	450
	s. Specimen.	—	Unc	900

		Good	Fine	XF
120	**100 Mil Reis** *L. 1923. E. 1A.* Black on multicolor underprint. Portrait R. Feijo at center. 2 printed signatures. Back: Shoreline at right. Printer: ABNC.			
	a. Issued note.	35.00	275	650
	s. Specimen, punch hole cancelled. Red overprint: MODELO on both sides.	—	Unc	200
121	**200 Mil Reis** *L. 1923. E. 1A.* Black on multicolor underprint. Portrait Dom Pedro II at right. 2 printed signatures. Back: City and shoreline mountains behind at center. Printer: ABNC.	Good	Fine	XF
	a. Issued note.	35.00	275	650
	s. Specimen. Red overprint: MODELO twice on both sides. Punch hole cancelled.	—	Unc	400
122	**500 Mil Reis** *L. 1923. E. 1A.* Blue on yellow underprint. Man seated with locomotive in background. 2 printed signatures. Printer: CdM.	Good	Fine	XF
	a. Issued note.	100	750	1,500
	s. Specimen, punch hole cancelled. Blue overprint: MODELO on both sides.	—	Unc	1,250
122A	**500 Mil Reis** *L. 1923. E. 1A.* Black on multicolor underprint. Portrait J. Bonafacio at left. 2 printed signatures. Back: Deep orange. City and trees at center. Printer: ABNC. Specimen	—	Unc	2200

		Good	Fine	XF
123	**1000 Mil Reis = 1 Conto de Reis** *L. 1923. E. 1A.* Black on multicolor underprint. Portrait Dom Pedro I at center. 2 printed signatures. Back: Cavalry charge at center. Printer: ABNC.			
	a. Issued note.	100	750	1,500
	s. Specimen, punch hole cancelled. Red overprint: MODELO on both sides.	—	Unc	1,250

#124 Deleted. See #131A.

1942 Casa da Moeda Provisionallssue

#125-131 are 5-500 Mil Reis notes ovpt: *CASA DA MOEDA* and new Cruzeiro denominations in a blue rosette.

		Good	Fine	XF
125	**5 Cruzeiros on 5 Mil Reis** ND (1942). Dark blue on multicolor underprint. Portrait B. do Rio Branco (foreign minister) at center. Back: Three allegorical figures at center.	2.50	12.50	50.00
126	**10 Cruzeiros on 10 Mil Reis** ND (1942). Dark blue on multicolor underprint. Portrait Pres. Manuel Ferraz de Campos Salles at center.	4.00	25.00	85.00

		Good	Fine	XF
127	**20 Cruzeiros on 20 Mil Reis** ND (1942). Dark blue on multicolor underprint. First Pres. Manuel Deodoro do Fonseca at center. Back: Allegorical woman at center.	6.00	35.00	150

		Good	Fine	XF
128	**50 Cruzeiros on 50 Mil Reis** ND (1942). Violet on multicolor underprint. Portrait J. Xavier da Silveira, Jr. at left.	125	1,400	2,750

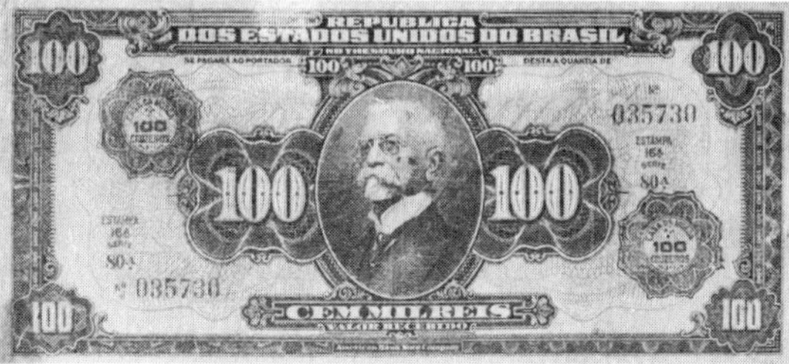

		Good	Fine	XF
129	**100 Cruzeiros on 100 Mil Reis** ND (1942). Dark blue on multicolor underprint. Portrait A. Augusto Moreira Pena at center.	20.00	100	400
130	**200 Cruzeiros on 200 Mil Reis** ND (1942). Dark blue on multicolor underprint. Portrait P. Jose de Moraes e Barros at center. Back: Building at center.	Good	Fine	XF
	a. overprint on #81b.	37.50	750	2,250
	b. overprint on #81c.	37.50	750	2,250
130A	**200 Cruzeiros on 200 Mil Reis** ND (1942). Red-brown on multicolor underprint. J. Saldanha Marinho at right.	—	—	—
131	**500 Cruzeiros on 500 Mil Reis** ND (1942). Dark blue on multicolor underprint. M. Peixoto at center.	Good	Fine	XF
	a. overprint on 92c.	25.00	400	850
	b. overprint on 92d.	20.00	150	400

1944 Emergency Issue

#131A, 1 Mil Reis of Banco do Brasil w/o ovpt. issued as 1 Cruzeiro.

		Good	Fine	XF
131A	**1 Mil Reis (Cruzeiro)** ND (1944). Black on green underprint. Portrait C. Salles at center. Like #110B but series #279-500. Back: Arms.	0.50	2.00	6.00

Tesouro Nacional, Valor Recebido
1943-1944, W/o Estampa (1A)

		VG	VF	UNC
132	**1 Cruzeiro** ND (1944). Blue on multicolor guilloches. Portrait Marquês de Tamandare at center. Series: #1-1000. Hand-signed. Back: Naval school at center. Printer: ABNC.			
	a. Issued note.	0.15	0.50	3.00
	s. Specimen.	—	—	75.00
133	**2 Cruzeiros** ND (1944). Blue on multicolor guilloches. Portrait Duque de Caxias at center. Series: #1-500. Hand-signed. Back: Military school at center. Printer: ABNC.	VG	VF	UNC
	a. Issued note.	0.20	0.75	4.00
	s. Specimen.	—	—	75.00
134	**5 Cruzeiros** ND (1943). Blue on multicolor guilloches. Portrait Barão do Rio Branco at center. Series: #1-500. Hand-signed. Back: *Amazonia* scene. Printer: ABNC.	VG	VF	UNC
	a. Issued note.	1.25	7.50	25.00
	s. Specimen.	—	—	125

		VG	VF	UNC
135	**10 Cruzeiros** ND (1943). Blue on multicolor guilloches. Portrait Getulio Vargas at center. Series: #1-330. Hand-signed. Back: Allegorical man with industrial implements at center. Printer: ABNC.			
	a. Issued note.	1.25	7.50	25.00
	s. Specimen.	—	—	125

		VG	VF	UNC
136	**20 Cruzeiros** ND (1943). Blue on multicolor guilloches. Portrait Deodoro da Fonseca at center. Series: #1-460. Hand-signed. Back: Allegory of the Republic at center. Printer: ABNC.			
	a. Issued note.	1.25	7.50	25.00
	s. Specimen.	—	—	125
137	**50 Cruzeiros** ND (1943). Blue on multicolor guilloches. Portrait Princesa Isabel at center. Series: #1-320. Hand-signed. Back: Allegory of Law at center. Printer: ABNC.	VG	VF	UNC
	a. Issued note.	2.50	10.00	45.00
	s. Specimen.	—	—	125
138	**100 Cruzeiros** ND (1943). Blue on multicolor guilloches. Dom Pedro II at center. Series: #1-235. Hand-signed. Back: Allegory of National Culture. Printer: ABNC.	VG	VF	UNC
	a. Issued note.	2.50	12.50	75.00
	s. Specimen.	—	—	150

		VG	VF	UNC
139	**200 Cruzeiros** ND (1943). Blue on multicolor guilloches. Portrait Dom Pedro I at center. Series: #1-320. Hand-signed. Back: Battle scene. Printer: ABNC.			
	a. Issued note.	4.00	15.00	100
	s. Specimen.	—	—	150
140	**500 Cruzeiros** ND (1943). Blue on multicolor guilloches. Portrait Joao VI at center. Series #1-160. Hand-signed. Back: Maritime allegory with ships at center. Printer: ABNC.	VG	VF	UNC
	a. Issued note.	10.00	100	375
	s. Specimen.	—	—	400
141	**1000 Cruzeiros** ND (1943). Blue on multicolor guilloches. Portrait Pedro Alvares Cabral at center. Series: #1-230. Hand-signed. Back: First Mass scene at center. Printer: ABNC.	VG	VF	UNC
	a. Issued note.	7.50	50.00	200
	s. Specimen.	—	—	250

1949-1950, Estampa 2A

		VG	VF	UNC
142	**5 Cruzeiros** ND (1950). Brown on multicolor underprint. Portrait B. do Rio Branco at center. Series: #1-500. Hand-signed. Back: *Amazonia* scene. Printer: TDLR.	0.50	2.00	10.00
143	**10 Cruzeiros** ND (1950). Green on multicolor underprint. Portrait G.Vargas at center. Series: #1-435. Hand-signed. Back: Allegorical man with industrial implements at center. Printer: TDLR.	0.50	2.50	12.50
144	**20 Cruzeiros** ND (1950). Red-brown on multicolor underprint. Portrait D. da Fonseca at center. Series: #1-370. Hand-signed. Back: Allegory of the Republic at center. Printer: TDLR.	1.25	5.00	25.00

145 50 Cruzeiros

ND (1949). Purple on multicolor underprint. Portrait Princesa Isabel at center. Series: #1-115. Hand-signed. Back: Allegory of Law at center. Printer: TDLR.

	VG	VF	UNC
	4.50	20.00	135

146 100 Cruzeiros

ND (1949). Red on multicolor underprint. Portrait Dom Pedro II at center. Series #1-115. Hand-signed. Back: Allegory of National Culture. Printer: TDLR.

	VG	VF	UNC
	6.00	50.00	175

147 200 Cruzeiros

ND (1949). Green. Portrait Dom Pedro I at center. Series: #1-30. Hand-signed. Back: Battle scene. Printer: TDLR.

	VG	VF	UNC
	37.50	300	900

148 500 Cruzeiros

ND (1949). Dark green. Portrait Joao VI at center. Series: #1-120. Hand-signed. Back: Maritime allegory with ships at center. Printer: TDLR.

	VG	VF	UNC
	12.50	100	300

149 1000 Cruzeiros

ND (1949). Orange. Portrait P. Alvares Cabral at center. Series: #1-90. Hand-signed. Back: First Mass scene at center. Printer: TDLR.

	VG	VF	UNC
	17.50	250	900

1953-1959 W/o Estampa 1A

150 1 Cruzeiro

ND (1954-1958). Blue on multicolor guilloches. Portrait M. de Tamandare at center. Like #132. 2 printed signatures. Back: Naval school at center. Printer: ABNC.

	VG	VF	UNC
a. Signature 2. Series #1001-1800.	0.05	0.20	1.00
b. Signature 3. Series #1801-2700.	0.05	0.20	1.00
c. Signature 5. Series #2701-3450.	0.05	0.20	1.00
d. Signature 6. Series #3451-3690.	0.05	0.20	1.00
s. Specimen.	—	—	75.00

151 2 Cruzeiros

ND (1954-1958). Blue on multicolor guilloches. Portrait D. de Caxias at center. Like #133. 2 printed signatures. Back: Military school at center. Printer: ABNC.

	VG	VF	UNC
a. Signature 2. Series #501-900.	0.05	0.20	1.00
b. Signature 6. Series #901-1135.	0.05	0.20	1.00
s. Specimen.	—	—	75.00

152 50 Cruzeiros

ND (1956-1959). Blue on multicolor guilloches. Portrait Princesa Isabel at center. Like #137. 2 printed signatures. Back: Allegory of Law at center. Printer: ABNC.

	VG	VF	UNC
a. Signature 5. Series #321-470.	1.00	4.00	20.00
b. Signature 6. Series #471-620.	1.00	4.00	20.00
c. Signature 7. Series #621-720.	1.00	5.00	25.00
s. Specimen.	—	—	100

153 100 Cruzeiros

ND (1955-1959). Blue on multicolor guilloches. Portrait Dom Pedro II at center. Like #138. 2 printed signatures. Back: Allegory of National Culture. Printer: ABNC.

	VG	VF	UNC
a. Signature 3. Series #236-435.	1.00	5.00	22.50
b. Signature 5. Series #436-535.	1.00	5.00	25.00
c. Signature 6. Series #536-660.	1.00	5.00	22.50
d. Signature 7. Series #661-760.	1.50	7.00	35.00
s. Specimen.	—	—	200

154 200 Cruzeiros

ND (1955-1959). Blue on multicolor guilloches. Portrait Dom Pedro I at center. Like #139. 2 printed signatures. Back: Battle scene at center. Printer: ABNC.

	VG	VF	UNC
a. Signature 3. Series #321-520.	1.25	6.00	30.00
b. Signature 6. Series #521-620.	2.00	10.00	50.00
c. Signature 7. Series #621-670.	7.00	35.00	175
s1. As a, b. Specimen.	—	—	125
s2. As c. Specimen.	—	—	350

155 500 Cruzeiros

ND (1953). Blue on multicolor guilloches. Portrait Joao VI at center. Like #140. Signature 1. Series #161-260. 2 printed signatures. Back: Maritime allegory with ships at center. Printer: ABNC.

	VG	VF	UNC
a. Issued note.	9.00	45.00	225
s. Specimen.	—	—	400

156 1000 Cruzeiros

ND (1953-1959). Blue on multicolor guilloches. Portrait P. Alvares Cabral at center. Like #141. 2 printed signatures. Back: Scene of first mass at center. Printer: ABNC.

	VG	VF	UNC
a. Signature 1. Series #231-330.	9.00	45.00	225
b. Signature 3. Series #331-630.	2.00	12.50	65.00
c. Signature 4. Series #631-930.	2.00	12.50	55.00
d. Signature 6. Series #931-1000.	3.00	15.00	75.00
e. Signature 7. Series #1081-1330.	2.50	12.50	60.00
s1. As a. Specimen.	—	—	400
s2. As b-e. Specimen.	—	—	200

1953-1960 Estampa 2A

157 2 Cruzeiros

ND (1955). Turquoise on multicolor underprint. Portrait D. de Caxias at center. Like #133. Signature 3. Series #1-230. 2 printed signatures. Back: Military school at center. Printer: TDLR.

	VG	VF	UNC
	0.05	0.20	1.00

157A 2 Cruzeiros

ND (1956-1958). Turquoise on multicolor underprint. Portrait D. de Caxias at center. Like #157. 2 printed signatures. Back: Military school at center. Printer: TDLR.

	VG	VF	UNC
a. Signature 3. Series #231-600.	0.05	0.20	1.00
b. Signature 5. Series #601-900.	0.05	0.20	1.00
c. Signature 6. Series #901-1045.	0.05	0.20	1.50

158 5 Cruzeiros

ND (1953-1959). Brown on multicolor underprint. Portrait B. do Rio Branco at center. 2 printed signatures. Back: *Amazonia* scene. Printer: TDLR.

	VG	VF	UNC
a. Signature 1. Series #501-1000.	0.10	0.50	3.00
b. Signature 2. Series #1001-1300.	0.10	0.50	3.00
c. Signature 5. Series #1301-1800.	0.10	0.50	2.50
d. Signature 6. Series #1801-2050.	0.10	0.50	3.00
e. Signature 7. Series #2051-2301	0.10	0.50	2.50

159 10 Cruzeiros

ND (1953-1960). Green on multicolor underprint. Portrait G. Vargas at center. Like #135. 2 printed signatures. Back: Allegorical man with industrial implements at center. Printer: TDLR.

	VG	VF	UNC
a. Signature 1. Series #436-735.	0.10	0.50	2.50
b. Signature 2. Series #736-1235.	0.10	0.40	2.00
c. Signature 5. Series #1236-1435.	0.10	0.40	2.00
d. Signature 6. Series #1436-1685.	0.10	0.40	2.00
e. Signature 7. Series #1686-1885.	0.10	0.50	2.50
f. Signature 8. Series #1886-2355.	0.05	0.20	1.00

160 20 Cruzeiros

ND (1955-1961). Red-brown on multicolor underprint. Portrait D. da Fonseca at center. Like #136. 2 printed signatures. Back: Allegory of the Republic at center. Printer: TDLR.

	VG	VF	UNC
a. Signature 3. Series #371-870.	0.10	0.50	3.00
b. Signature 6. Series #871-1175.	0.15	0.75	4.00
c. Signature 7. Series #1176-1225.	0.50	4.00	20.00
d. Signature 8. Series #1226-1575.	0.10	0.50	3.00

161 50 Cruzeiros

ND (1954-1961). Purple on multicolor underprint. Portrait Princesa Isabel at center. Like #137. 2 printed signatures. Printer: TDLR.

	VG	VF	UNC
a. Signature 2. Series #116-215.	2.00	10.00	50.00
b. Signature 3. Series #216-415.	0.25	1.50	7.50
c. Signature 8. Series #416-585.	0.25	1.50	7.50

162 100 Cruzeiros

	VG	VF	UNC
ND (1960). Red on multicolor underprint. Portrait Dom Pedro II at center. Signature 8. Series #116-215. Like #138. 2 printed signatures. Back: Allegory of National Culture. Printer: TDLR.	1.50	2.50	12.50

163 200 Cruzeiros

	VG	VF	UNC
ND (1960). Olive on multicolor underprint. Portrait Dom Pedro I at center. Signature 8. Series #31-110. Like #139. 2 printed signatures. Back: Battle scene at center. Printer: TDLR.	3.00	7.50	20.00

164 500 Cruzeiros

ND (1955-1960). Dark olive on multicolor underprint. Portrait Joao VI at center. Like #140. 2 printed signatures. Back: Maritime allegory with ships at center. Printer: TDLR.

	VG	VF	UNC
a. 3. #121-420.	1.50	6.50	32.50
b. 4. #421-720.	1.00	5.00	25.00
c. 6. #721-770.	3.50	17.50	85.00
d. 8. #771-1300.	1.00	5.00	15.00

165 1000 Cruzeiros

	VG	VF	UNC
ND (1960). Orange on multicolor underprint. Portrait P. Alvares Cabral at center. Signature 8. Series #91-790. 2 printed signatures. Back: Scene of first mass at center. Printer: TDLR.	0.50	2.50	12.50

Note: for similar issues but with *VALOR LEGAL* inscription, see listings in Volume 3.

The British Caribbean Territories (Eastern Group), a currency board formed in 1950, comprised the British West Indies territories of Trinidad and Tobago; Barbados; the Leeward Islands of Anguilla, St. Christopher, Nevis and Antigua; the Windward Islands of St. Lucia, Dominica, St. Vincent and Grenada; British Guiana and the British Virgin Islands. As time progressed, the members of this Eastern Group varied. For later issues see East Caribbean States listings in Volume 3, Modern Issues.

RULERS:
British

MONETARY SYSTEM:
1 Dollar = 100 Cents

BRITISH ADMINISTRATION

British Caribbean Territories, Eastern Group

1950-1951 Issue

No.	Description	VG	VF	UNC
1	**1 Dollar** 28.11.1950; 1.9.1951. Red on multicolor underprint. Map at lower left, portrait of King George VI at right. Signature varieties. Back: Arms of the various territories. Printer: BWC.	3.50	50.00	325
2	**2 Dollars** 28.11.1950; 1.9.1951. Blue on multicolor underprint. Map at lower left, portrait of King George VI at right. Signature varieties. Back: Arms of the various territories. Printer: BWC.	15.00	125	700

No.	Description	VG	VF	UNC
3	**5 Dollars** 28.11.1950; 1.9.1951. Green on multicolor underprint. Map at lower left, portrait of King George VI at right. Signature varieties. Back: Arms of the various territories. Printer: BWC.	12.50	100	650
4	**10 Dollars** 28.11.1950; 1.9.1951. Light brown on multicolor underprint. Map at lower left, portrait of King George VI at right. Signature varieties. Back: Arms of the various territories. Printer: BWC.	40.00	300	—
5	**20 Dollars** 28.11.1950; 1.9.1951. Purple on multicolor underprint. Map at lower left, portrait of King George VI at right. Signature varieties. Back: Arms of the various territories. Printer: BWC.	60.00	400	—
6	**100 Dollars** 28.11.1950. Black on multicolor underprint. Map at lower left, portrait of King George VI at right. Signature varieties. Back: Arms of the various territories. Printer: BWC.	400	1,500	—

1953 Issue

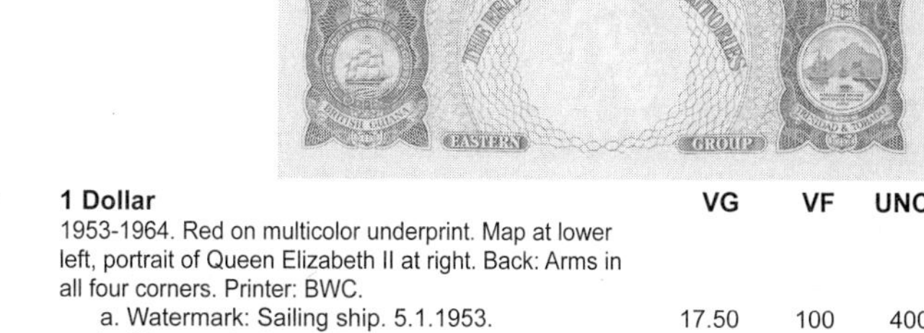

No.	Description	VG	VF	UNC
7	**1 Dollar** 1953-1964. Red on multicolor underprint. Map at lower left, portrait of Queen Elizabeth II at right. Back: Arms in all four corners. Printer: BWC.			
	a. Watermark: Sailing ship. 5.1.1953.	17.50	100	400
	b. Watermark: Queen Elizabeth II. 1.3.1954-2.1.1957.	10.00	40.00	275
	c. 2.1.1958-2.1.1964.	10.00	40.00	275

No.	Description	VG	VF	UNC
8	**2 Dollars** 1953-1964. Blue on multicolor underprint. Map at lower left, portrait of Queen Elizabeth II at right. Back: Arms in all four corners. Printer: BWC.			
	a. Watermark: Sailing ship. 5.1.1953.	100	550	1,750
	b. Watermark: Queen Elizabeth II. 1.3.1954-1.7.1960.	20.00	100	700
	c. 2.1.1961-2.1.1964.	20.00	100	700

No.	Description	VG	VF	UNC
9	**5 Dollars** 1953-1964. Green on multicolor underprint. Map at lower left, portrait of Queen Elizabeth II at right. Back: Arms in all four corners. Printer: BWC.			
	a. Watermark: Sailing ship. 5.1.1953.	50.00	300	1,250
	b. Watermark: Queen Elizabeth II. 3.1.1955-2.1.1959.	40.00	125	1,000
	c. 2.1.1961-2.1.1964.	35.00	100	900
	s. As b. Specimen. Perforated: *SPECIMEN*.	—	—	750
10	**10 Dollars** 1953-1964. Brown on multicolor underprint. Map at lower left, portrait of Queen Elizabeth II at right. Back: Arms in all four corners. Printer: BWC.			
	a. Watermark: Sailing ship. 5.1.1953.	60.00	400	—
	b. Watermark: Queen Elizabeth II. 3.1.1955-2.1.1959.	40.00	250	2,000
	c. 2.1.1961; 2.1.1962; 2.1.1964.	37.50	200	1,800
11	**20 Dollars** 1953-1964. Purple on multicolor underprint. Map at lower left, portrait of Queen Elizabeth II at right. Back: Arms in all four corners. Printer: BWC.			
	a. Watermark: Sailing ship. 5.1.1953.	90.00	600	—
	b. Watermark: Queen Elizabeth II. 2.1.1957-2.1.1964.	45.00	300	—
12	**100 Dollars** 1953-1963. Black on multicolor underprint. Map at lower left, portrait of Queen Elizabeth II at right. Back: Arms in all four corners. Printer: BWC.			
	a. Watermark: Sailing ship. 5.1.1953.	500	6,000	—
	b. Watermark: Queen Elizabeth II. 1.3.1954.	300	4,000	—
	c. 2.1.1957.	350	8,800	—
	d. 2.1.1963.	300	4,000	—
	s. As b. Specimen.	—	—	2,500

BRITISH GUIANA (Guyana)

British Guiana was situated on the northeast coast of South America, had an area of 83,000 sq. mi. (214,969 sq. km.). Capital: Georgetown. Now called Guyana, it formerly included present-day Surinam, French Guiana, and parts of Brazil and Venezuela. It was sighted by Columbus in 1498. The first European settlement was made late in the 16th century by the Dutch. For the next 150 years, possession alternated between the Dutch and the British, with a short interval of French control. The British exercised *de facto* control after 1796, although the area, which included the Dutch colonies of Essequebo, Demerary and Berbice, was not ceded to them until 1814. From 1803 to 1831, Essequebo and Demerary were administered separately from Berbice. The three colonies were united in the British Crown Colony of British Guiana in 1831. British Guiana won internal self-government in 1952 and full independence, under the traditional name of Guyana, on May 26, 1966. Notes of the British Caribbean Currency Board circulated from 1950-1965. For additional issues see Guyana in Modern Issues.

RULERS:

British to 1966

MONETARY SYSTEM:

1 Joe = 22 Guilders to 1836
1 Dollar = 4 Shillings 2 Pence, 1837-1965

DEMERARY AND ESSEQUEBO

Colonies of Demerary and Essequebo

1830s First Issue

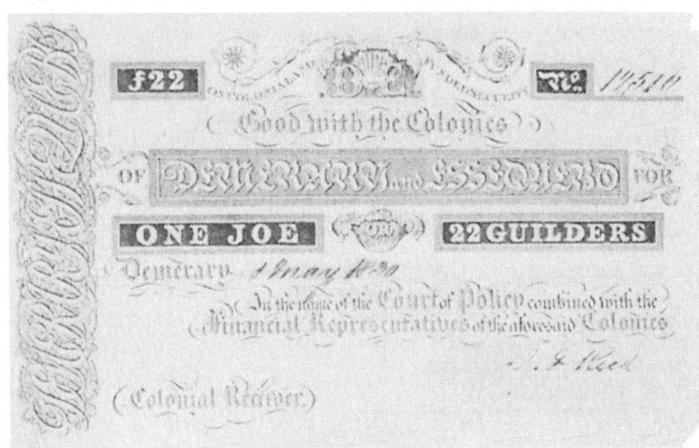

		Good	Fine	XF
A1	**1 Joe or 22 Guilders** 1.5.1830. Black. Ornate D-E at upper center. (Not issued).	—	250	750
A4	**10 Joes or 220 Guilders** ND (ca. 1830s). Reddish brown. Ornate D-E at upper center. (Not issued).	—	—	750

1830s Second Issue

		Good	Fine	XF
B1	**1 Joe of 22 Guilders** ND (1830s). Black. Woman with anchor at upper left. With or without counterfoil. (Not issued).	—	250	750
B2	**2 Joes of 22 Guilders Each** ND (1830s). Black. Woman with anchor at upper left. With or without counterfoil. (Not issued).	—	—	—
B3	**3 Joes of 22 Guilders Each** ND (1830s). Black. Woman with anchor at upper left. With or without counterfoil. (Not issued).	—	300	900
B4	**10 Joes of 22 Guilders Each** ND (1830s). Black. Woman with anchor at upper left. With or without counterfoil. (Not issued).	—	300	900

Color Abbreviation Guide

New to the *Standard Catalog of ® World Paper Money* are the following abbreviations related to color references:

BC: Back color
PC: Paper color

BRITISH ADMINISTRATION

Government of British Guiana

1916-1920 Issue

		Good	Fine	XF
1	**1 Dollar** 1.8.1916; 2.1.1918. Red-brown. Sailing ship at left. Signature varieties. 118x63mm.	225	750	—

		Good	Fine	XF
1A	**1 Dollar** 1.1.1920; 1.10.1924. Red-brown. Sailing ship at left. Signature varieties. Printer: TDLR. 150x85mm. PC: Tan or gray.	175	650	—
2	**2 Dollars** 1.8.1916; 2.1.1918. Blue. Sailing ship at upper center. Signature varieties. Back: Ship at center. Printer: TDLR. 115x73mm.	350	1,250	—

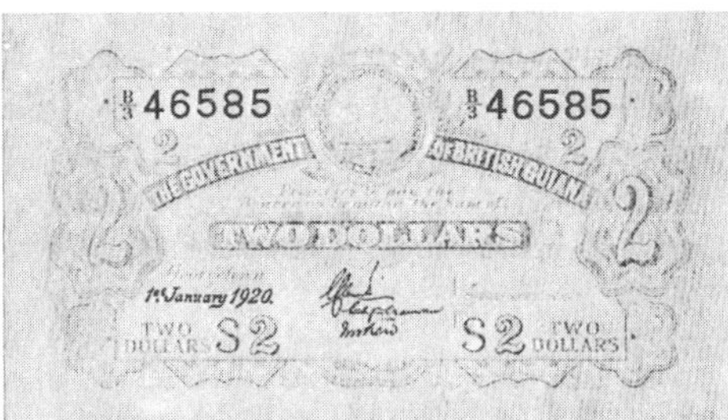

		Good	Fine	XF
2A	**2 Dollars** 1.1.1920; 1.10.1924. Blue. Sailing ship at upper center. Like #2, but larger format. Signature varieties. Printer: TDLR. 150x85mm.	250	900	—

#3-5 not assigned.

1929 Issue

		Good	Fine	XF
6	**1 Dollar** 1.1.1929; 1.1.1936. Red. Toucan at left, Kaieteur Falls at center, sailing ship seal at right. Back: Portrait of King George V at center. Printer: W&S.	450	2,750	—
7	**2 Dollars** 1.1.1929; 1.1.1936. Green. Toucan at left, Kaieteur Falls at center, sailing ship seal at right. Back: Portrait of King George V at center. Printer: W&S.	650	3,500	—

#8-11 not assigned.

1937-1942 Issue

Reduced size notes.

No.	Denomination	Good	Fine	XF
12	**1 Dollar** 1937-1942. Red. Toucan at left, Kaieteur Falls at center, sailing ship seal at right. Back: King George VI in 3/4 facing portrait. Printer: W&S.			
	a. 1.6.1937.	20.00	75.00	250
	b. 1.10.1938.	15.00	50.00	200
	c. 1.1.1942.	7.50	25.00	175
13	**2 Dollars** 1937-1942. Green. Toucan at left, Kaieteur Falls at center, sailing ship seal at right. Like #12. Back: King George VI in 3/4 facing portrait. Printer: W&S.			
	a. 1.6.1937.	40.00	300	1,750
	b. 1.10.1938.	40.00	300	1,750
	c. 1.1.1942.	40.00	300	1,750

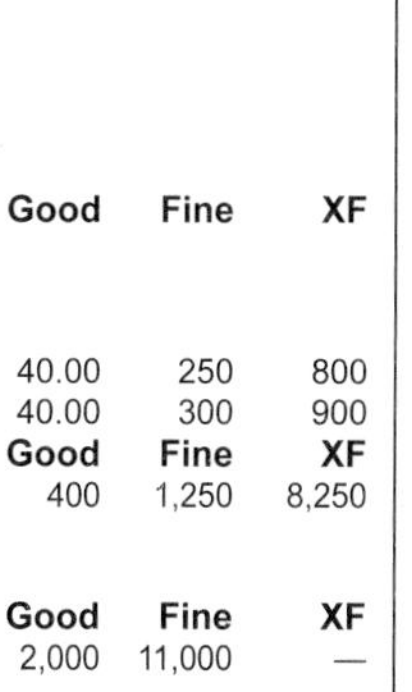

No.	Denomination	Good	Fine	XF
14	**5 Dollars** 1938; 1942. Olive. Toucan at left, Kaieteur Falls at center, sailing ship seal at right. Like #12. Back: King George VI in 3/4 facing portrait. Printer: W&S.			
	a. 1.10.1938.	40.00	250	800
	b. 1.1.1942.	40.00	300	900
15	**10 Dollars** 1.1.1942. Blue. Toucan at left, Kaieteur Falls at center, sailing ship seal at right. Back: King George VI in facing portrait. Printer: W&S.	400	1,250	8,250
16	**20 Dollars** 1.1.1942. Violet. Toucan at left, Kaieteur Falls at center, sailing ship seal at right. Like #15. Back: King George VI in facing portrait. Printer: W&S.	2,000	11,000	—
17	**100 Dollars** 1.1.1942. Rare. Yellow. Toucan at left, Kaieteur Falls at center, sailing ship seal at right. Like #12 & 15. Back: King George VI in facing portrait. Printer: W&S.	—	—	—

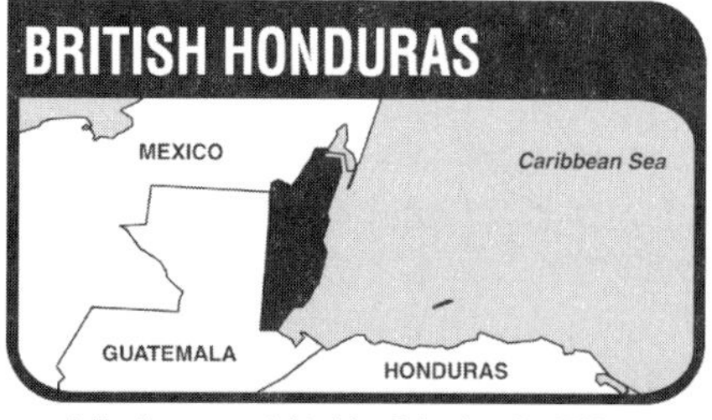

The former British colony of British Honduras is now Belize, a self-governing dependency of the United Kingdom situated in Central America south of Mexico and east and north of Guatemala, has an area of 8,867 sq. mi. (22,965 sq. km.) and a population of 209,000. Capital: Belmopan. Sugar, citrus fruits, chicle and hard woods are exported. The area, site of the ancient Mayan civilization, was sighted by Columbus in 1502, and settled by shipwrecked English seamen in 1638. British buccaneers settled the former capital of Belize in the 17th century. Britain claimed administrative right over the area after the emancipation of Central America from Spain, and declared it a colony subordinate to Jamaica in 1862. It established as the separate Crown Colony of British Honduras in 1884. The anti-British People's United Party, which attained power in 1954, won a constitution, effective in 1964 which established self-government under a British appointed governor. British Honduras became Belize on June 1, 1973, following the passage of a surprise bill by the Peoples United Party, but the constitutional relationship with Britain remained unchanged. In Dec. 1975, the U.N. General Assembly adopted a resolution supporting the right of the people of Belize to self-determination, and asking Britain and Guatemala to renew their negotiations on the future of Belize. Belize obtained independence on Sept. 21, 1981.

RULERS:

British

MONETARY SYSTEM:

1 Dollar = 100 Cents

BRITISH HONDURAS

Government of British Honduras

1894 Issue

No.	Denomination	Good	Fine	XF
1	**1 Dollar** 17.10.1894. Three recorded. Rare. Blue. Perforated at left. *BELIZE 1894* printed in circle at center. Uniface.	—	—	—
2	**2 Dollars** 1894. Requires confirmation.	—	—	—
3	**5 Dollars** 1894. Requires confirmation.	—	—	—
4	**10 Dollars** 1894. Requires confirmation.	—	—	—
5	**50 Dollars** 1894. Requires confirmation.	—	—	—
6	**100 Dollars** 1894. Requires confirmation.	—	—	—

1895 Issue

No.	Denomination	Good	Fine	XF
7	**1 Dollar** 1.1.1895; 3.9.1901. Blue and red. Perforated at left. Arms at top center. Printer: TDLR (without imprint).	1,000	3,500	—
8	**1 Dollar** 1.1.1895. Gray and dark red. Straight edge at left. Arms at top center. Printer: TDLR (without imprint).	1,000	3,250	—
9	**1 Dollar** 1.5.1912; 1.3.1920. Arms at top center. Printer: TDLR (without imprint).	1,000	2,500	—

No.	Description	Good	Fine	XF
10	**2 Dollars** 1895-1912. Brown and blue. Arms at top center. Printer: TDLR (without imprint).			
	a. 1.1.1895. Perforated left edge. Rare.	—	—	—
	b. 23.2.1904; 1.5.1912. Straight left edge.	1,250	3,500	—
12	**50 Dollars** 1.1.1895. Gray-blue and red. Arms at top center. Printer: TDLR (without imprint). Specimen. Rare.	—	—	—

#13 not assigned.

1924 Issue

No.	Description	Good	Fine	XF
14	**1 Dollar** 1.5.1924; 1.10.1928. Blue on brown and green underprint. Arms at top center. Printer: TDLR.	300	950	3,000
15	**2 Dollars** 1.5.1924; 1.10.1928. Brown on green underprint. Arms at top center. Printer: TDLR.	500	1,500	4,500

No.	Description	Good	Fine	XF
16	**5 Dollars** 1.5.1924; 1.10.1928. Green on brown underprint. Arms at top center. Printer: TDLR.	950	2,500	—

No.	Description	Good	Fine	XF
17	**10 Dollars** 1.5.1924; 1.10.1928. Purple on green and yellow underprint. Arms at top center. Printer: TDLR. Rare.	1,500	5,000	—
18	**50 Dollars** 1.5.1924; 1.10.1928. Arms at top center. Printer: TDLR. Rare.	—	—	—
19	**100 Dollars** 1.5.1924; 1.10.1928. Arms at top center. Printer: TDLR. Rare.	—	—	—

1939 Issue

No.	Description	VG	VF	UNC
20	**1 Dollar** 2.10.1939; 15.4.1942. Blue on multicolor underprint. Arms at left, portrait of King George VI at right.			
	a. 20.10.1939.	40.00	300	1,400
	b. 15.4.1942.	40.00	300	1,400
	s. As a. Specimen.	—	—	1,500
21	**2 Dollars** 2.10.1939; 15.4.1942. Brown on multicolor underprint. Arms at left, portrait of King George VI at right.			
	a. 2.10.1939.	75.00	700	2,500
	b. 15.4.1942.	75.00	700	2,500
	s. As a. Specimen. Perforated.	—	—	1,500
22	**5 Dollars** 2.10.1939; 15.4.1942. Purple on multicolor underprint. Arms at left, portrait of King George VI at right.	125	1,000	—
23	**10 Dollars** 2.10.1939; 15.4.1942. Dark olive-brown on multicolor underprint. Arms at left, portrait of King George VI at right.	250	1,500	—

1947 Issue

No.	Description	VG	VF	UNC
24	**1 Dollar** 1947-1952. Green on multicolor underprint. Arms at left, portrait of King George VI at right.			
	a. 30.1.1947.	50.00	350	1,500
	b. 1.11.1949; 1.2.1952.	40.00	325	1,250
25	**2 Dollars** 1947-1952. Purple on multicolor underprint. Arms at left, portrait of King George VI at right.			
	a. 30.1.1947.	75.00	700	2,000
	b. 1.11.1949; 1.2.1952.	75.00	700	2,000

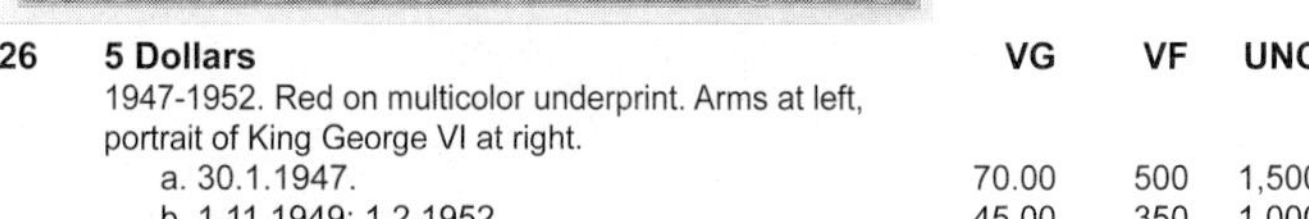

No.	Description	VG	VF	UNC
26	**5 Dollars** 1947-1952. Red on multicolor underprint. Arms at left, portrait of King George VI at right.			
	a. 30.1.1947.	70.00	500	1,500
	b. 1.11.1949; 1.2.1952.	45.00	350	1,000

No.	Description	VG	VF	UNC
27	**10 Dollars** 1947-1951. Black on multicolor underprint. Arms at left, portrait of King George VI at right.			
	a. 30.1.1947.	125	550	—
	b. 1.11.1949.	150	650	—
	c. 1.6.1951.	75.00	350	1,500

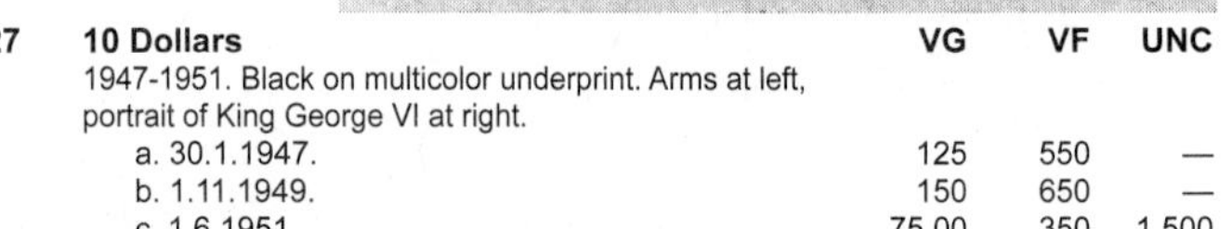

1952-1953 Issue

No.	Description	VG	VF	UNC
28	**1 Dollar** 1953-1973. Green on multicolor underprint. Arms at left, portrait of Queen Elizabeth II at right.			
	a. 15.4.1953-1.10.1958.	25.00	125	500
	b. 1.1.1961-1.5.1969.	15.00	75.00	400
	c. 1.6.1970-1.1.1973.	10.00	75.00	375
	s. As a, b, c. Specimen. Overprint: *SPECIMEN*, punch hole cancelled.	—	—	100

29	2 Dollars	VG	VF	UNC
	1953-1973. Purple on multicolor underprint. Arms at left, portrait of Queen Elizabeth II at right.			
	a. 15.4.1953-1.10.1958.	20.00	100	750
	b. 1.10.1960-1.5.1965.	12.50	60.00	550
	c. 1.1.1971-1.1.1973.	10.00	40.00	400
	s. As a, b, c. Specimen. Overprint: *SPECIMEN*, punch hole cancelled.	—	—	125

30	5 Dollars	VG	VF	UNC
	1953-1973. Red on multicolor underprint. Arms at left, portrait of Queen Elizabeth II at right.			
	a. 15.4.1953-1.10.1958.	30.00	150	1,000
	b. 1.3.1960-1.5.1965.	20.00	85.00	700
	c. 1.1.1970-1.1.1973.	15.00	75.00	600
	s. As a, c. Specimen. Overprint: *SPECIMEN*, punch hole cancelled.	—	—	150

31	10 Dollars	VG	VF	UNC
	1958-1973. Black on multicolor underprint. Arms at left, portrait of Queen Elizabeth II at right.			
	a. 15.4.1953-1.11.1961.	50.00	300	—
	b. 1.4.1964-1.5.1969.	35.00	175	1,300
	c. 1.1.1971-1.1.1973.	30.00	125	1,200
	s. As a, c. Specimen. Overprint: *SPECIMEN*, punch hole cancelled.	—	—	200

32	20 Dollars	VG	VF	UNC
	1952-1973. Brown on multicolor underprint. Arms at left, portrait of Queen Elizabeth II at right.			
	a. 1.12.1952-1.10.1958.	75.00	500	—
	b. 1.3.1960-1.5.1969.	50.00	350	2,800
	c. 1.1.1970-1.1.1973.	45.00	300	2,500
	s. As a, c. Specimen. Overprint: *SPECIMEN*, punch hole cancelled.	—	—	400

Note: For similar notes but with the *BELIZE* heading, see Belize country listings.

British North Borneo, a former British protectorate and crown colony, occupies the northern tip of the island of Borneo. The island of Labuan, which lies 6 miles off the northwest coast of the island of Borneo, was incorporated with British North Borneo in 1946. The Portuguese and Spanish established trading relations with Borneo early in the 16th century. Their monopoly was broken by the Dutch and British at the beginning of the 17th century. British North Borneo was administered by the North Borneo Company from 1877 to 1942, and later came under British military control, finally to become a British protectorate. Japan quickly eliminated the British and Dutch forces on Borneo and occupied the entire island during World War II. The island was retaken in 1945, and in July 1946, British North Borneo was made a crown colony. Britain relinquished its sovereignty over the colony in 1963. At that time it joined the Malaysian federation under the name of Sabah.

RULERS:

Japan, 1942-1945
British, 1945-1963

MONETARY SYSTEM:

1 Dollar = 100 Cents

BRITISH ADMINISTRATION

British North Borneo Company

1886-1896 Issue

#1-8 Dates partially or completely handwritten or handstamped on partially printed dates, i.e., 18xx, 189x, etc.

1	25 Cents	Good	Fine	XF
	11.6.1895; 19.8.1895. Brown. Arms at left. Uniface. Signature varieties. Printer: Blades, East & Blades Ltd., London.	250	750	—
2	50 Cents	Good	Fine	XF
	20.8.1895. Green. Uniface. Signature varieties. Printer: Blades, East & Blades Ltd., London. 176x95mm.	250	800	—

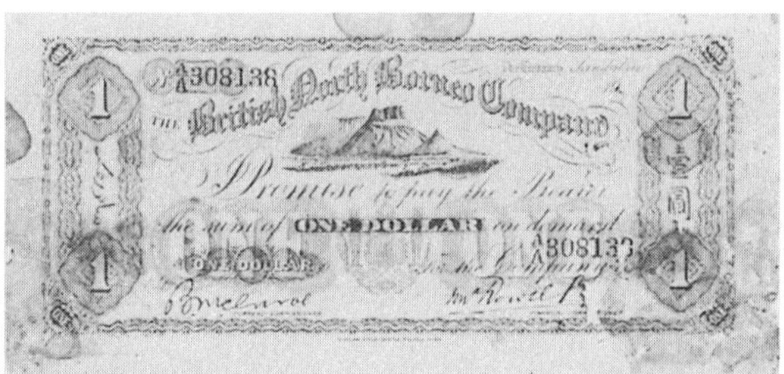

3	1 Dollar	Good	Fine	XF
	21.3.1886-8.10.1920. Black on red underprint. Mount Kinabalu at upper center. Signature varieties. Printer: Blades, East & Blades Ltd., London. 192x89mm.	150	500	—
3A	1 Dollar	Good	Fine	XF
	26.2.1920. Black on red underprint. Mount Kinabalu at upper center. Like #3. Signature varieties. Printer: Blades, East & Blades Ltd., London. 200x90mm.	250	—	—

4	5 Dollars	Good	Fine	XF
	189x-1926. Black on green underprint. Arms at upper center. Signature varieties. Printer: Blades, East & Blades Ltd., London. 200x102mm.			
	a. 14.5.189x; 1.10.1901.	350	1,000	—
	b. 10.1914; 14.1.1920; 26.2.1920; 1.12.1922; 7.8.1926.	250	750	—

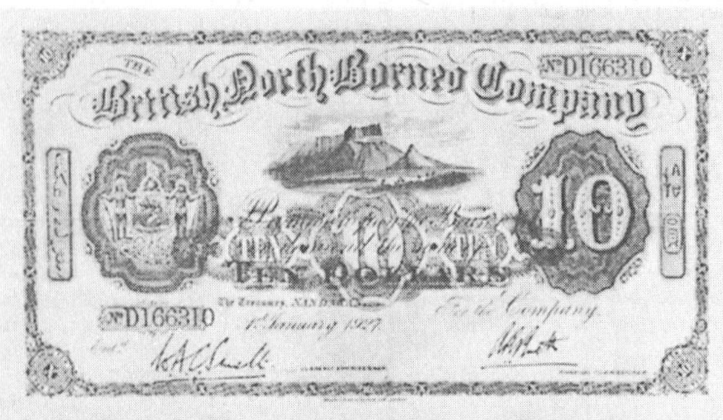

No.	Description	Good	Fine	XF
5	**10 Dollars** 1896-1926. Black on brown underprint. Mount Kinabalu at upper center, arms at left. Signature varieties. Printer: Blades, East & Blades Ltd., London. 215x115mm.			
	a. 3.3.1896; 11.8.1904; 3.1.1905; 25.10.1909; 1.7.1911.	500	1,250	—
	b. 13.3.1920; 5.3.1921.	325	850	—
	c. 1.12.1922; 1.12.1926.	300	750	—

1900; 1901 Issue

No.	Description	Good	Fine	XF
7	**25 Cents** 1900-1920. Deep red-brown. Arms at left. Uniface. Signature varieties. Printer: Blades, East & Blades Ltd., London. 161x82mm.			
	a. 17.10.1900; 1.10.1902; 24.1.1903; 26.11.1903; 5.10.1907.	200	750	—
	b. 1.1.1912; 13.10.1913; 3.11.1920.	150	500	—
8	**50 Cents** 11.2.1901; 26.11.1902; 9.5.1910. Green. Arms at left. Uniface. Signature varieties. Printer: Blades, East & Blades Ltd., London. 167x50mm.	200	750	—

1910 Issue

No.	Description	Good	Fine	XF
10	**50 Cents** 9.5.1910; 1.7.1911. Deep brown. Arms at left. Uniface. Printer: Blades, East & Blades Ltd., London. 174x91mm.	200	750	—

1916-1922 Issues

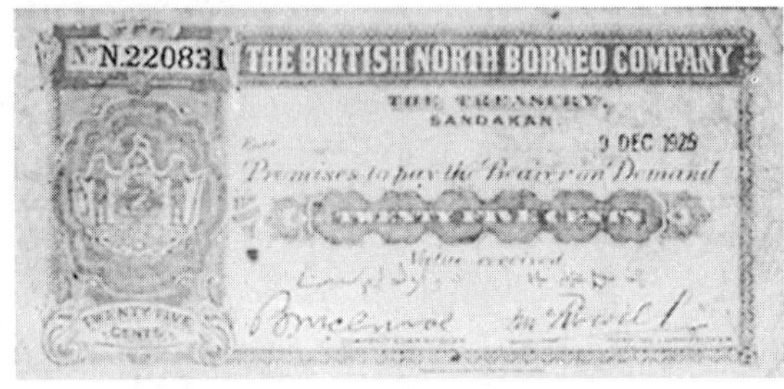

No.	Description	Good	Fine	XF
12	**25 Cents** 1917-1925. Red. Arms at left, Mt. Kinabalu at upper center. Uniface. 173x83mm.			
	a. 11.8.1917; 26.3.1919; 9.9.1920. Handstamped dates.	200	750	—
	b. 1.3.1921. Printed date.	100	350	900
	c. 9.12.1925. Handstamped date.	125	500	—
13	**50 Cents** 8.11.1916. Black. Arms at left. Uniface. Printer: Blades, East & Blades Ltd., London. 167x50mm.	200	750	—
14	**50 Cents** 1918-1929. Green. Arms at left. Printed or handstamped date.			
	a. 12.6.1918; 26.6.1918; 23.4.1919; 25.2.1920.	200	750	—
	b. 1.3.1921; 1.6.1929.	125	400	1,250

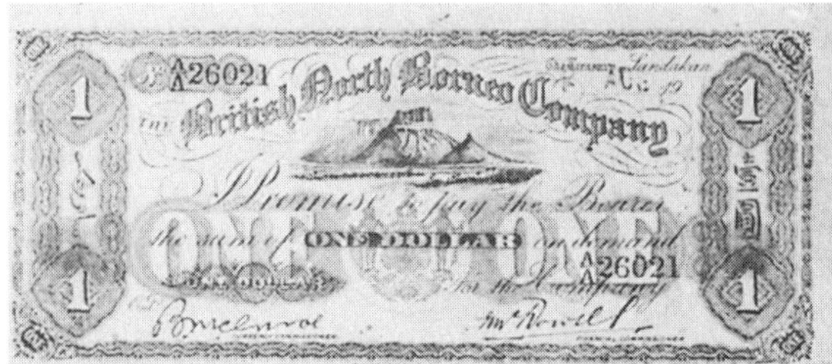

No.	Description	Good	Fine	XF
15	**1 Dollar** 30.7.1919; 2.1.1922; 2.5.1922. Black on red underprint. Mount Kinabalu at upper center. Printer: Blades, East & Blades Ltd., London. 184x82mm.	150	500	900

No.	Description	Good	Fine	XF
17	**25 Dollars** 1.12.1922-1.1.1927. Black on green underprint. Mount Kinabalu at upper center. Printer: Blades, East & Blades Ltd., London. 200x123mm.	500	4,000	—

1927 Issue

No.	Description	Good	Fine	XF
19	**1 Dollar** 1.1.1927. Black on dark green underprint. Mount Kinabalu at upper center. 205x93mm.	250	750	—

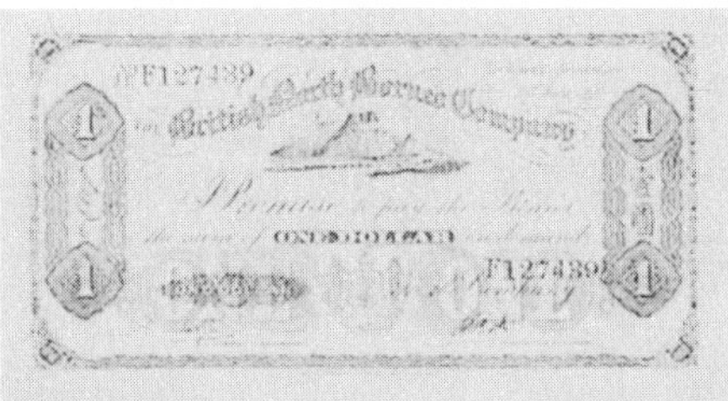

No.	Description	Good	Fine	XF
20	**1 Dollar** 29.7.1927; 1.1.1930. Black on dark green underprint. Mount Kinabalu at upper center. 135x77mm.	125	400	1,000

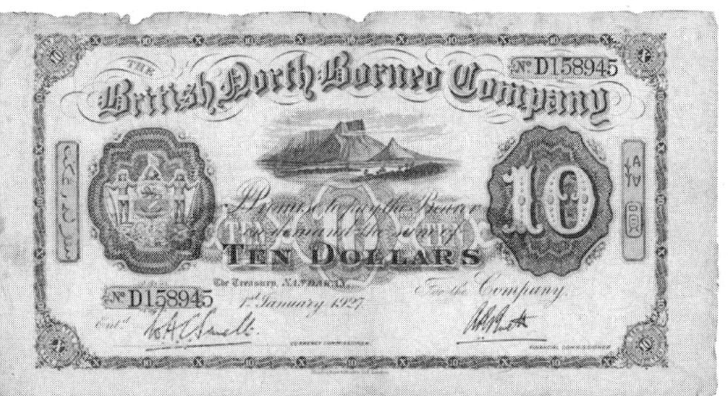

No.	Description	Good	Fine	XF
22	**10 Dollars** 1.1.1927. Black on red-brown underprint. Mount Kinabalu at upper center. 205x93mm.	350	850	—
23	**25 Dollars** 1.1.1927; 1.7.1929. Black on green. Mount Kinabalu at upper center. Arms at center. 201x126mm.	500	1,250	—

1930 Issue

No.	Description	Good	Fine	XF
25	**50 Cents** 1.1.1930. Green. Arms at left. 129x75mm.	75.00	200	750

1936; 1938 Issue

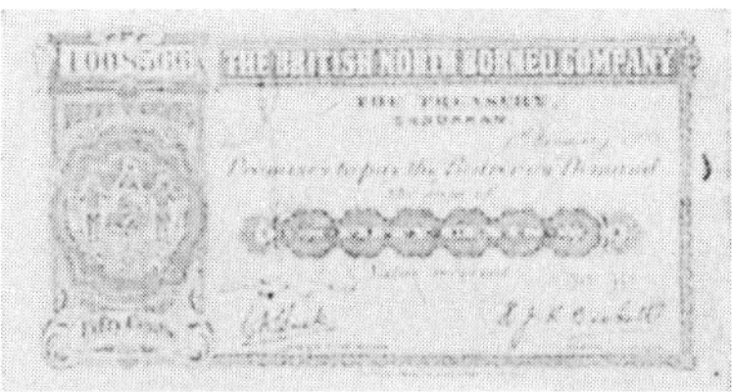

		Good	Fine	XF
27	**50 Cents** 1.1.1938. Olive-green. Arms at left, without *No.* at upper left. 119x63mm.	75.00	200	750

		Good	Fine	XF
28	**1 Dollar** 1.1.1936. Black on red underprint. Mount Kinabalu at upper center. Printer: Blades, East & Blades Ltd., London. 123x67mm.	27.50	75.00	400

1940 Issue

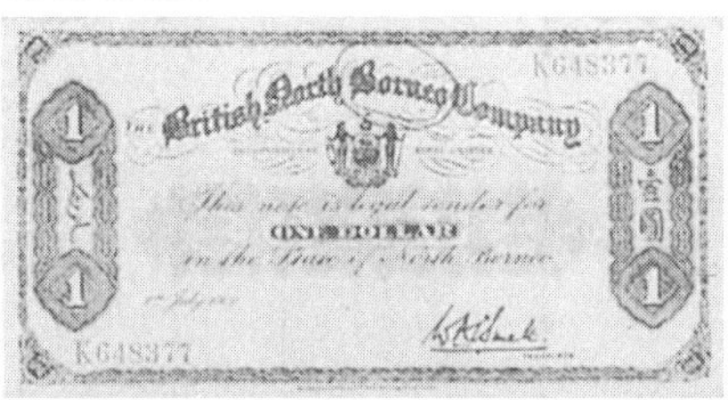

		Good	Fine	XF
29	**1 Dollar** 1.7.1940. Black on red underprint. Arms at center. 132x69mm.	35.00	100	350

		Good	Fine	XF
30	**5 Dollars** 1.1.1940. Black on dark green underprint. Arms at center. 145x76mm.	125	500	—

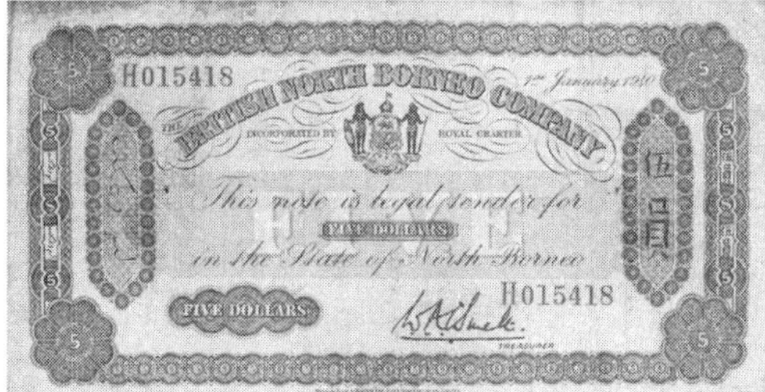

		Good	Fine	XF
31	**10 Dollars** 1.7.1940. Black on brown underprint. Arms at center. 160x82mm.	—	—	—
32	**25 Dollars** 1.7.1940. Black on green underprint. Arms at center. 170x98mm.	—	—	—

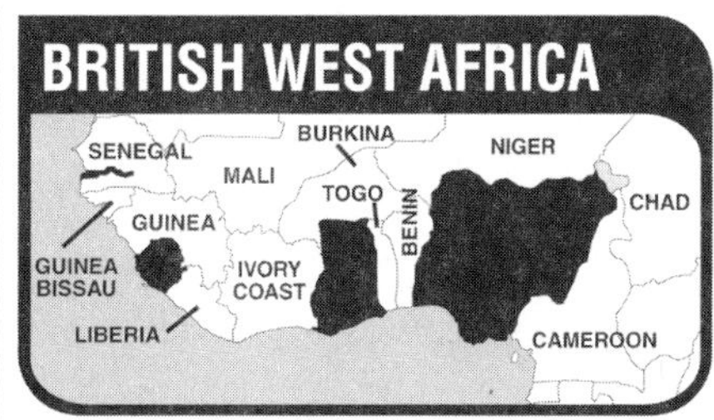

British West Africa was an administrative grouping of the four former British colonies of Gambia, Sierra Leone, Nigeria and Gold Coast (now Ghana). All are now independent republics and members of the British Commonwealth of Nations. These four colonies were supplied with a common currency by the West African Currency Board from 1907 through 1962. Also see Gambia, Ghana, Nigeria and Sierra Leone for related currency and for individual statistics and history.

RULERS:
British to 1952

MONETARY SYSTEM:
1 Shilling = 12 Pence
1 Pound = 20 Shillings

BRITISH ADMINISTRATION

West African Currency Board

1916-1920 Issue

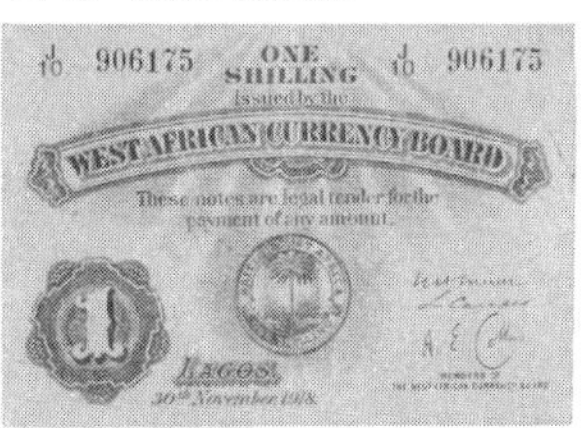

		Good	Fine	XF
1	**1 Shilling** 30.11.1918. Black. Coin with palm tree at lower center. Uniface. Signature varieties. PC: Salmon.			
	a. Issued note.	40.00	150	600
	s. Specimen.	—	Unc	750

		Good	Fine	XF
2	**2 Shillings** 1916-1918. Blue-gray. Palm tree at center. Signature varieties. Printer: W&S.			
	a. 30.6.1916. Uniface.	175	750	—
	b. 30.3.1918. Arabic script on back.	125	400	1,000
3	**5 Shillings** 1.3.1920. Red-brown. Palm tree at center. Signature varieties. Printer: W&S. (Not issued).	—	—	—
4	**10 Shillings** 1916-1918. Green. Palm tree at center, with *10* at left and right. Signature varieties. Printer: W&S.			
	a. 31.3.1916. Uniface.	—	—	—
	b. 30.3.1918. Arabic script on back.	175	750	—
	s. Specimen. Arabic script on back. 31.3.1916.	—	—	—

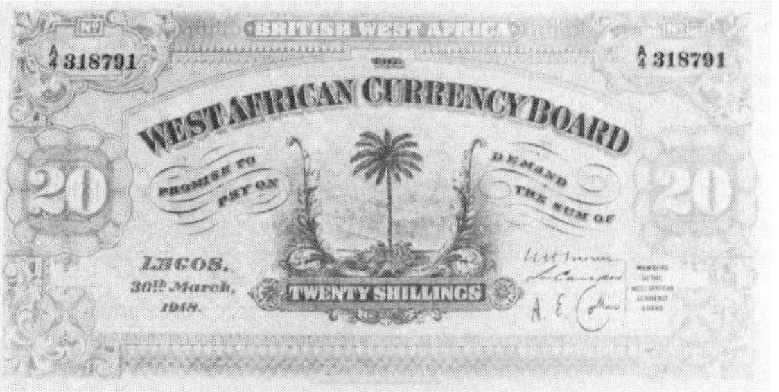

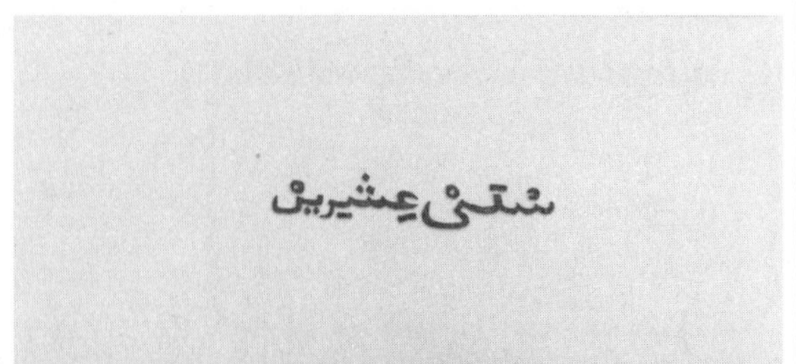

5	**20 Shillings**	Good	Fine	XF
	1916-1918. Black. Palm tree at center. Red *20* at left and right. Signature varieties. Printer: W&S.			
	a. 31.3.1916. Uniface.	—	—	—
	b. 30.3.1918. Back black, Denomination and Arabic script in black on back.	225	900	—
	s1. Specimen. Arabic script on back. 31.3.1916.	—		
	s2. Specimen perforated: *SPECIMEN.* 30.3.1918.	—	Unc	1,500

Note: Color trials exist for #4a and 5a but with Arabic inscription on back.

6	**100 Shillings = 5 Pounds**	Good	Fine	XF
	1.3.1919. Black. Palm tree at lower center. Printer: W&S. (Not issued).	—	—	—

1928 Issue

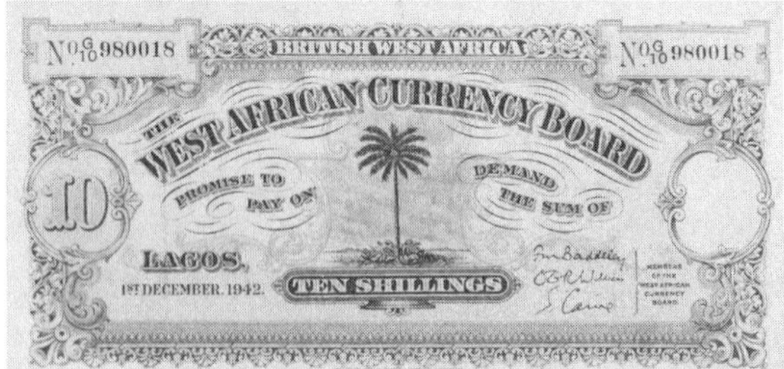

7	**10 Shillings**	Good	Fine	XF
	1928-1948. Green. Palm tree at center. *10* at left only. Watermark: *10* at right. Printer: W&S.			
	a. 2.1.1928-21.7.1930; 14.9.1934.	100	350	900
	b. 4.1.1937-24.12.1948.	25.00	100	400

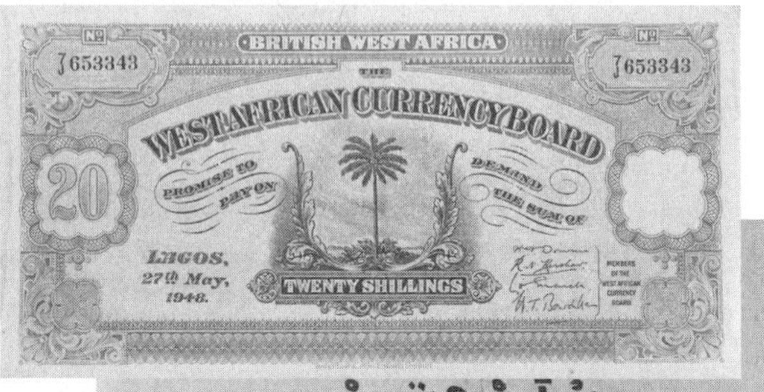

8	**20 Shillings**	Good	Fine	XF
	1928-1951. Black and red on light green and pink underprint. Palm tree at center. *20* at left only. Back: Denomination and Arabic script in black. Watermark: *20* at right. Printer: W&S.			
	a. 2.1.1928-21.7.1930; 14.9.1934.	75.00	300	650
	b. 4.1.1937-2.7.1951.	15.00	50.00	300

1953-1954 Issue

9	**10 Shillings**	VG	VF	UNC
	31.3.1953-4.2.1958. Black and green. River scene with palm trees at left. Back: Field workers. Printer: W&S.			
	a. Issued note.	15.00	75.00	450
	s. Specimen.	—	—	250

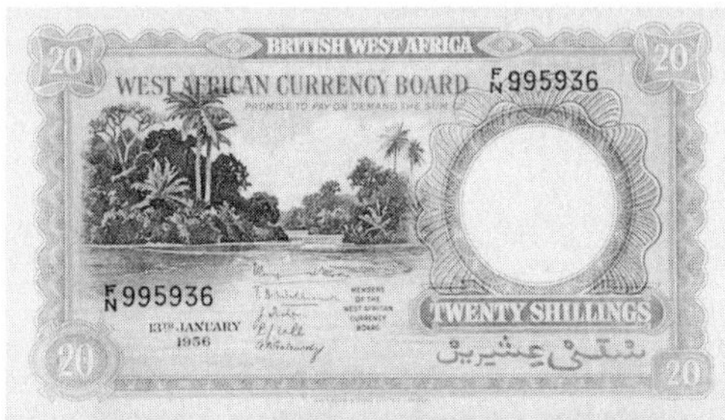

10	**20 Shillings**	VG	VF	UNC
	31.3.1953-20.1.1957. Black and red. River scene with palm trees at left. Back: Harvesting. Printer: W&S.			
	a. Issued note.	15.00	75.00	450
	s. Specimen.	—	—	350

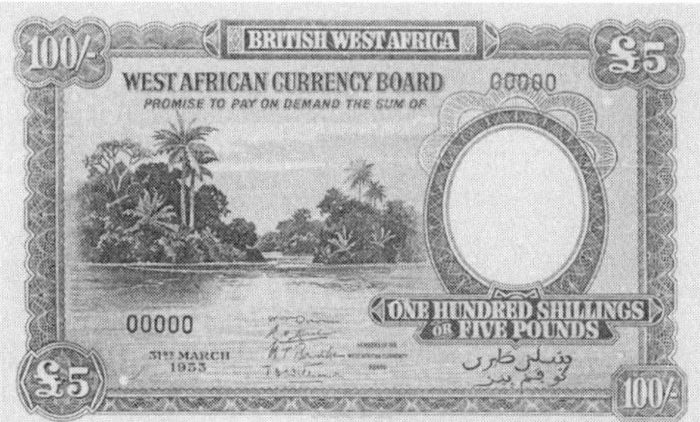

11	**100 Shillings = 5 Pounds**	VG	VF	UNC
	1953-1954. Blue. River scene with palm trees at left. Back: Man harvesting. Printer: W&S.			
	a. 31.3.1953.	—	—	—
	b. 26.4.1954.	—	—	—
	s. Specimen.	—	—	650

11A	**1000 Pounds**	Good	Fine	XF
	26.4.1954. Black. Uniface. Specimen.	—	Unc	6000.

The Republic of Bulgaria (formerly the Peoples Republic of Bulgaria), a Balkan country on the Black Sea in southeastern Europe, has an area of 110,910 sq. km. and a population of 7.26 million. Capital: Sofia. Agriculture remains a key component of the economy but industrialization, particularly heavy industry, has been emphasized since the late 1940s. Machinery, tobacco and cigarettes, wines and spirits, clothing and metals are the chief exports.

The Bulgars, a Central Asian Turkic tribe, merged with the local Slavic inhabitants in the late 7th century to form the first Bulgarian state. In succeeding centuries, Bulgaria struggled with the Byzantine Empire to assert its place in the Balkans, but by the end of the 14th century the country was overrun by the Ottoman Turks. Northern Bulgaria attained autonomy in 1878 and all of Bulgaria became independent from the Ottoman Empire in 1908. Having fought on the losing side in both World Wars, Bulgaria fell within the Soviet sphere of influence and became a People's Republic in 1946. Communist domination ended in 1990, when Bulgaria held its first multiparty election since World War II and began the contentious process of moving toward political democracy and a market economy while combating inflation, unemployment, corruption, and crime. The country joined NATO in 2004 and the EU in 2007.

RULERS:

Alexander I, 1879-1886
Ferdinand I, as Prince, 1887-1908
Ferdinand I, as King, 1908-1918
Boris III, 1918-1943
Simeon II, 1943-1946

MONETARY SYSTEM:

1 Lev = 100 Stotinki
1 Lev = 1,000 "Old" Lev, from 1999
Silver Lev = Lev Srebro
Gold Lev = Lev Zlato

SIGNATURES:

Boev
Chakalov
Geshov
Gikov
Karadjov
Tenev
Tropchiev
Urumov
Venkov

GOVERNORS:	CASHIERS:
Geshov 1883-1886	Tropchiev 1884-1900
Tenev 1887-1899	Urumov 1900-1908
Karadjov 1899-1905	Gikov 1908-1910
Boev 1906-1908	Venkov 1910-1919; 1923-1928
Chakalov 1908-1920	Popov 1920-1923
Damajanov 1920-1922	Nachev 1928-1935
Bojadjiev 1924-1926	Ivanov 1935-1945
Ivanov 1926-1931	Kalchev 1945-1953
Bojilov 1922-1944	
Gounev 1938-1944	
Stefanov 1944-1946	
Tzonchev 1946-1949	

PRINCIPALITY

Bulgarian National Bank

1885, 1887 Gold Issue

		Good	Fine	XF
A1	**20 Leva Zlato**			
	1.8.1885. Light ochre. Arms at upper left. Printer: Ekspedizia Zagotovlenia Gossudarstvennih Bumag, St. Petersburg, Russia. Rare.			
	a. Signatures: Geshov and Tropchiev.	2,000	—	—
	b. Signatures: Tenev and Tropchiev.	1,200	2,750	—
	c. Signatures: Karadjov and Tropchiev.	1,000	2,000	—

		Good	Fine	XF
A2	**50 Leva Zlato**			
	1.8.1885. Light green. Arms at upper left. Signatures: Geshov and Tropchiev. Printer: Ekspedizia Zagotovlenia Gossudarstvennih Bumag, St. Petersburg, Russia. Rare.	2,000	5,000	—

		Good	Fine	XF
A3	**100 Leva Zlato**			
	1887. Blue-gray and ochre. Arms at left, woman seated with child at right. Back: Blue, pale blue and ochre. Back: Floral spray at center. Printer: Ekspedizia Zagotovlenia Gossudarstvennih Bumag, St. Petersburg, Russia. Rare.			
	a. Signatures: Tenev and Tropchiev.	3,000	8,000	—
	b. Signatures: Karadjov and Tropchiev.	4,000	9,000	—

1890 ND Gold Issue

A4 5 Leva Zlato — Good / Fine / XF

ND (1890). Black on brown underprint. Arms at left. Signatures Tenev and Tropchiev. Like #A6. Back: Dark brown. Back: Farmer plowing with two horses at center. Printer: BWC.

	Good	Fine	XF
a. Issued note.	500	1,200	—
p. Die proof front on card.	—	—	2,000
s. Specimen. 000001 - 1000000. Perforated: *SPECIMEN*. See A6.	—	Unc	6,000
ct. Color Trial. Back.	—	—	1,000

A5 10 Leva Zlato — Good / Fine / XF

ND (1890). Black on blue and ochre underprint. Farm girl carrying roses at left, arms at right. Signatures: Tenev and Tropchiev. Like #A7. Back: Blue. Back: Shepherd tending flock of sheep at center. Printer: BWC.

	Good	Fine	XF
a. Issued note.	1,000	3,000	—
p. Die proof front on card.	—	—	2,000
s. Specimen 000001 - 500000. Perforated: *SPECIMEN*. See A7.	—	Unc	8,000
ct. Color Trial.	—	Unc	6,000

1899 ND Silver Issue

A6 5 Leva Srebro — Good / Fine / XF

ND (1899). Black on brown underprint. Arms at left. Signatures: Karadjov and Tropchiev. Like #A4. Back: Dark brown. Back: Farmer plowing with two horses. Printer: BWC.

Good	Fine	XF
120	500	1,000

A7 10 Leva Srebro — Good / Fine / XF

ND (1899). Black on blue and ochre underprint. Farm girl carrying roses at left, arms at right. Like #A5. Back: Blue. Back: Shepherd tending flock of sheep at center. Printer: BWC.

	Good	Fine	XF
a. Signatures: Karadjov and Tropchiev. 6 digit serial #.	120	350	1,600
b. Signatures: Karadjov and Tropchiev. 7 digit serial #.	100	300	1,500
c. Signatures: Karadjov and Urumov.	140	400	1,700
s1. Specimen 000001 - 500000. Perforated *SPECIMEN*. See A5.	—	Unc	8,000
s2. Specimen 500001 - 1500000. Perforated *SPECIMEN*.	—	Unc	8,000
s3. Specimen 1500001 - 2500000. Perforated *SPECIMEN*.	—	Unc	8,000

A8 50 Leva Srebro — Good / Fine / XF

ND (1899 -old date 1.8.1885). Light green. Arms at upper left. Signatures: Karadjov and Tropchiev. Printer: Ekspedizia Zagotovlenia Gossudarstvennih Bumag, St. Petersburg, Russia. Overprint: *ЗЛАТО* crossed out, *СРЕБРО* on #A2. Rare.

Good	Fine	XF
4,000	9,000	—

1904-1909 ND Silver Issue

#1-6 Denomination in *LEVA SREBRO* signature varieties. Vertical format.

1 5 Leva Srebro — Good / Fine / XF

ND (1904). Black on red, gray-green and multicolor underprint. Back: Arms without inscription at center. Printer: Orlov, St Petersburg, Russia (without imprint).

	Good	Fine	XF
a. Signatures: Karadjov and Urumov. 1 letter serial # prefix.	120	300	1,200
b. Signatures: Boev and Urumov. 1 letter serial # prefix.	140	350	1,300
c. Signatures: Boev and Urumov. 2 letter serial # prefix.	60.00	180	800
d. Signatures: Chakalov and Urumov. 2 letter serial # prefix.	60.00	200	900
s. Specimen. As a. Perforated *SPECIMEN*.	—	Unc	2,000

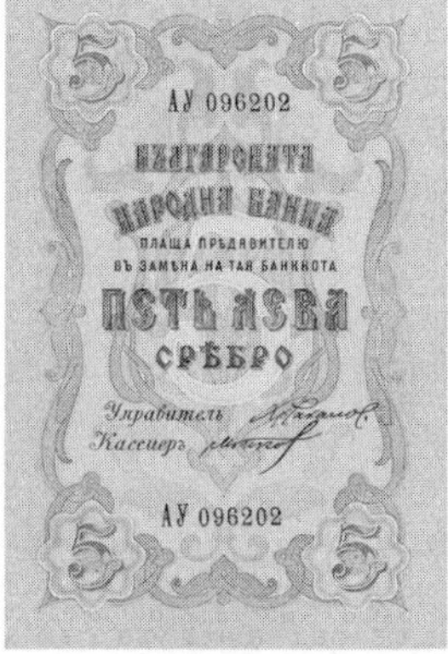

2 5 Leva Srebro — Good / Fine / XF

ND (1910). Black on green, lilac and multicolor underprint. Back: Arms with ЦАРСТВО БЪЛГАРИЯ. Printer: Orlov, St Petersburg, Russia (without imprint).

	Good	Fine	XF
a. Signatures: Chakalov and Gikov. 1 letter serial # prefix. 2 serial #.	5.00	25.00	110
b.Signatures: Chakalov and Gikov. 2 letter serial # prefix. 2 serial #.	4.00	20.00	95.00
c. Signatures: Chakalov and Venkov. 2 letter serial # prefix. 4 serial #.	4.00	20.00	95.00

3	10 Leva Srebro	Good	Fine	XF
	ND (1906). Dark green on multicolor underprint. Back: Arms at upper center. Printer: Orlov, St Petersburg, Russia (without imprint).			
	a. Signatures: Boev and Urumov. 1 letter serial # prefix. 2 serial #.	20.00	80.00	300
	b1. Signatures Chakalov and Urumov. 1 letter serial # prefix. 2 serial number.	50.00	150	450
	b2. Signatures: Chakalov and Urumov. 2 letter serial # prefix. 2 serial #.	15.00	70.00	250
	c. Signatures: Chakalov and Gikov. 2 letter serial # prefix. 2 serial #.	5.00	30.00	150
	d. Signatures: Chakalov and Gikov. 2 letter serial # prefix. 4 serial #.	5.00	30.00	120
	e. Signatures: Chakalov and Venkov. 2 letter serial # prefix. 4 serial #.	5.00	25.00	110

4	50 Leva Srebro	Good	Fine	XF
	ND (1904). Multicolor. Back: Arms at center. Printer: Orlov, St Petersburg, Russia (without imprint).			
	a. Signatures: Karadjov and Urumov.	30.00	100	400
	b. Signatures: Chakalov and Venkov.	25.00	80.00	350
	s. Specimen. As a. Perforated *SPECIMEN*.	—	Unc	2,500

Color Abbreviation Guide

New to the *Standard Catalog of® World Paper Money* are the following abbreviations related to color references:

BC: Back color
PC: Paper color

5	100 Leva Srebro	Good	Fine	XF
	ND (1904). Multicolor. Back: Arms at upper center. Printer: Orlov, St Petersburg, Russia (without imprint).			
	a. Signatures: Karadjov and Urumov.	70.00	300	1,000
	b. Signatures: Chakalov and Venkov.	50.00	200	800
	s. Specimen. As a. Perforated *SPECIMEN*.	—	Unc	3,500

6	500 Leva Srebro	Good	Fine	XF
	ND (1910). Multicolor. Signatures: Chakalov and Venkov. Back: Arms at upper center. Printer: Orlov, St Petersburg, Russia (without imprint).	400	1,400	4,500

1907 ND Silver Overprinted in Gold Issue

#	5 Leva Zlato	Good	Fine	XF
7	ND (1907). Black on red, gray-green and multicolor underprint. Like #1 but with СРЕБРО crossed out. Signatures: Boev and Urumov. Back: Arms at center. Overprint: ЗЛАТО at left and right.			
	a. 1 letter serial # prefix.	20.00	60.00	300
	b. 2 letter serial # prefix.	30.00	100	350

#	10 Leva Zlato	Good	Fine	XF
8	ND (1907). Dark green on multicolor. Like #3 but with СРЕБРО crossed out. Signatures: Boev and Urumov. Back: Arms at center. Overprint: ЗЛАТО at left and right.	40.00	120	450

1904-1907 ND Gold Issue

#9-12 Denomination in *LEVA ZLATO*, signature varieties. Horizontal format.

#	20 Leva Zlato	Good	Fine	XF
9	ND (1904). Black text and arms, edge pink, frame red and blue. Arms at upper center. Printer: Orlov, St Petersburg, Russia (without imprint).			
	a. Signatures: Karadjov and Urumov. 1 letter serial # prefix.	40.00	100	350
	b. Signatures: Boev and Urumov. 1 letter serial # prefix.	20.00	50.00	200
	c. Signatures: Chahalov and Urumov. 1 letter serial # prefix.	20.00	50.00	200
	d. Signatures: Chakalov and Gikov. 1 letter serial # prefix.	10.00	40.00	150
	e. Signatures: Chakalov and Gikov. 2 letter serial # prefix.	5.00	20.00	85.00
	f. Signatures: Chakalov and Venkov. 1 letter serial # prefix.	30.00	80.00	250
	g. Signatures: Chakalov and Venkov. 2 letter serial # prefix.	5.00	25.00	90.00
	s. Specimen. As a. Perforated *SPECIMEN*.	—	Unc	3,000

#	50 Leva Zlato	Good	Fine	XF
10	ND (1906). Black text and arms, edge pink, frame blue and green. Arms at upper center. Printer: Orlov, St Petersburg, Russia (without imprint).			
	a. Signatures: Boev and Urumov.	60.00	250	1,300
	b. Signatures: Chakalov and Gikov. 6 digit serial #. 1 dash in No.	20.00	80.00	250
	c. Signatures: Chakalov and Gikov. 6 or 7 digit serial #. 2 dash in No.	10.00	50.00	200
	d. Signatures: Chakalov and Venkov. 7 digit serial #.	10.00	50.00	200

#	100 Leva Zlato	Good	Fine	XF
11	ND (1906). Black text and arms, edge pink, frame light blue. Arms at upper center. Back: Arms at left center. Printer: Orlov, St Petersburg, Russia (without imprint).			
	a. Signatures: Boev and Urumov.	70.00	300	1,500
	b. Signatures: Chakalov and Urumov.	80.00	350	1,600
	c. Signatures: Chakalov and Gikov.	25.00	100	550
	d. Signatures: Chakalov and Venkov.	30.00	150	650

12	500 Leva Zlato	Good	Fine	XF
	ND (1907). Black text and arms, edge green, frame pink and green. Arms at upper center. Printer: Orlov, St Petersburg, Russia (without imprint).			
	a. Signatures: Boev and Urumov.	500	1,400	4,500
	b. Signatures: Chakalov and Gikov.	300	1,000	3,500
	c. Signatures: Chakalov and Venkov.	300	1,000	3,500

KINGDOM

1916 Cashier's Bond (КАСОВ БОНЪ) Issue

13	1000 Leva Zlatni	Good	Fine	XF
	10.5.1916. Blue on light blue-green underprint. Bulgarian printing. Back: Light blue-green. Watermark: Cross and curl pattern.	100	300	1,200

1916 ND Silver Issue

14	1 Lev Srebro	VG	VF	UNC
	ND (1916). Black on green and blue underprint. Cross and curl pattern. Signatures: Chakalov and Venkov. Back: Blue on lilac underprint. Watermark: Cross and curl pattern. Printer: RDK (without imprint).			
	a. 1 digit serial # prefix.	1.00	6.00	35.00
	b. 2 digit serial # prefix.	1.00	5.00	30.00
	s. Specimen. Red overprint: *SPECIMEN.*	—	—	800

15	2 Leva Srebro	VG	VF	UNC
	ND (1916). Black on green and pink underprint. Value 2 in lower corners. Signatures: Chakalov and Venkov. Back: Red on tan underprint. Back: Value 2 in four corners Watermark: Cross and curl pattern. Printer: RDK (without imprint).			
	a. 1 digit serial # prefix.	2.00	12.00	80.00
	b. 2 digit serial # prefix. (#10 only).	5.00	20.00	120
	s. Specimen. Red overprint: *SPECIMEN.*	—	—	400

16	5 Leva Srebro	VG	VF	UNC
	ND (1916). Black on blue and gray underprint. Signatures: Chakalov and Venkov. Back: Arms at upper center. Watermark: Cross and curl pattern. Printer: RDK (without imprint).			
	a. Issued note.	2.00	25.00	240
	s. Specimen. Red overprint: *SPECIMEN.*	—	—	400

17	10 Leva Srebro	VG	VF	UNC
	ND (1916). Black text, edge blue-green, ornament red and lilac. Back: Dark brown on green underprint. Back: Arms at upper center. Watermark: Cross and curl pattern. Printer: RDK (without imprint).			
	a. Issued note.	2.00	25.00	200
	s. Specimen. Red overprint: *SPECIMEN.*	—	—	400

1916 ND Gold Issue

		VG	VF	UNC
18	**20 Leva Zlato** ND (1916). Black on green underprint. Arms at upper center, value in lower corners. Signatures: Chakalov and Venkov. Back: Value flanking center text. Watermark: Cross and curl pattern. Printer: RDK (without imprint).			
	a. Issued note.	5.00	40.00	250
	s. Specimen. Red overprint: *SPECIMEN.*	—	—	400

		VG	VF	UNC
19	**50 Leva Zlato** ND (1916). Black on orange-brown underprint. Arms at upper center. Signatures: Chakalov and Venkov. Back: Brown and blue. Back: Arms at center. Watermark: Cross and curl pattern. Printer: RDK (without imprint).			
	a. Issued note.	20.00	100	450
	s. Specimen. Red overprint: *SPECIMEN.*	—	—	750

		VG	VF	UNC
20	**100 Leva Zlato** ND (1916). Black text and arms, edge green, ornament blue, lilac and violet. Arms at upper center. Signatures: Chakalov and Venkov. Watermark: Cross and curl pattern. Printer: RDK (without imprint).			
	a. Serial # without prefix letter.	3.00	30.00	180
	b. Serial # with prefix letter.	3.00	30.00	180
	c. As b, with СЕРИЯ А (Series A) red overprint at upper left and lower right. Only on series Д.	80.00	300	1,200
	d. Without overprint. Series Д.	100	350	1,200
	s. As a. Specimen. Red overprint: *SPECIMEN.*	—	—	1,500

1917 ND Issue

		VG	VF	UNC
21	**5 Leva Srebrni** ND (1917). Black on olive and lilac underprint. Arms at top center. Signatures: Chakalov and Venkov. Back: Lilac on green underprint. Back: Crown at center. Watermark: BNB. Printer: G&D, Leipzig.			
	a. 1 serial # prefix letters.	3.00	25.00	150
	b. 2 serial # prefix letter.	2.00	20.00	200
	s. Specimen. Red overprint: ОБРАЗЕЦЪ.	—	—	400

		VG	VF	UNC
22	**10 Leva Zlatni** ND (1917; 1919). Black on light green and pink underprint. Arms at top center. Back: Green on pink underprint. Watermark: BNB. Printer: G&D, Leipzig.			
	a. Arms with supporters without flags. (1917). 1 letter serial # prefix. Signatures: Chakalov and Venkov.	2.00	20.00	125
	b. New arms with supporters and flags. 2 letter serial # prefix. (1919). Signatures: Chakalov and Popov.	3.00	25.00	140
	s. As a. Specimen. Red overprint: ОБРАЗЕЦЪ.	—	—	400

23	20 Leva Zlatni	VG	VF	UNC
	ND (1917). Brown on light blue-green and pink underprint. Arms at top center. Initials (BNB) in underprint at center. Back: Lilac on green underprint. Watermark: BNB. Printer: G&D, Leipzig.			
	a. Issued note.	5.00	25.00	180
	s. Specimen. Red overprint: ОБРАЗЕЦЪ.	—	—	400

24	50 Leva Zlatni	VG	VF	UNC
	ND (1917). Brown on blue, green and salmon underprint. Arms at upper left. Back: Brown on green underprint. Watermark: BNB. Printer: G&D, Leipzig.			
	a. Serial # begins with *No.*	6.00	40.00	250
	b. Serial # begins with prefix letter.	5.00	30.00	200
	p1. Proof front.	—	—	1,000
	p2. Proof back.	—	—	800
	s. Specimen. Red overprint: ОБРАЗЕЦЪ.	—	—	450

25	100 Leva Zlatni	VG	VF	UNC
	ND (1917). Green, ochre, purple and pink. Portrait woman with sheaf at left. Watermark: BNB. Printer: G&D, Leipzig.			
	a. 6 digit serial #.	30.00	100	800
	b. 7 digit serial #.	40.00	120	900
	p. Proof front. Rare.	—	—	1,500
	s. Specimen. Red overprint: ОБРАЗЕЦЪ.	—	—	1,500

1918 Cashier's Bond Issue

26	1000 Leva Zlatni	VG	VF	UNC
	ND (1918). Blue-green and tan. Arms at left. Printer: Gebr. Parcus, Munich.			
	a. Issued note.	10.00	70.00	300
	s. Series B. Specimen. Red overprint: ОБРАЗЕЦЪ.	—	—	1,000

1917 State Treasury Bonds

26A	1000 Leva Zlatni	VG	VF	UNC
	15.12.1917-15.12.1919. 2 year bond. Rare.	—	2,000	—
26B	**10,000 Leva Zlatni**	**VG**	**VF**	**UNC**
	8.9.1917-8.3.1918. 6 month bond. Rare.	—	2,000	—

1919 Fixed Term Cashier's Bond

26C	2000 Leva	VG	VF	UNC
	25.10.1919-31.12.1919. Green			
	a. Issued note. Rare.	—	1,500	—
	s. Specimen. Red overprint: ОБРАЗЕЦЪ. Rare.	—	1,500	—
26D	**5000 Leva**	**VG**	**VF**	**UNC**
	25.10.1919-31.12.1919. Violet.			
	a. Issued note. Rare.	—	1,500	—
	s. Specimen. Red overprint: ОБРАЗЕЦЪ. Rare.	—	1,500	—

26E	10,000 Leva	VG	VF	UNC
	25.10.1919-31.12.1919. Red.			
	a. Issued note. Rare.	—	2,000	—
	s. Specimen. Green overprint: ОБРАЗЕЦЪ. Rare.	—	2,000	—
26F	**500 Leva**	**VG**	**VF**	**UNC**
	25.12.1919-31.03.1920. Red.			
	a. Issued note. Rare.	—	1,500	—
	s. Specimen. Red overprint: ОБРАЗЕЦЪ. Rare.	—	1,500	—

		VG	VF	UNC
26G	**1000 Leva**	VG	VF	UNC
	25.12.1919-31.03.1920. Green.			
	a. Issued note. Rare.	—	1,500	—
	s. Specimen. Red overprint: ОБРАЗЕЦЪ. Rare.	—	1,500	—
26H	**2000 Leva**	VG	VF	UNC
	25.12.1919-31.03.1920. Blue.			
	a. Issued note. Rare.	—	1,500	—
	s. Specimen. Red overprint: ОБРАЗЕЦЪ. Rare.	—	1,500	—
26I	**5000 Leva**	VG	VF	UNC
	25.12.1919-31.03.1920. Yellow-green.			
	a. Issued note. Rare.	—	2,000	—
	s. Specimen. Red overprint: ОБРАЗЕЦЪ. Rare.	—	2,000	—

1922 Overprinted State Treasury Bond Issue

		VG	VF	UNC
27	**500 Leva Zlatni**	VG	VF	UNC
	1922. Overprint: Green diagonal on invalidated state treasury bill issue of 10.8.1918 (2 year bond). Rare.	—	3,000	—

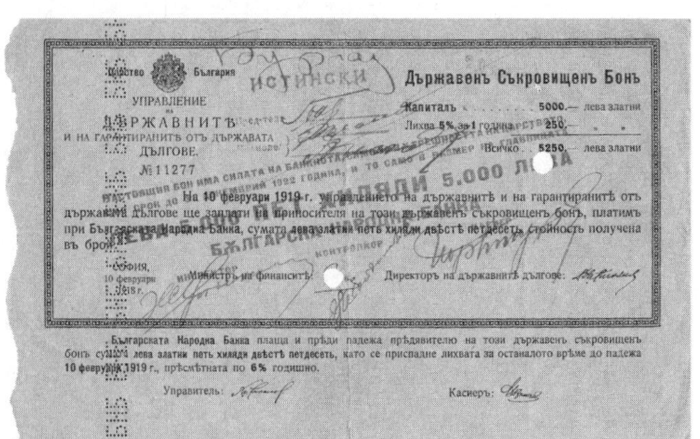

		VG	VF	UNC
27A	**5000 Leva Zlatni**	VG	VF	UNC
	1922. Rare. Overprint. Blue diagonal on invalidated state treasury bill issue of 10.2.1918 (1 year bond). Rare.	—	3,000	—
28	**5000 Leva Zlatni**	VG	VF	UNC
	1922. Overprint: Blue diagonal on invalidated state treasury bill issue of 10.8.1918 (1 year bond). Rare.	—	3,000	—
28A	**10,000 Leva Zlatni**	VG	VF	UNC
	1922. Overprint: Red diagonal on invalidated state treasury bill issue of 10.2.1918 (1 year bond). Rare.	—	3,000	—

		VG	VF	UNC
29	**10,000 Leva Zlatni**	VG	VF	UNC
	1922. Overprint: Red diagonal on invalidated state treasury bill issue of 10.8.1918 (1 or 2 year bond). Rare.	—	3,500	—

1918-1921 Proposed Issues

		VG	VF	UNC
29A	**500 Leva**	VG	VF	UNC
	1920. Arms at left. Back: Lakeside building with tower at center. Printer: O-FZ. (not issued).			
	a. Violet on beige underprint. Rare.	—	—	2,500
	b. Blue on yellow underprint. Rare.	—	—	2,500
	c. Violet on yellow-green underprint. Rare.	—	—	2,500
	d. Blue on light green underprint. Rare.	—	—	2,500

		VG	VF	UNC
29B	**500 Leva**	VG	VF	UNC
	1920. Arms at left. Back: Lakeside town view at center. Printer: O-FZ.			
	a. Violet on beige underprint. Rare.	—	—	2,500
	b. Blue on yellow underprint. Rare.	—	—	2,500
	c. Violet on yellow-green underprint. Rare.	—	—	2,500
	d. Red-brown on yellow underprint (without back vignette). Rare.	—	—	2,500

29C	1000 Leva Zlatni	VG	VF	UNC
	1918. Green on green and tan underprint. King Ferdinand at right. Signatures: Chakalov and Venkov BC: Green and ochre. Back: Value at center. Printer: G&D. (Not issued). Rare.	—	—	—

29D	1000 Leva Zlatni	VG	VF	UNC
	1921 King Boris at right. Signatures: Damjanov and Popov Back: Value at center. Printer: G&D. (not issued).			
	a. Green on green and tan underprint. Without serial #. Perforated *GIESECKE&DEVRIENT MUSTER LEIPZIG BERLIN.* Rare.	—	—	25,000
	b. Brown on green and tan underprint. Red all zero serial #. Rare.	—	12,000	—

1920 ND Silver Issue

30	1 Lev Srebro	VG	VF	UNC
	ND (1920). Dark green and brown. Arms at left, woman at right. Signatures: Damjanov and Popov. Back: Brown. Back: Old Bank building at center. Printer: W&S.			
	a. 1 digit serial # prefix.	—	3.00	30.00
	b. 2 digit serial # prefix.	—	2.00	20.00

31	2 Leva Srebro	VG	VF	UNC
	ND (1920). Dark brown and yellow. Woman at left, arms at right. Back: Light green. Back: National Assembly building at center. Printer: W&S.			
	a. 1 digit serial # prefix.	—	4.00	40.00
	b. 2 digit serial # prefix.	—	4.00	40.00

1920 ND Gold Issue

32	500 Leva Zlato	VG	VF	UNC
	ND (1920). Black on green and ochre. Portrait King Boris III at left, his sister Knyaginya Edokiya at right in national costumes. Signatures: Chakalov and Popov. Back: Arms at center. Printer: BG			
	a. Unissued note.	—	—	2,500
	p. Proof front. Rare.	—	1,000	—
	s. Specimen. Red overprint: ОБРАЗЕЦЪ.	—	—	2,500

1920 Cashier's Bond Issue

33	1000 Leva Zlatni	VG	VF	UNC
	ND (1920). Blue-green and tan. Arms at left. Signatures: Chakalov and Venkov. Like #26. Printer: BWC.			
	a. Issued note.	10.00	70.00	300
	s1. Specimen. With prefix letter Д-О.	—	—	1,000
	s2. Specimen. With prefix letter П - Ф.	—	—	1,000

1922 Internal Payment Checks

33A	20,000 Leva	VG	VF	UNC
	1922. Printer: Vienna, Austria. Rare.	—	2,000	—

33B	50,000 Leva	VG	VF	UNC
	1922. Printer: Vienna, Austria. Rare.	—	2,000	—

33C	100,000 Leva	VG	VF	UNC
	1922. Printer: Vienna, Austria. Rare.	—	3,000	—

1922 Issue

34	5 Leva	VG	VF	UNC
	1922. Brown on light orange and green underprint. Arms at center. Signatures: Damjanov and Popov. Back: Brown and green. Back: Beehives at center. Printer: ABNC.			
	a. Issued note.	5.00	20.00	140
	s1. Specimen. Overprint: *SPECIMEN* and punch hole cancelled.	—	—	120
	s2. Specimen: Overprint: *SPECIMEN* and perforated: *CANCELLED.*	—	—	600
	ct1. Color Trial front. Rare.	—	—	1,000
	ct2. Color Trial back. Rare.	—	—	1,000

35	10 Leva	VG	VF	UNC
	1922. Purple on orange and green underprint. Arms at center. Signatures: Damjanov and Popov. Back: Purple and brown. Back: Farm woman with turkey at center. Printer: ABNC.			
	a. Issued note.	5.00	25.00	150
	s1. Specimen. Overprint: *SPECIMEN* and punch hole cancelled.	—	—	150
	s2. Specimen. Overprint: *SPECIMEN* and perforated: *CANCELLED.*	—	—	150
	ct1. Color Trial front. Rare.	—	—	1,100
	ct2. Color Trial back. Rare.	—	—	1,100

36	20 Leva	VG	VF	UNC
	1922. Green on blue, light green and orange underprint. Arms at center. Back: Orange and olive-gray. Back: Farm women working at center. Printer: ABNC.			
	a. Issued note.	8.00	40.00	350
	s1. Specimen. Overprint: *SPECIMEN* and punch hole cancelled.	—	—	160
	s2. Specimen. Overprint: *SPECIMEN* and perforated: *CANCELLED.*	—	—	160
	ct1. Color Trial front. Rare.	—	—	1,200
	ct2. Color Trial back. Rare.	—	—	1,200

37	50 Leva	VG	VF	UNC
	1922. Green and multicolor. Arms at center. Signatures: Damjanov and Popov. Back: Green. Back: Boy shepherd with flute at center. Printer: ABNC.			
	a. Issued note.	20.00	80.00	300
	s1. Specimen. Overprint: *SPECIMEN* and punch hole cancelled.	—	—	250
	s2. Specimen. Overprint: *SPECIMEN* and perforated: *CANCELLED.*	—	—	250

38	100 Leva	VG	VF	UNC
	1922. Brown and multicolor. Arms at center. Signatures: Damjanov and Popov. Back: Brown. Back: Man plowing with oxen at center. Printer: ABNC.			
	a. Issued note.	30.00	110	420
	s1. Specimen. Overprint: *SPECIMEN* and punch hole cancelled.	—	—	300
	s2. Specimen. Overprint: *SPECIMEN* and perforated: *CANCELLED.*	—	—	300

39	500 Leva	VG	VF	UNC
	1922. Blue and multicolor. Arms at center. Back: Blue. Back: Harbor scene. Printer: ABNC.			
	a. Issued note.	60.00	300	1,500
	s1. Specimen. Red overprint: *SPECIMEN* and punch hole cancelled.	—	—	400
	s2. Specimen. Overprint: *SPECIMEN* and perforated: *CANCELLED.*	—	—	400

40	1000 Leva	VG	VF	UNC
	1922. Red-brown, green and pink. Arms at center. Back: Brown. Back: Rose harvest at center. Printer: ABNC.			
	a. Issued note.	50.00	300	1,500
	s1. Specimen. Overprint: *SPECIMEN* and punch hole cancelled.	—	—	800
	s2. Specimen. Overprint: *SPECIMEN* and perforated: *CANCELLED.*	—	—	1,200
	s3. Specimen. Overprint: ОБРАЗЕЦ and punch hole cancelled. Rare.	—	—	1,500
	ct1. Color Trial front. Rare.	—	—	2,500
	ct2. Color Trial back. Rare.	—	—	2,500

1924 ND Issue

41	5000 Leva	VG	VF	UNC
	1924. Green, brown-violet and multicolor. Arms at left, portrait King Boris III at right. Signatures: Bojadjiev and Venkov. Back: Portrait Botev at left.			
	a. Issued note.	400	2,000	4,500
	b. Perforated: БНБ.	—	—	3,500
	s. Specimen. Red overprint: ОБРАЗЕЦЪ.	—	—	4,000

1924 ND Overprinted Cashier's Bond Issue

42	1000 Leva Zlatni	VG	VF	UNC
	ND (1924). Blue-green and tan. Arms at left. Overprint: Red cyrillic: *"This note is only valid within the kingdom"* with additional red series on #26.	250	500	—

		VG	VF	UNC
43	**1000 Leva Zlatni** ND (1924). Blue-green and tan. Arms at left. Overprint: Red cyrillic: *"This note is only valid within the kingdom"* with additional red series on #33.	100	200	—

1925 Issue

		VG	VF	UNC
45	**50 Leva** 1925. Brown on multicolor underprint. Portrait King Boris III at right, arms at left. Signatures: Bojadjiev and Venkov. Back: Blue. Back: Farm women working at center. Printer: BWC.			
	a. Issued note.	8.00	60.00	260
	s1. Specimen. Red overprint: *SPECIMEN* punch hole cancelled.	—	—	300
	s2. Specimen with prefix letter. (A to Ч). Rare.	—	—	1,000
	ct. Color Trial. (A, B, or C). Rare.	—	—	1,000

		VG	VF	UNC
46	**100 Leva** 1925. Dark blue on multicolor underprint. Portrait King Boris III at right, arms at left. Back: Dark green. Back: People gathered in front of house at center. Printer: BWC.			
	a. Issued note.	5.00	40.00	130
	s1. Specimen. Red overprint: *SPECIMEN* punch hole cancelled.	—	—	300
	s2. Specimen with prefix letter. (A to C). Rare.	—	—	1,000
	ct. Color Trial. (A, B, or C). Rare.	—	—	1,000

		VG	VF	UNC
47	**500 Leva** 1925. Dark green on multicolor underprint. Portrait King Boris III at right. Back: Red on light blue underprint. Back: Man with oxen. Printer: BWC.			
	a. Issued note.	20.00	100	500
	s1. Specimen. Red overprint: *SPECIMEN* and punch hole cancelled.	—	—	450
	s2. Specimen with prefix letter. (A to K). Rare.	—	—	1,000
	ct. Color Trial. (A, B, or C). Rare.	—	—	1,000

		VG	VF	UNC
48	**1000 Leva** 1925. Brown on multicolor underprint. Portrait King Boris III at right. Back: Female seated at center pouring water; two male farmers at left, two women at loom at right, all in national costumes. Printer: BWC.			
	a. Issued note.	20.00	100	800
	s1. Specimen. Red overprint: *SPECIMEN* and punch hole cancelled.	—	—	600
	s2. Specimen with prefix letter. (A to П). Rare.	—	—	1,200
	ct. Color Trial. (A, B, or C). Rare.	—	—	1,200

		VG	VF	UNC
49	**5000 Leva** 1925. Purple on multicolor underprint. Portrait King Boris III at right, arms at left. Signatures: Bojilov and Venkov. Back: Brown on light blue underprint. Back: Aleksandr Nevski Cathedral, Sofia. Printer: BWC.			
	a. Issued note.	120	500	3,500
	s1. Specimen. Red overprint: *SPECIMEN* and punch hole cancelled.	—	—	1,000
	s2. Specimen with prefix letter. (A-Ж, 3). Rare.	—	—	3,500
	ct. Color Trial. (A, B, or C). Rare.	—	—	2,500

1925 ND Issue

		VG	VF	UNC
49A	**10 Leva** ND (1925). Ochre and green-brown. Portrait Rakovski at center. Signatures Bojilov and Venkov. Back: Green-gray. Man with oxen. Printer: BG (not issued).			
	a. Unissued note. Rare.	—	—	4,000
	s. Specimen. Red overprint: ОБРАЗЕЦЪ. Rare.	—	—	4,000

		VG	VF	UNC
49B	**20 Leva** ND (1925). Ochre and brown. Portrait King Boris III at center. Signatures: Bojilov and Venkov. Back: Salt-cellars. Printer: BG			
	a. 1 suffix letter serial #.	50.00	200	800
	b. 2 suffix letter serial #.	50.00	200	800
	s. Specimen. Red overprint: ОБРАЗЕЦЪ.	—	—	400

1929 Issue

		VG	VF	UNC
50	**200 Leva** 1929. Black on olive and light blue underprint. King Boris III at right, arms at bottom center. Signatures: Ivanov and Nachev. Back: Green. Back: Old man at center. Watermark: Rampant lion. Printer: TDLR.			
	a. Issued note.	4.00	15.00	80.00
	s. Specimen. Red overprint: *SPECIMEN.*	—	—	300
	ct. Color Trial.	—	—	900

		VG	VF	UNC
51	**250 Leva** 1929. Black and purple on peach underprint. King Boris III at right, arms at left. Signatures: Ivanov and Nachev. Back: Purple. Back: Aerial view of Tirnovo at center. Printer: TDLR.			
	a. Issued note.	5.00	20.00	140
	s. Specimen. Red overprint: *SPECIMEN.*	—	—	300
	ct. Color Trial.	—	—	1,000

		VG	VF	UNC
52	**500 Leva** 1929. Blue and multicolor. King Boris III at right, arms at left. Signatures: Ivanov and Nachev. Back: River canyon. Printer: TDLR.			
	a. Issued note.	10.00	60.00	360
	s. Specimen. Red overprint: *SPECIMEN.*	—	—	400
	ct. Color Trial.	—	—	1,200

		VG	VF	UNC
53	**1000 Leva** 1929. Red-brown on light green and tan underprint. King Boris III at right, arms at left. Signatures: Ivanov and Nachev. Back: Mountain lake. Printer: TDLR.			
	a. Issued note.	20.00	100	1,000
	s. Specimen. Red overprint: *SPECIMEN.*	—	—	1,200
	ct. Color Trial.	—	—	1,500

54	5000 Leva	VG	VF	UNC
	1929. Brown and brown-violet. King Boris III at right, arms at left. Signatures: Ivanov and Nachev. Back: Monastery. Printer: TDLR.			
	a. Issued note.	100	300	2,000
	s. Specimen. Red overprint: *SPECIMEN.*	—	—	1,000
	ct. Color Trial.	—	—	2,000

1938 Issue

55	500 Leva	VG	VF	UNC
	1938. Lilac, brown and green. Portrait King Boris III at left, arms at right. Signatures: Bojilov and Ivanov. Back: Sheaf of wheat at right. Watermark: Maria-Louiza Knyaginya in circle. Printer: G&D.			
	a. Issued note.	8.00	40.00	140
	s. Specimen. Red overprint: SPECIMEN.	—	—	1,500

56	1000 Leva	VG	VF	UNC
	1938. Lilac, brown and green. Portrait King Boris III at left. Signatures: Bojilov and Ivanov. Back: Flowers. Watermark: Simeon Knyaz in circle. Printer: G&D.			
	a. Issued note.	10.00	60.00	300
	s1. Specimen. Red overprint: *SPECIMEN.* All zero serial #.	—	—	600
	s2. Specimen. Serial # at top left and bottom right. Rare	—	—	2,000

57	5000 Leva	VG	VF	UNC
	1938. Green. Portrait King Boris III at left. Back: New bank building. Watermark: King Boris III and Queen Joanna. Printer: G&D.			
	a. Issued note.	150	550	3,000
	s1. Specimen. Red overprint: *SPECIMEN.* All zero serial #.	—	—	1,500
	s2. Specimen. Serial # at top left and bottom right. Rare.	—	—	4,000

1940 Issue

58	500 Leva	VG	VF	UNC
	1940. Blue on green underprint. Portrait King Boris III at right, arms at left. Signatures: Gounev and Ivanov. Back: Port Varna scene, boat at dockside. Printer: RDK.			
	a. Issued note.	5.00	15.00	100
	s1. Specimen. Red overprint: *SPECIMEN.*	—	—	350
	s2. Specimen. Perforated: *DRUCKPROBE* all zero serial #.	—	—	1,200

59	1000 Leva	VG	VF	UNC
	1940. Red and brown. Portrait King Boris III at right. Signatures: Gounev and Ivanov. Back: Man plowing with oxen. Printer: RDK.			
	a. Issued note.	5.00	30.00	350
	s1. Specimen. Red overprint: *SPECIMEN.*	—	—	350
	s2. Specimen. Perforated: *DRUCKPROBE* with all zero serial #.	—	—	1,200

1942 Issue

60	500 Leva	VG	VF	UNC
	1942. Black and blue on green and brown underprint. Portrait King Boris III at left. Signatures: Gounev and Ivanov. Back: Woman at right. Watermark: BNB. Printer: G&D.			
	a. Issued note.	2.00	15.00	70.00
	s. Specimen. Red overprint: *SPECIMEN.*	—	—	400

61	1000 Leva	VG	VF	UNC
	1942. Light and dark brown on orange and blue underprint. Portrait King Boris III at left. Signatures: Gounev and Ivanov. Back: Monastery at right. Watermark: BNB. Printer: G&D.			
	a. Issued note.	3.00	25.00	130
	s. Specimen. Red overprint: *SPECIMEN.*	—	—	400

62	5000 Leva	VG	VF	UNC
	1942. Brown and multicolor. Portrait King Boris III at left. Back: National Assembly building. Watermark: BNB. Printer: G&D.			
	a. Issued note.	60.00	150	450
	s. Specimen. Red overprint: *SPECIMEN.*	—	—	500

1943 Issue

63	20 Leva	VG	VF	UNC
	1943. Blue-black on light red underprint. Year date in lower right margin. Signatures: Gounev and Ivanov. Back: Brown. Back: Arms at left. Printer: BG.			
	a. 1 letter serial # prefix.	1.00	5.00	50.00
	b. 2 letters serial # prefix.	1.00	5.00	50.00
	s. Specimen. Red overprint: ОБРАЗЕЦЪ.	—	—	300

64	200 Leva	VG	VF	UNC
	1943. Brown and black. Portrait young King Simeon II at left, arms at right. Signatures: Gounev and Ivanov. Back: View of Tirnovo. Printer: RDK.			
	a. 1 letter serial # prefix.	2.00	10.00	40.00
	b. AO serial # prefix.	20.00	50.00	300
	s1. Specimen perforated: *MUSTER.*	—	—	1,000
	s2. Red overprint: *SPECIMEN.*	—	—	400

65	250 Leva	VG	VF	UNC
	1943. Green and brown. Portrait young King Simeon II at left, arms at right. Signatures: Gounev and Ivanov. Back: Man with oxen. Printer: RDK.			
	a. 1 letter serial # prefix.	2.00	10.00	40.00
	b. AO serial # prefix.	20.00	50.00	300
	s1. Specimen perforated: *MUSTER*.	—	—	1,000
	s2. Red overprint: *SPECIMEN*.	—	—	400

66	500 Leva	VG	VF	UNC
	1943. Blue on brown underprint. Portrait young King Simeon II at left, arms at right. Signatures: Gounev and Ivanov. Back: Blue and brown. Back: Boy shepherd with flute. Printer: RDK.			
	a. 1 letter serial # prefix.	2.00	10.00	60.00
	b. AO serial # prefix.	20.00	50.00	300
	s1. Specimen perforated: *DRUCKPROBE*.	—	—	400
	s2. Red overprint: *SPECIMEN*.	—	—	400

67	1000 Leva	VG	VF	UNC
	1943. Red and dark brown on purple underprint. Portrait King Simeon II at right, arms at left. Signatures: Gounev and Ivanov. Back: Nevski Cathedral. Printer: RDK.			
	a. With normal serial #. (Not issued).	—	—	150
	s. Specimen perforated: *MUSTER*. Rare.	—	—	5,000

67A	5000 Leva	VG	VF	UNC
	1943. Brown and red. Portrait King Simeon II at right, arms at left. Signatures: Gounev and Ivanov. Back: Orange and green. Back: Rose harvest scene. Printer: RDK.			
	s. Specimen perforated: *MUSTER*. Rare.	—	—	25,000

State Treasury
1942 Bond Issue

67B	1000 Leva	VG	VF	UNC
	25.3.1942. Arms at right. Printer: BG. Rare.	—	2,500	—

67C	5000 Leva	VG	VF	UNC
	15.12.1942. Red on blue and pink underprint. Arms at right. Back: Red on green and brown underprint. Printer: BG. Rare.	—	1,500	—

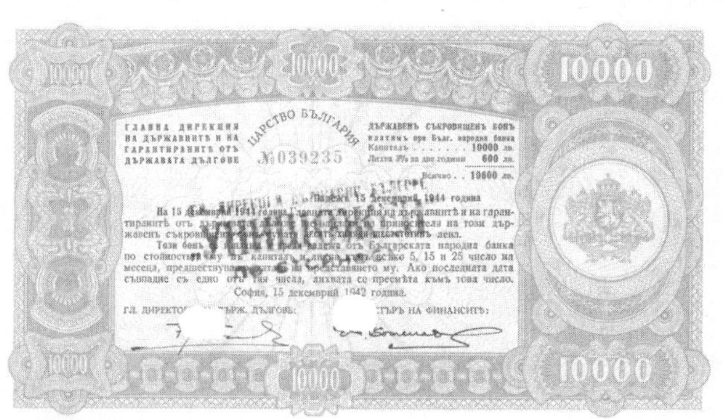

67D **10,000 Leva** | VG — | VF 2,000 | UNC —

15.12.1942. Brown on blue and pink underprint. Arms at right. Printer: BG. Rare.

67E **20,000 Leva** | VG — | VF 3,000 | UNC —

5.12.1942. Gray on green and purple underprint. Arms at right. Printer: BG. Rare.

67F **50,000 Leva** | VG — | VF 3,000 | UNC —

5.12.1942. Blue on green and purple underprint. Arms at right. Printer: BG. Rare.

1943 Bond Issue

Note: Reportedly used as currency during and after WWII.

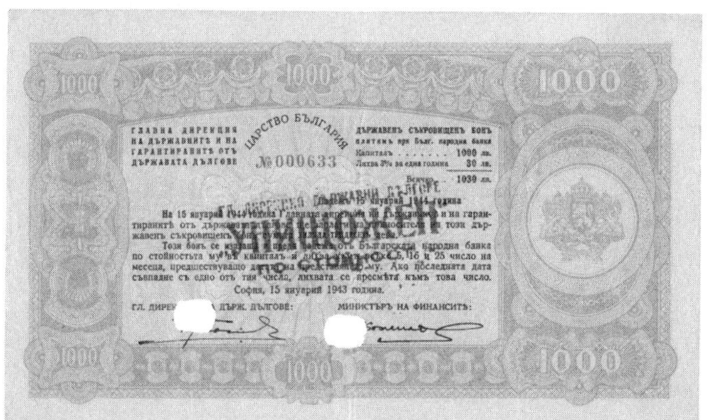

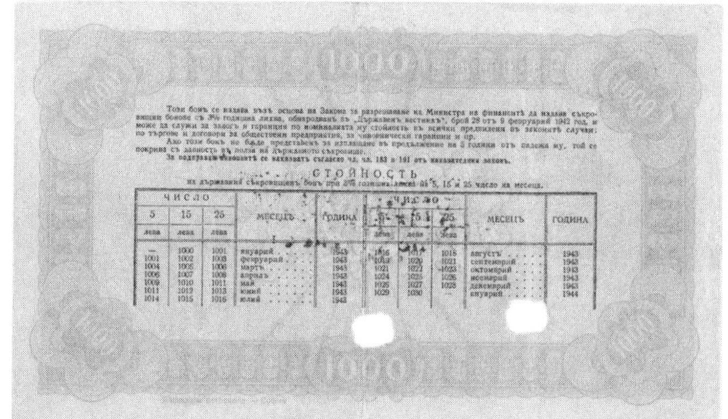

67G **1000 Leva** | VG — | VF 1,500 | UNC —

15.1.1943. Orange on light blue and ochre underprint. Arms at right. Back: Orange on green underprint. Printer: BG. Rare.

67H **1000 Leva** | VG 15.00 | VF 60.00 | UNC 200

25.1.1943. Green on light blue and orange underprint. Arms at right. Back: Green on grayish green and ochre underprint. Printer: BG.

67I **1000 Leva** | VG 10.00 | VF 40.00 | UNC 120

15.6.1943. Brownish orange on multicolor underprint. Arms at right. Back: Blue on orange and blue underprint. Printer: BG.

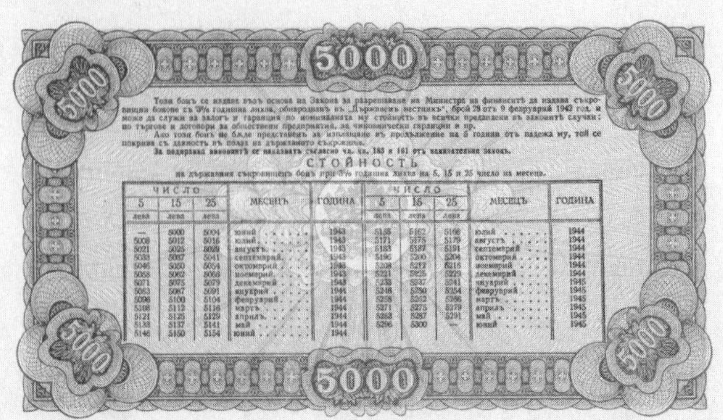

67J	5000 Leva	VG	VF	UNC
	15.6.1943. Green on multicolor underprint. Arms at right. Back: Blue on orange and blue underprint. Printer: BG.	30.00	150	500

1944 Bond Issue

Note: Reportedly used as currency during and after WWII.

67K	1000 Leva	VG	VF	UNC
	15.1.1944. Blue on green and purple underprint. Arms at right. Printer: BG.	20.00	60.00	250
67L	**1000 Leva**	**VG**	**VF**	**UNC**
	5.7.1944. Light brown on green and ochre underprint. Arms at right. Printer: BG.	10.00	30.00	120

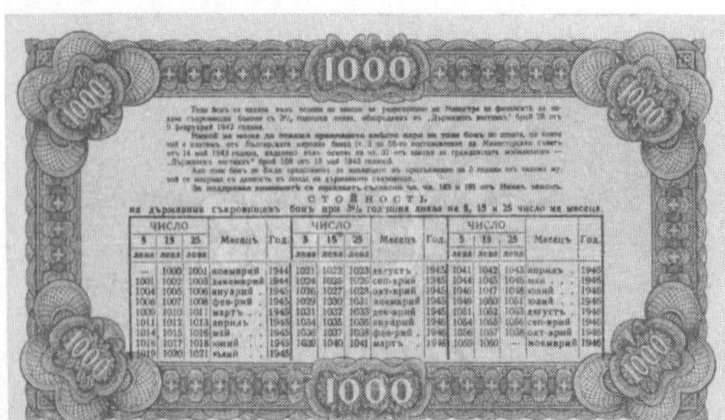

67M	1000 Leva	VG	VF	UNC
	15.11.1944. Ochre on pink and yellow. Arms at right. Back: Dark brown on light blue and ochre underprint. Printer: BG.			
	a. Issued note.	10.00	50.00	200
	s1. Specimen. Red overprint: ОБРАЗЕЦЪ.	—	—	250

67N	5000 Leva	VG	VF	UNC
	15.11.1944. Brown on gray and light brown. Arms at right. Back: Orange on light blue and ochre underprint.			
	a. Issued note.	10.00	50.00	150
	s. Specimen. Red overprint: ОБРАЗЕЦЪ.	—	—	200

1945 Bond Issue

Note: Reportedly used as currency during and after WWII.

67O	1000 Leva	VG	VF	UNC
	5.3.1945. Brown on light brown and light blue underprint. Arms at upper center. Back: Green on light brown underprint. Printer: BG.			
	a. Issued note.	8.00	40.00	120
	s. Specimen. Red overprint: ОБРАЗЕЦ.	—	—	200

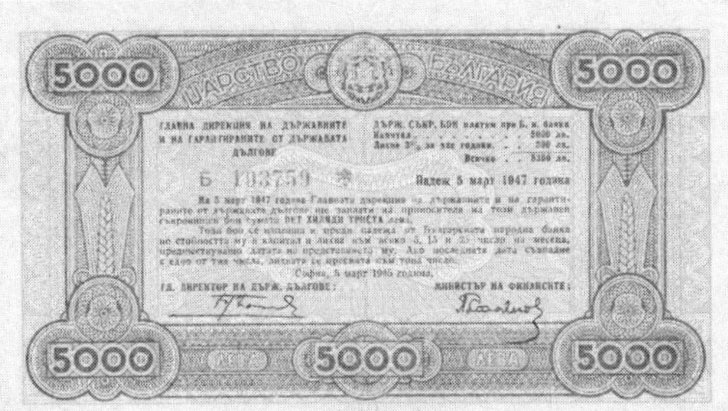

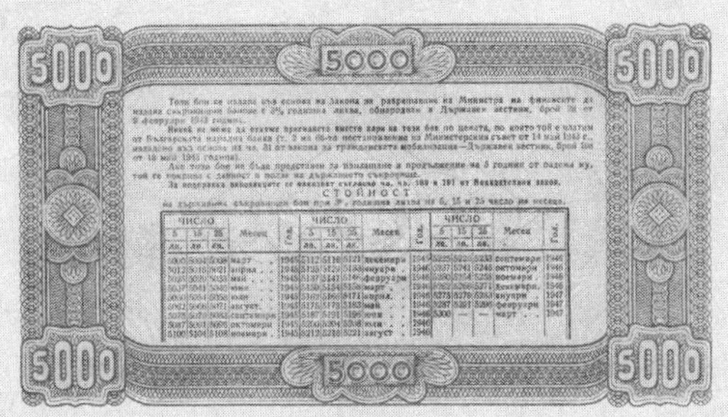

67P	5000 Leva	VG	VF	UNC
	5.3.1945. Purple on yellow and gray underprint. Arms at upper center. Back: Ochre on light brown and yellow underprint.			
	a. Issued note.	10.00	50.00	120
	s. Specimen. Red overprint: ОБРАЗЕЦ.	—	—	200

1946 Bond Issue

Note: Reportedly used as currency after WWII.

67Q	1000 Leva	VG	VF	UNC
	5.11.1946. Dark blue on light blue and pink underprint. Modified arms at upper center.			
	a. Issued note.	5.00	30.00	120
	s. Specimen. Red overprint: ОБРАЗЕЦ.	—	—	200

67R	5000 Leva	VG	VF	UNC
	5.11.1946. Red on light green and pink underprint. Modified arms at upper center. Printer: BG.			
	a. Issued note.	1.00	5.00	40.00
	s. Specimen. Red overprint: ОБРАЗЕЦ.	—	—	200

БЪЛГАРСКАТА НАРОДНА БАНКА

Bulgarian National Bank

1944-1945 Issue

68	20 Leva	VG	VF	UNC
	1944. Brown. Year date in lower right margin. Signatures: Stefanov and Kalchev. Back: Arms at center.			
	a. 1 letter serial # prefix. Red serial #.	—	2.00	25.00
	b. 2 letter serial # prefix. Red serial #.	—	2.00	25.00
	c. Brown serial #.	—	1.00	15.00
	s. As a. Specimen. Red overprint: ОБРАЗЕЦ.	—	—	250

69	200 Leva	VG	VF	UNC
	1945. Dark brown on green and tan underprint. Arms at center. Signatures: Stefanov and Ivanov. Printer: Goznak.			
	a. 1 letter serial # prefix.	3.00	12.00	120
	b. 2 letter serial # prefix.	3.00	12.00	140
	s. Specimen. Red overprint: ОБРАЗЕЦ. Punch hole cancelled. (Only on Series M #489xxx.)	—	—	300

70	250 Leva	VG	VF	UNC
	1945. Green on light brown underprint. Arms at upper center. Printer: Goznak.			
	a. 1 letter serial # prefix.	3.00	12.00	120
	b. 2 letter serial # prefix.	3.00	12.00	120
	s. As a. Specimen. Red overprint: ОБРАЗЕЦ. Punch hole cancelled. Only on Series АГ serial # range starting with 118xxx.	—	—	400

71	500 Leva	VG	VF	UNC
	1945. Blue on multicolor underprint. Arms at left. Signatures: Stefanov and Ivanov. Back: Brown on blue and orange underprint. Printer: Goznak.			
	a. 1 letter serial # prefix.	2.00	10.00	50.00
	b. 2 letter serial # prefix.	2.00	10.00	50.00
	s. Specimen. Red overprint: ОБРАЗЕЦ.	—	—	300

72	1000 Leva	VG	VF	UNC
	1945. Brown on light blue and salmon underprint. Arms at left. Signatures: Stefanov and Ivanov. Back: Wine on multicolor underprint. Printer: Goznak.			
	a. 1 letter serial # prefix.	4.00	20.00	130
	b. 2 letter serial # prefix.	10.00	30.00	200
	s. Specimen.	—	—	300

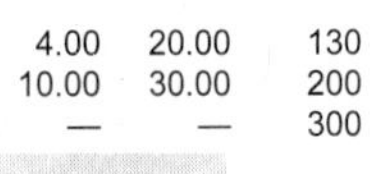

73	5000 Leva	VG	VF	UNC
	1945. Brown on multicolor underprint. Arms at upper center. Signatures: Stefanov and Ivanov. Printer: Goznak.			
	a. 1 letter serial # prefix.	6.00	30.00	200
	b. 2 letter serial # prefix.	30.00	100	450
	s. Specimen. Red overprint: ОБРАЗЕЦ.	—	—	400

PEOPLES REPUBLIC

НАРОДНА РЕПУБЛИКА БЪЛГАРИЯ

Bulgarian National Bank

1947-1948 Issues

74	20 Leva	VG	VF	UNC
	1947. Dark gray on pale blue underprint. Year after imprint in lower margin. Signatures: Tzonchev and Kalchev. Like #79. Back: Bank building at center. Printer: BG.			
	a. Issued note.	—	2.00	10.00
	s. Specimen. Red overprint: ОБРАЗЕЦ. Punch hole cancelled. (Only on Series Щ 4134.)	—	—	350

Note: For similar design note but dated 1950 see #79.

75	200 Leva	VG	VF	UNC
	1948. Brown. Year date with printer's name in lower margin. Arms with *9.IX.1944* at left. Signatures: Tzonchev and Kalchev.. Back: Miner. Printer: BG			
	a. Issued note.	1.00	5.00	20.00
	s. Specimen. Red overprint: ОБРАЗЕЦ.	—	—	250

76	250 Leva	VG	VF	UNC
	1948. Green on light brown underprint. Arms with *9.IX.1944* at left. Signatures: Tzonchev and Kalchev.. Back: Steam passenger train at center. Printer: BG.			
	a. Issued note.	1.00	5.00	30.00
	s. Specimen. Red overprint: ОБРАЗЕЦ.	—	—	250

77	500 Leva	VG	VF	UNC
	1948. Blue-black on brown underprint. Arms with *9.IX.1944* at left. Back: Tobacco harvesting. Printer: BG.			
	a. Issued note.	1.00	5.00	20.00
	s. Specimen. Red overprint: ОБРАЗЕЦ.	—	—	400

78	1000 Leva	VG	VF	UNC
	1948. Brown on blue underprint. Soldier at right. Arms with *9.IX.1944* at left. Back: Tractor and factory scene at lower center. Printer: BG.			
	a. Normal serial #. (Not issued).	—	20.00	120
	s. Specimen. Red overprint: ОБРАЗЕЦ.	—	—	350

1950 Issue

		VG	VF	UNC
79	**20 Leva** 1950. Brown on light tan underprint. Year after imprint in lower margin. Like #74. Back: Bank building at center. Printer: BG.			
	a. Issued note.	—	—	5.00
	s. Specimen. Red overprint: ОБРАЗЕЦ. (Only on Series E 3252).	—	—	200

Note: For similar note but dated 1947 see #74.

1951 State Note Issue

		VG	VF	UNC
80	**1 Lev** 1951. Brown on pale olive-green and orange underprint. Arms at left. Back: Upright hands holding hammer and sickle. Watermark: BNB with hammer and sickle. Printer: Goznak.			
	a. Issued note.	—	2.00	25.00
	s. Specimen. Red overprint: ОБРАЗЕЦ.	—	—	150

		VG	VF	UNC
81	**3 Leva** 1951. Deep olive-green on green and orange underprint. Arms at left. Back: Upright hands holding hammer and sickle. Watermark: BNB with hammer and sickle. Printer: Goznak.			
	a. Issued note.	—	—	1.50
	s. Specimen. Red overprint: ОБРАЗЕЦ.	—	—	150

		VG	VF	UNC
82	**5 Leva** 1951. Blue and green. Arms at left center. Back: Upright hands holding hammer and sickle. Watermark: BNB with hammer and sickle. Printer: Goznak.			
	a. Issued note.	—	—	1.50
	s. Specimen. Red overprint: ОБРАЗЕЦ.	—	—	150

		VG	VF	UNC
83	**10 Leva** 1951. Red-brown on multicolor underprint. G. Dimitrov at left, arms at right. Back: Farm tractor at right. Watermark: BNB with hammer and sickle. Printer: Goznak.			
	a. Issued note.	—	—	1.50
	s. Specimen. Red overprint: ОБРАЗЕЦ.	—	—	150

		VG	VF	UNC
84	**25 Leva** 1951. Gray blue on multicolor underprint. G. Dimitrov at left, arms at right. Back: Railroad construction at center. Watermark: BNB with hammer and sickle. Printer: Goznak.			
	a. Issued note.	—	—	1.50
	s. Specimen. Red overprint: ОБРАЗЕЦ.	—	—	150

		VG	VF	UNC
85	**50 Leva** 1951. Brown on multicolor underprint. G. Dimitrov at left, arms at right. Back: Peasant woman with baskets of roses at center. Watermark: BNB with hammer and sickle. Printer: Goznak.			
	a. Issued note.	—	—	1.50
	s. Specimen. Red overprint: ОБРАЗЕЦ.	—	—	150

86	100 Leva	VG	VF	UNC
	1951. Green and blue on multicolor underprint. G. Dimitrov at left, arms at right. Back: Woman picking grapes in vineyard. Watermark: Hammer and sickle. Printer: Goznak.			
	a. Issued note.	—	—	1.50
	s. Specimen. Red overprint: ОБРАЗЕЦ.	—	—	180

87	200 Leva	VG	VF	UNC
	1951. Gray-blue and black on multicolor underprint. G. Dimitrov at left, arms at right. Back: Farmers harvesting tobacco at center. Watermark: Hammer and sickle.			
	a. Issued note.	—	—	2.00
	s. Specimen. Red overprint: ОБРАЗЕЦ.	—	—	1,000

87A	500 Leva	VG	VF	UNC
	1951. Purple and multicolor. G. Dimitrov at left, arms at right. Back: River valley scene. Watermark: Hammer and sickle. Printer: Goznak.			
	a. With normal serial #. (Not issued).	—	5.00	60.00
	s. Specimen. Red overprint: ОБРАЗЕЦ.	—	—	1,200

BURMA

The Socialist Republic of the Union of Burma (now called Myanmar), is a country of Southeast Asia fronting on the Bay of Bengal and the Andaman Sea, has an area of 261,228 sq. mi. (676,577 sq. km.) and a population of 49.34 million. Capital: Rangoon. The first European to reach Burma, about 1435, was Nicolo Di Conti, a merchant of Venice. During the beginning of the reign of Bodawpaya (1782-1819AD) the kingdom comprised most of the same area as it does today including Arakan which was taken over in 1784-85. The British East India Company, while unsuccessful in its 1612 effort to establish posts along the Bay of Bengal, was enabled by the Anglo-Burmese Wars of 1824-86 to expand to the whole of Burma and to secure its annexation to British India. In 1937, Burma was separated from India, becoming a separate British colony with limited self-government. The Japanese occupied Burma in 1942, and on Aug. 1, 1943 Burma became an "independent and sovereign state" under Dr. Ba Maw who was appointed the Adipadi (head of state). This puppet state later collapsed with the surrender of Japanese forces. Burma became an independent nation outside the British Commonwealth on Jan. 4, 1948, the constitution of 1948 providing for a parliamentary democracy and the nationalization of certain industries. However, political and economic problems persisted, and on March 2, 1962, Gen. Ne Win took over the government, suspended the constitution, installed himself as chief of state, and pursued a socialistic program with nationalization of nearly all industry and trade. On Jan. 4, 1974, a new constitution adopted by referendum established Burma as a "socialist republic" under one-party rule. The country name was changed formally to the Union of Myanmar in 1989. For later issues refer to Myanmar.

RULERS:

British to 1948
Japanese, 1942-1945

MONETARY SYSTEM:

1 Rupee (Kyat) = 10 Mu = 16 Annas (Pe) to 1942, 1945-1952
1 Rupee = 100 Cents, 1942-1943
1 Kyat = 100 Pyas, 1943-1945, 1952-1989

BRITISH ADMINISTRATION

Government of India

Rangoon

1897-1915 Issue

Note: For similar notes from other branch offices see India.

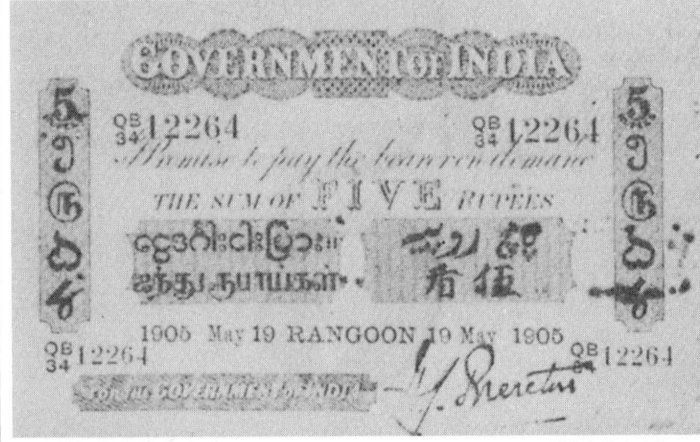

A1	5 Rupees	Good	Fine	XF
	1904-1905. Black on green underprint. Colonial type with four language panels. Uniface.			
	a. Signature F. Atkinson. 1.6.1904.	150	750	—
	b. Signature H. J. Brereton. 19.5.1905.	150	750	—

Color Abbreviation Guide

New to the *Standard Catalog of ® World Paper Money* are the following abbreviations related to color references:

BC: Back color
PC: Paper color

		Good	Fine	XF
A2	**10 Rupees** 1897-1907. Black on green underprint. Colonial type with four language panels. Uniface.			
	a. Signature R. E. Hamilton. 3.4.1897.	250	1,000	—
	b. Signature M. F. Gauntlett. 16.8.1907; 6.9.1907.	200	800	—
A3	**100 Rupees** 1915-1922. Black on green underprint. Colonial type with four language panels. Uniface.	Good	Fine	XF
	a. Signature M. M. S. Gubbay. 27.11.1915; 30.11.1915. Rare.	—	—	—
	b. Signature H. Denning. 18.8.1922. Rare.	—	—	—

1911-1914 Issue

		Good	Fine	XF
A4	**5 Rupees** 21.9.1914. Black on red underprint. Colonial type with eight language panels. Uniface. Signature M. M. S. Gubbay.	125	500	1,000

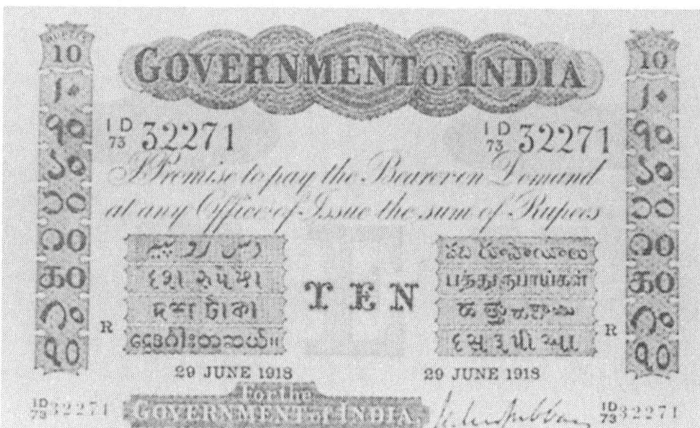

		Good	Fine	XF
A5	**10 Rupees** 1911-1918. Black on red underprint. Colonial type with eight language panels. Uniface.			
	a. Signature R. W. Gillan. 7.7.1911-30.11.1912.	650	2,000	3,500
	b. Signature H. F. Howard. 2.1.1915.	650	2,000	3,500
	c. Signature M. M. S. Gubbay. 28.3.1916-20.11.1918.	650	2,000	3,500

1917 ND Provisional Issue

		Good	Fine	XF
A6	**2 Rupees 8 Annas** ND (1917). Black on green and red-brown underprint. Portrait King George V in octagonal frame at upper left.	—	—	—

1927 ND Provisional Issue

		Good	Fine	XF
A7	**50 Rupees** ND (1927). Lilac and brown. Portrait King George V at right. Signature J. B. Taylor. Watermark: King George V.	2,500	7,000	—

		Good	Fine	XF
A8	**100 Rupees** ND (1927-1937). Violet and green. Portrait King George V at right. Watermark: King George V.			
	a. Signature H. Denning. Overprint: *RANGOON* in small black letters. Series S.	2,500	5,000	—
	b. Signature H. Denning. Overprint: *RANGOON* in small green letters. Series S.	2,500	5,000	—
	c. Signature H. Denning. Overprint: *RANGOON* in large green letters. Series S. Reported not confirmed.	—	—	—
	d. Signature J. B. Taylor. Overprint: *RANGOON* in large green letters. Series S.	2,500	5,000	—
	e. Signature J. B. Taylor. Overprint: *RANGOON* in large green letters. Series T.	2,500	5,000	—
	f. Signature J. W. Kelly. Overprint: *RANGOON* in small green letters. Series T.	2,500	5,000	—

Reserve Bank of India

Burma

1937 ND Provisional Issue

		Good	Fine	XF
1	**5 Rupees** ND (1937). Brown-violet on tan underprint. Portrait King George V at right. Signature J. W. Kelly. Watermark: King George V.			
	a. Red overprint in margins.	50.00	150	450
	b. Black overprint on face at center and on back at bottom.	50.00	150	450

		Good	Fine	XF
2	**10 Rupees** ND (1937). Dark blue. Portrait King George V at right. Signature J. W. Kelly. Watermark: King George V.			
	a. Red overprint in margins.	350	1,250	2,500
	b. Black overprint near center on face and back.	350	1,250	2,500

		Good	Fine	XF
3	**100 Rupees** ND (1937). Violet and green. Portrait King George V at right. Signature J. W. Kelly. Watermark: King George V.			
	a. *LEGAL TENDER IN BURMA ONLY* on Burma #A8f on face and back in margins.	4,500	10,000	—
	b. *LEGAL TENDER IN BURMA ONLY* on Burma #A8f on face above "I promise to Pay," and on back in lower border.	9,000	—	—

1938-1939 ND Issue

		Good	Fine	XF
4	**5 Rupees** ND (1938). Violet and green. Portrait King George VI at right, peacock at center. Back: Elephant. Watermark: King George VI.	1.00	5.00	25.00

		Good	Fine	XF
5	**10 Rupees** ND (1938). Green and multicolor. Portrait King George VI at right, ox plow and cart at center. Back: Dhow. Watermark: King George VI.	2.00	10.00	40.00

		Good	Fine	XF
6	**100 Rupees** ND (1939). Blue and multicolor. Portrait King George VI at right, peacock at center. Back: Elephant with logs. Watermark: King George VI.	500	2,750	5,500

		Good	Fine	XF
7	**1000 Rupees** ND (1939). Brown and multicolor. Portrait King George VI at center. Back: Tiger. Watermark: King George VI.	500	2,500	—
8	**10,000 Rupees** ND (1939). Green and multicolor. Portrait King George VI at center. Back: Waterfall. Watermark: King George VI.	—	—	—

JAPANESE OCCUPATION - WWII

Japanese Government

1942-1944 ND Issue

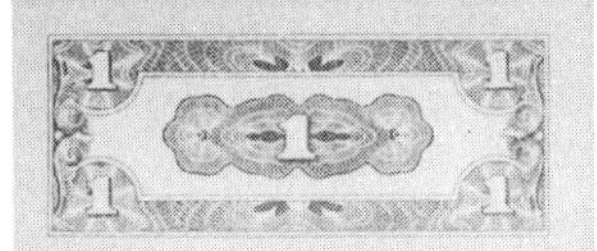

		VG	VF	UNC
9	**1 Cent** ND (1942). Red and light blue.			
	a. Block letters: BA-BP; BR-BZ.	0.10	0.20	0.60
	b. Fractional block letters: B/AA-B/EX.	0.10	0.25	0.75
	s. Specimen overprint: *Mihon.*	—	—	80.00

		VG	VF	UNC
10	**5 Cents** ND (1942). Violet and light green.			
	a. Block letters: BA-BV.	0.15	0.35	1.00
	b. Fractional block letters: B/AB-B/BX.	0.05	0.15	0.50
	s. Specimen overprint: *Mihon.*	—	—	80.00
11	**10 Cents** ND (1942). Brown and tan.			
	a. Block letters: BA-BZ.	0.15	0.35	1.00
	b. Fractional block letters: B/AA-B/AR.	0.25	1.00	4.00
	s. Specimen overprint: *Mihon.*	—	—	80.00
12	**1/4 Rupee** ND (1942). Blue and tan.			
	a. Block letters: BA-BV.	0.15	0.35	1.00
	s. Specimen overprint: *Mihon.*	—	—	100

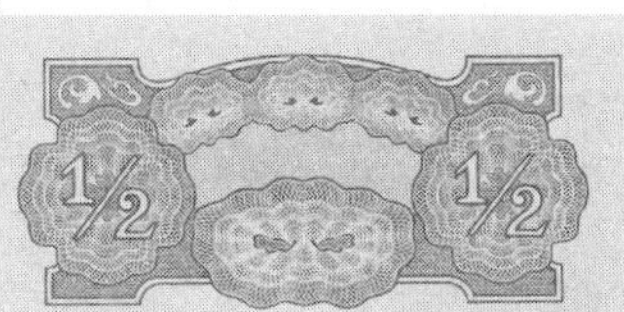

		VG	VF	UNC
13	**1/2 Rupee** ND (1942). Olive and green. Ananda Temple in Pagan at right.			
	a. Block letters: BA-BC.	0.20	0.65	3.00
	b. Block letters: BD.	0.10	0.25	0.75
	s. Specimen overprint: *Mihon.*	—	—	100

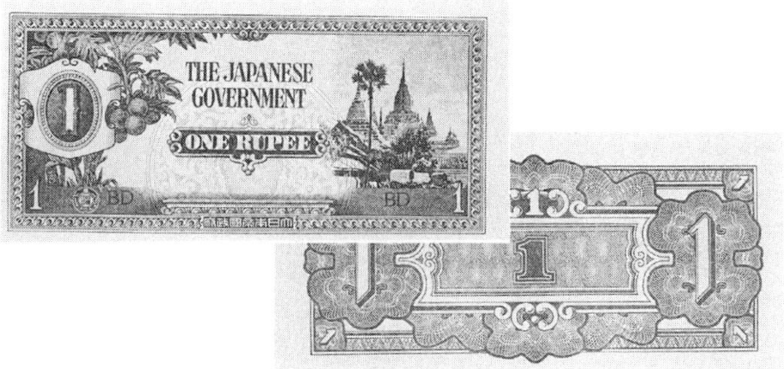

14	1 Rupee	VG	VF	UNC
	ND (1942). Green and pink. Ananda Temple in Pagan at right.			
	a. Block letters: BA-BD closely spaced. Off-white paper.	0.25	0.75	4.00
	b. Block letters: BD spaced farther apart.	0.10	0.25	0.75
	s. Specimen overprint: *Mihon.*	—	—	110

15	5 Rupees	VG	VF	UNC
	ND (1942-1944). Violet and yellow. Ananda Temple in Pagan at right.			
	a. Block letters: BA.	1.00	2.50	8.00
	b. Block letters: BB.	0.10	0.25	1.00
	s. Specimen overprint: *Mihon.*	—	—	120

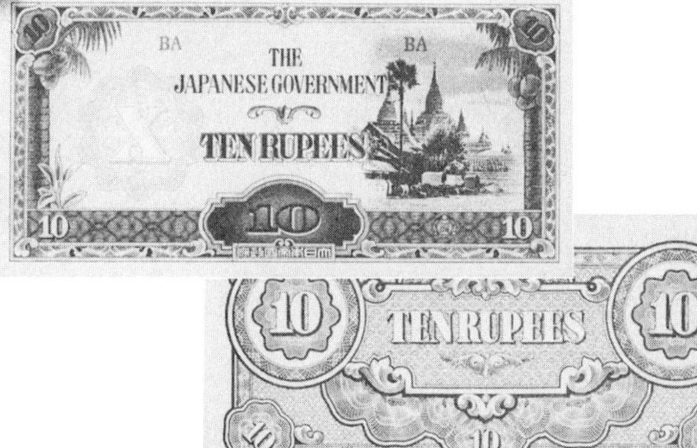

16	10 Rupees	VG	VF	UNC
	ND (1942-1944). Dull red and light green. Ananda Temple in Pagan at right.			
	a. Watermark. Block letters: BA. 8mm wide.	0.20	0.65	3.00
	b. Without watermark. Block letters: BA. 6.5mm wide. Silk threads.	0.15	0.50	2.00
	s. Specimen overprint: *Mihon.*	—	—	130

17	100 Rupees	VG	VF	UNC
	ND (1944). Dark green and gray-violet. Ananda Temple in Pagan at right.			
	a. Watermark. Block letters: BA. 7.5mm wide.	0.50	1.00	4.00
	b. Without watermark. Block letters: BA. 6.5mm wide. Silk threads.	0.10	0.40	1.00
	s. Specimen overprint: *Mihon.*	—	—	140

STATE OF BURMA

Burma State Bank

Instituted by the Japanese with Dr. Ba Maw in charge.

1944 ND Issue

18	1 Kyat	VG	VF	UNC
	ND (1944). Blue, pink and violet. Back: Peacock at left, scene in Mandalay at right. Watermark: Three Burmese characters.			
	a. Block #3; 17; 21; 22; 26; 29.	—	275	450
	s1. Red overprint: *Specimen* in script. Block #21.	—	—	450
	s2. Red Japanese characters. Overprint: *Mihon* (Specimen) on face only.	—	—	500

19	5 Kyats	VG	VF	UNC
	ND (1944). Red, purple and gray-green. Block #0. Back: Peacock at left, scene in Mandalay at right. Watermark: Three Burmese characters. Specimens only.	—	750	1,600

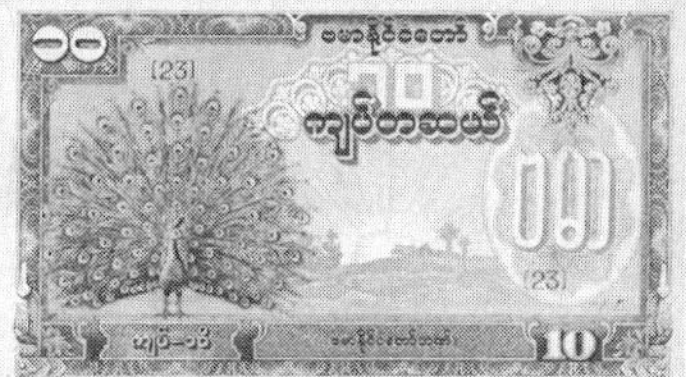

20	10 Kyats	VG	VF	UNC
	ND (1944). Green, orange and violet. Back: Peacock at left, scene in Mandalay at right. Watermark: Three Burmese characters.			
	a. Block #0; 1; 23; 24.	—	350	600
	s. Overprint: *Specimen* in script on face and back. Block #0.	—	—	600

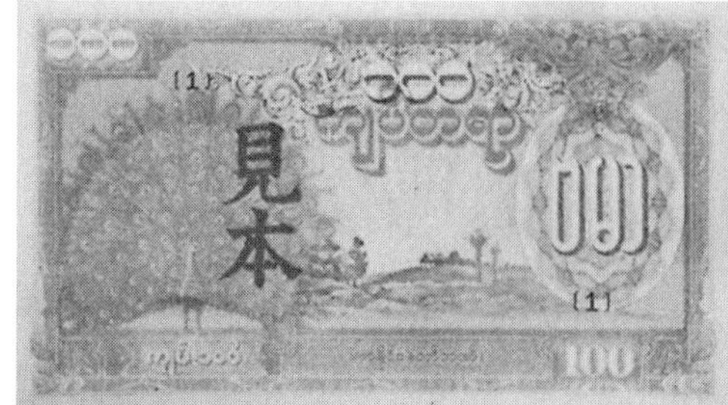

21	100 Kyats	VG	VF	UNC
	ND (1944). Orange, blue and light green. Back: Peacock at left, scene in Mandalay at right. Watermark: Three Burmese characters.			
	a. Block #1.	—	175	350
	s1. Red overprint: *Specimen* on face and back. Block #1.	—	—	300
	s2. Red Japanese characters. Overprint: *Mihon* (Specimen) on face only. Block #1.	—	—	400

1945 ND Issue

		VG	VF	UNC
22	**100 Kyats** ND (1945). Stylized peacock at lower left, portrait Ba Maw at upper right. Like #21. Back: Stylized peacock at bottom center. Printer: Rangoonian. PC: Dark blue on green underprint.			
	a. Serial # in open box directly below center.	—	35.00	125
	b. Without serial #.	—	—	70.00
	c. Sheet of 4.	—	—	—

MILITARY

Military Administration of Burma

1943 ND Provisional Issue

#23 and 24 prepared in booklet form.

		VG	VF	UNC
23	**4 Annas** ND (1943). Green. Portrait King George VI at right. Specimen.	—	—	—

		VG	VF	UNC
24	**8 Annas** ND (1943). Purple. Portrait King George VI at center. Specimen.	—	—	—

1945 ND Issue

		VG	VF	UNC
25	**1 Rupee** ND (1945 - old date 1940). Blue-gray on multicolor underprint. Coin with King George VI at upper right. Back: Coin with date at upper left. Watermark: King George VI.			
	a. Without Large *A* after black serial #.	60.00	80.00	100
	b. Large *A* after green serial #.	30.00	40.00	50.00
	s. As a. Specimen.	—	—	400

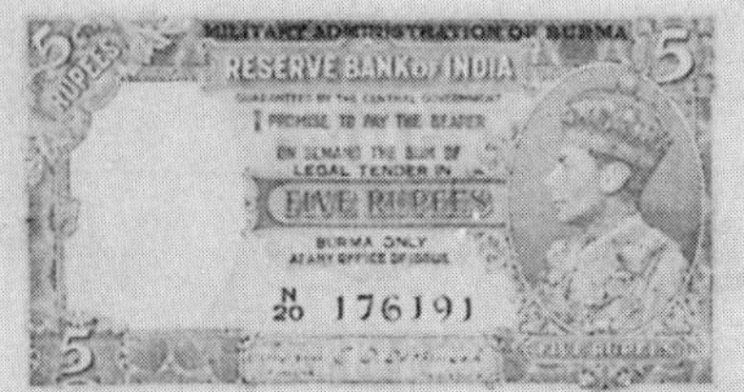

		VG	VF	UNC
26	**5 Rupees** ND (1945). Brown and green. Portrait King George VI at right. Watermark: King George VI.			
	a. Signature J. B. Taylor.	60.00	80.00	125
	b. Signature C. D. Deshmukh.	50.00	75.00	110
	s. As a. Specimen.	—	—	400

		VG	VF	UNC
27	**10 Rupees** ND (1945). Blue-violet on olive underprint. Portrait King George VI at right. Watermark: King George VI.			
	s. Specimen.	—	—	1,250

		VG	VF	UNC
28	**10 Rupees** ND (1945). Violet on multicolor underprint. Portrait King George VI at right. Signature C. D. Deshmukh. Watermark: King George VI.	75.00	125	200

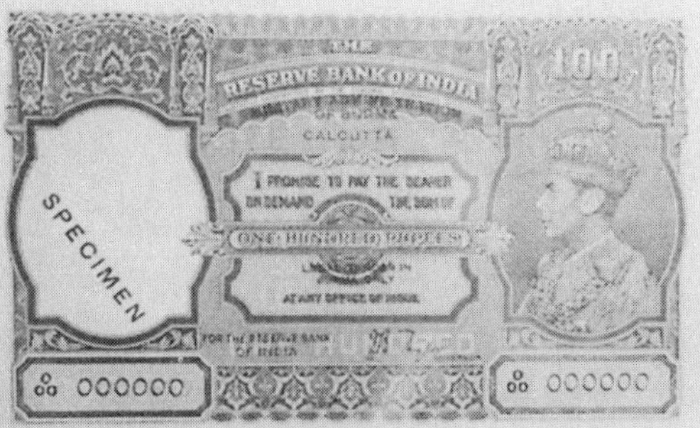

		VG	VF	UNC
29	**100 Rupees** ND (1945). Dark green on lilac underprint. Portrait King George VI at right. Watermark: King George VI.			
	a. Signature J. B. Taylor.	150	300	1,000
	b. Signature C. D. Deshmukh.	75.00	250	750
	s. As a. Specimen.	—	—	400

STATE OF BURMA - POST WWII

Burma Currency Board

1947 ND Provisional Issue

30 **1 Rupee** — VG 30.00 — VF 40.00 — UNC 50.00
ND (1947 - old date 1940). Blue-gray on multicolor underprint. Coin with King George VI at upper right.

31 **5 Rupees** — VG 60.00 — VF 80.00 — UNC 125
ND (1947). Brown and green. Back: Peacock at left, scene in Mandalay at right.

32 **10 Rupees** — VG 125 — VF 200 — UNC 350
ND (1947). Blue-violet on olive underprint. Portrait King George VI at center.

33 **100 Rupees** — VG 150 — VF 400 — UNC 1,250
ND (1947). Dark green on lilac underprint. Back: Peacock at left, scene in Mandalay at right.

Government of Burma

1948 ND Issue

34 **1 Rupee** — VG 1.00 — VF 4.00 — UNC 20.00
ND (1948). Gray, light green and pink. Peacock at right. Back: Dhows at center. Watermark: Peacock. Printer: TDLR.

35 **5 Rupees** — VG 75.00 — VF 150 — UNC 350
ND (1948). Brown and multicolor. Chinthe statue at right. Back: Woman and spinning wheel. Watermark: Peacock. Printer: TDLR.

Government of the Union of Burma

Issued by the Burma Currency Board although w/new titles on this issue.

1948-1950 ND Issue

36 **10 Rupees** — VG 2.00 — VF 7.50 — UNC 30.00
ND (1949). Blue and multicolor. Peacock at right. Back: Elephant lifting log at center.

37 **100 Rupees** — VG 10.00 — VF 35.00 — UNC 125
1.1.1948 (1950). Green. Peacock at center, chinthe head at right. Back: Worker with oxen.

Union Bank of Burma

1953 ND Rupee Issue

38 **1 Rupee** — VG 0.25 — VF 0.75 — UNC 3.00
ND (1953). Gray, light green and pink. Peacock at right. Similar to #34. Back: Dhows at center. Watermark: Peacock.

39 **5 Rupees** — VG 2.50 — VF 7.50 — UNC 25.00
ND (1953). Brown and multicolor. Chinthe statue at right. Similar to #35. Back: Woman and spinning wheel. Watermark: Peacock.

40 **10 Rupees** — VG 2.50 — VF 7.50 — UNC 25.00
ND (1953). Blue and multicolor. Peacock at right. Similar to #36. Back: Elephant lifting log at center. Watermark: Peacock.

41 100 Rupees — VG / VF / UNC
ND (1953). Green on pink underprint. Peacock at center, chinthe head at right. Similar to #37. Back: Worker with oxen. Watermark: Peacock. — 5.00 / 15.00 / 50.00

1953 ND Issue

42 1 Kyat — VG / VF / UNC
ND (1953). Gray, light green and pink. Peacock at right. Like #38. Back: Dhows at center. Watermark: Peacock. — 0.25 / 0.50 / 3.00

43 5 Kyats — VG / VF / UNC
ND (1953). Brown and multicolor. Chinthe statue at right. Like #39. Back: Woman and spinning wheel. Watermark: Peacock. — 0.50 / 2.00 / 8.50

44 10 Kyats — VG / VF / UNC
ND (1953). Blue and multicolor. Peacock at right. Like #40. Back: Elephant lifting log at center. Watermark: Peacock. — 0.75 / 2.50 / 12.50

45 100 Kyats — VG / VF / UNC
ND (1953). Green on light pink underprint. Peacock at center, chinthe head at right. Like #41. Back: Worker with oxen. Watermark: Peacock. — 1.00 / 5.00 / 35.00

1958 ND Issue

46 1 Kyat — VG / VF / UNC
ND (1958). Black, green and pink. General Aung San with hat at right. Back: Dhows at center. Similar to #42. Watermark: General Aung San.

	VG	VF	UNC
a. Issued note.	0.15	0.30	1.50
s1. Specimen. Overprint in red: *SPECIMEN* on both sides.	—	—	25.00
s2. Specimen. Red TDLR oval overprint.	—	—	50.00

47 5 Kyats — VG / VF / UNC
ND (1958). Brown and multicolor. General Aung San with hat at right. Back: Woman and spinning wheel. Similar to #43. Watermark: General Aung San.

	VG	VF	UNC
a. Issued note.	0.25	0.75	3.50
s1. Specimen. Red overprint *SPECIMEN* on both sides.	—	—	25.00
s2. Specimen. Red TDLR oval overprint.	—	—	50.00

48 10 Kyats — VG / VF / UNC
ND (1958). Blue and multicolor. General Aung San with hat at right. Back: Elephant lifting log at center. Similar to #44. Watermark: General Aung San.

	VG	VF	UNC
a. Issued note.	0.50	1.50	4.00
s1. Specimen. Red overprint: *SPECIMEN* on both sides.	—	—	25.00
s2. Specimen. Red TDLR overprint.	—	—	50.00

49 20 Kyats — VG / VF / UNC
ND (1958). Purple and multicolor. General Aung San with hat at right. 2 serial # varieties. Back: Field workers. Watermark: General Aung San.

	VG	VF	UNC
a. Issued note.	0.50	2.00	9.00
s. Specimen. Red overprint: *SPECIMEN* on both sides.	—	—	25.00

		VG	VF	UNC
50	**50 Kyats** ND (1958). Light brown and multicolor. General Aung San with hat at right. Back: Mandalay Temple. Watermark: General Aung San.			
	a. Issued note.	0.50	1.50	5.00
	s. Specimen. Red overprint: *SPECIMEN* on both sides.	—	—	25.00

		VG	VF	UNC
51	**100 Kyats** ND (1958). Green and multicolor. General Aung San with hat at right. Back: Worker with oxen. Similar to #45. Watermark: General Aung San.			
	a. Issued note.	0.50	1.50	5.00
	s. Specimen.	—	—	25.00

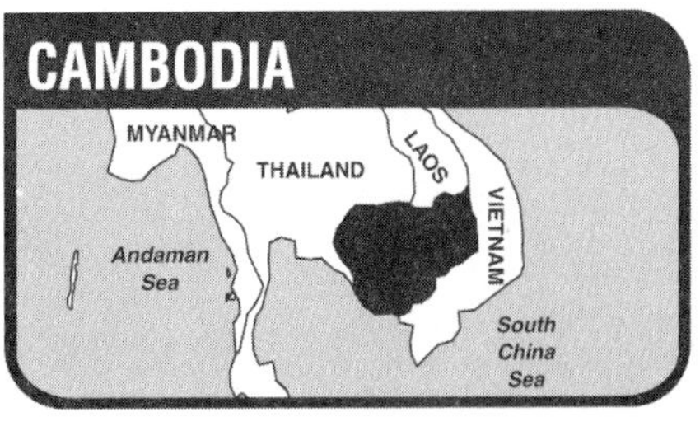

Kingdom of Cambodia, formerly known as Democratic Kampuchea, People's Republic of Kampuchea, and the Khmer Republic, a land of paddy fields and forest-clad hills located on the Indo-Chinese peninsula fronting on the Gulf of Thailand, has an area of 181,040 sq. km. and a population of 14.24 million. Capital: Phnom Penh. Agriculture is the major part of the economy, with rice the chief crop. Native industries include cattle breeding, weaving and rice milling. Rubber, cattle, corn, and timber are exported.

Most Cambodians consider themselves to be Khmers, descendants of the Angkor Empire that extended over much of Southeast Asia and reached its zenith between the 10th and 13th centuries. Attacks by the Thai and Cham (from present-day Viet Nam) weakened the empire, ushering in a long period of decline. The king placed the country under French protection in 1863 and it became part of French Indochina in 1887. Following Japanese occupation in World War II, Cambodia gained full independence from France in 1955

In April 1975, after a five-year struggle, communist Khmer Rouge forces captured Phnom Penh and evacuated all cities and towns. At least 1.5 million Cambodians died from execution, forced hardships, or starvation during the Khmer Rouge regime under Pol Pot. A December 1978 Vietnamese invasion drove the Khmer Rouge into the countryside, began a 10-year Vietnamese occupation, and touched off almost 13 years of civil war.

The 1991 Paris Peace Accords mandated democratic elections and a ceasefire, which was not fully respected by the Khmer Rouge. UN-sponsored elections in 1993 helped restore some semblance of normalcy under a coalition government. Factional fighting in 1997 ended the first coalition government, but a second round of national elections in 1998 led to the formation of another coalition government and renewed political stability. The remaining elements of the Khmer Rouge surrendered in 1998.

The colition governments parliament decided to restore the constitutional monarchy on September 24, 1993 and King Sihanouk became chief of state. He abdicated on October 6, 2004 and one of his sons, Prince Norodom Sihamoni, now sits on the throne.

RULERS:

Norodom Sihanouk, 1941-1955
Norodom Suramarit, 1955-1960
Norodom Sihanouk (as Chief of State), 1960-1970
Lon Nol, 1970-1975
Pol Pot, 1975-1979
Heng Samrin, 1979-1985
Hun Sen, 1985-1991
Norodom Sihanouk (as Chairman, Supreme National Council), 1991-1993
Norodom Sihanouk (as King), 1993-2002
Boromneath Norodom Sihamoni, 2004-

MONETARY SYSTEM:

1 Riel = 100 Sen

REPLACEMENT NOTES:

#4b-c, 5b, 7b use 3 special Cambodian prefix characters (equivalent to Z90).

SIGNATURE VARIETIES

	Chief Inspector	Governor	Advisor	Date
1				28.10.1955
2				1956
3				1956
4				Late 1961
5				Mid 1962
6				1963
7				1965
8				1968
9				1968
10				1969
11				1970
12				1972
13				1972

KINGDOM OF CAMBODIA

Banque Nationale du Cambodge

1955-1956 ND Issue

		VG	VF	UNC
1	**1 Riel** ND (1955). Blue. Figure "Kinnari" with raised arms at left. Signature 1. Back: Royal houseboat at left. Similar to French Indochina #94. Watermark: Elephant. Printer: TDLR (without imprint).			
	a. Issued note.	10.00	100	200
	s. TDLR Specimen (red oval).	—	—	—

		VG	VF	UNC
2	**5 Riels** ND (1955). Purple. Sculpture (Bayon head) at left. Signature 1. Back: Royal palace entrance at Chanchhaya at right. Watermark: Buddha. Printer: BWC (without imprint).			
	a. Issued note.	2.00	15.00	65.00
	ct. Color trial. Blue. Specimen overprint.	—	—	200

		VG	VF	UNC
3	**10 Riels** ND (1955). Brown. Temple of Banteal Srei at right. Signature 1. Back: Central market at Phnom-Penh. Watermark: Buddha. Printer: TDLR (without imprint).			
	a. Issued note.	2.00	15.00	70.00
	s1. Specimen.	—	—	—
	s2. Specimen TDLR (red oval).	—	—	—

		VG	VF	UNC
3A	**50 Riels** ND (1956). Multicolor. Cambodian with bamboo water vessels at left. Signature 1. Back: Stupas at Botoum-Waddei. Watermark: Buddha. Printer: BdF (without imprint).			
	a. Issued note.	80.00	300	850
	s. Specimen.	—	—	2,000

1956; 1958 ND Second Issue

		VG	VF	UNC
4	**1 Riel** ND (1956-1975). Grayish green on multicolor underprint. Boats dockside in port of Phnom-Penh. Back: Royal palace throne room. Printer: BWC (without imprint).			
	a. Signature 1; 2.	0.50	3.00	15.00
	b. Signature 6; 7; 8; 10; 11.	0.15	0.25	3.00
	c. Signature 12.	0.10	0.15	1.00
	r. Replacement note. As b, c. Cambodian characters equivalent to Z90.	0.10	2.00	5.00
	s. Specimen. Signature 1. Perforated and printed: *SPECIMEN.*	—	—	150
	ct. Color trial. Purple and blue. Specimen.	—	—	—

		VG	VF	UNC
5	**20 Riels** ND (1956-1975). Brown on multicolor underprint. Combine harvester at right. Back: Phnom Penh pagoda. Watermark: Buddha. Printer: BWC (without imprint).			
	a. Signature 3.	0.25	1.00	10.00
	b. Signature 6.	0.25	0.75	4.00
	c. Signature 7; 8; 10.	0.20	0.50	3.00
	d. Signature 12.	0.10	0.25	1.00
	r. Replacement note. As b. Cambodian characters equivalent to Z90.	0.10	2.00	5.00
	ct. Color trial. Green. Specimen.	—	—	—

#6 not assigned.

7	**50 Riels**	VG	VF	UNC
	ND (1956-1975). Blue and orange. Fishermen fishing from boats with Large nets in Lake Tonle Sap at left and right. Back: Angkor Wat complex. Watermark: Buddha. Printer: TDLR (without imprint).			
	a. Western numeral in plate block designator. Signature 3.	0.50	3.00	20.00
	b. Cambodian numeral in plate block designator. 5-digit serial #. Signature 7; 10.	0.25	1.00	4.00
	c. As b. Signature 12.	0.25	0.50	1.00
	d. Cambodian serial # 6-digits. Signature 12.	0.10	0.20	1.00
	r. Replacement note. As b. Cambodian characters equivalent to Z90.	0.10	—	5.00
	s1. As a. Specimen.	—	—	150
	s2. As c. Specimen. (TDLR).	—	—	150

8	**100 Riels**	VG	VF	UNC
	ND (1957-1975). Brown and green on multicolor underprint. Statue of Lokecvara at left. Back: Long boat. Watermark: Buddha.			
	a. Imprint: *Giesecke & Devrient AG, Munchen.* Signature 3.	0.50	3.00	20.00
	b. As a. Signature 7; 8; 11.	0.50	1.00	4.00
	c. Imprint: *Giesecke & Devrient-Munchen.* Signature 12; 13; 15.	0.20	0.50	2.00
	s. Specimen. As a. Signature 3. Perforated *Specimen. Uniface printings.*	—	—	200

9	**500 Riels**	VG	VF	UNC
	ND (1958-1970). Green and brown on multicolor underprint. Sculpture of two royal women dancers - *Devatas* at left. Back: Two royal dancers in ceremonial costumes. Watermark: Buddha. Printer: G&D.			
	a. Signature 3.	15.00	50.00	150
	b. Signature 6.	10.00	35.00	100
	c. Signature 9.	1.00	3.00	12.50
	s. As a. Signature 3. Specimen.	—	—	—
	x. Counterfeit.	—	2.00	5.00

Note: This banknote was withdrawn in March 1970 due to extensive counterfeiting.

1962-1963 ND Third Issue

10	**5 Riels**	VG	VF	UNC
	ND (1962-1975). Red on multicolor underprint. Bayon stone 4 faces of Avalokitesvara at left. Back: Royal Palace Entrance - Chanchhaya at right. Watermark: Buddha. Printer: BWC (without imprint).			
	a. Signature 4; 6.	0.50	3.00	20.00
	b. Signature 7; 8; 11.	0.20	0.50	4.00
	c. Signature 12.	0.10	0.25	1.00
	s. Specimen. Signature 4, 8. Perforated *SPECIMEN.*	—	—	200
	ct. Color trial. Green. Specimen.	—	—	—

11	**10 Riels**	VG	VF	UNC
	ND (1962-1975). Red-brown on multicolor underprint. Temple of Banteay Srei at right. Back: Central Market building at Phnom-Penh at left. Watermark: Buddha. Printer: TDLR (without imprint).			
	a. Signature 5; 6.	0.50	3.00	20.00
	b. Signature 7; 8; 11.	0.20	0.50	3.00
	c. Signature 12. 5 digit serial #.	0.10	0.25	1.00
	d. As c. 6 digit serial #.	0.20	0.50	2.00
	s. Specimen. Signature 5, 6, 8. TDLR.	—	—	125

12	**100 Riels**	VG	VF	UNC
	ND (1963-1972). Blue-black, dark green and dark brown on multicolor underprint. Sun rising behind Temple of Preah Vihear at left. Back: Aerial view of the Temple of Preah Vihear. Watermark: Buddha. Printer: G&D.			
	a. Signature 6.	0.50	3.00	20.00
	b. Signature 13. (Not issued).	0.10	0.20	1.00
	s. Specimen. Signature 6.	—	—	200

13	100 Riels	VG	VF	UNC
	ND (1956-1972). Blue on light blue underprint. Two oxen at right. Back: Three ceremonial women.			
	a. Printer: ABNC with imprint on lower margins, face and back. Signature 3.	3.00	20.00	100
	b. Without imprint on either side. Signature 12.	0.10	0.25	2.00
	p. Uniface proofs.	FV	FV	75.00
	s. As a. Specimen. Signature 3.	—	—	300

14	500 Riels	VG	VF	UNC
	ND (1958-1970). Multicolor. Farmer plowing with two water buffalo. Back: Pagoda at right, doorway of Preah Vihear at left. Watermark: Buddha. Printer: BdF (without imprint).			
	a. Signature 3.	0.50	4.00	30.00
	b. Signature 5; 7.	0.50	2.00	10.00
	c. Signature 9.	0.50	1.50	9.00
	d. Signature 12.	0.15	1.00	5.00
	x1. Lithograph counterfeit; watermark. barely visible. Signature 3; 5.	30.00	70.00	120
	x2. As x1. Signature 7; 9.	20.00	60.00	100
	x3. As x1. Signature 12.	15.00	45.00	80.00

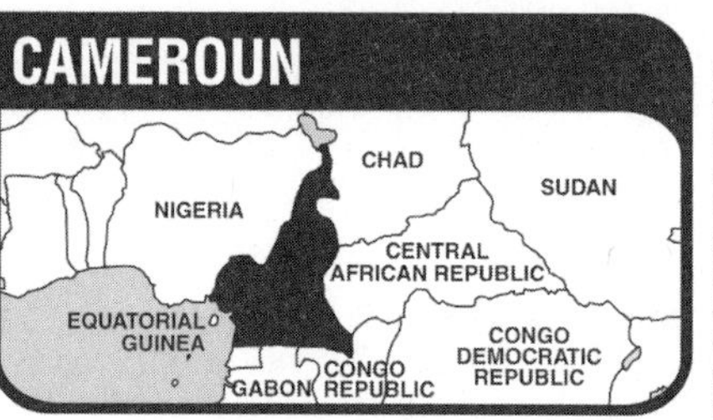

The United Republic of Cameroun, located in west-central Africa on the Gulf of Guinea, has an area of 475,440 sq. km. and a population of 18.46 million. Capital: Yaounde. About 90 percent of the labor force is employed on the land; cash crops account for 80 percent of the country's export revenue. Cocoa, coffee, aluminum, cotton, rubber and timber are exported.

The former French Cameroon and part of British Cameroon merged in 1961 to form the present country. Cameroon has generally enjoyed stability, which has permitted the development of agriculture, roads, and railways, as well as a petroleum industry. Despite a slow movement toward democratic reform, political power remains firmly in the hands of President Paul Biya.

MONETARY SYSTEM:

1 Franc = 100 Centimes

Note: German Reichsbanknoten and Reichkassenscheine circulated freely until 1914.

GERMAN KAMERUN

Kaiserliches Gouvernement

Treasury Notes

Duala

1914 Schatzscheine

1	5 Mark	Good	Fine	XF
	12.8.1914. Black on blue underprint.			
	a. Issued note.	400	1,225	2,450
	b. Cancelled.	150	400	725

Note: 10 and 20 Mark notes may possibly have been printed but they were not issued and no examples survive.

2	50 Mark	Good	Fine	XF
	12.8.1914. Gray-brown cardboard.			
	a. Light brown eagle; 2 varieties of eagles.	100	300	500
	b. Red-brown eagle.	100	300	500
	c. Cancelled.	150	400	725

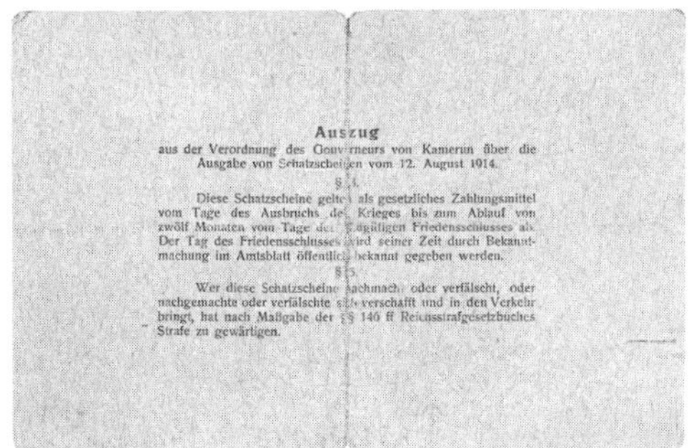

3	100 Mark	Good	Fine	XF
	12.8.1914. Gray-brown cardboard.			
	a. Blue eagle.	100	300	500
	b. Green-blue eagle.	100	300	500
	c. Cancelled.	20.00	80.00	225

FRENCH MANDATE POST WWI

1922 Territoire du Cameroun

1922 Issue

4	50 Centimes	VG	VF	UNC
	ND (1922). Red. TC monogram at top center. Back: Palm fronds at left and right.	200	600	1,500
5	1 Franc	VG	VF	UNC
	ND (1922). Brown and pink. TC monogram at top center. Back: Palm fronds at left and right.	265	800	2,000

CANADA

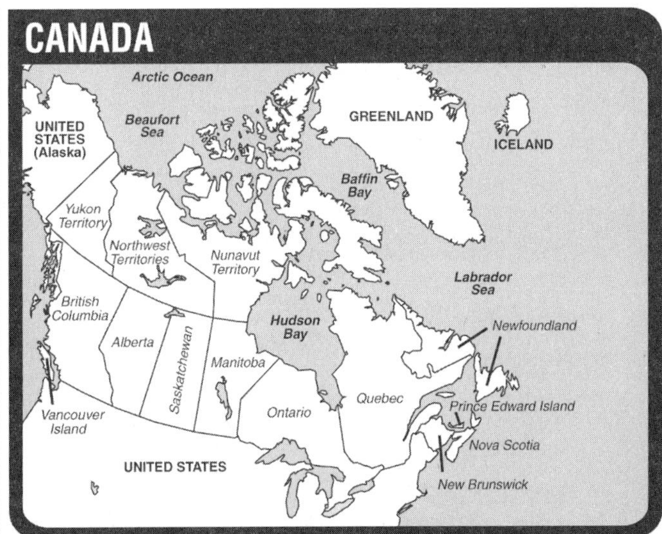

Canada is located to the north of the United States, and spans the full breadth of the northern portion of North America from Atlantic to Pacific oceans, except for the State of Alaska. It has a total area of 9,984,670 sq. km. and a population of 33.21 million. Capital: Ottawa.

A land of vast distances and rich natural resources, Canada became a self-governing dominion in 1867 while retaining ties to the British crown. Economically and technologically the nation has developed in parallel with the US, its neighbor to the south across an unfortified border. Canada faces the political challenges of meeting public demands for quality improvements in health care and education services, as well as responding to separatist concerns in predominantly francophone Quebec. Canada also aims to develop its diverse energy resources while maintaining its commitment to the environment.

RULERS:

French 1534-1763
British 1763-

MONETARY SYSTEM:

French:
12 Deniers = 1 Sou (sols)
20 Sous or Sols = 1 Livre Coloniale
1 Liard = 3 Deniers
1 Ecu = 6 Livres
1 Louis D'or = 4 Ecus
English:
4 Farthings = 1 Penny
12 Pence = 1 Shilling
20 Shillings = 1 Pound
Canadian Decimal Currency
100 Cents = 1 Dollar

PROVINCE OF CANADA

Province of Canada

1866 Issue

#1-7A Province of Canada notes w/additional ovpt.

1	1 Dollar	Good	Fine	XF
	1.10.1866. Black on light green underprint. Portrait Samuel de Champlain at lower left, arms at top center, flanked by farmer at left, and sailor at right, J. Cartier at lower right.			
	a. Overprint *PAYABLE AT MONTREAL.*	1,250	4,000	—
	b. Overprint *PAYABLE AT TORONTO.*	1,600	5,000	—
	c. Overprint *PAYABLE AT ST. JOHN.*	3,500	12,500	—

Color Abbreviation Guide

New to the *Standard Catalog of® World Paper Money* are the following abbreviations related to color references:

BC: Back color
PC: Paper color

2 **2 Dollars** | Good | Fine | XF
1.10.1866. Black on light green underprint. Indian woman at lower left, Britannia at top center flanked by a woman with agricultural produce at left and woman playing harp at right, sailor and lion at lower right.

	Good	Fine	XF
a. Overprint: *PAYABLE AT MONTREAL.*	2,000	6,500	—
b. Overprint: *PAYABLE AT TORONTO.*	3,000	8,500	—
c. Overprint: *PAYABLE AT ST. JOHN.*	4,250	—	—

3 **5 Dollars**
1.10.1866. Black on light green underprint. Queen Victoria at left, arms with lion and woman seated at top center, sailing ship at lower right.

	Good	Fine	XF
a. Overprint: *PAYABLE AT MONTREAL.*	5,000	15,000	—
b. Overprint: *PAYABLE AT TORONTO.*	—	—	—
c. Overprint: *PAYABLE AT HALIFAX.*	7,500	—	—
d. Overprint: *PAYABLE AT ST. JOHN.*	—	—	—

4 **10 Dollars**
1.10.1866. Black on light green underprint. Columbus and explorers at left, lion at center, beaver at right.

	Good	Fine	XF
a. Overprint: *PAYABLE AT MONTREAL.*	8,000	20,000	—
b. Overprint: *PAYABLE AT TORONTO.* Face proof.	—	Unc	2,500
c. Overprint: *PAYABLE AT ST. JOHN.* Reported not confirmed.	—	—	—

5 **20 Dollars**
1.10.1866. Black on light green underprint. Portrait Princess of Wales at left, beaver repairing dam at center, Prince Consort Albert at right.

	Good	Fine	XF
a. Overprint: *PAYABLE AT MONTREAL.* Rare.	—	—	—
b. Overprint: *PAYABLE AT TORONTO.* Reported not confirmed.	—	—	—
c. Overprint *PAYABLE AT ST. JOHN.* Reported not confirmed.	—	—	—

6 **50 Dollars**
1.10.1866. Black on light green underprint. Mercury with map of British America, harbor with ships and train in background.

	Good	Fine	XF
a. Overprint: *PAYABLE AT MONTREAL.* Face proof. Rare.	—	—	—
b. Overprint: *PAYABLE AT TORONTO.* Face proof.	—	Unc	3,000
c. Overprint: *PAYABLE AT ST. JOHN.* Reported not confirmed.	—	—	—

DOMINION

Dominion of Canada

Fractional Issues

#8-11 are commonly referred to as "shinplasters."

8 **25 Cents**
1.3.1870. Black on green underprint. Britannia with spear at center. Printer: BABNC.

	VG	VF	UNC
a. Without plate letter.	30.00	200	1,600
b. Plate letter *A* below date.	375	1,200	4,750
c. Plate letter *B* below date.	50.00	250	3,250

9 **25 Cents**
2.1.1900. Black on light brown underprint. Britannia seated with shield and trident at right, sailing ship in background. Printer: ABNC.

	VG	VF	UNC
a. Signature Courtney.	12.00	30.00	550
b. Signature Boville.	8.00	25.00	450
c. Signature Saunders.	12.00	40.00	650

10 **25 Cents**
2.7.1923. Black on brown underprint. Britannia with trident at center with text *AUTHORIZED BY R.S.C. CAP. 31.* across lower left and right. Signature Hyndman-Saunders. Printer: CBNC.

	VG	VF	UNC
a. Issued note.	17.00	45.00	700
p. Proof.	—	—	500

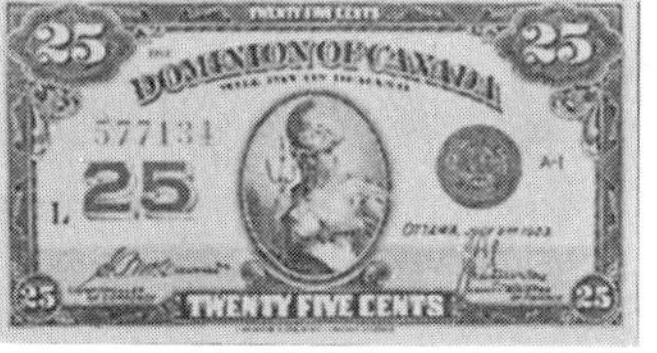

11 **25 Cents**
2.7.1923. Black on brown underprint. Britannia with trident at center. Like #10 without text *AUTHORIZED BY...* but with letters A-E, H, or J-L at left of large *25.* Printer: CBNC.

	VG	VF	UNC
a. Signature Hyndman-Saunders.	17.00	45.00	600
b. Signature McCavour-Saunders.	8.00	25.00	275
c. Signature Campbell-Clark.	8.00	25.00	275

1870 Issue

12 **1 Dollar**
1.7.1870. Black on green underprint. Portrait J. Cartier at upper left, reclining woman with child and globe at center. Printer: BABNC.

	Good	Fine	XF
a. *PAYABLE AT MONTREAL* on back.	425	2,500	15,000
b. *PAYABLE AT TORONTO* on back.	425	2,500	15,000
c. Overprint: *MANITOBA* on face. *PAYABLE AT TORONTO* on back.	5,000	—	—
d. *PAYABLE AT HALIFAX* on back.	2,250	6,000	—
e. *PAYABLE AT ST. JOHN* on back.	2,250	6,000	—
f. *PAYABLE AT VICTORIA* on back.	5,500	17,500	—
g. Overprint: *MANITOBA* on face. *PAYABLE AT MONTREAL* on back. Rare.	5,500	17,500	—

		Good	Fine	XF
13	**2 Dollars** 1.7.1870. Black on green underprint. Portrait Gen. de Montcalm at lower right, seated Indian chief overlooking steam train at center, portrait Gen. J. Wolfe at lower left. Printer: BABNC.			
	a. *PAYABLE AT MONTREAL* on back.	4,500	7,250	20,000
	b. *PAYABLE AT TORONTO* on back.	4,500	7,250	20,000
	c. Overprint: *MANITOBA* on face. *PAYABLE AT TORONTO* on back.	—	—	—
	d. *PAYABLE AT HALIFAX* on back.	6.00	10,000	—
	e. *PAYABLE AT ST. JOHN* on back.	—	—	—
	f. *PAYABLE AT VICTORIA* on back. Reported not confirmed.	—	—	—
	g. Overprint: *MANITOBA* on face. *PAYABLE AT MONTREAL* on back. Unknown	—	—	—

1871 Issue

#14 and 15 face and back proofs are known. All are rare.

		Good	Fine	XF
14	**500 Dollars** 1.7.1871. Black on green underprint. Portrait young Queen Victoria at center. Printer: BABNC.			
	a. *PAYABLE AT MONTREAL.*	—	—	—
	b. *PAYABLE AT TORONTO.*	—	—	—
	c. *PAYABLE AT HALIFAX.*	—	—	—
	d. *PAYABLE AT ST. JOHN.*	—	—	—
	e. *PAYABLE AT VICTORIA.*	—	—	—
	f. *PAYABLE AT WINNIPEG.*	—	—	—
	g. *PAYABLE AT CHARLOTTETOWN.*	—	—	—
	h. *PAYABLE AT OTTAWA* overprint.	—	—	—
	p. Face and back proof.	—	Unc	5,000

		Good	Fine	XF
15	**1000 Dollars** 1.7.1871. Black on green underprint. Canadian arms at center flanked by woman with lion at left, agricultural produce at right. Printer: BABNC.			
	a. *PAYABLE AT MONTREAL.*	—	—	—
	b. *PAYABLE AT TORONTO.*	—	—	—
	c. *PAYABLE AT HALIFAX.*	—	—	—
	d. *PAYABLE AT ST. JOHN.*	—	—	—
	e. *PAYABLE AT VICTORIA.*	—	—	—
	f. *PAYABLE AT WINNIPEG.*	—	—	—
	g. *PAYABLE AT CHARLOTTETOWN.*	—	—	—
	h. *PAYABLE AT OTTAWA* overprint.	—	—	—
	p. Face and back proof.	—	Unc	7,500

1872 Issue

#16 and 16A face and back proofs are known. All are rare.

		Good	Fine	XF
16	**50 Dollars** 1.3.1872. Black on green underprint. Mercury with map of British America at center, harbor with ships and train in background. Printer: BABNC.			
	a. *PAYABLE AT MONTREAL.*	—	—	—
	b. *PAYABLE AT TORONTO.*	—	—	—
	c. *PAYABLE AT OTTAWA.*	—	—	—
	p. Face and back proof.	—	Unc	3,000

		Good	Fine	XF
16A	**100 Dollars** 1.3.1872. Parliament building at center. Printer: BABNC.			
	a. *PAYABLE AT MONTREAL.*	—	—	—
	b. *PAYABLE AT TORONTO.*	—	—	—
	c. *PAYABLE AT OTTAWA.*	—	—	—
	p. Face and back proof.	—	Unc	3,000

1878 Issue

		Good	Fine	XF
17	**1 Dollar** 1.6.1878. Black on green underprint. Portrait Countess of Dufferin at center. Scalloped borders, corners without numeral. Printer: BABNC.			
	a. *PAYABLE AT MONTREAL* on back.	400	1,600	8,000
	b. *PAYABLE AT TORONTO* on back.	325	1,800	10,000
	c. *PAYABLE AT HALIFAX* on back.	2,750	8,500	—
	d. *PAYABLE AT ST. JOHN* on back.	1,300	5,500	—
	p. Face and back proof.	—	Unc	3,000

		Good	Fine	XF
18	**1 Dollar** 1.6.1878. Black on green underprint. Portrait Countess of Dufferin at center. Scalloped and lettered borders, with *1* in a circle at corners. Like #17. Printer: BABNC.			
	a. Without series letter; Series A-C. *PAYABLE AT MONTREAL* on back.	275	700	4,500
	b. Without series letter; Series A. *PAYABLE AT TORONTO* on back.	350	900	5,000
	c. *PAYABLE AT HALIFAX* on back.	1,500	5,000	—
	d. *PAYABLE AT ST. JOHN* on back.	1,250	5,000	—

		Good	Fine	XF
19	**2 Dollars** 1.6.1878. Black on green underprint. Portrait Earl of Dufferin (Governor General) at center. Printer: BABNC.			
	a. *PAYABLE AT MONTREAL* on back.	1,550	6,000	15,000
	b. *PAYABLE AT TORONTO* on back.	1,550	6,000	15,000
	c. *PAYABLE AT HALIFAX* on back.	4,000	—	—
	d. *PAYABLE AT ST. JOHN* on back.	6,000	15,000	—

1882 Issue

		Good	Fine	XF
20	**4 Dollars** 1.5.1882. Black on green underprint. Portrait Duke of Argyll (Governor General Marquis of Lorne) at center. Printer: BABNC.	800	3,500	15,000

1887 Issue

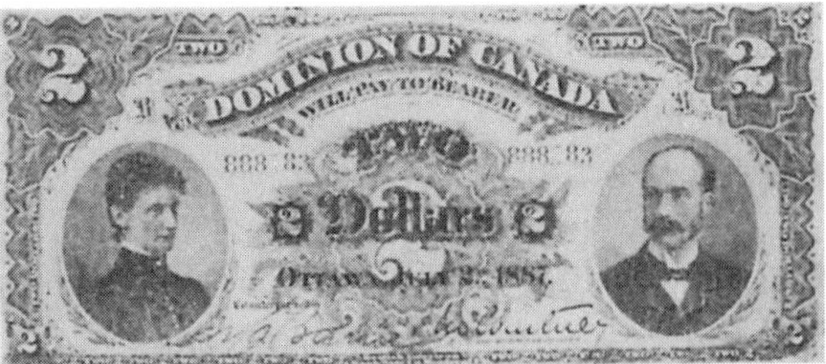

		Good	Fine	XF
21	**2 Dollars** 2.7.1887. Black and green. Portrait Marchioness and Marquis of Lansdowne (Governor General) at lower left and lower right. Printer: BABNC.			
	a. Without series letter.	400	1,750	6,500
	b. Series Letter *A.*	2,500	7,250	18,000

1896 Bank Legal Issue

#21A-21C used in bank transactions only.

		VG	VF	UNC
21A	**500 Dollars** 2.7.1896. Black on peach underprint. Genius at lower left, portrait Marquis of Lorne at center, Parliament building tower at lower right. Back: Seal of Canada at center. Printer: BABNC.			
	a. Issued note, cancelled.	—	—	—
	p1. Face proof.	—	—	20,000
	p2. Back proof.	—	—	35,000
	s. Specimen.	—	—	—

		VG	VF	UNC
21B	**1000 Dollars** 2.7.1896. Black. Portrait Queen Victoria at left. Back: Seal of Canada at center. Printer: BABNC.			
	a. Issued note, cancelled.	—	—	—
	p1. Face proof.	—	—	20,000
	p2. Back proof.	—	—	—
	s. Specimen.	—	—	—

		VG	VF	UNC
21C	**5000 Dollars** 2.7.1896. Black on yellow-orange underprint. Portrait J. A. MacDonald at left. Back: Seal of Canada at top center. Printer: BABNC.			
	a. Issued note, cancelled.	—	—	—
	p1. Face proof.	—	—	25,000
	p2. Back proof.	—	—	3,500
	s. Specimen.	—	—	—

1897-1900 Issue

		VG	VF	UNC
22	**1 Dollar** 2.7.1897. Black on green underprint. Portrait Countess and Earl of Aberdeen (Governor General) at left and right, lumberjacks at center. Back: Parliament building at center. Printer: ABNC-Ottawa.	600	2,650	15,000

#23 deleted.

		VG	VF	UNC
24	**1 Dollar** 31.3.1898. Black on green underprint. Portrait Countess and Earl of Aberdeen (Governor General) at left and right, lumberjacks at center. Signature: Courtney. Series A-D. Back: Parliament building at center. Like #22 but *ONE's* at left and right edge on back curved inward. Printer: ABNC-Ottawa.	200	2,500	8,000

		VG	VF	UNC
24A	**1 Dollar** 31.3.1898. Black on green underprint. Portrait Countess and Earl of Aberdeen (Governor General) at left and right, lumberjacks at center. Back: Parliament building at center. Like #24 but *ONE's* at left and right edge on back curved outward Printer: ABNC-Ottawa.			
	a. Signature Courtney. Series D-K.	50.00	850	6,750
	b. Signature Boville. Series L-S.	115	750	6,000

		VG	VF	UNC
24B	**2 Dollars** 2.7.1897. Black on green underprint. Portrait Edward, Prince of Wales (King Edward VII), at left, boat with fisherman at center. Signature: Courtney. Back: Farmers threshing wheat at center. Printer: ABNC-Ottawa.	5,500	16,000	—

		VG	VF	UNC
24C	**2 Dollars** 2.7.1897. Black on green underprint. Portrait Edward, Prince of Wales (King Edward VII), at left, boat with fisherman at center. Like #24B. Back: Farmers threshing wheat at center. Printer: ABNC-Ottawa.			
	a. Signature Courtney. without Series or with Series A-C.	400	2,750	16,000
	b. Signature Boville. Series D-L.	350	1,850	15,000

		VG	VF	UNC
25	**4 Dollars** 2.7.1900. Black on green underprint. Portrait Countess and Earl of Minto (Governor General) at left and right, ship in locks at Sault Ste. Marie (error: view of U.S. side of locks) at center. Back: Parliament building and library at left center. Printer: ABNC-Ottawa.	1,250	4,000	20,000

1901 Bank Legal Issue

#25A-25B used in bank transactions only.

		VG	VF	UNC
25A	**1000 Dollars** 2.1.1901. Black on green underprint. Portrait Lord E. Roberts at left. Printer: ABNC-Ottawa.			
	a. Issued note, cancelled.	—	—	—
	p1. Face proof.	—	—	20,000
	p2. Back proof.	—	—	3,000
	s. Specimen.	—	—	35,000

		VG	VF	UNC
25B	**5000 Dollars** 2.1.1901. Yellow-brown. Portrait Queen Victoria at left. Printer: ABNC-Ottawa.			
	a. Issued note, cancelled.	—	—	—
	p1. Face proof.	—	—	22,000
	p2. Back proof.	—	—	3,000
	s. Specimen.	—	—	35,000

1902 Issues

		VG	VF	UNC
26	**4 Dollars** 2.1.1902. Black on green underprint. Similar to #25 but vignette at center changed to show ship in Canadian side of locks at Sault Ste. Marie, with 4s on top, *Four* on bottom. Back: Parliament building and library at left center. Printer: ABNC-Ottawa.	2,000	6,000	—

		VG	VF	UNC
26A	**4 Dollars** 2.1.1902. Black on green underprint. Similar to #25 but vignette at center changed to show ship in Canadian side of locks at Sault Ste. Marie, with *Four* twice on top, 4s on bottom. Back: Parliament building and library at left center. Printer: ABNC-Ottawa.	875	5,500	1,500

1911 Issue

27	1 Dollar	VG	VF	UNC
	3.1.1911. Black on green underprint. Portrait Earl (Governor General) and Countess of Grey at center. Back: Parliament building at center. Printer: ABNC-Ottawa.			
	a. Green line above signature Series A-L.	125	600	5,000
	b. Black line above signature Series L-Y.	100	400	2,750

28	500 Dollars	VG	VF	UNC
	3.1.1911. Black on green underprint. Portrait young Queen Mary at center. Printer: ABNC-Ottawa.			
	a. Issued note.	200,000	350,000	—
	s. Specimen.	—	—	20,000

29	1000 Dollars	VG	VF	UNC
	3.1.1911. Black on blue underprint. Portrait King George V at center. Printer: ABNC-Ottawa.			
	a. Issued note.	250,000	—	—
	s. Specimen.	—	—	22,000

1912-1914 Issue

30	2 Dollars	VG	VF	UNC
	2.1.1914. Black on light brown and olive underprint. Portrait Duke and Duchess of Connaught at left and right. Back: Nine provincial shields around Royal arms at center. Printer: ABNC-Ottawa.			
	a. Text: *WILL PAY...* curved above center *2*. Signature Boville at right.	125	575	6,000
	b. Text: *WILL PAY...* straight above center *2*. Signature Boville at right.	150	675	6,000
	c. Without seal over right *TWO*. Signature Saunders at right.	150	1,000	6,500
	d. Black seal over right *TWO*. Signature Hyndman-Saunders.	225	750	5,250
	e. Black seal, without *TWO* at right. Signature Hyndman-Saunders.	200	1,100	6,750

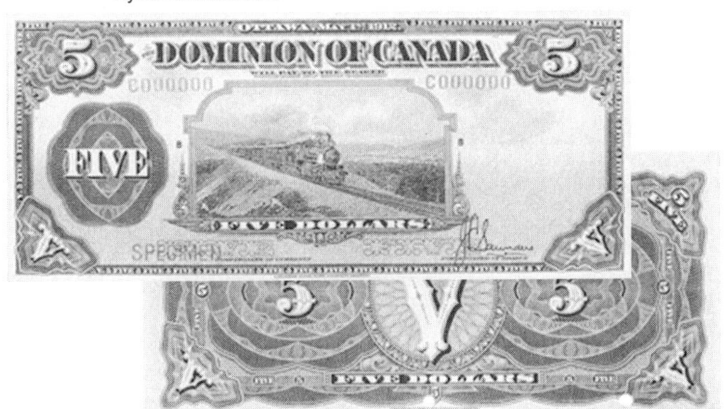

31	5 Dollars	VG	VF	UNC
	1.5.1912. Black on blue underprint. Steam passenger train *Ocean Limited* in Nova Scotia at center. Printer: ABNC-Ottawa.			
	a. Without seal over *FIVE* at right. Signature Boville at right.	800	2,000	9,000
	b. Without seal over *FIVE* at right. Signature Boville at right. B after sheet no.	1,200	2,750	—
	c. Without seal over *FIVE* at right. Signature Boville at right. B before sheet no.	850	1,400	5,750
	d. Blue seal over *FIVE* at right. Signature Hyndman-Boville.	900	1,600	7,500
	e. Blue seal over *FIVE* at right. Signature Hyndman-Saunders.	1,200	1,850	7,500
	f. Blue seal only at right. Signature Hyndman-Saunders.	850	1,375	6,000
	g. Like d. Signature McCavour-Saunders. Rare.	—	—	—
	s. Specimen.	—	—	5,500

1917 Issue

32	1 Dollar	VG	VF	UNC
	17.3.1917. Black on green underprint. Portrait Princess Patricia Ramsey (Princess of Connaught) at center without seal over right. *ONE*. Back: Parliament building at center. Printer: ABNC-Ottawa.			
	a. Without *ABNCo.* imprint. Signature Boville at right.	75.00	275	3,500
	b. With *ABNCo.* imprint. Signature Boville at right.	70.00	250	3,250
	c. With *ABNCo.* imprint. Signature Saunders at right.	100	325	3,250
	d. Black seal over right *ONE*. Signature Hyndman-Saunders.	75.00	425	3,700
	e. Without *ONE* at right. Signature Hyndman-Saunders.	75.00	275	3,250

1918 Bank Legal Issue

#32A-32B used in bank transactions only.

32A	5000 Dollars	VG	VF	UNC
	2.1.1918. Black on brown underprint. Portrait Queen Victoria at left. Printer: ABNC.			
	a. Issued note: Cancelled.	—	—	—
	p1. Face proof.	—	—	9,000
	p2. Back proof.	—	—	1,750
	s. Specimen.	—	—	—

32B	50,000 Dollars	VG	VF	UNC
	2.1.1918. Black on olive-green underprint. Portrait King George V and Queen Mary at center. Printer: ABNC.			
	a. Issued note: Cancelled.	—	—	—
	p1. Face proof.	—	—	30,000
	p2. Back proof.	—	—	4,000
	s. Specimen.	—	—	45,000

1923-1925 Regular Issue

#	Denomination	VG	VF	UNC
33	**1 Dollar** 2.7.1923. Black on green underprint. Portrait King George V at center; seal at right. Back: Library of Parliament at center. Printer: CBNC.			
	a. Black seal. Signature Hyndman-Saunders. Group 1.	65.00	250	3,500
	b. Red seal. Signature McCavour-Saunders. Group 1.	55.00	200	3,000
	c. Blue seal. Signature McCavour-Saunders. Group 1.	55.00	250	3,500
	d. Green seal. Signature McCavour-Saunders. Group 1.	40.00	175	2,750
	e. Bronze seal. Signature McCavour-Saunders. Group 1.	40.00	175	2,750
	f. Black seal. Signature McCavour-Saunders. Group 2.	40.00	150	2,500
	g. Red seal. Signature McCavour-Saunders. Group 2.	35.00	100	2,400
	h. Blue seal. Signature McCavour-Saunders. Group 2A.	40.00	125	2,400
	i. Bronze seal. Signature McCavour-Saunders. Group 2B.	100	1,000	2,750
	j. Green seal. Signature McCavour-Saunders. Group 2C.	40.00	125	1,750
	k. Purple seal. Signature McCavour-Saunders. Group 1.	175	800	5,750
	l. Purple seal. Signature Campbell-Sellar. Group 1.	400	1,250	7,500
	m. Black seal. Signature McCavour-Saunders. Group 3.	400	1,250	5,750
	n. Black seal. Signature Campbell-Sellar. Group 3.	30.00	100	950
	o. Black seal. Signature Campbell-Clark. Group 4A-4E.	28.00	75.00	650
	p. Black seal. Signature Campbell-Clark. Group 4F-.	65.00	250	1,800
	s. Specimen.	—	—	7,500

Note: The Group # for 2, 3 and 4 is found to the right of the seal.

#	Denomination	VG	VF	UNC
33A	**1 Dollar** 2.7.1923. Black on green underprint. Portrait King George V at center; seal at right. Like #33g. Serial # 1000001-1078500 on special Howard Smith Paper Co. stock. Back: Library of Parliament at center.	900	2,750	—

#	Denomination	VG	VF	UNC
34	**2 Dollars** 23.6.1923. Black on olive underprint. Portrait Edward, Prince of Wales (King Edward VII) at center. Back: Arms of Canada at center. Printer: CBNC.			
	a. Black seal. Signature Hyndman-Saunders. Group 1.	150	500	4,000
	b. Red seal. Signature McCavour-Saunders. Group 1.	115	450	3,400
	c. Blue seal. Signature McCavour-Saunders. Group 1.	150	500	4,300
	d. Green seal. Signature McCavour-Saunders. Group 1.	150	450	3,600
	e. Bronze seal. Signature McCavour-Saunders. Group 1.	115	450	3,400
	f. Black seal. Signature McCavour-Saunders. Group 2.	115	450	3,000
	g. Red seal. Signature McCavour-Saunders. Group 2.	115	450	3,200
	h. Blue seal. Signature McCavour-Saunders. Group 2.	115	675	4,500
	i. Blue seal. Signature Campbell-Seller. Group 2.	145	450	2,600
	j. Black seal. Signature Campbell-Sellar. Group 3.	125	450	3,200
	k. Black seal. Signature Campbell-Clark. Group 3.	125	400	2,800
	l. Black seal. Signature Campbell-Clark. Group 4.	125	375	2,600
	s. Specimen.	—	—	3,500

Note: The Group # is found to the right of the seal.

1924 Bank Legal Issue

#34A-34C used in bank transactions only.

#	Denomination	VG	VF	UNC
34A	**1000 Dollars** 2.1.1924. Black on green underprint. Portrait Lord E. Roberts at left. Printer: CBNC.			
	a. Issued note: Cancelled.	—	—	—
	p1. Face proof.	—	—	25,000
	p2. Back proof.	—	—	4,000
	s. Specimen.	—	—	35,000
34B	**5000 Dollars** 2.1.1924. Black on brown underprint. Portrait Queen Victoria at left. Printer: CBNC.	VG	VF	UNC
	a. Issued note: Cancelled.	—	—	—
	p1. Face proof.	—	—	25,000
	p2. Back proof.	—	—	4,000
	s. Specimen.	—	—	35,000
34C	**50,000 Dollars** 2.1.1924. Black on olive-green underprint. Portrait King George V and Queen Mary at center. Printer: CBNC.	VG	VF	UNC
	a. Issued note: Cancelled.	—	—	—
	p1. Face proof.	—	—	30,000
	p2. Back proof.	—	—	4,000
	s. Specimen.	—	—	45,000

1924-1925 Regular Issue

#	Denomination	VG	VF	UNC
35	**5 Dollars** 26.5.1924. Black on blue underprint. Portrait Queen Mary at center. Back: East view of Parliament buildings at center. Printer: CBNC.			
	a. Issued note.	5,000	8,500	20,000
	s. Specimen.	—	—	9,000

36 500 Dollars — VG | VF | UNC

2.1.1925. Black on blue underprint. Portrait King George V at center. Printer: CBNC.

	VG	VF	UNC
a. Issued note. Rare.	40,000	85,000	—
s. Specimen.	—	—	20,000

37 1000 Dollars — VG | VF | UNC

2.1.1925. Black and orange. Portrait Queen Mary at center. Printer: CBNC.

	VG	VF	UNC
a. Issued note. Rare.	45,000	100,000	—
s. Specimen.	—	—	20,000

Banque du Canada / Bank of Canada
1935 Issue

		VG	VF	UNC
38	**1 Dollar** 1935. Black on green underprint. Portrait King George V at left. English text. Series A; B. Back: Agriculture seated at center. Printer: CBNC.	35.00	125	1,000
39	**1 Dollar** 1935. Black on green underprint. Portrait King George V at left. Like #38 but French text. Series F. Back: Agriculture seated at center. Printer: CBNC.	70.00	250	3,000

		VG	VF	UNC
40	**2 Dollars** 1935. Black on blue underprint. Portrait Queen Mary at left. English text. Series A. Back: Mercury standing with various modes of transportation at center.	100	500	3,000

		VG	VF	UNC
41	**2 Dollars** 1935. Black on blue underprint. Portrait Queen Mary at left. Like #40 but French text. Series F. Back: Mercury standing with various modes of transportation at center.	225	1,500	11,500
42	**5 Dollars** 1935. Black on orange underprint. Portrait Edward, Prince of Wales (King Edward VII) at left. English text. Series A. Back: Electric Power seated at center.	100	500	4,500

		VG	VF	UNC
43	**5 Dollars** 1935. Black on orange underprint. Portrait Edward, Prince of Wales (King Edward VII) at left. Like #42 but French text. Series F. Back: Electric Power seated at center.	150	850	10,000

		VG	VF	UNC
44	**10 Dollars** 1935. Black on purple underprint. Portrait Princess Mary at left. English text. Series A. Back: Harvest seated at center.	100	500	4,000
45	**10 Dollars** 1935. Black on purple underprint. Portrait Princess Mary at left. Like #44 but French text. Series F. Back: Harvest seated at center.	175	900	8,500

		VG	VF	UNC
46	**20 Dollars** 1935. Black on rose underprint. Portrait Princess Elizabeth at left. English text. Series A. Back: Agriculture with farmer at center. Printer: CBNC.			
	a. Large seal.	650	2,750	23,000
	b. Small seal.	550	2,000	16,000
47	**20 Dollars** 1935. Black on rose underprint. Portrait Princess Elizabeth at left. Like #46 but French text. Series F. Back: Agriculture with farmer at center. Printer: CBNC.	1,200	4,500	30,000

1935 Commemorative Issue

#48 and 49, Silver Jubilee of Accession of George V. Printer: CBNC.

		VG	VF	UNC
48	**25 Dollars** 6.5.1935. Black on purple underprint. Portrait King George V and Queen Mary at center. English text. Series A. Back: Windsor Castle at center. Printer: CBNC. Silver Jubilee of Accession of George V.	3,000	5,600	18,500
49	**25 Dollars** 6.5.1935. Black on purple underprint. Portrait King George V and Queen Mary at center. Like #48 but French text. Series F. Back: Windsor castle at center. Printer: CBNC. Silver Jubilee of Accession of George V.	3,750	7,500	32,500

1935 Regular Issue

#	Denomination / Description	VG	VF	UNC
50	**50 Dollars** 1935. Black on brown underprint. Portrait Prince George, Duke of York (later King George VI) at left. English text. Series A. Back: Allegorical figure with modern inventions at center. Printer: CBNC.	1,800	4,250	25,000
51	**50 Dollars** 1935. Black on brown underprint. Portrait Prince George, Duke of York (later King George VI) at left. Like #50 but French text. Series F. Back: Allegorical figure with modern inventions at center. Printer: CBNC.	2,700	7,500	36,000

#	Denomination / Description	VG	VF	UNC
52	**100 Dollars** 1935. Black on dark brown underprint. Portrait Prince Henry, Duke of Gloucester at left. English text. Series A. Back: Commerce seated with youth standing at center. Printer: CBNC.	1,500	3,250	22,000
53	**100 Dollars** 1935. Black on dark brown underprint. Portrait Prince Henry, Duke of Gloucester at left. Like #52 but French text. Series F. Back: Commerce seated with youth standing at center. Printer: CBNC.	2,600	7,500	45,000
54	**500 Dollars** 1935. Black on brown underprint. Portrait Sir John A. MacDonald at left. English text. Series A. Back: Fertility reclining at center. Printer: CBNC.	35,000	75,000	—
55	**500 Dollars** 1935. Black on brown underprint. Portrait Sir John A. MacDonald at left. Like #54 but French text. Series F. Back: Fertility reclining at center. Printer: CBNC.	—	—	—
56	**1000 Dollars** 1935. Black on olive-green underprint. Portrait Sir Wilfred Laurier at left. English text. Series A. Back: Security with shield kneeling with child at center. Printer: CBNC.	3,750	6,000	15,000
57	**1000 Dollars** 1935. Black on olive-green underprint. Portrait Sir Wilfred Laurier at left. Like #56 but French text. Series F. Back: Security with shield kneeling with child at center. Printer: CBNC.	7,500	13,500	35,000

1937 Issue

#	Denomination / Description	VG	VF	UNC
58	**1 Dollar** 2.1.1937. Black on green underprint. Portrait King George VI at center. Back: Allegorical figure. Printer: CBNC.			
	a. Signature Osborne-Towers. Narrow (9mm) Signature panels.	25.00	75.00	500
	b. Signature Gordon-Towers. Narrow (9mm) Signature panels. Prefix H/A.	100	350	1,150
	c. Signature Gordon-Towers. as b1. Prefix J/A.	300	1,000	4,000
	d. Signature Gordon-Towers. Wide (11mm) Signature panels. Prefix K/A-O/M.	15.00	40.00	150
	e. Signature Coyne-Towers.	12.50	30.00	125
59	**2 Dollars** 2.1.1937. Black on red-brown underprint. Portrait King George VI at center. Back: Allegorical figure. Printer: BABNC.	VG	VF	UNC
	a. Signature Osborne-Towers.	75.00	300	2,000
	b. Signature Gordon-Towers.	30.00	75.00	325
	c. Signature Coyne-Towers.	40.00	100	500

#	Denomination / Description	VG	VF	UNC
60	**5 Dollars** 2.1.1937. Black on blue underprint. Portrait King George VI at center. Back: Allegorical figure. Printer: BABNC.			
	a. Signature Osborne-Towers.	200	700	9,000
	b. Signature Gordon-Towers.	25.00	75.00	450
	c. Signature Coyne-Towers.	25.00	75.00	400
61	**10 Dollars** 2.1.1937. Black on purple underprint. Portrait King George VI at center. Back: Allegorical figure. Printer: BABNC.	VG	VF	UNC
	a. Signature Osborne-Towers.	40.00	250	3,750
	b. Signature Gordon-Towers.	25.00	50.00	200
	c. Signature Coyne-Towers.	25.00	50.00	300
62	**20 Dollars** 2.1.1937. Black on olive-green underprint. Portrait King George VI at center. Back: Allegorical figure. Printer: CBNC.	VG	VF	UNC
	a. Signature Osborne-Towers.	100	300	3,750
	b. Signature Gordon-Towers.	25.00	50.00	500
	c. Signature Coyne-Towers.	25.00	50.00	500
63	**50 Dollars** 2.1.1937. Black on orange underprint. Portrait King George VI at center. Back: Allegorical figure. Printer: CBNC.	VG	VF	UNC
	a. Signature Osborne-Towers	450	1,850	30,000
	b. Signature Gordon-Towers.	100	200	1,600
	c. Signature Coyne-Towers.	100	225	1,900

#	Denomination / Description	VG	VF	UNC
64	**100 Dollars** 2.1.1937. Black on brown underprint. Portrait Sir John A. MacDonald at center. Back: Allegorical figure. Printer: CBNC.			
	a. Signature Osborne-Towers.	425	1,000	5,500
	b. Signature Gordon-Towers.	125	200	1,000
	c. Signature Coyne-Towers.	125	200	1,000
65	**1000 Dollars** 2.1.1937. Black on rose underprint. Portrait Sir Wilfred Laurier at center. Signature Osborne-Towers. Back: Allegorical figure. Printer: CBNC.	3,250	6,000	16,000

REPLACEMENT NOTES:
#66-70A and 74b, asterisk in front of fractional prefix letters. #76, 78-81, triple letter prefix ending in X (AAX, BAX, etc.). Exceptions: #82, no asterisk but serial number starts with 510 or 516; #83, serial number starts with 31 (instead of 30). #84-90, as #76 and 78-81.

1954 'Devil's Face Hairdo' Issue

Devil's Face Hairdo

Modified Hairdo

#	Denomination / Description	VG	VF	UNC
66	**1 Dollar** 1954. Black on green underprint. "Devil's face" in Queen's hairdo. Back: Western prairie scene. Printer: CBNC.			
	a. Signature Coyne-Towers.	12.50	25.00	150
	b. Signature Beattie-Coyne.	15.00	40.00	200

		VG	VF	UNC
67	**2 Dollars** 1954. Black on red-brown underprint. "Devil's face" in Queen's hairdo. Back: Quebec scenery. Printer: BABNC.			
	a. Signature Coyne-Towers.	20.00	55.00	400
	b. Signature Beattie-Coyne.	15.00	50.00	400

		VG	VF	UNC
68	**5 Dollars** 1954. Black on blue underprint. "Devil's face" in Queen's hairdo. Back: Otter Falls along the Alaska Highway. Printer: BABNC.			
	a. Signature Coyne-Towers.	25.00	60.00	400
	b. Signature Beattie-Coyne.	25.00	75.00	525
69	**10 Dollars** 1954. Black on purple underprint. "Devil's face" in Queen's hairdo. Back: Mt. Burgess, British Columbia. Printer: BABNC.	VG	VF	UNC
	a. Signature Coyne-Towers.	20.00	40.00	325
	b. Signature Beattie-Coyne.	25.00	50.00	525
70	**20 Dollars** 1954. Black on olive green underprint. "Devil's face" in Queen's hairdo. Back: Laurentian Hills in winter. Printer: CBNC.	VG	VF	UNC
	a. Signature Coyne-Towers.	35.00	60.00	400
	b. Signature Beattie-Coyne.	30.00	75.00	500
71	**50 Dollars** 1954. Black on orange underprint. "Devil's face" in Queen's hairdo. Back: Atlantic coastline in Nova Scotia. Printer: CBNC.	VG	VF	UNC
	a. Signature Coyne-Towers.	80.00	140	1,250
	b. Signature Beattie-Coyne.	90.00	160	1,500
72	**100 Dollars** 1954. Black on brown underprint. "Devil's face" in Queen's hairdo. Back: Okanagan Lake, British Columbia. Printer: CBNC.	VG	VF	UNC
	a. Signature Coyne-Towers.	140	175	1,025
	b. Signature Beattie-Coyne.	150	200	1,500
73	**1000 Dollars** 1954. Black on rose underprint. "Devil's face" in Queen's hairdo. Signature Coyne-Towers. Back: Central Canadian landscape. Printer: CBNC.	VG 2,000	VF 4,250	UNC 15,000

1954 Modified Hair Style Issue

		VG	VF	UNC
74	**1 Dollar** 1954 (1955-1972). Black on green underprint. Like #66 but Queen's hair in modified style. Back: Western prairie scene. Printer: CBNC.			
	a. Signature Beattie-Coyne. (1955-61).	1.25	2.50	15.00
	b. Signature Beattie-Rasminsky. (1961-72).	1.25	2.00	12.50

		VG	VF	UNC
75	**1 Dollar** 1954 (1955-1974). Black on green underprint. Queen's hair in modified style. Like #74. Back: Western prairie scene. Printer: BABNC.			
	a. Signature Beattie-Coyne. (1955-61).	1.25	2.50	40.00
	b. Signature Beattie-Rasminsky. (1961-72).	1.25	2.00	12.50
	c. Signature Bouey-Rasminsky. (1972-73).	1.25	2.00	10.00
	d. Signature Lawson-Bouey. (1973-74).	1.25	2.00	10.00

		VG	VF	UNC
76	**2 Dollars** 1954 (1955-1975). Black on red-brown underprint. Like #67 but Queen's hair in modified style. Back: Quebec scenery. Printer: BABNC. UV: planchettes fluoresce blue.			
	a. Signature Beattie-Coyne. (1955-61).	4.00	8.00	55.00
	b. Signature Beattie-Rasminsky. (1961-72).	2.25	3.00	12.50
	c. Signature Bouey-Rasminsky. (1972-73).	2.25	3.00	15.00
	d. Signature Lawson-Bouey. (1973-75).	2.25	3.00	15.00

		VG	VF	UNC
77	**5 Dollars** 1954 (1955-1972). Black on blue underprint. Like #68 but Queen's hair in modified style. Back: River in the north country. Printer: CBNC.			
	a. Signature Beattie-Coyne. (1955-61).	7.00	15.00	70.00
	b. Signature Beattie-Rasminsky. (1961-72).	6.00	10.00	45.00
	c. Signature Bouey-Rasminsky. (1972).	6.00	10.00	35.00
78	**5 Dollars** 1954 (1955-1961). Black on blue underprint. Queen's hair in modified style. Like #77. Signature Beattie-Coyne. Back: River in the north country. Printer: BABNC.	VG 7.50	VF 12.50	UNC 70.00

		VG	VF	UNC
79	**10 Dollars** 1954 (1955-1971). Black on purple underprint. Like #69 but Queen's hair in modified style. Back: Rocky Mountain scene. Printer: BABNC.			
	a. Signature Beattie-Coyne. (1955-1961).	12.00	15.00	85.00
	b. Signature Beattie-Rasminsky. (1961-1971).	12.00	13.00	60.00

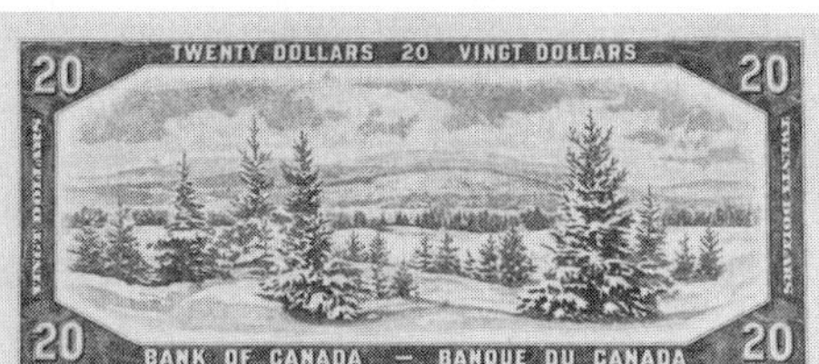

		VG	VF	UNC
80	**20 Dollars** 1954 (1955-1970) Black on olive olive-green underprint. Like #70 but Queen's hair in modified style. Back: Laurentian hills in winter. Printer: CBNC.			
	a. Signature Beattie-Coyne. (1955-1961).	22.00	25.00	150
	b. Signature Beattie-Rasminsky. (1961-1970).	22.00	25.00	100

		VG	VF	UNC
81	**50 Dollars** 1954 (1955-1975). Black on orange underprint. Like #71 but Queen's hair in modified style. Back: Atlantic coastline. Printer: CBNC.			
	a. Signature Beattie-Coyne. (1955-1961).	52.50	75.00	400
	b. Signature Beattie-Rasminsky. (1961-1972).	52.50	75.00	300
	c. Signature Lawson-Bouey. (1973-1975).	52.50	75.00	350

		VG	VF	UNC
82	**100 Dollars** 1954 (1955-1976). Black on brown underprint. Queen's hair in modified style. Back: Mountain lake. Printer: CBNC.			
	a. Signature Beattie-Coyne. (1955-1961).	110	125	375
	b. Signature Beattie-Rasminsky. (1961-1972).	110	125	300
	c. Signature Lawson-Bouey. (1973-1976).	110	125	350

		VG	VF	UNC
83	**1000 Dollars** 1954 (1955-1987). Black on rose underprint. Like #73 but Queen's hair in modified style. Back: Central Canadian landscape.			
	a. Signature Beattie-Coyne. (1955-1961).	1,100	1,400	4,500
	b. Signature Beattie-Rasminsky. (1961-1972).	1,025	1,100	2,750
	c. Signature Bouey-Rasminsky. (1972).	1,025	1,100	2,250
	d. Signature Lawson-Bouey. (1973-1984).	1,025	1,075	1,500
	e. Signature Thiessen-Crow. (1987).	1,025	1,250	2,250

1967 Commemorative Issue

#84, Centennial of Canadian Confederation

		VG	VF	UNC
84	**1 Dollar** 1967. Black on green underprint. Queen Elizabeth II at right. Signature Beattie-Rasminsky. Back: First Parliament Building. UV: planchettes fluoresce blue. Centennial of Canadian Confederation.			
	a. Centennial dates: *1867-1967* replaces serial #.	1.25	1.50	4.00
	b. Regular serial #'s.	1.25	2.00	7.50

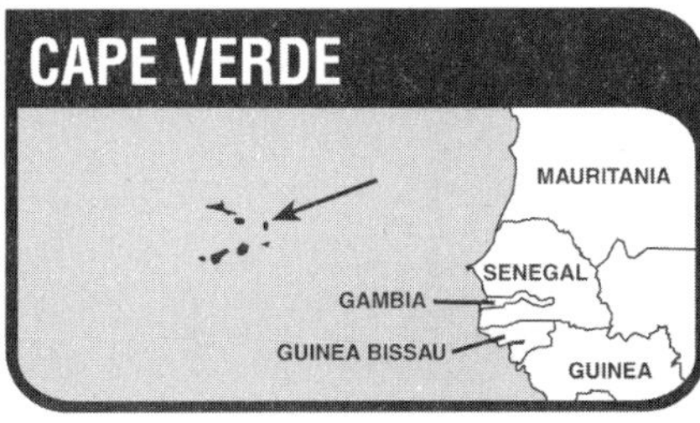

The Republic of Cape Verde, is located in the Atlantic Ocean, about 370 miles (595 km.) west of Dakar, Senegal off the coast of Africa. The 14-island republic has an area of 4,033 sq. km. and a population of 427,000. Capital: Praia. Fishing is important and agriculture is widely practiced, but the Cape Verdes are not self-sufficient in food. Fish products, salt, bananas, coffee, peanuts and shellfish are exported.

The uninhabited islands were discovered and colonized by the Portuguese in the 15th century; Cape Verde subsequently became a trading center for African slaves and later an important coaling and resupply stop for whaling and transatlantic shipping. Following independence in 1975, and a tentative interest in unification with Guinea-Bissau, a one-party system was established and maintained until multi-party elections were held in 1990. Cape Verde continues to exhibit one of Africa's most stable democratic governments. Repeated droughts during the second half of the 20th century caused significant hardship and prompted heavy emigration. As a result, Cape Verde's expatriate population is greater than its domestic one. Most Cape Verdeans have both African and Portuguese antecedents.

RULERS:

Portuguese to 1975

MONETARY SYSTEM:

1 Mil Reis = 1000 Reis
1 Escudo = 100 Centavos, 1911-

STEAMSHIP SEALS

Type I	Type II	Type III
LOANDA	LISBOA	C,C,A

C,C,A = Colonias, Commercio, Agricultura.

PORTUGUESE ADMINISTRATION

Banco Nacional Ultramarino

S. Thiago de Cabo Verde

1897 Issue

#1-3 ***Agencia de S. Thiago de Cabo Verde.***

#		Good	Fine	XF
1	**1 Mil Reis** 2.1.1897. Brown. Man standing with bow and arrow at left, embossed steamship seal at lower right. 125x91mm.	—	—	—
2	**2 1/2 Mil Reis** 2.1.1897. Blue. Woman standing next to embossed steamship seal at lower right. 141x104mm.	—	—	—
3	**5 Mil Reis** 2.1.1897. Bush at left, embossed steamship seal at lower right. 170x124mm.	—	—	—

S. Thiago

1909 Issue

#		Good	Fine	XF
4	**1000 Reis** 1.3.1909. Black on green and yellow underprint. Steamship seal at right. Printer: BWC. 137x81mm.			
	a. Steamship seal Type I.	100	250	750
	b. Steamship seal Type III.	75.00	200	600

#		Good	Fine	XF
5	**2500 Reis** 1.3.1909. Black on multicolor underprint. Portrait Vasco da Gama at left. Sailing ships at right. Back: Seated allegorical woman looking out at sailing ships. Printer: BWC. 147x93mm.			
	a. Steamship seal Type I.	125	300	900
	b. Steamship seal Type III.	100	250	750
6	**5 Mil Reis** 1.3.1909. Black on multicolor underprint. Portrait Vasco da Gama at left. Sailing ships at right. Back: Seated allegorical woman looking out at sailing ships. Printer: BWC. 159x101mm.			
	a. Steamship seal Type I.	150	500	1,250
	b. Steamship seal Type III.	150	500	1,250

Note: For #6b w/rectangular overprint: *PAGAVEL... GUINÉ* see Portuguese Guinea #5F.

#		Good	Fine	XF
7	**10 Mil Reis** 1.3.1909. Black on multicolor underprint. Portrait Vasco da Gama at left. Sailing ship at left and right. Back: Seated allegorical woman looking out at sailing ships. Printer: BWC. 176x106mm.			
	a. Steamship seal Type I.	200	750	—
	b. Steamship seal Type III.	175	650	—
8	**20 Mil Reis** 1.3.1909. Black on multicolor underprint. Portrait Vasco da Gama at left. Vasco da Gama embarking at right, palm fronds at lower left and right. Back: Seated allegorical woman looking out at sailing ships. Printer: BWC. 181x114mm.			
	a. Steamship seal Type I.	225	800	—
	b. Steamship seal Type III.	200	750	—
	s. As a. Specimen. Punch hole cancelled.	—	Unc	1,000
9	**50 Mil Reis** 1.3.1909. Black on multicolor underprint. Portrait Vasco da Gama at left. Palm trees at left, Vasco da Gama embarking at right. Back: Seated allegorical woman looking out at sailing ships. Printer: BWC. 200x121mm.			
	a. Steamship seal Type I.	300	1,250	—
	b. Steamship seal Type III.	300	1,000	—

1914 Provisional Issue

#		Good	Fine	XF
9A	**10 Centavos** 5.11.1914. Purple. Arms at right, steamship seal Type II at bottom center. 120x71mm.	125	600	—

1914 Regular Issue

#10-17 Red ovpt: ***S. Tiago.***

#		Good	Fine	XF
10	**4 Centavos** 5.11.1914. Blue-green on multicolor underprint. Arms at right, steamship seal Type III at lower center. Back: Allegorical woman looking out at sailing ships at center. Printer: BWC.	15.00	75.00	300
11	**5 Centavos** 5.11.1914. Rose on multicolor underprint. Arms at right, steamship seal Type I at lower center. Back: Allegorical woman looking out at sailing ships at center. Printer: BWC.	15.00	75.00	300
11A	**5 Centavos** 5.11.1914. Rose on multicolor underprint. Arms at right, steamship seal Type III at lower center. Back: Allegorical woman looking out at sailing ships at center. Printer: BWC.	15.00	75.00	300

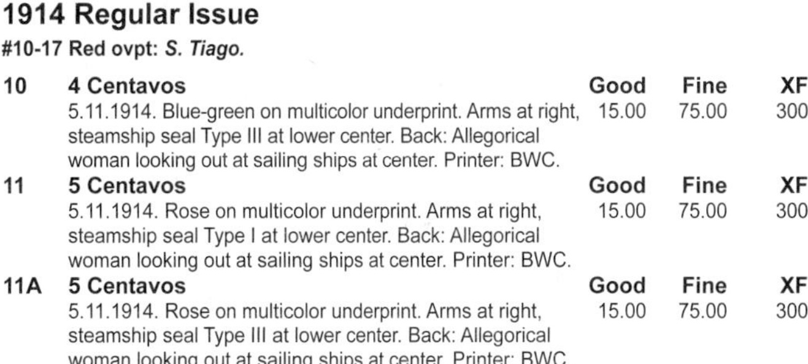

#		Good	Fine	XF
11B	**5 Centavos** 5.11.1914. Bluish purple on multicolor underprint. Arms at right, steamship seal Type III at lower center. Back: Allegorical woman looking out at sailing ships at center. Printer: BWC.	15.00	50.00	225
12	**10 Centavos** 5.11.1914. Purple on multicolor underprint. Arms at right, steamship seal Type I at lower center. Back: Allegorical woman looking out at sailing ships at center. Printer: BWC.	15.00	75.00	300
12A	**10 Centavos** 5.11.1914. Purple on multicolor underprint. Arms at right, steamship seal Type II at lower center. Back: Allegorical woman looking out at sailing ships at center. Printer: BWC.	7.50	60.00	250
13	**10 Centavos** 5.11.1914. Purple on multicolor underprint. Arms at right, steamship seal Type III at lower center. Back: Allegorical woman looking out at sailing ships at center. Printer: BWC.	12.50	50.00	200

No.	Denomination	Good	Fine	XF
14	**20 Centavos** 5.11.1914. Blue on multicolor underprint. Arms at right, steamship seal Type II at lower center. Back: Allegorical woman looking out at sailing ships at center. Printer: BWC.	20.00	125	350
15	**20 Centavos** 5.11.1914. Blue on multicolor underprint. Arms at right, steamship seal Type III at lower center. Back: Allegorical woman looking out at sailing ships at center. Printer: BWC.	15.00	50.00	200

No.	Denomination	Good	Fine	XF
16	**50 Centavos** 5.11.1914. Green on multicolor underprint. Arms at right, steamship seal Type II at lower center. Back: Allegorical woman looking out at sailing ships at center. Printer: BWC.	17.50	100	400
17	**50 Centavos** 5.11.1914. Green on multicolor underprint. Arms at right, steamship seal Type III at lower center. Back: Allegorical woman looking out at sailing ships at center. Printer: BWC.	17.50	100	400

W/o Branch name

1920 ND Porto Issue

No.	Denomination	Good	Fine	XF
18	**10 Centavos** 1.1.1920. Red. Sailing ship at left and right. 107x68mm.	100	400	—
19	**50 Centavos** 1.1.1920. Blue. Mercury at left, ships at lower left, farmer and allegory at right. Back: Sailing ship at center. 109x66mm.	125	600	—
19A	**50 Centavos** 1.1.1920. Dark blue. Arms at top center. 121x77mm. Rare.	—	—	—

1921 Provisional Issue

No.	Denomination	Good	Fine	XF
20	**10 Centavos** ND (1921 - old date 5.11.1914). Purple on multicolor underprint. Arms at right, steamship seal at lower center. Signature varieties. Back: Allegorical woman looking out at sailing ships at center. Printer: BWC.	8.00	30.00	200
21	**20 Centavos** ND (1921 - old date 5.11.1914). Blue on multicolor underprint. Arms at right, steamship seal at lower center. Signature varieties. Back: Allegorical woman looking out at sailing ships at center. Printer: BWC.	25.00	100	450
22	**50 Centavos** ND (1921 - old date 5.11.1914). Green on multicolor underprint. Arms at right, steamship seal at lower center. Signature varieties. Back: Allegorical woman looking out at sailing ships at center. Printer: BWC.	30.00	125	550
22A	**50 Centavos** ND (1921 - old date 1.1.1921). Green on multicolor underprint. Arms at right, steamship seal at lower center. Back: Allegorical woman looking out at sailing ships at center. Printer: BWC. Rare.	—	—	—

1922 ND First Provisional Issue

No.	Denomination	Good	Fine	XF
23	**1000 Reis** ND (1922 - old date 1.3.1909). Black on green and yellow underprint. Steamship seal Type III at right.	300	1,250	—
24	**2500 Reis** ND (1922 - old date 1.3.1909). Black on multicolor underprint. Vasco da Gama at left, sailing ships at right. Back: Seated allegorical woman looking out at sailing ships. Rare.	—	—	—
25	**5 Mil Reis** ND (1922 - old date 1.3.1909). Black on multicolor underprint. Vasco da Gama at left, sailing ships at right. Back: Seated allegorical woman looking out at sailing ships. Rare.	—	—	—
26	**10 Mil Reis** ND (1922 - old date 1.3.1909). Black on multicolor underprint. Vasco da Gama at left, sailing ship at left and right. Back: Seated allegorical woman looking out at sailing ships. Rare.	—	—	—
27	**20 Mil Reis** ND (1922 - old date 1.3.1909). Black on multicolor underprint. Vasco da Gama at left. Vasco da Gama embarking at right, palm fronds at lower left and right. Back: Seated allegorical woman looking out at sailing ships. Rare.	—	—	—
28	**50 Mil Reis** ND (1922 - old date 1.3.1909). Black on multicolor underprint. Vasco da Gama at left. Palm trees at left, Vasco da Gama embarking at right. Back: Seated allegorical woman looking out at sailing ships. Rare.	—	—	—

1922 ND Second Provisional Issue

No.	Denomination	Good	Fine	XF
29	**20 Escudos** ND (1922 - old date 1.1.1921). Dark blue on multicolor underprint. Portrait Francisco de Oliveira Chamico at left, steamship seal at right, arms at bottom center.	300	1,250	—
30	**50 Escudos** ND (1922 - old date 1.1.1921). Blue on multicolor underprint. Portrait Francisco de Oliveira Chamico at left, steamship seal at right, arms at bottom center. Rare.	—	—	—
31	**100 Escudos** ND (1922 - old date 1.1.1921). Brown on multicolor underprint. Portrait Francisco de Oliveira Chamico at left, steamship seal at right, arms at bottom center. Rare.	—	—	—

Cabo Verde

1921 Issue

No.	Description	Good	Fine	XF
32	**1 Escudo** 1.1.1921. Green on multicolor underprint. Portrait Francisco de Oliveira Chamico at left, steamship seal at right, arms at bottom center. Back: Allegorical woman looking out at sailing ships at center. Printer: BWC. 130x81mm.	7.50	50.00	150
33	**5 Escudos** 1.1.1921. Green on multicolor underprint. Portrait Francisco de Oliveira Chamico at left, steamship seal at right, arms at bottom center. Back: Allegorical woman looking out at sailing ships at center. Printer: BWC. 154x94mm. Overprint on #32.	50.00	250	900

No.	Description	Good	Fine	XF
34	**5 Escudos** 1.1.1921. Black on multicolor underprint. Portrait Francisco de Oliveira Chamico at left, steamship seal at right, arms at bottom center. Back: Allegorical woman looking out at sailing ships at center. Printer: BWC.	25.00	150	750
35	**10 Escudos** 1.1.1921. Brown on multicolor underprint. Portrait Francisco de Oliveira Chamico at left, steamship seal at right, arms at bottom center. Back: Allegorical woman looking out at sailing ships at center. Printer: BWC. 160x106mm.	25.00	200	—
36	**20 Escudos** 1.1.1921. Dark blue on multicolor underprint. Portrait Francisco de Oliveira Chamico at left, steamship seal at right, arms at bottom center. Back: Allegorical woman looking out at sailing ships at center. Printer: BWC. 172x114mm.	75.00	450	—
37	**50 Escudos** 1.1.1921. Red on multicolor underprint. Portrait Francisco de Oliveira Chamico at left, steamship seal at right, arms at bottom center. Back: Allegorical woman looking out at sailing ships at center. Printer: BWC. 185x121mm.	—	—	—
38	**100 Escudos** 1.1.1921. Purple on multicolor underprint. Portrait Francisco de Oliveira Chamico at left, steamship seal at right, arms at bottom center. Back: Allegorical woman looking out at sailing ships at center. Printer: BWC. 192x125mm.	—	—	—

1941 Issue

No.	Description	Good	Fine	XF
39	**50 Escudos** 1.8.1941. Red on multicolor underprint. Portrait Francisco de Oliveira Chamico at left, steamship seal at right, arms at bottom center. Back: Allegorical woman looking out at sailing ships at center. 185x121mm.	—	—	—
40	**100 Esucdos** 1.8.1941. Purple on multicolor underprint. Portrait Francisco de Oliveira Chamico at left, steamship seal at right, arms at bottom center. Back: Allegorical woman looking out at sailing ships at center. 192x125mm.			
	a. Issued note.	—	—	—
	s. Specimen. Punch hole cancelled.	—	—	—

1945 Issue

No.	Description	VG	VF	UNC
41	**5 Escudos** 16.11.1945. Olive-brown. Portrait Bartolomeu Dias at right, steamship seal at left, arms at upper center. Back: Allegorical woman looking out at sailing ships at center. Printer: BWC. 140x74mm.	10.00	50.00	150
42	**10 Escudos** 16.11.1945. Purple. Portrait Bartolomeu Dias at right, steamship seal at left, arms at upper center. Back: Allegorical woman looking out at sailing ships at center. Printer: BWC. 146x77mm.	15.00	100	300
43	**20 Escudos** 16.11.1945. Green. Portrait Bartolomeu Dias at right, steamship seal at left, arms at upper center. Back: Allegorical woman looking out at sailing ships at center. Printer: BWC. 150x80mm.	25.00	300	—
44	**50 Escudos** 16.11.1945. Blue. Portrait Bartolomeu Dias at right, steamship seal at left, arms at upper center. Back: Allegorical woman looking out at sailing ships at center. Printer: BWC. 156x82mm.	50.00	400	—
45	**100 Escudos** 16.11.1945. Red. Portrait Bartolomeu Dias at right, steamship seal at left, arms at upper center. Back: Allegorical woman looking out at sailing ships at center. Printer: BWC. 161x85mm.	75.00	650	—

No.	Description	Good	Fine	XF
46	**500 Escudos** 16.11.1945. Brown and violet. Portrait Bartolomeu Dias at right, steamship seal at left, arms at upper center. Back: Allegorical woman looking out at sailing ships at center. Printer: BWC. 166x87mm.	—	—	—

1958 Issue

Decreto Lei 39221

		VG	VF	UNC
47	**20 Escudos** 16.6.1958. Green on multicolor underprint. Portrait Serpa Pinto at right, sailing ship seal at left. Signature titles: *O-ADMINISTRADOR* and *O-GOVERNADOR*. Back: Allegorical woman looking out at sailing ships at center. Printer: BWC. 150x80mm.			
	a. Issued note.	1.00	7.50	40.00
	s. Specimen.	—	—	50.00
	ct. Color trial. Blue on multicolor underprint.	—	—	175

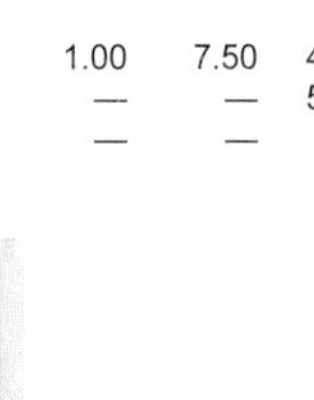

		VG	VF	UNC
48	**50 Escudos** 16.6.1958. Blue on multicolor underprint. Portrait Serpa Pinto at right, sailing ship seal at left. Signature titles: *O-ADMINISTRADOR* and *O-GOVERNADOR*. Back: Allegorical woman looking out at sailing ships at center. Printer: BWC. 155x83mm.			
	a. Issued note.	4.00	35.00	175
	s. Specimen.	—	—	50.00
	ct. Color trial. Green on multicolor underprint.	—	—	300

		VG	VF	UNC
49	**100 Escudos** 16.6.1958. Red on multicolor underprint. Portrait Serpa Pinto at right, sailing ship seal at left. Signature titles: *O-ADMINISTRADOR* and *O-GOVERNADOR*. Back: Allegorical woman looking out at sailing ships at center. Printer: BWC. 160x85mm.			
	a. Issued note.	2.00	15.00	50.00
	s. Specimen.	—	—	50.00
	ct. Color trial. Brown on multicolor underprint.	—	—	175

		VG	VF	UNC
50	**500 Escudos** 16.6.1958. Brown-violet on multicolor underprint. Portrait Serpa Pinto at right, sailing ship seal at left. Signature titles: *O-ADMINISTRADOR* and *O-GOVERNADOR*. Back: Allegorical woman looking out at sailing ships at center. Printer: BWC. 165x88mm.			
	a. Issued note.	12.50	50.00	200
	s. Specimen.	—	—	50.00
	ct. Color trial. Red on multicolor underprint.	—	—	350

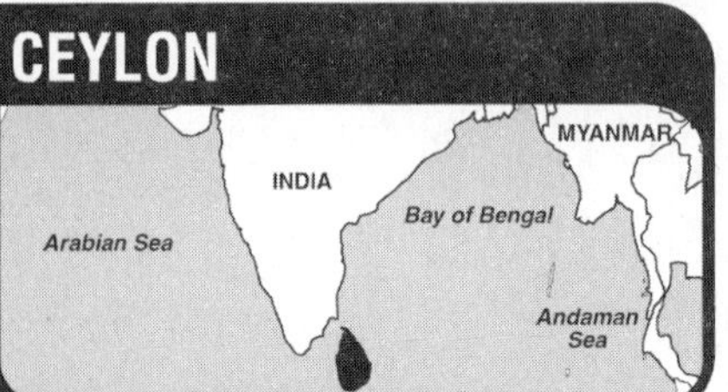

Ceylon (later to become The Democratic Socialist Republic of Sri Lanka) is an island situated in the Indian Ocean 18 miles (29 km.) southeast of India. It has an area of 65,610 sq. km. and a population of 21.13 million. Capital: Colombo. The economy is chiefly agricultural. Tea, rubber and coconut products are exported. The earliest known inhabitants are the Veddahs. The first Sinhala arrived in Lanka late in the 5th century BCE, probably from northern India. The coastal areas of the island were controlled by China for 30 years from 1408, the Portuguese from 1505 and the Dutch from 1658. The island was ceded to the British in 1796, became a crown colony in 1802, and the independent Kingdom of Kandy in the central part of the island was united under British rule by 1815, as Ceylon. Constitutional changes in 1931 g ranted Ceylon a parliamentary form of government. It became independent in 1948. Its name in English was changed to Sri Lanka on 1972 May 22 with the adoption of a Republican constitution. For later issues, see Sri Lanka.

RULERS:

Dutch to 1796
British, 1796-1972

MONETARY SYSTEM:

1 Rix Dollar = 48 Stivers
1 Rupee = 100 Cents

BRITISH ADMINISTRATION

General Treasury

1827-1856 Issue

#1, 2 and 6 Not assigned.

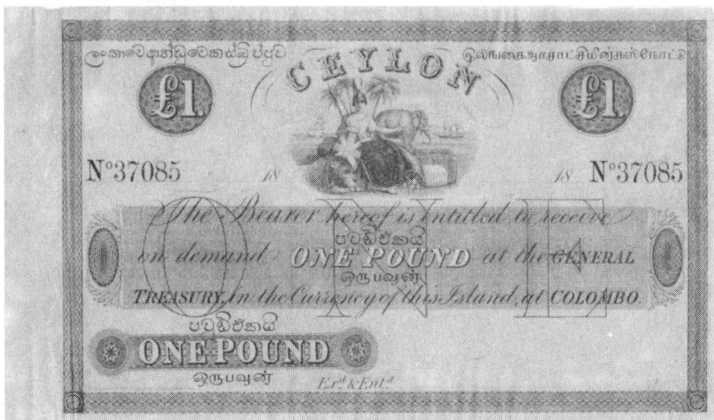

		Good	Fine	XF
3	**1 Pound** 18xx (1827-1856). Britannia seated at center with lion and shield, elephant and palm trees in background. Colombo. Like #4. Printer: PB&P.			
	r. Unsigned remainder.	—	—	350
	s. Overprint: *SPECIMEN.*	—	—	475
4	**2 Pounds** 18xx (1827-1856). Britannia seated at center with lion and shield, elephant and palm trees in background. Colombo. Printer: PB&P.			
	r. Unsigned remainder.	—	—	400
	s. Overprint: *SPECIMEN.*	—	—	525

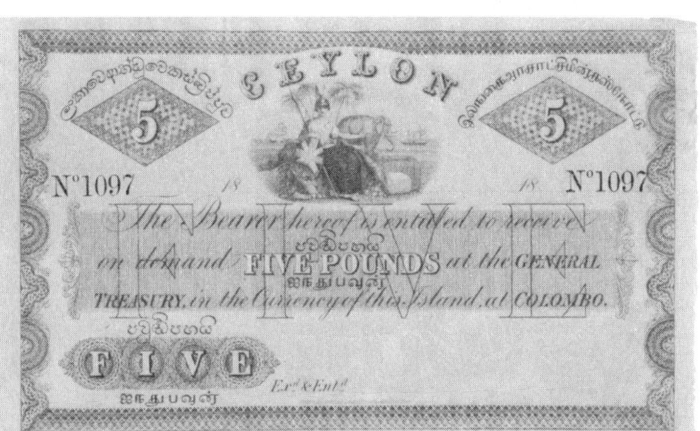

		Good	Fine	XF
5	**5 Pounds** 18xx (1827-1856). Britannia.seated at center with lion and shield, elephant and palm trees in background. Colombo. Like #4. Printer: PB&P.			
	r. Unsigned remainder.	—	—	400
	s. Overprint: *SPECIMEN.*	—	—	600

Government

1809-1826 Issue

7	**2 Rix Dollars**	Good	Fine	XF
	1.11.1826. Britania seated with shield and trident at upper left. Uniface.	—	—	—

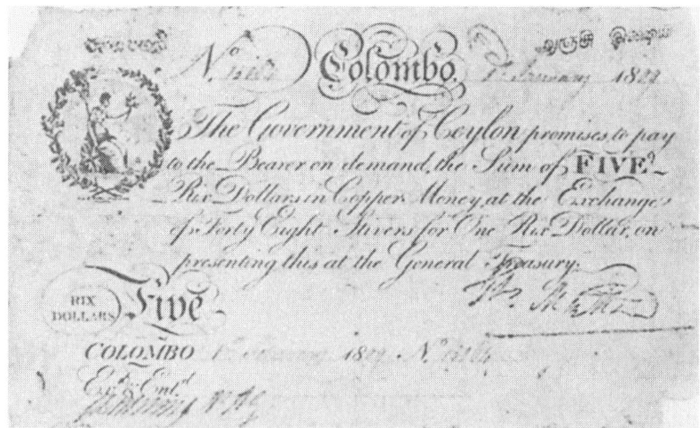

8	**5 Rix Dollars**	Good	Fine	XF
	1.1.1809; x.2.1809. Britania seated with shield and trident at upper left. Uniface.	—	—	—

1885-1899 Issue

#9, 10, 13 and 14 not assigned.

11	**5 Rupees**	Good	Fine	XF
	1885-1925. Black on green underprint. Uniface. 173x130mm.			
	a. 1885-1.11.1909.	200	425	1,000
	b. 2.1.1913-8.12.1919.	125	250	650
	c. 1.9.1922; 1.9.1923; 1.10.1924; 1.10.1925.	100	200	600

Color Abbreviation Guide

New to the *Standard Catalog of ® World Paper Money* are the following abbreviations related to color references:

BC: Back color

PC: Paper color

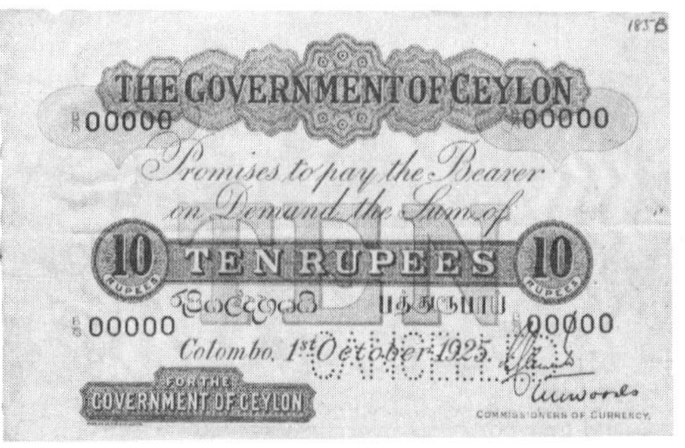

12	**10 Rupees**	Good	Fine	XF
	1894-1926. Black on green underprint. Uniface. 210x127mm.			
	a. 1.1.1894; 1.9.1894.	200	450	1,200
	b. 18.5.1908.	160	350	1,000
	c. 1.4.1914-1.6.1926.	100	300	900
	s. Specimen. 1.10.1925.	—	Unc	1,500
15	**1000 Rupees**	**Good**	**Fine**	**XF**
	1.8.1899; 1.4.1915. Rare. Uniface. 234x145mm.	—	—	—

1914-1919 Issues

16	**1 Rupee**	Good	Fine	XF
	1917-1939. Blue on green, gray and lilac underprint. Perforated or straight edge at left. Signature varieties. Printer: TDLR.			
	a. 1.5.1917-1.10.1924.	15.00	30.00	100
	b. 1.10.1925-18.6.1936.	8.50	22.00	75.00
	c. 24.7.1937-2.10.1939.	7.50	12.00	50.00
17	**2 Rupees**	**Good**	**Fine**	**XF**
	1.3.1917. Reddish brown on green and ochre underprint. *2* in circle at left and right. Uniface.Signature varieties. Printer: TDLR.	40.00	175	700

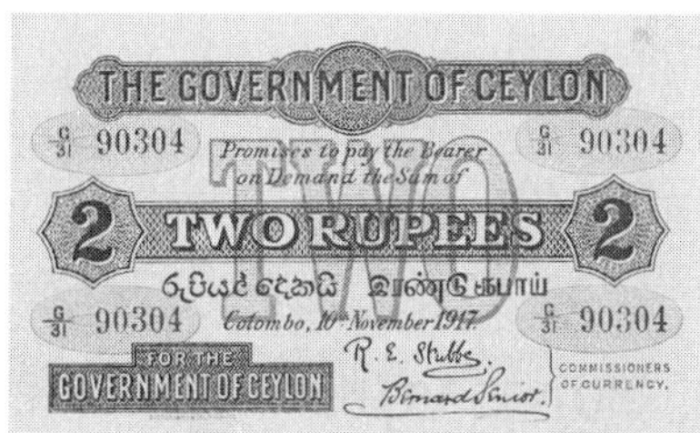

18	**2 Rupees**	Good	Fine	XF
	10.11.1917; 23.3.1918; 1.10.1921. Black on green underprint. Uniface. Signature varieties. Printer: TDLR.	30.00	75.00	400

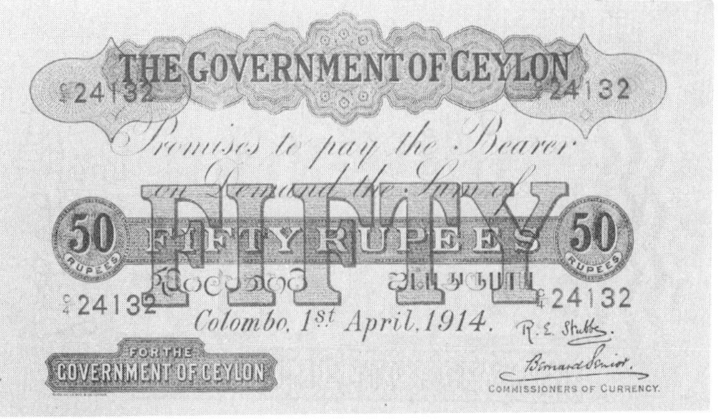

19	**50 Rupees**	Good	Fine	XF
	1.4.1914. Black on green underprint. Uniface. Signature varieties. Printer: TDLR. 233x125mm. Rare.	—	—	—

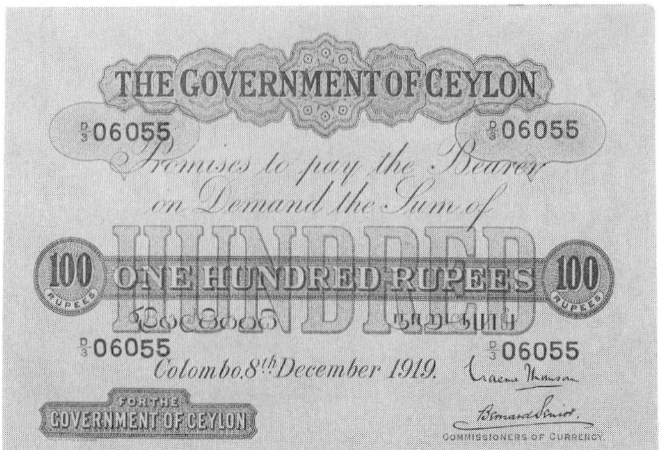

		Good	Fine	XF
20	**100 Rupees** 8.12.1919. Black on green underprint. Uniface. Signature varieties. Printer: TDLR. 216x145mm. Rare.	—	—	—

1926-1932 Issue

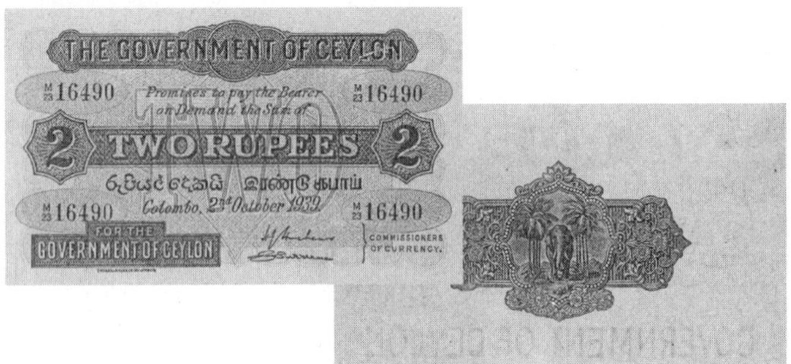

		Good	Fine	XF
21	**2 Rupees** 1925-1939. Black on green and lilac underprint. Perforated or straight edge at left. Signature varieties. Back: Palm trees and elephant in central vignette. Printer: TDLR.			
	a. Red serial #, yellow underprint. 1.10.1925; 1.6.1926; 1.9.1928; 1.7.1929.	6.00	40.00	150
	b. Green serial #, dark green underprint. 10.9.1930-2.10.1939.	3.00	15.00	65.00

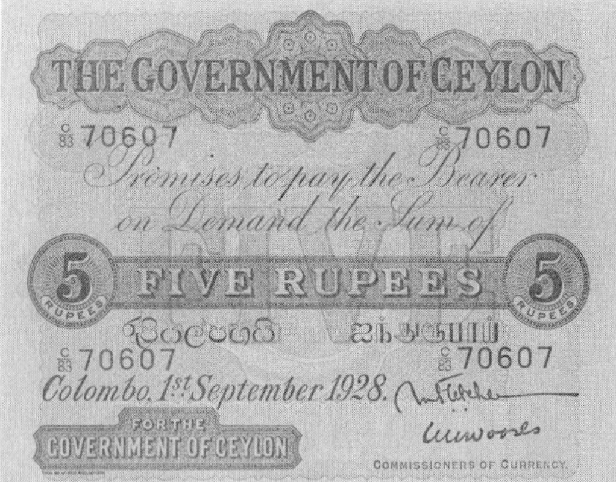

		Good	Fine	XF
22	**5 Rupees** 1.12.1925; 1.6.1926; 1.9.1927; 1.9.1928. Black on green and orange underprint. Signature varieties. Back: Palm trees and elephant in central vignette. Like #21. Printer: TDLR. 170x130mm.	60.00	150	450

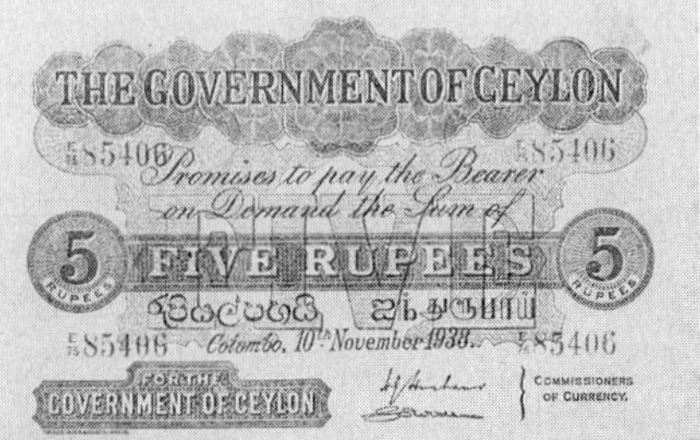

		Good	Fine	XF
23	**5 Rupees** 1.7.1929-2.10.1939. Black on green, orange and lilac underprint. Perforated or straight edge at left. Signature varieties. Back: Palm trees and elephant in central vignette. Like #21. Printer: TDLR. 136x88mm.			
	a. 13.7.1929.	32.00	100	200
	b. 18..6.1936-10.11.1938.	25.00	75.00	175
	c. 2.10.1939.	20.00	60.00	120

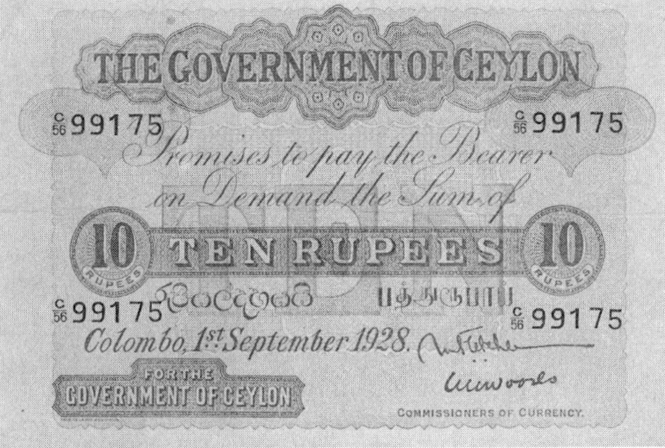

		Good	Fine	XF
24	**10 Rupees** 6.1.1927; 1.9.1928. Black on dull red and yellow-green underprint. Signature varieties. Back: Palm trees and elephant in central vignette. Like #21. Printer: TDLR. 198x127mm.			
	a. Issued note.	150	300	700
	s. Specimen. 1.10.1925.	—	Unc	1,000

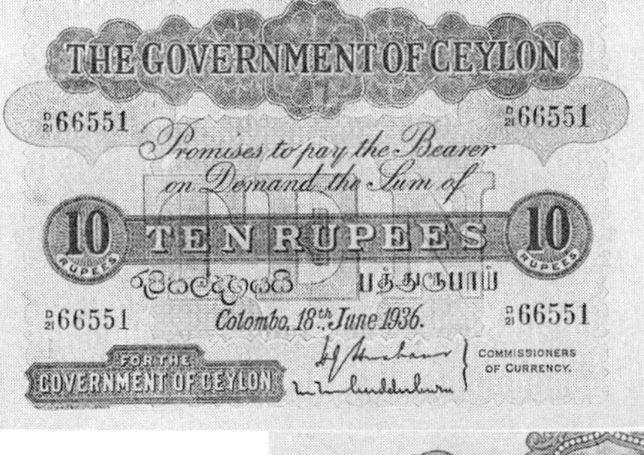

		Good	Fine	XF
25	**10 Rupees** 1.7.1929-2.10.1939. Gray on violet and yellow-green underprint. Signature varieties. Printer: TDLR. 152x102mm.			
	a. 1.7.1929-1936.	75.00	150	240
	b. 18.6.1936-10.11.1938.	40.00	100	220
	c. 2.10.1939.	30.00	75.00	200

		Good	Fine	XF
26	**50 Rupees** 1922-1939. Gray on violet and yellow-green underprint. Similar to #25 but reduced size. Signature varieties. Printer: TDLR.	125	300	1,000

		Good	Fine	XF
27	**100 Rupees** 1926-1939. Black on green underprint. Uniface. Similar to #20 but reduced size. Signature varieties. Printer: TDLR.	250	600	—

		Good	Fine	XF
28	**500 Rupees** 1.6.1926. Signature varieties. Printer: TDLR. 233x145mm. Rare.	—	—	—

		Good	Fine	XF
29	**1000 Rupees** 1.7.1929. Similar to #28 but reduced size. Signature varieties. Printer: TDLR. Rare.	—	—	—

1941 First Issue

		VG	VF	UNC
30	**1 Rupee** 1.2.1941. Olive, lilac and blue. Portrait King George VI at left, text at upper center begins: *PROMISES TO PAY...* Title on face begins: *THE GOVERNMENT...* Perforated or straight edge at left. Back: Elephant head. Watermark: Chinze. Printer: Indian.	10.00	25.00	100

		VG	VF	UNC
31	**2 Rupees** 1.2.1941. Violet on brown, blue and green underprint. Portrait King George VI at left, text at upper center begins: *PROMISES TO PAY...* Title on face begins: *THE GOVERNMENT...* Perforated or straight edge at left. Back: Sigiriya Rock. Watermark: Chinze. Printer: Indian.			
	a. Issued note.	15.00	40.00	200
	s. Specimen. Red overprint: *SPECIMEN.*	—	—	—

		VG	VF	UNC
32	**5 Rupees** 1.2.1941. Brown on lilac and blue underprint. Portrait King George VI at left, text at upper center begins: *PROMISES TO PAY...* Title on face begins: *THE GOVERNMENT...* Perforated or straight edge at left. Back: Thuparama Dagoba. Watermark: Chinze. Printer: Indian.	25.00	90.00	300

		VG	VF	UNC
33	**10 Rupees** 1.2.1941. Blue and multicolor. Portrait King George VI at left, text at upper center begins: *PROMISES TO PAY...* Title on face begins: *THE GOVERNMENT...* Perforated or straight edge at left. Back: Temple of the Tooth. Watermark: Chinze. Printer: Indian.			
	a. Issued note.	30.00	150	500
	s. Specimen. Red overprint: *SPECIMEN.*	—	—	—

		VG	VF	UNC
33A	**1000 Rupees** 1.7.1938. Specimen. Printer: Indian.	—	—	—

1941 Second Issue

		VG	VF	UNC
34	**1 Rupee** 20.12.1941-1.3.1949. Olive, lilac and blue. Portrait King George VI at left, text at upper center begins: *THIS NOTE IS LEGAL TENDER...* Perforated or straight edge at left. Similar to #30. Back: Elephant head. Watermark: Chinze. Printer: Indian.	7.50	20.00	60.00

		VG	VF	UNC
35	**2 Rupees** 20.12.1941-1.3.1949. Violet and brown on blue and green underprint. Portrait King George VI at left, text at upper center begins: *THIS NOTE IS LEGAL TENDER...* Perforated or straight edge at left. Similar to #31. Back: Sigiriya Rock. Watermark: Chinze. Printer: Indian.			
	a. Issued note.	20.00	30.00	120
	s. Specimen. Red overprint: *SPECIMEN.*	—	—	—

36	5 Rupees	VG	VF	UNC
	20.12.1941-1.3.1949. Lilac and brown on green and blue underprint. Portrait King George VI at left, text at upper center begins: *THIS NOTE IS LEGAL TENDER...* Perforated or straight edge at left. Similar to #32. Back: Thuparama Dagoba. Watermark: Chinze. Printer: Indian.			
	a. Issued note.	7.50	60.00	200
	s. Specimen. Red overprint: *SPECIMEN.*	—	—	—

36A	10 Rupees	VG	VF	UNC
	20.12.1941-7.5.1946. Blue and multicolor. Portrait King George VI at left, text at upper center begins THIS NOTE IS LEGAL TENDER... Similar to #33. Back: Temple of the Tooth. Watermark: Chinze.			
	a. Issued note.	30.00	75.00	350
	s. Specimen. Red overprint: *SPECIMEN.*	—	—	—

37	50 Rupees	VG	VF	UNC
	1941-1945. Purple on green, blue and brown underprint. Portrait King George VI at left, text at upper center begins: *THIS NOTE IS LEGAL TENDER...* Back: Farmer plowing with water buffalo in rice paddy field. Printer: Indian.			
	a. Issued note. 4.8.1943; 12.7.1944; 24.6.1945.	175	700	—
	s. Specimen. 1.9.1941.	—	—	850

38	100 Rupees	VG	VF	UNC
	1941-1945. Green on brown and red underprint. Portrait King George VI at left, text at upper center begins: *THIS NOTE IS LEGAL TENDER...* Back: Laxapana Waterfall. Printer: Indian.			
	a. Issued note. 4.8.1943; 24.6.1945.	200	550	1,200
	s. Specimen. 1.9.1941.	—	—	525

39	1000 Rupees	VG	VF	UNC
	1.9.1941. Violet, green and light blue. Portrait King George VI at left, text at upper center begins: *THIS NOTE IS LEGAL TENDER...* Back: Native and coastal scene. Printer: Indian. 195x141mm. Specimen.	—	—	3,000

Color Abbreviation Guide

New to the *Standard Catalog of® World Paper Money* are the following abbreviations related to color references:

BC: Back color
PC: Paper color

39A **10,000 Rupees**

15.10.1947. Green on multicolor underprint. Portrait King George VI at left, text at upper center begins: *THIS NOTE IS LEGAL TENDER...* Back: Kandy Lake scene. 195x145mm. Specimen. Intended for inter-bank transactions only.

VG	VF	UNC
—	—	25,000

1942 First Issue

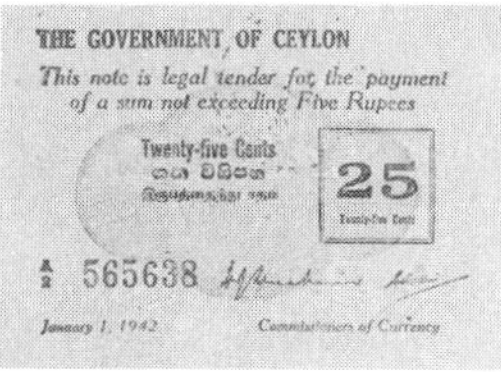

40 **25 Cents**

1.1.1942. Black text on green underprint. Uniface.

Good	Fine	XF
30.00	80.00	150

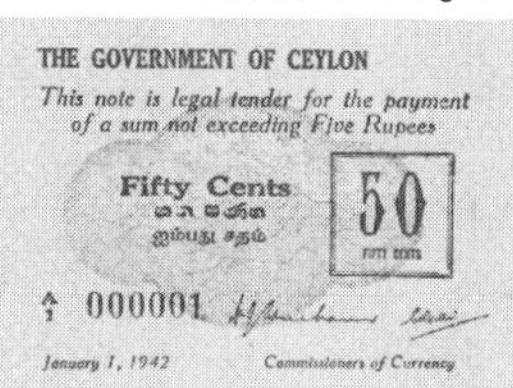

41 **50 Cents**

1.1.1942. Black text on red underprint. Uniface. Like #40.

Good	Fine	XF
50.00	125	300

1942 Second Issue

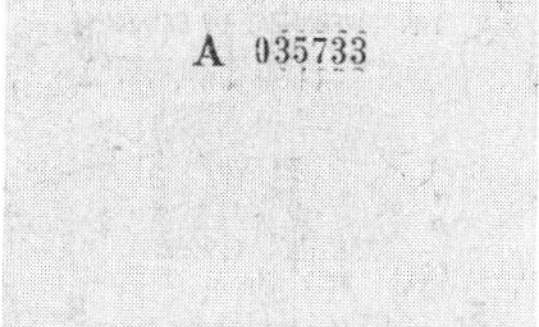

42 **5 Cents**

1.6.1942. Blue-gray. 2 and 3 cent postal card impressions with portrait King George VI. Uniface. Printer: Indian. (Sometimes rouletted down center for ease of separation.)

	VG	VF	UNC
a. Without roulettes down center.	30.00	60.00	150
b. Rouletted 7 (7 dashes per 20mm) down center.	50.00	75.00	250

43 **10 Cents**

1942-1943. Blue and multicolor. Portrait King George VI at center. Text begins THIS NOTE IS LEGAL TENDER... Uniface. Back: Serial #. Printer: Indian.

	VG	VF	UNC
a. 1.2.1942; 14.7.1942.	5.00	12.00	30.00
b. 23.12.1943.	6.00	15.00	30.00

44 **25 Cents**

1942-1949. Brown and multicolor. Portrait King George VI at center. Text begins THIS NOTE IS LEGAL TENDER... Uniface. Back: Serial #. Printer: Indian.

	VG	VF	UNC
a. 1.2.1942; 14.7.1942.	7.00	15.00	40.00
b. 7.5.1946; 1.3.1947; 1.6.1948; 1.12.1949.	8.00	17.50	40.00

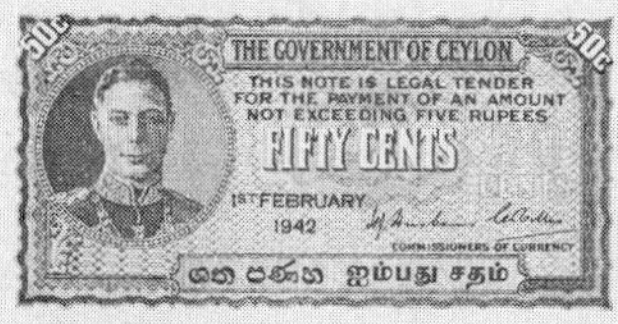

45 **50 Cents**

1942-1949. Lilac and multicolor. Portrait King George VI at left. Text begins THIS NOTE IS LEGAL TENDER... Uniface. Back: Serial #. Printer: Indian.

	VG	VF	UNC
a. 1.2.1942; 14.7.1942; 7.5.1946; 1.6.1948.	10.00	30.00	80.00
b. 1.12.1949.	18.00	35.00	90.00

Central Bank of Ceylon

1951 Issue

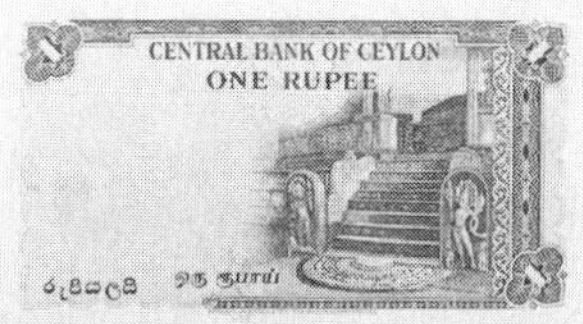

47 **1 Rupee**

20.1.1951. Blue on orange and green underprint. Portrait King George VI at left. Back: Ornate stairway. Watermark: Chinze. Printer: BWC.

VG	VF	UNC
7.50	30.00	125

48 **10 Rupees**

20.1.1951. Green on violet, brown and blue underprint. Portrait King George VI at left. Back: Ceremonial figures. Watermark: Chinze. Printer: BWC.

VG	VF	UNC
20.00	90.00	450

1952 Issue

		VG	VF	UNC
49	**1 Rupee** 3.6.1952; 16.10.1954. Blue on orange and green underprint. Portrait Queen Elizabeth II at left. Similar to #47. Back: Ornate stairway. Watermark: Chinze. Printer: BWC.			
	a. 3.6.1952.	7.50	30.00	80.00
	b. 16.10.1954.	7.50	30.00	80.00
	s. As a. Specimen.	—	—	3,000

		VG	VF	UNC
50	**2 Rupees** 3.6.1952; 16.10.1954. Brown and lilac on blue and green underprint. Portrait Queen Elizabeth II at left. Back: Pavilion. Watermark: Chinze. Printer: BWC.	15.00	45.00	150

		VG	VF	UNC
51	**5 Rupees** 3.6.1952. Purple on blue, green and orange underprint. Portrait Queen Elizabeth II at left. Back: Standing figure. Watermark: Chinze. Printer: BWC.	60.00	200	800
52	**50 Rupees** 3.6.1952; 12.5.1954. Blue, purple and multicolor. Portrait Queen Elizabeth II at left. Back: Ornate stairway. Watermark: Chinze. Printer: BWC.	100	300	—

		VG	VF	UNC
53	**100 Rupees** 3.6.1952; 16.10.1954. Brown on purple, green and orange underprint. Portrait Queen Elizabeth II at left. Back: Women in national dress. Watermark: Chinze. Printer: BWC.	70.00	250	1,600

1953-1954 Issue

		VG	VF	UNC
54	**5 Rupees** 16.10.1954. Orange on aqua, green and brown underprint. Portrait Queen Elizabeth II at left. Like #51. Back: Standing figure. Watermark: Chinze. Printer: BWC.	12.00	65.00	400

		VG	VF	UNC
55	**10 Rupees** 1.7.1953; 16.10.1954. Green on violet, brown and blue underprint. Portrait Queen Elizabeth II at left. Similar to #48. Back: Ceremonial figures. Watermark: Chinze. Printer: BWC.	18.00	65.00	400

STATE

Central Bank of Ceylon

1956 Issue

		VG	VF	UNC
56	**1 Rupee** 1956-1963. Blue on orange, green and brown underprint. Arms of Ceylon at left. Back: Ornate stairway. Watermark: Chinze. Printer: BWC. 108x60mm.			
	a. 30.7.1956. Signature: Stanley de Soysa and A. G. Ranasingha.	2.00	7.00	25.00
	b. 31.5.1957; 9.4.1958; 7.11.1958.	1.50	5.00	15.00
	c. With security strip. 11.9.1959.	1.50	2.00	7.50
	d. 18.8.1960; 29.1.1962. Signatures: Felix R. Dias Bandaranaike and W. Rajapatirana.	1.50	2.00	7.50
	e. 6..5.1963. Signature: T. B. Illangaratne and W. Rajapatirana.	1.50	2.00	7.50

		VG	VF	UNC
57	**2 Rupees** 1956-1962. Brown and lilac on blue and green underprint. Arms of Ceylon at left. Back: Pavilion. Watermark: Chinze. Printer: BWC. 121x67mm.			
	a. 30.7.1956; 31.5.1957; 6.10.1958; 7.11.1958. Signature: Stanley de Soysa and A. G. Ranasingha. Without security strip.	5.00	12.00	40.00
	b. 11.9.1959; Signature: Stanley de Soysa and W. Rajapatirana. With security strip.	5.00	12.00	40.00
	c. 18.8.1960; 29.1.1962. Signature: Felix R. Dias Bandaranaike and W. Rajapatirana.	5.00	10.00	30.00

#	Denomination	VG	VF	UNC
58	**5 Rupees** 1956-1962. Orange on aqua, green and brown underprint. Arms of Ceylon at left. Back: Standing figure. Watermark: Chinze. Printer: BWC. 133x73mm.			
	a. 30.7.1956; 31.5.1957; 10.6.1958. Signature: Stanley de Soysa and A. G. Ranasingha. Without security strip.	8.00	20.00	120
	b. 1.7.1959; 11.9.1959. Signature: Stanley de Soysa and W. Rajapatirana. With security strip.	8.00	20.00	120
	c. 18.8.1960; 29.1.1962. Signarues: Felix R. Dias Bandaranaike and W. Rajapatirana.	7.50	15.00	75.00

#	Denomination	VG	VF	UNC
59	**10 Rupees** 1956-1963. Green on violet, brown and blue underprint. Arms of Ceylon at left. Back: Ceremonial figures. Watermark: Chinze. Printer: BWC. 146x76mm.			
	a. 30.7.1956; 7.11.1957; 7.11.1958. Signatures Stanley de Soysa and A. G. Ranasingha. Without security strip.	10.00	25.00	100
	b. 11.9.1959. With security strip.	10.00	25.00	100
	c. 18.8.1960; 7.4.1961; 5.6.1963. Signatures Felix R. Dias Bandaranaike and W. Rajapatirana.	3.00	15.00	75.00

#	Denomination	VG	VF	UNC
60	**50 Rupees** 30.7.1956; 9,4,1958; 7.11.1958; 11.9.1959. Blue and violet on multicolor underprint. Arms of Ceylon at left. Back: Ornate stairway. Watermark: Chinze. Printer: BWC. 159x89mm.			
	a. 30.7.1956; 9.4.1958; 7.11.1958. Signatures: Stanley de Soysa and A. G. Ranasingha.	35.00	90.00	300
	b. 11.9.1959. Signatures: Stanley de Soysa and W. Rajapatirana.	35.00	90.00	300
61	**100 Rupees** 24.10.1956. Brown on multicolor underprint. Arms of Ceylon at left. Signature: Stanley de Soysa and A. G. Ranasingha. Back: Two women in national dress. Watermark: Chinze. Printer: BWC. 171x98mm.	50.00	200	800

The Republic of Chile, a ribbonlike country on the Pacific coast of southern South America, has an area of 756,950 sq. km. and a population of 16.45 million. Capital: Santiago. Copper, of which Chile has about 25 percent of the world's reserves, has accounted for a major portion of Chile's export earnings in recent years. Other important exports are iron ore, iodine, fruit and nitrate of soda.

Prior to the coming of the Spanish in the 16th century, northern Chile was under Inca rule while Araucanian Indians (also known as Mapuches) inhabited central and southern Chile. Although Chile declared its independence in 1810, decisive victory over the Spanish was not achieved until 1818. In the War of the Pacific (1879-83), Chile defeated Peru and Bolivia and won its present northern regions. It was not until the 1880s that the Araucanian Indians were completely subjugated. A three-year-old Marxist government of Salvador Allende was overthrown in 1973 by a military coup led by Augusto Pinochet, who ruled until a freely elected president was installed in 1990. Sound economic policies, maintained consistently since the 1980s, have contributed to steady growth, reduced poverty rates by over half, and have helped secure the country's commitment to democratic and representative government. Chile has increasingly assumed regional and international leadership roles befitting its status as a stable, democratic nation.

MONETARY SYSTEM:

1 Peso = 100 Centavos
1 Condor = 100 Centavos = 10 Pesos to 1960
1 Escudo = 100 Centesimos, 1960-75
1 Peso = 100 "old" Escudos, 1975-

REPLACEMENT NOTES:

#140, 143, 145-148 w/*R* next to serial #.
#149-158 w/*R* near to plate position #.

VALIDATION HANDSTAMPS:

The Regional and Republic issues are found with or without various combinations of round validation handstamps.

Type I: *DIRECCION DEL TESORO-SANTIAGO* around National Arms (large and small size).

Type II: *DIRECCION DE CONTABILIDAD-SANTIAGO* around plumed shield on open book.

Type III: *SUPERINTENDENCIA DE LA CASA DE MONEDA* around screwpress/SANTIAGO.

Type IV: *CONTADURIA MAYOR* around plumed shield on open book.

REPUBLIC

República de Chile

1880-1881 Issue

#	Denomination	Good	Fine	XF
1	**1 Peso** 5.4.1881. Black on orange underprint. Two women seated at left, one holding a caduceus, building at center right, portrait Prat at lower right. Handstamps Type III and IV. With text: *convertible en oro o plata.* Back: Text with law date 10.4.1879 at right. Printer: ABNC.	120	400	—

#	Denomination	Good	Fine	XF
2	**2 Pesos** 3.5.1880-19.2.1881. Black on green underprint. Man in uniform at upper left, village landscape at center right, national arms at lower right. Handstamps Type III and IV. With text: *convertible en oro o plata.* Back: Text with law date 10.4.1879 at right. Printer: ABNC.	120	400	—

#	Denomination	Good	Fine	XF
3	**5 Pesos** 13.6.1880-12.11.1881. Black on brown underprint. Village landscape at upper left, plumed shield at center right, portrait Gen. R. Freire at lower right. Handstamps Type III and IV. With text: *convertible en oro o plata*. Back: Text with law date 10.4.1879 at right. Printer: ABNC.	150	450	—
4	**10 Pesos** 4.1.1881-12.11.1881. Black on pink underprint. Towered bridge at upper left, portrait Pres. J. J. Perez at right. Handstamps Type III and IV. With text: *convertible en oro o plata*. Back: Text with law date 10.4.1879 at right. Printer: ABNC. 185x80mm.	200	550	—
5	**20 Pesos** ND (ca.1879). Black on brown underprint. Flower girl at left, man at left center, building at right, *VEINTE PESOS* without fringe along bottom margin. With text: *convertible en oro o plata*. Back: Text with law date 10.4.1879 at right. Printer: ABNC. Specimen or proof.	—	—	—
6	**50 Pesos** ND (ca.1879). Black on blue underprint. Man in uniform left, building at center, national arms at lower right, with one plate letter at upper left and upper right. With text: *convertible en oro o plata*. Back: Text with law date 10.4.1879 at right. Printer: ABNC. Specimen or proof.	—	—	—
7	**100 Pesos** 4.1.1881; 26.1.1881; 12.11.1881. Black on orange underprint. Portrait B. O'Higgins at lower left, monument at center, two women seated with shield at right, without double border. Handstamps Type III and IV. With text: *convertible en oro o plata*. Back: Text without border. With law date 10.4.1879 at right. Printer: ABNC. 183x78mm.	250	650	—
8	**1000 Pesos** 12.11.1881. Black on olive underprint. Monument at left, national arms at center right, man at lower right, without double border. Handstamps Type III and IV. With text: *convertible en oro o plata*. Back: Text without border. With law date 10.4.1879 at right. Printer: ABNC.	—	—	—

1883-1891 Issue

#	Denomination	Good	Fine	XF
9	**20 Centavos** ND (1891). Black on brown underprint. Portrait Liberty at upper left. Back: Arms at center. Printer: ABNC. (Not issued).	15.00	40.00	85.00

#	Denomination	Good	Fine	XF
10	**50 Centavos** 10.6.1891. Black on green underprint. Portrait Liberty at top center, two date style varieties. Back: Arms at center. Printer: ABNC.			
	a. Handstamp Type I.	5.00	25.00	75.00
	r. Remainder without date, signature or hand-stamp.	—	—	30.00
11	**1 Peso** 1883-1898. Black on red-orange underprint. Similar to #1 but with arms at left and 1s in corners. Back green. Reduced size.			
	a. Handstamps Type III and IV. 17.2.1883.	20.00	75.00	160
	b. Handstamps Type I and II. 17.5.1884-1.5.1895.	15.00	55.00	120
	c. Handstamps Type I and III. 17.8.1898.	—	—	—
	s. ND. Specimen.	—	—	—
12	**2 Pesos** 17.11.1885-1.5.1895. Black on green underprint. Man in uniform at upper left, village landscape at center right, national arms at lower right. Handstamps Type I and II. With text: *convertible en oro o plata*. Similar to #2. Back: Text with law date 10.4.1879 at right. Printer: ABNC. Reduced size.			
	a. Issued note.	30.00	100	250
	s. Specimen.	—	Unc	600
13	**100 Pesos** ca.1880-1890. Black on orange underprint. Portrait B. O'Higgins at lower left, monument at center, two women seated with shield at right, with double border on face, single plate letter. With text: *convertible en oro o plata*. Similar to #7. Back: Text with law date 10.4.1879 at right. Printer: ABNC.			
	p. Proof.	—	—	—
	s. Specimen.	—	—	—
14	**1000 Pesos** 18.8.1891. Black on olive underprint. Monument at left, national arms at center right, man at lower right, with double border on face, single plate letter. With text: *convertible en oro o plata*. Similar to #8. Back: Text with law date 10.4.1879 at right. Printer: ABNC.	—	—	—

1898-1920 Issue

#	Denomination	Good	Fine	XF
15	**1 Peso** 1898-1919. Black on red-orange underprint. Two women seated at left, one holding a caduceus, building at center right, portrait Prat at lower right. With arms at left and 1s in corners. Printer: ABNC. Similar to #11 but reduced in size.			
	a. Handstamps Type I and III. 17.11.1898-7.6.1911.	2.00	10.00	35.00
	b. Handstamps Type I and II. 8.11.1911-13.8.1919.	1.00	5.00	20.00
	s. Specimen.	—	Unc	85.00
16	**2 Pesos** 17.11.1898-22.2.1912. Black on green underprint. Man in uniform at upper left, village landscape at center right, national arms at lower right. Handstamps Type I and II. Back: Denomination numeral at right. Printer: ABNC. Similar to #12 but reduced in size.			
	a. Issued note.	5.00	25.00	60.00
	s. Specimen.	—	Unc	150
17	**2 Pesos** 22.2.1912-26.3.1919. Black on green underprint. Man in uniform at upper left, village landscape at center right, national arms at lower right. Handstamps Type I and II. Like #16. Back: Denomination numeral at right. Printer: W&S.	5.00	25.00	60.00

18	5 Pesos	Good	Fine	XF
	1899-1918. Black on brown underprint. Village landscape at upper left, plumed shield at center right, portrait Gen. R. Freire at lower right. Similar to #3. Back: Denomination numeral at right. Printer: W&S.			
	a. Handstamps Type I and III. 3.4.1899-25.4.1906.	25.00	100	325
	b. Handstamps Type I and II. 21.7.1916-20.6.1918.	12.50	50.00	150

19	5 Pesos	Good	Fine	XF
	1906-1916. Black on brown underprint. Village landscape at upper left, plumed shield at center right, portrait Gen. R. Freire at lower right. Similar to #18 but with modified guilloches around *5s*, and other plate changes. Back: Denomination numeral at right. Printer: ABNC.			
	a. Handstamps Type I and III. 23.5.1906-18.10.1910.	10.00	40.00	125
	b. Handstamps Type I and II. 31.1.1911-21.7.1916.	8.00	35.00	100
	s. Specimen.	—	Unc	250

20	10 Pesos	Good	Fine	XF
	19.11.1899-6.6.1905. Black on red-brown underprint. Towered bridge at upper left, portrait Pres. J. J. Perez at right. Handstamps Type I and III. Similar to #4. Back: Denomination numeral at right. Printer: W&S.	40.00	150	350

21	10 Pesos	Good	Fine	XF
	1905-1918. Black on pink underprint. Towered bridge at upper left, portrait Pres. J. J. Perez at right. Similar to #20 but with modified guilloches and other plate changes. Back: Denomination numeral at right. Printer: ABNC.			
	a. Handstamps Type I and III. 28.9.1905-23.11.1910.	30.00	125	275
	b. Handstamps Type I and II. 7.6.1911-20.6.1918.	20.00	60.00	150
	s. Specimen.	—	Unc	375

22	20 Pesos	Good	Fine	XF
	1906-1914. Black on brown underprint. Flower girl at left, man at left center, building at right. Similar to #5 but with fringe around *VEINTE PESOS* along bottom margin. Back: Denomination numeral at right. Printer: ABNC.			
	a. Handstamps Type I and III. 31.3.1906-21.6.1910.	30.00	125	300
	b. Handstamps Type I and II. 13.5.1912-1.8.1914.	20.00	60.00	150
	s. Specimen.	—	Unc	450

23	20 Pesos	Good	Fine	XF
	1900-1904. Black on red underprint. Flower girl at left, man at left center, building at right, with fringe around *VEINTE PESOS* along bottom margin. Similar to #22. Back: Denomination numeral at right. Printer: W&S.			
	a. Handstamps Type I and III. 6.12.1900; 31.8.1903; 27.10.1904.	30.00	125	300
	b. Handstamps Type I and II. 18.11.1903; 30.4.1904.	30.00	125	300

24	50 Pesos	Good	Fine	XF
	1899-1914. Black on blue underprint. Man in uniform left, building at center, national arms at lower right, with one plate letter at upper left and upper right. Similar to #6. Back: Denomination numeral at right. Printer: ABNC.			
	a. Handstamps Type I and III. 16.12.1899; 30.12.1904; 4.3.1905.	50.00	150	450
	b. Handstamps Type I and II. 18.7.1912, 25.9.1912, 31.10, 1912, 1.8.1914, 18.7.1912-1.8.1914.	45.00	125	350
	s1. Specimen.	—	Unc	900
	s2. Specimen. Overprint: *MUESTRA*.	—	Unc	950

25	100 Pesos	Good	Fine	XF
	1920. Black on blue and gold underprint. Portrait B. O'Higgins at lower left, monument at center, two women seated with shield at right, with double border on face. Similar to #13, with double plate letter. Back: Denomination numeral at right. Printer: ABNC.			
	a. Handstamps Type I and III.	100	350	—
	b. Handstamps Type I and II. 29.3.1920.	80.00	300	—
	s. Specimen.	—	Unc	800

		Good	Fine	XF
26	**100 Pesos** 1906-1916. Black on blue and red underprint. B. O'Higgins at left, monument at right. Back: Denomination numeral at right. Printer: ABNC.			
	a. Handstamps Type I and III. 23.5.1906.	90.00	325	—
	b. Handstamps Type I and II. 4.3.1912; 31.3.1913; 22.12.1916.	75.00	250	—
	s1. Specimen.	—	Unc	725
	s2. Specimen. Overprint: *MUESTRA*.	—	Unc	800

		Good	Fine	XF
27	**500 Pesos** 14.5.1912; 12.8.1912; 15.5.1917. Black on green and yellow underprint. Man at left center, building at right. Handstamps Type I and II. Back: Denomination numeral at right. Printer: ABNC.			
	a. Issued note.	300	700	—
	s1. Specimen.	—	Unc	1,650
	s2. Specimen. Overprint: *MUESTRA*.	—	Unc	2,750
27a	**1000 Pesos** 12.11.1881. Monument at left, arms at center right, men at lower right. Back: Text at right and without border. Printer: ABNC. 185x80mm.	—	—	—
28a	**1000 Pesos** 12.8.1912. Black on olive underprint. Monument at left, national arms at center right, man at lower right, with double border on face. Similar to #14 but without *plata,* with double plate letter. Back: Denomination numeral at right. Printer: ABNC.			
	a. Issued note.	350	1,000	—
	s. Specimen.	—	—	—

1898 Provisional Issue on Banco de José Bunster

Lei 1054 de 31 de Julio de 1898.

		Good	Fine	XF
29	**1 Peso** 17.8.1898. Black on yellow underprint. Woman leaning on wheel ("Fortune") at left, "Raphael's Angel" at upper center, portrait man at right. Rare.	—	—	—

1898 Provisional Issue on Banco Comercial de Chile

		Good	Fine	XF
30	**1 Peso** 17.8.1898. Black on yellow and pink underprint. Woman with basket on head at left, arms at right. Back: Condor at center. Rare.	—	—	—

		Good	Fine	XF
31	**2 Pesos** 17.8.1898. Black on green and pink underprint. Arms at left, seated woman with bales at center. Back: Woman at center. Rare.	—	—	—

		Good	Fine	XF
32	**10 Pesos** 17.8.1898 (- old date 8.6.1893). Black on green and rose underprint. Liberty at left, bridge at center, arms at right. Series B. Back: Ox-cart on back. Rare.	—	—	—
33	**20 Pesos** 1.8.1898 (-old date 8.6.1893). Rare.	—	—	—

1898 Provisional Issue on Banco de Concepción

		Good	Fine	XF
34	**1 Peso** 14.9.1898. Black on green and multicolor underprint. Reclining allegorical woman with globe ("Science") at left, portrait Pinto at right. Back: Standing Indian at center.	300	750	—

1898 Provisional Issue on Banco de Curicó

		Good	Fine	XF
35	**5 Pesos** 14.9.1898. Black on green and peach underprint. Portrait Comandante E. Ramirez in uniform at center. Back: Christopher Columbus sighting land at center. Rare.	—	—	—
36	**20 Pesos** 18.8.1898; 14.9.1898. Black on blue and yellow underprint. Woman with sheaf ("The Reaper") at left, portrait Capt. A. Prat at left center, bank above arms at lower right. Back: Two ships engaged in warfare. Rare.	—	—	—

1898 Provisional Issue on Banco de Escobar Ossa y Ca

Spurious Issue.

		Good	Fine	XF
37	**5 Pesos** 14.9.1898. Black on blue underprint. Seated woman with sword at left, miners at center, woman and shoreline ("Sea Side") at right. Rare.	—	—	—

		Good	Fine	XF
38	**10 Pesos** 14.9.1898. Black on brown underprint. Boy ("Oscar") at left, girl miners at center. Rare.	—	—	—

		Good	Fine	XF
39	**20 Pesos** 14.9.1898. Black on rose-pink underprint. Standing woman at left, miners at upper center, girl at right. Rare.	—	—	—

1898 Provisional Issue on Banco de D. Matte y Ca

		Good	Fine	XF
40	**10 Pesos** 1.8.1898. Black on yellow and green underprint. Farmer harvesting corn at left, girl and dog at right. ("The Pets"). Rare.	—	—	—

1898 Provisional Issue on Banco de Matte, Mac-Clure y Ca

		Good	Fine	XF
41	**1 Peso** 14.7.1898. Blue. Gathering hay at left, man at center, ships at right. Rare. PC: Violet.	—	—	—

1898 Provisional Issue on Banco de Melipilla

		Good	Fine	XF
42	**5 Pesos** 1.8.1898. Black on tan underprint. Seated girl ("Lucy's Pets") at left, gathering hay at center, ducks at right. Back: Seated woman. Rare.	—	—	—

1898 Provisional Issue on Banco de Mobiliario

		Good	Fine	XF
43	**1 Peso** 17.8.1898. Black on green and gold underprint. Two women at lower left, boy at top center, woman at lower right. Rare.	—	—	—

		Good	Fine	XF
44	**10 Pesos** 14.9.1898. Black. Boy at left, men with llamas at lower right. Rare.	—	—	—

1898 Provisional Issue on Banco Nacional de Chile, Valparaiso

#	Denomination	Good	Fine	XF
45	**1 Peso** 17.8.1898. Black on green and peach underprint. Bull's head at left, Valdivia at center, arms at right.	300	700	—
46	**2 Pesos** 17.8.1898. Black on red-brown and green underprint. Valdivia at left, arms at center, girl with flowers at right. Rare.	—	—	—
47	**5 Pesos** 31.7.1898. Black on green and orange underprint. Valdivia at lower left, arms at center, head at right. Rare.	—	—	—
48	**10 Pesos** 17.8.1898. Black on green and brown underprint. Valdivia at lower left, condor at upper center, arms at right. Rare.	—	—	—
49	**500 Pesos** 17.8.1898. Black on green and yellow underprint. Portrait Valdivia at left, cherub at upper center, allegorical woman with hammer and anvil at upper right, arms at lower right. Back: Valdivia at left, cattle watering in pond. Rare.	—	—	—

1898 Provisional Issue on Banco San Fernando

#	Denomination	Good	Fine	XF
50	**5 Pesos** 16.5.1899. Black on green underprint. Indian woman seated at left, horse's head ("My Horse") at right. Rare.	—	—	—

Note: Some authorities believe that all notes from this bank appearing to have been issued are in reality fraudulently dated and signed.

1898 Provisional Issue on Banco de Santiago

#	Denomination	Good	Fine	XF
51	**1 Peso** 14.9.1898. (- old date 25.2.1896). Black on brown underprint. Woman with fasces and portrait Tocornal at upper left, cherub at upper right. Back: Sailing ship "Esmeralda" at center.	60.00	275	—

Note: Regular commercial bank issues of #29-51 including other denominations without overprint: *EMISION FISCAL* are listed in the *Standard Catalog of World Paper Money, Specialzed Issues volume.*

1898 Provisional Issue on República de Chile

#	Denomination	Good	Fine	XF
52	**1 Peso** 17.8.1898; 26.9.1898. Black on red-orange underprint. Two women seated at left, one holding a caduceus, building at center right, portrait Prat at lower right. Back: Text with law date 10.4.1879 at right.	60.00	275	—

#	Denomination	Good	Fine	XF
53	**2 Pesos** 17.8.1898. Black on green underprint. Man in uniform at upper left, village landscape at center right, national arms at lower right. Back: Text with law date 10.4.1879 at right.	50.00	150	—
54	**5 Pesos** 1.8.1898. Black on brown underprint. Village landscape at upper left, plumed shield at center right, portrait Gen. R. Freire at lower right. Back: Denomination numeral at right. Rare.	—	—	—
55	**100 Pesos** 1.8.1898. Black on blue and gold underprint. Portrait B. O'Higgins at lower left, monument at center, two women seated with shield at right, with double border on face. Back: Denomination numeral at right. Rare.	—	—	—
56	**1000 Pesos** 1.8.1898. Black on olive underprint. Monument at left, national arms at center right, man at lower right, with double border on face. Back: Denomination numeral at right. Rare.	—	—	—

1918-1925 Regular Issue

#	Denomination	Good	Fine	XF
57	**2 Pesos** ND. Black on blue and light brown underprint. Heading in 1 line. Condor at right. Handstamps Type I and II. Back: Seated woman with shield at center. (Not issued).	—	—	—

#	Denomination	Good	Fine	XF
58	**2 Pesos** 19.10.1920-30.1.1922. Blue on green and red underprint. Woman seated with shield at right. Red serial #. Handstamps Type I and II.	2.50	7.50	45.00
59	**2 Pesos** 1922-1925. Blue on yellow underprint. Woman seated with shield at right. Red serial #. Handstamps Type I and II. Similar to #58.	Good	Fine	XF
	a. Brown serial #. 5.5.1922.	2.50	7.50	45.00
	b. Blue serial #. 20.12.1922-22.9.1925.	2.00	6.00	30.00

#	Denomination	Good	Fine	XF
60	**5 Pesos** 14.8.1918-2.1.1922. Blue. Woman seated with shield at left, value at right. Red serial #. Handstamps Type I and II. Back: Allegorical figures at left and right.	4.00	20.00	60.00
61	**5 Pesos** 16.8.1922-22.9.1925. Blue on yellow underprint. Woman seated with shield at left, value at right. Date in 1 or 2 lines. Blue serial #. 2 signature varieties. Handstamps Type I and II. Like #60. Back: Allegorical figures at left and right.	2.50	10.00	45.00

#	Denomination	Good	Fine	XF
62	**10 Pesos** 11.12.1918-2.1.1922. Brown on pink underprint. Condor at left, woman seated with shield at center. Handstamps Type I and II.	7.50	30.00	80.00
63	**10 Pesos** 31.7.1922-22.9.1925. Brown in green underprint. Condor at left, woman seated with shield at center. 2 signature varieties. Handstamps Type I and II. Like #62.	4.00	20.00	65.00
64	**20 Pesos** 1919-1924. Green on rose underprint. Condor at left, woman seated with shield at right. Handstamps Type I and II.			
	a. Red serial #. Series A. 24.6.1919-10.6.1920.	20.00	60.00	200
	b. Blue serial #. Series B. 25.2.1924.	20.00	60.00	200

#	Denomination	Good	Fine	XF
65	**50 Pesos** 4.5.1917-17.6.1923. Blue-green. Woman seated with shield at left, ships at right. Handstamps Type I and II.	30.00	100	350
66	**100 Pesos** 1917-1924. Blue. Woman seated with shield at left, three women reclining at right. Handstamps Type I and II. Back: Woman and globe at center. PC: Light blue.			
	a. Red underprint. and serial #. Date placement higher or lower. 19.9.1917-30.6.1921.	45.00	225	600
	b. Blue underprint. and serial #. 17.7.1923-31.10.1924.	40.00	200	500
66A	**500 Pesos** ND (ca. 1919). Dark blue on purple underprint. Seated figure at left, woman seated with shield at right. Back: Allegorical figures of Agriculture at left, Music at right. Specimen.	—	—	—
66B	**1000 Pesos** 4.3.1921. Dark brown on purple and yellow underprint. Seated woman at left, seated woman with shield at right. Back: Seated woman at left and right.	450	950	—

Color Abbreviation Guide

New to the *Standard Catalog of® World Paper Money* are the following abbreviations related to color references:

BC: Back color
PC: Paper color

Vale Del Tesoro

1921-1924 Issues

#67-70 special issue backed by saltpeter instead of gold.

#	Denomination	Good	Fine	XF
67	**50 Pesos** 1921; 1924. Light blue. Woman reclining at left. Handstamps Type I and II.			
	a. Series B. 7.9.1921. White paper.	150	400	—
	b. Series C. 2.12.1924. Blue paper. Watermark different from a.	150	400	—
68	**100 Pesos** 1921; 1924. Brown and ochre. Woman at left.			
	a. Series B. Face ochre, back gold. Ochre paper. 7.9.1921.	150	400	—
	b. Series C. Dark brown on light brown paper. 2.12.1924. Watermark different from a.	150	400	—
69	**500 Pesos** 25.4.1921; 2.12.1924. Black on lilac underprint. Seated woman at left. Rare.	—	—	—
70	**1000 Pesos** 4.3.1921; 2.12.1924. Seated allegorical figure at left and right. Rare.	—	—	—

Banco Central de Chile

1925 First Provisional Issue

#	Denomination	Good	Fine	XF
71	**5 Pesos = 1/2 Condor** 10.12.1925. Blue on yellow underprint. Woman seated with shield at left.	2.50	10.00	35.00
72	**5 Pesos = 1/2 Condor** 10.12.1925. Dark blue on light blue and yellow underprint. Woman seated with shield at left. Back: Condor at center, allegorical figure at right.	2.50	10.00	35.00
73	**10 Pesos = 1 Condor** 10.12.1925. Brown. Woman seated with shield at left.	3.00	12.50	50.00

#	Description	Good	Fine	XF
74	**10 Pesos = 1 Condor** 10.12.1925. Brown on green underprint. Condor at left, seated woman with shield at center.	3.00	12.50	50.00
75	**100 Pesos = 10 Condores** 10.12.1925. Black on blue underprint. Woman seated with shield at left, three women reclining at right. PC: Blue.	45.00	150	350

#	Description	Good	Fine	XF
76	**500 Pesos = 50 Condores** 10.12.1925. Brown on orange underprint. Woman reclining at left, woman seated with shield at right.	80.00	250	650
77	**1000 Pesos = 100 Condores** 10.12.1925. Dark brown on violet and yellow underprint. Woman seated with horns at left, woman seated with shield at right.	—	—	—

1925 Second Provisional Issue

#78-81 printed bank name.

#	Description	Good	Fine	XF
78	**50 Pesos** 10.12.1925. Blue. Woman reclining at left. Series D. Similar to #67.	—	—	—
79	**100 Pesos** 10.12.1925. Brown. Woman at left. Series D. Similar to #68.	—	—	—
80	**500 Pesos** 10.12.1925. Brown on orange underprint. Woman reclining at left, woman seated with shield at right. Similar to #76. Rare.	—	—	—
81	**1000 Pesos** 10.12.1925. Dark brown on violet and yellow underprint. Woman seated with horns at left, woman seated with shield at right. Similar to #77. Rare.	—	—	—

1927-1929 Billete Provisional Issue

#	Description	Good	Fine	XF
82	**5 Pesos = 1/2 Condor** 18.4.1927-2.6.1930. Black on green underprint. Signature varieties. Large or small serial # varieties. Series B-E. Watermark: BANCO CENTRAL DE CHILE. PC: Blue.	1.50	7.50	25.00

#	Description	Good	Fine	XF
83	**10 Pesos = 1 Condor** 1927-1930. Black on salmon underprint. Signature varieties. Large or small serial # varieties. Series B-C. Watermark: BANCO CENTRAL DE CHILE. PC: Yellow.			
	a. Printer's name in margin. 18.4.1927.	2.00	10.00	30.00
	b. Printer's name in frame. 14.5.1928-2.6.1930.	1.50	7.50	25.00

#	Description	Good	Fine	XF
84	**50 Pesos = 5 Condores** 1927-1930. Black on brown underprint. Condor at upper left. Signature varieties. Large or small serial # varieties. Series E-K. Watermark: BANCO CENTRAL DE CHILE. PC: Pink.			
	a. Printer's name in margin. 28.3.1927.	10.00	25.00	75.00
	b. Printer's name in frame. 14.5.1928-2.6.1930.	5.00	20.00	50.00

#	Description	Good	Fine	XF
85	**100 Pesos = 10 Condores** 28.3.1927-2.6.1930. Black on light blue and red-brown underprint. Signature varieties. Large or small serial # varieties. Series E-H. Watermark: BANCO CENTRAL DE CHILE.	10.00	25.00	75.00
86	**500 Pesos = 50 Condores** 29.1.1929. Green on purple underprint. Condor at upper left. Signature varieties. Large or small serial # varieties. Series D. Watermark: BANCO CENTRAL DE CHILE.	50.00	150	300

#	Description	Good	Fine	XF
87	**1000 Pesos = 100 Condores** 29.1.1929. Blue on pink and purple underprint. Andean condor at upper left. Signature varieties. Large or small serial # varieties. Watermark: BANCO CENTRAL DE CHILE.	90.00	200	500

1932 Billete Provisional Issue

#	Description	VG	VF	UNC
88	**1 Peso = 1/10 Condor** 1932-1933. Black frame, blue center with wide diagonal pink stripe. 120x60mm.			
	a. Tan paper. 12.9.1932.	1.00	4.00	15.00
	b. Peach paper. 7.3.1933.	1.00	4.00	15.00

1942-1943 Billete Provisional Issues

#	Description	VG	VF	UNC
89	**1 Peso = 1/10 Condor** 11.2.1942. Black on green underprint with blue frame. Series B-E. Like #82. 124x62mm. PC: Pink.	1.00	3.00	10.00

		VG	VF	UNC
90	**1 Peso = 1/10 Condor** 3.3.1943. Blue on yellow underprint. 88x50mm.			
	a. Back light orange; with A-A.	0.50	2.00	5.00
	b. Back purple; with B-B.	0.50	2.00	5.00
	c. Back green; with C-C.	0.50	2.00	5.00
	d. Back red-orange; with D-D.	0.50	2.00	5.00
	e. Back blue; with E-E. (Not issued). Rare.	—	—	—

1931-1942 Issue

		VG	VF	UNC
91	**5 Pesos = 1/2 Condor** 1932-1942. Blue on light orange underprint. Portrait B. O'Higgins at right, without name under portrait. Signature varieties.			
	a. 26.9.1932.	6.00	15.00	30.00
	b. 17.6.1933.	3.00	7.00	15.00
	c. 3.7.1935-8.7.1942.	1.00	3.00	10.00

		VG	VF	UNC
92	**10 Pesos = 1 Condor** 1931-1942. Red-brown on light yellow underprint. Portrait Bulnes at right, without name under portrait. Signature varieties.			
	a. Month in letters. 9.2.1931.	2.50	10.00	30.00
	b. Month in Roman numerals. 29.9.1932.	2.00	8.00	25.00
	c. 7.6.1933; 22.11.1933.	1.00	6.00	20.00
	d. 31.12.1934-8.7.1942.	1.00	3.00	10.00

		VG	VF	UNC
93	**20 Pesos = 2 Condores** 1939-1947. Portrait Capt. Valdivia at center, without name under portrait. Signature varieties. Back: Statue in park with trees and building at center.			
	a. Purple-brown. Back vignette lilac. 22.11.1939.	1.50	5.00	15.00
	b. Brown. Back vignette brown. 2.4.1947; 24.12.1947.	1.00	4.00	12.50
	s. Specimen.	—	—	—

		VG	VF	UNC
94	**50 Pesos = 5 Condores** 1932-1942. Green. Portrait Pinto at right, without name under portrait. Signature varieties. Back: German-style lettering and numerals at corners and left center.			
	a. 22.8.1932.	3.00	15.00	40.00
	b. 22.11.1933.	2.50	12.00	30.00
	c. 3.7.1935-8.7.1942.	1.00	8.00	20.00

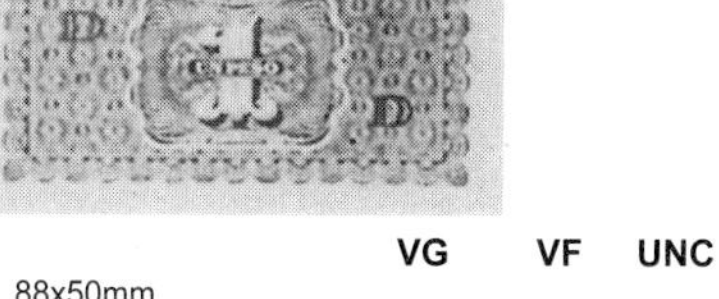

		VG	VF	UNC
95	**100 Pesos = 10 Condores** 7.6.1933-10.3.1937. Red with white underprint. Portrait Prat at right, without name under portrait. Signature varieties.	3.00	20.00	50.00
96	**100 Pesos = 10 Condores** 19.4.1939-20.1.1943. Red underprint. Portrait Prat at right, without name under portrait. Signature varieties. Different plate from #95.	2.00	10.00	35.00

		VG	VF	UNC
97	**500 Pesos = 50 Condores** 7.6.1933; 3.7.1935; 1.4.1936. Black on yellow underprint. Portrait Montt at center, without name under portrait. Signature varieties. Back: Explorer on horseback at left.	6.00	40.00	90.00
98	**500 Pesos = 50 Condores** 8.7.1942; 18.8.1943. Red-brown. Portrait Montt at center, without name under portrait. Signature varieties. Back: Spaniards at left.	5.00	30.00	70.00

		VG	VF	UNC
99	**1000 Pesos = 100 Condores** 7.6.1933-18.8.1943. Brown on green underprint. Portrait Blanco at right, without name under portrait. Signature varieties. Back: Spaniards at center.	25.00	60.00	175

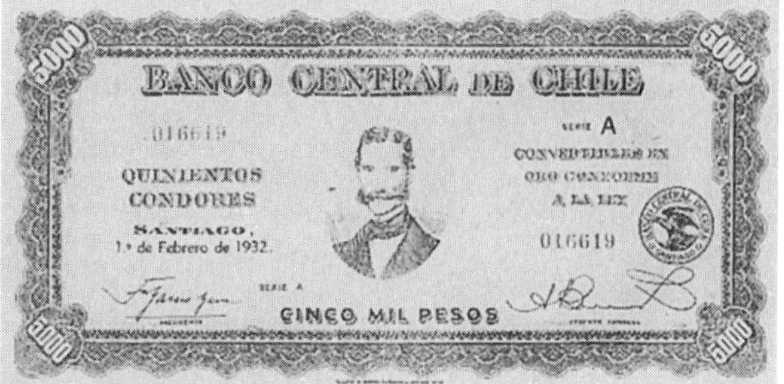

		VG	VF	UNC
100	**5000 Pesos = 500 Condores** 1.2.1932. Brown on yellow underprint. Portrait M. A. Tocornal at center, without name under portrait. Signature varieties. Back: Large *5000.*	75.00	250	550
101	**10,000 Pesos = 1000 Condores** 1.2.1932. Blue on multicolor underprint. Portrait M. Balmaceda at center, without name under portrait. Signature varieties. Back: Large *10,000.*	400	1,000	—

1940-1945 Issue

		VG	VF	UNC
102	**5 Pesos = 1/2 Condor** 19.4.1944; 3.7.1946; 30.4.1947. Blue. Portrait B. O'Higgins at right, with name under portrait. Signature varieties.	0.50	2.00	6.00

		VG	VF	UNC
103	**10 Pesos = 1 Condor** 18.8.1943-20.11.1946. Red-brown. Portrait Bulnes at right, with name under portrait. Signature varieties.	1.00	3.00	10.00
104	**50 Pesos = 5 Condores** 19.1.1944-1.10.1947. Green. Portrait Pinto at right, with name under portrait. Signature varieties. Back: German-style lettering and numerals at corners and left center.	1.50	4.00	15.00

		VG	VF	UNC
105	**100 Pesos = 10 Condores** 1943-1948. Red. Portrait Prat at right, with name under portrait. Signature varieties.			
	a. Without security thread. 29.5.1943-28.5.1947.	1.50	4.00	15.00
	b. With security thread. 24.11.1948.	1.50	4.00	15.00
106	**500 Pesos = 50 Condores** 28.2.1945. Orange-brown. Portrait Montt at center, with name under portrait. Signature varieties. Back: Spaniards at left.	6.00	20.00	60.00

		VG	VF	UNC
107	**1000 Pesos = 100 Condores** 28.2.1945; 1.10.1947. Brown on green underprint. Portrait Blanco at right, with name under portrait. Signature varieties. Back: Spaniards at center.	6.00	20.00	65.00
108	**5000 Pesos = 500 Condores** 2.10.1940. Blue. Portrait M. A. Tocornal at center, with name under portrait. Signature varieties. Back: Battle scene.	25.00	80.00	225

		VG	VF	UNC
109	**10,000 Pesos = 1000 Condores** 2.10.1940. Violet on brown underprint. Portrait M. Balmaceda at center, with name under portrait. Signature varieties. Back: Military horseman.	40.00	125	350

1947-1948 ND Issue

		VG	VF	UNC
110	**5 Pesos = 1/2 Condor** ND (1947-1958). Blue. Portrait B. O'Higgins at right. Like #91. Small or large signature varieties, with or without security thread. 2 signature varieties. Watermark: D. Diego Portales. Printer: Talleres de Especies Valoradas, Santiago, Chile.	0.15	0.50	2.00

		VG	VF	UNC
111	**10 Pesos = 1 Condor** ND (1947-1958). Red-brown. Portrait Bulnes at right. Like #92. Small or large signature varieties, with or without security thread. 2 block # varieties. 2 signature varieties. Watermark: D. Diego Portales. Printer: Talleres de Especies Valoradas, Santiago, Chile.	0.15	0.50	2.00

		VG	VF	UNC
112	**50 Pesos = 5 Condores** ND (1947-1958). Green. Portrait Pinto at right. Like #94. Small or large signature varieties, with or without security thread. 2 signature varieties. Back: German-style lettering and numerals at corners and left center. Watermark: D. Diego Portales. Printer: Talleres de Especies Valoradas, Santiago, Chile.	0.25	1.25	5.00

113 100 Pesos = 10 Condores VG VF UNC
ND (1947-1956). Red. Portrait Prat at right. Similar to #95. Small or large signature varieties, with or without security thread. 2 signature varieties. Back: Small black seal at center. Watermark: D. Diego Portales. Printer: Talleres de Especies Valoradas, Santiago, Chile. 0.50 2.00 8.00

114 100 Pesos = 10 Condores VG VF UNC
ND (1947-1958). Red. Portrait Prat at right. Like #113. Small or large signature varieties, with or without security thread. 2 serial # varieties. Back: Different design with Large red seal at bottom. Watermark: D. Diego Portales. Printer: Talleres de Especies Valoradas, Santiago, Chile. 0.50 1.50 7.50

115 500 Pesos = 50 Condores VG VF UNC
ND (1947-1959). Blue. Portrait Montt at center. Small or large signature varieties, with or without security thread. 4 signature varieties. Back: Explorer on horseback. Watermark: D. Diego Portales. Printer: Talleres de Especies Valoradas, Santiago, Chile. 1.00 3.50 15.00

116 1000 Pesos = 100 Condores VG VF UNC
ND (1947-1959). Dark brown. Portrait Encalada at center. Small or large signature varieties, with or without security thread. 3 signature varieties. Back: Founding of Santiago. Watermark: D. Diego Portales. Printer: Talleres de Especies Valoradas, Santiago, Chile. 2.00 6.00 20.00

117 5000 Pesos = 500 Condores VG VF UNC
ND (1947-1959). Brown-violet. Portrait M. A. Tocornal at center. Small or large signature varieties, with or without security thread. Back: Battle of Rancagua. Watermark: D. Diego Portales. Printer: Talleres de Especies Valoradas, Santiago, Chile. Smaller size than #100.

a. Large size, printed portion 169mm horizontally. 3.00 10.00 30.00
b. Small size, printed portion 166mm horizontally. 3.00 10.00 30.00

118 10,000 Pesos = 1000 Condores VG VF UNC
ND (1947-1959). Violet. Portrait M. Balmaceda at center. Small or large signature varieties, with or without security thread. 3 signatures. Back: Soldiers meeting. Watermark: D. Diego Portales at left, words *DIEZ varieties. MIL* at right. Printer: Talleres de Especies Valoradas, Santiago, Chile. 3.00 15.00 50.00

1958 ND Issue

119 5 Pesos = 1/2 Condor VG VF UNC
ND (1958-1959). Blue. Portrait B. O'Higgins at right. Like #91. 2 large size signature varieties. Printer: CdM-Chile. 0.10 0.25 1.00

120 10 Pesos = 1 Condor VG VF UNC
ND (1958-1959). Red-brown. Portrait Bulnes at right. Like #92. 2 large size signature varieties. Printer: CdM-Chile. 0.10 0.25 1.00

121 50 Pesos = 5 Condores VG VF UNC
ND (1958-1959). Green. Portrait Pinto at right. Like #94. 2 large size signature varieties. Back: Green seal at bottom center. Printer: CdM-Chile.

a. Imprint length 23mm. 0.25 0.50 2.00
b. Imprint length 26mm. 0.25 0.50 2.00

122 100 Pesos = 10 Condores VG VF UNC
ND (1958-1959). Red. Portrait Prat at right. Like #114. 3 large size signature varieties. Back: Large red seal at bottom. Printer: CdM-Chile. 0.25 0.50 3.00

		VG	VF	UNC
123	**50,000 Pesos = 5000 Condores** ND (1958-1959). Dark green. Portrait Alessandri at center. 2 large size signature varieties. Printer: CdM-Chile.	25.00	50.00	150

1960 ND Provisional Issue

1 Escudo = 1000 Pesos (= 100 Centesimos)

		VG	VF	UNC
124	**1/2 Centesimo on 5 Pesos** ND (1960-1961). Blue. Portrait Bernard O'Higgins at left, signature titles: *PRESIDENTE* and *GERENTE GENERAL*. Watermark: D. Diego Portales. Printer: CdM-Chile. Rare.	—	—	—

		VG	VF	UNC
125	**1 Centesimo on 10 Pesos** ND (1960-1961). Red-brown. Portrait Manuel Bulnes at left. Series F. Signature titles: *PRESIDENTE* and *GERENTE GENERAL*. Watermark: D. Diego Portales. Printer: CdM-Chile.	1.00	2.50	12.50

		VG	VF	UNC
126	**5 Centesimos on 50 Pesos** ND (1960-1961). Green. Portrait Anibal Pinto at left. Series C. 3 signature varieties. Signature titles: *PRESIDENTE* and *GERENTE GENERAL*. Watermark: D. Diego Portales. Printer: CdM-Chile.			
	a. Imprint on face 25mm wide.	0.25	1.00	2.50
	b. Imprint on face 22mm wide.	0.10	0.20	2.00
	s. Specimen.	—	—	12.50

		VG	VF	UNC
127	**10 Centesimos on 100 Pesos** ND (1960-1961). Red. Portrait Arturo Prat at left. 3 signature varieties. Series C-K. Signature titles: *PRESIDENTE* and *GERENTE GENERAL*. Watermark: D. Diego Portales. Printer: CdM-Chile.			
	a. Issued note.	0.25	1.00	3.00
	s. Specimen.	—	—	12.50

		VG	VF	UNC
128	**50 Centesimos on 500 Pesos** ND (1960-1961). Blue. Portrait Manuel Montt at right. Series A. Signature titles: *PRESIDENTE* and *GERENTE GENERAL*. Watermark: D. Diego Portales. Printer: CdM-Chile.	0.50	2.50	15.00

		VG	VF	UNC
129	**1 Escudo on 1000 Pesos** ND (1960-1961). Dark brown. Portrait Manuel Blanco Encalada at left. Series A. Signature titles: *PRESIDENTE* and *GERENTE GENERAL*. Watermark: D. Diego Portales. Printer: CdM-Chile.	0.50	2.00	12.50
130	**5 Escudos on 5000 Pesos** ND (1960-1961). Brown-violet. Portrait Manuel Antonio Tocornal at left. 2 signature varieties. Series J. Signature titles: *PRESIDENTE* and *GERENTE GENERAL*. Watermark: D. Diego Portales. Printer: CdM-Chile.	1.00	5.00	25.00
131	**10 Escudos on 10,000 Pesos** ND (1960-1961). Purple on light blue underprint. Portrait Jose Manuel Balmaceda at left. Series F. Signature titles: *PRESIDENTE* and *GERENTE GENERAL*. Watermark: D. Diego Portales at left, words *DIEZ MIL* at right. Printer: CdM-Chile.	2.00	10.00	40.00
132	**10 Escudos on 10,000 Pesos** ND (1960-1961). Red-brown. Portrait Jose Manuel Balmaceda at left. Similar to #131. Series F. Signature titles: *PRESIDENTE* and *GERENTE GENERAL*. Watermark: D. Diego Portales. Printer: CdM-Chile.	2.00	15.00	55.00
133	**50 Escudos on 50,000 Pesos** ND (1960-1961). Blue-green and brown on multicolor underprint. Portrait Arturo Alessandri at left. Series A. Signature titles: *PRESIDENTE* and *GERENTE GENERAL*. Watermark: D. Diego Portales. Printer: CdM-Chile.	4.50	25.00	75.00

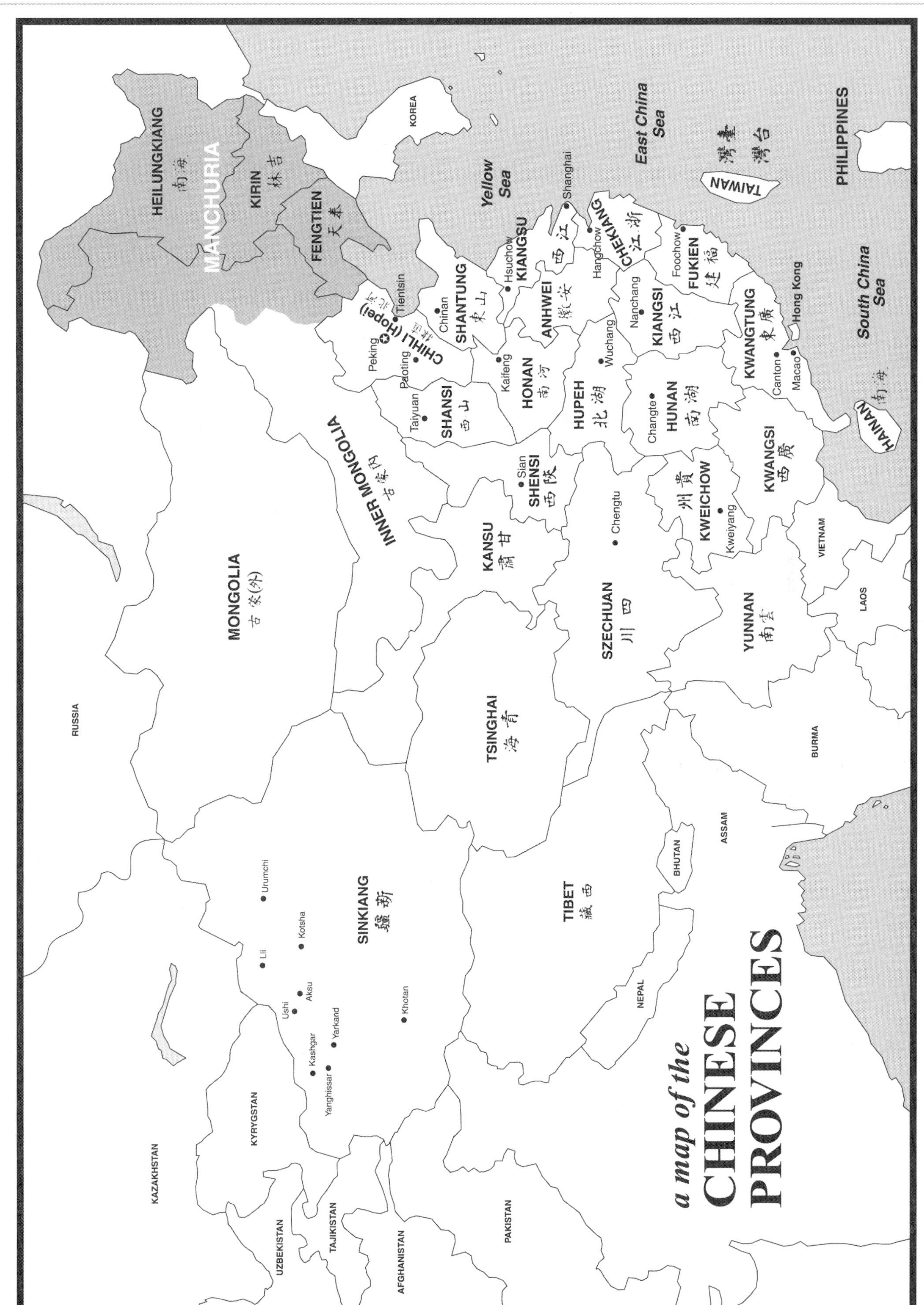
a map of the
CHINESE
PROVINCES
MANCHURIA
HEILUNGKIANG
KIRIN
FENGTIEN
KOREA
Yellow Sea
East China Sea
TAIWAN
PHILIPPINES
South China Sea
Hong Kong
Macao
Canton
HAINAN
CHIHLI (Hopei)
Peking
Tientsin
Paoting
SHANTUNG
Chinan
KIANGSU
Hsuchow
Shanghai
ANHWEI
CHEKIANG
Hangchow
FUKIEN
Foochow
KIANGSI
Nanchang
KWANGTUNG
HONAN
Kaifeng
HUPEH
Wuchang
HUNAN
Changte
SHANSI
Taiyuan
SHENSI
Sian
KWANGSI
KWEICHOW
Kweiyang
INNER MONGOLIA
KANSU
SZECHUAN
Chengtu
YUNNAN
VIETNAM
LAOS
BURMA
MONGOLIA
TSINGHAI
RUSSIA
SINKIANG
Urumchi
Kotsha
Lii
Aksu
Ushi
Khotan
Yarkand
Kashgar
Yanghissar
TIBET
BHUTAN
ASSAM
NEPAL
PAKISTAN
AFGHANISTAN
TAJIKISTAN
UZBEKISTAN
KYRYGSTAN
KAZAKHSTAN

PLACE NAMES

The following list is designed for users unfamiliar with written Chinese who wish to check place names appearing on notes, usually as overprints. For this reason, the arrangement is based on the number of strokes in the first character, normally found at the right or top. This is a selected list. Some obscure locations have been omitted.

English names are a mixture of popular names or variants thereon, which appear on notes, and Wade-Giles romanizations for places which lack well established English names.

Chinese place names tend to be simple descriptive terms relating to a geographical feature, e.g., "north of the lake" (Hupei), "southern capital" (Nanking) or "on the sea" (Shanghai". Most provincial names show this characteristic. In the latter case, many are paired, which has the disadvantage to the western eye and ear of making them look and sound much the same. Hunan-Hupei, Hunan-Hopei, Kwangtung-Kwangsi, Kiangsu-Kiangsi (plus Kiangnan on older notes) and Shantung-Shansi are not difficult to confuse. The most serious problem, however, is Shansi-Shensi. Here, the last characters are the same rather than the first but the first characters, if pronounced correctly, differ only in tone. Even the meanings are close. Shansi, literally, is "mountains west," while Shensi is "mountain passes west," although the first character in this instance is not often used in this meaning. The difference in English spelling is generally accepted convention. Chinese find no difficulty in keeping the two separated because the tonal difference is sufficient in the spoken language and written forms for the first characters are totally dissimilar.

Westerners who might be tempted to consider these or other problems in terminology as resulting from mysterious oriental mental processes should first appraise their own place names, which are rarely as logical or as simple. Inconsistent spellings of place names in romanization too, are primarily western rather than Chinese errors. If confusion does arise, the reasons are complex, and in any event, no satisfactory solution has yet been found.

Kiukiang, Kiangsi	江九
Pa Pu, Kwangsi	步八
Szechuan (alt)	川
Ch'uan Sha, Kiangsi	沙川
Ch'uan K'ang, Szechuan	康川
Shansi	西山
Shantung	東山
Shanhaikuan Chihli/Hopei	關海山
Shanghai, Kiangsu	海上
Shang Jao, Kiangsi	饒上
Ta T'ung Shansi	同大
Ta Cheng Chihli/Hopei	城大
Ta Ch'en Fukien	陳大
Dairen, Liaoning	連大
Honan (alt)	州中
China (alt)	華中
China	國中
Newchwang Liaoning	莊牛
Niu T'ou Chihli/Hopei	頭牛
T'ai Ku Shansi	谷太
T'ai Yuan, Shansi	原太
Tientsin, Chihli/Hopei	津天
Wen An, Chihli/Hope	安文
Wu Ch'ang, Kirin	常五
Cheng yang, Honan	陽正
Tibet	藏西
Hsien Yu, Fukien	遊仙
Kansu	肅甘
Paotow, Suiyuan	頭包
Peiping, Chihli/Hopei	平北
Peking, Chihli/Hopei	京北
Pakhoi, Kwangtung	海北
Shih I, Chihli/Hopei	邑石
Shihkiachwang, Chihli/Hopei	莊家石
Szechuan	川四
T'ai T'ou Chihli/Hopei	頭台
Taiwan (alt)	灣台
Yung Ch'ing, Chihli/Hopei	清永
Yung Ning, Chihli/Hopei	寧永
Anhwei	徽安
Chengtu, Szechuan	都成
Kirin	林吉
Chi Hsien, Chihli/Hopei	縣吉
Kiangsi	西江
Kiangnan	南江
Kiangsu	蘇江
Sian, Shensi	安西
Sikang	康西
Ili, Sinkiang	犁伊
Swatow, Kwangtung	頭汕
Tulunnoerh, Chahar	倫多
Ch'ih Feng, Jehol	峯赤
Hsin Tien, Chihli/Hopei	店辛
Li Chia K'ou, Kwangsi	口家李
Sha P'ing, Shansi	坪沙
Kiangsu (al (literary)	吳
Changsha, Hunan	沙長
Changchun, Kirin	春長
Ch'ang Cheng (Great Wall)	城長
Ch'ang Li, Chihli/Hopei	黎昌
Chihli	隸直
Quemoy (Kinmen) Fukien	門金
Peking/Peiping, Chihli/Hopei	京北
Tsingtao, Shantung	島青
Chinghai (or Tsinghai)	海青
Fengtien	天奉
Feng Hsin, Kiangsi	新奉
Fou Cheng, Chihli/Hopei	城阜
Hangchow, Chekiang	州杭
Hopei	北河
Honan	南河
Ho Chien, Chihli/Hopei	間河
Hulun, Heilungkiang	倫呼
Kunming, Yunnan	明昆
Manchuria	省三東
Manchuria (alt.)	九北東
Wu Ning, Szechuan	寧武
Wu Han, Hupei	漢武
Yenan Shensi	安延
Chekiang	江浙
Chien Ch'ang, Kiangsi	昌建
Chien Yang, Kiangsu	陽建
Chungking, Szechuan	慶重
Harbin, Heilungkiang	賓爾哈
Hsin An, Chihli/Hopei	安信
Kuling, Kiangsi	嶺牯
Liuchow, Kwangsi	州柳
Nan Chiang, Szechuan	江南
Nanchang, Kiangsi	昌南
Nanking, Kiangsu	京南
Nan Kuan Chen, Chihli/Hopei	鎮關南
Nan Hsiung, Kwangtung	雄南
Nanning, Kwangsi	(寗)寧南
Paoting, Chihli/Hopei	定保
T'ai An, Shantung	安泰
Tihua, Sinkiang	化廸
Weihaiwei, Shantung	衛海威
Shansi (literary)	(晋)晉
Chin Tz'u Shansi	祠晉
Shensi (Literary)	秦
Chinwangtao, Shantung	島皇秦
Haikow Kwangtung	口海
Hailar, Heilungkiang	爾拉海
Hainan, Kwangtung	南海
Hong Kong	港香
Hsuchow, Kiangsu	州徐
Kwangsi (literary)	桂
Kweilin, Kwangsi	林桂
Urga, Mongolia	倫庫
Matsu, Fukien	祖馬
Ma T'ou Chen Shantung	鎮頭馬
Hupei (literary)	鄂
P'u T'ien Fukien	田莆
Shensi	西陝
Tongshan, Chihli/Hopei	山唐
T'ao Yuan Hunan	源桃
Chefoo, Shantung	台烟
Kalgan, Chihli/Hopei	口家張
Ch'ang Te, Hunan	德常
Tsingkiangpu, Kiangsu	浦江清
Ch'ung Ming, Kiangsu	明崇
Huai Hai, Kiangsu	海淮
Kuo Hsien, Shansi	縣崞
Liao Cheng, Shantung	城聊
Pi'ng Hsien, Kiangsi	縣萍
Pukow, Kiangsu	口浦
Mukden, Liaoning	京盛
Su Hsien, Anhwei	縣宿
Ts'ao Ts'un, Shantung	村曹
T'ung Cheng, Hopei	城通
Wuchow, Kwangsi	州梧
Yeh Hsien, Shantung	縣掖
Chi Ning, Chahar	寧集
Chingtechen, Kiangsi	鎮德景
Hei Ho, Heilungkiang	河黑
Heilungkiang	江龍黑
Hunan (literary)	湘
Hupei	北湖
Hunan	南湖
Anhwei (literary)	皖
Kaifeng, Honan	封開
Kweichow	州貴
Kweiyang, Kwangsi	陽貴
Lung Ch'ang Szechuan	昌隆
Ningpo, Chekiang	波寧
Sheng Fang Chihli/Hopei	芳勝
Wusih, Kiangsu	錫無
Yu Tz'u, Shansi	次榆
Kwangtung/ Kwangsi (lit)	粵
Yunnan	南雲
Fu An, Fukien	安福
Foochow, Fukien	州福
Fu I, Fukien	邑福
Fukien	建福
Fu Ch'ing, Fukien	清福
Amoy, Fukien	門廈
Sinkiang	疆新
Jui Ch'ang Kiangsi	昌瑞
Fukien (literary)	閩
P'eng Lai, Shantung	萊蓬
Po Hai, Chihli/Hopei	海渤
Suiyuan	遠綏
Tan Hsien, Shantung	縣單
Yangchow, Kiangsu	州揚
Chefoo (alt) Shantung	台煙
Chahar	爾哈察
Chao Hsien, Chihli/Hopei	縣趙
Chia Ting, Kiangsu	定嘉
Hankow, Hupei	口漢
Ningpo (alt) Chekiang	波寧
Ninghsia	夏寧
Pinkiang, Heilungkiang	江賓
Shou Kuang, Shantung	光壽
Tainan, Taiwan	南臺
Taiwan (alt)	灣臺
Yunnan	滇
Chengchow, Honan	州鄭
Jehol	河熱
Kuang An Chen Chihli/Hopei	鎮安廣
Kwangsi	西廣
Canton, Kwangtung	州廣
Kwangtung	東廣
Manchukuo	國洲滿
Manchouli, Heilungkiang	里洲滿
Shantung (literary)	魯
Hopei (literary)	冀
Kweichow (literary)	黔
Chui Tzu Shan, Jehol	山字錐
Liaoning (al	東遼
Liaoning	寧遼
Lungkow, Shantung	口龍
Lungchow, Kwangsi	州龍
Mongolia	古蒙
Meng Chiang (Mongolia)	疆蒙
Honan (literary)	豫
Macao	門澳
Chinan (Tsinan) Shantung	南濟
Yingkow, Liaoning	口營
Chenkiang, Kiangsu	江鎮
Fengchen, Suiyuan	鎮豐
Li Chiang Chihli/Hopei	港鯉
Kuantung, Liaoning	東關
Lanchow, Kansu	州蘭
Kansu (literary)	隴
Kiangsu (literary)	蘇
Soochow, Kiangsu	州蘇
Su Ch'ao Chen Honan	鎮橋蘇
Hsien Hsien Chihli/Hopei	縣獻
Lu Hsien Szechuan	縣瀘
Pa Hsien Chihli / Hopei	縣霸
Li Hsien Chihli / Hopei	縣蠡
Kiangsi (literary)	贛
Watlam, Kwangsi	林鬱
Yungtsun	遵永

The above chart listings are taken from "CHINESE BANKNOTES" by Ward D. Smith and Brian Matravers (published 1970).

EMPIRE

China's ancient civilization began in the Huang Ho basin about 1500 BC. The warring feudal states comprising early China were first united under Emperor Ch'in Shih Huang Ti (246-210 BC) who gave China its name and first central government. Subsequent dynasties alternated brilliant cultural achievements with internal disorder until the Empire was brought down by the revolution of 1911, and the Republic of China installed in its place. Chinese culture attained a pre-eminence in art, literature and philosophy, but a traditional backwardness in industry and administration ill prepared China for the demands of 19th century Western expansionism which exposed it to military and political humiliations, and mandated a drastic revision of political practice in order to secure an accommodation with the modern world.

The Republic of 1911 barely survived the stress of World War I, and was subsequently all but shattered by the rise of nationalism and the emergence of the Chinese Communist movement. Moscow, which practiced a policy of cooperation between Communists and other parties in movements for national liberation, sought to establish an entente between the Chinese Communist Party and the Kuomintang (National People's Party) of Dr. Sun Yat-sen. The ensuing cooperation was based on little more than the hope each had of using the other.

An increasingly uneasy association between the Kuomintang and the Chinese Communist Party developed and continued until April 12, 1927, when Chiang Kai-shek, Dr. Sun Yat-sen's political heir, instituted a bloody purge to stamp out the Communists within the Kuomintang and the government and virtually paralyzed their ranks throughout China. Some time after the mid-1927 purges, the Chinese Communist Party turned to armed force to resist Chiang Kai-shek and during the period of 1930-34 acquired control over large parts of Kiangsi, Fukien, Hunan and Hupeh. The Nationalist Nanking government responded with a series of campaigns against the soviet power bases and, by October of 1934, succeeded in driving the remnants of the Communist army to a refuge in Shensi Province.

Subsequently, the Communists under the leadership of Mao Tse-tung defeated the Nationalists and on September 21, 1949 formally established the People's Republic.

EMPERORS

Reign title: Hsien Feng 咸 豐 — 文 宗 WENTSUNG 1851-1861

1st Reign title: Ch'i-hsiang
2nd Reign title: T'ung Chih 憲 洪 — 穆 宗 MUTSUNG 1861
1862-1875

Reign title: Kuang Hsu 光 緒 — 德 宗 TETSUNG 1875-1908

(Hsun Ti)
Reign title: Hsuan T'ung 宣 統 — 宣 統 帝 遜 帝 HSUAN T'UNG TI 1908-1911

Proposed Reign title: Hung Hsien 憲 洪 — YUAN SHIH-KAI Dec. 15, 1915- March 21, 1916

MONETARY SYSTEMS

1 Tael = 800-1600 Cash*

***NOTE: In theory, 1000 cash were equal to a tael of silver, but in actuality the rate varied from time to time and from place to place.**

Dollar System

1 Cent (fen, hsien) = 10 Cash (wen)
1 Chiao (hao) = 10 Cents
1 Dollar (yuan) = 100 Cents

Tael System

1 Fen (candareen) = 10 Li
1 Ch'ien (mace) = 10 Fen
1 Liang (tael) = 10 Ch'ien (mace)

NOTE: Many listings encompassing issues circulated by provincial, military, including early Communist, larger commercial and foreign banking authorities are contained in *Standard Catalog of World Paper Money, Specialized Issues*.

ARRANGEMENT

- Imperial .... #AA2-AA3, AA10, A1-A83J
- Republican .... #A84-A138, 1-643
- Peoples Republic .... #800-876
- Taiwan .... #900-970
- Taiwan - Offshore Islands .... #R102-R143
- Japanese Puppet .... #J1-J146
- Japanese Military .... #M1-M30
- Russian Military .... #M30A-M36

ISSUER IDENTIFICATION

Ming Dynasty, 1368-1644
#AA2-AA3, AA10
Ta Ming T'ung Hsing Pao Ch'ao

Ch'ing Dynasty, 1644-1911
#A1-A
行銀清大
Ta Ch'ing Pao Ch'ao

Board of Revenue
#A9-A13
票官部户
Hu Pu Kuan P'iao

General Bank of Communications
#A13A-A19E
行銀通交
Chiao T'ung Yin Hang

Bureau of Engraving and Printing
#A20-A23
局刷印部政財
Ts'ai Cheng Pu Yin Shua Chü

Hu Pu Bank, Peking
#A24-A35
行銀部户
Hu Pu Yin Hang
票銀換兌
Tui Huan Yin P'iao
行銀部户京北
Pei Ching Hu Pu Yin Hang

Imperial Bank of China
#A36-A55A
行銀商通國中
Chung Kuo T'ung Shang Yin Hang

Imperial Chinese Railways
#A56-A61
局總路官軌鐵洋北
Pei Yang T'ieh Kuei Kuan Lu Tsung Chü

Ningpo Commercial Bank, Limited
#A61A-A61D
Shang Hai Szu Ming Yin Hang

Ta Ch'ing Government Bank
#A62-A82
行銀清大
Ta Ch'ing Yin Hang

Ta Ch'ing Government Bank, Shansi
#A83-A83J
Shan Hsi Ta Ch'ing Yin Hang
行銀部户清大
Ta Ch'ing Hu Pu Yin Hang

Agricultural Bank of the Four Provinces
#A84-A91E
行銀民農省四
Szu Sheng Nung Min Yin Hang
行銀民農省四贛皖鄂豫
Yü O Huan Kan Szu Sheng Nung Min Yin Hang

Agricultural and Industrial Bank of China
#A92-A112
行銀工農國中
Chung Kuo Nung Kung Yin Hang

Bank of Agriculture and Commerce
#A113-A120
行銀商農
Nung Shang Yin Hang

China Silk and Tea Industrial Bank
#A120A-A120C
行銀茶絲國中
Chung Kuo Szu Ch'a Yin Hang

China and South Sea Bank
#A121-A133
行銀南中
Chung Nan Yin Hang

Commercial Bank of China
#A133A-A138, 1-15
行銀商通國中
Chung Kuo T'ung Shang Yin Hang

Bank of China, КИТАЙСКІЙ БАНКЪ
#16-100
行銀國中
Chung Kuo Yin Hang
Chung Kuo Yin Hang Tui Huan Ch'uan

Bank of Communications, БАНКЪ ПЧТИ СООЩЕНІЯ
#102-166
行銀通交
Chiao T'ung Yin Hang

Central Bank of China (National)
#167-170
行銀央中
Chung Yan Yin Hang

Central Bank of China (Quasi-national)
#171-192
行銀央中
Chung Yan Yin Hang

Central Bank of China (National - Cont.)
#193-450T
行銀央中
Chung Yun Yin Hang

Farmers Bank of China
#451-484
行銀民農國中
Chung Kuo Nung Min Yin Hang

Great Northwestern Bank
#485-490
行銀疆蒙
Men Tsang Yin Hang

Industrial Development Bank of China
#491-500
行銀業勸
Ch'üan Yeh Yin Hang

Land Bank of China, Limited
#501-506
行銀業墾國中
Chung Kuo K'en Yeh Yin Hang

National Bank of China, Nanking
#507-510
行銀家國華中
Chung Hua Kuo Chia Yin Hang

National Bank of China, Canton
#511-516
行銀民國華中
Chung Hua Kuo Min Yin Hang

The National Commercial Bank, Limited
#516A-519C
行銀業興江浙
Che Chiang Hsing Yeh Yin Hang

National Industrial Bank of China
#520-534
行銀業實國中
Chung Kuo Shih Yeh Yin Hang

Ningpo Commercial Bank
#539-550
行銀明四
Szu Ming Yin Hang

Tah Chung Bank 行銀中大
#551-565 Ta Chung Yin Hang

Bank of Territorial Development, 行銀邊殖
ТЕРРИТОРIАЛЬНО ПРОМЫШЛЕННЫЙ БАНКЪ ВЪКИТАБ
#566-585B Chih Pien Yin Hang

Ministry of Communications - Peking-Hankow Railway 付支路鐵漢京部通
#585C-594 Chiao T'ung Pu Ching Han T'ieh Lu Chih Fu Ch'üan

Military Exchange Bureau 局兑滙需軍部政財
#595 Ts'ai Cheng Pu Chün Hsu Hui Tui Chü

Market Stabilization Currency Bureau 局錢官市平部政財
#597-622 Ts'ai Cheng Pu P'ing Shih Kuan Ch'ien Chü

Ministry of Finance - Special Circulating Notes 券通流別特部政財
#623-625 Ts'ai Cheng Pu T'e Pieh Liu T'ung Ch'üan

Ministry of Finance - Fixed Term Treasury Notes 券庫國利有期定部政財
#626-637 Ts'ai Cheng Pu Ting Ch'i Yu Li Kuo K'u Ch'üan

Ministry of Finance - Short Term Exchange Notes 券換兑利有期短部政財
#638-640 Ts'ai Cheng Pu Tuan Ch'i Yu Li Tui Huan Ch'üan

Ministry of Finance - Circulating Notes 券通流利有部政財
#641-643 Ts'ai Cheng Pu Yu Li Liu T'ung Ch'üan

Peoples Bank of China 中國人民銀行
#800-858A Chung Kuo Jen Min Yin Hang / Zhong Guo Ren Min Yin Hang

行銀民人國中
#859-876 Chung Kuo Jen Min Yin Hang

T'ai-nan Kuan Yin P'iao 票銀官南臺
#900-906 Tai Nan Kuan Yin P'iao

Hu Li T'ai Nan Fu Cheng Tang Chung

Bank of Taiwan - Japanese Influence
#907-913 T'ai Wan Yin Hang

Bank of Taiwan - Taiwan Government General
#914-920
Bank of Taiwan Limited - Taiwan Bank
#921-934 Tai Wan Yin Hang Ch'üan

Bank of Taiwan - Chinese Administration 行銀灣臺
#935-970 T'ai Wan Yin Hang

Bank of Taiwan 行銀灣臺
#R102-R108, R113-R116, R119-R121, R140-R143 T'ai Wan Yin Hang

Central Reserve Bank of China 行銀備儲央中
#J1-J44 Chung Yang Ch'u Pei Yin Hang

Federal Reserve Bank of China 行銀備準合聯國中
#J45-J92 Chung Kuo Lien Ho Chun Pei Yin Hang

Hua Hsing Commercial Bank 行銀業商興華
#J93-J100 Hua Hsing Shang Yeh Yin Hang

Mengchiang Bank 行銀疆蒙
#J101-J112 Meng Chiang Yin Hang

Chi Tung Bank 行銀東冀
#J113-J117 Chi Tung Yin Hang

Chanan Bank 行銀南察
#J118-J119 Ch'a Nan Yin Hang

Central Bank of Manchukuo 行銀央中洲滿
#J120-J146 Man Chou Chung Yang Yin Hang

Japanese Imperial Government, Military 府政國帝本日大
#M1-M30 Ta Jih Pen Ti Kuo Cheng Fu

South China Expeditionary Army
M30A
Soviet Red Army Headquarters 蘇聯紅軍司令部
#M31-M36 Su Lien Hung Chün Szu Ling Pu

EMPIRE DATING

The mathematical discrepancy in this is accounted for by the fact that the first year is included in the elapsed time.

Most struck Chinese banknotes are dated by year within a given period, such as the regional eras or the republican periods. A 1907 issue, for example, would be dated in the 33rd year of the Kuang Hsu era (1875 + 33 - 1 = 1907).

CYCLICAL DATING

Another method of dating is a 60-year, repeating cycle, outlined in the table below. The date is shown by the combination of two characters, the first from the top row and the second from the column at left, in this catalog, when a cyclical date is used, the abbreviation CD appears before the AD date.

	庚	辛	壬	癸	甲	乙	丙	丁	戊	己
戌	1850 1910		1862 1922		1874 1934		1886 1946		1838 1898	
亥		1851 1911		1863 1923		1875 1935		1887 1947		1839 1899
子	1840 1900		1852 1912		1864 1924		1876 1936		1888 1948	
丑		1841 1901		1853 1913		1865 1925		1877 1937		1889 1949
寅	1830 1890		1842 1902		1854 1914		1866 1926		1878 1938	
卯		1831 1891		1843 1903		1855 1915		1867 1927		1879 1939
辰	1880 1940		1832 1892		1844 1904		1856 1916		1868 1928	
巳		1881 1941		1833 1893		1845 1905		1857 1917		1869 1929
午	1870 1930		1882 1942		1834 1894		1846 1906		1858 1918	
未		1871 1931		1883 1943		1835 1895		1847 1907		1859 1919
申	1860 1920		1872 1932		1884 1944		1836 1896		1848 1908	
酉		1861 1921		1873 1933		1885 1945		1837 1897		1849 1909

This chart has been adopted from *Chinese Banknotes* by Ward Smith and Brian Matravers. Calligraphy by Marian C. Smith.

REPUBLIC DATING

A modern note of 1926 issue is dated in the 15th year of the Republic (1912 + 15 - 1 = 1926). The mathematical discrepancy again is accounted for by the fact that the first year is included in the elapsed time.

Years of the Republic

Year		AD	Year		AD	Year		AD	Year		AD
1	一	= 1912	11	一十	= 1922	21	一十二	= 1932	31	一十三	= 1942
2	二	= 1913	12	二十	= 1923	22	二十二	= 1933	32	二十三	= 1943
3	三	= 1914	13	三十	= 1924	23	三十二	= 1934	33	三十三	= 1944
4	四	= 1915	14	四十	= 1925	24	四十二	= 1935	34	四十三	= 1945
5	五	= 1916	15	五十	= 1926	25	五十二	= 1936	35	五十三	= 1946
6	六	= 1917	16	六十	= 1927	26	六十二	= 1937	36	六十三	= 1947
7	七	= 1918	17	七十	= 1928	27	七十二	= 1938	37	七十三	= 1948
8	八	= 1919	18	八十	= 1929	28	八十二	= 1939	38	八十三	= 1949
9	九	= 1920	19	九十	= 1930	29	九十二	= 1940	39	九十三	= 1950
10	十	= 1921	20	十二	= 1931	30	十三	= 1941	40	十四	= 1951

NOTE: Chinese dates are normally read from right to left, except for the modern issues of the Peoples Republic of China from 1953 where the Western date is read from left to right.

Color Abbreviation Guide

New to the *Standard Catalog of® World Paper Money* are the following abbreviations related to color references:

BC: Back color
PC: Paper color

MONETARY UNITS

Dollar Amounts		
Dollar (*Yuan*)	元 or 員	圓 or 圜
Half Dollar (*Pan Yuan*)	圓半	
50¢ (*Chiao/Hao*)	角伍	毫伍
10¢ (*Chiao/Hao*)	角壹	毫壹
1¢ (*Fen/Hsien*)	分壹	仙壹

Tael Amounts	
Tael (*Liang*)	兩
Half Tael (*Pan Liang*)	兩半
5 Mace (*Wu Ch'ien*)	錢伍
1 Mace (*I Ch'ien*)	錢壹
Ku Ping (*Tael*)*	平庫

Copper and Cash Coin Amounts			
Copper (*Mei*)	枚	String (*Tiao*)	吊
Cash (*Wen*)	文	String (*Tiao*)	弔
String (*Kuan*)	貫	String (*Ch'uan*)	串

Common Prefixes			
Copper (*T'ung*)	銅	"Small money"	洋小
Silver (*Yin*)	銀	"Big money"	洋大
Gold (*Chin*)	金	"Big money"	洋英

These tables have been adopted from *CHINESE BANKNOTES* by Ward Smith and Bria Matravers. Calligraphy in special instances by Marian C. Smith.

NUMERICAL CHARACTERS

A. CONVENTIONAL

B. FORMAL

C. COMMERCIAL

No.	A			B		C
1	一	正	元	壹	弌	〡
2	二			弍	貳	〢
3	三			弎	叁	〣
4	四			肆		〤
5	五			伍		〥
6	六			陸		〦
7	七			柒		〧
8	八			捌		〨
9	九			玖		〩

No.	A		B		C
10	十		拾	什	十
20	十二	廿	拾貳	念	〢十
25	五十二	五廿	伍拾貳		〢十〥
30	十三	卅	拾叁		〣十
100	百一		佰壹		〡百
1,000	千一		仟壹		〡千
10,000	萬一		萬壹		〡万
100,000	萬十	億一	萬拾	億壹	十万
1,000,000	萬百一		萬佰壹		〡百万

REPUBLIC ISSUES

PORTRAIT ABBREVIATIONS

SYS = Dr. Sun Yat-sen, 1867-1925
President of Canton Government, 1917-25

CKS = Chiang Kai-shek 1886-1975
President in Nanking, 1927-31
Head of Formosa Government, Taiwan, 1949-1975

NOTE: Because of the frequency of the above appearing in the following listings, their initials are used only in reference to their portraits.

OVERPRINTS

The various city or regional overprints are easily noted, being normally two or three Chinese characters usually in two or more places on a note and sometimes found in English on the other side of the note.

Various single Chinese control characters were applied, and appear in two or more places on a note. Sometimes western numerals were utilized and appear in circles, or outlined squares, etc.

The most frequently encountered overprint in the Three Eastern Provinces and Manchurian series is a four Chinese character overprint in a 21mm square outline. This *Official Controller's Seal* overprint supervised the amount of issue of certain banks and guaranteed the notes.

In certain cases we find available an original printers' specimen, an issued note, an issued note with the official overprint along with a "local" specimen of a circulated note bearing normal serial numbers. The purpose of this overprint at present eludes the authors at this writing.

S/M # is in reference to *CHINESE BANKNOTES* by Ward D. Smith and Brian Matravers.

EMPIRE

Ming Dynasty, 1368-1644

鈔寶行通明大

Ta Ming T'ung Hsing Pao Ch'ao

The Ming Dynasty was characterized by a tapering off in note production and circulation, terminating in the complete suspension of official issues, probably in about 1450. The *Chüan Pu T'ung Chih* specifically refers to some 60 isues in three out of the four earliest reigns, covering the period from 1368 to 1426. This is almost certainly an understatement of the probable volume, although it is a larger total than in any other known source and, of course, few of the notes themselves have survived. The conspicuous exception is the 1-kuan note of the *Hung Wu* era (1368-99), listed below as #AA10 *(S/M #T36-20)*. In addition to this note below, issues reported for the *Hung Wu* reign include 100, 200, 300, 400 and 500 cash denominations and for the *Yung Lo* reign (1403-25), a tael series in 26 denominations from 1 through 20, plus 25, 30, 35, 40, 45 and 50 taels, none of which have surfaced.

1368-1375 Circulating Note Issue

Note: Other issues and denominatins have been reported, but not confirmed. Note: S/M#s are in reference to *Chinese Banknotes,* by Ward D. Smith and Brian Matravers.

		Good	Fine	XF
AA2	**20 Cash** 1375. Black with red seal handstamps. 2 strings of 10 cash coins at upper center. 270x165mm. *(S/M #T36-2)*. Rare. PC: Blue-gray mulberry.	—	—	—

		Good	Fine	XF
AA3	**300 Cash** 1368-1399. *(S/M #T36-3).* Black with red seal handstamps. 3 strings of cash coins at upper center. 110x193mm. PC: Blue-gray mulberry.	—	—	—

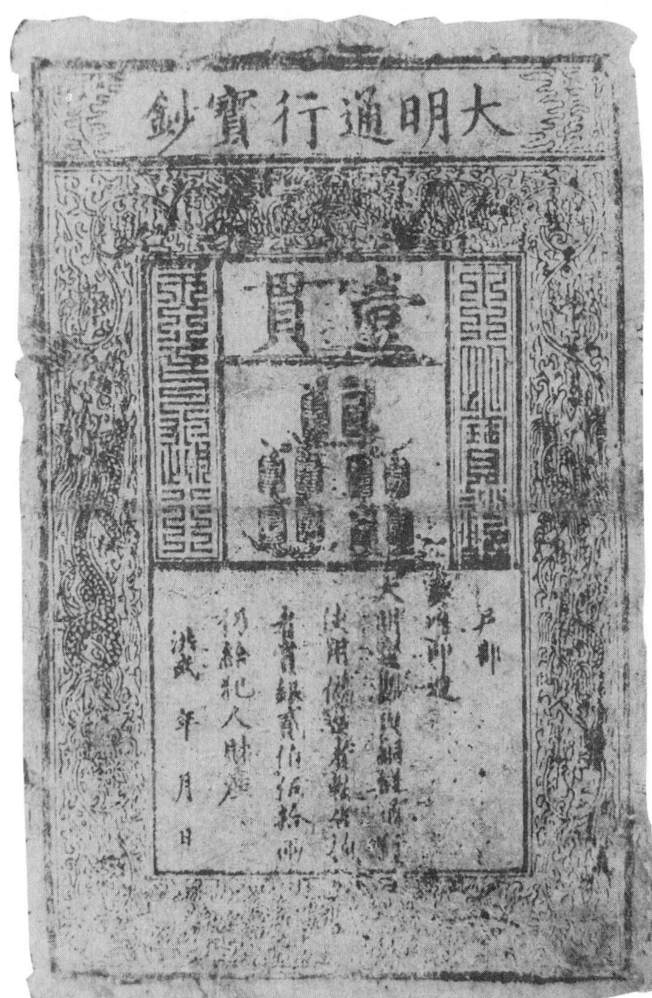

		Good	Fine	XF
AA10	**1 Kuan** 1368-1399. Black with 2 red square seal hand-stamps. 10 strings of cash coins at center. Uniface. Back: 1 red and 1 black square seal overprint. 209x320mm. (S/M #T36-20). PC: Deep gray mulberry.	1,500	3,000	9,000

Note: Other issues and denominations have been reported but not confirmed.

Note: *S/M#s* are in reference to *Chinese Banknotes,* by Ward D. Smith and Brian Matravers.

Ch'ing Dynasty, 16 44-1911

鈔寶清大

Ta Ch'ing Pao Ch'ao

1853 Issue

IDENTIFICATION Top: ***Ta Ch'ing Pao Ch'ao*** **= Ch'ing Dynasty note. Right Side:** ***T'ien Hsia T'ung Hsing*** **= Circulates everywhere (i.e. under the heavens). Left side:** ***Chun P'ing Ch'u Ju*** **= (Pay) equally when paying or receiving. (In other words, payable at face value; no discounts for buyers or sellers.) Center right:** ***Tzu*** **identifies the block character as** ***Ti . . . Hoa*** **= serial number less than the block numerical character. Center:** ***Chun Tsu Chih Ch'ien Erh Ch'ien Wen*** **= Equivalent to 2000 cash (payable in) standard (or regulated) coins. Or plain legal tender. (Getting into just what constituted Chih ch'ien in 1859 would be more than slightly complex.) Center at left:** ***Hsien Feng Chiuc Nien Chih*** **= Made (issued) in the 9th year of the Hsien Feng reign. #A1-A8 uniface except for occasional endorsements on back.**

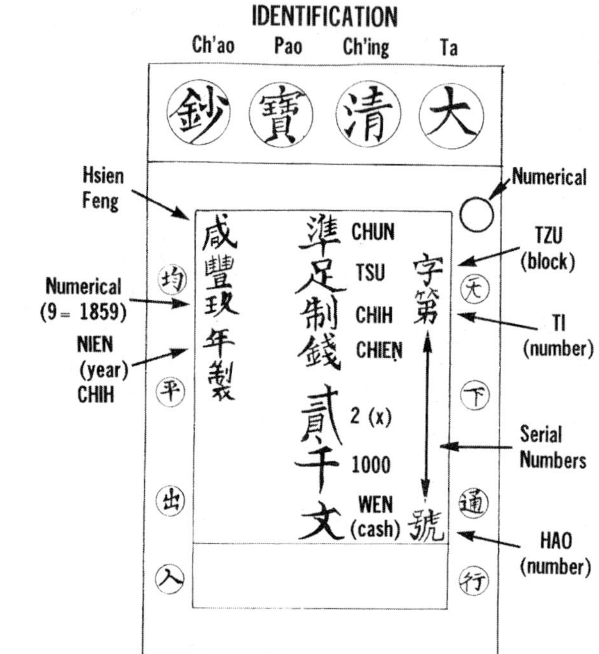

1853 Issue

IDENTIFICATION Top: *Ta Ch'ing Pao Ch'ao* = Ch'ing Dynasty note.

Right Side: *T'ien Hsia T'ung Hsing* = Circulates everywhere (i.e. under the heavens).

Left side: *Chun P'ing Ch'u Ju* = (Pay) equally when paying or receiving. (In other words, payable at face value; no discounts for buyers or sellers.)

Center right: *Tzu* identifies the block character as *Ti . . . Hoa* = serial number less than the block numerical character.

Center: *Chun Tsu Chih Ch'ien Erh Ch'ien Wen* = Equivalent to 2000 cash (payable in) standard (or regulated) coins. Or plain legal tender. (Getting into just what constituted Chih ch'ien in 1859 would be more than slightly complex.)

Center at left: *Hsien Feng*

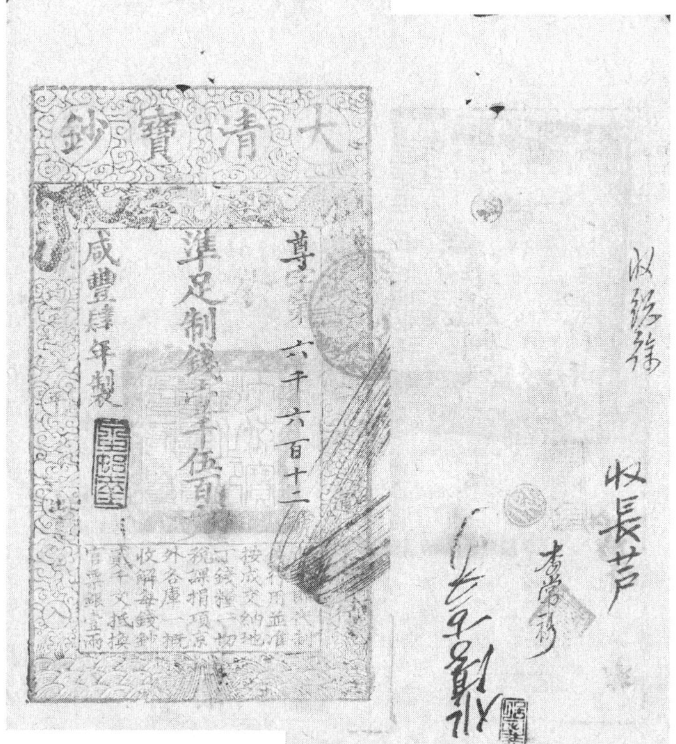

		Good	Fine	XF
A1	**500 Cash** 1853-1858. Blue and red.			
	a. Yr. 3 (1853). *(S/M #T6-1).*	160	375	2,200
	b. Yr. 4 (1854). *(S/M #T6-10).*	160	375	2,200
	c. Yr. 5 (1855). *(S/M #T6-20).*	160	375	2,200
	d. Yr. 6 (1856). *(S/M #T6-30).*	160	375	2,200
	e. Yr. 7 (1857). *(S/M #T6-40).*	160	375	2,200
	f. Yr. 8 (1858). *(S/M#T6-).*	160	375	2,200
	g. Reissue. CD1861-64. *(S/M#T6-).*	160	4500	2,600

A2	1000 Cash	Good	Fine	XF
	1853-1858. Blue and red. Similar to #A1.			
	a. Yr. 3 (1853). *(S/M #T6-2).*	175	425	2,600
	b. Yr. 4 (1854). *(S/M #T6-11).*	175	425	2,600
	c. Yr. 5 (1855). *(S/M #T6-21).*	175	425	2,600
	d. Yr. 6 (1856). *(S/M #T6-31).*	175	425	2,600
	e. Yr. 7 (1857). *(S/M #T6-41).*	175	425	2,600
	f. Yr. 8 (1858). *(S/M #T6-50).*	175	425	2,600
	g. Reissue. CD 1861-64 *(S/M#T6-).*	175	500	2,900

A3	1500 Cash	Good	Fine	XF
	1854. Blue and red. Similar to #A1.			
	a. Yr.4 (1854). *(S/M #T6-12).*	180	550	3,600
	b. Reissue. CD1861-64. *(S/M #T6-).* Requires confirmation.	—	—	—

A4	2000 Cash	Good	Fine	XF
	1853-1859. Blue and red. Similar to #A1.			
	a. Yr. 3 (1853). *(S/M #T6-4).*	120	350	1,500
	b. Yr. 4 (1854). *(S/M #T6-13).*	120	350	1,500
	c. Yr. 5 (1855). *(S/M #T6-22).*	120	350	1,500
	d. Yr. 6 (1856). *(S/M #T6-32).*	120	350	1,500
	e. Yr. 7 (1857). *(S/M #T6-42).*	120	350	1,500
	f. Yr. 8 (1858). *(S/M #T6-51).*	120	350	1,500
	g. Yr. 9 (1859). *(S/M #T6-60).*	120	350	1,500
	h. Reissue. CD1861-64. *(S/M#T6-).*	120	375	2,250

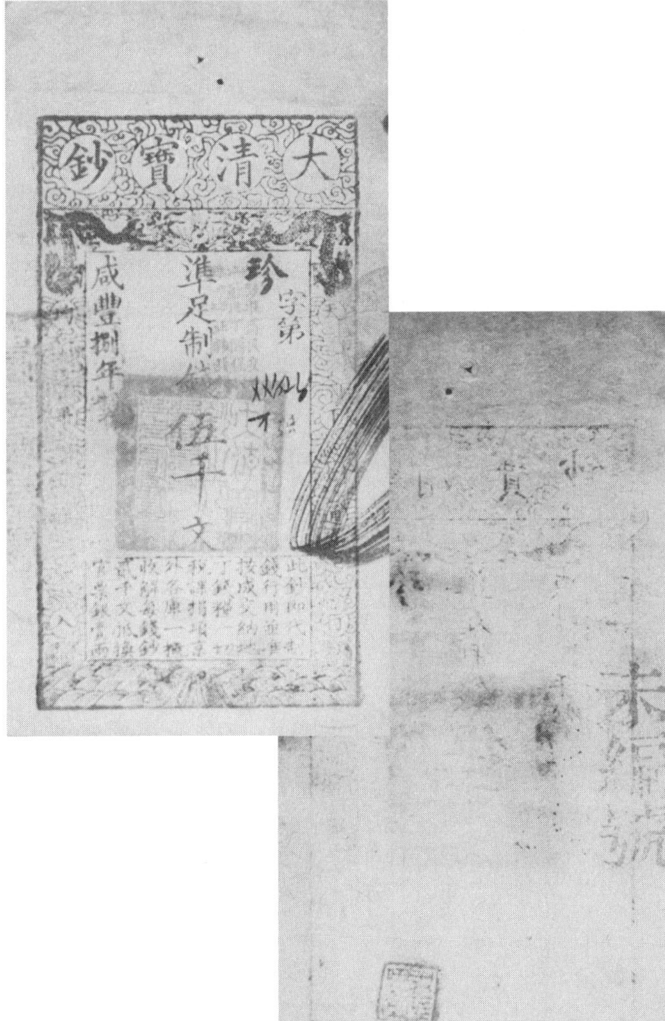

A5	5000 Cash	Good	Fine	XF
	1856-1859. Blue and red. Similar to #A1.			
	a. Yr. 6 (1856). *(S/M #T6-33).*	225	650	3,800
	b. Yr. 7 (1857). *(S/M #T6-43).*	225	650	3,800
	c. Yr. 8 (1858). *(S/M #T6-52).*	225	650	3,800
	d. Yr. 9 (1859). *(S/M#T6-).*	225	650	3,800
	e. Reissue. CD1861-64. *(S/M#T6-).*	275	700	4,200
	f. Handstamp: *Kiangsu Province* (21 Characters). Yr. 8 (1858). *(S/M#T6-).*	300	750	4,600

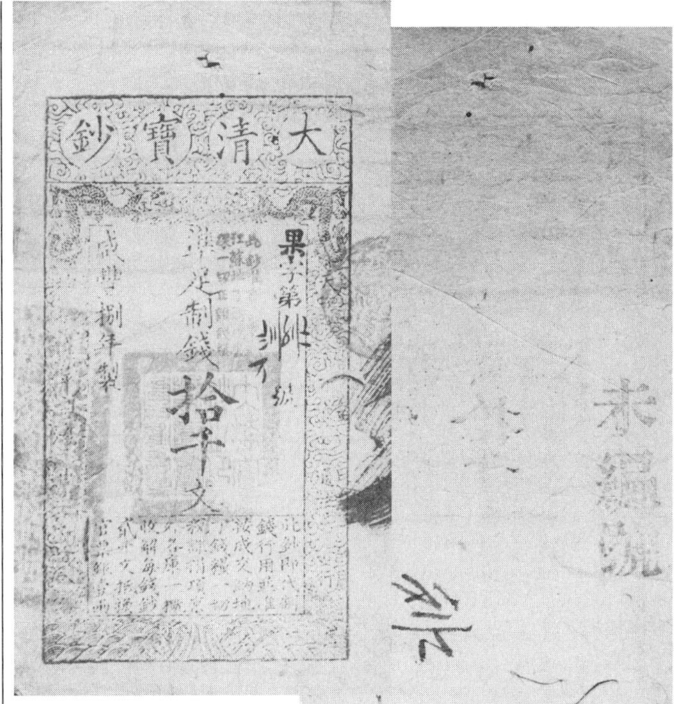

A6	10,000 Cash	Good	Fine	XF
	1857-1859. Blue and red. Similar to #A1.			
	a. Yr. 7 (1857). *(S/M #T6-44).*	350	1,050	6,500
	b. Yr. 8 (1858). *(S/M #T6-53).*	350	1,050	6,500
	c. Yr. 9 (1859). *(S/M#T6-).*	350	1,050	6,500
	d. Reissue. CD1861-64. *(S/M#T6-).*	400	1,200	6,500
	e. Handstamp: *Kiangsu Province* (21 Characters). Yr. 8 (1858). *(S/M#T6-).*	400	1,200	6,500

A7	50,000 Cash	Good	Fine	XF
	1857-1859. Blue and red. Similar to #A1.			
	a. Yr. 7 (1857). *(S/M #T6-45).*	1,400	4,000	24,000
	b. Yr. 8 (1858). *(S/M #T6-54).*	1,400	4,000	24,000
	c. Yr. 9 (1859). *(S/M#T6-).*	1,400	4,000	24,000

A8	100,000 Cash	Good	Fine	XF
	1857-1859. Blue and red. Similar to #A1.			
	a. Yr. 7 (1857). *(S/M #T6-46).*	1,500	5,000	26,000
	b. Yr. 8 (1858). *(S/M #T6-55).*	1,500	5,000	26,000
	c. Yr. 9 (1859). *(S/M#T6-).*	1,500	5,000	26,000
	d. Reissue. CD1861-64. *(S/M#T6-).*	1,500	5,000	26,000
	e. Handstamp: *Kiangsu Province* (21 characters). Yr. 8 (1858). *(S/M#T6-).*	1,500	5,000	26,000

Board of Revenue

票官部户

Hu Pu Kuan P'iao

The title in the upper center frame reads *Hu Pu Kuan P'iao* (Board of Revenue Official Note) in Chinese at right and Manchu at left. The Board of Revenue notes are issues of the central government but were placed in circulation by several government-appointed private banks. The date is found in the left vertical column, the value in the center column and the serial # on the right. The reissue w/CD 1861-64 is a 8 character vertical handstamp placed at the right of the original date at upper l.

1853-1857 Issue

#A9-A13 Occasional endorsements on back.

A9	1 Tael	Good	Fine	XF
	1853-1856. Blue and red. Uniface.			
	a. Yr. 3 (1853). *(S/M #H176-1).*	325	1,000	6,000
	b. Yr. 4 (1854). *(S/M #H176-10).*	325	1,000	6,000
	c. Yr. 5 (1855). *(S/M #H176-20).*	325	1,000	6,000
	d. Yr. 6 (1856). *(S/M #H176-30).*	325	1,000	6,000
	e. Reissue. CD1861-64. *(S/M#H176-).*	500	1,050	6,500

A10	3 Taels	Good	Fine	XF
	1853-1858. Blue and red. Uniface.			
	a. Yr. 3 (1853). *(S/M #H176-2).*	600	1,800	10,600
	b. Yr. 4 (1854). *(S/M #H176-11).*	600	1,800	10,600
	c. Yr. 5 (1855). *(S/M #H176-21).*	600	1,800	10,600
	d. Yr. 6 (1856). *(S/M #H176-31).*	600	1,800	10,600
	e. Yr. 7 (1857). *(S/M #H176-40).*	600	1,800	10,600
	f. Yr. 8 (1858). *(S/M#H176-).*	600	1,800	10,600
	g. Reissue. CD1861-64. *(S/M#H176-).*	750	2,000	12,000

A11	5 Taels	Good	Fine	XF
	1853-1857. Blue and red. Uniface.			
	a. Yr. 3 (1853). *(S/M #H176-3).*	450	1,350	8,000
	b. Yr. 4 (1854). *(S/M #H176-12).*	450	1,350	8,000
	c. Yr. 5 (1855). *(S/M #H176-22).*	450	1,350	8,000
	d. Yr. 6 (1856). *(S/M #H176-32).*	450	1,350	8,000
	e. Yr. 7 (1857). *(S/M #H176-41).*	450	1,350	8,000
	f. Reissue. CD1861-64. *(S/M#H176-).*	500	1,500	8,800

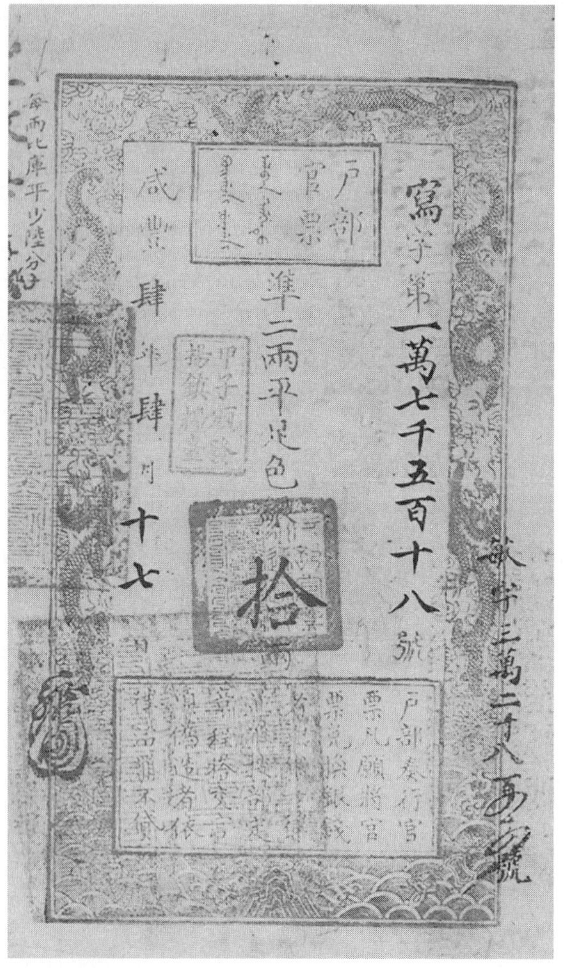

		Good	Fine	XF
A12	**10 Taels**			
	1853-1856. Blue and red. Uniface.			
	a. Yr. 3 (1853). *(S/M #H176-4).*	1,200	4,000	23,000
	b. Yr. 4 (1854). *(S/M #H176-13).*	1,200	4,000	23,000
	c. Yr. 5 (1855). *(S/M #H176-23).*	1,200	4,000	23,000
	d. Yr. 6 (1856). *(S/M #H176-33).*	1,200	4,000	23,000
	e. Reissue. CD1861-64. *(S/M#H176-).*	1,200	4,000	23,000
A13	**50 Taels**	Good	Fine	XF
	1853-1856. Blue and red. Uniface.			
	a. Yr. 3 (1853). *(S/M #H176-5).*	2,200	6,500	40,000
	b. Yr. 4 (1854). *(S/M #H176-14).*	2,200	6,500	40,000
	c. Yr. 5 (1855). *(S/M #H176-24).*	2,200	6,500	40,000
	d. Yr. 6 (1856). *(S/M #H176-34).*	2,200	6,500	40,000
	e. Reissue. CD1861-64. *(S/M #H176-).*	2,200	6,500	40,000

General Bank of Communications

行銀通交

Chiao T'ung Yin Hang

Note: For later issues see Bank of Communications #102-166.

W/o Branch

1909 General Issue

		Good	Fine	XF
A13A	**10 Cents**			
	1909. Requires confirmation. *(S/M #C126-).*	—	—	—

Canton Branch

1909 Issue

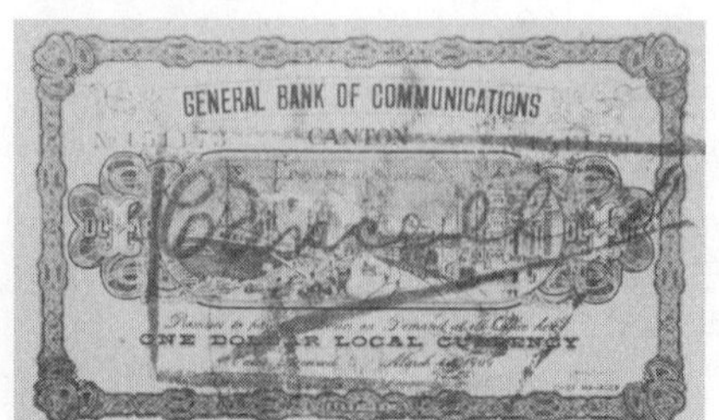

		Good	Fine	XF
A14	**1 Dollar**			
	1.3.1909. Brown with black text on yellow underprint. Two dragons facing value at center. Back: Ship dockside, steam passenger train at center. Printer: CMPA. *(S/M #C126-1a).*			
	a. Issued note.	300	1,100	6,000
	b. Cancelled with perforated Chinese characters.	—	180	650
	c. Hand cancelled.	—	150	450

		Good	Fine	XF
A15	**5 Dollars**			
	1.3.1909. Green and multicolor. Two dragons facing value at center, ship, station and train below. Printer: CMPA. *(S/M #C126-).*			
	a. Issued note.	650	2,700	9,000
	b. Cancelled with perforated Chinese characters.	—	225	750
A16	**10 Dollars**	Good	Fine	XF
	1.3.1909. Blue and red. Two dragons facing value at center, ship, station and train below. Printer: CMPA. *(S/M #C126-4).*			
	a. Issued note.	800	3,500	7,500
	b. Cancelled with perforated Chinese characters.	—	225	1,350

Hankow Branch

1909 Issue

		Good	Fine	XF
A16A	**1 Dollar**	3,000	12,000	—
	1.3.1909.Brown with black text on yellow underprint. Two dragons facing value at center. Like #A14. Back: Ship dockside, steam passenger train at center. Printer: CMPA. *(S/M #C126-)*			
A16B	**5 Dollars**	Good	Fine	XF
	1.3.1909. Green and multicolor. Two dragons facing value at center, ship, station and train below. Like #A15. Printer: CMPA. *(S/M #C126-).*	—	—	—
A16C	**5 Dollars**	Good	Fine	XF
	1.3.1909. Reported not confirmed. Green and red. Two dragons facing value at center, ship, station and train below. Like #A15. Printer: CMPA. *(S/M #C126-).*	—	—	—

		Good	Fine	XF
A16D	**10 Dollars** 1.3.1909. Blue, orange and green. Two dragons facing value at center, ship, station and train below. Like #A16. Printer: CMPA. *(S/M #C126-).*	—	—	—

Shanghai Branch 海上

1909 Issue

		Good	Fine	XF
A17	**1 Dollar** 1.3.1909. Brown and yellow. Two dragons facing value at center. Like #A14. Back: Ship dockside, steam passenger train at center. Printer: CMPA. *(S/M #C126-1b).*			
	a. Issued note.	1,100	3,300	15,000
	b. Cancelled with perforated Chinese characters.	—	600	4,350

Kaifeng Branch 封開

1909 Issue

		Good	Fine	XF
A17C	**5 Dollars** 1.3.1909. Reported not confirmed. Green and red. Two dragons facing value at center, ship, station and train below. Like #A15. Printer: CMPA. *(S/M #C126-).*	—	—	—
A17D	**10 Dollars** 1.3.1909. Blue, yellow and green. Printer: CMPA. Unsigned remainder. *(S/M #C126-).*	—	—	—

Shanghai Branch 海上

1909 Issue

		Good	Fine	XF
A18	**5 Dollars** 1.3.1909. Green and red. Two dragons facing value at center, ship, station and train below. Like #A15. Printer: CMPA. *(S/M #C126-3).*			
	a. Issued note.	1,450	3,600	21,750
	b. Cancelled with perforated Chinese characters.	—	1,100	6,250

Swatow Branch 頭汕

1909 Issue

		Good	Fine	XF
A18A	**1 Dollar** 1.3.1909. Requires confirmation. Brown and yellow. Two dragons facing value at center. Like #A14. Back: Ship dockside, steam passenger train at center. Printer: CMPA. *(S/M #C126-).*	—	—	—

Shanghai Branch 海上

1909 Issue

		Good	Fine	XF
A19	**10 Dollars** 1.3.1909. Blue and green. Two dragons facing value at center, ship, station and train below. Like #A16. Printer: CMPA. *(S/M #C126-5).*			
	a. Issued note.	2,200	6,500	33,750
	b. Cancelled with perforated Chinese characters.	—	725	9,375

Wusih Branch 錫無

1909 Issue

		Good	Fine	XF
A19B	**5 Dollars** 1.3.1909. Green and multicolor. Two dragons facing value at center, ship, station and train below. Like #A15. Printer: CMPA. *(S/M #C126-).*	—	—	—
A19C	**5 Dollars** 1.3.1909. Green and red. Two dragons facing value at center, ship, station and train below. Like #A15. Printer: CMPA. *(S/M #C126-).*	—	—	—

Yingkow Branch 口營

1909 Issue

		Good	Fine	XF
A19E	**1 Dollar** 1.3.1909. Brown and yellow. Two dragons facing value at center. Like #A14. Back: Ship dockside, steam passenger train at center. Printer: CMPA. *(S/M #C126-).*	1,200	—	—

Bureau of Engraving and Printing 局刷印部政財

Ts'ai Cheng Pu Yin Shua Chü

Not a Chinese note-issuing agency in the usual sense, but the Chinese name is used on what are samples of the work proposed by this organization. This same series, which was designed first for the Ta Ch'ing Government Bank #A79-A82, later turned up as the first issue of the Japanese puppet issuer known as the Federal Reserve Bank of China.

1909 ND Issue

		VG	VF	UNC
A20	**1 Dollar** ND (1909). Green. Regent Prince Chun at left, dragon at upper center. Junks at lower right. *(S/M #T190-1).* Proof.	—	—	10,000
A21	**5 Dollars** ND (1909). Orange. Regent Prince Chun at left, dragon at upper center. Mounted patrol at lower right. *(S/M #T190-2).* Proof.	—	—	19,200
A22	**10 Dollars** ND (1909). Blue. Regent Prince Chun at left, dragon at upper center. Great Wall at lower right. *(S/M #T190-3).* Proof.	—	—	29,000

		VG	VF	UNC
A23	**100 Dollars** ND (1909). Purple. Regent Prince Chun at left, dragon at upper center. Farm workers at lower right. *(S/M T190-4).* Proof.	—	—	19,200

Hu Pu Bank, Peking

行銀部户
Hu Pu Yin Hang

票銀換兌
Tui Huan Yin P'iao

行銀部户京北
Pei Ching Hu Pu Yin Hang

In 1906 the Hu Pu Bank changed its name to the Ta Ch'ing Bank.

1905 Dollar Issue

		VG	VF	UNC
A24	**1 Dollar** 12.11.yr. 31 (1905). Black text, orange on green underprint. Two facing dragons at upper left and right. Uniface. *(S/M #H177-1).*	—	—	—

1909 Tael Issue

		VG	VF	UNC
A25	**1 Tael** ca. 1909. Specimen. Orange and brown. *(S/M #H177-10).*	—	—	—

No.	Description	VG	VF	UNC
A26	**2 Taels**	VG	VF	UNC
	ca. 1909. Orange and brown. Specimen. *(S/M #H177-11).*	—	—	—
A27	**3 Taels**	VG	VF	UNC
	ca. 1909. Orange and brown. Specimen. *(S/M #H177-1).*	—	—	—
A28	**4 Taels**	VG	VF	UNC
	ca. 1909. Orange and brown. Specimen. *(S/M #H177-13).*	—	—	—
A29	**5 Taels**	VG	VF	UNC
	ca. 1909. Orange and brown. Specimen. *(S/M #H177-14).*	—	—	—
A30	**6 Taels**	VG	VF	UNC
	ca. 1909. Green and brown. Specimen. *(S/M #H177-15).*	—	—	—
A31	**8 Taels**	VG	VF	UNC
	ca. 1909. Green and brown. Specimen. *(S/M #H177-16).*	—	—	—
A32	**10 Taels**	VG	VF	UNC
	ca. 1909. Green and brown. Specimen. *(S/M #H177-17).*	—	—	—
A33	**50 Taels**	VG	VF	UNC
	ca. 1909. Gray and blue. Specimen. *(S/M #H177-20).*	—	—	—
A34	**100 Taels**	VG	VF	UNC
	1909. Green on light blue underprint. *(S/M #H177-21).*	—	—	—
A35	**500 Taels**	VG	VF	UNC
	ca. 1909. Green on light green underprint. *(S/M #H177-22).*			
	r. Remainder.	—	—	—
	s. Specimen.	—	—	—

Imperial Bank of China

Chung Kuo T'ung Shang Yin Hang

The Imperial Bank of China was the first half-hearted attempt at a central bank for China. Following the revolution of 1911-1912, the bank changed its name to Commercial Bank of China, but its role as a government bank had ended in 1905 with the creation of the Hu Pu Bank.

Canton Branch

1898 Issue

No.	Description	VG	VF	UNC
A36	**1 Dollar**	VG	VF	UNC
	22.1.1898. Two dragons supporting shield at upper center. Printer: BFL. *(S/M #C293-10b).*			
	a. Issued note.	3,600	18,000	—
	r. Remainder perforated: *CANCELLED.*	—	—	18,000

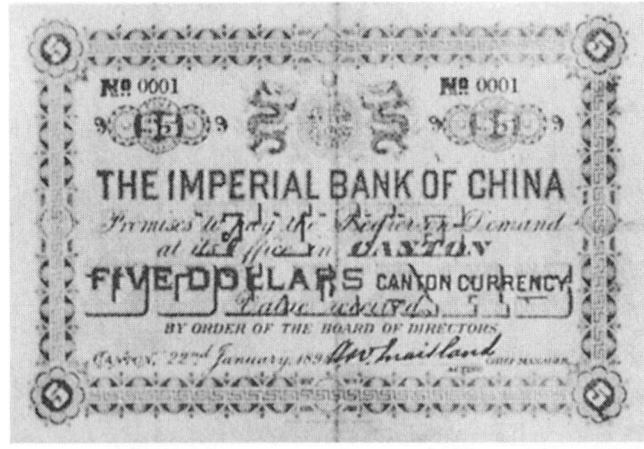

No.	Description	VG	VF	UNC
A37	**5 Dollars**	VG	VF	UNC
	22.1.1898. Two dragons supporting shield at upper center. Printer: BFL. *(S/M #C293-11b).*			
	a. Issued note.	9,000	22,000	—
	r. Remainder perforated: *CANCELLED.*	—	—	35,000
A38	**10 Dollars**	VG	VF	UNC
	22.1.1898. Two dragons supporting shield at upper center. Printer: BFL. *(S/M #C293-12b).*			
	a. Issued note.	—	—	—
	r. Remainder perforated: *CANCELLED.*	—	—	22,000

Peking Branch

1898 Issue

No.	Description	VG	VF	UNC
A39	**5 Mace**	VG	VF	UNC
	14.11.1898. Dark blue, brown and red on orange underprint. Two dragons supporting shield at upper center. Printer: BFL. *(S/M #C293-1b).*			
	a. Issued note.	1,400	3,600	—
	r. Remainder perforated: *CANCELLED.*	—	—	1,250

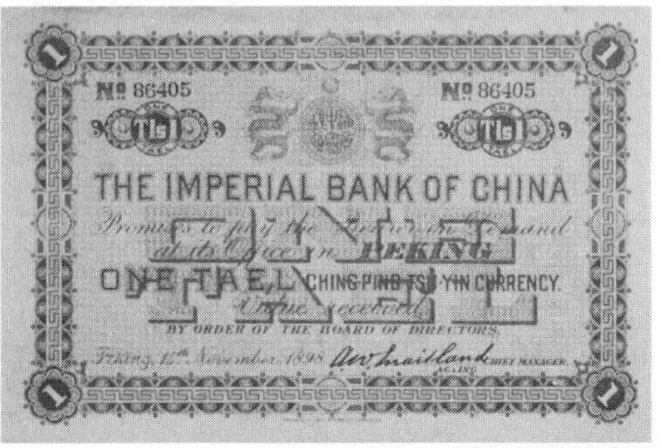

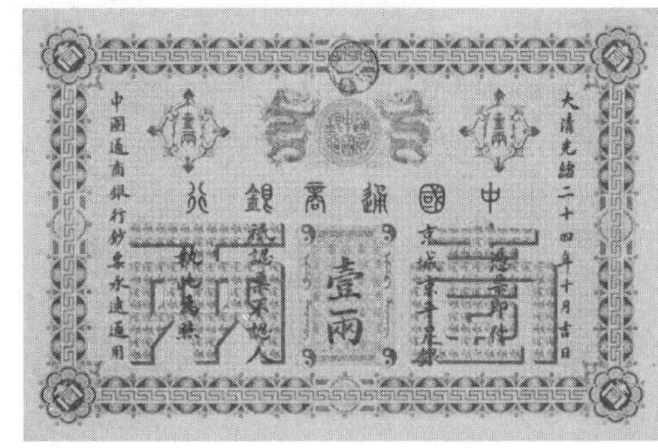

No.	Description	VG	VF	UNC
A40	**1 Tael**	VG	VF	UNC
	14.11.1898. Two dragons supporting shield at upper center. Printer: BFL. *(S/M #C293-2b).*			
	a. Issued note.	1,150	3,600	12,500
	r. Remainder perforated: *CANCELLED.*	—	—	3,600
A41	**5 Taels**	VG	VF	UNC
	14.11.1898. Two dragons supporting shield at upper center. Printer: BFL. *(S/M #C293-3b).*			
	a. Issued note.	3,300	14,500	—
	r. Remainder perforated: *CANCELLED.*	—	—	4,320
A42	**10 Taels**	VG	VF	UNC
	14.11.1898. Two dragons supporting shield at upper center. Printer: BFL. *(S/M #C293-4b).*			
	a. Issued note.	3,240	14,500	—
	r. Remainder perforated: *CANCELLED.*	—	—	4,900
A43	**50 Taels**	VG	VF	UNC
	14.11.1898. Two dragons supporting shield at upper center. Printer: BFL. *(S/M #C293-5b).*			
	a. Issued note. Requires confirmation.	—	—	—
	r. Remainder perforated: *CANCELLED.*	—	—	14,500
A44	**100 Taels**	VG	VF	UNC
	14.11.1898. Two dragons supporting shield at upper center. Printer: BFL. *(S/M #C293-6b).*			
	a. Issued note. Requires confirmation.	—	—	—
	r. Remainder perforated: *CANCELLED.*	—	—	30,000

Shanghai Branch

1898 Tael Issue

No.	Description	VG	VF	UNC
A45	**1/2 Tael**	VG	VF	UNC
	22.1.1898. Two dragons supporting shield at upper center. Printer: BFL. *(S/M #C293-1a).*			
	a. Issued note.	2,700	8,200	—
	r. Remainder perforated: *CANCELLED.*	—	—	2,400
A46	**1 Tael**	VG	VF	UNC
	22.1.1898. Purple, brown and red on yellow underprint. Two dragons supporting shield at upper center. Printer: BFL. *(S/M #C293-2a).*			
	a. Issued note.	4,800	12,000	—
	r. Remainder perforated: *CANCELLED.*	—	—	4,100
A47	**5 Taels**	VG	VF	UNC
	22.1.1898. Two dragons supporting shield at upper center. Printer: BFL. *(S/M #C293-3a).*			
	a. Issued note.	5,500	17,000	—
	r. Remainder perforated: *CANCELLED.*	—	—	3,250
A48	**10 Taels**	VG	VF	UNC
	22.1.1898. Two dragons supporting shield at upper center. Printer: BFL. *(S/M #C293-4a).*			
	a. Issued note.	8,000	24,000	—
	r. Remainder perforated: *CANCELLED.*	—	—	5,200
A49	**50 Taels**	VG	VF	UNC
	22.1.1898. Two dragons supporting shield at upper center. Printer: BFL. *(S/M #C293-5a).*			
	a. Issued note. Requires confirmation.	—	—	—
	r. Remainder perforated: *CANCELLED.*	—	—	14,500

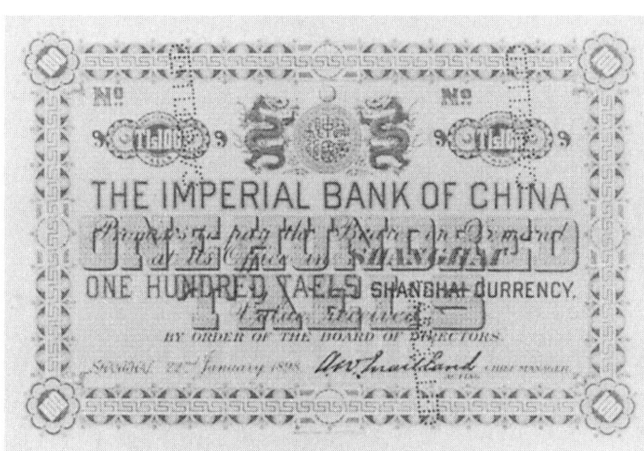

		VG	VF	UNC
A50	**100 Taels**	VG	VF	UNC
	22.1.1898. Purple, brown and red on yellow underprint. Two dragons supporting shield at upper center. Printer: BFL. *(S/M #C293-6a).*			
	a. Issued note.	32,500	80,000	—
	r. Remainder perforated: *CANCELLED.*	—	—	30,000

1898 Dollar Issue

		VG	VF	UNC
A51	**1 Dollar**	VG	VF	UNC
	22.1.1898. Two dragons supporting shield at upper center. Printer: BFL. *(S/M #C293-10a).*			
	a. Issued note.	3,250	10,000	—
	r. Remainder perforated: *CANCELLED.*	—	—	2,750
A52	**5 Dollars**	VG	VF	UNC
	22.1.1898. Two dragons supporting shield at upper center. Printer: BFL. *(S/M #C293-11a).*			
	a. Issued note.	5,500	16,000	—
	r. Remainder perforated: *CANCELLED.*	—	—	2,750
A53	**10 Dollars**	VG	VF	UNC
	22.1.1898. Two dragons supporting shield at upper center. Printer: BFL. *(S/M #C293-12a).*			
	a. Issued note.	7,550	22,000	—
	r. Remainder perforated: *CANCELLED.*	—	—	5,000

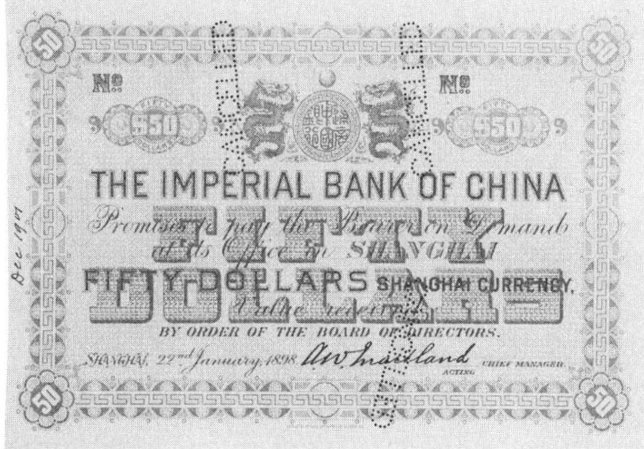

		VG	VF	UNC
A54	**50 Dollars**	VG	VF	UNC
	22.1.1898. Red and brown on orange underprint. Two dragons supporting shield at upper center. Printer: BFL. *(S/M #C293-).*			
	a. Issued note.	25,000	54,000	—
	r. Remainder perforated: *CANCELLED.*	—	—	14,000
A54A	**100 Dollars**	VG	VF	UNC
	22.1.1898. Red on yellow underprint. Two dragons supporting shield at upper center. Printer: BFL. *(S/M #C293-).*			
	a. Issued note.	29,000	58,000	—
	r. Remainder perforated: *CANCELLED.*	—	—	20,000

Note: See also #A133.

Color Abbreviation Guide

New to the *Standard Catalog of® World Paper Money* are the following abbreviations related to color references:

BC: Back color
PC: Paper color

1904 Issue

Note: For similar issues w/Worthy see Commercial Bank of China, #A133A-A138, #1-15.

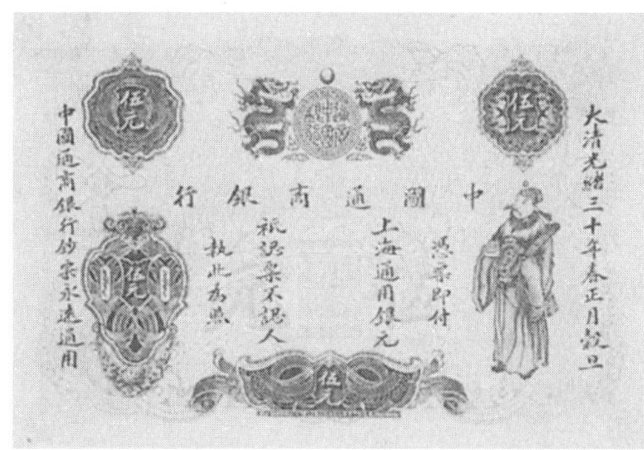

		VG	VF	UNC
A55	**5 Dollars**	VG	VF	UNC
	16.2.1904. Black on multicolor underprint. Two dragons supporting shield at upper center. Confucius standing at lower right. Printer: BFL. *(S/M #C293-20).*			
	a. Small signature. Printer: BWC.	2,400	6,000	36,000
	b. Large signature. Without imprint.	2,400	6,000	36,000
	r. Remainder perforated: *CANCELLED.*	—	—	7,500

		VG	VF	UNC
A55A	**10 Dollars**	VG	VF	UNC
	16.2.1904. Black on multicolor underprint. Two dragons supporting shield at upper center. Confucius standing at lower right. Similar to #A55. Printer: BFL. *(S/M #C293-21).*			
	a. Small signature. Printer: BWC.	6,000	27,750	—
	b. Large signature. Without imprint.	6,000	27,750	—
	r. Remainder perforated: *CANCELLED.*	—	—	9,000

Imperial Chinese Railways 北洋鐵軌官路總局

Pei Yang T'ieh Kuei Kuan Lu Tsung Chü

Peiyang Branch 北洋

1895 Issue

#A56, handwritten dates exist over printed date.

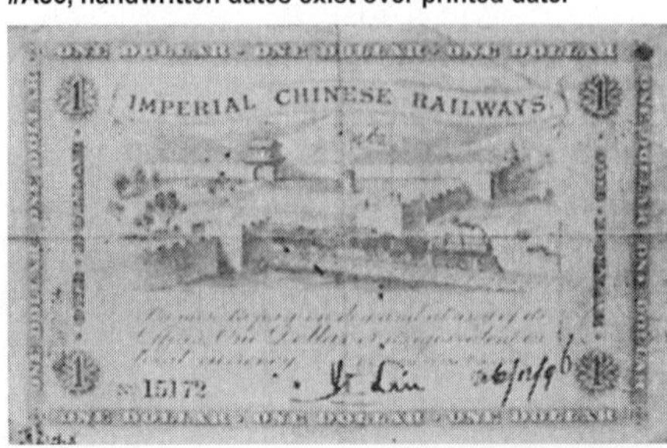

		Good	Fine	XF
A56	**1 Dollar** 22.4.1895. Blue on orange underprint. Train passing through fortress at center. Back: Boat, shoreline with mountains in background. Printer: BFL. *(S/M #P34-1).*			
	a. Issued note.	425	1,250	3,250
	r. Unsigned remainder.	—		

#A57-A58 *Not assigned.*

Shanghai Branch 上海

1899 Issue

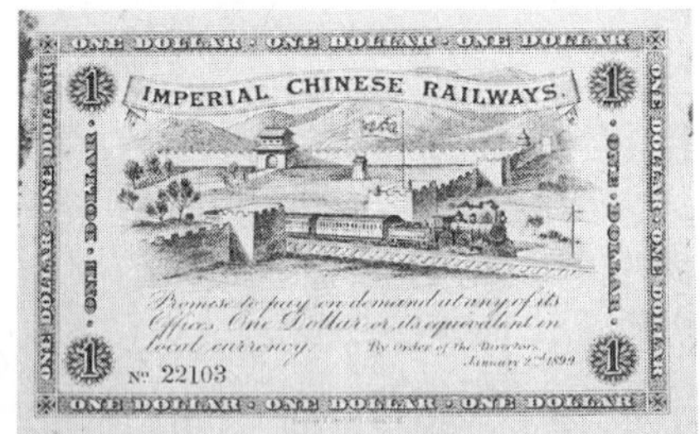

		Good	Fine	XF
A59	**1 Dollar** 2.1.1899. Blue on orange underprint. Train passing through fortress at center. Without signature. *(S/M #S13-1).*	125	450	1,325
A60	**5 Dollars** 2.1.1899. Blue on orange underprint. Train passing through fortress at center. Without signature. *(S/M #S13-2).*	1,325	3,250	10,875
A61	**10 Dollars** 2.1.1899. Train passing through fortress at center. Without signature. *(S/M #S13-3).*			
	a. Issued note.	1,600	5,000	15,000
	r. Remainder perforated: *CANCELLED.*	—	Unc	4,800

Ningpo Commercial Bank, Limited 上海四明銀行

Shang Hai Szu Ming Yin Hang

1909 Issue

		Good	Fine	XF
A61A	**1 Dollar** 22.1.1909. Gray. Dragons at upper center. Back: Dragons at upper center. Printer: TSPC. *SHANGHAI. (S/M #S107-1).*			
	a. Issued note.	200	200	1,625
	b. *HK* monogram (Hankow)/*SHANGHAI.*	250	250	3,750
	c. *NP* (Ningpo)/*SHANGHAI.*	350	350	2,200
	d. *SH* monogram *SHANGHAI.*	350	350	2,200

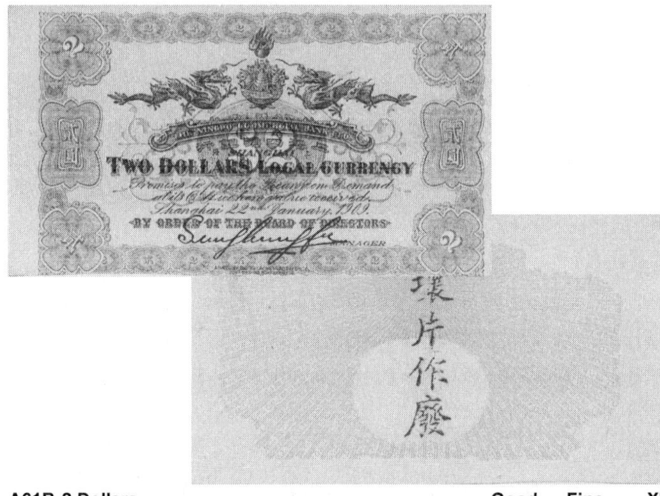

		Good	Fine	XF
A61B	**2 Dollars** 22.1.1909. Green and yellow. Dragons at upper center. Back: Dragons at upper center. Printer: TSPC. *SHANGHAI. (S/M #S107-2).*			
	a. Issued note.	425	425	3,600
	r. Partly printed remainder.	—	Unc	800
A61C	**5 Dollars** 22.1.1909. Black and yellow. Dragons at upper center. Back: Dragons at upper center. Printer: TSPC. *SHANGHAI. (S/M #S107-3).*	1,000	2,300	7,000
A61D	**10 Dollars** 22.1.1909. Black and brown. Dragons at upper center. Back: Dragons at upper center. Printer: TSPC. *SHANGHAI. (S/M #S107-4).*	1,100	2,400	6,000

Note: For later issues see #539-550.

Ta Ch'ing Government Bank 大清銀行

Ta Ch'ing Yin Hang

Chinanfu Branch 濟南福

1906 Issue

		Good	Fine	XF
A62	**1 Dollar** 1.9.1906. Green and lilac. Back: Supported arms at upper center. Printer: CMPA. *(S/M #T10-).*	4,250	13,200	—

Fengtien Branch 奉天

1907 Issue

		Good	Fine	XF
A62A	**50 Cents** 1907. *(S/M #T10-).* Purple and blue. Back: Supported arms at upper center. Printer: CMPA.	4,250	17,250	—

Foochow Branch 州福

1906 Provisional Issue

		VG	VF	UNC
A62B	**1 Dollar** 1.9.1906. Back: Supported arms at upper center. Printer: CMPA. *(S/M #T10-).*	7,500	21,750	—

Hangchow Branch 州杭

1906 Issue

		VG	VF	UNC
A63	**1 Dollar** 1.9.1906. Back: Supported arms at upper center. Printer: CMPA. *(S/M #T10-1b).*	—	—	—

Hankow Branch 口漢

1906 Issue

		VG	VF	UNC
A63A	**1 Dollar** 1.9.1906. Back: Supported arms at upper center. Printer: CMPA. *(S/M #T10-).*	175	500	1,200

		VG	VF	UNC
A64	**5 Dollars** 1.9.1906. Blue and orange. Crossed flags at center. Back: Supported arms at upper center. Printer: CMPA. *(S/M #T10-2a).*	1,800	5,775	—

		VG	VF	UNC
A65	**10 Dollars** 1.9.1906. Lilac and yellow. Crossed flags at top center. Back: Supported arms at upper center. Printer: CMPA. *(S/M #T10-3a).*			
	a. Issued note.	1,800	6,375	—
	r. Unsigned remainder.	—	—	3,000

1907 Issue

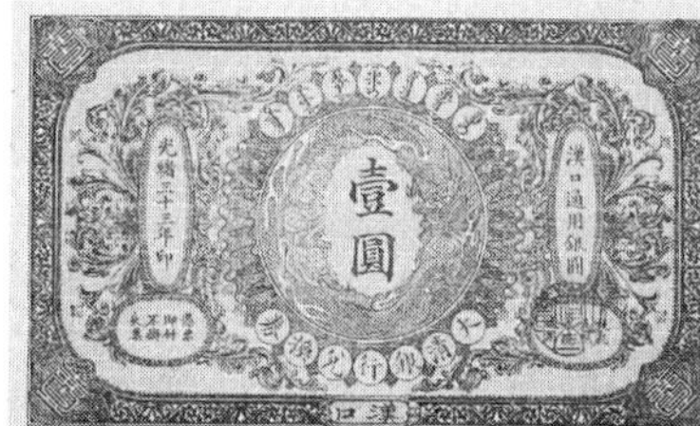

		VG	VF	UNC
A66	**1 Dollar** 1.6.1907. Green and lilac. Back: Supported arms at upper center. Printer: CMPA. *(S/M #T10-10a).*			
	a. Issued note.	150	725	—
	r. Unsigned remainder.	—	—	500

Hunan Branch 南湖

1906-1907 Issue

		VG	VF	UNC
A66A	**1 Dollar** 1.9.1906. Back: Supported arms at upper center. Printer: CMPA. *(S/M #T10-).*	—	—	—
A67	**5 Dollars** 1.6.1907. Blue and orange. Crossed flags at center. Back: Supported arms at upper center. Printer: CMPA. *(S/M #T10-11).*	—	—	—
A68	**10 Dollars** 1.6.1907. Lilac and yellow. Crossed flags at top center. Back: Supported arms at upper center. Printer: CMPA. *(S/M #T10-12).*	—	—	—

Kaifong Branch 封開

1906 Provisional Issue

		VG	VF	UNC
A69	**1 Dollar** 1.9.1906. Back: Supported arms at upper center. Printer: CMPA. *(S/M #T10-1c).*			
	a. Issued note. Rare.	—	—	—
	r. Unsigned remainder.	—	—	3,300

		VG	VF	UNC
A70	**5 Dollars** 1.9.1906. Back: Supported arms at upper center. Printer: CMPA. *(S/M #T10-2c).*			
	a. Issued note.	—	—	—
	r. Unsigned remainder.	—	725	3,300

		VG	VF	UNC
A71	**10 Dollars** 1.9.1906. Back: Supported arms at upper center. Printer: CMPA. *(S/M #T10-3c).*			
	a. Issued note.	—	—	—
	r. Unsigned remainder.	—	950	3,975

Kalgan Branch 口家張

1906 Issue

		VG	VF	UNC
A71A	**1 Dollar** 1.9.1906. Dark green and lilac on yellow underprint. Back: Supported arms at upper center. Printer: CMPA. *(S/M #T10-).*	—	—	—

Kwangchow (Canton) Branch 州廣

1908 Issue

		VG	VF	UNC
A71B	**1 Dollar** 1.3.1908. Dark green and lilac on yellow underprint. Back: Supported arms at upper center. Printer: CMPA. *(S/M #T10-).*	2,500	6,500	27,000
A71C	**10 Dollars** 1.3.1908. Brown and yellow. Crossed flags at top center. Back: Supported arms at upper center. Printer: CMPA. *(S/M #T10-).*	—	—	—

Peking Branch 京北

1906 Issue

		VG	VF	UNC
A71D	**1 Dollar** 1.9.1906. Back: Supported arms at upper center. Printer: CMPA. *(S/M #T10).*	—	—	—

Notes numbered A71H to A75E have been rearranged to follow alphabetically by branch.

Shanghai Branch 海上

1906 Issue

		VG	VF	UNC
A71H	**5 Dollars** 1.9.1906. Red-violet on green underprint. Nine seal characters in frame at bottom center. Supported arms at upper center. Back: Supported arms at upper center. Printer: CMPA. *(S/M #T10-).*	—	—	—

1907 Issue

		VG	VF	UNC
A71J	**1 Dollar** 1.9.1907. Back: Supported arms at upper center. Printer: CMPA. *(S/M #T10-).*	—	—	—

Tientsin Branch 倫庫

1906 Issue

		VG	VF	UNC
A72	**1 Dollar** 1.9.1906. Green and lilac. Back: Supported arms at upper center. Printer: CMPA. *(S/M #T10-1a).*	—	—	6,400
A73	**5 Dollars** 1.9.1906. Blue and orange. Crossed flags at center. Back: Supported arms at upper center. Printer: CMPA. *(S/M #T10-2a).*			
	a. Issued note.	—	—	—
	r. Unsigned remainder.	—	—	—
A74	**10 Dollars** 1.9.1906. Lilac and yellow. Crossed flags at center. Back: Supported arms at upper center. Printer: CMPA. *(S/M #T10-3a).*	—	—	—

Urga Branch 倫庫

1907 Issue

		VG	VF	UNC
A74A	**1 Dollar** 1.6.1907. Back: Supported arms at upper center. Printer: CMPA. *(S/M #T10-).*	—	—	—
A74C	**10 Dollars** 1.6.1907. Back: Supported arms at upper center. Printer: CMPA. *(S/M #T10-).*	—	—	—

1908 Issue

		VG	VF	UNC
A75	**1 Dollar** 1.3.1908. Green and lilac. Back: Supported arms at upper center. Printer: CMPA. *(S/M #T10-20).*	—	—	—

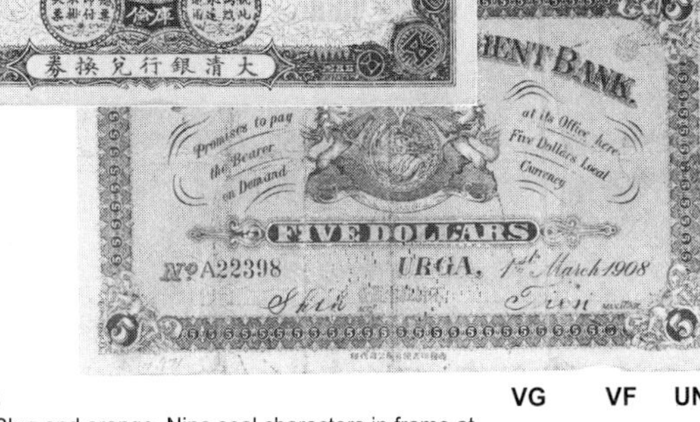

		VG	VF	UNC
A75A	**5 Dollars** 1.3.1908. Blue and orange. Nine seal characters in frame at bottom center. Supported arms at upper center. Back: Supported arms at upper center. Printer: CMPA. *(S/M #T10-).*	—	—	—
A75B	**10 Dollars** 1.3.1908. *(S/M #T10-).*	—	—	—

Wuhu Branch

1906 Provisional Issue

		VG	VF	UNC
A75E	**1 Dollar** 1.9.1906. Back: Supported arms at upper center. Printer: CMPA. *(S/M #T10-).*	—	—	—

Yingkow Branch 口營

1906 Issue

		VG	VF	UNC
A75J	**1 Dollar** 1.6.1906. Specimen. Uniface pair. *(S/M #T10-).*	—	—	—
A75K	**5 Dollars** 1.6.1906. Specimen. Uniface pair. *(S/M #T10-).*	—	—	—
A75L	**10 Dollars** 1.6.1906. Specimen. Uniface pair. *(S/M #T10-).*	—	—	—

Yunnan Branch 南雲

1906 Provisional Issue

		VG	VF	UNC
A75P	**1 Dollar** 1.9.1906. Back: Supported arms at upper center. *(S/M #T10-).*	—	—	—

W/o Branch

1909 General Issue

Note: See also Bank of China provisional issue #16-18.

		VG	VF	UNC
A76	**1 Dollar** 1.10.1909. Olive-brown on red-orange underprint; black text. Portrait Li Hung Chan at left. Hillside village, railroad at right. Without office of issue or signature. Back: Waterfront park at center. Printer: ABNC. (Not issued). *(S/M #T10-30).*	4,400	13,000	—
A77	**5 Dollars** 1.10.1909. Brown on blue and multicolor underprint; black text. Portrait Li Hung Chan at left. Gazebo at right. Without office of issue or signature. Back: Hillside pagoda, village at center. Printer: ABNC. (Not issued). *(S/M #T10-31).*	3,600	8,650	22,000
A78	**10 Dollars** 1.10.1909. Black text. Portrait Li Hung Chan at left. Teahouse at right. Without office of issue or signature. Back: Great Wall at center. Printer: ABNC. (Not issued). *(S/M #T10-32).*	4,800	11,000	24,000

		VG	VF	UNC
A78A	**50 Dollars** 1.10.1909. Specimen only. Fortified city gates at right. Back: Pagodas atop monastery at center right. *(S/M #T10-33).*	—	—	30,000

		VG	VF	UNC
A78B	**100 Dollars** 1.10.1909. Temple of Heaven at right. Back: Teahouse with gazebos at center. *(S/M #T10-34).*	—	—	60,000

Note: See also Bank of China provisional issue, #16-18.

1910 ND Issue

Note: Crudely printed, but deceptive, souvenir copies exist.

		VG	VF	UNC
A79	**1 Dollar** ND (1910). Green. Portrait Prince Chun at left, dragon at upper center. Junks at lower right. Without signature or serial #. *(S/M #T10-40).* (Not issued).	1,100	2,400	16,500

		VG	VF	UNC
A80	**5 Dollars** ND (1910). Red. Portrait Prince Chun at left, dragon at upper center. Mounted patrol at lower right. Without signature or serial #. *(S/M #T10-41).* (Not issued).	1,800	5,550	22,600

		VG	VF	UNC
A81	**10 Dollars** ND (1910). Black. Portrait Prince Chun at left, dragon at upper center. Great Wall at lower right. Without signature or serial #. *(S/M #T10-42).*			
	a. Issued note.	10,800	24,000	—
	r. Unsigned remainder. Without seal stamps on back.	—	—	14,500

		VG	VF	UNC
A82	**100 Dollars** ND (1910). Dark green. Portrait Prince Chun at left, dragon at upper center. Field workers at lower right. Without signature or serial #. *(S/M #T10-43).* (Not issued).	—	—	—

Ta Ch'ing Government Bank, Shansi 陝西大清銀行

Shan Hsi Ta Ch'ing Yin Hang

Note: Prefixing a provincial or city name to that of a bank's name in the heading was not an uncommon practice during the banking days of the Empire.

1911 Issue

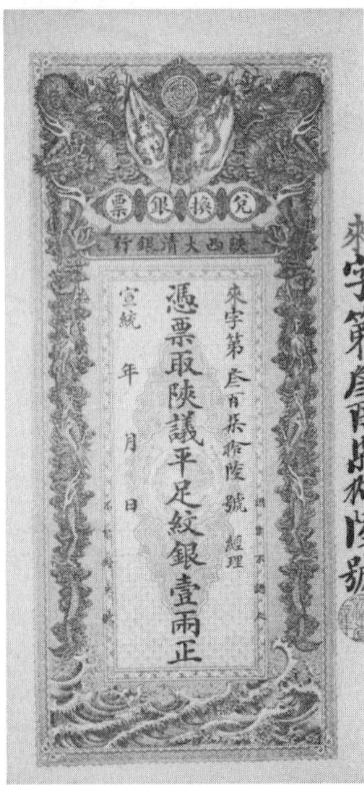

		VG	VF	UNC
A83	**1 Tael** ca.1911. Purple on light green underprint. Facing dragons with crossed flags at top center. With or without counterfoils. Unissued remainder. *(S/M #T10-50).*	—	—	2,500
A83A	**3 Taels** ca.1911. Facing dragons with crossed flags at top center. With or without counterfoils. Unissued remainder. *(S/M #T10-51).*	—	—	3,000
A83H	**100 Taels** ca.1909. Purple on light green underprint. Facing dragons with crossed flags at top center. With or without counterfoils. Unissued remainder. *(S/M #T10-54).*	—	—	4,600
A83J	**1000 Taels** ca.1911. Brown-orange on pale olive-green underprint. Facing dragons with crossed flags at top center. With or without counterfoils. Unissued remainder. *(S/M #T10-60).*	—	—	5,750

Note: Beware of remainders missing red validation seal stampings over the denomination which were "created" in recent times for collectors.

REPUBLIC

Agricultural Bank of the Four Provinces

四省農民銀行

Szu Sheng Nung Min Yin Hang

豫鄂皖贛四省農民銀行

Yü O Huan Kan Szu Sheng Nung Min Yin Hang

This bank was established in 1933 with strong connections to the Chinese nationalist administration and an assigned area of operations in Honan, Hupei, Anhwei and Kiangsi. Two years later, in June 1935, it was reorganized into the Farmers Bank of China and given national bank status. See #451-482. The succeeding bank took over the small existing note issue.

1933 Issue

		Good	Fine	XF
A84	**10 Cents** ND (1933). Red. Farmer at center. Printer: TYPC. *(S/M #S110-1).*			
	a. Issued note.	90.00	330	1,000
	s. Specimen.	—	Unc	600
A84A	**20 Cents** 1933. Purple and yellow. Printer: TYPC. *(S/M #S110-).*	**Good**	**Fine**	**XF**
	a. Issued note.	—	—	—
	s. Specimen.	—	Unc	900
A84B	**20 Cents** 1933. Purple. *(S/M #S110-).*	—	—	—

		Good	Fine	XF
A85	**20 Cents** 1933. Green and purple. Farmers carrying baskets at right. Printer: CCCA. *(S/M #S110-2).*			
	a. Issued note.	50.00	300	775
	r. Remainder. Without signature or serial #.	—	Unc	350
	s. Specimen.	—	Unc	550

		Good	Fine	XF
A86	**50 Cents** ND (1933). Blue. Farmer plowing with ox at center. Back: Farm workers at right. Printer: CCCA. *(S/M #S110-3).*			
	a. Issued note.	240	600	1,800
	r. Remainder. Without signature or serial #.	—	Unc	975

		Good	Fine	XF
A87	**1 Dollar** 1933. Brown on yellow underprint. Farm workers at left and right. Back: Farm workers at center. Printer: TYPC. *(S/M #S110-10).*			
	a. Issued note.	220	720	2,000
	b. Overprint: *SIAN.*	275	840	2,600
	s. As a. Specimen.	—	Unc	675

1933 Provisional Issue

#A88-A90 joint issue with the Hupeh Provincial Bank. New issuer overprint on notes of Hupeh Provincial Bank.

		VG	VF	UNC
A88	**1 Dollar**	VG	VF	UNC
	ND (1933 - old date 1929). Violet on multicolor underprint. Pagoda at right. *(S/M #S110-20).*	175	1,100	—
A89	**5 Dollars**	VG	VF	UNC
	ND (1933 - old date 1929). Green on multicolor underprint. Pagoda at center. *(S/M #S110-21).*	200	1,200	—
A90	**10 Silver Yüan**	VG	VF	UNC
	ND (1933 - old date 1929). *(S/M #S110-22).* Red on multicolor underprint. Pagoda at left.	200	1,200	—

1934 Issue

		Good	Fine	XF
A91A	**10 Cents**	Good	Fine	XF
	1934. Orange and blue. Printer: TYPC. *(S/M #S110-).*	—	—	—
A91B	**20 Cents**	Good	Fine	XF
	1934. Purple and yellow. Printer: TYPC. *(S/M #S110-).*	—	—	—

		Good	Fine	XF
A91E	**1 Dollar**			
	1.5.1934. Red. Farm workers at upper left. Back: Ox at center. Printer: TYPC.			
	a. *Foochow. (S/M #S110-30a).*	100	250	1,000
	b. *HANG CHOW. (S/M #S110-30b).*	150	650	1,400
	c. Control overprint: *Yu.*	100	400	1,200
	s. As a, b. Specimen.	—	Unc	725

Agricultural and Industrial Bank of China

中國農工銀行

Chung Kuo Nung Kung Yin Hang

1927 Dollar Issue

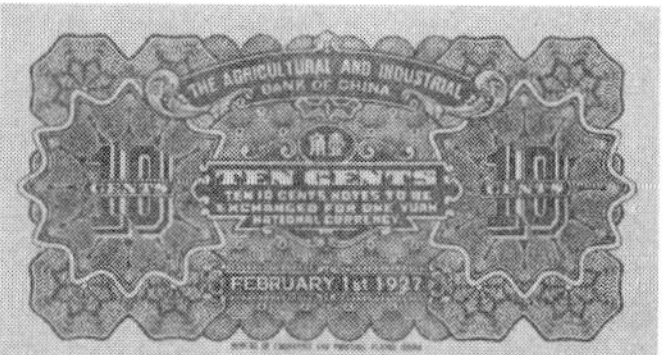

		Good	Fine	XF
A92	**10 Cents**			
	1.2.1927. Purple. Bridge over water at center. Printer: BEPP (Peiping or Peking).			
	a. *Peking. (S/M #C287-1a).*	15.00	35.00	125
	b. *Tientsin. (S/M #C287-1c).*	16.00	55.00	150

		Good	Fine	XF
A93	**10 Cents**			
	1.2.1927. Purple. Bridge over water at center. Like #A92. Printer: BEP-Peking.			
	a. *Peking. (S/M #C287-2).*	20.00	55.00	175
	b. *Tientsin (S/M #C287-1b).*	30.00	200	600
	s1. As a. Peking. Specimen	—	Unc	200
	s2. As b. Tientsin. Specimen.	—	Unc	300

		Good	Fine	XF
A94	**20 Cents**			
	1.2.1927. Green. Bridge over water at center. Printer: BEPP (Peiping or Peking).			
	a. *Peking. (S/M #C287-3a).*	12.00	35.00	150
	b. *Tientsin. (S/M #C287-3c).*	16.00	55.00	300

		Good	Fine	XF
A94A	**20 Cents**			
	1.2.1927. Green. Bridge over water at center. Like #A94. Printer: BEP-Peiping.			
	a. *Peking. (S/M #C287-).*	12.00	35.00	200
	b. *Tientsin. (S/M #C287-3b).*	16.00	55.00	300
	s. As a, specimen.	—	Unc	175

		Good	Fine	XF
A94B	**50 Cents**	Good	Fine	XF
	1.2.1927. Orange. Bridge over water at center. Printer: BEP-Peking. *(S/M #C287-).*	90	300	1,200

		Good	Fine	XF
A95	**1 Dollar**			
	1.9.1927. Brown and multicolor. Great Wall at center. 2 signature varieties. Printer: BEPP-Peking.			
	a. Peking. *(S/M #C287-10).*	100	400	1,250
	b. *TIENTSIN.*	—	—	—
	s. Specimen.	—	Unc	1,350

		Good	Fine	XF
A98	**5 Dollars**			
	1.9.1927. Red-orange on multicolor underprint. Sailing ships at center. Like #A99. Printer: BEPP-Peking. (S/M #C287-13).			
	a. Issued note.	100	425	1,400
	s. 2 part specimen.	—	Unc	360

		Good	Fine	XF
A99	**5 Dollars**			
	1.9.1927. Red and multicolor. Sailing ships at center. Printer: BEPP.			
	a. *HANKOW. (S/M #C287-14a).*	100	300	1,200
	b. *HANKOW.* Overprint. *PAYABLE AT CHANGSHA (S/M #C287-14b).*	100	350	1,680
	s. As b. Specimen.	—	Unc	350

		Good	Fine	XF
A100	**5 Dollars**			
	1.9.1927. Orange and multicolor. Printer: BEPP. *TIEN-TSIN. (S/M #C287-15).*	125	350	1,400

		Good	Fine	XF
A101	**5 Dollars**			
	1.9.1927. Green and multicolor. Sailing ships at center. Like #A99. Printer: BEPP. *SHANGHAI.* (S/M #C287-16).			
	a. Issued note.	100	500	2,220
	s. Specimen.	—	Unc	350

A102 Not assigned.

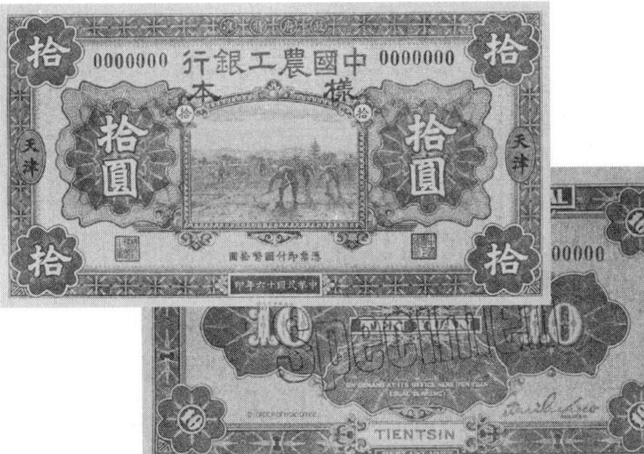

		Good	Fine	XF
A105	**10 Dollars**			
	1.9.1927. Green and multicolor. Farm workers at center. Like #A104. Printer: BEPP.			
	a. *SHANGHAI. (S/M #C287-22a).*	125	375	1,950
	b. *TIENTSIN. (S/M #C287-22b).*	100	300	1,620
	s. As b. Specimen.	—	Unc	500
A106	**10 Dollars**	**Good**	**Fine**	**XF**
	1.9.1927. Brown and multicolor. Farm workers at center. Like #A104. Printer: BEPP. *SHANGHAI. (S/M #C287-23).*	60.00	125	750

1927 Yüan Issues

		Good	Fine	XF
A96	**1 Yüan**			
	1.9.1927. Green and multicolor. Great Wall at center. Like #A95. Printer: BEPP.			
	a. *HANKOW. (S/M #C287-11a).*	125	300	1,050
	b. *HANKOW.* Overprint. *PAYABLE AT CHANGSHA(S/M #C287-11b).*	125	500	2,100
	s1. 2 part specimen.	—	Unc	375
	s2. Specimen. Overprint: *SPECIMEN.* and punch hole cancelled.	—	Unc	300

		Good	Fine	XF
A97	**1 Yüan**			
	1.9.1927. Red and multicolor. Great Wall at center. Like #A95. Printer: BEPP. *SHANGHAI. (S/M #C287-12).*	50.00	175	1,200
A103	**10 Yüan**	**Good**	**Fine**	**XF**
	1927. Printer: BEPP. *PEKING. (S/M #C287-20).* Requires confirmation.	—	—	—

A104 10 Yüan	Good	Fine	XF
1.9.1927. Purple and multicolor. Farm workers at center. Printer: BEPP.			
a. *HANKOW. (S/M #C287-21a).*	175	600	2,000
b. *HANKOW.* Overprint: *PAYABLE AT CHANG-SHA. (S/M #C287-21b).*	200	720	2,250
s. As a, b. Specimen.	—	Unc	750

1932 Issue

A107 10 Cents	Good	Fine	XF
1.1.1932. Brown and red. Bridge over water at center. Printer: BEPP. *HANKOW. (S/M #C287-31).*	22.50	85.00	350

A108 20 Cents	Good	Fine	XF
1.1.1932. Yellow. Printer: BEPP. *HANKOW. (S/M #C287-31).*	120	300	1,200

A109 1 Dollar	Good	Fine	XF
1932. Red and multicolor. Farmer plowing with water buffalo at center. Signature varieties. Printer: ABNC. *SHANGHAI. (S/M #C287-40).*			
a. Issued note.	100	295	1,350
b. With various numerical overprints.	100	275	1,500

A110 5 Yüan	Good	Fine	XF
1932. Green and multicolor. Farmer plowing with water buffalo at left. Signature varieties. Printer: ABNC.			
a. *HANKOW.* with various numerical overprint: 11; 21; 22. *(S/M #C287-41a).*	175	375	2,300
b. *SHANGHAI.* with various numerical overprint: 11-43, etc. *(S/M #C287-41b).*	100	300	1,500
c. *PEIPING. (S/M #C287-41c).*	100	300	1,500
d. *HANKOW.* Overprint: *PAYABLE AT CHANG-SHA. (S/M #C287-41d).*	175	375	2,300
s1. As b. 2 part specimen.	—	Unc	450
s2. Specimen. Without place name.	—	Unc	425
s3. Specimen. *Hankow.* Pinhole cancelled.	—	Unc	450

A111 10 Yüan	Good	Fine	XF
1932. Purple and multicolor. Farmer plowing with water buffalo at right. Signature varieties. Printer: ABNC.			
a. *HANKOW.* with various numerical overprint: 3; 4; 7, etc. *(S/M #C287-42a).*	275	800	2,400
b. *SHANGHAI.* with various numerical overprint: 33; 40; 43 etc. *(S/M #C287-42b).*	200	700	2,000
s. Specimen. Uniface face and back attached, perforated.	—	Unc	325

1934 Issue

A112 1 Yüan	Good	Fine	XF
1934. Red and multicolor. Farmer plowing with water buffalo at center. Printer: W&S.			
a. *SHANGHAI. (S/M #C287-50a).*	75.00	200	900
b. *PEIPING. (S/M #C287-50b).*	75.00	200	900
c. Without place name. *(S/M #C287-50c).*	75.00	150	750
d. *TIENTSIN (S/M #C287-50d).*	75.00	200	850
s1. As a. 2 part specimen.	—	Unc	375
s2. As b. 2 part specimen.	—	Unc	375
s3. Specimen. *Shanghai.* Overprint and pinhole cancelled.	—	Unc	375

Bank of Agriculture and Commerce

農商銀行

Nung Shang Yin Hang

1921 Issue

For former #A112A-A112C see A114A or A117C, D.

A113 1 Yüan	Good	Fine	XF
Yr.11 (1921). Red-brown and blue. Harvesting grain. Printer: Yu Foong Industrial Development Co. Ltd., Peking.			
a. *SHANGHAI.* Specimen. *(S/M #N23-1).*	—	—	—
b. *PEKING.* Specimen. *(S/M #N23-).*	—	—	—
c. *HANKOW. (S/M #N23-).*	3,300	7,500	—

		Good	Fine	XF
A114	**5 Yüan** Yr. 11 (1921). Gray and multicolor. Harvesting grain. Similar to #A113. Printer: Yu Foong Industrial Development Co. Ltd., Peking.			
	a. *SHANGHAI.* Specimen. *(S/M #N23-).*	—	—	—
	b. *PEKING. (S/M #N23-).* Requires confirmation.	—	—	—
A115	**10 Yüan** Yr. 11 (1921). Printer: Yu Foong Industrial Development Co. Ltd., Peking.	**Good**	**Fine**	**XF**
	a. *SHANGHAI. (S/M #N23-3).*	750	2,500	11,250
	b. *PEKING. (S/M #N23-).*	—	—	—
	s. As a. Specimen.	—	Unc	7,500
A116	**50 Yüan** Yr. 11 (1921). Printer: Yu Foong Industrial Development Co. Ltd., Peking. *SHANGHAI. (S/M #N23-).* Requires confirmation.	**Good** —	**Fine** —	**XF** —

		VG	VF	UNC
A117	**100 Yüan** Yr. 11 (1921). Printer: Yu Foong Industrial Development Co. Ltd., Peking.			
	s1. *SHANGHAI.* Specimen. *(S/M #N23-).*	—	—	11,250
	s2. *HANKOW.* Specimen. Overprint and pinhole cancelled.	—	—	11,250

1922 Dollar Issue

		Good	Fine	XF
A117A	**1 Dollar** 1.5.1922. Red and blue. Printer: BEPP. *(S/M #N23-).*			
	a. Issued note.	—	—	—
	s. 2 part specimen, *Shanghai*, red and yellow, back red.	—	Unc	750

		Good	Fine	XF
A117B	**5 Dollars** 1.5.1922. Green and yellow. River scene at center. Printer: BEPP.			
	a. *SHANGHAI. (S/M #N23-).*	250	750	3,750
	b. *HANKOW. (S/M #N23-).*	200	500	2,625

1922 Yuan Issue

		VG	VF	UNC
A117C	**1 Yüan** 1922. Red. Agricultural workers. Printer: Wu Foong Industrial Development Co. Ltd., Peking. *(S/M #N23-).*			
	s1. Specimen.	—	—	800
	s2. Specimen perforated: *UNGÜLTIG.*	—	—	800
A117D	**5 Yüan** 1922. Dark brown and violet. Agricultural workers. Similar to #A117C. Printer: Wu Foong Industrial Development Co. Ltd., Peking. Specimen. *(S/M #N23-).*	**VG** —	**VF** —	**UNC** 800

1926 Issue

		Good	Fine	XF
A118	**1 Yüan** 1.12.1926. Brown and multicolor. Pagoda on hilltop, shoreline at center. Printer: ABNC. *SHANGHAI. (S/M #N23-10).*			
	a. Issued note.	125	400	1,350
	s. Specimen. Uniface face and back.	—	Unc	750

A119 5 Yüan	Good	Fine	XF
1.12.1926. Green and multicolor. Pagoda on hilltop, shoreline at center. Printer: ABNC.			
a. *SHANGHAI.* with various numerical overprint: 3; 6; 10; 21. *(S/M #N23-11a).*	100	275	1,400
b. *CHANGSHA. (S/M #N23-11b).*	100	275	1,600
c. *HANKOW. (S/M #N23-11c).*	100	275	1,400
s1. As a. Specimen. Uniface face and back.	—	Unc	1,300
s2. As c. Specimen. Uniface face and back.	—	Unc	1,300
s3. Peking. Specimen. Uniface face and back.	—	Unc	1,300

A120 10 Yüan	Good	Fine	XF
1.12.1926. Purple and blue. Pagoda on hilltop, shoreline at center. Printer: ABNC. *SHANGHAI. (S/M #N23-12).*			
a. Issued note.	125	400	2,600
s1. Specimen. Uniface face and back.	—	Unc	1,300
s2. *Hanken.* Specimen uniface face and back.	—	Unc	1,300
s3. Peking. Specimen.	—	Unc	1,300

China Silk and Tea Industrial Bank

中國絲茶銀行

Chung Kuo Szu Ch'a Yin Hang

1925 Issue

A120A 1 Dollar	Good	Fine	XF
15.8.1925. Blue on multicolor underprint. Harvesting tea at center. Back: Weaving at center. Printer: BEPP.			
a. *PEKING. (S/M #C292-1a).*	75.00	200	650
b. *TIENTSIN. (S/M #C292-1b).*	50.00	150	450
c. *CHENGCHOW / PEKING. (S/M #C292-1c).*	125	400	1,250

A120B 5 Dollars	Good	Fine	XF
15.8.1925. Orange on multicolor underprint. Harvesting tea at center. Back: Weaving at center. Printer: BEPP.			
a. *PEKING. (S/M #C292-2a).*	125	350	1,500
b. *TIENTSIN. (S/M #C292-2b).*	100	250	1,275
c. *CHENGCHOW / PEKING. (S/M #C292-2c).*	150	450	2,475

A120C 10 Dollars	Good	Fine	XF
15.8.1925. Green on multicolor underprint. Harvesting tea at center. Back: Weaving at center. Printer: BEPP.			
a. *PEKING. (S/M #C292-3a).*	200	600	3,375
b. *TIENTSIN. (S/M #C292-3b).*	200	600	3,000
c. *CHENGCHOW / PEKING. (S/M #C292-3c).*	225	850	6,000

China and South Sea Bank, Limited

中南銀行

Chung Nan Yin Hang

Established 1921. Though bearing only the China and South Sea Bank's name, all these notes were backed and circulated by a coalition of four major Shanghai banks, of which the issuer was one. These notes achieved wide circulation and acceptance.

1921 Issue

A121 1 Yüan	Good	Fine	XF
1.10.1921. Blue on multicolor underprint. Monument at center. Signature varieties.			
a. *SHANGHAI.* Title: *CHAIRMAN* below signature on back. *(S/M #C295-1a).*	50.00	250	700
b. *SHANGHAI.* Without title: *CHAIRMAN* below signature on back. *(S/M #C295-1a).*	50.00	175	600
c. *HANKOW.* Title: *CHAIRMAN* below signature on back. *(S/M #295-1b).*	100	350	1,000
d. *TIENTSIN. (S/M #C295-1c).*	150	600	2,000
e. *AMOY.*	100	425	2,100

A122 5 Yüan	Good	Fine	XF
1.10.1921. Common with various letter and numerical control overprint. Purple on multicolor underprint. Monument at left. Back: Title: *CHAIRMAN* below signature on back. Printer: ABNC. *SHANGHAI. (S/M #C295-2).*	100	275	800

A123 10 Yüan	Good	Fine	XF
1.10.1921. Common with various letter and numerical control overprint. Black and multicolor. Monument at right. Printer: ABNC.			
a. *SHANGHAI. (S/M #C295-3a).*	125	400	1,400
b. *TIENTSIN. (S/M #C295-3b).*	300	800	2,750
c. *HANKOW. (S/M #C295-3c).*	225	600	1,900

A123A 50 Yüan	Good	Fine	XF
1.10.1921. Common with various letter and numerical control overprint. Monument at center. Printer: ABNC. *SHANGHAI. (S/M #C295-4).*	—	—	—

A123B 100 Yüan	Good	Fine	XF
1.10.1921. Monument at left. Proof.	—	—	—

1924 Issue

A124 5 Yüan	Good	Fine	XF
1924. Purple and multicolor. Monument at left. Like #A122. Printer: ABNC. Common with letter control overprint: SK or SY.			
a. *SHANGHAI. (S/M #C295-10a).*	100	225	2,000
b. *TIENTSIN. (S/M #C295-10b).*	100	200	1,500
c. *HANKOW. (S/M #C295-10c).*	120	300	2,200
d. *AMOY. (S/M #C295-10d).*	120	300	2,200

A125 10 Yüan	Good	Fine	XF
1924. Black and multicolor. Monument at right. Like #A123. Printer: ABNC. Common with letter control overprint: SK or SY.			
a. *SHANGHAI. (S/M #C295-11a).*	75.00	175	550
b. *TIENTSIN. (S/M #C295-11b).*	75.00	225	600
c. *HANKOW. (S/M #C295-11c).*	75.00	225	600
d. *AMOY. (S/M #C295-11d).*	90.00	300	1,000

1927 Issue

A126 1 Yüan	Good	Fine	XF
1927. Purple and multicolor. Three women's busts over dollar coin at center. Back: Two women's busts over Yuan Shih Kai dollar coin. Printer: W&S.			
a. *SHANGHAI.* With various control overprints. *(S/M #C295-20a).*	100	400	2,250
b. *TIENTSIN. (S/M #C295-20b).*	200	600	3,000

A127 5 Yüan	Good	Fine	XF
1927. Red and multicolor. Monument at left. Similar to #A124. Printer: ABNC. With various numerical, letter or Chinese character control overprints.			
a. *HANKOW. (S/M #C295-21b).*	125	500	1,400
b. *SHANGHAI. (S/M #C295-21a).*	125	500	1,400
c. *TIENTSIN.*	225	600	—

A128 5 Yüan	Good	Fine	XF
1927. Purple and multicolor. Two women's busts at left and right. Similar to #A129. Back: Three women's busts at left, center and right. Printer: ABNC. *SHANGHAI.* With various letter or Chinese character control overprints. *(S/M #C295-22).*	125	500	1,750

A129 10 Yüan	VG	VF	UNC
1927. Brown and red. Two women's busts at left and right. 2 signature varieties. Back: Three women's busts at left, center and right. Printer: W&S.			
a. *SHANGHAI.* With various letter or Chinese character control overprints. *(S/M #C295-23).*	—	—	—
s. Specimen. Punch hole Cancelled.	—	—	850

A130 50 Yüan	Good	Fine	XF
1927. Purple. Printer: ABNC. *(S/M #C295-24).* Requires confirmation.	—	—	—

A131 100 Yüan	Good	Fine	XF
1927. Red. Printer: ABNC. *(S/M #C295-25).* Requires confirmation.	—	—	—

1931-1932 Issue

A132 1 Yüan	Good	Fine	XF
1931. Blue and multicolor. Monument at left. Printer: W&S.			
a. *SHANGHAI. (S/M*	75	150	975
b. *TIENTSIN. (S/M #C295-30b).*	150	500	1,800

A133 5 Yüan	Good	Fine	XF
Jan. 1932. Purple and multicolor. Printer: TDLR. *SHANGHAI. (S/M #C295-40).*	125	500	1,750

Commercial Bank of China 中國通商銀行

Chung Kuo T'ung Shang Yin Hang

Formerly the Imperial Bank of China. Earlier issues have been reported to exist w/ Republic period ovpts. The issues of the Commercial Bank are also found w/various numerical, letter or Chinese character ovpt.

1913 Provisional Tael Issue

A133A 1 Tael	Good	Fine	XF
ND. (1913-old date 22.1.1898). Purple, brown and red on yellow underprint. Two dragons supporting shield at upper center. *(S/M #C293-).*	1,750	7,000	25,000

1913 Provisional Dollar Issue

		Good	Fine	XF
A133B	**5 Dollars** ND (1913-old date 16.2.1904). Black and multicolor. Two dragons supporting shield at upper center. *(S/M #C293-).*	2,000	8,000	30,000

		Good	Fine	XF
A133C	**10 Dollars** ND (1913-old date 16.2.1904). Black on multicolor underprint. Two dragons supporting shield at upper center. *(S/M #C293-).*	2,400	9,000	37,500

1920 Shanghai Tael Issue

		Good	Fine	XF
A134	**1 Tael** 15.1.1920. Blue on multicolor underprint. Confucius standing at center. Back: Medallion supported by two lions. Printer: ABNC. *(S/M #C293-30).*			
	a. Issued note.	250	400	1,400
	p. Proof.	—	Unc	400
	s. Specimen.	—	Unc	225
A135	**5 Taels** 15.1.1920. Yellow-orange on multicolor underprint. Confucius standing at center. Back: Medallion supported by two lions. Printer: ABNC. *(S/M #C293-31).*	Good	Fine	XF
	a. Issued note.	300	750	4,000
	p. Proof.	—	Unc	500
	s. Specimen.	—	Unc	500

		Good	Fine	XF
A136	**10 Taels** 15.1.1920. Purple on multicolor underprint. Confucius standing at center. Back: Medallion supported by two lions. Printer: ABNC. *(S/M #C293-32).*			
	a. Issued note.	450	1,100	4,000
	p. Proof.	—	Unc	600
	s. Specimen.	—	Unc	550
A137	**50 Taels** 15.1.1920. Confucius standing at center. Back: Medallion supported by two lions. Printer: ABNC. *(S/M #C293-33).* Requires confirmation.	Good —	Fine —	XF —
A138	**100 Taels** 15.1.1920. Requires confirmation. Confucius standing at center. Back: Medallion supported by two lions. Printer: ABNC. *(S/M #C293-34).*	Good —	Fine —	XF —

1920 Dollar Issue

		Good	Fine	XF
1	**1 Dollar** 15.1.1920. Black and multicolor. Worthy standing at center. Back: Medallion supported by two lions. Printer: ABNC. *(S/M #C293-40).*			
	a. Issued note.	80.00	350	1,000
	p. Proof.	—	Unc	400
	s. Specimen.	—	Unc	300
2	**1 Dollar** 15.1.1920. Blue and multicolor. Worthy standing at center. Back: Medallion supported by two lions. Printer: ABNC. *(S/M #C293-41).*	Good	Fine	XF
	a. Issued note.	75.00	200	600
	b. With character overprint: *Yuan.*	75.00	200	550
	p. Proof.	—	Unc	250
	s. Specimen.	—	Unc	200

		Good	Fine	XF
3	**5 Dollars** 15.1.1920. Purple and multicolor. Worthy standing at center. Back: Medallion supported by two lions. Printer: ABNC. *(S/M #C293-42).*			
	a. Issued note.	25.00	275	700
	b. With character overprint: *Yuan.*	25.00	200	500
	s. Specimen.	—	Unc	300
4	**5 Dollars** 15.1.1920. Yellow and multicolor. Worthy standing at center. Back: Medallion supported by two lions. Printer: ABNC. *(S/M #C293-43).*	Good 75	Fine 225	XF 1,125

		Good	Fine	XF
4A	**5 Dollars** 15.1.1920. Brown and multicolor. Worthy standing at center. Back: Medallion supported by two lions. Printer: ABNC. *(S/M #293-).*			
	a. Issued note.	275	750	3,000
	p. Proof.	—	Unc	800
	s. Specimen.	—	Unc	550

		Good	Fine	XF
5	**10 Dollars** 15.1.1920. Yellow and multicolor. Worthy standing at center. Back: Medallion supported by two lions. Printer: ABNC. *(S/M #C293-44).*			
	a. Issued note.	200	600	2,640
	b. With character overprint	100	300	1,000
	p. Proof.	—	Unc	750
	s. Specimen.	—	Unc	600

		Good	Fine	XF
6	**10 Dollars** 15.1.1920. Red and multicolor. Worthy standing at center. Back: Medallion supported by two lions. Printer: ABNC. *(S/M #C293-45).*			
	a. Issued note.	100	250	1,425
	b. With character overprint.	100	250	1,125
	p. Proof.	—	Unc	500
	s. Specimen.	—	Unc	600

		Good	Fine	XF
7	**50 Dollars** 15.1.1920. Blue and multicolor. Worthy standing at center. Back: Medallion supported by two lions. Printer: ABNC. *(S/M #C293-46).*			
	a. Issued note.	1,400	3,500	—
	p. Proof.	—	Unc	800
	s. Specimen.	—	Unc	750

		Good	Fine	XF
8	**100 Dollars** 15.1.1920. Olive-green and multicolor. Worthy standing at center. Back: Medallion supported by two lions. Printer: ABNC. *(S/M #C293-47).*			
	a. Issued note.	2,160	9,600	—
	p. Proof.	—	Unc	2,200
	s. Specimen.	—	Unc	2,000

1926 Shanghai Issue

		Good	Fine	XF
9	**5 Dollars** Jan. 1926. Green and multicolor. Harbor scene at left, Confucius standing at right. Back: Medallion supported by two lions. Printer: W&S. *(S/M #C293-50).*	100	250	1,000

		Good	Fine	XF
10	**10 Dollars** Jan. 1926. Brown and multicolor. Harbor scene at left, Confucius standing at right. Back: Medallion supported by two lions. Printer: W&S. *(S/M #C293-51).*	150	500	1,200

1929 National Currency Issue

#	Denomination	Good	Fine	XF
11	**1 Dollar** Jan. 1929. Black and green. Medallion supported by lions at top center, Confucius standing at right. Back: Medallion supported by two lions.			
	a. *SHANGHAI. (S/M #C292-60a).*	50.00	150	660
	b. *SHANGHAI/AMOY. (S/M #C293-60b).*	75.00	225	900
	c. *HANKOW. (S/M #C293-60c).*	125	350	1,080
	d. *AMOY. (S/M #C293-60d).*	150	750	1,800

1929 Shanghai Currency Issue

#	Denomination	Good	Fine	XF
12	**1 Dollar** Jan. 1929. Black and yellow. Medallion supported by lions at top center, Confucius standing at right. Similar to #13. Back: Medallion supported by two lions. *SHANGHAI. (S/M #C293-61).*	100.00	250	800

#	Denomination	Good	Fine	XF
13	**1 Dollar** Jan. 1929. Blue and multicolor. Medallion supported by lions at top center, Confucius standing at right. Back: Medallion supported by two lions. *SHANGHAI. (S/M #C293-62).*	60.00	175	1,200
13A	**1 Dollar** 1929. Purple. *(S/M #C293-63).*	60	175	600

1932 Issue

#14-15 with and without various Chinese character control overprints.

#	Denomination	Good	Fine	XF
14	**5 Dollars** June 1932. Purple and multicolor. Harbor scene at left, Confucius standing at right. Similar to #9. Back: Medallion supported by two lions. Printer: W&S.			
	a. *SHANGHAI. (S/M #C293-70a).*	100	350	1,020
	b. *AMOY. (S/M #C293-70b).*	150	450	1,560
	s. Specimen. As b.	—		

#	Denomination	Good	Fine	XF
15	**10 Dollars** June 1932. Red and multicolor. Harbor scene at left, Confucius standing at right. Similar to #10. Printer: W&S. *SHANGHAI. (S/M #C293-71).*	75.00	225	900

Bank of China

КИТАЙСКIЙ БАНКЪ

中國銀行

Chung Kuo Yin Hang

1912 Provisional Issue

#16-18 overprint of new issuer name on Ta Ching Government Bank notes.

#	Denomination	Good	Fine	XF
16	**1 Dollar** ND (1912 - old date 1.10.1909). Olive-brown on red-orange underprint. Portrait Li Hung Chan at left. Hillside village, railroad at right. Signature varieties. Back: Water-front park at center.			
	a. Overprint: *Chung Kuo* at left and *Yin Hang* at right. Dated yr. 1. *(S/M #C294-1a).*	1,500	7000	24,750
	b. *HANKOW. (S/M #C294-1b).*	1,500	7000	30,000
	c. *HONAN. (S/M #C294-1c).*	1,500	7000	29,250
	d. *PEKING. (S/M #C294-1d).*	1,250	8,000	26,250
	e. *SHANTUNG. (S/M #C294-1e).*	1,500	10,000	30,000
	f. *SHANTUNG/CHIHLI. (S/M #C294-1f).*	1,750	10,000	33,000
	g. *TIENTSIN* overprint in red on #16a. *(S/M #C294-1g).*	2,000	10,000	30,000
	h. *SHANGHAI. (S/M #C294-1h).*	2,100	10,000	33,000
	i. *MANCHURIA (S/M #C294-1i).*	2,300	12,500	37,500
	j. *CHIHLI (S/M #C294-1j).*	2,200	10,000	30,000

17	**5 Dollars**	Good	Fine	XF
	ND (1912 - old date 1.10.1909). Brown on blue and multicolor underprint. Portrait Li Hung Chan at left. Gazebo at right. Signature varieties. Back: Hillside pagoda, village at center.			
	a. Overprint: *Chung Kuo* at left and *Yin Hang* at right. *(S/M #C294-2a).*	1,800	7,000	30,000
	b. *HANKOW. (S/M (S/M #C294-2b).*	2,250	10,000	37,500
	c. *HONAN. (S/M #C294-2c).*	6750	10,000	37,500
	d. *PEKING. (S/M #C294-2d).*	1,800	7,000	30,000
	e. *SHANTUNG. (S/M #C294-2e).*	2,250	1,000	37,500
	f. *SHANTUNG/CHIHLI. (S/M #C294-2f).).*	3,600	13,000	41,250
	g. *TIENTSIN. (S/M #C294-2g).*	3,600	7,500	30,000
	h. *TIENTSIN/PEKING. (S/M #C294-2h).*	3,600	13,000	41,250
	i. *SHANGHAI. (S/M #C294-2i).*	2,250	10,000	37,500
	j. *MANCHURIA. (S/M #C294-2j).*	2,250	10,000	37,500

18	**10 Dollars**	Good	Fine	XF
	ND (1912 - old date 1.10.1909). Portrait Li Hung Chan at left. Teahouse at right. Signature varieties. Back: Great Wall at center.			
	a. Overprint: *Chung Kuo* at left. *Yin Hang* at right. (S/M #C294-3a).	4,250	15,000	41,250
	b. *HANKOW. (S/M #C294-3b).*	5,500	15,000	45,000
	c. *HONAN. (S/M #C294-3c).*	5,500	15,000	45,000
	d. *PEKING. (S/M #C294-3d).*	4,250	13,000	41,250
	e. *SHANTUNG. (S/M #C294-3e).*	3,250	15,000	45,000
	f. *SHANTUNG/CHIHLI. (S/M #C294-3f).*	3,250	13,000	41,250
	g. *TIENTSIN. (S/M #C294-3g).*	3,250	13,000	41,250

#19-24 *Not assigned.*

1912 Issue

25	**1 Dollar**	Good	Fine	XF
	1.6.1912. Dark green on multicolor underprint. Portrait Emperor Huang-ti at left. Hillside village, railroad at right. Back: Waterfront park at center. Printer: ABNC.			
	a. *ANHWEI. (S/M #C294-30a).*	400	1,800	7,500
	b. *CANTON. (S/M #C294-30b).*	125	350	1,300
	c. *CHEFOO. (S/M #C294-30c).*	600	2,500	12,000
	d. *CHEHKIANG. (S/M #C294-30d).*	500	2,200	10,500
	e. *FUHKIEN* (Fukien). *(S/M #C294-30e).*	500	2,200	11,250
	f. *HANKOW. (S/M #C294-30f).*	400	1,800	7,500
	g. *HONAN. (S/M #C294-30g).*	500	2,000	9,000
	h. *KIANGSI. (S/M #C294-30h).*	400	1,800	7,500
	i. *KIANGSU. (S/M #C294-30i).*	400	1,800	7,500
	j. *KUEISUI. (S/M #C294-30j).*	500	2,400	8,625
	k1. *KWANGTUNG.* Overprint: *N.B. Payable in subsidiary (silver) coins... on back. (S/M #C294-30k).*	200	450	1,440
	k2. *KWEICHOW.*	500	1,200	—
	l. *MANCHURIA. (S/M #C294-30l).*	300	900	3,000
	m. *MUKDEN. (S/M #C294-30m).*	300	1,350	4,500
	n. *SHANSI. (S/M #C294-30n).*	500	3,300	11,250
	o. *SHANTUNG. (S/M #C294-30o).*	500	3,300	11,250
	p. *Szechuen* in Chinese characters in oval frames at left and right edge on face. Large *SZECHUEN* below date at bottom center on back. *(S/M #C294-30p).*	500	2,700	6,750
	q. *One Dollar* in Chinese characters in oval frames at left and right edge on face. *One Dollar* / small *SZECHUEN* below date at bottom center on back. *(S/M #C294-30p).*	500	2,700	6,000
	r. *THREE EASTERN PROVINCES. (S/M #C294-30q).*	800	2,400	8,250
	s. *YUNNAN. (S/M #C294-30r).*	300	600	3,600
	t. *SHANGHAI. (S/M #C294-30s).*	400	1,000	7,500
	u. *TIENTSIN. (S/M #C294-30t).*	500	2,000	7,500
	v. КАЛГАНъ (Kalgan). *(S/M #C294-30u).*	500	2,500	7,500
	w. *PEKING. (S/M #C294-30w).*	500	2,750	9,000

26	**5 Dollars**	Good	Fine	XF
	1.6.1912. Black on multicolor underprint. Portrait Emperor Huang-ti at left, gazebo at right. Back: Hillside pagoda, village at center. Printer: ABNC.			
	a. *ANHWEI. (S/M #C294-31a).*	800	2,400	13,500
	b. *CANTON. (S/M #C294-31b).*	180	900	3,300
	c. *CHEFOO. (S/M #C294-31c).*	600	2,400	11,250
	d. *CHEHKIANG. (S/M #C294-31d).*	1,000	4,000	18,750
	e. *FUHKIEN* (Fukien). *(S/M #C294-31e).*	1,000	4,000	18,750
	f. *HANKOW. (S/M #C294-31f).*	900	3,600	17,250
	g. *HONAN. (S/M #C294-31g).*	1,000	4,800	18,750
	h. *KIANGSI. (S/M #C294-31h).*	750	3,000	13,500
	i. *KIANGSU. (S/M #C294-31i).*	600	2,400	12,000
	j. *KUEISUI. (S/M #C294-31j).*	1,500	8,000	24,750
	k. *KWANGTUNG.* Overprint *N.B. Payable in subsidiary (silver) coins on back. (S/M #C294-31k).*	300	900	6,000
	l. *MANCHURIA. (S/M #C294-31l).*	600	800	5,250
	m. *MUKDEN. (S/M #C294-31m).*	800	2,000	12,000
	n. *SHANSI. (S/M #C294-31n).*	800	3,000	15,000
	o. *SHANTUNG. (S/M #C294-31o).*	600	2,200	11,250
	p. *SZECHUAN. (S/M #C294-31p).*	600	2,400	12,750
	q. *THREE EASTERN PROVINCES. (S/M #C294-31q).*	1,200	5,400	14,000
	r. *YUNNAN. (S/M #C294-31r).*	150	600	2,200
	s. *KWEICHOW. (S/M #C294-).*	450	2,100	6,500
	t. Without place name. Specimen. *(S/M #C294-).*	—	Unc	750
	u. *SHANGHAI.*	300	1,500	—
	v. *TIENTSIN.*	300	1,500	—

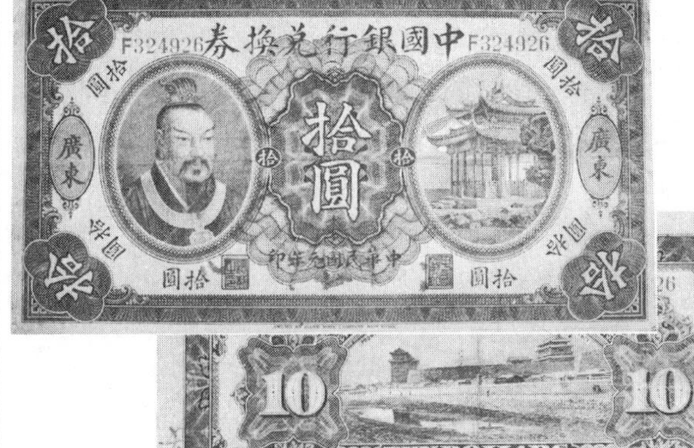

27	**10 Dollars**	Good	Fine	XF
	1.6.1912. Deep blue on multicolor underprint. Portrait Emperor Huang-ti at left, teahouse at right. Back: Great Wall at center. Printer: ABNC.			
	a. *ANHWEI. (S/M #C294-32a).*	900	5,250	10,250
	b. *CANTON. (S/M #C294-32b).*	225	800	2,640
	c. *CHEFOO. (S/M #C294-32c).*	1,000	6,500	19,875
	d. *CHEHKIANG. (S/M #C294-32d).*	900	6,500	36,000
	e. *FUHKIEN* (Fukien). *(S/M #C294-32e).*	900	6,500	36,000
	f. *HANKOW. (S/M #C294-32f).*	950	7,000	19,875
	g. *HONAN. (S/M #C294-32g).*	900	5,500	16,500
	h. *KIANGSI. (S/M #C294-32h).*	750	4,500	13,125
	i. *KIANGSU. (S/M #C294-32i).*	750	5,000	14,400
	j. *KUEISUI. (S/M #C294-32j).*	1,100	6,500	18,900
	k. *KWANGTUNG.* Overprint: *N.B. Payable in subsidiary (silver) coins...* on back. *(S/M #C294-32k).*	300	1,600	4,320
	l. *MANCHURIA. (S/M #C294-32l).*	450	2,000	4,500
	m. *MUKDEN. (S/M #C294-32m).*	450	1,800	9,900

		Good	Fine	XF
	n. *SHANSI. (S/M #C294-32n).*	750	5,000	14,625
	o. *SHANTUNG. (S/M #C294-32o).*	600	3,750	11,250
	p. *SZECHUAN. (S/M #C294-32p).*	650	3,750	11,250
	q. *THREE EASTERN PROVINCES. (S/M #C294-32q).*	1,100	6,600	18,900
	r. *YUNNAN. (S/M #C294-32r).*	125	500	2,400
	s. *SHANGHAI. (S/M #C294-32s).*	600	3,000	6,600
	t. Without place name. Specimen. *(S/M #C294-).*	—	Unc	2,200

#28 Not assigned.

1913 Provisional Issue

#29 and 29A overprint new bank name on notes of the Provincial Bank of Kwangtung Province.#28 ***Deleted.***

		Good	Fine	XF
29	**5 Dollars** ND (-old date 1.1.1913). Dark green on multicolor underprint. Large building at center. *(S/M #C294-41).*	175	650	2,400
29A	**10 Dollars** ND (-old date 1.1.1913). *(S/M #C294-42).*	375	1,600	5,300

1913 Regular Issue

		Good	Fine	XF
30	**1 Dollar** 1.6.1913. Olive and red. Portrait Emperor Huang-ti at left. Hillside village, railroad at right. Similar to #25. Back: Waterfront park at center. Printer: ABNC.			
	a. *CANTON. (S/M #C294-42a).*	250	1,000	2,500
	b. *FUKIEN. (S/M #C294-42b).*	900	5,000	16,500
	c. *SHANTUNG. (S/M #C294-42c).*	150	850	1,800
	d. *SHANSI. (S/M #C294-42d).*	1,100	6,000	18,000
	e. Without place name. (S/M #C294-42).	175	1,000	2,200
31	**5 Dollars** 1.6.1913. Black and brown on blue and multicolor underprint. Portrait Emperor Huang-ti at left, gazebo at right. Similar to #26. Back: Hillside pagoda, village at center. Printer: ABNC.	**Good**	**Fine**	**XF**
	a. *CANTON. (S/M #C294-43a).*	1,500	6,500	3,000
	b. *FUKIEN. (S/M #C294-43b).*	1,800	8,750	32,400
	c. *SHANTUNG. (S/M #C294-43c).*	1,800	9,600	34,800
32	**10 Dollars** 1.6.1913. Portrait Emperor Huang-ti at left, teahouse at right. Similar to #27. Back: Great Wall at center. Printer: ABNC.	**Good**	**Fine**	**XF**
	a. *CANTON. (S/M #C294-44a).*	1,800	8,050	28,800
	b. *FUKIEN. (S/M #C294-44b).*	1,800	13,000	31,800
	c. *SHANTUNG. (S/M #C294-44c).*	2,400	8,700	3,000
32A	**50 Dollars** 1.6.1913. Purple on multicolor underprint. Portrait Emperor Huang-ti at left, large building at right. Printer: ABNC. *PEKING.* Specimen perforated with Chinese characters. *(S/M #C294-45a).*	**Good** —	**Fine** Unc	**XF** 32,500

		Good	Fine	XF
32B	**100 Dollars** 1.6.1913. Dark olive-green on multicolor underprint. Portrait Emperor Huang-ti at left, Temple of Heaven at right. Printer: ABNC. *PEKING.* Specimen perforated with Chinese characters. *(S/M #C294-46a).*	—	Unc	8,000

1914 Provisional Issue

		Good	Fine	XF
32C	**1 Dollar** 1914 (-old date-1.10.1909). Olive-brown on red-orange underprint. Portrait Li Hung Chan at left. Hillside village, railroad at right. Back: Waterfront park at center. *CHIHLI. (S/M #C294-46).*	—	—	—

1914 "Yuan Shih-kai" Issue

		VG	VF	UNC
33	**1 Yüan** 4.10.1914. Black on multicolor underprint. Portrait Yuan Shih-kai at center. Printer: ABNC. Unsigned remainder with or without perforated "cancelled" in Chinese characters. *(S/M #294-50).*	—	2,200	6,000
34	**5 Yüan** 4.10.1914. Black on multicolor underprint. Portrait Yuan Shih-kai at center. Printer: ABNC. Unsigned remainder with or without perforated "cancelled" in Chinese characters. *(S/M #294-51).*	**VG** —	**VF** 3,600	**UNC** 10,800
35	**10 Yüan** 4.10.1914. Black on multicolor underprint. Portrait Yuan Shih-kai at center. Printer: ABNC. Unsigned remainder with or without perforated "cancelled" in Chinese characters. *(S/M #294-52).*	**VG** —	**VF** 4,400	**UNC** 10,800

		VG	VF	UNC
35A	**50 Yüan** 4.10.1914. Black on multicolor underprint. Portrait Yuan Shih-kai at center. Printer: ABNC. Unsigned remainder with or without perforated "cancelled" in Chinese characters. *(S/M #294-53).*	—	—	—

		VG	VF	UNC
35B	**100 Yüan** 4.10.1914. Black on multicolor underprint. Portrait Yuan Shih-kai at center. Printer: ABNC. Unsigned remainder with or without perforated "cancelled" in Chinese characters. *(S/M #C294-54).*	—	—	—

1914 "Small Change" Issue

		VG	VF	UNC
36	**20 Cents** 1.12.1914. Great Wall at center. Printer: BEPP.			
	a. Black on green underprint. Back red. *MANCHURIA.*	140	3500	720
	b. As a, but back brown.	300	660	—
	c. Back orange. Black on green underprint. *MANCHURIA. (S/M #C294-60).* 2 signature varieties.	75.00	175	420

		VG	VF	UNC
37	**50 Cents** 1.12.1914. Brown on red underprint. Great Wall at center. Printer: BEPP. *MANCHURIA. (S/M #C294-61).*	100	425	1,200

1915 "Small Change" Issue

		Good	Fine	XF
37C	**50 Cents** 1.1.1915. *YUNNAN. (S/M #C294-).*	—	—	—

1915 "Huang Ti" Issue

#37A-37C *Renumbered.* See #37D-37F.

		VG	VF	UNC
37D	**1 Dollar** 1.7.1915. Green. Portrait Emperor Huang Ti at left. Printer: ABNC. Proof without signature or office of issue. *(S/M #C294-62).*	—	—	14,400

		VG	VF	UNC
37E	**5 Dollars** 1.7.1915. Black. Portrait Emperor Huang Ti at left. Printer: ABNC. Proof without signature or office of issue. *(S/M #C294-63).*	—	—	17,250

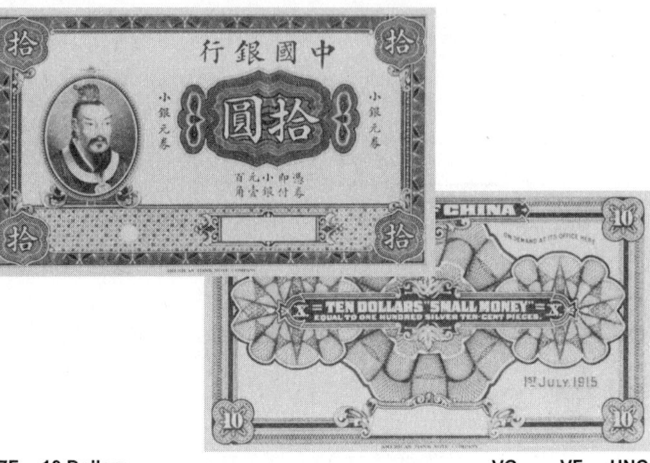

		VG	VF	UNC
37F	**10 Dollars** 1.7.1915. Blue. Portrait Emperor Huang Ti at left. Printer: ABNC. Proof without signature or office of issue. *(S/M #C294-64).*	—	—	40,500

1917 "Tsao Kuan" Issue

		VG	VF	UNC
37J	**1 Dollar** 1.5.1917. Black on blue, red and purple underprint. Portrait Tsao Kuan at left or right. Printer: ABNC. Proof without signature or office of issue. *(S/M #C294-65).*	—	—	25,125

		VG	VF	UNC
37K	**5 Dollars** 1.5.1917. Black on blue, red and green underprint. Portrait Tsao Kuan at left or right. Printer: ABNC. Proof without signature or office of issue. *(S/M #C294-66).*	—	—	40,500

		VG	VF	UNC
37L	**10 Dollars** 1.5.1917.. Black on red, blue and ochre underprint. Portrait Tsao Kuan at left or right. Printer: ABNC. Proof without signature or office of issue. *(S/M #C294-67)*	—	—	45,000

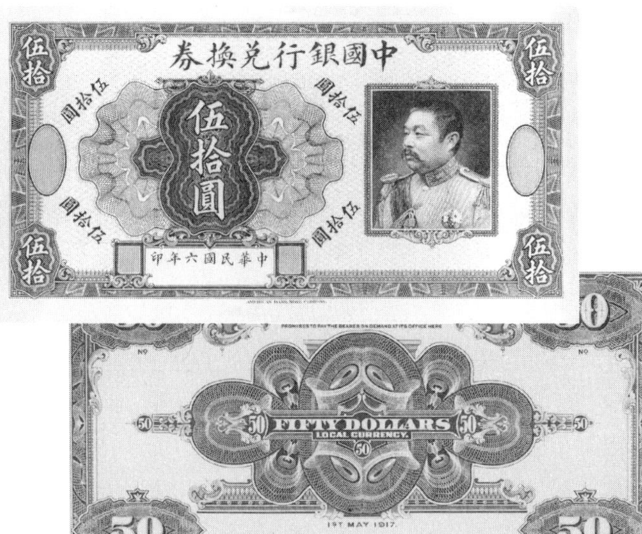

37M 50 Dollars | VG — | VF — | UNC 66,000

1.5.1917. Black on olive-green, red and blue underprint. Portrait Tsao Kuan at left or right. Printer: ABNC. Proof without signature or office of issue. *(S/M # #C294-68).*

37N 100 Dollars | VG — | VF — | UNC 54,000

1.5.1917. Black on blue, brown and green underprint. Portrait Tsao Kuan at left or right. Printer: ABNC. Proof without signature or office of issue. *(S/M #C294-69).*

1917 "Tientsin" Issue

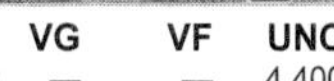

38 1 Dollar | VG — | VF — | UNC 4,400

Yr. 6//1.5.1917. Black on brown, purple and green underprint. Gateway at right. Printer: ABNC. *TIENTSIN.* Proof. *(S/M #C294-80).*

39 5 Dollars | VG — | VF — | UNC 5,300

Yr. 6//1.5.1917. Blue-black on red, blue and brown underprint. Gateway. Printer: ABNC. *TIENTSIN.* Proof. *(S/M #C294-81).*

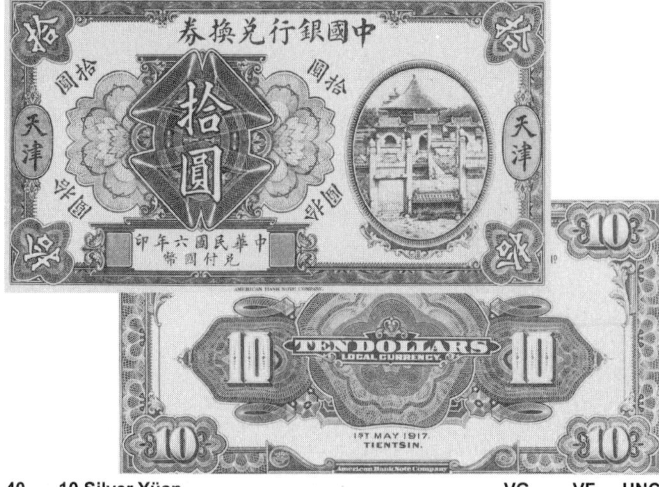

40 10 Silver Yüan | VG — | VF — | UNC 6,500

Yr. 6//1.5.1917. Black on blue, purple and green underprint. Gateway. Printer: ABNC. *TIENTSIN.* Proof. *(S/M #C294-82).*

Note: For similar notes dated year 7 / 1.5.1917 see #54A and 54C.

#40A *Deleted.* See #54.

1917 "Small Change" Issue

45A and 45B *Renumbered.* See #58 and 59.

41 5 Cents | Good 300 | Fine 975 | XF 2,550

1.10.1917. Brown. Printer: BEPP. *HARBIN.* *(S/M #C294-70).*

		Good	Fine	XF
42	**10 Cents = 1 Chiao**			
	1.10.1917. Green. Temple at left. Printer: BEPP.			
	a. *HARBIN. (S/M #C294-71).*	275	675	2,000
	b. *MANCHURIA. (S/M #C294-).*	180	425	4,200
	r. Remainder, without serial #, signature or place name. *(S/M #C294-).*	—	Unc	1,400

#	Description	Good	Fine	XF
43	**10 Cents = 1 Chiao**	**Good**	**Fine**	**XF**
	1.10.1917. Bridge at center. Printer: BEPP.			
	b. *HARBIN.* Orange. Exchange clause blocked out on face and back. Overprint new exchange clause in Chinese at left and right on back. *(S/M #C294-72b).*	175	600	3,975
	c. КАЛГАНъ *Kalgan in Chinese at left and right. Brown.(S/M #C294-72c).*	125	450	2,438
	d. *KIANGSI. (S/M #C294-72d).*	175	550	3,300
	e. *KUEISUI.* Green. *(S/M #C294-72e).*	450	1,800	8,100
	f. *MANCHURIA.* Orange. *(S/M #C294-72f).*	125	450	2,175
	g. *PAOTING.* Green. *(S/M #C294-72g).*	450	1,200	6,300
	h. *SHANSI.* Brown. *(S/M #C294-72h).*	125	350	3,300
	i. *SHANGTUNG.* Purple. Back green. *(S/M #C294-72i).*	125	350	3,300
	j. *TSINGKIANGPU.* Red. *(S/M #C294-72j).*	450	1,800	8,100
	k. *TSINGTAO.* Brown. *(S/M #C294-72k).*	175	700	3,300
	l. *TSINGTAO/SHANTUNG. (S/M #C294-72l).*	200	900	3,960
	m. КАЛГАНъ in Manchu at left, Chinese at right on face. Green. Back purple; Russian text. (S/M #C294-72m).	150	600	2,700
	r. Remainder, without serial #, signature or place name. Green. Back purple. *(S/M #C294-72a).*	—	Unc	1,650

#	Description	Good	Fine	XF
44	**20 Cents = 2 Chiao**	**Good**	**Fine**	**XF**
	1.10.1917. Pagoda on hill at shoreline at center. Printer: BEPP.			
	b. *HARBIN.* Violet. Exchange clause blocked out on face and back. Overprint new exchange clause in Chinese at left and right on back. *(S/M #C294-73b).*	150	450	2,700
	c. КАЛГАНъ (Kalgan). Black. Back dark brown. *(S/M #C294-73c).*	200	900	3,600
	d. *KIANGSI.* Red. *(S/M #C294-73d).*	300	1,200	5,400
	e. *KUEISUI.* Brown. *(S/M #C294-73e).*	400	1,800	8,250
	f. *MANCHURIA. (S/M #C294-73f).*	200	1,100	4,125
	g. *PAOTING.* Orange. *(S/M #C294-73g).*	450	1,800	8,288
	h. *SHANSI.* Green. *(S/M #C294-73h).*	300	1,600	6,000
	i. *SHANGTUNG. (S/M #C294-73i).*	300	1,500	6,000
	j. *TSINGKIANGPU. (S/M #C294-73j).*	450	2,300	9,750
	k. *TSINGTAO.* Orange. *(S/M #C294-73k).*	300	1,500	6,600
	l. *TSINGTAO/SHANTUNG. (S/M #C294-73l).*	350	1,500	6,600
	r. Remainder without serial #, signature or place name. Green. Back violet. *(S/M #C294-73a).*	—	Unc	1,650

#	Description	Good	Fine	XF
45	**50 Cents = 5 Chiao**	**Good**	**Fine**	**XF**
	1.10.1917. Various colors. Bridge with building in background at center. Printer: BEPP.			
	b. *HARBIN.* Exchange clause blocked out on face and back. Overprint new exchange clause in Chinese at left and right on back. *(S/M #C294-74b).*	60.00	175	1,500
	c. КАЛГАНъ (Kalgan). *(S/M #C294-74c).*	450	2,200	8,250
	d. *KIANGSI. (S/M #C294-74d).*	350	1,900	6,600
	e. *KUEISUI. (S/M #C294-74e).*	350	1,800	6,600
	f. *MANCHURIA. (S/M #C294-74f).*	300	1,325	5,100
	g. *PAOTING. (S/M #C294-74g).*	550	2,750	9,750
	h. *SHANSI. (S/M #C294-74h).*	550	2,750	9,750
	i. *SHANTUNG. (S/M #C294-74i).*	450	2,650	9,375
	j. *TSINGKIANGPU. (S/M #C294-74j).*	550	2,750	9,900
	k. *TSINGTAO. (S/M #C294-74k).*	550	2,750	9,900
	l. *TSINGTAO/SHANTUNG. (S/M #C294-74l).*	450	2,650	7,650
	r. Remainder without serial #, signature or place name. *(S/M #C294-74a).*	—	Unc	1,650

1918 ND Issue

#	Description	Good	Fine	XF
46	**5 Fen**	**Good**	**Fine**	**XF**
	ND (1918). Blue on red underprint. Chinese printer. *HARBIN. (S/M #C294-90).*	100	350	1,100

#	Description	Good	Fine	XF
46A	**5 Fen**	**Good**	**Fine**	**XF**
	ND (1918). Blue and red. Printer: BEPP. *HARBIN. (S/M #C294-91).*	150	350	2,160

1918 Issues

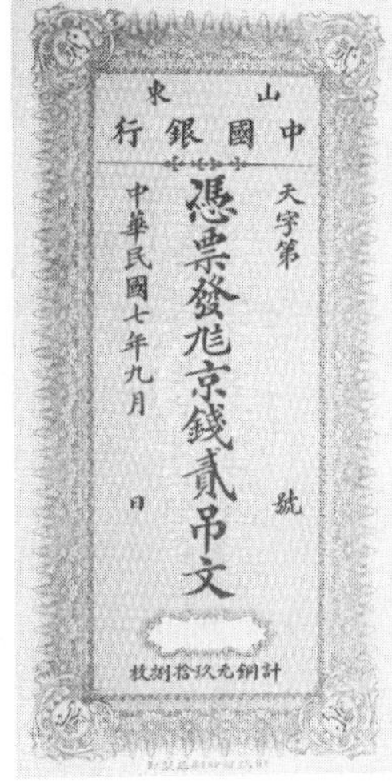

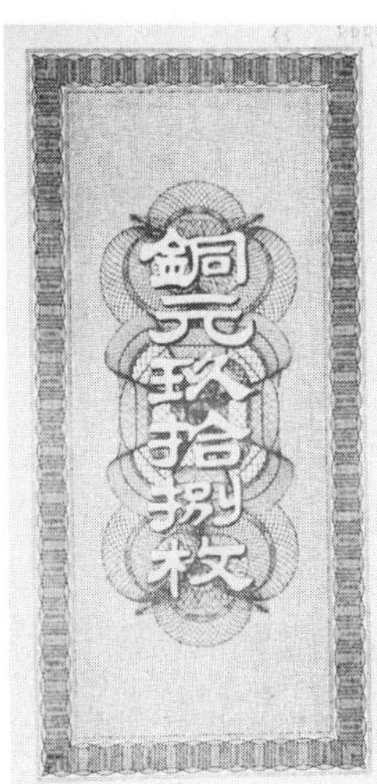

#	Description	Good	Fine	XF
47	**2 Tiao = 98 Copper Coins**	**Good**	**Fine**	**XF**
	Sept. 1918. Gray-green and orange.			
	r. Remainder without signature or serial #. *SHANTUNG. (S/M #C294-).*	—	Unc	8,100

#	Description	Good	Fine	XF
48	**10 Cents = 1 Chiao**	**Good**	**Fine**	**XF**
	Sept. 1918. Black and multicolor. Temple of Heaven at right. Signature varieties. Back: Bank name in Russian. Printer: ABNC. With various Chinese character or western numeral or letter control overprints.			
	a. *HARBIN. (S/M #C294-93a).*	15.00	32.50	185
	b. *SHANGHAI/HARBIN.* 2 signature varieties. *(S/M #C294-93b).*	15.00	32.50	185
	c. As a. But with red official 4-Chinese character overprint *(S/M #C294-93c).*	15.00	32.50	185
	s. As a. Specimen.	—	Unc	200

#	Description	Good	Fine	XF
49	**20 Cents = 2 Chiao**	**Good**	**Fine**	**XF**
	Sept. 1918. Black and multicolor. Temple of Heaven at left. Signature varieties. Back: Bank name in Russian. Printer: ABNC. With various Chinese character or western numeral or letter control overprints.			
	a. *HARBIN. (S/M #C294-94a).*	12.50	45.00	203
	b. *SHANGHAI/HARBIN. (S/M #C294-94b).*	9.00	45.00	188
	c. As a. But red official 4-Chinese character overprint *(S/M #C294-94c).*	12.50	45.00	203
	s. As a. Specimen.	—	Unc	225

50	50 Cents = 5 Chiao	Good	Fine	XF
	Sept. 1918. Green and multicolor. Temple of Heaven at left. Signature varieties. Back: Bank name in Russian. Printer: ABNC. With various Chinese character or western numeral or letter control overprints.			
	a. *HARBIN. (S/M #C294-95a).*	80.00	350	1,875
	b. *SHANGHAI/HARBIN. (S/M #C294-95b).*	30.00	150	675

51	1 Dollar or Yüan	Good	Fine	XF
	Sept. 1918. Color varieties. Temple of Heaven at center. Signature and serial # varieties. Printer: ABNC. With various Chinese character or western numeral or letter control overprints.			
	a. *AMOY-FUKIEN.* Green on multicolor underprint. Back green. *(S/M #C294-100d).*	25.00	90.00	225
	b. *ANHWEI.* Back red-orange. *(S/M #C294-100a).*	175	900	4,050
	c. *CHEFOO-SHANTUNG.* Orange. *(S/M #C294-100-).*	175	900	4,050
	d. *CHEKIANG.* Orange on multicolor underprint. Back dark green. *(S/M #C294-100q).*	175	900	4,050
	e. *CHENGTU-SZECHUAN.* Back orange. *(S/M #C294-100q).*	350	1,500	5,400
	f. *FUKIEN.* Green. *(S/M #C294-100c).*	75.00	350	1,125
	g. *HANKOW.* Green. Back orange. *(S/M #C294-100e).*	150	800	3,300
	h. *KALGAN.* Green. *(S/M #C294-100g).*	70.00	350	1,125
	i. *KIANGSI.* Orange on multicolor underprint. Back orange. *(S/M #C294-100h).*	175	800	3,300
	j. *KIANGSU.* Brown. Back brown. *(S/M #C294-100i).*	150	800	3,300
	k. *PEKING.* Blue-black. Back black. *(S/M #C294-100j).*	150	700	2,625
	l. *SHANGHAI/PEKING.* Blue-black. Back blue-black. *(S/M #C294-100k).*	100	450	1,100
	m. *SHANGHAI.* Brown. Back blue. 3 signature varieties. *(S/M #C294-100k).*	25.00	50.00	150
	n. *SHANSI.* Back purple. *(S/M #C294-100m).*	240	1,200	4,500
	o. *SHANTUNG.* Orange on multicolor underprint. Back orange. *(S/M #C294-100n).*	75.00	500	1,950
	p. *SZECHUAN.* Back red-orange. *(S/M #C294-100p).*	350	1500	5,100
	q. *TIENTSIN.* Brown. 2 signature varieties. *(S/M #C294-100r).*	25.00	70.00	175
	r. *TIENTSIN/KALGAN.* Green. Back green. *(S/M #C294-100s).*	60.00	275	975
	s. *TIENTSIN/PEKING.* Blue-black. *(S/M #C294-100-).*	100	450	1,650
	s1. *KIATING/SZECHUAN.* Orange. Specimen. *(S/M #C294-).*	—	Unc	1,650
	t. *TSINGTAO.* Back Orange. *(S/M #C294-100-).*	250	1,100	4,500
	u. *TSINGTAO/SHANTUNG.* Orange. (S/M #C294-100-).	200	900	3,300
	v. *KIUKIANG. (S/M #C294-100-).*	350	1,550	6,000
	w. *SHANTUNG WEIHAIWEI. (S/M #C294-100-).*	175	1,100	3,750

51A	1 Dollar	Good	Fine	XF
	Sept. 1918. Color varieties. Temple of Heaven at center. Signature and serial # varieties. Similar to #51. Back: Bank name in Russian text. Printer: ABNC. With various Chinese character or western numeral or letter control overprints.			
	a. *HARBIN. (S/M #C294-100f).*	600	2,400	7,200
	s. Specimen.	—	Unc	3,000

51B	1 Dollar	Good	Fine	XF
	Sept. 1918. Orange on multicolor underprint. Two buildings at right. Signature varieties. Printer: ABNC. With various Chinese character or western numeral or letter control overprints. *Shanghai.* Proof. *(S/M #C294-100.5).*	—	Unc	5,300

52	5 Dollars or Yüan	Good	Fine	XF
	Sept. 1918. Color varieties. Houses with Peking pagoda at center. Signature and serial # varieties. Printer: ABNC. Local or National Currency. With various Chinese character or western numeral or letter control overprints.			
	a. *AMOY-FUKIEN.* Purple. *(S/M #C294-101d).*	15.00	75.00	200
	b. *ANHWEI.* Blue-black. Back olive-green. *(S/M #C294-101a).*	175	800	2,625
	c. *CHEKIANG.* Green. Back blue. *(S/M #C294-101b).*	150	725	2,400
	d. *CHENGTU-SZECHUAN.* Back green. *(S/M #C294-101q).*	225	1,300	3,600
	e. *FUKIEN.* Purple. Back purple. Signature varieties. *(S/M #C294-101c).*	50.00	225	550
	f. *HANKOW.* Back brown. *(S/M #C294-101e).*	200	900	2,700
	g. *KALGAN.* Back purple. *(S/M #C294-101g).*	225	1,300	3,975
	h. *KIANGSI.* Back gray-brown. *(S/M #C294-101h).*	175	850	3,000
	i. *KIANGSU.* Brown. Back red-orange. *(S/M #C294-101i).*	150	725	2,700
	j. *PEKING.* Brown. *(S/M #C294-101j).*	175	850	3,000
	k. *SHANGHAI.* Dark blue. Signature varieties. *(S/M #C294-101k).*	75.00	275	1,200
	l. *SHANGHAI/PEKING.* Brown. *(S/M #C294-101l).*	125	550	2,000
	m. *SHANSI.* Back orange. *(S/M #C294-101m).*	175	900	3,300
	n. *SHANTUNG.* Green. Back dark green. *(S/M #C294-101n).*	150	725	2,700
	o. *SZECHUAN.* Back green. *(S/M #C94-101p).*	225	1,500	4,350
	p. *TIENTSIN.* Back orange. Signature vareities. *(S/M #C294-101r).*	50.00	120	450
	q. *TIENTSIN/KALGAN. (S/M #C294-101s).*	50.00	175	400
	r. *TIENTSIN/PEKING.* Brown. *(S/M #C294-101-).*	50.00	175	400
	s. *TSINGTAO/SHANTUNG.* Green. *(S/M #C294-100o).*	75.00	275	1,000

52A	5 Dollars	Good	Fine	XF
	Sept. 1918. Color varieties. Houses with Peking pagoda at center. Signature and serial # varieties. Similar to #52. Back: Bank name in Russian text. Printer: ABNC. With various Chinese character or western numeral or letter control overprints.			
	a. *HARBIN. (S/M #C294-101f).*	1,200	3,000	8,500
	s. Specimen.	—	Unc	3,000

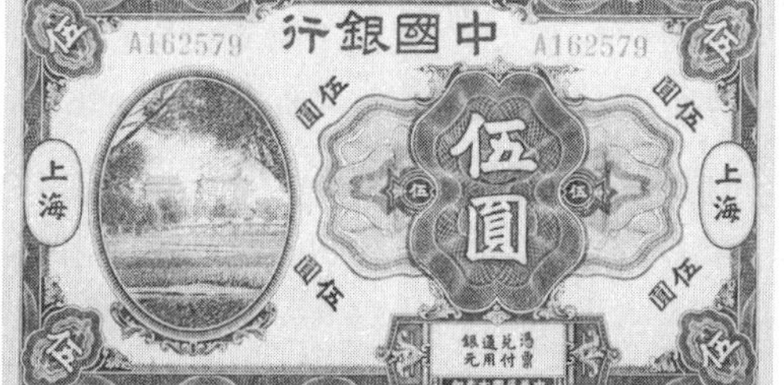

52B	5 Dollars	Good	Fine	XF
	Sept. 1918. Green on multicolor underprint. Two buildings at left. Signature varieties. Printer: ABNC. With various Chinese character or western numeral or letter control overprints.			
	a. *SHANGHAI. (S/M #C294-101.5).*	250	1,350	4,000
	s. Specimen.	—	Unc	1,320

53	10 Dollars	Good	Fine	XF
	Sept. 1918. Various colors. Temple behind trees at center. Signature varieties. Printer: ABNC. With various Chinese character or western numeral or letter control overprints.			
	a. *AMOY-FUKIEN.* Orange. *(S/M #C294-102d).*	10.00	30.00	125
	b. *ANHWEI.* Back green. *(S/M #C294-102a).*	125	550	1,300
	c. *CHEFOO-SHANTUNG.* Brown. *(S/M #C294-102-).*	100	550	1,200
	d. *CHEKIANG.* Orange. Back red-brown. *(S/M #C294-102b)*	125	550	1,300
	e. *CHENGTU-SZECHUAN.* Back brown. *(S/M #C294-102q).*	175	775	1,800
	f. *FUKIEN.* Orange. Back red-orange. Signature varieties. *(S/M #C294-102c).*	20.00	75.00	200
	g. *HANKOW.* Dark green. Back purple. *(S/M #C294-102e).*	175	900	2,200
	h. *KALGAN.* Back orange. *(S/M #C294-102g).*	180	900	2,200
	i. *KIANGSI.* Back blue. *(S/M #C294-102h).*	150	650	1,500
	j. *KIANGSU.* Back blue-gray. *(S/M #C294-102i).*	150	650	1,600
	k. *PEKING.* Green. *(S/M #C294-102j).*	175	800	1,900
	l. *SHANGHAI/PEKING.* Back orange. *(S/M #C294-102l).*	175	800	1,900
	m. *SHANGHAI.* Back red-orange. Signature varieties. *(S/M #C294-102k).*	150	725	1,800
	n. *SHANTUNG.* Brown. Back brown. *(S/M #C294-102n).*	75.00	275	550
	o. *SZECHUAN.* Back red-brown. *(S/M #C294-102p).*	150	725	1,500
	p. *TIENTSIN.* Green. Signature varieties. *(S/M #C294-102r).*	20.00	125	225
	q. *TIENTSIN/KALGAN. (S/M #C294-102s).*	60.00	275	550
	r. *TIENTSIN/PEKING.* Green. *(S/M #C294-102-).*	60.00	275	550
	s. *TSINGTAU/SHANTUNG.* Brown. *(S/M #C294-102o).*	150	725	1,600
	t. *WEIHAWAI-SHANTUNG. (S/M #C294-).*	175	900	1,650
	u. *SHANSI.* Back green. *(S/M #C294-102m).*	225	1,100	2,250
	v. *SHANTUNG/CHEEFOO//WEIHAWAI. Brown. (S/M #C294-102-).*	200	—	—

53A	10 Dollars	Good	Fine	XF
	Sept. 1918. Blue. Temple behind trees at center. Signature varieties. Similar to #53. Back: Bank name in Russian text. Printer: ABNC. With various Chinese character or western numeral or letter control overprints. *HARBIN. (S/M #C294-102f).*			
	a. Issued note.	1,800	5,000	15,000
	s. Specimen.	—	Unc	5,760

53B	10 Dollars	Good	Fine	XF
	Sept. 1918. Brown on multicolor underprint. Two buildings at right. Signature varieties. Printer: ABNC. With various Chinese character or western numeral or letter control overprints. *SHANGHAI.* Specimen. *(S/M #C294-102.3).*	—	Unc	2,300

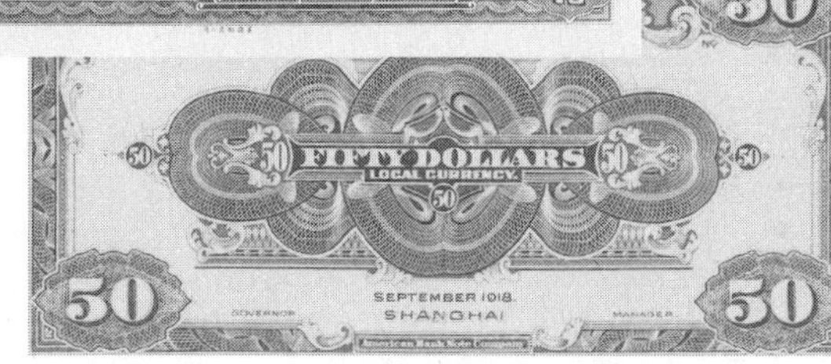

54	50 Dollars	Good	Fine	XF
	Sept. 1918. Purple on multicolor underprint. Two buildings at left. Signature varieties. Printer: ABNC. With various Chinese character or western numeral or letter control overprints. *SHANGHAI.* Proof. *(S/M #C294-102.4).*	—	Unc	5,000

54A	50 Dollars	Good	Fine	XF
	Yr. 7//1.5.1917. Black on brown, green and purple underprint. Gateway at left. Signature varieties. Printer: ABNC. With various Chinese character or western numeral or letter control overprints. *TIENTSIN.* Proof. *(S/M #C294-102.5).*	—	Unc	5,300

Note: Often confusing as the face is dated yr. 7 while the back is dated 1st May 1917. For similar notes dated Yr. 6 1.5.1917, see #38-40.

		Good	Fine	XF
54B	**100 Dollars** Sept. 1918. Olive-green on multicolor underprint. Signature varieties. Printer: ABNC. With various Chinese character or western numeral or letter control overprints. *SHANGHAI.* Proof. *(S/M #C294-102.5).*	—	Unc	4,000

		Good	Fine	XF
54C	**100 Dollars** Yr. 7 1.5.1917. Black on multicolor underprint. Gateway at right. Signature varieties. Printer: ABNC. With various Chinese character or western numeral or letter control overprints. *TIENTSIN. (S/M #C294-103).*	1,100	3,000	6,500

1919 Issue

		Good	Fine	XF
56	**10 Copper Coins** March 1919.Brown. Temple and trees at shoreline at left. Printer: BEPP. *Kiukiang. (S/M #C294-110).*	75	375	1,275

		Good	Fine	XF
57	**50 Copper Coins** March 1919. Violet. Printer: BEPP.			
	a. *Kiukiang. (S/M #C294-111a).*	75.00	750	2,500
	b. *Kalgan. (S/M #C294-111b).*	75.00	350	1,000

		Good	Fine	XF
58	**1 Yüan** May 1919. Dark blue-black. Pavilion in park at center. Printer: BEPP. *HARBIN, MANCHURIA. (S/M #C294-120).*			
	a. Issued note.	75.00	325	1,000
	r. Remainder, without serial #, signature seals, with or without place name.	—	Unc	550

		Good	Fine	XF
59	**5 Yüan** May 1919. Orange. Pavilion in park at center. Printer: BEPP.			
	a. *HARBIN, MANCHURIA. (S/M #C294-121).*	100	375	1,100
	r. Remainder, without serial #, signature seals or place name.	—	Unc	450

		Good	Fine	XF
60	**10 Yüan** May 1919. Dark brown. Printer: BEPP.			
	a. *HARBIN, MANCHURIA. (S/M #C294-122).*	125	725	2,200
	r. Remainder, without serial #, signature seals or place name.	—	Unc	525

1920 Issue

		Good	Fine	XF
61	**100 Copper Coins** 1920. Orange. Printer: BEPP. *Kiukiang. (S/M #C294-130).* Reported not confirmed.	—	—	—

1924 Issue

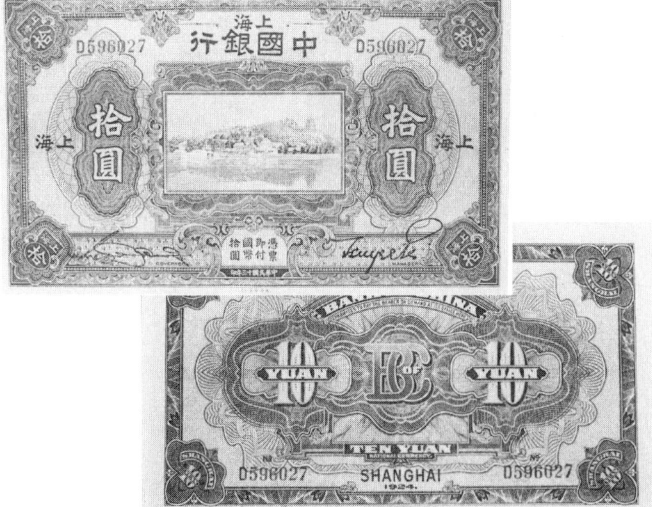

		Good	Fine	XF
62	**10 Yüan** 1924. Purple. Houses and pagoda at shoreline at center. 3 signature varieties. Printer: ABNC. *Shanghai. (S/M #C294-140).*	100	300	1,100

1925 Issue

		Good	Fine	XF
62A	**10 Cents** 1925. Brown. Printer: W&S. *Chenkiang. (S/M #C294-150).* Reported not confirmed.	—	—	—

		VG	VF	UNC
63	**10 Cents** 1.7.1925. Brown. Pagoda by house at water's edge. 7 signature varieties. Printer: W&S. *SHANGHAI. (S/M #C294-151).*	7.50	27.50	65.00

		VG	VF	UNC
64	**20 Cents** 1.7.1925. Dark blue on olive. Monument of Bull with bridge in background at top. 4 signature varieties. Printer: W&S.			
	a. *SHANGHAI. (S/M #C294-152).*	8.00	25.00	90.00
	s. Specimen.	15.00	60.00	200

		VG	VF	UNC
65	**50 Cents** 1.7.1925. Orange. Stag and man with beard at top. Printer: W&S.			
	a. *SHANGHAI. (S/M #C294-153).*	30.00	100	275
	s. Specimen.	18.00	50.00	150

1925 Provisional Issue

		VG	VF	UNC
65A	**1 Dollar** 1.7.1925. Green on multicolor underprint. Temple of Heaven at center. Printer: ABNC. Fengtien-MUKDEN, MANCHURIA office. Proof. *(S/M #C294-154).*	—	—	4,500

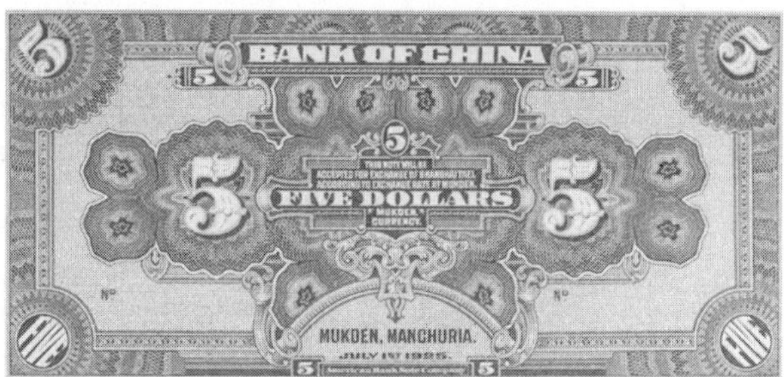

		VG	VF	UNC
65B	**5 Dollars** 1.7.1925. Orange on multicolor underprint. Temple and Peking pagoda at center. Printer: ABNC. Fengtien-MUKDEN, MANCHURIA office. Proof. *(S/M #C294-155).*	—	—	7,500

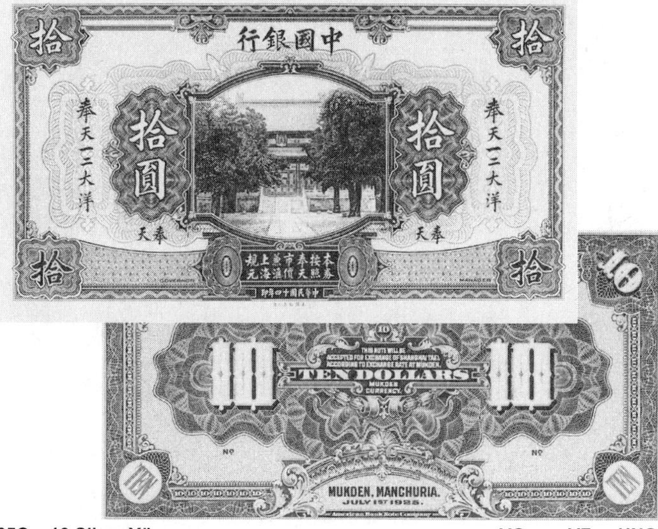

		VG	VF	UNC
65C	**10 Silver Yüan** 1.7.1925. Blue on multicolor underprint. Temple in woods at center. Printer: ABNC. Fengtien-MUKDEN, MANCHURIA office. Proof. *(S/M #C294-156).*	—	—	8,500

1925 ND Provisional Issue

#65E and 65F overprint: *Liaoning* on face; *Promises to pay...Silver dollars...* on back.

		VG	VF	UNC
65E	**5 Dollars** ND (old date - 1.7.1925). Orange on multicolor underprint. Temple and Peking pagoda at center. Specimen. *(S/M #C294-158).*	—	—	8,000

		VG	VF	UNC
65F	**10 Silver Yüan** ND (old date - 1.7.1925). Blue on multicolor. Temple in woods at center. Specimen. *(S/M C294-159).*	—	—	9,000

1926 Issue

66	5 Yüan	Good	Fine	XF
	1926. Black on multicolor underprint. Temple and Peking Pagoda on hilltop at center. Back: Bank at center. Printer: ABNC. *SHANGHAI.* Also various letter, numeral and Chinese character control overprints.			
	a. Black signature (3 varieties). *(S/M #C294-160a).*	25.00	80.00	375
	b. Red signature (5 varieties). *(S/M #C294-160b/i).*	15.00	75.00	250

1930 Issue

67	1 Dollar	Good	Fine	XF
	Oct. 1930. Dark green on red and multicolor underprint. Temple of Heaven at center. Printer: ABNC. *AMOY. (S/M #C294-170).*	5.00	25.00	100

68	5 Dollars	Good	Fine	XF
	Oct. 1930. Purple on multicolor underprint. Temple and Peking Pagoda at center. 2 signature varieties. Printer: ABNC. *AMOY.(S/M #C294-171).*	5.00	20.00	75.00

69	10 Silver Yüan	Good	Fine	XF
	Oct. 1930. Orange on multicolor underprint. Temple behind trees at center. 2 sign varieties. Printer: ABNC. *AMOY. (S/M #C294-172).*	5.00	20.00	75.00

1931 Issue

70	5 Yüan	VG	VF	UNC
	Jan. 1931. Orange and black. Temple of Heaven at left, landscape, mountains at right. Back: Bank. Printer: TDLR. *TIENTSIN.(S/M #C294-180).*			
	a. Serial # face only.	6.00	30.00	100
	b. Serial # face and back.	2.50	5.00	30.00

1934 Issue

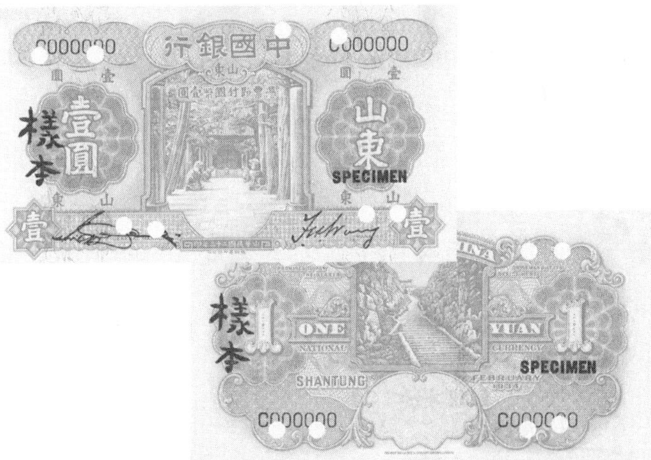

71	1 Yüan	VG	VF	UNC
	Feb. 1934. Yellow-brown. Colonnade, animal figures at center. Back: Long stairway. Printer: TDLR.			
	a. *SHANTUNG. (S/M #C294-190).*	5.00	15.00	50.00
	s. Specimen as above, 2 part.	—	—	175

71A	1 Yüan	VG	VF	UNC
	1934. Red and brown. Farmer plowing with oxen. Printer: TDLR. *TIENTSIN. (S/M #C294-191).*	500	2,750	6,500

		VG	VF	UNC
72	**5 Yüan**	VG	VF	UNC
	Feb. 1934. Green. Portico behind trees at center. Back: House in rocks. Printer: TDLR.			
	a. *SHANTUNG. (S/M #C294-192a).*	12.50	60.00	200
	b. *TSINGTAU/SHANTUNG. (S/M #C294-192b).*	75	400	1,275
	c. *CHEF OO/SHANTUNG. (S/M #C294-192c).*	175	750	2,700
	d. *WEI HAI WEI/SHANTUNG. (S/M #C294-192d).*	175	750	2,700
	s. As a, 2 part specimen.	—	—	415
72A	**5 Yüan**	VG	VF	UNC
	1934. Printer: TDLR. *TIENTSIN. (S/M #C294-193).*	20.00	90.00	200

		VG	VF	UNC
73	**10 Yüan**	VG	VF	UNC
	Oct. 1934. Dark green. Shepherd, sheep at center. Back: Great Wall, pavilion at right. Printer: TDLR. *TIENTSIN. (S/M #C294-194).*			
	a. Issued note.	10.00	30.00	150
	s. Two part specimen.	—	—	300

1935 First Issue

		VG	VF	UNC
74	**1 Yüan**	VG	VF	UNC
	1935. Dark brown. Temple of Heaven at center. Back: Junk 1 Yuan coin at center. Printer: W&S.			
	a. *SHANGHAI.* Without overprint *(S/M #C294-200).*	4.00	13.00	50.00
	b. Overprint: *TN* on face.	5.00	20.00	75.00
	c. Overprint: *TN* on face and back.	5.00	20.00	75.00

		VG	VF	UNC
75	**10 Yüan**	VG	VF	UNC
	Jan. 1935. Brown. Temple behind trees at center. Printer: TDLR. *SHANTUNG.(S/M #C294-204).*	15.00	40.00	215

1935 Second Issue

		VG	VF	UNC
76	**1 Yüan**	VG	VF	UNC
	March 1935. Brown. Farmer plowing with horse at left, irrigation system at right. Back: Junk 1 Yuan coin at center. Printer: TDLR. *TIENTSIN. (S/M #C294-201).*	5.00	18.00	66.00

		VG	VF	UNC
77	**5 Yüan**	VG	VF	UNC
	March 1935. Black on multicolor underprint. SYS at left, bridge to Bottle Pagoda at right. Back: Bank building at center. Printer: TDLR. Note: The "Bottle Pagoda" structure was erected in Peking as a complimentary gesture towards Tibet.			
	a. *SHANGHAI. (S/M #C294-202).*	10.00	25.00	100
	b. Without *SHANGHAI. (S/M #C294-203).*	3.00	7.50	45.00

1936 Issue

		VG	VF	UNC
78	**1 Yüan**	VG	VF	UNC
	May 1936. Green on multicolor underprint. SYS at left. Back: Junk 1-Yuan coin at center. Printer: TDLR. *(S/M #C294-210).*	1.00	5.00	40.00

1937 Issue

		VG	VF	UNC
79	**1 Yüan**	VG	VF	UNC
	1937. Blue. SYS at left. Back: Skyscraper at right. Printer: TDLR. *(S/M #C294-220).*	0.75	2.25	11.00

		VG	VF	UNC
80	**5 Yüan** 1937. Violet on multicolor underprint. SYS at left. Back: Skyscraper at center. Printer: TDLR. *(S/M #C294-221).*	0.25	.50	10.00

		VG	VF	UNC
81	**10 Yüan** 1937. Green on multicolor underprint. SYS at left. Back: Skyscraper at right. Printer: TDLR. *(S/M #C294-222).*	0.25	.50	10.00

1939 Issue

		VG	VF	UNC
81A	**1 Yüan** 1939. Purple on multicolor underprint. Portrait Liao Chung-kai at left. Back: Bank building at right. Printer: ABNC. *(S/M #C294-223).*			
	p. Proof.	—	—	2,250
	r. Unsigned remainder.	500	2,750	5,400

		VG	VF	UNC
81B	**5 Yüan** 1939. Proof. Brown and multicolor. Portrait Liao Chung-kai at left. Back: Bank building at right. Printer: ABNC. *(S/M #C294-224).*	—	—	4,300

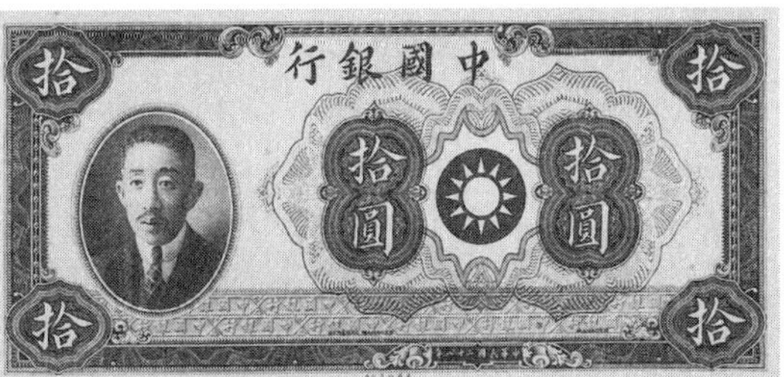

		VG	VF	UNC
81C	**10 Yüan** 1939. Proof. Black and multicolor. Portrait Liao Chung-kai at left. Back: Bank building at right. Printer: ABNC. *(S/M #C294-225).*	—	—	6,600

1940 Issue

		VG	VF	UNC
82	**10 Cents** ND (1940). Red. Temple of Heaven at right. Printer: TTBC. *(S/M #C294-230).*	0.75	2.00	9.50

		VG	VF	UNC
83	**20 Cents** ND (1940). Blue. Great Wall at left. Printer: TTBC. *(S/M #C294-231).*	0.90	2.40	9.50

		VG	VF	UNC
84	**5 Yüan** 1940. Blue on multicolor underprint. Portrait SYS at left. Back: Temple of Heaven at right. Printer: ABNC. *(S/M #C294-240).*	.50	2.00	10.00

85	10 Yüan	VG	VF	UNC
	1940. Red on multicolor underprint. Portrait SYS at left. Back: Temple of Heaven at right. Printer: ABNC.			
	a. Serial # on face. *(S/M #C294-241a).*	0.25	2.00	14.00
	b. Serial # on face and back. *(S/M #C294-241b).*	0.25	1.50	8.00

Note: # 85 with overprint: *SHENSI PROVINCE* and *CHUNGKING* have been determined to be modern fantasies.

86	25 Yüan	VG	VF	UNC
	1940. Green on multicolor underprint. Portrait SYS at left. Back: Temple of Heaven at right. Printer: ABNC. *(S/M #C294-242).*	20.00	75.00	450

87	50 Yüan	VG	VF	UNC
	1940. Brown on multicolor underprint. Portrait SYS at left. Back: Temple of Heaven at right. Printer: ABNC.			
	a. Serial # on face. *(S/M #C294-243c).*	8.00	25.00	135
	b. Serial # on face and on back. *(S/M #C294-243d).*	8.00	25.00	135
	c. Serial # and *CHUNGKING* on face. *CHUNGKING* on back. *(S/M #C294-243b).*	3.00	7.50	55.00
	d. Serial # and *CHUNGKING* on face. Serial # and *CHUNGKING* on back. *(S/M #C294-243b).*	3.00	7.50	55.00

88	100 Yüan	VG	VF	UNC
	1940. Purple on multicolor underprint. Portrait SYS at left. Back: Temple of Heaven at right. Printer: ABNC.			
	a. Serial # on face and back. *(S/M #C294-244d).*	7.50	30.00	115
	b. Serial # and *Chungking* at left and right on face. *CHUNGKING* on back. *(S/M #C294-244a).*	4.00	20.00	50.00
	c. Serial # and *Chungking* at left and right on face. Serial # and *CHUNGKING* on back. *(S/M #C294-244b).*	3.00	15.00	40.00

Note: # 88 with overprint: *SHENSI PROVINCE* is believed to be a modern fantasy.

1941 Issue

89	10 Cents	VG	VF	UNC
	1941. Green. Temple of Heaven at top. Vertical format. *(S/M #C294-250).*			
	a. Issued note.	50.00	200	400
	s. Specimen.	—	—	175

90	20 Cents	VG	VF	UNC
	1941. Red on yellow and pink underprint. Temple of Heaven at top. Vertical format. *(S/M #C294-251).*			
	a. Issued note.	50.00	150	300
	s. Specimen.	—	—	175

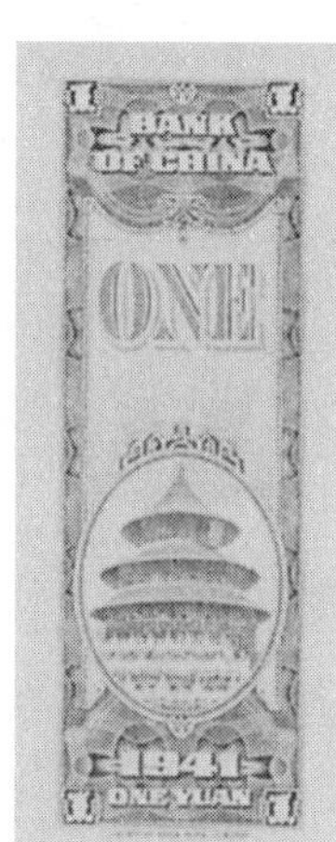

91	1 Yüan	VG	VF	UNC
	1941. Blue on multicolor underprint. SYS at top. Back: Celestial Temple at bottom. Printer: ABNC. *(S/M #C294-260).*			
	a. Issued note.	50.00	250	500
	s. Specimen.	—	—	250

92	5 Yüan	VG	VF	UNC
	1941. Red on multicolor underprint. SYS at top. Like #91. Back: Celestial Temple at bottom. Printer: ABNC. *(S/M #C294-261).*			
	a. Issued note.	50.00	200	400
	s. Specimen.	—	—	200

Color Abbreviation Guide

New to the *Standard Catalog of® World Paper Money* are the following abbreviations related to color references:

BC: Back color

PC: Paper color

93	**5 Yüan**	VG	VF	UNC
	1941. Blue on multicolor underprint. Temple at right. Back: Gateway at right. Printer: CMPA. *(S/M #C294-262).*	30.00	100	600

Note: For #93 with overprint: *HONG KONG GOVERNMENT* see Hong Kong #7.

94	**10 Yüan**	VG	VF	UNC
	1941. Purple on multicolor underprint. SYS at top. Similar to #91. Back: Celestial Temple at bottom. Printer: ABNC. *(S/M #C294-264).*			
	a. Issued note.	75.00	350	750
	s. Specimen.	—	—	275

95	**10 Yüan**	VG	VF	UNC
	1941. Red on multicolor underprint. SYS at center. Printer: DTBC. *(S/M #C294-263).*	23.00	125	225

96	**100 Yüan**	VG	VF	UNC
	1941. Blue on multicolor underprint. SYS at top. Similar to #91. Back: Celestial Temple at bottom. Printer: ABNC. *(S/M #C294-265).*			
	a. Issued note.	75.00	350	750
	s. Specimen.	—	—	300

97	**500 Yüan**	VG	VF	UNC
	1941. Brown on multicolor underprint. SYS at top. Similar to #91. Back: Celestial Temple at bottom. Printer: ABNC. *(S/M #C294-266).*			
	a. Issued note.	100	400	1,100
	s. Specimen.	—	—	375

1942 Issue

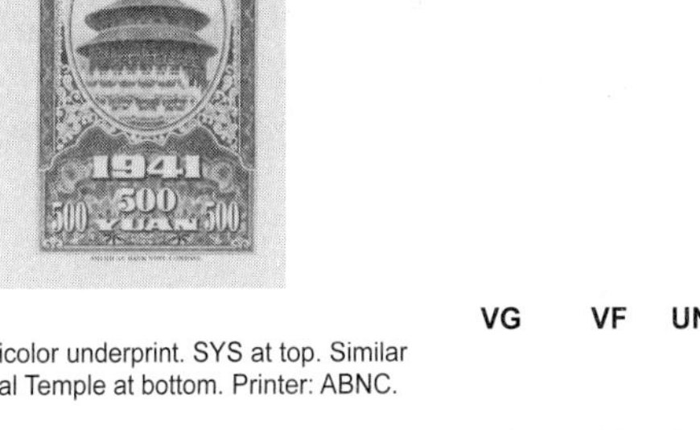

98	**50 Yüan**	VG	VF	UNC
	1942. Green and multicolor. Steam passenger train at left. Printer: TTBC. *(S/M #C294-270).*	30.00	180	325

		VG	VF	UNC
99	**500 Yüan** 1942. Olive-green and multicolor. SYS at left. Printer: ABNC. *(S/M #C294-271).*	28.00	90.00	275

		VG	VF	UNC
100	**1000 Yüan** 1942. Green and multicolor. SYS at left. Like #99. Printer: ABNC. *(S/M #C294-272).*			
	a. Issued note.	150	725	1,750
	s. Specimen.	—	—	750

Bank of Communications

БАНКЪ ПУТИ СООБШЕНІЯ

行銀通交

Chiao T'ung Yin Hang

Formerly the General Bank of Communications. Also see #A13A-A19D.

1912 Issue

		Good	Fine	XF
102	**50 Cents** 1912. Sailing ships dockside by depot and train at bottom center. *YINGKOW. (S/M #C126-10).*	350	1,800	3,600

		Good	Fine	XF
103	**100 Cents** 1912. Sailing ships dockside by depot and train at bottom center.			
	a. *MUKDEN. (S/M #C126-11).*	725	3,600	15,000
	b. *CHANGCHUN. (S/M #C126-).*	900	4,500	18,000
	c. *YINGKOW. (S/M #C126-).*	360	—	—

		Good	Fine	XF
104	**1 Dollar** 1912. Green and yellow. Sailing ships dockside by depot and train at bottom center.			
	a. *PEKING. (S/M #C126-20a).*	2,525	5,400	22,500
	b. *SHANGHAI. (S/M #C126-20b).*	2,525	5,400	22,500
	c. *TSINAN (S/M #C126-20c).*	—	—	—
	d. *TIENTSIN.*	2,400	6,000	29,000
	e. *HONAN.* Perforated and overprint: *SPECIMEN. (S/M #C126-).*	—	Unc	14,500
105	**1 Dollar** 1.9.1912. Green and multicolor. Sailing ships dockside by depot and train at bottom center. Specimen. *(S/M #C126-21).*	—	Unc	7,500
106	**500 Cents** 1.9.1912. Purple and blue on yellow underprint. Sailing ships dockside by depot and train at bottom center. *Mukden* handstamp.*(S/M #C126-215).*	—	—	—

		Good	Fine	XF
107	**5 Dollars** 1.9.1912. Blue and multicolor. Sailing ships dockside by depot and train at bottom center.			
	a. *CHANGCHUN.* Cancelled remainder. *(S/M #C126-24a).*	—	Unc	14,000
	b. *HONAN.* Perforated and overprint *SPECIMEN. (S/M # C126-24b).*	—	Unc	28,000
	c. *PEKING. (S/M #C126-23).*	1,800	3,300	43,500
	d. *YINGKOW.* Specimen. *(S/M #C126-22).*	—	Unc	30,000
	e. Without place name. Specimen. *(S/M #C126-24c).*	—	Unc	7,200
107A	**1000 Cents** 1.9.1912. Green with black text. Sailing ships dockside by depot and train at bottom center. *FENGTIEN. (S/M #C126-).*	—	—	—

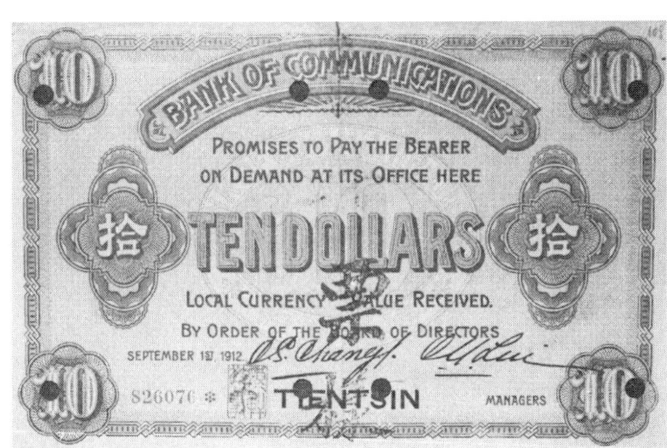

		Good	Fine	XF
108	**10 Dollars** 1.9.1912. Blue. Sailing ships dockside by depot and train at bottom center.			
	a. *HONAN.* Perforated and overprint: *SPECIMEN. (S/M #C126-25a).*	—	Unc	6,000
	b. *KALGAN. (S/M #C126-25b)*	—	—	—
	c. *TIENTSIN. (S/M #C126-25c).*	2,700	6,500	8,100
	d. Without place name. Specimen. *(S/M #C126-25d).*	—	Unc	13,250

		Good	Fine	XF
109	**100 Dollars** 1.9.1912. Sailing ships dockside by depot and train at bottom center. *(S/M #C126-26).*	8,750	21,750	54,000

1913 Issue

#110-111C Specimens were also prepared from notes w/normal serial numbers.

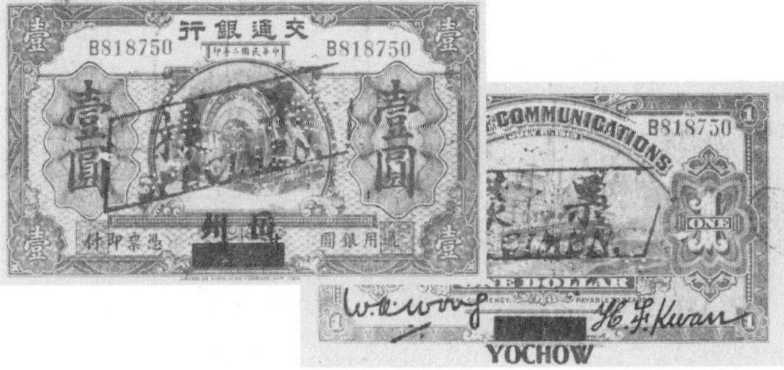

		Good	Fine	XF
110	**1 Dollar** 1.7.1913. Red-orange on multicolor underprint. Electric direct current generator at center. Back: Sailing ship at center. Printer: ABNC.			
	a. *CHANGCHUN.* Chinese overprint on face. English overprint: *N.B. Payable in subsidiary (silver) coins* on back. *(S/M #C126-31d).*	450	2,160	8,800
	b. *CHUNGKING.* Specimen. *(S/M #C126-31d).*	—	Unc	14,500
	c. *HUNAN. (S/M #C126-31a).*	700	3,250	13,200
	d. *Fengtien//MUKDEN.* Chinese overprint on face. English overprint: *N.B. This note is exchangeable...* on back. *(S/M #C126-).*	750	4,320	18,000
	e. *PUKOW. (S/M #C126-31e).*	750	4,325	18,000
	f. *TIENTSIN. (S/M #C126-30a).*	550	3,450	13,200
	g. *TSITSIHAR.* Chinese overprint on face. English overprint: *N.B. Payable in subsidiary (silver) coins* on back. Specimen. *(S/M #C126-31f).*	—	Unc	6,000
	h. *YOCHO with KALGAN.* Specimen. *(S/M #C126-31f).*	—	Unc	5,300
	i. *PEKING (S/M #C126-31g).*	350	2,650	6,500
	j. *WUSIH.* Specimen. *(S/M #C126-30b).*	—	Unc	5,300
	k. *CHEFOO. (S/M #C126-31h).*	—	—	—
	l. *LUNGKO with CHEFOO. (S/M #C126-30i).*	700	7,200	15,400
	m. *HANKOW. (S/M #C126-30m).*	700	7,200	15,400
	n. *TSINAN.*	—	—	—

		Good	Fine	XF
111	**5 Dollars** 1.7.1913. Green on multicolor underprint. Steam passenger train in ravine at left. Back: Steam passenger train at center. Printer: ABNC.			
	a. *CHANGCHUN.* Chinese overprint on face. English overprint: *N.B. Payable in subsidiary (silver) coins...* on back. Specimen. *(S/M #C126-32b).*	—	Unc	9,000
	b. *CHUNGKING.* Specimen. *(S/M #C126-32c).*	—	Unc	9,000
	c. *HUNAN.* Specimen *(S/M #C126-32a).*	—	Unc	9,000
	d. *TIENTSIN.* Specimen. *(S/M #C126-32d).*	—	Unc	9,000
	e. *CHEFOO.* Specimen. *(S/M #C126-32e).*	—	Unc	9,000
	f. *HANKOW.* Specimen. *(S/M #C126-32f).*	—	Unc	9,000
	g. *HONAN.* Specimen. *(S/M #C126-32g).*	—	Unc	9,000
	h. *KALGAN.* Specimen. *(S/M #C126-32h)*	—	Unc	9,000
	i. *Fengtien//MUKDEN.* Chinese overprint on face. English overprint: *N.B. This note is exchangeable...* on back. Specimen. *(S/M #C126-32i).*	—	Unc	9,000
	j1. *PEKING.* Issued note.	750	2,200	13,200
	j2. *PEKING.* Specimen. *(S/M #C126-32j).*	—	Unc	4,300
	k1. *PUKOW.* Specimen. *(S/M #C126-32k).*	—	Unc	6,500
	k2. *TSINAN.*	750	4,000	16,000
	l. *TSITSIHAR.* Chinese overprint on face. English overprint: *N.B. Payable in subsidiary (silver) coins...* on back. Specimen. *(S/M #C126-326).*	—	Unc	6,500
	m. *YOCHOW.* Specimen. *(S/M #C126-32m).*	—	Unc	6,500
	n. *SHANGHAI. (S/M #C126-32n).*	750	3,000	13,200

		Good	Fine	XF
111A	**10 Dollars** 1.7.1913. Purple and multicolor. Steam passenger train in ravine at left. Back: Steam passenger train at center. Printer: ABNC.			
	a. *HUNAN. (S/M #C126-40a).*	1,000	6,500	26,400
	b. *CHANGCHUN.* Chinese overprint on face. English overprint: *N.B. Payable in subsidiary (silver) coins...* on back. *(S/M #C126-40b).*	—	Unc	13,000
	c. *ANHUI.* Specimen. *(S/M #C126-40c).*	—	Unc	13,000
	d. *LUNGKOwith CHEFOO. (S/M #C126-40d).*	—	Unc	15,000
	e. *CHUNGKING.* Specimen. *(S/M #126-40e).*	—	Unc	13,000
	f. *Fengtien//MUKDEN.* Chinese on face. English overprint: *N.B. this note is exchangeable...* on back. *(S/M #C126-40f).*	—	Unc	13,000
	g. *HANKOW.* Specimen. *(S/M #C126-40g).*	—	Unc	13,000
	h. *KALGAN.* Specimen. *(S/M #C126-40h).*	—	Unc	13,000
	i. *PEKING.*	3,500	20,000	—
	j. *TIENTSIN.* Specimen. *(S/M #C126-40i).*	—	Unc	13,000
	k. *TSITSIHAR.* Chinese overprint on face. English overprint: *N.B. Payable in subsidiary (silver) coins...* on back. Specimen. *(S/M #C126-40j).*	—	Unc	16,000
	l. *WUSIH.* Specimen. *(S/M #C126-40k).*	—	Unc	15,000

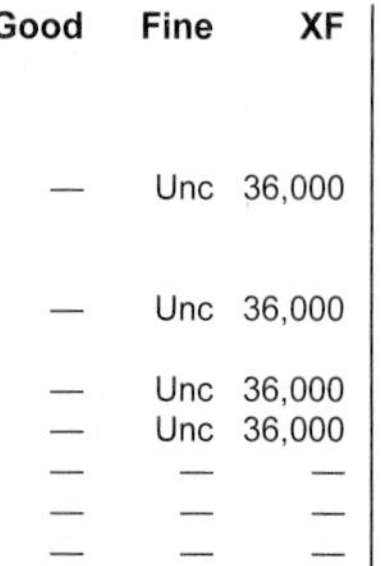

111B	50 Dollars	Good	Fine	XF
	1.7.1913. Blue and multicolor. Steam passenger train at center. Back: Maritime Customs building, street car at center. Printer: ABNC.			
	a. *CHANGCHUN*. Chinese overprint on face. English overprint: *N.B. Payable in subsidiary (silver) coins...* on back. Specimen. *(S/M #C126-40.5a)*.	—	Unc	36,000
	b. *LUNGKOwith CHEFOO*. Specimen. *(S/M #C126-40.5b)*.	—	Unc	36,000
	c. *KALGAN*. Specimen. *(S/M #C126-40.5c)*.	—	Unc	36,000
	d. *FENGTIEN*. Specimen. *(S/M #C126-40.5d)*.	—	Unc	36,000
	e. *HSUCHOW*. *(S/M #C126-40.5e)*.	—	—	—
	f. *SHANTUNG*. Brown and multicolor.	—	—	—
	g. *PEKING*.	—	—	—

111C	100 Dollars	Good	Fine	XF
	1.7.1913. Blue and multicolor. Ship at dockside, steam train at center. Back: Sailing ships at center. Printer: ABNC.			
	a. *CHANGCHUN*. Chinese overprint on face. English overprint: *N.B. Payable in subsidiary (silver) coins...* on back. *(S/M #C126-41b)*.	—	Unc	50,000
	b. *Fengtien/MUKDEN*. Chinese overprint on face. English overprint: *N.B. This note is exchangeable...* on back. Specimen. *(S/M #C126-41d)*.	—	Unc	50,000
	c. *HANKOW*. Specimen. *(S/M #C126-41d)*.	—	Unc	50,000
	d. *HUNAN*. Specimen. *(S/M #C126-41a)*.	—	Unc	50,000
	e. *KIANGSU*. *(S/M #C126-41e)*.	—	—	—
	f. *TSINAN*.	—	—	—

1914 Issue

The original issues have Chinese script signatures while the more common reissues have red Chinese signatures seal on face. All have handwritten English signatures (i.e. *S.M. Tong - T.S. Wong)* on back. Various Western control letter, numeral or Chinese characters are encountered on earlier issues, but rarely on the WWII reissues. In addition, earlier issues w/various banking commercial and private handstamps are encountered and command a small premium.

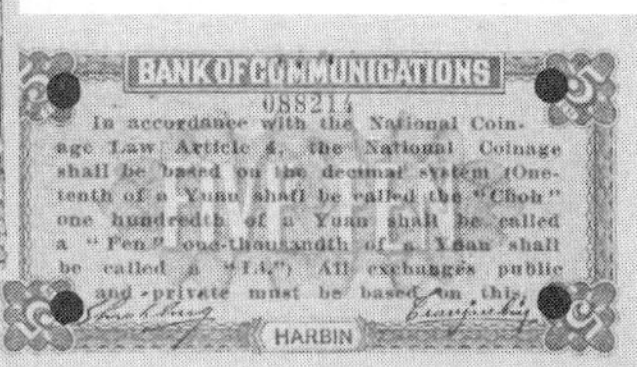

112	5 Fen	Good	Fine	XF
	ND (1914). Green and multicolor. Printer: BEPP.			
	a. *HARBIN*. Specimen. *(S/M #C126-50a)*.	—	Unc	900
	b. *KALGAN*. *(S/M #C126-50b)*.	100	375	2,500
	c. *TAIHEIHO*. *(S/M #C126-50c)*.	180	600	4,800
	d. *TULUNNOERH*. *(S/M #C126-50d)*	180	600	4,800
	e. Without place name. Specimen. *(S/M #C126-50)*.	—	Unc	1,100

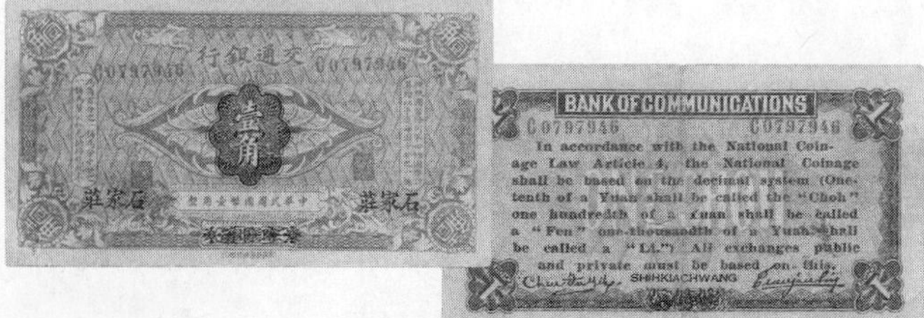

113	1 Choh (Chiao)	Good	Fine	XF
	ND (1914). Black and red-brown on light green underprint. Printer: BEPP.			
	a. *HARBIN*. *(S/M #C126-51d)*.	100	225	750
	b. *KALGAN*. *(S/M #C126-51e)*.	100	225	750
	c. *SHIHKIACHWANG*. *(S/M #C126-51a)*.	125	550	2,625
	d. *TSINGTAU*. *(S/M #C126-51b)*.	125	550	2,625
	e. *TULUNNOERH*. *(S/M #C126-51c)*.	125	150	2,625
	f. *WEIHAIWEI*. *(S/M #C126-f)*.	50.00	100	825
	g. *WEIHAIWEI/HARBIN*. *(S/M #C126-51g)*.	40.00	150	600
	h. Without place name. Specimen. *(S/M #C126-51)*.	—	Unc	400
	i. *PAOTOW*. *(S/M #C126-51)*	—	—	—
	j. *SHIHKIACHWANG/HARBIN*. (S/M #C126-51)	400	1,000	—

114	2 Choh (Chiao)	Good	Fine	XF
	ND (1914). Blue-black and blue-gray on pink underprint. Similar to #113. Printer: BEPP.			
	a. *HARBIN*. Specimen. *(S/M #C126-52c)*.	—	Unc	450
	b. *KALGAN*. *(S/M #C126-52a)*.	35.00	100	300
	c. *TAIHEIHO*. *(S/M #C126-52d)*.	50.00	225	825
	d. *TSINGTAU*. *(S/M #C126-52e)*.	45.00	175	825
	e. *TULUNNOERH*. *(S/M #C126-52f)*.	45.00	175	825
	f. *WEIHAIWEI/HARBIN*. *(S/M #C126-52b)*.	25.00	100	413
	g. *PAOTOW*. *(S/M #C126-52g)*.	50.00	225	825
	h. *WEIHAIWEI*. *(S/M #C126-52h)*.	45.00	175	675
	i. Without place name. Specimen. *(S/M #C126-52)*.	—	Unc	525
	j. *SHIHKIACHWANG/HARBIN*. *(S/M #C126-52)*	500	1,200	—

115	5 Choh (Chiao)	Good	Fine	XF
	ND (1914). Brown. Similar to #113. Printer: BEPP.			
	a. *HARBIN*. Specimen. *(S/M #C126-53a)*.	—	Unc	780
	b. *KALGAN*. *(S/M #C126-54b)*.	150	600	3,000
	c. *TSINGTAU*. *(S/M #C126-54c)*.	150	600	3,000
	d. *WEIHAIWEI*. *(S/M #C126-54d)*.	150	600	3,000
	e. Without place name. Specimen. *(S/M #C126-54)*.	—	Unc	975

116	1 Yüan	Good	Fine	XF
	1.10.1914. With various overprints. Brown on multicolor underprint. Steam passenger train in ravine at center. Back: Sailing ship. Printer: ABNC.			
	a. *AMOY*. *(S/M #C126-60)*.	175	800	1,800
	b. *CHANGCHUN*. *(S/M #C126-63)*.	175	900	1,800
	c. *CHEFOO*. Dark brown and multicolor. *(S/M #C126-61)*.	200	900	2,400
	d. *CHEKIANG*. *(S/M #C126-62)*.	300	1,300	3,000
	e. *CHUNGKING*. Violet and multicolor. *(S/M #C126-64)*.	10.00	50.00	150
	f. *HANKOW*. Brown and multicolor. *(S/M #C126-65)*.	200	900	2,000
	g. *HONAN*. *(S/M #C126-66)*.	400	1,500	5,400
	h. *KALGAN*. Orange and multicolor. *(S/M #C126-67)*.	400	2,000	6,240
	i. *KIANGSU*. *(S/M #C126-70)*.	300	1,800	5,040
	k. *KIUKIANG*. Dark brown and multicolor. *(S/M #C126-71)*.	350	1,900	5,280

	Good	Fine	XF
l. *PUKOW.* Dark brown and multicolor. *(S/M #C126-72).*	400	2,000	5,750
m. *SHANGHAI.* Purple and multicolor. *(S/M #C126-73).*	5.00	10.00	20.00
n. *SHANGHAI.* Dark brown and multicolor. 2 signature varieties. *(S/M #C126-74).*	350	1,800	3,600
o. *SHANGHAI.* Blue and multicolor. *(S/M #C126-75).*	45.00	240	600
p. *SHANTUNG. (S/M #C126-76).*	5.00	20.00	60.00
q. *SIAN.* Violet and multicolor. *(S/M #C126-77).*	140	700	1,600
r1. *TIENTSIN.* Purple and multicolor. *(S/M #C126-78).*	5.00	15.00	40.00
r2. *TIENTSIN.* Brown and multicolor.	250	1,200	2,600
s. *TSINGTAO.* Dark brown and multicolor. *(S/M #C126-79).*	350	1,800	4,320
t. *SHANGHAI.* Violet and multicolor. Red control letter *P* at left and right. *(S/M #C126-73a).*	10.00	40.00	120
u. *TULUNNOERH.* Brown and multicolor. Mongol text at left and right. *(S/M #C126-79.6).*	—	—	—
v. Without place name. Specimen. *(S/M #C126-).*	—	Unc	250
w. *FOOCHOW-AMOY.* Purple and multicolor.	400	1,000	—
x. *KIUKIANG.* Blue and multicolor.	1,000	2,500	—

117 5 Yüan	Good	Fine	XF
1.10.1914. With various overprints. Steam passenger train at center. Back: Post Office at center. Printer: ABNC.			
a. *AMOY.* Dark Brown (black) and multicolor. *(S/M #C126-80).*	75.00	270	550
b. *CHANGCHUN. (S/M #C126-84).*	120	600	1,200
c. *CHEFOO. (S/M #C126-82).*	450	2,200	5,400
d. *CHEKIANG. (S/M #C126-83).*	500	2,500	6,000
e. *CHUNGKING.* Dark brown and multicolor. *(S/M #C126-85).*	10.00	35.00	100
f. *FOOCHOW/AMOY.* Dark brown and multicolor. *(S/M #C126-81).*	275	1,400	3,350
g. *HANKOW. (S/M #C126-86).*	350	1,800	4,300
h. *HONAN.* Blue-black and multicolor. *(S/M #C126-87).*	600	3,000	7,200
i. *KALGAN.* Green on multicolor underprint. *(S/M #C126-88).*	800	4,000	9,600
k. *KIANGSU. (S/M #C126-90).*	600	3,000	7,200
l. *KIUKIANG.* Blue and multicolor. *(S/M #C126-91).*	800	4,000	9,600
m. *PUKOW. (S/M #C126-92).*	1,100	5,400	13,200
n. *SHANGHAI.* Dark brown and multicolor. *Shanghai* overprint in black with red signature seals. *(S/M #C126-93a).*	—	Unc	25.00
o. *SHANGHAI.* Dark brown and multicolor. *Shanghai* overprint and script signature in blue-black. *(S/M #C126-93).*	5.00	25.00	75.00
p. *SHANTUNG.* Dark brown and multicolor. *(S/M #C126-).*	5.00	15.00	50.00
q. *SHANTUNG.* Blue-black and multicolor. *(S/M #C126-94).*	50.00	250	550
r. *SIAN.* Orange and multicolor. *(S/M #C126-95).*	200	1,000	2,400
s1. *TIENTSIN.* Red and multicolor. Seal signatures. *(S/M #C126-96).*	5.00	25.00	75.00
s2. *TIENTSIN.* Red and multicolor. Script signatures. *(S/M #C126-).*	10.00	25.00	100
t. *TIENTSIN.* Dark brown and multicolor. *(S/M #C126-99).*	3.00	13.00	30.00
u. *TSINGTAU.* Dark blue and multicolor. *(S/M #C126-97).*	400	2,000	4,800
v. *TULUNNOERH.* Mongol text at left and right. *(S/M #C126-98).*	—	—	—
w. *SHANGHAI.* Blue and multicolor. *(S/M #C126-).*	150	800	2,000
x. *SHANGHAI.* Dark brown and multicolor. Red control letter *P* at left and right. *(S/M #C126-93b).*	—	Unc	25.00
y. *SHANGHAI.* Black and multicolor. *(S/M #C126-).*	325	1,750	4,000
z. *AMOY.* Light brown and multicolor.	200	450	1,500
aa. *FOOCHOW/AMOY.* Light brown on multicolor.	350	1,200	—
ab. *KIUKIANG.* Dark brown and multicolor.	2,500	6,000	—
ac. *TIENTSIN.* Black and multicolor.	—	—	—

118 10 Yüan	Good	Fine	XF
1.10.1914. With various overprints. Maritime Customs building, streetcar at center. Back: Ship at dockside, steam passenger train at center. Printer: ABNC.			
a. *AMOY.* Blue and multicolor. *(S/M #C126-100).*	120	600	1,450
b. *AMOY.* Red and multicolor. *(S/M #C126-101).*	50.00	175	450
c. *CHANGCHUN. (S/M #C126-104).*	100	400	1,000
d. *CHEFOO. (S/M #C126-102).*	500	2,500	7,200
e. *CHEKIANG. (S/M #C126-103).*	500	2,500	7,200
f. *CHUNGKING.* Red and multicolor. *(S/M #C126-105).*	7.50	25.00	75.00
g. *HANKOW. (S/M #C126-106).*	500	3,000	6,750
h. *HONAN. (S/M #C126-107).*	825	4,000	10,800
i. *KALGAN.* Orange and multicolor. *(S/M #C126-110).*	825	4,500	11,520
j. *KALGAN.* Green and multicolor. *(S/M #C126-111).*	750	4,000	10,500
k. *KANSU. (S/M #C126-109).*	350	2,250	5,400
l. *KIUKIANG.* Green and multicolor. *(S/M #C126-112).*	825	4,500	11,500
m. *PUKOW. (S/M #C126-113).*	1,200	6,000	17,400
n. *SHANGHAI.* Green and multicolor. *(S/M #C126-114).*	350	1,750	4,800
o. *SHANGHAI.* Red and multicolor. *Shanghai* and signature in blue-black. *(S/M #C126-115).*	—	Unc	45.00
p. *SHANGHAI.* Red and multicolor. *Shanghai* in black with red signature seals. *(S/M #C126-115a).*	—	Unc	15.00
q. *SHANGHAI.* Red and multicolor. *Shanghai* in blue-black with red signature seals. *(S/M #C126-115b).*	—	Unc	10.00
r1. *SHANTUNG.* Red and multicolor. Seal signatures. *(S/M #C126-116).*	10.00	50.00	125
r2. *SHANTUNG.* Red and multicolor. Script signatures. *(S/M #C126-116).*	25.00	60.00	—
s. *SIAN. (S/M #C126-117).*	675	3,300	7,500
t1. *TIENTSIN.* Purple and multicolor. Seal signatures.*(S/M #C126-120).*	10.00	50.00	125
t2. *TIENTSIN.* Purple and multicolor. Script signatures.*(S/M #C126-).*	20.00	60.00	150
u. *SHANGHAI.* Red and multicolor. *Shanghai* in black with red signature seals and red control letter *P* at left and right. *(S/M #C126-115a).*	—	Unc	100
v. *NANKING.* Green and multicolor. Overprint: *SPECIMEN* on issued note.	—	—	—
w. *FOOCHOW-AMOY.* Blue and multicolor.	500	1,400	—

Note: #118q with overprint: *KANSU PROVINCE / SHANGHAI* is a modern fabrication.

119	50 Yüan	Good	Fine	XF
	1.10.1914. Orange on multicolor underprint. Mountain landscape with two steam freight trains at center. Back: Ships at center. Printer: ABNC.			
	a. *CHUNGKING.* Orange and multicolor. *(S/M #C126-121).*	25.00	100	275
	b. *KALGAN.* Orange and multicolor. *(S/M #C126-122).*	375	2,000	10,200
	c. *SHANGHAI.* Orange and multicolor. *(S/M #C126-123).*	25.00	100	275
	d. *TIENTSIN. (S/M #C126-).*	150	800	2,175
	e. *KIUKIANG.* Orange and multicolor. Specimen. *(S/M #C126-).*	—	Unc	5,400
	f. *PEKING.* Orange and multicolor. Specimen. *(S/M #C126-).*	50.00	225	550

120	100 Yüan	Good	Fine	XF
	1.10.1914. Purple and multicolor. Steam passenger train crossing bridge at center. Back: Steam passenger train at center. Printer: ABNC.			
	a. *CHUNGKING. (S/M #C126-124).*	20.00	100.00	2,200
	b. *KALGAN. (S/M #C126-125).*	400	1,300	10,800
	c. *SHANGHAI. (S/M #C126-126).*	15.00	75.00	175
	d. *TIENTSIN. (S/M #C126-).*	125	600	3,300
	e. *KIUKIANG.* Specimen. *(S/M #C126-).*	—	Unc	3,600
	f. *PEKING.* Overprint: Specimen on issued note. *(S/M #C126-).*	35.00	150	300

1915 Issue

121	50 Cents	Good	Fine	XF
	1.1.1915. Black. Ship at left. Printer: ABNC.			
	a. *CHANGCHUN. (S/M #C126-).*	450	2,400	10,800
	b. *CHANGCHUN/YINGKOW.*	600	2,900	12,975

122	100 Cents	Good	Fine	XF
	1.1.1915. Black. Steam locomotive at right. Printer: ABNC.			
	a. *CHANGCHUN (S/M #C126-).*	400	1,800	10,800
	b. *CHANGCHUN/YINGKOW.*	350	1,400	6,488

122A	500 Cents	Good	Fine	XF
	1.1.1915. Gray. Steam passenger train in mountain pass at left. Printer: ABNC.			
	a. *YINGKOW.*	600	2,000	12,975
	s. *YINGKOW.* Specimen. *(S/M #C126-).*	—	Unc	2,700

122B	1000 Cents	Good	Fine	XF
	1.1.1915. Gray. Steam passenger train at right. Printer: ABNC. *(S/M #C126-).*			
	a. *YINGKOW.*	1,000	3,500	9,375
	s. As a. Specimen.	—	Unc	3,600

1917 Issue

123	10 Cents	Good	Fine	XF
	1.8.1917. Orange. *CHANGCHUN. (S/M #C126-).*	225	500	2,700

124	20 Cents	Good	Fine	XF
	1.8.1917. Black. River view at center. *CHANGCHUN. (S/M #C126-).*	225	950	3,000

124A	50 Cents	Good	Fine	XF
	1.8.1917. Green. Steam passenger train at center. *MUKDEN.* Specimen. *(S/M #C126-).*	—	Unc	1,800

1919 Issue

125	1 Yüan	Good	Fine	XF
	1.7.1919. Blue. Village near mountain at center. 2 signature varieties. Printer: BEPP. *HARBIN.(S/M #C126-131).*			
	a. Issued note.	125	425	1,800
	r. Remainder. Without serial # or place name.	—	Unc	450
	s. Specimen. *TAHEIHO.*	—	Unc	3,500

		Good	Fine	XF
126	**5 Yüan**			
	1.7.1919. Green. Bridge across brook. Printer: BEPP.			
	a. *HARBIN. (S/M #C126-132).*	175	550	2,700
	b. *TAHEIHO.* Specimen. *(S/M #C126-).*	—	Unc	3,600
	r. Remainder. Without place name. *(S/M #C126-).*	—	Unc	600

		Good	Fine	XF
127	**10 Yüan**			
	1.7.1919. Pagoda near mountain. Printer: BEPP.			
	a. *HARBIN.* Cancelled. *(S/M #C126-133).*	100	300	1,800
	b. *TAHEIHO.* Specimen. *(S/M #C126-).*	—	Unc	3,975

1920 Harbin Issue

		VG	VF	UNC
128	**1 Yüan**			
	1.12.1920. Black. Steam passenger train in ravine at center. 2 signature varieties. Similar to #116. Back: Sailing ship. Bank name, office of issue and denomination also in Russian. Printer: ABNC. *HARBIN. (S/M #C126-140).*			
	a. Issued note.	1,000	3,600	12,000
	s. Specimen.	—	—	2,880

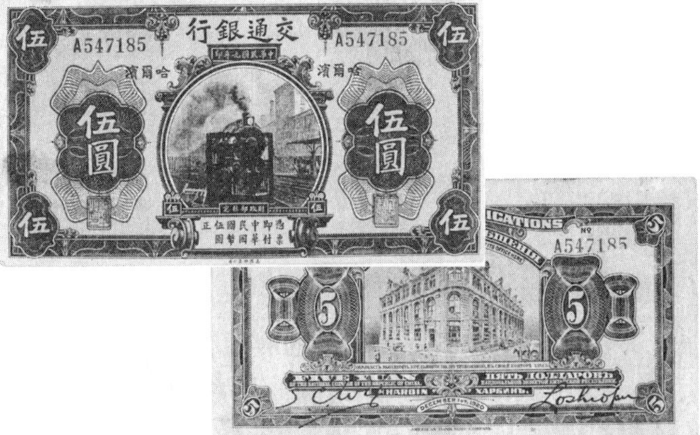

		VG	VF	UNC
129	**5 Yüan**			
	1.12.1920. Steam passenger train at center. Similar to #117. Back: Post Office at center. Bank name, office of issue and denomination also in Russian. Printer: ABNC. *HARBIN. (S/M #C126-141).*			
	a. Issued note.	1,200	4,500	17,400
	s. Specimen.	—	—	1,800

		VG	VF	UNC
130	**10 Yüan**			
	1.12.1920. Maritime Customs building, streetcar at center. Similar to #118. Back: Ship at dockside, steam passenger train at center. Bank name, office of issue and denomination also Printer: ABNC. *HARBIN. (S/M #C126-142).*			
	a. Issued note.	2,200	4,800	9,600
	s. Specimen.	—	—	1,325

		VG	VF	UNC
130A	**50 Yüan**			
	1.12.1920. Orange on multicolor underprint. Mountain landscape with two steam freight trains at center. Similar to #119. Back: Ships at center. Bank name, office of issue and denomination also in Russian. Printer: ABNC. *HARBIN.* Proof. *(S/M #C126-143).*	—	—	8,000

		VG	VF	UNC
130B	**100 Yüan**			
	1.12.1920 Purple and multicolor. Steam passenger train crossing bridge at center. Similar to #120. Back: Steam passenger train at center. Bank name, office of issue and denomination also in Russian. Printer: ABNC.. *HARBIN.* Proof. *(S/M #C126-144).*	—	—	5,000

1923 Issue

#131-133 printer: ABNC.

		VG	VF	UNC
131	**1 Dollar** 1.1.1923. Orange and multicolor. Electric direct current generator at center. Back: Sailing ship. Printer: ABNC. *FENGTIEN PROVINCE.* Specimen. *(S/M #C126-150).*			
	a. Issued note.	350	900	3,600
	s. Specimen. *(S/M #C126-150).*	—	—	1,000

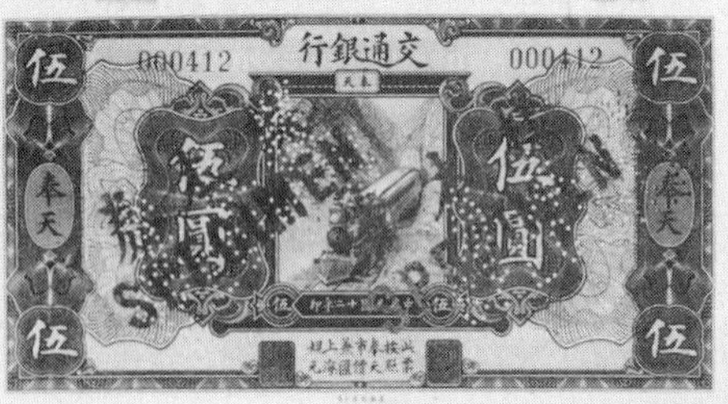

		VG	VF	UNC
132	**5 Dollars** 1.1.1923. Green and multicolor. Steam passenger train at center. Back: Steam passenger train at center. Printer: ABNC. *FENGTIEN PROVINCE.*			
	a. Issued note.	1,200	3,000	—
	s. Specimen. *(S/M #C126-151).*	—	—	1,450

		VG	VF	UNC
133	**10 Dollars** 1.1.1923. Purple and multicolor. Steam passenger train at center. Back: Bank building at center. Printer: ABNC.			
	a. *FENGTIEN PROVINCE. (S/M #C126-152).*	550	3,000	8,250
	b. *FENGTIEN PROVINCE/TIENTSIN.* Brown and multicolor.	2,700	6,300	—
	s. Specimen.	—	—	—

1924 Issue

		Good	Fine	XF
134	**1 Yüan** 1.7.1924. Brown. Steam passenger train at center. Back: Bank building at center. Printer: W&S. *SHANGHAI. (S/M #C126-160).*			
	a. Issued note.	525	1,450	3,200
	s. Specimen.	—	Unc	900

		Good	Fine	XF
135	**5 Yüan** 1.7.1924. Black-brown. Steam passenger train at center. Back: Bank building at center. Printer: W&S.			
	a. *KIUKIANG. (S/M #C126-).*	275	1,200	2,900
	b. *SHANGHAI. (S/M #C126-161).*	175	850	1,800
	s. No place name.	—	Unc	500

		Good	Fine	XF
136	**10 Yüan** 1.7.1924. Green. Ship dockside. Steam passenger train at center. Back: Bank building at center. Printer: W&S. *SHANGHAI. (S/M #C126-162).*	325	1,625	3,250

137 20 Yüan	Good	Fine	XF
1.7.1924. Blue. Ship, airplane, steam locomotive and truck at center. Printer: W&S.			
a. *SHANGHAI. (S/M #C126-).*	1,255	5,600	18,000
s. Without place name. Specimen. *(S/M #C126-163).*	—	Unc	8,100

1925 Issue

138 10 Cents	Good	Fine	XF
1.7.1925. Green. Steamship at center. Printer: BEPP.			
a. *HARBIN. (S/M #C126-170a).*	120	550	1,500
b. *SHANGHAI. (S/M #C126-).*	100	450	1,200
c. *TSINGTAU. (S/M #C126-170b).*	125	675	1,750
d. *WEIHAIWEI. (S/M #C126-170c).*	100	450	1,100
e. *SHIH-KIA CHUANG. (S/M #C126-).*	275	1,350	3,500
f. *WEI HAI WEI / PEKING & TIENTSIN CURRENCY.*	—	700	2,200
g. *TSINAN*	—	1,500	—
s. Specimen, 2 part.	—		

139 20 Cents	Good	Fine	XF
1.7.1925. Orange. Steam passenger train at center. Printer: BEPP.			
a. *HARBIN. (S/M #C126-171b).*	250	1,200	2,900
b. *SHANGHAI. (S/M #C126-171a).*	100	300	1,100
c. *TSINGTAU. (S/M #C126-).*	140	450	1,750
d. *WEIHAIWEI. (S/M #C126-).*	140	450	1,750
e. *WEIHAIWEI / PEKING & TIENTSIN CURRENCY.*	—	650	3,500

1927 First Issues

140 5 Cents	Good	Fine	XF
1.1.1927. Printer: BEPP. *HARBIN. (S/M #C126-180).*	250	1,200	3,600

141 10 Cents	Good	Fine	XF
1.1.1927. Blue. Steamship at left, steam locomotive at right. Similar to #143. Printer: W&S.			
a. *SHANGHAI. (S/M #C126-181a).*	35.00	225	500
b. *TSINGTAU. (S/M #C126-181b).*	55.00	400	850
s. Without place name. Specimen uniface face and back. *(S/M #C126-181-).*	—	Unc	450

142 10 Cents	Good	Fine	XF
1.1.1927. Red. Steamship at left, steam locomotive at right. Similar to #143. Printer: W&S. *TSINGTAU. (S/M #C126-182).*			
a. Issued note.	35.00	225	500
s. 2 part specimen.	—	Unc	450

143 20 Cents	Good	Fine	XF
1.1.1927. Red-brown. Steamship left, steam locomotive at right. Printer: W&S.			
a. *KALGAN. (S/M #C126-183a).*	45.00	225	540
b. *SHANGHAI* in black. *(S/M #C126-183b).*	100	225	900
c. *SHIHKIACHWANG. (S/M #C126-183c).*	125	700	1,950
d. *TSINAN. (S/M #C126-183d).*	65.00	400	840
e. *TSINGTAU. (S/M #C126-183e).*	50.00	275	660
f. *SHANGHAI* in blue. Specimen. Uniface face and back. *(S/M #C126-183b-a).*	—	Unc	660
g. *TSINGTAUBlue. Back: red-brown. (S/M #C126-183).*	240	660	—
s. 2 part specimen.	—	Unc	175

144 50 Cents	Good	Fine	XF
1.1.1927. *HARBIN. (S/M #C126-184).*	250	750	4,350

1927 Second Issue

145 1 Yüan	Good	Fine	XF
1.11.1927. Multicolor. Steam passenger train in ravine at center. Printer: ABNC. *FENGTIEN. (S/M #C126-190).*			
a. Issued note. Purple. *FEINTIEN.*	125	550	1,200
b. *HANKOW.* Orange.	—	—	—
s. Specimen. Orange. *HANKOW.*	—	Unc	350

145A 1 Yüan	Good	Fine	XF
1.11.1927. Steam passenger train in ravine at center. Similar to #145 but different colors and guilloches. Printer: ABNC. *SHANGHAI.*			
a. Purple and multicolor. *(S/M #C126-191).*	45.00	225	900
b. Brown and multicolor. *(S/M #C126-192).*	45.00	225	900
c. Blue and multicolor. 2 English signatures on back. *(S/M #C126-193).*	18.00	75.00	200
d. Like c. 2 Chinese signatures on back.	18.00	75.00	175

145B 1 Yüan	**Good**	**Fine**	**XF**
1.11.1927. Yellow-orange and multicolor. Steam passenger train in ravine at center. Similar to #145 but different guilloches. Printer: ABNC.			
a. *SHANTUNG. (S/M #C126-194).*	18.00	75.00	200
b. *CHEFOO/SHANTUNG.* Black Chinese signature on face and back. *(S/M #C126-195).*	22.50	90	275
c. *CHEFOO/SHANTUNG.* Red signature seals. Black English signature on back. *(S/M #C126-195).*	22.50	90	275
d. *LUNGKOW with SHANTUNG. (S/M #C126-196).* 2 signatures.	22.50	90	275
e. *TSINAN/SHANTUNG. (S/M #C126-197).* 2 signatures.	22.50	90	275
f. *TSINGTAU/SHANTUNG. (S/M #C126-198).* 2 signatures	22.50	90	275
g. *WEIHAIWEI/SHANTUNG. (S/M #C126-199).* 2 signatures	30.00	135	375
s. As a, specimen.	—	Unc	150

145C 1 Yüan	**Good**	**Fine**	**XF**
1.11.1927. Green and multicolor. Steam passenger train in ravine at center. Similar to #145 but different guilloches. Printer: ABNC. *TIENTSIN. (S/M #C126-200).*	13.50	40.00	175

146 5 Yüan	**Good**	**Fine**	**XF**
1.11.1927. Brown and multicolor. Steam passenger train at center. Printer: ABNC. *FENGTIEN. (S/M #C126-201).*			
a. Issued note.	135	550	1,800
s. Specimen.	—	Unc	700

146A 5 Yüan	**Good**	**Fine**	**XF**
1.11.1927. Green and multicolor. Steam passenger train at center. Similar to #146 but different guilloches. Printer: ABNC. *HANKOW. (S/M #C126-202).*	60.00	275	575

146B 5 Yüan	**Good**	**Fine**	**XF**
1.11.1927. Olive-brown and multicolor. Steam passenger train at center. Similar to #146 but different guilloches. Printer: ABNC. *SHANGHAI. (S/M #C126-203).*	25.00	120	250

146C 5 Yüan	**Good**	**Fine**	**XF**
1.11.1927. Purple and multicolor. Steam passenger train at center. Similar to #146 but different guilloches. Printer: ABNC.			
a. *SHANTUNG.* English signature. *(S/M #C126-204).*	18.00	75.00	225
b. *CHEFOO/SHANTUNG. (S/M #C126-210).*	18.00	75.00	225
c. *LUNGKOW with SHANTUNG. (S/M #C126-211).*	18.00	75.00	225
d. *TSINAN/SHANTUNG. (S/M #C126-212).*	18.00	75.00	225
e. *TSINGTAU/SHANTUNG. (S/M #C126-213).*	18.00	75.00	225
f. *WEIHAIWEI/SHANTUNG. (S/M #C126-).*	18.00	75.00	225
g. *SHANTUNG.* Chinese signature. *(S/M #C126-).*	18.00	75.00	225
s. As a, specimen.	—	Unc	150

146D 5 Yüan	**Good**	**Fine**	**XF**
1.11.1927. Orange and multicolor. Steam passenger train at center. Similar to #146 but different guilloches. Printer: ABNC. *TIENTSIN. (S/M #C126-214).*	30.00	150	300

147 10 Yüan	**Good**	**Fine**	**XF**
1.11.1927. Maritime Customs building, street car at center. Similar to #A147A but blue and different guilloches. Printer: ABNC. *FENGTIEN. (S/M #C126-220).*			
a. Issued note.	180	900	3,150
s. Specimen.	—	Unc	500

147A 10 Yüan	**Good**	**Fine**	**XF**
1.11.1927. Red and multicolor. Maritime Customs building, street car at center. Printer: ABNC. *SHANGHAI. (S/M #C126-221).*	30.00	150	300

		Good	Fine	XF
147B	**10 Yüan** 1.11.1927. Green and multicolor. Maritime Customs building, street car at center. Similar to #147 but different guilloches. Printer: ABNC.			
	a. *SHANTUNG.* English signature. *(S/M #C126-222).*	15.00	45.00	150
	b. *CHEFOO/SHANTUNG. (S/M #C126-223).*	15.00	65.00	225
	c. *LUNGKO with SHANTUNG. (S/M #C126-224).*	15.00	65.00	225
	d. *TSINAN/SHANTUNG. (S/M #C126-225).*	15.00	65.00	225
	e. *TSINGTAU/SHANTUNG. (S/M #C126-226).*	15.00	45.00	150
	f. *WEIHAIWEI/SHANTUNG. (S/M #C126-).*	45.00	150	450
	g. *SHANTUNG.* Chinese signature. *(S/M #C126-).*	15.00	54.00	150
	s. As a, specimen.	—	Unc	300

		Good	Fine	XF
147C	**10 Yüan** 1.11.1927. Brown and multicolor. Maritime Customs building, street car at center. Similar to #147 but different guilloches. Printer: ABNC.			
	a. *TIENTSIN. (S/M #C126-227).*	50.00	110	425
	b. *HANKOW. (S/M #C126-).* Olive green.	55.00	165	550
	s. As a, 2 part specimen.	—	Unc	325

1931 Issue

		VG	VF	UNC
148	**1 Yüan** 1.1.1931. Red. Steam passenger train at center. Back: Houses and pagoda at center. Printer: TDLR. *SHANGHAI. (S/M #C126-230).*			
	a. English signature and red signature seals printed separately at lower left and right.	—	—	—
	b. Red signature seals printed separately at lower left and right.	2.50	10.00	60.00
	c. Red signature seals engraved in frame design at lower left and right.	0.50	2.00	6.00
	s1. Specimen without seals on front.	—	—	150
	s2. Specimen with seals on front.	—	—	150

1935 First Provisional Issue

New issuer overprint of 9-Chinese characters and/or English text on National Industrial Bank of China notes.

		VG	VF	UNC
149	**1 Yüan** ND (1935-old date 1931). Purple and multicolor. Running horse at center. Back: Bank building at center. *(S/M #C126-231).*	80.00	200	650

		VG	VF	UNC
150	**5 Yüan** ND (1935-old date 1931). Red and multicolor. Running horse at center. Back: Bank building at center. *(S/M #C126-232).*	50.00	180	500
151	**10 Yüan** ND (1935-old date 1931). Green and multicolor. Running horse at center. Back: Bank building at center. *(S/M #C126-233).*	40.00	100	300

1935 Second Provisional Issue

		VG	VF	UNC
152	**1 Yüan** Nov. 1935 (-old date 1935). Red and multicolor. *(S/M #C126-240).*	20.00	100	250

1935 Regular Issue

		VG	VF	UNC
153	**1 Yüan** 1935. Purple on green underprint. Steam locomotive at center. Back: Pagoda on hill, shoreline at center. Printer: TDLR. *(S/M #C126-241).*	0.50	2.00	15.00

		VG	VF	UNC
154	**5 Yüan** 1935. Dark green on pink underprint. Junks at center. Back: Pagoda on hill, shoreline at center. Printer: TDLR. *(S/M #C126-242).*			
	a. Issued note.	0.10	0.50	5.00
	r. Remainder without red signature seals on face at lower left and right.	5.00	10.00	25.00

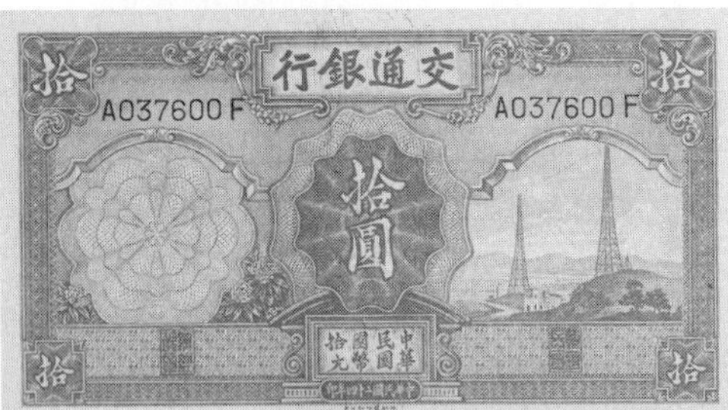

		VG	VF	UNC
155	**10 Yüan** 1935. Red on yellow-orange underprint. High voltage electric towers at right. Back: Pagoda on hill, shoreline at center. Printer: TDLR. *(S/M #C126-243).*	0.25	0.50	5.00

1941 Issue

#156-162 Nationalist issues with *CHUNGKING* while those without any place name were issued in Japanese controlled areas.

		VG	VF	UNC
156	**5 Yüan** 1941. Brown and multicolor. Steam passenger train at center. Back: Bank at center. Printer: ABNC. *(S/M #C126-252).*	2.00	7.50	35.00

		VG	VF	UNC
157	**5 Yüan** 1941. Brown and multicolor. Ship at center. Printer: CMPA. *(S/M #C126-#251).*			
	a. Issued note.	1.00	3.00	15.00
	s. 2 part specimen.	—	—	120

		VG	VF	UNC
158	**10 Yüan** 1941. Red and multicolor. Building with clock tower at center. Back: Dockside scene at center. Printer: ABNC. *(S/M #C126-253).*	2.00	7.50	25.00

	159 10 Yüan	VG	VF	UNC
	1941. Brown and multicolor. Steam passenger train at center. Printer: Dah Tung Book. *(S/M #C126-254).*			
	a. Serial # face and back.	.75	3.50	15.00
	b. Serial # on face only.	.75	3.50	15.00
	c. Without serial # or signature seals.	.75	3.50	15.00
	d. Mismatched serial #.	1.50	5.00	22.50
	e. Cancellation handstamp, serial # on face and back.	.75	3.50	15.00
	f. Cancellation handstamp, without serial # or signature seals.	.75	3.50	15.00
	g. Cancellation handstamp and mismatched serial #.	.40	1.00	7.50
	h. Serial # on back only.	.75	3.50	15.00
	s. Specimen.	—	—	100

	160 25 Yüan	VG	VF	UNC
	1941. Green and multicolor. Electric direct current generator, Zeppelin and plane at center. Back: Airplane at center. Printer: ABNC. *(S/M #C126-260).*	30.00	90.00	350

	161 50 Yüan	VG	VF	UNC
	1941. Brown and multicolor. Two railroad trains in a mountain pass. Back: Ships at center. Printer: ABNC.			
	a. *CHUNGKING. (S/M (S/M #C126-261b).*	5.00	20.00	90.00
	b. Without place name. *(S/M #C126-261a).*	5.00	20.00	55.00

	162 100 Yüan	VG	VF	UNC
	1941. Purple and multicolor. Steam passenger train on bridge at center. Back: Steam train at center. Printer: ABNC.			
	a. *CHUNGKING. (S/M #C126-262b).*	3.00	17.50	35.00
	b. Without place name. *(S/M #C126-262a).*	2.00	12.00	25.00

	163 500 Yüan	VG	VF	UNC
	1941. Blue on multicolor underprint. Ship at dockside at center. Back: Steam passenger train, high voltage electrical towers across landscape. Printer: ABNC. *(S/M #C126-263).*			
	a. Issued note.	200	900	2,100
	s. Specimen.	—	—	1,100

1942 Issue

	164 50 Yüan	VG	VF	UNC
	1942. Steam passenger train at left. Printer: Ta Tung (Dah Tung) Printing. *(S/M #C126-270).*			
	a. Purple.	45.00	90.00	400
	b. Brown-violet.	30.00	60.00	250

	165 100 Yüan	VG	VF	UNC
	1942. Brown. Steam train at left, ships at right. Back: Large value *100.* Printer: Ta Tung (Dah Tung) Printing. *(S/M #C126-271).*	20.00	90.00	225

1949 Circulating Cashier's Checks Issue

		VG	VF	UNC
165A	**500 Yüan** ND (1949). Light brown on light green. Back: Steam passenger train at upper center. Specimen. *(S/M #C126-).*	—	—	200

		Good	Fine	XF
165B	**1000 Yüan** ND (1949). Green. Back: Steam passenger train at upper center. *(S/M #C126-).*			
	a. Issued note.	45.00	225	450
	s. Specimen.	—	Unc	200

		Good	Fine	XF
165C	**2000 Yüan** ND (1949). Red. Back: Steam passenger train at upper center. *(S/M #C126-).*			
	a. Issued note.	45.00	225	450
	s. Specimen.	—	Unc	200

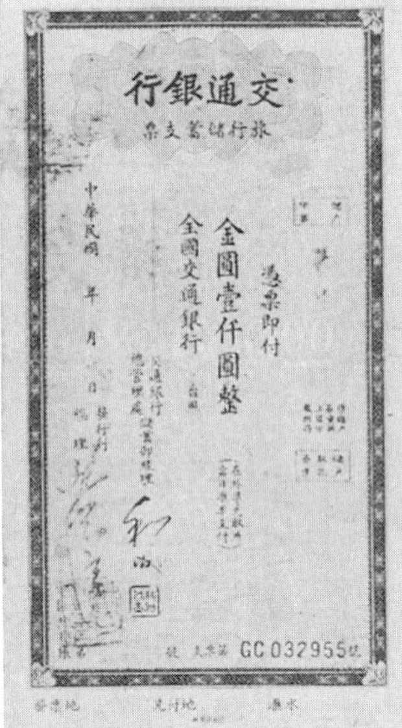

		Good	Fine	XF
166	**1000 Gold Yüan** ND (1949). Green. Printer: CPF. *(S/M #C126-280).*	18.00	75.00	175

Central Bank of China (National) 行銀央中

Chung Yan Yin Hang

Established in November 1928 as the primary note issuing agency for the Chinese Nationalist Government in Nanking. Not to be confused with the other Central Bank of China (quasi-national) which was based in Kwangtung Province w/issues dated 1923-27. See #171-192. For other national issues see #193-450. Note: Numerous sign. varieties exist for issues prior to 1940.

1928 (ND) Coin Note Issue

		VG	VF	UNC
167	**10 Coppers** ND (1928). Violet and green underprint. Pagoda at left.			
	a. Black overprint: *SHENSI.*	12.00	50.00	125
	b. Red Chinese overprint: *5 Fen* (5 Cents) (Legal tender for circulation in Szechuan Province).	7.50	18.00	45.00
	c. Similar to #167b. With additional black Chinese overprint: *5 Fen.*	12.50	45.00	125

		VG	VF	UNC
168	**20 Coppers** ND (1928). Dark blue on red underprint. Pagoda at right.			
	a. Black overprint: *SHENSI.*	18.00	60.00	200
	b. Red overprint: *1 CHIAO* (10 Cents). Similar to #167b.	5.00	23.00	50.00
	c. Similar to #168b. With additional Chinese overprint: *1 Chiao* over *20 Coppers.*	7.50	30.00	90.00

		VG	VF	UNC
169	**50 Coppers** ND (1928). Lilac-brown on light brown. Pagoda at right.			
	a. Black overprint: *SHENSI.*	30.00	150	300
	b. Red overprint: *2 CHIAO 5 FEN* (25 Cents). Similar to #167b and #168b.	15.00	60.00	175

1920 Provisional Issue

		Good	Fine	XF
170	**5 Dollars** ND (1928-old date 1.9.1920). Red and multicolor. Bank at center. Back: Floral pot at center.			
	a. English overprint 80mm on back.	40.00	200	450
	b. English overprint 83mm on back.	40.00	200	450

Central Bank of China (Quasi-national) 行銀央中

Chung Yan Yin Hang

Not to be confused w/the national bank of the same name, this issuer was located in Kwangtung Province. Included are many military issues of the Kuomintang forces during the 1926-27 Northern Expedition.

1923 Issue

171	1 Dollar	Good	Fine	XF
	1923. Green and multicolor. Portrait SYS at center. Printer: ABNC.			
	a. English signature.	5.00	23.00	45.00
	b. Chinese signature.	5.00	23.00	45.00
	c. Overprint: *HUNAN, KIANGSI & KWANGSI* on back. English signature.	50.00	225	675
	d. Red overprint: 4-Chinese characters in circles at corners, (Kwangchow) on face. English signature.	60.00	350	900
	e. Overprint: *Swatow* at left and right. SWATOW at lower center with Swatow diagonally at left and right on back. English signature.	6.25	22.50	60.00
	f. SWATOW with circular violet Central Bank handstamp.	7.50	40.00	80.00
	g. Red overprint: *HUPEH, HUNAN, & KWANGSI* on back.	90.00	450	1,100
	h. Overprint: *Kwangtung* above portrait.	12.50	45.00	125
	i. Large oval branch office handstamp: *HUNAN, KIANGSI & KWANGSI.* With Chinese characters on face.	—		
	s. Specimen.	—	Unc	150

171A	1 Dollar	Good	Fine	XF
	1923. Dark green and multicolor. Portrait SYS at center. Printer: ABNC.			
	a. *Haikow* at left and right. *HAI KOW* at lower left and right on back. Specimen.	—	Unc	1,000
	b. *Kongmoon* at left and right. *KONG MOON* at lower left and right on back. Specimen.	—	Unc	1,000
	c. *Meiluck* at left and right. *MEI LUCK* at lower left and right on back. Specimen.	—	Unc	1,000
	d. *Pakhoi* at left and right. *PAK HOI* at lower left and right on back. Specimen.	—	Unc	1,000
	e. *Suichow* at left and right. *SUI CHOW* at lower left and right on back. Specimen.	—	Unc	1,000
	f. *Swatow* at left and right. *SWATOW* at lower left and right on back. Specimen.	—	Unc	1,000
	g. *Swatow* with additional circular violet Central Bank handstamp on face.	—	Unc	1,000

172	1 Dollar	Good	Fine	XF
	1923. Yellow-orange and multicolor. Portrait SYS at center. Similar to #171. Printer: ABNC.			
	a. English signature.	14.00	60.00	150
	b. Chinese signature.	12.50	60.00	125
	c. Overprint: *Kwangtung* at left and right of portrait.	14.00	60.00	150
	d. 4-Chinese character overprint: *Kwang-Chung-Tsung-Hang* for Kwangchow head office. Chinese signature.	90	450	1,100
	e. Overprint: *Kwangchow* and *Kwangtung.*	54.00	270	550
	f. English signatures and overprint: *KWANGTUNG.*	200	550	—
	g. English signatures.	—	600	—
	s. Specimen.	—	Unc	300

173	5 Dollars	Good	Fine	XF
	1923. Brown and multicolor. Portrait SYS at center. Printer: ABNC.			
	a. English signature.	15.00	70.00	175
	b. Chinese signature.	15.00	70.00	175
	c. Overprint: *HUNAN, KIANGSI & KWANGSI* on back. English signature.	115	450	1,325
	d. 4 character Chinese overprint: *Kwang-Chung-Tsung-Hang* for Kwang-chow head office in circles in corners. English signature.	100	550	1,325
	e. Red overprint: *HUPEH, HUNAN & KIANGSI* on back.	225	1,200	2,700
	f. Large oval branch office handstamp: *HUNAN, KIANGSI, & KWANGSI.* With Chinese characters on face.	—	—	—
	g. Overprint: *PAKHOI.*	60.00	300	875
	h. *PAKHOI.* English signature.	60.00	300	875
	s. Specimen.	—	Unc	275

174	5 Dollars	Good	Fine	XF
	1923. Red. Portrait SYS at center. Similar to #173. Printer: ABNC.			
	a. Chinese and English signature.	125	600	2,400
	b. Overprint: *Kwangtung* above portrait Chinese and English signature.	125	600	2,400
	c. Overprint: *Kwangtung* above portrait English signature	125	600	2,400
	d. 4 character Chinese overprint: *Kwang-Chung-Tsung-Hang* for Kwanchow head office.	165	1,050	2,400
	s. Specimen.	—	Unc	450

175	5 Dollars	Good	Fine	XF
	1923. Green and multicolor. Portrait SYS at center. Similar to #174. Printer: ABNC.			
	a. *Haikow* at left and right. *KAI KOW* on back. Specimen.	—	Unc	2,200
	b. *Kongmoon* at left and right. *KONG MOON* at left and right on back. Specimen.	—	Unc	1,350
	c. *Meiluck* at left and right. *MEI LUCK* at left and right on back. Specimen.	—	Unc	1,350
	d. *Pakhoi* at left and right. *PAK HOI* at left and right on back. Specimen.	—	Unc	1,350
	e. *Suichow* at left and right. *SUI CHOW* at left and right on back. Specimen.	—	Unc	1,350
	f. *Swatow* at left and right. *SWATOW* at left and right on back. Specimen.	—	Unc	1,350

176	10 Dollars	Good	Fine	XF
	1923. Brown on multicolor underprint. Portrait SYS at center. Printer: ABNC.			
	a. Overprint: *Kwangtung* in Chinese on face (single black characters at upper left and right center), English signature. 152x76mm.	2.00	15.00	35.00
	b. As a. Chinese and English signature. 152x76mm.	4.00	20.00	50.00
	c. As a. 157x78mm.	2.00	15.00	35.00
	d. As b. 157x78mm.	2.00	15.00	35.00
	e. Without overprint: *Kwangtung* on face. Chinese signature. 157x78mm.	2.00	12.40	30.00
	s. Specimen.	—	Unc	250

176A	10 Dollars	Good	Fine	XF
	1923. Pink and multicolor. Portrait SYS at center. Similar to #176. Printer: ABNC.			
	a. *Haikow* at left and right. *HAI KOW* on back. Specimen.	—	Unc	1,750
	b. *Kongmoon* at left and right. *KONG MOON* at left and right on back. Specimen.	—	Unc	1,750
	c. *Meiluck* at left and right. *MEI LUCK* at left and right on back. Specimen.	—	Unc	1,750
	d. *Suichow* at left and right. *SUI CHOW* at left and right on back. Specimen.	—	Unc	1,750
	e. *Pakhoi* at left and right. *Pak Hoi* at left and right on back. Specimen.	—	Unc	2,700
	f. *Swatow* at left and right. *SWATOW* at left and right on back. Specimen.	—	Unc	2,700

No.	Description	Good	Fine	XF
177	**10 Dollars** 1923. Green and multicolor. Portrait SYS at center. Similar to #176 but with *10* in large outlined Chinese characters. Printer: ABNC.			
	a. Red overprint: *HUPEH, HUNAN & KIANGSI* and *TEN STANDARD DOLLARS* on back.	180	900	3,800
	b. Blue 4 character Chinese overprint: *Kwang-Chung-Tsung-Hang* for Kwangchow head office in circles.	135	675	2,625
	c. Large oval branch office handstamp: *HUNAN, KIANGSI, & KWANGSI*. With Chinese characters on face.	—	—	—
	s. Specimen.	—	Unc	450
178	**50 Dollars** 1923. Orange and multicolor. Portrait SYS at center. Printer: ABNC.	Good	Fine	XF
	a. English signature.	225	1,050	3,900
	b. *SWATOW*. With circular violet *Central Bank* handstamp on face.	225	1,050	4,875
	c. Overprint: *The Central Bank of China - SWATOW* on face and back.	300	1,700	6,750
	s. Specimen.	—	Unc	3,750

No.	Description	Good	Fine	XF
179	**100 Dollars** 1923. Brown. Portrait SYS at center. Printer: ABNC.			
	a. Issued note.	350	1,775	6,500
	b. Overprint: *HUNAN, KIANGSI & KWANGSI* on back.	350	1,775	6,500
	c. Overprint: *SWATOW on back*.	—	Unc	12,000
	s. Specimen.	—	Unc	3,900
179A	**100 Dollars** 1923. Green and multicolor. Portrait SYS at center. Printer: ABNC. Specimen.	VG —	VF —	UNC 1,625
179B	**100 Dollars** 1923. Violet and multicolor. *Suichow* at left and right. Back: *SUI CHOW* at left and right. Specimen.	VG —	VF —	UNC 1,625

1923 Commemorative Issue

#180 and 180A death of Sun Yat Sen.

No.	Description	VG	VF	UNC
180	**5 Dollars** 1923. Brown and multicolor. SYS at center.	200	750	3,000
180A	**10 Dollars** 1923. Green and multicolor. SYS at center.	225	1,000	4,100

1926 Provisional Issue

No.	Description	Good	Fine	XF
181	**1 Dollar** ND (1926). Orange and multicolor.	75.00	225	725

1926 Issue

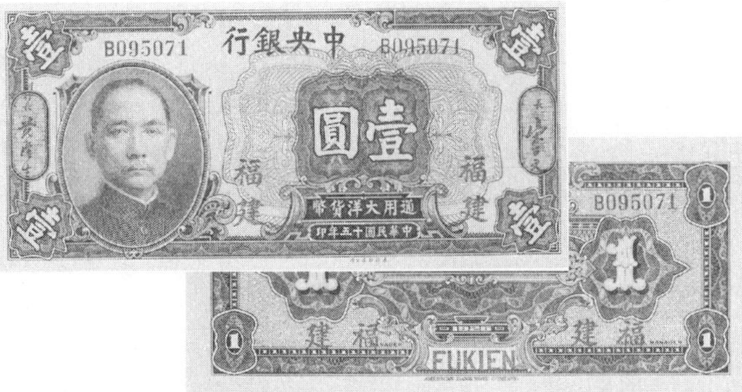

No.	Description	Good	Fine	XF
182	**1 Dollar** 1926. Blue on multicolor underprint. Portrait SYS at left. Printer: ABNC.			
	a. *CHUNGKING* and *ONE YUAN LOCAL CURRENCY...* overprint on back.	50.00	225	550
	b. *FUKIEN*.	15.00	75.00	200
	c. *HANKOW*.	50.00	250	675

No.	Description	Good	Fine	XF
183	**5 Dollars** 1926. Orange on multicolor underprint. Portrait SYS at right. Printer: ABNC.			
	a. *CHUNGKING*. Green overprint: *FIVE YUAN LOCAL CURRENCY* ... on back.	90.00	250	1,100
	b. *FUKIEN*.	40.00	190	675
	c. *HANKOW* with control letters *TH*.	90.00	350	1,450
	d. *HOIKOW*.	100	450	1,950
	e. *SHANGHAI*.	100	450	1,950

No.	Description	Good	Fine	XF
184	**10 Dollars** 1926. Red on multicolor underprint. Portrait SYS at center. Printer: ABNC.			
	a. *CHUNGKING. Overprint: TEN YUAN LOCAL CURRENCY...*	100	550	2,650
	b. *FUKIEN*.	125	450	2,200
	c. *HANKOW*.	360	840	—
	s. Specimen.	—	Unc	300

		Good	Fine	XF
184A	**50 Dollars**	**Good**	**Fine**	**XF**
	1926. Black and multicolor. Portrait SYS. Printer: ABNC.			
	a. *HANKOW.*	150	750	3,900
	b. *SHANGHAI.*	150	750	3,900
	s. Specimen. Without office of issue.	—	Unc	2,000
184B	**100 Dollars**	**Good**	**Fine**	**XF**
	1926. Printer: ABNC.			
	p. Proof.	—	Unc	1,325
	s. Specimen.	—	Unc	1,600

1926 Military Issue

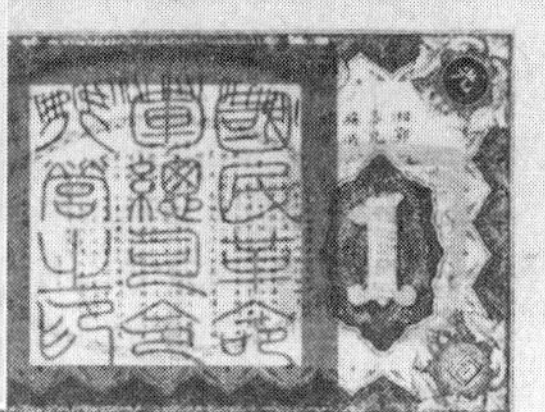

		Good	Fine	XF
185	**1 Dollar**	**Good**	**Fine**	**XF**
	1926. Lilac-brown. Sailing ship at left, steamer at right. Back: Large red handstamp.			
	a. Red serial #.	50.00	350	650
	b. Blue serial #.	50.00	350	650
	c. Cancelled. With Chinese handstamp.	45.00	225	500

		Good	Fine	XF
186	**5 Dollars**	**Good**	**Fine**	**XF**
	1926. Gray-green. Temple at center. Back: Large red handstamp.			
	a. Issued note.	75.00	350	1,250
	b. Cancelled. With Chinese handstamp.	75.00	350	1,250

		Good	Fine	XF
187	**10 Dollars**	**Good**	**Fine**	**XF**
	1926. Brown. Ship at center. Back: Large red handstamp.			
	a. Issued note.	75.00	400	1,625
	b. Cancelled. With Chinese handstamp.	75.00	400	1,625

1927 Issue

#188 ***Renumbered.*** **See #193.#190** ***Renumbered.*** **See #194.**

		Good	Fine	XF
189	**1 Chiao = 10 Cents**	**Good**	**Fine**	**XF**
	1927. Green. Temple of Heaven. Printer: CHB.	180	750	3,263
191	**2 Chiao = 20 Cents**	**Good**	**Fine**	**XF**
	1927. Red. Temple of Heaven. Printer: CHB.	180	750	3,263

		Good	Fine	XF
192	**5 Chiao = 50 Cents**	**Good**	**Fine**	**XF**
	1927. Orange. Temple of Heaven at center. Printer: CHB.	75	300	1,500

Central Bank of China (National-Continued) 中央銀行

Chung Yuan Yin Hang

SIGNATURE/TITLE VARIETIES		
1	GENERAL MANAGER	MANAGER
2	ASST. MANAGER	GENERAL MANAGER
3	ASST. MANAGER	GENERAL MANAGER
4	ASST. MANAGER	GENERAL MANAGER
5	ASST. MANAGER	GENERAL MANAGER
6	ASST. GENERAL MANAGER	GENERAL MANAGER
7	ASST. GENERAL MANAGER	GENERAL MANAGER
8	ASST. GENERAL MANAGER	GENERAL MANAGER
9	ASST. GENERAL MANAGER	GENERAL MANAGER
10	GENERAL MANAGER	GOVERNOR
11	GENERAL MANAGER	GOVERNOR
12	ASST. GENERAL MANAGER	GENERAL MANAGER

1924 Issue

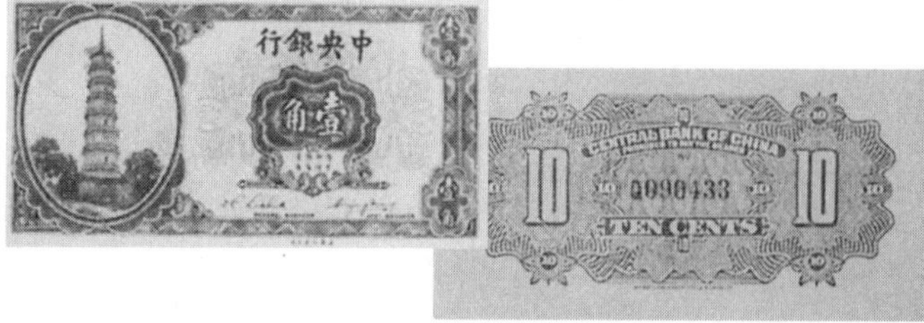

193	1 Chiao = 10 Cents	VG	VF	UNC
	ND (1924). Black on multicolor underprint. Back: Pagoda at left. Printer: ABNC.			
	a. Signature 1.	1.50	7.50	22.50
	b. Signature 5.	1.50	7.50	22.50
	s. As a. Specimen.	—	—	75.00

194	2 Chiao = 20 Cents	VG	VF	UNC
	ND (1924). Black on multicolor underprint. Pagoda at right. Printer: ABNC.			
	a. Signature 1.	5.50	23.00	60.00
	b. Signature 2.	5.50	23.00	60.00
	c. Signature 5. Requires confirmation.	—	—	—
	s. Specimen.	—	—	125

1928 Issue

195	1 Dollar	VG	VF	UNC
	1928. Green. Back: Portrait SYS at left. Printer: ABNC. Serial # on face and back. *SHANGHAI*. Various control overprints: symbols, numerals and Chinese characters.			
	a. Signature 2.	15.00	75.00	—
	b. Signature 3.	15.00	75.00	—
	c. Signature 5.	0.75	3.00	15.00

196	5 Dollars	VG	VF	UNC
	1928. Olive and multicolor. Back: Portrait SYS at right. Printer: ABNC. Serial # on face and back. Black signature. *SHANGHAI*. Various control overprints: symbols, numerals and Chinese characters.			
	a. Signature 2.	100	350	2,000
	b. Signature 3.	100	350	2,000
	c. Signature 5.	50.00	225	1,100
	d. Signature 8.	50.00	225	1,100

197	10 Dollars	VG	VF	UNC
	1928. Dark blue and multicolor. Back: Portrait SYS at center. Printer: ABNC. *SHANGHAI*.			
	a. Signature 2.	3.00	13.00	40.00
	b. Signature 3.	3.00	7.50	25.00
	c. Signature 4.	3.00	13.00	40.00
	d. Signature 5a. Small black Signature	3.00	5.00	10.00
	e. Signature 5b. Large black Signature	3.00	5.00	10.00
	f. Signature 7 in black. Serial # on face and back.	3.00	5.00	12.50
	g. As f. Serial # on face only.	3.00	5.00	10.00
	h. Signature 7 in green as part of plate.	3.00	5.00	10.00

198	50 Dollars	VG	VF	UNC
	1928. Orange and multicolor. Back: Portrait SYS at center. Printer: ABNC. *SHANGHAI*.			
	a. Signature 5.	5.00	8.00	18.00
	b. Signature 5. Overprint: *CHUNGKING/SHANGHAI*.	5.00	13.00	30.00
	c. Signature 6. Serial numbers front and back.	5.00	15.00	50.00
	d. Signature 7 in blue.	5.00	23.00	65.00
	e. Signature 7 in black. Serial # on face and back.	5.00	12.00	35.00
	f. As e. Serial # on face only.	5.00	12.00	45.00
	g. As e. Signature thinner, as part of plate.	5.00	12.00	35.00
	h. As c. Serial number on back only.	5.00	—	—

Note: #198a-g with various control overprints are considered spurious.

199	100 Dollars	VG	VF	UNC
	1928. Olive and multicolor. Back: Portrait SYS at center. Printer: ABNC. *SHANGHAI*.			
	a. Signature 5. Serial # on face and back.	4.00	12.00	40.00
	b. As a. Serial # on face only.	4.00	12.00	40.00
	c. As a. Overprint: *CHUNGKING/SHANGHAI*.	4.00	12.00	40.00
	d. Signature 6. Serial numbers on face only.	4.00	9.00	35.00
	e. Signature 7. Black. Serial numbers on face only.	4.00	12.00	40.00
	f. Signature 7. Purple as part of plate.	4.00	12.00	35.00
	g. As d. Serial numbers on face and back.	4.00	12.00	35.00
	h. As e. Serial numbers on face and back.	4.00	12.00	40.00

Note: #199a-g with various control overprints are considered spurious.

1930 Issue

200	5 Dollars	VG	VF	UNC
	1930. Dark green and multicolor. SYS at center. Back: Temple at center. Printer: ABNC. *SHANGHAI*. With various control overprints.			
	a. Signature 2.	4.00	12.00	45.00
	b. Signature 3.	4.00	12.00	40.00
	c. Signature 4.	4.00	12.00	45.00

	VG	VF	UNC
d. Signature 5.	4.00	6.00	12.00
e. Signature 7 in black. Serial # on face and back.	4.00	6.00	12.00
f. Signature 7 in green as part of plate. Serial # on back only.	4.00	6.00	9.00
s1. Specimen	—	—	200
s2. As b, 2 part specimen	—	—	200
s3. As f, specimen	—	—	225

201 *Deleted.* Renumbered to #205A.

1931 Issue

202	10 Cents = 1 Chiao	VG	VF	UNC
	ND (1931). Green. Temple behind trees at left. Printer: CHB.	2.00	3.00	5.00

203	20 Cents = 2 Chiao	VG	VF	UNC
	ND (1931). Blue. Chu-Shui-Bridge at right. Printer: CHB.	3.00	5.00	8.00

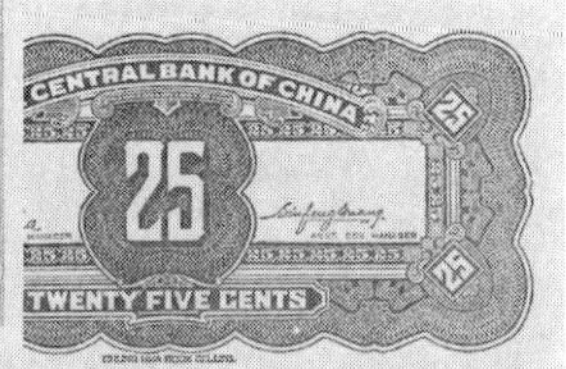

204	25 Cents	VG	VF	UNC
	ND (1931). Lilac. P'ai-lou (commemorative archway) at left. Printer: CHB.	5.00	20.00	70.00

205	50 Cents	VG	VF	UNC
	ND (1931). Purple. Temple of Confucius at left. Printer: CHB. Paper and 3 serial # varieties.	3.00	15.00	60.00

1934 Provisional Issue

205A	1 Dollar	VG	VF	UNC
	ND (-old date 1934). Red and multicolor. Farmer plowing with water buffalo at center. Printer: CHB.			
	a. *SHANGHAI.*	140	450	1,400
	b. *TIENTSIN.*	140	450	1,400
	c. *PEIPING.*	140	250	1,400
	d. Without place name.	100	300	1,000

1935 Regular Issue

205B	10 Cents	VG	VF	UNC
	ND (1935). Dark blue. Portrait SYS at upper center. *SZECHUEN.*	125	600	1,750

205C	20 Cents	VG	VF	UNC
	ND (1935). Brown. Portrait SYS at upper center. *SZECHUEN.*	125	550	2,000
206	1 Yüan	VG	VF	UNC
	1935. Orange on yellow and light blue underprint. Ships at center. Printer: CHB. *CHUNGKING.*	135	700	2,400
207	5 Yüan	VG	VF	UNC
	1935. Red on pink underprint. Multicolor guilloche at center. Portrait SYS at left. Printer: BEPP. *CHUNGKING.*	75.00	450	2,040

208	10 Yüan	VG	VF	UNC
	1935. Green on light green and brown underprint. Portrait SYS at left. Printer: BEPP. *CHUNGKING.*	75.00	375	1,000

1936 "CHB" Issues

209	1 Yüan	VG	VF	UNC
	1936. Orange on multicolor underprint. Wan Ku Chang Ch'un monument at right. Back: 2 signature varieties. Printer: CHB.	75.00	338	900

		VG	VF	UNC
210	**1 Yüan** 1936. Orange and black. Similar to #209 but monument in black at right. Back: Signature 5. Printer: CHB. 135x65mm.	3.00	15.00	40.00

		VG	VF	UNC
211	**1 Yüan** 1936. Orange on multicolor underprint. Vessel at left, SYS at right. Back: Confucius meeting Lao Tzu; men with two horse-drawn carts. Printer: CHB.			
	a. Signature 10.	3.00	4.00	10.00
	b. Signature 11.	3.00	5.00	20.00

1936 "TDLR" Issues

		VG	VF	UNC
212	**1 Yüan** 1936. Orange and black on multicolor underprint. SYS at left. Back: Gateway and temple behind trees at center. Watermark: SYS. Printer: TDLR.			
	a. Signature 5.	3.00	5.00	10.00
	b. Signature 8.	3.00	5.00	12.00
	c. Signature 9.	2.00	5.00	10.00

		VG	VF	UNC
212A	**1 Yüan** ND (-old date 1936). Dark green and black on multicolor underprint. SYS at left. Lithograph like #213. Back: Chinese text. (Pass for Nanking Military Government).	275	450	—

		VG	VF	UNC
213	**5 Yüan** 1936. Dark green and black on multicolor underprint. SYS at left. Back: Gateway and temple behind trees at center. Watermark: SYS. Printer: TDLR.			
	a. Signature 5.	3.00	5.00	8.00
	b. Signature 8.	3.00	8.00	15.00
	c. Signature 9.	3.00	4.00	8.00

		VG	VF	UNC
214	**10 Yüan** 1936. Dark blue and black on multicolor underprint. SYS at left. Back: Gateway and temple behind trees at center. Watermark: SYS. Printer: TDLR.			
	a. Signature 5.	3.00	5.00	10.00
	b. Signature 8.	3.00	5.00	15.00
	c. Signature 9.	3.00	5.00	10.00

#215 Deleted.

1936 "W&S" Issue

		VG	VF	UNC
216	**1 Yüan** 1936. Orange. SYS at left. Back: Temple (Palace of China in Peking). Printer: W&S. 2 serial # varieties.			
	a. Signature 5.	3.00	5.00	10.00
	b. Signature 7.	3.00	5.00	10.00
	c. Signature 8.	3.00	5.00	10.00
	d. Signature 9.	3.00	5.00	10.00
	e. Overprint: Tibetan characters on face and back. Signature 5; 7-9.	135	—	—
	s1. Specimen (2 part).	—	—	225
	s2. Specimen - 2 part, as a.	—	—	225

Note: The Tibetan overprint occurs on #216e, 217d, 218f, 219c and 220c, although the authenticity of the last two overprints is questionable. There are also many examples of the 1 to 10 year notes, 216e, 217d and 218f when the overprints have been later additions. Great care must be excercised to establish authenticity.

		VG	VF	UNC
217	**5 Yüan** 1936. Green on multicolor underprint. SYS at left. Back: Palace of China in Peking. Printer: W&S. 2 serial # varieties.			
	a. Signature 5.	3.00	5.00	10.00
	b. Signature 8.	3.00	5.00	15.00
	c. Signature 9.	3.00	5.00	10.00
	d. Overprint: Tibetan characters on face and back. Signature 5.	45.00	125	—

		VG	VF	UNC
218	**10 Yüan** 1936. Dark blue and black on multicolor underprint. SYS at left. Back: Palace of China in Peking at right. Watermark: SYS. Printer: W&S.			
	a. Signature 5.	3.00	5.00	8.00
	b. Signature 6.	3.00	5.00	8.00
	c. Signature 7.	3.00	5.00	15.00
	d. Signature 8 (heavier or lighter print).	3.00	5.00	15.00
	e. Signature 9.	3.00	5.00	10.00
	f. Overprint: Tibetan characters on face and back. Signature 5; 7.	30.00	75.00	—

		VG	VF	UNC
219	**50 Yüan** 1936. Dark blue and brown on multicolor underprint. SYS at left. Back: Palace of China in Peking at center. Watermark: SYS. Printer: W&S.			
	a. Issued note. Signature 11 in red.	5.00	15.00	30.00
	b. Overprint: *Chungking* in Chinese at left and right and in English at upper center on back. Signature 10 in black.	25.00	—	—
	c. Overprint: Tibetan characters on face and back.	—	—	—

Note: #219 b-c are controversial.

		VG	VF	UNC
220	**100 Yüan**			
	1936. Olive-green and dark brown on multicolor underprint. SYS at left. Back: Palace of China in Peking at center. Watermark: SYS. Printer: W&S.			
	a. Signature 11 in purple.	10.00	20.00	120
	b. Overprint: *Chungking* in Chinese at left and right and in English at upper center on back. Signature 10 in black.	150	—	—
	c. Overprint: Tibetan characters on face and back. Signature 11 in black.	375	—	—
	d. Signature 11 in black. No overprint.	10.00	20.00	120

		VG	VF	UNC
221	**500 Yüan**			
	1936. Red-brown. SYS at left. Back: Palace of China in Peking at center. Printer: W&S.			
	a. Issued note. Signature 11.	100	300	1,440
	s. Specimen.	—	—	225

1937 Issue

		VG	VF	UNC
222	**5 Yüan**			
	1937. Green on multicolor underprint. Antique bronze tripod at left, portrait SYS at right. Back: Confucius meeting Lao Tzu; men with two horse-drawn carts. Like #211. Printer: CHB.	8.00	35.00	90.00

		VG	VF	UNC
223	**10 Yüan**			
	1937. Blue and green. SYS at left, vessel at right. Back: Confucius meeting Lao Tzu; men with two horse-drawn carts. Like #211. Printer: CHB.			
	a. Issued note.	15.00	75.00	175
	b. Without signature.	10.00	40.00	90.00

1939 Issue

		VG	VF	UNC
224	**1 Fen = 1 Cent**			
	1939. Red. Pagoda at left. Back: Coin at right.			
	a. Printer: Union Publishers & Printers.	2.00	3.00	5.00
	b. Printer: Union Printing Co.	2.00	3.50	8.00

		VG	VF	UNC
225	**5 Fen = 5 Cents**			
	1939. Green. Pagoda at left. Back: Coin at center.			
	a. Printer: Union Publishers & Printers.	2.00	3.00	5.00
	b. Printer: Union Printing Co.	2.00	3.50	15.00

		VG	VF	UNC
225A	**5 Fen = 5 Cents**			
	1939. Green. Pagoda at left. Like #225. Back: With date 1936 and Chinese text (Pass for the Nanking Military Government).	—	125	250

1940 Issue

		VG	VF	UNC
226	**1 Chiao = 10 Cents**			
	1940. Green. Portrait SYS at right. Printer: CHB.	2.00	3.00	4.00

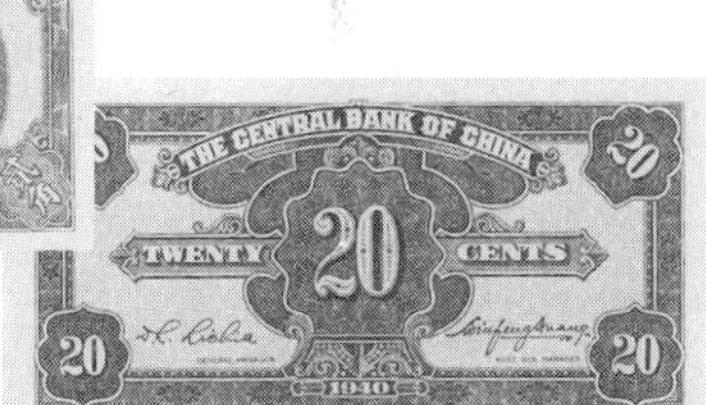

		VG	VF	UNC
227	**2 Chiao = 20 Cents**			
	1940. Blue. Portrait SYS at right. Like #226. Printer: CHB.			
	a. Issued note.	2.00	3.00	6.00
	r. Remainder without signature.	—	—	—

		VG	VF	UNC
228	**10 Yüan**			
	1940. Blue-gray. Portrait SYS at right. Printer: CHB.	0.30	0.75	4.00

229	50 Yüan	VG	VF	UNC
	1940. Orange. Portrait SYS at right. Printer: CHB. *CHUNG-KING*.			
	a. Signature 5.	7.50	20.00	90.00
	b. Signature 8.	6.00	20.00	75.00

1941 Issue

230	2 Yüan	VG	VF	UNC
	1941. Purple on light orange and blue underprint. SYS at right. Printer: CHB.	5.00	7.50	15.00

231	2 Yüan	VG	VF	UNC
	1941. Blue and multicolor. SYS at left. 3 serial # varieties. Back: Temple behind trees at center. Printer: TDLR.	5.00	7.50	30.00

232	2 Yüan	VG	VF	UNC
	1941. Blue and multicolor. SYS at left. Back: Pagoda near Wang He Lou mountain slope. Printer: TDLR.	8.00	25.00	75.00

233	5 Yüan	VG	VF	UNC
	1941. Green. SYS at left. Back: Similar to #237. Printer: W&S.	5.50	15.00	50.00

234	5 Yüan	VG	VF	UNC
	1941. Green on multicolor underprint. Portrait SYS at lower right. 2 serial # varieties. Printer: CHB.			
	a. Issued note.	3.00	5.00	12.00
	b. overprint: *Chungking* in Chinese at left and right on face. *CHUNGKING* in English on back.	3.00	15.00	45.00

235	5 Yüan	VG	VF	UNC
	1941. Lilac-brown. SYS at left. 2 serial # varieties. Back: Pagoda near Wang He Lou mountain slope. Printer: TDLR.	2.00	3.00	6.00

236	5 Yüan	VG	VF	UNC
	1941. Dark brown. SYS at left. 3 serial # varieties. Back: Temple behind trees at center. Printer: TDLR.	1.00	3.00	15.00

237	10 Yüan	VG	VF	UNC
	1941. Dark blue. SYS at left. Printer: W&S.			
	a. Signature 5.	3.00	7.00	18.00
	b. Signature 6.	3.00	5.00	15.00
	c. Signature 7.	3.00	5.00	15.00
	d. Signature 8.	3.00	7.00	18.00
	e. Signature 9.	2.50	3.00	9.00

238	10 Yüan	VG	VF	UNC
	1941. Blue. P'ai-Lou Gate at left. 2 serial # varieties. Printer: Chinese.			
	a. Signature 7.	9.00	25.00	110
	b. Signature 9.	7.00	25.00	80.00

239	10 Yüan	VG	VF	UNC
	1941. Blue. SYS at left. Printer: SBNC.			
	a. Signature 7 in black.	3.00	6.00	12.00
	b. Signature 12 in green as part of plate.	3.00	10.00	30.00
	s. 2 part specimen.	—	—	60.00

240	20 Yüan	VG	VF	UNC
	1941. Red and multicolor. Portrait SYS at left. Printer: SBNC.			
	a. Signature 7 in black. Blue serial # and signature seals.	3.00	7.50	30.00
	b. As a but with red serial # and signature seals.	3.00	6.00	25.00
	c. Signature 12 in brown as part of plate.	1.00	3.00	15.00
	s. 2 part specimen.	—	—	120

#241 *Deleted.*

242	50 Yüan	VG	VF	UNC
	1941. Green. P'ai-Lou Gate at right. 2 serial # varieties.			
	a. Chinese printer 8 characters.	13.00	25.00	90.00
	b. Chinese printer 7 characters.	25.00	60.00	180
	c. Chinese printer 6 characters.	25.00	60.00	180

243	100 Yüan	VG	VF	UNC
	1941. Greenish gray on multicolor underprint. Portrait SYS at left. Printer: SBNC.			
	a. Issued note.	1.00	2.00	4.00
	b. Without serial #.	3.00	13.00	30.00
	s. 2 part specimen.	—	—	80.00

1942 Issue

244	5 Yüan	VG	VF	UNC
	1942. Green. SYS at left. Back: Airplane. Printer: TDLR.			
	a. Signature 6.	3.00	6.00	30.00
	b. Signature 7.	3.00	6.00	30.00
	s. 2 part specimen.	—	—	100

245	10 Yüan	VG	VF	UNC
	1942. Blue. Portrait SYS at left. Back: Military trumpeter near Great Wall. Printer: TDLR.			
	a. Signature 5.	3.00	7.50	30.00
	b. Signature 6.	3.00	3.50	15.00
	c. Signature 7.	3.00	4.50	18.00
	d. Overprint: *Chungking*. Signature 7.	23.00	75.00	225

246	10 Yüan	VG	VF	UNC
	1942. Blue. SYS at left. Back: Without vignette. Printer: Dah Tung Book Company.	3.00	8.00	35.00

247	10 Yüan	VG	VF	UNC
	1942. Brown. P'ai-lou Gate at right. Printer: Chinese. 2 serial # and 2 paper varieties.	7.50	30.00	120

248	20 Yüan	VG	VF	UNC
	1942. Brown. P'ai-lou Gate at right. Printer: Chinese.	7.50	35.00	140

		VG	VF	UNC
249	**100 Yüan**			
	1942. Red. Victory Gate at center.			
	a. Chinese printer 8 characters. Signature 7.	6.50	18.00	75.00
	b. As a. Signature 9.	4.50	12.00	45.00
	c. Chinese printer 7 characters. Signature 7.	6.50	23.00	90.00

		VG	VF	UNC
250	**100 Yüan**			
	1942. Red. SYS at right. Printer: Chinese.	12.00	50.00	120

		VG	VF	UNC
251	**500 Yüan**			
	1942. Red on gold underprint. SYS at left. Back: Ship at center. Printer: TDLR.	0.50	2.00	10.00

		VG	VF	UNC
252	**1000 Yüan**			
	1942. Lilac on light green underprint. SYS at left. Back: Great Wall at center. Printer: TDLR.	0.50	2.00	10.00

		VG	VF	UNC
253	**2000 Yüan**			
	1942. Red on light green underprint. SYS at left. Back: Pagoda at shoreline. Printer: TDLR.	0.75	2.50	8.00

1943 Issue

		VG	VF	UNC
254	**100 Yüan**			
	1943. Green-black. Victory Gate at left. Printer: Chinese.	5.00	30.00	100

1944 Issue

		VG	VF	UNC
255	**50 Yüan**			
	1944. Deep purple on multicolor underprint. SYS at left. Watermark: SYS. Printer: TDLR.	1.00	4.00	15.00

		VG	VF	UNC
256	**100 Yüan**			
	1944. Dark brown on multicolor underprint. SYS at left. Watermark: SYS. Printer: TDLR.	0.75	3.00	15.00

		VG	VF	UNC
257	**100 Yüan**			
	1944. Green on red underprint. SYS at left. Back: SYS memorial at right. Printer: W&S.	150	700	2,000

		VG	VF	UNC
258	**100 Yüan**			
	1944. Gray on light blue and pale orange underprint. P'ai-lou gateway at center. Printer: Chinese. 150x64mm.	7.50	35.00	120

		VG	VF	UNC
259	**100 Yüan**			
	1944. Blue. P'ai-lou gateway at left. Printer: Chinese. 151x77mm.	7.50	35.00	120

		VG	VF	UNC
260	**100 Yüan**			
	1944. Black on light gray and pale violet underprint. P'ai-lou gateway at left. Printer: Chinese. 165x65mm.	7.50	35.00	120

		VG	VF	UNC
260A	**100 Yüan**			
	1944. Dark gray on pale green underprint. Portrait SYS at right. Printer: Chinese 6 characters.	2.50	15.00	40.00

		VG	VF	UNC
261	**100 Yüan**			
	1944. Dark brown. P'ai-lou gateway at center. Printer: Chinese 8 characters. 165x63mm.	5.00	30.00	80.00

262 200 Yüan VG VF UNC
1944. Dark green. Portrait SYS at lower left. Printer: Chinese 6 characters. 5.00 40.00 90.00

263 400 Yüan VG VF UNC
1944. Green. Portrait SYS at lower left. Printer: Chinese 6 characters. 10.00 75.00 180

264 500 Yüan VG VF UNC
1944. Red. SYS at left. Watermark: SYS. Printer: TDLR. 0.75 3.00 20.00

265 500 Yüan VG VF UNC
1944. Red-brown on pale orange and light yellow-green underprint. SYS at left. Watermark: SYS. Printer: W&S. 3.00 15.00 40.00

266 500 Yüan VG VF UNC
1944. Black on yellow-green and tan underprint. P'ai-lou gateway at left, portrait SYS at right. Printer: Chinese 8 characters. 179x79mm. 10.00 40.00 100

267 500 Yüan VG VF UNC
1944. Dark brown on pale orange and light olive-green underprint. Portrait SYS at left. Printer: BABNC. 2 serial # varieties. 1.50 7.50 15.00

268 1000 Yüan VG VF UNC
1944. Deep brown on purple and multicolor underprint. Portrait SYS at left. P'ai-lou gateway at right. Printer: Chinese 8 characters.

	VG	VF	UNC
a. Issued note.	2.00	10.00	30.00
b. With 2 red Chinese handstamps: "Army Command Northeast" and *Tung Pei* on face.	30.00	150	450

269 1000 Yüan VG VF UNC
1944. Blue-gray. Portrait SYS at lower right. Printer: Chinese 6 characters. 12.00 35.00 90.00

Note: Also see special issues for Manchuria #375-379.

1945 Issues

No.	Description	VG	VF	UNC
269A	**5 Yüan** 1945. Green on red underprint. Portrait SYS at lower left. Vietnam. *(S/M #C300-).*	—	—	—
269B	**5 Yüan** 1945. Blue. SYS at left. Taiwan. *(S/M #C300-219).*	—	—	—

No.	Description	VG	VF	UNC
270	**10 Yüan** 1945. Green on pale green underprint. Portrait SYS at lower left. Printer: Chinese.	0.50	2.50	10.00

No.	Description	VG	VF	UNC
271	**10 Yüan** 1945. Orange. SYS at left. Back: Naval battle. Taiwan. (Not issued).	—	—	—

No.	Description	VG	VF	UNC
272	**10 Yüan** 1945. Burgundy. Portrait SYS at lower left. Vietnam.	—	—	—

No.	Description	VG	VF	UNC
273	**50 Yüan** 1945. Red on pale red underprint. Portrait SYS at left. Printer: Chinese.	0.50	2.50	8.00

Note: #273 with 5 character overprint for Vietnam is believed to be a modern fabrication.

No.	Description	VG	VF	UNC
274	**50 Yüan** 1945. Olive. SYS at left. Printer: CPF. Sinkiang.	75.00	400	1,500
275	**50 Yüan** 1945. Red. SYS at left. Back: Mirror printing of naval battle. Taiwan. (Not issued).	—	—	—

No.	Description	VG	VF	UNC
276	**50 Yüan** 1945. Portrait SYS at lower left. Vietnam. Rare. Blue.	—	—	—
277	**50 Yüan** 1945. Green. Victory Gate.	20.00	100	300

No.	Description	VG	VF	UNC
277A	**100 Yüan** 1945 Blue-gray. Portrait SYS at lower left. Printer: CPF.. Sinkiang.	125	600	7,500
277B	**100 Yüan** 1945. Taiwan.	—	—	—

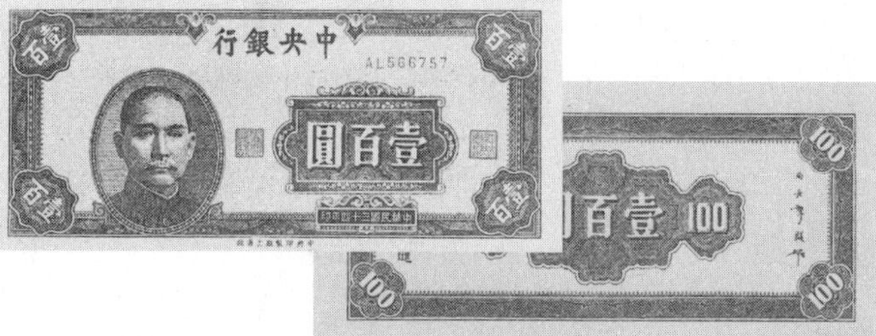

No.	Description	VG	VF	UNC
278	**100 Yüan** 1945. Blue on pale blue underprint. Portrait SYS at lower left. Printer: Chinese.	2.00	8.00	20.00

No.	Description	VG	VF	UNC
279	**200 Yüan** 1945. Gray-blue. SYS at left. Printer: Chinese.	4.00	18.00	40.00

No.	Description	VG	VF	UNC
280	**400 Yüan** 1945. Lilac. Portrait SYS at lower left. Printer: Chinese.	5.00	18.00	125
281	**400 Yüan** 1945. Dark blue-black on light blue-green and pink underprint. SYS at left in underprint.	20.00	100	250

No.	Description	VG	VF	UNC
282	**500 Yüan** 1945. Blackish green on light blue underprint. Portrait SYS at lower left. Printer: Chinese 8 characters.	2.00	8.00	40.00

		VG	VF	UNC
283	**500 Yüan**			
	1945. Black with light blue national sunbursts in underprint at left and right. Portrait SYS at center. Printer: Chinese 8 characters.			
	a. Issued note.	1.00	2.50	10.00
	b. 2 Chinese handstamps: "Army Command North-east" and *Tung Pei* on face.	13.00	75.00	150

		VG	VF	UNC
284	**500 Yüan**			
	1945. Green. SYS at left. Printer: Chinese 5 characters.	2.00	7.50	25.00

		VG	VF	UNC
285	**500 Yüan**			
	1945. Brown on lilac underprint. P'ai-lou Gate at right. Printer: Chinese 7 characters.	10.00	50.00	140

		VG	VF	UNC
286	**500 Yüan**			
	1945. Red. Printer: Chinese 8 characters.	10.00	50.00	180

		VG	VF	UNC
287	**1000 Yüan**			
	1945. Red-orange on lilac underprint. Portrait SYS at lower left. Printer: Chinese 8 characters.	3.50	15.00	50.00

		VG	VF	UNC
288	**1000 Yüan**			
	1945. Brown-violet on pink underprint. Portrait SYS at lower left. Printer: Chinese 8 characters.	2.50	13.00	40.00

		VG	VF	UNC
289	**1000 Yüan**			
	1945. Brown. Portrait SYS at center. Printer: Chinese 8 characters.	1.00	4.00	15.00

		VG	VF	UNC
290	**1000 Yüan**			
	1945. Purple. SYS at center. Back: National sunburst at left and right. Printer: SBNC.	0.40	2.00	5.00

		VG	VF	UNC
291	**1000 Yüan**			
	1945. Black. SYS at right. Printer: Chinese 7 characters. PC: Gray.	2.50	10.00	35.00

291A Deleted. See #290.
291B Deleted. See #294.

		VG	VF	UNC
292	**1000 Yüan**			
	1945. Brown on lilac underprint. SYS at left. Printer: Chinese 5 characters.	2.50	10.00	40.00

293	1000 Yüan	VG	VF	UNC
	1945. Blue-gray on pale blue and lilac underprint. SYS at left. Printer: Chinese 5 characters.	2.50	10.00	40.00

294	1000 Yüan	VG	VF	UNC
	1945. Brown on red-brown underprint. SYS at left. Printer: Chinese 10 characters.	1.50	7.50	25.00

295	1000 Yüan	VG	VF	UNC
	1945. Dark blue on pale blue and lilac underprint. Printer: Chinese 5 characters.	2.50	13.00	40.00

296	1000 Yüan	VG	VF	UNC
	1945. Red on pink underprint. P'ai-lou Gate at center. Printer: Chinese 7 characters.	10.00	50.00	150

297	1000 Yüan	VG	VF	UNC
	1945. Green. SYS at left. Printer: Chinese 6 characters.	3.50	15.00	50.00

298	1000 Yüan	VG	VF	UNC
	1945. Blue. Portrait SYS at lower left. Chinese signature in thick or thin characters. Printer: Chinese 6 characters. PC: White to gray.	2.50	13.00	35.00

299	2000 Yüan	VG	VF	UNC
	1945. Green. Great Wall at right. Printer: Chinese 7 characters.	20.00	100	260

300	2000 Yüan	VG	VF	UNC
	1945. Brown-violet. SYS at right. Printer: Chinese 5 characters.	2.50	10.00	40.00

301	2000 Yüan	VG	VF	UNC
	1945. Violet. SYS at left. Printer: Chinese 5 character.			
	a. Issued note.	2.00	10.00	40.00
	b. With 2 Chinese handstamps: "Army Command Northeast" and *Tung Pei* on face.	25.00	100	375

302	2000 Yüan	VG	VF	UNC
	1945. Green. SYS at left. Printer: Chinese 6 characters.	7.50	35.00	90.00

303	2500 Yüan	VG	VF	UNC
	1945. Blue-light blue. Portrait SYS at left. 3 serial # varieties. Printer: Chinese 7 characters.	5.00	30.00	80.00

304	2500 Yüan	VG	VF	UNC
	1945. Blue on green underprint. SYS at left. Printer: Chinese 6 characters.	12.50	60.00	225

305	5000 Yüan	VG	VF	UNC
	1945. Blue-black on multicolor underprint. Portrait SYS at left. P'ai-lou Gate at right. Printer: Chinese 5 characters.	2.50	10.00	60.00

306	5000 Yüan	VG	VF	UNC
	1945. Brown. SYS at left. 2 Chinese signature varieties. 2 serial # varieties. Printer: Chinese 6 characters.	2.00	8.00	40.00

1946 Issue

307	2000 Yüan	VG	VF	UNC
	1946. Purple on gold underprint. SYS at left. Back: SYS Mausoleum at center right. Printer: W&S.	2.00	6.00	20.00

1947 Issue

No.	Description	VG	VF	UNC
308	**2000 Yüan** 1947. Green on pale green and pink underprint. Portrait SYS at lower left. P'ai-lou Gate at right. Printer: Chinese 8 characters.	5.00	30.00	70.00
309	**5000 Yüan** 1947. Dark blue on light green underprint. SYS at left. Printer: Chinese 8 characters.	1.50	6.50	30.00
310	**5000 Yüan** 1947. Purple. SYS at left. Printer: TDLR.	1.25	5.00	25.00
311	**5000 Yüan** 1947. Dark lilac on gold underprint. SYS at left. Back: SYS Mausoleum at center.	1.50	7.50	25.00

No.	Description	VG	VF	UNC
312	**5000 Yüan** 1947. Blue on green underprint. Portrait SYS at lower left. Like #309. Printer: Chinese 5 characters.	1.50	7.50	20.00
313	**5000 Yüan** 1947. Green on light violet underprint. SYS at center. Printer: Chinese 6 characters.	1.50	7.50	20.00
314	**10,000 Yüan** 1947. Brown. SYS at left, mountains and river at right. Printer: Chinese 8 characters.	0.75	5.00	15.00

No.	Description	VG	VF	UNC
315	**10,000 Yüan** 1947. Olive on multicolor underprint. Portrait SYS at left, mountains and river at right. Printer: Chinese 8 characters. 159x75mm.	7.50	40.00	90.00

#316 *Deleted.* See #320c.

No.	Description	VG	VF	UNC
317	**10,000 Yüan** 1947. Red on pale blue and light green underprint. Portrait SYS at center. Printer: TDLR.	1.50	4.00	15.00

No.	Description	VG	VF	UNC
318	**10,000 Yüan** 1947. Gray-blue. SYS at left. Printer: Chinese 8 characters. 164x74mm.	1.50	6.00	20.00

No.	Description	VG	VF	UNC
319	**10,000 Yüan** 1947. Red-brown. SYS at center. Printer: SBNC.			
	a. Issued note.	0.75	2.50	15.00
	s. 2 part specimen.	—	—	70.00

No.	Description	VG	VF	UNC
320	**10,000 Yüan** 1947. Blue-violet. Portrait SYS at lower left.			
	a. Chinese printer 5 characters. 2 paper and serial # varieties.	1.25	5.00	25.00
	b. Chinese printer 6 characters.	1.25	5.00	20.00
	c. Chinese printer 8 characters.	1.25	5.00	20.00
321	**10,000 Yüan** 1947. Dark brown on multicolor underprint. SYS at left. Printer: Chinese 6 characters.	5.00	25.00	90.00

No.	Description	VG	VF	UNC
322	**10,000 Yüan** 1947. Lilac. Portrait SYS at lower left. Printer: Chinese 8 characters. 162x74mm.	5.00	25.00	90.00
322A	**50,000 Yüan** 1947. Brown on green underprint. SYS at right. Back: Small house at center. Printer: HBNC.			
	a. Finished note (not issued).	—	—	—
	p. Proof.	—	—	750

1930 Shanghai Customs Gold Units Issue

Note: This issue was primarily intended to facilitate customs payments, but during and after World War II the notes were used for general circulation. The 1930 issue was printed into the 1940s.

		VG	VF	UNC
323	**10 Cents** 1930. Purple with multicolor guilloche. Portrait SYS at top center. Back: Bank building at left center. Printer: ABNC. Vertical format.			
	a. Signature 4.	10.00	55.00	250
	b. Signature 5.	5.00	15.00	90.00

		VG	VF	UNC
324	**20 Cents** 1930. Green with multicolor guilloche. Portrait SYS at top center. Back: Bank building at left center. Printer: ABNC. Vertical format.			
	a. Signature 4.	10.00	45.00	135
	b. Signature 5.	5.00	27.50	75.00

		VG	VF	UNC
325	**1 Customs Gold Unit** 1930. Brown with multicolor guilloche. Portrait SYS at top center. Back: Bank building at left center. Printer: ABNC. Vertical format.			
	a. Signature 4.	5.50	20.00	110
	b. Signature 5.	3.50	15.00	45.00
	c. Signature 7 in black. Signature title: *ASSISTANT MANAGER* at right. Serial # on face and back.	5.50	20.00	110
	d. Signature 7 in brown as part of plate. Signature title: *ASST. GENERAL MANAGER* at right. Serial # on back only.	0.75	3.50	15.00

		VG	VF	UNC
326	**5 Customs Gold Units** 1930. Black with multicolor guilloche. Portrait SYS at top center. Back: Bank building at left center. Printer: ABNC. Vertical format.			
	a. Signature 4.	5.00	18.00	75.00
	b. Signature 5.	3.50	11.00	45.00
	c. Signature 7. Sign title: *ASSISTANT MANAGER* at right. Serial # on face and on back.	3.50	11.00	45.00
	d. Signature 7 in plate. Signature title: *ASST. GENERAL MANAGER* at right. Serial # on back only.	0.40	1.25	3.50

		VG	VF	UNC
327	**10 Customs Gold Units** 1930. Olive-gray with multicolor guilloche. Portrait SYS at top center. Back: Bank building at left center. Printer: ABNC. Vertical format.			
	a. Signature 4.	5.50	20.00	110
	b. Signature 5.	2.25	9.00	20.00
	c. Signature 7 in black. Signature title: *ASSISTANT MANAGER* at right. Serial # on face and on back.	2.25	9.00	20.00
	d. Signature 7 in plate. Signature title: *ASST. GENERAL MANAGER* at right. Serial # on back only.	0.50	1.75	5.00
	s. Specimen as c.	—	—	200

		VG	VF	UNC
328	**20 Customs Gold Units** 1930. Dark green with multicolor guilloche. Portrait SYS at top center. Back: Bank building at left center. Printer: ABNC.Vertical format.	0.50	3.50	7.50

		VG	VF	UNC
329	**50 Customs Gold Units** 1930. Purple with multicolor guilloche. Portrait SYS at top center. Back: Bank building at left center. Printer: ABNC. Vertical format.	0.50	2.50	6.00

		VG	VF	UNC
330	**100 Customs Gold Units** 1930. Red with multicolor guilloche. Portrait SYS at top center. Back: Bank building at left center. Printer: ABNC. Vertical format.			
	a. Issued note.	0.60	2.00	7.50
	b. With 2 red Chinese handstamps: "Army Command Northeast" and *Tung Pei.*	—	—	—

		VG	VF	UNC
331	**250 Customs Gold Units** 1930. Brown with multicolor guilloche. Portrait SYS at top center. Back: Bank building at left center. Printer: ABNC. Vertical format.	1.50	7.50	35.00

Color Abbreviation Guide

New to the *Standard Catalog of® World Paper Money* are the following abbreviations related to color references:

BC: Back color

PC: Paper color

1930 (1947) Customs Gold Units Issue

		VG	VF	UNC
332	**500 Customs Gold Units** 1930 (1947). Blue. Portrait SYS at top center. Back: Bank building at left center. Printer: ABNC. Vertical format.	1.00	5.00	20.00

Note: #332, though dated 1930 these notes were issued in 1947.

1947 Customs Gold Units Issue

		VG	VF	UNC
333	**100 Customs Gold Units** 1947. Violet with multicolor guilloche. Portrait SYS at top center. Back: Bank building at left center. Horizontal format. Specimen.	—	—	600

		VG	VF	UNC
334	**500 Customs Gold Units** 1947. Blue on multicolor underprint with multicolor guilloche. Portrait SYS at top center. Back: Bank building at left center. Horizontal format.	5.00	18.00	45.00

		VG	VF	UNC
335	**500 Customs Gold Units** 1947. *SHANGHAI*. Blue. Portrait SYS at top center. Back: Bank building at left center. Printer: ABNC. Vertical format.	1.00	4.00	12.50

		VG	VF	UNC
336	**500 Customs Gold Units** 1947. Light green. Portrait SYS at top center. Back: Bank building at left center. Printer: SBNC. Vertical format.			
	a. Issued note.	1.00	5.00	15.00
	s. Specimen.	—	—	—

#337 *Deleted*. See #339c.

		VG	VF	UNC
338	**1000 Customs Gold Units** 1947. Olive. Olive guilloche. Portrait SYS at top center. Back: Bank building at left center. Printer: CHB. Vertical format.	0.50	4.50	10.00

		VG	VF	UNC
339	**1000 Customs Gold Units** 1947. Gray. Brown and lilac guilloche. Portrait SYS at top center. Back: Bank building at left center. Vertical format.			
	a. Chinese printer 8 characters. Serial # 2mm tall.	0.50	4.00	12.50
	b. Chinese printer 6 characters. Serial # 3mm tall.	0.50	4.00	12.50
	c. Chinese printer 5 characters. 2 serial # varieties.	1.00	3.50	15.00
	s. Specimen. Face and back uniface.	—	—	200

		VG	VF	UNC
340	**2000 Customs Gold Units** 1947. Orange. Portrait SYS at top center. Back: Bank building at left center. Printer: ABNC. Vertical format.	1.00	5.00	15.00

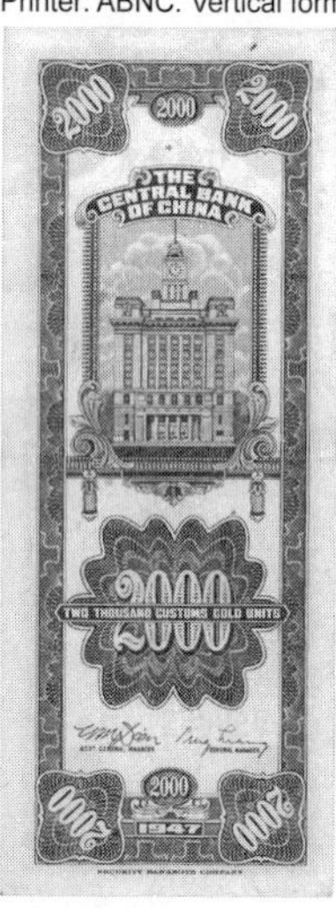

		VG	VF	UNC
341	**2000 Customs Gold Units** 1947. Light olive-brown. Portrait SYS at top center. Back: Bank building at left center. Printer: SBNC. Vertical format.	0.50	3.50	12.50

#341A *Deleted.* See #342c.

		VG	VF	UNC
342	**2000 Customs Gold Units** 1947. Green. Portrait SYS at top center. Back: Bank building at left center. Vertical format.			
	a. Chinese printer 5 characters.	1.00	3.50	20.00
	b. Chinese printer 6 characters.	1.00	3.50	20.00
	c. Chinese printer 9 characters.	1.00	3.50	20.00

		VG	VF	UNC
343	**2000 Customs Gold Units** 1947. Dark brown. Portrait SYS at top center. Back: Bank building at left center. Printer: CHB. Vertical format.	1.00	3.50	20.00

		VG	VF	UNC
344	**2000 Customs Gold Units** 1947. Blue-violet. Portrait SYS at top center. Back: Bank building at left center. Printer: TDLR. Vertical format.	1.00	3.00	15.00

		VG	VF	UNC
345	**2500 Customs Gold Units** 1947. Olive. Portrait SYS at top center. Back: Bank building at left center. Printer: CHB. Vertical format.	3.50	18.00	60.00
346	**2500 Customs Gold Units** 1947. Violet. Portrait SYS at top center. Back: Bank building at left center. Printer: Chinese 5 characters. Vertical format. Requires confirmation.	—	—	—

		VG	VF	UNC
347	**5000 Customs Gold Units** 1947. Brown. Portrait SYS at top center. Back: Bank building at left center. Printer: TDLR. Vertical format.	3.00	10.00	40.00
348	**5000 Customs Gold Units** 1947. Green. Portrait SYS at top center. Back: Bank building at left center. Printer: TDLR. Vertical format.	—	—	—
349	**5000 Customs Gold Units** 1947. Blue. Portrait SYS at top center. Back: Bank building at left center. Printer: SBNC.Vertical format.	2.50	10.00	30.00

		VG	VF	UNC
350	**5000 Customs Gold Units** 1947. Green. Portrait SYS at top center. Back: Bank building at left center. Printer: Chinese 5 characters. Vertical format.	1.25	5.00	25.00

		VG	VF	UNC
351	**5000 Customs Gold Units** 1947. Red. Portrait SYS at top center. Back: Bank building at left center. Printer: Chinese 5 characters. Vertical format.			
	a. Issued note.	1.25	3.50	18.00
	p. Proof.	—	—	275

		VG	VF	UNC
352	**5000 Customs Gold Units** 1947. Brown on gold underprint. Portrait SYS at top center. Large or small serial #. Back: Bank building at left center. Printer: Chinese 5 characters. Vertical format.	1.25	5.00	25.00

		VG	VF	UNC
353	**5000 Customs Gold Units** 1947. Brown. Portrait SYS at top center. Back: Bank building at left center. Printer: CHB. Vertical format.	1.00	3.50	15.00

		VG	VF	UNC
354	**10,000 Customs Gold Units** 1947. Blue. Portrait SYS at top center. Back: Bank building at left center. Printer: TDLR. Vertical format.	1.00	3.50	15.00
355	**10,000 Customs Gold Units** 1947. Portrait SYS at top center. Back: Bank building at left center. Printer: SBNC. Vertical format. Requires confirmation.	—	—	—

#356 not assigned.

1948 Customs Gold Units Issue

		VG	VF	UNC
357	**2000 Customs Gold Units** 1948. Orange. Portrait SYS at top center. Back: Bank building at left center. Printer: Chinese 5 characters. Vertical format.	0.50	3.00	15.00

358 2500 Customs Gold Units
1948. Lilac-brown. Portrait SYS at top center. Large or small serial #. Back: Bank building at left center. Printer: Chinese 5 characters. Vertical format.

VG	VF	UNC
2.00	9.00	25.00

359 5000 Customs Gold Units
1948. Purple. Portrait SYS at top center. Back: Bank building at left center. Printer: ABNC. Vertical format.

VG	VF	UNC
3.00	9.00	50.00

360 5000 Customs Gold Units
1948. Blue. Portrait SYS at top center. Back: Bank building at left center. Printer: SBNC. Vertical format.

VG	VF	UNC
2.00	7.50	30.00

361 5000 Customs Gold Units
1948. Purple. Portrait SYS at top center. Large or small serial # . Back: Bank building at left center. Printer: Chinese 5 characters. 2 paper varieties. Vertical format.

VG	VF	UNC
1.25	3.50	15.00

362 5000 Customs Gold Units
1948. Blue. Portrait SYS at top center. Back: Bank building at left center. Printer: CHB. Vertical format.

VG	VF	UNC
1.25	3.50	15.00

363 10,000 Customs Gold Units
1948. Blue. Portrait SYS at top center. Back: Bank building at left center. Printer: SBNC. Vertical format.

VG	VF	UNC
1.50	7.50	25.00

364 10,000 Customs Gold Units
1948. Blue. Portrait SYS at top center. 2 serial # varieties. Back: Bank building at left center. Printer: Chinese 5 characters. Vertical format.

VG	VF	UNC
1.25	3.50	15.00

364A 10,000 Customs Gold Units
1948. Portrait SYS at top center. Back: Bank building at left center. Printer: W&S. Vertical format.

VG	VF	UNC
—	—	—

365 25,000 Customs Gold Units
1948. Brown. Portrait SYS at top center. Back: Bank building at left center. Printer: ABNC. Vertical format.

VG	VF	UNC
12.50	50.00	250

Color Abbreviation Guide

New to the *Standard Catalog of ® World Paper Money* are the following abbreviations related to color references:

BC: Back color
PC: Paper color

		VG	VF	UNC
366	**25,000 Customs Gold Units** 1948. Green. Portrait SYS at top center. Large or small serial #. Back: Bank building at left center. Printer: Chinese 5 characters. Vertical format.	3.00	14.00	60.00
367	**25,000 Customs Gold Units** 1948. Lilac-brown. Portrait SYS at top center. Back: Bank building at left center. Printer: CHB. Vertical format.	9.00	25.00	150
368	**50,000 Customs Gold Units** 1948. Red. Portrait SYS at top center. Back: Bank building at left center. Printer: CHB. Vertical format.			
	a. Issued note.	60.00	225	800
	s. Specimen.	—	—	275
369	**50,000 Customs Gold Units** 1948. Pink. Portrait SYS at top center. Similar to #368 but different guilloche. Back: Bank building at left center. Printer: CHB. Vertical format. Specimen.	—	—	250
369A	**50,000 Customs Gold Units** 1948. Purple. Portrait SYS at top center. Back: Bank building at left center. Printer: SBNC. Vertical format. (Not issued).	—	—	—

		VG	VF	UNC
370	**50,000 Customs Gold Units** 1948. Red. Portrait SYS at top center. 2 serial # varieties. Back: Bank building at left center. Printer: Chinese 5 characters. 64x154mm. Vertical format.	2.50	9.00	45.00
371	**50,000 Customs Gold Units** 1948. Orange. Portrait SYS at top center. Back: Bank building at left center. Printer: Chinese 5 characters. 70x162mm. Vertical format.			
	a. Issued note.	3.00	15.00	60.00
	p. Proof.	—	—	300
372	**50,000 Customs Gold Units** 1948. Deep purple on light blue underprint. Portrait SYS at top center. Back: Bank building at left center. Printer: Chinese 5 characters. Vertical format.	5.00	25.00	110

		VG	VF	UNC
373	**50,000 Customs Gold Units** 1948. Brown-violet. Portrait SYS at top center. Back: Bank building at left center. Printer: Chinese 5 characters. Vertical format.	6.00	25.00	125

		VG	VF	UNC
374	**250,000 Customs Gold Units** 1948. Red and multicolor. Portrait SYS at top center. Back: Bank building at left center. Vertical format.	25.00	125	600

1945-1948 "9 Northeastern Provinces" Branch Issue

Issued at a rate of 20 to 1 current yuan. #375-386 Under the bank title are 7 Chinese characters which translates "note for circulation in the northeast 9 provinces."

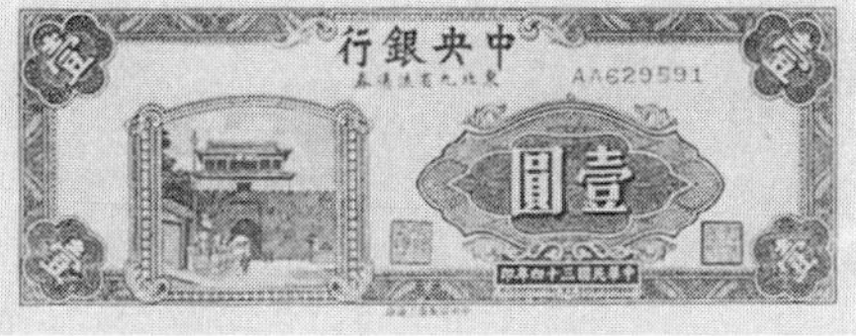

		VG	VF	UNC
375	**1 Yüan** 1945. Brown on pink underprint. City gate at left. 7 Chinese characters under bank title. *(S/M #C303-1).*	7.50	30.00	90.00
376	**5 Yüan** 1945. Orange. City gate at left. 7 Chinese characters under bank title. *(S/M #C303-2).*	6.00	20.00	60.00
376A	**5 Yüan** 1945. Red. City gate at left. 7 Chinese characters under bank title. *(SM #C303-2.5).*	—	800	1,750
377	**10 Yüan** 1945. Blue on purple underprint. City gate at left. 7 Chinese characters under bank title. *(S/M #C303-3).*	3.00	12.00	60.00
378	**50 Yüan** 1945. Purple on green underprint. City gate at left. 7 Chinese characters under bank title. *(S/M #C303-4).*	6.00	15.00	75.00
379	**100 Yüan** 1945. Olive-green on light tan underprint. City gate at left. 7 Chinese characters under bank title. 2 serial # varieties. *(S/M #C303-5).*	.75	3.00	10.00

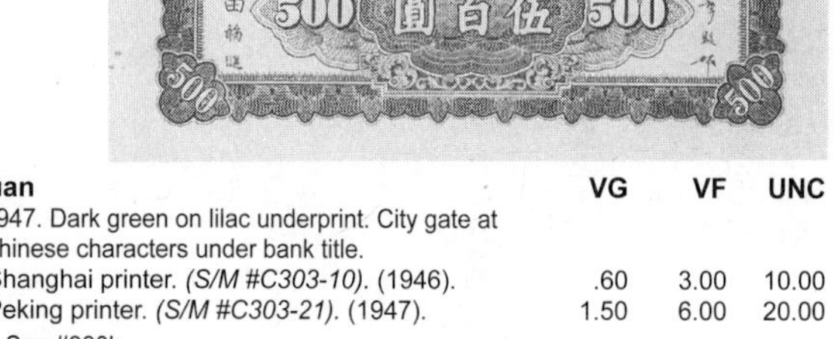

		VG	VF	UNC
380	**500 Yüan**			
	1946; 1947. Dark green on lilac underprint. City gate at left. 7 Chinese characters under bank title.			
	a. Shanghai printer. *(S/M #C303-10)*. (1946).	.60	3.00	10.00
	b. Peking printer. *(S/M #C303-21)*. (1947).	1.50	6.00	20.00

#380A *Deleted*. See #380b.

		VG	VF	UNC
381	**500 Yüan**			
	1947. Dark brown on orange underprint. City gate at left. 7 Chinese characters under bank title. Back: Great Wall at center. *(S/M #C303-20)*.	1.00	3.50	10.00

		VG	VF	UNC
382	**1000 Yüan**			
	1947. Blue-black on pink underprint. City gate at left. 7 Chinese characters under bank title. Back: Great Wall at center.			
	a. Chinese printer 5 characters. *(S/M #C303-22)*.	6.00	15.00	55.00
	b. Chinese printer 8 characters. *(S/M #C303-23)*.	0.60	2.00	10.00
	c. As b but without underprint.	3.00	7.00	20.00
383	**2000 Yüan**	VG	VF	UNC
	1947. Brown. City gate at left. 7 Chinese characters under bank title. Back: Great Wall center. *(S/M #C303-24)*.	1.25	3.50	15.00
384	**2000 Yüan**	VG	VF	UNC
	1948. Brown-violet on multicolor underprint. City gate at left. 7 Chinese characters under bank title. Back: Great Wall at center. *(S/M #C303-30)*.	0.40	2.25	6.00

		VG	VF	UNC
385	**5000 Yüan**			
	1948. Dark blue-black on red and tan guilloche. City gate at left. 7 Chinese characters under bank title. 2 serial # varieties. Back: Great Wall at center. *(S/M #C303-31a)*.	0.60	2.75	7.00

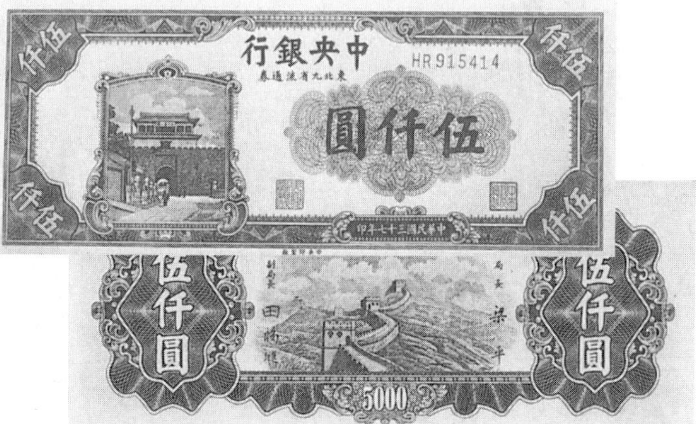

		VG	VF	UNC
385A	**5000 Yüan**			
	1948. Greenish blue-black on brown and olive-green guilloche. City gate at left. 7 Chinese characters under bank title. Back: Great Wall at center. *(S/M #C303-31b)*.	1.25	6.00	15.00

		VG	VF	UNC
386	**10,000 Yüan**			
	1948. Brown on multicolor underprint. City gate at left. 7 Chinese characters under bank title. Back: Great Wall at center. *(S/M #C303-32)*.	0.60	2.25	7.00

1948 (1945 Dated) Gold *Chin Yuan* Issue

This system was introduced in August 1948, to replace the previous currency at an exchange rate of GY$1 for $3,000,000 in the old currency.

#387 - 394 Fa Pi currency withheld because of high inflation and later issued as gold yuan.

		VG	VF	UNC
387	**1 Yüan**			
	1945 (1948). Blue on multicolor underprint. CKS at center. Printer: ABNC. *(S/M #C302-1)*.	0.60	3.50	10.00

		VG	VF	UNC
388	**5 Yüan**			
	1945 (1948). Olive-green on multicolor underprint. Lin Sun at left. 3 signature varieties. Printer: ABNC. *(S/M #C302-2)*.	0.60	3.50	10.00

389 5 Yüan — VG | VF | UNC
1945 (1948). Blue. SYS at center. National sunbursts at left and right. Back: Junks at center. Printer: SBNC. Specimen. *(S/M #C302-3).*

	VG	VF	UNC
a. Issued note.	—	—	250
s. Specimen.	—	—	—

389A 5 Yüan — VG | VF | UNC
1945. Black. SYS at center. National sunbursts at left and right. Like #389. Back: Junks at center. Wide margin. Specimen. — — —

390 10 Yüan — VG 1.25 | VF 6.00 | UNC 20.00
1945 (1948). Brown on multicolor underprint. CKS at right. 3 signature varieties. Back: Bridge at left. Printer: ABNC. *(S/M #C302-4).*

391 20 Yüan — VG 2.25 | VF 9.00 | UNC 25.00
1945 (1948). Green. Lin Sun at center. Printer: ABNC.

392 50 Yüan — VG 0.60 | VF 2.00 | UNC 12.50
1945 (1948). Black on multicolor underprint. SYS at center. 2 signature varieties. Printer: ABNC. *(S/M #C302-6).*

393 50 Yüan — VG 0.60 | VF 2.50 | UNC 20.00
1945 (1948). Black on multicolor underprint. CKS at center. 3 signature varieties. Printer: ABNC. *(S/M #C302-7)*

394 100 Yüan — VG 1.25 | VF 5.00 | UNC 30.00
1945 (1948). Red on multicolor underprint. Lin Sun at left. CKS at right. 2 signature varieties. Printer: ABNC. *(S/M #C302-8).*

1948 (1946 Dated) Gold *Chin Yuan* Issue

395 10 Cents — VG 0.50 | VF 2.25 | UNC 6.00
1946. Brown. Portrait CKS at right. Back: Shoreline village, pagoda at center. Printer: TDLR. *(S/M #C302-10).*

395A 20 Cents — VG — | VF — | UNC 60.00
1946. Black. Portrait CKS at right. Back: Sampans at anchor. Printer: TDLR. Specimen.

396 20 Cents — VG 0.60 | VF 3.25 | UNC 9.00
1946. Orange. Portrait CKS at right. Back: Sampans at anchor. Printer: TDLR. *(S/M #C302-11).*

1948 Gold *Chin Yuan* Issue

396A 10 Cents — VG — | VF — | UNC —
1948. CKS at center. Printer: CPF. (Not issued).

397 50 Cents — VG 0.60 | VF 3.25 | UNC 10.00
1948. Brown on yellow underprint. CKS at right. Printer: CPF. *(S/M #C302-20).*

398 50 Cents — VG 15.00 | VF 50.00 | UNC 180
1948. Violet. CKS at right. Printer: SBNC. *(S/M #C302-21).*

399 10 Yüan — VG 0.60 | VF 3.25 | UNC 10.00
1948. Green on multicolor underprint. CKS at right. Printer: CPF. *(S/M #C302-30).*

400 20 Yüan — VG 3.00 | VF 9.00 | UNC 30.00
1948. Brown on multicolor underprint. CKS at right. Printer: CHB. *(S/M #C302-32).*

		VG	VF	UNC
401	**20 Yüan** 1948. Red on multicolor underprint. CKS at right. Printer: CPF. *(S/M #C302-31).*	1.00	5.00	15.00

		VG	VF	UNC
402	**50 Yüan** 1948. Deep red on gold and light blue underprint. CKS at center. Printer: CHB. *(S/M #C302-41).*	1.25	4.50	18.00

		VG	VF	UNC
403	**50 Yüan** 1948. Violet on multicolor underprint. CKS at right. Printer: CPF. *(S/M #C302-40).*	0.60	2.25	10.00

		VG	VF	UNC
404	**50 Yüan** 1948. Black on multicolor underprint. CKS at center. Back: Yangtze Ganges at center. Printer: TDLR. *(S/M #C302-42).*	45.00	180	600
405	**50 Yüan** 1948. Red. CKS at right. Printer: SBNC. *(S/M #C302-43).*	12.00	50.00	150

		VG	VF	UNC
406	**100 Yüan** 1948. Green. CKS at center. Printer: CHB. *(S/M #C302-45).*	2.00	9.00	25.00
407	**100 Yüan** 1948. Dark blue on multicolor underprint. CKS at right. Printer: CPF. *(S/M #C302-44).*	1.25	3.50	15.00

1949 Gold *Chin Yuan* Issues

		VG	VF	UNC
408	**100 Yüan** 1949. Orange on multicolor underprint. CKS at right. Printer: CPF. *(S/M #C302-50).*	1.25	3.50	15.00

		VG	VF	UNC
409	**500 Yüan** 1949. Dark green on multicolor underprint. CKS at right. Printer: CPF. *(S/M #C302-51).*	2.00	9.00	25.00

		VG	VF	UNC
410	**500 Yüan** 1949. Violet on multicolor underprint. CKS at right. Printer: CHB. *(S/M #C302-52).*	3.00	6.00	25.00

		VG	VF	UNC
411	**1000 Yüan** 1949. Brown. CKS at right. Back: Temple at right. Printer: CHB. *(S/M #C302-55).*	3.00	6.00	25.00

412	1000 Yüan	VG	VF	UNC
	1949. Blue-gray on multicolor underprint. CKS at right.			
	a. Printer: CPF. *(S/M #C302-54a).*	1.50	3.50	20.00
	b. Printer: CPF1. *(S/M #C302-54b).*	1.50	4.00	22.50
	c. Printer: CPF2. *(S/M #C302-54c).*	1.50	4.00	22.50
	d. Printer: CPF3. *(S/M #C302-54d).*	1.50	4.00	22.50
	e. Printer: CPF4. *(S/M #C302-54e).*	1.50	4.00	22.50

413	1000 Yüan	VG	VF	UNC
	1949. Brown. CKS at right. Printer: CPF. *(S/M #C302-55).*	1.00	5.00	12.00

414	5000 Yüan	VG	VF	UNC
	1949. Red. CKS at right. Back: Bridge. Printer: CHB. *(S/M #C302-57).*	0.60	3.25	10.00

415	5000 Yüan	VG	VF	UNC
	1949. Red on multicolor underprint. CKS at right. Back: Bank at left.			
	a. Printer: CPF. *(S/M #C302-56a).*	1.00	5.00	12.00
	b. Printer: CPF3. *(S/M #C302-56b).*	2.00	9.00	25.00

416	10,000 Yüan	VG	VF	UNC
	1949. Blue on multicolor underprint. CKS at right. Back: Bridge. Printer: CHB. *(S/M #C302-61).*	1.50	8.50	25.00

417	10,000 Yüan	VG	VF	UNC
	1949. Blue on multicolor underprint. CKS at right. Back: Bank at left.			
	a. Printer: CPF. *(S/M #C302-60a).*	1.50	6.00	20.00
	b. Printer: CPF1. *(S/M #C302-60b).*	2.00	7.50	35.00
	c. Printer: CPF2. *(S/M #C302-60c).*	2.00	7.50	35.00

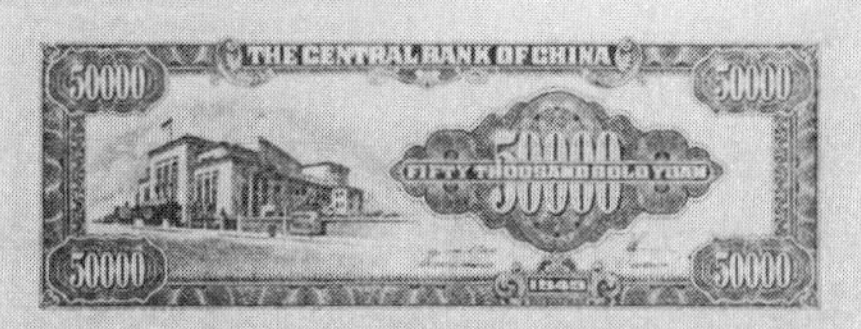

418	50,000 Yüan	VG	VF	UNC
	1949. Red-orange on multicolor underprint. CKS at right. Printer: CPF. *(S/M #C302-62).*	1.50	8.50	25.00

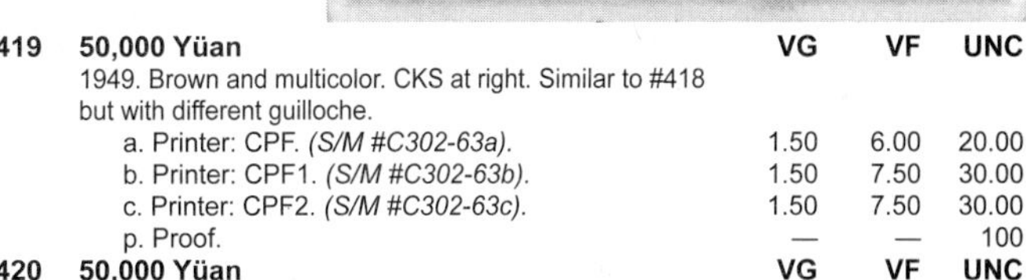

419	50,000 Yüan	VG	VF	UNC
	1949. Brown and multicolor. CKS at right. Similar to #418 but with different guilloche.			
	a. Printer: CPF. *(S/M #C302-63a).*	1.50	6.00	20.00
	b. Printer: CPF1. *(S/M #C302-63b).*	1.50	7.50	30.00
	c. Printer: CPF2. *(S/M #C302-63c).*	1.50	7.50	30.00
	p. Proof.	—	—	100

420	50,000 Yüan	VG	VF	UNC
	1949. Red. CKS at center. Printer: TDLR. *(S/M #C302-64).*	15.00	55.00	270

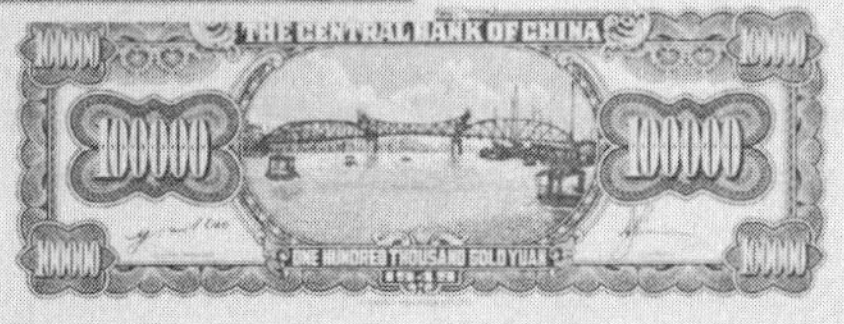

421	100,000 Yüan	VG	VF	UNC
	1949. Lilac. CKS at right. Printer: CHB. *(S/M #C302-71).*	1.50	4.00	15.00

422	100,000 Yüan	VG	VF	UNC
	1949. Grayish green. CKS at right.			
	a. Printer: CPF. *(S/M # #C302-72a).*	1.00	2.50	12.00
	b. Printer: CPF1. *(S/M #C302-72b).*	2.00	7.50	25.00
	c. Printer: CPF2. *(S/M #C302-72c).*	2.00	7.50	30.00
	d. Printer: CPF3. *(S/M #C302-72d).*	2.00	7.50	30.00
	e. Printer: CPF4. *(S/M #C302-72e).*	2.00	7.50	30.00
	f. Printer: CPF-Taipei. *(S/M #C302-72f).*	25.00	100	250

423	500,000 Yüan	VG	VF	UNC
	1949. Greenish black on multicolor underprint. Back: Temple at center. Printer: CHB. *(S/M #C302-73).*	2.50	6.00	20.00

424	500,000 Yüan	VG	VF	UNC
	1949. Lilac-brown on multicolor underprint. Back: Bank at center.			
	a. Printer: CPF. *(S/M #C302-72a).*	2.50	6.00	20.00
	b. Printer: CPF1. *(S/M #C302-72b).*	2.50	8.50	25.00
	c. Printer: CPF2.*(S/M #C302-72c).*	2.50	8.50	30.00
	d. Printer: CPF3. *(S/M #C302-72d).*	2.50	8.50	30.00
	e. Printer: CPF4. *(S/M # #C302-72e).*	2.50	8.50	30.00
	f. Printer: CPF-Taipei. *(S/M #C302-72f).*	15.00	55.00	300

425	500,000 Yüan	VG	VF	UNC
	1949. Green. CKS at right. Printer: SBNC. *(S/M #C302-74).*	18.00	55.00	360

426	1,000,000 Yüan	VG	VF	UNC
	1949. Brown and blue. CKS at right. Printer: CHB. *(S/M #C302-75).*	7.50	22.50	150

427	5,000,000 Yüan	VG	VF	UNC
	1949. Red and blue. CKS at right. Printer: CHB. *(S/M #C302-77).*	375	1,050	3,000

1949 Silver *Yin Yuan* Issue

428	1 Cent	VG	VF	UNC
	1949. Green. CKS at center. Printer: CPF-Chungking. Vertical format. *(S/M #C304-1).*	10.00	65.00	225

429	5 Cents	VG	VF	UNC
	1949.Red. CKS at center. Printer: CPF-Chungking. Vertical format. *(S/M #C304-2).*	30.00	165	5752

430	5 Cents	VG	VF	UNC
	1949. Green. SYS at right. Back: Temple of Heaven. Printer: CPF-Taipei. *(S/M #C304-3).*	27.50	150	575

431	5 Cents	VG	VF	UNC
	1949. Red-violet. Pier at center.*Tsingtao. (S/M #C304-4).*	28.00	150	375

432	10 Cents	VG	VF	UNC
	1949. Blue on red underprint. CKS at center. Printer: CPF-Chungking. Vertical format. *(S/M #C304-5).*	27.50	150	525

		VG	VF	UNC
433	**10 Cents**	VG	VF	UNC
	1949. Purple. SYS at right. Printer: CHB. *(S/M #C304-6).*	1.00	5.00	12.00

		VG	VF	UNC
434	**10 Cents**	VG	VF	UNC
	1949. Gray-green. Pier at center. *Tsingtao. (S/M #C304-7).*	30.00	165	350
435	**20 Cents**	VG	VF	UNC
	1949. Orange. CKS at center. Printer: CPF-Chungking. Vertical format. *(S/M #C304-10).*	30.00	165	500

		VG	VF	UNC
436	**20 Cents**	VG	VF	UNC
	1949. Green. SYS at right. Printer: CHB. *(S/M #C304-11).*	125	5.00	15.00

		VG	VF	UNC
437	**50 Cents**	VG	VF	UNC
	1949. Lilac. CKS at center. Printer: CPF-Chungking.Vertical format. *(S/M #C304-12).*	27.50	150	525
438	**50 Cents**	VG	VF	UNC
	1949. Brown. SYS at right. Printer: CPF-Taipei. *(S/M #C304-13).*	17.50	55.00	425
438A	**50 Cents**	VG	VF	UNC
	1949. Yellow-green.*Tsingtao. (S/M #C304-14).* Requires confirmation.	—	—	—

		VG	VF	UNC
439	**1 Dollar**	VG	VF	UNC
	1949. Blue on multicolor underprint. Portrait SYS at right. Back: Silver "junk" 1-Yuan coin at center. Printer: CHB. *(S/M #C304-20).*	2.50	9.00	20.00

		VG	VF	UNC
440	**1 Dollar**	VG	VF	UNC
	1949. Lilac-brown. SYS at right. Back: Silver "junk" 1-Yuan coin at center. Printer: CHB. *CHUNGKING. (S/M #C304-22).*	2.00	5.00	20.00

		VG	VF	UNC
441	**1 Dollar**	VG	VF	UNC
	1949. Black-blue. SYS at right. Back: Silver "junk" 1-Yuan coin at center. Printer: CHB. *CANTON. (S/M #C304-21).*	2.00	6.00	35.00
442	**5 Dollars**	VG	VF	UNC
	1949. SYS at right. Back: Silver "junk" 1-Yuan coin at center. Printer: CHB. *(S/M #C304-23).*	3.00	12.00	50.00
443	**5 Dollars**	VG	VF	UNC
	1949. Dark brown on multicolor underprint. SYS at right. Back: Silver "junk" 1-Yuan coin at center. Printer: CHB. *CHUNGKING. (S/M #C304-25).*	1.25	5.00	20.00
444	**5 Dollars**	VG	VF	UNC
	1949. Brown and red. SYS at right. Back: Silver "junk" 1-Yuan coin at center. Printer: CHB.			
	a. *CANTON. (S/M #C304-24).*	1.25	3.00	15.00
	b. Signature on back.	22.00	75.00	—

		VG	VF	UNC
445	**10 Dollars**	VG	VF	UNC
	1949. Red. SYS at right. Back: Silver "junk" 1-Yuan coin at center. Printer: CHB. *(S/M #C304-30).*	3.50	12.00	60.00
446	**10 Dollars**	VG	VF	UNC
	1949. Pink. SYS at right. Back: Silver "junk" 1-Yuan coin at center. Printer: CHB. *CHUNGKING. (S/M #C304-32).*	6.00	25.00	120
447	**10 Dollars**	VG	VF	UNC
	1949. Black on multicolor underprint. SYS at right. Back: Silver "junk" 1-Yuan coin at center. Printer: CHB.			
	a. *CHUNGKING. (S/M #C304-31).*	0.60	3.50	12.00
	b. *CANTON.*	2.00	5.00	20.00
448	**100 Dollars**	VG	VF	UNC
	1949. Green. SYS at right. Printer: CHB.*CHUNGKING.* Specimen. *(S/M #C304-33).*	—	—	110

Central Bank of China (Branches - National)

Note: The following section, beginning with number 449G, has been restructured to run alpabetically by branch,

General Issue - Shanghai Checks Branch

1949 General Gold *Chin Yuan* Issue

Circulating Bearer Cashier's Checks.

		Good	Fine	XF
449	**50,000 Yüan**	Good	Fine	XF
	1949. Green on blue underprint. *(S/M #C302-).*	15.00	60.00	250
449A	**100,000 Yüan**	Good	Fine	XF
	1949. Red on pink underprint. *(S/M #C302-).*	15.00	60.00	250
449B	**300,000 Yüan**	Good	Fine	XF
	Green. 1949.*(S/M #C302-).*	15.00	90.00	225
449C	**500,000 Yüan**	Good	Fine	XF
	28.4.1949.Blue on pink underprint. *(S/M #C302-).*	15.00	90.00	225
449D	**1,000,000 Yüan**	Good	Fine	XF
	1949.Violet on green underprint. *(S/M #C302-).*	15.00	90.00	225

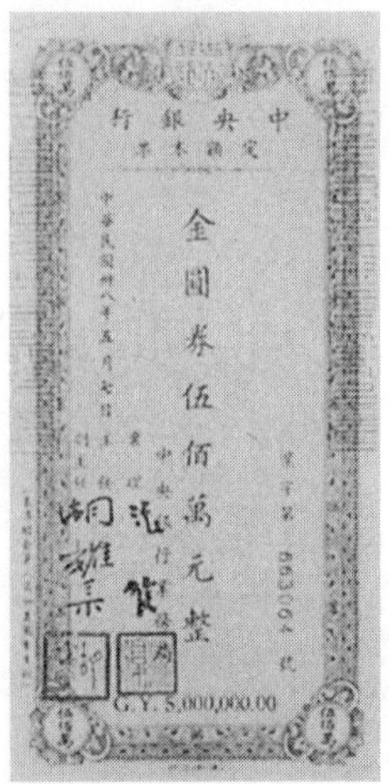

No.	Denomination	Good	Fine	XF
449E	**5,000,000 Yüan** 7.5.1949. Brown on yellow underprint. *(S/M #C302-93).*	15.00	90.00	225
449F	**10,000,000 Yüan** 1949. (Not issued). *(S/M #C302-).*	—	—	—

Changchung Branch

1948 First Issue

No.	Denomination	Good	Fine	XF
449G	**100,000 Yüan** 1948. Green on violet underprint. *(S/M #C302-).*	15.00	90.00	225
449GE	**200,000 Yüan** 1948. *(S/M #C302-).*	12.50	75.00	200
449GF	**500,000 Yüan** 1948. *(S/M #C302-).*	12.50	75.00	200
449GG	**1,000,000 Yüan** 1948. *(S/M #C302-).*	12.50	75.00	200
449GH	**2,000,000 Yüan** 1948. *(S/M #C302-).*	12.50	75.00	200
449H	**10,000,000 Yüan** 1948. *(S/M #C302-).*	12.50	75.00	200
449HH	**15,000,000 Yüan** 1948. *(S/M #C302-).*	12.50	75.00	200
449I	**30,000,000 Yüan = 50 Gold Yüan** 1948.Gray on blue underprint. *(S/M #C302-).*	12.50	75.00	200
449J	**50,000,000 Yüan** 1948. Gray on blue underprint. *(S/M #C302-).*	12.50	75.00	200

No.	Denomination	Good	Fine	XF
449K	**60,000,000 Yüan = 10 Gold Yüan** 1948. Purple on lilac underprint. *(S/M #C302-95).*	6.00	20.00	80.00
449L	**120,000,000 Yüan** 1948. Blue on gray underprint. *(S/M #C302-).*	7.50	20.00	80.00
449M	**180,000,000 Yüan** 1948.Purple on brown underprint. *(S/M #C302-).*	7.50	20.00	80.00

1948 Second Issue

No.	Denomination	Good	Fine	XF
449N	**5,000,000 Yüan** 24.8.1948. *(S/M #C302-).*	7.50	35.00	125
449O	**50,000,000 Yüan** 1948. *(S/M #C302-).*	7.50	30.00	100

1948 Provisional Issue

No.	Denomination	Good	Fine	XF
449P	**4,500,000 Yüan** 1948. *(S/M #C302-).*	7.50	35.00	125
449Q	**30,000,000 Yüan = 50 Gold Yüan** 1948. *(S/M #C302-).*	7.50	30.00	120

Chengtu Branch

1949 Gold *Chin Yuan* First Issue

No.	Denomination	Good	Fine	XF
449Z	**5000 Yüan** 7.4.1949-18.4.1949.Brown on yellow underprint, black text. *(S/M #C302-).*			
	a. Issued note.	9.00	35.00	150
	b. Remainder with counterfoil.	6.00	20.00	90.00

1949 Gold *Chin Yuan* Second Issue

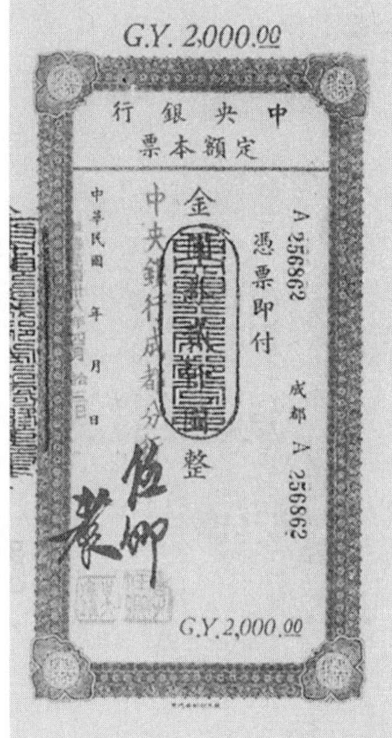

No.	Denomination	Good	Fine	XF
449Y	**2000 Yüan** 30.3.1949-13.4.1949. Violet-brown on light blue underprint, black text. *(S/M #C302-).*	9.00	35.00	150
449AA	**10,000 Yüan** 25.4.1949-28.4.1949. Red-violet on light green underprint. *(S/M #C302-).*	12.00	45.00	175
449R	**10,000,000 Yüan** 1949. *(S/M #C302-).*	10.00	35.00	150

Chungking Branch

1949 Gold *Chin Yuan* Issue

No.	Denomination	Good	Fine	XF
449S	**50,000 Yüan** 1949. Brown. *(S/M #C302-).*	12.50	50.00	150
449T	**500,000 Yüan** 1949. Red. *(S/M #C302-).*	12.50	50.00	150
449U	**1,000,000 Yüan** 14.6.1949. Red on yellow underprint. *(S/M #C302-91).*	12.50	50.00	150
449V	**5,000,000 Yüan** 1.6.1949. Green. *(S/M #C302-92).*	12.50	50.00	150
449W	**5,000,000 Yüan** 1949. Purple on yellow underprint. *(S/M #C302-94).*	7.50	30.00	125

		Good	Fine	XF
449X	**10,000,000 Yüan** 14.6.1949. Red on light blue underprint. *(S/M #C302-).*	7.50	30.00	120

Foochow Branch

1949 Gold *Chin Yuan* First Issue

		Good	Fine	XF
449AF	**50,000 Yüan** 1.9.1949. Bank title in seal script with flower bud outline in all 4 corners. *(S/M #C302-).*	2.00	3.00	20.00

1949 Gold *Chin Yuan* Second Issue

		Good	Fine	XF
450	**1000 Yüan** April 1949. Purple. *(S/M #C302-80).*	7.50	30.00	120

450A Deleted.

		Good	Fine	XF
450B	**20,000 Yüan** April 1949. Red-brown. *(S/M #C302-).*	7.50	30.00	120
450BB	**50,000 Yüan** April 1949. *(S/M #C302-).*	7.50	30.00	120

1949 National *Kuo Pi Yuan* Issue

		Good	Fine	XF
450C	**20,000 Yüan** ND (1949). Red. Printer: CPF. (Not issued). *(S/M #C302-).*	—	—	—
450D	**30,000 Yüan** ND (1949).Green. Printer: CPF. (Not issued). *(S/M #C302-).*	—	—	—
450E	**40,000 Yüan** ND (1949). (Not issued). *(S/M #C302-).* Light blue. Printer: CPF.	—	—	—
450F	**50,000 Yüan** ND (1949). (Not issued). *(S/M #C302-).* Dark blue. Printer: CPF.	—	—	—

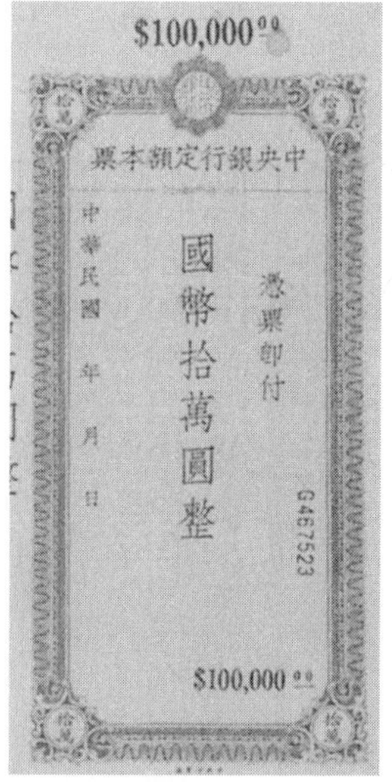

		Good	Fine	XF
450G	**100,000 Yüan** ND (1949). Brown on yellow underprint. Printer: CPF. (Not issued). *(S/M #C302-).*	—	—	90.00

1949 Gold *Chin Yuan* Provisional Issue

		Good	Fine	XF
450H	**20,000 Yüan** 25.4.1949. Red. *(S/M #C302-81).*	9.00	30.00	110
450I	**30,000 Yüan** 25.4.1949. Green. *(S/M #C302-82).*	9.00	30.00	110

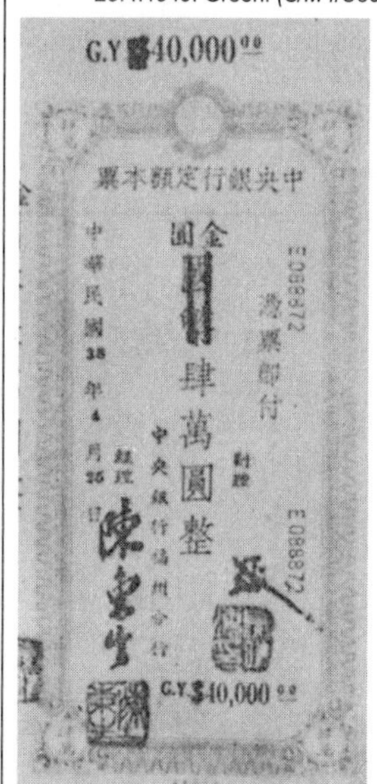

		Good	Fine	XF
450J	**40,000 Yüan**	Good	Fine	XF
	25.4.1949. Light blue. *(S/M #C302-83).*	9.00	30.00	110
450K	**50,000 Yüan**	Good	Fine	XF
	25.4.1949. Dark blue. *(S/M #C302-84).*	9.00	30.00	110
450L	**100,000 Yüan**	Good	Fine	XF
	25.4.1949. Brown on yellow underprint. *(S/M #C302-85).*	9.00	30.00	110

1949 Gold *Chin Yuan* Fourth Issue

		Good	Fine	XF
450M	**100,000 Yüan**	Good	Fine	XF
	April 1949. Brown on light blue underprint. SYS at upper center. *(S/M #C302-).*	7.50	30.00	110

		Good	Fine	XF
450N	**500,000 Yüan**	Good	Fine	XF
	April 1949. Blue on yellow underprint. SYS at upper center. *(S/M #C302-90).*	7.50	25.00	95.00

Kunming Branch

1945-1947 Issue

		Good	Fine	XF
450O	**100,000 Yüan**	Good	Fine	XF
	1945.Violet on yellow underprint. *(S/M #C302-).*	10.00	28.00	110
450P	**300,000 Yüan**	Good	Fine	XF
	1947.Green on brown underprint. *(S/M #C302-).*	10.00	28.00	110

Mukden, Manchuria Branch

1948 Northwest *Yuan* Issue

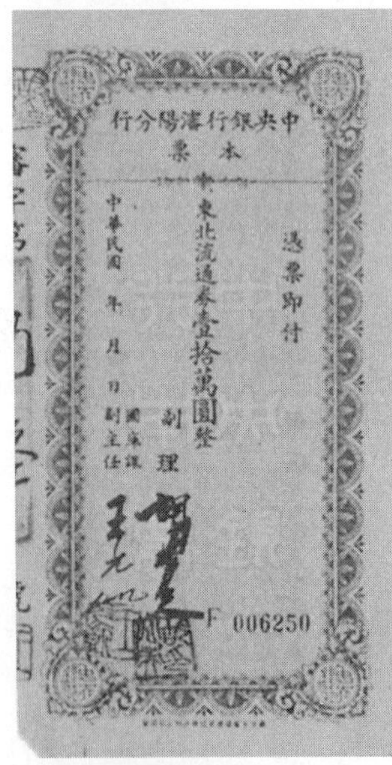

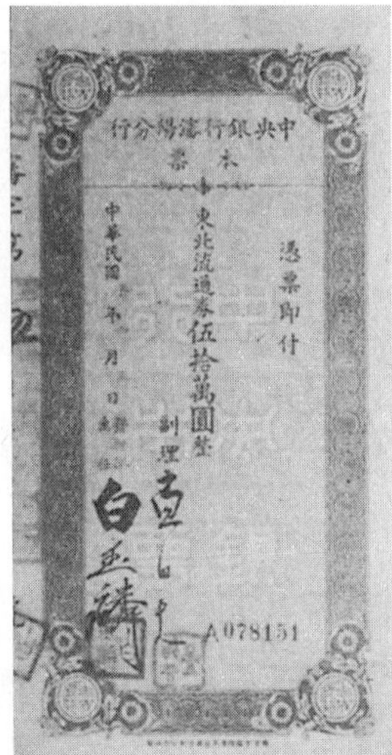

		Good	Fine	XF
450Q	**100,000 Yüan**	Good	Fine	XF
	1948. Dark brown on light gray underprint, black text. *(S/M #C303-).*	9.50	30.00	120
450R	**500,000 Yüan**	Good	Fine	XF
	1948. Blue on yellow-orange underprint, black text. *(S/M #C303-).*	9.50	30.00	120
450S	**5,000,000 Yüan**	Good	Fine	XF
	2.4.1948. *(S/M #C30-).*	9.50	30.00	120

Yibin Branch

1944 National *Kuo Pi Yuan* Issue

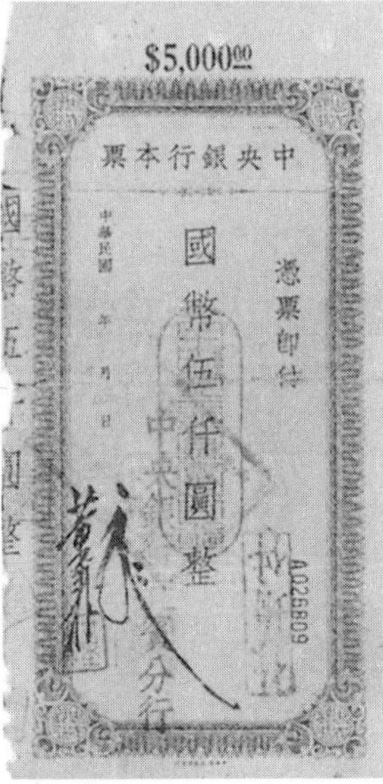

		Good	Fine	XF
450T	**5000 Yüan**	Good	Fine	XF
	12.9.1944. Brown-violet on light blue underprint, black text. *(S/M #C302-).*	12.00	35.00	145

Farmers Bank of China

中國農民銀行

Chung Kuo Nung Min Yin Hang

1934 Issue

		Good	Fine	XF
451	**1 Chiao = 10 Cents**	Good	Fine	XF
	ND (1934). Red. Farm laborer at center. Signature varieties. Printer: TYPC. Vertical format. *(S/M #C290-1).*	12.50	40.00	150
452	**2 Chiao = 20 Cents**	Good	Fine	XF
	ND. (1934) Red. Signature varieties. Printer: TYPC. *(S/M #C290-2).*	15.00	50.00	200

		Good	Fine	XF
453	**1 Yüan**	Good	Fine	XF
	1934. Red on light green and lilac underprint. Three farm laborers at left. Signature varieties. Back: Farmer plowing with ox. Printer: TYPC.			
	a. *CHENGCHOW. (S/M #C290-10c).*	60.00	275	1,200
	b. *FOOCHOW. (S/M #C290-10a).*	22.50	75.00	220
	c. *LANCHOW. (S/M #C290-10d).*	60.00	270	650
	d. Without place name. *(S/M #C290-10b).*	27.50	100	350
	e. *CHANGSHA. (S/M #C290-10e).*	60.00	270	1,100
	f. *HANKOW. (S/M #C290-10f).*	60.00	270	825
	g. *KWEIYANG. (S/M #C290-10g).*	75.00	350	1,350
	h. *SIAN. (S/M #C290-10h).*	50.00	225	550
	s. 2 part specimen as d.	—	Unc	225

		Good	Fine	XF
453A	**1 Yüan** 1934. Dark blue. Three farm laborers at left. Similar to #453. Signature varieties. Back: Farmer plowing with ox. Printer: TYPC. *(S/M #C290-)*.	55.00	275	675

1935 First Issue

		VG	VF	UNC
454	**20 Cents = 2 Chiao** Feb. 1935. Red. Farmer plowing with ox at top. 2 signature varieties. Printer: TYPC. *(S/M #C290-20)*.	18.00	75.00	200

1935 Second Issue

		VG	VF	UNC
455	**10 Cents = 1 Chiao** 1.3.1935. Red. Farmer in irrigation system at top. 2 signature varieties. Printer: TYPC. *(S/M #C290-21)*.			
	a. Issued note.	5.00	22.50	72.00
	s. 2 part specimen.	—	—	110

		VG	VF	UNC
456	**20 Cents = 2 Chiao** 1.4.1935. Black and red. Farmer plowing with ox at top. 2 signature varieties. Printer: TYPC. *(S/M #C290-22)*.	7.50	37.50	110

		VG	VF	UNC
457	**1 Yüan** 1.4.1935. Red on green and multicolor underprint. Farming scenes at left and right. 2 signature varieties. Back: House at center, sheep at right. Printer: TDLR. *(S/M #C290-30)*.			
	a. Issued note.	2.00	10.00	25.00
	b. With various numerical overprint	2.25	10.00	35.00

		VG	VF	UNC
457A	**1 Yüan** 1935. Red without underprint. Farming scenes at left and right. Like #457. Back: House at center, sheep at right. Printer: TDLR. Specimen.	—	—	200

		VG	VF	UNC
458	**5 Yüan** 1935. Green and multicolor. Agricultural occupations at left and right. 2 signature varieties. Back: Temple at center, ox at right. Printer: TDLR. *(S/M #C290-31)*.			
	a. Issued note.	6.00	30.00	60.00
	b. With various numerical overprint	12.50	30.00	90.00
	s. 2 part specimen.	—	—	200

		VG	VF	UNC
459	**10 Yüan** 1935. Purple and multicolor. Agricultural occupations at left and right. 3 signature varieties. Back: Pagoda at center, horse at right. Printer: TDLR. *(S/M #C290-32)*.			
	a. Issued note.	4.00	13.00	25.00
	b. With various numerical overprints.	7.50	25.00	60.00

1936 Issue

		VG	VF	UNC
460	**50 Cents** 1936. Blue. Agricultural occupations at left and right. Back: Hillside pagoda at center, goat head at right. Printer: TDLR. *(S/M #C290-40)*.	1.50	7.50	30.00

1937 Issue

		VG	VF	UNC
461	**10 Cents** 1937. Blue. Landscape. Printer: TYPC. 2 serial # varieites. *(S/M #C290-50).*	0.50	2.00	15.00
461A	**10 Cents** 1937. Blue. Landscape. Like #461. Back: Chinese text (Pass for the Nanking Military Government). Printer: TYPC.	90.00	330	—

		VG	VF	UNC
462	**20 Cents** 1937. Green. Agricultural scene. Printer: TYPC. 2 serial # varieties. *(S/M #C290-51).*	1.25	6.00	25.00

1940 Regular Issue

		VG	VF	UNC
463	**1 Yüan** 1940. Red. Workers at lower right. Printer: TYPC. *(S/M #C290-60).*	1.25	6.00	25.00

		VG	VF	UNC
464	**10 Yüan** 1940. Red. Farmer working in irrigation system. Printer: TYPC. 2 serial # varieites. *(S/M #C290-65).*	3.00	12.50	35.00

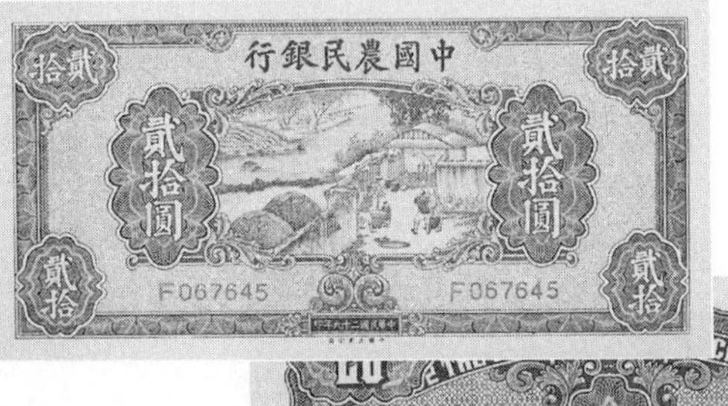

		VG	VF	UNC
465	**20 Yüan** 1940. Blue. Worker by houses along river. Printer: TYPC. 2 serial # varieties. *(S/M #C290-70).*	9.00	37.50	200

1940 First Provisional Issue

#466-468 new issuer name overprint on notes of the Hupeh Provincial Bank.

		Good	Fine	XF
466	**1 Yüan** ND (1940 - old date 1929). Purple and multicolor. Pagoda at right. *(S/M #C290-62).*	75.00	400	1,450

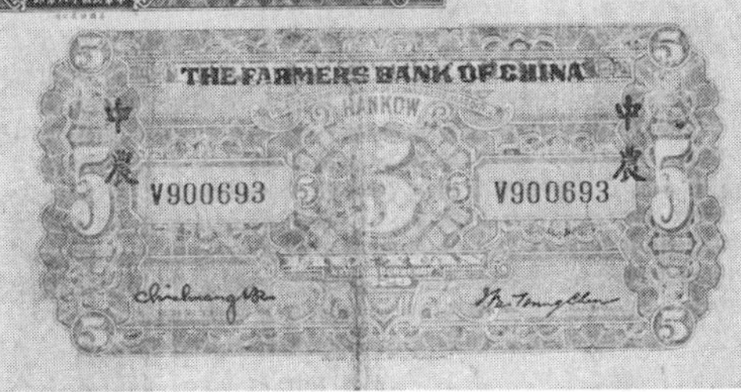

		Good	Fine	XF
467	**5 Yüan** ND (1940 - old date 1929). Green and multicolor. Pagoda at center.			
	a. *HANKOW. (S/M #C290-63b).*	55.00	250	900
	b. *HUPEH. (S/M #C290-63c).*	75.00	375	1,100
	c. *SHANTUNG. (S/M #C290-63d).*	75.00	375	1,800
	d. Without place name. *(S/M #C290-63a).*	50.00	225	950

		Good	Fine	XF
468	**10 Yüan** ND (1940 - old date 1929). Red and multicolor. Pagoda at left. *(S/M #C290-66).*	75.00	375	1,100

1940 Second Provisional Issue

#469. New issuer name overprint on notes of the Provincial Bank of Kwangtung Province. It is considered spurious by some authorities.

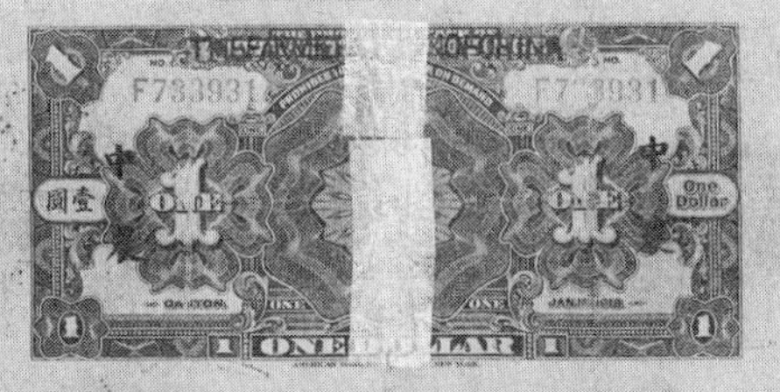

		Good	Fine	XF
469	**1 Yüan** ND (1940 - old date 1.1.1918). Blue and multicolor. Pagoda at center. *(S/M #C290-61).*	—	—	—

1940 Third Provisional Issue

#470 and 471 new issuer name overprint on notes of the Szechuan Provincial Bank.

		Good	Fine	XF
470	**5 Yüan** ND (1940 - old date 1.7.1937). Green and multicolor. Mountains, tower at upper center. *(S/M #C290-64).*	32.50	165	1,100

		Good	Fine	XF
471	**10 Yüan** ND (1940 - old date 1.7.1937). Purple and multicolor. *(S/M #C290-67).*	45.00	225	1,350

1940 Fourth Provisional"Reconstruction" Issue

#472 and 473 new issuer multi-color name overprint on notes of the Szechuan Provincial Government.

		Good	Fine	XF
472	**50 Yüan** ND (1940 - old date 1937). Blue and green. Buildings at center. *Chungking. (S/M #C290-71).*	75	400	2,000

		Good	Fine	XF
473	**100 Yüan** ND (1940 - old date 1937). Orange and yellow. Buildings at left and right. *Chungking. (S/M #C290-72).*	125	550	2,250

1941 Issue

		VG	VF	UNC
474	**1 Yüan** 1941. Brown on multicolor underprint. SYS at left. 3 serial # varieties. Back: House at center, sheep at right. Printer: TDLR. *(S/M #C290-80).*	1.00	3.00	15.00

		VG	VF	UNC
475	**5 Yüan** 1941. Blue on multicolor underprint. SYS at left. 3 serial # varieties. Back: Temple at center, ox at right. Printer: TDLR. *(S/M #C290-81).*	1.50	5.00	22.00

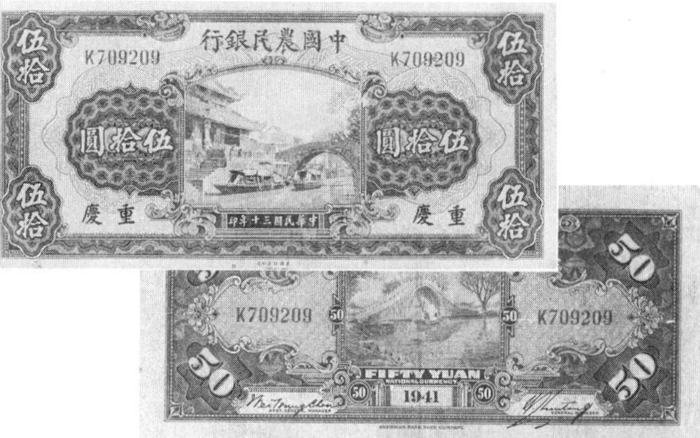

		VG	VF	UNC
476	**50 Yüan**			
	1941. Brown on green and multicolor underprint. Boats near bridge at center. Back: Bridge center. Printer: ABNC.			
	a. Issued note. Reported not confirmed. *(S/M #C290-82b).*	—	—	—
	b. Overprint: *Chungking (S/M #C290-82a).*	2.50	7.50	30.00
	s. As b, 2 part specimen.	—	—	—

		VG	VF	UNC
477	**100 Yüan**			
	1941. Purple on green and multicolor underprint. Boats near bridge at center. Back: Bridge at center. Printer: ABNC.			
	a. Serial # on face only. *(S/M #C290-83b).*	2.50	5.00	30.00
	b. Overprint: *Chungking.* Serial # on face and back. *(S/M #C290-83a).*	2.00	5.00	27.50

		VG	VF	UNC
478	**500 Yüan**			
	1941. Green on brown and multicolor underprint. Boats near bridge at center. Similar to #476. Back: Bridge at center. Printer: ABNC.			
	a. Issued note. *(S/M #C290-84b).*	14.00	70.00	275
	b. Black overprint: *Chungking.* Specimen *(S/M #C290-84a).*	—	—	275

1942 Issue

		VG	VF	UNC
479	**50 Yüan**			
	1942. Brown. Steam passenger train at left. Printer: TTBC. *(S/M #C290-90).*	18.00	90.00	338

		VG	VF	UNC
480	**100 Yüan**			
	1942. Green. Landscape and agricultural scene at right. Printer: TYPC. *(S/M #C290-91).*	15.00	60.00	300

1943 Issue

		Good	Fine	XF
480A	**5 Yüan**			
	1.10.1943. Agricultural scenes at left and right. Printer: CTPA. *(S/M #C290-97).*	50.00	90.00	300

		Good	Fine	XF
480B	**10 Yüan**			
	1.10.1943. Purple. Agricultural scenes at left and right. Printer: CTPA. Uniface. *(S/M #C290-98).*	17.50	60.00	192
481	**50 Yüan**			
	1.10.1943. Red. Agricultural scenes at left and right. Like #480A. Printer: CTPA. *(S/M #C290-100).*	20.00	75.00	300
482	**100 Yüan**			
	1.10.1943. Brown. Agricultural scenes at left and right. Like #480A. Printer: CTPA. *(S/M, #C290-101).*	20.00	50.00	300

1945 Circulating Cashiers Check Issue

		Good	Fine	XF
483	**500 Yüan**			
	1945. Orange. Printer: YAWY. *(S/M #C290-110).*	10.00	60.00	120
484	**1000 Yüan**			
	1945. *Shang Jao.* Purple. Printer: YAWY. *(S/M #C290-111).*	10.00	60.00	120

Great Northwestern Bank

行銀疆蒙

Men Tsang Yin Hang

Its Chinese name means "Mongolian-Tibetan Bank" but its issues had limited circulation.

1924 Issue

		Good	Fine	XF
485	**10 Cents**			
	1924. Red. *TIENTSIN. (S/M #M14-1).*	30.00	100	750

		Good	Fine	XF
486	**20 Cents**			
	1924. Dark brown. *TIENTSIN. (S/M #M14-2).*	40.00	125	1,050
487	**50 Cents**			
	1924. *TIENTSIN. (S/M #M14-3).* Requires confirmation.	—	—	—

		Good	Fine	XF
488	**1 Dollar**	Good	Fine	XF
	1924. *(S/M #M14-10).* Requires confirmation.	—	—	—
489	**5 Dollars**	Good	Fine	XF
	1924. *(S/M #M14-11).* Requires confirmation.	—	—	—
490	**10 Silver Yüan**	Good	Fine	XF
	1924. *(S/M #M14-12).* Requires confirmation.	—	—	—

Industrial Development Bank of China

勸業銀行

Ch'uan Yeh Yin Hang

1921 Issues

		Good	Fine	XF
491	**1 Yüan**	Good	Fine	XF
	1.2.1921. Red and multicolor. Village gateway, building at center. Printer: ABNC.			
	a. *PEKING. (S/M #C245-1a).*	40.00	300	1,163
	b. *CHENGCHOW. (S/M #C245-1b).*	65.00	150	900
	p. Proof.	—	Unc	195
	r. Remainder without place name. *(S/M #C245-1c).*	—	Unc	180
	s. Specimen.	—	Unc	150
492	**1 Yüan**	Good	Fine	XF
	1921. Green and black. Building at center. Printer: BEPP.			
	a. *PEKING. (S/M #C245-2a).*	75	180	1,200
	r. Remainder without place name. *(S/M #C245-2b).*	—	Unc	225

		Good	Fine	XF
493	**5 Yüan**	Good	Fine	XF
	1.2.1921. Dark blue and multicolor. Village gateway, building at center. Printer: ABNC. With various control letter overprints.			
	a. *PEKING. (S/M #C245-3a).*	60.00	180	1,000
	b. *CHENGCHOW. (S/M #C245-3b).*	45.00	135	975
	c. *TIENTSIN.*	60.00	185	1,000
	p. Proof.	—	Unc	225
	s. Specimen.	—	Unc	120
494	**5 Yüan**	Good	Fine	XF
	1.5.1921. Black and multicolor. Printer: BEPP.			
	a. *PEKING. (S/M #C245-4a).*	27.50	125	825
	b. *NANKING. (S/M #C245-4b).*	75.00	300	1,400
	c. *TIENTSIN. (S/M #C245-4c).*	45.00	275	825

		Good	Fine	XF
495	**10 Yüan**	Good	Fine	XF
	1.2.1921. Dark green and multicolor. Village gateway, building at center. Printer: ABNC.			
	a. *PEKING. (S/M #C245-5b).*	70.00	400	1,100
	p. Proof.	—	Unc	200
	r. Remainder without place name. *(S/M #C245-5b).*	—	Unc	275
	s. Specimen.	—	Unc	175

		Good	Fine	XF
496	**10 Yüan**	Good	Fine	XF
	1.7.1921. Green and multicolor. Printer: BEPP.			
	a. *PEKING. (S/M #C245-6).*	75	400	1,350
	b. *TIENTSIN. (S/M #C245-).*	185	675	1,875

		Good	Fine	XF
496A	**50 Yüan**	Good	Fine	XF
	1.2.1921. Orange on red and green underprint. Village gateway at center. *(S/M #C245-7).*			
	p. Proof without office of issue.	—	Unc	3,600
	s. Specimen without office of issue.	—	Unc	2,700
496B	**100 Yüan**	Good	Fine	XF
	1.2.1921. Light blue on orange and olive-green underprint. Village gateway at center. *PEKING. (S/M #C245-8).*			
	a. Issued note. Requires confirmation.	—	—	—
	p. Proof without office of issue.	—	Unc	6,000
	s. Specimen without office of issue.	—	Unc	4,500

1927 Issue

		Good	Fine	XF
497	**10 Cents**	Good	Fine	XF
	1927. Dark green. Waterfront palace at top center. Printer: BEPP.			
	a. *TIENTSIN. (S/M #C245-10a).*	45.00	225	875
	r. Remainder, without place name *(S/M #C245-10b).*	—	Unc	180

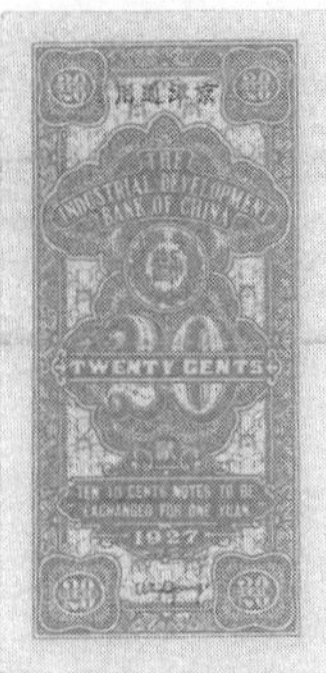

498	20 Cents	Good	Fine	XF
	1927. Orange. Hillside pagoda at top center. Printer: BEPP.			
	a. *TIENTSIN/PEKING. (S/M #C245-11a).*	60.00	1353	525
	b. *TIENTSIN. (S/M #C245-11)*	150	450	—
	r. Remainder, without place name. *(SM #C245-11b).*	—	Unc	135

1928 Issue

499	10 Cents	Good	Fine	XF
	1.9.1928. Red. Fortress city at left. Back: Temple of Heaven at center. Printer: BEPP. *PEIPING. (S/M #C245-20a).*			
	a. Issued note.	18.00	37.50	675
	r. Remainder. Without place name.	—	Unc	200
499A	**10 Cents**	**Good**	**Fine**	**XF**
	1.9.1928.Brown. Fortress city at left. Back: Temple of Heaven at center. Printer: BEPP. *TIENTSIN. (S/M #C245-20b).*			
	a. Issued note.	22.50	7	825
	r. Remainder. Without place name.	—	Unc	225

500	20 Cents	Good	Fine	XF
	1.9.1928. Purple. Fortress city at left. Back: Temple of Heaven at center. Printer: BEPP.			
	a. *PEIPING. (S/M #C245-21a).*	25.00	125	750
	b. *TIENTSIN. (S/M #C245-21b).*	20.00	100	525
	r. Remainder. Without place name. *(S/M #C245-21c).*	—	Unc	300

Land Bank of China, Limited

中國墾業銀行

Chung Kuo K'en Yeh Yin Hang

1926 Issue

501	1 Dollar	Good	Fine	XF
	1.6.1926. With various numerical, letter and Chinese character control overprints. Brown and multicolor. Cliffs at left, shoreline temple at center. Back: Shoreline at left. Printer: W&S.			
	a. *SHANGHAI. (S/M #C285 1a).*	225	1,200	3,750
	b. *TIENTSIN. (S/M #C285-1b).*	300	1,800	5,400

502	5 Dollars	Good	Fine	XF
	1.6.1926. Purple and green. Cliffs at left, shoreline temple at center. Back: Shoreline at left. Printer: W&S. With various numerical, letter and Chinese character control overprints.			
	a. *SHANGHAI. (S/M #C285-2a).*	150	600	4,875
	b. *TIENTSIN. (S/M #C285-2b).*	150	1,000	7,500

503	10 Dollars	Good	Fine	XF
	1.6.1926. Green and multicolor. Cliffs at left, shoreline temple at center. Back: Shoreline at left. Printer: W&S. With various numerical, letter and Chinese character control overprints.			
	a. *SHANGHAI. (S/M #C285-3a).*	175	725	5,200
	b. *TIENTSIN. (S/M #C285-3b).*	400	1,950	8,850

1931 Issue

504	1 Dollar	Good	Fine	XF
	1.6.1931. With various numerical, letter and Chinese character control overprints. Red and green. Cliffs at left, shoreline temple at center. Back: Shoreline at left. Printer: W&S. *SHANGHAI. (S/M #C285-10).*	125	250	1,500
505	**5 Dollars**	**Good**	**Fine**	**XF**
	1.6.1931. With various numerical, letter and Chinese character control overprints. Green and red. Cliffs at left, shoreline temple at center. Back: Shoreline at left. Printer: W&S. *SHANGHAI. (S/M #C285-11).*	125	225	1,350
506	**10 Dollars**	**Good**	**Fine**	**XF**
	1.6.1931. With various numerical, letter and Chinese character control overprints. Yellow. Cliffs at left, shoreline temple at center. Back: Shoreline at left. Printer: W&S. *SHANGHAI. (S/M #C285-12).*	175	400	2,500

National Bank of China - Nanking

中華國家銀行

Chung Hua Kuo Chia Yin Hang

Established 1930 by Marshal Yen Hsi-shan at Peking in opposition to the Kuomintang in Nanking.

1930 Issue

		VG	VF	UNC
507	**20 Cents** 1930.Temple of Heaven at center. Printer: BEPP. PEKING. Specimen. *(S/M #C260-1).*	—	—	10,000

		VG	VF	UNC
508	**1 Dollar** 1930. Brown. Temple of Heaven at center. Printer: BEPP. PEKING. Specimen. *(S/M #C260-10).*	—	—	8,700
509	**5 Dollars** 1930. Deep olive-green. Temple of Heaven at center. Printer: BEPP. PEKING. Specimen. *(S/M #C260-11).*	—	—	8,700
510	**10 Dollars** 1930. Orange. Temple of Heaven at center. Printer: BEPP. PEKING. Specimen. *(S/M #C260-12).*	—	—	8,700

National Bank of China - Canton

Established by Kuomintang Party in 1920-21 at Canton. Merged into Central Bank of China about 1923. It had no affiliation w/the previous bank, which has a similar English name.

1921 Issue

		Good	Fine	XF
511	**10 Cents** 1921. Blue and black on pink underprint. SYS at center with palm trees at left and right. Back: Three men and a farmer with an ox at center. *(S/M #C261-1).*	600	1,800	10,800
512	**20 Cents** 1921. Requires confirmation. SYS at center with palm trees at left and right. Back: Three men and a farmer with an ox at center. *(S/M #C261-2).*	—	—	—
513	**50 Cents** 1921. Requires confirmation. SYS at center with palm trees at left and right. Back: Three men and a farmer with an ox at center. *(S/M #C261-3).*	—	—	—
514	**1 Dollar** 1921. Blue and black on pink underprint. SYS at center with palm trees at left and right. Back: Three men and a farmer with an ox at center. *(S/M #C261-10).*	1,300	5,400	21,000
515	**5 Dollars** 1921. Green and black on pink underprint. SYS at center with palm trees at left and right. Back: Three men and a farmer with an ox at center. *(S/M #C261-11).*	900	4,500	16,500

		Good	Fine	XF
516	**10 Dollars** 1921. Red and black on yellow underprint. SYS at center with palm trees at left and right. Back: Three men and a farmer with an ox at center. *(S/M #C261-12).*	1,950	8,500	28,875

The National Commercial Bank, Limited

浙江興業銀行

Che Chiang Hsing Yeh Yin Hang

Established 1908.

Law 4.7.1907

		Good	Fine	XF
516A	**1 Dollar** ND. Mandarin at left. Back: Rooster at right.			
	a. *HUPEH. (S/M #C22-).*	1,000	4,500	18,000
	b. *SHANGHAI. (S/M #C22-).*	1,000	4,500	18,000

		Good	Fine	XF
516B	**5 Dollars** ND.Orange. Mandarin at right. *(S/M #C22-).*			
	a. *HUPEH. (S/M #C22-).*	1,000	4,325	18,000
	b. *SHANGHAI. (S/M #C22-).*	1,200	4,800	19,800

		Good	Fine	XF
516C	**10 Dollars** ND. Brown. Mandarin at left. Back: Rooster at right. *SHANGHAI*. Specimen. *(S/M #C22-)*.	1,625	5,400	22,500

1923 Issue

		Good	Fine	XF
517	**1 Dollar** 1.10.1923. Black and multicolor. Mandarin at right. Back: Rooster. Printer: ABNC. Various control letter overprints.			
	a. *SHANGHAI. (S/M #C22-1a).*	75.00	250	950
	b. *TIENTSIN. (S/M #C22-1b).*	75.00	250	950
	c. *HUPEH. (S/M #C22-1c).*	90.00	300	1,600
	s. 2 part specimen as a.	—	Unc	600

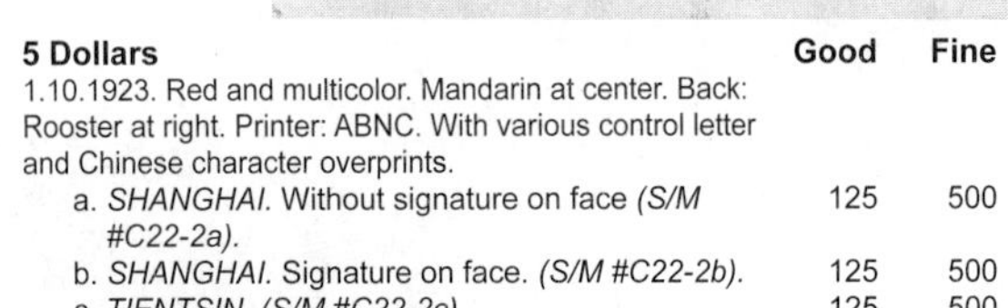

		Good	Fine	XF
518	**5 Dollars** 1.10.1923. Red and multicolor. Mandarin at center. Back: Rooster at right. Printer: ABNC. With various control letter and Chinese character overprints.			
	a. *SHANGHAI.* Without signature on face *(S/M #C22-2a).*	125	500	1,450
	b. *SHANGHAI.* Signature on face. *(S/M #C22-2b).*	125	500	1,450
	c. *TIENTSIN. (S/M #C22-2c).*	125	500	1,600
	d. *NANKING. (S/M #C22-2d).*	150	775	2,300
	e. *HUPEH. (S/M #C22-2e).*	125	500	2,300

		Good	Fine	XF
519	**10 Dollars** 1.10.1923. Green and multicolor. Old man at center. Back: Rooster at left. Printer: ABNC.			
	a. *HUPEH. (S/M #C22-3c).*	350	1,925	6,300
	b. *SHANGHAI. (S/M #C22-3a).*	275	1,650	4,900
	c. *TIENTSIN. (S/M #C22-3b).*	225	1,400	4,350

		Good	Fine	XF
519C	**10 Dollars** 1.10.1929. *SHANGHAI.* Specimen. *(S/M #C22-).* Fortress at left.	—	Unc	840

National Industrial Bank of China

中國實業銀行

Chung Kuo Shih Yeh Yin Hang

1922 Issue

		Good	Fine	XF
520	**1 Yüan** 1.6.1922. Landscape at left. Back: Landscape at center. Printer: BEPP.			
	a. *HANKOW. (S/M #C291-).*	250	1,000	—
	b. *PEKING.* Specimen. *(S/M #C291-).*	—	Unc	1,000
	c. *SHANGHAI.* Specimen. *(S/M #C291-).*	—	Unc	1,000
	d. *TIENTSIN. (S/M #C291-).*	250	1,000	—

		Good	Fine	XF
521	**5 Yüan** 1.6.1922. Landscape at left. Back: Landscape at center. Printer: BEPP.			
	a. *HANKOW.* Specimen. *(S/M #C291-).*	—	Unc	1,875
	b. *PEKING.* Specimen. *(S/M #C291-).*	—	Unc	1,875
	c. *SHANGHAI.* 2 part specimen Shanghai.	—	Unc	1,875

		Good	Fine	XF
522	**10 Yüan** 1.6.1922. Landscape at left. Back: Landscape at center. Printer: BEPP.			
	a. *PEKING. (S/M #C291-1).*	135	675	2,500
	s1. Without place name. Specimen. *(S/M #C291-).*	—	Unc	2,000
	s2. 2 part specimen Shanghai.	—	Unc	2,000

523	50 Yüan	Good	Fine	XF
	1.6.1922. Landscape at left. Back: Landscape at center. Printer: BEPP.			
	a. *PEKING.* Specimen. *(S/M #C291-).*	—	Unc	5,400
	s1. Without place name. Specimen. *(S/M #C291-).*	—	Unc	3,300
	s2. 2 part specimen Shanghai.	—	Unc	3,600

524	100 Yüan	Good	Fine	XF
	1.6.1922. Landscape at left. Back: Landscape at center. Printer: BEPP.			
	a. *PEKING.* Specimen. *(S/M #C291-).*	—	Unc	5,000
	b. *SHANGHAI.* Specimen.	—	Unc	5,000
	s1. Without place name. Specimen. *(S/M #C291-).*	—	Unc	3,150
	s2. 2 part specimen. Shanghai.	—	Unc	3,600

1924 Issue

525	1 Yüan	Good	Fine	XF
	1924. Violet on multicolor underprint. Running horse at upper left. Signature varieties. Back: Great Wall at center. Printer: ABNC. With various numerical, letter and Chinese character overprints.			
	a. *SHANGHAI. (S/M #C291-1c).*	36.00	225	650
	b. *TSINGTAO. (S/M #C291-1a).*	60.00	180	1,100
	c. *WEIHAIWEI. (S/M #C291-1b).*	90	325	2,400
	d. *PEKING. (S/M #C291-1e).*	90	180	850
	e. *TIENTSIN (S/M #C291-1d).*	60.00	180	850
	f. *SHANTUNG. (S/M #C291-1f).*	120	350	1,600

526	5 Yüan	Good	Fine	XF
	1924. Red and multicolor. Running horse at center. Signature varieties. Back: Great Wall at center. Printer: ABNC. With various numerical, letter and Chinese character overprints.			
	a. *HANKOW. (S/M #C291-2b).*	180	900	2,650
	b. *SHANGHAI. (S/M #C291-2a).*	90	350	1,100
	c. *TIENTSIN. (S/M #C291-2c).*	90	275	1,450
	d. *TSINGTAO. (S/M #C291-2d).*	150	550	2,600
	e. *PEKING. (S/M #C291-2e).*	150	450	2,200
	f. *WEIHAIWEI. (S/M #C291-2f).*	225	1,325	3,250
	g. *SHANGTUNG/TSINAN (S/M #C291-).*	—	—	—

527	10 Yüan	Good	Fine	XF
	1924. Green and multicolor. Running horse at right. Signature varieties. Back: Great Wall at center. Printer: ABNC. With various numerical, letter and Chinese character overprints.			
	a. *SHANGHAI. (S/M #C291-3a).*	135	700	1,950
	b. *TIENTSIN. (S/M #C291-3b).*	180	700	2,650
	c. *PEKING. (S/M #C291-3c).*	180	700	2,650
	d. *SHANTUNG. (S/M #C291-3d).*	330	1,950	4,000
	e. *TSINGTAO. (S/M #C291-3)*	600	2,000	—

528	50 Yüan	Good	Fine	XF
	1924. Orange. Running horse at center. Signature varieties. Back: Great Wall at center. Printer: ABNC. With various numerical, letter and Chinese character overprints.			
	a. *PEKING. (S/M #C291-4a).*	350	2,200	6,500
	b. *SHANTUNG. (S/M #C291-4b).*	350	2,200	6,500
	c. *SHANGHAI. (S/M #C291-4c).*	225	900	4,950
	s. Specimen. *(S/M #C291-4).*	—	Unc	1,625

529	100 Yüan	Good	Fine	XF
	1924. Blue and multicolor. Running horse at center. Signature varieties. Back: Great Wall at center. Printer: ABNC. With various numerical, letter and Chinese character overprints.			
	a. *PEKING. (S/M #C291-5b).*	600	3,600	7,200
	b. *SHANGHAI. (S/M #C291-5a).*	700	4,325	8,700
	s. Specimen. *(S/M #C291-5).*	—	Unc	2,400

530	100 Yüan	Good	Fine	XF
	1924. Red. Signature varieties. Back: Great Wall at center. Printer: ABNC. With various numerical, letter and Chinese character overprints. Specimen. *(S/M #C291-6).*	—	Unc	1,800

1931 Issue

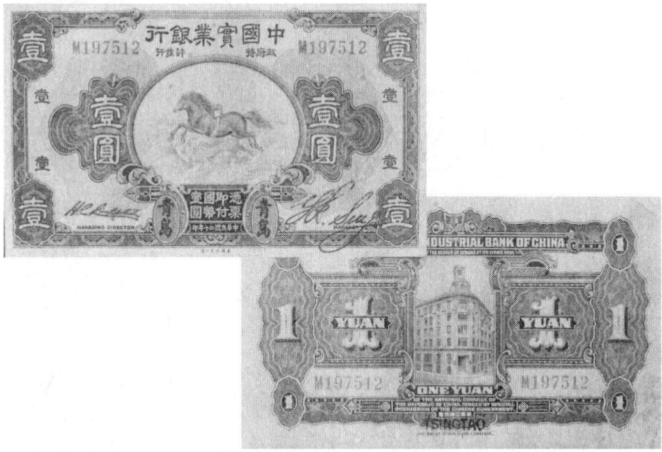

531	1 Yüan	Good	Fine	XF
	1931. Purple on multicolor underprint. Running horse at center. 2 signature varieties. Back: Bank building at center. Printer: ABNC. With various numerical, letter and Chinese character overprints.			
	a. *FUKIEN. (S/M #C291-).*	90.00	450	900
	b. *Shanghai* on face; *SHANGHAI* on back. *(S/M #C291-10a).*	60.00	325	675
	c. *Shanghai* on face only. *(S/M #C291-10b).*	55.00	250	500
	d. *SHANTUNG. (S/M #C291-10c).*	120	650	1,900
	e. *TSINGTAO. (S/M #C291-10d).*	115	500	1,600
	f. *TIETSION.*	80.00	225	1,900
	g. *HANKOW.*	250	450	—
	r. Remainder. Without place name. *(S/M #C291-10).*	—	Unc	350

532	5 Yüan	Good	Fine	XF
	1931. Red and multicolor. Running horse at center. Back: Bank building at center. Printer: ABNC. With various numerical, letter and Chinese character overprints.			
	a. *SHANGHAI.* 2 signature varieties. *(S/M #C291-11a).*	50.00	240	825
	b. *TIENTSIN. (S/M #C291-11b).*	60.00	375	900
	c. *FUKIEN. (S/M #C291-11c).*	90.00	425	1,350
	d. *FOOCHOwith FUKIEN. (S/M #C291-11d).*	90.00	425	1,350
	e. *AMOY/FUKIEN.*	110	500	1,800
	f. *Tsinan/SHANTUNG.*	450	975	—
	r. Remainder. Without place name. *(S/M #C291-11).*	—	Unc	275

533	10 Yüan	Good	Fine	XF
	1931. Green and multicolor. Running horse at center. Back: Bank building at center. Printer: ABNC. With various numerical, letter and Chinese character overprints.			
	a. *SHANGHAI. (S/M #C291-12).*	60.00	160	700
	b. *TSINGTAO.*	60.00	300	1,800
	c. *AMOY/FUKIEN. (S/M#C291-12)*	—	—	1,000

1935 Issue

534	1 Yüan	Good	Fine	XF
	1935. *Shanghai. (S/M #C291-20).* Red. Printer: W&S.	40.00	180	750

Ningpo Commercial and Savings Bank Limited

行銀明四

Szu Ming Yin Hang

Note: For earlier issues see #A61A-A61D. Shanghai office.

1920 Issue

539	1 Dollar	Good	Fine	XF
	1920. Blue and multicolor. *Shanghai. (S/M #S107-10).*			
	a. Issued note.	225	1,325	2,700
	b. Overprint: *SH.*	275	1,625	3,240

540	1 Dollar	Good	Fine	XF
	1.9.1920. With various Chinese character overprints. *Shanghai. (S/M #S107-11).* Blue. Printer: ABNC.			
	a. Issued note.	275	1,620	3,800
	b. Overprint: *SH.*	275	1,500	3,800

541	5 Dollars	Good	Fine	XF
	1.9.1920. Red and multicolor. Bank at center. Back: Floral pot at center. Printer: ABNC. With various Chinese character overprints. *SHANGHAI. (S/M #S107-12).*			
	a. Issued note.	80.00	350	750
	b. Overprint: *NP.*	90.00	350	900
	c. Overprint: *SH.*	90.00	350	900
	d. Overprint: *Y.*	90.00	350	900

Note: For #541 with additional *CENTRAL BANK* overprint see #170.

#	Description	Good	Fine	XF
542	**10 Dollars** 1.9.1920.Green. Printer: ABNC. With various Chinese character overprints. *SHANGHAI. (S/M #S107-13).*	350	1,625	4,350
543	**50 Dollars** 1.9.1920. Red and multicolor. Printer: ABNC.With various Chinese character overprints. *SHANGHAI. (S/M #S107-14).*	900	4,325	11,000
544	**100 Dollars** 1.9.1920. Blue and multicolor. Printer: ABNC.With various Chinese character overprints. *SHANGHAI. (S/M #S107-15).*	1,625	5,400	14,500

1921 Issue

#	Description	Good	Fine	XF
545	**1 Dollar** 1.11.1921. Red. Bank at center. Printer: BEPP. *SHANGHAI. (S/M #S107-20).*			
	a. Issued note.	150	500	1,625
	s. Specimen.	—	Unc	825

1925 Issue

#	Description	Good	Fine	XF
546	**1 Dollar** 1.9.1925. Brown. Mountain landscape at center. Printer: G&D. *SHANGHAI (S/M #S107-30).*			
	a. Issued note.	250	1,200	2,650

#	Description	Good	Fine	XF
546A	**1 Dollar** 1.9.1925. Red on black underprint. Bank at center. Back: Similar to #546. Printer: G&D. *SHANGHAI (S/M #S107-).*	100	500	1,000
547	**5 Dollars** 1.9.1925. Green. Mountain landscape at center. Printer: G&D. *SHANGHAI (S/M #S107-31).*	250	1,200	2,700

Deceptive forgeries exist.

#	Description	Good	Fine	XF
547A	**5 Dollars** 1.9.1925. Green on multicolor underprint. Back: Bank at center. Printer: G&D. Specimen. *(S/M #S107-).*			
	a. Issued note.	—	Unc	600
	b. As a. Brown back.	—	—	—

#	Description	Good	Fine	XF
548	**10 Dollars** 1.9.1925. Black and red. Mountain landscape at center. Printer: G&D. *SHANGHAI. (S/M #S107-32).*	150	700	2,200
548A	**10 Dollars** 1.9.1925. Black and red. Bank at center. Printer: G&D. *(S/M #S107-33).*	225	1,300	2,800
548B	**100 Dollars** 1.9.1925. Violet and multicolor. Mountain landscape. Back: Floral pot at center. Similar to #541. Printer: G&D. *SHANGHAI (S/M #S107-35).*	270	1,625	4,500

1932-1934 Issue

#	Description	Good	Fine	XF
549	**1 Dollar** Jan. yr. 21 (1932) 11.1.1933. Red-brown. Mountain landscape at left. Printer: W&S. *SHANGHAI.*			
	a. Green serial #. *(S/M #S107-40a).*	20.00	175	700
	b. Blue serial #. *(S/M #S107-40b).*	20.00	175	700
	c. Without serial # on face. *(S/M #S107-40c).*	20.00	175	700

Mismatched dates on face and back.

		Good	Fine	XF
550	**10 Dollars** January 1934. Red. Mountain landscape at left. Printer: W&S. *SHANGHAI. (S/M #S107-50).*	75.00	450	900

Mismatched dates on face and back.

Tah Chung Bank

行銀中大

Ta Chung Yin Hang

1921 First Issue

		VG	VF	UNC
551	**10 Cents** 1921. Green. Landscape at left, Great Wall at right. Printer: BEPP.			
	a. *HANKOW.* Specimen. *(S/M #T12-1b).*	—	—	550
	b. *TIENTSIN. (S/M #T12-1a).*	60.00	250	600
	c. *TSINGTAU.* Specimen. *(S/M #T12-1c).*	—	—	550
552	**20 Cents** 1921. Orange. Landscape at left, Great Wall at right. Printer: BEPP.	VG	VF	UNC
	a. *HANKOW.* Specimen. *(S/M #T12-2b).*	—	—	660
	b. *TIENTSIN. (S/M #T12-2a).*	72.00	300	720
	c. *TSINGTAU.* Specimen. *(S/M #T12-2c).*	—	—	660
553	**50 Cents** 1921. Purple. Landscape at left, Great Wall at right. Printer: BEPP.	VG	VF	UNC
	a. *HANKOW.* Specimen. *(S/M #T12-3b).*	—	—	660
	b. *TIENTSIN.* Specimen. *(S/M #T12-3a).*	—	—	660
	c. *TSINGTAU.* Specimen. *(S/M #T12-3c).*	—	—	660

		VG	VF	UNC
554	**1 Yüan** 15.7.1921. Green and black. Landscape at left, Great Wall at right. Printer: BEPP.			
	a. *HANKOW.* Specimen. *(S/M #T12-10a).*	—	—	525
	b. *TSINGTAU.* Specimen. *(S/M #T12-10b).*	—	—	525
	c. *TIENTSIN. (S/M #T12-10c).*	55.00	150	800
555	**5 Yüan** 15.7.1921. Orange and black. Landscape at left, Great Wall at right. Printer: BEPP.	VG	VF	UNC
	a. *HANKOW.* Specimen. *(S/M #T12-11a).*	—	—	600
	b. *TSINGTAU.* Specimen. *(S/M #T12-11b).*	—	—	600
556	**10 Yüan** 15.7.1921. Purple and black. Landscape at left, Great Wall at right. Printer: BEPP.	VG	VF	UNC
	a. *HANKOW.* Specimen. *(S/M #T12-12a).*	—	—	850
	b. *TSINGTAU.* Specimen. *(S/M #T12-12b).*	—	—	850
	c. *TIENTSIN. (S/M #T12-).*	120	660	1,600
	d. *CHUNGKING. (S/M #T12-).*	180	870	1,750

1921 Second Issue

		VG	VF	UNC
557	**1 Dollar** 1.1.1921. Brown. Landscape at center. Printer: BEPP. *CHUNGKING.* Specimen. *(S/M #T12-).*	—	—	1,800

Color Abbreviation Guide

New to the *Standard Catalog of® World Paper Money* are the following abbreviations related to color references:

BC: Back color
PC: Paper color

		VG	VF	UNC
557A	**10 Dollars** 1.1.1921. Green and multicolor. Landscape at center. Printer: BEPP.			
	a. *PEKING.* Specimen. *(S/M #T12-13a).*	—	—	2,400
	b. *CHUNGKING. (S/M #T12-13b).*	—	—	—

1932 Issue

		VG	VF	UNC
558	**10 Cents** 1932. Brown. Bell at center. *Tientsin. (S/M #T12-20).*	60.00	300	850

		VG	VF	UNC
559	**20 Cents** 1932. Green. Bell at center. *Tientsin. (S/M #T12-21).*	75.00	375	1,100
560	**50 Cents** 1932. *(S/M #T12-22).*	VG 75.00	VF 375	UNC 1,350

		VG	VF	UNC
561	**1 Yüan** 1.9.1932. Green. Back: Dollar coin at center. *SHANGHAI.* Specimen. *(S/M #T12-30).*	—	—	2,000

		VG	VF	UNC
562	**5 Yüan** 1.9.1932. Black on multicolor underprint. Bell at center. Back: Five 1-Yuan coins. *SHANGHAI.* Specimen. *(S/M #T12-31).*	—	—	1,988
563	**10 Yüan** 1.9.1932. *SHANGHAI. (S/M #T12-32).*	—	—	2,175

1938 Issue

#	Denomination	VG	VF	UNC
564	**1 Yüan** 15.1.1938. Green and black. Landscape at left, Great Wall at right. Printer: BEPP. PEKING. *(S/M #T12-40).*	30.00	135	375
565	**5 Yüan** 15.1.1938. Orange and black. Printer: BEPP. PEKING. *(S/M #T12-41).*	30.00	150	325

Bank of Territorial Development

ТЕРРИТОРIАЛЬНО IIРОМЫШЛЕННЫЙ БАНКЪ В'Ъ КИТА Ъ

殖邊銀行

Chih Pien Yin Hang

This institution collapsed in 1917, leaving behind quantities of unpaid notes and shares. Its branches, however, enjoyed considerable autonomy and not all were immediately affected. The Yunnan office was still in operation and probably issuing notes in the mid-1920s although none of the latter has been seen.

1914 Issue

#566-572 Changchun issues with overprint: *N.B. Payable in subsidiary (silver) coins at par...*on back.

#	Denomination	Good	Fine	XF
566	**1 Dollar** 1.12.1914. Green and black. Workers and camels along road at center. Printer: BEPP.			
	a. *CHANGCHUN.* Without overprint: *N.B. Payable by Ten Coins to The Dollar,* on back. *(S/M #C165-1a).*	27.50	200	600
	b. *CHANGCHUN/CHEKIANG. (S/M #C165-2a).*	27.50	200	600
	c. *CHANGCHUN/DOLONOR. (S/M #C165-2b).*	75.00	275	775
	d. *CHANGCHUN/HANKOW. (S/M #C165-2c).*	27.50	200	600
	e. CHANGCHUN/KIANGSU. (S/M #C165- 2d).	27.50	200	600
	f. *CHANGCHUN/SHANGHAI. (S/M #C165-2e).*	15.00	50.00	275
	g. *CHANGCHUN/TIENTSIN. (S/M #C165-2f).*	15.00	50.00	275
	h. *CHEKIANG. (S/M #C165-1b).*	27.50	200	600
	i. *HARBIN. (S/M #C165-1c).*	75.00	300	1,000
	j. *KIANGSU. (S/M #C165-1d).*	27.50	200	600
	k. *KIRIN. (S/M #C165-1e).*	27.50	200	600
	l. *Fengtien//MOUKDEN. (S/M #C165-1f).*	27.50	200	600
	m. *Fengtien/ /MOUKDEN/CHANGCHUN. (S/M #C165-3a).*	27.50	200	600
	n. *Fengtien//MOUKDEN/YUNNAN. (S/M #C165-3b).*	27.50	200	600
	o. *SHANGHAI. (S/M #C165-1g).*	15.00	55.00	275
	p. *TIENTSIN. (S/M #C165-1h).*	15.00	55.00	275
	q. *CHANGCHUN/MUKDEN. (S/M #C165-).*	27.50	200	600
	r. Remainder. Without place name or signature *(S/M #C165-1i).*	15.00	50.00	200
	s. *MANCHURIA.*	75.00	275	870
	t. *MOUKDEN/KUNGSU.*	120	400	—
	u. *CHANGCHUN/KALGAN. (S/M #C165-)*	50.00	150	—
	v. *CHANGCHUN/PAOTING/TIENTSIN. (S/M #C165-)*	130	400	—
	w. *MOUKDEN, FENGTIEN/KIANGU.*	70.00	220	—

#	Denomination	Good	Fine	XF
567	**5 Dollars** 1.12.1914. Purple on yellow underprint. Hut along shoreline, ships at center. Printer: BEPP.			
	a. *CHANGCHUN. (S/M #C165-4a).*	27.50	110	500
	b. *CHANGCHUN/CHEKIANG. (S/M #C165-5a).*	27.50	110	500
	c. *CHANGCHUN/HANKOW. (S/M #C165-5b).*	27.50	110	500
	d. *CHANGCHUN/HARBIN. (S/M #C165-5c).*	60.00	200	675
	e. *CHANGCHUN/KIANGSU. (S/M #C165-5d).*	27.50	110	500
	f. *CHANGCHUN/SHANGHAI. (S/M #C165-5e).*	27.50	110	500
	g. *DOLONOR. (S/M #C165-4b).*	90.00	400	1,450
	h. *HARBIN. (S/M #C165-4c).*	90.00	400	1,450
	i. *MANCHURIA.* with *N.B. payable in silver...* and *To be converted into silver dollars...* on back. *(S/M #C165-4d).*	50.00	200	600
	k. *Fengtien-MOUKDEN. (S/M #C165-4e).*	27.50	90.00	500
	l. *Fengtien-MOUKDEN/SHANGHAI. (S/M #C165-6a).*	27.50	90.00	500
	m. *Fengtien-MOUKDEN/YUNNAN. (S/M #C165-6b).*	27.50	90.00	500
	n. *SHANGHAI. (S/M #C165-4f).*	27.50	90.00	500
	o. *TIENTSIN. (S/M #C165-4g).*	27.50	90.00	500
	p. *CHEKIANG. (S/M #C165-).*	27.50	90.00	500
	q. *KIANGSI. (S/M #C165-).*	27.50	90.00	500
	r. *KIANGSU. (S/M #C165-).*	27.50	90.00	500
	s. *YUNNAN. (S/M #C165-).*	27.50	90.00	500
	t. Remainder. Without place name or signature *(S/M #C165-).*	25.00	75.00	350
	u. *KIRIN.*	50.00	180	—
	v. *CHANGCHUN/DOLONOR.*	100	220	—
	w. Overprint. *FENGTIEN-MOUKDEN with military overprint.*	70.00	200	600
	x. *CHANGCHUN/KALGAN. (S/M #C165-)*	50.00	150	450
	y. *CHANGCHUN/MOUKDEN*	30.00	100	300
	z. *SHANGHAI/MOUKDEN. (S/M #C165-)*	—	200	650

#	Denomination	Good	Fine	XF
568	**10 Dollars** 1.12.1914. Yellow and red border, black center. Road-building at center. Printer: BEPP.			
	a. *CHANGCHUN. (S/M #C165-7a).*	37.50	150	450
	b. *CHANGCHUN/HANKOW. (S/M #C165-8a).*	37.50	150	450
	c. *CHANGCHUN/KIANGSU. (S/M #C165-8b).*	37.50	150	450
	d. *DOLONOR. (S/M #C165-7b).*	80.00	250	900
	e. *KIANGSU. (S/M #C165-7c).*	37.50	150	450
	f. *KIRIN. (S/M #C165-7d).*	37.50	150	450
	g. *MANCHURIA. (S/M #C165-7e).*	50.00	165	600

	Good	Fine	XF
h. *SHANGHAI. (S/M #C165-7f).*	20.00	180	450
i. *TIENTSIN. (S/M #C165-7g).*	20.00	180	450
j. *CHANGCHUN/KALGAN. (S/M #C165-).*	20.00	180	450
k. *CHANGCHUN/Fengtien/ /MOUKDEN. (S/M #C165-).*	20.00	180	450
l. *CHANGCHUN/SHANGHAI.*	20.00	180	450
m. *CHANGCHUN/TIENTSIN. (S/M #C165-).*	20.00	180	450
n. *Fengtien/MOUKDEN.*	70.00	240	600
o. *CHANGCHUN - KALGAN/MOUKDEN. (S/M #C165-)*	70.00	220	—
p. *CHANGCHUN/DOLONOR. (S/M #C165-)*	120	350	—
r. Remainder. Without place name or signature *(S/M #C165-7h).*	20.00	80.00	300

1915 Issue

		Good	Fine	XF
569	**5 Cents** 1915. Red. Printer: BEPP. *(S/M #C165-10).*	35.00	100	900

		Good	Fine	XF
570	**10 Cents** 1915. Purple. Printer: BEPP. *(S/M #C165-11).*	30.00	75.00	675

		Good	Fine	XF
571	**20 Cents** 1.11.1915. Green. Farm workers at left. Printer: BEPP. *MANCHURIA. (S/M #C165-12).*	12.50	30.00	220

		Good	Fine	XF
572	**50 Cents** 1.11.1915. Black. Landscape at left. Printer: BEPP. *MANCHURIA. (S/M #C165-13).*	22.50	90.00	375

		Good	Fine	XF
573	**1 Dollar** 1915. Green. Back: Russian text. Printer: CMN. *(S/M #C165-20).* Requires confirmation.	—	—	—

		VG	VF	UNC
574	**5 Dollars** 1915. Brown and black on pink underprint. Similar to #575. Back: Russian text. Printer: CMN. *Urga.* Remainder. Without signature *(S/M #C165-21).*	—	—	2,775

		VG	VF	UNC
575	**10 Dollars** 1915. Blue. Back: Russian text. Printer: CMN. *Urga.* Remainder. Without signature *(S/M #C165-22).*	—	—	6,500

1916 Issue

		VG	VF	UNC
576	**100 Coppers** 1916. Red and yellow. Remainder. Without place name, serial # or signature *(S/M #C165-30).*	—	—	300

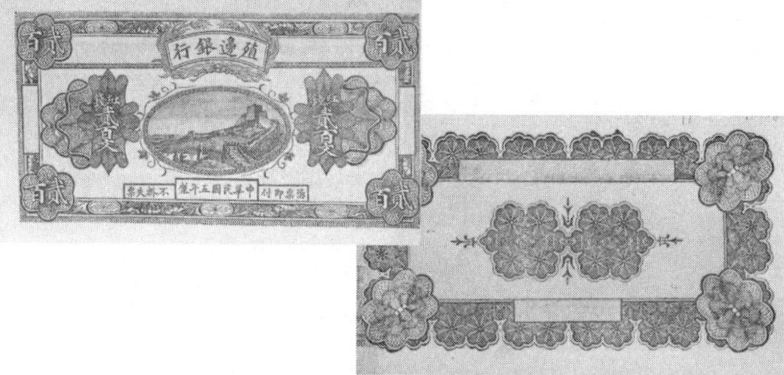

		VG	VF	UNC
577	**200 Coppers** 1916. Dark green. Remainder. Without place name, serial # or signature *(S/M #C165-31).*	—	—	450

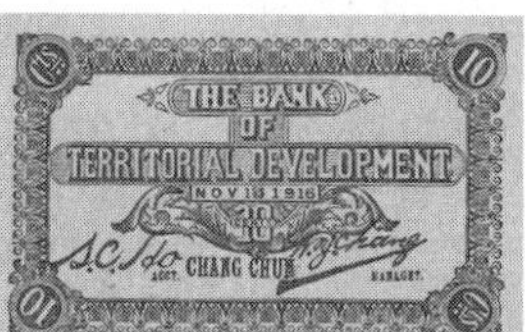

		VG	VF	UNC
578	**10 Cents** 1.11.1916. Purple. Cows at left.			
	a. *CHANGCHUN. (S/M #C165-40b).*	20.00	90.00	375
	b. *MANCHURIA. (S/M #C165-40a).*	30.00	175	600
	r. Remainder. Without serial #. *(S/M #C165-40).*	—	—	175

		VG	VF	UNC
579	**20 Cents** 1916. Requires confirmation. *(S/M #C165-41).*	—	—	—

		VG	VF	UNC
580	**40 Cents** 1.11.1916. Black and red. Houses along shoreline at left. *CHANGCHUN. (S/M #C165-42).*	25.00	125	450

		VG	VF	UNC
581	**50 Cents** 1916. Black. Printer: BEPP. *MANCHURIA. (S/M #C165-43).*	30.00	165	475

582	1 Dollar	VG	VF	UNC
	ND. (1916) Black on multicolor underprint. City gate at left. Printer: ABNC.			
	a. *KALGAN. (S/M #C165-50a).*	40.00	180	650
	b. *CHANGCHUN.* Without overprint: *N.B. payable in sudsidiary (silver) coins...* on back. *(S/M #C165-50c).*	40.00	180	675
	c. *TIENTSIN. (S/M #C165-50d).*	40.00	150	675
	r. Remainder. Without place name. *(S/M #C165-50b).*	—	—	375

583	5 Dollars	VG	VF	UNC
	ND. (1916) Black on multicolor underprint. Building at shoreline at right. Printer: ABNC.			
	a. *KALGAN. (S/M #C165-51b).*	45.00	225	825
	b. *TIENTSIN. (S/M #C165-51a).*	45.00	225	825
	c. *ANHWEI. (S/M #C165-51c).*	125	525	2,200
	d. *CHANGCHUN.* Without overprint: *N.B. payable in subsidiary (silver) coins...* on back. *(S/M #C165-51).*	40.00	225	675
	r. Remainder. Without place name. *(S/M #C165-51).*	—	—	300

584	10 Dollars	VG	VF	UNC
	ND. (1916) Black on multicolor underprint. Building at left. Printer: ABNC.			
	a. *SHANGHAI. (S/M #C165-52b).*	45.00	300	900
	b. *TIENTSIN. (S/M #C165-52a).*	45.00	300	900
	c. *ANHWEI*	—	—	—
	r. Remainder. Without place name. *(S/M #C165-52).*	—	—	575

585	50 Dollars	VG	VF	UNC
	ND. (1916) Black on multicolor underprint. Building right. Printer: ABNC. Remainder. Without place name. *(S/M #C165-53).*	—	—	4,350

1918 Issue

585A	1 Dollar	VG	VF	UNC
	1918. Green and black. Temple at left, rural buildings at right. Back: Rural buildings center. *KIRIN. (S/M #C165-61).*	150	600	4,350

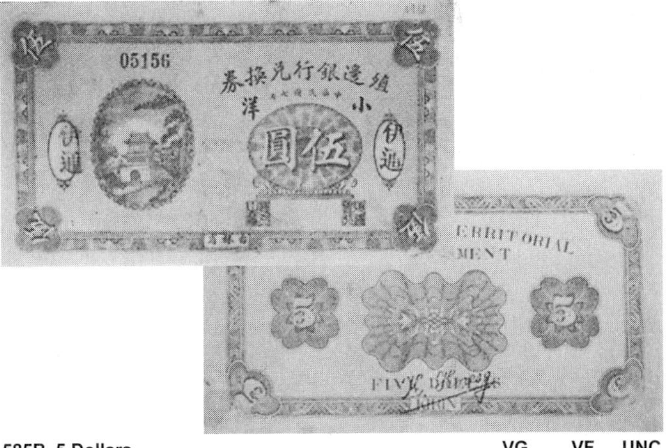

585B	5 Dollars	VG	VF	UNC
	1918. Lilac and green. Temple at left. *Kirin. (S/M #C165-).*	200	1,000	6,600

Ministry of Communications - Peking-Hankow Railway 交通部京漢鐵路支付券

Chiao T'ung Pu Ching Han T'ieh Lu Chih Fu Ch'üan

#585C-594 similar except for denomination and period in months in Chinese below bank name. Printer: BEPP.

16 Month Series 第十六期

585C	10 Dollars	VG	VF	UNC
	Feb. 1922. Blue and red. *(S/M #C125-2c).*	2.50	15.00	30.00

24 Month Series 第二十四期

586	5 Dollars	VG	VF	UNC
	Feb. 1922. Purple and red. *(S/M #C125-1a).*	2.25	7.50	25.00

		VG	VF	UNC
587	**10 Dollars** Feb. 1922. Blue and red. *(S/M #C125-2a).*	2.50	9.00	30.00
588	**50 Dollars** Feb. 1922. Green and red. *(S/M #C125-3a).*	18.00	45.00	200

25 Month Series

第二十五期

		VG	VF	UNC
588B	**10 Dollars** Feb. 1921. Blue and red. *(S/M #C125-2d).*	2.00	4.75	20.00

32 Month Series

第三十二期

		VG	VF	UNC
589	**5 Dollars** Feb. 1922. Purple and red. *(S/M #C125-1b).*	2.25	7.50	22.50
590	**10 Dollars** Feb. 1922. Blue and red. *(S/M #C125-2b).*	2.50	9.00	30.00
591	**50 Dollars** Feb. 1922. Green and red. *(S/M #C125-3b).*	18.00	75.00	180

36 Month Series

第三十六期

		VG	VF	UNC
592	**5 Dollars** Feb. 1922. Purple and red. *(S/M #C125-1e).*	3.00	9.00	30.00
593	**10 Dollars** Feb. 1922. Blue and red. *(S/M #C125-2e).*	3.00	9.00	30.00
594	**50 Dollars** Feb. 1922. Green and red. *(S/M #C125-3e).*	18.00	75.00	180

Military Exchange Bureau

財政部軍需滙兌局

Ts'ai Cheng Pu Chün Hsü Hui Tui Chü

1927 Issue

		VG	VF	UNC
595	**1 Yüan** 1927. Black and multicolor. Junks at upper left, ships at upper right. Back: Great Wall at center. *(S/M #T181-1).*	135	550	1,350

Market Stabilization Currency Bureau

財政部平市官錢局

Ts'ai Cheng Pu P'ing Shih Kuan Ch'ien Chü

1910s (ND) Issue

		VG	VF	UNC
597	**20 Coppers** ND. Brown. Temple of Heaven at center. *Peking. (S/M #T183-).*	—	—	—
598	**50 Coppers** ND. (1910) Brown and blue. Printer: BEPP. *Honan. (S/M #T183-).*	1,575	3,600	—
598A	**100 Coppers** ND (1910). Brown and blue. Similar to #598.	—	—	—

1915 Issue

		VG	VF	UNC
599	**10 Coppers** 1915. Black, blue and yellow. Hillside pagoda at left, Temple of Heaven at right.			
	a. *Ching Chao* (Peking). *(S/M #T183-1a).*	18.00	45.00	270
	b. *Ching Chao/Three Eastern Provinces. (S/M #T183-1c).*	20.00	55.00	300
	c. *Tientsin/Chihli. (S/M #T183-1b).*	20.00	55.00	300
	d. *Kiangsi. (S/M #T183-1d).*	14.00	37.50	200

		VG	VF	UNC
600	**20 Coppers** 1915. Black, purple and blue. Hillside pagoda at left, Temple of Heaven at right.			
	a. *Ching Chao. (S/M #T183-2a).*	20.00	70.00	300
	b. *Ching Chao/Chihli. (S/M #T183-2d).*	18.00	55.00	275
	c. *Ching Chao/Honan. (S/M #T183-2f).*	18.00	55.00	275
	d. *Ching Chao/Kiangsi. (S/M #T183-2c).*	18.00	55.00	275
	e. *Ching Chao/Shantung. (S/M #T183-2e).*	18.00	55.00	275
	f. *Ching Chao/Three Eastern Provinces. (S/M #T183-2g).*	18.00	55.00	275
	g. *Tientsin/Chihli. (S/M #T183-2b).*	18.00	55.00	275

No.	Description	VG	VF	UNC
601	**40 Coppers**			
	1915. Black, brown and green. Hillside pagoda at left, Temple of Heaven at right.			
	a. *Chihli. (S/M #T183-3b).*	27.00	90.00	270
	b. *Ching Chao. (S/M #T183-3a).*	21.60	66.00	216
	c. *Ching Chao/Anhwei. (S/M #T183-3d).*	27.00	90.00	270
	d. *Ching Chao/Chihli. (S/M #T183-3e).*	27.00	90.00	270
	e. *Ching Chao/Honan. (S/M #T183-3f).*	27.00	90.00	270
	f. *Ching Chao/Kiangsi. (S/M #T183-3g).*	27.00	90.00	270
	g. *Ching Chao/Shantung. (S/M #T183-3h).*	27.00	90.00	270
	h. *Kiangsu. (S/M #T183-3c).*	27.00	90.00	270
	i. *Ching Chao/Peking. (S/M #T183-3i).*	27.00	90.00	270
	j. *Shantung. (S/M #T183-3).*	27.00	90.00	270

No.	Description	VG	VF	UNC
602	**50 Coppers**			
	1915. Black, red and green. Hillside pagoda at left, Temple of Heaven at right.			
	a. *Chihli. (S/M #T183-4b).*	16.00	45.00	165
	b. *Ching Chao. (S/M #T183-4a).*	11.00	27.50	90.00
	c. *Ching Chao/Heilungkiang. (S/M #T183-4f).*	16.00	35.00	125
	d. *Ching Chao/Honan. (S/M #T183-4g).*	16.00	35.00	125
	e. *Ching Chao/Kiangsi. (S/M #T183-4h).*	16.00	35.00	125
	f. *Ching Chao/Kiangsu. (S/M #T183-4i).*	16.00	35.00	125
	g. *Honan. (S/M #T183-4c).*	16.00	35.00	125
	h. *Kiangsu. (S/M #T183-4d).*	16.00	35.00	125
	i. *Kiangsu/Heilungkiang. (S/M #T183-4j).*	16.00	35.00	125
	j. *Shantung. (S/M #T183-4e).*	16.00	35.00	125
	k. *Peking. (S/M #T183-4k).*	16.00	35.00	125
	l. *KIANGSI/HONAN. (S/M #T183-41).*	16.00	35.00	125
	r. Remainder. Without place name. *(S/M T183-4).*	16.00	35.00	125

No.	Description	VG	VF	UNC
603	**100 Coppers**			
	1915. Black, green and orange. Hillside pagoda at left, Temple of Heaven at right.			
	a. *Anhwei. (S/M #T183-5b).*	42.00	125	500
	b. *Chihli. (S/M #T183-5c).*	42.00	100	450
	c. *Ching Chao. (S/M #T183-5a).*	42.00	100	450
	d. *Ching Chao/Heilungkiang. (S/M #T183-5h).*	42.00	100	450
	e. *Honan. (S/M #T183-5d).*	42.00	100	450
	f. *Kiangsi. (S/M #T183-5d).*	42.00	100	450
	g. *Shansi. (S/M #T183-5f).*	42.00	100	450
	h. *Shantung. (S/M #T183-5g).*	42.00	100	450
	i. *Peking. (S/M #T183-5i).*	42.00	100	450

1919 First Issue

No.	Description	VG	VF	UNC
603A	**10 Coppers**			
	Jan. 1919. *Ching Chao. (S/M #T183-).* Blue on green underprint.	18.00	90.00	216
603B	**20 Coppers**			
	Jan. 1919. *Tientsin. (S/M #T183-).* Blue-green on orange underprint.	16.00	85.00	204

1919 Second Issue

No.	Description	VG	VF	UNC
604	**10 Coppers**			
	1919. Black and dark blue-violet on light orange underprint. Printer: BEPP.			
	a. *Ching Chao. (S/M #T183-10a).*	13.00	70.00	145
	b. *Ching Chao/Yen T'ai. (S/M #T183-10b).*	23.00	90.00	265
	c. *Ching Chao/Peking. (S/M #T183-10c).*	23.00	90.00	265
	d. *ChiNan. (S/M #T183-10d).*	23.00	90.00	265

1919 Third Issue

No.	Description	VG	VF	UNC
604A	**10 Coppers**			
	1919. Black and dark blue-violet on light orange underprint. Like #604.			
	a. *Chefoo, Shantung. (S/M #T183-).*	22.50	90.00	398
	b. *Peking/? (S/M #T183-).*	22.50	90.00	398
605	**20 Coppers**			
	1919. Black, purple and blue. Printer: BEPP.			
	a. *Ching Chao. (S/M #T183-11a).*	22.00	45.00	216
	b. *Ching Chao/Yen T'ai. (S/M #T183-11b).*	22.00	55.00	270
	c. *Ching Chao/Peking. (S/M #T183-11c).*	22.00	55.00	270
	d. *ChiNan. (S/M #T183-11d).*	27.50	110	360

1920 Issue

No.	Description	VG	VF	UNC
606	**20 Coppers**			
	1920. Black, blue and multicolor. Printer: ABNC.			
	a. *Chihli. (S/M #T183-20b).*	17.50	45.00	198
	b. *Ching Chao. (S/M #T183-20a).*	16.50	45.00	210

1921 First Issue

No.	Description	VG	VF	UNC
607	**10 Coppers**			
	1921. Black, blue and orange. Back: Without English.			
	a. *Chihli. (S/M #T183-30b).*	7.50	22.50	110
	b. *Ching Chao. (S/M #T183-30a).*	7.50	22.50	1110
	c. *Peking. (S/M #T183-30c).*	7.50	22.50	108
607A	**10 Coppers**			
	1921. Black, blue and orange. Similar to #607. Back: *10 COPPER COINS. Ching Chao. (S/M #T183-).*	7.50	22.50	110
608	**20 Coppers**			
	1921. Black, purple and blue.			
	a. *Ching Chao. (S/M #T183-31a).*	7.50	22.50	90.00
	b. *Ching Chao/Chihli. (S/M #T183-31b).*	7.50	27.50	90.00

1922 Issues

No.	Description	VG	VF	UNC
609	**10 Coppers**			
	1922. Black, blue and yellow. Printer: BEPP. *Ching Chao. (S/M #T183-40).*	9.00	27.50	90.00

#	Description	VG	VF	UNC
610	**20 Coppers**	VG	VF	UNC
	1922. Black, purple and blue. Printer: BEPP. 120x72mm.			
	a. *Ching Chao. (S/M #T183-41a).*	7.50	18.00	70.00
	b. *Ching Chao/Kiangsu. (S/M #T183-41b).*	7.50	18.00	70.00
	c. *Shantung. (S/M #T183-41c).*	7.50	18.00	70.00
611	**20 Coppers**	VG	VF	UNC
	1922. Black, purple and blue. 139x82mm. *Ching Chao. (S/M #T183-42).*	6.00	18.00	60.00

1923 Issue

#	Description	VG	VF	UNC
612	**10 Coppers**	VG	VF	UNC
	1923. Black, blue and yellow. 112x60mm.			
	a. *Ching Chao. (S/M #T183-50a).*	4.00	13.00	25.00
	b. *Shantung. (S/M #T183-50b).*	4.00	15.00	35.00
	c. *Tientsin. (S/M #T183-50c).*	4.00	15.00	35.00
613	**10 Coppers**	VG	VF	UNC
	1923. Black, blue and yellow. 110x55mm. *Ching Chao. (S/M #T183-51).*	4.50	18.00	45.00

#	Description	VG	VF	UNC
614	**20 Coppers**	VG	VF	UNC
	1923. Black, purple and blue.			
	a. *Ching Chao. (S/M #T183-52a).*	4.00	13.00	30.00
	b. *SHANTUNG. (S/M #T183-52b).*	7.50	28.00	75.00
615	**40 Coppers**	VG	VF	UNC
	1923. Black, brown and green. *Ching Chao. (S/M #T183-53).*	7.00	23.00	65.00

1923 Second Issue

#	Description	VG	VF	UNC
616	**10 Cents**	VG	VF	UNC
	1.6.1923. Blue. Palace at center. Printer: BEPP.			
	a. *Peking. (S/M #T183-60b).*	2.25	9.00	28.00
	r. Remainder. Without place name. *(S/M #T183-60a).*	2.00	4.50	25.00
617	**20 Cents**	VG	VF	UNC
	1.6.1923. Purple. Similar to #531. Printer: BEPP.			
	a. *Peking. (S/M #T183-61b).*	2.25	9.00	28.00
	r. Remainder. Without place name. *(S/M #T183-61a).*	2.00	4.50	25.00
618	**50 Cents**	VG	VF	UNC
	1.6.1923. Green. Similar to #531. Printer: BEPP.			
	a. *Kalgan. (S/M #T183-62c).*	10.00	28.00	100
	b. *Peking. (S/M #T183-62b).*	10.00	28.00	100
	r. Remainder. Without place name. *(S/M #T183-62a).*	4.50	11.00	45.00
619	**1 Yüan**	VG	VF	UNC
	ND. (1923) Brown. Shrine at center. Printer: BEPP. Remainder. Without place name. *(S/M #T183-70).*	—	—	340
620	**5 Yüan**	VG	VF	UNC
	ND. (1923) Purple. Printer: BEPP. *(S/M #T183-71).*	22.50	90.00	400
621	**10 Yüan**	VG	VF	UNC
	ND. (1923) Requires confirmation. Printer: BEPP. *(S/M #T183-72).*	—	—	—
622	**100 Yüan**	VG	VF	UNC
	ND. (1923) Requires confirmation. Printer: BEPP. *(S/M #T183-73).*	—	—	—

Special Circulating Notes 券通流別特部政財

Ts'ai Cheng Pu T'e Pieh Liu T'ung Ch'üan

#623-625 various dates 1923-1924 w/an elongated purple hand stamped seal diagonally. This indicates that they were once presented for payment and then affixed to a separate document providing for redemption on a monthly installment basis through 1926. The full sheet has 39 stamp-sized coupons for the holder to clip and turn in. Peking: Printer: BEPP.

1923 Issue

#	Description	VG	VF	UNC
623	**1 Yüan**	VG	VF	UNC
	1923. Blue. Arched bridge over stream at center. *(S/M #T184-1).*	3.75	14.00	35.00
624	**5 Yüan**	VG	VF	UNC
	1923. Brown. Arched bridge over stream at center. *(S/M #T184-2).*	4.50	18.00	45.00
625	**10 Yüan**	VG	VF	UNC
	1923. Red. Temple at center. *(S/M #T184-3).*	9.00	23.00	80.00

Fixed Term, Interest-bearing Treasury Notes

券庫國利有期定部政財

Ts'ai Cheng Pu Ting Ch'i Yu Li Kuo K'u Chüan

1919-1920 Issue

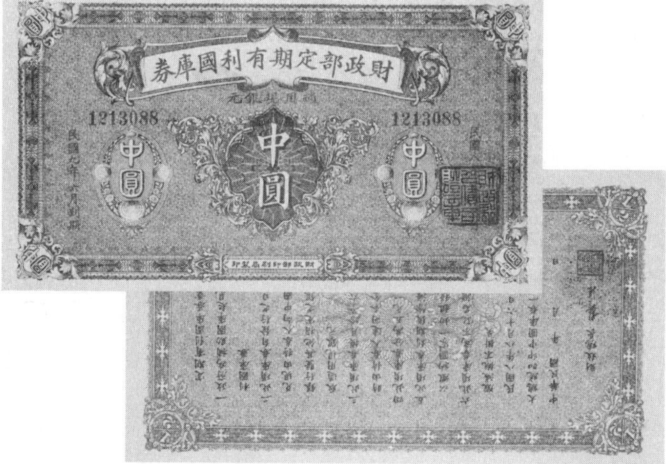

#	Description	VG	VF	UNC
626	**1/2 Yüan**	VG	VF	UNC
	1919-1920. Blue. Original date vertically at lower right and reissue date vertically at lower left. Printer: BEPP.			
	a. Aug., Oct., Dec. 1919. *(S/M #T185-1a).*	1.80	3.50	25.00
	b. April 1920. *(S/M #T185-1b).*	1.80	3.50	25.00
	c. June 1920. *(S/M #T185-1c).*	1.80	3.50	25.00
	r. Remainder. Without date. *(S/M #T185-1d).*	—	—	23.00

		VG	VF	UNC
627	**1 Yüan** 1919-20. Orange. Original date vertically at lower right and reissue date vertically at lower left. Printer: BEPP.			
	a. Aug. 1919. *(S/M #T185-10a).*	1.80	3.50	25.00
	b. April 1920. *(S/M #T185-10b).*	1.80	3.50	25.00
	c. June 1920. *(S/M #T185-10c).*	1.80	3.50	25.00
	r. Remainder. Without date. *(S/M #T185-10d).*	—	—	23.00

		VG	VF	UNC
628	**5 Yüan** 1919-20. Green. Original date vertically at lower right and reissue date vertically at lower left. Printer: BEPP.			
	a. Aug., Oct., Dec. 1919. *(S/M #T185-11a).*	2.50	5.50	30.00
	b. Feb., April, June, July 1920. *(S/M #T185-11b).*	2.50	5.50	30.00
	c. Aug., Oct. 1920. *(S/M #T185-11c).*	2.50	5.50	30.00
	r. Remainder. Without date. *(S/M #T185-11d).*	—	—	22.50

1922 Issue

		VG	VF	UNC
629	**1 Yüan** 1922. Brown. Printer: BEPP. Peking. *(S/M #T185-20).*	2.50	7.50	30.00
630	**5 Yüan** 1922. Purple. Printer: BEPP. Peking. *(S/M #T185-21).*	3.50	15.00	50.00
631	**10 Yüan** 1922. Green. Printer: BEPP. Peking. *(S/M #T185-22).*	5.50	18.00	60.00

1923 Issues

#632-637 Peking. Printer: BEPP.

		VG	VF	UNC
632	**1 Yüan** Feb. 1923. Red. Printer: BEPP. Peking. *(S/M #T185-30).*	2.50	7.50	30.00
633	**1 Yüan** June 1923. Blue. Printer: BEPP. Peking. *(S/M #T185-31).*	2.50	7.50	30.00
634	**5 Yüan** Feb. 1923. Blue. Printer: BEPP. Peking. *(S/M #T185-32).*	5.00	12.00	50.00
635	**5 Yüan** June 1923. Brown. Printer: BEPP. Peking. *(S/M #T185-33).*	5.00	12.00	50.00
636	**10 Yüan** Feb. 1923. Purple. Printer: BEPP. Peking. *(S/M #T185-34).*	5.50	18.00	60.00
637	**10 Yüan** June 1923. Red. Printer: BEPP. Peking. *(S/M #T185-35).*	5.50	18.00	60.00

Short Term, Interest-bearing Exchange Notes

財政部短期有利兌換券

Ts'ai Cheng Pu Tuan Ch'i Yu Li Tui Huan Ch'üan

#638-640 Peking. Printer: BEPP.

1922 Issue

		VG	VF	UNC
638	**1 Yüan** 1922. Brown. Temple at center. *(S/M #T186-1).*	4.00	9.00	35.00

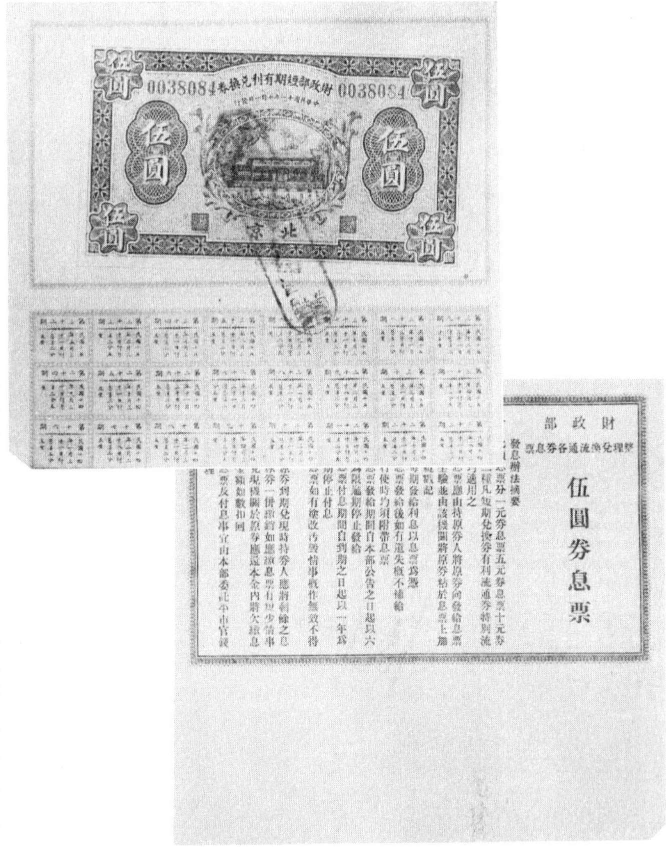

		VG	VF	UNC
639	**5 Yüan** 1922. Purple. *(S/M #T186-2).*	4.25	18.00	45.00
640	**10 Yüan** 1922. Green. *(S/M #T186-3).*	4.25	18.00	45.00

Interest-bearing, Circulating Notes

財政部有利流通券

Ts'ai Cheng Pu Yu Li Liu T'ung Ch'üan

#641-643 Peking. Printer: BEPP.

1923 Issue

		VG	VF	UNC
641	**1 Yüan** 1.2.1923. Red. Pagoda on hill, shoreline at center. *(S/M #T187-1).*			
	a. Issued note.	3.00	6.00	30.00
	b. Overprint: 2 vertical columns, twenty Chinese characters at left on back.	4.25	13.00	35.00
	c. Punch hole cancelled.	—	—	20.00

		VG	VF	UNC
642	**5 Yüan** 1.2.1923. Blue. Arched bridge over stream at center. *(S/M #T187-2).*	3.50	7.25	30.00

643	10 Yüan	VG	VF	UNC
	1.2.1923. Purple. House, bridge at center. *(S/M #T187-3).*	3.00	9.00	35.00

PEOPLES REPUBLIC OF CHINA

Peoples Bank of China

中國人民銀行

Chung Kuo Jen Min Yin Hang
Zhong Guo Ren Min Yin Hang

The Peoples Republic of China notes of 1948-1953 have been replicated extensively. Because most of the earlier notes were lithographed, they are easily replicated. Some of these notes were printed in multiple places using different raw materials. Become educated on the qualities that differentiate the original notes.

1948 Issue

800	1 Yüan	VG	VF	UNC
	1948. Blue and light red. Two workers at left. *(S/M #C282-1).*	7.50	22.50	135

801	5 Yüan	VG	VF	UNC
	1948. Dark blue. Junks at left. *(S/M #C282-3).*	9.00	45.00	180

802	5 Yüan	VG	VF	UNC
	1948. Green. Sheep at left. *(S/M #C282-2).*	7.50	45.00	180

803	10 Yüan	VG	VF	UNC
	1948. Blue-green and black on light green underprint. Farm laborers at left, coal mine at right. *(S/M #C282-4).*	15.00	75.00	225

804	20 Yüan	VG	VF	UNC
	1948. Brown. Chinese with donkeys at left, steam passenger trains at right. *(S/M #C282-5).*	20.00	150	725

805	50 Yüan	VG	VF	UNC
	1948. Red-brown and black on light green underprint. Donkey operated well at left, coal mine at right. *(S/M #C282-6).*	18.00	250	825

806	100 Yüan	VG	VF	UNC
	1948. Dark green. Hillside pagoda, shoreline at right. Back: Steam passenger train at center. *(S/M #C282-11).*	30.00	150	700

807	100 Yüan	VG	VF	UNC
	1948. Brown-violet with olive green guilloche at center. Factory at left, steam passenger trains at right. *(S/M #C282-10).*			
	a. Blue underprint on face.	25.00	135	1,200
	b. Without underprint on face.	25.00	135	1,200

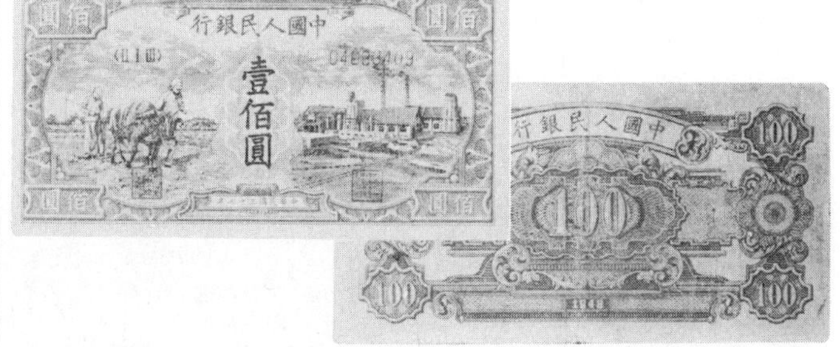

808	100 Yüan	VG	VF	UNC
	1948. Black and brownish red. Farm couple plowing with ox at left, factory at right. *(S/M #C282-9).*	25.00	150	400

#809 not assigned.

810	1000 Yüan	VG	VF	UNC
	1948. Gray-violet. Farmer plowing with horses at left. 2 serial # varieties. Back: Temple of Heaven at center. *(S/M #C282-14).*	35.00	180	500

1949 ND Provisional Issue

811	150 Yüan	VG	VF	UNC
	ND (-old date 1949). Green with brown and black guilloche. Factory, bridge and steam passenger train at left.	50.00	250	800

1949 Issue

812	1 Yüan	VG	VF	UNC
	1949. Dark purple on light blue underprint. Factory at left. *(S/M #C282-20).*	4.50	22.50	90.00

813	5 Yüan	VG	VF	UNC
	1949. Brown on light yellow underprint. Two women weaving at left. *(S/M #C282-21).*	3.75	20.00	75.00
813A	5 Yüan	VG	VF	UNC
	1949. Red. Vertical format. *Kiangsi. (S/M #C282-22).*	85.00	375	3,000
814	5 Yüan	VG	VF	UNC
	1949. Light blue. Plow at left, man with donkey cart at center, steer at right. *(S/M #C282-).*	90.00	375	3,000
814A	5 Yüan	VG	VF	UNC
	1949. Blue. Factory at left. Back: Hydro-electric plant at center. Specimen. *(S/M #C282-).*	—	—	8.700
814B	5 Yüan	VG	VF	UNC
	1949. Purple. Sawing wood, planting rice, steam passenger train at left. Without serial #. *(S/M #C282-).*	—	—	—

815	10 Yüan	VG	VF	UNC
	1949. Red and black. Workers at left, farmer plowing with ox at right. 2 serial # varieties. *(S/M #C282-25).*	4.50	22.50	90.00

816	10 Yüan	VG	VF	UNC
	1949. Gray-blue on green underprint. Farmer and worker at left. *(S/M #C282-23).*	4.50	22.50	90.00

817	10 Yüan	VG	VF	UNC
	1949. Brown on yellow and olive-green underprint. Steam passenger train in front of factory at left. *(S/M #C282-24).*			
	a. Issued note. Letterpress, plain paper.	30.00	165	725
	s. Specimen.	—	—	—
818	10 Yüan	VG	VF	UNC
	1949. Vertical format. *Kiangsi. (S/M #C282-26).*	—	—	1,800
818A	10 Yüan	VG	VF	UNC
	1949. Purple and yellow. Truck by factory at left, ox drawn irrigation system at right. Without serial #. *(S/M #C282-).*	—	—	—

819	20 Yüan	VG	VF	UNC
	1949. Lilac-brown. Pagoda at shoreline in foreground at left. *(S/M #C282-31).*	30.00	150	720

820	20 Yüan	VG	VF	UNC
	1949. Blue. Pagoda at shoreline in foreground at left. Similar to #819. *(S/M #C282-30).*	22.50	120	600

821	20 Yüan	VG	VF	UNC
	1949. Green with brown and black guilloche. Factory, bridge and steam passenger train at left. *(S/M #C282-32).*	6.00	30.00	120

Note: For issues with 5 Chinese character overprint at right see 150 Yuan, #811.

821A	20 Yüan	VG	VF	UNC
	1949. Blue and orange. Steam passenger train passing under viaduct, factories at center right. Without serial #. *(S/M #C282-).*	—	—	—
821B	20 Yüan	VG	VF	UNC
	1949. Blue, yellow and green. Steam passenger train passing under viaduct, factories at center right. Like #821A. *(S/M #C282-).*	40.00	225	900

		VG	VF	UNC
822	**20 Yüan** 1949. Violet on light ochre underprint. Junks at left, coal mine at right. *(S/M #C282-27).*	60.00	200	675
823	**20 Yüan** 1949. Blue on light blue underprint. Agricultural occupations. *(S/M #C282-).*	40.00	180	600

		VG	VF	UNC
824	**20 Yüan** 1949. Bluish purple on light green underprint. Two workers pushing ore car at center. *(S/M #C282-33).*	10.00	50.00	400

		VG	VF	UNC
825	**20 Yüan** 1949. Blue. Vertical format. *Kiangsi. (S/M #C282-34).*	100	200	1,100

Note 825A and 825B have been renumbered. See #821A and 821B.

		VG	VF	UNC
826	**50 Yüan** 1949. Dark blue with purple guilloche at center. Steam passenger train at left, bridge at right. *(S/M #C282-41).*	60.00	300	900
827	**50 Yüan** 1949. Red with orange guilloche at center. Steam passenger train at left, bridge at right. Similar to #826. *(S/M #C282-41).*	115	500	1,500

		VG	VF	UNC
828	**50 Yüan** 1949. *(S/M #C282-37).* Gray-olive with brown guilloche at left. Steam roller at right. *(S/M #C282-37).*	45.00	180	575

		VG	VF	UNC
829	**50 Yüan** 1949. Dark blue and black on light gold underprint. Steam passenger train at center. 2 serial # varieties. *(S/M #C282-35).*	5.00	25.00	150

		VG	VF	UNC
830	**50 Yüan** 1949. Red-brown. Farmer and laborer at center. 2 serial # varieties. *(S/M #C282-36).*	5.00	20.00	225

		VG	VF	UNC
831	**100 Yüan** 1949. Red on orange underprint. Brown and red guilloche. Ship dockside at right. *(S/M #C282-43).*	7.00	40.00	140

		VG	VF	UNC
832	**100 Yüan** 1949. Dark brown and black on blue underprint. Bridge and Peking pagoda at left, shrine at right. 3 serial # varieties. Back: Like #833. *(S/M #C282-44).*	20.00	90	400
833	**100 Yüan** 1949. Brown and black on orange underprint. Bridge and Peking pagoda at left, shrine at right. 3 serial # varieties. Similar to #832. Watermark: Both seal spacing varieties with a horizontal or vertical wavy line pattern spaced at 6mm apart, or open white stars. *(S/M #C282-45).*			
	a. Red signature seals 20mm apart.	20.00	90.00	400
	b. Red signature seals 42mm apart.	20.00	90.00	400

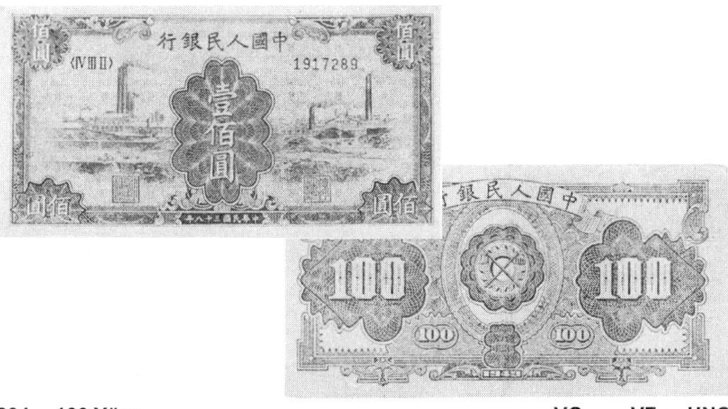

834 **100 Yüan**
1949. Red on purple underprint. Factories at left and right. *(S/M #C282-42).*

VG	VF	UNC
4.00	30.00	600

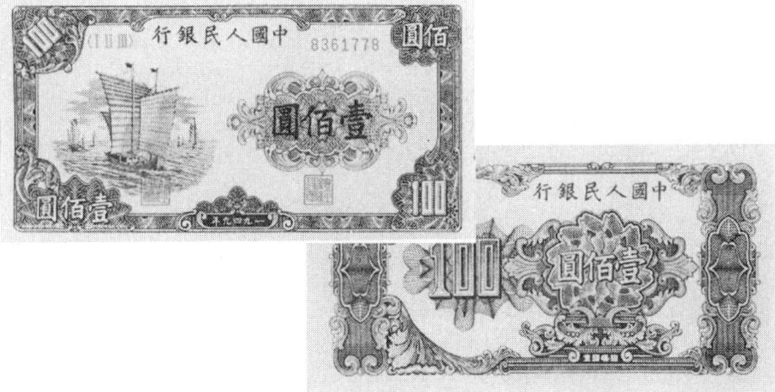

835 **100 Yüan**
1949. Brown on green underprint. Sampans at left. *(S/M #C282-).*

VG	VF	UNC
1,200	3,800	10,000

836 **100 Yüan**
1949. Brown and black on light gold underprint. Donkey train with factories behind at left center, peasants hoeing at right. *(S/M #C282-46).*

VG	VF	UNC
10.00	60.00	220

837 **200 Yüan**
1949. Lilac-brown with green guilloche at left. Pagoda near shoreline at right. 2 serial # varieties. *(S/M #C282-51).*

VG	VF	UNC
20.00	100	400

838 **200 Yüan**
1949. Purple on green underprint. Great Wall at right. *(S/M #C282-47).*

VG	VF	UNC
15.00	70.00	300

839 **200 Yüan**
1949. Blue-green. Harvesting at left. *(S/M #C282-52).*

VG	VF	UNC
90.00	425	1,800

840 **200 Yüan**
1949. Brown with blue and black guilloche on orange underprint. Steel plant at left. *(S/M #C282-53).* PC: White or tan.

VG	VF	UNC
15.00	70.00	300

841 **200 Yüan**
1949. Blue on light orange underprint. House at left behind bronze cow, bridge at right. *(S/M #C282-50).*

VG	VF	UNC
50.00	250	750

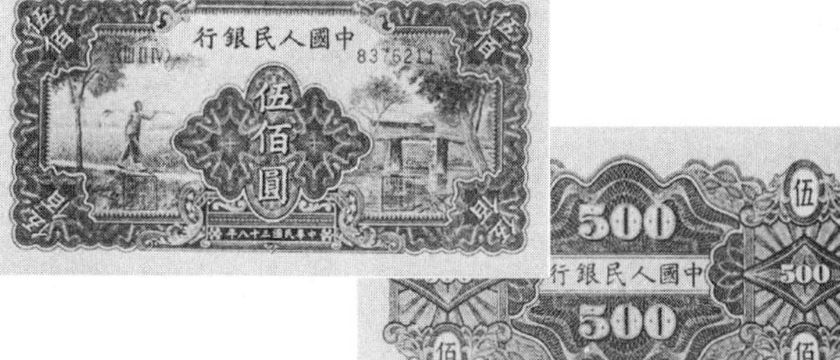

842 **500 Yüan**
1949. Reddish-brown. Peasant walking at left, small bridge at right. *(S/M #C282-56).*

VG	VF	UNC
45.00	220	675

843 **500 Yüan**

1949. Brown and black. Steam shovel at right. *(S/M #C282-55).*

VG	VF	UNC
30.00	150	450

844 **500 Yüan**

1949. Dark brown on lilac and light blue underprint. City gate at center. *(S/M #C282-57).*

VG	VF	UNC
60	300	1,950

845 **500 Yüan**

1949. Violet and black on brown and light blue underprint. Farmer plowing with mule at center. *(S/M #C282-).*

VG	VF	UNC
100	500	2,400

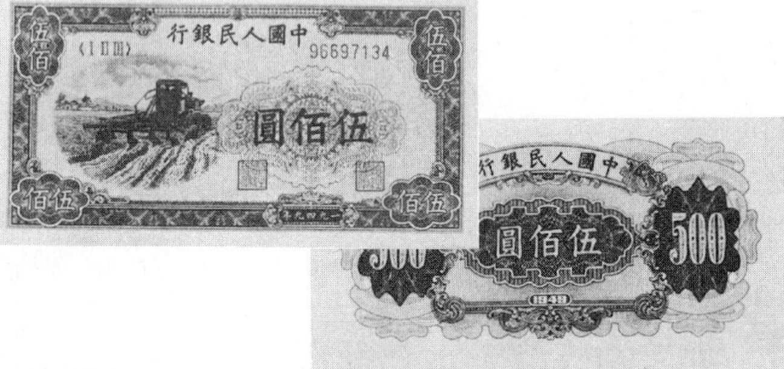

846 **500 Yüan**

1949. Green on light green and red underprint. Tractor plowing at left. *(S/M #C282-54).*

VG	VF	UNC
15.00	45.00	450

847 **1000 Yüan**

1949. Black with multicolor guilloche at left. Town view and bridge at right. *(S/M #C282-61).*

VG	VF	UNC
10.00	45.00	200

848 **1000 Yüan**

1949. Blue-black. Tractors at left and at right. Back: Farmer at center. *(S/M #C282-63).*

VG	VF	UNC
60.00	300	1,125

849 **1000 Yüan**

1949. Dark green and brown on light blue underprint. Harvesting scene with donkey cart at right. *(S/M #C282-60).*

VG	VF	UNC
30.00	70.00	360

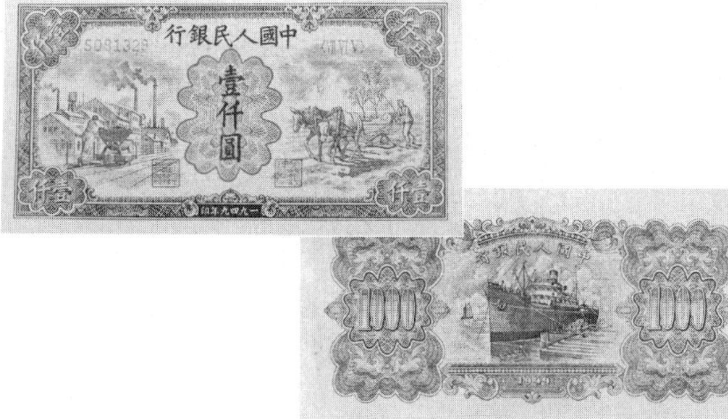

850 **1000 Yüan**

1949. Lilac-brown on gray and brown underprint. Factory at left with man pushing ore hopper in foreground, farmer plowing with two donkeys at right. Back: Ship dockside at center. *(S/M #C282-62).*

VG	VF	UNC
30.00	150	600

851 **5000 Yüan**

1949. Dark gray-green on light green and blue underprint. Tractor tilling at center. *(S/M #C282-65).*

VG	VF	UNC
23.00	120	500

		VG	VF	UNC
852	**5000 Yüan** 1949. Black-green. Three tractors at left, factory at right. *(S/M #C282-64).*	45.00	225	450

		VG	VF	UNC
853	**10,000 Yüan** 1949. Dark brown and yellow on light brown underprint. Farmers plowing with horses at center. Back: Boy with farm animals at center. *(S/M #C282-67).*	25.00	60.00	275

		VG	VF	UNC
854	**10,000 Yüan** 1949. Green on multicolor underprint. Warship at center. *(S/M #C282-66).*	30.00	150	300

1950 Issue

		VG	VF	UNC
855	**50,000 Yüan** 1950.Dark green. Combine harvester at left. Back: Foundry workers at center. *(S/M #C282-).*	3,600	9,000	—

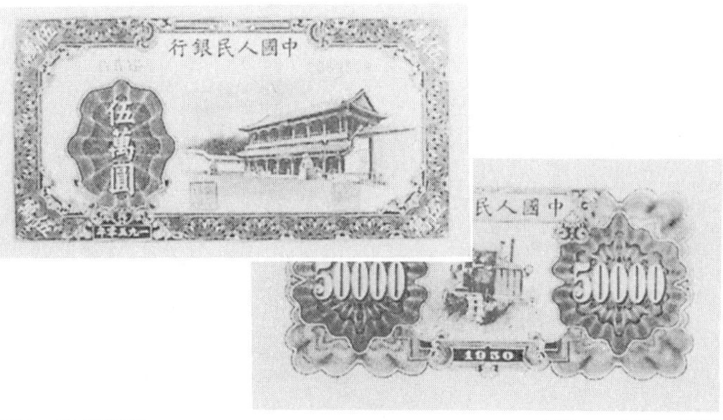

		VG	VF	UNC
856	**50,000 Yüan** 1950.Blue on light green underprint. Building at right. *(S/M #C282-).*	1,000	3,000	8,000

1951 Issue

Note: Specimen books of #857-859 were *liberated* from the Peoples Bank. They usually have glue stains on the back at left and right edges.

		VG	VF	UNC
857	**500 Yüan** 1951. Violet. City gate. Back: Arabic legends with *Sinkiang. (S/M #C282-70).*			
	a. Issued note. Lithographed, paper not observed.	1,800	8,000	24,000
	s. Specimen.	—	—	3,600

		VG	VF	UNC
857A	**1000 Yüan** 1951. Horses grazing by tents. Back: Arabic legends with *Singkiang. (S/M #C282-).*			
	a. Issued note. Shallow intaglio, plain paper.	700	3,600	7,250
	s. Specimen.	—	—	2,400

		VG	VF	UNC
857B	**5000 Yüan** 1951. Blue-green and black. Tents and camel at right. *(S/M #C282-).*			
	a. Issued note. Intaglio, plain paper.	5,400	18,900	—
	b. Specimen.	—	—	2,400

		VG	VF	UNC
857C	**5000 Yüan** 1951.Purple and black on yellow underprint. Sheep grazing at right. Back: Arabic legends with *Sinkiang* at center. *(S/M #C282-).*			
	a. Issued note. Lithographed, plain paper.	750	4,320	10,800
	s. Specimen.	—	—	3,600

		VG	VF	UNC
858	**10,000 Yüan** 1951. Red-brown on purple. Camel caravan. Back: Arabic legends with *Sinkiang*. *(S/M #C282-).*			
	a. Issued note. Lithographed, paper not observed.	1,260	5,400	25,000
	s. Specimen.	—	—	2,400

		VG	VF	UNC
858A	**10,000 Yüan** 1951. Brown-violet on black underprint. Herdsman with horses at left center. *(S/M #C282-).*			
	a. Issued note. Shallow intaglio, somewhat mottled paper.	4,800	19,250	—
	s. Specimen.	—	—	3,000

1953 First Issue

		VG	VF	UNC
859	**5000 Yüan** 1953. Brown-violet on multicolor underprint. Steam passenger train crossing bridge at left center. *(S/M #C282-).*			
	a. Issued note. Lithographed, plain paper with vertical screen lines on back.	100	450	2,175
	s. Specimen.	—	—	450

1953 Second Issue

All notes are intaglio except #860-862, which are lithographed on plain paper.

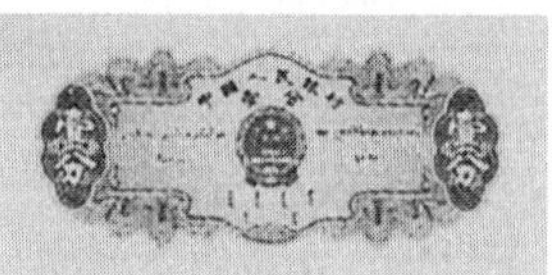

		VG	VF	UNC
860	**1 Fen** 1953. Brown on yellow-orange underprint. Produce truck at right. Back: Arms at center.			
	a. Roman control numerals and serial #.	0.50	2.00	10.00
	b. 3 Roman control numerals only.	—	—	0.50
	c. 2 Roman control numerals.	—	—	0.25

		VG	VF	UNC
861	**2 Fen** 1953. Dark blue on light blue underprint. Airplane at right. Back: Arms at center.			
	a. Roman control numerals and serial #.	1.00	5.00	35.00
	b. Roman control numerals only.	—	0.20	0.50

		VG	VF	UNC
862	**5 Fen** 1953. Dark green on green underprint. Cargo ship at right. Back: Arms at center.			
	a. Roman control numerals and serial #.	5.00	20.00	135
	b. Roman control numerals only.	—	0.20	0.50

		VG	VF	UNC
863	**1 Jiao** 1953. Brown-violet. Farm tractor at left. Back: Arms at center. *(S/M #C283-4).*	1.505	8.00	45.00

		VG	VF	UNC
864	**2 Jiao** 1953. Black on dark green and multicolor underprint. Steam passenger train at left. Back: Arms at center. *(S/M #C283-5).*	4.00	25.00	120

		VG	VF	UNC
865	**5 Jiao** 1953. Violet on lilac and light blue underprint. Dam at left. Back: Arms at center. *(S/M #C283-6).*	0.50	2.50	30.00

		VG	VF	UNC
866	**1 Yüan** 1953. Red on orange and pink underprint. Great Hall at center. Back: Arms at center. *(S/M #C283-10).*	4.50	25.00	325

		VG	VF	UNC
867	**2 Yüan** 1953. Blue on light tan underprint. Pagoda near rock at center. Back: Arms at center. *(S/M #C283-10).*	5.50	60.00	500

		VG	VF	UNC
868	**3 Yüan** 1953. Green and black on light orange underprint. Old bridge at center. Back: Arms at center. *(S/M #C283-12).*	50.00	400	2,625
869	**5 Yüan** 1953. Red-brown on light lilac underprint. Demonstrators at center. Back: Arms at center. *(S/M #C283-13).*	100	450	1,250

		VG	VF	UNC
870	**10 Yüan** 1953. Gray-black. Farm couple at center. Back: Coat of arms at center. *(S/M #C283-14).*	900	4,500	13,500

1956 Issue

Both notes are intaglio.

		VG	VF	UNC
871	**1 Yüan** 1956. Black on light orange and blue underprint. Great Hall at center. Similar to #866. *(S/M #C283-40).*	12.00	60.00	240

		VG	VF	UNC
872	**5 Yüan** 1956. Dark brown and multicolor. Demonstrators at center. Similar to #869. *(S/M #C283-43).*	15.00	75.00	300

1960 Issue

All notes are intaglio.

		VG	VF	UNC
873	**1 Jiao** 1960. Red-brown. Workers at center. Back: Arms at right. Watermark: Stars. *(S/M #C284-1).*	40.00	120	480

		VG	VF	UNC
874	**1 Yüan** 1960. Red-brown and red-violet on multicolor underprint. Woman driving tractor at center. Back: Arms at right. *(S/M #C284-).*			
	a. Watermark: Large star and 4 small stars.	.75	4.00	50.00
	b. Watermark: Stars and ancient *Pu* (pants) coins.	1.25	6.00	160
	c. Serial # prefix: 2 Roman numerals. Watermark of #874a.	.75	4.00	80.00

875	2 Yüan	VG	VF	UNC
	1960. Black and green on multicolor underprint. Machinist working at lathe at center. Back: Arms at right.			
	a. Watermark: Large star and 4 small stars. Serial # prefix: 2 or 3 Roman numerals.	7.50	65.00	600
	b. Watermark: Stars and ancient *Pu* (pants) coins. *(S/M #C284-106).*	7.50	40.00	350

876	5 Yüan	VG	VF	UNC
	1960. Brown and black on multicolor underprint. Foundry worker at center. Back: Arms at right. Watermark: Large star and 4 small stars. *(S/M #C284-11).*			
	a. Serial # prefix: 3 Roman numerals.	3.00	12.50	45.00
	b. Serial # prefix: 2 Roman numerals.	7.00	25.00	110

REPUBLIC OF CHINA - TAIWAN

The Republic of China, comprising Taiwan (an island located 90 miles (145 km.) off the southeastern coast of mainland China), the offshore islands of Quemoy and Matsu and nearby islets of the Pescadores chain, has an area of 14,000 sq. mi. (35,981 sq. km.) and a population of 20.2 million. Capital: Taipei. During the past decade, manufacturing has replaced agriculture in importance. Fruits, vegetables, plywood, textile yarns and fabrics and clothing are exported.

Chinese migration to Taiwan began as early as the sixth century. The Dutch established a base on the island in 1624 and held it until 1661, when they were driven out by supporters of the Ming dynasty who used it as a base for their unsuccessful attempt to displace the ruling of Manchu dynasty of mainland China. After being occupied by Manchu forces in 1683, Taiwan remained under the suzerainty of China until its cession to Japan in 1895. It was returned to China following World War II. On December 8, 1949, Taiwan became the last remnant of Sun Yatsen's Republic of China when Chiang Kai-shek moved his army and government from mainland China to the island following his defeat by the Communist forces of Mao Tse-tung.

RULERS:

Japanese, 1895-1945

MONETARY SYSTEM:

Chinese:

1 Chiao = 10 Fen (Cents)
1 Yuan (Dollar) = 10 Chiao

Japanese:

1 Yen = 100 Sen

Note: S/M # in reference to *CHINESE BANKNOTES* by Ward D. Smith and Brian Matravers.

T'ai-nan Official Silver Notes

票銀官南臺

T'ai-nan Kuan Yin P'iao

票銀官南臺

Tai Nan Kuan Yin P'iao

1895 First Issue

#1900-1902 are dated in the 21st year of the reign of Kuang Hsu and are in the Chinese lunar calendar. Add approximately 7 weeks for western dates.

1900	1 Dollar	Good	Fine	XF
	June Yr. 21 (1895). Blue. Red seal. *(S/M #T63-1).* Uniface.			
	a. Issued note.	120	325	1,000
	b. Reissue with 2 additional smaller vertical chinese character overprint. *(S/M #T63-1-).*	100	300	900

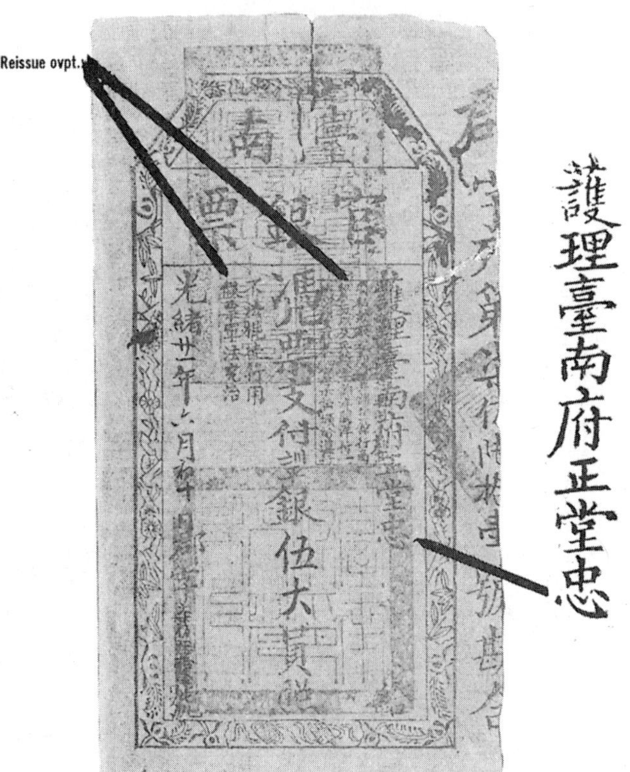

1901	5 Dollars	Good	Fine	XF
	June Yr. 21 (1895). Blue. Red seal. *(S/M #T63-2).* Uniface.			
	a. Issued note.	120	325	1,000
	b. Reissue with 2 additional smaller vertical Chinese character overprint. *(S/M #T63-2-).*	100	300	900

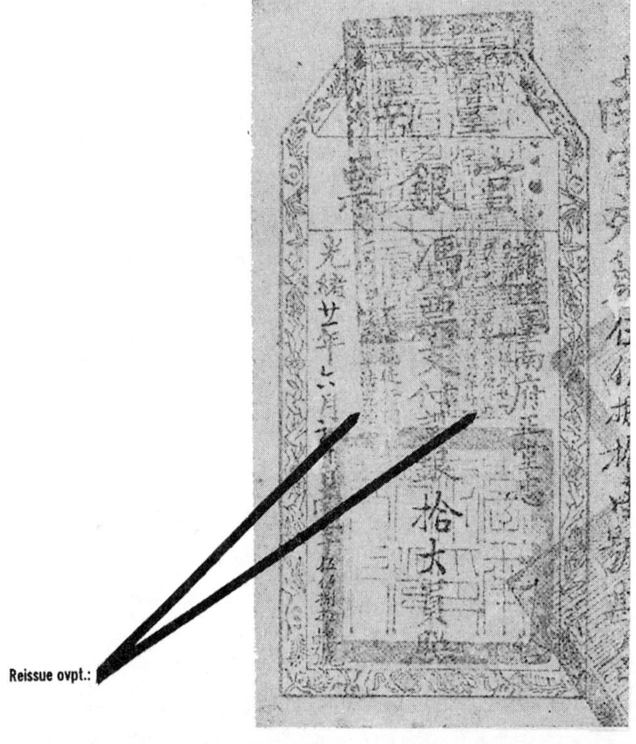

1902	10 Dollars	Good	Fine	XF
	June Yr. 21 (1895). Blue. Red seal. *(S/M #T63-3).* Uniface.			
	a. Issued note.	125	350	1,200
	b. Reissue with 2 additional smaller vertical Chinese character overprint. *(S/M #T63-3-).*	110	325	900

1895 Second Issue

#1903-1906 dated June or August in the 21st year of the reign of Kuang Hsu and are in the Chinese lunar calendar. Add approximately 7 weeks for western dates.

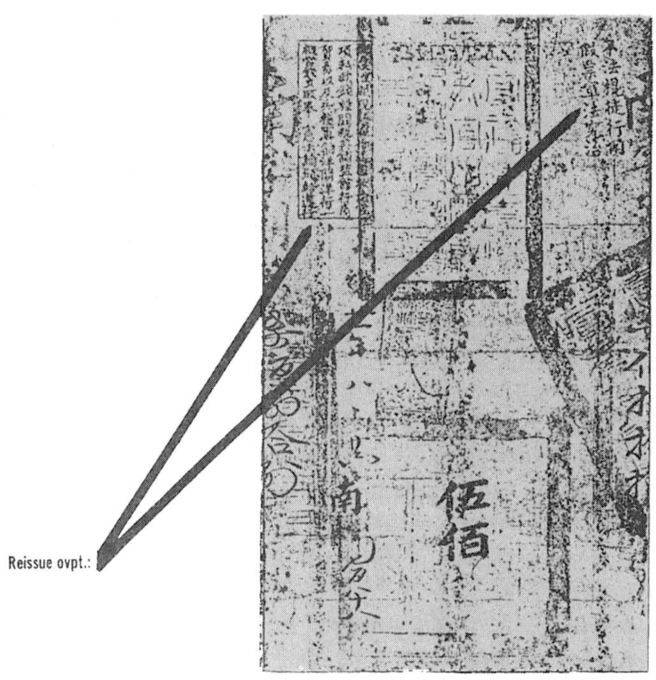

1903	**500 Cash**	Good	Fine	XF
	Aug. Yr. 21 (1895). Green. Red seals. Uniface.			
	a. 131 x 237mm. *(S/M #T63-10).*	125	350	1,200
	b. 128 x 246mm. *(S/M #T63-11).*	110	325	900
	c. Reissue with 2 additional smaller vertical Chinese character overprint. *(S/M #T63-).*	100	300	850

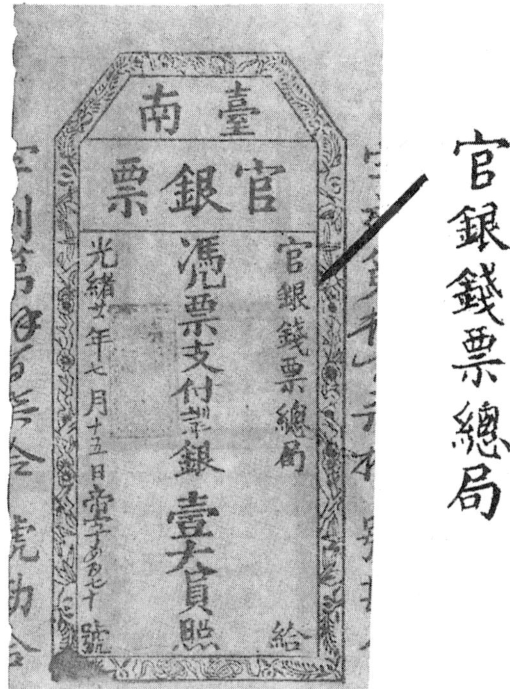

1904	**1 Dollar**	Good	Fine	XF
	June/July Yr. 21 (1895). Blue. Red handstamped seals. Uniface.			
	a. Thick paper. *(S/M #T63-20b).*	100	300	850
	b. Thin paper. *(S/M #T63-20a).*	90.00	275	800
	c. Reissue with 2 additional smaller vertical Chinese character overprint. *(S/M #T63-20-).*	85.00	250	750

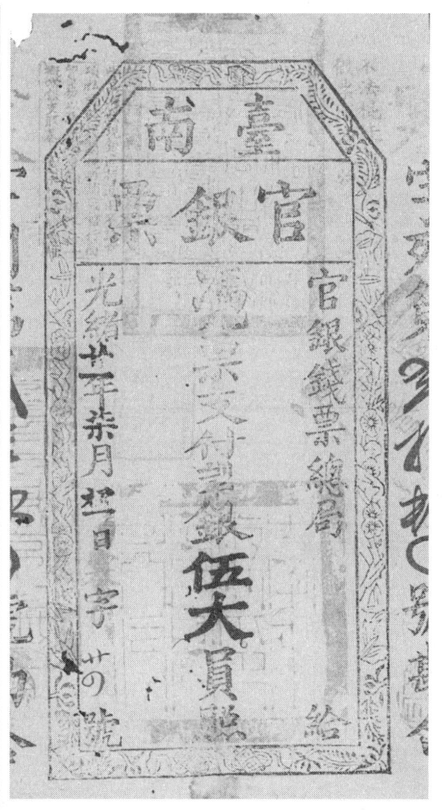

1905	**5 Dollars**	Good	Fine	XF
	June/July Yr. 21 (1895). Blue. Red handstamped seals. Uniface.			
	a. Thick paper. *(S/M #T63-21b).*	120	300	900
	b. Thin paper. *(S/M #T63-21a).*	120	300	900
	c. Reissue with 2 additional smaller vertical Chinese character overprint. *(S/M #T63-21-).*	100	250	850
1906	**10 Dollars**	**Good**	**Fine**	**XF**
	June/July Yr. 21 (1895.) Blue. 2 red handstamped seals. Uniface.			
	a. Thick paper. *(S/M #T63-22b).*	140	350	1,000
	b. Thin paper. *(S/M #T63-22a).*	140	350	1,000
	c. Reissue with 2 additional smaller vertical Chinese character overprint. *(S/M #T63-22-).*	100	250	800

JAPANESE INFLUENCE

Bank of Taiwan

行銀灣臺

T'ai Wan Yin Hang

1899-1901 ND Silver Note Issue

#1907-1910 vertical format with 2 facing Onagadori cockerels at upper center and 2 facing dragons below. With text: *THE BANK OF TAIWAN Promises to pay the bearer on demand...Yen in Silver* on back.

1907	**1 Yen**	Good	Fine	XF
	ND (1899). Black on light green underprint. Two Onagadori cockerels at upper center, two facing dragons below. Back: Text: THE BANK OF TAIWAN Promises to pay the bearer on demand... Yen in Silver.Vertical format. *(S/M #T70-1).*	1,400	1,900	4,500

1908 5 Yen | Good 3,000 | Fine 6,000 | XF —
ND (1899). Black on brown-orange underprint. Two Onagadori cockerels at upper center, two facing dragons below. Back: Text: THE BANK OF TAIWAN Promises to pay the bearer on demand... Yen in Silver. Vertical format. *(S/M #T70-2).*

1909 10 Yen | Good — | Fine — | XF —
ND (1901). Black on gray-violet underprint. Two Onagadori cockerels at upper center, two facing dragons below. Back: Text: THE BANK OF TAIWAN Promises to pay the bearer on demand... Yen in Silver. Vertical format. *(S/M #T70-3).*

1910 50 Yen | Good — | Fine — | XF —
ND (1900). Black on light orange underprint. Two Onagadori cockerels at upper center, two facing dragons below. Back: Text: THE BANK OF TAIWAN Promises to pay the bearer on demand... Yen in Silver. Vertical format. Specimen. *(S/M #T70-4).*

1904-1906 ND Gold Note Issue

#1911-1913 vertical format w/2 Onagadori cockerels at upper center 2 facing dragons below. W/text: *THE BANK OF TAIWAN Promises to pay the bearer on demand ... Yen in Gold* on back.

1911 1 Yen | Good 20.00 | Fine 100 | XF 200
ND (1904). Black on yellow-orange underprint. Two Onagadori cockerels at upper center, two facing dragons below. Back: Text: THE BANK OF TAIWAN Promises to pay the bearer on demand... Yen in Gold. Vertical format. *(S/M #70-10).*

1912 5 Yen | Good 125 | Fine 500 | XF 1,200
ND (1904). Black on blue underprint. Two Onagadori cockerels at upper center, two facing dragons below. Back: Text: THE BANK OF TAIWAN Promises to pay the bearer on demand... Yen in Gold. *(S/M #T70-11).*

1913 10 Yen | Good 200 | Fine 750 | XF 1,800
ND (1906). Black on pale gray underprint. Two Onagadori cockerels at upper center, two facing dragons below. Back: Text: *THE BANK OF TAIWAN* Promises to pay the bearer on demand... Yen in Gold. *(S/M #T70-12).*

Taiwan Government General

1917 Emergency Postage Stamp Subsidiary Coinage

Japanese postage stamps (Type Tazawa) pasted on special forms called *Tokubetsu Yubin Kitte Daishi* (Special Postage Stamp Cards).

1914 5 Sen | Good 300 | Fine 500 | XF 775
ND (1917). Purple adhesive stamp on blue form. Back: Black text and circle. *(S/M #T70-).*

1915 10 Sen | Good 300 | Fine 500 | XF 775
ND (1917). Blue adhesive stamp on pink form. Back: Black text and circle. *(S/M #T70-).*

1916 20 Sen | Good 300 | Fine 500 | XF 775
ND (1917). Purple adhesive stamp on green form. Back: Black text and circle. *(S/M #T70-).*

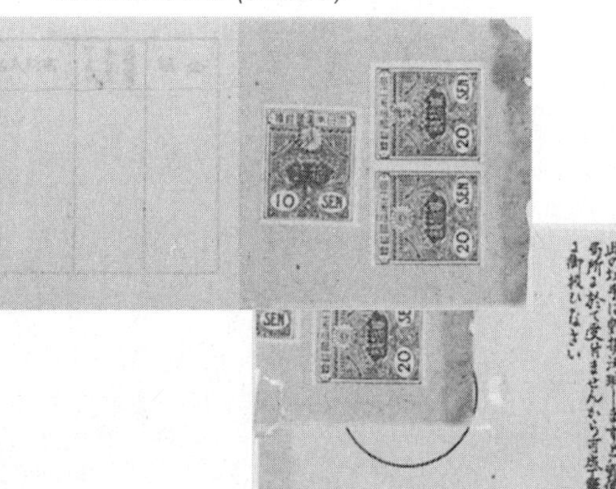

1917 50 Sen | Good 500 | Fine 700 | XF 1,000
ND (1917). Two *20 Sen* plus one *10 Sen* adhesive stamps on orange form. Back: Black text and circle. *(S/M #T70-).*

1918 Emergency Postage Stamp Subsidiary Coinage Issue

		Good	Fine	XF
1918	**1 Sen** ND (1918). Orange adhesive stamp on orange form. Back: Black circle. *(S/M #T70-1).*	300	500	775

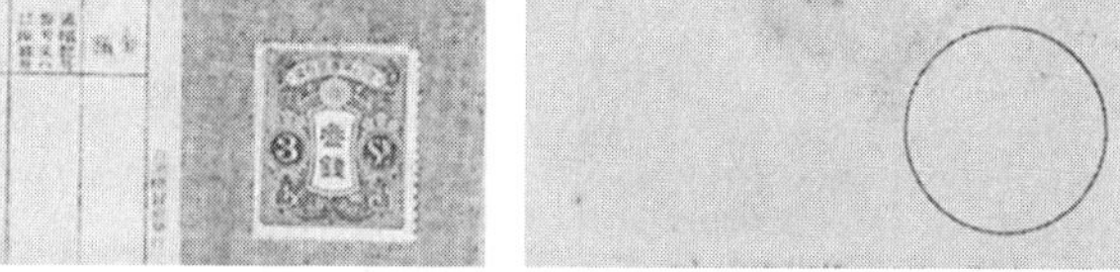

		Good	Fine	XF
1919	**3 Sen** ND (1918). Red adhesive stamp on purple form. Back: Black circle. *(S/M #T70-).*	300	500	775

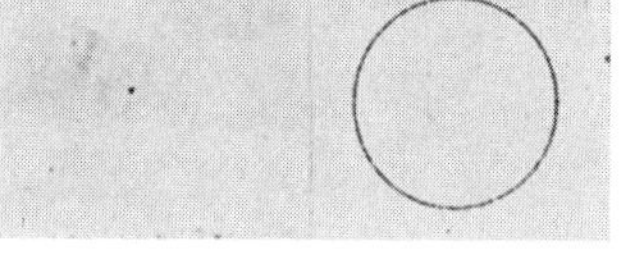

		Good	Fine	XF
1920	**5 Sen** ND (1918). Purple adhesive stamp on red form. Back: Black circle. *(S/M #T70-).*	300	500	775

Bank of Taiwan Limited - Taiwan Bank

Tai Wan Yin Hang Ch'uan

1914-1916 ND Issue

#1921-28, 1930, 1931 and 1933 engraved.

		VG	VF	UNC
1921	**1 Yen** ND (1915). Blue on lilac and light green underprint. Temple and stairs at right. Back: Seascape of a lighthouse point. *(S/M #T70-20).*	13.00	50.00	150
1922	**5 Yen** ND (1914). Gray on ochre and pink underprint. Temple and stairs at right. Back: Seascape of a lighthouse point. *(S/M #T70-21).*	150	350	900

		VG	VF	UNC
1923	**10 Yen** ND (1916). Black on tan underprint. Temple and stairs at right. Back: Seascape of a lighthouse point. *(S/M #T70-22).*	150	350	1,000

1921 Issue

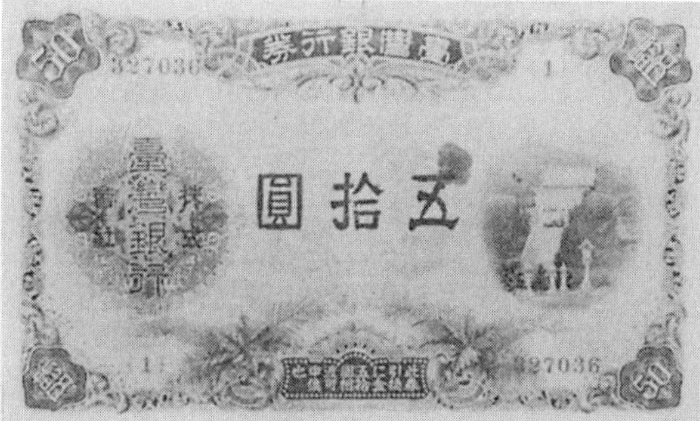

		VG	VF	UNC
1924	**50 Yen** 1921. Black on ochre and light brown underprint. Temple and stairs at right. Back: Seascape of a lighthouse point. *(S/M #T70-23).*	400	1,100	3,600

1932-1937 ND Issue

		VG	VF	UNC
1925	**1 Yen** ND (1933; 1944). Black on gray, ochre and olive-green underprint. Temple and stairs at left. Back: Seascape of a lighthouse point.			
	a. Serial # and block # (1933). *(S/M #T70-30).*	1.00	4.00	15.00
	b. Block # only (1944). *(S/M #T70-40).*	1.00	5.00	18.00
	s1. As a. Specimen.	—	—	175
	s2. As b. Specimen.	—	—	425

		VG	VF	UNC
1926	**5 Yen** ND (1934). Black on pink and green underprint. Pillared portico at left. Shrine and stairs in background. Back: Seascape of a lighthouse point. Japanese characters *5 YEN* at right. *(S/M #T70-31).*			
	a. Issued note.	6.00	50.00	150
	s1. Specimen.	—	—	400
	s2. Specimen with normal serial #.	—	—	150

1927 10 Yen	VG	VF	UNC
ND (1932). Black on dark green, gray and ochre underprint. Lanterns on road to Taiwan Jinja. Back: Seascape of a lighthouse point. *10 YEN* at lower center.			
a. Issued note.	6.00	50.00	150
s1. Specimen.	—	—	400
s2. Specimen with normal serial #.	—	—	150

1928 100 Yen	VG	VF	UNC
ND (1937). Black on light green, ochre and purple underprint. Temple and stairs at left. Black serial #. Back: Seascape of a lighthouse point. *100's* in border. *(S/M #T70-33).*			
a. Issued note.	40.00	100	300
s1. Specimen.	—	—	400
s2. Specimen with normal serial #.	—	—	200

1944 ND Issue

1929 5 Yen	VG	VF	UNC
ND (1944). Black on green, purple and brown underprint. Pillared portico at left. Shrine and stairs in background. Like #1926. Back: Seascape of a lighthouse point. Golden kite over *5* at right. *(S/M #T70-42).*			
a. Issued note.	10.00	60.00	150
s1. Specimen.	—	—	400
s2. Specimen with normal serial #.	—	—	150

1930 10 Yen	VG	VF	UNC
ND (1944-45). Black on light green and lilac underprint. Lanterns on road to Taiwan Jinja. Like #1927. Back: Seascape of a lighthouse point. Golden kite at right, palm trees at center right, *10's* in border.			
a. Black serial # and block # (1944). *(S/M #T70-).*	10.00	60.00	150
b. Red block # only (1945). *(S/M #T70-43).*	10.00	60.00	150
s1. Specimen. Watermark: Bank of Taiwan logos. *(S/M #T70-).*	—	—	175
s2. As a. Specimen	—	—	400
s3. As a. Specimen with normal serial #.	—	—	150
s4. As b. Specimen.	—	—	150

1945 ND Issue

1931 10 Yen	VG	VF	UNC
ND (1945). Black on olive underprint with green at center (color shade varieties). Lanterns on road to Taiwan Jinja. Like #1927. Back: Seascape of a lighthouse point. Crude paper. Red block # only.			
a. Issued note. *(S/M #T70-45).*	13.00	60.00	175
s. Specimen.	—	—	175

1932 100 Yen	VG	VF	UNC
ND (1945). Black on light blue and blue-violet to gray underprint. Temple and stairs at left. Black serial #. Like #1928. Back: Seascape of a lighthouse point. Golden kite at lower left, *100* at bottom center. Crude paper.			
a. Without watermark. Block #1-2. *(S/M #T70-46b).*	15.00	100	300
b. Watermark: Bank of Taiwan logos. Block #2-7. *(S/M #T70-46b).*	10.00	60.00	150
s1. As a. Specimen	—	—	175
s2. As b. Specimen.	—	—	175

1933 1000 Yen	VG	VF	UNC
ND (1945). Back: Red seal of the Bank of Taiwan and vertical characters; *Tai Wan Yin Hang* at center.			
a. Issued note. *(S/M #T70-).*	1,500	2,900	5,000
s. Specimen.	—	—	3,000

1934 1000 Yen	VG	VF	UNC
ND (1945). Black on yellow-green and gray underprint. Shrine at right. Back: Mountain range. Specimen. *(S/M #T70-47).* Rare.	—	—	—

TAIWAN - CHINESE ADMINISTRATION

Bank of Taiwan

臺灣銀行

T'ai Wan Yin Hang

PRINTERS, 1946-

CPF: (Central Printing Factory) 中央印製廠

CPFT: (Central Printing Factory, Taipei) 中央印製廠台北廠

FPFT: (First Printing Factory) 第一印刷廠

PFBT: (Printing Factory of Taiwan Bank) 臺灣銀行印刷所

1946 Issue

		VG	VF	UNC
1935	**1 Yüan** 1946.Blue. Bank building at left, portrait SYS at center. Back: Naval battle scene at center. Printer: CPF. *(S/M #T72-1).*	1.50	6.00	15.00
1936	**5 Yüan** 1946.Red. Bank building at left, portrait SYS at center. Back: Naval battle scene at center. Printer: CPF. *(S/M #T72-2).*	1.75	7.50	18.00
1937	**10 Yüan** 1946. Gray. Bank building at left, portrait SYS at center. Back: Naval battle scene center. Printer: CPF. *(S/M #T72-3).*	1.75	7.50	18.00
1938	**50 Yüan** 1946. Brown. Bank building at left, portrait SYS at center. Back: Naval battle scene at center. Printer: CPF. *(S/M #T72-4).*	25.00	125	250

		VG	VF	UNC
1939	**100 Yüan** 1946.Green. Bank building at left, portrait SYS at center. Back: Naval battle scene at center. Printer: CPF. *(S/M #T72-5).*	2.25	7.50	22.50
1940	**500 Yüan** 1946. 2 serial # varieties. Red. Bank building at left, portrait SYS at center. Back: Naval battle scene at center. Printer: CPF. *(S/M #T72-6).*	3.50	20.00	50.00

1947-1949 Issue

		VG	VF	UNC
1941	**100 Yüan** 1947. Green. Like #1939 but bank building without car, with flag at top of front of building. Portrait SYS at center. Back: Naval battle scene in circular ornament. Printer: FPFT. *(S/M #T72-10).*	3.00	6.00	30.00
1942	**1000 Yüan** 1948. Blue. Like #1939 with car in front of building, flag over left side of building. Portrait SYS at center. Back: Naval battle scene in oval ornament. Printer: CPF. *(S/M #T72-20).*	3.00	15.00	50.00
1943	**1000 Yüan** 1948. Blue. Like #1942 but bank building without car at left, with flag on top of front of building. Portrait SYS at center. Back: Naval battle scene in circular ornament. Printer: FPFT. *(S/M #T72-21).*	7.50	35.00	80.00

		VG	VF	UNC
1944	**10,000 Yüan** 1948. Dark green. Bank building at left, portrait SYS at center. Back: Naval battle scene at center. Printer: FPFT. *(S/M #T72-23).*	100	100	200

		VG	VF	UNC
1945	**10,000 Yüan** 1949. Red and green. Portrait SYS at left. Back: Bank building. Printer: CPF. *(S/M #T72-30).*	4.00	20.00	40.00
1945A	**100,000 Yüan** 1949. SYS at center. Printer: FPFT. *(S/M #T72-).* (Not issued.)	—	—	—

1949 Issue

		VG	VF	UNC
1946	**1 Cent** 1949. Blue. Bank building at upper center. Back: Taiwan outlined. Printer: CPF. *(S/M #T73-1).*	1.50	4.00	10.00

		VG	VF	UNC
1947	**5 Cents** 1949. Brown. Bank building at upper center. Back: Taiwan outlined. Printer: CPF. *(S/M #T73-2).*	1.50	4.50	15.00
1948	**10 Cents** 1949. Green. Portrait SYS at upper center. Back: Bank at upper center. Printer: CPF. *(S/M #T73-3).*	9.00	45.00	90.00

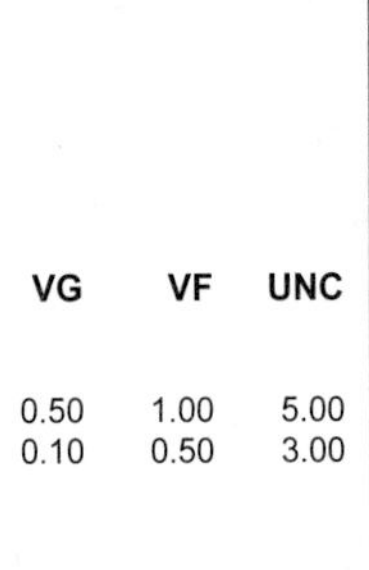

1949 50 Cents
1949. Orange. Portrait SYS at upper center. Back: Bank at upper center. Printer: CPF. *(S/M #T73-4).*

	VG	VF	UNC
a. Serial # with 2 letter prefix.	0.50	1.00	5.00
b. Serial # with 1 letter prefix and suffix.	0.10	0.50	3.00

1950 1 Yüan
1949.Brown-violet. Portrait SYS at upper center. Back: Bank at upper center in circular frame. Printer: FPFT. 2 serial # varieties. *(S/M #T73-11).*

VG	VF	UNC
9.00	45.00	100

1951 1 Yüan
1949. Red. Portrait SYS at upper center. Back: Bank at upper center. Printer: CPF. *(S/M #T73-10).*

VG	VF	UNC
30.00	140	300

1952 5 Yüan
1949. Green. Portrait SYS at upper center. Back: Bank at upper center. *1949* above lower frame. Printer: FPFT. *(S/M #T73-13).* Rare.

VG	VF	UNC
—	—	—

1953 5 Yüan
1949. Red with red and purple guilloche. Portrait SYS at upper center. Back: Bank at upper center. *1949* within lower frame. Printer: FPFT. *(S/M #T73-12).*

VG	VF	UNC
18.00	120	200

1954 10 Yüan
1949. Blue on light blue underprint. Portrait SYS at upper center. Back: Bank at upper center. *1949* above lower frame. Printer: FPFT. *(S/M #T73-15).*

VG	VF	UNC
50.00	150	900

		VG	VF	UNC
1955	**10 Yüan** 1949. Blue-black on light green and pink underprint. Portrait SYS in simple oval frame at upper center. Back: Bank at upper center. *1949* in lower ornamental frame. Printer: CPF. *(S/M #T73-14).*	13.00	75.00	150

		VG	VF	UNC
1956	**100 Yüan** 1949. Brown-violet with blue and pink guilloche. Portrait SYS at upper center. Back: Bank at upper center. Printer: CPF. *(S/M #T73-17).*	150	775	2,400

		VG	VF	UNC
1957	**100 Yüan** 1949. Brown-violet with brown-violet guilloche. Portrait SYS at upper center. Back: Bank at upper center. Printer: CPF. *(S/M #T73-16).*	125	775	1,950

1948-1949 Circulating Bank Cashier's Check Issue

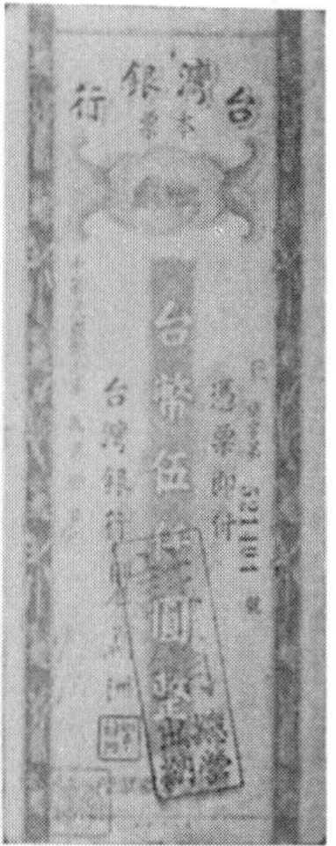

5000 Yuan

10,000 Yuan

100,000 Yuan

		Good	Fine	XF
1958	**5000 Yüan** (1948). Orange. Bank at upper center. Printer: FPFT. Vertical format.*(S/M #T72-22).* Uniface.	18.00	75.00	200
1959	**10,000 Yüan** (1948). Blue. Bank at upper center. Printer: FPFT. Vertical format. *(S/M #T72-24).* Uniface.	18.00	75.00	200
1960	**100,000 Yüan** (1949). Red. Bank at upper center. Printer: FPFT. Vertical format. *(S/M #T72-31).* Uniface.	15.00	60.00	175
1961	**1,000,000 Yüan** (1949). Brown. Bank at upper center. Printer: FPFT. Vertical format. *(S/M #T72-32).* Uniface.	22.00	90.00	225

1950 Issue

		VG	VF	UNC
1962	**10 Yüan** 1950. Multicolor. Portrait SYS at upper center. Similar to #R105. Specimen. *(S/M #T73-).*	—	—	150

1954 Issue

		VG	VF	UNC
1963	**1 Cent** 1954. Blue. Bank. Printer: CPF. *(S/M #T73-20).*	0.50	2.50	7.50
1964	**1 Yüan** 1954. Blue. Printer: PFBT. *(S/M #T73-31).*	1.50	4.00	15.00
1965	**1 Yüan** 1954. Deep green on light blue-green underprint. Printer: PFBT. *(S/M #T73-30).*	1.75	5.00	25.00

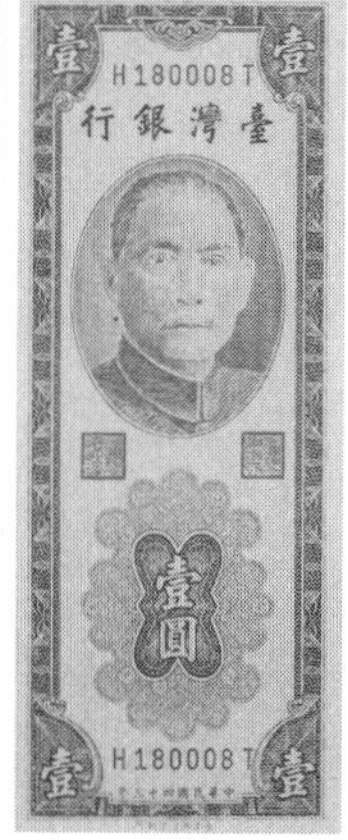

		VG	VF	UNC
1966	**1 Yüan** 1954. Deep green on light green underprint. Printer: PFBT. (litho). *(S/M #T73-31).*	1.75	10.00	35.00

Color Abbreviation Guide

New to the *Standard Catalog of® World Paper Money* are the following abbreviations related to color references:

BC: Back color
PC: Paper color

		VG	VF	UNC
1967	**10 Yüan** 1954. Blue. Printer: PFBT. *(S/M #T73-32).*	1.75	10.00	35.00

1955 Issue

		VG	VF	UNC
1968	**5 Yüan** 1955. Red with red and blue guilloche. Printer: PFBT. *(S/M #T73-40).*	1.75	10.00	35.00

1960 Issue

		VG	VF	UNC
1969	**10 Yüan** 1960. Blue on multicolor underprint. SYS at left, bridge at right. Printer: PFBT. *(S/M#T73-50).*	1.25	5.00	18.00
1970	**10 Yüan** 1960. Red on yellow and light green underprint. SYS at left, bridge at right. Like #1969 but without printer. *(S/M #T73-51).*	1.25	4.00	10.00

JAPANESE PUPPET BANKS

Japan's attempt to assert political and economic control over East Asia, an expansionist program called "Asia for the Asiatics," and later the "Co-Prosperity Sphere for East Asia," was motivated by economic conditions and the military tradition of the Japanese people. Living space, food, and raw materials were urgently needed. To secure them and also markets for their manufactured goods, the Japanese thought they had to establish control over the markets and resources of East Asia. They planned: (1) to add nearby islands to the islands of Japan, (2) to obtain possession of Korea, (3) to absorb the Malay Peninsula, Indo-China, Thailand, the Philippines, and the numerous Southwest Pacific islands into the Empire of Japan, and (4) to assert at least economic control over China.

By the eve of World War I, the Japanese had succeeded in occupying the Bonin Islands (1874), annexing Formosa and the Pescadores Islands (1895), annexing the Liaotung peninsula and the southern half of Sakhalin island (Russo-Japanese War), and annexing Korea (1910).

During World War I, Japan managed to gain economic control over Manchuria and Inner Mongolia, and to take the Shantung Peninsula from Germany. Further territorial expansion was achieved by the Paris Peace Settlement (1919) which mandated to Japan all of the Caroline, Marshall, and Mariana islands except Guam. The Japanese were, however, forced to give the Shantung Peninsula back to China.

Japan's military thrust against mainland China began in earnest on Sept. 18, 1931, when with a contrived incident for an excuse, the Japanese army seized the strategic centers in Manchuria and set up (1932) the puppet nation of Manchukuo with Henry Pu-Yi, ex-emperor of China, as emperor under the protection and control of the Japanese army. Not content with the seizure of Manchuria, the Japanese army then invaded the Chinese province of Jehol and annexed it to Manchukuo (1933). In 1934, Japan proclaimed Manchukuo an independent nation and the Japanese army penetrated into Inner Mongolia and some of China's northern provinces, and established a garrison near Peiping. Although determined to resist the invasion of their country, the Chinese were able to do little more than initiate a boycott of Japanese goods.

War between the two powers quickened in July 1937, when Japanese and Chinese troops clashed at the Marco Polo Bridge near Peiping, an incident Japanese leaders used as an excuse to launch a full-fledged invasion of China without a declaration of war. Peiping and Tientsin were taken in a month. Shanghai fell in Nov. 1937. Nanking fell in Dec. 1937 and was established as a puppet state under a Chinese president. Canton fell in 1938.

Though badly mauled and weakened by repeated Japanese blows, the Chinese continued to fight, and to meet defeat, while Japanese armies overran large sections of Eastern China and occupied the essential seaports. Trading space for time, Chiang Kai-shek kept his army intact and moved his capital from Nanking to Chungking behind the mountains in western China. Factory machinery, schools and colleges were moved to the west. With the aid of the Flying Tigers, a volunteer force of American aviators commanded by General Claire Chennault, and military supplies from the United States and Great Britain moved slowly over the dangerous Burma Road, the Chinese continued to resist the hated invader. The war came to a stalemate. The Japanese made no attempt to take Chungking. The Chinese could not drive the Japanese armies from the provinces they had conquered.

The defeat of Japan was brought about by the decision of the Japanese government to execute their plan to drive the United States, France, Great Britain, and the Netherlands out of the East, a plan initiated by an air attack on U.S. military installations at Pearl Harbor, Hawaii. Japan's dream of dominance in East Asia began to fade with the defeat of a powerful Japanese fleet at the Battle of Midway (June 3, 1942), and flickered out at Hiroshima and Nagasaki in Aug. 1945 in the wake of "a rain of ruin from the air, the like of which had never been seen on this earth." Upon the defeat of Japan by the Allies, control of the China-Japanese puppet states reverted to Chinese factions.

During the existence of the China-Japanese puppet states, Japanese occupation authorities issued currency through Japanese puppet banks, the most important of which were the Central Reserve Bank of China, Federal Reserve Bank of China, Hua-Hsing Commercial Bank, and Chi Tung Bank.

Operations of the Central Reserve Bank of China, the state bank of the puppet Republic of China government at Nanking, began sometime in 1940, although the official inauguration date is Jan. 1, 1941. To encourage public acceptance, the notes of this puppet bank carried, where size permitted, the portrait of Sun Yat-sen, Chinese nationalist revolutionary leader and founder of the Chinese republic, on the face, and his mausoleum on the back. The number of notes issued by the Central Reserve Bank of China exceeds the total number issued by all other Japanese puppet banks in China.

An interesting feature of the issues of the Central Reserve Bank of China is the presence of clandestine propaganda messages engraved on some of the plates by patriotic Chinese engravers. The 50-cent notes of 1940 carry a concealed propaganda message in Chinese. The initials "U S A C" and the date 1945 ("U.S. Army Coming, 1945") appear on the 1944 200-yuan note. Two varieties of the 1940 10-yuan note include in the face border design devices resembling bisected turtles, an animal held in low esteem in China.

A small number of notes issued by the Central Reserve Bank of China carry overprints, the exact purpose of which is unclear, with the exception of those which indicate a circulation area. Others are thought to be codes referring to branch offices or Japanese military units.

The Federal Reserve Bank of China, located in Peiping, was the puppet financial agency of the Japanese in northeast China. This puppet bank issued both coins and currency, but in modest amounts. The first series of notes has a curious precedent. The original plates were prepared by two American engravers who journeyed to China in 1909 to advise officials of the Bureau of Engraving and Printing, Peking (BEPP) on engraving techniques of the Western World. The Chinese gentleman appearing on the 1-yuan notes of 1938 is said to be making an obscene gesture to indicate Chinese displeasure with the presence of the Japanese.

The Hua Hsing Commercial Bank was a financial agency created and established by the government of Japan and its puppet authorities in Nanking. Notes and coins were issued until sometime in 1941, with the quantities restricted by Chinese aversion to accepting them.

The Chi Tung Bank was the banking institution of the "East Hopei Autonomous Government" established by the Japanese in 1938 to undermine the political position of China in the northwest provinces. It issued both coins and notes between 1937 and 1939 with a restraint uncharacteristic of the puppet banks of the China-Japanese puppet states. The issues were replaced in 1940 by those of the Federal Reserve Bank of China.

Central Reserve Bank of China

中央儲備銀行

Chung Yang Ch'u Pei Yin Hang

1940 Issue

All notes are intaglio except for J1 and J2.

		VG	VF	UNC
J1	**1 Fen = 1 Cent** 1940. Red on light brown underprint.			
	a. Imprint and serial #.	1.50	8.00	30.00
	b. Without imprint, With block letters and #.	0.50	2.00	7.50
	s1. As a. Specimen with blue overprint: *Yang Pen. Specimen* on back. Uniface pair.	—	—	150
	s2. As b. Specimen without overprint: *Yang Pen. Specimen* on back.	—	—	150
J2	**5 Fen = 5 Cents** 1940. Green on pale green underprint.			
	a. Imprint and serial #.	1.00	4.00	15.00
	b. Without imprint, With block letters and #.	0.25	1.50	6.00
	s1. As a. Specimen with red overprint: *Yang Pen. Specimen* on back. Uniface pair.	—	—	150
	s2. As b. Specimen with red overprint: *Yang Pen. Specimen* on back.	—	—	150

		VG	VF	UNC
J3	**10 Cents = 1 Chiao** 1940. Green.			
	a. Issued note.	0.25	1.50	7.50
	s1. Specimen with red overprint: *Yang Pen. Specimen* on back. Uniface pair.	—	—	150
	s2. Specimen with red overprint: *Yang Pen. Specimen* on back.	—	—	150

		VG	VF	UNC
J4	**20 Cents = 2 Chiao** 1940. Blue.			
	a. Issued note.	0.25	1.25	9.00
	s1. Specimen with red overprint: *Yang Pen. Specimen* on back. Uniface pair.	—	—	150
	s2. Specimen with red overprint: *Yang Pen. Specimen* on back.	—	—	150

J5	50 Cents = 5 Chiao	VG	VF	UNC
	1940. (1941). Red-brown.			
	a. Issued note.	0.50	2.50	20.00
	s. Specimen with blue overprint: *Yang Pen.* Red *Specimen* on back.	—	—	150

J6	50 Cents = 5 Chiao	VG	VF	UNC
	1940. Orange.			
	a. Issued note.	1.00	5.00	22.50
	b. Specimen with blue overprint: *Yang Pen* Red *Specimen* on back.	—	—	—

J7	50 Cents = 5 Chiao	VG	VF	UNC
	1940. Purple.			
	a. Issued note.	0.50	3.00	20.00
	s1. Specimen with red overprint: *Yang Pen. Specimen* on back. Uniface pair.	—	—	150
	s2. Specimen with red overprint: *Yang Pen. Specimen* on back.	—	—	150

J8	1 Yüan	VG	VF	UNC
	1940. Green on yellow underprint. Portrait SYS at left, mausoleum of SYS at center. 150x78mm.			
	a. Issued note.	0.50	2.50	10.00
	b. Red overprint: *HSING* twice on face and back.	3.00	8.00	20.00
	c. Control overprint: *I (Yi)* or 218 twice on face and back.	15.00	40.00	100
	s. Specimen with red overprint: *Yang Pen. Specimen* on back.	—	—	125

J9	1 Yüan	VG	VF	UNC
	1940. Purple on light blue underprint. Portrait SYS at left, mausoleum of SYS at center. Like #J8.			
	a. Black signature on back 151 x 79mm. (1.5.1942).	2.00	6.00	18.00
	b. Purple signature Serial # format: LL123456L. 151 x 79mm.	1.00	3.50	12.50
	c. Purple signature Serial # format: L/L 123456L. 146 x 78mm.	1.00	3.50	10.00
	s1. As a. Specimen with red overprint: *Yang Pen. Specimen* on back.	—	—	150
	s2. As b. Specimen with red overprint: *Yang Pen. Specimen* on back.	—	—	150

J10	5 Yüan	VG	VF	UNC
	1940. Red. Portrait SYS at center. Back: Mausoleum at center.			
	a. Face with yellow and blue-green underprint. Serial # on face and back. Black signature (6.1.1941).	5.00	15.00	45.00
	b. As a. Black control overprint on face and back.	10.00	35.00	100
	c. Face with pink and blue underprint. Serial # on face only. Black signature (19.12.1941).	1.50	4.00	10.00
	d. As c. Black control overprint on face and back.	3.00	10.00	30.00
	e. As c. Red signature	0.25	1.50	4.00
	f. As e. Red overprint: *Wuhan* over seals on face.	3.00	10.00	30.00
	g. As e. Black overprint: *Kwangtung* horizontally on lower corners of face.	3.00	10.00	30.00
	h. Without serial #; black signature.	—	—	75.00
	s1. As a. Specimen.	—	—	125
	s2. As c. Specimen with blue overprint: *Yang Pen. Specimen* on back.	—	—	125
	s3. As c. Specimen with red overprint: *Mi-hon.*	—	—	125

Note: Many are of the opinion that overprint: *Wuhan* and *Kwangtung* on #J10 are fantasies.

J11	5 Yüan	VG	VF	UNC
	1940. Red with repeated gold Chinese 4 character underprint. Proof.	—	—	400

J12 10 Yüan	VG	VF	UNC
1940. Blue on blue-green and light brown underprint. Portrait SYS at center. Similar to #J10. Back: Mausoleum at center.			
a. Bright blue face and back. Serial # on face and back. Black signature (6.1.1941).	13.00	38.00	150
b. As a. Red control overprint on face and back.	38.00	150	—
c. Dark blue face and back. Serial # on face only, black signature	1.00	4.00	10.00
d. As c. Red control overprint on face and back.	5.00	20.00	60.00
e. As c. Black overprint: *Kwangtung* vertically at left and right.	2.50	7.50	25.00
f. As e. Smaller blue overprint: *Kwangtung.*	2.50	7.50	25.00
g. As c. Light blue overprint: *Wuhan* over red seals on face.	2.50	7.50	25.00
h. Color similar to c. Serial # on face only, blue signature (19.12.1941).	0.50	1.50	4.00
i. As h. Overprint: *Wuhan* over signature seals at lower left and right. (as g.).	2.50	7.50	25.00
j. As h. Overprint: *Wuhan* vertically at sides on face.	2.50	7.50	25.00
k. As h. Black overprint: *Kwangtung* at left and right. (as e.).	2.50	7.50	25.00
l. As h. Blue overprint: *Kwangtung* at left and right in different style of type.	2.50	7.50	25.00
s1. As a. Specimen with red overprint: *Yang Pen. Specimen* on back.	—	—	150
s2. As c. Specimen with red overprint: *Yang Pen. Specimen* on back.	—	—	125
s3. As c. Specimen with red overprint: *Mi-hon.* Regular serial #.	—	—	100
s4. As h. Specimen with red overprint: *Yang Pen. Specimen* on back.	—	—	125
s5. As h. Specimen with red overprint: *Mi-hon.* Regular serial #.	—	—	100

Note: Many are of the opinion that the overprint: *Wuhan* and *Kwangtung* on #J12 are fantasies.

1942 Issue

#J13 *Deleted.* See #J12.

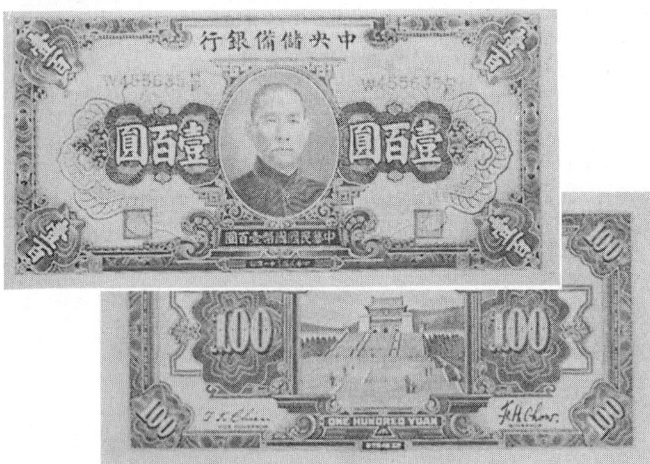

J14 100 Yüan	VG	VF	UNC
1942. Dark green on multicolor underprint. Portrait SYS at center. Back: SYS Mausoleum at center.			
a. Blue signature	1.50	7.50	20.00
b. Black signature (17.6.1942).	10.00	33.00	100
s. As b. Specimen with red overprint: *Yang Pen. Specimen* on back.	—	—	150

J15 500 Yüan	VG	VF	UNC
1942. Brown on multicolor underprint. Lithographed face and back. Portrait SYS at left. *Kwangtung* at lower left and right. Back: SYS Mausoleum at right on back.			
a. Watermark: *500 Yuan.*	6.00	30.00	100
b. Without watermark.	6.00	20.00	60.00
s. Specimen with red overprint: *Yang Pen. Specimen* on back. Without *Kwangtung.*	—	—	300

1943 Issue

All notes lithographed except noted.

J16 10 Cents = 1 Chiao	VG	VF	UNC
1943. Green. SYS Mausoleum at center. Without imprint, with block #.			
a. Issued note.	1.00	5.00	10.00
s. Specimen with red overprint: *Yang Pen.* Uniface pair.	—	—	100

J17 20 Cents = 2 Chiao	VG	VF	UNC
1943. Blue. SYS Mausoleum at center. Without imprint, with block #.			
a. Issued note.	1.00	5.00	10.00
s. Specimen with red overprint: *Yang Pen.* Uniface pair.	—	—	100

J18 50 Cents = 5 Chiao	VG	VF	UNC
1943. Red-brown. SYS Mausoleum at center.			
a. Without imprint, With block #.	1.00	4.00	10.00
b. Without imprint, With block letter and #.	1.25	5.00	15.00
s. As a. Specimen with blue overprint: *Yang Pen.* Uniface pair.	—	—	100

J19 1 Yüan	VG	VF	UNC
1943. Green on light blue underprint. Portrait SYS at center. Back: SYS Mausoleum at center.			
a. Issued note.	1.00	4.00	10.00
s. Specimen with red overprint: *Yang Pen.*	—	—	150

J20 10 Yüan	VG	VF	UNC
1943. Purple on multicolor underprint. Portrait SYS at left. Back: SYS Mausoleum at center.			
a. Issued note.	4.00	16.00	40.00
b. Overprint: *Kwangtung.* vertically at left and right.	6.00	20.00	70.00
s. As a. Specimen with red overprint: *Yang Pen.*	—	—	150

J21 100 Yüan	VG	VF	UNC
1943. Dark olive-green on multicolor underprint. Portrait SYS at center. Back: SYS Mausoleum at center. With serial #.			
a. Issued note. Intaglio.	2.00	8.00	20.00
b. Red overprint: *Wuhan.*	6.00	30.00	70.00

#J22 *Deleted.* See #J21.

J23 100 Yüan	VG	VF	UNC
1943 (1944). Blue on multicolor underprint. Portrait SYS at center. Back: SYS Mausoleum at center. With block letters.			
a. Watermark: Clouds.	1.00	5.00	17.50
b. Without watermark.	0.50	2.50	8.00
s. Specimen overprint: *Yang Pen.*	—	—	150

J24 500 Yüan	VG	VF	UNC
1943 (1944). Brown on multicolor underprint. Portrait SYS at center. Block letters. Back: SYS Mausoleum at center. 180x96mm.			
a. Watermark: *500* in Chinese characters.	3.25	10.00	30.00
b. Without watermark.	1.00	4.00	12.50
c. Red overprint: *Kwangtung*.	2.50	7.50	25.00
d. Red overprint: *Wuhan* vertically at left and right.	2.50	7.50	25.00
s1. Specimen with red overprint: *Yang Pen. Specimen* on back.	—	—	150
s2. Specimen with red overprint: *Mi-hon.*	—	—	150
s3. As d. Specimen with red overprint: *Yang Pen. Specimen* on back.	—	—	150

J24A 500 Yüan	VG	VF	UNC
1943 (1944). Dark brown on multicolor underprint. Portrait SYS at center. Serial #. Back: SYS Mausoleum at center. 187x95mm.			
a. Issued note. Intaglio.	5.00	20.00	60.00
s. Specimen with red overprint: *Yang Pen. Specimen* on back.	—	—	150

J25 500 Yüan	VG	VF	UNC
1943 (1944). Violet on multicolor underprint. Guilloche in the underprint. Portrait SYS at center. Serial #. Back: SYS Mausoleum at center. 187x95mm. Intaglio.			
a. Watermark: *500* in Chinese characters.	5.00	25.00	55.00
b. Watermark: Cloud forms.	4.00	18.00	40.00
c. Without watermark.	3.00	15.00	30.00
s1. Specimen with red overprint: *Yang Pen. Specimen* on back.	—	—	150
s2. Specimen with red overprint: *Mi-hon.*	—	—	150

J26 500 Yüan	VG	VF	UNC
1943 (1944). Pale purple on pink underprint. Portrait SYS at center. Like #J25. Back: SYS Mausoleum at center. With plate varieties. Watermark: Cloud form.			
a. Issued note.	3.50	15.00	35.00
s. Specimen with red overprint: *Yang Pen. Specimen* on back.	—	—	140

J27 500 Yüan	VG	VF	UNC
1943 (1945). Brown on light brown underprint. Brown guilloche. Portrait SYS at center. Block letters. Back: SYS Mausoleum at center. 169x84mm.			
a. Issued note.	2.50	15.00	30.00
s. Specimen with red overprint: *Yang Pen. Specimen* on back.	—	—	150

J28 500 Yüan	VG	VF	UNC
1943. Brown on lilac. Multicolor guilloche. Portrait SYS at center. Block letters. Back: SYS Mausoleum at center. 169x84mm.			
a. Watermark: Cloud forms.	3.00	15.00	30.00
b. Without watermark.	2.50	10.00	25.00
s. Specimen with red overprint: *Yang Pen. Specimen* on back.	—	—	150

1944 Issue

All notes are lithographed except noted.

J29 100 Yüan	VG	VF	UNC
1944 (1945). Blue on pale green underprint. Portrait SYS at center. Back: SYS Mausoleum at center. Watermark: Cloud forms.			
a. Issued note.	3.00	15.00	60.00
s. Specimen with red overprint: *Yang Pen. Specimen* on back.	—	—	150

J30 200 Yüan	VG	VF	UNC
1944. Red-brown on pink underprint. Portrait SYS at center. Back: SYS Mausoleum at center. Watermark: Cloud forms.			
a. Issued note. Intaglio.	2.00	10.00	30.00
s. Specimen overprint: *Yang Pen. Specimen* on back.	—	—	150

Note: #J30 has letters *USAC* hidden in frame design.

		VG	VF	UNC
J31	**1000 Yüan** 1944 (1945). Dark blue on multicolor underprint. Portrait SYS at center. Serial #. Back: SYS Mausoleum at center. Watermark: Cloud forms. 185x94mm.			
	a. Issued note. Intaglio.	5.00	20.00	60.00
	s. Specimen with red overprint: *Yang Pen. Specimen* on back.	—	—	150

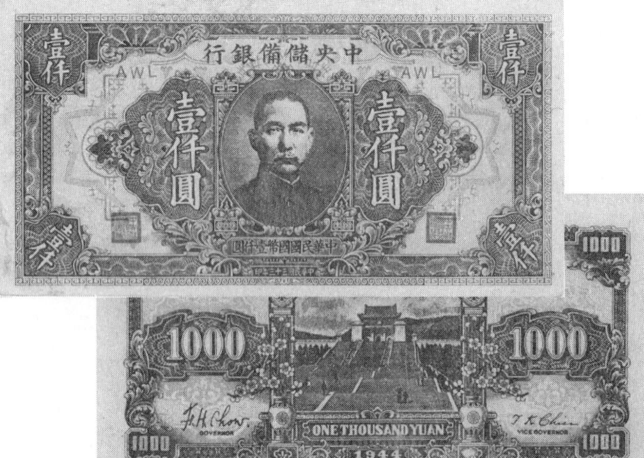

		VG	VF	UNC
J32	**1000 Yüan** 1944 (1945). Deep gray-blue on multicolor underprint. Portrait SYS at center. Block letters. Back: SYS Mausoleum at center. Watermark: Cloud forms. 185x94mm.			
	a. Watermark: Cloud forms.	1.50	7.50	15.00
	b. Without watermark.	1.00	5.00	10.00
	c. Red overprint: *Wuhan.*	3.00	10.00	35.00
	s. Specimen with red overprint: *Yang Pen. Specimen* on back.	—	—	150
J33	**1000 Yüan** 1944 (1945). Deep gray-blue on ochre underprint. Portrait SYS at center. Block letters. Back: SYS Mausoleum at center. Watermark: Cloud forms. 169x84mm.			
	a. Issued note.	1.50	7.50	15.00
	s. Specimen with red overprint: *Yang Pen. Specimen* on back.	—	—	150
J34	**1000 Yüan** 1944 (1945). Gray. Portrait SYS at center. Block letters. Back: SYS Mausoleum at center. Watermark: Cloud forms. 163x65mm.			
	a. Issued note.	5.00	20.00	80.00
	s. Specimen with red overprint: *Yang Pen. Specimen* on back.	—	—	150
J35	**1000 Yüan** 1944 (1945). Green on light blue underprint. Portrait SYS at center. Block #. Back: SYS Mausoleum at center. Watermark: Cloud forms. 149x79mm.			
	a. Issued note.	15.00	70.00	140
	s1. Specimen with red overprint: *Yang Pen. Specimen* on back.	—	—	150
	s2. As s1. Without *Specimen* on back.	—	—	150
	s3. Specimen with red overprint: *Mi-hon.*	—	—	150

		VG	VF	UNC
J36	**10,000 Yüan** 1944 (1945). Dark brown on pink underprint. Portrait SYS at center. Serial #. Back: SYS Mausoleum at center. Watermark: Cloud forms. 184x94mm.			
	a. Issued note. Intaglio.	30.00	150	375
	s. Specimen with red overprint: *Yang Pen. Specimen* on back.	—	—	250

		VG	VF	UNC
J37	**10,000 Yüan** 1944 (1945). Dark green on tan or pale yellow-brown underprint. Portrait SYS at center. Serial #. Back: SYS Mausoleum at center. With vignette varieties. Watermark: Cloud forms. 184x94mm. Intaglio.			
	a. Back with pink sky in center.	20.00	140	275
	b. Back with green sky in center.	30.00	180	375
	s1. Specimen with red overprint: *Yang Pen. Specimen* on back.	—	—	400
	s2. Specimen with red overprint: *Mi-hon.*	—	—	450
J38	**10,000 Yüan** 1944 (1945). Green on pale yellow-brown underprint. Portrait SYS at center. Block letters. Back: SYS Mausoleum at center. Watermark: Cloud forms. 170x83mm.			
	a. Issued note.	20.00	140	275
	s. Specimen with red overprint: *Yang Pen. Specimen* on back.	—	—	400

		VG	VF	UNC
J39	**10,000 Yüan** 1944 (1945). Green on pale yellow-brown underprint. Portrait SYS at center. Block letters. Back: SYS Mausoleum at center. Watermark: Cloud forms. 166x65mm.			
	a. Issued note.	20.00	140	275
	s. Specimen with red overprint: *Yang Pen. Specimen* on back.	—	—	450

1945 Issue

All notes are lithographed except as noted.

		VG	VF	UNC
J40	**5000 Yüan** 1945. Intaglio. Gray-green on pale green underprint. Portrait SYS at center. Serial #. Back: SYS Mausoleum at center. 166x90mm.			
	a. Printer: CRBCPW.	13.00	60.00	120
	b. Without imprint.	15.00	75.00	150
	s. As a. Specimen with red overprint: *Yang Pen. Specimen* on back.	—	—	175

		VG	VF	UNC
J41	**5000 Yüan** 1945. Dark gray-green on pale green underprint. Portrait SYS at center. Block letters. Like #J40. Back: SYS Mausoleum at center. 170x84mm.			
	a. Issued note.	13.00	55.00	125
	s. Specimen with red overprint: *Yang Pen. Specimen* on back.	—	—	175

J42	5000 Yüan	VG	VF	UNC
	1945. Black. Portrait SYS at center. Block letters. Back: SYS Mausoleum at center. 166x65mm.			
	a. Issued note.	18.00	90.00	175
	s. Specimen with red overprint: *Yang Pen. Specimen* on back.	—	—	225

J43	100,000 Yüan	VG	VF	UNC
	1945. Red-violet on pale green underprint. Portrait SYS at center. Serial #. Back: SYS Mausoleum at center. 185x95mm.			
	a. Issued note. Intaglio.	225	1,250	4,000
	s. Specimen with overprint: *Mi-hon.*	—	—	675

J44	100,000 Yüan	VG	VF	UNC
	1945. Purple on yellow-brown underprint. Portrait SYS at center. Back: SYS Mausoleum at center. 168x64mm.			
	a. Block letters.	200	600	4,000
	r. Remainder without block letters or signature seals. Back purple to red-violet.	75.00	225	750

Federal Reserve Bank of China 中國聯合準備銀行

Chung Kuo Lien Ho Chun Pei Yin Hang

1938 First Issue

All notes are lithographed except as noted.

J45	1/2 Fen	VG	VF	UNC
	1938. Light blue on yellow underprint. Seventeen arch bridge at summer palace at center. *(S/M #C286-1).*			
	a. Issued note.	3.50	10.00	55
	s. Specimen with overprint: *Yang Pen. Specimen* on back. Uniface pair.	—	—	100

J46	1 Fen	VG	VF	UNC
	1938. Light brown on pale green underprint. Seventeen arch bridge at summer palace at center. *(S/M #C286-2).*			
	a. Issued note.	1.50	7.00	15.00
	s. Specimen with overprint: *Yang Pen. Specimen* on back. Uniface pair.	—	—	100

J47	5 Fen	VG	VF	UNC
	1938; 1939. Red on pink underprint. Seventeen arch bridge at summer palace at center.			
	a. 1938. *(S/M #C286-3).*	1.00	4.00	10.00
	b. 1939. *(S/M #C286-30).*	0.50	2.00	5.00
	s. As a. Specimen with red overprint: *Yang Pen* on face. Blue overprint on back. Uniface pair.	—	—	100

J48	10 Fen = 1 Chiao	VG	VF	UNC
	1938; 1940. Red-brown on pink underprint. Tower of summer palace at right.			
	a. 1938. *(S/M #C286-4).*	0.50	2.00	5.00
	b. 1940. *(S/M #C286-31).*	1.00	4.00	10.00
	s. As a. Specimen with red overprint: *Yang Pen* on face and back. Uniface pair.	—	—	100

J49	20 Fen = 2 Chiao	VG	VF	UNC
	1938; 1940. Blue on pale blue underprint. Temple of Heaven at right.			
	a. 1938. *(S/M #C286-5).*	0.75	2.50	8.00
	b. 1940. *(S/M #C286-32).*	1.00	3.25	10.00
	s. As a. Specimen with red overprint: *Yang Pen* on face and back. Uniface pair.	—	—	100

J50	50 Fen = 5 Chiao	VG	VF	UNC
	ND (1938). Orange on pale green underprint. Marco Polo bridge at center. *(S/M #C286-60).*			
	a. Issued note. Intaglio.	3.50	10.00	35.00
	s. Specimen with overprint: *Yang Pen. Specimen* on back.	—	—	150

1938 Second Issue

All notes are intaglio except #J55.

J51	10 Cents = 1 Chiao	VG	VF	UNC
	1938. Brown-violet. Dragon at right. Printer: BEPP. *(S/M #C286-5).*			
	a. Issued note.	23.00	60.00	150
	s. Specimen with red overprint: *Yang Pen. Specimen* on back. Uniface pair.	—	—	200

J52	20 Cents = 2 Chiao	VG	VF	UNC
	1938. Green. Dragon at right. Printer: BEPP. *(S/M #C286-7).*			
	a. Issued note.	15.00	75.00	200
	s. Specimen with overprint: *Yang Pen. Specimen* on back. Uniface pair.	—	—	200

J53	**50 Cents = 5 Chiao**	**VG**	**VF**	**UNC**
	1938. Orange. Dragon at right. Printer: BEPP.			
	a. Issued note. *(S/M #C286-8).*	20.00	100	250
	s. Specimen with overprint: *Yang Pen. Specimen* on back. Uniface pair.	—	—	200

J54	**1 Dollar**	**VG**	**VF**	**UNC**
	1938. Green. Portrait Confucius at left, junks at lower center right, dragon above. 183x93mm.			
	a. Issued note. *(S/M #C286-10).*	38.00	175	550
	s. Specimen with overprint: *Yang Pen. Specimen* on back.	—	—	550

J55	**1 Dollar**	**VG**	**VF**	**UNC**
	1938. Green. Portrait Confucius at left, junks at lower center right, dragon above. Like #J54 but poor printing. *(S/M #C286-11).*	25.00	80.00	275

Note: Doubtful whether war printing or forgery.

J56	**5 Dollars**	**VG**	**VF**	**UNC**
	1938. Orange. Portrait Yüeh Fei at left, horseback patrol at lower right, dragon above. 184x97mm.			
	a. Issued note. *(S/M #C286-13).*	170	650	2,300
	s. Specimen with overprint: *Yang Pen. Specimen* on back.	—	—	1,100

J57	**10 Dollars**	**VG**	**VF**	**UNC**
	1938. Blue. Portrait Kuan-yü at left, Great Wall at lower right, dragon above. 190x102mm.			
	a. Issued note. *(S/M #C286-15).*	170	600	2,000
	s. Specimen with overprint: *Yang Pen. Specimen* on back.	—	—	750

J58	**100 Dollars**	**VG**	**VF**	**UNC**
	1938. Purple. Portrait Huang Ti at left, farm laborer at lower right, dragon above. 190x107mm.			
	a. Issued note. *(S/M #C286-20).*	200	700	3,600
	s. Specimen with overprint: *Yang Pen. Specimen* on back.	—	—	1,200

		VG	VF	UNC
J59	**100 Yüan** 1938 (1944). Brown. Great Wall at center, dragon above, portrait Huang Ti at right. Like #J63. Back: Plain pattern. Outer frame has color varieties. *(S/M #C286-22).*	10.00	45.00	135

1938 (1939) Issue

#J60 deleted. All notes are intaglio.

		VG	VF	UNC
J61	**1 Yüan** 1938 (1939). Yellow-green. Boats at center, dragon above, portrait Confucius at right. Back: Pagoda at center. 148x78mm.			
	a. Issued note. *(S/M #C286-12).*	3.00	15.00	50.00
	s. Specimen with red overprint: *Yang Pen. Specimen* on back. Uniface pair.	—	—	150
J62	**5 Yüan** 1938 (1939). Orange. Horseback patrol at center, dragon above, portrait Yüeh Fei at right. 155x76mm.Engraved..	**VG**	**VF**	**UNC**
	a. Issued note. *(S/M #C286-14)*	4.00	20.00	60.00
	s. Specimen with red overprint: *Yang Pen. Specimen* on back. Uniface pair.	—	—	150
	x. Lithograph counterfeit. Block #4.	—	—	30.00

		VG	VF	UNC
J63	**10 Yüan** 1938 (1939). Blue. Great Wall at center, dragon above, portrait Huang Ti at right. 164x83mm.Paper with many or few fibers.			
	a. Issued note. *(S/M #C286-16).*	7.00	30.00	80.00
	s. Specimen with red overprint: *Yang Pen. Specimen* on back. Uniface pair.	—	—	150
J64	**100 Yüan** 1938 (1939). Purple. Ships along shoreline at left, farm laborers at right center, with dragon above, portrait Huang Ti at right. Back: Pagoda at center. 178x95mm.	**VG**	**VF**	**UNC**
	a. Issued note. *(S/M #C286-21).*	120	400	1,000
	s. Specimen with red overprint: *Yang Pen. Specimen* on back. Uniface pair.	—	—	300

#J65 *Deleted.* See #J47.
#J66 *Deleted.* See #J48.

1944 Issue

#J67 deleted. See #J49. Notes are lithographed.

		VG	VF	UNC
J68	**50 Fen = 5 Chiao** 1944. Violet on ochre and violet underprint. Temple of the clouds at left.			
	a. Issued note. *(S/M #C286-40).*	1.00	3.00	10.00
	s. Specimen perforated: *Yang Pen.* Uniface pair.	—	—	100

		VG	VF	UNC
J69	**1 Yüan** 1944. Dark gray on dark olive-green or olive-brown (shades) underprint. Partial view of temple, Confucius at right. 125x65mm.			
	a. Issued note. *(S/M #C286-50).*	1.25	4.00	10.00
	s. Specimen perforated: *Yang Pen.* Uniface pair.	—	—	100

1941 ND Issue

#J70 deleted. See #J50. #J71 deleted. See #J73. All notes are intaglio.

		VG	VF	UNC
J72	**1 Yüan** ND (1941). Gray-green on green and pink overprint. Partial view of temple at left, Confucius at right. 149x70mm.			
	a. Issued note. *(S/M #C286-70).*	1.50	5.00	15.00
	s. Specimen with red overprint and perforated: *Yang Pen. Specimen* on back.	—	—	120

		VG	VF	UNC
J73	**5 Yüan** ND (1941). Orange on multicolor underprint. Temple at left, Yüeh Fei at right.			
	a. Issued note. *(S/M #C286-71).*	3.00	13.00	30.00
	s. Specimen with overprint and perforated: *Yang Pen. Specimen* on back. Uniface pair.	—	—	120

J74	10 Yüan	VG	VF	UNC
	ND (1941). Blue on multicolor underprint. Wu Ying Hall at left, man with cap at right.			
	a. Issued note. *(S/M #C286-74).*	2.50	10.00	25.00
	s. Specimen with red overprint and perforated: *Yang Pen. Specimen* on back.	—	—	150

J75	100 Yüan	VG	VF	UNC
	ND (1941). Chinese printer. Brown on green and purple underprint. House with stairs at left, Huang Ti at right. 174x93mm.			
	a. Issued note. *(S/M #C286-84).*	8.00	30.00	95.00
	s. Specimen with red overprint and perforated: *Yang Pen. Specimen* on back.	—	—	200

1943 ND Issue

All notes are intaglio.

J76	10 Yüan	VG	VF	UNC
	ND (1943). Dark blue-gray on green and brown underprint. Kuan Yü at left. Jade Peak Pagoda at right. 160x85mm.			
	a. Issued note. *(S/M #C286-73).*	5.00	20.00	50.00
	s. Specimen perforated: *Yang Pen.* Uniface pair.	—	—	160

J77	100 Yüan	VG	VF	UNC
	ND (1943). Brown on multicolor underprint. Huang Ti at left. Temple near mountainside at right. 176x95mm.			
	a. Issued note. *(S/M #C286-83).*	5.00	20.00	50.00
	s. Specimen with overprint and perforated *Yang Pen. Yang Pen* on back. Uniface pair.	—	—	150

J78	500 Yüan	VG	VF	UNC
	ND (1943). Brownish black on pale green and olive underprint. Temple of Heaven at left. Confucius at right. Onagadori cocks underprint at left and at right of vertical denomination at center. Block letters and serial #. Back: *500* once. 179x98mm. *(S/M #C286-90).*			
	a. Back frame brown. Imprint 26mm.	10.00	35.00	100
	b. Back frame brown. Imprint 29mm.	5.00	20.00	60.00
	s. Back frame red-brown. Imprint 24mm. Specimen perforated: *Yang Pen.* Uniface pair.	—	—	150

1944 ND Issue

All notes are lithographed except as noted.

J79	5 Yüan	VG	VF	UNC
	ND (1944). Brown on yellow underprint. Small house at left, Yüeh Fei with book at right. *(S/M #C286-72).*			
	a. Black on yellow underprint. Seal 8mm high at left. Watermark: Clouds and *FRB* logo.	2.00	7.50	20.00
	b. Watermark: *FRB* logo.	2.00	7.50	20.00
	c. Dark brown on light brown underprint. Seal 7mm high at left. Without watermark.	3.00	10.00	27.50
	s. Specimen perforated: *Yang Pen.* Uniface pair.	—	—	150

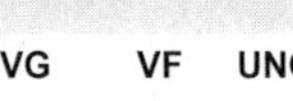

J80	10 Yüan	VG	VF	UNC
	ND (1944). Blue on light brown underprint. Kuan-yü at left, wall of house with tree and rock at right. Back: *10 YUAN* at bottom center. 158x78mm.			
	a. Issued note. *(S/M #C286-75).*	2.00	7.50	20.00
	s1. Specimen with red overprint: *Yang Pen. Yang Pen* on back. Uniface pair.	—	—	150
	s2. Specimen perforated: *Yang Pen.* Uniface pair.	—	—	150

		VG	VF	UNC
J81	**10 Yüan** ND (1944). Purple on multicolor underprint. Man with mustache at right.			
	a. Issued note. *(S/M #C286-80).*	3.00	15.00	40.00
	s. Specimen with red overprint and perforated: *Yang Pen.*	—	—	150

		VG	VF	UNC
J82	**10 Yüan** ND (1944). Blue on multicolor underprint. Man with mustache at right. Similar to #J81.			
	a. Issued note. *(S/M #C286-81).*	4.00	15.00	40.00
	s1. Specimen with red overprint and perforated: *Yang Pen.*	—	—	150
	s2. Specimen with red overprint: *Mi-hon.*	—	—	150

		VG	VF	UNC
J83	**100 Yüan** ND (1944). Dark brown on green-blue and violet. House with stairs at left, Huang Ti at right. 178x95mm. Without imprint. Intaglio.			
	a. Issued note. *(S/M #C286-85).*	6.00	20.00	60.00
	b. Horizontal quadrille paper.	6.00	20.00	60.00
	s1. Specimen with red overprint and perforated: *Yang Pen.*	—	—	200
	s2. Specimen with red overprint: *Mi-hon.*	—	—	200

		VG	VF	UNC
J84	**500 Yüan** ND (1944). *(S/M #C286-91).* Dark green on tan and purple underprint. Temple of Heaven at left, Confucius at right. Underprint with Onagadori cock above guilloche at center. Back: *500* five times. 181x99mm. Intaglio.			
	a. Horizontal quadrille paper.	15.00	45.00	140
	b. Non-quadrille paper.	15.00	45.00	140
	s1. Specimen with red overprint and perforated: *Yang Pen.* Uniface pair.	—	—	150
	s2. Specimen with red overprint: *Mi-hon.*	—	—	150

		VG	VF	UNC
J84A	**500 Yüan** ND (1944). Blue on light blue-green and yellow-brown underprint. Temple of Heaven at left. Like #J89 but lithographed. Block #1. Specimen.	—	—	300

1945 ND Issue

All notes are lithographed except as noted.

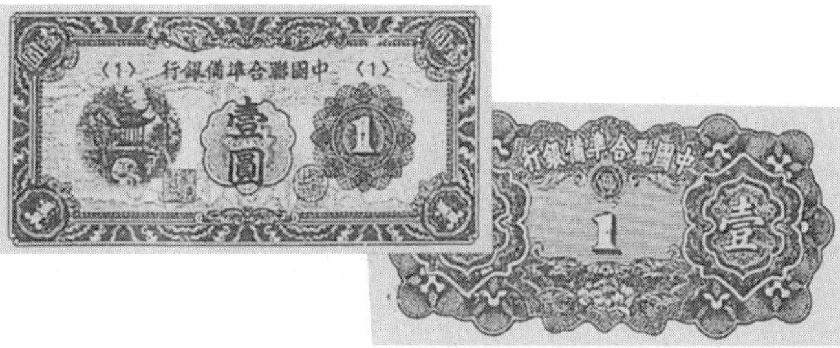

		VG	VF	UNC
J85	**1 Yüan** ND (1945). Dark brown on light orange-brown underprint. Bridge and pavilion at left, numeral at right. 123x63mm. (Not issued).			
	a. Block #. *(S/M #C286-65).*	—	200	750
	s. Specimen perforated: *Yang Pen.* Uniface pair.	—	—	500

		VG	VF	UNC
J86	**10 Yüan** ND (1945). Violet on light brown underprint. Kuan-yü at left, wall of house with tree and rock at right. Back: Without *10 YUAN.* 143x72mm.			
	a. Chinese printer (11 characters). *(S/M #C286-77).*	2.00	7.50	20.00
	b. Chinese printer (14 characters). *(S/M #C286-76).*	2.00	7.50	20.00
	s. As b. Specimen perforated: *Yang Pen.*	—	—	150

		VG	VF	UNC
J87	**50 Yüan** ND (1945). Violet-brown. Man with beard at left. *(S/M #C286-82).*			
	a. Watermark. *FRB* logo and clouds. Block #1.	10.00	50.00	110
	b. Without watermark. Block #2.	10.00	25.00	100
	s. As a. Specimen perforated: *Yang Pen.* Uniface pair.	—	—	150

		VG	VF	UNC
J88	**100 Yüan** ND (1945). Brown to red-brown. Imperial Resting Quarters near mountainside at at left, Huang Ti at right. 170x90mm.			
	a. Issued note. *(S/M #C286-86).*	2.50	10.00	25.00
	s. Specimen perforated: *Yang Pen.* Uniface pair.	—	—	150

		VG	VF	UNC
J88A	**100 Yüan** ND (1945). Gray and red-brown. Imperial Resting Quarters near mountainside at at left, Huang Ti at right. Like #J88. Block #16.	6.00	20.00	60.00

		VG	VF	UNC
J89	**500 Yüan**	VG	VF	UNC
	ND (1945). Blue on light blue-green and yellow-brown underprint. Temple of Heaven at left. Watermark: *FRB* logo and clouds. 185x83mm. *(S/M #C286-92).*			
	a. Issued note.	20.00	120	300
	s. Specimen perforated: *Yang Pen.* Uniface pair.	—	—	150
J90	**500 Yüan**	VG	VF	UNC
	ND (1945). Blue-gray on orange-yellow to salmon underprint. Man with beard at left. Like #J87. 168x78mm. *(S/M #C286-93).*	10.00	40.00	100

		VG	VF	UNC
J91	**1000 Yüan**	VG	VF	UNC
	ND (1945). Dark green. Great Wall at center right. Back: Ch'ien Men fortress at center. *(S/M #C286-94).* Intaglio.			
	a. Engraved, with serial # and block #1-3. Watermark: *1* in oval, ovals horizontal.	15.00	75.00	150
	b. Engraved, with serial # and block #1-3. Watermark: *1* in oval, ovals vertical.	15.00	75.00	150
	c. Watermark: *FRB* logo repeated.	23.00	125	225
	r. Remainder, without serial #, block #, or signature seals.	—	—	150
	s. As b. Specimen perforated: *Yang Pen.* Uniface pair.	—	—	225

		VG	VF	UNC
J92	**5000 Yüan**	VG	VF	UNC
	ND (1945). Brown. State stone barge at left. (Empress Dowager's summer palace, *I Ho Yuan*). Watermark: *FRB* logo. *(S/M #C286-95).*			
	a. Issued note. Intaglio.	50.00	250	550
	r. Remainder without serial # or block #.	—	125	300

Note: The "State Barge" is a marble boat in the Empress dowager's summer palace *(I Ho Yuan).*

Hua-Hsing Commercial Bank

華興商業銀行

Hua Hsing Shang Yeh Yin Hang

1938 Issue

		VG	VF	UNC
J93	**10 Cents = 1 Chiao**	VG	VF	UNC
	1938. Green on pink and light blue underprint. Junks at left. *(S/M #H184-1).*			
	a. Issued note.	225	650	2,700
	s. Specimen with overprint: *Yang Pen. Specimen* on back.	—	—	2,700

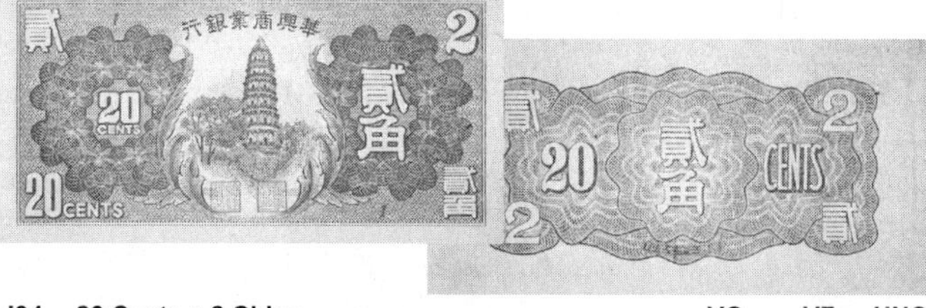

		VG	VF	UNC
J94	**20 Cents = 2 Chiao**	VG	VF	UNC
	1938. Brown. Pagoda at center. *(S/M #H184.2).*			
	a. Issued note.	125	425	1,800
	s. Specimen with overprint: *Yang Pen. Specimen* on back.	—	—	1,650

J95 *Deleted.*

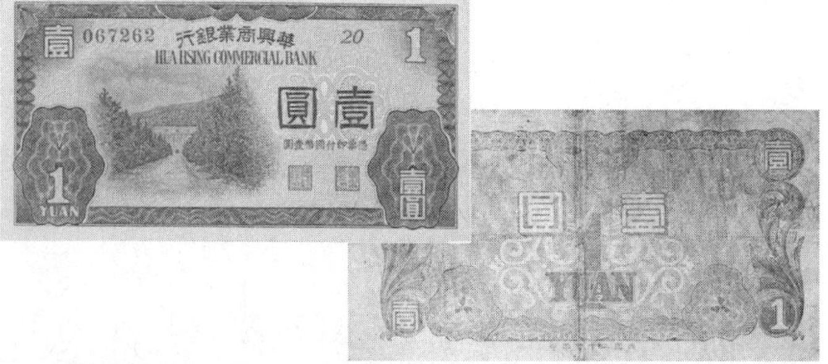

		VG	VF	UNC
J96	**1 Yüan**	VG	VF	UNC
	1938. Green on yellow and gray underprint. Trees along roadway at left center. *(S/M #H184-10).*			
	a. Issued note.	325	900	3,900
	s. Specimen with overprint: *Yang Pen. Specimen* on back.	—	—	2,000
J97	**5 Yüan**	VG	VF	UNC
	ND (1938). Blue on multicolor underprint. Liu Ho Pagoda at left, Yüeh Fei at right. *(S/M #184H-11).*			
	a. Issued note. Rare.	—	—	—
	s. Specimen with overprint: *Yang Pen. Specimen* on back.	—	—	3,500

		VG	VF	UNC
J98	**5 Yüan**			
	1938. Dark green and black on ochre and gray. House, arch, bridge, and pagoda at center. *(S/M #H184-12).*			
	a. Black overprint signature of bank president Ch'en Chin Tao on back.	—	—	1,800
	s. Specimen with overprint: *Yang Pen* on face and back.	—	—	1,500

		VG	VF	UNC
J99	**10 Yüan**			
	ND (1938). Black on multicolor underprint. Ta Ch'eng Tien building at left. Confucius at right.			
	a. Issued note. (Sea salvaged). *(S/M #H184-13).*	2,700	—	—
	s. Specimen with overprint: *Yang Pen* on face and back.	—	—	3,300

		VG	VF	UNC
J100	**10 Yüan**			
	1938. Brown-orange and black on ochre and light green underprint. Temple at center.			
	a. Issued note. *(S/M #H184-14).*	325	850	2,400
	r. Remainder without signature	—	—	1,650
	s. Specimen with overprint: *Yang Pen* on face and back.	—	—	1,650

Mengchiang Bank

行銀疆蒙

Meng Chiang Yin Hang

All notes are intaglio except J101 and J101A.

1938-1945 ND Issue

		VG	VF	UNC
J101	**5 Fen**			
	ND (1940). Gray. Herd of sheep at center.			
	a. Issued note. *(S/M #M11-1).*	125	3.00	12.50
	s. Specimen with overprint: *Yang Pen.* on face and back.	—	—	75.00

		VG	VF	UNC
J101A	**1 Chiao**			
	ND (1940). Brown and black on light blue underprint. Herd of camels at center.			
	a. Issued note. *(S/M #M11-2).*	2.00	6.00	20.00
	s. Specimen with red overprint: *Yang Pen* on face and back.	—	—	60.00

		VG	VF	UNC
J102	**5 Chiao**			
	ND (1944). Black on yellow-brown underprint. Temple courtyard.			
	a. Issued note. *(S/M #M11-4).*	40.00	125	575
	s. Specimen with red-orange overprint: *Mi-hon.*	—	—	300

		VG	VF	UNC
J103	**5 Chiao = 50 Fen**			
	ND (1940). Dark purple and black on green and pale blue underprint. Herd of camels at center.			
	a. Issued note. *(S/M #M11-3).*	5.00	20.00	100
	s. Specimen with red overprint: *Yang Pen* on face and back.	—	—	120

		VG	VF	UNC
J104	**1 Yüan**			
	ND. Dark green on ochre underprint. Great Wall at left center. *(S/M #M11-10).*	1.50	5.00	20.00

		VG	VF	UNC
J105	**1 Yüan**			
	ND (1938). Dark green and black on ochre and multicolor underprint. Herd of sheep at center.			
	a. Issued note. *(S/M #M11-11).*	4.00	13.00	50.00
	s. Specimen with red overprint: *Yang Pen* on face and back. Toppan Printing Co. imprint. Uniface pair.	—	—	150

J106	5 Yüan	VG	VF	UNC
	ND (1938). Orange-brown and black with violet guilloche. Pagoda at left, fortress at right. Back: Rural building at center.			
	a. Issued note. *(S/M #M11-12).*	3.00	13.00	30.00
	s. Specimen with red overprint: *Yang Pen* on face and back. Toppan Printing Co. imprint. Uniface pair.	—	—	150

J107	5 Yüan	VG	VF	UNC
	ND (1944). Purple on pale purple and orange underprint. Lama monastery at left center. Specimen. *(S/M #M11-13).* Rare.	—	—	—

J108	10 Yüan	VG	VF	UNC
	ND (1944). Dark blue-gray on yellow underprint. Camel at left, men on horseback, with oxen and horses at center. Back: Buddhas at center.			
	a. Watermark: Bank logo. Serial # and block #. *(S/M #M11-15).*	15.00	50.00	150
	b. Without watermark. Serial # and block #. *(S/M #M11-).*	5.00	18.00	60.00
	c. Block # only. *(S/M #M11-).*	8.00	25.00	75.00

J108A	10 Yüan	VG	VF	UNC
	ND (1944).Brown and black on ochre underprint. Camel at left, men on horseback, with oxen and horses at center. Like #J108. Back: Buddhas at center. *(S/M #M11-).*			
	r. Remainder. Block # only.	8.00	25.00	75.00
	s. Specimen with red-orange overprint.	—	—	125

J109	10 Yüan	VG	VF	UNC
	ND (1938). Dark brown. Sheep at center.			
	a. Issued note. *(S/M #M11-14).*	5.00	25.00	75.00
	s. Specimen with red overprint: *Yang Pen* on face and back. Toppan Printing Co. imprint. Uniface pair.	—	—	150

J110	100 Yüan	VG	VF	UNC
	ND (1945). Dark green on light brown underprint. Herdsman with goats.			
	a. Issued note. *(S/M #M11-22).*	3.00	10.00	30.00
	s. Specimen with red-orange overprint: *Mi-hon.*	—	—	125

J111	100 Yüan	VG	VF	UNC
	ND (1945). Black on yellow-green underprint. Lama monastary. *(S/M #M11-21).*	5.00	15.00	40.00

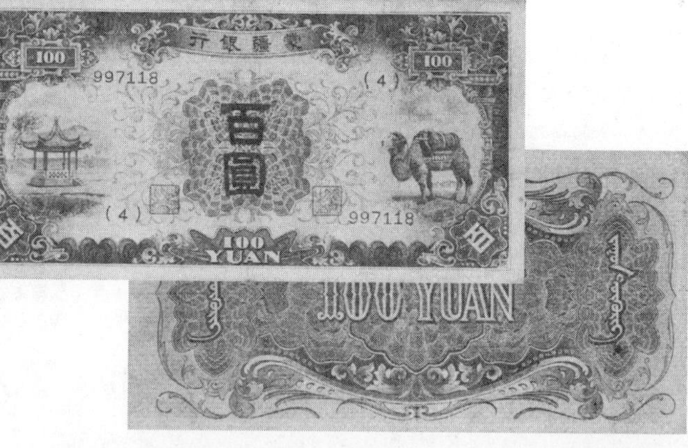

J112 100 Yüan
ND (1938). Purple and black on olive-geen and multicolor underprint. Pavilion at left, camel at right.

	VG	VF	UNC
a. Issued note. *(S/M #M11-21).*	4.00	13.00	55.00
s. Specimen with red overprint: *Yang Pen* on face and back. Toppan Printing Co. imprint. Uniface pair.	—	—	150

Chi Tung Bank

冀東銀行

Chi Tung Yin Hang

All notes are intaglio.

1937 Issue

J113 5 Chiao = 50 Fen
ND (1937). Dark green on light blue and pink underprint. Gateway at left center.

	VG	VF	UNC
a. Issued note. *(S/M #C84-1).*	450	1,250	4,725
s1. Specimen with overprint: *Yang Pen.* and *SPECIMEN.*	—	—	2,025
s2. As a. Specimen with overprint: *Yang Pen* and *Specimen* on face and back, perforated serial #.	—	—	2,025

J114 1 Yüan
ND (1937). Orange on light green and ochre underprint. Great Wall at right.

	VG	VF	UNC
a. Issued note. *(S/M #C284-2).*	450	1,250	4,725
s1. Specimen (English).	—	—	2,025
s2. As a. Specimen with overprint: *Yang Pen* and *Specimen* on face and back, perforated serial #.	—	—	1,875

J115 5 Yüan
ND (1937). Purple on multicolor underprint. Tower at Tunghsien at right. *(S/M #C84-3).*

	VG	VF	UNC
s1. Specimen (English).	—	—	4,050
s2. Specimen with overprint: *Yang Pen* and *Specimen* on face and back, perforated serial #.	—	—	3,775

J116 10 Yüan
ND (1937). Black on multicolor underprint. Temple at right. *(S/M #C84-4).*

	VG	VF	UNC
s1. Specimen (English).	—	—	6,750
s2. Specimen with overprint: *Yang Pen* and *Specimen* on face and back. Perforated serial #.	—	—	6,500

J117 100 Yüan
ND (1937). Dark blue on multicolor underprint. Building at right. *(S/M #C84-5).*

	VG	VF	UNC
s1. Specimen (English).	—	—	10,800
s2. Specimen with overprint: *Yang Pen* and *Specimen* on face and back. Perforated serial #.	—	—	10,800

Chanan Bank

察南銀行

Ch'a Nan Yin Hang

All notes are intaglio.

Provisional Issue

#J118-J119 overprint on notes of the Central Bank of Manchukuo. This is the second overprint with *Ch'a Nan Yin Hang* in Chinese vertically at left and right on the face. The first overprint is for the Central Bank of Manchukuo. Chanan Bank notes have the face overprint for CBM lined out, but without any new overprint on back leaving the CBM overprint.

J118 1 Yüan
ND (1937- old date 1929). Black and multicolor. *(S/M #C4-1).*

	VG	VF	UNC
a. Double line through red overprint below pavilion.	450	1,000	3,600
b. Single line through red overprint below pavilion.	450	1,000	3,600
s. Specimen with red handstamp: *Yang Pen.* Punch hole cancelled.	—	—	1,000

J119 10 Yüan
ND (1937- old date 1929). Green and multicolor.

	VG	VF	UNC
a. Issued note. *(S/M #C4-3).*	2,700	4,500	—
s. Specimen with red handstamp: *Yang Pen.* Punch hole cancelled.	—	—	4,500

MANCHUKUO

Under the lax central government of the Republic of China, Manchuria attained a relatively large measure of automony. This occurred in 1917, under the leadership of Marshal Chang Tso-lin and his son, Chang Hsueh-liang. Following the Japanese occupation, the State of Manchukuo was established on February 18, 1932, with the annexation of the Chinese Province of Jehol. UnderJapanese auspices, Manchukuo was ruled by Pu Yi, the last emperor of the Manchu (Ching) Dynasty. In 1934, Manchukuo was declared an empire; an Pu Yi proclaimed emperor. The empire was dissolved when Soviet troops occupied the territory in August, 1945. Following the Soviet evacuation, Manchukuo was re-incorporated into China. Capital: Hsinking.

RULERS:

Ta Tung, Years 1-3, 1932-1934
Kang Teh, Years 1-12, 1934-1945

MONETARY SYSTEM:

1 Yuan = 10 Chiao = 100 Fen

Central Bank of Manchukuo

滿洲中央銀行

Man Chou Chung Yang Yin Hang

All notes are intaglio except as noted.

Formed in 1932 by a merger of the following banks: Provincial Bank of the Three Eastern Provinces, Frontier Bank, Heilungkiang Provincial Bank and Kirin Provincial Bank.

Provisional Issue

#J120-J122 overprint new bank name on notes of the Provincial Bank of the Three Eastern Provinces. Dated first year of Ta Tung (1932). Note: For #J120 and J122 w/ additional vertical Chinese overprint: *Cha Nan Yin Hang*, see Chanan Bank #J118 and #J119.

J120 1 Yüan	**VG**	**VF**	**UNC**
1932 (-old date Nov. 1929). Black and multicolor.			
a. Issued note. *(S/M #M2-1).*	400	1,200	3,600
s1. Specimen with overprint: *Yang Pen* and *Specimen. Specimen* on back. Uniface pair.	—	—	1,200
s2. As a. Specimen with overprint: *Yang Pen* and *Specimen.* Punch hole cancelled.	—	—	800

J121 5 Yüan	**VG**	**VF**	**UNC**
1932 (- old date Nov. 1929). Brown and multicolor. Specimen. Uniface pair. *(S/M #M2-).*	—	—	1,450

J122 10 Yüan	**VG**	**VF**	**UNC**
1932 (- old date Nov. 1929). Green and multicolor.			
a. Issued note. *(S/M #M2-2).*	1,450	3,600	—
s1. Specimen with overprint: *Yang Pen* and *Specimen* on back. Uniface pair.	—	—	1,200
s2. As a. Specimen with overprint: *Yang Pen.* Punch hole cancelled.	—	—	850

#J123 *Deleted.*

1932 Issue

J124 5 Chiao = 50 Fen	**VG**	**VF**	**UNC**
ND (1932). Dark blue on ochre underprint.			
a. Issued note. Lithographed. *(S/M #M2-10).*	50.00	200	825
s. Specimen with overprint: *Yang Pen* and *Specimen* on face and back. Uniface pair.	—	—	500

1932-1933 ND Issue

J125 1 Yüan	**VG**	**VF**	**UNC**
ND (1932). Blue on yellow yellow underprint. Multicolor flag at left, building at right.			
a. Issued note. *(S/M #M2-20).*	37.50	200	725
s. Specimen with overprint: *Yang Pen* and *Specimen* on face and back. Uniface pair.	—	—	400

J126 5 Yüan	**VG**	**VF**	**UNC**
ND (1933). Dark brown on tan underprint. Multicolor flag at left, building at right.			
a. Issued note. *(S/M #M2-21).*	150	500	1,800
s. Specimen with overprint: *Yang Pen* and *Specimen* on face and back. Punch hole cancelled. Uniface pair.	—	—	500

J127 10 Yüan	**VG**	**VF**	**UNC**
ND (1932). Blue on orange underprint. Multicolor flag at left, building at right.			
a. Issued note. *(S/M #M2-22).*	150	575	1,950
s. Specimen with overprint: *Yang Pen* and *Specimen* on face and back. Uniface pair.	—	—	625

	VG	VF	UNC
J128 100 Yüan			
ND (1933). Blue on yellow-orange underprint. Multicolor flag at left, building at right.			
a. Issued note. *(S/M #M2-23).*	200	500	1,325
s. Specimen with overprint: *Yang Pen* and *Specimen* on face and back. Uniface pair.	—	—	550

1935-1938 ND Issue

	VG	VF	UNC
J129 5 Chiao = 50 Fen			
ND (1935). Brown on green and lilac underprint. Ch'ien Lung at right.			
a. Issued note. *(S/M #M2-30).*	3.00	8.00	40.00
s. Specimen with overprint: *Yang Pen* and *Specimen* on face and back. Uniface pair.	—	—	100

	VG	VF	UNC
J130 1 Yüan			
ND (1937). Black on green and yellow underprint at center. T'ien Ming at right. *(S/M #M2-40).*			
a. 6-digit serial #.	3.00	10.00	30.00
b. 7-digit serial #.	2.00	5.00	13.00
s. Specimen with overprint: *Yang Pen* and *Specimen* on face and back. Uniface pair.	—	—	100

	VG	VF	UNC
J131 5 Yüan			
ND (1938). Black on brown underprint at center. Man with beard wearing feather crown at right. *(S/M #M2-41).*			
a. 6-digit serial #.	15.00	50.00	150
b. 7-digit serial #.	8.00	25.00	75.00
s. Specimen with overprint: *Yang Pen* and *Specimen* on face and back. Punch hole cancelled. Uniface pair.	—	—	100

	VG	VF	UNC
J132 10 Yüan			
ND (1937). Black on brown underprint at center. Emperor Ch'ien Lung at right. *(S/M #M2-42).*			
a. 6-digit serial #.	7.50	20.00	50.00
b. 7-digit serial #.	3.00	8.00	25.00
s. Specimen with overprint: *Yang Pen* and *Specimen* on face and back. Uniface pair.	—	—	100

	VG	VF	UNC
J133 100 Yüan			
ND (1938). Black on green underprint at center. Confucius at right, Ta Ch'eng Tien building at left. Back: Sheep. *(S/M #M2-43).*			
a. 6-digit serial #.	30.00	100	225
b. 7-digit serial #.	6.00	15.00	35.00
s. Specimen with overprint: *Yang Pen* and *Specimen* on face and back. Uniface pair.	—	—	100

1944 ND Issue

#J135-J138 w/block # and serial #. New back designs.

	VG	VF	UNC
J134 5 Chiao = 50 Fen ND (1944). Blue-green on pale blue underprint. Ta Ch'eng Tien building at left center. *(S/M #M2-50).*	10.00	35.00	90.00

J135 1 Yüan	VG	VF	UNC
ND (1944). Black on green and violet underprint at center. T'ien Ming at right.			
a. Block # and serial #. *(S/M #M2-60).*	1.50	7.50	15.00
b. Block # only. *(S/M #M2-80).*	2.00	7.50	20.00
s1. As a. Specimen with overprint: *Yang Pen. Specimen* on back. Uniface pair.	—	—	100
s2. As b. Specimen with overprint: *Yang Pen.*	—	—	100

J136 5 Yüan	VG	VF	UNC
ND (1944). Black on orange underprint at center. Man with beard wearing feather crown at right.			
a. Block # and serial #. *(S/M #M2-61).*	2.50	7.50	20.00
s. Block # only. Specimen with overprint: *Yang Pen. (S/M #M2-81).*	—	—	175

J137 10 Yüan	VG	VF	UNC
ND (1944). Black on green underprint at center. Emperor Ch'ien Lung at right.			
a. Block # and serial #. Watermark: *MANCHU CENTRAL BANK. (S/M #M2-62).*	2.00	10.00	20.00
b. Revalidation *10 Yuan* adhesive stamp on face. See #M35.	—	—	—
c. Block # only. Watermark. as a. *(S/M #M2-82).*	2.50	13.00	25.00
d. Revalidation *10 Yuan* adhesive stamp on face. See #M35.	—	—	—
e. Block # only. Watermark: Chinese character: *Man* in clouds repeated.	2.50	13.00	30.00
s1. As a. Specimen with overprint: *Yang Pen. Specimen* on back. Uniface pair.	—	—	100
s2. As e. Specimen with overprint: *Yang Pen.*	—	—	100

J138 100 Yüan	VG	VF	UNC
ND (1944). Black on blue underprint at center. Confucius at right, Ta Ch'eng Tien building at left. Back: Men and donkey carts by storage silos at center. *(S/M #M2-63).*			
a. Watermark: *MANCHU CENTRAL BANK.*	5.00	15.00	55.00
b. Watermark: Chinese character: *Man* in clouds repeated.	4.00	10.00	35.00
s1. As a. Specimen with overprint: *Yang Pen. Specimen* on back. Block #1. Uniface pair.	—	—	60.00
s2. As b. Specimen with overprint: *Yang Pen.*	—	—	100
s3. Specimen. Uniface face and back.	—	—	250

1941-1945 Issue

#J139-J141; J145-J146 without serial #, only block letters.

J139 5 Fen	VG	VF	UNC
ND (1945). Blue-green. Back: Tower at center. *(S/M #M2-70).*	20.00	100	300

J140 10 Fen = 1 Chiao	VG	VF	UNC
ND (1944). Yellow-orange underprint. Back: House at center. *(S/M #M2-71).*	1.50	5.00	15.00

J141 5 Chiao = 50 Fen	VG	VF	UNC
ND (1941). Green on pink and orange underprint. Ch'ien Lung at right.			
a. Issued note. *(S/M #M2-72).*	1.00	3.00	12.00
s. Specimen with overprint: *Yang Pen* and *Specimen.* Uniface pair.	—	—	75.00

#J142-J144 *Deleted.* See #J135b, J136s, J137c.

J145 100 Yüan	VG	VF	UNC
ND (1945). Black on blue underprint at center. Confucius at right, Ta Ch'eng Tien building at left. Like #J138. Back: Men and donkey carts by storage silos at center. 1 serial #. Local printer. *(S/M #M2-83).*	375	1,200	—

J146 1000 Yüan	VG	VF	UNC
ND (1944). Dark brown and violet. Confucius at right, Ta Ch'eng Tien building at left. Back: Bank building at center. *(S/M #M2-84).*	300	1,000	4,000

COLOMBIA

The Republic of Colombia, located in the northwestern corner of South America, has an area of 1.139 million sq. km. and a population of 45.01 million. Capital: Bogotá. The economy is primarily agricultural with a mild, rich coffee the chief crop. Colombia has the world's largest platinum deposits and important reserves of coal, iron ore, petroleum and limestone; precious metals and emeralds are also mined. Coffee, crude oil, bananas, sugar, coal and flowers are exported.

Colombia was one of the three countries that emerged from the collapse of Gran Colombia in 1830 (the others are Ecuador and Venezuela). A 40-year conflict between government forces and anti-government insurgent groups and illegal paramilitary groups - both heavily funded by the drug trade - escalated during the 1990s. The insurgents lack the military or popular support necessary to overthrow the government, and violence has been decreasing since about 2002, but insurgents continue attacks against civilians and large swaths of the countryside are under guerrilla influence. More than 32,000 former paramilitaries had demobilized by the end of 2006 and the United Self Defense Forces of Colombia (AUC) as a formal organization had ceased to function. Still, some renegades continued to engage in criminal activities. The Colombian Government has stepped up efforts to reassert government control throughout the country, and now has a presence in every one of its administrative departments. However, neighboring countries worry about the violence spilling over their borders.

MONETARY SYSTEM:

1 Real = 1 Decimo = 10 Centavos, 1870s
1 Peso = 10 Decimos = 10 Reales, 1880s
1 Peso = 100 Centavos 1993
1 Peso Oro = 100 Centavos to 1993

REPUBLIC

República de Colombia

1819 Issue

#	Note	Good	Fine	XF
1	**6 1/4 Centavos = Medio Real** ND (ca. 1819) Black. Pineapple at upper center. Printer: Peter Maverick, New York, U.S.A.	40.00	100	300
2	**12 1/2 Centavos = 1 Real** ND ca.(1819). Black. Uniface. Loaded burro at upper center. Similar to #1. Printer: Peter Maverick, New York, U.S.A.	40.00	100	300

#	Note	Good	Fine	XF
3	**25 Centavos = 2 Reales** ND (ca. 1819). Black. Uniface. Loaded burro at upper center. Printer: Peter Maverick, New York, U.S.A.	40.00	100	300
4	**50 Centavos = 4 Reales** ND (ca. 1819). Black. Uniface. Similar to #3. Printer: Peter Maverick, New York, U.S.A.	40.00	100	—

1820s Issue

#5-8 *BOLIVAR* above arms at ctr. Uniface. Printer: Peter Maverick, New York, U.S.A. (From cut up 4-subject sheets of unissued remainders.)

#	Note	VG	VF	UNC
5	**1 Peso** 182x Black. Uniface. BOLIVAR above arms at center. Printer: Peter Maverick, New York, U.S.A.	—	—	200

From cut up 4-subject sheets of unissued remainders.

#	Note	VG	VF	UNC
6	**2 Pesos** 182x. Black. Uniface. BOLIVAR above arms at center. Printer: Peter Maverick, New York, U.S.A.	—	—	200

From cut up 4-subject sheets of unissued remainders.

#	Note	VG	VF	UNC
7	**3 Pesos** 182x. Black. Uniface. BOLIVAR above arms at center. Printer: Peter Maverick, New York, U.S.A.	—	—	200

From cut up 4-subject sheets of unissued remainders.

#	Note	VG	VF	UNC
8	**5 Pesos** 182x. Black. Uniface. BOLIVAR above arms at center. Printer: Peter Maverick, New York, U.S.A.	—	—	200

From cut up 4-subject sheets of unissued remainders.
#9-58 not assigned.

Tesorería Jeneral de los Estados Unidos de Nueva Granada

1860s Issue

#	Note	Good	Fine	XF
59	**20 Centavos = 2 Reales** (ca.1860) Printer: Lit. Ayala.	40.00	125	300

#60 not assigned.

#	Note	Good	Fine	XF
61	**1 Peso = 10 Reales** 186x. Pink underprint. Steamship at upper left and right. Printer: Lit. Ayala.	60.00	200	400

#	Note	Good	Fine	XF
62	**2 Pesos = 20 Reales** December 1862. Yellow underprint. Steamship at upper left and right. Printer: Lit. Ayala.	75.00	225	550

#	Note	Good	Fine	XF
63	**3 Pesos = 30 Reales** 186x. Implements. Printer: Lit. Ayala.	80.00	250	600
64	**10 Pesos = 100 Reales** 186x. Implements. Printer: Lit. Ayala.	90.00	275	650
65	**20 Pesos = 200 Reales** 186x. Implements. Printer: Lit. Ayala.	110	300	750
66	**100 Pesos = 1000 Reales** 1.3.1861. Blue underprint. Implements. Printer: Lit. Ayala. Rare.	—	—	—

Tesorería Jeneral de los Estados Unidos de Colombia

1860s Issue

#	Note	Good	Fine	XF
67	**25 Centavos = 2 1/2 Reales** ND (ca. 1860s). Black. Standing allegorical woman with cornucopia at center.	—	—	—

Estados Unidos de Colombia

1863 Treasury Issue

#	Description	Good	Fine	XF
71	**5 Centavos** ND. Blue. Farm tools at center.	80.00	200	500
72	**10 Centavos** ND. Blue. Horse.	80.00	200	500
73	**20 Centavos** ND. Black. Seated woman with shield at center. Back: Printer signature.	80.00	200	500

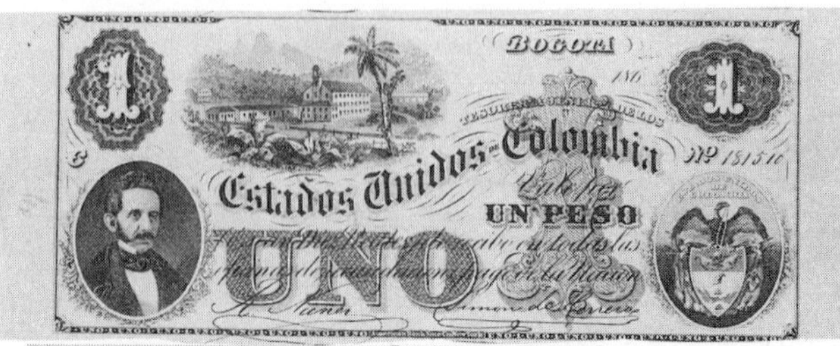

#	Description	Good	Fine	XF
74	**1 Peso** 2.1.1863. Black on brown underprint. Portrait man at lower left, building at upper left center, arms at lower right. Printer: ABNC.	65.00	175	500

#	Description	Good	Fine	XF
75	**2 Pesos** 2.1.1863. Black on red underprint. Arms at lower left, horse and rider at top center, portrait Bolívar at lower right. Series A-C. Printer: ABNC.	90.00	250	700

#	Description	Good	Fine	XF
76	**5 Pesos** 2.1.1863. Black on green underprint. Portrait man at lower left, standing woman at center, arms at right. Printer: ABNC.	100	300	750
77	**10 Pesos** 2.1.1863. Black on green underprint. Arms at left, steamboat at right center, portrait man at lower right. Printer: ABNC.	125	350	900
78	**20 Pesos** 2.1.1863. Black on yellow underprint. Arms at left, man with mule cart at center, portrait Caldas at right. Printer: ABNC. Rare.	—	—	—

#79 Not assigned.

1869 Issue

#	Description	Good	Fine	XF
80	**3 Pesos** 28.8.1869. Rare.	—	—	—

1876 Issue

#	Description	Good	Fine	XF
81	**5 Centavos** 24.11.1876. Black. Tobacco, beehive, plow and shovel at center. Back: Printed signature and dark red oval stamping. Printer: Ayala i Medrano.	80.00	200	500

#82-121 not assigned.

Banco Nacional de los Estados Unidos de Colombia

ND Issue

#	Description	Good	Fine	XF
122	**20 Centavos** ND. Black on blue underprint. Portrait right. Nuñez at upper center. Series Y. Printer: Chaix.	30.00	75.00	200

#	Description	Good	Fine	XF
123	**20 Centavos** ND. Black on blue underprint. Like #122. Printer: Litografia de Villaveces, Bogotá.	—	—	—

#124-133 not assigned.

1881 First Issue

#	Description	Good	Fine	XF
134	**1 Peso** 1.3.1881. Partially printed. Blue. Liberty seal at left, arms at top center right. Series A. Printer: Lit. D. Paredes, Bogota.	100	250	600
135	**5 Pesos** 1.3.1881. Partially printed. Black and red. Liberty seated at left, arms at top center right. Back: Stamping and handwritten signature. Printer: Lit. D Paredes, Bogota.	100	250	600
136	**10 Pesos** 1.5.1881. Liberty seated at left, arms at top center right. Printer: Lit. D Paredes, Bogota.	—	—	—
138	**20 Pesos** 1.3.1881. Partially handwritten. Rare. Liberty seated at left, arms at top center right. Printer: Lit. D. Paredes, Bogota.	—	—	—

#137, 139-140 not assigned.

1881 Second Issue

#	Description	Good	Fine	XF
141	**1 Peso** 1.3.1881. Black on brown underprint. Portrait helmeted Athena at lower left, portrait S. Bolívar at upper center, arms at lower right. Series A. Printer: ABNC.			
	a. Issued note	100	250	600
	s. Specimen.	—		

		Good	Fine	XF
142	**5 Pesos** 1.3.1881. Black on green underprint. Woman at left, man in uniform at center, arms at right. Printer: ABNC.			
	a. Issued note.	100	250	600
	s. Specimen.	—	—	—

		Good	Fine	XF
143	**10 Pesos** 1.3.1881. Black on orange underprint. Arms at lower left, steam locomotive at center, portrait Caldas at right. Printer: ABNC.	125	300	750

		Good	Fine	XF
144	**20 Pesos** 1.3.1881. Black on blue underprint. Arms at left, unloading bales at center, portrait Nariño at right. Printer: ABNC.	150	360	900
145	**50 Pesos** 1.3.1881. Black on brown underprint. Arms at left, globe with ship and train at center, portrait Torres at right. Printer: ABNC.	300	750	—
146	**100 Pesos** 1.3.1881. Black on brown-orange underprint. Miners at lower left, allegorical woman flanking shield at center, portrait Santander at lower right. Printer: ABNC.	375	950	—

#147-152 not assigned.

1882 Issue

		Good	Fine	XF
153	**50 Centavos** 1.3.1882. Orange and black. Arms at center. Back: Purple stamping.	35.00	90.00	225

#154-160 not assigned.

1885 Issue

		Good	Fine	XF
161	**10 Centavos** 1885. Black on orange-gold underprint. Arms at upper center. Series Z. Back: Printed signature and stamping. Printer: Lit. D. Paredes.			
	a. 15.3.1885.	7.50	20.00	60.00
	b. 5.8.1885.	7.50	20.00	60.00

		Good	Fine	XF
162	**20 Centavos** 15.3.1885. Black on aqua underprint. Similar to #161. Series Y. Back: Printed signature and stamping. Printer: Lit. D. Paredes.	7.50	20.00	60.00

#163 not assigned.

		Good	Fine	XF
164	**1 Peso** 6.10.1885. Black on green underprint. Arms at upper center. Series A. Back: Signature and stamping. Printer: Lit. D. Paredes.	7.50	20.00	60.00
165	**1 Peso** 6.10.1885. Black on pink underprint. Like #164. Printer: Lit. D. Paredes.	7.50	20.00	60.00

#155-169 not assigned.

		Good	Fine	XF
170	**50 Pesos** 22.7.1885. Condor.	—	—	—
171	**100 Pesos** 3.3.1885. Black on orange underprint. Woman.	—	—	—

#172-180 not assigned.

Banco Nacional de Colombia

1885 Issue

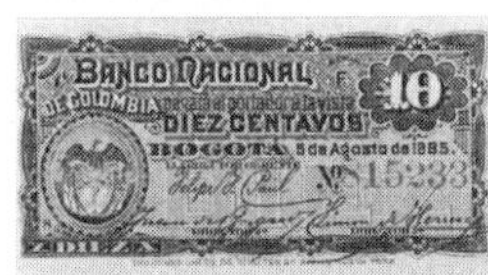

		Good	Fine	XF
181	**10 Centavos = 1 Real** 5.8.1885. Black on green underprint. Arms at left. Red seal at center. Series C; D; E; F; G; H; I; K; M; O; Back: Printed signature across. Printer: HLBNC.	2.50	10.00	25.00
182	**10 Centavos = 1 Real** 5.8.1885. Like #181. Blue seal. Series F; K; O; Q; T; Back: Blue seal. Printer: CABB (ABNC).			
	a. Issued note.	2.50	10.00	25.00
	s. Specimen.	—	Unc	200

#183-185 not assigned.

1886 Issue

		Good	Fine	XF
186	**20 Centavos** ND (1886). Black on orange underprint. Man at left. Printer: Villaveces, Bogotá.	8.00	25.00	50.00

187-188 not assigned.

1887 Issue

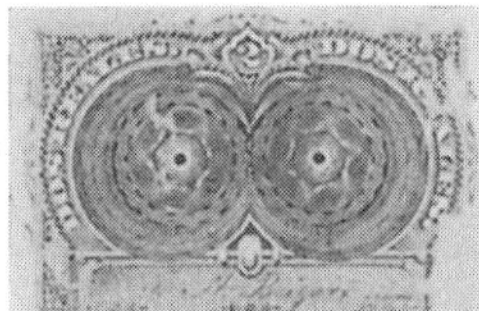

		Good	Fine	XF
189	**20 Centavos = 2 Reales** 1.1.1887. Black on gold underprint. Portrait man at lower left, arms at lower right. Series B; D; E; H; I; J; L; N. Printer: HLBNC.	5.00	20.00	50.00
190	**50 Centavos** 1.5.1887. Printer: Villaveces, Bogotá.	—	—	—

Banco Nacional de la República de Colombia

1886 Issue

		Good	Fine	XF
191	**50 Centavos** 1.9.1886. Green. Justice at upper left, shield at lower right. Series 1. Printer: HLBNC.	7.50	30.00	110

		Good	Fine	XF
192	**1 Peso** 1.9.1886. Green. Helmeted woman at upper left, arms at upper right. Series 2A. Printer: HLBNC.			
	a. Issued note.	6.00	25.00	100
	s. Uniface Specimen.	—	Unc	500
193	**1 Peso** 1.9.1886. Like #192-Helmeted woman at upper left, arms at upper right. Printer: HLBNC.	7.50	30.00	110

		Good	Fine	XF
194	**5 Pesos** 1.9.1886. Green on orange underprint. Shield at lower left, helmeted Minerva at upper center. Series 2A. Printer: HLBNC.	27.50	120	425

		Good	Fine	XF
195	**10 Pesos** 1.9.1886. Brown. Reclining allegorical seated figures with arms at center. Series 2A. Printer: HLBNC.	35.00	150	500

#196-210 not assigned.

1888 Issue

		Good	Fine	XF
211	**10 Centavos = 1 Real** 1.3.1888. Black on yellow underprint. Arms at lower left. Back: Circular red bank seal. Printed signature. At least eleven Greek and English series letters. Printer: ABNC.			
	a. Issued note.	3.00	15.00	45.00
	s. Specimen.	—	Unc	150

#212-213 not assigned.

		Good	Fine	XF
214	**1 Peso** 1.3.1888. Black on orange and yellow underprint. Arms at left, portrait S. Bolívar at right. At least 15 Greek and English series letters. Back: Circular red bank seal. Printer: ABNC.			
	a. Issued Note.	4.50	20.00	55.00
	s. Specimen.	—	Unc	250

		Good	Fine	XF
215	**5 Pesos** 1.3.1888. Black on orange and yellow underprint. Arms at left, allegorical woman with bale seated at left center, portrait S. Bolívar at right. Series A. Back: Circular red bank seal. Printer: ABNC.			
	a. Issued note.	8.00	32.50	150
	s. Specimen.	—	Unc	650
216	**10 Pesos** 1.3.1888. Black on brown and yellow underprint. Standing allegorical woman and pedestal of Liberty at left, portrait S. Bolívar at center, arms at right. Series A. Back: Circular red bank seal. Printer: ABNC.			
	a. Issued note.	12.50	50.00	200
	s. Specimen.	—	Unc	800

		Good	Fine	XF
217	**50 Pesos** 1.3.1888. Black on blue and yellow underprint. Portrait S. Bolívar at left, arms at center, seated allegorical woman at lower right. Series A. Back: Circular red bank seal. Printer: ABNC.			
	a. Issued note.	22.00	90.00	400
	s. Specimen.	—	Unc	1,000

		Good	Fine	XF
218	**100 Pesos** 1.3.1888. Black on green and yellow underprint. Arms at left, cherub at center, portrait S. Bolívar at right. Series A. Back: Circular red bank seal. Printer: ABNC.			
	a. Issued note.	37.50	150	550
	s. Specimen.	—	Unc	2,750

1893 Issue

#222, 223, 225, 226, 229-233 not assigned.

		Good	Fine	XF
221	**10 Centavos = 1 Real** 2.1.1893. Like #211-arms at lower left. At least 16 Greek and English series letters. Printer: ABNC.			
	a. Issued note.	1.00	4.00	12.00
	s. Specimen.	—	Unc	125

		Good	Fine	XF
224	**1 Peso** 2.1.1893. Black on orange and yellow underprint. Arms at left, portrait S.Bolivar at right, like #214. At least 13 Greek and English series letters. Back: Circular red bank seal.			
	a. Issued note.	2.50	10.00	35.00
	s. Specimen.	—	Unc	150

		Good	Fine	XF
227	**50 Pesos**	Good	Fine	XF
	2.1.1893. Black on blue and yellow underprint. Portrait S. Bolívar at left, arms at center, seated allegorical woman at lower right. Series A. Like #217. Back: Circular red bank seal.			
	a. Issued note.	17.50	70.00	300
	s. Specimen.	—	Unc	2,500
228	**100 Pesos**	Good	Fine	XF
	2.1.1893. Black on green and yellow underprint. Arms at left, cherub at center, portrait S. Bolívar at right. Series A. Like #218. Back: Circular red bank seal.			
	a. Issued note.	30.00	125	450
	s. Specimen.	—	Unc	3,000

1895 Issue

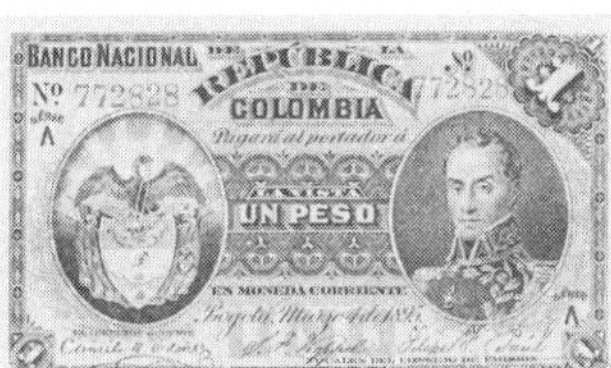

		Good	Fine	XF
234	**1 Peso**	Good	Fine	XF
	4.3.1895. Black on orange and yellow underprint. Arms at left, portrait S. Bolívar at right. Like #214. At least 21 Greek and English series letters. Back: Circular red bank seal.			
	a. Issued note.	1.50	6.00	30.00
	s. Specimen.	—	Unc	100

		Good	Fine	XF
235	**5 Pesos**	Good	Fine	XF
	4.3.1895. Black on orange and yellow underprint. Arms at left, allegorical woman with bale seated at left center, portrait S. Bolívar at right. Series A. Like #215. Back: Circular red bank seal.			
	a. Issued note.	5.50	22.50	135
	s. Specimen.	—	Unc	450

		Good	Fine	XF
236	**10 Pesos**	Good	Fine	XF
	4.3.1895. Black on brown and yellow underprint. Standing allegorical woman and pedestal of Liberty at left, portrait S. Bolívar at center, arms at right. Series A. Like #216. Back: Circular red bank seal.			
	a. Issued note.	7.50	30.00	175
	s. Specimen.	—	Unc	600

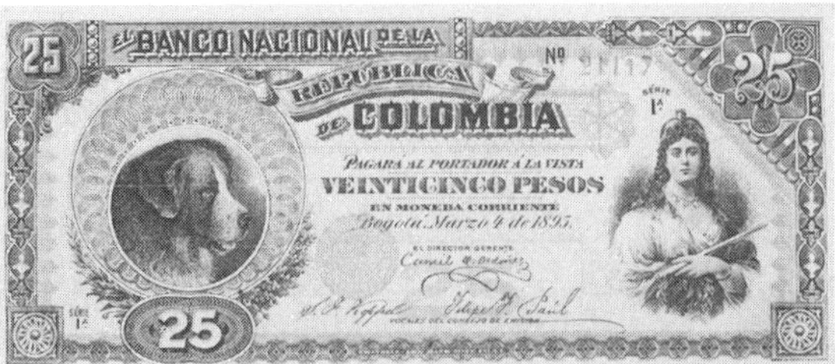

		Good	Fine	XF
237	**25 Pesos**	Good	Fine	XF
	4.3.1895. Black on orange and green underprint. Dog at left, Liberty at lower right. Series 1. Printer: FLBN.	32.50	150	450

		Good	Fine	XF
238	**50 Pesos**	Good	Fine	XF
	4.3.1895. Black on blue and yellow underprint. Portrait S. Bolívar at left, arms at center, seated allegorical woman at lower right. Series A. Like #217. Back: Circular red bank seal.	15.00	75.00	325
239	**100 Pesos**	Good	Fine	XF
	4.3.1895. Black on green and yellow underprint. Arms at left, cherub at center, portrait S. Bolívar at right. Series A. Like #218. Back: Circular red bank seal.			
	a. Issued note.	32.50	135	450
	s. Specimen.	—	Unc	1,500

#240 not assigned.

		Good	Fine	XF
241	**1000 Pesos**	Good	Fine	XF
	4.3.1895. Black on pink and blue underprint. Woman at left. Back: Woman with head covered on red back. Printer: FLBN.	—	725	2,000

#242-250 not assigned.

1899 Civil War Issue

Notes of 1899 and 1900 show great variance in printing quality, color shades, types of paper used. There was also a considerable amount of forgery of these notes.

		Good	Fine	XF
251	**2 Pesos**	Good	Fine	XF
	28.10.1899. Black on pink underprint. Liberty facing left at left. Series A-C; G; K; M; N.			
	a. Issued note.	2.00	10.00	42.00
	b. Punch hole cancelled.	2.00	8.00	35.00

		Good	Fine	XF
252	**2 Pesos** 28.10.1899. Black on pink underprint. Liberty facing right at left. *SEGUNDA EDICION* at lower left. Series A-L. Printer: LN.	2.00	15.00	50.00
253	**5 Pesos** 29.10.1899. Black on blue underprint. Arms and allegorical seated figures at center. Series B; D; E; F. Printer: Otto Schroeder.	5.00	25.00	72.00
254	**5 Pesos** 29.10.1899. Arms and allegorical seated figures at center with Otto Schroeder imprint. Series A; D. Back: *SEGUNDA EDICION* at lower right. Printer: LN.	4.00	20.00	60.00

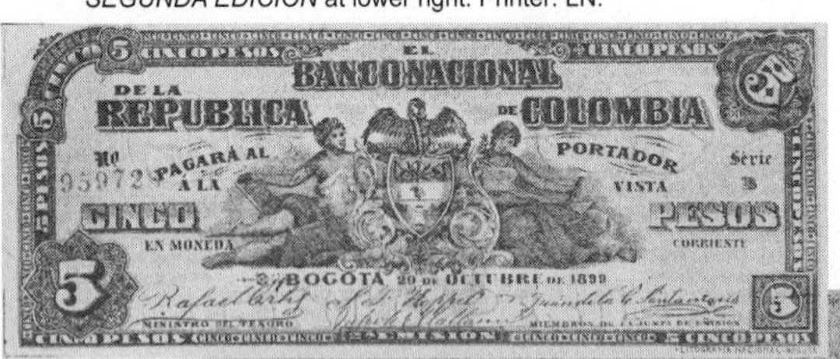

		Good	Fine	XF
255	**5 Pesos** 29.10.1899. Black on blue underprint. Arms and allegorical seated figures at center; *A EMISION* at lower center and *LN* imprint at lower right. Series A; B; E.	4.00	20.00	80.00
256	**5 Pesos** 29.10.1899. Black on blue underprint. Arms and allegorical seated figures at center;#A EMISION at lower center. Series A-C; E; F.	4.50	22.00	85.00

#257-259, 261 not assigned.

		Good	Fine	XF
260	**100 Pesos** 29.10.1899. Black on orange-tan underprint. Portrait S. Bolivar at left, Spaniards landing at center, arms at right. Series A. Printer: Otto Schroeder.	40.00	125	425

1900 Civil War Issue

		VG	VF	UNC
262	**10 Centavos** 2.1.1900. Black on green underprint. Arms at left. Series A. Printer: Villaveces, Bogotá. Plain edge.			
	a. Serial # across lower center.	1.00	4.50	20.00
	b. Without serial #.	1.00	4.50	20.00
	c. Numeral 2 for day in date missing. Perforated edge.	—	—	—
	d. Without serial #. Perforated edge.	—	—	—

		VG	VF	UNC
263	**10 Centavos** 30.9.1900. Blue on orange underprint. Arms at upper left. Back: Series A-C; E-F; H-J; L-M; O-P at left or right. Printer: LN.	1.00	5.00	22.00

		VG	VF	UNC
264	**20 Centavos** 25.3.1900. Black on light blue-gray underprint. Arms at left. At least 13 series letters.	1.00	4.50	20.00

		VG	VF	UNC
265	**20 Centavos** 30.9.1900. Black on wine or lilac underprint. Arms at lower left. Back: Arms at center. Printer: LN. At least 17 series letters.	0.75	3.00	15.00
265A	**20 Centavos** 30.9.1900. Black without underprint. Arms at lower left. Back: Arms at center.	2.50	10.00	35.00

		Good	Fine	XF
266	**50 Centavos** 20.7.1900. Black on blue underprint. Arms at upper right. Series B; E. Imprint: Otto Schroeder. Back: Imprint: Otto Schroeder.	2.25	10.00	40.00
267	**50 Centavos** 20.7.1900. Black on blue underprint. Like #266: Arms at upper right; 2A EMISION at lower left and no Schroeder imprint at lower right. Series F. Back: Schroeder imprint at bottom and is not inverted.	2.25	10.00	40.00
268	**50 Centavos** 20.7.1900. Blue or green underprint. Like #267-arms at upper right.Series B-P; V. Back: *2A EMISION* at bottom margin, and no Schroeder imprint. Series H; L have inverted backs.	1.75	7.50	30.00

		Good	Fine	XF
269	**1 Peso** 25.4.1900 Black on light red underprint. Arms at center. Series B; E; G; I; O; P. Printer: Lit. D Paredes.	3.00	15.00	50.00

		Good	Fine	XF
270	**1 Peso** 30.9.1900. At least 12 series letters. Black on light red underprint. Man at left. Back: Arms at center. Printer: LN.	1.75	7.50	35.00

		Good	Fine	XF
271	**1 Peso**			
	30.9.1990. Black on red-orange underprint. Man and woman watering horses at left, blue bank seal at right center. *2A EMISION* at lower left margin. Series A; H; I; K; N. Back: *2A EMISION* at lower center in margin. Printer: LN.	3.00	12.50	50.00

		Good	Fine	XF
273	**5 Pesos**			
	30.9.1900. Requires confirmation. *2A EMISION.*	—	—	—

		Good	Fine	XF
274	**10 Pesos**			
	30.9.1900. Black on orange-brown underprint. Miners at left, arms at center. Printer: LN.			
	a. No imprint at lower right. Back purple. Series A; B; I.	7.50	30.00	90.00
	b. Like a., but back blue. Series A; B.	8.00	32.00	100
	c. Imprint at lower right. Back purple. Series H; M.	6.50	27.50	80.00
	d. Like a.; back inverted and blue. Series M.	6.50	27.50	80.00

		Good	Fine	XF
275	**10 Pesos**			
	30.9.1900. Black on orange-brown underprint. Like #274-miners at left, arms at center, but *2A EMISION* at lower center. Series A; N; O. Back: *LEHNER* at left, LN imprint at bottom right.	6.50	27.50	85.00

		Good	Fine	XF
276	**20 Pesos**			
	30.9.1900. Black. Arms at center, farmer at right. Back: Mules and boys on mountain trail at center. Printer: LN.			
	a. Blue underprint. Series B.	7.50	30.00	95.00
	b. Green underprint. Series A; C; F; M; O; P; Q.	6.50	27.50	85.00

		Good	Fine	XF
278	**50 Pesos**			
	15.2.1900. Black on green underprint. Arms at upper left, sailing ship and steam passenger train at upper center, portrait of man at upper right. Back: Arms at center. Imprint: Otto Schroeder.			
	a. Series A; C.	17.50	70.00	250
	b. Perforated *B de B (Banco de Bogotá)* at center Series B.	17.50	70.00	250

		Good	Fine	XF
279	**50 Pesos**			
	30.9.1900. Black on dull orange underprint. Woman and trough at lower left, arms at upper center. Portrait of S.Bolívar at lower right. Series A; C; D. Back: Woman at center. Printer: LN.	17.50	70.00	250

		Good	Fine	XF
280	**50 Pesos**			
	30.9.1900. Blue on dull orange underprint. Woman and trough at lower left, arms at upper center, portrait of S. Bolivar at lower right-like #279. Series A-D. Back: Woman at center. Printer: LN.	17.50	70.00	250

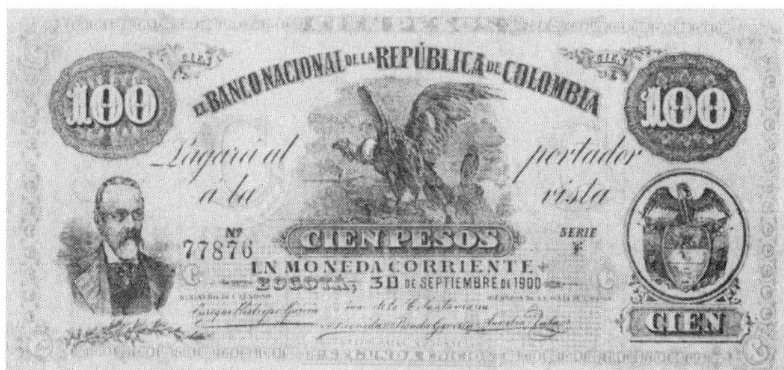

		Good	Fine	XF
281	**100 Pesos**			
	30.9.1900. Black on orange underprint. Man at lower left, condor at upper center, arms at lower right. *SEGUNDA EDICION* at lower center. Series A; C; F. Back: Funeral of Atahualpa scene at center. Printer: LN.	25.00	100	400

		Good	Fine	XF
282	**500 Pesos**			
	28.2.1900. Brown. Arms at upper left. Series A. Back: Black text. Large blue eagle at center. 4 hand signature below.	800	1,250	2,000

Estados Unidos de Colombia

1864-1869 *Bono Flotante al 3 Por 100 Anual* Issue

(3% Annual Bonds)

		Good	Fine	XF
283	**10 Pesos**			
	16.8.1864. Black on light orange underprint. Arms at upper center.	—	—	—

283D 1000 Pesos — Good — Fine — XF
13.2.1869. Black on light blue underprint. Arms at upper center. — — —

1878 *Lei 57 de 1878 Vale Por Indemnizacion de Estranjeros* Issue

284 10 Pesos — Good — Fine — XF
18xx. 18xx. Printer: Paredes. — — —

284A 50 Pesos — Good — Fine — XF
18xx. 18xx. Printer: Paredes. — — —

284B 100 Pesos — Good — Fine — XF
18xx. Black on orange underprint. Allegorical woman reclining at upper center. Printer: Paredes. Unsigned remainder. — — —

284C 500 Pesos — Good — Fine — XF
187x. Black on green underprint. Train at upper center. Printer: Paredes. Unsigned remainder. — — —

1880 *Libranza Contra las Aduanas* Issue

285 100 Pesos — Good — Fine — XF
11.1880. — — —

1883 *Bonos Especiales de 4%* Issue

286 10 Pesos — Good — Fine — XF
1.12.1883. Black on blue underprint. Arms at center. — — —

286B 1000 Pesos — Good — Fine — XF
1.12.1883. Black on red underprint. Arms at center. — — —

1884 *Billete de Tesorería* Issue

287 10 Pesos — Good — Fine — XF
1884. Arms at upper center. — — —

287A 10 Pesos — Good — Fine — XF
188x. Black on pink and blue underprint. Arms at upper left. Printer: Villa Veces, Bogota. — — —

1884 *Libranzas de la Empresa de la Ferrería de la Pradera* Issue

288 5 Pesos — Good — Fine — XF
1884. Printer: Paredes. — — —

288A 10 Pesos — Good — Fine — XF
1884. Printer: Paredes. — — —

288B 50 Pesos — Good — Fine — XF
1884. Printer: Paredes. — — —

288C 100 Pesos — Good — Fine — XF
1884. Printer: Paredes. — — —

288D 500 Pesos — Good — Fine — XF
1884. Printer: Paredes. — — —

1884 *Tesorería General de la Union* Issue

289 5 Pesos — Good — Fine — XF
188x. Green and black. Arms at upper left. — — —

289D 500 Pesos — Good — Fine — XF
1884. Brown and black. Arms at upper left. — — —

1884 *Vale de Tesorería al Portador* Issue

Articulo 12, Ley 53 de 1884

290 5 Pesos — Good — Fine — XF
188x. Black on green underprint. Arms at upper left. Printer: Paredes. Interest-bearing note. Unsigned remainder. — — —

290D 100 Pesos — Good — Fine — XF
188x Black on orange underprint. Arms at upper left. Printer: Paredes. Interest-bearing note. Unsigned remainder. — — —

República de Colombia

1880s *Billete de Dos Unidades* Issue

290E 50 Pesos — Good — Fine — XF
188x. Black and green. Dog's head at upper left. Arms in underprint at center. Printer: Villaveces, Bogota. — — —

1886 *Administración General de las Salinas Maritimas* Issue

291 **50 Pesos** Good Fine XF
1886. Brown on gold underprint. Woman at lower right. Unsigned remainder. — — —

1888 *Libranza Contra las Oficinas de Espendio de Sal Marino* Issue

291A **10 Pesos** Good Fine XF
April 1888. Black on light brown underprint. Portrait of man at left. Printer: Villaveces, Bogota. — — —

1888 *Libranza Contra las Aduanas de la Costa Atlántica* Issue

292 **500 Pesos** Good Fine XF
1.11.1888. Train at center. Printer: Paredes. — — —

1889 *Bono Colombiano* Issue

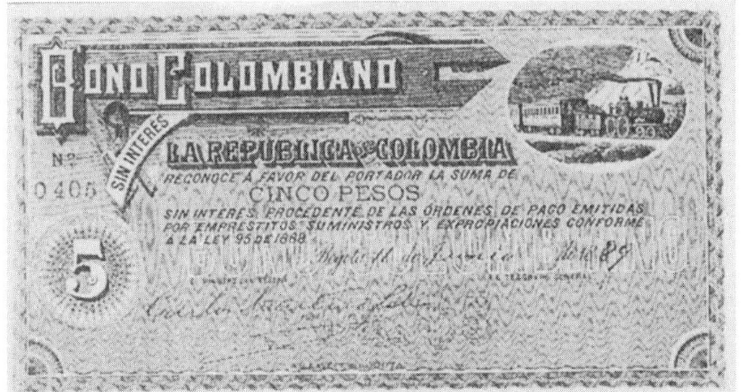

293 **5 Pesos** Good Fine XF
11.6.1889. Black on blue underprint. Steam passenger train at upper right. Printer: Villaveces, Bogota. — — —

293A **10 Pesos** Good Fine XF
20.3.1889. Black on pink underprint. Dog head at upper right. Printer: Villaveces, Bogota. — — —

293B **50 Pesos** Good Fine XF
18xx. Black. Romping horses at upper right. Printer: Villaveces, Bogota. Unsigned remainder. — — —

Color Abbreviation Guide

New to the *Standard Catalog of® World Paper Money* are the following abbreviations related to color references:

BC: Back color
PC: Paper color

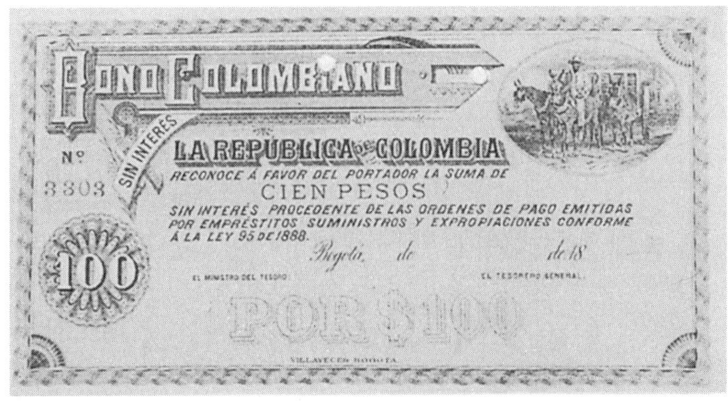

293C **100 Pesos** Good Fine XF
18xx. Black. Horses with rider and wagon at upper right. Printer: Villaveces, Bogota. Unsigned remainder. — — —

República de Colombia

Vale por Exacciones en la Guerra de 1895 Issue

Property Expropriation Voucher

294 **5 Pesos** Good Fine XF
L. 1896. Black on green underprint. Waterfalls at left. Unsigned remainder. — — —

294A **10 Pesos** Good Fine XF
6.6.1907. Black on green underprint. Agriculture with cherubs at left. — — —

294B **50 Pesos** Good Fine XF
L.1896. Black on gray underprint. Justice seated at lower left. Unsigned remainder. — — —

294C 100 Pesos — Good — | Fine — | XF —
9.5.1906. Black on light orange underprint. Standing woman with sheaf at left.

294E 1000 Pesos — Good — | Fine — | XF —
21.3.1899. 2 allegorical women with fasces at left. Arms at lower right. Similar to #298. Printer: Paredes.

1900 *Tesorería del Gobierno* Provisional Issue

Notes of the "Thousand Day War" issued by Liberal forces under Gen. Uribe at Ocaña.

295 20 Centavos — Good — | Fine — | XF —
ND. (1900). Black on red underprint. Arms at right. Back: Printed signature.

295A 1 Peso — Good 75.00 | Fine 175 | XF 275
15.6.1900. Justice standing at left. Back: Footbridge over river at left. PC: Heavy white lined paper.

295B 5 Pesos — Good 100 | Fine 150 | XF 250
15.6.1900. Soldier with flag and cannon at left center. Back: Center Steamship *Peralonso* at left. PC: Heavy white lined paper.

295C 10 Pesos — Good 100 | Fine 175 | XF 300
15.6.1900. Soldier with flag and cannon at left center. Back: Center Steamship *Peralonso* at left. PC: Heavy white lined paper.

1905 *Deuda Exterior Consolidada* Issue

296 100 Pesos — Good — | Fine — | XF —
1905. Black on orange underprint. Seated figure with globe at upper left. Unsigned remainder.

1905 *Pagaré del Tesoro* Issue

297 25 Centavos — Good — | Fine — | XF —
1.5.1905. Green on orange underprint. Arms at center.

297A 50 Centavos — Good — | Fine — | XF —
1.5.1905. Black on orange underprint. Arms at center.

297B 1 Peso — Good — | Fine — | XF —
1.5.1905. Black on purple underprint. Arms at upper left and in underprint.

297D 25 Pesos — Good — | Fine — | XF —
1.2.1905. Black on light red underprint. Arms at center. Dog's head at upper left. Printer: Lit. Nacional.

1906-07 *Vale por Exacciones en la Guerra de 1899* Issue

Issued as payment for property forcibly taken by the military during the revolution of 1899-1902. Each voucher states that no interest will be paid on the principal.

298 5 Pesos — Good — | Fine — | XF —
1.5.1907. Issued as payment for property forcibly taken by the military during the revolution of 1899-1902. Voucher states that no interest will be paid on the principal. Black. 2 allegorical women with fasces at left. Arms at lower right. Back: Imprint (Paredes) blocked out at bottom. Some with cancellation. PC: Peach.

298A 10 Pesos — Good — | Fine — | XF —
6.6.1907. Issued as payment for property forcibly taken by the military during the revolution of 1899-1902. Voucher states that no interest will be paid on the principal. Black. 2 allegorical women with fasces at left. Arms at lower right. Back: Imprint (Paredes) blocked out at bottom. Some with cancellation. PC: Peach.

298B 50 Pesos — Good — | Fine — | XF —
18xx. Issued as payment for property taken by the military during the revolution of 1899-1902. Voucher states that no interest will be paid on the principal. 2 allegorical women with fasces at left. Arms at lower right. Back: Imprint (Paredes) blocked out at bottom. Some with cancellation.

298C 100 Pesos — Good — | Fine — | XF —
6.5.1906. Issued as payment for property taken by the military during the revolution of 1899-1902. Voucher states that no interest will be paid on the principal. 2 allegorical women with fasces at left. Arms at lower right. Back: Imprint (Paredes) blocked out at bottom. Some with cancellation.

298D 500 Pesos — Good — Fine — XF

1.5.1907. Issued as payment for property taken by the military during the revolution of 1899-1902. Voucher states that no interest will be paid on the principal. Black on gold underprint. 2 allegorical women with fasces at left. Arms at lower right. Back: Imprint (Paredes) blocked out at bottom. Some with cancellation. — — —

298E 1000 Pesos — Good — Fine — XF

1.5.1907. Issued as payment for property taken by the military during the revolution of 1899-1902. Voucher states that no interest will be paid on the principal. 2 allegorical women with fasces at left. Arms at lower right. Back: Imprint (Paredes) blocked out at bottom. Some with cancellation. — — —

298F 5000 Pesos — Good — Fine — XF

25.7.1907. Issued as payment for property taken by the military during the revolution of 1899-1902. Voucher states that no interest will be paid on the principal. 2 allegorical women with fasces at left. Arms at lower right. Back: Imprint (Paredes) blocked out at bottom. Some with cancellation. — — —

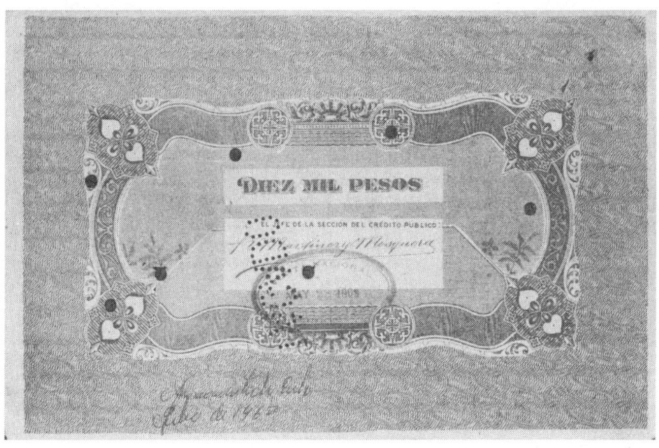

298G 10,000 Pesos — Good — Fine — XF

1.5.1907. Issued as payment for property taken by the military during the revolution of 1899-1902. Voucher states that no interest will be paid on the principal. Rare. Black on gold underprint. 2 allegorical women with fasces at left. Arms at lower right. Back: Imprint (Paredes) blocked out at bottom. Some with cancellation. — — —

1907 *Vale de Tesorería Sin Interés* Issue

299 1 Peso — Good — Fine — XF

April 1907. Purple on green underprint. Arms at lower left. Printer: Lit. Nacional. — — —

299A 5 Pesos — Good — Fine — XF

April 1907. Purple on blue-green underprint. Arms at lower left. Printer: Lit. Nacional. — — —

1908 *Vale Especial por Primas de Exportación* Issue

300 1 Peso — Good — Fine — XF

2.6.1908. Blue on green underprint. Arms at upper center. Printer: Lit. Nacional. — — —

300B 10 Pesos — Good — Fine — XF

2.6.1908. Black on light red underprint. Arms at upper center. Printer: Lit. Nacional. — — —

300C 50 Pesos — Good — Fine — XF

2.6.1908. Blue on green underprint. Arms at upper center. Printer: Lit. Nacional. — — —

300D 100 Pesos — Good — Fine — XF

2.5.1908. Black on light orange underprint. Arms at upper center. Printer: Lit. Nacional. — — —

190x *Ministerio del Tesoro - Tesorería General de la Republica* Issue

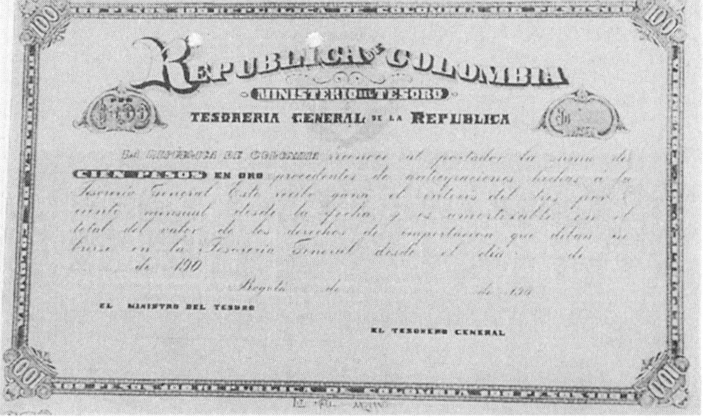

301 100 Pesos — Good — Fine — XF

190x. Black on light blue-green underprint. Unsigned remainder. — — —

1914-1918 *Bono Colombiano* Issue

302 10 Pesos — Good — Fine — XF

L. 1918. Black and red. Arms at upper left. Allegorical woman at lower right. — — —

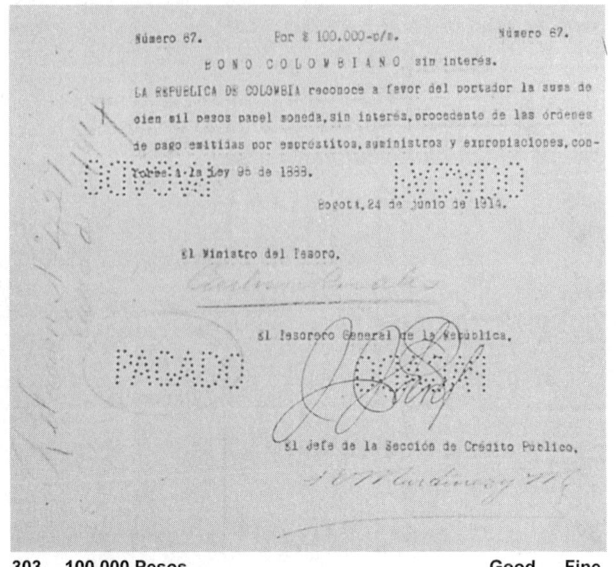

Número 67. Por $ 100.000-c/m. Número 67.

BONO COLOMBIANO sin interés.

LA REPUBLICA DE COLOMBIA reconoce a favor del portador la suma de cien mil pesos papel moneda, sin interés, procedente de las órdenes de pago emitidas por empréstitos, suministros y expropiaciones, conforme a la Ley 95 de 1888.

Bogotá, 24 de junio de 1914.

El Ministro del Tesoro.

El Tesorero General de la República.

El Jefe de la Sección de Crédito Público.

		Good	Fine	XF
303	**100,000 Pesos** 24.6.1914. Typed text in blue. Perforated *PAGADO* cancellation 4 times.	—	—	—

1917 *Vale de Tesorería* Issue

		Good	Fine	XF
304	**1 Peso** 17.12.1917. Black on red-orange underprint. Arms at left. Back: Red vertical overprint at left, handstamped date: *6 JUL 1918* at center. Imprint (Paredes) blocked out. Perforated: *PAID.*	30.00	85.00	150
304A	**5 Pesos** 17.12.1917. Black on orange underprint. Arms at left.	—	—	—
304B	**10 Pesos** 17.12.1917. Black on green underprint. Arms at left.	—	—	—
304C	**50 Pesos** 17.12.1917. Black on violet underprint. Arms at left.	—	—	—
304D	**100 Pesos** 17.12.1917. Black. Arms at left.	—	—	—

1921-1922 *Vale del Tesoro* Issue

		Good	Fine	XF
305	**1 Peso** Requires confirmation.	—	—	—
305A	**5 Pesos** 31.12.1921. Eagle. Printer: Lit. Nacional.	—	—	—

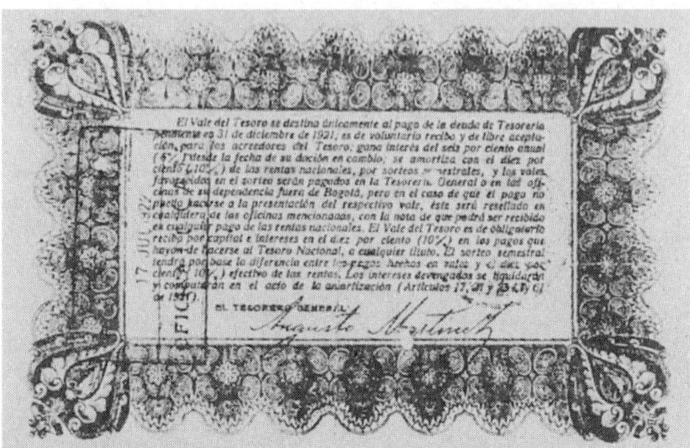

		Good	Fine	XF
305B	**20 Pesos** 8.5.1922. Black on red underprint. Eagle at upper left. Arms at lower center. Back: 17.7.1922 stamp. Printer: Lit. Nacional.	20.00	70.00	150

Banco de la República

República de Colombia

Treasury and Junta de Conversion issues leading to the establishment of the Banco de la Républica in 1923. Also the re-emergent República issues of 1938-1953.

1904 Issue

		Good	Fine	XF
309	**1 Peso** April 1904. Black on gold underprint. Arms at left. Cordoba at center. Back: Plantation scene. Printer: W&S.	2.50	15.00	65.00

		Good	Fine	XF
310	**2 Pesos** April 1904. Black on blue underprint. Arms at left. Sheep at center. Back: Rigaurte at center. Printer: W&S.	3.00	20.00	85.00

		Good	Fine	XF
311	**5 Pesos** April 1904. Black on green underprint. Arms at upper left. Church at center. Back: Portrait of Torres at center. Printer: W&S.	5.00	30.00	100
312	**10 Pesos** April 1904. Black on red underprint. Portrait Gen. A. Nariño at left, arms at right. Back: Standing helmeted woman at left. Riverboats at center. Printer: W&S.	7.50	50.00	150

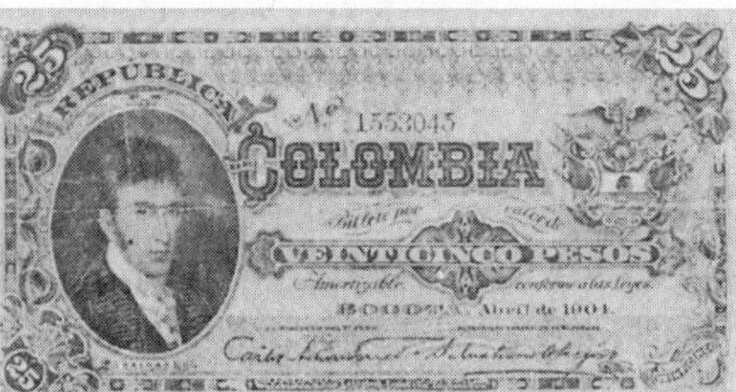

		Good	Fine	XF
313	**25 Pesos** April 1904. Black on orange underprint. Portrait of Caldas at left. Arms at right. Back: Observatory at center. Printer: W&S.	10.00	75.00	225

314	50 Pesos	Good	Fine	XF
	April 1904. Black on green underprint. Portrait of General Santander at left. Arms and cherubs at center. Plantation scene at right. Back: Standing Liberty and eagle at left. Bridge scene at center. Printer: W&S.	22.50	100	300

315	100 Pesos	Good	Fine	XF
	April 1904. Black on red underprint. Standing Simon Bolívar at left, arms at center. Back: Plaza de Bolívar at center. Printer: W&S.	17.50	70.00	250

1908 Issue

316	1000 Pesos	Good	Fine	XF
	March 1908. Black on green underprint. Portrait Simon Bolívar at center between seated allegorical woman at left, Mercury at right. Printer: W&S. Rare.	—	—	—

1910 *Junta de Conversion* Issue

317	50 Pesos	Good	Fine	XF
	August 1910. Black on olive underprint. Arms at left. Portrait of Simon Bolívar at right. Series A; B; C; D. Back: Printed signature across center. Printer: ABNC.			
	a. Issued note.	8.00	50.00	150
	s. Specimen.	—	Unc	600

318	100 Pesos	Good	Fine	XF
	August 1910. Black on orange and yellow underprint. Arms at left. Portrait of Simon Bolívar at center right. Printer: ABNC.			
	a. Issued note.	20.00	100	300
	s. Specimen.	—	Unc	1,000

1915 Pesos Oro Issue

321	1 Peso Oro	Good	Fine	XF
	20.7.1915. Black on green and multicolor underprint. Portrait S. Bolívar at left. Series A-J. Back: Arms at center. Large heading at top with 10-line text in square at center. Printer: ABNC.			
	a. Issued note.	8.00	40.00	225
	s. Specimen.	—	Unc	800

322	2 Pesos Oro	Good	Fine	XF
	20.7.1915. Black on blue and multicolor underprint. Portrait of General A. Nariño at center. Series A-E. Back: Arms at center. Printer: ABNC.			
	a. Issued note.	20.00	100	400
	s. Specimen.	—	Unc	1,000

323	5 Pesos Oro	Good	Fine	XF
	20.7.1915. Series F was actually issued by the Banco de la Republica. Black on orange and multicolor underprint. Portrait Córdoba at left center. Condor at right. Series A-F. Back: Arms at center. Printer: ABNC.			
	a. Issued note.	10.00	50.00	300
	s. Specimen.	—	Unc	700

324	10 Pesos Oro	Good	Fine	XF
	20.7.1915. Series D was actually issued by the Banco de la República. Black on green, purple and orange underprint. Portrait General Santander at left. Large dollar sign at center. Arms at right. Series A-D. Back: National capitol. 3 printed signatures beneath. Printer: ABNC.			
	a. Issued note.	18.00	125	400
	s. Specimen.	—	Unc	750

1919 *Cédula de Tesorería* Provisional Issue

		Good	Fine	XF
325	**1 Peso** 1.4.1919; 1.6.1919. Overprint on #S366 or S367. Bank name and portrait obscured. Back: Bank name partially obscured at bottom.	35.00	100	250

		Good	Fine	XF
326	**5 Pesos** 1.4.1919. Overprint on #S368. Bank name and portrait obscrued. Back: Bank name partially obscured at bottom	—	—	—

		Good	Fine	XF
327	**10 Pesos** 1.4.1919. Overprint on #S369. Bank name and portrait obscured. Back: Bank name partially obscured.	—	—	—

1922 *Bono del Tesoro* Treasury Bond Provisional Issue

#331-332 Junta de Conversion issue authorized by Law 6 and Decree #166 of 1922, and Public Notice #206 of 8.2.1922.

		VG	VF	UNC
331	**1 Peso Oro** 1922 (-old date 20.7.1915). Junta de Conversion issue authorized by Law 6 and Decree #166 of 1922, and Public Notice #206 of 8.2.1922. Red overprint *BONO DEL TESORO* across face. Series J.	50.00	175	—

		VG	VF	UNC
332	**5 Pesos Oro** 1922 (- old date 20.7.1915). Overprint on face and back of #323 as above. Red overprint *BONO DEL TESORO*. Back: Red overprint large heading at top with 10-line text in square at center.	100	300	—

1938 Pesos Oro Issue

		VG	VF	UNC
341	**5 Pesos Oro** 22.3.1938. Black on multicolor underprint. Córdoba at center. Series A. Back: Arms at center. Printer: ABNC.			
	a. Issued note.	7.50	30.00	120
	s. Specimen.	—	—	175

		VG	VF	UNC
342	**10 Pesos Oro** 22.3.1938. Black on multicolor underprint. Portrait General Santander at left. Bust of S. Bolívar at right. Series B. Back: Arms at center. Printer: ABNC.			
	a. Issued note.	10.00	50.00	140
	s. Specimen.	—	—	250

Note: Since the Banco de la República could not issue notes without gold backing after 1923, the Treasury issued the 5 and 10 Pesos dated 1938 and the 1/2 Pesos of 1948 and 1953. These notes were signed by the Minister of Finance, the Treasurer and the Comptroller, and were designed to contravene the law concerning issuance of notes w/o gold backing. The notes were needed because of the worldwide depression of the 1930's. In reality these notes are emergency issues that eventually became legal tender within the Banco de la República system.

1948-1953 Pesos Oro Issue

		VG	VF	UNC
345	**1/2 Peso Oro** 1948; 1953. Brown on multicolor underprint. Portrait of Gen. A. Nariño at center. Series C. Back: Arms at center. Printer: ABNC.			
	a. Prefix letter A; B. 16.1.1948.	1.00	4.00	50.00
	b. Prefix letter C. 18.2.1953.	1.00	4.00	50.00
	s. As a or b. Specimen.	—	—	125

Banco de la República

1923 *Certificados Sobre Consignación de Oro*

Gold Certificates Provisional Issue

		VG	VF	UNC
351	**2 1/2 Pesos** ND (- old date 1.5.1920). Black on green and multicolor underprint. Printer: ABNC. Rare.	—	—	—

		VG	VF	UNC
352	**5 Pesos** ND (-old date 15.9.1919). Black on brown and multicolor underprint. Printer: ABNC. Rare.	—	—	—

		VG	VF	UNC
353	**10 Pesos** ND. Black on orange and multicolor underprint. Printer: ABNC. Rare.	—	—	—

		VG	VF	UNC
354	**20 Pesos** ND. Black on blue and multicolor underprint. Printer: ABNC. Rare.	—	—	—

#355-360 not assigned.

1923 Pesos Oro Issue

		VG	VF	UNC
361	**1 Peso Oro** 20.7.1923. Blue on multicolor underprint Bank name below upper frame in Gothic lettering. Portrait Caldas at center. Series A. Back: Liberty head at center, printed signature below. Printer: ABNC.			
	a. Issued note.	20.00	100	450
	s. Specimen.	—	—	675

362	2 Pesos Oro	VG	VF	UNC
	20.7.1923. Green on multicolor underprint. Bank name below upper frame in Gothic lettering. Porteait C. Torres at center. Series B. Back: Liberty head at center, printed signature below. Printer: ABNC.			
	a. Issued note.	45.00	150	750
	s. Specimen.	—	—	1,000

363	5 Pesos Oro	VG	VF	UNC
	20.7.1923. Brown on multicolor underprint. Bank name below upper frame in Gothic lettering. Portrait Córdoba at left. Series C. Back: Liberty head at center, printed signature below. Printer: ABNC.			
	a. Issued note.	45.00	150	800
	s. Specimen.	—	—	1,500

364	10 Pesos Oro	VG	VF	UNC
	20.7.1923. Black on multicolor underprint. Portrait Gen. A. Nariño at right. Series D. Bank name below upper frame in Gothic lettering. Back: Liberty head at center, printed signature below. Printer: ABNC.			
	a. Issued note.	42.50	140	800
	p1. Face proof. Without series or serial #. Punch hole cancelled.	—	—	175
	p2. Back proof. Punch hole cancelled.	—	—	100
	s. Specimen.	—	—	1,750

365	50 Pesos Oro	VG	VF	UNC
	20.7.1923. Dark brown on multicolor underprint. Portrait A.J. de Sucre at left. Series E. Back: Liberty head at center, printed signature below. Printer: ABNC.			
	a. Issued note.	150	600	—
	s. Specimen.	—	—	3,000

366	100 Pesos Oro	VG	VF	UNC
	20.7.1923. Purple on multicolor underprint. Portrait Gen. Santander at center. Series F.Bank name below upper frame in Gothic lettering. Back: Liberty head at center, printed signature below. Printer: ABNC.			
	a. Issued note.	125	500	—
	s. Specimen.	—	—	3,250

367	500 Pesos Oro	VG	VF	UNC
	20.7.1923. Olive green on multicolor underprint. Bank name below upper frame in Gothic lettering. Portrait S. Bolívar at right. Series G. Back: Liberty head at center, printed signature below. Printer: ABNC.			
	a. Rare.	—	—	—
	s. Specimen.	—	—	5,000

1926-1928 Issue

371	1 Peso Oro	VG	VF	UNC
	1.1.1926. Orange on multicolor underprint. Bank name as part of upper frame in standard lettering. Portrait S. Bolívar at center. Series H. Back: Liberty head at center, printed signature below. Printer: ABNC.			
	a. Issued note.	9.00	37.50	225
	s. Specimen.	—	—	400

372	2 Pesos Oro	VG	VF	UNC
	1.1.1926. Olive on multicolor underprint. Bank name as part of upper frame in standard lettering. Portrait C. Torres at center. Series I. Back: Liberty head at center, printed signature below. Printer: ABNC.			
	a. Issued note.	30.00	125	600
	s. Specimen.	—	—	1,100

373	5 Pesos Oro	VG	VF	UNC
	1926; 1928. Blue on multicolor underprint. Bank name as part of upper frame in standard lettering. Portrait Córdoba at left. Back: Liberty head at center, printed signature below. Printer: ABNC.			
	a. Series J. 1.1.1926.	25.00	100	500
	b. Series M. 1.1.1928.	3.50	17.50	125
	p1. As a. Face proof. Without series or serial #.	—	—	175
	p2. As a. Back proof.	—	—	100
	s1. As a. Specimen.	—	—	1,250
	s2. As b. Specimen.	—	—	250

374	10 Pesos Oro	VG	VF	UNC
	1926; 1928. Purple on multicolor underprint. Portrait Gen. A. Nariño at right.			
	a. Series K. 1.1.1926.	30.00	100	575
	b. Series N. 1.1.1928.	10.00	35.00	250
	p1. As a. Face proof. Without series or serial #.	—	—	175
	p2. Back proof.	—	—	100
	s1. As a. Specimen.	—	—	1,250
	s2. As b. Specimen.	—	—	550

375	50 Pesos Oro	VG	VF	UNC
	1926; 1928. Green on multicolor underprint. Portrait A.J. de Sucre at left.			
	a. Series L. 1.1.1926.	50.00	200	700
	b. Series P. 20.7.1928.	30.00	110	525
	p1. As a. Face proof. Without series or serial #.	—	—	125
	p2. Back proof.	—	—	100
	s. Specimen.	—	—	1,500

375A	100 Pesos Oro	VG	VF	UNC
	20.7.1928. Brown on multicolor underprint. Bank name as part of upper frame in standard lettering. Portrait Gen. Santander at center. Series Q. Back: Liberty head at center, printed signature below. Printer: ABNC.			
	a. Issued note.	50.00	300	850
	p1. Face proof. without series or serial #.	—	—	175
	p2. Back proof.	—	—	100
	s. Specimen.	—	—	1,750

1927 Issue

376	5 Pesos Oro	VG	VF	UNC
	20.7.1927. Green on multicolor underprint. Portrait Córdoba and seated allegorical woman at left. Watermark area at right. Series M. Back: Older bank at Bogota. Signature below. Printer: TDLR.	10.00	50.00	225

377	10 Pesos Oro	VG	VF	UNC
	20.7.1927. Blue on multicolor underprint. Watermark area at right. Portrait Gen. A. Nariño and Mercury at left. Series N. Back: Bank at Medelin, printed signature below. Printer: TDLR.	20.00	125	475

378	20 Pesos Oro	VG	VF	UNC
	20.7.1927. Violet on multicolor underprint. Watermark area at right. Portrait Caldas and allegorical woman at left. Series O. Back: Older bank at Barranquilla, printed signature below. Printer: TDLR.	25.00	125	475

1929 Issue

380	1 Peso Oro	VG	VF	UNC
	1929-54. Blue on multicolor underprint. Portrait Gen. Santander and standing allegorical male at left, bust of S.Bolívar at right. Back: Liberty at center. Printer: ABNC.			
	a. Series R in red. 20.7.1929.	0.75	3.50	25.00
	b. Signature and series like a. 20.7.1940.	0.25	2.00	20.00
	c. Series R in red. 20.7.1942; 20.7.1943.	0.25	1.50	15.00
	d. Series R in blue. 20.7.1944; 1.1.1945.	0.25	2.00	18.00

	VG	VF	UNC
e. Series R in blue. 20.7.1946; 7.8.1947 (prefixes A-F).	0.25	2.00	18.00
f. Series HH. 1.1.1950.	0.25	1.00	7.00
g. Series HH. 1.1.1954.	0.25	1.00	7.00
p. Face proof. ND, no series. Punch hole cancelled.	—	—	75.00
s1. As e. Specimen.	—	—	125

1931 ND *Certificados de Plata*

Silver Certificates Provisional Issue

CERTIFICADO DE PLATA
CAMBIABLE A SU PRESENTACION EN EL
BANCO DE LA REPUBLICA
POR IGUAL VALOR EN MONEDAS
LEGALES DE PLATA

		VG	VF	UNC
381	**5 Pesos** ND (1931- old date 20.7.1915).	75.00	200	650

1932 Issue

		VG	VF	UNC
382	**1 Peso** 1.1.1932. Green on multicolor underprint. Portrait Gen. Santander at center. Back: Liberty at center. Printer: ABNC.	6.50	40.00	225

		VG	VF	UNC
383	**5 Pesos** 1.1.1932. Blue on multicolor underprint. Portrait Gen. A. Nariño at center. Back: Liberty at center. Printer: ABNC.			
	a. Issued note.	25.00	200	600
	p1. Face proof. Without serial #.	—	—	175
	p2. Back proof.	—	—	100

1935 Peso Oro Issue

		VG	VF	UNC
384	**1/2 Peso Oro** 20.7.1935. Brown on multicolor underprint. Bust of Caldas at left center. Bust of S. Bolívar at right. Series S. Back: Liberty at center. Printer: ABNC.	20.00	125	475

1938 Pesos Oro Commemorative Issue

#385, 400th Anniversary - Founding of Bogotá 1538-1938

		VG	VF	UNC
385	**1 Peso Oro** 6.8.1938. 400th Anniversary-Founding of Bogota 1538-1938. Blue on multicolor underprint. Portrait G. Ximenez de Quesada in medallion supported with two allegorical angels at center. Series T. Back: Scene of founding of Bogotá at center. Printer: ABNC.			
	a. Issued note.	15.00	50.00	375
	p1. Face proof. Without series or serial #.	—	—	175
	p2. Back proof.	—	—	125
	s. Specimen.	—	—	650

1940 Issue

		VG	VF	UNC
386	**5 Pesos Oro** 1940-1950. Blue on multicolor underprint. Portrait Cordoba at left-Like #373. Back: Without title: *CAJERO* and signature.			
	a. Series M in red. 20.7.1940.	1.00	6.00	40.00
	b. Series M in red. 20.7.1942; 20.7.1943.	0.50	3.00	35.00
	c. Series M in blue. 20.7.1944; 1.1.1945; 20.7.1946; 7.8.1947.	0.50	3.00	35.00
	d. Series M. 12.10.1949.	0.25	1.50	22.50
	e. Series FF. 1.1.1950.	0.25	1.50	22.50
	p1. As b. 20.7.1942. Face proof. Without series or serial #.	—	—	175
	p2. Back proof.	—	—	100
	p3. Face proof. As e. 1.1.1950. Series FF.	—	—	90.00
	s. As c. Specimen.	—	—	125

1941 *Certificados de Plata* Silver Certificates Issue

		VG	VF	UNC
387	**1 Peso** 1.1.1941. Green on multicolor underprint. Portrait Gen. Santander at left. Back: Liberty at center.	7.00	25.00	200

		VG	VF	UNC
388	**5 Pesos** 1.1.1941. Black on multicolor underprint. Portrait Gen. A. Nariño at left. Back: Liberty at center-like #387.			
	a. Issued note.	4.00	15.00	100
	p1. Face proof. Without series #, punch hole cancelled.	—	—	175
	p2. Back proof.	—	—	75.00

1941 Pesos Oro Issue

		VG	VF	UNC
389	**10 Pesos Oro** 1941-1963. Purple on multicolor underprint. Portrait Gen. A. Nariño at lower right. Back: Without title: *CAJERO* and signature on back.			
	a. Series N in red. 20.7.1941.	1.50	8.00	50.00
	b. Series N. 20.7.1943; 20.7.1944; 7.8.1947.	1.00	5.00	30.00
	c. Series N. 1.1.1945.	1.25	7.50	40.00
	d. Series N. 12.10.1949.	0.75	3.00	18.00
	e. Series EE. 1.1.1950.	0.25	0.75	7.50
	f. Series EE. 2.1.1963.	0.25	0.75	7.50
	p. Face proof. Without serial #. Punch hole cancelled.	—	—	90.00
	s. As b. Specimen.	—	—	125

1942 Pesos Oro Issue

		VG	VF	UNC
390	**2 Pesos** 1942-1955. Portrait of Torres. Like #372. Back: Without title: *CAJERO* and signature on back.			
	a. Series I in red. 20.7.1942; 20.7.1943.	0.50	4.00	35.00
	b. Series I in olive. 20.7.1944; 1.1.1945; 7.8.1947.	0.50	3.00	30.00
	c. Series GG. 1.1.1950.	0.50	2.50	25.00
	d. Series GG. 1.1.1955.	0.25	1.00	8.00
	p1. As a. 20.7.1942. Face proof. Without series or serial #.	—	—	175
	p2. Back proof.	—	—	100
	s. As b. Specimen.	—	—	125
391	**500 Pesos** 1942-1953. Portrait S. Bolivar at right. Back: Without title: *CAJERO* and signature.	VG	VF	UNC
	a. Series G in red. 20.7.1942.	50.00	225	850
	b. Series G in olive. 20.7.1944; 1.1.1945; 7.8.1947 (prefix A).	40.00	100	385
	c. Series AA. 1.1.1950.	15.00	60.00	325
	d. Series AA. 1.1.1951; 1.1.1953.	10.00	30.00	90.00
	p1. As a. Face proof. Without series or serial #. Punch hole cancelled.	—	—	150
	p2. As d. 1.1.1951. Face proof. Without serial #. Punch hole cancelled.	—	—	150
	p3. As d. 1.1.1953. Face proof. Without serial #. Punch hole cancelled.	—	—	150
	s1. As a. Specimen.	—	—	1,250
	s2. As b. Specimen.	—	—	550

Note: For 500 Pesos dated 1964, see #408 in Volume 3, Modern Issues.

1943 Pesos Oro Issue

		VG	VF	UNC
392	**20 Pesos Oro** 1943-1963. Purple and multicolor. Bust of Francisco José de Caldas at left, bust of Simon Bolívar at right. Back: Liberty at center. Printer: ABNC.			
	a. Series U in red. 20.7.1943.	20.00	200	500
	b. Series U in purple. 20.7.1944; 1.1.1945.	10.00	60.00	200
	c. Series U. Prefix A. 7.8.1947.	3.00	15.00	80.00
	d. Series DD. 1.1.1950; 1.1.1951.	1.50	7.50	50.00
	e. Series DD. 2.1.1963.	1.50	7.50	50.00
	s. Specimen.	—	—	65.00

		VG	VF	UNC
393	**50 Pesos Oro** 1944-1958. Green on multicolor underprint. Back: Like #375, but without title: *CAJERO* and signature. Printer: ABNC.			
	a. Series P. 20.7.1944; 1.1.1945.	6.00	20.00	110
	b. Series P. Prefix A. 7.8.1947.	1.00	5.00	60.00
	c. Series CC. 1.1.1950; 1.1.1951.	1.00	4.00	30.00
	d. Series CC. 1.1.1953.	1.00	4.00	30.00
	e. Series CC. 1.1.1958.	1.00	3.00	25.00
	p1. As a. 20.7.1944. Face proof. Without series or serial #.	—	—	150
	p2. As c. 1.1.1951. Face proof.Without serial #. Punch hole cancelled.	—	—	150
	p3. As d. 1.1.1953. Face proof. Without serial #. Punch hole cancelled.	—	—	150
	s. Specimen.	—	—	375

1943 Issue

394	100 Pesos Oro	VG	VF	UNC
	1944-1957. Like #375A. Back: Without *CAJERO* title and signature. Printer: ABNC.			
	a. Series Q. 20.7.1944; 1.1.1945; 7.8.1947. Prefix A.	6.00	40.00	135
	b. Series BB. 1.1.1950.	5.00	25.00	125
	c. Series BB. 1.1.1951.	2.00	12.50	60.00
	d. Series BB. 1.1.1953; 20.7.1957.	1.50	6.00	35.00
	p1. As a. 20.7.1944. Face proof. Without series or serial #.	—	—	150
	p2. As c. Face proof. Without serial #. Punch hole cancelled.	—	—	150
	p3. As d. 1.1.1953. Face proof. Without serial #. Punched hole cancelled.	—	—	150
	p4. As d. 20.7.1957. Face proof. Without serial #. Punched hole cancelled.	—	—	150
	s. Specimen.	—	—	350

1946 ND Provisional Issue

As a result of a scarcity of coins in circulation, the Banco de la República took certain quantities of *R* series 1 Peso notes dated 1942 and 1943, sliced them in half and overprint each half as a Half Peso. The 1942 dated notes are Serial #57 000 001 - 58 000 000 (Group 1), while the 1943 dated notes are Serial # 70 000 001 - 70 250 000 (Group 2).

397	1/2 Peso	VG	VF	UNC
	ND (1946-old dates 20.7.1942 and 20.7.1943). Back: Halves of *R* series of #380c overprint in black squares as Half Peso on face, words *MEDIO*			
	a. Printer's name: *LITOGRAFIA COLOMBIA, S.A. - BOGOTA* as part of black overprint on face of l. half. ND. Group 1.	75.00	250	600
	b. Overprint as a. on face of right half (old date 20.7.1942). Group 1.	75.00	250	600
	c. Without local printer's name as part of black overprint on left half of face. ND. Group 1.	75.00	250	600
	d. As c, on right half (old date 20.7.1942). Group 1.	75.00	250	600
	e. As c, but Group 2.	75.00	300	700
	f. As d, but old date 20.7.1943. Group 2.	100	350	700

1953 Pesos Oro Issue

398	1 Peso Oro	VG	VF	UNC
	7.8.1953. Blue on multicolor underprint. Standing S. Bólivar statue at left, bridge of Boyaca at center, portrait Gen. Santander at right. Series A. Printer: W&S.	0.25	0.75	4.50

399	5 Pesos Oro	VG	VF	UNC
	1.1.1953. Green on multicolor underprint. Portrait Cordoba and seated allegorical woman at left-similar to #376 but numeral in guilloche instead of watermark at right. Series M. Back: Long view of older bank building at Bogotá. Printer: TDLR.			
	a. Issued note.	0.25	2.50	17.50
	s. Specimen. With red TDLR oval stamp and *SPECIMEN*.	—	—	200

1953 Pesos Oro Issue

400	10 Pesos Oro	VG	VF	UNC
	1953-1961. Blue on multicolor underprint. Similar to #377, but palm trees at right instead of watermark. Portrait General Antonio Nariño with Mercury alongside at left. Back: Bank building at Cali. Series N. Printer: TDLR.			
	a. 1.1.1953.	1.00	7.50	50.00
	b. 1.1.1958; 1.1.1960.	1.00	7.50	50.00
	c. 2.1.1961.	1.00	7.50	50.00
	s1. Specimen. With red TDLR and *SPECIMEN* overprint. Punch hole cancelled.	—	—	100
	s2. Specimen. Red overprint: *SPECIMEN*.	—	—	100

401	20 Pesos Oro	VG	VF	UNC
	1953-1965. Red-brown on multicolor underprint. Similar to #378, but Liberty in circle at right instead of watermark. Portrait Francisco José de Caldas and allegory at left. Series O. Back: Newer bank building at Barranquilla on back. Printer: TDLR.			
	a. 1.1.1953.	1.00	7.50	45.00
	b. 1.1.1960.	1.00	7.50	45.00
	c. 2.1.1961; 2.1.1965.	1.00	6.00	40.00
	s1. Specimen. With red TDLR overprint and *SPECIMEN*. Punch hole cancelled.	—	—	100
	s2. Specimen. Red overprint: *SPECIMEN*. Punch hole cancelled.	—	—	65.00

1958 Pesos Oro Issue

402	50 Pesos Oro	VG	VF	UNC
	1958-1967. Light brown on multicolor underprint. Portrait Antonio José de Sucre at lower left. Series Z. Back: Liberty at center. Printer: ABNC.			
	a. 20.7.1958; 7.8.1960.	1.00	10.00	100
	b. 1.1.1964; 12.10.1967.	1.00	8.00	70.00
	s1. Specimen.	—	—	135
	s2. Specimen. Red overprint: *SPECIMEN*. Punch hole cancelled.	—	—	150

403	100 Pesos Oro	VG	VF	UNC
	1958-1967. Gray on multicolor underprint. Portrait General Francisco de Paula Santander at right. Series Y. Back: Liberty at center. Printer: ABNC.			
	a. 7.8.1958.	1.00	8.00	70.00
	b. 1.1.1960; 1.1.1964.	1.00	6.00	90.00
	c. 20.7.1965; 20.7.1967.	1.00	6.00	90.00
	p1. Face proof. Without date, signatures, series or serial #. Punch hole cancelled.	—	—	150
	s. Specimen.	—	—	125

1959-1960 Pesos Oro Issue

404	1 Peso Oro	VG	VF	UNC
	1959-1977. Blue on multicolor underprint. Portrait Simón Bolívar at left, portrait General Francisco de Paula Santander at right. Back: Liberty head and condor with waterfall and mountain at center. Printer: Imprenta de Billets-Bogota.			
	a. Security thread. 12.10.1959.	0.25	2.50	12.50
	b. Security thread. 2.1.1961; 7.8.1962; 2.1.1963; 12.10.1963; 2.1.1964; 12.10.1964.	0.20	2.00	9.00
	c. As b. 20.7.1966.	1.25	10.00	40.00
	d. Without security thread. 20.7.1966; 20.7.1967; 1.2.1968; 2.1.1969.	0.15	1.25	6.00
	e. Without security thread. 1.5.1970; 12.10.1970; 7.8.1971; 20.7.1972; 7.8.1973; 7.8.1974.	0.10	0.50	4.00
	f. As e. 1.1.1977.	0.75	5.00	35.00
	s1. Specimen.	—	—	60.00
	s2. Specimen. Red overprint: *ESPECIMEN.* on face	—	—	60.00

1959-1960 Pesos Oro Issue

405	5 Pesos Oro	VG	VF	UNC
	20.7.1960. Green on multicolor underprint. Portrait José María Córdoba and seated allegory at left. Like #399. Series M. Back: Tall view of new bank building at Bogotá. Printer: TDLR.	1.00	3.00	12.50

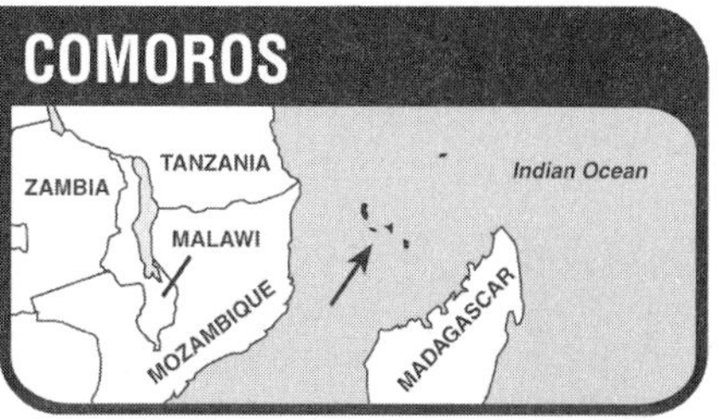

The Union of the Comoros, a volcanic archipelago located in the Mozambique Channel of the Indian Ocean 483 km. northwest of Madagascar, has an area of 2,170 sq. km. and a population of 731,800. Capital: Moroni. The economy of the islands is based on agriculture. There are practically no mineral resources. Vanilla, essence for perfumes, copra and sisal are exported.

Comoros has endured more than 20 coups or attempted coups since gaining independence from France in 1975. In 1997, the islands of Anjouan and Moheli declared independence from Comoros. In 1999, military chief Col. Azali seized power in a bloodless coup, and helped negotiate the 2000 Fomboni Accords power-sharing agreement in which the federal presidency rotates among the three islands, and each island maintains its own local government. Azali won the 2002 Presidential election, and each island in the archipelago elected its own president. Azali stepped down in 2006 and President Sambi took office. Since 2006, Anjouan's President Mohamed Bacar has refused to work effectively with the Union presidency. In 2007, Bacar effected Anjouan's de-facto secession from the Union, refusing to step down in favor of fresh Anjouanais elections when Comoros' other islands held legitimate elections in July. The African Union (AU) initially attempted to resolve the political crisis by applying sanctions and a naval blockade on Anjouan, but in March 2008, AU and Comoran soldiers seized the island. The move was generally welcomed by the island's inhabitants. Its present status is that of a French Territorial Collectivity. Euro coinage and currency circulates there.

RULERS:

French to 1975

MONETARY SYSTEM:

1 Franc = 100 Centimes

FRENCH ADMINISTRATION

Government of the Comoros

1920 ND Emergency Postage Stamp Issue

#A1-1C small adhesive postage stamps of Madagascar depicting Navigation and Commerce, Scott #32, 43, 44, and 46; Moheli, Scott #12 affixed to rectangular pressboard w/animals printed on the back (similar to the Madagascar stamps, Scott #A7).

A1	0.05 Franc	Good	Fine	XF
	ND (1920). Green adhesive stamp. Blue legend at bottom *MADAGASCAR ET DEPENDANCES.* Back: Dog. Requires confirmation.	—	—	—

1	0.50 Franc	Good	Fine	XF
	ND (1920). Pink adhesive stamp. Blue legend at bottom *MADAGASCAR ET DEPENDANCES.* Back: Dog.	350	750	—

1A	0.50 Franc	Good	Fine	XF
	ND (1920). Brown adhesive stamp. Red legend at bottom *MOHELI.* Back: Dog.	350	750	—
1B	**0.50 Franc**	**Good**	**Fine**	**XF**
	ND (1920). Dark pink adhesive stamp. Blue legend at bottom *MADAGASCAR ET DEPENDANCES.* Back: Zebu.	—	—	—
1C	**1 Franc**	**Good**	**Fine**	**XF**
	ND (1920). Green adhesive stamp. Red legend at bottom *MADAGASCAR ET DEPENDANCES.* Back: Dog.	—	—	—

REPUBLIC

Banque de Madagascar et des Comores

1960 ND Provisional Issue

2	**50 Francs**	VG	VF	UNC
	ND (1960-1963). Brown and multicolor. Woman with hat at right. Back: Man.			
	a. Signature titles: *LE CONTROLEUR GAL.* and *LE DIRECTEUR GAL.* ND (1960).	—	—	—
	b. Signature titles: *LE DIRECTEUR GAL. ADJOINT* and *LE PRESIDENT DIRECTEUR GAL.* ND (1963). 2 sign varieties.	5.00	30.00	105
	s. Specimen.	—	—	—

3	**100 Francs**	VG	VF	UNC
	ND (1960-1963). Multicolor. Woman at right, palace of the Queen of Tananariva in background. Back: Woman, boats and animals.			
	a. Signature titles: *LE CONTROLEUR GAL.* and *LE DIRECTEUR GAL.* ND (1960).	8.00	60.00	175
	b. Signature titles: *LE DIRECTEUR GAL. ADJOINT* and *LE PRESIDENT DIRECTEUR GAL.* ND (1963).	3.00	18.00	70.00
	s. Specimen.	—	—	—

Color Abbreviation Guide

New to the *Standard Catalog of ® World Paper Money* are the following abbreviations related to color references:

BC: Back color
PC: Paper color

4	**500 Francs**	VG	VF	UNC
	ND (1960-1963). Multicolor. Man with fruit at center.			
	a. Signature titles: *LE CONTROLEUR GAL* and *LE DIRECTEUR GAL.* - old date 30.6.1950; 9.10.1952 (1960).	25.00	170	550
	b. Signature titles: *LE DIRECTEUR GAL. ADJOINT* and *LE PRESIDENT DIRECTEUR GAL.* ND (1963).	12.50	110	380

5	**1000 Francs**	VG	VF	UNC
	ND (1960-1963). Multicolor. Woman and man at left center. Back: Center Ox cart.			
	a. Signature titles: *LE CONTROLEUR GAL.* and *LE DIRECTEUR GAL.* - old date 1950-52; 9.10.1952 (1960).	35.00	220	650
	b. Signature titles: *LE DIRECTEUR GAL. ADJOINT* and *LE PRESIDENT DIRECTEUR GAL.* ND (1963).	20.00	130	425

6	**5000 Francs**	VG	VF	UNC
	ND (1960-1963). Multicolor. Portrait Gallieni at upper left, young woman at right. Back: Huts at left, woman with baby at right.			
	a. Signature titles: *LE CONTROLEUR GAL.* and *LE DIRECTEUR GAL.* - old date 30.6.1950 (1960).	150	450	1,000
	b. Signature titles: *LE DIRECTEUR GAL. ADJOINT* and *LE PRESIDENT DIRECTEUR GAL.* ND (1963).	100	350	850
	c. Signature titles: *LE DIRECTEUR GÉNÉRAL* and *LE PRÉSIDENT DIRECTEUR GAL.*	125	350	850

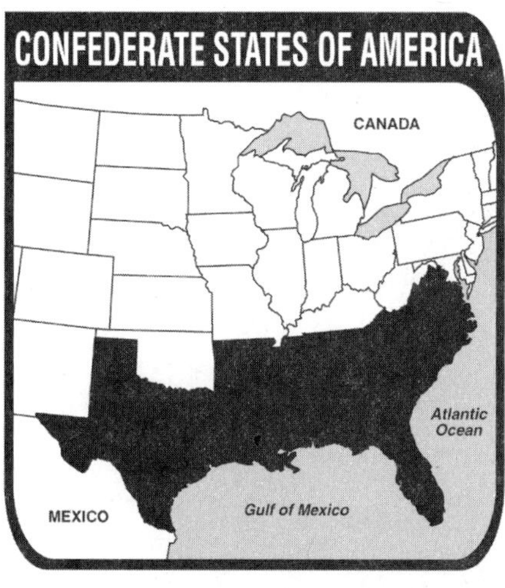

The Confederate States of America (1861-1865) was a federal republic constituted by the 11 Southern states which seceded from the United States after the election of Abraham Lincoln as President. In the order of their secession, the 11 members of the Confederate States of America were South Carolina, Mississippi, Florida, Alabama, Georgia, Louisiana, Texas, Arkansas, North Carolina, Virginia and Tennessee. The seceded states had left the Union separately and were in effect separate nations, each too small to withstand economic pressures or attack by the Union Army. On Feb. 4, 1861, delegations from South Carolina, Mississippi, Florida, Alabama, Georgia, and Louisiana - Texas arrived later - met in Montgomery, Alabama to organize a Southern nation dedicated to states' rights and the protection of slavery. A provisional government was formed and Jefferson Davis was elected President. The secession crisis precipitated the Civil War - officially known as the War of the Rebellion and, in the South, as the War Between the States - which ended in Union victory and the collapse of the Confederate States of America. The secession states were eventually readmitted to the Union. To finance the war, both the Confederacy and its constituent states issued paper currency, the redemption of which is specifically forbidden by Section 4 of the 14th Amendment to the U.S. Constitution. WATERMARKS "NY" "TEN" "FIVE" "CSA" in Block letters "CSA" in Script letters "J. WHATMAN 1862" "HODGKINSON & CO. WOOKEY HOLE MILL" "CSA" in block letters with wavy borderline.

MONETARY SYSTEM

1 Dollar = 100 Cents

Note: *SL#* in the listings refer to the *Confederate States Paper Money book*.

SECESSIONIST STATES

Confederate States of America

Montgomery, Alabama

Note: Punch cancelled notes are worth less than values shown.

1861 Issue

#1-4 Handwritten dates of May-June, 1861. Interest Bearing Notes. Printer: NBNC.

		Good	Fine	XF
1	**50 Dollars** 5.6.1861. Green and black. Males hoeing cotton at center. Plate letter A. Printer: NBNC. 1,606 issued. *(SL #1).* Interest bearing note. Handwritten.	5,000	12,000	30,000

		Good	Fine	XF
2	**100 Dollars** 5.6.1861. Green and black. Columbia at left, steam train depot scene at center. Plate letter A. Printer: NBNC. 1,606 issued. *(SL #1).* Interest bearing note. Handwritten.	4,000	9,000	20,000

		Good	Fine	XF
3	**500 Dollars** 5.6.1861. Green and black. Steam passenger train crossing viaduct, cattle below. Plate letter A. Printer: NBNC. 607 issued. *(SL #3).* Interest bearing note. Handwritten.	10,000	20,000	45,000

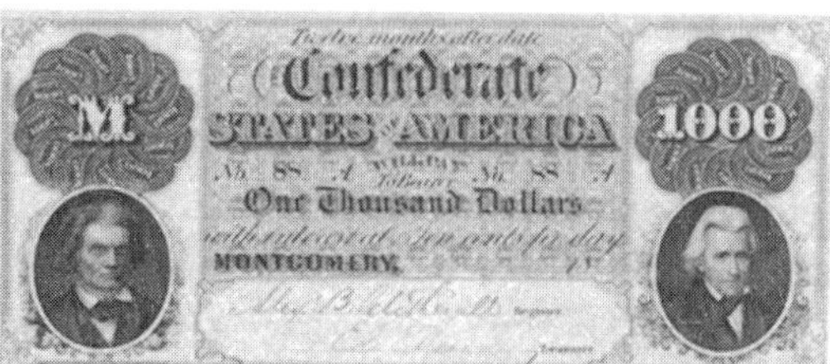

		Good	Fine	XF
4	**1000 Dollars** 5.6.1861. Green and black. Portrait Calhoun at lower left, Jackson at lower right. Plate letter A. Printer: NBNC. 607 issued. *(SL #4).* Interest bearing note. Handwritten.	12,500	22,000	45,000

Richmond, Virginia

Note: Punch cancelled notes are worth less than values shown.

1861 (First) Issue, Aug.-Sept.

#5-6 usually have handwritten dates of Aug.-Sept. 1861. Printer: Southern BNC. Interest Bearing Notes.

		Good	Fine	XF
5	**50 Dollars** 8.9.1861. Green and black. Justice at left, Pallas and Ceres seated on cotton bale at center, portrait Washington at right. Plate letter B. *(SL #5).* Printer: Southern BNC. *(SL #5).* 5,798 issued. Interest bearing note. Usually handwritten.	350	1,500	4,000

		Good	Fine	XF
6	**100 Dollars** 8.9.1861. Green and black. Justice at lower left, steam passenger train at center, Minerva at right. Plate letter B. Printer: Southern BNC. *(SL #6).* 5,798 issued. Interest bearing note. Usually handwritten.	500	2,000	5,000

1861 (Second) Issue, July

		Good	Fine	XF
7	**5 Dollars** 25.7.1861. *FIVE* at left, *Confederate States of America* in blue. Plate letters F-I. Printer: J. Manouvrier. *(SL #7).*	500	4,000	7,000

		Good	Fine	XF
8	**5 Dollars** 25.7.1861. Sailor at lower left, Liberty seated above *5* with eagle at center. Plate letters B; Bb. Printer: H & L. *(SL #8).*	300	2,000	—

#	Description	Good	Fine	XF
9	**10 Dollars** 25.7.1861. Woman at lower left, Liberty seated above shield with flag and eagle at center. Plate letters A; B; C. Printer: H & L. *(SL #9).*	140	750	4,000

#	Description	Good	Fine	XF
10	**20 Dollars** 25.7.1861. Sailing ship at center. Plate letters B, C; Cc; Ccc; D. Printer: H & L. *(SL #10).*	70.00	135	550

#	Description	Good	Fine	XF
11	**50 Dollars** 25.7.1861. Tellus at left, portrait Washington at center. Plate letters B; Bb; C. Printer: H & Lt. *(SL #11).*	90.00	225	350

#	Description	Good	Fine	XF
12	**100 Dollars** 25.7.1861. Portrait Washington at left, Ceres and Proserpine in flight at center. Plate letters B; C. Printer: H & L. *(SL #12).*	500	1,500	2,500

1861 (Third) Issue, Sept.

Note: #13 was incorrectly dated for an 1862 Issue.

#	Description	Good	Fine	XF
13	**2 Dollars** 2.9.1861. Incorrectly dated for an 1862 issue. Portrait Benjamin at upper left, personification of the South striking down the Union with a sword at top center. Series 1-10. Printer: B. Duncan (S.C.). *(SC #26).*	500	2,250	—

#	Description	Good	Fine	XF
14	**5 Dollars** 2.9.1861. Black and red on red fibre paper. Minerva at left, Commerce, Agriculture, Justice, Liberty and Industry at upper center, Washington statue at right. Plate letters A; B; C. Printer: Southern BNC. *(SL #22).*	250	800	3,500

#	Description	Good	Fine	XF
15	**5 Dollars** 2.9.1861. Black and orange. Boy at lower left, blacksmith with hammer, steam passenger train at lower right. Plate letters A; AA. Printer: Leggett, Keatinge & Ball. *(SL #31).*	350	2,000	6,000

#	Description	Good	Fine	XF
16	**5 Dollars** 2.9.1861. Black with blue-green or yellow-green ornamentation. Portrait C. G. Memminger at center, Minerva at right above Roman numeral V. *(SL #32).*			
	a. Printer: Leggett, Keatinge & Ball.	175	450	2,000
	b. Printer: K & B(V.).	175	450	2,000

#	Description	Good	Fine	XF
17	**5 Dollars** 2.9.1861. Black. C. G. Memminger at center, Minerva at right. *(SL #33).*			
	a. Printer: K & B (V.).	75.00	200	750
	b. Without imprint.	75.00	200	750

#	Description	Good	Fine	XF
18	**5 Dollars** 1.9.1861. Loading cotton at dockside at lower left, Indian Princess at right. Printer: H & L. *(SL #14).*	14,000	37,000	—

		Good	Fine	XF
19	**5 Dollars** 2.9.1861. Sailor at lower left, Ceres seated on a bale of cotton at top center. Serial #9A-16A without series, also *SECOND* and *THIRD SERIES.* (SL #19).			
	a. Printer: H & L.	20.00	75.00	150
	b. Printer: J. T. Paterson.	20.00	75.00	150
	c. Printer: J. T. Paterson & C.	20.00	75.00	150

		Good	Fine	XF
20	**5 Dollars** 2.9.1861. Portrait C. G. Memminger at lower left, sailor reclining by cotton bales at upper center, Justice standing with Ceres kneeling at right. *(SL #27).*			
	a. Plate letters A-H. Printer: B. Duncan (V.).	30.00	75.00	500
	b. *SECOND SERIES,* serial #1-8. Printer: B. Duncan (S.C.)	30.00	75.00	500

		Good	Fine	XF
21	**10 Dollars** 2.9.1861. Black and red. Thetis at upper left, Indian family at top center, Indian maiden at upper right. Plate letters A; B; C. Printer: Southern BNC. *(SL #23).*	350	900	3,500

		Good	Fine	XF
22	**10 Dollars** 2.9.1861. Black and orange-red. Portrait J. E. Ward at lower left, horse cart loaded with cotton at center, man carrying sugar cane at lower right. Plate letters, A, A1. Printer: Leggett, Keatinge & Ball. *(SL #34).*	1,000	2,700	7,000

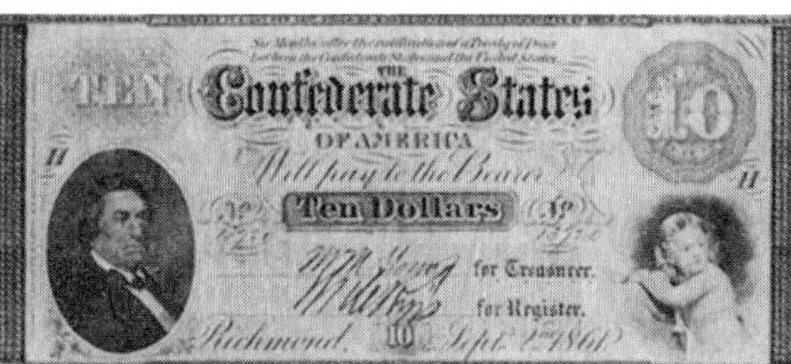

		Good	Fine	XF
23	**10 Dollars** 2.9.1861. Black and orange-red. Portrait right. M. T. Hunter at lower left, child at lower right. Plate letters: H-K. *(SL #35).*			
	a. Printer: Leggett, Keatinge & Ball.	140	350	1,150
	b. Printer: K & B.	140	350	1,150

		Good	Fine	XF
24	**10 Dollars** 2.9.1861. Portrait right. M. T. Hunter at lower left, Hope with anchor at lower center, portrait C. G. Memminger at lower right. Plate letters W-Z. Printer: K & B. *(SL #36).*	80.00	225	600

		Good	Fine	XF
25	**10 Dollars** 2.9.1861. Red or orange. *X - X* protector in underprint. Portrait right. M.T. Hunter at lower left, Hope with anchor at lower center, portait C.G. Memminger at lower right. Plate letters W-Z. Printer: K & B. *(SL #37).*	65.00	200	700

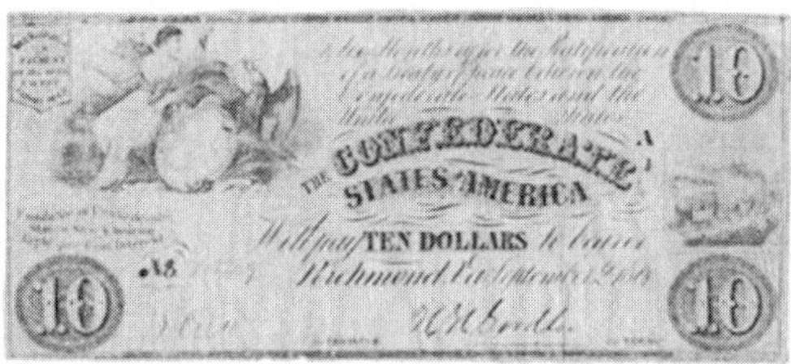

		Good	Fine	XF
26	**10 Dollars** 2.9.1861. Liberty seated by shield and eagle at upper left, train at right. Printer: H & L (litho). *(SL #15).*			
	a. Plate letter Ab.	6,000	10,000	—
	b. Plate letters A9-A16. Rare.	—	—	—

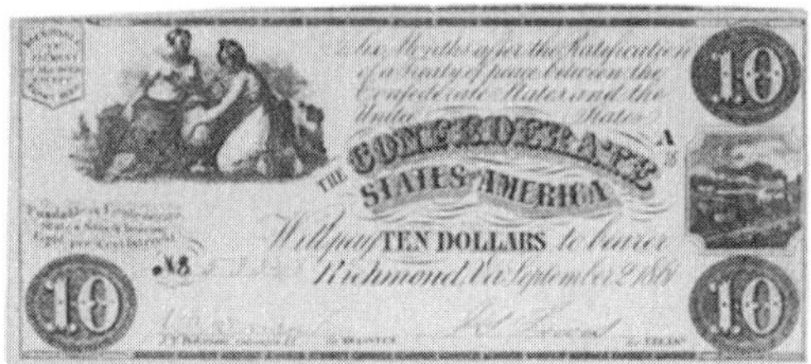

		Good	Fine	XF
27	**10 Dollars** 2.9.1861. Ceres and Commerce seated by an urn at upper left, train at right. Plate letters A9-A16. *(SL #20).*			
	a. Printer: J. T. Paterson.	25.00	50.00	175
	b. Printer: H & L.	30.00	100	850

		Good	Fine	XF
28	**10 Dollars** 2.9.1861. Male picking cotton at top center. Plate letters A-H. Printer: B. Duncan (V.). *(SL #28).*	150	1,000	2,000

		Good	Fine	XF
29	**10 Dollars** 2.9.1861. Portrait right. M. T. Hunter at left, Gen. F. Marion's "Sweet Potato Dinner" scene at center, Minerva standing at right. *FIRST - FOURTH SERIES.* (SL #29).			
	a. Printer: B. Duncan (S.C.).	25.00	60.00	350
	b. Without imprint.	25.00	60.00	350

		Good	Fine	XF
30	**20 Dollars** 2.9.1861. Black with green ornamentation. Liberty at left, Ceres seated between Commerce and Navigation at upper right center. Serial letter A. Printer: H & L. *(SL #16).*	350	1,000	2,300

		Good	Fine	XF
31	**20 Dollars** 2.9.1861. Sailor leaning on capstan at lower left, sailing ship at upper center. *(SL #21).*			
	a. Printer: H & L.	75.00	200	700
	b. Printer: J. T. Paterson.	25.00	45.00	125

		Good	Fine	XF
32	**20 Dollars** 2.9.1861. Minerva reclining with shield at lower left, Navigation kneeling at top center, blacksmith by anvil at lower right. Plate letter A. Printer: Southern BNC. *(SL #24).*	2,500	5,000	10,000

		Good	Fine	XF
33	**20 Dollars** 2.9.1861. Portrait Vice-Pres. A. H. Stevens at left, Industry seated between Cupid and beehive at center, Navigation at right. Plate #1-10. *FIRST-THIRD SERIES.* Printer: B. Duncan (V or SC). *(SL #30).*	25.00	50.00	250

		Good	Fine	XF
34	**20 Dollars** 2.9.1861. Portrait A. H. Stephens at center between industrial and agricultural goods. Plate letters W-Z. Printer: K & B. (S.C.) *(SL #38).*	150	700	2,000

		Good	Fine	XF
35	**50 Dollars** 2.9.1861. 2 sailors at lower lower left, Moneta seated with chest at upper center. Various serial letters and #'s. Printer: H & L. *(SL #17).*	40.00	100	175

		Good	Fine	XF
36	**50 Dollars** 2.9.1861. Hope with anchor at lower left, steam passenger train at top center, Justice at right. Plate letter A. Printer: Southern BNC. *(SL #25).*	2,500	5,000	16,000

		Good	Fine	XF
37	**50 Dollars** 2.9.1861. Black and green. Portrait Pres. Jefferson Davis at center without series, also *SECOND SERIES #.* Plate letters WA-ZA. Printer: K & B (V.). *(SL #39).*	75.00	200	700

		Good	Fine	XF
38	**100 Dollars** 2.9.1861. Sailor with anchor at lower left, slaves loading cotton on wagon at upper center. Various serial letters and #'s. Printer: H & L. *(SL #18).*	60.00	120	220

1862 (Fourth) Issue, June

		Good	Fine	XF
39	**1 Dollar** 2.6.1862. Liberty standing at left, steam powered sailing ships at top center right, portrait left. H. Pickens at lower right, *FIRST-THIRD SERIES.* Printer: B. Duncan (S.C.). *(SL #43).*	40.00	85.00	2,000

		Good	Fine	XF
40	**1 Dollar** 2.6.1862. Liberty standing at left, steam powered sailing ships at top center right, portrait left. H. Pickens at lower right, like #39, but with green *1* and *ONE* protector underprint. *FIRST, SE* Printer: B. Duncan (S.C.). *(SL #44).*	50.00	200	1,100

		Good	Fine	XF
41	**2 Dollars** 2.6.1862. Portrait J. Benjamin at upper left, personification of the South striking down the Union with a sword at top center *FIRST-THIRD SERIES*. Printer: B. Duncan (S.C.). *(SL #45)*.	25.00	60.00	160

		Good	Fine	XF
42	**2 Dollars** 2.6.1862. Portrait J. Benjamin at upper left, personification of the South striking down the Union with a sword at top center *FIRST-THIRD SERIES*. With green *2* and *TWO* protector underprint. Printer: B. Duncan. (S.C.). *(SL #46)*.	40.00	400	9,000

Notes: #43-48 have been reorganized by denomination.

		Good	Fine	XF
46	**10 Dollars** 2.9.1862. Ceres reclining on cotton bales at top center with sailing ship in background, portrait right. M. T. Hunter at lower right. Printer: H. & L. (without imprint). *(SL #47)*. Should probably have been dated 1861.			
	a. Terms of redemption read: *Six Months after...*	30.00	90.00	300
	b. Error: terms of redemption read: *Six Month after...*	30.00	90.00	300

		Good	Fine	XF
47	**10 Dollars** 2.9.1862. Ceres holding sheaf of wheat at top center, portrait right. M. T. Hunter at lower right. Printer: K & B (S.C.). (Not regularly issued.)*(SL #48)*. Should probably have been dated 1861.	2,000	4,000	—

		Good	Fine	XF
48	**20 Dollars** 2.9.1862. Liberty seated with shield on bale of cotton top center, portrait right. M. T. Hunter at lower right. *(SL #49)*. Should probably have been dated 1861.	3,500	6,000	—

		Good	Fine	XF
43	**100 Dollars** 1862. Milkmaid at lower left, steam passenger train at top center with straight steam blowing out of locomotive boiler. Back: With or without various interest paid markings. *(SL #40)*.			
	a. Plate letters A, Ab-Ah. Printer: H & L. 5.5.1862-5.9.1862.	25.00	60.00	200
	b. Plate letters Aa-Ah. Printer: J. T. Paterson. 8.4.1862; May, 1862.	20.00	50.00	150

		Good	Fine	XF
44	**100 Dollars** Milkmaid at lower left, steam passenger train at top center with diffused steam blowing out of locomotive boiler. Plate letters Aa-Ah. Back: With or without various interest paid markings. Printer: T. Paterson & C. *(SL #41)*.	30.00	75.00	150

		Good	Fine	XF
45	**100 Dollars** 26.8.1862. Portrait Calhoun at lower left, people hoeing cotton at top center, Columbia at right. Back: With or without various interest paid markings. Printer: K & B (S.C.). *(SL #42)*.	40.00	100	200

1862 (Fifth) Issue, Dec.

		VG	VF	UNC
49	**1 Dollar** 2.12.1862. Portrait Clement C. Clay at top center. *(SL #50)*.			
	a. *FIRST* or *SECOND* SERIES Printer: K & B. (S.C.).	40.00	150	250
	b. Without Series. Printer: B. Duncan.	60.00	175	250

		VG	VF	UNC
50	**2 Dollars** 2.12.1862. Judah P. Benjamin at right. *(SL #51)*.			
	a. *FIRST* or *SECOND SERIES*. Printer: K & B (S.C.).	50.00	130	200
	b. Without series. Printer: J. T. Paterson & C.	50.00	130	200

51	**5 Dollars**	VG	VF	UNC
	2.12.1862. Capital at Richmond, Va. at top center, portrait C. G. Memminger at lower right. *(SL #52).*			
	a. *FIRST* or *SECOND SERIES*, without imprint.	40.00	75.00	200
	b. *FIRST* or *SECOND SERIES*. Printer: J. T. Paterson & C.	40.00	75.00	200
	c. *FIRST-THIRD SERIES, Lithog'd by* J. T. Paterson & C.	40.00	75.00	200
	d. *SECOND SERIES.* Printer: E & C.	40.00	75.00	200
	e. *SECOND SERIES, Ptd. by* Evans & Cogswell and *Lithog'd by* J. T. Paterson & C.	40.00	75.00	200
	f. *SECOND SERIES, Ptd. by* E & C. and J. T. Paterson & C.	40.00	75.00	200

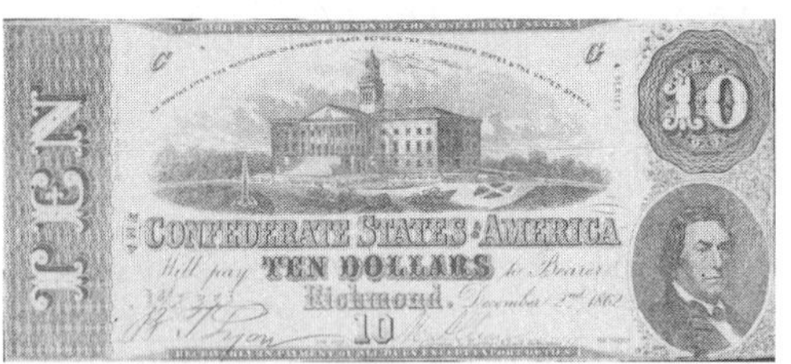

52	**10 Dollars**	VG	VF	UNC
	2.12.1862. Capital at Columbia, S.C., at top center, portrait right. M. T. Hunter at lower right. *(SL #53).*			
	a. Without series. Printer: B. Duncan, K & B (S.C.).	40.00	90.00	175
	b. *SECOND, THIRD* or *FOURTH SERIES*, Printer: B. Duncan.	40.00	90.00	175
	c. Without series, also *THIRD SERIES* Printer: E & C.	40.00	90.00	175
	d. *THIRD* or *FOURTH SERIES.* Printer: E & C, B. Duncan.	40.00	90.00	175

53	**20 Dollars**	VG	VF	UNC
	2.12.1862. Capital at Nashville, Tenn. at top center, portrait Alexander H. Stephens at lower right. *(SL #54).*			
	a. *FIRST SERIES. Printed by* J. T. Paterson & C.	200	500	1,100
	b. *FIRST SERIES.* Printer: J. T. Paterson & C.	200	500	1,100
	c. *FIRST SERIES.* without imprint.	200	500	1,100
	d. *FIRST SERIES.* Printer: B. Duncan.	200	500	1,100
	e. *FIRST SERIES. Printed by* Duncan.	200	500	1,100

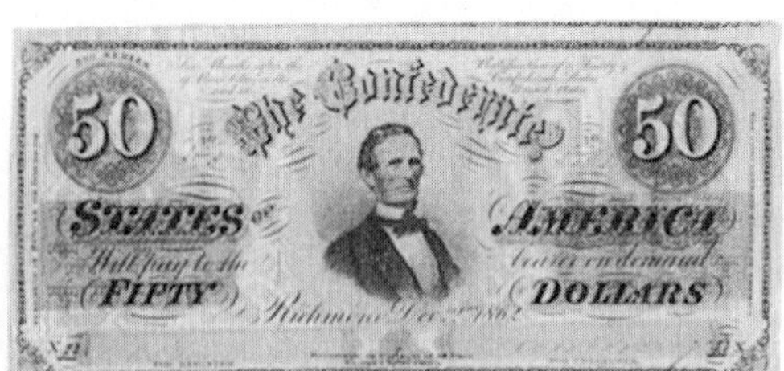

54	**50 Dollars**	VG	VF	UNC
	2.12.1862. Portrait Pres. Jefferson Davis at center. Engravers' names above or below *FUNDABLE...* at left. *(SL #55).*			
	a. Printer: K & B (V).	200	450	1,350
	b. Printer: K & B (S.C.).	200	450	1,350

55	**100 Dollars**	VG	VF	UNC
	2.12.1862. *(SL #56).* 2 soldiers at lower left, portrait left. Lucy Pickens at center, portrait George W. Randolph at lower right without series; also *SECOND SERIES.* Printer: K & B (S.C.).	200	350	600

1863 (Sixth) Issue, April

56	**50 Cents**	VG	VF	UNC
	6.4.1863. Black on pink paper. Portrait Pres. Jefferson Davis at top center. Printed signature *FIRST* or *SECOND SERIES.* Printer: Archer & Daly. *(SL #57).*	20.00	30.00	75.00

57	**1 Dollar**	VG	VF	UNC
	6.4.1863. Portrait Clement C. Clay at top center. *(SL #58).*			
	a. *FIRST* or *SECOND SERIES.* Printer: K & B. (S.C.).	35.00	80.00	175
	b. Without series, also *SECOND SERIES.* Printer: E & C. (litho).	35.00	80.00	175

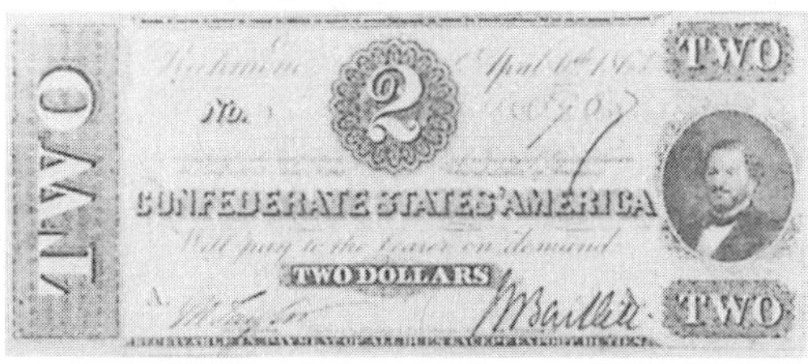

58	**2 Dollars**	VG	VF	UNC
	6.4.1863. Portrait Judah P. Benjamin at right. *(SL #59).* PC: Pink.			
	a. *FIRST* or *SECOND SERIES.* Printer: K & B (S.C.).	75.00	275	700
	b. Without series, also *SECOND SERIES.* Printer: E & C (litho) and K & B. (S.C.).	75.00	275	700

59	**5 Dollars**	VG	VF	UNC
	6.4.1863. Capital at Richmond, Va. at top center, portrait C. G. Memminger at lower right. Date overprint from April, 1863 - Feb. 1864. *(SL #60).*			
	a. *SECOND-THIRD SERIES.* Printer: K & B. (S.C.).	25.00	45.00	150
	b. *FIRST-THIRD SERIES.* Printer: K & B and J. T. Paterson & C.	25.00	45.00	150
	c. Without series, *THIRD SERIES.* Printer: K & B, E & C.	25.00	45.00	150
	d. Without series, *FIRST SERIES.* Printer: K & B, J. T. Paterson & C., E & C.	25.00	45.00	150

60	10 Dollars	VG	VF	UNC
	6.4.1863. Capital at Columbia, S.C. at top center, portrait right. M. T. Hunter at lower right. Date overprint from April,1863 - Feb. 1864. *(SL #61).*			
	a. Without series, *FIRST* and *FIFTH SERIES.* Printer: K & B (S.C.), E & C.	25.00	100	300
	b. *FIRST, SECOND, FIFTH SERIES.* Printer: K & B, B. Duncan.	25.00	100	300
	c. *SECOND SERIES.* Printer: K & B, J. T. Paterson & C.	25.00	100	300

61	20 Dollars	VG	VF	UNC
	6.4.1863. Capital at Nashville, Tenn. at top center, portrait A. H. Stephens at lower right. Date overprint from April - Oct. 1863. *(SL #62).*			
	a. *FIRST SERIES.* Printer: K & B. (S.C.).	30.00	60.00	235
	b. Without series, *FIRST-THIRD SERIES.* Printer: K & B, E & C.	30.00	60.00	235
	c. *FIRST SERIES.* Printer: K & B, J. T. Paterson & C.	30.00	60.00	235

62	50 Dollars	VG	VF	UNC
	6.4.1863. Portrait Pres. Jefferson Davis at center Date overprint from April, 1863 - Feb., 1864. Plate letters WA-ZA. without series, also *FIRST SERIES.* Imprint above or below *FUNDABLE...* at left. *(SL #63).*			
	a. Printer: K & B (Va.).	75.00	150	270
	b. Printer: K & B (S.C.).	75.00	150	270

63	100 Dollars	VG	VF	UNC
	6.4.1863. 2 soldiers at left. Portrait left. Lucy Pickens at center, portrait George W. Randolph at lower right. Date overprint from May, 1863 - Jan., 1864. without series, also *FIRST SERIES.* Printer: K & B (S.C.). *(SL #64).*	90.00	225	400

1864 (Seventh) Issue, Feb.

64	50 Cents	VG	VF	UNC
	17.2.1864. Portrait Pres. Jefferson Davis at top center. Printed signature. Printer: Archer & Halpin. *(SL #65).* PC: Pink.			
	a. *FIRST SERIES.*	20.00	30.00	75.00
	b. *SECOND SERIES.*	20.00	30.00	75.00

65	1 Dollar	VG	VF	UNC
	17.2.1864. Red underprint. Portrait Clement C. Clay at top center. *(SL #66).*			
	a. *ENGRAVED BY* K & B. (S.C.).	45.00	100	175
	b. *ENGRAVED & PRINTED BY* K & B. (S.C.).	45.00	100	175
	c. *ENGRAVED BY* K & B (S.C.) & *LITHOG'D BY* E & C.	45.00	100	175

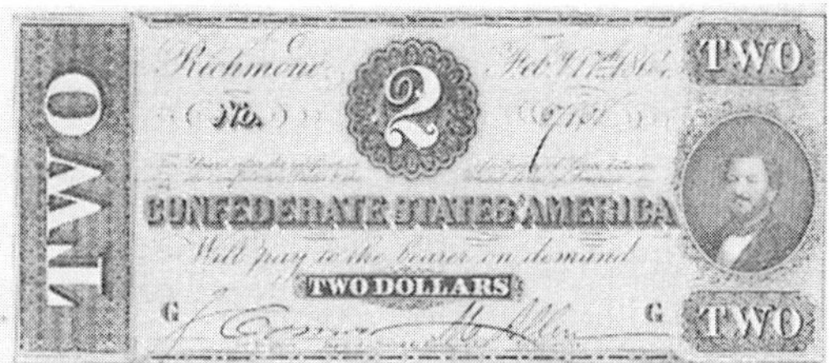

66	2 Dollars	VG	VF	UNC
	17.2.1864. Red underprint. Portrait J. P. Benjamin at right. *(SL #67).*			
	a. *ENGRAVED BY* K & B. (S.C.).	35.00	90.00	150
	b. *ENGRAVED & PRINTED BY* K & B. (S.C.).	35.00	90.00	150
	c. *ENGRAVED BY* K & B. (S.C.) *LITHOG'D BY* E & C.	35.00	90.00	150

67	5 Dollars	VG	VF	UNC
	17.2.1864. Red underprint. Capital at Richmond, Va. at top center, portrait C. G. Memminger at lower right. Without series, also *SERIES 1-7.* Back: Blue *FIVE* Printer: K & B. (S.C.). *(SL #68).*	25.00	50.00	100

68	10 Dollars	VG	VF	UNC
	17.2.1864. Red underprint. Artillery horseman pulling cannon at upper center, portrait right. M. T. Hunter at lower right. Without series, also *FIRST-TENTH SERIES.* Back: Blue *TEN.* Printer: K. & B. (S.C.). *(SL #69).*	20.00	45.00	85.00

69 **20 Dollars** | VG 25.00 | VF 50.00 | UNC 90.00

17.2.1864. Red underprint. Capital at Nashville, Tenn. at top center, portrait A. H. Stephens at lower right. Date overprint from April - Oct., 1863. Without series, also *SERIES 1-5*, also *VI-XI*. Back: Blue *TWENTY*. Printer: K & B (S.C.). *(SL #70)*.

70 **50 Dollars** | VG 50.00 | VF 75.00 | UNC 150

17.2.1864. Red underprint. Portrait Pres. Jefferson Davis at center. Without series, also *FIRST - FOURTH SERIES*. Back: Blue *FIFTY*. (SL #71).

71 **100 Dollars** | VG 50.00 | VF 85.00 | UNC 150

17.2.1864. Red underprint. 2 soldiers at left. Portrait left. Lucy Pickens at center, portrait George W. Randolph at lower right. Without series, also *SERIES I, II*. Back: Blue *HUNDRED*. (SL #72).

72 **100 Dollars** | VG 50.00 | VF 85.00 | UNC 150

17.2.1864. 2 soldiers at left. Portrait left. Lucy Pickens at center, portrait George W. Randolph at lower right. Like #71, but reduced size. Plate letter D. "Havana counterfeit". *(SL #-)*.

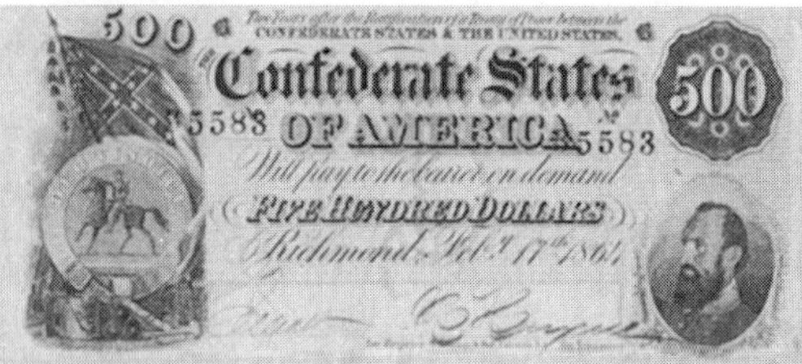

73 **500 Dollars** | VG 200 | VF 450 | UNC 800

17.2.1864. Red underprint. Confederate seal with equestrian statue of George Washington below Confederate flag at left, portrait Gen. T. J. "Stonewall" Jackson at lower right. *(SL #73)*.

COOK ISLANDS

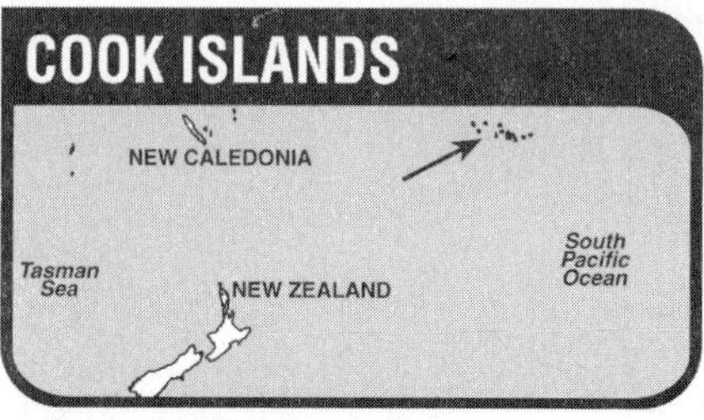

Cook Islands, a political dependency of New Zealand consisting of 15 islands located in the South Pacific Ocean about 3,218 km. northeast of New Zealand, has an area of 236.7 sq. km. and a population of 12,270. Capital: Avarua. The United States claims the islands of Danger, Manahiki, Penrhyn and Rakahanga atolls. Citrus, canned fruits and juices, copra, clothing, jewelry and mother-of-pearl shell are exported.

Named after Captain Cook, who sighted them in 1770, the islands became a British protectorate in 1888. By 1900, administrative control was transferred to New Zealand; in 1965, residents chose self-government in free association with New Zealand. The emigration of skilled workers to New Zealand and government deficits are continuing problems.

RULERS:

New Zealand, 1901-

MONETARY SYSTEM:

1 Shilling = 12 Pence
1 Pound = 20 Shillings, to 1967
1 Dollar = 100 Cents, 1967-

NEW ZEALAND ADMINISTRATION

Government of the Cook Islands

1894 Issue

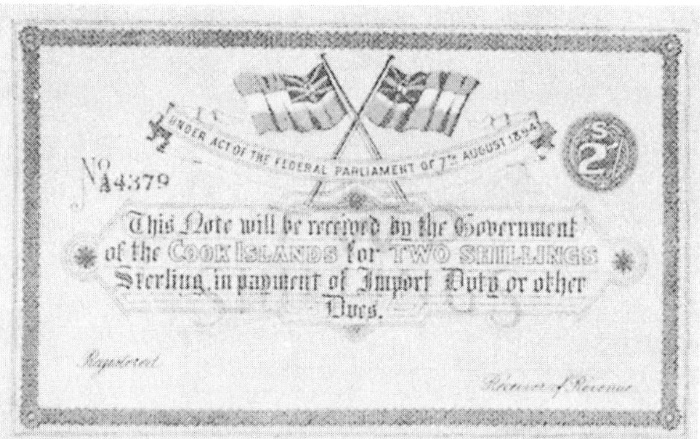

1 **2 Shillings** | Good — | Fine — | XF 4,500

7.8.1894. Blue on pink underprint. Crossed flags of Cook Island at top center. Not issued.

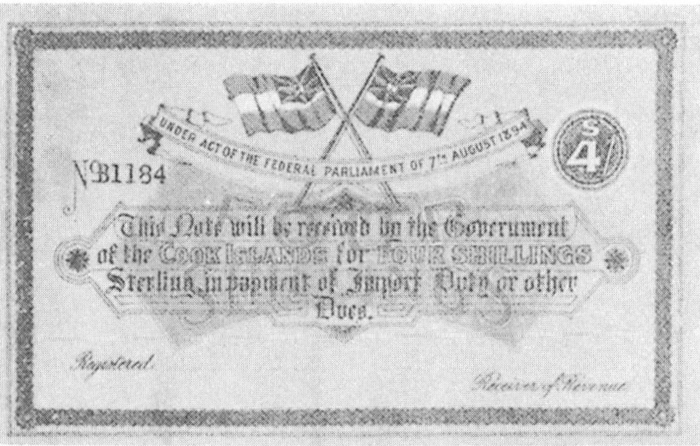

2 **4 Shillings** | Good — | Fine — | XF 4,500

7.8.1894. Blue on green and orange underprint. Crossed flags of Cook Island at top center. Not issued.

The Republic of Costa Rica, located in southern Central America between Nicaragua and Panama, has an area of 51,100 sq. km. and a population of 4.19 million. Capital: San Jose. Agriculture predominates; coffee, bananas, beef and sugar contribute heavily to the country's export earnings.

Although explored by the Spanish early in the 16th century, initial attempts at colonizing Costa Rica proved unsuccessful due to a combination of factors, including: disease from mosquito-infested swamps, brutal heat, resistance by natives, and pirate raids. It was not until 1563 that a permanent settlement of Cartago was established in the cooler, fertile central highlands. The area remained a colony for some two and a half centuries. In 1821, Costa Rica became one of several Central American provinces that jointly declared their independence from Spain. Two years later it joined the United Provinces of Central America, but this federation disintegrated in 1838, at which time Costa Rica proclaimed its sovereignty and independence. Since the late 19th century, only two brief periods of violence have marred the country's democratic development. Although it still maintains a large agricultural sector, Costa Rica has expanded its economy to include strong technology and tourism industries. The standard of living is relatively high. Land ownership is widespread.

MONETARY SYSTEM:

1 Peso = 100 Centavos to 1896
1 Colon = 100 Centimos

REPUBLIC

República de Costa Rica

1865-1871 Issue

101	1 Peso	Good	Fine	XF
	2.1.1865. Black on green underprint. Arms at left, Mercury with bales at right. Printer: BWC. Uniface.			
	a. Without circular stampings on back.	150	550	—
	b. Circular stampings on back: *EMISION DE GUERRA...* with arms at center embossed at left. *SECRETARIA DE HACIENDA Y COMERCIO...* stamped with arms at center right.	125	500	—

102	2 Pesos	Good	Fine	XF
	27.3.1871. Black on brown underprint. Arms at left, portrait young woman at right. Printer: BWC. Uniface.			
	a. Without circular stampings on back.	—	—	—
	b. With stampings as #101b above on back.	300	1,200	—

103	5 Pesos	Good	Fine	XF
	2.1.1865. Black on reddish tan underprint. Arms at left, sailing boat at right. Back: Without stampings. Printer: BWC. Uniface. Rare.	—	—	—

103A	5 Pesos	Good	Fine	XF
	2.1.1865 (1883). Gen. Prospero Fernandez vignette at right. Printer: BWC. Uniface. Rare.	—	—	—

104	10 Pesos	Good	Fine	XF
	2.1.1865. Black on green underprint. Arms at left, vignette at right. Printer: BWC. Uniface. Rare.	—	—	—

104A	10 Pesos	Good	Fine	XF
	2.1.1865 (1883). Black on green underprint. Gen. Prospero Fernandez vignette at right. Printer: BWC. Uniface. Rare.	—	—	—

105	25 Pesos	Good	Fine	XF
	2.1.1865. Black on blue underprint. Arms at left, oxen and cart at right. Printer: BWC. Uniface. Rare.	—	—	—

106	50 Pesos	Good	Fine	XF
	2.1.1865. Black on orange underprint. Arms at left, standing woman with fruit basket at right. Rare.	—	—	—

107	50 Pesos	Good	Fine	XF
	2.1.1865. Black on olive underprint. Arms at left, building at right. Rare.	—	—	—

1877 Issue

111	1 Peso	Good	Fine	XF
	4.4.1877. Black and red. Arms at lower center. Uniface. Rare.	—	—	—

1880s Issue

120	5 Pesos	Good	Fine	XF
	5.5.1884-1.5.1885. Black on red-orange underprint. Standing woman at left, arms at lower center, Raphael's Angel at right. Printer: ABNC.			
	a. Issued note. Rare.	—	—	—
	s. Specimen.	—	Unc	350

121	10 Pesos	Good	Fine	XF
	4.5.1884-1.5.1885. Black on green underprint. Seated woman with globe at left, arms at center, seated woman with plants at right. Printer: ABNC.			
	a. Circular black cancellation stamp: *JEFATURA DE SECCION DEL SELLO NACIONAL 26 DIC 89,* and hand signature. Back green; flowers. Rare.	—	—	—
	b. Punch hole cancelled. Rare.	—	—	—
	p. Without circular black stamp or handsignature. Proof.	—	Unc	400

122	25 Pesos	Good	Fine	XF
	20.3.1885-9.10.1885. Black on orange underprint. Arms at left, Prospect Point, Niagara Falls and Canadian Horseshoe Falls at center, Prospero Hernandes at right. Printer: ABNC.			
	a. Issued note, text like #121a. Rare.	—	—	—
	p1. Brown underprint. Uniface proof.	—	Unc	350
	p2. Blue underprint. Uniface proof.	—	Unc	350

123	50 Pesos	Good	Fine	XF
	20.3.1885-14.11.1888. Black on green underprint. Building at left, Prospero Hernandes at center, arms at lower right. Printer: ABNC.			
	a. Circular black cancellation hand stamp and hand signature on face like #121. Back olive. Rare.	—	—	—
	b. Punch hole cancelled. Rare.	—	—	—
	p. Without stamping. Proof.	—	—	—

124	100 Pesos	Good	Fine	XF
	20.3.1885-14.11.1888. Black on light orange underprint. Building at at left, Prospero Hernandes at center, arms at right. Printer: ABNC.			
	a. Issued note. Rare.	—	—	—
	s. Specimen.	—	Unc	450

1897 Gold Certificate Issue

131	5 Colones	Good	Fine	XF
	1.1.1897. Black on yellow and green underprint. Portrait Christopher Columbus at center. Series A. Back: Arms at center. Printer: ABNC.			
	p. Proof. Rare.	—	—	—
	s. Specimen.	—	Unc	4,000

132	10 Colones	Good	Fine	XF
	1.1.1897. Black on green and yellow underprint. Portrait Christopher Columbus at center. Series B. Back: Arms at center. Printer: ABNC.			
	p. Proof. Rare.	—	—	—
	s. Specimen.	—	Unc	2,500

133	25 Colones	Good	Fine	XF
	1.1.1897. Black on blue and yellow underprint. Portrait Christopher Columbus at center. Series C. Back: Arms at center. Printer: ABNC. Proof. Rare.	—	—	—

134	50 Colones	Good	Fine	XF
	1.1.1897. Black on orange and yellow underprint. Portrait Christopher Columbus at left, seated Agriculture at center. Series D. Back: Arms at center. Printer: ABNC.			
	p. Proof. Rare.	—	—	—
	s. Specimen.	—	Unc	5,000

135	100 Colones	Good	Fine	XF
	1.1.1897. Black on brown and yellow underprint. Portrait Christopher Columbus at left, allegorical woman with globe and lute at center. Series E. Back: Arms at center. Printer: ABNC.			
	p. Proof. Rare.	—	—	—
	s. Specimen.	—	Unc	6,000

1902-1910 Silver Certificate Issue

Payable in 25 and 50 Centimos coins.

141	1 Colón	Good	Fine	XF
	1.11.1902; 5.11.1902; 1.10.1903. (filled in by hand). Black on green and yellow underprint. Portrait Christopher Columbus at left, arms with flags at right. Back: Black circular stamping of arms at center. Printer: ABNC. Uniface.			
	a. Issued note.	75.00	350	—
	s. Specimen.	—	Unc	1,200

142	1 Colón	Good	Fine	XF
	1.10.1905; 1.7.1906; 1.11.1906. Portrait Christopher Columbus at left, arms with flags at right. Back: Black circular stamping of arms at left. Printer: ABNC.			
	a. Issued note.	15.00	80.00	275
	s. Specimen.	—	Unc	500

143	1 Colón	Good	Fine	XF
	23.5.1910; 10.11.1910; 1.12.1912; 1.10.1914. Portrait Christopher Columbus at left, arms without flags at right. Back: Black stamping of arms without circle at right. Printer: ABNC.			
	a. Issued note.	6.00	70.00	250
	s. Specimen.	—	—	—

144	2 Colones	Good	Fine	XF
	1.11.1902; 5.11.1902; 1.10.1903; 1.10.1905. Black on yellow and orange underprint. Portrait Christopher Columbus at left, arms with flags at right. Back: Black circular stamping of arms. Plain. Printer: ABNC.			
	a. Issued note.	100	400	—
	s. Specimen.	—	Unc	800

145	2 Colones	Good	Fine	XF
	1.10.1905; 1.7.1906. Black on yellow and orange underprint. Portrait Christopher Columbus at left, arms with flags at right. Printer: ABNC.			
	a. Issued note.	25.00	100	350
	s. Specimen.	—	Unc	700

146	2 Colones	Good	Fine	XF
	1.11.1910; 1.12.1912; 1.10.1914. Portrait Christopher Columbus at left, arms without flags at right. Back: Black stamping of arms without circle at right. Printer: ABNC.			
	a. Issued note.	15.00	80.00	275
	s. Specimen.	—	Unc	500

1917 Silver Certificate Issue

Notes backed by coined silver.

147	50 Centimos	Good	Fine	XF
	11.10.1917-21.11.1921. Black on olive underprint. Portrait Christopher Columbus at center. Back: Black stamped arms at right. Printer: ABNC.			
	a. Issued note.	5.00	25.00	75.00
	p. Proof.	—	Unc	350
	s. Specimen.	—	Unc	100

148	1 Colón	Good	Fine	XF
	22.9.1917; 11.10.1917; 24.10.1917; 5.6.1918; 3.7.1918. Portrait Christopher Columbus at left, arms without flags at right. (Like #143, but with different text below heading and different signature titles.) Printer: ABNC.			
	a. Issued note.	7.50	35.00	150
	p. Proof.	—	Unc	450
	s. Specimen.	—	Unc	500

149	2 Colones	Good	Fine	XF
	Portrait Christopher Columbus at left, arms without flags at right. Different text below heading and different signature titles than #146. Printer: ABNC.			
	a. Issued note.	50.00	250	—
	p. Proof.	—	Unc	850
	s. Specimen.	—	Unc	1,000

150	50 Colones	Good	Fine	XF
	ND (1917). Black on brown and multicolor underprint. Portrait Christopher Columbus at center. Back: Arms at center. Printer: ABNC.			
	a. Proof.	—	Unc	1,250
	s. Specimen.	—	Unc	1,750

150A	100 Colones	Good	Fine	XF
	ND (1917). Black on blue and multicolor underprint. Portrait Christopher Columbus at center. Like #150. Back: Arms at center.			
	p. Proof.	—	Unc	1,500
	s. Specimen.	—	Unc	2,000

1918-1920 Provisional Issues

151	2 Colones	Good	Fine	XF
	19.6.1918-22.12.1919. Red. Red signature. Printer: ABNC.	15.00	70.00	150

152	2 Colones	Good	Fine	XF
	11.8.1920. Black. Black signature. Portrait Christopher Columbus at left, arms without flags at right. Back: Black stamping of arms without circle at right. Printer: ABNC.	15.00	70.00	150

Banco Internacional de Costa Rica

Series A

156	25 Centimos	Good	Fine	XF
	9.10.1918-25.7.1919. Dark green. Portrait Liberty at left.			
	a. Issued note.	5.00	20.00	75.00
	s. Specimen.	—	Unc	100

157	50 Centimos	Good	Fine	XF
	18.1.1918-24.10.1921. Black on brown underprint. Portrait woman at center.			
	a. Issued note.	5.00	20.00	85.00
	s. Specimen.	—	—	—

158	1 Colón	Good	Fine	XF
	1918-1935. Black on multicolor underprint. Seated woman at center. Back: Liberty head.			
	a. 18.1.1918; 9.10.1918; 21.10.1918.	7.00	25.00	75.00
	b. 17.11.1922; 18.4.1923.	7.00	20.00	65.00
	c. 27.9.1929; 12.4.1935-9.10.1935.	6.00	17.50	60.00
	s. Specimen.	—	Unc	125

159	2 Colones	Good	Fine	XF
	1918-1931. Black on multicolor underprint. Reclining Liberty with lion and book at center. Back: Liberty head.			
	a. 16.1.1918; 28.6.1919.	25.00	75.00	250
	b. 24.5.1923-8.7.1931.	20.00	60.00	225
	p. Proof.	—	Unc	450
	s. Specimen.	—	Unc	500

160	5 Colones	Good	Fine	XF
	1.11.1914. Black. Indian girl with pineapple basket at left, banana tree at right. Back: Large V5.			
	a. Issued note.	35.00	115	550
	s. Specimen.	—	Unc	1,100

161	10 Colones	Good	Fine	XF
	1.11.1914. Black. Five coffee bean pickers at center. Signature title overprint at left: *EL SECRETARIO DE HACIENDA*.			
	a. Issued note.	45.00	225	650
	s. Specimen.	—	Unc	1,000

162	20 Colones	Good	Fine	XF
	1.11.1914. Black. Draped woman with ship's wheel at right. Like #169B. Signature title overprint at left: *EL SECRETARIO DE HACIENDA*.			
	a. Issued note. Rare.	—	—	—
	s. Specimen.	—	Unc	1,750
	x. Counterfeit.	—	—	—

Note: For years only counterfeits for #162 were known. A genuine piece has now been confirmed.

163	50 Colones	Good	Fine	XF
	1.11.1914. Black. Woman playing mandolin at center. Signature title overprint at left: *EL SECRETARIO DE HACIENDA*.			
	a. Issued note. Rare.	—	—	—
	s. Specimen.	—	Unc	1,750

164	100 Colones	Good	Fine	XF
	1.11.1914. Black. Seated female ("Study") at left. Signature title overprint at left: *EL SECRETARIO DE HACIENDA*.			
	a. Issued note.	75.00	200	650
	p. Proof.	—	Unc	1,750
	s. Specimen.	—	Unc	1,500

A modern proof reprint exisits of #164, value about $100.

Series B - Provisional Issue (1935)

		Good	Fine	XF
165	**50 Centimos** 12.4.1935. Portrait C. Columbus at center. Back: Black stamped arms at right.	5.00	27.50	75.00

Series B 1916-1935 Issue

		Good	Fine	XF
166	**1 Colón** 9.10.1935. Green on multicolor underprint. Seated woman at center. Like #158. Back: Liberty head. Printer: ABNC.			
	a. Issued note.	6.00	30.00	110
	s. Specimen.	—	Unc	200

		Good	Fine	XF
167	**2 Colones** 10.12.1931-31.10.1936. Brown on red, blue and green underprint. Portrait Mona Lisa at center. Back: Ox-cart. Printer: W&S.			
	a. Issued note.	25.00	200	600
	ct. Color trial. Black on green underprint. Punch hole cancelled.	—	Unc	1,000

		Good	Fine	XF
168	**5 Colones** 1.12.1916. Black on multicolor underprint. Portrait Pres. A. Gonzalez Flores at center. Printer: ABNC.			
	a. Issued note.	60.00	375	—
	p. Proof.	—	Unc	1,250
	s. Specimen.	—	Unc	1,250

		Good	Fine	XF
169	**10 Colones** 1.12.1916; 9.10.1918. Black on multicolor underprint. Portrait W. J. Field Spencer, first director of the Banco, at center. Printer: ABNC.			
	a. Issued note.	70.00	400	—
	p. Proof.	—	Unc	650
	s. Specimen.	—	Unc	700

		Good	Fine	XF
169A	**20 Colones** 1.12.1916. Deep blue on multicolor underprint. Liberty seated with sword and shield at center. Series B. Back: French Marianne at center. Printer: ABNC.			
	a. Issued note with date. Rare.	—	—	—
	p. Proof.	—	Unc	1,250
	s. Black on blue underprint. Back green. ND. Specimen.	—	Unc	1,750
169B	**20 Colones** 21.10.1918. Black. Draped woman with ship's wheel at right. Like #162. Printer: ABNC. Rare.	—	—	—
170A	**50 Colones** 1.3.1916. Black. Seated woman playing mandolin at center Like #163. Printer: ABNC.			
	a. Issued note.	—	2,000	—
	b. Punch hole cancelled.	—	—	—
170B	**100 Colones** 17.3.1916. Black. Seated female ("Study") at left. Like #164. Printer: ABNC. Rare.	—	—	—

1918-1919 Provisional Issue

		Good	Fine	XF
171	**5 Colones** 9.10.1918 (- old date 1.12.1916).	45.00	300	—
172	**10 Colones** 9.10.1918 (- old date 1.12.1916).	45.00	300	—

Series C

		Good	Fine	XF
173	**50 Centimos** 21.6.1935; 21.7.1935; 1.8.1935. Blue on tan underprint. Portrait woman at center. Like #157. Printer: ABNC.			
	a. Issued note.	10.00	25.00	85.00
	s. Specimen.	—	Unc	125

174	5 Colones	Good	Fine	XF
	1919-1930. Dark blue on multicolor underprint. Indian girl with pineapple basket at left, banana tree at right. Printer: ABNC.			
	a. 4.1.1919; 28.6.1919.	17.50	75.00	450
	b. 17.7.1925-22.12.1930.	12.50	60.00	350
	p. Proof.	—	Unc	950
	s. Specimen. Red overprint: *SPECIMEN* and punch hole cancelled.	—	Unc	500

175	10 Colones	Good	Fine	XF
	1919-1932. Blue on multicolor underprint. 5 coffee bean pickers at center-like #161. Printer: ABNC.			
	a. Date at lower right. 4.1.1919.	25.00	100	500
	b. Date at lower center 13.9.1927-20.1.1932.	20.00	75.00	450
	s. Specimen.	—	Unc	500

176	20 Colones	Good	Fine	XF
	1919-1936. Dark blue on multicolor underprint. People cutting sugar cane at center. Printer: ABNC.			
	a. 4.1.1919-24.3.1924.	25.00	200	600
	b. Signature title: *EL SUBDIRECTOR* overprint at right. 31.7.1933.	22.50	150	500
	c. Without signature title changes. 17.4.1928-3.7.1936.	20.00	140	450
	p. Proof.	—	Unc	950
	s. Specimen.	—	Unc	500

177	50 Colones	Good	Fine	XF
	1919-1932. Dark blue on multicolor underprint. Woman playing mandolin at center-like #163. Printer: ABNC.			
	a. 4.1.1919-23.6.1927.	40.00	250	650
	b. 8.4.1929-5.11.1932.	30.00	200	550
	p. Proof.	—	Unc	1,250
	s. Specimen.	—	Unc	800

178	100 Colones	Good	Fine	XF
	1919-1932. Dark blue on multicolor overprint. Seated female ("Study") at left. Like #164. Printer: ABNC.			
	a. 4.1.1919-23.6.1927.	35.00	225	600
	b. 22.4.1930-11.2.1932.	30.00	150	500
	s. Specimen.	—	Unc	400
	x. Error date: 14.12.2931.	60.00	275	650

A modern proof exisits of #178, value about $100.

Series D Provisional Issue

179	10 Colones	Good	Fine	XF
	7.11.1931. Red. Red signature. Olive and blue on pink underprint. Three workers on horseback at center. Back: Portrait Columbus at center. Large red overprint:*CERTIFICADO DE PLATA* across center. Printer: TDLR.			
	a. Issued note.	90.00	375	850
	s. Specimen. Red overprint: *MUESTRA*.	—	Unc	1,000

1931-1933 Series D

		Good	Fine	XF
180	**5 Colones** 1931-1936. Red-orange and blue on tan underprint. Three coffee bean workers at right. Back: Monument. Printer: TDLR.			
	a. 8.7.1931-31.10.1936.	10.00	85.00	350
	b. Signature title: *EL SUBDIRECTOR* overprint at right. 27.8.1936.	10.00	85.00	350

		Good	Fine	XF
181	**10 Colones** 20.1.1932; 3.12.1935-17.12.1936. Black. Red, olive and blue on pink underprint. Three workers on horseback at center. Black signature. Like #179 but without overprint. Back: Portrait C. Columbus at center.			
	a. Issued note.	20.00	125	450
	s. Specimen. Perforated: *CANCELLED* and punch hole cancelled.	—	Unc	500

		Good	Fine	XF
182	**100 Colones** 1933-1935. Blue on multicolor underprint. Woman standing with basket of vegetables at left. Back: Large building. Printer: W&S.			
	a. Signature title: *EL SUBDIRECTOR* overprint at right. 2.6.1933-4.9.1933.	25.00	125	450
	b. Without signature title changes. 17.1.1933; 30.10.1934; 26.3.1935.	25.00	125	450
	s. Specimen. Red overprint: *SPECIMEN* twice on face, punch hole cancelled.	—	Unc	1,200

1933 Series E

		Good	Fine	XF
183	**50 Colones** 1933. Dark green on multicolor underprint. Woman standing at left. Back: Monument at center. Printer: W&S.			
	a. Signature title: *EL SUBDIRECTOR* overprint at right. 31.7.1933.	22.50	175	550
	b. Without signature title changes. 17.1.1933; 24.11.1933.	22.50	175	550
	s. Specimen. Red overprint: *SPECIMEN* twice on face, punch hole cancelled.	—	Unc	1,000

Caja de Conversion

1924-1925 Issue

		Good	Fine	XF
184	**2 Colones** 18.7.1924-5.2.1929. Dark blue on multicolor underprint. Allegorical woman standing with model airplane by woman seated at right. Series A. Printer: ABNC.			
	a. Issued note.	15.00	75.00	300
	s. Specimen.	—	Unc	300

		Good	Fine	XF
185	**5 Colones** 4.11.1925-12.12.1928. Dark blue on multicolor underprint. Woman seated at right. Series A. Printer: ABNC.			
	a. Issued note.	20.00	200	—
	s. Specimen.	—	Unc	500

186	10 Colones	Good	Fine	XF
	15.7.1924; 6.1.1925; 6.7.1927; 27.12.1927. Dark Blue on multicolor underprint. Woman holding steam locomotive and woman seated at left. Series A. Printer: ABNC.			
	a. Issued note.	40.00	350	—
	p. Proof.	—	Unc	950
	s. Specimen.	—	Unc	600

187	20 Colones	Good	Fine	XF
	15.7.1924-12.4.1928. Dark blue multicolor underprint. Seated woman holding book and wreath at right. Series A. Printer: ABNC.			
	a. Issued note.	70.00	450	—
	s. Specimen.	—	Unc	1,500

188	50 Colones	Good	Fine	XF
	15.7.1924-10.1.1927. Dark blue on multicolor underprint. Helmeted woman seated holding sword and palm branch at left. Series A. Printer: ABNC.			
	a. Issued note. Rare.	—	—	—
	p. Proof.	—	Unc	1,750
	s. Specimen.	—	Unc	2,500

189	100 Colones	Good	Fine	XF
	24.12.1924-21.10.1927. Dark blue on multicolor underprint. Seated woman holding branch at right. Series A. Printer: ABNC.			
	a. Issued note. Rare.	—	—	—
	p. Proof.	—	Unc	1,750
	s. Specimen.	—	Unc	1,750

Note: The 2, 5 and 10 Colones of Series B were used with provisional oveprints of the Banco Nacional, as were some of #184 and #187.

1929 Issue

189A	5 Colones	Good	Fine	XF
	5.2.1929. Purple. Workers loading bananas on train. Like #198 but without overprint. Back: National arms at center. Printer: TDLR. Rare.	—	—	2,500

189B	10 Colones	Good	Fine	XF
	5.2.1929. Orange on yellow underprint. Workers in field drying coffee beans. Like #199 but without overprint. Back: Large building. Printer: TDLR.	—	—	—

Banco Nacional de Costa Rica

Provisional issues consist of 4 diff. types of ovpt. found on various notes.

1937-1943 Provisional Issue, Ovpt. Type A, W/o Ley

190	1 Colón	Good	Fine	XF
	23.6.1943. Red signature. Red. Series C/B.	5.00	15.00	85.00

191	10 Colones	Good	Fine	XF
	10.3.1937.	15.00	85.00	450

192	20 Colones	Good	Fine	XF
	1937-1938.			
	a. Signature titles: *PRESIDENTE* and *GERENTE*. 10.3.1937; 7.7.1937; 2.3.1938.	25.00	200	425
	b. Signature title: *VICEPRESIDENTE* at left. 22.6.1938.	25.00	200	425

193	50 Colones	Good	Fine	XF
	8.4.1941; 4.2.1942. Red signature. Red.	25.00	250	550

194	100 Colones	Good	Fine	XF
	1937-1942. Red signature. Red.			
	a. Signature title: *GERENTE* at right. 3.11.1937; 29.3.1939; 30.10.1940; 4.2.1942.	15.00	100	350
	b. Signature title: *SUB-GERENTE* at right. 9.7.1941.	15.00	100	350

1937-1938 Provisional Issue, Ovpt. Type B, Ley No. 16 de 5 de Noviembre de 1936

195	2 Colones	Good	Fine	XF
	1937-1938. Red-orange and purple on gold underprint. Portrait Columbus at left. Series C/B. Back: Plantation workers. Printer: TDLR.			
	a. 4 lines of overprint added. signature titles: *PRESIDENTE* and GERENTE 4.1.1937-3.11.1937.	5.00	30.00	90.00
	b. Signature titles: *VICE PRESIDENTE* at left. 22.6.1938.	5.00	30.00	90.00
	c. 5 lines of overprint added. signature title: *PRESIDENTE* at left. 2.3.1938.	5.00	30.00	90.00

1939-1940 Provisional Issue, Ovpt. Type C, Ley No. 16 de 5 de Noviembre de 1936

196	2 Colones	Good	Fine	XF
	15.2.1939-at end of overprint text. Series C/B.	5.00	30.00	90.00

197	2 Colones	Good	Fine	XF
	1940. Series D/A.			
	a. 7.2.1940.	10.00	35.00	100
	b. 9.5.1940.	7.00	15.00	75.00

1937-1939 Provisional Issue, Ovpt. Type D, Ley No. 16 de 5 de Noviembre de 1936

198	5 Colones	Good	Fine	XF
	1937-1938. Purple. Workers loading train with bananas at left, mountain view at right. Series E/B. Back: Arms on back. Printer: TDLR.			
	a. Signature title: *PRESIDENTE* at left. 10.3.1937-2.3.1938.	20.00	125	400
	b. Signature title: *VICE PRESIDENTE* at left. 22.6.1938.	20.00	125	400

		Good	Fine	XF
199	**10 Colones** 11.8.1937; 3.11.1937; 2.3.1938. Orange on yellow underprint. Workers in field drying coffee beans at left center. Series E/B. Back: Large building. Printer: TDLR.	25.00	200	450

		Good	Fine	XF
200	**20 Colones** 1.2.1939. Red signature. Red. Series D/A.	30.00	250	550

1941 Series E

		VG	VF	UNC
201	**2 Colones** 1941-1945. Brown on multicolor underprint. Portrait Juan V. de Coronado at center. Back: Rescue scene with Coronado at center. Printer: W&S.			
	a. Without signature title changes. 5.2.1941; 4.2.1942; 20.1.1943-16.2.1944.	3.00	10.00	45.00
	b. Signature title: *SUB-GERENTE* overprint at right. 18.6.1941; 12.11.1941; 15.7.1942.	2.00	9.00	40.00
	c. Signature title: *VICE-PRESIDENTE* overprint at left. 10.12.1942; 18.11.1942.	2.00	9.00	40.00
	d. Both signature titles overprint 28.2.1945.	2.00	9.00	40.00

		VG	VF	UNC
202	**20 Colones** 1941-1944. Red on multicolor underprint. Portrait Juan de Cavallon at center. Back: Church at Orosi. Printer: W&S.			
	a. Signature title: *SUB-GERENTE* overprint at right. 10.9.1941; 21.7.1943.	20.00	175	500
	b. Signature title: *VICE-PRESIDENTE* overprint at left. 12.11.1942.	20.00	175	500
	c. Without signature title changes: 5.2.1941; 17.3.1942; 12.1.1944.	20.00	175	500
	s. Specimen. Red overprint: *SPECIMEN* twice on face, punch hole cancelled.	—	—	1,000

1939-1946 Series F

		VG	VF	UNC
203	**2 Colones** 1946-1949. Red on multicolor underprint. Portrait Joaquin B. Calvo at center. Back: Plaza in San José. Printer: ABNC.			
	a. Both signature titles overprint 18.9.1946; 13.11.1946; 14.12.1949.	2.00	7.50	40.00
	b. Signature title: *SUB-GERENTE* overprint at right. 23.4.1947-13.8.1947; 7.12.1949.	2.00	6.00	35.00
	c. Signature title: *VICE-PRESIDENTE* overprint at left. 28.1.1948.	2.00	6.00	35.00
	s. Specimen.	—	—	125

		VG	VF	UNC
204	**5 Colones** 5.7.1939-28.10.1942. Green on multicolor underprint. Portrait Juan Mora Fernandez at center. Back: Ruins in Cartago. Printer: W&S.	5.00	35.00	150

		VG	VF	UNC
205	**10 Colones** 1939-1941. Blue on multicolor underprint. Portrait Florencio del Castillo at center. Back: Cacique Indian at center. Printer: W&S.			
	a. Without signature title changes. 8.9.1939-26.3.1941.	10.00	75.00	350
	b. Signature title: *SUB-GERENTE* overprint at right. 10.9.1941.	10.00	75.00	350

206	20 Colones	VG	VF	UNC
	1945-1948. Olive on multicolor underprint. Portrait Gregorio J. Ramirez at right. Back: View of Poas Volcano at center. Printer: ABNC.			
	a. Both signature titles overprint 28.2.1945.	15.00	175	550
	b. Signature title: *SUB-GERENTE* overprint at right. 23.4.1947.	15.00	175	550
	c. Without signature title changes. 3.3.1948.	15.00	175	550
	d. Signature title: *VICE PRESIDENTE*. 4.6.1947.	15.00	175	550
	s. Specimen.	—	—	600

207	50 Colones	VG	VF	UNC
	1942. Black on green and gold underprint. Portrait C. Columbus at center. Back: Scene of Columbus at Cariari in 1502. Printer: W&S.			
	a. Without signature title changes. 9.9.1942.	15.00	150	500
	b. Signature title: *VICE-PRESIDENTE* at left. 1.12.1942.	15.00	150	500
	s. Specimen. Red overprint: *SPECIMEN* twice on face, punch hole cancelled.	—	—	1,000

208	100 Colones	VG	VF	UNC
	3.6.1942; 19.8.1942; 26.8.1942. Olive on multicolor underprint. Vaso Policromo artifact at center. Back: Ceremonial alter. Printer: W&S.			
	a. Issued note.	25.00	175	600
	s. Specimen. Red overprint: *SPECIMEN* twice on face, punch hole cancelled.	—	—	1,250

1942-1944 Series G

209	5 Colones	VG	VF	UNC
	1943-1949. Brown on multicolor underprint. Portrait B. Carillo at right. Back: Bridge at center. Printer: ABNC.			
	a. Without signature title changes. 3.3.1943; 28.1.1948; 3.3.1948.	1.50	7.50	40.00
	b. Both signature titles overprint 28.2.1945; 14.12.1949.	1.50	7.50	40.00
	c. Signature title: *SUB-GERENTE* overprint at right. 16.10.1946; 13.8.1947; 31.8.1949; 30.11.1949; 14.12.1949.	1.50	7.50	40.00
	s. Specimen.	—	—	125

210	10 Colones	VG	VF	UNC
	1942-1949. Light orange on multicolor underprint. Portrait Manuel J. Carazo at left. Back: Large sailing ship at center. Printer: ABNC.			
	a. Without signature title changes. 28.10.1942-12.1.1944; 28.1.1948-3.3.1948.	5.00	40.00	200
	b. Signature title: *SUB-GERENTE* overprint at right. 16.10.1946; 13.8.1947-10.12.1947; 31.8.1949; 30.11.1949.	5.00	40.00	200
	c. Both signature titles overprint 14.12.1949.	5.00	40.00	200
	p1. Proof. Uniface face.	—	—	—
	s. Specimen.	—	—	250

211	50 Colones	VG	VF	UNC
	1944-1948. Grayish green on multicolor underprint. Portrait Manuel G. Escalante at left. Back: Church in Heredia at center. Printer: ABNC.			
	a. Both signature titles overprint 24.5.1944; 7.6.1944.	10.00	70.00	300
	b. Signature title: *VICE-PRESIDENTE* overprint at left. 4.6.1947.	10.00	70.00	300
	c. Without signature title changes. 3.3.1948.	10.00	70.00	300
	s. Specimen.	—	—	500

No.	Description	VG	VF	UNC
212	**100 Colones**	VG	VF	UNC
	1943-1949. Green on multicolor underprint. Portrait Dr. José M. Castro Madriz at left. Back: Old University of Santo Tomas. Printer: ABNC.			
	a. Signature title: *SUB-GERENTE* overprint at right. 17.3.1943; 21.7.1943; 21.12.1949.	15.00	120	400
	b. Without signature title changes. 10.10.1943; 20.10.1943; 16.2.1944; 22.10.1947; 3.3.1948.	15.00	120	400
	c. Signature title: *VICE PRESIDENTE*. 17.3.1943.	15.00	120	400
	s. Specimen.	—	—	425

Banco Central de Costa Rica

1950-1967 Provisional Issue

No.	Description	VG	VF	UNC
215	**5 Colones**	VG	VF	UNC
	1950-1951. Series G.			
	a. Without signature title changes. 20.7.1950; 5.10.1950; 6.12.1950.	3.00	35.00	175
	b. *POR* (for) added to left of signature title at left. 8.8.1951.	3.00	35.00	175
	c. Signature title: *VICE-PRESIDENTE* overprint at left. 5.9.1951.	1.00	6.00	30.00
216	**10 Colones**	VG	VF	UNC
	1950-1951. Series G.			
	a. Without signature title changes. 3.4.1950; 8.8.1951.	10.00	60.00	300
	b. *SUB-GERENTE* signature overprint at right. 20.0.1950.	10.00	60.00	300
217	**20 Colones**	VG	VF	UNC
	3.4.1950; 8.11.1950; 7.3.1951. Series F.	6.00	30.00	375

No.	Description	VG	VF	UNC
218	**50 Colones**	VG	VF	UNC
	1950-1953. Series G.			
	a. Without signature title changes. 3.4.1950-5.3.1952.	8.00	45.00	400
	b. *POR* (for) added to left of signature title on left. 10.10.1951; 5.12.1951; 25.3.1953.	8.00	45.00	400
219	**100 Colones**	VG	VF	UNC
	1952-1955. Series.			
	a. Without signature title changes. 23.4.1952; 28.10.1953; 16.6.1954.	15.00	120	425
	b. Signature title: *SUB-GERENTE* overprint at right. 2.3.1955.	15.00	120	425

Note: For 2 Colones 1967 overprint for Banco Central, see #235 in Volume 3.

1951; 1952 Issue - Series A

No.	Description	VG	VF	UNC
220	**5 Colones**	VG	VF	UNC
	1951-1958. Green on multicolor underprint. Portrait B. Carillo at right. Back: Coffee worker. Printer: ABNC.			
	a. *POR* (for) added to left of signature title at right. 20.11.1952.	3.00	15.00	66.00
	b. Without signature title changes. 2.7.1952-6.8.1958.	3.00	15.00	60.00
	c. Signature title: *SUB-GERENTE* overprint at right. 11.7.1956.	3.00	15.00	50.00
	d. *POR* added to left of signature title at left. 12.9.1951; 26.5.1954.	3.00	15.00	50.00
	s. Specimen. Punch hole cancelled.	—	—	150

No.	Description	VG	VF	UNC
221	**10 Colones**	VG	VF	UNC
	1951-1962. Blue on multicolor underprint. Portrait A. Echeverria at center. Back: Ox-cart at center. Printer: W&S.			
	a. *POR* added to left of sign title at left. 24.10.1951; 8.11.1951; 19.11.1951; 5.12.1951; 29.10.1952.	6.00	25.00	120
	b. *POR* added to both signature titles. 28.11.1951.	6.00	25.00	100
	c. Without *POR* title changes. 2.7.1952; 28.10.1953-27.6.1962.	6.00	25.00	100
	d. *POR* added to left of signature title at right. 20.11.1952.	6.00	25.00	100

No.	Description	VG	VF	UNC
222	**20 Colones**	VG	VF	UNC
	1952-1964. Red on multicolor underprint. Portrait C. Picado at center. Back: University building at center. Printer: W&S.			
	a. Date at left center, without signature title changes. 26.2.1952; 11.6.1952; 11.8.1954; 14.10.1955; 13.2.1957; 10.12.62.	15.00	50.00	200
	b. Signature title: *SUB-GERENTE* overprint at right. 20.4.1955.	15.00	50.00	175
	c. Date at lower left 7.11.1957-9.9.1964.	15.00	50.00	175
	d. *POR* added at left of signature title at left. 25.3.1953; 25.2.1954.	15.00	50.00	175

No.	Description	VG	VF	UNC
223	**50 Colones**	VG	VF	UNC
	1952-1964. Olive on multicolor underprint. Portrait right. F. Guardia at center. Back: National Library at center. Printer: W&S.			
	a. 10.6.1952-25.11.1959.	15.00	50.00	225
	b. 14.9.1960-9.9.1964.	15.00	45.00	200
224	**100 Colones**	VG	VF	UNC
	1952-1960. Black on multicolor underprint. Portrait J. R. Mora at center. Back: Statue of J. Santamaría at center.			
	a. Without signature title changes: 11.6.1952-29.4.1960.	15.00	35.00	240
	b. Signature title: *SUB-GERENTE* overprint at right. 27.3.1957.	15.00	35.00	200

		VG	VF	UNC
225	**500 Colones** 1951-1977. Purple on multicolor underprint. Portrait M. M. Gutiérrez at right. Back: National Theater at center. Printer: ABNC.			
	a. 10.10.1951-6.5.1969.	60.00	300	850
	b. 7.4.1970-26.4.1977.	50.00	250	500
	s. Specimen. Punch hole cancelled.	—	—	1,000

		VG	VF	UNC
226	**1000 Colones** 1952-1974. Red on multicolor underprint. Portrait J. Pena at left. Back: Central and National Bank at center. Printer: ABNC.			
	a. 11.6.1952-6.10.1959.	125	500	1,350
	b. 25.4.1962-6.5.1969.	100	350	850
	c. 7.4.1970-12.6.1974.	60.00	150	300
	s. Specimen. Punch hole cancelled.	—	—	600

1958 Issue

		VG	VF	UNC
227	**5 Colones** 29.10.1958-8.11.1962. Green on multicolor underprint. Portrait B. Carrillo at center. Series B. Back: Coffee worker at center. Printer: W&S.	3.50	25.00	65.00

The Republic of Croatia (Hrvatska), has an area of 56,542 sq. km. and a population of 4.49 million. Capital: Zagreb.

The lands that today comprise Croatia were part of the Austro-Hungarian Empire until the close of World War I. In 1918, the Croats, Serbs, and Slovenes formed a kingdom known after 1929 as Yugoslavia. Following World War II, Yugoslavia became a federal independent Communist state under the strong hand of Marshal Tito. Although Croatia declared its independence from Yugoslavia in 1991, it took four years of sporadic, but often bitter, fighting before occupying Serb armies were mostly cleared from Croatian lands. Under UN supervision, the last Serb-held enclave in eastern Slavonia was returned to Croatia in 1998.

Local Serbian forces supported by the Yugoslav Federal Army had developed a military stronghold and proclaimed an independent "SRPSKE KRAJINA" state in the area around Knin, located in southern Croatia. In August 1995 Croat forces overran this political-military enclave.

RULERS:

Austrian, 1527-1918
Yugoslavian, 1918-1941

MONETARY SYSTEM:

1 Dinar = 100 Para 1918-1941, 1945-
1 Kuna = 100 Banica 1941-1945
1 Kuna = 100 Lipa, 1994-
1 Dinar = 100 Para

REVOLUTION OF 1848

Croatia-Slavonia-Dalmatia

1848 Assignat Issue

		Good	Fine	XF
A1	**25 Forint** 5.5.1848. Grayish blue. Arms at upper center. Hand signature of Count Jelacic, governor of the triple kingdom. (Not issued). Rare.	—	—	—
A2	**100 Forint** 5.5.1848. Arms at upper center. Hand signature of Count Jelacic, governor of the triple kingdom. (Not issued). Requires confirmation.	—	—	—
A3	**1000 Forint** 5.5.1848. Olive green. Arms at upper center. Hand signature of Count Jelacic, governor of the triple kingdom. 240x170mm. (Not issued). Rare.	—	—	—

Note: In 1850 all but 8 pieces were apparently burned.

KINGDOM, WWII AXIS INFLUENCE

Nezavisna Drzava Hrvatska

Independent State of Croatia

Government Notes

1941 Issue

		VG	VF	UNC
1	**50 Kuna** 26.5.1941. Red-brown. Arms at upper left. Printer: G&D, Berlin.			
	a. Issued note.	1.00	7.00	25.00
	s. Specimen. Red overprint: *UZORAK*. Serial # A0000000.	—	—	300
2	**100 Kuna** 26.5.1941. Dark blue on light brown underprint. Ustasha emblem. Printer: G&D, Berlin.			
	a. Issued note.	0.75	2.00	10.00
	s. Specimen. Red overprint: *UZORAK*.	—	—	350
3	**500 Kuna** 26.5.1941. Green on pale yellow underprint. Corn sheaves at right center. Ustasha emblem underprint at left. Back: Ustasha emblem in underprint at left. Printer: G&D, Berlin.			
	a. Issued note.	4.00	12.50	50.00
	s. Specimen. Red overprint: *UZORAK*.	—	—	350

#	Description	VG	VF	UNC
4	**1000 Kuna** 26.5.1941. Brown. Croatian farmer's wife at left. Ustasha emblem in underprint at center. Back: Low mountain range across center. Printer: G&D, Berlin.			
	a. Issued note.	0.75	2.00	10.00
	s. Specimen. Red overprint: *UZORAK*.	—	—	400

1941 Second Issue

#	Description	VG	VF	UNC
5	**10 Kuna** 30.8.1941. Brown on olive underprint. Ustasha emblem at lower right. Printer: Rozankowski.			
	a. Single letter prefix.	1.00	5.00	20.00
	b. Double letter prefix.	0.75	3.50	15.00
	s. Specimen. Red overprint: *UZORAK*. Prefix C.	—	—	300

1942 Issue

#	Description	VG	VF	UNC
6	**50 Banica** 25.9.1942. Blue on light brown underprint. Back: Arms at upper center on back. Printer: Croat Mint, Zagreb. Vertical format.			
	a. Single letter prefix.	0.75	3.00	12.50
	b. Double letter prefix.	0.50	2.00	10.00
	s. Specimen. Red overprint: *UZORAK*.	—	—	200
7	**1 Kuna** 25.9.1942. Dark blue on brown. Arms at right. Printer: Croat Mint, Zagreb. Vertical format.	VG	VF	UNC
	a. Single letter prefix.	0.50	2.00	10.00
	b. Double letter prefix.	0.50	2.00	8.00
	s. Specimen. Red overprint: *UZORAK*.	—	—	200

#	Description	VG	VF	UNC
8	**2 Kune** 25.9.1942. Dark brown on red-brown underprint. Arms at right. Vertical format.			
	a. Single letter prefix.	0.50	2.00	10.00
	b. Double letter prefix.	0.50	2.00	8.00

1944 Issue

#	Description	VG	VF	UNC
9	**20 Kuna** 15.1.1944. Brown on tan underprint. Arms at right. Printer: G&D, Berlin. (Not issued).			
	a. Single letter prefix.	—	20.00	60.00
	b. Double letter prefix.	—	15.00	50.00
	s. Specimen. Red overprint: *UZORAK*.	—	—	—
10	**50 Kuna** 15.1.1944. Black on green and light orange underprint. Arms at right. Printer: G&D, Berlin. (Not issued).	VG	VF	UNC
	a. Without serial #.	—	180	250
	b. With normal serial #.	—	200	600
	s. Specimen. Red overprint: *UZORAK*.	—	—	—

Hrvatska Drzavna Banka

Croatian State Bank

1943 Issue

#	Description	VG	VF	UNC
11	**100 Kuna** 1.9.1943. Dark blue on light brown underprint. Round design of birds and flowers at right. Back: Mother and child in Croatian dress at center. Printer: G&D, Leipzig.			
	a. 7-digit serial #.	2.00	7.50	25.00
	s. Specimen. Red overprint: *UZORAK*.	—	—	—

#	Description	VG	VF	UNC
11A	**500 Kuna** 1.9.1943. Lilac on violet and rose underprint. Printer: G&D, Leipzig. (Not issued).			
	a. Serial #C055000-C0575000.	—	400	1,000
	s. Specimen. Red overprint: *UZORAK*.	—	—	650

		VG	VF	UNC
12	**1000 Kuna** 1.9.1943. Brown on yellow and green underprint. Frieze at center. Back: Two Croatian women. Printer: G&D, Leipzig.			
	a. Issued note. 7-digit serial #.	0.50	2.00	8.00
	s. Specimen. Red overprint: *UZORAK*.	—	—	—

		VG	VF	UNC
13	**5000 Kuna** 1.9.1943. Brown on red-brown and blue underprint. Hexagonal receptacle at right. Back: Croatian couple. Printer: G&D, Leipzig.			
	a. Issued note. 7-digit serial #.	1.00	2.50	10.00
	s. Specimen. Red overprint: UZORAK.	—	—	—

		VG	VF	UNC
14	**5000 Kuna** 15.7.1943. Brown on violet and dull green underprint. Woman in national costume at left. Printer: G&D, Leipzig.			
	a. Single letter prefix.	2.00	10.00	25.00
	b. Double letter prefix.	2.00	7.00	20.00
	r. Remainder. Without serial #. Cross-cancelled.	—	10.00	30.00
	s. Specimen. Red overprint: *UZORAK*.	—	—	—

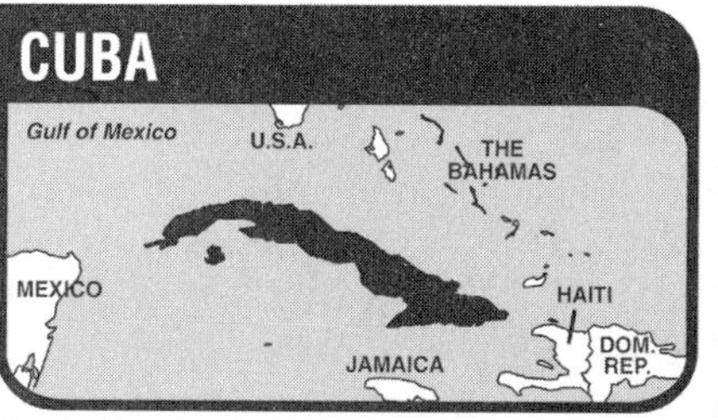

The Republic of Cuba, situated at the northern edge of the Caribbean Sea about 145 km. south of Florida, has an area of 110,860 sq. km. and a population of 11.4 million. Capital: Havana. The Cuban economy is based on the cultivation and refining of sugar, which provides 80 percent of export earnings.

The native Amerindian population of Cuba began to decline after the European discovery of the island by Christopher Columbus in 1492 and following its development as a Spanish colony during the next several centuries. Large numbers of African slaves were imported to work the coffee and sugar plantations, and Havana became the launching point for the annual treasure fleets bound for Spain from Mexico and Peru. Spanish rule, marked initially by neglect, became increasingly repressive, provoking an independence movement and occasional rebellions that were harshly suppressed. It was US intervention during the Spanish-American War in 1898 that finally overthrew Spanish rule. The subsequent Treaty of Paris established Cuban independence, which was granted in 1902 after a three-year transition period. Fidel Castro led a rebel army to victory in 1959; his iron rule held the subsequent regime together for nearly five decades. He stepped down as president in February 2008 in favor of his younger brother Raul Castro. Cuba's Communist revolution, with Soviet support, was exported throughout Latin America and Africa during the 1960s, 1970s, and 1980s. The country is now slowly recovering from a severe economic downturn in 1990, following the withdrawal of former Soviet subsidies. Cuba portrays its difficulties as the result of the US embargo in place since 1961.

RULERS:

Spanish to 1898

MONETARY SYSTEM:

1 Peso = 100 Centavos
1 Peso Convertible = 1 U.S.A. Dollar, 1995-

SPANISH ADMINISTRATION

El Banco Español de la Habana

Cardenas

1860s Issue

		Good	Fine	XF
33A	**10 Pesos** 186x. Rare.	—	—	—
33B	**25 Pesos** 186x. Rare.	—	—	—
33C	**50 Pesos** 186x. Rare.	—	—	—
33D	**100 Pesos** 186x. Rare.	—	—	—
33E	**300 Pesos** 186x. Rare.	—	—	—
33F	**500 Pesos** 186x. Rare.	—	—	—
33G	**1000 Pesos** 186x. Rare.	—	—	—

Matanzas

1860s Issue

		Good	Fine	XF
34	**5 Pesos** 186x. Printer: NBNC. Requires confirmation.	—	—	—

		Good	Fine	XF
35	**10 Pesos** 186x Light blue. Printer: NBNC.. Rare.	—	—	—
36	**25 Pesos** 186x. Printer: NBNC. Requires confirmation.	—	—	—

		Good	Fine	XF
37	**50 Pesos** 186x. Printer: NBNC. a. Issued note. Rare.	—	—	—
	b. Punch hole cancelled. Rare.	—	—	—
38	**100 Pesos** 186x. Requires confirmation. Printer: NBNC.	—	—	—

Sagua La Grande

1860s Issue

#38A-38G similar to #12-17. Printer: NBNC.

		Good	Fine	XF
38A	**10 Pesos** 186x. Printer: NBNC.Rare.	—	—	—
38B	**25 Pesos** 186x. Printer: NBNC. Rare.	—	—	—
38C	**50 Pesos** 186x. Printer: NBNC. Rare.	—	—	—
38D	**100 Pesos** 186x. Red and black. Printer: NBNC. Rare.	—	—	—
38E	**300 Pesos** 186x. Printer: NBNC.Rare.	—	—	—
38F	**500 Pesos** 186x. Brown and black. Printer: NBNC. Rare.	—	—	—
38G	**1000 Pesos** 186x. Printer: NBNC. Rare.	—	—	—

Habana

1857 Issue

		Good	Fine	XF
A1	**50 Pesos** 18xx. Allegorical woman seated with Indian, lion and symbols of commerce at top center. Signature varieties.	—	—	—
1	**100 Pesos** 1857-1859. Black on blue paper. Rare. PC: Blue.	—	—	—
2	**300 Pesos** 1857-1859. Black. Allegorical woman seated with Indian, lion and symbols of commerce at top center. Signature varieties. Rare.	—	—	—

		Good	Fine	XF
3	**500 Pesos** 1.2.1857-1859. Black on pink paper. Allegorical woman seated with Indian, lion and symbols of commerce at top center. Signature varieties. Rare. PC: Pink.	—	—	—
4	**1000 Pesos** 1857-1859. Black. Allegorical woman seated with Indian, lion and symbols of commerce at top center. Signature varieties. Rare.	—	—	—

1867 Issue

		Good	Fine	XF
5	**25 Pesos** 1867-1868. Black on green underprint. Allegorical woman seated with Indian, lion and symbols of commerce at top center. Signature varieties. Rare.	—	—	—
6	**50 Pesos** 1867-1868. Black on tan underprint. Allegorical woman seated with Indian, lion and symbols of commerce at top center. Signature varieties. Rare. PC: Green.	—	—	—
7	**100 Pesos** 1867-1868. Black on green underprint. Allegorical woman seated with Indian, lion and symbols of commerce at top center. Signature varieties. Rare. PC: Yellow.	—	—	—

		Good	Fine	XF
8	**300 Pesos** 13.7.1867-1869. Black on tan underprint. Allegorical woman seated with Indian, lion and symbols of commerce at top center. Signature varieties. Rare. PC: Light purple.	—	—	—
9	**500 Pesos** 1867-1868. Black on green underprint. Allegorical woman seated with Indian, lion and symbols of commerce at top center. Signature varieties. Rare. PC: Red,	—	—	—

Color Abbreviation Guide

New to the *Standard Catalog of ® World Paper Money* are the following abbreviations related to color references:

BC: Back color
PC: Paper color

10 **1000 Pesos** — Good — Fine — XF
26.8.1867-1868. Black on green underprint. Allegorical woman seated with Indian, lion and symbols of commerce at top center. Signature varieties. Rare. PC: White.

Good	Fine	XF
—	—	—

1869 Issue

11 **5 Pesos**
1869-1879. Rust and black. Seated allegorical figure at upper center. Signature varieties. Printer: NBNC. Rare.

Good	Fine	XF
—	—	—

12 **10 Pesos**
1869-1879. Rust and black. Seated allegorical figure at upper center. Signature varieties. Printer: NBNC. Rare.

Good	Fine	XF
—	—	—

13 **25 Pesos**
1869-1879. Blue and black. Seated allegorical figure at upper center. Signature varieties. Printer: NBNC. Rare.

Good	Fine	XF
—	—	—

14 **50 Pesos**
1869-1879. Yellow and black. Seated allegorical figure at upper center. Signature varieties. Printer: NBNC. Rare.

Good	Fine	XF
—	—	—

15 **100 Pesos**
1869-1879. Red and black. Seated allegorical figure at upper center. Signature varieties. Printer: NBNC. Rare.

Good	Fine	XF
—	—	—

16 **300 Pesos**
1869-1879. Brown and black. Seated allegorical figure at upper center. Signature varieties. Printer: NBNC. Rare.

Good	Fine	XF
—	—	—

17 **500 Pesos**
1869-1879. Tan and black. Seated allegorical figure at upper center. Signature varieties. Printer: NBNC. Rare.

Good	Fine	XF
—	—	—

18 **1000 Pesos**
1869-1879. Green and black. Seated allegorical figure at upper center. Signature varieties. Printer: NBNC. Rare.

Good	Fine	XF
—	—	—

1872 First Issue

19 **5 Pesos**
1872-1887. Black on pink and green underprint. Woman at upper center. Signature varieties. Printer: BWC (without imprint). Uniface.

Good	Fine	XF
600	2,000	—

20 **10 Pesos**
1872-1892. Woman by beehive at upper center. Signature varieties. Printer: BWC (without imprint). Uniface.

Good	Fine	XF
600	2,000	—

		Good	Fine	XF
21	**25 Pesos** 1872-1891. Uniface. Mercury holding a caduceus at upper center. Signature varieties. Printer: BWC (without imprint).	1,000	3,250	—

		Good	Fine	XF
22	**50 Pesos** 1872-1890. Youth carrying a bundle of sugar cane at upper center. Signature varieties. Printer: BWC (without imprint). Uniface.	1,200	3,750	—
23	**100 Pesos** 1872-1887. Black on light purple and green underprint. Woman at upper center. Signature varieties. Printer: BWC (without imprint). Uniface.	—	—	—
24	**300 Pesos** 1872-1887. Printer: BWC (without imprint). Uniface. Requires confirmation.	—	—	—
25	**500 Pesos** 1872-1887. Printer: BWC (without imprint). Uniface. Requires confirmation.	—	—	—

		Good	Fine	XF
26	**1000 Pesos** 1872-1887. Portrait Queen Isabella I of Castile at upper center. Signature varieties. Printer: BWC (without imprint). Uniface. Rare.	—	—	—

1872 Second Issue

		Good	Fine	XF
27	**1 Peso** 1872-1883. Seated allegorical figure at upper center. Signature varieties. Back: Columbus in sight of land. Printer: CNBB. Various varieties.			
	a. 15.6.1872.	30.00	125	400
	b. 1.7.1872.	30.00	125	400
	c. 15.5.1876.	30.00	125	400
	d. 31.5.1879.	30.00	125	400
	e. 6.8.1883.	30.00	125	400
	p. As e. Uniface Proof	—	Unc	350

		Good	Fine	XF
28	**3 Pesos** 1872-1883. Black. Seated allegorical figure at upper center. Signature varieties. Back: Columbus in sight of land. Printer: CNBB.			
	a. 15.6.1872.	60.00	300	1,000
	b. 1.7.1872.	60.00	300	1,000
	c. 1.12.1877.	60.00	300	1,000
	d. 7.3.1879. Requires confirmation.	—	—	—
	e. 31.5.1879.	60.00	300	1,000
	f. 6.8.1883.	60.00	300	1,000

1872 Third Issue

		Good	Fine	XF
29	**5 Centavos** 1872-1883. Black. Crowned shields at left. Signature varieties. Back: Seated allegorical figure. Printer: NBNC. PC: Light tan or yellow.			
	a. 1.7.1872.	2.50	10.00	35.00
	b. 15.5.1876. With ABNC monogram.	1.75	7.50	25.00
	c. 15.5.1876. Without imprint.	—	—	—
	d. 6.8.1883.	1.75	7.50	25.00
	s1. 1876. Specimen.	—	Unc	250
	s2. 1883. Specimen.	—	Unc	300
30	**10 Centavos** 1872-1883. Black. Crowned shields at left. Signature varieties. Back: Seated allegorical figure. Printer: NBNC. PC: Light tan.			
	a. 1.7.1872.	3.00	12.00	40.00
	b. Imprint. 15.5.1876.	2.50	10.00	35.00
	c. Without imprint. 15.5.1876.	2.50	10.00	35.00
	d. 6.8.1883.	2.50	10.00	35.00
	s1. 1876. Specimen.	—	Unc	300
	s2. 1883. Specimen.	—	Unc	300

31	25 Centavos	Good	Fine	XF
	1872-1876. Black. Crowned shields at left. Signature varieties. Back: Seated allegorical figure. Printer: NBNC.			
	a. 1.7.1872.	6.00	25.00	85.00
	b. 15.5.1876. Reported not confirmed.	—	—	—

32	50 Centavos	Good	Fine	XF
	1872-1876. Black. Crowned shield at left center. Signature varieties. Back: Seated allegorical figure. Printer: NBNC.			
	a. 1.7.1872.	8.00	30.00	125
	b. 15.5.1876.	6.00	25.00	100

1889 Issue

33	50 Centavos	Good	Fine	XF
	28.10.1889. Black. Spaniard and Indian at right. Back: Noble Havana fountain at center. Printer: ABNC. PC: Tan.			
	a. With counterfoil.	35.00	125	350
	b. Without counterfoil.	10.00	40.00	150
	s. As b. Specimen.	—	Unc	400

Bonos del Tesoro

1865 Issue

38J	500 Pesos	Good	Fine	XF
	24.9.1865. Black. Arms in underprint at center. Interest-bearing note payable to bearer. Punch hole cancellation at left.	—	—	—

1866 Provisional Issue

38K	20 Pesos	Good	Fine	XF
	1866 (- old date 1848). Black on light red underprint. Printer: Durand, Baldwin & Co., New York.	—	—	—

Many authorities currently beleive this item to be spurious.

38L	50 Pesos	Good	Fine	XF
	1866 (- old date 1848). Brown. Printer: Durand, Baldwin & Co., New York.	—	—	—

Many authorities currently believe this item to be spurious.

Billete del Tesoro

1874 Issue

38M	100 Pesos	Good	Fine	XF
	30.6.1874. Black. Interest-bearing note payable to bearer. Arms in underprint at center.	—	—	—
38N	500 Pesos	Good	Fine	XF
	30.6.1874. Black. Arms in underprint at center. Similar to #38M.	—	—	—

El Tesoro de la Isla de Cuba

1891 Treasury Note Issue

39	5 Pesos	Good	Fine	XF
	12.8.1891. Black on blue and orange underprint. Winged woman with trumpet by woman with book at left. Printer: BWC.			
	a. Signed.	—	—	—
	b. Unsigned.	35.00	100	250

Color Abbreviation Guide

New to the *Standard Catalog of ® World Paper Money* are the following abbreviations related to color references:

BC: Back color
PC: Paper color

40	10 Pesos	Good	Fine	XF
	12.8.1891. Black on blue-green underprint. Mercury with shield at right. Printer: BWC.			
	a. Signed.	—	—	—
	b. Unsigned.	50.00	125	325

41	20 Pesos	Good	Fine	XF
	12.8.1891. Black on purple and green underprint. Woman seated with shield at left. Printer: BWC.			
	a. Signed.	—	—	—
	b. Unsigned.	52.50	135	350

42	50 Pesos	Good	Fine	XF
	12.8.1891. Black on purple and orange underprint. Mercury and youth seated at left. Printer: BWC.			
	a. Signed.	—	—	—
	b. Unsigned.	65.00	175	450

43	100 Pesos	Good	Fine	XF
	12.8.1891. Black on purple and orange underprint. Young boy seated with lamb at left, young girl seated at right. Printer: BWC.			
	a. Signed.	—	—	—
	b. Unsigned.	75.00	200	550

44	200 Pesos	Good	Fine	XF
	12.8.1891. Black on brown and red underprint. Justice standing at left, young farm couple at right. Printer: BWC.			
	a. Signed.	—	—	—
	b. Unsigned.	120	350	950

Banco Español de la Isla de Cuba

1896 Issue

45	5 Centavos	VG	VF	UNC
	15.5.1896. Black. Arms at left. Series J. Back: Tobacco plants at center. Printer: ABNC.			
	a. Issued note without overprint.	0.25	1.25	4.50
	b. Red overprint: *PLATA* across face on a.	2.00	10.00	35.00
	s. As a. Specimen.	—	—	300

46	50 Centavos	VG	VF	UNC
	15.5.1896. Black. Arms at right. Series H. Back: Tobacco plants at center. Printer: ABNC.			
	a. Issued note without overprint.	0.50	3.00	9.00
	b. Red overprint: *PLATA* across face on a.	2.50	15.00	45.00
	s. As a. Specimen.	—	—	250

47	1 Peso	VG	VF	UNC
	15.5.1896. Black. Arms at center. Series G. Back: Queen Regent María Cristina at center. Printer: ABNC.			
	a. Issued note without overprint.	1.00	5.00	15.00
	b. Red overprint: *PLATA* across face on a.	2.50	15.00	45.00
	s. As a. Specimen.	—	—	275

48	5 Pesos	VG	VF	UNC
	1896-1897. Black on orange and gold underprint. Woman seated with bales at center. Back: Arms at center. Printer: ABNC.			
	a. Issued note without overprint 15.5.1896.	0.75	3.50	12.50
	b. Overprint: PLATA in red on back of a. 15.5.1896.	0.75	3.50	12.50
	c. Without overprint 15.2.1897.	0.75	3.50	12.50
	s. As a. Specimen.	—	—	500

49	10 Pesos	VG	VF	UNC
	15.5.1896. Black on green underprint. Ox cart at top center. Back: Arms at center.			
	a. Handwritten or hand stamped partially printed date, without overprint.	1.00	5.00	17.50
	b. Handwritten date and month, handstamped signature.	75.00	200	—
	c. Printed date, without overprint.	1.00	4.00	12.50
	d. Printed date, overprint: red *PLATA* on back of c.	1.00	5.00	15.00
	s. Specimen.	—	—	500

#	Denomination	VG	VF	UNC
50	**50 Pesos**	VG	VF	UNC
	15.5.1896. Black on red and green underprint. Allegorical woman at left. Printer: BWC (without imprint.)			
	a. Issued note without overprint	27.50	65.00	175
	b. overprint: red PLATA on back of a.	20.00	50.00	150
51	**100 Pesos**	VG	VF	UNC
	15.5.1896. Black on orange and green underprint. Woman and cow at left. Printer: BWC (without imprint.)	75.00	200	750
51A	**500 Pesos**	VG	VF	UNC
	15.5.1896. Black on orange and blue underprint. Winged woman and spear at left. Back: Columbus at center. Printer: BWC (without imprint.)	—	—	—

#	Denomination	VG	VF	UNC
51B	**1000 Pesos**	VG	VF	UNC
	15.5.1896. Black on brown and gray underprint. Justice with scales at left. Printer: BWC (without imprint.)	—	—	—

1897 Issue

#52-53 Note: For 5 Pesos dated 1897, see #48c.

#	Denomination	VG	VF	UNC
52	**10 Centavos**	VG	VF	UNC
	15.2.1897. Black. Arms at right. Series K. Back: Ship at center. Printer: ABNC.			
	a. Issued note.	0.25	1.50	7.50
	s. Specimen.	—	—	300

#	Denomination	VG	VF	UNC
53	**20 Centavos**	VG	VF	UNC
	15.2.1897. Black. Arms at center. Series I. Back: Harvesting sugar cane at center. Printer: ABNC.			
	a. Issued note.	0.25	1.50	7.50
	s. Specimen.	—	—	300

1868-1876 REVOLUTION

La Republica de Cuba

1869 Issue

#	Denomination	Good	Fine	XF
54	**50 Centavos**	Good	Fine	XF
	1869. Black on gray underprint. Flag at center. Uniface.	6.00	15.00	50.00

#55-60 day and month handwritten on some notes.

> **Color Abbreviation Guide**
>
> New to the *Standard Catalog of ® World Paper Money* are the following abbreviations related to color references:
>
> BC: Back color
>
> PC: Paper color

#	Denomination	Good	Fine	XF
55	**1 Peso**	Good	Fine	XF
	1869. Black. Arms at upper left. Uniface.			
	a. Without signature Red seal.	8.00	25.00	65.00
	b. As a. without red seal.	10.00	35.00	90.00
	c. Signed note, signature stamped.	35.00	125	275

#	Denomination	Good	Fine	XF
56	**5 Pesos**	Good	Fine	XF
	1869. Black. Draped shield at left. Uniface.			
	a. Without signature.	12.50	37.50	125
	b. Hand signature.	25.00	75.00	225
	c. Stamped signature.	25.00	75.00	225

#	Denomination	Good	Fine	XF
57	**10 Pesos**	Good	Fine	XF
	1869. Black. Draped shield at left. Uniface.			
	a. Without signature.	60.00	175	550
	b. Hand signature of Céspedes.	125	500	1,000
58	**50 Pesos**	Good	Fine	XF
	1869. Black. Draped shield at left. Uniface. Rare.	—	—	—

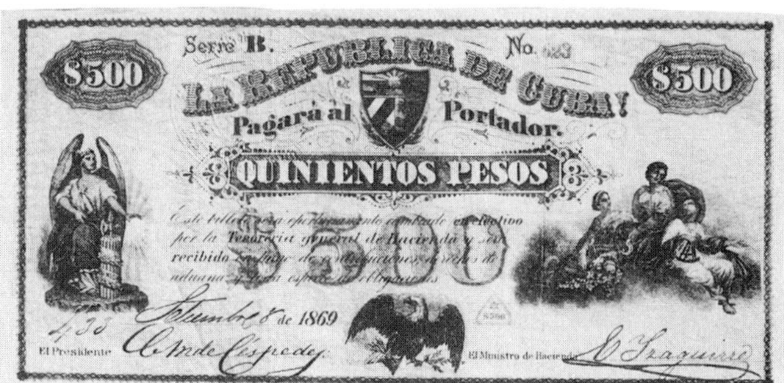

#	Denomination	Good	Fine	XF
59	**500 Pesos**	Good	Fine	XF
	8.9.1869. Black. Angel at left, three women seated at right, eagle at lower center.	500	1,500	—

#	Denomination	Good	Fine	XF
60	**1000 Pesos**	Good	Fine	XF
	6.9.1869. Red and brown. Angel at left, three women seated at right, eagle at lower center.	250	950	1,850

Junta Central Republicana de Cuba y Puerto Rico

1869 Issue

#61-64 issued by a military revolutionist group located in New York City. Uniface.

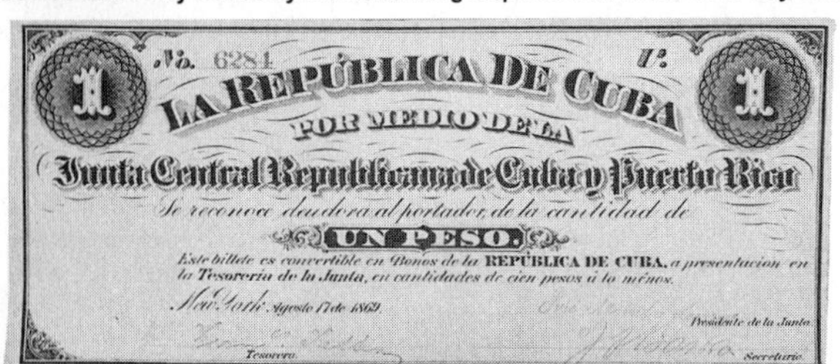

		Good	Fine	XF
61	**1 Peso** 17.8.1869. Black. Uniface.	10.00	50.00	150

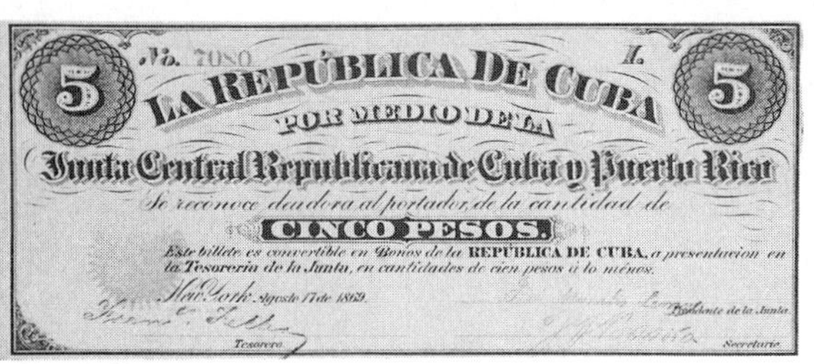

		Good	Fine	XF
62	**5 Pesos** 17.8.1869. Blue. Like #61.	60.00	250	650

		Good	Fine	XF
63	**10 Pesos** 17.8.1869. Green.	450	1,500	—

		Good	Fine	XF
64	**20 Pesos** 17.8.1869. Red. Rare.	—	—	—

REPUBLIC

Banco Nacional de Cuba

National Bank of Cuba

1905 First Issue

		VG	VF	UNC
65	**1 Peso** ND (1905). Black. Portrait D. Méndez Capote at center. Back: Fortress at center. Printer: ABNC.			
	a. Not Issued. Rare.	—	—	—
	s. Specimen.	—	—	5,000

		VG	VF	UNC
66	**2 Pesos** ND (1905). Black. Portrait M. Gomez at right. Back: Fortress at center. Printer: ABNC.			
	a. Not issued. Rare.	—	—	—
	s. Specimen.	—	—	6,000

		VG	VF	UNC
67	**5 Pesos** ND (1905). Black. Text: *EN ORO DEL CUÑO ESPAÑOL PAGARA AL PORTADOR A LA PRESENTACION.* Portrait J. Montes at left. Back: Fortress at center. Printer: ABNC.			
	a. Not issued. Rare.	—	—	—
	s. Specimen.	—	—	6,000

		VG	VF	UNC
68	**10 Pesos** ND (1905). Black. Text: *EN ORO DEL CUÑO ESPAÑOL PAGARA AL PORTADOR A LA PRESENTACION.* Portrait T. Estrada Palma at center. Back: Fortress at center. Printer: ABNC.			
	a. Issued note. Rare.	—	—	—
	s. Specimen.	—	—	7,500

1905 Second Issue

		VG	VF	UNC
68A	**1 Dollar** ND (ca.1905). Black. Portrait D. Mendez Capote at center. Text: *EN ORO DEL CUNO ESPANOL PAGARA AL PORTADOR A LA PRESENTACION.* Printer: ABNC. Proof.	—	—	—
68B	**2 Dollars** ND (ca.1905). Black. Portrait M. Gomez at right. Text: *EN ORO DEL CUNO ESPANOL PAGARA AL PORTADOR A LA PRESENTACION.* Printer: ABNC. Proof.	—	—	—
68C	**5 Dollars** ND (ca.1905). Black. Portrait J. Montes at left. Printer: ABNC. Proof.	—	—	—
68D	**10 Dollars** ND (ca.1905). Black. Portrait T. Estrada Palma at center. Printer: ABNC. Proof.	—	—	—

República de Cuba
Certificados de Plata (Silver Certificates)

		Good	Fine	XF
69	**1 Peso** 1934-1949. Black on blue underprint. Port. J. Martí at center. Back: Arms at center. Printer: BEP, United States.			
	a. 1934.	4.00	20.00	75.00
	b. 1936.	4.00	32.50	125
	c. 1936A.	4.00	25.00	90.00
	d. 1938.	4.00	18.00	70.00
	e. 1943.	4.00	18.00	70.00
	f. 1945.	4.00	18.00	70.00
	g. 1948.	4.00	18.00	70.00
	h. 1949.	4.00	22.50	85.00

		Good	Fine	XF
70	**5 Pesos** 1934-1949. Black on orange underprint. Portrait M. M. Gomez at center. Back: Arms at center. Printer: BEP, United States.			
	a. 1934.	15.00	45.00	175
	b. 1936.	15.00	45.00	175
	c. 1936A.	15.00	45.00	175
	d. 1938.	15.00	40.00	160
	e. 1943.	15.00	45.00	165
	f. 1945.	15.00	40.00	160
	g. 1948.	15.00	40.00	160
	h. 1949.	15.00	45.00	175

		Good	Fine	XF
71	**10 Pesos** 1934-1948. Black on brown underprint. Portrait C. Manuel de Céspedes at center. Back: Arms at center. Printer: BEP, United States.			
	a. 1934.	25.00	82.50	300
	b. 1936.	25.00	82.50	300
	c. 1936A.	25.00	82.50	300
	d. 1938.	25.00	80.00	300
	e. 1943.	25.00	82.50	300
	f. 1945.	25.00	80.00	300
	g. 1948.	25.00	80.00	300

		Good	Fine	XF
72	**20 Pesos** 1934-1948. Black on olive underprint. Portrait A. Maceo at center. Back: Arms at center. Printer: BEP, United States.			
	a. 1934.	40.00	135	450
	b. 1936.	40.00	135	450
	c. 1936A.	40.00	135	450
	d. 1938.	40.00	125	450
	e. 1943.	40.00	135	450
	f. 1945.	40.00	125	450
	g. 1948.	40.00	125	450

		Good	Fine	XF
73	**50 Pesos** 1934-1948. Black on light orange underprint. Portrait Calixto García Iñíguez center. Back: Arms at center. Printer: BEP, United States.			
	a. 1934.	100	300	900
	b. 1936.	100	300	900
	c. 1936A.	100	300	900
	d. 1938.	100	300	900
	e. 1943.	100	300	900
	f. 1948.	100	300	900

		Good	Fine	XF
74	**100 Pesos** 1936-1948. Black on purple underprint. Portrait F. Aguilera at center. Back: Capitol at left, cathedral at right.			
	a. 1936.	125	400	1,250
	b. 1938.	125	400	1,250
	c. 1943.	125	400	1,250
	d. 1945.	125	400	1,250
	e. 1948.	125	400	1,250
		VG	**VF**	**UNC**
75	**500 Pesos** 1944. Black on red and violet underprint. Portrait S. Betancourt at center. Back: Arms at center. Printer: ABNC. Specimen.	—	—	2,500

		Good	Fine	XF
75A	**500 Pesos** 1947. Black on red and violet underprint. Portrait S. Betancourt at center, with *LEY NO. 5 DE 2 DE MAYO DE 1942* beneath left signature title. Back: Arms at center. Printer: ABNC.			
	a. Issued note. Rare.	—	—	—
	s. Specimen.	—	Unc	2,750
		Good	**Fine**	**XF**
76	**1000 Pesos** 1944; 1945. Black on dark green underprint. Portrait T. E. Palma at center. Back: Arms at center. Printer: ABNC.			
	a. Issued note. 1944.	1,650	3,350	—
	b. Issued note. 1945.	750	1,500	3,750
	s. Specimen. 1944; 1945.	—	Unc	7,500
		Good	**Fine**	**XF**
76A	**1000 Pesos** 1947. Black on dark green underprint. Portrait T.E. Palma at center, with *LEY NO. 5 DE 2 DE MAYO DE 1942* beneath left signature title. Back: Arms at center. Printer: ABNC.			
	a. Issued note.	1,250	2,500	6,000
	s. Specimen.	—		

Banco Nacional de Cuba

This is not the same institution that attempted to issue notes in 1905.

1949-1950 Issue

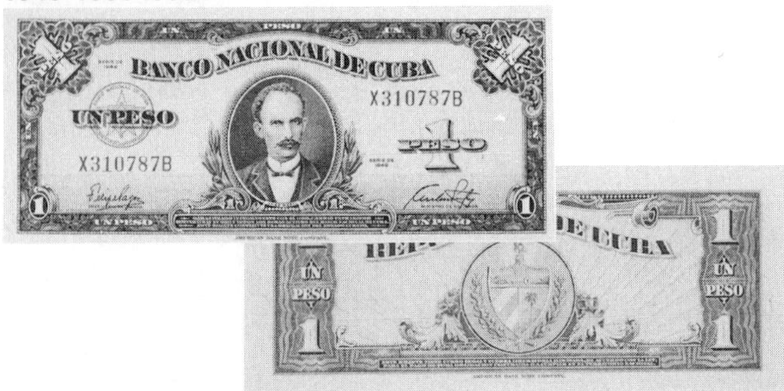

77	1 Peso	VG	VF	UNC
	1949; 1960. Black on blue underprint. Portrait J. Martí at center. Back: Arms at center. Printer: ABNC.			
	a. Red serial #. 1949.	0.50	4.00	20.00
	b. Black serial #. 1960.	0.75	4.50	22.50
	s1. As a. Specimen overprint: *MUESTRA*.	—	—	325
	s2. As b. Specimen overprint: *MUESTRA*.	—	—	300

78	5 Pesos	VG	VF	UNC
	1949-1950. Black on orange underprint. Portrait M. Gómez at center. Back: Arms at center. Printer: ABNC.			
	a. 1949.	2.00	10.00	50.00
	b. 1950.	2.00	12.00	55.00
	s1. As a. Specimen overprint: *MUESTRA*.	—	—	325
	s2. As b. Specimen overprint: *MUESTRA*.	—	—	300

79	10 Pesos	VG	VF	UNC
	1949; 1960. Black on brown underprint. Portrait C. de Céspedes at center. Back: Arms at center. Printer: ABNC.			
	a. Red serial #. 1949.	0.50	4.00	20.00
	b. Black serial #. 1960.	0.50	4.00	20.00
	s1. As a. Specimen overprint: *MUESTRA*.	—	—	275
	s2. As b. Specimen overprint: *MUESTRA*.	—	—	250

80	20 Pesos	VG	VF	UNC
	1949-1960. Black on olive underprint. Portrait A. Maceo at center. Back: Arms at center. Printer: ABNC.			
	a. Red serial #. 1949.	0.75	5.00	22.50
	b. Red serial #. 1958.	0.50	4.00	20.00
	c. Black serial #. 1960.	0.50	4.00	20.00
	s1. As a. Specimen overprint: *MUESTRA*.	—	—	275
	s2. As b. Specimen overprint: *MUESTRA*.	—	—	300
	s3. As c. Specimen overprint: *MUESTRA*.	—	—	275

81	50 Pesos	VG	VF	UNC
	1950-1960. Black on yellow underprint. Portrait Calixto García Iñíguez center. Back: Arms at center. Printer: ABNC.			
	a. Red serial #. 1950.	1.00	6.00	30.00
	b. Red serial #. 1958.	1.00	6.00	30.00
	c. Black serial #. 1960.	2.00	10.00	55.00
	s1. As a. Specimen overprint: *MUESTRA*.	—	—	300
	s2. As b. Specimen. Red overprint: *MUESTRA* twice on both sides. Some punch hole cancelled.	—	—	100
	s3. As c. Specimen overprint: *MUESTRA*.	—	—	300

82	100 Pesos	VG	VF	UNC
	1950-1958. Black on purple underprint. Portrait F. Aguilera at center. Red serial #. Back: Arms at center. Printer: ABNC.			
	a. 1950.	2.00	10.00	55.00
	b. 1954.	1.00	6.00	30.00
	c. 1958.	2.00	10.00	55.00
	s1. As a. Specimen overprint: *MUESTRA*.	—	—	275
	s2. As b. Specimen overprint: *MUESTRA*.	—	—	275
	s3. As c. Specimen overprint: *MUESTRA*.	—	—	250

83	500 Pesos	VG	VF	UNC
	1950. Black on red underprint. Portrait S. Cisneros Betancourt at center. Back: Arms at center. Printer: ABNC.			
	a. Issued note.	15.00	50.00	200
	s. Specimen.	—	—	700

		VG	VF	UNC
84	**1000 Pesos**			
	1950. Black on dark green underprint. Portrait T. Estrada Palma at center. Back: Arms at center. Printer: ABNC.			
	a. Issued note.	5.00	20.00	75.00
	s. Specimen.	—	—	400

		VG	VF	UNC
85	**10,000 Pesos**			
	1950. Black on olive underprint. Portrait I. Agramonte at center. Back: Arms at center. Printer: ABNC.			
	a. Issued note (2 known). Rare.	—	—	—
	p. Proofs, face and back.	—	—	1,000
	s. Specimen.	—	—	3,500

1953 Commemorative Issue

#86, Centennial Birth of José Marti

		VG	VF	UNC
86	**1 Peso**			
	1953. Black on blue underprint. Portrait J. Martí at lower left. *MANIFIESTO DE MONTECRISTI 1895* at center. Back: Map of Cuba over arms at center, commemorative dates at left. Printer: ABNC.			
	a. Issued note.	10.00	45.00	150
	s. Specimen.	—	—	300

1956 Issue

		VG	VF	UNC
87	**1 Peso**			
	1956-1958. Black on blue underprint. Monument at center, portrait J. Martí at right. Back: Farm scene at left, arms at center, factory at right. Printer: TDLR.			
	a. 1956.	0.75	5.00	25.00
	b. 1957.	0.75	4.00	20.00
	c. 1958.	0.75	4.00	20.00
	r. Replacement note. Small crosslet design in place of prefix letter.	—	—	—
	s1. As a. Specimen perforated: *SPECIMEN.*	—	—	225
	s2. As b. Specimen perforated: *SPECIMEN.*	—	—	225

		VG	VF	UNC
88	**10 Pesos**			
	1956-1960. Black on brown underprint. Ruins of the Demajagua Sugar Mill, portrait C. de Céspedes at right. Back: Cows at left, arms at center, milk bottling factory at right. Printer: TDLR.			
	a. 1956.	0.50	4.00	30.00
	b. 1958.	0.50	4.00	20.00
	c. 1960.	0.50	3.00	15.00
	r. Replacement note. Small crosslet design in place of prefix letter.	—	—	—
	s1. As a. Specimen perforated: *SPECIMEN.*	—	—	225
	s2. As b. Specimen perforated: *SPECIMEN.*	—	—	225
	s3. As c. Specimen perforated: *SPECIMEN.*	—	—	225

1958-1960 Issues

		VG	VF	UNC
90	**1 Peso**			
	1959. Black on blue underprint. J. Martí addressing assembly at center, portrait J. Martí at right. Back: Farm scene at left, arms at center, factory at right. Printer: TDLR.			
	a. Issued note.	0.75	4.00	20.00
	r. Replacement note. Small crosslet design in place of prefix letter.	—	—	—
	s. Specimen perforated: *SPECIMEN.*	—	—	325
91	**5 Pesos**			
	1958-1960. Black on green underprint. Riders on horseback at center, portrait M. Gómez at right. Back: Plantation at left, arms at center, cigar factory at right. Printer: TDLR.			
	a. 1958.	1.00	5.00	25.00
	b. 1959. (Not issued).	—	—	—
	c. 1960.	1.00	5.00	25.00
	r. Replacement note. Small crosslet design in place of prefix letter.	—	—	—
	s1. As a. Specimen perforated: *SPECIMEN.*	—	—	225
	s2. As c. Specimen perforated: *SPECIMEN.*	—	—	225

		VG	VF	UNC
92	**5 Pesos**			
	1960. Black on green underprint. Back: Portrait M. Gómez at center. Arms at center. Printer: ABNC.			
	a. Issued note.	0.75	4.00	20.00
	s. Specimen. Perforated: *SPECIMEN.*	—	—	250

		VG	VF	UNC
93	**100 Pesos**			
	1959-1960. Black on orange underprint. Portrait F. Aguilera at center. Black serial #. Back: Arms at center. Printer: ABNC.			
	a. 1959.	0.50	3.00	15.00
	s1. As a. Specimen perforated: *SPECIMEN.*	—	—	225
	s2. Specimen perforated: *SPECIMEN.* 1960.	—	—	325

Note: Several examples of #93s2 in "issued" form (with serial #) have been verified.

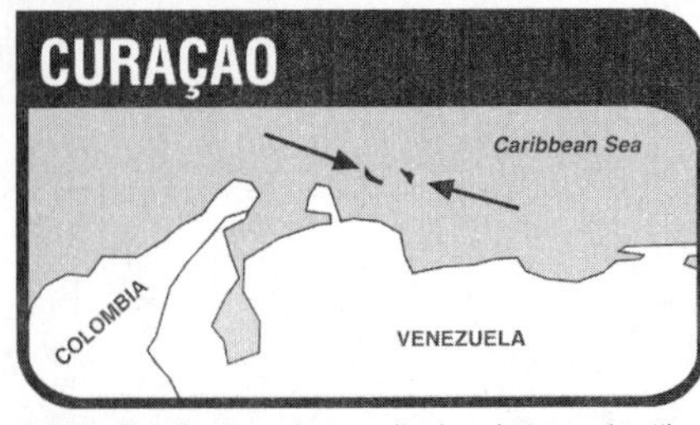

The island of Curaçao, the largest of the Netherlands Antilles, is an autonomous part of the Kingdom of the Netherlands located in the Caribbean Sea 40 miles off the coast of Venezuela. It has an area of 173 sq. mi. (472 sq. km.) and a population of 150,000. Capital: Willemstad. The chief industries are the refining of crude oil imported from Venezuela and Colombia, and tourism. Petroleum products, salt, phosphates and cattle are exported. Curaçao was discovered by Spanish navigator Alonso de Ojeda in 1499 and was settled by Spain in 1527. The Dutch West India Company took the island from Spain in 1634 and administered it until 1787, when it was surrendered to the crown. The Dutch held it thereafter except for two periods during the Napoleonic Wars, 1800-1803 and 1807-1816, when it was occupied by the British. During World War II, Curaçao refined 60 percent of the oil used by the Allies; the refineries were protected by U.S. forces after Germany invaded the Netherlands in 1940.

RULERS:
Dutch

MONETARY SYSTEM:
1 Gulden = 100 Cents

DUTCH ADMINISTRATION

Curaçaosche Bank

1855 Issue

No.	Description	Good	Fine	XF
A11	**5 Gulden** 1855. Black. Ornate border, value at lower center. Printer: Local. Rare.	—	—	—
A12	**10 Gulden** 1855. Black. Ornate border, value at lower center. Printer: Local. Rare.	—	—	—
A13	**25 Gulden** 1855. Black. Ornate border, value at lower center. Printer: Local. Rare.	—	—	—

No.	Description	Good	Fine	XF
A14	**50 Gulden** 1855. Black. Ornate border, value at lower center. Printer: Local. Rare.	—	—	—

1879 Issue

No.	Description	Good	Fine	XF
A31	**5 Gulden** 1879. Black on orange underprint. Ornate border. Printer: JEZ. Rare.	—	—	—
A32	**10 Gulden** 1879. Black on green underprint. Ornate border. Printer: JEZ. Rare.	—	—	—

No.	Description	Good	Fine	XF
A33	**25 Gulden** 1879. Black on red-brown underprint. Ornate border. Printer: JEZ. Rare.	—	—	—

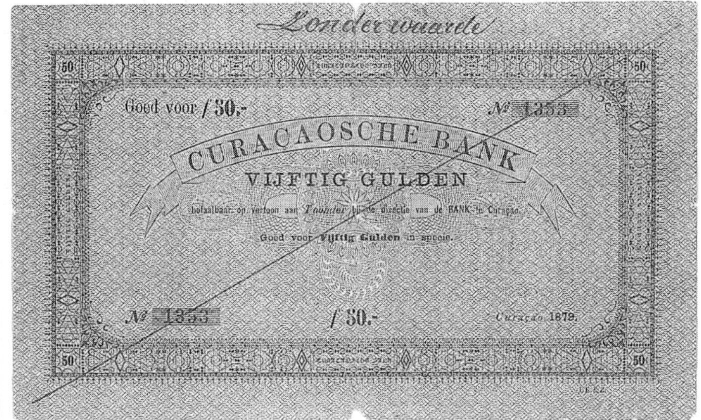

No.	Description	Good	Fine	XF
A34	**50 Gulden** 1879. Black on blue underprint. Ornate border. Printer: JEZ. Rare.	—	—	—

1892 Issue

No.	Description	Good	Fine	XF
A51	**25 Centen** 1892. Black on green underprint. Uniface. Back: Hand-signed. Printer: HBNC. Rare.	—	10,000	—
A52	**50 Centen** 1892. Black on blue underprint. Uniface. Back: Hand-signed. Printer: HBNC. Rare.	—	—	—
A53	**1 Gulden** 1892. Black on yellow underprint. Uniface. Back: Hand-signed. Printer: HBNC. Rare.	—	—	—
A54	**2 1/2 Gulden** 1892. Black on red underprint. Uniface. Back: Hand-signed. Printer: HBNC. Rare.	—	—	—

1900s Issue

No.	Description	Good	Fine	XF
1	**5 Gulden** Ca. 1900. Rare.	—	—	—
2	**10 Gulden** Ca. 1900. Rare.	—	—	—
3	**25 Gulden** Ca. 1900. Rare.	—	—	—
4	**50 Gulden** Ca. 1900. Rare.	—	—	—
5	**100 Gulden** Ca. 1900. Rare.	—	—	—
6	**250 Gulden** Ca. 1900. Rare.	—	—	—
7	**500 Gulden** Ca. 1900. Rare.	—	—	—

1918; 1920 Issue

No.	Description	Good	Fine	XF
7A	**1 Gulden** ND; 1918. Black on yellow underprint.	100	475	—

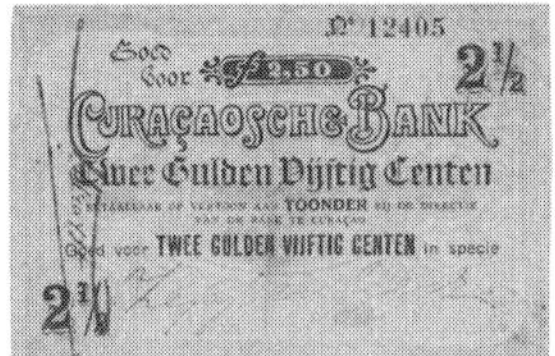

		Good	Fine	XF
7B	**2 1/2 Gulden**	**Good**	**Fine**	**XF**
	ND (ca.1918). Black on red underprint.	—	—	—

		Good	Fine	XF
7C	**2 1/2 Gulden**	**Good**	**Fine**	**XF**
	1.7.1918; 1920. Red and yellow.			
	a. Issued note.	200	750	—
	r. Unsigned remainder.	—	125	250

		Good	Fine	XF
7E	**5 Gulden**	**Good**	**Fine**	**XF**
	1918; 1920. Rare.	—	—	—

1920 Issue

		Good	Fine	XF
7F	**1 Gulden**	**Good**	**Fine**	**XF**
	1920. Black on yellow underprint.	—	—	—
7G	**10 Gulden**	**Good**	**Fine**	**XF**
	1920. Rare.	—	—	—

1925 Issue

		Good	Fine	XF
8	**5 Gulden**	**Good**	**Fine**	**XF**
	1925. Purple. City view at lower center.	300	1,250	—
9	**10 Gulden**	**Good**	**Fine**	**XF**
	1925. Rare. City view at lower center.	—	—	—
11	**50 Gulden**	**Good**	**Fine**	**XF**
	1925. Rare.	—	—	—
12	**100 Gulden**	**Good**	**Fine**	**XF**
	1925. Rare.	—	—	—
13	**250 Gulden**	**Good**	**Fine**	**XF**
	1925. Rare.	—	—	—
14	**500 Gulden**	**Good**	**Fine**	**XF**
	1925. Rare.	—	—	—

1930 Issue

		Good	Fine	XF
15	**5 Gulden**	**Good**	**Fine**	**XF**
	1930. Green on red and green underprint. Woman seated with scroll and flag at left. Back: Arms. Printer: JEZ.	15.00	125	—
16	**10 Gulden**	**Good**	**Fine**	**XF**
	1930. Green. Woman seated with scroll and flag at left. Back: Arms. Printer: JEZ.	40.00	350	—
17	**25 Gulden**	**Good**	**Fine**	**XF**
	1930. Green. Woman seated with scroll and flag at left. Back: Arms. Printer: JEZ.	—	—	—
18	**50 Gulden**	**Good**	**Fine**	**XF**
	1930. Green. Woman seated with scroll and flag at left. Back: Arms. Printer: JEZ.	—	—	—
19	**100 Gulden**	**Good**	**Fine**	**XF**
	1930. Green. Woman seated with scroll and flag at left. Back: Arms. Printer: JEZ.	—	—	—
20	**250 Gulden**	**Good**	**Fine**	**XF**
	1930. Green. Woman seated with scroll and flag at left. Back: Arms. Printer: JEZ.	—	—	—
21	**500 Gulden**	**Good**	**Fine**	**XF**
	1930. Green. Woman seated with scroll and flag at left. Back: Arms. Printer: JEZ.	—	—	—

1939 Issue

		Good	Fine	XF
22	**5 Gulden**	**Good**	**Fine**	**XF**
	1939. Green. Coastline city at center. Printer: JEZ.	5.00	40.00	200

		Good	Fine	XF
23	**10 Gulden**	**Good**	**Fine**	**XF**
	1939. Green. Ships dockside at center. Printer: JEZ.	12.50	100	—
24	**25 Gulden**	**Good**	**Fine**	**XF**
	1939. Printer: JEZ.	40.00	350	—

1943 Issue

		Good	Fine	XF
25	**5 Gulden**	**Good**	**Fine**	**XF**
	1943. Green. Coastline city at center, with printing in watermark area at lower center. Printer: ABNC (without imprint.)			
	a. Issued note.	10.00	60.00	250
	s. Specimen.	—	Unc	400
26	**10 Gulden**	**Good**	**Fine**	**XF**
	1943. Green. Ships dockside at center, with printing in watermark area at lower center. Printer: ABNC (without imprint.)			
	a. Issued note.	15.00	80.00	375
	s. Specimen.	—	Unc	500
27	**25 Gulden**	**Good**	**Fine**	**XF**
	1943. Green. View of city at center, with printing in watermark area at lower center. Printer: ABNC (without imprint.)			
	a. Issued note.	35.00	150	500
	s. Specimen.	—	Unc	1,000

#28 *Deleted.*

1948 Issue

#	Denomination	Good	Fine	XF
29	**5 Gulden** 1948. Green. Building on the waterfront at center. Back: Arms at center. Printer: JEZ.	7.50	50.00	250
30	**10 Gulden** 1948. Green. Building with tower at center. Back: Arms at center. Printer: JEZ.	12.50	75.00	350
31	**50 Gulden** 1948. Green. Building with flag at center. Back: Arms at center. Printer: JEZ.	40.00	250	—
32	**100 Gulden** 1948. Green. View of city at center. Back: Arms at center. Printer: JEZ.	60.00	325	—

Curacao Muntbiljetten

Currency Notes

1942 Issue

#	Denomination	VG	VF	UNC
35	**1 Gulden** 1942; 1947. Red. Mercury seated between ships at center. Back: Arms at center. Printer: ABNC.			
	a. 1942. 2 signature varieties.	2.50	20.00	100
	b. 1947.	3.00	25.00	135
	s1. As a. Specimen.	—	—	200
	s2. As b. Specimen.	—	—	500

#	Denomination	VG	VF	UNC
36	**2 1/2 Gulden** 1942. Blue. Ship at dockside at center. Back: Arms at center. Printer: ABNC.	5.00	30.00	225

Curaçaosche Bank (Resumed)

1954 Issue

#	Denomination	VG	VF	UNC
38	**5 Gulden** 25.11.1954. Blue. View of Curacao at center. Woman seated with scroll and flag at left. Back: Title: *NEDERLANDSE ANTILLEN* over crowned supported arms at center. Printer: JEZ.	6.00	35.00	200

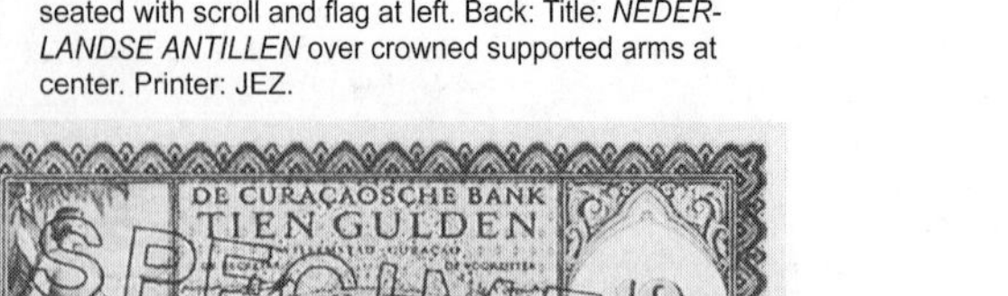

#	Denomination	VG	VF	UNC
39	**10 Gulden** 25.11.1954. Green. Beach in Aruba at center. Woman seated with scroll and flag at left. Back: Title: *NEDERLANDSE ANTILLEN* over crowned supported arms at center. Printer: JEZ.	10.00	50.00	250
40	**25 Gulden** 25.11.1954. Black-gray. View of Bonaire at center. Woman seated with scroll and flag at left. Back: Title: *NEDERLANDSE ANTILLEN* over crowned supported arms at center. Printer: JEZ.	15.00	75.00	300
41	**50 Gulden** 25.11.1954. Red-brown. Coastline city of St. Maarten at center. Woman seated with scroll and flag at flag. Back: Title: *NEDERLANDSE ANTILLEN* over crowned supported arms at center. Printer: JEZ.	50.00	250	—
42	**100 Gulden** 25.11.1954. Violet. Monument in St. Eustatius at center. Woman seated with scroll and flag at left. Back: Title: *NEDERLANDSE ANTILLEN* over crowned supported arms at center. Printer: JEZ.	75.00	350	—
43	**250 Gulden** 25.11.1954. Olive. Boats on the beach in Saba at center. Woman seated with scroll and flag at left. Back: Title: *NEDERLANDSE ANTILLEN* over crowned supported arms at center. Printer: JEZ.	—	—	—
44	**500 Gulden** 25.11.1954. Red. Oil refinery in Curacao at center. Woman seated with scroll and flag at left. Back: Title: *NEDERLANDSE ANTILLEN* over crowned supported arms at center. Printer: JEZ.	—	—	—

1958 Issue

#	Denomination	VG	VF	UNC
45	**5 Gulden** 1958. Blue. View of Curacao at center. Woman seated with scroll and flag at left. Back: Title: *NEDERLANDSE ANTILLEN* over crowned supported arms at center.	8.00	25.00	125
46	**10 Gulden** 1958. Green. Beach in Aruba at center. Back: Title: *NEDERLANDSE ANTILLEN* over crowned supported arms at center.	10.00	40.00	150

#	Denomination	VG	VF	UNC
47	**25 Gulden** 1958. Black-gray. View of Bonaire at center. Back: Title: *NEDERLANDSE ANTILLEN* over crowned supported arms at center.	17.50	75.00	300
48	**50 Gulden** 1958. Brown. Coastline city of St. Maarten at center. Woman seated with scroll and flag at left. Back: Title: *NEDERLANDSE ANTILLEN* over crowned supported arms at center.	35.00	175	—
49	**100 Gulden** 1958. Violet. Monument in St. Eustatius at center. Woman seated with scroll and flag at left. Back: Title: *NEDERLANDSE ANTILLEN* over crowned supported arms at center.	70.00	325	—
50	**250 Gulden** 1958. Olive. Boats on the beach in Saba at center. Woman seated with scroll and flag at left. Back: Title: *NEDERLANDSE ANTILLEN* over crowned supported arms at center.	—	—	—

1960 Issue

#	Denomination	VG	VF	UNC
51	**5 Gulden** 1960. Blue. View of Curacao at center. Woman seated with scroll and flag at left. Back: Title: *NEDERLANDSE ANTILLEN* over crowned supported arms at center.	7.00	20.00	100
52	**10 Gulden** 1960. Green. Beach in Aruba at center. Woman seated with scroll and flag at left. Back: Title: *NEDERLANDSE ANTILLEN* over crowned supported arms at center.	10.00	25.00	120
53	**25 Gulden** 1960. Black-gray. View of Bonaire at center. Woman with scroll and flag at left. Back: Title: *NEDERLANDSE ANTILLEN* over crowned supported arms at center.	15.00	60.00	250

		VG	VF	UNC
54	**50 Gulden** 1960. Brown. Coastline city of St. Maarten at center. Back: Title: *NEDERLANDSE ANTILLEN* over crowned supported arms at center.	35.00	175	—

		VG	VF	UNC
55	**100 Gulden** 1960. Violet. Monument in St. Eustatius at center. Back: Title: *NEDERLANDSE ANTILLEN* over crowned supported arms at center.	70.00	325	—

Note: For later issues see Netherlands Antilles in Volume 3.

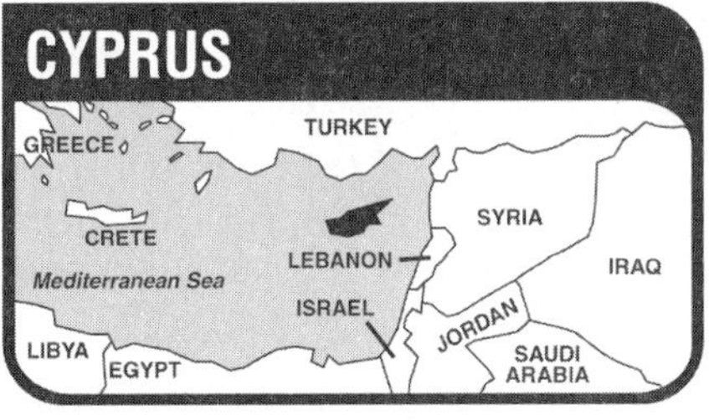

The Republic of Cyprus lies in the eastern Mediterranean Sea 71 km. south of Turkey and 97 km. west of Syria. It is the third largest island in the Mediterranean Sea, having an area of 9,250 sq. km. and a population of 792,600. Capital: Nicosia. Agriculture and mining are the chief industries. Asbestos, copper, citrus fruit, iron pyrites and potatoes are exported.

A former British colony, Cyprus became independent in 1960 following years of resistance to British rule. Tensions between the Greek Cypriot majority and Turkish Cypriot minority came to a head in December 1963, when violence broke out in the capital of Nicosia. Despite the deployment of UN peacekeepers in 1964, sporadic intercommunal violence continued forcing most Turkish Cypriots into enclaves throughout the island. In 1974, a Greek Government-sponsored attempt to seize control of Cyprus was met by military intervention from Turkey, which soon controlled more than a third of the island. In 1983, the Turkish-held area declared itself the "Turkish Republic of Northern Cyprus" (TRNC), but it is recognized only by Turkey. The latest two-year round of UN-brokered talks - between the leaders of the Greek Cypriot and Turkish Cypriot communities to reach an agreement to reunite the divided island - ended when the Greek Cypriots rejected the UN settlement plan in an April 2004 referendum. The entire island entered the EU on 1 May 2004, although the EU acquis - the body of common rights and obligations - applies only to the areas under direct government control, and is suspended in the areas administered by Turkish Cypriots. However, individual Turkish Cypriots able to document their eligibility for Republic of Cyprus citizenship legally enjoy the same rights accorded to other citizens of European Union states. The election of a new Cypriot president in 2008 served as the impetus for the UN to encourage both the Turkish and Cypriot Governments to reopen unification negotiations.

RULERS:

British to 1960

MONETARY SYSTEM:

1 Shilling = 9 Piastres
1 Pound = 20 Shillings to 1963
1 Shilling = 50 Mils
1 Pound = 1000 Mils, 1963-83
1 Pound = 100 Cents, 1983-2007.
1 Euro = 100 cents, 2008 -

BRITISH ADMINISTRATION

Government of Cyprus

1914 First Issue

		Good	Fine	XF
1	**1 Pound** 10.9.1914. Black. Arms at center.	—	—	—

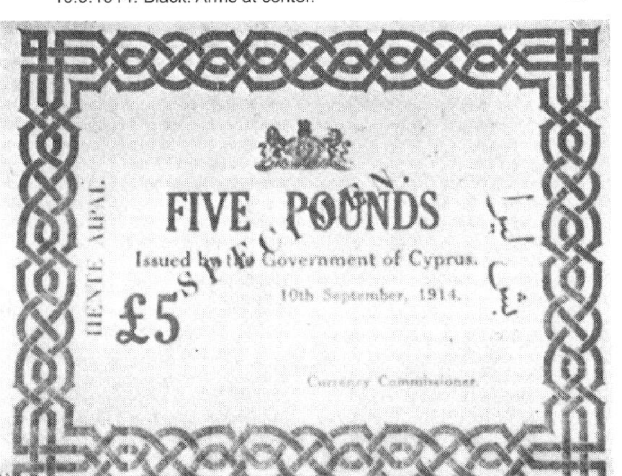

		Good	Fine	XF
2	**5 Pounds** 10.9.1914. Red. Arms at upper center. Rare.	—	—	—

1914 Second Issue

		Good	Fine	XF
3	**5 Shillings** 30.10.1914; 6.11.1914. Blue. Portrait King George V at left. Rare.	—	—	—
4	**10 Shillings** 30.10.1914; 6.11.1914. Green. Portrait King George V at left. Uniface. Rare.	—	—	—
5	**1 Pound** 30.10.1914; 6.11.1914. Black. Portrait King George V at center. Rare.	—	—	—
6	**5 Pounds** 30.10.1914; 6.11.1914; 1.9.1916. Red-brown. Portrait King George V at center. Rare.	—	—	—

1917 Issue

		Good	Fine	XF
7	**5 Shillings** 1.12.1917; 1.3.1918. Brown on blue and gray underprint. Portrait King George V at center.	250	1,000	—
8	**10 Shillings** 30.6.1917; 1.3.1918; 1.4.1922. Blue. Portrait King George at top center. Uniface.	300	1,250	—

		Good	Fine	XF
9	**1 Pound** 1917-1928. Purple on blue and green underprint. Portrait King George V at right. Uniface.			
	a. Date at left. 30.6.1917-1.7.1925.	250	1,000	—
	b. Date at center 1.4.1926; 1.5.1926; 1.7.1927; 1.10.1928.	250	1,000	—

		Good	Fine	XF
10	**10 Pounds** 30.6.1917; 1.9.1919. Red. Portrait King George V at right. Rare.	—	—	—

		Good	Fine	XF
11	**100 Pounds** 1.11.1917. Arms in upper frame at center. (Not issued). Rare.	—	—	—

1919 Emergency Issue

		Good	Fine	XF
12	**1 Shilling** ND (12.11.1919).			
	a. Printed on 1/3 cut piece of #7 (- old date 1918). Rare.	—	—	—
	p. Proof of overprint text for back of #7. 38 x 64mm. 1.11.1919. Rare.	—	—	—

		Good	Fine	XF
13	**2 Shillings** 1.11.1919. Proof. Rare. 42x78mm.	—	—	—

1920; 1926 Issue

		Good	Fine	XF
14	**1 Shilling** 1.3.1920. Dark green. Portrait King George V at right. Printer: TDLR.	200	800	—

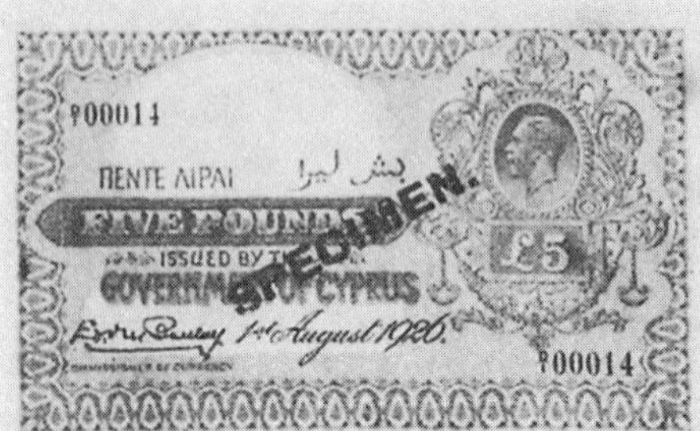

		Good	Fine	XF
15	**2 Shillings** 1.3.1920. Dark red on blue underprint., green border. Portrait King George V at center. Printer: TDLR.	300	1,250	—

		Good	Fine	XF
16	**5 Pounds** 1.8.1926; 1.11.1927. Green. Portrait King George V at right. Uniface. Printer: TDLR.	—	—	—

1930; 1933 Issue

		Good	Fine	XF
17	**10 Shillings** 1.8.1933; 1.9.1934; 2.1.1936. Gray and violet. Portrait King George V at top center. Back: Text: *GOVERNMENT OF CYPRUS.* Arms.	150	600	2,000

		Good	Fine	XF
18	**1 Pound** 2.1.1930; 1.9.1934; 3.9.1935; 2.1.1936. Gray-violet and brown. Portrait King George V at upper right. Back: Text: *GOVERNMENT OF CYPRUS.* Arms.	125	500	1,250
19	**5 Pounds** 2.1.1930; 2.1.1936. Green. Portrait King George V at right. Back: Text:*GOVERNMENT OF CYPRUS.* Arms.	300	1,000	—

1937-1939 Issue

		VG	VF	UNC
20	**1 Shilling** 3.1.1939-25.8.1947. Brown and green. Portrait King George VI at center. Signature varieties.	10.00	45.00	100

		VG	VF	UNC
21	**2 Shillings** 3.1.1939-25.8.1947. Green and violet. Portrait King George VI at center. Signature varieties.	20.00	100	450
22	**5 Shillings** 3.1.1939-1.11.1950. Brown-violet and blue. Portrait King George VI at center Values in Greek and Arabic characters. Signature varieties.	15.00	75.00	350

		VG	VF	UNC
23	**10 Shillings** 12.5.1937-1.11.1950. Maroon on pink and olive underprint. Portrait King George VI at top center. Values in Greek and Arabic characters. Signature varieties. Printer: TDLR.	35.00	125	600

		VG	VF	UNC
24	**1 Pound** 12.5.1937-30.9.1951. Brown on green underprint. Portrait King George VI at upper right. Signature varieties. Printer: TDLR.	25.00	100	400
25	**5 Pounds** 1.9.1938-30.9.1951. Green. Portrait King George VI at upper right. Values in Greek and Arabic characters. Signature varieties. Printer: TDLR.	100	500	1,500

1943 Provisional Issue

Note: Previously listed variety #26b (ex #23b), back with overprint: *3* at lower left and upper right corners only; also large *3* at center, is now believed to be altered from #26.

26	**3 Piastres on 1 Shilling**	VG	VF	UNC
	ND (1943 - old date 30.8.1941). Brown and green.	75.00	200	550

27	**3 Piastres**	VG	VF	UNC
	1.3.1943. Brown on green.	50.00	125	350

1943 Regular Issue

28	**3 Piastres**	VG	VF	UNC
	1943-44. Blue. Portrait King George VI at center.			
	a. 18.6.1943; 6.4.1944.	2.00	10.00	40.00
	b. 15.9.1944; 25.9.1944. (Not issued).	—	—	—

1952-1953 Issue

29	**5 Shillings**	VG	VF	UNC
	1.2.1952. Brown-violet and blue. Portrait King George VI at center. Similar to #22 but values in Greek and modern Turkish characters.	25.00	125	425

30	**5 Shillings**	VG	VF	UNC
	1.9.1952. Brown-violet and blue. Portrait Queen Elizabeth II at center.	20.00	100	475

31	**10 Shillings**	VG	VF	UNC
	1.9.1953; 31.7.1954. Maroon on pink and olive underprint. Portrait King George VI at top center. Similar to #23 but values in Greek and modern Turkish characters.	50.00	175	700

32	**5 Pounds**	VG	VF	UNC
	1.11.1953. Green. Portrait King George VI at upper right. Similar to #25 but values in Greek and modern Turkish characters.	125	600	1,750

1955 Issue

33	**250 Mils**	VG	VF	UNC
	1.6.1955; 1.2.1956; 1.3.1957; 1.3.1960. Blue on multicolor underprint. Portrait Queen Elizabeth II at right. Map at lower right. Signature varieties. Back: Arms at right.			
	a. Issued note.	10.00	75.00	400
	s. Specimen.	—	—	75.00

34	**500 Mils**	VG	VF	UNC
	1.6.1955; 1.2.1956; 1.3.1957. Green on multicolor underprint. Portrait Queen Elizabeth II at right. Map at lower right. Signature varieties. Back: Arms at right.			
	a. Issued note.	30.00	200	750
	s. Specimen.	—	—	75.00

35	**1 Pound**	VG	VF	UNC
	1.6.1955; 1.2.1956; 1.3.1957. Brown on multicolor underprint. Portrait Queen Elizabeth II at right. Map at lower right. Signature varieties. Back: Arms at right.			
	a. Issued note.	12.50	100	450
	s. Specimen.	—	—	75.00

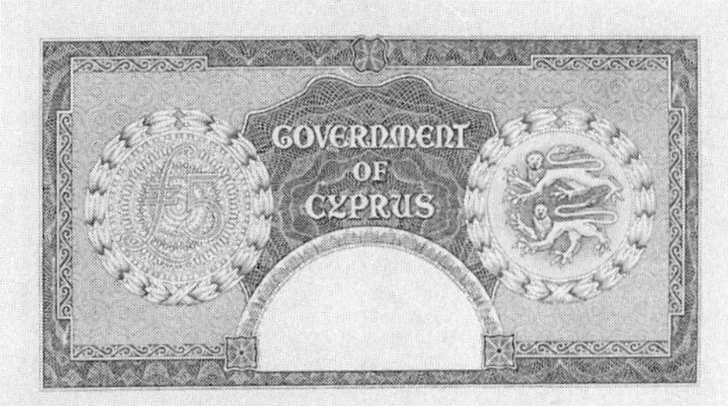

36	**5 Pounds**	VG	VF	UNC
	1.6.1955; 1.2.1956; 1.3.1957; 15.3.1958; 1.3.1960. Green on multicolor underprint. Portrait Queen Elizabeth at right. Map at lower right. Signature varieties. Back: Arms at right.			
	a. Issued note.	25.00	150	600
	s. Specimen.	—	—	75.00

The Republic of Czechoslovakia, located in central Europe, had an area of 49,365 sq. mi. (127,859 sq. km.). Capital: Prague (Praha). Industrial production in the cities and agriculture and livestock in the rural areas were the chief occupations. The Czech lands to the west were united with the Slovak to form the Czechoslovak Republic on October 28, 1918 upon the dissolution of the Austrian-Hungarian Empire. Tomas G. Masaryk was the first president. In the 1930s Hitlet provoked Czechoslovakia's German minority in the Sudetenland to agitate for autonomy. The territory was broken up for the benefit of Germany, Poland and Hungary by the Munich agreement signed by the United Kingdom, France, Germany and Italy on September 29, 1938. On March 15, 1939, Germany invaded Czechoslovakia and incorporated the Czech lands into the Third Reich as the "Protectorate of Bohemia and Moravia." eastern Slovakia, was constituted as a republic under Nazi infulence. A government-in-exile was set up in London in 1940. The Soviet and American forces liberated the area by May 1945. After World War II the physical integrity and independence of Czechoslovakia was re-established, while bringing it within the Russian sphere of influence. On February 23-25, 1948, the Communists seized control of the government in a *coup d'etat,* and adopted a constitution making the country a "people's republic." A new constitution adopted June 11, 1960, converted the country into a "socialist republic." Communist infulence increased steadily while pressure for liberalization culminated in the overthrow of the Stalinist leader Antonçin Novotny and his associates in January, 1968. The Communist Party then introduced far reaching reforms which received warnings from Moscow, followed by occupation of Warsaw Pact forces on August 21, 1968 resulting in stationing of Soviet troops. Student demonstrations for reform began in Prague on November 17, 1989. The Federal Assembly abolished the Communist Party's sole right to govern. In December, 1989, communism was overthrown. In January, 1990 the Czech and Slovak Federal Republic (CSFR) was formed. The movement for a democratic Slovakia was apparent in the June 1992 elections with the Slovak National Council adopting a declaration of sovereignty. The CSFR was disolved on December 31, 1992, and both new republics came into being on January 1, 1993. See the Czech Republic and Slovakia sections for additional listings.

MONETARY SYSTEM:

1 Koruna = 100 Haleru

SPECIMEN NOTES:

Large quantities of specimens were made available to collectors. Notes issued after 1945 are distinguished by a perforation consisting of three small holes or a letter S (for Solvakia). Since the difference in value between issued notes and specimen notes is frequently very great, both types of notes are valued. Earlier issues recalled from circulation were perforated: *SPECIMEN* or *NEPLATNE* or with a letter *S* for collectors. Caution should be exercised while examining notes as examples of perforated notes having the holes filled in are known.

NOTE AVAILABILITY:

The Czech National Bank in 1997 made available to collectors uncirculated examples of #78-98, as a full set or in issue groups. As the notes were demonetized they had no cancellation holes nor were overprinted. These notes have regular serial #'s and thus can not be distinguished from regular uncirculated notes of the period.

REPUBLIC

Republika Ceskoslovenská

1919 Provisional Issue

		Good	Fine	XF
1	**10 Korun** 1919 (- old date 2.1.1915). In circulation 3.3.1919 - 20.6.1920. Blue imperforate 10 Haleru adhesive stamp on Austria #19. Large state emblem on stamp.			
	a. Imperforate stamp.	5.00	15.00	40.00
	b. Perforated stamp.	20.00	50.00	125
	x. Cancelled stamp (false).	10.00	30.00	60.00

		Good	Fine	XF
2	**20 Korun** 1919 (- old date 2.1.1913). In circulation 3.3.1919 - 20.6.1920. Red perforated 20 Haleru adhesive stamp on Austria #13. Small state emblem on stamp.	5.00	15.00	30.00
2A	**20 Korun** 1919 (- old date 2.1.1913). In circulation 3.3.1919 - 20.6.1920. Red 20 Haleru adhesive stamp on Austria #14.	15.00	40.00	80.00

Not officially stamped. Some officially stamped by mistake.

		Good	Fine	XF
3	**50 Korun** 1919 (- old date 2.1.1914). In circulation 3.3.1919 - 20.2.1920. Brown perforated 50 Haleru adhesive stamp on Austria #15. Stamp with small state emblem.	5.00	20.00	40.00

4 **100 Korun**
1919 (- old date 2.1.1912). In circulation 3.3.1919 - 15.11.1919. Red imperforate 1 Koruna adhesive stamp on Austria #12. Large state emblem on stamp.

	Good	Fine	XF
a. Stamp with straight edge.	5.00	15.00	35.00
b. Stamp with perforations.	20.00	70.00	150

5 **1000 Korun**
1919 (- old date 2.1.1902). In circulation 3.3.1919 - 31.12.1919 Reddish black 10K(orun) stamplike printed overprint on Austria #8. Frantisek Palacky on stamp.

Good	Fine	XF
15.00	35.00	80.00

Note: Some notes have an additional hand stamp, indicating in many cases that the adhesive stamp is forged. It reads: *BANK.UR.MIN.FIN / PRAHA.* (Banking Office of the Ministry of Finance, Prague).

1919 Issue

6 **1 Koruna**
15.4.1919. In circulation 24.9.1919 - 31.12.1924. Blue. Back: Arms at center. Value in 6 languages. Printer: Haase, Praha. 100x60mm.

	Good	Fine	XF
a. Issued note.	1.00	5.00	10.00
s. Specimen.	—	—	20.00
x. Error date: 5.4.1919 (Series 014).	100	250	600

7 **5 Korun**
15.4.1919. In circulation 24.9.1919 - 31.12.1922. Red and black. Woman at left and right. Back: Red text. Printer: Haase, Praha. 122x78mm.

	Good	Fine	XF
a. Issued note.	5.00	25.00	70.00
s. Specimen.	—	12.50	30.00

8 **10 Korun**
15.4.1919. In circulation 26.2.1920 - 31.5.1944; in Slovakia until 23.10.1939, and again 25.8.1945 - 31.10.1945. Purple on brown underprint. Helmeted Husite soldier at lower left and lower right. Series H, O. Back: Girl at left and right. Watermark: Curves. Printer: Otto a Ruzicka, Pardubice and Haase, Praha. 143x84mm.Artists Alfons Mucha, Rössler, Mudruňka.

	Good	Fine	XF
a. Issued note.	15.00	70.00	180
s. Specimen.	—	30.00	60.00

9 **20 Korun**
15.4.1919. In circulation 31.1.1920 - 30.6.1928. Blue and brown. Heads of Czech Legionnary soldiers in France. Series P, U. Back: Head at left and right. Watermark: As in #8. Printer: Narodni politika, Praha and Graficka unie, Praha. 152x93mm.

	Good	Fine	XF
a. Issued note.	15.00	75.00	300
s. Specimen.	—	20.00	40.00
x. Error: back without blue-green printed legend.	—	—	—

10 **50 Korun**
15.4.1919. In circulation 8.11.1919 - 31.12.1924. Brown and dark red on light brown and green underprint. Woman at left and right. Back: Arms at center. Watermark: RCS. Printer: Haase, Praha 180x90mm.

	Good	Fine	XF
a. Issued note.	25.00	150	450
s. Specimen.	—	35.00	75.00

11	100 Korun	Good	Fine	XF
	15.4.1919. Blue and violet. Four arms across lower center. Back: Woman at left and right of falcon. Watermark: Grid-like. Printer: Narodni politika, Praha. 165x95mm. Artist Alfons Mucha. In circulation 7.7.1919 - 31.1.1921.			
	a. Issued note.	40.00	200	550
	s. Specimen.	—	30.00	60.00

Note: 60,000 pieces of #11` were counterfeited by Meczarosz in Graz, Austria.

12	500 Korun	Good	Fine	XF
	15.4.1919. In circulation 20.10.1919 - 31.8.1922. Red and brown. Seated figures at center. Back: Arms at upper left and woman at upper right above falcons. Watermark: Grid-like. Printer: Ceska Graficka Unie, Praha. 172x122mm.			
	a. Issued note. Rare.	—	—	—
	s. Specimen.	1,000	1,750	—
	x. Counterfeit.	125	300	500

Note: Artist Alfons Mucha, 60,000 pieces of #12 were counterfeited by Meczarosz in Graz, Austria shortly after it was released for circulation. Most of the pieces seen in collections today are counterfeits. These are distinguished easily by a printed imitation of the watermark and the lack of the hacek accent mark (resembling a small latter "v") over the letter "c" of the text "C.187," on the line of text that crosses the top the back. Genuine notes are seldom encountered. Most forgeries are Series: 020, 021, 022 and 023.

13	1000 Korun	Good	Fine	XF
	15.4.1919. In circulation 12.12.1919 - 30.6.1937. Blue on multicolor underprint. Allegorical figure with globe at right. Seris A-E. Back: Two standing women at left. Paper with fibers. Printer: ABNC (without imprint). 193x102mm.			
	a. Issued note. Series D.	125	375	850
	s1. Perforated: *SPECIMEN.*	—	150	450
	s2. Brown. Special uniface print by ABNC from their "archive series" for collectors.	—	Unc	30.00

14	5000 Korun	Good	Fine	XF
	15.4.1919. In circulation 7.8.1919 - 15.4.1921. Red. Woman at right. Like Austria #8. Printer: Austrian printing office, Wein. 192x128mm.			
	a. Issued note. Unknown.	—	—	—
	s. Perforated: *NEPLATNÉ* (invalid). Less than 10 known. Rare.	—	—	—

A specimen sold in a Prague auction in 2005 for about $45,000. There are 12 known pieces, all perforated.

1920-1923 Issue

15	5 Korun	Good	Fine	XF
	28.9. 1921. In circulation 26.5.1924 - 30.6.1933. Blue and red-brown. Portrait J. A. Komensky at left. Back: Arms at center. Printer: Ceska graficka unie, Praha. 120x60mm. Artist Jaroslav Benda.	5.00	20.00	75.00

16	50 Korun	Good	Fine	XF
	12.7.1922. In circulation 26.5.1924 - 30.6.1933. Brown, red and blue. Arms at upper left, woman's head at lower right. Back: Farmer with Trencin castle in background. Printer: Haase, Praha and Tiskarna bankovek NBCS, Praha. 162x81mm. Artist František Kysela.	50.00	175	550

		Good	Fine	XF
17	**100 Korun** 14.1.1920. In circulation 10.11.1920 - 30.4.1939; in Slovakia until 6.6.1939. Green on multicolor underprint. Arms at left center, Pagan priestess at right. Woman in Czech costume of Kyjov at left, Slovak costume of Piestany at right. Series A-Z; Aa-Zz. Back: View of Hradcany and Charles bridge across Vltava River at center. Printer: ABNC (without imprint.) 170x85mm.Note: Artist Alfons Mucha; fibres in paper.			
	a. Issued note.	30.00	100	275
	s. Perforated: *SPECIMEN.*	—	40.00	80.00

		Good	Fine	XF
18	**500 Korun** 6.10.1923. In circulation 25.01.1924 - 31.12.1931. Brown. Arms at left, WWI Czech Legionnaire at right. Series A, B. Back: Lion, Liberty head and child on back. Printer: ABNC (without imprint.) 181x92mm. Artist Alfons Mucha.			
	a. Issued note.	200	750	2,000
	s. Perforated: *SPECIMEN.*	—	400	800

		Good	Fine	XF
19	**5000 Korun** 6.7.1920. In circulation 10.2.1921 - 31.8.1944; in Slovakia until 26.4.1939 and again May 1945 - 31.10.1945. Brown-violet on multicolor underprint. River Labe with Rip mountain at left center, girl in costume of Tabor at right. Back: Standing allegorical woman at center. Paper with fibres. Printer: TB, Praha. 203x112mm.			
	a. Issued note. Series A.	60.00	250	750
	s. Perforated: *SPECIMEN.* Series B; C.	—	15.00	100

Note: Some of #19 are overprint for Bohemia-Moravia (see #16 under that heading).

Narodni (a) Banka Ceskoslovenská

Czechoslovak National Bank

1926-1934 Issue

		VG	VF	UNC
20	**10 Korun** 2.1.1927. In circulation 11.4.1927 - 31.5.1944; in Slovakia until 23.10.1939 and again 25.8.1945 - 31.10.1945. Dark purple on lilac underprint. Helmeted Husite soldier at lower left and lower right. Series B, N, O, P, R. Back: Girl at left and right. Watermark: Curves. Printer: Otto a Ruzicka, Pardubice and TB, Prague. 143x84mm. Artists Alfons Mucha, Rössler, Mudruňka.			
	a. Issued note.	5.00	15.00	50.00
	s. Perforated: *SPECIMEN* or *NEPLATNÉ.*	—	5.00	20.00

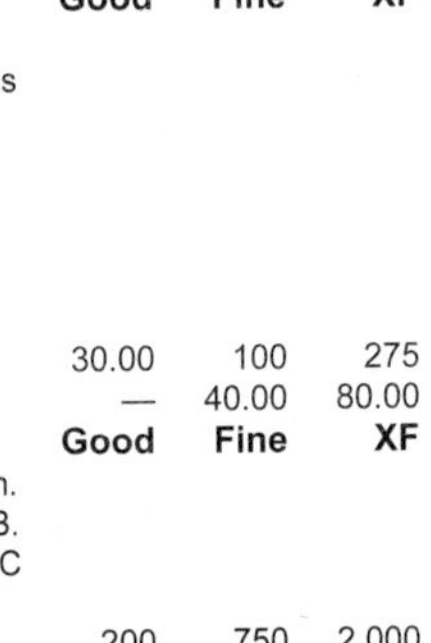

		VG	VF	UNC
21	**20 Korun** 1.10.1926. In circulation 26.3.1927 - 31.1.1945; in Slovakia until 9.12.1939 and again 25.8.1945 - 31.10.1945. Blue-violet, brown and red. Portrait General Milan Rastislav Stefanik at left, arms at right. Series A-Z, Aa-Zh. Back: Portrait Dr. A. Rasin at right. Watermark: 20 on edge. Printer: Haase Praha, TBNEČS, Praha. 149x74mm. Artist Alois Mudruňka and Karel Wolf.			
	a. Issued note.	4.00	10.00	35.00
	s. Perforated: *SPECIMEN.*	—	4.00	22.50

		VG	VF	UNC
22	**50 Korun** 1.10.1929. In circulation 27.4.1931 - 30.11.1944; in Slovakia until 24.7.1939 and again, 25.8.1945 - 31.10.1945. Red-violet on brown underprint. Girl at upper left, ornate arms at center. Series A-Z, Aa-Zb. Back: Farmer, wife and tools of industry and agriculture on back. Watermark: Rhombuses with crosses. Printer: TB, Prague. 162x81mm. Artists Alfons Mucha and Karel Wolf.			
	a. Issued note.	10.00	20.00	65.00
	s. Perforated: *SPECIMEN.*	—	10.00	32.50

23	100 Korun	VG	VF	UNC
	10.1.1931. In circulation 25.10. 1932 - 30.10.1944; in Slovakia until 6.6.1939 and again, 25.8.1945 - 31.10.1945. Dark green on multicolor underprint. Boy with falcon at left, arms at center, Liberty at right. Series A-Z, Aa-Zb, Ac-Zc. Back: Allegorical figures at left, portrait Pres. T. Masaryk at right. Paper with fibres. Watermark: Garland. Printer: TBNEČS, Praha. 170x88mm. Artists: Max Švabinský and Ferdinand Schirnböck.			
	a. Issued note.	5.00	30.00	150
	p. Black proofs. Uniface pair.	—	—	45.00
	s. Perforated: *SPECIMEN.*	—	—	45.00

24	500 Korun	VG	VF	UNC
	2.5.1929. In circulation 16.3.1931 - 31.7.1944; in Slovakia until 26.4.1939. Red on multicolor underprint. Arms at left, WWI Czech Legionnaire at right. Back: Lion, Liberty head and child. Paper with fibres. Printer: ABNC (without imprint). 185x94mm.			
	a. Issued note. Series A, B-A,B-C, H.	7.00	20.00	120
	s. Perforated: *SPECIMEN.* Series D; G.	—	3.50	45.00

25	1000 Korun	VG	VF	UNC
	8.4.1932. In circulation 16.3.1931 - 31.7.1944; in Slovakia until 26.4.1939. Blue on multicolor underprint. Allegorical figure with globe at right. Back: Two standing women at left. Paper with fibres. Printer: ABNC (without imprint). 197x113mm.			
	a. Issued note. Series A-C.	12.00	75.00	500
	s. Perforated: *SPECIMEN.*	—	4.00	20.00

26	1000 Korun	VG	VF	UNC
	25.5.1934. In circulation 7.12.1935 - 31.12.1944; in Slovakia until 26.4.1939. Blue on light blue and green underprint. Woman with book and two children at left. Back: Portrait F. Palacky at right. Watermark: Head of woman at edge. Printer: TB, Prague. 200x105mm. Artists Alfons Mucha and Karel Wolf.			
	a. Issued note. Series A-H, J-R.	6.00	20.00	115
	s. Perforated: *SPECIMEN.*	—	5.00	75.00

Republika Ceskoslovenská

Republic of Czechoslovakia

1938 ND Issue

#27 and 28 were prepared for use by the mobilized Czech army in 1938, but were not released. After the Nazis occupied Czechoslovakia, these notes were ovpt. for the new Bohemia and Moravia Protectorate (refer to those listings #1 and 2). Printer: TB, Prague.

27	1 Koruna	VG	VF	UNC
	ND (1938). Blue. Lettering in underprint in left circle, Liberty wearing cap at right circle. Back: Arms at left, *RADA* (series) in white rectangle and 5 lines of text. Printer: TB, Prague. 105x59mm. (Not issued). Purported to have been in circulation by mistake / without reprint. Artists: Bohumil-Heinz and Bedřich Vojtášek.			
	a. Issued note. Series A001-080.	8.00	20.00	75.00
	s. Perforated: *SPECIMEN.*	—	1.50	10.00

Note: For similar design issue see #58.

		VG	VF	UNC
28	**5 Korun**			
	ND (1938). Lilac and purple. Portrait J. Jungmann at right. Back: Woman's head at left. Watermark: Stars. Printer: TB, Prague. 98x55mm. (Not issued). Purported to have been in circulation by mistake.Artists Jindra Schmidt, Bedřich Vojtášek, and Antonín Machek.			
	a. Issued note. Series A001-084.	20.00	60.00	180
	s. Perforated: *SPECIMEN.*	—	2.00	15.00

#29-43 are now listed under Bohemia and Moravia as #3-17.

1944-1945 Issue

		VG	VF	UNC
45	**1 Koruna**			
	1944 In circulation 19.5.1945 - 13.4.1946. Red-brown on brown underprint. Watermark: Stars. Printer: Goznak, Moscow. 98x55mm.			
	a. Issued note. Series AA-Xc.	0.50	1.50	15.00
	s. Perforated: *SPECIMEN.*	—	1.00	7.50

		VG	VF	UNC
46	**5 Korun**			
	1944 In circulation 19.5.1945 - 31.10.1945, in Slovakia 23.3.1945 - 31.10.1945. Dark blue on light blue underprint. Watermark: Stars. Printer: Goznak, Moscow. 120x60mm.			
	a. Underprint: horizontal wavy lines.	0.25	2.50	22.50
	b. Underprint: vertical wavy lines.	0.25	2.50	22.50
	s. Perforated: *SPECIMEN* (a or b).	—	1.50	7.50

		VG	VF	UNC
47	**20 Korun**			
	1944 In circulation 19.5.1945 - 31.10.1945, in Slovakia 23.3.1945 - 31.10.1945. Blue-black on tan underprint. 2 serial # varieties. Watermark: Stars. Printer: Goznak, Moscow. 160x76mm.			
	a. Issued note.	1.00	3.00	27.50
	s. Perforated: *SPECIMEN* or *NEPLATNÉ.*	—	1.75	15.00

		VG	VF	UNC
48	**100 Korun**			
	1944 In circulation 19.5.1945 - 31.10.1945, in Slovakia 23.3.1945 - 31.10.1945. Green on light green underprint. 2 serial # varieties. Watermark: Stars. Printer: Goznak, Moscow. 166x84mm.			
	a. Issued note.	1.50	5.00	25.00
	s. Perforated: *SPECIMEN.*	—	1.75	17.50

		VG	VF	UNC
49	**500 Korun**			
	1944 In circulation 19.5.1945 - 31.10.1945, in Slovakia 23.3.1945 - 31.10.1945. Red on light brown underprint. Watermark: Stars. Printer: Goznak, Moscow. 183x93mm.			
	a. Issued note. Series A, X.	5.00	15.00	50.00
	s. Perforated: *SPECIMEN* or *NEPLATNÉ.*	—	2.50	25.00

		VG	VF	UNC
50	**1000 Korun**			
	1944 In circulation 19.5.1945 - 31.10.1945, in Slovakia 23.3.1945 - 31.10.1945. Dark blue on green underprint. Watermark: Stars. Printer: Goznak, Moscow. 191x100mm.			
	a. Issued note. Series AA, CK, TA.	4.00	25.00	75.00
	s. Specimen. Perforated: *SPECIMEN.*	—	2.50	25.00

		VG	VF	UNC
50A	**2000 Korun**			
	1945 Circulated in Slovakia only 24.8.1931 - 31.10.1945. Blue and black on green underprint. Arms with produce at right. Watermark: Double cross and linden leaf. Printer: Neografia Turciansky Sv. Martin. 150x73mm.			
	a. Issued note.	100	450	1,000
	s. Perforated: *SPECIMEN.*	—	3.50	35.00

1945 ND Provisional Issues

#51-57 issues of Slovakia and Republic w/Czechoslovak revalidation adhesive stamps portraying Pres. T. G. Masaryk (w/or w/o cap) affixed.

		VG	VF	UNC
51	**100 Korun**			
	ND (1945 - old date 7.10.1940). Circulated in Slovakia only 24.8.1931 - 31.10.1945. Orange *K* adhesive stamp on Slovakia #10.			
	a. Issued note.	2.00	8.00	50.00
	s. Perforated: *SPECIMEN.*	—	1.00	3.00

52	**100 Korun**	VG	VF	UNC
	ND (1945 - old date 7.10.1940). *II. Emisia* at left margin. Circulated in Slovakia only 24.8.1931 - 31.10.1945. Orange *K* adhesive stamp on Slovakia #11.			
	a. Issued note.	2.00	15.00	150
	s. Perforated: *SPECIMEN.*	—	2.50	22.50

53	**100 Korun**	VG	VF	UNC
	ND (1945 - old date 1944). In circulation 3.7.1945 - 31.10.1945. Blue *E* adhesive stamp with black overprint: *100* on #48. 2 serial # varieties.			
	a. Issued note.	2.00	7.50	65.00
	s. Perforated: *SPECIMEN.*	—	3.00	27.50

54	**500 Korun**	VG	VF	UNC
	ND (1945 - old date 12.7.1941). In circulation 3.7.1945 - 31.10.1945. Orange-red *B* adhesive stamp on Slovakia #12.			
	a. Issued note.	6.00	25.00	60.00
	s. Perforated: *SPECIMEN.*	—	2.50	22.50

55	**500 Korun**	VG	VF	UNC
	ND (1945 - old date 1944). In circulation 3.7.1945 - 31.10.1945. Blue *E* adhesive stamp with red overprint: *500* on #49.			
	a. Issued note.	4.00	15.00	40.00
	s. Perforated: *SPECIMEN.*	—	3.00	27.50

56	**1000 Korun**	VG	VF	UNC
	ND (1945 - old date 25.11.1940). In circulation 3.7.1945 - 31.10.1945. Red *Y* adhesive stamp on Slovakia #13.			
	a. Issued note.	10.00	35.00	200
	s. Perforated: *SPECIMEN.*	—	3.00	30.00

57	**1000 Korun**	VG	VF	UNC
	ND (1945 - old date 1944). In circulation 3.7.1945 - 31.10.1945. Blue *E* adhesive stamp with red overprint: *1000* on #50.			
	a. Issued note.	5.00	20.00	60.00
	s. Perforated: *SPECIMEN.*	—	3.50	35.00

Note: Originally the above issues were considered to be worth more with the adhesive stamps affixed as noted but quantities of unused adhesive stamps have made their way into today's market.

1945-1946 ND Issue

58	**1 Koruna**	VG	VF	UNC
	ND (1946). Blue. Liberty wearing cap at right circle. LIke #27 but without underprint in left circle. Back: Arms at left. Like #27, but with different underprint design without *RADA* (series), and 4 lines of text on back. (Not issued.)			
	a. Without perforation holes.	0.25	3.00	30.00
	s. Perforated with 3 holes.	—	1.50	12.50

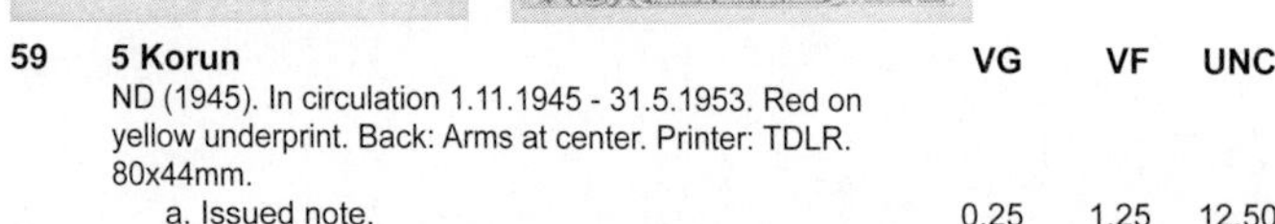

59	**5 Korun**	VG	VF	UNC
	ND (1945). In circulation 1.11.1945 - 31.5.1953. Red on yellow underprint. Back: Arms at center. Printer: TDLR. 80x44mm.			
	a. Issued note.	0.25	1.25	12.50
	s. Perforated with 3 holes, *S*, or *SPECIMEN.*	—	1.00	7.50

60	10 Korun	VG	VF	UNC
	ND (1945). In circulation 1.11.1945 - 31.5.1953. Green on pink and green underprint. Printer: TDLR. 103x54mm.			
	a. Issued note.	0.25	1.25	12.50
	s. Perforated with 3 holes, *S*, or *SPECIMEN*.	—	1.00	7.50

61	20 Korun	VG	VF	UNC
	ND (1945). In circulation from 1.1.1945 - 31.5.1953. Blue on yellow and green underprint. Portrait Karel Havlicek Borovsky at left. Back: Arms at lower center. Printer: W&S. 117x67mm. Artist: J.A.C. Harrison.			
	a. Issued note.	0.25	2.50	22.50
	s. Perforated with 3 holes, *S*, or *SPECIMEN*.	—	1.25	12.50

62	50 Korun	VG	VF	UNC
	ND (1945). In circulation from 1.11.1945 - 1953. Purple on light green underprint. Portrait Gen. Milan R. Stefanik at left. Back: Ornate arms at center on back. Printer: W&S. 140x60mm. Artist: J.A.C. Harrison.			
	a. Issued note.	0.25	3.50	32.50
	s. Perforated with 3 holes, *S*, or *SPECIMEN*.	—	2.50	25.00

63	100 Korun	VG	VF	UNC
	ND (1945). In circulation 1.11.1945 - 31.5.1953. Black-green on orange and green underprint. Portrait Pres. Tomas G. Masaryk at left. Back: Hradcany and Charles Bridge at center. Printer: BWC. 153x83mm.			
	a. Issued note.	0.50	5.00	50.00
	s. Perforated with 3 holes, *S*, or *SPECIMEN*.	—	3.00	27.50

64	500 Korun	VG	VF	UNC
	ND (1945). In circulation 1.11.1945 - 31.5.1953. Brown on orange and multicolor underprint. Portrait J. Kollar at left. Black serial # and *MINISTER FINANCI* signature and title. Back: Lake Strbske Pleso and High Tatra mountains. Watermark: Man's head. Printer: BWC. 165x95mm.			
	a. Issued note. Series CA, CB, CD, CE.	3.00	15.00	50.00
	s. Perforated with 3 holes, *S*, or *SPECIMEN*.	—	4.00	40.00

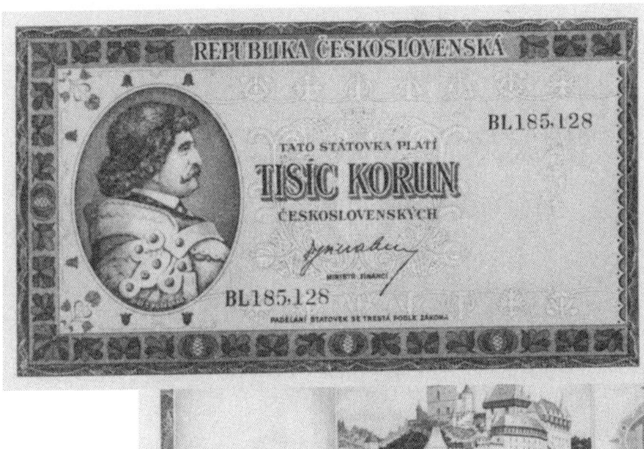

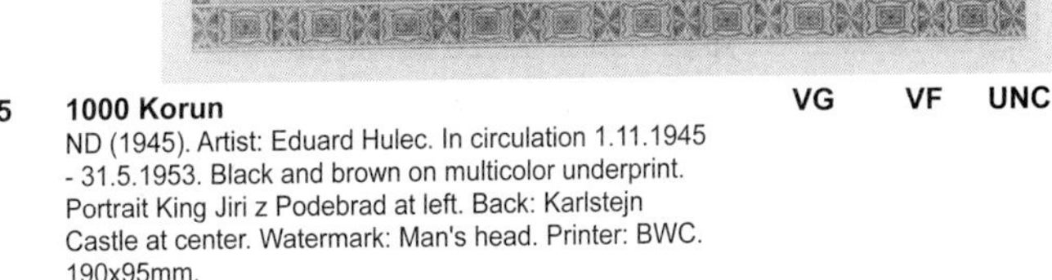

65	1000 Korun	VG	VF	UNC
	ND (1945). Artist: Eduard Hulec. In circulation 1.11.1945 - 31.5.1953. Black and brown on multicolor underprint. Portrait King Jiri z Podebrad at left. Back: Karlstejn Castle at center. Watermark: Man's head. Printer: BWC. 190x95mm.			
	a. Issued note.	0.50	5.00	47.50
	s. Perforated with 3 holes, *S*, or *SPECIMEN*.	—	1.75	9.00

1945-1948 Dated Issue

66	50 Korun	VG	VF	UNC
	3.7.1948. In circulation 1.11.1945 - 31.5.1953. Deep blue on gray underprint. Gen. Milan R. Stefanik at right. 3 serial # varieties. Back: Scene of Banska Bystrica village and Lower Tatar mountains. Printer: TB, Prague. 140x75mm.			
	a. Issued note.	0.50	7.50	65.00
	s. Perforated with 3 holes, *S*, or *SPECIMEN*.	—	—	3.00

		VG	VF	UNC
67	**100 Korun** 16.5.1945. Gray-brown on blue and peach underprint. Liberty wearing cap at right. 3 serial # varieties. Watermark: Rhombuses with crosses. Printer: TB, Prague. 146x76mm. Artists: Max Švabinský and Jindra Smith.			
	a. Issued note.	0.50	3.00	30.00
	s. Perforated with 3 holes, *S*, or *SPECIMEN*.	—	1.00	9.00

1949-1950 Issue

		VG	VF	UNC
68	**5 Korun** 25.1.1949. In circulation 25.5.1949 - 31.5.1953. Red on light brown underprint. Back: Arms at center, like #59. Printer: TB, Prague. 80x44mm.			
	a. Issued note.	0.25	1.50	12.50
	s. Perforated with 3 holes or *SPECIMEN*.	—	1.00	9.00
69	**10 Korun** 4.4.1950. In circulation 27.6.1949 - 31.5.1953. Green. Large 10 at center. Similar to #60. Back: Large 10 at center. Printer: TB, Prague.	VG	VF	UNC
	a. Issued note.	0.25	1.50	12.50
	s. Perforated with 3 holes, *S*, or *SPECIMEN*.	—	1.00	10.00

		VG	VF	UNC
70	**20 Korun** 1.5.1949. In circulation 21.12.1949 - 31.5.1953. Orange-brown and multicolor. Girl with floral wreath at right. Back: Farm woman and vase of flowers. Printer: TB, Prague. 127x60mm. Artist: First edition, Bedřich Fojtašek.			
	a. Margin with fibers at left, bluish paper. Series A. Printer: TB, Prague.	0.25	2.50	25.00
	b. Margin without fibers at left, yellowish paper. Series B. Tiskarna bankovek Statni Banky ceskoslovenske.	0.25	2.50	22.50
	s. Perforated with 3 holes, *S*, or *SPECIMEN* (a or b).	—	2.50	24.00

		VG	VF	UNC
71	**50 Korun** 29.8.1950. In circulation 31.12.1950 - 31.5.1953. Dark brown on tan underprint. Miner at right. Printer: TB, Prague. 145x65mm. Artist: First edition, L. Ilečko and L. Jindra.			
	a. Margin with fibers at left, bluish paper. Series A.	0.50	2.50	25.00
	b. Margin without fibers at left, yellowish paper. Series B.	0.50	2.75	27.50
	s. Perforated with 3 holes, *S*, or *SPECIMEN* (a or b).	—	1.25	12.00

1953 Issue

		VG	VF	UNC
72	**10 Korun** 25.2.1953. Second edition in circulation 6.12.1951 - 31.5.1953. Brown. 98x44mm. (Not issued).	—	—	—

		VG	VF	UNC
72A	**20 Korun** 25.2.1953. Blue. 130x60mm. (Not issued). Artists: Bedřich Fojtašek, J. Houštěk.	—	—	400

Narodni (a) Banka Ceskoslovenská (resumed)

1945-1946 Issue

		VG	VF	UNC
73	**500 Korun** 12.3.1946. In circulation. 1.11.1945 - 31.5.1953. Brown on orange and multicolor underprint. Portrait J. Kollar at left. Orange serial # and 3 signature without title. Brown. Watermark: Man's head. Printer: TB, Prague. 165x95mm.			
	a. Issued note. Series A-Z, Aa-Za.	1.00	3.25	32.50
	s. Perforated with 3 holes, *S*, or *SPECIMEN*.	—	2.75	27.50

		VG	VF	UNC
74	**1000 Korun** 16.5.1945. Dark grayish brown on gray underprint. Head of Jana Dvoraková by Josef Manes at right. Back: Arms at center right. Watermark: Rhombuses with crosses. Printer: TB, Prague. 180x87mm. Artist: First edition, Bedřich Fojtašek and L. Jirka.			
	a. Watermark: dark "X" repeated between light colored lines. Paper yellowish and dense.	1.00	4.50	42.50
	b. Watermark like a. Paper bluish and transparent.	1.00	4.00	40.00
	c. Watermark: Squarish pattern without "X" at center. Paper yellowish and dense.	1.00	4.00	40.00
	d. Watermark like c. Paper bluish and transparent.	1.00	3.00	30.00
	s. Perforated: with 3 holes, *S*, *S-S*, or *SPECIMEN* (a, b, c, or d).	—	2.50	30.00

		VG	VF	UNC
75	**5000 Korun** 1.11.1945. In circulation 3.5.1946 - 31.5.1953. Black on brownish gray underprint. Portrait Bedrich Smetana at right. Three signatures without titles at bottom center. Back: National Theater in Prague at center, wreath at right. Paper with fibres. 190x87mm. Artists: Max Švabinský, J. Mráček and Bedřich Fojtašek			
	a. Issued note.	1.50	4.00	90.00
	s. Perforated with 3 holes, *S*, or *SPECIMEN*.	—	2.50	60.00

Státní Banka Ceskoslovenská

Czechoslovak State Bank

1951 Issue

		VG	VF	UNC
76	**100 Korun** 24.10.1951. Brown. Woman at right. 2 signatures without titles at bottom center. Back: Arms with lion on multicolor back. Printer: STC, Prague. 150x68mm. (Not issued). Artists: Karel Svolinsky, L. Jirke, and Bedřich Fojtašek.	—	—	300

Note: The whole edition was destroyed in 1953; several pieces were pinched.

		VG	VF	UNC
77	**1000 Korun** 9.5.1951. Brown. Girl at right. 2 signatures without title at bottom center. Like #74. Back: Arms at center right. Watermark: Ring and spindle. Printer: STC, Prague. 180x87mm. (Not issued). Artists: Bedřich Fojtašek and L. Jirke.	—	—	500

Note: As 76, the whole edition was destroyed in 1953; several pieces were pinched.

PEOPLES REPUBLIC

Státovky Republiky Ceskoslovenské

State Notes of the Republic of Czechoslovakia

1953 Issue

#78-82 w/o pictorial design on face, arms at ctr. on back. #78-80 were printed by either Gosnak, Moscow (Russian serial #) or TB, Praha (Western serial #). Replacement notes: Z prefix.

		VG	VF	UNC
78	**1 Koruna** 1953. In circulation 1.6.1953 - 31.5.1960. Brown on tan underprint. Value flanking central text. Back: Arms at center. Watermark: Star in circle. 101x56mm.			
	a. Series prefix A, B, C, D. Printer: Gosnak, Moscow.	0.25	1.00	6.00
	b. Other series prefixes. Printer: TB, Prague.	0.20	0.50	4.00
	r. Replacement note. Series Z. Printer: Gosnak, Moscow.	—	—	—
	s. Perforated: *SPECIMEN*.	—	0.50	2.00

		VG	VF	UNC
79	**3 Koruny** 1953. Blue on light blue underprint. Value at center. Watermark: Star in circle. Printer: Series A, B, C, Z -Goznak, Moscow the others STC Praha. 110x56mm.			
	a. Series prefix: A, B, C.	0.50	2.50	12.50
	b. Other series prefixes.	0.25	1.00	6.00
	r. Replacement note: Series Z.	—	—	—
	s. Perforated with 1 hole or *SPECIMEN*.	—	0.50	2.00

		VG	VF	UNC
80	**5 Korun** 1953. In circulation 1.6.1953 - 31.12.1972. Olive on light green underprint. Value in center. 2 serial # varieties. Watermark: Star in circle. Printer: Series A, B, C, Z -Goznak, Moscow the others STC Praha. 120x61mm.			
	a. Series prefix A, B, C.	1.00	3.50	12.50
	b. Other series prefixes.	0.50	1.50	6.50
	r. Replacement note. Series Z.	—	—	—
	s. Perforated: *SPECIMEN*.	—	0.50	6.00

SOCIALIST REPUBLIC

Státní Banka Ceskoslovenská

Czechoslovak State Bank

1953 Issue

83	10 Korun	VG	VF	UNC
	1953. In circulation 1.6.1953 - 31.12.1963. Brown on light green and orange underprint. Back: Arms at left. Watermark: Star in circle. 129x65mm.			
	a. Series prefix A, B, C. Printer: Goznak, Moscow.	0.50	2.00	10.00
	b. Other series prefixes.	0.25	1.00	6.00
	r. Replacement note. Series Z. Printer: Goznak, Moscow.	—	—	—
	s. Perforated with 3 holes.	—	—	7.50

84	25 Korun	VG	VF	UNC
	1953. In circulation 1.6.1953 - 31.12.1962. Blue on light blue underprint. Equestrian statue of Jan Zizka at left. Back: Scene of Tábor. Watermark: Star in circle. Printer: Series A, B Goznak, Moscow (Russian series prefix) or the others STC Praha. 138x70mm.			
	a. Series prefix A, B, C.	6.00	15.00	37.50
	b. Other series prefixes.	0.75	4.00	20.00
	r. Replacement note. Series Z.	—	—	—
	s. Perforated with 3 holes.	—	—	15.00

85	50 Korun	VG	VF	UNC
	1953. In circulation 1.6.1953 - 31.12.1967. Green on light green underprint. Statue of partisan with Russian soldier at left. Back: Scene of Banská Bystrica at center. 147x74mm.			
	a. Series prefix A, B. Printer: Goznak, Moscow.	1.00	6.00	22.50
	b. Other series prefixes. Printer: STC Praha.	0.50	3.00	17.50
	r. Replacement note. Series Z. Printer: Goznak, Moscow.	—	—	—
	s. Perforated with 3 holes.	—	—	17.50

86	100 Korun	VG	VF	UNC
	1953. Brown on tan and pink underprint. Worker and farmer at left. Back: Scene of Prague. Watermark: Star in circle. Printer: Series A, B, C, D Goznak, Moscow or the others STC Praha. 156x80mm.			
	a. Series prefix A, B, C, D. Printer: Goznak, Moscow.	1.00	5.00	20.00
	b. Other series prefixes. Printer: STC Praha.	0.50	2.50	12.50
	r. Replacement note. Series Z. Printer: Goznak, Moscow.	—	—	—
	s. Perforated with 3 holes.	—	—	5.00

1958 Issue

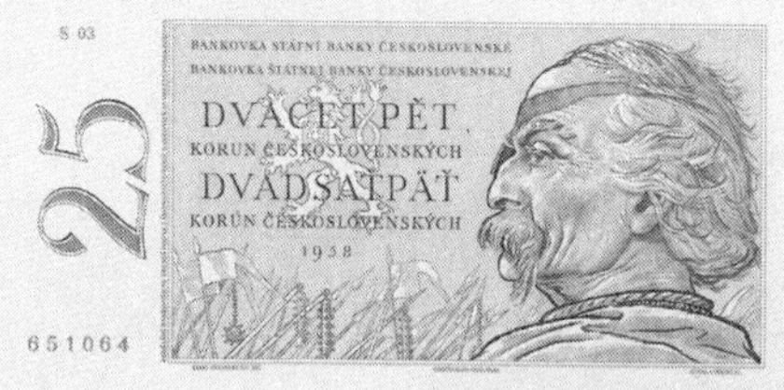

87	25 Korun	VG	VF	UNC
	1958. In circulation 1.12.1958 - 31. 12.1971. Blue-black on light blue underprint. Arms at left center. Portrait Jan Zizka at right. Series S 01-40 Back: Tábor town square. Watermark: Star in leaf of lime tree. Printer: STC Praha 140x69mm. Artists: Karel Svolinsky, Jindra Schmidt.			
	a. Issued note.	2.00	8.00	25.00
	s. Perforated with 1 hole or *SPECIMEN.*	—	—	12.50

1960-1964 Issue

88	10 Korun	VG	VF	UNC
	1960. In circulation from 1.12.1962. Brown on multicolor underprint. Two girls with flowers at right. Back: Orava Dam. Watermark: Star in leaf of lime tree. Printer: STC-Prague. 133x65mm. Artists : M. Merdveská, L. Jirka and Bedřich Fojtašek.			
	a. Series prefix: H; F (wet photogravure printing). (Smaller image area).	10.00	20.00	50.00
	b. Series prefixes: E, J, L, M, S, X (dry photogravure printing).	0.50	1.50	6.00
	s. Specimen.	—	—	3.00

DAHOMEY

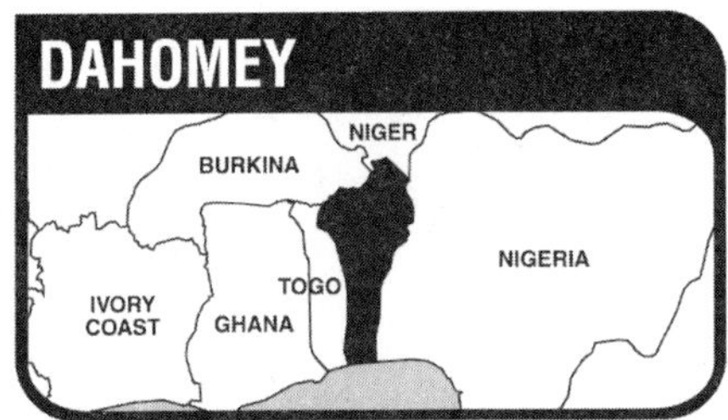

The Peoples Republic of Benin (former French colony that became the Republic of Dahomey), located on the south side of the West African bulge between Togo and Nigeria, has an area of 43,484 sq. mi. (112,622 sq. km.) and and a population of 6.22 million. Capital: Porto-Novo. The principal industry of Benin, one of the poorest countries of West Africa, is the processing of palm oil products. Palm kernel oil, peanuts, cotton and coffee are exported. Porto-Novo, on the Bight of Benin, was founded as a trading post by the Portuguese in the 17th century. At that time, Benin was composed of an aggregation of mutually suspicious tribes, the majority of which were tributary to the powerful northern Kingdom of Abomey. In 1863, the King of Porto-Novo petitioned France for protection from Abomey. The French subjugated other militant tribes as well, and in 1892 organized the area as a protectorate of France; in 1904 it was incorporated into French West Africa as the Territory of Dahomey. After the establishment of the Fifth French Republic, the Territory of Dahomey became an autonomous state within the French community. On Aug. 1, 1960, it became the fully independent Republic of Dahomey. In 1974, the republic began a transition to a socialist society with Marxism-Leninism as its revolutionary philosophy. On Nov. 30, 1975, the name of the Republic of Dahomey was changed to the Peoples Republic of Benin. Benin is a member of the "Union Monetaire Ouest-Africaine" with other West African states. Also see French West Africa, West African States.

RULERS:

French to 1960

MONETARY SYSTEM:

1 Franc = 100 Centimes

FRENCH ADMINISTRATION

Gouvernement Général de l'A.O.F. (Afrique Occidentale Francaise) Colonie du Dahomey

1917 Emergency Issue

#1-2 Décret du 11.2.1917.

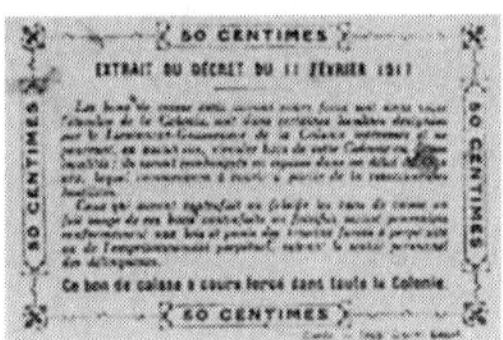

		Good	Fine	XF
1	**0.50 Franc** *D.1917.* Orange and black. French coin design at left and right. Back: Black text.			
	a. Watermark: Bees.	27.50	60.00	175
	b. Watermark: Laurel leaves.	27.50	60.00	175

		Good	Fine	XF
2	**1 Franc** *D.1917.* Black on orange and yellow underprint. French coin design at left and right.			
	a. Watermark: Bees.	27.50	60.00	175
	b. Watermark: Laurel leaves.	30.00	65.00	200

DANISH WEST INDIES

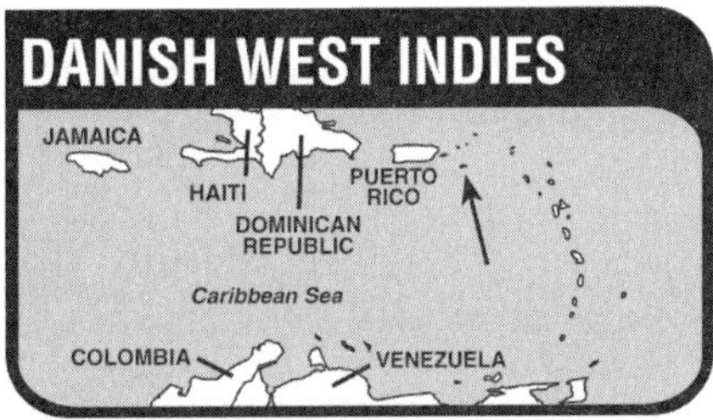

The Danish West Indies (now the organized unincorporated territory of the Virgin Islands of the United States) consists of the islands of St. Thomas, St. John, St. Croix, and 62 islets located in the Caribbean Sea 40 miles (64 km.) east of Puerto Rico. The islands have a combined area of 133 sq. mi (344 sq. km.) and a population of 110,000. Capital: Charlotte Amalie. Tourism is the principal industry. Watch movements, costume jewelry, pharmaceuticals and rum are exported. The Virgin Islands were discovered by Columbus in 1493, during his second voyage to America. During the 17th century the islands, actually the peaks of a submerged mountain range, were held at various times by Spain, Holland, England, France and Denmark, and during the same period were favorite resorts of the buccaneers operating in the Caribbean and the coastal waters of eastern North America. Control of the 100-island chain finally passed to Denmark and England. The Danish islands were purchased by the United States in 1917 for $25 million, mainly because they command the Anegada Passage into the Caribbean Sea, a strategic point on the defense perimeter of the Panama Canal. Currency of the United States of America is now in circulation.

RULERS:

Danish to 1917

MONETARY SYSTEM:

25 West Indies Rigsdaler Courant = 20 Danish Rigsdaler Courant
1 Franc = 20 Cents
1 Daler = 5 Francs
1 Dollar = 100 Cents

DANISH ADMINISTRATION

Treasury

St. Croix

1784-1785 Provisional Issue

#A1 reissue of 1775 Danish State notes.

		Good	Fine	XF
A1	**6 1/4 Rigsdaler** 4.9.1784; 2.3.1785 (- old date 1775). Black. Printed on back of Denmark 5 Rigsdaler #A29a. PC: White.	—	—	—

Note: For similar revalued Danish notes refer to Faeroe Islands and Iceland listings.

1788 Issue

		Good	Fine	XF
A2	**20 Rigsdaler** 1788. Black text. Uniface. Various hand signatures across bottom. Rare.	—	—	—
A3	**50 Rigsdaler** 1788. Black text. Uniface. Various hand signatures across bottom. Rare.	—	—	—
A4	**100 Rigsdaler** 1788. Black text. Uniface. Various hand signatures across bottom. Rare.	—	—	—

1799 Issue

No.	Description	Good	Fine	XF
A11	**20 Rigsdaler** 1799. Black text. Uniface. Various hand signatures across bottom. Rare.	—	—	—
A12	**50 Rigsdaler** 1799. Black text. Uniface. Various hand signatures across bottom. Rare.	—	—	—
A13	**100 Rigsdaler** 1799. Black text. Uniface. Various hand signatures across bottom. Rare.	—	—	—

1806 Issue

No.	Description	Good	Fine	XF
A21	**5 Rigsdaler** 1806. Black text. Uniface. Various hand signatures across bottom. Rare.	—	—	—
A22	**10 Rigsdaler** 1806. Black text. Uniface. Various hand signatures across bottom. Rare.	—	—	—
A23	**50 Rigsdaler** 1806. Black text. Uniface. Various hand signatures across bottom. Rare.	—	—	—
A24	**100 Rigsdaler** 1806. Black text. Uniface. Various hand signatures across bottom. Rare.	—	—	—

1814-1815 Issue

No.	Description	Good	Fine	XF
A31	**5 Rigsdaler** 1814-1815. Black text. Uniface. Various hand signatures across bottom. Rare.	—	—	—
A32	**10 Rigsdaler** 1814-1815. Black text. Uniface. Various hand signatures across bottom. Rare.	—	—	—
A33	**50 Rigsdaler** 1814-1815. Black text. Uniface. Various hand signatures across bottom. Rare.	—	—	—
A34	**100 Rigsdaler** 1814-1815. Black text. Uniface. Various hand signatures across bottom. Rare.	—	—	—

1822 Issue

No.	Description	Good	Fine	XF
A41	**5 Rigsdaler** 1822. Black text. Uniface. Various hand signatures across bottom. Rare.	—	—	—
A42	**10 Rigsdaler** 1822. Black text. Uniface. Various hand signatures across bottom. Rare.	—	—	—
A43	**50 Rigsdaler** 1822. Black text. Uniface. Various hand signatures across bottom. Rare.	—	—	—
A44	**100 Rigsdaler** 1822. Black text. Uniface. Various hand signatures across bottom. Rare.	—	—	—

1829 Issue

No.	Description	Good	Fine	XF
A51	**5 Rigsdaler** 1829. Black text. Uniface. Various hand signatures across bottom. Rare.	—	—	—
A52	**10 Rigsdaler** 1829. Black text. Uniface. Various hand signatures across bottom. Rare.	—	—	—
A53	**50 Rigsdaler** 1829. Black text. Uniface. Various hand signatures across bottom. Rare.	—	—	—
A54	**100 Rigsdaler** 1829. Black text. Uniface. Various hand signatures across bottom. Rare.	—	—	—

1836 Issue

No.	Description	Good	Fine	XF
A61	**5 Rigsdaler** 1836. Black text. Uniface. Various hand signatures across bottom. Rare.	—	—	—
A62	**10 Rigsdaler** 1836. Black text. Uniface. Various hand signatures across bottom. Rare.	—	—	—
A63	**50 Rigsdaler** 1836. Black text. Uniface. Various hand signatures across bottom. Rare.	—	—	—
A64	**100 Rigsdaler** 1836. Black text. Uniface. Various hand signatures across bottom. Rare.	—	—	—

1842 Issue

No.	Description	Good	Fine	XF
A71	**5 Rigsdaler** 1842. Uniface, with text in Gothic lettering. Various hand signatures across bottom. Black denomination line across top. Rare.	—	—	—
A72	**10 Rigsdaler** 1842. Uniface, with text in Gothic lettering. Various hand signatures across bottom. Black denomination line across top. Rare.	—	—	—
A73	**50 Rigsdaler** 1842. Uniface, with text in Gothic lettering. Various hand signatures across bottom. Black denomination line across top. Rare.	—	—	—
A74	**100 Rigsdaler** 1842. Uniface, with text in Gothic lettering. Various hand signatures across bottom. Black denomination line across top. Rare.	—	—	—

State Treasury

Law of 4.4.1849

#1-6 Denominations in *VESTINDISKE DALERE* (West Indies dollars). Note: Issued examples required 7 signatures.

No.	Description	Good	Fine	XF
1	**2 Dalere** *L. 1849.* Portrait Mercury in frame at left, portrait Zeus at right, arms at lower center. Signature varieties. PC: Pink.	200	500	1,250
2	**3 Dalere** *L. 1849.* Portrait Mercury in frame at left, portrait Zeus at right, arms at lower center. Signature varieties. PC: Pink.	300	700	—
3	**5 Dalere** *L. 1849.* Portrait Mercury in frame at left, portrait Zeus at right, arms at lower center. Signature varieties. PC: Light violet.	300	700	—
4	**10 Dalere** *L. 1849* (1900). 1.6.1901 (hand dated). Portrait Mercury in frame at left, portrait Zeus at right, arms at lower center. Signature varieties. PC: Light blue.	150	450	1,000
5	**50 Dalere** *L. 1849.* Portrait Mercury in frame at left, portrait Zeus at right, arms at lower center. Signature varieties. Rare. PC: Light blue.	—	—	—
6	**100 Dalere** *L. 1849.* Portrait Mercury in frame at left, portrait Zeus at right, arms at lower center. Signature varieties. Rare.	—	—	—

Laws of 4.4.1849 and 1860

No.	Description	Good	Fine	XF
7	**2 Dalere** *L. 1860.* Portrait Mercury in frame at left, portrait Zeus at right, arms at lower center. Signature varieties.	200	500	1,250

Laws of 4.4.1849 and 1898

No.	Description	Good	Fine	XF
8	**2 Dalere** *L. 1898.* Portrait Mercury in frame at left, portrait Zeus at right, arms at lower center. Signature varieties. Back: Large 2. PC: Brown.			
	a. Issued note with 7 signatures. 1.8.1899.	125	250	700
	r. Remainder with 3 signatures.	25.00	50.00	125

Bank of St. Thomas

1837 Issue

#	Note	Good	Fine	XF
9	**5 Dollars** 1837. Harbor scene at center, allegorical figures at left and right. Printer: New England Bank Note Co. Boston. Rare.	—	—	—
10	**10 Dollars** 1837. Harbor scene at center, allegorical figures at left and right. Similar to #9. Printer: New England Bank Note Co. Boston. Rare.	—	—	—
11	**100 Dollars** 1837. Columbus and steamship at left, landing of Columbus at center, allegorical figures at right. Printer: New England Bank Note Co. Boston. Rare.	—	—	—
12	**500 Dollars** 1837. 4 women seated on globe, allegorical figures at left and right. Printer: New England Bank Note Co. Boston. Rare.	—	—	—

Note: Reprints of #11 and #12 were inserted in a reference volume on Danish money by J. Wilcke. These are valued at $400.-$500. each.

1860 Issue

#	Note	Good	Fine	XF
13	**5 Dollars** 1860. Blue and red. Bank arms at top center. Back: Denomination: *$5* Printer: ABNC. Rare.	—	—	—

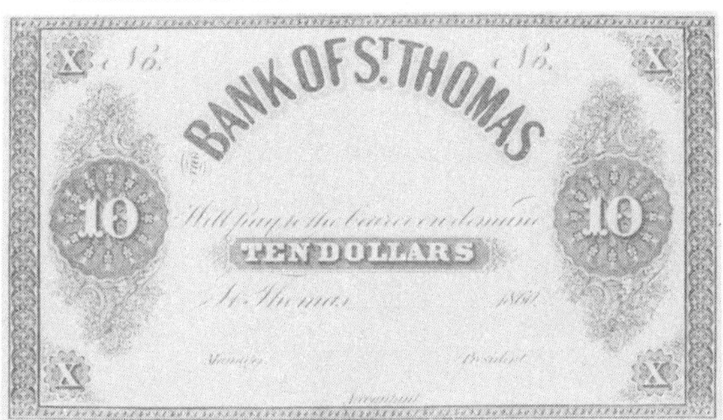

#	Note	Good	Fine	XF
14	**10 Dollars** 1860. Black. Uniface. Rare.	—	—	—
14A	**10 Dollars** 1860. Orange. Uniface. Rare.	—	—	—
14B	**100 Dollars** 1860. Brown. Bank arms at upper center. Uniface. Rare.	—	—	—

1889 Issue

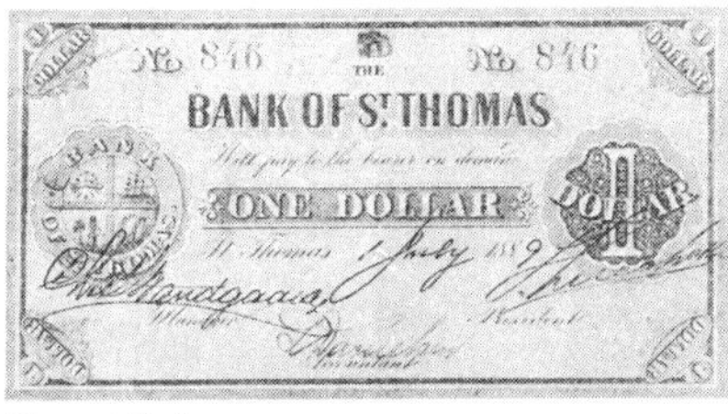

#	Note	Good	Fine	XF
15	**1 Dollar** 1.7.1889. Light green. Bank arms at left. Back: Large value. Printer: Hoffensberg & Trap Etab.			
	a. Issued note. Rare.	—	—	—
	r. Unsigned remainder. 188x. Rare.	—	—	—
16	**2 Dollars** 1889. Bank arms at left. Back: Large value. Printer: Hoffensberg & Trap Etab.			
	a. Issued note. Rare.	—	—	—
	r. Unsigned remainder. 188x. Rare.	—	—	—

Dansk-Vestindiske Nationalbank

National Bank of the Danish West Indies

1905 Issue

#	Note	Good	Fine	XF
17	**5 Francs** 1905. Green and gray. Portrait King Christian IX at lower left, palm tree at right. Back: Village. Printer: BWC.	150	350	1,250

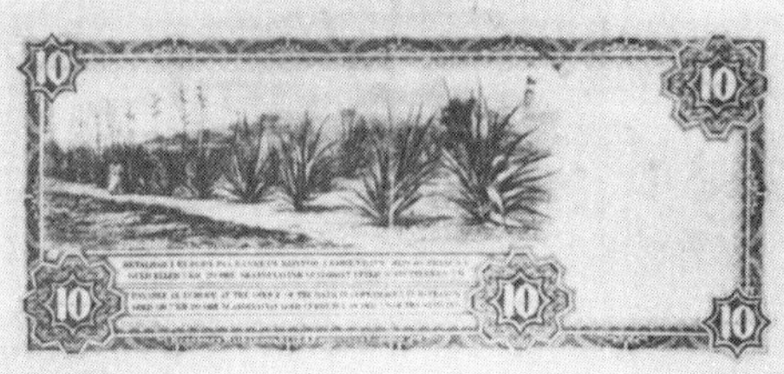

#	Note	Good	Fine	XF
18	**10 Francs** 1905. Black and red. Palm tree at left, portrait King Christian IX at top center, village scene at right. Back: Plants. Printer: BWC.			
	a. Issued note.	550	1,250	3,000
	b. Cut and handstamped: *CANCELLED.*	150	350	650

#	Note	Good	Fine	XF
19	**20 Francs** 1905. Red and light green. Palm tree at left, portrait King Christian IX at center, harbor scene at right. Back: Several local scenes at left and center. Printer: BWC.			
	a. Issued note. Rare.	—	—	—
	b. Cut and handstamped: *CANCELLED.*	200	450	1,250

#	Note	Good	Fine	XF
20	**100 Francs** 1905. Gray and black. Portrait King Christian IX at left, street scene at upper center, palm tree at right. Back: Town scene. Printer: BWC.			
	a. Issued note. Rare.	—	—	—
	b. Cut and handstamped: *CANCELLED.*	1,000	2,500	—

Danzig (Gdansk), the capital of Gdansk province, north-central Poland, is situated at the mouth of the Vistula River on the Baltic Sea. Danzig was first mentioned in 997 as belonging to Poland. It began its development as a trade center in 1260, upon the attainment of municipal autonomy. In 1308, the city was seized by the Teutonic Knights who held it until it was regained by Poland in 1466. It reached its peak during the Renaissance, becoming the most prosperous port on the Baltic. Danzig's decline began during the Swedish wars of the 17th century. In 1772 it was seized by Prussia and in 1793 was incorporated as part of Prussia. Napoleon granted it the status of a free city in 1807, which it didn't want because it had a German majority, and later was relegated to the province of West Prussia. From 1919 to 1939, Danzig again had the status of a free city. It was given to Poland in March 1945, following the defeat of the Axis powers. Polish currency is now in circulation.

MONETARY SYSTEM:

1 Mark = 100 Pfennige
1 MO (Million) = 1,000,000
1 MD (Milliarde) = 1,000,000,000 to 1923
1 Gulden = 100 Pfennig, 1923-1937

Note: Issues w/*UNGÜLTIG* marking are worth less than the values shown.

DANZIG

City Council

1914 Emergency Issue

Note: #1-12 were issued by the city before its free city status began in 1919.

#	Denomination	VG	VF	UNC
1	**50 Pfennig**	VG	VF	UNC
	10.8.1914. Violet.			
	a. Watermark: Scales.	150	375	575
	b. Watermark: Wavy lines.	125	325	550
	c. Watermark: Spades.	150	375	575

#	Denomination	VG	VF	UNC
2	**1 Mark**	VG	VF	UNC
	10.8.1914. Brown.			
	a. Watermark: Wavy lines.	100	200	375
	b. Watermark: Spades.	100	200	375
3	**2 Mark**	VG	VF	UNC
	10.8.1914. Pink.	150	325	550
4	**3 Mark**	VG	VF	UNC
	10.8.1914. Green.			
	a. Watermark: Spades.	100	300	500
	b. Watermark: Crosses in squares.	100	300	600

1916 Issue

#	Denomination	VG	VF	UNC
5	**10 Pfennig**	VG	VF	UNC
	9.12.1916. Black on blue underprint.	20.00	30.00	50.00
6	**50 Pfennig**	VG	VF	UNC
	9.12.1916. Black on orange underprint.	30.00	40.00	75.00

1918 First Issue

#	Denomination	VG	VF	UNC
7	**5 Mark**	VG	VF	UNC
	12.10.1918. Black on green underprint.			
	a. Watermark: Drops.	100	175	325
	b. Without watermark.	100	175	325
8	**20 Mark**	VG	VF	UNC
	12.10.1918. Black on brown underprint.			
	a. Watermark: Drops.	100	250	400
	b. Watermark: Spades.	100	250	400
	c. Watermark: Crosses in squares.	100	250	400
	d. Without watermark.	75.00	175	275

1918 Second Issue

#	Denomination	VG	VF	UNC
9	**50 Pfennig**	VG	VF	UNC
	1.11.1918. Brown. City Hall. Back: Two stylized lions and arms.	40.00	90.00	150

#	Denomination	VG	VF	UNC
10	**20 Mark**	VG	VF	UNC
	15.11.1918. Black on lilac-brown underprint. Hanseatic galleon at left. Back: Town view, two stylized lions and arms.	150	300	450

1919 Issue

#	Denomination	VG	VF	UNC
11	**50 Pfennig**	VG	VF	UNC
	15.4.1919. Brown and violet. Back: Town view.	20.00	35.00	70.00
12	**50 Pfennig**	VG	VF	UNC
	15.4.1919. Dark green and olive-green. Back: Town view on back. Like #11.	20.00	40.00	80.00

Senate of the Municipality - Free City 1919

Post-WWI Inflation Issues

1922 Issue

13 **100 Mark**

31.10.1922. Green on gray underprint. St. Mary's Church at center. Back: Building at left and right.

VG	VF	UNC
150	250	400

14 **500 Mark**

31.10.1922. Blue. Arms at left, tall church at right. Back: Krantor.

VG	VF	UNC
175	350	600

15 **1000 Mark**

31.10.1922. Olive-green and dark brown. Arms at left, Hanseatic galleon at right. Back: Town view.

VG	VF	UNC
150	300	600

1923 First Issue

16 **1000 Mark**

15.3.1923. Dark green. Arms at left, Hanseatic galleon at right. Similar to #15. Back: Town view.

VG	VF	UNC
150	300	600

17 **10,000 Mark**

20.3.1923. Dark blue on light brown underprint. Town view at left and right. Back: Large building on back.

VG	VF	UNC
200	400	700

18 **10,000 Mark**

26.6.1923. Dark brown and blue. Portrait Danzig merchant at left. (painting by Hans Holbein the younger), ship at right. Back: City view at left and right on back.

VG	VF	UNC
175	300	500

19 **50,000 Mark**

20.3.1923. Light green on pale yellow underprint. St. Mary's Church at left. Back: Arms at left, buildings at center on back.

VG	VF	UNC
300	600	900

20 **50,000 Mark**

20.3.1923. Dark brown. St. Mary's Church at left. Like #19. Back: Arms at left, buildings at center on back.

VG	VF	UNC
300	600	900

1923 Provisional Issue

21 **1 Million on 50,000 Mark**

8.8.1923 (- old date 20.3.1923).

VG	VF	UNC
350	650	1,000

#	Description	VG	VF	UNC
22	**1 Million on 50,000 Mark**			
	8.8.1923 (- old date 20.3.1923).	400	700	1,300

#	Description	VG	VF	UNC
23	**5 Millionen on 50,000 Mark**			
	15.10.1923 (- old date 20.3.1923).	400	700	1,200

1923 Inflation Issues

#	Description	VG	VF	UNC
24	**1 Million Mark**			
	8.8.1923. Lilac and green. Arms at left, Chodowieki at right. Back: Ornate gateway.			
	a. 5-digit serial #.	50.00	100	200
	b. 6-digit serial #.	50.00	100	200

#	Description	VG	VF	UNC
25	**10 Millionen Mark**			
	31.8.1923. Green. Portrait J Hevelius at upper left, arms at right. Margin printing upright. Back: City view.			
	a. Large *A* at lower right corner.	150	300	500
	b. Without *A* at lower right corner.	200	400	700
26	**10 Millionen Mark**			
	31.8.1923. Green. Portrait J. Hevelius at upper left, arms at right. Margin printing inverted. Back: City view.	250	500	900
27	**100 Millionen Mark**			
	22.9.1923. Black on light orange underprint. Uniface.			
	a. Watermark: Triangles.	300	600	1,100
	b. Watermark: Tear drops.	350	700	1,300
28	**500 Millionen Mark**			
	26.9.1923. Dark brown on violet underprint. Portrait Schopenhauer at top center. Back: City view.			
	a. Upright light blue margin inscription.	350	600	900
	b. Upright light yellow margin inscription.	350	600	900
29	**500 Millionen Mark**			
	26.9.1923. Dark brown on violet underprint. Portrait Schopenhauer at top center. Back: City view.			
	a. Inverted light blue margin inscription.	350	600	900
	b. Inverted light yellow margin inscription.	350	600	900
30	**5 Milliarden Mark**			
	11.10.1923. Black on blue underprint. Uniface.	375	700	1,000
31	**10 Milliarden Mark**			
	11.10.1923. Black on brown underprint.			
	a. Watermark: Interlaced lines.	375	700	1,000
	b. Watermark: Tear drops.	375	700	1,000

Danziger Zentralkasse

Danzig Central Finance Department

1923 First Gulden Issue, Oct.

#	Description	VG	VF	UNC
32	**1 Pfennig**			
	22.10.1923. Dark blue on light brown underprint. Uniface.	50.00	100	200

#	Description	VG	VF	UNC
33	**2 Pfennige**			
	22.10.1923. Dark green on orange underprint. Uniface.			
	a. Issued note.	150	300	500
	s. Specimen. Overprint: *UNGULTIG.*	—	—	300

#	Description	VG	VF	UNC
34	**5 Pfennige**			
	22.10.1923. Black on green underprint. Uniface.			
	a. Watermark: Interlaced lines.	150	300	500
	b. Watermark: Octagons.	150	300	500

No.	Description	VG	VF	UNC
35	**10 Pfennige**	VG	VF	UNC
	22.10.1923. Dark red on blue underprint. Uniface.			
	a. Watermark: Interlaced lines.	150	300	600
	b. Watermark: Hanseatic galleon.	150	300	600
	s. Specimen. Overprint: *UNGULTIG.*	—	—	250
36	**25 Pfennige**	VG	VF	UNC
	22.10.1923. Black on lilac-brown underprint. Uniface.	250	700	1,000
37	**50 Pfennige**	VG	VF	UNC
	22.10.1923. Black on gray underprint. Uniface. 2 serial # varieties.	300	800	1,200
38	**1 Gulden**	VG	VF	UNC
	22.10.1923. Black on green underprint.			
	a. Watermark: Interlaced lines.	200	400	700
	b. Watermark: Hanseatic galleon.	300	500	900
39	**2 Gulden**	VG	VF	UNC
	22.10.1923. Lilac-brown. Hanseatic galleon at center. 2 serial # varieties.	400	800	1,200
40	**5 Gulden**	VG	VF	UNC
	22.10.1923. Black on light brown and gray-green underprint. Hanseatic galleon at center.			
	a. Watermark: Interlaced lines.	800	1,350	2,250
	b. Watermark: Hanseatic galleon.	800	1,350	2,250

No.	Description	VG	VF	UNC
41	**10 Gulden**	VG	VF	UNC
	22.10.1923. Black on reddish brown underprint. Hanseatic galleon at left.	800	1,500	2,500
42	**25 Gulden**	VG	VF	UNC
	22.10.1923. Black on olive underprint. Hanseatic galleon at left.	2,200	5,000	10,000

1923 Second Gulden Issue, Nov.

No.	Description	VG	VF	UNC
43	**1 Pfennig**	VG	VF	UNC
	1.11.1923. Dark blue on light brown underprint. Uniface.	200	400	600
43A	**2 Pfennige**	VG	VF	UNC
	1.11.1923. Dark green on orange underprint.	300	700	1,500
44	**5 Pfennige**	VG	VF	UNC
	1.11.1923. Black on green underprint. Uniface.	300	700	1,500
45	**10 Pfennige**	VG	VF	UNC
	1.11.1923. Dark red on blue underprint. Uniface.	300	700	1,500
46	**25 Pfennige**	VG	VF	UNC
	1.11.1923. Black on lilac-brown underprint. Uniface.	400	900	1,500
47	**50 Pfennige**	VG	VF	UNC
	1.11.1923. Black on gray underprint. Uniface.	400	900	1,500
48	**1 Gulden**	VG	VF	UNC
	1.11.1923. Black on green underprint.	700	1,500	3,000
49	**2 Gulden**	VG	VF	UNC
	1.11.1923. Lilac-brown. Hanseatic galleon at center.	500	900	1,500
50	**5 Gulden**	VG	VF	UNC
	1.11.1923. Black on light brown & gray-green underprint. Hanseatic galleon at center in underprint.	800	1,500	2,250
51	**50 Gulden**	VG	VF	UNC
	1.11.1923. Black on reddish brown underprint. Hanseatic galleon at center.	4,000	7,500	11,500
52	**100 Gulden**	VG	VF	UNC
	1.11.1923. Black on olive underprint. Hanseatic galleon at center.	6,500	10,000	—

Bank von Danzig

Bank of Danzig

1924 Issue

No.	Description	VG	VF	UNC
53	**10 Gulden**	VG	VF	UNC
	10.2.1924. Brown. *Artushof* (Artus' courtyard) at center. Arms at left.	1,000	1,800	5,000
54	**25 Gulden**	VG	VF	UNC
	10.2.1924. St. Mary's Church at center. Arms at left.	1,500	2,500	—
55	**100 Gulden**	VG	VF	UNC
	10.2.1924. Blue. River Mottlau dock scene at center. Arms at left.	1,700	3,000	—

No.	Description	VG	VF	UNC
56	**500 Gulden**	VG	VF	UNC
	10.2.1924. Green. *Zeughaus* (the arsenal) at center. Arms at left.	750	1,500	2,500

No.	Description	VG	VF	UNC
57	**1000 Gulden**	VG	VF	UNC
	10.2.1924. Red-orange on blue underprint. City Hall at center. Arms at left.	750	1,500	2,500

1928-1930 Issue

No.	Description	VG	VF	UNC
58	**10 Gulden**	VG	VF	UNC
	1.7.1930. Brown. *Artushof* (Artus' courtyard) at center.	500	1,000	1,800
59	**25 Gulden**	VG	VF	UNC
	1.10.1928. Dark green. St. Mary's Church at center.	1,000	2,000	4,000

1931-1932 Issue

No.	Description	VG	VF	UNC
60	**20 Gulden**	VG	VF	UNC
	2.1.1932. Lilac-brown. *Stockturm* (local tower) at center 2 serial # varieties. Back: Neptune at right on back.	400	800	1,600
61	**25 Gulden**	VG	VF	UNC
	2.1.1931. Dark green. St. Mary's Church at center.	800	1,500	3,500

No.	Description	VG	VF	UNC
62	**100 Gulden**	VG	VF	UNC
	1.8.1931. Blue. River Mottlau dock scene at center. Back: Allegorical man at right.	250	500	8,500

1937-1938 Issue

#	Denomination / Description	VG	VF	UNC
63	**20 Gulden** 1.11.1937. Dark green. *Artushof* (Artus' courtyard) at center. 2 serial # varieties. Back: Allegorical man at right.	600	900	1,500
64	**20 Gulden** 2.1.1938. Blue-green and orange. Specimen. Rare.	—	—	—
65	**50 Gulden** 5.2.1937. Brown. The *Vorlaubenhaus* (building) at center. Back: Allegorical man at right.	450	850	1,700

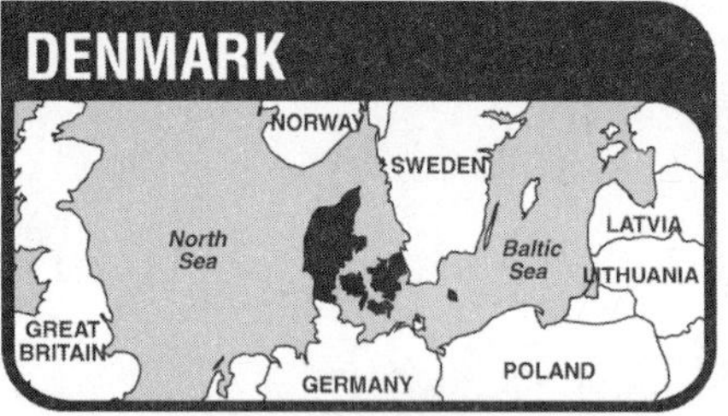

The Kingdom of Denmark, a constitutional monarchy located at the mouth of the Baltic Sea, has an area of 43,094 sq. km. and a population of 5.48 million. Capital: Copenhagen. Most of the country is arable. Agriculture, which used to employ the majority of the people, is now conducted by large farms served by cooperatives. The largest industries are food processing, iron and metal, and shipping. Machinery, meats (chiefly bacon), dairy products and chemicals are exported.

Once the seat of Viking raiders and later a major north European power, Denmark has evolved into a modern, prosperous nation that is participating in the general political and economic integration of Europe. It joined NATO in 1949 and the EEC (now the EU) in 1973. However, the country has opted out of certain elements of the European Union's Maastricht Treaty, including the European Economic and Monetary Union (EMU), European defense cooperation, and issues concerning certain justice and home affairs.

RULERS:

Frederik IV, 1699-1730
Christian VI, 1730-1746
Frederik V, 1746-1766
Christian VII, 1766-1808
Frederik VI, 1808-1839
Christian VIII, 1839-1848
Frederik VII, 1848-1863
Christian IX, 1863-1906
Frederik VIII, 1906-1912
Christian X, 1912-1947
Frederik IX, 1947-1972
Margrethe II, 1972-

MONETARY SYSTEM:

1 Rigsdaler dansk Courant = 96 Skilling Courant = 6 Mark; at the same time, 1 Rigsdaler Species = 120 Skilling Courant, 1713-1813
1 Rigsbankdaler = 96 Rigsbankskilling (= 1/2 Rigsdaler Species), 1813-1854
1 Daler Rigsmnt = 96 Skilling Rigsmnt (= 1 Rigsbankdaler), 1854-1874
1 Krone = 100 re
1 Krone (1/2 Rigsdaler) = 100 re 1874-

REPLACEMENT NOTES:

#42-45 although dated (19)50, they were issued from 1952 onwards.
#42-47, suffix OJ (for whole sheets) or OK (for single notes).

REVALUED NOTES:

For early Danish notes with additional printing and signatures on back refer to Danish West Indies, Faeroe Islands and Iceland.

KINGDOM

Treasury

Decree of 8.4.1713 - "Authorized Notes"

#	Denomination / Description	Good	Fine	XF
A1	**1 Rigsdaler** 1713. Crowned double monogram F4 printed at top left, handwritten denomination, 6 hand signatures.	—	—	—
A2	**5 Rigsdaler** 1713. Crowned double monogram F4 printed at top left, handwritten denomination, 6 hand signatures.	—	—	—

The one known note is a counterfeit 1 Rigsdaler note.

#	Denomination / Description	Good	Fine	XF
A3	**10 Rigsdaler** 1713. Unknown. Crowned double monogram F4 printed at top left, handwritten denomination, 6 hand signatures.	—	—	—
A4	**25 Rigsdaler** 1713. Unknown. Crowned double monogram F4 printed at top left, handwritten denomination, 6 hand signatures.	—	—	—
A5	**50 Rigsdaler** 1713. Unknown. Crowned double monogram F4 printed at top left, handwritten denomination, 6 hand signatures.	—	—	—
A6	**100 Rigsdaler** 1713. Unknown. Crowned double monogram F4 printed at top left, handwritten denomination, 6 hand signatures.	—	—	—

Decree of 8.4.1713 - 2nd Group

#	Denomination / Description	Good	Fine	XF
A7	**1 Rigsdaler** 1713. Unknown. Crowned double monogram F4 printed at top left, printed denominations, 6 hand signatures.	—	—	—
A8	**5 Rigsdaler** 1713. Unique. Crowned double monogram F4 printed at top left, printed denominations, 6 hand signatures.	—	—	—
A9	**10 Rigsdaler** 1713. Unknown. Crowned double monogram F4 printed at top left, printed denominations, 6 hand signatures.	—	—	—
A9A	**100 Rigsdaler** 1713. Crowned double monogram F4 printed at top left, printed denominations, 6 hand signatures.	—	—	—

Decree of 8.4.1713 - 3rd Group

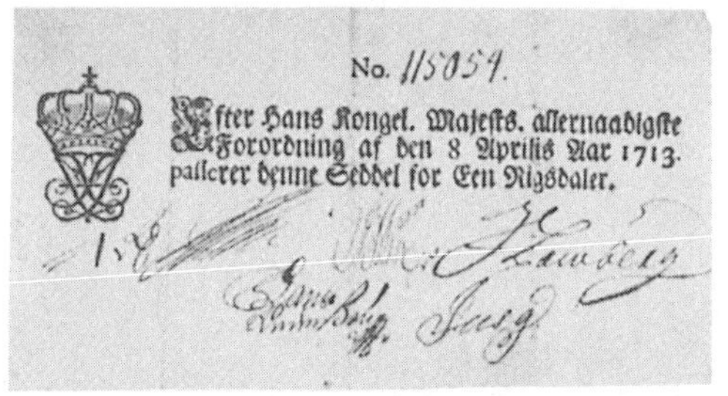

#	Denomination / Description	Good	Fine	XF
A10	**1 (Een) Mark** 1713. Crowned double monogram F4 printed at top left, printed denominations, 5 hand signatures.	5,000	—	—
A11	**2 (Toe) Mark** 1713. Crowned double monogram F4 printed at top left, printed denominations, 5 hand signatures.			
	a. Issued note.	4,500	—	—
	r. Remainder.	2,000	—	—
A12	**3 Mark** 1713. Crowned double monogram F4 printed at top left, printed denominations, 5 hand signatures.			
	a. Value expressed as: *Tree Mark.*	3,200	—	—
	b. Value expressed as: *Tre Mark.*	3,500	8,000	—
	r. Remainder.	1,000	2,000	—
A13	**1 (Een) Rigsdaler** 1713. Crowned double monogram F4 printed at top left, printed denominations, 5 hand signatures.			
	a. Issued note.	2,500	—	—
	r. Remainder.	—	500	1,000

Decree of 8.4.1713 - 4th Group

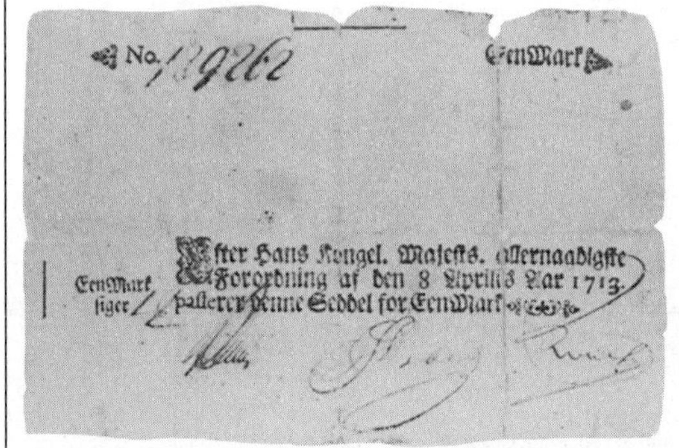

#	Denomination / Description	Good	Fine	XF
A14	**1 (Een) Mark** 1713. Without monogram, impressed stamp with imperial arms. 3 hand signatures.	900	2,000	—

		Good	Fine	XF
A15	**2 (Toe) Mark** 1713. Crowned double monogram F4 printed at top left, printed denominations, 5 hand signatures.	2,000	4,000	—

		Good	Fine	XF
A16	**3 (Tree) Mark** 1713. Crowned double monogram F4 printed at top left, printed denominations, 5 hand signatures.	2,500	5,000	—

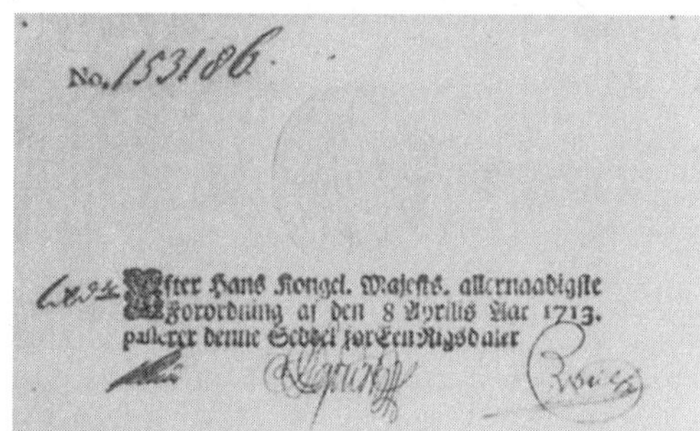

		Good	Fine	XF
A17	**1 (Een) Rigsdaler** 1713. Crowned double monogram F4 printed at top left, printed denominations, 5 hand signatures. Denominations in Mark and Rigsdaler.	700	2,000	8,000

Note: In a June, 1999 auction, #A17 brought $6,750 in XF.

Kiöbenhavnske Assignation-, Vexel- og Laane-Banque

Copenhagen Notes, Exchange and Mortgage Bank

Copenhagen

1737 Issue

		Good	Fine	XF
A18	**10 Rigsdaler Courant** 1737-1740. Ornate column at left, handwritten denomination.			
	a. *Rixdaler* in lines 2 and 6. 1737; 1740.	—	—	—
	b. *Rdl* in lines 2 and 6. Unknown.	—	—	—

		Good	Fine	XF
A19	**20 Rigsdaler Courant** 1737. Ornate column at left, handwritten denomination.	—	—	—

		Good	Fine	XF
A20	**30 Rigsdaler Courant** 1737. Ornate column at left, handwritten denomination. Unknown.	—	—	—

		Good	Fine	XF
A21	**40 Rigsdaler Courant** 1737; 1740. Ornate column at left, handwritten denomination. Unknown.	—	—	—

		Good	Fine	XF
A22	**50 Rigsdaler Courant** 1737; 1740. Ornate column at left, handwritten denomination.	—	—	—

		Good	Fine	XF
A23	**100 Rigsdaler Courant** 1737; 1739; 1740. Ornate column at left, handwritten denomination. Unknown.	—	—	—

1748-1762 Issue

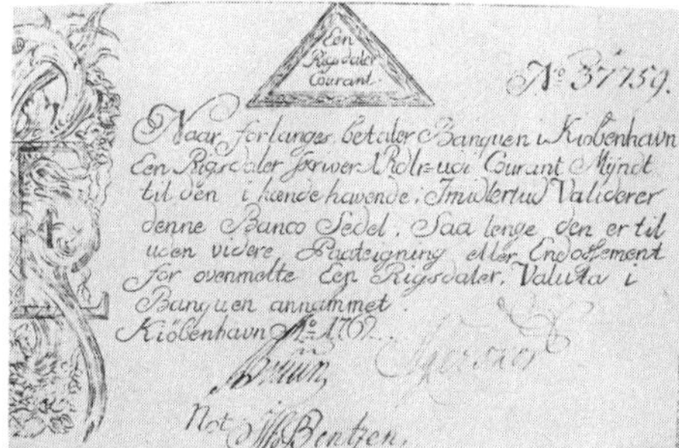

		Good	Fine	XF
A24	**1 Rigsdaler Courant** 1762-1792. Black. Printed denomination, design at left in 3 styles, includes a large E. 3 hand signatures.			
	a. 1762-1763 (only 1762 and 1763 known). No watermark.	—	—	—
	b. 1766-1767 (only 1766 known). Watermark: crowned monogram *F5* with letters A-F, *C7* with impressed stamp.	—	—	—
	c. 1769-1792. Watermark: crowned monogram with impressed stamp *C7*.	150	350	1,200

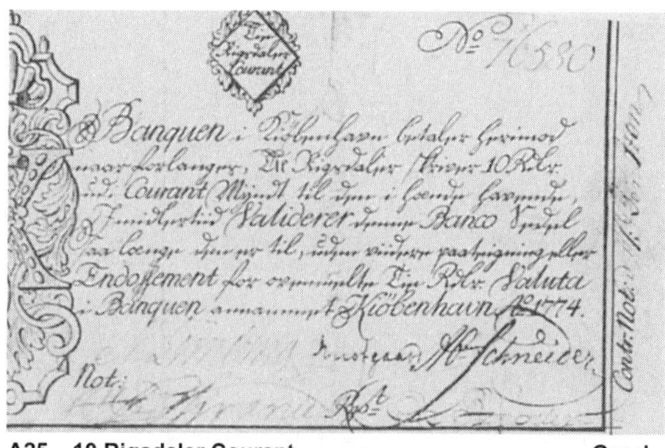

		Good	Fine	XF
A25	**10 Rigsdaler Courant** 1748-1788. Black. Printed denomination, design at left in 3 styles, includes a large X. 3 hand signatures.			
	a. 1748-1763. Watermark: crowned monogram *F5* with impressed stamp *F5*. No examples known.	—	—	—
	b. 1768-1780. Watermark: crowned monogram *F5* with impressed stamp *C7*.	—	—	—
	c. 1772-1788. Watermark: crowned monogram *C7* and impressed stamp *C7*.	—	—	—

		Good	Fine	XF
A26	**50 Rigsdaler Courant** 1748-1787. Black. Printed denomination, design at left in 3 styles, includes a large L. 5 hand signatures.			
	a. 1748-1761. Watermark and impressed stamp with *F5*. Only 1748 date known.	—	—	—
	b. 1770-1787. Watermark and impressed stamp with *C7*. Unknown.	—	—	—

		Good	Fine	XF
A27	**100 Rigsdaler Courant** 1748-1788. Black. Printed denomination, design at left in 3 styles, includes a large C. 5 hand signatures.			
	a. 1748-1761. Watermark and impressed stamp with *F5*. ,Unknown	—	—	—
	b. 1768. Watermark: *F5*, impressed stamp *C7*. Unknown.	—	—	—
	c. 1772-1788 (only 1773; 1782 known). Watermark and impressed stamp with *C7*.	—	—	—

1775-1788 Issue

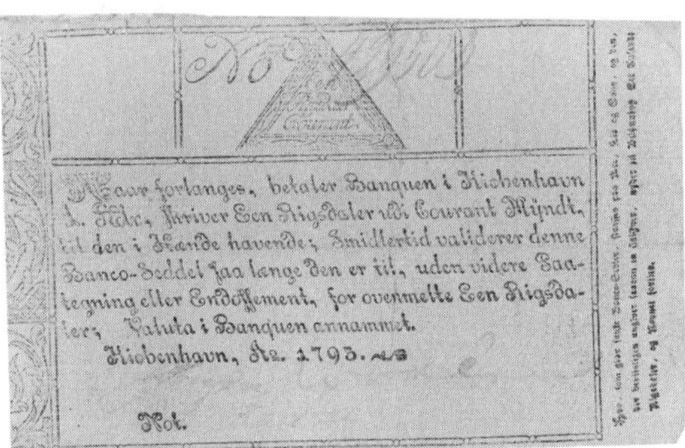

		Good	Fine	XF
A28	**1 Rigsdaler Courant** 1788-1808. Issued until 1813. Anti-counterfeiting text added vertically at right. Large E at left. PC: Blue.	50.00	200	800

		Good	Fine	XF
A29	**5 Rigsdaler Courant** 1775-1800. Anti-counterfeiting text added vertically at right. Large V at left.			
	a. White paper. 1775-91. Issued until 1793.	250	800	1,200
	b. Blue paper. 1786-1800. Issued until 1813.	125	350	1,250

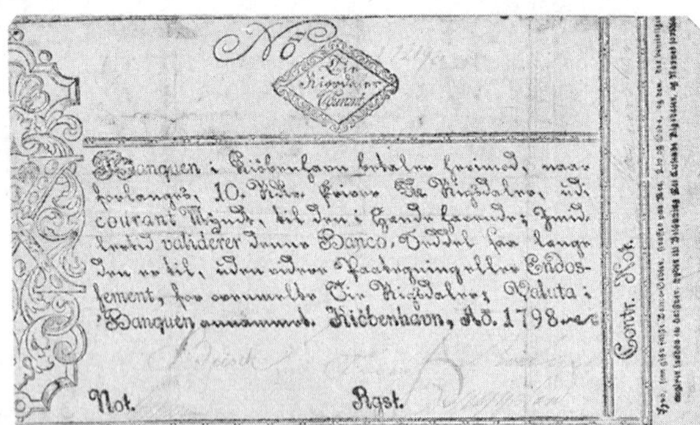

		Good	Fine	XF
A30	**10 Rigsdaler Courant** 1778-1798. Issued until 1813. Anti-counterfeiting text added vertically at right. Large X at left. PC: Blue.	400	1,000	3,000
A31	**50 Rigsdaler Courant** 1785-1794. Issued until 1812. Anti-counterfeiting text added vertically at right. Large L at left. PC: Blue.	2,500	7,000	—

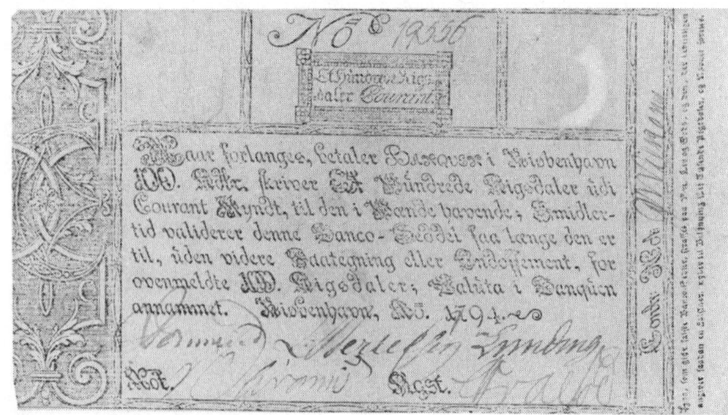

		Good	Fine	XF
A32	**100 Rigsdaler Courant** 1785-1798. Issued until 1813. Anti-counterfeiting text added vertically at right. Large C at left. PC: Blue.	1,800	5,000	—

Danske og Norske Species Banke i Kiöbenhavn

Danish-Norwegian Specie Bank in Copenhagen

1791-1798 Issue

		Good	Fine	XF
A33	**8 Rigsdaler Specie** 1791; 1797.	—	—	—
A34	**20 Rigsdaler Specie** 1791.	—	—	—
A35	**40 Rigsdaler Specie** 1792-1796. Unknown.	—	—	—
A36	**80 Rigsdaler Specie** 1791-1797. Only a *formular* of 1791 and a regular issue of 1796 are known.	—	—	—
A37	**4 Rigsdaler Specie** 1798-1800. Only 1798 is known.	—	5,000	—

Drafts on the Revenue of the Treasury - Compensation Fund

Decree of 8.4.1808

		Good	Fine	XF
A38	**2 Rigsdaler D.C.** *D.1808.*	500	1,200	—

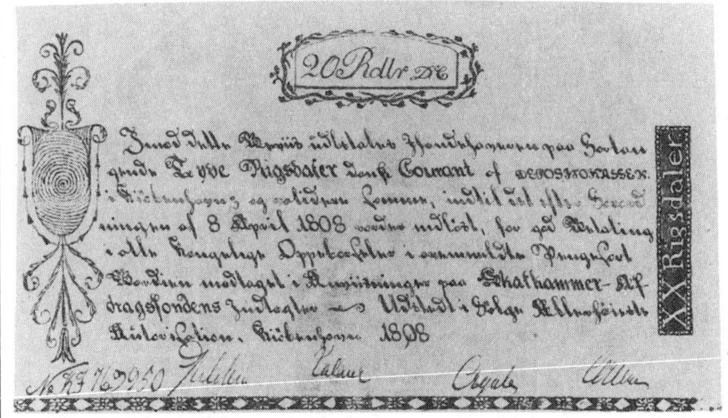

		Good	Fine	XF
A39	**20 Rigsdaler D.C.** *D.1808.*	400	900	—

Decrees of 28.8.1809 and 6.6.1810

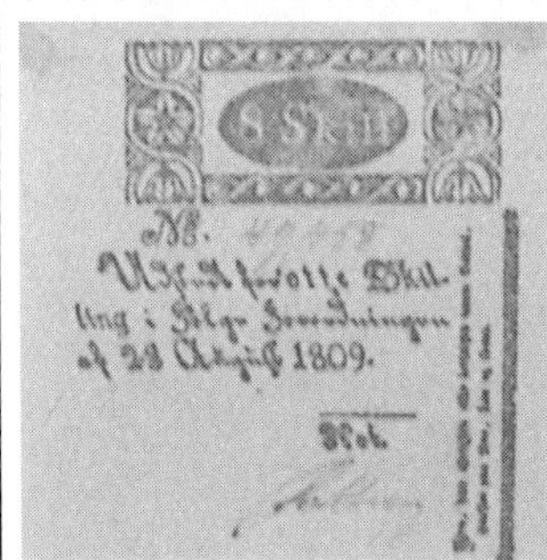

		Good	Fine	XF
A40	**8 Skilling** *D.1809.* PC: Blue.	25.00	120	450

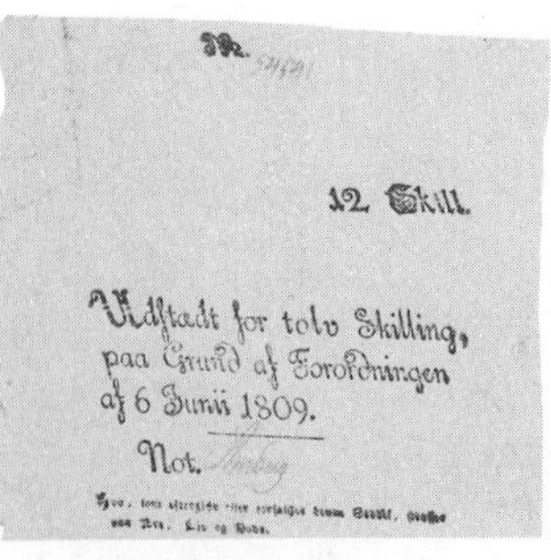

		Good	Fine	XF
A41	**12 Skilling** *D.1809.* PC: Blue.	25.00	135	500

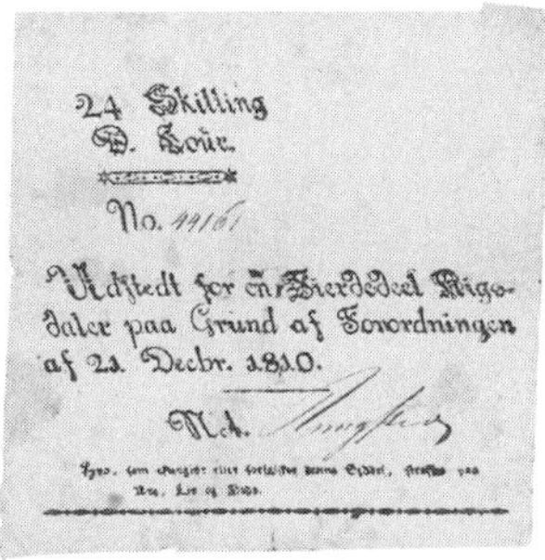

		Good	Fine	XF
A42	**24 Skilling**	Good	Fine	XF
	D.1810. PC: White.	30.00	140	500

Notes of the "Committee for the Advantage of Commerce" of the Wholesalers' Society of 1799 (100, 400 and 800 Rigsdaler interest-bearing at 3 3/4%), 1806 (100 and 500 Rigsdaler Courant interest-bearing at 5%) and 1814 (5, 25 and 100 Rigsbankdaler interest-bearing at 3.55%), though issued with government sanction, cannot be included as true government issues.

Royal Bank

1813 Drafts

		Good	Fine	XF
A43	**100 Rigsbankdaler**	Good	Fine	XF
	6.2.1813. Unknown.	—	—	—
A44	**250 Rigsbankdaler**	Good	Fine	XF
	6.2.1813.	—	—	—
A45	**500 Rigsbankdaler**	Good	Fine	XF
	6.2.1813. Unknown.	—	—	—

Danish State

Drafts - Royal Decree of 30.9.1813

		Good	Fine	XF
A46	**100 Rigsbankdaler**	Good	Fine	XF
	1813. Unknown.	—	—	—
A47	**200 Rigsbankdaler**	Good	Fine	XF
	1813. Unknown.	—	—	—

Rigsbanken i Kiøbenhavn

Rigsbank in Copenhagen

1813 Issue

		Good	Fine	XF
A48	**1 Rigsbankdaler**	Good	Fine	XF
	1813-1815. Uniface.	150	400	—
A49	**5 Rigsbankdaler**	Good	Fine	XF
	1813-1814. Uniface.	400	1,500	3,000
A50	**10 Rigsbankdaler**	Good	Fine	XF
	1814. Uniface.	2,250	5,000	—

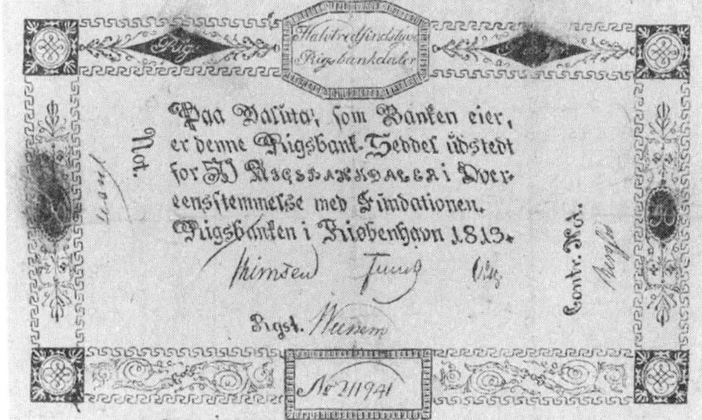

		Good	Fine	XF
A51	**50 Rigsbankdaler**	Good	Fine	XF
	1813. Uniface.	2,500	5,500	—
A52	**100 Rigsbankdaler**	Good	Fine	XF
	1813. Uniface.	2,500	5,500	—

Color Abbreviation Guide

New to the *Standard Catalog of ® World Paper Money* are the following abbreviations related to color references:

BC: Back color
PC: Paper color

Nationalbanken i Kiøbenhavn

National Bank in Copenhagen

1819 Issue

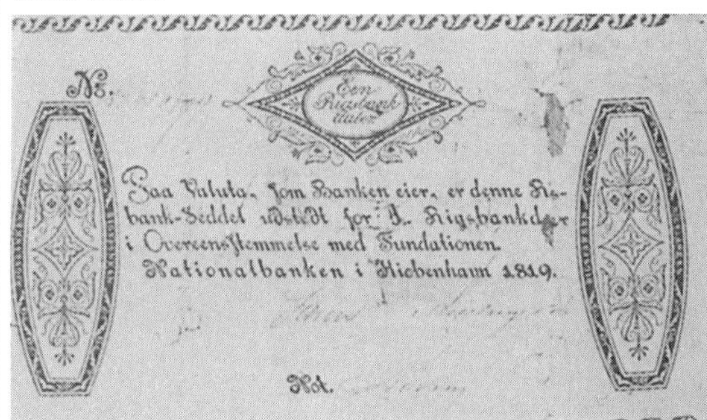

		Good	Fine	XF
A53	**1 Rigsbankdaler**	Good	Fine	XF
	1819. Uniface.	40.00	100	500
A54	**5 Rigsbankdaler**	Good	Fine	XF
	1819. Uniface.	600	2,000	—
A55	**10 Rigsbankdaler**	Good	Fine	XF
	1819. Uniface.	1,000	6,000	—
A56	**50 Rigsbankdaler**	Good	Fine	XF
	1819. Uniface.	1,750	7,000	12,000

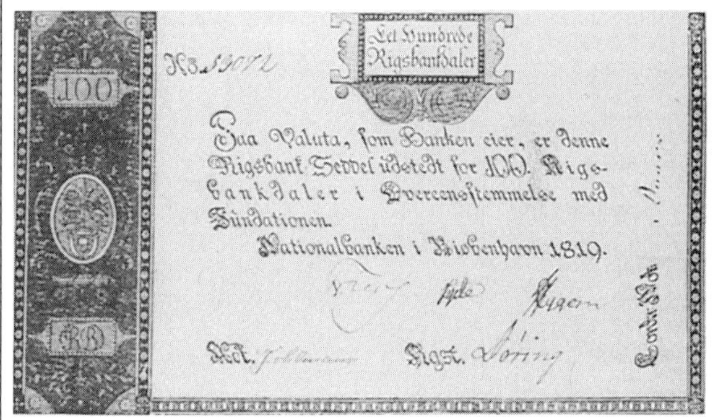

		Good	Fine	XF
A57	**100 Rigsbankdaler**	Good	Fine	XF
	1819. Uniface.	2,000	8,000	15,000

1834-1851 Issue

		Good	Fine	XF
A58	**5 Rigsbankdaler**	Good	Fine	XF
	1835.	200	550	—
A59	**20 Rigsbankdaler**	Good	Fine	XF
	1851.			
	a. Hand serial #, impressed stamps, back with 3 hand signatures.	7,000	14,000	—
	b. Printed serial #, no impressed stamps, no signature on back (issued 1872).	—	—	—
A60	**50 Rigsbankdaler**	Good	Fine	XF
	1834.			
	a. Plain back, impressed stamps, 5 hand signature.	—	—	—
	b. Brown back, impressed stamps, 5 hand signature. (issued 1850).	—	—	—
	c. Like b. but no impressed stamp, 2 hand signature (issued 1870). Unknown.	—	—	—
A61	**100 Rigsbankdaler**	Good	Fine	XF
	1845.	—	—	—

1860-1874 Issue

No.	Description	Good	Fine	XF
A62	**5 Rigsdaler**	Good	Fine	XF
	1863-1874.			
	a. Watermark without wavy lines, impressed stamp, hand serial #. 1863.	600	1,800	5,000
	b. Watermark has wavy lines, no impressed stamp, printed serial #. 1872-74.	900	3,000	—
A63	**10 Rigsdaler**	Good	Fine	XF
	1860-1874.			
	a. Impressed stamp, hand serial #, back with 3 hand signature 1860.	1,500	5,000	—
	b. No impressed stamp, printed serial #, no signature 1872-74.	—	—	—
A64	**50 Rigsdaler**	Good	Fine	XF
	1873-1874.	—	—	—
A65	**100 Rigsdaler**	Good	Fine	XF
	1870-1874.	—	—	—

Interest-bearing Credit Notes 1848-1870

Various Decrees and Laws

No.	Description	Good	Fine	XF
A66	**5 Rigsbankdaler**	Good	Fine	XF
	D.1848.	1,000	2,500	—
A67	**5 Rigsbankdaler**	Good	Fine	XF
	L.1850.	1,250	3,000	—

Law of 27.1.1851

No.	Description	Good	Fine	XF
A68	**5 Rigsbankdaler**	Good	Fine	XF
	L.1851.	1,250	3,000	—
A69	**50 Rigsbankdaler**	Good	Fine	XF
	L.1851. Unknown.	—	—	—
A70	**100 Rigsbankdaler**	Good	Fine	XF
	L.1851. Unknown.	—	—	—

Law of 26.8.1864

No.	Description	Good	Fine	XF
A71	**20 Rigsdaler**	Good	Fine	XF
	L.1864.	—	—	—
A72	**50 Rigsdaler**	Good	Fine	XF
	L.1864.	—	—	—
A73	**100 Rigsdaler**	Good	Fine	XF
	L.1864.	—	—	—

Law of 27.3.1866

No.	Description	Good	Fine	XF
A74	**20 Rigsdaler**	Good	Fine	XF
	L.1866.	—	—	—
A75	**50 Rigsdaler**	Good	Fine	XF
	L.1866.	—	—	—
A76	**100 Rigsdaler**	Good	Fine	XF
	L.1866.	—	—	—
A77	**500 Rigsdaler**	Good	Fine	XF
	L.1866.	—	—	—

Law of 1.8.1870

No.	Description	Good	Fine	XF
A78	**50 Rigsdaler**	Good	Fine	XF
	L.1870.	—	—	—
A79	**100 Rigsdaler**	Good	Fine	XF
	L.1870.	—	—	—
A80	**500 Rigsdaler**	Good	Fine	XF
	L.1870.	—	—	—

1875-1903 Issue

No.	Description	Good	Fine	XF
A81	**10 Kroner**	Good	Fine	XF
	1875-1890. Arms at upper center.	900	2,000	5,500
A82	**50 Kroner**	Good	Fine	XF
	1875-1881. Ornate panels at sides.	—	—	—
A83	**100 Kroner**	Good	Fine	XF
	1875-1887. Head at left and right, ornate oval design between.	—	—	—

No.	Description	Good	Fine	XF
A84	**500 Kroner**	Good	Fine	XF
	1875; 1889; 1903; 1907. Head of Mercury at left and Ceres at right, arms at bottom center.			
	a. Issued note. Rare.	10,000	22,500	—
	b. Handstamped: *MAKULATUR* (waste paper) with 2 punch holes.	7,000	18,000	—

1898-1904 Issue

No.	Description	Good	Fine	XF
1	**5 Kroner**	Good	Fine	XF
	1899-1903. Blue. Ornamental design of *5s* and *FEM KRONER*. Serial # at bottom left and right. Watermark: *NATIONALBANKEN i KJOBENHAVN*.	400	900	2,000
2	**10 Kroner**	Good	Fine	XF
	1891-1903. Black on brown underprint. Shield at left, ten 1 krone coins along bottom. Watermark: 2 heads facing.	750	1,250	3,000
3	**50 Kroner**	Good	Fine	XF
	1883-1902. Violet. Woman seated at left.			
	a. Issued note.	—	—	—
	b. Handstamped: *MAKULATUR.*	4,000	8,000	15,000
4	**100 Kroner**	Good	Fine	XF
	1888-1902. Green. Woman standing with scrolls at center.			
	a. Issued note.	—	—	—
	b. Handstamped: *MAKULATUR.*	4,000	8,000	15,000

1904-1911 Issue

No.	Description	Good	Fine	XF
6	**5 Kroner**	Good	Fine	XF
	1904-1910. Blue. Ornamental design of *5s* and *FEM KRONER*. Serial # at top left and right. Watermark: Wavy lines around *NATIONALBANKEN I KJBENHAVN.*			
	a. 1904 Prefix A.	450	850	1,450
	b. 1905 Prefix A.	900	1,500	2,200
	c. 1906 Prefix A.	450	850	1,450
	d. 1907 Prefix A. Left signature: J.C.L. Jensen.	450	850	1,450
	e. 1908 Prefix A. Left signature: Lange.	700	1,300	1,800
	f. 1908 Prefix B.	350	625	1,200
	g. 1909 Prefix B.	275	425	900
	h. 1910 Prefix B.	400	775	1,300
	i. 1910 Prefix C.	200	325	750

No.	Description	Good	Fine	XF
7	**10 Kroner**	Good	Fine	XF
	1904-1911. Black on brown underprint. Shield at left. Back: Ten 1 krone coins along bottom. Watermark: Wavy lines.			
	a. 1904 Prefix A.	450	800	1,800
	b. 1905 Prefix A.	—	—	—
	c. 1906 Prefix A.	—	—	—
	d. 1906 Prefix B.	250	800	1,800
	e. 1907 Prefix B. Left signature: J.C.L. Jensen.	300	500	1,100

		Good	Fine	XF
	f. 1908 Prefix C. Left signature: Lange.	250	400	850
	g. 1909 Prefix C.	300	500	1,100
	h. 1909 Prefix D.	250	400	850
	i. 1910 Prefix D.	250	400	850
	j. 1910 Prefix E.	250	400	850
	k. 1911 Prefix E.	175	275	725
	l. 1911 Prefix F.	150	225	650
8	**50 Kroner**	**Good**	**Fine**	**XF**
	1904; 1905; 1907. Brown. Woman seated at left. Cancelled note. Handstamped:*MAKULATUR*. Like #3. Watermark: Wavy lines.			
	a. Issued note.	3,000	10,000	—
	b. Cancelled note.	1,500	4,500	—

		Good	Fine	XF
9	**100 Kroner**			
	1905; 1905; 1907; 1908; 1910. Green. Woman standing with scrolls at center. Cancelled note. Watermark: Wavy lines.			
	a.	—	25,000	—
	b. Cancelled note. Handstamped: MAKULATUR.	—	11,000	22,500

1914-1916 Issues

		VG	VF	UNC
10	**1 Krone**			
	1914. Black on red paper. Large 1 and denomination above center text. Back: Arms in shield with dried fish at lower left for Iceland.			
	a. 6-digit serial #. Large digits.	4.50	25.00	120
	b. 7-digit serial #. Smaller digits.	5.50	30.00	140
11	**1 Krone**	**VG**	**VF**	**UNC**
	1914. Black. Large 1 and denomination above center text. 7-digit serial #. Smaller digits. Back: Arms in shield with falcon at lower left for Iceland. PC: Red.	3.50	20.00	110

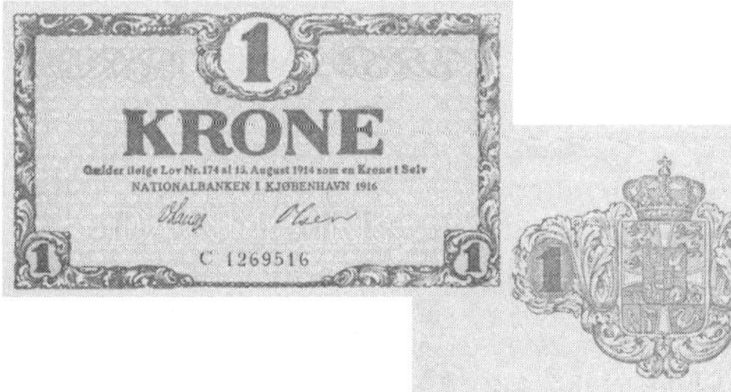

		VG	VF	UNC
12	**1 Krone**			
	1916; 1918; 1920; 1921. Blue on blue-green underprint. Back: Arms.			
	a. 1916. Without prefix letter.	1.00	4.50	22.50
	b. 1916. Prefix letter A-C.	1.50	5.50	22.50
	c. 1918. Prefix letter C.	20.00	0.50	22.50
	d. 1918. Prefix letter D-M.	2.75	9.00	30.00
	e. 1920. Prefix letter N-S.	3.50	10.00	35.00
	f. 1921. Prefix letter T-.	2.75	9.00	30.00
	g. 1921. Prefix letter 2A-2N.	2.75	7.00	25.00
	h. 1921. Prefix letter 2O.	1.00	3.50	18.00

Statsbevis

State Treasury Notes

1914 Issue

5% interest bearing notes that passed as legal tender.

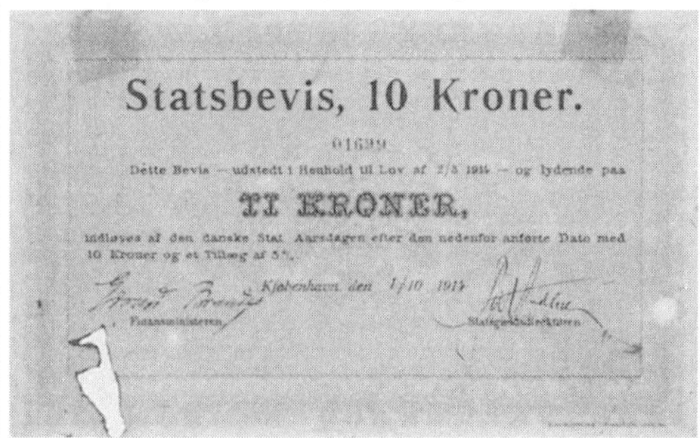

		Good	Fine	XF
16	**10 Kroner**			
	1.10.1914.			
	a. Series 1. 5 digit number.	450	800	1,400
	b. Series 2. 6 digit number.	550	1,000	—
17	**50 Kroner**	**Good**	**Fine**	**XF**
	1.10.1914.	—	—	—
18	**100 Kroner**	**Good**	**Fine**	**XF**
	1.10.1914.	—	—	—
19	**500 Kroner**	**Good**	**Fine**	**XF**
	1.10.1914.	—	—	—

Nationalbanken i Kjøbenhavn

National Bank, Copenhagen

1910-1931 Issue

Wmk: Dark numerals of the notes' denominations. #20-24 first signature V. Lange. Second signature changes.

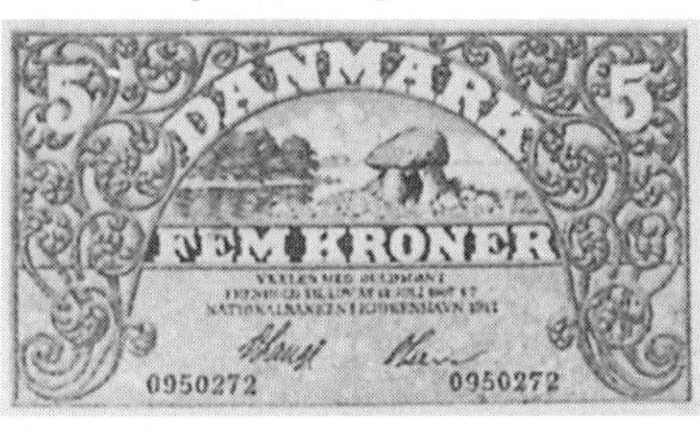

		VG	VF	UNC
20	**5 Kroner**			
	1912-1929. Dark blue. Landscape with stone-age burial site in center, surrounded by ornamentation of chrysanthemum flowers. First signature V. Lange. Second signature changes. Back: Arms within birch branches. Watermark: Dark numeral #5.			
	a. 1912.	90.00	250	1,150
	b. 1915. Prefix A.	145	400	1,450
	c. 1917. Prefix A.	210	575	2,100
	d. 1917. Prefix B.	145	400	1,450
	e. 1918. Prefix B.	110	340	1,175
	f. 1918. Prefix C.	200	520	1,600
	g. 1920. Prefix C.	45.00	130	600
	h. 1920. Prefix D.	145	400	1,450
	i. 1922. Prefix D.	40.00	125	550
	j. 1922. Prefix E.	145	400	1,450
	k. 1924. Prefix E.	45.00	130	600
	l. 1924. Prefix F.	55.00	150	725
	m. 1926. Prefix F.	45.00	130	600
	n. 1926. Prefix G.	250	700	2,250
	o. 1928. Prefix G.	30.00	100	450
	p. 1929. Prefix G.	45.00	130	600
	q. 1929. Prefix H.	30.00	100	450

21 10 Kroner

1913-1928. Brown. Lettering and denomination surrounded by ornamentation of seaweed. First signature V. Lange. Second signature changes. Back: Mercury head, surrounded by three lions. Watermark: Dark # 10.

	VG	VF	UNC
a. 1913.	40.00	120	600
b. 1913. Prefix A.	50.00	135	600
c. 1915. Prefix A.	130	320	1,350
d. 1915. Prefix B.	65.00	160	725
e. 1915. Prefix C.	55.00	145	680
f. 1917. Prefix C.	130	290	1,275
g. 1917. Prefix D.	35.00	110	550
h. 1919. Prefix E.	35.00	110	550
i. 1919. Prefix F.	45.00	125	580
j. 1920. Prefix F.	55.00	145	680
k. 1920. Prefix G.	55.00	145	680
l. 1921. Prefix G.	65.00	160	725
m. 1921. Prefix H.	90.00	250	900
n. 1922. Prefix H.	45.00	125	580
o. 1922. Prefix I.	55.00	145	680
p. 1923. Prefix I.	55.00	145	680
q. 1923. Prefix J.	45.00	125	580
r. 1924. Prefix J.	55.00	145	680
s. 1924. Prefix K.	35.00	110	550
t. 1925. Prefix K.	55.00	145	680
u. 1925. Prefix L.	35.00	110	550
v. 1925. Prefix M.	65.00	160	725
w. 1927. Prefix M.	35.00	110	550
x. 1927. Prefix N.	30.00	90.00	375
y. 1927. Prefix O.	300	600	2,000
z. 1928. Prefix O.	27.50	75.00	325
aa. 1928. Prefix P.	27.50	75.00	325
ab. 1928. Prefix Q.	22.50	65.00	290

22 50 Kroner

1911-1928. Blue-green. Three fishermen in boat pulling in a net, surrounded by ornamentation of hops. First signature V. Lange. Second signature changes. Back: Arms surrounded by oak branches to left, and beach to right. Watermark: Dark #50.

	VG	VF	UNC
a. 1911.	1,800	4,000	—
b. 1914.	1,625	3,650	—
c. 1919.	550	1,350	—
d. 1923.	625	1,550	—
e. 1925.	625	1,550	—
f. 1926.	625	1,550	—
g. 1928.	1,500	4,500	—
h. 1928. Prefix A.	220	675	—

23 100 Kroner

1910-1928. Brown-yellow. Lettering and denomination surrounded by ornamentation of dolphins. First signature V. Lange. Second signature changes. Back: Arms surround by seaweed, held by two mermen in waves. Watermark: Dark #100.

	VG	VF	UNC
a. 1910.	1,800	3,500	—
b. 1912.	1,800	3,500	—
c. 1914.	1,450	3,200	—
d. 1917.	1,450	3,200	—
e. 1920.	900	2,250	—
f. 1922.	325	1,000	—
g. 1924.	—	—	—
h. 1924. Prefix A.	325	1,000	—
i. 1926. Prefix A.	180	550	—
j. 1928. Prefix A.	80.00	275	—

24 500 Kroner

1910-1925. Gray-blue. Farmer plowing field with two horses surrounded by ornamentation of leaves. First signature V. Lange. Second signature changes. Back: Arms surrounded by branches of oak at left and beech at right. Watermark: Dark #500.

	VG	VF	UNC
a. 1910.	6,500	13,500	—
b. 1916.	—	—	—
c. 1919.	4,500	7,500	—
d. 1921.	3,250	5,500	—
e. 1925.	2,250	4,000	—

1930-1931 Issue

#25-29 first signature: V. Lange to 31.3.1935. Svendsen from 1.4.1935. Second signature changes.

25 5 Kroner

1931-1936. Blue-green. *NATIONALBANKENS SEDLER INDLSES MED GULD EFTER GAELDENDE LOV.* Landscape with Stone Age burial site at center, surrounded by ornamentation of chrysanthemum flowers. Back: Arms with birch branches. Watermark: Light #5.

	VG	VF	UNC
a. 1931.	25.00	75.00	350
b. 1931. Prefix A.	35.00	120	450
c. 1933. Prefix A.	25.00	75.00	350
d. 1933. Prefix B.	25.00	75.00	350
e. 1935. Prefix B.	30.00	105	400
f. 1935. Prefix C. First signature A. Lange to 31.3.1935.	25.00	75.00	300
g. 1935. Prefix C. First signature Svendsen from 1.4.1935.	18.00	65.00	300
h. 1935. Prefix D.	25.00	75.00	350
i. 1936. Prefix D.	25.00	75.00	350

26 10 Kroner

1930-1936. Brown. *NATIONALBANKENS SEDLER INDLSES MED GULD EFTER GAELDENDE LOV.* Lettering and denomination surrounded by ornamentation of seaweed. Back: Mercury head, surrounded by three lions. Watermark: Light #10. First signature V. Lange (1930-1934), Svendsen (1935-1936).

	VG	VF	UNC
a. 1930.	22.50	60.00	300
b. 1930. Prefix A.	25.00	70.00	325
c. 1932. Prefix B.	30.00	90.00	380
d. 1932. Prefix C.	30.00	90.00	380
e. 1933. Prefix C.	250	550	1,500
f. 1933. Prefix D.	27.50	75.00	325
g. 1933. Prefix E.	37.50	115	600
h. 1934. Prefix E.	27.50	75.00	325
i. 1934. Prefix F.	27.50	75.00	325
j. 1934. Prefix G.	37.50	115	600
k. 1935. Prefix G.	18.00	55.00	290
l. 1935. Prefix H.	11.00	40.00	200
m. 1936. Prefix H.	90.00	250	800
n. 1936. Prefix I.	13.50	45.00	220

27 50 Kroner

1930-1936. Blue-green. *NATIONALBANKENS SEDLER INDLSES MED GULD EFTER GAELDENDE LOV.* Three fishermen in boat pulling in a net, surrounded by ornamentation of hops. Back: Arms surrounded by oak branches at left and beach at right. Watermark: Light #50. First signature V. Lange to (1930-1935), Svendsen (1936).

	VG	VF	UNC
a. 1930.	125	360	1,100
b. 1933.	160	400	1,300
c. 1935.	125	360	1,100
d. 1936.	145	380	1,200

28 100 Kroner

1930-1936. Brown. *NATIONALBANKENS SEDLER INDLSES MED GULD EFTER GAELDENDE LOV.* Lettering and denomination surrounded by ornamentation of dolphins. Back: Arms surrounded by seaweed, held by two mermen in waves. Watermark: Light #100. First signature V. Lange (1930-1932), Svendsen (1935-1936).

	VG	VF	UNC
a. 1930.	75.00	235	775
b. 1932.	75.00	235	775
c. 1935.	180	525	1,200
d. 1936.	180	525	1,200

		VG	VF	UNC
29	**500 Kroner** 1931 Gray-blue. *NATIONALBANKENS SEDLER INDLSES MED GULD EFTER GAELDENDE LOV.* Farmer plowing field with two horses surrounded by ornamentation of leaves. Back: Arms surrounded by branches of oak at left and beech at right. Watermark: Light #500.	725	1,275	2,750

Danmarks Nationalbank

1937-1938 Issue

		VG	VF	UNC
30	**5 Kroner** 1937-1943. Blue-green. Landscape with Stone Age burial site at center, surrounded by ornamentation of chrysanthemum flowers. First signature Svendsen. Second signature changes (18 different.) Back: Arms within birch branches.			
	a. 1937. Prefix E.	9.00	27.50	130
	b. 1939. Prefix E.	11.00	20.00	170
	c. 1939. Prefix F.	9.00	27.50	130
	d. 1940. Prefix F.	5.50	9.00	80.00
	e. 1940. Prefix G.	4.50	12.75	70.00
	f. 1942. Prefix G.	4.50	12.75	70.00
	g. 1942. Prefix H.	3.50	5.50	60.00
	h. 1942. Prefix J.	3.50	5.50	60.00
	i. 1943. Prefix J.	3.50	5.50	60.00
	j. 1943. Prefix J. Signature Svendsen - Lund.	3.00	5.00	50.00
	k. 1943. Prefix K.	4.50	12.75	70.00

		VG	VF	UNC
31	**10 Kroner** 1937-1943. Brown. Lettering and denomination surrounded by ornamentation of seaweed. First signature Svendsen. Second signature changes (14 different.) Back: Mercury head, surrounded by three lions.			
	a. 1937. Prefix K.	10.00	30.00	180
	b. 1937. Prefix L.	9.00	25.00	155
	c. 1937. Prefix M.	8.00	22.00	130
	d. 1937. Prefix N.	200	400	2,000
	e. 1939. Prefix N.	5.50	18.00	100
	f. 1939. Prefix O.	4.50	14.50	90.00
	g. 1939. Prefix P.	3.50	10.00	75.00
	h. 1939. Prefix Q.	9.00	30.00	200
	i. 1941. Prefix Q.	3.50	10.00	75.00
	j. 1941. Prefix R.	3.50	10.00	75.00
	k. 1942. Prefix R.	3.50	10.00	75.00
	l. 1942. Prefix S.	1.75	3.50	45.00
	m. 1942. Prefix T.	90.00	250	800
	n. 1943. Prefix T.	1.75	3.50	45.00
	o. 1943. Prefix U.	1.75	3.50	45.00
	p. 1943. Prefix V.	1.75	3.50	45.00
	q. 1943. Prefix X.	—	—	2,000

		VG	VF	UNC
32	**50 Kroner** 1938-1942. Blue-green. Three fishermen in boat pulling in a net, surrounded by ornamentation of hops. First signature Svendsen. Second signature changes (13 different.) Back: Arms surrounded by oak branches at left and beech to right.			
	a. 1938. Prefix C.	130	360	1,500
	b. 1939. Prefix C.	35.00	105	360
	c. 1941. Prefix C.	27.50	80.00	275
	d. 1942. Prefix C.	17.50	45.00	160
	e. 1946. Prefix C.	—	—	225

#32e is a counterfeit. Signatures: Svendesen-Ingerslevgaard.

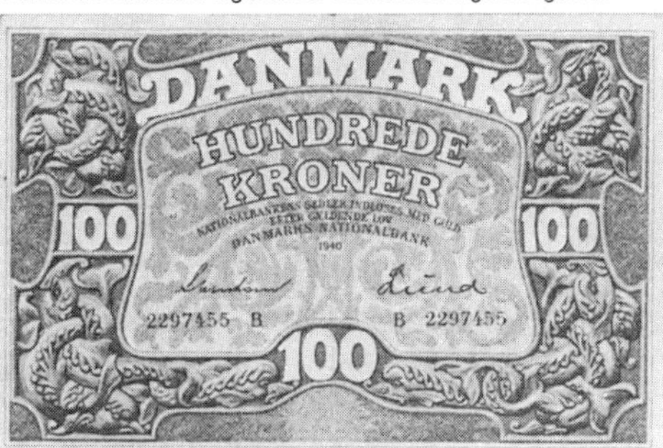

		VG	VF	UNC
33	**100 Kroner** 1938-1943. Brown-yellow. Lettering and denomination surrounded by ornamentation of dolphins. First signature Svendsen. Second signature changes (13 different.) Back: Arms surrounded by seaweed, held by two mermen in waves.			
	a. 1938. Prefix B.	65.00	110	775
	b. 1940. Prefix B.	27.50	67.50	360
	c. 1941. Prefix B.	36.00	80.00	500
	d. 1943. Prefix B.	22.50	50.00	325

		VG	VF	UNC
34	**500 Kroner** 1938-1941. Gray-blue. Farmer plowing field with two horses surrounded by ornamentation of leaves. First signature Svendsen. Second signature changes (11 different.) Back: Arms surrounded by branches of oak at left and beech at right.			
	a. 1939. Prefix A.	550	1,100	3,650
	b. 1941. Prefix A.	550	1,100	3,650
	s. Specimen.	—	—	2,100

Note: For issues with overprint:...*FAERO. AMT, JUNI 1940.* See Faeroe Islands listings.

1944-1946 Issue

#35-41 first signature: Svendsen for 1944-45. Halberg for 1945-49. Riim for 1948-1962.

		VG	VF	UNC
35	**5 Kroner** 1944-1950. Blue. *KRO 5 NER.* Back: Arms.			
	a. 1944. Prefix AA-AP. Engraved.	18.00	50.00	225
	b. 1945. Prefix BA-BH. Lithographed. Left signature: Svendsen.	21.00	60.00	275
	c. 1946. Prefix BH-BO. Left signature: Halberg.	27.50	72.50	360
	d. 1947. Prefix BO-BV.	24.00	65.00	325
	e. 1948. Prefix BX-CH.	24.00	65.00	325
	f. 1949. Prefix CH-DB.	13.50	40.00	250
	g. 1950. Prefix DC-DAE. Left signature: Riim.	11.00	35.00	180
	s. Specimen.	—	—	—

36	10 Kroner	VG	VF	UNC
	1944 Prefix AA-CM. Brown. *10 TI KRONER 10.* Back: Arms.			
	a. Issued note. Engraved. Prefix AB-CM.	7.50	22.50	110
	s. Specimen.	—	—	450

37	10 Kroner	VG	VF	UNC
	1945-1948. Dark green. Lettering and denomination surrounded by ornamentation of seaweed. Back: Arms.			
	a. Hand-made paper, watermark: Floral ornaments at left and right. 1945. Prefix A. Left signature: Svendsen.	22.50	72.50	425
	b. 1945. Prefix A. Left signature: Halberg.	55.00	160	575
	c. 1945. Prefix B-C.	21.00	65.00	360
	d. 1945. Prefix D.	27.50	110	490
	e. Watermark: Wavy lines and crowns. 1947. Prefix E-H.	15.00	42.50	185
	f. 1948. Prefix H-O.	22.50	72.50	300
	g. 1948. Prefix O-U. Left signature: Riim.	18.00	65.00	250
	h. 1948. Prefixes M-N.	18.00	65.00	250
	i. 1948. Prefix O. Left signature: Halberg.	18.00	65.00	250
	j. 1948. Prefix O. Left signature:Riim.	24.50	80.00	325
	k. 1948. Prefixes R-T.	13.50	40.00	175
	l. 1948. Prefix U.	18.00	65.00	250
	s. As c-e. Specimen.	—	—	500

38	50 Kroner	VG	VF	UNC
	1944-1954. Purple. Fishermen in boat, pulling in net. Like #32. Back: Arms at center.			
	a. 1944. Prefix F. Left signature: Svendsen.	120	250	825
	b. 1945. Prefix F. Left signature: Svendsen.	220	450	1,350
	c. 1945. Prefix F. Left signature: Halberg.	220	500	1,550
	d. 1948. Prefix F. Left signature: Halberg.	250	550	1,625
	e. 1948. Prefix K. Left signature: Halberg.	200	410	1,175
	f. 1948. Prefix K. Left signature: Riim.	275	600	1,800
	g. 1951. Prefix K. Left signature: Riim.	180	360	1,100
	h. 1951. Prefix M. Left signature: Riim.	275	600	1,800
	i. 1953. Prefix M. Left signature: Riim.	275	600	1,800
	j. 1954. Prefix M. Left signature: Riim.	160	325	950
	k. 1954. Prefix N. Left signature: Riim.	200	410	1,175
	s. Specimen. Left signature: Riim.	—	—	1,200

39	100 Kroner	VG	VF	UNC
	1944-1960. Green. Lettering and denomination surrounded by ornamentation of dolphins, like#33. Back: Arms.			
	a. 1944. Prefix E.	40.00	105	320
	b. 1946. Prefix E. Left signature Svendsen.	120	275	1,000
	c. 1946. Prefix E. Left signature: Halberg.	105	220	775
	d. 1946. Prefix H. Left signature: Halberg.	110	250	900
	e. 1948. Prefix H. Left signature: Halberg.	105	220	775
	f. 1948. Prefix H. Left signature: Riim.	120	275	1,000
	g. 1948. Prefix K.	90.00	190	680
	h. 1951. Prefix K.	85.00	175	590
	i. 1953. Prefix K.	120	275	1,000
	j. 1953. Prefix M.	40.00	125	450
	k. 1953. Prefix N.	90.00	190	680
	l. 1955. Prefix N.	35.00	110	360
	m. 1955. Prefix O.	650	1,100	2,500
	n. 1956. Prefix O.	35.00	110	360
	o. 1957. Prefix O.	105	220	775
	p. 1957. Prefix R.	40.00	125	450
	q. 1958. Prefix R.	45.00	135	500
	r. 1958. Prefix S.	45.00	135	500
	s. 1959. Prefix S.	45.00	135	500
	t. 1959. Prefix T.	650	1,100	2,500
	u. 1960. Prefix T.	45.00	135	500

#40 *Deleted.* Merged into #39.

41 500 Kroner

1944-1962. Orange-red. Farmer with horses at center, plowing a field. Back: Arms. 175x108mm.

	VG	VF	UNC
a. 1944. Prefix D. Left signature: Svendsen.	400	625	1,650
b. 1945. Prefix D. Left signature: Halberg.	510	900	2,300
c. 1948. Prefix D. Left signature: Halberg.	510	900	2,300
d. 1948. Prefix D. Left signature: Riim.	510	900	2,300
e. 1951. Prefix D. Left signature: Riim.	650	1,200	2,750
f. 1953. Prefix D. Left signature: Riim.	650	1,200	2,750
g. 1954. Prefix D. Left signature: Riim.	700	1,400	3,200
h. 1956. Prefix D. Left signature: Riim.	475	850	2,300
i. 1959. Prefix D. Left signature: Riim.	400	625	1,650
j. 1961. Prefix D. Left signature: Riim.	650	1,200	2,750
k. 1962. Prefix D. Left signature: Riim.	475	825	2,300
s. Specimen.	—	—	—

1950 (1952)-1963 Issue

Law of 7.4.1936 #42-47 first signature changes. Usually there are 3 signature combinations per prefix A0, A1, A2 etc. Second signature Riim, (19)51-68 for #42, 43, 44a-f, (19)51-68 for #42, 43, 44a-f, 45a-b, 46a-b, 47. Valeur for (19)69 for #44g-h, 45c and 46b. The prefixes mentioned in the listings refer to the first two characters of the left serial #. The middle two digits indicate the year date of issue, and the last two characters indicate the sheet position of the note. Replacement Notes: #42-47, Serial # suffix: *OJ* (for whole sheet replacements) or *OK* (for single note replacements).

42 5 Kroner

(19)50; (19)52; (19)54-1960. Blue-green. Portrait Bertil Thorvaldsen at left, three Graces at right. Back: Kalundborg city view with five spire church at center. Watermark: *5* repeated. 125x65mm.

	VG	VF	UNC
a. 5 in the watermark 11mm high. Without dot after 7 in law date. (19)52. Prefix A0; A1.	4.50	16.00	125
b. As a. (19)52. Prefix A2.	13.50	45.00	225
c. As a, but with dot after 7 in law date. (19)52. Prefix A2.	7.25	27.50	175
d. As c. (19)52. Prefix A3.	13.50	45.00	225
e. As c. (19)54. Prefixes A3-A5.	7.25	27.50	175
f. As c. (19)54. Prefix A6.	8.25	30.00	190
g. As c. (19)55. Prefixes A7-A8.	7.25	27.50	175
h. As c. (19)55. Prefix A9.	8.25	30.00	190
i. 5 in the watermark 13mm high. Prefix B0.	3.75	13.50	80.00
j. As i. (19)55. Prefix B1.	10.00	25.00	175
k. As i. (19)56. Prefix B1.	6.50	20.00	120
l. As i. (19)56. Prefixes B2-B3.	4.00	16.00	90.00
m. As i. (19)56. Prefix B4.	13.50	45.00	225
n. As i. (19)57. Prefixes B4-B6.	2.75	7.25	55.00
o. As i. (19)58-59. Prefixes B7-B9, C0.	2.25	6.50	45.00
p. As i. (19)59. Prefix C1.	2.00	5.50	32.50
q. As i. (19)59. Prefix C3.	200	400	800
r. As i. (19)60. Prefixes C3.	2.00	5.50	32.50
r1. Replacement note. (19)50. Prefixes as e, g. suffix 0J.	35.00	90.00	275
r2. Replacement note. (19)50. Prefixes as f, h, j, m,q, suffix 0J.	45.00	100	290
r3. Replacement note. (19)50. Prefixes as i, l, suffix 0J.	30.00	70.00	225
r4. Replacement note. (19)50. Prefixes as n, o, suffix 0J.	25.00	60.00	210
r5. Replacement note. (19)60. Prefixes as p, r, s, suffix 0J.	12.00	30.00	80.00
r6. Replacement note. (19)50. Prefixes as a, suffix 0K.	10.00	25.00	70.00
r7. Replacement note. (19)50. Prefixes as e, suffix 0K.	13.50	32.50	85.00
r8. Replacement note. (19)60. Prefixes as f, suffix 0K.	200	450	—
r9. Replacement note (19)50. Prefixes as o, suffix 0K.	200	450	—
r10. Replacement note. (19)60. Prefixes as s, suffix 0K.	200	450	—
r11. Replacement note. (19)50. Prefix as o, suffix 0K.	200	450	900
r12. Replacement note (19)60. Prefix as s, suffix 0K.	200	450	—
s. As i. (19)60. Prefix C4.	2.25	6.50	45.00
s1. Specimen.	—	—	400

43 10 Kroner

(19)50-52. Black and olive-brown. Portrait Hans Christian Andersen at left, white storks in nest at right. Back: Green landscape of Egeskov Mølle Fyn at center. Watermark: *10* repeated. 125x65mm.

	VG	VF	UNC
a. (19)51. Prefix A0.	22.50	60.00	220
b. (19)51. Prefix A3.	60.00	135	410
c. (19)51. Prefix A4.	22.50	60.00	220
d. (19)52. Prefix A1-A2; A5-A8.	22.50	60.00	220
e. (19)52. Prefix A9.	300	600	—
f. (19)52. Prefix B0.	60.00	135	410
g. (19)52. Prefix B1.	90.00	225	550
r1. (19)51. Replacement note. Suffix 0K.	300	650	—
r2. (19)52. Replacement note. Suffix 0K.	275	550	—

44 10 Kroner

(19)50; (19)54-1974. Black and brown. Portrait Hans Christian Andersen at left, white storks in nest at right, text line added in upper and lower frame. Portrait Hans Christian Andersen at left. Back: Black landscape at center. 125x71mm.

	VG	VF	UNC
a. Top and bottom line in frame begins with *10*. Watermark: *10* repeated, 11mm high. (19)54. Prefix C0.	10.00	30.00	125
b. As a. Prefix C1.	22.50	55.00	225
c. As a. Watermark 13mm high. (19)54. Prefix C1.	22.50	55.00	225
d. As c. (19)54-55. Prefixes C2-D5.	9.00	27.00	110
e. As c. (19)55. Prefix D6.	35.00	90.00	350
f. As c. (19)56. Prefix D6.	22.50	55.00	225
g. As a. (19)56. Prefix D6.	22.50	55.00	225
h. As a. (19)56. Prefix D7.	18.00	45.00	165
i. As a. (19)56. Prefix D8.	16.00	40.00	145
j. As c. (19)56. Prefixes D8-E1.	9.00	27.50	110
k. As c. (19)56. Prefix E2.	290	450	1,250
l. As c. (19)57. Prefixes E2-E4.	9.00	27.50	110
m. Top and bottom line in frame begins with *TI*. (19)57. Prefix E4.	290	450	1,250
n. As m. (19)57. Prefixes E5-E6.	7.25	22.50	90.00
o. As m. (19)58. Prefixes E7-F3.	90.00	275	900
o. As m. (19)57. Prefix E7.	6.50	14.50	75.00
q. As m. (19)58. Prefix F4.	6.50	14.50	75.00
r. As m. (19)59. Prefix F4.	7.25	22.00	90.00
r1. Replacement note. (19)50. Prefixes as d. Suffix 0J.	35.00	100	275
r2. Replacement note. (19)50. Prefixes as e-i, m. Suffix 0J.	55.00	150	400
r3. Replacement note. (19)50. Prefixes as j, l. Suffix 0J.	20.00	55.00	220
r4. Replacement note. (19)50, (19)60. Prefixes as n, p-s. Suffix 0J.	16.00	40.00	150
r5. Replacement note. (19)60. Prefixes as t. Suffix 0J.	16.00	45.00	175
r6. Replacement note. (19)61-64. Prefixes as u, w. Suffix 0J.	9.00	27.50	90.00
r7. Replacement note. (19)62. Prefixes as v. Suffix 0J.	12.00	35.00	125
r8. Replacement note. (19)64. Prefixes as x. Suffix 0J.	9.00	27.50	90.00
r9. Replacement note. (19)65-69 Prefixes as y-ac. Suffix 0J.	4.50	10.00	35.00
r10. Replacement note. (19)70-71. Prefixes as ae. Suffix 0J.	3.50	9.00	28.00

	VG	VF	UNC
r11. Replacement note. (19)69, (19)71. Prefixes as ad, af. Suffix 0J.	90.00	225	500
r12. Replacement note. (19)74. Prefixes as ag, ai. Suffix 0J.	3.50	10.00	25.00
r13. Replacement note. (19)74. Prefix as aj. Suffix 0J.	3.50	10.00	25.00
r14. Replacement note. (19)50. Prefixes as b. Suffix 0K.	350	750	—
r15. Replacemnet note. (19)50. Prefixes as d. Suffix 0K.	300	650	—
r16. Replacement note. (19)65-69. Prefix as y-ac. Suffix 0K.	260	550	—
r17. Replacement note. (19)62-64. Prefixes as u-w. Suffix 0K.	260	550	—
r18. Replacement note. (19)69, (19)71. Prefixes as ad, af. Suffix 0K.	225	400	—
r19. Replacement note. (19)70-73. Prefixes as ae, ag. Suffix 0K.	90.00	175	350
r20. Replacement note. (19)74. Prefixes as ai-aj. Suffix 0K.	120	250	450
s. As m. (19)59. Prefixes F5-F8.	5.50	12.50	65.00
s1. Specimen.	—	—	500
t. As m. (19)60. Prefixes F9-G3.	5.50	12.50	65.00
u. As m. (19)61-62. Prefixes G4-H1.	4.50	10.50	45.00
v. As m. (19)62. Prefix H2.	9.00	18.00	72.50
w. As m. (19)63-64. Prefixes H2-J3.	4.25	9.00	40.00
x. As m. (19)64. Prefix J4.	5.00	14.50	60.00
y. As m. (19)65-67. Prefixes J5-K9.	3.50	7.50	27.50
z. As m. (19)68. Prefixes A0-A3.	3.25	6.50	23.00
aa. As m. (19)68. Second signature: Riim. Prefix A4.	4.00	9.00	32.00
ab. As m. (19)69. Second signature: Valear. Prefix A4.	4.00	9.00	32.00
ac. As aa. (19)69. Prefixes A5-A8.	3.25	6.50	25.00
ad. As aa. (19)69. Prefix A9.	37.50	90.00	360
ae. As aa. (19)70-71. Prefixes A9-B9.	—	5.00	18.00
af. As aa. (19)71. Prefix C0.	32.00	75.00	325
ag. As aa. (19)72-73. Prefixes C0-C9.	—	3.50	16.00
ah. As aa. (19)74. Prefix C9.	37.50	90.00	360
ai. As aa. (19)74. Prefixes D0-D5.	—	2.50	11.00
aj. As aa. (19)74. Prefix D6.	—	2.75	13.00

45 50 Kroner

(19)50; (19)56-1970. Blue on green underprint. Portrait Ole Rømer at left, Round Tower in Copenhagen at right. Back: Stone Age burial site Dolmen of Stenvad, Djursland at center. 153x78mm.

	VG	VF	UNC
a. Handmade paper. Watermark: Crowns and *50* (19)56, Prefix A1.	50.00	100	300
b. As a. (19)57. Prefix A1.	50.00	100	300
c. As a. (19)57. Prefix A2.	65.00	125	400
d. As a. (19)58. Prefix A2.	40.00	75.00	275
e. As a. (19)58. Prefix B0.	275	600	1,800
f. As a. (19)60. Prefix A2.	—	1,500	—
g. Machine made paper. Watermark: Rhombuses and 50. (19)61/1962. Prefix A4.	32.00	70.00	220
h. As f. (19)62. Prefix A4.	32.00	70.00	220
i. As f. (19)63. Prefix A4.	35.00	80.00	250
j. As f. (19)63. Prefix A5.	22.00	60.00	200
k. As f. (19)66. Prefix A6-A7.	40.00	80.00	160
l. As f. (19)66. Prefix A8.	16.00	22.00	165
m. As g. (19)70. Prefix A8-A9.	—	20.00	80.00
r1. As a. Replacement note. (19)50/1956. Suffix OJ.	50.00	100	300
r2. As b. Replacement note. (19)50/1957. Suffix OJ.	50.00	100	300
r3. As c. Replacement note. (19)57 Suffix OJ.	65.00	125	400
r4. As d. Replacement note. (19)50/1958. Suffix OJ.	45.00	90.00	275
r5. As f. Replacement note. Prefixes A2-A3. (19)60.	45.00	90.00	300
r6. As g-j. Replacement note. (19)61-63. Suffix OJ.	40.00	85.00	240
r7. As k. Replacement note. (19)66. Suffix OJ.	18.00	35.00	125
r8. As l. Replacement note. (19)66. Suffix OJ.	22.00	60.00	165
r9. As m. Replacement note. (19)70. Suffix OJ.	—	20.00	75.00
r10. As b. Replacement note. (19)50/1957. Suffix OK.	300	550	1,500
r11. As d. Replacement note. (19)50/1958. Suffix OK.	350	700	1,750
r12. As f. Replacement note. (19)60. Suffix OK.	300	550	1,500
r13. As k-l. Replacement note. (19)66. Suffix OK.	250	450	1,250
r14. As m. Replacement note. (19)70 Suffix 0K.	200	400	1,000
s. Specimen.	—	—	600

#45g shows date in lower left corner as 1962, while the date in the left serial number shows (19)61. On the replacements r1-r4 and r10-r11, the date in the lower left corner shows the actual date, while the date in the left serial number shows (19)50.

46 100 Kroner

(19)61-1970. Red-brown on red-yellow underprint. Portrait Hans Christian Ørsted at left, compass card at right. Back: Kronborg castle in Elsinore. 155x84mm.

	VG	VF	UNC
a. Handmade paper. Watermark: Close wavy lines and compass. (19)61. Prefix A0.	225	420	1,100
b. Machine made paper. Watermark: *100.* (19)61. Prefix A2- A3.	23.00	45.00	165
c. (19)62. Prefix A4-A5.	27.00	60.00	225
d. (19)65. Prefix A6-B1.	21.00	35.00	125
e. (19)65. Prefix B2.	40.00	100	360
f. (19)70. Prefix B2-B4.	—	27.00	80.00
r1. As a. Replacement note. (19)61. Suffix 0J.	30.00	85.00	325
r2. As b. Replacement note. (19)62. Suffix 0J.	25.00	55.00	190
r3. As c. Replacement note. (19)62. Suffix 0J.	32.00	80.00	250
r4. As d. Replacement note. (19)65. Suffix 0J.	23.00	45.00	145
r5. As e. Replacement note. (19)65. Suffix 0J.	36.00	80.00	320
r6. As f. Replacement note. (19)70. Suffix 0J.	—	27.00	80.00
r7. As a. Replacement note. (19)61. Suffix 0K.	550	1,000	1,800
r8. As d. Replacement note. (19)65. Suffix 0K.	550	1,000	1,800
r9. As f. Replacement note. (19)70. Suffix 0K.	550	1,000	1,800
s. Specimen.	—	—	650

47 500 Kroner

1963-1967. Green. Portrait C.D.F. Reventlow at left, farmer plowing at right. Small date at lower right. Back: Roskilde city view. 175x90mm.

	VG	VF	UNC
a. 1963. Prefix A0.	150	325	900
b. 1965. Prefix A0.	180	400	1,200
c. 1967. Prefix A0.	110	225	700
d. 1967. Prefix A1.	125	275	825
r1. As a. Replacement note. (19)63. Suffix 0J.	220	480	1,350
r2. As b. Replacement note. (19)65. Suffix 0J.	200	450	1,275
r3. As c. Replacement note. (19)67. Suffix 0J.	125	245	775
r4. As d. Replacement note. (19)67. Suffix 0J.	135	300	900
s. Specimen.	—	—	900

The Dominican Republic, occupying the eastern two-thirds of the island of Hispañiola, has an area of 48,730 sq. km. and a population of 9.50 million. Capital: Santo Domingo. The agricultural economy produces sugar, coffee, tobacco and cocoa.

Explored and claimed by Christopher Columbus on his first voyage in 1492, the island of Hispaniola became a springboard for Spanish conquest of the Caribbean and the American mainland. In 1697, Spain recognized French dominion over the western third of the island, which in 1804 became Haiti. The remainder of the island, by then known as Santo Domingo, sought to gain its own independence in 1821, but was conquered and ruled by the Haitians for 22 years; it finally attained independence as the Dominican Republic in 1844. In 1861, the Dominicans voluntarily returned to the Spanish Empire, but two years later they launched a war that restored independence in 1865. A legacy of unsettled, mostly non-representative rule followed, capped by the dictatorship of Rafael Leonidas Trujillo from 1930-61. Juan Bosch was elected president in 1962, but was deposed in a military coup in 1963. In 1965, the United States led an intervention in the midst of a civil war sparked by an uprising to restore Bosch. In 1966, Joaquin Balaguer defeated Bosch in an election to become president. Balaguer maintained a tight grip on power for most of the next 30 years when international reaction to flawed elections forced him to curtail his term in 1996. Since then, regular competitive elections have been held in which opposition candidates have won the presidency. Former President (1996-2000) Leonel Fernandez Reyna won election to a second term in 2004 following a constitutional amendment allowing presidents to serve more than one term.

MONETARY SYSTEM:

1 Peso Oro = 100 Centavos Oro
1 Peso Dominicano = 100 Centavos, 2010-

SPECIMEN NOTES:

In 1998 the Banco Central began selling various specimens over the counter to the public.

REPLACEMENT NOTES:

#53-61: Z prefix and suffix (TDLR printings).
#117-124: Z prefix and suffix (TDLR printings).

SPANISH ADMINISTRATION

República Dominicana

1848 Provisional Issue

#6 and 7 overprint:...*del decreto Congreso Nacional de 19 de Mayo de 1853...* on blank back.

		Good	Fine	XF
6	**20 Pesos on 1 Peso = 40 Centavos** 1848. Black. Printer: Durand, Baldwin & Co. N.Y.	50.00	175	—

		Good	Fine	XF
7	**40 Pesos on 2 Pesos = 80 Centavos** 1848. Brown. Farm boy raking at left, arms at top center. Printer: Durand, Baldwin & Co. N.Y.	50.00	225	—

Note: #6 and 7 are most often encountered with punched hole cancellations. Uncancelled notes are worth 30% more.

#8 not assigned.

Decreto 23.7.1849 Regular Issue

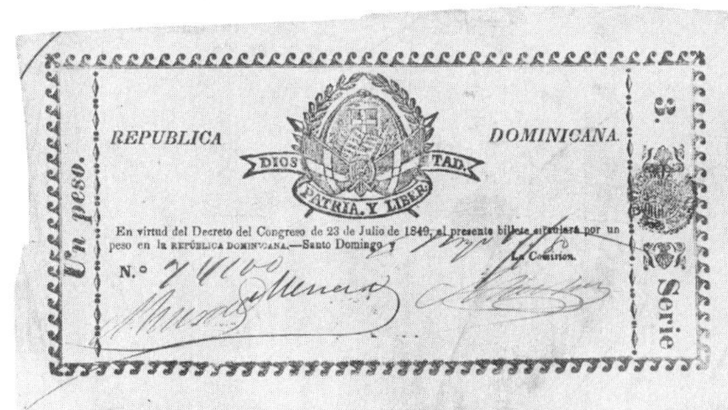

		Good	Fine	XF
9	**1 Peso** D.1849. Black. Arms at upper center.	150	400	—
10	**2 Pesos** D.1849. Black.	150	400	—

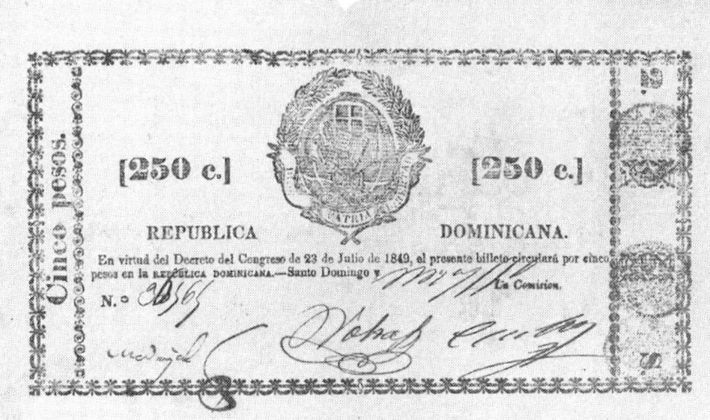

		Good	Fine	XF
11	**5 Pesos** D.1849. Black.	175	450	—

#12 and 13 not assigned.

Decreto 19.5.1853

		Good	Fine	XF
14	**1 Peso** D.1853. Arms at upper center.	150	400	—

		Good	Fine	XF
15	**2 Pesos** D.1853. Black. Arms at upper center.	150	400	—

#17 not assigned.

Decreto 16.8.1858

		Good	Fine	XF
16	**5 Pesos** ND (1858). Black. Arms at upper center.	—	—	—

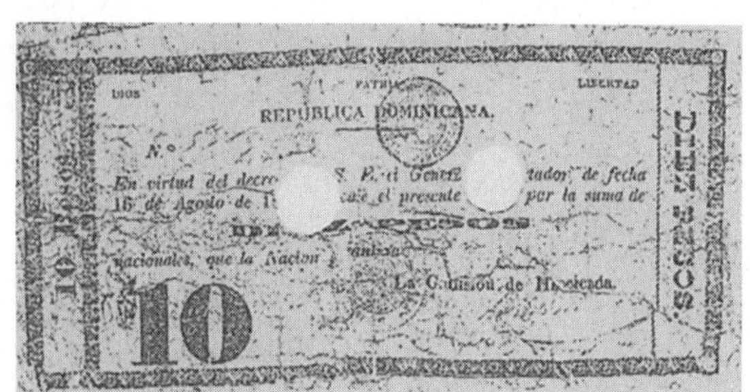

#	Denomination	Good	Fine	XF
18	**10 Pesos** D.1858. Black.	—	—	—
19	**50 Pesos** D.1858. Black.	—	—	—

1860 Issue

#	Denomination	Good	Fine	XF
20	**50 Pesos** 17.5.1860; 28.12.1860. Black. 2 circular handstamps.	500.	800.	—

1864 Issue

#	Denomination	Good	Fine	XF
21	**10 Pesos** 20.9.1864. Issued at Santiago de los Caballeros. Black.	—	—	—
22	**20 Pesos** 1864. Black. PC: White.	—	—	—

#23 not as signed.

Comisión de Hacienda

Decreto 12 Julio 1865

#25 and 27 held in reserve.

#	Denomination	Good	Fine	XF
24	**50 Pesos** D.1865.	—	—	—

#	Denomination	Good	Fine	XF
26	**200 Pesos** D.1865. 2 circular handstamps. Series J.	—	—	—

Junta de Credito

Decreto 23 Octobre 1865

#	Denomination	Good	Fine	XF
28	**10 Centavos Fuertes** D.1865. Arms in rectangular frame at upper center, oval handstamp below. Series C.	—	—	—

#	Denomination	Good	Fine	XF
29	**20 Centavos Fuertes** D.1865. Black. Arms at upper center. Uniface.	—	—	—

#30 not assigned.

#	Denomination	Good	Fine	XF
30	**40 Centavos Fuertes** D.1865. Black on brown paper. Small allegorical figure in oval at left, arms at upper center. Uniface.	—	—	—

Decreto 12 Marzo 1866

#	Denomination	Good	Fine	XF
31	**40 Centavos Fuertes** D.1866. Design in vertical guilloche at left, large arms at upper center right, oval handstamp below. Uniface. Series B.	—	—	—

#32 not assigned.

Decreto 29 Julio 1866

#	Denomination	Good	Fine	XF
33	**5 Centavos Fuertes** ND. Arms at top center. Uniface.	85.00	200	350

#	Denomination	Good	Fine	XF
34	**10 Centavos Fuertes** D.1866. Black. Arms at top center, circular handstamp below. Uniface. Series D; E.	—	—	—
35	**10 Centavos Fuertes** 29.7.1866. Black. Arms at top center. Uniface.	50.00	200	—

#	Denomination	Good	Fine	XF
36	**20 Centavos Fuertes** ND. Large arms at center right, circular handstamp below to right. Series B. Uniface.	75.00	225	—

#37 not assigned.

Decreto 26 Marzo 1867

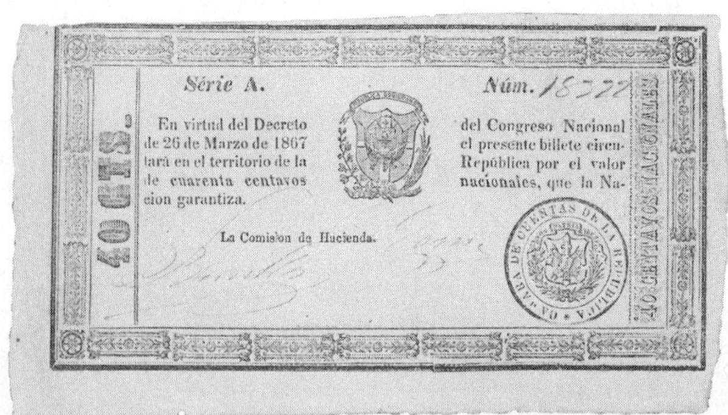

		Good	Fine	XF
38	**40 Centavos**	Good	Fine	XF
	D.1867. Small arms at top center, handstamp below to right. Uniface. Series A; B.	75.00	225	—
39	**1 Peso**	Good	Fine	XF
	ND.	75.00	225	—
40	**2 Pesos**	Good	Fine	XF
	1867.	75.00	225	—
42	**5 Pesos**	Good	Fine	XF
	1867.	75.00	225	—
43	**10 Pesos**	Good	Fine	XF
	D.1867.	75.00	225	—

#44 not assigned.

Decreto 30.9.1867

		Good	Fine	XF
45	**20 Pesos**	Good	Fine	XF
	D.1867. Black.	—	—	—

#46 not assigned.

Intendencia de Santo Domingo

1860s Issue

Issued during the period Spain considered Santo Domingo as a Spanish territory, March 3, 1861 to July 11, 1865.

		Good	Fine	XF
47	**1/2 Peso Fuerte**	Good	Fine	XF
	1.5.1862. Blue. Red handstamped oval seal:*MINISTERIO LA GUERRA Y...* around crowned Spanish arms. Series A.	250	550	—

		Good	Fine	XF
48	**2 Pesos Fuertes**	Good	Fine	XF
	1.5.1862. Green. Red handstamped oval seal:*MINISTERIO LA GUERRA Y...* around crowned Spanish arms. Series B.	250	550	—
49	**5 Pesos Fuertes**	Good	Fine	XF
	ca.1862. Red handstamped oval seal:*MINISTERIO LA GUERRA Y...* around crowned Spanish arms. Series C.	300	650	—
50	**15 Pesos Fuertes**	Good	Fine	XF
	ca.1862. Red handstamped oval seal:*MINISTERIO LA GUERRA Y...* around crowned Spanish arms. Series D.	400	900	—
51	**25 Pesos Fuertes**	Good	Fine	XF
	ca.1862. Red handstamped oval seal:*MINISTERIO LA GUERRA Y...* around crowned Spanish arms. Series E.	600	1,350	—

Treasury

Restoration of 16.8.1863

		Good	Fine	XF
55	**1 Peso Fuerte**	Good	Fine	XF
	1870. Red. Allegorical figure of the Republic at left, arms at upper center. Uniface.	—	—	—

REPUBLICA DOMINICANA

Banco Central de la República Dominicana

1947 ND Issue

		VG	VF	UNC
60	**1 Peso Oro**	VG	VF	UNC
	Black. Orange seal with text over seal: *CIUDAD TRUJILLO / DISTRITO DE SANTO DOMINGO / REPUBLICA DOMINICANA.* Portrait Duarte at center. Back: Indian (Liberty) head and national arms. Printer: ABNC.			
	a. Signature title: *Secretario de Estado del Tesoro y Credito Publico* at right.	2.00	8.00	35.00
	b. Signature title: *Secretario de Estado de Finanzas* at right.	2.00	8.00	35.00
	s. Specimen.	—	—	70.00
61	**5 Pesos Oro**	VG	VF	UNC
	ND (1947-1950). Black. Orange seal with text over seal: *CIUDAD TRUJILLO / DISTRITO DE SANTO DOMINGO / REPUBLICA DOMINICANA.* Portrait Sanchez at center. Back: Indian (LIberty) head and national arms on back. Printer: ABNC.			
	a. Issued note.	7.00	25.00	80.00
	s. Specimen.	—	—	125

		VG	VF	UNC
62	**10 Pesos Oro**	VG	VF	UNC
	ND (1947-1950). Black. Orange seal with text over seal: *CIUDAD TRUJILLO / DISTRITO DE SANTO DOMINGO / REPUBLICA DOMINICANA.* Portrait Mella at center. Back: Indian (Liberty) head and national arms. Printer: ABNC.			
	a. Issued note.	15.00	40.00	150
	s. Specimen.	—	—	175

		VG	VF	UNC
63	**20 Pesos Oro**	VG	VF	UNC
	ND (1947-1950). Black. Orange seal with text over seal: *CIUDAD TRUJILLO / DISTRITO DE SANTO DOMINGO / REPUBLICA DOMINICANA. Puerta del Conde* (Gate) at center. Back: Indian (Liberty) head and national arms. Printer: ABNC.			
	a. Issued note.	30.00	150	375
	s. Specimen.	—	—	600

		VG	VF	UNC
64	**50 Pesos Oro** ND (1947-1950). Black. Orange seal with text over seal: *CIUDAD TRUJILLO / DISTRITO DE SANTO DOMINGO / REPUBLICA DOMINICANA.* Tomb of Columbus at center. Back: Indian (Liberty) head and national arms. Printer: ABNC.			
	a. Issued note.	60.00	200	450
	s. Specimen.	—	—	700
65	**100 Pesos Oro** ND (1947-1950). Black. Orange seal with text over seal: *CIUDAD TRUJILLO / DISTRITO DE SANTO DOMINGO / REPUBLICA DOMINICANA.* Woman with coffeepot and cup at center. Back: Indian (Liberty) head and national arms. Printer: ABNC.	VG	VF	UNC
	a. Issued note.	120	300	650
	s. Specimen.	—	—	750

		VG	VF	UNC
66	**500 Pesos Oro** ND (1947-1950). Black. Orange seal with text over seal: *CIUDAD TRUJILLO / DISTRITO DE SANTO DOMINGO / REPUBLICA DOMINICANA. Obelisco de Ciudad Trujillo* (Tower) at center. Back: Indian (Liberty) head and national arms. Printer: ABNC.			
	a. Issued note.	—	—	—
	s. Specimen.	—	—	1,250

		VG	VF	UNC
67	**1000 Pesos Oro** ND (1947-1950). Black. Orange seal with text over seal: *CIUDAD TRUJILLO / DISTRITO DE SANTO DOMINGO / REPUBLICA DOMINICANA. Basilica Menor de Santa Maria* at center. Back: Indian (Liberty) head and national arms. Printer: ABNC.			
	a. Issued note.	—	—	—
	s. Specimen.	—	—	1,000

1952 ND Issue

		VG	VF	UNC
68	**5 Pesos Oro** ND (1952). Portrait Sanchez at center, similar to #61. Printer: TDLR.	8.00	30.00	100

		VG	VF	UNC
69	**10 Pesos Oro** ND (1952). Portrait Mella at center. Similar to #62 but many major differences. Printer: TDLR.	20.00	50.00	185

		VG	VF	UNC
70	**20 Pesos Oro** ND (1952). Portrait Trujillo at center. Back: Trujillo's Peace Monument at center between Indian head and arms. Printer: TDLR.	50.00	175	425

1956 ND Issue

		VG	VF	UNC
71	**1 Peso Oro** ND (1956-1958). Black with orange seal. Text over seal: *CIUDAD TRUJILLO / DISTRITO NACIONAL / REPUBLICA DOMINICANA.* Signature varieties. Portrait Duarte at center, like #60. Printer: ABNC.			
	a. Issued note.	1.50	6.00	27.50
	s. Specimen.	—	—	70.00

		VG	VF	UNC
72	**5 Pesos Oro** ND (1956-1958). Black with orange seal. Text over seal: *CIUDAD TRUJILLO / DISTRITO NACIONAL / REPUBLICA DOMINICANA.* Signature varieties. Portrait Sanchez at center, similar to #61. Printer: ABNC.			
	a. Issued note.	3.50	15.00	55.00
	s. Specimen.	—	—	85.00
73	**10 Pesos Oro** ND (1956-1958). Black with orange seal. Text over seal: *CIUDAD TRUJILLO / DISTRITO NACIONAL / REPUBLICA DOMINICANA.* Signature varieties. Portrait Mella at center, similar to #62. Printer: ABNC.	VG	VF	UNC
	a. Issued note.	8.00	25.00	95.00
	s. Specimen.	—	—	110
74	**20 Pesos Oro** ND (1956-1958). Black with orange seal. Text over seal: *CIUDAD TRUJILLO / DISTRITO NACIONAL / REPUBLICA DOMINICANA.* Signature varieties. *Puerta del Conde* (Gate) at center, like #63. Printer: ABNC.	VG 20.00	VF 50.00	UNC 155
75	**50 Pesos Oro** ND (1956-1958). Black with orange seal. Text over seal: *CIUDAD TRUJILLO / DISTRITO NACIONAL / REPUBLICA DOMINICANA.* Signature varieties. Tomb of Columbus at center, like #64. Printer: ABNC.	VG 60.00	VF 140	UNC 275
76	**100 Pesos Oro** ND (1956-1958). Black with orange seal. Woman with coffeepot and cup at center, like #65. Printer: ABNC.	VG	VF	UNC
	a. Issued note.	40.00	100	250
	s. Specimen.	—	—	600

Color Abbreviation Guide

New to the *Standard Catalog of® World Paper Money* are the following abbreviations related to color references:

BC: Back color

PC: Paper color

No.	Description	VG	VF	UNC
77	**500 Pesos Oro** ND (1956-1958). Black with orange seal. Text over seal: *CIUDAD TRUJILLO / DISTRITO NACIONAL / REPUBLICA DOMINICANA.* Signature varieties. *Obelisco de Ciudad Trujillo* at center, like #66. Printer: ABNC.	—	—	—
78	**1000 Pesos Oro** ND (1956-1958). Black with orange seal. Text over seal: *CIUDAD TRUJILLO / DISTRITO NACIONAL / REPUBLICA DOMINICANA.* Signature varieties. *Basilica Menor de Santa Maria* at center, like #67. Printer: ABNC.	VG	VF	UNC
	a. Issued note.	—	—	—
	s. Specimen.	—	—	700

1956 ND Commemorative Issue

No.	Description	VG	VF	UNC
79	**20 Pesos Oro** ND (1956). Black. Portrait Trujillo at center. Printer: ABNC.			
	a. Issued note. Rare.	—	—	—
	s. Specimen.	—	—	850

1958 ND Issue

No.	Description	VG	VF	UNC
80	**1 Peso Oro** ND (1958-1959). Portrait Duarte at center, like #71. Printer: W&S.	2.00	8.00	35.00
81	**5 Pesos Oro** ND (1959). Portrait Sanchez at center, like #72. Printer: W&S.	5.00	25.00	85.00
82	**10 Pesos Oro** ND (1959). Portrait Mella at center, like #73. Printer: W&S.	10.00	32.50	110
83	**20 Pesos Oro** ND (ca.1958). Black. Portrait Trujillo at center. Like #79 but without commemorative text on face. Printer: ABNC.	VG	VF	UNC
	a. Issued note.	—	—	—
	s. Specimen.	—	—	1,500
84	**100 Pesos Oro** ND (1959). Woman with coffeepot and cup at center, like #76. Printer: W&S.	25.00	90.00	200

Note: For fractional notes ND (1961) and ABNC issue similar to #80-84 but printed in red, ND (1962-63) see Volume 3.

East Africa was an administrative grouping of several neighboring British territories: Kenya, Tanganyika, Uganda and Zanzibar. The common interest of Kenya, Tanzania and Uganda invited cooperation in economic matters and consideration of political union. The territorial governors, organized as the East Africa High Commission, met periodically to administer such common activities as taxation, industrial development and education. The authority of the Commission did not infringe upon the constitution and internal autonomy of the individual colonies. The common monetary system circulated for the territories by the East African Currency Board and was also used in British Somaliland and the Aden Protectorate subsequent to the independence of India (1947) whose currency had previously circulated in these two territories. Also see British Somaliland, Zanzibar, Kenya, Uganda and Tanzania. Also see Somaliland Republic, Kenya, Uganda and Tanzania.

RULERS:

British

MONETARY SYSTEM:

1 Rupee = 100 Cents to 1920
1 Florin = 100 Cents, 1920-1921
1 Shilling = 100 Cents

BRITISH ADMINISTRATION

Government of the East Africa Protectorate

Mombasa Issue

1905 Issue

No.	Description	Good	Fine	XF
1A	**5 Rupees** 1.9.1905. Black on green underprint. Printer: TDLR.	450	1,200	—
1B	**10 Rupees** 1.9.1905. Black on yellow underprint. Printer: TDLR.	550	2,000	—
1C	**20 Rupees** 1.9.1905. Black on red underprint. Printer: TDLR.	1,250	3,500	—

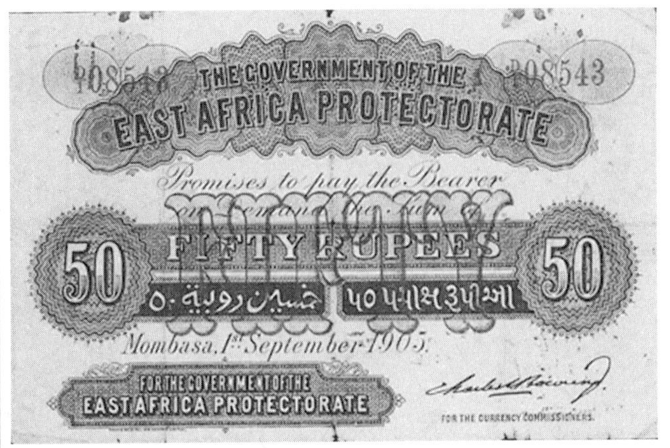

No.	Description	Good	Fine	XF
1D	**50 Rupees** 1.9.1905. Black on purple underprint. Printer: TDLR. Rare.	—	—	—

No.	Description	Good	Fine	XF
1E	**100 Rupees** 1.9.1905. Black on reddish brown underprint. Printer: TDLR. Rare.	—	—	—
1F	**500 Rupees** 1.9.1905. Printer: TDLR. Rare.	—	—	—

1912-1916 Issue

No.	Description	Good	Fine	XF
2	**5 Rupees** 1.5.1916; 1.12.1918. Brown on green underprint. Various signatures. Printer: TDLR. Various.	275	700	1,750
2A	**10 Rupees** 1.7.1912; 15.1.1914; 1.5.1916; 1.12.1918.	350	1,200	2,250
3	**20 Rupees** 1.7.1912; 1.5.1916; 1.12.1918. Brown on red underprint. Various signatures. Printer: TDLR. Various.	800	2,500	—
4	**50 Rupees** 1.7.1912. Brown on purple underprint. Various signatures. Printer: TDLR. Various.	1,000	3,000	—
5	**100 Rupees** 1.7.1912. Brown on reddish-brown underprint. Various signatures. Printer: TDLR. Various. Rare.	—	—	—
6	**500 Rupees** 1.7.1912; 1.5.1916. Various signatures. Printer: TDLR. Various. Rare.	—	—	—

East African Currency Board

Mombasa Issue

1920 First Issue

No.	Description	Good	Fine	XF
7	**1 Rupee** 7.4.1920. Olive-brown and red. Portrait King George V at right. Back: Hippo at center. Printer: TDLR.	75.00	350	1,000

1920 Second Issue

No.	Description	Good	Fine	XF
8	**1 Florin** 1.5.1920. Olive-brown and red. Portrait King George V at right, similar to #7. Back: Hippo at center.			
	a. Issued note.	35.00	150	550
	s. Specimen. Pin hole cancelled.	—	Unc	5,000
9	**5 Florins** 1.5.1920. Blue and green. Portrait King George V at right. Back: Hippo at center.	400	1,000	2,500

No.	Description	Good	Fine	XF
10	**10 Florins = 1 Pound** 1.5.1920. Blue and orange. Portrait King George V at top center. Printer: BWC.	—	—	—
11	**20 Florins = 2 Pounds** 1.5.1920. Portrait King George V at top center. Printer: BWC. Rare.	—	—	—
12	**50 Florins = 5 Pounds** 1.5.1920. Portrait King George V at top center. Printer: BWC. Rare.	—	—	—
12A	**100 Florins = 10 Pounds** 1.5.1920. Portrait King George V at top center. Printer: BWC. Rare.	—	—	—
12B	**500 Florins = 50 Pounds** 1.5.1920. Portrait King George V at top center. Printer: BWC. Rare.	—	—	—

1921 Issue

No.	Description	Good	Fine	XF
13	**5 Shillings** 15.12.1921. Blue-black on brown and orange underprint. Portrait King George V at right. Back: Lion at center. Printer: TDLR.	60.00	250	750
14	**10 Shillings** 15.12.1921. Blue-black on green and pink underprint. Portrait King George V at right. Back: Lion at center. Printer: TDLR.	80.00	300	1,000
15	**20 Shillings = 1 Pound** 15.12.1921. Blue-black on yellow and orange underprint. Portrait King George V at right. Back: Lion at center. Printer: TDLR.	150	550	1,600

No.	Description	Good	Fine	XF
16	**100 Shillings = 5 Pounds** 15.12.1921. Blue-black on lilac underprint. Portrait king George V at right. Back: Lion at center. Printer: TDLR.	300	1,000	—

17 200 Shillings = 10 Pounds
15.12.1921. Blue-black on gray-blue underprint. Portrait King George V at right. Back: Lion at center. Printer: TDLR.

Good	Fine	XF
1,200	4,000	—

18 1000 Shillings = 50 Pounds
15.12.1921. Blue-black on light brown underprint. Portrait King George V at right. Back: Lion at center. Rare.

Good	Fine	XF
—	—	—

19 10,000 Shillings = 500 Pounds
15.12.1921. Blue-black on blue underprint. Portrait King George V at right. Back: Lion at center. Printer: TDLR. Rare.

Good	Fine	XF
—	—	—

Nairobi Issue

1933 Issue

20 5 Shillings
1.1.1933. Blue-black on brown and orange underprint. Portrait King George V at right. Back: Lion at center. Printer: TDLR.

Good	Fine	XF
25.00	100	400

21 10 Shillings
1.1.1933. Blue-black on green and pink underprint. Portrait King George V at right. Back: Lion at center. Printer: TDLR.

Good	Fine	XF
40.00	160	700

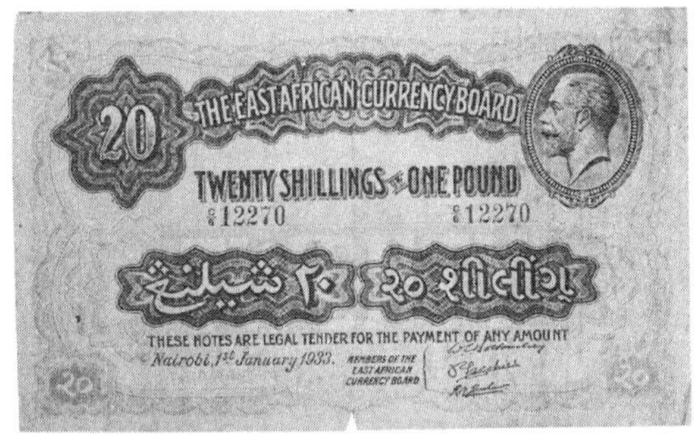

22 20 Shillings = 1 Pound
1.1.1933. Blue-black on yellow and orange underprint. Portrait King George V at right. Back: Lion at center. Printer: TDLR.

Good	Fine	XF
85.00	300	900

23 100 Shillings = 5 Pounds
1.1.1933. Blue-black on green and lilac underprint. Portrait King George V at right. Back: Lion at center. Printer: TDLR.

Good	Fine	XF
200	475	1,750

24 200 Shillings = 10 Pounds
1.1.1933. Blue-black on gray underprint. Portrait King George V at right. Back: Lion at center. Printer: TDLR. Rare.

Good	Fine	XF
—	—	—

25 1000 Shillings = 50 Pounds
1.1.1933. Blue-black on light brown underprint. Portrait King George V at right. Back: Lion at center. Printer: TDLR. Rare.

Good	Fine	XF
—	—	—

26 10,000 Shillings = 500 Pounds
1.1.1933. Blue-black on blue underprint. Portrait King George V at right. Back: Lion at center. Printer: TDLR. Rare.

Good	Fine	XF
—	—	—

1938-1952 Issue

27 1 Shilling
1.1.1943. Blue-black on purple underprint. Portrait King George VI at left. Signature and serial # varieties. Back: Lion at center.

VG	VF	UNC
2.00	20.00	90.00

28 5 Shillings
1938-52. Blue-black on brown underprint. Portrait King George VI at left. Signature and serial # varieties. Printer: TDLR.

	VG	VF	UNC
a. 3 signature 1.1.1938-42.	7.00	50.00	225
b. 4 signature 1943-1.1.1952.	6.00	40.00	175
s. Specimen. Pin hole cancelled.	—	—	1,000

28A 5 Shillings
1.8.1942. Portrait King George VI at left. Signature and India style serial #. Without imprint.

VG	VF	UNC
60.00	400	—

29 10 Shillings
1938-1952. Dark blue on green and pink underprint. Portrait King George VI at left. Signature and serial # varieties. Printer: TDLR.

	VG	VF	UNC
a. 3 signature 1.1.1938-42.	9.00	75.00	350
b. 4 signature 1943-1.1.1952.	8.00	60.00	300
s1. As a. Specimen. Serial # 000000.	—	—	500
s2. As b. Specimen. Serial #000000.	—	—	500

29A	10 Shillings	VG	VF	UNC
	1.8.1942. Dark blue on green and pink underprint. Portrait King George VI at left. Signature and India style serial #. Without imprint.			
	a. Issued note.	50.00	350	—

30	20 Shillings = 1 Pound	VG	VF	UNC
	1938-1952. Blue-black on yellow and orange underprint. Portrait King George VI at left. Signature and serial # varieties. Printer: TDLR.			
	a. 3 signature 1.1.1938-42.	15.00	125	650
	b. 4 signature 1943-1.1.1952.	10.00	75.00	450
	s. As a. Specimen. Pinhole cancelled.	—	—	1,000
	ct. Color trial. Purple on light green.	—	—	1,000

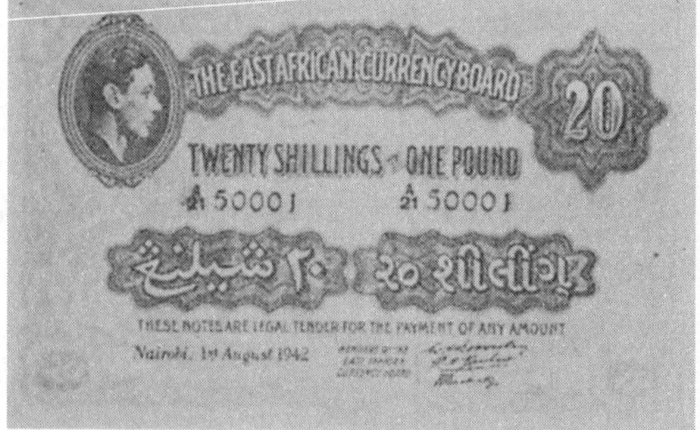

30A	20 Shillings = 1 Pound	VG	VF	UNC
	1.8.1942. Blue-black on yellow and orange underprint. Portrait King George VI at left. Signature and with India style serial #. Without imprint.	100	750	3,000

31	100 Shillings = 5 Pounds	VG	VF	UNC
	1938-51. Blue-black on gree. and lilac underprint. Portrait King George VI at left. Signature and serial # varieties. Printer: TDLR.			
	a. 3 signature 1.1.1938-42.	80.00	450	1,200
	b. 4 signature 1943-1.8.1951.	75.00	350	1,000
	s. Specimen. Pin hole cancelled.	—	—	1,250

31B	1000 Shillings = 50 Pounds	Good	Fine	XF
	2.1.1939. Blue-black on pale orange and light blue underprint. Portrait King George VI at left. Signature and serial # varieties. Specimen.	—	—	—

31C	100 Shillings = 5 Pounds	VG	VF	UNC
	1.8.1942. Blue-black on green and lilac underprint. Portrait King George VI at left. Signature and with India style serial #. Without imprint. Specimen.	—	—	5,000

32	10,000 Shillings = 500 Pounds	VG	VF	UNC
	1.1.1947; 1.8.1951. Blue-black on blue underprint. Portrait King George VI at left. Signature and serial # varieties. Printer: TDLR.			
	a. Issued note.	—	—	—
	s. Specimen.	—	—	—

1939 Issue

26A	5 Shillings	Good	Fine	XF
	1.6.1939. Blue-black on brown underprint. Portrait King George VI at left. Back: Lion at center.			
	a. Printer: TDLR. Serial # somewhat larger than later issues.	35.00	75.00	250
	b. Without imprint. Serial # same size as later issues.	30.00	70.00	200
	s. As a. Specimen. Perforated: *CANCELLED*.	—	Unc	500

26B	10 Shillings	Good	Fine	XF
	1.6.1939. Blue-black on green and pink underprint. Portrait King George VI at left. Without BWC imprint. Back: Lion at center.	35.00	90.00	350

26C	20 Shillings = 1 Pound	Good	Fine	XF
	1.6.1939. Blue-black on yellow and orange underprint. Portrait King George VI at left. Without BWC imprint. Back: Lion at center.	30.00	90.00	350

1953 Issue

33	5 Shillings	VG	VF	UNC
	31.3.1953-1.10.1957. Blue-black on light brown underprint. Portrait Queen Elizabeth II at right. Signature varieties. Printer: TDLR.	5.00	50.00	400

34	10 Shillings	VG	VF	UNC
	31.3.1953-1.10.1957. Blue-black on green and pink underprint. Portrait Queen Elizabeth II at right. Signature varieties. Printer: TDLR.	12.00	175	850

No.	Description	VG	VF	UNC
35	**20 Shillings = 1 Pound** 31.3.1953-1.2.1956. Blue-black on yellow and orange underprint. Portrait Queen Elizabeth II at right. Signature varieties. Printer: TDLR.	7.00	50.00	350
36	**100 Shillings = 5 Pounds** 31.3.1953-1.2.1956. Blue black on green and lilac underprint. Portrait Queen Elizabeth II at right. Signature varieties. Printer: TDLR.	50.00	300	1,200

East African Currency Board, Nairobi

1958 ND Issue, W/o Office of Issue

No.	Description	VG	VF	UNC
37	**5 Shillings** ND (1958-1960). Brown multicolor underprint. Portrait Queen Elizabeth II at upper left. 4 signatures at lower right. Printer: TDLR.	2.50	20.00	175
38	**10 Shillings** ND (1958-1960). Green on multicolor underprint. Portrait Queen Elizabeth II at upper left. 4 signatures at lower right. Printer: TDLR.	2.50	25.00	250

No.	Description	VG	VF	UNC
39	**20 Shillings** ND (1958-1960). Blue on multicolor underprint. Portrait Queen Elizabeth II at upper left. 4 signatures at lower right. Printer: TDLR.	3.00	45.00	400
40	**100 Shillings** ND (1958-1960). Red on multicolor underprint. Portrait Queen Elizabeth II at upper left. 4 signatures at lower right. Printer: TDLR.			
	a. Issued note.	20.00	200	900
	s. Specimen. Overprint: *SPECIMEN* and punch hole cancelled.	—	—	—

1961 ND Issue

No.	Description	VG	VF	UNC
41	**5 Shillings** ND (1961-1963). Brown on light red underprint. Portrait Queen Elizabeth II at upper left. Three signatures at left and four at right. Printer: TDLR. Various.			
	a. Top left signature: E. B. David. (1961).	5.00	20.00	250
	b. Top left sign: A. L. Adu. (1962-1963).	3.50	15.00	200

No.	Description	VG	VF	UNC
42	**10 Shillings** ND (1961-1963). Green on multicolor underprint. Portrait Queen Elizabeth II at upper left. Three signatures at left and four at right. Printer: TDLR.Various.			
	a. Top left signature: E. B. David. (1961).	9.00	25.00	350
	b. Top left signature: A. L. Adu. (1962-1963).	6.00	20.00	300
43	**20 Shillings** ND (1961-1963). Blue on light pink underprint. Portrait Queen Elizabeth II at upper left. Three signatures at left and four at right. Printer: TDLR.Various.			
	a. Top left signature: E. B. David. (1961).	10.00	75.00	500
	b. Top left signature: A. L. Adu. (1962-1963).	7.00	50.00	350

		VG	VF	UNC
44	**100 Shillings** ND (1961-1963). Red on multicolor underprint. Portrait Queen Elizabeth II at upper left. Three signatures at left and four at right. Printer: TDLR. Various.			
	a. Top left signature: E. B. David. (1961).	25.00	150	1,000
	b. Top left signature: A. L. Adu. (1962-63).	20.00	100	750

1964 ND Issue

		VG	VF	UNC
45	**5 Shillings** ND (1964). Brown on multicolor underprint. Sailboat at left center. Back: Various plants. Watermark: Rhinoceros.	3.00	15.00	100

ECUADOR

North Pacific Ocean · COLOMBIA · BRAZIL · PERU

The Republic of Ecuador, located astride the equator on the Pacific coast of South America, has an area of 283,560 sq. km. and a population of 13.93 million. Capital: Quito. Agriculture is the mainstay of the economy but there are appreciable deposits of minerals and petroleum. It is the world's largest exporter of bananas and balsa wood. Coffee, cacao and shrimp are also valuable exports.

What is now Ecuador formed part of the northern Inca Empire until the Spanish conquest in 1533. Quito became a seat of Spanish colonial government in 1563 and part of the Viceroyalty of New Granada in 1717. The territories of the Viceroyalty - New Granada (Colombia), Venezuela, and Quito - gained their independence between 1819 and 1822 and formed a federation known as Gran Colombia. When Quito withdrew in 1830, the traditional name was changed in favor of the "Republic of the Equator." Between 1904 and 1942, Ecuador lost territories in a series of conflicts with its neighbors. A border war with Peru that flared in 1995 was resolved in 1999. Although Ecuador marked 25 years of civilian governance in 2004, the period has been marred by political instability. Protests in Quito have contributed to the mid-term ouster of Ecuador's last three democratically elected Presidents. In 2007, a Constituent Assembly was elected to draft a new constitution; Ecuador's twentieth since gaining independence.

MONETARY SYSTEM:

1 Peso = 8 Reales
1 Peso = 100 Centavos
1 Sucre = 10 Decimos = 100 Centavos
1 Condor = 25 Sucres
1 USA Dollar = 25,000 Sucres (March 2001)

GOVERNMENT

La Caja Central de Emisión y Amortización

In February 1926, the Caja Central de Emisión y Amortización was established as a preliminary move towards the creation of the Banco Central del Ecuador. The main task of the Caja Central was the transferrance of notes and metallic reserves of the private banks. The Caja Central operated until August 12, 1927. Unissued notes of the private banks were ovpt. in the name of the Caja Central and the issuing place of Quito. Faces were ovpt. with medium large text across, either straight or at an angle, and in upper and lower case or all upper case letters. Backs were ovpt. in much larger letters at ctr. in curved or straight lines.

1926-1927 Issue

		Good	Fine	XF
21	**1 Sucre** 30.11.1926.	150	500	—
31	**2 Sucres** 30.11.1926; 19.1.1927.	150	500	—
41	**5 Sucres** 19.1.1927.	150	500	—
51	**5 Sucres** 30.11.1926.	150	500	—
61	**10 Sucres** 30.11.1926; 19.1.1927.	150	500	—
71	**50 Sucres** 6.4.1927; 1.6.1927.	—	—	—
72	**1000 Sucres** 6.4.1927.	—	—	—

REPUBLIC

Banco Central del Ecuador

Multiple signature varieties.

1928 Issue

		Good	Fine	XF
84	**5 Sucres** 1928-1938. Black on multicolor underprint. Woman seated ("Agriculture") at center. With text: *CAPITAL AUTHORIZADO 10,000,000 SUCRES* 2 signatures. Back: Arms. Printer: ABNC.			
	a. 14.1.1928; 6.11.1928; 9.11.1932; 21.12.1933; 7.11.1935; 5.10.1937.	7.50	30.00	100
	b. Signature title overprint: *Delegado de la Superintendencia de Bancos* across center 27.10.1938. Title overprint: *TESORERO/GERENTE* at right.	7.50	30.00	100
	s. As a. Specimen.	—	Unc	150

	85 **10 Sucres**	Good	Fine	XF
	1928-1938. Woman at center. Steam locomotive at left, ox-carts at right in background. With text: *CAPITAL AUTHORIZADO 10,000,000 SUCRES.* 2 signatures. Back: Arms. Printer: ABNC.			
	a. 30.5.1928; 6.11.1928; 9.11.1932; 21.12.1933; 7.11.1935; 5.10.1937.	10.00	65.00	150
	b. Signature title overprint: *Delegado de la Superintendencia de Bancos* across center 27.10.1938. Title overprint: *TESORERO/GERENTE* at right.	15.00	75.00	175
	s. As a. Specimen.	—	Unc	200

	86 **20 Sucres**	Good	Fine	XF
	30.5.1928; 6.11.1928; 9.11.1932; 21.12.1933; 7.11.1935; 12.2.1937. Woman seated with symbols of commerce and industry at center. With text: *CAPITAL AUTHORIZADO 10,000,000 SUCRES.* 2 signatures. Back: Arms. Printer: ABNC.			
	a. Issued note.	25.00	100	250
	s. Specimen.	—	Unc	400

	87 **50 Sucres**	Good	Fine	XF
	30.5.1928; 6.11.1928; 9.11.1932; 21.12.1933; 8.8.1934; 1.10.1936. Ship at left, woman seated with globe and anvil at center, train at right. With text: *CAPITAL AUTHORIZADO 10,000,000 SUCRES.* 2 signatures. Back: Arms. Printer: ABNC.			
	a. Issued note.	30.00	125	300
	s. Specimen.	—	Unc	400

	88 **100 Sucres**	Good	Fine	XF
	30.5.1928; 6.11.1928; 9.11.1932; 21.12.1933; 8.8.1934; 1.10.1936. Woman seated with globe at center. With text: *CAPITAL AUTHORIZADO 10,000,000 SUCRES.* 2 signatures. Back: Arms. Printer: ABNC.			
	a. Issued note.	50.00	200	450
	s. Specimen.	—	Unc	500

1939-1944 Issue

	91 **5 Sucres**	VG	VF	UNC
	1940-1949. Woman seated ("Agriculture") at center. With text: *CAPITAL AUTORIZADO 20,000,000 SUCRES.* 3 signatures. Printer: ABNC.			
	a. Printed signature title: *TESORERO DE RESERVA* at right. 12.3.1940-28.11.1941.	4.50	20.00	70.00
	b. Signature title overprint: *GERENTE GENERAL* at right. 3.2.1945-1.4.1947.	4.00	17.50	60.00
	c. Like b., but signature title printed. 21.10.1947-21.6.1949.	3.00	15.00	50.00
	s1. Specimen. Blue overprint: *SPECIMEN* twice on face. ND, Series FA, FD (3.2.1945). Punch hole cancelled.	—	—	125
	s2. As c. Specimen. Pin hole perforated: *SPECIMEN A.B.N. Co.* in two lines on face. ND. Without series or serial #. Punch hole cancelled.	—	—	125
	s3. As s2 but pin hole perforated on back.	—	—	50.00

	92 **10 Sucres**	VG	VF	UNC
	1939-1949. Woman with basket at center. Steam locomotive at left, ox-carts at right in background. With text: *CAPITAL AUTORIZADO 20,000,000 SUCRES.* 3 signatures. Printer: ABNC.			
	a. Signature title overprint: *PRESIDENTE* at left. Date at right. 17.10.1939-6.6.1944.	5.00	25.00	100
	b. Printed signature titles. 6.2.1942; 4.6.1943; 30.6.1947; 21.6.1949; 30.6.1949.	4.50	20.00	90.00
	c. Signature title overprint: *PRESIDENTE* at left, *GERENTE GENERAL* at right. Date at left. 5.10.1944; 19.12.1944; 23.1.1945.	4.00	15.00	80.00
	d. Sign title overprint: *GERENTE GENERAL* at right. 22.8.1945; 7.11.1945; 8.2.1946; 25.7.1946; 22.11.1948; 21.6.1949.	3.00	12.50	75.00
	s1. Specimen. Signature title: *TESORERO DE RESERVA.*	—	—	125
	s2. Specimen. Signature title: *GERENTE GENERAL.*	—	—	150

	93 **20 Sucres**	VG	VF	UNC
	1939-1949. Woman seated with symbols of commerce and industry at center. With text: *CAPITAL AUTORIZADO 20,000,000 SUCRES.* 3 signatures. Similar to #86. Printer: ABNC.			
	a. Date at upper right center 17.10.1939.	8.00	35.00	160
	b. Printed signature titles. Date at lower right. 5.7.1940-27.3.1944.	8.00	35.00	160
	c. Signature title overprint: *PRESIDENTE* at left. Date at lower right. 5.7.1940-27.3.1944.	6.00	25.00	125
	d. Signature title overprint: *PRESIDENTE* at left, *GERENTE GENERAL* at right. 25.10.1944.	6.00	25.00	125
	e. Sign title overprint: *GERENTE GENERAL* at right. Date at upper right. 21.9.1945; 26.12.1945; 12.7.1947; 22.11.1948; 17.3.1949.	5.00	20.00	110
	f. Printed signature titles with *GERENTE GENERAL* at right. 24.3.1949; 6.5.1949.	5.00	20.00	110
	s1. Specimen. Signature title: *TESORERO DE RESERVA.*	—	—	175
	s2. Specimen. Signature title: *GERENTE GENERAL.*	—	—	200

		VG	VF	UNC
94	**50 Sucres** 1939-1949. Ship at left, woman seated with globe and anvil at center, train at right. With text: *CAPITAL AUTORIZADO 20,000,000 SUCRES.* 3 signatures. Printer: ABNC.			
	a. 17.10.1939-3.12.1943.	25.00	110	325
	b. Signature title overprint: *GERENTE GENERAL* at right. 16.10.1946; 12.7.1947; 22.11.1948; 27.1.1949.	20.00	100	300
	s. As a. Specimen.	—	—	300

		VG	VF	UNC
95	**100 Sucres** 1939-1949. Woman seated with globe at center. With text: *CAPITAL AUTORIZADO 20,000,000 SUCRES.* 3 signatures. Like # 88. Printer: ABNC.			
	a. 17.10.1939-19.11.1943.	30.00	125	300
	b. 31.7.1944; 7.9.1944.	25.00	85.00	250
	c. 7.11.1945-1.27.1949.	20.00	60.00	150
	s. Specimen.	—	—	250

1944-1967 Issue

		VG	VF	UNC
96	**500 Sucres** 1944-1966. Black on multicolor underprint. Mercury seated at center. With text: *CAPITAL AUTORIZADO 20,000,000 SUCRES.* 3 signatures. Printer: ABNC.			
	a. Signature title overprint: *PRESIDENTE* at left. 12.5.1944; 27.6.1944.	175	400	—
	b. Signature title overprint: *GERENTE GENERAL* at left, *VOCAL* at right. 31.7.1944; 7.9.1944.	150	375	—
	c. Signature title overprint: *GERENTE GENERAL* at right. 12.1.1945-12.7.1947.	125	300	—
	d. As c. 21.4.1961-17.11.1966.	125	300	—
	s. Specimen. ND.	—	—	700

		VG	VF	UNC
97	**1000 Sucres** 1944-1967. Black on multicolor underprint. Woman reclining ("Telephone Service") at center. With text: *CAPITAL AUTORIZADO 20,000,000 SUCRES.* 3 signatures. Printer: ABNC.			
	a. Signature title overprint: *PRESIDENTE* at left. 12.5.1944; 27.6.1944.	300	650	—
	b. Signature title overprint: *GERENTE GENERAL* at left, *VOCAL* at right. 31.7.1944; 7.9.1944.	275	550	—
	c. Signature title overprint: *PRESIDENTE* at left, *GERENTE GENERAL* at right. 12.1.1945.	250	500	—
	d. Signature title overprint: *GERENTE GENERAL* at right. 16.10.1945; 12.7.1947.	225	450	—
	e. As d. 21.4.1961; 27.2.1962; 4.3.1964; 23.7.1964; 17.11.1966; 6.4.1967.	150	350	—
	s. Specimen. ND.	—	—	850

The following reduced size notes are listed by printer.1950 Issue (1950-59) (TAB)#98-99 printer: W&S. 1950-71 Issue (1950-74) (TAB)#100-107 printer: ABNC. 1975-80 Issue (1975-83) (TAB)#108-112 printer: ABNC. 1957-71 Issue (1957-82) (TAB)#113-118 printer: TDLR.

1950 Issue - Reduced Size Notes

		VG	VF	UNC
98	**5 Sucres** 1950-1955. Black on green underprint. Portrait Antonio Jose de Sucre at center. Date at left or right. Back: Arms at center. Printer: W&S.			
	a. 11.5.1950-13.7.1953.	2.25	15.00	75.00
	b. Signature title overprint: *SUBGERENTE GENERAL* at left. 21.9.1953.	4.50	20.00	85.00
	c. 31.5.1954-28.11.1955.	2.00	12.50	55.00
99	**50 Sucres** 1950-1959. Black on green underprint. National monument at center with buildings in background. Back: Arms at center. Printer: W&S.	**VG**	**VF**	**UNC**
	a. 11.5.1950; 26.7.1950; 13.10.1950; 3.4.1951; 26.9.1951.	7.50	50.00	150
	b. Signature title overprint: *SUBGERENTE GENERAL* at left. 3.9.1952; 8.10.1954; 24.9.1957.	7.50	50.00	150
	c. 10.12.1953; 19.6.1956; 25.11.1957; 25.11.1958; 8.4.1959.	6.00	40.00	125
	s1. Specimen. Black overprint: *ESPÉCIMEN* on both sides. ND, with 0000 serial #, unsigned.	—	—	175
	s2. Specimen. Red overprint: *MUESTRA* twice on both sides. ND, without serial # or signs. Punch hole cancelled.	—	—	175

1950-1971 Issue

		VG	VF	UNC
100	**5 Sucres** 1956-1973. Black on multicolor underprint. Portrait Antonio Jose de Sucre at center. Back: Arms 31mm. wide, without flagpole stems below. Printer: ABNC. Several varieties in signature title overprints and serial # styles.			
	a. 19.6.1956; 28.8.1956; 2.4.1957; 19.6.1957; 19.7.1957.	1.00	5.00	40.00
	b. Signature title overprint: *SUBGERENTE GENERAL.* 24.9.1957; 2.1.1958.	0.75	5.00	40.00
	c. 2.2.1958; 1.1.1966.	0.50	2.50	20.00
	d. 27.2.1970; 3.9.1973. Serial # varieties.	0.25	1.50	3.50
101	**10 Sucres** 1950-1955. Black on multicolor underprint. Portrait Sebastian de Benalcazar at center. Plain background. Back: Arms 31mm. wide, without flagpole stems below. Printer: ABNC. Several varieties in signature title overprints and serial # styles.	**VG**	**VF**	**UNC**
	a. 14.1.1950-28.11.1955.	2.00	8.00	45.00
	b. 21.9.1953; 16.3.1954; 3.10.1955. Overprint: *SUB GERENTE GENERAL.*	2.00	10.00	50.00
	s. Specimen.	—	—	150

		VG	VF	UNC
101A	**10 Sucres** 1956-74; 24.12.1957. Black on multicolor underprint. Portrait Sebastian de Benalcazar at center, with different guilloches and ornate background. Signature title overprint varieties. Serial # varieties. Back: Arms 31 mm. wide, without flagpole stems below. Printer: ABNC. UV: fibers fluoresce blue and yellow.			
	a. 15.6.1956-27.4.1966.	1.00	7.50	35.00
	b. 24.5.1968-2.1.1974.	0.50	3.00	15.00
	s. Specimen.	—	—	150

Note: #101A with date of 24.12.1957 has signature title overprint: ***SUB GERENTE GENERAL.***

		VG	VF	UNC
102	**20 Sucres** 28.2.1950-28.7.1960. Black on multicolor underprint. Church façade at center. Back: Arms 31 mm. wide, without flagpole stems below. Printer: ABNC. Several varieties in signature title overprints and serial # styles.			
	a. Issued note.	2.50	15.00	50.00
	s. Specimen. Overprint: *SPECIMEN* in red on face.	—	—	80.00
103	**20 Sucres** 1962-1973. Black on multicolor underprint. Church façade at center, different guilloches and darker underprint. Back: Arms 31 mm. wide, without flagpole stems below. Printer: ABNC. Several varieties in signature title overprints, and serial # styles.	**VG**	**VF**	**UNC**
	a. 12.12.1962-4.10.1967.	2.00	5.00	25.00
	b. 24.5.1968-3.9.1973.	1.00	3.00	15.00
	s. Specimen. ND.	—	—	175

		VG	VF	UNC
104	**50 Sucres** 1968-1976. Black on multicolor underprint. National monument at center with buildings in background. Signature title overprint varieties. Serial # varieties. Back: Arms 31 mm. wide, without flagpole stems below. Printer: ABNC. UV: planchettes fluoresce pink.			
	a. 24.5.1968; 5.11.1969.	2.00	5.00	30.00
	b. 20.5.1971; 10.8.1976.	1.00	4.00	20.00
	s. Specimen. ND.	—	—	50.00
104A	**100 Sucres** 1952-1957. Black on multicolor underprint. Portrait Simón Bolívar at center. Back: Arms 31 mm. wide, without flagpole stems below. Printer: ABNC. Several varieties, signature title overprints, and serial # styles.	**VG**	**VF**	**UNC**
	a. 3.9.1952-19.6.1957.	15.00	75.00	220
	b. Signature title: *SUBGERENTE*. 3.9.1952; 10.12.1953.	15.00	75.00	220

		VG	VF	UNC
105	**100 Sucres** 27.6.1964-7.7.1970. Black on multicolor underprint. Portrait Simón Bolívar at center with different guilloches. Back: Arms 31 mm. wide, without flagpole stems below. Printer: ABNC. Several varieties, signature title overprints, and serial # styles.			
	a. Issued note.	5.00	10.00	50.00
	s. Specimen. Overprint: *SPECIMEN* in red on face.	—	—	80.00

		VG	VF	UNC
107	**1000 Sucres** 30.5.1969-20.9.1973. Black on multicolor underprint. Banco Central building at center. Back: Arms 31 mm. wide, without flagpole stems below. Printer: ABNC. Several varieties, signature title overprints, and serial # styles.			
	a. Issued note.	20.00	85.00	250
	s. Specimen. ND.	—	—	75.00

1957-1971 Issue

		VG	VF	UNC
113	**5 Sucres** 1958-1988. Black on multicolor underprint. Portrait Antonio Jose de Sucre at center. Back: New rendition of arms. Printer: TDLR.			
	a. 2.1.1958-7.11.1962.	0.75	4.00	17.50
	b. 23.5.1963-27.2.1970.	0.50	1.00	12.50
	c. 25.7.1979-24.5.1980.	0.25	0.50	7.50
	d. 20.4.1983; 22.11.1988.	0.10	0.25	3.00
	s. Specimen. ND; 24.5.1968; 25.7.1979; 24.5.1980. Overprint: *MUESTRA SIN VALOR* in red on both sides.	—	—	125

		VG	VF	UNC
116	**50 Sucres** 1957-1982. Black on multicolor underprint. National monument at center. Back: New rendition of arms. Printer: TDLR.			
	a. 2.4.1957; 7.7.1959.	2.50	15.00	60.00
	b. 7.11.1962; 29.10.1963; 27.6.1964; 29.1.1965; 6.8.1965.	1.00	8.00	35.00
	c. 1.1.1966; 27.4.1966; 17.11.1966.	1.00	4.00	25.00
	d. 4.10.1967; 30.5.1969; 17.7.1974.	0.75	2.00	15.00
	e. 24.5.1980; 20.8.1982.	0.50	1.25	10.00
	s1. Specimen. ND; 1.1.1966. Overprint: *SPECIMEN* in red on both sides.	—	—	80.00
	s2. Specimen. 20.8.1982. Overprint: *MUESTRA SIN VALOR* in red on both sides.	—	—	100

1975-1980 Issue

		VG	VF	UNC
108	**5 Sucres** 1975-1983. Black on multicolor underprint. Portrait Antonio Jose de Sucre at center. Back: New rendition of arms. 29mm. wide with flagpole stems below. Printer: ABNC. UV: planchettes fluoresce red, fibers yellow.			
	a. 14.3.1975; 29.4.1977.	0.25	1.50	9.00
	b. 20.8.1982; 20.4.1983.	0.25	1.00	6.00

		VG	VF	UNC
109	**10 Sucres** 14.3.1975; 10.8.1976; 29.4.1977; 24.5.1978. Black on multicolor underprint. Portrait Sebastian de Benalcazar at center. Back: New rendition of arms. 29mm. wide with flagpole stems below. Printer: ABNC.	0.25	2.00	12.50

		VG	VF	UNC
110	**20 Sucres** 10.8.1976. Black on multicolor underprint. Church facade at center. Back: New rendition of arms. 29mm. wide with flagpole stems below. Printer: ABNC.	0.25	2.50	17.50

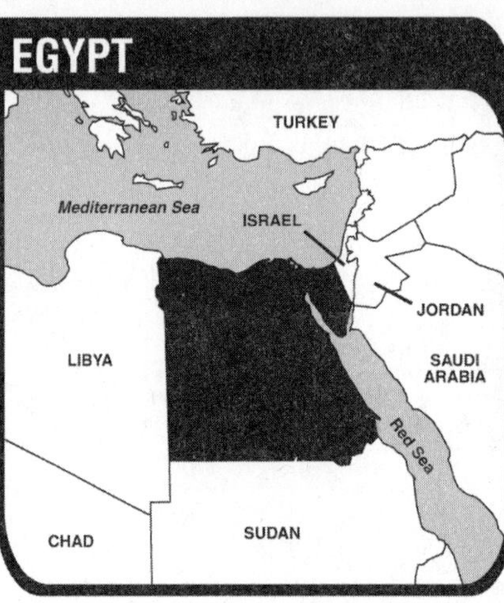

The Arab Republic of Egypt, located on the northeastern corner of Africa, has an area of 1,001,450 sq. km. and a population of 81.71 million. Capital: Cairo. Although Egypt is an almost rainless expanse of desert, its economy is predominantly agricultural. Cotton, rice and petroleum are exported.

The regularity and richness of the annual Nile River flood, coupled with semi-isolation provided by deserts to the east and west, allowed for the development of one of the world's great civilizations. A unified kingdom arose circa 3200 B.C., and a series of dynasties ruled in Egypt for the next three millennia. The last native dynasty fell to the Persians in 341 B.C., who in turn were replaced by the Greeks, Romans, and Byzantines. It was the Arabs who introduced Islam and the Arabic language in the 7th century and who ruled for the next six centuries. A local military caste, the Mamluks took control about 1250 and continued to govern after the conquest of Egypt by the Ottoman Turks in 1517. Following the completion of the Suez Canal in 1869, Egypt became an important world transportation hub, but also fell heavily into debt. Ostensibly to protect its investments, Britain seized control of Egypt's government in 1882, but nominal allegiance to the Ottoman Empire continued until 1914. Partially independent from the UK in 1922, Egypt acquired full sovereignty with the overthrow of the British-backed monarchy in 1952. The completion of the Aswan High Dam in 1971 and the resultant Lake Nasser have altered the time-honored place of the Nile River in the agriculture and ecology of Egypt. A rapidly growing population (the largest in the Arab world), limited arable land, and dependence on the Nile all continue to overtax resources and stress society. The government has struggled to meet the demands of Egypt's growing population through economic reform and massive investment in communications and physical infrastructure.

RULERS:

OTTOMAN
- Abdul Mejid, AH1255-1277, 1839-1861AD
- Abdul Aziz, AH1277-1293, 1861-1876AD
- Abdul Hamid II, AH1293-1327, 1876-1909AD

EGYPTIAN
- Muhammad V, AH1327-1332, 1909-1914AD
- Hussein Kamil, AH1334-1336, 1915-1917AD
- Fuad I (Sultan), AH1336-1341, 1917-1922AD
- Fuad I (King), AH1341-1355, 1922-1936AD
- Farouk I, AH1355-1372, 1936-1952AD

MONETARY SYSTEM:
- 1 Piastre = 10 Ochr-El-Guerches
- 1 Pound = 100 Piastres, to 1916
- 1 Piastre (Guerche) = 10 Milliemes
- 1 Pound (Junayh) = 100 Piastres, 1916-

OTTOMAN ADMINISTRATION

National Bank of Egypt

Bank notes issued since 1899. Many signature, serial # and date varieties. Valuations are for the most common dates; earlier dates of a long date-run issue usually deserve higher values.

Decree of 25.6.1898

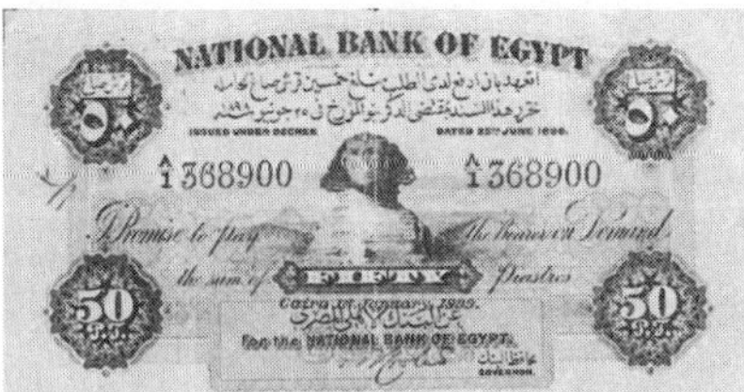

		VG	VF	UNC
1	**50 Piastres** 1.1.1899. Black on green and pink underprint. Sphinx at center.			
	a. Signature Palmer.	8,000	20,000	—
	b. Signature Rowlatt.	6,000	18,000	—
	s. Specimen.	—	—	15,000

2	1 Pound	VG	VF	UNC
	5.1.1899. Black on red and orange underprint. 2 camels at center. Printer: BWC.			
	a. Signature: Palmer.	10,000	25,000	—
	b. Signature: Rowlatt.	10,000	25,000	—
	s. Specimen.	—	—	25,000

3	5 Pounds	VG	VF	UNC
	10.1.1899. Yellow, green and rose. Pyramids and palms at left. Specimen.			
	a. Signature: Palmer. One known.	—	—	—
	b. Signature: Rowlat. Unknown.	—	—	—
	s. As a. Specimen. Perforated: *SPECIMEN.*	—	—	8,000

4	10 Pounds	VG	VF	UNC
	13.1.1899. Rose and light blue. Philae Temple with two sailboats at left. Specimen.	—	—	9,000

5	50 Pounds	VG	VF	UNC
	15.1.1899 (21.3.1904). Blue, yellow and rose. Philae Temple at left. Specimen.	—	—	15,000

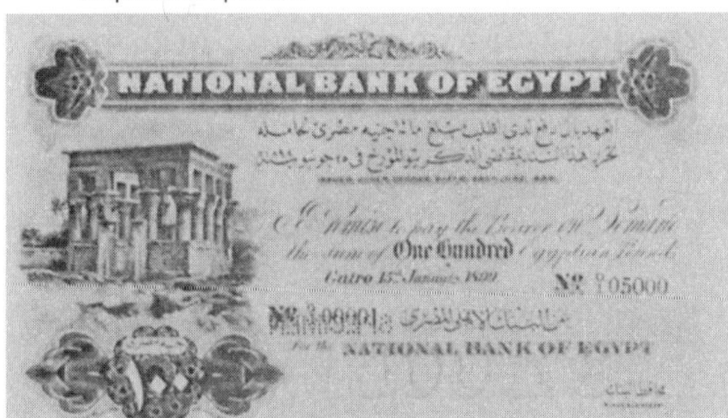

6	100 Pounds	VG	VF	UNC
	15.1.1899; 17.7.1906; 2.10.1912. Black on green and multicolor underprint. Philae Temple at left.			
	s1. 15.1.1899. Specimen.	—	—	15,000
	s2. 17.7.1906. Specimen.	—	—	15,000
	s3. 2.10.1912. Specimen.	—	—	15,000

1912 Issue

8	10 Pounds	VG	VF	UNC
	1.1.1912. Rose and dark blue. Philae Temple with two sailboats at left. Specimen.	—	—	10,000

1913-1917 Issue

10	25 Piastres	VG	VF	UNC
	1917-1951. Deep purple on multicolor underprint. Banks of the Nile at center. Printer: BWC.			
	a. Signature Rowlatt. 5.8.1917-18.6.1918.	250	1,000	2,500
	b. Signature Cook. 6.6.1940; 7.6.1940.	200	800	2,500
	c. Signature Nixon. 18.12.1940-1946.	20.00	75.00	250
	d. Signature Leith-Ross. 5.12.46; 1.12.1947-7.7.1950.	20.00	75.00	250
	e. Signature Saad (Arabic). 15.5.1951-21.5.1951.	20.00	75.00	250
	f. As e, but with Arabic serial #. 22.5.1951-23.5.1951.	20.00	75.00	250

11	50 Piastres	VG	VF	UNC
	1.8.1914-12.12.1920. Brown. Sphinx at left.			
	a. Issued note.	300	1,250	—
	s. Specimen.	—	—	1,800

12	1 Pound	VG	VF	UNC
	1914-1924. Blue on pink and light green underprint. Ruins at left.			
	a. Signature Rowlatt. 21.9.1914-1920.	200	1,000	2,500
	b. Signature Hornsby. 1923-20.1.1924.	250	1,200	2,500
	s. Specimen.	—	—	2,000

13	**5 Pounds**	VG	VF	UNC
	1.9.1913-1920. Pink and black. Small sailing ship at left.	—	—	3,500
	a. Issued note.	600	2,250	5,000

14	**10 Pounds**	VG	VF	UNC
	2.9.1913-30.5.1920. Brown and multicolor. Mosque of Sultan Qala'un and street in Cairo. Printer: BWC.			
	a. Issued note.	400	1,600	—
	s. Specimen.	—	—	3,500

15	**50 Pounds**	VG	VF	UNC
	1913-1945. Purple and multicolor. Mameluke tombs with caravan in front.			
	a. Signature Rowlatt. 4.9.1913.	650	3,000	—
	b. Signature Rowlatt 14.11.1918-21.1.1920.	500	2,500	—
	c. Signature Nixon. 6.2.1942-2.5.1945.	200	500	1,800

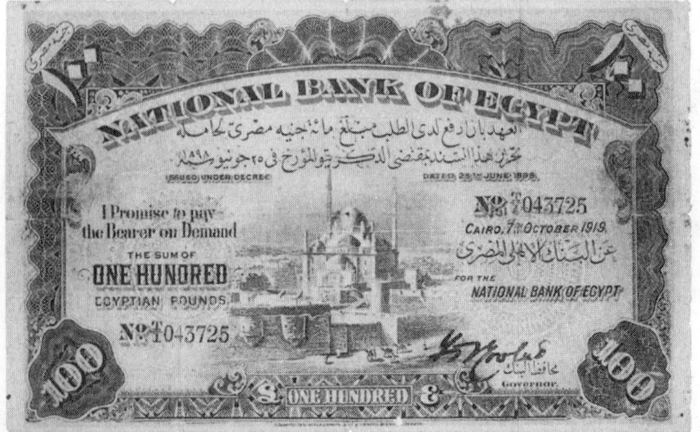

16	**100 Pounds**	VG	VF	UNC
	5.9.1913; 7.10.1919. Green. Citadel and mosque of Mohammed Ali at center. Rare. (three known).	25,000	—	—

1921 Issue

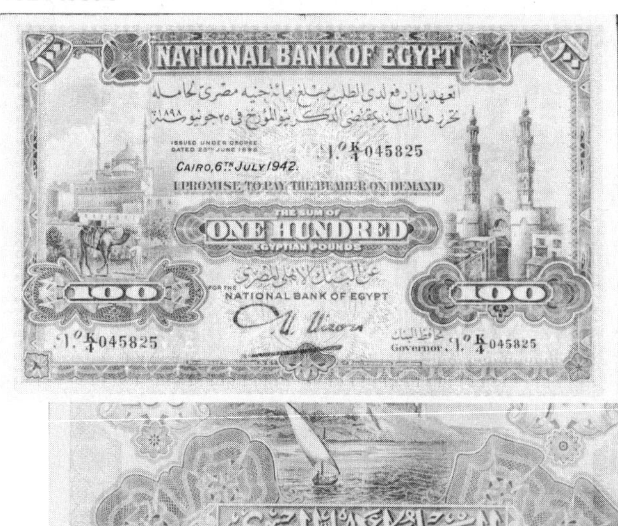

17	**100 Pounds**	VG	VF	UNC
	1921-1945. Brown, red and green. Citadel of Cairo at left. Mosque at right. Back: Small sailing boat and island of Philae.			
	a. Signature Hornsby. 1.3.1921.	—	—	—
	b. Signature Hornsby. 1.9.1921.	2,000	10,000	—
	c. Signature Cook. 4.6.1936.	250	800	—
	d. Signature Nixon. 1942-45.	200	600	2,000
	s. Specimen.	—	—	4,500

1924 Issue

18	**1 Pound**	VG	VF	UNC
	1.6.1924-20.9.1924. Red and blue. Camel at center.			
	a. Issued note.	250	800	3,000
	s. Specimen.	—	—	3,000

		VG	VF	UNC
19	**5 Pounds** 1924-1945. Green and purple. Bank at center. Back: Palms and building at center.			
	a. Signature Hornsby. 1.8.1924-13.1.1929.	150	600	1,900
	b. Signature Cook. 1930-1940.	100	350	1,000
	c. Signature Nixon. 1940-1945.	15.00	40.00	250
	s. Specimen.	—	—	2,000

1926 Issue

		VG	VF	UNC
20	**1 Pound** 1.7.1926-10.1.1930. Green and dark blue. Portrait Fellah at right.			
	a. Issued note.	250	800	2,500
	s. Specimen.	—	—	2,500

1930-1935 Issue

		VG	VF	UNC
21	**50 Piastres** 1935-1951. Green and multicolor. Tutankhamen profile at left. Back: Crescent and stars at left. Watermark: Scarab.			
	a. Signature Cook. 7.5.1935-1940.	100	250	800
	b. Large signature Nixon. 1940-1943.	75.00	200	600
	c. Small signature Nixon. 1945-1947.	20.00	60.00	350
	d. Signature Leith-Ross. 1947-1950.	20.00	60.00	350
	e. Signature Saad (Arabic). 17.5.1951; 18.5.1951.	20.00	60.00	350
	s. Specimen.	—	—	2,000

		VG	VF	UNC
22	**1 Pound** 1930-1948. Blue and brown circle over watermark at left unprinted. Portrait Tutankhamen in brown at right. Back: Mosque at center. Watermark: Sphinx.			
	a. Signature Hornsby. 23.4.1930; 24.4.1930; 25.4.1930.	150	700	1,400
	b. Signature Cook. 5.12.1931-10.6.1940.	100	250	800
	c. Signature Nixon. 25.11.1940-31.1.1945.	10.00	35.00	100
	d. Signature Leith-Ross. 26.5.1948-10.6.1948.	10.00	35.00	100
	s. Specimen. Pinhole cancelled.	3.00	—	2,000

		VG	VF	UNC
23	**10 Pounds** 1931-1951. Brown, yellow-green and multicolor. Mosque of Sultan Qala'un and street in Cairo at right. Back: Farm scene and trees. Printer: BWC.			
	a. Signature Cook. 3.3.1931-1940.	80.00	250	800
	b. Signature Nixon. 1940-1947.	30.00	150	400
	c. Signature Leith-Ross. 1947-1950.	30.00	150	400
	d. Signature Saad (Arabic). 24.5.1951.	30.00	150	400
	s. Specimen.	—	—	2,500

1946-1950 Issue

		VG	VF	UNC
24	**1 Pound** 1950-1952. Blue and lilac. Portrait King Farouk at right.			
	a. European and Arabic serial #. 1.7.1950-13.7.1950.	20.00	100	500
	b. Arabic serial #. 15.5.1951-22.5.1951.	20.00	100	500
	c. Like b. Without imprint. 8.5.1952-10.5.1952.	20.00	100	500
	s. Specimen.	—	—	2,500

		VG	VF	UNC
25	**5 Pounds** 1946-1951. Blue-green, violet and brown. Portrait King Farouk at right. Citadel of Cairo at left.			
	a. Signature Leith-Ross. 1.5.1946-1950.	50.00	250	800
	b. Signature Saad (Arabic). 6.6.1951.	50.00	250	800

26	50 Pounds	VG	VF	UNC
	1949-1951. Green and brown. Portrait King Farouk at right. Ruins at lower left center. Back: City scene.			
	a. Signature Leith-Ross. 1.11.1949-1950.	100	500	2,500
	b. Signature Saad (Arabic). 16.5.1951.	100	500	2,500
	s. Specimen.	—	—	3,000

27	100 Pounds	VG	VF	UNC
	1948-1951. Light violet and green. Portrait King Farouk at right. Minaret at left. Back: Mosque.			
	a. Signature Leith-Ross. 1.7.194819-50.	100	500	2,500
	b. Signature Saad (Arabic). 16.5.1951.	100	500	2,500
	s. Specimen.	—	—	3,500

1952 Issue

28	25 Piastres	VG	VF	UNC
	8.5.1952-14.12.1957. Green. Tutankhamen facing at right. Back: Mosque.			
	a. Signature Fekry.	1.00	5.00	25.00
	b. Signature Saad.	—	—	20.00
	c. Signature El-Emano.	—	—	20.00

29	50 Piastres	VG	VF	UNC
	8.5.1952-3.8.1960. Brown on multicolor underprint. Tutankhamen at right. Back: Ruins. Watermark: Sphinx.			
	a. Signature Fekry.	1.00	5.00	40.00
	b. Signature Saad.	—	—	20.00
	c. Signature El-Emano.	—	—	20.00
	d. Signature El-Refay.	—	—	—

30	1 Pound	VG	VF	UNC
	12.5.1952-23.8.1960. Blue and lilac. Tutankhamen at right. Circle over watermark at left with underprint. Back: Ruins. Watermark: Sphinx.			
	a. Signature Fekry.	1.00	5.00	40.00
	b. Signature Saad.	—	—	20.00
	c. Signature El-Emano.	—	—	20.00
	d. Signature El-Refay.	—	—	20.00

31	5 Pounds	VG	VF	UNC
	8.5.1952-11.8.1960. Dark green, gray-blue and brown. Tutankhamen facing at right. Mosque at left. Back: Allegorical figures. Watermark: Flower.			
	a. Signature Fekry.	5.00	12.00	50.00
	b. Signature Saad.	—	—	25.00
	c. Signature El-Emano.	—	—	25.00
	d. Signature El-Refay.	—	—	25.00

32	10 Pounds	VG	VF	UNC
	1.11.1952-31.5.1960. Red and lilac. Tutankhamen facing at right. Back: Ruins. Watermark: Sphinx.			
	a. Signature Fekry.	7.50	20.00	50.00
	b. Signature Saad.	—	—	25.00
	c. Signature El-Emano.	—	—	25.00
	d. Signature El-Refay.	—	—	25.00

33	50 Pounds	VG	VF	UNC
	29.10.1952; 30.10.1952. Green and brown. Tutankhamen at right. Back: City scene, like #26.			
	a. Issued note.	150	400	3,000
	s1. Specimen. Overprinted in Arabic and French *ANNULE*. Perforated: *CANCELLED*.	—	—	4,000
	s2. Specimen. Perforated: *SPECIMEN*.	—	—	4,000

34	100 Pounds	VG	VF	UNC
	29.10.1952; 30.10.1952. Violet and green. Tutankhamen facing at right. Minaret at left. Back: Mosque on back. Like #27.			
	a. Issued note.	30.00	200	1,000
	s. Specimen.	—	—	3,000

Egyptian Government

1916-1917 Issue

		VG	VF	UNC
158	**5 Piastres** 27.5.1917. Blue on green and tan underprint. Back: Ruins at center. (Not issued).	—	—	1,200

		VG	VF	UNC
159	**10 Piastres** ND (ca. 1917). Green and black. Specimen.	—	—	—

		VG	VF	UNC
160	**10 Piastres** 1916-1917. Green on tan and light green underprint. Back: Colossi of Memnon at center. Printer: TDLR.			
	a. 17.7.1916.	500	2,000	3,000
	b. 27.5.1917.	100	300	800
	s. Specimen. Perforated: *CANCELLED.*	—	—	1,000

1918 Issue

		VG	VF	UNC
161	**5 Piastres** 1.5.1918-10.6.1918. Purple on green and orange underprint. Back: Ruins at center. Printer: Survey of Egypt. Varities exist in the series print on different dates.	200	600	2,000

		VG	VF	UNC
162	**5 Piastres** 1.6.1918. Lilac-brown on green underprint. Caravan at lower center. Printer: BWC.	25.00	100	750

		VG	VF	UNC
162A	**5 Piastres** 22.5.1920. Yellow-brown on multicolor underprint. Signature Fekry. Specimen, punch hole cancelled.	—	—	4,500

Law 50/1940 ND Issues

		VG	VF	UNC
163	**5 Piastres** ND. Green on brown underprint. Signature varieties. Back: Aswan Dam.	20.00	100	400

		VG	VF	UNC
164	**5 Piastres** ND. Brown on yellow underprint. Mosque of Emir Khairbak at left. Signature varieties.			
	a. Issued note.	10.00	40.00	200
	b. Serie crossover C4.	50.00	200	800

		VG	VF	UNC
165	**5 Piastres** ND. Brown on yellow underprint. Portrait King Farouk at left. Signature varieties.			
	a. Signature title: *MINISTER OF FINANCE* on back.	50.00	150	600
	b. Signature title: *MINISTER OF FINANCE AND ECONOMY* on back.	20.00	100	400

		VG	VF	UNC
166	**10 Piastres** ND. Brown on lilac underprint. Signature varieties. Back: Nile scene with Citadel.			
	a. Without watermark. Arabic serial #.	30.00	150	600
	b. Watermark: Geometric shape. Arabic serial #.	30.00	150	600
	c. Watermark: Geometric shape. Arabic and Western serial #'s.	20.00	75.00	350

		VG	VF	UNC
167	**10 Piastres** ND. Blue on green underprint. Temple of Philae at center. Color shading varieties. Signature varieties. Back: Placement of series letter varies.			
	a. Single letter to left of signature.	20.00	100	400
	b. Letter and number above signature.	20.00	100	400

		VG	VF	UNC
168	**10 Piastres** ND. Blue on green underprint. Portrait King Farouk at right. Signature varieties.			
	a. Signature title: *MINISTER OF FINANCE* on back.	50.00	200	800
	b. Signature title: *MINISTER OF FINANCE AND ECONOMY* on back.	20.00	80.00	600

Egyptian Royal Government

1952 Revolutionary Provisional Issue

		VG	VF	UNC
169	**5 Piastres**			
	ND. (1952). Portrait Queen Nefertiti at right, like #170 but different heading at top.			
	a. Issued note. Rare.	—	—	—
	s. Specimen.	—	—	2,500

		VG	VF	UNC
169A	**10 Piastres**			
	ND. (1952). Group of people and flag with three stars and crescent at right. Like #171 but different heading at top. Dhow at riverbank at center.			
	a. Issued note. Rare.	—	—	—
	s. Specimen.	—	—	2,000

Egyptian State

1952 ND Issue

		VG	VF	UNC
170	**5 Piastres**			
	ND. (1952). Lilac on gray-olive underprint. Portrait Queen Nefertiti at right. Overprint pattern on King Farouk watermark at left.	100	400	1,500

		VG	VF	UNC
171	**10 Piastres**			
	ND (1952). Gray-blue on brown underprint. Group of people and flag with three stars and crescent at right. Overprint pattern on Farouk watermark at left.	200	800	3,500

Egyptian Republic

1952 Provisional Issue

		VG	VF	UNC
172	**5 Piastres**			
	ND (1952). Portrait Queen Nefertiti at right with overprint pattern on Farouk watermark at left.	50.00	150	500

1952 Regular Issue

		VG	VF	UNC
174	**5 Piastres**			
	ND (1952-1958). Lilac. Portrait Queen Nefertiti at right. Like #172 but without pattern overprint on watermark area.			
	a. Watermark: Pyramids. 3 signature varieties.	1.00	15.00	50.00
	b. Watermark: Crown and letters (paper from #165 and #168).	1.00	20.00	80.00

		VG	VF	UNC
175	**10 Piastres**			
	ND (1952-1958). Gray-blue to black. Group of people and flag with three stars and crescent at right. Like #171 but without overprint pattern on watermark area.			
	a. Watermark: Pyramids. 3 signature varieties.	1.00	20.00	85.00
	b. Watermark: Crown and letters (paper as on #174b).	1.00	15.00	45.00

UNITED ARAB REPUBLIC

Arab Republic of Egypt

1958-1971 ND Issue

		VG	VF	UNC
176	**5 Piastres**			
	ND. Red-lilac to violet. Portrait Queen Nefertiti at right. Like # 174.			
	a. Watermark: Pyramids.	5.00	10.00	40.00
	b. Watermark: Eagles. 2 signature varieties.	5.00	10.00	50.00
	c. Watermark: *U A R* letters in Arabic and English. Lilac or dark purple.	3.00	5.00	20.00

		VG	VF	UNC
177	**10 Piastres**			
	ND. Blue-black to black. Group of people and flag with two stars. No crescent.			
	a. Watermark: Pyramids. 2 signature varieties.	1.50	5.00	40.00
	b. Watermark: Eagles.	1.50	5.00	30.00
	c. Watermark: *U A R* letters in Arabic and English.	1.50	5.00	30.00

		VG	VF	UNC
178	**10 Piastres**			
	ND. Mule note combining Face 3 with back 1A.	40.00	150	400

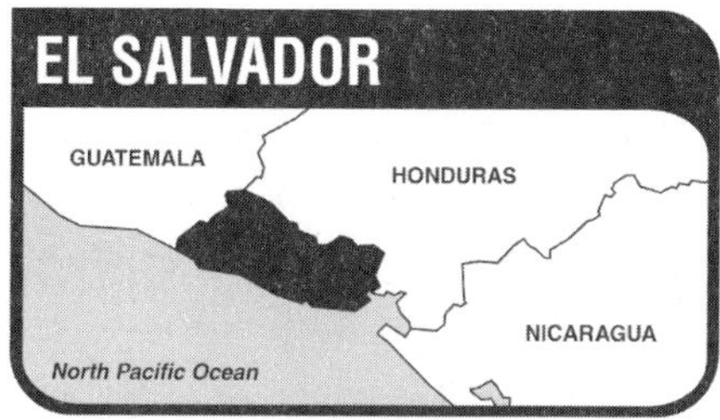

The Republic of El Salvador, a Central American country bordered by Guatemala, Honduras and the Pacific Ocean, has an area of 21,040 sq. km. and a population of 7.07 million. Capital: San Salvador. This most intensely cultivated country of Latin America produces coffee (the major crop), sugar and balsam for export. Gold, silver and other metals are largely unexploited.

El Salvador achieved independence from Spain in 1821 and from the Central American Federation in 1839. A 12-year civil war, which cost about 75,000 lives, was brought to a close in 1992 when the government and leftist rebels signed a treaty that provided for military and political reforms.

On January 1, 2001, a monetary reform established the U.S. dollar as the accounting unit for all financial transactions, and fixed the exchange rate as 8.75 colones per dollar. In addition, the Central Reserve Bank has indicated that it will cease issuing coins and notes.

MONETARY SYSTEM:

1 Peso = 100 Centavos to 1919
1 Colón = 100 Centavos 1919-

DATING SYSTEM:

Dates listed for notes are those found on the face, regardless of the overprint issue dates on back which were applied practically on a daily basis as notes were needed for circulation.

REPUBLIC

Gobierno del Salvador

Government of El Salvador
1877 Issue

No.	Description	VG	VF	UNC
1	**1 Peso** 1.4.1877. Blue and black. Arms at upper center. Back: Arms at center. Printer: NBNC. 180x82mm.			
	a. Issued note.	—	—	300
	s. Specimen.	—	—	300
2	**2 Pesos** 1.4.1877. Brown and black. Arms at upper center. Back: Arms at center. Printer: NBNC. 180x82mm.	—	—	300
3	**5 Pesos** 1.4.1877. Green and black. Arms at upper center. Back: Arms at center. Printer: NBNC. 180x82mm. Specimen.	—	—	300
4	**10 Pesos** 1.4.1877. Orange and black. Arms at upper center. Back: Arms at center. Printer: NBNC. 180x82mm. Specimen.	—	—	300
5	**25 Pesos** 1.4.1877. Orange-brown and black. Arms at upper center. Back: Arms at center. Printer: NBNC. 180x82mm. Specimen.	—	—	400
6	**50 Pesos** 1.4.1877. Red-orange and black. Arms at upper center. Back: Arms at center. Printer: NBNC. 180x82mm. Specimen.	—	—	400
7	**100 Pesos** 1.4.1877. Blue and black. Arms at upper center. Back: Arms at center. Printer: NBNC. 180x82mm. Specimen.	—	—	500
8	**500 Pesos** 1.4.1877. Gold and black. Arms at upper center. Back: Arms at center. Printer: NBNC. 180x82mm. Specimen.	—	—	500

Color Abbreviation Guide

New to the *Standard Catalog of® World Paper Money* are the following abbreviations related to color references:

BC: Back color
PC: Paper color

Deuda Interior del Pais

Circulating Interior Debt Notes

No.	Description	VG	VF	UNC
9	**1 Peso** 1.4.1877. Blue and black. Arms at upper center. Back: Arms at center. Printer: NBNC. 215x127mm.			
	a. Issued note.	—	—	—
	s. Specimen.	—	—	300
10	**2 Pesos** 1.4.1877. Brown and black. Arms at upper center. Back: Arms at center. Printer: NBNC. 215x127mm. Specimen.	—	—	300
11	**5 Pesos** 1.4.1877. Green and black. Arms at upper center. Back: Arms at center. Printer: NBNC. 215x127mm. Specimen.	—	—	300
12	**10 Pesos** 1.4.1877. Orange and black. Arms at upper center. Back: Arms at center. Printer: NBNC. 215x127mm. Specimen.	—	—	300
13	**25 Pesos** 1.4.1877. Orange-brown and black. Arms at upper center. Back: Arms at center. Printer: NBNC. 215x127mm. Specimen.	—	—	—
14	**50 Pesos** 1.4.1877. Red-orange and black. Arms at upper center. Back: Arms at center. Printer: NBNC. 215x127mm.			
	a. Issued note.	—	—	—
	s. Specimen.	—	—	—
15	**100 Pesos** 1.4.1877. Blue and black. Arms at upper center. Back: Arms at center. Printer: NBNC. 215x127mm. Specimen.	—	—	—
16	**200 Pesos** 1.4.1877. Black on brown underprint. Arms at upper center. Back: Arms at center. Printer: NBNC. 215x127mm. Specimen.	—	—	—
17	**500 Pesos** 1.4.1877. Gold and black. Arms at upper center. Back: Arms at center. Printer: NBNC. 215x127mm. Specimen.	—	—	—
18	**1000 Pesos** 1.4.1877. Black on deep red underprint. Arms at upper center. Back: Arms at center. Printer: NBNC. 215x127mm. Specimen.	—	—	—

Deuda Publica del Salvador

Circulating Public Debt Notes. Ca. 1880

No.	Description	VG	VF	UNC
35	**25 Pesos** 18xx. Brown and black. Mercury left, arms at upper center. Printer: BWC. Specimen.	—	—	—
38	**500 Pesos** 18xx. Brown on light orange. Mercury left, arms at upper center. Printer: BWC.			
	a. Issued note.	—	—	—
	s. Specimen.	—	—	—

Banco Central de Reserva de El Salvador

VALIDATION OVERPRINTS

The Government decreed that after 1907 all issued banknotes should have a validation stamp with the text: *TOMADO RAZON* accompanied by the official seal and sign. Varieties of sign. and numerous dates may exist for some issues. Later issues have only the seal, sign. and date after San Salvador. The dates listed throughout are only those found on the face of the note.

TRIBUNAL DE CUENTAS

Sergio Castellanos . . 1907-1910

TRIBUNAL SUPERIOR DE CUENTAS

Sergio Castellanos . .	1910-1916	Alb. Galindo	1924-1927
Jose E. Suay	1917-1918	D. Rosales Sol	1928-1929
Luis Valle M.	1919	C.V. Martinez	1939

JUNTA DE VIGILANCIA DE BANCOS Y S.A.

V.C. Barriere	1935-1944	B. Glower V.	1952
C. Valmore M.	1940 M.	Ant. Ramirez	1954-1958
V.M. Valdes	1946-1948	Antonio Serrano L.	1956 -1958
M.E. Hinds	1949	Pedro A. Delgado.	1959
Jorge Sol	1950-1953	R. Rubino	1961

CORTE DE CUENTAS

M.E. Hinds 1940-1943

SUPERINTENDENCIA DE BANCOS Y OTRAS INSTITUCIONES FINANCIERAS

Juan S. Quinteros . . .	1962-1975	Marco T. Guandique . .	1977-Feb. 1981
Jose A. Mendoza	1968-1975	Rafael T. Carbonell . . .	1981-
Jorge A. Dowson	1975-1977	Raul Nolasco	1981-

Note: Certain listings encompassing issues circulated by various bank and regional authorities are contained in Volume 1.

1934 Issue

75	1 Colón	VG	VF	UNC
	31.8.1934; 4.9.1941; 14.1.1943. Black on pale blue and multicolor underprint. Allegorical woman reclining with fruits and branch at center. Back: Portrait Christopher Columbus at center. Printer: ABNC.			
	a. Issued note.	7.50	25.00	135
	s. Specimen.	—	—	200

76	2 Colones	VG	VF	UNC
	31.8.1934-14.5.1952. Black on multicolor underprint. Allegorical woman reclining with fruits and branch at center. Back: Portrait Christopher Columbus at center. Printer: ABNC.			
	a. Issued note.	12.50	40.00	145
	s. Specimen.	—	—	250

77	5 Colones	VG	VF	UNC
	31.8.1934. Black on multicolor underprint. Allegorical woman reclining with fruits and branch at center. Back: Portrait Christopher Columbus at center. Printer: ABNC.			
	a. Issued note.	15.00	50.00	175
	s. Specimen.	—	—	300

78	10 Colones	VG	VF	UNC
	31.8.1934. Black on multicolor underprint. Allegorical woman reclining with fruits and branch at center. Back: Portrait Christopher Columbus at center. Printer: ABNC.			
	a. Issued note.	25.00	75.00	225
	s. Specimen.	—	—	500

79	25 Colones	VG	VF	UNC
	31.8.1934; 14.2.1951; 17.3.1954. Black on multicolor underprint. Allegorical woman reclining with fruits and branch at center. Back: Portrait Christopher Columbus at center. Printer: ABNC.			
	a. Issued note.	30.00	85.00	275
	s. Specimen.	—	—	400

80	100 Colones	VG	VF	UNC
	31.8.1934; 9.2.1937. Brown and green underprint. Allegorical woman reclining with fruits and branch at center. Back: Portrait Christopher Columbus at center. Printer: ABNC.			
	a. Issued note.	30.00	100	325
	s. Specimen.	FV	FV	450

		VG	VF	UNC
81	**1 Colón** 10.5.1938. Black on multicolor underprint. Black on multicolor underprint. Back: Portrait Christopher Columbus at center. Printer: W&S.	6.00	20.00	100

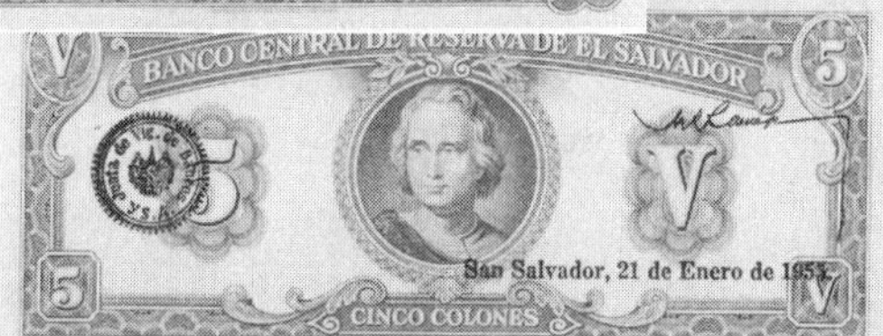

		VG	VF	UNC
82	**5 Colones** 10.5.1938-17.3.1954. Black on multicolor underprint. Woman with basket of fruit on her head at left. Back: Portrait Christopher Columbus at center. Printer: W&S.			
	a. Issued note.	10.00	35.00	150
	s. Specimen. Overprint: *SPECIMEN* in red. Punch hole cancelled.	—	—	1,000

1942-1944 Issue

		VG	VF	UNC
83	**1 Colón** 26.9.1944-14.5.1952. Black on pale blue and multicolor underprint. Farmer plowing with oxen at center. Back: Portrait Christopher Columbus at center. Printer: ABNC.			
	a. Issued note.	4.00	15.00	75.00
	s. Specimen.	—	—	125

		VG	VF	UNC
84	**5 Colones** 11.8.1942-14.5.1952. Black on multicolor underprint. Delgado addressing crowd at center. Back: Portrait Christopher Columbus at center. Printer: ABNC.			
	a. Issued note.	7.50	25.00	150
	s. Specimen.	—	—	175

		VG	VF	UNC
85	**10 Colones** 14.3.1943-14.5.1952. Black on multicolor underprint. Portrait M.J. Arce at left. Back: Portrait Christopher Columbus at center. Printer: ABNC.			
	a. Issued note.	10.00	50.00	200
	s. Specimen.	—	—	225
86	**100 Colones** 1942-1954. Black on multicolor underprint. Independence monument at center. Back: Portrait Christopher Columbus at center. Printer: ABNC.	VG	VF	UNC
	a. Brown and green underprint. 11.8.1942-31.1.1951.	30.00	75.00	250
	b. Green underprint. 17.3.1954.	30.00	75.00	250
	s. As a. Specimen.	—	—	275

1950; 1954 Issue

		VG	VF	UNC
87	**1 Colón** 10.1.1950; 6.11.1952; 17.3.1954. Black on multicolor underprint. Coffee bush at left, Lake Coatepeque at right. Printer: W&S.	6.00	15.00	50.00

		VG	VF	UNC
88	**10 Colones** 17.3.1954. Black on dull purple and multicolor underprint. M.J. Arce at upper center. Series ZA. Printer: W&S.	12.50	50.00	225

#89 Renumbered, see #86b.

1955 Issue

		VG	VF	UNC
90	**1 Colón** 1955-1960. Black on multicolor underprint. Coffee bush at lower left, bank at right. Back: Portrait Christopher Columbus at center. Printer: W&S.			
	a. Paper without metal thread. 13.4.1955.	2.50	5.00	25.00
	b. Paper with metal thread. 15.2.1956-17.8.1960.	1.00	2.50	17.50

#	Denomination / Description	VG	VF	UNC
91	**2 Colones** 1955-1958. Black on multicolor underprint. Coffee bush at left with field workers in background. Back: Portrait Christopher Columbus at center. Printer: W&S.			
	a. Plain paper without security thread. 13.4.1955.	5.00	15.00	60.00
	b. Paper with metal thread. watermark: *BANCO CENTRAL*. 27.8.1958.	4.50	10.00	50.00

#	Denomination / Description	VG	VF	UNC
92	**5 Colones** 1955-1959. Black on multicolor underprint. Woman with basket of fruit on her head. Back: Portrait Christopher Columbus at center. Printer: W&S.			
	a. Plain paper without security thread. 13.4.1955.	4.00	15.00	65.00
	b. Paper with metal thread. watermark: *BANCO CENTRAL*. 25.1.1957-25.11.1959.	4.00	15.00	65.00

1957-1958 Issue

#	Denomination / Description	VG	VF	UNC
93	**1 Colón** 4.9.1957. Black on pink and pale green underprint. *SAN SALVADOR* at lower left, farmer plowing with oxen at center. Red serial # and series letters. Back: Portrait Christopher Columbus at center. Printer: ABNC.			
	a. Issued note.	3.00	8.00	27.50
	s. Specimen.	—	—	150

#	Denomination / Description	VG	VF	UNC
94	**2 Colones** 9.11.1960. Black on multicolor underprint. Allegorical woman reclining with fruits and branch at center. Like #76 but reduced size. Back: Portrait Christopher Columbus at center. Printer: ABNC.			
	a. Issued note.	4.00	15.00	65.00
	s. Specimen.	—	—	150

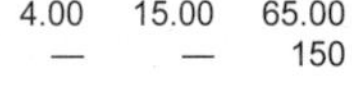

#	Denomination / Description	VG	VF	UNC
95	**5 Colones** 15.2.1956; 9.11.1960. Black on multicolor underprint. *SAN SALVADOR* at lower left, Delgado addressing crowd at center. Red serial # at upper left and right. Back: Portrait Christopher Columbus at center. Printer: ABNC.			
	a. Issued note.	4.00	10.00	50.00
	s. Specimen.	—	—	150

#	Denomination / Description	VG	VF	UNC
96	**10 Colones** 4.9.1957. Black on multicolor underprint. Portrait M.J. Arce at left. Back: Portrait Christopher Columbus at center. Printer: ABNC.			
	a. Issued note.	7.50	30.00	100
	s. Specimen.	—	—	140

#	Denomination / Description	VG	VF	UNC
97	**25 Colones** 29.12.1958; 9.11.1960. Black on multicolor underprint. Reservoir in frame at center. Back: Portrait Christopher Columbus at center. Printer: ABNC.			
	a. Issued note.	8.00	30.00	100
	s. Specimen.	—	—	150

#	Denomination / Description	VG	VF	UNC
98	**100 Colones** 29.12.1958; 9.11.1960. Black on multicolor underprint. *SAN SALVADOR* at lower left, Independence monument at center. Serial # at upper left and upper right. Printer: ABNC.			
	a. Issued note.	25.00	90.00	300
	s. Specimen.	—	—	400

1959 Issue

#	Denomination / Description	VG	VF	UNC
99	**10 Colones** 25.11.1959. Reduced size. Black on pale green and multicolor underprint. Portrait M.J. Arce at upper center. Back: Portrait Christopher Columbus at center. Printer: W&S. 67x156mm.	4.00	20.00	80.00

The Republic of Estonia is the northernmost of the three Baltic states in eastern Europe. It has an area of 45,226 sq. km. and a population of 1.31 million. Capital: Tallinn. Agriculture and dairy farming are the principal industries. Butter, eggs, bacon, timber are exported.

After centuries of Danish, Swedish, German, and Russian rule, Estonia attained independence in 1918. Forcibly incorporated into the USSR in 1940 - an action never recognized by the US - it regained its freedom in 1991, with the collapse of the Soviet Union. Since the last Russian troops left in 1994, Estonia has been free to promote economic and political ties with Western Europe. It joined both NATO and the EU in the spring of 2004.

MONETARY SYSTEM

1 Mark = 100 Penni to 1928
1 Kroon = 100 Senti

REPUBLIC

Tallinna Arvekoja Maksutäht

Payment notes of the Clearing House of Tallinn

1919 First Issue

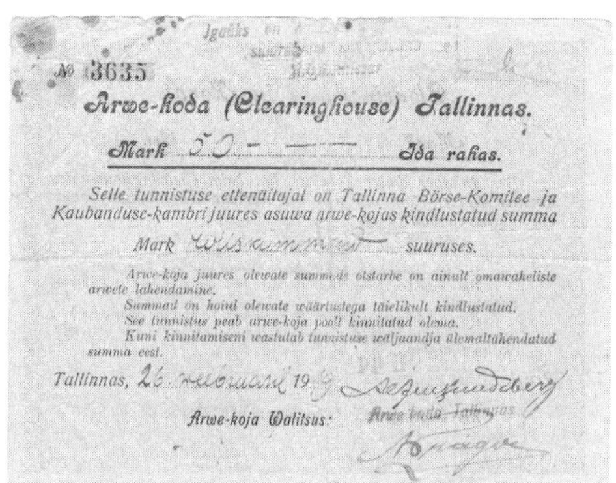

		Good	Fine	XF
A1	**50 Ost. Marka**			
	1919-1922. Black on green underprint.			
	a. Issued note. Rare.	—	—	—
	s. Specimen. Handwritten on both sides: *PROOV.*	—	—	—

1919 Second Issue

		Good	Fine	XF
A2	**50 Marka**			
	1919. Blue on light blue underprint.			
	a. Without issued branch stamp.	250	450	900
	b. With issued branch stamp.	200	400	800
	s. Specimen. Red overprint: *PROOV.*	—	—	—
A3	**100 Marka**	Good	Fine	XF
	1919. Brown.			
	a. Issued note.	350	700	1,350
	s. Specimen. Red overprint stamped: *PROOV* on face and handwritten on back.	—	—	—

1920 Issue

		Good	Fine	XF
A4	**5000 Marka**			
	192x (1920-1923). Brown and green on light green underprint. Arms at center.			
	a. Issued note. Rare.	—	—	—
	s. Specimen. Handwritten: *PROOV* on both sides.	—	—	—
A5	**10,000 Marka**	Good	Fine	XF
	192x (1920-1923). Black and brown on rose underprint. Coat of arms.			
	a. Issued note. Rare.	—	—	—
	s. Specimen. Handwritten: *PROOV* on both sides.	—	—	—
	ct. Color trial. Black and brown on yellow underprint.	—	—	—
A6	**25,000 Marka**	Good	Fine	XF
	192x (1920-1923). Black and brown on grey underprint. Coat of arms.			
	a. Issued note. Rare.	—	—	—
	s. Specimen. Handwritten: *PROOV* on both sides.	—	—	—

Eesti Wabariigi 5% Wõlakohustus

Republic Debt Obligations of 5% Interest

#1-38 bonds w/o pictorial design that were declared legal tender on 20.1.1919. Dates given are redemption dates.

1919 Series A Issues

		Good	Fine	XF
1	**50 Marka**			
	1.5.1919. Gray. Uniface.	30.00	150	—
1A	**50 Marka**	Good	Fine	XF
	1.5.1919. Gray. Printed on both sides.	70.00	200	—
2	**100 Marka**	Good	Fine	XF
	1.5.1919. Gray. Uniface.	100	250	—
2A	**100 Marka**	Good	Fine	XF
	1.5.1919. Gray. Printed on both sides.	100	200	—
3	**200 Marka**	Good	Fine	XF
	1.5.1919. Gray. Uniface.	150	350	—
3A	**200 Marka**	Good	Fine	XF
	1.5.1919. Gray. Printed on both sides.	150	300	—
4	**500 Marka**	Good	Fine	XF
	1.5.1919. Uniface.	150	400	—
5	**500 Marka**	Good	Fine	XF
	1.5.1919. Gray. Printed on both sides.	150	400	—
6	**1000 Marka**	Good	Fine	XF
	1.5.1919. Gray. Uniface.	400	900	—
6A	**5000 Marka**	Good	Fine	XF
	1.5.1919 Gray. Uniface. Rare.	—	—	—
6B	**10,000 Marka**	Good	Fine	XF
	1.5.1919. Gray. Uniface. Rare.	—	—	—

1919 Series B Issues

		Good	Fine	XF
7	**50 Marka**			
	1.6.1919. Yellow-brown. Uniface.	80.00	200	—
8	**50 Marka**	Good	Fine	XF
	1.6.1919. Yellow-brown. Printed on both sides.	70.00	150	—

		Good	Fine	XF
9	**100 Marka**			
	1.6.1919. Yellow-brown. Uniface.	100	200	—
9A	**100 Marka**	Good	Fine	XF
	1.6.1919. Yellow-brown. Printed on both sides.	100	200	—
10	**200 Marka**	Good	Fine	XF
	1.6.1919. Yellow. Uniface.	200	400	—
11	**200 Marka**	Good	Fine	XF
	1.6.1919. Black and light brown on rose underprint. Printed on both sides.	200	400	—
12	**500 Marka**	Good	Fine	XF
	1.6.1919. Yellow-brown. Uniface.	300	600	—
12A	**500 Marka**	Good	Fine	XF
	1.6.1919. Yellow-brown. Printed on both sides. Rare.	—	—	—
13	**1000 Marka**	Good	Fine	XF
	1.6.1919. Black and light brown on rose underprint. Uniface.	400	900	—

		Good	Fine	XF
13A	**1000 Marka**	Good	Fine	XF
	1.6.1919. Yellow-brown. Printed on both sides. Rare.	—	—	—
13B	**5000 Marka**	Good	Fine	XF
	1.6.1919. Yellow-brown. Uniface. Rare.	—	—	—
13C	**10,000 Marka**	Good	Fine	XF
	1.6.1919. Yellow-brown. Uniface. Rare.	—	—	—

1919 Series D Issues

		Good	Fine	XF
14	**50 Marka**	Good	Fine	XF
	1.7.1919. Green. Uniface.	50.00	125	—
14A	**100 Marka**	Good	Fine	XF
	1.7.1919. Green. Printed on both sides.	50.00	100	—
15	**100 Marka**	Good	Fine	XF
	1.7.1919. Green. Uniface.	100	250	—
15A	**100 Marka**	Good	Fine	XF
	1.7.1919. Black on green underprint. Printed on both sides.			
	a. Issued note.	100	200	—
	s. Specimen. Red overprint: *PROOV* on both sides.	—	—	—
16	**200 Marka**	Good	Fine	XF
	1.7.1919. Green. Uniface.	150	300	—
17	**200 Marka**	Good	Fine	XF
	1.7.1919. Green. Printed on both sides.	150	350	—
18	**500 Marka**	Good	Fine	XF
	1.7.1919. Black and light green on rose underprint. Uniface.	200	600	—
19	**500 Marka**	Good	Fine	XF
	1.7.1919. Black on green underprint. Printed on both sides.	200	600	—
20	**1000 Marka**	Good	Fine	XF
	1.7.1919. Green. Uniface.	350	900	—
20A	**1000 Marka**	Good	Fine	XF
	1.7.1919. Green. Printed on both sides. Rare.	—	—	—
20B	**5000 Marka**	Good	Fine	XF
	1.7.1919. Green. Uniface. Rare.	—	—	—
20C	**10,000 Marka**	Good	Fine	XF
	1.7.1919. Green. Uniface. Rare.	—	—	—

1919 W/o Series First Issue

		Good	Fine	XF
21	**50 Marka**	Good	Fine	XF
	1.11.1919. Black on gray underprint.	40.00	120	—
22	**100 Marka**	Good	Fine	XF
	1.11.1919. Black on light brown and rose underprint.	60.00	180	—
23	**200 Marka**	Good	Fine	XF
	1.11.1919. Orange.	100	300	—
24	**500 Marka**	Good	Fine	XF
	1.11.1919. Green.	200	600	—

1919 W/o Series Second Issue

		Good	Fine	XF
25	**50 Marka**	Good	Fine	XF
	1.12.1919. Black on gray underprint.	40.00	150	—
26	**100 Marka**	Good	Fine	XF
	1.12.1919. Yellow-brown.	70.00	200	—
27	**200 Marka**	Good	Fine	XF
	1.12.1919. Black on rose underprint.	80.00	300	—
28	**500 Marka**	Good	Fine	XF
	1.12.1919. Green.	350	800	—

1920 First Issue

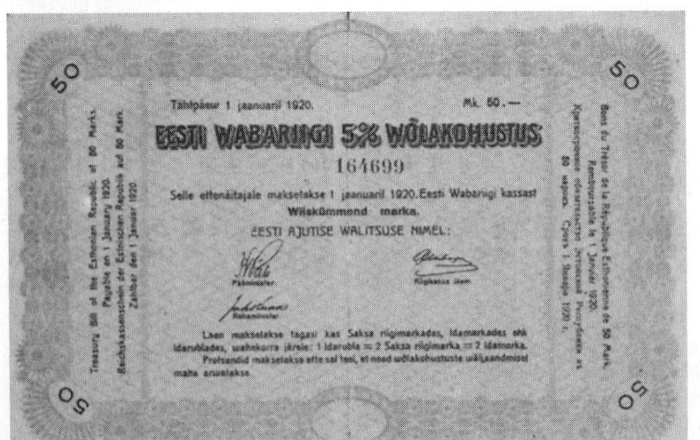

		Good	Fine	XF
29	**50 Marka**	Good	Fine	XF
	1.1.1920. Black on gray underprint.			
	a. Issued note.	40.00	100	—
	s. Specimen. Red overprint: *PROOV* on both sides.	—	—	—
30	**50 Marka**	Good	Fine	XF
	1.1.1920. Blue.	40.00	100	—
31	**100 Marka**	Good	Fine	XF
	1.1.1920. Black on gray underprint.			
	a. Issued note.	80.00	180	—
	s. Specimen. Red overprint: *PROOV* on both sides.	—	—	—
32	**100 Marka**	Good	Fine	XF
	1.1.1920. Black on light brown and rose underprint.	80.00	180	—
33	**200 Marka**	Good	Fine	XF
	1.1.1920. Black on rose underprint.	—	—	—
34	**500 Marka**	Good	Fine	XF
	1.1.1920. Black on gray underprint.	—	—	—
35	**500 Marka**	Good	Fine	XF
	1.1.1920. Green.			
	a. Issued note.	—	—	—
	s. Specimen. Red overprint: *PROOV* on both sides.	—	—	—

#36 and 37, not assigned.

1920 Second Issue

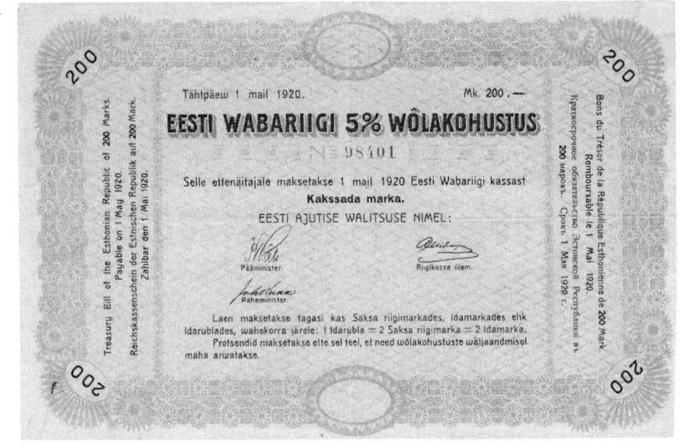

		Good	Fine	XF
38	**200 Marka**	Good	Fine	XF
	1.5.1920. Black on gray underprint.			
	a. Issued note.	—	—	—
	s. Specimen. Red overprint: *PROOV* on both sides.	—	—	—
38A	**200 Marka**	Good	Fine	XF
	1.5.1920. Orange.			
	a. Issued note.	100	300	—
	s. Specimen.	—	—	—

Eesti Vabariigi 6%-line Kassa-veksel

Promissory Notes of the Treasury of the Republic of Estonia

1920 Series A

Issue of 4.5% interest.

		Good	Fine	XF
38B	**1000 Marka**	Good	Fine	XF
	1.7.1920. Lilac.			
	a. Issued note.	400	1,000	—
	s. Specimen.	—	—	—
38C	**5000 Marka**	Good	Fine	XF
	1.7.1920. Blue-gray.			
	a. Issued note.	700	1,500	—
	s. Specimen.	—	—	—
38D	**10,000 Marka**	Good	Fine	XF
	1.7.1920. Blue.			
	a. Issued note.	900	2,000	—
	s. Specimen.	—	—	—
38E	**25,000 Marka**	Good	Fine	XF
	1.7.1920. Black on rose underprint.			
	a. Issued note. Rare.	—	—	—
	s. Specimen.	—	—	—

38F	100,000 Marka	Good	Fine	XF
	1.7.1920. Yellow.			
	a. Issued note. Rare.	—	—	—
	s. Specimen.	—	—	—

1920 Series B

Issue of 5% interest.

38G	1000 Marka	Good	Fine	XF
	1.9.1920. Blue on rose underprint.			
	a. Issued note.	400	900	—
	s. Specimen.	—	—	—

38H	5000 Marka	Good	Fine	XF
	1.9.1920. Blue-gray.			
	a. Issued note.	700	1,500	—
	s. Specimen. Red overprint: *PROOV* on both sides.	—	—	—

38I	10,000 Marka	Good	Fine	XF
	1.9.1920. Blue.			
	a. Rare.	—	—	—
	s. Specimen.	—	—	—

38J	25,000 Marka	Good	Fine	XF
	1.9.1920. Pink.			
	a. Issued note. Rare.	—	—	—
	s. Specimen.	—	—	—

38K	100,000 Marka	Good	Fine	XF
	1.9.1920. Black on yellow underprint.			
	a. Issued note. Rare.	—	—	—
	s. Specimen.	—	—	—

1920 Series D

Issue of 5.5% interest.

38L	1000 Marka	Good	Fine	XF
	1.12.1920. Lilac.			
	a. Issued note.	400	900	—
	s. Specimen.	—	—	—

38M	5000 Marka	Good	Fine	XF
	1.12.1920. Blue on gray underprint.			
	a. Issued note.	700	1,500	—
	s. Specimen.	—	—	—

38N	10,000 Marka	Good	Fine	XF
	1.12.1920. Blue.			
	a. Issued note.	900	2,000	—
	s. Specimen.	—	—	—

38O	25,000 Marka	Good	Fine	XF
	1.12.1920. Pink.			
	a. Issued note. Rare.	—	—	—
	s. Specimen.	—	—	—

38P	100,000 Marka	Good	Fine	XF
	1.12.1920. Yellow.			
	a. Issued note. Rare.	—	—	—
	s. Specimen.	—	—	—

1921 Series E

Issue of 6% interest.

38Q	1000 Marka	Good	Fine	XF
	1.2.1921. Black on rose underprint.			
	a. Issued note.	400	900	—
	s. Specimen. Red overprint: *PROOV* on both sides.	—	—	—

38R	5000 Marka	Good	Fine	XF
	1.2.1921. Blue on gray underprint.			
	a. Issued note.	700	1,500	—
	s. Specimen. Red overprint: *PROOV* on both sides.	—	—	—

38S	10,000 Marka	Good	Fine	XF
	1.2.1921. Blue.			
	a. Issued note.	900	2,000	—
	s. Specimen.	—	—	—

38T	25,000 Marka	Good	Fine	XF
	1.2.1921. Pink.			
	a. Issued note. Rare.	—	—	—
	s. Specimen.	—	—	—

38U	100,000 Marka	Good	Fine	XF
	1.2.1921. Black on yellow underprint.			
	a. Issued note. Rare.	—	—	—
	s. Specimen. Red overprint: *PROOV* on both sides.	—	—	—

Eesti Vabariigi Kassatäht

Republic of Estonia Treasury Notes

1919-1920 Issue

39	5 Penni	VG	VF	UNC
	ND (1919). Green. Owl in tree at center.			
	a. Issued note.	5.00	10.00	25.00
	s. Specimen. Red overprint: *PROOV* on both sides.	20.00	50.00	115

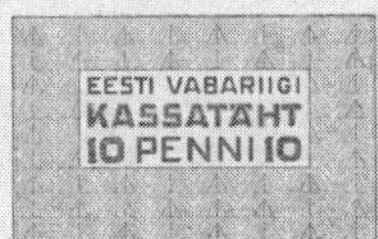

40	10 Penni	VG	VF	UNC
	ND (1919). Ship at center.			
	a. Gray. Printer: Bergmann, Tartu.	8.00	15.00	35.00
	b. Brown. Printer: Riigi Trkikoda, Tallinn.	5.00	10.00	25.00
	s. Specimen. As b. Red overprint: *PROOV* on both sides.	20.00	50.00	115

41	20 Penni	VG	VF	UNC
	ND (1919). Yellow. Windmill at center.			
	a. Issued note.	10.00	15.00	35.00
	s. Specimen. Red overprint: *PROOV* on both sides.	10.00	25.00	50.00

42	50 Penni	VG	VF	UNC
	1919. Blue on light blue underprint. Ornamental design at center.			
	a. Issued note.	10.00	20.00	40.00
	p. Proof. Black print on white paper.	—	125	250
	s. Specimen. Red overprint: *PROOV* on both sides.	—	—	200

Numerious color trials exist for #42.

43	1 Mark	VG	VF	UNC
	1919. Brown on gold underprint. Sheaves of wheat and sickles at center.			
	a. Issued note.	10.00	30.00	50.00
	p1. Proof. Black overprint on white paper.	—	75.00	150
	p2. Proof. Green overprint on yellow paper.	—	75.00	150
	s. Specimen.	25.00	60.00	125

Note: #42 and 43 also exist w/overprint: *POHJAN POJAT RYKMENTIN...* See #M1 and M3. in the *Specialized* volume.

44	3 Marka	VG	VF	UNC
	1919. Green on light green underprint. Agricultural symbols at center.			
	a. White paper.	5.00	15.00	30.00
	b. Cream paper.	10.00	20.00	40.00
	s. Specimen. Red overprint: *PROOV.*	25.00	60.00	125

45	5 Marka	VG	VF	UNC
	1919. Blue and light brown. Farmer plowing at center. Back: Field scene. Thin or thick paper.			
	a. Issued note.	50.00	70.00	100
	s. Specimen. Red overprint: *PROOV* on both sides.	20.00	40.00	80.00

46	10 Marka	VG	VF	UNC
	1919. Brown. Shepherd blowing a horn while standing between a cow and some sheep. Back: Man with horse between cornucopiae on back.			
	a. *KÜMME MARKA* in blue border on back. watermark: light horizontal lines (blue).	60.00	80.00	120
	b. *KÜMME MARKA* with blue border. Watermark: light vertical lines.	40.00	80.00	120
	c. *KÜMME MARKA* without border. Watermark: light horizontal lines.	40.00	80.00	120
	d. *KÜMME MARKA* without border. Watermark: light vertical lines.	40.00	80.00	120
	s. Specimen. Red overprint: *PROOV* on both sides.	—	50.00	100

47	25 Marka	VG	VF	UNC
	1919. Blackish purple and brown. Tree at left and right, harvesting potatoes at center. Back: Fishermen with boats and nets.			
	a. Watermark: Horizontal wavy lines.	50.00	100	200
	b. Watermark: Vertical wavy lines.	50.00	100	200
	s. Specimen. Red overprint: *PROOV* on both sides.	—	50.00	100

48	100 Marka	VG	VF	UNC
	1919. Brown on tan underprint. Woman at spinning wheel at center. Man at left, woman at right.			
	a. Watermark: Horizontal wavy lines.	60.00	100	200
	b. *SEERIA II.*	60.00	100	200
	c. *SEERIA III.*	60.00	100	200
	d. Watermark: Vertical lines.	60.00	100	200
	s. Specimen. Red overprint: *PROOV* on both sides.	—	100	180

49	500 Marka	VG	VF	UNC
	ND (1920-1921). Bluish green and violet. Light green eagle and shield at center.			
	a. Watermark: *500.* (1920).	100	250	500
	b. *SEERIA II.* (1920).	100	250	500
	c. *SEERIA III.* (1920).	90.00	200	300
	d. *SEERIA A.* Watermark: *EV.* (1920)	90.00	200	300
	e. *SEERIA B.* (1920).	90.00	200	300
	f. *SEERIA D.* (1921).	90.00	200	300
	s. Specimen. Red overprint: *PROOV* on both sides.	—	100	200

		VG	VF	UNC
50	**1000 Marka**	VG	VF	UNC
	ND (1920-1921). Green and brown. Back: *Birth of Liberty* Watermark: *EV.*			
	a. Without series prefix letters. (1920).	600	1,000	2,000
	b. *SEERIA A.* Watermark: *EV.* (1921).	600	1,000	2,000
	c. *SEERIA B.* (1921).	600	1,000	2,000
	s. Specimen. Red overprint: *PROOW* on both sides.	—	800	1,500

1923 Issue

		VG	VF	UNC
51	**100 Marka**	VG	VF	UNC
	1923. Green and brown. Bank at center. Watermark: *EV.*			
	a. Without series.	50.00	150	300
	b. *SEERIA A.* (1927).	50.00	150	300
	s. Specimen. Red overprint: *PROOV* on both sides.	—	150	300

		VG	VF	UNC
52	**500 Marka**	VG	VF	UNC
	1923. Gray-blue and brown. Toompea Castle at center. Watermark: Rhombic patterns.			
	a. Issued note.	200	600	1,000
	s. Specimen. Red overprint: *PROOV* on both sides.	200	600	1,000

Eesti Vabariigi Vahetustäht

Republic of Estonia Exchange Note

1922 Issue

		VG	VF	UNC
53	**10 Marka**	VG	VF	UNC
	1922. Blackish green on red-brown underprint.			
	a. Without serial # prefix letters. Watermark: *EV.*	25.00	45.00	90.00
	b. Series A. Watermark: Squares (1924).	25.00	45.00	90.00
	s. Specimen. Red overprint: *PROOV* on both sides.	—	50.00	90.00

		VG	VF	UNC
54	**25 Marka**	VG	VF	UNC
	1922. Lilac on mauve underprint.			
	a. Without serial # prefix letter. Watermark: Horizontal wavy lines.	20.00	50.00	150
	b. Series A. Serial # in red. Waterkmark: Horizontal wavy lines.Different signature (1926).	20.00	50.00	150
	c. Series A. Serial # in red. Watermark: Vertical wavy lines. (1926).	20.00	50.00	150
	d. Series A. Serial # in brown. Watermark: Horizontal wavy lines.	15.00	60.00	180
	s. Specimen. Red overprint: *PROOV* on both sides.	—	70.00	160

Eesti Pangatäht

Estonian Banknote

1919-1921 Issue

		VG	VF	UNC
55	**50 Marka**	VG	VF	UNC
	1919. Brown on olive underprint. Back: Globe at center.			
	a. Watermark: Horizontal light lines.	70.00	150	300
	b. Watermark: Vertical light lines.	70.00	150	300
	s. Specimen. Red overprint: *PROOV* on both sides.	70.00	150	300

		VG	VF	UNC
56	**100 Marka**	VG	VF	UNC
	1921. Brown. 2 blacksmiths at center. Back: Monogram at center.			
	a. Watermark: Horizontal light lines.	100	200	400
	b. Watermark: Vertical light lines.	100	200	400
	s. Specimen. Red overprint: *PROOV* on both sides.	—	200	400
57	**500 Marka**	VG	VF	UNC
	1921. Light green and gray. Ornamental design. Watermark: *EV.*			
	a. Issued note.	500	1,500	3,000
	s. Specimen. Red overprint: *PROOV* on both sides.	500	1,500	3,000

1922-1923 Issue

58 100 Marka

1922. Black on lilac, brown and green underprint. Back: Galleon. Watermark: Light and dark keys.

	VG	VF	UNC
a. Issued note. Serial letter A; B; D or E.	300	500	1,000
s. Specimen. Red overprint: *PROOW* on both sides.	300	500	1,000

59 1000 Marka

ND (1922). Black on lilac and green underprint. Back: Port view of the city of Tallinn (Reval). Watermark: Light and dark keys.

	VG	VF	UNC
a. Without serial letter.	400	700	1,500
b. Serial letter A in black.	400	700	1,500
c. Serial letter B in red.	400	700	1,500
d. Serial letter B in black.	400	700	1,500
e. Serial letter D in blue.	500	800	1,700
f. Serial letters Aa, 1927.	500	800	1,700
s1. Specimen. Red overprint: *PROOV* on both sides.	—	—	1,700
s2. Specimen. Red overprint: *PROOW* on both sides.	—	—	1,700

Numerous partial prints and color trials exist of #59.

60 5000 Marka

1923. Blue, brown and green. Arms at center right. Back: Bank at left center. Watermark: *5000, EV.*

	VG	VF	UNC
a. Issued note.	2,000	3,000	—
s1. Specimen. Red overprint: *PROOV* on both sides.	—	1,300	2,700
s2. Specimen. Red overprint: *PROOW* on back.	—	1,300	2,700
s3. Specimen. Punch hole cancelled.	—	1,300	2,700

Eesti Vabariigi Kassatäht (resumed)

1928 Provisional Issue

61 1 Kroon on 100 Marka

ND. (1928-old date 1923).

	VG	VF	UNC
a. Issued note. Without series.	100	150	300
b. Series A.	100	150	300
s. Specimen. As b. Red overprint: *PROOV* on both sides.	—	90.00	180

Eesti Pank

Bank of Estonia

1928-1935 Issue

62 5 Krooni

1929. Red-brown. Fisherman holding oar at left. Back: Arms at upper left. Watermark: *5* between wavy lines.

	VG	VF	UNC
a. Issued note.	30.00	50.00	80.00
s. Specimen. Red overprint: *PROOV* on both sides.	—	50.00	80.00

63	10 Krooni	VG	VF	UNC
	1928. Blue. Woman in national costume carrying sheaf of wheat and sickle at left. 2 signatures. Back: Arms at upper left. Watermark: *10* between wavy lines.			
	a. Issued note.	30.00	50.00	80.00
	p1. Proof. Uniface face.	—	—	—
	p2. Proof. Uniface back.	—	—	—
	s1. Specimen. Red overprint: *PROOV* on face, large "X" on back.	—	50.00	80.00
	s2. Specimen. Red overprint: *PROOV* on both sides.	—	50.00	80.00
	s3. Specimen. Red overprint: *PROOV* on both sides. Perforated numbers at right end.	—	50.00	80.00

64	20 Krooni	VG	VF	UNC
	1932. Green and brown. Shepherd blowing horn at left. Back: Arms at upper left. Watermark: *20* between zigzag lines.			
	a. Issued note.	25.00	50.00	60.00
	s. Specimen. Red overprint: *PROOV* on both sides.	—	20.00	40.00

65	50 Krooni	VG	VF	UNC
	1929. Brown. Coastline of Rannamoisa at left. Back: Arms at upper left. Watermark: *Eesti Pank* and *L*.			
	a. Issued note.	40.00	80.00	150
	s. Specimen. Red overprint: *PROOV* on both sides.	—	30.00	70.00

Color Abbreviation Guide

New to the *Standard Catalog of® World Paper Money* are the following abbreviations related to color references:

BC: Back color
PC: Paper color

66	100 Krooni	VG	VF	UNC
	1935. Blue. Blacksmith working at an anvil at left. Watermark: *100* surrounded by oak leaves and acorns.			
	a. Issued note.	100	150	300
	s. Specimen. Red overprint: *PROOV* on both sides.	—	100	150

1937 Issue

67	10 Krooni	VG	VF	UNC
	1937. Blue. Like #63, but 3 signatures. Woman in national costume carrying sheaf of wheat and sickle at left. Series A. Back: Arms at upper left.			
	a. Issued note.	15.00	35.00	70.00
	s. Specimen. Red overprint: *PROOV* on both sides.	—	70.00	80.00

1940 Issue

68	10 Krooni	VG	VF	UNC
	1940. (Not issued). Blue. Woman in national costume carrying sheaf of wheat and sickle at left. 3 signatures. Series B. Back: Arms at upper left.			
	a. Finished printing.	—	300	500
	p1. Back printing only. Wide or narrow margins. Full color print.	—	300	500
	p2. Back printing only. Wide or narrow margins. Two color print.	—	300	500
	s. Specimen. Red overprint: *PROOV* on both sides.	—	300	500

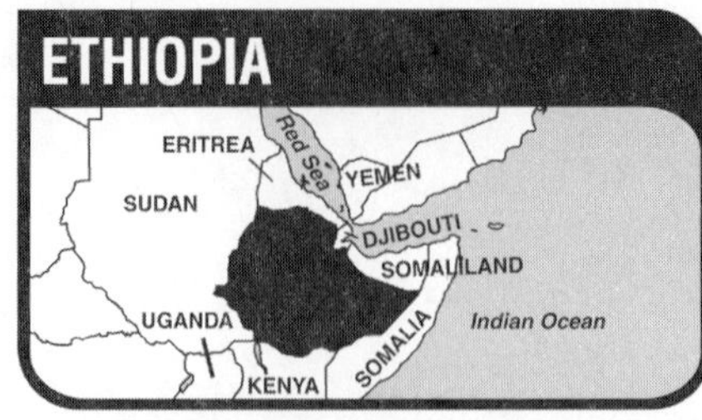

The Federal Republic of Ethiopia is located in east-central Africa. The country has an area of 1.13 million sq. km. and a population of 82.54 million people. Capital: Addis Ababa. The economy is predominantly agricultural and pastoral. Gold and platinum are mined and petroleum fields are being developed. Coffee, oil, seeds, hides and cereals are exported.

Unique among African countries, the ancient Ethiopian monarchy maintained its freedom from colonial rule with the exception of the 1936-41 Italian occupation during World War II. In 1974, a military junta, the Derg, deposed Emperor Haile Selassie (who had ruled since 1930) and established a socialist state. Torn by bloody coups, uprisings, wide-scale drought, and massive refugee problems, the regime was finally toppled in 1991 by a coalition of rebel forces, the Ethiopian People's Revolutionary Democratic Front (EPRDF). A constitution was adopted in 1994, and Ethiopia's first multiparty elections were held in 1995. A border war with Eritrea late in the 1990s ended with a peace treaty in December 2000. The Eritrea-Ethiopia Border Commission in November 2007 remotely demarcated the border by geographical coordinates, but final demarcation of the boundary on the ground is currently on hold because of Ethiopian objections to an international commission's finding requiring it to surrender territory considered sensitive to Ethiopia.

RULERS:

Menelik II, 1889-1913
Lij Yasu, 1913-1916
Zauditu, Empress, 1916-1930
Haile Selassie I, 1930-1936, 1941-1974

MONETARY SYSTEM:

1 Birr = 1 Thaler = 16 Gersh (Piastres) to 1930
1 Birr = 1 Thaler = 100 Matonas, 1931-1935
1 Birr (Dollar) = 100 Santeems (Cents), since 1944

EMPIRE

Bank of Abyssinia

1915 Issue

		VG	VF	UNC
1	**5 Thalers** 1915-1.6.1929. Purple on lilac and light green underprint. Greater Kudu at center. Back: Large value at center. Printer: BWC. 153x83mm.			
	a. Handwritten date. 1915-1926. Rare.	—	—	—
	b. Handstamped date. 1926-1927. Rare.	—	—	—
	c. Printed date. 1.6.1929. Rare.	—	—	—
	s. Specimen.	—	—	1,250

		VG	VF	UNC
2	**10 Thalers** 1915-1.6.1929. Purple on rose and light green underprint. Leopard at center. Back: Value flanking center text. Printer: BWC. 169x88mm.			
	a. Handwritten date. 1915-1926. Rare.	—	—	—
	b. Handstamped date. 1926-1927. Rare.	—	—	—
	c. Printed date. 1.6.1929. Rare.	—	—	—
	s. Specimen.	—	—	1,500

		VG	VF	UNC
3	**50 Thalers** 1915-1.6.1929. Slate blue on multicolor underprint. Lion at center. Back: Large value and ornate design featuring palm. Printer: BWC. 187x87mm.			
	a. Handwritten date. 1915-1926. Rare.	—	—	—
	b. Handstamped date. 1926-1927. Rare.	—	—	—
	c. Printed date. 1.6.1929. Rare.	—	—	—
	s. Specimen.	—	—	2,000

		VG	VF	UNC
4	**100 Thalers** 1915-1.6.1929. Slate blue on rose underprint. Elephant at right. Back: Value at top and bottom of center text. Palm leaf motif. Printer: BWC. 194x102mm.			
	a. Handwritten date. 1915-1926. Rare.	—	—	—
	b. Handstamped date. 1926-1927. Rare.	—	—	—
	c. Printed date. 1.6.1929. Rare.	—	—	—
	s. Specimen.	—	—	2,750

		VG	VF	UNC
5	**500 Thalers** 1915-1.6.1929. Warrior standing at left. Printer: BWC. 153x83mm.			
	a. Handwritten date. 1915-1926. Rare.	—	—	—
	b. Handstamped date. 1926-1927. Rare.	—	—	—
	c. Printed date. 1.6.1929. Rare.	—	—	—
	s. Specimen.	—	—	3,500

Bank of Ethiopia

These notes were recalled by the Italian authorities in 1936.

1932-1933 Issue

#	Denomination	Good	Fine	XF
6	**2 Thalers** 1.6.1933. Dark blue on green and multicolor underprint. Jugate busts of Emperor Haile Selassie and Empress at center. Printer: BWC.	7.50	35.00	120

#	Denomination	Good	Fine	XF
7	**5 Thalers** 1.5.1932; 29.4.1933. Purple on multicolor underprint. Greater Kudu head at center, bank building at left, arms at right. Printer: BWC.	15.00	80.00	325

#	Denomination	Good	Fine	XF
8	**10 Thalers** 1.5.1932; 29.4.1933; 31.5.1935. Blue-green on multicolor underprint. Leopard at center, arms at left, bank building at right. Printer: BWC.	20.00	100	350

#	Denomination	Good	Fine	XF
9	**50 Thalers** 1.5.1932; 29.4.1933. Blue-green on multicolor underprint. Lion at center, bank building at upper left, arms at upper right. Printer: BWC.	40.00	125	400

#	Denomination	Good	Fine	XF
10	**100 Thalers** 1.5.1932; 29.4.1933. Blue on multicolor underprint. Elephant at right, bank building at left, arms at upper left center. Printer: BWC.	50.00	250	600

#	Denomination	Good	Fine	XF
11	**500 Thalers** 1.5.1932; 29.4.1933. Purple on multicolor underprint. Warrior standing at left, arms at top center, bank building at right. Printer: BWC.	250	600	1,500

State Bank of Ethiopia

1945 Issue

#12-17 The notes were originally issued on 23.7.1945, the emperor's birthday.

#	Denomination	VG	VF	UNC
12	**1 Dollar** ND (1945). Black on orange underprint. Emperor Haile Selassie at left. Farmer plowing with oxen at center. Back: Arms at center. Printer: SBNC.			
	a. Signature 1. Blowers.	4.00	25.00	100
	b. Signature 2. Bennett.	3.00	17.50	65.00
	c. Signature 3. Rozell.	3.00	12.50	45.00
	p. Proof. Uniface back.	—	—	—
	s1. Specimen. Paper with planchets.	—	—	300
	s2. Specimen. Paper without planchets.	—	—	300

13	5 Dollars	VG	VF	UNC
	ND (1945). Black and lilac on orange underprint. Emperor Haile Selassie at left. Acacia tree with beehives at center right. Back: Arms at center. Printer: SBNC.			
	a. Signature 1. Blowers.	7.50	50.00	300
	b. Signature 2. Bennett.	5.00	40.00	175
	c. Signature 3. Rozell.	3.50	30.00	125
	s1. Specimen. Paper with planchets.	—	—	250
	s2. Specimen. Paper without planchets.	—	—	250

14	10 Dollars	VG	VF	UNC
	ND (1945). Black on orange and blue underprint. St. George's Square with equestrian monument to Menelik II with domed building in background at center. Emperor Haile Selassie at left. Back: Arms at center. Printer: SBNC.			
	a. Signature 1. Blowers.	25.00	100	400
	b. Signature 2. Bennett.	15.00	80.00	250
	c. Signature 3. Rozell.	10.00	50.00	175
	s. Specimen.	—	—	375

15	50 Dollars	VG	VF	UNC
	ND (1945). Black on green and yellow underprint. Parliament building at center. Emperor Haile Selassie at left. Back: Arms at center. Printer: SBNC.			
	a. Signature 1. Blowers.	40.00	200	900
	b. Signature 2. Bennett.	30.00	150	550
	c. Signature 3. Rozell.	25.00	125	350
	s. Specimen.	—	—	725

16	100 Dollars	VG	VF	UNC
	ND (1945). Black on green underprint. Imperial Palace of Haile Selassie I (now a university) at center. Back: Arms at center. Printer: SBNC.			
	a. Signature 1. Blowers.	75.00	350	1,200
	b. Signature 2. Bennett.	50.00	250	750
	c. Signature 3. Rozell.	35.00	175	450
	p. Proof. Uniface back.	—	—	—
	s1. Specimen. Paper with planchets.	—	—	900
	s2. Specimen. Paper without planchets.	—	—	900

17	500 Dollars	VG	VF	UNC
	ND (1945). Black on yellow and olive underprint. Holy Trinity Church in Addis Ababa at center. Emperor Haile Selassie at left. Back: Arms at center. Printer: SBNC.			
	a. Signature 1. Blowers.	300	700	2,000
	b. Signature 2. Bennett.	225	500	1,100
	c. Signature 3. Rozell.	150	350	750
	s1. Specimen. Paper with planchets.	—	—	1,250
	s2. Specimen. Paper without planchets.	—	—	1,250

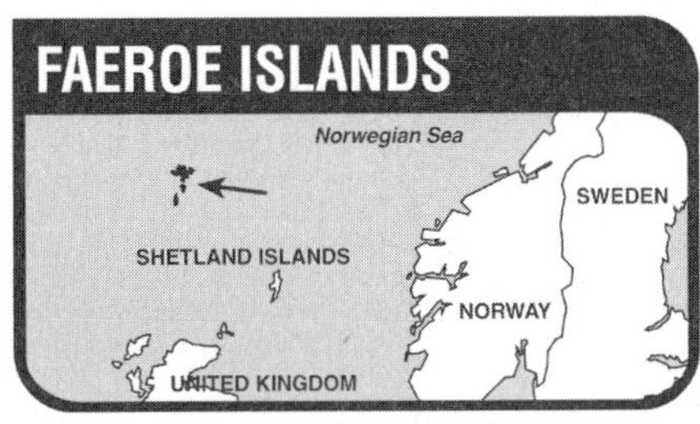

The Faeroe, a self-governing community within the kingdom of Denmark, are situated in the North Atlantic between Iceland and the Shetland Islands. The 17 inhabited islets and reefs have an area of 1,399 sq. km. and a population of 46,668. Capital: Thorshavn. The principal industries are fishing and grazing. Fish and fish products are exported.

The population of the Faeroe Islands is largely descended from Viking settlers who arrived in the 9th century. The islands have been connected politically to Denmark since the 14th century. A high degree of self government was attained in 1948.

RULERS:

Danish

MONETARY SYSTEM:

1 Króne = 100 re

DANISH ADMINISTRATION

Government

1809-1812 Emergency Issue

A1, A2 and A10 not assigned.

A3	**3 Skilling**	Good	Fine	XF
	1809. Handwritten on oval card stock or paper. Uniface. Printer: Thorshavn.	—	—	—
A4	**4 Skilling**	Good	Fine	XF
	1809 Handwritten on oval card stock or paper. Uniface. Printer: Thorshavn.	—	—	—
A5	**5 Skilling**	Good	Fine	XF
	1812 Handwritten on oval card stock or paper. Uniface. Printer: Thorshavn.	—	—	—
A6	**6 Skilling**	Good	Fine	XF
	1809 Handwritten on oval card stock or paper. Uniface. Printer: Thorshavn.	—	—	—
A9	**5 Mark**	Good	Fine	XF
	1810 Handwritten on oval card stock or paper. Uniface. Printer: Thorshavn.	—	—	—

1815 Provisional Issue

#A11 reissue of Danish Rigsbanken i Kibenhavn notes dated 1814.

A11	**1 Rigsbankdaler**	Good	Fine	XF
	15.4.1815 (-old date 1814). Printed on back of Denmark #A48.	—	—	—

Note: For similar provisional issues refer to Danish West Indies and Iceland listings.

Faerø Amt

1940 WWII Provisional Issue

1	**5 Kroner**	Good	Fine	XF
	June 1940. Blue-green. Printed signature: Hilbert. Overprint: red:*KUN GYLDIG PAA FAERØERNE FAERØ AMT JUNI 1940.*			
	a. Overprint on Denmark #30b.	600	1,000	—
	b. Overprint on Denmark #30c.	—	700	1,200

2	**10 Kroner**	VG	VF	UNC
	June 1940. Brown. Handwritten signature: Hilbert. Serial # M9627001-M9627500.	—	120	280

Note: #2 is rarely seen below XF.

3	**10 Kroner**	Good	Fine	XF
	June 1940. Brown. Printed signature: Hilbert. Overprint: Red:*KUN GYLDIG PAA FAERØERNE FAERØ AMT JUNI 1940.*			
	a. Overprint on Denmark #21.	3,250	—	—
	b. Overprint on Denmark #26.	1,000	2,000	—
	c. Overprint on Denmark #31a or #31b.	500	1,500	—
	d. Overprint on Denmark #31c.	100	275	—
4	**50 Kroner**	Good	Fine	XF
	June 1940. Blue. Printed signature: Hilbert. Overprint: Red: *KUN GYLDIG PAA FAERØERNE FAERØ AMT JUNI 1940.*			
	a. Overprint on Denmark #22.	12,000	20,000	—
	b. Overprint on Denmark #32.	4,000	9,000	—
5	**100 Kroner**	Good	Fine	XF
	June 1940. Brown. Printed signature: Hilbert. Overprint: Red: *KUN GYLDIG PAA FAERØERNE FAERØ AMT JUNI 1940.*			
	a. Overprint on Denmark #23.	10,000	—	—
	b. Overprint on Denmark #28.	8,000	—	—
	c. Overprint on Denmark #33a.	5,000	8,000	—
6	**500 Kroner**	Good	Fine	XF
	June 1940. Rare. Gray-blue. Printed signature of *HILBERT.* Overprint: red: *KUN GYLDIG PAA FAERØERNE FAERØ AMT JUNI 1940* on Denmark #29.	—	—	—

Faerøerne

1940 First Emergency Issue

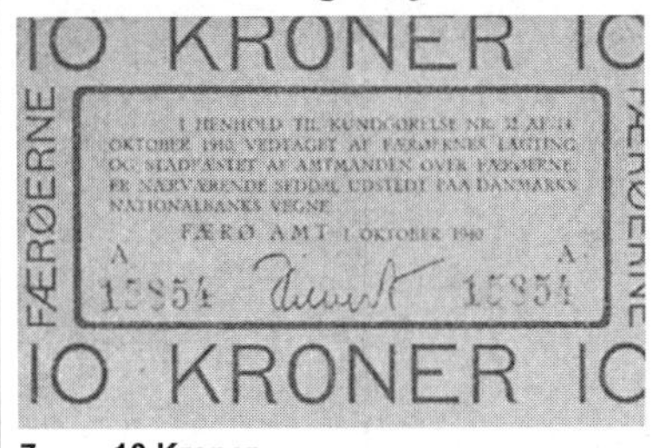

7	**10 Kroner**	Good	Fine	XF
	1.10.1940. Brown on light brown underprint. Serial # prefix A-L. Printer: H.N. Jacobsen, Thorshavn.	500	1,100	2,300
8	**100 Kroner**	Good	Fine	XF
	1.10.1940. Dark gray-green on red-brown underprint. Ram's head at upper right. Printer: H.N. Jacobsen, Thorshavn.	2,500	4,500	9,000

1940 Second Emergency Issue

9	**1 Krone**	VG	VF	UNC
	Nov. 1940. Blue on lilac and light red underprint. Serial # suffix A.	10.00	35.00	200

10	**5 Kroner**	VG	VF	UNC
	Nov. 1940. Green and blue-green. Serial # suffix B.	—	275	1,000
11	**10 Kroner**	VG	VF	UNC
	Nov. 1940. Like #10. Brown on lilac and green underprint.			
	a. Serial # suffix C.	25.00	100	600
	b. Serial # suffix G.	50.00	200	850
12	**100 Kroner**	VG	VF	UNC
	Nov. 1940. Like #10. Green and brown. Serial # suffix D.			
	a. Issued note.	800	3,000	6,500
	s. Specimen. Perforated.	—	—	4,500

Føroyar

1951-1954 Issue

Law of 12.4.1949

13	**5 Krónur**	VG	VF	UNC
	L.1949 (1951-1960). Black on green underprint. Coin with ram at left. Back: Fishermen with boat.			
	a. Signature C. A. Vagn-Hansen and Kr. Djurhuus.	60.00	150	700
	b. Signature N. Elkaer-Hansen and Kr. Djurhuus.	35.00	90.00	425

14	10 Krónur	VG	VF	UNC
	L.1949 (1954). Black on orange underprint. Shield with ram at left. Back: Rural scene.			
	a. Signature C. A. Vagn-Hansen and Kr. Djurhuus. Watermark: *10*. 10.5mm.	20.00	40.00	180
	b. As a. but 13mm watermark.	15.00	35.00	150
	c. Signature M. Wahl and P. M. Dam. Watermark: *10*. 13mm.	7.00	16.00	30.00
	d. Signature M. Wahl and A. P. Dam.	5.00	8.00	16.00

15	100 Krónur	VG	VF	UNC
	L.1949 (1952-1963). Blue-green. Irregular margins at left and right. (straight margins are trimmed). Back: Porpoises.			
	a. Signature C. A. Vagn-Hansen and Kr. Djurhuus.	150	400	850
	b. Signature N. Elkaer-Hansen and Kr. Djurhuus.	125	350	750
	c. Signature M. Wahl and P. M. Dam.	200	500	1,000

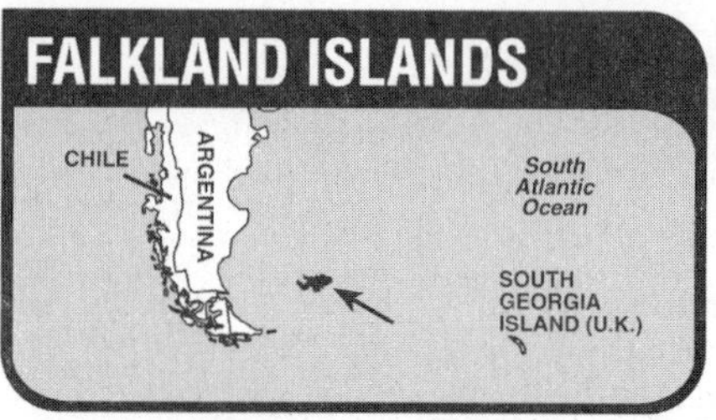

The Colony of the Falkland Islands and Dependencies, a British colony located in the South Atlantic about 500 miles northeast of Cape Horn, has an area of 12,173 sq. km. and a population of 3,140. East Falkland, West Falkland, South Georgia, and South Sandwich are the largest of the 200 islands. Capital: Port Stanley. Fishing and sheep are the industry. Wool, whale oil, and seal oil are exported.

Although first sighted by an English navigator in 1592, the first landing was by the English almost a century later in 1690, and the first settlement was by the French in 1764. The colony was turned over to Spain two years later and the islands have since been the subject of a territorial dispute, first between Britain and Spain, then between Britain and Argentina. The UK asserted its claim to the islands by establishing a naval garrison there in 1833. The Islands were important in the days of sail and steam shipping as a location to re-stock fresh food and fuel, and make repairs after trips around Cape Horn. In April 1982 Argentine forces invaded and after a short military campaign Britain regained control in June 1982. In 1990 the Argentine congress declared the Falklands and Dependencies as the province Tierra del Fuego.

RULERS:
British

MONETARY SYSTEM:
1 Shilling = 12 Pence
1 Pound = 20 Shillings to 1966
1 Pound = 100 Pence, 1966-

BRITISH ADMINISTRATION

Government of the Falkland Islands

1899-1905 Issue

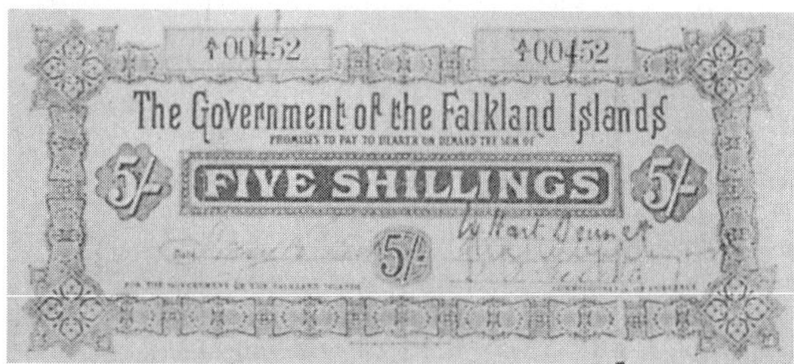

A1	5 Shillings	Good	Fine	XF
	12.1.1901; 15.1.1901. Green on pink underprint. Uniface. Printer: TDLR.	—	—	—
A1A	**5 Shillings**	**Good**	**Fine**	**XF**
	1.2.1905; 12.10.1908; 27.11.1916. Like #A1. Brown on pink underprint. Uniface. Printer: TDLR.	1,000	2,750	—
A2	**10 Shillings**	**Good**	**Fine**	**XF**
	Like #A1. Requires confirmation. Green on pink underprint. Uniface. Printer: TDLR.	—	—	—

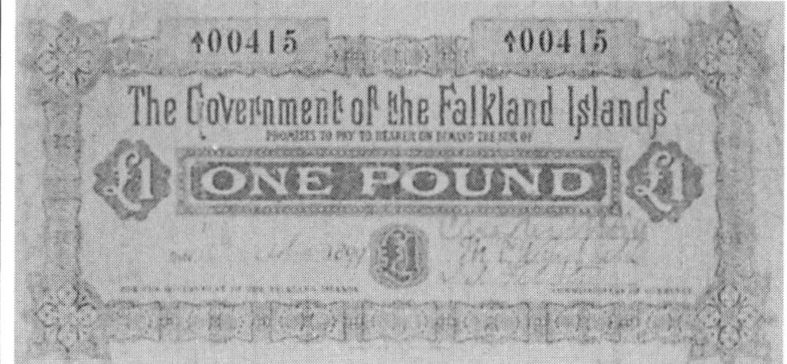

A3	1 Pound	Good	Fine	XF
	16.10.1899; 28.8.1915. Blue on pink underprint. Uniface. Printer: TDLR.	1,750	4,000	—
A4	**5 Pounds**	**Good**	**Fine**	**XF**
	ND. Like #A3. Red on gray underprint. Color trial. Uniface. Printer: TDLR. Rare.	—	—	—

1921 Issue

		Good	Fine	XF
1	**10 Shillings** 1921-1932. Brown on gray underprint. Portrait King George V at right. Printer: TDLR.			
	a. 2 signatures. 1.2.1921; 10.1.1927.	550	2,000	—
	b. 1 signature. 10.2.1932.	400	1,500	—

		Good	Fine	XF
2	**1 Pound** 1921-1932. Blue on green underprint. Portrait King George V at right. Printer: TDLR.			
	a. 2 signatures. 1.2.1921; 10.1.1927.	800	2,500	—
	b. 1 signature. 10.2.1932.	600	1,500	—

		Good	Fine	XF
3	**5 Pounds** 1.2.1921; 10.2.1932. Red on green underprint. Portrait King George V at right. Printer: TDLR. Rare.	—	—	—

1938-1951 Issue

		VG	VF	UNC
4	**10 Shillings** 19.5.1938. Brown on gray underprint. Portrait King George VI at right. Printer: TDLR.	12.50	70.00	200

		VG	VF	UNC
5	**1 Pound** 19.5.1938. Blue on green and lilac underprint. Portrait King George VI at right. Printer: TDLR.	15.00	100	425

		VG	VF	UNC
6	**5 Pounds** 20.2.1951. Red on green, blue and light tan underprint. Portrait King George VI at right. Printer: TDLR.	65.00	250	900

1960-1967 Issue

		VG	VF	UNC
7	**10 Shillings** 10.4.1960. Brown on gray underprint. Portrait of Queen Elizabeth II at right. Printer: TDLR.			
	a. Issued note.	70.00	300	900
	s. Specimen.	—	—	850

		VG	VF	UNC
9	**5 Pounds** 1960; 1975. Red on green underprint. Portrait of Queen Elizabeth II at right. Printer: TDLR.			
	a. Signature L. Gleadel. 10.4.1960.	60.00	250	1,000
	b. Signature H. T. Rowlands. 30.1.1975.	50.00	200	900
	s. Specimen. As a, b.	—	—	1,075

Color Abbreviation Guide

New to the *Standard Catalog of® World Paper Money* are the following abbreviations related to color references:

BC: Back color
PC: Paper color

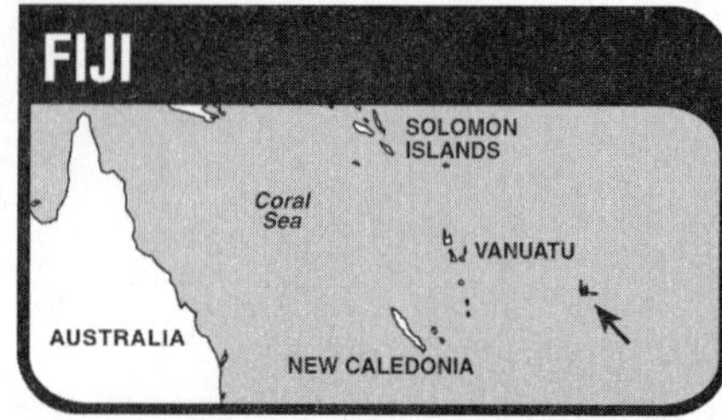

The republic of Fiji consists of about 320 islands located in the southwestern Pacific 1,770 km. north of New Zealand. The islands have a combined area of 18,270 sq. km. and a population of 931,750. Capital: Suva, on the island of Viti Levu. Fiji's economy is based on agriculture, tourism and mining. Sugar, fish, timber, coconut products, and gold are exported.

Fiji became independent in 1970, after nearly a century as a British colony. Democratic rule was interrupted by two military coups in 1987, caused by concern over a government perceived as dominated by the Indian community (descendants of contract laborers brought to the islands by the British in the 19th century). The coups and a 1990 constitution that cemented native Melanesian control of Fiji, led to heavy Indian emigration; the population loss resulted in economic difficulties, but ensured that Melanesians became the majority. A new constitution enacted in 1997 was more equitable. Free and peaceful elections in 1999 resulted in a government led by an Indo-Fijian, but a civilian-led coup in May 2000 ushered in a prolonged period of political turmoil. Parliamentary elections held in August 2001 provided Fiji with a democratically elected government led by Prime Minister Laisenia Qarase. Re-elected in May 2006, Qarase was ousted in a December 2006 military coup led by Commodore Voreqe Bainimarama, who initially appointed himself acting president. In January 2007, Bainimarama was appointed interim prime minister. In September 2009 Fiji was suspended from the British Commonwealth.

RULERS:

Thakombau (Cakobau), until 1874
British, 1874-1970.

MONETARY SYSTEM:

1 Dollar = 100 Cents, 1871-1873
1 Shilling = 12 Pence
1 Pound = 20 Shillings to 1969
1 Dollar = 100 Cents, 1969-

REPLACEMENT NOTES:

#64-85: Z/1 prefix; #96-108: Z prefix; #109-114: ZA prefix.

KINGDOM

C.R. - Cakobau Rex

1871 Treasury Note Issue

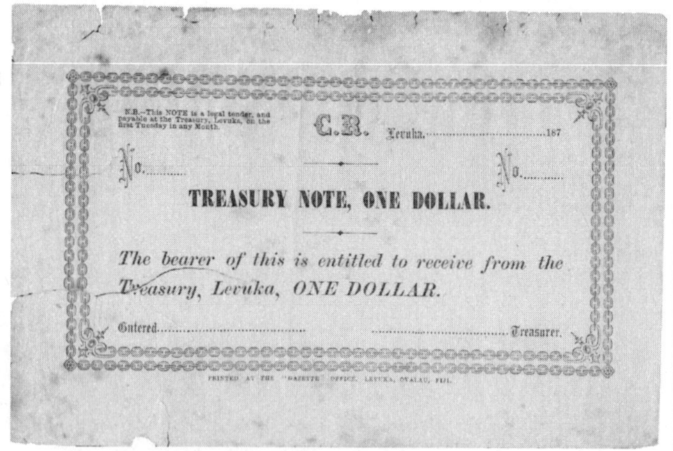

#		Good	Fine	XF
1	**1 Dollar** 1871. Black on buff paper. C.R. top center. Handwritten dates and serial #. Handsigned. Uniface. Double chain border. Printer: Gazette Office, Levuka, Ovalau, Fiji.			
	a. Signature: S.C. Burt.	1,500	3,000	6,500
	b. Signature: F.W. Hennings.	1,200	2,000	4,000
	r. Unissued remainder.	750	1,000	2,500

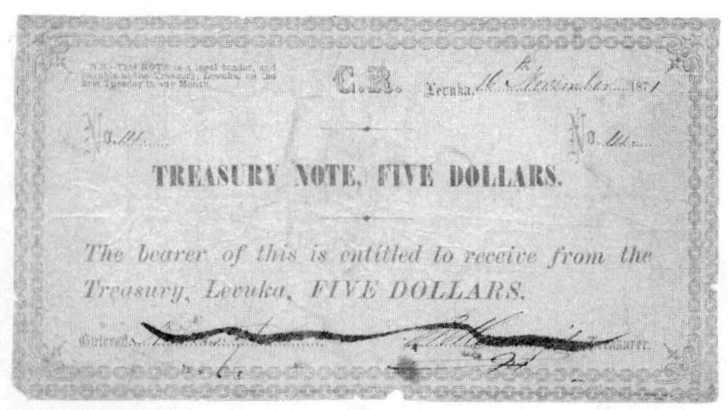

#		Good	Fine	XF
2	**5 Dollars** 1871. Brown on buff paper. C.R. top center. Handwritten dates and serial #. Handsigned. Uniface. Double chain border. Printer: Gazette Office, Levuka, Ovalau, Fiji.			
	a. Signature: S.C. Burt.	1,000	3,000	7,500
	b. Signature: F.W. Hennings.	800	2,500	5,000
	r. Unissued remainder.	600	1,250	2,500
3	**10 Dollars** 1871. C.R. top center. Handwritten dates and serial #. Handsigned. Uniface. Double chain border. Printer: Gazette Office, Levuka, Ovalau, Fiji.			
	a. Signature: S.C. Burt.	1,850	5,000	10,000
	b. Signature: F. W. Hennings.	1,250	3,000	8,000
	r. Unissued remainder.	1,000	1,750	6,000

1871 Government Debentures

Public Loans Act 1871

#		Good	Fine	XF
4	**5 Dollars** 1871-1872. Black on buff paper. Arms at top center, handwritten dates, handsigned. Uniface. Printer: Gazette Office, Levuka, Ovalau, Fiji.			
	a. Signature F.W. Hennings.	150	450	1,000
	b. Signature Smith or Clarkson.	185	650	1,500
	c. *FIVE* altered to *TEN* by hand.	500	1,000	3,000
	r. Unissued remainder.	125	475	1,000

#		Good	Fine	XF
5	**10 Dollars** 1871-1873. Black on buff paper. Arms at top center, handwritten dates, handsigned. Uniface. Value entered by hand. Printer: Gazette Office, Levuka, Ovalau, Fiji.			
	a. Without *No.* at top right. Signature: F.W. Hennings.	100	200	800
	b. With *No.* at top right. Signature: F.W. Hennings.	125	250	900
	c. Without *No.* at top right. Signature: Smith or Clarkson.	150	350	1,000
	d. With *No.* at top right. Signature: Smith or Clarkson.	175	400	1,100
	r. Unissued remainder.	125	300	850
6	**10 Dollars** 1871-1873. Black on buff paper. Arms at top center, handwritten dates, handsigned. Uniface. Value printed. Printer: Gazette Office, Levuka, Ovalau, Fiji.			
	a. Signature: F.W. Hennings.	135	250	900
	b. Signature: Smith or Clarkson.	175	450	1,200
	c. Unissued remainder.	140	400	950

1872-1873 Vakacavacava Fractional Tax Notes

#7-13 Spurious signatures exist - e.g. "Page."

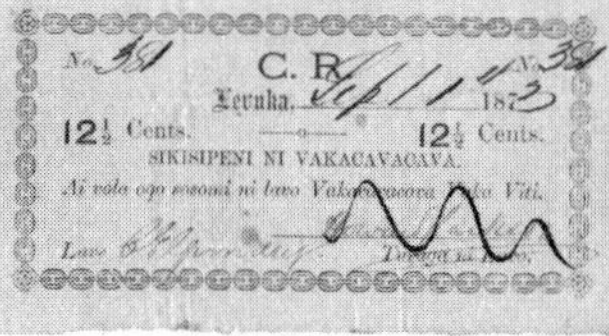

#		Good	Fine	XF
7	**12 1/2 Cents** 1872-1873. Blue. C.R. top center, handwritten dates and serial #. Handsigned (Lave). Single chain border. Uniface. Printer: Gazette Office, Levuka, Ovalau.			
	a. Issued note.	100	300	800
	b. Cancelled note.	75.00	200	425
	r. Unissued remainder.	175	275	—

		Good	Fine	XF
8	**25 Cents** 1872-1873. Black on dark blue paper. C.R. top center, handwritten dates and serial #. Handsigned (Lave). Single chain border. Uniface. Printer: Gazette Office, Levuka, Ovalau.			
	a. Issued note.	300	—	—
	b. Cancelled note.	125	400	—
	r. Unissued remainder.	200	300	—

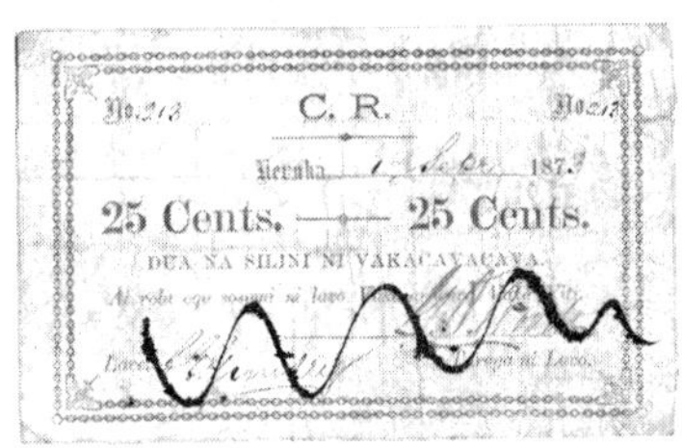

		Good	Fine	XF
9	**25 Cents** 1872-1873. Red. C.R. top center, handwritten dates and serial #. Handsigned (Lave). Double chain border. Uniface. Printer: Gazette Office, Lavuka, Ovalau.			
	a. Issued note.	200	550	1,000
	b. Cancelled note.	90.00	200	450
	r. Unissued remainder.	175	300	—
10	**50 Cents** 1872-1873. Black. C.R. top center, handwritten dates and serial #. Handsigned (Lave). Single chain border. Uniface. Printer: Gazette Office, Levuka, Ovalau.	Good	Fine	XF
	a. Issued note.	350	1,000	1,500
	b. Cancelled note.	275	750	1,000
	r. Unissued remainder.	250	400	800

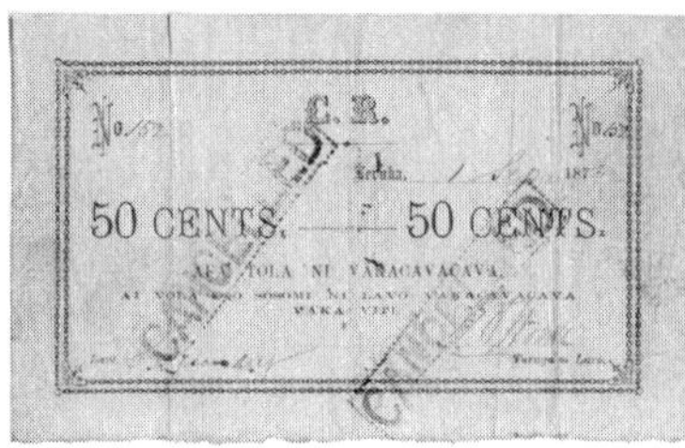

		Good	Fine	XF
11	**50 Cents** 1872-1873. Green. C.R. top center, handwritten dates and serial #. Handsigned (Lave). Double chain border. Uniface. Printer: Gazette Office, Levuka, Ovalau.			
	a. Issued note.	300	750	1,250
	b. Cancelled note.	200	600	950
	r. Unissued note.	225	350	1,000

		Good	Fine	XF
12	**100 Cents** 1872. Brown. C.R. top center, handwritten dates and serial #. Handsigned (Lave). Single chain border. Uniface. Printer: Gazette Office, Levuka, Ovalau.			
	a. Issued note.	750	1,250	2,000
	b. Cancelled note.	500	1,000	1,500
	r. Unissued remainder.	700	1,000	1,750
13	**100 Cents** 1872-1873. C.R. top center, handwritten dates and serial #. Handsigned (Lave). Double chain border. Uniface. Printer: Gazette Office, Levuka, Ovalau.	Good	Fine	XF
	a. Issued note.	950	1,750	3,000
	b. Cancelled note.	750	1,250	2,000
	r. Unissued note.	600	850	1,250

1872 Treasury Note Issue

#14-18 Spurious signatures exist - e.g."Page." Most available notes are cancelled by handstamp or by pen through signature.

		Good	Fine	XF
14	**1 Dollar** 1872-1873. Various dates. Black on off-white paper. C.R. monogram at top center, arms below, engraved, various handwritten dates and serial #, handsigned (Treasurer). Handstamped: *CANCELLED.* Printer: S.T. Leigh & Co., Sydney.			
	a. Signature: J.C. Smith.	600	1,200	1,800
	b. Signature: Howard Clarkson.	450	1,000	1,650
	c. Signature: G.A. Woods.	700	1,250	1,900
	d. Uncancelled note.	900	1,350	2,000
	r. Unissued remainder.	450	950	1,450

		Good	Fine	XF
15	**5 Dollars** 1872-1873. Mauve on off-white paper. C.R. monogram at top center, arms below, engraved, various handwritten dates and serial #, handsigned (Treasurer). Printer: S.T. Leigh & Co., Sydney.			
	a. Signature: J.C. Smith.	700	1,250	2,100
	b. Signature: Howard Clarkson.	525	1,100	1,900
	c. Signature: G.A. Woods.	850	1,400	2,250
	d. Uncancelled note.	1,000	1,600	2,750
	r. Unissued remainder.	600	1,200	2,000

		Good	Fine	XF
16	**10 Dollars** 1872-1873. Brown on off-white paper. C.R. monogram at top center, arms below, engraved, various handwritten dates and serial #, handsigned (Treasurer). Printer: S.T. Leigh & Co., Sydney.			
	a. Signature: J.C. Smith.	400	900	1,500
	b. Signature: Howard Clarkson.	325	700	1,250
	c. Signature: G.A. Woods.	500	1,000	1,750
	d. Uncancelled note.	650	1,200	1,950
	r. Unissued remainder.	400	900	1,600

17	25 Dollars	Good	Fine	XF
	1872-1873. Blue on off-white paper. C.R. monogram at top center, arms below, engraved, various handwritten dates and serial #, handsigned (Treasurer). Printer: S.T. Leigh & Co., Sydney.			
	a. Signature: J.C. Smith.	900	1,400	2,800
	b. Signature: Howard Clarkson.	500	1,000	2,200
	c. Signature: G.A. Woods.	700	1,300	2,500
	d. Uncancelled note.	1,000	1,600	3,000
	r. Unissued remainder.	700	1,250	2,000

18	50 Dollars	Good	Fine	XF
	1872-1873. Pink on off-white paper. C.R. monogram at top center, arms below, engraved, various handwritten dates and serial #, handsigned (Treasurer). Printer: S.T. Leigh & Co., Sydney.			
	a. Signature: J.C. Smith.	450	950	1,750
	b. Signature: Howard Clarkson.	350	800	1,400
	c. Signature: G.A. Woods.	525	1,100	1,600
	d. Uncancelled note.	650	1,200	1,900
	r. Unissued remainder.	450	950	1,500

Fiji Banking & Commercial Company

1873 Issue

19	5 Shillings	Good	Fine	XF
	1873. Green and black. Printer: Schmidt & Co., Auckland, New Zealand.			
	a. Issued note. Rare.	—	—	—
	r. Unissued remainder.	—	850	1,650
20	10 Shillings	Good	Fine	XF
	1873. Green and black. Printer: Schmidt & Co., Auckland, New Zealand.			
	a. Issued note. Rare.	—	—	—
	r. Unissued remainder.	—	—	—
21	1 Pound	Good	Fine	XF
	1873. Black. Printer: Schmidt & Co., Auckland, New Zealand.			
	a. Issued note. Rare.	—	—	—
	r. Unissued remainder.	—	500	1,600
22	5 Pounds	Good	Fine	XF
	1873. Blue and black. Printer: Schmidt & Co., Auckland, New Zealand.			
	a. Issued note. Rare.	—	—	—
	r. Unissued remainder.	—	—	1,750
23	10 Pounds	Good	Fine	XF
	1873. Maroon and black. Printer: Schmidt & Co., Auckland, New Zealand.			
	a. Issued note. Rare.	—	—	—
	r. Unissued remainder.	—	500	1,900

Ad-Interim Administration

1874 Certificate of Indebtedness

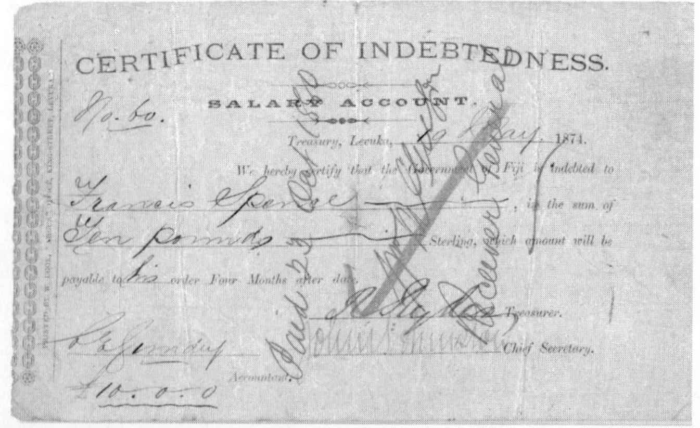
CERTIFICATE OF INDEBTEDNESS.
SALARY ACCOUNT.
No. 60.
Treasury, Levuka, 1874.
We hereby certify that the Government of Fiji is indebted to Francis Spence, in the sum of Ten Pounds Sterling, which amount will be payable to his order Four Months after date.
Treasurer.
Chief Secretary.
Accountant.
£10.0.0

24		Good	Fine	XF
	1874. Various handwritten denominations. Grey or green on white laid paper. Various dates.			
	a. Issued note. Currency of forty days.	250	450	950
	b. As a. Cancelled issue.	125	200	550
	c. Issued note. Currency of four months.	200	400	750
	d. As c. Cancelled issue.	150	250	400
	e. Issued note. Currency of six months.	250	450	1,000
	f. As e. Cancelled issue.	150	275	700
	g. Issued note. Currency of twelve months.	300	500	1,250
	h. As g. Cancelled issue.	175	300	750
	r1. As a. Unissued remainder.	135	250	500
	r2. As c. Unissued remainder.	125	200	400
	r3. As e. Unissued remainder.	150	300	800
	r4. As g. Unissued remainder.	200	400	700

BRITISH ADMINISTRATION

Fiji Government

1914-1933 Issue

25	5 Shillings	Good	Fine	XF
	1918-1933. Green on brown underprint. Arms at top center. Uniface. Printer: TDLR.			
	a. 1.1.1920. Signature Rankine, Brabant, Marks.	250	900	3,000
	b. 1.8.1920. Signature Fell, Brabant, Marks.	250	900	3,000
	c. 1.9.1920. Signature Fell, Brabant, Marks.	200	800	2,750
	d. 4.2.1923.	250	850	3,000
	e. 10.11.1924. Signature Stewart, Rushton, Marks.	175	800	2,750
	f. 5.12.1925. Signature Stewart, Rushton, Marks.	175	800	2,750
	g. 1.1.1926. Signature Stewart, Rushton, Marks.	175	800	2,750
	h. 1.12.1926. Signature Stewart, Rushton, Marks.	175	800	2,750
	i. 4.2.1928. Signature McOwan, Harcourt, Marks.	175	800	2,750
	j. 1.7.1929. Signature Rushton, Harcourt, Marks.	175	800	2,750
	k. 14.7.1932. Seymour, Craig, Boyd.	150	750	2,500
	l. 23.9.1932. Signature Seymour, Craig, Boyd.	150	750	2,500
	m. 31.10.1932. Signature Seymour, Craig, Boyd.	150	750	2,500
	n. 14.9.1933. Signature Seymour, Chamberlain, Boyd.	150	750	2,500
	o. 9.11.1933. Signature Seymour, Chamberlain, Boyd.	150	750	2,500
	r. Unissued remainder.	400	900	3,500
	s. Specimen. Various dates.	500	1,100	4,000

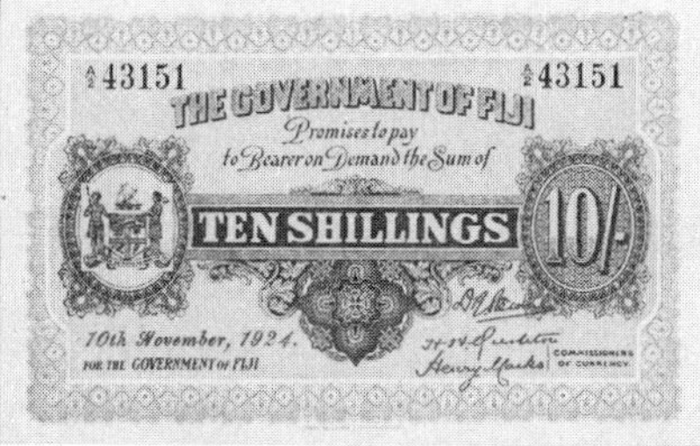

26	10 Shillings	Good	Fine	XF
	1918-1933. Blue on green underprint. Arms at left. Uniface. Printer: TDLR.			
	a. 29.10.1918. Signature Rushton, Rankine, Marks.	750	3,000	—
	b. 1.1.1920. Signature Rankine, Brabant, Marks.	750	3,000	—
	c. 1.8.1920. Signature Fell, Brabant, Marks.	750	3,000	—
	d. 10.11.1924. Signature Stewart, Rushton, Marks.	750	3,000	—
	e. 5.12.1925. Signature Stewart, Rushton, Marks.	750	5,000	3,000
	f. 1.1.1926. Signature Stewart, Rushton, Marks.	750	3,000	—
	g. 4.2.1928. Signature McOwan, Harcourt, Marks.	750	3,000	—
	h. 14.7.1932. Signature Seymour, Craig, Boyd.	750	3,000	—
	i. 23.9.1932.	900	4,000	—
	j. 8.12.1933. Signature Seymour, Chamberlain, Boyd.	750	3,000	—
	r. Unsigned remainder.	1,000	7,500	10,000
	s. Specimen. Various dates.	700	5,000	7,000

27	1 Pound	Good	Fine	XF
	1914-1930. Green on pink underprint. Arms at center. Uniface. Printer: TDLR.			
	a. 4.12.1914. Signature Hutson, Rankine, Marks.	750	2,000	—
	b. 1.3.1917. Signature Hutson, Montgomerie, Marks.	450	1,750	6,000
	c. 1.1.1920. Signature Rankine, Brabant, Marks.	450	1,750	5,000
	d. 5.12.1925. Signature Stewart, Rushton, Marks.	450	1,700	5,000
	e. 20.8.1926. Signature McOwan, Rushton, Marks.	450	1,650	5,000
	f. 4.2.1928. Signature McOwan, Harcourt, Marks.	450	1,650	5,000
	g. 21.12.1930. Signature Seymour, Rushton, Marks.	450	1,650	4,500
	r. Unsigned remainder.	750	2,000	7,000
	s. Specimen. Various dates.	650	1,900	6,000

28	5 Pounds	Good	Fine	XF
	1914-1930. Mulberry on orange underprint. Arms at center. Uniface. Printer: TDLR.			
	a. 4.12.1914. Signature Hutson, Rankine, Marks.	1,000	—	—
	b. 1.3.1917. Signature Hutson, Montgomerie, Marks.	750	—	—
	c. 20.8.1926. Signature McOwan, Rushton, Marks.	750	—	—
	d. 4.2.1928. Signature McOwan, Harcourt, Marks.	750	—	—
	r. Unsigned remainder.	1,000	—	—
	s. Specimen.	900	1,750	7,000

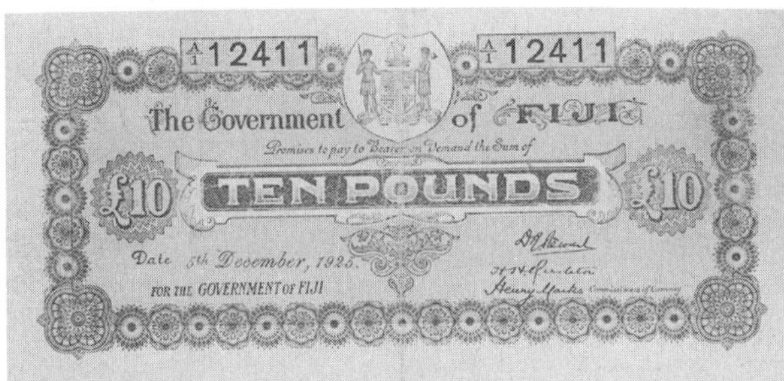

29	10 Pounds	Good	Fine	XF
	1914-1928. Blue on grey underprint. Arms at center. Uniface. Printer: TDLR.			
	a. 4.12.1914. Signature Hutson, Rankine, Marks.	2,000	—	—
	b. 1.3.1917. Signature Hutson, Montgomerie, Marks.	1,000	—	—
	c. 5.12.1925. Signature Stewart, Rushton, Marks.	1,000	—	—
	d. 20.8.1926. Signature McOwan, Rushton, Marks.	1,000	—	—
	e. 4.2.1928. Signature McOwan, Harcourt, Marks.	1,000	—	—
	r. Unissued remainder.	1,400	—	—
	s. Specimen. Various dates.	1,200	2,750	8,500

30	20 Pounds	Good	Fine	XF
	1914-1928. Arms at center. Uniface. Printer: TDLR.			
	a. 4.12.1914. Signature Hutson, Rankine, Marks.	3,000	—	—
	b. 1.3.1917. Signature Hutson, Montgomerie, Marks.	1,300	—	—
	c. 20.8.1926. Signature McOwan, Rushton, Marks.	1,300	—	—
	r. Unissued remainder.	1,750	—	—
	s. Specimen. Various dates.	1,500	3,500	10,000

1934 Issue

31	5 Shillings	Good	Fine	XF
	1934-1935 Blue on blue and brown underprint. Portrait King George V at right, arms at top center. Printer: BWC.			
	a. 1.1.1934. Signature Seymour, Chamberlain, Boyd.	200	700	1,500
	b. 1.6.1934. Signature Wright, Craig, Boyd.	200	700	1,500
	c. 1.3.1935. Signature Wright, Craig, Boyd.	200	700	1,500
	s. Specimen. Various dates.	450	900	1,900
	cs. Commercial (false color) specimen.	300	800	1,600

32	10 Shillings	Good	Fine	XF
	1934-1935. Brown on blue underprint. Portrait King George V at right, arms at top center. Printer: BWC.			
	a. 1.1.1934. Signature Seymour, Chamberlain, Boyd.	750	2,000	5,500
	b. 1.6.1934. Signature Wright, Craig, Boyd.	750	2,000	5,500
	c. 1.3.1935. Signature Wright, Craig, Boyd.	750	2,000	5,500
	s. Specimen. Various dates.	—	2,500	6,500
	cs. Commercial (false color) specimen.	—	1,850	4,000

33	1 Pound	Good	Fine	XF
	1934-1935. Green on pink underprint. Portrait King George V at right, arms at top center. Printer: BWC.			
	a. 1.1.1934. Signature Seymour, Chamberlain, Boyd.	600	1,250	3,500
	b. 1.6.1934. Signature Wright, Craig, Boyd.	600	1,250	3,500
	c. 1.3.1935. Signature Wright, Craig, Boyd.	600	1,250	3,500
	s. Specimen. Various dates.	—	1,500	4,500
	cs. Commercial (false color) specimen.	—	950	3,000

34	5 Pounds	Good	Fine	XF
	1934-1935. Purple on green underprint. Portrait King George V at right, arms at top center. Printer: BWC.			
	a. 13.9.1934. Signature Wright, Craig, Boyd.	900	2,000	6,500
	b. 1.3.1935. Signature Wright, Craig, Boyd.	900	2,000	6,500
	s. Specimen. Various dates.	1,100	3,000	7,500
	cs. Commercial (false color) specimen.	—	1,900	4,500

35	10 Pounds	Good	Fine	XF
	1934-1935. Black and blue on grey underprint. Portrait King George V at right, arms at top center. Printer: BWC.			
	a. 1.1.1934. Signature Seymour, Chamberlain, Boyd.	1,100	3,000	7,500
	b. 12.7.1934. Signature Wright, Craig, Boyd.	1,100	3,000	7,500
	c. 13.9.1934. Signature Wright, Craig, Boyd.	1,100	3,000	7,500
	d. 1.3.1935. Signature Wright, Craig, Boyd.	1,100	3,000	7,500
	s. Specimen.	—	4,000	8,500
	cs. Commercial (false color) specimen.	—	2,500	6,000

36	20 Pounds	Good	Fine	XF
	1934. Black on purple underprint. Portrait King George V at right, arms at top center. Printer: BWC.			
	a. 12.7.1934. Signature Wright, Craig, Boyd.	1,500	5,000	10,000
	b. 3.8.1934. Signature Wright, Craig, Boyd.	1,500	5,000	10,000
	c. 2.9.1934. Signature Wright, Craig, Boyd.	1,500	5,000	10,000
	s. Specimen. Various dates.	—	6,500	12,500
	cs. Commercial (false color) specimen.	—	4,000	9,000

1937-1951 Issue

37	5 Shillings	VG	VF	UNC
	1937-1951. Blue on brown and blue underprint. Portrait King George VI at right, facing 3/4 left. Printer: BWC.			
	a. 1.3.1937. Signature Barton, Craig, Savage.	20.00	175	1,100
	b. 1.3.1938. Signature Barton, Craig, Savage.	20.00	175	1,100
	c. 1.10.1940. Signature Robertson, Hayward, Ackland.	20.00	160	1,000
	d. 1.1.1941. Signature Robertson, Hayward, Banting.	20.00	150	1,000
	e. 1.1.1942. Signature Robertson, Hayward, Banting.	20.00	150	1,000
	f. 1.7.1943. Signature Robertson, Banting, Allen.	20.00	140	1,000
	g. 1.1.1946. Signature Robertson, Banting, Hayward.	20.00	130	950
	h. 1.9.1948. Signature Taylor, Banting, Smith.	20.00	130	900
	i. 1.8.1949. Signature Taylor, Banting, Smith.	20.00	125	900
	j. 1.7.1950. Signature Taylor, Banting, Smith.	20.00	125	900
	k. 1.6.1951. Signature Taylor, Donovan, Smith.	15.00	160	850
	s. Specimen. Various dates.	—	—	1,100
	cs. Commercial (false color) specimen.	—	—	950

38	10 Shillings	VG	VF	UNC
	1937-1951. Brown on blue underprint. Portrait King George VI at right, facing 3/4 left. Printer: BWC.			
	a. 1.3.1937. Signature Barton, Craig, Savage.	30.00	275	1,600
	b. 1.3.1938. Signature Barton, Craig, Savage.	30.00	275	1,300
	c. 1.7.1940. Signature Robertson, Hayward, Ackland.	30.00	250	1,200
	d. 1.10.1940. Signature Robertson, Hayward, Ackland.	30.00	250	1,200
	e. 1.1.1941. Signature Robertson, Hayward, Banting.	30.00	250	1,200
	f. 1.7.1943. Signature Robertson, Banting, Allen.	30.00	250	1,200
	g. 1.1.1946. Signature Robertson, Banting, Hayward.	30.00	225	1,100
	h. 1.9.1948. Signature Taylor, Banting, Smith.	25.00	225	1,050
	i. 1.8.1949. Signature Taylor, Banting, Smith.	25.00	225	1,050
	j. 1.7.1950. Signature Taylor, Banting, Smith.	25.00	225	1,050
	k. 1.6.1951. Signature Taylor, Donovan, Smith.	20.00	185	950
	s. Specimen. Various dates.	—	—	1,500
	cs. Commercial (false color) specimen.	—	—	900

39	1 Pound	VG	VF	UNC
	1937-1940. Green on red underprint. Portrait King George VI at right, facing 3/4 left. Printer: BWC.			
	a. 1.3.1937. Signature Barton, Craig, Savage.	35.00	475	1,450
	b. 1.3.1938. Signature Barton, Craig, Savage.	35.00	475	1,300
	c. 1.7.1940. Signature Robertson, Hayward, Ackland.	35.00	450	1,200
	s. Specimen. Various dates.	—	—	1,500
	cs. Commercial (false color) specimen.	—	—	1,200

40	1 Pound	VG	VF	UNC
	1941-1951. Green on red underprint. Portrait King George VI at right facing front. Printer: BWC.			
	a. 1.1.1941. Signature Robertson, Hayward, Banting.	35.00	425	1,200
	b. 1.1.1946. Signature Robertson, Banting, Hayward.	35.00	425	1,000
	c. 1.9.1948. Signature Taylor, Banting, Smith.	35.00	400	1,100
	d. 1.8.1949. Signature Taylor, Banting, Smith.	35.00	400	1,050
	e. 1.7.1950. Signature Taylor, Banting, Smith.	30.00	375	1,000
	f. 1.6.1951. Signature Taylor, Donovan, Smith.	25.00	350	950
	s. Specimen. Various dates.	—	—	1,500
	cs. Commercial (false color) specimens.	—	—	1,100

41	5 Pounds	VG	VF	UNC
	1941-1951. Purple on green underprint. Portrait King George VI at right, facing front. Printer: BWC.			
	a. 1.1.1941. Signature Robertson, Hayward, Banting.	175	1,000	1,850
	b. 1.7.1943. Signature Robertson, Banting, Allen.	175	1,000	1,750
	c. 1.1.1946. Signature Robertson, Banting, Hayward.	150	975	1,500
	d. 1.8.1949. Signature Taylor, Banting, Smith.	125	900	1,500
	e. 1.7.1950. Signature Taylor, Banting, Smith.	125	900	1,500
	f. 1.6.1951. Signature Taylor, Donovan, Smith.	110	850	1,250
	s. Specimen. Various dates.	—	—	1,950
	cs. Commercial (false color) specimen.	—	—	1,200

42	10 Pounds	VG	VF	UNC
	1942-1951. Blue on grey underprint. Portrait King George VI at right, facing front. Printer: BWC.			
	a. 1.1.1942. Signature Robertson, Hayward, Banting.	350	1,750	2,500
	b. 1.7.1943. Signature Robertson, Banting, Allen.	350	1,750	2,500
	c. 1.1.1946. Signature Robertson, Banting, Hayward.	300	1,450	2,000
	d. 1.8.1948. Signature Taylor, Banting, Smith.	250	1,300	2,000
	e. 1.8.1949. Signature Taylor, Banting, Smith.	250	1,300	2,000
	f. 1.6.1951. Signature Taylor, Donovan, Smith.	225	1,200	1,800
	s. Specimen. Various dates.	—	—	3,000
	cs. Commercial (false color) specimen.	—	—	1,800

43	20 Pounds	VG	VF	UNC
	1937-1951. Black on purple underprint. Portrait King George VI at right, facing front. Printer: BWC.			
	a. 1.3.1937. Signature Barton, Craig, Savage.	750	2,000	5,000
	b. 1.3.1938. Signature Barton, Craig, Savage.	750	2,000	5,000
	c. 1.7.1943. Signature Robertson, Banting, Allen.	750	2,000	5,000
	d. 1.9.1948. Signature Taylor, Banting, Smith.	600	1,750	4,000
	e. 1.6.1951. Signature Taylor, Donovan, Smith.	500	1,500	3,500
	s. Specimen. Various dates.	—	—	7,000
	cs. Commercial (false color) specimen.	—	—	3,500

1942 Emergency Overprint Issues

44	10 Shillings	VG	VF	UNC
	ND (1947 - old date 1.8.1934).			
	a. Issued note. Rare, one known.	—	—	—
	s. Specimen.	—	—	9,000

45	1 Pound	VG	VF	UNC
	ND (1942-old date 1.8.1934).			
	a. RBNZ watermark, 1D prefix serial #.	150	750	2,350
	b. RBNZ watermark, 6D prefix serial #.	125	550	1,500
	c. Crown/A watermark repeated. F 1/O prefix serial #.	100	400	1,100
	s. Specimen.	—	—	2,000

46	5 Pounds	VG	VF	UNC
	ND (1942 - old date 1.8.1934).			
	a. RBNZ watermark, 4K prefix serial #.	2,250	5,500	20,000
	b. RBNZ watermark, 5K prefix serial #.	2,000	4,500	15,000
	s. Specimen.	—	—	—

1942 Emergency Issues

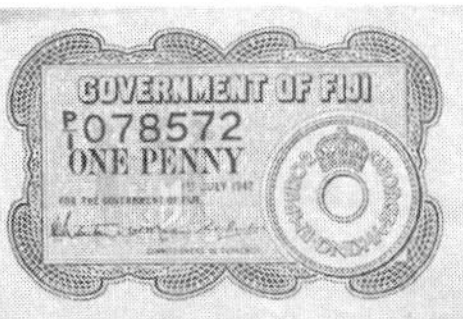

47	1 Penny	VG	VF	UNC
	1.7.1942. Partial watermark on some notes. Black on green underprint. Arms in underprint. at left, penny coin at lower right. Back: Penny coin at lower left. Printer: Commonwealth Printer, Australia.			
	a. Issued note.	0.50	2.00	8.50
	s. Specimen.	—	75.00	125

48	1 Shilling	VG	VF	UNC
	1.1.1942. Partial watermark on some notes. Black on gray laid paper. Arms at top center. Uniface. Printer: Commonwealth Printer, Australia.			
	a. Issued note.	2.00	15.00	160
	b. Issued note with rampant leopard watermark.	4.00	25.00	225
	r1. Remainder, without serial #.	—	35.00	125
	r2. Remainder; 6 note sheet.	—	—	950
	s. Specimen.	—	45.00	185

49	1 Shilling	VG	VF	UNC
	1.9.1942. Partial watermark on some notes. Black on yellow underprint. Arms at top center. Printer: Government Printer, Fiji. PC: Yellow.			
	a. Issued note. Block letter A.	2.00	15.00	165
	b. Issued note. Block letter B.	2.00	15.00	150
	s1. As a. Specimen.	—	—	200
	s2. As b. Specimen.	—	—	190

2s. Nº 929 Nº 929 GOVERNMENT OF FIJI TWO SHILLINGS 1st January, 1942.

50	2 Shillings	VG	VF	UNC
	1.1.1942. Partial watermark on some notes. Black on red underprint. Portrait King George VI at right facing left, arm at top right. Printer: Government Printer, Fiji.			
	a. Issued note.	2.00	35.00	210
	r1. Remainder, without serial #.	—	40.00	140
	r2. Remainder; 6 note sheet.	—	—	950
	s. Specimen.	—	45.00	185

1953-1967 Issue

51	5 Shillings	VG	VF	UNC
	1957-1965. Gray-blue on lilac, green and blue underprint. Arms at upper center, portrait of Queen Elizabeth II at right. Watermark: Fijian youth's bust. Printer: BWC.			
	a. 1.6.1957. Signature Davidson, Griffiths, Marais.	10.00	75.00	550
	b. 28.4.1961. Signature Bevington, Griffiths, Cruickshank.	10.00	75.00	550
	c. 1.12.1962. Signature Ritchie, Griffiths, Cruickshank.	8.00	60.00	525

	VG	VF	UNC
d. 1.9.1964. Signature Ritchie, Griffiths, Cruickshank.	7.50	50.00	475
e. 1.10.1965. Signature Ritchie, Griffiths, Cruickshank.	7.50	40.00	400
s. Specimen. Various dates.	—	—	750
cs. Commercial (false color) specimen.	—	—	550

52 **10 Shillings**

1957-1965. Brown on green, pink and yellow underprint. Arms at upper center, portrait of Queen Elizabeth II at right. Watermark: Fijian youth's bust. Printer: BWC.

	VG	VF	UNC
a. 1.6.1957. Signature Davidson, Griffiths, Marais.	17.50	100	750
b. 28.4.1961. Signature Bevington, Griffiths, Cruickshank.	17.50	120	800
c. 1.12.1962. Signature Ritchie, Griffiths, Cruickshank.	10.00	80.00	750
d. 1.9.1964. Signature Ritchie, Griffiths, Cruickshank.	12.50	125	500
e. 1.10.1965. Signature Ritchie, Griffiths, Cruickshank.	10.00	75.00	600
s. Specimen. Various dates.	—	—	850
cs. Commercial (false color) specimen.	—	—	700

53 **1 Pound**

1954-1967. Green on yellow and blue underprint. Arms at upper center, portrait of Queen Elizabeth II at right. Watermark: Fijian youth's bust. Printer: BWC.

	VG	VF	UNC
a. 1.7.1954. Signature Davidson, Donovan, Davis.	20.00	130	825
b. 1.6.1957. Signature Davidson, Griffiths, Marais.	25.00	145	875
c. 1.9.1959. Signature Bevington, Griffiths, Marais.	20.00	130	825
d. 1.12.1961. Signature Ritchie, Griffiths, Cruickshank.	27.50	145	900
e. 1.12.1962. Signature Ritchie, Griffiths, Cruickshank.	25.00	145	925
f. 20.1.1964. Signature Ritchie, Griffiths, Cruickshank.	22.50	140	825
g. 1.5.1965. Signature Ritchie, Griffiths, Cruickshank.	20.00	130	750
h. 1.12.1965. Signature Ritchie, Griffiths, Cruickshank.	25.00	135	725
i. 1.1.1967. Signature Ritchie, Griffiths, Cruickshank.	17.50	125	725
s. Specimen. Various dates.	—	—	1,050
cs. Commercial (false color) specimen.	—	—	900

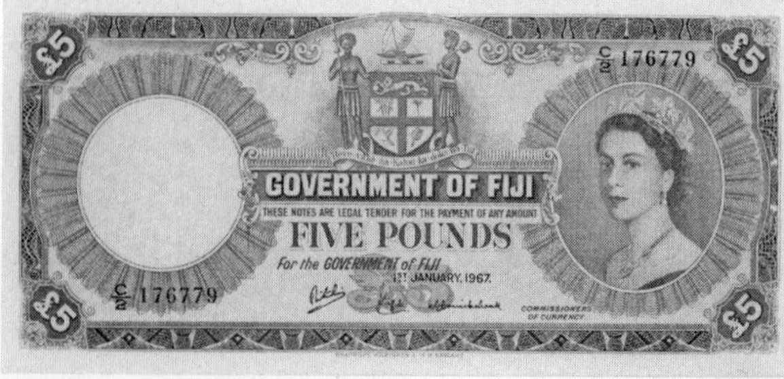

54 **5 Pounds**

1954-1967. Purple on orange, green and purple underprint. Arms at upper center, portrait of Queen Elizabeth II at right. Watermark: Fijian youth's bust. Printer: BWC.

	VG	VF	UNC
a. 1.7.1954. Signature Davidson, Donovan, Davis.	125	850	1,950
b. 1.9.1959. Signature Bevington, Griffiths, Marais.	125	900	2,150
c. 1.10.1960. Signature Bevington, Griffiths, Cruickshank.	95.00	850	1,950
d. 1.12.1962. Signature Ritchie, Griffiths, Cruickshank.	85.00	825	1,900
e. 20.1.1964. Signature Ritchie, Griffiths, Cruickshank.	85.00	800	1,950
f. 1.1.1967. Signature Ritchie, Griffiths, Cruickshank.	80.00	800	1,800
s. Specimen. Various dates.	—	—	1,400
cs. Commercial (false color) specimen.	—	—	1,050

55 **10 Pounds**

1954-1965. Blue on blue, orange and green underprint. Arms at upper center, portrait of Queen Elizabeth II at right. Watermark: Fijian youth's bust. Printer: BWC.

	VG	VF	UNC
a. 1.7.1954. Signature Davidson, Donovan, Davis.	250	1,250	2,750
b. 1.9.1959. Signature Bevington, Griffiths, Marais.	250	1,250	2,500
c. 1.10.1960. Signature Bevington, Griffiths, Cruickshank.	180	1,100	3,250
d. 20.1.1964. Signature Ritchie, Griffiths, Cruickshank.	170	1,000	2,250
e. 11.6.1964. Signature Ritchie, Griffiths, Cruickshank.	160	900	2,100
f. 1.5.1965. Signature Ritchie, Griffiths, Cruickshank. Not released.	—	—	—
s. Specimen. Various dates.	—	—	2,250
cs. Commercial (false color) specimen.	—	—	1,100

56 **20 Pounds**

1953. Black and purple on purple underprint. Arms at upper center, portrait of Queen Elizabeth II at right. Watermark: Fijian youth's bust. Printer: BWC.

	VG	VF	UNC
a. 1.1.1953. Signature Davidson, Donovan, Smith.	950	1,850	8,250
s. Specimen.	—	—	4,250
cs. Commercial (false color) specimen.	—	—	2,750

57 **20 Pounds**

1954-1958. Red on red and green underprint. Arms at upper center, portrait of Queen Elizabeth II at right. Watermark: Fijian youth's bust. Printer: BWC.

	VG	VF	UNC
a. 1.7.1954. Signature Davidson, Donovan, Davis.	850	2,000	6,500
b. 1.11.1958. Signature Bevington, Griffiths, Marais.	700	2,000	5,500
s. Specimen.	—	—	4,000
cs. Commercial (false color) specimen.	—	—	2,000

The Republic of Finland, the second most northerly state of the European continent, has an area of 338,145 sq. km. and a population of 5.24 million. Capital: Helsinki. Electrical, optical equipment, shipbuilding, metal and woodworking are the leading industries. Paper, wood pulp, plywood and telecommunication equipment are exported.

Finland was a province and then a grand duchy under Sweden from the 12th to the 19th centuries, and an autonomous grand duchy of Russia after 1809. It won its complete independence in 1917. During World War II, it was able to successfully defend its freedom and resist invasions by the Soviet Union - albeit with some loss of territory. In the subsequent half century, the Finns made a remarkable transformation from a farm/forest economy to a diversified modern industrial economy; per capita income is now among the highest in Western Europe. A member of the European Union since 1995, Finland was the only Nordic state to join the euro system at its initiation in January 1999.

RULERS:

Gustaf III, 1771-1792, of Sweden
Gustaf IV Adolph, 1792-1809
Alexander I, 1809-1825, of Russia
Nicholas I, 1825-1855
Alexander II, 1855-1881
Alexander III, 1881-1894
Nicholas II, 1894-1917

MONETARY SYSTEM:

(With Sweden to 1809)
1 Riksdaler Specie = 48 Skilling Specie
(With Russia 1809-1917)
1 Ruble = 100 Kopeks, 1809-1860
1 Markka = 100 Penniä, 1860-1963
1 Markka = 100 "Old" Markkaa, 1963-2001
1 Euro = 100 Cents, 2002-

REPLACEMENT NOTES:

Replacement notes were introduced in 1955. Until 1980, replacement notes have an asterisk after the serial number. Series 1986 show 2nd and 3rd digits of serial # as 99.

SWEDISH ADMINISTRATION

Kongl. General Krigs Commissariatet

King's General War Commissariat

1790 Issue

		Good	Fine	XF
A1	**8 Skilling Specie** Various handwritten dates; 1790 printed. Uniface. Minor varieties exist. Embossed seal with legend: K. FINSKA G: KRIGS COMMISARIATET around crowned arms at top center. Printed signature of Fahnehjelm with an additional handwritten signature.	500	1,500	—
A2	**12 Skilling Specie** Various handwritten dates; 1790 printed. Uniface. Minor varities exist. Embossed seal with legend: K. FINSKA G: KRIGS COMMISARIATET around crowned arms at top center. Printed signature of Fahnehjelm with an additional handwritten signature.	500	1,500	—
A3	**16 Skilling Specie** Various handwritten dates; 1790 printed. Uniface. Minor varieties exist. Embossed seal with legend: K. FINSKA G: KRIGS COMMISARIATET around crowned arms at top center. Printed signature of Fahnehjelm with an additional handwritten signature.	500	1,500	—
A4	**24 Skilling Specie** Various handwritten dates; 1790 printed. Uniface. Minor varities exist. Embossed seal with legend: K. FINSKA G: KRIGS COMMISARIATET around crowned arms at top center. Printed signature of Fahnehjelm with an additional handwritten signature.	500	1,500	—
A5	**32 Skilling Specie** Various handwritten dates; 1790 printed Uniface. Minor varities exist. Embossed seal with legend: K. FINSKA G: KRIGS COMMISARIATET around crowned arms at top center. Printed signature of Fahnehjelm with an additional handwritten signature.	—	—	—
A6	**1 Riksdaler Specie** Various handwritten dates; 1790 printed. Uniface. Minor varities exist. Embossed seal with legend: K. FINSKA G: KRIGS COMMISARIATET around crowned arms at top center. Printed signature of Fahnehjelm with an additional handwritten signature.	—	—	—
A7	**1 Riksdaler 8 Skilling Specie** Various handwritten dates; 1790 printed. Uniface. Minor varities exist. Embossed seal with legend: K. FINSKA G: KRIGS COMMISARIATET around crowned arms at top center. Printed signature of Fahnehjelm with an additional handwritten signature.	—	—	—
A8	**1 Riksdaler 16 Skilling Specie** Various handwritten dates; 1790 printed. Uniface. Minor varities exist. Embossed seal with legend: K. FINSKA G: KRIGS COMMISARIATET around crowned arms at top center. Printed signature of Fahnehjelm with an additional handwritten signature.	—	—	—
A9	**1 Riksdaler 24 Skilling Specie** Various handwritten dates; 1790 printed. Uniface. Minor varieties exist. Embossed seal with legend: K. FINSKA G: KRIGS COMMISARIATET around crowned arms at top center. Printed signature of Fahnehjelm with an additional handwritten signature.	—	—	—
A10	**1 Riksdaler 32 Skilling Specie** Various handwritten dates; 1790 printed. Uniface. Minor varieties exist. Embossed seal with legend: K. FINSKA G: KRIGS COMMISARIATET around crowned arms at top center. Printed signature of Fahnehjelm with an additional handwritten signature.	—	—	—
A11	**1 Riksdaler 40 Skilling Specie** Various handwritten dates; 1790 printed. Uniface. Minor varieties exist. Embossed seal with legend: K. FINSKA G: KRIGS COMMISARIATET around crowned arms at top center. Printed signature of Fahnehjelm with an additional handwritten signature.	—	—	—
A12	**2 Riksdaler Specie** Various handwritten dates; 1790 printed. Uniface. Minor varieties exist. Embossed seal with legend: K. FINSKA G: KRIGS COMMISARIATET around crowned arms at top center. Printed signature of Fahnehjelm with an additional handwritten signature.	—	—	—

RUSSIAN ADMINISTRATION

GRAND DUCHY OF FINLAND

Storfurstendömet Finlands Wäxel-Låne-och Depositions-Contor

ÅBO

1812 Assignates Issue

		Good	Fine	XF
A13	**20 Kopeks** 1812-1818. Handwritten with printed 18. Denominations in oval, without pictorial design. Various signatures. Watermark: Various designs or none.	800	1,700	4,500
A14	**50 Kopeks** 1812-1819. Handwritten with printed 18. Denomination in oval, without pictorial design. Various signatures. Watermark: Various designs or none.	700	1,350	3,500
A15	**75 Kopeks** 1812-1821. Handwritten with printed 18. Denomination in oval, without pictorial design. Various signatures. Watermark: Various designs or none.	700	1,350	3,500

Storfurstendömet Finlands Wäxel-Depositions-och Låne-Bank

ÅBO

1818-1821 Assignates Issue

		Good	Fine	XF
A16	**20 Kopeks** 1818-1819.	1,000	2,000	5,500
A17	**50 Kopeks** 1819-1820.	1,000	2,000	5,500
A18	**75 Kopeks** 1821. Rare.	—	—	—

Helsingfors

1819-1822 Assignates Issue

		Good	Fine	XF
A19	**20 Kopeks** 1820-1822. With or without watermark.	1,000	2,000	6,000
A20	**50 Kopeks** 1822. Rare.	—	—	—
A21	**1 Ruble** 1819-1820. 136x160mm. Rare.	—	—	—

Note: An example of #A21 sold in a 1992 auction for $40,000.

		Good	Fine	XF
A22	**2 Rubles** 1819-1820. 136x160mm. Rare.	—	—	—
A23	**4 Rubles** 1819-1820. 160x136mm. Rare.	—	—	—

Note: An example of #A23 sold in a 1993 auction for $26,000.

Storfurstendömet Finlands Wäxel-Depositions-och Låne-Bank

1822-1824 Assignates Issue

No.	Description	Good	Fine	XF
A24	**20 Kopeks**	Good	Fine	XF
	1824-1826; 1829-1838; 1840. Double-headed eagle at top center. Uniface.	200	500	1,200
A25	**50 Kopeks**	Good	Fine	XF
	1824-1826; 1830; 1835-1837; 1839-1840. Double-headed eagle at top center. Uniface.	200	700	1,500
A26	**75 Kopeks**	Good	Fine	XF
	1824-1826; 1831; 1836; 1839-1840. Double-headed eagle at top center. Uniface.	300	700	1,500
A27	**1 Ruble**	Good	Fine	XF
	1822-1829. Handwritten dates. Double-headed eagle at top center. Uniface.			
	a. Handwritten serial #. 1822-1824.	700	1,250	3,500
	b. Printed serial #. 1826; 1828-1829.	500	950	3,500
A28	**2 Rubles**	Good	Fine	XF
	1823-1828. Handwritten dates. Double-headed eagle at top center. Uniface.			
	a. Handwritten serial #. 1823-1824.	1,000	1,800	6,000
	b. Printed serial #. 1827. Rare.	—	—	—
	c. Printed serial #. 1828.	700	1,250	4,500

Finska Banken

Bank of Finland

1841 Ruble Issue

No.	Description	Good	Fine	XF
A29	**3 Rubles**	Good	Fine	XF
	1840-1862. Green. Double-headed eagle at top center. Various signature varieties. Backed by silver. Russian and Swedish text. Back: Finnish text. 150x98mm.			
	a. 1841; 1843; 1845-46; 1848; 1852-53; 1857; 1862. Rare.	—	—	—
	b. 1842; 1847; 1855-56; 1859-61.	1,000	2,000	4,000
A30	**5 Rubles**	Good	Fine	XF
	1841-1862. Blue. Double-headed eagle at top center. Backed by silver. Various signatures. Russian and Swedish text. Back: Finnish text. 167x100mm.			
	a. 1841-43; 1847-48; 1851-53; 1860; 1862. Rare.	—	—	—
	b. 1855-57; 1861.	2,500	5,000	8,500
A31	**10 Rubles**	Good	Fine	XF
	1841-1842; 1847; 1849; 1852-1853; 1855-1857. Red. Double-headed eagle at top center. Backed by silver. Various signature varities. Russian and Swedish text. Back: Finnish text. 175x127mm. Rare.	—	—	—
A32	**25 Rubles**	Good	Fine	XF
	1841-1857. Olive. Double-headed eagle at top center. Backed by silver. Various signature varieties. Russian and Swedish text. Back: Finnish text. 184x137mm.			
	a. 1841	1,500	3,000	5,000
	b. 1842-43.	200	3,500	6,000
	c. 1844; 1846-47; 1851-52; 1855-56. Rare.	—	—	—

Finlands Bank

Suomen Pankki

1860-1862 Markka Issue

No.	Description	Good	Fine	XF
A32A	**1 Markka**	Good	Fine	XF
	1860-1861. Red-brown on light blue. Embossed arms at top. Signature varieties.			
	a. 1860. Without watermark.	350	1,000	3,500
	b. Watermark: *COUPON.*	350	700	3,500
	c. 1860. Watermark: Arms.	350	1,000	3,500
	d. 1861	300	850	2,500
A33	**1 Markka**	Good	Fine	XF
	1864; 1866. Signature varieties. White arms.			
	a. 1864	1,200	2,500	4,500
	b. 1866	450	1,000	3,500
A34	**3 Markkaa**	Good	Fine	XF
	1860-1861. Green on yellow. Signature varieties. Embossed arms at top.			
	a. 1860. Without watermark.	750	1,500	5,000
	b. 1860. Watermark: *COUPON.*	750	1,500	5,000
	c. 1860. Watermark: Arms.	750	1,500	5,000
	d. 1861	2,000	4,500	12,000
A34A	**3 Markkaa**	Good	Fine	XF
	1864; 1866. Signature varieties. White arms.			
	a. 1864	1,500	4,000	10,000
	b. 1866. Rare.	—	—	—

No.	Description	Good	Fine	XF
A35	**12 Markkaa**	Good	Fine	XF
	1862. Green. Man with stick and cap at left, young woman with scarf at right. Signature varieties. 136x72mm.			
	a. Without series. 7 digit serial #.	400	750	2,500
	b. Series B. 6 digit serial #.	500	1,250	4,000
	c. Series C. 6 digit serial #.	400	800	3,000
A36	**20 Markkaa**	Good	Fine	XF
	1862. Red. Crowned mantled arms consisting of crowned double-headed eagle between man and woman at left. Signature varieties. 141x77mm.			
	a. Without series.	500	1,000	2,000
	b. Series B.	750	1,500	4,000
	c. Series C.	500	1,000	2,500
A37	**40 Markkaa**	Good	Fine	XF
	1862. Yellow. Crowned mantled arms consisting of crowned double-headed eagle at left, seated woman with anchor and caduceus at right. Signature varieties. 150x85mm.	5,000	12,000	20,000

No.	Description	Good	Fine	XF
A38	**100 Markkaa**	Good	Fine	XF
	1862. Multicolor. Young man with stick and cap at left, young woman at right. Signature varieties. 154x90mm.			
	a. Without series.	1,200	2,500	5,000
	b. Series B.	1,500	3,000	8,000
	c. Series C.	1,250	2,200	6,000

1866-1875 Issue

No.	Description	Good	Fine	XF
A39	**1 Markka**	Good	Fine	XF
	1866. Black arms overprint on white arms. Like #33A.	350	750	2,500
A39A	**1 Markka**	Good	Fine	XF
	1867. Blue-green and red-brown. Black arms.			
	a. 1867. Signature R. Frenckell.	250	600	1,500
	b. 1867. Signature V. Von Haartman.	200	350	850
A40	**3 Markkaa**	Good	Fine	XF
	1866-1875. Black arms.			
	a. 1866. Black arms overprint on blind embossed arms.	1,250	3,500	8,000
	b. 1867. Signature R. Frenckell. Rare.	—	—	—
	c. 1867. Signature V. Von Haartman.	200	450	1,000
	d. 1869-70; 1872.	400	800	3,000
	e. 1873-75.	300	600	1,500

Note: #A40e, 1874 comes in thick or thin paper varieties.

No.	Description	Good	Fine	XF
A41	**5 Markkaa**	Good	Fine	XF
	1875. Bluish-gray. Arms at left. *I SILFVER* below *FEM MARK.*			
	a. Serial #0000001-0186000.	750	1,500	5,000
	b. Watermark slightly changed. Serial #0186001-1788000.	450	900	3,000
A42	**10 Markkaa**	Good	Fine	XF
	1875. Red and gray. Arms at left. *I SILFVER* below *TIO MARK.*	1,500	3,500	10,000

1878 Issue

No.	Description	Good	Fine	XF
A43	**5 Markkaa**	Good	Fine	XF
	1878. Bluish-gray. Arms at left, like #A41, but *FINSKT MYNT* below *FEM MARK.*			
	a. Signature handwritten. Serial #0000001-1926000.	250	700	1,500
	b. Signature printed. Serial #1926001-4876900.	200	500	1,200
A44	**10 Markkaa**	Good	Fine	XF
	1878. Red and gray. Arms at left, like #A42, but *I GULD* below *TIO MARK.*	500	1,200	3,500

		Good	Fine	XF
A45	**500 Markkaa**	Good	Fine	XF
	1878. Yellow and gray. Arms with 2 cherubs.			
	a. Printed in Copenhagen. Serial #000001-079000.	3,000	5,000	9,000
	b. Printed in Helsinki. Serial #079001-150400.	2,500	4,000	7,500

1882-1884 Issue

		Good	Fine	XF
A46	**10 Markkaa**	Good	Fine	XF
	1882. Black and yellow. Arms at left, like #A44, but slightly altered design.			
	a. With lines under signature.	150	400	1,000
	b. Without lines under signature.	150	400	1,000
A47	**20 Markkaa**	Good	Fine	XF
	1882; 1883. Black and brown. Arms at left.			
	a. 1882	650	1,500	4,500
	b. 1883	300	700	1,750
A49	**50 Markkaa**	Good	Fine	XF
	1884. Black and blue. Arms at center.	300	800	2,200
A48	**100 Markkaa**	Good	Fine	XF
	1882. Black and red. Arms at center.			
	a. Printed in Copenhagen. 3mm serial #000001-481300.	350	750	2,500
	b. Printed in Helsinki. 3.8mm serial #481301-683000.	500	1,000	3,000

1886-1894 Issue

		Good	Fine	XF
A50	**5 Markkaa**	Good	Fine	XF
	1886. Black and blue. Arms at center.			
	a. Watermark at center right.	100	200	500
	b. Watermark at center.	80.00	150	400
A51	**10 Markkaa**	Good	Fine	XF
	1889. Dark brown and red. Arms at center.	100	200	600
A52	**20 Markkaa**	Good	Fine	XF
	1894. Black and dark brown. Arms at center watermark at left and right.			
	a. Dark red. Serial # up to 0096584.	175	350	1,250
	b. Red-brown. Serial #123023-324770.	150	200	1,100
	c. Brown. Serial #403209-0981274.	120	175	900

1897-1898 Issue

		Good	Fine	XF
1	**5 Markkaa**	Good	Fine	XF
	1897. Vertical format. Blue on brown underprint. Arms at left, woman at center, head at right. Back: Shield surrounded by spruce twigs on dark background.			
	a. Serial #0000001-7092000.	30.00	100	250
	b. Serial #7092001-7143000. Test paper.	—	1,000	—

		Good	Fine	XF
2	**5 Markkaa**	Good	Fine	XF
	1897. Vertical format. Blue on brown underprint. Arms at left, woman at center, head at right. 7 and 8 digit serial #. Back: Shield surrounded by pine twigs on light background.	30.00	80.00	200
3	**10 Markkaa**	Good	Fine	XF
	1898. Purple on brown underprint. Woman standing at left.			
	a. Serial #0000001-4065000.	30.00	90.00	250
	b. Serial #4065001-4114000. Test paper.	—	1,000	—
	c. Serial #4114001-8560000.	25.00	70.00	200
	d. Serial #8560001-8563000. Test paper.	—	400	—

#4, not assigned.

		Good	Fine	XF
5	**20 Markkaa**	Good	Fine	XF
	1898. Woman with youth and globe.			
	a. Back green. Serial #0000001-2026000.	75.00	200	750
	b. Back red. (Not issued). Serial #2026001-4196000.	35.00	100	500
6	**50 Markkaa**	Good	Fine	XF
	1898. Blue. Woman with tablet at left.			
	a. Serial # 1-0001000. Handwritten signature.	1,000	2,500	—
	b. Serial #1000-341000. Lines under signature.	250	500	2,000
	c. Printed signature.	120	250	900
7	**100 Markkaa**	Good	Fine	XF
	1898. Young farming couple at left.			
	a. Handwritten signature to #86000.	700	1,500	2,500
	b. Lines under signature. Serial #86001-659000.	200	500	1,500
	c. Without lines under signature.	150	300	1,000

		Good	Fine	XF
8	**500 Markkaa** 1898. Blue. Woman with lion at left.			
	a. Handwritten signature to #23000.	1,500	2,700	6,000
	b. Lines under signature. Serial #23001-99000.	800	1,500	5,000
	c. Without lines under signature. Serial #99001-205000.	700	1,250	4,500

1909 First Issue

Beginning w/#9, issues are affected by WWI and many reissues of earlier dates.

		VG	VF	UNC
9	**5 Markkaa** 1909. Blue. Czarist eagle at upper center. Back: Rowboat in river in black.			
	a. Watermark: *SPFB.*	3.00	15.00	45.00
	b. Without watermark. 7 or 8 digit serial #.	3.00	15.00	50.00
	c. Serial # prefix A, B or C.	350	650	1,250
	d. Double rings in eagle's wing.	750	1,500	3,000

Note: The watermark is found on only about half of the printings of #9a. Notes with prefix letters A, B & C are believed to be test printings.

		VG	VF	UNC
10	**10 Markkaa** 1909. Lilac. Czarist eagle at upper center. Stylized tree at center. Back: House/w 2 cows in black on back.			
	a. Serial # 2.5 mm high.	5.00	20.00	75.00
	b. Serial # 3.5 mm high.	10.00	30.00	120

		VG	VF	UNC
11	**20 Markkaa** 1909. Orange on gray underprint. Czarist eagle at upper center. Caduceus at center. Serial # varieties. Back: Stylized tree on back.			
	a. Watermark: *SPFB.*	20.00	70.00	150
	b. Without watermark.	20.00	70.00	150
12	**50 Markkaa** 1909. Blue. Czarist eagle at upper center. Back: Lighthouse.	VG	VF	UNC
	a. Without watermark.	100	200	700
	b. Watermark: *FINLANDS BANK.*	200	700	2,000
13	**100 Markkaa** 1909. Violet. Czarist eagle at upper center. Farmer plowing at left and right. Serial # varieties.	VG	VF	UNC
	a. Without watermark.	100	250	750
	b. Watermark: *FINLANDS BANK*	250	750	2,200
14	**500 Markkaa** 1909. Orange and brown. Czarist eagle at upper center. Two blacksmiths at anvil at center.	1,000	2,500	4,500

#14 is for serial # range below 170,000; if higher see #23.

		VG	VF	UNC
15	**1000 Markkaa** 1909. Blue and brown. Czarist eagle at upper center. Two men holding a caduceus at center.	1,200	3,000	8,000

1915 Issue

		VG	VF	UNC
16	**1 Markka** 1915. Red. Czarist eagle at upper center. Uniface. Serial # varieties.			
	a. Without series.	1.00	5.00	15.00
	b. Series A.	0.50	2.00	10.00

1916 Issue

		VG	VF	UNC
17	**25 Penniä** 1916. (Not issued). Yellow-brown. Czarist eagle at upper center.	—	600	1,200
18	**50 Penniä** 1916. (Not issued). Gray-blue. Czarist eagle at upper center.	—	600	1,200

		VG	VF	UNC
19	**1 Markka** 1916. Dark brown on light brown underprint. Czarist eagle at upper center. 7 and 8 digit serial #.	0.25	1.50	5.00

1917 Senate Issue

Notes printed and issued under Senate control, December 6, 1917-January 28, 1918.

		VG	VF	UNC
19A	**1 Markka** 1916. Printed 6.12.1917-26.1.1918. Dark on light brown underprint. Czarist eagle at upper center. Serial #18288001-20232000. Similar to # 19.	0.50	2.00	5.00
19B	**5 Markkaa** 1909. Printed 10.12.1917-25.1.1918. Blue. Czarist eagle at upper center. Serial #18573001-19397000. Like #9. Back: Rowboat in river in black.	2.00	15.00	40.00
19C	**10 Markkaa** 1909. Lilac. Czarist eagle at upper center. Similar to #10b, stylized tree at center. Back: House with 2 cows in black.	VG	VF	UNC
	a. 7 digit serial #9946100-9999999. Printed 20.12.1917-3.1.1918.	3.00	30.00	100
	b. 8 digit serial #10000000-10231000. Printed 3.1.1918-17.1.1918.	75.00	150	450
19D	**20 Markkaa** 1909. Orange on gray underprint. Czarist eagle at upper center. Caduceus at center, similar to #11. Serial #9646001-9870000. Back: stylized tree.	10.00	60.00	175
19E	**100 Markkaa** 1909. Violet. Czarist eagle at upper center. Farmer plowing at left and right, similar to #13. Serial #2575001-2775000.	125	300	750

1918 Peoples Commissariat Issue

Notes printed and issued under Peoples Commissariat control, January 28, 1918-May 20, 1918.

		VG	VF	UNC
19F	**1 Markka** 1916. Dark brown on light brown underprint. Czarist eagle at upper center. Serial #20232001-20880000.	15.00	35.00	100
19G	**1 Markka** 1916. Dark brown on light brown underprint. Czarist eagle at upper center. Serial #20880001-24795000.	1.00	2.00	5.00

		VG	VF	UNC
20	**5 Markkaa** 1909 (1918). Blue. Czarist eagle at upper center. Serial #19397001-20789000. Back: Rowboat in river in black.	1.00	5.00	25.00
21	**20 Markkaa** 1909 (1918). Orange-brown. Czarist eagle at upper center. Caduceus at center. Back: Stylized tree.	VG	VF	UNC
	a. 7 digit serial #9874001-9999999.	7.00	50.00	150
	b. 8 digit serial #10000000-10019001.	25.00	250	1,000
22	**100 Markkaa** 1909 (1918). Violet. Czarist eagle at upper center. Farmer plowing at left and right. Serial #2775001-2983000.	10.00	30.00	100

Color Abbreviation Guide

New to the *Standard Catalog of® World Paper Money* are the following abbreviations related to color references:

BC: Back color
PC: Paper color

23 **500 Markkaa** — VG 20.00, VF 70.00, UNC 150
1909 (1918). Orange and brown. Czarist eagle at upper center. Two blacksmiths at anvil at center. Serial #170001-262000.

REPUBLIC OF FINLAND

Finlands Bank

1909 Dated Issue (1918), Litt. A

No.	Description	VG	VF	UNC
24	**5 Markkaa** 1909 (1918). Blue. Czarist eagle at upper center. Back: Row boat in river in black.			
	a. Without watermark.	5.00	25.00	70.00
	b. With watermark.	5.00	25.00	70.00
25	**10 Markkaa** 1909 (1918). Lilac. Czarist eagle at upper center. Stylized tree at center. Back: Hose with 2 cows in black.	10.00	20.00	75.00
26	**20 Markkaa** 1909 (1918). Orange-brown. Czarist eagle at upper center. Caduceus at center. Back: Stylized tree.	200	850	1,750
27	**50 Markkaa** 1909 (1918). Blue. Czarist eagle at upper center. Back: Lighthouse.	100	200	500
28	**100 Markkaa** 1909 (1918). Violet. Czarist eagle at upper center. Farmer plowing at left and right.	1,000	2,500	5,000
29	**500 Markkaa** 1909 (1918). Orange and brown. Czarist eagle at upper center. Two blacksmiths at anvil at center. Rare.	—	—	—

1909 Dated Issue (1918), *Sarja II* (Series II)

No.	Description	VG	VF	UNC
30	**5 Markkaa** 1909 (1918). Green. Czarist eagle at upper center. Back: Rowboat in river in black.	3.00	15.00	30.00
31	**100 Markkaa** 1909 (1918). Orange and gray. Czarist eagle at upper center. Farmer plowing at left and right. Serial # varieties.	75.00	175	300
32	**500 Markkaa** 1909 (1918). Gray and yellow. Czarist eagle at upper center. Two blacksmiths at anvil at center.	250	1,000	2,500

1918 Issue

No.	Description	VG	VF	UNC
33	**25 Penniä** 1918. Dark brown on light brown underprint. Without Czarist eagle at upper center.	0.50	1.50	3.00

No.	Description	VG	VF	UNC
34	**50 Penniä** 1918. Dark brown on blue underprint. Without czarist eagle at upper center.	0.50	1.50	3.00

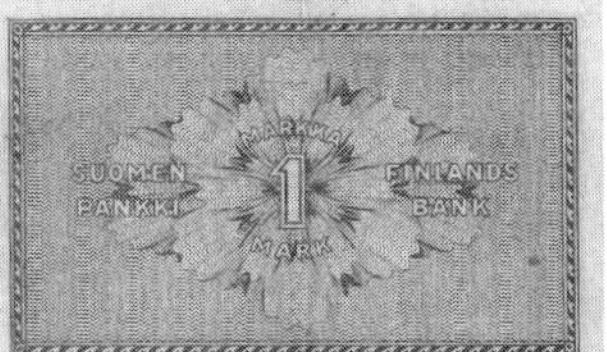

No.	Description	VG	VF	UNC
35	**1 Markka** 1918. Dark brown on light brown underprint. Without czarist eagle at upper center. Similar to #19.	0.50	1.50	5.00

No.	Description	VG	VF	UNC
36	**5 Markkaa** 1918. Green. Without czarist eagle at upper center. Back: Rowboat in river in black.	3.00	12.00	35.00
37	**10 Markkaa** 1918. Lilac. Without czarist eagle at upper center. Stylized tree at center. Back: 2 cows in black.	5.00	20.00	60.00

No.	Description	VG	VF	UNC
38	**20 Markkaa** 1918. Blue. Without czarist eagle at upper center. Caduceus at center. Back: Stylized tree.	10.00	60.00	150

No.	Description	VG	VF	UNC
39	**50 Markkaa** 1918. Blue. Without czarist eagle at upper center. Back: Lighthouse.	70.00	170	500
40	**100 Markkaa** 1918. Light brown on gray nderprint. Without czarist eagle at upper center. Farmer plowing at left and right.	70.00	200	500
41	**1000 Markkaa** 1918. Blue and brown. Without czarist eagle at upper center. Two men holding a caduceus at center.	900	3,000	5,500

1922 Dated Issue

#	Description	VG	VF	UNC
42	**5 Markkaa**	VG	VF	UNC
	1922. Green. Fir tree at center. Back: Arms.	2.00	15.00	60.00
43	**10 Markkaa**	VG	VF	UNC
	1922. Brown. Pine tree at center. Back: Arms.	2.00	15.00	60.00
44	**20 Markkaa**	VG	VF	UNC
	1922 (1926). Violet. Pine tree at center. Back: Arms.	20.00	125	250
45	**50 Markkaa**	VG	VF	UNC
	1922 (1926). Dark blue. Allegorical group of six people. Back: Arms.	100	500	900

#	Description	VG	VF	UNC
46	**100 Markkaa**	VG	VF	UNC
	1922. Dark brown. Allegorical group of six people. Back: Arms.	90.00	400	1,000
47	**500 Markkaa**	VG	VF	UNC
	1922 (1924). Brown on green underprint. Allegorical group of eleven people. Back: Arms.			
	a. Without plate # at lower left.	200	600	1,750
	b. Plate # at lower left.	200	500	1,500
48	**1000 Markkaa**	VG	VF	UNC
	1922 (1923). Brown. Allegorical group of thirteen people. Back: Arms.			
	a. Without plate # at lower left.	250	900	2,000
	b. Plate # at lower left.	200	750	1,500

1922 Dated Issue, Litt. A

#	Description	VG	VF	UNC
49	**5 Markkaa**	VG	VF	UNC
	1922 (1926). Green. Fir tree at center. Back: Arms.	2.00	15.00	100
50	**10 Markkaa**	VG	VF	UNC
	1922 (1926). Brown. Pine tree at center. Back: Arms.	5.00	20.00	80.00
51	**20 Markkaa**	VG	VF	UNC
	1922 (1927). Red. Pine tree at center. Back: Arms.	40.00	150	450
52	**50 Markkaa**	VG	VF	UNC
	1922 (1925). Dark blue. Allegorical group of six people. Back: Arms.	75.00	500	900
53	**100 Markkaa**	VG	VF	UNC
	1922 (1923). Dark brown. Allegorical group of six people. Back: Arms.			
	a. Without plate # at lower left.	100	250	1,200
	b. Plate # at lower left .	75.00	200	650
54	**500 Markkaa**	VG	VF	UNC
	1922 (1930). Brown on green underprint. Allegorical group of eleven people. Back: Arms.	500	1,750	4,500
55	**1000 Markkaa**	VG	VF	UNC
	1922 (1929). Brown. Allegorical group of thirteen people. Back: Arms.	350	1,200	3,000

1922 Dated Issue, Litt. B

#	Description	VG	VF	UNC
56	**5 Markkaa**	VG	VF	UNC
	1922 (1929). Green. Fir tree at center. Back: Arms.	5.00	30.00	120
57	**10 Markkaa**	VG	VF	UNC
	1922 (1929). Brown. Pine tree at center. Back: Arms.	10.00	50.00	110
58	**20 Markkaa**	VG	VF	UNC
	1922 (1929). Violet. Pine tree at center. Back: Arms.	100	300	750
59	**50 Markkaa**	VG	VF	UNC
	1922 (1929). Dark blue. Allegorical group of six people. Back: Arms.	250	850	2,000
60	**100 Markkaa**	VG	VF	UNC
	1922 (1929). Dark brown. Allegorical group of six people. Back: Arms.	100	400	1,200

1922 Dated Issue, Litt. C

#	Description	VG	VF	UNC
61	**5 Markkaa**	VG	VF	UNC
	1922 (1930). Green. Fir tree at center. Back: Arms.			
	a. Issued note.	2.00	10.00	40.00
	s. Specimen.	—	—	500
62	**10 Markkaa**	VG	VF	UNC
	1922 (1930). Brown. Pine tree at center. Back: Arms.			
	a. Issued note.	3.00	20.00	50.00
	s. Specimen.	—	—	300
63	**20 Markkaa**	VG	VF	UNC
	1922 (1931). Red. Pine tree at center. Back: Arms.			
	a. Issued note.	2.00	15.00	40.00
	s. Specimen.	—	—	300

#	Description	VG	VF	UNC
64	**50 Markkaa**	VG	VF	UNC
	1922 (1931). Dark blue. Allegorical group of six people. Back: Arms.			
	a. Issued note.	10.00	30.00	100
	s. Specimen.	—	—	500

#	Description	VG	VF	UNC
65	**100 Markkaa**	VG	VF	UNC
	1922 (1932-1945). Dark brown. Allegorical group of six people. Back: Arms.			
	a. Issued note.	10.00	35.00	120
	s. Specimen.	—	—	350

		VG	VF	UNC
66	**500 Markkaa** 1922 (1931-1942). Brown on green underprint. Allegorical group of eleven people. Serial #varieties. Back: Arms.			
	a. Issued note.	35.00	150	500
	s. Specimen.	—	—	1,000

		VG	VF	UNC
67	**1000 Markkaa** 1922 (1931-1945). Brown. Allegorical group of thirteen people. Serial # varieties. Back: Arms.			
	a. Issued note.	25.00	75.00	200
	s. Specimen.	—	—	250

1922 Dated Issue, Litt. D

		VG	VF	UNC
67A	**1000 Markkaa** 1922 (1939). Green. *Litt. D.* Allegorical group of thirteen people. Back: Arms.	250	1,000	2,000

1939 Provisional Issue

		VG	VF	UNC
68	**5000 Markkaa** 1922 (1939). Brown. *Litt. A.* Allegorical group of eleven people. Back: Arms.	5,000	12,000	35,000

1939-41 Dated Issue

		VG	VF	UNC
69	**5 Markkaa** 1939 (1942-1945). Green. Fir tree at center. Back: Arms.			
	a. Issued note.	1.00	3.00	10.00
	s. Specimen.	—	—	170

		VG	VF	UNC
70	**10 Markkaa** 1939 (1939-1945). Brown. Pine tree at center. Back: Arms.			
	a. Issued note.	1.00	3.00	10.00
	s. Specimen.	—	—	170

		VG	VF	UNC
71	**20 Markkaa** 1939 (1939-1945). Purple. Pine tree at center. Back: Arms.			
	a. Issued note.	1.00	3.00	10.00
	s. Specimen.	—	—	200

		VG	VF	UNC
72	**50 Markkaa** 1939 (1939-1945). Dark blue. Allegorical group of six people. Back: Arms.			
	a. Issued note.	5.00	30.00	100
	s. Specimen.	—	—	220

		VG	VF	UNC
73	**100 Markkaa** 1939 (1940-1945). Dark brown. Allegorical group of six people. Back: Arms.			
	a. Issued note.	5.00	15.00	60.00
	s. Specimen.	—	—	250
74	**1000 Markkaa** 1941(1944-1945). Brown. *Litt. E.* Allegorical group of thirteen people. Back: Arms.	1,000	3,000	6,000

		VG	VF	UNC
75	**5000 Markkaa** 1939 (1940). Dark blue and violet. Snellman at left.			
	a. Denomination at center and at right. Without reddish underprint. (1940-1943) .	400	1,200	2,500
	b. Denomination at center and at right. With reddish underprint. (1945).	450	1,250	2,700
	s. Specimen.	—	—	2,000

1945 Dated Issue, Litt. A

		VG	VF	UNC
76	**5 Markkaa** 1945 (1946). Yellow. Fir at center.			
	a. Issued note.	1.00	3.00	8.00
	s. Specimen.	—	—	250

		VG	VF	UNC
77	**10 Markkaa**	VG	VF	UNC
	1945. Red. Pine at center.			
	a. Issued note.	1.00	3.00	10.00
	s. Specimen.	—	—	350

		VG	VF	UNC
78	**20 Markkaa**	VG	VF	UNC
	1945. Blue. Pine at center.			
	a. Issued note.	1.00	5.00	15.00
	s. Specimen.	—	—	250
79	**50 Markkaa**	VG	VF	UNC
	1945. Brown. Back: Young farm couple.			
	a. Printed area on face 93 x 96mm. (A serial #).	5.00	30.00	100
	b. Printed area on face 88 x 92mm.	3.00	15.00	70.00
	s. Specimen.	—	—	300
80	**100 Markkaa**	VG	VF	UNC
	1945. Blue-green. Back: Woman with lion.			
	a. Issued note.	3.00	15.00	35.00
	s. Specimen.	—	—	175

		VG	VF	UNC
81	**500 Markkaa**	VG	VF	UNC
	1945. Blue. Allegorical group of eleven people.			
	a. Issued note.	45.00	250	700
	s. Specimen.	—	—	900

		VG	VF	UNC
82	**1000 Markkaa**	VG	VF	UNC
	1945. Blue-violet. Allegorical group of thirteen people.			
	a. Issued note.	30.00	100	250
	s. Specimen.	—	—	500

		VG	VF	UNC
83	**5000 Markkaa**	VG	VF	UNC
	1945. Dark brown. Juhana Vilhelm Snellman at left.			
	a. One letter in serial #.	200	450	900
	b. Two letters in serial #.	250	600	1,200
	s. Specimen.	—	—	500

1945 Dated Issue, Litt. B

		VG	VF	UNC
84	**5 Markkaa**	VG	VF	UNC
	1945 (1948). Yellow. Fir at center.	2.00	7.00	25.00
85	**10 Markkaa**	VG	VF	UNC
	1945 (1948). Red. Pine at center.	1.00	2.00	7.00

		VG	VF	UNC
86	**20 Markkaa**	VG	VF	UNC
	1945 (1948). Blue. Allegorical group of six people, like #78.	1.00	3.00	7.00

		VG	VF	UNC
87	**50 Markkaa**	VG	VF	UNC
	1945 (1948). Brown. Back: Young farm couple, like #79.	2.00	10.00	30.00

		VG	VF	UNC
88	**100 Markkaa**	VG	VF	UNC
	1945 (1948). Blue-green. Back: Woman with lion, like #80.	2.00	10.00	20.00
89	**500 Markkaa**	VG	VF	UNC
	1945 (1948). Blue. Allegorical group of eleven people, like #81.	30.00	100	300

		VG	VF	UNC
90	**1000 Markkaa** 1945 (1948). Violet. Allegorical group of thirteen people, like #82.	25.00	75.00	300

1955 Issue

		VG	VF	UNC
91	**100 Markkaa** 1955. Brown on olive underprint. Ears of wheat at center.			
	a. Issued note.	1.00	5.00	15.00
	r. Replacement.	5.00	20.00	50.00
	s. Specimen.	—	—	150
92	**500 Markkaa** 1955. Brown on blue underprint. Conifer branch at center. 2 signature varieties.	VG	VF	UNC
	a. Issued note.	30.00	150	220
	r. Replacement.	50.00	250	450
	s. Specimen.	—	—	450
93	**1000 Markkaa** 1955. Dark green. Juho Kusti Paasikivi at left.	VG	VF	UNC
	a. Issued note.	10.00	35.00	75.00
	r. Replacement.	50.00	120	300
	s. Specimen.	—	—	500

		VG	VF	UNC
94	**5000 Markkaa** 1955. Brown and lilac. Kaarlo Juho Ståhlberg at left.			
	a. Issued note.	50.00	150	300
	b. Issued note. Inverted watermark.	350	1,500	2,500
	s. Specimen.	—	—	500

		VG	VF	UNC
95	**10,000 Markkaa** 1955. Lilac. Juhana Vilhelm Snellman at left center.			
	a. Issued note.	75.00	250	400
	b. Issued note. Inverted watermark.	80.00	300	450
	s. Specimen.	—	—	650

1956 Issue

		VG	VF	UNC
96	**500 Markkaa** 1956. Blue. Conifer branch at center. 2 signature varieties. Like #92.			
	a. Issued note.	5.00	25.00	65.00
	r. Replacement.	100	300	700
	s. Specimen.	—	—	300

1957 Issue

		VG	VF	UNC
97	**100 Markkaa** 1957. Dark red on light brown underprint. Ears of wheat, like #91.			
	a. Issued note.	1.00	3.00	10.00
	r. Replacement.	7.50	25.00	50.00
	s. Specimen.	—	—	200

FRANCE

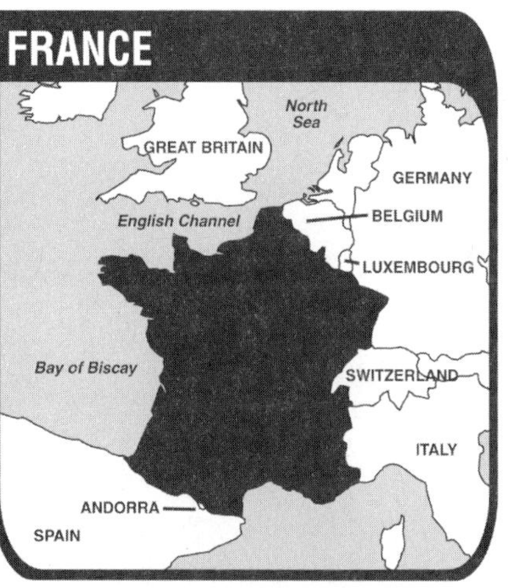

The French Republic, largest of the West European nations, has an area of 547,026 sq. km. and a population of 64.05 million. Capital: Paris. Agriculture, manufacturing and tourism are the most important elements of France's diversified economy. Textiles and clothing, iron and steel products, machinery and transportation equipment, agricultural products and wine are exported.

Although ultimately a victor in World Wars I and II, France suffered extensive losses in its empire, wealth, manpower, and rank as a dominant nation-state. Nevertheless, France today is one of the most modern countries in the world and is a leader among European nations. Since 1958, it has constructed a hybrid presidential-parliamentary governing system resistant to the instabilities experienced in earlier more purely parliamentary administrations. In recent years, its reconciliation and cooperation with Germany have proved central to the economic integration of Europe, including the introduction of a common exchange currency, the euro, in January 1999. At present, France is at the forefront of efforts to develop the EU's military capabilities to supplement progress toward an EU foreign policy.

MONETARY SYSTEM:

1 Livre = 20 Sols (Sous)
1 Ecu = 6 Livres
1 Louis D'or = 4 Ecus to 1794
1 Franc = 10 Decimes = 100 Centimes, 1794-1959
1 Nouveau Franc = 100 "old" Francs, 1959-1962

KINGDOM

Billets de Monoye

1701-1710 Issue

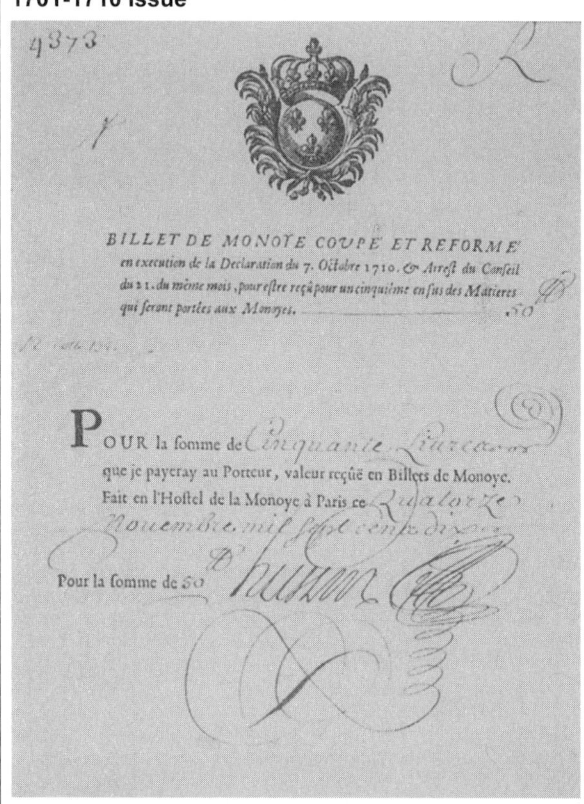

BILLET DE MONOYE COUPÉ ET REFORMÉ en execution de la Declaration du 7. Octobre 1710. & Arreſt du Conſeil du 21. du même mois, pour eſtre reçû pour un cinquiéme en ſus des Matieres qui ſeront portées aux Monoyes.

POUR la ſomme de Cinquante Livres que je payeray au Porteur, valeur reçûë en Billets de Monoye. Fait en l'Hoſtel de la Monoye à Paris ce Quatorze Novembre mil ſept cent dix

Pour la ſomme de 50

		Good	Fine	XF
A1	**25-10,000 Livres** 1701-1710. Black.			
	a. Crowned double *L* monogram. 1701-1707.	4,000	7,000	12,000
	b. Crowned fleur-de-lis. 1709-1710.	4,000	7,000	12,000

Billets de l'Estat

1716 Issue

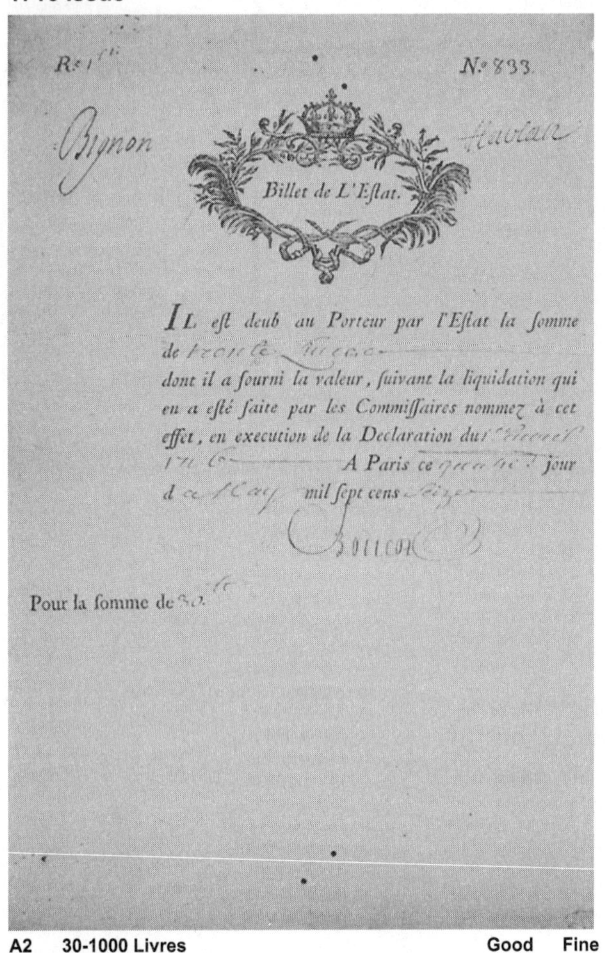

		Good	Fine	XF
A2	**30-1000 Livres** 1716. Black.	4,000	7,000	12,000

La Banque Générale

Issued by John Law in Louisiana. In 1720 a 50% devaluation occurred causing a great panic.

1716 Issue

		Good	Fine	XF
A3	**10 Ecus** 16.6.1716-9.11.1717. Black.	—	—	—
A4	**40 Ecus** 13.10.1716-9.11.1717 Black.	—	—	—
A5	**100 Ecus** 16.6.1716-8.3.1718. Black.	—	—	—
A6	**400 Ecus** 13.10.1716-8.3.1718. Black.	—	—	—
A7	**1000 Ecus** 16.6.1716-8.3.1718. Black.	—	—	—

1718 Issue

		Good	Fine	XF
A8	**10 Ecus** 8.6.1718; 30.8.1718. Black.	—	—	—
A9	**50 Ecus** 8.6.1718; 30.8.1718; 18.10.1718. Black.	—	—	—
A10	**500 Ecus** 8.6.1718; 30.8.1718; 18.10.1718. Black.	—	—	—

La Banque Royale

Issued by John Law in Louisiana. In 1720 a 50% depreciation occurred and caused a great panic.

1719-1720 Issue

		Good	Fine	XF
A12	**10 Livres** 1.4.1719; 25.7.1719. Black. Engraved ornamented monogram at left edge.	600	1,300	2,600

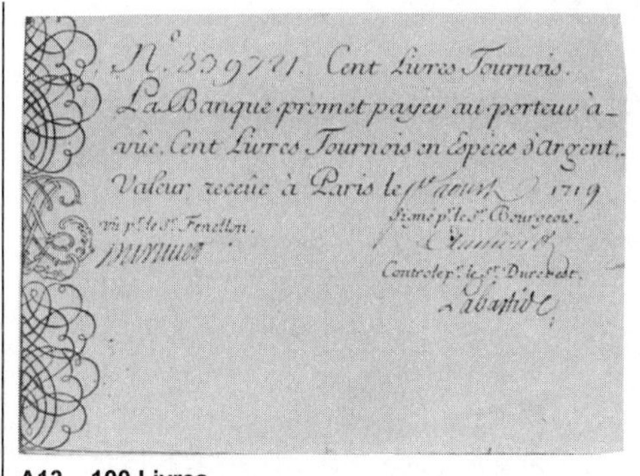

		Good	Fine	XF
A13	**100 Livres** 10.1.1719-1.1.1720. Black. Engraved ornamented monogram at left edge.	800	1,800	3,800
A14	**1000 Livres** 10.1.1719-1.1.1720. Black. Engraved ornamented monogram at left edge.	1,400	2,800	5,000
A15	**10,000 Livres** 1.1.1720. Black. Engraved ornamented monogram at left edge.	—	—	—

1720 First Issue

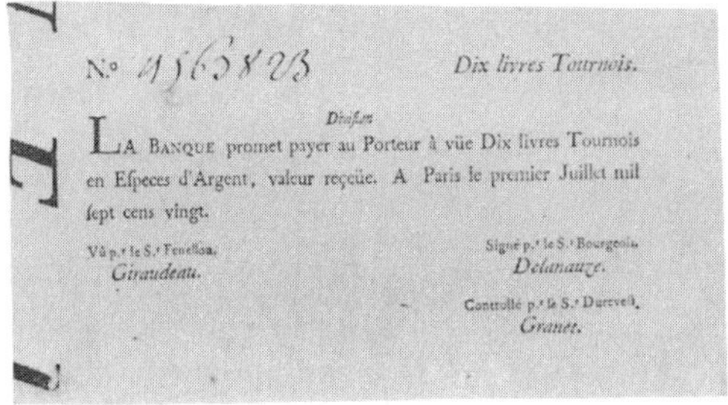

		Good	Fine	XF
A16	**10 Livres** 1.1.1720. Black. Lettered left edge.			
	a. Without text: *...en Espèces d'Argent.*	500	1,200	2,300
	b. With text: *...en Espèces d'Argent.*	200	300	500
A17	**100 Livres** 1.1.1720. Black. Lettered left edge.			
	a. Without text: *...en Espèces d'Argent.*	700	1,400	2,800
	b. With text: *...en Espèces d'Argent.*	120	300	5,500

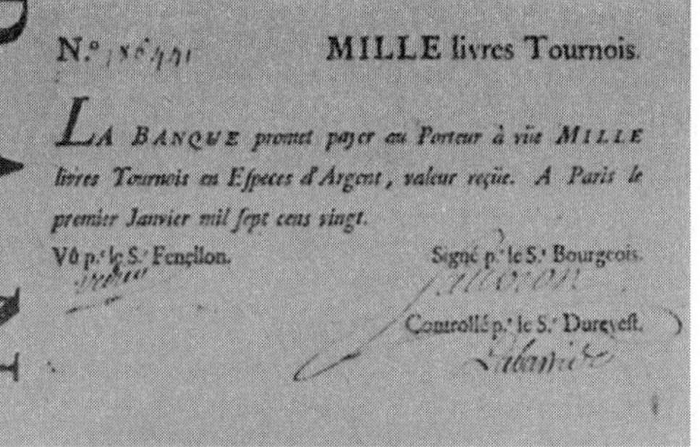

		Good	Fine	XF
A18	**1000 Livres** 1.1.1720. Black. Lettered left edge.			
	a. Without text: *...en Espèces d'Argent.*	—	—	—
	b. With text: *...en Espèces d'Argent.*	300	600	1,200
A19	**10,000 Livres** 1.1.1720. Black. Lettered left edge.	—	—	—

1720 Second Issue

		Good	Fine	XF
A20	**10 Livres** 1.7.1720. Black. Large letters at left edge. Blind embossed seal. 151x82mm.			
	a. With text: *...payer au Porteur à vüe Dix livres Tournois...*	120	300	450
	b. With text: *...payer au Porteur Dix livres a vue Tournois...*	500	1,000	2,200
	c. With text: *...espèces* (instead of *Espèces*).	—	—	—
A21	**100 Livres** 1.7.1720. Black. Lettered left edge.	300	700	1,200

1720 Third Issue

		Good	Fine	XF
A22	**10 Livres** 2.9.1720. Black. Lettered left edge.	200	500	900
A23	**50 Livres** 2.9.1720. Black. Lettered left edge.	200	400	950

Caisse d'Escompte

1776 Issue

		Good	Fine	XF
A24	**200 Livres** 1776-1790. Black. Without text: *Promesse d'Assignat.* PC: Green	900	2,400	4,500
A25	**300 Livres** 1776-1790. Black. Without text: *Promesse d'Assignat.* PC: Blue.	1,000	2,200	4,700
A26	**600 Livres** 1776-1790. Black. Without text: *Promesse d'Assignat.*	—	—	—
A27	**1000 Livres** 1776-1790. Black. Without text: *Promesse d'Assignat.*	900	2,200	4,500

1790 Issue

		Good	Fine	XF
A24A	**200 Livres** 1790-1793. Black. With text: *Promesse d'Assignat.*	—	—	—
A25A	**300 Livres** 1790-1793. Black. With text: *Promesse d'Assignat.*	—	—	—
A26A	**600 Livres** 1790-1793. Black. With text: *Promesse d'Assignat.*	—	—	—
A27A	**1000 Livres** 1790-1793. Black. With text: *Promesse d'Assignat.*	—	—	—

ASSIGNATS

Domaines Nationaux

1789 Issue

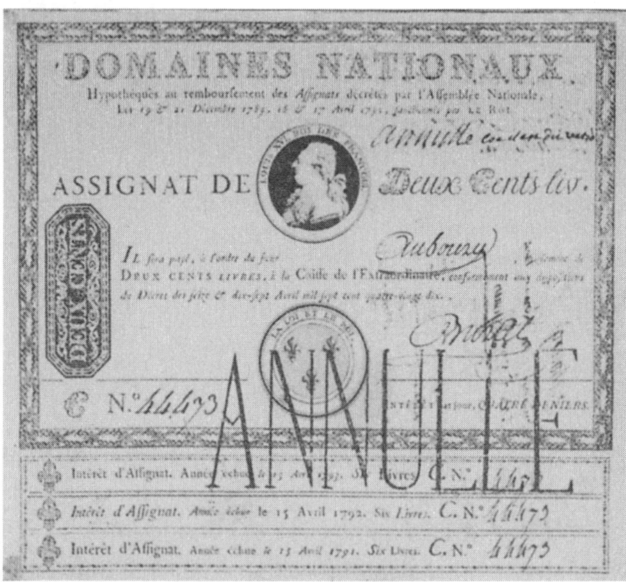

		Good	Fine	XF
A28	**200 Livres** 19&21.12.1789 and 16&17.4.1790. Black. Bust King Louis XVI at upper center.			
	a. Issued note complete with 3 coupons.	—	—	—
	b. Issued note without coupons.	800	2,200	4,500
	c. Cancelled with overprint: *ANNULE.*	—	—	—
A29	**300 Livres** 19&21.12.1789 and 16&17.4.1790. Black. Bust King Louis XVI at upper center. PC: Pink.			
	a. Issued note complete with 3 coupons.	—	—	—
	b. Issued note without coupons.	900	2,400	5,000
A30	**1000 Livres** 19&20.12.1789 and 16&17.4.1790. Red. Bust King Louis XVI at upper center.			
	a. Issued note complete with 3 coupons.	—	—	—
	b. Issued note without coupons.	1,800	4,000	7,000

1790 Interest Coupons

		Good	Fine	XF
A31	**6 Livres** 16/17.4.1790. Coupon of #A28. Black.	—	—	—
A32	**9 Livres** 16/17.4.1790. Coupon of #A29. Black.			
	a. Single coupon. Rare.	—	—	—
	b. Sheet of 3 coupons. Rare.	—	—	—
A33	**30 Livres** 16/17.1790. Coupon of #A30. Black.			
	a. Single coupon. Rare.	—	—	—
	b. Sheet of 3 coupons. Rare.	—	—	—

1790 Issue

		Good	Fine	XF
A34	**50 Livres** 29.9.1790. Black. King Louis XVI at top center.	45.00	125	200
A35	**60 Livres** 29.9.1790. Black. King Louis XVI at top center.	150	300	600
A36	**70 Livres** 29.9.1790. Black. King Louis XVI at top center.	220	400	600
A37	**80 Livres** 29.9.1790. Black. King Louis XVI at top center.	220	400	600
A38	**90 Livres** 29.9.1790. Black. King Louis XVI at top center.	250	500	750
A39	**100 Livres** 29.9.1790. Black. King Louis XVI at top center.	250	500	750

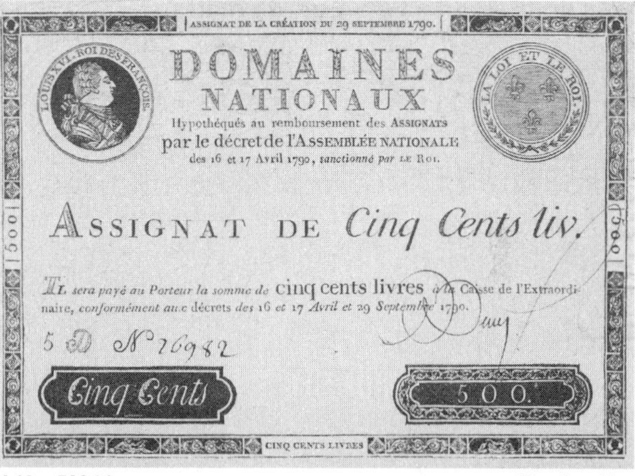

		Good	Fine	XF
A40	**500 Livres** 29.9.1790. Black. King Louis XVI at top left.	70.00	225	350
A41	**2000 Livres** 29.9.1790. Red. King Louis XVI at top left.	1,400	2,400	5,000

1791 First Issue

		Good	Fine	XF
A42	**5 Livres** 6.5.1791. Black.	5.00	12.50	30.00
A43	**50 Livres** 19.6.1791. Black. King Louis XVI at top center.	30.00	100	150

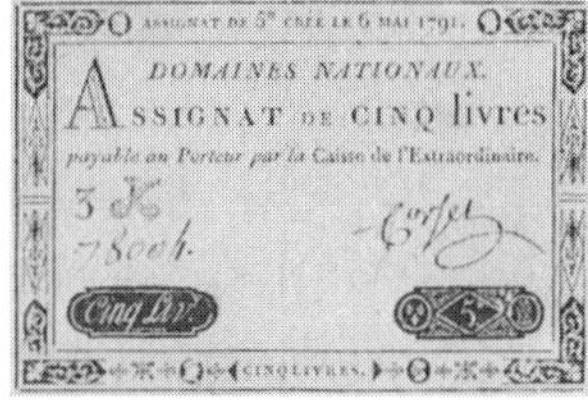

		Good	Fine	XF
A44	**60 Livres** 19.6.1791. Black. King Louis XVI at top center.	40.00	120	175

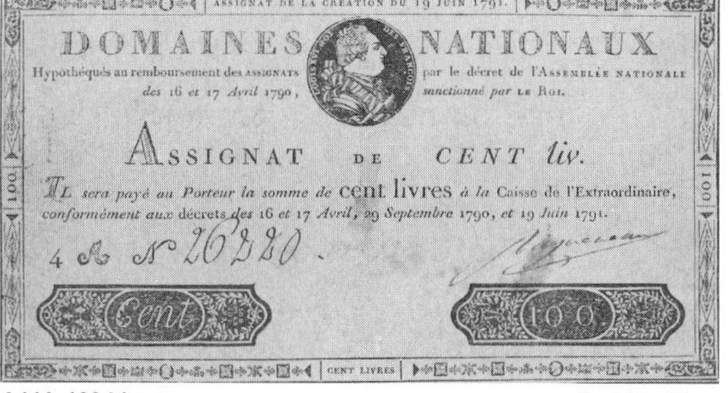

		Good	Fine	XF
A44A	**100 Livres** 19.6.1791. Black. King Louis XVI at top center.	30.00	100	150
A46	**500 Livres** 19.6.1791. Black. King Louis XVI at top center.	250	600	1,000

1791 Second Issue

		Good	Fine	XF
A47	**200 Livres** 19.6/12.9.1791. Black. King Louis XVI at top center.	100	200	400

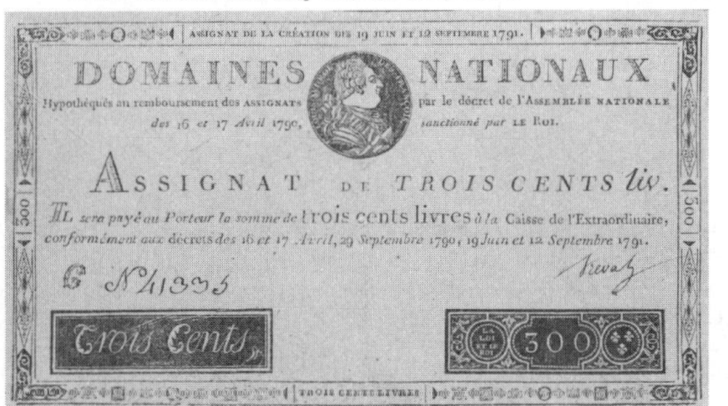

		Good	Fine	XF
A48	**300 Livres** 19.6/12.9.1791. Black. King Louis XVI at top center.	100	200	400

1791 Third Issue

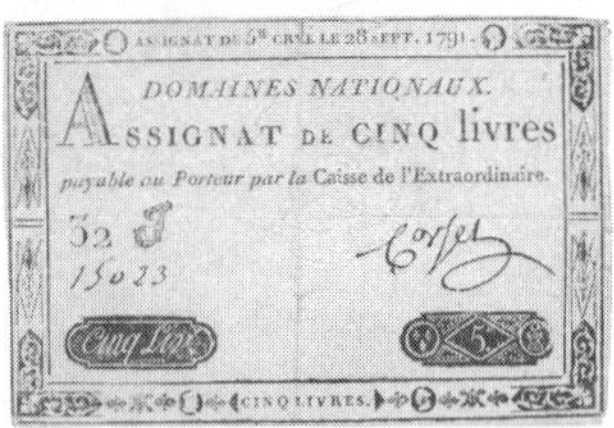

		Good	Fine	XF
A49	**5 Livres** 28.9.1791. Black. Like #A42.	5.00	10.00	30.00
A50	**5 Livres** 1.11.1791. Black. Like #A42.	5.00	10.00	30.00

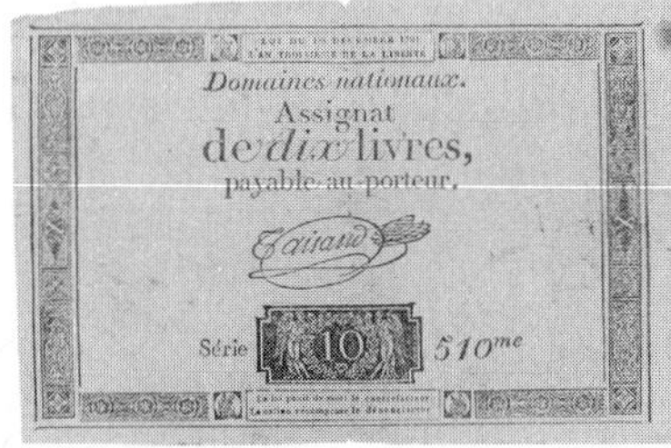

		Good	Fine	XF
A51	**10 Livres** 16.12.1791. Black.	4.00	8.00	20.00

		Good	Fine	XF
A52	**25 Livres** 16.12.1791. Black. King Louis XVI at top right, standing figure with Constitution at top left.	12.00	25.00	60.00

1792 First Issue

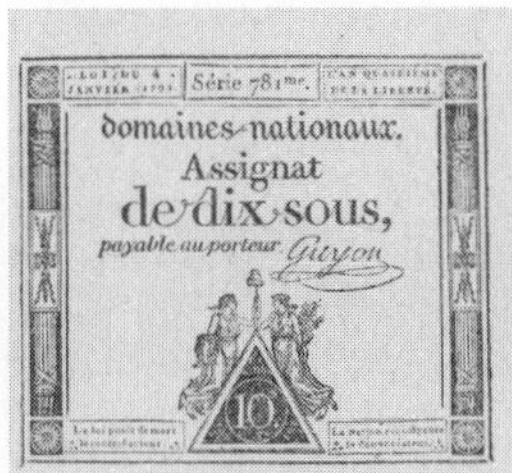

		VG	VF	UNC
A53	**10 Sous** 4.1.1792. Black. Fasces left and right, two women with Liberty cap on pole at lower center.	5.00	10.00	30.00

		VG	VF	UNC
A54	**15 Sols** 4.1.1792. Black. Two seated women with Liberty cap on pole at lower center.	5.00	10.00	30.00

		VG	VF	UNC
A55	**25 Sols** 4.1.1792. Black. Eye at upper center, rooster at lower center.	5.00	12.50	35.00

		VG	VF	UNC
A56	**50 Sols** 4.1.1792. Black. Allegorical woman at lower left and right.	5.00	10.00	30.00
A57	**5 Livres** 30.4.1792. Black. Like #A42.	5.00	12.50	35.00
A58	**50 Livres** 30.4.1792. Black. King Louis XVI at top center.	50.00	100	225
A59	**200 Livres** 30.4.1792. Black. King Louis XVI at top center.	150	300	600

1792 Second Issue

		VG	VF	UNC
A60	**5 Livres** 27.6.1792. Black. Like #A42.	5.00	10.00	30.00
A61	**5 Livres** 31.7.1792. Black. Like #A42.	5.00	10.00	30.00
A62	**50 Livres** 31.8.1792. Black. King Louis XVI at top center.	60.00	125	225
A63	**200 Livres** 31.8.1792. Black. King Louis XVI at top center.	150	300	600

1792 Third Issue

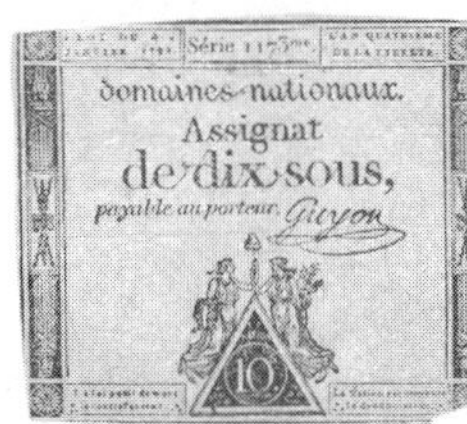

		VG	VF	UNC
A64	**10 Sous** 24.10.1792. Black. Fasces left and right, two women with Liberty cap on pole at lower center.			
	a. Issued note.	5.00	10.00	30.00
	b. Error note with text: *La loi punit...* at lower left, repeated at lower right.	50.00	200	400

		VG	VF	UNC
A65	**15 Sols** 24.10.1792. Black. Two seated women with Liberty cap on pole at lower center.	5.00	10.00	20.00

		VG	VF	UNC
A66	**10 Livres**			
	24.10.1792. Black. Like #A51.			
	a. Watermark: Fleur-de-lis.	10.00	25.00	50.00
	b. Watermark. *RP-FR* top left. *X.*	5.00	10.00	25.00

		VG	VF	UNC
A67	**25 Livres**			
	24.10.1792. Black. Standing figure with Constitution at top left, King Louis XVI at top right.	12.50	35.00	75.00

1793 Issue

		VG	VF	UNC
A68	**10 Sous**			
	23.5.1793. Black. Fasces left and right.			
	a. Watermark: *LA NATION...* Series 1/16.	8.00	15.00	40.00
	b. Watermark: *RF/Xs.*	5.00	10.00	25.00
	c. Error note with text: *La loi puni...*at lower left, repeated at lower right.	50.00	200	400

		VG	VF	UNC
A69	**15 Sols**			
	23.5.1793. Black. Two seated women with Liberty cap on pole at lower center.			
	a. Watermark: *LA NATION...* Series 1/42.	8.00	15.00	40.00
	b. Watermark: *RF/15s.*	5.00	10.00	30.00
	c. Error note with text: *LA NATION...*at lower right, repeated at lower left	50.00	200	400

		VG	VF	UNC
A70	**50 Sols**			
	23.5.1793. Black. Allegorical women at lower left and right.			
	a. Watermark: *LA NATION...* Series 1/36.	8.00	15.00	35.00
	b. Watermark. *RF/50s.*	5.00	10.00	25.00

		VG	VF	UNC
A71	**25 Livres**			
	6.6.1793. Black. Small standing figures at left and right border.	5.00	10.00	30.00

République Française

1792 Issue

		VG	VF	UNC
A72	**50 Livres**			
	14.12.1792. Black. Seated figure with shovel on pedestal at lower center.	15.00	40.00	85.00

		VG	VF	UNC
A73	**400 Livres**			
	21.11.1792. Black. Eagle and Liberty cap at lower center, sun with rays behind.	20.00	50.00	100

1793 First Issue

		VG	VF	UNC
A74	**125 Livres**			
	7 Vendemiaire An II (28.9.1793). Black.	20.00	60.00	125

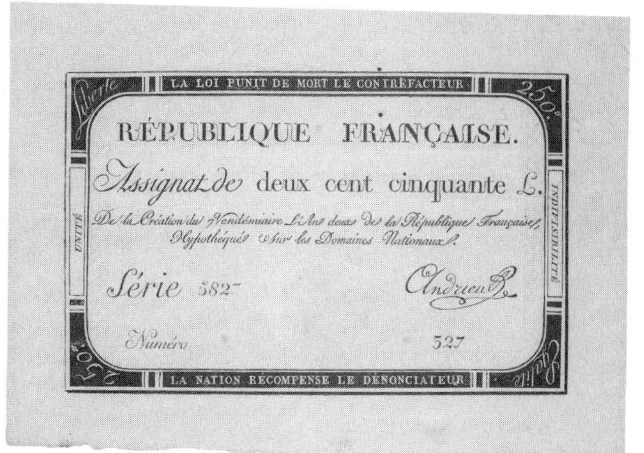

		VG	VF	UNC
A75	**250 Livres**			
	7 Vendemiaire An II (28.9.1793). Black.	25.00	75.00	180

1793 Second Issue

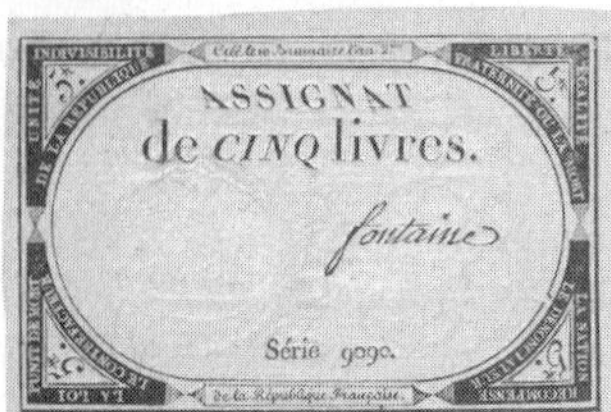

		VG	VF	UNC
A76	**5 Livres** 10 Brumaire An II (31.10.1793). Black.	5.00	10.00	20.00

1794 Issue

		VG	VF	UNC
A77	**500 Livres** 20 Pluviôse An II (8.2.1794). Black.	15.00	45.00	110

1795 Franc Issue

		Good	Fine	XF
A78	**100 Francs** 18 Nivôse An III (7.1.1795). Black.	5.00	10.00	25.00

		Good	Fine	XF
A79	**750 Francs** 18 Nivôse An III (7.1.1795). Black.	400	1,100	1,800

		Good	Fine	XF
A80	**1000 Francs** 18 Nivôse An III (7.1.1795). Redish orange.	30.00	85.00	225

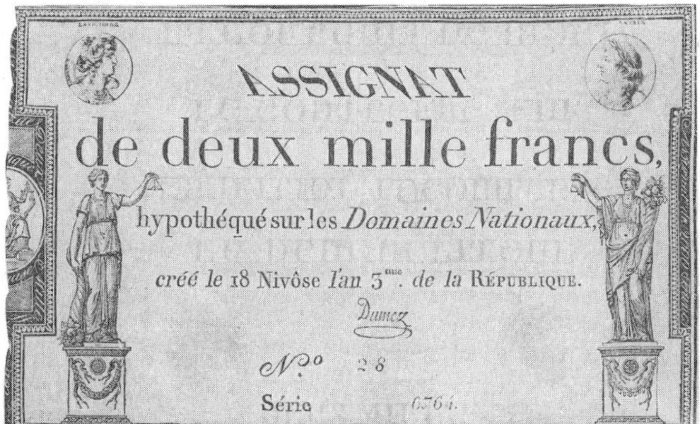

		Good	Fine	XF
A81	**2000 Francs** 18 Nivôse An III (7.1.1795). Black.	45.00	125	300

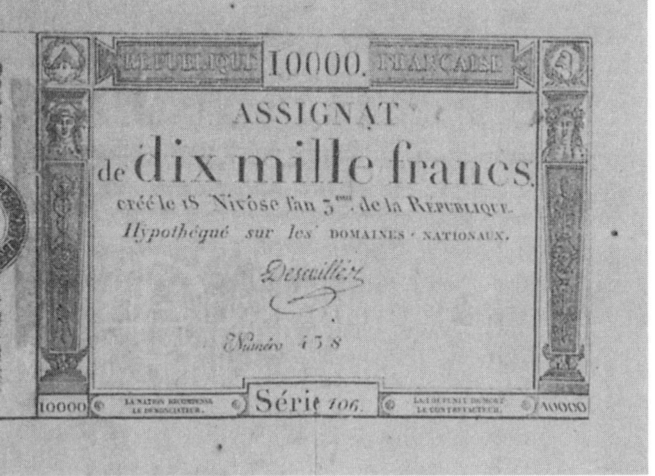

		Good	Fine	XF
A82	**10,000 Francs** 18 Nivôse An III (7.1.1795). Black.	100	200	400

Promesses de Mandats Territoriaux

1796 Issue

		Good	Fine	XF
A83	**25 Francs** 28 Ventôse An IV (18.3.1796). Black and olive. Signature varieties.			
	a. Without *Serie.*	15.00	30.00	60.00
	b. With *Serie.*	10.00	20.00	35.00
A84	**100 Francs** 28 Ventôse An IV (18.3.1796). Red and blue-gray. Signature varieties.	Good	Fine	XF
	a. Without *Serie.*	30.00	70.00	125
	b. With *Serie.*	8.00	25.00	50.00
A85	**250 Francs** 28 Ventôse An IV (18.3.1796). Olive and black. Signature varieties.	Good	Fine	XF
	a. Without *Serie.*	25.00	70.00	125
	b. With *Serie.*	15.00	40.00	90.00

		Good	Fine	XF
A86	**500 Francs** 28 Ventôse An IV (18.3.1796). Gray-blue and red. Signature varieties.			
	a. Without *Serie.*	30.00	70.00	125
	b. With *Serie.*	15.00	30.00	65.00

Mandats Territoriaux

1796 Issue

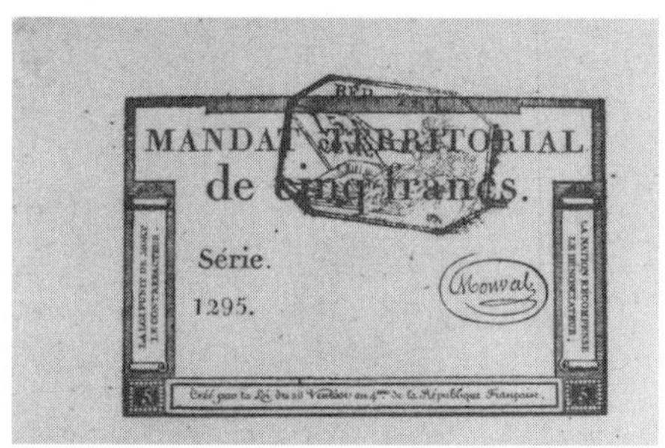

		Good	Fine	XF
A87	**5 Francs** 28 Ventôse An IV (18.3.1796). Black.			
	a. Without handstamp.	400	800	1,300
	b. Black handstamp: *Rep. Fra.*	50.00	100	200
	c. Red handstamp: *Rep. Fra.*	50.00	100	200

Rescriptions de l'Emprunt Forcé

1796 Issue

		Good	Fine	XF
A88	**25 Francs** 21 Nivôse An IV (11.1.1796). Black.	175	400	650
A89	**50 Francs** 21 Nivôse An IV (11.1.1796). Black.	300	700	1,100

		Good	Fine	XF
A90	**100 Francs** 21 Nivôse An IV (11.1.1796). Black.	175	400	650
A91	**250 Francs** 21 Nivôse An IV (11.1.1796). Black.	350	750	1,200
A92	**500 Francs** 21 Nivôse An IV (11.1.1796). Black.	500	1,200	2,000
A93	**1000 Francs** 21 Nivôse An IV (11.1.1796). Black.	650	1,500	2,500

Armée Catholique et Royale

1793 Issue

		Good	Fine	XF
A94	**Sous or Livres** 2.8.1793. Black. Assignats with handwritten notice: *Au nom du Roi bon pour...* (In the name of the King good for...)	—	—	—

1793-1794 Bons de Manlevrier

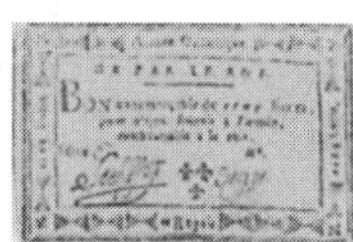

		Good	Fine	XF
A94A	**10 Sous** ND (1794). Black.	35.00	100	250
A94B	**15 Sous** ND (1794). Black.	35.00	100	250
A95	**5 Livres** ND (Nov. 1793). Black.	35.00	100	250
A96	**10 Livres** ND (Nov. 1793). Black.	50.00	150	400
A97	**25 Livres** ND (Nov. 1793). Black.	65.00	200	500
A98	**50 Livres** ND (Nov. 1793). Black.	75.00	225	550
A99	**100 Livres** ND (Nov. 1793). Black.	85.00	250	600

1794 Bons de Passage

		Good	Fine	XF
A100	**Livres - various handwritten amounts** ND (1794). Deep red. Louis XVII at top center. Uniface.			
	a. Issued note.	750	1,500	—
	r. Remainder without signature or value filled in.	500	1,000	—
	x. Printed *500 Livre* (counterfeit).	25.00	50.00	100

DIRECTORATE & CONSULATE THROUGH SECOND REPUBLIC

Bons Porteur (Directorate, 1795-1799)

1798 Issue

		Good	Fine	XF
A121	**25 Francs** An VII (1798). Black.			
	a. Without red text: *TRESIE NATL* at upper right.	75.00	150	325
	b. With red text: *TRESIE NATL* at upper right.	85.00	200	450

Bon Au Porteur (Consulate, 1799-1804)

1799 Issue

		Good	Fine	XF
A131	**25 Francs** (1799-1801). Black.			
	a. An VIII (1799).	75.00	150	325
	c. An X (1801).	75.00	150	325

Banque de France

1800 Provisional Issue

		Good	Fine	XF
1	**500 Francs** 1800. Blue and red. Overprint: *Payable a la Banque de France* on Caisse de Comptes Courants notes.	—	—	—

No.	Description	Good	Fine	XF
2	**1000 Francs** 1800. Black and red. Overprint: *Payable a La Banque de France* on Caisse de Compte Courants notes. Rare.	—	—	—

1800 Regular Issue

No.	Description	Good	Fine	XF
5	**500 Francs** 21.6.1800-27.10.1802. Blue and red. Name as *Banque de France.* Rare.	—	—	—
10	**1000 Francs** 21.6.1800-28.4.1802. Black and red. Name as *Banque de France.* Rare.	—	—	—

1803-1806 Issue

No.	Description	Good	Fine	XF
15	**500 Francs** 19.2.1806-29.8.1806. Allegorical figures at left and right. Rare.	—	—	—
16	**1000 Francs** 14.4.1803-16.4.1812. Allegorical figures at left and right. 4 signature varieties. Rare.	—	—	—

1810-1814 Issue

No.	Description	Good	Fine	XF
20	**250 Francs** 27.9.1810-2.1.1812. With text: *Comptoir de Lille...* Rare. PC: Green.	—	—	—
21	**1000 Francs** 25.4.1814-4.4.1816. Printed seal at upper left and right. Rare.	—	—	—

1817-1818 Issue

No.	Description	Good	Fine	XF
25	**500 Francs** 2.1.1818-3.7.1828. Women at top center and at left, Mercury at right.			
	a. Watermark: *Cinq Cents 500 Fr.* Date handwritten. 6 signature varieties. Up to 8.8.1822. Rare.	—	—	—
	b. Watermark: *Cinq Cents Fr. Banque de France BF.* Date handwritten. 8.4.1824-22.5.1825. Rare.	—	—	—
	c. Date printed. 19.4.1827-3.7.1828. Rare.	—	—	—
26	**1000 Francs** 1817-1829. Woman in chariot drawn by lions at top center, seated allegorical figures at left and right.			
	a. Watermark: *Mille Francs 1000 Fr.* Rose field. 3 signature varieties. 17.4.1817-8.4.1824. Rare.	—	—	—
	b. Watermark: Like "a", but rusty-brown field. 6 signature varieties. 27.11.1817-13.3.1823. Rare.	—	—	—
	c. Watermark: *Mille Francs - Banque de France.* 20.1.1825-14.5.1829. Rare.	—	—	—

1829 Issue

No.	Description	Good	Fine	XF
30	**500 Francs** 5.3.1829-15.9.1831. Women at top center and left, Mercury at right. Top left and right text in circle.			
	a. Signature title: *LE DIRECTEUR.* 2 Signature varieties. Up to 22.4.1830. Rare.	—	—	—
	b. Signature title: *LE SECRÉTAIRE DU GOUVERNEMENT DE LA BANQUE.* 2 Signature varieties. 15.9.1831. Rare.	—	—	—
31	**1000 Francs** 26.11.1829-3.2.1831. Women in chariot drawn by lions at top center. Seated allegorical figures at left and right. *Banque de France* stamped.			
	a. Signature title: *LE DIRECTEUR.* 3 Signature varieties. 25.3.1830. Rare.	—	—	—
	b. Signature title: *LE SECRÉTAIRE DU GOUVERNEMENT DE LA BANQUE.* Rare.	—	—	—

1831-1837 Issue

No.	Description	Good	Fine	XF
35	**250 Francs** 9.6.1836-13.8.1846. Women at top center and at left, Mercury at right, two reclining women at bottom center. PC: Green.			
	a. Signature title: *Secrétaire du Gouvernement de la Banque.* Up to 14.10.1841. Rare.	—	—	—
	b. Signature title: *Secrétaire Général 14.12.1843.* Rare.	—	—	—
36	**500 Francs** 1831-1843. Like #30 but back printed in reverse. Women at top center and left. Mercury at right. Top left and right text in circle.			
	a. Signature title: *LE SECRÉTAIRE DU GOUVERNEMENT DE LA BANQUE.* 3 Signature varieties. 15.9.1831-25.11.1841. Rare.	—	—	—
	b. Signature title: *LE SECRÉTAIRE GÉNÉRAL.* 25.6.1842-13.7.1843. Rare.	—	—	—
37	**1000 Francs** 15.9.1831-25.11.1841. Like #31, but back printed in reverse. Women in chariot drawn by lions at top center, seated allegorical figures at left and right. *Banque de France* stamped. 3 signature varieties. Rare.	—	—	—
38	**1000 Francs** 28.2.1837-17.2.1848. Like #37, but *Comptoir de ...* (name of place) stamped. Women in chariot drawn by lions at top center, seated allegorical figures at left and right. Rare.	—	—	—

1842-1846 Issue

No.	Description	Good	Fine	XF
40	**500 Francs** 1844-1863. Woman at left, man at right, woman seated at bottom center with two cherubs.			
	a. Watermark: *Cinq Cents Fr. Banque de France.* 22.2.1844. Rare.	—	—	—
	b. Watermark: *Cinq Cents Fr. Banque de France BF.* 5.9.1844-21.10.1847. Rare.	—	—	—
	c. Watermark: *500 F. Cinq Cents Fr. Banque de France.* 6 signature varieties. 21.4.1848-15.1.1863. Rare.	—	—	—
41	**1000 Francs** 25.6.1842-13.11.1862. Two female allegorical figures at left, right, top center and at bottom center.			
	a. Watermark: *Mille Francs - Banque de France.* 25.6.1842-24.10.1844. Rare.	—	—	—
	b. Watermark: *1000 Fr. Mille Francs - Banque de France.* 7 signature varieties. From 24.10.1844. Rare.	—	—	—
	c. Name of branch bank below *Banque de France.* 12.10.1848-27.9.1849. Rare.	—	—	—
	d. Name of branch bank on counterfoil at right. 28.1.1850-23.8.1860. Rare.	—	—	—
42	**5000 Francs** 28.5.1846. Red. Women in chariot drawn by lions at top center. Seated allegorical figure at left and right. 2 signature varieties. Rare.	—	—	—

1848 Provisional Issue

No.	Description	Good	Fine	XF
44	**100 Francs** 1848. Black on green underprint.			
	a. Signature in script. 16.3.1848. Rare.	—	—	—
	b. Printed signature. Serial # at left and r. 4.5.1848. Rare.	—	—	—
	c. Printed signature. Serial # at right, series letter at left. 15.7.1848. Rare.	—	—	—

1847-1848 Regular Issues

No.	Description	Good	Fine	XF
45	**100 Francs** 1848-1863. Woman at top center, woman at left, two recumbent women at bottom.			
	a. Signature black. 14.9.1848-24.1.1856. Rare.	—	—	—
	b. Signature blue. 2 Signature varieties. 25.1.1856-8.1.1863. Rare.	—	—	—
46	**200 Francs** 10.6.1847-27.10.1864. Woman at left, Mercury at right, two recumbent women at bottom center. Oval frame. Various succursales (branches).			
	a. Without name of branch bank below *BANQUE DE FRANCE* and with 3 signature varieties. Rare.	—	—	—
	b. Name of branch bank below *BANQUE DE FRANCE* and with 4 signature Rare.	—	—	—
	c. Name of branch bank in blue printing on counterfoil at right. Rare.	—	—	—

		Good	Fine	XF
47	**200 Francs** 9.3.1848-30.3.1848. Woman in chariot drawn by lions at top center. Square frame. Rare. PC: Yellowish.	—	—	—

1862-1868 Issue

		Good	Fine	XF
50	**50 Francs** 1864-1866. Blue. Two cherubs, coat of arms at bottom center.			
	a. Watermark: *B-F.* 2.3.1864-6.6.1864.	2,800	5,000	12,000
	b. Watermark: Head of Mercury. 7.6.1864-8.6.1866.	2,800	5,000	12,000
51	**50 Francs** 26.11.1868-16.11.1883. Blue and black. Two cherubs, arms at bottom center. Like #50.	Good	Fine	XF
	a. Printed serial # at upper left and lower right. 4 signature varieties. Paris printing.	1,000	2,000	6,250
	b. Handwritten serial # at upper left and lower right, star at left, right, and above denomination. Clermont-Ferrand printing. 15.9.1870-27.10.1870.	—	—	—
52	**100 Francs** 1863-1882. Blue. Allegorical figures of four women and numerous cherubs.	Good	Fine	XF
	a. Blue serial #, date on back. 8.1.1863-19.6.1866.	—	—	—
	b. Black serial #, date on face, 4 signature varieties. 23.8.1866-13.4.1882.	1,175	3,800	10,000
53	**500 Francs** 1863-1887. Back and face with same imprint. Woman at left, man at right, woman seated at bottom center with two cherubs.	Good	Fine	XF
	a. Blue serial #. 5.11.1863-2.4.1868.	—	—	—
	b. Black serial #. Signature title: *LE CONTROLEUR.* 5 signature varieties. 25.6.1868-19.6.1882.	4,165	12,450	—
	c. Signature title: *LE CONTROLEUR GÉNÉRAL.* 3 Signature varieties. 20.6.1882-20.8.1887.	4,000	11,000	—
54	**1000 Francs** 1862-1889. Blue. Two female allegorical figures at left, right, top and bottom center.	Good	Fine	XF
	a. Blue serial #. 4.12.1862-2.11.1866. Rare.	—	—	—
	b. Like a., but name of branch bank below *Banque de France.* Rare.	—	—	—
	c. Black serial #. Signature title: *LE CONTROLEUR.* 20.6.1867-16.8.1882. Rare.	2,780	8,300	—
	d. Like c., but signature title: *LE CONTROLEUR GÉNÉRAL.* Foursignature varieties. 17.8.1882-28.6.1889. Rare.	2,340	7,300	—
	e. Name of branch bank below *BANQUE DE FRANCE* and in red on counterfoil at right. Rare.	—	—	—

1870 Issue

		Good	Fine	XF
55	**20 Francs** 23.12.1870-29.5.1873. Blue. Seated woman at lower center.	215	875	3,550

		Good	Fine	XF
56	**25 Francs** 1870-1873. Blue. Seated woman at lower center. Like #55.			
	a. Printed serial # at upper left and lower right. Paris printing. 16.8.1870-17.11.1870; 10.3.1873.	2,280	6,800	—
	b. Handwritten serial # at upper left and lower right, star at left, right and above denomination (in letters). Clermont-Ferrand printing. 18.11.1870-15.9.1870.	1,300	4,000	—

THIRD REPUBLIC THRU WWII

Banque de France

1871-1874 Issue

Consecutive dates of the day of printing, thus many varieties of dates and also of signature quoted were the first and last date of printing (not the date of issue). Listings are given by sign. combination for each note, w/values according to relative scarcity. The signs of the zodiac are used in place of the date on some notes.

		VG	VF	UNC
60	**5 Francs** 1.12.1871-19.1.1874. Blue, denomination in black. Man standing at left, woman standing with staff at right. Back: Three allegorical figures.	350	1,130	3,200
61	**20 Francs** 1874-1905. Blue on ochre underprint., denomination in black. Mercury seated at left, woman seated at right. Back: Woman's head at left and right.	VG	VF	UNC
	a. A. Mignot and Marsaud. 1.7.1874-7.8.1875.	500	1,900	—
	b. V. d'Anfreville and Giraud. 1.6.1904.	395	1,350	—

1882-1884 Issue

		VG	VF	UNC
62	**50 Francs** 1884-1889. Blue. Women at left and right, two small angels above, caduceus at each corner. Back: Allegorical figures.			
	a. Signature A. Mignot and F. Carre. 1.8.1884-23.10.1885.	3,150	8,550	—
	b. Signature E. Bertin and F. Carre. 2.1.1886-15.2.1886.	3,400	9,100	—
	c. Signature E. Bertin and Billotte. 18.10.1888-4.3.1889.	3,400	9,100	—
63	**100 Francs** 1882-1888. Blue. Two women seated.	VG	VF	UNC
	a. Signature A. Mignot and de Jancigny. 2.1.1882-10.1.1882.	9,100	17,000	—
	b. Signature A. Mignot and F. Carre. 11.1.1882-31.12.1885.	1,600	4,700	—
	c. Signature C. Bertin and F. Carre. 2.1.1886-13.1.1888.	1,750	5,000	—
	d. Signature C. Bertin and Billotte. 16.7.1888-11.9.1888.	2,500	7,400	—

1888-1889 Issue

64	50 Francs	VG	VF	UNC
	1889-1927. Blue on lilac underprint. Similar to #62. Women at left and right, two small angels above, caduceus at each corner. Five women in medallions at center. Back: Allegorical figures.			
	a. Signature E. Bertin and Billotte. 1.5.1889-3.8.1889. Rare.	1,600	4,000	—
	b. Signature V. d'Anfreville and Billotte. 27.2.1890-26.5.1900.	420	1,250	—
	c. Signature V. d'Anfreville and Giraud. 2.1.1901-30.12.1905.	195	820	—
	d. Signature V. d'Anfreville and E. Picard. 2.1.1906-13.7.1907.	160	770	—
	e. Signature J. Laferriere and E. Picard. 16.7.1907-8.11.1919.	30.00	175	—
	f. Signature J. Laferriere and A. Aupetit. 15.11.1920-6.6.1921.	80.00	480	—
	g. Signature L. Platet and A. Aupetit. 1.5.1922-20.4.1925.	23.50	135	—
	h. Signature L. Platet and P. Strohl. 1.7.1926-25.3.1927.	28.50	135	—

65	100 Francs	VG	VF	UNC
	1888-1909. Blue on pink underprint. Like #63 but four women at center.			
	a. Signature C. Bertin and Billotte. 12.9.1888-31.12.1889.	700	2,850	—
	b. Signature V. d'Anfreville and Billotte. 2.1.1890-5.7.1900.	390	1,450	—
	c. Signature V. d'Anfreville and Giraud. 18.7.1900-30.12.1905.	245	890	—
	d. Signature V. d'Anfreville and E. Picard. 2.1.1906-12.3.1907.	215	850	—
	e. Signature J. Laferriere and E. Picard. 1.8.1907-29.1.1909.	205	900	—

Note: For the four provisional overprint issues which are found on #65b (old dates 1892-93), see French West Africa #3, Guadeloupe #15, Madagascar #34, and Tunisia #31.

66	500 Francs	VG	VF	UNC
	1888-1937. Blue on lilac underprint. Woman at left, Mercury at right. Ornate oval border with cherubs, animals and three figures at bottom. Back: Allegorical figures. Signature title: *LE CAISSIER PRINCIPAL* added.			
	a. Signature A. Delmotte, C. Bertin and Billote. 2.11.1888-8.7.1889.	4,000	10,250	—
	b. Signature A. Delmotte, V. d'Anfreville and Billotte. 9.1.1890-24.4.1897.	3,000	6,900	—
	c. Signature Bouchet, V. d'Anfreville and Billotte. 23.3.1899-30.6.1900.	2,950	6,400	—
	d. Signature Panhard, V. d'Anfreville and Giraud. 7.2.1901-17.4.1902.	2,750	6,500	—
	e. Signature Frachon, V. d'Anfreville and Giraud. 27.8.1903-26.12.1904.	2,500	5,700	—
	f. Signature Frachon, V. d'Anfreville and E. Picard. 22.2.1906-10.9.1906.	1,800	5,100	—
	g. Signature Frachon, J. Laferriere and E. Picard. 24.10.1907-4.10.1917.	120	475	—
	h. Signature A. Aupetit, J. Laferriere and E. Picard. 1.4.1920-21.6.1920.	90.00	500	—
	i. Signature J. Emmery, J. Laferriere and A. Aupetit. 3.1.1921-9.2.1921.	100	625	—
	j. Signature J. Emmery, L. Platet and A. Aupetit. 1.5.1922-11.9.1924.	50.00	250	—
	k. Signature J. Emmery, L. Platet and P. Strohl. 1.7.1926-26.10.1929.	35.00	225	—
	l. Signature Roulleau, L. Platet and P. Strohl. 1.4.1930-29.12.1932.	22.50	200	—
	m. Signature Roulleau, J. Boyer and P. Strohl. 12.1.1933-10.6.1937.	24.50	210	—

67	1000 Francs	VG	VF	UNC
	1889-1926. Blue on lilac underprint. Mercury at left, woman in medallion at right, many allegorical figures in border. Back: Allegorical figures.			
	a. Signature A. Delmotte, C. Bertin and Billotte. 7.11.1889-29.11.1889. Rare.	—	—	—
	b. Signature A. Delmotte, V. d'Anfreville and Billotte. 23.1.1890-14.3.1898.	2,150	4,550	—
	c. Signature Bouchet, V. d'Anfreville and Billotte. 27.10.1898-21.6.1900.	1,700	4,100	—
	d. Signature Panhard, V. d'Anfreville and Giraud. 9.4.1901-10.2.1902.	1,900	4,200	—
	e. Signature Frachon, V. d'Anfreville and Giraud. 23.10.1902-30.12.1905.	1,700	4,000	—
	f. Signature Frachon, V. d'Anfreville and E. Picard. 2.1.1906-23.5.1907.	1,650	3,900	—
	g. Signature Frachon, J. Laferriere and E. Picard. 7.5.1908-24.1.1919.	75.00	285	—
	h. Signature A. Aupetit, J. Laferriere and E. Picard. 15.5.1919-27.2.1920.	60.00	240	—
	i. Signature J. Emmery, J. Laferriere and A. Aupetit. 15.11.1920-29.4.1921.	57.00	205	—
	j. Signature J. Emmery, L. Platet and A. Aupetit. 1.5.1922-26.6.1926.	45.00	180	—
	k. Signature J. Emmery, L. Platet and P. Strohl. 1.7.1926-16.9.1926.	57.00	250	—

1906-1908 Issue

68	20 Francs	VG	VF	UNC
	1906-1913. Blue on ochre underprint. Mercury seated at left, woman seated at right. Denomination in blue. Back: Woman's head at left and right.			
	a. Signature V. d'Anfreville and E. Picard. 2.1.1906-25.10.1906.	100	315	2,850
	b. Signature J. Laferriere and E. Picard. 2.1.1912-12.2.1913.	57.00	230	1,700

69	100 Francs	VG	VF	UNC
	2.1.1908-10.5.1909. Multicolor. Woman with child at left and right. Bale marked *LOM 02* at right. Back: Blacksmith at left, woman and child at right.	140	880	—

1909-1912 Issue

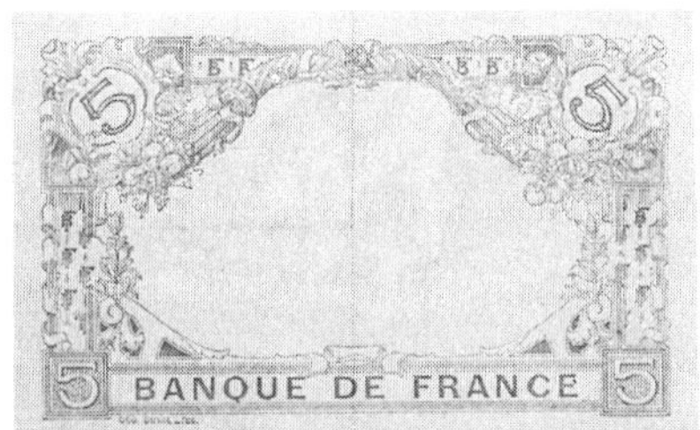

		VG	VF	UNC
70	**5 Francs** 2.1.1912-2.2.1917. Blue. Man standing at left, woman standing with staff at right. Back: Ornaments.	35.00	135	600

		VG	VF	UNC
71	**100 Francs** 1909-1923. Multicolor. Woman with child at left and right. Without *LOM 02*. Back: Blacksmith at left, woman and child at right.			
	a. Signature J. Laferriere and E. Picard. 11.5.1909-12.4.1920.	8.00	65.00	—
	b. Signature J. Leferriere and A. Aupetit. 15.11.1920-21.9.1921.	19.00	140	—
	c. Signature L. Platet and A. Aupetit. 1.5.1922-29.11.1923.	12.50	90.00	—

1916-1918 Issue

		VG	VF	UNC
72	**5 Francs** 1917-1933. Lilac. Woman wearing helmet at left. Back: Dock worker and sailing ship. Signature titles: *LE CAISSIER PRINCIPAL* and *LE SECRÉTAIRE GÉNÉRAL*.			
	a. Signature J. Laferriere and E. Picard. 1.12.1917-23.1.1919.	20.00	85.00	300
	b. Signature J. Laferriere and A. Aupetit. 15.11.1920-16.6.1921.	27.00	110	540
	c. Signature L. Platet and A. Aupetit. 1.5.1922-21.7.1925.	7.50	40.00	190
	d. Signature L. Platet and P. Strohl. 1.7.1926-29.12.1932.	5.00	30.00	155
	e. Signature J. Boyer and P. Strohl. 5.1.1933-14.9.1933.	3.00	17.00	80.00

		VG	VF	UNC
73	**10 Francs** 1916-1937. Blue. Minerva at upper left. Back: Sitting farm woman. Signature titles: *LE CAISSIER PRINCIPAL* and *LE SECRÉTAIRE GÉNÉRAL*.			
	a. Signature J. Laferriere and E. Picard. 3.1.1916-15.11.1918.	11.00	57.00	350
	b. Signature J. Laferriere and A. Aupetit. 15.11.1920-6.6.1921.	35.00	170	1,000
	c. Signature L. Platet and A. Aupetit. 1.5.1922-26.6.1926.	7.00	34.00	260
	d. Signature L. Platet and P. Strohl. 1.7.1926-8.9.1932.	4.50	40.00	155
	e. Signature J. Boyer and P. Strohl. 17.12.1936-25.2.1937.	20.00	85.00	650

Note: For 5 and 10 Francs similar to #72 and 73 but w/later dates, see #83 and 84.

		VG	VF	UNC
74	**20 Francs** 1.7.1916-21.2.1919. Blue. Portrait Bayard at left. Back: Farmer with scythe.	55.00	260	2,450

		VG	VF	UNC
75	**100 Francs** ND (1917). Black on multicolor underprint. Standing woman at center. Printer: ABNC. Face proof. Rare.	—	—	—

		Good	Fine	XF
76	**5000 Francs** 2.1.1918-29.1.1918 (1938). Multicolor. Worker seated with Mercury at upper left, angelic child figure with symbols of agriculture and painting at upper right. Back: Paris.	550	2,250	9,650

1923-1927 Issue

		VG	VF	UNC
77	**50 Francs** 11.2.1927-17.7.1930. Brown, blue and multicolor. Two angels above, Mercury below. Artist's name *Luc-Olivier Merson* below frame. Back: Woman and man in two wreaths. Artist's name *Luc-Olivier Merson* below frame.			
	a. 11.2.1927-13.12.1929.	43.00	265	—
	b. 10.7.1930-24.7.1930.	135	740	—

		VG	VF	UNC
78	**100 Francs** 1923-1937. Multicolor. Woman with child at left and right. Recess in the frame for serial number expanded from 20 to 23 mm. Signature title: *LE CAISSIER PRINCIPAL.*			
	a. Signature L. Platet and A. Aupetit. 29.11.1923-26.6.1926.	4.50	34.00	—
	b. Signature L. Platet and P. Strohl. 1.7.1926-29.12.1932.	2.50	15.00	685
	c. Signature J. Boyer and P. Strohl. 12.1.1933-30.6.1937.	2.50	11.00	625

		VG	VF	UNC
79	**1000 Francs** 1927-1937. Light brown, blue and multicolor. Ceres at left, Mercury at right, two small angels below. Signature title: *LE CAISSIER PRINCIPAL.* Back: Four different craftsmen.			
	a. Signature J. Emmery, L. Platet and P. Strohl. 11.2.1927-5.2.1930.	9.00	65.00	—
	b. Signature Roulleau, L. Platet and P. Strohl. 1.4.1930-29.12.1932.	7.50	50.00	—
	c. Signature Roulleau, J. Boyer and P. Strohl. 12.1.1933-30.6.1937.	8.00	65.00	—

1930 Issue

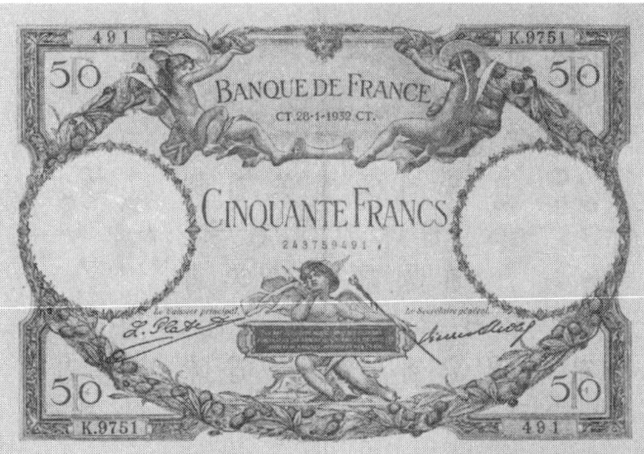

		VG	VF	UNC
80	**50 Francs** 1930-1934. Brown, blue and multicolor. Two angels above, Mercury below. Back: Woman and man in Two wreaths.			
	a. Signature L. Platet and P. Strohl. 24.7.1930-29.12.1932.	32.00	180	—
	b. Signature J. Boyer and P. Strohl. 12.1.1933-16.8.1934.	37.00	200	—

1934 Issue

		VG	VF	UNC
81	**50 Francs** 15.11.1934-30.6.1937. Brown and multicolor. Ceres and Park of Versailles at left, reclining figure at right. Signature title: *LE CAISSIER PRINCIPAL.* Back: Mercury at right with caduceus.	15.00	95.00	1,050

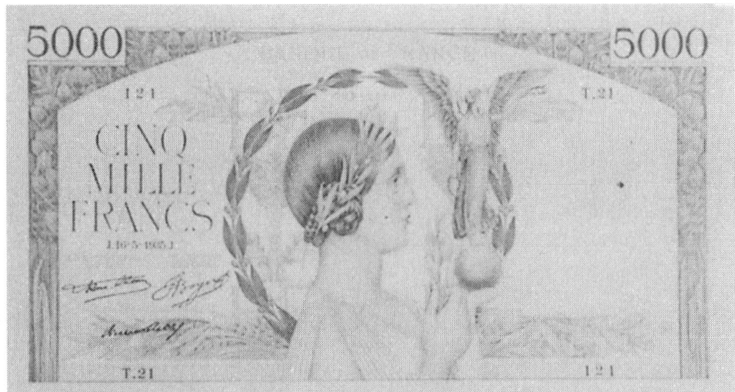

82	5000 Francs	VG	VF	UNC
	1934-1935. Purple and multicolor. Woman with Victory statuette and olive branch at center. Signature title: *LE CAISSIER PRINCIPAL.* Back: Statuette in rotogravure.			
	a. 8.11.1934.	180	800	—
	b. 16.5.1935; 11.7.1935.	165	770	—

1937-1939 Issue

83	5 Francs	VG	VF	UNC
	13.7.1939-26.12.1940. Lilac. Woman wearing helmet at left. Signature title: *LE CAISSIER GÉNÉRAL.* Back: Dock worker and sailing ship.	2.00	10.00	80.00
84	10 Francs	VG	VF	UNC
	2.2.1939-5.3.1942. Blue. Minerva at upper left. Signature title: *LE CAISSIER GÉNÉRAL.* Back: Sitting farm woman.	2.00	10.00	100

85	50 Francs	VG	VF	UNC
	1937-1940. Ceres and Park of Versailes at left, reclining figure at right. Signature title: *LE CAISSIER GÉNÉRAL.* Back: Mercury at right with caduceus.			
	a. Signature J. Boyer and R. Favre-Gilly. 5.8.1937-9.9.1937.	23.00	110	1,350
	b. Signature P. Rousseau and R. Favre-Gilly. 4.11.1937-18.4.1940.	8.50	45.00	850

86	100 Francs	VG	VF	UNC
	1937-1939. Multicolor. Minerva at upper left. Signature title: *LE CAISSIER GÉNÉRAL.* Back: Sitting farm woman. Thin or thick paper.			
	a. Signature J. Boyer and R. Favre-Gilly. 9.9.1937-2.12.1937.	16.00	88.00	1,350
	b. Signature P. Rousseau and R. Favre-Gilly. 9.12.1937-14.9.1939.	3.00	15.00	550

87	300 Francs	VG	VF	UNC
	ND (1938). Brown and multicolor. Ceres at left. Back: Mercury at right.			
	a. Issued note.	90.00	400	2,850
	r. Replacement note. With *W* prefix. 24.11.1938.	225	900	3,950

88	500 Francs	VG	VF	UNC
	1937-1940. Blue on pink underprint. Woman at left, Mercury at right. Signature title: *LE CAISSIER GÉNÉRAL.* Back: Ornate oval border with cherubs, animals and three figures at bottom.			
	a. Signature P. Strohl, J. Boyer and R. Favre-Gilly. 5.8.1937-9.9.1937.	23.00	285	—
	b. Signature P. Strohl, P. Rousseau and R. Favre-Gilly. 2.12.1937-9.12.1937.	23.00	285	—
	c. Signature H. de Bletterie, P. Rousseau and R. Favre-Gilly. 24.3.1938-18.1.1940.	14.50	180	—

		VG	VF	UNC
89	**500 Francs**	VG	VF	UNC
	ND. Ceres at left. Back: Mercury at right. Proof.	—	—	—
90	**1000 Francs**	VG	VF	UNC
	1937-1940. Ochre, blue and multicolor. Ceres at left, Mercury at right, two small angels below. Signature title: *LE CAISSIER GÉNÉRAL*. Back: Four different craftsmen. Thin or thick paper.			
	a. Signature P. Strohl, J. Boyer and R. Favre-Gilly. 8.7.1937-26.8.1937.	30.00	155	—
	b. Signature P. Strohl, P. Rousseau and R. Favre-Gilly. 4.11.1937-23.12.1937.	18.50	95.00	—
	c. Signature H. de Bletterie, P. Rousseau and R. Favre-Gilly. 24.3.1938-18.7.1940.	7.50	35.00	320
91	**5000 Francs**	VG	VF	UNC
	13.10.1938. Woman with Victory statuette and olive branch at center. Signature title: *LE CAISSIER GÉNÉRAL*. Back: Statuette in rotogravure.	180	625	—

1939-1940 Issue

		VG	VF	UNC
92	**20 Francs**	VG	VF	UNC
	1939-1942. Blue on multicolor underprint. Allegories of Science and Labor at right. Back: Scientist and city view with bridge at left.			
	a. 7.12.1939-3.10.1940.	20.00	115	950
	b. 17.10.1940-4.12.1941.	12.00	60.00	700
	c. 8.1.1942.	35.00	170	1,700

		VG	VF	UNC
93	**50 Francs**	VG	VF	UNC
	13.6.1940-15.5.1942. Brown, green and multicolor. Jacques Coeur at left. Back: Scene in Bourges, woman at right.	3.00	17.50	90.00

		VG	VF	UNC
94	**100 Francs**	VG	VF	UNC
	19.5.1939-23.4.1942. Brown and multicolor. Woman and child with background of Paris. Back: Maximilien de Béthune, Duc de Sully, looking over field scene with farm, castle, rivers.	2.50	10.00	90.00

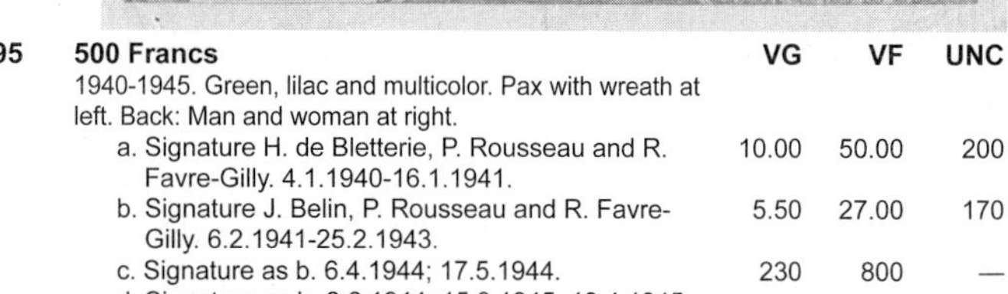

		VG	VF	UNC
95	**500 Francs**	VG	VF	UNC
	1940-1945. Green, lilac and multicolor. Pax with wreath at left. Back: Man and woman at right.			
	a. Signature H. de Bletterie, P. Rousseau and R. Favre-Gilly. 4.1.1940-16.1.1941.	10.00	50.00	200
	b. Signature J. Belin, P. Rousseau and R. Favre-Gilly. 6.2.1941-25.2.1943.	5.50	27.00	170
	c. Signature as b. 6.4.1944; 17.5.1944.	230	800	—
	d. Signature as b. 8.6.1944; 15.3.1945; 19.4.1945.	—	—	—

		VG	VF	UNC
96	**1000 Francs**	VG	VF	UNC
	1940-1944. Multicolor. Woman at left and right. Back: Blacksmith and Mercury.			
	a. Signature H. de Bletterie, P. Rousseau and R. Favre-Gilly. 24.10.1940-19.12.1940.	20.00	62.50	295
	b. Signature J. Belin, P. Rousseau and R. Favre-Gilly. 6.2.1941-29.6.1944.	24.00	95.00	375
	c. Signature as b. 6.7.1944-20.7.1944.	20.00	70.00	300
	d. Signature as b. 10.8.1944; 12.10.1944. Rare.	—	—	—

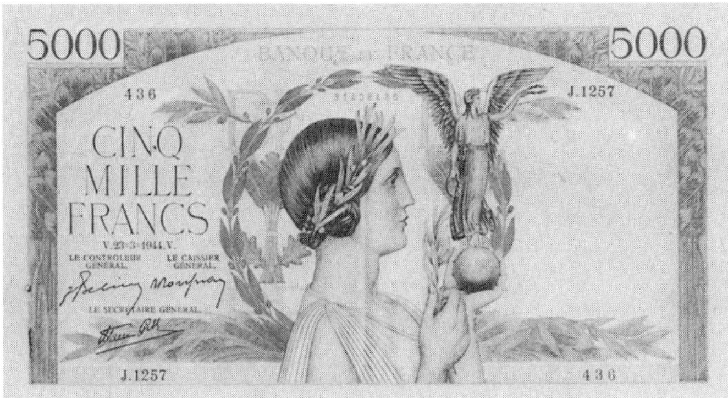

97	5000 Francs	VG	VF	UNC
	1938-1944. Woman with Victory statuette and olive branch at center.			
	a. Signature H. de Bletterie, P. Rousseau and R. Favre-Gilly. 8.12.1938-26.12.1940.	16.00	80.00	—
	b. Signature as a. 19.1.1939.	17.00	80.00	—
	c. Signature J. Belin, P. Rousseau, and R. Favre-Gilly. 10.4.1941-10.12.1942.	15.50	80.00	—
	d. Signature as c. 7.1.1943-18.3.1943.	30.00	125	—
	e. Signature as c. 23.3.1944-6.4.1944.	105	310	—

1941-1943 Issue

98	5 Francs	VG	VF	UNC
	1943-1947. Blue, green and multicolor. Pyrenean shepherd at right. Back: Woman and flowers.			
	a. Signature P. Rousseau and R. Favre-Gilly. 2.6.1943-5.4.1945.	2.00	8.00	40.00
	b. Signature P. Rousseau and P. Gargam. 30.10.1947.	2.00	9.00	45.00

99	10 Francs	VG	VF	UNC
	1941-1949. Brown and multicolor. Miners at left, another at right. Back: Cows at left, farm woman and child at right.			
	a. Signature P. Rousseau and R. Favre-Gilly. 11.9.1941.	5.50	28.50	250
	b. Sign as a. 9.10.1941; 19.11.1942; 14.1.1943; 19.4.1945.	3.50	19.00	115
	c. Signature as a. 11.6.1942; 20.1.1944.	2.50	10.50	62.50
	d. Signature as a. 15.10.1942; 9.9.1943.	1.00	8.00	48.50
	e. Signature as a. 26.11.1942; 25.3.1943; 13.1.1944; 22.6.1944-9.1.1947.	1.00	6.00	38.00
	f. Signature P. Rousseau and P. Gargam. 30.10.1947-30.6.1949.	1.25	6.50	43.00

100	20 Francs	VG	VF	UNC
	1942-1950. Red and multicolor. Breton fisherman at right. Back: Two women at left center, Breton calvary statuary at right.			
	a. Signature P. Rousseau and R. Favre-Gilly. 12.2.1942-17.5.1944.	1.50	7.00	65.00
	b. Signature as a. 5.7.1945; 9.1.1947.	2.00	8.50	65.00
	c. Signature P. Rousseau and P. Gargam. 29.1.1948-3.11.1949.	1.50	7.00	60.00
	d. Signature as c. 9.2.1950.	17.00	45.00	180

101	100 Francs	VG	VF	UNC
	1942-1944. Multicolor. Descartes at right. Allegorical female reclining at left. Back: Angel.			
	a. 15.5.1942-12.10.1944.	19.50	67.00	280
	b. 7.1.1943.	68.00	340	1,365
101A	500 Francs	VG	VF	UNC
	14.1.1943. Black, brown and multicolor. Portrait Colbert with globe at left, statue of Mercury at right, and early sailing ships in background. Back: Allegorical figure at right with dockside scene in background. Watermark: Ceres. Rare.	—	—	28,500

		VG	VF	UNC
102	**1000 Francs** 28.5.1942-20.1.1944. Brown and multicolor. Ceres/Demeter seated with Hermes at right. Back: Mercury.	6.00	25.00	165

Note: A few notes dated 1943 and all those dated 1944 were not issued.

		VG	VF	UNC
103	**5000 Francs** 1942-1947. Brown, red and multicolor. Allegory of France with three men (French colonies) at center. Back: Same woman alone, but with scenes from colonies.			
	a. Signature J. Belin, P. Rousseau and R. Favre-Gilly. 5.3.1942-12.11.1942.	27.50	130	—
	b. Signature as a. 27.4.1944; 28.9.1944.	65.00	250	—
	c. Signature as a. 18.1.1945-9.1.1947.	17.00	78.00	—
	e. Signature J. Belin, P. Rousseau and P. Gargam. 20.3.1947-25.9.1947.	23.00	130	710

ND 1938 Provisional Issue

		VG	VF	UNC
104	**3000 Francs** ND. Green. Large value at center. Provisional printing. Proof.	—	—	—

WWII

Tresor Central

Government Notes

		VG	VF	UNC
105	**100 Francs** 2.10.1943. Blue on green and violet underprint. Portrait Marianne at center. Back: Anchor, barrel, bale, other implements at center. Printer: BWC without imprint. Issued in Corsica.			
	a. Issued note.	26.50	115	300
	s. Specimen.	—	—	1,140

		VG	VF	UNC
106	**500 Francs** ND (1944). Brown. Portrait Marianne at left. 2 serial # varieties. Printer: TDLR (without imprint).	17.00	50.00	180

		VG	VF	UNC
107	**1000 Francs** ND (1944). Green. Portrait Marianne at center. Two serial # varieties. Printer: TDLR without imprint.	13.00	60.00	175
108	**1000 Francs** 2.10.1943. Green. Phoenix rising at center. Similar to French Equatorial Africa #14. Printer: BWC (without imprint).	VG	VF	UNC
	a. (Not issued). Rare.	—	—	11,400
	s. Specimen.	—	—	7,950

		VG	VF	UNC
109	**5000 Francs** ND. Blue. Portrait Marianne at right. Printer: TDLR (without imprint).			
	a. Issued note. Rare.	—	—	13,650
	s. Specimen. Rare.	—	—	8,550
110	**5000 Francs** 2.10.1943. Marianne with flag and torch. Specimen. Rare.	—	—	9,100

1945 Provisional Issue

		VG	VF	UNC
111	**500 Francs** ND (1945). Blue on green underprint. Printer: French. Issued in Corsica.	370	1,600	—

		VG	VF	UNC
112	**1000 Francs** ND (1945). Multicolor. Printer: French. Issued in Corsica.			
	a. Overprint on #86. Watermark: Head. (-old date 2.7.1942).	115	420	—
	b. Overprint on #89. Watermark: lettering: *Banque de l'Algérie* (-old dates 14.8.1942; 17.8.1942; 2.11.1942).	210	760	—

		VG	VF	UNC
113	**5000 Francs** 1945. Brown-violet on pink underprint. Printer: French. All notes were destroyed. No examples known. Issued in Corsica.	—	—	—

Allied Military Currency

1944 First Issue - Supplemental French Franc Currency

		VG	VF	UNC
114	**2 Francs** 1944. Green with black border. Torch at left and right in green underprint. With text: *EMIS EN FRANCE.* Printer: Forbes Lithograph Manufacturing Co., Boston. Replacement notes with X near serial #.			
	a. Issued note.	2.50	8.00	57.00
	b. Block #2.	2.50	8.00	57.00
	s. Specimen.	—	—	305

		VG	VF	UNC
115	**5 Francs** 1944. Blue and black on green underprint. Torch at left and right in green underprint. With text: *EMIS EN FRANCE.* Printer: Forbes Lithograph Manufacturing Co., Boston. Replacement notes with X near serial #.			
	a. Issued note.	2.50	13.50	68.00
	b. Block #2.	3.50	17.00	115
	s. Specimen.	—	—	305

		VG	VF	UNC
116	**10 Francs** 1944. Lilac and black on green underprint. Torch at left and right in green underprint. With Text: *EMIS EN FRANCE.* Printer: Forbes Lithograph Manufacturing Co., Boston. Replacement notes with X near serial #.			
	a. Issued note.	2.50	13.50	80.00
	s. Specimen.	—	—	365

		VG	VF	UNC
117	**50 Francs** 1944. Lilac and black on green and blue underprint. Text: *EMIS EN FRANCE.* Printer: Forbes Lithograph Manufacturing Co., Boston. Replacement notes with X near serial #.			
	a. Issued note.	11.50	51.00	250
	s. Specimen.	—	—	740

		VG	VF	UNC
118	**100 Francs** 1944. Dark blue and black on green and blue underprint. Text: *EMIS EN FRANCE.* Printer: Forbes Lithograph Manufacturing Co., Boston. Replacement notes with X near serial #.			
	a. Issued note.	14.00	62.50	260
	b. Block #2.	17.00	85.00	400
	s. Specimen.	—	—	740

		VG	VF	UNC
119	**500 Francs** 1944. Brown and black on green and blue underprint. With text: *EMIS EN FRANCE.* Printer: Forbes Lithograph Manufacturing Co., Boston. Replacement notes with X near serial #.			
	a. Issued note.	57.00	205	795
	s. Specimen.	—	—	685

		VG	VF	UNC
120	**1000 Francs** 1944. Red and black on green and blue underprint. Text:*EMIS EN FRANCE.* Printer: Forbes Lithograph Manufacturing Co., Boston. Replacement notes with X near serial #.			
	a. Issued note.	510	1,365	—
	s. Specimen.	—	—	1,365

		VG	VF	UNC
121	**5000 Francs** 1944. Green and black on green and blue underprint. Text:*EMIS EN FRANCE.* Printer: Forbes Lithograph Manufacturing Co., Boston. Replacement notes with X near serial #.	—	—	7,950

1944 Second Issue - Provisional French Franc Currency

Note: Authorized by French Committee of National Liberation.#122-126 replacement notes with *X* near serial #.

		VG	VF	UNC
122	**50 Francs** 1944. Similar to #117.			
	a. Issued note.	3.50	16.00	100
	b. Block #2.	3.50	16.00	68.00
	c. Block #3.	4.00	17.00	90.00
	s. Specimen perforated: *SPECIMEN.*	—	—	795

		VG	VF	UNC
123	**100 Francs** 1944. Similar to #118.			
	a. Issued note.	2.50	11.00	45.00
	b. Block #2. Numbered at USA-BEP; position of small #2 at left. is at left. center.	2.00	9.00	34.00
	c. Blocks #3-8. Numbered at Forbes; position of larger run # at left. is nearer to l. border.	2.00	9.00	34.00
	d. Block #9.	17.00	75.00	285
	e. Block #10.	11.00	50.00	160
	s. Specimen.	—	—	740

		VG	VF	UNC
124	**500 Francs** 1944. Similar to #119.			
	a. Not officially issued.	—	5,700	—
	s. Specimen perforated: *SPECIMEN.*	—	—	2,100

		VG	VF	UNC
125	**1000 Francs** 1944. Similar to #120.			
	a. Issued note.	57.00	225	625
	b. Block #2.	57.00	225	570
	c. Block #3.	62.50	250	625
	s. Specimen with *X.*	—	—	1,140

		VG	VF	UNC
126	**5000 Francs** 1944. Similar to #121. Specimen perforated: *SPECIMEN.*	—	—	4,330

REPUBLIC

Banque de France

1945-1949 Issue

For notes dated after 1945 in the old Franc currency see #98, 99, 100 and 103.

		VG	VF	UNC
126A	**10 Francs** ND (1946). Proof. Blue. Mercury at left, Ceres at right. Back: Ceres at center.	—	—	—

		VG	VF	UNC
127	**50 Francs** 1946-1951. Red, blue and multicolor. Leverrier at right. Back: Neptune and date *1846*.			
	a. Signature P. Rousseau and R. Favre-Gilly. 14.3.1946-3.10.1946.	4.50	19.00	150
	b. Signature P. Rousseau and P. Gargam. 20.3.1947-2.3.1950.	3.25	13.00	110
	c. Signature J. Cormier and P. Gargam. 29.6.1950-1.2.1951.	4.50	60.00	160
	d. Signature G. Gouin d'Ambrieres and P. Gargam. 7.6.1951.	57.00	230	685

Note: #59 was first issued to coinside with the centennial of Leverrier's discovery of Neptune in 1846.

		VG	VF	UNC
128	**100 Francs** 1945-1954. Brown, red and multicolor. Farmer with two oxen. Back: Man, woman and children at dockside. Watermark: Woman with hair parted on her left.			
	a. Signature P. Rousseau and R. Favre-Gilly. 7.11.1945-9.1.1947.	2.50	10.50	100
	b. Signature P. Rousseau and P. Gargam. 3.4.1947-19.5.1949.	2.50	10.50	85.00
	c. Signature J. Cormier and P. Gargam. 29.6.1950-16.11.1950.	5.00	23.00	190
	d. Signature G. Gouin d'Ambrieres and P. Gargam. 6.9.1951-1.4.1954.	3.00	13.00	90.00
	e. Watermark reversed, hair parted on her right. 2.10.1952; 6.8.1953; 1.10.1953; 7.1.1954; 4.3.1954; 1.4.1954.	3.50	17.00	112
	f. Signature as a. 17.7.1947, #203 & 204.	200	750	2,000

		VG	VF	UNC
129	**500 Francs** 1945-1953. Purple and multicolor. Chateaubriand at center with musical instrument. Back: Allegorical figures.			
	a. Signature J. Belin, P. Rousseau and R. Favre-Gilly. 19.7.1945-9.1.1947.	15.50	65.00	650
	b. Signature J. Belin, P. Rousseau and P. Gargam. 13.5.1948.	57.00	285	1,700
	c. Signature J. Belin, G. Gouin d'Ambrieres and P. Gargam. 3.7.1952-2.7.1953.	15.00	45.00	600

		VG	VF	UNC
130	**1000 Francs** 1945-1950. Blue and multicolor. Minerva and Hercules at center. Back: Woman at center.			
	a. Signature J. Belin, P. Rousseau and R. Favre-Gilly. 12.4.1945-9.1.1947.	6.50	30.00	250
	b. Signature J. Belin, P. Rousseau and P. Gargam. 11.3.1948-20.4.1950.	5.50	26.50	200
	c. Signature J. Belin, J. Cormier and P. Gargam. 29.6.1950.	17.00	68.00	685

		VG	VF	UNC
131	**5000 Francs** 1949-1957. Multicolor. Two allegorical figures (Sea and Countryside) at center. Back: Mercury and allegorical woman.			
	a. Signature J. Belin, P. Rousseau and P. Gargam. 10.3.1949-3.11.1949.	15.50	90.00	—
	b. Signature J. Belin, J. Cormier and P. Gargam. 1.2.1951-5.4.1951.	15.50	90.00	1,140
	c. Signature J. Belin, G. Gouin d'Ambrieres and P. Gargam. 16.8.1951-6.12.1956.	14.50	73.00	1,180
	d. Signature G. Gouin d'Ambrieres, R. Favre-Gilly and P. Gargam. 7.3.1957-7.11.1957.	20.00	95.00	—

		VG	VF	UNC
132	**10,000 Francs** 1945-1956. Multicolor. Young woman with book and globe.			
	a. Signature J. Belin, P. Rousseau and R. Favre-Gilly. 27.12.1945-9.1.1947.	150	485	—
	b. Signature J. Belin, P. Rousseau and P. Gargam. 3.11.1949-16.2.1950.	155	530	—
	c. Signature J. Belin, J. Cormier and P. Gargam. 8.6.1950-5.4.1951.	70.00	265	—
	d. Signature J. Belin, G. Gouin d'Ambrieres and P. Gargam. 4.5.1951-7.6.1956.	35.00	155	—
	s. Specimen.	—	—	3,400

1953-1957 Issue

		VG	VF	UNC
133	**500 Francs** 1954-158. Blue, orange and multicolor. Building at left, Victor Hugo at right. Back: Hugo at left, Panthéon in Paris.			
	a. Signature J. Belin, G. Gouin d'Ambrieres and P. Gargam. 7.1.1954-4.8.1955.	17.00	95.00	1,150
	b. Signature G. Gouin d'Ambrieres, R. Favre-Gilly and P. Gargam. 7.2.1957-30.10.1958.	25.00	130	1,490

Note: #133 dated 1959 with overprint: *5 NF* is #137.

		VG	VF	UNC
134	**1000 Francs** 1953-1957. Multicolor. Palais Cardinal across, Armand du Plessis, Cardinal Richelieu at right. Back: Town gate (of Richelieu, in Indre et Loire) at right.			
	a. Signature J. Belin, G. Gouin d'Ambrieres and P. Gargam. 2.4.1953-6.12.1956.	10.50	50.00	500
	b. Signature G. Gouin d'Ambrieres, R. Favre-Gilly and P. Gargam. 7.3.1957-5.9.1957.	30.00	125	570
135	**5000 Francs** 1957-1958. Multicolor. Henry IV at center, Paris' *Pont Neuf* bridge in background. Back: Henry IV at center, Château de Pau at left.	**VG**	**VF**	**UNC**
	a. Signature G. Gouin d'Ambrieres, R. Favre-Gilly, and P. Gargam. 7.2.1957-10.7.1958.	90.00	340	2,475
136	**10,000 Francs** 1955-1958. Multicolor. Arc de Triomphe at left, Napoléon Bonaparte at right. Back: *Church of the Invalides* in Paris at right, Bonaparte at left.	**VG**	**VF**	**UNC**
	a. Signature J. Belin, G. Gouin d'Ambrieres and P. Gargam. 1.12.1955-6.12.1956.	14.00	120	550
	b. Signature G. Gouin d'Ambrieres, R. Favre-Gilly, P. Gargam. 4.4.1957-2.10.1958.	11.50	110	520

		VG	VF	UNC
136A	**50,000 Francs** ND (1956). Specimen. (Not issued). Multicolor. Molière at center. Back: Molière at center.	—	—	—

1958 Provisional Issue

		VG	VF	UNC
137	**5 Nouveaux Francs on 500 Francs** ND (1960-old dates 1958).			
	a. 30.10.1958.	200	800	3,200

		VG	VF	UNC
138	**10 Nouveaux Francs on 1000 Francs** ND (-old date 7.3.1957).	80.00	320	1,820

139	50 Nouveaux Francs on 5000 Francs	VG	VF	UNC
	ND (-old dates 1958-1959).			
	a. 30.10.1958.	115	455	2,850
	b. 5.3.1959.	170	685	—

140	100 Nouveaux Francs on 10,000 Francs	VG	VF	UNC
	ND (-old date 30.10.1958).	140	515	—

140A	500 Nouveaux Francs on 50,000 Francs	VG	VF	UNC
	ND. Multicolor.			
	a. (Not Issued). Rare.	—	—	—
	s. Specimen. 0s in serial # and date. Rare.	—	—	—

1959 Issue

141	5 Nouveaux Francs	VG	VF	UNC
	5.3.1959-5.11.1965. Blue, orange and multicolor. Panthéon in Paris at left, Victor Hugo at right,denomination: *NOUVEAUX FRANCS* (NF). Back: Vosges place at right, Victor Hugo at left.			
	a. Issued note.	9.00	52.00	530
	s. Specimen.	—	340	1,250

142	10 Nouveaux Francs	VG	VF	UNC
	5.3.1959-4.1.1963. Multicolor. *Palais Royal* across bottom, Armand du Plessis, Cardinal Richelieu at right,denomination: *NOUVEAUX FRANCS* (NF). Back: Town gate (of Richelieu, in *Indre et Loire*) at right.			
	a. Issued note.	6.00	21.50	370
	s. Specimen.	—	340	1,250
143	50 Nouveaux Francs	VG	VF	UNC
	5.3.1959-6.7.1961. Multicolor. Henry IV at center, Paris' *Pont Neuf* bridge in background, denomination: *NOUVEAUX FRANCS* (NF). Back: Henry IV at center, *Château de Pau* at left.			
	a. Issued note.	42.00	175	1,520
	s. Specimen.	—	455	2,850
144	100 Nouveaux Francs	VG	VF	UNC
	5.3.1959-2.4.1964. Multicolor. Arc de Triomphe at left, Napoléon Bonaparte at right, denomination: *NOUVEAUX FRANCS* (NF). Back: Paris' *Church of the Invalides* at right, Bonaparte at left.			
	a. Issued note.	15.00	52.00	1,280
	s. Specimen.	—	455	2,050
145	500 Nouveaux Francs	VG	VF	UNC
	1959-1966. Multicolor. Jean Baptiste Poquelin called Molière at center Paris' *Palais Royal* in background, denomination: *NOUVEAUX FRANCS* (NF). Back: Theater in Versailles.			
	a. Signature G. Gouin D'Ambrières, R. Tondu and P. Gargam. 2.7.1959-8.1.1965.	145	460	—
	b. Signature H. Morant, R. Tondu and P. Gargam. 6.1.1966.	160	510	—
	s. Specimen. As b.	—	625	2,280

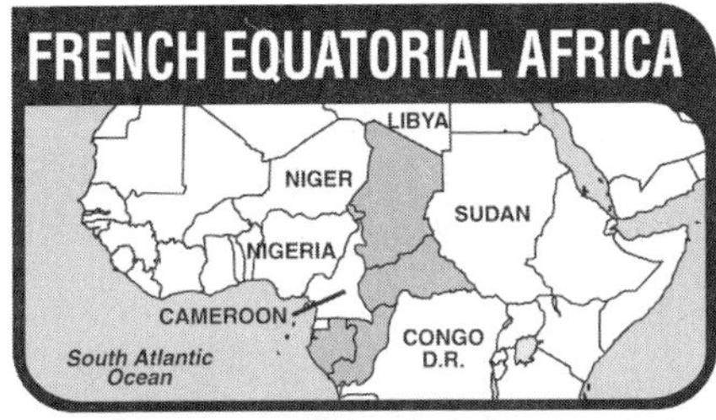

French Equatorial Africa, an area consisting of four self governing dependencies (Middle Congo, Ubangi-Shari, Chad and Gabon) in west-central Africa, has an area of 969,111 sq. mi. (2,509,987 sq. km.) and a population of 3.5 million. Capital: Brazzaville. The area, rich in natural resources, exported cotton, timber, coffee, cacoa, diamonds and gold. Little is known of the history of these parts of Africa prior to French occupation - which began with no thought of territorial acquisition. France's initial intent was simply to establish a few supply stations along the west coast of Africa to service the warships assigned to combat the slave trade in the early part of the 19th century. French settlement began in 1839. Gabon (then Gabun) and the Middle Congo were secured between 1885 and 1891; Chad and the Ubangi-Shari between 1894 and 1897. The four colonies were joined to form French Equatorial Africa in 1910. The dependencies were changed from colonies to territories within the French Union in 1946, and all the inhabitants were made French citizens. In 1958, they voted to become autonomous republics within the new French Community, and attained full independence in 1960.

RULERS:
French to 1960

MONETARY SYSTEM:
1 Franc = 100 Centimes

FRENCH ADMINISTRATION

Gouvernement Général

1917 ND Emergency Issue

		VG	VF	UNC
1	**50 Centimes** ND (1917). Green on blue underprint.			
	a. Without watermark. 3 signature varieties.	20.00	90.00	175
	b. Watermark: Laurel leaves.	20.00	90.00	175

		VG	VF	UNC
2	**1 Franc** ND (1917). Red on blue underprint.			
	a. Without watermark. 3 signature varieties.	25.00	100	225
	b. Watermark: Laurel leaves.	25.00	100	225

		VG	VF	UNC
3	**2 Francs** ND (1917). Blue on yellow underprint. Like #2. 2 signature varieties.	40.00	140	350

1925 Provisional Issue

		VG	VF	UNC
3A	**25 Francs** 9.7.1925. Rare.	—	—	—

Bons de Caisse

1940 Emergency WWII Issue

		VG	VF	UNC
4	**1000 Francs** 25.10.1940; 20.12.1940. Green on yellow paper. Man rowing boat at center. Rare.	—	—	—

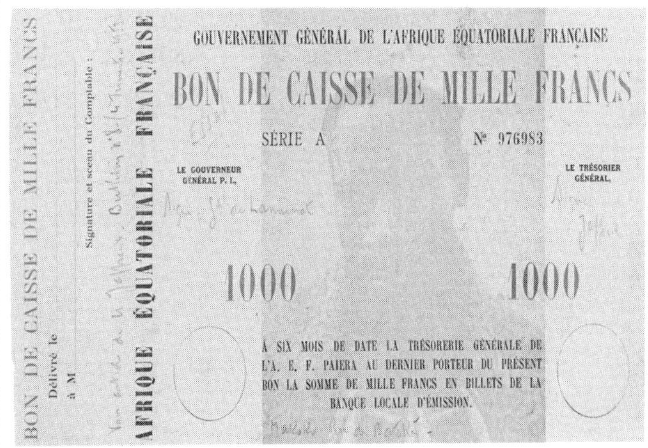

		VG	VF	UNC
4A	**1000 Francs** ND (1940). Man at center. Specimen. Rare.	—	—	—

		VG	VF	UNC
5	**5000 Francs** 25.10.1940. Red. Dancer at center. Specimen. Rare.	—	—	—

Afrique Française Libre
ND 1941 Issue

		VG	VF	UNC
6	**5 Francs** ND (1941). Green, brown and multicolor. Man at center. Flag in upper right corner. Back: Man weaving.			
	a. Issued note.	5.00	25.00	75.00
	s. Specimen. Overprinted: *SPECIMEN.*	—	—	400
7	**25 Francs** ND (1941). Red, blue and multicolor. Flag in upper right corner. Man wearing turban with horse. Back: Lion.	VG	VF	UNC
	a. Issued note.	17.50	90.00	300
	s. Specimen. Overprinted: *SPECIMEN.*	—	—	400

		VG	VF	UNC
8	**100 Francs** ND (1941). Dark brown, lilac and multicolor. Flag in upper right corner. Two women at center. Back: Woman with basket.			
	a. Issued note.	65.00	275	—
	s. Specimen. Overprinted: *SPECIMEN.*	—	—	400
9	**1000 Francs** ND (1941). Brown, yellow and green. Flag in upper right corner. French woman with African woman and child. Printer: BWC.	VG	VF	UNC
	a. Issued note.	1,000	2,250	—
	s. Specimen.	—	—	2,500

Note: For issues similar to #6-9 but with heading: *Afrique Occidentale*, see French West Africa #21-24.

Caisse Centrale de la France Libre
Ordonnance du 2 Dec. 1941

		VG	VF	UNC
10	**5 Francs** *L.1941.* Red on orange and lilac underprint. Portrait Marianne at center. Printer: BWC (without imprint).			
	a. Issued note.	20.00	80.00	240
	s. Specimen, punch hole cancelled.	—	—	175
11	**10 Francs** *L.1941.* Purple on light brown and light blue underprint. Like #10. Printer: BWC (without imprint).	VG	VF	UNC
	a. Issued note.	22.50	125	—
	s. Specimen, punch hole cancelled.	—	—	200
12	**20 Francs** *L.1941.* Green on lilac and olive underprint. Like #10. Printer: BWC (without imprint).	VG	VF	UNC
	a. Issued note.	30.00	150	—
	s. Specimen, punch hole cancelled.	—	—	225
13	**100 Francs** *L.1941.* Blue-green on gold and orange underprint. Similar to #10. Back: Anchor, barrel, bale and other implements. Like France #105. Printer: BWC (without imprint).	VG	VF	UNC
	a. Issued note.	45.00	200	—
	s. Specimen, punch hole cancelled.	—	—	300

		VG	VF	UNC
14	**1000 Francs** *L.1941.* Dark blue. Phoenix rising from flames. Like #19. Printer: BWC (without imprint).			
	a. Issued note.	300	1,200	—
	p. Red. Proof.	—	—	750
	s1. Specimen, punch hole cancelled.	—	—	950
	s2. As a. Specimen without overprint and perforated: *SPÉCMEN.*	—	—	950

		VG	VF	UNC
14A	**5000 Francs** *L.1941.* Violet. Marianne advancing with torch in left hand and flag in right hand. Printer: BWC (without imprint). Proof. Rare.	—	—	—

Note: #10, 13, 14 issues for Reunion with special serial # ranges, see Reunion.
Note: #10, 11, 12, 13, 14 issues for St. Pierre with special serial # ranges, see St. Pierre.

Caisse Centrale de la France d'Outre-Mer

Ordonnance du 2 Feb. 1944

#15-19 without imprinted name of colony. For notes with imprinted name see Guadeloupe, French Guiana or Martinique.

#	Denomination	VG	VF	UNC
15	**5 Francs** *L.1944.* Red. Portrait Marianne at center. Similar to #10. Printer: BWC (without imprint).			
	a. Signature A. Duval. Blue serial #.	5.00	25.00	100
	b. Signature A. Postel-Vinay. Blue serial #.	4.00	20.00	80.00
	c. Signature A. Postel-Vinay. without serial #.	6.00	30.00	120
	d. Black serial # with prefix A (in plate).	7.00	35.00	140
	e. Black serial # with prefix B (in plate).	6.00	30.00	120
	f. Black serial # with prefix C (in plate).	6.00	30.00	120
	g. Black serial # with prefix D (in plate).	6.00	30.00	120

#	Denomination	VG	VF	UNC
16	**10 Francs** *L.1944.* Purple. Portrait Marianne at center. Printer: BWC (without imprint).			
	a. Signature A. Duval. Red Serial #.	7.50	35.00	110
	b. Signature A. Postel-Vinay. Red serial #.	7.50	35.00	110
	c. Signature A. Postel-Vinay. Black serial #.	10.00	45.00	125
	d. Black serial # with prefix A (in plate).	10.00	50.00	200
	e. Black serial # with prefix B (in plate).	10.00	55.00	220

#	Denomination	VG	VF	UNC
17	**20 Francs** *L.1944.* Green. Portrait Marianne at center. Printer: BWC (without imprint).			
	a. Signature A. Duval. Red serial #.	15.00	70.00	280
	b. Signature A. Postel-Vinay. Red serial #.	12.50	65.00	260
	c. Signature A. Postel-Vinay. Black serial #.	12.50	65.00	260
	d. Black serial # with prefix A (in plate).	12.50	65.00	260
	s. As a. Specimen. Overprint: *SPECIMEN.*	—	—	400

#	Denomination	VG	VF	UNC
18	**100 Francs** *L.1944.* Green. Portrait Marianne at center. Back: Anchor, barrel, bale and other implements. Printer: BWC (without imprint).	40.00	125	500

#	Denomination	VG	VF	UNC
19	**1000 Francs** *L.1944.* Dark blue. Phoenix rising from flames. Back: War-scarred landscape at left, peaceful landscape at right. Printer: BWC (without imprint).			
	a. Black serial #.	450	1,000	—
	s1. As a. Specimen overprint: *SPÉCIMEN.*	—	—	1,200
	s2. Specimen overprint and perforated. *SPÉCIMEN.* Red serial #.	—	—	1,350

#	Denomination	VG	VF	UNC
20	**5000 Francs** *L. 1944.* Proof. Rare. Violet. Marianne advancing with torch in left hand and flag in right hand. Printer: BWC (without imprint).	—	—	—

Note: #15, 16, 17, 19 issues for St. Pierre with special serial # ranges, see St. Pierre.

Note: #18, 19 issues for Reunion with special serial # ranges, see Reunion.

1947-1952 Issue

#20B-27 without imprinted name of colony. For notes with imprinted name see French Antilles, French Guiana, Guadeloupe, Martinique, Reunion or Saint Pierre et Miquelon.

#	Denomination	VG	VF	UNC
20B	**5 Francs** ND (1947). Blue and multicolor. Ship at left, Bougainville at right. Back: Woman with fruits. Printed in France.	2.50	12.00	45.00

#	Denomination	VG	VF	UNC
21	**10 Francs** ND (1947). Blue and multicolor. Colbert at left. Back: River scene. Printed in France.	3.00	15.00	55.00

#	Denomination	VG	VF	UNC
22	**20 Francs** ND (1947). Brown and multicolor. E. Gentil at right, villagers at left center. Back: Man at left and right. Printed in France.	4.00	17.50	75.00

#	Denomination	VG	VF	UNC
23	**50 Francs** ND (1947). Multicolor. Belain d'Esnambuc at left, sailing ship at right. Back: Woman at left. Printed in France.	7.50	25.00	115

		VG	VF	UNC
24	**100 Francs** ND (1947). Multicolor. La Bourdonnais at left, women at right. Back: Woman at right, mountain scenery in background on back. 2 serial # varieties. Printed in France.	15.00	45.00	150
25	**500 Francs** ND (1949). Multicolor. Two girls at right. Printed in France.	50.00	200	525
26	**1000 Francs** ND (1947). Multicolor. Two women (symbol of the "Union Francaise") at right. 2 serial # varieties. Printed in France.	45.00	165	425

		VG	VF	UNC
27	**5000 Francs** ND (1952). Brown. Gen. Schoelcher at center right. Printed in France.	95.00	350	850

Note: #20B, 21, 22, 23 issues for St. Pierre with special serial # ranges, see St. Pierre.

Institut d'Emission de l'Afrique Equatoriale Française et du Cameroun

1957 Issue

		VG	VF	UNC
28	**5 Francs** ND. Multicolor. Ship at left, Bougainville at right. Back: Woman with fruits.	15.00	45.00	140
29	**10 Francs** ND. Multicolor. Colbert at left. Back: River scene.	20.00	55.00	150
30	**20 Francs** ND. Olive-brown. E. Gentil at right, villagers at left center. Back: Man at left and right.	25.00	75.00	185

		VG	VF	UNC
31	**50 Francs** ND (1957). Green and multicolor. Woman picking coffee beans at left. Back: Men logging in river.	6.00	17.50	75.00

		VG	VF	UNC
32	**100 Francs** Nd (1957). Blue and multicolor. Gov. Gen. Felix Eboue at center. Back: Cargo ships, man.	10.00	30.00	110

		VG	VF	UNC
33	**500 Francs** ND (1957). Brown and multicolor. Woman in front of huts. Back: Freight train crossing bridge at center.	35.00	140	400

		VG	VF	UNC
34	**1000 Francs** ND (1957). Multicolor. Woman with harvest of cocoa. Back: Man picking cotton.	45.00	150	425

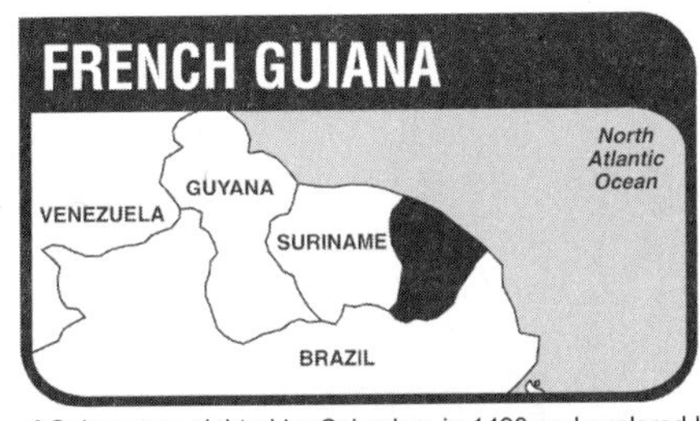

The French Overseas Department of French Guiana, located on the northeast coast of South America, bordered by Surinam and Brazil, has an area of 32,252 sq. mi. (91,000 sq. km.) and a population of 173,000. Capital: Cayenne. Placer gold mining and shrimp processing are the chief industries. Shrimp, lumber, gold, cocoa and bananas are exported. The coast of Guiana was sighted by Columbus in 1498 and explored by Amerigo Vespucci in 1499. The French established the first successful trading stations and settlements, and placed the area under direct control of the French Crown in 1674. Portuguese and British forces occupied French Guiana for five years during the Napoleonic Wars. Devil's Island, the notorious penal colony in French Guiana where Capt. Alfred Dreyfus was imprisoned, was established in 1852 - and finally closed in 1947. When France adopted a new constitution in 1946, French Guiana voted to remain within the French Union as an overseas department. Note: For later issues see French Antilles.

RULERS:

French

MONETARY SYSTEM:

1 Franc = 10 Decimes = 100 Centimes to 1960
1 Nouveau (new) Franc = 100 "old" Francs, 1961-
1 Euro = 100 Cents

FRENCH ADMINISTRATION

Treasury

1795 Emergency Issue

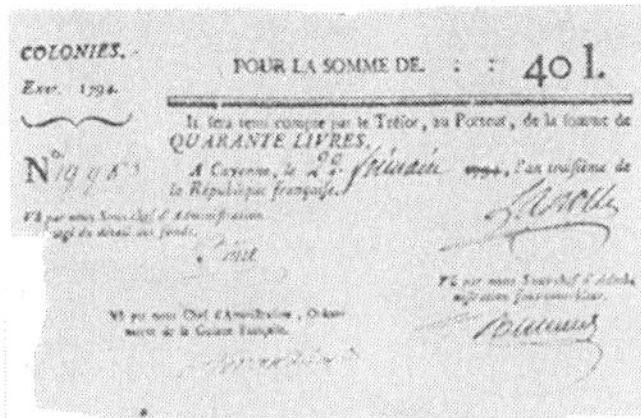

		Good	Fine	XF
A5	**40 Livres** 13.12.1795. Black. Uniface.	250	500	—

Note: #A5 is dated *22 frimare an 3 eme* which relates to the 3rd month, 3rd year of the First French Republic.

Banque de la Guyane

1888-1922 Issues

		Good	Fine	XF
1	**5 Francs** *L.1901* (1922-1947). Blue. Man at left, woman at right.			
	a. Signature title: *Directeur* H. Poulet (1922).	20.00	50.00	170
	b. Signature title: *Directeur* P. L. Lamer (1933).	18.00	45.00	150
	c. Signature titles: *Directeur* C. Halleguen and *Caissier* E. Brais (1939).	15.00	35.00	125
	d. Signature titles: *Directeur* C. Halleguen, and *Caissier* ? (1942).	10.00	30.00	125
	e. Signature title: *Directeur* M. Buy (1947).	10.00	25.00	115
		Good	**Fine**	**XF**
2	**25 Francs** ND (1910). Black and green.	200	725	—
		Good	**Fine**	**XF**
3	**100 Francs** ND. Rare. Red and blue.	—	—	—
		Good	**Fine**	**XF**
4	**500 Francs** ND (1888-1889). Red. Rare.	—	—	—

1916 Emergency Issue

		Good	Fine	XF
5	**1 Franc** 16.12.1916 (1917-1919). Blue and gray. 2 signature varieties.	25.00	80.00	275
		Good	**Fine**	**XF**
6	**2 Francs** 16.12.1916 (1917-1919). Red and blue. 2 signature varieties.	30.00	90.00	350

1933-1938 ND Issue

		Good	Fine	XF
7	**25 Francs** ND (1933-1945). Purple and multicolor. Woman with wreath at center. Back: Trees left and right, ship in water at center. 5 signature varieties.	35.00	175	500

		Good	Fine	XF
8	**100 Francs** ND (1933-1942). Multicolor. Woman holding staff at left. 4 signature varieties.	110	350	800
		Good	**Fine**	**XF**
9	**500 Francs** nd (1938-1940). Multicolor. Woman holding staff at left. 2 signature varieties.	250	850	—

#10 not assigned.

1942; 1945 ND WWII Emergency Issues

		VG	VF	UNC
11	**1 Franc** ND (1942). Red. Border with design element at upper and lower center. Back: Bank name stamped in oval, 40 mm long. Handstamped signature. 2 signature varieties. Local printing.	60.00	135	250

		VG	VF	UNC
11A	**2 Francs** ND (1942). Blue-green. Border with design element at upper and lower center. Back: Bank name stamped in oval, 40 mm long. Handstamped signature. 2 signature varieties. Local printing.	70.00	150	300
11B	**1 Franc** ND (1945). Red. Unbroken pattern without design element in upper and lower border. Local printing. Bank name 51 mm long.	70.00	150	300
11C	**2 Francs** ND (1945). ND (1945). Blue-green. Bank name 51 mm long. Blue-green. Unbroken pattern without design element in upper and lower border. Back: Bank name 51 mm long.			
	a. Hand signature	75.00	175	350
	b. Stamped signature	70.00	150	300

1942 ND Issue

		VG	VF	UNC
12	**5 Francs** ND (1942). Black on green underprint. Justice at left. Signature varieties. Printer: E.A. Wright, Philadelphia, Penn. U.S.A.			
	r. Unsigned remainder.	—	—	2,000
	s. Specimen.	—	—	1,500

		VG	VF	UNC
13	**100 Francs** ND (1942). Black on red underprint. Map of Guiana at left. Two signature varieties. Printer: E.A. Wright, Philadelphia, Penn. U.S.A.			
	a. Signature Halleguen as *LE DIRECTEUR.*	200	650	1,600
	b. Signature Buy as *LE DIRECTEUR.*	240	775	1,850

		VG	VF	UNC
14	**500 Francs** ND (1942). Black on yellow underprint. Seaplane at center. Two signature varieties. Back: Caravelle *Santa Maria* at center. Printer: E.A. Wright, Philadelphia, Penn. U.S.A.			
	a. Signature Collat as *UN CENSEUR.*	1,250	2,750	—
	b. Signature St.-Clair as *UN CENSEUR.*	1,250	2,750	—
	s. Specimen.	—	—	1,150
15	**1000 Francs** ND (1942). Green. Seated woman at left and right. Three signature varieties. Back: Liberty at center. Printer: E.A. Wright, Philadelphia, Penn. U.S.A.	1,750	3,500	—

Caisse Centrale de la France Libre
Ordonnance du 2 Dec. 1941

		VG	VF	UNC
16	**100 Francs** *L.1941.* Green on orange underprint. Marianne at center. Back: Anchor, barrel, bale and other implements. English printing.			
	a. Issued note.	110	275	700
	s. Specimen.	—	—	450

		VG	VF	UNC
16A	**1000 Francs** *L.1941.* Blue. Phoenix rising from flames. Black handstamp: *GUYANE FRANÇAISE* twice. Handstamp: *ANNULE* (cancelled). English printing.	—	850	2,250

Caisse Centrale de la France d'Outre-Mer
Ordonnance du 2 Feb. 1944

#	Description	VG	VF	UNC
17	**100 Francs** *L.1944*. Green on orange underprint. Marianne at center. Overprint or handstamped: *GUYANE*. Back: Anchor, barrel, bale and other implements. English printing.			
	a. Issued note.	50.00	200	575
	s. Specimen.	—	—	400
18	**1000 Francs** *L.1944*. Blue. Phoenix rising from flames. English printing.	VG	VF	UNC
	a. Dark blue serial #.	750	1,650	—
	b. Blue serial #. Overprint: *GUYANE*. without watermark.	750	1,650	—
	c. Red serial #. Handstamped: *GUYANE FRANÇAISE*. watermark. paper.	850	1,750	—
	d. As c. Cancelled with black stamp *ANNULÉ*.	—	—	—
	s. As a. Specimen.	—	—	1,250

1947 Issue

#	Description	VG	VF	UNC
19	**5 Francs** ND (1947-1949). Multicolor. Bougainville at right. French printing.			
	a. Issued note.	7.50	25.00	85.00
	s. Specimen.	—	—	90.00
20	**10 Francs** ND (1947-1949). Multicolor. Colbert at left. French printing.	VG	VF	UNC
	a. Issued note.	10.00	30.00	110
	s. Specimen.	—	—	90.00
21	**20 Francs** ND (1947-1949). Multicolor. E. Gentil at right. French printing.	VG	VF	UNC
	a. Issued note.	12.50	35.00	135
	s. Specimen.	—	—	100

#	Description	VG	VF	UNC
22	**50 Francs** ND (1947-1949). Multicolor. B. d'Esnambuc at left, sailing ship at right. French printing.			
	a. Issued note.	25.00	75.00	285
	s. Specimen.	—	—	125
23	**100 Francs** ND (1947-1949). Multicolor. La Bourdonnais at left, women at right. French printing.	VG	VF	UNC
	a. Issued note.	35.00	100	350
	s. Specimen.	—	—	150
24	**500 Francs** ND (1947-1949). Multicolor. Two women at right. French printing.	VG	VF	UNC
	a. Issued note.	75.00	250	800
	s. Specimen.	—	—	250
25	**1000 Francs** ND (1947-1949). Multicolor. Two women at right. French printing.	VG	VF	UNC
	a. Issued note.	100	300	900
	s. Specimen.	—	—	275
26	**5000 Francs** ND (1947-1949). Multicolor. Gen. Schoelcher at center right. French printing.	VG	VF	UNC
	a. Issued note.	100	450	1,100
	s. Specimen.	—	—	325

1960 Issue

#	Description	VG	VF	UNC
27	**1000 Francs** ND (1960). Multicolor. Fishermen. Specimen.	—	—	850
28	**5000 Francs** ND (1960). Multicolor. Woman with fruit bowl.	VG	VF	UNC
	a. Issued note.	400	750	1,850
	s. Specimen.	—	—	500

Note: For notes overprint in *Nouveaux Francs* see Volume 3.

French India consisted of five settlements in India that formerly constituted a territory of France: Pondicherry (Pondichery), Chandemagor, Karikal and Yanam on the east coast, and Mahe on the west coast. The combined settlements had an area of 197 sq. mi. (500 sq. km). Capital: Pondicherry. French interest in the East was evident as early as the opening of the 16th century, but initial individual efforts were checked by the Portuguese. After a number of false starts, they acquired Pondicherry, 85 miles (137 Km.) south of Madras, in 1654. Chandernagor, 16 miles (26 km) north of Calcutta, was acquired in 1690-92. Mahe was acquired in 1725 and Karikai in 1739. Yanam was founded in 1750. The French enclaves were captured (by the Dutch and British) and restored several times before French possession was established, by treaties, 1914-17. Chandernagor voted in 1949 to join India and became part of the Republic of India in 1950. Pondicherry, Karikal, Yanam and Mahe formed the Pondicherry Union Territory and joined the Republic of India in 1954.

RULERS

French to 1954

MONTETARY SYSTEM

1 Roupie = 8 Fanons = 16 Annas

FRENCH ADMINISTRATION

Banque de L'Indochine, Pondichery

Note: Emergency *Bons de Caisse* are reported to have been issued during 1918-1819.

Décret du 21.1.1875

#	Description	Good	Fine	XF
A1	**10 Roupies** 1.1.1874; 3.4.1901; 24.5.1909. Blue. Neptune reclining holding trident at lower left. Signature varieties. Back: Multiple language texts.			
	a. Issued note. Rare.	—	—	—
	s1. 0.5.1910. Specimen. Rare.	—	—	—
	s2. 13.3.1. Specimen.	—	—	12,500
A2	**50 Roupies** (1877-). Rare. Blue-gray and red-brown. Elephant columns left and right, two reclining women with ox left, tiger right. at lower border. Decree in ribbon in border at top center. Signature varieties.	—	—	—

Décrets des 21.1.1875 et 20.2.1888

	50 Roupies	Good	Fine	XF
A3	10.9.1898. Blue-gray and red-brown. Elephant columns left and right, two reclining women with ox left, tiger right at lower border. Decree in ribbon in border at top center. Rare.	—	—	—

Décrets des 21.1.1875, 20.2.1888 et 16.5.1900

	50 Roupies	Good	Fine	XF
1	(1902-). Blue-gray and red-brown. Elephant columns left and right, two reclining women with ox left, tiger right at lower border. Printed decree, with counterfeiting clause replacing decrees in ribbon border at top center.			
	a. Issued note.	—	—	—
	s. 22.2.1902. Specimen. Perforated: *ANNULE.*	—	Unc	17,500

Décrets des 21.1.1875, 20.2.1888, 16.5.1900 et 3.4.1901

	10 Roupies	Good	Fine	XF
2	3.11.1919; 4.11.1919. Printed. Blue. Neptune reclining holding trident at lower left. Back: Multiple language texts.			
	a. Issued note. Rare.	—	—	—
	b. Cancelled with handstamp: *ANNULÉ.*	—	—	2,500

	50 Roupies	Good	Fine	XF
3	17.6.1915. Blue-gray and red-brown. Elephant columns left and righ, two reclining women with ox left, tiger right at lower border. Printed decree. With counterfeiting clause replacing decrees in ribbon in border at top center.			
	a. Issued note. Rare.	—	—	—
	b. Cancelled with handstamp: *ANNULÉ.* Rare.	—	—	—

W/o Décrets

	1 Roupie	Good	Fine	XF
4	1919-45. Blue and brown on light orange underprint. Helmeted woman at left.			
	a. Signature titles: *L'ADMININSTRATEUR-DIRECTEUR* and *UN ADMINISTRATEUR.* 12.11.1919.	400	900	3,000
	b. Signature titles: *UN ADMINISTRATEUR* and *LE DIRECTEUR.* 2 sign varieties. 1.8.1923; 1.1.1928.	325	750	2,200
	c. Signature titles: *UN ADMININSTRATEUR* and *LE DIRECTEUR GÉNÉRAL.* 5.4.1932.	300	650	2,000
	d. Signature titles: *LE PRÉSIDENT* and *LE DIRECTEUR GÉNÉRAL.* 2 Signature varieties. 13.2.1936; 8.3.1938; 8.9.1945.	250	500	1,800
	e. As d. Punch hole cancelled with handstamp: *ANNULÉ.* 8.9.1945.	—	—	—

	1 Roupie	Good	Fine	XF
4A	8.9.1945. Helmeted woman at left. Back: Guilloche with three cross-shapes instead of two.	300	750	—

Color Abbreviation Guide

New to the *Standard Catalog of ® World Paper Money* are the following abbreviations related to color references:

BC: Back color

PC: Paper color

1936-1937 ND Issue

	5 Roupies	Good	Fine	XF
5	ND (1937). Brown and orange on multicolor underprint. Women wearing helmet holding lance at left, denomination numeral *5* over wreath at upper right. Back: Woman with headress at left, ancient statues at right.			
	a. Signature titles: *LE PRÉSIDENT* and *LE DIRECTEUR GÉNÉRAL.* (1937).	400	750	3,000
	b. Signature titles: *LE PRÉSIDENT and LE DIRECTEUR GAL. ADJOINT.* (1946).	350	675	2,750
	c. As b. Punch hole cancelled with handstamp: *ANNULÉ.*	—	—	—
	s. As b. Specimen perforated *SPECIMEN.*	—	—	2,300

	50 Roupies	Good	Fine	XF
7	ND (1936). Multicolor. Ornamental stove at left. Back: Portrait Dupleix.			
	a. Signature Thion de la Chaume as *LE PRÉSIDENT* and Baudouin as *LE DIRECTEUR GÉNÉRAL* (1936). Rare.	—	—	—
	b. Signature Borduge-Baudouin. (1937-1940).	2,000	6,000	—
	c. Signature Minost-Laurent. (1945).	2,000	6,000	—
	d. Punch hole cancelled with handstamp: *ANNULÉ.*	—	—	—
	s. Specimen perforated: *SPECIMEN.*	—	—	3,500

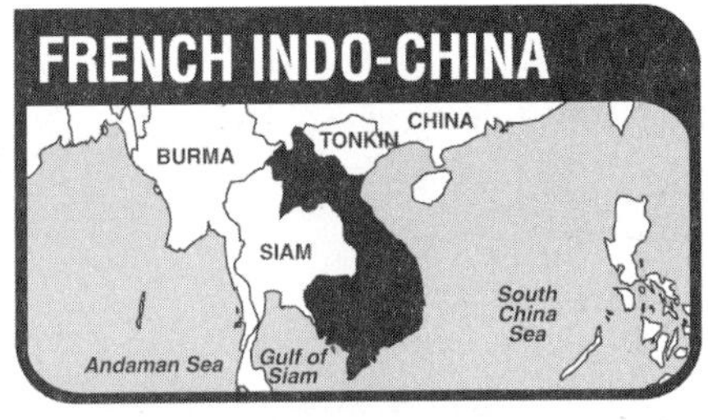

French Indo-China (l'Indo-Chine) was located on the Indo-Chinese peninsula of Southeast Asia. It was a French colonial possession from the later 19th century until 1954. A French Governor-General headed a federal-type central government and colonial administration, but reported directly to France which retained exclusive authority over foreign affairs, defense, customs, finance and public works. The colony covered 286,194 sq. mi. (741,242 sq. km.) and had a population of 24 million. It consisted of 5 protectorates: Tonkin (northern Vietnam), Annam (central Vietnam), Cochin-China (southern Vietnam), Laos and Cambodia. Principal cities were: Saigon, Hanoi, Haiphong, Pnom-Penh and Vientiane. From 1875 to 1951, the exclusive right to issue banknotes within the colony was held by the Bank of Indochina (Banque de l'Indochine). On December 31, 1951 this privilege was transferred to the Issuing Authority of the States of Cambodia, Laos and Vietnam (Institut d'Emission des Etats du Cambodge, du Laos et du Vietnam). From the moment of their conquest, the Indochinese people resisted French rule. The degree of resistance varied, being strongest in central and northern Vietnam, but was evident throughout Indochina. There were unsuccessful attempts by Vietnamese nationals, headed by Nguyen Ai Quoc (later known as Ho Chi Minh), to gain recognition/independence at the Versailles Peace Conference following World War I. Japan occupied French Indochina at the start of World War II, but allowed the local French (Vichy) government to remain in power until March 1945. Meanwhile, many nationalists (communist and non-communist alike) followed Ho Chi Minh's leadership in the formation of the League for Independence of Vietnam (Viet-Minh) which took an active anti-Japanese part during the war. France reoccupied the area after the Japanese surrender, and established the Associated States of Indochina, with each of the five political subdivisions having limited independence within the French Union. Disagreement over the degree of independence and the reunification of the three Vietnamese subdivisions led to armed conflict with the Viet-Minh and a protracted war (The First Indochina War). In 1949/1950, in an attempt to retain her holdings, France recognized Laos, Cambodia and Vietnam as semi-independent self governing States within the French Union, but retained financial and economic control. Fighting continued and culminated with the French military disaster at Dien Bien Phu in May 1954. The subsequent Geneva Agreement brought full independence to Laos, Cambodia and Vietnam (*temporarily* divided at the 17th parallel of latitude), and with it, an end to French rule in Indochina. See also Vietnam, South Vietnam, Laos and Cambodia.

RULERS:

French to 1954

MONETARY SYSTEM:

1 Piastre = 1 (Mexican Silver) Dollar = 100 Cents,1875-1903
1 Piastre = 100 Cents, 1903-1951
1 Piastre = 100 Cents = 1 Riel (Cambodia), 1951-1954
1 Piastre = 100 Cents = 1 Kip (Laos)
1 Piastre = 100 Cents = 1 Dong (Vietnam)

SIGNATURE VARIETIES/TITLE COMBINATIONS
BANQUE DE L'INDOCHINE, 1875–1951

1	Edwuoard Delessert Un Administrateur a Paris NOTE: Also handsigned by Le Cassier and Le Directeur de la Succursale	
2	Aduoard Delessert Un Administrateur	Stanislas Simon Le Directeur
3	Ernest Denormandie Un Administrateur	Stanislas Simon Le Directeur
4	Baron Hely D'Oissel Un Administrateur	Stanislas Simon Le Directeur
5	Baron Hely D'Oissel Un Administrateur	Stanislas Simon Le Administrateur-Directeur
6	Albert de Monplanet Un Administrateur	René Thion de la Chaume Le Directeur
7	Stanislas Simon Un Administrateur	René Thion de la Chaume Le Directeur
8	René Thion de la Chaume Le President	Paul Baudouin Le Directeur-General
9	Macel Borduge Le President	Paul Baudouin Le Directeur-General
10	Paul Gannay L'Inspecteur-General	Edmond Bruno Le Directeur de la Succursale de Saigon
11	Emile Minost Le President	Jean Laurent Le Directeur-General Adjoin

FRENCH ADMINISTRATION

Banque de l'Indo-Chine

Haiphong

Décret du 21.1.1875

		Good	Fine	XF
1	**5 Dollars = 5 Piastres** 1876-1896 (17.10.1896). Rare.	600	1,800	—
1A	**20 Dollars = 20 Piastres** (1876-1892). Rare.	1,000	3,000	—

Décrets des 21.1.1875 et 20.2.1888

		Good	Fine	XF
2	**1 Dollar = 1 Piastre** ND (1892-1899). Blue. Oriental woman seated below France seated holding caduceus at left. Handstamped city of issue. Text:*Emission autorisee 3 Aôut 1891.*	400	1,500	—
3	**20 Dollars = 20 Piastres** 1892-1893 (25.4.1893; 28.4.1893.) Blue. Elephant columns left and right. Two reclining women with ox left, tiger right at lower border. Handstamped city name of issue. LIke #25. Rare.	800	2,500	—
4	**100 Dollars = 100 Piastres** 1893-1907 (5.5.1893.) Blue. Vasco da Gama at left, sailing ships at lower center. Polynesian man with paddle by dragon boat at right. Handstamped city of issue. Like #26. Printed. Rare.	1,500	4,500	—

1897-1899 Issue

		Good	Fine	XF
5	**1 Dollar = 1 Piastre** ND (1900-1903). Red-brown. Oriental woman seated below France seated holding caduceus at left. Text: *Emission autorisee 3 Aôut 1891.*	300	900	—
6	**5 Dollars = 5 Piastres** 1897-1900 (4.2.1897; 6.2.1897.) Blue. Neptune reclining holding trident at lower left. Printed city of issue. Like #28. Rare.	600	1,750	—

#7 *Deleted,* see #1A and 3.

1899-1900 Issue

		Good	Fine	XF
8	**5 Dollars = 5 Piastres** 19.9.1900; 20.9.1900. Red. Neptune reclining holding trident at lower left.	400	1,200	—
9	**20 Dollars = 20 Piastres** 12.9.1898; 13.9.1898; 14.9.1898; 15.9.1898. Red. Elephant columns left and right. Two reclining women with ox left, tiger right at lower border. Rare.	600	1,750	—
10	**100 Dollars = 100 Piastres** 17.2.1899. Red. Vasco da Gama at left, sailing ships at lower center, Polynesian man with paddle by dragon boat at right. Signature left. Rare.	1,000	3,000	—

Décrets des 21.1.1875, 20.2.1888 et 16.5.1900

		Good	Fine	XF
11	**100 Dollars = 100 Piastres** (1903). Red. Vasco da Gama at left, sailing ships at lower center, Polynesian man with paddle by dragon boat at right. Like #10. Reported not confirmed.	—	—	—

#	Description	Good	Fine	XF
12	**100 Piastres** 3.7.1903-22.3.1907. Red. Vasco da Gama at left, sailing ships at lower center, Polynesian man with paddle by dragon boat at right. Signature 4 at left. Like #11. Rare.	800	2,000	—

Décrets des 21.1.1875, 20.2.1888, 16.5.1900 et 3.4.1901

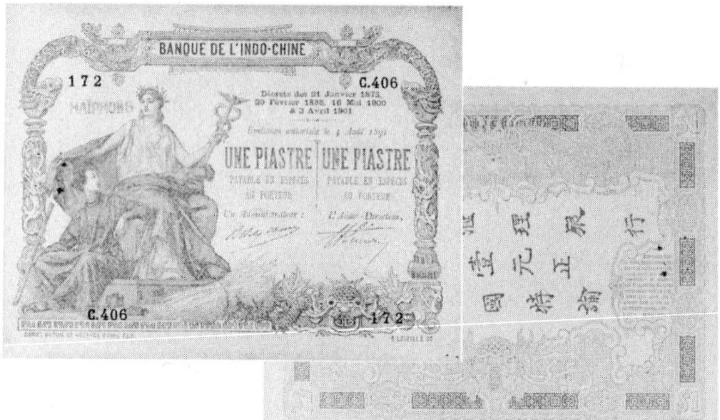

#	Description	Good	Fine	XF
13	**1 Piastre** ND (1903-1921). Red-brown. Oriental woman seated below France seated holding caduceus at left. City of issue handstamped. With text:*Emission autorisee 3 Aôut 1891.*			
	a. Signature 4 with titles: *Un Administrateur* and *Le Directeur.* (1903-09).	100	200	800
	b. Signature 5 with titles: *Un Administrateur* and *L'Administrateur - Directeur.*(1909-21).	30.00	100	400

#	Description	Good	Fine	XF
14	**5 Piastres** 9.6.1905; 10.6.1905; 1.3.1907; 2.3.1907. Red. Neptune reclining holding trident at lower left. Signature 4.	200	1,200	200
15	**20 Piastres** 10.6.1905; 11.3.1907. Red. Elephant columns left and right. Two reclining women with ox left, tiger right at lower border. Signature 4.			
	a. Issued note.	300	1,200	2,000
	s. Specimen. 30.2.1905.	—		

1909-1919 Issue

#	Description	Good	Fine	XF
16	**5 Piastres** 1.9.1910-29.11.1915. Green. Ships in background at left, flowers at center. Like #37. Back: Dragon.			
	a. Signature 4 with titles: *Un Administrateur* and *Le Directeur.* (1910).	125	500	1,200
	b. Signature 5 with titles: *Un Administrateur* and *L'Administrateur - Directeur.* (1910-15).	60.00	350	900

#	Description	Good	Fine	XF
17	**20 Piastres** 12.1.1909-6.4.1917. Green. Seated woman with sword at left, coupe at right. Like #38. Back: Two dragons.			
	a. Signature 4 with titles: *Un Administrateur* and *Le Directeur.* (1909).	300	900	1,800
	b. Signature 5 with titles: *Un Administrateur* and *L'Administrateur - Directeur* (1917).	100	400	900

#	Description	Good	Fine	XF
18	**100 Piastres** 6.5.1911-11.4.1919. Green and brown. Woman with branch and wreath at right, mandarin in front. Signature 5 with titles: *Un Administrateur* and *L'Administrateur - Directeur.* Like #39. Back: Dragon design.	300	1,000	1,800

1920; 1925 Issue

#	Description	Good	Fine	XF
19	**5 Piastres** 27.5.1920. (1926-1927). Green. Ships in background at left, flowers at center. Signature #5. Without dÉcrets or autograph signature. Without signature titles: *Le Caissier...* Back: Dragon.	75.00	200	600

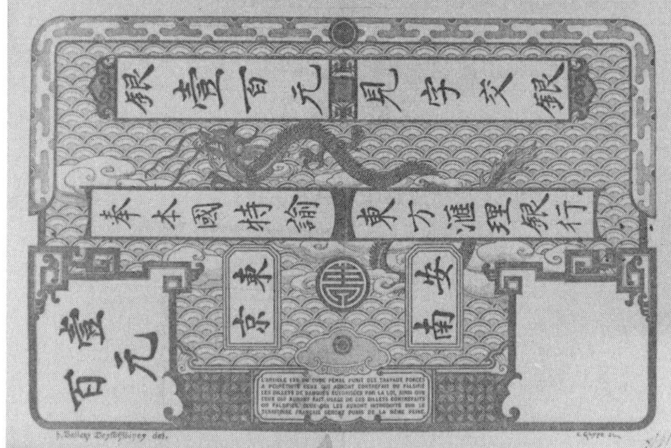

		Good	Fine	XF
20	**100 Piastres** 1.9.1925. Green and brown. Woman with branch and wreath at right, mandarin in front. Without dÈcrats or autograph signature. Without signature titles: *Le Caissier...* Signature 6. Back: Dragon design.	200	600	1,750

Saigon

Notes in Dollars and Piastres

Décret du 21.1.1875

		Good	Fine	XF
21	**5 Dollars = 5 Piastres** 1876-96 (19.7.1893; 8.2.1895; 30.1.1896). Blue. Neptune reclining holding trident at lower left. Signature left. City of issue printed. Handwritten or handstamped.	750	2,500	3,500

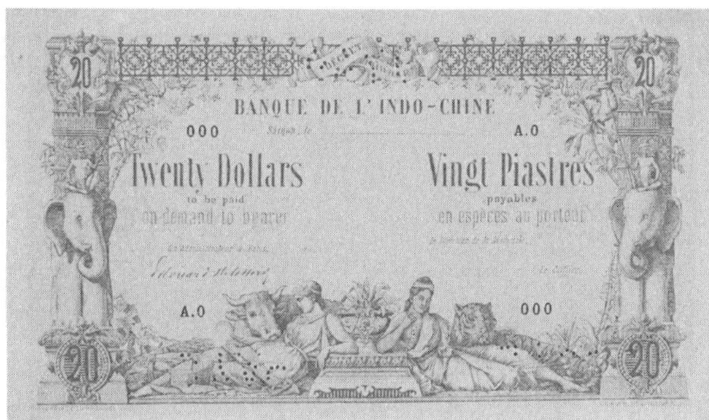

		Good	Fine	XF
22	**20 Dollars = 20 Piastres** (1876-1892). Blue. Elephant columns left and right. Two reclining women with ox left, tiger right at lower border. Signature left. City of issue printed. Handwritten or handstamped.	750	3,000	4,500

		Good	Fine	XF
23	**100 Dollars = 100 Piastres** (1877-1893). 22.2.1879; 24.6.1890. Blue. Vasco da Gama at left, sailing ships at lower center, Polynesian man with paddle by dragon boat at right. Signature left. City of issue printed. Handwritten or handstamped.	1,000	4,000	6,000

Décrets des 21.1.1875 et 20.2.1888

		Good	Fine	XF
24	**1 Dollar = 1 Piastre** ND (1892-1899). Blue. Oriental woman seated below France seated holding caduceus at left. Signature 2. Handstamped city of issue. With text: *Emission autorisee 3 Aôut 1891.*	200	700	1,200
25	**20 Dollars = 20 Piastres** 25.4.1893. Elephant columns left and right. Two reclining women with oxleft, tiger right at lower border. Text: *Emission autorisee 3 Aôut 1891.* Signature 2.	500	1,600	—
26	**100 Dollars = 100 Piastres** 2.5.1893; 5.5.1893; 9.5.1893; 12.5.1893. Blue. Vasco da Gama at left, sailing ships at lower center, Polynesian man with paddle by dragon boat at right. Signature 2. Handstamped city of issue. Text:*Emission autorisee 3 Aôut 1891.* Like #23.			
	a. Issued note.	1,000	3,000	—
	b. Cancelled with handstamp: *ANNULÉ.* 2.5.1893; 9.5.1893.	1,000	3,000	—

1897-1900 Issue

		Good	Fine	XF
27	**1 Dollar = 1 Piastre** ND (1900-1903). Red-brown. Oriental woman seated below France seated holding caduceus at left. Signature 3. Text:*Emission autorisee 3 Aôut 1891.* Printed city of issue.	275	700	1,250

		Good	Fine	XF
28	**5 Dollars = 5 Piastres** 9.1.1897; 23.1.1897. Blue. Neptune reclining holding trident at lower left. Text: *Emission autorisee 3 Aout 1891.* Printed city name. Signature 2. Printed.			
	a. Issued note.	300	850	1,750
	s. Specimen. 30.2.1899.	—	—	—

1900 Issue

		Good	Fine	XF
29	**5 Dollars = 5 Piastres** 26.9.1900; 27.9.1900; 1.10.1900; 4.10.1900; 5.10.1900. Handwritten or handstamped. Blue. Neptune reclining holding trident at lower left. Signature 3 at left. Like #28.	550	2,250	—
30	**20 Dollars = 20 Piastres** 3.9.1898; 5.9.1898; 6.9.1898; 7.9.1898. Blue. Elephant columns left and right. Two reclining women with ox left, tiger right at lower border, like #22. Signature 3 at left.	850	2,750	—

		Good	Fine	XF
31	**100 Dollars = 100 Piastres** 16.2.1899. Blue. Vasco da Gama at left, sailing ships at lower center, Polynesian man with paddle by dragon boat at right. Signature 3 at left. Like #23.	1,100	4,500	—

Décrets des 21.1.1875, 20.2.1888 et 16.5.1900

		Good	Fine	XF
32	**100 Dollars = 100 Piastres** 9.3.1903. Blue. Vasco da Gama at left, sailing ships at lower center, Polynesian man with paddle by dragon boat at right. Signature 4 at left.	675	2,250	—

1903 "Piastres" Issue

		Good	Fine	XF
33	**100 Piastres** 4.7.1903-20.3.1907. Blue with black text. Vasco da Gama at left, sailing ships at lower center, Polynesian man with paddle by dragon boat at right. Signature 4 at left. Like #32.	550	2,250	—

Décrets des 21.1.1875, 20.2.1888, 16.5.1900 et 3.4.1901

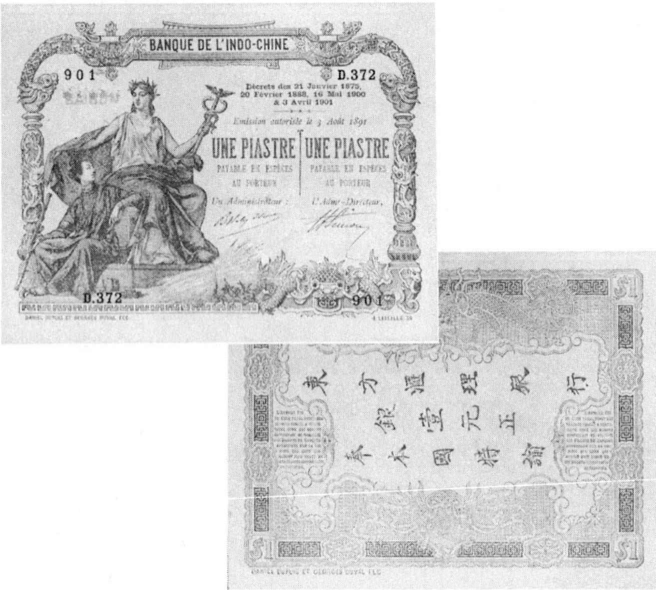

		Good	Fine	XF
34	**1 Piastre** ND (1903-1921). Red-brown. Oriental woman seated below France seated holding caduceus at left. Hand-stamped city of issue. Text: *Emission autorisee 3 Aôut 1891*.			
	a. Signature 4 with titles: *Un Administrateur* and *Le Directeur*. (1903-09).	30.00	150	600
	b. Signature 5 with titles: *Un Administrateur* and *L'Administrateur - Directeur.* (1909-21).	12.50	60.00	175
35	**5 Piastres** 5.6.1905; 7.6.1905; 8.6.1905; 4.3.1907; 5.3.1907; 6.3.1907. Neptune reclining holding trident at lower left. Printed city of issue. Signature 4.	225	675	1,750

		Good	Fine	XF
36	**20 Piastres** 5.6.1905; 6.6.1905; 14.3.1907; 15.3.1907; 16.3.1907. Blue. Elephant columns left and right. Two reclining women with ox left, tiger right at lower bottom. Like #22. Signature 4.	400	900	1,750

1909-1919 Issue

		Good	Fine	XF
37	**5 Piastres** 2.1.1909-15.11.1916. Purple. Ships in background at left, flowers at center. Back: Dragon.			
	a. Signature 4 with titles: *Un Administrateur* and *Le Directeur.* (1909).	125	350	1,250
	b. Signature 5 with titles: *Un Administrateur* and *L'Administrateur - Directeur.* (1910-1916).	30.00	125	500
38	**20 Piastres** 3.3.1913;23.5.1917. (1909). Purple. Seated woman with sword at left, coupe at right. Back: Two dragons.			
	a. Signature 4 with titles: *Un Administrateur* and *Le Directeur.* (1909).	150	350	1,500
	b. Signature 5 with titles: *Un Administrateur* and *L'Administrateur - Directeur.* (1913-1917).	60.00	225	700

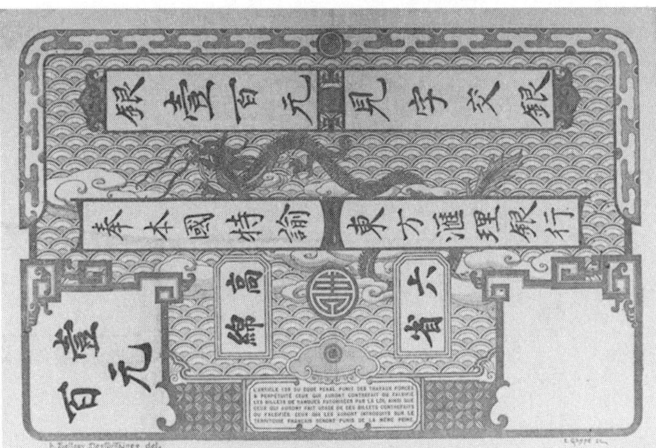

		Good	Fine	XF
39	**100 Piastres** 3.5.1911-14.4.1919. Purple. Woman with branch and wreath at right, mandarin in front. Signature 5 with titles: *Un Administrateur* and *L'Administrateur - Directeur.* Back: Dragon design.	90.00	225	1,250

1920 Issue

#40-42 without décrets or autograph signature, without titles: *Le Caissier...*

#	Denomination	Good	Fine	XF
40	**5 Piastres** 5.1.1920-15.3.1920. Purple. Ships in background at left, flowers at center, like #37. Signature 5.	20.00	85.00	350

#	Denomination	Good	Fine	XF
41	**20 Piastres** 1.8.1920. Purple. Seated woman with sword at left, coupe at right. Like #38. Signature 6. Back: Two dragons.	30.00	125	500

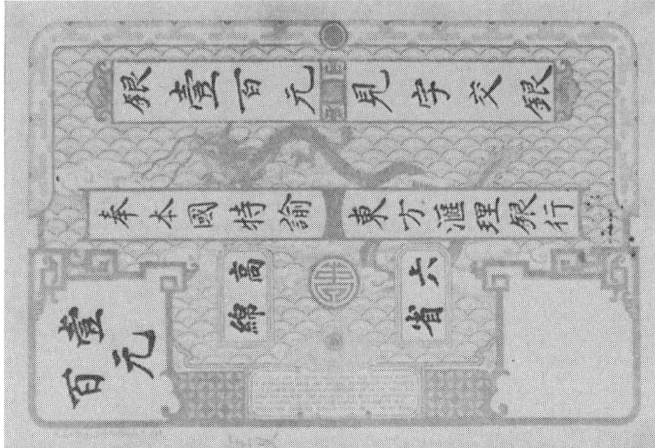

#	Denomination	Good	Fine	XF
42	**100 Piastres** 5.1.1920-27.1.1920. Purple. Woman with branch and wreath at right, mandarin in front. Signature 5. Back: Dragon design.	60.00	225	900

Banque de l'Indo-Chine (1920s)

1920 Fractional Issue

Décret of 3.4.1901 and authorization date 6.10.1919 on back.

#	Denomination	VG	VF	UNC
43	**10 Cents** *L.1919* (1920-1923). Blue. Black serial #. Signature 5. Printer: Chaix.	15.00	35.00	125

#	Denomination	VG	VF	UNC
44	**10 Cents** *L.1919* (1920-1923). Blue. Red serial #. Signature 6. Back: Red Chinese and Vietnamese denomination overprint. Printer: Chaix.	10.00	40.00	125

#	Denomination	VG	VF	UNC
45	**20 Cents** *L.1919* (1920-1923) Purple on gold underprint. Black serial #. Signature 5. Printer: Chaix.			
	a. Printer's name at lower right on back.	10.00	40.00	150
	b. Without imprint.	10.00	40.00	150

#	Denomination	VG	VF	UNC
46	**50 Cents** *L.1919* (1920-1923). Red. Black serial #. Signature 6. Printer: Chaix.	25.00	75.00	300

#	Denomination	Good	Fine	XF
47	**50 Cents** *L.1919* (1920). Red. Like #46. Black serial #.			
	a. Issued note.	200	400	—
	s. Specimen perforated: *SPECIMEN / IMPRIMERIE CHAIX.*	—	Unc	500

1921-1928 ND Issue

#	Denomination	VG	VF	UNC
48	**1 Piastre** ND (1921-1931). Brown and blue on light tan underprint. Helmeted woman at left. Back: Large *$1* on back.			
	a. Signature 6. (1921-1926).	5.00	20.00	60.00
	b. Signature 7. (1927-1931).	1.00	10.00	30.00

#	Denomination	VG	VF	UNC
49	**5 Piastres** ND (1926-1931). Multicolor. Woman with wreath at right. Back: Peacock.			
	a. Signature 6. (1926).	25.00	100	300
	b. Signature 7. (1927-1931).	12.50	75.00	200

50	20 Piastres	VG	VF	UNC
	ND (1928-1931). Multicolor. Woman with wreath holding branch and golden sphere at center. Signature 7. Back: Ancient statue.	40.00	175	800

51	100 Piastres	VG	VF	UNC
	ND (1925-1939). Multicolor. Golden vessel with dog on top at left. Back: Bust statue of Duplex at center, head at right.			
	a. Signature 6. (1925-1926).	50.00	150	500
	b. Signature 7. (1927-1931).	40.00	125	400
	c. Signature 8. (1932-1935).	50.00	150	500
	d. Signature 9. (1936-1939).	25.00	100	250

Banque de l'Indo-Chine (1930s)

Issues starting in 1932 when the Piastre was removed from silver standard and defined in terms of gold with a de facto exchange rate of 1 Piastre = 10 French Francs.

1932 ND Issue

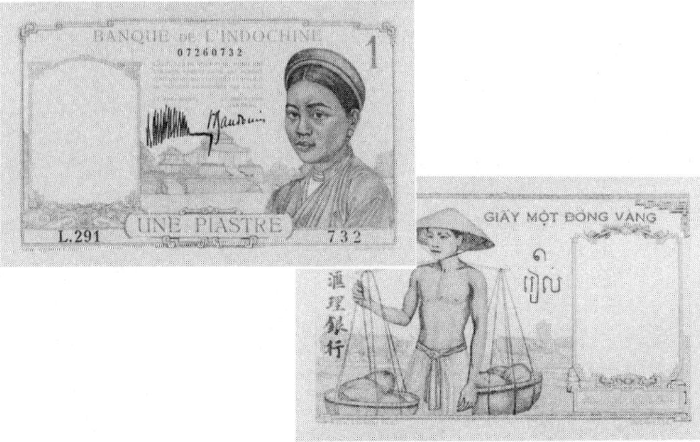

52	1 Piastre	VG	VF	UNC
	ND (1932). Brown, red, and multicolor. Woman at right, building at center, blue denomination numeral *1*. Signature 8. Back: Man with baskets. Without Lao text.	7.50	45.00	150

53	5 Piastres	VG	VF	UNC
	ND (1932). Brown, orange and multicolor. Woman with helmet and lance at left, denomination numeral *5* over wreath at upper right. Signature 8. Back: Women with headdress at left, ancient statues at right. Without Lao text.			
	a. Issued note.	25.00	50.00	200
	x. Contemporary counterfeit on genuine watermarked paper.	—	—	10.00

1932-1939 ND Issue

54	1 Piastre	VG	VF	UNC
	ND (1932-1939). Brown, red, and multicolor. Woman at right, building at center, red denomination numeral *1*. Signature 8. Back: Man with baskets. With Lao text.			
	a. Lao text Type I (Old Lao). Signature 8. (1932).	5.00	20.00	120
	b. Lao text Type I. Signature 9. (1936).	0.50	2.00	10.00
	c. Lao text Type I. Signature 11. (1946).	0.75	3.00	12.50
	d. Lao text Type II (New Lao). with dot under *O* in *MOT* on back. Signature 11. (1949).	1.50	5.00	20.00
	e. As d but without dot under *O* in *MOT* on back.	0.25	1.00	5.00

Note: For note of similar design but different heading see #92.

55	5 Piastres	VG	VF	UNC
	ND. (1932-1939). Brown, orange and multicolor. Woman with helmet and lance at left, large denomination numeral *5* over wreath at upper right on white background. Signature 8. Back: omen with headdress at left, ancient statues at right. With Lao text.			
	a. Lao text Type I (Old Lao). Signature 8. (1932).	3.00	15.00	70.00
	b. Lao text Type I. Signature 9. (1936).	1.00	5.00	25.00
	c. Lao text Type I. Signature 11. (1946).	1.00	4.00	15.00
	d. Lao text Type II (New Lao). Signature 11. (1949).	1.00	5.00	25.00

56	20 Piastres	VG	VF	UNC
	ND (1936-1939). Purple, blue and multicolor. Helmeted woman holding wreath at center, Athens standing in background, maroon bank name and denomination *20*, blue *VINGT PIASTRES*. Back: Helmeted woman holding wreath at center right.			
	a. Signature 8. (1936). Specimen only.	—	—	400
	b. Signature 9. (1936-39).	10.00	30.00	100

57	500 Piastres	VG	VF	UNC
	ND (from 1939). Multicolor. Woman and child examining globe; blue bank name and denomination numerals. Signature 9. Back: Two elephants behind woman and child.	25.00	75.00	400

1942-1945 ND Issues

#58-73 printed in French Indochina by the Imprimerie de l'Extreme Orient (I.D.E.O.) in Hanoi. Signature 10.

58	1 Piastre	VG	VF	UNC
	ND (1942-1945). Dark blue-black on orange underprint. Sampans at left. Back: Figure with hands together.			
	a. 7-digit serial #, 2.4mm tall.	1.00	4.00	25.00
	b. 7-digit serial #, 2.0mm tall.	1.00	4.00	25.00
	c. Letter and 6 digits in serial #, without serifs.	1.00	4.00	25.00

59	1 Piastre	VG	VF	UNC
	ND (1942-1945). Black on blue underprint. Sampans at left. Back: Figure with hands together.			
	a. 7-digit serial #.	1.00	4.00	25.00
	b. Letter and 6 digits in serial #, without serifs.	1.00	4.00	25.00
60	1 Piastre	VG	VF	UNC
	ND (1942-1945). Dark brown on purple underprint. (Color shades). Sampans at left. 7-digit serial #. Back: Figure with hands together.	0.50	2.50	10.00

61	5 Piastres	VG	VF	UNC
	ND (1942-1945). Dark green on red and multicolor underprint. Back: Pavillion at water's edge.	10.00	25.00	75.00
62	5 Piastres	VG	VF	UNC
	ND (1942-1945). Dark green on red and multicolor underprint. Back: Pavillion at water's edge.			
	a. Serial # 4mm tall, with serifs.	12.50	65.00	150
	b. Serial # 4.5mm tall, without serifs.	12.50	65.00	150
63	5 Piastres	VG	VF	UNC
	ND (1942-1945). Dark brown on pinkish brown and multicolor underprint. Back: Pavillion at water's edge.	10.00	25.00	60.00

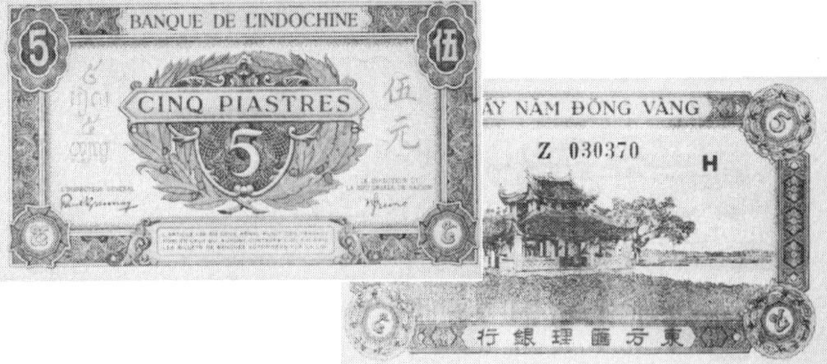

64	5 Piastres	VG	VF	UNC
	ND (1942-1945). Violet, bright pink and multicolor underprint. Back: Pavillion at water's edge.	10.00	50.00	125
65	20 Piastres	VG	VF	UNC
	ND (1942-1945). Blue on gray underprint. Autograph signature with titles:*LE CAISSIER DE LA SUCCURSALE*. Walled fortress at right. Back: Seated figure. Letters: A-F.	2.00	15.00	40.00

		VG	VF	UNC
66	**100 Piastres** ND (1942-1945). Lilac and orange frame and vignette. Market scenes at left and right. Autograph signature with titles:*LE CAISSIER DE LA SUCCURSALE*. Letters: A-G.	2.00	12.50	30.00
67	**100 Piastres** ND (1942-1945). Violet frame, green and violet vignette. Market scenes at left and right. Autograph signature with titles:*LE CAISSIER DE LA SUCCURSALE*. Letters: A-G.	3.00	15.00	40.00

		VG	VF	UNC
68	**500 Piastres** ND (1944-1945). Blue on yellow underprint. Red value at center right, six men on irrigation work. Autograph signature with titles: *LE CAISSIER DE LA SUCCURSALE*. Back: Dragon.	25.00	75.00	200
69	**500 Piastres** ND (1945). Dark green and gray. Red value at center right, six men on irrigation work. Autograph signature with titles: *LE CAISSIER DE LA SUCCURSALE*.	25.00	75.00	200

1942-1945 ND Second Issues

		VG	VF	UNC
70	**20 Piastres** ND (1942-1945). Green and yellow. Walled fortress at right. Printed signature with titles: *LE CAISSIER...* Back: Seated figure. Letters: A-E.	2.00	15.00	30.00

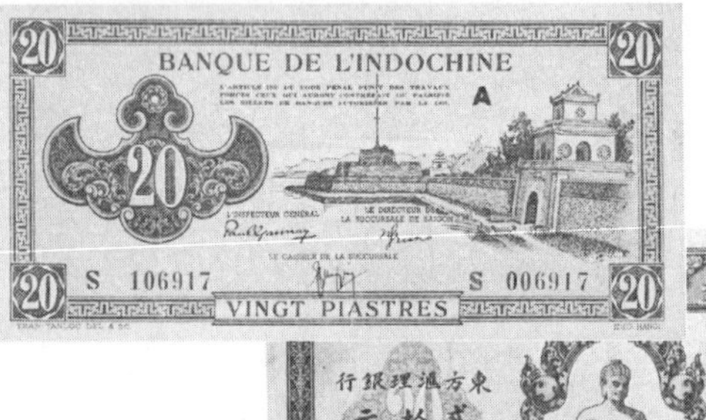

		VG	VF	UNC
71	**20 Piastres** ND (1942-1945). Black and gray on brown underprint. Walled fortress at right. Printed signature with titles: *LE CAISSIER...* Back: Seated figure. Letters: A-L.	1.00	5.00	20.00
72	**20 Piastres** ND (1942-1945). Pink and black. Walled fortress at right. Printed signature with titles: *LE CAISSIER...* Back: Seated figure. Letters: A-E.	10.00	40.00	100

		VG	VF	UNC
73	**100 Piastres** ND (1942-1945). Black-green frame, orange, brown and yellow vignette. Market scenes at left and right. Printed signature with titles: *LE CAISSIER..* .Letters: A-Q.	2.00	12.50	30.00

1949; 1951 ND Issue

#74-75 printed in Japan in 1944 for issue in Indochina.

		VG	VF	UNC
74	**1 Piastre** ND (1949). Green, orange and multicolor. Two farmers with ox. Signature 10. Back: Two women with branches.			
	a. Issued note.	2.50	10.00	30.00
	s. Specimen.	—	150	300

		VG	VF	UNC
75	**5 Piastres** ND. (1951). Green and multicolor. Farmers working in rice fields. Signature 10. Back: Temple with Buddhists.			
	a. Issued note with regular serial #.	—	—	500
	s1. Unfinished specimen, without signatures or serial #.	—	—	400
	s2. Finished specimen with 2 signatures and serial # all zeros. Overprint: *MIHON*.	—	—	800

1945 ND Issue

#76-79 printed in the U.S. and England for issue in Indochina after WW II.

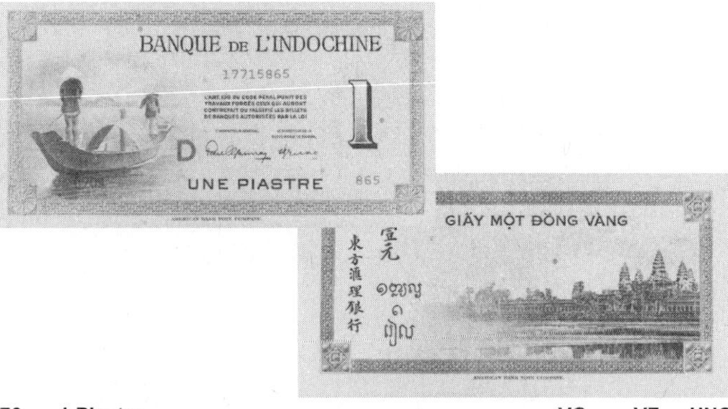

		VG	VF	UNC
76	**1 Piastre** ND (1945). Brown on light green underprint. Two men with boat. Signature 10. Back: Angkor Wat at right. Printer: ABNC.			
	a. Red letter B (Possibly not officially released).	0.10	0.50	2.50
	b. Red letters A; C; D; E (1951).	1.00	2.00	15.00
	c. Red letter F (1951).	1.00	4.00	20.00
	s. As b. Specimen.	—	—	125
77	**50 Piastres** ND (1945). Green. Man with straw hat and baskets at right. Signature 10. Back: Frieze from Angkor Wat. Printer: ABNC (without imprint).			
	a. Issued note.	10.00	40.00	200
	s. Specimen.	—	—	375

		VG	VF	UNC
78	**100 Piastres** ND (1945). Blue. Statues at Angkor Wat at left. Signature 10. Back: Five workers carrying baskets. Printer: ABNC (without imprint).			
	a. Issued note.	2.00	12.50	100
	s. Specimen.	—	—	175

1946 ND Issue

		VG	VF	UNC
79	**100 Piastres** ND (1946). Blue on multicolor underprint. BIC bank building at center. Signature 10. Back: Two sampans. Printer: TDLR (without imprint).			
	a. Issued note.	10.00	50.00	300
	s. Specimen.	—	—	500
	x. Contemporary counterfeit, brown paper.	2.50	10.00	30.00

1947-1951 ND Issue

		VG	VF	UNC
80	**10 Piastres** ND (1947). Dark purple on multicolor underprint. Angkor Wat at left. Signature 11. 2 serial # varieties. Back: Field worker. Printer: TDLR (without imprint).			
	a. Issued note.	3.00	8.00	40.00
	s. Specimen. TDLR oval.	—	—	400

		VG	VF	UNC
81	**20 Piastres** ND (1949). Multicolor. Helmeted woman holding wreath at center, Athens standing in background, white bank name and value *20* on red background, red *VINGT PIASTRES*. Signature 11.			
	a. Issued note.	5.00	30.00	125
	s. Specimen.	—	—	—

		VG	VF	UNC
82	**100 Piastres** ND (1947-1954). Multicolor. Mercury at left. Back: Man with two elephants at left, man at right. Signature 11.			
	a. Type I Lao text on back. (1947-1949).	2.50	20.00	100
	b. Type II Lao text on back. (1949-1954).	1.50	7.50	50.00
	s. Specimen.	—	—	250

		VG	VF	UNC
83	**500 Piastres** ND (1951). Multicolor. Woman and child examining globe; white bank name and value numerals on red background. Back: Two elephants behind woman and child. Signature 11.			
	a. Issued note.	45.00	175	500
	s. Specimen.	—	—	1,000

		VG	VF	UNC
84	**1000 Piastres** ND (printed 1951). Gray, orange and multicolor. Elephant at left, water buffaloes at right. With title: *Le Directeur General*. Back: Bayon head (Angkor) at left, tree at right. Watermark: Woman in Cambodian dancer's headdress.			
	s1. Specimen (serial # all Os).	—	—	2,000
	s2. Note with regular serial # perforated: *SPECIMEN*. Rare.	—	—	—

Note: For issued notes of similar design see #98 and #109.

Gouvernement Général de l'Indochine

SIGNATURE VARIETIES/TITLE COMBINATIONS BANQUE DE L'INDOCHINE ISSUES, 1939–43		
12	Emile Henry — Le Tresorier Payeur General	Yves Cazaux — Le Directeur des Finances
13	Louis Mayet — Le Tresorier General	Yves Cazaux — Le Directeur des Finances
14	Louis Mayet — Le Tresorier General	Jean Cousin — Le Directeur des Finances

1939 ND Issue

		VG	VF	UNC
85	**10 Cents** ND (1939). Red-brown. Sculptures at left, dancer at right. Back: Market scene with elephants.			
	a. *Le Tresorier Payeur General* in 2 lines at lower left. Denominations in Chinese, Cambodian and Vietnamese on back. Signature 12.	6.50	25.00	75.00
	b. Like #85a, but denomination in Lao added on back. Signature 12.	6.50	25.00	75.00
	c. *Le Tresorier General* in 1 line at lower left. Signature 13.	1.00	2.00	12.50
	d. Like #85c, serial # format 123456LL. signature 14.	0.25	1.50	7.50
	e. Like #85d, but serial # format LL 1236. Color is dark brown.	0.25	1.00	4.00

		VG	VF	UNC
86	**20 Cents** ND (1939). Red-brown and green. Women with conical hat at left. Back: Boat at center.			
	a. Like #85a. Signature 12.	7.00	27.50	100
	b. *Deleted.*	—	—	—
	c. Like #85c. Signature 13.	1.00	3.00	15.00
	d. Like #85d. Signature 14.	1.00	3.00	15.00

		VG	VF	UNC
87	**50 Cents** ND (1939). Red-brown and purple. Back: Woman with pole.			
	a. Like #85a. Signature 12.	3.00	20.00	100
	b. *Deleted.*	—	—	—
	c. Like #85c. Signature 13.	2.00	7.50	20.00
	d. Like #85d. Signature 14.	2.00	7.50	20.00
	e. Like #87d, but coffee-brown and black.	4.00	15.00	40.00

1942 ND Issue

#89-91, (from 1942-1943) Pham-Ngoc-Khue, designer. Color shades vary. Signature 14.

		VG	VF	UNC
88	**5 Cents** ND (1942). Green on pale blue underprint.			
	a. Signatures, titles and penalty clause in black. Serial # format: 123456L.	0.25	2.00	6.00
	b. Green underprint. Signature, titles and penalty clause in green. Serial # format: LL123456.	0.25	1.00	3.00

		VG	VF	UNC
89	**10 Cents** ND (1942). Brown on tan underprint.			
	a. Serial # format: LL1236.	0.25	1.00	2.00
	b. Serial # format: 1LL2347.	1.25	5.00	15.00

		VG	VF	UNC
90	**20 Cents** ND (1942). Red-violet on pinkish underprint. Dragons and flames at center.	0.50	1.75	4.00

		VG	VF	UNC
91	**50 Cents** ND (1942). Green on light green underprint. Dragons in underprint at left and right. Back: Rice underneath.			
	a. Serial # format: LL1236.	0.50	2.00	5.00
	b. Serial # format: 1LL2347.	1.25	5.00	15.00

Institut d'Emission des Etats du Cambodge,

SIGNATURE VARIETIES/TITLE COMBINATIONS ON INSTITUT D'EMISSION NOTES			
15	Gaston Cusin — Le President	M. Lacoutre — Le Caissier Central	ALL THREE STATES
16		Le Caissier General (unidentified)	ALL THREE STATES
17		Chhean Vam	CAMBODIA
18		Son Sann	CAMBODIA
19		Khun One Voravong — Un Administrateur	LAOS
20		Le Ky Huong	LAOS
21		Nghiem Van Tri — Un Administrateur	VIET-NAM

Cambodia, Laos and Viet Nam Combined Issue

1953 ND Issue

		VG	VF	UNC
92	**1 Piastre** ND (1953). Signature 15. Brown, red and multicolor. Woman at right. Similar to #54, but modified legends in red.	0.50	4.00	15.00

Cambodia Issue

Piastre-Riel System

1953-1954 ND Issues

		VG	VF	UNC
93	**1 Piastre = 1 Riel** ND (1953). Green and blue on yellow and multicolor underprint. Young King Sihanouk at center. Back: Cambodian title. Watermark: Elephant head. Signature 16.	10.00	40.00	100

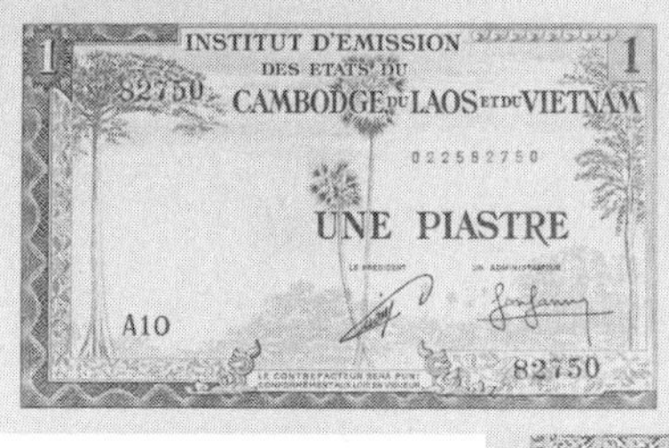

		VG	VF	UNC
94	**1 Piastre = 1 Riel** ND (1954). Blue and green. LIke #100 and #105 with trees. Signature 18. Back: Royal houseboat at left. Cambodian title. Watermark: Elephant head.	3.00	20.00	75.00

		VG	VF	UNC
95	**5 Piastres = 5 Riels** ND (1953). Green on pink and green underprint. Like #101 and #106 with banana trees at left, palms at right. Signature 18. Back: Naga (mythical snake) head at left. Cambodian title. Watermark: Elephant head.	3.00	25.00	80.00

		VG	VF	UNC
96	**10 Piastres = 10 Riels** ND (1953). Red on blue and gold underprint. Face like #102 and #107 with stylized sunburst at center. Back: Two dancers at left. Cambodian title. Watermark: Elephant head.			
	a. Signature 17.	3.00	6.00	40.00
	b. Signature 18.	3.00	30.00	100

		VG	VF	UNC
97	**100 Piastres = 100 Riels** ND (1954). Orange and multicolor. Like #103 and #108 with three women at left representing Cambodia, Laos & Vietnam. Signature 18. Back: Temple of Angkor. Watermark: Elephant head.	10.00	50.00	200

		VG	VF	UNC
98	**200 Piastres = 200 Riels** ND (1953). Green and brown. Like #84 and #109. Elephant at left, two water buffaloes at right. Signature 17. Back: Bayon head (Angkor) at left, tree at right. Cambodian title. Watermark: Elephant head.	50.00	100	300

Note: For later issues see Cambodia.

Laos Issue

Piastre-Kip System

1953-54 ND Issues

		VG	VF	UNC
99	**1 Piastre = 1 Kip** ND (1953). Blue-black on green, pale yellow and multicolor underprint. King Sisavang Vong at center. Signature 16. Back: Laotian title. Watermark: Elephant head.	3.00	12.50	75.00

		VG	VF	UNC
100	**1 Piastre = 1 Kip** ND (1954). Blue and green. Face Like #94 and #105. Signature 19. Back: Pagoda with three roots at left. Luang-Prabang at left. Laotian title. Watermark: Elephant head.	15.00	50.00	100

101 **5 Piastres = 5 Kip**

ND (1953). Green on pink and green underprint. Like #96 and #106. Signature 19. Back: Stupa at That Luang at left. Laotian title. Watermark: Elephant head.

VG	VF	UNC
5.00	40.00	100

102 **10 Piastres = 10 Kip**

ND (1953). Red on blue and gold underprint. Face Like #96 and #107. Signature 19. Back: Laotian woman at left. Laotian title. Watermark: Elephant head.

VG	VF	UNC
3.00	20.00	75.00

103 **100 Piastres = 100 Kip**

ND (1954). Multicolor. Like #97 and #108. Signature 20. Back: Pagoda at Vientiane at center, Laotian woman with bowl of roses at right. Laotian title. Watermark: Elephant head.

VG	VF	UNC
25.00	75.00	200

Note: For later issues see Laos.

Viet Nam Issue

Piastre-Dong System

1953-1954 ND Issues

104 **1 Piastre = 1 Dong**

ND (1953). Blue-black on green, pale yellow and multicolor underprint. Bao Dai at center. Signature 16. Back: Vietnamese title: VIN PHÁT-HÀNH. Watermark: Tiger head.

VG	VF	UNC
1.00	5.00	20.00

105 **1 Piastre = 1 Dong**

ND (1954). Blue and green. Like # 94 and #100. Signature 21. Back: Dragon at left. Vietnamese title: VIN PHÁT-HÀNH. Watermark: Tiger head. PC: Thin white or white/tan.

VG	VF	UNC
1.00	2.00	8.00

106 **5 Piastres = 5 Dong**

ND (1953). Green on pink and green underprint. Like #95 and #101. Signature 21. Back: Bao Dai at left. Vietnamese title: VIN PHÁT-HÀNH. Watermark: Tiger head.

VG	VF	UNC
1.00	4.00	20.00

107 **10 Piastres = 10 Dong**

ND (1953). Red on blue and gold underprint. Like #96 and #102. Signature 21. Back: Rock in the Bay of Along at left. Vietnamese title: VIN PHÁT-HÀNH. Watermark: Tiger head.

VG	VF	UNC
1.00	6.00	30.00

108 **100 Piastres = 100 Dong**

ND (1954). Multicolor. Like #97 and #103. Signature 21. Back: Small building at center, Bao Dai at right. Vietnamese title: VIN PHÁT-HÀNH. Watermark: Tiger head.

VG	VF	UNC
20.00	50.00	125

109 **200 Piastres = 200 Dong**

ND (1953). Green, brown and pink. Like #98. Signature 21. Back: Bao Dai at left, pagoda at center. Vietnamese title: VIN PHÁT-HÀNH. Watermark: Tiger head.

VG	VF	UNC
20.00	100	250

Note: For later issues see Viet Nam.

The colony of French Oceania (now the Territory of French Polynesia), comprising 130 basalt and coral islands scattered among five archipelagoes in the South Pacific, had an area of 1,544 sq. mi. (3,999 sq. km.) and a population of about 185,000, mostly Polynesians. Capital: Papeete. The colony produced phosphates, copra and vanilla. Tahiti of the Society Islands, the hub of French Oceania, was visited by Capt. Cook in 1769 and by Capt. Bligh in the Bounty 1788-89. The Society Islands were claimed by France in 1768, and in 1903 grouped with the Marquesas Islands, the Tuamotu Archipelago, the Gambier Islands and the Astral Islands under a single administrative head located at Papeete, Tahiti, to form the colony of French Oceania.

RULERS:
French

MONETARY SYSTEM:
1 Franc = 100 Centimes

FRENCH ADMINISTRATION

Chambre de Commerce des Etablissements Français de L'Océanie

1919 First Issue

Arrété du 29 Decembre 1919

		Good	Fine	XF
1	**25 Centimes** *L.1919.* Brown. Woman leaning on arch at left and right. Back: Helmeted head at left and right. Printer: Halpin Lithograph Co., San Francisco.	35.00	125	500

		Good	Fine	XF
2	**50 Centimes** *L.1919.* Green. Woman leaning on arch at left and right. Back: Helmeted head at left and right. Printer: Halpin Lithograph Co., San Francisco.	35.00	125	500

		Good	Fine	XF
3	**1 Franc** *L.1919.* Orange. Black or red serial #. Woman leaning on arch at left and right. Back: Helmeted head at left and right. Printer: Halpin Lithograph Co., San Francisco.	35.00	135	550

		Good	Fine	XF
4	**2 Francs** *L.1919.* Purple. Woman leaning on arch at left and right. Back: Helmeted head at left and right. Printer: Halpin Lithograph Co., San Francisco.	35.00	135	550

1919 Second Issue

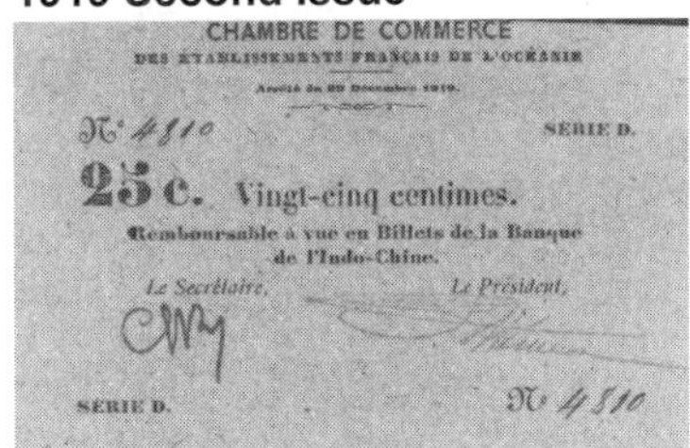

		Good	Fine	XF
4A	**25 Centimes** *L.1919.* Brown. Printer: Local.	60.00	200	550

		Good	Fine	XF
4B	**50 Centimes** *L.1919.* Blue. Printer: Local.	60.00	200	550

		Good	Fine	XF
5	**1 Franc** *L.1919.* Black. Without design. Printer: Local. PC: Dark brown.	60.00	200	550

		Good	Fine	XF
6	**2 Francs** *L.1919.* Black. Without design. Printer: Local. PC: Tan	60.00	200	550

Bons de Caisse des Etablissements Français Libres de L'Océanie

1941 Emergency WWII Issue

Arrété du 18 Aut 1941

		VG	VF	UNC
6A	**1 Franc** *D.1941.* PC: Cardboard. Rare. Black. Back: Soccer player at center.	—	—	—

		VG	VF	UNC
6B	**1 Franc** *D. 1941.* Black. Back: Plow at center.	—	—	—

		VG	VF	UNC
10A	**2 Francs** *D.1941.* Rare.	—	—	—

1942 Issue

Arrté No. 300 A.G.F. du 7 Avril 1942

		VG	VF	UNC
7	**50 Centimes** *L.1942.* Orange and green. Upright hand holding torch of freedom behind shield of Lorraine at center. Two signature varieties.	65.00	275	650
8	**1 Franc** *L.1942.* Green and red. Upright hand holding torch of freedom behind shield of Lorraine at center. Two signature varieties.	75.00	300	700

		VG	VF	UNC
9	**2 Francs** *L.1942.* Blue and black. Upright hand holding torch of freedom behind shield of Lorraine at center. Two signature varieties.	85.00	325	750

Bons de Caisse des Etablissements Français de L'Océanie

1943 Emergency WWII Issue

Arrté No. 698 S.G. du 25 Septembre 1943

		VG	VF	UNC
10	**50 Centimes** *L.1943.* Orange and black. Back: Map outline with text inside.			
	a. Circular violet handstamp.	37.50	125	300
	b. Wreath in circular violet handstamp.	40.00	135	350
	c. Embossed seal.	37.50	125	325
11	**1 Franc** *L.1943.* Green and purple. Back: Map outline with text inside.	VG	VF	UNC
	a. Circular violet handstamp.	37.50	135	325
	b. Wreath in circular violet handstamp.	40.00	165	400
	c. Embossed seal.	37.50	125	300
12	**2 Francs** *L.1943.* Blue and green. Flora and waves border; green text within. Back: Map outline with text inside.	VG	VF	UNC
	a. Circular violet handstamp.	50.00	165	375
	b. Wreath in circular violet handstamp.	60.00	200	500
	c. Embossed seal.	50.00	165	375
	d. Without seal.	60.00	165	350

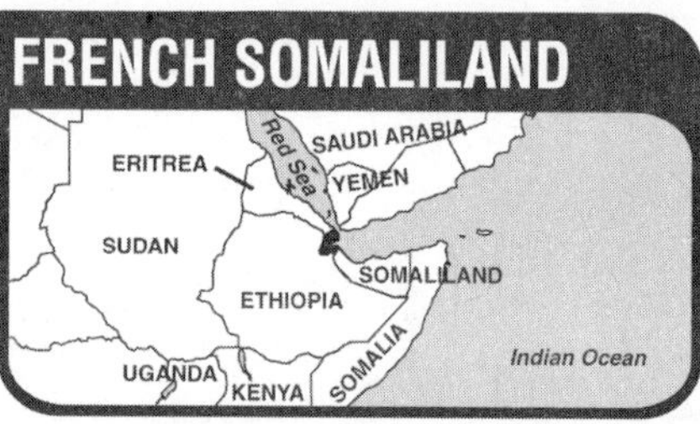

		VG	VF	UNC
13	**2.50 Francs** *L.1943.* Black and red. Back: Map outline with text inside.			
	a. Circular violet handstamp.	50.00	165	375
	b. Wreath in circular violet handstamp.	60.00	200	500
	c. Embossed seal.	50.00	165	375

French Somaliland (later to become the French Overseas Territory of Afars and Issas, and then independent Dijbouti) was located in northeast Africa at the Bab el-Mandeb Strait connecting the Suez Canal and the Red Sea with the Gulf of Aden and the Indian Ocean. It had an area of 8,494 sq. mi. (22,000 sq. km.). Capital: Djibouti. French interest in the area began in 1839 with concessions obtained by a French naval lieutenant from the provincial sultans. French Somaliland was made a protectorate in 1884 and its boundaries were delimited by the Franco-British and Ethiopian accords of 1887 and 1897. It became a colony in 1896 and a territory within the French Union in 1946. In 1958, it voted to join the new French Community as an overseas territory, and reaffirmed that choice by a referendum in March 1967. Its name was changed from French Somaliland to the French Territory of Afars and Issas on July 5, 1967. On June 27, 1977 French Afars and Issas became Africa's 49th independent state as the republic of Djibouti.

RULERS:

French to 1977

MONETARY SYSTEM:

1 Franc = 100 Centimes

FRENCH SOMALILAND

Banque de l'Indo-chine

Djibouti

Decrets des 21.1.1875, 20.2.1888, 16.5.1900 et 3.4.1901

		Good	Fine	XF
1	**5 Francs** 1913; 1919. Blue. Oriental woman seated below FRANCE seated holding caduceus at left. Signature varieties.			
	a. Issued note. 14.3.1913; 26.8.1919.	250	850	—
	b. Cancelled note handstamped: *ANNULÉ*. 26.8.1919.	100	400	—

		Good	Fine	XF
2	**20 Francs** 1.5.1910; 4.5.1910. Blue. Neptune reclining holding trident at lower left. Signature varieties.			
	a. Issued note.	375	1,650	—
	b. Cancelled note handstamped: *ANNULÉ*.	125	700	—

No.	Description	Good	Fine	XF
3	**100 Francs** 1909; 1915. Elephant columns at left and right, two women reclining with ox and tiger at bottom. Signature varieties.			
	a. 1.5.1909. signature titles: *UN ADMINISTRATEUR* and *LE DIRECTEUR*. Rare.	—	—	—
	b. 10.6.1915. signature titles: *UN ADMINISTRATEUR* and *L'ADM- DIRECTEUR*.	375	1,800	—
	c. Cancelled note handstamped: *ANNULÉ*.	125	650	—

1920 Provisional Issue

No.	Description	Good	Fine	XF
4	**100 Francs** 2.1.1920 (-old date 10.3.1914). Elephant columns at left and right, two women reclining with ox and tiger at bottom. Overprint: Red, on Tahiti #3.			
	a. Issued note.	50.00	125	350
	b. Cancelled note handstamped: *ANNULÉ*.	20.00	65.00	135

1920-1923 Regular Issue

No.	Description	Good	Fine	XF
4A	**5 Francs** 1.8.1923. Blue. Oriental woman seated below FRANCE seated holding caduceus at left.			
	a. Issued note.	200	800	—
	s. Perforated: *SPECIMEN*.	—	Unc	200
4B	**20 Francs** 3.1.1921. Blue. Neptune reclining holding trident at lower left.	325	1,250	—

No.	Description	Good	Fine	XF
5	**100 Francs** 2.1.1920. Brown. Elephant columns at left and right, two women reclining with ox and tiger at bottom.	35.00	85.00	250

1928-1938 Issues

#6-10 issued ca. 1926-1938.

No.	Description	Good	Fine	XF
6	**5 Francs** ND. Blue and red on light gold underprint. Woman wearing helmet at left.			
	a. Signature titles: *UN ADMINISTRATEUR* and *LE DIRECTEUR*.	2.00	7.00	37.50
	b. Signature titles: *LE PRÉSIDENT* and *LE DIRECTEUR GÉNÉRAL*.	2.00	7.00	37.50

No.	Description	Good	Fine	XF
7	**20 Francs** ND. Lilac-brown and dark lilac on light green underprint. Dark blue text. Woman at right. Back: Peacock at left center.			
	a. Run # through 18.	3.00	12.50	70.00
	b. Similar coloring but much lighter lilac and more visible light green underprint. Run #19-20 only.	4.00	15.00	85.00
7A	**20 Francs** ND. Blue and light lilac on light gold underprint. Woman at right. Back: Peacock at left center. Run #21-23.	4.00	15.00	85.00
7B	**20 Francs** ND. Woman at right. Legend in black, and circle at bottom center is red with white numeral. Back: Peacock at left. Red *20*. Different from #7 or 7A. Specimen.	—	Unc	750
8	**100 Francs** ND. Multicolor. Woman with head inlaurel wreath holding small figure of Athena at center.	8.00	20.00	90.00
8A	**100 Francs** ND. Multicolor. Woman with head in laurel wreath holding small figure of Athena at center. With circle at bottom right is red with white numeral. Specimen.	—	Unc	900

No.	Description	Good	Fine	XF
9	**500 Francs** 1927; 1938. Woman with coat of arms and branch at left, ships in background.			
	a. Signature titles: *UN ADMINISTRATEUR* and *LE DIRECTEUR*. 20.7.1927.	17.50	55.00	200
	b. Signature titles: *LE PRÉSIDENT* and *LE DIRECTEUR GÉNÉRAL*. 8.3.1938.	15.00	50.00	185

No.	Description	Good	Fine	XF
10	**1000 Francs** ND (1938). Multicolor. Market scene at left and in background, woman sitting at right. Signature titles: *LE PRÉSIDENT and LE DIRECTEUR GÉNÉRAL.*	20.00	50.00	250
10A	**1000 Francs** ND (1938). Market scene at left and in background, woman sitting at right. Bank title and denomination *1000* with red background. Signature titles: *LE PRÉSIDENT* and *LE DIRECTEUR GÉNÉRAL* Back: Bank title and denomination *1000* with red background. Rare.	—	—	—

1943 Provisional Issues

No.	Description	Good	Fine	XF
11	**5 Francs** ND (1943). Overprint: Double cross of Lorraine and head of antelope on #6.	40.00	150	350

No.	Description	Good	Fine	XF
12A	**20 Francs** ND (18.2.1943). Blue and red. Overprint: *COTE FRANCAISE DES SOMALIS. B.I.C. DJIBOUTI* in rectangle on #7.	75.00	175	550
13	**100 Francs** ND (1943). Overprint: Double cross of Lorraine and head of antelope on #8.	100	250	650
13A	**100 Francs** ND (18.2.1943). Overprint: *COTE FRANCAISE...* on #8.	100	250	650
13B	**500 Francs** ND (1943). Overprint: Double cross of Lorraine and head of antelope on #9.	—	—	—
13C	**500 Francs** ND (18.2.1943). Overprint: *COTE FRANCAISE...* on #9.	—	—	—
13D	**1000 Francs** ND (1943). Overprint: Double cross of Lorraine and head of antelope on #10.	—	—	—
13E	**1000 Francs** ND (18.2.1943). Overprint: *COTE FRANCAISE...* on #10.	—	—	—

Note: Dangerous counterfeits of #12 and 13A have appeared in the market recently. All genuine overprint B.I.C. notes can be verified by the alphabets appearing on them by refering to *Les billets de la Banque de l'Indochine* by Kolsky and Muszynski.

1945 Issue

No.	Description	Good	Fine	XF
14	**5 Francs** ND (19.2.1945). Light brown. Back: Boat at center. Printer: Government Printer, Palestine.	10.00	70.00	275

No.	Description	Good	Fine	XF
15	**20 Francs** ND (19.2.1945). Red on yellow underprint. Back: Building. Printer: Government Printer, Palestine.	15.00	100	350
16	**100 Francs** ND (19.2.1945). Green. Back: Palms. Printer: Government Printer, Palestine.	40.00	250	—
17	**500 Francs** ND (19.2.1945). Purple and multicolor. Back: Swords and spears. Printer: Government Printer, Palestine.	125	850	—
18	**1000 Francs** ND (19.2.1945). Green, yellow and blue. Back: Fish at center. Printer: Government Printer, Palestine.	200	1,200	—

1946 Issue

No.	Description	Good	Fine	XF
19	**10 Francs** ND (1946). Multicolor. Youth at left. Back: Camel caravan. Watermark: Winged head of Mercury.	10.00	50.00	200

No.	Description	Good	Fine	XF
19A	**100 Francs** ND (1946). Multicolor. Woman at left, farmer plowing with oxen at right.	15.00	90.00	275
20	**1000 Francs** ND (1946). Multicolor. Woman holding jug at left center. Back: Woman holding jug at left center.	40.00	175	600

Chambre de Commerce, Djibouti

1919 Emergency Issue

No.	Description	Good	Fine	XF
21	**5 Centimes** ND (1919). Green cardboard. With or without perforations at left.	20.00	50.00	200
22	**10 Centimes** ND (1919). Light brown cardboard. With or without perforations at left.	20.00	50.00	200
23	**50 Centimes** 30.11.1919. Violet. 3 signature varieties.	25.00	75.00	250

		Good	Fine	XF
24	**1 Franc** 30.11.1919. Brown. 3 signature varieties.	30.00	90.00	300

Trésor Public, Cóte Française des Somalis

1952 Issue

		VG	VF	UNC
25	**50 Francs** ND (1952). Light brown and multicolor. Boat anchored at right. Back: Camels.	1.00	8.00	45.00

		VG	VF	UNC
26	**100 Francs** ND (1952). Multicolor. Stylized corals. Back: Trunk of palm tree.			
	a. Issued note.	2.00	25.00	100
	s. Specimen. Perforated *SPECIMEN*.	—	—	—

		VG	VF	UNC
27	**500 Francs** ND (1952). Ochre and multicolor. Ships at left center. Back: Jumping gazelle.	10.00	80.00	350

		VG	VF	UNC
28	**1000 Francs** ND (1952). Multicolor. Woman holding jug at left center. Back: Woman holding jug at right center.	25.00	120	450

		VG	VF	UNC
29	**5000 Francs** ND (1952). Multicolor. Aerial view of harbor at Djibouti at center.			
	a. Issued note.	75.00	275	800
	s. Specimen. Perforated *SPECIMEN*.	—	—	500

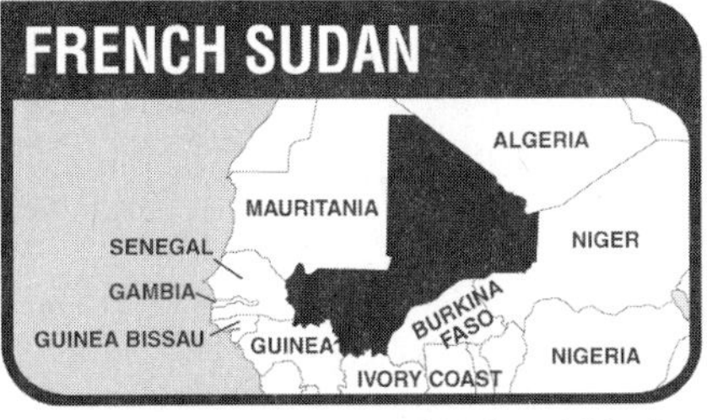

The French Sudan, a landlocked country in the interior of West Africa southwest of Algeria, has an area of 478,764 sq. mi. (1,240,000 sq. km.). Capital: Bamako. Livestock, fish, cotton and peanuts are exported. French Sudanese are descendants of the ancient Malinke Kingdom of Mali that controlled the middle Niger from the 11th to the 17th centuries. The French penetrated the Sudan (now Mali) about 1880, and established their rule in 1898 after subduing fierce native resistance. In 1904 the are became the colony of Upper Senegal-Niger (changed to French Sudan in 1920), and became part of the French Union in 1946. In 1958 French Sudan became the Sudanese Republic with complete internal autonomy. Senegal joined with the Sudanese Republic in 1959 to form the Mali Federation which, in 1960, became a fully independent member of the French Community. Upon Senegal's subsequent withdrawal from the Federation, the Sudanese, on Sept. 22, 1960, proclaimed their nation the fully independent Republic of Mali and severed all ties with France.

RULERS:

French to 1960

MONETARY SYSTEM:

1 Franc = 100 Centimes

FRENCH ADMINISTRATION

Gouvernement Général de l'Afrique Occidentale Française Colonie du Soudan Française

1917 Emergency WWI Issue

Décret du 11.2.1917 Soudan Française

		VG	VF	UNC
A1	**0.50 Franc** *D.1917.*			
	a. Watermark: Bees.	650	1,600	3,750
	b. Watermark: Laurel leaves.	550	1,500	3,500

Note: Denominations of 1 Franc and 2 Francs probably exist but have not been reported. For later issues see Mali in Volume 3.

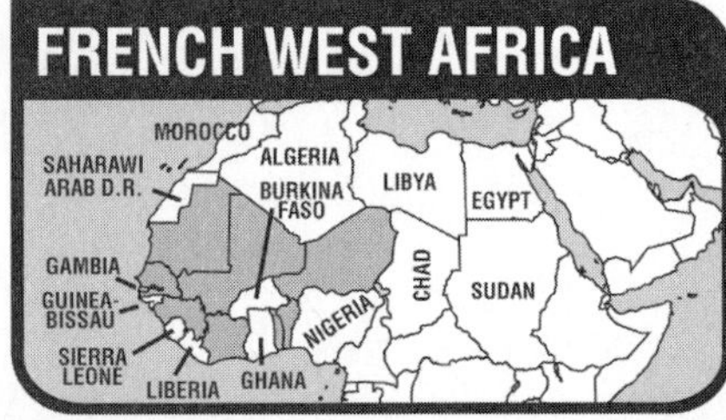

French West Africa (Afrique Occidentale Francaise), a former federation of French colonial territories on the northwest coast of Africa, has an area of 1,831,079 (4,742,495 sq. km.) and a population of about 17 million. Capital: Dakar. The constituent territories were Mauritania, Senegal, Dahomey, French Sudan, Ivory Coast, Upper Volta, Niger, French Guinea, and later on the mandated area of Togo. Peanuts, palm kernels, cacao, coffee and bananas were exported. Prior to the mid-19th century, France, as the other European states, maintained establishments on the west coast of Africa for the purpose of trading in slaves and gum, but made no serious attempt at colonization. From 1854 onward, the coastal settlements were gradually extended into the interior until, by the opening of the 20th century, acquisition ended and organization and development began. French West Africa was formed in 1895 by grouping the several colonies under one administration (at Dakar) while retaining a large measure of autonomy to each of the constituent territories. The inhabitants of French West Africa were made French citizens in 1946. With the exception of French Guinea, all of the colonies voted in 1958 to become autonomous members of the new French Community. French Guinea voted to become the fully independent Republic of Guinea. The present-day independent states are members of the "Union Monetaire Ouest-Africaine." Also see West African States.

MONETARY SYSTEM:

1 Franc = 100 Centimes
1 Unit = 5 Francs

SIGNATURE TITLES:

a, c, f, h, j, l: ***Un Administrateur, Le Directeur***

b, e: ***Un Administrateur, Le Directeur, Le Caissier***

d, g, i, k: ***Le Président, L'Administrateur- Directeur***

m: ***Le Président, Le Directeur General***

CITIES OF ISSUE:

In addition to city of issue designation, the back color is the same for all denominations within a city.

A - Conakri, Conakry (French Guinea) Back: green.

B - Dakar (Senegal) Back: red (5 Francs green)

C - Duala (Cameroon) Overprint on Conakry or Dakar notes.

D - Grand-Bassam (Ivory Coast) Back: blue.

E - Porto Novo (Dahomey) Back: dark brown or red.

F - St. Louis (Senegal) Back: red.

NOTE: The first issue of the bank also circulated in Equatorial Africa, Togo and Cameroon. Dakar is most frequenty encountered. Notes with Lome (Togo) imprint allegedly exist but no examples have been reported.

FRENCH ADMINISTRATION

Banque de l'Afrique Occidentale

Conakry

1903-1924 Issue

		Good	Fine	XF
5A	**5 Francs** 1904-1919. Blue and yellow. Lion at left; bowl, drum and other objects at right.			
	a. *CONAKRI.* Signature titles: a. 13.1.1904; 5.2.1904.	85.00	225	500
	b. *CONAKRY.* Signature titles: c. 10.7.1919.	75.00	200	450

		Good	Fine	XF
9A	**50 Francs** 1920-1924. Blue and yellow. Elephant head and tree at left and right. *CONAKRY.* Signature titles: h.			
	a. Signature titles: e. 12.2.1920.	—	—	—
	b. Signature titles: h. 12.6.1924.	100	350	650

		Good	Fine	XF
10A	**100 Francs** 1903-1924. Red and green. Elephant head and tree at left and right. *CONAKRY.*			
	a. Signature titles: a. 3.1.1903.	140	500	—
	b. Signature titles: e. 12.2.1920.	100	350	650
	c. Signature titles: i. 13.11.1924.	110	375	700
	s. Specimen. As a.	—		

		Good	Fine	XF
13A	**500 Francs** 1912-1924. Blue and yellow. Elephant head and tree at left and right. *CONAKRY.*			
	a. Signature titles: b. 12.9.1912.	350	850	—
	b. Signature titles: g. 10.11.1921.	300	750	—
	c. Signature titles: i. 10.4.1924.	300	750	—

		Good	Fine	XF
15A	**1000 Francs** 10.4.1924. Red and green. Elephant head and tree at left and right. *CONAKRY.* Signature titles: i.	375	1,000	—

Dakar

1892 ND Provisional Issue

		Good	Fine	XF
3	**100 Francs** ND (old dates 26; 30.11.1892). Rare. Blue on pink underprint.	—	—	—

1916-1924 Issue

		Good	Fine	XF
5B	**5 Francs** 1916-1932. Blue and yellow. Lion at left; bowl, drum and other objects at right.			
	a. Signature titles: c. 8.6.1916; 28.5.1918; 10.7.1919.	17.50	55.00	135
	b. Signature titles: h. 14.12.1922; 10.4.1924.	15.00	40.00	125
	c. Signature titles: j. 1.8.1925; 17.2.1926; 21.10.1926.	12.00	35.00	120
	d. Signature titles: k. 10.6.1926.	12.00	35.00	120
	e. Signature titles: l. 13.1.1928.	17.50	55.00	135
	f. Signature titles: m. 16.5.1929; 1.9.1932.	17.50	55.00	135

		Good	Fine	XF
7B	**25 Francs** 1920-1926. Gray-brown and green. Elephant head and tree at left and right.	Good	Fine	XF
	a. Signature titles: d. 15.4.1920.	50.00	150	425
	b. Signature titles: i. 9.7.1925.	30.00	125	300
	c. Signature titles: k. 10.6.1926.	30.00	125	300
9B	**50 Francs** 1919; 1926; 1929. Blue and yellow. Elephant head and tree at left and right.	Good	Fine	XF
	a. Signature titles: b. 11.9.1919.	50.00	150	425
	b. Signature titles: k. 11.2.1926.	35.00	115	300
	c. Signature titles: m. 14.3.1929.	50.00	150	425

		Good	Fine	XF
10B	**100 Francs** 15.4.1920. Red and green. Elephant head and tree at left and right. Signature titles: f.	100	250	550
11B	**100 Francs** 1924; 1926. Elephant head and tree at left and right. Normally printed city of issue.	Good	Fine	XF
	a. Signature titles: i. 13.11.1924.	50.00	150	425
	b. Signature titles: k. 24.9.1926.	50.00	150	425

		Good	Fine	XF
12B	**500 Francs** 10.11.1921. Blue and yellow. Signature titles: g.	300	650	—
13B	**500 Francs** 1919-1924. Blue and yellow. Elephant head and tree at left and right.	Good	Fine	XF
	a. Signature titles: d. 11.9.1919.	350	850	—
	b. Signature titles: g. 10.11.1921.	300	750	—
	c. Signature titles: i. 10.4.1924.	275	675	—
15B	**1000 Francs** 10.4.1924. Red and green. Elephant head and tree at left and right. Signature titles: i.	325	900	—

Duala

1919-1921 Issue

		Good	Fine	XF
6C	**25 Francs** 15.4.1920. Signature titles: f.	250	550	—
13C	**500 Francs** 10.11.1921. Blue and yellow. Signature titles: g.	500	1,500	—
14C	**1000 Francs** 11.9.1919. Signature titles: d.	600	1,750	—

Grand-Bassam

1904-1924 Issues

		Good	Fine	XF
5D	**5 Francs** 1904-1919. Lion at left; bowl, drum and other objects at right.	Good	Fine	XF
	a. Signature titles: a. 26.2.1904; 1.3.1904.	90.00	250	600
	b. Signature titles: c. 8.6.1916; 18.5.1918; 28.5.1918; 10.7.1919.	85.00	235	475
6D	**25 Francs** 12.7.1923. Gray-brown. Elephant head and tree at left and right. Signature titles: h.	265	550	—
7D	**25 Francs** 1920; 1923. Elephant head and tree at left and right. Normally printed city of issue.	Good	Fine	XF
	a. Signature titles: f. 12.2.1920.	180	500	1,000
	b. Signature titles: i. 12.7.1923.	180	500	1,000
9D	**50 Francs** 1920; 1924. Elephant head and tree at left and right.	Good	Fine	XF
	a. Signature titles: f. 12.2.1920.	275	675	—
	b. Signature titles: i. 12.6.1924.	275	675	—
11D	**100 Francs** 1910-1924. Elephant head and tree at left and right. Normally printed city of issue.	Good	Fine	XF
	a. Signature titles: b. 18.8.1910; 9.3.1916.	325	750	—
	b. Signature titles: e. 12.2.1920.	325	750	—
	c. Signature titles: f. 15.4.1920.	325	750	—
	d. Signature titles: i. 13.11.1924.	325	750	—
12D	**100 Francs** 15.4.1920. Elephant head and tree at left and right. Signature titles: f.	375	750	—
13D	**500 Francs** 15.4.1924. Elephant head and tree at left and right. Signature titles: f.	450	950	—
14D	**1000 Francs** 15.4.1924. Elephant head and tree at left and right. Signature titles: f.	600	1,500	—

Porto-Novo

1916-1924 Issue

		Good	Fine	XF
5E	**5 Francs** 8.6.1916; 28.5.1918; 10.7.1919. Lion at left; bowl, drum and other objects at right. Signature titles: c.	85.00	225	500
7E	**25 Francs** 1920; 1923. Elephant head and tree at left and right.	Good	Fine	XF
	a. Signature titles: e. 12.2.1920.	180	500	950
	b. Signature titles: i. 12.7.1923.	180	500	950
10E	**50 Francs** 1920; 1924. Elephant head and tree at left and right.	Good	Fine	XF
	a. Signature titles: e. 12.2.1920.	300	675	—
	b. Signature titles: i. 12.6.1924.	300	675	—
11E	**100 Francs** 1920; 1924. Elephant head and tree at left and right. Normally printed city of issue.	Good	Fine	XF
	a. Signature titles: f. 15.4.1920.	325	750	—
	b. Signature titles: i. 13.11.1924.	325	750	—
12E	**100 Francs** 9.3.1916. Signature titles: b.	325	750	—
13E	**500 Francs** 10.4.1924. Elephant head and tree at left and right. Signature titles: f.	450	1,100	—
14E	**1000 Francs** 11.9.1919. Red and green. Signature titles: d.	600	1,500	—
15E	**1000 Francs** 10.4.1924. Elephant head and tree at left and right. Signature titles: i.	600	1,500	—

Saint-Louis

1904-1917 Issues

#	Denomination	Good	Fine	XF
5F	**5 Francs** 1904; 1916. Blue, red and tan. Lion at top left; bowl, drum and other objects at top right.			
	a. Signature titles: a. 1.2.1904; 1.5.1904.	200	550	—
	b. Signature titles: c. 8.6.1916; 15.8.1918.	140	400	650
7F	**25 Francs** 9.11.1917. Signature titles: b.	250	600	—
9F	**50 Francs** 9.10.1905. Elephant head and tree at left and right. Signature titles: b.	275	750	—
13F	**500 Francs** 12.9.1912; 11.9.1913. Blue and yellow. Elephant head and tree at left and right. Signature titles: b.	500	1,150	—
14F	**1000 Francs** 14.10.1905. Signature titles: a.	600	1,500	—

W/o Branch Name

1919 Issue

#	Denomination	Good	Fine	XF
5G	**5 Francs** 10.7.1919. Signature titles: c. Blue and yellow. Lion at left; bowl, drum and other objects at right.	100	275	575

1934-1937 Issue

#21-27 w/o city of issue. Printed by the Banque de France (w/o imprint).

#	Denomination	VG	VF	UNC
21	**5 Francs** 17.7.1934-22.4.1941. Brown, green and multicolor. Man at center. Value in dark blue. Signature varieties. Back: Man weaving.	1.50	7.50	27.50
22	**25 Francs** 1.5.1936-9.3.1939. Multicolor. Young man wearing turban with horse at left center. Value in blue. Signature varieties. Back: Lion at right.	5.00	17.50	55.00

#	Denomination	VG	VF	UNC
23	**100 Francs** 17.11.1936; 11.1.1940; 10.9.1941. Blue and brown. 2 women with fancy hairdress. Signature varieties. Back: Woman with basket.	25.00	85.00	265
24	**1000 Francs** 21.10.1937; 28.9.1939; 5.6.1941; 28.4.1945. Multicolor. French woman with African women with child. Signature varieties.	150	525	—

Note: For issues similar to #21-24 but with heading: *Afrique Française Libre,* see French Equatorial Africa #6-9.

1941-1943 Issues

#	Denomination	VG	VF	UNC
25	**5 Francs** 6.3.1941-1.10.1942. Multicolor. Man at center. Value in light blue. Signature varieties. Back: Man weaving.	1.50	8.50	30.00
26	**5 Francs** 2.3.1943. Multicolor. Man at center. Value, date and signature in red. Signature varieties. Back: Man weaving.	6.00	20.00	57.50

#	Denomination	VG	VF	UNC
27	**25 Francs** 9.1.1942; 24.2.1942; 22.4.1942; 1.10.1942. Multicolor. Young man wearing turban with horse at left center. Value in red. Signature varieties.	7.00	27.50	65.00

Note: For #25-27 with: *RF-FEZZAN* overprint. see Libya.

1942-1943 WWII Issue

#	Denomination	VG	VF	UNC
28	**5 Francs** 14.12.1942. Black on gold underprint. Woman at center. Signature varieties. Printer: E.A. Wright. Phila.			
	a. Serial #. Wide V in left signature.	3.00	10.00	25.00
	b. As a. Narrow V in left signature.	2.00	7.50	20.00
	c. Without serial #.	10.00	30.00	75.00
	s1. As a. Specimen.	—	—	100
	s2. As b. Specimen.	—	—	85.00

#	Denomination	VG	VF	UNC
29	**10 Francs** 2.1.1943. Violet on gold underprint. Woman at right. Printer: Algerian.	25.00	75.00	225

#	Denomination	VG	VF	UNC
30	**25 Francs** 14.12.1942. Black on green underprint. Woman at left. Signature varieties. Back: Plane and palms at center. Printer: E.A. Wright. Phila.			
	a. Serial # at center, block letter at upper left and right.	4.50	15.00	60.00
	b. Block letter and # at upper left and lower right, # at lower left and upper right, serial # at center.	7.00	25.00	90.00
	c. Without serial #.	17.50	60.00	175
	s. Specimen.	—	—	150

31 **100 Francs**
14.12.1942. Black on pink underprint. Baobab tree at center. Signature varieties. Back: Huts and palms at center. Printer: E.A. Wright. Phila.

	VG	VF	UNC
a. Serial #.	15.00	45.00	150
b. Without serial #.	30.00	90.00	200
s. Specimen.	—	—	175

32 **1000 Francs**
14.12.1942. Purple on light green and pinkish underprint. Ships and train at center. Back: *BAO* in wreath. Printer: ABNC.

	VG	VF	UNC
a. Issued note.	225	675	1,200
p. Proof. Seperate face and back on cards.	—	—	2,500
s. Specimen.	—	—	2,000

Afrique Occidentale Française
1944 ND Issue

33 **0.50 Franc**
ND (1944). Orange. Fortress at center.

	VG	VF	UNC
a. Without security thread.	2.00	6.00	20.00
b. With security thread.	2.00	6.00	20.00

Sometimes red in color.

34 **1 Franc**
ND (1944). Dark brown. Fisherman in boat at left, woman at right.

	VG	VF	UNC
a. Light blue paper.	2.00	6.00	20.00
b. Light brown on yellow paper.	2.00	6.00	20.00

35 **2 Francs**
ND (1944). Blue. Beach with palm tree at left.

	VG	VF	UNC
	20.00	60.00	225

Banque de l'Afrique Occidentale (resumed)
1943-1948 Issue

36 **5 Francs**
17.8.1943 (1945)-28.10.1954. Multicolor. 2 women, one in finery the other with jug. Back: Men poling in long boats at left center. Printer: French printing (without imprint.)

	VG	VF	UNC
	2.00	7.50	20.00

37 **10 Francs**
18.1.1946-28.10.1954. Multicolor. 2 male bow hunters at center. Back: Man carring gazelle. Printer: French printing (without imprint.)

	VG	VF	UNC
	2.50	10.00	30.00

38 **25 Francs**
17.8.1943(1945)-28.10.1954. Multicolor. Woman at center. Back: Man with bull at center. Printer: French printing (without imprint.)

	VG	VF	UNC
	4.00	17.50	75.00

39 **50 Francs**
27.9.1944(1945)-28.10.1954. Multicolor. Women at center, old man wearing fez at right. Back: Man with stalk of bananas at center Printer: French printing (without imprint.)

VG	VF	UNC
5.00	25.00	100

40 **100 Francs**
10.5.1945-28.10.1954. Multicolor. Woman with fruit bowl at center. Back: Family. Printer: French printing (without imprint.)

VG	VF	UNC
7.50	27.50	110

41 **500 Francs**
6.2.1946-21.11.1953. Multicolor. Woman with flag at center. Back: Colonial soldiers. Printer: French printing (without imprint.)

VG	VF	UNC
35.00	175	650

42 **1000 Francs**
16.4.1948-28.10.1954. Multicolor. Woman holding 2 jugs at left center. Back: Woman with high headdress at center. Printer: French printing (without imprint.)

VG	VF	UNC
60.00	185	750

43 **5000 Francs**
10.4.1947; 15.11.1948; 27.12.1948; 22.12.1950. Multicolor. France with 2 local women at center. Printer: French printing (without imprint.)

VG	VF	UNC
150	350	850

Institut d'Emission de l'A.O.F. et du Togo
1955-1956 Issue

44 **50 Francs**
5.10.1955. Multicolor. Women at center, old man wearing fez at right.

VG	VF	UNC
60.00	225	500

45 **50 Francs**
ND (1956). Black and multicolor. Three women at center. Back: Woman with headdress, city in background at center.

VG	VF	UNC
3.50	15.00	75.00

46 **100 Francs**
23.10.1956; 20.5.1957. Multicolor. Mask at left, woman with braids at right. Back: Woman at left.

VG	VF	UNC
6.00	25.00	100

47 **500 Francs**
23.10.1956. Multicolor. People at field work at left, mask at right.

VG	VF	UNC
30.00	100	350

48 **1000 Francs**
5.10.1955. Multicolor. Woman with 2 jugs at left center. Back: Woman with high headdress at center.

VG	VF	UNC
125	225	550

Georgia is bounded by the Black Sea to the west and by Turkey, Armenia and Azerbaijan. It occupies the western part of Transcaucasia covering an area of 69,700 sq. km. and a population of 4.63 million. Capital: Tbilisi. Hydro-electricity, minerals, forestry and agriculture are the chief industries.

The region of present-day Georgia contained the ancient kingdoms of Colchis and Kartli-Iberia. The area came under Roman influence in the first centuries A.D. and Christianity became the state religion in the 330s. Domination by Persians, Arabs, and Turks was followed by a Georgian golden age (11th-13th centuries) that was cut short by the Mongol invasion of 1236. Subsequently, the Ottoman and Persian empires competed for influence in the region. Georgia was absorbed into the Russian Empire in the 19th century. Independent for three years (1918-1921) following the Russian revolution, it was forcibly incorporated into the USSR until the Soviet Union dissolved in 1991. An attempt by the incumbent Georgian government to manipulate national legislative elections in November 2003 touched off widespread protests that led to the resignation of Eduard Shevardnadze, president since 1995. New elections in early 2004 swept Mikheil Saakashvili into power along with his National Movement party. Progress on market reforms and democratization has been made in the years since independence, but this progress has been complicated by Russian assistance and support to the breakaway regions of Abkhazia and South Ossetia. Georgian military action in South Ossetia in early August 2008 led to a Russian military response that not only occupied the breakaway areas, but large portions of Georgia proper as well. Russian troops pulled back from most occupied Georgian territory, but in late August 2008 Russia unilaterally recognized the independence of Abkhazia and South Ossetia. This action was strongly condemned by most of the world's nations and international organizations.

MONETARY SYSTEM:

1 Lari = 100 Thetri to 1995

1 Lari = 1,000,000 'old' Laris, 1995-

ГРYЗИНСКОИ РЕСПYБЛИКИ

GEORGIA, AUTONOMOUS REPUBLIC

Treasury

1919 ОБЯЗАТЕЛЬСТВО КАЗНАЧЕИСТВА Debenture Bonds

#	Denomination	VG	VF	UNC
1	**25 Rubles** 15.1.1919.	5.00	10.00	30.00

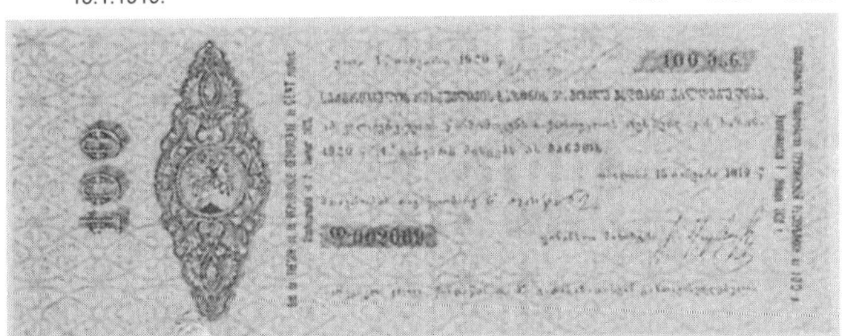

#	Denomination	VG	VF	UNC
2	**100 Rubles** 15.1.1919.	3.00	12.00	37.50
3	**500 Rubles** 15.1.1919.	3.00	15.00	48.00
4	**1000 Rubles** 15.1.1919.	3.00	15.00	45.00
5	**5000 Rubles** 15.1.1919.	5.00	25.00	75.00

1919-1921 State Notes

#	Denomination	VG	VF	UNC
6	**50 Kopeks** ND (1919). Blue on light brown underprint. Back: St. George on horseback.	1.00	3.00	6.00

#	Denomination	VG	VF	UNC
7	**1 Ruble** 1919. Brown on pink underprint. Back: St. George on horseback.	2.00	5.00	10.00
8	**3 Rubles** 1919. Black on green underprint. Back: St. George on horseback.	2.00	5.00	10.00

#	Denomination	VG	VF	UNC
9	**5 Rubles** 1919. Black on orange underprint. Back: St. George on horseback.	2.00	5.00	10.00
10	**10 Rubles** 1919. Brown on red-brown underprint. Back: St. George on horseback.	2.00	5.00	10.00
11	**50 Rubles** 1919. Violet on brown underprint. Back: St. George on horseback.	3.00	6.00	12.00

#	Denomination	VG	VF	UNC
12	**100 Rubles** 1919. Green. Back: St. George on horseback.	3.00	8.00	15.00

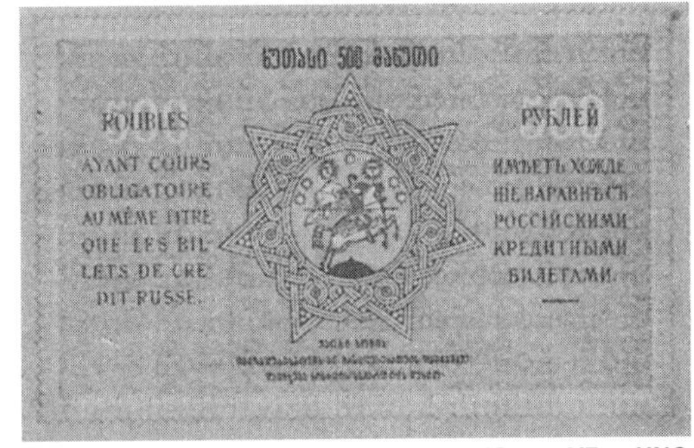

#	Denomination	VG	VF	UNC
13	**500 Rubles** 1919. Black-green on red-brown underprint. Woman seated with shield and lance at center. Back: St. George on horseback.			
	a. Watermark: plaited lines.	3.00	10.00	30.00
	b. Thick or thin paper without watermark.	3.00	8.00	15.00
14	**1000 Rubles** 1920. Brown on blue and tan underprint. Back: St. George on horseback.			
	a. Watermark: Plaited lines.	5.00	20.00	40.00
	b. Without watermark.	3.00	10.00	20.00

		VG	VF	UNC
15	**5000 Rubles** 1921. Lilac to brown. Building with flags at center. Margin circles around corner numerals are ringed once at each side. Back: St. George on horseback.			
	a. Watermark: Monograms.	5.00	15.00	30.00
	b. Without watermark.	3.00	8.00	15.00
	c. Ruled on back.	5.00	20.00	40.00

GERMAN EAST AFRICA

UGANDA
KENYA
BELGIAN CONGO
Indian Ocean
NORTHERN RHODESIA
MOZAMBIQUE

German East Africa (Tanganyika), located on the coast of east-central Africa between British East Africa (now Kenya) and Portuguese East Africa (now Mozambique) had an area of 362,284 sq. mi. (938,216 sq. km.) and a population of about 6 million. Capital: Dar es Salam. Chief products prior to German control were ivory and slaves; after German control, sisal, coffee and rubber. The East African coast first felt the impact of foreign influence in the eighth century, when Arab traders arrived. By the 12th century, traders and immigrants from the Near East and India had built highly developed city/trading states along the coast. By 1506, Portugal claimed control along the entire coast, but made no attempt to establish a colony or to explore the interior. Germany acquired control of the area by treaties in 1884, and established it as a protectorate administered by the German East Africa Company. In 1891, the German government assumed direct administration of the area, which was proclaimed the Colony of German East Africa in 1897. German colonial domination of Tanganyika ended with World War I. Control of most of the territory passed to Great Britain, under a League of Nations mandate. British control was continued after World War II, under a United Nations trusteeship. Thereafter, Tanganyika moved gradually toward self-government. It became autonomous in May 1961. Full independence was achieved on Dec. 9 of the same year.

RULERS:

German, 1884-1918
British, 1918-1961

MONETARY SYSTEM:

1 Rupie = 100 Heller

GERMAN ADMINISTRATION

Deutsch-Ostafrikanische Bank

1905-1912 Issue

		Good	Fine	XF
1	**5 Rupien** 15.6.1905. Blue on brown and multicolor underprint. 2 lions at bottom center. Printer: G&D.	125	300	1,750

		Good	Fine	XF
2	**10 Rupien** 15.6.1905. Black on red underprint. Dar es Salam Harbor at lower center. Printer: G&D. 133x86mm.	125	300	1,750

		Good	Fine	XF
3	**50 Rupien** 15.6.1905. Black on blue underprint. Portrait Kaiser Wilhelm II in cavalry uniform at left. Printer: G&D.			
	a. 2 serial # on face only.	150	500	3,000
	b. 2 serial # each on face and back.	125	450	2,750

Color Abbreviation Guide

New to the *Standard Catalog of® World Paper Money* are the following abbreviations related to color references:

BC: Back color
PC: Paper color

		Good	Fine	XF
4	**100 Rupien** 15.6.1905. Black on green underprint. Portrait Kaiser Wilhelm II in cavalry uniform at center. Printer: G&D.	200	900	3,800

		Good	Fine	XF
5	**500 Rupien** 2.9.1912. Black on purple underprint. Portrait Kaiser Wilhelm II in admiral's uniform at left. Printer: G&D.	2,000	5,000	10,500

1915-1917 Emergency WWI Issues

Many varieties of signatures, serial #, watermarks, eagle types and letters.

		VG	VF	UNC
6	**1 Rupie** 1.9.1915. Letter A. No eagle. PC: Blue-gray.	25.00	100	200
7	**1 Rupie** 1.11.1915. Back: Letter A with text: *Gebucht von* below date at left. PC: Blue-gray.			
	a. With bank handstamp.	85.00	350	550
	b. Without bank handstamp.	15.00	45.00	110

		VG	VF	UNC
8	**1 Rupie** 1.11.1915. Letter B. Without text: *Gebucht von*. PC: Light green.	35.00	135	210

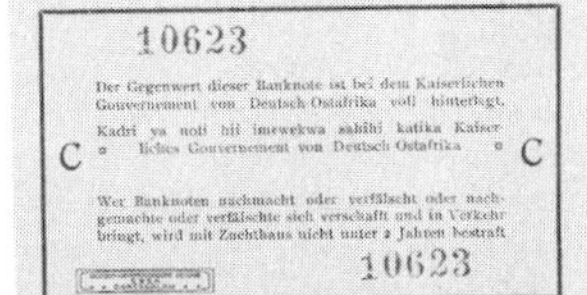

		VG	VF	UNC
9	**1 Rupie** 1.11.1915. With text: *Kraft besonderer Ermächtigung* below date at left. Both signature handwritten.			
	a. Light green paper. Letter B.	15.00	55.00	85.00
	b. Gray-brown paper. Letters B; C.	7.50	30.00	50.00
	c. Gray-brown paper. Letter P.	60.00	275	425
9A	**1 Rupie** 1.11.1915. With text:*Kraft besonderer Ermächtigung* below date at left. Stamped signature at right.			
	a. Gray-brown paper. Letter B, C.	7.50	30.00	50.00
	b. Gray-white paper. Letters P, Q (2 different types), R, S, T, U, V, Y, A2, B2, C2, D2, E2, F2.	5.00	20.00	30.00

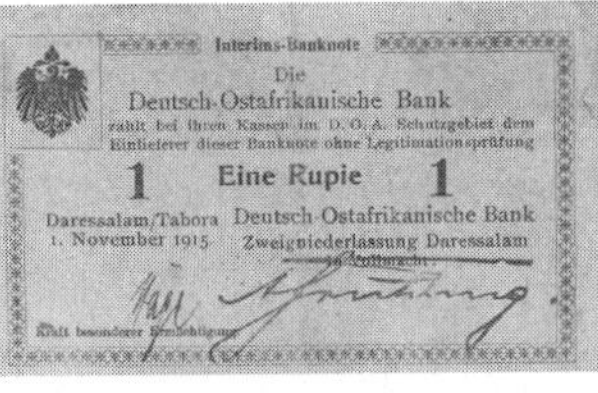

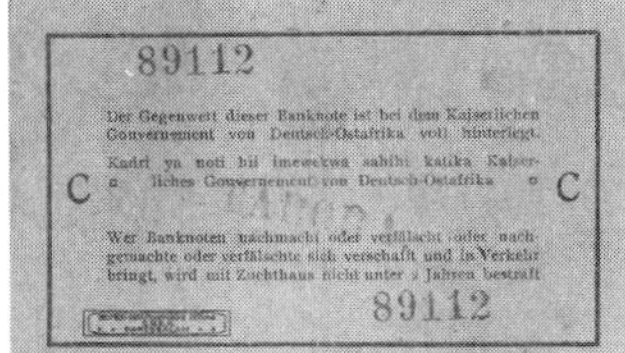

		VG	VF	UNC
10	**1 Rupie** 1.11.1915. With text: *Kraft besonderer Ermächtigung* below signature at left. Stamped signature at right.			
	a. Gray-brown paper. Letter C.	5.00	25.00	40.00
	b. Thick olive-brown paper. Letter D.	5.00	45.00	70.00
	c. Thick gray paper. Letter D.	15.00	55.00	85.00
11	**1 Rupie** 1.11.1915. *Gez.: A Frühling* printed at right.			
	a. Thick gray paper. Letter E.	5.00	20.00	35.00
	b. Thin gray-white paper. Letters E; F; G.	5.00	20.00	40.00

		VG	VF	UNC
12	**1 Rupie** 1.11.1915. *A. Frühling (without gez.)* printed at right.			
	a. Without watermark. Letter H.	5.00	20.00	35.00
	b. With watermark. Letter H.	15.00	45.00	70.00
	c. Watermark: Meander stripe. Letters H; P.	15.00	55.00	85.00
13	**1 Rupie** 1.12.1915. With text: *Gebucht von...* below date at left. Letter H.	5.00	25.00	50.00
14	**1 Rupie** 1.12.1915. Without text: *Gebucht von...* Letters H; J.	10.00	40.00	65.00
15	**1 Rupie** 1.12.1915. With text: *Kraft besonderer Ermächtigung* below date at left, *gez. A. Frühling* printed at right.			
	a. Red-brown paper. Letter J.	5.00	25.00	40.00
	b. Gray-brown paper. Letters J; K (K left & right in same positions).	20.00	80.00	125
	c. As b. Letters K left high, right below.	50.00	215	350
	d. As b. Letters left high and center below.	50.00	215	350

		VG	VF	UNC
16	**1 Rupie** 1.12.1915. With text: *Kraft besonderer Ermächtigung* below date at left. *A. Frühling* (without *gez.*) printed at right.			
	a. Gray-brown paper. Letter K (3 different positions).	30.00	115	180
	b. Dark brown wrapping paper. Letters K; L.	7.50	30.00	50.00
17	**1 Rupie** 1.12.1915. With text: *Kraft besonderer Ermächtigung* below date at left, printed signature at right. Letter left.	17.50	70.00	55.00
18	**1 Rupie** 1.2.1916. Without text: *Gebucht von* at left, eagle on face 20mm high.			
	a. Brown transparent oil paper. Letters L; M; N.	2.50	10.00	25.00
	b. Thick gray-brown paper. Letter N.	65.00	250	400
	c. Norman light-brown paper. Serie N. Rare.	—	—	—
	ax. Error, without signature. Letter L.	65.00	250	400

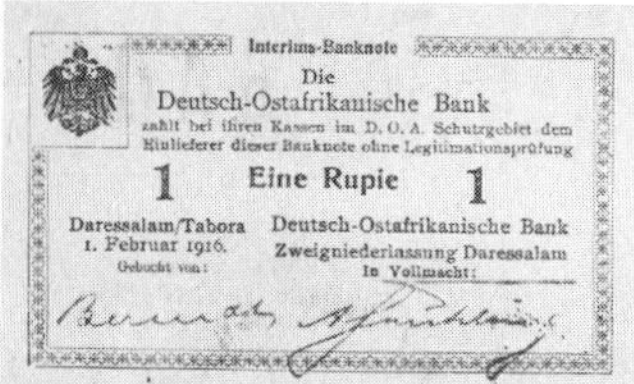

#	Description	VG	VF	UNC
19	**1 Rupie** 1.2.1916. Letters F2; G2; H2; J2; K2; L2; M2; N2; O2; P2; Q2; R2; S2, T2, U2, V2, W2, X2, Y2, Z2, A3, B3, C3, D3, E3, F3, G3. With text: *Gebucht von* at left, eagle on face 15mm high; frame at upper left. has 7 stars and at upper right. 14 stars. Black printing.	4.00	15.00	20.00

#	Description	VG	VF	UNC
20	**1 Rupie** 1.2.1916. With text: *Gebucht von* at left, eagle on face 15mm high; frame at upper left has 6 stars and at upper right 13 stars. Black printing.			
	a. Letters: G3; H3; J3; K3; L3; M3; N3; O3; P3; Q3, (normal paper, 4 different types); R3; S3; T3; U3; V3.	3.50	12.50	20.00
	b. Square lined paper. Letter Q3 (4 different types).	17.00	70.00	125
	x. Error: 3 instead of N3.	4.00	14.00	—
	y. Error without signature (V).	10.00	17.50	—
	z. Error with word on back: *Kaiserl ches* with letter "i" dropped out.	10.00	17.50	—
21	**1 Rupie** 1.2.1916. With text: *Gebucht von* at left, eagle on face 15mm high; frame at upper left. has 7 stars and at upper right. 14 stars. Blue and blue-green printing. Letter A4.	5.00	25.00	40.00

#	Description	VG	VF	UNC
22	**1 Rupie** 1.7.1917. Printed with rubber type (so-called "bush notes"). Eagle stamp on back in different sizes.			
	a. Eagle on back 15mm high. Letters EP.	15.00	45.00	70.00
	b. Eagle on back 23mm high. Letters EP.	10.00	35.00	55.00
	c. Letters ER.	10.00	35.00	55.00
	d. Eagle on back 15mm high. Letters FP.	15.00	70.00	100
	e. Eagle on back 19mm high. Letters FP.	15.00	70.00	100
	f. Letters IP.	15.00	70.00	140
	ax. Error with back inverted.	15.00	70.00	100
	bx. Error with back inverted.	15.00	70.00	100
	by. Error: *Daressalan* on face.	10.00	35.00	55.00
	cx. Error with back inverted.	12.50	25.00	—
	cy. Error with letters EP on face, ER on back. Rare.	—	—	—
	dx. Error with back inverted.	15.00	70.00	100
	ex. Error with back inverted. Error with letters Ep on face, ER on back. Rare.	15.00	70.00	100
23	**1 Rupie** ND. #15b (J) and #18a (N) on back with large violet stamp: *W* over original letter.	10.00	40.00	85.00
24	**1 Rupie** ND. #10f (Q, V, Y) on back with violet stamp: *X* over original letter, 1 serial # crossed out and 2 new serial # added.	7.50	15.00	30.00
24A	**1 Rupie** ND. Violet. Handstamp: *Z* on back over original letter, 1 serial # crossed out and 2 new serial # added. The following notes are known with stamp: 10 (P, Q, R, S, T, U, V); 18 (N); 19 (N2, O2, P2, Q2, R2, A	10.00	20.00	45.00
25	**1 Rupie** ND. Stamp: *X* as on #24 but 2 serial # crossed out and 2 new serial # added. The following notes are known: 7b (A); 8 (B); 10f (T, V, Y, A2, B2, C2, D2); 11a (E); 18a (M); 19 (X2, B3, C3).	7.50	17.50	30.00
25A	**1 Rupie** ND. Violet. Handstamp: *Z* 2 serial #'s crossed out and 2 serial # added. The following notes are known with stamp: 10 (P, Q, R, T, U,V); 18 (L, M, N); 19 (F2, N2, O2, P2, R2, S2, T2, X2, Z2, A3).	7.50	17.50	30.00

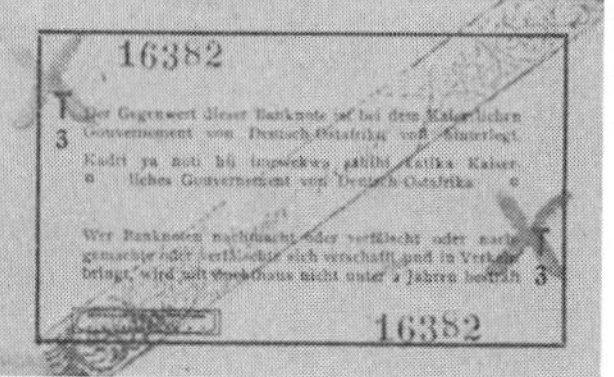

#	Description	VG	VF	UNC
26	**1 Rupie** ND. Stamp: *X* as on #24 but without change of serial #. The following notes are known: 8 (B); 10d (P, Q, R, T, U, Y, B2, C2, E2, F2); 11b (F, G); 12a (H); 14 (J); 15a (J); 16b (K, L); 17 (L); 18a (M	15.00	30.00	60.00
26A	**1 Rupie** ND. Violet. Handstamp *Z* over original letter without change of serial #. The following notes are known with stamp: 10 (C, S, U); 11 (E, F, G); 12 (H); 14 (H); 15 (J); 16 (K); 17 (L); 18 (M, N); 19 (J2, M	7.50	17.50	30.00

#26B and 26C deleted, see #24A and 25A.

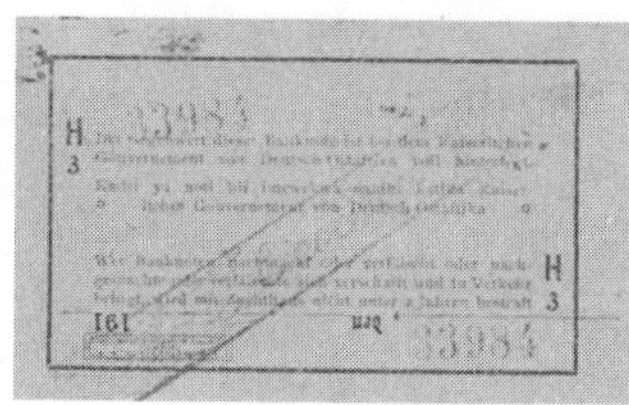

#	Description	VG	VF	UNC
27	**1 Rupie** ND.Date (from stationery used as printing paper). 5 different dateline types exist.			
	a. Dateline on back of the following notes: 19 (F3, G3); 20 (H3, J3, K3, L3, M3, N3, O3, P3, Q3, R3, S3, T3, U3, V3).	30.00	75.00	200
	b. Dateline on back of the following notes: 22a (EP); 22b (EP); 22c (ER); 22e (FP); 22f (IP); 26 (M3, V3).	30.00	75.00	200
	c. Dateline on front of the following notes: 22b (EP); 22c (ER).	30.00	75.00	200

#	Description	VG	VF	UNC
28	**1 Rupie** ND. 14 different types of letterheads exist on the following notes: 22a (EP); 22b (EP); 22c (ER); 22d (FP); 22e (FP); 22f (IP). Back: Letterhead (from stationery used as printing paper), so-called "letterhead notes".	50.00	120	250
29	**5 Rupien** 15.8.1915. Value in letters only, both signature handwritten without series letter.	30.00	110	175
30	**5 Rupien** 15.8.1915. Value in letters only. Handwritten signature at right. Facsimile stamped. Without series letter.	30.00	110	175

#	Description	VG	VF	UNC
31	**5 Rupien** 15.8.1915. Value in letters and #, both signature handwritten. Series letters B (2 varieties); C.	35.00	135	225
32	**5 Rupien** 15.8.1915. Value in letters and #. Signature at right. Facsimile stamped. Letter C.	25.00	90.00	175
33	**5 Rupien** 1.11.1915. *Daressalam/Tabora* in 2 lines. Letter D.	30.00	110	175

		VG	VF	UNC
34	**5 Rupien** 1.11.1915. *Daressalam/Tabora* in 1 line. Text: *Kraft besonderer Ermächtigung* at lower left. Signature at left, handwritten.			
	a. Gray-green cardboard with blue fibres. Letters D; E.	15.00	55.00	100
	b. Gray-green cardboard with blue fibres (darker than #34a) and impressed jute texture. Letters D; E.	15.00	65.00	110
	c. Gray-green cardboard without blue fibres. Letter E.	15.00	65.00	110
	d. Dark green cardboard without impressed jute texture. Letters E; F.	35.00	125	250

		VG	VF	UNC
35	**5 Rupien** 1.11.1915. *Daressalam/Tabora* in 1 line. Text: *Kraft besonderer Ermächtigung* at lower left. Both signatures facsimile stamped. Letters E; F.	100	300	500

		VG	VF	UNC
36	**5 Rupien** 1.2.1916. *Gebucht von* below date at left.			
	a. Stiff gray-blue cardboard. Letter F.	25.00	90.00	140
	b. Soft dark blue cardboard. Letters F; G.	15.00	60.00	100
	c. Stiff dark gray cardboard. Letter F.	25.00	100	170
	d. Green cardboard. Letters G; F.	25.00	90.00	140
	e. Green paper. Letters G; H.	25.00	90.00	140
	f. Letter X/F, new serial #. dark blue. Rare.	—	—	—

		VG	VF	UNC
37	**5 Rupien** 1.7.1917. Printed with rubber type (so-called *bush notes*).			
	a. Value *5* 3.5mm high.	35.00	150	200
	b. Value *5* 5mm high.	25.00	100	170

#38-49 serial # and signature varieties.

		VG	VF	UNC
38	**10 Rupien** 1.10.1915. Dark brown cardboard.			
	a. Without serial letter.	15.00	45.00	75.00
	b. Handwritten B.	85.00	350	550

		VG	VF	UNC
39	**10 Rupien** 1.10.1915. Dark brown cardboard. Back: Violet stamp: *Z*	10.00	45.00	70.00

		VG	VF	UNC
40	**10 Rupien** 1.2.1916. Dark brown cardboard. Back: Without letter or with B. *DOAB* in ornamental letters on top right and bottom left.	25.00	100	200

		VG	VF	UNC
41	**10 Rupien** 1.6.1916. Letter B. PC: Yellow-brown.	10.00	35.00	70.00

		VG	VF	UNC
42	**10 Rupien** 1.6.1916. Back: Violet stamp: *X* over B. PC: Yellow-brown.	50.00	100	200

		VG	VF	UNC
43	**10 Rupien** 1.7.1917. Printed with rubber type (so-called *bush notes*).			
	a. Value 3mm high and 4mm wide.	35.00	135	250
	b. Value 5mm high and 4-5mm wide.	50.00	180	275
	c. Value 5mm high and 7mm wide.	65.00	225	350

		VG	VF	UNC
44	**20 Rupien** 15.3.1915. White cardboard.			
	a. Both signature handwritten. Serial # on face handwritten.	—	—	—
	b. British forgery on thick cardboard. Serial # on face and back do not match. Rare.	—	—	—

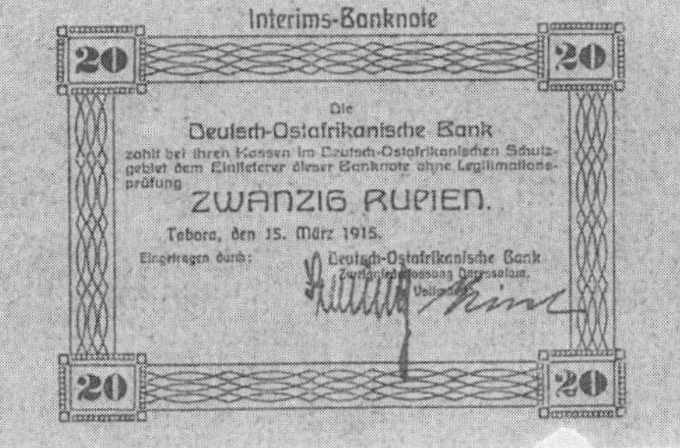

		VG	VF	UNC
45	**20 Rupien** 15.3.1915. Lilac cardboard. Both signature handwritten. Back: Serial #.			
	a. Both signature handwritten.	50.00	100	200
	b. Left signature handwritten, right signature facsimile stamped.	50.00	100	200

		VG	VF	UNC
46	**50 Rupien**			
	1.10.1915.			
	a. Soft gray cardboard.	65.00	135	175
	b. Stiff brown cardboard.	350	600	800

		VG	VF	UNC
47	**50 Rupien**			
	1.10.1917. Printed with rubber type (so-called *bush notes*).			
	a. With signature, back printed.	2,500	5,400	—
	b. Without signature Back not printed. (Not issued).	2,500	5,400	—
48	**200 Rupien**	VG	VF	UNC
	15.4.1915. Watermark: None.	1,250	2,500	5,250

		VG	VF	UNC
49	**200 Rupien**			
	15.6.1915. Watermark: Wavy lines.	1,000	2,000	3,250

German New Guinea (also known as Neu Guinea or Kaiser Wilhelmsland, now part of Papua New Guinea) included the northeast corner of the island of New Guinea, the islands of the Bismarck Archipelago, Bougainville and Buka Islands, and about 600 small offshore islands. Bounded on the west coast by West Irian, to the north and east by the Pacific Ocean and to the south by Papua, it had an area of 92,159 sq. mi. (238,692 sq. km.) and, under German administration, had a population of about 250,000. Capital: Herbertshohe, later moved to Rabaul. Copra was the chief export. Germany took formal possession of German New Guinea in 1884. It was administered by the German New Guinea Company until 1899, when control was assumed by the German imperial government. On the outbreak of World War I in 1914, Australia occupied the territory and it remained under military control until 1921, when it became an Australian mandate of the League of Nations. During World War II, between 1942 and 1945, the territory was occupied by Japan. Following the Japanese surrender, it was administered by Australia under the United Nations trusteeship system. In 1949, Papua and New Guinea were combined as one administrative unit known as Papua New Guinea, which attained internal autonomy on Dec. 1, 1973. Papua New Guinea achieved full independence on Sept. 16, 1975. German Reichsbanknoten and Reichskassenscheine circulated until 1914.

RULERS:

German, 1884-1914
Australian, 1914-1942, 1945-1975
Japanese, 1942-1945

MONETARY SYSTEM:

1 Mark = 100 Pfennig

AUSTRALIAN OCCUPATION - WWI

Treasury Notes

1914-1915 Issue

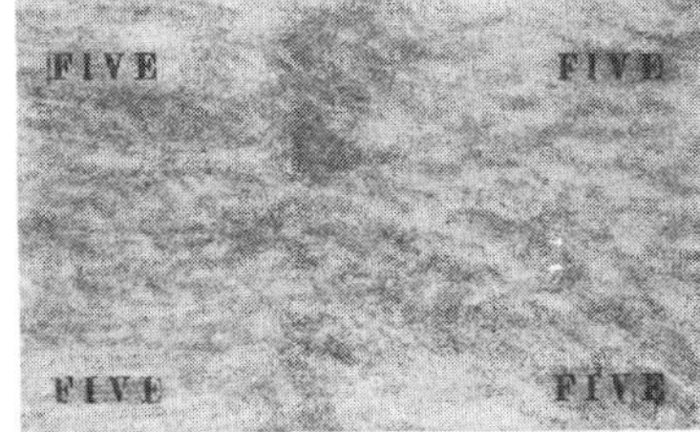

		VG	VF	UNC
1	**5 Marks**			
	1914-1915. Without pictorial design, with text: *Payable in coin at the Treasury, Rabaul.* 123x82mm.			
	a. 14.10.1914. Rare.	—	—	—
	b. Pen *cancelled* 1.1.1915. Rare.	—	—	—

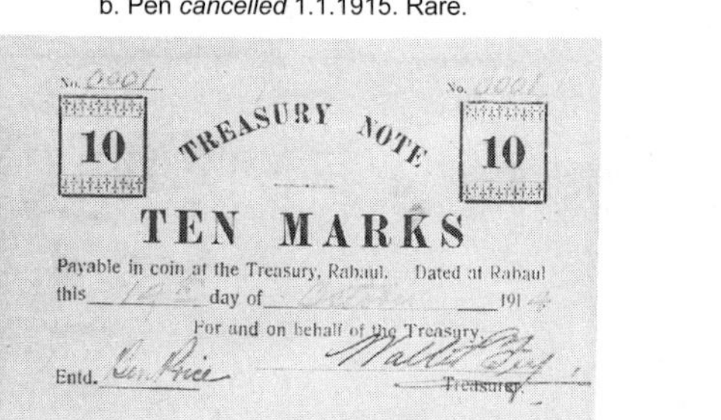

		Good	Fine	XF
2	**10 Marks** 1914-1915. Without pictorial design, with text: *Payable in coin at the Treasury, Rabaul.* 140x90mm.			
	a. 14.10.1914. Rare.	5,000	8,000	—
	b. Pen *cancelled* 1.1.1915. Rare.	—	—	—

		VG	VF	UNC
3	**20 Marks** 1914. Without pictorial design, with text: *Payable in coin at the Treasury, Rabaul.* 147x98mm.			
	a. 1914. Rare.	—	—	—
	b. Pen *cancelled* 1.1.1915. Rare.	—	—	—

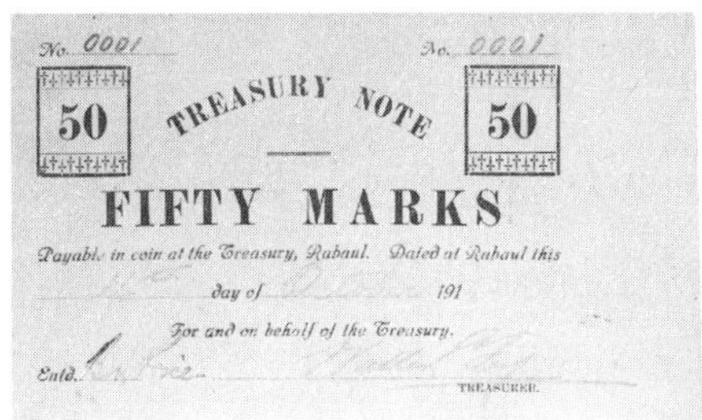

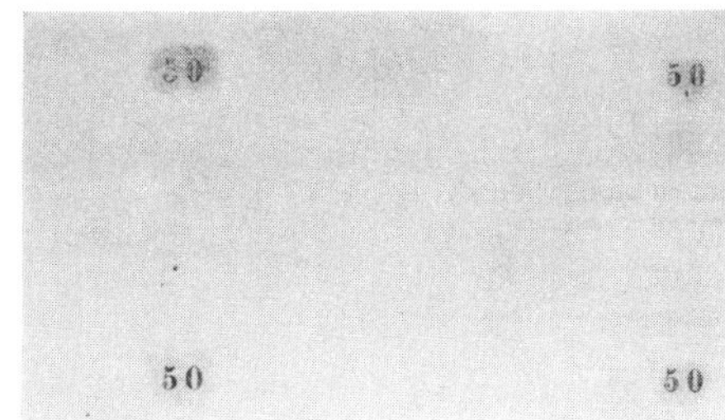

		VG	VF	UNC
4	**50 Marks** 1914. Without pictorial design, with text: *Payable in coin at the Treasury, Rabaul.* 161x85mm.			
	a. 16.10.1914	3,500	7,500	—
	b. Pen *cancelled* 1.1.1915. Rare.	—	—	—

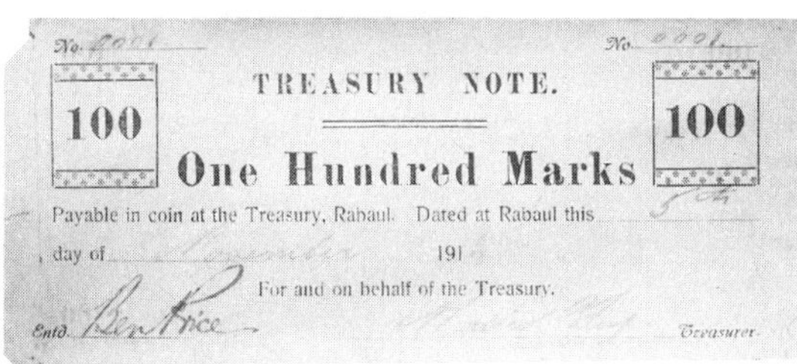

		VG	VF	UNC
5	**100 Marks** 5.11.1914. Without pictorial design, with text: *Payable in coin at the Treasury, Rabaul.* 200x85mm.	—	—	—

Note: A primitive 20 Mark note printed with boot polish is also reputed to have existed which was used for paying the wages of the German Voluntary Brigade.

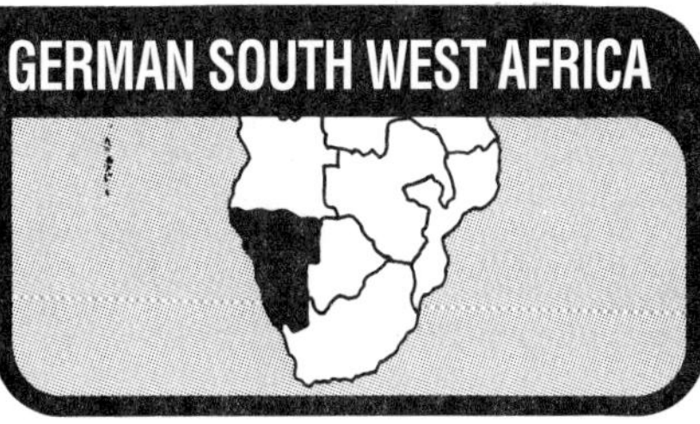

German South West Africa (Deutsch-Sudwestafrika) is a former German territory situated on the Atlantic coast of southern Africa. The colony had an area of 318,261 sq. mi. (824,293 sq. km.). Capital: Windhoek. The first Europeans to land on the shores of the area were 15th-century Portuguese navigators. The interior, however, was not explored until the middle of the 18th century. Great Britain annexed the Walvis Bay area in 1878; it was incorporated into the Cape of Good Hope in 1884. The rest of the coastal area was annexed by Germany in 1885. South African forces occupied German South West Africa during World War I. South Africa received it as a League of Nations mandate on Dec. 17, 1920. South Africa's mandate was terminated by the United Nations on Oct. 27, 1966. In June 1968 the UN General Assembly voted to rename the country Namibia. South Africa found both actions unacceptable. After many years of dispute, independence of Namibia was finally achieved on March 21, 1990. German Reichsbanknoten and Reichskassenscheine circulated until 1914.

RULERS:

German to 1914

MONETARY SYSTEM:

1 Mark = 100 Pfennig

GERMAN ADMINISTRATION

Kassenschein

1914 Issue

#1-5 are so-called *Seitz notes,* named after the Imperial Governor whose signature is printed on some of the notes.

		Good	Fine	XF
1	**5 Mark** 8.8.1914. Green.			
	a. Issued note.	750	1,500	6,000
	b. Cancelled.	750	1,500	6,000

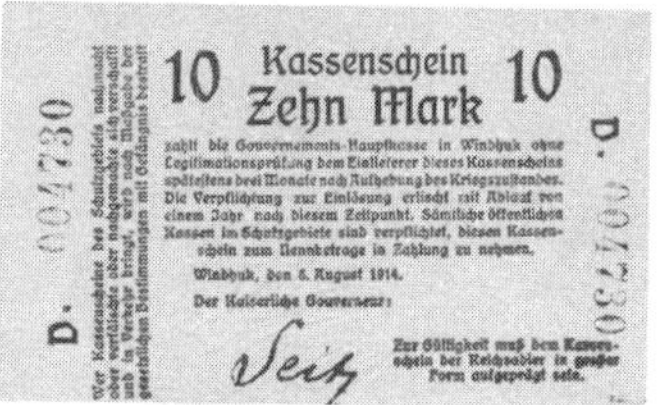

		Good	Fine	XF
2	**10 Mark** 8.8.1914. Red-brown.			
	a. Issued note.	750	1,500	6,000
	b. Cancelled.	750	1,500	6,000
3	**20 Mark** 8.8.1914. Brown-violet.			
	a. Issued note.	750	1,500	6,000
	b. Cancelled.	750	1,500	6,000

		Good	Fine	XF
4	**50 Mark** 8.8.1914. Red.			
	a. Issued note.	750	1,500	6,000
	b. Cancelled.	750	1,500	6,000

		Good	Fine	XF
5	**100 Mark** 8.8.1914. Blue.			
	a. Issued note.	1,000	3,000	9,000
	b. Cancelled.	1,000	2,500	6,000

Swakopmunder Buchhandlung

These notes were issued by order of the Windhoek Chamber of Commerce and used for payment by the authorities and public institutions (police, post office, railroad, etc.). They circulated all over the colony.

1915-1918 ND Issue

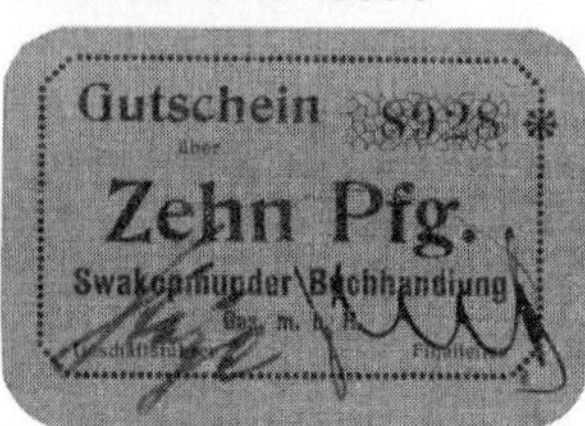

		Good	Fine	XF
6	**10 Pfennig** ND (1916-1918). Green linen. Value: *Zehn Pfg.*; without *NUMMER* at upper right.			
	a. 1 signature	75.00	175	325
	b. 2 signature	50.00	150	250

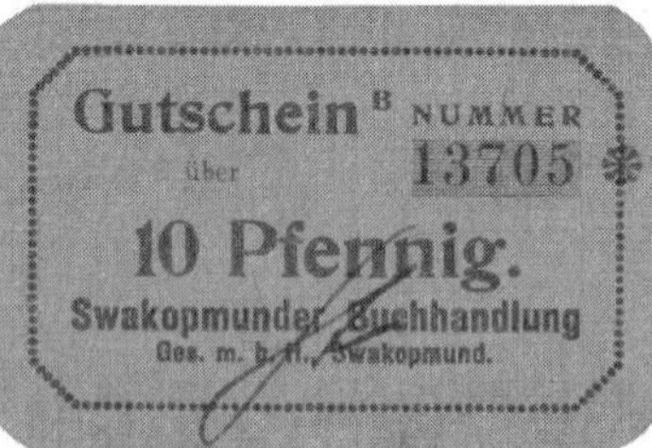

		Good	Fine	XF
7	**10 Pfennig** ND (1916-1918). Green linen. Value: *10 Pfennig; NUMMER* at upper right. With or without letter *B*.	75.00	150	250

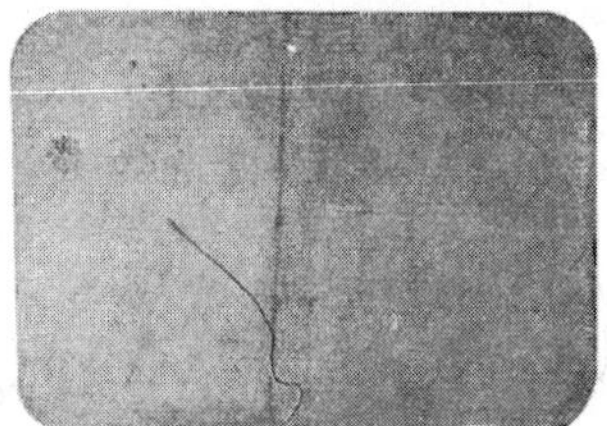

		Good	Fine	XF
8	**25 Pfennig** ND (1916-1918). Red-brown text, green value (diagonal). Without *NUMMER* at upper right. PC: Pale blue or white (fabric between paper layers).			
	a. Rounded corners. 2 handwritten signature.	100	200	350
	b. Square corners. 1 facsimile signature.	125	225	425
9	**25 Pfennig** ND (1916-1918). Red-brown text, black value on green underprint. *NUMMER* at upper right. PC: Pale blue (cloth fabric between paper layers).	125	225	425

		Good	Fine	XF
10	**50 Pfennig** ND (1916-1918). Blue on light blue linen. Value: *Funfzig Pfg;* without *NUMMER* at upper right.			
	a. Rounded corners. 2 handwritten signature.	100	200	350
	b. Square corners. 1 facsimile signature.	125	225	425

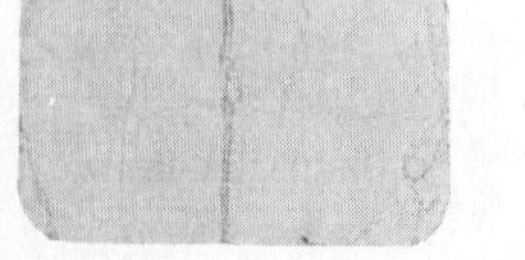

		Good	Fine	XF
11	**50 Pfennig** ND (1916-1918). Blue-green on white linen. Value: *0,50 Mark; NUMMER* at upper right. (2 varieties of *M* in *Mark*; with or without period after *Mark*).	75.00	150	325

		Good	Fine	XF
12	**1 Mark** ND (1916-1918). Yellowish cardboard. Black text on green underprint.Without *NUMMER* at upper right. 2 signature varieties.	100	200	350
13	**1 Mark** ND (1916-1918). Light green cardboard. Black and red-brown on dark green underprint. *NUMMER* at upper left.	100	200	350

		Good	Fine	XF
14	**1 Mark** ND (1916-1918). Rose linen. Red-brown underprint extending over entire note. *Ausgabe B* at upper right.	75.00	180	325

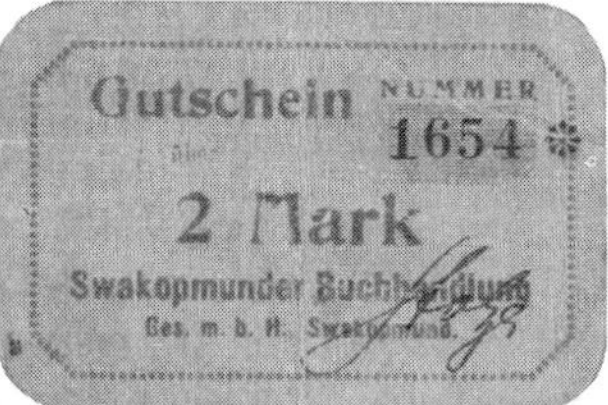

		Good	Fine	XF
15	**2 Mark** ND (1916-1918). Black and salmon text. Value: *Zwei;* without *NUMMER* at right 1 or 2 signatures.			
	a. Rose colored cardboard with impressed linen texture.	35.00	90.00	225
	b. Yellowish cardboard with impressed linen texture.	35.00	90.00	225

		Good	Fine	XF
16	**2 Mark** ND (1916-1918). Brown. Value: *2; NUMMER* at upper right. (2 varieties of *M* in *Mark*).			
	a. Light gray cardboard with impressed linen texture.	20.00	65.00	190
	b. Light brown cardboard with impressed linen texture.	30.00	90.00	225

		Good	Fine	XF
17	**3 Mark** ND (1916-1918). Green underprint. Light green cardboard with linen texture. Without *NUMMER* at upper right.	32.50	100	275
18	**3 Mark** ND (1916-1918). Brown underprint. Light brown cardboard. *NUMMER* at upper right. (2 varieties of *M* in *Mark*).	37.50	110	300

Germany, a nation of north-central Europe which from 1871 to 1945 was, successively, an empire, a republic and a totalitarian state, attained its territorial peak as an empire when it comprised a 208,780 sq. mi. (540,740 sq. km.) homeland and an overseas colonial empire. As the power of the Roman Empire waned, several warlike tribes residing in northern Germany moved south and west, invading France, Belgium, England, Italy and Spain. In 800 AD the Frankish King Charlemagne, who ruled most of present-day France and Germany, was crowned Emperor of the Holy Roman Empire. Under his successors, this empire was divided into France in the West and Germany (including the Emperor's title) in the East. Over the centuries the German part developed into a loose federation of an estimated 1,800 German States that lasted until 1806. Modern Germany was formed from the eastern part of Charlemagne's empire. In 1815, the German States were reduced to a federation of 32, of which Prussia was the strongest. In 1871, Prussian Chancellor Otto Von Bismarck united the German States into an empire ruled by Wilhelm I, the Prussian king. The empire initiated a colonial endeavor and became one of the world's greatest powers. Germany disintegrated as a result of World War I, and was reestablished as the Weimar Republic. The humiliation of defeat, economic depression, poverty and discontent gave rise to Adolf Hitler in 1933, who reconstituted Germany as the Third Reich and after initial diplomatic and military triumphs, led it to disaster in World War II. During the postwar era, the western provinces were occupied by the Allied forces while the eastern provinces were occupied and administered by the Soviet Union. East Germany and West Germany were established in 1949. The post-WWII division of Germany ended on Oct. 3, 1990, when the German Democratic Republic (East Germany) ceased to exist and its five constituent provinces were formally admitted to the Federal Republic of Germany. An election held on Dec. 2, 1990 chose representatives to the united federal parliament (Bundestag), which then conducted its opening session in Berlin in the old Reichstag building. The Capital remained in Bonn until 1999. For subsequent history, see German Federal Republic and German Democratic Republic.

RULERS:

Wilhelm I, 1871-1888
Friedrich III, 1888
Wilhelm II, 1888-1918

MONETARY SYSTEM:

1 Mark = 100 Pfennig
1 Mark = 100 Pfennig to 1923
1000 Milliarden Mark = 1 Billion Mark = 1 Rentenmark = 100 Rentenpfennig, 1923-1924
1 Rentenmark = 1 Reichsmark = 100 Reichspfennig, 1924-1948
1 AMC Mark = 100 AMC Pfennig, 1945-1948
1 Million = 1,000,000
10 Millionen = 10,000,000
1 Milliarde = 1,000,000,000 (English 1 Billion)
10 Milliarden = 10,000,000,000
1 Billion = 1,000,000,000,000 (English 1 Trillion)
10 Billionen = 10,000,000,000,000

REPLACEMENT NOTES:

#191-198,-prefix, 8-digit serial number, and small F printer's mark in scrollwork. (These are partially listed as #191b, 192c, 193c, 194c, 195c, 196c and 197c.)

NOTE: The below watermarks are from "Papiergeld-Spezialkatalog Deutschland, 1874-1980" by Pick/Rixen (published by Battenberg Verlag, Munich).

WATERMARK VARIETIES

A. Wavy lines diagonally-congruent	B. Pattern of triangles with concave sides within circles	C. 6-pointed stars within rounded triangle pattern	D. Small crucifera blossoms	E. G, D within 6-pointed stars and Z's
F. Greek pattern	G. Lattice	H. Knotted rope and EKAHA	I. Thorns	J. Horizontally opposed wavy lines
K. Diamonds in maze	L. Small circles	M. S in 6-pointed stars within clouds	N. Diamond pattern	O. Tuning fork H's pattern

WATERMARK VARIETIES

	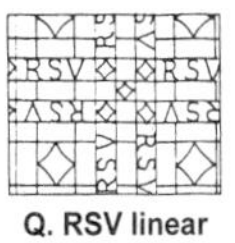	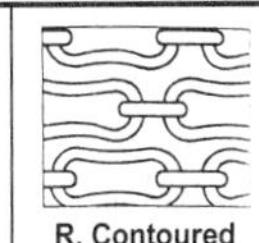	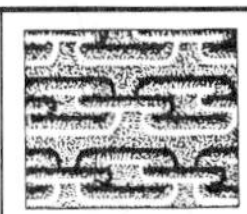
P. HUDS in circular pattern	Q. RSV linear pattern	R. Contoured chain pattern	S. Straight chain pattern

EMPIRE

Reichskassenscheine

Imperial Treasury Notes

1874 Issue

#	Denomination	Good	Fine	XF
1	**5 Mark** 11.7.1874. Dark blue and gray-blue. 2 children seated at lower center with arms between them. 125x80mm.	2,250	3,275	—

#	Denomination	Good	Fine	XF
2	**20 Mark** 11.7.1874. Green and yellow. Allegorical man wearing shirt with arms and holding a staff with arms at left center. 140x90mm. Rare.	15,500	—	—
3	**50 Mark** 11.7.1874. Dark violet, brown and dark green. 2 allegorical figures at center, arms at each corner. 150x100mm. Rare.	—	—	—

1882 Issue

#	Denomination	Good	Fine	XF
4	**5 Mark** 10.1.1882. Dark blue. Knight in armor with shield of arms at right. 125x80mm.	250	400	2,000

		Good	Fine	XF
5	**20 Mark** 10.1.1882. Green. 2 small boys with fruit at left and right. 140x90mm.	1,250	2,500	6,500
6	**50 Mark** 10.1.1882. Dark brown. Allegorical winged figure at right.	3,500	7,500	—

1899 Issue

		Good	Fine	XF
7	**50 Mark** 5.1.1899. Dark green and brown-olive. Germania seated at left. 150x100mm.	5,000	10,000	—

1904-1906 Issue

		Good	Fine	XF
8	**5 Mark** 31.10.1904. Blue and blue-green. Germania with child and dove at left. Back: Dragon.			
	a. 6 digit serial #.	5.00	10.00	25.00
	b. 7 digit serial #.	5.00	10.00	25.00

		Good	Fine	XF
9	**10 Mark** 6.10.1906. Dark green and olive-green. Woman standing holding palm branch at right. 140x90mm.			
	a. 6 digit serial #.	35.00	60.00	225
	b. 7 digit serial #.	10.00	20.00	100

Reichsbanknote

Imperial Bank Notes

1876 Issue

		Good	Fine	XF
10	**100 Mark** 1.1.1876. Dark blue and gray-blue. Arms at left, Minerva in wreath at right. 160x103mm. Rare.	15,000	—	—
10A	**500 Mark** 1.1.1876. Black. Crowned eagle at center, heads at ends facing inwards. 173x110mm. Proof. Rare.	—	—	—

		Good	Fine	XF
11	**1000 Mark** 1.1.1876. Brown. Arms at left. Back: Woman with small angels on back. 187x100mm. Specimen. (Not issued). Rare.	—	—	—

1883-1884 Issue

		Good	Fine	XF
12	**100 Mark** 3.9.1883. Dark blue on light blue underprint. 1 red seal. Back: Medallic woman's head supported by two women. 160x105mm.	750	1,500	—

		Good	Fine	XF
13	**1000 Mark** 2.1.1884. Brown. 1 red seal. Back: Allegorical figures of Navigation and Agriculture. 187x110mm.	2,500	5,000	—

1891 First Issue

		Good	Fine	XF
14	**1000 Mark** 1.1.1891. Brown. 1 red seal. Back: Allegorical figures of Navigation and Agriculture. 187x110mm.	—	—	—

1891 Second Issue

		Good	Fine	XF
15	**100 Mark** 1.5.1891. Blue. 1 red seal. Back: Medallic woman's head supported by two women. 160x105mm.	750	1,400	3,000

1895 Issue

		Good	Fine	XF
16	**100 Mark** 1.3.1895. Blue. Two red seals. Back: Medallic woman's head supported by two women. 160x105mm.			
	a. Issued note. 2 red seals.	750	1,750	—
	s. Specimen. 1 red seal.	—	—	—
17	**1000 Mark** 1.3.1895. Brown. 2 red seals. Back: Allegorical figures of Navigation and Agriculture. 187x110mm. Rare.	—	—	—

1896 Issue

		Good	Fine	XF
18	**100 Mark** 10.4.1896. Blue. 2 red seals. Back: Medallic woman's head supported by two women. 160x105mm.	400	1,000	2,000

		Good	Fine	XF
19	**1000 Mark** 10.4.1896. Brown. 2 red seals. Back: Allegorical figures of Navigation and Agriculture. 187x110mm.	1,500	3,500	—

1898 Issue

		Good	Fine	XF
20	**100 Mark** 1.7.1898. 2 seals. Back: Medallic woman's head supported by two women. 160x105mm.			
	a. Issued note.	75.00	400	1,500
	b. With overprint: *Im usland ungiltig, nur zahlbar bei der Staatsbank Munchen.*	—	—	—
21	**1000 Mark** 1.7.1898. Brown. 2 red seals. Back: Allegorical figures of Navigation and Agriculture. 187x110mm.	50.00	150	1,300

1903 Issue

		VG	VF	UNC
22	**100 Mark** 17.4.1903. Blue. 2 seals. Back: Medallic woman's head supported by two women. 160x105mm.	200	500	2,000
23	**1000 Mark** 10.10.1903. Brown. 2 red seals. Back: Allegorical figures of Navigation and Agriculture. 187x110mm.	100	400	1,400

1905 Issue

		VG	VF	UNC
24	**100 Mark** 18.12.1905. Blue. 2 seals. Back: Medallic woman's head supported by two women. 160x105mm.			
	a. 24mm serial #.	15.00	100	850
	b. 29mm serial #.	15.00	100	850

1906 Issue

		VG	VF	UNC
25	**20 Mark** 10.3.1906. Blue. Eagle at upper right. 136x90mm.			
	a. 6 digit serial #.	50.00	200	450
	b. 7 digit serial #.	50.00	200	450

		VG	VF	UNC
26	**50 Mark** 10.3.1906. Green on pink underprint. Germania at upper left and right. 150x100mm.			
	a. 6 digit serial #.	30.00	150	650
	b. 7 digit serial #.	30.00	150	650
27	**1000 Mark** 26.7.1906. Brown. 2 red seals. Back: Allegorical figures of Navigation and Agriculture. 187x110mm.	150	400	1,400

1907 Issue

		VG	VF	UNC
28	**20 Mark** 8.6.1907. Blue. Eagle at upper right. 136x90mm.	20.00	80.00	250
29	**50 Mark** 8.6.1907. Green. Germania at upper left and right. 7 digit serial #. 150x100mm.	300	1,000	2,250
30	**100 Mark** 8.6.1907. Blue. Back: Medallic woman's head supported by two women. 160x105mm.	150	400	1,500

1908 Issue

No.	Description	VG	VF	UNC
31	**20 Mark** 7.2.1908. Blue. Eagle at upper right. 7 digit serial #. 136x90mm.	25.00	100	250
32	**50 Mark** 7.2.1908. Green. Germania at upper left and right. 7 digit serial #. 150x100mm.	30.00	150	350

No.	Description	VG	VF	UNC
33	**100 Mark** 7.2.1908. Dark blue on light blue underprint. Red serial # and seal. Back: Medallic woman's head supported by two women. 160x105mm.			
	a. Serial # 29mm long.	2.50	10.00	20.00
	b. Serial # 24mm long.	60.00	200	550
34	**100 Mark** 7.2.1908. Dark blue on light blue underprint. Green serial # and seal (reissue 1918-22). Back: Medallic woman's head supported by two women. 160x105mm.	5.00	10.00	20.00
35	**100 Mark** 7.2.1908. Blue. Mercury at left, Ceres at right. Back: Germania seated with shield and sword on back. Watermark: Wilhelm I and *100.* 207 x 102mm. 160x105mm.	30.00	150	350
36	**1000 Mark** 7.2.1908. Brown. 2 red seals. Back: Allegorical figures of Navigation and Agriculture. 207x102mm.	25.00	150	1,000

1909 Issue

No.	Description	VG	VF	UNC
37	**20 Mark** 10.9.1909. Blue. Eagle at upper right. 7 digit serial #. 136x90mm.	30.00	150	400

No.	Description	VG	VF	UNC
38	**100 Mark** 10.9.1909. Blue. Mercury at left, Ceres at right. Back: Germania seated with shield and sword. 207x102mm.	35.00	150	400
39	**1000 Mark** 10.9.1909. Brown. 2 red seals. Back: Allegorical figures of Navigation and Agriculture. 187x110mm.	75.00	500	1,100

Color Abbreviation Guide

New to the *Standard Catalog of ® World Paper Money* are the following abbreviations related to color references:

BC: Back color
PC: Paper color

1910 Issue

No.	Description	VG	VF	UNC
40	**20 Mark** 21.4.1910. Blue. Eagle at upper right. 136x90mm.			
	a. Without watermark. 6 digit serial #.	20.00	50.00	350
	b. Without watermark. 7 digit serial #.	15.00	30.00	80.00
	c. Watermark: *20 Mark.*	60.00	150	1,750

No.	Description	VG	VF	UNC
41	**50 Mark** 21.4.1910. Green. Germania at upper left and right. 7 digit serial #. 150x100mm.	15.00	25.00	75.00

No.	Description	VG	VF	UNC
42	**100 Mark** 21.4.1910. Dark blue on light blue-gray underprint. Mercury at left, Ceres at right. Red serial # and seal. Back: Germania seated with shield and sword. 207x102mm.	7.00	15.00	50.00

		VG	VF	UNC
43	**100 Mark**	VG	VF	UNC
	21.4.1910. Dark blue on light blue underprint. Mercury at left, Ceres at right. Green serial # and seal. (Reprinted 1918-22). Back: Germania seated with shield and sword. 207x102mm.	10.00	20.00	60.00
44	**1000 Mark**	VG	VF	UNC
	21.4.1910. Brown. Red serial # and seal. Back: Allegorical figures of Navigation and Agriculture. 187x110mm.			
	a. 6 digit serial # (until 1916).	10.00	20.00	40.00
	b. 7 digit serial #.	5.00	10.00	20.00

		VG	VF	UNC
45	**1000 Mark**	VG	VF	UNC
	21.4.1910. Dark brown on tan underprint. Green serial # and seal. (Reprinted 1918-1922). Back: Allegorical figures of Navigation and Agriculture. 187x110mm.			
	a. 6 digit serial #.	10.00	30.00	50.00
	b. 7 digit serial #.	2.00	4.00	8.00

1914 Issue

		VG	VF	UNC
46	**20 Mark**	VG	VF	UNC
	19.2.1914. Blue. Eagle at upper right. 136x90mm.			
	a. 6 digit serial #.	20.00	80.00	200
	b. 7 digit serial #.	8.00	15.00	30.00

Darlehenskassenschein

State Loan Currency Note

1914 First Issue

		VG	VF	UNC
47	**5 Mark**	VG	VF	UNC
	5.8.1914. Black on gray-violet underprint. Back: Germania at left and right. 125x80mm.			
	a. 6 digit serial #.	30.00	100	300
	b. 7 digit serial #.	15.00	40.00	100
	c. 8 digit serial #.	15.00	40.00	100

		VG	VF	UNC
48	**20 Mark**	VG	VF	UNC
	5.8.1914. Dark brown on brown and lilac underprint. Back: Minerva at left, Mercury at right. 140x90mm.			
	a. 6 digit serial #.	30.00	100	250
	b. 7 digit serial #.	30.00	100	220

		VG	VF	UNC
49	**50 Mark**	VG	VF	UNC
	5.8.1914. Black and lilac-red on gray underprint. Back: Germania at left and right. 150x100mm.			
	a. 6 digit serial #.	30.00	100	250
	b. 7 digit serial #.	10.00	15.00	30.00

1914 Second Issue

		VG	VF	UNC
50	**1 Mark**	VG	VF	UNC
	12.8.1914. Black on light green and lilac underprint. Red serial # and seal. 95x60mm. PC: White.	1.00	2.50	4.00

		VG	VF	UNC
51	**1 Mark**	VG	VF	UNC
	12.8.1914. (1917). Black on light green and lilac underprint. Red serial # and seal. Light brown pattern over entire note. 95x60mm. PC: White.	1.00	2.50	4.00
52	**1 Mark**	VG	VF	UNC
	12.8.1914. (1920). Black on light green and lilac underprint. Blue serial # and seal. Light brown pattern over entire note. 95x60mm.	1.00	2.50	4.00

#	Note	VG	VF	UNC
53	**2 Mark** 12.8.1914. Black on red underprint. Red serial # and seal. 110x70mm. PC: White.	1.00	3.00	5.00
54	**2 Mark** 12.8.1914. Black on red underprint. Red serial # and seal. Light red pattern over entire note. 110x70mm.	1.00	3.00	5.00
55	**2 Mark** 12.8.1914. Black on red underprint. Blue serial # and seal. Light red pattern over entire note. 110x70mm.	2.00	4.00	7.00

1917-1918 Issue

Note: Spelling of heading changed to *Darlehnskassenschein* from 1917 onwards.

#	Note	VG	VF	UNC
56	**5 Mark** 1.8.1917. Black and purplish blue. Girl at upper right. 125x80mm.			
	a. 7 digit serial #.	3.00	6.00	15.00
	b. 8 digit serial #.	2.00	4.00	8.00

#	Note	VG	VF	UNC
57	**20 Mark** 20.2.1918. Dark brown on carmine underprint. Minerva at left, Mercury at right. Back: Man in armor at left, allegorical woman at right. 140x90mm.	8.00	15.00	30.00

1920 Issues (Weimar Republic)

#	Note	VG	VF	UNC
58	**1 Mark** 1.3.1920. Dark brown on green and olive underprint. 90x60mm.	0.50	1.00	5.00

#	Note	VG	VF	UNC
59	**2 Mark** 1.3.1920. Red on light brown underprint. Brown serial # and seal. 100x65mm.	0.50	1.00	5.00
60	**2 Mark** 1.3.1920. Dark brown on blue and light brown underprint. Red serial # and seal. 100x65mm.	0.50	1.00	5.00

1922 Issue

#	Note	VG	VF	UNC
61	**1 Mark** 15.9.1922. Dark green on light green underprint. Large value at center, two seals below. Back: Large value at center. 85x60mm.			
	a. Light green paper.	1.00	2.00	5.00
	b. Gray paper.	50.00	125	250

#	Note	VG	VF	UNC
62	**2 Mark** 15.9.1922. Reddish-brown on rose underprint. Large value at center, two seals below Back: Large value at center. 90x65mm.	1.00	2.00	5.00

Reichsbanknote (resumed)

Imperial Bank Note

NOTE ON VARIETIES: There are many differences in serial #, sheet mark letters and paper among the inflation period notes in addition to the wmk. varieties quoted.

1915-1919 Issue

#	Note	VG	VF	UNC
63	**20 Mark** 4.11.1915. Dark blue on light blue underprint. Two men with cornucopias filled with money at upper center. Back: Man and woman. 140x90mm.	5.00	10.00	20.00

64	50 Mark	VG	VF	UNC
	20.10.1918. Dark brown on gray-violet underprint. Green guilloche at left. Dark line margin (known as the "Mourning Note"). 140x110mm.			
	a. Watermark: J.	100	200	350
	b. Watermark: A.	80.00	150	300
	c. Watermark: B.	80.00	150	300

65	50 Mark	VG	VF	UNC
	30.11.1918. Olive-brown on gray underprint. Back: Broad margin, with egg-shaped white area (known as the "Egg Note"). 144x114mm.	25.00	50.00	100

66	50 Mark	VG	VF	UNC
	24.6.1919. Green on light brown underprint. Woman at upper right. Reihe 1-4 (at upper left). 153x102mm.	5.00	10.00	25.00

WEIMAR REPUBLIC

Reichsbanknote

Republic Treasury Notes

1920 Issue

67	10 Mark	VG	VF	UNC
	6.2.1920. Dark green and black on olive underprint. 126x84mm.			
	a. Underprint letters in red on back.	2.00	5.00	9.00
	b. Without underprint letters on back.	300	750	1,750

68	50 Mark	VG	VF	UNC
	23.7.1920. Dark green and green. Woman with flowers and fruit at right. Back: Farmer and worker.	8.00	15.00	30.00

69	100 Mark	VG	VF	UNC
	1.11.1920. Dark brown with black text on blue and red underprint. "Bamberg Horseman" (in Bamberg Cathedral) at upper left and right. 162x108mm.			
	a. 7 digit serial #.	5.00	10.00	20.00
	b. 8 digit serial #.	5.00	10.00	20.00
	c. Without underprint. letters. Rare.	—	—	—

1922 First Issue

70	**10,000 Mark**	VG	VF	UNC
	19.1.1922. Blue-green on olive-green underprint. Male portrait at right by Albrecht Durer, like #71. Back: Eagle in rectangular ornament. 210x124mm.	6.00	10.00	25.00

71	**10,000 Mark**	VG	VF	UNC
	19.1.1922. Blue-green on olive-green underprint. Male Portrait at right by Albrecht Durer. Back: Monochrome below eagle. 210x124mm.	6.00	12.00	30.00

72	**10,000 Mark**	VG	VF	UNC
	19.1.1922. Blue-green on olive-brown underprint. Male portrait at right by Albrecht Durer. Back: Monochrome below eagle; 10000 vertical at right. 180x100mm.	4.00	8.00	20.00

1922 Second Issue

73	**500 Mark**	VG	VF	UNC
	27.3.1922. Dark blue and olive-green. Portrait J. Mayer at upper right. 175x112mm.	15.00	40.00	70.00

74	**500 Mark**	VG	VF	UNC
	7.7.1922. Black. Right margin tinted. Uniface. 173x90mm.			
	a. Red serial # (valid until 1.1.1923).	20.00	60.00	250
	b. Green 7-digit serial # (valid until 1.4.1923).	5.00	15.00	25.00
	c. Green 8-digit serial # (valid until 1.4.1923).	3.00	8.00	15.00

1922 Third Issue

75	**100 Mark**	VG	VF	UNC
	4.8.1922. Black-blue. Left and right margins tinted.	5.00	10.00	22.00

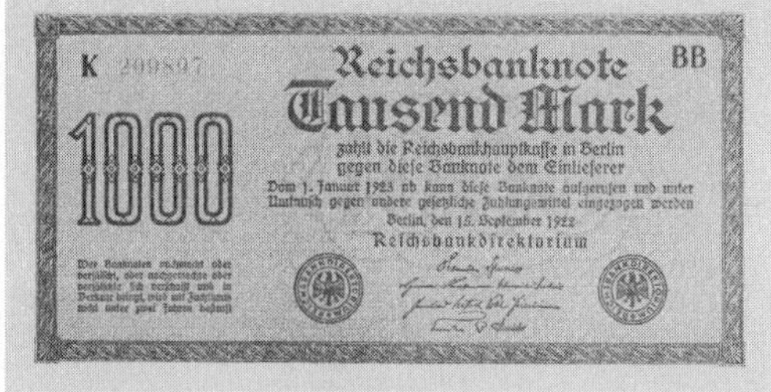

		VG	VF	UNC
76	**1000 Mark** 15.9.1922. Dark green on green and lilac underprint. 160x85mm.			
	a. Watermark: E. White paper.	1.00	2.00	10.00
	b. Watermark: I. Yellow paper.	1.00	2.00	7.00
	c. Watermark: F. White paper.	1.00	2.00	7.00
	d. Watermark: D. White paper.	1.00	2.00	10.00
	e. Watermark: G. White paper.	1.00	2.00	8.00
	f. Watermark: H. White paper.	1.00	2.00	10.00
	g. Watermark: J. Pale green paper.	1.00	2.00	12.00
	h. Watermark: K. Pale green paper.	1.00	2.00	12.00

		VG	VF	UNC
77	**5000 Mark** 16.9.1922. Blue and brown on gray and green underprint. Portrait mintmaster Spinelli at right by Memling. 130x90mm.	40.00	75.00	200

		VG	VF	UNC
78	**5000 Mark** 19.11.1922. Dark brown on brown underprint. Chamberlain H. Urmiller at left. 198x107mm.	30.00	50.00	125

		VG	VF	UNC
79	**50,000 Mark** 19.11.1922. Black on white with green tint at right. Portrait Burgermaster Brauweiler at upper left by B. Bruyn, without underprint. 190x110mm.	5.00	10.00	20.00
80	**50,000 Mark** 19.11.1922. Dark brown on pink and green. Portrait Burgermaster Brauweiler at upper left by Bruyn, with underprint. 190x110mm.	5.00	10.00	25.00

1922 Fourth Issue

		VG	VF	UNC
81	**5000 Mark** 2.12.1922. Brown on green and light brown underprint. Portrait merchant Imhof at right by A. Durer. 130x90mm.			
	a. Watermark: G/D in stars, E.	3.00	5.00	10.00
	b. Watermark: Lattice, G.	3.00	5.00	10.00
	c. Watermark: Thorns, I.	3.00	5.00	10.00
	d. Watermark: Greek pattern, F.	3.00	5.00	10.00
	e. Watermark: Wavy lines, J.	5.00	10.00	40.00

1922 Fifth Issue

		VG	VF	UNC
82	**1000 Mark** 15.12.1922. (Not issued). Black on dark brown underprint. Portrait mintmaster J. Herz at upper left by G. Penz. 140x90mm.			
	a. Various styles of serial #, 4mm or less.	25.00	50.00	100
	b. Serial # 4.5mm with single prefix letter.	—	250	500

Note: For #82 with overprint: *EINE MILLIARDE*, see #113.

1923 First Issue

#	100,000 Mark	VG	VF	UNC
83	1.2.1923. Dark brown on lilac with lilac tint at right. Portrait merchant Gisze at left by H. Holbein. 190x115mm.			
	a. Without *T* at left of portrait.	5.00	10.00	20.00
	b. With *T* at left of portrait Two serial #.	7.00	15.00	30.00
	c. With *T* at left of portrait One serial #.	5.00	10.00	20.00

1923 Second Issue

#	10,000 Mark	VG	VF	UNC
84	3.2.1923. (Not issued). Dark blue on green and red underprint. 130x90mm.			
	r. Remainder.	—	2,000	4,000
	s. Specimen overprint: *MUSTER.*	—	—	2,750

#	20,000 Mark	VG	VF	UNC
85	20.2.1923. Blue-black on pink and green underprint. 160x95mm.			
	a. Watermark: Small circles, L. 2 serial # varieties.	5.00	10.00	17.00
	b. Watermark: *G/D* in stars, E.	5.00	10.00	17.00
	c. Watermark: Lattice, G.	5.00	10.00	15.00
	d. Watermark: Thorns, I.	8.00	15.00	35.00
	e. Watermark: Greek pattern, F.	8.00	15.00	30.00
	f. Watermark: Wavy lines, J.	8.00	15.00	30.00

#	1 Million Mark	VG	VF	UNC
86	20.2.1923. Dark brown on light brown and dark green underprint. Uniface. 160x110mm.			
	a. Series letters and serial # at left and right.	10.00	25.00	45.00
	b. Series letters and serial # at upper left and upper right.	10.00	25.00	50.00

1923 Third Issue

#	5000 Mark	VG	VF	UNC
87	15.3.1923. (Not issued). Dark olive-brown. Chamberlain H. Urmiller. 148x90mm.	—	400	750

Note: #87 w/overprint: *500 MILLIARDEN,* see #124.

#	500,000 Mark	VG	VF	UNC
88	1.5.1923. Dark green on lilac and green underprint. Portrait man wearing Jacobite cap at left and right. 170x95mm.			
	a. Serial # on face and back.	10.00	20.00	55.00
	b. Serial # on face only.	10.00	20.00	40.00

89 2 Millionen Mark VG VF UNC

23.7.1923. Dark brown on pink and green underprint. Merchant Gisze at left and right by H. Holbein. 162x87mm.

	VG	VF	UNC
a. Issued note.	10.00	25.00	50.00
b. Error: *MULIONEN.*	500	1,000	2,000

90 5 Millionen Mark VG VF UNC

1.6.1923. Brown on lilac and green with yellow tint at right. Portrait woman (Constitutional Medallion) at upper left center. 30.00 80.00 150

1923 Fourth Issues

91 100,000 Mark VG VF UNC

25.7.1923. Black on green underprint. Uniface. 110x80mm.

	VG	VF	UNC
a. Watermark: *G/D* in stars, E, green paper.	2.00	4.00	8.00
b. Watermark: Wavy lines, J, white paper.	2.00	7.50	15.00

92 500,000 Mark VG VF UNC

25.7.1923. Carmine with violet tint at right. Uniface. 175x80mm. 3.00 10.00 15.00

93 1 Million Mark VG VF UNC

25.7.1923. Dark blue on lilac and light brown underprint. Denomination field like #85 with new denomination overprint at left. Back: Printed. 160x95mm. 20.00 35.00 80.00

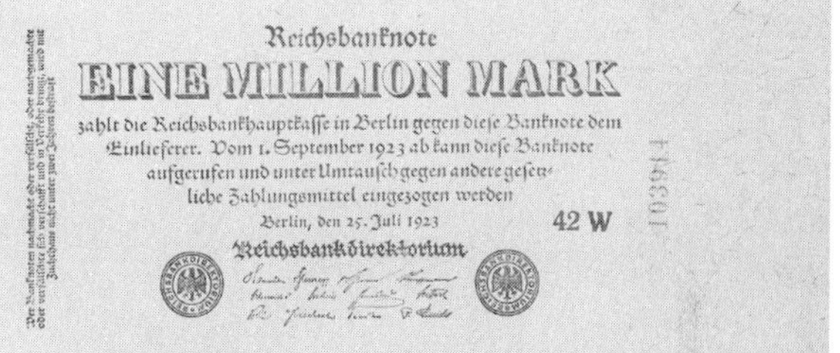

94 1 Million Mark VG VF UNC

25.7.1923. Black on white with yellow tint at right. Uniface. 175x80mm. 6.00 15.00 55.00

95 5 Millionen Mark VG VF UNC

25.7.1923. Black on white with blue-green tint at left. 190x80mm. 8.00 20.00 35.00

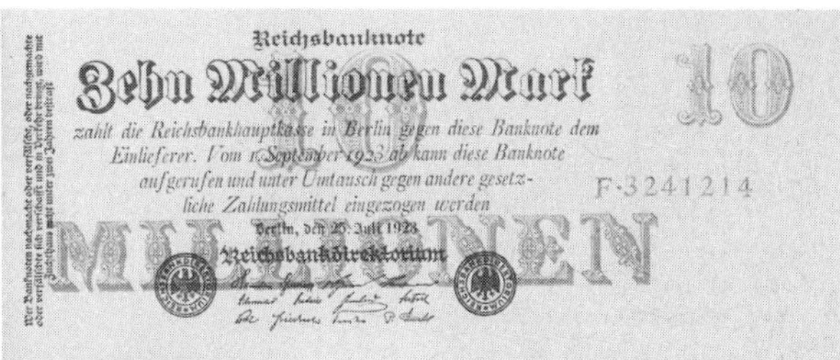

96 10 Millionen Mark VG VF UNC

25.7.1923. Black and dark green with yellow tint at right. 195x80mm. 7.00 15.00 25.00

97 20 Millionen Mark VG VF UNC

25.7.1923. Black and light blue with lilac tint at right. 195x83mm.

	VG	VF	UNC
a. 7 digit serial #.	5.00	10.00	20.00
b. 6 or 8 digit serial #.	5.00	10.00	20.00

98	**50 Millionen Mark**	VG	VF	UNC
	25.7.1923. Black and lilac-brown with lilac tint at right. Uniface. 195x86mm.			
	a. 7 digit serial #.	7.00	10.00	20.00
	b. 8 digit serial #.	3.00	5.00	10.00

1923 Fifth Issues

99	**50,000 Mark**	VG	VF	UNC
	9.8.1923. Black on light brown underprint. Uniface. 105x70mm.	5.00	10.00	20.00

100	**200,000 Mark**	VG	VF	UNC
	9.8.1923. Black on gray underprint. Uniface. 115x70mm.	3.00	5.00	10.00

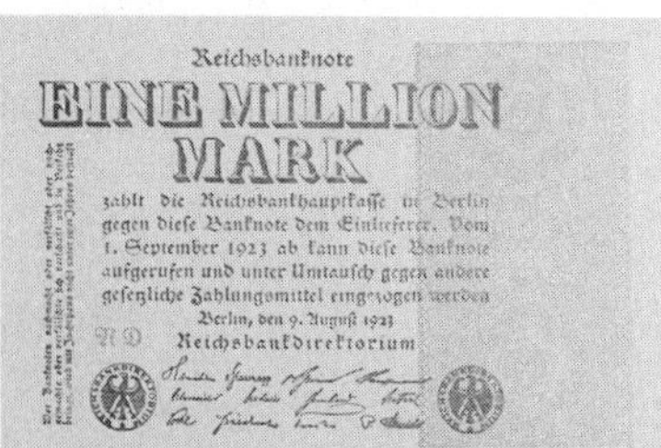

101	**1 Million Mark**	VG	VF	UNC
	9.8.1923. Black. Serial # at bottom. Uniface. Watermark: Oak leaves. 120x80mm. PC: White, with green tint at right.	3.00	5.00	10.00

102	**1 Million Mark**	VG	VF	UNC
	9.8.1923. Black. Green underprint panel at right. Without serial #. Uniface. 120x80mm.			
	a. Watermark: *G/D* in stars, E.	3.00	5.00	10.00
	b. Watermark: Small circles, L.	3.00	5.00	10.00
	c. Watermark: Lattice, G.	3.00	5.00	10.00
	d. Watermark: Wavy lines, J.	5.00	10.00	20.00

103	**2 Millionen Mark**	VG	VF	UNC
	9.8.1923. Black. White paper, with lilac tint at right. Serial # at bottom. Uniface. Watermark: Oak leaves. 125x80mm.	4.00	10.00	18.00

104	**2 Millionen Mark**	VG	VF	UNC
	9.8.1923. Black. Lilac guilloche at right. Without serial #. Uniface. 125x80mm.			
	a. Watermark: *G/D* in stars, E.	2.00	4.00	8.00
	b. Watermark: Small circles, L.	2.00	4.00	8.00
	c. Watermark: Lattice with *8*, G.	2.00	4.00	8.00
	d. Watermark: Wavy lines, J.	3.00	5.00	10.00

105	**5 Millionen Mark**	VG	VF	UNC
	20.8.1923. Black on gray-green underprint. Uniface. 128x80mm. PC: Pink.	5.00	10.00	20.00

106	**10 Millionen Mark**	VG	VF	UNC
	22.8.1923. Black on pale olive-green and blue-gray underprint. Serial # varieties. Uniface. 125x80mm.			
	a. Watermark: *G/D* in stars, E.	3.00	7.00	10.00
	b. Watermark: Small circles, L.	3.00	7.00	10.00
	c. Watermark: Lattice with *8*, G.	3.00	5.00	10.00
	d. Watermark: Wavy lines, J.	3.00	5.00	10.00

107	**100 Millionen Mark**	VG	VF	UNC
	22.8.1923. Black on blue-green and olive-brown underprint. Uniface. 150x85mm.			
	a. Watermark: Oak leaves, gray tint at right.	3.00	5.00	10.00
	b. Watermark: Small crucifera blossoms, D. With embedded fibre strips in paper on back.	3.00	5.00	10.00

	VG	VF	UNC
c. Watermark: Small crucifera blossoms, D. Without embedded fibre strips in paper on back.	4.00	10.00	20.00
d. Watermark: *G/D* in stars, E.	4.00	10.00	20.00
e. Watermark: Small circles, L.	4.00	10.00	20.00
f. Watermark: *S* in stars, M.	4.00	10.00	20.00
g. Watermark: Lozenges, N.	4.00	8.00	15.00

1923 Sixth Issue

108 20 Millionen Mark

1.9.1923. Black on olive-brown and dark green underprint. Uniface. 125x82mm.

	VG	VF	UNC
a. Watermark: Small circles. L.	3.00	5.00	10.00
b. Watermark: Lozenges, N.	3.00	5.00	10.00
c. Watermark: *G/D* in stars, E.	3.00	5.00	10.00
d. Watermark: Wavy lines, J.	3.00	5.00	10.00
e. Watermark: Lattice, G.	3.00	5.00	10.00
f. Watermark: *S* in stars, M.	10.00	25.00	50.00

109 50 Millionen Mark

1.9.1923. Black on gray and lilac underprint. Uniface. 124x84mm.

	VG	VF	UNC
a. Watermark: Small crucifera blossoms, gray paper. D.	3.00	5.00	10.00
b. Watermark: *G/D* in stars, E. White paper.	3.00	5.00	10.00
c. Watermark: Small circles, L. White paper.	3.00	5.00	10.00
d. Watermark: Lozenges, N. White paper.	3.00	5.00	10.00
e. Watermark: *S* in stars, M. White paper.	3.00	5.00	10.00
f. Watermark: Lattice, G. White paper.	3.00	5.00	10.00

110 500 Millionen Mark

1.9.1923. Dark brown on light brown and lilac underprint. *500* facing inwardly at right margin. Uniface. 155x85mm.

	VG	VF	UNC
a. Watermark: Thistle leaves, lilac tint at right.	2.00	5.00	10.00
b. Watermark: Small crucifera blossoms, *500* facing inwardly at right. margin.	2.00	5.00	10.00
c. Like b, but *500* facing outwardly at right. margin, D.	250	450	700
d. Watermark: *G/D* in stars, E.	2.00	5.00	10.00
e. Watermark: Small circles, L.	2.00	5.00	10.00
f. Watermark: *S* in stars. M.	2.00	5.00	12.00
g. Watermark: Lozenges. N.	150	325	550
h. Watermark: Lattice. G.	10.00	20.00	35.00

111 500 Milliarden Mark

	VG	VF	UNC
1.9.1923. Specimen only. Rare. Blue, lilac and green. Allegorical head at upper right. Printer: Vienna printing. 155x85mm.	—	—	—

112 1 Billion Mark

	VG	VF	UNC
1.9.1923. Specimen only. Rare. Violet and lilac. Allegorical head at right. Printer: Vienna printing.	—	—	—

1923 Seventh Issues

113 1 Milliarde Mark on 1000 Mark

ND (Sept. 1923 - old date 15.12.1922). Black on dark brown. 140x90mm.

	VG	VF	UNC
a. Watermark: *1000,* brown tint at right. White paper.	5.00	10.00	20.00
b. Watermark: Small crucifera blossoms, D. Brown paper.	5.00	10.00	20.00
c. Watermark: Small crucifera blossoms, D. White paper.	5.00	10.00	20.00
d. Overprint inverted.	50.00	100	200
e. Overprint on back only.	50.00	100	200
f. Overprint on face only.	50.00	100	200

114 1 Milliarde Mark

	VG	VF	UNC
5.9.1923. Black on dark green, lilac and blue. Blue-green tint at right. Uniface. 160x86mm.	7.00	15.00	30.00

115 5 Milliarden Mark

10.9.1923. Black on olive-brown underprint. Uniface. 165x85mm.

	VG	VF	UNC
a. Lilac tint at right. Watermark: Oak leaves.	15.00	30.00	50.00
b. Without tint at right. Watermark: Small crucifera blossoms, D.	15.00	30.00	50.00

116	**10 Milliarden Mark**	VG	VF	UNC
	15.9.1923. Black on gray-lilac and blue-green underprint. Format similar to #114. Uniface. 170x85mm.			
	a. Watermark: Thistle leaves, yellow tint at right.	15.00	35.00	50.00
	b. Watermark: Small crucifera blossoms, D.	15.00	35.00	50.00

117	**10 Milliarden Mark**	VG	VF	UNC
	1.10.1923. Black-green (shades) on lilac and green underprint. Format similar to #118. Uniface. 160x105mm.			
	a. Watermark: *G/D* in stars, E.	10.00	30.00	80.00
	b. Watermark: Small circles, L.	10.00	30.00	80.00
	c. Watermark: *S* in stars, M.	25.00	50.00	110
	d. Watermark: Lozenges, N.	150	300	535
	e. Watermark: Lattice, G.	20.00	50.00	100

118	**20 Milliarden Mark**	VG	VF	UNC
	1.10.1923. Dark green on blue and orange underprint. Format similar to 117. Uniface. 140x90mm.			
	a. Watermark: *G/D* in stars. 5 or 6 digit serial #. E.	15.00	30.00	50.00
	b. Watermark: *G/D* in stars, E. Error with *20 MILLIARDEN* on l. edge. Format 175 x 85mm.	125	250	535
	c. Watermark: Small circles. L.	15.00	30.00	60.00
	d. Watermark: Small circles, L. with error *20 MILLIARDEN* on l. edge.	150	275	600
	e. Watermark: Lozenges, N.	20.00	40.00	80.00
	f. Watermark: Lattice, G.	20.00	40.00	80.00
	g. Watermark: *S* in stars, M.	20.00	40.00	70.00

119	**50 Milliarden Mark**	VG	VF	UNC
	10.10.1923. Black on orange and blue underprint. Uniface. 183x57mm.			
	a. Watermark: Oak leaves, green tint at right.	25.00	55.00	100
	b. Watermark: Small crucifera blossoms, D. White paper.	25.00	50.00	100
	c. Watermark: Small crucifera blossoms, D. White paper. without serial #.	25.00	55.00	100
	d. Watermark: Small crucifera blossoms, D. Gray paper. without serial #.	25.00	45.00	85.00

120	**50 Milliarden Mark**	VG	VF	UNC
	10.10.1923. Black on orange, blue and green. Like #119b but green rectangular underprint at right. Uniface. 176x86mm.			
	a. Watermark: *G/D* in stars, E.	35.00	55.00	100
	b. Watermark: Small circles, L.	20.00	40.00	80.00
	c. Watermark: *S* in stars, M.	25.00	50.00	100

121	**200 Milliarden Mark**	VG	VF	UNC
	15.10.1923. Black on violet and green underprint. Uniface. 140x80mm.			
	a. Watermark: *G/D* in stars, E.	25.00	50.00	100
	b. Watermark: Small circles, L.	25.00	50.00	100
	c. Watermark: *S* in stars, M.	25.00	50.00	100
	d. Watermark: Lattice, G.	150	450	625
	e. Watermark: Lozenges. Rare.	—	—	—

1923 Eighth Issue

122	**1 Milliarde Mark**	VG	VF	UNC
	20.10.1923. Black on blue-green underprint. Uniface. 127x61mm.	5.00	10.00	20.00

123	**5 Milliarden Mark**	VG	VF	UNC
	20.10.1923. Black on violet-brown underprint. Uniface. 130x64mm.			
	a. With serial #.	10.00	15.00	30.00
	b. Without serial #.	5.00	10.00	20.00

124	**500 Milliarden Mark on 5000 Mark**	VG	VF	UNC
	ND (Oct. 1923 - old date 15.3.1923). Dark brown on olive-brown underprint. 145x90mm.			
	a. Overprint on face and back.	80.00	150	300
	b. Overprint on back only (error).	750	1,500	2,250
	c. Overprint on face only (error).	750	1,500	2,250

1923 Ninth Issue

		VG	VF	UNC
125	**50 Milliarden Mark** 26.10.1923. Black on blue-green underprint. Uniface. 130x64mm.			
	a. Gray paper.	20.00	40.00	80.00
	b. Green paper.	20.00	40.00	80.00

		VG	VF	UNC
126	**100 Milliarden Mark** 26.10.1923. Dark blue on white, blue tint at right. Uniface. 135x65mm.	20.00	40.00	80.00

		VG	VF	UNC
127	**500 Milliarden Mark** 26.10.1923. Dark brown on white. Uniface. 137x65mm.			
	a. Watermark: Oak leaves, green tint at right.	50.00	100	200
	b. Watermark: *500M*, blue or violet tint at right.	50.00	100	200

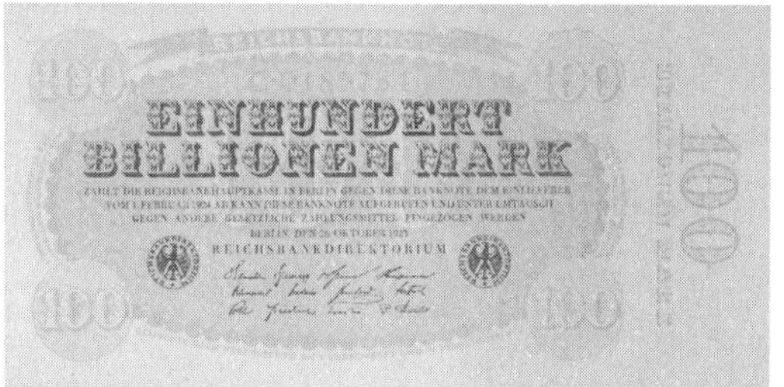

		VG	VF	UNC
128	**100 Billionen Mark** 26.10.1923. Black on lilac and gray, brown tint at right. Uniface. 174x86mm.	1,000	2,250	3,250

1923 Tenth Issue

		VG	VF	UNC
129	**1 Billion Mark** 1.11.1923. Brown-violet, lilac tint at right. Uniface. 137x65mm.	100	200	500

		VG	VF	UNC
130	**5 Billionen Mark** 1.11.1923. Black on light blue and pink underprint. Uniface. 168x86mm.			
	a. Watermark: Thistles, yellow tint at right.	200	400	900
	b. Watermark: Small crucifera blossoms, D.	200	400	900

		VG	VF	UNC
131	**10 Billionen Mark** 1.11.1923. Black on green and light brown underprint. Uniface. 171x86mm.			
	a. Watermark: Thistles, blue-green tint at right.	300	500	1,000
	b. Watermark: Small crucifera blossoms, D.	400	1,000	1,500

		VG	VF	UNC
132	**10 Billionen Mark** 1.11.1923. Black on brown and blue-green underprint. Uniface. 120x82mm.			
	a. Watermark: *G/D* in stars, E.	300	600	1,200
	b. Watermark: Small circles, L.	300	600	1,200

1923 Eleventh Issue

		VG	VF	UNC
133	**100 Milliarden Mark** 5.11.1923. Red-brown on olive and blue-green underprint. Uniface. 135x65mm.	20.00	40.00	90.00

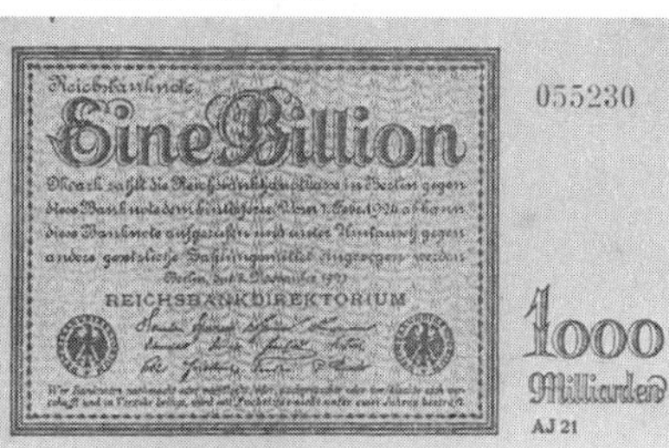

		VG	VF	UNC
134	**1 Billion Mark** 5.11.1923. Black on violet and brown underprint. Uniface. 143x86mm.	100	200	450

		VG	VF	UNC
135	**2 Billionen Mark** 5.11.1923. Black on green and pink underprint. Uniface. 120x71mm.			
	a. Watermark: *G/D* in stars, E.	120	250	550
	b. Watermark: Small circles, L.	120	250	550
	c. Watermark: *S* in stars, M.	120	250	550

		VG	VF	UNC
136	**5 Billionen Mark** 7.11.1923. Black on blue and pink underprint. Uniface. 165x86mm.			
	a. Watermark: Thistles. Yellow tint at right.	300	800	1,400
	b. Watermark: Small crucifera blossoms, D.	300	800	1,400
	c. Watermark: *G/D* in stars, E.	300	800	1,400
	d. Watermark: Small circles, L.	300	800	1,400

1924 First Issue

		VG	VF	UNC
137	**10 Billionen Mark** 1.2.1924. Brown on green, lilac tint at right. Uniface. 140x72mm.	450	900	1,600

		VG	VF	UNC
138	**20 Billionen Mark** 5.2.1924. Blue-green and violet, light violet tint at right. Portrait woman at upper right by A. Durer. 160x95mm.	750	1,400	2,500

		VG	VF	UNC
139	**50 Billionen Mark** 10.2.1924. Brown and olive, green tint at right. Portrait Councillor J. Muffel at center right by A. Durer.	1,250	2,250	4,500

		VG	VF	UNC
140	**100 Billionen Mark** 15.2.1924. Red-brown and blue, light blue tint at right. Portrait W. Pirkheimer at right by A. Durer. 180x95mm.	3,500	7,500	12,000

1924 Second Issue

		VG	VF	UNC
141	**5 Billionen Mark** 15.3.1924. Dark brown on green and lilac underprint. 120x72mm.	200	500	1,000

Reichsschuldenverwaltung

Imperial Debt Administration

1915 Emergency Interest Coupon Issue

In October 1918 all interest coupons of war loans, due on 2.1.1919 (letter q), were temporarily declared legal tender.

		VG	VF	UNC
142	**2.50 Mark** Year of loan: 1915; 1916; 1917; 1918.	15.00	40.00	75.00
143	**5.00 Mark** Year of loan: 1915; 1916; 1917; 1918.	20.00	50.00	100

		VG	VF	UNC
144	**12.50 Mark** Year of loan: 1915; 1916; 1917; 1918.	75.00	225	350
145	**25.00 Mark** Year of loan: 1915; 1916; 1917; 1918.	40.00	100	200
146	**50.00 Mark** Year of loan: 1915; 1916; 1917; 1918.	100	200	300
147	**125.00 Mark** Year of loan: 1915; 1916; 1917; 1918.	200	500	900

Zwischenscheine - Schatzanweisungen

Imperial Treasury

1923 Interim Note Issue

In October 1923, interim notes of the Reichsbank for Treasury certificates, partial bonds of the treasury certificates of the German Reich were declared legal tender.

		VG	VF	UNC
148	**0.42 Goldmark = 1/10 Dollar (U.S.A.)** 23.10.1923. Watermark: O.	45.00	90.00	150
149	**1.05 Goldmark = 1/4 Dollar (U.S.A.)** 23.10.1923. Uniface. Watermark: *5.*	50.00	100	175
150	**1.05 Goldmark = 1/4 Dollar (U.S.A.)** 23.10.1923. Back: Capital letters. Watermark: *50.*	60.00	125	250

		VG	VF	UNC
151	**2.10 Goldmark = 1/2 Dollar (U.S.A.)** 23.10.1923. Watermark: *20 MARK.*	125	300	525

1923 Partial Bond of Treasury Certificates Issues

No.	Denomination	VG	VF	UNC
152	**0.42 Goldmark = 1/10 Dollar (U.S.A.)** 26.10.1923. Watermark: Oak and thistles.	40.00	90.00	170
153	**1.05 Goldmark = 1/4 Dollar (U.S.A.)** 26.10.1923. Watermark: *5.*	50.00	100	190

No.	Denomination	VG	VF	UNC
154	**1.05 Goldmark = 1/4 Dollar (U.S.A.)** 26.10.1923. Watermark: *10.*	75.00	125	220
155	**1.05 Goldmark = 1/4 Dollar (U.S.A.)** 26.10.1923. Watermark: *50.*	75.00	150	290
156	**2.10 Goldmark = 1/2 Dollar (U.S.A.)** 26.10.1923. Watermark: *5.*	100	200	290

No.	Denomination	VG	VF	UNC
157	**2.10 Goldmark = 1/2 Dollar (U.S.A.)** 26.10.1923. Watermark: *20.*	125	250	300

1923 Whole Treasury Certificates Issues

3 different issues of each:

1. Watermark: Ornaments.
2. *Ausgefertigt*, at lower right, watermark of lines and *RSV.*
3. Like #2 but without *Ausgefertigt* at lower right.

No.	Denomination	VG	VF	UNC
158	**4.20 Goldmark = 1 Dollar (U.S.A.)** 25.8.1923.			
	a. Watermark: P.	200	450	750
	b. Watermark: Q.	200	450	750
159	**8.40 Goldmark = 2 Dollars (U.S.A.)** 25.8.1923.			
	a. Watermark: P.	750	1,750	4,000
	b. Watermark: Q.	750	1,575	4,000

No.	Denomination	VG	VF	UNC
160	**21.00 Goldmark = 5 Dollars (U.S.A.)** 25.8.1923.			
	a. Watermark: P.	1,500	3,000	5,000
	b. Watermark: Q.	1,000	3,000	5,000

Rentenbank - Stabilization Bank

1923 Rentenmarkschein Issue

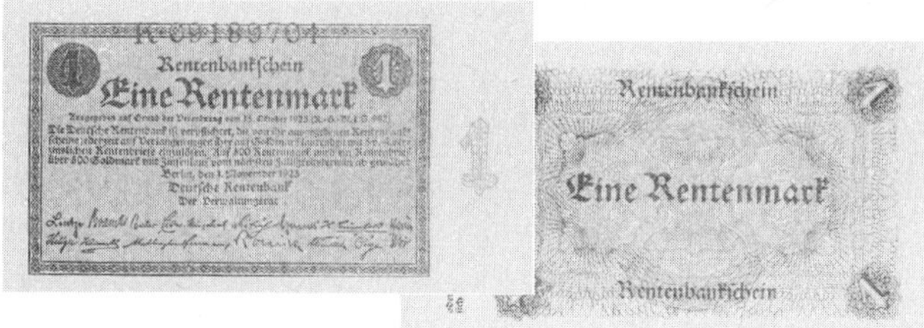

No.	Denomination	VG	VF	UNC
161	**1 Rentenmark** 1.11.1923. Olive.	20.00	50.00	100

No.	Denomination	VG	VF	UNC
162	**2 Rentenmark** 1.11.1923. Red and green.	80.00	150	375

No.	Denomination	VG	VF	UNC
163	**5 Rentenmark** 1.11.1923. Blue-green and violet.	100	200	550

No.	Denomination	VG	VF	UNC
164	**10 Rentenmark** 1.11.1923. Lilac and green.	250	575	1,150

No.	Denomination	VG	VF	UNC
165	**50 Rentenmark** 1.11.1923. Brown and violet.	1,750	3,250	5,500

No.	Denomination	VG	VF	UNC
166	**100 Rentenmark** 1.11.1923. Brown and blue-green.	700	1,250	3,250

		VG	VF	UNC
167	**500 Rentenmark** 1.11.1923. Blue-gray and green.			
	a. Issued note. Rare.	—	—	10,500
	s. Specimen overprint: *MUSTER*.	—	—	8,500
168	**1000 Rentenmark** 1.11.1923. Brown and light green.	VG	VF	UNC
	a. Issued note.	1,500	3,500	7,000
	s. Specimen overprint: *MUSTER*.	—	—	3,250

1925-1926 Issue

		VG	VF	UNC
169	**5 Rentenmark** 2.1.1926. Dark green and olive. Portrait farm girl at upper center right. 7 or 8 digit serial #. 133x74mm.	40.00	100	200

		VG	VF	UNC
170	**10 Rentenmark** 3.7.1925. Green and brown. Portrait farm woman at left. 145x78mm.	550	1,100	3,000

		VG	VF	UNC
171	**50 Rentenmark** 20.3.1925. Brown, green and lilac. Farmer at right. 155x85mm.	750	1,250	3,275

1934 Issue

		VG	VF	UNC
172	**50 Rentenmark** 6.7.1934. Dark brown on olive. Freiherr vom Stein at right. 155x85mm.	240	500	1,300

1937 Issue

#173 and 174 blind embossed seal at lower right.

		VG	VF	UNC
173	**1 Rentenmark** 30.1.1937. Olive. Yellow stripe at right. Large or small size numerals in serial #. 120x65mm.			
	a. 7 digit serial #.	30.00	70.00	150
	b. 8 digit serial #.	5.00	10.00	20.00

		VG	VF	UNC
174	**2 Rentenmark** 30.1.1937. Brown. Yellow strip at right. Large or small size numerals in serial #. 125x70mm.			
	a. 7 digit serial #.	25.00	50.00	100
	b. 8 digit serial #.	5.00	10.00	20.00

Deutsche Golddiskontbank

German Gold Discount Bank

1924 Issue

		VG	VF	UNC
174A	**5 Pounds** 20.4.1924. Brown. Youth. 144x80mm. Specimen. Rare.	—	—	—

		VG	VF	UNC
174B	**10 Pounds** 20.4.1924. Gray-green. Portrait youth with wreath at upper center right. 155x80mm. Specimen. Rare.	—	—	—

Reichsbanknote

1924 Issue

		VG	VF	UNC
175	**10 Reichsmark** 11.10.1924. Dark green and red-lilac. Portrait of a man by H. Holbein at upper center right. 150x75mm.	500	850	2,650

		VG	VF	UNC
176	**20 Reichsmark** 11.10.1924. Brown and red-lilac. Portrait of a woman by H. Holbein at upper center right. 160x80mm.	500	1,100	3,275

		VG	VF	UNC
177	**50 Reichsmark** 11.10.1924. Brown and dark green. Portrait of merchant Dietrich Born by H. Holbein at upper center right. 170x85mm.	70.00	125	400

		VG	VF	UNC
178	**100 Reichsmark** 11.10.1924. Brown and blue-green. Portrait English Lady by H. Holbein at upper center right. 180x90mm.	75.00	135	400

		VG	VF	UNC
179	**1000 Reichsmark** 11.10.1924. Brown and blue. Portrait Patrician Wedigh by H. Holbein at upper center right. 190x95mm.	175	275	700

1929-1936; (1945) Issue

#180-183 serial # on face and back for first variety; serial # on face only for second variety.

		VG	VF	UNC
180	**10 Reichsmark** 22.1.1929. Dark green and black on tan and gray underprint. Portrait Albrecht D. Thaer at right. 150x75mm.			
	a. Watermark: Head of Thaer at left with underprint letter.	5.00	10.00	20.00
	b. Watermark: Ornament at left without underprint letter. (1945).	12.00	30.00	50.00

181	20 Reichsmark	VG	VF	UNC
	22.1.1929. Dark brown on multicolor underprint. Portrait Werner von Siemens at right. 160x80mm.			
	a. Watermark: W. von Siemens at left. With underprint letter.	6.00	15.00	30.00
	b. Watermark: Ornament at left. Without underprint letter (1945).	15.00	35.00	60.00

182	50 Reichsmark	VG	VF	UNC
	30.3.1933. Green and black on multicolor underprint. Portrait David Hansemann at right. 7 or 8 digit serial #. 170x85mm.			
	a. Watermark: David Hansemann at left. With underprint letter.	8.00	15.00	35.00
	b. Watermark: Ornament at left. Without underprint letter (1945).	15.00	35.00	70.00

183	100 Reichsmark	VG	VF	UNC
	24.6.1935. Blue. Portrait Justus von Liebig at right, swastika in underprint at center. 7 or 8 digit serial #. 180x90mm.			
	a. Watermark: J. von Liebig at left. With underprint letter.	10.00	20.00	40.00
	b. Watermark: Ornament at left. Without underprint letter (1945).	20.00	40.00	80.00

184	1000 Reichsmark	VG	VF	UNC
	Brown and olive. Portrait Karl-Friedrich Schinkel at right, swastika underprint at center. 190x95mm.	30.00	60.00	150

1939 Issue

185	20 Reichsmark	VG	VF	UNC
	16.6.1939. Brown. Portrait of a woman holding edelweiss at right. (Similar to Austria #101). 160x80mm.	20.00	35.00	70.00

1942 Issue

186	5 Reichsmark	VG	VF	UNC
	1.8.1942. Red-brown. Portrait young man at right. Watermark: *5* straight up at left, either frontwards or backwards. 140x70mm.			
	a. Issued note.	8.00	15.00	30.00
	b. Watermark: *5* upside down at left.	75.00	135	250

Color Abbreviation Guide

New to the *Standard Catalog of ® World Paper Money* are the following abbreviations related to color references:

BC: Back color
PC: Paper color

LOCAL

The territory of Eupen-Malmedy was part of the German Reich until 1919, when as a result of the Treaty of Versailles it was given to Belgium. After occupation of Belgium in WW II (1940) this territory was re-united with the Reich - therefore the circulation of German banknotes. After the entry of Allied troops the circulating German notes were hand-stamped by the returning Belgian authorities. In the territory of Eupen-Malmedy, before the entry of the Allied troops in 1944, the locally valid German banknotes, occasionally also Reich's Credit Treasury Notes, were handstamped by various municipalities, previously Belgian. The handstamped notes were legal tender until exchanged for Belgian notes. Almost all handstamped notes of this type are very scarce.

Sudetenland and lower Silesia

1945 Kassenschein Emergency Issue

		VG	VF	UNC
187	**20 Reichsmark**			
	28.4.1945. Red-brown on tan underprint.	25.00	50.00	100

Reichsbank Offices in Graz, Linz and Salzburg

1945 Emergency Reissue

Photo-mechanically produced notes, following the pattern of the notes already in circulation. All notes of a particular denomination have identical serial #.

		VG	VF	UNC
187A	**5 Reichsmark**			
	ND (1945-old date 1/8/1942). Red-brown. Portrait young man at right. Serial #G.13663932. Reported not confirmed.	—	—	—

		VG	VF	UNC
188	**10 Reichsmark**			
	ND (1945-old date 22.1.1929). Blue-green. Like #180. Portrait A. D. Thaer at right, blurred printing. Serial #D.02776733.			
	a. Without holes.	200	500	1,000
	b. With holes.	140	400	600

		VG	VF	UNC
189	**50 Reichsmark**			
	ND (1945-old date 30.3.1933). Green. Like #182. Portrait D. Hansemann at right, blurred printing. Serial #E.06647727.			
	a. Without holes.	125	400	700
	b. With holes.	50.00	125	175

		VG	VF	UNC
190	**100 Reichsmark**			
	ND (1945-old date 24.6.1935). Blue. Like #183. Portrait J. von Liebig at right, blurred printing. Serial #T.7396475.			
	a. Without holes.	75.00	175	350
	b. With holes.	30.00	60.00	120

ALLIED OCCUPATION - WWII

Allied Military Currency

1944 Issue

		VG	VF	UNC
191	**1/2 Mark**			
	1944. Green on light blue underprint. Back: Large M at center.			
	a. 9 digit serial # with F.	15.00	30.00	60.00
	b. 8 digit serial # with dash, with F.	40.00	125	250
	c. 8 digit serial # with dash, without F.	20.00	55.00	250

		VG	VF	UNC
192	**1 Mark**			
	1944. Blue on light blue underprint. Back: Large M at center.			
	a. 9 digit serial # with F.	8.00	15.00	25.00
	b. 9 digit serial # without F.	8.00	15.00	25.00
	c. 8 digit serial # with dash, with F.	15.00	100	250
	d. 8 digit serial # with dash, without F.	10.00	20.00	30.00

		VG	VF	UNC
193	**5 Mark**			
	1944. Lilac on light blue underprint. Back: Large M at center.			
	a. 9 digit serial # with F.	5.00	10.00	20.00
	b. 9 digit serial # without F.	8.00	12.00	30.00
	c. 8 digit serial # with dash, with F.	100	250	350
	d. 8 digit serial # with dash, without F.	7.00	15.00	30.00

		VG	VF	UNC
194	**10 Mark**			
	1944. Blue on light blue underprint. Back: Large M at center.			
	a. 9 digit serial # with F.	15.00	30.00	60.00
	b. 9 digit serial # without F.	20.00	40.00	80.00
	c. 8 digit serial # with dash, with F.	200	450	850
	d. 8 digit serial # with dash, without F.	10.00	20.00	55.00

		VG	VF	UNC
195	**20 Mark** 1944. Red on light blue underprint. Back: Large M at center.			
	a. 9 digit serial # with *F.*	20.00	40.00	80.00
	b. 9 digit serial # without *F.*	25.00	50.00	100
	c. 8 digit serial # with dash, with *F.*	150	300	550
	d. 8 digit serial # with dash, without *F.*	10.00	15.00	30.00

		VG	VF	UNC
196	**50 Mark** 1944. Blue on light blue underprint. Back: Large M at center.			
	a. 9 digit serial # with *F.*	20.00	40.00	80.00
	b. 9 digit serial # without *F.*	10.00	30.00	50.00
	c. 8 digit serial # with dash, with *F.*	250	525	1,000
	d. 8 digit serial # w dash, without *F.*	20.00	40.00	80.00

		VG	VF	UNC
197	**100 Mark** 1944. Lilac on light blue underprint. Back: Large M at center.			
	a. 9 digit serial # with *F.*	20.00	40.00	80.00
	b. 9 digit serial # without *F.*	10.00	30.00	50.00
	c. 8 digit serial # with dash, with *F.*	300	900	1,750
	d. 8 digit serial # with dash, without *F.*	5.00	15.00	50.00
198	**1000 Mark** 1944. Green on light blue underprint. Back: Large M at center.	**VG**	**VF**	**UNC**
	a. 9 digit serial # with *F.*	250	500	900
	b. 8 digit serial # with dash, without *F.*	30.00	90.00	180
	c. 8 digil serial # with dash, with *F.*	2,000	4,000	7,000

THIRD REICH

Konversionskasse für Deutsche

Conversion Fund for German Foreign Debts

1933 Issue

		VG	VF	UNC
199	**5 Reichsmark** 28.8.1933. Black, green and brown.	50.00	100	200

		VG	VF	UNC
200	**10 Reichsmark** 28.8.1933. Black and lilac.	50.00	100	200
201	**30 Reichsmark** 28.8.1933. Black, red and brown.	100	200	400
202	**40 Reichsmark** 28.8.1933. Black, blue and brown.	150	375	675
203	**50 Reichsmark** 28.8.1933. Black, brown and blue.	100	200	335
204	**100 Reichsmark** 28.8.1933. Black, brown and green.	150	300	450
205	**500 Reichsmark** 28.8.1933.	—	—	—
206	**1000 Reichsmark** 28.8.1933.	—	—	—

1934 Issue

#207-214 overprint 2 red guilloches at left, the lower one containing the date 1934.

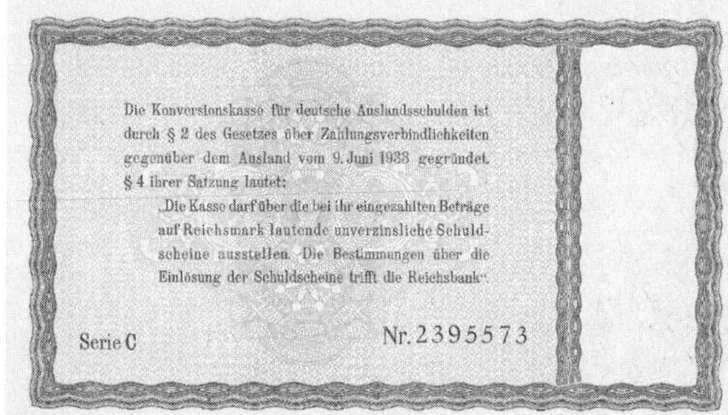

		VG	VF	UNC
207	**5 Reichsmark** 1934. Black, green and brown.	50.00	100	200

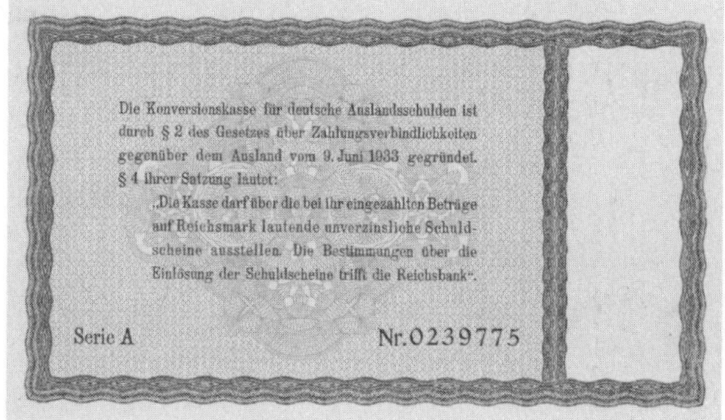

		VG	VF	UNC
208	**10 Reichsmark** 1934.	50.00	100	200

		VG	VF	UNC
209	**30 Reichsmark**	VG	VF	UNC
	1934.	125	290	400
210	**40 Reichsmark**	VG	VF	UNC
	1934.	125	290	475

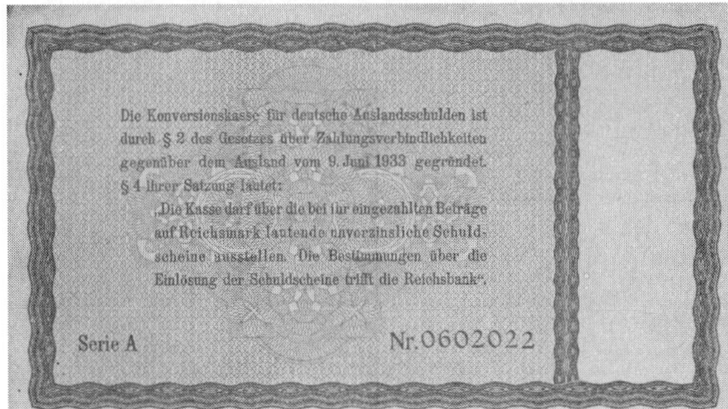

		VG	VF	UNC
211	**50 Reichsmark**	VG	VF	UNC
	1934.	50.00	130	350
212	**100 Reichsmark**	VG	VF	UNC
	1934.	60.00	280	350
213	**500 Reichsmark**	VG	VF	UNC
	1934.	—	—	—
214	**1000 Reichsmark**	VG	VF	UNC
	1934.	—	—	—

The German Democratic Republic (East Germany), located on the great north European plain, ceased to exist in 1990. During the closing days of World War II in Europe, Soviet troops advancing into Germany from the east occupied the German provinces of Mecklenburg, Brandenburg, Saxony-Anhalt, Saxony and Thuringia. These five provinces comprised the occupation zone administered by the Soviet Union after the cessation of hostilities. The other three zones were administered by the United States, Great Britain and France. Under the Potsdam agreement, questions affecting Germany as a whole were to be settled by the commanders in chief of the occupation zones acting jointly and by unanimous decision. When Soviet intransigence rendered the quadripartite commission inoperable, the three western zones were united to form the Federal Republic of Germany, May 23, 1949. Thereupon the Soviet Union dissolved its occupation zone and established it as the Democratic Republic of Germany, Oct. 7, 1949. East and West Germany became reunited as one country on Oct. 3, 1990.

MONETARY SYSTEM:

1 Mark = 100 Pfennig

SOVIET OCCUPATION - POST WW II

Treasury

1948 Currency Reform Issue

Introduction of the Deutsche Mark-Ost (East).

		VG	VF	UNC
1	**1 Deutsche Mark**	VG	VF	UNC
	1948 (- old date 30.1.1937). Blue adhesive stamp on Germany 1 Rentenmark #173. 120x65mm.	5.00	10.00	15.00

		VG	VF	UNC
2	**2 Deutsche Mark**	VG	VF	UNC
	1948 (- old date 30.1.1937). Green adhesive stamp on Germany 2 Rentenmark #174. 125x70mm.	8.00	12.50	20.00

		VG	VF	UNC
2A	**5 Deutsche Mark**	VG	VF	UNC
	1948 (-old date 2.1.1926). Brown adhesive stamp on Germany 5 Rentenmark #169. 133x74mm.	30.00	65.00	215

		VG	VF	UNC
3	**5 Deutsche Mark** 1948 (- old date 1.8.1942). Brown adhesive stamp on Germany 5 Reichsmark #186. 140x70mm.	8.00	12.50	25.00

		VG	VF	UNC
4	**10 Deutsche Mark** 1948 (- old date 22.1.1929). Lilac adhesive stamp. 150x75mm.			
	a. On Germany 10 Reichsmark #180a.	10.00	20.00	40.00
	b. On Germany 10 Reichsmark #180b.	10.00	20.00	40.00

		VG	VF	UNC
5	**20 Deutsche Mark** 1948 (- old dates 1929; 1939). Brown adhesive stamp. 160x80mm.			
	a. On Germany 20 Reichsmark #181a. (-old date 22.1.1929).	12.00	25.00	50.00
	b. On Germany 20 Reichsmark #181b. (-old date 22.1.1929).	12.00	25.00	50.00
5A	**20 Deutsche Mark** 1948 (-old date 16.6.1939). Brown adhesive stamp on Germany 20 Reichsmark #185. 160x80mm.	25.00	37.50	75.00

		VG	VF	UNC
6	**50 Deutsche Mark** 1948 (- old date 30.3.1933). Blue-gray adhesive stamp. 170x85mm.			
	a. On Germany 50 Reichsmark #182a.	10.00	20.00	40.00
	b. On Germany 50 Reichsmark #182b.	10.00	20.00	40.00

		VG	VF	UNC
7	**100 Deutsche Mark** 1948 (- old date 24.6.1935). Blue-green adhesive stamp. 180x90mm.			
	a. On Germany 100 Reichsmark #183a.	25.00	50.00	90.00
	b. On Germany 100 Reichsmark #183b.	30.00	50.00	95.00

Note: Germany #171, 172, 177 and 178 are also encountered with these adhesive stamps although they were not officially issued as such.

DEMOCRATIC REPUBLIC

Deutsche Notenbank

1948 Issue

#8a-13a printer: Goznak, Moscow, Russia.#8b-13b printer: East German.

		VG	VF	UNC
8	**50 Deutsche Pfennig** 1948. Blue on brown underprint. Without pictorial design. 100x65mm.			
	a. 6 digit serial #.	12.00	35.00	75.00
	b. 7 digit serial #.	6.00	10.00	15.00
	s. Specimen.	—	—	500

9	1 Deutsche Mark	VG	VF	UNC
	1948. Olive-brown on olive and brown underprint. Without pictorial design. 120x65mm.			
	a. 6 digit serial #.	10.00	20.00	85.00
	b. 7 digit serial #.	3.00	5.00	10.00
	s. Specimen.	—	—	500

10	2 Deutsche Mark	VG	VF	UNC
	1948. Brown on light brown and green underprint. Without pictorial design. 130x70mm.			
	a. 6 digit serial #.	5.00	10.00	85.00
	b. 7 digit serial #.	4.00	8.00	15.00
	s. Specimen.	—	—	420

11	5 Deutsche Mark	VG	VF	UNC
	1948. Dark brown on green and light brown underprint. Without pictorial design. 142x72mm.			
	a. 6 digit serial #, without plate #.	5.00	15.00	55.00
	b. 7 digit serial #, with plate #.	5.00	10.00	15.00
	s. Specimen.	—	—	200

12	10 Deutsche Mark	VG	VF	UNC
	1948. Black on green and light brown underprint. Without pictorial design. 150x75mm.			
	a. 6 digit serial #, without plate #.	15.00	35.00	70.00
	b. 7 digit serial #, with plate #.	4.00	8.00	12.00
	s. Specimen.	—	—	250

13	20 Deutsche Mark	VG	VF	UNC
	1948. Dark brown on red-brown and green underprint. Without pictorial design. 163x83mm.			
	a. 6 digit serial #, without plate #.	15.00	50.00	130
	b. 7 digit serial #, with plate #.	4.00	8.00	15.00
	s. Specimen.	—	—	240

14	50 Deutsche Mark	VG	VF	UNC
	1948. Green on brown underprint. Without pictorial design. 171x87mm.			
	a. Without plate #. Single letter prefix.	25.00	50.00	100
	b. With plate #. Double letter prefix.	5.00	10.00	15.00
	s. Specimen.	—	—	210

15	100 Deutsche Mark	VG	VF	UNC
	1948. Blue on green and light brown underprint. Without pictorial design. 180x90mm.			
	a. Issued note.	10.00	25.00	75.00
	s. Specimen.	—	—	140

16	1000 Deutsche Mark	VG	VF	UNC
	1948. Brown on green and light brown underprint. Without pictorial design. 191x97mm.			
	a. Issued note.	15.00	35.00	85.00
	s. Specimen.	—	—	350

1955 Issue

		VG	VF	UNC
17	**5 Deutsche Mark** 1955. Gray and black on brown and red-brown underprint. Without pictorial design. 142x73mm.	5.00	10.00	35.00

		VG	VF	UNC
18	**10 Deutsche Mark** 1955. Light purple on olive and dark orange underprint. Without pictorial design. 147x75mm.			
	a. Issued note.	8.00	15.00	30.00
	s. Specimen overprint: *MUSTER*.	—	—	100

		VG	VF	UNC
19	**20 Deutsche Mark** 1955. Dark blue on tan and red-brown underprint. Without pictorial design, like #13. 162x82mm.			
	a. Issued note.	10.00	15.00	25.00
	s. Specimen overprint: *MUSTER*.	—	—	100

		VG	VF	UNC
20	**50 Deutsche Mark** 1955. Dark red on orange and light green underprint. Without pictorial design, like #14. 171x86mm.			
	a. Issued note.	5.00	9.00	20.00
	s. Specimen overprint: *MUSTER*.	—	—	100

		VG	VF	UNC
21	**100 Deutsche Mark** 1955. Brown on light blue, green and pink underprint. Without pictorial design, like #15. 180x90mm.	12.00	20.00	30.00

The Federal Republic of Germany (formerly West Germany), located in north-central Europe, since 1990 with the unification of East Germany, has an area of 137,782 sq. mi. (356,854 sq. km.) and a population of 82.69 million. Capital: Berlin. The economy centers about one of the world's foremost industrial establishments. Machinery, motor vehicles, iron, steel, chemicals, yarns and fabrics are exported. During the post-Normandy phase of World War II, Allied troops occupied the western German provinces of Schleswig-Holstein, Hamburg, Lower Saxony, Bremen, North Rhine-Westphalia, Hesse, Rhineland-Palatinate, Baden-Wurttemberg, Bavaria and Saarland. The conquered provinces were divided into American, British and French occupation zones. Five eastern German provinces were occupied and administered by the forces of the Soviet Union. The western occupation forces restored the civil status of their zones on Sept. 21, 1949, and resumed diplomatic relations with the provinces on July 2, 1951. On May 5, 1955, nine of the ten western provinces, organized as the Federal Republic of Germany, became fully independent. The tenth province, Saarland, was restored to the republic on Jan. 1, 1957. The post-WW II division of Germany ended on Oct. 3, 1990, when the German Democratic Republic (East Germany) ceased to exist and its five constituent provinces were formally admitted to the Federal Republic of Germany. An election Dec. 2, 1990, chose representatives to the united federal parliament (Bundestag), which then conducted its opening session in Berlin in the old Reichstag building.

MONETARY SYSTEM:

1 Deutsche Mark (DM) = 100 Pfennig, 1948-2001
1 Euro = 100 Cents, 2002-

ALLIED OCCUPATION - POST WW II

U.S. Army Command

1948 First Issue

#1-10 were issued under military authority and w/o name of country. #1-10, also #13-17 may come with stamped: *B* in circle, perforated: *B* or with both varieties on the same note. These markings were made as a temporary check on currency circulating in West Berlin.

#	Denomination	VG	VF	UNC
1	**1/2 Deutsche Mark** 1948. Green on light green and light brown underprint. Printer: Forbes Litho (without imprint). 112x67mm.			
	a. Issued note.	10.00	45.00	175
	b. Stamped: *B* in circle.	10.00	55.00	225
	c. Perforated: *B*.	40.00	80.00	420
	d. Stamped and perforated: *B* on the same note.	40.00	200	600
	s1. As a. perforated: *SPECIMEN*.	—	—	250
	s2. Specimen with red overprint: *MUSTER*.	—	—	250

#	Denomination	VG	VF	UNC
2	**1 Deutsche Mark** 1948. Blue on blue-green and lilac underprint. Printer: Forbes Litho (without imprint). 112x67mm.			
	a. Issued note.	10.00	40.00	155
	b. Stamped: *B* in circle.	12.50	55.00	210
	c. Perforated: *B*.	25.00	100	350
	d. Stamped and perforated: *B* on the same note.	40.00	145	525
	s1. As a. perforated: *SPECIMEN*.	—	—	250
	s2. Specimen with red overprint: *MUSTER*.	—	—	250

#	Denomination	VG	VF	UNC
3	**2 Deutsche Mark** 1948. Lilac on blue-green underprint. Allegorical woman seated at left holding tablet. Printer: Tudor Press, Boston, Mass. U.S.A. (Without imprint). 112x67mm.			
	a. Issued note.	100	250	600
	b. Stamped: *B* in circle.	100	250	600
	c. Perforated: *B*.	50.00	300	1,400
	d. Stamped and perforated: *B* on the same note.	75.00	300	1,450
	s1. As a. perforated: *SPECIMEN*.	—	—	300
	s2. Specimen with red overprint: *MUSTER*.	—	—	300

#	Denomination	VG	VF	UNC
4	**5 Deutsche Mark** 1948. Brown on green and gold underprint. Man seated at right. Printer: Tudor Press, Boston, Mass. U.S.A. (Without imprint). 112x67mm.			
	a. Issued note.	50.00	200	625
	b. Stamped: *B* in circle.	75.00	275	625
	c. Perforated: *B*.	85.00	350	1,000
	d. Stamped and perforated: *B* on the same note.	100	450	1,250
	s1. As a. perforated: *SPECIMEN*	—	—	250
	s2. Specimen with 44mm red overprint: *MUSTER*.	—	—	250
	s3. Specimen with 54mm red overprint: *MUSTER*.	—	—	250

#	Denomination	VG	VF	UNC
5	**10 Deutsche Mark** 1948. Blue on multicolor underprint. Allegorical figures of 2 women and a man at center. Printer: ABNC. (Without imprint). 140x67mm.			
	a. Issued note.	35.00	135	500
	b. Handstamped: *B* in circle.	35.00	145	600
	c. Perforated: *B*.	50.00	225	750
	d. Handstamped and perforated: *B* on the same note.	75.00	275	1,000
	s1. As a. perforated: *SPECIMEN*.	—	—	250
	s2. Specimen with red overprint: *MUSTER*.	—	—	250
	s3. As s2. perforated *SPECIMEN*.	—	—	250

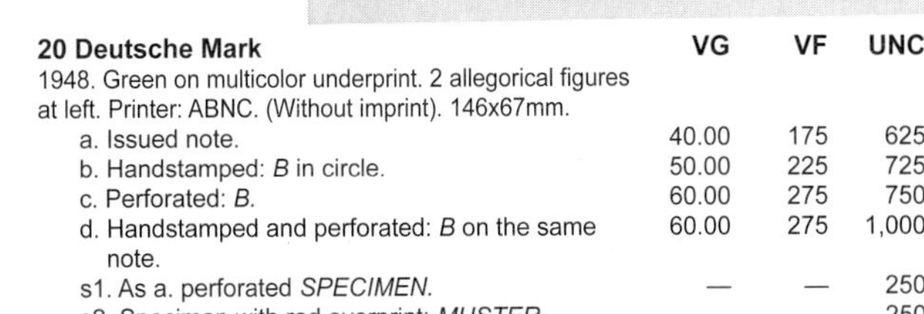

#	Denomination	VG	VF	UNC
6	**20 Deutsche Mark** 1948. Green on multicolor underprint. 2 allegorical figures at left. Printer: ABNC. (Without imprint). 146x67mm.			
	a. Issued note.	40.00	175	625
	b. Handstamped: *B* in circle.	50.00	225	725
	c. Perforated: *B*.	60.00	275	750
	d. Handstamped and perforated: *B* on the same note.	60.00	275	1,000
	s1. As a. perforated *SPECIMEN*.	—	—	250
	s2. Speciman with red overprint: *MUSTER*.	—	—	250

#	Denomination	VG	VF	UNC
7	**50 Deutsche Mark** 1948. Purple on multicolor underprint. Allegorical woman at center. Printer: ABNC. (Without imprint). 151x67mm.			
	a. Issued note.	35.00	150	1,650
	b. Handstamped: *B* in circle.	50.00	250	2,250
	c. Perforated: *B*.	100	450	2,350
	d. Handstamped and perforated: *B* on the same note.	175	750	2,500
	s1. Specimen with red overprint: *MUSTER*.	—	—	250

#	Denomination	VG	VF	UNC
8	**100 Deutsche Mark** 1948. Red on multicolor underprint. Allegorical woman with globe at center. Printer: ABNC. (Without imprint). 156x67mm.			
	a. Issued note.	350	1,450	3,750
	b. Handstamped: *B* in circle.	500	2,000	5,000
	c. Perforated: *B*.	650	2,700	5,500
	d. Handstamped and perforated: *B* on the same note.	850	3,750	6,250
	s1. As d. perforated *SPECIMEN*.	—	—	300
	s2. Specimen with red overprint: *MUSTER* perforated *SPECIMEN*.	—	—	300

1948 ND Second Issue

#	Denomination	VG	VF	UNC
9	**20 Deutsche Mark** ND (1948). Blue on blue-green and orange underprint. Medallic woman's head at left. Printer: Tudor Press, Boston Mass. U.S.A. (without imprint) 156x67mm.			
	a. Issued note.	300	800	1,750
	b. Handstamped: *B* in circle.	400	1,000	2,000
	c. Perforated: *B*.	450	1,350	2,500
	d. Handstamped and perforated: *B* on the same note.	250	1,500	3,000
	s1. As a. perforated *SPECIMEN*.	—	—	200
	s2. Specimen with red overprint: *MUSTER*.	—	—	200
	s3. As s2. perforated: *SPECIMEN*.	—	—	200
10	**50 Deutsche Mark** ND (1948). Green-blue. Allegorical woman's head at center. Printer: Tudor Press, Boston Mass. U.S.A. (without imprint) 156x67mm.			
	a. Issued note.	2,000	5,500	7,000
	b. Handstamped: *B* in circle. Rare.	—	—	—
	s1. Specimen.	—	—	1,000
	s2. Specimen with red overprint: *MUSTER*.	—	—	1,000
	s3. Specimen perforated: *B*. Rare.	—	—	—

Note: #10 was in circulation for only a very few days.

Bank Deutscher Länder

1948 Issue

#	Denomination	VG	VF	UNC
11	**5 Pfennig** ND (1948). Green on lilac underprint. 60x40mm.			
	a. Issued note.	5.00	10.00	25.00
	s. Specimen with red overprint: *MUSTER*.	—	—	60.00

#	Denomination	VG	VF	UNC
12	**10 Pfennig** ND (1948). Blue on brown underprint. Back brown. 60x40mm.			
	a. Issued note.	5.00	10.00	25.00
	s. Specimen with red overprint: *MUSTER*.	—	—	60.00

#	Denomination	VG	VF	UNC
13	**5 Deutsche Mark** 9.12.1948. Black on green and yellow underprint. Woman (Europa) on the bull at right. Watermark: Woman's head. 120x60mm.			
	a. Single series letter. Printer: TDLR (without imprint).	50.00	200	1,250
	b. As a. handstamped *B* in circle.	125	550	1,300
	c. As a. perforated *B*.	50.00	250	900
	d. As a. handstamped and perforated *B* on same note.	90.00	250	1,000
	e. Number with series letter in front of serial #.	35.00	180	900
	f. As e. handstamped *B* in circle.	50.00	200	1,250
	g. As e. perforated *B*.	15.00	75.00	275
	h. As e. handstamped and perforated *B* on same note.	25.00	90.00	300
	i. Number with series letter 7A-(?). Printer: BDK (without imprint).	50.00	170	425
	s1. Series letter A with red overprint: *SPECIMEN* perforated *SPECIMEN*.	—	—	200
	s2. Series letter 7A with red overprint: *MUSTER* on face and back.	—	—	200

#	Denomination	VG	VF	UNC
14	**50 Deutsche Mark** 9.12.1948. Brown and black on yellow-green underprint. Merchant Hans Imhof by Albrecht Dürer at right. Back: Imhof at left, men with ship at right. Watermark: Hans Imhof Printer: Banque de France 150x75mm.			
	a. Issued note.	50.00	100	300
	b. Handstamped: *B* in circle.	150	300	500
	s. Specimen with red overprint: *MUSTER*.	—	—	300

15	100 Deutsche Mark	VG	VF	UNC
	9.12.1948. Black and brown on blue underprint. Councillor Jakob Muffel by Albrecht Dürer at right. Back: Muffel at left, old city view of Nürnberg at center. Watermark: Jakob Muffel Printer: Banque de France 160x80mm.			
	a. Issued note.	100	225	425
	b. Stamped: *B* in circle.	200	425	900
	s1. Specimen with 89mm red overprint: *MUSTER.*	—	—	250
	s2. Specimen with 99mm red overprint: *MUSTER.*	—	—	250

1949 Issue

16	10 Deutsche Mark	VG	VF	UNC
	22.8.1949. Blue. Allegorical figures of 2 women and a man at center. With bank name. Printer: ABNC. (Without imprint). 141x67mm.			
	a. Issued note.	17.50	45.00	90.00
	b. Stamped: *B* in circle.	50.00	180	420
	s1. As a. with red overprint: *MUSTER.*	—	—	200
	s2. As s1. perforated *SPECIMEN.*	—	—	200

17	20 Deutsche Mark	VG	VF	UNC
	22.8.1949. Green. 2 allegorical figures at left. With bank name. Printer: ABNC. (Without imprint). 146x67mm.			
	a. Issued note.	55.00	115	325
	b. Handstamped: *B* in circle.	100	250	600
	s1. As a. perforated: *SPECIMEN.*	—	—	200
	s2. As s1. with red overprint: *MUSTER.*	—	—	200

FEDERAL REPUBLIC

Deutsche Bundesbank

1960 Issue

#18-24 Replacement notes: Serial # prefix *Y, Z.* #18-22 with or without ultraviolet sensitive features.

18	5 Deutsche Mark	VG	VF	UNC
	2.1.1960. Green on multicolor underprint. *Young Venetian Woman* by Albrecht Dürer (1505) at right. Back: Oak sprig at left center. Watermark: Young Venetian woman. 120x60mm.			
	a. Issued note.	5.00	10.00	20.00
	s. Specimen.	—	—	150

19	10 Deutsche Mark	VG	VF	UNC
	2.1.1960. Blue on multicolor underprint. *Young Man* by Albrecht Dürer at right. Back: Sail training ship *Gorch Fock.* Watermark: Young man. 130x65mm.			
	a. Issued note.	8.00	15.00	50.00
	s. Specimen.	—	—	150

20	20 Deutsche Mark	VG	VF	UNC
	2.1.1960. Black and green on multicolor underprint. *Elsbeth Tucher* by Albrecht Dürer (1499) at right. Back: Violin, bow and clarinet. Watermark: Elsbeth Tucher. 140x70mm.			
	a. Issued note.	25.00	65.00	100
	s. Specimen.	—	—	150

21	50 Deutsche Mark	VG	VF	UNC
	2.1.1960. Brown and olive-green on multicolor underprint. *Hans Urmiller* by Barthel Beham (about 1525) at right. Back: Holsten-Tor gate in Lübeck. Watermark: Hans Urmiller. 150x75mm.			
	a. Issued note.	30.00	60.00	140
	s. Specimen.	—	—	150

22	100 Deutsche Mark	VG	VF	UNC
	2.1.1960. Blue on multicolor underprint. *Master Sebastian Münster* by Christoph Amberger (1552) at right. Back: Eagle. Watermark: Sebastian Münster. 160x80mm.			
	a. Issued note.	60.00	125	250
	s. Specimen.	—	—	250

23	500 Deutsche Mark	VG	VF	UNC
	2.1.1960. Brown-lilac on multicolor underprint. Male portrait by Hans Maler zu Schwaz. Back: Eltz Castle. Watermark: Male portrait. 170x85mm.			
	a. Issued note.	300	750	1,500
	s. Specimen.	—	—	800

24	1000 Deutsche Mark	VG	VF	UNC
	2.1.1960. Dark brown on multicolor underprint. Astronomer Johann Schöner by Lucas Cranach the Elder (1529) at right. Back: Cathedral of Limburg on the Lahn. Watermark: Johan Schöner. 180x90mm.			
	a. Issued note.	500	1,250	2,000
	s. Specimen.	—	—	1,200

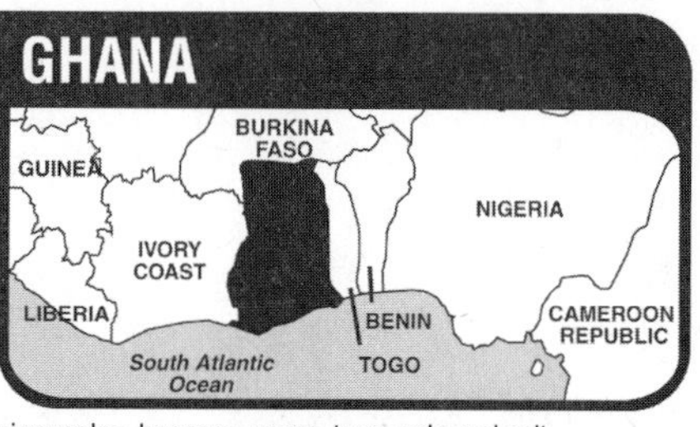

The Republic of Ghana, a member of the British Commonwealth situated on the West Coast of Africa between the Ivory Coast and Togo, has an area of 239,460 sq. km. and a population of 23,38 million, almost entirely African. Capital: Accra. Traditional exports include cocoa, coffee, timber, gold, industrial diamonds, maganese and bauxite. Additional exports include pineapples, bananas, yams, tuna, cola and salt.

Formed from the merger of the British colony of the Gold Coast and the Togoland trust territory, Ghana in 1957 became the first sub-Saharan country in colonial Africa to gain its independence. Ghana endured a long series of coups before Lt. Jerry Rawlings took power in 1981 and banned political parties. After approving a new constitution and restoring multiparty politics in 1992, Rawlings won presidential elections in 1992 and 1996, but was constitutionally prevented from running for a third term in 2000. John Kufuor succeeded him and was reelected in 2004. Kufuor is constitutionally barred from running for a third term in upcoming Presidential elections, which are scheduled for December 2008.

Ghana's monetary denomination of "cedi" is derived from the word "sedie" meaning cowrie, a shell money commonly employed by coastal tribes.

MONETARY SYSTEM:

1 Shilling = 12 Pence
1 Pound = 20 Shillings to 1965
1 Cedi = 100 Pesewas, 1965-

REPUBLIC

Bank of Ghana

1958-1963 Issue

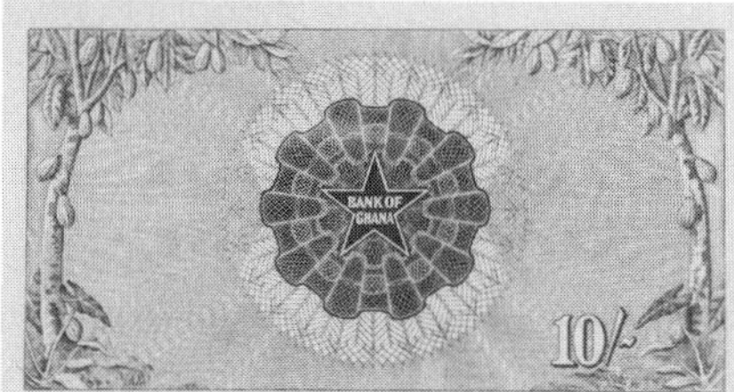

1	10 Shillings	VG	VF	UNC
	1958-1963. Green and brown on multicolor underprint. Bank of Ghana building in Accra at center right. Back: Star. Watermark: *GHANA* in star.			
	a. 1.7.1958. 2 signatures. Printer: TDLR.	6.00	30.00	90.00
	b. 1.7.1961. Without imprint.	4.00	22.50	70.00
	c. 1.7.1962. Without imprint.	7.00	35.00	100
	d. 1.7.1963. 1 signature.	1.75	15.00	50.00
	s. As a. Specimen.	—	—	200

2 **1 Pound**

1958-1962. Red-brown and blue on multicolor underprint. Bank of Ghana building in Accra at center. Back: Cocoa pods in two heaps. Watermark: *GHANA* in star.

	VG	VF	UNC
a. 1.7.1958. Printer: TDLR.	4.75	18.00	60.00
b. 1.4.1959. Printer. TDLR.	3.75	15.00	45.00
c. 1.7.1961. Without imprint.	5.00	12.50	45.00
d. 1.7.1962. Without imprint.	3.00	8.00	25.00
s. As a. Specimen.	—	—	75.00

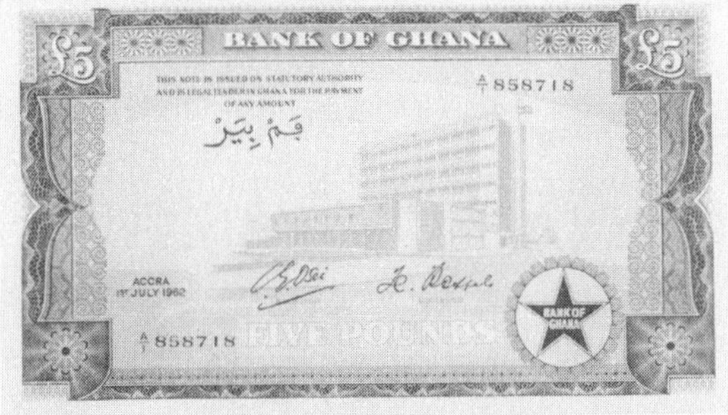

3 **5 Pounds**

1.7.1958-1.7.1962. Purple and orange on multicolor underprint. Bank of Ghana building in Accra at center. Back: Cargo ships, logs in water. Watermark: *GHANA* in star.

	VG	VF	UNC
a. 1.7.1958.	25.00	75.00	250
b. 1.4.1959.	22.50	60.00	225
c. 1.7.1961.	17.50	50.00	200
d. 1.7.1962.	7.50	20.00	70.00
s1. Specimen. 1.7.1958.	—	—	225
s2. Specimen. Perforated: *CANCELLED.*	—	—	350

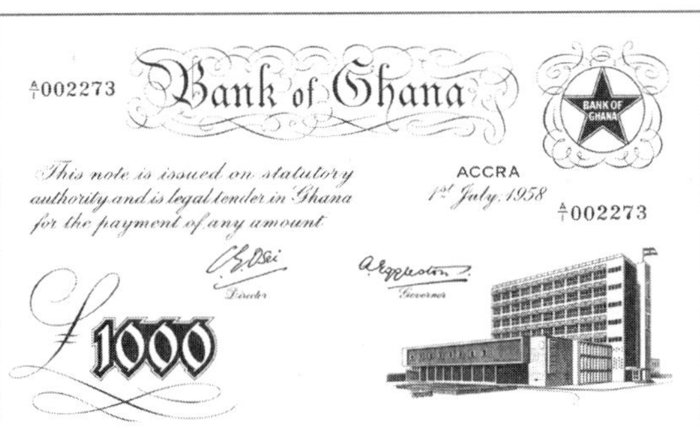

4 **1000 Pounds**

1.7.1958. Blackish brown. Bank of Ghana building in Accra at lower right. Back: Ornate design. Watermark: *GHANA* in star. Used in interbank transactions only.

VG	VF	UNC
—	150	500

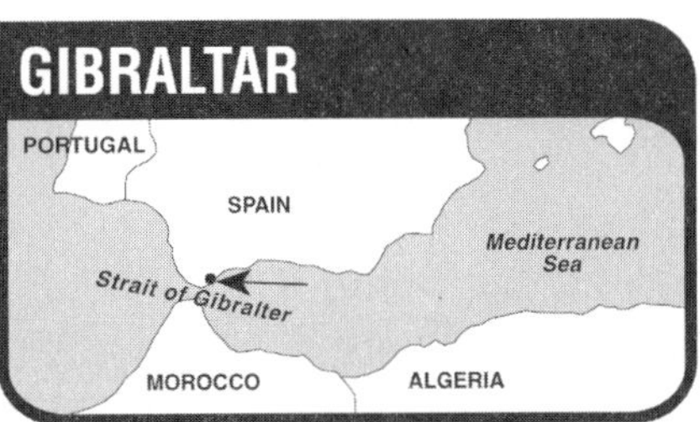

The British Colony of Gibraltar, located at the southernmost point of the Iberian Peninsula, has an area of 6.5 sq. km. and a population of 28,000. Capital (and only town): Gibraltar.

Strategically important, Gibraltar was reluctantly ceded to Great Britain by Spain in the 1713 Treaty of Utrecht; the British garrison was formally declared a colony in 1830. In a referendum held in 1967, Gibraltarians voted overwhelmingly to remain a British dependency. The subsequent granting of autonomy in 1969 by the UK led to Spain closing the border and severing all communication links. A series of talks were held by the UK and Spain between 1997 and 2002 on establishing temporary joint sovereignty over Gibraltar. In response to these talks, the Gibraltar Government called a referendum in late 2002 in which the majority of citizens voted overwhelmingly against any sharing of sovereignty with Spain. Since the referendum, tripartite talks on other issues have been held with Spain, the UK, and Gibraltar, and in September 2006 a three-way agreement was signed. Spain agreed to remove restrictions on air movements, to speed up customs procedures, to implement international telephone dialing, and to allow mobile roaming agreements. Britain agreed to pay increased pensions to Spaniards who had been employed in Gibraltar before the border closed. Spain will be allowed to open a cultural institute from which the Spanish flag will fly. A new noncolonial constitution came into effect in 2007, but the UK retains responsibility for defense, foreign relations, internal security, and financial stability.

RULERS:

British

MONETARY SYSTEM:

1 Shilling = 12 Pence
1 Pound = 20 Shillings to 1971
1 Pound = 100 New Pence, 1971-

BRITISH ADMINISTRATION

Government of Gibraltar

1914 Emergency WW I Series A

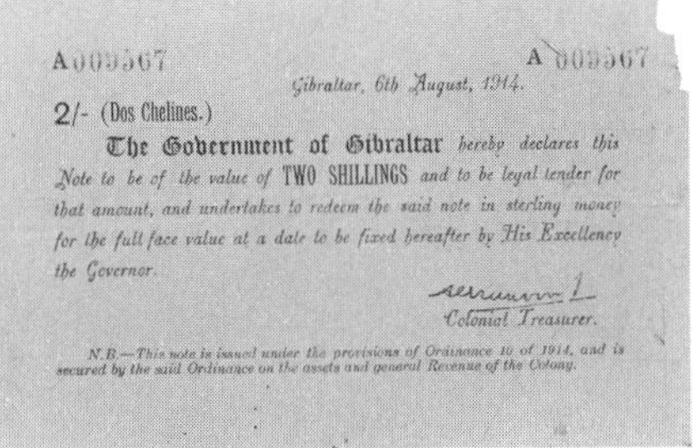

No.	Denomination	Good	Fine	XF
1	**2 Shillings = 2 Chelines** 6.8.1914. Red. Embossed stamp of the *Anglo-Egyptian Bank, Ltd., Gibraltar.* Typeset.	425	1,500	—
2	**10 Shillings = 10 Chelines** 6.8.1914. Blue. Embossed stamp of the *Anglo-Egyptian Bank, Ltd., Gibraltar.* Typeset.	850	2,500	—
3	**1 Pound = 1 Libra** 6.8.1914. Black. Embossed stamp of the *Anglo-Egyptian Bank, Ltd., Gibraltar.* Typeset. PC: Yellow.	1,250	3,750	—
4	**5 Pounds = 5 Libras** 6.8.1914. Black. Embossed stamp of the *Anglo-Egyptian Bank, Ltd., Gibraltar.* Typeset. Rare. PC: Blue.	—	—	—
5	**50 Pounds = 50 Libras** 6.8.1914. Black. Embossed stamp of the *Anglo-Egyptian Bank, Ltd., Gibraltar.* Typeset. Rare. PC: Blue.	—	—	—

1914 Series B

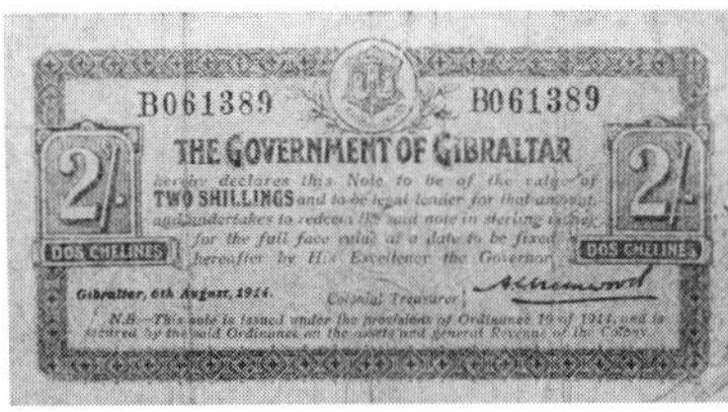

No.	Denomination	Good	Fine	XF
6	**2 Shillings = 2 Chelines** 6.8.1914. Green on pink. Arms at top center.	100	250	750

Color Abbreviation Guide

New to the *Standard Catalog of® World Paper Money* are the following abbreviations related to color references:

BC: Back color
PC: Paper color

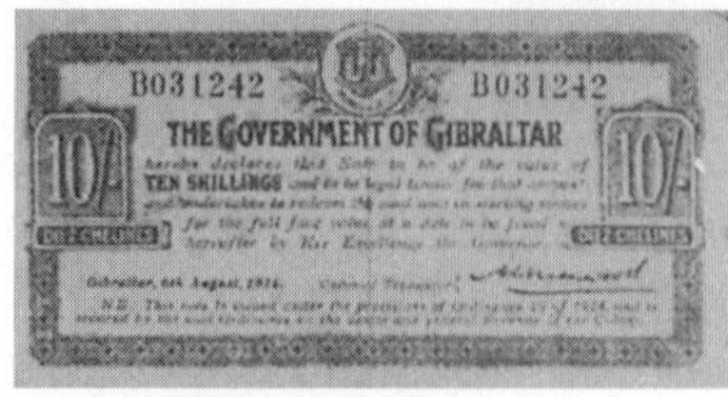

No.	Description	Good	Fine	XF
7	**10 Shillings = 10 Chelines** 6.8.1914. Lilac on pink.	200	650	—
8	**1 Pound = 1 Libra** 6.8.1914. Blue on green.	275	1,000	—
9	**5 Pounds = 5 Libras** 6.8.1914. Rare. Brown on green.	—	—	—
10	**50 Pounds = 50 Libras** 6.8.1914. Rare. Pink on green.	—	—	—

1927 Ordinance, Regular Issue

No.	Description	VG	VF	UNC
11	**10 Shillings** 1.10.1927. Blue on yellow-brown underprint. Rock of Gibraltar at upper left. Back: Arms at center. Printer: W&S.	30.00	125	600
12	**1 Pound** 1.10.1927. Green on yellow-brown underprint. Rock of Gibraltar at bottom center. Back: Arms at center. Printer: W&S.	30.00	125	600
13	**5 Pounds** 1.10.1927. Brown. Rock of Gibraltar at bottom center. Back: Arms at center. Printer: W&S.	60.00	300	—

1934 Ordinance, 1938-1942 Issue

No.	Description	VG	VF	UNC
14	**10 Shillings** 1937-1958. Blue on yellow-brown underprint. Rock of Gibraltar at upper left. 2 serial # varieties and 4 signature varieties. Back: Arms at center. Printer: W&S.			
	a. Signature title: *TREASURER.* 1.2.1937.	15.00	75.00	450
	b. Signature title: *FINANCIAL SECRETARY.* 1.6.1942; 1.7.1954; 3.10.1958.	5.00	25.00	200
	c. As b. 1.7.1954. with security thread.	5.00	25.00	200

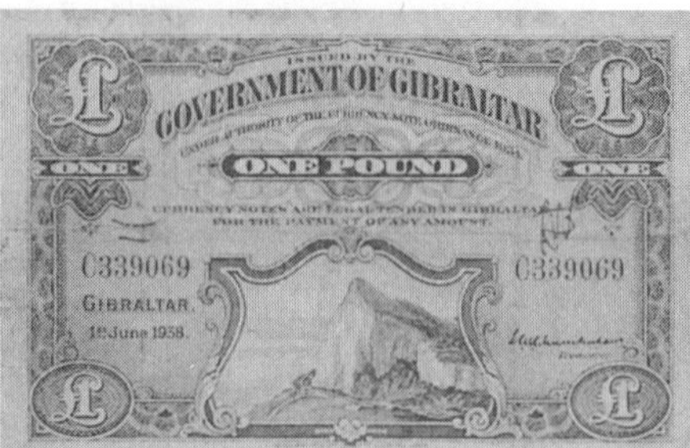

No.	Description	VG	VF	UNC
15	**1 Pound** 1938-1958. Green on yellow-brown underprint. Rock of Gibraltar at bottom center. 2 serial varieties and 5 signature varieties. Back: Arms at center. Printer: W&S.			
	a. Signature title: *TREASURER.* 1.6.1938.	25.00	100	600
	b. Signature title: *FINANCIAL SECRETARY.* 1.6.1942; 1.12.1949.	5.00	25.00	200
	c. As b. 1.7.1954; 3.10.1958.	3.00	15.00	150
16	**5 Pounds** 1942-1958. Brown. Rock of Gilbraltar at bottom center. 2 serial # varieties and 4 signature varieties. Back: Arms at center. Printer: W&S.			
	a. 1.6.1942.	20.00	90.00	500
	b. 1.12.1949.	15.00	70.00	450
	c. 1.7.1954; 3.10.1958.	12.50	60.00	425

1934 Ordinance; 1958 Issue

No.	Description	VG	VF	UNC
17	**10 Shillings** 3.10.1958; 1.5.1965. Blue on yellow-brown underprint. Rock of Gilbraltar at left. Back: Arms at center. Printer: TDLR.	20.00	100	380

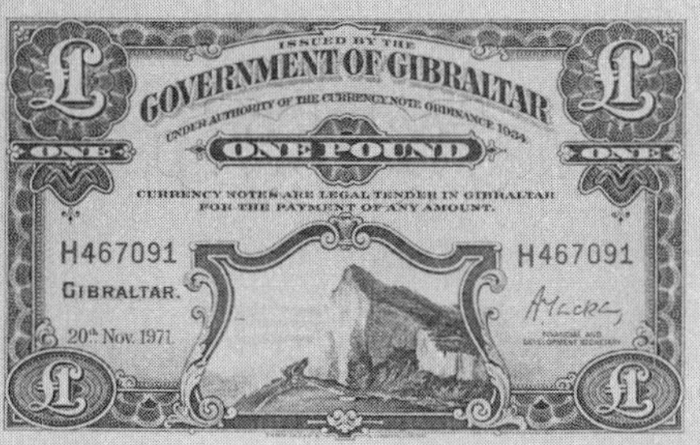

No.	Description	VG	VF	UNC
18	**1 Pound** 1958-1975. Green on yellow-brown underprint. Rock of Gibraltar at bottom center. Back: Arms at center. Printer: TDLR.			
	a. Signature title: *FINANCIAL SECRETARY.* 3.10.1958; 1.5.1965.	6.00	27.50	150
	b. Signature title: *FINANCIAL AND DEVELOPMENT SECRETARY.* 20.11.1971.	5.00	22.50	115
	c. 20.11.1975.	10.00	45.00	230
	s. Specimen. As a-c.	—	—	—

No.	Description	VG	VF	UNC
19	**5 Pounds** 1958-1975. Brown. Rock of Gibraltar at bottom center. Back: Arms at center. Printer: TDLR.			
	a. Signature title: *FINANCIAL SECRETARY.* 3.10.1958; 1.5.1965.	35.00	155	800
	b. Signature title: *FINANCIAL AND DEVELOPMENT SECRETARY.* 1.5.1965; 20.11.1971; 20.11.1975.	30.00	120	640
	s. Specimen. As a-b.	—	—	—

The Gilbert and Ellice Islands comprised a British colony made up of 40 atolls and islands in the western Pacific Ocean. The colony consisted of the Gilbert Islands, the Ellice Islands, Ocean Island, Fanning, Washington and Christmas Island in the Line Islands, and the Phoenix Islands. The principal industries were copra production and phosphate mining. Early inhabitants were Melanesian but the Ellice Islands were occupied in the 16th century by the Samoans, who established the Polynesian culture there. The first Europeans to land in the islands came in 1764. James Cook visited in 1777. Britain declared a protectorate over the islands in 1892 and made it a colony in 1915. In World War II the Gilberts were occupied by the Japanese from Dec. 1941 to Nov. 1943. The colony adopted a new constitution and became self-governing in 1971. The Ellice Islands became Tuvalu in 1976 with independence in 1978. The balance of the colony became Kiribati in 1979. Australian currency is currently used in circulation.

RULERS:

British until 1978-1979

MONETARY SYSTEM:

1 Pound = 20 Shillings
1 Shilling = 12 Pence

BRITISH ADMINISTRATION

Gilbert and Ellice Islands Colony

1942 Emergency WWII Issue

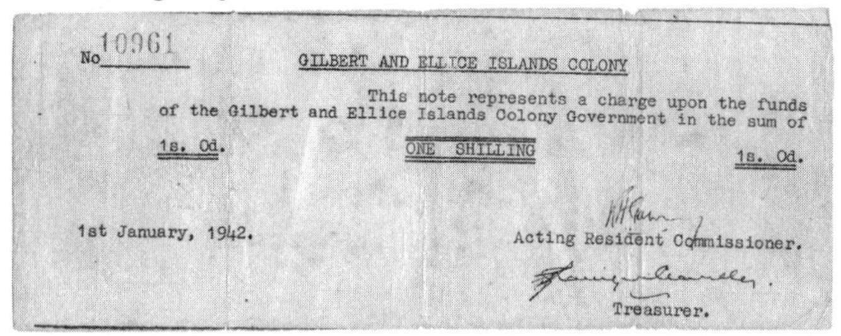

#	Denomination	Good	Fine	XF
1	**1 Shilling** 1.1.1942. Made by mimeograph process. Embossed seal: *COURT OF H.B.M. HIGH COMMISSIONER FOR WESTERN PACIFIC* at left. Uniface. PC: White.	5,000	14,000	—
2	**2 Shillings** 1.1.1942. Made by mimeograph process. Embossed seal: *COURT OF H.B.M. HIGH COMMISSIONER FOR WESTERN PACIFIC* at left. Uniface.	5,000	14,000	—
4	**10 Shillings** 1.1.1942. Made by mimeograph process. Embossed seal: *COURT OF H.B.M. HIGH COMMISSIONER FOR WESTERN PACIFIC* at left. Uniface.	5,000	14,000	—

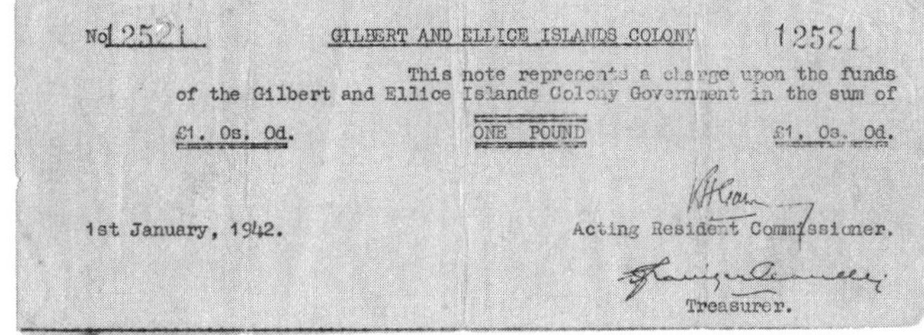

#	Denomination	Good	Fine	XF
5	**1 Pound** 1.1.1942. Made by mimeograph process. Embossed seal: *COURT OF H.B.M. HIGH COMMISSIONER FOR WESTERN PACIFIC* at left. Uniface. PC: Pink.	5,000	14,000	—

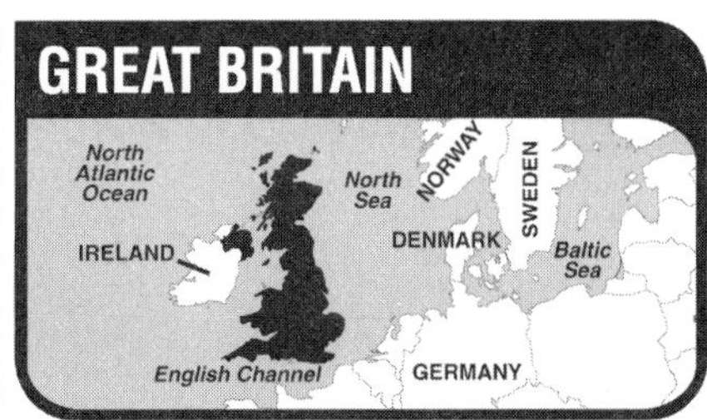

The United Kingdom of Great Britain and Northern Ireland, (including England, Scotland, Wales and Northern Ireland) is located off the northwest coast of the European continent, has an area of 94,227 sq. mi. (244,046 sq. km.), and a population of 59.45 million. Capital: London. The economy is based on industrial activity, trading and financial services. Machinery, motor vehicles, chemicals and textile yarns and fabrics are exported. After the departure of the Romans, who brought Britain into an active relationship with Europe, Britain fell prey to invaders from Scandinavia and the Low Countries who drove the original Britons into Scotland and Wales, and established a profusion of kingdoms that finally united in the 11th century under the Danish King Canute. Norman rule, following the conquest of 1066, stimulated the development of those institutions which have since distinguished British life. Henry VIII (1509-47) turned Britain from continental adventuring and faced it to the sea - a decision that made Britain a world power during the reign of Elizabeth I (1558-1603). Strengthened by the Industrial Revolution and the defeat of Napoleon, 19th century Britain turned to the remote parts of the world and established a colonial empire of such extent and prosperity that the world has never seen its like. World Wars I and II sealed the fate of the Empire and relegated Britain to a lesser role in world affairs by draining her resources and inaugurating a worldwide movement toward national self-determination in her former colonies. By the mid-20th century, most of the former British Empire had gained independence and had evolved into the Commonwealth of Nations. This association of equal and and autonomous states, set out to agree views and special relationships with one another (appointing High Commissioners rather than Ambassadors) for mutual benefit, trade interests, etc. The Commonwealth is presently (1999) composed of 54 member nations, including the United Kingdom. All recognize the monarch as Head of the Commonwealth; 16 continue to recognize Queen Elizabeth II as Head of State. In addition to the United Kingdom, they are: Antigua & Barbuda, Australia, The Bahamas, Barbados Belize, Canada, Grenada, Paupa New Guinea, St. Christopher & Nevis, St. Lucia, St. Vincent & the Grenadines, Solomon Islands.

RULERS:

William III, 1694-1702
Anne, 1702-1714
George I, 1714-1727
George II, 1727-1760
George III, 1760-1820
George IV, 1820-1830
William IV, 1830-1837
Victoria, 1837-1901
Edward VII, 1901-1910
George V, 1910-1936
Edward VIII, 1936
George VI, 1936-1952
Elizabeth II, 1952-

MONETARY SYSTEM:

1 Shilling = 12 Pence
1 Pound = 20 Shillings to 1971
1 Pound = 100 (New) Pence, 1971-

REPLACEMENT NOTES:

#368, ##A series prefix. #369, S-S or S-T, #373-376, letter M as one of the letters in series prefix. #377-380, Page sign. only, M## or ##M series p refix.

KINGDOM

Bank of England

Founded in 1694, the earliest recorded notes were all handwritten promissory notes and certificates of deposit. The first partially printed notes were introduced ca. 1696 with handwritten amounts. By 1745 all notes were printed with partial denominations of round figures in denominations of 20 Pounds through 1000 Pounds, allowing handwritten denominations of shillings to be added on. In 1759 the word *POUNDS* was also printed on the notes. From 1752 the Chief Cashier's handwritten name as payee is usually found and from 1782 it was used exclusively. From 1798 until 1855 it was actually printed on the notes. In 1855 notes were produced made simply payable to *bearer. For specialized listings of Bank of England notes refer to English Paper Money,* by Vincent Duggleby; published by Pam West, www.westbanknotes.co.uk.

1694-1695 Issue

#	Denomination	Good	Fine	XF
25	**5 Pounds** 1695-1699. Black. Handwritten signature of Thomas Speed.			
	a. 1695-1697. Without watermark in paper.	—	—	—
	b. 1697-1699. With watermark in paper. Rare.	—	—	—
26	**10 Pounds** 1694-1699. Black. Handwritten signature of Thomas Speed. Rare.	—	—	—
27	**20 Pounds** 1694-1699. Black. Handwritten signature of Thomas Speed. Rare.	—	—	—
28	**50 Pounds** 1694-1699. Black. Handwritten signature of Thomas Speed. Rare.	—	—	—
29	**100 Pounds** 1694-1699. Black. Handwritten signature of Thomas Speed. Rare.	—	—	—

1699 Issue

No.	Denomination	Good	Fine	XF
35	**5 Pounds** 1699-1707. Black. Medallion of Britannia with spear and olive branch. Handwritten denominations. Signature of Thomas Madocks. Rare.	—	—	—
36	**10 Pounds** 1699-1707. Black. Medallion of Britannia with spear and olive branch. Handwritten denominations. Signature of Thomas Madocks. Rare.	—	—	—
37	**20 Pounds** 1699-1707. Black. Medallion of Britannia with spear and olive branch. Handwritten denominations. Signature of Thomas Madocks. Rare.	—	—	—
38	**50 Pounds** 1699-1707. Black. Medallion of Britannia with spear and olive branch. Handwritten denominations. Signature of Thomas Madocks. Rare.	—	—	—
39	**100 Pounds** 1699-1707. Black. Medallion of Britannia with spear and olive branch. Handwritten denominations. Signature of Thomas Madocks. Rare.	—	—	—

1707 Issue

No.	Denomination	Good	Fine	XF
40	**5 Pounds** 1707-1725. Black. Medallion of Britannia within foliate border. Signature of Thomas Madocks. Rare.	—	—	—
41	**10 Pounds** 1707-1725. Black. Medallion of Britannia within foliate border. Signature of Thomas Madocks. Rare.	—	—	—
42	**20 Pounds** 1707-1725. Black. Medallion of Britannia within foliate border. Signature of Thomas Madocks. Rare.	—	—	—
43	**50 Pounds** 1707-1725. Black. Medallion of Britannia within foliate border. Signature of Thomas Madocks. Rare.	—	—	—
44	**100 Pounds** 1707-1725. Black. Medallion of Britannia within foliate border. Signature of Thomas Madocks. Rare.	—	—	—

1725 Issue

No.	Denomination	Good	Fine	XF
50	**20 Pounds** 1725-1739. Black. Rare.	—	—	—
51	**30 Pounds** 1725-1739. Black. Rare.	—	—	—
52	**40 Pounds** 1725-1739. Black. Rare.	—	—	—
53	**50 Pounds** 1725-1739. Black. Rare.	—	—	—
54	**60 Pounds** 1725-1739. Black. Rare.	—	—	—
55	**70 Pounds** 1725-1739. Black. Rare.	—	—	—
56	**80 Pounds** 1725-1739. Black. Rare.	—	—	—
57	**90 Pounds** 1725-1739. Black. Rare.	—	—	—
58	**100 Pounds** 1725-1739. Black. Rare.	—	—	—
59	**200 Pounds** 1725-1739. Black. Rare.	—	—	—
60	**300 Pounds** 1725-1739. Black. Rare.	—	—	—
61	**400 Pounds** 1725-1739. Black. Rare.	—	—	—
62	**500 Pounds** 1725-1739. Black. Rare.	—	—	—
63	**1000 Pounds** 1725-1739. Black. Rare.	—	—	—

1739 Issue

No.	Denomination	Good	Fine	XF
65	**20 Pounds** 1739-1751. Black. Rare.	—	—	—
66	**30 Pounds** 1739-1751. Black. Signature of James Collier and Daniel Race.	—	—	—
67	**40 Pounds** 1739-1751. Black. Signature of James Collier and Daniel Race.	—	—	—
68	**50 Pounds** 1739-1751. Black. Signature of James Collier and Daniel Race.	—	—	—
69	**60 Pounds** 1739-1751. Black. Signature of James Collier and Daniel Race.	—	—	—
70	**70 Pounds** 1739-1751. Black. Signature of James Collier and Daniel Race.	—	—	—
71	**80 Pounds** 1739-1751. Black. Signature of James Collier and Daniel Race.	—	—	—
72	**90 Pounds** 1739-1751. Black. Signature of James Collier and Daniel Race.	—	—	—
73	**100 Pounds** 1739-1751. Black. Signature of James Collier and Daniel Race.	—	—	—
74	**200 Pounds** 1739-1751. Black. Signature of James Collier and Daniel Race.	—	—	—
75	**300 Pounds** 1739-1751. Black. Signature of James Collier and Daniel Race.	—	—	—
76	**400 Pounds** 1739-1751. Black. Signature of James Collier and Daniel Race.	—	—	—
77	**500 Pounds** 1739-1751. Black. Signature of James Collier and Daniel Race.	—	—	—
78	**1000 Pounds** 1739-1751. Black. Signature of James Collier and Daniel Race.	—	—	—

1751; 1759 Issue

No.	Denomination	Good	Fine	XF
80	**10 Pounds** 1759. Black. Signature of Daniel Race and Elias Simes. Rare.	—	—	—
81	**15 Pounds** 1759. Black. Signature of Daniel Race and Elias Simes. Rare.	—	—	—
82	**20 Pounds** 1751-1759. Black. Signature of Daniel Race and Elias Simes. Rare.	—	—	—
83	**30 Pounds** 1751-1759. Black. Signature of Daniel Race and Elias Simes. Rare.	—	—	—
84	**40 Pounds** 1751-1759. Black. Signature of Daniel Race and Elias Simes. Rare.	—	—	—
85	**50 Pounds** 1751-1759. Black. Signature of Daniel Race and Elias Simes. Rare.	—	—	—
86	**60 Pounds** 1751-1759. Black. Signature of Daniel Race and Elias Simes. Rare.	—	—	—
87	**70 Pounds** 1751-1759. Black. Signature of Daniel Race and Elias Simes. Rare.	—	—	—
88	**80 Pounds** 1751-1759. Black. Signature of Daniel Race and Elias Simes. Rare.	—	—	—
89	**90 Pounds** 1751-1759. Black. Signature of Daniel Race and Elias Simes. Rare.	—	—	—
90	**100 Pounds** 1751-1759. Black. Signature of Daniel Race and Elias Simes. Rare.	—	—	—
91	**200 Pounds** 1751-1759. Black. Signature of Daniel Race and Elias Simes. Rare.	—	—	—
92	**300 Pounds** 1751-1759. Black. Signature of Daniel Race and Elias Simes. Rare.	—	—	—
93	**400 Pounds** 1751-1759. Black. Signature of Daniel Race and Elias Simes. Rare.	—	—	—
94	**500 Pounds** 1751-1759. Black. Signature of Daniel Race and Elias Simes. Rare.	—	—	—
95	**1000 Pounds** 1751-1759. Black. Signature of Daniel Race and Elias Simes. Rare.	—	—	—

1759; 1765 Issue

No.	Denomination	Good	Fine	XF
100	**10 Pounds** 1759-1775. Black. Signature of Daniel Race. Rare.	—	—	—
101	**15 Pounds** 1759-1775. Black. Signature of Daniel Race. Rare.	—	—	—
102	**20 Pounds** 1759-1775. Black. Signature of Daniel Race. Rare.	—	—	—
103	**25 Pounds** 1765-1775. Black. Signature of Daniel Race. Rare.	—	—	—
104	**30 Pounds** 1759-1775. Black. Signature of Daniel Race. Rare.	—	—	—
105	**40 Pounds** 1759-1775. Black. Signature of Daniel Race. Rare.	—	—	—
106	**50 Pounds** 1759-1775. Black. Signature of Daniel Race. Rare.	—	—	—
107	**60 Pounds** 1759-1775. Black. Signature of Daniel Race. Rare.	—	—	—
108	**70 Pounds** 1759-1775. Black. Signature of Daniel Race. Rare.	—	—	—
109	**80 Pounds** 1759-1775. Black. Signature of Daniel Race. Rare.	—	—	—
110	**90 Pounds** 1759-1775. Black. Signature of Daniel Race. Rare.	—	—	—
111	**100 Pounds** 1759-1775. Black. Signature of Daniel Race. Rare.	—	—	—
112	**200 Pounds** 1759-1775. Black. Signature of Daniel Race. Rare.	—	—	—
113	**300 Pounds** 1759-1775. Black. Signature of Daniel Race. Rare.	—	—	—
114	**400 Pounds** 1759-1775. Black. Signature of Daniel Race. Rare.	—	—	—
115	**500 Pounds** 1759-1775. Black. Signature of Daniel Race. Rare.	—	—	—
116	**1000 Pounds** 1759-1775. Black. Signature of Daniel Race. Rare.	—	—	—

1775 Issue

#	Denomination	Good	Fine	XF
130	**10 Pounds**	Good	Fine	XF
	1775-1778. Black. Signature of Charles Jewson. Rare.	—	—	—
131	**15 Pounds**	Good	Fine	XF
	1775-1778. Black. Signature of Charles Jewson. Rare.	—	—	—
132	**20 Pounds**	Good	Fine	XF
	1775-1778. Black. Signature of Charles Jewson. Rare.	—	—	—
133	**25 Pounds**	Good	Fine	XF
	1775-1778. Black. Signature of Charles Jewson. Rare.	—	—	—
134	**30 Pounds**	Good	Fine	XF
	1775-1778. Black. Signature of Charles Jewson. Rare.	—	—	—
135	**40 Pounds**	Good	Fine	XF
	1775-1778. Black. Signature of Charles Jewson. Rare.	—	—	—
136	**50 Pounds**	Good	Fine	XF
	1775-1778. Black. Signature of Charles Jewson. Rare.	—	—	—
137	**60 Pounds**	Good	Fine	XF
	1775-1778. Black. Signature of Charles Jewson. Rare.	—	—	—
138	**70 Pounds**	Good	Fine	XF
	1775-1778. Black. Signature of Charles Jewson. Rare.	—	—	—
139	**80 Pounds**	Good	Fine	XF
	1775-1778. Black. Signature of Charles Jewson. Rare.	—	—	—
140	**90 Pounds**	Good	Fine	XF
	1775-1778. Black. Signature of Charles Jewson. Rare.	—	—	—
141	**100 Pounds**	Good	Fine	XF
	1775-1778. Black. Signature of Charles Jewson. Rare.	—	—	—
142	**200 Pounds**	Good	Fine	XF
	1775-1778. Black. Signature of Charles Jewson. Rare.	—	—	—
143	**300 Pounds**	Good	Fine	XF
	1775-1778. Black. Signature of Charles Jewson. Rare.	—	—	—
144	**400 Pounds**	Good	Fine	XF
	1775-1778. Black. Signature of Charles Jewson. Rare.	—	—	—
145	**500 Pounds**	Good	Fine	XF
	1775-1778. Black. Signature of Charles Jewson. Rare.	—	—	—
146	**1000 Pounds**	Good	Fine	XF
	1775-1778. Black. Signature of Charles Jewson. Rare.	—	—	—

1778 Issue

#	Denomination	Good	Fine	XF
150	**10 Pounds**	Good	Fine	XF
	1778-1797. Black. Signature of Abraham Newland. Rare.	—	—	—
151	**15 Pounds**	Good	Fine	XF
	1778-1807. Black. Signature of Abraham Newland. Rare.	—	—	—
152	**20 Pounds**	Good	Fine	XF
	1778-1807. Black. Signature of Abraham Newland. Rare.	—	—	—
153	**25 Pounds**	Good	Fine	XF
	1778-1807. Black. Signature of Abraham Newland. Rare.	—	—	—
154	**30 Pounds**	Good	Fine	XF
	1778-1807. Black. Signature of Abraham Newland. Rare.	—	—	—
155	**40 Pounds**	Good	Fine	XF
	1778-1807. Black. Signature of Abraham Newland. Rare.	—	—	—
156	**50 Pounds**	Good	Fine	XF
	1778-1807. Black. Signature of Abraham Newland. Rare.	—	—	—
157	**60 Pounds**	Good	Fine	XF
	1778-1807. Black. Signature of Abraham Newland. Rare.	—	—	—
158	**70 Pounds**	Good	Fine	XF
	1778-1807. Black. Signature of Abraham Newland. Rare.	—	—	—
159	**80 Pounds**	Good	Fine	XF
	1778-1807. Black. Signature of Abraham Newland. Rare.	—	—	—
160	**90 Pounds**	Good	Fine	XF
	1778-1807. Black. Signature of Abraham Newland. Rare.	—	—	—
161	**100 Pounds**	Good	Fine	XF
	1778-1807. Black. Signature of Abraham Newland. Rare.	—	—	—
162	**200 Pounds**	Good	Fine	XF
	1778-1807. Black. Signature of Abraham Newland. Rare.	—	—	—
163	**300 Pounds**	Good	Fine	XF
	1778-1807. Black. Signature of Abraham Newland. Rare.	—	—	—
164	**400 Pounds**	Good	Fine	XF
	1778-1807. Black. Signature of Abraham Newland. Rare.	—	—	—
165	**500 Pounds**	Good	Fine	XF
	1778-1807. Black. Signature of Abraham Newland. Rare.	—	—	—
166	**1000 Pounds**	Good	Fine	XF
	1778-1807. Black. Signature of Abraham Newland. Rare.	—	—	—

1793 Issue

#	Denomination	Good	Fine	XF
168	**5 Pounds**	Good	Fine	XF
	1793-1807. Black.	8,500	25,000	—

Color Abbreviation Guide

New to the *Standard Catalog of® World Paper Money* are the following abbreviations related to color references:

BC: Back color
PC: Paper color

1797 Issue

#170-172 handwritten date, serial # and Cashier's name.

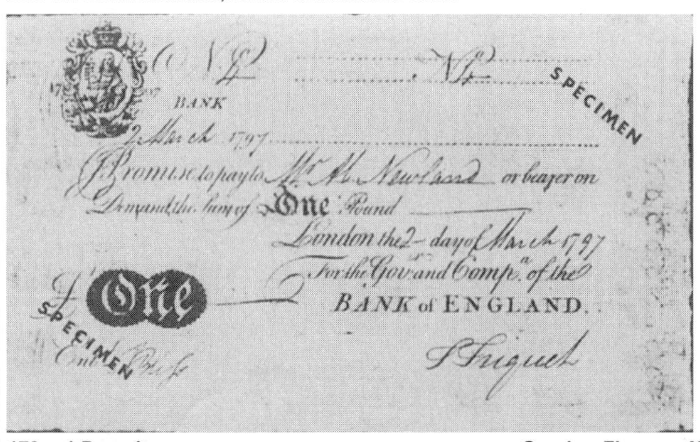

#	Denomination	Good	Fine	XF
170	**1 Pound**	Good	Fine	XF
	1797. Handwritten. Black. Handwritten serial # and Cashier's name.	3,500	10,000	—

No. 4 realized $42,256 in Spink's October 2012 sale.

#	Denomination	Good	Fine	XF
171	**2 Pounds**	Good	Fine	XF
	1797. Handwritten. Black. Handwritten serial # and Cashier's name.	5,500	15,000	—
172	**10 Pounds**	Good	Fine	XF
	1797. Handwritten. Black. Handwritten serial # and Cashier's name. Rare.	—	—	—

1798 Issue

#175-177 printed Cashier's name. Smaller size.

#	Denomination	Good	Fine	XF
175	**1 Pound**	Good	Fine	XF
	1798-1801. Black. Printed Cashier's name. Smaller size.	2,850	8,000	—
176	**2 Pounds**	Good	Fine	XF
	1798-1801. Black. Printed Cashier's name. Smaller size.	4,750	13,000	—
177	**10 Pounds**	Good	Fine	XF
	1798-1805. Black. Printed Cashier's name. Smaller size. Rare.	16,000	45,000	—

1801 Issue

#180-181 new watermark, standard size.

#	Denomination	Good	Fine	XF
180	**1 Pound**	Good	Fine	XF
	1801-1803. Black.	2,750	7,500	—
181	**2 Pounds**	Good	Fine	XF
	1801-1803. Black.	4,000	10,000	—

1803 Issue

#184-185 denomination in watermark.

#	Denomination	Good	Fine	XF
184	**1 Pound**	Good	Fine	XF
	1803-1807. Black. Watermark: Denomination.	2,500	7,000	—
185	**2 Pounds**	Good	Fine	XF
	1803-1805. Black. Watermark: Denomination.	4,500	12,500	—

1805 Issue

#187-188 Bank of England head.

#	Denomination	Good	Fine	XF
187	**2 Pounds**	Good	Fine	XF
	1805-1807. Black. Bank of England head.	3,250	9,000	—
188	**10 Pounds**	Good	Fine	XF
	1805-1807. Black. Bank of England head. Rare.	16,000	45,000	—

1807 Issue

#190-204 Henry Hase as Chief Cashier. Branch as London. Additional branches opened: 1826 - Gloucester, Manchester, Swansea; 1827 - Birmingham, Bristol, Exter, Leeds, Liverpool; 1828 - Newcastle.

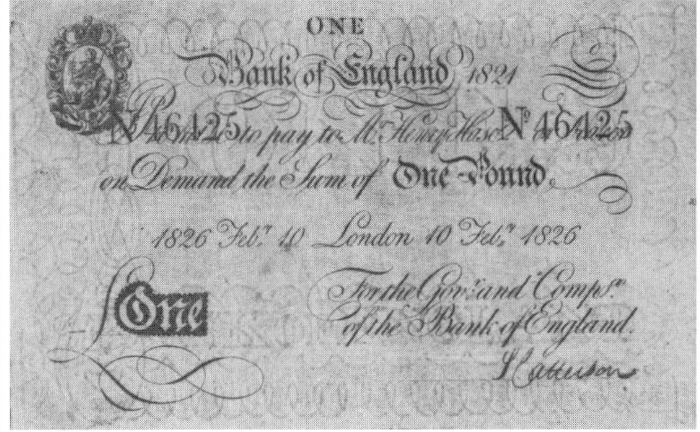

#	Denomination	Good	Fine	XF
190	**1 Pound**	Good	Fine	XF
	1807-1821; 1825-1826. Black.			
	a. Handwritten date, with countersignature.	2,850	8,000	—
	b. Handwritten date, without countersignature.	2,350	6,000	—
	c. Printed date and serial #.	1,000	3,000	—

No.	Description	Good	Fine	XF
	d. As c. but dated 1821 at top and 1826 or 1826 in center (reissue).	1,000	3,000	—
191	**2 Pounds**	Good	Fine	XF
	1807-1821. Black.			
	a. Handwritten date, with countersignature.	3,350	9,500	—
	b. Handwritten date, without countersignature.	3,250	9,000	—
	c. Printed date and serial #.	2,750	7,500	—
192	**5 Pounds**	Good	Fine	XF
	1807-1829. Black.			
	a. Handwritten date.	6,500	18,500	—
	b. Printed date and serial #.	5,750	16,000	—
193	**10 Pounds**	Good	Fine	XF
	1807-1829. Black. Rare.	—	—	—
194	**15 Pounds**	Good	Fine	XF
	1807-1822. Black. Rare.	—	—	—
195	**20 Pounds**	Good	Fine	XF
	1807-1829. Black. Rare.	—	—	—
196	**25 Pounds**	Good	Fine	XF
	1807-1822. Black. Rare.	—	—	—
197	**30 Pounds**	Good	Fine	XF
	1807-1829. Black. Rare.	—	—	—
198	**40 Pounds**	Good	Fine	XF
	1807-1829. Black. Rare.	—	—	—
199	**50 Pounds**	Good	Fine	XF
	1807-1829. Black. Rare.	—	—	—
200	**100 Pounds**	Good	Fine	XF
	1807-1829. Black. Rare.	—	—	—
201	**200 Pounds**	Good	Fine	XF
	1807-1829. Black. Rare.	—	—	—
202	**300 Pounds**	Good	Fine	XF
	1807-1829. Black. Rare.	—	—	—
203	**500 Pounds**	Good	Fine	XF
	1807-1829. Black. Rare.	—	—	—
204	**1000 Pounds**	Good	Fine	XF
	1807-1829. Black. Rare.	—	—	—

1829 Issue

#210-220 Thomas Rippon as Chief Cashier. Branch as London. Additional Branches were opened at Hull and Norwich (1829); Portsmouth (1834). Exeter closed in 1834.

No.	Description	Good	Fine	XF
210	**5 Pounds**	Good	Fine	XF
	1829-1835. Black.	4,250	12,000	—

A Manchester issue dated 8.6.1832 realized $49,936 in Spink's October 2012 sale.

No.	Description	Good	Fine	XF
211	**10 Pounds**	Good	Fine	XF
	1829-1835. Black.	8,000	22,000	—
212	**20 Pounds**	Good	Fine	XF
	1829-1835. Black. Rare.	—	—	—
213	**30 Pounds**	Good	Fine	XF
	1829-1835. Black. Rare.	—	—	—
214	**40 Pounds**	Good	Fine	XF
	1829-1835. Black. Rare.	—	—	—
215	**50 Pounds**	Good	Fine	XF
	1829-1835. Black. Rare.	—	—	—

A Manchester Branch issue in GVF sold for $67,000 in Spink's 10/2008 sale.

No.	Description	Good	Fine	XF
216	**100 Pounds**	Good	Fine	XF
	1829-1835. Black. Rare.	—	—	—
217	**200 Pounds**	Good	Fine	XF
	1829-1835. Black. Rare.	—	—	—
218	**300 Pounds**	Good	Fine	XF
	1829-1835. Black. Rare.	—	—	—
219	**500 Pounds**	Good	Fine	XF
	1829-1835. Black. Rare.	—	—	—
220	**1000 Pounds**	Good	Fine	XF
	1829-1835. Black. Rare.	—	—	—

1835 Issue

#221-231 payable to Matthew Marshall as Chief Cashier.

No.	Description	Good	Fine	XF
221	**5 Pounds**	Good	Fine	XF
	1835-1853. Black.	3,500	10,000	—

Note: An example of #221 dated 26.10.1849, from the Portsmouth Branch, graded VF was auctioned by Spink's in October 2012 for $63,380.

No.	Description	Good	Fine	XF
222	**10 Pounds**	Good	Fine	XF
	1835-1853. Black.	4,750	13,500	—
223	**20 Pounds**	Good	Fine	XF
	1835-1853. Black. Rare.	—	—	—
224	**30 Pounds**	Good	Fine	XF
	1835-1852. Black. Rare.	—	—	—
225	**40 Pounds**	Good	Fine	XF
	1835-1851. Black. Rare.	—	—	—
226	**50 Pounds**	Good	Fine	XF
	1835-1853. Black. Rare.	—	—	—
227	**100 Pounds**	Good	Fine	XF
	1835-1853. Black. Rare.	—	—	—
228	**200 Pounds**	Good	Fine	XF
	1835-1853. Black. Rare.	—	—	—
229	**300 Pounds**	Good	Fine	XF
	1835-1853. Black. Rare.	—	—	—
230	**500 Pounds**	Good	Fine	XF
	1835-1853. Black. Rare.	—	—	—
231	**1000 Pounds**	Good	Fine	XF
	1835-1853. Black. Rare.	—	—	—

1853 Issue

#232-240 payable to Matthew Marshall as Chief Cashier. Printed signature of Bank officials: J. Vautin, H. Bock, J. Ferraby, J. Williams and J. Luson.

No.	Description	Good	Fine	XF
232	**5 Pounds**	Good	Fine	XF
	1853-1855. Black.	3,500	10,000	—
233	**10 Pounds**	Good	Fine	XF
	1853-1855. Black.	4,750	13,500	—
234	**20 Pounds**	Good	Fine	XF
	1853-1855. Black. Rare.	—	—	—
235	**50 Pounds**	Good	Fine	XF
	1853-1855. Black. Rare.	—	—	—
236	**100 Pounds**	Good	Fine	XF
	1853-1855. Black. Rare.	—	—	—
237	**200 Pounds**	Good	Fine	XF
	1853-1855. Black. Rare.	—	—	—
238	**300 Pounds**	Good	Fine	XF
	1853-1855. Black. Rare.	—	—	—
239	**500 Pounds**	Good	Fine	XF
	1853-1855. Black. Rare.	—	—	—
240	**1000 Pounds**	Good	Fine	XF
	1853-1855. Black. Rare.	—	—	—

1855 Issue

#241-249 *Pay to the bearer* notes, London. Modified Britannia vignette. The watermark includes the bank name, value and signature of Matthew Marshall.

No.	Description	Good	Fine	XF
241	**5 Pounds**	Good	Fine	XF
	1855. Black.			
	a. Signature J. Vautin.	3,500	10,000	—
	b. Signature H. Bock.	3,500	10,000	—
	c. Signature J. Ferraby.	3,500	10,000	—
242	**10 Pounds**	Good	Fine	XF
	1855. Black.			
	a. Signature J. Vautin.	4,750	13,500	—
	b. Signature H. Bock.	4,750	13,500	—
	c. Signature J. Ferraby.	4,750	13,500	—
243	**20 Pounds**	Good	Fine	XF
	1855. Black. Signature J. Williams.	—	—	—
244	**50 Pounds**	Good	Fine	XF
	1855; 1858. Black. Signature J. Williams.	—	—	—

A London issue in VF sold for $31,750 in Spink's 10/2008 sale.

No.	Description	Good	Fine	XF
245	**100 Pounds**	Good	Fine	XF
	1855. Black. Signature J. Williams.	—	—	—
246	**200 Pounds**	Good	Fine	XF
	1855. Black. Signature J. Luson. Rare.	—	—	—
247	**300 Pounds**	Good	Fine	XF
	1855. Black. Signature J. Luson.	—	—	—
248	**500 Pounds**	Good	Fine	XF
	1855. Black. Signature J. Luson. Rare.	—	—	—
249	**1000 Pounds**	Good	Fine	XF
	1855. Black. Signature J. Luson. Rare.	—	—	—

1860 Issue

#250-258 additional branch office of this series is: Leicester (1843-1872).

No.	Description	Good	Fine	XF
250	**5 Pounds**	Good	Fine	XF
	1860. Black. Signature W. P. Gattie. London.	3,500	10,000	—
251	**10 Pounds**	Good	Fine	XF
	1860. Black. Signature W. P. Gattie. London.	4,750	13,500	—
252	**20 Pounds**	Good	Fine	XF
	1860. Black. Signature T. Kent. London. Rare.	—	—	—
253	**50 Pounds**	Good	Fine	XF
	1860. Black. Signature T. Kent. London. Rare.	—	—	—
254	**100 Pounds**	Good	Fine	XF
	1860. Black. Signature T. Kent. London. Rare.	—	—	—
255	**200 Pounds**	Good	Fine	XF
	1860. Black. Signature C. T. Whitmell. London. Rare.	—	—	—
256	**300 Pounds**	Good	Fine	XF
	1860. Black. Signature C. T. Whitmell. London. Rare.	—	—	—
257	**500 Pounds**	Good	Fine	XF
	1860. Black. Signature C. T. Whitmell. London. Rare.	—	—	—

No.	Note	Good	Fine	XF
258	**1000 Pounds** 1860. Black. Signature C. T. Whitmell. London. Rare.	—	—	—

1864 Issue

#259-267 William Miller as Chief Cashier.

No.	Note	Good	Fine	XF
259	**5 Pounds** 1864-1866. Black. William Miller as Chief Cashier. Signature W. P. Gattie. London.	7,500	20,000	—
260	**10 Pounds** 1864-1866. Black. William Miller as Chief Cashier. Signature W. P. Gattie. London.	12,000	35,000	—
261	**20 Pounds** 1864-1866. Black. William Miller as Chief Cashier. Signature T. Kent. London. Rare.	—	—	—
262	**50 Pounds** 1864-1866. Black. William Miller as Chief Cashier. Signature T. Kent. London. Rare.	—	—	—
263	**100 Pounds** 1864-1866. Black. William Miller as Chief Cashier. Signature T. Kent. London. Rare.	—	—	—
264	**200 Pounds** 1864-1866. Black. William Miller as Chief Cashier. Signature C. T. Whitmell. London. Rare.	—	—	—
265	**300 Pounds** 1864-1866. Black. William Miller as Chief Cashier. Signature C. T. Whitmell. London. Rare.	—	—	—
266	**500 Pounds** 1864-1866. Black. William Miller as Chief Cashier. Signature C. T. Whitmell. London. Rare.	—	—	—
267	**1000 Pounds** 1864-1866. Black. William Miller as Chief Cashier. Signature C. T. Whitmell. London. Rare.	—	—	—

1866 Issue

#268-276 signature of George Forbes in watermark.

No.	Note	Good	Fine	XF
268	**5 Pounds** 1866-1870. Black. Signature Hy Dixon. London. Watermark: Signature of George Forbes.	4,000	11,500	—
269	**10 Pounds** 1866-1870. Black. Signature Hy Dixon. London. Watermark: Signature of George Forbes. Rare.	9,000	25,000	—
270	**20 Pounds** 1866-1870. Black. Signature T. Puzey. London. Watermark: Signature of George Forbes. Rare.	—	—	—
271	**50 Pounds** 1866-1870. Black. Signature T. Puzey. London. Watermark: Signature of George Forbes. Rare.	—	—	—
272	**100 Pounds** 1866-1870. Black. Signature T. Puzey. London. Watermark: Signature of George Forbes. Rare.	—	—	—
273	**200 Pounds** 1866-1870. Black. Signature W. O. Wheeler. London. Watermark: Signature George Forbes. Rare.	—	—	—
274	**300 Pounds** 1866-1870. Black. Signature W. O. Wheeler. London. Watermark: Signature George Forbes. Rare.	—	—	—
275	**500 Pounds** 1866-1870. Black. Signature W. O. Wheeler. London. Watermark: Signature George Forbes. Rare.	—	—	—
276	**1000 Pounds** 1866-1870. Black. Signature W. O. Wheeler. London. Watermark: Signature George Forbes. Rare.	—	—	—

1870 Issue

No.	Note	Good	Fine	XF
277	**5 Pounds** 1870-1873. Black. Printed signature. Signature title: *Chief Cashier*. London.	7,550	20,000	—
278	**10 Pounds** 1870-1873. Black. Printed signature. Signature title: Chief *Cashier. London*. Rare.	—	—	—
279	**20 Pounds** 1870-1873. Black. Printed signature. Signature title: Chief *Cashier. London*. Rare.	—	—	—
280	**50 Pounds** 1870-1873. Black. Printed signature. Signature title: Chief *Cashier. London*. Rare.	—	—	—
281	**100 Pounds** 1870-1873. Black. Printed signature. Signature title: Chief *Cashier. London*. Rare.	—	—	—
282	**200 Pounds** 1870-1873. Black. Printed signature. Signature title: Chief *Cashier. London*. Rare.	—	—	—
283	**300 Pounds** 1870-1873. Black. Printed signature. Signature title: Chief *Cashier. London*. Rare.	—	—	—
284	**500 Pounds** 1870-1873. Black. Printed signature. Signature title: Chief *Cashier. London*. Rare.	—	—	—
285	**1000 Pounds** 1870-1873. Black. Printed signature. Signature title: Chief *Cashier. London*. Rare.	—	—	—

1873 Issue

No.	Note	Good	Fine	XF
286	**5 Pounds** 1873-1893. Black. Frank May as Chief Cashier. London.	2,500	6,000	—

#286 from Bristol brought $46,500 at auction.

No.	Note	Good	Fine	XF
287	**10 Pounds** 1873-1893. Black. Frank May as Chief Cashier. London.	5,500	15,000	—
288	**20 Pounds** 1873-1893. Black. Frank May as Chief Cashier. London. Rare.	—	—	—
289	**50 Pounds** 1873-1893. Black. Frank May as Chief Cashier. London. Rare.	—	—	—
290	**100 Pounds** 1873-1893. Black. Frank May as Chief Cashier. London. Rare.	—	—	—
291	**200 Pounds** 1873-1893. Black. Frank May as Chief Cashier. London. Rare.	—	—	—
292	**300 Pounds** 1873-1893. Black. Frank May as Chief Cashier. London. Rare.			
	a. Issued note.	—	—	—
	s. Specimen.	—	—	50,000
293	**500 Pounds** 1873-1893. Black. Frank May as Chief Cashier. London. Rare.	—	—	—
294	**1000 Pounds** 1873-1893. Black. Frank May as Chief Cashier. London. Rare.	—	—	—

1893 Issue

No.	Note	Good	Fine	XF
295	**5 Pounds** 1893-1902. Black. Horace G. Bowen as Chief Cashier. London.	2,500	6,000	13,000
296	**10 Pounds** 1893-1902. Black. Horace G. Bowen as Chief Cashier. London.	5,250	14,000	—
297	**20 Pounds** 1893-1902. Black. Horace G. Bowen as Chief Cashier. London. Rare.	—	—	—
298	**50 Pounds** 1893-1902. Black. Horace G. Bowen as Chief Cashier. London. Rare.	—	—	—
299	**100 Pounds** 1893-1902. Black. Horace G. Bowen as Chief Cashier. London. Rare.	—	—	—
300	**200 Pounds** 1893-1902. Black. Horace G. Bowen as Chief Cashier. London. Rare.	—	—	—
301	**500 Pounds** 1893-1902. Black. Horace G. Bowen as Chief Cashier. London. Rare.	—	—	—
302	**1000 Pounds** 1893-1902. Black. Horace G. Bowen as Chief Cashier. London. Rare.	—	—	—

1902 Issue

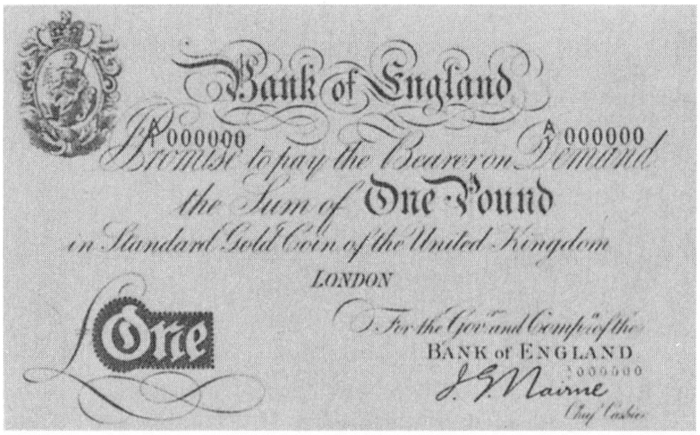

No.	Note	Good	Fine	XF
304	**5 Pounds** 1902-1918. Black. John G. Nairne as Chief Cashier. London.	225	550	1,400
305	**10 Pounds** 1902-1918. Black. John G. Nairne as Chief Cashier. London.	475	1,200	2,850
306	**20 Pounds** 1902-1918. Black. Signature of John G. Nairne as Chief Cashier. London.			
	a. London.	1,350	3,250	8,000
	b. Manchester.	1,600	4,000	10,000

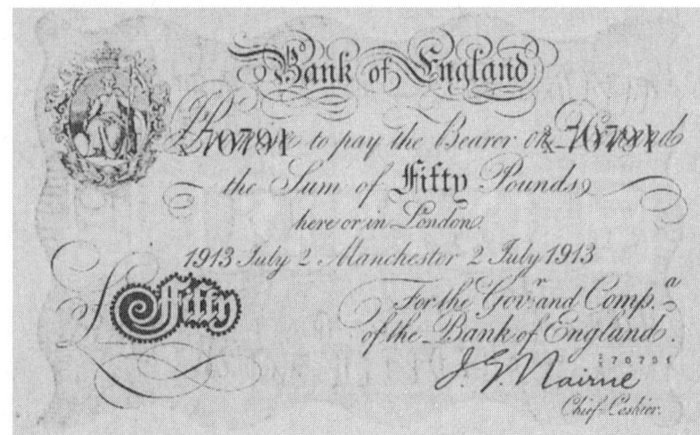

No.	Denomination / Description	Good	Fine	XF
307	**50 Pounds**	Good	Fine	XF
	1902-1918. Black. John G. Nairne as Chief Cashier. London.			
	a. London. Rare.	1,400	3,500	8,500
	b. Manchester.	1,200	2,850	7,500
308	**100 Pounds**	Good	Fine	XF
	1902-1918. Black. John G. Nairne as Chief Cashier. London.			
	a. London. Rare.	1,500	3,600	9,000
	b. Manchester.	1,000	2,500	6,500
309	**200 Pounds**	Good	Fine	XF
	1902-1918. Black. John G. Nairne as Chief Cashier. London.Rare.	—	—	—
310	**500 Pounds**	Good	Fine	XF
	1902-1918. Black. John G. Nairne as Chief Cashier. London. Rare.	—	—	—
311	**1000 Pounds**	Good	Fine	XF
	1902-1918. Black. John G. Nairne as Chief Cashier. London. Rare.	—	—	—

1918 Issue

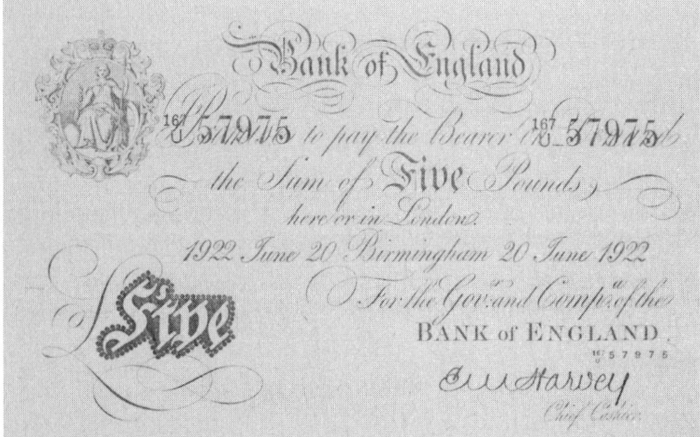

No.	Denomination / Description	Good	Fine	XF
312	**5 Pounds**	Good	Fine	XF
	1918-1925. Black. Ernest M. Harvey as Chief Cashier.			
	a. London.	140	385	900
	b. Leeds.	225	550	1,400
	c. Liverpool.	250	600	1,500
	d. Manchester.	275	650	1,600
	e. Hull.	400	1,000	2,500
	f. Birmingham.	500	1,200	2,850
	g. Newcastle.	625	1,500	4,000
	h. Plymouth.	1,150	2,750	7,000
	i. Bristol.	2,500	6,000	14,000
313	**10 Pounds**	Good	Fine	XF
	1918-1925. Black. Ernest M. Harvey as Chief Cashier. London.	200	500	1,250
314	**20 Pounds**	Good	Fine	XF
	1918-1925. Black. Ernest M. Harvey as Chief Cashier. London.	800	2,000	5,000
315	**50 Pounds**	Good	Fine	XF
	1918-1925. Black. Ernest M. Harvey as Chief Cashier. London.	900	2,200	5,500

No.	Denomination / Description	Good	Fine	XF
316	**100 Pounds**	Good	Fine	XF
	1918-1925. Black. Ernest M. Harvey as Chief Cashier. London.	950	2,400	6,000
317	**200 Pounds**	Good	Fine	XF
	1918-1925. Black. Ernest M. Harvey as Chief Cashier. London. Rare.	—	—	—

A note dated 20.6.1918 in VF sold for $42,250 in Spink's October 2012 sale.

No.	Denomination / Description	Good	Fine	XF
318	**500 Pounds**	Good	Fine	XF
	1918-1925. Black. Ernest M. Harvey as Chief Cashier. London. Rare.	—	—	—

A Manchester Branch issue in VF sold for $40,600 in Spink's October 2008 sale.

No.	Denomination / Description	Good	Fine	XF
319	**1000 Pounds**	Good	Fine	XF
	1918-1925. Black. Ernest M. Harvey as Chief Cashier. London. Rare.	—	—	—

1925 Issue

No.	Denomination / Description	Good	Fine	XF
320	**5 Pounds**	Good	Fine	XF
	1925-1929. Black. Cyril P. Mahon as Chief Cashier.			
	a. London.	175	475	1,200
	b. Manchester.	285	700	1,750
	c. Leeds.	285	700	1,750
	d. Liverpool.	375	900	2,350
	e. Hull.	575	1,400	3,500
	f. Birmingham.	750	1,750	4,500
	g. Newcastle.	750	1,750	4,500
	h. Plymouth. Rare.	2,000	4,750	11,000
	i. Bristol. Rare.	3,500	7,500	20,000
321	**10 Pounds**	Good	Fine	XF
	1925-1929. Black. Cyril P. Mahon as Chief Cashier.			
	a. London.	275	650	1,600
	b. Leeds.	650	1,500	3,750
	c. Manchester.	700	1,650	4,250
	d. Liverpool.	700	1,650	4,250
322	**20 Pounds**	Good	Fine	XF
	1925-1929. Black. Cyril P. Mahon as Chief Cashier. London.	750	1,850	4,750
323	**50 Pounds**	Good	Fine	XF
	1925-1929. Black. Cyril P. Mahon as Chief Cashier. London.	700	1,650	4,750
324	**100 Pounds**	Good	Fine	XF
	1925-1929. Black. Cyril P. Mahon as Chief Cashier. London.	900	2,250	5,500
325	**200 Pounds**	Good	Fine	XF
	9.4.1925. Black. Cyril P. Mahon as Chief Cashier. London. Specimen only.	—	-3.00	—
326	**500 Pounds**	Good	Fine	XF
	1925-1929. Black. Cyril P. Mahon as Chief Cashier. London. Rare.	—	—	—

No.	Denomination / Description	Good	Fine	XF
327	**1000 Pounds**	Good	Fine	XF
	1925-1929. Black. Cyril P. Mahon as Chief Cashier. London. Rare.	—	—	—

This note in XF sold for $48,000 in Spink's October 2012 sale.

Color Abbreviation Guide

New to the *Standard Catalog of ® World Paper Money* are the following abbreviations related to color references:

BC: Back color
PC: Paper color

1929 Issue

		Good	Fine	XF
328	**5 Pounds**			
	1929-1934. Black. Basil G. Catterns as Chief Cashier.			
	a. London.	120	325	800
	b. Leeds.	175	475	1,200
	c. Liverpool.	200	535	1,350
	d. Manchester.	250	600	1,500
	e. Birmingham.	350	850	2,200
	f. Newcastle.	350	850	2,200
	g. Hull.	500	1,200	3,000
	h. Plymouth.	1,500	3,750	9,000
	i. Bristol.	2,250	5,500	13,000
329	**10 Pounds**	**Good**	**Fine**	**XF**
	1929-1934. Black. Basil G. Catterns as Chief Cashier.			
	a. London.	200	500	1,200
	b. Liverpool.	285	725	1,800
330	**20 Pounds**	**Good**	**Fine**	**XF**
	1929-1934. Black. Basil G. Catterns as Chief Cashier. London.	600	1,500	3,750

		Good	Fine	XF
331	**50 Pounds**			
	1929-1934. Black. Basil G. Catterns as Chief Cashier. London.	500	1,200	3,000
332	**100 Pounds**	**Good**	**Fine**	**XF**
	1929-1934. Black. Basil G. Catterns as Chief Cashier. London.	725	1,750	4,500
333	**500 Pounds**	**Good**	**Fine**	**XF**
	1929-1934. Black. Basil G. Catterns as Chief Cashier. London. Rare.	—	—	—
334	**1000 Pounds**	**Good**	**Fine**	**XF**
	1929-1934. Black. Basil G. Catterns as Chief Cashier. London. Rare.	—	—	37,500

A London issue in about EF sold for $53,000 in Spink's October 2008 sale.

1934 Issue

OPERATION BERNHARD FORGERIES During World War II *almost perfect* forgeries of Bank of England Pound notes were produced by prisoners in a German concentration camp. The enterprise was code named "Operation Bernhard". The following occur: 5, 10, 20 and 50 Pound notes with different dates, also including branch office issues such as Leeds and Bristol. They come with signatures of Catterns or Peppiatt. There are a number of very small but discernible differences between the Operation Bernhard counterfeits and genuine notes. For example, most counterfeits have a dull look in Britannia's eyes and less clarity on the cross at top of her crown. For further information and details, see *Nazi Counterfeiting of British Currency During World War II* by Bryan Burke, and *World War II Remembered* by C. Frederick Schwan and Joseph E. Boling.

		Good	Fine	XF
335	**5 Pounds**			
	1934-1944. Black. Kenneth O. Peppiatt as Chief Cashier.			
	a. London.	85.00	185	450
	b. Liverpool.	150	400	1,000
	c. Manchester.	150	400	1,000
	d. Leeds.	150	400	1,000
	e. Birmingham.	285	725	1,800
	f. Newcastle.	365	875	2,150
	g. Hull.	365	875	2,150
	h. Plymouth.	900	2,250	5,500
	i. Bristol.	2,400	6,000	15,000

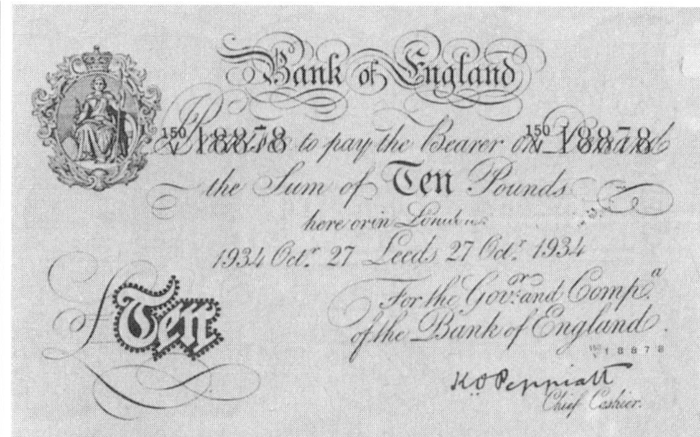

		Good	Fine	XF
336	**10 Pounds**			
	Aug. 1934-Aug.1943. Black. Kenneth O. Peppiatt as Chief Cashier. London.			
	a. London.	125	300	750
	b. Liverpool.	275	700	1,750
	c. Birmingham.	350	850	2,100
	d. Manchester.	350	850	2,100
337	**20 Pounds**	**Good**	**Fine**	**XF**
	Aug. 1934-Aug.1943. Black. Kenneth O. Peppiatt as Chief Cashier.			
	a. London.	400	1,000	2,500
	b. Liverpool.	750	1,850	4,800
	c. Manchester.	750	1,850	4,800
	d. Leeds.	1,150	2,750	7,000
338	**50 Pounds**	**Good**	**Fine**	**XF**
	1934-1938. Black. Kenneth O. Peppiatt as Chief Cashier.			
	a. London.	365	875	2,150
	b. Manchester.	625	1,600	4,000
	c. Liverpool.	750	1,850	4,800
339	**100 Pounds**	**Good**	**Fine**	**XF**
	1934-1943. Black. Kenneth O. Peppiatt as Chief Cashier.			
	a. 1934-43. London.	500	1,200	3,000
	b. 1934-38. Liverpool.	450	1,150	2,800
340	**500 Pounds**	**Good**	**Fine**	**XF**
	Aug. 1934-Aug. 1943. Kenneth O. Peppiatt as Chief Cashier. London.	2,000	5,500	13,000

		Good	Fine	XF
341	**1000 Pounds**			
	April 1934-Aug.1943. Black. Kenneth O. Peppiatt as Chief Cashier. London.	—	—	35,000

A London issue in EF sold for $38,400 in Spink's October 2012 sale.

1944-1947 Issue

		Good	Fine	XF
342	**5 Pounds**			
	1944-1947. Black. Kenneth O. Peppiatt as Chief Cashier. Thick paper. London.	45.00	110	275

#	Denomination	Good	Fine	XF
343	**5 Pounds** 1947. Black. Kenneth O. Peppiatt as Chief Cashier. Thin paper. London.	40.00	90.00	225

1949 Issue

Bank of England R71 051330
I Promise to pay the Bearer on Demand
the Sum of Five Pounds
R71 051330 1950 June 7 London 7 June 1950
Five For the Gov. and Comp. of the
BANK of ENGLAND.
R71 051330
Chief Cashier.

#	Denomination	Good	Fine	XF
344	**5 Pounds** 1949-1955. Black. P.S. Beale as Chief Cashier. London.	40.00	90.00	225

1955 Issue

#	Denomination	Good	Fine	XF
345	**5 Pounds** 1955-1956. Black. L.K. O'Brien as Chief Cashier. London.	40.00	90.00	225

Treasury Notes

1914 ND Issue

#	Denomination	Good	Fine	XF
346	**10 Shillings** ND (Aug. 1914). Red. Portrait King George V at left. Signature John Bradbury. 3 serial # varieties. Uniface.	165	450	1,100

#	Denomination	Good	Fine	XF
347	**1 Pound** ND (Aug. 1914). Black. Portrait King George V at left. Signature John Bradbury. 13 serial # varieties. Uniface.	200	550	1,550

1914-1915 Issue

#	Denomination	Good	Fine	XF
348	**10 Shillings** ND (Jan. 1915). Red. Portrait King George V at upper left, St. George at upper right. Signature John Bradbury. 5 serial # varieties. Uniface.			
	a. Issued note.	120	260	800
	b. With black overprint in Turkish: *60 silver piastres.*	275	700	2,750

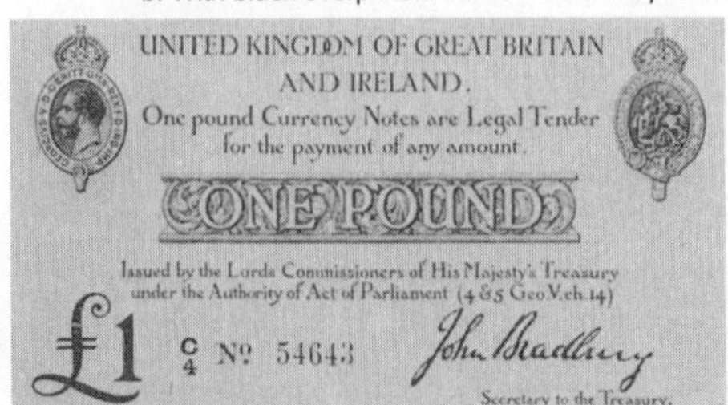

#	Denomination	Good	Fine	XF
349	**1 Pound** ND (23.10.1914.) Black. Portrait King George V at upper left, St. George at upper right. Signature John Bradbury. 5 serial # varieties. Uniface.			
	a. Issued note.	130	285	875
	b. With red overprint in Turkish: *120 silver piastres.*	2,000	5,500	18,000

Note: #348b and 349b withTurkish overprint were formerly listed as Turkey #M1 and M2. Counterfeits exist.

1917-1918 ND Issue

#	Denomination	Good	Fine	XF
350	**10 Shillings** ND (1918). Green. Portrait King George V at right. Britannia at left. Signature John Bradbury. Uniface.			
	a. Black serial #. (Nov.)	160	400	1,100
	b. Red serial #. (Dec.)	135	325	900

#	Denomination	Good	Fine	XF
351	**1 Pound** ND (Feb. 1917). Brown and green. Portrait King George V at right. St. George slaying dragon at left. Signature John Bradbury.	50.00	120	375

1919 ND First Issue

#	Denomination	Good	Fine	XF
352	**5 Shillings** ND (1919). Red-violet and green. Portrait King George V at center. Signature John Bradbury. Rare.	—	—	—

1919 ND Second Issue

#	Denomination	Good	Fine	XF
353	**1 Shilling** ND (1919). Green and Brown. Portrait King George V at center. Signature N. K. Waren Fisher. Back: Shilling coin. Not issued.	3,000	7,500	—

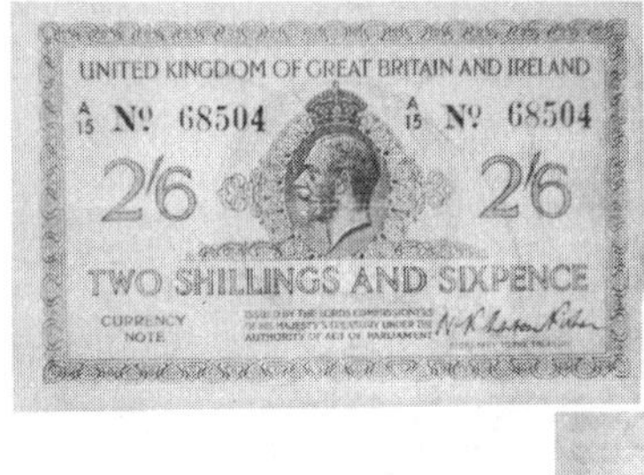

#	Denomination	Good	Fine	XF
354	**2 Shillings - 6 Pence** ND (1919). Olive-green and deep brown. Portrait King George V at center. Signature N. K. Waren Fisher. Back: Half Crown coin. Not issued.	3,000	7,500	—
355	**5 Shillings** ND (1919). Deep violet and green. Portrait King George V at right. Signature John Bradbury. Back: One Crown coin. Not issued.	2,500	6,000	—

1919 ND Third Issue

#	Denomination	Good	Fine	XF
356	**10 Shillings** ND (Oct. 1919). Green. Portrait King George V at right, Britannia at left. 2 serial # varieties. Signature N. K. Waren Fisher.	55.00	165	575
357	**1 Pound** ND (Oct. 1919). Brown and green. Signature N.K. Waren Fisher. Watermark: *ONE POUND* at center in one line.	20.00	65.00	240

1922 ND Issue

#	Denomination / Description	Good	Fine	XF
358	**10 Shillings** ND (1922-1923). Green. Serial # without *No.* Signature N. K. Waren Fisher.	45.00	140	425
359	**1 Pound** ND (1922-1923). Brown. Signature N. K. Warren Fisher. Watermark: *ONE POUND* in two lines at center.			
	a. Letter and figure *1* over number (dot).	20.00	70.00	240
	b. Letter and figure *1* over number (square dot).	65.00	220	600

1928 ND Issue

#	Denomination / Description	Good	Fine	XF
360	**10 Shillings** ND (1928). Green. Britannia at left, portrait King George V at right. Signature N. K. Warren Fisher.	45.00	140	475
361	**1 Pound** ND (1928). Brown. St. George slaying dragon at left, portrait King George V at right. Signature N. K. Warren Fisher.			
	a. Letter and figure *1* over number (dot).	25.00	75.00	300
	b. Letter and figure *1* over number (square dot).	65.00	220	600

1948 Issue

#	Denomination / Description	VG	VF	UNC
361A	**1,000,000 Pounds** 30.8.1948. Green. Arms at top center. Eight printed, two available. Punch hole cancelled.	—	—	140,000

Bank of England (resumed)

1928-1948 ND Issue

#	Denomination / Description	VG	VF	UNC
362	**10 Shillings** ND (1928-1948). Brown. Seated Britannia at left. Paper without security thread.			
	a. Signature C. P. Mahon (1928-1929).	50.00	150	500
	b. Signature B. G. Catterns (1929-1934).	30.00	90.00	300
	c. Signature K. O. Peppiatt (1934-1939).	25.00	70.00	240
	d. Signature like c. Series with L (1948).	40.00	120	400

#	Denomination / Description	VG	VF	UNC
363	**1 Pound** ND (1928-1948). Green. Seated Britannia at upper left. Paper without security thread.			
	a. Signature C. P. Mahon (1928-1929).	30.00	90.00	300
	b. Signature B. G. Catterns (1929-1934).	16.00	47.50	150
	c. Signature K. O. Peppiatt (1934-1939).	12.50	35.00	120
	d. Signature like c. Series letters R-A; S-A (1948).	12.50	35.00	120
	e. Overprint: *Withdrawn from circulation September 18th, 1941.* on a.	275	825	—
	f. Overprint as e on b.	250	750	—
	g. Overprint as e on c, with serial prefix letters: B; C; D; E; H; J; K; L; M; N; O; R; S; T; U; W; X; Y; Z.	215	650	—
	h. Overprint as e on c, with serial # prefix A-A; B-A; C-A; D-A; E-A; H-A; J-A; K-A.	120	300	925
	i. Overprint: *Withdrawn from circulation November 10th 1941* on c. Period on face and back. Serial E03A only.	225	675	1,800
	j. Overprint as i on c. No period on face but period on back. Serial E15A only.	140	425	1,250

Note: During the WW II German occupation of Guernsey, 5000 pieces of #363 were withdrawn and replaced with new small change notes. Before the notes were turned over to the occupation forces, local officials had them overprinted on face and back, quickly ending any further redeemability.

1940-1941 ND Emergency Issue

#	Denomination / Description	VG	VF	UNC
364	**2 Shillings - 6 Pence** ND (1941). Black on light blue underprint. Signature K. O. Peppiatt. (Not issued).	2,500	6,500	—

#	Denomination / Description	VG	VF	UNC
365	**5 Shillings** ND (1941). Olive on pink underprint. Signature K. O. Peppiatt. (Not issued).	2,500	6,500	—

#	Denomination / Description	VG	VF	UNC
366	**10 Shillings** ND (1940-1948). Mauve. Seated Britannia at left. Signature K. O. Peppiatt. Paper with security thread.	14.00	40.00	150
367	**1 Pound** ND (1940-1948). Light or dark blue and pink. Seated Britannia at upper left. Signature K. O. Peppiatt. Paper with security thread.			
	a. Issued note.	4.00	12.50	45.00
	b. Overprint: *Withdrawn from circulation September 18th, 1941.* Serial prefix A-D.	375	900	2,500
	c. Overprint: *Withdrawn from circulation September 18th 1941.* Serial prefix C-D.	275	750	2,000

Note: Many shade varieties exist such as pale blue and pink, blue and deep pink or deep blue and buff. The back shade varieties range from pale blue to blue-green.

Note: #367b Guernsey withdrawal, for other issues see also #363e-363g.

1948 ND Issue

#	Denomination / Description	VG	VF	UNC
368	**10 Shillings** ND (1948-1960). Brown-violet and brown on gray and pink underprint. Seated Britannia at left. Watermark: Head of Minerva. Paper with security thread.			
	a. Signature K. O. Peppiatt. (1948-1949).	12.50	35.00	140
	b. Signature P. S. Beale. (1949-1955).	7.50	20.00	90.00
	c. Signature L. K. O'Brien. (1955-1960).	7.00	18.00	75.00
	s. Specimen.	—	—	1,000

		VG	VF	UNC
369	**1 Pound**			
	ND (1948-1960). Green. Seated Britannia at upper left. Paper with security thread.			
	a. Signature K. O. Peppiatt. (1948-1949).	9.00	27.50	90.00
	b. Signature P. S. Beale. (1949-1955).	5.00	8.00	25.00
	c. Signature L. K. O'Brien. (1955-1960).	5.00	8.00	25.00
	d. As a but with light blue cross at end of *Demand* on face.	20.00	60.00	175
	s. Specimen.	—	—	1,000

Note: #369d was most likely used to track movement of notes from Jersey and England in the immediate post-WWII era (1948-49).

#370 not assigned.

1957-1961 ND Issue

		VG	VF	UNC
371	**5 Pounds**			
	ND (1957-1961). Blue and multicolor. Helmeted Britannia head at left, St. George and dragon at lower center. Signature L.K. O'Brien. Back: Lion standing left. Denomination *5* in blue print on back. 159x88mm.			
	a. Issued note.	20.00	65.00	150
	s. Specimen.	—	—	1,500
372	**5 Pounds**	**VG**	**VF**	**UNC**
	ND (1961-1963). Blue and multicolor. Helmeted Britannia head at left, St. George and dragon at lower center. Signature L. K. O'Brien at left. Back: Denomination *£5* in white on back. 159x88mm.			
	a. Issued note.	20.00	65.00	150
	s. Specimen.	—	—	1,500

1960-1964 ND Issue

		VG	VF	UNC
374	**1 Pound**			
	ND (1960-1978). Deep green on multicolor underprint. Portrait Queen Elizabeth II at right. Watermark: Laureate heads in continuous vertical row at left. Back: Britannia seated with shield in circle at center right. Watermark: Laureate heads in continuous vertical row at left. 150x72mm.			
	a. Signature L. K. O'Brien. (1960-1961).	2.50	5.00	14.00
	b. Signature as a. Small letter *R* (for Research) at lower left center on back. (Notes printed on web press.) Serial # prefixes A01N; A05N; A06N.	150	400	1,250
	c. Signature J. Q. Hollom. (1962-1966).	FV	4.00	12.00
	d. Signature as c. Letter *G* at lower left center on back. (Printed on the experimental German Goebel Press.)	4.00	12.50	27.50
	e. Signature J. S. Fforde. (1966-1970).	FV	4.00	12.00
	f. Signature as e. Letter *G* at lower center on back.	4.00	14.00	32.50
	g. Signature J. B. Page. (1970-1977).	FV	4.00	10.00
	s. Specimen. As a, e, g.	—	—	1,100

The Hellenic Republic of Greece is situated in southeastern Europe on the southern tip of the Balkan Peninsula. The republic includes many islands, the most important of which are Crete and the Ionian Islands. Greece (including islands) has an area of 131,940 sq. km. and a population of 10.72 million. Capital: Athens. Greece is still largely agricultural. Tobacco, cotton, fruit and wool are exported.

Greece achieved independence from the Ottoman Empire in 1829. During the second half of the 19th century and the first half of the 20th century, it gradually added neighboring islands and territories, most with Greek-speaking populations. In World War II, Greece was first invaded by Italy (1940) and subsequently occupied by Germany (1941-44); fighting endured in a protracted civil war between supporters of the king and Communist rebels. Following the latter's defeat in 1949, Greece joined NATO in 1952. A military dictatorship, which in 1967 suspended many political liberties and forced the king to flee the country, lasted seven years. The 1974 democratic elections and a referendum created a parliamentary republic and abolished the monarchy. In 1981, Greece joined the EC (now the EU); it became the 12th member of the European Economic and Monetary Union in 2001.

RULERS:

John Capodistrias, 1827-1831
Othon (Otto of Bavaria) 1832-1862
George I, 1863-1913
Constantine I, 1913-1923
George II, 1922-1923, 1935-1947
Paul I, 1947-1964
Constantine II, 1964-1973

MONETARY SYSTEM:

1 Phoenix = 100 Lepta, 1828-1831
1 Drachma = 100 Lepta, 1841-2001
1 Euro = 100 Cents, 2002-

REPLACEMENT NOTES:

#195-: OOA prefix.

DENOMINATIONS

1 - ΜΙΑ
2 - ΔΥΟ
5 - ΠΕΝΤΕ
10 - ΔΕΚΑ
20 - ΕΙΚΟΣΙ
25 - ΕΙΚΟΣΙΠΕΝΤΕ
50 - ΠΕΝΤΗΚΟΝΤΑ
100 - ΕΚΑΤΟΝ
200 - ΔΙΑΚΟΣΙΑ
250 - ΔΙΑΚΟΣΙΑ ΠΕΝΤΗΚΟΝΤΑ
500 - ΠΕΝΤΑΚΟΣΙΑΙ
750 - ΕΠΤΑΚΟΣΙΑ ΠΕΝΤΗΚΟΝΤΑ
1000 - ΧΙΛΙΑΙ
2000 - ΔΥΟ ΧΙΛΙΑΔΕΣ
5000 - ΠΕΝΤΕ ΧΙΛΙΑΔΕΣ
10,000 - ΔΕΚΑ ΧΙΛΙΑΔΕΣ
20,000 - ΕΙΚΟΣΙ ΧΙΛΙΑΔΕΣ
25,000 - ΕΙΚΟΣΙ ΠΕΝΤΕ ΧΙΛΙΑΔΕΣ
50,000 - ΠΕΝΤΗΚΟΝΤΑ ΧΙΛΙΑΔΕΣ
100,000 - ΕΚΑΤΟΝ ΧΙΛΙΑΔΕΣ
500,000 - ΠΕΝΤΑΚΟΣΙΑΙ ΧΙΛΙΑΔΕΣ
1,000,000 - ΕΝ ΕΚΑΤΟΜΜΥΡΙΟΝ
5,000,000 - ΠΕΝΤΕ ΕΚΑΤΟΜΜΥΡΙΑ
10,000,000 - ΔΕΚΑ ΕΚΑΤΟΜΜΥΡΙΑ
25,000,000 - ΕΙΚΟΣΙ ΠΕΝΤΕ ΕΚΑΤΟΜΜΥΡΙΑ
50,000,000 - ΠΕΝΤΗΚΟΝΤΑ ΕΚΑΤΟΜΜΥΡΙΑ
100,000,000 - ΕΚΑΤΟΝ ΕΚΑΤΟΜΜΥΡΙΑ
200,000,000 - ΔΙΑΚΟΣΙΑ ΕΚΑΤΟΜΜΥΡΙΑ
500,000,000 - ΠΕΝΤΗΑΚΟΝΤΑ ΕΚΟΤΟΜΜΥΡΙΑ
2,000,000,000 - ΔΥΟ ΧΙΛΙΑΔΕΣ ΕΚΑΤΟΜΜΥΡΙΑ
10,000,000,000 - ΔΕΚΑ ΔΙΣΕΚΑΤΟΜΜΥΡΙΑ
100,000,000,000 - ΕΚΑΤΟΝ ΔΙΣΕΚΑΤΟΜΜΥΡΙΑ

EKDOSIS ISSUES

Many notes can be differentiated by the designation of the Ekdosis (EK.) on the back of the notes. The issue numbers quoted here are found on the note in Greek letters in each case following “ ” i.e.

1	ΠΡΩΤΗ	**6**	ΕΚΤΗ	**11**	ΕΝΔΕΚΑΤΗ
2	ΔΕΥΤΕΡΑ	**7**	ΕΒΔΟΜΗ	**12**	ΔΩΔΕΚΑΤΗ
3	ΤΡΙΤΗ	**8**	ΟΓΔΟΗ	**13**	ΔΕΚΑΤΗ ΤΡΙΤΗ
4	ΤΕΤΑΡΤΗ	**9**	ΕΝΑΤΗ (ΕΝΝΑΤΗ)	**14**	ΔΕΚΑΤΗ ΤΕΤΑΡΤΗ
5	ΠΕΜΠΤΗ	**10**	ΔΕΚΑΤΗ		

		GREEK ALPHABET									
Α	α	Alpha	(ä)	Ι	ι	Iota	(ē)	Ρ	ρ	Rho	(r)
Β	β	Beta	(b)	Κ	κ	Kappa	(k)	Σ	σ	Sigma	(s)6
Γ	γ	Gamma	(g)	Λ	λ	Lambda	(l)	Τ	τ	Tau	(t)
Δ	δ	Delta	(d)	Μ	μ	Mu	(m)	Υ	υ	Upsilon	(o͞o)
Ε	ε	Epsilon	(e)	Ν	ν	Nu	(n)	Φ	φ	Phi	(f)
Ζ	ζ	Zeta	(z)	Ξ	ξ	Xi	(ks)	Χ	χ	Chi	(H)
Η	η	Eta	(ā)	Ο	ο	Omicron	(o)	Ψ	ψ	Psi	(ps)
Θ	θ	Theta	(th)	Π	π	Pi	(p)	Ω	ω	Omega	(ō)

Note: Certain listings encompassing issues circulated by various bank and regional authorities are contained in Volume 1.

INDEPENDENT GREECE

ΠΡΟΣΩΡΙΝΗ ΔΙΟΙΚΗΣΙΣ ΤΗΣ ΕΛΛΑΔΟΣ

Provisional Administration of Greece

1822 Issue

#1-5 bonds that circulated as currency. Issued in Corinth and Nauplion. Denominations in Gr. (Grossi = Piastres).

		Good	Fine	XF
1	**100 Grossi** 1822. Black.	120	300	800
2	**250 Grossi** 1822. Black.	100	300	800
3	**500 Grossi** 1822. Black.	100	300	800
4	**750 Grossi** 1822. Black.	250	500	1,000

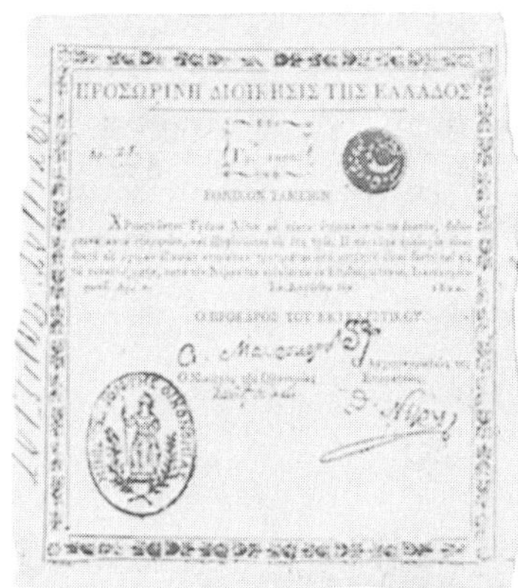

		Good	Fine	XF
5	**1000 Grossi** 1822. Black.	300	500	1,500

National Finance Bank

1831 Issue

		Good	Fine	XF
6	**5 Phoenix** 30.6.1831. Red.	350	1,200	2,400

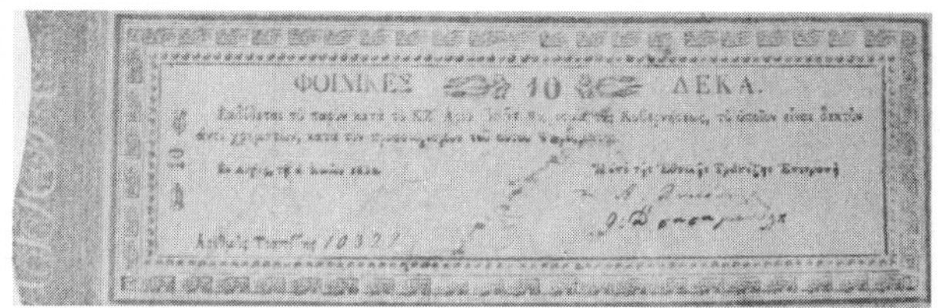

		Good	Fine	XF
7	**10 Phoenix** 30.6.1831. Red.	800	2,200	4,600

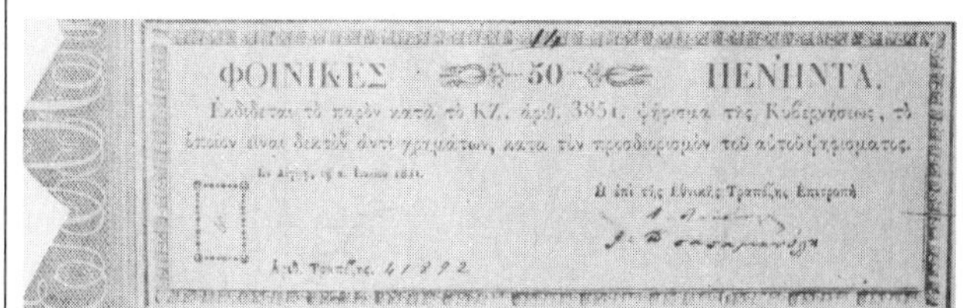

		Good	Fine	XF
8	**50 Phoenix** 30.6.1831. Light blue. Rare.	—	—	7,500

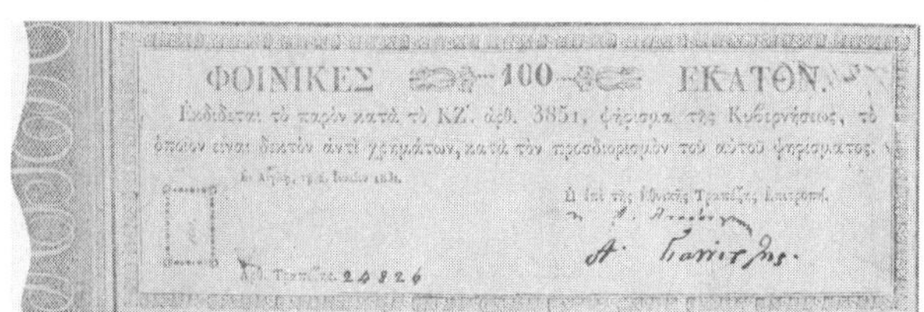

		Good	Fine	XF
9	**100 Phoenix** 30.6.1831. Light blue. Rare.	—	—	—

KINGDOM

ΕΛΛΗΝΙΚΗ ΤΡΑΠΕΖΑ

Bank of Greece

1841 Issue

		Good	Fine	XF
10	**25 Drachmai** 30.3.1841. Black. Arms of King Othon at upper center. Uniface. Rare. PC: Green.	—	—	—
11	**50 Drachmai** 30.3.1841. Black. Arms of King Othon at upper center. Uniface. Rare. PC: Green.	—	—	—

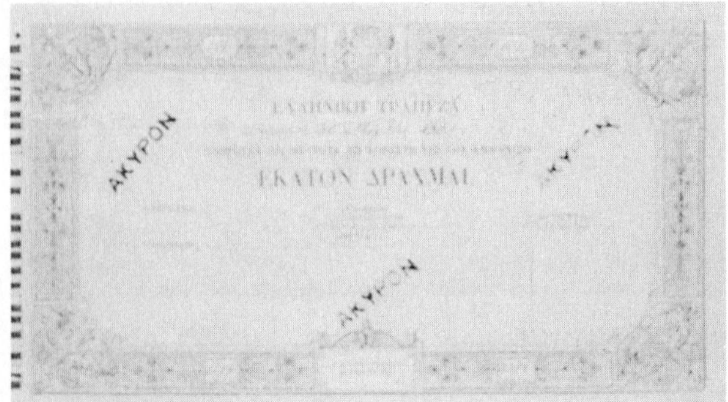

#	Denomination	Good	Fine	XF
12	**100 Drachmai** 30.3.1841. Black. Arms of King Othon at upper center. Oval at center. Uniface. Rare. PC: Light brown.	—	—	—
13	**500 Drachmai** 30.3.1841. Black. Arms of King Othon at upper center. Uniface. Rare. PC: Green.	—	—	—

ΕΘΝΙΚΗ ΤΡΑΠΕΖΑ ΤΗΣ ΕΛΛΑΔΟΣ

National Bank of Greece

1852 Issue

#	Denomination	Good	Fine	XF
19	**10 Drachmai** 1852. Arms of King Othon at top center. Uniface. Rare.	—	—	—
20	**25 Drachmai** 1852. Arms of King Othon. Uniface. Rare.	—	—	—

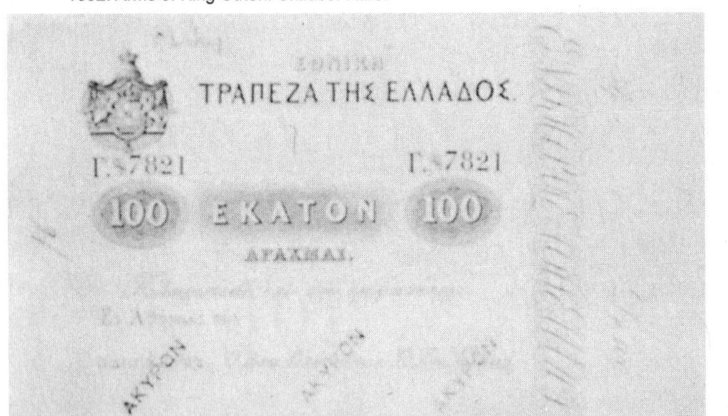

#	Denomination	Good	Fine	XF
21	**100 Drachmai** 1852. Green denomination guilloches. Arms of King Othon at upper left. Uniface. Rare.	—	—	—

#22 not assigned.

1863-1867 Issue

#	Denomination	Good	Fine	XF
23	**10 Drachmai** 15.7.1863; 10.3.1867. Black on red and green underprint. Arms of King Othon at left, portrait G. Stavros at top center, Nereid at lower right. Uniface. Printer: ABNC.	1,500	4,000	—

Color Abbreviation Guide

New to the *Standard Catalog of® World Paper Money* are the following abbreviations related to color references:

BC: Back color
PC: Paper color

#	Denomination	Good	Fine	XF
24	**25 Drachmai** Black on red and green underprint. Portrait G. Stavros at upper left, two women at upper center, arms of King Othon at lower right. Uniface. Printer: ABNC.			
	p. Proof on card. Punch hole cancelled.	—	—	1,500
	s. Specimen.	—	—	5,000
25	**100 Drachmai** Black on red and green underprint. Portrait G. Stavros at upper left, woman reclining with shield at upper center, arms of King Othon at bottom right. Uniface. Printer: ABNC. Specimen.	—	—	5,000

#26 not assigned.

1867-1869 Issue

#	Denomination	Good	Fine	XF
27	**10 Drachmai** ca. 1867. Arms of King George I at left, portrait G. Stavros at top center, Nereid at lower right. Uniface. Printer: ABNC. Requires confirmation.	—	—	—

#	Denomination	Good	Fine	XF
28	**25 Drachmai** 3.7.1867; 8.3.1868; 28.6.1868. Black, red and green. Portrait G. Stavros at upper left, two women at upper center, arms of King George I at lower right. Uniface. Printer: ABNC.	1,200	2,000	3,500

#	Denomination	Good	Fine	XF
29	**100 Drachmai** 4.8.1867; 25.8.1869. Rare. Black, red and green. Portrait G. Stavros at upper left, woman reclining with shield at upper center, arms of King George I at bottom right. Uniface. Printer: ABNC.	—	—	—
29A	**500 Drachmai** Green and brown. Arms of King George I at upper left, women at lower right. Similar to #33. Requires confirmation.	—	—	—

1870-1878 Issue

No.	Description	Good	Fine	XF
30	**10 Drachmai** 18.8.1878-3.8.1883. Black, blue and red. Arms of King George I at left, G. Stavros at top center, Nereid at lower right. 2 large *N*'s (for New Drachmai of Latin Monetary Union). Printer: ABNC.	1,200	2,200	3,600
31	**25 Drachmai** 30.12.1871; 20.5.1882-12.8.1886. Black on blue and green underprint. G. Stavros at upper left. Two women at upper center, arms of King George I at lower right. 2 large *N*s (for New Drachmai of Latin Monetary Union). Printer: ABNC.	450	1,200	2,400

No.	Description	Good	Fine	XF
32	**100 Drachmai** 1870-20.5.1882. Black, red and green. G. Stavros at upper left, woman reclining with shield at upper center, arms of King George at bottom right. 2 large *N*s (for New Drachmai of Latin Monetary Union). Printer: ABNC.	400	600	1,200
33	**500 Drachmai** 1872-5.8.1886. Green and brown. Arms of King George I at upper left, women at lower right. 2 large *N*s (for New Drachmai of Latin Monetary Union). Printer: ABNC. Rare.	—	—	—

1885 ND Provisional Issue

No.	Description	Good	Fine	XF
36	**5 Drachmai** ND (-old dates 1878-1900). Left or right half of 10 Drachmai #30, 37, 43 and 46.	50.00	100	300

Note: Regarding #36, demand for the 5 Drachmai denomination was satisfied by cutting the 10 Drachmai notes in half. The practice continued apparently beyond 1910 despite the issuance of 5 Drachmai notes in 1897 as these were not enough to satisfy the demand.

Law of 30.2.1841

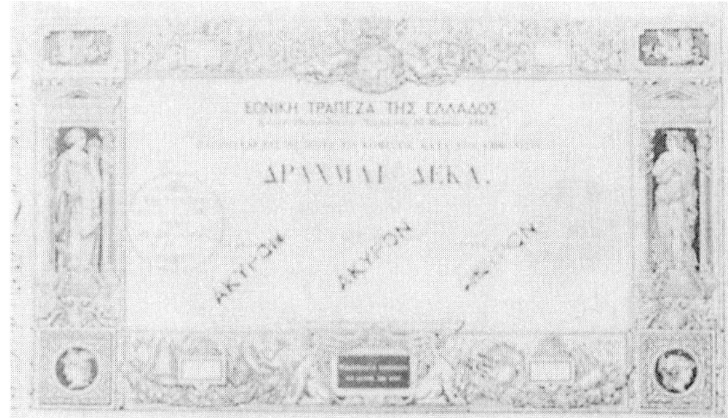

No.	Description	Good	Fine	XF
14	**10 Drachmai** *L.1841.* Blue. Statue at left and right. Embossed seal at right. Rare.	—	—	—
15	**25 Drachmai** *L.1841.* Statue at left and right. Embossed seal at right. Rare.	—	—	—
16	**50 Drachmai** *L.1841.* Statue at left and right. Embossed seal at right. Rare.	—	—	—
17	**100 Drachmai** *L.1841.* Statue at left and right. Embossed seal at right. Rare.	—	—	—
18	**500 Drachmai** *L.1841.* Black. Statue at left and right. Embossed seal at right. Rare.	—	—	—

Law of 21.12.1885

No.	Description	Good	Fine	XF
34	**1 Drachma** *L.1885.* Black on blue yellow underprint. Portrait Hermes at lower left. Back: Arms of King George I at center. Printer: BWC.	20.00	65.00	175

No.	Description	Good	Fine	XF
35	**2 Drachmai** *L.1885.* Black on blue and yellow underprint. Portrait Hermes at left, Athena at right. Back: Arms of King George I at center. Printer: BWC.	30.00	100	200

1886-1897 Issue

No.	Description	Good	Fine	XF
36A	**2 Drachmai** 1.3.1886. Black on pink and green underprint. Back: Athena bust right at center. Printer: G&D (without imprint). Proof.	—	—	—

No.	Description	Good	Fine	XF
37	**10 Drachmai** 18.9.1889-5.8.1893. Orange and blue. Arms of King George I at center, Hermes at right. G. Stavros at left. Back: Woman and sheep. Printer: ABNC.	500	1,200	2,200
38	**25 Drachmai** 30.5.1888-12.6.1897. Black on red and green underprint. Reclining woman at center, arms of King George I at right. G. Stavros at left. Back: Woman at center. Printer: ABNC.	600	1,300	2,500
39	**100 Drachmai** 25.2.1886; 6.3.1886; 18.9.1887. Black, red and green with red denomination in underprint. Arms of King George I. G. Stavros at left. Printer: ABNC. Rare.	—	—	—

1897 ND Issue

Law of 21.12.1885

No.	Description	Good	Fine	XF
40	**1 Drachma** *L.1885* (1897). Black on blue and orange underprint. Athena at left. Back: Arms of King George I at center. Printer: BWC.	10.00	40.00	90.00

Note: For #40 overprint: *1917* in red, see #301.

No.	Description	Good	Fine	XF
41	**2 Drachmai** *L.1885* (1897). Black on blue and orange underprint. Hermes at right. Back: Arms of King George I at center. Printer: BWC.	17.50	75.00	175

Note: For #41 overprint: *1917* in red, see #302.

1892; 1897 Issue

No.	Description	Good	Fine	XF
43	**10 Drachmai** 14.9.1892-June 1900. Purple on tan underprint. Mercury at left, arms of King George I at center. Printed in Vienna.	600	2,000	5,000

44	25 Drachmai	Good	Fine	XF
	12.8.1897-31.8.1900. Black on orange and blue underprint. Athena at left, male portrait at center right, arms of King George I at right Back: Hermes at center. Printer: W&S.	500	1,500	5,000

45	100 Drachmai	Good	Fine	XF
	12.2.1892-12.4.1893; 20.5.1899. Purple. Athena reclining on lion chair at left, arms of King George I at top center, male portrait at right. Printed in Vienna.	500	2,000	8,000

1897 Issue

42	5 Drachmai	Good	Fine	XF
	2.10.1897; 10.11.1897; 12.12.1897. Black on orange and purple underprint. Arms of King George I at left, portrait G. Stavros at top center. Back: Athena at center.	50.00	150	800

1900; 1903 Issue

46	10 Drachmai	Good	Fine	XF
	1.6.1900; 20.6.1900; 15.7.1900. Green. Portrait G. Stavros at left, arms of King George I at right. Back: Hermes at center. Printer: BWC.	100	300	1,000
47	**25 Drachmai**	**Good**	**Fine**	**XF**
	1.5.1903-2.9.1903.EK. 8. Black on red and blue underprint. Portrait G. Stavros at left, arms of King George I at right. Two women at center. Back: Child and fish at center. Printer: ABNC.			
	a. Issued note.	75.00	150	800
	s. Specimen.	—	Unc	400
48	**100 Drachmai**	**Good**	**Fine**	**XF**
	10.6.1900; 1.7.1900; 15.7.1900. Black on purple and orange underprint. Portrait G. Stavros at left, arms of King George I at right. Back: Athena at center. Printer: BWC.	200	700	1,600

1901 Issue

49	500 Drachmai	Good	Fine	XF
	2.1.1901. Brown and green. Portrait Athena at center. Portrait G. Stavros at left, arms of King George at right. Back: Woman and sheep. Printer: ABNC. EK. 6.			
	a. Issued note.	150	300	1,500
	s. Specimen.	—	Unc	750

50	1000 Drachmai	VG	VF	UNC
	30.3.1901; 30.5.1901. Black on multicolor underprint. Portrait G. Stavros at left, arms of King George I at right. Hermes at center. Back: Woman at center. Printer: ABNC.			
	a. Issued note.	—	—	—
	s. Specimen.	—	—	1,500

1905-1910 Issue

51	10 Drachmai	Good	Fine	XF
	12.3.1910-24.3.1917. Black on purple and green undeprint. Portrait G. Stavros at left, arms of King George I at right. Signature varieties. Back: Hermes at center. Printer: ABNC.			
	a. Issued note.	25.00	100	350
	s. Specimen. Rare.	—	—	—

52	25 Drachmai	Good	Fine	XF
	2.1.1909-14.2.1918. Portrait G. Stavros at left, arms of King George I at right. Similar to #47 but different guilloches. Signature varieties. Printer: ABNC. EK. 9.			
	a. Issued note.	10.00	50.00	250
	s. Specimen.	—	Unc	150

53	100 Drachmai	Good	Fine	XF
	1.10.1905-12.11.1917. EK. 9. Black on purple and green underprint. Portrait G. Stavros at left, arms of King George I at right. Signature varieties. Back: Woman holding child at center. Printer: ABNC.			
	a. Issued note.	12.50	100	350
	s. Specimen.	—	Unc	300

1905-1917 Issue

54	5 Drachmai	Good	Fine	XF
	1.10.1905-15.3.1918. Black on purple and green underprint. Portrait G. Stavros at left, arms of King George I at right. Back: Athena at center. Printer: ABNC. EK. 2.			
	a. Issued note.	12.00	38.00	155
	s. Speicmen.	—	Unc	150

55	100 Drachmai	Good	Fine	XF
	10.12.1917-Sept.1918. Black on purple and green underprint. Portrait G. Stavros at left, arms of King George I at right. Similar to #53 but different guilloches. Back: Temple at center. Printer: ABNC. EK. 10.			
	a. Issued note.	50.00	150	300
	s. Specimen.	—	Unc	400

56	500 Drachmai	Good	Fine	XF
	5.5.1914-20.12.1918. Black on multicolor underprint. Portrait G. Stavros at left, arms of King George I at right. Similar to #49 but different guilloches. Printer: ABNC. EK. 7.			
	a. Issued note.	100	200	750
	s. Specimen.	—	Unc	750

57	1000 Drachmai	Good	Fine	XF
	15.4.1917-16.12.1918. Black on multicolor underprint. Portrait G. Stavros at left, arms of King George I at right. Hermes at center. Similar to # 50. Back: Woman at center. Printer: ABNC.			
	a. Issued note.	300	600	1,500
	s. Specimen.	—	Unc	1,200

1922 Emergency Issue

Law of 25.3.1922

Note: Many National Bank notes in circulation were cut in half. The left half remained legal tender until 1927 at half face value. The right half was considered a compulsory loan, equally valued at half face value.

		Good	Fine	XF
58	**5 Drachmai = 2 1/2 Drachmai**	Good	Fine	XF
	L.1922. EK. 2 (#54).	2.00	8.00	25.00
59	**10 Drachmai = 5 Drachmai**	Good	Fine	XF
	L.1922. EK. 8, 9 (#46, 51).	3.00	11.00	35.00

		Good	Fine	XF
60	**25 Drachmai = 12 1/2 Drachmai**	Good	Fine	XF
	L.1922. EK. 7, 8, 9 (#44, 47, 52).	4.00	12.00	40.00
61	**100 Drachmai = 50 Drachmai**	Good	Fine	XF
	L.1922. EK. 8, 9, 10 (#48, 53, 55).	13.00	52.00	180
62	**500 Drachmai = 250 Drachmai**	Good	Fine	XF
	L.1922. EK. 5, 6, 7 (#33, 49, 56).	25.00	80.00	250
63	**1000 Drachmai = 500 Drachmai**	Good	Fine	XF
	L.1922. EK. 1 (#50, 57).	35.00	115	325

1922 *NEON* Issue

64	5 Drachmai	Good	Fine	XF
	31.5.1918-8.1.1919 (1922). Black on red and multicolor underprint. Portrait G. Stavros at left, arms of King George I at right. Back: Athena at center. Printer: ABNC. Overprint: Black: *NEON* over arms.			
	a. Issued note.	6.00	20.00	75.00
	s. Specimen.	—	Unc	100

65	25 Drachmai	Good	Fine	XF
	2.5.1918-25.11.1919 (1922). Black on blue underprint. Seated figure at center. Portrait G. Stavros at left, arms og King George I at right. Back: Two allegorical women. Printer: ABNC. Overprint: Red: *NEON* over arms.			
	a. Issued note.	18.00	65.00	195
	s. Specimen.	—	Unc	1,000

66	50 Drachmai	Good	Fine	XF
	16.9.1921-24.2.1922 (1922) Brown on green underprint. Relief from Sarcophagus at center. Portrait G. Stavros at left, arms of King George I at right. Back: Alexander at center. Printer: ABNC. Overprint: Red: *NEON* over arms.			
	a. Issued note.	27.00	110	420
	s. Specimen.	—	Unc	300

67	100 Drachmai	Good	Fine	XF
	8.2.1922; 17.2.1922. Blue on light green and red-orange underprint. Two women reclining at center. Portrait G. Stavros at left, arms og King George I at right. Back: Temple at center. Printer: BWC. Overprint: Red: *NEON* over arms.			
	a. Issued note.	40.00	160	480
	s. Specimen.	—	Unc	300

68	500 Drachmai	Good	Fine	XF
	13.10.1921; 25.1.1922 (1922). Black on brown and green underprint. Woman at center. Portrait G. Stavros at left, arms of King George I at right. Back: Statue at left and right, temple at center. Printer: ABNC. Overprint: Red: *NEON* over arms.			
	a. Issued note.	45.00	180	520
	s. Specimen.	—	Unc	300

69	1000 Drachmai	Good	Fine	XF
	15.6.1921-25.1.1922 (1922). Blue on multicolor underprint. Woman at center, arms of King George I at right. Back: Urn at left and right, temple at center. Printer: ABNC. Overprint: Red: *NEON* over arms.			
	a. Issued note.	55.00	220	750
	s. Specimen.	—	Unc	1,200

1923 First Issue

		Good	Fine	XF
70	**5 Drachmai** 24.3.1923. Green on orange underprint. Portrait G. Stavros at left. Back: Alexander at center. Printer: BWC.			
	a. Issued note.	4.00	14.00	50.00
	s. Specimen.	—	Unc	50.00

		Good	Fine	XF
71	**25 Drachmai** 5.3.1923. Brown. Portrait G. Stavros at left. Back: Temple at center. Printer: BWC.			
	a. Issued note.	15.00	60.00	140
	s. Specimen.	—	—	—

		Good	Fine	XF
72	**1000 Drachmai** 5.1.1923. Blue on brown underprint. Portrait G. Stavros at left. Back: Parthenon at center. Printer: BWC.			
	a. Issued note. Rare.	—	—	—
	ct. Color trial. Specimen.	—	Unc	600

1923 Second Issue

		Good	Fine	XF
73	**5 Drachmai** 28.4.1923. Black on orange and green underprint. Back: Athena at center. Printer: ABNC.			
	a. Issued note.	6.00	22.00	85.00
	s. Specimen.	—	Unc	100

		Good	Fine	XF
74	**25 Drachmai** 15.4.1923. Black on green and multicolor underprint. Back: Ancient coin at left and right. Printer: ABNC.			
	a. Issued note.	20.00	140	350
	s. Specimen.	—	Unc	300
75	**50 Drachmai** 12.3.1923. Black on multicolor underprint. Back: Hermes at center. Printer: ABNC.	Good	Fine	XF
	a. Issued note.	18.00	65.00	280
	s. Specimen.	—	Unc	1,250

		Good	Fine	XF
76	**100 Drachmai** 1.3.1923. Black and multicolor. Back: Relief of Elusis at center. Printer: ABNC.			
	a. Issued note.	100	280	900
	ct. Color trial. Specimen.	—	Unc	300
77	**500 Drachmai** 8.1.1923. Black on yellow and green underprint. Back: Church at center. Printer: ABNC.	Good	Fine	XF
	a. Issued note. Rare.	—	—	—
	ct. Color trial. Specimen.	—	Unc	800
78	**500 Drachmai** 8.1.1923. Black on yellow and green underprint. Back: Ruins at center. Printer: Gebr. Parcus, Munich (without imprint). Specimen.	Good —	Fine —	XF 600
79	**1000 Drachmai** 4.4.1923; 14.7.1923. Black on multicolor underprint. Statue at left and right. Back: Four columns and view of ruins at center. Printer: ABNC.	Good	Fine	XF
	a. Rare.	—	—	—
	s. Specimen.	—	Unc	1,250

REPUBLIC - 1920S

ΕΘΝΙΚΗ ΤΡΑΠΕΖΑ ΤΗΣ ΕΛΛΑΔΟΣ

National Bank of Greece (continued)

1926 Emergency Issue

Law of 23.1.1926 Older National Bank 50-1000 Drachmai notes were cut w/the left-hand portion 3/4 of the width leaving the right-hand portion 1/4 in width. Later on, the large left-hand pieces were exchanged at 3/4 of original face value and at 1/4 of the 3/4 face value for debentures of compulsory loan. The smaller 1/4 right-hand pieces were also exchanged for debentures.

		Good	Fine	XF
80	**50 Drachmai** *L.1926.* EK. 3, 4 (#66, 75).	4.00	15.00	60.00

		Good	Fine	XF
81	**100 Drachmai** *L.1926.* EK. 11, 12 (#67, 76).	6.00	25.00	75.00
82	**500 Drachmai** *L.1926.* EK. 8, 9 (#68, 77).	Good 16.00	Fine 75.00	XF 175

		Good	Fine	XF
83	**1000 Drachmai** *L.1926.* EK. 2, 3, 4 (#69, 72, 79).	30.00	100	250

Note: #83 illustrates two different notes which have been pieced together.

1926 *NEON* Issue

		Good	Fine	XF
84	**50 Drachmai** ND(1926-old date 6.5.1923). Purple on green and orange underprint. Portrait G. Stavros at left. Back: Statue at ccenter. Printer: BWC. Overprint: Red: *NEON* in circle.			
	a. Issued note.	35.00	120	290
	ct. Specimen.	—	—	200

		Good	Fine	XF
85	**100 Drachmai** ND(1926-old date 20.4.1923). Green. Portrait G. Stavros at center. Back: Church at center. Printer: BWC. Overprint: Red: *NEON* in circle.			
	a. Black signature of Royal Commissioner.	80.00	200	—
	b. Red signature of Royal Commissioner.	45.00	145	—
	ct. Color trial. Specimen.	—	Unc	300

		Good	Fine	XF
86	**500 Drachmai** ND(1926-old date 12.4.1923). Brown. Portrait G. Stavros at center. Back: City at center. Printer: BWC. Overprint: Red: *NEON* in circle.			
	a. Issued note.	120	200	—
	ct. Color trial. Specimen.	—	Unc	300

1926 Third Issue

		Good	Fine	XF
87	**5 Drachmai** 17.12.1926. Brown on green underprint. Back: Ancient coin at left and right.			
	a. Issued note.	18.00	55.00	160
	s. Specimen.	—	Unc	100

#87 was issued as a provisional note of the Bank of Greece. See #94.

		Good	Fine	XF
88	**10 Drachmai** 15.7.1926; 5.8.1926. Blue on yellow and orange underprint. Portrait G. Stavros at center. Back: Ancient coin at left and right. Printer: ABNC.			
	a. Issued note.	16.00	52.00	130
	s. Specimen.	—	Unc	150

		Good	Fine	XF
89	**500 Drachmai** 21.11.1926. Purple on multicolor underprint. Portrait G. Stavros at center. Back: Church at center, mythical animal at left and right. Printer: ABNC.			
	a. Black signature of Commissioner.	80.00	340	—
	b. Red signature of Commissioner.	65.00	310	—
	s. Specimen.	—	Unc	750

1927 Issue

		Good	Fine	XF
90	**50 Drachmai** 30.4.1927; 13.5.1927; 24.5.1927. Brown on orange and green underprint. Columns at left and right, portrait G. Stavros at center. Back: Ancient coin at left and right Printer: ABNC. (Not issued).			
	a. Issued note.	2.00	11.00	45.00
	s. Specimen.	—	Unc	175

Note: #90 was issued as a provisional note of the Bank of Greece. See #97.

		Good	Fine	XF
91	**100 Drachmai** 25.5.1927; 6.6.1927; 14.6.1927. Green on orange and brown underprint. Portrait G. Stavros at left, ancient coin at right. Back: Coin with Apollo at center. Printer: ABNC. (Not issued).			
	a. Issued note.	1.50	6.00	25.00
	s. Specimen.	—	Unc	175

Note: #91 was issued only as provisional notes of the Bank of Greece. See #98.

ΤΡΑΠΕΖΑ ΤΗΣ ΕΛΛΑΔΟΣ

Bank of Greece

ca. 1928 First Provisional Issue

#92 and 93 overprint: new bank name on notes of the National Bank of Greece.

		Good	Fine	XF
92	**50 Drachmai** ND (-old date 6.5.1923). Overprint: New bank name on #84.			
	a. Issued note.	10.00	45.00	160
	s. Specimen.	—	Unc	300

		Good	Fine	XF
93	**100 Drachmai** ND (-old date 20.4.1923). Overprint: New bank name on #85.			
	a. Issued note.	7.50	50.00	250
	s. Specimen.	—	Unc	200

ca. 1928 Second Provisional Issue

#94-101 overprint: new bank name on notes of the National Bank of Greece.

		Good	Fine	XF
94	**5 Drachmai** ND (-old date 17.11.1926). Overprint: Black new bank name at lower right on #87.			
	a. Issued note.	15.00	40.00	125
	s. Specimen.	—	Unc	100

Note: The overprint is often very weak and hardly discernible.

ca. 1928 Third Provisional Issue

#95-101 red overprint. new bank name in curved line across upper center.

		Good	Fine	XF
95	**20 Drachmai** ND (-old dates 19.10.1926; 5.11.1926. Brown on multicolor underprint. G. Stavros at left. Back: Woman at center. Overprint: Red new bank name in curved line across upper center.			
	a. Issued note.	35.00	120	395
	s. Specimen.	—	Unc	250
96	**25 Drachmai** ND (-old date 15.4.1923). Overprint: Red new bank name on #74.	Good	Fine	XF
	a. Issued note.	30.00	115	380
	s. Specimen.	—		
97	**50 Drachmai** ND (-old date 30.4.1927). Overprint: Red new bank name on #90.	Good	Fine	XF
	a. Issued note.	1.25	5.00	22.00
	s. Specimen.	—	Unc	500

		Good	Fine	XF
98	**100 Drachmai** ND (-old date 6.6.1927). Overprint: Red new bank name on #91.			
	a. Issued note.	1.50	7.00	28.00
	s. Specimen.	—	Unc	200
99	**500 Drachmai** ND (-old date 21.11.1926). Overprint: Red new bank name on #89a or #89b.	Good	Fine	XF
	a. Issued note.	8.00	18.00	70.00
	s. Specimen.	—	Unc	200

		Good	Fine	XF
100	**1000 Drachmai** ND (-old date 1926). Black on green and multicolor underprint. Portrait G. Stavros at center. Back: Stone carving at center. Overprint: Red new bank name in curved line across upper center.			
	a. Without signature under red bar at lower right. Old date 15.10.1926.	2.50	8.00	20.00
	b. Without signature under red bar at lower right. Old date 4.11.1926.	0.75	3.00	14.00
	c. Red bar overprint over signature at lower right.	18.00	65.00	260
	s. Specimen without overprint.	—	Unc	300

		Good	Fine	XF
101	**5000 Drachmai** ND (-old date 5.10.1926). Brown on green underprint. Frieze at top, portrait G. Stavros at center. Back: Stone carving at center. Overprint: Red new bank name in curved line across upper center.			
	a. Issued note.	75.00	300	—
	s. Specimen.	—	Unc	500

1932 Issue

		VG	VF	UNC
102	**500 Drachmai** 1.10.1932. Multicolor. Portrait Athena at center. Back: Stone carving at center. Printer: ABNC.			
	a. Issued note.	1.00	4.00	15.00
	s. Specimen.	—	—	200

		VG	VF	UNC
103	**5000 Drachmai** 1.9.1932. Brown. Portrait Athena at center. Back: Griffin at center. Printer: ABNC.			
	a. Issued note.	1.00	3.00	25.00
	s. Specimen.	—	—	350

KINGDOM 1935-1941

ΤΡΑΠΕΖΑ ΤΗΣ ΕΛΛΑΔΟΣ

Bank of Greece (continued)

1935 Issue

		VG	VF	UNC
104	**50 Drachmai** 1.9.1935. Multicolor. Girl with sheaf of wheat at left. Back: Relief of Elusis at center, woman at right. Printed in France.			
	a. Issued note.	1.50	6.00	25.00
	s. Specimen.	—	—	350

105 **100 Drachmai** | VG | VF | UNC
1.9.1935. Multicolor. Hermes at center. Back: Woman holding basket at center. Printed in France.

	VG	VF	UNC
a. Issued note.	7.00	28.00	120
s. Specimen.	—	—	400

106 **1000 Drachmai**
1.5.1935. Multicolor. Girl in national costume at center. Back: Workman at left and right, girl in national costume at center. Printed in France.

	VG	VF	UNC
a. Issued note.	1.50	6.00	50.00
s. Specimen.	—	—	500

1939 Issue

107 **50 Drachmai**
1.1.1939. Green. Hesiod at left. Back: Frieze at center. Printer: TDLR (without imprint).

	VG	VF	UNC
a. Issued note.	2.00	7.00	20.00
s. Specimen.	—	—	100

Note: For a note similar to #107 in red-brown and dated 1941, see #168.

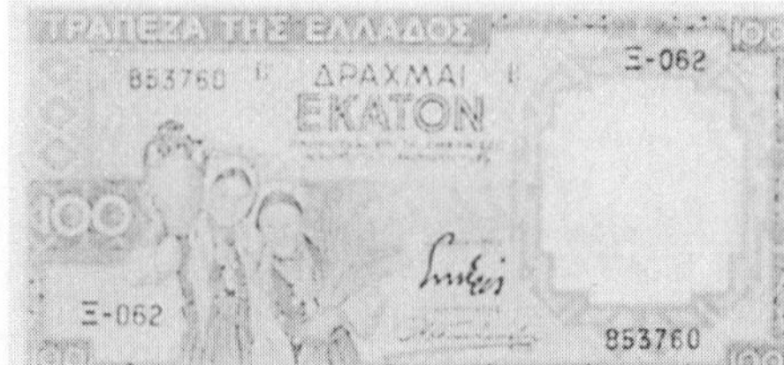

108 **100 Drachmai**
1.1.1939. Green and yellow. Two peasant women at lower left. Back: Stone carving in country scene. Printer: W&S (without imprint). (Not issued).

	VG	VF	UNC
a. Issued note.	0.50	2.50	10.00
s. Specimen.	—	—	40.00

109 **500 Drachmai**
1.1.1939. Purple and lilac. Portrait woman in national costume at left. Back: View of city and woman in oval. Printer: BWC (without imprint).

	VG	VF	UNC
a. ΕΠΙ in line below Greek denomination.	1.00	4.50	25.00
b. Error: ΕΝΙ instead of ΕΠΙ .	1.00	4.50	30.00
s. Specimen.	—	—	100

110 **1000 Drachmai**
1.1.1939. Green. Woman in national costume at right. Back: Athena at left and view of Parthenon ruins at center. Printer: BWC (without imprint).

	VG	VF	UNC
a. Issued note.	1.00	4.00	15.00
s. Specimen.	—	—	100

1939 Provisional Issue

111 **1000 Drachmai on 100 Drachmai**
1939.

	VG	VF	UNC
a. Issued note.	0.75	3.00	16.00
s. Specimen.	—	—	50.00

GERMAN / ITALIAN OCCUPATION - WWII

Bank of Greece

1941 Emergency Reissue

Because of a shortage of notes caused by the German-Italian occupation, Greek authorities on April 25, 1941 reissued cancelled notes readied for destruction. These were in use for about a year, and were redeemed on 1.4.1942 by exchanging them for new notes. Some are hole cancelled (probably issued in Athens), while others also bear local stamps of branches of the Bank of Greece. Clear stamps are worth considerably more. The condition of all these notes is usually very low.

112 **50 Drachmai**

	Good	Fine	XF
(1941). Reissue of #97, 104.	6.00	20.00	—

		Good	Fine	XF
113	**100 Drachmai**	Good	Fine	XF
	(1941). Reissue of #98, 105.	5.00	18.00	—
114	**500 Drachmai**	Good	Fine	XF
	(1941). Reissue of #102.	4.00	17.00	—
115	**1000 Drachmai**	Good	Fine	XF
	(1941). Reissue of #100a, 100b, 106.	2.50	10.00	—
115A	**5000 Drachmai**	Good	Fine	XF
	(1941). Reissue of #103. Rare.	—	—	—

1941 Inflation Issue

Serial # varieties including positioning.

		VG	VF	UNC
116	**100 Drachmai**	VG	VF	UNC
	10.7.1941. Brown. Bird frieze at left and right. Back: Kapnikarea Church at center.			
	a. Issued note.	0.50	2.50	8.00
	s. Specimen.	—	—	50.00

		VG	VF	UNC
117	**1000 Drachmai**	VG	VF	UNC
	1.10.1941. Blue and brown. Coin of Alexander at left.			
	a. Title of picture on illustration.	0.50	3.00	12.00
	b. Title of picture on white background.	0.50	2.75	8.00
	s. Specimen.	—	—	100

1942 Inflation Issue

		VG	VF	UNC
118	**1000 Drachmai**	VG	VF	UNC
	21.8.1942. Black on blue-gray and pale orange underprint. Bust of young girl from Thasos at center. Back: Statue of Lion of Amphipolis at center.			
	a. Issued note.	—	1.25	3.75
	s. Specimen.	—	—	100

		VG	VF	UNC
119	**5000 Drachmai**	VG	VF	UNC
	20.6.1942. Black on pale red, blue and multicolor underprint. Factories and ships at lower left, statue of Nike of Samothrace between male workers at center, fisherman and shoreline at lower right. Back: Farmers sowing and plowing with horses at center.			
	a. Paper without watermark.	—	1.25	7.00
	b. Watermarked paper (same paper used for Agricultural Bonds #136-144).	0.50	2.00	9.00
	s. Specimen.	—	—	100
120	**10,000 Drachmai**	VG	VF	UNC
	29.12.1942. Brown. Young farm couple from Delphi at left. Back: Treasure of the Athenians in Delphi.			
	a. Title of picture on illustration.	3.00	12.00	50.00
	b. Title of picture in light background.	3.00	12.00	50.00
	s. Specimen.	—	—	100

1943 Inflation Issue

		VG	VF	UNC
121	**50 Drachmai**	VG	VF	UNC
	1.2.1943. Brown on blue underprint. Woman from Paramithia at left. Back: Ancient coin at left and right.			
	a. Issued note.	—	1.50	7.50
	s. Specimen.	—	—	100

		VG	VF	UNC
122	**5000 Drachmai**	VG	VF	UNC
	19.7.1943. Green and brown. Frieze at left and right, Athena at center. Back: Relief at center.			
	a. Issued note.	2.00	9.00	42.00
	s. Specimen.	—	—	100

123	25,000 Drachmai	VG	VF	UNC
	12.8.1943. Black on brown and light blue-green underprint. Bust of Nymph Deidamia at left. Back: Ruins of Olympian Temple of Zeus at center.			
	a. Issued note.	1.75	7.50	35.00
	s. Speicmen.	—	—	100

1944 Inflation Issue

124	50,000 Drachmai	VG	VF	UNC
	14.1.1944. Blue. Athlete at center.			
	a. Issued note.	3.50	14.00	55.00
	s. Specimen. Rare.	—	—	—

125	100,000 Drachmai	VG	VF	UNC
	21.1.1944. Black on brown and light blue-green underprint. Ancient silver tetradrachm coin of Athens at left and right. Back: Ruins of the Temple of Aphaea Athena in Aegina at center on back.			
	a. Serial number with prefix letters.	0.50	2.50	10.00
	b. Serial number with suffix letters.	0.50	2.50	10.00
	s. Specimen.	—	—	100

126	500,000 Drachmai	VG	VF	UNC
	20.3.1944. Black on dull violet-brown underprint. Head of Zeus at left. Back: Ears of wheat at center.			
	a. Serial #with prefix letters.	0.50	2.00	7.50
	b. Serial # with suffix letters.	0.50	2.00	7.50
	s. Specimen.	—	—	100

127	1,000,000 Drachmai	VG	VF	UNC
	29.6.1944. Black on blue-green and pale orange underprint. Bust of youth from Antikythera at center. Back: Ruins of Temple of Poseidon in Sounion at center.			
	a. Serial # with prefix letters.	—	1.50	4.00
	b. Serial # with suffix letters.	—	1.50	4.00
	s. Specimen.	—	—	100

128	5,000,000 Drachmai	VG	VF	UNC
	20.7.1944. Brown. Arethusa on dekadrachm of Syracuse at left.			
	a. Serial # with prefix letters.	—	1.75	5.00
	b. Serial # with suffix letters.	—	1.75	5.00
	s. Specimen.	—	—	100

129	10,000,000 Drachmai	VG	VF	UNC
	29.7.1944. Brown. Dark brown fringe around denomination guilloche and signature.			
	a. Serial # with prefix letters.	0.50	2.00	6.00
	b. Serial # with suffix letters.	0.50	2.00	6.00
	s. Specimen.	—	—	100

130	25,000,000 Drachmai	VG	VF	UNC
	10.8.1944. Green. Ancient Greek coin at left and right.			
	a. Serial # with prefix letters.	—	0.25	2.50
	b. Serial # with suffix letters.	—	0.25	2.50
	s. Specimen.	—	—	100

131	200,000,000 Drachmai	VG	VF	UNC
	9.9.1944. Brown and red-brown. Parthenon frieze at center.			
	a. Underprint in tightly woven pattern without circles.	0.50	2.00	12.00
	b. Underprint interconnecting circles with dots.	2.50	10.00	35.00
	s. Specimen.	—	—	100

		VG	VF	UNC
132	**500,000,000 Drachmai** 1.10.1944. Notes exist with duplicate serial #. Blue-green. Apollo at left. Back: Relief at center.			
	a. Serial # with prefix letters.	0.50	3.50	7.50
	b. Serial # with suffix letters.	0.50	3.50	7.50
	s. Specimen.	—	—	100

		VG	VF	UNC
133	**2,000,000,000 Drachmai** 11.10.1944. Notes exist with duplicate serial #. Black on pale light green underprint. Parthenon frieze at center.			
	a. Serial # with prefix letters.	—	0.75	3.00
	b. Serial # with suffix letters.	—	0.75	3.00
	s. Specimen.	—	—	100

		VG	VF	UNC
134	**10,000,000,000 Drachmai** 20.10.1944. Notes exist with duplicate serial #. Black and blue-black on tan underprint. Arethusa on dekadrachm of Syracuse at left.			
	a. Serial # with prefix letters.	—	1.00	4.50
	b. Serial # with suffix letters.	—	1.00	4.50
	s. Specimen.	—	—	100

		VG	VF	UNC
135	**100,000,000,000 Drachmai** 3.11.1944. Notes exist with duplicate serial #. Red-brown. Nymph Deidamia at left. Back: Ancient coin at left and right.			
	a. Issued note.	0.75	3.00	15.00
	s. Specimen.	—	—	100

ΤΑΜΕΙΑΚΟΝ ΓΡΑΜΜΑΤΙΟΝ

Agricultural Treasury Bonds

Note: There is some question as to whether or not this series of Agricultural Treasury Bonds circulated as banknotes.

1942 Issue

		VG	VF	UNC
136	**25,000 Drachmai** 26.11.1942. Series 1. Light orange.			
	a. Issued note.	25.00	70.00	160
	s. Specimen.	—	—	150
137	**100,000 Drachmai** 27.11.1942. Series 1. Dark green.	VG	VF	UNC
	a. Issued note.	—	—	95.00
	s. Specimen.	—	—	150
138	**500,000 Drachmai** 27.11.1942. Series 1. Brown and green	VG	VF	UNC
	a. Issued note.	—	—	350
	s. Specimen.	—	—	300

1943 First Issue

		VG	VF	UNC
139	**25,000 Drachmai** 5.3.1943. Series 2. Blue and gray.			
	a. Issued note.	—	—	75.00
	s. Specimen.	—	—	100
140	**100,000 Drachmai** 5.3.1943. Series 2. Blue and red.	VG	VF	UNC
	a. Issued note.	—	—	95.00
	s. Specimen.	—	—	150

		VG	VF	UNC
141	**500,000 Drachmai** 5.3.1943. Series 2. Light orange.			
	a. Issued note.	—	—	150
	s. Specimen.	—	—	300

1943 Second Issue

		VG	VF	UNC
142	**25,000 Drachmai** 15.5.1943. (Not issued). Gray, blue and green.			
	a. Issued note.	—	—	250
	s. Specimen.	—	—	500
143	**100,000 Drachmai** 15.5.1943. Series 3. (Not issued). Green.	VG	VF	UNC
	a. Issued note.	—	—	250
	s. Specimen.	—	—	500
144	**500,000 Drachmai** 15.5.1943. Series 3. (Not issued). Green and brown.	VG	VF	UNC
	a. Issued note.	—	—	250
	s. Specimen.	—	—	500

REGIONAL - WWII

Bank of Greece

ΑΓΡΙΝΙΟΥ - Agrinion

1944 Treasury Notes

#145-150 bank name in capital or small letters. Uniface.

		VG	VF	UNC
145	**100,000,000 Drachmai** Oct. 1944. Bank name in capital or small letters. Uniface.	15.00	60.00	175
146	**200,000,000 Drachmai** Oct. 1944. Bank name in capital or small letters. Uniface.	20.00	80.00	225
147	**300,000,000, Drachmai** Oct. 1944. Bank name in capital or small letters. Uniface.	20.00	80.00	225
148	**500,000,000 Drachmai** 9.10.1944. Blue text. Bank name in capital or small letters. Uniface.	20.00	80.00	225
149	**1,000,000,000 Drachmai** Oct. 1944. Bank name in capital or small letters. Uniface.	20.00	80.00	225
150	**2,000,000,000 Drachmai** 2.10.1944. Bank name in capital or small letters. Uniface.	VG	VF	UNC
	a. Bank name with capital letters.	17.00	60.00	225
	b. Bank name with small letters.	17.00	60.00	225

Color Abbreviation Guide

New to the *Standard Catalog of® World Paper Money* are the following abbreviations related to color references:

BC: Back color
PC: Paper color

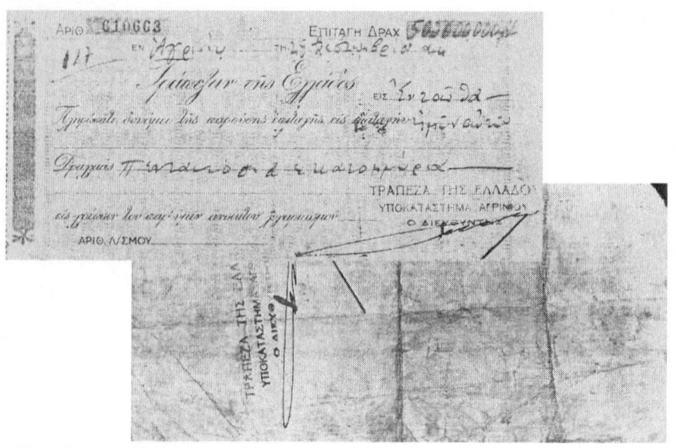

		VG	VF	UNC
150A	**Various Amounts** Sept.-Oct. 1944. Regular checks of the Agrinion branch made payable to *Ourselves* by bank manager. Amounts in millions of drachmai.	70.00	160	340

ΚΕΦΑΛΛΝΙΑ - ΙΘΑΚΑ Cephalonia - Ithaka

1944 Treasury Notes

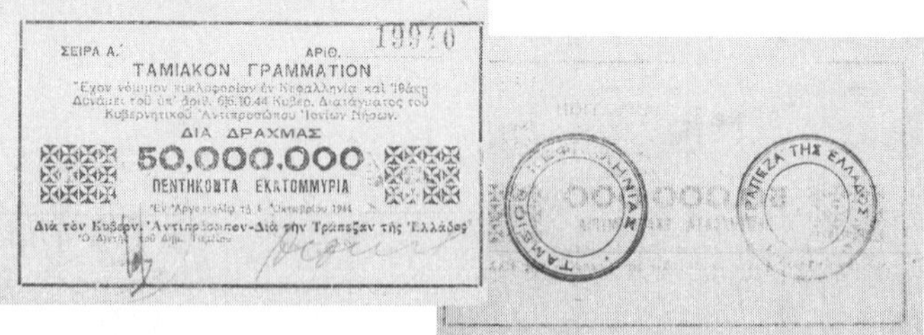

		VG	VF	UNC
151	**50,000,000 Drachmai** 6.10.1944. PC: Yellowish.	18.00	95.00	200

		VG	VF	UNC
152	**100,000,000 Drachmai** 6.10.1944. PC: Bluish	9.00	28.00	110

ΚΕΡΚΨΡΑ - Corfu

1944 Provisional Issue

Red overprint on Ionian Islands notes #M14, M15 and M16 for use in Corfu.

		VG	VF	UNC
153	**20 Drachmai on 50 Drachmai** 18.12.1944. Rare.	100	—	2,000

		VG	VF	UNC
154	**100 Drachmai on 100 Drachmai** 18.12.1944. Rare.	200	—	—
155	**500 Drachmai on 1000 Drachmai** 18.12.1944.	300	—	2,000

1944 Treasury Note w/Kerkyra Name

		VG	VF	UNC
156	**100,000,000 Drachmai** 17.10.1944. Green on yellow.	6.00	20.00	75.00

ΚΑΛΑΜΑΤΑ - Kalamata

1944 First Issue Treasury Notes

		VG	VF	UNC
157	**25,000,000 Drachmai** 20.9.1944. Brown. Flag at left and right. Uniface.	12.00	50.00	125
158	**50,000,000 Drachmai** 20.9.1944. Violet. Flag at left and right. Uniface.	12.00	35.00	125

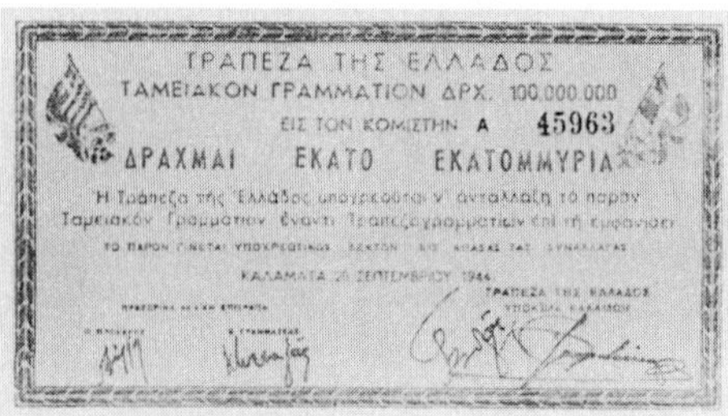

		VG	VF	UNC
159	**100,000,000 Drachmai** 20.9.1944. Light blue. Flag at left and right. Uniface.	9.00	28.00	110
160	**500,000,000 Drachmai** 20.9.1944. Green. Flag at left and right. Uniface.	16.00	65.00	175

1944 Second Issue

		VG	VF	UNC
161	**200,000,000 Drachmai** 5.10.1944. Orange.			
	a. Greek handstamp on back.	50.00	215	—
	b. French handstamp on back.	55.00	230	—
	c. Stamp for *TRIPOLIS* branch on back.	75.00	300	—

ΝΑΥΠΛΙΟΥ - Nauplia

1944 Provisional Treasury Notes

		VG	VF	UNC
162	**100,000,000 Drachmai** 19.9.1944.	25.00	80.00	160

		VG	VF	UNC
163	**500,000,000 Drachmai** 19.9.1944. Rare.	500	—	—

ΤΡΙΚΑΛΩΝ - Trikala

1944 Provisional Treasury Notes

Note for #166: All overprint. on #118 are believed to be spurious.

		VG	VF	UNC
167	**200,000,000 Drachmai** 29.9.1944.	150	450	2,000

Note: A 500 Million Drachmai issue from the Zakinthos branch dated Oct. 1944 requires confirmation.

ΥΠΟΚΑΤΑΣΤΗΜΑ ΠΑΤΡΩΝ - Patras

1944 Treasury Notes

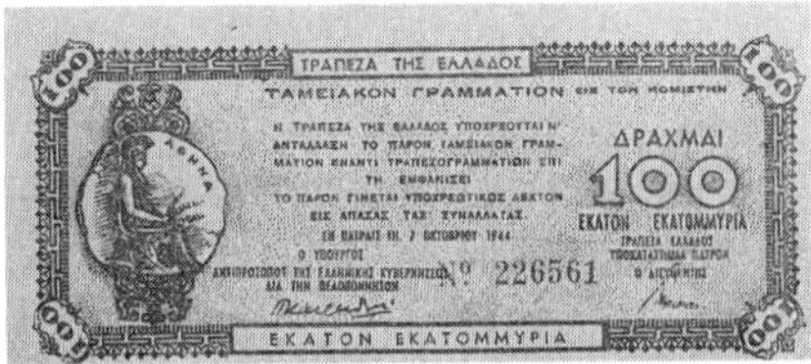

		VG	VF	UNC
164	**100,000,000 Drachmai** 7.10.1944. Brown. Ancient Greek coin at left. Uniface.	5.00	18.00	70.00

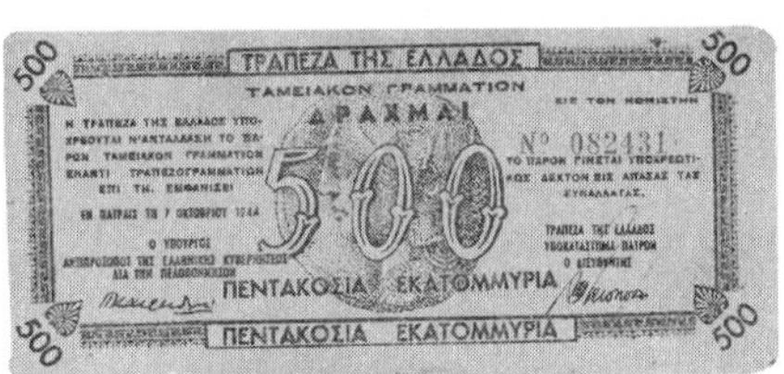

		VG	VF	UNC
165	**500,000,000 Drachmai** 7.10.1944. Blue-gray. Ancient Greek coin at center. Uniface.	5.00	18.00	65.00

KINGDOM - POST WWII

ΤΡΑΠΕΖΑ ΤΗΣ ΕΛΛΑΔΟΣ

Bank of Greece

1941-1944 Issue

		VG	VF	UNC
168	**50 Drachmai** 1.1.1941 (2.1.1945). Red-brown on lilac underprint. Hesiod at left. Back: Frieze at center. Watermark: Young male head. Printer: TDLR (without imprint).			
	a. Issued note.	0.50	2.50	15.00
	s. Specimen.	—	—	100

Note: For similar note to #168 in green and dated 1939, see #107.

		VG	VF	UNC
169	**50 Drachmai** 9.11.1944. Brown on blue and gold underprint. Statue of Nike of Samothrake at left. Back: Phoenix at center.			
	a. Issued note.	5.00	12.00	45.00
	s. Specimen.	—	—	150

1944-1946 ND Issue

		VG	VF	UNC
170	**100 Drachmai** ND (1944). Blue on gold underprint. Canaris (maritime hero) at right. Back: Goddess at center. Printer: W&S (without imprint).			
	a. Issued note.	3.00	12.00	45.00
	s. Specimen.	—	—	100

		VG	VF	UNC
171	**500 Drachmai** ND (1945). Green. Portrait Capodistrias (statesman) at left. Back: University of Athens at bottom center. Printer: BWC (without imprint).			
	a. Issued note.	2.00	8.50	35.00
	s. Specimen.	—	—	100

		VG	VF	UNC
172	**1000 Drachmai** ND (1944). Brown. Portrait Kolokotronis (hero of freedom) at left. Back: Soldier at center. Printer: BWC (without imprint). 161x80mm.			
	a. Issued note.	6.00	22.00	80.00
	s. Specimen.	—	—	100

173	5000 Drachmai	VG	VF	UNC
	ND (1945). Red. Woman with children at center. Back: Two women with mythical horse at center. Printer: BWC (without imprint). 170x84mm.			
	a. Issued note.	22.00	110	450
	s. Specimen.	—	—	500

174	10,000 Drachmai	VG	VF	UNC
	ND (1945). Orange. Aristotle at left, ancient coins around border. Back: Standing male figure at center. Printer: BWC (without imprint). 180x90mm.			
	a. Issued note.	15.00	60.00	250
	s. Specimen.	—	—	300

175	10,000 Drachmai	VG	VF	UNC
	ND (1946). Blue. Aristotle at left, ancient coins around border. Back: Standing male figure at center. 180x90mm.			
	a. Issued note.	18.00	80.00	320
	s. Specimen.	—	—	500

176	20,000 Drachmai	VG	VF	UNC
	ND (1946). Dark green. Athena at left, ancient coin at bottom. Back: Medusa at upper center, chicken at lower center Printer: BWC (without imprint). 180x90mm.			
	a. Issued note.	45.00	195	500
	s. Specimen.	—	—	500

1947 ND Issue

177	5000 Drachmai	VG	VF	UNC
	ND (1947). Purple on orange underprint. Women with children at center. 2 signatures. Back: Two women with mythical horse at center. 153x80mm.			
	a. Issued note.	30.00	120	450
	s. Specimen.	—	—	300

178	10,000 Drachmai	VG	VF	UNC
	ND (1947). Orange. Aristotle at left, ancient coins around border. 2 signatures. Back: Standing male figure at center. 153x80mm.			
	a. Issued note.	25.00	125	450
	s. Specimen.	—	—	500

179	20,000 Drachmai	VG	VF	UNC
	ND (1947). Dark green. Athena at left, ancient coin at bottom. 2 signatures. Back: Medusa at upper center, chicken at lower center. 153x80mm.			
	a. Without security strip.	17.00	80.00	300
	b. With security strip.	22.00	100	400
	s. Specimen.	—	—	650

1947; 1949 Issue

180	1000 Drachmai	VG	VF	UNC
	1947. Brown. Portrait Kolokotronis (hero of freedom) at left. 3 signatures. Back: Soldier at center. 145x75mm.			
	a. 9.1.1947. Watermark: Ancient warrior with helmet.	2.50	10.00	70.00
	b. 14.11.1947. Without watermark.	12.50	50.00	175
	s. Specimen.	—	—	100

181	5000 Drachmai	VG	VF	UNC
	9.6.1947. Brown. Woman with children at center. 3 signatures. Back: Two women with mythical horse at center. 153x80mm.			
	a. Issued note.			
	s. Specimen.	—	—	300

182	10,000 Drachmai	VG	VF	UNC
	29.12.1947. Orange. Aristotle at left, ancient coins around border. 3 signatures. Back: Standing male figure at center. 150x79mm.			
	a. Without printer's name at bottom on back. (Printer: BWC.)	8.00	35.00	130
	b. Greek printer's name at bottom on back. Same numeral style as a.	16.00	70.00	280
	c. Printer like b., but small serial # prefix letters.	12.00	55.00	200
	s. Specimen.	—	—	300

183	20,000 Drachmai	VG	VF	UNC
	29.12.1949. Blue on multicolor underprint. Athena at left, ancient coin at bottom. 3 signatures. Back: Medusa at upper center, chicken at lower center. 147x78mm.			
	a. Issued note.	4.00	35.00	150
	s. Specimen.	—	—	300

1950 Issue

184	5000 Drachmai	VG	VF	UNC
	28.10.1950. Brown. Portrait Solomos at left. Back: Battle of Mesolonghi.			
	a. Issued note.	5.00	20.00	160
	s. Specimen.	—	—	500

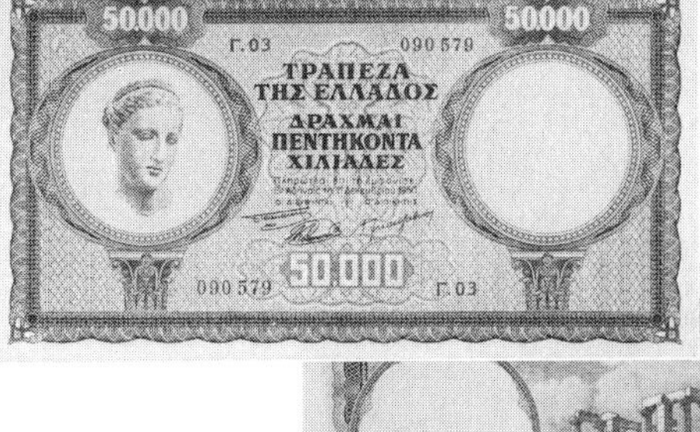

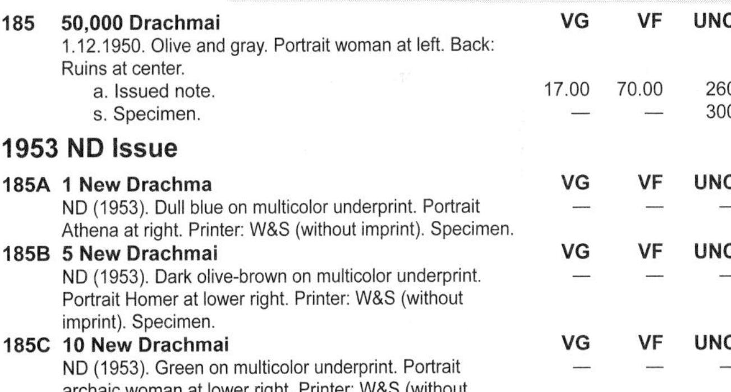

185	50,000 Drachmai	VG	VF	UNC
	1.12.1950. Olive and gray. Portrait woman at left. Back: Ruins at center.			
	a. Issued note.	17.00	70.00	260
	s. Specimen.	—	—	300

1953 ND Issue

185A	1 New Drachma	VG	VF	UNC
	ND (1953). Dull blue on multicolor underprint. Portrait Athena at right. Printer: W&S (without imprint). Specimen.	—	—	—

185B	5 New Drachmai	VG	VF	UNC
	ND (1953). Dark olive-brown on multicolor underprint. Portrait Homer at lower right. Printer: W&S (without imprint). Specimen.	—	—	—

185C	10 New Drachmai	VG	VF	UNC
	ND (1953). Green on multicolor underprint. Portrait archaic woman at lower right. Printer: W&S (without imprint). Specimen.	—	—	—

1954 Issue

#186-188 ΝΕΑ ΕΚΔΟΣΙΣ (New Issue) at r.

186 10 Drachmai
15.1.1954. Orange. Aristotle at left, ancient coins around border. Back: Standing male figure at center. 150x79mm.

	VG	VF	UNC
a. Issued note.	120	470	—
s. Specimen.	—	—	800

187 20 Drachmai
15.1.1954. Blue. Athena at left, ancient coin at bottom. Back: Medusa at upper center, chicken at lower center. 147x78mm.

	VG	VF	UNC
a. Issued note.	40.00	135	550
s. Specimen.	—	—	800

188 50 Drachmai
15.1.1954. Green and gray. Portrait woman at left. Back: ruins at center.

	VG	VF	UNC
a. Issued note.	15.00	45.00	280
s. Specimen.	—	—	800

1954-1956 Issue

189 10 Drachmai
1954-1955. Orange. King George I at left. Back: Church at center.

	VG	VF	UNC
a. 15.5.1954.	8.00	35.00	—
b. 1.3.1955.	3.00	15.00	85.00
s. Specimen.	—	—	300

190 20 Drachmai
1.3.1955. Blue. Demokritos at left. Back: Mythical scene.

	VG	VF	UNC
a. Issued note.	4.00	20.00	130
s. Specimen.	—	—	300

191 50 Drachmai
1.3.1955. Dark green. Pericles at center. Back: Pericles speaking.

	VG	VF	UNC
a. Issued note.	4.00	20.00	90.00
s. Specimen.	—	—	45.00

192 100 Drachmai
1954-1955. Red on multicolor underprint. Themistocles at left, galley at bottom right. Back: Sailing ships.

	VG	VF	UNC
a. 31.3.1954.	22.00	90.00	300
b. 1.7.1955.	8.00	35.00	145
s1. As a. Specimen.	—	—	300
s2. As b. Specimen.	—	—	300

193 500 Drachmai
8.8.1955. Green on multicolor underprint. Socrates at center. Back: Apostle Paul speaking to assembly.

	VG	VF	UNC
a. Issued note.	35.00	160	—
s. Specimen.	—	—	300

		VG	VF	UNC
194	**1000 Drachmai** 16.4.1956. Brown. Alexander at left, frieze at bottom. Back: Alexander in battle.			
	a. Issued note.	30.00	145	500
	s. Specimen.	—	—	750

MINISTRY OF FINANCE

Greek State

1917 Provisional Issue

		VG	VF	UNC
301	**1 Drachma** 1917 (-old date 21.12.1885). Printer: BWC.	8.00	35.00	125
302	**2 Drachmai** 1917 (-old date 21.12.1885).	11.00	45.00	150

ΒΑΣΙΛΕΙΟΝ ΤΗΣ ΕΛΛΑΔΟΣ

Kingdom of Greece

1917-1920 ND Issue

		VG	VF	UNC
303	**50 Lepta** ND (1920). Blue. Standing Athena at center. Arms of King George I. Back: Ancient coin at left and right. Printer: Aspiotis Freres.			
	a. Square perforations.	8.50	35.00	100
	b. Zig-zag perforations.	7.50	30.00	95.00

		VG	VF	UNC
304	**1 Drachma** 27.10.1917. Brown. Hermes seated at center.			
	a. Brown on gold underprint. Without inner line in diamond surrounding Hermes, diamond dark brown.	5.00	25.00	85.00
	b. Darker brown without underprint. Inner line in diamond surrounding Hermes, diamond brown.	4.50	20.00	75.00

		VG	VF	UNC
305	**1 Drachma** ND (1918). Brown. Pericles at right. Back: Medal at center.	3.00	15.00	50.00
306	**2 Drachmai** 27.10.1917. Blue and brown. Hermes seated at center.	15.00	52.00	140
307	**2 Drachmai** ND (1918). Black on gold underprint. Pericles at left. Back: Ancient coin at middle left and right.	60.00	200	—

1917 (1918) Issue

Note: All issues with a 1917 date were released in 1918.

		VG	VF	UNC
308	**1 Drachma** 27.10.1917 (1918). Black on light green and pink underprint. Homer at center. Printer: BWC.	10.00	35.00	90.00

		VG	VF	UNC
309	**1 Drachma** 27.10.1917 (1918). Purple on lilac and multicolor underprint. Hermes seated at right. Printer: BWC.	10.00	35.00	90.00

		VG	VF	UNC
310	**2 Drachmai** 27.10.1917 (1918). Blue on brown and orange underprint. Zeus at left. Printer: BWC.	15.00	55.00	145

		VG	VF	UNC
311	**2 Drachmai** 27.10.1917 (1918). Red-brown on multicolor underprint. Orpheus with lyre at center. Printer: BWC.	15.00	60.00	170

1918 Issue

		VG	VF	UNC
312	**5 Drachmai** 14.6.1918. Green and multicolor. Athena at left. (Not issued).	220	600	1,500

ΕΛΛΑΣ

1922 ND Postage Stamp Currency Issue

		VG	VF	UNC
313	**10 Lepta** ND (1922). Postage stamp of the 1911-1921 issue (Michel #162, Scott #202). Brown. Hermes. Back: Same design as front in reverse.			
	a. Square perforations.	2.00	7.50	20.00
	b. Zig-zag perforations.	2.00	6.00	15.00

ΒΑΣΙΛΕΙΟΝ ΤΗΣ ΕΛΛΑΔΟΕ

1940 Issue

No.	Denomination	VG	VF	UNC
314	**10 Drachmai** 6.4.1940. Blue on green and light brown underprint. Ancient coin with Demeter at left. Back: University at center.	—	1.50	7.00

No.	Denomination	VG	VF	UNC
315	**20 Drachmai** 6.4.1940. Green on light lilac and orange underprint. Ancient coin with Poseidon at left. Back: Parthenon at center.	—	1.50	7.00

ΕΛΛΗΝΙΚΝ ΠΟΛΙΤΕΙΑ

Greek State (resumed)

1941 Issue

No.	Denomination	VG	VF	UNC
316	**50 Lepta** 18.6.1941. Red and black on light brown underprint. Nike of Samothrake at left. Back: Church. Printer: Aspiotis-ELKA.	—	1.50	7.00

No.	Denomination	VG	VF	UNC
317	**1 Drachma** 18.6.1941. Red and blue on gray underprint. Aristotle at left. Back: Ancient coin at center. Printer: Aspiotis-ELKA.	—	1.50	7.00

No.	Denomination	VG	VF	UNC
318	**2 Drachmai** 18.6.1941. Purple and black on light brown underprint. Ancient coin of Alexander III at left. Back: Ancient coin at center. Printer: Aspiotis-ELKA.	—	1.75	8.00

No.	Denomination	VG	VF	UNC
319	**5 Drachmai** 18.6.1941. Black and red on pale yellow underprint. Three women of Knossos at center. Back: Column at center. Printer: Aspiotis-ELKA.	—	1.75	8.00

ΒΑΣΙΛΕΙΟΝ ΤΗΣ ΕΛΛΑΔΟΣ

Kingdom of Greece (resumed)

1944; 1945 Issue

No.	Denomination	VG	VF	UNC
320	**1 Drachma** 9.11.1944. Blue on green underprint. Back: Phoenix at center.	—	1.75	8.00

No.	Denomination	VG	VF	UNC
321	**5 Drachmai** 15.1.1945. Brown and yellow-orange.	—	1.75	8.00

No.	Denomination	VG	VF	UNC
322	**10 Drachmai** 9.11.1944. Brown on green and orange underprint. Laborer at left and right. Back: Church at center.	—	1.75	8.00

No.	Denomination	VG	VF	UNC
323	**20 Drachmai** 9.11.1944. Blue on orange underprint. Zeus on ancient coin at center. Back: Angel at center.	0.50	2.50	12.00

1950 Issue

No.	Denomination	VG	VF	UNC
324	**100 Drachmai** 1950-1953. Blue on orange underprint. Constantine at center. Back: Church at center.			
	a. 10.7.1950.	1.00	4.00	20.00
	b. 1.11.1953.	0.75	3.00	18.00

No.	Denomination	VG	VF	UNC
325	**500 Drachmai** 1950-1953. Green on brown underprint. Byzantine coin at left. Back: Church at center.			
	a. 10.7.1950.	2.00	8.00	50.00
	b. 1.11.1953.	2.00	8.00	50.00

No.	Denomination	VG	VF	UNC
326	**1000 Drachmai** 1950-1953. Brown on orange and green underprint. Ancient coin at left and right. Back: Stone carving of a lion at center.			
	a. 10.7.1950.	2.50	10.00	60.00
	b. 1.11.1953.	1.50	7.50	40.00

GREENLAND

Greenland, an integral part of the Danish realm, is a huge island situated between the North Atlantic Ocean and the Polar Sea, almost entirely within the Artic Circle. It has an area of 2.166 million sq. km. and a population of 57,564. Capital: Nuuk (Godthab). Greenland is the world's only source of natural cryolite, a fluoride of sodium and aluminum important in making aluminum. Fish products and minerals are exported.

Greenland, the world's largest island, is about 81% ice-capped. Vikings reached the island in the 10th century from Iceland; Danish colonization began in the 18th century, and Greenland was made an integral part of Denmark in 1953. It joined the European Community (now the EU) with Denmark in 1973, but withdrew in 1985 over a dispute centered on stringent fishing quotas. Greenland was granted self-government in 1979 by the Danish parliament; the law went into effect the following year. Denmark continues to exercise control of Greenland's foreign affairs in consultation with Greenland's Home Rule Government.

RULERS:
Danish

MONETARY SYSTEM:
1 Rigsbankdaler = 96 Skilling to 1874
1 Krone = 48 Skilling
1 Krone = 100 Óre, 1874-

DANISH ADMINISTRATION

Kongel. Grønlandske Handel

1803 Issue

		Good	Fine	XF
A1	**12 Skilling** 1803. Value text at upper right. Julianehaab District.	950	2,250	4,100

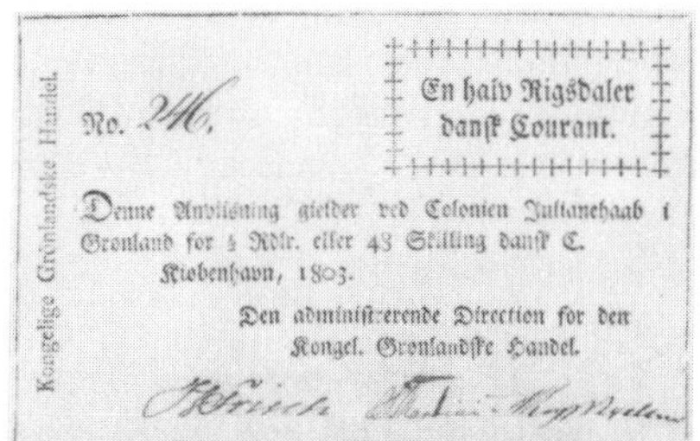

		Good	Fine	XF
A2	**24 Skilling** 1803. Value text at upper right. Julianehaab District.	1,000	2,500	4,250

		Good	Fine	XF
A3	**1/2 Rigsdaler** 1803. Value text at upper right. Julianehaab District.	900	2,100	4,000
A4	**1 Rigsdaler** 1803. Value text at upper right. Julianehaab District.	800	1,750	3,750

Note: An 1801 issue (possibly handwritten) requires confirmation.

Handelsstederne i Grønland

1804 Issue

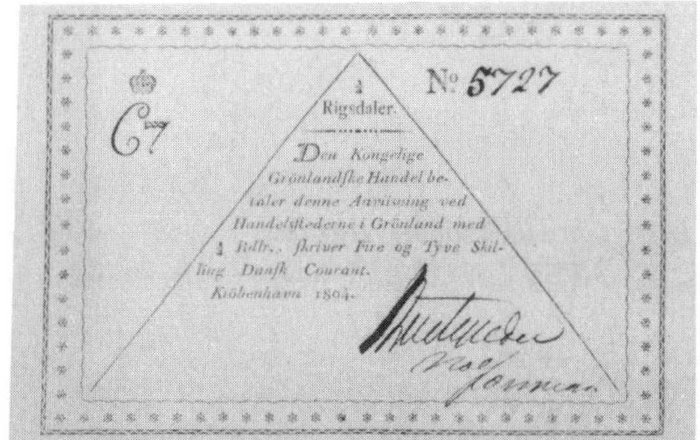

		Good	Fine	XF
A5	**6 Skilling** 1804. Blue. Denomination at top of text in diamond at center.	500	1,100	2,000
A6	**12 Skilling** 1804. Red. Denomination at top of text in diamond at center.	575	1,200	2,150
A7	**1/4 Rigsdaler** 1804. Blue. Denomination at top of text in triange at center.	625	1,275	2,250
A8	**1/2 Rigsdaler** 1804. Red. Denomination at top of text in triangle at center.	625	1,275	2,250
A9	**1 Rigsdaler** 1804. Blue. Denomination at top of text in large frame.	700	1,350	2,450

		Good	Fine	XF
A10	**5 Rigsdaler** 1804. Red. Denomination at top of text in large frame.	700	1,350	2,450

1819 Issue

		Good	Fine	XF
A11	**6 Skilling** 1819. Black. Crowned F6R monogram at left and crowned polar bear at right ends. Denomination in frame at top center.	3,000	—	—
A12	**12 Skilling** 1819. Black. Crowned F6R monogram at left and crowned polar bear at right ends. Denomination in script in oval at top center.	—	9,000	—
A13	**24 Skilling** 1819. Black. Crowned F6R monogram at left and crowned polar bear at right ends. Denomination in frame at top center and in diamond at left.	—	—	—
A14	**1 Rigsbankdaler** 1819. Black. Crowned F6R monogram at left and crowned polar bear at right ends. Denomination and serial number in each corner.	—	—	—

1837 Issue

		Good	Fine	XF
A15	**6 Skilling** 1837. Black. Crowned F6R monogram at left and crowned polar bear at right ends. Denomination in frame at top center.	—	—	—
A16	**12 Skilling** 1837. Black. Crowned F6R monogram at left and crowned polar bear at right ends. Denomination in script oval frame at top center.	—	—	—
A17	**24 Skilling** 1837. Black. Crowned F6R monogram at left and crowned polar bear at right ends. Denomination in frame at top center and in diamond at left.	—	—	—
A18	**1 Rigsbankdaler** 1837. Black. Crowned F6R monogram at left and crowned polar bear at right ends. Denomination and serial number in each corner.	—	—	—

1841 Issue

		Good	Fine	XF
A19	**6 Skilling** 1841. Black. Crowned C8R monogram at left and crowned polar bear at right ends. Denomination in frame at top center.			
	a. Issued note.	—	—	—
	r. Remainder.	—	Unc	8,000
A20	**12 Skilling** 1841. Black. Crowned C8R monogram at left and crowned polar bear at right ends. Denomination in oval at top center.	—	—	—

		Good	Fine	XF
A21	**24 Skilling**			
	1841. Black. Crowned C8R monogram at left and crowned polar bear at right ends. Denomination in frame at top center.	—	—	—
A22	**1 Rigsbankdaler**			
	1841. Black. Crowned C8R monogram at left and crowned polar bear at right ends. Denomination and serial number in each corner.	—	—	—

1844 Issue

		Good	Fine	XF
A23	**6 Skilling**			
	1844. Blue in red frame. As A15.	—	—	—
A24	**12 Skilling**			
	1844. Blue in red frame. As A16.			
	a. Issued note.	—	19,000	—
	r. Remainder.	—	—	4,250
A25	**24 Skilling**			
	1844. Blue in red frame. As A17.	—	—	—
A26	**1 Rigsbankdaler**			
	1844. Blue in red frame. As A18.	—	—	—

1848 Issue

		Good	Fine	XF
A27	**6 Skilling**			
	1848. Blue in red frame. As A23, F7R monogram at upper left.	—	—	9,500
A28	**12 Skilling**			
	1848. Blue in red frame. As A24, F7R monogram at upper left.	—	—	—
A29	**24 Skilling**			
	1848. Blue in red frame. As A25, F7R monogram at upper left.	—	—	—
A30	**1 Rigsbankdaler**			
	1848. Blue in red frame. As A26, F7R monogram at upper left.	—	—	—

1853 Issue

		Good	Fine	XF
A31	**6 Skilling**			
	1853. Blue in red frame. As A27.	—	—	—
A31A	**12 Skilling**			
	1853. Blue in red frame.	—	—	—
A31B	**24 Skilling**			
	1853. Unknown. Blue in red frame.	—	—	—
A32	**1 Rigsbankdaler**			
	1853. Blue in red frame. As A30.	—	—	—

1856 Issue

		Good	Fine	XF
A33	**6 Skilling R.M.**			
	1856. Blue in red frame. F7R monogram at center left.			
	a. Issued note.	700	1,800	3,200
	r. Unsigned remainder.	—	Unc	5,000

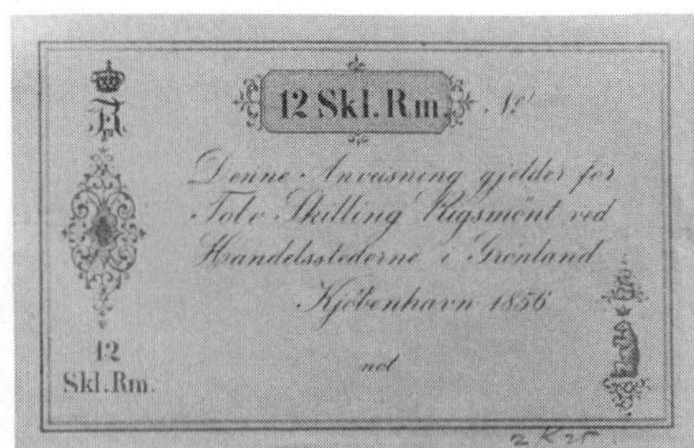

		Good	Fine	XF
A34	**12 Skilling R.M.**			
	1856. Blue in red frame. F7R monogram at upper left.			
	a. Issued note.	800	2,000	3,800
	r. Unsigned remainder.	—	Unc	500
A35	**24 Skilling R.M.**			
	1856. Blue in red frame. F7R monogram at upper left.			
	a. Issued note.	900	2,100	4,000
	r. Unsigned remainder.	—	Unc	500
A36	**1 Rigsdaler**			
	1856. Blue in red frame. F7R monogram at upper left.			
	a. Issued note.	1,200	2,400	5,000
	r. Remainder.	—	Unc	500

1874 Issue

		Good	Fine	XF
A37	**50 Øre**			
	1874. Gray. Value in scroll at center, C9R monogram at left, crowned small polar bear at right.			
	a. Signature H. Rink - Nyholm.	500	1,200	2,750
	b. Signature Hørring - Nyholm.	—	—	—
	c. Signature Hørring - Stibget.	—	—	—
	d. Signature Hørring - Stephensen.	600	1,500	3,000
	r. Unsigned remainder.	—	Unc	500

		Good	Fine	XF
A38	**1 Krone**			
	1874. Blue. Value in scroll at center, C9R monogram at left, crowned small polar bear at right.			
	a. Signature: H. Rink - Nyholm.	750	1,750	3,500
	b. Signature: Hørring - Nyholm.	—	—	—
	c. Signature: Hørring - Stibget.	—	—	—
	r. Unsigned remainder.	—	Unc	500

1875 Issue

		Good	Fine	XF
A39	**25 Øre**			
	1875. Light brown. Value in scroll at center, C9R monogram at left, crowned small polar bear at right.			
	a. Signature: H. Rink - Nyholm.	400	1,400	2,900
	b. Signature: Hørring -Stephensen.	500	1,500	3,000
	c. Signature: Stephensen - Petersen.	—	—	—
	d. Signature: Stephensen - Ryberg.	—	—	—
	r. Unsigned remainder.	—	Unc	3,500

1883; 1887 Issue

		Good	Fine	XF
A40	**1 Krone**			
	1883. Blue. Crowned polar bear at left and right. Printer: V. Søborgs Stent.			
	a. Signature: Hørring - Stephensen.	700	1,600	3,400
	b. Signature: Stephensen - Petersen.	900	2,100	4,000
	c. Signature: Stephensen - Ryberg.	700	1,600	3,400
	r. Remainder.	—	—	500

		Good	Fine	XF
A41	**5 Kronen**			
	1887. Green. Crowned polar bear shield at left and right, both facing left. Printer: V. Søborgs Stentr.			
	a. Handwritten serial #. Signature: Hørring - Stephensen.	2,000	4,000	8,000
	b. Handwritten serial #. Signature: Stephensen - Ryberg.	2,000	4,000	8,000
	c. Printed serial #. Signature: Ryberg - Krenchel.	4,500	8,000	—
	d. Printed serial #. Signature: Krenchel - Bergh.	—	—	—
	e. Printed serial #. Signature: Ryberg - Bergh.	5,000	10,000	—
	r. Unsigned remainder.	—	Unc	800

1888 Issue

		Good	Fine	XF
1	**50 Øre** 1888. Brown. Greenland seal on ice slab at center. Polar bear in left shield facing right. Printer: V. Söborgs Stentr.			
	a. Handwritten serial #. Signature: Hørring - Stephensen.	350	700	1,800
	b. Handwritten serial #. Signature: Stephensen - Petersen.	—	—	—
	c. Handwritten serial #. Signature: Stephensen - Ryberg.	350	700	1,800
	d. Printed serial #. Signature: Stephensen - Ryberg.	600	1,200	2,500
	e. Printed serial #. Signature: Ryberg - Krenchel.	250	600	1,600
	f. As b. With star (Ivigtut).	1,400	2,350	4,000
	r. Unsigned remainder.	—	—	400

1892 Issue

		Good	Fine	XF
2	**25 Øre** 1892. Black. Polar bear in left shield facing right. Printer: V. Söborgs Lit. Etabl.			
	a. Serial # handwritten. Signature: Stephensen - Ryberg.	300	600	1,500
	b. Serial # printed. Signature: Stephensen - Ryberg.	350	700	1,600
	c. Serial # printed. Signature: Ryberg - Krenchel.	250	500	900
	d. Serial # printed. Signature: Ryberg - Bergh.	400	800	1,750
	r. Unsigned remainder.	—	—	350

1897 Issue

		Good	Fine	XF
5	**1 Krone** 1897; 1905. Blue. Polar bear in left shield facing left.			
	a. 1897. Handwritten serial #. Signature: Stephensen - Ryberg. Printer imprint as: Vilh. Søborgs Eftfs Etabl.	2,000	4,000	—
	b. 1897. Serial # printed. Signature: Stephensen - Ryberg.	800	1,600	4,000
	c. 1897. Serial # printed. Signature: Ryberg - Krenchel.	800	1,600	4,000
	d. 1905. Signature: Ryberg - Krenchel. Without printer imprint.	800	1,600	4,000
	e. 1905. Signature: Ryberg - Bergh.	90.00	280	600
	f. As e. 1905. With star. (Ivigtut).	—	—	—
	r. As a. Unsigned remainder.	—	—	250

1905 Issue

		Good	Fine	XF
4	**25 Øre** 1905. Red. Polar bear in left shield facing left.			
	a. Signature Ryberg-Krenchel.	250	450	600
	b. Signature Ryberg-Bergh.	25.00	55.00	150
	c. As a. With star. (Ivigtut).	600	1,250	2,250
	r. Remainder.	—	Unc	100

Den Kongelige Grønlandske Handel

1911 Provisional Issue

		Good	Fine	XF
6	**1 Krone** 1911 (-old date 1905). Blue.			
	a. Overprint: *Den kgl. grønlandske Handel 1911* across lower center on #5d or e. Signature Oskar Wesche-Munch.	1,000	2,250	3,500
	b. With additional overprint.: *Kolonien Holstensborg* at top.	2,000	3,500	5,500

1911 Issue

		Good	Fine	XF
7	**25 Øre** 1911. Red. Eider duck on rock in water at center. Signature Oskar Wesche-Munch.			
	a. Perforated edges.	1,100	2,500	—
	b. Straight cut edges. Watermark: *DKGH.*	800	1,800	2,800

		Good	Fine	XF
8	**50 Øre** 1911. Brown. Greenland seal on ice at center. Signature Oskar Wesche-Munch.			
	a. Perforated edges.	1,000	3,400	6,000
	b. Straight cut edges. Watermark: *DKGH.*	1,200	3,800	6,500

		Good	Fine	XF
9	**1 Krone** 1911. Straight cut edges. Blue. Reindeer in mountains at center. Signature Oskar Wesche-Munch. Watermark: *DKGH.*	800	2,000	4,000

		Good	Fine	XF
10	**5 Kroner** 1911. Green. Polar bear on ice at center.			
	a. Perforated edges.	3,000	4,750	—
	b. Straight cut edges. Watermark: *DKGH.*	3,250	5,250	—
	c. As a. Overprint at top: *Kolonien Holstensborg.*	3,500	6,000	—
	r. Remainder.	—	2,000	3,000

Styrelsen af Kolonierne i Grønland

State Notes

1913 Issue

		VG	VF	UNC
11	**25 Øre** ND (1913). Red. Common eider duck on rock in water at center. 2 signature varieties. Printer: Andreasen & Lachmann Lit.			
	a. Signature: Daugaard Jensen - Munch (straight dash over u in Munch).	180	350	700
	b. Signature: Daugaard Jensen - Munch. (curved dash over u in Munch).	40.00	75.00	150
	c. Signature: Daugaard Jensen-Barner Rasmussen (Large signature).	40.00	75.00	150
	d. Signature: Daugaard Jensen-Barner Rasmussen (Small signature).	300	700	1,100
	r. Unsigned remainder.	—	—	100

		VG	VF	UNC
12	**50 Øre** ND (1913). Brown. Saddleback seal on ice at center. 2 signature varieties. Printer: Andreasen & Lachmann Lit.			
	a. Signature: Daugaard Jensen - Munch (straight dash over u in Munch).	250	500	1,000

		VG	VF	UNC
	b. Signature: Daugaard Jensen - Munch (curved dash over u in Munch).	75.00	150	300
	c. Signature: Daugaard Jensen - Barner Rasmussen (large signature).	125	275	500
	d. Signature: Daugaard Jensen - Barner Rasmussen (small signature).	140	325	650
	r. Unsigned remainder.	—	—	250

		VG	VF	UNC
13	**1 Krone** ND (1913). Blue. Reindeer in mountains at center. 2 signature varieties. Printer: Andreasen & Lachmann Lit.			
	a. Signature: Daugaard Jensen - Munch (straight dash over u in Munch).	250	500	1,000
	b. Signature: Daugaard Jensen - Munch. (curved dash over u in Munch).	85.00	165	325
	c. Signature: Daugaard Jensen - Barner Rasmussen (large signature).	300	600	1,200
	d. Signature: Daugaard Jensen - Barner Rasmussen (small signature).	140	350	725
	r. Unsigned remainder.	—	—	300
14	**5 Kroner** ND (1913). Dark green on blue-green underprint. Polar bear on ice at center. Signature Daugaard Jensen - Munch. Printer: Andreasen & Lachmann Lit.	300	900	2,000
14A	**5 Kroner** ND (1913). (500 pieces made available in 1981). Dark green on blue-green underprint. Polar bear on ice at center. Signature Daugaard Jensen - Barner Rasmussen. Printer: Andreasen & Lachmann Lit.	—	—	200

Grønlands Styrelse

State Notes

1926-1952 Issue

		VG	VF	UNC
15	**5 Kroner** ND (1926-1945). Green. Polar bear on ice at center. *GRØNLANDS STYRELSE* on all sides. Back: *GRØNLANDS STYRELSE* around GS at center. 125x83mm.			
	a. Signature Daugaard Jensen - Barner Rasmussen.	—	—	—
	b. Signature: Daugaard Jensen - P.O. Sveistrup.	250	550	975
	c. Small signature: Oldendow - P.P. Sveistrup.	1,000	2,250	4,000
	d. Large signature: Oldendow - P.P. Sveistrup.	100	200	500
	e. Signature: Eske Brun - P.P. Sveistrup.	125	250	625
	f. Large signature - Eske Brun - Ole Pedersen.	350	650	—
15A	**5 Kroner** ND (1945-1952). Green. Polar bear on ice at center. Green underprint of diagonal lines, white border.			
	a. Small signature: Eske Brum - Ole Pedersen.	100	200	500

		VG	VF	UNC
16	**10 Kroner** ND (1926-1945). Brown. *GRØNLANDS STYRELSE* on all sides. Hump-back whale at center. Green underprint fine screening through border. Back: *GRØNLANDS STYRELSE* around GS at center. 131x83mm.			
	a. Signature: Daugaard Jensen - Barner Rasmussen.	—	—	—
	b. Signature: Daugaard Jensen - P.P. Sveistrup.	275	—	—
	c. Small signature: Oldendow - P.P. Sveistrup.	—	—	—
	d. Large signature: Oldendow - P.P. Sveistrup.	125	350	800
	e. Signature: Eske Brun - P.P. Sveistrup.	125	350	800
	f. Large signature: Eske Brun - Ole Pedersen.	200	500	—
16A	**10 Kroner** ND (1945-1952). Brown. Humpback whale at center. Brown underprint of diagonal lines, white border.			
	a. Small signature: Eske Brun - Ole Pedersen.	100	200	500
17	**50 Kroner** ND (1926-1945). Lilac. *GRØNLANDS STYRELSE* on all sides. Clipper ship at center. Back: *GRØNLANDS STYRELSE* around map at center.			
	a. Signature: Daugaard Jensen - P.P. Sveistrup.	2,000	4,000	17,000
	b. Large signature: Oldendow - P.P. Sveistrup.	2,250	4,500	22,000
	c. Signature: Eske Brun - P.P. Sveistrup.	—	—	—
17A	**50 Kroner** ND (1945-1952). Lilac. Clipper ship at center. Lilac underprint of diagonal lines, white border.			
	a. Small signature: Eske Brun - Ole Pedersen.	200	2,250	4,000

Den Kongelige Grønlandske Handel (resumed)

1953 Issue

		VG	VF	UNC
18	**5 Kroner** ND (1953-1967). Green. Polar bear on ice at center. *DEN KONGELIGE GRØNLANDSKE HANDEL* at left and right margin, across bottom. Back: *DEN KONGELIGE GRØNLANDSKE HANDEL* around map at center.			
	a. Signature: Hans C. Christensen. Size: 84x125mm.	35.00	90.00	200
	b. Signature: Hans C. Christensen. Size: 84x130mm.	35.00	90.00	200
	s. Specimen.	—	—	200

19	10 Kroner	VG	VF	UNC
	ND (1953-1967). Brown. Humpback whale at center. *DEN KONGELIGE GRØNLANDSKE HANDEL* at left and right margin, across bottom. Back: *DEN KONGELIGE GRØNLANDSKE HANDEL* around map at center.			
	a. Serial number with serifs. Signature: Hans C. Christensen.	75.00	180	400
	b. Serial number without serifs. Signature: Hans C. Christensen.	40.00	100	250
	s1. Specimen. As a.	100	200	—
	s2. Specimen. As b.	—	—	200

20	50 Kroner	VG	VF	UNC
	ND (1953-1967). Lilac. Clipper ship at center. *DEN KONGELIGE GRØNLANDSKE HANDEL* at left and right margin, across bottom. Back: *DEN KONGELIGE GRØNLANDSKE HANDEL* around map at center.			
	a. Signature: Hans C. Christensen.	125	375	700
	s. Specimen.	—	—	475

Kreditseddel

Credit Notes

1953 Issue

21	100 Kroner	VG	VF	UNC
	16.1.1953. Black, orange and blue-green. Portrait Knud Rasmussen (1879-1933) at left, dog sled at Thule-rock at lower right. Back: Crown and title at left center, map at right.			
	a. Signature: A.W. Nielsen.	600	1,200	2,400
	b. Signature: Hans C. Christensen. Serial # type as a.	400	800	1,600
	c. Signature: Hans C. Christensen. Serial # type in "print" style.	250	450	900
	s1. Specimen. As a.	—	—	600
	s2. Specimen. As b.	—	—	600
	s3. Specimen. As c.	—	—	400

Note: Since 1968 only Danish currency is in circulation.

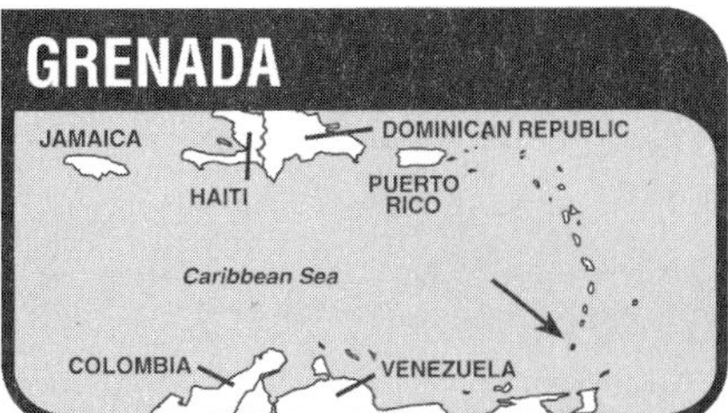

Grenada, located in the Windward islands of the Caribbean Sea 145 km. north of Trinidad, has (with Carriacou and Petit Martinique) an area of 344 sq. km. and a population of 90,343. Capital: St. George's.

Carib Indians inhabited Grenada when COLUMBUS discovered the island in 1498, but it remained uncolonized for more than a century. The French settled Grenada in the 17th century, established sugar estates, and imported large numbers of African slaves. Britain took the island in 1762 and vigorously expanded sugar production. In the 19th century, cacao eventually surpassed sugar as the main export crop; in the 20th century, nutmeg became the leading export. In 1967, Britain gave Grenada autonomy over its internal affairs. Full independence was attained in 1974, making Grenada one of the smallest independent countries in the Western Hemisphere. Grenada was seized by a Marxist military council on 19 October 1983. Six days later the island was invaded by US forces and those of six other Caribbean nations, which quickly captured the ringleaders and their hundreds of Cuban advisers. Free elections were reinstituted the following year and have continued since that time. Hurricane Ivan struck Grenada in September of 2004 causing severe damage.

RULERS:

British

MONETARY SYSTEM:

1 Shilling = 12 Pence
1 Pound = 20 Shillings to 1970
1 Dollar = 100 Cents
1 British West Indies Dollar = 4 Shillings-2 Pence

BRITISH ADMINISTRATION

Government of Grenada

1920 Issue

1	2 Shillings 6 Pence	Good	Fine	XF
	1.7.1920. Red and olive-gray. Portrait King George V at right. Back: Sailing ship at center. Printer: TDLR. Rare.	—	—	—

2	5 Shillings	Good	Fine	XF
	1.7.1920. Blue and green. Portrait King George V at right. Back: Sailing ship at center. Printer: TDLR. Rare.	—	—	—
3	**10 Shillings**	**Good**	**Fine**	**XF**
	1.7.1920. Blue-gray and green. Portrait King George V at right. Back: Sailing ship at center. Printer: TDLR. Rare.	—	—	—

Note: For later issues see British Caribbean Territories and East Caribbean States.

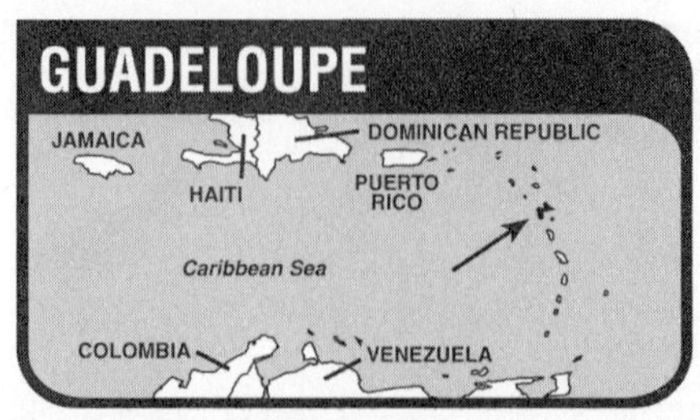

The French Overseas Department of Guadeloupe, located in the Leeward Islands of the West Indies about 300 miles (493 km.) southeast of Puerto Rico, has an area of 687 sq. mi. (1,779 sq. km.) and a population of 425,000. Actually it is two islands separated by a narrow salt water stream: volcanic Basse-Terre to the west and the flatter limestone formation of Grande-Terre to the east. Capital: Basse-Terre, on the island of that name. The principal industries are agriculture, the distillation of liquors, and tourism. Sugar, bananas and rum are exported. Guadeloupe was discovered by Columbus in 1493 and settled in 1635 by two Frenchmen, L'Olive and Dupiessis, who took possession in the name of the French Company of the Islands of America. When repeated efforts by private companies to colonize the island failed, it was relinquished to the French crown in 1674, and established as a dependency of Martinique. The British occupied the island on two occasions, 1759-1763 and 1810-1816, before it passed permanently to France. A colony until 1946, Guadeloupe was then made an overseas territory of the French Union. In 1958 it voted to become an Overseas Department within the new French Community. Grande-Terre, as noted in the first paragraph, is the eastern member of two-island Guadeloupe. Isle Desirade (La Desirade), located east of Grande-Terre, and Les Saintes (Iles des Saintes), located south of Basse-Terre, are dependencies of Guadeloupe.

RULERS

French

MONETARY SYSTEM

1 Franc = 100 Centimes
1 Nouveau Franc = 100 "old" Francs, 1960-

FRENCH ADMINISTRATION

Banque de Pret

1848 Issue

		Good	Fine	XF
A1	**5 Francs** 1848. Rare.	—	—	—
A2	**10 Francs** 1848. Rare.	—	—	—
A3	**50 Francs** 1848. Rare.	—	—	—
A4	**100 Francs** 1848. Rare.	—	—	—
A5	**500 Francs** 1848. Rare.	—	—	—
A6	**1000 Francs** 1848. Rare.	—	—	—

1851 Issue

		Good	Fine	XF
A7	**5 Francs** 13.5.1851. Rare.	—	—	—
A8	**10 Francs** 13.5.1851. Rare.	—	—	—

Guadeloupe Trésor Colonial Bons de Caisse

Décret du 25.5.1854

		Good	Fine	XF
A12	**1 Franc** 1.6.1854. Black. Uniface. Rare. PC: Light green.	—	—	—

Décrets des 13.4.1855 et 3.3.1858

		Good	Fine	XF
A12A	**1 Franc** 6.11.1863. Red. Rare.	—		

Décrets des 23.4.1855, 3.3.1858 et 2.6.1863

		Good	Fine	XF
A13	**1 Franc** 6.3.1863; 13.11.1863; 15.11.1863. Red. Sailing ship at lower left. Border of trees, barrels, arms etc. Uniface. Signature varieties. Rare.	—	—	—
A14	**2 Francs** 9.12.1864. Red. Sailing ship at lower left. Border of trees, barrels, arms etc. Uniface. Signature varieties. Rare.	—	—	—
A15	**5 Francs** ND. Sailing ship at lower left. Border of trees, barrels, arms etc. Uniface. Signature varieties. (Not issued). Rare.	—	—	—

Guadeloupe et Dependances, Trésor Colonial

Décret du 18.8.1884

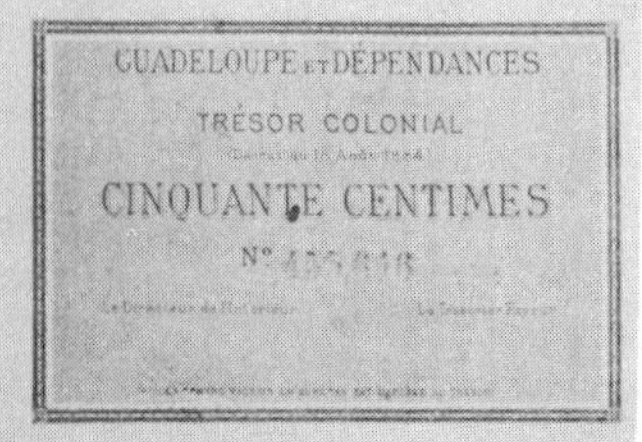

		Good	Fine	XF
1	**50 Centimes** *D.1884*. Brown.			
	a. Issued note.	—	—	—
	r. Unsigned remainder.	100	400	—
1A	**1 Franc** *D.1884*. Format as #1. Black on gray underprint.	—	—	—

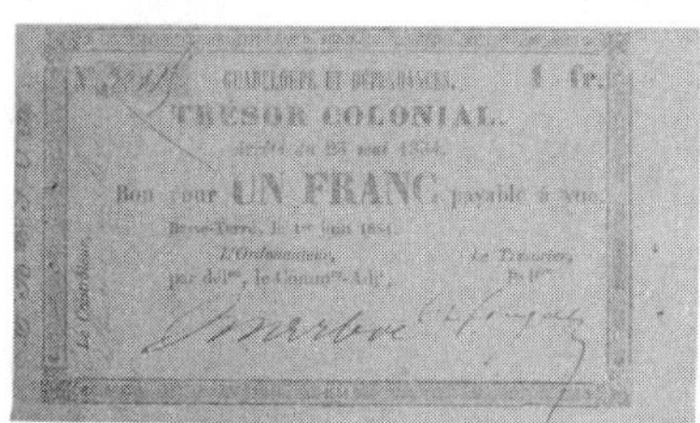

		Good	Fine	XF
2	**1 Franc** *D.1884*. Different format.			
	a. Issued note.	—	—	—
	r. Unsigned remainder.	150	425	—
3	**2 Francs** *D.1884*. Brown underprint. Uniface.			
	a. Issued note.	—	—	—
	r. Unsigned remainder.	175	500	—

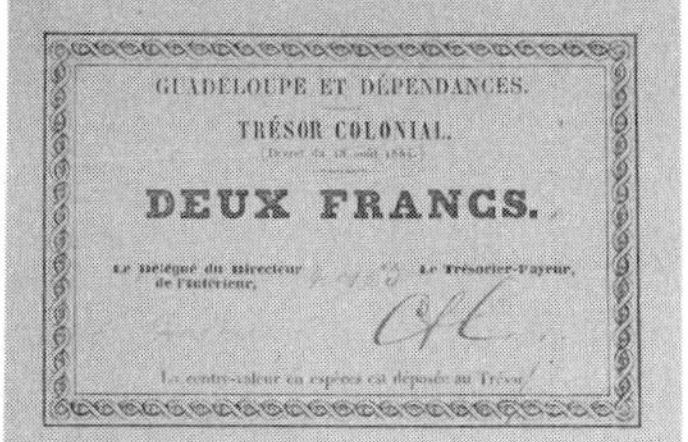

		Good	Fine	XF
3A	**2 Francs** *D.1884*. Black. Uniface. Rare. PC: Purple	—	—	—

		Good	Fine	XF
4	**5 Francs** *D.1884*. Format as #1. Uniface.			
	a. Blue on green underprint.	—	—	—
	b. Black on green paper. Rare.	—	—	—
	r. Unsigned remainder.	250	650	—
5	**10 Francs** *D.1884*. Black.			
	a. Cream paper. Rare.	—	—	—
	b. Brown paper. Rare.	—	—	—

Banque de la Guadeloupe

Law of 1874

		Good	Fine	XF
6	**5 Francs** *L.1874*. Blue. Man at left, woman at right. Back: Law date. Rare.	—	—	—

Law of 1901

		Good	Fine	XF
7	**5 Francs** *L.1901* (1928-1945). Red. Man at left, woman at right. Back: Law date.			
	a. Signature A. Mollenthiel.	30.00	75.00	200
	b. Signature C. Damoiseau. (1928).	30.00	70.00	175
	c. Signature H. Marconnet. (1934, 1943).	15.00	40.00	130
	d. Signature G. Devineau. (1944).	20.00	55.00	150
	e. Signature A. Boudin. (1945).	10.00	30.00	120

		Good	Fine	XF
8	**25 Francs** ND (1920-1944). Black and red. Scales and cornucopias at center of lower frame. 6 signature varieties.	150	500	—

		Good	Fine	XF
9	**100 Francs** ND (1920-1921; 1925). Red and blue. Scales and cornucopias at center of lower frame. 2 signature varieties.	225	800	—
9A	**250 Francs** ND. Rare. Black. Scales and cornucopias at center of lower frame. 6 signature varieties.	—	—	—
10	**500 Francs** ND (1887-1929). Black and red. Standing figures at left and right. 5 signature varieties.			
	a. Watermark: Lion and snake. *COLONIES* text. Rare.	—	—	—
	b. Watermark: Numerals of value *500*. Rare.	—	—	—

Law of 1901, 1920 Issue

		VG	VF	UNC
11	**50 Centimes** 1920. Blue on purple underprint.	35.00	200	450

		Good	Fine	XF
12	**1 Franc** 1920. Brown on aqua underprint.	45.00	225	500

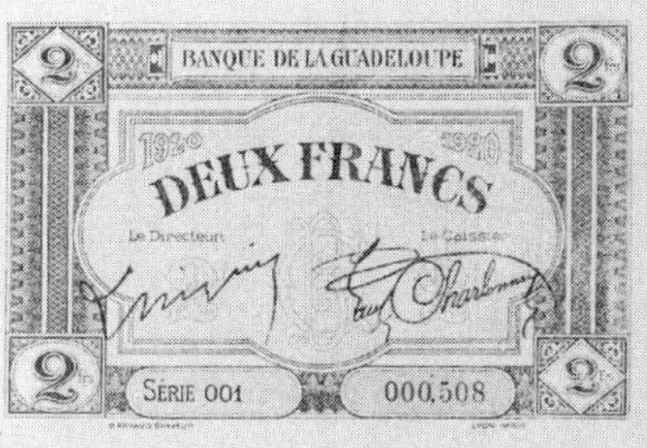

		Good	Fine	XF
13	**2 Francs** 1920. Green on orange underprint.	65.00	300	650

		Good	Fine	XF
14	**25 Francs** ND (1934; 1944). Multicolor. Woman with wreath at center, flowers on top, fruit on bottom. 2 signature varieties.	40.00	150	500

1920 (ND) Provisional Issue

		Good	Fine	XF
14	**100 Francs** ND (1920-old dates 1892-1893). Violet, blue and brown. Woman seated at left and right. Overprint: BANQUE DE LA GUADELOUPE on unissued Banque de France notes. Rare.	—	—	—

1934 ND Issue

#	Denomination	Good	Fine	XF
16	**100 Francs** ND (1934; 1944). Multicolor. Woman with staff at left, ship in background at lower center right. 2 signature varieties.	150	400	1,500

#	Denomination	Good	Fine	XF
17	**500 Francs** ND (1934). Multicolor. Woman with staff at left, ship in background at lower center right. 2 signature varieties.	250	750	—

#18-19 Not assigned.

Emergency Bank Check Issues

#20A-20E early bank checks (ca. 1870-1900).

#	Denomination	Good	Fine	XF
20A	**50 Centimes** ca. 1870-1900. Printed partial dates 187x, 189x, 190x. Rare. Blue-green.	—	—	—

#	Denomination	Good	Fine	XF
20B	**50 Centimes** ca. 1890-1900. Printed partial dates 189x, 190x. Rare. Orange-brown.	—	—	—

Color Abbreviation Guide

New to the *Standard Catalog of® World Paper Money* are the following abbreviations related to color references:

BC: Back color

PC: Paper color

#	Denomination	Good	Fine	XF
20C	**1 Franc** ca. 1870-1900. Printed partial dates 187x, 190x. (1902 reported). Rare. Blue.	—	—	—
20D	**2 Francs** 189x; 190x. Rare. Red.	—	—	—
20E	**5 Francs** 187x; 2.4.1890. Black and red on tan underprint. Rare.	—	—	—

1940 Emergency WWII Bank Check Issue

#	Denomination	Good	Fine	XF
20F	**1000 Francs** 24.6.1940; 27.1.1942. Purple. View of island with two sailing ships sideways at left. Printer: Forlin, Paris. Rare.	—	—	—

1942 Issue

#	Denomination	VG	VF	UNC
21	**5 Francs** ND (1942). Black on yellow underprint. Columbus at center. Printer: E.A. Wright, Philadelphia, Pa.			
	a. Signature G. Devineau with title: *LE DIRECTEUR.*	35.00	175	450
	b. Signature A. Boudin with title: *LE DIRECTEUR.*	30.00	150	400
	s. Specimen.	—	—	185

#	Denomination	VG	VF	UNC
22	**25 Francs** ND (1942). Black on green underprint. Map of Guadeloupe at left. Back: Woman at center. Printer: E.A. Wright, Philadelphia, Pa.			
	a. Signature G. Devineau with title: *LE DIRECTEUR.*	45.00	225	550
	b. Signature A. Boudin with title: *LE DIRECTEUR.*	40.00	175	500
	s. Specimen.	—	—	235

		VG	VF	UNC
23	**100 Francs** ND (1942). Black on red-orange underprint. Oxcart at center. Back: Small sailing boat at center. Printer: E.A. Wright, Philadelphia, Pa.			
	a. Signature G. Devineau with title: *LE DIRECTEUR.*	125	375	950
	b. Signature A. Boudin with title: *LE DIRECTEUR.*	110	350	850
	s. Specimen.	—	—	475

		VG	VF	UNC
24	**500 Francs** ND (1942). Black on red underprint. Sailing ship "Santa Maria" at left. Back: Flying boat Printer: E.A. Wright, Philadelphia, Pa. 158x114mm.			
	a. Signature H. Marconnet with title: *LE DIRECTEUR.*	750	1,850	—
	b. Signature G. Devineau with title: *LE DIRECTEUR.*	675	1,600	—
	s. Specimen.	—	—	2,000

		VG	VF	UNC
25	**500 Francs** ND (1942). Sailing ship *Santa Maria* at left. Printer: E.A. Wright, Philadelphia, Pa. 150x85mm.			
	a. Issued note.	900	2,500	—
	s. Specimen.	—	—	1,500

		VG	VF	UNC
26	**1000 Francs** ND (1942). Black on blue underprint. Bust of Karukera at center. Printer: E.A. Wright, Philadelphia, Pa. 178x117mm.			
	a. Signature H. Marconnet with title: *LE DIRECTEUR.*	750	1,500	3,000
	b. Signature G. Devineau with title: *LE DIRECTEUR.*	675	1,350	2,250
	s. Specimen.	—	—	1,250

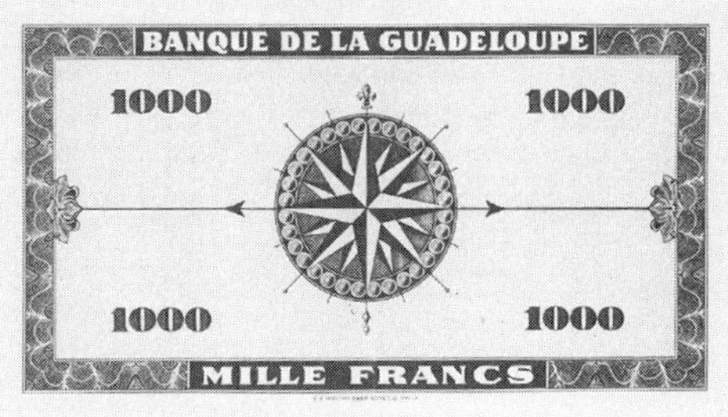

		VG	VF	UNC
26A	**1000 Francs** ND (1942). Black on blue underprint.. Bust of Karukera at center. Like #26 but reduced size. Printer: E.A. Wright, Philadelphia, Pa.			
	a. Issued note.	1,200	3,000	—
	s. Specimen.	—	—	1,750

Caisse Centrale de la France d'Outre-Mer

Guadeloupe

1944 Issue

		VG	VF	UNC
27	**10 Francs** 2.2.1944. Purple. Marianne at center. Printer: English printer (without imprint).			
	a. Issued note.	15.00	40.00	150
	s. Specimen. with regular serial #.	—	—	225

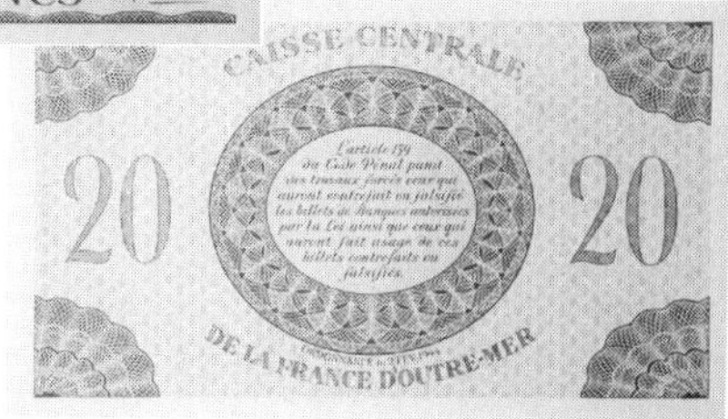

		VG	VF	UNC
28	**20 Francs** 2.2.1944. Green. Marianne at center. Printer: English printer (without imprint).			
	a. Issued note.	25.00	75.00	225
	s. Specimen.	—	—	225

29	100 Francs	VG	VF	UNC
	2.2.1944. Green on orange underprint. Marianne at center. Printer: English printer (without imprint).			
	a. Issued note.	50.00	200	650
	s. Specimen.	—	—	450

30	1000 Francs	VG	VF	UNC
	2.2.1944. Blue. Phoenix rising from flames. Back: War/peace scenes. Printer: English printer (without imprint).			
	a. Without watermark.	400	1,400	—
	b. Watermark: Marianne.	400	1,400	—
	s. As a. Specimen.	—	—	1,200

1947-1952 ND Issue

31	5 Francs	VG	VF	UNC
	ND (1947-1949). Multicolor. Bougainville at right. Printer: French printer (without imprint).	5.00	20.00	110

32	10 Francs	VG	VF	UNC
	ND (1947-1949). Multicolor. Colbert at left, sailing ships at center right. Printer: French printer (without imprint).	8.50	22.50	135

33	20 Francs	VG	VF	UNC
	ND (1947-1949). Multicolor. E. Gentil at right, four people with huts at left center. Printer: French printer (without imprint).	15.00	40.00	175

34	50 Francs	VG	VF	UNC
	ND (1947-1949). Multicolor. B. d'Esnambuc at left, sailing ship at right. Printer: French printer (without imprint).	25.00	125	350

35	100 Francs	VG	VF	UNC
	ND (1947-1949). Multicolor. La Bourdonnais at left, two women at right. Printer: French printer (without imprint).	35.00	150	400

36	500 Francs	VG	VF	UNC
	ND (1947-1949). Multicolor. Two women at right, sailboat at left. Printer: French printer (without imprint).	100	350	900

		VG	VF	UNC
37	**1000 Francs** ND (1947-1949). Multicolor. Two women at right. Printer: French printer (without imprint).			
	a. Issued note.	150	400	1,050
	s. Specimen.	—	—	350

		VG	VF	UNC
38	**5000 Francs** ND (1952). Multicolor. Gen. Schoelcher. Printer: French printer (without imprint).			
	a. Issued note.	275	750	—
	s. Specimen.	—	—	325

1960 ND Issue

		VG	VF	UNC
39	**1000 Francs** ND (1960). Multicolor. Fishermen from the Antilles. Printer: French printer (without imprint).			
	a. Issued note.	100	350	850
	s. Specimen.	—	—	325

		VG	VF	UNC
40	**5000 Francs** ND (1960). Multicolor. Woman with fruit bowl at center right, palm trees at left. Printer: French printer (without imprint).			
	a. Issued note.	250	750	—
	s. Specimen.	—	—	—

1960 ND Provisional Issue

		VG	VF	UNC
41	**1 Nouveau Franc on 100 Francs** ND (1960).	40.00	150	500

		VG	VF	UNC
42	**5 Nouveaux Francs on 500 Francs** ND (1960).	75.00	275	825

		VG	VF	UNC
43	**10 Nouveaux Francs on 1000 Fracs** ND (1960).	100	350	1,000

		VG	VF	UNC
44	**50 Nouveaux Francs on 5000 Francs** ND (1960).	200	900	—

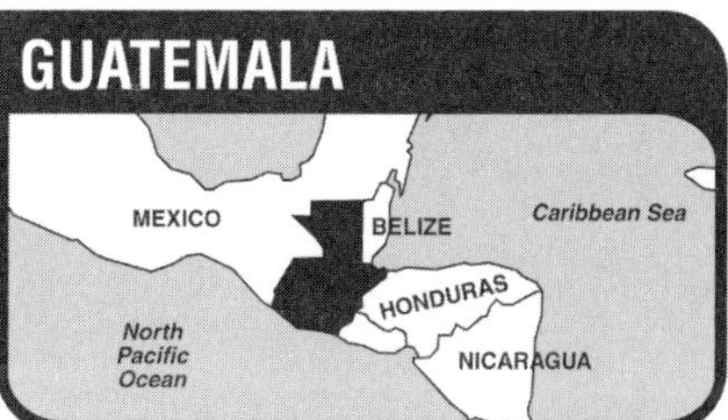

The Republic of Guatemala, the northernmost of the five Central American republics, has an area of 108,890 sq. km. and a population of 13 million. Capital: Guatemala City. The economy of Guatemala is heavily dependent on resources which are being developed. Coffee, cotton and bananas are exported.

The Mayan civilization flourished in Guatemala and surrounding regions during the first millennium A.D. After almost three centuries as a Spanish colony, Guatemala won its independence in 1821. During the second half of the 20th century, it experienced a variety of military and civilian governments, as well as a 36-year guerrilla war. In 1996, the government signed a peace agreement formally ending the conflict, which had left more than 100,000 people dead and had created, by some estimates, some 1 million refugees.

MONETARY SYSTEM:

1 Peso = 100 Centavos to 1924
1 Quetzal = 100 Centavos, 1924-

AVAILABILITY OF EARLY BANK ISSUES

A rising inflation from about 1900 to 1924 created a need for more and more bank notes to be issued. Their value decreased, higher denominations were introduced, and by the time of the 1924 currency reform it took 60 old pesos to equal 1 new quetzal. The Caja Reguladora reissued notes of 20 Pesos or more into the new system but all lower peso values ceased to circulate. Many notes of these earlier banks are still readily available today.

GOVERNMENT

Tesorería Nacional de Guatemala

1881-1885 ND First Issue

		Good	Fine	XF
A1	**1 Peso** ND (ca.1881). Black on red underprint. Seated allegorical woman at lower left and right, portrait Pres. J. Rufino Barrios at left center, arms at center right. Back: Treasury seal. Printer: CCBB.			
	a. Overprint: *PAGADERO EN LA ADMINISTRACION DE COBAN* on back.	—	—	—
	b. Overprint: *PAGADERO EN LA ADMINISTRACION DE ESQUINTLA* on back.	—	—	—
	c. Overprint: *PAGADERO EN LA ADMINISTRACION DE MAZATENANGO* on back.	—	—	—
	d. Overprint: *PAGADERO EN LA ADMINISTRACION DE QUEZAL TENANGO* on back.	—	—	—

		Good	Fine	XF
A2	**5 Pesos** ND. Black. Portrait Pres. J. R. Barrios at lower left, allegorical woman at center, arms at lower right. Printer: CCBB.	—	—	—

		Good	Fine	XF
A3	**10 Pesos** ND. Black. Portrait Pres. J. R. Barrios at upper left, arms at lower left, standing allegorical woman with tablet inscribed: *30 DE JUNIO DE 1871.* Printer: CCBB.	—	—	—

1882 ND Second Issue

A4	1 Peso	Good	Fine	XF
	ND (ca.1882). Black on orange and olive underprint. Reclining woman with book at left, arms at center, woman with scales and cornucopia filled with coin at right. Back: Denomination at center. Printer: ABNC.			
	a. Black signature without series, series A; B; C; E; plate A.	15.00	100	400
	b. Red signature Plate A.	20.00	125	500
	p. Proof.	—	Unc	400
	s. Specimen.	—	Unc	800

A5	5 Pesos	Good	Fine	XF
	ND (ca.1882). Black on orange and blue underprint. Steam locomotive at left, arms at right. Series A; B: E. Black signature. Printer: ABNC.			
	a. Issued note.	75.00	300	750
	s. Specimen.	—	Unc	1,400

A6	10 Pesos	Good	Fine	XF
	ND (ca.1882). Black on green and red underprint. Two cherubs at left, woman's head at center, arms at right. Printer: ABNC.			
	a. Red signature Plate C.	125	500	—
	b. Black signature Series B; C; D; plate E.	125	500	—
	p. Proof.	—	Unc	750
	s. Specimen.	—	Unc	2,500

A7	25 Pesos	Good	Fine	XF
	ND (ca.1888). Black on orange and yellow underprint. Arms at left, house in forest scene beneath, cherub at top center, allegorical woman holding wheat and sickle at center right. Printer: ABNC.			
	a. Issued note.	—	—	—
	p. Proof.	—	—	—
	s. Specimen.	—	Unc	1,750

1890s Cedulas Fiscales (Fiscal Notes) Issue

#A21-A24 issued to facilitate payment of taxes.

A21	1 Peso Plata	Good	Fine	XF
	189x. Arms at center.	—	—	—

A22	5 Pesos Plata	Good	Fine	XF
	189x. Requires confirmation.	—	—	—

A23	25 Pesos Plata	Good	Fine	XF
	189x. Requires confirmation.	—	—	—

A24	100 Pesos Plata	Good	Fine	XF
	189x. Requires confirmation.	—	—	—

1902 Vales al Portador (Notes Payable to bearer) Issue

#A31-A34 issued to pay customs duties on exportation of coffee.

A31	1 Peso	Good	Fine	XF
	6.8.1902. Requires confirmation.	—	—	—

A32	6 Pesos	Good	Fine	XF
	6.8.1902. Requires confirmation.	—	—	—

A33	100 Pesos	Good	Fine	XF
	6.8.1902. Requires confirmation.	—	—	—

A34	1000 Pesos	Good	Fine	XF
	6.8.1902. Arms at upper center.	—	—	—

REPUBLIC

Banco Central de Guatemala

Ley 7 de Julio de 1926

6	1 Quetzal	Good	Fine	XF
	21.4.1927; 29.4.1927; 13.6.1927; 31.10.1928. Green on orange underprint. Portrait Gen J. María Orellana at left, workers loading bales with steam crane in background. Engraved law date 7.7.1926. Back: Monolith of Quirigua at center. Printer: TDLR.			
	a. Issued note.	75.00	300	900
	s. Specimen. Overprint: *SPECIMEN* and punch hole cancelled.	—	Unc	1,000

7	2 Quetzales	Good	Fine	XF
	29.4.1927; 13.4.1928. Orange on light green and lilac underprint. Portrait Gen. J. María Orellana, palm trees at left, mountains at center. Engraved law date 7.7.1926. Back: Seascape and mountains at center. Printer: TDLR.			
	a. With law date.	150	600	—
	b. With *Acuerdo de* and issue date, Without law date.	150	600	—
	c. Without *Acurdo de.*	150	600	—

8	5 Quetzales	Good	Fine	XF
	13.6.1927. 21.11.1927; 13.4.1928; 7.4.1934. Purple on light green and blue underprint. Workers by Gen. J. María Orellana at left. Engraved law date 7.7.1926. Back: Town and mountains. Printer: TDLR.	125	500	—

9	20 Quetzales	Good	Fine	XF
	1927-1945. Blue on yellow and green underprint. Portrait Gen. J. María Orellana at lower left, with Mercury reclining at upper right. Engraved law date 7.7.1926. Back: Palace of the Captains General. Printer: TDLR.			
	a. Without *Acuerdo de.* signature title *GERENTE* at right. 25.7.1927; 13.4.1928.	225	1,000	—
	b. *Acuerdo de.* signature title: *SUB-GERENTE* at right. 1.2.1945.	175	800	—

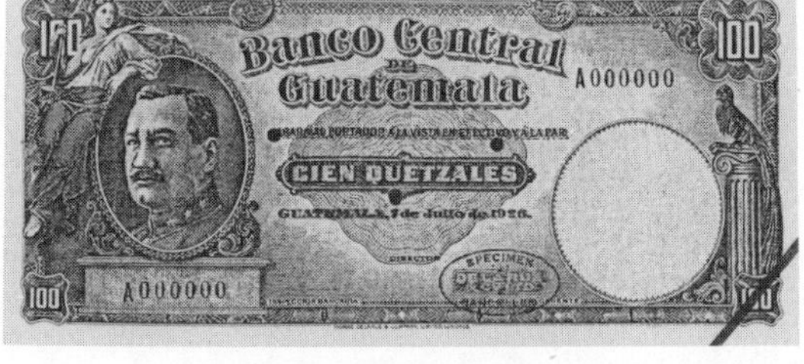

No.	Description	Good	Fine	XF
10	**100 Quetzales** *L.1926.* Dark green on orange and yellow underprint. Portrait Gen. J. María Orellana at left. Engraved law date 7.7.1926. Printer: TDLR. Specimen.	—	—	—

1928 Issue

No.	Description	Good	Fine	XF
11	**1 Quetzal** 13.4.1928; 31.10.1928; 17.3.1934. Green. Portrait Gen. J. Maria Orellana at left, workers loading bales with steam crane in background. Back: Monolith of Quirigua at center. Printer: W&S.			
	a. Issued note.	70.00	250	800
	s. Specimen.	—	Unc	125

No.	Description	Good	Fine	XF
12	**10 Quetzales** 24.12.1929; 11.5.1931; 21.4.1934; 21.5.1935. Red on yellow and green underprint. Portrait Gen. J. María Orellana at left. Back: Ornate bridge. Printer: W&S.			
	a. Issued note.	200	900	—
	s. Specimen.	—	Unc	400

1933-1936 Issue

No.	Description	Good	Fine	XF
13	**1/2 Quetzal** 1933-1942. Brown on blue underprint. Banana plantation at right. Back: Lake and mountain. Printer: W&S.			
	a. Signature title: *GERENTE* at right. 26.1.1933; 2.12.1938; 19.2.1941; 21.10.1942.	6.00	17.50	80.00
	b. Signature title: *SUB-GERENTE* at right. 21.10.1942.	6.00	22.00	95.00

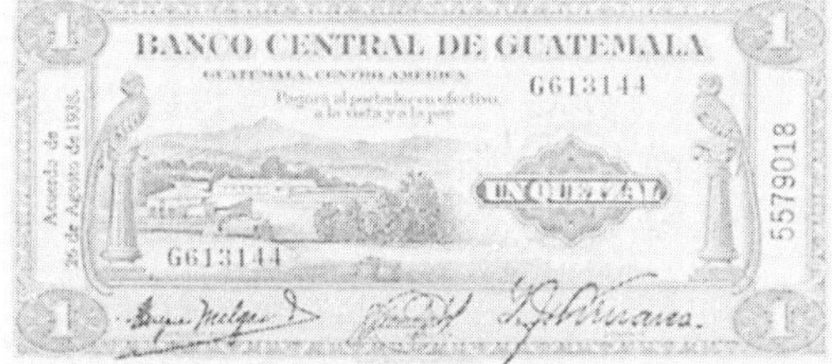

No.	Description	Good	Fine	XF
14	**1 Quetzal** 1934-1945. Deep green on lilac and ochre underprint. Farm buildings and truck at left center. Quetzal bird at left and right. Back: Monolith of Quirigua at center. Printer: W&S.			
	a. Signature title: *GERENTE* at right. 17.3.1934-19.9.1942.	6.00	25.00	95.00
	b. Signature title: *SUB-GERENTE* at right. 19.9.1942; 31.10.1945.	6.00	25.00	110

Color Abbreviation Guide

New to the *Standard Catalog of® World Paper Money* are the following abbreviations related to color references:

BC: Back color
PC: Paper color

No.	Description	Good	Fine	XF
15	**2 Quetzales** 1936-1942. Orange on green and violet underprint. Mountains and lake at left. Quetzal bird at left and right. Back: Seascape and mountains at center. Printer: W&S.			
	a. Signature title: *GERENTE* at right. 25.1.1936; 4.2.1942.	30.00	150	600
	b. Signature title: *SUB-GERENTE* at right. 4.2.1942.	30.00	150	650

No.	Description	Good	Fine	XF
16	**5 Quetzales** 1934-1945. Purple on orange and green underprint. Ship at dockside at left. Quetzal bird at left and right. Back: Quetzal. Printer: W&S.			
	a. Signature title: *GERENTE* at right. 7.4.1934-8.1.1943.	30.00	150	600
	b. Signature title: *SUB-GERENTE* at right. 29.1.1945.	30.00	150	650

No.	Description	Good	Fine	XF
17	**10 Quetzales** 1935-1945. Dark red on green underprint. Mountains and lake at left. Quetzal bird at left and right. Back: Ornate bridge. Printer: W&S.			
	a. Signature title: *GERENTE* at right. 21.5.1935-12.6.1943.	30.00	150	600
	b. Signature title: *SUB-GERENTE* at right. 1.2.1945; 22.5.1945.	30.00	175	850
18	**20 Quetzales** 1936-1944. Blue on green and multicolor underprint. Dock workers at left. Quetzal bird at left and right. Signature title: *GERENTE* at right. Back: Palace of the Captains General. Printer: W&S.			
	a. 2.5.1936.	75.00	425	1,500
	b. 14.1.1937/2.5.1936.	400	1,500	—
	c. 4.2.1942; 3.9.1943; 3.2.1944; 9.8.1944.	75.00	425	1,500

1936 Issue

No.	Description	Good	Fine	XF
18A	**2 Quetzales** 25.1.1936. Orange on light green and lilac underprint. Mountains and lake at left. Printer: TDLR.			
	a. Issued note.	60.00	400	1,200
	s. Specimen.	—	Unc	350

Banco de Guatemala

1946 Provisional Issue

		VG	VF	UNC
19	**1/2 Quetzal** 1946; 1948. Signature title overprint:*PRESIDENTE TRIBUNAL DE CUENTAS* at left, *PRESIDENTE DEL BANCO* at right.			
	a. 12.8.1946.	6.00	25.00	125
	b. 10.3.1948.	17.50	110	325

		VG	VF	UNC
20	**1 Quetzal** 12.8.1946. Signature title overprint:*PRESIDENTE TRIBUNAL DE CUENTAS* at left, *PRESIDENTE DEL BANCO* at right.	12.00	40.00	200

		VG	VF	UNC
21	**5 Quetzales** 12.8.1946. Signature title overprint:*PRESIDENTE TRIBUNAL DE CUENTAS* at left, *PRESIDENTE DEL BANCO* at right.	65.00	400	1,500

		VG	VF	UNC
22	**20 Quetzales** 12.8.1946;28.3.1947. Signature title overprint:*PRESIDENTE TRIBUNAL DE CUENTAS* at left, *PRESIDENTE DEL BANCO* at right.	250	1,250	—

1948 Issue

		VG	VF	UNC
23	**1/2 Quetzal** 15.9.1948-5.1.1954. Brown. Quetzal bird in flight above denomination. Signature title: *PRESIDENTE DEL...* at right. Hermitage of Cerro del Carmen at left. Signature varieties. Back: Two Guatemalans. Printer: ABNC.	3.00	14.00	85.00

		VG	VF	UNC
24	**1 Quetzal** 1948-1955. Green. Quetzal bird in flight above denomination. Signature title: *PRESIDENTE DEL...* at right. Palace of the Captains General at left. Signature varieties. Back: Lake Atitlan. Printer: ABNC.			
	a. Date alone at right. 15.9.1948-5.1.1954.	3.00	14.00	85.00
	b. With *Autorizacion de.* 5.1.1955.	5.00	25.00	120
25	**5 Quetzales** 15.9.1948-5.1.1954. Purple. Quetzal bird in flight above denomination. Signature title: *PRESIDENTE DEL...* at right. Vase (Vasija de Uaxactun) at left. Signature varieties. Back: Mayan-Spanish conflict. Printer: ABNC.	17.50	50.00	150
26	**10 Quetzales** 1948-1955. Red. Quetzal bird in flight above denomination. Signature title: *PRESIDENTE DEL...* at right. Round stone carving (Ara de Tikal) at left. Signature varieties. Back: Founding of old Guatemala Printer: ABNC.			
	a. Date alone at right. 15.9.1948-5.1.1954.	25.00	60.00	200
	b. With *Autorizacion de.* 5.1.1955.	25.00	75.00	225
27	**20 Quetzales** 15.9.1948; 18.2.1949; 7.9.1949; 3.5.1950; 5.1.1954. Blue. Quetzal bird in flight above denomination. Signature title: *PRESIDENTE DEL...* at right. Portrait right. Landivar at left. Signature varieties. Back: Meeting of Independence. Printer: ABNC.	30.00	115	350
28	**100 Quetzales** 1948-1952. Black on multicolor underprint. Quetzal bird in flight above denomination. Signature title: *PRESIDENTE DEL...* at right. Indio de Nahuala at left. Signature varieties. Back: Valley and mountain. Printer: ABNC.			
	a. 15.9.1948; 21.5.1952.	65.00	225	600
	b. 3.8.1949.	100	275	750

1955-1956 Issue

		VG	VF	UNC
29	**1/2 Quetzal** 5.1.1955; 22.2.1956; 16.1.1957. Brown. Building at right. Hermitage of Cerro del Carmen at left. Signature varieties. Printer: W&S.	2.00	14.00	65.00

		VG	VF	UNC
30	**1 Quetzal** 5.1.1955; 22.2.1956; 16.1.1957. Green. Palace of the Captains General at left, building at center right. Signature varieties. Back: Lake Atitlan. Printer: W&S.	2.00	14.00	65.00

No.	Description	VG	VF	UNC
31	**5 Quetzales** 5.1.1955; 22.2.1956; 16.1.1957 Purple. Vase at right. Signature varieties. Back: Mayan-Spanish conflict. Printer: W&S.	5.00	35.00	150
32	**10 Quetzales** 22.2.1956; 16.1.1957; 22.1.1958. Red. Round stone at right. Signature varieties. Back: Founding of old Guatemala. Printer: W&S.	12.50	50.00	250
33	**20 Quetzales** 5.1.1955-18.2.1959. Blue. Portrait right. Landivar at center. Signature varieties. Back: Meeting of Independence. Printer: W&S.	25.00	100	350

No.	Description	VG	VF	UNC
34	**100 Quetzales** 5.1.1955; 22.2.1956; 16.1.1957; 22.1.1958. Dark blue. Indio de Nahuala at center. Signature varieties. Back: Valley and mountain. Printer: W&S.			
	a. Issued note.	100	250	600
	s. Specimen. Punch hole cancelled.	—	—	500

1957-1963 Issue

No.	Description	VG	VF	UNC
35	**1/2 Quetzal** 22.1.1958. Brown on multicolor underprint. Hermitage of Cerro del Carmen at left. Signature title: *JEFE DE...* Back: Two Guatemalans. Printer: ABNC.	3.00	20.00	100
36	**1 Quetzal** 1957-1958. Green on multicolor underprint. Palace of the Captains General at left. Signature title: *JEFE DE...* Back: Lake Atitlan. Printer: ABNC.			
	a. 16.1.1957.	3.00	15.00	90.00
	b. 22.1.1958.	3.00	15.00	90.00

No.	Description	VG	VF	UNC
37	**5 Quetzales** 22.1.1958. Purple. Vase *Vasija de Uaxactum* at left. Signature title: *JEFE DE...* Back: Mayan-Spanish battle scene. Printer: ABNC.			
	a. Issued note.	8.00	35.00	175
	s. Specimen.	—	—	50.00
38	**10 Quetzales** 1958; 1962-1964. Red. Round stone carving *Ara de Tikal* at left. Signature title: *JEFE DE...* Back: Founding of old Guatemala. Printer: ABNC.			
	a. 22.1.1958.	12.50	65.00	225
	b. 12.1.1962.	12.50	65.00	225
	c. 9.1.1963.	12.50	65.00	225
	d. 8.1.1964.	12.50	65.00	225

No.	Description	VG	VF	UNC
39	**20 Quetzales** 1963-1965. Blue. Landivar at left. Signature title: *JEFE DE...* Back: Meeting of Independence. Printer: ABNC.			
	a. 9.1.1963.	20.00	75.00	275
	b. 8.1.1964.	20.00	75.00	275
	c. 15.1.1965.	20.00	75.00	275

1959-1960 Issues

No.	Description	VG	VF	UNC
40	**1/2 Quetzal** 18.2.1959. Lighter brown shadings around value guilloche at left. 6-digit serial #. Signature varieties. Printer: W&S. Printed area 2mm smaller than #41. Signature title: *JEFE DE...* at right.	5.00	15.00	100

No.	Description	VG	VF	UNC
41	**1/2 Quetzal** 1959-1961. Darker brown shadings around value guilloche at left. 7-digit serial #. Signature varieties. Printer: W&S. Signature title: *JEFE DE...* at right.			
	a. 18.2.1959.	3.00	10.00	45.00
	b. 13.1.1960.	3.00	10.00	45.00
	c. 18.1.1961.	3.00	10.00	45.00
	s. Specimen.	—	—	30.00
42	**1 Quetzal** 18.2.1959. Signature title: *JEFE DE...* at right. Building at center right. Green palace. 6-digit serial #. Signature varieties. Printer: W&S.			
	a. Issued note.	2.00	10.00	75.00
	s. Specimen.	—	—	80.00
43	**1 Quetzal** 1959-1964. Signature title: *JEFE DE...* at right. Black palace. 7-digit serial #. Signature varieties. Printer: W&S.			
	a. 18.2.1959.	2.00	7.50	50.00
	b. 13.1.1960.	2.00	7.50	50.00
	c. 18.1.1961.	2.00	7.50	50.00
	d. 12.1.1962.	2.00	7.50	50.00
	e. 9.1.1963.	2.00	7.50	50.00
	f. 8.1.1964.	2.00	7.50	50.00
	s. Specimen.	—	—	80.00

No.	Description	VG	VF	UNC
44	**5 Quetzales** 18.2.1959. Value at left center. Vase in purple. Signature title: *JEFE DE...* at right. Signature varieties. Printer: W&S.	8.00	50.00	200

No.	Description	VG	VF	UNC
45	**5 Quetzales** 1959-1964. Redesigned guilloche. Value at center. Vase in brown. Signature title: *JEFE DE...* at right. Signature varieties. Printer: W&S.			
	a. 18.2.1959.	5.00	25.00	100
	b. 13.1.1960.	5.00	25.00	100
	c. 18.1.1961.	5.00	25.00	100

		VG	VF	UNC
	d. 12.1.1962.	5.00	25.00	100
	e. 9.1.1963.	5.00	25.00	100
	f. 8.1.1964.	5.00	25.00	100
	s. Specimen.	—	—	—

		VG	VF	UNC
46	**10 Quetzales** 18.2.1959. Signature title: *JEFE DE...* at right. Round red stone at right. Signature varieties. Printer: W&S.			
	a. Issued note.	15.00	70.00	250
	s. Specimen.	—	—	135

		VG	VF	UNC
47	**10 Quetzales** 1959-1961. Similar to #46 but redesigned guilloche. Round stone in brown. Signature title: *JEFE DE...* at right. Signature varieties. Printer: W&S.			
	a. 18.2.1959.	15.00	35.00	175
	b. 13.1.1960	15.00	35.00	175
	c. 18.1.1961.	15.00	35.00	175
	s. Specimen.	—	—	—

		VG	VF	UNC
48	**20 Quetzales** 1960-1965. Blue. Signature title: *JEFE DE...* at right. Portrait at right Landivar at right. Signature varieties. Printer: W&S.			
	a. 13.1.1960.	20.00	65.00	200
	b. 18.1.1961.	20.00	65.00	200
	c. 12.1.1962.	20.00	65.00	200
	d. 9.1.1963.	20.00	65.00	200
	e. 8.1.1964.	20.00	65.00	200
	f. 15.1.1965.	20.00	65.00	200
	s. Specimen.	—	—	—

		VG	VF	UNC
49	**100 Quetzales** 18.2.1959. Dark blue. Signature title: *JEFE DE...* at right. *Indio de Nahuala* in blue at center. Signature varieties. Printer: W&S.	115	250	650

		VG	VF	UNC
50	**100 Quetzales** 1960-1965. Dark blue. Signature title: *JEFE DE...* at right. Portrait *Indio de Nahuala* in brown at right. Signature varieties. Printer: W&S.			
	a. 13.1.1960.	115	250	500
	b. 18.1.1961.	115	250	500
	c. 12.1.1962.	115	250	500
	d. 9.1.1963.	115	250	500
	e. 8.1.1964.	115	250	500
	f. 15.1.1965.	115	250	500
	s. Specimen.	—	—	—

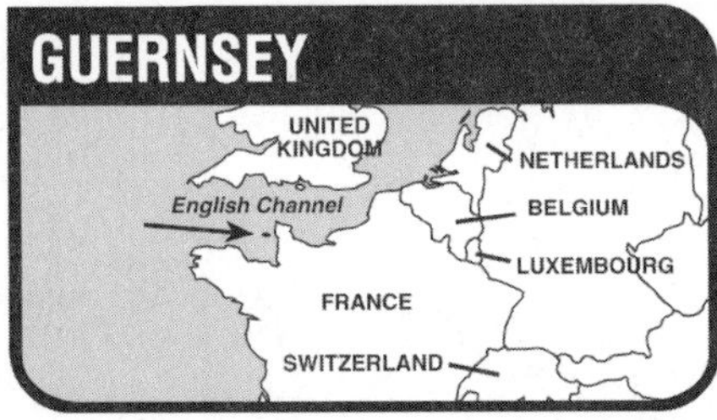

The Bailiwick of Guernsey, a British crown dependency located in the English Channel 48 km. west of Normandy, France, has an area of 78 sq. km., including the Isles of Alderney, Jethou, Herm, Brechou and Sark, and a population of 58,681. Capital: St. Peter Port. Agriculture and cattle breeding are the main occupations.

Guernsey and the other Channel Islands represent the last remnants of the medieval Dukedom of Normandy, which held sway in both France and England. The islands were the only British soil occupied by German troops in World War II. Guernsey is a British crown dependency, but is not part of the UK. However, the UK Government is constitutionally responsible for its defense and international representation. United Kingdom bank notes and coinage circulate concurrently with Guernsey money as legal tender.

RULERS:

British to 1940, 1944-
German Occupation, June 1940-June 1944

MONETARY SYSTEM:

1 Penny = 8 Doubles
1 Shilling = 12 Pence
5 Shillings = 6 Francs
1 Pound = 20 Shillings to 1971
1 Pound = 100 New Pence 1971-

BRITISH ADMINISTRATION

States of Guernsey

1825; 1857 Government Notes

		Good	Fine	XF
A1	**1 Pound** 1827-1836. Britannia standing with shield and lion at upper left, allegorical woman standing at upper right. Large *ONE* in guilloche at lower left.			
	a. 21.11.1827; 15.4.1828. Rare.	—	—	—
	b. 10.7.1829; 1.12.1829; 1.10.1836. Rare.	—	—	—

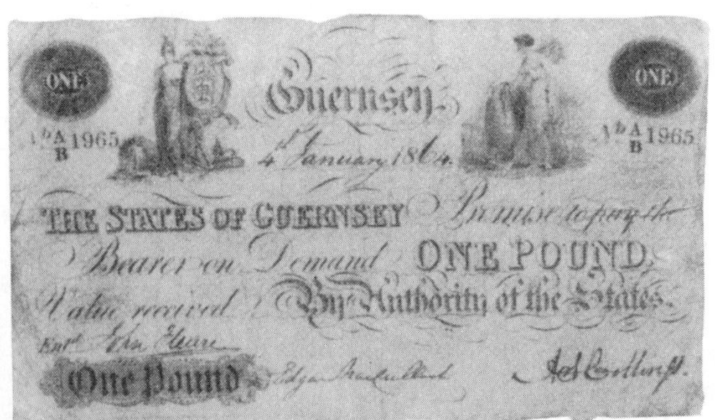

		Good	Fine	XF
A2	**1 Pound** 28.3.1857-22.5.1894. Britannia standing with shield and lion at upper left, allegorical woman standing at upper right. Large *One Pound* in guilloche at lower left. Rare.	—	—	—

1895; 1903 Government Notes

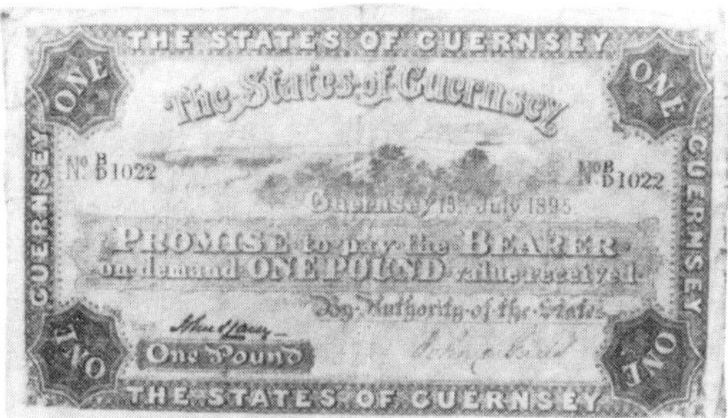

No.	Description	Good	Fine	XF
1	**1 Pound** 15.7.1895. Sailing ships anchored along coastline across upper center (St. Sampson's Harbor). Back: Arms medallion at center in ornate pattern. Printer: PBC. Rare.	—	—	—
1A	**1 Pound** 23.3.1903. Rare.	—	—	—
2	**5 Pounds** Requires confirmation.	—	—	—

1914 Emergency WWI Issue

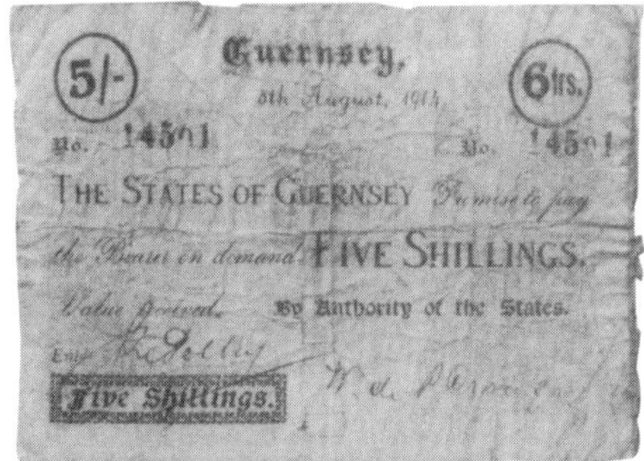

No.	Description	Good	Fine	XF
3	**5 Shillings = 6 Francs** 5.8.1914. Arms at center in underprint. Printer: The Star, Guernsey. Rare.	—	—	—
4	**10 Shillings = 12 Francs** 7.8.1914. Arms at center in underprint. Back: The Evening Press, Guernsey. Rare.	—	—	—

1914 Issue

No.	Description	Good	Fine	XF
5	**5 Shillings = 6 Francs** 1.9.1914. Black on red underprint. Back: Arms medallion at center in guilloche. Printer: PBC. Rare.	—	—	—
6	**10 Shillings = 12 Francs** 1.9.1914; 19.7.1919. Black on red underprint. Back: Arms medallion at center in guilloche. Printer: PBC. Rare.	—	—	—
7	**1 Pound** 3.4.1914; 1.9.1916; 1.9.1917; 1.8.1919. Sailing ships anchored along coastline across upper center (St. Sampson's Harbor). Back: Arms medallion at center in ornate pattern. Rare.	—	—	—

Note: The date 1.9.1914 for #7 requires confirmation.

1921 Provisional Issue

No.	Description	Good	Fine	XF
8	**5 Shillings = 6 Francs** ND (Apr. 1921-old date 1.9.1914). Overprint: Red: *BRITISH* on #5. Rare.	—	—	—
9	**10 Shillings = 12 Francs** ND (Apr. 1921-old date 1.9.1914). Overprint: Red: *BRITISH* on #6. Rare.	—	—	—

No.	Description	Good	Fine	XF
9A	**1 Pound** ND (Apr. 1921-old date 1.8.1919). Overprint: Red: *BRITISH* on #7. Rare.	—	—	—

1921-1924 Issue

No.	Description	Good	Fine	XF
10	**10 Shillings** 17.5.1924. Black and gray. St. Sampson's Harbor scene across upper center. Without denomination in numerals at center.	150	450	—
11	**1 Pound** 1.3.1921; 9.2.1924; 17.5.1924. Black and gray on orange underprint. St. Sampson's Harbor scene across upper center. Without denomination in numerals at center. Rare.	—	—	—

1927 Issue

No.	Description	Good	Fine	XF
12	**1 Pound** 6.12.1927; 12.4.1928. Black and gray on red underprint. Denomination *£1* in underprint at center.	150	450	1,000

1933 Issue

No.	Description	Good	Fine	XF
13	**10 Shillings** 18.11.1933. Light blue and brown. Denomination *10/-* underprint at center. Back: Only 1 signature English wording.	100	400	900
14	**1 Pound** 3.1.1933-18.11.1933. Gray on red underprint. Without denomination in numerals at center. Back: Only 1 signature English wording.	100	400	950

Note: Additional dates for #10-13 require confirmation. *All* dates for #14 require confirmation.

1934 Issue

No.	Description	Good	Fine	XF
15	**10 Shillings** 29.3.1934; 5.6.1937; 1.7.1939; 9.3.1940. Light blue and orange. Denomination *10/-* underprint at center. Back: *S'BALLIVIE INSULE DEGERNEREYE* (Seal of the Island of Guernsey).	100	500	1,250

No.	Description	Good	Fine	XF
16	**1 Pound** 1934-1940. Gray. Denomination in underprint at center, like #14. Back: *S'BALLIVIE INSULE DEGERNEREYE* (Seal of the Island of Guernsey).			
	a. 29.3.1934-1.7.1939.	185	600	1,400
	b. 9.3.1940.	75.00	300	750

GERMAN OCCUPATION - WW II

States of Guernsey

1941 First Issue

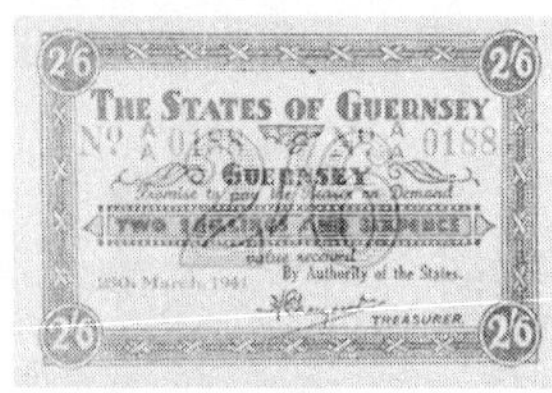

No.	Description	Good	Fine	XF
18	**2 Shillings 6 Pence** 25.3.1941. Blue on orange underprint. 92x59mm.	35.00	100	225

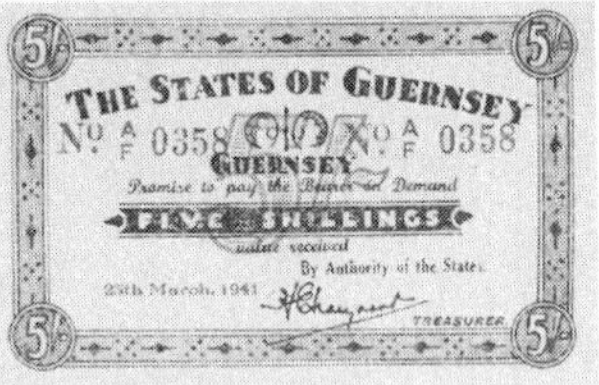

No.	Description	Good	Fine	XF
19	**5 Shillings** 25.3.1941. Black on red underprint. 100x63mm.	40.00	140	325

1941 Second Issue

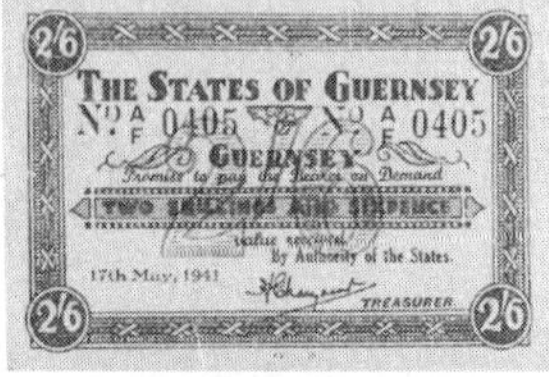

No.	Description	Good	Fine	XF
20	**2 Shillings 6 Pence** 17.5.1941. Blue on orange underprint.	35.00	125	275
21	**5 Shillings** 17.5.1941. Black on red underprint.	50.00	150	400

1941 Third Issue

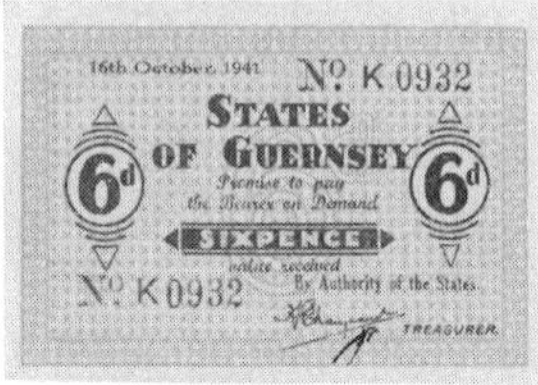

No.	Description	Good	Fine	XF
22	**6 Pence** 16.10.1941. Black on light blue and orange underprint. 92x59mm.	25.00	100	200

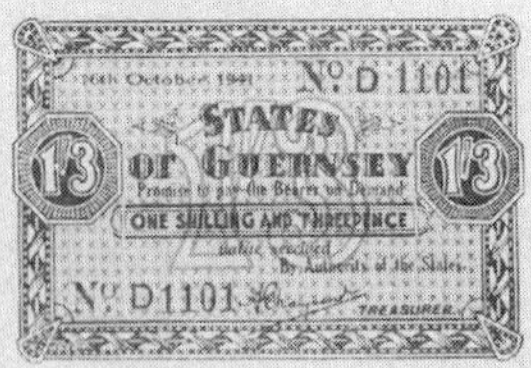

No.	Description	Good	Fine	XF
23	**1 Shilling 3 Pence** 16.10.1941. Black on yellow and brown underprint. 92x59mm.	45.00	175	400

1942 First Issue

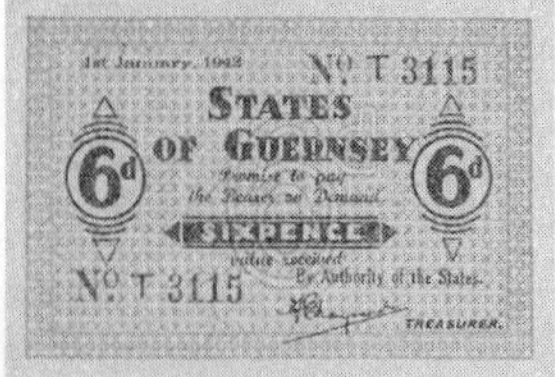

No.	Description	Good	Fine	XF
24	**6 Pence** 1.1.1942. Black on light blue and orange underprint. PC: Blue	40.00	140	325
25	**1 Shilling on 1/3d** 1.1.1942. Orange overprint of new denomination. 90x60mm. PC: Blue.	15.00	80.00	175

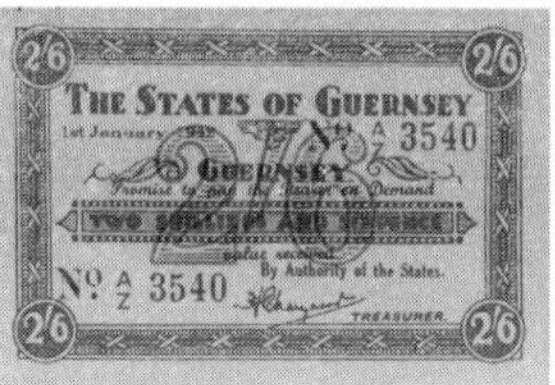

No.	Description	Good	Fine	XF
25A	**2 Shillings 6 Pence** 1.1.1942. Blue on orange underprint. PC: Blue.	15.00	80.00	175
25B	**5 Shillings** 1.1.1942.	25.00	100	225

1942 Second Issue

No.	Description	Good	Fine	XF
26	**1 Shilling 3 Pence** 18.7.1942. Black on yellow underprint. 92x59mm. PC: Blue.	20.00	90.00	200
27	**1 Shilling on 1/3d** 18.7.1942. Overprint: Orange on #26.	25.00	100	250

1943 Issue

No.	Description	Good	Fine	XF
28	**6 Pence** 1.1.1943. Black on light blue and orange underprint. PC: White	25.00	100	200
29	**1 Shilling on 1/3d** 1.1.1943. Overprint: Orange, on #26.	30.00	110	250
30	**2 Shillings 6 Pence** 1.1.1943. Blue.	30.00	110	250

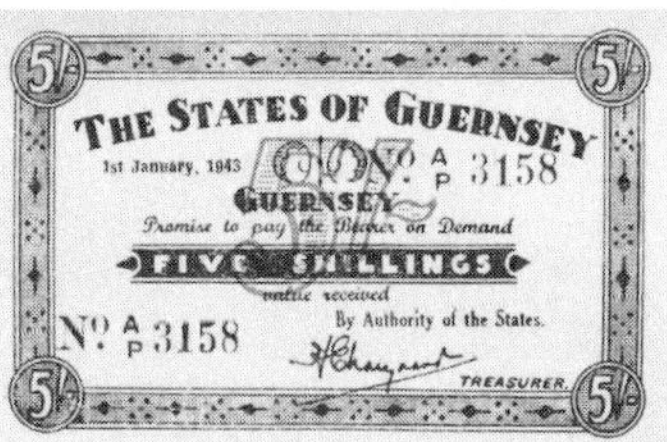

No.	Description	Good	Fine	XF
31	**5 Shillings** 1.1.1943. Black on red denomination. 98x63mm.	30.00	175	450

No.	Description	Good	Fine	XF
32	**10 Shillings** 1.1.1943. Blue on red denomination. 134x79mm.	75.00	275	700

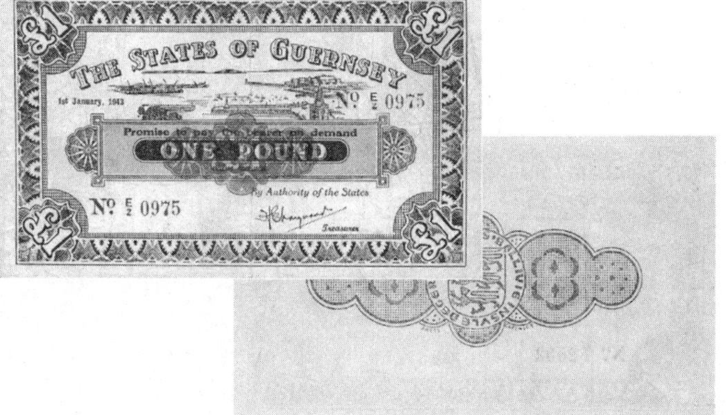

No.	Description	Good	Fine	XF
33	**1 Pound** 1.1.1943. Black on red underprint. Sailing ships and coastline St. Sampson's Harbor across upper center. 151x89mm.	80.00	300	750

BRITISH ADMINISTRATION - POST WWII

States of Guernsey

1945 First Issue

		Good	Fine	XF
33A	**1 Pound** 1.1.1945. Sailing ships and coastline St. Sampson's Harbor across upper center.	75.00	275	700

Note: A blue paper variety of #33A requires confirmation.

		Good	Fine	XF
33B	**5 Pounds** 1.1.1945. Withdrawn shortly after release. Green. Arms at upper left. Rare. PC: Green.	—	—	—

1945 Second Issue

		VG	VF	UNC
34	**5 Shillings** 1.1.1945. Text:...*backed by Guernsey Notes.* Rare. PC: Blue French paper.	—	—	—
35	**10 Shillings** 1.1.1945. Text:...*backed by Guernsey Notes.* Rare. PC: Blue French paper.	—	—	—
36	**1 Pound** 1.1.1945. Text:...*backed by Guernsey Notes.* Sailing ships and coastline St. Sampson's Harbor across center. Rare. PC: Blue French paper.	—	—	—
37	**5 Pounds** 1.1.1945. Text:...*backed by Guernsey Notes.* Rare. PC: Blue French paper.	—	—	—

1945 Third Issue

		VG	VF	UNC
38	**5 Shillings** 1.1.1945. Text:...*backed by British Notes.* Rare.	—	—	—
39	**10 Shillings** 1.1.1945. Text:...*backed by British Notes.* Rare.	—	—	—
40	**1 Pound** 1.1.1945. Text:...*backed by British Notes.* Rare.	—	—	—
41	**5 Pounds** 1.1.1945. Text:...*backed by British Notes.* Rare.	—	—	—

1945; 1956 Issue

		VG	VF	UNC
42	**10 Shillings** 1945-1966. Lilac on light green underprint. Value at center and in underprint. Printer: PBC.			
	a. 1.8.1945-1.9.1957.	50.00	225	600
	b. 1.7.1958-1.3.1965.	20.00	100	325
	c. 1.7.1966.	8.00	45.00	125
	s. As c. Specimen.	—	—	—

		VG	VF	UNC
43	**1 Pound** 1945-1966. Purple on green underprint. Harbor entrance across top center. Printer: PBC.			
	a. 1.8.1945-1.3.1957.	150	650	1,250
	b. 1.9.1957-1.3.1962; 1.6.1963; 1.3.1965.	25.00	120	375
	c. 1.7.1966.	15.00	90.00	300
	s. As c. Specimen.	—	—	—

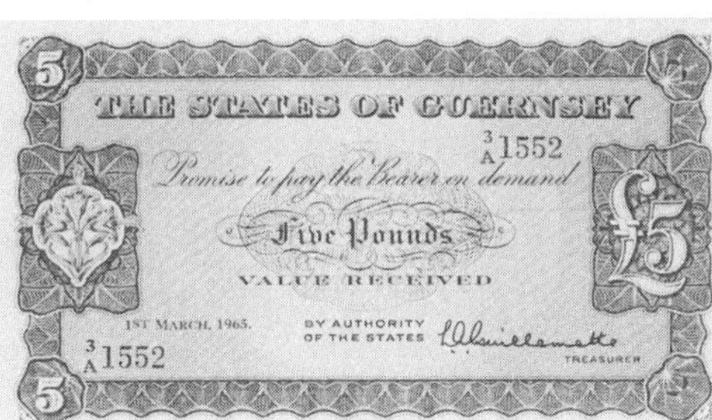

		VG	VF	UNC
44	**5 Pounds** 1956; 1965-1966. Green and blue. Flowers at left. Printer: PBC.			
	a. 1.12.1956.	150	650	1,500
	b. 1.3.1965.	150	650	1,500
	c. 1.7.1966.	150	650	1,500

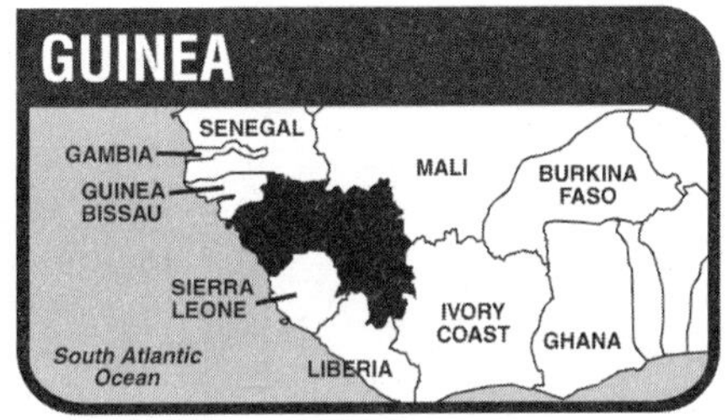

The Republic of Guinea (formerly French Guinea), situated on the Atlantic coast of Africa between Sierra Leone and Guinea-Bissau, has an area of 245,857 sq. km. and a population of 9.8 million. Capital: Conakry. Although Guinea contains one-third of the world's reserves of bauxite and significant deposits of iron ore, gold and diamonds, the economy is still dependent on agriculture. Aluminum, bananas, copra and coffee are exported.

Guinea has had only two presidents since gaining its independence from France in 1958. Lansana Conte came to power in 1984 when the military seized the government after the death of the first president, Sekou Toure. Guinea did not hold democratic elections until 1993 when Gen. Conte (head of the military government) was elected president of the civilian government. He was reelected in 1998 and again in 2003, though all the polls have been marred by irregularities. Guinea has maintained its internal stability despite spillover effects from conflict in Sierra Leone and Liberia. As those countries have rebuilt, Guinea's own vulnerability to political and economic crisis has increased. Declining economic conditions and popular dissatisfaction with corruption and bad governance prompted two massive strikes in 2006; a third nationwide strike in early 2007 sparked violent protests in many Guinean cities and prompted two weeks of martial law. To appease the unions and end the unrest, Conte named a new prime minister in March 2007.

RULERS:

French to 1958

MONETARY SYSTEM:

1 Franc = 100 Centimes to 1971
1 Syli = 10 Francs, 1971-1980
Franc System, 1985-

FRENCH ADMINISTRATION

Gouvernement Général de l'Afrique Occidentale Française Colonie de la Guinée Française

Décret du 11.2.1917

		VG	VF	UNC
1	**0.50 Franc** *D.1917.* Dark brown on light brown underprint. Reverse and obverse of 50 Centimes coin.			
	a. Watermark: Bees. Imprint on back 23mm long.	50.00	175	400
	b. Watermark: Bees. Imprint on back 26mm long.	60.00	225	550
	c. Watermark: Laurel leaves.	60.00	225	550
	d. Without watermark.	50.00	175	400

		VG	VF	UNC
2	**1 Franc** *D.1917.* Blue on green underprint. Reverse and obverse of 1 Franc coin.			
	a. Watermark: Bees.	75.00	300	650
	b. Watermark: Laurel leaves.	85.00	350	750
	c. Without watermark.	85.00	350	750

1920 Emergency Postage Stamp Issue

#3-5 adhesive postage stamps (Michel #66, 67 and 70, or Scott #54, 56 and 61) affixed to colored cardboard with overprint: *VALEUR D'ECHANGE* in two lines on face. Value in ornate frame at center on back.

		VG	VF	UNC
3	**5 Centimes** ND (1920). Green. Back: Value in ornate frame at center. Adhesive postage stamps affixed to orange-colored cardboard with overprint.	85.00	200	350
4	**10 Centimes** ND (1920). Rose. Adhesive postage stamps affixed to green-colored cardboard with overprint.	85.00	200	350
5	**25 Centimes** ND (1920). Blue. Adhesive postage stamps affixed to red-colored cardboard with overprint.	100	225	400

REPUBLIC

Banque de la République de Guinée

1958 Issue

		VG	VF	UNC
6	**50 Francs** 2.10.1958. Brown. Pres. Sekou Toure at left. Back: Mask at center.	8.00	50.00	225

		VG	VF	UNC
7	**100 Francs** 2.10.1958. Lilac. Pres. Sekou Toure at left. Back: Woman and child with village.	15.00	50.00	250
8	**500 Francs** 2.10.1958. Red-orange. Pres. Sekou Toure at left. Back: Pineapple field.	30.00	150	500

		VG	VF	UNC
9	**1000 Francs** 2.10.1958. Blue. Pres. Sekou Toure at left. Back: Small boats at shore, man at center right.	20.00	110	475

		VG	VF	UNC
10	**5000 Francs** 2.10.1958. Green. Pres. Sekou Toure at left. Back: Banana harvesting.	75.00	400	—

		VG	VF	UNC
11	**10,000 Francs** 2.10.1958. Dark brown. Pres. Sekou Toure at left. Back: Mining.	125	500	—

Banque Centrale de la République de Guinée

1960 Issue

		VG	VF	UNC
12	**50 Francs** 1.3.1960. Brown on multicolor underprint. President Sekou Toure at left. Back: Heavy machinery. Watermark: Dove.			
	a. Issued note.	1.00	4.00	20.00
	s. Specimen.	—	—	25.00

13	100 Francs	VG	VF	UNC
	1.3.1960. Dark brown on pale olive-green, pale orange, pink and lilac underprint. President Sekou Toure at left. Back: Pineapple field workers. Watermark: Dove.			
	a. Issued note.	2.00	6.00	35.00
	s. As a. Specimen.	—	—	25.00
	x. (Error). dark brown and pale olive-green, light blue and pale yellow-orange underprint. Back dark brown on yellow underprint.	—	—	—

14	500 Francs	VG	VF	UNC
	1.3.1960. Blue on multicolor underprint. President Sekou Toure at left. Back: Men pulling long boats ashore. Watermark: Dove.			
	a. Issued note.	3.00	20.00	150
	s. Specimen.	—	—	35.00

15	1000 Francs	VG	VF	UNC
	1.3.1960. Green on multicolor underprint. President Sekou Toure at left. Back: Banana harvesting. Watermark: Dove.			
	a. Issued note.	3.00	15.00	75.00
	s. Specimen.	—	—	35.00

Banque Centrale de la République de Guinée

1960 Issue

15A	5000 Francs	VG	VF	UNC
	1.3.1960. Purple on green and multicolor underprint. Pres. Sekou Toure at left. Back: Woman in headdress at left, huts at right. Watermark: Dove. Specimen. (Not issued).	—	—	400

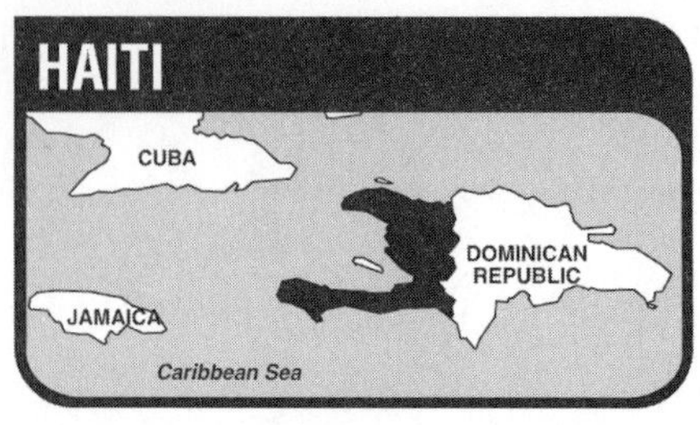

The Republic of Haiti, occupying the western one third of the island of Hispañola in the Caribbean Sea between Puerto Rico and Cuba, has an area of 27,750 sq. km. and a population of 8.92 million. Capital: Port-au-Prince. The economy is based on agriculture, light manufacturing and tourism which is becoming increasingly important. Coffee, bauxite, sugar, essential oils and handicrafts are exported.

The native Taino Amerindians - who inhabited the island of Hispañiola when it was discovered by Columbus in 1492 - were virtually annihilated by Spanish settlers within 25 years. In the early 17th century, the French established a presence on Hispaniola, and in 1697, Spain ceded to the French the western third of the island, which later became Haiti. The French colony, based on forestry and sugar-related industries, became one of the wealthiest in the Caribbean, but only through the heavy importation of African slaves and considerable environmental degradation. In the late 18th century, Haiti's nearly half million slaves revolted under Toussaint L'Ouverture. After a prolonged struggle, Haiti became the first black republic to declare its independence in 1804. The poorest country in the Western Hemisphere, Haiti has been plagued by political violence for most of its history. After an armed rebellion led to the forced resignation and exile of President Jean-Bertrand Aristide in February 2004, an interim government took office to organize new elections under the auspices of the United Nations Stabilization Mission in Haiti (Minustah). Continued violence and technical delays prompted repeated postponements, but Haiti finally did inaugurate a democratically elected president and parliament in May of 2006.

MONETARY SYSTEM:

1 Gourde = 100 Centimes
1 Piastre = 300 Gourdes, 1873
5 Gourdes = 1 U.S. Dollar, 1919-89

FRENCH ADMINISTRATION

St. Domingue

1810s Issue

		Good	Fine	XF
A11	**4 Escalins** ND. Arms at center. Uniface.	—	—	—

Department of Port-du-Paix

1790s ND Issue

		Good	Fine	XF
A1	**4 Escalins** ND. Arms at center. Uniface.	—	—	—

REPUBLIC (FIRST)

République d'Haiti

Billets de Caisse

Decret du 8 Mai 1813

		Good	Fine	XF
A31	**5 Gourdes** Requires confirmation.	—	—	—
A33	**50 Gourdes** Requires confirmation.	—	—	—
A34	**100 Gourdes** Requires confirmation.	—	—	—

Arreté du 26 Septembre 1826

		Good	Fine	XF
A51	**1 Gourde** Requires confirmation.	—	—	—
A52	**2 Gourdes** Requires confirmation.	—	—	—
A53	**5 Gourdes** 3.10.1826. Rare.	—	—	—

Loi du 10 Avril 1827

		Good	Fine	XF
A64	**10 Gourdes** *L.1827.* Rare.	—	—	—

Loi du 16 Avril 1827 - First Issue

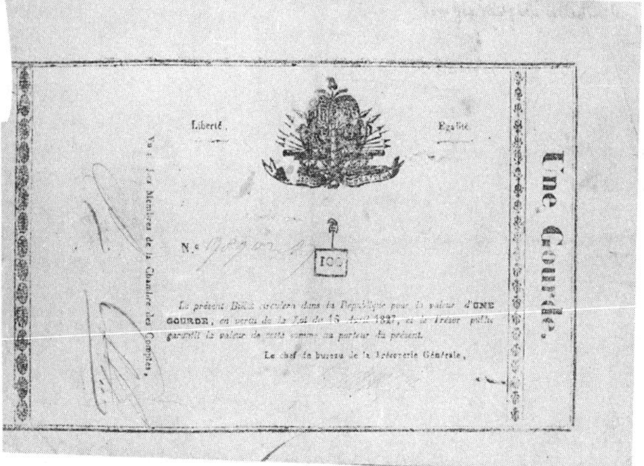

		Good	Fine	XF
1	**1 Gourde** *L.1827.* Black or gray. Very wide margins (often trimmed). Arms at upper center. Print frame ca. 204 x 112mm. PC: Large, thin white or off-white.	40.00	100	200
2	**2 Gourdes** *L.1827.* Arms at upper center.			
	a. Thin paper. Without watermark.	20.00	50.00	130
	b. Thick paper. Without watermark.	20.00	50.00	130
	c. Thin yellow paper. Watermark: *REPUBLIQUE D'HAITI.*	20.00	50.00	130
3	**5 Gourdes** *L.1827.* Arms at upper center. Rare.	—	—	—

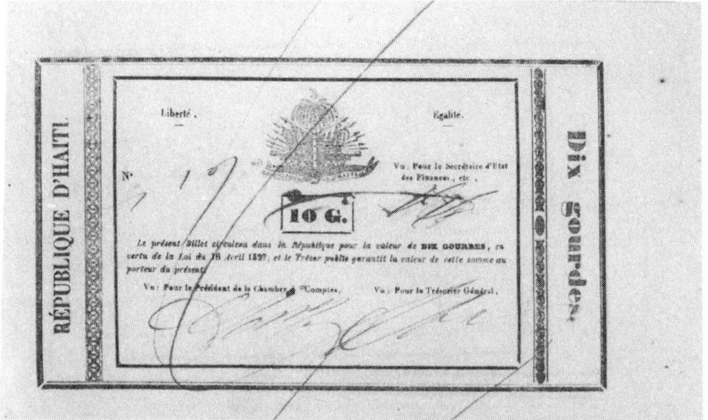

		Good	Fine	XF
4	**10 Gourdes** *L.1827.* Value *10 G.* in center box. Arms at upper center. Watermark: None.			
	a. Thin paper.	25.00	80.00	225
	b. Thick paper.	25.00	80.00	225

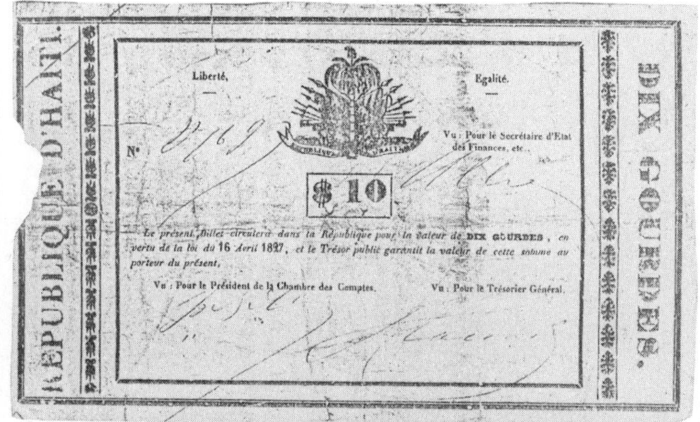

		Good	Fine	XF
5	**10 Gourdes** *L.1827.* Value *$10* in center box. Arms at upper center.			
	a. Thin paper. Watermark: *REPUBLIQUE D'HAITI.*	25.00	80.00	225
	b. Thick paper without watermark.	25.00	80.00	225

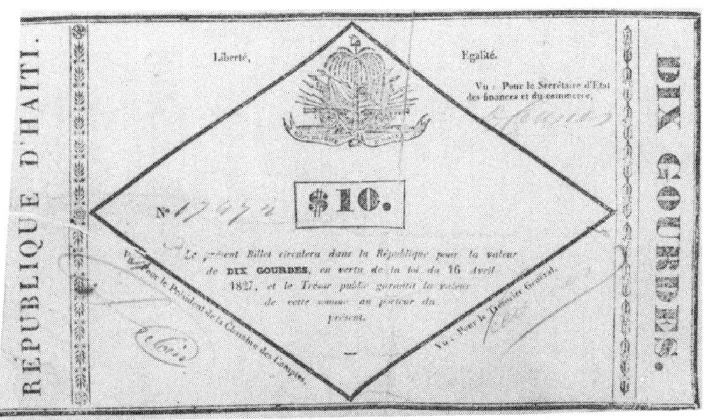

		Good	Fine	XF
6	**10 Gourdes** *L.1827.* Large lozenge around center watermark in two lines. Arms at upper center. PC: Thin, yellow.	100	250	—

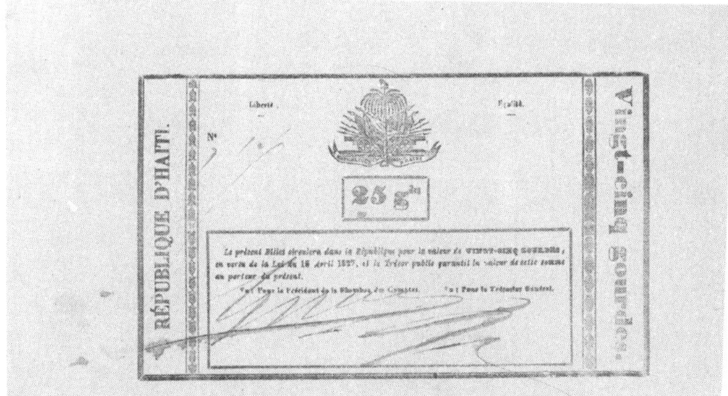

		Good	Fine	XF
7	**25 Gourdes** *L.1827.* Numeral 2 has straight bottom. Arms at upper center. PC: Thin, white.	25.00	80.00	225

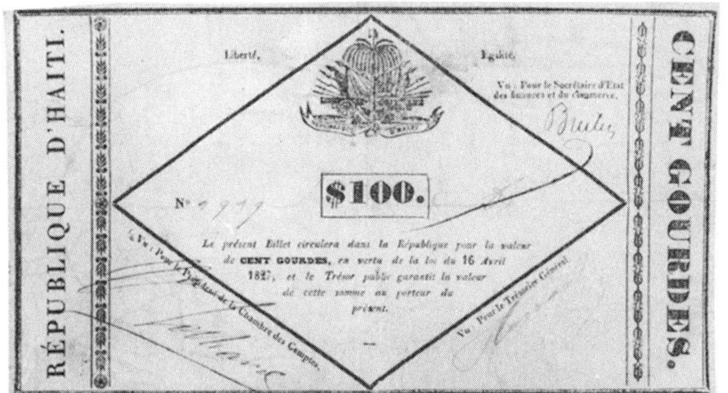

		Good	Fine	XF
8	**25 Gourdes** *L.1827.* Numeral 2 has curved bottom. Arms at upper center. PC: Thick, brown.	20.00	75.00	200

		Good	Fine	XF
10	**100 Gourdes** *L.1827.* Large lozenge around center. Arms at upper center. Watermark: Large oval.	30.00	100	250

Arreté du 31 Juillet 1849

		Good	Fine	XF
11	**50 Centimes** *L.1849.* Black. Arms at upper center. Rare.	—	—	—

EMPIRE D'HAITI

Treasury

Loi du 16 Avril 1851

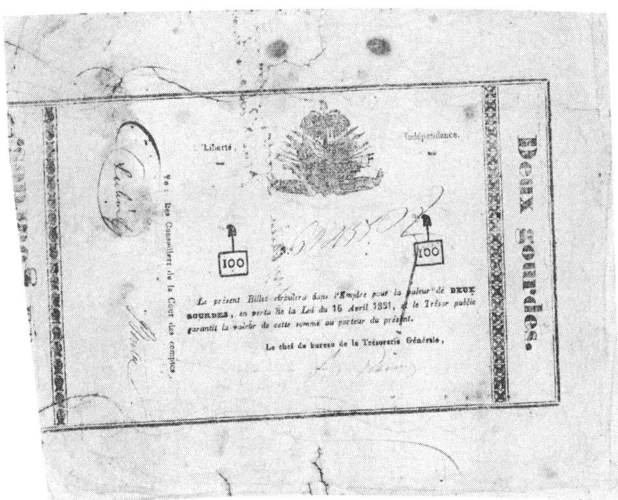

		Good	Fine	XF
15	**2 Gourdes** *L.1851.* Black. Arms at upper center. Very wide margins (often trimmed). Frame 200 x 112mm.			
	a. Yellow paper. Large 2-line watermark: *EMPIRE D'HAYTI* (sometimes with crown in watermark).	40.00	100	250
	b. Watermark: *REPUBLIQUE D'HAYTI.*	50.00	120	275
	c. Pale blue-green paper without watermark.	50.00	120	275

RÉPUBLIQUE D'HAITI

Treasury (1827)

Loi du 16 Avril 1827 - Second Issue

		Good	Fine	XF
18	**2 Gourdes** *L.1827.* Arms at upper center. Watermark: None. Frame about 134 x 75mm. Simple format style. PC: Thin, white.	100	250	—
20	**10 Gourdes** *L.1827.* With or without printed *Serie A* and *No.1.* Arms at upper center. Simple format style.	100	250	—

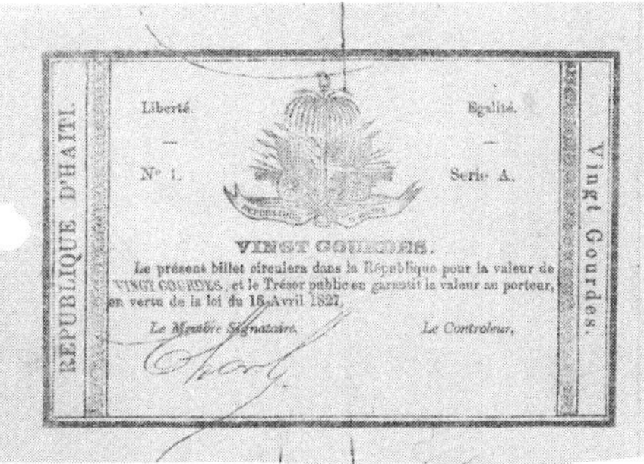

		Good	Fine	XF
21	**20 Gourdes** *L.1827.* With or without printed *Serie A* and No. 1. Arms at upper center. Simple format style.	120	300	—

Loi du 16 Avril 1827 - Third Issue

		Good	Fine	XF
25	**20 Gourdes** *L.1827.* Arms at upper center. Printed *Serie A* and *No 1.* Long format style. Frame about 174 x 74mm.	120	300	—

Loi du 16 Avril 1827 - Fourth Issue

		Good	Fine	XF
27	**4 Gourdes** *L.1827.* Value *400* in box at upper center without arms. *Le Membre Signataire* in italics. Rare.	—	—	—

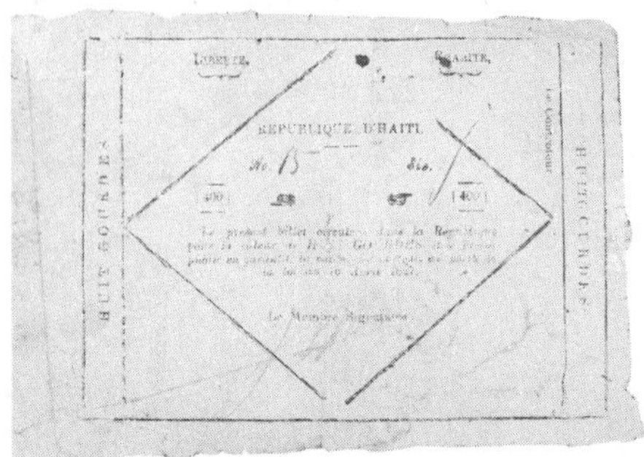

		Good	Fine	XF
28	**8 Gourdes** *L.1827.* Without arms. Diamond frame format style. Frame about 120 x 84mm.			
	a. *HUIT GOURDES* at left reads bottom to top.	200	400	—
	b. *HUIT GOURDES* at left reads top to bottom.	200	400	—

		Good	Fine	XF
30	**16 Gourdes** *L.1827.* Without arms. Diamond frame format style.			
	a. Le Membre Signataire in standard type.	80.00	150	—
	b. *Le Membre Signataire* in italics.	80.00	150	—

Loi du 16 Avril 1827 - Fifth Issue

		Good	Fine	XF
33	**2 Gourdes** *L.1827.* Black. Ornate format with oval arms at top center. Series A-D. Watermark: Yes. Printer: CS&E. Frame about 94 x 61mm. PC: Yellow.	8.00	20.00	60.00

		Good	Fine	XF
35	**2 Gourdes** *L.1827.* Black. Ornate format with oval arms at top center. Series D11-K12. Watermark: Yes. Printer: W&S. PC: White.	8.00	20.00	60.00

		Good	Fine	XF
34	**5 Gourdes** *L.1827.* Black. Ornate format with oval arms at center. Series A-D. Watermark: Yes. Printer: CS&E. PC: White.	10.00	25.00	70.00

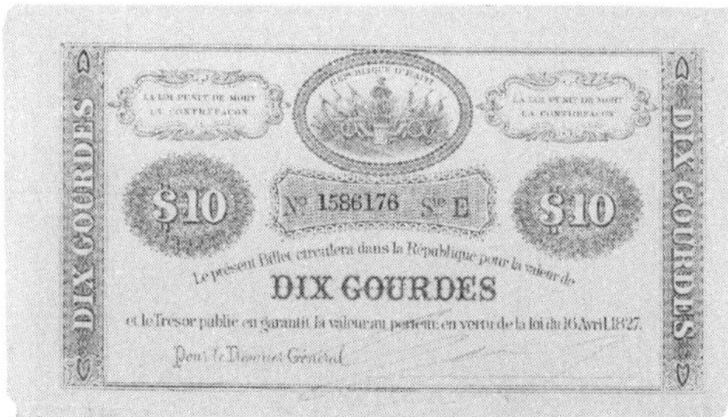

		Good	Fine	XF
36	**10 Gourdes** *L.1827.* Black. Ornate format with oval arms at top center. Series A-F. Back: Printed. Watermark: Yes. Printer: CS&E. PC: Blue.	10.00	25.00	70.00

		Good	Fine	XF
37	**25 Gourdes** *L.1827.* Black. Series G. Watermark: Yes. Printer: CS&E. PC: Green.	15.00	50.00	110

Loi du 16 Avril 1827 - Sixth Issue

		Good	Fine	XF
41	**1 Gourde** *L.1827.* Black. Portrait Pres. Geffard at upper left. Wide margins (sometimes trimmed). Watermark: Fancy, rarely without. Printer: W&S. Frame about 94 x 62mm. Fancy format style. PC: Pink or rose.	5.00	20.00	60.00

		Good	Fine	XF
42	**2 Gourdes** *L.1827.* Black. Portrait Pres. Geffrard at upper left and right. Series A1-U10. Watermark: Yes. Printer: W&S. Fancy format style. PC: White.	5.00	20.00	60.00

		Good	Fine	XF
45	**2 Gourdes** *L.1827.* Blue. Printer: TDLR. Specimen. Rare. PC: White.	—	—	—

Gouvernement du Sud d'Haiti

Government of South Haiti

En date du 13 Octobre 1868

No.	Description	Good	Fine	XF
51	**2 Gourdes** *L.1868.* Black. Arms at upper center. Series A-D.	200	—	—
52	**4 Gourdes** *L.1868.* Black. Arms at upper center. Series A; C; F; L; N; O; P.			
	a. White or off-white paper.	150	250	—
	b. Blue paper.	150	250	—

No.	Description	Good	Fine	XF
54	**12 Gourdes** *L.1868.* Black. Arms at upper center. Without Series, or Series E-V. Paper varieties: orange, yellow, blue, pink, green, violet. Many typographic varieties.	150	250	—
55	**24 Gourdes** *L.1868.* Black. Arms at center. Series B.	300	—	—

No.	Description	Good	Fine	XF
56	**25 Gourdes** *L.1868.* Black. Arms at upper center. Series D.	400	1,000	—

No.	Description	Good	Fine	XF
57	**48 Gourdes** *L.1868.* Black. Arms at upper center. Without series.	300	—	—
58	**100 Gourdes** *L.1868.* Black. Arms at upper center. Frame ca. 196x72mm.	350	—	—

Loi du 28 Octobre 1869

No.	Description	Good	Fine	XF
60	**10 Piastres Fortes** *L.1869.* Arms at upper center. Frame 170x75mm. Rare. PC: Thin, white.	—	—	—

Loi du 22 Juillet 1871

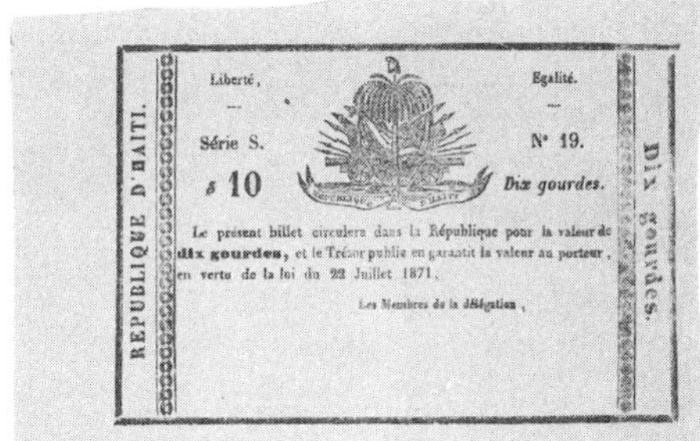

No.	Description	Good	Fine	XF
64	**10 Gourdes** *L.1871.* Black. Arms at upper center. Series E-X4. PC: Green or blue-green	30.00	120	225
65	**20 Gourdes** *L.1871.* Black. Arms at upper center. Series A-Q5. PC:White or off-white.	30.00	120	225

La Banque Nationale d'Haiti

Septre. 1875 Issue

#68-72 without signatures (but some have had fraudulent signatures added later). Some have irregular edges from having been torn from uncut sheets.

No.	Description	Good	Fine	XF
68	**25 Centimes** Sept.1875. Black on pink underprint. Portrait Pres. Michel Domingue at left, arms at right. Printer: ABNC. 112x56mm.	8.00	20.00	60.00

No.	Description	Good	Fine	XF
70	**1 Piastre** Sept. 1875. Black on blue and orange underprint. Portrait Pres. Michel Domingue at left, arms at center, allegorical woman (Agriculture) at right. Printer: ABNC. 155x77mm.	10.00	35.00	100

No.	Description	Good	Fine	XF
72	**5 Piastres** Sept. 1875. Black on light green and pink underprint. Woman ("Justice") at left, arms at center, portrait Pres. Michel Domingue at right. Printer: ABNC.	12.50	50.00	125

1880s Issue

No.	Description	Good	Fine	XF
74	**5 Gourdes** ND. Blue and buff. Justice at left, arms in orange at right. Printer: Imp. Filigranique G. Richard et Cie., Paris. 139x79mm.	1,000	—	—
74A	**10 Gourdes** ND. Rare.	—	—	—

Treasury (1883-1889)

Loi du 28 Aout 1883

		Good	Fine	XF
75	**1 Gourde** *L.1883.* Black on blue underprint. Arms at upper center, female portrait (Majesty No. 2) at right. Series through A48. Printer: ABNC. 177x77mm. *Salomon Jeune* (first issue.)			
	a. Issued note.	250	650	—
	s. Specimen.	—	Unc	1,000

		Good	Fine	XF
76	**2 Gourdes** *L.1883.* Black on pink underprint. Dog at upper left, arms at upper right. Series through B14. Printer: ABNC. *Salomon Jeune* (first issue.)			
	a. Issued note.	300	800	—
	s. Specimen.	—	Unc	1,250

Loi du 6 Octobre 1884

		Good	Fine	XF
77	**1 Gourde** *L.1884.* Black on orange and blue underprint. Naiad reclining at left, arms at right. Series through C54. Printer: ABNC. 170x74mm. *Salomon Jeune* (second issue.)			
	a. Issued note.	200	500	—
	s. Specimen.	—	Unc	850
78	**2 Gourdes** *L.1884.* Black on green and orange underprint. Agriculture" at left. Series through D32. Printer: ABNC. *Salomon Jeune* (second issue.)	Good	Fine	XF
	a. Issued note.	300	800	—
	s. Specimen.	—	Unc	1,250

Loi du 3 Novembre 1887

		Good	Fine	XF
79	**1 Gourde** *L.1887.* Black on orange and blue underprint. Arms at upper left, Ceres reclining at right. Series through E100. Printer: CS&E. *Salomon Jeune* (third issue.)			
	a. Issued note.	200	500	—
	s. Specimen.	—	Unc	750

		Good	Fine	XF
80	**2 Gourdes** *L.1887.* Black on green and orange underprint. Farmers and horse at left, portrait girl at upper right, arms at lower right. Series through F50. Printer: CS&E. *Salomon Jeune* (third issue.)			
	a. Issued note.	300	700	—
	s. Specimen.	—	Unc	1,250

Decret ... du 28 Juin 1889

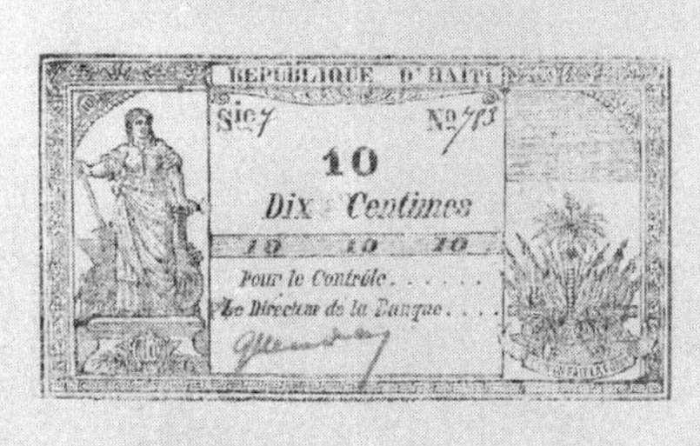

		Good	Fine	XF
83	**10 Centimes** ND. Issued in Port-au-Prince by Pres. François Denis Légitime. Frame 11861mm. PC: Heavy gray watermark paper.			
	a. Black print.	250	—	—
	b. Blue print.	250	—	—

		Good	Fine	XF
84	**20 Centimes** ND. Issued in Port-au-Prince by Pres. François Denis Légitime. Frame 118x61mm. PC: Green on heavy gray watermark paper.	250	—	—

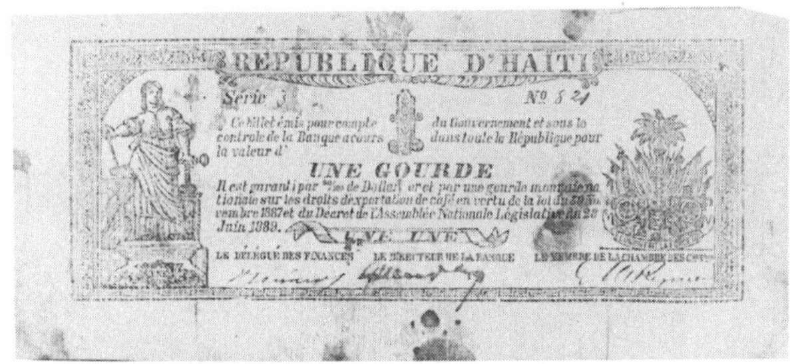

		Good	Fine	XF
85	**1 Gourde** *D.1889.* Issued in Port-au-Prince by Pres. François Denis Légitime. Frame 166x61mm. PC: Green on heavy white watermark paper.	1,000	—	—

République Septentrionale d'Haiti

1888 ND Issue

Government of General Floraville Hippolyte 1888-1889 in North Haiti.

		Good	Fine	XF
88	**10 Centimes** ND (1888). Black on gray underprint. Arms at upper left. Series A. Printer: HILBNC. 82x42mm.	200	400	—

		Good	Fine	XF
89	**25 Centimes** ND (1888). Black on light blue underprint. Arms at right. Series A. Printer: HLBNC. 110x62mm.	175	350	—

		Good	Fine	XF
90	**50 Centimes** ND (1888). Black on pale orange underprint. Arms at left. Series A. Printer: HLBNC. 110x64mm.	250	450	—

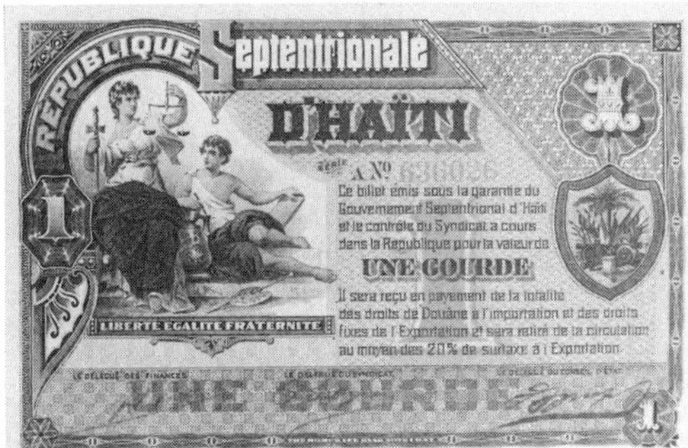

		Good	Fine	XF
91	**1 Gourde** ND (1888). Black on pink and green underprint. Justice and Youth at upper left, arms at right. Series A. Printer: HLBNC. 154x100mm.			
	a. Issued note.	200	400	—
	s. Specimen.	—	Unc	800

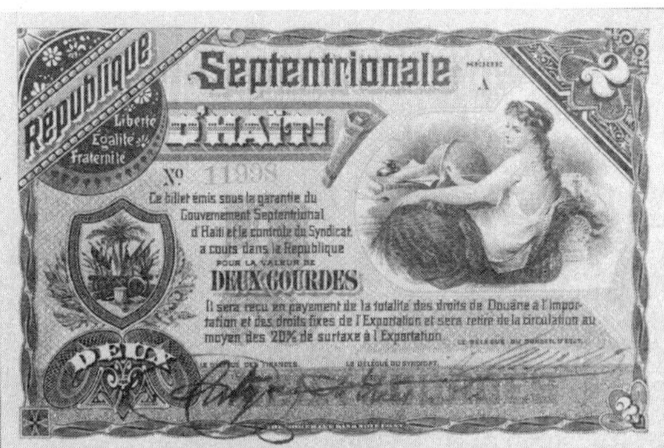

		Good	Fine	XF
92	**2 Gourdes** ND (1888). Black on orange and blue underprint. Arms at left, woman seated with globe at right. Series A. Printer: HLBNC. 154x100mm.			
	a. Issued note.	250	500	—
	s. Specimen.	—	Unc	1,000

1889 ND Issue

		Good	Fine	XF
95	**1 Gourde** ND (1889). Woman at left. Serial # and 2 of 3 signatures in red. Series T. Printer: HLBNC. 165x74mm.	250	600	—

Treasury (1892)

Loi du 29 Septembre 1892

		Good	Fine	XF
101	**1 Gourde** *L.1892.* Black on yellow and blue underprint. Portrait J.J. Dessalines at left, arms at right. Series B-V. Printer: ABNC. 182x80mm.			
	a. Issued note.	20.00	100	300
	s. Specimen.	—	Unc	350

		Good	Fine	XF
102	**2 Gourdes**			
	L.1892. Black on yellow and pink underprint. Series AB; BC-OP. Portrait J.J. Dessalines at left, arms at right. Printer: ABNC.			
	a. Issued note.	25.00	150	425
	s. Specimen.	—	Unc	400

Treasury (1903-1908)

Loi Du 10 Aout 1903 - Commemorative

#110 and 111, Centennial of Haitian Independence, 1804-1904.

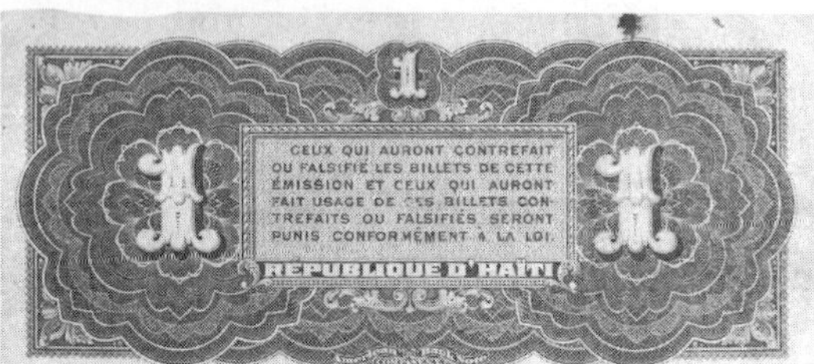

		Good	Fine	XF
110	**1 Gourde**			
	L.1903. Black on blue-gray underprint. Series A-G. Portrait J.J. Dessalines and date 1804 at left, arms at center. Portrait Nord Alexis and date 1904 at right. 176x80mm.			
	a. Issued note.	7.50	60.00	225
	s. Specimen.	—	Unc	250

		Good	Fine	XF
111	**2 Gourdes**			
	L.1903. Black on green-gray underprint. Series AA-JJ. Portrait J.J. Dessalines and date 1804 at left, arms at center. Portrait Nord Alexis and date 1904 at right. Printer: ABNC.			
	a. Issued note.	10.00	70.00	250
	s. Specimen.	—	Unc	300

Loi Du 27 Fevrier 1904 - Commemorative

#120 and 121, Centennial of Haitian Independence, 1804-1904.

		Good	Fine	XF
120	**1 Gourde**			
	L.1904. Black on blue-gray underprint. Series A-R.			
	a. Issued note.	6.00	40.00	200
	s. Specimen.	—	Unc	250

		Good	Fine	XF
121	**2 Gourdes**			
	L.1904. Black on green-gray underprint. Series BB-OO.			
	a. Issued note.	7.50	60.00	225
	s. Specimen.	—	Unc	300

Loi du 14 Mai 1908

		Good	Fine	XF
125	**5 Gourdes**			
	L.1908. Black on pink underprint. Portrait Nord Alexis at both left and right. Series C3-19. Printer: ABNC. 169x73mm.			
	a. Issued note.	150	550	—
	s. Specimen.	—	Unc	750

Note: It is probable that #125 was issued upon the death of Nord Alexis in 1908.

Bon du Tresor

Treasury

Loi du 22 Decembre 1914 (Issued Feb. 1915)

		Good	Fine	XF
131	**1 Gourde** *L.1914.* Black on blue underprint. Portrait J.J. Dessalines and date 1804 at left, arms at center. Portrait Nord Alexis and date 1904 at right. Without overprint. Series A. Back: Farming scene at center. Printer: ABNC.			
	a. Issued note.	8.00	50.00	150
	p. Proof.	—	Unc	1,000
	s. Specimen.	—	Unc	400

		Good	Fine	XF
132	**2 Gourdes** *L.1914.* Black on green underprint. Portrait J.J. Dessalines and date 1804 at left, arms at center. Portrait Nord Alexis and date 1904 at right. Without overprint. Series AA-FF. Back: Mining scene at center. Printer: ABNC.			
	a. Issued note.	10.00	60.00	165
	p. Proof.	—	Unc	1,250
	s. Specimen.	—	Unc	500

l'Arrete du 22 Janvier 1915

		Good	Fine	XF
127	**1 Gourde** *L.1915.* Black. Arms at center. Series A; B. Printer: Local. Heavy manilla paper.	10.00	40.00	100
128	**2 Gourdes** *L.1915.* Black. Arms at center. Series AA. Printer: Local. Heavy manilla paper.	25.00	100	250
129	**5 Gourdes** *L.1915.* Arms at center. Series AAA. Printer: Local. Heavy manilla paper.			
	a. Red serial #.	10.00	50.00	150
	b. Black serial #.	8.00	40.00	120

1916 ND Issue

		Good	Fine	XF
134	**1 Gourde** ND (1916). Black and orange. Series A. Printer: Local.	150	300	650
135	**1 Gourde** ND (1916). Blue and black with red title and text. Series D; E; J. Printer: Local. 184x82mm.	125	250	550

		Good	Fine	XF
136	**2 Gourdes** ND (1916). Red and black with blue title and text. K-O. Printer: Local.	150	275	600

Banque Nationale de la République d'Haiti

1916 Provisional Issue

#137-141 with vertical red overprint lines of French text on unsigned notes of the Eighteenth Issue of République (1914). Red dates either 1916 and 1913, or 1919 and 1913. The distinguishing 1916 or 1919 date is vertical in red near the top center of the note.

		Good	Fine	XF
137	**1 Gourde** *L.1916.* Series A-D. Overprint: 1916 on #131.	15.00	50.00	200
138	**2 Gourdes** *L.1916.* Series AA-II. Overprint: 1916 on #132. Rare.	—	—	—

1919 Provisional Issue

		Good	Fine	XF
140	**1 Gourde** *L.1919.* Series D-M. Overprint: 1919 on #131.			
	a. Issued note.	8.00	30.00	150
	s. Specimen.	—	Unc	120

141	2 Gourdes	Good	Fine	XF
	L.1919. Series HH-RR. Overprint: 1919 on #132.			
	a. Issued note.	10.00	35.00	175
	s. Specimen.	—	Unc	140

Convention du 2 Mai 1919 - First Issue (ca.1920-1924)

150	1 Gourde	Good	Fine	XF
	L.1919. Black on green and brown underprint. Banana plant at left. Prefix letters. A-L. 2 signature varieties. Back: Coffee plant. Printer: ABNC. 163x87mm.			
	a. Issued note.	5.00	35.00	175
	s. Specimen.	—	Unc	150

151	2 Gourdes	Good	Fine	XF
	L.1919. Black on green and brown underprint. Banana plant at right. Prefix letters A-J. 2 signature varieties. Back: Coffee plant. Printer: ABNC.			
	a. Issued note.	15.00	100	350
	s. Specimen.	—	Unc	225

152	5 Gourdes	Good	Fine	XF
	L.1919. Black on red, blue and green underprint. Banana plant at right center. Prefix letters A and B. 2 signature varieties. Back: Coffee plant. Printer: ABNC.			
	a. Issued note.	50.00	250	750
	s. Specimen.	—	Unc	450
153	10 Gourdes	Good	Fine	XF
	L.1919. Black on green and brown underprint. Banana plant at right center. Prefix letter A. Back: Coffee plant. Printer: ABNC.			
	a. Issued note.	125	600	—
	s. Specimen.	—	Unc	750
154	20 Gourdes	Good	Fine	XF
	L.1919. Black on blue and multicolor underprint. Banana plant at right center. Back: Coffee plant. (Not issued). Archive example.	—	—	—

Convention du 12 Avril 1919 - Second Issue (ca.1925-1932)

160	1 Gourde	VG	VF	UNC
	L.1919. Dark brown and multicolor. Distant aerial view of Citadel le Ferriere at center. Black signature. Prefix letters M-AC (but without W). 5 signature varieties. Third signature title:*Pour Controle...* Back: Arms. Printer: ABNC. 121x60mm.			
	a. Issued note.	1.50	10.00	40.00
	p. Proof.	—	—	250
	s. Specimen.	—	—	45.00

161	2 Gourdes	VG	VF	UNC
	L.1919. Deep blue and multicolor. Distant aerial view of Citadel le Ferriere at center. Black signature. Prefix letters K-M; P-R. 5 signature varieties. Printer: ABNC.			
	a. Issued note.	2.00	15.00	50.00
	p. Proof.	—	—	225
	s. Specimen.	—	—	125

162	5 Gourdes	VG	VF	UNC
	L.1919. Orange on light green and multicolor underprint. Women harvesting coffee at left. Third signature title:*Pour Controle...* Black signature. Prefix letters C; D. 3 signature varieties. Printer: ABNC. 162x70mm.			
	a. Issued note.	1.50	10.00	75.00
	s. Specimen.	—	—	150
163	10 Gourdes	VG	VF	UNC
	L.1919. Green and multicolor. Third signature title:*Pour Controle...* Coffee plant at center. Prefix letter B. 2 signature varieties. Printer: ABNC.			
	a. Issued note.	5.00	30.00	100
	p. Proof.	—	—	650
	s. Specimen.	—	—	175

No.	Description	VG	VF	UNC
164	**20 Gourdes** *L.1919.* Red-brown and multicolor. Palm tree at right. Prefix letter A. Third signature title:*Pour Controle...* Printer: ABNC.	VG	VF	UNC
	a. Issued note.	200	600	—
	s. Specimen.	—	—	500
165	**50 Gourdes** *L.1919.* Dark olive and multicolor. Cotton balls at center. Prefix letter A. Third signature title:*Pour Controle...* Printer: ABNC.	VG	VF	UNC
	a. Issued note.	50.00	300	—
	s. Specimen.	—	—	400
166	**100 Gourdes** *L.1919.* Purple and multicolor. Field workers at left. Prefix letter A. Third signature title:*Pour Controle...* Printer: ABNC.	VG	VF	UNC
	a. Issued note.	50.00	300	—
	s. Specimen.	—	—	400

Convention du 12 Avril 1919 - Third Issue (ca.1935-1942)

No.	Description	VG	VF	UNC
167	**1 Gourde** *L.1919.* Dark brown and multicolor. Portrait Pres. Stenio Vincent at center. Prefix letter W. Printer: ABNC.	VG	VF	UNC
	a. Issued note.	30.00	150	300
	s. Specimen.	—	—	175
168	**2 Gourdes** *L.1919.* Blue and multicolor. Portrait Pres. Stenio Vincent at center. Prefix letter N.	VG	VF	UNC
	a. Issued note.	30.00	175	375
	s. Specimen.	—	—	250

Convention du 12 Avril 1919 - Fourth Issue (ca.1946-1950)

No.	Description	VG	VF	UNC
170	**1 Gourde** *L.1919.* Distant aerial view of Citadel le Ferriere at center. Brown signature. Prefix letters AD-AR. 4 signature varieties. First and third signature title each:*Un Administrateur.* Printer: ABNC.	VG	VF	UNC
	a. Issued note.	1.00	4.00	25.00
	s. Specimen.	—	—	40.00

No.	Description	VG	VF	UNC
171	**2 Gourdes** *L.1919.* Dark brown and multicolor. Distant aerial view of Citadel le Ferriere at center. Blue signature. Prefix letters S-Y. 4 signature varieties. First and third signature title each:*Un Administrateur.* Printer: ABNC.	VG	VF	UNC
	a. Issued note.	1.00	5.00	30.00
	s. Specimen.	—	—	75.00
172	**5 Gourdes** *L.1919.* Orange on light green and multiclor underprint. Women harvesting coffee at left. Prefix letters D; E. 3 signature varieties. First and third signature title each: *Un Administrateur.* Printer: ABNC.	VG	VF	UNC
	a. Orange signature. Prefix letter D.	2.00	12.50	45.00
	b. Black signature. Prefix letter E.	1.50	10.00	30.00
	s1. Like a. Specimen.	—	—	75.00
	s2. Like b. Specimen.	—	—	60.00
173	**10 Gourdes** *L.1919.* Green and multicolor. Coffee plant at center. Prefix letter B. First and third signature title: *Un Administrateur.* Printer: ABNC.	VG	VF	UNC
	a. Issued note.	5.00	25.00	60.00
	s. Specimen.	—	—	80.00

Convention du 12 Avril 1919 - Fifth Issue (ca.1950)

No.	Description	VG	VF	UNC
174	**1 Gourde** *L.1919.* Dark brown and multicolor. Closeup view of Citadel Rampart at center. Prefix letters WA-WD. 2 signature varieties. Printer: W&S.	20.00	70.00	200
175	**2 Gourdes** *L.1919.* Blue and multicolor. Closeup view of Citadel Rampart at center. Prefix letters WA and WB. 2 signature varieties. Printer: W&S.	40.00	125	350

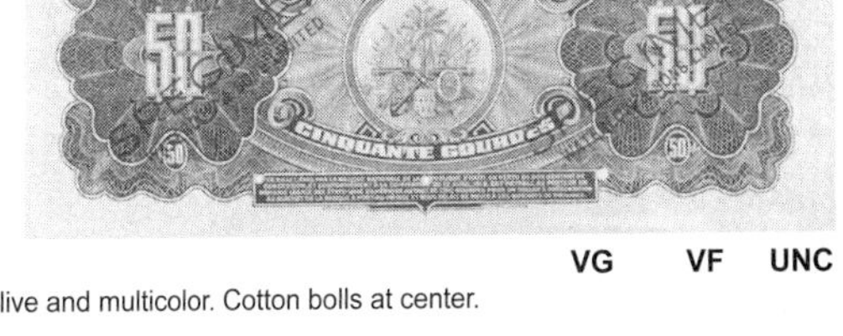

No.	Description	VG	VF	UNC
176	**50 Gourdes** *L.1919.* Dark olive and multicolor. Cotton bolls at center. Printer: W&S.	VG	VF	UNC
	a. Issued note.	—	—	—
	s. Specimen, with or without punch hole cancels.	—	—	200
177	**100 Gourdes** *L.1919.* Brown. Field workers at left. Printer: W&S. Uniface specimen pair.	—	—	250

REPUBLIC (SECOND)

Banque Nationale de la République d'Haiti

Convention du 12 Avril 1919 - Sixth Issue (ca.1951-1964)

		VG	VF	UNC
178	**1 Gourde** *L.1919.* Dark brown on light blue and multicolor underprint. Closeup view of Citadel Rampart at center. Prefix letters AS-BM. 5 signature varieties. First signature title: *Le President.* Back: Arms at center. Printer: ABNC.			
	a. Issued note.	0.75	2.00	17.50
	s. Specimen. Punch hole cancelled.	—	—	35.00

		VG	VF	UNC
179	**2 Gourdes** *L.1919.* Blue and multicolor. Light green in underprint. Citadel rampart at center. Prefix letters Y-AF. 6 signature varieties. First signature title: *Le President.* Back: Arms at center. Printer: ABNC.			
	a. Issued note.	1.00	4.00	25.00
	s. Specimen. Punch hole cancelled. SPECIMEN twice on face.	—	—	65.00
180	**5 Gourdes** *L.1919.* Orange and multicolor. Green in underprint. Woman harvesting coffee at left. Prefix letters G-M. 3 signature varieties. First signature title:*Le President.* Back: Arms at center. Printer: ABNC.	VG	VF	UNC
	a. Issued note.	1.25	6.00	35.00
	s. Specimen. Punch hole cancelled.	—	—	55.00
181	**10 Gourdes** *L.1919.* Green on multicolor underprint. Coffee plant at center. Prefix letters B-D. 2 signature varieties. First signature title: *Le President.* Back: Arms at center. Printer: ABNC.	VG	VF	UNC
	a. Issued note.	3.00	12.50	55.00
	s. Specimen. Punch hole cancelled.	—	—	70.00

#182 not assigned.

		VG	VF	UNC
183	**50 Gourdes** *L.1919.* Olive-green on multicolor underprint. Cotton bolls at center. First signature title: *Le President.* Back: Arms at center. Printer: ABNC. Specimen.	—	—	225

		VG	VF	UNC
184	**100 Gourdes** *L.1919.* Purple on multicolor underprint. Field workers at left. Prefix letter A. First signature title: *Le President.* Back: Arms at center. Printer: ABNC.			
	a. Issued note.	30.00	125	350
	s. Specimen. Punch hole cancelled.	—	—	175

HAWAII

North Pacific Ocean

U.S.A

MEXICO

Hawaii consists of eight main islands and numerous smaller islands of coral and volcanic origin situated in the central Pacific Ocean 2,400 miles (3,862 km.) from San Francisco. The archipelago has an area of 6,471 sq. mi. (16,641 sq. km.) and a population of 1.1 million. Capital: Honolulu. The principal industries are tourism and agriculture. The islands, originally populated by Polynesians who traveled from the Society Islands, were discovered by British navigator Capt. James Cook in 1778. He named them the Sandwich Islands. King Kamehameha the Great united the islands under one kingdom (1795-1810) which endured until 1893 when Queen Liliuokalani, the gifted composer of "Aloha Oe" and other songs, was deposed and a provisional government established. This was followed by a republic which governed Hawaii until 1898 when it ceded itself to the United States. Hawaii was organized as a territory in 1900 and became the 50th state of the United States on Aug. 21, 1959.

RULERS

King Kalakaua, 1874-1891
Queen Liliuokalani, 1891-1893
Provisional Govt., 1893-1894
Republic, 1894-1898
Annexed to U.S., 1898-1900
Territory, 1900-1959
Statehood, 1959

MONETARY SYSTEM

1 Dollar = 100 Cents

KINGDOM

Department of Finance

1879 (1880) Silver Certificate of Deposit - Series A

		Fine	XF	CU
1	**10 Dollars** ND (1880). Black on orange underprint. Sailing ship at left, cowboy roping steers at center, steam locomotive at right. Back: Arms at center. Printer: ABNC.			
	a. Issued note. 1 known in private hands (serial # 1).	—	200,000	—
	b. Punch hole or cut cancelled. 2 known in private hands.	17,500	—	—
	p. Proof pair, face and back.	—	—	9,000

		Fine	XF	CU
2	**20 Dollars** ND (1879). Black on brown underprint. Portrait girl with dog at lower left, portrait woman between steam paddle-wheel ship and steam passenger train at center, anchor at lower right. Back: Arms at center. Printer: ABNC.			
	a. Issued note. Unknown.	—	—	—
	b. Punch hole or cut cancelled. Rare. 3 known in private hands.	20,000	—	—
	p. Proof pair, face and back.	—	—	15,000

		Fine	XF	CU
3	**50 Dollars** ND (1879). Black on green underprint. Ram at left, allegorical woman at center, girl at right. Back: Arms at center. Printer: ABNC.			
	a. Issued note. Rare. 1 known in private hands.	50,000	—	—
	b. Punch hole or cut cancelled. Unknown in private hands.	—	—	—
	p. Proof pair, face and back.	—	—	17,500

4	100 Dollars	Fine	XF	CU
	ND (1879). Black on blue underprint. Galloping horse at lower left, globe between steam passenger train and sailing ship at center, cow at lower right. Back: Arms at center. Printer: ABNC.			
	a. Issued note. Rare. Unknown in private hands.	—	—	—
	b. Punch hole or cut cancelled. 3 known in private hands.	25,000	—	—
	p. Proof pair, face and back.	—	—	20,000

5	500 Dollars	Fine	XF	CU
	ND (1879). Black on orange underprint. Portrait King Kalakaua I at left, steam locomotive between sailing ships at center, farmer carrying produce at right. Back: Arms at center. Printer: ABNC. Proof pair, face and back. Rare.			
	a. Unknown.	—	—	—
	p. Proof pair.	—	—	55,000

REPUBLIC OF HAWAII

Department of Finance

1895 (1899) Gold Certificate of Deposit Issue - Series B

6	5 Dollars	Fine	XF	CU
	1895 (1899). Black on gold underprint. Woman "Haidee" at left, building and trees at center, steer at right. Back: Arms in circle. Printer: ABNC.			
	a. Issued note. Rare. 3 known in private hands.	25,000	—	—
	b. Cancelled. 1 known in private hands.	—	—	—
	p. Proof pair, face and back.	—	—	10,000

7	10 Dollars	Fine	XF	CU
	1895 (1899). Black on gold underprint. Steamship at left, sugar cane harvest at center, woman at right. Back: Arms in circle. Printer: ABNC.			
	a. Issued note. 1 known in private hands.	—	—	—
	b. Cancelled. 2 known in private hands.	—	—	—
	p. Proof pair, face and back.	—	—	75,000

8	20 Dollars	Fine	XF	CU
	1895 (1899). Black on gold underprint. Woman standing at left, sugar cane harvest at center, horse's head at right. Back: Arms in circle. Printer: ABNC.			
	a. Issued note. Rare. 1 known in private hands (3/4 of a note)	—	—	—
	b. Cancelled. 1 known in private hands.	—	—	15,000
	p. Proof pair, face and back.	—	—	10,000

9	50 Dollars	Fine	XF	CU
	1895 (1899). Black on gold underprint. Woman at left, longhorns with cowboy on horseback at center, tree at right. Back: Arms in circle. Printer: ABNC.			
	a. Issued note. Unknown in private hands.	—	—	—
	b. Cancelled. Unknown in private hands.	—	—	—
	p. Proof pair, face and back.	—	—	10,000

10	100 Dollars	Fine	XF	CU
	1895 (1899). Black on gold underprint. Two allegorical women at left, cowboys and steam passenger train at center, horse at right. Back: Arms in circle. Printer: ABNC.			
	a. Issued note. Unknown in private hands.	—	—	—
	b. Cancelled. 2 known in private hands.	—	—	17,500
	p. Proof pair, face and back.	—	—	10,000

1895 (1897) Silver Certificate of Deposit Issue - Series C

11	5 Dollars	VG	VF	UNC
	1895 (1897). Black on blue underprint. Palm tree at left, Iolani Palace at center, kneeling man at right. Back: Arms at center. Printer: ABNC.			
	a. Issued note. 14 known in private hands.	10,000	15,000	—
	b. Cancelled.1 known in private hands.	12,000	—	—
	p. Proof pair, face and back.	—	—	5,000

#	Description	VG	VF	UNC
12	**10 Dollars**	VG	VF	UNC
	1895 (1897). Black on blue underprint. Sailing ship at left, cowboy roping steers at center, steam locomotive at right. Back: Arms at center.			
	a. Issued note. Rare. 3 known in private hands.	20,000	—	—
	b. Cancelled. 1 known in private hands.	15,000	—	—
	p. Proof pair, face and back.	—	—	7,500
13	**20 Dollars**	VG	VF	UNC
	1895 (1897). Black on blue underprint. Portrait girl with dog at lower left, portrait woman between steam paddle-wheel ship and steam passenger train at center, anchor at lower right. Back: Arms at center. Printer: ABNC.			
	a. Issued note. Unknown.	—	—	—
	b. Cancelled. 1 known in private hands.	25,000	—	—
	p. Proof pair, face and back.	—	—	10,000
14	**50 Dollars**	VG	VF	UNC
	1895 (1897). Black on blue underprint. Ram at left, allegorical woman at center, girl at right. Back: Arms at center. Printer: ABNC.			
	a. Issued note. Unknown.	—	—	—
	b. Cancelled. Unknown in private hands.	—	—	—
	p. Proof pair, face and back.	—	—	10,000
15	**100 Dollars**	VG	VF	UNC
	1895 (1897). Black on blue underprint. Galloping horse at lower left, globe between steam passenger train and sailing ship at center, cow at lower right. Back: Arms at center. Printer: ABNC.			
	a. Issued note. Unknown.	—	—	—
	b. Cancelled. Unknown in private hands.	—	—	—
	p. Proof pair, face and back.	—	—	10,000

UNITED STATES OF AMERICA - TERRITORIAL

Treasury

1935 A (1942) Emergency Silver Certificate Issue

#36, overprint: *HAWAII* on face and back of 1935 A series.

#	Description	VG	VF	UNC
36	**1 Dollar**	VG	VF	UNC
	1935 A (1942). Black. Portrait G. Washington at center. Brown serial # and seal at right.			
	a. Issued note.	45.00	70.00	75.00
	r. Replacement note. * at start of serial #.	300	450	500

Federal Reserve

1934 (1942) Emergency Issue

#	Description	VG	VF	UNC
37	**5 Dollars**	VG	VF	UNC
	1934 (1942). Black. Portrait A. Lincoln at center. Brown serial # and seal at right. Back: Lincoln Memorial at center. Series 'L' notes.			
	a. Issued note.	90.00	125	500
	r. Replacement note. * at end of serial #.	1,200	2,500	8,000
38	**5 Dollars**	VG	VF	UNC
	1934 A (1942). Black. Portrait A. Lincoln at center. Brown serial # and seal at right. Back: Lincoln Memorial at center. Series 'L' notes.			
	a. Issued note.	80.00	100	525
	r. Replacement note. * at end of serial #.	5,000	9,000	18,500

#	Description	VG	VF	UNC
39	**10 Dollars**	VG	VF	UNC
	1934 A (1942). Black. Portrait A. Hamilton at center. Brown serial # and seal at right. Back: Treasury Building at center. Series 'L' notes.			
	a. Issued note.	75.00	200	550
	r. Replacement note. * at end of serial #.	550	1,500	5,000
40	**20 Dollars**	VG	VF	UNC
	1934 (1942). Black. Portrait A. Hamilton at center. Brown serial # and seal at right. Back: Treasury Building at center. Series 'L' notes.			
	a. Issued note.	600	800	8,500
	r. Replacement note. * at end of serial #.	1,500	5,000	20,000
41	**20 Dollars**	VG	VF	UNC
	1934 A (1942). Black. Portrait A. Jackson at center. Brown serial # and seal at right. Back: White House at center. Series 'L' notes.			
	a. Issued note.	80.00	150	800
	r. Replacement note. * at end of serial #.	300	3,000	9,000

Hejaz, a province of Saudi Arabia and a former vilayet of the Ottoman Empire, occupies an 800-mile-long (1,287 km.) coastal strip between Nejd and the Red Sea. Population: 1.4 million. Hejaz contains the holy cities of Mecca and Medina. The economy is based on pilgrimage spending, light industries, limited agriculture production and the wealth generated by the oil deposits of Saudi Arabia. The province was a Turkish dependency until freed in World War I. Husain Ibn Ali, Amir of Mecca, opposed the Turkish control and, with the aid of Lawrence of Arabia, wrested much of Hejaz from the Turks and in 1916 assumed the title of King of Hejaz. Ibn Sa'ud of Nejd conquered Hejaz in 1925, and in 1932 combined it with Nejd and other provinces under his control to form the Kingdom of Saudi Arabia.

RULERS

Husain Ibn Ali, AH1334-1373 (AD 1916-1924)
Abd Al-Aziz Ibn Sa'ud, AH1342-1373 (AD 1924-1953)

MONETARY SYSTEM

1 Pound (Riyal) = 20 Ghirsh (Piastres)

HEJAZ

Arabian National Bank of Hedjaz

Decree of 23 Shawal AH1343 (1924)

#	Description	Good	Fine	XF
1	**1/2 Pound**	Good	Fine	XF
	D. AH1343 (1924). Red. Kaaba (or Ka'bah-Moslem shrine in Mecca). Back: Indian coin. Rare.	—	—	—

#	Description	Good	Fine	XF
2	**1 Pound**	Good	Fine	XF
	D. AH1343 (1924). Green, brown and multicolor. City view at center. Back: Arms at center. Rare.	—	—	—
3	**5 Pounds**	Good	Fine	XF
	D. AH1343 (1924). Brown, gold and multicolor. Ornate building at upper right. Back: Arms at center. Rare.	—	—	—

		Good	Fine	XF
4	**10 Pounds** *D. AH1343* (1924). Brown, blue, pink and multicolor. Temple at center, columns at left and right. Back: Arms at center. Rare.	—	—	—

		Good	Fine	XF
5	**50 Pounds** D. AH1343 (1924). Blue, orange and multicolor. Cedar tree at left, ruins at right. Back: Arms at center. Rare.	—	—	—
6	**100 Pounds** *D. AH1343* (1924). Brown, blue, lilac and multicolor. Oasis at center, facing ancient winged statues at left and right of archway. Back: Arms at center. Rare.	—	—	—

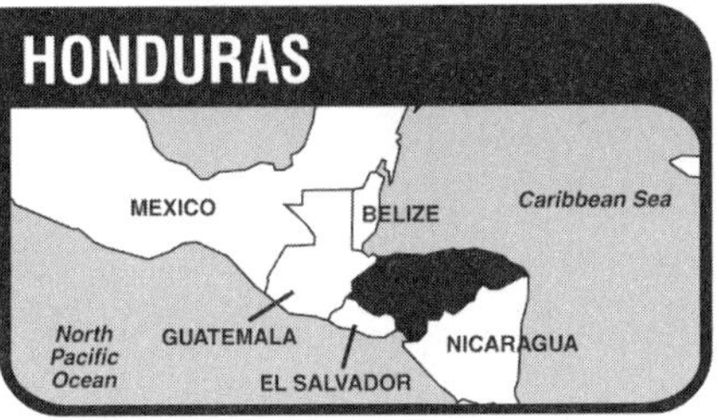

The Republic of Honduras, situated in Central America between El Salvador, Nicaragua and Guatemala, has an area of 43,277 sq. mi. (112,088 sq. km.) and a population of 6.48 million. Capital: Tegucigalpa. Tourism, agriculture, mining (gold and silver), and logging are the chief industries. Bananas, timber and coffee are exported.

Once part of Spain's vast empire in the New World, Honduras became an independent nation in 1821. After two and a half decades of mostly military rule, a freely elected civilian government came to power in 1982. During the 1980s, Honduras proved a haven for anti-Sandinista contras fighting the Marxist Nicaraguan Government and an ally to Salvadoran Government forces fighting leftist guerrillas. The country was devastated by Hurricane Mitch in 1998.

MONETARY SYSTEM:

I Peso = 100 Centavos, 1871-1926
1 Lempira = 100 Centavos, 1926-

REPÚBLICA DE HONDURAS

Vales of 1848

1848 Issue

#1-6 authorized by Decree of 9.9.1848. Some may be found with written cancellation on back, along with punched holes.

		Good	Fine	XF
1	**1 Peso** *D. 1848.* Black. Wreath at center. Uniface. Large format. PC: Off-white.	—	—	750
2	**2 Pesos** *D. 1848.* Black. Wreath at center. Uniface. Large format. PC: Off-white.	—	—	750
3	**10 Pesos** *D. 1848.* Black. Wreath at center. Uniface. Large format. PC: off-white.	—	—	1,000

		Good	Fine	XF
4	**15 Pesos** *D. 1848.* Black. Wreath at center. Uniface. Large format. PC: Off-white.	—	—	750
5	**25 Pesos** *D. 1848.* Black. Uniface. Large format. PC: Off-white.	—	—	1,200
6	**100 Pesos** *D. 1848.* Black. Uniface. Large format. PC: Off-white.	—	—	1,500

Vales of 1863

1863 Issue

		Good	Fine	XF
7	**5 Pesos** *D. 1863.* Black. Arms at upper center, ribbon at left and right. Punch cancelled. PC: Off-white.	—	—	1,500

Vale al Portador

Billete del Tesoro

1889 Issue

#9-13 receipts issued by the Bogran government w/circular handstamp: *REPUBLICA DE HONDURAS* at left, embossed circular seal:...*PUBLICO*...at center; with or without oval handstamp: *OFICINA GENERAL* at right.

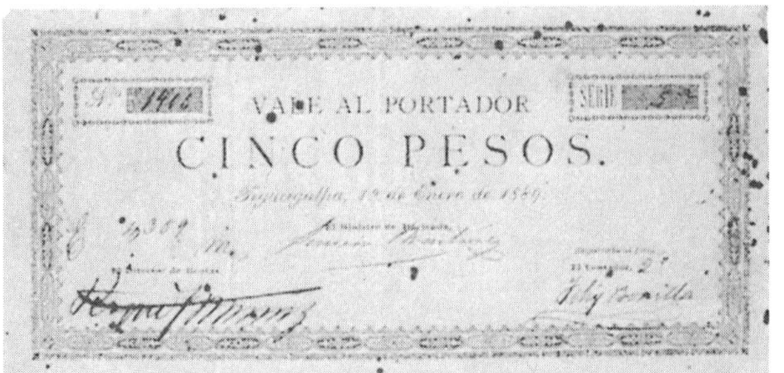

		Good	Fine	XF
9	**5 Pesos** 1.1.1889.	—	—	—

		Good	Fine	XF
10	**10 Pesos** 1.1.1889.	—	—	—
11	**25 Pesos** 1.1.1889.	—	—	—
12	**50 Pesos** 1.1.1889. Gray with maroon denomination at left and right with 2 red handstamps.	—	—	—

		Good	Fine	XF
13	**100 Pesos** 1.1.1889. Orange-brown with 2 handstamps.	—	—	—

Billete Privilegiado

Exemption Notes

1891 Issue

		Good	Fine	XF
14	**2 Pesos** 15.7.1891. Brown. Arms at center.	—	—	—

		Good	Fine	XF
15	**25 Pesos** 15.7.1891. Gray-green. Arms at center.	—	—	—

Vale al Portador Reissue

Billete del Tesoro

1889 Issue

#16-20 like #9-13.

		Good	Fine	XF
16	**5 Pesos** 1889.	—	—	—
17	**10 Pesos** 1889.	—	—	—
18	**25 Pesos** 1889.	—	—	—
19	**50 Pesos** 1889.	—	—	—
20	**100 Pesos** 1889.	—	—	—

Banco de Honduras

1889 Issue

#22-24 various dates including authorization dates on backs.

		Good	Fine	XF
22	**5 Pesos** 1.10.1889. Black on orange and yellow underprint. Steer head at left, arms at right. Signature varieties. Printer: ABNC.			
	a. Rare.	—	—	—
	s. Specimen.	—	Unc	1,500

		Good	Fine	XF
23	**50 Pesos** 1.10.1889. Black on brown and yellow underprint. Allegorical woman with three children and globe at left, arms at lower left, Indian with bow at right. Signature varieties. Printer: ABNC. Archive copy.	—	—	—

		Good	Fine	XF
24	**100 Pesos** 1.10.1889. Black on orange and yellow underprint. Seated woman at left, steer head at center, arms at right. Signature varieties. Printer: ABNC.			
	a. Issued note, cancelled. Rare.	—	—	—
	s. Specimen.	—	Unc	2,750

1913 Issue

		Good	Fine	XF
25	**10 Pesos**			
	1.10.1913. Black on multicolor underprint. Steers head at left. Series A. Back: Arms at center. Printer: ABNC.			
	a. Issued note. Rare.	—	—	—
	p. Proof.	—	Unc	2,500
	s. Specimen.	—	Unc	1,500

		Good	Fine	XF
26	**20 Pesos**			
	1.10.1913. Black on multicolor underprint. Steer head at right. Back: Arms at center. Printer: ABNC.			
	a. Issued note. Rare.	—	—	—
	p. Proof.	—	Unc	2,500
	s. Specimen.	—	Unc	1,500

		Good	Fine	XF
27	**50 Pesos**			
	1.10.1913. Black on multicolor underprint. Steer head at at center. Back: Green. Arms at center. Printer: ABNC.			
	p. Proof.	—	Unc	2,500
	s. Specimen.	—	Unc	1,500

1922 Issue

		Good	Fine	XF
28	**50 Centavos**			
	27.5.1922. Multicolor. Steer head at left, church at center. Back: Arms. Printer: W&S. Specimen, punch hole cancelled.	—	—	—

		Good	Fine	XF
29	**1 Peso**			
	27.5.1922. Black on purple and multicolor underprint. Steer head at right. Back: Arms at center. New authorization date of 13.7.1925 and text overprint in upper margin. Printer: ABNC.			
	a. Issued note.	—	—	—
	s. Specimen.	—	Unc	600

#30-33 not assigned.

1932 Issue

		Good	Fine	XF
34	**1 Lempira**			
	11.2.1932. Blue on multicolor underprint. Lempira at left, arms at right. Series A. Back: Bank at center. Printer: W&S.	40.00	200	600
35	**2 Lempiras**			
	11.2.1932. Green on multicolor underprint. Lempira at left, arms at right. Series A. Back: Bank at center. Printer: W&S.	80.00	600	—
36	**5 Lempiras**			
	11.2.1932. Brown on multicolor underprint. Lempira at left, arms at right. Series A. Back: Bank at center. Printer: W&S.	125	1,000	—

		Good	Fine	XF
37	**10 Lempiras**			
	11.2.1932. Black on light green and multicolor underprint. Lempira at left, arms at right. Series A. Back: Bank at center. Printer: W&S.			
	a. Issued note.	250	1,500	—
	s. Specimen. Red overprint: *SPECIMEN* and punch hole cancelled.	—	Unc	1,000

#38-41 *not assigned.*

1941 Issue

		Good	Fine	XF
42	**5 Lempiras**			
	5.3.1941. Brown on red underprint. Portrait Morazán at left. Series B. Back: Steer head. Printer: ABNC.			
	a. Without green overprint on back.	70.00	250	750
	b. Green overprint: *Autorizada su circulacion...25.5.1948* in three lines of text and signature on back.	400	1,200	—
	s. Specimen.	—	Unc	600

43	10 Lempiras	Good	Fine	XF
	5.3.1941. Green on brown underprint. Portrait S. Soto at right. Series B. Back: Steer head. Printer: ABNC.			
	a. Without red overprint on back.	200	800	—
	b. Red overprint: *Autorizada su circulacion...25.5.1948* in 3 lines of text and signature on back.	400	1,200	—
	s. Specimen.	—	Unc	900

44	20 Lempiras	Good	Fine	XF
	5.3.1941. Black on olive underprint. Portrait I. Agurcia at left. Series A. Back: Steer head at center. Printer: ABNC.			
	a. Without red overprint on back.	300	1,500	—
	b. Red overprint: *Autorizada su circulacion...25.5.1948* in 3 lines of text and signature on back.	300	1,500	—
	s. Specimen.	—	Unc	1,000

Banco Central de Honduras

Established July 1, 1950 by merger of Banco Atlantida and Banco de Honduras. Various date and signature varieties.

1950-1951 Issue

45	1 Lempira	VG	VF	UNC
	1951. Red on light tan underprint. Lempira at left, arms at right. Red serial #. Back: Monolith. Printer: W&S.			
	a. 16.3.1951; 4.5.1951.	3.00	14.00	65.00
	b. 28.12.1951.	1.50	6.00	35.00
	s. Specimen, punch hole cancelled.	—	6.00	40.00

46	5 Lempiras	VG	VF	UNC
	1950-1951. Dark blue-gray on multicolor underprint. Morazán at left. Back: Arms at center. Printer: ABNC.			
	a. 1.7.1950; 11.7.1950; 22.9.1950; 22.12.1950.	12.50	90.00	—
	b. 16.2.1951.	8.50	75.00	—
	s. Specimen, punch hole cancelled.	—	—	400

47	10 Lempiras	VG	VF	UNC
	25.5.1951-26.3.1954. Brown on multicolor underprint. Cabañas at left. Back: Plantation work. Printer: W&S.			
	a. Issued note.	25.00	150	550
	s. Specimen, punch hole cancelled.	—	—	135

48	20 Lempiras	VG	VF	UNC
	25.5.1951-4.6.1954. Purple on multicolor underprint. D. Herrera at left. Back: Cattle. Printer: W&S.			
	a. Issued note.	25.00	185	650
	s. Specimen, punch hole cancelled.	—	—	175

49	100 Lempiras	VG	VF	UNC
	1951-1973. Yellow on multicolor underprint. Valle at left, arms at right. Back: Village and bridge.			
	a. Without security thread, lilac-pink underprint. Printer: W&S. 16.3.1951; 8.3.1957.	70.00	300	1,500
	b. Without security thread, With fibers at right center, light green and light orange underprint. Printer: W&S. 5.2.1964; 5.11.1965; 22.3.1968; 10.12.1969.	100	300	1,500
	c. With security thread, yellow underprint. 13.10.1972. Reported not confirmed.	—	—	—
	d. As c. but without security thread. 13.10.1972; 23.3.1973.	45.00	175	500
	s. Specimen, punch hole cancelled.	—	—	250

#50 not assigned.

1953-1956 Issue

		VG	VF	UNC
51	**5 Lempiras** 1953-1968. Gray on multicolor underprint. Morazán at left, arms at right. Serial # at upper left and upper right. Back: Battle of Trinidad. Printer: ABNC. 156x67mm.			
	a. Date horizontal. 17.3.1953; 19.3.1954; 26.3.1954; 7.5.1954.	6.00	50.00	300
	b. Date horizontal. 22.11.1957-7.1.1966.	4.00	35.00	225
	c. Date vertical. 15.4.1966; 29.9.1967; 22.3.1968.	3.50	20.00	150
	s. Specimen.	—	—	300

		VG	VF	UNC
52	**10 Lempiras** 1954-1969. Brown on multicolor underprint. Cabañas at left, arms at right. Back: Old bank building. Printer: TDLR. 156x67mm. Date and signature style varieties.			
	a. Right signature title: *MINISTRO DE HACIENDA...* 19.11.1954.	15.00	75.00	550
	b. Right signature title: *MINISTRO DE ECONOMIA...* 19.2.1960-10.1.1969.	10.00	50.00	400

		VG	VF	UNC
53	**20 Lempiras** 1954-1972. Green. D. de Herrera at left, arms at right. Back: Waterfalls. Printer: TDLR. 156x67mm.			
	a. 4.6.1954; 26.11.1954; 5.4.1957; 6.3.1959; 8.5.1959.	22.50	90.00	600
	b. 19.2.1960; 27.4.1962; 19.4.1963; 6.3.1964.	17.50	60.00	450
	c. 7.1.1966; 3.3.1967; 8.3.1968; 5.4.1968; 10.1.1969; 11.4.1969; 13.1.1970; 2.4.1971; 18.2.1972.	15.00	60.00	400
54	**50 Lempiras** 20.1.1956. Deep blue on multicolor underprint. Dr. J. Trinidad Reyes at left, arms at right. Back: University of Honduras. 156x67mm.	VG	VF	UNC
	a. Issued note.	50.00	200	800
	s. Specimen, punch hole cancelled.	—	—	275

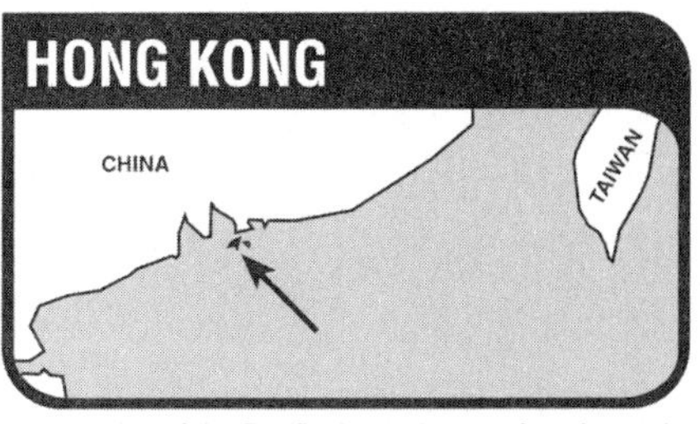

Hong Kong S.A.R., a former British Colony, is situated at the mouth of the Canton or Pearl River 90 miles (145 km.) southeast of Canton, has an area of 1,092 sq. km. and a population of 7.01 million. Capital: Central (formerly Victoria). The port of Hong Kong had developed as the commercial center of the Far East, a transshipment point for goods destined for China and the countries of the Pacific rim. Light manufacturing and tourism are important components of the economy.

Occupied by the UK in 1841, Hong Kong was formally ceded by China the following year; various adjacent lands were added later in the 19th century. Pursuant to an agreement signed by China and the UK on 19 December 1984, Hong Kong became the Hong Kong Special Administrative Region (SAR) of China on 1 July 1997. In this agreement, China promised that, under its "one country, two systems" formula, China's socialist economic system would not be imposed on Hong Kong and that Hong Kong would enjoy a high degree of autonomy in all matters except foreign and defense affairs for the next 50 years.

RULERS:
British (1842-1997)

MONETARY SYSTEM:
1 Dollar = 100 Cents

BRITISH ADMINISTRATION

Agra & United Service Bank, Limited

行銀理匯剌加呵

A Jai La Hui Li Yin Hang

1862 Issue

		Good	Fine	XF
5	**100 Dollars** ca.1862. Royal arms at top center. Printer: John Biden, London. Rare.	—	—	—
6	**200 Dollars** ca.1862. Royal arms at top center. Printer: John Biden, London. Proof. Rare.	—	—	—
7	**300 Dollars** ca.1862. Royal arms at top center. Printer: John Biden, London. Proof. Rare.	—	—	—
8	**500 Dollars** ca.1862. Royal arms at top center. Printer: John Biden, London. Proof. Rare.	—	—	—

Asiatic Banking Corporation

行銀理匯特鴉西亞

Ya Hsi Ya De Hui Li Yin Hang

1800s Issue

		Good	Fine	XF
11	**10 Dollars** 18xx. Specimen. Rare.	—	—	—
13	**50 Dollars** 18xx. Arms at upper center. Rare.	—	—	—

Color Abbreviation Guide

New to the *Standard Catalog of ® World Paper Money* are the following abbreviations related to color references:

BC: Back color
PC: Paper color

#	Denomination	Good	Fine	XF
14	**100 Dollars** 18xx. Arms at upper center. Specimen. Rare.	—	—	—
15	**500 Dollars** 18xx. Specimen. Rare.	—	—	—

Bank of Hindustan, China & Japan

行銀理匯本日國中丹士度慳

Keng Tu Shi Dan Chung Kuo Jih Ben Hui Li Yin Hang

Hong Kong

1863 Issue

#	Denomination	Good	Fine	XF
20	**1000 Dollars** 18xx. Arms at upper center. Printer: Batho, Sprague & Co., London. Remainder. Rare.	—	—	—

Chartered Bank of India, Australia & China

行銀理滙國中山金新度印

Yin Tu Hsin Chin Shan Chung Kuo Hui Li Yin Hang

行銀利加麥國中山金新度印

Yin Tu Hsin Chin Shan Chung KuoTa Cha Yin Hang

Hong Kong

1863 Issue

#	Denomination	Good	Fine	XF
17	**10 Dollars** 1863. Gray frame. Arms at upper center. Two handwritten signatures.	—	—	—

1865 Issue

#	Denomination	Good	Fine	XF
21	**5 Dollars** 1865-1879. Gray frame. Arms at upper center. 2 handwritten signatures. Printer: Batho, Sprague & Co.			
	a. 2.1.1865. Rare.	—	—	—
	b. 1.1.1874; 1.1.1879. Rare.	—	—	—
22	**10 Dollars** 18xx. Gray frame. Arms at upper center. Printer: Batho, Sprague & Co. Proof.	—	—	—

Note: A forgery of #22 dated 15.1.1906 is known.

#	Denomination	Good	Fine	XF
23	**25 Dollars** 18xx. Blue. Arms at upper center. Printer: Batho, Sprague & Co. Proof. Rare.	—	—	—
24	**50 Dollars** 18xx. Light blue frame. Arms at upper center. Printer: Batho, Sprague & Co. Proof. Rare.	—	—	—

#	Denomination	Good	Fine	XF
25	**100 Dollars** 18xx. Red-orange. Arms at upper center. Printer: Batho, Sprague & Co. Proof. Rare.	—	—	—
26	**500 Dollars** 18xx. Gray frame. Arms at upper center. Gray *500* below arms. Back: Large *500* in guilloche. Printer: Batho, Sprague & Co. 195x118mm. Proof. Rare.	—	—	—

1879 Issue

#	Denomination	VG	VF	UNC
27	**5 Dollars** 1.1.1879. Blue-gray frame. Arms at upper center. Printer: WWS. Proof.	—	—	37,500
28	**10 Dollars** 1.1.1879. Brown frame. Arms at upper center. Printer: WWS. Proof.	—	—	37,500
29	**25 Dollars** 1.1.1879. Green on red underprint. Arms at upper center. Printer: WWS. Proof.	—	—	60,000
30	**50 Dollars** 1.1.1879. Orange on red underprint. Arms at upper center. Printer: WWS. Proof.	—	—	52,500
31	**100 Dollars** 1.1.1879. Black on red underprint. Arms at upper center. Printer: WWS. Proof.	—	—	52,500
32	**500 Dollars** 1.1.1879. Black. Arms at upper center. Back: Dragon at center. Printer: WWS. Proof.	—	—	37,500

1897-1910 Issues

#	Denomination	Good	Fine	XF
33	**5 Dollars** 1.11.1897; 15.11.1897. Gray frame. Arms at upper or top center. Signature at right printed. Printer: Batho, Sprague & Co.	8,000	39,000	—

		Good	Fine	XF
34	**5 Dollars** 1.10.1903; 1.1.1905; 19.1.1910; 1.7.1911; 1.10.1912. Blue-green frame on brown-orange underprint. Last 2 digits of year stamped on printed *190x*. Printer: WWS. 201x121mm.	2,750	17,500	45,000
35	**10 Dollars** 190x. 19.1.1905; 19.1.1906; 19.1.1910. Brown frame on brown-orange underprint. Purple *TEN* at lower center. Printer: WWS. 198x121mm.	14,000	32,000	—
36	**25 Dollars** 1.1.1897. Green. Arms at upper center. Printer: Batho, Sprague & Co. 185x118mm. Rare.	—	—	—
37	**25 Dollars** 189x.; 1903. Green on purple and red underprint. Arms at upper center. Printer: WWS. 220x122mm. Rare.	—	—	—
38	**50 Dollars** 8.9.1910; 6.10.1910. Yellow-orange on purple and yellow underprint. Printer: WWS. 204x124mm. Rare.	—	—	—
39	**100 Dollars** 8.9.1910. Gray on purple and pink underprint. Printer: WWS. 204x122mm.	9,000	24,000	112,500

		Good	Fine	XF
40	**500 Dollars** 8.9.1910; 6.10.1910; 20.10.1910; 1.7.1911. Red on olive-green and pink underprint. Arms at top center; Large *500* below. Printer: WWS. 198x120mm. Rare.	—	—	—

1911-1923 Issues

		Good	Fine	XF
41	**5 Dollars** 1.11.1911-1.7.1922. Blue and black. Workmen at left, arms at upper center, river scene at right. Large blue *5* in underprint at bottom center. Back: Building at center. Printer: W&S. 208x126mm.	1,200	4,500	26,000

		Good	Fine	XF
42	**10 Dollars** 1.12.1911-1.7.1922. Black and red-violet on multicolor underprint. Boats and pagoda at left, boats in cove at right. Back: Building at center. Printer: W&S. 190x125mm.	1,500	4,500	21,000

		Good	Fine	XF
43	**50 Dollars** 1.1.1912. Black and orange-brown. *50* at upper left and at each side of vignette. Back: Old bank building at center. Printer: W&S. 185x122mm.	4,000	12,000	72,000
43A	**50 Dollars** ND. Black and orange-brown on light blue underprint. 50 at upper left and at each side of vignette. Back: Old bank building at center. Printer: W&S. 185x122mm.	—	—	—

		Good	Fine	XF
43B	**50 Dollars** 1.5.1923. Black and orange-brown on light blue underprint. 50 at upper right and at each side of vignette. Back: Old bank building at center. Printer: W&S. 185x122mm.	—	—	—

		Good	Fine	XF
44	**50 Dollars** 1.11.1923; 1.5.1924; 1.11.1929. Black and orange-brown on multicolor underprint. Red *FIFTY* at each side of central vignette. Back: Old bank building at center. Printer: W&S. 185x122mm.	2,000	8,000	48,000

		Good	Fine	XF
45	**100 Dollars** 1.2.1912; 1.5.1924; 1.2.1926; 1.9.1927. Black and green on multicolor underprint. Bridge at upper left, pavilion at upper right. Back: Old bank building at center. Printer: W&S. 201x127mm.	5,000	18,000	50,000
46	**500 Dollars** 1912-1926. Pale red and blue-black on multicolor underprint. Boat, coastline at center. Back: Old bank building at center. Printer: W&S. 202x125mm.			
	a. 1.3.1912; 1.7.1912.	5,000	15,000	90,000
	b. 1.2.1921; 1.7.1922; 1.10.1926.	4,000	10,000	68,000

1923-1929 Issues

		Good	Fine	XF
47	**5 Dollars** 1.9.1923; 1.11.1923. Blue and black. Workmen at left, arms at upper center, river scene at right. Red *FIVE* at lower center. Printer: W&S. 208x126mm.	750	2,250	7,000
48	**5 Dollars** 1.5.1924; 1.9.1927. Blue. Workmen at left, arms at upper center, river scene at right. Chinese character *Wu* (5) in red in either side of arms. Printer: W&S. 208x126mm.	675	1,800	5,500
49	**10 Dollars** 1.3.1923-1.11.1923. Black and violet underprint. Boats and pagoda at left, boats in cove at right. Red *TEN* at lower center. Printer: W&S. 190x125mm.	775	2,100	7,250

		Good	Fine	XF
50	**10 Dollars** 1.5.1924; 1.9.1927; 1.8.1929. Purple and green on red underprint. Boats and pagoda at left, boats in cove at right. Red *TEN* between red Chinese characters *Shih* (ten) at lower center. Printer: W&S. 190x125mm.	500	1,250	4,250
51	**50 Dollars** 1.5.1923; 1.11.1923; 1.5.1924; 1.11.1929. Black and orange-brown on multicolor underprint. *50* at upper right. Printer: W&S. 185x122mm.	2,250	6,000	15,000
52	**100 Dollars** 2.12.1929; 2.6.1930. Black and dark blue on multicolor underprint. Britannia at left. Back: Junk and sampan at center. Printer: W&S. 180x106mm.	1,000	3,000	7,750

1930-1934 Issues

		Good	Fine	XF
53	**5 Dollars** 18.8.1930; 1.9.1931. Dark green on rose underprint. Short red 30mm *5* in underprint. at center. Helmeted warrior's head at left. Printer: W&S. 167x96mm.	600	1,350	4,250

54	5 Dollars	Good	Fine	XF
	1934-1956. Black and green on red underprint. Helmeted warrior's head at left. 50mm tall red *5* in underprint at center. Printer: W&S. 167x96mm.			
	a. Signature at right printed. 2.4.1934-20.9.1940.	125	500	1,250
	b. Both signatures printed. 28.10.1941; 26.2.1948.	75.00	175	750

55	10 Dollars	Good	Fine	XF
	1931-1956. Black and red on green underprint. Helmeted warrior's head at left, arms at center. Back: Woman harvesting rice at center. Printer: W&S. 166x95mm.			
	a. Signature at right. printed. 1.7.1931.	125	400	1,500
	b. 2.4.1934-20.9.1940.	100	325	1,000
	c. 2 signature printed. 18.11.1941-1.9.1956.	35.00	125	450

56	50 Dollars	Good	Fine	XF
	1.7.1931; 2.4.1934; 1.11.1934. Black and brown on multicolor underprint. Helmeted warrior's head at left. Back: Woman harvesting rice at right. Printer: W&S. 179x108mm.	550	1,500	5,500

57	100 Dollars	Good	Fine	XF
	1934-1956. Dark green and dark brown on multicolor underprint. Britannia seated holding trident with shield and lion at center, arms at upper right. Back: Statue Square, Supreme Court building at center right. Printer: W&S. 184x113mm.			
	a. Signature at right printed. 1.5.1934; 2.7.1934.	600	2,000	6,000
	b. 28.3.1936-1.11.1939.	500	1,250	3,000
	c. 2 signature printed. 8.12.1941-1.9.1956.	275	750	1,800

58	500 Dollars	Good	Fine	XF
	1.8.1930. Dark blue on multicolor underprint. Helmeted warrior's head at lower center. Back: Sampan at right. Printer: W&S. 192x122mm. Rare.	—	—	—

59	500 Dollars	Good	Fine	XF
	1934-1952. Black and dark brown on multicolor underprint. Man at left. Back: Boat, harbor view at center right. Printer: W&S. 190x120mm.			
	a. 1.6.1934.	500	1,200	7,500
	b. 14.9.1936.	400	1,200	6,000
	c. 1.11.1939.	400	1,250	6,000
	d. 6.8.1947.	300	1,150	6,000
	e. 1.7.1949.	300	1,150	6,000
	f. 1.8.1951; 1.11.1952.	200	1,000	4,125

Chartered Bank

行銀打渣[1]

Cha Ta Yin Hang

1956-1959 Issues

62	5 Dollars	VG	VF	UNC
	9.4.1959. Black and dark green on multicolor underprint. Arms at lower left. Back: Chinese junk and sampan at center. Watermark: Helmeted warrior's head. Printer: W&S. 142x80mm.	15.00	50.00	425

63	10 Dollars	VG	VF	UNC
	6.12.1956. Black and red. Helmeted warrior's head at left. Back: Woman harvesting rice at center. Watermark: Helmeted warrior's head. Printer: W&S. 166x95mm.	40.00	125	1,200

		VG	VF	UNC
64	**10 Dollars** 9.4.1959. Black and red-violet on red underprint. Arms at left. Back: Bank building at center. Watermark: Helmeted warrior's head. Printer: W&S. 166x95mm.	15.00	40.00	225

		VG	VF	UNC
65	**100 Dollars** 6.12.1956. Dark green and brown on multicolor underprint. Britannia seated holding trident with shield and lion at center, arms at upper right. Back: Statue Sqaure, Supreme Court building at center right. Watermark: Helmeted warrior's head. Printer: W&S. 159x89mm.	400	1,800	5,000

		VG	VF	UNC
66	**100 Dollars** 9.4.1959. Dark green and brown on multicolor underprint. Arms at center. Back: Harbor view. Watermark: Helmeted warrior's head. Printer: W&S. 184x113mm.	65.00	200	1,300

		VG	VF	UNC
67	**500 Dollars** 1.9.1957; 14.12.1959. Black and dark brown on multicolor underprint. Man at left. Back: Boat, harbor view at center right. Watermark: Helmeted warrior's head. Printer: W&S. 190x120mm.	300	750	4,500

Chartered Mercantile Bank of India, London & China

行銀理匯處三國中頓倫度印

Yin Tu Lun Dun Chung Kuo San Zhu Hui Li Yin Hang

Hong Kong

1858 Issue

		Good	Fine	XF
82	**5 Dollars** 18xx. Black. Britannia seated with crowned shield at upper center. Large blue *FIVE* in underprint. Uniface. Printer: Batho & Co. Proof.	—	—	—

		Good	Fine	XF
83	**10 Dollars** 18xx. Black. Britannia seated with crowned shield at upper center. Large gray *TEN* in underprint. Uniface. Printer: Batho & Co. Proof.	—	—	—

		Good	Fine	XF
84	**25 Dollars** 18xx. Black. Britannia seated with crowned shield at upper center. Large red-orange *TWENTY FIVE* in underprint. Uniface. Printer: Batho & Co. Proof.	—	—	—

		Good	Fine	XF
85	**50 Dollars** 18xx. Black. Large green *FIFTY* in underprint. Britannia seated with crowned shield at upper center Uniface. Printer: Batho & Co. Proof.	—	—	—

		Good	Fine	XF
86	**100 Dollars** 18xx. Britannia seated with crowned shield at upper center. Uniface. Large red-orange *ONE HUNDRED* in underprint. Printer: Batho & Co. Proof.	—	—	—

1873-1890 Issue

		Good	Fine	XF
87	**5 Dollars** 1873-1890. Arms at upper center. Red *FIVE* in underprint. Printer: PBC.			
	a. Perforated: *CANCELLED*. 8.1.1873; 1.9.1880; 1.5.1882. Rare.	—	—	—
	b. 1.12.1888; 1.9.1889; 1.1.1890. Rare.	—	—	—

		Good	Fine	XF
88	**10 Dollars** 16.7.1883; 16.12.1887; 16.5.1889. Arms at upper center. Printer: PBC. Rare.	—	—	—

		VG	VF	UNC
89	**25 Dollars** 1.1.1880; 1.9.1880; 1.1.1890. Arms at upper center. Printer: PBC. Proof.	—	—	70,000

		VG	VF	UNC
90	**50 Dollars** 1.9.1888; 1.1.1890. Arms at upper center. Printer: PBC. Proof.	—	—	54,000

		VG	VF	UNC
91	**100 Dollars** 18xx; 1.9.1880; 1.9.1888. Arms at upper center. Printer: PBC. Proof.	—	—	54,000

Hong Kong & Shanghai Banking Company, Limited

行銀豐滙海上港香商英

Ying Shang Hsian g K'ang Shang Hai Hui Feng Yin Hang

1865 Issue

		VG	VF	UNC
96	**5 Dollars** 18xx. Arms at upper center. Printer: Ashby & Co. Proof.	—	—	30,000

		VG	VF	UNC
97	**10 Dollars** 18xx. Arms at upper center. Printer: Ashby & Co. Proof.	—	—	10,000

No.	Denomination / Description	VG	VF	UNC
98	**25 Dollars** 18xx. Black. Arms at upper center. Printer: Ashby & Co. Proof. Rare.	—	—	—
99	**50 Dollars** 16.4.1865. Arms at upper center. Printer: Ashby & Co. Rare.	—	—	—
100	**100 Dollars** 18xx. Arms at upper center. Printer: Ashby & Co. Proof.	—	—	45,000
101	**500 Dollars** 18xx. Arms at upper center. Printer: Ashby & Co. Proof.	—	—	60,000

Hong Kong & Shanghai Banking Corporation

行銀理滙海上港香

Hsiang K'ang Shang Hai Hui Li Yin Hang

Hong Kong

1867-1889 Issues

No.	Denomination / Description	Good	Fine	XF
111	**1 Dollar** 1.10.1872-30.11.1872. Gray on red-orange underprint. *$1 - Chinese character - 1$* in underprint. Arms at upper center. Back: Bank arms at center. Printer: Ashby & Co. 186x123mm.	2,200	5,500	24,000
112	**1 Dollar** 1.4.1873-1.6.1874. Gray on red-orange underprint. Arms at upper center. *$1- Chinese character-1$* in underprint. Back: Bank arms at center. Printer: Ashby & Co.	1,500	3,500	16,000
113	**1 Dollar** 30.6.1879-1.9.1879. Grey on red-orange underprint. *$1 - Chinese character - 1$* in underprint. Arms at upper center. Back: Bank arms at center. Printer: Ashby & Co.	1,500	3,500	12,000

No.	Denomination / Description	Good	Fine	XF
114	**1 Dollar** 1.6.1884-20.9.1888. Grey on red-orange underprint. *$1 - Chinese character - 1$* in underprint. Arms at upper center. Printer: Ashby & Co. 204x122mm.	1,500	4,500	9,750
115	**5 Dollars** 1.1.1867. Grey on light green underprint. Arms at upper center. Back: Bank arms at center. Printer: Ashby & Co. Rare.	—	—	—
116	**5 Dollars** 16.7.1877. Grey on green underprint. Arms at upper center. Back: Bank arms at center. Printer: Ashby & Co. 198x117mm. Rare.	—	—	—

No.	Denomination / Description	Good	Fine	XF
117	**5 Dollars** 3.1.1882; 1.2.1883; 6.2.1883. Gray on green and dark blue underprint. Dark blue *$5 - 5$* at left and right in underprint. Arms at upper center. Back: Bank arms at center. Printer: Ashby & Co. Rare.	—	—	—
119	**10 Dollars** 16.7.1877. Blue and black. Arms at upper center. Back: Bank arms at center. Printer: Ashby & Co. 206x122mm. Proof.	—	—	—

		Good	Fine	XF
121	**25 Dollars** 18xx; 1880; 1884. Black on blue-black underprint. *$25-25$* at left and right in underprint. Arms at upper center. Back: Bank arms at center. Printer: Ashby & Co. 202x124mm.			
	a. 1.11.1880; 1.12.1884. Rare.	—	—	—
	p. Proof. 18xx.	—	—	—
	r. Remainder with oval handstamp: *CANCELLED-JUL 16 1877*. 18xx. Rare.	—	—	—

123, 124, 126, 128, 130, 133 not assigned.

1884-1896 Issues

		Good	Fine	XF
136	**1 Dollar** 1889-1899. Black frame on light blue and brown underprint. Printer: BFL. 129x86mm.			
	a. Handwritten date. 1.11.1889.	250	1,250	13,500
	b. 2.1.1890.	200	700	6,000
	c. Printed dates. 18.11.1895; 2.1.1899.	150	500	4,500
137	**5 Dollars** 1.5.1884-1.12.1889. Gray frame on green underprint. Red-orange *$5-5$* at left and right. Printer: BFL. 204x122mm. Rare.	—	—	—
138	**5 Dollars** 2.1.1890-1.9.1893. Gray frame on light green underprint. Printer: BFL. 204x122mm.	4,500	9,000	30,000

		Good	Fine	XF
139	**5 Dollars** 1.3.1897; 1.9.1897; 1.3.1898. Gray frame on yellow underprint. Printer: BFL. 204x122mm.	3,400	7,500	24,000
141	**10 Dollars** 26.4.1888. Light blue. Printer: BFL. 206x122mm. Rare.	—	—	—
142	**10 Dollars** 1.3.1890; 15.12.1890. Light green. Printer: BFL. 206x122mm. Rare.	—	—	—

		Good	Fine	XF
143	**10 Dollars** 1.4.1893-1.3.1898. Blue-gray on pink underprint. Printer: BFL. 206x122mm.	4,500	10,000	30,000

		Good	Fine	XF
145	**50 Dollars** 2.1.1890; 1.3.1897; 1.3.1898. Violet on red underprint. Printer: BFL. 206x114mm. Rare.	—	—	—

		Good	Fine	XF
146	**100 Dollars** 18xx. Black on brown underprint. Queen Victoria at left, colony arms at right. Printer: BFL. 206x124mm. Specimen. Rare.	—	—	—

		Good	Fine	XF
147	**100 Dollars** 1895-1896. Red on blue underprint. Arms at top center. Printer: BFL. 206x124mm.			
	a. 1.1.1895. Rare.	—	—	—
	b. 1.3.1896.	3,000	9,000	45,000

		VG	VF	UNC
149	**500 Dollars** 1896-1897. Red-orange on light green underprint. Back: Colony arms at center. Printer: BFL. 207x122mm.			
	a. Issued note. 1.3.1896. Rare.	—	—	—
	r. Remainder, perforated: *CANCELLED*. 1.3.1897.	—	—	60,000

1900-1901 Issue

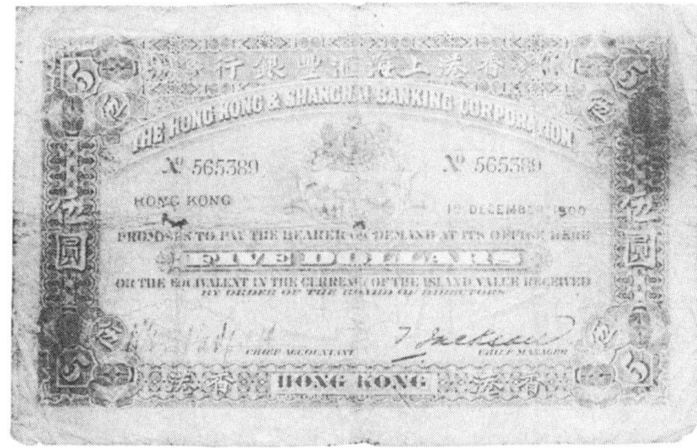

		Good	Fine	XF
150	**5 Dollars** 1.12.1900; 1.1.1901. Olive-green on yellow underprint. Large curved *FIVE* in underprint below arms at upper center. Printer: BWC. 196x124mm.	1,500	5,000	18,000

		Good	Fine	XF
151	**10 Dollars** 1.12.1900; 1.1.1901; 1.7.1902. Dark blue on red underprint. Large *TEN* in underprint below arms at upper center. Printer: BWC. 196x123mm.	1,500	5,000	30,000

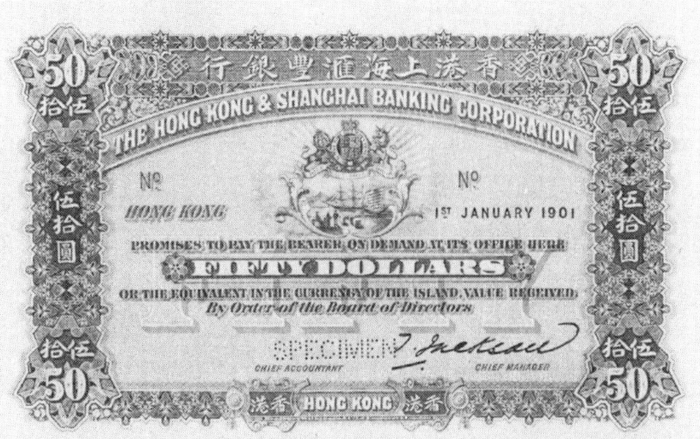

		Good	Fine	XF
152	**50 Dollars** 1.1.1901. Violet on tan underprint. Large *FIFTY* below arms at upper center. Arms at upper center under arched bank name. Back: Allegorical woman reclining at center. Printer: BWC. 200x123mm. Specimen.	—	Unc	33,000

		Good	Fine	XF
153	**100 Dollars** 1.1.1901. Red on green. Large curved *ONE HUNDRED* in underprint below arms at upper center. Back: Allegorical woman artist seated at center. Printer: BWC. 196x121mm. Specimen.	—	Unc	24,000

		Good	Fine	XF
154	**500 Dollars** 1.1.1901. Brown on blue underprint. Large curved *FIVE HUNDRED* in underprint under arms at upper center. Back: Seated allegorical woman with three cherubs at center. Printer: BWC. 200x124mm.	—	Unc	32,000

1904-1905 Issue

155	1 Dollar	Good	Fine	XF
	1904-1906; 1913. Black on blue and yellow underprint. Helmeted woman at left, port scene and arms at lower right. Bank name in curved line. Back: Seated allegorical woman with lyre at center. Printer: BWC. 132x90mm.			
	a. 1 printed signature. 1.1.1904; 1.5.1906.	200	1,200	6,000
	b. 2 printed signatures. 1.7.1913.	90.00	350	1,000

156	5 Dollars	Good	Fine	XF
	1.5.1904; 1.6.1905. Olive on yellow underprint. Arms at upper center. Printer: BWC. 196x124mm.	1,150	3,750	18,000

157	10 Dollars	Good	Fine	XF
	1.5.1904; 1.1.1905; 1.6.1905. Dark blue on tan underprint. Arms at upper center. 196x123mm.	1,500	6,000	21,000

#158 has been renumbered to #162A.

159	100 Dollars	Good	Fine	XF
	1.5.1904; 1.1.1906. Red on multicolor underprint. Arms at upper center. Printer: BWC. 196x121mm.	3,750	12,000	75,000

160	500 Dollars	Good	Fine	XF
	1.5.1904; 1.1.1905; 1.6.1907. Brown on multicolor underprint. Arms at upper center. Printer: BWC. 200x124mm.	5,500	13,500	84,000

1905-1915 Issue

		Good	Fine	XF
161	**5 Dollars** 1.1.1906; 1.1.1909. Olive and brown on orange underprint. Water carrier and sedan bearers at left, ship at right. Back: Old bank building at center. Printer: W&S. 196x124mm.	750	2,250	12,000
162	**10 Dollars** 1.1.1909. Black and dark blue on light blue and pink underprint. Waterfront at left, horseman and walkers at right, ships and houses in background. Back: Old bank building at center. 196x123mm.	750	2,250	12,000
162A	**50 Dollars** 1905; 1909. Black, purple and dark green on light green underprint. Bank shield at left, head of Greek male statue at center, Great Wall of China vignette at right. Back: Old bank building at center. Printer: W&S. 208x128mm.	Good	Fine	XF
	a. 1.1.1905.	3,000	12,000	55,000
	b. 1.1.1909.	1,800	9,000	36,000

		Good	Fine	XF
163	**100 Dollars** 1906-1909. Orange and black on light blue underprint. Bank shield at upper left, Chinese laborers with baskets at left and right. Back: Old bank building at center. Printer: W&S. 202x126mm.			
	a. Issued note. 1.1.1909.	4,500	13,500	62,000
	s. Specimen. 1.1.1906.	—	Unc	30,000

		Good	Fine	XF
164	**500 Dollars** 1909; 1912. Black and brown on light blue underprint. Farmer with ox at left, arms at center, Botanic Garden at right. Back: Old bank building at center. Printer: W&S. 213x124mm.			
	a. 1.1.1909.	—	—	—
	b. 1.1.1912.	—	—	—
165	**500 Dollars** 1.1.1915. Deep brown and black on light blue underprint. Farmer with ox at left, arms at center, Botanic Garden at right. Printer: W&S. 213x124mm.	—	—	—

1912-1921 Issue

		Good	Fine	XF
166	**5 Dollars** 1.7.1916; 1.1.1921; 1.1.1923; 1.5.1923. Olive and brown on orange underprint. Water carrier and sedan bearers at left, ship at right. Printer: W&S.	1,000	2,700	10,000

		Good	Fine	XF
167	**10 Dollars** 1.7.1913; 1.1.1921; 1.1.1923. Blue on red underprint. Waterfront at left, horseman and walkers at right, ships and houses in background. Printer: W&S. 206x126mm.	450	2,250	9,000

		Good	Fine	XF
168	**50 Dollars** 1.1.1921; 1.1.1923. Bank shield at left, head of Greek male statue at center. Great Wall of China vignette at right. Printer: W&S. 208x128mm.	8,000	12,000	90,000

169	100 Dollars	Good	Fine	XF
	1912-1923. Orange and black on light blue underprint. Bank shield at upper left, Chinese laborers with baskets at left and right. Printer: W&S. 202x126mm.			
	a. 1.1.1912.	3,600	14,500	120,000
	b. 1.1.1921; 1.1.1923.	3,000	12,000	108,000
170	500 Dollars	Good	Fine	XF
	1.1.1921; 1.7.1925. Farmer with ox at left, arms at center, Botanic Garden at right. Printer: W&S. 213x124mm.	4,000	15,000	120,000

Note: Bank records show that all 1.7.1925 dated notes have been redeemed.

1923 Issue

171	1 Dollar	VG	VF	UNC
	1.1.1923; 1.1.1925. Black on blue and yellow underprint. Helmeted woman at left, port scene and arms at lower right. Bank name in straight line. Back: Seated allegorical woman with lyre at center. Printer: BWC. 131x93mm.	75.00	325	1,500

1926-1927 Issue

172	1 Dollar	VG	VF	UNC
	1926-1935. Blue on yellow and light green underprint. Helmeted woman at left. Back: Allegorical woman with torch at center. Printer: BWC.			
	a. 1.1.1926.	75.00	325	1,500
	b. 1.1.1929.	50.00	150	750
	c. 1.6.1935.	25.00	65.00	450

173	5 Dollars	VG	VF	UNC
	1927-1946. Dark brown on multicolor underprint. Woman seated at right. *HONGKONG* at date not divided. Back: With 4 serial #s. Old bank building below angel playing trumpet at center. Printer: BWC. 178x102mm.			
	a. 1 printed signature. 1.10.1927; 1.1.1929; 1.9.1930.	75.00	375	900
	b. 1.1.1930-1.1.1938.	45.00	225	600
	c. 2 printed signatures. Additional vertical serial # on face and back. 1.4.1940; 1.4.1941.	50.00	200	600
	d. Without serial # on back. 1.4.1941.	22.50	45.00	300
	e. 30.3.1946.	22.50	37.50	275
174	10 Dollars	VG	VF	UNC
	1927-1930. Dark blue on multicolor underprint. Woman holding sheaf of grain at left, *HONGKONG* at date not divided. Back: With 4 serial #s. Old bank building below angel playing trumpet at center. Printer: BWC. 183x108mm.			
	a. 1.10.1927. Green.	115	375	2,000
	b. 1.1.1929; 1.1.1930.	100	300	2,000
	c. 1.9.1930.	150	425	4,200

175	50 Dollars	VG	VF	UNC
	1927-1937. Dark green on multicolor underprint. Woman standing on winged wheel with vines and fruit at left, arms at top center. Printer: BWC. 188x112mm.			
	a. 1.10.1927.	275	750	3,300
	b. 1.10.1930.	250	700	2,700
	c. 1.1.1934.	200	500	1,950
	d. "Duress" note issued during Japanese occupation with serial #B350,001 to B550,000. 1934-37.	200	500	1,950
176	100 Dollars	VG	VF	UNC
	1927-1959. Red. Woman seated with book at left, arms at upper center. Back: Old bank building below angel playing trumpet at center. Printer: BWC. 194x118mm.			
	a. 1 printed signature. 1.10.1927; 1.9.1930; 2.1.1933.	180	600	3,000
	b. 2.1.1934; 1.1.1936.	150	425	2,700
	c. 1.7.1937.	150	360	2,700

	VG	VF	UNC
d. "Duress" note issued during Japanese occupation with serial #B485,001 to B650,000. 1934-37.	160	425	3,000
e. 1.4.1941-1.3.1955.	125	300	1,400
f. 5.9.1956; 25.2.1958; 24.9.1958.	100	275	1,275
g. 4.2.1959.	125	360	1,650

177 500 Dollars
1927; 1930. Dark brown on purple and multicolor underprint. Woman seated holding tablet at right. Back: Old bank building below angel playing trumpet at center. Printer: BWC. 199x126mm.

	VG	VF	UNC
a. 1.10.1927.	2,200	6,000	50,000
b. 1.7.1930.	900	2,500	10,000
c. "Duress" note issued during Japanese occupation with serial #C126,001 to C300,000. 1.7.1930.	900	2,500	10,000

1932-1935 Issue

178 10 Dollars
1930-1948. Dark green on multicolor underprint. Woman holding sheaf of grain at left. Printer: BWC. 183x108mm.

	VG	VF	UNC
a. 1 printed signature. 4 serial # on back. 1.10.1930-1.1.1938.	8.50	75.00	500
b. With additional small serial # printed vertically on face and back. 1.4.1941.	35.00	125	400
c. 2 printed signatures. Without serial # on back. 1.4.1941.	6.00	25.00	300
d. 30.3.1946; 31.3.1947; 1.4.1948.	5.00	20.00	200

179 500 Dollars
1935-1969. Brown and blue. Arms at top center, Sir T. Jackson at right. Back: Allegorical female head at left, bank building at center. Printer: BWC. 201x123mm.

	VG	VF	UNC
a. 11.7.1960-1.8.1966.	375	2,250	5,250
b. 31.7.1967.	250	700	2,700
c. 11.2.1968.	250	700	2,700
d. 27.3.1969.	180	180	900
e. 11.2.1968.	—	180	700
f. 27.3.1969.	—	160	825

1949 Issue

179A 10 Dollars
1949-1959. Dark green on multicolor underprint. Woman holding sheaf of grain at left. With *HONG KONG* at date divided. Printer: BWC. 183x108mm.

	VG	VF	UNC
a. 1.7.1949; 31.12.1953.	20.00	30.00	300
b. 1.7.1954-14.1.1958.	15.00	25.00	250
c. 26.3.1958.	17.50	75.00	525
d. 24.9.1958.	15.00	25.00	300
e. 4.2.1959.	18.00	30.00	300

1954 Issue

180 5 Dollars
1954-1959. Brown. Woman seated at right. With *HONG KONG* at date divided. Printer: BWC. 178x102mm.

	VG	VF	UNC
a. 1.7.1954-7.8.1958.	15.00	30.00	300
b. 4.2.1959.	18.00	35.00	325

1959 Issue

181	5 Dollars	VG	VF	UNC
	1959-1975. Brown on multicolor underprint. Woman seated at right. Back: New bank building at center. Watermark: Helmeted warrior's head. Printer: BWC. 142x79mm.			
	a. Signature titles: *CHIEF ACCOUNTANT* and *CHIEF MANAGER*. 2.5.1959-29.6.1960.	3.00	15.00	45.00
	b. 1.5.1963.	50.00	175	750
	c. 1.5.1964-27.3.1969.	2.50	5.00	25.00
	d. Signature titles: *CHIEF ACCOUNTANT* and *GENERAL MANAGER*. 1.4.1970-18.3.1971.	2.00	5.00	18.00
	e. 13.3.1972; 31.10.1972.	1.00	2.00	13.00
	f. Small serial #. 31.10.1973; 31.3.1975.	1.00	1.25	11.00
	s. Specimen.	—	—	—

182	10 Dollars	VG	VF	UNC
	1959-1983. Dark green on multicolor underprint. Dark green on multicolor underprint. Back: New bank building at left center. Watermark: Helmeted warrior's head. Printer: BWC. 152x85mm.			
	a. Signature titles: *CHIEF ACCOUNTANT* and *CHIEF MANAGER*. 21.5.1959-1.9.1962.	5.00	15.00	45.00
	b. 1.5.1963; 1.9.1963.	6.00	20.00	60.00
	c. 1.5.1964; 1.9.1964.	5.00	15.00	55.00
	d. 1.10.1964.	40.00	200	800
	e. 1.2.1965; 1.8.1966; 31.7.1967.	2.00	6.00	25.00
	f. 20.3.1968; 23.11.1968; 27.3.1969.	2.00	6.00	25.00
	g. Signature titles: *CHIEF ACCOUNTANT* and *GENERAL MANAGER*. 1.4.1970-31.3.1976.	2.00	3.75	15.00
	h. Signature titles: *CHIEF ACCOUNTANT* and *EXECUTIVE DIRECTOR*. 31.3.1977; 31.3.1978; 31.3.1979.	2.00	3.00	15.00
	i. Signature titles: *CHIEF ACCOUNTANT* and *GENERAL MANAGER*. 31.3.1980; 31.3.1981.	2.00	3.00	12.50
	j. Signature titles: *MANAGER* and *GENERAL MANAGER*. 31.3.1982; 31.3.1983.	2.00	3.00	12.50
	s. Specimen.	—	—	—

183	100 Dollars	VG	VF	UNC
	1959-1972. Red on multicolor underprint. Woman seated at left with open book, arms at upper center. Watermark: Helmeted warrior's head and denomination. Printer: BWC. 160x89mm.			
	a. Signature titles: *CHIEF ACCOUNTANT* and *CHIEF MANAGER*. 12.8.1959-1.10.1964.	20.00	100	650
	b. 1.2.1965-27.3.1969.	20.00	50.00	500
	c. Signature titles: *CHIEF ACCOUNTANT* and *GENERAL MANAGER*. 1.4.1970; 18.3.1971; 13.3.1972.	15.00	40.00	350

Mercantile Bank of India, Limited

香港有利銀行

Hsiang K'ang Yu Li Yin Hang

Hong Kong

1912 Issue

235	5 Dollars	Good	Fine	XF
	1912-1941. Olive on tan underprint. Boats at center with houses and towers in background. Back: Mercury at center. Printer: W&S. 196x114mm.			
	a. 2 serial # on back. 1.3.1912.	2,000	5,000	15,000
	b. As a. 1.5.1924; 1.1.1930.	1,500	4,000	10,000
	c. 4 serial # on back. 1.7.1936; 1.12.1937.	1,500	3,400	9,000
	d. 2 serial # on back. 29.11.1941.	900	2,000	5,250

236 10 Dollars

1912-1941. Red-brown on light yellow-green underprint. Houses and mountains near water, bridge at center. Back: Mercury at center. Printer: W&S. 196x113mm.

	Good	Fine	XF
a. 2 serial # on back. 1.3.1912.	2,000	6,500	22,000
b. As a. 1.1.1930.	1,125	3,000	10,000
c. 4 serial # on back. 1.7.1936.	1,200	3,000	10,000
d. As c. 1.12.1937.	2,000	4,250	16,500
e. 2 serial # on back. 29.11.1941.	850	2,400	7,000

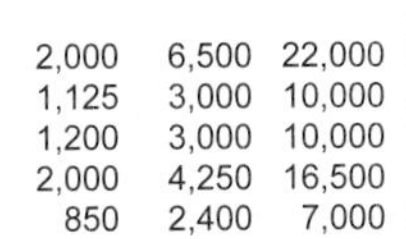

237 25 Dollars

1.3.1912. Blue on yellow underprint. River view with boats and houses at left. Back: Mercury at center. Printer: W&S. 196x114mm.

Good	Fine	XF
6,750	18,000	56,000

238 50 Dollars

1.3.1912; 1.5.1924; 1.1.1930. Brown and black. Ships at center, mountains in background. Back: Mercury at center. Printer: W&S. 194x114mm.

Good	Fine	XF
5,500	12,000	33,000

1935 Issue

240 50 Dollars

1935-1941. Dark brown on multicolor underprint. Male bust at left. Back: Chinese mansion. Watermark: Male bust. Printer: W&S. 195x114mm.

	Good	Fine	XF
a. With 2 serial # on back. 1.7.1935.	900	2,750	15,500
b. With 4 serial # on back. 1.12.1937.	6,000	—	—
c. With 2 serial # on back. 29.11.1941.	1,800	4,500	18,750

1912 Issue

239 100 Dollars

1912-1956. Red-violet on orange and light blue underprint. Houses below mountains at water's edge at center. Back: Mercury at center. Printer: W&S. 192x114mm.

	Good	Fine	XF
a. 1.3.1912.	1,800	5,000	24,000
b. 1.5.1924; 1.1.1930.	1,500	3,600	19,000
c. 4 serial # on back. 1.7.1936; 1.12.1937.	1,500	3,600	14,400
d. 2 serial # on back. 24.8.1948; 28.3.1950; 10.3.1953; 26.10.1954; 4.10.1955; 2.1.1956.	625	1,500	10,000

1948 Issue

241 500 Dollars

24.8.1948. Dark blue on yellow and light blue underprint. Mercury at right. Handsigned. Back: Gateway. Watermark: *500*. Printer: W&S. 194x115mm. Rare.

Good	Fine	XF
—	20,000	—

Mercantile Bank Limited

行銀利有港香

Hsiang K'ang Yu Li Yin Hang

Formerly The Mercantile Bank of India Limited. In 1959 this bank was absorbed by the Hong Kong & Shanghai Banking Corporation. In July 1984 it was sold to Citibank N.A. which resold the Mercantile's Hong Kong banking license to the Mitsubishi Bank in January 1987.

1958-1960 Issue

		VG	VF	UNC
242	**100 Dollars** 1958-1960. Brown-violet on orange and light blue underprint. Houses below mountains at water's edge at center. Printer: W&S. 192x114mm.			
	a. 3.1.1958; 12.8.1958; 26.5.1959.	675	2,700	6,500
	b. 20.9.1960; 6.12.1960.	675	2,400	6,000

		VG	VF	UNC
243	**500 Dollars** 26.5.1959. Blue on yellow and light blue underprint. Mercury at right. Printed signature. Back: Gateway. Watermark: *500*. Printer: W&S. 194x115mm. Rare.	—	—	—

National Bank of China Limited

行銀理滙華中港香

Hsiang K'ang Chung Hua Hui Li Yin Hang

Hong Kong

1892 Issue

		Good	Fine	XF
247	**5 Dollars** 1894. Deep red on yellow and orange underprint. Black text. Arms at upper center. Back: Junks over harbor view at center. Printer: W&S.			
	a. Issued note with printed date. 2.5.1894.	14,500	44,000	—
	b. Partially printed date, 2 handwritten signature 189x. Rare.	—	—	—
	r1. Remainder with partially printed date, printed signature at right, punch hole cancelled and perforated: *CANCELLED*. 189x. Rare.	—	—	—
	r2. Remainder without signature 189x. Rare.	—	—	—
	s. Salesman's sample punch hole cancelled, with W&S printer's seal, overprint: *SPECIMEN*. Rare.	—	—	—

		Good	Fine	XF
248	**10 Dollars** 2.5.1894. Green on light green and yellow underprint. Black text. Arms at upper center. Back: Junks over harbor view at center. Printer: W&S.	16,500	54,000	—

		VG	VF	UNC
249	**50 Dollars** 189x. Black and red on yellow underprint. Arms at upper center. Back: Junks over harbor view at center. Printer: W&S. Unsigned remainder punch hole cancelled and perforated: *CANCELLED*.	—	—	60,000
250	**100 Dollars** 189x. Black and purple on lilac and yellow underprint. Arms at upper center. Back: Junks over harbor view at center. Printer: W&S. Unsigned remainder punch hole cancelled and perforated: *CANCELLED*.	—	—	47,250
251	**500 Dollars** 189x. Black on multicolor underprint. Arms at upper center. Back: Junks over harbor view at center. Printer: W&S. Unsigned remainder punch hole cancelled and perforated: *CANCELLED*.	—	—	54,000

Oriental Bank Corporation

行銀理滙藩東

Tung Fan Hui Li Yin Hang

Victoria, Hong Kong

1860s Issue

		Good	Fine	XF
260	**5 Dollars** 18xx. Black. Royal crowned shield between lion and unicorn at upper center. Proof handstamped: *SPECIMEN.* Printer: PBC.	—	—	—

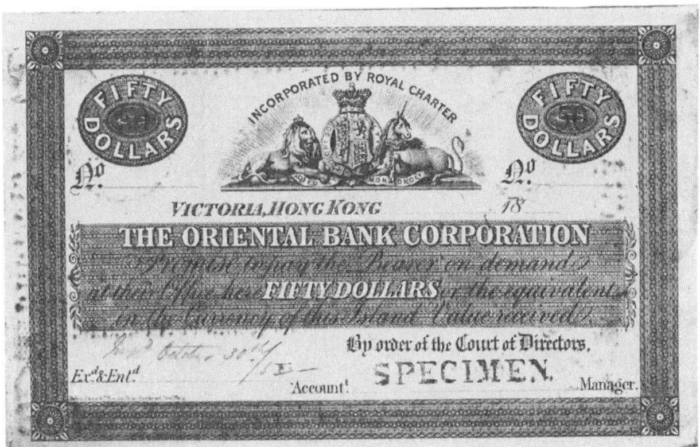

		Good	Fine	XF
263	**50 Dollars** 18xx. Black. Royal crowned shield between lion and unicorn at upper center. Proof handstamped: *SPECIMEN.* Printer: PBC.	—	—	—

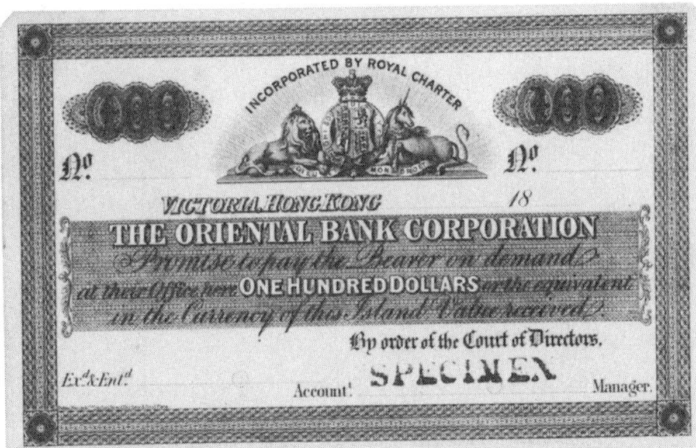

		Good	Fine	XF
264	**100 Dollars** 18xx. Black. Royal crowned shield between lion and unicorn at upper center. Proof handstamped: *SPECIMEN.* Printer: PBC.	—	—	—

Hong Kong

1866 Issue

		Good	Fine	XF
267	**5 Dollars** 1866-1882. Crowned shield between lion and unicorn at upper center. Printer: PBC.			
	a. Issued note. 7.3.1866.	25,500	90,000	—
	b. Issued note. 7.3.1879. Rare.	—	—	—
	s. Specimen. 4.9.1866; 1.9.1882. Rare.	—	—	—

		Good	Fine	XF
268	**25 Dollars** 7.5.1866; 7.5.1879/1866. Orange on yellow underprint. Crowned shield between lion and unicorn at upper center. Printer: PBC. Rare.	—	—	—
269	**50 Dollars** 7.3.1866; 1.5.1883. Black. Crowned shield between lion and unicorn at upper center. Printer: PBC. Proof. Rare.	—	—	—

		Good	Fine	XF
270	**100 Dollars** 7.3.1866; 1.5.1883. Crowned shield between lion and unicorn at upper center. Printer: PBC. Proof. Rare.	—	—	—

Government of Hong Kong

Hsiang K'ang Cheng Fu

1935 ND Issue

		VG	VF	UNC
311	**1 Dollar** ND (1935). Purple on multicolor underprint. Portrait King George V at right. Printer: BWC. 126x79mm.	25.00	350	1,500

1936 ND Issue

#	Denomination	VG	VF	UNC
312	**1 Dollar** ND (1936). Purple on multicolor underprint. Portrait King George VI at right. Printer: BWC. 126x79mm.	15.00	50.00	300

Note: For similar issues in blue, see #316; in green, see #324.

1940-1941 ND Issues

#	Denomination	VG	VF	UNC
313	**1 Cent** ND (1941). Brown on ochre underprint. 75x42mm.			
	a. Without serial # prefix.	0.25	1.50	18.00
	b. Prefix A.	0.25	1.00	6.00
	c. Prefix B.	0.25	0.50	4.50

#	Denomination	VG	VF	UNC
314	**5 Cents** ND (1941). Green on pale orange underprint. 85x48mm.	5.00	20.00	80.00
315	**10 Cents** ND (1941). Red on yellow underprint. 95x55mm.			
	a. Without serial # prefix.	0.50	3.00	35.00
	b. Prefix A.	0.25	2.50	35.00
316	**1 Dollar** ND (1940-1941). Dark blue on multicolor underprint. Portrait King George VI at right. Printer: BWC. 126x79mm.	15.00	30.00	250

Note: For similar issue in purple see #312; in green see #324.

1941 ND Emergency Issue

#	Denomination	VG	VF	UNC
317	**1 Dollar on 5 Yuan** ND (Dec. 1941 - old date 1941). Dark blue on multicolor underprint.	70.00	400	1,500

Note: #317 was in circulation for less than 2 weeks prior to the surrender of British and Hong Kong defense forces on Dec. 25, 1941.

1945 ND Emergency Issue

#318-320 prepared by the British Military Administration to replace the "duress" notes of the Hong Kong and Shanghai Banking Corporation in circulation immediately following the Japanese surrender. (Not issued).

#	Denomination	VG	VF	UNC
318	**1 Dollar on 1000 Yen** ND. Red, with or without underprint. Temple at left, man at right. Plate includes all legends and lineout bar.	100	500	1,400

#	Denomination	VG	VF	UNC
319	**5 Dollars on 1000 Yuan** ND (1945 - old date 1944). Blue.	150	1,000	2,500

#	Denomination	VG	VF	UNC
320	**10 Dollars on 5000 Yuan** ND (1945 - old date 1945). Gray.	150	900	3,000

Note: Other notes with these overprints have been reported, but their authenticity is doubtful.

1945-1949 ND Issue

		VG	VF	UNC
321	**1 Cent** ND (1945). Brown on light blue underprint. Portrait King George VI at right. Uniface. 89x41mm.	0.15	0.30	2.00
322	**5 Cents** ND (1945). Green on lilac underprint. Portrait King George VI at right. Uniface. 85x48mm.	0.25	3.00	30.00

		VG	VF	UNC
323	**10 Cents** ND (1945). Red on grayish underprint. Portrait King George VI at right. Uniface. 95x55mm.	0.25	1.00	18.00

		VG	VF	UNC
324	**1 Dollar** 1949; 1952. Dark green on multicolor underprint. Portrait King George VI at right. Printer: BWC. 126x79mm.			
	a. 9.4.1949.	2.50	6.00	100
	b. 1.1.1952.	2.00	5.00	125

Note: for similar issue in purple see #312; in blue see #316.

1952 ND Issue

		VG	VF	UNC
324A	**1 Dollar** 1952-1959. Dark green on multicolor underprint. Portrait Queen Elizabeth II at right. Printer: BWC. 126x79mm.			
	a. 1.7.1952; 1.7.1954; 1.7.1955.	2.50	6.00	60.00
	b. 1.6.1956-1.7.1959.	2.00	5.00	45.00

The Hungarian Republic, located in central Europe, has an area of 93,030 sq. km. and a population of 9.93 million. Capital: Budapest. The economy is based on agriculture and a rapidly expanding industrial sector. Machinery, chemicals, iron and steel, and fruits and vegetables are exported.

Hungary became a Christian kingdom in A.D. 1000 and for many centuries served as a bulwark against Ottoman Turkish expansion in Europe. The kingdom eventually became part of the polyglot Austro-Hungarian Empire, which collapsed during World War I. The country fell under Communist rule following World War II. In 1956, a revolt and an announced withdrawal from the Warsaw Pact were met with a massive military intervention by Moscow. Under the leadership of Janos Kadar in 1968, Hungary began liberalizing its economy, introducing so-called *Goulash Communism.* Hungary held its first multiparty elections in 1990 and initiated a free market economy. It joined NATO in 1999 and the EU in 2004.

RULERS:

Austrian to 1918

MONETARY SYSTEM:

1 Korona = 100 Fillér to 1926
1 Pengö = 100 Fillér to 1946
1 Milpengö = 1 Million Pengö
1 B(illió) Pengö = 1 Billion Pengö
1 Adopengö = 1 Tax Pengö
1 Forint = 100 Fillér 1946- 1 Forint (Florin) = 60 Krajczar

AUSTRO-HUNGARIAN EMPIRE

Magyar Király Kölcsönpénztár-Jegy

Royal Hungarian War Loan Bank

1914 Issue

		VG	VF	UNC
1	**250 Korona** 27.9.1914. Specimen perforated: *MINTA.*	—	—	850

		VG	VF	UNC
2	**2000 Korona** 27.9.1914. Portrait Empress Zita at right. Specimen perforated: *MINTA.*	—	—	850

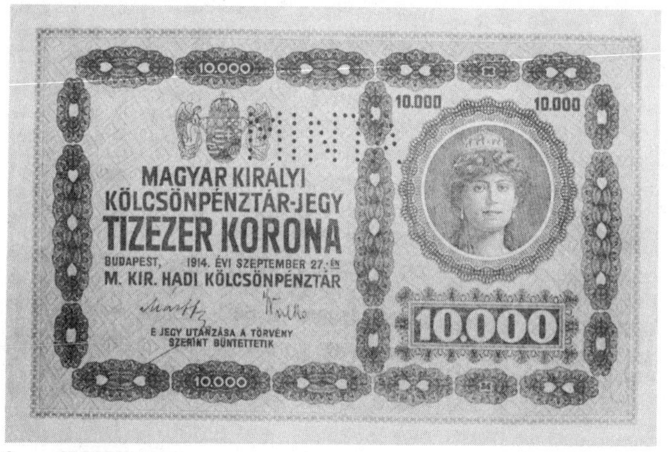

#	Denomination	VG	VF	UNC
3	**10,000 Korona** 27.9.1914. Specimen perforated: *MINTA.*	—	—	900

Az Osztrák-Magyar Bank Pénztárjegye

Austro-Hungarian Bank

#4-9, non-interest bearing Treasury notes of Hungarian branches. Text in Hungarian, various dates (ca.1918) and place names handstamped.

Kolozsvár

1918 Issue

#	Denomination	VG	VF	UNC
4	**1000 Korona** 1918.	500	1,000	2,000
5	**5000 Korona** 1918.	500	1,000	2,000
6	**10,000 Korona** 1918.	500	1,000	2,000

Szatmár-Németi

1918 Issue

#	Denomination	VG	VF	UNC
7	**1000 Korona** 29.11.1918.	550	1,100	2,200
8	**5000 Korona** 29.11.1918.	550	1,100	2,200
9	**10,000 Korona** 29.11.1918.	550	1,100	2,200

Budapest

1919 Issue

#10-16, notes printed in Budapest in 1919 with variations from the regular notes printed in Austria. Bilingual text.

#	Denomination	VG	VF	UNC
10	**1 Korona** 1.12.1916. (1919). Red. Helmeted warrior's head at center. Back: Woman's head at upper left and right. Like Austria #20. Series # above 7000 with and without star after the numbers. (Communist regime in Budapest).	3.00	7.00	15.00
11	**2 Korona** 1.3.1917 (1919). Red. Like Austria #21 but series # above 7000.			
	a. Issued note.	3.00	6.00	12.00
	x. Error: with *Genenalsekretar.*	5.00	15.00	35.00
12	**25 Korona** 27.10.1918 (1919). Blue on light brown underprint. Uniface. 137x82mm. Like Austria #23 but series # above 3000. 2 serial # varieties. (Soviet Republic of Bela Kun. 21.3.1919-4.8.1919).	5.00	10.00	20.00
13	**25 Korona** 27.10.1918 (1919). Blue on light brown underprint. 137x82mm. Like #12 but wavy lines on back. Series #1001-1999. 3 serial # varieties.	5.00	12.00	25.00
14	**200 Korona** 27.10.1918 (1919). Green on red-brown underprint. 166x101mm. Like Austria #24 but series A up to 2000. (People's Republic, 16.11.1918-21.3.1919).	5.00	12.00	25.00
15	**200 Korona** 27.10.1918 (1919). Green on red-brown underprint. Uniface. 166x101mm. Like #14 but series A above 2000. (Soviet Republic of Bela Kun 21.3.1919-4.8.1919).	5.00	10.00	20.00
16	**200 Korona** 27.10.1918 (1919). Green on red-brown underprint. 166x101mm. Like #15 but wavy lines on back. Series A2101; Series B1001-B1999.	5.00	10.00	20.00

Az Osztrák-Magyar Bank - Budapesti Föintezete

Treasury Note of the Budapest Head Office

1918 Issue

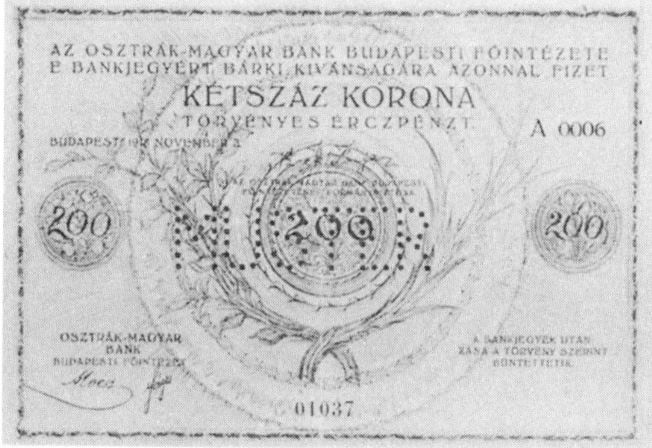

#	Denomination	VG	VF	UNC
17	**200 Korona** 3.11.1918. Hungarian legends. Specimen only.	—	350	750

1920 ND Provisional Issue

#18-32 Overprint notes issued as state notes with seal upright or turned to left. Only the 1000 and 10,000 Korona with seal turned to the right are rare.

#	Denomination	VG	VF	UNC
18	**10 Korona** ND (1920-old date 2.1.1904).	5.00	15.00	30.00
19	**10 Korona** ND (1920-old date 2.1.1915).	1.00	2.00	5.00

		VG	VF	UNC
20	**20 Korona** ND (1920- old date 2.1.1913).	1.00	2.00	5.00
21	**20 Korona** ND.	1.00	2.00	5.00

		VG	VF	UNC
21A	**20 Korona** ND (1920-old date 2.1.1913). (2nd issue).	1.00	2.00	5.00
22	**25 Korona** ND (1920- old date 27.10.1918). Series up to 3000.	3.00	15.00	40.00

		VG	VF	UNC
23	**25 Korona** ND (1920-old date 27.1.1918). Series above 3000.	4.00	20.00	50.00
24	**50 Korona** ND (1920- old date 2.1.1902).	45.00	120	300
25	**50 Korona** ND (1920-old date 2.1.1914).	1.00	2.00	5.00

		VG	VF	UNC
26	**100 Korona** ND (1920-old date 2.1.1910).	100	250	600
27	**100 Korona** ND (1920-old date 2.1.1912).	1.00	2.00	4.00

		VG	VF	UNC
28	**200 Korona** ND (1920-old date 27.10.1918). Series A.			
	a. Wavy lines on back.	30.00	75.00	175
	b. Without wavy lines on back.	30.00	75.00	175
29	**200 Korona** ND (1920-old date 27.10.1918). Series B.	40.00	100	250
30	**200 Korona** ND (1920-old date 27.10.1918). 6 digit serial #.	40.00	100	250
31	**1000 Korona** ND (1920-old date 2.1.1902).	3.00	6.00	12.00

		VG	VF	UNC
32	**10,000 Korona** ND (1920-old date 2.11.1918).	5.00	15.00	40.00

Note: #18-32 are also found with additional South Slavonian or Romanian handstamps. Notes with forged MAGYARORSZÁG overprint. were given a black, thick-ruled cross (#18-23, 25, 27-32) w/handstamp: *Stempel wurde von ... als unecht befunden.*

Note: The numerous local or military overprint and cancellations are beyond the scope of this catalog.

REGENCY

Magyar Postatakarékpénztár

Hungarian Post Office Savings Bank

1919 First Issue

		VG	VF	UNC
33	**5 Korona** 1.5.1919. 132x82mm. Specimen. (1 known).	—	—	—
34	**5 Korona** 15.5.1919. Blue on green underprint. Man sowing at right. *AZ OSZTRÁK-MAGYAR BANK BANKJEGYEIRE* 132x82mm.	2.00	5.00	10.00

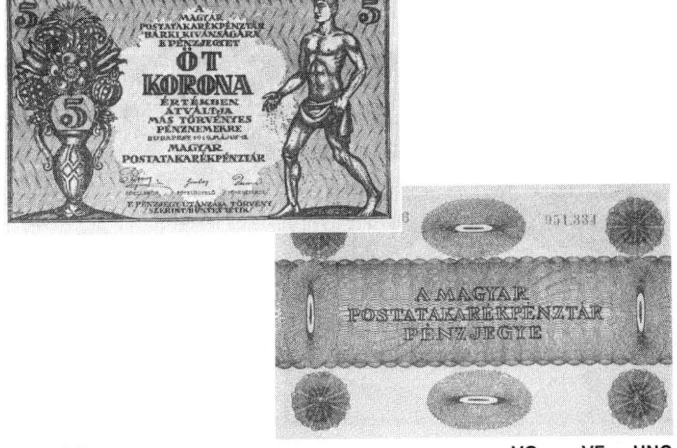

		VG	VF	UNC
35	**5 Korona** 15.5.1919. Blue on green underprint. Man sowing at right. *MÁS TÖRVÉNYES PENZNEMEKRE* 143x86mm.	2.00	5.00	10.00

		VG	VF	UNC
37	**10 Korona** 15.7.1919. Blue on green-blue underprint. Woman wearing Phrygian cap at left. 143x86mm.	3.00	10.00	35.00

		VG	VF	UNC
38	**20 Korona** 15.7.1919. Dark blue. Woman with two small children at center. 2 serial # varieties. 148x91mm.			
	a. Olive underprint.	2.00	10.00	40.00
	b. Yellow underprint.	2.00	10.00	40.00

#37-38 color trials also exist.

		VG	VF	UNC
39	**100 Korona** 15.7.1919. Blue and olive. Man seated with sword at center. (Not issued.) (2 known.)	—	—	—

		VG	VF	UNC
39A	**1000 Korona** 15.7.1919. Specimen.	—	—	—

1919 Second Issue

		VG	VF	UNC
40	**5 Korona** 9.8.1919. Specimen. (1 known).	—	—	—

		VG	VF	UNC
41	**10 Korona** 9.8.1919. Gray-blue on brown underprint. Woman without cap. 3 serial # varieties. 143x86mm.	5.00	20.00	70.00

		VG	VF	UNC
42	**20 Korona** 9.8.1919. Dark blue on green and pink underprint. Woman with two small children at center. 2 serial # varieties. Back: Black on light red underprint.	2.00	10.00	40.00

1920 Issue

		VG	VF	UNC
43	**20 Fillér** 2.10.1920. Brown. Arms at upper center. 88x53mm.	0.50	2.00	4.00

No.	Description	VG	VF	UNC
44	**50 Fillér** 2.10.1920. Blue. Arms at left. 88x53mm.	0.50	2.00	4.00

1921 Issue

No.	Description	VG	VF	UNC
45	**10 Million Korona** 1.5.1921. Specimen.	—	—	—

Magyar Nemzeti Bank

Hungarian National Bank

1919 First Issue

No.	Description	VG	VF	UNC
46	**50 Korona** 15.3.1919. Specimen.	—	—	—
47	**1000 Korona** 15.3.1919. Specimen.	—	—	—

1919 Second Issue

No.	Description	VG	VF	UNC
48	**25 Korona** 2.5.1919. Specimen. (1 known)	—	—	—

1919 Third Issue

No.	Description	VG	VF	UNC
49	**2 Korona** 2.6.1919. Specimen.	—	—	—
50	**20 Korona** 2.6.1919. Specimen.	—	—	—

1919 Fourth Issue

No.	Description	VG	VF	UNC
51	**10 Korona** 1.8.1919. Specimen.	—	—	—
52	**100 Korona** 15.8.1919. Specimen. (2 known)	—	—	—
53	**1000 Korona** 15.8.1919. Specimen.	—	—	—

Pénzügyminisztérium

State Notes of the Ministry of Finance

1920 First Issue

No.	Description	VG	VF	UNC
54	**50 Fillér** 1920. Circular, 30mm. Specimen.	—	—	—
55	**1 Korona** 1920. Circular, 35mm. Specimen.	—	—	—
56	**2 Korona** 1920. Circular, 40mm. Specimen.	—	—	—
56A	**5 Korona** 1920. Circular, 44mm. Specimen.	—	—	—

1920 Second Issue

No.	Description	VG	VF	UNC
57	**1 Korona** 1.1.1920. Blue. Woman at right. Serial # red or dark red. Printer: Magyar penzjegynyomd Rt., Budapest 132x66mm.	0.50	1.00	3.00

No.	Description	VG	VF	UNC
58	**2 Korona** 1.1.1920. Red on light brown underprint. Arms at left, reaping farmer at right. 2 serial # varieties. Printer: Magyar penzjegynyomd Rt., Budapest and Orell Fussl 134x77mm.	0.20	0.50	2.50
59	**5 Korona** 1.1.1920. Face specimen.	—	—	—

No.	Description	VG	VF	UNC
60	**10 Korona** 1.1.1920. Brown on blue-green underprint. Chain bridge, Budapest at upper center. 2 serial # varieties(with and without decimal point within). Back: Arms at right. 137x81mm.	1.00	2.00	4.00

No.	Description	VG	VF	UNC
61	**20 Korona** 1.1.1920. Black on green and pale orange underprint. Mátyás Church in Budapest at right. 2 serial # varieties: 000000; 000.000. Back: Arms at upper center. 147x86mm.	1.00	2.00	4.00

No.	Description	VG	VF	UNC
62	**50 Korona** 1.1.1920. Dark brown on brown and tan underprint. Portrait Prince F. Rákóczi at right. Printer: OFZ. 152x96mm.	1.00	3.00	6.00

		VG	VF	UNC
63	**100 Korona** 1.1.1920. Brown on light brown underprint. Portrait King Mátyás wearing wreath at right. Printer: OFZ. 156x101mm.	1.00	3.00	6.00
64	**100 Korona** 1.1.1920. 119 x 70mm. Specimen perforated: *MINTA.*	—	—	—

#65-68 printer: OFZ.

		VG	VF	UNC
65	**500 Korona** 1.1.1920. Dark green on brown-olive underprint. Portrait Prince Árpád wearing helmet at right. Printer: OFZ. 171x111mm.	2.00	7.00	14.00

		VG	VF	UNC
66	**1000 Korona** 1.1.1920. Dark brown on brown underprint. Portrait St. Stephan at right. Printer: OFZ. 196x127mm.			
	a. Issued note.	2.00	5.00	20.00
	s. Specimen perforated: *MINTA.*	—	—	50.00

		VG	VF	UNC
67	**5000 Korona** 1.1.1920. Dark brown on green and gray underprint. Hungária at right. Printer: OFZ. 204x135mm.	3.00	8.00	40.00

		VG	VF	UNC
68	**10,000 Korona** 1.1.1920. Dark green and violet. "Patrona Hungariae" at right. Printer: OFZ. 215x147mm.	4.00	14.00	50.00

1922 Issue

		VG	VF	UNC
69	**25,000 Korona** 15.8.1922. Violet. "Patrona Hungariae" at right. Printer: OFZ. 213x145mm.			
	a. Paper without silk thread.	10.00	30.00	100
	b. Paper with silk thread.	20.00	50.00	150
	s. As a. perforated: *MINTA.*	—	—	100
70	**50,000 Korona** 15.8.1922. Proof.	—	—	—

1923 First Issue

		VG	VF	UNC
71	**50,000 Korona** 1.5.1923. Red. Portrait young woman at right. Printer: OFZ. 163x105mm.			
	a. Imprint: Orell Füssli.	10.00	30.00	90.00
	b. Without imprint.	10.00	30.00	100
	s. Specimen. Perforated: *MINTA/*	—	—	1,000

72	100,000 Korona	VG	VF	UNC
	1.5.1923. Dark blue. Portrait young woman at right. 195x163mm.			
	a. Imprint: Orell Füssli.	20.00	75.00	225
	b. Imprint: Magyar Pénzjegynyomda Rt.	25.00	85.00	250
	s. As a. perforated: *MINTA*.	—	—	125

1923 Second Issue

73	100 Korona	VG	VF	UNC
	1.7.1923. Brown. Portrait King Mátyáas wearing a wreath at right. 121x70mm.			
	a. Imprint: Magyar Pénzjegynyomda Rt.	1.00	2.00	4.00
	b. Without imprint.	1.00	2.00	4.00

74	500 Korona	VG	VF	UNC
	1.7.1923. Dark green on light brown underprint. Portrait Prince Árpád wearing helmet at right. 129x75mm.			
	a. Imprint: Magyar Pénzjegynyomda Rt.	1.00	2.00	4.00
	b. Without imprint.	1.00	2.00	3.00

75	1000 Korona	VG	VF	UNC
	1.7.1923. Black on brown underprint. Portrait St. Stephan at right. 137x77mm.			
	a. Imprint: Magyar Pénzjegynyomda Rt.	1.00	2.00	5.00
	b. Without imprint.	1.00	2.00	5.00

76	5000 Korona	VG	VF	UNC
	1.7.1923. Dark brown on tan and light blue underprint. Hungária at right. 139x83mm.			
	a. Imprint: Magyar Pénzjegynyomda Rt.	1.00	3.00	8.00
	b. Without imprint.	1.00	3.00	8.00

77	10,000 Korona	VG	VF	UNC
	1.7.1923. Dark green on tan and lilac underprint. "Patrona Hungariae" at right. 148x90mm.			
	a. Imprint: Magyar Pénzjegynyomda Rt.	2.00	4.00	12.00
	b. Without imprint.	2.00	4.00	12.00
	c. Imprint: Orell Füssli, Zürich.	2.00	4.00	12.00

78	25,000 Korona	VG	VF	UNC
	1.7.1923. Violet. Portrait St. Ladislaus wearing crown at right. Printer: Orell Füssli, Zürich. 148x90mm.	15.00	50.00	150

79	500,000 Korona	VG	VF	UNC
	1.7.1923. Violet and brown. Portrait woman wearing a wreath at right. 163x105mm.			
	a. Imprint: Magyar Pénzjegynyomda Rt.	40.00	150	400
	b. Imprint: Orell Füssli.	60.00	200	500

		VG	VF	UNC
80	**1,000,000 Korona** 4.9.1923. Blue on green underprint. Portrait woman wearing wreath at right. 185x84mm.			
	a. Imprint: Magyar Pénzjegynyomda Rt.	150	350	750
	b. Without imprint.	150	350	750
	c. Without portrait and Without serial # (half-finished printing).	—	—	500

Note: Treasury certificates of the State Note Issuing Office (5, 10, 50 and 100 million Korona dated 14.7.1923) are reputed to have been printed, but have not been confirmed.

1925 ND Provisional Issue

Monetary reform. 1 Pengo = 12,500 "old" Korona. #81-88 new denomination overprinted on old notes.

		VG	VF	UNC
81	**8 Fillér on 1000 Korona** ND (1925 - old date 1.7.1923).			
	a. Imprint: Magyar Pénzjegynyomda Rt.	8.00	20.00	45.00
	b. Without imprint.	8.00	20.00	40.00

		VG	VF	UNC
82	**40 Fillér on 5000 Korona** ND (1925 - old date 1.7.1923).			
	a. Imprint: Magyar Pénzjegynyomda Rt.	10.00	20.00	80.00
	b. Without imprint.	10.00	20.00	80.00

		VG	VF	UNC
83	**80 Fillér on 10,000 Korona** ND (1925 - old date 1.7.1923).			
	a. Imprint: Magyar Pénzjegynyomda Rt.	10.00	25.00	90.00
	b. Without imprint.	10.00	25.00	90.00
	c. Imprint: Orell Füssli.	12.00	30.00	100
84	**2 Pengö on 25,000 Korona**	VG	VF	UNC
	ND (1925 - old date 1.7.1923).	20.00	60.00	175
85	**4 Pengö on 50,000 Korona**	VG	VF	UNC
	ND (1925 - old date 1.5.1923).			
	a. Imprint: Orell Füssli.	35.00	100	250
	b. Without imprint.	35.00	100	250
86	**8 Pengö on 100,000 Korona**	VG	VF	UNC
	ND (1925 - old date 1.5.1923).			
	a. Imprint: Orell Füssli.	75.00	175	400
	b. Imprint: Magyar Pénzjegynyomda Rt.	75.00	175	400
87	**40 Pengö on 500,000 Korona**	VG	VF	UNC
	ND (1925 - old date 1.7.1923).			
	a. Imprint: Magyar Pénzjegynyomda Rt.	—	—	—
	b. Without imprint.	—	—	—
88	**80 Pengö on 1,000,000 Korona**	VG	VF	UNC
	ND (1925 - old date 4.9.1923).			
	a. Imprint: Magyar Pénzjegynyomda Rt.	—	—	—
	b. Without imprint.	—	—	—

Magyar Nemzeti Bank (resumed)

Hungarian National Bank

1926-1927 Issue

		VG	VF	UNC
89	**5 Pengö** 1.3.1926. Brown. Portrait Count I. Széchenyi at right. Back: Bridge. 149x74mm.			
	a. Issued note.	15.00	40.00	175
	s. Specimen perforated: *MINTA.*	—	—	85.00

		VG	VF	UNC
90	**10 Pengö** 1.3.1926. Green on light tan underprint. Portrait F. Deák at right. Back: Parliament House. 159x79mm.			
	a. Issued note.	50.00	200	600
	s. Specimen perforated: *MINTA.*	—	—	350

		VG	VF	UNC
91	**20 Pengö** 1.3.1926. Brown on green underprint. Portrait L. Kossuth at right. 165x83mm.			
	a. Issued note.	100	450	1,100
	s. Specimen perforated: *MINTA.*	—	—	475

		VG	VF	UNC
92	**50 Pengö** 1.3.1926. Blue. Portrait Prince F. Rákóczi II at right. Back: Horses in field with dark clouds above by painter K. Lotz. 175x89mm.			
	a. Issued note.	200	675	1,700
	s. Specimen perforated: *MINTA.*	—	—	750

#		VG	VF	UNC
93	**100 Pengö** 1.3.1926. Brown-lilac. Portrait King Mátyáas at right. Back: Royal Palace at Budapest at center. 181x95mm.			
	a. Issued note.	300	800	1,700
	s. Specimen perforated: *MINTA*.	—	—	750

#		VG	VF	UNC
94	**1000 Pengö** 1.7.1927. Blue, green and red. Portrait Hungaria at upper right. Back: Gyula Benczúr's painting *Baptism of Vajk* at center. 195x114mm.			
	a. Issued note.	400	1,000	2,700
	s. Specimen perforated: *MINTA*.	—	—	850

1928-1930 Issue

#		VG	VF	UNC
95	**5 Pengö** 1.8.1928. Blue. Portrait Count I. Széchenyi at right. Back: Bridge. 151x75mm.	10.00	30.00	80.00

#		VG	VF	UNC
96	**10 Pengö** 1.2.1929. Green. Portrait F. Deák at right. Back: Parliament House. 160x80mm.	5.00	15.00	40.00

#		VG	VF	UNC
97	**20 Pengö** 2.1.1930. Dark blue. Portrait L. Kossuth at right. Back: Hungarian National Bank building. 166x85mm.	2.00	5.00	16.00

#		VG	VF	UNC
98	**100 Pengö** 1.7.1930. Violet. Portrait King Mátyás at right. Series # without asterisk. Back: Royal Palace at Budapest at center. 180x92mm.	1.00	2.00	4.00

Note: Also see #112.

1932 Issue

#		VG	VF	UNC
99	**50 Pengö** 1.10.1932. Red-brown on green and blue underprint. Arms at upper left, portrait S. Petófi at right. Back: János Visky's painting *Horse driving in Hortobágy*. 173x89mm.	1.00	3.00	5.00

1936 Issue

#		VG	VF	UNC
100	**10 Pengö** 22.12.1936. Green on orange, green and purple underprint. *Patrona Hungariae* at left, girl at at right. Series # without asterisk. Back: Equestrian statue of St. Stephan. 163x72mm.	1.00	2.00	3.00

Note: Also see #113.

1938 Issue

#		VG	VF	UNC
101	**50 Fillér** 15.1.1938. 86x50mm. Proof.	—	—	—
102	**1 Pengö** 15.1.1938. Dark blue on brown underprint. Arms at left, portrait girl at right. Series # without asterisk. 100x57mm.	2.00	5.00	10.00

Note: Also see #114.

		VG	VF	UNC
103	**2 Pengö** 15.1.1938. 111x61mm. Specimen.	—	—	65.00

		VG	VF	UNC
104	**5 Pengö** 15.1.1938. Brown on green underprint. Girl at right. 119x65mm.			
	a. Issued note. With *MINTA*.	10.00	30.00	80.00
	b. 1938. Without *MINTA*.	—	—	—

		VG	VF	UNC
105	**20 Pengö on 50 Fillér** 15.1.1938. Proof.	—	—	—

1939 Issue

		VG	VF	UNC
106	**5 Pengö** 25.10.1939. Brown on green underprint. Arms at lower left center, portrait girl at right. Back: Man with balalaika. 120x53mm.	2.00	5.00	15.00

		VG	VF	UNC
107	**100 Pengö on 5 Pengö** 25.10.1939. Proof.	—	—	—

1940-1945 Issue

		VG	VF	UNC
108	**2 Pengö** 15.7.1940. Green on peach underprint. Arms at left, portrait Valeria Rudas at right. Back: Woman and child at center. 115x58mm. PC: White or yellow.	2.00	5.00	12.00

		VG	VF	UNC
109	**20 Pengö** 15.1.1941. Blue on tan and light green underprint. Shepherd and sheep at lower center, portrait woman wearing national costume at right. Back: Old man and young woman at center. 165x76mm.	1.00	2.00	4.00

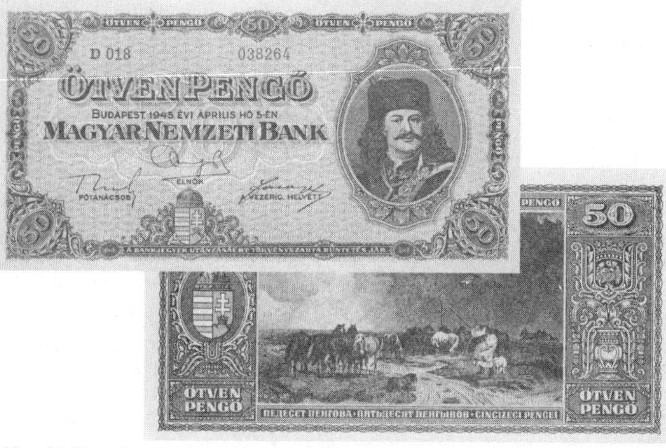

		VG	VF	UNC
110	**50 Pengö** 5.4.1945. Brown on green underprint. Portrait Prince F. Rákóczi II at right. Back: Horses in field with dark clouds above by painter K. Lotz. 177x91mm.			
	a. Printed on both sides.	1.00	3.00	6.00
	x. Printed on face only.	—	—	4.00

		VG	VF	UNC
111	**100 Pengö** 5.4.1945. Purple on light blue and lilac underprint. Portrait King Mátyás at right. Back: Royal Palace at Budapest. 185x98mm.			
	a. BÜÑTETÉS. With lauer leaves watermark.	1.00	3.00	8.00
	b. BÜÑTETÉS. Without watermark.	8.00	20.00	70.00
	c. BÜNTETÉS. With lauer leaves watermark.	4.00	24.00	40.00
	d. BÜNTETÉS. Without watermark.	10.00	120	160

SZÁLASI GOVERNMENT IN VESZPRÉM, 1944-1945

Magyar Nemzeti Bank

1930-Dated Issue

		VG	VF	UNC
112	**100 Pengö** 1.7.1930. Violet. Portrait King Matyás at right. Series # with asterisk.	1.00	3.00	8.00

1936-Dated Issue

		VG	VF	UNC
113	**10 Pengö** 22.12.1936. Green on orange, green and purple underprint. *Patrona Hungariae* at left, girl at right. Series # with asterisk.	4.00	10.00	25.00

1938-Dated Issue

		VG	VF	UNC
114	**1 Pengö** 15.1.1938. Blue on brown underprint. Arms at left, portrait girl at right. Series # with asterisk.	5.00	15.00	30.00

1943 Issue

		VG	VF	UNC
115	**100 Pengö** 24.2.1943. Lilac-brown on light brown underprint. Young man with fruits and doves at left, portrait girl at right. Back: Allegorical figures to left and right of arms at center. 150x95mm.			
	a. Printed on both sides.	15.00	30.00	90.00
	x1. Printed on face only.	—	—	—
	x2. Printed on back only.	5.00	10.00	35.00

		VG	VF	UNC
116	**1000 Pengö** 24.2.1943. Brown on lilac and green underprint. Portrait *Hungária* at right. Back: Arms at left, city scene with bridge at center. 185x103mm.	2.00	4.00	8.00

Magyar Nemzeti Bank

Hungarian National Bank

1945-1946 Pengö Issue

		VG	VF	UNC
117	**500 Pengö** 15.5.1945. Blue on dull lilac and orange underprint. Portrait woman wearing wreath at right. Back: First Russian word at upper left correctly spelled ПЯТЬСОТ. 180x90mm.			
	a. Issued note. First letter П.	1.00	5.00	15.00
	x. Error with word incorrectly spelled NЯТЬСОТ.	2.00	7.50	20.00

#118, 119 and 121 adhesive stamps have 2 types of letter *B* in MNB.

		VG	VF	UNC
118	**1000 Pengö** 15.7.1945. Dark green on red-brown underprint. Portrait woman wearing flowers at right. 2 serial # varieties. 185x90mm.			
	a. Without adhesive stamp.	1.00	2.00	4.00
	b. Red adhesive stamp.	1.00	2.00	4.00

		VG	VF	UNC
119	**10,000 Pengö** 15.7.1945. Lilac-brown on green underprint. Portrait woman at right. 170x83mm.			
	a. Without adhesive stamp.	1.00	2.00	5.00
	b. Brown on light green adhesive stamp.	1.00	2.00	5.00

119c has been removed from the catalog.

120	100,000 Pengö	VG	VF	UNC
	23.10.1945. Blue. Portrait Valeria Rudas wearing national costume at right. Back: Arms at center. 182x82mm.			
	a. Without adhesive stamp.	25.00	60.00	150
	b. Green adhesive stamp.	35.00	75.00	200

121	100,000 Pengö	VG	VF	UNC
	23.10.1945. Brown on green-blue underprint. Portrait woman wearing national costume at right. Back: Arms at center. 182x82mm.			
	a. Without adhesive stamp.	1.00	2.00	4.00
	b. Red adhesive stamp.	1.00	2.00	4.00

122	1,000,000 Pengö	VG	VF	UNC
	16.11.1945. Blue on brown and green underprint. Portrait L. Kossuth at right. Back: Painting *At the shore of Lake Balaton* (by G. Mészöly). 168x85mm.	1.00	2.00	4.00

123	10,000,000 Pengö	VG	VF	UNC
	16.11.1945. Dark green on multicolor underprint. Portrait L. Kossuth at right. Back: Dove with olive branch. 185x87mm.	1.00	3.00	6.00

124	100,000,000 Pengö	VG	VF	UNC
	18.3.1946. Brown on green underprint. Portrait woman wearing headscarf at right. Back: Parliament House. 162x80mm.	1.00	3.00	6.00

125	1 Milliard Pengö	VG	VF	UNC
	18.3.1946. Violet on light orange underprint. Portrait woman at right. 175x85mm.	1.00	3.00	6.00

1946 Milpengö Issues

126	10,000 Milpengö	VG	VF	UNC
	29.4.1946. Dark blue and red. Portrait woman at right. 170x83mm.	1.00	3.00	6.00

127	100,000 Milpengö	VG	VF	UNC
	29.4.1946. Dark green and red. Portrait woman wearing national costume at right. Back: Arms at center. 182x82mm.	1.00	3.00	6.00

128	1 Million Milpengö	VG	VF	UNC
	24.5.1946. Brown on yellow underprint. Portrait L. Kossuth at right. Without serial #. Back: Painting *At the shore of Lake Balaton* (by G. Mészóly). 168x85mm.	1.00	3.00	6.00

129	10 Million Milpengö	VG	VF	UNC
	24.5.1946. Brown on blue underprint. Portrait L. Kossuth at right. Without serial #. Back: Dove with olive branch. 185x87mm.	1.00	3.00	6.00

130	100 Million Milpengö	VG	VF	UNC
	3.6.1946. Green. Portrait woman wearing headscarf at right. Without serial #. Back: Parliament house. 162x80mm.	1.00	3.00	6.00

131	1 Milliard Milpengö	VG	VF	UNC
	3.6.1946. Blue. Portrait woman at right. Without serial #. 175x85mm.	1.00	3.00	6.00

1946 "B.-Pengö" Issues

132	10,000 B.-Pengö	VG	VF	UNC
	3.6.1946. Brown on violet underprint. Portrait woman at right. Without serial #. 170x83mm.	1.00	3.00	6.00

133	100,000 B.-Pengö	VG	VF	UNC
	3.6.1946. Red-brown. Portrait woman wearing national costume at right. Without serial #. Back: Arms at center. 182x82mm.	1.00	3.00	6.00

134	1,000,000 B.-Pengö	VG	VF	UNC
	3.6.1946. Dark brown. Portrait L. Kossuth at right. Without serial #. Back: Painting *At the shore of Lake Balaton* (by G. Meszoly). 168x85mm.	1.00	3.00	6.00

		VG	VF	UNC
135	**10,000,000 B.-Pengö** 3.6.1946. Purple. Portrait L. Kossuth at right. Without serial #. Back: Dove with olive branch. 185x87mm.	2.00	4.00	8.00

		VG	VF	UNC
136	**100,000,000 B.-Pengö** 3.6.1946. Blue. Portrait woman wearing headscarf at right. Without serial #. Back: Parliament House. 162x80mm.	2.00	5.00	14.00

		VG	VF	UNC
137	**1 Milliard B.-Pengö** 3.6.1946. Green. Portrait woman at right. Without serial #. 175x85mm. (Not issued.)	15.00	50.00	160

1951 Issue

		VG	VF	UNC
167	**50 Forint** 1.9.1951. Brown on blue and orange underprint. Portrait Prince F. Rákóczi at right. Back: Battle of the Hungarian insurrectionists (kuruc) against pro-Austrian soldiers (labanc) at center.			
	a. Issued note.	1.00	5.00	15.00
	s. Specimen with red overprint and perforated: *MINTA*.	—	—	50.00

Ministry of Finance

1946 Adópengö (Tax Pengö) System - First Issue

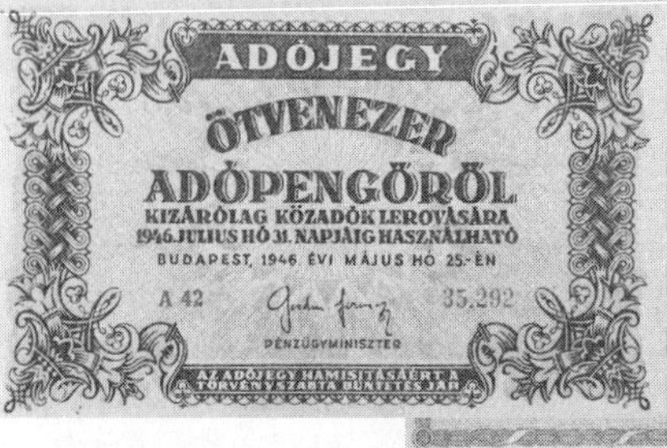

		VG	VF	UNC
138	**50,000 (Ötvenezer) Adópengö** 25.5.1946. Green. Back: Arms in underprint at center.			
	a. Gray paper with watermark and serial #.	1.00	3.00	7.00
	b. Gray paper with watermark, without serial #.	1.00	3.00	7.00
	c. White paper without watermark,without serial #.	1.00	3.00	7.00

		VG	VF	UNC
139	**500,000 (Ötszazezer) Adópengö** 25.5.1946. Dark blue. Back: Arms in underprint at center.			
	a. Gray paper with watermark and serial #.	1.00	3.00	8.00
	b. White paper without watermark, without serial #.	1.00	3.00	8.00
140	**1,000,000 (Egymillió) Adópengö** 25.5.1946. Red on gray underprint. Back: Arms in underprint at center.	VG	VF	UNC
	a. Gray paper with watermark and serial #.	1.00	3.00	8.00
	b. Like a, but arms in underprint on back reversed (cross at l.).	1.00	3.00	8.00
	c. White paper without watermark, without serial #.	1.00	3.00	8.00

		VG	VF	UNC
141	**10,000,000 (Tizmillió) Adópengö** 25.5.1946. Blue on yellow underprint. Back: Arms in underprint at center.			
	a. White paper without watermark, without serial #.	2.00	5.00	10.00
	b. Like a, but arms in underprint on back reversed (cross at l.).	4.00	10.00	20.00
	c. Gray paper with watermark, without serial # but arms in underprint on back reversed (cross at l.).	4.00	10.00	20.00

		VG	VF	UNC
142	**100,000,000 (Szazmillio) Adópengö** 25.5.1946. Gray-blue on pink underprint. Back: Arms in underprint at center.			
	a. White paper without watermark, without serial #.	3.00	7.00	20.00
	b. Like a, but arms in underprint on back at left and right reversed (cross at left).	4.00	15.00	40.00
	c. Gray paper, without serial #.	3.00	6.00	20.00
142A	**1 Md. (Egymilliárd) Adópengö** 25.5.1946. Lilac on light blue underprint. Back: Arms in underprint at center. (Not issued).	—	—	—

1946 Adópengö (Tax Pengö) System - Second Issue

		VG	VF	UNC
143	**10,000 (Tizezer) Adópengö**			
	28.5.1946. Brown. Back: Arms in underprint at center.			
	a. Gray paper with watermark and serial #. *5.970/1946, M.E.* on back.	1.00	3.00	6.00
	b. Gray paper with watermark, without serial #.	1.00	3.00	6.00
	c. White paper without watermark, without serial #. *5.600/1946 M.E.* on back.	5.00	15.00	40.00

		VG	VF	UNC
144	**100,000 (Egyszázezer) Adópengö**			
	28.5.1946. Brown-lilac on pink underprint. Back: Arms in underprint at center.			
	a. Gray paper with watermark and serial #. *5.970/1946. M.E.* on back.	1.00	3.00	6.00
	b. Gray paper with watermark, without serial #. *5.970/1946. M.E.* on back.	1.00	3.00	6.00
	c. Like b, but arms in underprint on back reversed (cross at left).	5.00	20.00	50.00
	d. Gray paper with watermark and serial #. *5.600/1946. M.E.* on back.	5.00	20.00	50.00
	e. White paper without watermark, without serial #. *5.600/1946. M.E.* on back.	2.00	8.00	20.00

In accordance with an ordinance by the Ministry of Finance, numerous tax-accounting letters of credit, law court fee, and deed stamps were declared legal tender.

Magyar Postatakarékpénztár

Hungarian Postal Savings Bank

Non-Interest Bearing Certificates

1946 First Issue

#145-148 Issued 29.6.1946.

		VG	VF	UNC
145	**10,000 (Tizezer) Adópengö**			
	22.4.1946. Black. *Kir.* Back: Regulations.	10.00	25.00	50.00
146	**10,000 (Tizezer) Adópengö**			
	22.4.1946. Black. Without *Kir.* Back: Regulations.	8.00	20.00	50.00
147	**100,000 (Százezer) Adópengö**			
	22.4.1946. Red. *Kir.* Back: Regulations.	10.00	20.00	50.00
148	**100,000 (Százezer) Adópengö**			
	22.4.1946. Red. Without *Kir.* Back: Regulations.	10.00	20.00	50.00

1946 Second Issue

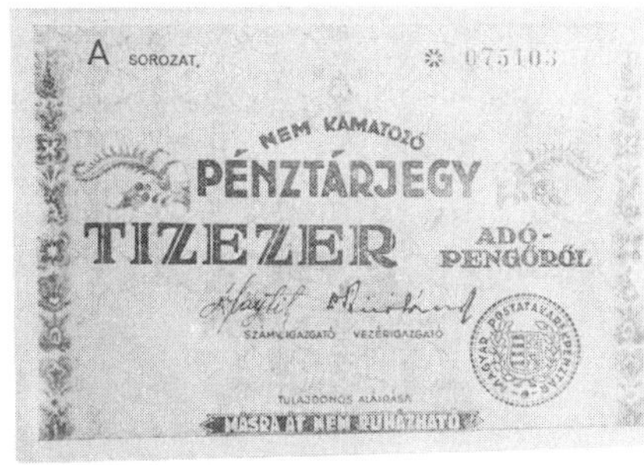

		VG	VF	UNC
149	**10,000 (Tizezer) Adópengö**			
	1946. Black on gray underprint. *MASRA AT NEM RUHAZHATO* at bottom. Back: Text.	4.00	8.00	20.00

		VG	VF	UNC
150	**100,000 (Százezer) Adópengö**			
	1946. Red on light red underprint. *MASRA AT NEM RUHAZHATO* at bottom. Back: Text.	4.00	8.00	20.00

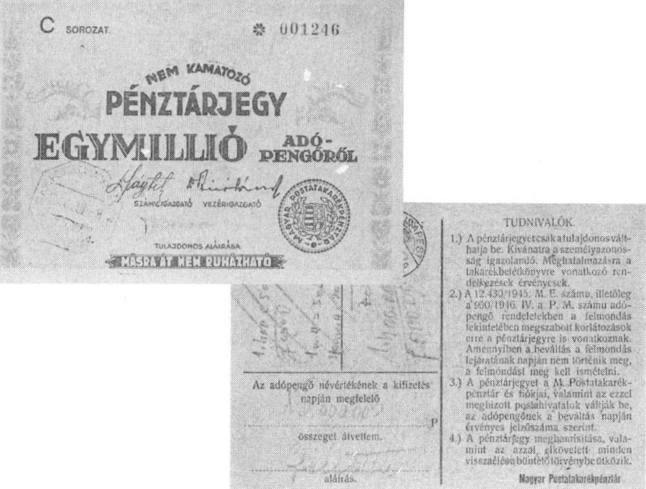

		VG	VF	UNC
151	**1,000,000 (Egymillió) Adópengö**			
	1946. Dark blue on light blue underprint. *MASRA AT NEM RUHAZHATO* at bottom. Back: Text.	4.00	8.00	20.00

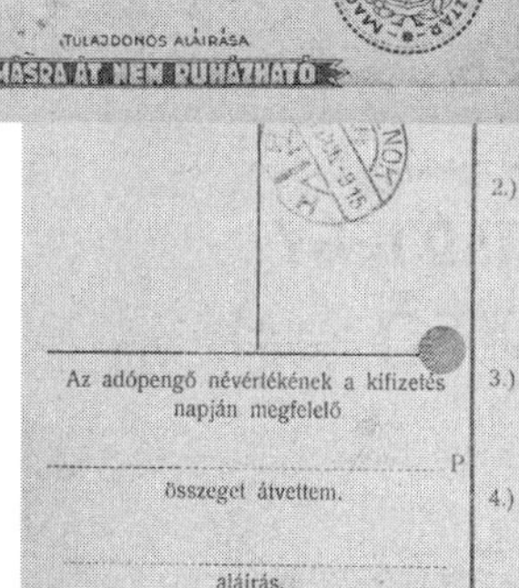

		VG	VF	UNC
152	**10,000,000 (Tizmillió) Adópengö**			
	1946. Dark green on light green underprint. *MASRA AT NEM RUHAZHATO* at bottom. Back: Text.	4.00	8.00	20.00

1946 Third Issue

		VG	VF	UNC
153	**100,000 (Százezer) Adópengö**			
	1946. Uniface.			
	a. With serial #.	—	—	—
	b. Without serial #.	5.00	10.00	30.00
154	**1,000,000 (Egymillió) Adópengö**			
	1946. Uniface.			
	a. With serial #.	—	—	—
	b. Without serial #.	5.00	10.00	30.00

1946 Fourth Issue

		VG	VF	UNC
155	**10,000 (Tizezer) Adópengö**			
	1946. Black on gray underprint. Back: Text.			
	a. With serial #.	—	—	—
	b. Without serial #.	5.00	10.00	30.00
156	**1,000,000 (Egymillió) Adópengö**			
	1946. Black on gray underprint. Back: Text.			
	a. With serial #.	—	—	—
	b. Without serial #.	5.00	10.00	30.00

1946 Fifth Issue

		VG	VF	UNC
157	**10,000 (Tizezer) Adópengö**			
	1946. Black on gray underprint. *MASRA AT NEM RUHAZHATO* at bottom. Uniface.	3.00	8.00	20.00
158	**10,000,000 (Tizmillió) Adópengö**			
	1946. Black on gray underprint. *MASRA AT NEM RUHAZHATO* at bottom. Uniface.	3.00	8.00	20.00

Note: #149-158 exist with postal handstamp on lower left or without handstamp. Unfinished, partially printed notes exist for #157 and 158.

Magyar Nemzeti Bank (resumed)

Hungarian National Bank

1946 Forint Issue

No.	Description	VG	VF	UNC
159	**10 Forint** 3.6.1946. Green on light tan underprint. Blue denomination guilloche at right. Portrait young man with hammer at left. Back: Arms. 156x72mm.			
	a. Issued note.	10.00	30.00	70.00
	s. Specimen perforated: *MINTA*.	—	—	50.00

No.	Description	VG	VF	UNC
160	**100 Forint** 3.6.1946. Blue on green underprint. Red denomination guilloche at right. Portrait young woman with sickle and ear of corn at at left. Back: Hands grasping hammer and wheat. 159x73mm.			
	a. Issued note.	10.00	30.00	70.00
	s. Specimen perforated: *MINTA*.	—	—	50.00

1947 Issue

No.	Description	VG	VF	UNC
161	**10 Forint** 27.2.1947. Green and blue-black on orange and lilac underprint. Portrait S. Petőfi at right. Signature with titles. Back: Painting *Birth of the Song* by J. Jankó.			
	a. Issued note.	8.00	30.00	70.00
	s. Specimen perforated: *MINTA*.	—	—	50.00
162	**20 Forint** 27.2.1947. Blue and green on light green and pink underprint. Portrait Gy. Dózsa at right. Back: Penthathlete Csaba Hegedüs with hammer and wheat at center.			
	a. Issued note.	8.00	35.00	80.00
	s. Specimen perforated: *MINTA*.	—	—	50.00

No.	Description	VG	VF	UNC
163	**100 Forint** 27.2.1947. Red-brown on blue and orange underprint. Arms at upper center, portrait L. Kossuth at right. Back: Horse-drawn wagon scene from *Took Refuge from the Storm* by K. Lotz at center.			
	a. Issued note.	8.00	35.00	80.00
	s. Specimen perforated: *MINTA*.	—	—	50.00

POST WWII INFLATIONARY ERA

Magyar Nemzeti Bank

Hungarian National Bank

1949 Issue

No.	Description	VG	VF	UNC
164	**10 Forint** 24.10.1949. Green and blue-black on orange and lilac underprint. Portrait S. Petofi at right. Arms with star. Signature without titles. Back: Painting *Birth of the Song* by J. Janko.			
	a. Issued note.	2.00	6.00	20.00
	s. Specimen perforated: *MINTA*.	—	—	50.00

No.	Description	VG	VF	UNC
165	**20 Forint** 24.10.1949. Blue and green on light green and pink underprint. Portrait Gy. Dozsa at right. Arms with tar. Signature without titles. Back: Penthathlete Csaba Hegedus with hammer and wheat at center.			
	a. Issued note.	2.00	6.00	14.00
	s. Specimen.	—	—	50.00
166	**100 Forint** 24.10.1949. Red-violet on blue and orange underprint. Arms with star at upper center. Portrait left, Kossuth at right. Signature without titles.			
	a. Issued note.	1.00	5.00	15.00
	s. Specimen with red overprint and perforated: *MINTA*.	—	—	50.00

PEOPLES REPUBLIC

Magyar Nemzeti Bank

HUNGARIAN NATIONAL BANK

1957-1883 Issue

#168-171 The variety in the serial # occurs in 1975 when the letter and numbers are narrower and larger.

168 10 Forint

1957-1975. Green and slate black on orange and lilac underprint. Portrait Sándar Petőfi at right. Value at left. Arms of 3-bar shield. Back: Trees and river, *Birth of the Song* by János Jankó at center. 174x80mm.

	VG	VF	UNC
a. 23.5.1957.	1.00	4.00	10.00
b. 24.8.1960.	1.00	2.00	12.00
c. 12.10.1962.	0.50	2.00	8.00
d. 30.6.1969. Blue-green center on back.	0.50	2.00	8.00
e. 26.10.1975. Serial # varieties.	0.50	2.00	8.00
s1. As a, b, c. Specimen with red overprint and perforated: *MINTA*.	—	—	45.00
s2. As d, e. Specimen.	—	—	27.50

169 20 Forint

1957-1980. Blue and green on light green and pink underprint. Arms of 3-bar shield. Portrait György Dózsa at right. Value at left. Back: Penthathlete Csaba Hegedüs with hammer and wheat at center. 174x80mm.

	VG	VF	UNC
a. 23.5.1957.	1.00	5.00	15.00
b. 24.8.1960.	3.00	10.00	50.00
c. 12.10.1962.	0.50	2.00	15.00
d. 3.9.1965.	0.50	2.00	15.00
e. 30.6.1969.	0.50	2.00	15.00
f. 28.10.1975. Serial # varieties.	0.50	2.00	15.00
g. 30.9.1980.	0.50	2.00	15.00
s1. As a; c; d. Specimen with red overprint and perforated: *MINTA*.	—	—	27.50
s2. As b. Specimen.	—	—	35.00
s3. As e; f; g. Specimen.	—	—	25.00

170 50 Forint

1965-1989. Brown on blue and orange underprint. Value at left. Arms of 3-bar shield with star. Portrait Prince Ferencz Rákóczi II at right. Back: Battle of the Hungarian insurrectionists (Kuruc) against pro-Austrian soldiers (Labanc) scene at center. 174x80mm.

	VG	VF	UNC
a. 3.9.1965.	1.00	3.00	30.00
b. 30.6.1969.	1.00	3.00	30.00
c. 28.10.1975. Serial # varieties.	2.00	5.00	15.00
d. Serial # prefix D. 30.9.1980.	1.00	3.00	12.50
e. Serial # prefix H. 30.9.1980.	2.00	4.00	20.00
f. 10.11.1983.	0.50	1.00	12.00
g. 4.11.1986.	0.50	1.00	30.00
h. 10.1.1989.	0.50	1.00	20.00
s1. As a. Specimen. Overprint *MINTA*.	—	—	50.00
s2. As b-h. Specimen. Overprint: MINTA.	—	—	25.00

171 100 Forint

1957-1989. Red-violet on blue and orange underprint. Arms of 3-bar shield with star. Value at left, portrait Lajos Kossuth at right. Back: Horsedrawn wagon from *Took Refuge from the Storm* by Károly Lotz at center. 174x80mm.

	VG	VF	UNC
a. 23.5.1957.	3.00	5.00	18.00
b. 24.8.1960.	3.00	5.00	18.00
c. 12.10.1962.	3.00	5.00	15.00
d. 24.10.1968.	1.00	2.00	15.00
e. 28.10.1975. Serial # varieties.	1.00	3.00	12.00
f. 30.9.1980.	1.00	2.00	12.00
g. 30.10.1984.	1.00	2.00	12.00
h. 10.1.1989.	1.00	2.00	12.00
s1. As a. Specimen with red overprint and perforted: *MINTA*.	—	—	65.00
s2. As b; c. Specimen.	—	—	—
s3. As d; e. Specimen.	—	—	35.00
s4. As f; g. Specimen.	—	—	30.00
s5. As h. Specimen.	—	—	30.00

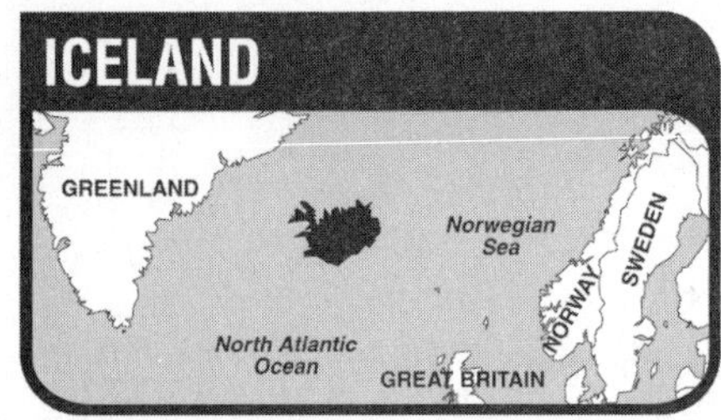

The Republic of Iceland, an island of recent volcanic origin in the North Atlantic east of Greenland and immediately south of the Arctic Circle, has an area of 103,000 sq. km. and a population of 304,367. Capital: Reykjavík. Fishing is the chief industry and accounts for more than 60 percent of the exports.

Settled by Norwegian and Celtic (Scottish and Irish) immigrants during the late 9th and 10th centuries A.D., Iceland boasts the world's oldest functioning legislative assembly, the Althing, established in 930. Independent for over 300 years, Iceland was subsequently ruled by Norway and Denmark. Fallout from the Askja volcano of 1875 devastated the Icelandic economy and caused widespread famine. Over the next quarter century, 20% of the island's population emigrated, mostly to Canada and the US. Limited home rule from Denmark was granted in 1874 and complete independence attained in 1944. Literacy, longevity, income, and social cohesion are first-rate by world standards.

RULERS:

Danish until 1873
Christian IX, 1863-1906
Frederik VIII, 1906-1912
Christian X, 1912-1944

MONETARY SYSTEM:

1 Krona = 100 Aurar, 1874-

DANISH ADMINISTRATION

Courant Bank

1778-1792 Provisional Issues

#A1, A2, A5, A6 and A11 reissue of early Danish State notes.

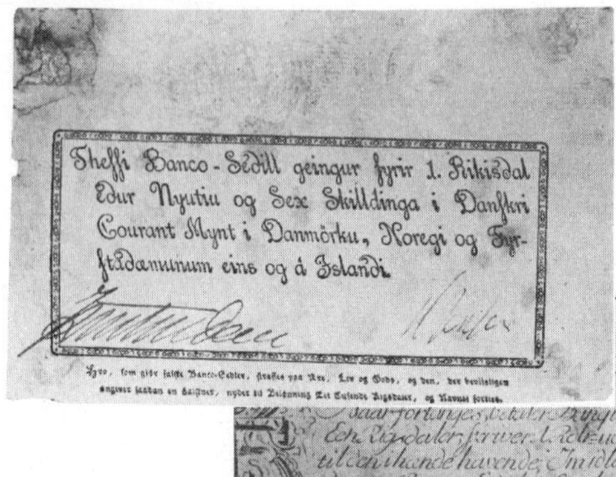

		Good	Fine	XF
A1	**1 Rigsdaler** 1777-1780; 1783-1784; 1788-1789; 1791-1792. Black. Printed on the back of Denmark #A24c.	450	1,350	—

1795-1801 Provisional Issues

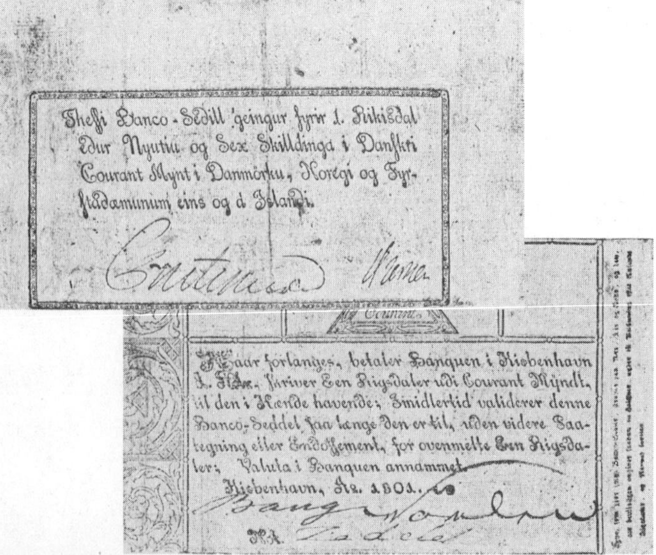

		Good	Fine	XF
A5	**1 Rigsdaler** 1792-1794; 1801. Black. Printed on the back of Denmark #A28.			
	a. Issued note.	425	1,050	—
	b. Handstamped: "A" in circle. 1792-94.	625	1,275	—
	c. Handstamped: "B" in circle. 1794.	850	2,250	—
	d. Handstamped: "C" in circle. 1801.	625	1,275	—
	e. Handstamped: "D" in circle. 1801.	625	1,275	—

Note: The stamping *A, B, C, D* was a precautionary measure during the Napoleonic War. A lot of money had been seized by the Allies against Napoleon, as Denmark was one of his supporters. All notes (dates and types) that exist with the handstamp are also found without the handstamp.

		Good	Fine	XF
A6	**5 Rigsdaler** 1800-1801. Black. Printed on the back of Denmark #A29b. Handstamped: "C" in circle. PC: Blue.	—	3,750	—

Rigsbank

1815 Provisional Issue

		Good	Fine	XF
A11	**1 Rigsbankdaler** 20.3.1815 (- old date 1814). Printed on the back of Rigsbanken i København notes. Rare.	—	—	—

Note: For similar issues refer to Danish West Indies and Faeroe Islands listings.

Landssjod Íslands

Law of 18.9.1885

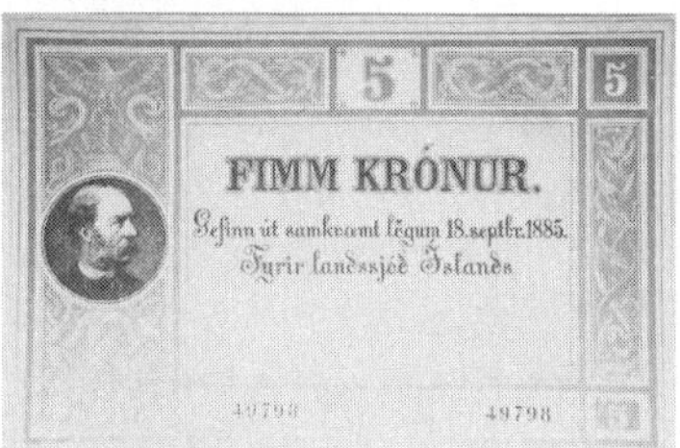

		Good	Fine	XF
1	**5 Krónur** *L.1885.* Gray-brown and black. Uniface. Portrait King IX at left in profile.			
	a. Issued note.	650	1,400	1,800
	r. Unissued remainder.	—	Unc	1,300
2	**10 Krónur** *L.1885.* Blue. Uniface. Portrait King Christian IX at left in profile.	**Good**	**Fine**	**XF**
	a. Issued note.	675	1,550	2,200
	r. Unissued remainder.	—	Unc	1,300
3	**50 Krónur** *L.1885.* Gray-green and light brown. Portrait King Christian IX at left in profile. Back: Allegorical figure at center.	**Good**	**Fine**	**XF**
	a. Issued note. Rare.	—	—	—
	r. Unissued remainder. Requires confirmation.	—	—	—

Laws of 18.9.1885 and 12.1.1900 - First Issue

		Good	Fine	XF
4	**5 Krónur** *L.1885* and *1900* (1900-06). Brown and gray. Portrait King Christian IX at left. Back: Bird at center.			
	a. Issued note.	375	1,050	—
	b. Punch hole cancelled.	—	235	—
5	**10 Krónur** *L.1885* and *1900* (1900-06). Blue and brown. Portrait King Christian IX at left. Back: Allegorical figure at center.	**Good**	**Fine**	**XF**
	a. Issued note.	250	575	2,100
	b. Punch hole cancelled.	—	325	—
6	**50 Krónur** *L.1885* and *1900* (1906-12). Gray-green and brown. Portrait King Frederik VIII at left. Back: Allegorical figure at center.	**Good**	**Fine**	**XF**
	a. Issued note. Rare.	—	—	—
	b. Punch hole cancelled.	—	2,550	—

Laws of 18.9.1885 and 12.1.1900 - Second Issue

		Good	Fine	XF
7	**5 Krónur** *L.1885* and *1900* (1912). Brown and green-gray. Portrait King Christian X at left.			
	a. Issued note.	400	1,250	—
	b. Punch hole cancelled.	—	175	—

No.	Description	Good	Fine	XF
8	**10 Krónur**	Good	Fine	XF
	L.1885 and *1900* (1912). Blue and brown. Portrait King Christian X at left.			
	a. Issued note.	400	1,250	—
	b. Punch hole cancelled.	—	225	—
9	**50 Krónur**	Good	Fine	XF
	L.1885 and *1900* (1912). Gray-green and light brown. Portrait King Christian X at left.			
	a. Issued note. Rare.	—	—	—
	b. Punch hole cancelled.	—	435	—

Íslands Banki

1904 Issue

No.	Description	Good	Fine	XF
10	**5 Krónur**	Good	Fine	XF
	1904. Black on red and violet underprint. Portrait King Christian IX at left. Back: Bird at left.	150	465	1,400

No.	Description	Good	Fine	XF
11	**10 Krónur**	Good	Fine	XF
	1904. Black on blue and tan underprint. Portrait King Christian IX at left. Back: Bird at right.	200	600	1,800
12	**50 Krónur**	Good	Fine	XF
	1904. Black on red and violet underprint. Volcano and river at right. Portrait King Christian IX at left. Back: Bird at right. Rare.	—	—	—

No.	Description	Good	Fine	XF
13	**100 Krónur**	Good	Fine	XF
	1904. Black on blue and tan underprint. Portrait King Christian IX at left. Geyser at right. Back: Bird at center. Rare.	—	—	—

1919 Provisional Issue

No.	Description	Good	Fine	XF
14	**100 Krónur**	Good	Fine	XF
	1919. Blue and gray. Portrait King Christian IX at left. Overprint: On back of #1.			
	a. Issued note. Rare.	—	—	—
	r. Unissued remainder.	—	Unc	1,450

1920 Issue

No.	Description	Good	Fine	XF
15	**5 Krónur**	Good	Fine	XF
	1920. Black on red and violet underprint. Geyser at left. Printer: G&D.			
	a. Issued note.	275	950	2,000
	r. Remainder (1 signature).	—	Unc	435

No.	Description	Good	Fine	XF
16	**10 Krónur**	Good	Fine	XF
	1920. Black on blue and tan underprint. Volcano and river at left. Printer: G&D.	275	750	2,000

Rikissjod Íslands

Laws of 18.9.1885 and 12.1.1900 (1921)

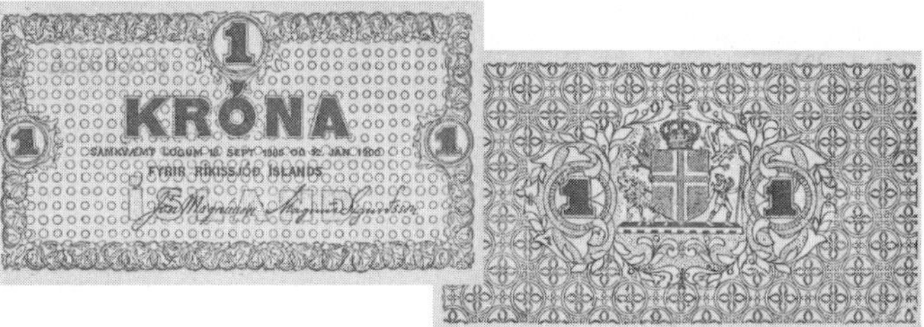

No.	Description	Good	Fine	XF
17	**1 Króna**	Good	Fine	XF
	L.1885 and *1900.* Dark blue. Underprint of double-line circles. Back: Arms. Printer: R. Gutenberg, Reykjavik.			
	a. Blue serial # at bottom center (1921).	30.00	80.00	200
	b. Dark blue serial # at upper left. (1922).	30.00	50.00	175

No.	Description	Good	Fine	XF
18	**1 Króna**	Good	Fine	XF
	L.1885 and *1900.* Dark blue. Underprint of simple circles. Back: Arms. Printer: R. Gutenberg, Reykjavik.			
	a. Black serial #. (1922-1923).	12.00	40.00	115
	b. Prefix A, circles behind red serial #. (1924-1925).	18.00	50.00	150
	c. Prefix B, without circles behind red serial #. (1925).	18.00	50.00	150
19	**5 Krónur**	Good	Fine	XF
	ND. Brown and green. Portrait King Christian X at left. *Fyrir Rikissjod Íslands.*	220	550	1,500
20	**10 Krónur**	Good	Fine	XF
	ND. Dark green on green underprint. Portrait King Christian X at left. *Fyrir Rikissjod Íslands.*	225	560	1,500
21	**50 Krónur**	Good	Fine	XF
	ND. Gray-green and light brown. Portrait King Christian X at left. *Fyrir Rikissjod Íslands.*	875	2,300	—

1941 Emergency WW II Issue

No.	Description	VG	VF	UNC
22	**1 Króna**	VG	VF	UNC
	1941 (1941-1947). Back: Arms. Printer: R. Gutenberg, Reykjavik. All on very thin paper, with short (3.5mm) or large serial numbers (4mm).			
	a. Dark green on light green paper. 000001-200000, (1941).	10.00	30.00	80.00
	b. Green on light green paper. 200001-250000, (1942).	22.00	85.00	200
	c. Brown on light brown paper. 250001-350000, (1942-1943).	10.00	30.00	85.00
	d. Brown on white paper. 350001-500000, (1944-1947).	15.00	40.00	120
	e. Brown on white paper. 500001-636000, (1944-1945).	15.00	40.00	120
	f. Brown on white paper. 636001-1000000, (1945).	10.00	35.00	80.00

	VG	VF	UNC
g. Blue-green on white paper. Serial # 3.5mm tall. 000001S-216000S, (1947).	10.00	30.00	85.00
h. Dark blue on white paper. 216001-332000, (1944).	10.00	30.00	85.00
i. Dark blue on white paper. 332001-452000, (1944-1945).	15.00	40.00	120
j. Dark blue on white paper. 452001-576000, (1945).	10.00	20.00	55.00
k. Dark blue on yellow paper. 576001-760000, (1945).	10.00	20.00	55.00
l. Blue-green on white paper. 760001-1000000, (1946).	10.00	30.00	80.00
m. Blue-green on white paper. Serial # 4mm tall. 000001-260000, (1946-1947).	10.00	25.00	65.00
n. Blue-green on white paper. 260001-558000, (1947).	10.00	20.00	55.00
o. Light blue on white paper. 558001-806000, (1947).	10.00	20.00	55.00

Note: Varieties a-f compose the first printing; g-l the second; m-o the third.

Landsbanki Íslands

Laws of 31.5.1927 and 15.4.1928

#		Good	Fine	XF
23	**5 Krónur** *L.1928* (1929). Brown on green underprint. Like #19 but with Landsbanki Íslands. Portrait King Christian X at left. Varieties in right signature. Mentions 1928 law date.	200	350	800
24	**10 Krónur** *L.1928* (1929). Dark blue on light blue underprint. Like #20 but with Landsbanki Íslands. Portrait King Christian X at left. Varieties in right signature. Mentions 1928 law date.	225	400	975
25	**50 Krónur** *L.1928* (1929). Gray-green on light brown underprint. Portrait King Christian X at left. Varieties in right signature. Like #21 but with Landsbanki Íslands. Mentions 1928 law date.	325	700	1,750

Note: For similar notes but ND see #19-21.

#		Good	Fine	XF
26	**100 Krónur** 31.5.1927. Gray-blue on gray underprint. Portrait King Christian X at left. Varieties in right signature. Back: Like #24.	535	1,200	3,750

Law of 15.4.1928

#27-31 notes issued 1934-1947.

SIGNATURE VARIETIES	
1	Jón Árnason – Magnús Sigurthsson, 1917-1945
2	Jón Árnason – Lúthvik Kaaber, 1918–1940
3	Jón Árnason – Georg Ólafsson, 1921–1941
4	Jón Árnason – Vilhjálmur Thor, 1940–1945
5	Jón Árnason – Pétur Magnússon, 1941–1944

#		VG	VF	UNC
27	**5 Krónur** *L.1928.* Brown and violet on multicolor underprint. Portrait J. Eriksson at left. Signature of Bank Director at left, Bank Governor at right. Back: Building at right. Printer: BWC.			
	a. Without serial # prefix. Signature 1-3.	30.00	80.00	175
	b. Serial # prefix A. signature 1, 3, 4.	25.00	50.00	110
	c. Serial # prefix B. signature 1.	25.00	50.00	100
	s. Specimen.	—	—	300

#		VG	VF	UNC
28	**10 Krónur** *L.1928.* Blue on multicolor underprint. Portrait J. Sigurdsson at left. Signature of Bank Director at left, Bank Governor at right. Back: Waterfalls at right. Printer: BWC.			
	a. Without serial # prefix. signature 1-3.	25.00	50.00	160
	b. Serial # prefix A. signature 1, 3, 4.	20.00	40.00	115
	c. Serial # prefix B. signature 1, 4, 5.	20.00	40.00	105
	s. Specimen.	—	—	300
29	**50 Krónur** *L.1928.* Violet. Portrait J. Eriksson at left. Signature of Bank Director at left, Bank Governor at right. Back: Men with fishing boats and freighter. Printer: BWC.	VG	VF	UNC
	a. Without serial # prefix. Signature 1-3.	100	235	700
	b. Serial # prefix A. signature 1, 3, 4.	100	220	550
	c. Serial # prefix B. signature 1, 4, 5.	100	220	450
	s. Specimen.	—	—	750
30	**100 Krónur** *L.1928.* Red on multicolor underprint. Portrait J. Sigurdsson at left. Signature of Bank Director at left, Bank Governor at right. Back: Flock of sheep. Printer: BWC.	VG	VF	UNC
	a. Without serial # prefix. Signature 3.	150	285	700
	b. Serial # prefix A. Signature 1, 3, 4.	120	250	650
	c. Serial # prefix B. Signature 1, 4, 5.	120	250	550
	d. Serial # prefix C. Signature 1, 4, 5.	120	250	525
	e. Serial # prefix D. Signature 1, 4, 5.	120	250	480
	s. Specimen.	—	—	1,100
31	**500 Krónur** *L.1928.* Green on multicolor underprint. Portrait J. Sigurdsson at left. Signature of Bank Director at left, Bank Governor at right. Signature 1, 4-5. Back: River, rocks and mountains. Printer: BWC.	VG	VF	UNC
	a. Without serial # prefix. Signature 1, 4, 5.	250	700	2,300
	s. Specimen.	—	—	2,150

REPUBLIC

Landsbanki Íslands

Law of 15.4.1928

#32-36 issued 1948-1956.

SIGNATURE VARIETIES	
6	Magnús Jónsson – Magnús Sigurthsson, 1946-1947
7	Magnús Jónsson – Vilhjálmur Thor, 1955–1957
8	Magnús Jónsson – Jón Árnason, 1946–1954
9	Magnús Jónsson – Jón G. Maríasson, 1943-1957
10	Magnús Jónsson – Gunnar Vithar, 1948–1955
11	Magnús Jónsson – Pétur Benediktsson, 1956–1957

32 5 Krónur

L.1928. Green on multicolor underprint. Portrait J. Eriksson at left. Signature of Bank Director at left; Bank Governor at right. Back: Building at right. Printer: BWC. Issued 1948-1956.

	VG	VF	UNC
a. Without serial # prefix. Signature 6, 8-11.	8.00	15.00	30.00
b. Serial # prefix C. Signature 7, 9, 11.	8.00	15.00	30.00
s. Specimen.	—	—	175

33 10 Krónur

L.1928. Red on multicolor underprint. Portrait J. Sigurdsson at left. Signature of Bank Director at left, Bank Governor at right. Back: Waterfalls at right. Printer: BWC. Issued 1948-1956.

	VG	VF	UNC
a. Without serial # prefix. Signature 6, 8-11.	10.00	18.00	30.00
b. Serial # prefix C. Signature 8-11.	10.00	18.00	30.00
s. Specimen.	—	—	185

34 50 Krónur

L.1928. Green on multicolor underprint. Portrait J. Eriksson at left. Signature of Bank Director at left, Bank Governor at right. Back: Men with fishing boats and freighter. Printer: BWC. Issued 1948-1956.

	VG	VF	UNC
a. Without serial # prefix. Signature 6, 8, 9, 11.	30.00	80.00	200
s. Specimen.	—	—	220

35 100 Krónur

L.1928. Blue on multicolor underprint. Portrait J. Sigurdsson at left. Signature of Bank Director at left, Bank Governor at right. Back: Flock of sheep. Printer: BWC. Issued 1948-1956.

	VG	VF	UNC
a. Without serial # prefix. Signature 6, 8-11.	50.00	100	200
b. Serial # prefix C. Signature 7, 9, 11.	50.00	100	200
s. Specimen.	—	—	265

36 500 Krónur

L.1928. Brown on multicolor underprint. Portrait J. Sigurdsson at left. Signature of Bank Director at left, Bank Governor at right. Back: River, rocks and mountains. Printer: BWC. Issued 1948-1956.

	VG	VF	UNC
a. Without serial # prefix. Signature 6, 8-11.	100	250	500
b. Serial # prefix C. Signature 8-10.	100	250	500
s. Specimen.	—	—	800

Landsbanki Íslands-Sedlabankinn

Law of 21.6.1957

37 5 Krónur

L.1957. Orange-brown on multicolor underprint. Viking I. Arnarson at left. Back: Farm buildings. Printer: BWC (without imprint).

	VG	VF	UNC
a. Buff paper (first printing).	3.00	5.00	10.00
b. White paper (second printing).	3.00	5.00	10.00
s1. As a. Specimen.	—	—	135
s2. As b. Specimen.	—	—	160

38 10 Krónur

L.1957. Violet-brown on green and orange underprint. Portrait J. Eiriksson at left. Back: Dock scene. Printer: BWC (without imprint).

	VG	VF	UNC
a. Letter O in *REYKJAVIKURHOFN* on back without umlaut (error).	4.00	8.00	18.00
b. Letter Ö with umlaut on top. (corrected).	5.00	10.00	25.00
s1. As a. Specimen.	—	—	180
s2. As b. Specimen.	—	—	180

39	25 Krónur	VG	VF	UNC
	L.1957. Purple on multicolor underprint. Portrait M. Stephensen Logmadur at left, fjord at center. Back: Fishing boats near large rock formation in water. Printer: BWC (without imprint).			
	a. Issued note.	4.00	8.00	15.00
	s. Specimen.	—	—	170

40	100 Krónur	VG	VF	UNC
	L.1957. Blue-green on multicolor underprint. Portrait T. Gunnarsson at left. Back: Herd of sheep and mountain at center. Printer: BWC (without imprint).			
	a. Issued note.	4.00	7.00	18.00
	s. Specimen.	—	—	170

41	1000 Krónur	VG	VF	UNC
	L.1957. Blue and green on multicolor underprint. Building at lower center, portrait J. Sigurdsson at right. Back: Rock formations. Printer: BWC (without imprint).			
	a. Issued note.	30.00	80.00	250
	s. Specimen.	—	—	285

Note: For notes similar to above but dated 1961 see Volume 3.

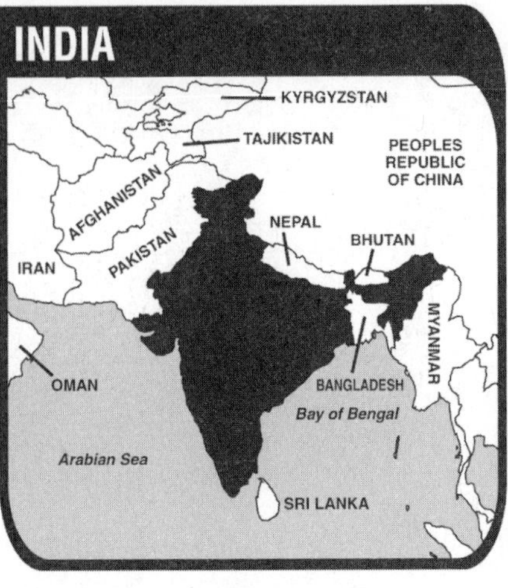

The Republic of India, a subcontinent jutting southward from the mainland of Asia, has an area of 3,287,590 sq. km. and a population of 1,147.9 million, second only to that of the Peoples Republic of China. Capital: New Delhi. India's economy is based on agriculture and industrial activity. Engineering goods, cotton apparel and fabrics, handicrafts, tea, iron and steel are exported.

Aryan tribes from the northwest infiltrated onto the Indian subcontinent about 1500 B.C.; their merger with the earlier Dravidian inhabitants created the classical Indian culture. The Maurya Empire of the 4th and 3rd centuries B.C. - which reached its zenith under Ashoka - united much of South Asia. The Golden Age ushered in by the Gupta dynasty (4th to 6th centuries A.D.) saw a flowering of Indian science, art, and culture. Arab incursions starting in the 8th century and Turkic in the 12th were followed by those of European traders, beginning in the late 15th century. By the 19th century, Britain had assumed political control of virtually all Indian lands. Indian armed forces in the British army played a vital role in both World Wars. Nonviolent resistance to British colonialism led by Mohandas Gandhi and Jawaharlal Nehru brought independence in 1947. The subcontinent was divided into the secular state of India and the smaller Muslim state of Pakistan. A third war between the two countries in 1971 resulted in East Pakistan becoming the separate nation of Bangladesh. India's nuclear weapons testing in 1998 caused Pakistan to conduct its own tests that same year. The dispute between the countries over the state of Kashmir is ongoing, but discussions and confidence-building measures have led to decreased tensions since 2002. Despite impressive gains in economic investment and output, India faces pressing problems such as significant overpopulation, environmental degradation, extensive poverty, and ethnic and religious strife.

RULERS:

British to 1947

Note: Staple holes and condition: Perfect uncirculated notes are rarely encountered without having at least two tiny holes made by staples, stick pins or stitching having been done during age old accounting practices before and after a note is released to circulation. Staples were officially discontinued in 1998.

COLONIAL OFFICES			
	Allahabad	K	Karachi
B	Bombay	L	Lahore
C	Calcutta	M	Madras
	Calicut	R	Rangoon, refer to Myanmar listings
A	Cawnpore		

DENOMINATION LANGUAGE PANELS	
Bengali	Marathi
Burmese	Tamil
Gujarati	Telugu
Gujarati (variation)	Persian (Farsi)
Hindi	Urdu
Kannada	

SIGNATURE VARIETIES

Dates appearing on notes are not when the notes were printed. Dates of manufacture may be deduced from a wmk. code, i.e. A 41 06 means Vat A, week 41, year 1906. This date is sometimes one or two years later than the printed date. Signatures are left off until the notes are actually issued, sometimes many years after the notes were printed. Therefore, the dates below do not correspond exactly with the years the signers held office.

A.V.V. Alyar, 1919	Stephen Jacob, 1886–1896
J.A. Ballard, 1861–1863	E. Jay, 1884
O.T. Barrow, 1899–1906	C.E. Jones, 1941
C.W.C. Cassog, 1913–1915	J.W. Kelly, 1935
A.F. Cox, 1891–1905	A. Kingstocke, 1913
H. Denning, 1920–1925	R. Logan, 1887–1899
C.D. Deshmukh, 1943–1947	A.C. McWatters, 1916–1922
R.W. Gillan, 1907–1913	W.H. Michael, 1906
M.M.S. Gubbay, 1913–1919	Hugh Sandeman, 1872

BRITISH ADMINISTRATION

Government of India

1850s Issue

		Good	Fine	XF
AA1	**5 Rupees** 26.3.1858. Queen Victoria in sprays at upper left. Two language panels. *CALCUTTA*. Uniface.	—	—	—

1861-1865 Issue

		Good	Fine	XF
AA2	**5 Rupees** 1861-1867. Queen Victoria in sprays at upper left. Two language panels. *CALCUTTA*. Signature H. Hydes. Uniface. Rare.	—	—	—

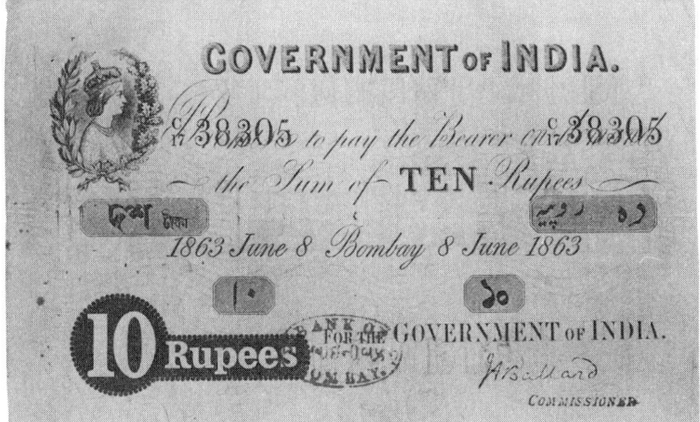

		Good	Fine	XF
A1	**10 Rupees** 6.8.1861; 9.5.1862; 7.6.1862; 8.6.1863; 14.6.1864; 6.6.1865. Queen Victoria in sprays at upper left. Two language panels. Uniface. Signature J. A. Ballard with title:*COMMISSIONER*. Rare.	—	—	—
A1A	**20 Rupees** 1861-1867. 10.6.1864. Queen Victoria in sprays at upper left. Two language panels. Uniface. Signature J.A. Ballard with title:*COMMISSIONER*.			
	a. Signature J. A. Ballard and S. K. Lambert.	—	—	—
	b. Signature J. A. Ballard and H. Hydes.	—	—	—
	c. Signature H. Hydes and C. W. Clerdin.	—	—	—
	d. Signature H. Hydes and L. Berkeley.	—	—	—
	e. Signature H. Hydes and C. Wilson.	—	—	—

Issued in Calcutta, Calcutta or Allahabad, Calcutta or Lahore, Bombay, Bombay or Karachi, Madras.

		Good	Fine	XF
A1D	**500 Rupees** 1861-1867. Queen Victoria in sprays at upper left. Two language panels. Uniface. Requires confirmation.	—	—	—

Issued from Calcutta, Calcutta or Nagpore, Calcutta or Lahore, Bombay.

		Good	Fine	XF
A1E	**1000 Rupees** 1861-1867. Queen Victoria in sprays at upper left. Two language panels. Signature H. Hydes. Uniface.	—	—	—

1872-1927 Issue

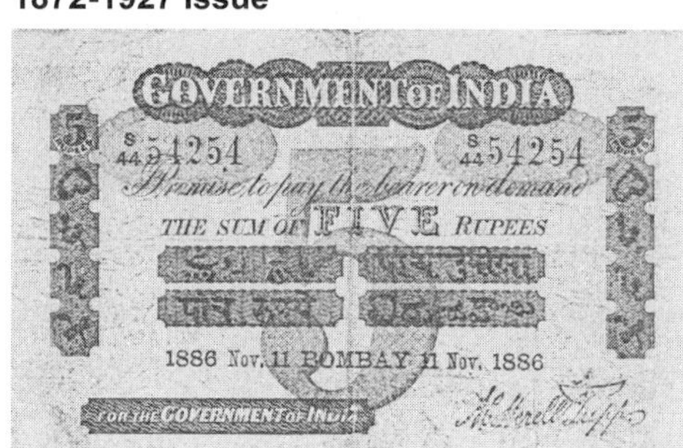

		Good	Fine	XF
A2	**5 Rupees** 1872-1901. Green underprint. Four language panels, 2 serial #.			
	a. *ALLAHABAD* or *CALCUTTA*. Signature Edward A. Harrison. 19.1.1872.	250	800	1,500
	b. *ALLAHABAD* or *CALCUTTA*. Signature R.A. Sterndales.	250	800	1,500
	c. *ALLAHABAD* or *CALCUTTA*. Signature A.F. Cox.	250	800	1,500
	d. *ALLAHABAD* or *CALCUTTA*. Signature Stephen Jacob.	250	800	1,500
	e. *BOMBAY*. Signature A. C. Merell Tupps. 27.5.1872; 11.11.1886.	250	800	1,500
	f. *BOMBAY*. Signature A. F. Cox. 7.5.1891; 5.2.1899-8.6.1899.	250	800	1,500
	g. *BOMBAY*. Signature O. T. Barrow. 1.11.1894-9.1.1901.	250	800	1,500
	h. *BOMBAY*. Signature R. Logan.	250	800	1,500
	i. *BOMBAY*. Signature G. L. Lushington.	250	800	1,500
	j. *BOMBAY*. Signature E. Gay.	250	800	1,500
	k. *CALCUTTA*. Signature E. Gay. 10.5.1884.	250	800	1,500
	l. *CALCUTTA*. Signature Edward F. Harrison.	250	800	1,500
	m. *CALCUTTA*. Signature R. A. Sterndales.	250	800	1,500
	n. *CALCUTTA*. Signature Stephen Jacob. 1.10.1886; 1.6.1888.	250	800	1,500
	o. *CALCUTTA*. Signature J. Westland.	250	800	1,500
	p. *CALCUTTA*. Signature A. F. Cox.	250	800	1,500
	q. *LAHORE* or *CALCUTTA*. Signature Stephen Jacob.	250	800	1,500
	r. *LAHORE* or *CALCUTTA*. Signature A. F. Cox.	250	800	1,500
	s. *AKOLA* or *BOMBAY*. Signature G. L. Lushington.	250	800	1,500
	t. *MADRAS*. Signature H. Clogstown.	250	800	1,500
	u. *MADRAS*. Signature F. C. Harrison.	250	800	1,500
	v. *MADRAS*. Signature T. Haskell Biggs.	250	800	1,500
	w. *MADRAS*. Signature W. H. Dobbie.	250	800	1,500
	x. *CALICUT* or *MADRAS*. Signature F. Lushington.	250	800	1,500
	y. *CALICUT* or *MADRAS*. Signature F. C. Harrison.	250	800	1,500

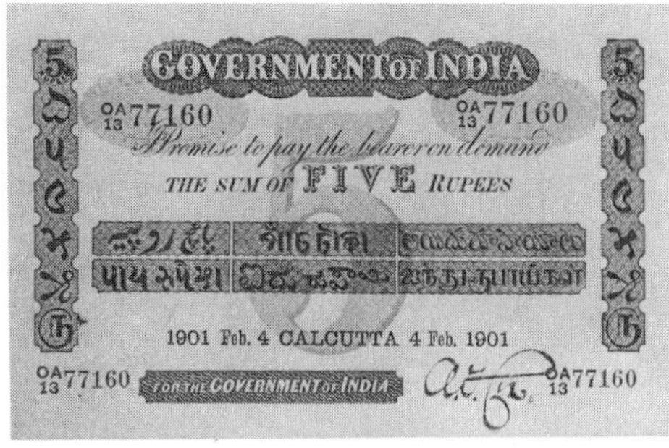

		Good	Fine	XF
A3	**5 Rupees** 1901-1903. Green underprint. Six language panels, 4 serial #.			
	a. *BOMBAY*. Signature A. F. Cox. 3.3.1902-1.8.1903.	650	800	1,500
	b. *BOMBAY*. Signature O. T. Barrow. 9.1.1901; 1.3.1902.	650	800	1,500
	c. *CALCUTTA*. Signature A. F. Cox. 4.2.1901.	650	800	1,500
	d. *CALICUT* or *LAHORE* or *CALCUTTA*. Signature A. F. Cox.	650	800	1,500

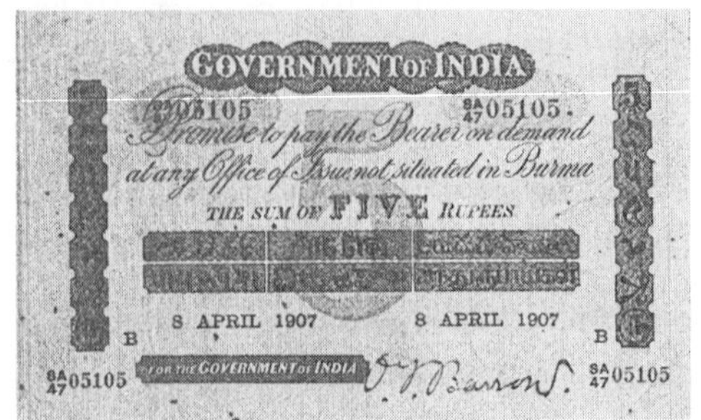

A4	5 Rupees	Good	Fine	XF
	1903. Black and pink. Eight language panels and 4 serial #. Text: *at any Office of Issue not situated in Burma* added. Letter for city of issue.			
	a. L (Lahore). Signature A. F. Cox. Requires confirmation.	—	—	—
	b. B (Bombay). Signature O. T. Barrow. 12.7.1905; 1.8.1905; 6.4.1907; 8.4.1907.	600	800	1,300
	c. C (Calcutta). Signature A. F. Cox.	600	800	1,300

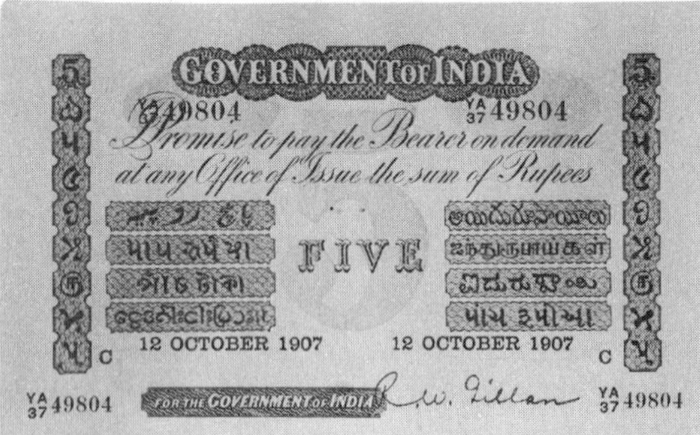

A5	5 Rupees	Good	Fine	XF
	1907-1915. Red-pink underprint. Eight language panels, 4 serial #. Text: *at any Office of Issue* added. Letter for city of issue.			
	a. B (Bombay). Signature H. F. Howard. 9.11.1907; 7.2.1912; 13.10.1913; 14.10.1913; 31.10.1913.	250	650	1,200
	b. B (Bombay). Signature M. M. S. Gubbay. 7.1.1914; 28.4.1914; 1.5.1914; 18.5.1914; 19.5.1914; 8.4.1915.	250	650	1,200
	c. B (Bombay). Signature R. W. Gillan. 8.2.1909; 2.10.1909.	250	650	1,200
	d. B (Bombay). Signature O. T. Barrow.	250	650	1,200
	e. B (Bombay). Without signature (sea salvage).	250	650	1,200
	f. C (Calcutta). Signature H. F. Howard. 23.9.1912; 25.10.1912; 30.10.1912; 31.7.1913.	250	650	1,200
	g. C (Calcutta). Signature M. M. S. Gubbay. 4.3.1914.	250	650	1,200
	h. C (Calcutta). Signature R. W. Gillan. 20.5.1907; 12.10.1907.	250	650	1,200
	i. C (Calcutta). Signature O. T. Barrow.	250	650	1,200
	j. A (Cawnpore). Signature H. F. Howard. 2.10.1912.	250	650	1,200
	k. A (Cawnpore). Signature M. M. S. Gubbay.	250	650	1,200
	l. A (Cawnpore). Signature R. W. Gillen.	250	650	1,200
	m. A (Cawnpore). Signature O. T. Barrow.	250	650	1,200
	n. A (Cawnpore). Without signature (sea salvage).	250	650	1,200
	o. M (Madras). Signature H. F. Howard.	250	650	1,200
	p. M (Madras). Signature M. M. S. Gubbay. 22.7.1914.	250	650	1,200
	q. M (Madras). Signature R. W. Gillen.	250	650	1,200
	r. M (Madras). Signature O. T. Barrow.	250	650	1,200
	s. L (Lahore). Signature H. F. Howard.	250	650	1,200
	t. L (Lahore). Signature M. M. S. Gubbay.	250	650	1,200
	u. L (Lahore). Signature R. W. Gillen.	250	650	1,200
	v. L (Lahore). Signature O. T. Barrow.	250	650	1,200

A6	5 Rupees	Good	Fine	XF
	1914-1924. Black on pink underprint. Three serial #. With or without letter for city of issue.			
	a. B (Bombay). Signature M. M. S. Gubbay. 8.4.1915-8.8.1916.	300	450	600
	b. C (Calcutta). Signature M. M. S. Gubbay. 9.1.1915-21.7.1916.	300	450	600
	c. C (Calcutta). Signature H. F. Howard. 4.5.1916; 13.7.1916.	300	450	600
	d. A (Cawnpore). Signature M. M. S. Gubbay. 2.2.1915; 28.12.1915.	300	450	600
	e. L (Lahore). Signature M. M. S. Gubbay. 31.7.1916.	300	450	600
	f. M (Madras). Signature M. M. S. Gubbay. 12.8.1914-23.10.1918.	300	450	600
	g. Without letter. Signature M. M. S. Gubbay. 26.10.1918-23.1.1920.	250	350	600
	h. Without letter. Signature A. C. McWatters. 12.1.1922-8.2.1924.	250	350	600
	i. Without letter. Signature H. Denning. 24.1.1924; 25.1.1924; 8.2.1924; 11.2.1924.	250	350	600

For notes with letters R or K, for Rangoon or Kurrachee, see Burma or Pakistan listings.

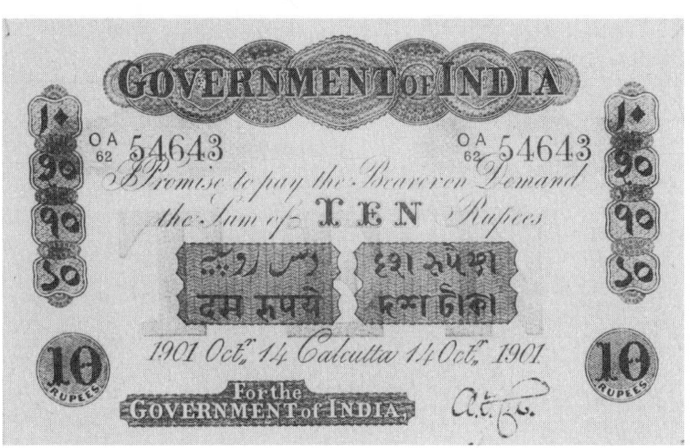

A7	10 Rupees	Good	Fine	XF
	1872-1901. Green underprint. Four languages on 2 panels, 2 serial #.			
	a. *ALLAHABAD* or *CALCUTTA*. Signature E. Jay. 24.3.1884.	800	1,100	2,000
	b. *ALLAHABAD* or *CALCUTTA*. Signature A. F. Cox.	800	1,100	2,200
	c. *BOMBAY*. Signature I. L. Sundtrayton. 7.5.1872. Rare.	—	—	—
	d. *BOMBAY*. Signature J. A. Ballard with title: *Commissioner*.	800	1,100	2,200
	e. *BOMBAY*. Signature R. Logan. 10.3.1887; 16.6.1899.	800	1,100	2,200
	f. *BOMBAY*. Signature G. L. Lushington.	800	1,100	2,200
	g. *BOMBAY*. Signature O. T. Barrow. 1.7.1899; 2.2.1900; 11.10.1900.	800	1,100	2,200
	h. *BOMBAY*. Signature A. F. Cox.	800	1,100	2,200
	i. *BOMBAY*. Signature A. C. Tupps.	800	1,100	2,200
	j. *CALCUTTA*. Signature H. Hydes.	800	1,100	2,200
	k. *CALCUTTA*. Signature H. D. Sanderman. 1872.	800	1,100	2,200
	l. *CALCUTTA*. Signature R. A. Sterndales.	800	1,100	2,200
	m. *CALCUTTA*. Signature J. Westland. 15.4.1882; 10.12.1883.	800	1,100	2,200
	n. *CALCUTTA*. Signature R. Logan.	800	1,100	2,200
	o. *CALCUTTA*. Signature Stephen Jacob. 6.1.1893; 10.2.1893.	800	1,100	2,200
	p. *CALCUTTA*. Signature A. F. Cox. 17.1.1898-14.10.1901.	800	1,100	2,200
	q. *CALCUTTA*. Signature W. H. Dobbie.	800	1,100	2,200
	r. *CALCUTTA*. Signature E. F. Harrison.	800	1,100	2,200
	s. *LAHORE* or *CALCUTTA*. Signature Stephen Jacob. 25.11.1896. Rare.	—	—	—
	s1. Specimen. *ALLAHABAD* or *CALCUTTA*.	800	1,100	2,200
	s2. Specimen. *CALCUTTA*.	—	—	—
	s3. Specimen. *LAHORE* or *CALCUTTA*.	—	—	—
	s4. Specimen. *MADRAS*.	—	—	—
	s5. Specimen. *CALICUT* or *MADRAS*.	—	—	—
	s6. Specimen. *TRICHINOPOLY* or *MADRAS*.	—	—	—
	s7. Specimen. *VIZAGAPATAM* or *MADRAS*.	—	—	—
	t. *MADRAS / Rangoon*. 1896. Rare.	—	—	—
	u. *MADRAS / L*. 1896. Rare.	—	—	—

A8	10 Rupees	Good	Fine	XF
	1903-1906. Green underprint. Four language panels, 4 serial #. BOMBAY.			
	a. Signature O. T. Barrow. 14.8.1903; 19.8.1903; 1.9.1905.	700	1,000	1,600
	b. Signature F. C. Harrison. 2.9.1905; 6.9.1905; 3.10.1905; 12.10.1905.	700	1,000	1,600
	c. Signature W. H. Michael. 3.1.1906.	700	1,000	1,600
	d. Signature R. W. Gillen.	700	1,000	1,600

A9	10 Rupees	Good	Fine	XF
	1903-1906. Green underprint. Four languages on 2 panels, 4 serial #. CALCUTTA.			
	a. Signature A. F. Cox. 10.6.1903; 5.8.1904; 20.12.1904.	800	1,000	1,600
	b. Signature O. T. Barrow. 1.11.1904-3.12.1906.	800	1,000	1,600
	c. Signature R. W. Gillen.	800	1,000	1,600
	d. *CAWNPORE* or *CALCUTTA.* Signature R. W. Gillan. 29.8.1906.	800	1,000	1,600
	e. *LAHORE* or *CALCUTTA.* Signature O. T. Barrow.	800	1,000	1,600
	f. *MADRAS.* Signature W. H. Dobbie.	800	1,000	1,600

A10	10 Rupees	Good	Fine	XF
	1910-1920. Red underprint. Eight language panels, 4 serial #. *at any Office of Issue* added to text. Letter for city of issue.			
	a. B (Bombay). Signature R. W. Gillan. 24.8.1910; 26.8.1910; 16.11.1911.	250	450	850
	b. B (Bombay). Signature H. F. Howard. 1914-26.4.1916; 29.5.1916.	250	450	850
	c. B (Bombay). Signature M. M. S. Gubbay. 1916-17.2.1919.	250	450	850
	d. B (Bombay). Signature A. M. Brigstocke.	600	800	1,200
	e. C (Calcutta). Signature R. W. Gillan. 21.2.1910; 31.5.1912.	250	450	850
	f. C (Calcutta). Signature H. F. Howard. 31.5.1912-6.4.1916.	250	450	850
	g. C (Calcutta). Signature M. M. S. Gubbay. 3.8.1916-1919.	250	450	850
	h. C (Calcutta). Without signature (sea salvage).	—	—	—
	i. A (Cawnpore). Signature R. W. Gillen.	500	1,000	1,500
	j. A (Cawnpore). Signature H. W. Howard.	500	1,000	1,500
	k. A (Cawnpore). Signature M. M. S. Gubbay. 23.12.1915-1919.	250	450	850
	l. K (Karachi). Signature R. W. Gillen.	500	1,000	1,500
	m. K (Karachi). Signature H. F. Howard.	250	450	850
	n. K (Karachi). Signature M. M. S. Gubbay. 27.2.1918.	250	450	850
	o. L (Lahore). Signature R. W. Gillen.	250	450	850
	p. L (Lahore). Signature H. F. Howard.	250	450	850
	q. L (Lahore). Signature M. M. S. Gubbay. 10.10.1917.	250	450	850
	r. M (Madras). Signature M. M. S. Gubbay. 1914-19.	250	450	850
	s. M (Madras). Signature R. W. Gillen.	250	450	850
	t. M (Madras). Signature H. F. Howard.	250	450	850
	u. M (Madras). Signature A. M. Brigstocke.	500	800	1,800
	v. Without letter. Signature M. M. S. Gubbay. 27.2.1919-16.8.1920.	250	800	850
	w. Without letter. Signature A. C. McWatters. 10.2.1920.	250	800	850

Note: For issues with letter R for Rangoon, see Burma.

A11	20 Rupees	Good	Fine	XF
	5.7.1899; 1.1.1901. Green underprint. Four language panels, 2 serial #.			
	a. *BOMBAY.* Signature O. T. Barrow.	2,500	3,500	5,000
	b. *BOMBAY.* Signature A. C. Tupps.	2,500	3,500	5,000
	c. *BOMBAY.* Signature G. L. Lushington.	2,500	3,500	5,000
	d. *KURRACHEE* or *BOMBAY.* Signature O. T. Barrow.	2,500	3,500	5,000
	e. *NAGPORE* or *BOMBAY.* Signature not known.	—	—	—
	s. Specimen.	—	Unc	7,500

A12	20 Rupees	Good	Fine	XF
	1904-1906. Green underprint. Four language panels, 4 serial #.			
	a. *BOMBAY.* Signature O. T. Barrow.	—	—	—
	b. *BOMBAY.* Signature F. C. Harrison. 11.1.1904; 12.1.1904; 17.10.1905.	200	650	—
	c. *BOMBAY.* Signature W. H. Michael. 18.10.1905; 16.1.1906.	200	650	—
	d. *KURRACHEE* or *BOMBAY.* Signature F. C. Harrison.	—	—	—
	e. *MADRAS.* Signature W. H. Dobbie.	650	—	—
	f. *MADRAS.* Signature A. M. Brigstocke.	650	—	—

A13	20 Rupees	Good	Fine	XF
	1894-1901. Green underprint. Four languages on 2 panels, 2 serial #.			
	a. *CALCUTTA.* Signature J. Westland.	3,500	4,500	6,000
	b. *CALCUTTA.* Signature Stephen Jacob.	3,000	4,000	5,000
	c. *CALCUTTA.* Signature A. F. Cox.	3,500	4,500	6,000
	d. *CALCUTTA.* Signature E. F. Harrison.	3,500	4,500	6,000
	e. *ALLAHABAD* or *CALCUTTA.* Signature A. F. Cox. 26.6.1894; 26.2.1901. 4 serial #.	3,000	4,500	6,000
	f. *ALLAHABAD* or *CALCUTTA.* Signature E. Gay.	3,000	4,500	6,000
	g. *LAHORE* or *CALCUTTA.* Signature A. F. Cox. 28.8.1900.	3,000	4,500	6,000
	h. *MADRAS.* Signature W. Dobbie.	—	—	—
	s1. Specimen. *CALCUTTA.*	—	—	—
	s2. Specimen. *MADRAS.*	—	—	—

A14	20 Rupees	Good	Fine	XF
	1902-1905. Green underprint. Four languages on 2 panels, 4 serial #.			
	a. *CALCUTTA.* Signature A. F. Cox. 3.2.1902.	600	—	—
	b. *CALCUTTA.* Signature O. T. Barrow. 10.3.1905.	600	—	—
	c. *LAHORE* or *CALCUTTA.* Signature A. A. Cox. 27.3.1902.	600	—	—
	d. *LAHORE* or *CALCUTTA.* Signature O. T. Barrow. 30.8.1905.	600	—	—
	e. *ALLAHABAD* or *CALCUTTA.* Signature A. F. Cox.	600	—	—
	f. *ALLAHABAD* or *CALCUTTA.* Signature O. T. Barrow.	600	—	—
	g. *CAWNPORE* or *CALCUTTA.* Signature O. T. Barrow.	600	—	—

A14A	50 Rupees	Good	Fine	XF
	1867-1901. Green underprint. Four Language panels, 2 serial #.			
	a. *BOMBAY.* Signature O. T. Barrow.	1,000	—	—
	b. *CALCUTTA.* Signature O. T. Barrow.	1,000	—	—
	c. *CALCUTTA.* Signature Stephen Jacob.	1,000	—	—
	d. *CALCUTTA.* Signature A. F. Cox.	1,000	—	—
	e. *CALCUTTA.* Signature H. D. Sanderman.	1,000	—	—
	f. *MADRAS.* Signature J. W. Larkins.	1,000	—	—
	g. *CALICUT* or *MADRAS.* Signature W. Dobbie.	1,000	—	—
	s1. Specimen. *CALCUTTA.*	—	—	—
	s2. Specimen. *MADRAS.*	—	—	—

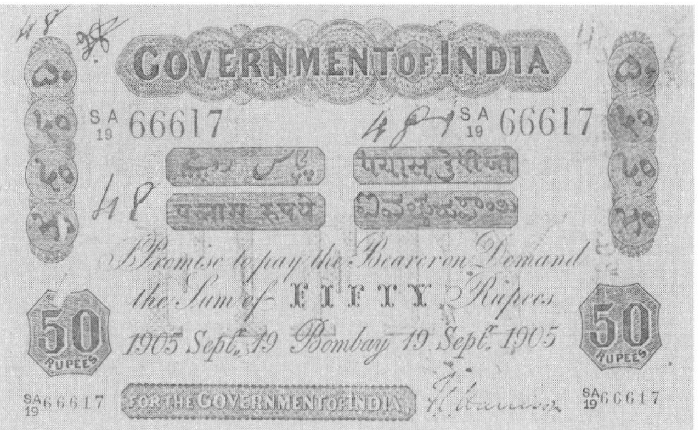

A14B	50 Rupees	Good	Fine	XF
	1901-1910. Green underprint. Four language panels, 4 serial #.			
	a. *BOMBAY.* Signature F. C. Harrison. 19.9.1905.	825	—	—
	b. *BOMBAY.* Signature O. T. Barrow.	825	—	—
	c. *BOMBAY.* Signature R. W. Gillen.	825	—	—
	d. *BOMBAY.* Signature RW. H. Michael.	825	—	—

	Good	Fine	XF
e. *CALCUTTA.* Signature O. T. Barrow.	825	—	—
f. *MADRAS.* Signature R. W. Gillen.	1,000	—	—
g. *CAWNPORE* or *CALCUTTA.* H. F. Howard.	1,200	—	—
h. *CAWNPORE* or *CALCUTTA.* M. M. S. Gubbay.	1,200	—	—

A15 50 Rupees

1913-1922. Red underprint. Eight language panels, 4 serial #. Text: *at any Office of Issue.* Letter for city of issue.

	Good	Fine	XF
a. B (Bombay). Signature H. F. Howard. 11.6.1913; 17.6.1913; 10.6.1920.	1,750	2,500	3,500
b. B (Bombay). Signature A. C. McWatters. 8.2.1916.	1,750	2,500	3,500
c. B (Bombay). Signature H. Denning. 8.6.1920.	1,750	2,500	3,500
d. B (Bombay). Signature M. M. S. Gubbay.	1,750	2,500	3,500
e. C (Calcutta). Signature H. F. Howard.	1,750	2,500	3,500
f. C (Calcutta). Signature A. C. McWatters. 11.1.1918. Rare.	1,750	2,500	3,500
g. C (Calcutta). Signature H. Denning. 15.1.1918; 9.3.1920; 10.3.1920; 28.10.1922.	1,750	2,500	3,500
h. C (Calcutta). Signature M. M. S. Gubbay.	1,750	2,500	3,500
i. A (Cawnpore). Signature A. C. McWatters. 29.4.1919.	2,500	3,500	4,200
j. A (Cawnpore). Signature H. Denning.	2,500	3,500	4,200
k. K (Karachi). Signature M. M. S. Gubbay. 1.12.1913.	2,500	3,500	4,200
l. K (Karachi). Signature A. C. McWatters.	2,500	3,500	4,200
m. K (Karachi). Signature H. Denning.	2,500	3,500	4,200
n. L (Lahore). A. C. McWatters.	2,500	3,500	4,200
o. L (Lahore). H. Denning.	2,500	3,500	4,200
p. L (Lahore) M. M. S. Gubbay. 21.3.1918. Rare.	2,500	3,500	4,200
q. M (Madras). Signature H. F. Howard. 23.6.1913. Rare.	2,500	3,500	4,200
r. M (Madras). Signature H. Denning.	2,500	3,500	4,200
s1. Specimen. L (Lahore).	—	—	—
ct. Color Trial. Purple underprint. *CALCUTTA.*	—	—	—

A16 100 Rupees

1867-1901. Green underprint. Four language panels, 2 serial #.

	Good	Fine	XF
a. *BOMBAY.* Signature O. T. Barrow. 1.7.1900; 15.10.1900.	2,500	3,000	3,500
b. *BOMBAY.* Signature A. C. Tupps.	2,500	3,000	3,500
c. *CALCUTTA.* Signature J. A. Ballard.	2,500	3,000	3,500
d. *CALCUTTA.* Signature A. F. Cox.	2,500	3,000	3,500
e. *CALCUTTA.* Signature Stephen Jacob.	2,500	3,000	3,500
f. *LAHORE* or *CALCUTTA.* Signature A. F. Cox.	2,750	3,500	4,000
g. *LAHORE* or *CALCUTTA.* Signature Stephen Jacob.	2,750	3,500	4,000
h. *LAHORE* or *CALCUTTA.* Signature J. Westland.	2,750	3,500	4,000
i. *MADRAS.* Rare.	—	—	—
j. *CALCUT* or *MADRAS.* Signature F. C. Harrison.	2,750	3,500	4,000
s1. Specimen. *CALCUTTA.*	—	—	—
s2. Specimen. *MADRAS.*	—	—	—

A17 100 Rupees

1904-1927. Green underprint. Four language panels, 4 serial #.

	Good	Fine	XF
a. *BOMBAY.* Signature H. F. Howard. 26.2.1913.	2,000	2,500	3,000
b. *BOMBAY.* Signature M. M. S. Gubbay. 14.7.1914; 26.4.1916; 16.7.1916.	2,000	2,500	3,000
c. *BOMBAY.* Signature A. C. McWatters. 10.6.1918-12.9.1919.	2,000	2,500	3,000
d. *BOMBAY.* Signature H. Denning. 3.7.1920; 17.7.1920; 26.7.1920; 4.1.1923; 24.1.1925.	2,000	2,500	3,000
e. *CALCUTTA.* Signature A. F. Cox. 22.9.1904; 23.3 1905.	2,000	2,500	3,000
f. *CALCUTTA.* Signature A. C. McWatters. 31.1.1918-22.11.1925.	2,000	2,500	3,000
g. *CALCUTTA.* Signature O. T. Barrow. 23.3.1905.	2,000	2,500	3,000
h. *CALCUTTA.* Signature H. Denning. 27.3.1920; 30.10.1922; 31.10.1922.	2,000	2,500	3,000
i. *CALCUTTA.* Signature R. W. Gillen.	2,000	2,500	3,000
j. *CALCUTTA.* Signature H. F. Howard.	2,000	2,500	3,000
k. *CALCUTTA.* Signature M. M. S. Gubbay.	2,000	2,500	3,000
l. *CAWNPORE* or *CALCUTTA.* Signature O. T. Barrow.	2,000	2,500	3,000
m. *CAWNPORE.* Signature M. M. S. Gubbay.	2,000	2,500	3,000
n. *CAWNPORE.* Signature A. C. McWatters.	2,000	2,500	3,000
o. *CAWNPORE.* Signature H. Denning. 11.3.1918; 6.6.1919; 14.6.1919; 15.4.1920.	2,000	2,500	3,000
p. *CAWNPORE.* Signature H. F. Howard.	2,000	2,500	3,000
q. *LAHORE* or *CALCUTTA.* Signature O. T. Barrow.	2,000	2,500	3,000
r. *KARACHI.* Signature M. M. S. Gubbay.	2,500	3,000	3,500
s. *KARACHI.* Signature H. Denning. 30.12.1915.	2,500	3,000	3,500
t. *KARACHI.* Signature A. C. McWatters. 6.9.1913-24.5.1920.	2,500	3,000	3,500
u. *LAHORE.* Signature D. Hastings.	2,500	3,000	3,500
v. *LAHORE.* Signature M. M. S. Gubbay.	2,500	3,000	3,500
w. *LAHORE.* Signature A. C. McWatters. 30.3.1916; 25.4.1918.	2,500	3,000	3,500
x. *LAHORE.* Signature H. Denning.	2,500	3,000	3,500
y. *MADRAS.* Signature H. Denning. 3.9.1920-16.2.1925.	2,000	2,500	3,000
z. *MADRAS.* Signature W. Dobbie.	2,000	2,500	3,000
aa. *MADRAS.* Signature M. M. S. Gubbay.	2,000	2,500	3,000
ab. *MADRAS.* Signature A. C. McWatters.	2,000	2,500	3,000

A18 500 Rupees

1867-1900. Green underprint. Four language panels at top, 2 serial #.

	Good	Fine	XF
s1. Specimen. *BOMBAY.*	—	—	—
s2. Specimen. *CALCUTTA.*	—	—	—
s3. Specimen. *MADRAS.*	—	—	—

A18A 500 Rupees

1901-1930. Green underprint. Four language panels at top, 4 serial #.

	Good	Fine	XF
a. *BOMBAY.* Signature A. Kingstocke. 8.5.1913.	—	—	—
b. *BOMBAY.* Signature H. Denning. 10.5.1913.	—	—	—
c. *BOMBAY.* Signature C. W. C. Casson. 9.5.1913.	—	—	—
d. *BOMBAY.* Signature A. V. V. Aiyar.	—	—	—
e. *BOMBAY.* Signature J. W. Kelly.	—	—	—
f. *CALCUTTA.* Signature A. V. V. Aiyar. 22.4.1919. Rare.	—	—	—
g. *CALCUTTA.* Signature H. Denning. 2.5.1922; 29.5.1922. Rare.	—	—	—
h. *CALCUTTA.* Signature O. T. Barrow.	—	—	—
i. *CALCUTTA.* Signature A. F. Cox.	—	—	—
j. *CALCUTTA.* Signature J. W. Kelly.	—	—	—
k. *CALCUTTA.* Signature Cyril Gwyther.	—	—	—
l. *CAWNPORE* or *CALCUTTA.* Signature J. W. Kelly. 26.6.1907; 27.6.1907. Rare.	—	—	—
m. *CAWNPORE* or *CALCUTTA.* Signature H. Denning.	—	—	—
n. *LAHORE* or *CALCUTTA.* Signature A. F. Cox.	—	—	—
o. *LAHORE* or *CALCUTTA.* Signature J. W. Kelly.	—	—	—
p. *LAHORE* or *CALCUTTA.* Signature O. T. Barrow.	—	—	—
q. *MADRAS.* Signature W. H. Dobbie.	—	—	—
r. *MADRAS.* Signature J. W. Kelly.	—	—	—

	A19 1000 Rupees	Good	Fine	XF
	1867-1900. Green underprint. Four language panels at top, 2 serial #.			
	a. *CALCUTTA*. Signature Stephen Jacob.	—	—	—
	b. *CALCUTTA*. Signature A. F. Cox.	—	—	—
	c. *ALLAHABAD* or *CALCUTTA*. Signature Stephen Jacob.	—	—	—
	d. *LAHORE* or *CALCUTTA*. Signature Stephen Jacob.	—	—	—
	e. *BOMBAY*. Signature J.A. Ballard.	—	—	—
	f. *BOMBAY*. Signature Stephen Jacob.	—	—	—
	g. *BOMBAY*. Signature A. F. Cox.	—	—	—
	s1. *CALCUTTA*. Specimen.	—	—	—
	s2. *MADRAS*. Specimen.	—	—	—

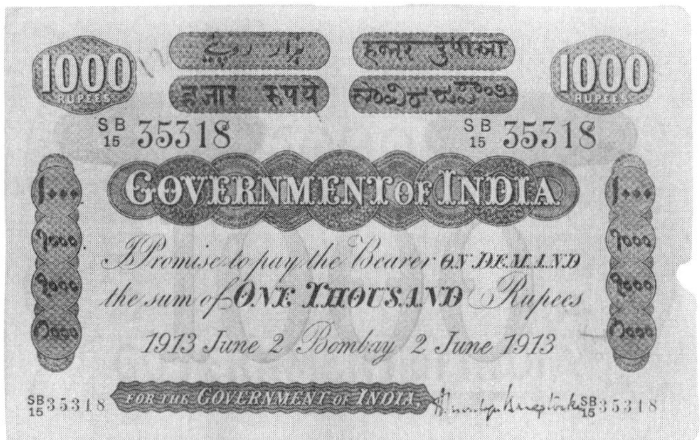

A19A	1000 Rupees	Good	Fine	XF
	1909-1927. Light green underprint. Four language panels at top, 4 serial #.			
	a. *BOMBAY*. Signature A. M. Brigstocke. 1909; 2.6.1913.	—	—	4,000
	b. *BOMBAY*. Signature E. M. Cook.	—	—	4,000
	c. *BOMBAY*. Signature H. Denning. 20.9.1915; 9.8.1918; 10.8.1918; 12.8.1925; 14.8.1925; 7.7.1926.	—	—	4,000
	d. *BOMBAY*. Signature A. V. V. Aiyar. 22.9.1919; 12.8.1925-7.7.1926.	—	—	4,000
	e. *BOMBAY*. Signature A. C. McWatters.	—	—	4,000
	f. *BOMBAY*. Signature C. W. C. Carson. 20.9.1915.	—	—	4,000
	g. *BOMBAY*. Signature W. H. Michael.	—	—	4,000
	h. *CALCUTTA*. Signature A. F. Cox.	—	—	4,000
	i. *CALCUTTA*. Signature M. M. S. Gubbay.	—	—	4,000
	j. *CALCUTTA*. Signature H. Denning. 6.4.1920; 19.8.1927; 22.8.1927.	—	—	4,000
	k. *CALCUTTA*. Signature C. J. Rivett Carnac.	—	—	4,000
	l. *CALCUTTA*. Signature A V. V. Aiyar.	—	—	4,000
	m. *CALCUTTA*. Signature Cyril Gwyther.	—	—	4,000
	n. *ALLAHABAD* or *CALCUTTA*. Signature A. F. Cox.	—	—	4,000
	o. *LAHORE*. Signature H. Denning.	—	—	4,000
	p. *LAHORE*. Signature J. B. Taylor.	—	—	4,000

A20	10,000 Rupees	Good	Fine	XF
	1899. Green underprint. Four languages on 1 panel, 4 serial #.			
	a. *CALCUTTA*. Signature A. F. Cox.	—	—	—
	b. *CALCUTTA*. Signature Cyril Gwyther.	—	—	—
	c. *CALCUTTA*. Signature H. Denning.	—	—	—
	s. Specimen. *CALCUTTA*. 22.4.1899.	—	—	—

1917-1930 Issue

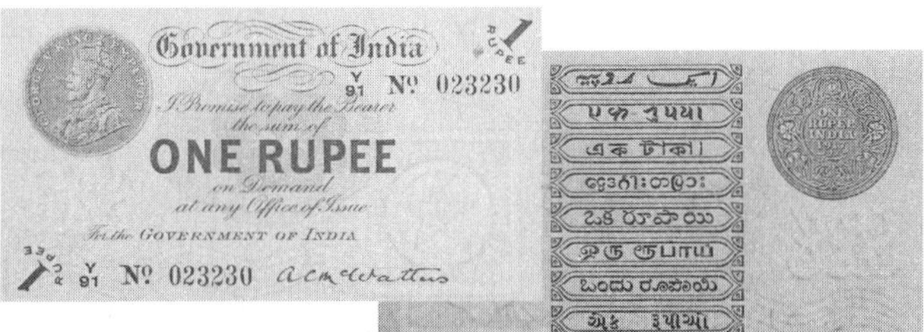

1	1 Rupee	VG	VF	UNC
	1917. Black on red underprint. Coin depicting King George V at upper left. With or without perforation on left border. Also isssued in booklets of 25 notes.			
	a. Watermark: Rayed star in plain field at right. Signature M. M. S. Gubbay.	250	500	1,250
	b. Watermark: Rayed star in plain field at right. Signature A. C. McWatters.	250	500	1,250
	c. Watermark: Rayed star in plain field at right. Signature H. Denning.	350	600	1,500
	d. Watermark: Rayed star in square at right. Smaller letters in last line (Gujarati) on back. Signature H. Denning.	250	500	1,250
	e. Watermark: Rayed star in square at right. Larger letters in last line on back. Signature A. C. McWatters.	250	500	1,250
	f. Watermark: Rayed star in square at right. Larger letters in last line on back. Signature H. Denning.	250	500	1,250
	g. Watermark: Rayed star in square. Signature M. M. S. Gubbay.	250	500	1,250

First issued with prefix letters: A for Cawnpore, B for Bombay, C for Calcutta, K for Karachi, L for Lahore, M for Madras, R for Ragoon. Later universalized and other prefixes used.

1A	1 Rupee	VG	VF	UNC
	1920. Light green. King George V in oval.			
	s. Specimen.	—	—	5,000

2	2 Rupees 8 Annas	VG	VF	UNC
	ND (1917). Black on green and red-brown underprint. King George V in octagon at upper left. Signature M. M. S. Gubbay.			
	a. Issued note.	1,250	3,750	10,000
	s1. Specimen.	—	—	—

First issued with prefix letter A for Cawnpore, B for Bombay, C for Calcutta, K for Karachi, L for Lahore, M for Madras, R for Ragoon.

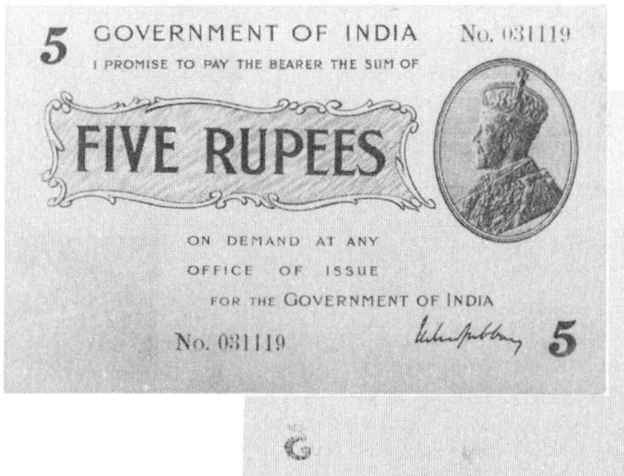

3	5 Rupees	VG	VF	UNC
	ND. Oval portrait of King George V at upper right. Signature M. M. S. Gubbay. Back: Retrograge 5 at lower left.			
	a. Color trial. Green and brown.	—	—	—
	b. Color trial. Green.	—	—	—
	c. Color trial. Light Brown.	—	—	—
	d. Color trial. Purple.	—	—	—
	e. Color trial. Green and rust.	—	—	—
	f. Color trial. Red.	—	—	—
	g. Color trial. Dark Green.	—	—	—
	h. Color trial. Magenta.	—	—	—

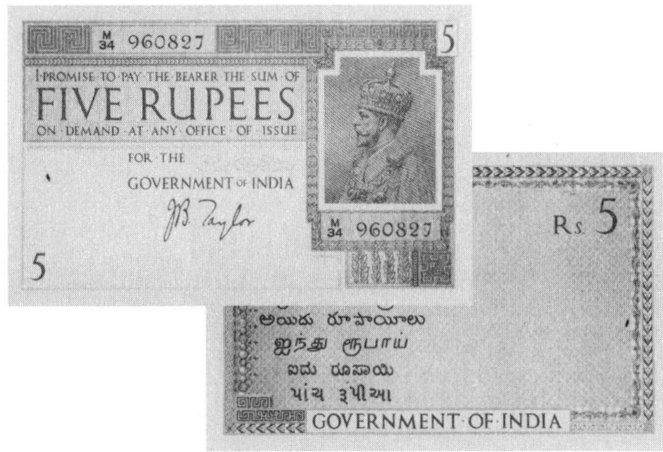

4	5 Rupees	VG	VF	UNC
	ND. Brown-violet, green and light brown. King George V at upper right.			
	a. Signature H. Denning. Watermark with wavy lines.	150	250	600
	b. Signature H. Denning. Watremark without wavy lines	150	250	600
	c. Signature J. B. Taylor. Watermark without wavy lines.	150	250	600

5	10 Rupees	VG	VF	UNC
	ND. Blue and brown. King George V at upper right. Serial # at upper left and lower right.			
	a. Signature A. C. McWatters.	300	400	1,200
	b. Signature H. Denning.	300	400	1,200

6	10 Rupees	VG	VF	UNC
	ND. Green and brown King George V at upper right. Similar to #5 but serial # at lower left and upper right. Signature H. Denning.			
	a. Issued note.	300	400	1,200
	s. Specimen. Rare.	—	—	—

Also souvenier gifted for inauguration of Security Printing Press, Nasik.

7	10 Rupees	VG	VF	UNC
	ND. Dark blue on gray and purple underprint. King George V at right.			
	a. Signature H. Denning.	200	250	1,000
	b. Signature J. B. Taylor.	200	250	1,000
	s. Specimen. Unique.	—	—	—

8	50 Rupees	VG	VF	UNC
	ND. Coin depicting King George V at upper right. *CAWNPORE* without signature. Uniface. Perforated: *SPECIMEN*.			
	s1. Blue, green and brown.	—	—	30,000
	s2. Brown, red and yellow.	—	—	30,000
	s3. Green, brown and blue. Without circle of issue. Unique.	—	—	—

9	50 Rupees	VG	VF	UNC
	ND (1930). Lilac and brown. King George V in oval at right.			
	a. *BOMBAY.* Signature H. Denning.	6,000	7,000	20,000
	b. *BOMBAY.* Signature J. B. Taylor.	6,000	7,000	20,000
	c. *CALCUTTA.* Signature H. Denning.	6,000	7,000	20,000
	d. *CALCUTTA.* Signature J. B. Taylor.	6,000	7,000	20,000
	e. *CAWNPORE.* Signature H. Denning.	6,000	7,000	20,000
	f. *CAWNPORE.* Signature J. B. Taylor.	6,000	7,000	20,000
	g. *KARACHI.* Signature H. Denning.	6,000	7,000	20,000
	h. *KARACHI.* Signature J. B. Taylor.	6,000	7,000	20,000
	i. *LAHORE.* Signature H. Denning.	6,000	7,000	20,000
	j. *LAHORE.* Signature J. B. Taylor.	6,000	7,000	20,000
	k. *MADRAS.* Signature H. Denning.	6,000	7,000	20,000
	l. *MADRAS.* Signature J. B. Taylor.	6,000	7,000	20,000
	m. Dark green color trial. Signature H. Denning. Without circle of issue. Unique.	—	—	—

Note: For similar 50 Rupees with *RANGOON,* see Burma.

10	100 Rupees	VG	VF	UNC
	Violet and green. Oval portrait of King George V at upper right.			
	a. Small *BOMBAY* in black. Signature H. Denning.	1,500	2,000	5,000
	b. Small *BOMBAY* in green. Signature H. Denning.	1,500	2,000	5,000
	c. Large (13mm) *BOMBAY* in green. Signature H. Denning.	1,500	2,000	5,000
	d. Large (13mm) *BOMBAY* in green. Signature J. B. Taylor.	1,500	2,000	5,000
	e. Large *BOMBAY* in green, prefix letter: T. Signature J. W. Kelly.	1,500	2,000	5,000
	f. Small *CALCUTTA* in black. Signature H. Denning.	1,500	2,000	5,000
	g. Small *CALCUTTA* in green. Signature H. Denning.	1,500	2,000	5,000
	h. Large *CALCUTTA* in green, prefix letter: T. Signature J. W. Kelly.	900	2,500	6,000
	i. Small *CAWNPORE* in green. Signature H. Denning.	900	2,500	6,000
	i. Large *CALCUTTA* in green. Signature J. B. Taylor.	900	2,500	6,000
	j. Large *CALCUTTA* in green, prefix letter: T. Signature J. B. Taylor.	900	2,500	6,000
	j. Large *CAWNPORE* in green. Signature J. B. Taylor.	900	2,500	6,000
	k. Large *CAWNPORE* in green, prefix letter: T. Signature J. W. Kelly.	900	2,500	6,000
	l. Large or small *KARACHI* in green. Signature H. Denning.	900	2,500	6,000
	m. Large *LAHORE* in green. Signature H. Denning.	900	2,500	6,000
	n. Large *LAHORE* in green. Signature J. B. Taylor.	900	2,500	6,000
	o. Large *LAHORE* in green, prefix letter: *T.* Signature J. W. Kelly.	900	2,500	6,000
	p. Small *MADRAS* in green. Signature H. Denning.	900	2,500	6,000
	q. Large *MADRAS* in green. Signature J. B. Taylor.	900	2,500	6,000
	r. Large *MADRAS* in green, prefix letter: *T.* Signature J. W. Kelly.	900	2,500	6,000

Note: For similar 100 Rupees with *RANGOON,* see Burma.

Note: Letter *T* may have been used officially for "thinner paper" as all notes w/*T* prefix are on thinner stock.

Note: Notes with small black city name only have wavy lines in the border of the watermark.

11	500 Rupees	VG	VF	UNC
	ND (1928). Greenish brown. Signature J. B. Taylor. Rare.	—	—	—

12	1000 Rupees	VG	VF	UNC
	ND (1928). Violet and green. Oval portrait of King George V in sprays at right. Back: Farmer plowing with oxen at center.			
	a. *BOMBAY.* Signature J. B. Taylor.	3,000	10,000	30,000
	b. *CALCUTTA.* Signature J. B. Taylor.	3,000	10,000	30,000
	c. *CALCUTTA.* Signature J. W. Kelly.	3,000	10,000	30,000
	d. *LAHORE.* Signature J. B. Taylor.	3,000	10,000	30,000
	e. *BOMBAY.* Signature J. W. Kelly.	3,000	10,000	30,000

13	10,000 Rupees	VG	VF	UNC
	ND (1928). Green and brown. Oval portrait of King George V at center, watermark at left and right.			
	a. *BOMBAY.* Signature J. B. Taylor. Rare.	—	—	—
	b. *CALCUTTA.* Signature J. B. Taylor. Rare.	—	—	—
	c. *KARACHI.* Signature J. W. Kelly. Rare.	—	—	—
	s. Specimen.	—	—	—

1928-1935 Issue

14	1 Rupee	VG	VF	UNC
	1935. Green-blue. Coin depicting King George V at right. Back: Reverse of coin with date. With or without perforation on left edge. Those with perforations were issued in booklets of 25 notes.			
	a. Watermark: portrait. Signature J. W. Kelly.	35.00	130	325
	b. Without portrait watermark. Signature J. W. Kelly.	45.00	180	450

15	5 Rupees	VG	VF	UNC
	ND (1928-1935). Brown-violet and light brown. Oval portrait King George V at right.			
	a. Signature J. B. Taylor.	85.00	350	1,000
	b. Signature J. W. Kelly.	85.00	350	1,000

16	10 Rupees	VG	VF	UNC
	ND. Blue or dark blue. Palm tree, lake and mountains at center. Back: Elephants.			
	a. Signature J. B. Taylor.	100	450	1,200
	b. Signature J. W. Kelly.	100	450	1,200

Reserve Bank of India

1937 Issue

#17-19 without place names.

17	2 Rupees	VG	VF	UNC
	ND. Lilac and Multicolor. King George VI at right.			
	a. Black serial #. Signature J. B. Taylor (1937).	14.00	60.00	180
	b. Black serial #. Signature C. D. Deshmukh (1943).	15.00	65.00	200
	c. Red serial #. Signature C. D. Deshmukh (1943).	60.00	250	700

18	5 Rupees	VG	VF	UNC
	ND. Brown and green. Oval portrait King George VI at right.			
	a. Signature J. B. Taylor (1937).	22.50	100	250
	b. Signature C. D. Deshmukh (1943).	22.50	100	250

19	10 Rupees	VG	VF	UNC
	ND. Blue-violet and olive. George VI at right. Palm tree, lake and mountain at center. Back: Elephants at center.			
	a. Signature J. B. Taylor (1937).	30.00	135	400
	b. Signature C. D. Deshmukh (1943).	30.00	135	400

#	Description	VG	VF	UNC
20	**100 Rupees** ND. Dark green and lilac. King George VI at right. Back: Tiger at center. Watermark: King George VI.			
	a. *BOMBAY.* Watermark: Profile. Signature J. B. Taylor (1937).	250	800	2,000
	b. *BOMBAY.* Watermark: Profile. Signature C. D. Deshmukh (1943).	250	800	2,000
	c. *BOMBAY.* Watermark: Facing portrait. Signature C. D. Deshmukh (1943).	325	1,000	2,500
	d. *CALCUTTA.* Watermark: Profile. Signature J. B. Taylor (1937).	250	800	2,000
	e. *CALCUTTA.* Watermark: Profile. Signature C. D. Deshmukh (1943).	250	800	2,000
	f. *CALCUTTA.* Watermark: Facing portrait. Signature C. D. Deshmukh (1943).	325	1,000	2,500
	g. *CAWNPORE.* Watermark: Profile. Signature J. B. Taylor (1937).	250	800	2,000
	h. *CAWNPORE.* Watermark: Profile. Signature C. D. Deshmukh (1943).	250	800	2,000
	i. *KANPUR (Cawnpore).* Watermark: Facing portrait. Signature C. D. Deshmukh (1943).	550	1,750	—
	j. *DELHI.* Watermark: Profile. Signature C. D. Deshmukh (1943).	375	1,200	3,000
	k. *KARACHI.* watermark: Profile. Signature C. D. Deshmukh (1943).	250	800	2,000
	l. *LAHORE.* Watermark: Profile. Signature J. B. Taylor (1937).	250	800	2,000
	m. *LAHORE.* watermark: Profile. Signature C. D. Deshmukh (1943).	250	800	2,000
	n. *MADRAS.* watermark: Profile. Signature J. B. Taylor (1937).	250	800	2,000
	o. *MADRAS.* watermark: Profile. Signature C. D. Deshmukh (1943).	250	800	2,000
	p. *MADRAS.* watermark: Facing. Signature C. D. Deshmukh (1943).	325	1,000	2,500
	q. *KARACHI.* watermark: Profile. Signature J. B. Taylor.	250	800	2,000

#	Description	VG	VF	UNC
21	**1000 Rupees** ND (1937). Lilac, violet and green. King George VI at right. Signature J.B. Taylor. Back: Mountain scene. Watermark: King George VI.			
	a. *BOMBAY.*	750	2,400	6,000
	b. *CALCUTTA.*	750	2,400	6,000
	c. *CAWNPORE.*	750	2,400	6,000
	d. *KARACHI.*	750	2,400	6,000
	e. *LAHORE.*	750	2,400	6,000
	f. *MADRAS.*	750	2,400	6,000

#	Description	VG	VF	UNC
22	**10,000 Rupees** ND (1938). King George VI at right. Rare.	—	—	—

ND 1943 Issue

#	Description	VG	VF	UNC
23	**5 Rupees** ND (1943). Green and multicolor. George VI facing at right. Signature C.D. Deshmukh. Back: Antelope.			
	a. Black serial #.	50.00	200	500
	b. Red serial #.	125	500	1,400
24	**10 Rupees** ND (1943). Purple and multicolor. George VI facing at right. Signature C.D. Deshmukh. Back: Dhow.	10.00	45.00	120

Government of India (resumed)

1940 Issue

#	Description	VG	VF	UNC
25	**1 Rupee** 1940. Blue-gray and multicolor. Dated coin depicting King George VI at right. Signature C. E. Jones.			
	a. Black serial #.	15.00	20.00	75.00
	b. Red serial #.	400	600	1,200
	c. Black serial #, letter A.	400	600	1,200
	d. Green serial #, letter A.	15.00	20.00	75.00

REPUBLIC OF INDIA

SIGNATURE VARIETIES

GOVERNORS, RESERVE BANK OF INDIA (all except 1 Rupee notes)

#	Governor	Signature
71	Sir C.D. Deshmukh August 1943 - June 1949	C.D. Deshmukh
72	Sir B. Rama Rue July 1949 - 1957	B Rama Rau
73	K. G. Ambegoankar January 1957 - February 1957	
74	H. V. R. Iengar March 1957 - February 1962	
75	P. C. Bhattacharyya March 1962 - June 1967	

Reserve Bank of India

First Series

Error singular Hindi = *RUPAYA*

Corrected plural Hindi = *RUPAYE*

VARIETIES: #27-28, 33, 38, 42, 46, 48 and 50 have large headings in Hindi expressing the value incorrectly in the singular form as: *Rupaya.* Note: For similar notes but in different colors, please see the Haj Pilgrim or the Persian Gulf listings at the end of this country listing.

#	Description	VG	VF	UNC
27	**2 Rupees** ND. Red-brown on violet and green underprint. Hindi numeral *2* at upper right. Signature 72. Asoka column at right. Large letters in underprint beneath serial number. Back: Tiger head at left. 8 value text lines. Watermark: Asoka column.	25.00	75.00	150
28	**2 Rupees** ND. Red-brown on violet and green underprint. English *2* at upper left and right. Redesigned panels. Asoka column at right. Large letters in underprint beneath serial number. Signature 72. Back: 7 value text lines; third line 18mm long. Watermark: Asoka column.	1.50	6.00	16.00

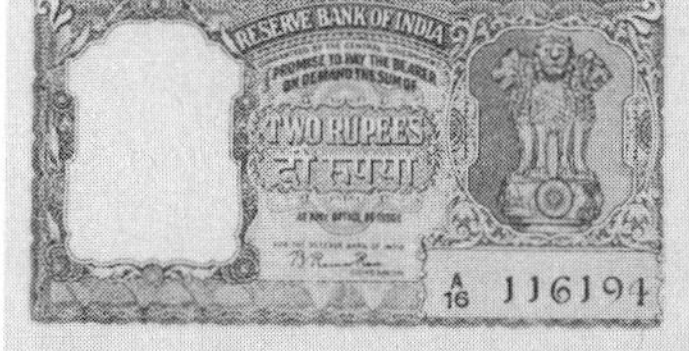

29 2 Rupees

ND. Red-brown on violet and green underprint. Value in English and corrected Hindi on both sides. Asoka column at right. Large letters in underprint beneath serial number. Back: Tiger head at left looking to left, third value text line 24mm long. Watermark: Asoka column.

	VG	VF	UNC
a. Signature 72.	3.00	12.00	40.00
b. Signature 74.	1.25	5.00	18.00

30 2 Rupees

ND. Red-brown on green underprint. Value in English and corrected Hindi. Signature 75. Back: Tiger head at left looking to right, with 13 value text lines at center.

VG	VF	UNC
2.25	9.00	30.00

31 2 Rupees

ND. Olive on tan underprint. Value in English and corrected Hindi. Signature 75. Back: Tiger head at left looking to right, with 13 value text lines at center. Watermark: Asoka column.

VG	VF	UNC
2.00	8.00	25.00

32 5 Rupees

ND. Green on brown underprint. English value only on face, serial number at center. Signature 72. Back: *Rs. 5* and antelope. Watermark: Asoka column.

VG	VF	UNC
7.00	30.00	125

33 5 Rupees

ND. Value in English and error Hindi , serial number at right. Signature 72. Back: 8 value lines; fourth line 21mm long. Watermark: Asoka column.

VG	VF	UNC
2.50	10.00	35.00

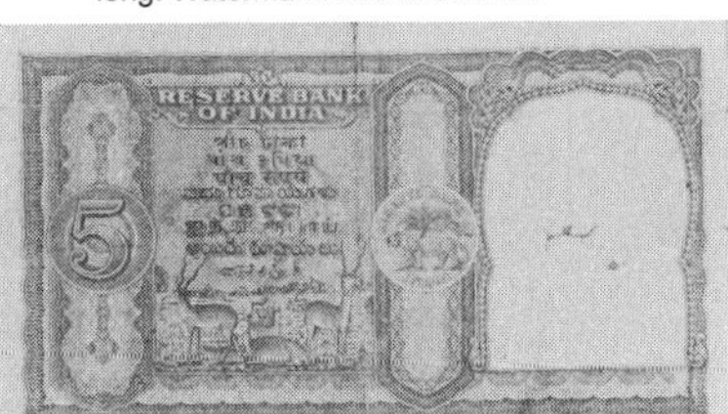

34 5 Rupees

ND. Hindi corrected. Signature 72. Back: Fourth value text line 26mm long. Watermark: Asoka column.

VG	VF	UNC
8.00	35.00	150

35 5 Rupees

ND. Green on brown underprint. Hindi corrected, redesigned panels at left and right. Asoka columns at right. Large letters in underprint beneath serial number. Watermark: Asoka column.

	VG	VF	UNC
a. Without letter. Signature 74.	2.50	10.00	35.00
b. Letter A. Signature 74.	1.50	6.00	20.00

Note: For similar note but in orange, see #R2 (Persian Gulf listings in the Specialized edition).

37 10 Rupees

ND. Purple on multicolor underprint. English value. Asoka column at right. Large letters in underprint beneath serial number. Back: *Rs. 10* at lower center, 1 serial number. English in both lower corners, dhow at center. Watermark: Asoka column.

	VG	VF	UNC
a. Signature 71.	50.00	225	750
b. Signature 72.	8.00	30.00	125

38 10 Rupees

ND. Value in English and error Hindi. Asoka column at right. Large letters in underprint beneath serial number. 2 serial numbers. Signature 72. Back: Third value text line 24mm long. Watermark: Asoka column.

VG	VF	UNC
1.50	6.00	20.00

39 10 Rupees

ND. Purple on multicolor underprint. Hindi corrected. Asoka column at right. Large letters in underprint beneath serial number. Back: Third value text line 29mm long. Watermark: Asoka column.

	VG	VF	UNC
a. Without letter. Signature 72.	2.25	9.00	30.00
b. Without letter. Signature 74.	2.25	9.00	30.00
c. Letter A. Signature 74.	1.25	5.00	18.00

Note: For similar note but in red, see #R3 (Persian Gulf listings in the Specialized edition); in blue, see #R5 (Haj Pilgrim listings in the Specialized edition).

40 10 Rupees

ND. Green on brown underprint. Hindi corrected. Asoka column at right. Large letters in underprint beneath serial number. Title: *GOVERNOR* centered. Back: Thirteen value text lines. Watermark: Asoka column.

	VG	VF	UNC
a. Letter A. Signature 75.	1.75	7.00	25.00
b. Letter B. Signature 75.	1.25	4.50	15.00

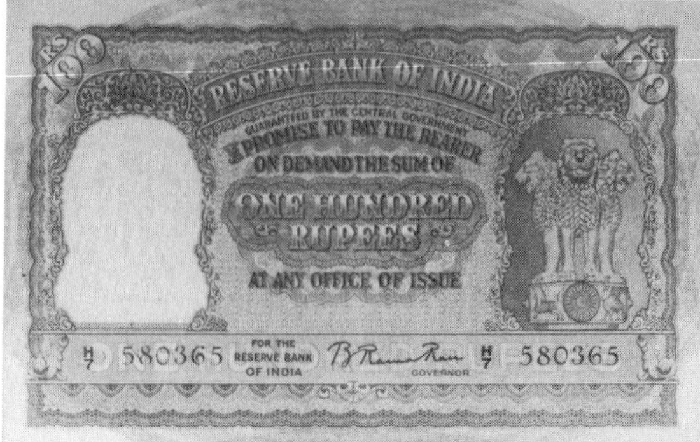

41 100 Rupees

ND. Blue on multicolor underprint. English value. Asoka column at right. Large letters in overprint beneath serial number. Back: Two elephants at center, 8 value text lines below and bank emblem at left. Watermark: Asoka column.

	VG	VF	UNC
a. Dark blue. Signature 72.	35.00	140	375
b. Light blue. Signature 72.	35.00	140	375

42 100 Rupees

ND. Purplish-blue on multicolor underprint. Value in English and error Hindi. Asoka column at right. Large letters in underprint beneath serial number. Back: Value in English and error Hindi. 7 value text lines; third 27mm long. Watermark: Asoka column.

	VG	VF	UNC
a. Black serial #. Signature 72.	30.00	120	325
b. Red serial #. Signature 72.	30.00	120	325

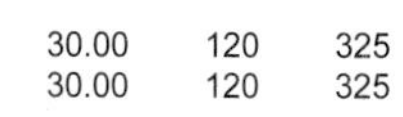

43 100 Rupees

ND. Purplish blue on multicolor underprint. Hindi corrected. Asoka column at right. Large letters in underprint beneath serial number. Back: Third value text line 40mm long. Watermark: Asoka column.

	VG	VF	UNC
a. Without letter, thin paper. Signature 72.	30.00	120	325
b. Without letter, thin paper. Signature 74.	25.00	100	275
c. Without letter, thick paper. Signature 74.	35.00	140	375

Note: For similar note but in green, see #R4 (Persian Gulf listings in the Specialized volume); in red, see #R6 (Haj Pilgrim listings in the Specialized volume).

44 100 Rupees

ND. Purple and multicolor. Heading in rectangle at top, serial numberat upper left and lower right. Asoka column at right. Large letters in underprint beneath serial number. Signature 74. Title: *GOVERNOR* at center right Back: Dam at center with 13 value text lines at left. Watermark: Asoka column.

VG	VF	UNC
20.00	90.00	250

48 5000 Rupees

ND. Green, violet and brown. Asoka column at left. Value in English and error Hindi. Back: Gateway of India. Value in English and error Hindi.

	VG	VF	UNC
a. *BOMBAY.* Signature 72. Rare.	—	30,000	50,000
b. *CALCUTTA.* Signature 72. Rare.	—	30,000	50,000
c. *DELHI.* Signature 72. Rare.	—	30,000	50,000

49 5000 Rupees

ND. Green, violet and brown. Value in English. Hindi corrected. Back: Gateway of India.

	VG	VF	UNC
a. *BOMBAY.* Signature 74.	—	30,000	50,000
b. *MADRAS.* Signature 74.	—	30,000	50,000
s. As a. Specimen. Red overprint: *SPECIMEN.*	—	—	17,500

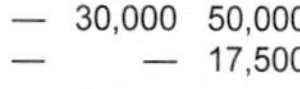

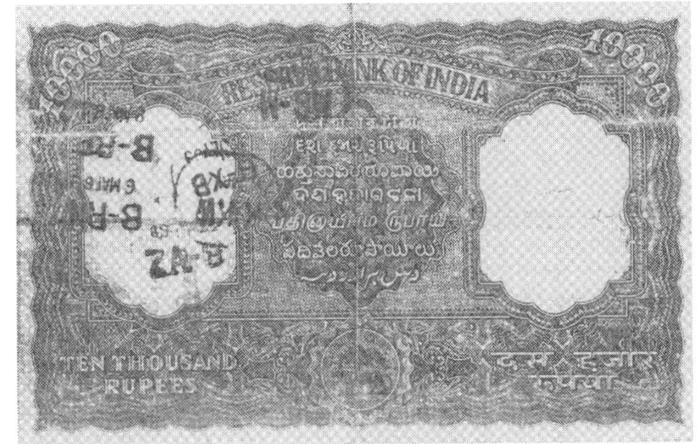

50 10,000 Rupees | VG | VF | UNC
ND. Blue, violet and brown. Asoka column at center. Value in English and error Hindi. Back: Value in English and error Hindi.

	VG	VF	UNC
a. *BOMBAY.* Signature 72.	—	35,000	60,000
b. *CALCUTTA.* Signature 72.	—	35,000	60,000
s. As B. Specimen. Signature 72.	—	—	—

50A 10,000 Rupees | Good | Fine | XF
ND. Asoka column at center. Value in English. Hindi corrected. Back: Value in English. Hindi corrected.

	Good	Fine	XF
a. *BOMBAY.* Signature 74.	35,000	45,000	60,000
b. *MADRAS.* Signature 74.	35,000	45,000	60,000
c. *NEW DELHI.* Signature 74.	35,000	45,000	60,000
d. *BOMBAY.* Signature 76.	35,000	45,000	60,000

Government of India

SIGNATURE VARIETIES
SECRETARIES, MINISTRY OF FINANCE (1 Rupee notes only)

K. R. K. Menon, 1949	A. K. Roy, 1957
K. G. Ambegaonkar, 1949-1951	L. K. Jha, 1957-1963
H. M. Patel, 1951-1957	

Note: The sign. H.M. Patel is often misread as "Mehta". There was never any such individual serving as Secretary. Also, do not confuse H.M. Patel with I.G. Patel who served later.

1949-1951 Issue

71 1 Rupee | VG | VF | UNC
ND (1949-1950). Green-gray and multicolor. Asoka column at right. Without coin design. Back: Without coin design.

	VG	VF	UNC
a. Signature K. R. K. Menon. (1949).	0.25	2.50	8.00
b. Signature K. G. Ambegaonkar. (1949-1950).	0.25	2.50	8.00

72 1 Rupee | VG | VF | UNC
1951. Green-gray and multicolor. Coin with Asoka column at right. Signature K. G. Ambegaonkar. Back: Reverse of coin dated 1951. | 0.25 | 2.00 | 6.50

73 1 Rupee | VG | VF | UNC
ND (- old date 1951). Violet and multicolor. Coin with asoka column at right. Signature K. G. Ambegaonkar. Back: Reverse of coin dated 1951. | 0.25 | 2.00 | 6.50

74 1 Rupee | VG | VF | UNC
ND (- old date 1951). Coin with Asoka column at right. Signature K. G. Ambegaonkar. Back: Reverse of coin dated 1951. Like #73 except different rendition of all value lines on back.

	VG	VF	UNC
a. Without letter. Signature H. M. Patel. (1956).	0.20	1.00	8.00
b. Letter A. Signature H. M. Patel.	0.20	1.00	8.00

1957; 1963 Issue

75 1 Rupee | VG | VF | UNC
1957. Violet on multicolor underprint. Redesigned coin with Asoka column at right. Back: Coin dated 1957 and *100 Naye Paise* in Hindi, 7 value text lines. Watermark: Asoka column.

	VG	VF	UNC
a. Letter A. Signature H. M. Patel with signature title: *SECRETARY...* (1957).	0.75	2.00	10.00
b. Letter A. Signature H. M. Patel with signature title: *PRINCIPAL SECRETARY...* 1957.	1.00	3.00	12.00
c. Letter B. Signature A. K. Roy. 1957.	0.50	1.00	4.00
d. Letter B. Signature L. K. Jha. 1957.	20.00	50.00	125
e. Letter C. Signature L. K. Jha. 1957.	—	0.60	3.00
f. Letter D. Signature L. K. Jha. 1957.	—	0.60	3.00

Note: For similar note but in red, see #R1 (Persian Gulf listings in the Specialized edition).

PERSIAN GULF

Reserve Bank of India

ND Issue

R2 5 Rupees | VG | VF | UNC
ND. Orange. Redesigned panels at left and right. Signature H. V. R. Iengar. | 400 | 1,000 | 2,500

R3 10 Rupees | VG | VF | UNC
ND. Red. Hindi corrected. Letter A. Signature H. V. R. Iengar. | 240 | 600 | 1,750

		VG	VF	UNC
R4	**100 Rupees** ND. Green. Hindi corrected. Signature H. V. R. lengar.	1,200	2,750	7,000

Government of India

ND Issue

		VG	VF	UNC
R1	**1 Rupee** ND. Red. Redesigned coin with Asoka column at right. Signature A. K. Roy; left K. Jha or H. V. R. lengar.	80.00	200	550

HAJ PILGRIM

Reserve Bank of India

(ND) Issue

		VG	VF	UNC
R5	**10 Rupees** ND. Blue. Asoka column at right. Letters *HA* near serial number, and *HAJ* at left and right of bank title at top. Like # 39c.	1,250	2,500	5,000

INDONESIA

The Republic of Indonesia, the world's largest archipelago, extends for more than 4,827 km. along the equator from the mainland of southeast Asia to Australia. The 13,667 islands comprising the archipelago have a combined area of 1,919,440 sq. km. and a population of 237.5 million, including East Timor. Capital: Jakarta. Petroleum, timber, rubber and coffee are exported.The Dutch began to colonize Indonesia in the early 17th century; the islands were occupied by Japan from 1942 to 1945. Indonesia declared its independence after Japan's surrender, but it required four years of intermittent negotiations, recurring hostilities, and UN mediation before the Netherlands agreed to relinquish its colony. Indonesia is the world's largest archipelagic state and home to the world's largest Muslim population. Current issues include: alleviating poverty, preventing terrorism, consolidating democracy after four decades of authoritarianism, implementing financial sector reforms, stemming corruption, holding the military and police accountable for human rights violations, and controlling avian influenza. In 2005, Indonesia reached a historic peace agreement with armed separatists in Aceh, which led to democratic elections in December 2006. Indonesia continues to face a low intensity separatist movement in Papua.

MONETARY SYSTEM:

1 Gulden = 100 Cents to 1948
1 Rupiah = 100 Sen, 1945-

REPUBLIC

Republik Indonesia

1945 Issue

#1-12 formerly listed here have been moved to listings under the Netherlands Indies. #13-29 many paper and printing varieties.

		VG	VF	UNC
13	**1 Sen** 17.10.1945. Green. Dagger in numeral at left.	0.25	0.75	2.00

		VG	VF	UNC
14	**5 Sen** 17.10.1945. Gray-violet.	0.25	0.75	2.00

		VG	VF	UNC
15	**10 Sen** 17.10.1945. Brown on tan underprint.			
	a. Printing size 94 x 43mm.	0.25	1.50	3.50
	b. Printing size 100 x 44mm.	0.25	1.00	3.00

		VG	VF	UNC
16	**1/2 Rupiah** 17.10.1945. Green on pale peach underprint.	2.00	5.00	14.00

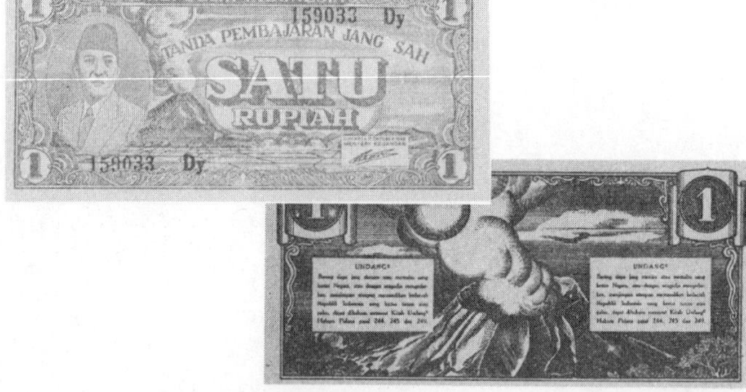

#	Denomination	VG	VF	UNC
17	**1 Rupiah** 17.10.1945. Gray-blue to dark blue. Sukarno at left. Back: Smoking volcano.			
	a. Serial # and letters.	0.50	2.00	6.00
	b. Letters only.	0.50	2.00	6.00

#	Denomination	VG	VF	UNC
18	**5 Rupiah** 17.10.1945. Green. Sukarno at left.	1.00	3.00	10.00

#	Denomination	VG	VF	UNC
19	**10 Rupiah** 17.10.1945. Blue. Volcano at right. Sukarno at left.	2.00	5.00	12.00

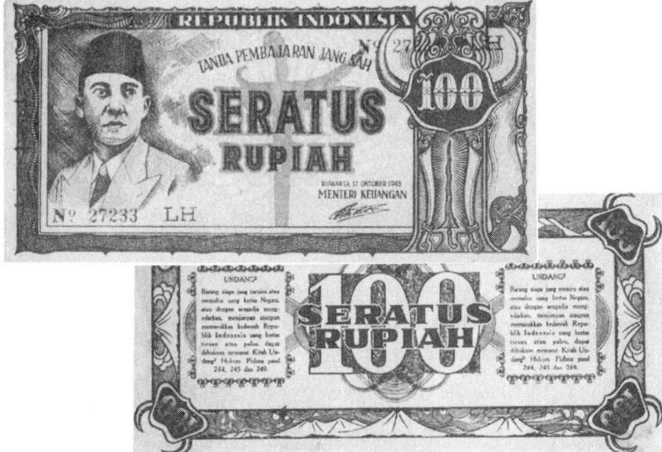

#	Denomination	VG	VF	UNC
20	**100 Rupiah** 17.10.1945. Green-blue. Sukarno at left. Back: Denomination at center.	7.50	20.00	60.00

1947 First Issue

#	Denomination	VG	VF	UNC
21	**5 Rupiah** 1.1.1947. Green. Sukarno at left, like #18.	2.00	5.00	10.00
22	**10 Rupiah** 1.1.1947. Blue. Volcano at right. Sukaro at left, like #19.	4.00	15.00	40.00

#	Denomination	VG	VF	UNC
23	**25 Rupiah** 1.1.1947. Brown. Portrait Sukarno at right, mountain scene at left center.	3.00	10.00	30.00

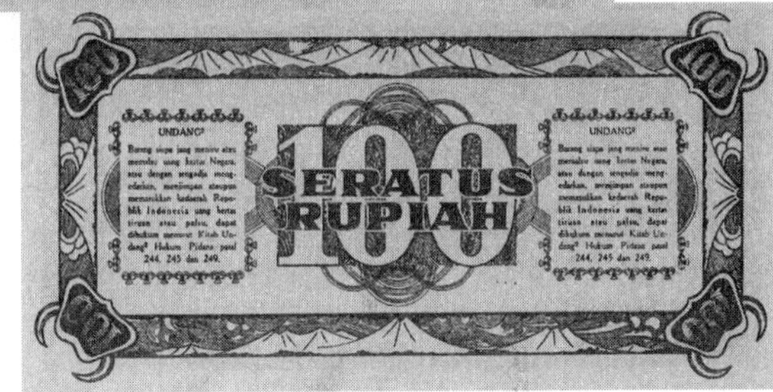

#	Denomination	VG	VF	UNC
24	**100 Rupiah** 1.1.1947. Green-blue. Sukarno at left. Back: Denomination at center.			
	a. With underprint.	12.00	30.00	80.00
	b. Without underprint.	12.00	30.00	75.00

1947 Second Issue

#	Denomination	VG	VF	UNC
25	**1/2 Rupiah** 26.7.1947. Red.	3.00	8.00	25.00

#	Denomination	VG	VF	UNC
26	**2 1/2 Rupiah** 26.7.1947. Brown.	3.00	12.00	30.00

Note: What purports to be #26 in red is a modern fantasy.

		VG	VF	UNC
27	**25 Rupiah** 26.7.1947. Dark blue on green underprint. Portrait Sukarno at rihgt mountain scene at left center. Like #23.	2.00	5.00	14.00

		VG	VF	UNC
28	**50 Rupiah** 26.7.1947. Brown on orange underprint. Portrait Sukarno at left. Workers in rubber plantation at right.	25.00	75.00	200

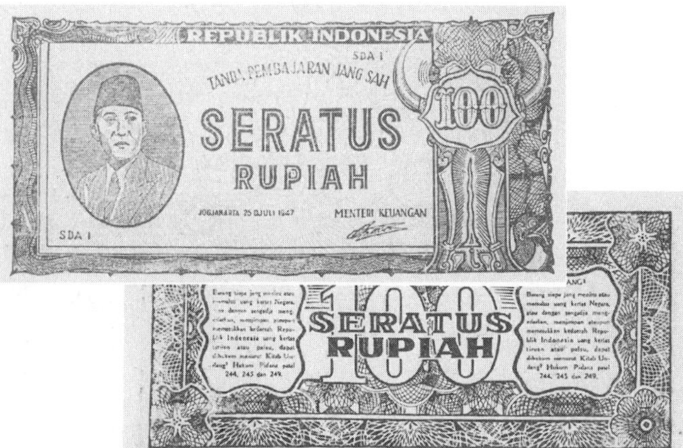

		VG	VF	UNC
29	**100 Rupiah** 26.7.1947. Brown on brown-orange or pink underprint. Portrait Sukarno at left. Block letters *SDA 1* part of plate.	1.50	6.00	17.50

		VG	VF	UNC
29A	**100 Rupiah** 26.7.1947. Green and brown. Portrait Sukarno at left. Tobacco field and mountain at right.	15.00	50.00	200

		VG	VF	UNC
30	**250 Rupiah** 26.7.1947. Brown on orange underprint. Portrait Sukarno at left. Peasant at right.			
	a. Serial # printed.	10.00	40.00	150
	b. Serial # typed.	25.00	75.00	250

1947 Third Issue

		VG	VF	UNC
31	**10 Sen** 1.12.1947. Dark green on gray underprint. Back: Palms at center.	0.25	1.00	3.00
32	**25 Sen** 1.12.1947. Brown. Back: Palms at center.	0.25	1.25	3.50

1948 Issue

		VG	VF	UNC
33	**40 Rupiah** 23.8.1948. Gray and lilac. Sukarno at left, female weaver at right.	10.00	25.00	75.00

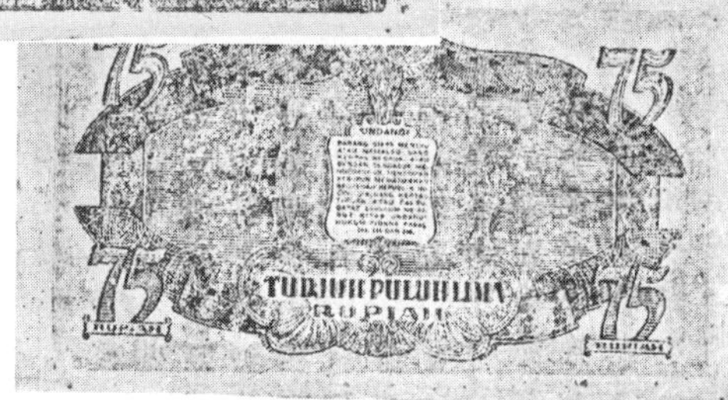

		VG	VF	UNC
33A	**75 Rupiah** 23.8.1948. Brown. Portrait Sukarno at left, 2 smiths at right.	25.00	75.00	250
34	**100 Rupiah** 23.8.1948. Dark brown. Portrait Sukarno at left. Tobacco field and mountain at right.	20.00	50.00	200

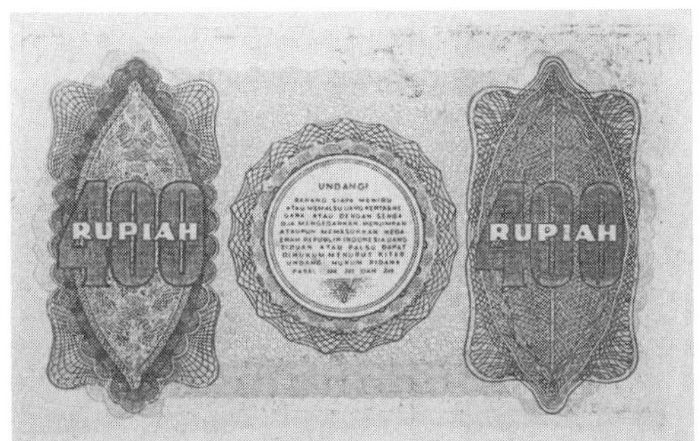

		VG	VF	UNC
35	**400 Rupiah**			
	23.8.1948. Portrait Sukarno at left. Sugar plantation at right.			
	a. Serial # printed.	2.00	5.00	12.00
	b. Serial # typed.	30.00	85.00	200

Note: Many examples of #35a in high grade are believed to be contemporary counterfeits.

		VG	VF	UNC
35A	**600 Rupiah**			
	23.8.1948. Orange. Portrait Sukarno at left, ornamental *RI* at right. Uniface proof.	—	—	2,000

1949 Revaluation Issue

#35B-35G prepared in sen and rupiah baru (new cents and rupiah).

		VG	VF	UNC
35B	**10 New Cents**			
	17.8.1949.			
	a. Dark blue. Red signature	7.00	15.00	60.00
	b. Red. Black signature	6.00	15.00	55.00

		VG	VF	UNC
35C	**1/2 New Rupiah**			
	17.8.1949.			
	a. Green. Red signature	5.00	15.00	50.00
	b. Red. Black signature	5.00	15.00	50.00
35D	**1 New Rupiah**	VG	VF	UNC
	17.8.1949.			
	a. Purple. Red signature	8.00	30.00	65.00
	b. Green. Requires confirmation.	—	—	—

		VG	VF	UNC
35E	**10 New Rupiah**			
	17.8.1949. Portrait Sukarno at upper left.			
	a. Black on yellow underprint. Red signature	15.00	50.00	100
	b. Brown on yellow underprint. Black signature.	10.00	40.00	100
35F	**25 New Rupiah**	VG	VF	UNC
	17.8.1949. Requires confirmation.	—	—	—
35G	**100 New Rupiah**	VG	VF	UNC
	17.8.1949. Purple on yellow underprint. Portrait Sukarno at upper left.	20.00	60.00	150

Note: Unfinished notes of the above series exist also.

REPUBLIK INDONESIA SERIKAT

UNITED STATES OF INDONESIA

Treasury

1950 Issue

		VG	VF	UNC
36	**5 Rupiah**			
	1.1.1950. Orange. Portrait Sukarno at right. Back: Paddy field and palms. Printer: TDLR.	1.50	5.00	20.00

		VG	VF	UNC
37	**10 Rupiah**			
	1.1.1950. Purple. Portrait Sukarno at right. Back: Paddy fields and palms. Printer: TDLR.			
	a. Issued note.	2.00	7.50	22.50
	s. Specimen. Red overprint of TDLR oval.	—	—	400

Note: The Javasche Bank notes cut in half (from 5 Gulden) and those of the Republic of Indonesia originate from the currency reform of 1950. The left half of a note was valid for exchange against new notes at 50% of nominal denomination; the right half was also accepted at half its face value for a 3% government bond issue. Verification of any of these pieces in collections is needed.

Republik Indonesia

1951 Issue

		VG	VF	UNC
38	**1 Rupiah**			
	1951. Blue. Beach with palms at left, terraced field at right. Back: Mountain. Printer: SBNC.	0.50	1.50	4.00

		VG	VF	UNC
39	**2 1/2 Rupiah**			
	1951. Orange. Steep coast at left, palm trees at right. Back: Arms at center. Printer: SBNC.	0.50	1.50	4.00

1953 Issue

40	1 Rupiah	VG	VF	UNC
	1953. Blue. Beach with palms at left, terraced field at right. Back: Mountain on back.	0.50	1.00	3.00

41	2 1/2 Rupiah	VG	VF	UNC
	1953. Orange. Steep coast at left, palm trees at right. Back: Arms at center.	0.50	1.75	4.00

Bank Indonesia

1952 Issue

42	5 Rupiah	VG	VF	UNC
	1952. Gray-blue. Portrait A. Kartini at left.	0.75	3.00	6.00

43	10 Rupiah	VG	VF	UNC
	1952. Brown. Statue of a goddess Prajñaparamita at left.			
	a. Printer: Joh. Enschede on face.	1.00	4.00	10.00
	b. Printer: Pertjetakan on back.	1.00	4.00	10.00

44	25 Rupiah	VG	VF	UNC
	1952. Dark blue. Cloth designs at left and right.			
	a. Printer: Joh. Enschede on face.	1.00	6.00	15.00
	b. Printer: Pertjetakan on back.	1.00	6.00	15.00

45	50 Rupiah	VG	VF	UNC
	1952. Green. Stylized trees with bird at left and right.	1.00	6.00	15.00

46	100 Rupiah	VG	VF	UNC
	1952. Brown. Lion at left, portrait Prince Diponegoro at right. Printer: JEZ.	2.00	8.00	20.00

47	500 Rupiah	VG	VF	UNC
	1952. Orange-brown, green and brown. Frieze at center right.	3.00	12.00	30.00

48	1000 Rupiah	VG	VF	UNC
	1952. Green and brown. Woman with ornamented helmet at right.	5.00	17.50	45.00

Note: For #42-#48 w/revolutionary overprint. see Volume 1.

1957 Issue

49	5 Rupiah	VG	VF	UNC
	ND (1957). Green on pink and yellow underprint. Orang-utan at left. Back: Prambanan temple in blue.			
	a. Issued note.	0.25	1.50	5.00
	s. Specimen.	—	—	50.00

49A	10 Rupiah	VG	VF	UNC
	ND (1957). Red-brown and multicolor. Stag at upper left. Back: Longboat.			
	a. Issued note (only in use for three days.)	100	250	500
	s. Specimen.	—	—	750

49B	25 Rupiah	VG	VF	UNC
	ND (1957). Purple and multicolor. Java rhinoceros at upper left. Back: Batak houses at center.			
	a. Issued note. Only in use for three days.	100	250	600
	s. Specimen.	—	—	800

50	50 Rupiah	VG	VF	UNC
	ND (1957). Maroon on green underprint. Crocodile at left. Back: Deli Mosque at upper left and right.			
	a. Issued note.	2.00	7.50	25.00
	s. Specimen.	—	—	100

51	100 Rupiah	VG	VF	UNC
	ND (1957). Gray-blue on pink underprint. Squirrel at left. Back: President's palace across center.			
	a. Issued note.	1.50	5.00	15.00
	s. Specimen.	—	—	150

52	500 Rupiah	VG	VF	UNC
	ND (1957). Brown. Tiger at left. Back: Paddy terraces and buffalos.			
	a. Issued note.	7.50	20.00	50.00
	s. Specimen. Serial # 0000.	—	—	150

53 **1000 Rupiah**

ND (1957). Gray-blue. Elephant at left. Back: Fishing.

	VG	VF	UNC
a. Issued note.	7.50	20.00	50.00
s. Specimen.	—	—	150

54 **2500 Rupiah**

ND (1957). Green. Leguan at left. Back: Village at lakeshore.

	VG	VF	UNC
a. Issued note.	8.00	25.00	65.00
s. Specimen.	—	—	150

54A **5000 Rupiah**

ND. Dark red and multicolor. Wild buffalo at left. Back: Tug boat with ship in harbor. Specimen.

VG	VF	UNC
—	—	5,000

1958 Issue

55 **5 Rupiah**

ND (1958). Green and red-brown. Woman applying wax to cloth (batiking) at left. Back: Indonesian house. Watermark: Buffalo.

VG	VF	UNC
0.10	0.30	0.50

56 **10 Rupiah**

1958. Dark blue and multicolor. Carver at left. Back: Mask at right. Indonesian house. Watermark: Buffalo.

VG	VF	UNC
0.10	0.30	1.00

57 **25 Rupiah**

1958. Green and brown. Woman weaver at left. Back: Indonesian house. Watermark: Buffalo.

VG	VF	UNC
0.25	0.75	2.00

58 **50 Rupiah**

1958. Dark brown. Woman spinner at left. Back: Indonesian house. Watermark: Buffalo.

VG	VF	UNC
0.25	1.00	3.00

59 **100 Rupiah**

1958. Red and red-brown. Worker on rubber plantation at left. Back: Indonesian house. Watermark: Buffalo.

VG	VF	UNC
0.25	0.75	2.50

		VG	VF	UNC
60	**500 Rupiah** 1958. Dark brown and red-brown. Man with coconuts at left. Back: Indonesian house. Watermark: Buffalo.	1.50	5.00	20.00

		VG	VF	UNC
61	**1000 Rupiah** 1958. Red-brown. Man making a silver plate at left. Back: Indonesian house. Watermark: Buffalo.	0.25	1.00	2.50
62	**1000 Rupiah** 1958. Purple and green. Man making a silver plate at left. Back: Indonesian house. Watermark: Buffalo.	0.50	1.50	5.00

		VG	VF	UNC
63	**5000 Rupiah** 1958. Dark green and brown. Woman gathering rice at left. Back: River and rice terraces. Watermark: Buffalo.	2.00	8.00	25.00

		VG	VF	UNC
64	**5000 Rupiah** 1958. Lilac. Woman gathering rice at left. Printed Indonesian arms in watermark area. Back: River and rice terraces. Watermark: Arms at center.	2.00	5.00	10.00

1959 Issue

		VG	VF	UNC
65	**5 Rupiah** 1.1.1959. Blue and yellow. Flowers at center. Back: Sunbirds. Watermark: Arms. Printer: TDLR. UV: center flower fluoresces yellow.	0.10	0.25	0.75

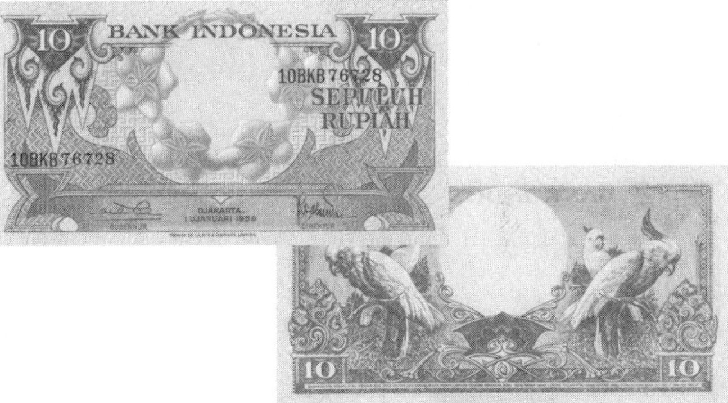

		VG	VF	UNC
66	**10 Rupiah** 1.1.1959. Red-violet on multicolor underprint. Flowers at center. Back: Salmon-crested cockatoos. Watermark: Arms. Printer: TDLR.	0.10	0.25	1.00

		VG	VF	UNC
67	**25 Rupiah** 1.1.1959. Green on multicolor underprint. Water lilies at left. Back: Great egrets. Watermark: Arms. Printer: TDLR.			
	a. Issued note.	0.25	0.50	2.50
	s. Specimen. Serial # 00000.	—	—	—

68	**50 Rupiah**	VG	VF	UNC
	1.1.1959. Dark brown, blue and orange. Sunflower at center. Back: White-bellied fish eagle. Watermark: Arms. Printer: TDLR.			
	a. Issued note.	0.25	1.00	3.50
	s. Specimen. Serial # 000000.	—	—	—

69	**100 Rupiah**	VG	VF	UNC
	1.1.1959. Dark brown and red on multicolor underprint. Giant Rafflessia Patma flowers at center. Back: Rhinoceros hornbills. Watermark: Arms. Printer: TDLR.	0.25	1.00	3.50

70	**500 Rupiah**	VG	VF	UNC
	1.1.1959. Blue on multicolor underprint. Flowers at center. Back: Crested fireback. Watermark: Arms. Printer: TDLR.			
	a. Issued note.	3.00	8.00	20.00
	s. Specimen. Serial # 00000.	—	—	—

71	**1000 Rupiah**	VG	VF	UNC
	1.1.1959. Black-green and lilac on multicolor underprint. Flowers at center. Back: Bird of Paradise. Watermark: Arms. Printer: TDLR.			
	a. Imprint TDLR at bottom center on face.	2.00	5.00	15.00
	b. Without imprint.	0.50	1.50	5.00

Republik Indonesia (resumed)

1954 Issue

72	**1 Rupiah**	VG	VF	UNC
	1954. Blue. Portrait Javanese girl at right. Back: Arms at center.	0.25	0.75	2.00
73	**2 1/2 Rupiah**	VG	VF	UNC
	1954. Red-brown. Portrait old Rotinese man at left. Back: Arms at center.	0.25	0.75	2.00

1956 Issue

74	**1 Rupiah**	VG	VF	UNC
	1956. Blue. Portrait Javanese girl at right. Back: Arms at center.	0.10	0.50	1.00

75	**2 1/2 Rupiah**	VG	VF	UNC
	1956. Red-brown. Portrait old Rotinese man at left. Back: Arms at center.	0.10	0.50	1.25

1960 Issue

76	**1 Rupiah**	VG	VF	UNC
	1960. Dark green on orange underprint. Rice field workers at left. Back: Farm produce.	0.25	0.50	1.25

77	2 1/2 Rupiah	VG	VF	UNC
	1960. Black, dark blue and brown on blue-green underprint. Corn field work at left.	0.25	0.75	1.75

1964 Issue (1960 dated)

82	5 Rupiah	VG	VF	UNC
	1960. Lilac on yellow underprint. President Sukarno at left. Back: Female dancer at right.			
	a. Watermark: Sukarno.	0.25	1.50	5.00
	b. Watermark: Water buffalo.	0.30	0.60	6.00

Bank Indonesia (resumed)

1960 Dated (1964) Issue

83	10 Rupiah	VG	VF	UNC
	1960. Green on light blue underprint. President Sukarno at left. Back: Two female dancers. Watermark: Sukarno.	0.50	2.00	6.50

84	25 Rupiah	VG	VF	UNC
	1960. Green on yellow underprint. President Sukarno at left. Back: Female dancer. Watermark: Sukarno.			
	a. Printer: TDLR. Watermark: Sukarno. 3 Letter varieties.	1.00	4.00	10.00
	b. Printer: Pertjetakan. Watermark: Water buffalo.	1.00	4.00	10.00

85	50 Rupiah	VG	VF	UNC
	1960. Dark blue on light blue underprint. President Sukarno at left. Back: Female dancer and two men.			
	a. Printer: TDLR. Watermark: Sukarno. 3 Letter varieties.	2.00	8.00	20.00
	b. Printer: Pertjetakan. Watermark: Water buffalo.	1.50	4.50	12.50

86	100 Rupiah	VG	VF	UNC
	1960. Red-brown. President Sukarno at left. Back: Batak man and woman dancer.			
	a. Printer: Pertjetakan. Watermark: Sukarno.	2.50	10.00	22.50
	b. Watermark: Water buffalo. Requires confirmation.	—	—	—

87	500 Rupiah	VG	VF	UNC
	1960. Black on green underprint. President Sukarno at left. Back: Two Javanese dancers.			
	a. Printer: TDLR. Watermark: Sukarno. 3 Letter varieties.	7.50	15.00	75.00
	b. Printer: Pertjetakan. Watermark: Sukarno.	7.50	15.00	75.00
	c. Printer like b. Watermark: Water buffalo.	7.50	15.00	75.00
	d. Printer like b. Watermark: Arms.	10.00	20.00	80.00
	s. Specimen. As a.	—	—	—

88	1000 Rupiah	VG	VF	UNC
	1960. Dark green on yellow. President Sukarno at left. Back: Two Javanese dancers.			
	a. Printer: TDLR. Watermark: Sukarno. 3 Letter varieties.	25.00	60.00	175
	b. Printer: Pertjetakan. Watermark: Water buffalo.	15.00	40.00	125

88A	5000 Rupiah	VG	VF	UNC
	1960. Back: Female dancer at right. Printer: TDLR.			
	p. Uniface back proof.	—	—	—

The Islamic Republic of Iran, located between the Caspian Sea and the Persian Gulf in southwestern Asia, has an area of 1,648,000 sq. km. and a population of 65.87 million. Capital: Tehran. Although predominantly an agricultural state, Iran depends heavily on oil for foreign exchange. Crude oil, carpets and agricultural products are exported.

Known as Persia until 1935, Iran became an Islamic republic in 1979 after the ruling monarchy was overthrown and the shah was forced into exile. Conservative clerical forces established a theocratic system of government with ultimate political authority vested in a learned religious scholar referred to commonly as the Supreme Leader who, according to the constitution, is accountable only to the Assembly of Experts. US-Iranian relations have been strained since a group of Iranian students seized the US Embassy in Tehran on 4 November 1979 and held it until 20 January 1981. During 1980-88, Iran fought a bloody, indecisive war with Iraq that eventually expanded into the Persian Gulf and led to clashes between US Navy and Iranian military forces between 1987 and 1988. Iran has been designated a state sponsor of terrorism for its activities in Lebanon and elsewhere in the world and remains subject to US and UN economic sanctions and export controls because of its continued involvement in terrorism and conventional weapons proliferation. Following the election of reformer Hojjat ol-Eslam Mohammad Khatami as president in 1997 and similarly a reformer Majles (parliament) in 2000, a campaign to foster political reform in response to popular dissatisfaction was initiated. The movement floundered as conservative politicians, through the control of unelected institutions, prevented reform measures from being enacted and increased repressive measures. Starting with nationwide municipal elections in 2003 and continuing through Majles elections in 2004, conservatives reestablished control over Iran's elected government institutions, which culminated with the August 2005 inauguration of hardliner Mahmud Ahmadi-Nejad as president.

RULERS:

Qajar Dynasty

Sultan Ahmad Shah, AH1327-44/1909-25AD

Pahlavi Dynasty

Reza Shah, SH1304-20/1925-41AD
Mohammad Reza Pahlavi, SH1320-58/1941-79AD

PRESIDENTS:

Islamic Republic of Iran
Abolhassan Bani Sadr, SH1358-60 (AD1979-Jun 81)
Mohammad Ali Rajai, SH1360 (AD-1981 Jun-Oct)
Hojjatoleslam Ali Khamene'i, SH1360-(AD1981-)

MONETARY SYSTEM:

1 Shahi = 50 Dinars
1 Kran (Qiran) = 20 Shahis
1 Toman = 10 Krans AH1241-1344, SH1304-09 (1825-1931)
1 Shahi = 5 Dinars
1 Rial 100 Dinars = 20 Shahis
1 Toman = 10 Rials SH1310- (1932-)

SIGNATURE/TITLE VARIETIES

	GENERAL DIRECTOR	MINISTER OF FINANCE
1	Mohammad Ali Bamdad	Abol Hossein Ebtehaj
2	Ahmad Razavi	Ebrahim Zand
3	Mohammad Ali Varesteh	Ebrahim Zand
4	Nezam-ed-Din Emani	Ali Asghar Nasser
5	Nasrullah Jahangir	Ali Asghar Nasser
6	Mohammad Reza Vishkai	Ebrahim Kashani

KINGDOM OF PERSIA

Imperial Bank of Persia

1890 First Issue

		VG	VF	UNC
A1	**1 Toman** 25.10.1890; 24.1.1894; 1.1.1896. Portrait Shah Nasr-ed-Din at right. *BUSHIRE*. Rare.	—	—	—

1890 Second Issue

#1-10 With or without places of redemption such as Abadan, Bushire, Meshed, Shiraz, Resht, Hamadan, Isfahan, Kermanshah, Basrah, Tabriz, Teheran. Varieties exist of the government seal w/lion. Various date and sign. varieties. #1-6 Dates in the 1890s command a premium.

		Good	Fine	XF
1	**1 Toman** 1890-1923. Black on pink and light green underprint. Portrait Nasr-ed-Din at right. Back: Lion at center. Printer: BWC.			
	a. Red serial #.	125	250	750
	b. Black serial #.	100	200	600

		Good	Fine	XF
2	**2 Tomans** 1890-1923. Pink and light green. Portrait Nasr-ed-Din at right. Back: Lion at center. Printer: BWC.	125	250	550

		Good	Fine	XF
2A	**3 Tomans** 1890-1923. Green. Portrait Nasr-ed-Din at right. Back: Lion at center. Printer: BWC.	1,500	3,000	4,000

		Good	Fine	XF
3	**5 Tomans** 1890-1923 (16.4.1912). Red-brown. Portrait Nasr-ed-Din at right. Back: Lion at center. Printer: BWC. *Teheran.*	150	325	950
4	**10 Tomans** 1890-1923. Black. Portrait Nasr-ed-Din at right. Back: Lion at center. Printer: BWC.	250	600	1,250
5	**20 Tomans** 1890-1923. Orange. Portrait Nasr-ed-Din at right. Back: Lion at center. Printer: BWC.	500	1,500	—
6	**25 Tomans** 1890-1923. Dark green. Portrait Nasr-ed-Din at right. Back: Lion at center. Printer: BWC. Rare.	—	—	—

		Good	Fine	XF
7	**50 Tomans** 1890-1923. (1.6.1918). Dark brown. Portrait Nasr-ed-Din at right. Back: Lion at center. Printer: BWC. *Teheran.* Rare.	—	—	—
8	**100 Tomans** 1890-1923. Red. Portrait Nasr-ed-Din at right. Back: Lion at center. Printer: BWC. Rare.	—	—	—
9	**500 Tomans** 1890-1923. Blue. Portrait Nasr-ed-Din at right. Back: Lion at center. Printer: BWC. Specimen. Rare.	—	—	—
10	**1000 Tomans** 1890-1923 (10.9.1904). Black on lilac and green underprint. Portrait Nasr-ed-Din at right. Back: Lion at center. Printer: BWC. *Teheran.* Rare.	—	—	—

Note: #9 and 10 were held in reserve at the National Treasury. A 30 Toman note requires confirmation.

1924 Issue

#11-17 with or without different places of redemption such as Abadan, Barfrush, Bunder-Abbas, Bushire, Dizful, Hamadan, Kazrin, Kermanshah, Meshed, Pehlevi, Shiraz, Tabriz, Muhammerah, Teheran. The redemption endorsement for Teheran was printed for the denominations of 1 to 10 Tomans #11-14; other place names and higher denominations for Teheran were handstamped. Various date and signature varieties.

		Good	Fine	XF
11	**1 Toman** 1924-1932. Black on pink and light green underprint. Portrait Muzaffar-al-Din upper left. Printer: W&S.	50.00	150	500

		Good	Fine	XF
12	**2 Tomans** 1924-1932. Green. Portrait Nasr-ed-Din at right. Back: Large *2* at center. Printer: BWC.	500	1,200	1,900

		Good	Fine	XF
13	**5 Tomans** 1924-1932. Light green and lilac. Portrait Muzaffar-al-Din at right. Back: Large *5* at center Printer: W&S.	750	1,250	1,500

		Good	Fine	XF
14	**10 Tomans** 1924-1932. Blue. Portrait Muzaffar-al Din at right. Back: Large *10* at center. Printer: W&S.	275	750	2,000

		VG	VF	UNC
15	**20 Tomans** 1924-1932. Red, green and purple. Portrait Nasr-ed-Din at right. Back: Lion at center. Printer: BWC.	2,750	4,000	—

		Good	Fine	XF
16	**50 Tomans** 1924-1932. Brown, green and light brown. Portrait Nasr-ed-Din at center right. Back: Lion at center. Printer: BWC.	700	1,750	—

		Good	Fine	XF
17	**100 Tomans** 1924-1932. Dark blue and brown. Portrait Nasr-ed-Din at right. Printer: BWC.	800	2,250	—

KINGDOM OF IRAN

Bank Melli Iran

Founded 1927.

ND Issue

		VG	VF	UNC
17A	**500 Rials = 5 Pahlevis** ND. Blue. Portrait Shah at right. Back: Palace of the 40 columns at center. Proof. Overprint in red on face: *SPECIMEN,* and in Arabic on the back.	—	—	—

1932 Issue

		VG	VF	UNC
18	**5 Rials** AH1311 (1932). Dark green on multicolor underprint. Portrait Shah Reza with high cap full face at left. Printer: ABNC.			
	a. Issued note.	300	750	1,500
	s. Specimen.	—	—	2,500

		VG	VF	UNC
19	**10 Rials** AH1311 (1932). Brown on multicolor underprint. Portrait Shah Reza with high cap full face at right. Printer: ABNC.			
	a. Issued note.	20.00	700	1,250
	s. Specimen.	—	—	2,000

No.	Description	VG	VF	UNC
20	**20 Rials**	VG	VF	UNC
	AH1311 (1932). Red on multicolor underprint. Portrait Shah Reza with high cap full face at center. Printer: ABNC.			
	a. Issued note.	500	1,250	2,000
	s. Specimen.	—	—	3,000

No.	Description	VG	VF	UNC
21	**50 Rials**	VG	VF	UNC
	AH1311 (1932). Olive on multicolor underprint. Portrait Shah Reza with high cap full face at upper left. Palace of the 40 columns at center. Printer: ABNC.			
	a. Issued note.	75.00	250	550
	s. Specimen.	—	—	900
22	**100 Rials**	VG	VF	UNC
	AH1311 (1932). Purple on multicolor underprint. Portrait Shah Reza with high cap full face at right. Persepolis at left. Printer: ABNC.			
	a. Issued note.	125	350	850
	s. Specimen.	—	—	1,400
23	**500 Rials**	VG	VF	UNC
	AH1311 (1932); AH1313 (1934). Blue on multicolor underprint. Portrait Shah Reza with high cap full face at left. Mount Demavand at right. Printer: ABNC.			
	a. Issued note.	300	800	—
	s. Specimen.	—	—	1,750

1933-1934 Issue

No.	Description	VG	VF	UNC
24	**5 Rials**	VG	VF	UNC
	ND (1933). Dark green on multicolor underprint. Portrait Shah Reza with high cap in three-quarter face (towards left) at left. Back: Various dates stamped.			
	a. Issued note.	200	500	1,000
	s. Specimen.	—	—	1,500
25	**10 Rials**	VG	VF	UNC
	AH1313 (1934). Brown on multicolor underprint. Portrait Shah Reza with high cap in three-quarter face (towards left) at right. Two signature varieties. Back: Various dates stamped. (AH1312; 1313; 1314) or ND.			
	a. Signatures in German and Farsi.	150	400	750
	b. Both signatures in Farsi.	15.00	65.00	200
	s. Specimen.	—	—	1,250
26	**20 Rials**	VG	VF	UNC
	AH1313 (1934). Red on multicolor underprint. Portrait Shah Reza with high cap in three-quarter face (towards left) at center. Two signature varieties. Back: Various dates stamped. (AH1312; 1313; 1314) or ND.			
	a. Signatures in German and Farsi.	250	750	1,500
	b. Both signatures in Farsi.	200	700	1,500
	s. Specimen.	—	—	2,400
27	**50 Rials**	VG	VF	UNC
	AH1313 (1934). Olive on multicolor underprint. Portrait Shah Reza with high cap in three-quarter face (towards left) at left. Two signature varieties. Back: Various dates stamped. (AH1312; 1313; 1314) or ND.			
	a. Signatures in German and Farsi.	85.00	200	500
	b. Both signatures in Farsi.	350	1,000	2,000
	s. Specimen.	—	—	2,500

No.	Description	VG	VF	UNC
28	**100 Rials**	VG	VF	UNC
	AH1313 (1934). Purple on multicolor underprint. Portrait Shah Reza with high cap in three-quarter face (towards left) at right. Two signature varieties. Back: Various dates stamped. (AH1312, 1313, 1314) or ND.			
	a. Signatures in German and Farsi.	135	300	700
	b. Both signatures in Farsi.	125	275	650
	s. Specimen. Punch hole cancelled.	—	—	1,400

No.	Description	VG	VF	UNC
28A	**100 Rials**	VG	VF	UNC
	ND (1935). Portrait Shah Reza with high cap in three-quarter face (towards left) at left. Two signature varieties. Back: French text. Various dates stamped. (AH1312; 1313; 1314) or ND.			
	t1. Color trial. Brown on multicolor underprint.	—	6,000	10,000
	t2. Color trial. Purple on multicolor underprint. Rare.	—	—	—
	t3. Color trial. Green on multicolor underprint.	—	6,000	10,000
29	**500 Rials**	VG	VF	UNC
	AH1313 (1934). Blue on multicolor underprint. Portrait Shah Reza with high cap in three-quarter face (towards left) at left. Mount Demavarst at right. Back: Various dates stamped.	250	750	1,750

No.	Description	VG	VF	UNC
30	**1000 Rials**	VG	VF	UNC
	AH1313 (1934). Green on multicolor underprint. Warrior killing fabulous creature at left. Two signature varieties. Back: Mythical figure with wings. (AH1313; 1314) or ND.			
	a. Signatures in German and Farsi.	1,000	1,750	2,250
	b. Both signatures in Farsi.	150	450	1,500
	s. Specimen.	—	—	3,600

1936 Issue

31	10 Rials	VG	VF	UNC
	AH1315 (1936). Purple on multicolor underprint. Portrait Shah Reza at right. Back: French text; mountains.			
	a. Issued note.	30.00	150	300
	s. Specimen. All zero serial #.	—	—	750

1937-1938 Issue

#32-38A AH1316 and 1317 dates printed on face. AH1319; 1320; 1321 dates stamped on back.

32	5 Rials	VG	VF	UNC
	AH1316 (1937). Red-brown on multicolor underprint. Portrait Shah Reza in three-quarter face towards left without cap at right. Serial # in Western or Persian numerals. Back: French text; Tomb of Daniel in Susa at center.			
	a. Red-brown overprint 17/5/15 (15 Mordad 1317) on back.	30.00	150	300
	s. Without overprint on back. Specimen.	—	—	—

32A	5 Rials	VG	VF	UNC
	AH1317 (1938). Red-brown on multicolor underprint. Portrait Shah Reza in three-quarter face towards left without cap at right. Serial # in Western or Persian numerals. Back: Persian text. Tomb of Daniel in Susa at center.			
	a. Without date stamp on back.	15.00	50.00	150
	b. Red-orange or purple date stamp 1319 on back.	30.00	75.00	300
	c. Outlined red-brown date stamp 1319 on back.	8.00	30.00	80.00
	d. Purple date stamp 1320 on back.	15.00	60.00	200
	e. Purple or slate blue date stamp 1321 on back.	25.00	75.00	250

33	10 Rials	VG	VF	UNC
	AH1316 (1937). Purple on multicolor underprint. Modified portrait Shah Reza in three-quarter face towards left without cap at right. Serial # in Western or Persian numerals. Back: French text.			
	a. Without overprint on back.	50.00	150	350
	b. Purple overprint 17/5/15 (15 Mordad 1317) on back.	25.00	100	350
	c. Purple date stamp 1319 on back.	50.00	150	350
	s. Specimen. Pinhole cancelled.	—	—	800

33A	10 Rials	VG	VF	UNC
	AH1317 (1938). Purple on multicolor underprint. Portrait Shah Reza in three-quarter face towards left without cap at right. Serial # in Western or Persian numerals. Back: Persian text.			
	a. Without date stamp on back.	20.00	100	200
	b. Violet or slate blue date stamp 1319 on back.	75.00	150	250
	c. Blue date stamp 1320 on back.	25.00	100	200
	d. Blue date stamp 1321 on back.	25.00	100	225

34	20 Rials	VG	VF	UNC
	AH1316 (1937). Orange on multicolor underprint. Portrait Shah Reza in three-quarter face towards left without cap at right. Serial # in Western or Persian numerals. Back: French text; bridges across river in valley at center.			
	a. Without overprint on back.	125	300	500
	b. Orange overprint 17/5/15 (15 Mordad 1317) on back.	125	300	500
	c. Orange date stamp 1319 on back.	17.50	85.00	225
	d. Purple date stamp 1320 on back.	150	350	550
	s. As a. Specimen. Overprint: TDLR oval	—	—	1,000

34A	20 Rials	VG	VF	UNC
	AH1317 (1938). Orange on multicolor underprint. Portrait Shah Reza in three-quarter face towards left without cap at right. Serial # in Western or Persian numerals. Back: Persian text.			
	a. Western serial #.	25.00	150	350
	b. Persian serial #. Without date stamp.	2.00	150	350
	c. Orange or purple date stamp 1319 on back.	8.00	35.00	130
	d. Blue (or purple) outlined date stamp on back.	2.50	15.00	110
	e. Purple date stamp 1320 on back.	50.00	175	450
	f. Purple date stamp 1321 on back.	50.00	175	450

		VG	VF	UNC
35	**50 Rials**			
	AH1316 (1937). Green on multicolor underprint. Portrait Shah Reza in three-quarter face towards left without cap at right. Serial # in Western or Persian numerals. Mount Damavand at left. Back: French text; ruins at center.			
	a. Without overprint on back.	20.00	85.00	375
	b. Green overprint 17/5/15 (15 Mordad 1317) on back.	175	500	1,000
	s. As a. Specimen. All zero serial #.	—	—	1,250

		VG	VF	UNC
35A	**50 Rials**			
	AH1317 (1938). Green on multicolor underprint. Portrait Shah Reza in three-quarter face towards left without cap at right. Serial # in Western or Persian numerals. Back: Persian text.			
	a. Western # on face.	75.00	250	600
	b. Persian # on face without date stamp on back.	50.00	200	550
	c. Green or red date stamp 1319 on back.	15.00	95.00	285
	d. Red outlined date stamp 1319 on back.	20.00	110	350
	e. Red date stamp 1320 on back.	75.00	250	650
	f. Red date stamp 1321 on back.	50.00	200	600
	s1. As a. Specimen. Perforated: *CANCELLED.*	—	—	750
	s2. As b. Specimen. Red overprint with TDLR oval.	—	—	1,250

		VG	VF	UNC
35B	**100 Rials**			
	AH1316 (1937). Shah Reza facing at right. Back: Fortress ruins at center, arms at left.			
	s. Specimen perforated: *SPECIMEN.* Dark blue and purple on multicolor underprint.	—	6,000	10,000
	t. Specimen perforated: *SPECIMEN.* Red on multicolor underprint. Color trial.	—	6,000	10,000

		VG	VF	UNC
35C	**100 Rials**			
	ND (1937). Brown on multicolor underprint. Shah Reza 3/4 facing, with short hair on top of head. Specimen. Punch hole cancelled.	—	6,000	10,000

		VG	VF	UNC
36	**100 Rials**			
	AH1316 (1937). Light brown on multicolor underprint. Portrait Shah Reza in three-quarter face towards left without cap at right. Serial # in Western or Persian numerals. Bank Melli at center. Back: French text; ship at center.			
	a. Without overprint on back.	15.00	125	400
	b. Brown overprint 17/5/15 (15 Mordad 1317) on back.	25.00	175	525
	c. Purple date stamp 1320 on back.	30.00	150	500
	s. Specimen.	—	—	3,000

		VG	VF	UNC
36A	**100 Rials**			
	AH1317 (1938). Light brown on multicolor underprint. Portrait Shah Reza in three-quarter face towards left without cap at right. Serial # in Western or Persian numerals. Back: Persian text.			
	a. Western serial #.	100	300	750
	b. Persian serial #. Without date stamp on back.	100	300	750
	c. Brown or purple date stamp 1319 on back.	25.00	75.00	300
	d. Purple or slate gray date stamp 1320 on back.	125	350	800
	e. Slate gray date stamp 1321 on back.	125	350	800
	s. Brown on multicolor underprint. Specimen. Pinhole cancelled.	—	—	1,200

36B	**500 Rials**	VG	VF	UNC
	ND (1937). Shah Reza at right facing front. Latin serial #. Back: French text. Specimen. Punch hole cancelled.	—	7,000	12,000

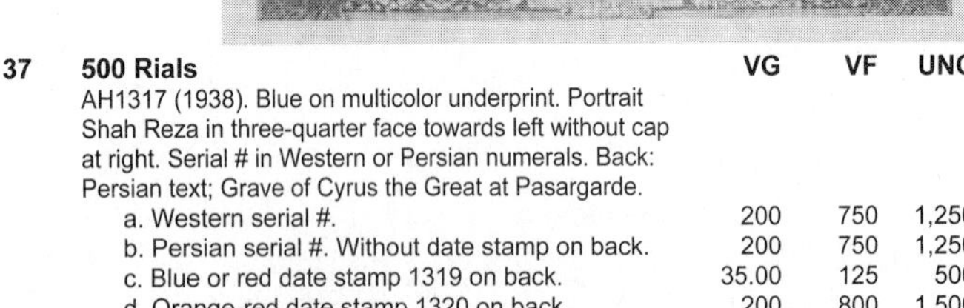

37	**500 Rials**	VG	VF	UNC
	AH1317 (1938). Blue on multicolor underprint. Portrait Shah Reza in three-quarter face towards left without cap at right. Serial # in Western or Persian numerals. Back: Persian text; Grave of Cyrus the Great at Pasargarde.			
	a. Western serial #.	200	750	1,250
	b. Persian serial #. Without date stamp on back.	200	750	1,250
	c. Blue or red date stamp 1319 on back.	35.00	125	500
	d. Orange-red date stamp 1320 on back.	200	800	1,500
	e. Red date stamp 1321 on back.	200	750	1,250

37A	**1000 Rials**	VG	VF	UNC
	ND (1937). Green on multicolor underprint. Portrait Shah Reza in three-quarter face towards left without cap at left. Latin serial #. Back: French text.			
	a. Issued note.	—	—	—
	s. Specimen. Punch hole cancelled.	—	—	15,000

38	**1000 Rials**	VG	VF	UNC
	AH1316 (1937). Green on multicolor underprint. Portrait Shah Reza in three-quarter face towards left without cap at right. Serial # in Western or Persian numerals. Back: French text; mountains at center.			
	a. Green overprint 17/5/15 (145 Mordad 1317) on back.	75.00	300	750
	b. Red date stamp 1320 on back.	300	1,000	2,500
	c. Red date stamp 1321 on back.	300	1,000	2,500
	s. Without overprint on back. Specimen.	—	—	—

38A	**1000 Rials**	VG	VF	UNC
	AH1317 (1938). Green on multicolor underprint. Portrait Shah Reza in three-quarter face towards left without cap at right. Serial # in Western or Persian numerals. Back: Persian text.			
	a. Western serial #.	250	1,000	2,500
	b. Persian serial #. Without date stamp on back.	250	1,000	2,500
	c. Date stamp 1319 on back. Rare.	—	—	—
	d. Red date stamp 1320 on back.	300	1,250	2,750
	e. Red date stamp 1321 on back.	300	1,250	2,750

38B	**10,000 Rials**	VG	VF	UNC
	AH1316 (1937). Blue on pink, yellow and multicolor underprint. Shah with short hair at center, building at left, ruins at right. 4 Western style serial #. Back: Pillar at left, long bridge across center, arms at upper right, French text. Watermark: Shah			
	a. Specimen. Rare.	—	—	—
	b. Same as above, but Shah facing and looking forward.	—	—	30,000
	s. Specimen. Punch hole cancelled.	—	—	—

		VG	VF	UNC
38C	**10,000 Rials** AH1317 (1938). Printed on face. Purple and yellow on multicolor underprint. Reza Shah 3/4 left at center. Persian serial #. Specimen.	—	—	—

Shah Mohammad Reza Pahlavi, SH1323-40/1944-61AD

Type 1. Imperial Iranian Army (IIA) Uniform. Three quarter view. SH1323.

Type II. Imperial Iranian Army (IIA) Uniform. Three view. SH1325-29

Type III. Civilian Attire. Full face. SH1330-32.

Type IV. Imperial Iranian Army (IIA) Uniform. Full left profile. SH1333.

Type V. Imperial Iranian Army (IIA). Uniform. Full face. SH1337-40.

1944 Issue

		VG	VF	UNC
39	**5 Rials** ND (1944). Reddish brown on light green and pink underprint. First portrait Shah Pahlavi in army uniform at right. Signature 1. Watermark: Imperial Crown. Printer: Harrison (without imprint). Large format.	5.00	15.00	35.00

		VG	VF	UNC
40	**10 Rials** ND (1944). Purple on light orange and multicolor underprint. First portrait Shah Pahlavi in army uniform at right. Ornate geometric design at center. Signature 1. Back: Caspian Seaside of Alborz Mountains. Watermark: Imperial Crown. Printer: Harrison (without imprint). Large format.	7.50	25.00	75.00
41	**20 Rials** ND (1944). Orange on multicolor underprint. First portrait Shah Pahlavi in army uniform at right. Scene from Persepolis at center. Signature 1. Back: Railroad tunnel and bridges. Watermark: Imperial Crown. Printer: Harrison (without imprint). Large format.			
	a. Issued note.	25.00	100	350
	s. Specimen. Black overprint: TDLR oval.	—	—	1,000

		VG	VF	UNC
42	**50 Rials** ND (1944). Dark green on lavender and violet underprint. First portrait Shah Pahlavi in army uniform at right. Stylized cock and ornate design at center. Signature 1. Back: Tomb of Cyrus at Pasargadae. Watermark: Imperial Crown. Printer: Harrison (without imprint). Large format.	35.00	150	500

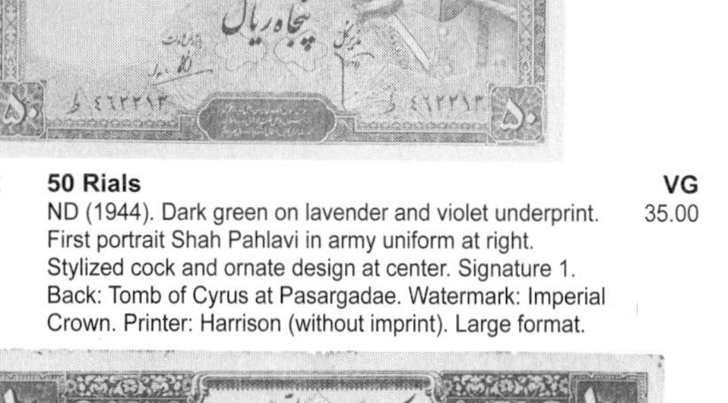

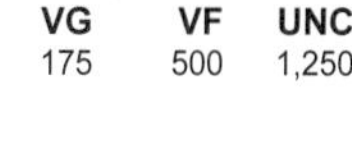

		VG	VF	UNC
43	**100 Rials** ND (1944). Brown and green. First portrait Shah Pahlavi in army uniform at right. Bank Melli and ornate design at center. Signature 1. Back: Steamship and dhow at Port of Enzely. Watermark: Imperial Crown. Printer: Harrison (without imprint). Large format.	175	500	1,250

		VG	VF	UNC
44	**100 Rials** ND (1944). Purple on orange underprint. First portrait Shah Pahlavi in army uniform at right. Stylized horse and ornate design at center. Signature 1. Back: Bridge and dam at Dezful. Watermark: Imperial Crown. Printer: Harrison (without imprint). Large format.	175	500	1,250

45 **500 Rials**

ND (1944). Dark blue and purple. First portrait Shah Pahlavi in army uniform at right. Multicolor design and winged horse at center. Signature 1. Back: Ruins of Persepolis. Watermark: Imperial Crown. Printer: Harrison (without imprint). Large format.

VG	VF	UNC
250	750	1,800

46 **1000 Rials**

ND (1944). Green, orange and blue. First portrait Shah Pahlavi in army uniform at right. Winged bull and floral design at center. Signature 1. Back: Mount Damavand. Watermark: Imperial Crown. Printer: Harrison (without imprint). Large format.

VG	VF	UNC
300	1,000	2,500

1948-1951 Issue

47 **10 Rials**

ND (1948). Dark blue on orange underprint. Second portrait Shah Pahlavi in army uniform at right. Multicolor design at center. Signature 1. Back: Winged Saurian from Tagh-I-Bostan. Watermark: Young Shah Mohammad Reza Pahlavi. Printer: Harrison (without imprint). Small format.

VG	VF	UNC
5.00	10.00	30.00

48 **20 Rials**

ND (1948). Dark brown, green and orange. Multicolor stone sculpture at center. Second portrait Shah Pahlavi in army uniform at right. Signature 1. Back: Lion biting stylized bull. Watermark: Young Shah Mohammad Reza Pahlavi. Printer: Harrison (without imprint). Small format.

VG	VF	UNC
10.00	25.00	100

49 **50 Rials**

ND (1948). Green on orange and green underprint. Sun disk at center. Second portrait Shah Pahlavi in army uniform at right. Signature 1. Back: Five Persian figures from Persepolis sculpture. Watermark: Young Shah Mohammad Reza Pahlavi. Printer: Harrison (without imprint). Small format.

VG	VF	UNC
20.00	50.00	150

50 **100 Rials**

ND (1951). Red-violet on light green underprint. Winged lion and multicolor design at center. Second portrait Shah Pahlavi in army uniform at right. Signature 1. Back: Ruins of Palace of Darius at Persepolis. Watermark: Young Shah Mohammad Reza Pahlavi. Printer: Harrison (without imprint). Small format.

VG	VF	UNC
20.00	50.00	150

51 **200 Rials**

ND (1951). Dark green and light yellow. Carved tray at center. Second portrait Shah Pahlavi in army uniform at right. Signature 1. Back: Railroad bridge and tunnels. Watermark: Young Shah Mohammad Reza Pahlavi. Printer: Harrison (without imprint). Small format.

VG	VF	UNC
30.00	75.00	250

52 **500 Rials**

ND (1951). Dark blue, purple and red. Rectangular design at center. Second portrait Shah Pahlavi in army uniform at right. Signature 1. Back: Four oriental figures in orchard. Watermark: Young Shah Mohammad Reza Pahlavi. Printer: Harrison (without imprint). Small imprint.

VG	VF	UNC
100	300	750

53 **1000 Rials**

ND (1951). Brown, red and light green. Second portrait Shah Pahlavi in army uniform at right. Multicolor floral design and birds at center. Signature 1. Back: Mount Damavand. Watermark: Young Shah Mohammad Reza Pahlavi. Printer: Harrison (without imprint). Small format.

VG	VF	UNC
150	400	1,250

1951 Issue

		VG	VF	UNC
54	**10 Rials** SH1330 (1951). Dark blue and multicolor. Shepherd and ram at center. Third portrait Shah Pahlavi in civilian attire at right. Yellow security thread runs vertically. Signature 2. Back: Royal seal of Darius. Printer: Harrison (without imprint).	2.00	7.00	15.00

		VG	VF	UNC
55	**20 Rials** SH1330 (1951). Dark brown on orange and multicolor underprint. Third portrait Shah Pahlavi in civilian attire at right. Yellow security thread runs vertically. Winged bull and spear bearer at center. Signature 2. Back: Ali Ghapoo in Isfahan. Watermark: None. Printer: Harrison (without imprint).	3.00	12.00	25.00

		VG	VF	UNC
56	**50 Rials** SH1330 (1951). Green on light orange and multicolor underprint. Third portrait Shah Pahlavi in civilian attire at right. Yellow security thread runs vertically. Pharaotic figure with urn at center. Signature 3. Back: Palace of Darius in Persepolis. Watermark: Young Shah Pahlavi. Printer: Harrison (without imprint).	3.00	12.00	30.00

		VG	VF	UNC
57	**100 Rials** SH1330 (1951). Maroon on multicolor underprint. Third portrait Shah Pahlavi in civilian attire at right. Yellow security thread runs vertically. Mythical figure at center. Signature 3. Back: Darius in royal coach. Watermark: Young Shah Pahlavi. Printer: Harrison (without imprint).	5.00	20.00	50.00

		VG	VF	UNC
58	**200 Rials** SH1330 (1951). Dark blue, light blue and brown. Third portrait Shah Pahlavi in civilian attire at right. Yellow security thread runs vertically. Ruins of Persepolis at center. Signature 2. Back: Allahverdikhan bridge in Isfahan. Watermark: Young Shah Pahlavi. Printer: Harrison (without imprint).			
	a. Issued note.	7.50	30.00	125
	s. TDLR specimen. Oval. Not Harrison imprint.	—	—	—

1953 Issue

		VG	VF	UNC
59	**10 Rials** SH1332 (1953). Dark blue and multicolor. Shepherd and ram at center. Signature 4. Back: Royal seal of Darius.	2.00	7.00	15.00

		VG	VF	UNC
60	**20 Rials** SH1332 (1953). Dark brown on orange and multicolor underprint. Winged bull and spear bearer at center. Signature 4. Back: Ali Ghapoo in Isfahan.	3.00	12.00	25.00

		VG	VF	UNC
61	**50 Rials** SH1332 (1953). Green on light orange and multicolor underprint. Pharaotic figure with urn at center. Signature N. Jahangir and A. A. Nasser. Back: Palace of Darius in Persepolis.	15.00	50.00	100

		VG	VF	UNC
62	**100 Rials** SH1332 (1953). Maroon on multicolor underprint. Mythical figure at center. Signature 4. Back: Darius in royal coach.	20.00	60.00	175

1954 Issue

		VG	VF	UNC
64	**10 Rials** SH1333 (1954). Dark blue on orange, green and multicolor underprint. Ruins of Persepolis at left. Fourth portrait Shah Pahlavi in army uniform at right. Yellow security thread runs vertically. Signature 4. Back: Tomb of Ibn Sina in Hamadan. Watermark: None. Printer: Harrison (without imprint).	2.00	7.00	15.00

		VG	VF	UNC
65	**20 Rials** SH1333 (1954). Dark brown on orange and multicolor underprint. Man slaying beast at left. Shah Pahlavi in army uniform at right. Yellow security thread runs vertically. Signature 4. Back: Bank Melli in Tehran at center. Watermark: None. Printer: Harrison (without imprint).	3.00	12.00	25.00

		VG	VF	UNC
66	**50 Rials** SH1333 (1954). Green on purple and multicolor underprint. Geometric design and floral motifs at center. Fourth portrait Shah Pahlavi in army uniform at right. Yellow security thread runs vertically. Signature 4. Back: Koohrang Dam and tunnel. Watermark: Young Shah Pahlavi. Printer: Harrison (without imprint).	3.00	12.00	30.00

		VG	VF	UNC
67	**100 Rials** SH1333 (1954). Maroon on light green and multicolor underprint. Geometric design and floral motifs at center. Fourth portrait Shah Pahlavi in army uniform at right. Yellow security thread runs vertically. Signature 4. Back: Oil refinery at Abadan. Watermark: Young Shah Pahlavi. Printer: Harrison (without imprint).	5.00	20.00	50.00

1958 Issue

		VG	VF	UNC
68	**10 Rials** SH1337 (1958). Dark blue on green and orange underprint. Fifth portrait Shah Pahlavi in army uniform at right. Yellow security thread runs vertically. Signature 6. Ornate floral design at center. Back: Amir Kabir Dam near Karaj. Watermark: Young Shah Pahlavi. Printer: Harrison (without imprint).	1.50	5.00	12.00

		VG	VF	UNC
69	**20 Rials** SH1337 (1958). Dark brown on light brown, lilac and multicolor underprint. Fifth portrait Saha Pahlavi in army uniform at right. Yellow security thread runs vertically. Signature 6. Ornate floral design at center. Back: Statue of Shah and Ramsar Hotel. Watermark: Young Saha Pahlavi. Printer: Harrison (without imprint).	2.50	7.50	20.00

		VG	VF	UNC
70	**200 Rials** SH1337 (1958). Blue on purple, orange and multicolor underprint. Fifth portrait Shah Pahlavi in army uniform at right. Yellow security thread runs vertically. Signature 6. Ruins of Persepolis at center. Back: Mehrabad Airport in Tehran. Watermark: Young Saha Pahlavi. Printer: Harrison (without imprint).	15.00	40.00	75.00

1952 Emergency Circulating Check

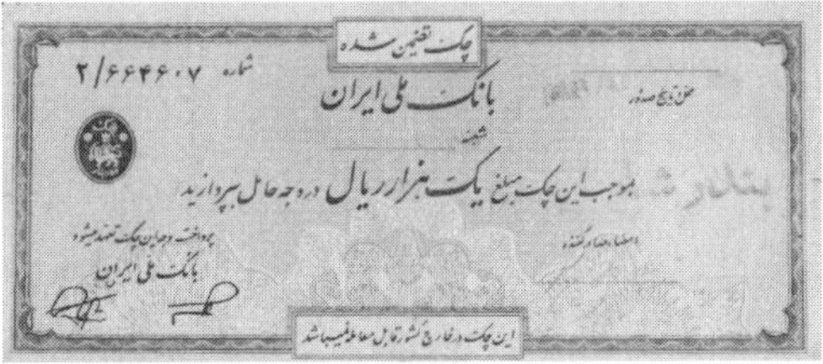

		VG	VF	UNC
70A	**1000 Rials** SH1331 (1952). Blue on gold and gray underprint. Stamped date and seal at left. Uniface. Issued at Bandar Shah.	15.00	50.00	150
70B	**5000 Rials** SH1331 (1952). Red on light red and blue underprint. Stamped date and seal at left. Uniface. Specimen.	—	—	150
70C	**10,000 Rials** SH1331 (1952). Dark green on blue and light red underprint. Stamped date and seal at left. Uniface. Specimen.	—	—	150

Note: For similar issues from Bank Markazi Iran, see Volume 3.

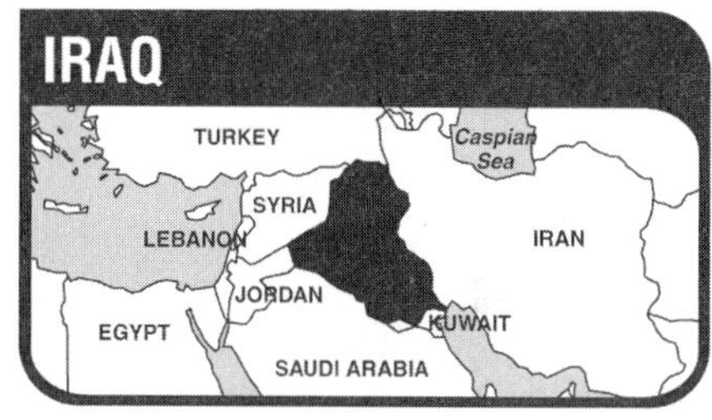

The Republic of Iraq, historically known as Mesopotamia, is located in the Near East and is bordered by Kuwait, Iran, Turkey, Syria, Jordan and Saudi Arabia. It has an area of 437,072 sq. km. and a population of 28.22 million. Capital: Baghdad. The economy of Iraq is based on agriculture and petroleum. Crude oil accounts for 94 percent of the exports before the war with Iran began in 1980.

Formerly part of the Ottoman Empire, Iraq was occupied by Britain during the course of World War I; in 1920, it was declared a League of Nations mandate under UK administration. In stages over the next dozen years, Iraq attained its independence as a kingdom in 1932. A "republic" was proclaimed in 1958, but in actuality a series of military strongmen ruled the country until 2003. The last was Saddam Husayn. Territorial disputes with Iran led to an inconclusive and costly eight-year war (1980-88). In August 1990, Iraq seized Kuwait but was expelled by US-led, UN coalition forces during the Gulf War of January-February 1991. Following Kuwait's liberation, the UN Security Council (UNSC) required Iraq to scrap all weapons of mass destruction and long-range missiles and to allow UN verification inspections. Continued Iraqi noncompliance with UNSC resolutions over a period of 12 years led to the US-led invasion of Iraq in March 2003 and the ouster of the Saddam Husayn regime. Coalition forces remain in Iraq under a UNSC mandate, helping to provide security and to support the freely elected government. The Coalition Provisional Authority, which temporarily administered Iraq after the invasion, transferred full governmental authority on 28 June 2004 to the Iraqi Interim Government, which governed under the Transitional Administrative Law for Iraq (TAL). Under the TAL, elections for a 275-member Transitional National Assembly (TNA) were held in Iraq on 30 January 2005. Following these elections, the Iraqi Transitional Government (ITG) assumed office. The TNA was charged with drafting Iraq's permanent constitution, which was approved in a 15 October 2005 constitutional referendum. An election under the constitution for a 275-member Council of Representatives (CoR) was held on 15 December 2005. The CoR approval in the selection of most of the cabinet ministers on 20 May 2006 marked the transition from the ITG to Iraq's first constitutional government in nearly a half-century.

RULERS:

Faisal I, 1921-1933
Ghazi I, 1933-1939
Faisal II, 1939-1958

MONETARY SYSTEM:

1 Dirham = 50 Fils
1 Riyal = 200 Fils
1 Dinar = 1000 Fils

KINGDOM

Government of Iraq

1931 Issue

		Good	Fine	XF
1	**1/4 Dinar** 1931-32. Green on multicolor underprint. Portrait King Faisal I with goatee at right. Back: English text. Watermark: King Faisal I. Printer: BWC.			
	a. 1.7.1931. Signatures: Sir E. Hilton Young, Ja'far Pasha al Askari, Sir Bertram Hornsby.	1,000	1,500	2,500
	b. 1.8.1932. Signatures: L.S. Amery, Husain Afnan, Viscount Goschen.	1,300	2,000	4,500

		Good	Fine	XF
2	**1/2 Dinar** 1931-1932. Brown on multicolor underprint. Portrait King Faisal I with goatee at right. Watermark: Portrait King Faisal I. Printer: BWC.			
	a. 1.7.1931. Signature: Sir E. Hilton Young, Ja'far Pasha al Askari, Sir Bertram Hornsby.	1,200	1,700	4,000
	b. 1.8.1932. Signature: L.S. Amery, Husain Afnan, Viscount Goschen.	1,500	2,000	5,500

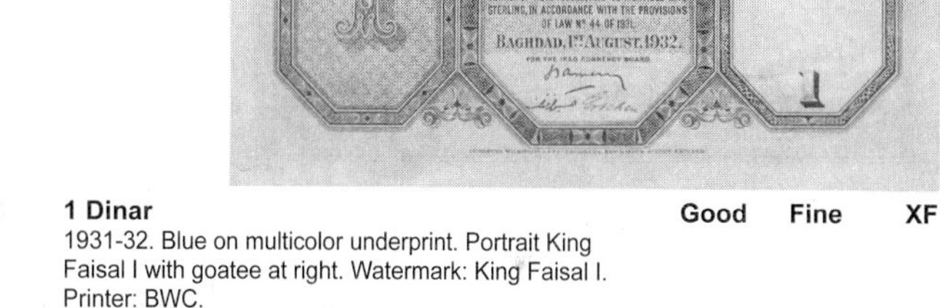

		Good	Fine	XF
3	**1 Dinar** 1931-32. Blue on multicolor underprint. Portrait King Faisal I with goatee at right. Watermark: King Faisal I. Printer: BWC.			
	a. 1.7.1931. Signature: Sir Hilton Young, Ja'far Pasha al Askari, Sir Bertram Hornsby.	500	1,000	1,750
	b. 1.8.1932. Signature: L.S. Amery, Husain Afnan, Viscount Goschen.	700	1,600	2,500

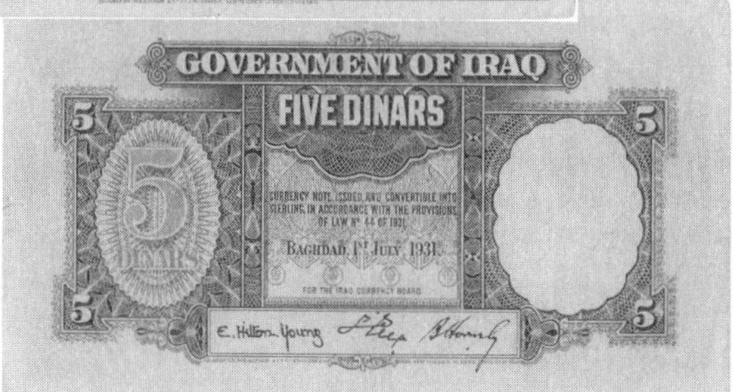

		Good	Fine	XF
4	**5 Dinars** 1.7.1931. Brown-violet on multicolor underprint. Portrait King Faisal I with goatee at right. Signature: Sir Hilton Young, Ja'far Pasha al Askari, Sir Bertram Hornsby. Watermark: King Faisal I. Printer: BWC.	7,500	10,000	20,000

#4 was approved on 14.9.1931.

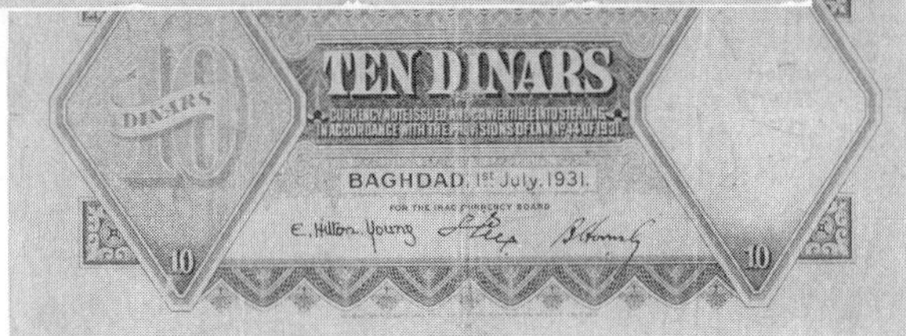

		Good	Fine	XF
5	**10 Dinars** 1.7.1931. Purple and blue on multicolor underprint. Portrait King Faisal I with goatee at right. Signature: Sir Hilton Young, Ja'far Pasha al Askari, Sir Bertram Hornsby. Watermark: King Faisal I. Printer: BWC. Rare.	—	—	—

#5 was approved on 21.9.1931.

		Good	Fine	XF
6	**100 Dinars** 1.7.1931. Blue and ochre on multicolor underprint. Portrait King Faisal I with goatee at right. Signature: Sir Hilton Young, Ja'far Pasha al Askari, Sir Bertram Hornsby. Watermark: King Faisal I. Printer: BWC. Rare.	—	—	—

#6 was approved on 2.10.1931.

Law #44 of 1931 (1933-1940 Issue)

		Good	Fine	XF
7	**1/4 Dinar** *L.1931.* (1935). Green on multicolor underprint. Portrait King Ghazi in military uniform at right. Watermark: King Ghazi. Printer: BWC.			
	a. Signature: L.S. Amery, Ja'far Pasha al Askari.	300	675	1,000
	b. Signature: L.S. Amery, Ata Amin.	250	600	850
	c. Signature: L.S. Amery, Ali Jawadat al Ayubi.	250	600	850
	d. Signature: L.S. Amery, Raouf al Chadirchi.	200	525	800
	e. Signature: Lord Kennet, Ata Amin.	150	400	700

		Good	Fine	XF
8	**1/2 Dinar** *L.1931.* (1935). Brown on multicolor underprint. Portrait King George Ghazi in military uniform at right. Watermark: King Ghazi. Printer: BWC.			
	a. Signature: L.S. Amery, Ja'Far Pasha al Askari.	500	1,000	1,800
	b. Signature: L.S. Amery, Ali Jawadat al Ayubi.	400	750	1,400
	c. Signature: L.S. Amery, Raouf al Chadirchi.	350	600	1,200
	d. Signature: Lord Kennet, Ata Amin.	300	500	1,000
	s. Specimen. Red overprint and punch hole cancelled.	—	Unc	3,000

		Good	Fine	XF
9	**1 Dinar** *L.1931.* (1934). Blue on multicolor underprint. Portrait King Ghazi in Military uniform at right. Watermark: King Ghazi. Printer: BWC.			
	a. Signature: L.S. Amery, Ja'far Pasha al Askari.	350	650	1,200
	b. Signature: L.S. Amery, Ata Amin.	300	600	1,000
	c. Signature: L.S. Amery, Ali Jawadat al Ayubi.	275	550	900
	d. Signature: L.S. Amery, Raouf al Chadirchi.	200	500	850
	e. Signature: Lord Kennet, Ata Amin.	175	475	800

10	5 Dinars	Good	Fine	XF
	L.1931. (1940). Brown-violet on multicolor underprint. Portrait Ghazi in military uniform at right. Watermark: King Ghazi. Printer: BWC.			
	a. Signature: L.S. Amery, Raouf al Chadirchi.	7,500	15,000	20,000
	b. Signature: Lord Kennet, Ata Amin.	7,500	15,000	20,000

11	10 Dinars	Good	Fine	XF
	L.1931. (1938). Purple and blue on multicolor underprint. Portrait King Ghazi in military uniform at right. Watermark: King Ghazi. Printer: BWC.			
	a. Signature: L.S. Amery, Raouf al Chadirchi.	1,500	3,000	7,000
	b. Signature: Lord Kennet, Ata Amin.	1,500	3,000	7,000

12	100 Dinars	Good	Fine	XF
	L.1931. (1936). Blue and ochre on multicolor underprint. Portrait King Ghazi in military uniform at right. Watermark: King Ghazi. Printer: BWC.			
	a. Signature: L.S. Amery, Ali Jawadat al Ayubi.	5,000	10,000	20,000
	b. Signature: Lord Kennet, Ata Amin.	5,000	10,000	20,000

Law #44 of 1931 (1941 Issue)

13	1/4 Dinar	Good	Fine	XF
	L.1931. (1941). Green on brown and blue underprint. Portrait King Faisal II as a child at right. Signature L.M. Swan at left. Ibrahim Kamal at right. Signature: L.M. Swan, Ibrahim Kamal. Printer: Nasik Security Printing Press (India).	3,500	5,000	7,500

14	1/2 Dinar	Good	Fine	XF
	L.1931. (1941). Brown. Portrait King Faisal II as a child at right. Signature L.M. Swan at left. Ibrahim Kamal at right. Signature: L.M. Swan, Ibrahim Kamal. Printer: Nasik Security Printing Press (India). Rare.	—	—	—

15	1 Dinar	Good	Fine	XF
	L.1931. (1941). Blue. Portrait King Faisal II as a child at right. Signature L.M. Swan at left. Ibrahim Kamal at right. L.M. Swan, Ibrahim Kamal. Printer: Nasik Security Printing Press (India).	250	750	2,000

Law #44 of 1931 (1942 Issue)

16	1/4 Dinar	Good	Fine	XF
	L.1931. (1942). Green on multicolor underprint. Portrait King Faisal II as child at right. Watermark: King Faisal. Printer: BWC.			
	a. Signature: Lord Kennet, Ata Amin.	100	250	500
	b. Signature: Lore Kennet, Daoud Al Haidari.	150	300	750
	c. Signature: Lord Kennet, Shakir al Wadi.	100	250	500

17	1/2 Dinar	Good	Fine	XF
	L.1931. (1942). Brown on multicolor underprint. Portrait King Faisal II as child at right. Watermark: King Faisal. Printer: BWC.			
	a. Signature: Lord Kennet, Ata Amin.	250	750	2,500
	b. Signature: Lord Kennet, Shakir al Wadi.	250	750	2,500

18	1 Dinar	Good	Fine	XF
	L.1931. (1942). Blue on multicolor underprint. Portrait King Faisal II as child at right. Watermark: King Faisal. Printer: BWC.			
	a. Signature: Lord Kennet, Ata Amin.	100	325	750
	b. Signature: Lord Kennet, Daoud al Haidari.	100	325	750

19	5 Dinars	Good	Fine	XF
	L.1931. (1942). Brown on multicolor underprint. Portrait King Faisal II as child at right. Watermark: King Faisal. Printer: BWC.			
	a. Signature: Lord Kennet, Ata Amin.	250	750	1,350
	b. Signature: Lord Kennet, Daoud al Haidari.	250	750	1,350

20	10 Dinars	Good	Fine	XF
	L.1931. (1942). Purple and blue on multicolor underprint. Portrait King Faisal II as child at right. Watermark: King Faisal. Printer: BWC.			
	a. Signature: Lord Kennet, Ata Amin.	750	1,300	2,000
	b. Signature: Lord Kennet, Daoud al Haidari.	750	1,300	2,000

21	100 Dinars	Good	Fine	XF
	L.1931. Dark blue and multicolor. Portrait King Faisal II as child at right. Watermark: King Faisal. Printer: BWC.			
	a. Signature: Lord Kennet, Ata Amin.	2,000	5,750	10,000
	b. Signature: Lord Kennet, Daoud al Haidari.	2,000	5,750	10,000

Note: Approval date of Nov. 1941 is known for #19-21.

Law #44 of 1931 (1944 Issue)

		Good	Fine	XF
A22	**50 Fils** *L.1931.* Green. Portrait young King Faisal II at left. Watermark: King Faisal II. Printer: BWC. Proof.	—	—	—

Note: #A22 was approved 6.3.1944 but apparently never issued.

Law #44 of 1931 (1945 Issue)

		Good	Fine	XF
22	**1/4 Dinar** *L. 1931.* Green on multicolor underprint. Portrait young King Faisal II at right. Signature Lord Kennet, Ibrahim al Khudhairi. Watermark: King Faisal II. Printer: BWC.	100	325	1,000

		Good	Fine	XF
23	**1/2 Dinar** *L.1931.* Brown on multicolor underprint. Portrait young King Faisal II at right. Signature Lord Kennet, Ibrahim al Khudhairi. Watermark: King Faisal II. Printer: BWC.	500	1,500	4,000

Note: #24-26 not assigned.

National Bank of Iraq

Law #42 of 1947

First Issue

		Good	Fine	XF
27	**1/4 Dinar** *L.1947.* (1950). Green on multicolor underprint. Portrait young King Faisal II at right. Back: Palm trees at center. Watermark: King Faisal II. Printer: BWC.	50.00	100	200

		Good	Fine	XF
28	**1/2 Dinar** *L.1947.* (1950). Brown on multicolor underprint. Portrait young King Faisal II at right. Back: Ruins of the mosque and spiral minaret at Samarra. Watermark: King Faisal II. Printer: BWC.	75.00	125	250

		Good	Fine	XF
29	**1 Dinar** *L.1947.* (1950). Blue on multicolor underprint. Portrait young King Faisal II at right. Back: Equestrian statue of King Faisal I Watermark: King Faisal II. Printer: BWC.	50.00	100	200

		Good	Fine	XF
30	**5 Dinars** *L.1947.* (1950). Red on multicolor underprint. Portrait young King Faisal II at right. Back: Ancient carving of Hammurabi receiving the laws. Watermark: King Faisal II. Printer: BWC.	200	300	500

31 **10 Dinars**
L.1947. (1950). Purple and blue on multicolor underprint. Portrait young King Faisal II at right. Back: Winged Assyrian ox and an Assyrian priest at center. Watermark: King Faisal II. Printer: BWC.

Good	Fine	XF
250	400	600

Second Issue

32 **1/4 Dinar**
L.1947 (1953). Green on multicolor underprint. Portrait young King Faisal II at right. Back: Palm trees at center. Watermark: King's head as a child. Printer: BWC.

Good	Fine	XF
45.00	90.00	180

33 **1/2 Dinar**
L.1947 (1953). Brown on multicolor underprint. Portrait young King Faisal II at right. Back: Ruins of the mosque and spiral minaret at Samarra. Watermark: King's head as a child. Printer: BWC.

Good	Fine	XF
55.00	110	220

34 **1 Dinar**
L.1947 (1953). Blue on multicolor underprint. Portrait young King Faisal II at right. Back: Equestrian statue of King Faisal I. Watermark: King's head as a child. Printer: BWC.

Good	Fine	XF
45.00	90.00	180

35 **5 Dinars**
L.1947 (1953). Red on multicolor underprint. Portrait young King Faisal II at right. Back: Ancient carving of Hammurabi receiving the laws. Watermark: King's head as a child. Printer: BWC.

Good	Fine	XF
500	1,000	2,000

36 **10 Dinars**
L.1947 (1953). Purple on multicolor underprint. Portrait young King Faisal II at right. Back: Winged Assyrian ox and an Assyrian priest at center. Watermark: King's head as a child. Printer: BWC.

Good	Fine	XF
1,000	2,000	3,000

Third Issue

37 **1/4 Dinar**
L.1947 (1955). Green on multicolor underprint. Portrait King Faisal II as an adolescent at right. Back: Palm trees at center. Watermark: King's head as a youth. Printer: BWC.

Good	Fine	XF
50.00	100	200

38 **1/2 Dinar**
L.1947 (1955). Brown on multicolor underprint. Portrait King Faisal II as an adolescent at right. Back: Ruins of the mosque and spiral minaret at Samarra. Watermark: King's head as a youth. Printer: BWC.

	Good	Fine	XF
a. Watermark: Large head.	100	200	400
b. Watermark: Small head.	100	200	400

39	1 Dinar	Good	Fine	XF
	L.1947 (1955). Blue on multicolor underprint. Portrait King Faisal II as an adolescent at right. Back: Equestrian statue of King Faisal I. Watermark: King's head as a youth. Printer: BWC.			
	a. Watermark: Large head.	65.00	125	250
	b. Watermark: Small head.	65.00	125	250

40	5 Dinars	Good	Fine	XF
	L.1947 (1955). Red on multicolor underprint. Portrait King Faisal II as an adolescent at right. Back: Ancient carving of Hammurabi receiving the laws. Watermark: King's head as a youth. Printer: BWC.			
	a. Watermark: Large head.	200	300	500
	b. Watermark: Small head.	200	300	500

41	10 Dinars	Good	Fine	XF
	L.1947 (1955). Purple on multicolor underprint. Portrait King Faisal II as an adolescent at right. Back: Winged Assyrian ox and an Assyrian priest at center. Watermark: King's head as a youth. Printer: BWC.			
	a. Watermark: Large head.	250	350	600
	b. Watermark: Small head.	250	350	600

Central Bank of Iraq

Law #42 of 1947

42	1/4 Dinar	Good	Fine	XF
	L.1947 (1959). Green on multicolor underprint. Portrait King Faisal II as an adolescent at right. Back: Palm trees at center. Watermark: King's head as a youth. Printer: BWC.	75.00	150	300

43	1/2 Dinar	Good	Fine	XF
	L.1947 (1959). Brown on multicolor underprint. Portrait King Faisal II as an adolescent at right. Back: Ruins of the mosque and spiral minaret at Samarra. Watermark: King's head as a youth. Printer: BWC.	50.00	100	200

#44 and 45 not assigned.

Second Issue

46	1/4 Dinar	Good	Fine	XF
	L.1947 (1959). Green on multicolor underprint. Portrait King Faisal II as a young man at right.	75.00	150	300

#47 not assigned.

48	1 Dinar	Good	Fine	XF
	L.1947 (1959). Blue on multicolor underprint. Portrait King Faisal II as a young man at right.	35.00	75.00	150

49	5 Dinars	Good	Fine	XF
	L.1947 (1959). Red on multicolor underprint. Portrait King Faisal II as a young man at right.	75.00	175	400

50	10 Dinars	Good	Fine	XF
	L.1947 (1959). Purple and blue on multicolor underprint. Portrait King Faisal II as a young man at right.	250	350	600

REPUBLIC

Central Bank of Iraq

1959 Issue

51	1/4 Dinar	VG	VF	UNC
	ND (1959). Green on multicolor underprint. Republic arms with 1958 at right. Back: Palm trees at center. Watermark: Republic arms with 1958.			
	a. Without security thread. Signature 13.	1.00	5.00	15.00
	b. With security thread. Signature 14, 16.	1.00	5.00	10.00
	s. Specimen. Punch hole cancelled.	—	—	500

52	1/2 Dinar	VG	VF	UNC
	ND (1959). Brown on multicolor underprint. Republic arms with 1958 at right. Back: Ruins of the mosque and spiral minaret at Samarra. Watermark: Republic arms.			
	a. Without security thread. Signature 13.	35.00	100	150
	b. With security thread. Signature 14, 16.	2.00	7.50	30.00
	s. Specimen. Punch hole cancelled.	—	—	500

53	1 Dinar	VG	VF	UNC
	ND (1959). Blue on multicolor underprint. Republic arms with 1958 at right. Back: The *Harp of Ur* at center. Watermark: Republic arms.			
	a. Without security thread. Signature 13.	1.50	8.00	30.00
	b. With security thread. Blue lines over watermark area. Signature 14, 15.	1.50	8.00	30.00
	s. Specimen. Punch hole cancelled.	—	—	500

54	5 Dinars	VG	VF	UNC
	ND (1959). Light purple on multicolor underprint. Republic arms with 1958 at right. Back: Ancient carving of Hammurabi receiving the laws. Watermark: Symbol of the Immortal Revolution.			
	a. Without security thread. 1 signature variety.	2.50	15.00	45.00
	b. With security thread.	2.50	15.00	45.00
	s. Specimen. Punch hole cancelled.	—	—	500

55	10 Dinars	VG	VF	UNC
	ND (1959). Purple on multicolor underprint. Republic arms with 1958 at right. Signature 10, 11 and 12. Back: Carvings of a winged Assyrian ox and an Assyrian priest. Watermark: Symbol of the Immortal Revolution.			
	a. Without security thread. 1 signature variety.	3.00	12.00	65.00
	b. With security thread. 2 signature varieties.	3.00	12.00	65.00
	s. Specimen. Punched hole cancelled.	—	—	500

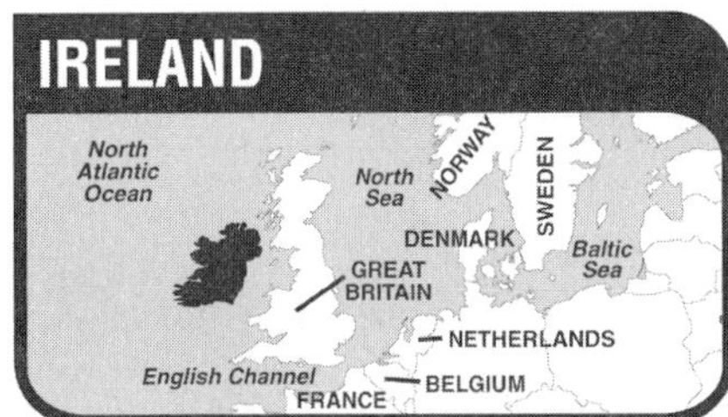

Ireland, the island located in the Atlantic Ocean west of Great Britain, was settled by dark and swarthy Celts from Gaul about 400 BC, but eventually they became known for their red hair and light complexions after frequent Viking invasions. The Celts assimilated the native Erainn and Picts and established a Gaelic civilization. After the arrival of St. Patrick in 432 AD, Ireland evolved into a center of Latin learning which sent missionaries to Europe and possibly North America. In 1154, Pope Adrian IV gave all of Ireland to English King Henry II to administer as a Papal fief. Because of the enactment of anti-Catholic laws and the awarding of vast tracts of Irish land to Protestant absentee landowners, English control did not become reasonably absolute until 1800 when England and Ireland became the "United Kingdom of Great Britain and Ireland." Religious freedom was restored to the Irish in 1829, but agitation for political autonomy continued until the Irish Free State was established as a dominion on Dec. 6, 1921 while Northern Ireland remained within the United Kingdom.

Additional information on bank notes of Northern Ireland can be found in *Paper Money of Ireland* by Bob Blake and Jonathan Callaway, published by Pam West.

RULERS:

British to 1921

MONETARY SYSTEM:

1 Shilling = 12 Pence
1 Pound = 20 Shillings to 1971
1 Guinea = 21 Shillings
1 Pound = 100 Pence 1971-2001. 1 Euro = 100 Euro Cents 2002-

BRITISH ADMINISTRATION

Bank of Ireland

Dublin

1797 Issue

No.	Description	Good	Fine	XF
4	**1 Guinea** 1797 Black. Hibernia seated with harp at upper left. ONE GUINEA in black panel.	—	—	—
5	**1 Guinea** 1797. Black. Hibernia seated with harp at upper left. ONE in black panel.	—	—	—

1798-1811 Issue

No.	Description	Good	Fine	XF
6	**1 Pound** 1798. Black. Hibernia seated in seal at top left. Rare.	—	—	—

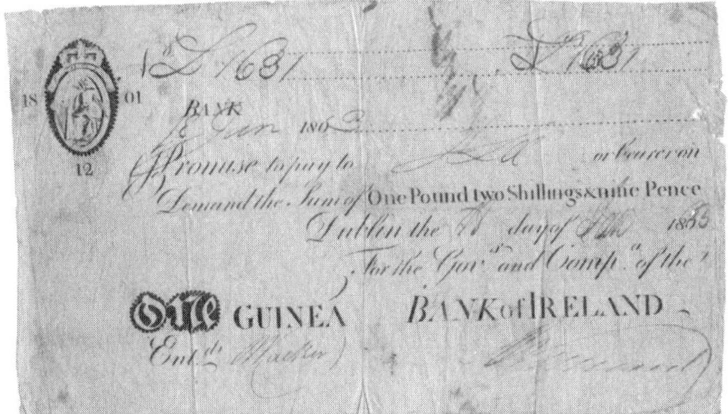

No.	Description	Good	Fine	XF
7	**1 Guinea** 1801-1803. Black. Hibernia seated within seal at top left.	2,000	4,000	8,000
8	**30 Shillings** 1798. Black. Hibernia seated within seal at top left. Rare.	—	—	—
9	**1 1/2 Guinea** 1798. Black. Hibernia seated within seal at top left. Rare.	—	—	—
10	**5 Guineas** 1798. Black. Hibernia seated within seal at top left. Rare.	—	—	—
11	**10 Pounds** 1798. Black. Hibernia seated within seal at top left. Rare.	—	—	—

1812-1815 Issue

No.	Description	Good	Fine	XF
12	**1 Pound** 1812. Black. Hibernia seated within seal at top left. Rare.	—	—	—
13	**1 Guinea** 1812. Black. Hibernia seated within seal at top left. Rare.	—	—	—
14	**25 Shillings** 1812. Black. Hibernia seated within seal at top left. Rare.	—	—	—
15	**30 Shillings** 1812. Black. Hibernia seated within seal at top left. Rare.	—	—	—
16	**5 Pounds** 1812. Black. Hibernia seated within seal at top left. Rare.	—	—	—

1815-1825 Issue

No.	Description	Good	Fine	XF
17	**1 Pound** 9.9.1816-3.3.1825. Black. Hibernia seated within seal at top left.			
	a. Issued note. Rare.	—	—	—
	p. Proof. Rare.	—	—	—
18	**1 Guinea** 6.9.1816; 3.2.1817. Black. Hibernia seated within seal at top left. Value in half moon device, reads ONE / GUINEA. Rare.	—	—	—
19	**1 Guinea** 8.4.1818-5.1.1821. Black. Hibernia seated within seal at top left. Value in oval device, reads ONE GUINEA. Rare.	—	—	—
20	**30 Shillings** 3.1.1816-3.12.1822. Black. Hibernia seated within seal at top left.			
	a. Issued note. Rare.	—	—	—
	p. Proof. Rare.	—	—	—
21	**2 Pounds** 2.12.1815. Black. Hibernia seated within seal at top left. Rare.	—	—	—
22	**5 Pounds** 7.2.1820. Black. Hibernia seated within seal at top left. Two oval panels, bank name in Roman typefont. Rare.	—	—	—
23	**5 Pounds** 1.5.1821-6.11.1824. Black. Hibernia seated within seal at top left. One oval panel, bank name in Gothic typefont. Rare.	—	—	—
24	**10 Pounds** 7.5.1824. Black. Hibernia seated within seal at top left. Rare.	—		
	7.5.1824. Black. Hibernia seated within seal at top left. Rare.	—	—	—

1820 Issue

No.	Description	Good	Fine	XF
25	**1 Pound** ND. Black and red. Hibernia seated within seal at left border. Color trial.	—	—	2,250

1825-1840 issue

No.	Description	Good	Fine	XF
26	**1 Pound** 3.12.1825-6.9.1827. Black. Hibernia seated within seal. Rare.	—	—	—
27	**1 Pound** 8.8.1832-8.9.1837. Black. Hibernia seated at upper left and right. Rare.			
	a. 8.8.1832; 8.10.1832.	—	—	—
	b. 9.9.1835-8.9.1837. Shading added to various parts of note design.	—	—	—
28	**30 Shillings** 9.12.1825-7.10.1828. Black. Hibernia seated at upper left and right. Rare.	—	—	—

No.	Description	Good	Fine	XF
29	**30 Shillings** 7.10.1828-17.5.1837. Black. Hibernia seated at upper left and right.			
	a. 7.10.1828-4.11.1831.	—	—	—
	b. 3.1.1833-17.5.1837.	—	—	—
	p. Proof. 12.1830.	—	Unc	2,000

No.	Description	Good	Fine	XF
30	**5 Pounds** 17.4.1838; 4.3.1840. Black. Hibernia seated at upper left and right.	—	—	—
31	**10 Pounds** ND. Black. Hibernia seated at upper left and right. Requires confirmation.	—	—	—
32	**20 Pounds** ND. Black. Hibernia seated at upper left and right.	—	—	—
33	**50 Pounds** ND. Black. Hibernia seated at upper left and right. Bank name in Roman typeface.	—	—	—
34	**50 Pounds** 7.1.1831. Black. Hibernia seated at upper left and right. Bank name in Gothic typeface.	—	—	—

Sold in 2006 for aprox. $33,500.

1838-1842 Issue

No.	Description	Good	Fine	XF
35	**1 Pound** 15.1.1838-4.1.1842. Black. Medusa heads across top, 75mm tall Hibernia standing at left and right.	2,000	6,000	—
36	**30 Shillings** 3.5.1838-7.9.1841. Black. Medusa heads across top, 75mm tall Hibernia standing at left and right.	4,000	10,000	—
37	**5 Pounds** ND. Black. Medusa heads across top, 75mm tall Hibernia standing at left and right. Requires confirmation.	—	—	—

1842-1849 issue

No.	Description	Good	Fine	XF
38	**1 Pound** 16.8.1849. Hibernia standing with harp at left and right, Medusa heads across top. *ONE* in protector at bottom.	1,000	3,000	—
39	**30 Shillings** 7.10.1843-16.8.1849. Black. Medusa heads across top, 68mm tall Hibernia standing at left and right.	4,000	10,000	—
40	**3 Pounds** 2.4.1846. Black. Medusa heads across top, 68mm tall Hibernia standing at left and right.	—	—	—
41	**5 Pounds** 1.1.1845; 8.9.1847. Black. Medusa heads across top, 68mm tall Hibernia standing at left and right. Rare.	—	—	—

Color Abbreviation Guide

New to the *Standard Catalog of® World Paper Money* are the following abbreviations related to color references:

BC: Back color
PC: Paper color

1852-1863 Issue

No.	Description	Good	Fine	XF
42	**1 Pound** 13.4.1852-6.11.1862. Black. Medusa heads across top, Hibernia standing at left and right. Wavy Security protector.	—	7,000	—
43	**3 Pounds** ND. Black. Medusa heads across top, Hibernia standing at left and right. Wavy Security protector. Requires confirmaiton.	—	—	—
44	**5 Pounds** 2.7.1856-2.8.1859. Black. Medusa heads across top, Hibernia standing at left and right. Wavy Security protector. Rare.	—	—	—
45	**10 Pounds** 8.6.1861. Black. Medusa heads across top, Hibernia standing at left and right. Wavy Security protector. Rare.	—	—	—

1863-1883 Issue

No.	Description	Good	Fine	XF
50	**1 Pound** 27.11.1869; 15.12.1869. Black and red. Medusa heads across top, Hibernia standing at left and right. Wavy Security protector. Serial #, date and branches in red. Three lines of branches. Rare.	4,000	10,000	—

No.	Description	Good	Fine	XF
51	**1 Pound** 10.3.1877; 23.8.1878. Hibernia standing with harp at left and right, Medusa heads across top. Wavy design protector at bottom. Offices of issue in 4 lines below *Dublin*.	1,500	6,000	—
52	**3 Pounds** ND. Black and red. Medusa heads across top, Hibernia standing at left and right. Wavy Security protector. Serial #, date and branches in red. Requires confirmation.	—	—	—
53	**5 Pounds** ND. Black and red. Medusa heads across top, Hibernia standing at left and right. Wavy Security protector. Serial #, date and branches in red. Requires confirmation.	—	—	—
54	**10 Pounds** ND. Black and red. Medusa heads across top, Hibernia standing at left and right. Wavy Security protector. Serial #, date and branches in red. Rare	—	—	—
55	**20 Pounds** ND. Black and red. Medusa heads across top, Hibernia standing at left and right. Wavy Security protector. Serial #, date and branches in red. Rare	—	—	—
56	**50 Pounds** ND. Black and red. Medusa heads across top, Hibernia standing at left and right. Wavy Security protector. Serial #, date and branches in red. Rare.	—	—	—
57	**100 Pounds** ND. Black and red. Medusa heads across top, Hibernia standing at left and right. Wavy Security protector. Serial #, date and branches in red. Rare.	—	—	—

#	Denomination	Good	Fine	XF
58	**500 Pounds** 13.12.1869. Black and red. Medusa heads across top, Hibernia standing at left and right. Wavy Security protector. Serial #, date and branches in red. Rare.	—	—	—

1883-1905 Issue

#	Denomination	Good	Fine	XF
62	**1 Pound** 1881-1905. Black and red. Medusa heads across top, Hibernia standing at left and right. Wavy Security protector. Serial #, date and branches in red.			
	a. 29.11.1881-29.7.1889. Signature J. Craig.	1,000	2,100	—
	b. 17.12.1890-12.3.1896. Signature Amos M. Vereker.	800	1,400	—
	c. 30.10.1900-18.11.1901. Signature Henry Evans.	800	1,750	—
	d. 20.1.1905. Signature William H. Baskin.	500	1,400	3,000
63	**3 Pounds** ND. Black and red. Medusa heads across top, Hibernia standing at left and right. Wavy Security protector. Serial #, date and branches in red. Requires confirmaiton.	—	—	—
64	**5 Pounds** 24.8.1887-13.10.1890. Black and red. Medusa heads across top, Hibernia standing at left and right. Wavy Security protector. Serial #, date and branches in red. Signature S. Foot.	1,800	3,500	—

#	Denomination	Good	Fine	XF
65	**10 Pounds** 23.7.1887-21.10.1904. Black and red. Medusa heads across top, Hibernia standing at left and right. Wavy Security protector. Serial #, date and branches in red.			
	a. 23.7.1887. Signature H. Henry.	—	5,000	—
	b. 10.11.1890. Signature Amos M. Vereker.	—	4,200	—
	c. 28.2.1901. Signature Henry Evans.	—	3,500	—
	d. 21.10.1904. Signature William H. Baskin.	—	2,800	—
66	**20 Pounds** ND. Black and red. Medusa heads across top, Hibernia standing at left and right. Wavy Security protector. Serial #, date and branches in red. Requires confirmation.	—	—	—
67	**50 Pounds** ND. Black and red. Medusa heads across top, Hibernia standing at left and right. Wavy Security protector. Serial #, date and branches in red. Requires confirmation.	—	—	—
68	**100 Pounds** ND. Black and red. Medusa heads across top, Hibernia standing at left and right. Wavy Security protector. Serial #, date and branches in red. Rare.	—	—	—
69	**500 Pounds** ND. Black and red. Medusa heads across top, Hibernia standing at left and right. Wavy Security protector. Serial #, date and branches in red. Requires confirmation.	—	—	—

1908-1919 Issue

#	Denomination	Good	Fine	XF
74	**1 Pound** 14.9.1910-20.12.1917. Black and red. Hibernia standing with harp at left and right, Medusa heads across top. Offices of issue in 5 lines of type below *Dublin*.			
	a. 14.9.1910-21.4.1917. 65 Branches.	300	800	2,000
	b. 12.7.1917-20.12.1917. 66 Branches (Newtonards added.)	300	800	2,000

#	Denomination	Good	Fine	XF
75	**3 Pounds** 17.9.1912; 10.10.1914. Hibernia standing with harp at left and right, Medusa heads across top.			
	a. Issued note.	5,000	10,000	—
	p. Proof.	—	—	700

#	Denomination	Good	Fine	XF
77	**5 Pounds** 12.3.1908-11.12.1918. Black and red. Medusa heads across top, Hibernia standing at left and right. Wavy Security protector. Serial #, date and branches in red.			
	a. 12.3.1908-14.12.1916. 65 Branches.	700	2,000	5,000
	b. 15.10.1917-11.12.1918. 66 Branches (Newtownards added).	700	2,100	5,000

		Good	Fine	XF
79	**10 Pounds** 1911-1918. Black and red. Medusa heads across top, Hibernia standing at left and right. Wavy Security protector. Serial #, date and branches in red.			
	a. 26.9.1911-11.11.1916. 65 Branches.	1,000	2,000	5,000
	b. 22.9.1917-23.11.1918. 66 Branches (Newtownards added).	1,000	2,000	5,000
	c. 23-11.1918-21.3.1919. Smaller sans-serif prefixes, thicker serial #.	1,000	2,000	5,000

		Good	Fine	XF
80	**20 Pounds** 10.11.1915. Black and red. Medusa heads across top, Hibernia standing at left and right. Wavy Security protector. Serial #, date and branches in red.			
	a. 66 Branches. Serif serial # prefix. Thin serial #.	—	5,000	7,000
	b. 66 Branches. Smaller serial # prefix. Thick serial #.	—	5,000	7,000

		Good	Fine	XF
81	**50 Pounds** 16.5.1908. Black and red. Medusa heads across top, Hibernia standing at left and right. Wavy Security protector. Serial #, date and branches in red.	—	—	—
82	**100 Pounds** ND. Black and red. Medusa heads across top, Hibernia standing at left and right. Wavy Security protector. Serial #, date and branches in red. Requires confirmation.	—	—	—
83	**500 Pounds** ND. Black and red. Medusa heads across top, Hibernia standing at left and right. Wavy Security protector. Serial #, date and branches in red. Requires confirmation.	—	—	—

1918-1919 Issue

		Good	Fine	XF
84	**1 Pound** 10.0.1918-14.4.1920. Black and red. Medusa heads across top. Hibernia standing at left and right. Wavy Security protector. Serial #, date, eight lines of branches in red at center. 150x100mm.			
	a. 10.8.1918-14.4.1920. Signature William H. Baskin.	200	800	2,300
	b. 12.1.1920-14.4.1920. Signature Alfred G. Fleming.	300	1,000	2,000

		Good	Fine	XF
85	**5 Pounds** 27.1.1919. Black and green. Medusa heads across top. Hibernia standing at left and right. Wavy Security protector. Serial #, date and branches in green.			
	a. 27.1.1919. Signature William M. Baskin	5,000	15,000	—
	b. 13.12.1919. Signature Alfred G. Fleming.	5,000	15,000	—

1920-1921 Issue

		Good	Fine	XF
86	**1 Pound** 12.8.1920-15.10.1921. Black and red. Medusa heads across top. Hibernia standing at left and right. Wavy Security protector. Serial #, date in red. 150x100mm.			
	a. 12.8.1920-17.1920. Signature A. G. Fleming.	300	1,000	2,300
	b. 12.9.1921-15.10.1921. Signature S. Hilton.	200	800	1,700
87	**5 Pounds** 10.8.1920-12.5.1921. Black and green. Medusa heads across top, Hibernia standing at left and right. Wavy Security protector. Serial # and date in green.			
	a. 10.8.1920; 10.9.1920. Signature Alfred G. Fleming.	—	2,800	—
	b. 11.4.1921; 12.5.1921. Signature S. Hilton.	—	2,800	—
88	**10 Pounds** 13.9.1920 Black and red. Medusa heads across top, Hibernia standing at left and right. Wavy Security protector. Serial # and date in red. Signature Alfred G. Fleming.	—	5,000	—

1922-1928 Issue

		Good	Fine	XF
95	**1 Pound** 10.4.1922-19.3.1924. Black on green underprint. Medusa heads across top, Hibernia standing at left and right. Value in sunburst underprint.			
	a. 10.4.1922. Signature S. Hilton.	300	500	1,000
	b. 10.4.1922-15.6.1922. Signature S. Hilton.	200	425	850

No.	Description	Good	Fine	XF
	c. 19.3.1924. Signature Joseph A. Gargan.	150	350	700
	d. 20.1.1925-16.2.1928. Signature Joseph A. Gargan.	100	300	600
96	**5 Pounds** 27.2.1922-14.12.1927. Black on red underprint. Medusa heads across top, Hibernia standing at left and right. Medusa head at center. Sunburst underprint. Back: Hibernia seated at center.			
	a. 27.2.1922. Signature S. Hilton. Small fraction prefix.	900	2,000	3,000
	b. 15.3.1922; 16.3.1922. Signature S. Hilton. In-line serial # prefix.	600	1,500	2,000
	c. 12.11.1923-12.11.1924. Signature Joseph A. Gargan. In-line serial # prefix.	300	900	1,500
	d. 24.9.1925-14.12.1927. Signature Joseph A. Gargan. Large fractional serial # prefix.	300	900	1,500
97	**10 Pounds** 14.1.1924-10.10.1925. Black on blue underprint. Medusa heads across top, Hibernia standing at left and right. Medusa head at center. Sunburst underprint. Back: Hibernia seated at center.			
	b. 10.1.1923. Signature Joseph S. Hinton. In-line Prefix.	1,500	3,000	4,500
	c. 14.1.1924. Signature Joseph A. Gargan. In-line serial # prefix.	900	2,200	3,500
	d. 10.10.1925. Signature Joseph A. Gargan. Fractional serial # prefix.	900	2,200	3,500
98	**20 Pounds** 14.1.1924-10.10.1925. Black on orange underprint. Medusa heads across top, Hibernia standing at left and right. Madusa head at center. Sunburst underprint. Back: Hibernia seated at center. Proof only.	—	—	—

Belfast Banking Company

Later became Belfast Banking Company Ltd.

Belfast

1827-1843 Issue

No.	Description	Good	Fine	XF
110	**1 Pound** ND. Black. Arms at top and right. Printer: Perkins & Heath. Proof.	—	—	1,400
111	**1 Pound** ND. Black. Arms at top and right. Numerals in each corner. Printer: Perkins, Bacon & Petch. Proof.	—	—	1,400
112	**1 Guinea** ND. Black. Requires confirmation.	—	—	—
113	**25 Shillings** ND. Black. Numerals in each corner. Proof.	—	—	1,400
114	**30 Shillings** ND. Black. Numerals in each corner. Printer: Perkins & heath. Proof.	—	—	1,400
115	**35 Shillings** ND. Black. Numerals in each corner. Proof.	—	—	1,400
116	**2 Pounds** ND. Black. Numerals in each corner. Requires confirmation.	—	—	—
118	**3 Pounds** ND. Black. Numerals in each corner. Requires confirmation.	—	—	—
119	**5 Pounds** ND. Black. Numerals in each corner. Proof.	—	—	1,400
120	**10 Pounds** ND. Black. Numerals in each corner. Proof	—	—	1,400
121	**20 Pounds** ND. Black. Numerals in each corner. Proof	—	—	1,400

1843-1850 Issue

No.	Description	Good	Fine	XF
122	**1 Pound** ND. Black. Rare.	—	—	—
123	**25 Shillings** ND. Black. Rare.	—	—	—
124	**30 Shillings** ND. Black. Rare.	—	—	—
125	**35 Shillings** ND. Black. Rare.	—	—	—
126	**2 Pounds** ND. Black. Rare.	—	—	—
127	**3 Pounds** ND. Black. Rare.	—	—	—
128	**5 Pounds** ND. Black. Rare.	—	—	—
129	**10 Pounds** ND. Black. Rare.	—	—	—
130	**20 Pounds** ND. Black. Rare.	—	—	—
131	**50 Pounds** ND. Black. Rare.	—	—	—

1851-1866 Issue

No.	Description	Good	Fine	XF
132	**1 Pound** ND. Black. Printer: Charles Skipper & East. Proof only.	—	—	1,000
133	**5 Pounds** ND. Black. Printer: Charles Skipper & East. Requires confirmation.	—	—	—
134	**10 Pounds** ND. Black. Printer: Charles Skipper & East. Requires confirmation.	—	—	—
135	**20 Pounds** ND. Black. Printer: Charles Skipper & East. Requires confirmation.	—	—	—
136	**50 Pounds** ND. Black. Printer: Charles Skipper & East. Requires confirmation.	—	—	—

1860s Montgomery Draft Issue

No.	Description	Good	Fine	XF
137	**1 Pound** ND. Black on green and red underprint. Printer: ABNC. Proof	—	—	750
138	**2 Pounds** ND. Black on green and red underprint. Printer: ABNC. Proof	—	—	750

1867-1878 Issue

No.	Description	Good	Fine	XF
139	**1 Pound** 4.12.1874. Arms at left and upper center right.	—	3,500	—
140	**5 Pounds** 1.3.1871-17.1.1877. Black. Arms at top and at left end.	—	3,500	—
141	**10 Pounds** ND. Black. Arms at top and at left end. Proof.	—	—	700
142	**20 Pounds** ND. Black. Arms at top and at left end. Requires confirmation.	—	—	—
143	**50 Pounds** ND. Black. Arms at top and at left end. Requires confirmation.	—	—	—
144	**100 Pounds** ND. Black. Arms at top and at left end. Requires confirmation.	—	—	—

1879-1882 Issue

No.	Description	Good	Fine	XF
145	**1 Pound** 22.7.1882. Black. Arms at top and at left end.	—	3,000	—
146	**5 Pounds** ND. Black. Arms at top and at left end. Requires confirmation.	—	—	—
147	**10 Pounds** ND. Black. Arms at top and at left end. Requires confirmation.	—	—	—

Belfast Banking Company Limited

See also Belfast Banking Co. Northern Ireland.

Belfast

1879-1920 Issue

No.	Description	Good	Fine	XF
149	**1 Pound** 1883-1905. Black. Value in each corner, arms at top center and left end.	—	1,500	—

#	Description	Good	Fine	XF
150	**1 Pound**	Good	Fine	XF
	1905-1920. Black on blue underprint. Oval in each corner, arms at top center and left end.			
	a. Black area under signature. 1905-1907.	—	1,400	—
	b. White area under signature. 1910-1920.	—	1,250	—
	p. Proof.	—	—	700

#	Description	Good	Fine	XF
151	**5 Pounds**	Good	Fine	XF
	1883-1918. Brown underprint. Arms at left and at center. Printer: CS&E.			
	a. Issued note.	1,000	2,500	—
	p. Proof.	—	—	700

#	Description	Good	Fine	XF
152	**10 Pounds**	Good	Fine	XF
	1883-1919. Black on rebdish brown underprint. Oval in each corner, arms at top center and left end.			
	a. Issued note.	1,100	3,000	—
	p. Proof.	—	—	700
153	**20 Pounds**	Good	Fine	XF
	1883-1916. Black on blue underprint. Oval in each corner, arms at top center flanked by large value.			
	a. Issued note.	1,500	5,000	—
	p. Proof.	—	—	700
154	**50 Pounds**	Good	Fine	XF
	1883-1919. Black on red underprint. Oval in each corner, arms at top center flanked by large value.			
	a. Issued note.	3,000	10,000	—
	p. Proof.	—	—	700
155	**100 Pounds**	Good	Fine	XF
	1885-1915. Black on green underprint. Female seated at shore. Value as underprint.			
	a. Issued note.	—	—	—
	p. Proof.	—	—	700

National Bank

Later became the National Bank Ltd.

Dublin

1835 Issue

#	Description	Good	Fine	XF
163	**1 Pound**	Good	Fine	XF
	2.4.1835. Black. Hibernia seated at center, shield at top left. Printer: Perkins, Bacon & Petch, London.			
	a. Issued note.	—	8,500	—
	p. Proof.	—	—	700
164	**30 Shillings**	Good	Fine	XF
	ND. Black. Hibernia seated at center, shield at top left. Printer: Perkins, Bacon & Petch, London. Proof.	—	—	1,500
165	**3 Pounds**	Good	Fine	XF
	ND. Black. Hibernia seated at center, shield at top left. Printer: Perkins, Bacon & Petch, London. Requires confirmation.	—	—	—
166	**5 Pounds**	Good	Fine	XF
	ND. Black. Hibernia seated at center, shield at top left. Printer: Perkins, Bacon & Petch, London. Proof	—	1,500	—

1835-1843 Issue

#	Description	Good	Fine	XF
167	**1 Pound**	Good	Fine	XF
	1.1.1836. Black. Hibernia seated at center, shield at top left supported by wolfhounds. Printer: Perkins, Bacon & Petch, London.	—	8,500	—
168	**30 Shillings**	Good	Fine	XF
	21.11.1843. Black. Hibernia seated at center, shield at top left supported by wolfhounds. Printer: Perkins, Bacon & Petch, London.	—	8,500	—

1835-1836 Issue

#	Description	Good	Fine	XF
169	**1 Pound**	Good	Fine	XF
	6.10.1835. Black. Hibernia seated at center, shield at top left supported by wolfhounds. Printer: Perkins, Bacon & Petch, London.			
	a. Issued note.	—	7,000	—
	p. Proof.	—	—	700
170	**30 Shillings**	Good	Fine	XF
	ND. Black. Hibernia seated at center, shield at top left supported by wolfhounds. Printer: Perkins, Bacon & Petch, London. Proof	—	1,000	—
171	**3 Pounds**	Good	Fine	XF
	ND. Black. Hibernia seated at center, shield at top left supported by wolfhounds. Printer: Perkins, Bacon & Petch, London. Requires confirmation.	—	—	—
172	**5 Pounds**	Good	Fine	XF
	ND. Black. Hibernia seated at center, shield at top left supported by wolfhounds. Printer: Perkins, Bacon & Petch, London. Proof.	—	1,000	—
173	**1 Pound**	Good	Fine	XF
	ND. Black. Hibernia seated at center, shield at top left supported by wolfhounds. Printer: Perkins, Bacon & Petch, London. Proof.	—	1,200	—
174	**30 Shillings**	Good	Fine	XF
	ND. Black. Hibernia seated at center, shield at top left supported by wolfhounds. Printer: Perkins, Bacon & Petch, London. Proof.	—	1,200	—
175	**3 Pounds**	Good	Fine	XF
	ND. Black. Hibernia seated at center, shield at top left supported by wolfhounds. Printer: Perkins, Bacon & Petch, London. Proof.	—	—	—
176	**5 Pounds**	Good	Fine	XF
	ND. Black. Hibernia seated at center, shield at top left supported by wolfhounds. Printer: Perkins, Bacon & Petch, London. Proof.	—	—	—
177	**10 Pounds**	Good	Fine	XF
	ND. Black. Hibernia seated at center, shield at top left supported by wolfhounds. Printer: Perkins, Bacon & Petch, London. Proof.	—	—	—
178	**20 Pounds**	Good	Fine	XF
	ND. Black. Hibernia seated at center, shield at top left supported by wolfhounds. Printer: Perkins, Bacon & Petch, London. Proof.			
	a. Value in white text.	—	1,500	—
	b. Value in white text with black center lines.	—	1,500	—

1836-1843 Issue

#	Description	Good	Fine	XF
179	**1 Pound**	Good	Fine	XF
	1841. Black. Hibernia seated at center, shield at top left supported by wolfhounds. Printer: Perkins, Bacon & Petch, London.			
	a. Issued note. 22.9.1841.	—	7,000	—
	p. Proof.	—	—	700
180	**30 Shillings**	Good	Fine	XF
	ND. Black. Hibernia seated at center, shield at top left supported by wolfhounds. Printer: Perkins, Bacon & Petch, London. Proof.	—	700	—
181	**3 Pounds**	Good	Fine	XF
	ND. Black. Hibernia seated at center, shield at top left supported by wolfhounds. Printer: Perkins, Bacon & Petch, London. Proof.	—	1,000	—

No.	Denomination / Description	Good	Fine	XF
182	**5 Pounds** ND. Black. Hibernia seated at center, shield at top left supported by wolfhounds. Printer: Perkins, Bacon & Petch, London. Proof.	—	700	—
183	**10 Pounds** ND. Black. Hibernia seated at center, shield at top left supported by wolfhounds. Printer: Perkins, Bacon & Petch, London. Proof.	—	900	—

1843-1856 Issue

No.	Denomination / Description	Good	Fine	XF
184	**1 Pound** 1844-1853. Black. Hibernia seated at center, shield at top left supported by wolfhounds. Printer: Perkins, Bacon & Petch, London.			
	a. Issued note. 1844-1853.	—	6,250	—
	p. Proof.	—	—	700
185	**30 Shillings** ND. Black. Hibernia seated at center, shield at top left supported by wolfhounds. Printer: Perkins, Bacon & Petch, London. Proof.	—	—	700
186	**3 Pounds** ND. Black. Hibernia seated at center, shield at top left supported by wolfhounds. Printer: Perkins, Bacon & Petch, London. Proof.	—	—	700
187	**5 Pounds** ND. Black. Hibernia seated at center, shield at top left supported by wolfhounds. Printer: Perkins, Bacon & Petch, London. Proof.	—	—	800
188	**10 Pounds** ND. Black. Hibernia seated at center, shield at top left supported by wolfhounds. Printer: Perkins, Bacon & Petch, London. Proof.	—	—	900

1856-1869 Issue

No.	Denomination / Description	Good	Fine	XF
189	**1 Pound** 1856-1866 Black. Hibernia seated at center, shield at top left supported by wolfhounds. Printer: Perkins, Bacon & Co., London.			
	a. Issued note. 1856-1866.	—	5,000	—
	p. Proof.	—	—	500
190	**3 Pounds** ND. Black. Hibernia seated at center, shield at top left supported by wolfhounds. Printer: Perkins, Bacon & Co., London. Proof.	—	—	700
191	**5 Pounds** ND. Black. Hibernia seated at center, shield at top left supported by wolfhounds. Printer: Perkins, Bacon & Co., London. Proof.	—	—	600
192	**10 Pounds** ND. Black. Hibernia seated at center, shield at top left supported by wolfhounds. Printer: Perkins, Bacon & Co., London. Proof.	—	—	650
193	**20 Pounds** ND. Black. Hibernia seated at center, shield at top left supported by wolfhounds. Printer: Perkins, Bacon & Co., London. Proof.	—	—	700
194	**50 Pounds** ND. Black. Hibernia seated at center, shield at top left supported by wolfhounds. Printer: Perkins, Bacon & Co., London. Proof.	—	—	—
195	**100 Pounds** ND. Black. Hibernia seated at center, shield at top left supported by wolfhounds. Printer: Perkins, Bacon & Co., London. Proof.	—	—	—

1870-1881 Issue

4 lines of branches now listed in center of each note.

No.	Denomination / Description	Good	Fine	XF
196	**1 Pound** ND. Black. Hibernia seated at center, shield at top left supported by wolfhounds. Printer: Perkins, Bacon & Co., London.			
	a. Issued note. 1874; 1879.	—	4,250	—
	p. Proof.	—	—	350
197	**3 Pounds** ND. Black. Hibernia seated at center, shield at top left supported by wolfhounds. Printer: Perkins, Bacon & Co., London.			
	a. Issued note. 1871.	—	7,000	—
	p. Proof.	—	—	500
198	**5 Pounds** ND. Black. Hibernia seated at center, shield at top left supported by wolfhounds. Printer: Perkins, Bacon & Co., London.	—	—	450
199	**10 Pounds** 10.1.1870. Black. Hibernia seated at center, shield at top left supported by wolfhounds. Printer: Perkins, Bacon & Co., London. Proof.	—	—	450
200	**20 Pounds** ND. Black. Hibernia seated at center, shield at top left supported by wolfhounds. Printer: Perkins, Bacon & Co., London. Proof.	—	—	550
201	**50 Pounds** ND. Black. Hibernia seated at center, shield at top left supported by wolfhounds. Printer: Perkins, Bacon & Co., London. Proof.	—	—	850
202	**100 Pounds** ND. Black. Hibernia seated at center, shield at top left supported by wolfhounds. Printer: Perkins, Bacon & Co., London. Proof.	—	—	1,000

National Bank Limited

See also Ireland-Republic and Northern Ireland.

Dublin

1882-1900 Issue

No.	Denomination / Description	Good	Fine	XF
203	**1 Pound** 1882; 1893. Black. Hibernia seated at center, shield at top left supported by wolfhounds. Printer: Perkins, Bacon & Co., London. Proof.			
	a. Issued note. 2.1.1882; 1.4.1893.	1,100	3,500	—
	p. Proof.	—	—	275

No.	Denomination / Description	Good	Fine	XF
204	**3 Pounds** 3.12.1891. Black. Hibernia seated at center, shield at top left supported by wolfhounds. Printer: Perkins, Bacon & Co., London.			
	a. Issued note. 3.12.1891.	4,000	7,000	—
	p. Proof.	—	—	500
205	**5 Pounds** ND. Black. Hibernia seated at center, shield at top left supported by wolfhounds. Printer: Perkins, Bacon & Co., London. Proof.	—	—	500
206	**10 Pounds** ND. Black. Hibernia seated at center, shield at top left supported by wolfhounds. Printer: Perkins, Bacon & Co., London. Proof.	—	—	425
207	**20 Pounds** ND. Black. Hibernia seated at center, shield at top left supported by wolfhounds. Printer: Perkins, Bacon & Co., London. Proof.	—	—	500
208	**50 Pounds** ND. Black. Hibernia seated at center, shield at top left supported by wolfhounds. Printer: Perkins, Bacon & Co., London. Proof.	—	—	775
208A	**100 Pounds** ND. Black. Hibernia seated at center, shield at top left supported by wolfhounds. Printer: Perkins, Bacon & Co., London. Proof.	—	—	1,000

1900-1915 Issue

		Good	Fine	XF
209	**1 Pound** 1911-1914. Black on green underprint. Hibernia seated at center, shield at top left supported by wolfhounds. Printer: Perkins, Bacon & Co., London.			
	a. Issued note. 1911-1914.	800	2,000	3,000
	p1. Proof of entire note.	—	—	200
	p2. Proof with bottom cut off.	—	—	30.00

		Good	Fine	XF
210	**3 Pounds** 1.10.1913. Black on green underprint. Arms at upper left. Hibernia seated with harp at upper center.			
	a. Issued note.	3,000	8,000	12,000
	p1. Proof.	—	—	200
	p2. Proof with bottom cut off.	—	—	30.00

		Good	Fine	XF
210A	**5 Pounds** ND. Black on green underprint. Hibernia seated at center, shield at top left supported by wolfhounds. Printer: Perkins, Bacon & Co., London.			
	a. Issued note.	1,000	2,500	4,000
	p. Proof.	—	—	200
	p2. Proof with bottom cut off.	—	—	30.00

		Good	Fine	XF
211	**10 Pounds** 1901-1915. Black on green underprint. Hibernia seated at center, shield at top left supported by wolfhounds. Printer: Perkins, Bacon & Co., London.			
	a. Issued note.	1,000	2,500	4,000
	p1. Proof.	—	—	200
	p2. Proof with bottom cut off.	—	—	30.00

		Good	Fine	XF
212	**20 Pounds** 1901-1915. Black on green underprint. Hibernia seated at center, shield at top left supported by wolfhounds. Printer: Perkins, Bacon & Co., London. Proof.			
	a.	—	—	8,000
	p1. Proof.	—	—	200
	p2. Proof with bottom cut off.	—	—	30.00
213	**50 Pounds** 1901-1915. Black on green underprint. Hibernia seated at center, shield at top left supported by wolfhounds. Printer: Perkins, Bacon & Co., London.	Good	Fine	XF
	p1. Proof.	—	—	200
	p2. Proof with cut off bottom.	—	—	30.00
214	**100 Pounds** 1901-1915. Black on green underprint. Hibernia seated at center, shield at top left supported by wolfhounds. Printer: Perkins, Bacon & Co., London. Proof.	Good	Fine	XF
	p1. Proof.	—	—	200
	p2. Proof with bottom cut off.	—	—	30.00

1915-1918 Issue

		Good	Fine	XF
215	**1 Pound** 1915-1918. Black on green underprint. Hibernia seated at center, shield at top left supported by wolfhounds. Signature of R. C. Wilson. Printer: Perkins, Bacon & Co., London.	800	2,000	3,000
216	**3 Pounds** 1915. Black on green underprint. Hibernia seated at center, shield at top left supported by wolfhounds. Signature of R. C. Wilson. Printer: Perkins, Bacon & Co., London. Specimen.	4,500	8,000	—

		Good	Fine	XF
217	**5 Pounds** 1918-1919. Black on green underprint. Hibernia seated at center, shield at top left supported by wolfhounds. Signature of R. C. Wilson. Printer: Perkins, Bacon & Co., London.	1,800	3,500	5,000

		Good	Fine	XF
218	**10 Pounds** 1915-1918. Black on green underprint. Hibernia seated at center, shield at top left supported by wolfhounds. Signature of R. C. Wilson. Printer: Perkins, Bacon & Co., London.	1,000	3,500	5,000
219	**20 Pounds** 1915-1916. Black on green underprint. Hibernia seated at center, shield at top left supported by wolfhounds. Signature of R. C. Wilson. Printer: Perkins, Bacon & Co., London.	3,000	6,000	8,000
220	**50 Pounds** ND. Black on green underprint. Hibernia seated at center, shield at top left supported by wolfhounds. Signature of R. C. Wilson. Printer: Perkins, Bacon & Co., London. Specimen.	—	—	300

		Good	Fine	XF
221	**100 Pounds** ND. Black on green underprint. Hibernia seated at center, shield at top left supported by wolfhounds. Signature of R. C. Wilson. Printer: Perkins, Bacon & Co., London. Specimen.	—	—	300

1918-1920 Issue

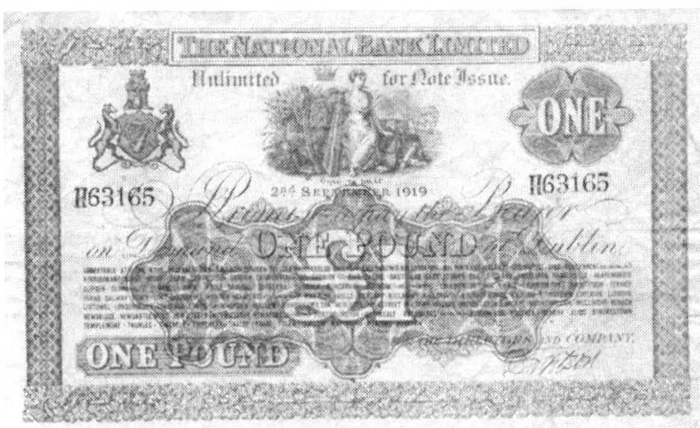

		Good	Fine	XF
222	**1 Pound** 1918-1920. Black on green underprint. Hibernia seated at center, shield at top left supported by wolfhounds. Signature of R. C. Wilson. Printer: Perkins, Bacon & Co., London.			
	a. 1.11.1918-1.10.1919. Uniface.	500	2,800	4,500
	b. 1.4.1920. Printed both sides.	800	3,500	4,800

		Good	Fine	XF
223	**5 Pounds** 1919. Blue on brown underprint. Hibernia seated at center, shield at top left supported by wolfhounds. Signature of R. C. Wilson. Printer: Perkins, Bacon & Co., London.	1,500	5,000	—

		Good	Fine	XF
224	**10 Pounds** 1919. Green on red underprint. Hibernia seated at center, shield at top left supported by wolfhounds. Signature of R. C. Wilson. Printer: Perkins, Bacon & Co., London.	1,500	5,000	7,000

1921-1927 Issue

		Good	Fine	XF
225	**1 Pound** 1.11.1924; 1.10.1925. Reduced size.			
	a. 1921-1924. Signature R. C. Wilson.	500	1,500	2,500
	b. 1924-1926. Signature J. Brown.	500	1,500	2,500

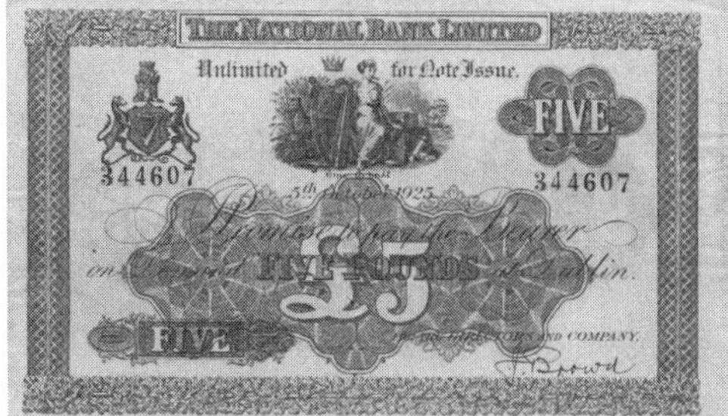

		Good	Fine	XF
226	**5 Pounds** 1921-1926. Black on green underprint. Hibernia seated at center, shield at top left supported by wolfhounds. Printer: Perkins, Bacon & Co., London.			
	a. 1921-1924. Signature R. C. Wilson.	600	1,700	3,500
	b. 1924-1926. Signature J. Brown.	600	1,700	3,500

		Good	Fine	XF
227	**10 Pounds** 10.2.1920; 10.2.1922; 10.11.1924. Green on brown underprint. *10* at center. Reduced size.			
	a. 1922-1924. Signature R.C. Wilson.	700	2,000	4,000
	b. 1924-1927. Signature J. Brown.	700	2,000	4,000
228	**20 Pounds** 20.11.1920. Black on green underprint. Hibernia seated at center, shield at top left supported by wolfhounds. Signature R. C. Wilson. Printer: Perkins, Bacon & Co., London.	—	—	—
229	**50 Pounds** 20.11.1920. Black on green underprint. Hibernia seated at center, shield at top left supported by wolfhounds. Signature R. C. Wilson. Printer: Perkins, Bacon & Co., London. Proof.	—	—	—
230	**100 Pounds** 20.11.1920. Black on green underprint. Hibernia seated at center, shield at top left supported by wolfhounds. Signature R. C. Wilson. Printer: Perkins, Bacon & Co., London. Proof.	—	—	—

Northern Banking Company

Later became the Northern Banking Company Limited.

Belfast

1825 Issue

		Good	Fine	XF
231	**1 Pound** ND. Black. Sailing ship at top center. Printer: Carpenter & Sons, London. Proof.	—	—	600
232	**1 Guinea** ND. Black. Sailing ship at top center. Printer: Carpenter & Sons, London. Proof.	—	—	—
233	**25 Shillings** ND. Black. Sailing ship at top center. Printer: Carpenter & Sons, London. Proof.	—	—	600
234	**30 Shillings** ND. Black. Sailing ship at top center. Printer: Carpenter & Sons, London. Proof.	—	—	—

1825-1850 Issue

		Good	Fine	XF
235	**1 Pound** ND. Black. Sailing ship at top center. Proof.	—	—	—
236	**1 Guinea** ND. Black. Sailing ship at top center.	—	—	600
237	**25 Shillings** ND. Black. Sailing ship at top center.			
	a. Issued note.	—	—	—
	p. Proof.	—	—	600
238	**25 Shillings** ND. Black. Sailing ship at top center. Ornate upper border.	—	—	1,100
239	**30 Shillings** ND. Black. Sailing ship at top center. Proof.			
	a. Issued note.	—	—	—
	p. Proof.	—	—	600
240	**35 Shillings** ND. Black. Sailing ship at top center. Proof.	—	—	600

#	Description	Good	Fine	XF
241	**4 Pounds**	Good	Fine	XF
	ND. Black. Sailing ship at top center. Proof.	—	—	600
242	**5 Pounds**	Good	Fine	XF
	ND. Black. Sailing ship at top center. Proof.	—	—	600
243	**10 Pounds**	Good	Fine	XF
	ND. Black. Sailing ship at top center. Proof.	—	—	600
244	**20 Pounds**	Good	Fine	XF
	ND. Black. Sailing ship at top center. Proof.	—	—	600

1850-1883 Issue

#	Description	Good	Fine	XF
244A	**1 Pound**	Good	Fine	XF
	ND. Black. Sailing ship at top center. Wavy borders. Proof.	—	—	—
245	**1 Pound**	Good	Fine	XF
	ND. Black. Sailing ship at top center.	—	—	600

#	Description	Good	Fine	XF
245A	**1 Pound**	Good	Fine	XF
	1.8.1866. Black. Sailing ship at top center.	5,000	7,000	—
246	**5 Pounds**	Good	Fine	XF
	1856-1883. Black. Sailing ship at top center.	—	500	—
247	**10 Pounds**	Good	Fine	XF
	1856-1883. Black. Sailing ship at top center.	—	750	—
248	**20 Pounds**	Good	Fine	XF
	1856-1883. Black. Sailing ship at top center.	—	—	750
249	**50 Pounds**	Good	Fine	XF
	1856-1883. Black. Sailing ship at top center. Proof.	—	—	600

Northern Banking Company Limited

Later became the Northern Bank Ltd.

Belfast

1883-1919 Issue

#	Description	Good	Fine	XF
250	**1 Pound**	Good	Fine	XF
	1883-1917. Black on blue underprint. Sailing ship at top center. Printer: Perkins, Bacon & Co., London.			
	a. 1889-1906. Uniface.	900	1,500	2,500
	b. 1907-1917. Back printed in blue.	700	1,000	2,000
	p. Proof. 1883.	—	—	300
251	**5 Pounds**	Good	Fine	XF
	1883-1917. Black on blue underprint. Sailing ship at top center. Printer: Perkins, Bacon & Co., London.			
	a. 1895-1907. Uniface.	900	2,000	3,500
	b. 1908-1918. Back printed in blue.	700	1,500	3,000
	p. Proof. 1883.	—	—	—
252	**10 Pounds**	Good	Fine	XF
	1883-1917. Black on blue underprint. Sailing ship at top center. Printer: Perkins, Bacon & Co., London.			
	a. 1897-1909. Uniface.	1,100	2,500	4,000
	b. 1910-1918. Back printed in blue.	900	2,000	3,500
	p. Proof. 1883.	—	—	—
253	**20 Pounds**	Good	Fine	XF
	1883-1917. Black on blue underprint. Sailing ship at top center. Printer: Perkins, Bacon & Co., London.			
	a. 1888-1917. Uniface.	—	—	—
	b. 1918. Back printed in blue.	—	—	—
	p. Proof. 1883.	—	—	—
254	**50 Pounds**	Good	Fine	XF
	1883-1917. Black on blue underprint. Sailing ship at top center. Printer: Perkins, Bacon & Co., London.			
	a. 1.5.1912, 5.8.1914. Red serial #s.	—	—	—
	b. 15.4.1918. Black serial #s.	—	—	—
	p. Proof.	—	—	—
255	**100 Pounds**	Good	Fine	XF
	1883-1917. Black on blue underprint. Sailing ship at top center. Printer: Perkins, Bacon & Co., London.			
	a. 1.5.1912, 5.8.1914, 25.4.1918-2.6.1919. Back printed in blue. Red serial #s.	—	—	—
	p. Proof	—	—	—

1918-1920 Issue

#	Description	Good	Fine	XF
256	**1 Pound**	Good	Fine	XF
	1918-1919. Black on blue underprint. Sailing ship at top center. Printer: Perkins, Bacon & Co., London.			
	a. 1.7.1918; 1.11.1918. Black prefix and serial #.	900	2,500	3,500
	b. 1.5.1919. Red prefix and serial #.	900	2,500	4,500
257	**5 Pounds**	Good	Fine	XF
	1918-1919. Black on blue underprint. Sailing ship at top center. Printer: Perkins, Bacon & Co., London.			
	a. 1.11.1918. Black prefix and serial #.	900	3,500	4,500
	b. Red prefix and serial #.	900	3,500	4,500
258	**10 Pounds**	Good	Fine	XF
	1918-1919. Black on blue underprint. Sailing ship at top center. Printer: Perkins, Bacon & Co., London.			
	a. 1.7.1918, 1.11.1918. Black prefix and serial #.	1,500	4,000	5,000
	b. 1.5.1919, 1.12.1919, 1.3.1920. Red prefix and serial #	1,500	4,000	5,000

1926-1927 Issue

#	Description	Good	Fine	XF
259	**1 Pound**	Good	Fine	XF
	1921-1927. Black on blue underprint. Sailing ship at top center. Printer: Perkins, Bacon & Co. Ltd.	—	500	750
260	**5 Pounds**	Good	Fine	XF
	1921-1927. Black on blue underprint. Sailing ship at top center. Printer: Perkins, Bacon & Co. Ltd.			
	a. 5.10.1921; 11.11.1925; 1.1.1926. Large size note.	900	2,000	3,000
	b. 1.9.1927. Reduced size note.	1,500	3,000	4,000
261	**10 Pounds**	Good	Fine	XF
	10.10.1921. Black on blue underprint. Sailing ship at top center. Printer: Perkins, Bacon & Co. Ltd.	—	—	—
262	**20 Pounds**	Good	Fine	XF
	20.10.1921. Black on blue underprint. Sailing ship at top center. Printer: Perkins, Bacon & Co. Ltd.	—	—	—

Provincial Bank of Ireland

Founded 1825. Later became Provincial Bank of Ireland Limited.

W/o Branch Name

1825 Issue

#	Description	Good	Fine	XF
270	**1 Pound**	Good	Fine	XF
	ND. Black. Britiania and Hibernia seated at top center. Printer: Perkins & Heath, London.			
	a. Issued note.	—	1,500	—
	p. Proof.	—	—	700
271	**30 Shillings**	Good	Fine	XF
	ND. Black. Britiania and Hibernia seated at top center. Printer: Perkins & Heath, London. Proof.	—	—	1,400

1825-1827 Issue

#	Description	Good	Fine	XF
272	**1 Pound**	Good	Fine	XF
	ND. Black. Portrait George IV at left. Printer: Perkins & Heath, London.	—	2,100	—
273	**25 Shillings**	Good	Fine	XF
	ND. Black. Portrait George IV at left. Printer: Perkins & Heath, London.	—	2,100	—
274	**30 Shillings**	Good	Fine	XF
	ND. Black. Portrait George IV at left. Printer: Perkins & Heath, London.			
	a. Issued note.	—	2,100	—
	p. Proof.	—	—	750

275 **3 Pounds** — Good Fine XF
ND. Black. Portrait George IV at left. Printer: Perkins & Heath, London. — — 1,400

276 **4 Pounds** — Good Fine XF
ND. Black. Portrait George IV at left. Printer: Perkins & Heath, London. Requires confirmation. — — —

277 **5 Pounds** — Good Fine XF
ND. Black. Portrait George IV at left. Printer: Perkins & Heath, London.
a. Issued note. — 2,100 —
p. Proof. — — 1,500

1826-1837 Issue

278 **1 Pound** — Good Fine XF
ND. Black. Profile portrait George IV at left. Britannia and Hibernia seated at top center. Printer: Perkins & Heath, London.
a. Issued note. — 1,000 —
p. Proof. — — 700

279 **25 Shillings** — Good Fine XF
ND. Black. Profile portrait George IV at left. Britannia and Hibernia seated at top center. Printer: Perkins & Heath, London.
a. Issued note. — 1,100 —
p. Proof. — 1,100 —

280 **30 Shillings** — Good Fine XF
ND. Black. Profile portrait George IV at left. Britannia and Hibernia seated at top center. Printer: Perkins & Heath, London.
a. Issued note. — 1,100 —
p. Proof. — — 750

281 **3 Pounds** — Good Fine XF
ND. Black. Profile portrait George IV at left. Britannia and Hibernia seated at top center. Printer: Perkins & Heath, London. —
ND. Black. Profile portrait George IV at left. Britannia and Hibernia seated at top center. Printer: Perkins & Heath, London.
a. Issued note. — 1,400 —
p. Proof. — — 800

282 **4 Pounds** — Good Fine XF
ND. Black. Profile portrait George IV at left. Britannia and Hibernia seated at top center. Printer: Perkins & Heath, London.
a. Issued note. — 2,100 —
p. Proof. — 1,100 —

283 **5 Pounds** — Good Fine XF
ND. Black. Profile portrait George IV at left. Britannia and Hibernia seated at top center. Printer: Perkins & Heath, London.
a. Issued note. — 1,100 —
p. Proof. — — 900

284 **10 Pounds** — Good Fine XF
ND. Black. Profile portrait George IV at left. Britannia and Hibernia seated at top center. Printer: Perkins & Heath, London.
a. Issued note. — 1,400 —
p. Proof. — — 900

285 **20 Pounds** — Good Fine XF
ND. Black. Profile portrait George IV at left. Britannia and Hibernia seated at top center. Printer: Perkins & Heath, London.
a. Issued note. — 2,100 —
p. Proof. — 2,100 —

286 **50 Pounds** — Good Fine XF
ND. Black. Profile portrait George IV at left. Britannia and Hibernia seated at top center. Printer: Perkins & Heath, London.
a. Issued note. — — —
p. Proof. — — —

287 **100 Pounds** — Good Fine XF
ND. Black. Profile portrait George IV at left. Britannia and Hibernia seated at top center. Printer: Perkins & Heath, London. — — —

1830-1846 Issue

288 **1 Pound** — Good Fine XF
15.6.1835. Portrait King William IV at upper left, Britannia and Hibernia seated at upper center.
a. Issued note. — — —
p. Proof. — — 700

289 **25 Shillings** — Good Fine XF
ND. Black. Profile portrait George IV at left. Britannia and Hibernia seated at top center. Printer: Perkins & Heath, London.
a. Issued note. — 750 —
p. Proof. — — 625

290 **30 Shillings** — Good Fine XF
ND. Black. Profile portrait William IV at left. Britannia and Hibernia seated at top center. Printer: Perkins, Bacon & Petch, London.
a. Issued note. — 1,000 —
p. Proof. — — 850

291 **3 Pounds** — Good Fine XF
ND. Black. Profile portrait William IV at left. Britannia and Hibernia seated at top center. Printer: Perkins, Bacon & Petch, London.
a. Issued note. — 1,400 —
p. Proof. — — 1,000

292 **4 Pounds** — Good Fine XF
ND. Black. Profile portrait William IV at left. Britannia and Hibernia seated at top center. Printer: Perkins, Bacon & Petch, London. Requires confirmation. — — —

293 **5 Pounds** — Good Fine XF
ND. Black. Profile portrait William IV at left. Britannia and Hibernia seated at top center. Printer: Perkins, Bacon & Petch, London.
a. Issued note. — 900 —
p. Proof. — — 1,200

294 **10 Pounds** — Good Fine XF
ND. Black. Profile portrait William IV at left. Britannia and Hibernia seated at top center. Printer: Perkins, Bacon & Petch, London.
a. Issued note. — 1,200 —
p. Proof. — — 1,000

295 **20 Pounds** — Good Fine XF
ND. Black. Profile portrait William IV at left. Britannia and Hibernia seated at top center. Printer: Perkins, Bacon & Petch, London.
a. Issued note. — 1,750 —
p. Proof. — — 1,100

296 **50 Pounds** — Good Fine XF
ND. Black. Profile portrait William IV at left. Britannia and Hibernia seated at top center. Printer: Perkins, Bacon & Petch, London.
a. Issued note. — 4,250 —
p. Proof. — — 1,400

297 **100 Pounds** — Good Fine XF
ND. Black. Profile portrait William IV at left. Britannia and Hibernia seated at top center. Printer: Perkins, Bacon & Petch, London.
a. Issued note. — 4,250 —
p. Proof. — — 1,400

1838-1857 Issue

298 **1 Pound** — Good Fine XF
ND. Black. Profile portrait Victoria at left. Britannia and Hibernia seated at top center. Printer: Perkins, Bacon & Petch, London. — 625 —

299 **30 Shillings** — Good Fine XF
ND. Black. Profile portrait Victoria at left. Britannia and Hibernia seated at top center. Printer: Perkins, Bacon & Petch, London. — 850 —

300 **5 Pounds** — Good Fine XF
ND. Black. Profile portrait Victoria at left. Britannia and Hibernia seated at top center. Printer: Perkins, Bacon & Petch, London. — 1,000 —

301 **10 Pounds** — Good Fine XF
ND. Black. Profile portrait Victoria at left. Britannia and Hibernia seated at top center. Printer: Perkins, Bacon & Petch, London. — 1,200 —

302 **20 Pounds** — Good Fine XF
ND. Black. Profile portrait Victoria at left. Britannia and Hibernia seated at top center. Printer: Perkins, Bacon & Petch, London. — 1,400 —

1841-1869 Issue

303 **1 Pound** — Good Fine XF
ND. Black. Profile portrait Victoria at left. Britannia and Hibernia seated at top center. Printer: Perkins, Bacon & Petch, London.
a. Issued note. — 500 —
p. Proof. — — 425

304 **1 Pound** — Good Fine XF
ND. Black. Profile portrait Victoria at left. Britannia and Hibernia seated at top center. Outline ONE over center panel. Printer: Perkins, Bacon & Petch, London.
a. Issued note. — 500 —
p. Proof. — — 425

305 **25 Shillings** — Good Fine XF
ND. Black. Profile portrait Victoria at left. Britannia and Hibernia seated at top center. Printer: Perkins, Bacon & Petch, London. Proof. — — 700

306 **30 Shillings** — Good Fine XF
ND. Black. Profile portrait Victoria at left. Britannia and Hibernia seated at top center. Printer: Perkins, Bacon & Petch, London. Proof.
a. Issued note. — 550 —
p. Proof. — — 500

307 **2 Pounds** — Good Fine XF
ND. Black. Profile portrait Victoria at left. Britannia and Hibernia seated at top center. Printer: Perkins, Bacon & Petch, London. — 900 —

308 **3 Pounds** — Good Fine XF
ND. Black. Profile portrait Victoria at left. Britannia and Hibernia seated at top center. Printer: Perkins, Bacon & Petch, London.
a. Issued note. — 1,000 —
p. Proof. — — 800

309 **3 Pounds** — Good Fine XF
ND. Black. Profile portrait Victoria at left. Britannia and Hibernia seated at top center. Outline THREE in center panel. Printer: Perkins, Bacon & Petch, London.
a. Issued note. — 750 —
p. Proof. — — 850

No.	Denomination / Description	Good	Fine	XF
310	**5 Pounds**	Good	Fine	XF
	ND. Black. Profile portrait Victoria at left. Britannia and Hibernia seated at top center. Printer: Perkins, Bacon & Petch, London.			
	a. Issued note.	—	630	—
	p. Proof.	—	—	550
311	**10 Pounds**	Good	Fine	XF
	ND. Black. Profile portrait Victoria at left. Britannia and Hibernia seated at top center. Printer: Perkins, Bacon & Petch, London.			
	a. Issued note.	—	900	—
	p. Proof.	—	—	750
312	**20 Pounds**	Good	Fine	XF
	ND. Black. Profile portrait Victoria at left. Britannia and Hibernia seated at top center. Printer: Perkins, Bacon & Petch, London.			
	a. Issued note.	—	1,400	—
	p. Proof.	—	—	850
313	**50 Pounds**	Good	Fine	XF
	ND. Black. Profile portrait Victoria at left. Britannia and Hibernia seated at top center. Printer: Perkins, Bacon & Petch, London.			
	a. Issued note.	—	3,500	—
	p. Proof.	—	3,500	—
314	**100 Pounds**	Good	Fine	XF
	ND. Black. Profile portrait Victoria at left. Britannia and Hibernia seated at top center. Printer: Perkins, Bacon & Petch, London.	—	—	1,200

1869-1870 Issue

No.	Denomination / Description	Good	Fine	XF
315	**1 Pound**	Good	Fine	XF
	ND. Black. Profile portrait Victoria at left. Britannia and Hibernia seated at top center. Printer: Perkins, Bacon & Petch, London. Proof.	—	1,200	—
316	**2 Pounds**	Good	Fine	XF
	ND. Black. Profile portrait Victoria at left. Britannia and Hibernia seated at top center. Printer: Perkins, Bacon & Petch, London.	—	1,400	—
317	**3 Pounds**	Good	Fine	XF
	ND. Black. Profile portrait Victoria at left. Britannia and Hibernia seated at top center. Printer: Perkins, Bacon & Petch, London.	—	1,400	—
318	**5 Pounds**	Good	Fine	XF
	ND. Black. Profile portrait Victoria at left. Britannia and Hibernia seated at top center. Printer: Perkins, Bacon & Petch, London.	—	1,400	—
319	**10 Pounds**	Good	Fine	XF
	ND. Black. Profile portrait Victoria at left. Britannia and Hibernia seated at top center. Printer: Perkins, Bacon & Petch, London.	—	1,000	—

1870-1881 Issue

No.	Denomination / Description	Good	Fine	XF
320	**1 Pound**	Good	Fine	XF
	ND. Black. Profile portrait Victoria at left. Britannia and Hibernia seated at top center. Printer: Perkins, Bacon & Co., London.	—	1,200	—
321	**3 Pounds**	Good	Fine	XF
	ND. Black. Profile portrait Victoria at left. Britannia and Hibernia seated at top center. Branch overprints at lower left. Printer: Perkins, Bacon & Co., London.	—	1,400	—
322	**5 Pounds**	Good	Fine	XF
	ND. Black. Profile portrait Victoria at left. Britannia and Hibernia seated at top center. Branch overprints at lower left. Printer: Perkins, Bacon & Co., London.	—	1,400	—
323	**10 Pounds**	Good	Fine	XF
	ND. Black. Profile portrait Victoria at left. Britannia and Hibernia seated at top center. Branch overprints at lower left. Printer: Perkins, Bacon & Co., London.	—	1,400	—
324	**20 Pounds**	Good	Fine	XF
	ND. Black. Profile portrait Victoria at top left, Britannia and Hibernia seated at top center. Printer: Perkins, Bacon & Co. London.	—	625	—
325	**50 Pounds**	Good	Fine	XF
	1871-1880. Black. Profile portrait Victoria at left end. Printer: Perkins, Bacon & Co. London. Proof.	—	—	1,100
326	**100 Pounds**	Good	Fine	XF
	1871-1880. Black. Profile portrait Victoria at left end. Printer: Perkins, Bacon & Co. London. Proof.	—	—	1,100

Provincial Bank of Ireland Limited

See also Ireland-Republic and Northern Ireland.

Dublin

1882-1902 Issue

No.	Denomination / Description	Good	Fine	XF
331	**1 Pound**	Good	Fine	XF
	1.8.1885-1.12.1894. Portrait Queen Victoria at left. Britannia and Hibernia seated at upper center.	—	—	—
331A	**3 Pounds**	Good	Fine	XF
	1882-1894. Portrait Queen Victoria at left. Britannia and Hibernia seated at upper center.			
	a. Intact issued note.	2,000	7,500	—
	b. Cut cancelled and rejoined.	—	200	—
	p. Proof.	—	—	300

No.	Denomination / Description	Good	Fine	XF
332	**5 Pounds**	Good	Fine	XF
	1882-1902. Black. Profile portrait Victoria at top left. Britannia and Hibernia seated at top center. Printer: Perkins, Bacon & Co. London.			
	a. Issued note.	—	400	—
	p. Proof.	—	—	425
333	**10 Pounds**	Good	Fine	XF
	1882-1899. Black. Profile portrait Victoria at top left. Britannia and Hibernia seated at top center. Printer: Perkins, Bacon & Co. London.			
	a. Issued note.	—	700	—
	p. Proof.	—	—	500
334	**20 Pounds**	Good	Fine	XF
	1883. Black. Profile portrait Victoria at top left. Britannia and Hibernia seated at top center. Printer: Perkins, Bacon & Co. London.			
	a. Issued note.	—	—	—
	p. Proof.	—	—	800
335	**50 Pounds**	Good	Fine	XF
	1883. Black. Profile portrait Victoria at top left. Britannia and Hibernia seated at top center. Printer: Perkins, Bacon & Co. London.			
	p. Proof.	—	—	900

Color Abbreviation Guide

New to the *Standard Catalog of® World Paper Money* are the following abbreviations related to color references:

BC: Back color
PC: Paper color

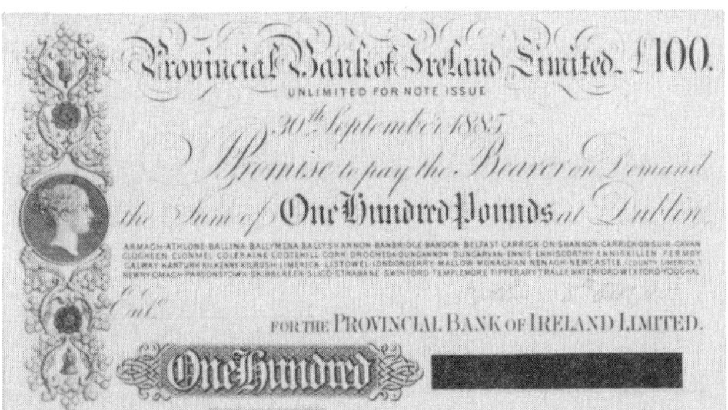

		Good	Fine	XF
336	**100 Pounds** 30.9.1885. Portrait Queen Victoria at left. Signature cut out. Remainder.	—	—	—

1903-1919 Issue

		Good	Fine	XF
337	**1 Pound** 1903-1918. Blue on tan underprint. Britannia and Hibernia seated at top center. Printer: Perkins, Bacon & Co. London.	300	700	2,000

		Good	Fine	XF
338	**3 Pounds** 1903-1918. Blue on tan underprint. Britannia and Hibernia seated at top center. Printer: Perkins, Bacon & Co. London.	2,000	7,500	—

		Good	Fine	XF
339	**5 Pounds** 5.2.1904. Blue. Britannia and Hibernia seated at upper center.	500	3,000	9,000

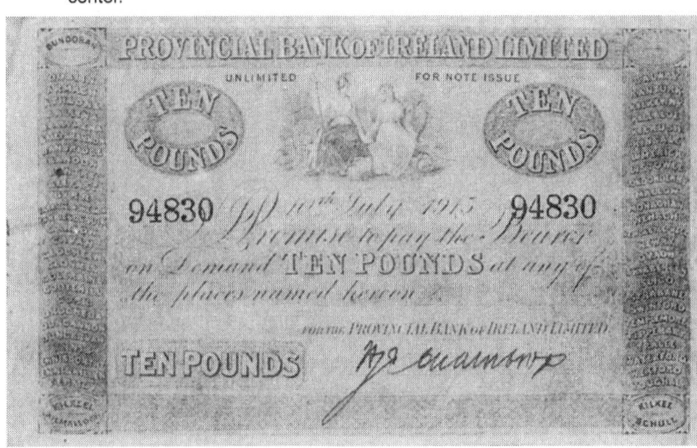

		Good	Fine	XF
340	**10 Pounds** 1904; 1915. Blue. Britannia and Hibernia seated at upper center.			
	a. 10.3.1904-10.7.1915.	500	2,500	5,000
	b. 10.7.1915.	500	2,500	5,000
341	**20 Pounds** 1904. Blue on tan underprint. Britannia and Hibernia seated at top center. Printer: Perkins, Bacon & Co. London.	2,000	7,500	—
342	**50 Pounds** 1905 Blue on tan underprint. Britannia and Hibernia seated at top center. Printer: Perkins, Bacon & Co. London.	—	—	900
343	**100 Pounds** 1905 Blue on tan underprint. Britannia and Hibernia seated at top center. Printer: Perkins, Bacon & Co. London. Requuires confirmation.	—	—	—

1919 Issue

		Good	Fine	XF
344	**1 Pound** 1.8.1918. Blue on tan underprint. Britannia and Hibernia seated at top center. Banknote reduced slightly in size and design altered.			
	a. Issued note.	1,300	3,500	5,000
	p. Proof. Issuing branch list from the Northern Bank.	—	—	2,000

NOTE:This is a separate issue, a re-design, which was dropped in favor of the 1919 Issue which is exactly the same design on a smaller note.

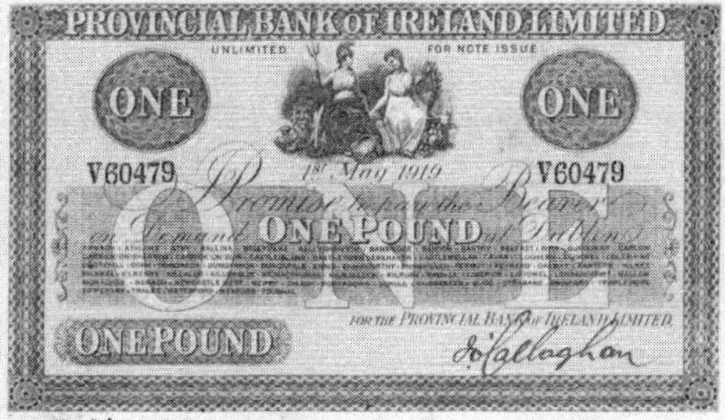

		Good	Fine	XF
345	**1 Pound** 1.5.1919; 1.8.1919. Black on green underprint. Britannia and Hibernia seated at upper center. Branches listed at center. Printer: Perkins, Bacon & Co., London. Small size.			
	a. Issued note.	500	2,500	4,500
	b. Proof.	—	—	500

1920-1927 Issue

		Good	Fine	XF
346	**1 Pound** 1.1.1920-1.9.1927. Green. Britannia and Hibernia seated at upper center. Without branches listed at center. Printer: Perkins, Bacon & Co., London. Reduced size.			
	a. 1.11.1920; 1.7.1921. Handwritten signature.	200	1,000	2,000
	b. 1.2.1922-1.9.1927. Signature printed: Hume Robinson.	100	500	2,000

No.	Description	Good	Fine	XF
	p1. 1.10.26. Punch cancelled unnumbered note.	—	—	130
	p2. 1.10.26. Punch cancelled numbered remainder.	—	—	150
347	**5 Pounds**	Good	Fine	XF
	5.11.20. Black and red. Center £5 in red.			
	a. 5.11.1920.	—	—	2,000
	b. 5.12.1926.	—	—	—
	p1. 5.12.1926. Punch cancelled unnumbered note.	—	—	200
	p2. 5.12.1926. Punch cancelled numbered remainder.	—	—	250

Ulster Banking Company

See also Ireland-Republic and Northern Ireland for issues dated after Dec. 6, 1921.

Belfast & Dublin

1836-1850 Issue

No.	Description	Good	Fine	XF
350	**1 Pound**	Good	Fine	XF
	1836. Black. Farm scene and sailing ship at top center.			
	a. Issued note.	—	—	—
	p. Proof.	—	—	700
351	**1 Pound**	Good	Fine	XF
	1836. Black. Farm scene and sailing ship at top center. ONE with serif.			
	a. Issued note. Rare.	—	—	—
	p. Proof.	—	—	700
352	**25 Shillings**	Good	Fine	XF
	1836-1842. Black. Farm scene and sailing ship.			
	a. Issued note.	—	—	—
	p. Proof.	—	—	—
353	**30 Shillings**	Good	Fine	XF
	1836-1842. Black. Farm scene and sailing ship.			
	a. Issued note.	—	—	—
	p. Proof.	—	—	—
354	**35 Shillings**	Good	Fine	XF
	1836-1842. Black. Farm scene and sailing ship.			
	a. Issued note.	—	—	—
	p. Proof.	—	—	—
355	**2 Pounds**	Good	Fine	XF
	1836-1842. Black. Farm scene and sailing ship. Requires confirmation.	—	—	—
356	**3 Pounds**	Good	Fine	XF
	1836-1842. Black. Farm scene and sailing ship. Requires confirmation.	—	—	—
357	**5 Pounds**	Good	Fine	XF
	1836-1842. Black. Farm scene and sailing ship. Proof.	—	—	—
358	**10 Pounds**	Good	Fine	XF
	1836-1842. Black. Farm scene and sailing ship. Requires confirmation.	—	—	—
359	**20 Pounds**	Good	Fine	XF
	1836-1842. Black. Farm scene and sailing ship. Proof.	—	—	—

1845-56 Issue

No.	Description	Good	Fine	XF
360	**1 Pound**	Good	Fine	XF
	1845-1846. Black. Farm scene and sailing ship. Back: Charles Skipper & East, London.	—	—	—
361	**2 Pounds**	Good	Fine	XF
	1845-1846. Black. Farm scene and sailing ship. Back: Charles Skipper & East, London.	—	—	—
362	**3 Pounds**	Good	Fine	XF
	1845-1846. Black. Farm scene and sailing ship. Back: Charles Skipper & East, London.	—	—	—
363	**5 Pounds**	Good	Fine	XF
	1845-1846. Black. Farm scene and sailing ship. Back: Charles Skipper & East, London. Requires confirmation.	—	—	—
364	**10 Pounds**	Good	Fine	XF
	1845-1846. Black. Farm scene and sailing ship. Back: Charles Skipper & East, London. Requires confirmation.	—	—	—
365	**20 Pounds**	Good	Fine	XF
	1845-1846. Black. Farm scene and sailing ship. Back: Charles Skipper & East, London. Requires confirmation.	—	—	—

1852-1861

No.	Description	Good	Fine	XF
366	**1 Pound**	Good	Fine	XF
	1.7.1852; 1.8.1860; 1.7.1861.. Black. Farm scene and sailing ship. Branches listed at ends, BELFAST in bottom border. Back: Perkins, Bacon & Co., London. Proof.	3,000	—	8,000
367	**1 Pound**	Good	Fine	XF
	1.7.1857. Black. Farm scene and sailing ship. Branches listed at ends, BELFAST in bottom border. Back: Perkins, Bacon & Co., London. Proof.	—	—	4,750
368	**5 Pounds**	Good	Fine	XF
	1.7.1857. Black. Farm scene and sailing ship. Branches listed at ends, BELFAST in bottom border. Back: Perkins, Bacon & Co., London. Proof.	—	—	550
369	**10 Pounds**	Good	Fine	XF
	1.7.1857. Black. Farm scene and sailing ship. Branches listed at ends, BELFAST in bottom border. Back: Perkins, Bacon & Co., London. Proof.	—	—	550
370	**20 Pounds**	Good	Fine	XF
	1.7.1857. Black. Farm scene and sailing ship. Branches listed at ends, BELFAST in bottom border. Back: Perkins, Bacon & Co., London. Proof.	—	—	575

1869-1878

No.	Description	Good	Fine	XF
371	**1 Pound**	Good	Fine	XF
	1869-1878 Black. Farm scene and sailing ship. Branches listed at ends, BELFAST & DUBLIN in bottom border. Back: Perkins, Bacon & Co., London.	—	3,500	—
373	**1 Pound**	Good	Fine	XF
	1874. Black on mauve underprint. Farm scene and sailing ship. Branches listed as ends, BELFAST & DUBLIN in bottom border. Back: Perkins, Bacon & Co., London.	—	4,800	—
372	**5 Pounds**	Good	Fine	XF
	1874. Black. Farm scene and sailing ship. Branches listed at ends, BELFAST & DUBLIN in bottom border. Back: Perkins, Bacon & Co., London.	—	700	—
374	**100 Pounds**	Good	Fine	XF
	1874. Black on blue underprint. Farm scene and sailing ship. Branches listed as ends, BELFAST & DUBLIN in bottom border. Back: Perkins, Bacon & Co., London. Color trial.	—	—	700

Ulster Bank Limited

Belfast & Dublin

1883-1906 Issue

No.	Description	Good	Fine	XF
376	**1 Pound**	Good	Fine	XF
	1887-1907. Black on blue underprint. Farm scene and sailing ship. Branches listed as ends, BELFAST & DUBLIN in bottom border. Back: Perkins, Bacon & Co., London.	—	2,800	—
377	**5 Pounds**	Good	Fine	XF
	1894-1906. Black on blue underprint. Farm scene and sailing ship. Branches listed as ends, BELFAST & DUBLIN in bottom border. Back: Perkins, Bacon & Co., London.	—	3,500	—
378	**10 Pounds**	Good	Fine	XF
	1894-1906. Black on blue underprint. Farm scene and sailing ship. Branches listed as ends, BELFAST & DUBLIN in bottom border. Back: Perkins, Bacon & Co., London.	—	5,600	—
379	**20 Pounds**	Good	Fine	XF
	1896-1900. Black on blue underprint. Farm scene and sailing ship. Branches listed as ends, BELFAST & DUBLIN in bottom border. Back: Perkins, Bacon & Co., London.	—	—	350
380	**50 Pounds**	Good	Fine	XF
	ND. Black on blue underprint. Farm scene and sailing ship. Branches listed as ends, BELFAST & DUBLIN in bottom border. Back: Perkins, Bacon & Co., London.	—	425	—

No.	Description	Good	Fine	XF
381	**100 Pounds**	Good	Fine	XF
	1.11.1904. Sailing ship, plow and blacksmiths at upper center. Printer: CS&E (without imprint). Proof without underprint, perforated: *SPECIMEN* and printer's name.	—	—	—

1906-1919 Issue

		Good	Fine	XF
382	**1 Pound** 1902-1918. Black on blue underprint. Sailing ship, plow and blacksmiths at upper center. Printer: CS&E (without imprint).			
	a. 1.6.1909; 1.3.1912.	300	100	250
	b. 1.6.1916; 2.7.1917; 1.10.1918.	300	80.00	175
	c. 2.6.1919.	300	800	1,500
	p. Proof without underprint. Perforated: *SPECIMEN* and printer's name. 1.12.1902; 1906; 2.5.1910; 1.12.1910.	—	—	—

		Good	Fine	XF
383	**5 Pounds** 1.5.1918. Black on green underprint. Sailing ship, plow and blacksmiths at upper center. Printer: CS&E (without imprint).			
	a. 1.8.1907-1.12.1910.	500	1,500	2,500
	b. 1.7.1911-1.5.1918.	500	1,500	2,500
	c. 2.6.1919.	600	2,000	3,300

		Good	Fine	XF
384	**10 Pounds** 1900-1917. Black on red underprint. Sailing ship, plow and blacksmiths at upper center. Printer: CS&E (without imprint).			
	a. 1.8.1900; 1.1.1908.	600	2,000	3,500
	b. 1.6.1916; 1.2.1917.	600	2,000	3,500

		Good	Fine	XF
385	**20 Pounds** 1906-1919. Black on blue underprint. Farm scene and sailing ship. Branches listed as ends, BELFAST & DUBLIN in bottom border. Printer: Perkins, Bacon & Co., London.	1,000	4,000	8,000

		Good	Fine	XF
386	**50 Pounds** 1906-1919. Black on underprint. Farm scene and sailing ship. Branches listed as ends, BELFAST & DUBLIN in bottom border. Printer: Perkins, Bacon & Co., London. Rare.	—	—	—

		Good	Fine	XF
387	**100 Pounds** 1906-1919. Black on underprint. Farm scene and sailing ship. Branches listed as ends, BELFAST & DUBLIN in bottom border. Printer: Perkins, Bacon & Co., London. Rare.	—	—	—

1920-1928 Issue

		Good	Fine	XF
388	**1 Pound** 1920-1924. Black on blue underprint. Without branch office listings at left or right. Reduced size.			
	a. Issued note. 1.10.1923; 1.10.1924.	30.00	100	400
	b. 1.3.1926-1.3.1928.	30.00	100	400
	p. Proof. 1.6.1920.	—	—	250

		Good	Fine	XF
390	**5 Pounds** 1.12.1924. Black on green underprint. Farm scene and sailing ship. BELFAST & DUBLIN in bottom border. Printer: Perkins, Bacon & Co., London.			
	a. Issued note.	500	2,100	3,000
	p. Proof.	—	—	250

		Good	Fine	XF
391	**10 Pounds** ND. Black on underprint. Farm scene and sailing ship. BELFAST & DUBLIN in bottom border. Printer: Perkins, Bacon & Co., London. Proof.	—	—	250

		Good	Fine	XF
392	**20 Pounds** ND. Black on underprint. Farm scene and sailing ship. BELFAST & DUBLIN in bottom border. Printer: Perkins, Bacon & Co., London. Proof.	—	—	350

		Good	Fine	XF
393	**50 Pounds** ND. Black on underprint. Farm scene and sailing ship. BELFAST & DUBLIN in bottom border. Printer: Perkins, Bacon & Co., London. Proof.	—	—	425

		Good	Fine	XF
394	**100 Pounds** ND. Black on underprint. Farm scene and sailing ship. BELFAST & DUBLIN in bottom border. Printer: Perkins, Bacon & Co., London. Proof.	—	—	500

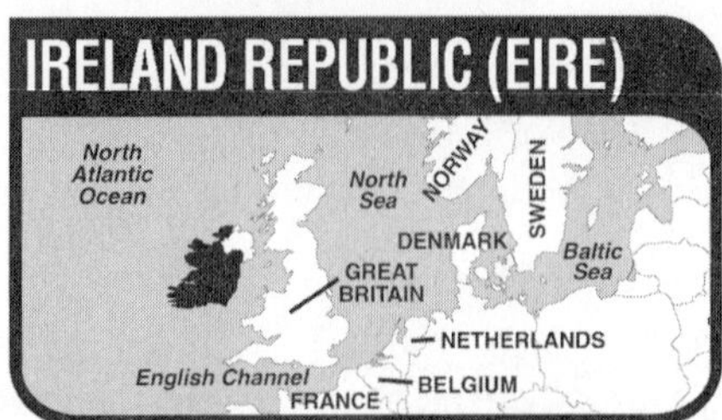

The Republic of Ireland (Éire) which occupies five-sixths of the Island of Ireland located in the Atlantic Ocean west of Great Britain, has an area of 70,280 sq. km. and a population of 4.16 million. Capital: Dublin. Agriculture and dairy farming are the principal industries. Meat, livestock, dairy products and textiles are exported.

Celtic tribes arrived on the island between 600-150 B.C. Invasions by Norsemen that began in the late 8th century were finally ended when King Brian Boru defeated the Danes in 1014. English invasions began in the 12th century and set off more than seven centuries of Anglo-Irish struggle marked by fierce rebellions and harsh repressions. Britian ruled Ireland directly since the Act of Union in 1800. The rule continued until a failed Raising on Easter Monday, April 24, 1916 touched off several years of guerrilla warfare that in 1921 resulted in independence, as the Irish Feree State, for 26 counties. Six of the nine counties of Ulster chose to remain part of the United Kingdom and became Northern Ireland. The constitution of 1937 mad the Irish Free State a republic in all but name. This is reflected on coins and currency with the change of "Irish Free State" to "Ireland." In 1949, Ireland declaired itself a republic, exiting the British Commonwealth. The country became a member of the Untied Nations in 1955 and the European Community in 1973.

Additional information on Irish bank notes can be found in the folowing references: www.irtishpapermoney.com; *Irish Banknotes, Irish Government Paper Money from 1928*; *Irish Banknotes, Irish Paper Money*; *Banknotes of the Irish Free State* all by Martain Mac Devitt and *Paper Money of Ireland* by Bob Blake and Jonathan Callaway, published by Pam West.

RULERS:

British to 1921.

MONETARY SYSTEM:

1 Shilling = 12 Pence
1 Pound = 20 Shillings to 1971
1 Pound = 100 New Pence, 1971-2001
1 Euro = 100 Cents, 2002-

REPLACEMENT NOTES:

#63-67, earlier dates use different letter than normal run of series letters. Later dates use different letter but have "OO" in front of the letter. #70-74 use a triple letter (3 of the same) to indicate replacement.

Printers: W&S 1928-1959, TDLR 1959-1976 (w/o imprint from either company on notes).

IRELAND

Coimisiún Airgid Reatha Saorstat Éireann

Currency Commission Irish Free State

1928 Issue

		Good	Fine	XF
1A	**10 Shillings** 10.9.1928-4.8.1937. Orange on purple and green underprint. Face portrait (Head only) of Lady Hazel Lavery at left. Back: River Blackwater river-mask.			
	a. 10.9.1928; 23.10.1928. Fractional serial # prefix.	100	600	1,800
	b. 31.12.1929-1.8.1937. Linear serial # prefix.	50.00	150	600

		Good	Fine	XF
2A	**1 Pound** 10.9.1928-23.12.1937. Green on orange and purple underprint. Face portrait (head only) of Lady Hazel Lavery at left. Back: Rive Lee river-mask.			
	a. 10.9.28; 23.10.1928. Fractional serial # prefix.	80.00	400	1,400
	b. 4.7.1930-23.12.1937. Linear serial # prefix.	15.00	50.00	400

		Good	Fine	XF
3A	**5 Pounds** 10.9.1928-19.8.1937. Brown on orange and pink underprint. Face portrait (head only) of Lady Hazel Lavery at left. Back: River Lagan river-mask.			
	a. 10.9.1928; 23.10.1928. Fractional serial # prefix.	200	600	1,500
	b. 7.6.1932-19.8.1937. Linear serial # prefix.	50.00	150	800

Color Abbreviation Guide

New to the *Standard Catalog of® World Paper Money* are the following abbreviations related to color references:

BC: Back color
PC: Paper color

		Good	Fine	XF
4A	**10 Pounds** 10.9.1928-16.1.1933. Blue on green and purple underprint. Lady Hazel Lavery in Irish national costume with chin resting on her hand and leaning on an Irish harp. Lakes and mountains in background. Back: River Bann river-mask.			
	a. 10.9.1928. Fractional serial # prefix.	300	1,500	4,000
	b. 6.7.1932; 16.1.1933. Linear serial # prefix.	100	300	2,000

		Good	Fine	XF
5	**20 Pounds** 10.9.1928. Red on orange and purple underprint. Lady Hazel Lavery in Irish national costume with chin resting on her hand and leaning on an Irish harp. Lakes and mountains in background. Fractional serial # prefix. Back: River Boyne river-mask.	900	2,000	7,000

		Good	Fine	XF
6	**50 Pounds** 10.9.1928. Purple on light brown and green underprint. Lady Hazel Lavery in Irish national costume with chin resting on her hand and leaning on an Irish harp. Lakes and mountains in background. Fractional serial # prefix. Back: River Shannon river-mask.	1,500	4,000	15,000

		Good	Fine	XF
7	**100 Pounds** 10.9.1928-20.12.1937. Olive on light and dark brown underprint. Lady Hazel Lavery in Irish national costume with chin resting on her hand and leaning on an Irish harp. Lakes and mountains in background. Back: River Erne river-mask.			
	a. 10.9.1928. Fractional serial # prefix.	1,500	4,000	18,000
	b. 9.12.1937-20.12.1937. Linear prefix.	700	1,500	6,000

Coimisiún Airgid Reatha Éire

Currency Commission Ireland

1938-1939 Issue

		Good	Fine	XF
1B	**10 Shillings** 17.1.1938-20.12.1939. Orange on purple and green underprint. Face portrait (head only) of Lady Hazel Lavery at left. Back: River Blackwater river-mask.	30.00	100	260
2B	**1 Pound** 9.1.1939-8.12.1939. Green on orange and purple underprint. Face portrait (head only) of Lady Hazel Lavery at left. Back: River Lee river-mask.	15.00	70.00	250
3B	**5 Pounds** 5.7.1938-1.1.1939. Brown on orange and pink underprint. Face portrait (head only) of Lady Hazel Lavery at left. Back: River Lagan river-mask.	30.00	100	400

		Good	Fine	XF
4B	**10 Pounds** 27.10.1938-2.7.1940. Blue on green and purple underprint. Face portrait (head only) of Lady Hazel Lavery at left. Back: River Bann river-mask.	40.00	250	700

Coimisiún Airgid Reatha Éire

Currency Commission Ireland

1940-1941 Issue

#1C-4C the identifying code letter in circle at top left and bottom right. Such letters were to aid in keeping track of notes en route from England to Ireland.

		Good	Fine	XF
1C	**10 Shillings** 30.7.1940-1.12.1941. Orange on purple and green underprint. Face portrait (head only) of Lady Hazel Lavery at left. Code letters: H (blue); K (green); J (brown). Back: River Blackwater river-mask.	30.00	100	300

		Good	Fine	XF
2C	**1 Pound** 14.3.1941-22.9.1942. Green on orange and purple underprint. Face portrait (head only) of Lady Hazel Lavery at left. Code letters in order of release: T (purple); B (red); P (brown); V (grey). Back: River Lee river-mask.	20.00	80.00	180

		Good	Fine	XF
3C	**5 Pounds** 12.9.1940-8.10.1942. Brown on orange and pink underprint. Face portrait (head only) of Lady Hazel Lavery at left. Code letters: A (green); C (purple); D (blue). Back: River Lagan river-mask.	30.00	130	400
4C	**10 Pounds** 9.10.1941-5.10.1942. Blue on green and purple underprint. Lady Hazel in Irish national costume with chin resting on her hand and leaning on an Irish harp. Lakes and mountains in background. Code letters E (brown); F (olive). Back: River Bann river-mask.	70.00	300	600

Banc Ceannais Na hÉireann

Central Bank of Ireland

1943-1944 Issue

		Good	Fine	XF
1D	**10 Shillings** 6.2.1943-28.3.1944. Orange on purple and green underprint. Face portrait (head only) of Lady Hazel Lavery at left. Code letters in order of release: L (orange); M (grey); R (black); E (purple). Back: River Blackwater river-mask.	30.00	100	200

		Good	Fine	XF
2D	**1 Pound** 3.2.1943-6.12.1944. Green on orange and purple underprint. Face portrait (head only) of Lady Hazel Lavery at left. Code letters in order of release: G (black); Y (blue); E (red); F (pink). Back: River Lee river-mask.	20.00	80.00	180

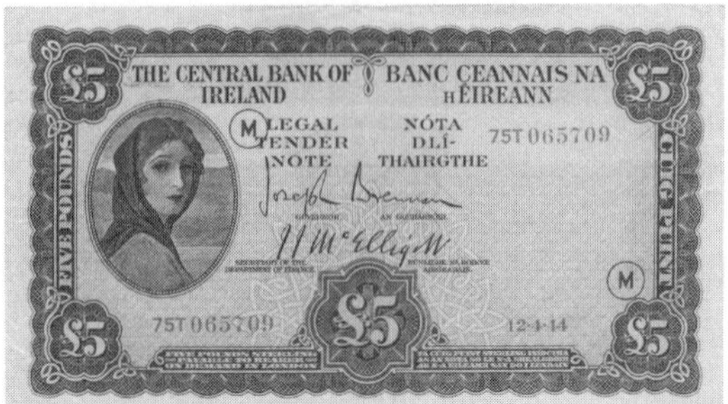

		Good	Fine	XF
3D	**5 Pounds** 3.2.1943-14.7.1944. Brown on orange and pink underprint. Face portrait (head only) of Lady Hazel Lavery at left. Code letters in order of release: N (black); R (red); M (brown). Back: River Lagan river-mask.	30.00	130	400

		Good	Fine	XF
4D	**10 Pounds** ND. Blue on green and purple underprint. Lady Hazel Lavery in Irish national costume with chin resting on her hand and leaning on an Irish harp. Lakes and mountains in background. Code letters in order of release: S (orange); W (blue); B (purple); G (black). Back: River Bann river-mask.	70.00	300	600

		Good	Fine	XF
5D	**20 Pounds** 11.2.1943- 10.1.1944. Red on orange and purple underprint. Lady Hazel Lavery in Irish national costume with chin resting on her hand and leaning on an Irish harp. Lakes and mountains in background. Code letter: A (blue). Back: River Boyne river-mask.	1,000	10,000	18,000

Color Abbreviation Guide

New to the *Standard Catalog of ® World Paper Money* are the following abbreviations related to color references:

BC: Back color

PC: Paper color

Currency Commission - Consolidated Bank Notes

CONSOLIDATED BANK NOTE ISSUES Uniform designs for the 8 "Shareholding Banks", only the bank name and the sign. change. Farmer w/plow and horses on face, different illustrations w/the different denominations. Various dates and sign. varieties between 1927 and 1942 circulated until 1953.

Bank of Ireland

1929 Issue

		Good	Fine	XF
8	**1 Pound** 1929-1939. Green on orange and purple underprint. Back: Government building.			
	a. Signature J. Brennan and J. A. Gargan. 6.5.1929-4.10.1938.	150	250	900
	b. Signature J. Brennan and H. J. Johnston. 10.1.1939; 9.2.1939; 3.7.1939; 2.1.1940.	150	250	900
	s. Specimen. As a.	—	Unc	1,300

		Good	Fine	XF
9	**5 Pounds** 1929-1939. Brown on green underprint. Back: Bridge with town behind.			
	a. Signature J. Brennan and J. A. Gargan. 6.5.1929; 29.1.1931; 8.5.1931.	300	900	2,000
	b. Signature J. Brennan and H. J. Johnston. 14.9.1939.	300	900	2,000
	s. Specimen. As a.	—	Unc	1,800
10	**10 Pounds** 6.5.1929. Blue on green and purple underprint. Back: Entrance to ornate building.	Good	Fine	XF
	a. Issued note.	1,300	2,700	6,000
	s. Specimen. As a.	—	Unc	3,500

		Good	Fine	XF
11	**20 Pounds** 6.5.1929. Deep red on pink and green underprint. Back: Medieval castle.			
	a. Issued note.	—	—	—
	s. Specimen.	—	Unc	5,000
12	**50 Pounds** 6.5.1929. Purple on gray and pink underprint. Back: Mountains and valley.	Good	Fine	XF
	a. Issued note.	—	—	—
	s. Specimen.	—	Unc	5,000

#	Description	Good	Fine	XF
13	**100 Pounds**	Good	Fine	XF
	6.5.1929. Olive on brown underprint. Back: Shoreline with mountain landscape.			
	a. Issued note.	—	—	—
	s. Specimen.	—	Unc	5,000

Hibernian Bank Ltd.

1929-1931 Issue

#	Description	Good	Fine	XF
14	**1 Pound**	Good	Fine	XF
	1929-1940. Green on orange and purple underprint. Back: Government building.			
	a. Signature J. Brennan and H. J. Campbell. 6.5.1929-4.5.1939.	200	400	1,000
	b. Signature J. Brennan and A. K. Hodges. 5.8.1939; 9.2.1940.	200	400	1,000

#	Description	Good	Fine	XF
15	**5 Pounds**	Good	Fine	XF
	1929-1939. Brown on green underprint. Back: Bridge with town behind.			
	a. Signature J. Brennan and H. J. Campbell. 6.5.1929; 15.3.1933; 4.1.1938; 5.8.1938.	400	1,200	2,500
	b. Signature J. Brennan and A. K. Hodges. 13.9.1939.	—	—	—
16	**10 Pounds**	Good	Fine	XF
	1931; 1939. Blue on green and purple underprint. Back: Entrance to ornate building.			
	a. Signature J. Brennan and H. J. Campbell. 5.12.1931.	1,500	3,000	5,000
	b. Signature J. Brennan and A. K. Hodges. 24.7.1939.	—	—	—
17	**20 Pounds**	Good	Fine	XF
	6.5.1929. Deep red on pink and green underprint. Back: Medieval castle.	—	—	—

#18 and 19 *not assigned.*

Munster and Leinster Bank Ltd.

1929 Issue

#	Description	Good	Fine	XF
20	**1 Pound**	Good	Fine	XF
	1929-1939. Green on orange and purple underprint. Back: Government building.			
	a. Signature J. Brennan and J. L. Gubbins. 6.5.1929-5.3.1935.	150	250	900
	b. Signature J. Brennan and A. E. Hosford. 7.2.1936-6.2.1940.	150	250	900
21	**5 Pounds**	Good	Fine	XF
	1929-1939. Brown on green underprint. Back: Bridge with town behind.			
	a. Signature J. Brennan and J. L. Gubbins. 6.5.1929-15.3.1933.	300	900	2,000
	b. Signature J. Brennan and A. E. Hosford. 7.4.1938-22.9.1939.	300	900	2,000

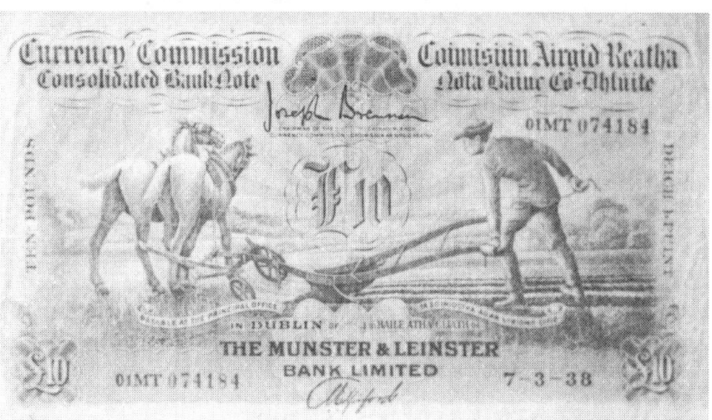

#	Description	Good	Fine	XF
22	**10 Pounds**	Good	Fine	XF
	1929-1939. Blue on green and purple underprint. Back: Entrance to ornate building.			
	a. Signature J. Brennan and J. L. Gubbins. 6.5.1929; 5.12.1931.	1,300	2,700	4,500
	b. Signature J. Brennan and A. E. Hosford. 7.3.1938; 4.8.1939.	1,300	2,700	4,500
23	**20 Pounds**	Good	Fine	XF
	6.5.1929. Deep red on pink and green underprint. Back: Medieval castle.	—	—	—
24	**50 Pounds**	Good	Fine	XF
	6.5.1929. Purple on gray and pink underprint. Back: Mountains and valley.	—	—	—
25	**100 Pounds**	Good	Fine	XF
	6.5.1929. Olive on brown underprint. Back: Shoreline with mountain landscape.	—	—	—

National Bank Ltd.

1929 Issue

#	Description	Good	Fine	XF
26	**1 Pound**	Good	Fine	XF
	6.5.1929-4.1.1940. Green on orange and purple underprint. Back: Government building.	150	250	900

#	Description	Good	Fine	XF
27	**5 Pounds**	Good	Fine	XF
	6.5.1929-16.9.1939. Brown on green underprint. Back: Bridge with town behind.	300	900	2,000
28	**10 Pounds**	Good	Fine	XF
	6.5.1929-31.7.1939. Blue on green and purple underprint. Back: Entrance to ornate building.	1,300	2,700	4,500

#29-31 *not assigned.*

Northern Bank Ltd.

1929 Issue

No.	Denomination	Good	Fine	XF
32	**1 Pound** 1929-1940. Green on orange and purple underprint. Back: Government building.			
	a. Signature J. Brennan and S. W. Knox. 6.5.1929; 10.6.1929.	1,500	4,000	9,000
	b. Signature J. Brennan and H. H. Stewart. 7.1.1931.	800	3,000	8,000
	c. Signature J. Brennan and A.P. Tibbey. 9.10.1939; 8.1.1940.	—	—	—

No.	Denomination	Good	Fine	XF
33	**5 Pounds** 1929-1939. Brown on green underprint. Back: Bridge with town behind.			
	a. Signature J. Brennan and S. W. Knox. 6.5.1929.	1,500	7,000	12,000
	b. Signature J. Brennan and H. H. Stewart. 29.1.1931; 8.5.1931; 15.3.1933.	1,000	4,000	10,000
	c. Signature J. Brennan and W.F. Scott. 15.9.1939.	—	—	—

No.	Denomination	Good	Fine	XF
34	**10 Pounds** 6.5.1929. Blue on green and purple underprint. Back: Entrance to ornate building.	8,000	20,000	30,000
35	**20 Pounds** 6.5.1929. Deep red on pink and green underprint. Back: Medieval castle.	—	—	—

#36 and 37 *not assigned.*

Provincial Bank of Ireland Ltd.

1929 Issue

No.	Denomination	Good	Fine	XF
38	**1 Pound** 1929-1940. Green on orange and purple underprint. Back: Government building.			
	a. Signature J. Brennan and H. Robertson. 6.5.1929; 10.6.1929.	200	400	1,100
	b. Signature J. Brennan and F. S. Forde. 7.1.1931-5.9.1936.	150	250	900
	c. Signature J. Brennan and G. A. Kennedy. 3.6.1937-19.4.1940.	150	250	900

No.	Denomination	Good	Fine	XF
39	**5 Pounds** 1929-1939. Brown on green underprint. Back: Bridge with town behind.			
	a. Signature J. Brennan and H. Robertson. 6.5.1929.	400	1,500	3,000
	b. Signature J. Brennan and F. S. Forde. 29.1.1931; 8.5.1831.	300	900	2,000
	c. Signature J. Brennan and G. A. Kennedy. 3.4.1939; 19.9.1939.	300	1,100	3,000
40	**10 Pounds** 1929-1939. Blue on green and purple underprint. Back: Entrance to ornate building.			
	a. Signature J. Brennan and H. Robertson. 6.5.1929.	1,400	3,000	5,000
	b. Signature J. Brennan and F. S. Forde. 2.10.1931.	1,300	2,700	4,500
	c. Signature J. Brennan and G.A. Kennedy. 17.7.1939	2,800	8,000	12,000
41	**20 Pounds** 6.5.1929. Deep red on pink and green underprint. Back: Medieval castle.	—	—	—

#42 and 43 *not assigned.*

Royal Bank of Ireland Ltd.

1929 Issue

No.	Denomination	Good	Fine	XF
44	**1 Pound** 1929-1941. Green on orange and purple underprint. Back: Government building.			
	a. Signature J. Brennan and G. A. Stanley. 6.5.1929; 10.6.1929; 7.1.1931.	250	550	1,500
	b. Signature J. Brennan and D. R. Mack. 8.12.1931-8.3.1939.	200	400	1,100
	c. Signature J. Brennan and J. S. Wilson. 2.5.1939; 5.6.1939; 6.9.1939; 5.2.1940; 30.4.1941.	200	400	1,100

#	Description	Good	Fine	XF
45	**5 Pounds** 1929-1939. Brown on green and purple underprint. Back: Bridge with town behind.			
	a. Signature J. Brennan and G. A. Stanley. 6.5.1929.	1,000	2,000	6,000
	b. Signature J. Brennan and D. R. Mack. 29.1.1931; 8.5.1931.	1,000	2,000	6,000
	c. Signature J. Brennan and J. S. Wilson. 21.9.1939.	—	—	—
46	**10 Pounds** 6.5.1929. Blue on green and purple underprint. Back: Entrance to ornate building.	2,000	5,000	10,000
47	**20 Pounds** 6.5.1929. Deep red on pink and green underprint. Back: Medieval castle.	—	—	—
48	**50 Pounds** 6.5.1929. Purple on gray and pink underprint. Back: Mountains and valley.	—	—	—
49	**100 Pounds** 6.5.1929. Olive on brown underprint. Back: Shoreline with mountain landscape.	—	—	—

Ulster Bank Ltd.

1929 Issue

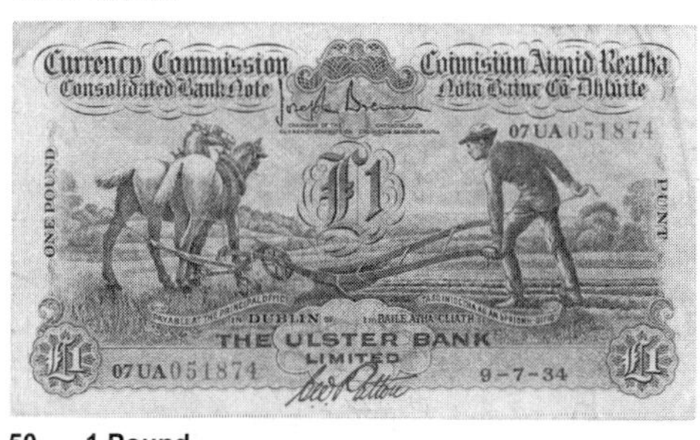

#	Description	Good	Fine	XF
50	**1 Pound** 1929-1940. Green on orange and purple underprint. Back: Government building.			
	a. Signature J. Brennan and C. W. Patton. 6.5.1929-17.6.1935.	500	1,000	1,700
	b. Signature J. Brennan and C. W. Lester. 3.11.1936-7.2.1940.	500	1,000	1,700
51	**5 Pounds** 1929-1939. Brown on green underprint. Back: Bridge with town behind.			
	a. Signature J. Brennan and C. W. Patton. 6.5.1929-15.3.1933.	700	1,400	4,000
	b. Signature J. Brennan and C. W. Lester. 3.5.1938; 7.2.1939.	700	1,400	4,000
52	**10 Pounds** 1929; 1938. Blue on green and purple underprint. Back: Entrance to ornate building.			
	a. Signature J. Brennan and C. W. Patton. 6.5.1929.	1,700	4,000	10,000
	b. Signature J. Brennan and C. W. Lester. 9.8.1938; 9.8.1939.	1,700	4,000	10,000
53	**20 Pounds** 6.5.1929. Deep red on pink and green underprint. Back: Medieval castle.	—	—	—
54	**50 Pounds** 6.5.1929. Purple on gray and pink underprint. Back: Mountains and valley.	—	—	—
55	**100 Pounds** 6.5.1929. Olive on brown underprint. Back: Shoreline with mountain landscape.	—	—	—

Banc Ceannais Na hÉireann

Central Bank of Ireland

1943-1945 Issue

#	Description	VG	VF	UNC
56	**10 Shillings** 1945-1959. Orange. Face portrait of Lady Hazel Lavery at left.			
	a. Deleted. See #1D.	—	—	—
	b1. Without letter overprint. Signature J. Brennan and J. J. McElligott. Lower signature title with *Runaidhe*. 15.5.1945-3.10.1950. Serial numbers 1-100,000.	20.00	80.00	100
	b2. As b1. 12.9.1951-22.10.1952. Serial numbers extended 1-1,000,000.	10.00	40.00	70.00
	c. Signature J. J. McElligott and K. Redmond, lower Signature title with *Runai*. 19.10.1955.	15.00	50.00	150
	d. Signature J. J. McElligott and T. K. Whitaker. 28.5.1957; 11.3.1959; 1.9.1959.	10.00	40.00	70.00

#	Description	VG	VF	UNC
57	**1 Pound** 1945-1960. Green. Face portrait of Lady Hazel Lavery at left.			
	a. Deleted. See #2D.	—	—	—
	b1. Without letter overprint. Signature J. Brennan and J. J. McElligott. Lower signature title with *Runaidhe*. 12.4.1945-11.12.1950. Serial # 1-100,000.	15.00	70.00	100
	b2. As b1. 11.9.1951-26.8.1952. Serial # extended 1-1,000,000.	3.00	25.00	60.00
	c. Signature J. J. McElligott and K. Redmond, lower signature title with *Runai*. 6.1.1954; 25.10.1955.	3.00	25.00	100
	d. Signature J. J. McElligott and T. K. Whitaker. 12.6.1957-18.5.1960.	3.00	25.00	60.00
58	**5 Pounds** 1945-1960. Brown. Face portrait of Lady Hazel Lavery at left.			
	a. Deleted. See #3D.	—	—	—
	b1. Without letter overprint. Signature J. Brennan and J. J. McElligott. Lower signature title with *Runaidhe*. 17.1.1945-24.4.1951. Serial # 1-100,000.	40.00	200	150
	b2. As b1. 16.8.1952-24.4.1953. Serial # extended 1-1,000,000.	15.00	50.00	100
	c. Signature J. J. McElligott and K. Redmond, lower signature title with *Runai*. 3.5.1954; 15.9.1955; 24.10.1955.	10.00	90.00	130
	d. Signature J. J. McElligott and T. K. Whitaker. 20.8.1956-12.5.1960.	10.00	90.00	130

59	10 Pounds	VG	VF	UNC
	1945-1960. Blue. Lady Hazel Lavery in Irish national costume with chin resting on her hand and leaning on an Irish harp.			
	a. Deleted. See #4D.	—	—	—
	b. Without letter overprint. Signature J. Brennan and J. J. McElligott. Lower signature title with *Runaidhe*. 6.9.1945-11.11.1952.	40.00	110	300
	c. Signature J. J. McElligott and K. Redmond, lower signature title with *Runai*. 3.12.1954-21.10.1955.	40.00	200	500
	d. Signature J. J. McElligott and T. K. Whitaker. 7.1.1957-6.12.1960.	30.00	55.00	110

60	20 Pounds	VG	VF	UNC
	1945-1957. Red. Lady Hazel Lavery in Irish national costume with chin resting on her hand and leaning on an Irish harp.			
	a. Deleted. See #5D.	—	—	—
	b. Without letter overprint. Signature J. Brennan and J. J. McElligott. Lower signature title with *Runaidhe*. 17.10.1945-25.3.1952.	150	500	1,800
	c. Signature J. J. McElligott and K. Redmond, lower signature title with *Runai*. 27.4.1954; 2.9.1955.	100	400	1,500
	d. Signature J. J. McElligott and T. K. Whitaker. 23.10.1957.	100	400	1,000
	s. As b. Specimen. Overprinted: *SPECIMEN* and punch hole cancelled.	—	—	1,500

61	50 Pounds	VG	VF	UNC
	1943-1960. Purple. Lady Hazel Lavery in Irish national costume with chin resting on her hand and leaning on an Irish harp.			
	a. Without identifying code letter. Signature J. Brennan and J. J. McElligott. Lower signature title with*Runaidhe*. 23.3.1943-13.2.1951.	400	1,000	3,000
	b. Signature J. J. McElligott and K. Redmond, lower signature title with*Runai*. 22.4.1954; 4.5.1954.	400	1,000	3,000
	c. Signature J. J. McElligott and T. K. Whitaker. 4.10.1957; 16.5.1960.	300	700	3,000
	s. As a. Specimen. Overprinted: *SPECIMEN* and punch hole cancelled.	—	—	1,500

62	100 Pounds	VG	VF	UNC
	1943-1959. Green. Lady Hazel Lavery in Irish national costume with chin resting on her hand and leaning on an Irish harp.			
	a. Without identifying code letter. Signature J. Brennan and J. J. McElligott. Lower signature title with *Runaidhe*. 3.2.1943-3.9.1949.	250	1,000	2,800
	b. Signature J. J. McElligott and K. Redmond, lower signature title with*Runai*. 21.4.1954; 1.5.1954.	200	1,000	2,800
	c. Signature J. J. McElligott and T. K. Whitaker. 14.10.1959; 11.11.1959.	200	700	2,200
	s. As a. Specimen. Overprinted: *SPECIMEN* and punch hole cancelled.	—	—	1,500

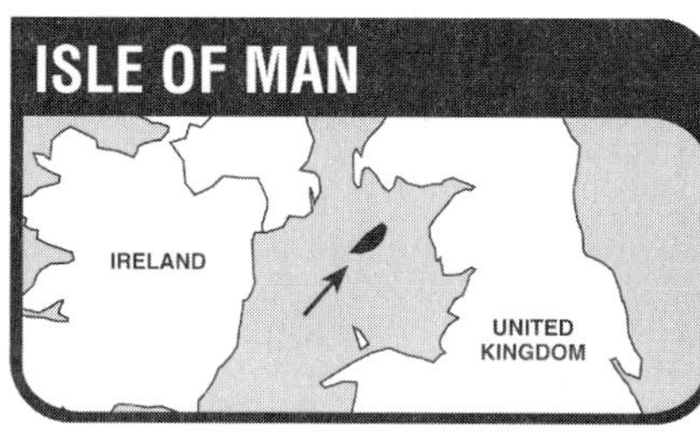

The Isle of Man, a dependency of the British Crown located in the Irish Sea equidistant from Ireland, Scotland and England, has an area of 572 sq. km. and a population of 76,220. Capital: Douglas. Agriculture, dairy farming, fishing and tourism are the chief industries.

Part of the Norwegian Kingdom of the Hebrides until the 13th century when it was ceded to Scotland, the isle came under the British crown in 1765. Current concerns include reviving the almost extinct Manx Gaelic language. Isle of Man is a British crown dependency but is not part of the UK. However, the UK Government remains constitutionally responsible for its defense and international representation. The Sovereign of the United Kingdom (currently Queen Elizabeth II) holds the title Lord of Man. The Isle of Man is ruled by its own legislative council and the House of Keys, one of the oldest legislative assemblies in the world. Acts of Parliament passed in London do not affect the island unless it is specifically mentioned. United Kingdom bank notes and coinage circulate concurrently with Isle of Man money as legal tender.

RULERS:

British

MONETARY SYSTEM:

1 Pound = 20 Shillings to 1971
1 Pound = 100 Pence, 1971-

BANKS:

Castle Rushen #S111
Douglas & Isle of Man Bank (Dumbell's) #S121-S122
Douglas & Isle of Man Bank (Holmes') #S121-S122
Dumbell's Banking Co. Ltd. #S141-S143

BRITISH ADMINISTRATION

Barclays Bank Limited

1924 Issue

		Good	Fine	XF
1	**1 Pound** 1924-1960. Brown and green. Triskele in underprint at center. Back: Douglas harbor. Printer: W&S.			
	a. 7.6.1924-7.4.1937.	375	750	1,500
	b. 17.12.1937-4.12.1953.	100	300	600
	c. 10.4.1954-10.3.1959.	80.00	150	400
	d. 30.3.1960.	100	200	450

Isle of Man Banking Co. Limited

In 1926 became Isle of Man Bank Limited.

1865 Issue

		Good	Fine	XF
2	**1 Pound** 1865-1915. Black and brown. Douglas harbor at upper center. Signature varieties. Back: Vertical blue lines and border. Triskele at center. Printer: W.& A.K. Johnston Ltd., Edinburgh.	500	1,250	—

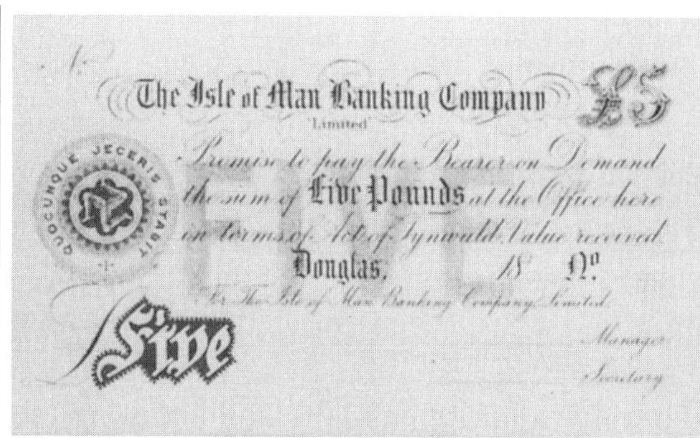

		Good	Fine	XF
3	**5 Pounds** 1894-1920. Black and blue. Seal of arms at left. Douglas harbor at upper center. Signature varieties. Back: Triskele at center. Printer: W.& A. K. Johnston Ltd., Edinburgh.			
	a. 1.11.1894; 1.1.1900; 4.12.1911; 7.8.1914; 1.3.1920.	2,500	5,000	—
	r. Unsigned remainder. ND.	—	—	—

1914 Issue

		Good	Fine	XF
3A	**1 Pound** 1914-1926. Black and brown. Douglas harbor at upper center. Back: Triskele at center, without vertical blue lines or border.			
	a. 1.8.1914.	250	600	1,500
	b. 8.1.1916-1.3.1926.	150	500	1,100

Isle of Man Bank Limited

Formerly the Isle of Man Banking Co. Limited.

1926-27 Issue

		Good	Fine	XF
4	**1 Pound** 1.12.1926-4.9.1933. Black and pink. Douglas harbor above bank title. Signature varieties. Back: Triskele at center. Printer: W.& A. K. Johnston Ltd., Edinburgh.	200	400	800

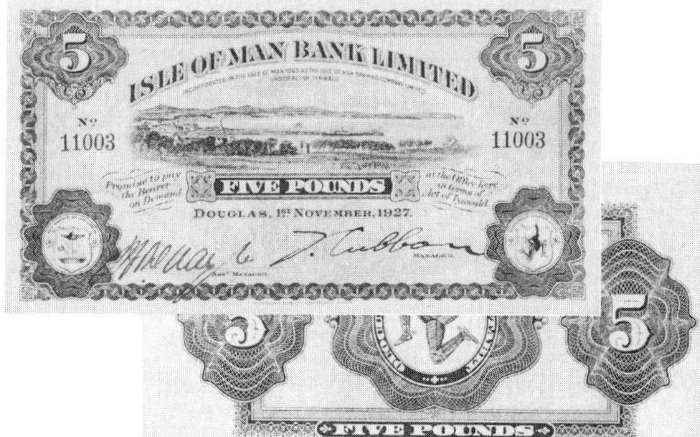

		Good	Fine	XF
5	**5 Pounds** 1.11.1927. Blue, green and pink. Douglas harbor above bank title. Two signature varieties. Back: Triskele at center. Printer: W&S.	40.00	175	400

1934-1936 Issue

		Good	Fine	XF
6	**1 Pound** 1934-1960. Blue, brown and green. Douglas harbor above bank title. Signature varieties. Back: Triskele at center. Printer: W&S.			
	a. 1.10.1934-5.5.1937.	40.00	100	275
	b. 4.2.1938-18.10.1952.	20.00	50.00	120
	c. 1.12.1953; 29.11.1954. 2 signature varieties.	40.00	90.00	175
	d. 5.1.1956-24.10.1960.	20.00	50.00	150

		Good	Fine	XF
6A	**5 Pounds** 1936-1960. Brown, pink and green. Douglas harbor above bank title. Signature varieties. Back: Triskele at center. Printer: W&S.			
	a. 1.12.1936.	50.00	175	550
	b. 3.1.1945; 7.4.1960.	150	400	1,000

Lancashire & Yorkshire Bank Limited

Taken over in 1928 by Martins Bank Limited.

Manx Bank

1904 Issue

		Good	Fine	XF
7	**1 Pound** 31.8.1904-30.10.1920. Slate gray. Tower of Refuge at center. Title: *MANX BANK / BRANCH OF THE / LANCASHIRE & YORKSHIRE BANK LIMITED.* Signature varieties. Back: Bank arms.	275	600	1,500

1920 W/o Branch Name Issue

		Good	Fine	XF
8	**1 Pound** 13.12.1920-28.12.1927. Slate gray. Bank arms at left, Tower of Refuge at right. Title: *LANCASHIRE & YORKSHIRE BANK LIMITED.* Signature varieties. Back: Castle Rushen at left, triskele at center, Laxey wheel at right.	375	850	1,750

Lloyds Bank Limited

1919-29 Issues

		Good	Fine	XF
9	**1 Pound** 23.4.1919-10.12.1920. Black and green. Signature varieties.	350	750	1,750
10	**1 Pound** 23.3.1921-21.1.1927. Pink underprint. *ONE POUND.* Signature varieties.	350	750	1,750
11	**1 Pound** 1.8.1929-14.2.1934. Black and green on pink underprint. Text: *INCORPORATED IN ENGLAND* in 1 line. Signature varieties.	300	600	1,500

1935 Issue

		Good	Fine	XF
12	**1 Pound** 1935-1954. Black and green on pink underprint. Text: *INCORPORATED IN ENGLAND* divided. Signature varieties. Back: Letters of bank name with shading.			
	a. 28.1.1935-27.4.1949.	175	350	850
	b. 27.2.1951-26.2.1954.	100	250	500

Color Abbreviation Guide

New to the *Standard Catalog of ® World Paper Money* are the following abbreviations related to color references:

BC: Back color
PC: Paper color

1955 Issue

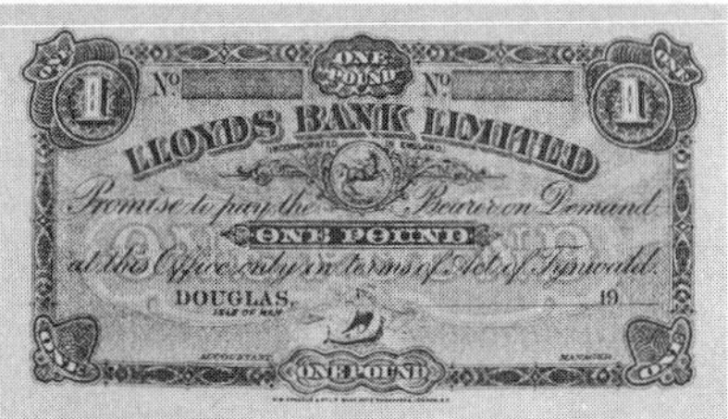

		Good	Fine	XF
13	**1 Pound** 21.1.1955-14.3.1961. Black on green underprint. Bank arms at upper center. Signature varieties. Back: Bank title enlarged.			
	a. Issued note.	180	350	750
	r. Unsigned remainder. ND.	—	—	200

London County Westminster and Parr's Bank Limited

In 1923 the name was changed to "Westminster Bank". See also #22-23.

1918 Provisional Issue

		Good	Fine	XF
14	**1 Pound** 28.3.1918-22.11.1918. Signature varieties. Overprint: *LONDON COUNTY WESTMINSTER* on #21.	500	1,000	2,400

1919 Regular Issue

		Good	Fine	XF
15	**1 Pound** 11.10.1919; 11.1.1921; 25.11.1921. Like #14 but newly printed bank name. Signature varieties. Printer: W&S.	500	1,000	2,400

Manx Bank Limited

Taken over in 1901 by the Mercantile Bank of Lancashire Limited.

1882 Issue

		Good	Fine	XF
16	**1 Pound** 11.11.1882-30.5.1900. Black. Tower of Rufuge at center. Signature varieties. Printer: W&S.	500	1,000	2,000

Martins Bank Limited

Absorbed the Lancashire & Yorkshire Bank Limited in 1928.

1928 Provisional Issue

		Good	Fine	XF
17	**1 Pound** 9.10.1928; 3.11.1928. Overprint: *MARTINS BANK LIMITED* on #8.	500	1,000	2,000

1928 Issue

		Good	Fine	XF
18	**1 Pound** 1929-1938. Black. Bird on dark hatched field in bank shield. Bank shield at left, Tower of Refuge at right. Back: Castle Rushen at left, Albert Tower at right.			
	a. Red serial #. 2.4.1929; 1.12.1931; 31.12.1932.	150	300	725
	b. Black serial #. 1.8.1934; 1.10.1938.	100	200	500

1946 Issue

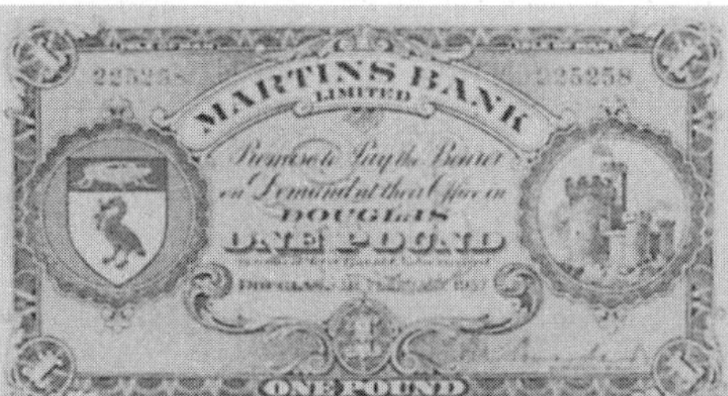

		Good	Fine	XF
19	**1 Pound** 1946-1957. Black. Bird on lightly stippled field in bank shield at left. Tower of Refuge at right. Back: Castle Rushen at left, Albert Tower at right.			
	a. 1.3.1946.	50.00	130	350
	b. 1.6.1950; 1.5.1953; 1.2.1957.	20.00	50.00	200

Mercantile Bank of Lancashire Limited

Absorbed Manx Bank Limited in 1901. Taken over in 1904 by the Lancashire and Yorkshire Bank.

1901 Issue

		Good	Fine	XF
20	**1 Pound** 13.6.1901-6.9.1902. Black. Tower of Refuge at center. Signature varieties. Printer: W&S.	500	1,000	2,000

Parr's Bank Limited

Amalgamated in 1918 with the London County and Westminster Bank.

1900 Issue

		Good	Fine	XF
21	**1 Pound** 1900-1916. Gray. Crowned triskele supported by lion left, unicorn right. Signature varieties.			
	a. Handwritten dates. 20.8.1900; 23.1.1901; 1.6.1906.	500	1,000	2,400
	b. Printed dates. 2.4.1909-10.11.1916.	500	1,000	2,400

Westminster Bank Limited

Formerly the London County Westminster and Parr's Bank Limited.

1923 Provisional Issue

		Good	Fine	XF
22	**1 Pound** 1923-1927. Signature varieties. Overprint: *WESTMINSTER BANK LIMITED* on #15.			
	a. 4.7.1923; 17.12.1923; 5.2.1924.	500	1,000	2,000
	b. 20.10.1924-4.4.1927.	500	1,000	2,000

1929 Regular Issue

		Good	Fine	XF
23	**1 Pound** 1929-1955. Black on light yellow underprint. Crowned triskele supported by lion left, unicorn right, at upper center. Signature varieties. Printer: W&S.			
	a. 9.1.1929; 24.10.1929; 14.11.1933.	150	300	750
	b. 22.1.1935-4.2.1943.	110	225	450
	c. 11.2.1944-18.3.1949.	80.00	160	400
	d. 7.11.1950-30.3.1955.	60.00	125	250

1955 Issue

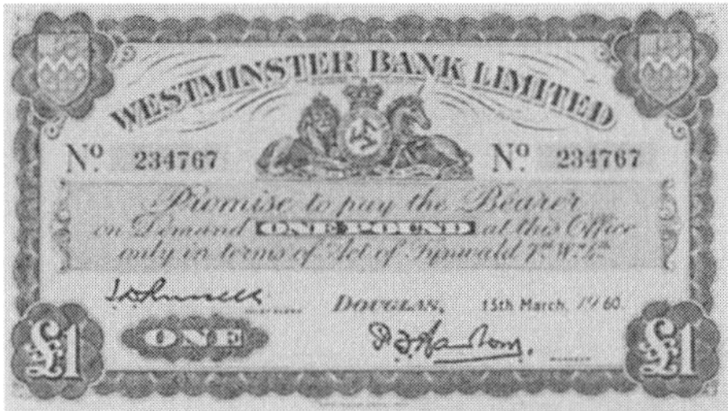

		Good	Fine	XF
23A	**1 Pound** 1955-1961. Black on light yellow underprint. Crowned triskele supported by lion left, unicorn right at upper center. Text: *INCORPORATED IN ENGLAND* added below bank name. Signature varieties. Printer: W&S.			
	a. 23.11.1955.	100	200	500
	b. 4.4.1956-10.3.1961.	40.00	100	225

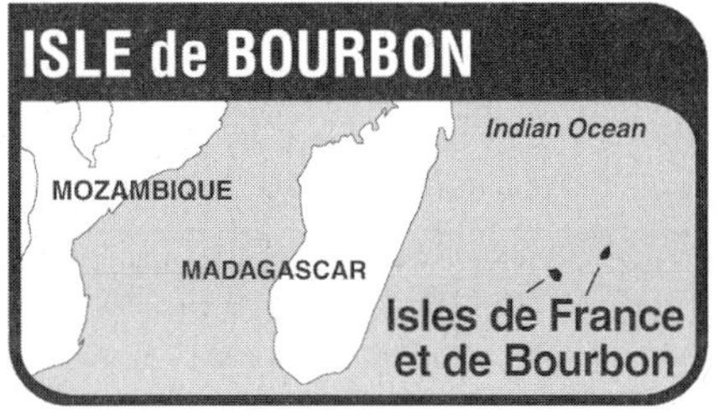

Isles of France and Bourbon (now the separate entities of Mauritius and Reunion), located in the Indian Ocean about 500 miles east of Madagascar, were at one time administered by France as a single colony, at which time they utilized a common currency issue. Ownership of Mauritius passed to Great Britain in 1810-14. Isle of Bourbon, renamed Reunion in 1793, remained a French possession and is now an overseas department.

RULERS:
French until 1810

MONETARY SYSTEM:
1 Livre = 20 Sols (Sous)

FRENCH ADMINISTRATION

Isle de Bourbon

1766 Issue

Note: Denominations of 10 Sous; 20 Sous and 3 Livres require confirmation.

		Good	Fine	XF
A1	**40 Sous Tournois** Dec. 1766. Crowned arms at top center. Uniface. Rare.	—	—	—

1793 Issue

		Good	Fine	XF
A3	**40 Sols Tournois** 11-13.4.1793. With text: *Papier de confiance et d'echange.*	—	—	—
A5	**50 Livres Tournois** 11-13.4.1793. With text: *Papier de confiance et d'echange.*	—	—	—

Isle de la Réunion

1793-1794 Issue

		Good	Fine	XF
A6	**20 Sols Tournois** 11.4.1793. With text: *Papier de confiance et d'echange.*	—	—	—
A7	**20 Sols Tournois** 10.5.1794. With text: *Papier de confiance et d'echange.*	—	—	—

		Good	Fine	XF
A9	**12 Livres Tournois** 10.5.1794. With text: *Papier de confiance et d'echange.*	—	—	—

Bure du Console

1768 Issue

		Good	Fine	XF
A12	**6 Livres** July 1768. Black. Uniface.	800	2,000	—

Isles de France et de Bourbon

1768 Issue

		Good	Fine	XF
A15	**3 Livres Tournois** July 1768. Rare.	—	—	—
A16	**6 Livres Tournois** July 1768. Rare.	—	—	—
A17	**12 Livres Tournois** July 1768. Rare.	—	—	—
A18	**24 Livres Tournois** July 1768. Rare.	—	—	—

ND Issue

Type I text: ***Intendant general des Colonies***

#	Description	Good	Fine	XF
1	**6 Livres Tournois** ND. With text: *Billet de...or Bon pour...*	350	600	1,100

#	Description	Good	Fine	XF
2	**20 Livres Tournois** ND. With text: *Billet de...or Bon pour...*	—	—	—

#	Description	Good	Fine	XF
3	**100 Livres Tournois** ND. With text: *Intendant general des Colonies*	—	—	—
4	**500 Livres Tournois** ND. With text: *Intendant general des Colonies*	—	—	—

1788 Issue

#5 not assigned. Type II text: *Intendant general des fonds de la Marine & des Colonies*

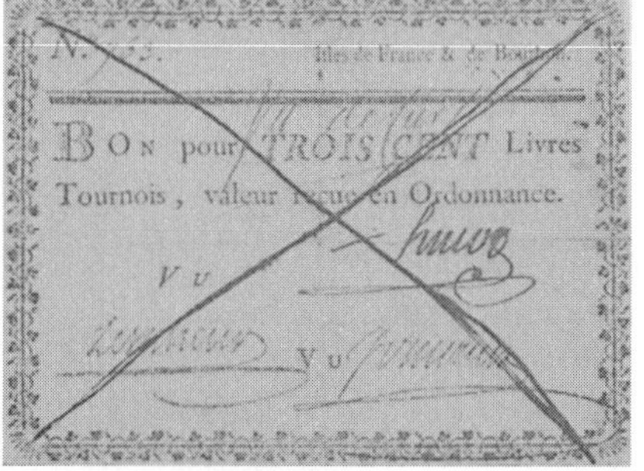

#	Description	Good	Fine	XF
6	**2 Livres 10 Sous Tournois** 10.6.1788. *Billet de...or Bon pour...* Text: *Intendant general des fonds de la Marine & des Colonies*	600	1,000	—
7	**5 Livres Tournois** 10.6.1788. *Billet de...or Bon pour...* Text: *Intendant general des fonds de la Marine & des Colonies*	—	—	—
8	**10 Livres Tournois** 10.6.1788. *Billet de...or Bon pour...* Text: *Intendant general des fonds de la Marine & des Colonies*	—	—	—
9	**50 Livres Tournois** 10.6.1788. *Billet de...or Bon pour...* Text: *Intendant general des fonds de la Marine & des Colonies*	—	—	—
10	**100 Livres Tournois** 10.6.1788. *Billet de...or Bon pour...* Text: *Intendant general des fonds de la Marine & des Colonies*	—	—	—

#	Description	Good	Fine	XF
11	**300 Livres Tournois** 10.6.1788. *Billet de...or Bon pour...* Text: *Intendant general des fonds de la Marine & des Colonies*	900	1,500	—

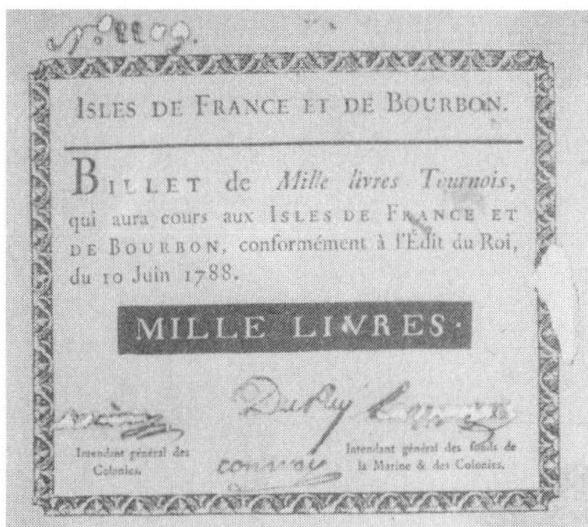

#	Description	Good	Fine	XF
12	**500 Livres Tournois** 10.6.1788. *Billet de...or Bon pour...* Text: *Intendant general des fonds de la Marine & des Colonies*	150	450	—

Note: Deceptive reprints created for collectors exist of the 500 Livres.

#	Description	Good	Fine	XF
13	**1000 Livres Tournois** 10.6.1788. *Billet de...or Bon pour...* Text: *Intendant general des fonds de la Marine & des Colonies*	—	—	—

Law of 28.7.1790

#	Description	Good	Fine	XF
16	**5 Livres** *L.1790.* With text: *Bon pour...*	—	—	—
17	**10 Livres** *L.1790.* With text: *Bon pour...*	—	—	—

Color Abbreviation Guide

New to the *Standard Catalog of® World Paper Money* are the following abbreviations related to color references:

BC: Back color
PC: Paper color

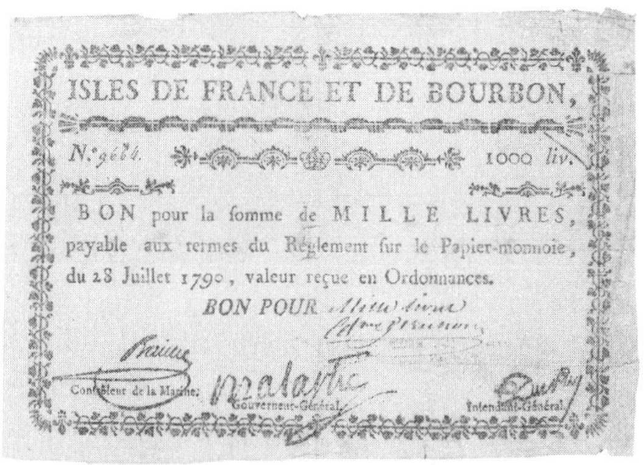

		Good	Fine	XF
22	**1000 Livres**	**Good**	**Fine**	**XF**
	L.1790. With text: *Bon pour...* Wavy bar under title.			
	a. Off-white paper.	400	800	1,600
	b. Bluish paper. Rare.	—	—	—
	x. Error: inverted *D* in *DE BOURBON*. Rare.	—	—	—
23	**1000 Livres**	**Good**	**Fine**	**XF**
	L.1790. With text: *Bon pour...* Straight bar under title.	400	800	1,600

		Good	Fine	XF
24	**10,000 Livres**	**Good**	**Fine**	**XF**
	L.1790. With text: *Bon pour...* Rare.	—	—	—

1795-1796 Issue

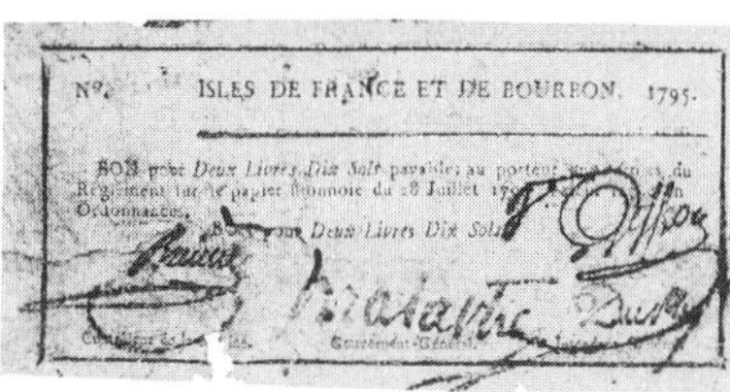

		Good	Fine	XF
26	**2 Livres 10 Sols**	**Good**	**Fine**	**XF**
	1795. Black. With text: *Bon pour...* Uniface.	—	—	—

		Good	Fine	XF
28	**10 Livres**	**Good**	**Fine**	**XF**
	1795-1796. Black. With text: *Bon pour...* Uniface.	—	—	—

Note: For later issues see Mauritius and Reunion.

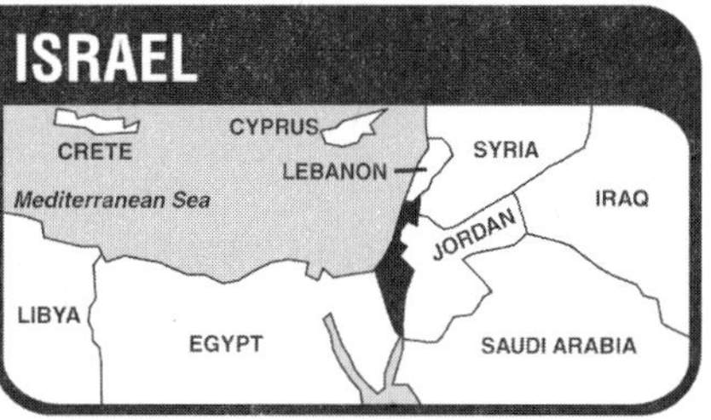

The State of Israel, at the eastern end of the Mediterranean Sea, bounded by Lebanon on the north, Syria on the northeast, Jordan on the east, and Egypt on the southwest, has an area of 20,770 sq. km. and a population of 7.11 million. Capital: Jerusalem. Diamonds, chemicals, citrus, textiles, and minerals are exported, local tourism to religious sites.

Following World War II, the British withdrew from their mandate of Palestine, and the UN partitioned the area into Arab and Jewish states, an arrangement rejected by the Arabs. Subsequently, the Israelis defeated the Arabs in a series of wars without ending the deep tensions between the two sides. The territories Israel occupied since the 1967 war are not included in the Israel country profile, unless otherwise noted. On 25 April 1982, Israel withdrew from the Sinai pursuant to the 1979 Israel-Egypt Peace Treaty. In keeping with the framework established at the Madrid Conference in October 1991, bilateral negotiations were conducted between Israel and Palestinian representatives and Syria to achieve a permanent settlement. Israel and Palestinian officials signed on 13 September 1993 a Declaration of Principles (also known as the "Oslo Accords") guiding an interim period of Palestinian self-rule.

MONETARY SYSTEM:

1 Palestine Pound = 1000 Mils to 1948
1 Lira = 1000 Prutot, 1948-1960
1 Lira = 100 Agorot, 1958-1980
1 Sheqel = 10 "old" Lirot, 1980-85
1 Sheqel = 100 New Agorot, 1980-1985
1 New Sheqel = 1000 "old" Sheqalim, 1985-
1 New Sheqel = 100 Agorot, 1985-

STATE OF ISRAEL

Anglo-Palestine Bank Limited

1948 Provisional Issue

Printed in the event that notes ordered might not be ready on time; destroyed in October, only a few sets preserved.

		VG	VF	UNC
1	**500 Mils**	**VG**	**VF**	**UNC**
	16.5.1948. Purple. Uniface.			
	a. Issued note.	—	—	1,500
	s. Specimen.	—	—	1,500
2	**1 Palestine Pound**	**VG**	**VF**	**UNC**
	16.5.1948. Green. Uniface.			
	a. Issued note.	—	—	1,500
	s. Specimen.	—	—	1,500
3	**5 Palestine Pounds**	**VG**	**VF**	**UNC**
	16.5.1948. Brown. Uniface.			
	a. Issued note.	—	—	1,500
	s. Specimen.	—	—	1,500
4	**10 Palestine Pounds**	**VG**	**VF**	**UNC**
	16.5.1948. Blue. Uniface.			
	a. Issued note.	—	—	1,500
	s. Specimen.	—	—	1,500
5	**50 Palestine Pounds**	**VG**	**VF**	**UNC**
	16.5.1948. Proof examples only.	—	—	—

Israel Government

1952-1953 ND Fractional Note Issues

Signature Varieties	
1. Zagaggi	E. Kaplan
2. Zagaggi	L. Eshkol
3. A. Neeman	L. Eshkol

6	50 Mils	VG	VF	UNC
	ND (printed 1948, issued 1952). Dark red and orange. Vertical format.	30.00	75.00	300

7	100 Mils	VG	VF	UNC
	ND (printed 1948, issued 1952). Green. Vertical format.	30.00	75.00	300

8	50 Pruta	VG	VF	UNC
	ND (1952). Blue-black. Horizontal format. Signature 1.	15.00	50.00	200

9	50 Pruta	VG	VF	UNC
	ND (1952). Red on pink underprint. Signature 1.	10.00	25.00	100

10	50 Pruta	VG	VF	UNC
	ND (1952). Red on red or orange underprint.			
	a. Signature 1.	10.00	25.00	100
	b. Signature 2.	10.00	25.00	100
	c. Signature 3.	0.75	3.00	7.50

11	100 Pruta	VG	VF	UNC
	ND (1952). Green on light green underprint. Signature 1.	10.00	25.00	100

12	100 Pruta	VG	VF	UNC
	ND (1952). Blue on green underprint.			
	a. Signature 1.	10.00	25.00	100
	b. Signature 2.	10.00	25.00	100
	c. Signature 3.	1.00	3.00	7.50
	d. Signature 3 with A. Neeman inverted (error).	500	1,200	3,000

Note: Paper thickness varies.

01005א *Aleph* 01004ב *Bet* 01011ג *Gimel*

13	250 Pruta	VG	VF	UNC
	ND (1953). Dark brown on green underprint. Back: Sea of Galilee with Arbel mountain at center right.			
	a. *Aleph* series with menorah.	3.00	15.00	65.00
	b. *Aleph* series without menorah.	2.50	12.50	45.00
	c. *Bet* series without menorah.	2.50	10.00	35.00
	d. *Gimel* series with menorah at left.	3.00	15.00	75.00
	e. *Gimel* series with menorah at right.	3.00	15.00	75.00
	f. *Aleph* series with *250* under guilloche on face.	—	—	—

Note: *Aleph, Bet* and *Gimel* series refer to the first 3 letters of the Hebrew alphabet. The series suffix letter follows the serial #. On some series, a very faint gold-colored Menorah appears on face at upper left or upper right when exposed to ultra-violet lighting.

Anglo-Palestine Bank Limited

1948-1951 ND Issue

14	500 Mils	VG	VF	UNC
	ND (1948-1951). Gray. Printer: ABNC (without imprint). Serial # varieties.			
	a. Issued note.	30.00	100	750
	s. Specimen.	—	—	300

15	1 Pound	VG	VF	UNC
	ND (1948-1951). Blue. Printer: ABNC (without imprint). Serial # varieties.			
	a. Issued note.	5.00	30.00	175
	s. Specimen.	—	—	300

16	5 Pounds	VG	VF	UNC
	ND (1948-1951). Brown. Printer: ABNC (without imprint). Serial # varieties.			
	a. Issued note.	10.00	35.00	200
	s. Specimen.	—	—	300

No.	Denomination	VG	VF	UNC
17	**10 Pounds** ND (1948-1951). Red. Printer: ABNC (without imprint). Serial # varieties.	VG	VF	UNC
	a. Issued note.	15.00	60.00	300
	s. Specimen.	—	—	300
18	**50 Pounds** ND (1948-1951). Lilac. Printer: ABNC (without imprint). Serial # varieties.	VG	VF	UNC
	a. Issued note.	2,000	3,250	—
	s. Specimen.	—	—	400

Bank Leumi Le-Israel B.M.

1952 ND Issue

No.	Denomination	VG	VF	UNC
19	**500 Prutah** ND (9.6.1952). Gray-green on light blue underprint. Printer: ABNC (without imprint).	VG	VF	UNC
	a. Issued note.	8.00	75.00	550
	s. Specimen.	—	—	300

No.	Denomination	VG	VF	UNC
20	**1 Pound** ND (9.6.1952). Olive on pink underprint. Printer: ABNC (without imprint).	VG	VF	UNC
	a. Issued note.	4.00	15.00	55.00
	s. Specimen.	—	—	300

No.	Denomination	VG	VF	UNC
21	**5 Pounds** ND (9.6.1952). Brown on yellow underprint. Printer: ABNC (without imprnt).	VG	VF	UNC
	a. Issued note.	12.00	45.00	250
	s. Specimen.	—	—	300

No.	Denomination	VG	VF	UNC
22	**10 Pounds** ND (9.6.1952). Gray on orange underprint. Printer: ABNC (without imprint).	VG	VF	UNC
	a. Issued note.	15.00	75.00	375
	s. Specimen.	—	—	300

No.	Denomination	VG	VF	UNC
23	**50 Pounds** ND (9.6.1952). Dark brown on light blue underprint. Printer: ABNC (without imprint).	VG	VF	UNC
	a. Issued note.	200	600	1,500
	s. Specimen.	—	—	400

Bank of Israel

1955 / 5715 Issue

No.	Denomination	VG	VF	UNC
24	**500 Pruta** 1955/5715. Red on green underprint. Ruin of an ancient synagogue near Bir'am at left, flowers at upper right. Back: Modernistic design. Watermark: Menorah. Printer: TDLR (without imprint).	VG	VF	UNC
	a. Issued note.	2.50	12.50	55.00
	s. Specimen.	—	—	300

25	1 Lira	VG	VF	UNC
	1955/5715. Blue on multicolor underprint. Landscape in Upper Galilee across bottom, flowers at upper right. Back: Geometric designs. Watermark: Menorah. Printer: TDLR (without imprint).			
	a. Issued note.	3.00	15.00	65.00
	s. Specimen.	—	—	350

26	5 Lirot	VG	VF	UNC
	1955/5715. Brown on light blue underprint. Negev landscape across center, flowers at upper right. Back: Geometric designs. Watermark: Menorah. Printer: TDLR (without imprint).			
	a. Issued note.	4.00	20.00	90.00
	s. Specimen.	—	—	400

27	10 Lirot	VG	VF	UNC
	1955/5715. Dark green on multicolor underprint. Landscape in the Plain of Jezreel across center, flowers at upper right. Back: Geometric designs. Watermark: Menorah. Printer: TDLR (without imprint).			
	a. Red serial #.	5.00	17.50	55.00
	b. Black serial #.	4.00	15.00	50.00
	s. Specimen.	—	—	500

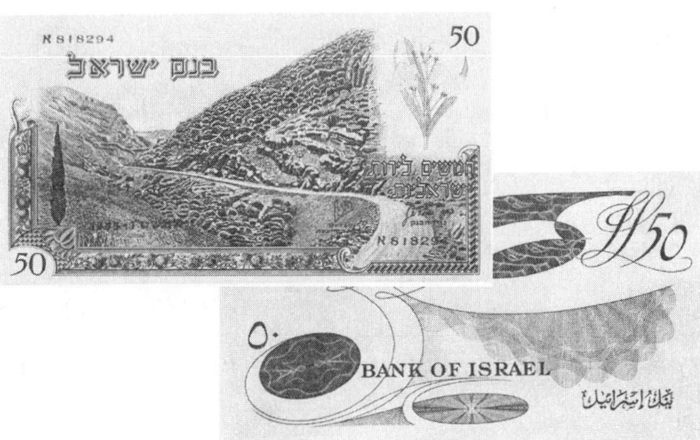

28	50 Lirot	VG	VF	UNC
	1955/5715. Dark blue and multicolor. Jerusalem Road between mountains, flowers at upper right. Watermark: Menorah. Printer: TDLR (without imprint).			
	a. Black serial #.	12.50	50.00	150
	b. Red serial #.	20.00	70.00	200
	s. Specimen.	—	—	600

1958-60 / 5718-20 Issue

29	1/2 Lira	VG	VF	UNC
	1958/5718. Green on green and peach underprint. Woman soldier with basket full of oranges at left. Back: Tombs of the Sanhedrin at right. Watermark: Woman soldier. Printer: JEZ (without imprint). UV: fibers fluoresce blue.			
	a. Issued note.	0.50	1.50	5.00
	s. Specimen.	—	—	275

30	1 Lira	VG	VF	UNC
	1958/5718. Blue on light blue and peach underprint. Fisherman with net and anchor at left. Back: Synagogue mosaic at right. Watermark: Fisherman. Printer: JEZ (without imprint). UV: fibers fluoresce blue.			
	a. Paper with security thread at left. Black serial #.	0.50	1.25	4.00
	b. Red serial #.	0.50	1.25	4.00
	c. Paper with security thread and morse tape, brown serial #.	0.50	1.00	3.00
	s. Specimen.	—	—	275

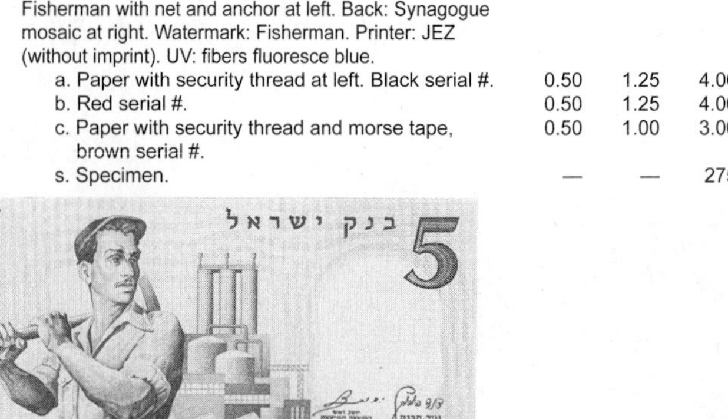

		VG	VF	UNC
31	**5 Lirot** 1958/5718. Brown on multicolor underprint. Worker with hammer in front of factory at left. Back: Seal of Shema at right. Watermark: Worker with hammer. Printer: TDLR (without imprint). UV: fibers fluoresce yellow.			
	a. Issued note.	0.50	2.00	5.00
	s. Specimen.	—	—	500

		VG	VF	UNC
32	**10 Lirot** 1958/5718. Lilac and purple on multicolor underprint. Scientist with microscope and test tube at left. Back: Dead Sea scroll and vases at right. Watermark: Scientist. Printer: TDLR (without imprint).			
	a. Paper with security thread. Black serial #.	0.50	2.00	12.00
	b. Paper with security thread and morse tape. Red serial #.	0.50	2.00	15.00
	c. Paper with security thread and morse tape. Blue serial #.	0.50	2.00	15.00
	d. Paper with security thread and morse tape. Brown serial #.	0.50	1.50	6.00
	s. Specimen.	—	—	500

		VG	VF	UNC
33	**50 Lirot** 1960/5720. Brown and multicolor. Boy and girl at left. Back: Mosaic of menorah at right. Watermark: Boy and girl. Printer: JEZ (without imprint).			
	a. Paper with security thread. Black serial #.	2.00	10.00	45.00
	b. Paper with security thread. Red serial #.	2.00	10.00	45.00
	c. Paper with security thread and morse tape. Blue serial #.	1.50	6.00	45.00
	d. Paper with security thread and morse tape. Green serial #.	1.50	6.00	30.00
	e. Paper with security thread and morse tape. Brown serial #.	1.50	5.00	30.00
	s. Specimen.	—	—	600

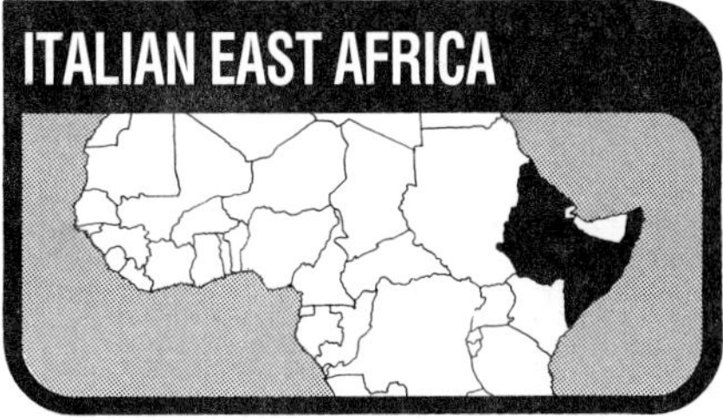

Italian East Africa was a former Italian possession made up of Eritrea (Italian colony since 1890), Ethiopia (invaded by Italy from Eritrea in 1935 and annexed in 1936) and Italian Somaliland (under Italian influence since 1889). Founded in 1936, it lasted until British-led colonial forces came into each of the areas in 1941.

ITALIAN OCCUPATION - WW II

Banca d'italia

Africa Orientale Italiana

1938-1939 Issue

Note: This issue circulated in all the Italian occupied areas and colonies in Africa.

		VG	VF	UNC
1	**50 Lire** 1938-1939. Green on light green underprint. Head of Italia seal at right. Back: Statue of she-wolf with Romulus and Remus at center. Watermark: Man's head facing right.			
	a. 14.6.1938-12.9.1938.	15.00	70.00	400
	b. 14.1.1939.	25.00	80.00	480

		VG	VF	UNC
2	**100 Lire** 1938-1939. Blue-green on orange underprint. Reclining Roma with shield and spear holding Victory, statue of she-wolf with Romulus and Remus at bottom center. Back: Eagle and wreath at center.			
	a. 14.6.1938-12.9.1938.	30.00	80.00	450
	b. 14.1.1939.	40.00	120	800

		VG	VF	UNC
3	**500 Lire** 1938-1939. Blue and green. Peasant woman with sheaf of grain and sickle at right. Back: Crowned arms at left, Roma seated between allegorical male figures at center, fasces seal below.			
	a. 14.6.1938-12.9.1938.	120	300	1,300
	b. 14.1.1939.	130	400	1,850

		VG	VF	UNC
4	**1000 Lire** 1938-1939. Violet, brown and blue. Two women (Venezia and Genova) reclining at bottom center. Back: Allegorical woman seated between reclining male and Mercury at center, fasces seal above.			
	a. 14.6.1938-12.9.1938.	120	480	1,800
	b. 14.1.1939.	150	600	2,000

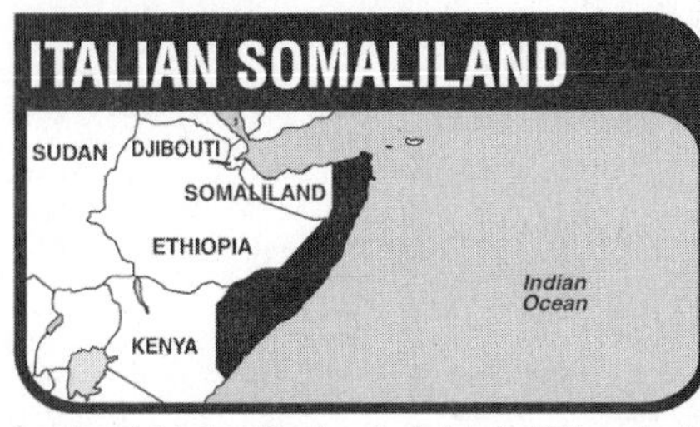

Italian Somaliland, a former Italian colony in East Africa, extended south from Ras Asir to Kenya. Area: 178,218 sq. mil. (461,585 sq. km.). Captial: Mogadisho. In 1885, Italy obtained commercial concessions in the area from the sultan of Zanzibar,and in 1905 purchased the coast from Warshek to Brava. The Italians then extended their occupation inward. Cession of Jubaland Province by Britain in 1924, and seizure of the sultanates of Obbia and Mijertein in 1925-27 brought direct Italian administration over the whole territory. Italian dominance continued until World War II. British troops occupied Italian Somaliland in 1941. Britain administered the colony until 1950, when it became a UN trust territory administered by Italy. On July 1, 1960, Italian Somaliland united with British Somaliland to form the independent Somali Democratic Republic.

RULERS:

Italian, 1892-1941, 1950-1960
British, 1941-1950

MONETARY SYSTEM:

1 Rupia = 100 Bese to 1925
1 Somali = 1 Lira = 100 Centesimi, 1925-1960
1 Shilling = 100 Cents, WW II British occupation

ITALIAN INFLUENCE

V. Filonardi & Co.

The Filonardi note appears to be a private issue; in reality it was sponsored by the Italian government to assist the company in overseeing the interests of Italy in the region. In other words, the Filonardi company was in all respects the *de facto* government in the designated Somali area.

1893 Issue

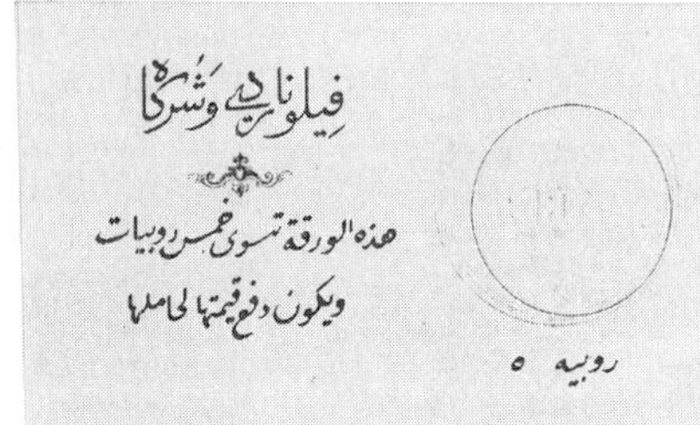

		VG	VF	UNC
1	**5 Rupias**			
	15.7.1893. Black on light green underprint. White 5-pointed star at center, embossed seal at left. Back: Red Arabic text at left, denomination at lower right.	170	800	—

Banca d'Italia

Somalia Italiana

1920 Buoni di Cassa Issue

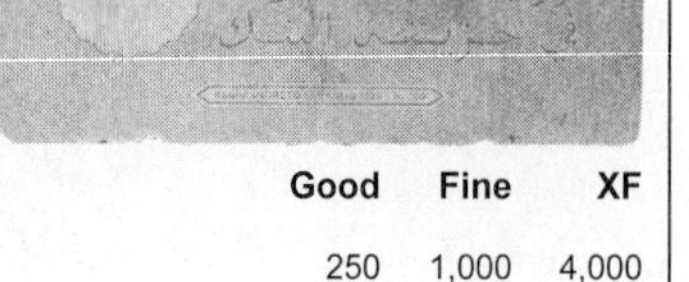

		Good	Fine	XF
2	**1 Rupia**			
	1920-1921. Black and red.			
	a. 8.9.1920.	250	1,000	4,000
	b. 2.6.1921.	600	2,500	—

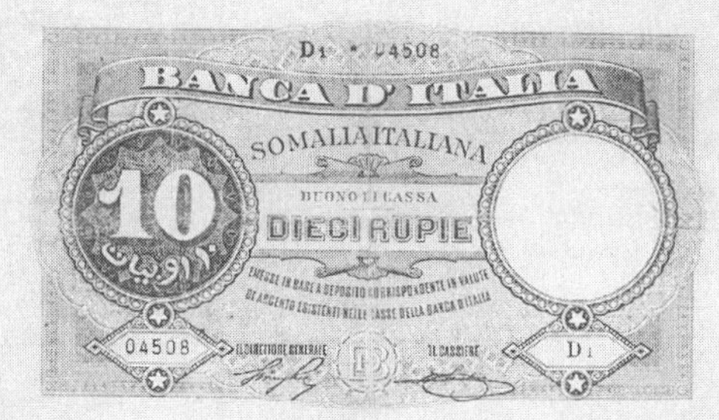

		Good	Fine	XF
3	**5 Rupias**			
	13.5.1920. Pink and brown.	2,200	9,000	—

		Good	Fine	XF
4	**10 Rupias**			
	13.5.1920. Yellowish brown and multicolor.	2,500	10,000	—

#5 and #6 *Deleted.*

Cassa per la Circolazione Monetaria della Somalia

1950 Issue

		VG	VF	UNC
11	**1 Somali**			
	1950. Brown and yellow. Leopard at center.			
	a. Issued note.	215	850	2,950
	s. Specimen.	—	—	2,000
12	**5 Somali**	VG	VF	UNC
	1950. Blue and yellow.			
	a. Issued note.	80.00	285	1,100
	s. Specimen.	—	—	800
13	**10 Somali**	VG	VF	UNC
	1950. Green and yellow. 3 signature varieties.			
	a. Issued note.	55.00	220	930
	s. Specimen.	—	—	800

		VG	VF	UNC
14	**20 Somali** 1950. Brown and yellow. 3 signature varieties.			
	a. Issued note.	50.00	195	870
	s. Specimen.	—	—	800

		VG	VF	UNC
15	**100 Somali** 1950. Violet and light brown. Lion at left. 3 signature varieties.			
	a. Issued note.	235	940	4,200
	s. Specimen.	—	—	2,950

1951 Issue

		VG	VF	UNC
16	**5 Somali** 1951. Brown-violet and light blue. Leopard at center. Watermark: Leopard.	70.00	250	1,000

The Italian Republic, a 700-mile-long peninsula extending into the heart of the Mediterranean Sea, has an area of 301,230 sq. km. and a population of 58.14 million. Captal: Rome. The economy centers about agriculture, manufacturing, forestry and fishing. Machinery, textiles, clothing and motor vehicles are exported.

Italy became a nation-state in 1861 when the regional states of the peninsula, along with Sardinia and Sicily, were united under King Victor Emmanuel II. An era of parliamentary government came to a close in the early 1920s when Benito Mussolini established a Fascist dictatorship. His alliance with Nazi Germany led to Italy's defeat in World War II. A democratic republic replaced the monarchy in 1946 and economic revival followed. Italy was a charter member of NATO and the European Economic Community (EEC). It has been at the forefront of European economic and political unification, joining the Economic and Monetary Union in 1999. Persistent problems include illegal immigration, organized crime, corruption, high unemployment, sluggish economic growth, and the low incomes and technical standards of southern Italy compared with the prosperous north.

RULERS:

Umberto I, 1878-1900
Vittorio Emanuele III, 1900-1946

MONETARY SYSTEM:

1 Lira = 100 Centesimi, to 2001
1 Euro = 100 Cents, 2001-

DECREES:

There are many different dates found on the following notes of the Banca d'Italia. These include ART. DELLA LEGGE (law date) and the more important DECRETO MINISTERIALE (D. M. date). The earliest D.M. date is usually found on the back of the note while later D.M. dates are found grouped together. The actual latest date (of issue) is referred to in the following listings.

PRINTERS:

Further differentiations are made in respect to the printers w/the place name *Roma* or *L'Aquila* (1942-44).

Note: Certain listings encompassing issues circulated by various bank and regional authorities are contained in Volume 1.

KINGDOM

Federal Biglietti Consorziale

A unified bank note issue imposed by the government to reduce the amount of coinage in circulation. These were released by the following banks: Banca Nazionale nel Regno d'Italia, Banco Nazionale Toscana, Banca Romana, Banca Toscana di Credito, Banco di Napoli and Banco di Sicilia.

Law of 30.4.1874

Note: All notes mention this law date, but Regal Decrees from 2.7.1875 to 3.11.1877 were the authorizing determinants.

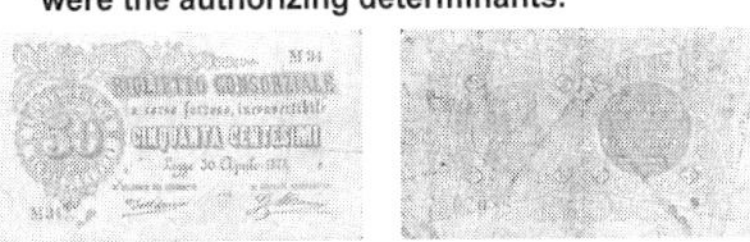

		Good	Fine	XF
1	**50 Centesimi** *L. 1874.* Black and blue on brown underprint. Back: Blue. Back: "Italia" at left.	3.00	10.00	35.00

		Good	Fine	XF
2	**1 Lira** *L. 1874.* Black and brown on green underprint. Back: Brown. Back: "Italia" at left.	2.00	8.00	30.00
3	**2 Lire** *L. 1874.* Green and black on peach underprint. Back: Dark green. Back: "Italia" at left.	2.00	8.00	40.00

		Good	Fine	XF
4	**5 Lire** *L. 1874.* Brown, tan and black on light orange underprint. Back: Brown. Back: "Italia" at left and right.	2.00	8.00	30.00

		Good	Fine	XF
5	**10 Lire** *L. 1874.* Blue and black on brown underprint. Back: Blue. Back: "Italia" at left and right.	3.00	10.00	35.00
6	**20 Lire** *L. 1874.* Black text, blue on orange underprint. Arms at upper center, cherubs at lower center, ornamental border. Back: Black. Back: Crowned "Italia" at center.	120	400	1,000

		Good	Fine	XF
7	**100 Lire** *L. 1874.* Black text, blue on gold underprint. Crowned supported arms at top center, allegorical figures around border. Back: Dark brown. Back: Crowned "Italia" at center.	120	500	1,200
8	**250 Lire** *L. 1874.* Black on brown underprint. Allegorical figures at bottom and around border. Back: Black on green underprint. Back: Crowned "Italia" at center.	300	1,000	1,250

		Good	Fine	XF
9	**1000 Lire** *L. 1874.* Black on light green underprint. Crowned supported arms at top center, allegorical women and cherubs at sides and bottom. Back: Black on light blue underprint. Back: Crowned "Italia" at center.	800	2,000	4,500

Federal Biglietti Già Consorziale
Law of 25.12.1881

Note: All notes mention this law date but Regal Decrees of 1881 and 1882 actually governed their issuance. Like previous issue, but different colors.

		Good	Fine	XF
10	**1 Lira** *L. 1881.* Black text, red on light tan underprint. Like #2. Back: Red. Back: "Italia" at left.	5.00	20.00	80.00

		Good	Fine	XF
11	**2 Lire** *L. 1881.* Black text, blue on blue-gray underprint. Like #3. Back: Blue. Back: "Italia" at left.	10.00	40.00	150
12	**5 Lire** *L. 1881.* Black text, light blue on gold underprint. Like #4. Back: Light blue. Back: "Italia" at left and right.	150	800	1,800
13	**10 Lire** *L. 1881.* Black text, orange on green underprint. Like #5. Back: Orange. Back: "Italia" at left and right.	150	800	1,800
14	**20 Lire** *L. 1881.* Gray on blue underprint. Like #6. Back: Gray. Back: Crowned "Italia" at center.	800	2,000	4,500
15	**100 Lire** *L. 1881.* Black and green on light blue underprint. Like #7. Back: Blue and green. Back: Crowned "Italia" at center.	800	2,000	4,500
16	**250 Lire** *L. 1881.* Blue and green. Like #8. Back: Black on green underprint. Back: Crowned "Italia" at center.	—	—	—
17	**1000 Lire** *L. 1881.* Black and green. Like #9. Back: Black on light blue underprint. Back: Crowned "Italia" at center.	500	3,500	10,000

Treasury Biglietti di Stato
1882-1895 Issues

		VG	VF	UNC
18	**5 Lire** *D.1882-1892.* Blue. Portrait King Umberto I at left.			
	a. Signature Dell'Ara and Crodara. 01.03.1883.	20.00	60.00	450
	b. Signature Dell'Ara and Pia. 6.8.1889.	30.00	120	750
	c. Signature Dell'Ara and Righetti. 25.10.1892.	15.00	50.00	350
19	**10 Lire** *D.11.3.1883.* Blue. Portrait King Umberto I at left on both sides. Signature Dell'Ara and Crodara.	130	500	2,200

		VG	VF	UNC
20	**10 Lire** 1888-1925. Blue on pink underprint. Portrait King Umberto I at left. Back: Only denomination in oval at left.			
	a. Signature Dell'Ara and Crodara. 28.2.1888.	100	200	800
	b. Signature Dell'Ara and Pia. 6.8.1889.	20.00	50.00	350
	c. Signature Dell'Ara and Righetti. 25.10.1892.	6.00	15.00	100
	d. Signature Dell'Ara and Altamura. 13.1.1911.	7.00	20.00	140
	e. Signature Dell'Ara and Righetti. 2.9.1914.	6.00	12.00	90.00
	f. Signature Giu. Dell'Ara and Righetti. 10.4.1915.	6.00	12.00	90.00
	g. Signature Giu. Dell'Ara and Porena. 28.12.1918.	6.00	12.00	90.00
	h. Signature Maltese and Rossolini. 19.5.1923.	6.00	12.00	90.00
	i. Signature Maltese and Rosi Bernardini. 3.6.1925.	6.00	15.00	120

		VG	VF	UNC
21	**25 Lire** 21.7.1895. Blue on pink underprint. Only denomination in oval at left. "Italia" at left. Back: Green.	1,000	2,800	6,000

1902 Issue

		VG	VF	UNC
22	**25 Lire** 23.3.1902. Blue on orange underprint. Portrait King Vittorio Emanuele III at left. Back: Heraldic eagle at right.	4,000	8,000	20,000

1904 Issue

		VG	VF	UNC
23	**5 Lire** 1904-1925. Blue and black on pink underprint. Portrait King Vittorio Emanuele III at right.			
	a. Signature Dell'Ara and Righetti. 8.11.1904.	2.00	6.00	60.00
	b. Signature Dell'Ara and Altamura. 27.12.1904.	4.00	10.00	80.00
	c. Signature Dell'Ara and Righetti. 22.1.1914.	2.00	10.00	90.00
	d. Signature Giu. Dell'Ara and Righetti. 5.11.1914.	2.00	10.00	90.00
	e. Signature G. Dell'Ara and Porena. 14.10.1917.	2.00	10.00	90.00
	f. Signature Maltese and Rossolini. 24.2.1922.	2.00	10.00	90.00
	g. Signature Maltese and Rosi Bernardini. 10.7.1924.	3.00	12.00	120

Regno D'Italia Biglietto di Stato

1923 Issue

		VG	VF	UNC
24	**25 Lire** 20.8.1923. Brown. Medallic head of "Italia" at right, eagle with flag above. Seals: Type A/E. Like#42. Back: Head of Minerva in oval at left. Watermark: Head of Minerva.			
	a. Signature Maltese and Rossolini. Series 001-116.	225	850	2,750
	b. Signature Maltese and Rosi Bernardini. Series 117-120.	800	2,400	6,500

Note: For similar type but headed *Banca d'Italia* and dated 1918-19, see #42.

1935 Issue

		VG	VF	UNC
25	**10 Lire** 1935; 1938-XVII; 1939-XVIII; 1944-XXII. Blue. Portrait King Vittorio Emanuele III at left. Date at bottom center edge. Back: Italia" at right. Watermark: Woman's head facing left.			
	a. Signature Grassi, Rosi Bernardini and Collari. 18.6.1935.	1.00	2.00	40.00
	b. Signature Grassi, Collari and Porena. 1938.	2.00	6.00	70.00
	c. Signature Grassi, Porena and Cossu. 1939; 1944.	1.00	2.00	35.00

1939; 1940 Issue

		VG	VF	UNC
26	**1 Lira** 14.11.1939. Dark brown on light brown underprint. Back: Caesar Augustus at center.	0.10	0.30	3.00

		VG	VF	UNC
27	**2 Lire** 14.11.1939. Blue-violet on pale lilac underprint. Back: Julius Caesar.	0.10	0.30	4.00

		VG	VF	UNC
28	**5 Lire** 1940; 1944. Violet on brown underprint. Portrait King Vittorio Emanuele III at left. Date at bottom center edge. Back: Blue on yellow underprint. Back: Eagle with sword at center.	1.00	2.00	20.00

Italia - Biglietto di Stato

1944 Issue

		VG	VF	UNC
29	**1 Lira** 23.11.1944. Brown on pink underprint. "Italia" at left. Back: Green.			
	a. Signature Ventura, Simoneschi and Giovinco.	0.10	0.25	3.00
	b. Signature Bolaffi, Cavallaro and Giovinco.	0.10	0.25	3.00
	c. Signature DiCristina, Cavallaro and Zaini.	0.10	0.25	5.00

		VG	VF	UNC
30	**2 Lire** 23.11.1944. Green on light orange underprint. "Italia" at left. Back: Orange or gold.			
	a. Signature Ventura, Simoneschi and Giovinco.	0.20	5.00	12.50
	b. Signature Bolaffi, Cavallaro and Giovinco.	0.20	0.50	12.50

		VG	VF	UNC
31	**5 Lire** 23.11.1944. Violet-brown. Archaic helmeted female at left.			
	a. Signature Ventura, Simoneschi and Giovinco.	0.10	0.35	5.00
	b. Signature Bolaffi, Simoneschi and Giovinco.	0.10	0.25	3.00
	c. Signature Bolaffi, Cavallaro and Giovinco.	0.10	0.25	3.00

		VG	VF	UNC
32	**10 Lire** 23.11.1944. Blue. Jupiter at left. Engraved or lithographed. (The lithographed note has a blue line design in the watermark area at center.) Back: Two allegorical men.			
	a. Signature Ventura, Simoneschi and Giovinco.	0.10	0.25	7.00
	b. Signature Bolaffi, Simoneschi and Giovinco.	0.10	0.30	5.00
	c. Signature Bolaffi, Cavallaro and Giovinco.	0.10	0.25	5.00

Treasury Buoni di Cassa

R. Decreto 4.8.1893/Decreto Ministeriale 22.2.1894

		VG	VF	UNC
33	**1 Lira** *D.1893* (1893-1894). Red-brown with black text on green underprint. Portrait King Umberto I at left. Back: Blue.	80.00	250	800

1894 Issue

		VG	VF	UNC
34	**1 Lira** *L.1894* (1894-1898). Red-brown with black text on green underprint. Portrait King Umberto I at left. Signature Dell'Ara and Righetti. Watermark: Waves. Series 033-119.	70.00	220	700

		VG	VF	UNC
35	**2 Lire** *D.1894* (1894-1898). Dark blue with black text on grayish brown underprint. Portrait King Umberto I at left. Back: Red-brown. Series 001-069.	150	400	2,000

1914 Issue

		VG	VF	UNC
36	**1 Lira** *D.1914* (1914-1921). Dark olive-brown on light blue underprint. Portrait King Vittorio Emanuele III at left. Back: Red. Back: Arms at center.			
	a. Signature Dell'Ara and Righetti. Series 001-150 (1914-1917).	2.00	5.00	30.00
	b. Signature Giu. Dell'Ara and Righetti. Series 151-200.	2.00	5.00	30.00
	c. Signature Giu. Dell'Ara and Porena. Series 200-266 (1921).	40.00	100	400

		VG	VF	UNC
37	**2 Lire** *D.1914* (1914-1922). Brown-violet on light red-brown underprint. King Vittorio Emanuele III at left. Back: Brown. Back: Arms at center.			
	a. Signature Dell'Ara and Righetti. Series 001-075 (1914-1917).	2.00	5.00	50.00
	b. Signature Giu. Dell'Ara and Righetti. Series 076-100.	2.00	5.00	50.00
	c. Signature Giu. Dell'Ara and Porena. Series 101-165 (1920-22).	2.00	5.00	50.00

Banca d'Italia

Bank of Italy

FACE SEAL VARIETIES

Type A
Italia facing l.

Type B
Facing head of Medusa

Type C
Winged lion of St. Mark of Venice above 3 shields of Genoa, Pisa and Amalfi

BACK SEAL VARIETIES

Type D
"Decreto Ministeriale De 30 Luglio 1896"
(17.7.1896-17.1.1930)

Type E
"Otto-Bre 1922"
w/fasces
(19.5.1926-6.8.1943)

Type F
Banco d'Italia monogram
(7.8.1943-21.3.1947)

Decreto Ministeriale 30.7.1896 and 12.9.1896

		VG	VF	UNC
38	**50 Lire** 1896-1926. Blue on green underprint with counterfoil. With counterfoil, large letter *L* and woman with three children at left. Back: Woman at right. Seals: Type A/D.			
	a. Signature Marchiori and Nazari. 12.9.1896; 9.2.1899.	300	1,000	4,000
	b. Signature Stringher and Accame. 9.12.1899; 9.6.1910.	50.00	100	750
	c. Signature Stringher and Sacchi. 2.1.1912-4.10.1918.	35.00	70.00	500
	d. Signature Canavai and Sacchi. 22.1.1919; 12.5.1919.	60.00	120	700
	e. Signature Stringher and Sacchi. 15.8.1919-29.6.1926.	30.00	60.00	450

		VG	VF	UNC
39	**100 Lire** 1897-1926. Brown and pink with counterfoil. Large *B* and woman seated with small angels at left. Watermark: Head of Mercury. Seals: Type A/D.			
	a. Signature Marchiori and Nazari. 30.10.1897.	400	1,200	4,000
	b. Signature Marchiori and Accame. 9.12.1899.	400	1,200	4,000
	c. Signature Stringher and Accame. 9.12.1899-9.6.1910.	40.00	100	650
	d. Signature Stringher and Sacchi. 10.9.1911-4.10.1918.	35.00	90.00	600
	e. Signature Canovai and Sacchi. 22.1.1919; 12.5.1919.	60.00	140	850
	f. Signature Stringher and Sacchi. 15.8.1919-8.9.1926.	35.00	90.00	600
40	**500 Lire** 1898-1921. Dark blue on pink-brown underprint . With counterfoil, oval ornament with allegorical figures. Watermark: Head of Roma. Seals: Type A/D.	VG	VF	UNC
	a. Signature Marchiori and Nazari. 25.10.1898.	2,000	5,000	12,000
	b. Signature Marchiori and Accame. 25.10.1898-9.12.1899.	2,200	6,000	14,000
	c. Signature Stringher and Accame. 9.12.1899-15.11.1909.	2,000	5,000	12,000
	d. Signature Stringher and Sacchi. 9.6.1910; 6.12.1918.	1,600	3,500	8,000
	e. Signature Canovai and Sacchi. 12.5.1919.	1,800	4,000	10,000
	f. Signature Stringher and Sacchi. 15.8.1919; 12.2.1921.	1,000	2,000	6,000
41	**1000 Lire** 1897-1920. Violet-brown and brown. With counterfoil, large *M* at left. Watermark: Head of "Italia" at right and *1000* at left. Seals: Type A/D.	VG	VF	UNC
	a. Signature Marchiori and Nazari. 6.12.1897.	3,000	8,000	—
	b. Signature Marchiori and Accame. 2.12.1899.	2,500	6,000	—
	c. Signature Stringher and Accame. 9.12.1899; 9.6.1910.	2,000	5,000	12,000
		VG	VF	UNC
	d. Signature Stringher and Sacchi. 13.11.1911-1.7.1918.	1,200	3,200	7,500
	e. Signature Canovai and Sacchi. 22.1.1919.	2,000	5,000	12,000
	f. Signature Stringher and Sacchi. 15.8.1919-17.8.1920.	1,200	3,000	7,000

1915-1921 Issues

		VG	VF	UNC
42	**25 Lire** 1918-1919. Deep brown on brown underprint. Medallic head of "Italia" at right, eagle with flag above. Back: Blue-black on blue-gray. Back: Head of Minerva at left. Watermark: Head of Minerva in oval at left. Seals: Type A/D.			
	a. Signature Stringher and Sacchi. 24.1.1918; 1.7.1918.	150	500	2,200
	b. Signature Canovai and Sacchi. 22.1.1919; 12.5.1919.	150	500	2,200

Note: For similar issue to #42 but headed *Regno d'Italia Biglietto di Stato* and dated 1923, see #24.

		VG	VF	UNC
43	**50 Lire** 1915-1920. Black on orange underprint. Seated "Italia" at right. Back: Farmer with oxen. Watermark: Dante. Seals: Type A/D.			
	a. Signature Stringher and Sacchi. 15.6.1915; 4.10.1918.	200	500	2,800
	b. Signature Canovai and Sacchi. 22.1.1919-12.5.1919.	200	500	2,800
	c. Signature Stringher and Sacchi. 15.8.1919; 7.6.1920.	200	500	2,800

#44 not assigned, see #43.

		VG	VF	UNC
45	**500 Lire** 16.7.1919-13.4.1926. Olive-brown on violet and multicolor underprint. Peasant woman with sickle and sheaf at right. Crowned arms at left. Roma seated between allegorical male figures at center. Signature Stringher and Sacchi. Watermark: Leonardo Da Vinci. Seals: Type A/D.	50.00	250	1,200

		VG	VF	UNC
46	**1000 Lire** 19.8.1921-8.8.1926. Voilet-brown and brown. Without counterfoil. Signature Stringher and Sacchi. Watermark: Banca d'Italia at left, head of "Italia" at right. Seals: Type A/D.	150	450	2,000

1926 Issue

		VG	VF	UNC
47	**50 Lire** 1926-1936. Blue on green underprint. Large letter*L* and woman with three children at left. With counterfoil at left. Back: Woman at right. Seals: Type A/D.			
	a. Signature Stringher and Sacchi. 8.9.1926-2.6.1928.	25.00	50.00	250
	b. Signature Stringher and Cima. 15.1.1929-17.11.1930.	25.00	50.00	250
	c. Signature Azzolini and Cima. 2.3.1931-17.3.1936.	25.00	50.00	250

		VG	VF	UNC
48	**100 Lire** 1927-1930. Brown and pink. With counterfoil. Seals: Type A/E.			
	a. Signature Stringher and Sacchi. 12.2.1927-2.6.1928.	45.00	140	600
	b. Signature Stringher and Cima. 15.1.1929-17.11.1930.	45.00	140	600

		VG	VF	UNC
49	**100 Lire** 2.2.1926; 8.8.1926. Blue. Without counterfoil. Signature Stringher and Sacchi. Watermark: Head of "Italia". Seals: Type A/D.	200	700	2,500

		VG	VF	UNC
50	**100 Lire** 1926-1934. Blue. Without counterfoil. Watermark: Head of "Italia". Seals: Type A/E.			
	a. Signature Stringher and Sacchi. 18.11.1926; 12.2.1927; 9.4.1928.	40.00	125	575
	b. Signature Stringher and Cima. 12.4.1929-22.4.1930.	40.00	125	575
	c. Signature Azzolini and Cima. 2.3.1931-17.10.1934.	40.00	125	575

		VG	VF	UNC
51	**500 Lire** 1926-1942. Violet and olive-brown. *ROMA* at end of imprint. Type A/E. Back: Back seal: Type E.			
	a. Signature Stringher and Sacchi. 6.12.1926-21.6.1928.	35.00	80.00	550
	b. Signature Stringher and Cima. 6.6.1929; 21.3.1930.	35.00	80.00	550
	c. Signature Azzolini and Cima. 18.2.1932-16.10.1935.	30.00	75.00	450
	d. Signature Azzolini and Urbini. 22.12.1937-23.3.1942.	30.00	75.00	425

Note: For similar type but green with overprint: *AFRICA ORIENTALE ITALIANA* see Italian East Africa #3.

		VG	VF	UNC
52	**1000 Lire** 1926-1932. Violet-brown and brown. Without counterfoil. Seals: A/E.			
	a. Signature Stringher and Sacchi. 18.11.1926-21.6.1928.	60.00	140	650
	b. Signature Stringher and Cima. 12.4.1929; 5.12.1929; 20.10.1930.	60.00	140	650
	c. Signature Azzolini and Cima. 2.1.1932.	80.00	160	900

1930-1933 Issue

		VG	VF	UNC
54	**50 Lire** 1933-1940. Blue-violet and yellow brown on orange and yellow underprint. Seals: Type A/E. Back: She/wolf with Romulus and Remus. *Roma* at end of imprint Watermark: Julius Caesar.			
	a. Signature Azzolini and Cima. 11.10.1933-16.12.1936.	3.00	12.00	120
	b. Signature Azzolini and Urbini. 30.4.1937; 19.8.1941.	3.00	12.00	100

Note: For similar type but green with overprint: *AFRICA ORIENTALE ITALIANA* see Italian East Africa #1.

		VG	VF	UNC
55	**100 Lire** 1931-1942. Olive and brown. Roma reclining with spear and shield holding Victory, wolf with twins at bottom center. *ROMA* at end of imprint. Back: Eagle and wreath at center. Watermark: "Italia" and Dante.			
	a. Signature Azzolini and Cima. 5.10.1931-16.12.1936.	5.00	12.50	240
	b. Signature Azzolini and Urbini. 13.3.1937-11.6.1942.	5.00	12.50	225

Note: For similar type but green with overprint: *AFRICA ORIENTALE ITALIANA* see Italian East Africa #2.

		VG	VF	UNC
56	**1000 Lire** 1930-1941. Black, blue, green, and brown. Two women reclining at bottom center (Venezia and Genova). Seals: Type A/D.*ROMA* at end of imprint. Back: Three allegorical figures at center. Watermark: "Italia" at left, Columbus at right.			
	a. Signature Stringher and Cima. 7.7.1930.	35.00	120	650
	b. Signature Azzolini and Cima. 28.6.1933-17.3.1936.	25.00	75.00	425
	c. Signature Azzolini and Urbini. 21.10.1938-13.11.1941.	25.00	75.00	425

Note: For similar type but green with overprint: *AFRICA ORIENTALE ITALIANA* see Italian East Africa #4.

1941-1942 Issue

		VG	VF	UNC
57	**50 Lire** 19.8.1941; 24.1.1942; 18.7.1942. Signature Azzolini and Urbini. Like # 54 but slightly reduced size. Back: She-wolf with Romulus and Remus. 120 x 70mm.	4.00	20.00	420
58	**50 Lire** 28.8.1942-6.8.1943. Blue-violet and yellow-brown on orange and yellow underprint. Like #54 but with *L'AQUILA* at end of imprint. Seals: Type A/E. Signature Azzolini and Urbini. Back: She-wolf with Romulus and Remus.	7.00	22.50	240
59	**100 Lire** 9.12.1942; 15.3.1943. Brown on yellow underprint. Seals: Type A/E. Signature Azzolini and Urbini.	8.00	25.00	180
60	**100 Lire** 28.8.1942-17.5.1943. Olive-green and brown. Seals: Type A/E. *L'AQUILA* at end of imprint. Signature Azzolini and Urbini	9.00	25.00	260

		VG	VF	UNC
61	**500 Lire** 21.10.1942; 18.1.1943; 17.5.1943. Olive-brown on violet and multicolor underprint. Seals: Type A/E. *L'AQUILA* at end of imprint. Signature Azzolini and Urbini.	60.00	125	700
62	**1000 Lire** 12.12.1942; 6.2.1943. Violet-brown and brown. Without counterfoil. Seals: Type A/E. Signature Azzolini and Urbini.	30.00	90.00	600

		VG	VF	UNC
63	**1000 Lire** 28.8.1942-6.8.1943. Blue and brown. *L'AQUILA* at end of imprint. Signature Azzolini and Urbini.	100	280	1,200

1943 Issues

		VG	VF	UNC
64	**50 Lire** 31.3.1943. Blue on green underprint. Without counterfoil. Large letter *L* and woman with three children at left. Seals: Type A/E. Signature Azzolini and Urbini. Back: Woman's head at right.	10.00	30.00	200
65	**50 Lire** 11.8.1943; 8.10.1943; 11.11.1944. Blue on green underprint. Like #64 but with seals: Type A/F. Signature Azzolini and Urbini.	10.00	30.00	220

		VG	VF	UNC
66	**50 Lire** 23.8.1943; 8.10.1943; 1.2.1944. Blue-violet and yellow-brown. Like #58. Seals: Type A/F. Signature Azzolini and Urbini.	15.00	35.00	220
67	**100 Lire** 1943-1944. Brown on yellow underprint. Seals: Type A/F.	VG	VF	UNC
	a. Signature Azzolini and Urbini. 23.8.1943-11.11.1944.	12.50	60.00	325
	b. Signature Introna and Urbini. 20.12.1944.	25.00	140	550
68	**100 Lire** 23.8.1943; 8.10.1943. Olive-green and brown. Seals: Type A/F. Signature Azzolini and Urbini.	15.00	60.00	425
69	**500 Lire** 31.3.1943. Dark red on pink underprint without counter-foil. Seals: Type A/E. Signature Azzolini and Urbini.	35.00	80.00	550

		VG	VF	UNC
70	**500 Lire** 1943-1947. Dark red on pink underprint. Ornate border of allegorical figures. Seals: Type A/F. Watermark: Mercury.			
	a. Signature Azzolini and Urbini. 23.8.1943-17.8.1944.	35.00	80.00	650
	b. Signature Introna and Urbini. 7.10.1944.	40.00	90.00	750
	c. Signature Azzolini and Urbini. 11.11.1944; 13.12.1945.	35.00	80.00	650
	d. Signature Einaudi and Urbini. 8.6.1945-19.2.1947.	35.00	80.00	650
71	**500 Lire** 23.8.1943. Olive-brown on violet and multicolor underprint. Seals: Type A/F. Signature Azzolini and Urbini.	150	350	1,500

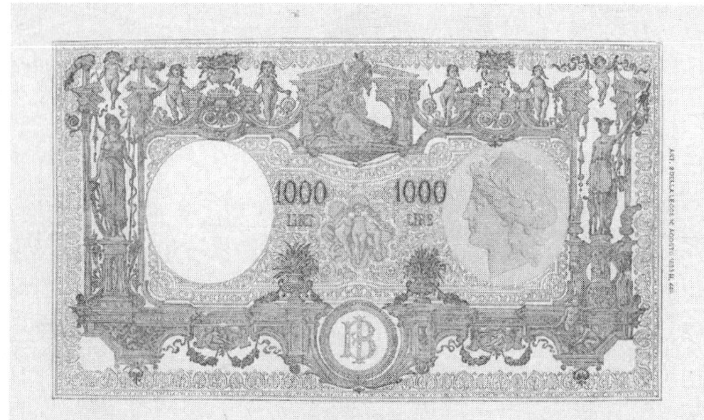

		VG	VF	UNC
72	**1000 Lire** 1943-1947. Violet-brown and brown. Ornate border with shield at upper center. Seals: Type A/F.			
	a. Signature Azzolini and Urbini. 11.8.1943-1.8.1944; 11.11.1944.	20.00	50.00	400
	b. Signature Introna and Urbini. 7.10.1944; 30.11.1944.	25.00	80.00	500
	c. Signature Einaudi and Urbini. 8.3.1945-12.7.1947.	20.00	70.00	440

		VG	VF	UNC
73	**1000 Lire** 23.8.1943; 8.10.1943. Blue and brown. Seals: Type A/F. Signature Azzolini and Urbini.	50.00	160	700

INTERIM GOVERNMENT

Banca d'Italia

1944 Issue

		VG	VF	UNC
74	**50 Lire** 10.12.1944. Green on pale orange underprint. Medallic head of "Italia" in oval at left. Seal: Type A. Signature Introna and Urbini. Watermark: *50*.			
	a. Issued note.	1.00	10.00	60.00
	s. Specimen. Red overprint: *SPECIMEN* four times on face.	—	—	—

		VG	VF	UNC
75	**100 Lire** 1944; 1946. Red on gray underprint. Medallic head of "Italia" at left. Seal: Type A. Watermark: *100*.			
	a. 10.12.1944. Signature Introna and Urbini.	1.00	7.50	50.00
	b. 20.4.1946. Signature Einaudi and Urbini. (Not issued)	1.00	7.50	50.00

		VG	VF	UNC
76	**500 Lire** 10.12.1944. Dark red on yellow underprint. Medallic head of "Italia" at left. (Not issued). Signature Introna and Urbini. Rare.	—	—	—

		VG	VF	UNC
77	**1000 Lire** 10.12.1944. Blue on blue-green underprint. Medallic head of "Italia" at left. (Not issued). Signature Introna and Urbini. Rare.			
	a. As an issued note. (Not Issued)	120	300	1,600
	r. As a replacement. Serial # prefix W. (Not issued)	100	200	1,200

REPUBLIC

Banca d'Italia

Bank of Italy

1945 Provisional Issue

		VG	VF	UNC
78	**5000 Lire** 1945-1947. Blue. Text: *Titolo provvisorio...* at left and right. in head of "Italia" underprint. Seal: Type A. Watermark: Head of "Italia".			
	a. Signature Einaudi and Urbini. 4.8.1945.	120	300	1,600
	b. Signature Einaudi and Urbini. 4.1.1947-12.7.1947.	100	200	1,200

		VG	VF	UNC
79	**10,000 Lire** 4.8.1945; 4.1.1947; 12.7.1947. Red-brown. Text: *Titolo provvisorio...* in head of "Italia" underprint at left and right. Seal: Type A. Signature Einaudi and Urbini. Watermark: Head of "Italia".	45.00	200	950

1947 Issues

		VG	VF	UNC
80	**500 Lire** 1947-1961. Purple on light brown underprint. "Italia" at left. Seal: Type B. Back: Purple on gray underprint. Watermark: Head of "Italia".			
	a. Signature Einaudi and Urbini. 20.3.1947; 10.2.1948.	4.00	30.00	200
	b. Signature Carli and Ripa. 23.3.1961.	4.00	35.00	275

		VG	VF	UNC
81	**1000 Lire** 1947-1950. Violet-brown and brown. Seals: Type B/F.			
	a. Signature Einaudi and Urbini. 22.11.1947; 14.4.1948.	60.00	120	850
	b. Signature Menichella and Urbini. 14.11.1950.	100	2,500	6,000

		VG	VF	UNC
82	**1000 Lire** 20.3.1947. Purple and brown. Italia" at left. Seal: Type A. Signature Einaudi and Urbini. Back: Blue on gray underprint. Watermark: Head of "Italia".	5.00	35.00	275

		VG	VF	UNC
83	**1000 Lire** 20.3.1947. Italia" at left. Seal: Type B. Signature Einaudi and Urbini. Back: Blue on gray underprint. Watermark: Head of "Italia".	4.00	15.00	150

		VG	VF	UNC
84	**5000 Lire** 17.1.1947. Green and brown. Two women seated at lower center (Venezia and Genova). Seal: Type A. Signature Einaudi and Urbini.	1,000	3,000	8,000

		VG	VF	UNC
85	**5000 Lire** 1947-1963. Green and brown. Two women seated at center (Venezia and Genova). Seals: Type A/F. Back: Woman at center. Watermark: Dante at left, "Italia" at right.			
	a. Signature Einaudi and Urbini. 17.1.1947; 27.10.1947; 23.4.1948.	70.00	250	1,200
	b. Signature Menichella and Urbini. 10.2.1949; 5.5.1952; 7.2.1953.	60.00	180	1,000
	c. Signature Menichella and Boggione. 27.10.1953-12.5.1960.	60.00	180	1,000
	d. Signature Carli and Ripa. 23.3.1961; 7.1.1963.	60.00	180	1,000

1947 Provisional Issue

		VG	VF	UNC
86	**5000 Lire** 1947-1949. Blue. Text: *Titolo provvisorio...* at left and right in head of "Italia" underprint. Seal: Type B. Watermark: Head of "Italia".			
	a. Signature Einaudi and Urbini. 8.9.1947; 18.11.1947; 17.12.1947; 28.1.1948.	60.00	180	1,000
	b. Signature Menichella and Urbini. 22.11.1949.	40.00	200	600

		VG	VF	UNC
87	**10,000 Lire** 1947-1950. Red-brown. Text: *Titolo provvisorio...* in head of "Italia" underprint at left and right. Seal: Type B.			
	a. Signature Einaudi and Urbini. 8.9.1947; 18.11.1947; 17.12.1947; 28.1.1948.	25.00	60.00	350
	b. Signature Menichella and Urbini. 6.9.1949; 12.6.1950.	25.00	60.00	350

1948 Issue

		VG	VF	UNC
88	**1000 Lire** 1948-1961. Purple and brown. Italia" at left. Seal: Type B. Back: Blue on gray underprint. Watermark: "Italia".			
	a. Signature Einaudi and Urbini. 10.2.1948.	3.00	15.00	175
	b. Signature Menichella and Urbini. 11.2.1949.	4.00	30.00	275
	c. Blue-gray. Signature Menichella and Boggione. 15.9.1959.	3.00	15.00	175
	d. Color like *c.* Signature Carli and Ripa. 25.9.1961.	3.00	15.00	175

		VG	VF	UNC
89	**10,000 Lire** 1948-1962. Brown, orange and multicolor. Two women seated at center (Venezia and Genova). Seal: Type B. Watermark: Verdi at left, Galilei at right.			
	a. Signature Einaudi and Urbini.23.4.1948.	60.00	140	900
	b. Signature Menichella and Urbini. 10.2.1949-7.2.1953.	60.00	140	900
	c. Signature Menichella and Boggione. 27.10.1953-12.5.1960.	60.00	140	900
	d. Signature Carli and Ripa. 23.3.1961-24.3.1962.	60.00	140	900

1950 Issue

		VG	VF	UNC
90	**500 Lire** 14.11.1950. Dark red on pink underprint. Seals: Type B/F. Signature Menichella and Urbini.	180	4,500	12,000

Repubblica Italiana - Biglietto di Stato

1951 Issue

		VG	VF	UNC
91	**50 Lire** 31.12.1951. Green on yellow underprint. "Italia" at left.			
	a. Signature Bolaffi, Cavallaro and Giovinco.	1.00	6.00	55.00
	b. Signature DiCristina, Cavallaro and Parisi.	1.50	10.00	90.00

		VG	VF	UNC
92	**100 Lire** 31.12.1951. Deep red, violet border on yellow underprint. "Italia" at left. Back: Red on yellow underprint.			
	a. Signature Bolaffi, Cavallaro and Giovinco.	1.00	6.00	55.00
	b. Signature DiCristina, Cavallaro and Parisi.	1.50	10.00	90.00

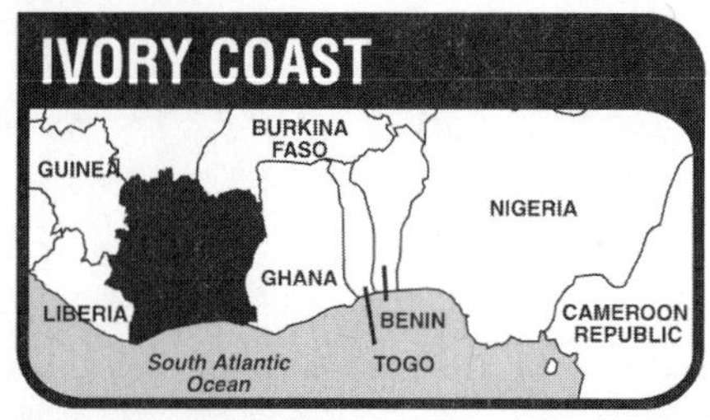

The Republic of Cote d'Ivoire (Ivory Coast), a former French overseas territory located on the south side of the African bulge between Nigeria and Ghana, has an area of 124,504 sq. mi. (322,463 sq. km.) and a population of 15.14 million. Capital: Abidjan. The predominantly agricultural economy is one of Africa's most prosperous. Coffee, tropical woods, cocoa, and bananas are exported. The Ivory Coast was first visited by French and Portuguese navigators in the 15th century. French traders set up establishments in the 19th century, and gradually extended their influence along the coast and inland. The area was organized as a territory in 1893, and from 1904 to 1958 was a constituent unit of the Federation of French West Africa - as a Colony under the Third Republic and an Overseas Territory under the Fourth. In 1958 the Ivory Coast became an autonomous republic within the French Community. Independence was attained on Aug. 7, 1960. Together with other West African states, the Cote d'Ivoire is a member of the "Union Monetaire Ouest-Africaine." Also see French West Africa and West African Monetary Union.

RULERS:

French to 1960

MONETARY SYSTEM:

1 Franc = 100 Centimes

FRENCH ADMINISTRATION

Gouvernement Général de l'Afrique Occidentale Française (A.O.F.)

Colonie de la Cote d'Ivoire

Décret du 11.2.1917

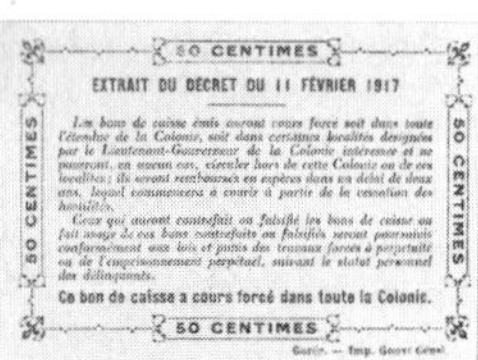

		VG	VF	UNC
1	**.50 Franc** *D.1917.* Black and orange on yellow underprint. Obverse and reverse of French 50 Centimes coin. Back: Black text.			
	a. Watermark: Bees.	15.00	65.00	175
	b. Watermark: Laurel leaves.	20.00	75.00	200
	c. Without watermark.	10.00	55.00	165

		VG	VF	UNC
2	**1 Franc** *D.1917.* Black and green on yellow underprint. Obverse and reverse of French 1 Franc coin.			
	a. Watermark: Bees.	15.00	65.00	200
	b. Watermark: Laurel leaves.	20.00	80.00	225
3	**2 Francs** *D.1917.* Red and black on light orange underprint. Obverse and reverse of French 2-Franc coin.			
	a. Watermark: Bees.	20.00	100	250
	b. Watermark: Laurel leaves.	20.00	100	250

1920 ND Postage Stamp Issue

#4-6 postage stamps of the Ivory Coast (Michel #44, 45, and 48, or Scott #45, 47 and 52 with men in boat) pasted on cardboard and wwith overprint: *Valeur d'echange* and value.

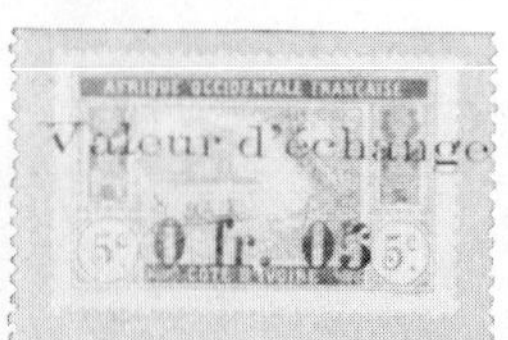

		VG	VF	UNC
4	**.05 Franc on 5 Centimes** ND (1920). Yellow-green and blue-green.	25.00	70.00	160

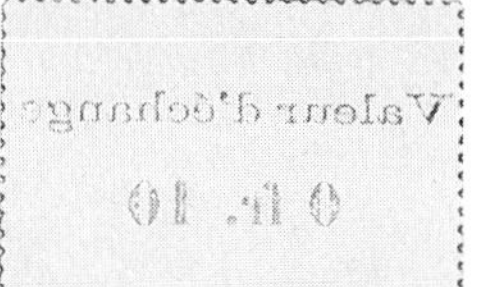

		VG	VF	UNC
5	**.10 Franc on 10 Centimes** ND (1920). Red-orange and rose.	25.00	70.00	160

		VG	VF	UNC
6	**.25 Franc on 25 Centimes** ND (1920). Ultramarine and blue.	25.00	70.00	160

Cote d'Ivoire

1943 ND Emergency WW II Issue

		VG	VF	UNC
6A	**50 Centimes** ND. Dark blue and yellow. Elephant head in underprint at center. Rare.	—	—	—

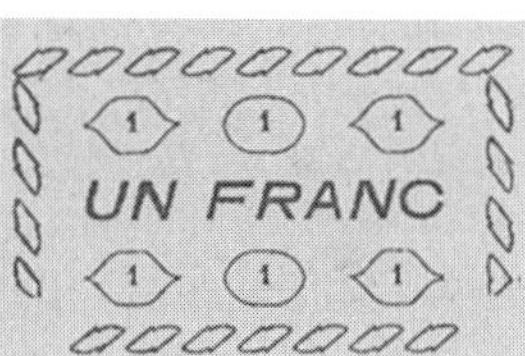

		VG	VF	UNC
7	**1 Franc** ND. Blue on yellow underprint. Rare.	—	—	—

		VG	VF	UNC
8	**2 Francs** ND. Blue on yellow underprint. Rare.	—	—	—

Note: Issues specially marked with letter *A* for Ivory Coast were made by the Banque Centrale des Etats de l'Afrique de l'Ouest. For listing see West African States.

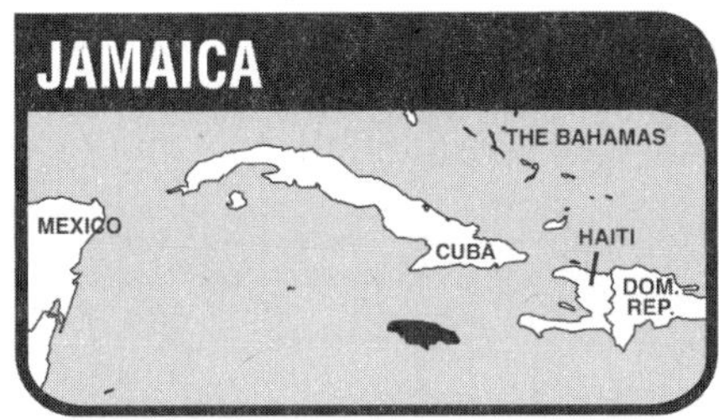

Jamaica, a member of the British Commonwealth situated in the Caribbean Sea 90 miles south of Cuba, has an area of 10,991 sq. km. and a population of 2.8 million. Capital: Kingston. The economy is founded chiefly on mining, tourism and agriculture. Alumina, bauxite, sugar, rum and molasses are exported.

The island - discovered by Christopher Columbus in 1494 - was settled by the Spanish early in the 16th century. The native Taino Indians, who had inhabited Jamaica for centuries, were gradually exterminated and replaced by African slaves. England seized the island in 1655 and established a plantation economy based on sugar, cocoa, and coffee. The abolition of slavery in 1834 freed a quarter million slaves, many of whom became small farmers. Jamaica gradually obtained increasing independence from Britain, and in 1958 it joined other British Caribbean colonies in forming the Federation of the West Indies. Jamaica gained full independence when it withdrew from the Federation in 1962. Deteriorating economic conditions during the 1970s led to recurrent violence as rival gangs affiliated with the major political parties evolved into powerful organized crime networks involved in international drug smuggling and money laundering. Violent crime, drug trafficking, and poverty pose significant challenges to the government today. Nonetheless, many rural and resort areas remain relatively safe and contribute substantially to the economy.

Jamaica is a member of the Commonwealth of Nations. Elizabeth II is the Head of State, as Queen of Jamaica. A decimal standard currency system was adopted on Sept. 8, 1969.

RULERS:
British

MONETARY SYSTEM:
1 Shilling = 12 Pence
1 Pound = 20 Shillings to 1969
1 Dollar = 100 Cents, 1969-

BRITISH ADMINISTRATION

Treasury

Law 27/1904 and 17/1918

No.	Denomination	Good	Fine	XF
27	**2 Shillings 6 Pence** *L.1904/18.* Green. Portrait King George V at right. Back: Woman with hat at center. Printer: TDLR.	500	1,250	2,500

No.	Denomination	Good	Fine	XF
28	**5 Shillings** *L.1904/18.* Red on green and brown underprint. Portrait King George V at upper right. Back: Sailing ship at center. Printer: TDLR.			
	a. 1 serial #, at upper center.	350	850	2,000
	b. 2 serial #, lower left and upper right. 2 signature varieties.	350	850	2,000

#29 not asigned.

No.	Denomination	Good	Fine	XF
30	**10 Shillings** *L.1904/18.* Blue. Portrait King George V at upper right. 2 signature varieties. Back: Lion at center.	400	950	2,250

Government of Jamaica

Law 27/1904 and 17/1918

#31, 34-36 not assigned.

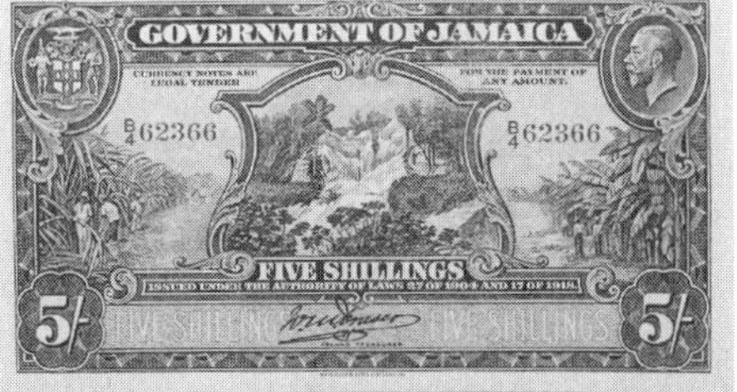

No.	Denomination	Good	Fine	XF
32	**5 Shillings** *L.1904/18.* Brown. Arms at upper left, waterfalls at center, portrait King George V at upper right. Back: River and bridge at center. Printer: W&S.			
	a. 2 serial #. 2 signature varieties.	125	400	950
	b. 1 serial #. Requires confirmation.	—	—	—

No.	Denomination	Good	Fine	XF
33	**10 Shillings** *L.1904/18.* Green. Arms at upper left, waterfalls at center, portrait King George V at upper right. Printer: W&S.			
	a. 2 serial #. 2 signature varieties.	350	750	1,750
	b. 1 serial #. Requires confirmation.	—	—	—
	s. Specimen. Punch hole cancelled.	—	—	—

1939-1952 Issues

No.	Denomination	VG	VF	UNC
37	**5 Shillings** 1939-1958. Orange. Portrait King George VI at left. Back: *FIVE SHILLINGS* in 2 lines. Printer: TDLR.			
	a. 2.1.1939-15.6.1950.	7.50	40.00	150
	b. 1.3.1953-15.8.1958.	5.00	27.50	120
38	**10 Shillings** 1939-1948. Blue. Portrait King George VI at left. Back: *TEN SHILLINGS* in 2 lines. Printer: TDLR.			
	a. 2.1.1939.	12.50	75.00	200
	b. 1.11.1940.	10.00	40.00	140
	c. 30.11.1942.	50.00	200	—
	d. 2.1.1948.	12.50	75.00	200

No.	Denomination	VG	VF	UNC
39	**10 Shillings** 15.6.1950-17.3.1960. Purple. Portrait King George VI at left. Back: *TEN SHILLINGS* in two lines. Printer: TDLR.	5.00	25.00	125

#	Denomination	VG	VF	UNC
40	**1 Pound**	VG	VF	UNC
	1.11.1940. Blue. Portrait King George VI at left. Printer: TDLR.			
	a. Red serial #.	40.00	150	—
	b. Black serial #.	40.00	125	—
41	**1 Pound**	VG	VF	UNC
	1942-1960. Green. Portrait King George VI at left. Back: *ONE POUND* in 2 lines. Printer: TDLR.			
	a. 30.11.1942; 2.1.1948.	15.00	75.00	375
	b. 15.6.1950-17.3.1960.	7.50	45.00	250
42	**5 Pounds**	VG	VF	UNC
	30.11.1942. Maroon. Portrait King George VI at left. Printer: TDLR.	250	800	—

#	Denomination	VG	VF	UNC
43	**5 Pounds**	VG	VF	UNC
	1.8.1952; 7.4.1955; 15.8.1957; 1.9.1957. Brown. Portrait King George VI at left. Printer: TDLR.	150	550	1,400

1960 Issue

#	Denomination	VG	VF	UNC
45	**5 Shillings**	VG	VF	UNC
	17.3.1960; 4.7.1960. Orange. Portrait King George VI at left. Back: *FIVE SHILLINGS* in 1 line. Printer: TDLR.	7.50	35.00	160

#	Denomination	VG	VF	UNC
46	**10 Shillings**	VG	VF	UNC
	4.7.1960. Purple. Portrait King George VI at left. Back: *TEN SHILLINGS* in 1 line. Printer: TDLR.	9.00	45.00	200
47	**1 Pound**	VG	VF	UNC
	19.5.1960. Green. Portrait King George VI at left. Back: *ONE POUND* in 1 line. Printer: TDLR.	12.00	65.00	250

#	Denomination	VG	VF	UNC
48	**5 Pounds**	VG	VF	UNC
	1960. Blue and multicolor. Queen Elizabeth II at left. Back: Factory and banana tree.			
	a. 17.3.1960.	200	500	—
	b. 4.7.1960.	60.00	250	1,000

JAPAN

Japan, a constitutional monarchy situated off the east coast of Asia, has an area of 377,835 sq. km. and a population of 127.29 million. Capital: Tokyo. Japan, one of the three major industrial nations of the free world, exports machinery, motor vehicles, textiles and chemicals.

In 1603, a Tokugawa shogunate (military dictatorship) ushered in a long period of isolation from foreign influence in order to secure its power. For more than two centuries this policy enabled Japan to enjoy stability and a flowering of its indigenous culture. Following the Treaty of Kanagawa with the US in 1854, Japan opened its ports and began to intensively modernize and industrialize. During the late 19th and early 20th centuries, Japan became a regional power that was able to defeat the forces of both China and Russia. It occupied Korea, Formosa (Taiwan), and southern Sakhalin Island. In 1931-32 Japan occupied Manchuria, and in 1937 it launched a full-scale invasion of China. Japan attacked US forces in 1941 - triggering America's entry into World War II - and soon occupied much of East and Southeast Asia. After its defeat in World War II, Japan recovered to become an economic power and a staunch ally of the US. While the emperor retains his throne as a symbol of national unity, elected politicians - with heavy input from bureaucrats and business executives - wield actual decisionmaking power. The economy experienced a major slowdown starting in the 1990s following three decades of unprecedented growth, but Japan still remains a major economic power, both in Asia and globally.

See also Burma, China (Japanese military issues, Central Reserve Bank, Federal Reserve Bank, Hua Hsing Commercial Bank, Mengchiang Bank, Chanan Bank, Chi Tung Bank and Manchukuo), Hong Kong, Indochina, Malaya, Netherlands Indies, Oceania, the Philippines, Korea and Taiwan.

RULERS:

Mutsuhito (Meiji), Years 1-45, (1868-1912)
Mutsuhito (Meiji), 1868-1912 — 明治

Yoshihito (Taisho), 1912-1926 — 大正

Hirohito (Showa), 1926-1989 — 昭和

Akihito (Heisei), 1989-

MONETARY SYSTEM:

1 Shu = 1000-1750 Mon (copper or iron "cash" coins)
1 Bu (fun) = 4 Shu
1 Ryo = 4 Bu to 1870
1 Sen = 10 Rin
1 Yen = 100 Sen, 1870-

厘 Rin; 銭 Sen; 圓 or 圓 or ¥ or 円 Yen

REPLACEMENT NOTES:

#49, 50, 51, 57, 89, notes w/first digit 9 are replacements. #62-75, H prefix, #67b, B prefix but no suffix letter; 90-94 blocks Z-Z and ZZ-Z.

PORTRAIT VARIETIES

#1 Takeuchi Sukune

#2 Sugawara Michizane

#3 Wakeno Kiyomaro

#4 Fujiwara Kamatari

#5 Wakeno Kiyomaro

#6 Shotoku-taishi

#7 Yamato Takeru No Mikoto

CONSTITUTIONAL MONARCHY

Great Japanese Government - Ministry of Finance

大日本政府大蔵省

Dai Nip-pon Sei-fu O-kura-sho

1872 Issue

#	Denomination	Good	Fine	XF
1	**10 Sen** ND (1872). Black on pink underprint. Meiji Tsuho-Satsu with facing Onagadori cockerels at top and two facing dragons at bottom. Back: Green. Printer: Dondorf and Naumann, Frankfurt, Germany.	20.00	35.00	70.00
2	**20 Sen** ND (1872). Black on brown underprint. Meiji Tsuho-Satsu with facing Onagadori cockerels at top and two facing dragons at bottom. Back: Blue. Printer: Dondorf and Naumann, Frankfurt, Germany.	40.00	75.00	150
3	**1/2 Yen** ND (1872). Black on green underprint. Meiji Tsuho-Satsu with facing Onagadori cockerels at top and two facing dragons at bottom. Back: Brown. Printer: Dondorf and Naumann, Frankfurt, Germany.	60.00	125	250

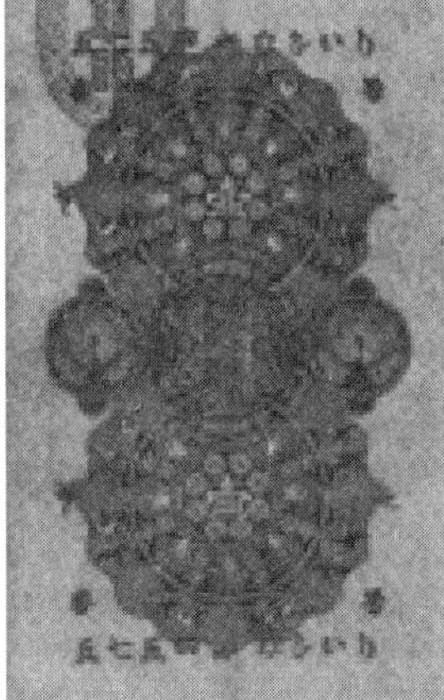

#	Denomination	Good	Fine	XF
4	**1 Yen** ND (1872). Black on brown underprint. Meiji Tsuho-Satsu with facing Onagadori cockerels at top and two facing dragons at bottom. Back: Blue. Printer: Dondorf and Naumann, Frankfurt, Germany.	50.00	100	200
5	**2 Yen** ND (1872). Black on blue underprint. Meiji Tsuho-Satsu with facing Onagadori cockerels at top and two facing dragons at bottom. Back: Brown. Printer: Dondorf and Naumann, Frankfurt, Germany.	200	400	800

#	Denomination	Good	Fine	XF
6	**5 Yen** ND (1872). Black on brown underprint. Meiji Tsuho-Satsu with facing Onagadori cockerels at top and two facing dragons at bottom. Back: Blue. Printer: Dondorf and Naumann, Frankfurt, Germany.	750	1,500	3,000
7	**10 Yen** ND (1872). Black on blue underprint. Meiji Tsuho-Satsu with facing Onagadori cockerels at top and two facing dragons at bottom. Back: Lilac. Printer: Dondorf and Naumann, Frankfurt, Germany.	450	900	1,750
8	**50 Yen** ND (1872). Black on lilac underprint. Meiji Tsuho-Satsu with facing Onagadori cockerels at top and two facing dragons at bottom. Back: Blue. Printer: Dondorf and Naumann, Frankfurt, Germany. Rare.	—	—	—
9	**100 Yen** ND (1872). Black on blue underprint. Meiji Tsuho-Satsu with facing Onagadori cockerels at top and two facing dragons at bottom. Back: Red. Printer: Dondorf and Naumann, Frankfurt, Germany. Rare.	—	—	—

Great Imperial Japanese Circulating Note

大日本帝國通用紙幣

Dai Nip-pon Tei-koku Tsu-yo Shi-hei

1873 "Paper Currency" Issue

#10-14 The number of the issuing national bank and location at lower center. Equivalent denomination gold coin at left and right on back.

#	Denomination	Good	Fine	XF
10	**1 Yen** ND (1873). Black. Prow of a ship at left. Warrior with bow and arrows at right. Back: Green and black. Back: Gold 1 yen coin at left and right, defeat of the Mongols in Hakata harbor at center. Printer: CONB.	800	1,750	3,500

#	Denomination	Good	Fine	XF
11	**2 Yen** ND (1873). Black. Warrior in armor at left and right. Back: Green and black. Back: Castle gateway. Printer: CONB.	1,750	3,500	—
12	**5 Yen** ND (1873). Field work at left and right. Back: Nihonbashi Bridge.	4,000	8,000	—

#	Denomination	Good	Fine	XF
13	**10 Yen** ND (1873). Black. Musicians at left and right. Back: Green and black. Back: Empress Jingu on horseback arriving on beach. Printer: CONB. Rare.	—	—	—

		Good	Fine	XF
14	**20 Yen** ND (1873). Black. Dragon at left, kneeling man at right. Back: Green and black. Back: Warriors at beach. Printer: CONB. Rare.	—	—	—

Great Imperial Japanese Government Note

大日本帝國政府紙幣

Dai Nip-pon Tei-koku Sei-fu Shi-hei

1881-1883 "Paper Money" Issue

		Good	Fine	XF
15	**20 Sen** 1881 (1882). Brown underprint. Brown seal at right.	30.00	75.00	150
16	**50 Sen** 1881 (1882). Brown underprint. Brown seal at right.	150	400	850

		Good	Fine	XF
17	**1 Yen** 1878 (1881). Brown underprint. Portrait Empress Jingu at right. Back: Ornate denomination with red seal.	150	300	600
18	**5 Yen** 1880 (1882). Brown underprint. Empress Jingu at right. Back: Ornate denomination with red seal.	800	1,500	3,000

		Good	Fine	XF
19	**10 Yen** 1881 (1883). Brown underprint. Empress Jingu at right. Back: Ornate denomination with red seal.	1,500	3,000	6,000

Great Imperial Japanese National Bank

大日本帝國國立銀行

Dai Nip-pon Tei-koku Koku-ritsu Gin-ko

1877-1878 Issue

		Good	Fine	XF
20	**1 Yen** ND (1877). Black on yellow-brown underprint. Two sailors at right. Issuing bank number. Back: Dark green. Back: Ebisu, god of household thrift and industry. Issue location and bank number.	300	600	1,200
21	**5 Yen** ND (1878). Black on green underprint. Three blacksmiths at right. Issuing bank number. Back: Black and green. Back: Ebisu. Issue location and bank number.	750	1,500	3,000

Bank of Japan

日本銀行兌換券

Nip-pon Gin-ko Da Kan Gin Ken

1885-1886 Convertible Silver Note Issue

		Good	Fine	XF
22	**1 Yen** ND (1885). Blue. Daikoku at right sitting on rice bales. Text: *Nippon Ginko Promises to Pay the Bearer on Demand 1Yen in Silver.*	125	300	600
23	**5 Yen** ND (1886). Blue. Text: *Nippon Ginko Promises to Pay the Bearer on Demand Five Yen in Silver.* and a guilloche. Back: Daikoku sitting on rice bales.	1,250	2,500	5,000
24	**10 Yen** ND (1885). Blue. Daikoku at right sitting on rice bales. Text: *Ten Yen.*	2,000	5,000	—
25	**100 Yen** ND (1885). Blue. Daikoku at right sitting on rice bales. Text: *Nippon Ginko Promises to Pay the Bearer on Demand 100 Yen in Silver.* Rare.	—	—	—

1889-1891 Convertible Silver Note Issue

		Good	Fine	XF
26	**1 Yen** ND (1889). Black on light orange underprint. Portrait #1 at right. 1 yen coin at center. Japanese character serial #. Back: 1 yen at left.	50.00	125	300
27	**5 Yen** ND (1888). Black on green underprint. Portrait #2 at right. Japanese character serial #. Back: Green.	800	2,000	5,000
28	**10 Yen** ND (1890). Black on light brown underprint. Portrait #3 at right. Japanese character serial #. Back: Light brown.	1,200	3,000	7,000
29	**100 Yen** ND (1891). Black on light brown underprint. Portrait #4 at right. Japanese character serial #. Back: Light blue. Rare.	—	—	—

1899-1900 Convertible Gold Note Issue

		Good	Fine	XF
31	**5 Yen** 1899-1910. Black on pale green underprint. Portrait #1 at center. Back: Orange.			
	a. Japanese block character.	250	500	1,000
	b. Western block #.	400	800	1,750

		Good	Fine	XF
32	**10 Yen** 1899-1913. Black on light brown underprint. Goo Shrine at left, portrait #3 at right. Back: Green. Back: Boar at center.			
	a. Japanese block character.	300	600	1,200
	b. Western block #.	350	750	1,500

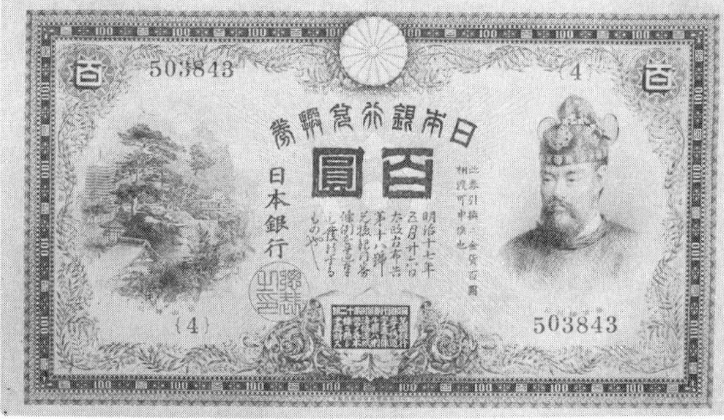

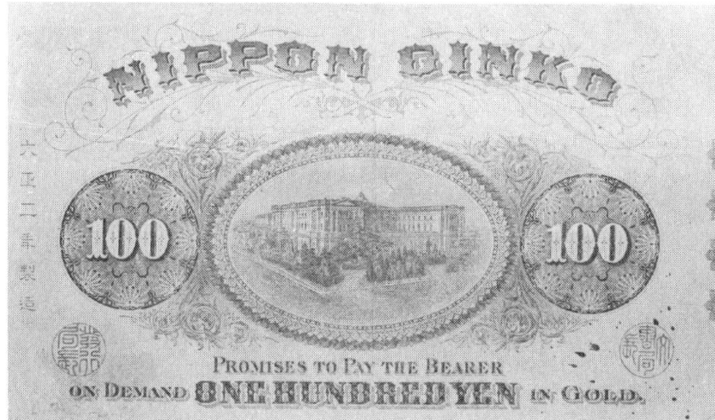

		Good	Fine	XF
33	**100 Yen** 1900-1913. Black on light brown underprint. Park with Danzan Shrine at left, portrait #4 at right. Back: Purple. Back: Bank of Japan.			
	a. Japanese block character.	3,500	8,000	—
	b. Western block #.	1,500	3,000	—

1910 Convertible Gold Note Issue

		Good	Fine	XF
34	**5 Yen** ND (1910). Green on violet underprint. Portrait #2 at right. Back: Violet. Watermark: Daikoku.	250	500	1,000

1916 Convertible Silver Note Issue

Issuer's name reads left to right or right to left.

		Good	Fine	XF
30	**1 Yen** ND (1916). Black on light orange underprint. Portrait #1 at right. 1 yen coin at center. Western character serial #. Back: 1 yen coin at left.			
	a. Block # below 200.	15.00	40.00	75.00
	b. Block #200-299.	4.00	8.00	15.00
	c. Block #300 and higher.	0.50	1.50	3.00
	s. As a, b or c. Small vermilion stamps: *Mi-hon.* Regular serial #.	—	Unc	150

1915-1917 Convertible Gold Note Issue

		Good	Fine	XF
35	**5 Yen** ND (1916). Black on light green underprint. Ube Shrine with stairs at left, portrait #1 at right. Back: Brown.	100	200	450

		Good	Fine	XF
36	**10 Yen** ND (1915). Gray. Portrait #5 at left, Goo Shrine at right. Back: Green and brown.	100	200	325
37	**20 Yen** ND (1917). Black on multicolor underprint. Portrait #2 at right. Back: Violet. Back: Kitano Shrine.	300	1,000	2,500

1927 Emergency Issue

		Good	Fine	XF
37A	**50 Yen** ND (1927). Guilloche at left and right of center. Uniface. Specimen. Rare.	—	—	—

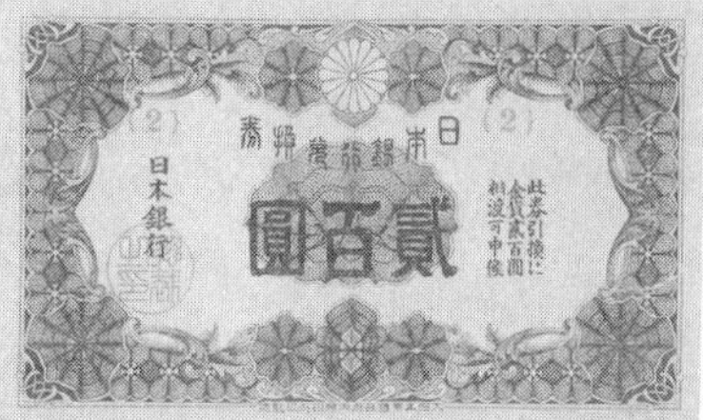

		Good	Fine	XF
37B	**200 Yen** ND (1927). Greenish black with black text. Guilloche at center without portrait. Uniface. Rare.	—	—	—

1927 ND Issue

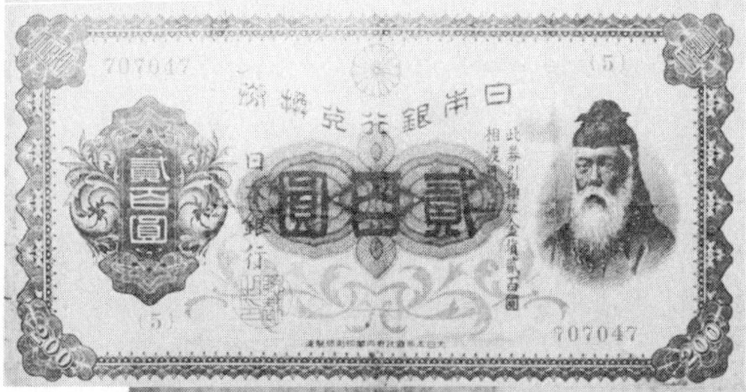

#	Denomination	Good	Fine	XF
38	**200 Yen** ND (1927). Black on green underprint. Portrait #1 at right. Back: Red. Specimen. Rare.	—	—	—

Note: For similar note but with pale blue underprint, see #43A.

1930-1931 ND Issue

#	Denomination	VG	VF	UNC
39	**5 Yen** ND (1930). Black on green and orange underprint. Kitano Shrine at left, green guilloche at center, portrait #2 at right. Curved main title. Back: Brown and olive. Back: Japanese text with denomination in English.			
	a. Issued note.	2.00	10.00	60.00
	s1. Specimen with overprint and perforated *Mi-hon.*	—	—	400
	s2. Specimen with small vermilion stamping: *Mi-hon.* Regular serial #.	—	—	75.00

#	Denomination	VG	VF	UNC
40	**10 Yen** ND (1930). Black on green and brown underprint. Portrait #3 at right. Back: Green and brown. Back: Japanese text with denomination in English.			
	a. Issued note.	1.50	4.00	20.00
	s1. Specimen with overprint and perforated: *Mi-hon.*	—	—	400
	s2. Specimen with small vermilion stamping: *Mi-hon.* Regular serial #.	—	—	75.00
	z. Face as a. Propaganda message in Japanese text on back. (4 varieties).	20.00	45.00	80.00

Note: 4 different propaganda notes with face of #40 and different messages on back in Japanese are frequently encountered.

#	Denomination	VG	VF	UNC
41	**20 Yen** ND (1931). Black on green underprint. Danzan Shrine at left, portrait #4 at right. Back: Blue and brown. Back: Another view of same shrine. Japanese text with denomination in English.			
	a. Issued note.	50.00	200	500
	s1. Specimen with overprint and perforated: *Mi-hon.*	—	—	1,200
	s2. Specimen with small vermilion stamping: *Mi-hon. SPECIMEN* on back. Regular serial #.	—	—	250
	s3. Specimen with blue stamping: *SPECIMEN* on face and back. Regular serial #.	—	—	200

#	Denomination	VG	VF	UNC
42	**100 Yen** ND (1930). Black on blue and brown underprint. Yumedono Pavillion at left, portrait #6 at right. Back: Green and brown. Back: Horyuji Temple at center. Japanese text with denomination in English.			
	a. Issued note.	15.00	50.00	125
	s. Specimen with small vermilion stamping: *Mi-hon.* Regular serial #.	—	50.00	125

1942 ND Issue

#	Denomination	VG	VF	UNC
43	**5 Yen** ND (1942). Black on green and orange underprint. Kitano Shrine at left, portrait #2 at right. Straight main title. Back: Red-brown and lilac. Back: Japanese text with denomination in English.			
	a. Issued note.	2.00	5.00	25.00
	s1. Specimen with overprint and perforated: *Mi-hon.*	—	—	400
	s2. Specimen with small vermilion stamping: *Mi-hon.* Regular serial #.	—	—	75.00
	s3. Specimen with red stamping: *SPECIMEN* on face and back. Regular serial #.	—	—	75.00

1945 ND Issue

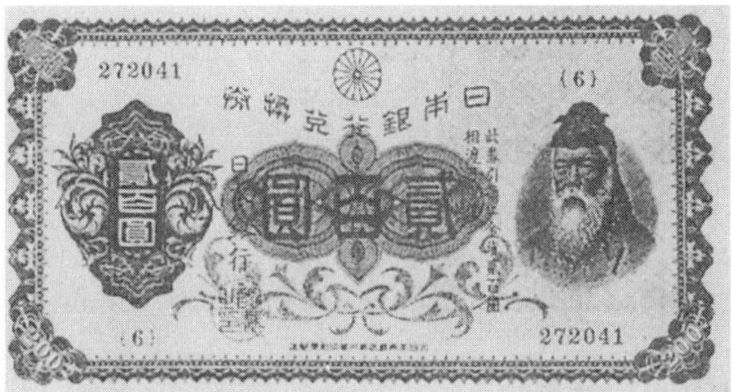

		Good	Fine	XF
43A	**200 Yen**			
	ND (1945). Black on pale blue underprint. Portrait #1 at right. Back: Red. Back: English denomination. (Originally printed in 1927).			
	a. Issued note.	300	700	1,500
	s1. Specimen with overprint and perforated *Mi-hon.*	—	Unc	4,000
	s2. Specimen with vermilion overprint: *Mi-hon. Specimen* on back. Regular serial #.	—	Unc	500
	s3. Specimen with small vermilion stamping: *Mi-hon.* Regular serial #.	—	Unc	500

		VG	VF	UNC
44	**200 Yen**			
	ND (1945). Black on gray and green underprint. Danzan Shrine at left, portrait #4 at right. Back: Blue. Back: Another view of same shrine. Japanese text with denomination in English.			
	a. Issued note.	100	300	550
	s1. Specimen with overprint and perforated: *Mi-hon.*	—	—	1,500
	s2. Specimen with vermilion overprint: *Mi-hon. SPECIMEN* on back. Regular serial #.	—	—	400
	s3. Specimen with small vermilion stamping: *Mi-hon.* Regular serial #.	—	—	500
	s4. Specimen with blue stamping: *SPECIMEN* on face and back. Regular serial #.	—	—	500

		VG	VF	UNC
45	**1000 Yen**			
	ND (1945). Black on brown, green and yellow underprint. Takebe Shrine at left, portrait #7 at right. Back: Brown and orange. Back: Japanese text with denomination in English.			
	a. Issued note.	750	1,600	3,250
	s1. Specimen with overprint and perforated: *Mi-hon.*	—	—	4,500
	s2. Specimen with vermilion overprint: *Mi-hon. SPECIMEN* on back. Regular serial #.	—	—	3,000
	s3. Specimen with small vermilion stamping: *Mi-hon.* Regular serial #.	—	1,500	3,000
	s4. Specimen with blue stamping: *SPECIMEN.* Regular serial #.	—	1,500	3,000

Great Imperial Japanese Government (Resumed)

1917 "Paper Money" Issue

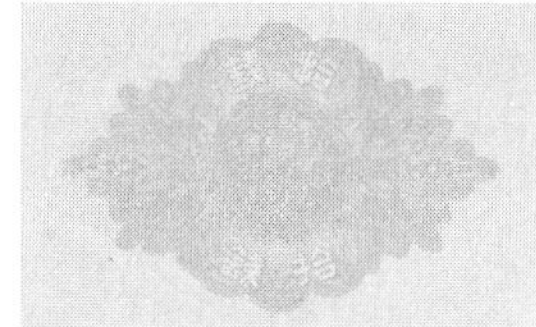

		VG	VF	UNC
46	**10 Sen**			
	1917-1921. Black on orange underprint. Red seal at left, denomination numeral at right.			
	a. Taisho yr. 6.	2.50	7.50	20.00
	b. Taisho yrs. 7; 8.	1.00	4.00	10.00
	c. Taisho yrs. 9; 10.	1.00	4.00	8.00

		VG	VF	UNC
47	**20 Sen**			
	1917-1919. Black on green underprint. Red seal at left, denomination numeral at right.			
	a. Taisho yr. 6.	8.00	30.00	100
	b. Taisho yrs. 7; 8.	5.00	20.00	60.00

		VG	VF	UNC
48	**50 Sen**			
	1917-1922. Black on pink underprint. Red seal at left, denomination numeral at right.			
	a. Taisho yr. 6.	7.00	25.00	100
	b. Taisho yrs. 7; 8.	4.00	15.00	60.00
	c. Taisho yrs. 9; 10; 11.	2.00	10.00	40.00

Bank of Japan (Continued)

券行銀本日

Nip-pon Gin-ko Ken

1943 ND Issue

		VG	VF	UNC
49	**1 Yen**			
	ND (1943). Black on light blue underprint. Portrait #1 at center, serial # and block #1-34. Japanese text only. Back: Ube Shrine at center.			
	a. Issued note.	0.50	3.00	10.00
	s1. Specimen with overprint and perforated: *Mi-hon.*	—	—	400
	s2. Specimen with red overprint: *SPECIMEN* on face and back.	—	—	700
	s3. Specimen with small stamping: *Mi-hon.*	—	—	75.00
	s4. Specimen with blue stamping: *SPECIMEN.*	—	—	75.00

50 **5 Yen**	VG	VF	UNC
ND (1943). Black on light green and purple underprint. Kitano Shrine at left, portrait #2 at right. Black serial # and block #. Japanese text only. Main title five characters. Back: Green and light brown.			
a. Issued note.	0.75	4.00	20.00
s. Specimen with overprint and perforated: *Mi-hon.*	—	—	100

51 **10 Yen**	VG	VF	UNC
ND (1943-1944). Black on brown and light blue underprint. Portrait #3 at right. Black serial # and block #. Japanese text only. Back: Blue. Back: Goo Shrine at center.			
a. Watermark: *10 Yen* in Japanese characters at top center (1943).	1.00	3.00	12.50
b. Watermark: Repeating characters *NICHI* and *JU. (10). (1944).*	2.00	4.00	15.00
s1. As a. Specimen with overprint and perforated: *Mi-hon.*	—	—	400
s2. As a. Specimen with blue stamping: *SPECIMEN.* Regular serial #.	—	—	75.00

1944 ND Issue

52 **5 Sen**	VG	VF	UNC
ND (1944). Black on yellow underprint. Equestrian statue at left. Japanese text only.			
a. Issued note.	0.10	25.00	1.50
s1. Specimen with overprint: *Mi-hon.* Block #1.	—	—	250
s2. Specimen with small stamping: *Mi-hon.* Regular block #.	—	—	75.00

53 **10 Sen**	VG	VF	UNC
ND (1944). Black on purple underprint. Tower monument at left. Japanese text only.			
a. Issued note.	0.10	0.50	2.00
s1. Specimen with overprint*Mi-hon.* Block #1.	—	—	250
s2. Specimen with small stamping: *Mi-hon.* Regular block #.	—	—	75.00

54 **1 Yen**	VG	VF	UNC
ND (1944-1945). Black on light blue underprint. Portrait #1 at center. Block # at upper left. Back: Ube Shrine at center.			
a. Watermark: Fancy floral design. Block #35-47 (1944).	0.50	3.00	15.00
b. Watermark: Outline of kiri leaf. Block #48-49 (1945).	1.50	4.00	20.00
s1. As a. Specimen with overprint and perforated: *Mi-hon.*	—	—	600
s2. As a. Specimen with red overprint: *SPECIMEN.*	—	—	750

55 **5 Yen**	VG	VF	UNC
ND (1944). Black on light green and purple underprint. Kitano Shrine at left, portrait #2 at right. Red block # only. Back: Green and light brown.			
a. Issued note.	5.00	20.00	65.00
s1. Specimen with overprint and perforated: *Mi-hon.*	—	—	600
s2. Specimen with small stamps: *Mi-hon.* Regular block #.	30.00	60.00	125

56 **10 Yen**	VG	VF	UNC
ND (1944-1945). Black on brown and light blue underprint. Portrait #3 at right. Red block # only. Back: Blue. Back: Goo Shrine at center.			
a. Watermark: Repeating characters *NICHI* and *JU. (10) (1944).*	2.00	6.00	20.00
b. Watermark: Repeating Bank of Japan logos (circles) (1945).	3.00	8.00	25.00
c. Watermark: Outline of Kiri leaf (1945).	4.00	10.00	35.00
s1. As a. Specimen with overprint and perforated: *Mi-hon.*	—	—	600
s2. As b. Specimen with overprint: *Mi-hon.* Regular block #.	—	—	250
s3. As B. Specimen with small vermilion stamping *Mi-hon*	—	—	—

57	100 Yen	VG	VF	UNC
	ND (1944). Black on brown underprint of leaves. Yumedono Pavilion at left, portrait #6 at right. Back: Lilac. Back: Temple.			
	a. Watermark: Arabesque phoenix design at left.	5.00	20.00	60.00
	b. Watermark: Kiri leaves.	9.00	25.00	75.00
	s1. As a. Specimen with overprint and perforated: *Mi-hon.*	—	—	400
	s2. As a. Specimen with small stamping: *Mi-hon.* Regular block #.	—	—	100
	s3. As b. Specimen with small stamping: *Mi-hon.*	—	—	—

Great Imperial Japanese Government (Cont.)

1938 "Paper Money" Issue

58	50 Sen	VG	VF	UNC
	1938. Black on yellow and blue underprint. Mt. Fuji and cherry blossoms. (Showa yr. 13 at l.) Back: Light green.			
	a. Issued note.	0.25	0.75	6.00
	s. Specimen with small stamping: *Mi-hon.* Regular block #.	—	—	75.00

Note: Date shown at right on #58 is 2598 years since foundation of Japan (old calendar year).

1942 "Paper Money" Issue

59	50 Sen	VG	VF	UNC
	1942-1944. Black on green and brown underprint. Yasukuni Shrine. Back: Green. Back: Mountain at center.			
	a. Showa yr. 17.	0.25	1.00	8.00
	b. Showa yr. 18.	0.25	0.75	2.50
	c. Showa yr. 19.	0.25	0.75	3.50
	s1. As c. Specimen with small stamping: *Mi-hon.* Regular block #.	—	—	75.00
	s2. As c. Specimen with red stamping: *SPECIMEN.* Regular block.	—	—	100

Imperial Japanese Government 日本帝國政府紙幣

Nip-pon Tei-koku Sei-fu Shi-hei

1945 "Paper Money" Issue

60	50 Sen	VG	VF	UNC
	1945. Black on lilac underprint. Yasukuni Shrine. Showa yr. 20. Back: Mountain at center.			
	a. Issued note.	0.25	0.75	4.00
	s1. Specimen with overprint: *MI-hon.* Block #1.	—	—	250
	s2. Specimen with red overprint: *SPECIMEN.* Block #22.	—	—	500

Japanese Government 日本政府紙幣

Nip-pon Sei-fu Shi-hei

1948 "Paper Money" Issue

#61, issuer's name reads l. to r.

61	50 Sen	VG	VF	UNC
	1948. Black on lilac underprint. Portrait Itagaki Taisuke at right. Back: Green. Back: Diet building at center.			
	a. Gray paper.	0.25	0.50	2.00
	b. White paper.	0.25	0.50	2.00

Allied Military Currency - WWII

Initially printed in the U.S.A., subsequently printed in Japan having different serial # style. Notes with *A* unpt. circulated only a few weeks in Japan in 1946 and were never legal tender for Japanese citizens. *A* notes were also legal tender in Korea from Sept., 1945 - June, 1946. Notes with *B* unpt. were legal tender for Japanese citizens from Sept. 1945 - July 1948. *B* yen were used in Okinawa until 1958.

1945-1951 ND Issue

62	10 Sen	VG	VF	UNC
	ND (1946). A in underprint. Black on light blue underprint. Back: Brown.	6.00	15.00	60.00

63	10 Sen	VG	VF	UNC
	ND (1945). Black on light blue underprint. B in underprint. Back: Brown.	0.50	1.50	3.50
64	**50 Sen**	**VG**	**VF**	**UNC**
	ND (1946). Black on light blue underprint. A in underprint. Back: Brown.	6.00	12.00	65.00

65	50 Sen	VG	VF	UNC
	ND (1945). Black on light blue underprint. B in underprint. Back: Brown.	0.75	2.00	4.50
66	**1 Yen**	**VG**	**VF**	**UNC**
	ND (1946). Black on light blue underprint. A in underprint. Back: Brown.	5.00	12.00	65.00

67	1 Yen	VG	VF	UNC
	ND. Black on light blue underprint. B in underprint. Back: Brown.			
	a. Serial # prefix - suffix A-A. (1945).	0.75	2.00	4.50
	b. Serial # prefix - suffix B-B. (1955).	6.00	15.00	50.00
	c. Serial # prefix - suffix C-C. (1956).	2.50	10.00	30.00
	d. Serial # prefix - suffix D-D. (1957).	2.50	10.00	30.00
68	**5 Yen**	**VG**	**VF**	**UNC**
	ND (1946). Black on light blue underprint. A in underprint. Back: Brown.	20.00	65.00	200

#	Denomination	VG	VF	UNC
69	**5 Yen** ND (1945). Black on light blue underprint. B in underprint. Back: Brown.			
	a. Serial # prefix - suffix A-A.	1.00	4.00	12.00
	b. Serial # prefix - suffix B-B.	4.00	15.00	50.00
70	**10 Yen** ND (1946). Black on light blue underprint. A in underprint. Back: Brown.	30.00	70.00	275
71	**10 Yen** ND (1945). Black on light blue underprint. B in underprint. Back: Brown.	1.00	4.00	15.00

#	Denomination	VG	VF	UNC
72	**20 Yen** ND (1946). Black on light blue underprint. A in underprint. Back: Brown.	125	300	750
73	**20 Yen** ND (1945). Black on light blue underprint. B in underprint. Back: Brown.	4.00	15.00	50.00

#	Denomination	VG	VF	UNC
74	**100 Yen** ND (1946). Black on light blue underprint. A in underprint. Back: Brown.	200	450	1,000
75	**100 Yen** ND (1945). Black on light blue underprint. B in underprint. Back: Brown.	4.00	15.00	50.00

#	Denomination	VG	VF	UNC
76	**1000 Yen** ND (1951). Black on blue-green underprint. B in underprint. Back: Brown.			
	a. Block letters A; B.	800	1,500	3,500
	b. Block letters C; D.	650	1,250	2,750
	c. Block letter E.	500	1,100	2,000

Color Abbreviation Guide

New to the *Standard Catalog of ® World Paper Money* are the following abbreviations related to color references:

BC: Back color

PC: Paper color

Bank of Japan (Continued)

券行銀本日

Nip-pon Gin-ko Ken

1945 ND Issue

#	Denomination	VG	VF	UNC
77	**10 Yen** ND (1945). Black. Portrait #3 at center. Back: Brown.			
	a. Green and gray underprint. Watermark: Quatrefoil. Blocks #1-69.	25.00	75.00	175
	b. Lilac underprint. Without watermark. Blocks #70-165.	35.00	125	300
	s1. As a. Specimen with overprint and perforated: *Mi-hon.*	—	—	400
	s2. As a. Specimen with small stamping: *Mi-hon.* Regular block #.	—	—	125
78	**10 Yen** ND (1945). Black, green, and lilac. Portrait #3 at right. Back: Green. Specimen.	—	—	3,500
78A	**100 Yen** ND (1945). Black on green underprint. Portrait #6 at center. Back: Dark green.			
	a. Watermark: Quatrefoil. Shaded gray to dull gray-green to gray underprint. Block #1-43.	35.00	75.00	175
	b. Watermark: Kiri leaves. Dull gray-green underprint. Block #44-190.	25.00	60.00	150
	s1. As a. Specimen with overprint and perforated: *Mi-hon.*	—	—	750
	s2. As b. Specimen with small stamping: *Mi-hon.* Regular block #.	—	—	125
78B	**500 Yen** ND (1945). Black on orange underprint. Portrait #1 at center. Back: Brown. Specimen.	—	—	3,500
78C	**1000 Yen** ND (1945). Black and blue. Takebe Shrine at left, portrait #7 at right. Lithographed. Back: Light blue. Specimen.	—	—	3,500

1946 Provisional Issue

#79-82 March 1946 Currency Reform. Old notes from 10 to 1000 Yen were revalidated with validation adhesive stamps (Shoshi) of corresponding values.

#	Denomination	VG	VF	UNC
79	**10 Yen** ND (1946). Blue stamp.			
	a. Affixed to 10 Yen #40.	7.50	10.00	25.00
	b. Affixed to 10 Yen #51.	5.00	8.00	17.50
	c. Affixed to 10 Yen #56.	10.00	20.00	30.00
	d. Affixed to 10 Yen #77.	25.00	75.00	250

		VG	VF	UNC
80	**100 Yen**	VG	VF	UNC
	ND (1946). Green stamp.			
	a. Affixed to 100 Yen #42.	20.00	60.00	125
	b. Affixed to 100 Yen #57.	15.00	35.00	70.00
	c. Affixed to 100 Yen #78A.	30.00	90.00	175
81	**200 Yen**	VG	VF	UNC
	ND (1946). Violet stamp.			
	a. Affixed to 200 Yen #43A.	—	—	—
	b. Affixed to 200 Yen #44.	—	—	—
82	**1000 Yen**	VG	VF	UNC
	ND (1946). Validation adhesive stamp affixed to 1000 Yen #45. Red stamp.	—	—	—

1946-1951 ND Issue

Red numbers are elaborate block numbers, not serial #s. Duplicate #s are not errors.

		VG	VF	UNC
83	**5 Sen**	VG	VF	UNC
	ND (1948). Black on yellow underprint. Plum blossoms at right. Back: Light brown.	0.25	1.00	3.00

		VG	VF	UNC
84	**10 Sen**	VG	VF	UNC
	ND (1947). Black on blue underprint. Doves at right. Back: Light red-brown. Back: Diet building at left.	0.10	0.25	1.50

		VG	VF	UNC
85	**1 Yen**	VG	VF	UNC
	ND (1946). Black on light brown underprint. Cockerel at lower center, portrait Ninomiya Sontoku at right. Back: Blue.			
	a. Issued note.	0.10	0.30	1.00
	s. Specimen with overprint: *Mi-hon. SPECIMEN* on back.	—	—	500

		VG	VF	UNC
86	**5 Yen**	VG	VF	UNC
	ND (1946). Dark brown on green underprint without vignette. Back: Blue.			
	a. Issued note.	0.50	1.50	5.00
	s. Specimen with overprint: *Mi-hon. SPECIMEN* on back.	—	—	500

		VG	VF	UNC
87	**10 Yen**	VG	VF	UNC
	ND (1946). Black on gray-blue underprint. Diet building at left. Back: Green.			
	a. Issued note.	0.25	1.25	4.00
	s1. Specimen with stamping: *SPECIMEN.*	—	—	600
	s2. Specimen with small stamping: *Mi-hon.* Regular block #.	—	—	100

		VG	VF	UNC
88	**50 Yen**	VG	VF	UNC
	ND (1951). Black on orange and olive underprint. Portrait Takahashi Korekiyo at right. Back: Brown. Back: Bank of Japan at building at left.	4.00	10.00	30.00

		VG	VF	UNC
89	**100 Yen** ND (1946). Black on lilac underprint of leaves. Yumedono Pavillion at left, portrait #6 at right. Black block # (upper right and lower left) and serial # (upper left and lower right). Back: Blue. Back: Horyuji Temple.			
	a. Watermark: Kiri leaves.	2.00	5.00	12.50
	b. Watermark: Arabesque - phoenix design.	4.00	10.00	25.00
	s1. As a. Specimen with overprint: *SPECIMEN.*	—	—	850
	s2. As a. Specimen with small stamping: *Mi-hon.* Regular block #.	—	—	100

		VG	VF	UNC
89A	**1000 Yen** ND. Black on rose underprint. Takebe Shrine at left, portrait #7 at right. Back: Green and light blue. Specimen. Rare.	—	—	3,500

1950-1958 ND Issue

		VG	VF	UNC
90	**100 Yen** ND (1953). Brown-violet on green and multicolor underprint. Portrait Itagaki Taisuke at right. Back: Diet building at right. 12 varieties exist.			
	a. Single letter serial # prefix.	4.00	12.50	40.00
	b. Double letter serial # prefix. Light brown paper.	0.75	2.00	5.00
	c. As b. White paper.	FV	FV	2.00
	s. As a. Specimen with red overprint and perforated: *Mi-hon.*	—	—	1,500

		VG	VF	UNC
91	**500 Yen** ND (1951). Blue on multicolor underprint. Portrait Iwakura Tomomi at right. Back: Gray and pale green. Back: Mt. Fuji at right.			
	a. Single letter serial # prefix.	6.00	12.50	35.00
	b. Double letter serial # prefix. Cream paper.	FV	6.00	12.50
	c. As b. White paper.	FV	5.00	10.00
	s. As a. Specimen with red overprint and perforated: *Mi-hon.*	—	—	1,500

		VG	VF	UNC
92	**1000 Yen** ND (1950). Black on green and multicolor underprint. Portrait #6 at right. Back: Brown and blue. Back: Yumedono Pavillion at left. 164x77mm.			
	a. Single letter serial # prefix.	10.00	30.00	75.00
	b. Double letter serial # prefix.	FV	15.00	30.00
	s. As a. Specimen with red overprint: *Mi-hon.* Punch hole cancelled.	—	—	1,500

		VG	VF	UNC
93	**5000 Yen** ND (1957). Dark green on multicolor underprint. Portrait #6 at center. Back: Green. Back: Bank of Japan at center. Watermark: Portrait #6.			
	a. Single letter serial # prefix.	FV	60.00	90.00
	b. Double letter serial # prefix.	FV	FV	65.00

		VG	VF	UNC
94	**10,000 Yen** ND (1958). Dark brown and dark green on multicolor underprint. Portrait #6 at right. Back: Brown. Back: Phoenix at left and right in underprint within ornate frame. Watermark: Yumedono Pavilion.			
	a. Single letter serial # prefix.	FV	125	200
	b. Double letter serial # prefix.	FV	FV	125

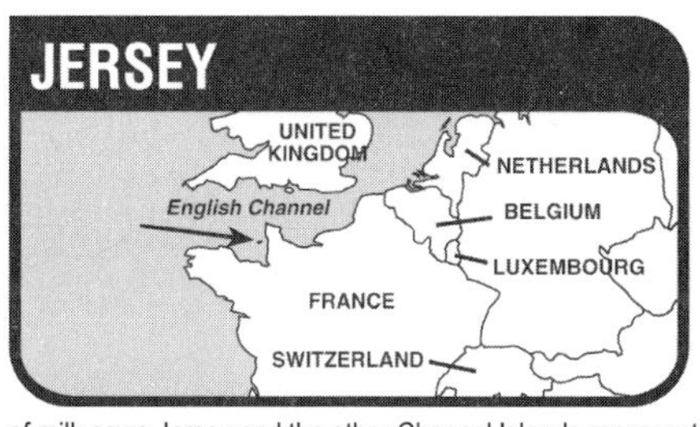

The Bailiwick of Jersey, a British Crown dependency located in the English Channel 12 miles (19 km.) west of Normandy, France, has an area of 45 sq. mi. (117 sq. km.) and a population of 90,000. Capital: St. Helier. The economy is based on agriculture and cattle breeding - the importation of cattle is prohibited to protect the purity of the island's world-famous strain of milk cows.Jersey and the other Channel Islands represent the last remnants of the medieval Dukedom of Normandy that held sway in both France and England. These islands were the only British soil occupied by German troops in World War II. Jersey is a British crown dependency but is not part of the UK. However, the UK Government is constitutionally responsible for its defense and international representation.

RULERS:

British

MONETARY SYSTEM:

1 Shilling = 12 Pence

1 Pound = 20 Shillings to 1971

1 Pound = 100 Pence, 1971-

From 1816 to 1941, only two notes circulated as government issues: a 5 Pound 1840 Bearer Bond (see #A1 in *SCWPM General Issues volume) and a 1 Pound 1874 Harbour Committee note. Some States politicians were bankers who apparently wanted fiscal control to remain with their banks. Eventually, over 100 banks, parishes and individuals became note issuers. Notes were often issued for road-building and other public works. Bank and parish issues sometimes became intertwined with those of private companies. The notes catalogued here are church, parish or bank issues which seemed to serve the general public in some capacity.*

BRITISH ADMINISTRATION

States of the Island of Jersey

1840 Interest Bearing Notes

A1	5 Pounds	Good	Fine	XF
	1.9.1840. Black. Arms at upper center. Back: *JERSEY STATES' BOND for FIVE POUNDS BRITISH.* Printer: W. Adams.			
	a. Issued note. Rare.	—	—	—
	b. Pen cancelled.	50.00	125	250
	r. Remainder. 18xx.	50.00	125	250

GERMAN OCCUPATION - WWII

States of Jersey

1941 ND Issues

1	6 Pence	VG	VF	UNC
	ND (1941-1942). Black on orange underprint. Arms at upper left. Watermark: Thick or thin chain.			
	a. Issued note.	25.00	65.00	175
	b. Cancelled.	15.00	40.00	100
	r. Remainder. Without serial #.	—	—	—

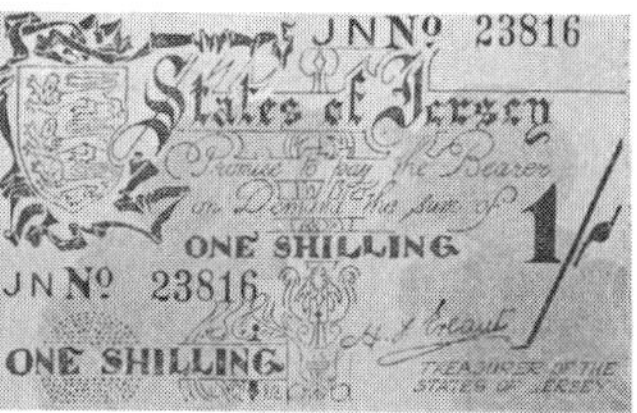

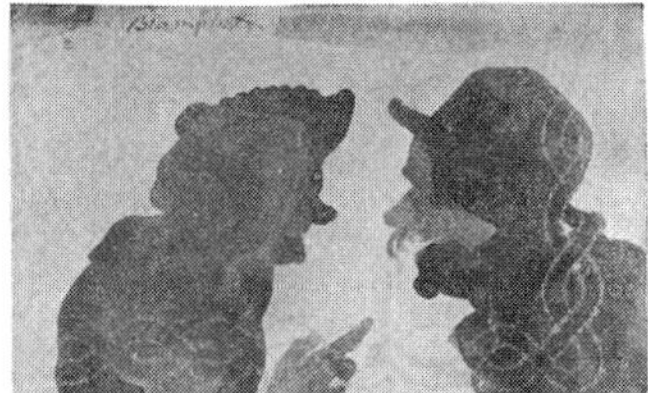

2	1 Shilling	VG	VF	UNC
	ND (1941-1942). Dark brown on blue underprint. Arms at upper left. Two men in underprint. Back: Same two men in brown. Watermark: Thick chain.			
	a. Issued note.	30.00	80.00	225
	b. Cancelled.	18.00	50.00	125
	r. Remainder. Without serial #.	—	—	—

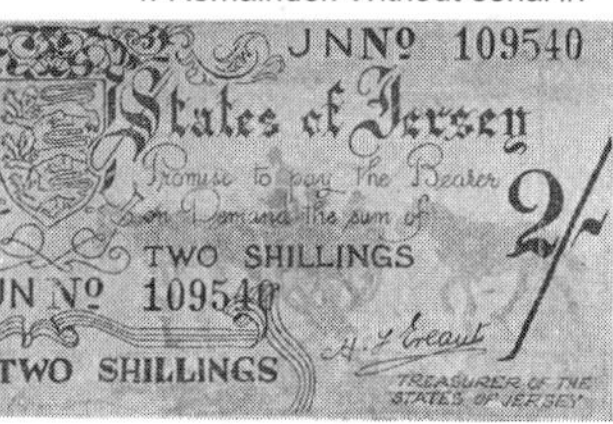

3	2 Shillings	VG	VF	UNC
	ND (1941-1942). Blue on light brown underprint. Arms at upper left. Horse-drawn cart in underprint. Back: Same cart in blue. Watermark: Thick chain.			
	a. Issued note.	50.00	130	350
	b. Cancelled.	25.00	65.00	175
	r. Remainder. Without serial #.	—	—	—

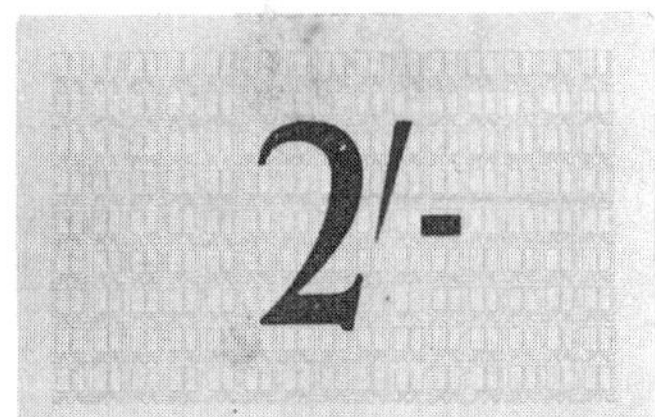

4	2 Shillings	VG	VF	UNC
	ND (1941-1942). Dark blue-violet on pale orange underprint. Arms at upper left. Back: No cart scene. Watermark: Thick chain.			
	a. Issued note.	85.00	225	550
	b. Cancelled.	45.00	110	275

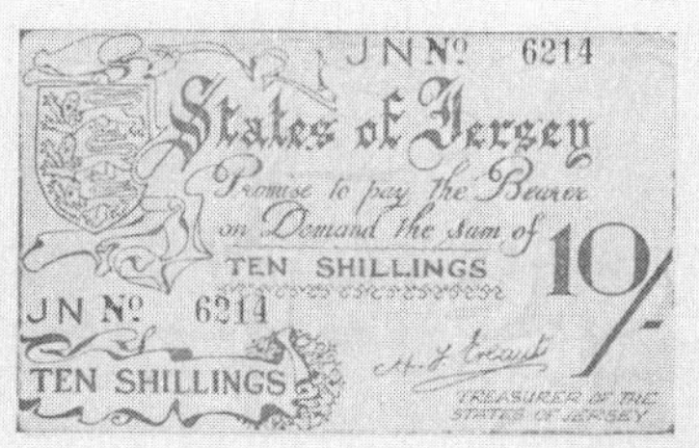

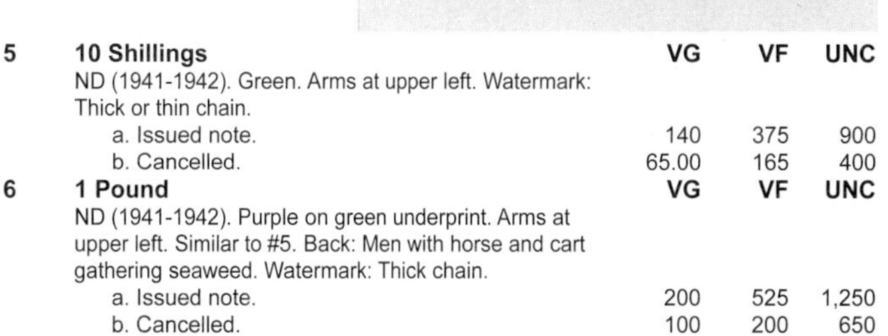

5	10 Shillings	VG	VF	UNC
	ND (1941-1942). Green. Arms at upper left. Watermark: Thick or thin chain.			
	a. Issued note.	140	375	900
	b. Cancelled.	65.00	165	400

6	1 Pound	VG	VF	UNC
	ND (1941-1942). Purple on green underprint. Arms at upper left. Similar to #5. Back: Men with horse and cart gathering seaweed. Watermark: Thick chain.			
	a. Issued note.	200	525	1,250
	b. Cancelled.	100	200	650

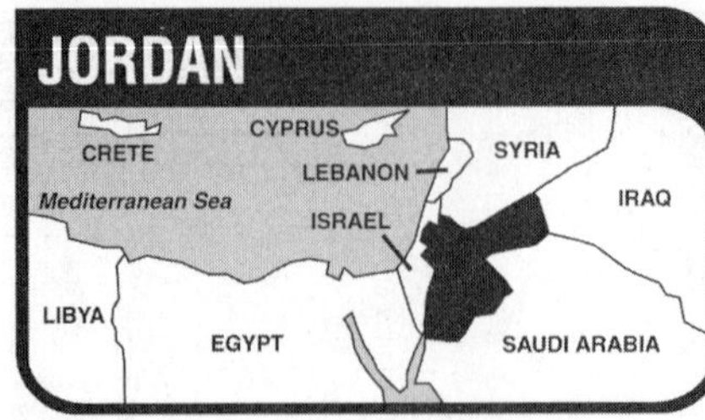

The Hashemite Kingdom of Jordan, a constitutional monarchy in southwest Asia, has an area of 37,738 sq. mi. (97,740 sq. km.) and a population of 5.46 million. Capital: Amman. Agriculture and tourism comprise Jordan's economic base. Chief exports are phosphates, tomatoes and oranges.Following World War I and the dissolution of the Ottoman Empire, the UK received a mandate to govern much of the Middle East. Britain separated out a semi-autonomous region of Transjordan from Palestine in the early 1920s, and the area gained its independence in 1946; it adopted the name of Jordan in 1950. The country's long-time ruler was King Hussen (1953-99). A pragmatic leader, he successfully navigated competing pressures from the major powers (US, USSR, and UK), various Arab states, Israel, and a large internal Palestinian population. Jordan lost the West Bank to Israel in the 1967 war and barely managed to defeat Palestinian rebels who threatened to overthrow the monarchy in 1970. Hussen in 1988 permanently relinquished Jordanian claims to the West Bank. In 1989, he reinstituted parliamentary elections and initiated a gradual political liberalization; political parties were legalized in 1992. In 1994, he signed a peace treaty with Israel. King Abdullah II, the son of King Hussein, assumed the throne following his father's death in February 1999. Since then, he has consolidated his power and undertaken an aggressive economic reform program. Jordan acceded to the World Trade Organization in 2000, and began to participate in the European Free Trade Association in 2001. In 2003, Jordan staunchly supported the Coalition ouster of Saddam in Iraq and following the outbreak of insurgent violence in Iraq, absorbed hundreds of thousands of displaced Iraqis, most of whom remain in the country. Municipal elections were held in July 2007 under a system in which 20% of seats in all municipal councils were reserved by quota for women. Parliamentary elections were held in November 2007 and saw independent pro-government candidates win the vast majority of seats. In November 2007, King Abdullah instructed his new prime minister to focus on socioeconomic reform, developing a healthcare and housing network for civilians and military personnel, and improving the educational system.

RULERS:

Abdullah I, 1946-1951
Hussein I, 1952-1999
Abdullah II, 1999-

MONETARY SYSTEM:

1 Dinar = 10 Dirhams
1 Dirham = 10 Piastres = 10 Qirsh
1 Piastre = 1 Qirsh = 10 Fils

REPLACEMENT NOTES:

#9-27, jj prefix (YY).

SIGNATURE VARIETIES			
1		6	
2		6A	
3		7	
4		8	
5		9	

KINGDOM

The Hashemite Kingdom of The Jordan

Jordan Currency Board First Issue

1	500 Fils	VG	VF	UNC
	L.1949. Lilac. Landscape with irrigation system. Back: Cows in hayfield. Watermark: King Abdullah. Printer: TDLR.			
	a. Issued note. Signature 1.	200	500	2,000
	b. Issued note. Signature 2.	200	500	2,000
	s1. Specimen perforated: *CANCELLED.* Signature 1.	—	—	3,000
	s2. Specimen overprinted: *SPECIMEN* or just with *TDLR specimen oval seal.* Signature 1.	—	—	3,000

2	1 Dinar	VG	VF	UNC
	L. 1949. Green and black. King Abdullah at right. Signature 1,2. Back: Ruins. Watermark: King Abdullah.			
	a. Signature 1.	75.00	300	1,700
	b. Signature 2.	75.00	350	1,500
	s1. Specimen perforated: *CANCELLED.* Signature 1, 2.	—	—	3,000
	s2. Specimen overprinted: *SPECIMEN* or just with *TDLR specimen oval seal.* Signature 1, 2.	—	—	3,000

3	5 Dinars	VG	VF	UNC
	L.1949. Red and black. King Abdullah at right. Signature 1. Back: El Hazne, Treasury of Pharaoh at Petra at center. Watermark: King Abdullah. Printer: TDLR.			
	a. Issued note.	400	800	1,400
	s1. Specimen perforated: *CANCELLED.*	—	—	3,000
	s2. Specimen overprinted: *SPECIMEN* or just with *TDLR oval seal.*	—	—	3,000

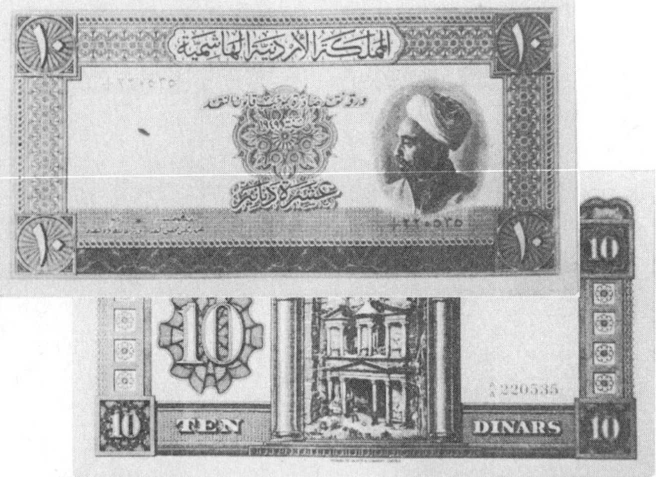

4	**10 Dinars**	VG	VF	UNC
	L.1949. Blue and black. King Abdullah at right. Signature 1. Back: El Hazne, Treasury of Pharaoh at Petra at center. Watermark: King Abdullah. Printer: TDLR.			
	a. Issued note.	500	1,000	2,500
	s1. Specimen perforated: *CANCELLED.*	—	—	3,000
	s2. Specimen overprinted: *SPECIMEN* or just with *TDLR oval seal.*	—	—	3,000

5	**50 Dinars**	VG	VF	UNC
	L. 1949. Brown. King Abdullah at right. Signature 2. Back: Aqaba beach. Watermark: King Abdullah. Printer: TDLR.			
	a. Issued note. Rare.	—	—	—
	s. Specimen. Punch hole cancelled and red TDLR oval.	—	—	15,000

The Hashemite Kingdom of Jordan
Jordan Currency Board Second Issue

5A	**500 Fils**	VG	VF	UNC
	L.1949. (1952) Lilac. Landscape with irrigation system. Back: Cows in hay field by water. Watermark: Young King Hussein. Printer: TDLR.			
	a. Signature 3.	50.00	175	800
	b. Signature 4.	50.00	175	800
	c. Signature 5.	50.00	175	800
	s. As c. Specimen. Red overprint: *SPECIMEN* on both sides.	—	—	750

6	**1 Dinar**	VG	VF	UNC
	L.1949. (1952). Green and black. King Hussein at right. Back: Ruins. Watermark: Young King Hussein. Printer: TDLR.			
	a. Signature 3.	50.00	125	800
	b. Signature 6.	50.00	125	800
	c. Signature 6A.	50.00	125	800

7	**5 Dinars**	VG	VF	UNC
	L.1949. (1952). Red and black. King Hussein at right. Back: El Hazne, Treasury of Pharaoh at Petra at center. Watermark: Young King Hussein. Printer: TDLR.			
	a. Signature 3.	100	250	900
	b. Signature 7.	100	250	900
	c. Signature 9.	100	250	900
	s. As b. Specimen. Red overprint: *SPECIMEN* on both sides.	—	—	750

8	**10 Dinars**	VG	VF	UNC
	L.1949. (1952). Blue and black. King Hussein at right. Back: El Hazne, Treasury of Pharaoh at Petra at center. Watermark: Young King Hussein. Printer: TDLR.			
	a. Signature 3.	200	350	1,100
	b. Signature 4.	200	350	1,100
	c. Signature 5.	200	350	1,100
	d. Signature 8.	200	350	1,100

Central Bank of Jordan
First Issue - Law 1959

9	**500 Fils**	VG	VF	UNC
	L.1959. (1965). Brown on multicolor underprint. King Hussein at left with law date 1959 (in Arabic *1909.*) Signature 10. Back: Jerash Forum. *FIVE HUNDRED FILS* at bottom margin. 140x70mm.			
	a. Issued note.	25.00	60.00	250
	s. Specimen.	—	—	500

10	**1 Dinar**	VG	VF	UNC
	L.1959. (1965). Green on multicolor underprint. King Hussein at left with law date 1959 (in Arabic *1909.*) Signature 10. Back: Dome of the Rock at center with columns at right. 150x75mm.			
	a. Issued note.	10.00	25.00	200
	s. Specimen.	—	—	500

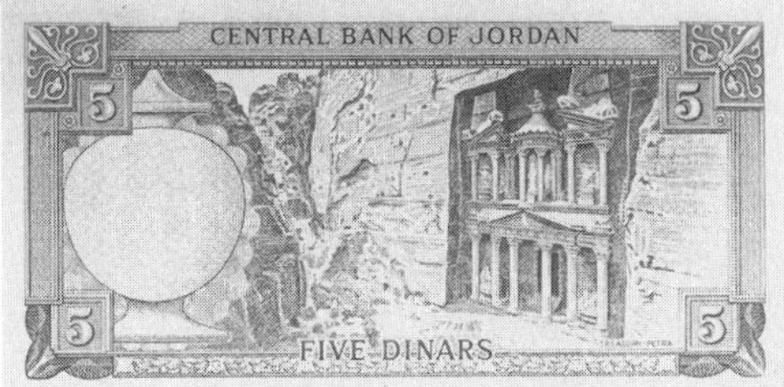

		VG	VF	UNC
11	**5 Dinars**			
	L.1959. (1965). Red-brown on multicolor underprint. Hussein at left with law date 1959 (in Arabic *1909.*) Back: Al-Hazne, Treasury of Pharaoh at Petra at center right. 164x82mm.			
	a. Signature 10.	15.00	45.00	200
	b. Signature 11.	15.00	45.00	200
	c. Signature 12.	15.00	45.00	200
	s. Specimen. Signature 10, 11, 12.	—	—	500

		VG	VF	UNC
12	**10 Dinars**			
	L.1959. (1965). Blue-gray on multicolor underprint. King Hussein at left with law date 1959 (in Arabic *1909.*) Back: Baptismal site on River Jordan. 175x88mm.			
	a. Signature 10.	40.00	95.00	275
	b. Signature 11.	40.00	95.00	275
	c. Signature 12.	40.00	95.00	275
	s. As a, b, c. Specimen. Red overprint: *SPECIMEN* on both sides. Punch hole cancelled.	—	—	750

Kiau Chau (Kiao Chau, Kiaochow, Kiautscho), a former German trading enclave, including the port of Tsingtao, was located on the Shantung Peninsula of eastern China. Following the murder of two missionaries in Shantung in 1897, Germany occupied Kiaochow Bay, and during subsequent negotiations with the Chinese government obtained a 99-year lease on 177 sq. mi. of land. The enclave was established as a free port in 1899, and a customs house set up to collect tariffs on goods moving to and from the Chinese interior. The Japanese took siege to the port on Aug. 27, 1914, as their first action in World War I to deprive German sea marauders of their east Asian supply and refitting base. Aided by British forces the siege ended on Nov. 7. Japan retained possession until 1922, when it was restored to China by the Washington Conference on China and naval armaments. It fell again to Japan in 1938, but not until the Chinese had destroyed its manufacturing facilities. Since 1949, it has been a part of the Peoples Republic of China.

RULERS:

German, 1897-1914
Japanese, 1914-1922, 1938-1945

MONETARY SYSTEM:

1 Dollar = 100 Cents

Note: *S/M #* refer to *Chinese Banknotes* by Ward D. Smith and Brian Matravers.

GERMAN ADMINISTRATION

Deutsch-Asiatische Bank

行銀華德
Te Hua Yin Hang

Tsingtao

1907; 1914 Issue

		Good	Fine	XF
1	**1 Dollar**			
	1.3.1907. Blue and rose. "Germania" standing at right with spear. *(S/M #T101-40).* Printer: G&D.			
	a. Watermark: 8 cornered crossflower.	7,500	12,500	—
	b. Watermark: *GD.*	7,500	12,500	—
2	**5 Dollars**	**Good**	**Fine**	**XF**
	1907; 1914. Dark green and violet. "Germania" standing at right with spear. *(S/M #T101-41).* Printer: G&D.			
	a. Watermark: 8 cornered crossflower. 1.3.1907.	5,000	8,000	—
	b. Watermark: *GD.* 1.3.1907.	5,000	8,000	—
	c. Watermark: *GD.* 1.7.1914. (Not issued). Rare.	—		

		Good	Fine	XF
3	**10 Dollars**			
	1907; 1914. Brown and blue. "Germania" standing at right with spear. *(S/M #T101-42).* Printer: G&D.			
	a. Watermark: 8 cornered crossflower.	5,000	8,000	—
	b. Watermark: *GD.* 1.3.1907. Reported not confirmed.	—	—	—
	c. Watermark: *GD.* 1.7.1914. (Not issued). Rare.	—	—	—

		Good	Fine	XF
4	**25 Dollars** 1.3.1907. Green and rose. "Germania" standing at right with spear. *(S/M #T101-43).* Printer: G&D.			
	a. Watermark: 8 cornered crossflower. Rare.	—	—	—
	b. Watermark: *GD.*	—	—	—

		Good	Fine	XF
5	**50 Dollars** 1.3.1907. Violet and gray. "Germania" standing at right with spear. *(S/M #T101-44).* Printer: G&D.			
	a. Watermark: 8 cornered crossflower. Rare.	—	—	—
	b. Watermark: *GD.* Requires confirmation.	—	—	—

		Good	Fine	XF
6	**200 Dollars** 1.7.1914. Blue and rose. "Germania" standing at right with spear. Watermark: *GD. (S/M #T101-45).* Printer: G&D.	—	—	—

		Good	Fine	XF
7	**500 Dollars** 1.7.1914. Blue and rose. "Germania" standing at right with spear. Watermark: *GD. (S/M #T101-46).* Printer: G&D.	—	—	—

Note: Denominations of 1, 50, 100 and 200 Dollars require confirmation.

1914 Tael Issue

		Good	Fine	XF
8	**50 Taels** 1.7.1914. Blue and rose. "Germania" standing at right with spear. Watermark: *GD. (S/M #T101-51).* Printer: G&D.	—	—	—

		Good	Fine	XF
9	**100 Taels** 1.7.1914. Blue and rose. "Germania" standing at right with spear. Watermark: *GD. (S/M #T101-52).* Printer: G&D.	—	—	—

		Good	Fine	XF
10	**500 Taels** 1.7.1914. Blue and rose. "Germania" standing at right with spear. *(S/M #T101-53).* Printer: G&D.	—	—	—

Note: Denominations of 1, 5, 10 and 20 Taels dated 1914 require confirmation.

Korea, "Land of the Morning Calm", occupies a mountainous peninsula in northeast Asia bounded by Manchuria, the Yellow Sea and the Sea of Japan. According to legend, the first Korean dynasty, that of the House of Tangun, ruled from 2333 BC to 1122 BC. It was followed by the dynasty of Kija, a Chinese scholar, which continued until 193 BC and brought a high civilization to Korea. The first recorded period in the history of Korea, the Period of the Three Kingdoms, lasted from 57 BC to 935 AD and achieved the first political unification on the peninsula. The Kingdom of Koryo, from which Korea derived its name, was founded in 935 and continued until 1392, when it was superseded by the Yi dynasty of King Yi, Sung Kye which was to last until the Japanese annexation in 1910. At the end of the 16th century Korea was invaded and occupied for 7 years by Japan, and from 1627 until the late 19th century it was a semi-independent tributary of China. Japan replaced China as the predominant foreign influence at the end of the Sino-Japanese War (1894-95), only to find its position threatened by Russian influence from 1896 to 1904. The Russian threat was eliminated by the Russo-Japanese War (1904-1905) and in 1905 Japan established a direct protectorate over Korea. On Aug. 22, 1910, the last Korean ruler signed the treaty that annexed Korea to Japan as a government general in the Japanese Empire. Japanese suzerainty was maintained until the end of World War II. The Potsdam conference (1945) set the 38th parallel as the line dividing the occupation forces of the United States in the South and the Soviet Union in the north. A contingent of the United States Army landed at Inchon to begin the acceptance of the surrender of Japanese forces in the South on Sept. 8, 1945. Unissued Japanese printed stock was released during the U.S. Army's administration for circulation in the southern sector. NOTE: For later issues see Korea/North and Korea/South.

RULERS:

Japanese, 1910-1945
Yi Hyong (Kojong), 1864-1897
as Kwangmu, 1897-1907
Yung Hi, 1907-1910

MONETARY SYSTEM:

1 Yang = 100 Fun
1 Whan = 5 Yang to 1902
1 Won = 100 Chon 1902-
1 Yen = 100 Sen

MONETARY UNITS:

REPLACEMENT NOTES:

#29-32, 34,35,37: notes w/first digit 9 in serial number.

KINGDOM OF KOREA

Treasury Department

Hojo

1893 Convertible Notes

#1-3 Printed in 1893 (30th year of King Kojong). Issuing Agency: Tai Whan Shou (Conversion Office). (Not issued).

		Good	Fine	XF
1	**5 Yang** Yr. 30 (1893). Dragons around text in circle at center. Rare.	—	—	—

		Good	Fine	XF
2	**10 Yang** Yr.30 (1893). Dragons around text in circle at center. Rare.	—	—	—
2A	**20 Yang** Yr. 30 (1893). Dragons around text in circle at center. Rare.	—	—	—

		Good	Fine	XF
3	**50 Yang** Yr. 30 (1893). Dragons around text in circle at center. Rare.	—	—	—

JAPANESE PROTECTORATE

Dai Ichi Ginko

First National Bank of Japan

1902 Issue

		Good	Fine	XF
4	**1 Yen** 1902; 1904. Black on blue-green underprint. With 10-pronged star at top center. S. Eiichi at right. Back: Dark blue.			
	a. Stars in corners on face. 1902. (Meiji yr. 35).	300	800	1,750
	b. Numerals in corners on face. 1904. (Meiji yr. 37).	225	700	1,500

		Good	Fine	XF
5	**5 Yen** 1902; 1904. Black on ochre underprint. With 10-pronged star at top center. S. Eiichi at right. Back: Grayish-green.			
	a. Stars in corners on face. 1902. (Meiji yr. 35).	600	1,500	—
	b. Numerals in corners on face. 1904. (Meiji yr. 37).	500	1,250	4,000

		Good	Fine	XF
6	**10 Yen** 1902; 1904. Black on light blue underprint. With 10-pronged star at top center. S. Eiichi at right. Back: Dark red-brown.			
	a. Stars in corners on face. 1902. (Meiji yr. 35).	700	2,000	—
	b. Numerals in corners on face. 1904. (Meiji yr. 37).	550	1,750	—

1904 Issue

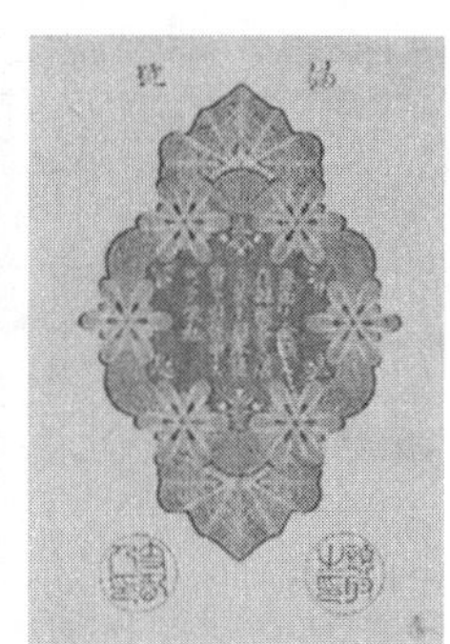

		Good	Fine	XF
7	**10 Sen** 1904. (Meiji yr. 37). Red. Two Onagadori cockerels at top with two dragons below. 10-pronged star at top center.	75.00	250	850
8	**20 Sen** 1904. (Meiji yr. 37). Blue. Two Onagadori cockerels at top with two dragons below. 10-pronged star at top center.	200	600	1,500
9	**50 Sen** 1904. (Meiji yr. 37). Yellow. Two Onagadori cockerels at top with two dragons below. 10-pronged star at top center. Back: Purple.	250	850	2,000

Note: For issues similar to #7-9 but with chrysanthemum crest above cockerels' heads see Japan - Military Issues #M1-M3.

1907 Issue

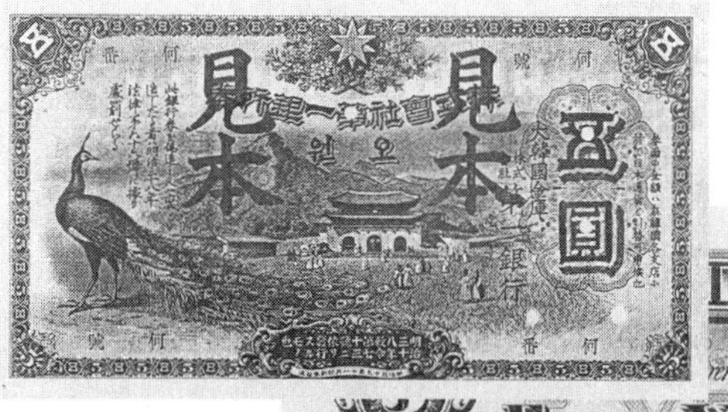

		Good	Fine	XF
9A	**5 Yen** 1907. (Meiji yr. 39). Black. Peacock at left, temple at center. 10-pronged star at top center. Back: Purple on ochre underprint. Specimen overprint: *Mi-hon*. Rare.	—	—	—

1908-1909 Issue

		Good	Fine	XF
10	**1 Yen** 1908. (Meiji yr. 40). Blue on pink underprint. Bridge shelter at left. 10-pronged star at top center. Back: Red on light blue underprint.	175	600	1,250

		Good	Fine	XF
11	**5 Yen** 1909. (Meiji yr. 41). Black on light orange-brown underprint. Shrine at right. 10-pronged star at top center. Back: Purple with black text on light green underprint. Rare.	—	—	—

#	Denomination	Good	Fine	XF
12	**10 Yen** 1909. (Meiji yr. 41). Green. 10-pronged star at top center. Back: Brown-violet. Back: House at right. Rare.	—	—	—

Bank of Korea

1909 Issue

#13-15 plum blossom at top center. Dated Yung Hi yr. 3.

#	Denomination	Good	Fine	XF
13	**1 Yen** 1909 (1910). Yung Hi yr. 3. Bridge shelter at left. Plum blossom at top center. Back: Brown-orange.	100	350	950
14	**5 Yen** 1909 (1911). Yung Hi yr. 3. Black on light violet-brown underprint. Shrine at right. Plum blossom at top center. Back: Blue-black on light green underprint.	375	1,250	4,000
15	**10 Yen** 1909 (1911). Yung Hi yr. 3. Dark gray-green on lilac underprint. Plum blossom at top center. Back: Brown. Back: House at right.	350	850	2,750

Bank of Chosen

1911 (1914) First Issue

#	Denomination	Good	Fine	XF
16	**100 Yen** Meiji yr. 44 (1911), (1914). Purple on lilac and ochre underprint. God of Fortune sitting on rice bales with sack over shoulder. Stylized serial # (Korean). Printer: Korean.	65.00	200	1,250

#	Denomination	Good	Fine	XF
16A	**100 Yen** Meiji yr. 44 (1911), (1914). Blue. God of Fortune sitting on rice bales with sack over shoulder. Regular style serial #. Printer: Japanese.	50.00	175	1,000

1911 (1915) Second Issue

#	Denomination	VG	VF	UNC
17	**1 Yen** Meiji yr. 44 (1911), (1915). Black on light red underprint. Man with beard. *ONE YEN* at left.			
	a. Stylized serial # (Korean).	15.00	60.00	300
	b. Regular style serial # (Japanese).	10.00	45.00	200

#	Denomination	VG	VF	UNC
18	**5 Yen** Meiji yr. 44 (1911), (1915). Brown. Man with beard at right.			
	a. Stylized serial # (Korean printer).	75.00	450	2,000
	b. Regular style serial # (Japanese printer).	60.00	400	1,750

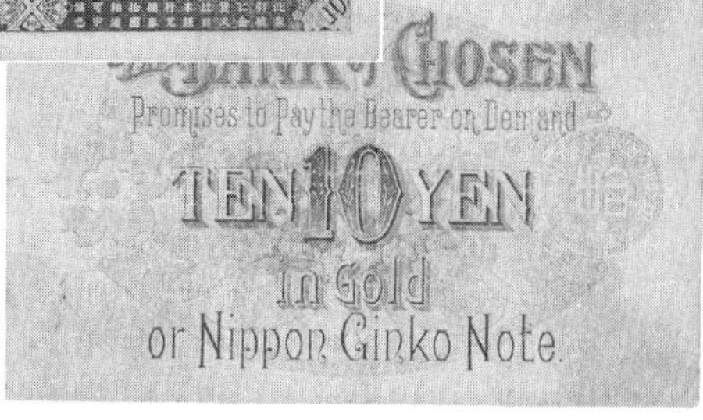

#	Denomination	VG	VF	UNC
19	**10 Yen** Meiji yr. 44 (1911), (1915). Green. *TEN YEN* at left, man with beard at right.			
	a. Stylized serial # (Korean).	60.00	400	1,600
	b. Regular style serial # (Japanese).	50.00	275	1,250

1916 Issue

#	Denomination	VG	VF	UNC
20	**10 Sen** 1916. Taisho yr. 5. Blue on pink underprint. Without Western numerals for denomination. Back: Red.	30.00	100	400
21	**20 Sen** 1916. Taisho yr.5. Blue on orange underprint. Without Western numerals for denomination.	135	475	1,500

		VG	VF	UNC
22	**50 Sen**	VG	VF	UNC
	1916. Taisho yr. 5. Blue on light green underprint. Without Western numerals for denomination.	135	475	1,500

1917 Provisional Postal Stamp Issue

		VG	VF	UNC
26	**5 Sen**	VG	VF	UNC
	1917 Japanese 5 Sen postal adhesive stamp (type Tazawa) affixed to a special form.	200	500	1,100

1919 Issue

#23-25 Russian, Japanese and English text: *payable in Japanese currency at any of its Manchurian offices.*

		VG	VF	UNC
23	**10 Sen**	VG	VF	UNC
	20.10.1919. Taisho yr. 8. Green on pink underprint. Western numerals for denomination at right. Russian, Japanese text: *payable in Japanese currency at any of its Manchurian offices.* Back: Pink. Back: Russian and English wording.			
	a. 7 character imprint (Korean).	12.50	50.00	175
	b. 14 character imprint (Japanese).	20.00	75.00	225

		VG	VF	UNC
24	**20 Sen**	VG	VF	UNC
	20.10.1919. Black on yellow underprint. Russian, Japanese text: *payable in Japanese currency at any of its Manchurian offices.* Western numerals for denomination at right. Back: Russian legends.	30.00	100	350
25	**50 Sen**	VG	VF	UNC
	20.10.1919. Taisho yr. 8. Black on green underprint. Russian, Japanese text: *payable in Japanese currency at any of its Manchurian offices.* Western numerals for denomination at right. Back: Russian legends.			
	a. 7 character imprint (Korean). Blocks 1-6.	20.00	125	375
	b. 14 character imprint (Japanese). Blocks 6-7.	30.00	175	500

1932-1938 ND and Dated Issue

		VG	VF	UNC
27	**10 Sen**	VG	VF	UNC
	1937. (Showa yr. 12). Western numerals for denomination at right.	12.50	50.00	200
28	**50 Sen**	VG	VF	UNC
	1937. (Showa yr. 12). Black on green underprint. Western numerals for denomination at right.			
	a. Issued note.	10.00	40.00	175
	s. Specimen with red overprint: *Mi-hon.*	—	—	200

#29 and following without bank name in English on back.

		VG	VF	UNC
29	**1 Yen**	VG	VF	UNC
	ND (1932). Black on light brown underprint. Brown guilloche at left, green guilloche at center, man with beard at right. Serial # and block #. 14 character imprint. Back: Without bank name in English.			
	a. Issued note.	0.25	2.00	7.50
	s1. Specimen with red overprint and perforated: *Mi-hon.*	—	—	200
	s2. Specimen with vermilion overprint: *Mi-hon.*	—	—	125
	s3. Specimen with red overprint: *Mi-hon,* punch hole cancelled.	—	—	75.00
30	**5 Yen**	VG	VF	UNC
	ND (1935). Black on light brown, green and lilac underprint. Man with beard at right. 7 character imprint. Back: Green. Back: *5 YEN* at bottom. Without bank name in English.			
	a. Issued note.	8.00	25.00	200
	s1. Specimen with red overprint and perforated: *Mi-hon.*	—	—	200
	s2. Specimen with red overprint: *Mi-hon,* punch hole cancelled.	—	—	100

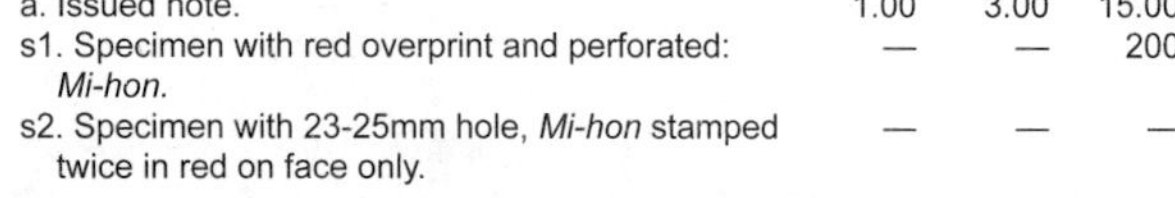

		VG	VF	UNC
31	**10 Yen**	VG	VF	UNC
	ND (1932). Black. Green and olive guilloche at center, man with beard at right. 14 character imprint. Back: Green and brown. Back: Bank of Chosen home office in Seoul at center. *10 YEN* at bottom.			
	a. Issued note.	1.00	3.00	15.00
	s1. Specimen with red overprint and perforated: *Mi-hon.*	—	—	200
	s2. Specimen with 23-25mm hole, *Mi-hon* stamped twice in red on face only.	—	—	—

		VG	VF	UNC
32	**100 Yen**	VG	VF	UNC
	ND (1938). Black on pink, green and violet underprint. Man with beard at right. Back: *100 YEN* at bottom. Without bank name in English. Watermark: Plum branches.			
	a. Issued note.	5.00	15.00	80.00
	s. Specimen with red overprint: *Mi-hon,* punch hole cancelled.	—	—	200

1944 ND Issues

		VG	VF	UNC
33	**1 Yen**	VG	VF	UNC
	ND (1944). Black on light brown underprint. Brown guilloche at left, green guilloche at center, man with beard at right. Block # only.			
	a. Issued note.	0.50	4.50	15.00
	s1. Specimen with red overprint: *Mi-hon.*	—	—	150
	s2. Specimen with vermilion overprint: *Mi-hon* on face and back.	—	—	100
	s3. Specimen with 23-25mm hole, *Mi-hon* stamped twice in red on face only.	—	—	—
34	**5 Yen**	VG	VF	UNC
	ND (1944). Black on light brown, green and lilac underprint. Man with beard at right. Serial # and block #. 10 character imprint. Back: Green. Back: Without 5 YEN at bottom.			
	a. Issued note.	4.00	25.00	135
	s1. Specimen with red overprint and perforated: *Mi-hon.*	—	—	250
	s2. Specimen with vermilion overprint: *Mi-hon* on face and back.	—	—	200
	s3. Specimen with vermilion overprint: *Mi-yo* in frame. *Specimen* on back.	—	—	100
35	**10 Yen**	VG	VF	UNC
	ND (1944). Black on blue underprint. Brown and green guilloche at center, man with beard at right. Serial # and block #. 7 character imprint. Back: Dull green. Back: Without *10 YEN* at bottom.			
	a. Issued note.	2.00	10.00	85.00
	s. Specimen with red overprint and perforated: *Mi-hon.*	—	—	225

		VG	VF	UNC
36	**10 Yen**	VG	VF	UNC
	ND (1944-1945). Black on blue underprint. Brown and green guilloche at center, man with beard at right. Block # only. 7 character imprint.			
	a. Watermark: *CHOSEN GINKO* (4 characters) at bottom, ornaments at center (1944).	3.00	10.00	50.00
	b. Watermark: *CHO* character and cherry blossoms repeated. (1945).	2.00	7.50	40.00
	s1. As a. Specimen with vermilion overprint: *Mi-hon* on face and back.	—	—	150
	s2. As a. Specimen with vermilion overprint: *Mi-hon.*	—	—	100
	s3. As a. Specimen with purple overprint: *Mi-yo* in frame. *Specimen* on back.	—	—	100
	s4. As b. Specimen with vermilion overprint: *Mi-hon* on face and back.	—	—	150
37	**100 Yen**	VG	VF	UNC
	ND (1944). Black on green, blue and violet underprint. Guilloche at center, man with beard at right. Serial and block #. 10 character imprint. Back: Without *100 YEN* at bottom. Watermark: With or without.			
	a. Issued note.	3.00	10.00	45.00
	s1. Specimen with red overprint: *Mi-hon.*	—	—	215
	s2. Specimen with vermilion overprint: *Mi-hon* on face and back.	—	—	150
	s3. Specimen with vermilion overprint: *Mi-hon.*	—	—	100

1945 ND Issue

		VG	VF	UNC
38	**1 Yen**	VG	VF	UNC
	ND (1945). Black on pale green and brown underprint. Guilloche brown at left. Without guilloche at center. Man with beard at right. Block # only. Back: Green. Lithographed.			
	a. Issued note.	0.25	2.00	7.50
	s1. Specimen with red overprint: *Mi-hon.* Special serial # on back.	—	—	125
	s2. Specimen with red overprint: *Mi-hon* in frame.	—	—	75.00
	s3. Specimen with vermilion overprint: *Mi-hon* in frame on face and back.	—	—	75.00
	s4. Specimen with vermilion overprint: *Mi-yo* in frame. *Specimen* on back.	—	—	75.00
39	**5 Yen**	VG	VF	UNC
	ND (1945). Black on light brown, green and lilac underprint. Man with beard at right. Block # only. Back: Green. Back: Without 5 YEN at bottom.			
	a. Issued note.	3.00	10.00	75.00
	s1. Specimen with vermilion overprint: *Mi-yo* in frame. *Specimen* on back.	—	—	100
	s2. Specimen with 23-25mm hole, *Mi-hon* stamped twice in red on face only.	—	—	—

		VG	VF	UNC
40	**10 Yen**	VG	VF	UNC
	ND (1945-1946). Black on purple underprint. Gray guilloche at center, man with beard at right, paulownia crest at top center. Block # only. 7 character imprint. Back: Gray to grayish purple.			
	a. Block # 1; 2 (1945).	10.00	45.00	325
	b. Block # 3; 4 (1946).	15.00	65.00	400
	s1. As a. Specimen with red overprint: *Mi-hon.* Special serial # on back.	—	—	200
	s2. As a. Specimen with vermilion overprint: *Mi-yo* in frame. *Specimen* on back.	—	—	125
	s3. As b. Specimen with vermilion overprint: *Mi-yo* in frame.	—	—	125

		VG	VF	UNC
41	**100 Yen**	VG	VF	UNC
	ND (1945). Black. Guilloche at center, man with beard at right. Lithographed. Light blue underprint and guilloche at left. Paulownia crest above portrait. Blocks 1 and 2 only. Back: Dull gray-brown. Back: Like #37.	350	1,000	3,500

		VG	VF	UNC
42	**1000 Yen**			
	ND (1945). Light purple. Man with beard at right. Back: Gray.			
	a. Block #1. (Not issued).	—	2,000	5,000
	s. Specimen with red overprint: *Mi-hon.*	—	2,500	6,000

1945 ND Provisional Issue

		VG	VF	UNC
42A	**1000 Yen**			
	ND (1945).	—	2,500	6,000

Note: #37 and 37A may have been issued by the South Korean government.

U.S. ARMY ADMINISTRATION

Bank of Chosen

1946-47 Issue

		VG	VF	UNC
43	**10 Yen = 10 Won**			
	ND (1946). Black on pale green underprint, blue-green guilloche at center. Man with beard at right. Five-petaled white hibiscus flower at upper center. Block # only. 12 character imprint. Back: Gray.	0.75	4.00	22.50
44	**100 Yen = 100 Won**			
	ND (1946). Blackon pale blue-green underprint, olive guilloche at left. Man with beard at right, paulownia crest above. Block # only. Back: Pale brown.	15.00	75.00	400

		VG	VF	UNC
45	**100 Yen = 100 Won**			
	ND (1946). Blue. Five-petaled white hibiscus flower above portrait. Back: Brown with orange guilloche. Color variations.	2.50	15.00	50.00

		VG	VF	UNC
46	**100 Yen = 100 Won**			
	ND (1947). Guilloche orange to yellow (varies). Five-petaled white hibiscus flower above portrait. Back: Green with violet guilloche. Watermark: Varieties.			
	a. Gray paper, with watermark.	0.50	2.00	10.00
	b. White paper, without watermark.	0.25	1.00	3.00

Note: For later issues see North Korea and South Korea.

The State of Kuwait, a constitutional monarchy located on the Arabian Peninsula at the northwestern corner of the Persian Gulf, has an area of 6,880 sq. mi. (17,818 sq. km.) and a population of 1.97 million. Capital: Kuwait. Petroleum, the basis of the economy, provides 95 percent of the exports. Britain oversaw foreign relations and defense for the ruling Kuwaiti Al-Sabah dynasty from 1899 until independence in 1961. Kuwait was attacked and overrun by Iraq on 2 August 1990. Following several weeks of aerial bombardment, a US-led, UN coalition began a ground assault on 23 February 1991 that liberated Kuwait in four days. Kuwait spent more than $5 billion to repair oil infrastructure damaged during 1990-1991. The Al-Sabah family has ruled since returning to power in 1991 and reestablished an elected legislature that in recent years has become increasingly assertive.

RULERS:

British to 1961
Abdullah, 1961-1965
Sabah Ibn Salim Al Sabah, 1965-1977
Jabir Ibn Ahmad Al Sabah, 1977-2006
Sabah Al Ahmad Al Sabah, 2006-

MONETARY SYSTEM:

1 Dinar = 1000 Fils

STATE

Kuwait Currency Board

Law of 1960, 1961 ND Issue

		VG	VF	UNC
1	**1/4 Dinar**			
	L.1960 (1961). Brown on multicolor underprint. Amir Shaikh Abdullah at right. Signature 1. Back: Aerial view, Port of Kuwait at center. Watermark: Amir Shaikh Abdullah.	5.00	25.00	75.00

		VG	VF	UNC
2	**1/2 Dinar**			
	L.1960 (1961). Purple on multicolor underprint. Amir Shaikh Abdullah at right. Signature 1. Back: School at center. Watermark: Amir Shaikh Abdullah.	7.50	35.00	125

		VG	VF	UNC
3	**1 Dinar** *L.1960* (1961). Red-brown on multicolor underprint. Amir Shaikh Abdullah at right. Signature 1. Back: Cement plant at center. Watermark: Amir Shaikh Abdullah.	12.50	50.00	175

		VG	VF	UNC
4	**5 Dinars** *L.1960* (1961). Blue on multicolor underprint. Amir Shaikh Abdullah at right. Signature 1. Back: Street scene. Watermark: Amir Shaikh Abdullah.	50.00	250	800

		VG	VF	UNC
5	**10 Dinars** *L.1960* (1961). Green on multicolor underprint. Amir Shaikh Abdullah at right. Signature 1. Back: Dhow. Watermark: Amir Shaikh Abdullah.	50.00	200	750

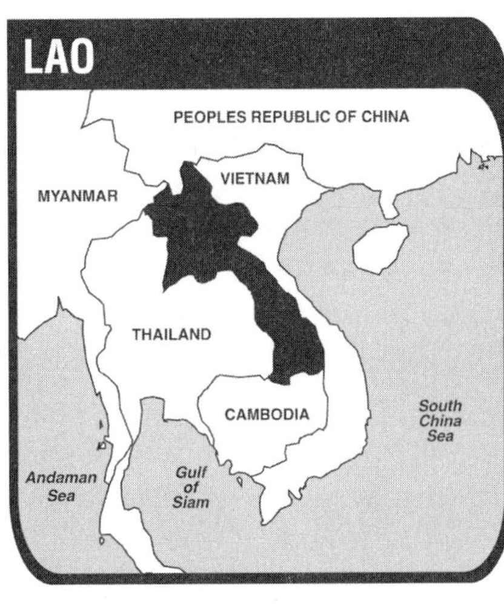

The Lao People's Democratic Republic is located on the Indo-Chinese Peninsula between the Socialist Republic of Viet Nam and the Kingdom of Thailand, has an area of 91,429 sq. mi. (236,800 sq. km.) and a population of 5.69 million. Capital: Vientiane. Agriculture employs 95 percent of the people. Tin, lumber and coffee are exported.

Modern-day Lao has its roots in the ancient Lao Kingdom of Lan Xang, established in the 14th Century under King Fa Ngum. For 300 years Lan Xang had influence reaching into present-day Cambodia and Thailand, as well as over all of what is now Lao. After centuries of gradual decline, Lao came under the domination of Siam (Thailand) and Viet Nam from the late 18th century until the late 19th century when it became part of French Indochina.

The Kingdome of Laos became fully independent of the French in 1955, and war soon ensued with the communist Pathet Lao. In 1975, the communist Pathet Lao took control of the government ending a six-century-old monarchy and instituting a strict socialist regime closely aligned to Viet Nam. A gradual return to private enterprise and the liberalization of foreign investment laws began in 1986. Lao became a member of ASEAN in 1997.

RULERS:

Sisavang Vong, 1949-1959
Savang Vatthana, 1959-1975

MONETARY SYSTEM:

1 Piastre = 100 Cents to 1955
1 Kip = 100 At, 1955-1975
1 (new) Kip = 100 Att, 1975-

FREE LAO GOVERNMENT

Government of 1945-1946 established in Vientiane after the Japanese surrender.

Lao Issara

1945-1946 Issue

		Good	Fine	XF
A1	**10 At** ND. Black. Kneeling Buddhist monk with parasol at center. Series 1. Plain paper.	80.00	200	325

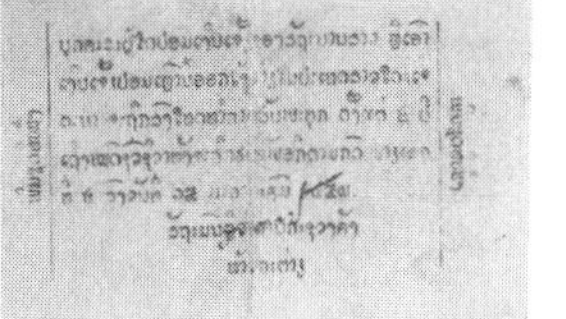

		Good	Fine	XF
A2	**20 At** ND. Black. Lao temple at center. Series 1. Plain paper.	75.00	175	300

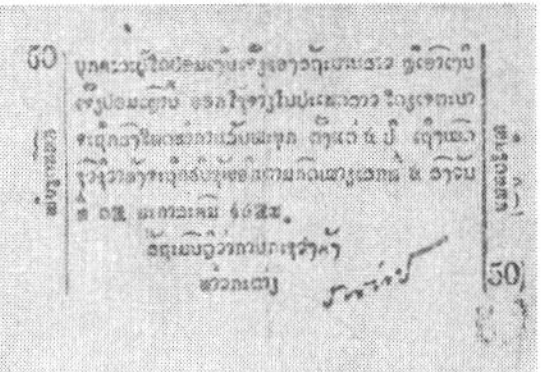

		Good	Fine	XF
A3	**50 At** ND. Black. Symbol of constitution at center. Minor varieties exist.			
	a. Without *50* on back. Plain paper. Series 1.	5.00	20.00	50.00
	b. Sm. *50* 4mm high on back, top of 5 curved. Plain paper. Series 2-7.	5.00	20.00	50.00
	c. Sm. *50* 4mm high on back, top of 5 straight, first character on fifth line is as illustration. Vertical lined paper. Series 2; 5; 6.	5.00	20.00	50.00
	d. Like #A3c but character as illustrated is last on fourth line. Vertical lined paper. Series 10.	5.00	20.00	50.00
	e. Large *50* 5.5mm high on back. Last character separated from last word of third line by a space. Verical lined paper. Series 10, 13.	5.00	20.00	50.00

	Good	Fine	XF
f. Large *50* 5.5mm high on back, but without printer's identification line on face. Vertical lined paper. Series 9.	5.00	20.00	50.00
g. Like #A3e but with designer name Phong on face on a vertical line inside the lower left Letters VS in lower corner. Series II.	—	—	—
h. Series # on face (Lao numeral) different from the # (in words - 7 on front, 4 on back) on back. Plain paper. Rare.	—	—	—
i. As b. but line 7 on back is missing : character. Series 4.	—	—	—
j. As b. Vertical lined paper. Series 2-7.	5.00	20.00	50.00
k. As d. Horizontal lined paper. Series 10.	—	—	—
l. As f. Horizontal lined paper. Series 9.	—	—	—
m. Like A3e. Character is part of last word of 3rd line on back. Vertical lined paper. Series 3, 12.	5.00	20.00	50.00
n. Like #A3e. 2nd line on back divided into 3 groups of characters. Character separated from last word of 4th line on back. Vertical lined paper. Series 5, 8.	5.00	20.00	50.00
o. Like A3e. Wrong character in 4th line on back. Vertical lined paper. Series 13.	5.00	20.00	50.00

A4	**10 Kip**	Good	Fine	XF
	ND. Purple. With or without underprint. Garuda bird at top center. Back: Temple.			
	a. Serial # in Western numerals. Signature Khammao Vilay.	80.00	200	400
	b. Serial # in Lao and European characters. Signature Katay Don Sasorith.	50.00	150	300

KINGDOM OF LAOS

Banque Nationale du Laos

SIGNATURE VARIETIES		
	LE GOUVERNEUR	UN CENSEUR
1		
2		
3		

1957 ND Issue

#1b-3b, and 5b were printed by the Pathet Lao during the Civil War. This second issue was printed in Bulgaria on paper w/o planchettes (security dots). Serial # style is different from notes printed by SBNC.

1	**1 Kip**	VG	VF	UNC
	ND (1957). Green. Lao Tricephalic Elephant Arms at upper center. Signature 1. That Ing Hang at left. Back: Farmer with water buffalo.			
	a. Security dots. Printer: SBNC.	0.25	1.00	15.00
	b. Without security dots (second issue).	0.25	1.00	4.00
	s. As a. Specimen.	—	—	250

2	**5 Kip**	VG	VF	UNC
	ND (1957). Brown on pale orange underprint. Lao Tricephalic Elephant Arms at upper center. Signature 1. That Makmo at right. Back: Ox cart.			
	a. Security dots. Printer: SBNC.	6.00	40.00	80.00
	b. Without security dots (second issue).	0.25	1.00	4.00
	s. As a. Specimen.	—	—	250

3	**10 Kip**	VG	VF	UNC
	ND (1957). Blue. Lao Tricephalic Elephant Arms at upper center. Signature 1. Pagoda Wat Ong Teu at right. Back: Workers in rice field.			
	a. Security dots. Printer: SBNC.	0.50	5.00	30.00
	b. Without security dots (second issue).	0.50	1.00	5.00
	s. As a. Specimen.	—	—	250

4	**20 Kip**	VG	VF	UNC
	ND (1957). Purple. Lao Tricephalic Elephant Arms at upper center. Signature 1. Government palace. Back: Woman weaving. Printer: SBNC.			
	a. Issued note.	5.00	55.00	110
	s. Specimen.	—	—	300

5	**50 Kip**	VG	VF	UNC
	ND (1957). Red-orange. Lao Tricephalic Elephant Arms at upper center. Signature 1. National Assembly building. Back: Orange. Back: Logger on elephant.			
	a. Security dots. Printer: SBNC.	7.50	50.00	250
	b. Without security dots (second issue).	1.00	2.00	6.00
	p. Proof. Back, uniface.	—	—	—
	s1. As a. Specimen.	—	—	450
	s2. As b. Specimen.	—	—	400

6	**100 Kip**	VG	VF	UNC
	ND (1957). Brown and multicolor. Lao Tricephalic Elephant Arms at upper center. Signature 1. Sisa Vang at left, vessels at center, dragons at right. Back: Woman with bowl of roses at right, building at center (like Fr. Indochina #103). Watermark: Tricephalic arms. Printer: Bank of France (without imprint).			
	a. Issued note.	5.00	10.00	25.00
	s. Specimen. Perforated.	—	—	300

1957 Commemorative Issue

#7, 2500th Year of Buddhist Era

7	**500 Kip**	VG	VF	UNC
	Yr. 2500 (1957). Red and multicolor. Sisa Vang at left, building at center. Signature 3. Back: Purple on blue underprint. Back: Buildings. Watermark: Tricephalic elephant arms.			
	a. Issued note.	8.00	80.00	150
	s1. Specimen.	—	—	250
	s2. Specimen. TDLR (red oval).	—	—	250

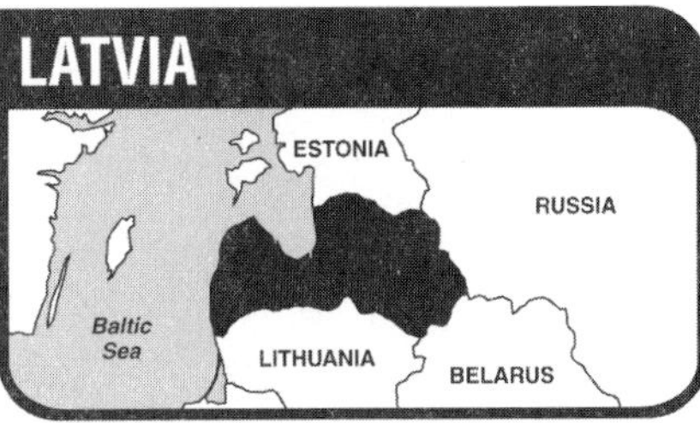

The Republic of Latvia, the central Baltic state in east Europe, has an area of 24,595 sq. mi. (43,601 sq. km.) and a population of 2.4 million. Capital: Riga. Livestock raising and manufacturing are the chief industries. Butter, bacon, fertilizers and telephone equipment are exported. The name "Latvia" originates from the ancient Latgalians, one of four eastern Baltic tribes that formed the ethnic core of the Latvian people (ca. 8th-12th centuries A.D.). The region subsequently came under the control of Germans, Poles, Swedes, and finally, Russians. A Latvian republic emerged following World War I, but it was annexed by the USSR in 1940 - an action never recognized by the US and many other countries. Latvia reestablished its independence in 1991 following the breakup of the Soviet Union. Although the last Russian troops left in 1994, the status of the Russian minority (some 30% of the population) remains of concern to Moscow. Latvia joined both NATO and the EU in the spring of 2004.

MONETARY SYSTEM:

1 Rublis = 100 Kapeikas, 1919-22
1 Lats = 100 Santimu, 1923-40; 1992
1 Lats = 200 Rublu, 1993
1 Rublis = 1 Russian Ruble, 1992

RUSSIAN ADMINISTRATION

Rigaer Borsen-Bank

Stock Exchange Bank of Riga

1863 Issue

		Good	Fine	XF
A1	**10 Kop.** 1863. Rare.	—	—	—
A2	**15 Kop.** 1863. Rare.	—	—	—
A3	**20 Kop.** 1863. Rare.	—	—	—
A4	**25 Kop.** 1863. Rare.	—	—	—

		Good	Fine	XF
A5	**50 Kop.** 1863. Rare.	—	—	—

REPUBLIC

Latwijas Walsts Kases Sihme

Latvian Government Currency Note

Sign. 1	Minister of Finance	J. Seskows
Sign. 2	Cashier of the State Treasury	J. Jakobsons
Sign. 3	Minister of Finance	K. Purinsch
Sign. 4	Manager of the State Treasury	K. Vanags
Sign. 5	Minister of Finance	R. Erhards
Sign. 6	Minister of Finance	Ringold Kalnings

1919-1920 Issue

		VG	VF	UNC
A21	**5 Kapeikas** ND (1919). Black. (Not issued). PC: Light beige.	—	—	—

		VG	VF	UNC
A22	**10 Kapeikas** ND (1919). Black on purple underprint. Back: Black on red-brown underprint. (Not issued).	—	—	—

No.	Description	VG	VF	UNC
A23	**50 Kapeikas**			
	ND (1919). Black on red-violet underprint. (Not issued).	—	—	—

No.	Description	VG	VF	UNC
1	**1 Rublis**			
	1919. Blue and brown. Flaming ball with L and three stars above legend. Signature 1 & 2. Series A. Watermark: Wavy lines.	50.00	100	250

No.	Description	VG	VF	UNC
2	**1 Rublis**			
	1919. Light and dark green. Flaming ball with L and three stars above legend.			
	a. Watermark: Wavy lines. Signature 3 & 4. Series B, C, D.	20.00	35.00	60.00
	b. Watermark: Light lines. Series E, F, G, H, K.	15.00	30.00	50.00
	s1. Specimen. Perforated: *PARAUGS* 10mm.	—	—	400
	s2. Specimen. Perforated: *PARAUGS* 14mm. Series F.	—	—	300

No.	Description	VG	VF	UNC
3	**5 Rubli**			
	ND (1919). Light and dark blue. Woman's head facing left at center.			
	a. Watermark: Wavy lines. Signature 4 & 5. Series Aa.	25.00	75.00	200
	b. As a, but Series A, B, C.	18.00	30.00	150
	c. Watermark: Light lines. Signature 5 & 4. Series D.	15.00	30.00	100
	d. As c. Signature 3 & 4.	30.00	100	250
	e. As d. Series E.	15.00	45.00	100
	f. Watermark: as c. Signature 6 & 4. Series F, G, H, K.	10.00	25.00	65.00
	s. Specimen. Overprint: *PARAUGS*. Several varieties exist.	—	—	500

No.	Description	VG	VF	UNC
4	**10 Rubli**			
	1919. Red-brown and green. Sailing ship at center.			
	a. Watermark: Wavy lines. Signature 5 & 4. Series Aa, Bb.	20.00	65.00	200
	b. Watermark: light lines. Signature 5 & 4. Series Ab, Ba, Bb, Bc, Bd, Be, Bk.	15.00	50.00	150
	c. Watermark: light lines. Signature 3 & 4. Series Bb, Bd, Bg, Bh, Bl, Bm.	20.00	50.00	150
	d. As c. Series A, B.	10.00	30.00	100
	e. As d, but 2 serial #. Series C, D, E.	10.00	30.00	100
	f. As e, but signature 6 & 4. Series F, G, H, K, L.	20.00	40.00	80.00
	s. Specimen. Overprint or perforated: *PARAUGS*. Several varieties exist.	—	—	500

No.	Description	VG	VF	UNC
5	**25 Rubli**			
	1919. Brown. Back: Three stylized ears of corn.			
	a. Watermark: Line groups. Black serial #. Signature 3 & 4. Rare.	—	—	—
	b. As a, but blue serial #. Rare.	—	—	—
	c. As a, but red serial #. Series A. Rare.	—	—	—
	d. As c, but green serial #. Series B.	150	500	—
	e. As d, but watermark: Stars & hexagons. Series C, D.	30.00	100	300
	f. As e, but watermark: light lines. Series E, F, G.	40.00	100	250
	g. As f, but signature 6 & 4. Series F, G.	30.00	80.00	200
	h. As g, but 2 serial #. Series H, K, L, M, N, P, R, S.	20.00	50.00	150
	s. Specimen. Overprint or perforated: *PARAUGS*. Several varieties exist.	—	—	550

No.	Description	VG	VF	UNC
6	**50 Rubli**			
	1919. Green and gray. Signature 5 & 4. Watermark: Wavy lines.	50.00	160	400

Note: Excellent Russian forgeries exist of #6.

7	**100 Rubli**	VG	VF	UNC
	1919. Brown and dark brown. Three legend varieties. Back: Oak tree.			
	a. Watermark: Light lines. signature 5 & 4. Series A, B, C.	40.00	120	300
	b. As a, but signature 3 & 4. Series C, D, E, F, G, H, K.	40.00	110	200
	c. As b, but signature 6 & 4. Series K. Rare.	—	—	—
	d. Signature 6 & 4. Series L. 2 serial #.	40.00	90.00	200
	e. As c, but single serial # with *No.* Series M.	40.00	90.00	200
	f. As c, but series N, P, R, S, T, U.	40.00	90.00	200
	g. As e. Paper without watermark. Series U. Rare.	—	—	—
	s. Specimen. Overprint or perforated: *PARAUGS.* Several varieties exist.	—	—	500

8	**500 Rubli**	VG	VF	UNC
	1920. Light and dark green. Back: Symbols of agriculture, industry and navigation.			
	a. Watermark: light lines. signature 3 & 4. Series A-F.	120	300	800
	b. As a, but signature 6 & 4. Series G, H, K.	120	300	800
	c. As b, but watermark: Interlocked wave-bands. Series L-N, P, R-W, Z.	120	200	550
	s. Specimen. Overprint or perforated: *PARAUGS.* Several varieties exist. Rare.	—	—	—

Note: Excellent Russian forgeries exist of #8.

Latwijas Mainas Sihme

Latvian Small Exchange Note

1920 ND Issue

9	**5 Kapeikas**	VG	VF	UNC
	ND (1920). Red. Like back. Back: Like face.			
	a. Issued note.	5.00	10.00	20.00
	s. Specimen. overprint: *PARAUGS.*	—	—	25.00

10	**10 Kapeikas**	VG	VF	UNC
	ND (1920). Blue. Like back. Back: Like face.			
	a. Issued note.	5.00	10.00	20.00
	s. Specimen. overprint: *PARAUGS.*	—	—	25.00

11	**25 Kapeikas**	VG	VF	UNC
	ND (1920). Brown. Like back. Back: Like face.			
	a. Issued note.	8.00	15.00	50.00
	s. Specimen. overprint: *PARAUGS.*	—	—	25.00

12	**50 Kapeikas**	VG	VF	UNC
	ND (1920). Purple. Like back. Back: Like face.			
	a. Issued note.	5.00	15.00	30.00
	s. Specimen. overprint: *PARAUGS.*	—	—	25.00

Latvijas Bankas

Bank of Latvia

Naudas Zime

Money Note

Provisional Issue

Individual sign. for #13-22:

Sign. 1	President of the Bank Council	Ringold Kalnings
Sign. 2	General Director	Edgars Schwede
Sign. 3	President of the Bank Council	J. Clems
Sign. 4	General Director	K. Vanags
Sign. 5	President of the Bank Council	A. Klive

13	**10 Latu on 500 Rubli**	VG	VF	UNC
	ND (-old date 1920).			
	a. Issued note. Series A-E.	400	800	1,500
	s1. Specimen. Perforated: *PARAUGS* 15mm. Face and back pair. Rare.	—	—	—
	s2. As s1, but single example printed on both sides. Rare.	—	—	—

1923 Issue

14	**100 Latu**	VG	VF	UNC
	1923. Blue. 2 legend varieties. Back: Two seated women in national costume.			
	a. Signature 1 & 2. #A 000001-110000.	400	800	1,500
	b. Signature 3 & 4. #A 110001-160000.	400	800	1,500
	s. Specimen. Overprint or perforated: *PARAUGS.* Several varieties exist. Rare.	—	—	—

1924 Issue

15	**20 Latu**	VG	VF	UNC
	1924. Black on orange underprint. Farmer sowing. Back: Red. Back: Arms at center. (Issued only briefly.) PC: Light tan.			
	a. Issued note. Rare.	600	1,200	2,500
	s. Specimen. Overprint: *PARAUGS BEZ VERTIBAS* in red. Rare.	—	—	—

16	50 Latu	VG	VF	UNC
	1924. Brown on green underprint. Back: River Dvina (Daugava) with view of Riga. Arms at left.			
	a. Issued note.	1,500	3,000	—
	s. Specimen. Overprint: *PARAUGS BEZ VERTI-BAS* in red. Rare.	—	—	—

1925 Issue

17	20 Latu	VG	VF	UNC
	1925. Black on yellow and green underprint. Portrait Pres. J. Cakste at top center. Back: Arms. Printer: W&S.			
	a. Issued note.	200	300	600
	s. Specimen. Overprint: *PARAUGS BEZ VERTI-BAS* in red. Rare.	—	—	—

1928-1929 Issue

18	25 Latu	VG	VF	UNC
	1928. Black on yellow underprint. K. Valdemars at top center, ships left and right. Back: Blue. Back: Arms at center. Printer: W&S.			
	a. Issued note.	100	200	400
	s1. Specimen. Overprint: *PARAUGS BEZ VERTI-BAS* in red.	—	—	—
	s2. Specimen. Overprint in red. Punch hole cancelled.	—	—	1,500

19	500 Latu	VG	VF	UNC
	1929. Blue and brown. Girl in national costume at right. Back: Cows and sheaves. Printer: BWC.			
	a. Issued note.	400	800	1,500
	s. Specimen. Overprint: *PARAUGS.* Several varieties exist. Rare.	—	—	—

1934 Issue

20	50 Latu	VG	VF	UNC
	1934. Blue. Prime Minister K. Ulmanis at right. Printer: TDLR.			
	a. Issued note.	30.00	50.00	100
	s1. Specimen. Perforated: *PARAUGS,* 9mm.	—	—	500
	s2. Specimen. TDLR oval seal.	—	—	400

1938-1939 Issue

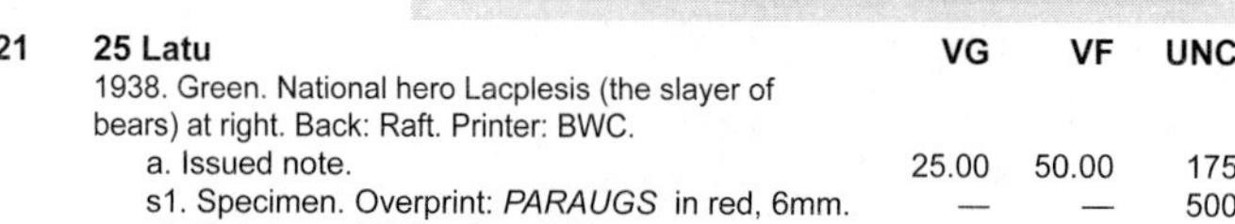

21	25 Latu	VG	VF	UNC
	1938. Green. National hero Lacplesis (the slayer of bears) at right. Back: Raft. Printer: BWC.			
	a. Issued note.	25.00	50.00	175
	s1. Specimen. Overprint: *PARAUGS* in red, 6mm.	—	—	500
	s2. Specimen. BWC red seal. Rare.	—	—	—

22	100 Latu	VG	VF	UNC
	1939. Red. Farm couple with daughter. Back: Cargo ship dockside.			
	a. Issued note.	40.00	70.00	150
	s. Specimen. Perforated: *PARAUGS.* 10mm. and overprint 6mm in green.	—	—	750

Latvijas Valsts Kases Zime

Latvian Government State Treasury Note

1925-1926 Issue

Individual sign. for #23-33:

Sign. 1	Director of the Credit Dept.	A. Karklins
Sign. 2	Vice-Director	Robert Baltgailis
Sign. 3	Minister of Finance	V. Bastjanis
Sign. 4	Substitute Director of the Credit Dept.	A. Kacens
Sign. 5	Minister of Finance	R. Leepinsch
Sign. 6	Substitute Director of the Credit Dept.	J. Miezis
Sign. 7	Minister of Finance	A. Petrevics
Sign. 8	Minister of Finance	M. Skujenieks
Sign. 9	Minister of Finance	J. Blumbergs
Sign. 10	Minister of Finance	J. Annuss
Sign. 11	Substitute Director of the State Economic Department	J. Skujevics
Sign. 12	Minister of Finance	E. Rimbenieks
Sign. 13	Minister of Finance	L. Ekis
Sign. 14	Minister of Finance	A. Valdmanis
Sign. 15	Minister of Finance	J. Kaminskis
Sign. 16	Minister of Finance	K. Karlsons
Sign. 17	Director of the State Economic Dept.	V. Bastjanis

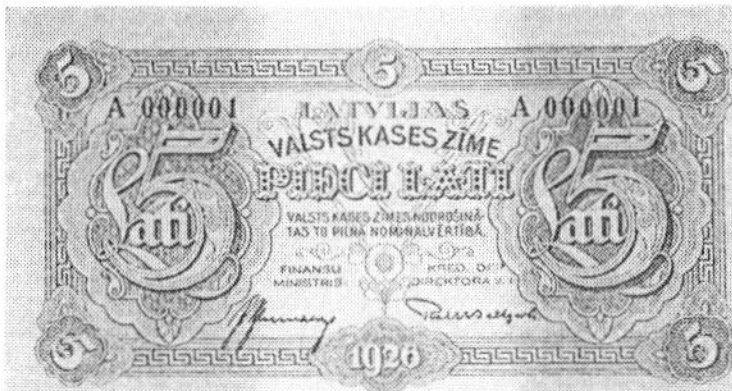

#		Good	Fine	XF
23	**5 Lati** 1926. Brown. Back: Symbols of commerce and navigation.			
	a. Issued note.	500	1,000	—
	s. Specimen. Perforated: *PARAUGS*. Two varieties exist. Rare.	—	—	—
24	**10 Latu** 1925. Red-brown. 5 signature varieties. Back: Oak tree and cornfield.	Good	Fine	XF
	a. Signature 1 & 2. Series A, B.	250	450	1,000
	b. Signature 3 & 4. Series C-K.	200	400	900
	c. Signature 5 & 6. Series K, L.	200	400	900
	d. Signature 7 & 6. Series M-T.	200	400	900
	e. Signature 8 & 6. Series T, U.	200	400	900
	s. Specimen. Perforated: *PARAUGS*. Several varieties exist. Rare.	—	—	—

1933 Issue

#		VG	VF	UNC
25	**10 Latu** 1933-1934. Blue-green. Back: Seated woman in national costume.			
	a. Signature 10 & 11. Series A-G. 1933.	40.00	100	200
	b. As a. Series H. 1933.	90.00	180	300
	c. Signature 10 & 11. Series H, J-N, P. 1934.	50.00	150	250
	d. Signature 12 & 11. Series R-U. 1934.	50.00	150	250
	e. Signature 13 & 11. Series V, Z. 1934.	50.00	150	250
	f. As e, but 2-letter series AA-AH, AJ. 1934.	50.00	150	250
	s1. Specimen. Perforated: *PARAUGS*, 19mm. Face and back pair. 1933.	—	—	750
	s2. As s1, but single example printed on both sides. 1933.	—	—	1,000

1935 Issue

#		Good	Fine	XF
26	**10 Latu** 1935. Deep brown and deep violet on multicolor underprint. Bondage (?) monument at left. Back: Blue-black on light blue. Back: Arms at center right. Specimen perforated: *PARAUGS*. Rare.	—	—	—

#		Good	Fine	XF
27	**20 Latu** 1935. Deep brown on gray underprint. Back: Lacplesis with bear at left, arms at upper center. Specimen perforated: *PARAUGS*. Rare.	—	—	—

#28 not assigned.

1935-1937 Issue

#		VG	VF	UNC
29	**10 Latu** 1937-1940. Dark brown and multicolor. Fishermen and net at center. Back: Blue-black. Back: Man sowing.			
	a. Signature 13 & 11. Series A-Z. 1937.	15.00	40.00	80.00
	b. Signature 13 & 11. Series AA-ZZ; BA-BD. 1938.	15.00	40.00	80.00
	c. Signature 13 & 11. Series BE-BK. 1939.	20.00	45.00	90.00
	d. Signature 14 & 11. Series BL-BZ; CA-CV. 1939.	15.00	50.00	100
	e. Signature 15 & 11. Series CZ; DA-DM. 1940.	15.00	50.00	100
	s1. Specimen. Like a. Perforated: *PARAUGS*. 1937.	—	—	750
	s2. Specimen. Like c. Perforated: *PARAUGS*. 1939.	—	—	750

#31-32 not assigned.

#		VG	VF	UNC
30	**20 Latu** 1935-1936. Brown. Castle of Riga. Back: Farmer at left, woman in national costume at right.			
	a. Signature 13 & 11. Series A-J. 1935.	150	225	350
	b. Signature 13 & 11. Series R-U. 1936.	50.00	150	300
	s1. Specimen. Like a. Perforated: *PARAUGS*. 1935.	—	—	750
	s2. Specimen. Like b. Perforated: *PARAUGS*. 1936. Rare.	—	—	—

1940 Issue

#	Denomination	Good	Fine	XF
33	**20 Latu** 1940. Blue. Academy of Agriculture in Jelgava.			
	a. Issued note.	300	800	1,500
	s. Specimen. Perforated: *PARAUGS*. With or without #. Rare.	—	—	—

Latvijas Valsts Kases Mainas Zime

Latvian Government Exchange Note

1940 Issue

Sign. 1	Minister of Finance	K. Karlsons
Sign. 2	Peoples Commissary of Finance	A. Tabaks
Sign. 3	Director of the State Economic Dept.	V. Bastjanis

Individual Sign. for #34 and 34A:

#	Denomination	VG	VF	UNC
34	**5 Lati** 1940. Blue, gray and brown. Bridge across the River Guaja. Back: Brown. Back: Arms at center.			
	a. Signature 1 & 3. Series A-D. Signature title at left: *Finansu Ministrs.*	90.00	170	300
	b. Signature 2 & 3. Series D. Signature title at left: *Finansu Tautas Komisars.*	120	200	400
	c. As b, but Series E.	200	500	1,000
	s. Specimen. Perforated: *PARAUGS*. Several varieties exist. Rare.	—	—	—

Latvijas Socialistiskas Padomju Republikas Kases Zime

Latvian Socialistic Soviet Republic Currency Note

1940 Issue

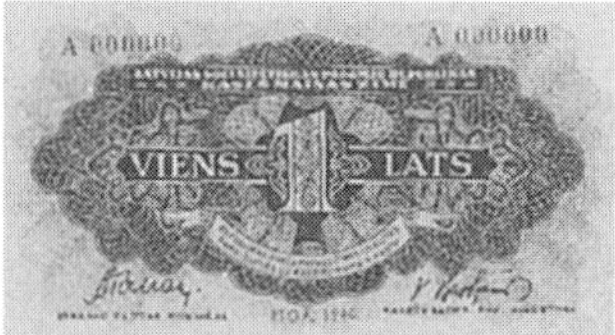

#	Denomination	VG	VF	UNC
34A	**1 Lats** 1940. Black on gray and light brown underprint. Serial #A. Specimen only. Face and back pair. Rare.	—	—	—

Note: A single set of notes was overprint. *LATVIJA 1941 1.JULIJS* possibly in anticipation of a new issue of Latvian notes in 1941. Notes thus overprint. included 5 Lati 1940 (#34), 10 Latu 1937 (#29), 20 Latu 1935 (#27), 100 Latu 1939, 2 var. of overprint. (#22), and 500 Latu 1929 (#19). They were never issued; instead, the German occupation forces issued Reichskreditkassen notes.

The Republic of Lebanon, situated on the eastern shore of the Mediterranean Sea between Syria and Israel, has an area of 4,015 sq. mi. (10,400 sq. km.) and a population of 3.29 million. Capital: Beirut. The economy is based on agriculture, trade and tourism. Fruit, other foodstuffs and textiles are exported. Following the capture of Syria from the Ottoman Empire by Anglo-French forces in 1918, France received a mandate over this territory and separated out the region of Lebanon in 1920. France granted this area independence in 1943. A lengthy civil war (1975-1990) devastated the country, but Lebanon has since made progress toward rebuilding its political institutions. Under the Ta'if Accord - the blueprint for national reconciliation - the Lebanese established a more equitable political system, particularly by giving Muslims a greater voice in the political process while institutionalizing sectarian divisions in the government. Since the end of the war, Lebanon has conducted several successful elections. Most militias have been disbanded, and the Lebanese Armed Forces (LAF) have extended authority over about two-thirds of the country. Hizballah, a radical Shia organization listed by the US State Department as a Foreign Terrorist Organization, retains its weapons. During Lebanon's civil war, the Arab League legitimized in the Ta'if Accord Syria's troop deployment, numbering about 16,000 based mainly east of Beirut and in the Bekaa Valley. Israel's withdrawal from southern Lebanon in May 2000 and the passage in October 2004 of UNSCR 1559 - a resolution calling for Syria to withdraw from Lebanon and end its interference in Lebanese affairs - encouraged some Lebanese groups to demand that Syria withdraw its forces as well. The assassination of former Prime Minister Rafiq Hariri and 22 others in February 2005 led to massive demonstrations in Beirut against the Syrian presence ("the Cedar Revolution"), and Syria withdrew the remainder of its military forces in April 2005. In May-June 2005, Lebanon held its first legislative elections since the end of the civil war free of foreign interference, handing a majority to the bloc led by Saad HARIRI, the slain prime minister's son. Lebanon continues to be plagued by violence - Hizballah kidnapped two Israeli soldiers in July 2006 leading to a 34-day conflict with Israel. The LAF in May-September 2007 battled Sunni extremist group Fatah al-Islam in the Nahr al-Barid Palestinian refugee camp; and the country has witnessed a string of politically motivated assassinations since the death of Rafiq Hariri. Lebanese politicians in November 2007 were unable to agree on a successor to Emile Lahud when he stepped down as president, creating a political vacuum until the election of Army Commander Michel Sulaymanin May 2008 and the formation of a new unity government in July 2008.

RULERS

French to 1943

MONETARY SYSTEM

1 Livre (Pound) = 100 Piastres

OVERPRINT VARIETIES

/	//	V	VV	◇
Type A	Type B	Type C	Type D	Type E

FRENCH ADMINISTRATION

Banque de Syrie et du Grand-Liban

1925 Issue

#1-8 *GRAND-LIBAN* heading on notes similar to some Syrian issues.

#	Denomination	Good	Fine	XF
1	**25 Piastres** 15.4.1925. Multicolor. Similar to Syria #21. Back: Water wheel and mill.	50.00	300	950
2	**50 Piastres** 15.4.1925. Multicolor. Similar to Syria #22.	100	500	—
3	**1 Livre** 15.4.1925. Multicolor.	200	800	—
4	**5 Livres** Blue, orange and multicolor.	250	1,000	—
5	**10 Livres** 15.4.1925. Multicolor.	—	—	—
6	**25 Livres** 15.4.1925. Multicolor.	—	—	—

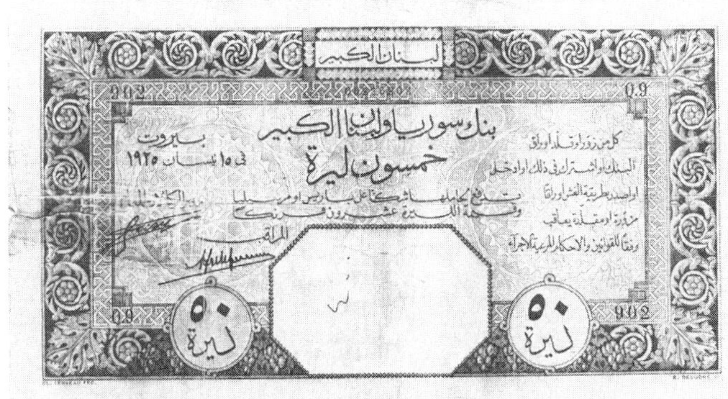

		Good	Fine	XF
7	**50 Livres** 15.4.1925. Multicolor. Back: Buildings across center.	—	—	—
8	**100 Livres** 15.4.1925. Multicolor.	—	—	—

1930 Issue

#8A-11 *GRAND-LIBAN* heading on notes similar to some Syrian issues.

		Good	Fine	XF
8A	**1 Livre** 1.11.1930. Multicolor. Similar to Syria #29A.	—	—	—

		Good	Fine	XF
9	**5 Livres** 1.11.1930. Multicolor. Similar to Syria #30. Back: Hillside fortress.	250	1,250	—
10	**10 Livres** 1.11.1930. Multicolor. Similar to Syria #31. Back: Ornate ruins at left center.	—	—	—
11	**25 Livres** 1.11.1930. Multicolor. Similar to Syria #32.	—	—	—

1935 Issue

		Good	Fine	XF
12	**1 Livre** 1.2.1935. Multicolor. Similar to Syria #34. Back: Harbor and mountain landscape across left and center panels.	50.00	250	700

		Good	Fine	XF
12A	**5 Livres** 1.2.1935. Multicolor. Similar to Syria #36. Back: Building across center, *LIBAN* at upper center.	125	850	—
12F	**100 Livres** 1.2.1935. Violet overprint. Type A. Printer: BWC.	—	—	—

1939 Provisional Issue

		Good	Fine	XF
A13	**1 Livre** 1939 (- old date 1935). *LIBAN 1939* on various earlier Lebanese and Syrian notes. Back: *SYRIE* at upper center. Overprint: *LIBAN 1939* on face of #12.			
	a. Overprint at upper center.	40.00	225	650
	b. Overprint at lower center.	40.00	225	650
13	**5 Livres** 1939 (- old date 1935). *LIBAN 1939* on various earlier Lebanese and Syrian notes. Back: *SYRIE* at upper center. Overprint: Across upper center on face of Syria #36.	75.00	325	—

		Good	Fine	XF
13A	**5 Livres** 1939 (- old date 1935). *LIBAN 1939* on various earlier Lebanese and Syrian notes. Back: *SYRIE* at upper center. Overprint: *LIBAN 1939* across lower center on Lebanon #12A.	100	450	—
13B	**10 Livres** 1939 (- old date 1930). *LIBAN 1939* on various earlier Lebanese and Syrian notes. Back: *SYRIE* at upper center. Overprint: *LIBAN 1939* at upper center on Lebanon #10.	225	1,000	—

		Good	Fine	XF
13C	**25 Livres** 1939 (- old date 1.2.1935). Multicolor. *LIBAN 1939* on various earlier Lebanese and Syrian notes. Back: Ornamented flower pattern at left and right. Bridge and buildings at center. Overprint: *LIBAN 1939* at upper center.	—	—	—
13D	**50 Livres** 1939 (- old date 1938). *LIBAN 1939* on various earlier Lebanese and Syrian notes. Back: *SYRIE* at upper center. Overprint: *LIBAN 1939* at upper center on Syria #39.	—	—	—
14	**100 Livres** 1939 (- old date 1935). *LIBAN 1939* on various earlier Lebanese and Syrian notes. Overprint: *LIBAN 1939* on Lebanon #12F.			
	a. Green overprint. Type A.	—	—	—
	b. Orange overprint. Type B.	—	—	—
	c. Lilac overprint. Type C.	—	—	—

Banque de Syrie et du Liban

1939 First Issue

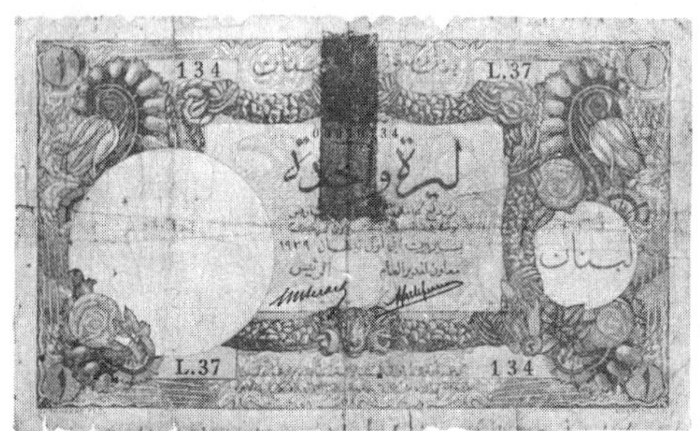

		Good	Fine	XF
15	**1 Livre** 1.9.1939. Blue and multicolor. Back: View of of Cyprus tree.	17.50	110	350
16	**5 Livres** 1.9.1939. Type C1. Serveau. Back: City views.	45.00	325	1,100
17	**10 Livres** 1.9.1939. Type C1. Back: Serveau with *Livres*, building.	—	—	—
18	**25 Livres** 1.9.1939. Type Seb. Laurent with *Livres*, columns.	—	—	—
19	**50 Livres** 1.9.1939. Type Seb. Laurent with *Livres*. City scene at center.	—	—	—

#20 not assigned.

		Good	Fine	XF
21	**250 Livres** 1.9.1939. Multicolor. Well with dome.	—	—	—

1939 Second Issue

#22-24 like #17-19 but with *Livres Libanaises*. 25 *Deleted*. See #21.

		Good	Fine	XF
22	**10 Livres** 1.9.1939. Type C1. Serveau with *Livres Libanaises*. Back: Building.	—	—	—
23	**25 Livres** 1.9.1939. Type Seb. Laurent with *Livres Libanaises*. Columns.	—	—	—
24	**50 Livres** 1.9.1939. Type Seb. Laurent with *Livres Libanaises*. City scene at center.	—	—	—

OVERPRINT VARIETIES

/	//	∨	⩔	◇
Type A	Type B	Type C	Type D	Type E

1939 Provisional Issue

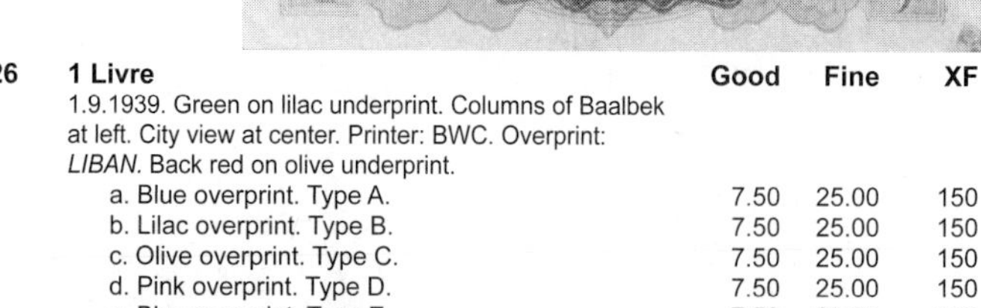

		Good	Fine	XF
26	**1 Livre** 1.9.1939. Green on lilac underprint. Columns of Baalbek at left. City view at center. Printer: BWC. Overprint: *LIBAN*. Back red on olive underprint.			
	a. Blue overprint. Type A.	7.50	25.00	150
	b. Lilac overprint. Type B.	7.50	25.00	150
	c. Olive overprint. Type C.	7.50	25.00	150
	d. Pink overprint. Type D.	7.50	25.00	150
	e. Blue overprint. Type E.	7.50	25.00	150

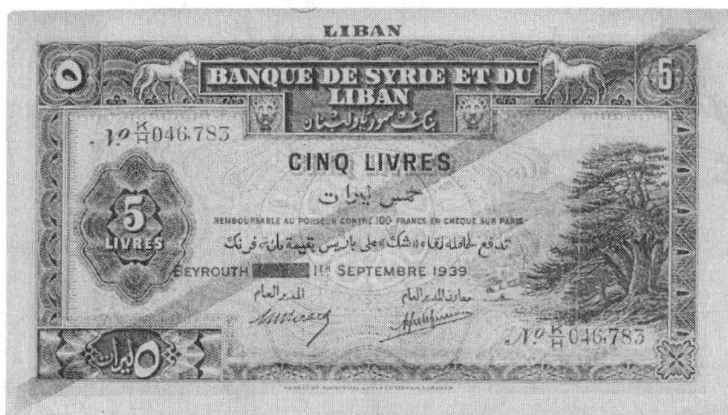

		Good	Fine	XF
27	**5 Livres** 1.9.1939. Brown. Cedar tree at right. Printer: BWC. Overprint: *LIBAN*.			
	a. Violet overprint. Type A.	22.50	110	350
	b. Pink overprint. Type B.	22.50	110	350
	c. Green overprint. Type C.	22.50	110	350
	d. Blue overprint. Type E.	22.50	110	350

Note: Notes w/*BEYROUTH* overprint on *DAMAS* are forgeries. In 1947, new Syrian notes were introduced and all former issues of Syria were cancelled whereas Lebanese notes remained valid (and were redeemable for many years afterwards); therefore, some attempts were made to "change" Syrian notes into Lebanese issues. These series, however, are different for the 2 countries and allow easy identification.

		Good	Fine	XF
28	**10 Livres** 1.9.1939. Brown-violet. Clock tower at left. Like Syria #42. Overprint: *LIBAN*.			
	a. Pink overprint. Type A.	50.00	250	650
	b. Green overprint. Type B.	50.00	250	650
	c. Blue overprint. Type C.	50.00	250	650
29	**25 Livres** 1.9.1939. Purple. Caravan at lower center. Like Syria #43. Overprint: *LIBAN*.			
	a. Blue-gray overprint. Type A.	75.00	375	1,000
	b. Orange overprint. Type C.	75.00	375	1,000

		Good	Fine	XF
30	**50 Livres** 1.9.1939. Brown and multicolor. Like Syria #44. Overprint: *LIBAN.*			
	a. Brown overprint. Type A.	150	750	—
	b. Olive overprint. Type E.	150	750	—

1942 Issue

		Good	Fine	XF
31	**5 Livres** 1.8.1942. Dark brown. Overprint: *BEYROUTH* on Syria #46.	75.00	350	1,000
32	**50 Livres** 1.8.1942. Dark brown. Overprint: *BEYROUTH* on Syria #47.	—	—	—
33	**100 Livres** 1.8.1942. Blue. Overprint: *BEYROUTH* on Syria #48.	—	—	—

RÉPUBLIQUE LIBANAISE

Government Banknotes

1942 Issue

		VG	VF	UNC
34	**5 Piastres** 15.7.1942. Purple and green. Cedar tree at left. Back: Dark blue.	1.50	10.00	35.00
35	**10 Piastres** 31.7.1942. Dark blue on light green. Back: Three Arabs sitting near coastline.	2.00	15.00	45.00

		VG	VF	UNC
36	**25 Piastres** 1.8.1942. Lilac and tan. Omayyad Mosque in Damascus at center. Back: Blue and light orange. Printer: BWC.	5.00	25.00	90.00

		VG	VF	UNC
37	**50 Piastres** 1.8.1942. Green and lilac. Trees at top center, mosque with two minarets at right. Printer: BWC.	10.00	30.00	100

1944 Issue

		VG	VF	UNC
38	**5 Piastres** 15.2.1944. Purple and green. Cedar tree at left. Back: Dark blue.	1.00	8.00	30.00

		VG	VF	UNC
39	**10 Piastres** 15.2.1944. Dark blue on light green underprint. Back: Three Araba sitting near coastline. BC: Brown.	2.00	15.00	45.00

1948 Issue

		VG	VF	UNC
40	**5 Piastres** 12.1.1948. Blue and yellow. Cedar tree at left. BC: Green.	1.00	3.50	25.00

		VG	VF	UNC
41	**10 Piastres** 12.1.1948. Lilac-brown on light blue underprint. Back: Three Arabs sitting near coastline. BC: Blue.	1.50	12.50	40.00

		VG	VF	UNC
42	**25 Piastres** 12.1.1948; 6.11.1950. Violet on green and orange underprint. Cedar tree at right. Back: Lion at center.	3.50	20.00	60.00

		VG	VF	UNC
43	**50 Piastres** 12.1.1948; 6.11.1950. Green on multicolor underprint. Columns of Baalbek at center. Back: Ruins.	10.00	30.00	100

1950 Issue

		VG	VF	UNC
46	**5 Piastres** 21.11.1950. Brown on red-brown underprint. Back: Krak des Chevaliers.	2.00	15.00	45.00

		VG	VF	UNC
47	**10 Piastres** 21.11.1950. Blue-violet on lilac underprint. Back: Blue. Back: Palais Beit-ed-Din.	1.50	10.00	30.00

Banque de Syrie et du Liban

1945 Issue

		Good	Fine	XF
48	**1 Livre** 1.12.1945; 1.8.1950. Blue and multicolor. Back: View of Cyprus.			
	a. Issued note.	17.50	100	325
	s. Specimen. Stars as punch hole cancelled.	—	—	—

		Good	Fine	XF
49	**5 Livres** 1.12.1945; 1.8.1950. Blue, orange and multicolor. Type C1. Serveau. Back: City views.			
	a. Issued note.	45.00	325	850
	s. Specimen. Stars as punch hole cancelled.	—	—	—

		Good	Fine	XF
50	**10 Livres** 1.12.1945; 1.8.1950. Multicolor. Type C1. Serveau with *Livres*. Back: Buildings on back.			
	a. Issued note.	60.00	500	—
	s. Specimen. Perforated.	—	—	—

		Good	Fine	XF
51	**25 Livres** 1.12.1945; 1.8.1950. Multicolor. Type "Seb. Laurent" with *Livres*. Columns.			
	a. Issued note.	90.00	475	1,150
	s. Specimen. Star punch hole cancelled.	—	—	—

52	50 Livres	Good	Fine	XF
	1.12.1945; 1.8.1950. Multicolor. Type "Seb. Laurent" with *Livres*. City scene at center.			
	a. Issued note.	100	400	1,000
	s. Specimen. Star punch hole cancelled.	—	—	—

53	100 Livres	Good	Fine	XF
	1.12.1945. Multicolor. Back: Cedar tree and mountain.	—	—	—

1952; 1956 Issue

55	1 Livre	VG	VF	UNC
	1.1.1952-1.1.1964. Crusader Castle at Saida (Sidon) at left. Signature varieties. Back: Columns of Baalbek. Printer: TDLR.			
	a. Without security strip.	2.00	10.00	60.00
	b. With security strip.	2.00	10.00	60.00
	s1. Specimen. Oval TDLR stamp, punch hole cancelled.	—	—	30.00
	s2. Specimen. Perforated: *SPECIMEN* and large double lined X inked on face.	—	—	150

56	5 Livres	VG	VF	UNC
	1.1.1952-1.1.1964. Blue on multicolor underprint. Courtyard of the Palais de Beit-ed-Din. Signature varieties. Back: Snowy mountains with trees. Printer: TDLR.			
	a. Without security strip.	5.00	45.00	160
	b. With security strip.	5.00	45.00	160
	s1. Specimen. Oval TDLR stamp, punch hole cancelled.	—	—	40.00
	s2. Specimen. Perforated: *SPECIMEN* and large double lined X inked on face.	—	—	250

57	10 Livres	VG	VF	UNC
	1.1.1956; 1.1.1961; 1.1.1963. Green on multicolor underprint. Ruins of Bacchus temple at Baalbek. Signature varieties. Back: Shoreline with city in hills. Printer: TDLR.			
	a. Issued note.	10.00	60.00	230
	s1. Speciemen. Oval TDLR stamp, punch hole cancelled.	—	—	100
	s2. Specimen. Perforated: *SPECIMEN* and large double lined X inked on face.	—	—	500

58	25 Livres	VG	VF	UNC
	1.1.1952; 1.1.1953. Blue-gray on multicolor underprint. Harbor town. Signature varieties. Back: Stone arch bridge at center right. Watermark: Lion's head. Printer: TDLR.			
	a. Issued note.	70.00	210	900
	s1. Specimen. Oval TDLR stamp, punch hole cancelled.	—	—	1,000
	s2. Specimen. Perforated: *SPECIMEN* and large double lined X inked on face.	—	—	1,250

		VG	VF	UNC
59	**50 Livres** 1.1.1952; 1.1.1953; 1.1.1964. Deep brown on multicolor underprint. Coast landscape. Signature varieties. Back: Large rock formations in water. Watermark: Lion's head. Printer: TDLR.			
	a. Issued note.	60.00	200	900
	s1. Specimen. Oval TDLR stamp, punch hole cancelled.	—	—	1,000
	s2. Specimen. Perforated: *SPECIMEN* and large double lined X inked on face.	—	—	1,250

		VG	VF	UNC
60	**100 Livres** 1.1.1952; 1.1.1953; 1.1.1958; 1.1.1963. Blue on multicolor underprint. View of Beirut and harbor. Signature varieties. Back: Cedar tree at center. Watermark: Cedar tree. Printer: TDLR.			
	a. Issued note.	25.00	50.00	250
	s1. Specimen. Oval TDLR stamp, punch hole cancelled.	—	—	1,000
	s2. Specimen. Perforated: *SPECIMEN* and large double lined X inked on face.	—	—	1,250

Leeward Islands is a geographical name, always distinguished from the Windward Islands. In English terminology, the term "Leeward Islands" applies to the northernmost Lesser Antilles, from the Virgin Islands to Guadeloupe, sometimes including Dominica. From 1871 to 1956, the British colonies of Antigua (with Barbuda and Redonda), St. Kitts-Nevis-Anguilla, Montserrat, and the British Virgin Islands were collectively administered as the Leeward Islands. See separate listings for the individual colonies; also see British East Caribbean Territories.

RULERS:
British

MONETARY SYSTEM:
1 Shilling = 12 Pence
1 Pound = 20 Shillings

BRITISH ADMINISTRATION

Government of the Leeward Islands

1921 Issue

		Good	Fine	XF
1	**5 Shillings** 1.1.1921. Red on gray underprint. Portrait King George V at top center. Back: Green. Back: Arms at center. Printer: TDLR. Rare.	—	—	—

		Good	Fine	XF
2	**10 Shillings** 1.1.1921. Green on blue underprint. Portrait King George V at top center. Back: Light brown. Back: Arms at center. Printer: TDLR. Rare.	—	—	—

Note: For later issues see East Caribbean States.

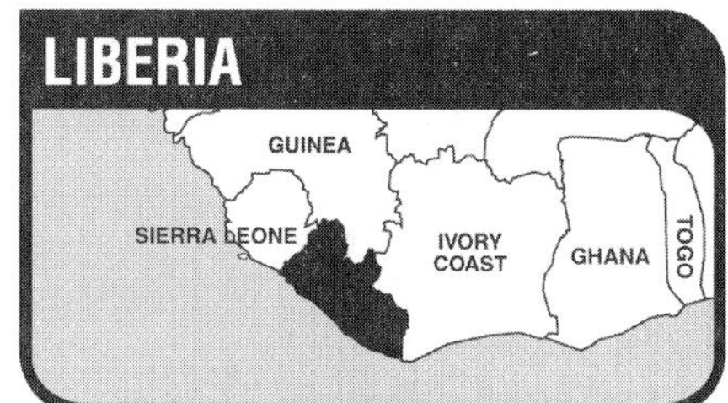

The Republic of Liberia, located on the southern side of the west African bulge between Sierra Leone and the Ivory Coast, has an area of 38,250 sq. mi. (111,369 sq. km.) and a population of 3.26 million. Capital: Monrovia. The major industries are agriculture, mining and lumbering. Iron ore, diamonds, rubber, coffee and cocoa are exported. Settlement of freed slaves from the US in what is today Liberia began in 1822; by 1847, the Americo-Liberians were able to establish a republic. William Tubman, president from 1944-1971, did much to promote foreign investment and to bridge the economic, social, and political gaps between the descendents of the original settlers and the inhabitants of the interior. In 1980, a military coup led by Samuel Doe ushered in a decade of authoritarian rule. In December 1989, Charles Taylor launched a rebellion against Doe's regime that led to a prolonged civil war in which Doe himself was killed. A period of relative peace in 1997 allowed for elections that brought Taylor to power, but major fighting resumed in 2000. An August 2003 peace agreement ended the war and prompted the resignation of former president Charles Taylor, who faces war crimes charges in The Hague related to his involvement in Sierra Leone's civil war. After two years of rule by a transitional government, democratic elections in late 2005 brought President Ellen Johnson Sirleaf to power. The UN Mission in Liberia (UNMIL) maintains a strong presence throughout the country, but the security situation is still fragile and the process of rebuilding the social and economic structure of this war-torn country will take many years.

MONETARY SYSTEM:

1 Dollar = 100 Cents

REPLACEMENT NOTES:

#19, 20: ZZ prefix.

Note: Certain listings encompassing issues circulated by various bank and regional authorities are contained in Volume 1.

REPUBLIC

Treasury Department

1857-1862 Issue

#6-9 various partly handwritten dates. Black printing; notes with center shore with plow and palm tree with sailing ship in background at center. TYPE I: With text: *Pay to bearer in Gold or Silver coin.*

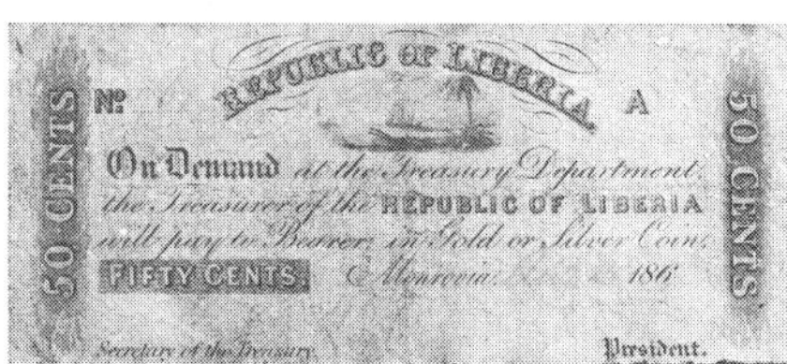

		Good	Fine	XF
6	**50 Cents** 1858-1866. Black type I: With text: *Pay to bearer in Gold or Silver coin.* Handstamped by Secretary of the Treasury and President.			
	a. 26.2.1858.	300	750	—
	b. *18__* in printing plate. 6.2.1862; 26.2.1862; 25.2.1863; 7.4.1863.	175	450	—
	c. *186_* in printing plate. 24.8.1863; 26.8.1863; 28.12.1863; 18.2.1864; 18.2.1866.	175	450	—

		Good	Fine	XF
7	**1 Dollar** 1857-1864. Black type I: With text: *Pay to bearer in Gold or Silver coin.* Handstamped by Secretary of the Treasury and President.			
	a. 25.4.1857.	300	800	—
	b. *18__* in printing plate. 26.2.1862; 26.7.1862; 21.8.1862; 26.2.1863.	200	500	—
	c. *186_* in printing plate. 7.8.1863; 24.8.1863; 28.12.1863; 18.2.1864.	200	500	—

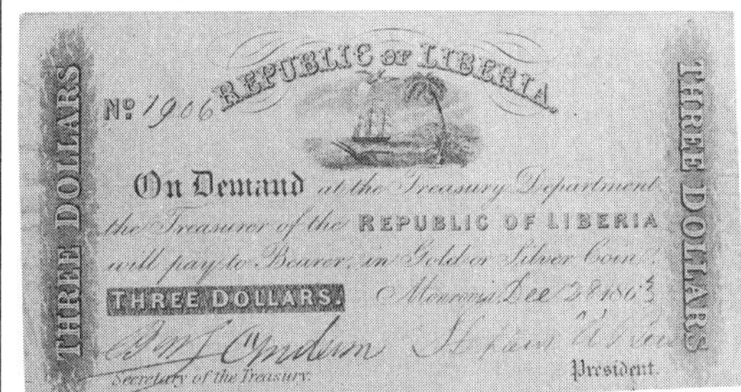

		Good	Fine	XF
8	**3 Dollars** 26.2.1862; 26.7.1862; 28.12.1863; 18.2.1864. Black type I: With text: *Pay to bearer in Gold or Silver coin.* Handstamped by Secretary of the Treasury and President.	250	550	—
9	**5 Dollars** 26.8.1858; 26.2.1862; 24.8.1863; 28.12.1863. Black type I: With text: *Pay to bearer in Gold or Silver coin.* Handstamped by Secretary of the Treasury and President.	275	600	—

Note: Sizes in both outer dimensions and printed areas may vary by as much as 8-10mm.

1876-1880 Issue

		Good	Fine	XF
10	**10 Cents** 26.8.1880. Black type II: Without specie payment clause. Handsigned by Treasurer and Secretary of the Treasury.	225	600	—
11	**50 Cents** 24.1.1876. Black type II: Without specie payment clause. Handsigned by Treasurer and Secretary of the Treasury. 141x63mm.	250	700	—
11A	**50 Cents** 26.8.1880. Black type II: Without specie payment clause. Handsigned by Treasurer and Secretary of the Treasury. 91x51mm.	250	700	—
12	**1 Dollar** 24.1.1876; 26.8.1880. Black type II: Without specie payment clause. Handsigned by Treasurer and Secretary of the Treasury.	250	700	—
13	**2 Dollars** 24.1.1876; 26.8.1880. Black type II: Without specie payment clause. Handsigned by Treasurer and Secretary of the Treasury.	300	750	—

		Good	Fine	XF
14	**3 Dollars** 26.8.1880. Black type II: Without specie payment clause. Handsigned by Treasurer and Secretary of the Treasury.	325	825	—
15	**5 Dollars** 24.1.1876; 1.3.1880; 26.8.1880. Black type II: Without specie payment clause. Handsigned by Treasurer and Secretary of the Treasury.	300	750	—

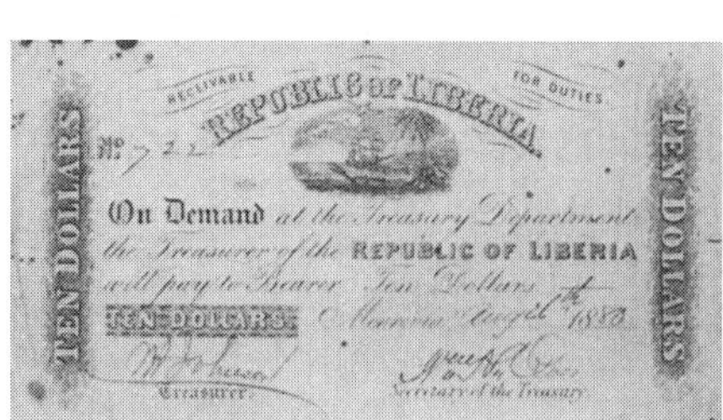

		Good	Fine	XF
16	**10 Dollars** 26.8.1880. Black type II: Without specie payment clause. Handsigned by Treasurer and Secretary of the Treasury.	375	1,000	—

Treasury Department Payment Certificates

MONROVIA

1880s Issue

		Good	Fine	XF
17	**Various Handwritten Denominations** Various handwritten dates.	50.00	125	275

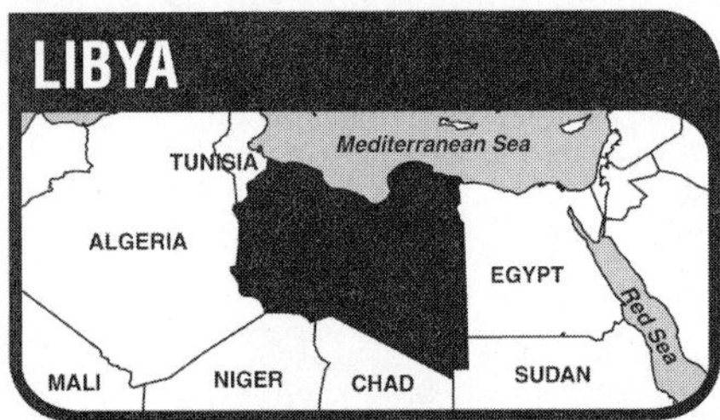

The Socialist People's Libyan Arab Jamahiriya, located on the north central coast of Africa between Tunisia and Egypt, has an area of 679,359 sq. mi. (1,759,540 sq. km.) and a population of 6.39 million. Capital: Tripoli. Crude oil, which accounts for 90 percent of the export earnings, is the mainstay of the economy. The Italians supplanted the Ottoman Turks in the area around Tripoli in 1911 and did not relinquish their hold until 1943 when defeated in World War II. Libya then passed to UN administration and achieved independence in 1951. Following a 1969 military coup, Col. Muammar Abu Minyar al-Qadhafi began to espouse his own political system, the Third Universal Theory. The system is a combination of socialism and Islam derived in part from tribal practices and is supposed to be implemented by the Libyan people themselves in a unique form of "direct democracy." Qadhafi has always seen himself as a revolutionary and visionary leader. He used oil funds during the 1970s and 1980s to promote his ideology outside Libya, supporting subversives and terrorists abroad to hasten the end of Marxism and capitalism. In addition, beginning in 1973, he engaged in military operations in northern Chad's Aozou Strip - to gain access to minerals and to use as a base of influence in Chadian politics - but was forced to retreat in 1987. UN sanctions in 1992 isolated Qadhafi politically following the downing of Pan AM Flight 103 over Lockerbie, Scotland. During the 1990s, Qadhafi began to rebuild his relationships with Europe. UN sanctions were suspended in April 1999 and finally lifted in September 2003 after Libya accepted responsibility for the Lockerbie bombing. In December 2003, Libya announced that it had agreed to reveal and end its programs to develop weapons of mass destruction and to renounce terrorism. Qadhafi has made significant strides in normalizing relations with Western nations since then. He has received various Western European leaders as well as many working-level and commercial delegations, and made his first trip to Western Europe in 15 years when he traveled to Brussels in April 2004. The US rescinded Libya's designation as a state sponsor of terrorism in June 2006. In January 2008, Libya assumed a nonpermanent seat on the United Nations Security Council for the 2008/09 term. In August 2008, the US and Libya signed a bilateral comprehensive claims settlement agreement to compensate claimants in both countries who allege injury or death at the hands of the other country, including the Lockerbie bombing, the LaBelle disco bombing, and the UTA 772 bombing. In October 2008, the US Government received $1.5 billion pursuant to the agreement to distribute to US national claimants, and as a result effectively normalized its bilateral relationship with Libya. The two countries then exchanged ambassadors for the first time since 1973 in January 2009.

RULERS:

Idris I, 1951-1969

MONETARY SYSTEM:

1 Piastre = 10 Milliemes
1 Pound = 100 Piastres = 1000 Milliemes, 1951-1971
1 Dinar = 1000 Dirhams, 1971-

UNITED KINGDOM

Treasury

Law of 24.10.1951

		VG	VF	UNC
5	**5 Piastres** *L.1951.* Red on light yellow underprint. Colonnade at left, palm tree at right.			
	a. Issued note.	1.00	15.00	45.00
	s. Specimen.	—	—	400

		VG	VF	UNC
6	**10 Piastres** *L.1951.* Green on light orange underprint. Ruins of gate at left, palm tree at right.			
	a. Issued note.	1.50	20.00	50.00
	s. Specimen.	—	—	400

7	**1/4 Pound** *L.1951.* Blue on light orange underprint. Ruins of columns at left, palm tree at right.	VG	VF	UNC
	a. Issued note.	6.00	120	250
	s. Specimen.	—	—	600
8	**1/2 Pound** *L.1951.* Purple on multicolor underprint. Arms at left. Denomination in large # at right over watermark area.	Good	Fine	XF
	a. Issued note.	700	1,500	2,500
	s. Specimen.	—	Unc	1,250
9	**1 Pound** *L.1951.* Blue on multicolor underprint. Arms at left. Denomination in large # at right over watermark area.	Good	Fine	XF
	a. Issued note.	250	550	1,000
	s. Specimen.	—	Unc	3,000
	ct. Color Trial.	—	Unc	4,500
10	**5 Pounds** *L.1951.* Green on multicolor underprint. Arms at left. Denomination in large # at right over watermark area.	Good	Fine	XF
	a. Issued note.	450	1,750	2,750
	s. Specimen.	—	Unc	4,000
	ct. Color Trial.	—	Unc	4,500
11	**10 Pounds** *L.1951.* Brown on multicolor underprint. Arms at left. Denomination in large # at right over watermark area.	Good	Fine	XF
	a. Issued note.	500	2,000	3,000
	s. Specimen.	—	Unc	4,000
	ct. Color Trial.	—	Unc	4,500

KINGDOM

Treasury

1952 Issue

		VG	VF	UNC
12	**5 Piastres** 1.1.1952. Red on light yellow underprint. Portrait King Idris at left, palm tree at right.			
	a. Issued note.	1.50	40.00	100
	s. Specimen.	—	—	800

		VG	VF	UNC
13	**10 Piastres** 1.1.1952. Green. Portrait King Idris at left, palm tree at right.			
	a. Issued note.	2.50	60.00	140
	s. Specimen.	—	—	800

No.	Description	VG	VF	UNC
14	**1/4 Pound**	**VG**	**VF**	**UNC**
	1.1.1952. Orange. Portrait King Idris at left, palm tree at right.			
	a. Issued note.	7.50	200	600
	s. Specimen.	—	—	1,800
	ct. Color Trial.	—	—	2,000
15	**1/2 Pound**	**VG**	**VF**	**UNC**
	1.1.1952. Purple. Portrait King Idris at left, bush at lower center.			
	a. Issued note.	8.00	40.00	150
	s. Specimen. Red overprint in Arabic.	—	—	500
	ct. Color Trial.	—	—	2,000
16	**1 Pound**	**Good**	**Fine**	**XF**
	1.1.1952. Blue. Portrait King Idris at left, bush at lower center.	—	Unc	2,500
	1.1.1952. Blue. Portrait King Idris at left, bush at lower center.			
	a. Issued note.	—	250	800
	s. Specimen. Red overprint in Arabic.	—	Unc	1,000
17	**5 Pounds**	**Good**	**Fine**	**XF**
	1.1.1952. Green. Portrait King Idris at left, bush at lower center.			
	a. Issued note.	1,000	2,000	5,000
	s. Specimen.	—	Unc	8,000
	ct. Color Trial.	—	Unc	9,000
18	**10 Pounds**	**Good**	**Fine**	**XF**
	1.1.1952. Brown. Portrait King Idris at left, bush at lower center.			
	a. Issued note.	800	2,000	5,000
	s. Specimen.	—	Unc	8,000
	ct. Color Trial.	—	Unc	9,000

National Bank of Libya

Law of 26.4.1955

1958-1959 Issue

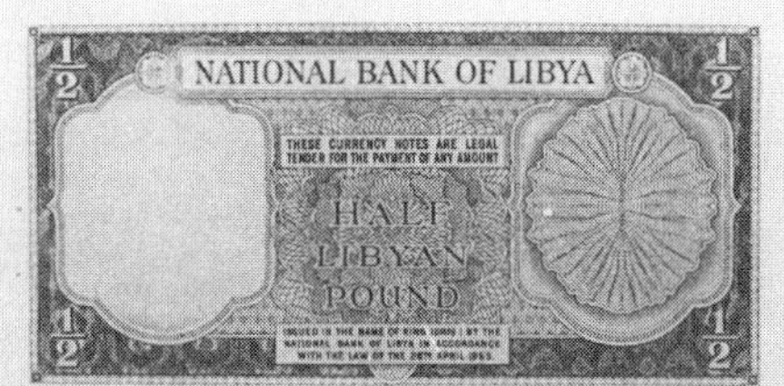

No.	Description	Good	Fine	XF
19	**1/2 Pound**	**Good**	**Fine**	**XF**
	L.1955 (1959). Purple. Arms at left. 2 Signature varieties.			
	a. Black serial #	20.00	75.00	150
	b. Red serial #.	15.00	50.00	100
	s. Specimen.	—	Unc	1,500
	ct. Color Trial.	—	Unc	1,500

No.	Description	Good	Fine	XF
20	**1 Pound**	**Good**	**Fine**	**XF**
	L.1955 (1959). Blue. Arms at left. 2 Signature varieties.			
	a. Issued note.	10.00	50.00	400
	s. Specimen.	—	Unc	1,700
	ct. Color Trial	—	Unc	1,900
21	**5 Pounds**	**Good**	**Fine**	**XF**
	L.1955 (1958). Green. Arms at left. 2 Signature varieties.			
	a. Issued note.	100	350	1,000
	s. Specimen.	—	Unc	4,000
	ct. Color Trial.	—	Unc	4,200
22	**10 Pounds**	**Good**	**Fine**	**XF**
	L.1955 (1958). Brown. Arms at left. 2 Signature varieties.			
	a. Issued note.	100	450	2,000
	s. Specimen.	—	Unc	5,200
	ct. Color Trial.	—	Unc	5,500

Note: For similar notes issued by the Bank of Libya, see Volume 3 listings.

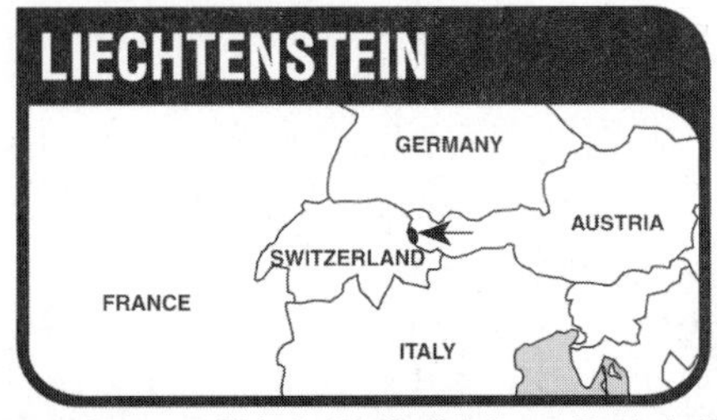

The Principality of Liechtenstein, located in central Europe on the east bank of the Rhine between Austria and Switzerland, has an area of 62 sq. mi. (157 sq. km.) and a population of 33,000. Capital: Vaduz. The ecomomy is based on agriculture and light manufacturing. Canned goods, textiles, ceramics and precision instruments are exported. The Principality of Liechtenstein was established within the Holy Roman Empire in 1719. Occupied by both French and Russian troops during the Napoleanic wars, it became a sovereign state in 1806 and joined the Germanic Confederation in 1815. Liechtenstein became fully independent in 1866 when the Confederation dissolved. Until the end of World War I, it was closely tied to Austria, but the economic devastation caused by that conflict forced Liechtenstein to enter into a customs and monetary union with Switzerland. Since World War II (in which Liechtenstein remained neutral), the country's low taxes have spurred outstanding economic growth. In 2000, shortcomings in banking regulatory oversight resulted in concerns about the use of financial institutions for money laundering. However, Liechtenstein implemented anti-money-laundering legislation and a Mutual Legal Assistance Treaty with the US went into effect in 2003.

RULERS:

Prince John II, 1858-1929
Prince Franz I, 1929-1938
Prince Franz Josef II, 1938-1989
Prince Hans Adam II, 1989-

MONETARY SYSTEM:

1 Krone = 100 Heller to 1924
1 Frank = 100 Rappen, 1924-

PRINCIPALITY

Furstentum Liechtenstein Gutscheine

Duchy of Leichtenstein Credit Notes

1920 Issue

#	Denomination	VF	UNC
1	**10 Heller** ND (1920). Red and blue. Arms at left. Back: Villa.	20.00	40.00

#	Denomination	VF	UNC
2	**20 Heller** ND (1920). Red and blue. Back: Castle at Vaduz.	20.00	40.00

#	Denomination	VF	UNC
3	**50 Heller** ND (1920). Red and blue. Arms in underprint at center. Back: Landscape.	20.00	40.00

The Republic of Lithuania southernmost of the Baltic states in east Europe, has an area of 26,173 sq. mi. (65,301 sq. km.) and a population of 3.69 million. Capital: Vilnius. The economy is based on livestock raising and manufacturing. Hogs, cattle, hides and electric motors are exported. Lithuanian lands were united under Mlinfaugas in 1236; over the next century, through alliances and conquest, Lithuania extended its territory to include most of present-day Belarus and Ukraine. By the end of the 14th century Lithuania was the largest state in Europe. An alliance with Poland in 1386 led the two countries into a union through the person of a common ruler. In 1569, Lithuania and Poland formally united into a single dual state, the Polish-Lithuanian Commonwealth. This entity survived until 1795, when its remnants were partitioned by surrounding countries. Lithuania regained its independence following World War I but was annexed by the USSR in 1940 - an action never recognized by the US and many other countries. On 11 March 1990, Lithuania became the first of the Soviet republics to declare its independence, but Moscow did not recognize this proclamation until September of 1991 (following the abortive coup in Moscow). The last Russian troops withdrew in 1993. Lithuania subsequently restructured its economy for integration into Western European institutions; it joined both NATO and the EU in the spring of 2004.

MONETARY SYSTEM:

1 Litas = 100 Centu

REPUBLIC

Lietuvos Ukio Bankas

1919 Issue

#A1-A4 circulating checks *Sio cekio pao...*

#	Denomination	VG	VF	UNC
A1	**50 Ost. Markiu** ND (1919-20). Rare.	—	—	—
A2	**100 Ost. Markiu** ND (1919-20). Black and gold. Rare.	—	—	—
A3	**500 Ost. Markiu** ND (1919-20). Black. Rare.	—	—	—

#	Denomination	VG	VF	UNC
A4	**1000 Ost. Markiu** ND (1919-20). Back: Multicolor. Rare.	—	—	—

Lietuvos Bankas

Bank of Lithuania

1922 September Issue

#	Denomination	VG	VF	UNC
1	**1 Centas** 10.9.1922. Blue. Back: Knight on horseback at center. Printer: Otto Elsner, Berlin.			
	a. Issued note.	30.00	60.00	140
	s1. Specimen perforated: *PAVYZDYS.*	—	—	75.00
	s2. Specimen overprint: *Ungiltig als Banknote!...* Rare.	—	—	—

#	Denomination	VG	VF	UNC
2	**5 Centai** 10.9.1922. Green. Back: Knight on horseback at center. Printer: Otto Elsner, Berlin.			
	a. Issued note.	30.00	70.00	150
	s1. Specimen perforated: *PAVYZDYS.*	—	—	75.00
	s2. Specimen overprint: *Ungiltig als Banknote!...* Rare.	—	—	—

3	20 Centu	VG	VF	UNC
	10.9.1922. Red-brown. Back: Knight on horseback at center. Printer: Otto Elsner, Berlin.			
	a. Issued note.	50.00	100	200
	s1. Specimen perforated: *PAVYZDYS.*	—	—	125
	s2. Specimen overprint: *Ungiltig als Banknote!...* Rare.	—	—	—

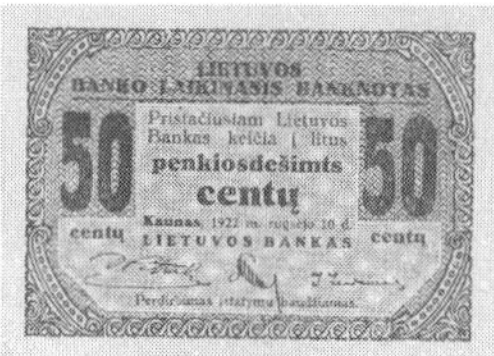

4	50 Centu	VG	VF	UNC
	10.9.1922. Purple. Back: Knight on horseback at center. Printer: Otto Elsner, Berlin.			
	a. Issued note.	60.00	120	270
	s1. Specimen perforated: *PAVYZDYS.*	—	—	135
	s2. Specimen overprint: *Ungiltig als Banknote!...* Rare.	—	—	—

5	1 Litas	VG	VF	UNC
	10.9.1922. Gray. Back: Knight on horseback at center. Printer: Otto Elsner, Berlin.			
	a. Watermark: Strands.	120	250	470
	b. Watermark: Loop.	120	200	430
	s1. Specimen perforated: *PAVYZDYS.*	—	—	265
	s2. Specimen overprint: *Ungiltig als Banknote!* Rare.	—	—	—

6	5 Litai	VG	VF	UNC
	10.9.1922. Dark brown. Back: Knight on horseback at center. Printer: Otto Elsner, Berlin.			
	a. Issued note.	150	400	600
	s1. Specimen perforated: *PAVYZDYS.*	—	—	500
	s2. Specimen overprint: *Ungiltig als Banknote!* Rare.	—	—	—

1922 November Issue

7	1 Centas	VG	VF	UNC
	16.11.1922. Blue and burgundy-red. Back: Green and dark red. Printer: Andreas Haase, Prague.			
	a. Issued note.	15.00	30.00	70.00
	s1. Specimen perforated: *PAVYZDYS.*	—	—	70.00
	s2. Specimen overprint: *VALEUR NON VALABLE! ECHANTILLON!*	—	—	70.00
	s3. Specimen overprint: *Pavyzdys-bevertis.*	—	—	70.00

8	2 Centu	VG	VF	UNC
	16.11.1922. Dark green on gray-violet. Back: Light and dark brown. Printer: Andreas Haase, Prague.			
	a. Issued note.	30.00	50.00	90.00
	s1. Specimen perforated: *PAVYZDYS.*	—	—	90.00
	s2. Specimen overprint: *VALEUR NON VALABLE! ECHANTILLON!*	—	—	90.00
	s3. Specimen overprint: *Pavyzdys-bevertis.*	—	—	90.00

9	5 Centai	VG	VF	UNC
	16.11.1922. Blue on green. Back: Brown and purple. Printer: Andreas Haase, Prague.			
	a. Issued note.	30.00	60.00	100
	s1. Specimen perforated: *PAVYZDYS.*	—	—	80.00
	s2. Specimen overprint: *VALEUR NON VALABLE! ECHANTILLON!*	—	—	80.00
	s3. Specimen overprint: *Pavyzdys-bevertis.*	—	—	80.00

10	10 Centu	VG	VF	UNC
	16.11.1922. Red-brown on gray-violet. Back: Red on brown. Printer: Andreas Haase, Prague.			
	a. Issued note.	30.00	50.00	100
	s1. Specimen perforated: *PAVYZDYS.*	—	—	90.00
	s2. Specimen overprint: *VALEUR NON VALABLE! ECHANTILLON!*	—	—	90.00
	s3. Specimen overprint: *Pavyzdys-bevertis.*	—	—	90.00

11	20 Centu	VG	VF	UNC
	16.11.1922. Dark blue on gray. Back: Dark and light brown. Printer: Andreas Haase, Prague.			
	a. Issued note.	40.00	80.00	150
	s1. Specimen perforated: *PAVYZDYS.*	—	—	110
	s2. Specimen overprint: *VALEUR NON VALABLE! ECHANTILLON!*	—	—	110
	s3. Specimen overprint: *Pavyzdys-bevertis.*	—	—	110

12	50 Centu	VG	VF	UNC
	16.11.1922. Purple and green. Back: Dark green and brown. Printer: Andreas Haase, Prague.			
	a. Issued note.	60.00	100	200
	s1. Specimen perforated: *PAVYZDYS.*	—	—	200
	s2. Specimen overprint: *VALEUR NON VALABLE! ECHANTILLON!*	—	—	200
	s3. Specimen overprint: *Pavyzdys-bevertis.*	—	—	200

13	**1 Litas**	VG	VF	UNC
	16.11.1922. Red-brown on gray. Back: Red and purple on tan. Printer: Andreas Haase, Prague.			
	a. Issued note.	100	220	400
	s1. Specimen perforated: *PAVYZDYS.*	—	—	300
	s2. Specimen overprint: *VALEUR NON VALABLE! ECHANTILLON!*	—	—	300
	s3. Specimen overprint: *Pavyzdys-bevertis.*	—	—	300

14	**2 Litu**	VG	VF	UNC
	16.11.1922. Blue on gray. Back: Dark blue and purple. Printer: Andreas Haase, Prague.			
	a. Issued note.	200	350	600
	s1. Specimen perforated: *PAVYZDYS.*	—	—	250
	s2. Specimen overprint: *VALEUR NON VALABLE! ECHANTILLON!*	—	—	250
	s3. Specimen overprint: *Pavyzdys-bevertis.*	—	—	250

15	**5 Litai**	VG	VF	UNC
	16.11.1922. Purple and blue. Farmer sowing at center. Black serial # at lower center. Back: Woman at right. Printer: Andreas Haase, Prague. BC: Green and brown.			
	a. Issued note.	250	500	1,000
	s1. Specimen perforated: *PAVYZDYS.*	—	—	600
	s2. Specimen overprint: *VALEUR NON VALABLE! ECHANTILLON!*	—	—	600
	s3. Specimen overprint: *Pavyzdys-bevertis.*	—	—	600

16	**5 Litai**	VG	VF	UNC
	16.11.1922. Olive-green, blue and black. Farmer sowing at center. Red serial # at upper right. Similar to #15 but ornamentation slightly changed. Back: Woman at right. Printer: Andreas Haase, Prague.			
	a. Issued note.	250	500	900
	s1. Specimen perforated: *PAVYZDYS.*	—	—	600
	s2. Specimen overprint: *VALEUR NON VALABLE! ECHANTILLON!*	—	—	600
	s3. Specimen overprint: *Pavyzdys-bevertis.*	—	—	600

17	**5 Litai**	VG	VF	UNC
	16.11.1922. Red-brown and dark gray. Farmer sowing at center. Green serial #. Back: Like #16, but ornamentation is changed. Printer: Andreas Haase, Prague.			
	a. Issued note.	250	500	1,000
	s1. Specimen perforated: *PAVYZDYS.*	—	—	425
	s2. Specimen overprint: *VALEUR NON VALABLE! ECHANTILLON!*	—	—	425
	s3. Specimen overprint: *Pavyzdys-bevertis.*	—	—	425

18	**10 Litu**	VG	VF	UNC
	16.11.1922. Blue, purple and brown. Raftsman at right. Back: Woman at left and right. Printer: Andreas Haase, Prague.			
	a. Issued note.	350	600	1,200
	s1. Specimen perforated: *PAVYZDYS.*	—	—	700
	s2. Specimen overprint: *VALEUR NON VALABLE! ECHANTILLON!*	—	—	700
	s3. Specimen overprint: *Pavyzdys-bevertis.*	—	—	700

19	**50 Litu**	VG	VF	UNC
	16.11.1922. Dark green and brown. City arms of Kaunas, Vilnius and Klaipeda from left to center, Lithuanian Grand Duke Gediminas at right. Back: Building behind ornamented gate. Printer: Andreas Haase, Prague.			
	a. Issued note.	500	900	1,500
	s1. Specimen perforated: *PAVYZDYS.*	—	—	1,000
	s2. Specimen overprint: *VALEUR NON VALABLE! ECHANTILLON!*	—	—	1,000
	s3. Specimen overprint: *Pavyzdys-bevertis.*	—	—	1,000

		VG	VF	UNC
20	**100 Litu** 16.11.1922. Blue and purple. Arms at left; Vytautas the Great at right. Printer: Andreas Haase, Prague.			
	a. Issued note.	500	1,000	2,000
	s1. Specimen perforated: *PAVYZDYS.*	—	—	1,100
	s2. Specimen overprint: *VALEUR NON VALABLE! ECHANTILLON!*	—	—	1,100
	s3. Specimen overprint: *Pavyzdys-bevertis.*	—	—	1,100

		VG	VF	UNC
20A	**500 Litu** 10.8.1924. Brown. Lithuanian emblem. Printer: Andreas Haase, Prague. (Not issued). Rare.	—	—	—

		VG	VF	UNC
20B	**1000 Litu** 10.8.1924. Blue and orange. Similar to #A21. Back: Map at left, snakes in limbs. Printer: Andreas Haase, Prague. (Not issued). Rare.	—	—	—

December 11, 1924 Issue

		VG	VF	UNC
21	**500 Litu** 11.12.1924. Dark brown. Back: Blue. Printer: BWC.			
	a. Issued note.	500	900	1,800
	s1. Specimen perforated: *PAVYZDYS.*	—	—	1,000
	s2. Specimen overprint: *PAVYZDYS.*	—	—	1,000

		VG	VF	UNC
22	**1000 Litu** 11.12.1924. Green. Arms at center. Back: Girl in Lithuanian national costume at left, seated youth at right. Printer: BWC.			
	a. Issued note.	1,200	2,300	3,800
	s1. Specimen perforated: *PAVYZDYS.*	—	—	1,500
	s2. Specimen overprint: *PAVYZDYS*	—	—	1,500

1927-1928 Issue

		VG	VF	UNC
23	**10 Litu** 24.11.1927. Green. Back: Farmers tilling the fields.			
	a. Issued note.	70.00	150	200
	s1. Specimen perforated: *PAVYZDYS.*	—	—	150
	s2. Specimen overprint: *PAVYZDYS.*	—	—	150

24 **50 Litu**

	VG	VF	UNC
31.3.1928. Dark blue. Dr. Jonas Basanavicius at left. Back: Ornate building.			
a. Issued note.	70.00	140	250
s1. Specimen perforated: *PAVYZDYS.*	—	—	150
s2. Specimen perforated. Cancelled and overprint: *PAVYZDYS.*	—	—	150

25 **100 Litu**

	VG	VF	UNC
31.3.1928. Dark purple. Seated woman at left, boy with staff of Mercury at right. Back: Building.			
a. Issued note.	70.00	140	250
s1. Specimen perforated: *PAVYZDYS.*	—	—	150
s2. Specimen overprint: *PAVYZDYS.*	—	—	150

1929-1930 Commemorative Issue

#26 and 27, 500th Anniversary Vytautas the Great.

26 **5 Litai**

	VG	VF	UNC
24.6.1929. Brown. Grand Duke Vytautas the Great at left. Back: Medieval warriors on horseback. Printer: BWC. 500th Anniversary Vytautas the Great.			
a. Issued note.	80.00	150	300
s1. Specimen perforated: *PAVYZDYS.*	—	—	200
s2. Specimen overprint: *PAVYZDYS.*	—	—	200

27 **20 Litu**

	VG	VF	UNC
5.7.1930. Brown on green and blue underprint. Grand Duke Vytautas the Great at left. Vytautas Church at center. Back: Cargo ship and statue. Printer: BWC. 500th Anniversary Vytautas the Great.			
a. Issued note.	90.00	150	300
s1. Specimen perforated: *PAVYZDYS.*	—	—	200
s2. Specimen overprint: *PAVYZDYS.*	—	—	200

1938 Commemorative Issue

#28, 20th Anniversary of Independence

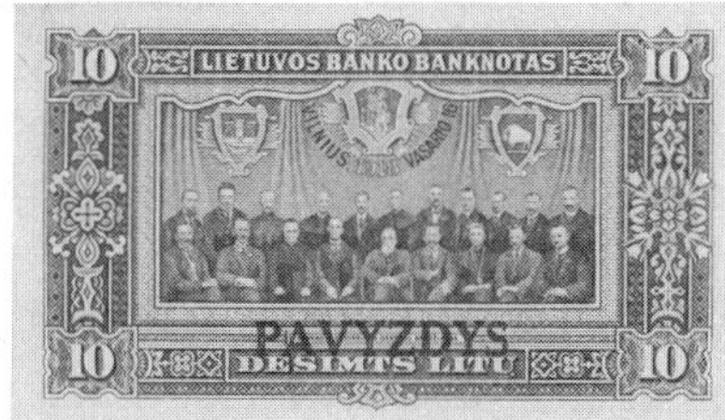

28 **10 Litu**

	VG	VF	UNC
16.2.1938. Green and orange. Pres. Antanas Smetona at left. Back: Council of Lithuania. Printer: BWC. Specimen overprint: *PAVYZDYS.* 20th Anniversary of Independence.	—	—	8,500

Note: For notes issued by the Darlehnskasse Ost at Kaunas in 1918 with Lithuanian language, see *Standard Catalog of World Paper Money, Volume 1, Specialized issues and they are under Germany, Occupied Territories WWI.*

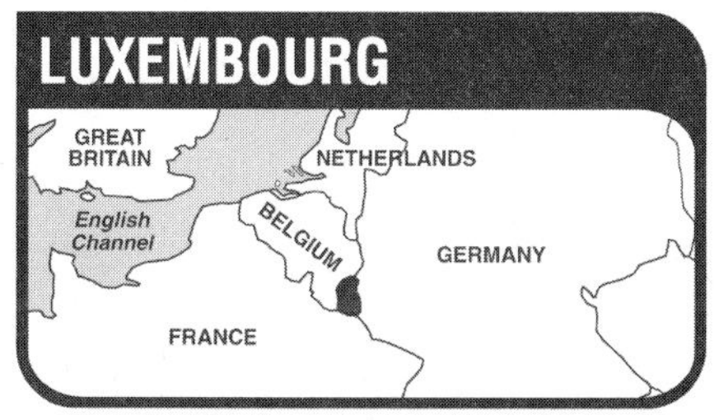

The Grand Duchy of Luxembourg is located in western Europe between Belgium, Germany and France. It has an area of 998 sq. mi. (2,586 sq. km.) and a population of 430,000. Capital: Luxembourg. The economy is based on steel - Luxembourg's per capita production of 16 tons is the highest in the world. Founded in 963, Luxembourg became a grand duchy in 1815 and an independent state under the Netherlands. It lost more than half of its territory to Belgium in 1839, but gained a larger measure of autonomy. Full independence was attained in 1867. Overrun by Germany in both World Wars, it ended its neutrality in 1948 when it entered into the Benelux Customs Union and when it joined NATO the following year. In 1957, Luxembourg became one of the six founding countries of the European Economic Community (later the European Union), and in 1999 it joined the euro currency area

RULERS:

William III (Netherlands), 1849-90 (represented by brother Henry)
Adolphe, 1890-1905
William IV, 1905-12
Marie Adelaide, 1912-19
Charlotte, 1919-64
Jean, 1964-

MONETARY SYSTEM:

1 Thaler = 30 Groschen
1 Mark = 100 Pfennig = 1 Franc (Franken) 25 Centimes
1 Franc = 100 Centimes, to 2001
1 Euro = 100 Cents, 2001-

GRAND DUCHY

Banque Internationale a Luxembourg

International Bank in Luxembourg

1856 Gulden Issue

		Good	Fine	XF
A1	**5 Gulden** 1.9.1856. Proof.	—	—	—
A2	**10 Gulden** 1.9.1856. Proof.	—	—	—
A3	**25 Gulden** 1.9.1856. Proof.	—	—	—

1856 Thaler Issue

		Good	Fine	XF
1	**10 Thaler** 1.9.1856; 30.9.1885; 15.9.1894. Black on yellow underprint. Back: Blue. Back: Seated woman and three cherubs. Rare.	—	—	—

1856 Franc/Mark Issue

		Good	Fine	XF
2	**25 Francs = 20 Mark** 1.9.1856; 30.9.1886; 15.4.1894. Brown on yellow underprint. Back: Blue. Back: Seated woman and three cherubs. Rare.	—	—	—
3	**100 Francs = 80 Mark** 1.9.1856; 30.9.1886; 15.9.1894. Brown on yellow underprint. Back: Blue. Back: Seated woman and three cherubs.	—	—	—

1900 Issue

		Good	Fine	XF
4	**20 Mark** 1.7.1900. Blue and brown on multicolor underprint. Foundry worker with factory in background at left. Printer: G&D.	500	1,200	2,750

		Good	Fine	XF
5	**50 Mark** 1.7.1900. Green and red-brown. Miner at left, farmer at right. Printer: G&D.	650	1,750	—

1914 WW I Emergency Issue

		Good	Fine	XF
6	**1 Mark** 5.8.1914. Blue. Back: Circular arms at left.	37.50	110	300

		Good	Fine	XF
7	**2 Mark** 5.8.1914. Brown. Back: Circular arms at left.	50.00	160	400
8	**5 Mark** 5.8.1914. Blue text (without vignette). Back: Black text.	100	325	650

1923 Issue

		Good	Fine	XF
9	**100 Francs** 10.2.1923; 1.4.1930. Yellow and blue. City of Luxembourg. Back: Red and blue. Back: Vianden Castle at right.	120	350	800
10	**100 Francs** 18.12.1930. Yellow and blue. City of Luxembourg. Back: Vainden Castle at right.	100	325	750

1936 Issue

		Good	Fine	XF
11	**100 Francs** 1.8.1936; 18.12.1940. Yellow and blue. City of Luxembourg. Back: Viaden castle at right.	125	400	900

1947 Issue

		VG	VF	UNC
12	**100 Francs** 15.5.1947. Brown and blue. Farm wife at left, portrait Grand Duchess Charlotte at center facing left, farmer at right. Back: Three steelworkers.	12.50	85.00	475

1956 Issue

		VG	VF	UNC
13	**100 Francs** 21.4.1956. Dark green. Farm wife at left, portrait Grand Duchess Charlotte at center facing right, farmer at right. Back: Three steelworkers.			
	a. Issued note.	6.00	35.00	275
	s. Specimen with red overprint: *SPECIMEN.*	—	—	165

Note: For #14 and 14A see Volume 3.

Grossherzoglich Luxemburgische National Bank

Grand Dukal Luxembourg National Bank

1873 Thaler Issue

		Good	Fine	XF
15	**5 Thaler** 1.7.1873. Brown. Arms at left and right.			
	a. Issued note. Rare.	—	—	—
	s. Specimen.	—	—	—
16	**10 Thaler** 1.7.1873. Gray.	Good	Fine	XF
	a. Issued note. Rare.	—	—	—
	s. Specimen.	—	—	—

		Good	Fine	XF
17	**20 Thaler** 1.7.1873. Light brown. Arms at left, allegorical figures at right.			
	a. Issued note. Rare.	—	—	—
	s. Specimen.	—	—	—

1873 Franc Issue

		Good	Fine	XF
17A	**20 Francs** 1.7.1873. Blue on pink underprint. Rare.	—	—	—
17B	**100 Francs** 1.7.1873. Rare.	—	—	—

1876 Mark Issue

		VG	VF	UNC
18	**5 Mark** 25.3.1876. Blue on violet underprint. Arms at left, bust at right.			
	a. Issued note. Rare.	—	—	—
	s. Specimen.	—	—	1,500

		Good	Fine	XF
19	**10 Mark** 25.3.1876. Brown.			
	a. Issued note. Rare.	—	—	—
	s. Specimen.	—	—	—
20	**20 Mark** 25.3.1876. Gray-green.	Good	Fine	XF
	a. Issued note. Rare.	—	—	—
	s. Specimen.	—	—	—

État du Grand-Duché de Luxembourg

Grossherzoglich Luxemburgischer Staat

State Treasury Notes - Bons de Caisse

Law of 28.11.1914

		Good	Fine	XF
21	**1 Frank = 80 Pfennig** *L. 1914.* Black on blue underprint. Signature varieties. Printer: G&D.	8.50	35.00	150

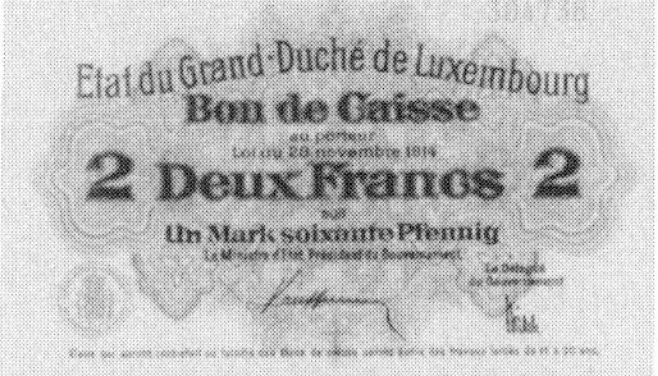

		Good	Fine	XF
22	**2 Franken = 1 Mark 60 Pfennig** *L.1914.* Dark brown on orange and green underprint. Signature varieties. Printer: G&D.	12.50	50.00	200

		Good	Fine	XF
23	**5 Franken = 4 Mark** *L.1914*. Brownish purple on lilac and green underprint. Signature title: *Le Directeur...Finances.* Printer: G&D.	20.00	85.00	300
23A	**5 Franken = 4 Mark** *L.1914*. Brownish purple on lilac and green underprint. Signature title: *Le Ministre d'État, President du Gouvernement.*	25.00	175	—
24	**25 Franken = 20 Mark** *L.1914*. Violet and green. Signature varieties. Printer: G&D.	65.00	150	550
25	**125 Franken = 100 Mark** *L.1914*. Lilac and green. Signature varieties. Printer: G&D.			
	a. Issued note.	125	375	—
	r. Remainder.	—	Unc	300

Law of 28.11.1914 and 11.12.1918

#26-33 have Law dates 28.11.1914-11.12.1918 but were issued in 1919.

		Good	Fine	XF
26	**50 Centimes** *L.1914-1918* (1919). Dark brown on lilac underprint. Signature varieties. Printer: G&D.	4.00	25.00	100

		Good	Fine	XF
27	**1 Franc** *L.1914-1918* (1919). Black on blue underprint. Like #21. Printer: G&D.	5.00	30.00	125

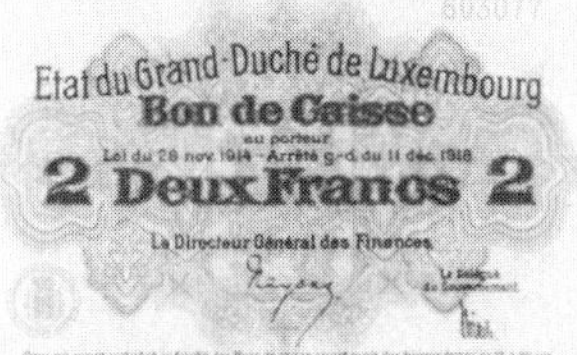

		Good	Fine	XF
28	**2 Francs** *L.1914-1918* (1919). Dark brown on orange and green underprint. Like #22. Printer: G&D.	7.50	40.00	200

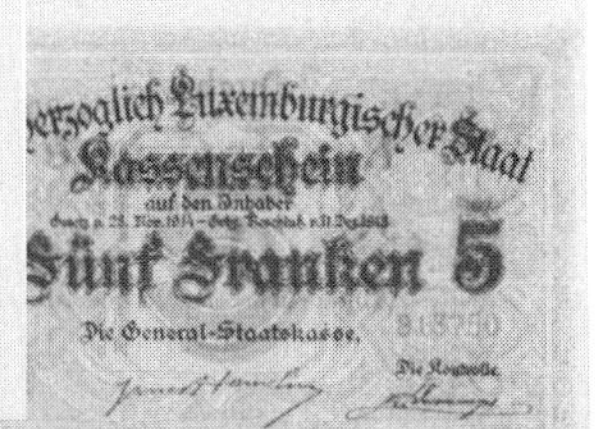

		Good	Fine	XF
29	**5 Francs** *L.1914-1918* (1919). Brownish purple on lilac and green underprint. Like #23; Signature title: *LeDirecteur... Finances.* Printer: G&D.			
	a. Red seal.	8.00	60.00	250
	b. Dark brown seal.	8.00	60.00	250
	c. Black seal.	8.00	60.00	250

		Good	Fine	XF
30	**10 Francs** *L.1914-1918* (1919). Blue on blue-gray. Allegorical woman at left and right. Printer: G&D.	325	850	—
31	**25 Francs** *L.1914-1918* (1919). Blue-green on light green underprint.			
	a. Without serial # (unfinished).	—	Unc	40.00
	b. With serial #, blue and green.	35.00	150	350

		Good	Fine	XF
32	**125 Francs** *L.1914-1918* (1919). Lilac and green. Printer: G&D.	100	500	—

		Good	Fine	XF
33	**500 Francs** *L.1914-1918* (1919).			
	a. Without seal or serial # on back (unfinished).	—	Unc	50.00
	b. With serial #, pink underprint.	150	500	—

1923-1927 Issue

34	10 Francs	Good	Fine	XF
	ND (1923). Blue. Farmer's wife at left, worker at right. Back: Portrait Grand Duchess Charlotte at left.	65.00	250	750

35	20 Francs	Good	Fine	XF
	L.1914-1918 (1926). Violet and green. Arms at center. Back: Portrait Grand Duchess Charlotte and buildings. Printer: G&D.	55.00	250	750

36	100 Francs	Good	Fine	XF
	ND (1927). Brown and green. Portrait Grand Duchess Charlotte at left. Back: Twelve coats of arms. Printer: G&D.	75.00	300	850

Grand Duché de Luxembourg

1929-1939 Issue

37	20 Francs	Good	Fine	XF
	1.10.1929 Blue. Grape harvest. Back: Farmer plowing. Printer: JEZ.			
	a. Issued note.	25.00	80.00	250
	s. Specimen with red overprint: *SPECIMEN*.	—	Unc	135

38	50 Francs	Good	Fine	XF
	1.10.1932. Green-blue on tan underprint. Grand Duchess Charlotte at upper right. Back: Palace in Luxembourg. Printer: JEZ.			
	a. Issued note.	20.00	70.00	225
	s1. As a. Specimen with red overprint: *SPECIMEN.*	—	Unc	110
	s2. Lilac. Specimen.	—	Unc	250

39	100 Francs	Good	Fine	XF
	ND (1934). Black on green, brown and multicolor underprint. Portrait Grand Duchess Charlotte at left, arms at center. Back: Seated woman with globe and anvil at center, Adolphe Bridge and city of Luxembourg behind. BC: Green. Printer: ABNC.			
	a. Issued note.	17.50	60.00	175
	s. Specimen.	—	Unc	85.00

40	1000 Francs	Good	Fine	XF
	1.9.1939. (Issued 1940). Dark brown and green. Arms in underprint. Printer: G&D.			
	a. Issued note.	250	825	—
	r. Remainder without date.	175	425	—
	s. Specimen.	—	Unc	1,250

GERMAN OCCUPATION - WW II

Letzeburg

1940 Issue

41	10 (zeng) Frang	Good	Fine	XF
	20.4.1940. Brown with pink underprint. P. Eyschen at left. Back: Arms on back. Printer: G&D. (Not issued). Rare.	—	—	—

41A	20 Frang	Good	Fine	XF
	ND (ca. 1939-1940). Blue and brown. Harvesting at left and right. (Not issued). Rare.	—	—	—

ALLIED OCCUPATION - WW II

Grand Duché de Luxembourg

Letzeburg

1943 Issue

		VG	VF	UNC
42	**20 Frang** 1943. Brown on multicolor underprint. Arms at left, portrait Grand Duchess Charlotte at right. Back: Farmer with sickle and corn. BC: Purple. Printer: W&S.			
	a. Issued note.	0.75	5.00	70.00
	s. Specimen with red overprint: *SPECIMEN,* punch hole cancelled.	—	—	140

1944 ND Issue

		VG	VF	UNC
43	**5 Francs** ND (1944). Olive-green. Portrait Grand Duchess Charlotte at center. Back: Arms at center. BC: Red. Printer: ABNC.			
	a. 000000-222222. Without serial # prefix,	0.50	5.00	60.00
	b. Serial # prefix A. 222223-.	0.50	3.00	45.00
	p. Proof. Uniface pair.	—	—	175
	s. Specimen with red overprint: *SPECIMEN.*	—	—	125

		VG	VF	UNC
44	**10 Francs** ND (1944). Purple. Portrait Grand Duchess Charlotte at center. Back: Arms at center. BC: Olive. Printer: ABNC.			
	a. Issued note.	0.50	3.00	45.00
	p. Proof. Uniface pair.	—	—	175
	s. Specimen with red overprint: *SPECIMEN.*	—	—	150

		VG	VF	UNC
45	**50 Francs** ND (1944). Dark green on multicolor underprint. Portrait Grand Duchess Charlotte at left. Arms at center. Serial # prefix A. Back: Vianden Castle at lower center, guilloche overprint covering German wording below. Watermark: Portrait Grand Duchess Charlotte. Printer: BWC.	2.00	12.50	175

		VG	VF	UNC
46	**50 Francs** ND (1944). Dark green on multicolor underprint. Serial number prefix A. Portrait Grand Duchess Charlotte at left. Arms at center. Serial # prefix B-D. Like #45 but back without wording at bottom and also without guilloche. Watermark: Grand Duchess Charlotte. Printer: BWC.			
	a. Issued note.	1.50	7.50	150
	s. Specimen with red overprint: *SPECIMEN,* punch hole cancelled.	—	—	225

		VG	VF	UNC
47	**100 Francs** ND (1944). Blue on multicolor underprint. Portrait Grand Duchess Charlotte at left, arms at center. Back: Seated woman with globe and anvil at center. BC: Red-brown. Printer: ABNC.			
	a. Issued note.	10.00	50.00	300
	p. Proof. Uniface pair.	—	—	225
	s. Specimen with red overprint: *SPECIMEN,* punch hole cancelled.	—	—	175

1954-1956 Issue

		VG	VF	UNC
48	**10 Francs** ND (1954). Green on multicolor underprint. Portrait Grand Duchess Charlotte at right. Signature varieties. Back: Vianden Castle at left, arms at center, hillside at right. Watermark: Grand Duchess Charlotte.			
	a. Issued note.	1.50	4.50	15.00
	s. Specimen with red overprint: *SPECIMEN* punch hole cancelled.	—	—	100

		VG	VF	UNC
49	**20 Francs** ND (1955). Blue on multicolor underprint. Grand Duchess Charlotte at right. Back: Moselle River with village of Ehnen. Watermark: Grand Duchess Charlotte.			
	a. Issued note.	1.00	4.00	12.00
	s. Specimen with red overprint: *SPECIMEN* punch hole cancelled.	—	—	150

		VG	VF	UNC
50	**100 Francs** 15.6.1956. Red-brown on blue and multicolor underprint. Portrait Grand Duchess Charlotte with tiara at right. Back: Differdange steelworks. Watermark: Grand Duchess Charlotte.			
	a. Issued note.	4.00	10.00	30.00
	s. Specimen with red overprint: *SPECIMEN* punch hole cancelled.	—	—	200

MACAU

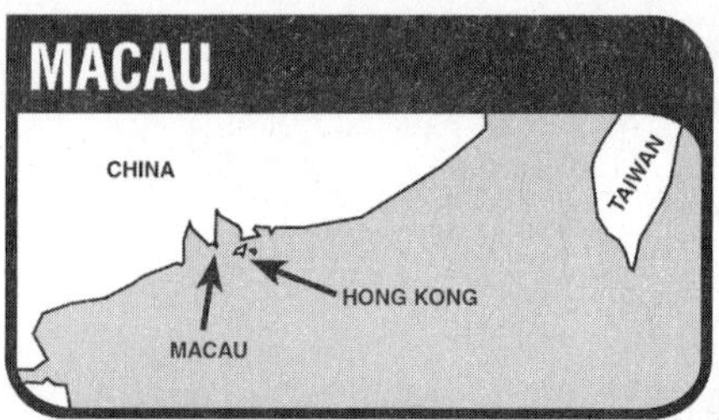

The Macau R.A.E.M., a former Portuguese overseas province located in the South China Sea 35 miles (56 km.) southwest of Hong Kong, consists of the peninsula and the islands of Taipa and Coloane. It has an area of 14 sq. mi. (21.45 sq. km.) and a population of 415,850. Capital: Macau. The economy is based on tourism, gambling, commerce and gold trading - Macau is one of the few entirely free markets for gold in the world. Cement, textiles, vegetable oils and metal products are exported. Established by the Portuguese in 1557, Macau is the oldest European settlement in the Far East. Pursuant to an agreement signed by China and Portugal on 13 April 1987, Macau became the Macau R.A.E.M. of the People's Republic of China on 20 December 1999. In this agreement, China promised that, under its *one country, two systems* formula, China's socialist economic system would not be practiced in Macau, and that Macau would enjoy a high degree of autonomy in all matters except foreign and defense affairs for the next 50 years.

RULERS:

Portuguese from 1849-1999

MONETARY SYSTEM:

1 Dollar = 100 Cents
1 Pataca = 100 Avos

DATING

Most notes were issued in the year of the Chinese Republic but occasionally the old Chinese lunar calendar was used. These dates are listed as "CD". Refer to China-introduction for Cyclical Date Chart.

PRIVATE BANKS

During the 1920s and early 1930s the private banks of Macao issued various circulating checks in dollars to facilitate trade with Chinese firms. These apparently circulated freely along with the Pataca issues of the Banco Nacional Ultramarino which quite obviously were in short supply. Most examples known have appropriate colonial revenue adhesive stamps affixed as found on bills of exchange and private checks. The additional large brush strokes or marks obliterating the denomination indicates the sum has been paid. A similar circulating check was issued in 1944 by the Tai Fong Cambista.

PORTUGUESE ADMINISTRATION

Banco Nacional Ultramarino

行銀理滙外海國洋西大

Ta Hsi Yang Kuo Hai Wai Hui Li Yin Hang

1905-1907 Issue

		Good	Fine	XF
1	**1 Pataca** 1905; 1911. Brown on blue underprint. Imprint: *Lisboa... 19...*, date partially handwritten. Back: Crowned arms at center. Printer: BFL. 126x88mm.			
	a. 4.9.1905.	300	900	4,500
	b. 1.8.1911.	375	1,200	—
2	**5 Patacas** 4.9.1905; 4.10.1910; 4.12.1910. Blue on orange underprint. Sailing ship at upper center. Printer: BFL.			
	a. 4.9.1905. 197x121mm	1,800	9,000	—
	b. 4.10.1910; 4.12.1910. 192x125mm	1,800	900	—

Note: Contemporary forgeries exist of the 4.9.1905 date ($250 value in Fine).

		Good	Fine	XF
3	**10 Patacas** 2.1.1907; 30.1.1922; 31.3.1924; 4.12.1924; 22.6.1925; 18.6.1936; 23.12.1941. Light red on green underprint. Crowned arms at upper left, sailing ship at upper center. Serrated left edge. Printer: BFL. 205x126mm.	3,000	7,000	20,000

		Good	Fine	XF
4	**25 Patacas** 2.1.1907; 22.1.1907. Black on rose underprint. Crowned arms at upper left, sailing ship at upper center. Serrated left edge. 201x123mm. Rare.	—	—	—

		Good	Fine	XF
5	**50 Patacas** 1.1.1906. Blue on rose underprint. Sailing ship at upper center, large red *50* in underprint at lower center. Printer: BFL. 207x135mm. Rare.	—	—	—

		Good	Fine	XF
6	**100 Patacas** 1.1.1906. Dark green on green, light brown and yellow underprint. Crowned arms at upper left, sailing ship at upper left center, large *100* in underprint at center. Printer: BFL. 205x129mm. Rare.	—	—	—

1912-1924 Issue

		Good	Fine	XF
7	**1 Pataca** 1.1.1912. Brown on blue underprint. Imprint:*Lisboa...19...* printed. Back: Arms without crown at center. Printer: BWC. 130x90mm.	100	350	1,500

		Good	Fine	XF
8	**5 Patacas** 1.1.1924. Green on yellow underprint. Steamship at left, junks at right. Printer: TDLR. 185x117mm.	800	4,000	15,000

		Good	Fine	XF
9	**100 Patacas** 22.7.1919. Brown on multicolor underprint. Arms at upper left, steamship at upper left center, steamship seal at lower right. Printer: BWC. 183x116mm. Rare.	—	25,000	—

1920 ND Subsidiary Note Issue

		VG	VF	UNC
10	**5 Avos** ND (1920). Brown on green underprint. Arms at upper left. Printer: HKP. 84x46mm.	30.00	100	400

		VG	VF	UNC
11	**10 Avos** ND (1920). Green on yellow underprint. Arms at upper left. Printer: HKP. 98x54mm.	20.00	50.00	200
12	**50 Avos** ND (1920). Black on green underprint. Arms at top center. Handwritten signature. Back: Orange. Printer: HKP. 122x66mm.	75.00	225	900

1942 ND Subsidiary Note Issue

		VG	VF	UNC
13	**1 Avo** ND (1942). Grayish brown. Arms at upper left. Printer: HKP. 47x72mm.	10.00	25.00	80.00
14	**5 Avos** ND (1942). Brown on green underprint. Arms at upper left, like #10. Printer: HKP. 84x46mm.	25.00	80.00	250

		VG	VF	UNC
15	**10 Avos** ND (1942). Blue on yellow underprint. Arms at upper left. Printer: HKP. 100x55mm.	25.00	80.00	250

Note: Also see #19.

		VG	VF	UNC
16	**20 Avos** ND (1942). Brown on green underprint. 104x60mm.	25.00	80.00	250
17	**50 Avos** ND (1942). Purple on green underprint. Arms at top center. Printer: HKP. 123x66mm.	60.00	150	450

Note: Also see #21.

JAPANESE ADMINISTRATION - WWII

Banco Nacional Ultramarino

1944 ND Subsidiary Note Issue

		VG	VF	UNC
18	**5 Avos** ND (1944). Red on green underprint. Arms at upper left. 87x47mm.	90.00	300	1,050

		VG	VF	UNC
19	**10 Avos** ND (1944). Blue on yellow underprint. Arms at upper left, like #15, but 100 x 55mm. 85x48mm.	5.00	30.00	225
20	**20 Avos** ND (1944). Red on light olive underprint. Back: Light orange. 100x55mm.	6.00	25.00	120

		VG	VF	UNC
21	**50 Avos** ND (1944). Purple on light green underprint. Arms at top center, like #17 but with letters A-J at left and right. Back: Orange. 125x66mm. Thin paper.	6.00	15.00	60.00

1944 Emergency Certificate Issue

Decreto No. 33:517

		VG	VF	UNC
22	**5 Patacas** *D.5.2.1944.* Black-blue with maroon guilloche. Arms at left, steamship seal at right. Signature varieties. Back: Vertical. BC: Green. Printer: Sin Chun and Co. 133x76mm.	15.00	80.00	660

		VG	VF	UNC
23	**10 Patacas** *D.5.2.1944.* Brown with maroon guilloche. Arms at left, steamship seal at right. Signature varieties. Back: Vertical. BC: Brown. Printer: Sin Chun and Co. 132x75mm.	25.00	150	780
24	**25 Patacas** *D.5.2.1944.* Brown. Arms at left, steamship seal at right. Signature varieties. Back: Vertical. Printer: Sin Cun and Co. 152x77mm.	4,500	16,500	—

		VG	VF	UNC
25	**50 Patacas** *D.5.2.1944.* Olive with maroon guilloche. Arms at left, steamship seal at right. Signature varieties. Back: Vertical. BC: Brown. Printer: Sin Chun and Co. 165x84mm.	600	2,400	—

		VG	VF	UNC
26	**100 Patacas** *D.5.2.1944.* Red-violet with light blue guilloche. Arms at left, steamship seal at right. Signature varieties. Back: Vertical. BC: Red. Printer: Sin Chun and Co. 170x97mm.	4,500	11,000	—
27	**500 Patacas** *D.5.2.1944.* Brown on multicolor underprint. Arms at left, steamship seal at right. Signature varieties. Back: Vertical. Printer: Sin Chun and Co. 205x100mm. Rare.	—	—	—

PORTUGUESE ADMINISTRATION - POST WWII

Banco Nacional Ultramarino

1945 Regular Issue

		VG	VF	UNC
28	**1 Pataca** 16.11.1945. Blue on red and green underprint. Temple at right. Signature varieties. Back: Steamship seal at center. Printer: W&S. 142x65mm.	4.00	20.00	150

		VG	VF	UNC
29	**5 Patacas** 16.11.1945. Green on green and red underprint. Temple at right. Signature varieties. Back: Steamship seal at center. Printer: W&S. 145x67mm.	20.00	55.00	800
30	**10 Patacas** 16.11.1945. Brown. Temple at right. Signature varieties. Back: Steamship seal at center. Printer: W&S. 151x70mm.	30.00	200	1,350
31	**25 Patacas** 16.11.1945. Red-orange on light green underprint. Temple at right. Signature varieties. Back: Steamship seal at center. Printer: W&S. 160x70mm.	1,200	4,800	—
32	**50 Patacas** 16.11.1945. Blue-gray. Temple at right. Signature varieties. Back: Steamship seal at center. Printer: W&S. 165x78mm.	225	1,125	—

		VG	VF	UNC
33	**100 Patacas** 16.11.1945. Violet. Temple at right. Signature varieties. Back: Steamship seal at center. Printer: W&S. 170x80mm.	2,750	5,750	—
34	**500 Patacas** 16.11.1945. Brown. Temple at right. Signature varieties. Back: Steamship seal at center. Printer: W&S. 147x90mm.	13,500	30,000	—

1946-1950 Issue

		VG	VF	UNC
35	**5 Avos** 6.8.1946. Dark brown on green underprint. Back: Green. Printer: HKP. 85x50mm.			
	a. Issued note.	1.50	7.50	100
	r. Remainder without serial #.	—	—	30.00

		VG	VF	UNC
36	**10 Avos** 6.8.1946. Red on blue underprint. Ship and light tower at center. Back: Gray. Printer: HKP. 98x56mm.			
	a. Issued note.	2.00	10.00	105
	r. Remainder without serial #.	—	—	22.50

		VG	VF	UNC
37	**20 Avos** 6.8.1946. Violet on gray underprint. Ruins of S. Paulo at left. Back: Red-brown. Printer: HKP. 110x58mm.			
	a. Issued note.	5.00	20.00	160
	r. Remainder without serial #.	—	—	30.00

		VG	VF	UNC
38	**50 Avos** 6.8.1946. Blue on tan underprint. Junks at left, steamship seal at right. Back: Violet. Printer: HKP. 118x60mm.			
	a. Issued note.	2.00	8.00	60.00
	r. Remainder without serial #.	—	—	22.50
39	**25 Patacas** 20.4.1948. Brown. Portrait L. de Camoes at right. *MACAU* below. 160x75mm.	150	900	4,125

		VG	VF	UNC
39A	**100 Patacas** 27.11.1950. Brown on multicolor underprint. Portrait Colonel J. M. Ferreira da Amabal at right. Printer: W&S. Specimen.	—	—	—

1952 First Issue

		VG	VF	UNC
39B	**1 Avo** 19.1.1952. Arms at lower center. Specimen.	—	—	—
40	**2 Avos** 19.1.1952. Purple. Green on light brown and blue underprint. Arms at lower center. Back: Steamship seal at center. 80x45mm. Specimen.	—	—	800
41	**5 Avos** 19.1.1952. Brown. Green on light brown and blue underprint. Arms at lower center. Back: Steamship seal at center. 90x50mm. Specimen.	—	—	700

		VG	VF	UNC
42	**10 Avos** 19.1.1952. Green on light brown and blue underprint. Arms at lower center. Back: Steamship seal at center. 100x55mm.			
	r. Remainder.	—	—	120
	s. Specimen.	—	—	700

Note: #42a was not officially released. A quantity of approximately 5000 notes have found its way into the market.

		VG	VF	UNC
43	**20 Avos** 19.1.1952. Olive. Arms at lower center. Like #42. Back: Steamship seal at center. 110x60mm. Specimen.	—	—	400

Decreto No. 17154

		VG	VF	UNC
44	**100 Patacas** 19.5.1952. Brown on light green underprint. Portrait M. de Arriaga Brum da Silveira at right. Signature varieties. Back: Archway with flag at center. Printer: W&S. 170x80mm.			
	a. Issued note.	500	1,200	4,800
	s. Specimen.	—	—	450

1958 Issue

Decreto - Lei No. 39,221

		VG	VF	UNC
45	**10 Patacas** 20.11.1958. Blue on multicolor underprint. Portrait L. de Camoes at right. Signature varieties. Watermark: L. de Camoes. Printer: BWC. 145x70mm.			
	a. Issued note.	70.00	180	850
	s. Specimen.	—	—	150

		VG	VF	UNC
46	**25 Patacas** 20.11.1958. Brown on multicolor underprint. Portrait L. de Camoes at right. Watermark: L. de Camoes. 160x75mm.			
	a. Issued note.	60.00	300	1,100
	s. Specimen.	—	—	400

		VG	VF	UNC
47	**50 Patacas** 20.11.1958. Dark green on multicolor underprint. Portrait L. de Camoes at right. Watermark: L. de Camoes. 166x75mm.			
	a. Issued note.	112	562	1,350
	s. Specimen.	—	—	300

		VG	VF	UNC
48	**500 Patacas** 20.11.1958. Olive-brown on multicolor underprint. Portrait L. de Camoes at right. Watermark: L. de Camoes. 176x85mm.			
	a. Issued note.	900	2,700	—
	s. Specimen.	—	—	1,600

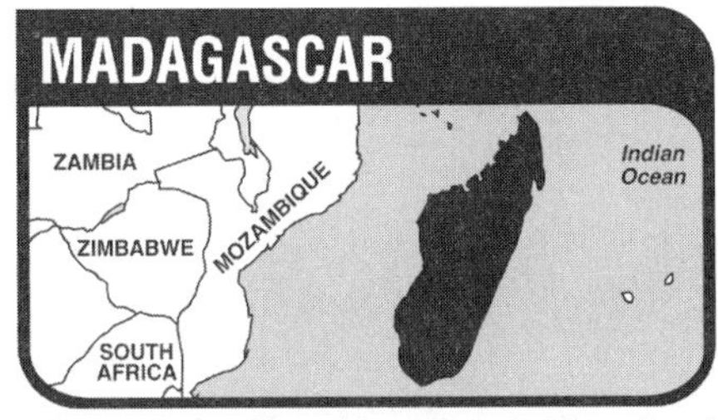

The Democratic Republic of Madagascar, an independent member of the French Community located in the Indian Ocean 250 miles (402 km.) off the southeast coast of Africa, has an area of 226,658 sq. mi. (587,041 sq. km.) and a population of 17.39 million. Capital: Antananarivo. The economy is primarily agricultural; large bauxite deposits are presently being developed. Coffee, vanilla, graphite and rice are exported.Formerly an independent kingdom, Madagascar became a French colony in 1896 but regained independence in 1960. During 1992-93, free presidential and National Assembly elections were held ending 17 years of single-party rule. In 1997, in the second presidential race, Didier Ratsiraka, the leader during the 1970s and 1980s, was returned to the presidency. The 2001 presidential election was contested between the followers of Didier Ratsiraka and Marc Ravalomanana, nearly causing secession of half of the country. In April 2002, the High Constitutional Court announced Ravalomanana the winner. Ravalomanana is now in his second term following a landslide victory in the generally free and fair presidential elections of 2006.

MONETARY SYSTEM:

1 French Franc = 100 Centimes to 1945
1 CFA Franc = 1.70 French Francs, 1945-1948
1 CFA Franc = 2 French Francs, 1948-1959
1 CFA Franc = 0.02 French Franc, 1959-1961
5 Malagasy Francs (F.M.G.) = 1 Ariary, 1961-2003
1 Ariary = 5 Francs, 2003-

REPUBLIC

Gouverneur Général, Tananarive

Décret du 17.9.1914

No.	Note	VG	VF	UNC
1	**5 Francs** *D.1914.*	—	—	—
2	**10 Francs** 29.3.1917.	—	—	—
3	**20 Francs** 29.3.1917.	—	—	—

Emergency Postage Stamp Issues

1916 Issue Type I

No.	Note	VG	VF	UNC
4	**0.25 Franc** ND (1916). Blue.	50.00	100	250
5	**0.50 Franc** ND (1916). Violet.	50.00	100	250
5A	**1 Franc** ND (1916). Brown and green. Requires confirmation.	—	—	—
6	**2 Francs** ND (1916). Blue and olive.	50.00	100	250

1916 Issue Type II

No.	Note	VG	VF	UNC
7	**0.10 Franc** ND (1916). Red and brown.	50.00	100	250

1916 Issue Type III

No.	Note	VG	VF	UNC
8	**0.05 Franc** ND (1916). Blue-green and olive.	50.00	100	250

1916 Issue Type IV

No.	Note	VG	VF	UNC
9	**0.05 Franc** ND (1916). Blue-green and olive.	50.00	100	250
10	**0.10 Franc** ND (1916). Red and brown.	50.00	100	250
11	**0.25 Franc** ND (1916). Blue.	50.00	100	250
11A	**0.50 Franc** ND (1916).	50.00	100	250
11B	**1 Franc** ND (1916).	50.00	100	250

No.	Note	VG	VF	UNC
11C	**2 Francs** ND (1916).	50.00	100	250

1916 Issue Type V

No.	Note	VG	VF	UNC
12	**0.05 Franc** ND (1916). Green.	50.00	100	250
13	**0.50 Franc** ND (1916). Violet.	50.00	100	250
14	**1 Franc** ND (1916). Brown and green.	50.00	100	250
15	**2 Francs** ND (1916). Blue and green.	50.00	100	250

1916 Issue Type VI

No.	Note	VG	VF	UNC
16	**0.05 Franc** ND (1916). Blue-green and olive.	50.00	100	250
17	**0.10 Franc** ND (1916). Red and brown.	50.00	100	250
18	**0.25 Franc** ND (1916). Blue.	50.00	100	250
19	**0.50 Franc** ND (1916). Violet.	50.00	100	250
20	**1 Franc** ND (1916). Brown and green.	50.00	100	250
21	**2 Francs** ND (1916). Blue and green.	50.00	100	250

1916 Issue Type VII

No.	Note	VG	VF	UNC
22	**0.05 Franc** ND (1916). Blue-green and olive. Requires confirmation.	—	—	—
23	**0.10 Franc** ND (1916). Red and brown.	50.00	100	250
24	**0.25 Franc** ND (1916). Blue.	50.00	100	250
25	**0.50 Franc** ND (1916). Violet.	50.00	100	250
26	**1 Franc** ND (1916). Brown and green.	50.00	100	250
27	**2 Francs** ND (1916). Blue and green. Requires confirmation.	—	—	—

1916 Issue Type VIII

No.	Note	VG	VF	UNC
28	**0.05 Franc** ND (1916). Blue-green and olive.	50.00	100	250
29	**0.10 Franc** ND (1916). Red and green.	50.00	100	250
30	**0.25 Franc** ND (1916). Blue.	50.00	100	250
31	**0.50 Franc** ND (1916). Violet.	50.00	100	250
32	**1 Franc** ND (1916). Brown and green.	50.00	100	250
33	**2 Francs** ND (1916). Blue and green.	50.00	100	250

1916 Issue Type IX

No.	Note	VG	VF	UNC
33A	**0.05 Franc** ND (1916). Blue-green and olive.	60.00	125	300
33B	**0.10 Franc** ND (1916). Red and green.	60.00	125	300
33C	**0.50 Franc** ND (1916). Violet.	60.00	125	300
33D	**1 Franc** ND (1916). Brown and green.	60.00	125	300

Note: For smaller stamps with *MADAGASCAR ET DEPENDANCES* or *MOHELI* pasted on square cardboard with dog on back, see Comoros.

Banque de Madagascar

1926 ND Provisional Issue

#	Denomination	Good	Fine	XF
34	**100 Francs** ND (1926 - old dates 3.12.1892-13.2.1893). Overprint: *BANQUE DE MADAGASCAR* on unissued notes of the Banque de France (#65b).	150	500	—

1930s Issue

#	Denomination	VG	VF	UNC
35	**5 Francs** ND (ca.1937). Red-brown on blue and green underprint. Goddess Juno at left. 2 signature varieties.	2.50	17.50	60.00

#	Denomination	VG	VF	UNC
36	**10 Francs** ND (ca. 1937-1947). Green and blue. Woman with fruit at right. 2 signature varieties. Back: Farmer plowing.	5.00	25.00	85.00

#	Denomination	VG	VF	UNC
37	**20 Francs** ND (ca. 1937-1947). Yellow-brown. France and African woman with child at right. 3 signature varieties. Back: Man at left.	8.50	35.00	125

#	Denomination	Good	Fine	XF
38	**50 Francs** ND (ca. 1937-1947). Light green and multicolor. Minerva at left, female allegory of science at right. 3 signature varieties.	25.00	100	350
39	**100 Francs** ND (ca. 1937-1947). Female allegory of wisdom at left, Fortuna and symbols of agriculture and industry at right. Requires confirmation.	—	—	—
40	**100 Francs** ND (ca.1937). Violet, brown and yellow. Man with woman and child. 2 signature varieties.	25.00	100	350

#	Denomination	Good	Fine	XF
41	**1000 Francs** 11.7.1933; 19.5.1945; 28.12.1948. Multicolor. Female allegory of the French Republic at left, African woman at right. 3 signature varieties.	100	400	1,200

		Good	Fine	XF
42	**1000 Francs**			
	ND (ca. 1937). Blue and multicolor. Female allegory of industry at left, female allegory of agriculture at right.	150	500	1,300

1941 Emergency Issue

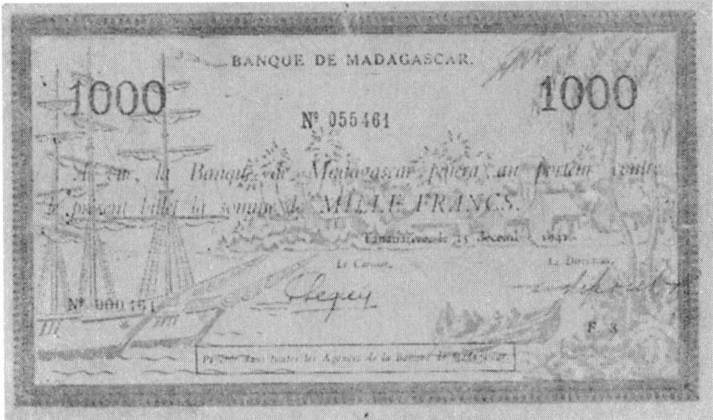

		Good	Fine	XF
43	**1000 Francs**			
	1941; 1946. Blue and brown. Sailing ships at left, coastal scenery.			
	a. Signature handwritten. 15.12.1941.	1,650	—	—
	b. Signature handwritten or stamped. 15.3.1946.	1,650	—	—

1942 Bons de Caisse

		Good	Fine	XF
44	**5000 Francs**			
	30.4.1942. Green. 2 oxen. Back: Animals, woman with fruit, and workers.			
	a. Issued note. Rare.	—	—	—
	s. Specimen.	—	Unc	3,000

Banque de Madagascar et des Comores

1950-1951 Issue

		VG	VF	UNC
45	**50 Francs**			
	ND. Brown and multicolor. Woman with hat at right. 2 signature varieties. Back: Man at center. Watermark: Woman's head.			
	a. Signature title: *LE CONTROLEUR GÉNÉRAL.*	2.50	22.50	75.00
	b. Signature title: *LE DIRECTOR GÉNÉRAL ADJOINT.*	2.50	22.50	75.00

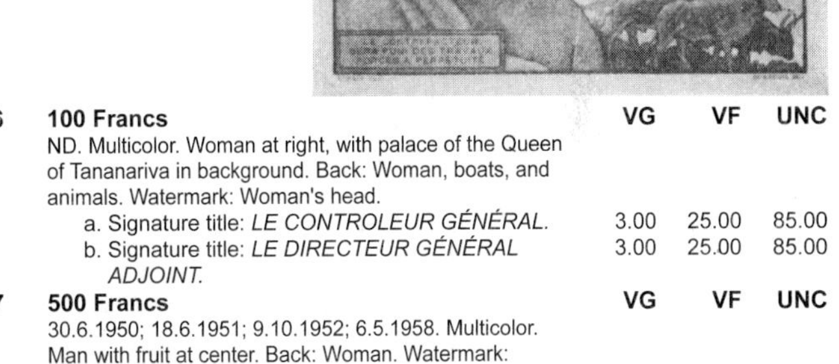

		VG	VF	UNC
46	**100 Francs**			
	ND. Multicolor. Woman at right, with palace of the Queen of Tananariva in background. Back: Woman, boats, and animals. Watermark: Woman's head.			
	a. Signature title: *LE CONTROLEUR GÉNÉRAL.*	3.00	25.00	85.00
	b. Signature title: *LE DIRECTEUR GÉNÉRAL ADJOINT.*	3.00	25.00	85.00
47	**500 Francs**	VG	VF	UNC
	30.6.1950; 18.6.1951; 9.10.1952; 6.5.1958. Multicolor. Man with fruit at center. Back: Woman. Watermark: Woman's head.			
	a. Signature title: *LE CONTROLEUR GÉNÉRAL.*	15.00	90.00	375
	b. Signature title: *LE DIRECTEUR GÉNÉRAL ADJOINT.*	15.00	90.00	375

		VG	VF	UNC
48	**1000 Francs**			
	14.3.1950; 1.2.1951; 15.10.1953. Multicolor. Woman and man at left center. Back: Ox cart. Watermark: Woman's head. 158x104mm.			
	a. Signature title: *LE CONTROLEUR GÉNÉRAL.*	30.00	175	550
	b. Signature title: *LE DIRECTEUR GÉNÉRAL ADJOINT.*	30.00	175	550

Note: For #48 dated 9.10.1952 with provisional overprint, see #54.

		VG	VF	UNC
49	**5000 Francs** 30.6.1950; 23.11.1955. Multicolor. Portrait Gallieni at upper left, portrait young woman at right. Back: Huts at left, woman with baby at right. Watermark: Woman's head.			
	a. Signature title: *LE CONTROLEUR GÉNÉRAL.*	175	450	1,000
	b. Signature title: *LE DIRECTEUR GÉNÉRAL ADJOINT.*	175	450	1,000
	s. Specimen. Perforated.	—	—	1,000

MALAGASY

Institut d'Emission Malgache

1961 ND Provisional Issue

#51-55 new bank name and new Ariary denominations overprint on previous issue of Banque de Madagascar et des Comores.

		VG	VF	UNC
51	**50 Francs = 10 Ariary** ND (1961). Multicolor. Woman with hat at center right. Back: Man at center. Watermark: Woman's head.			
	a. Signature title: *LE CONTROLEUR GENERAL.*	2.00	17.50	70.00
	b. Signature title: *LE DIRECTEUR GENERAL ADJOINT.*	2.50	20.00	75.00

		VG	VF	UNC
52	**100 Francs = 20 Ariary** ND (1961). Multicolor. Woman at center right, palace of the Queen of Tananariva in background. Back: Woman, boats and animals. Watermark: Woman's head.	3.00	30.00	110

		VG	VF	UNC
53	**500 Francs = 100 Ariary** ND (1961 - old date 9.10.1952). Multicolor. Man with fruit at center. Watermark: Woman's head.	15.00	90.00	400
54	**1000 Francs = 200 Ariary** ND (1961 - old date 9.10.1952). Multicolor. Man and woman at left center. Back: Ox cart at center right. Watermark: Woman's head.	20.00	175	500
55	**5000 Francs = 1000 Ariary** ND (1961). Multicolor. Gallieni at upper left, woman at right. Back: Woman and baby. Watermark: Woman's head.	50.00	325	800

Note: #53-55 some notes also have old dates of intended or original issue (1952-1955).

MADEIRA ISLANDS

The Madeira Islands, which belong to Portugal, are located 360 miles (492 km.) off the northwest coast of Africa. They have an area of 307 sq. mi. (795 sq. km.) and a population of 267,000. The group consists of two inhabited islands named Madeira and Porto Santo and two groups of uninhabited rocks named Desertas and Selvagens. Capital: Funchal. The three staple products are wine, flowers and sugar. Although the evidence is insufficient, it is thought that the Phoenicians visited Madeira at an early period. The Portuguese navigator Goncalvez Zarco first sighted Porto Santo in 1418, having been driven there by a storm while he was exploring the coast of West Africa. Madeira itself was discovered in 1420. The islands were uninhabited when visited by Zarco, but their colonization was immediately begun by Prince Henry the Navigator, aided by the knights of the Order of Christ. British troops occupied the islands in 1801, and again in 1807-14. Since 1976 Madeira is politically and administratively an autonomous region with a regional government and a parliament.

RULERS:

Portuguese

PORTUGUESE ADMINISTRATION

Banco de Portugal

Agencia no Funchal

1875 Issue

		Good	Fine	XF
1	**20,000 Reis** 2.3.1875-4.3.1876. Blue. Seated figure at left and right, arms at center. Oval overprint vertically at left and right. Uniface. Rare.	—	—	—

1878 Issue

		Good	Fine	XF
2	**10,000 Reis** 5.11.1878. Brown on blue-green underprint. Arms with two women in oval at center. Back: Green. Rare.	—	—	—

1879 Provisional Issue

		Good	Fine	XF
3	**10,000 Reis** ND (1879 -old date 5.11.1878). Overprint: *MOEDA FORTE* across bottom and at upper left and right on #2. Rare.	—	—	—

#4 Deleted, see #9.

1891 Provisional Issue

		Good	Fine	XF
5	**500 Reis** 18.7.1891. Overprint: Oval; at right. Requires confirmation.	—	—	—
6	**1000 Reis** 18.7.1891. Overprint: Oval; at right. Requires confirmation.	—	—	—
7	**2500 Reis** 18.7.1891. Overprint: Oval; at right. Requires confirmation.	—	—	—
8	**5000 Reis** 18.7.1891. Overprint: Oval; at right. Requires confirmation.	—	—	—

		Good	Fine	XF
9	**10,000 Reis** 18.7.1891. Overprint: Blue oval:*DOMICILIADA NA AGENCIA DO FUNCHAL....BANCO DE PORTUGAL* at right on #3. Punch hole cancelled: *SEM VALOR*. Rare.	—	—	—
10	**20,000 Reis** *DOMICILIADA NA AGENCIA DO FUNCHAL....BANCO DE PORTUGAL* at right on #3. Overprint: Oval; at right. Requires confirmation.	—	—	—
11	**50,000 Reis** 18.7.1891. Overprint: Oval; at right. Rare.	—	—	—

1892 Provisional Issue

		Good	Fine	XF
11A	**50 Reis** 3.2.1892 (- old date 6.8.1891). Overprint: Three line diagonal-like #12- on Portugal #87.	400	1,000	—

		Good	Fine	XF
12	**100 Reis** 3.2.1892 (- old date 6.8.1891). Overprint: Three line diagonal: *Domiciliada para circular no districto do Funchal em virtude do Decreto de 3*	300	700	—

Malaya, a former member of the British Commonwealth located in the southern part of the Malay Peninsula, consisted of 11 states: the unfederated Malay states of Johore, Kedah, Kelantan, Perlis and Trengganu; the federated Malay states of Negri Sembilan, Pahang, Perak and Selangor; and former members of the Straits Settlements, Malacca and Penang. The federation had an area of about 60,000 sq. mi. (155,400 sq. km.). Capital: Kuala Lumpur. It was occupied by Japan from 1941-1945. Malaya was organized February 1, 1948, was granted full independence on August 31, 1957, and became part of the Federation of Malaysia on September 16, 1963. See also Straits Settlements and Malaysia.

RULERS:
British

MONETARY SYSTEM:
1 Dollar = 100 Cents

BRITISH ADMINISTRATION

Board of Commissioners of Currency

1940 First Issue

		VG	VF	UNC
1	**10 Dollars** 1.1.1940. Violet on green underprint. Portrait King George VI at right. Back: Arms of the 11 states. Printer: W&S.	250	700	4,000

Note: A shipment of 1 and 5 Dollar bills dated 1940 was captured by the Germans. The bills were not issued. Later they were ovprinted in 1945 by the British Military Government. See #4 and 5.

1940 Second Issue

		VG	VF	UNC
2	**10 Cents** 15.8.1940. Dark blue on lilac and brown underprint. Portrait King George VI at left. Uniface. Printer: Survey Dept. F. M. S.	40.00	120	600

		VG	VF	UNC
3	**25 Cents** 1.9.1940. Aqua on blue, orange and lilac underprint. Portrait King George VI at right. Back: Arms of the 11 states. Printer: Survey Dept. F. M. S.	80.00	250	1,600

1940 (1945) Issue

		VG	VF	UNC
4	**1 Dollar** 1.1.1940 (Aug. 1945). Green and multicolor. Portrait King George VI at right. Back: States' arms. Printer: W&S.			
	a. Overprint as described.	500	2,000	8,000
	b. Without overprint	500	2,500	8,800
5	**5 Dollars** 1.1.1940 (Aug. 1945). Blue and Multicolor. Portrait King George VI at right. Back: States arms. Printer: W&S.	VG	VF	UNC
	a. Overprint: *NOT LEGAL...*	3,000	7,000	16,000
	b. Without overprint Rare.	—	—	—

1941-1942 (1945) Issue

Portrait Varieties

Type 1

Type 2

Type 3

		VG	VF	UNC
6	**1 Cent** 1.7.1941 (1945). Lilac on light orange underprint. Portrait King George VI at left. Uniface. Printer: TDLR.	2.00	8.00	22.00

		VG	VF	UNC
7	**5 Cents** 1.7.1941 (1945). Red on light green underprint. Portrait King George Vi at left. Uniface. Printer: TDLR.			
	a. Jawi script at lower left: ليم سين	3.00	10.00	30.00
	b. Jawi script at lower left: ليماسين	3.00	10.00	22.00

		VG	VF	UNC
8	**10 Cents** 1.7.1941 (1945). Blue on pink underprint. Portrait King George VI at left. Uniface. Three portrait varieties. Printer: TDLR.	3.00	10.00	22.00

		VG	VF	UNC
9	**20 Cents** 1.7.1941 (1945). Brown on orange and green underprint. Portrait King George VI at left. Back: States' arms. Printer: W&S.			
	a. Jawi script at lower left: سين	10.00	50.00	200
	b. Jawi script at lower left: سن	10.00	70.00	250

10	50 Cents	VG	VF	UNC
	1.7.1941 (1945). Violet on orange and blue underprint. Portrait King George VI at left. Portrait varieties. Printer: W&S.			
	a. Jawi script at lower left: ليما فوله	10.00	30.00	120
	b. Jawi script at lower left: ليمڤوله	10.00	30.00	120

11	1 Dollar	VG	VF	UNC
	1.7.1941 (1945). Blue on orange and multicolor underprint. Portrait King George VI at right. Back: States' arms. Printer: W&S.	10.00	30.00	120

12	5 Dollars	VG	VF	UNC
	1.7.1941 (1945). Green on gray and multicolor underprint. Portrait King George VI at right. Back: States' arms. Printer: W&S.	50.00	200	1,100

13	10 Dollars	VG	VF	UNC
	1.7.1941 (1945). Red and multicolor. Portrait King George VI at right. Back: States' arms. Printer: W&S.	50.00	220	1,300

14	50 Dollars	VG	VF	UNC
	1.1.1942 (1945). Blue. Portrait King George VI at right. Back: States' arms. Watermark: Lion's head. Printer: BWC.	500	2,000	17,000

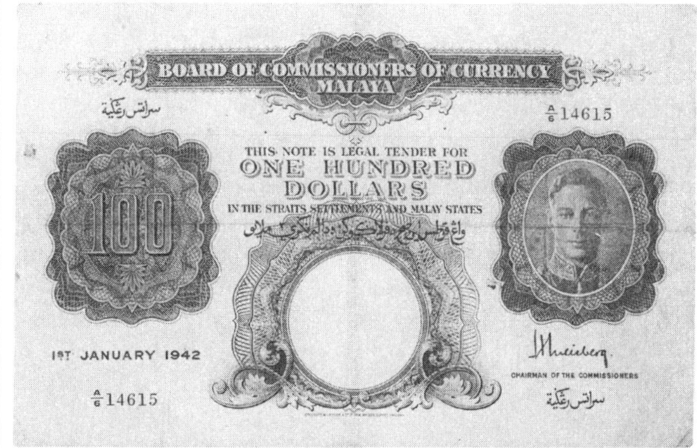

15	100 Dollars	VG	VF	UNC
	1.1.1942 (1945). Red and green. Portrait King George VI at right. Back: States' arms. Watermark: Lion's head. Printer: BWC.	600	2,200	17,000

16	1000 Dollars	VG	VF	UNC
	1.1.1942 (1945). Violet. Watermark: Lion's head. Printer: BWC. Rare.	—	—	—

17	10,000 Dollars	VG	VF	UNC
	1.1.1942 (1945).			
	a. Issued note. Requires confirmation.	—	—	—
	s. Specimen. Rare.	—	—	—

Color Abbreviation Guide

New to the *Standard Catalog of® World Paper Money* are the following abbreviations related to color references:

BC: Back color
PC: Paper color

JAPANESE OCCUPATION - WW II

Japanese Government

1942-1945 Issue

#M1-M10 block letters commencing with M. Note: Many modern *'replicas'* from paste-up plates in strange colors have entered the market from sources in Southeast Asia.

		VG	VF	UNC
M1	**1 Cent**			
	ND (1942). Dark blue on light green underprint.			
	a. 2 block letters, format: MA.	0.10	3.00	5.00
	b. Fractional block letters, format: M/AA.	0.05	0.50	3.00
	s. As a. Specimen with red overprint: *Mi-hon. SPECIMEN* on back.	—	—	120

		VG	VF	UNC
M2	**5 Cents**			
	ND (1942). Brown-violet and gray.			
	a. 2 block letters.	0.10	2.00	11.00
	b. Fractional block letters.	0.10	0.60	3.00
	s. As a. Specimen with red overprint: *Mi-hon. SPECIMEN* on back.	—	—	150

		VG	VF	UNC
M3	**10 Cents**			
	ND (1942). Green and light blue.			
	a. 2 block letters.	0.50	3.00	11.00
	b. Fractional block letters.	0.10	0.50	1.00
	s. As a. Specimen with red overprint: *Mi-hon. SPECIMEN* on back.	—	—	120

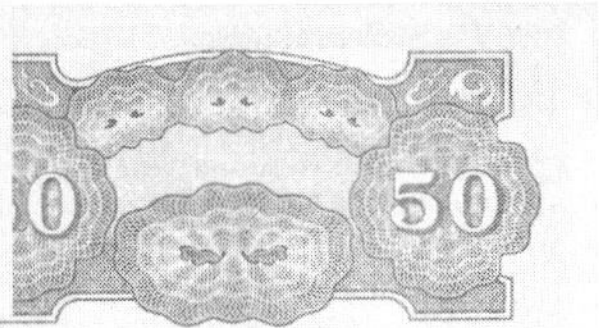

		VG	VF	UNC
M4	**50 Cents**			
	ND (1942). Brown. Fan-like tree at right.			
	a. Without watermark. Block letters: MA; MB.	1.00	5.00	30.00
	b. With watermark. Block letters: MC-MT.	0.10	0.50	5.00
	s. As a. Specimen with red overprint: *Mi-hon. SPECIMEN* on back.	—	—	150

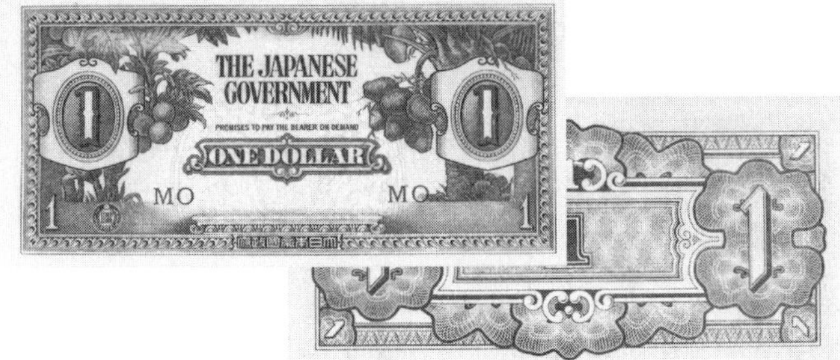

		VG	VF	UNC
M5	**1 Dollar**			
	ND (1942). Dark blue on pink underprint. Breadfruit tree at left, coconut palm at right.			
	a. Without watermark. Block letters: MA With serial #.	30.00	110	250
	b. With watermark. Block letters: MB-MH; MJ-MN; MR.	0.25	1.00	5.00
	c. With watermark. Block letters: MI; MO; MS.	0.20	0.40	4.00
	s. Block letters: MB. Specimen with red overprint: *Mi-hon. SPECIMEN* on back.	—	—	150

		VG	VF	UNC
M6	**5 Dollars**			
	ND (1942). Lilac on orange underprint. Coconut palm at left, paw-paw tree at right.			
	a. Block letters: MA with serial #.	15.00	30.00	210
	b. Block letters MB-MJ; MO; MP.	1.00	4.00	12.50
	c. Block letters MK; MR.	0.20	0.50	3.00
	d. Woven paper.	0.30	1.25	12.50
	s. As b. Specimen with red overprint: *Mi-hon. SPECIMEN* on back.	—	—	150

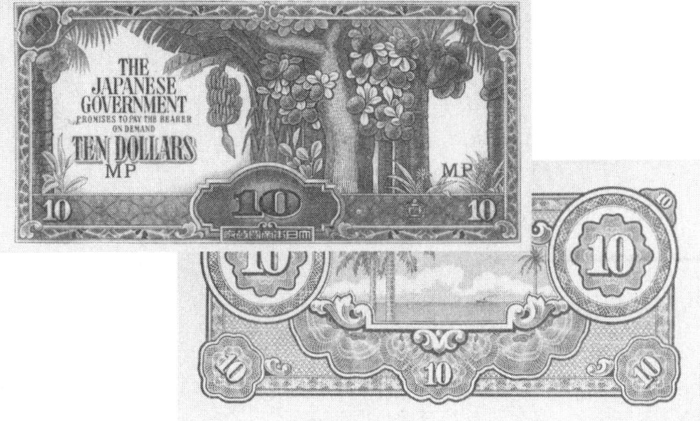

		VG	VF	UNC
M7	**10 Dollars**			
	ND (1942-1944). Blue-green on light yellow underprint. Trees and fruits. Back: Green to bluish green or light blue. Back: Ship on horizon.			
	a. Block letters with serial #.	10.00	40.00	220
	b. Block letters: MB-MP. M with vertical upstroke and downstroke. With watermark.	0.25	1.00	5.00
	c. Block letters without serial #. *M* with sloping upstroke and downstroke. Paper with silk threads, without watermark. MP. (1944).	0.10	0.25	3.00
	s. As b. Specimen with red overprint: *Mi-hon. SPECIMEN* on back.	—	—	150

		VG	VF	UNC
M8	**100 Dollars**			
	ND (1944). Brown. Hut and trees on the water. Back: Man with buffalos in river.			
	a. M with vertical upstroke and downstroke. Watermark. paper.	0.25	4.00	12.00
	b. *M* with sloping upstroke and downstroke. Paper with silk threads, without watermark.	0.15	0.50	6.00
	c. Block letters only. Watermark. woven paper.	0.50	3.00	12.00
	s. As a. Specimen with red overprint: *Mi-hon. SPECIMEN* on back.	—	—	150
	x. Purple face (probable error). Block letters MT.	5.00	20.00	60.00

		VG	VF	UNC
M9	**100 Dollars** ND (1945). Brown. Workers on a rubber estate at right. Back: Houses and seashore at center. BC: Green.	8.00	15.00	50.00

		VG	VF	UNC
M10	**1000 Dollars** ND (1945). Greenish black on green underprint. Ox cart at center. Back: Man with buffalos in river. BC: Green.			
	a. Black block letters. M with vertical upstroke and downstroke. With watermark.	100	500	1,200
	b. Red block letters. *M* with sloping upstroke and dowstroke. Paper with silk threads, without watermark.	3.00	10.00	40.00
	s. As a. Specimen with red overprint: *Mi-hon.*	—	—	900

Note: Many new "replicas" from paste-up plates in strange colors are entering the market from Southeast Asian sources.

MALAYA & BRITISH BORNEO

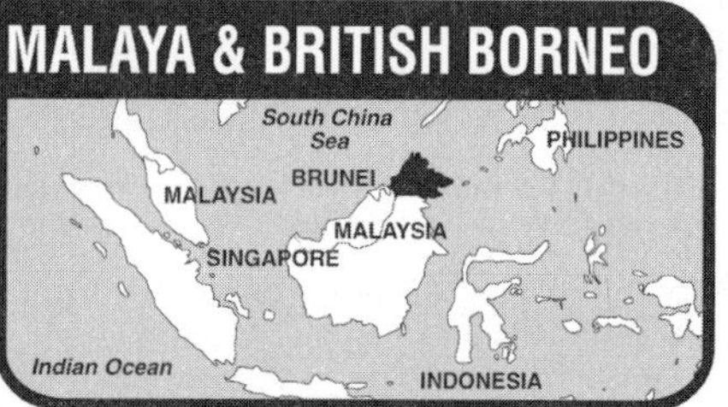

Malaya and British Borneo, a Currency Commission named the Board of Commissioners of Currency, Malaya and British North Borneo, was initiated on Jan. 1, 1952, for the purpose of providing a common currency for use in Johore, Kelantan, Kedah, Perlis, Trengganu, Negri Sembilan, Pahang, Perak, Salangor, Penang, Malacca, Singapore, North Borneo, Sarawak and Brunei. For later issues see Brunei, Malaysia and Singapore.

RULERS:
British

MONETARY SYSTEM:
1 Dollar = 100 Cents

BRITISH ADMINISTRATION

Board of Commissioners of Currency
1953 Issue

		VG	VF	UNC
1	**1 Dollar** 21.3.1953. Blue on red and multicolor underprint. Queen Elizabeth II at right. Back: Arms of the 16 states. Watermark: Tiger's head. Printer: W&S.			
	a. Issued note.	15.00	40.00	180
	s. Specimen.	—	—	6,000

		VG	VF	UNC
2	**5 Dollars** 21.3.1953. Green on brown and multicolor underprint. Queen Elizabeth II at right. Back: Arms of the 16 states. Watermark: Tiger's head. Printer: W&S.			
	a. Issued note.	50.00	150	1,000
	s. Specimen.	—	—	8,000

		VG	VF	UNC
3	**10 Dollars** 21.3.1953. Red on green and multicolor underprint. Queen Elizabeth II at right. Back: Arms of the 16 states. Watermark: Tiger's head. Printer: W&S.			
	a. Issued note.	50.00	180	850
	s. Specimen.	—	—	10,000

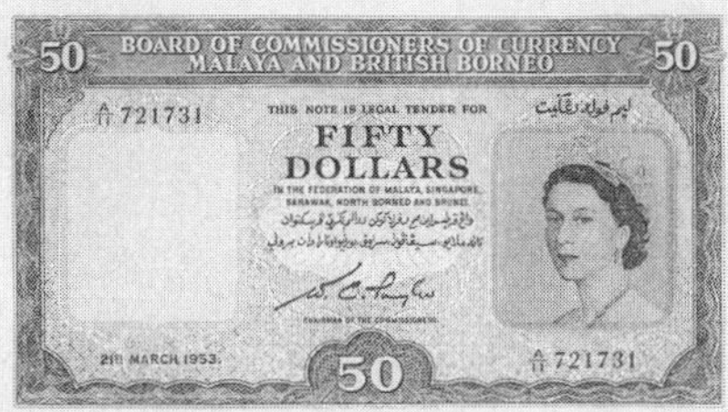

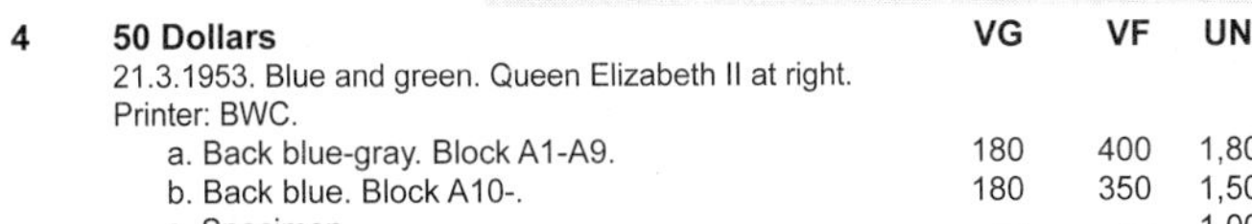

4 50 Dollars
21.3.1953. Blue and green. Queen Elizabeth II at right. Printer: BWC.

	VG	VF	UNC
a. Back blue-gray. Block A1-A9.	180	400	1,800
b. Back blue. Block A10-.	180	350	1,500
s. Specimen.	—	—	1,000

5 100 Dollars
21.3.1953. Violet and brown. Queen Elizabeth II at right. Printer: BWC.

	VG	VF	UNC
a. Issued note.	400	2,000	18,000
s. Specimen.	—	—	18,000

6 1000 Dollars
21.3.1953. Violet on multicolor underprint. Queen Elizabeth II at right. Printer: BWC.

	VG	VF	UNC
a. Issued note. Rare.	—	—	—
s. Specimen.	—	—	20,000

7 10,000 Dollars
21.3.1953. Green on multicolor underprint. Queen Elizabeth II at right. Printer: BWC.

	VG	VF	UNC
a. Issued note. Rare.	—	—	—
s. Specimen.	—	—	—

1959-1961 Issue

8 1 Dollar
1.3.1959. Blue on multicolor underprint. Sailing boat at left. Back: Men with boat and arms of five states. Watermark: Tiger's head. Printer: W&S.

	VG	VF	UNC
a. Issued note.	15.00	50.00	250
s. Specimen.	—	—	—

8A 1 Dollar
1.3.1959. Blue on multicolor underprint. Sailing boat at left. Back: Men with boat and arms of five states. Watermark: Tiger's head. Printer: TDLR.

	VG	VF	UNC
	6.00	50.00	150

THE MALDIVES

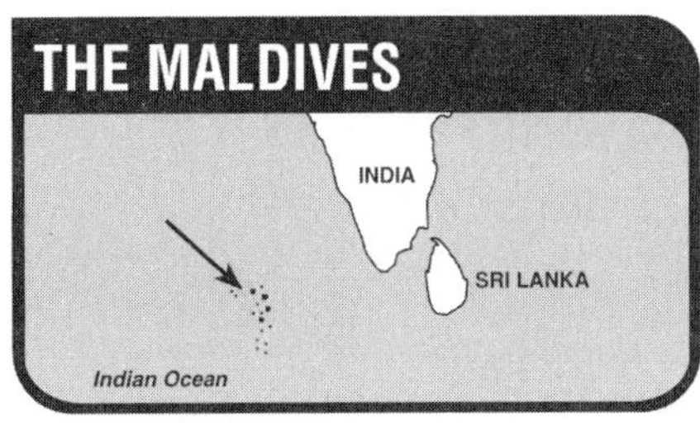

The Republic of Maldives, an archipelago of about 2,000 coral islets in the northern Indian Ocean 417 miles (671 km.) southwest of Ceylon, has an area of 115 sq. mi. (298 sq. km.) and a population of 302,000. Capital: Malé. Fishing employs 95 percent of the work force. Dried fish, copra and coir yarn are exported. The Maldives was long a sultanate, first under Dutch and then under British protection. It became a republic in 1968, three years after independence. President Maumoon Abdul Gayoom dominated the islands' political scene for 30 years, elected to six successive terms by single-party referendums. Following riots in the capital Male in August 2004, the president and his government pledged to embark upon democratic reforms including a more representative political system and expanded political freedoms. Progress was sluggish, however, and many promised reforms were slow to be realized. Nonetheless, political parties were legalized in 2005. In June 2008, a constituent assembly - termed the "Special Majlis" - finalized a new constitution, which was ratified by the president in August. The first-ever presidential elections under a multi-candidate, multi-party system were held in October 2008. Gayoom was defeated in a runoff poll by Mohamed Nasheed, a political activist who had been jailed several years earlier by the former regime. Challenges facing the new president include strengthening democracy and combating poverty and drug abuse.

RULERS:
British to 1965

MONETARY SYSTEM:
1 Rufiyaa (Rupee) = 100 Lari

REPUBLIC

Maldivian State, Government Treasurer

1947; 1960 Issue

1 1/2 Rupee
14.11.1947/AH1367. Orange and multicolor. Palm tree and dhow at center. Uniface. 107x57mm.

	VG	VF	UNC
	30.00	100	325

2 1 Rupee
1947; 1960. Blue and green on multicolor underprint. Palm tree and dhow at left, dhow at right. Back: Buildings at right.

	VG	VF	UNC
a. 14.11.1947/AH1367.	1.50	7.50	25.00
b. 4.6.1960/AH1379.	0.30	1.00	4.00

3 2 Rupees
1947; 1960. Brown and blue on multicolor underprint. Palm tree and dhow at left, dhow at right. Back: Pavilion at center right.

	VG	VF	UNC
a. 14.11.1947/AH1367.	15.00	80.00	200
b. 4.6.1960/AH1379.	0.50	1.50	5.00

		VG	VF	UNC
4	**5 Rupees** 1947; 1960. Violet and orange on multicolor underprint. Palm tree and dhow at left, dhow at right. Back: Building at center.			
	a. 14.11.1947/AH1367.	1.50	10.00	30.00
	b. 4.6.1960/AH1379.	0.75	4.00	15.00
	s. As a. Specimen. Overprinted: *SPECIMEN* in red. Punch hole cancelled.	—	—	500

		VG	VF	UNC
5	**10 Rupees** 1947; 1960. Brown on multicolor underprint. Palm tree and dhow at left, dhow at right. Back: Building at center.			
	a. 14.11.1947/AH1367.	3.00	12.50	45.00
	b. 4.6.1960/AH1379.	2.00	10.00	35.00

1951; 1960; 1980 Issue

		VG	VF	UNC
6	**50 Rupees** 1951-1980. Blue on multicolor underprint. Palm tree and dhow at left, dhow at right. Back: Royal Embarkation Gate at Malé at center.			
	a. 1951/AH1371.	35.00	150	400
	b. 4.6.1960/AH1379.	4.00	20.00	90.00
	c. Lithographed 1.8.1980/AH17.7.1400.	5.00	25.00	100
	s. As c. Specimen.	—	—	175

		VG	VF	UNC
7	**100 Rupees** 1951; 1960. Green on multicolor underprint. Palm tree and dhow at left, dhow at right. Back: Park and building complex at center. BC: Brown, violet and multicolor.			
	a. 1951/AH1371.	45.00	175	500
	b. 4.6.1960/AH1379.	15.00	50.00	200

#8 not assigned.

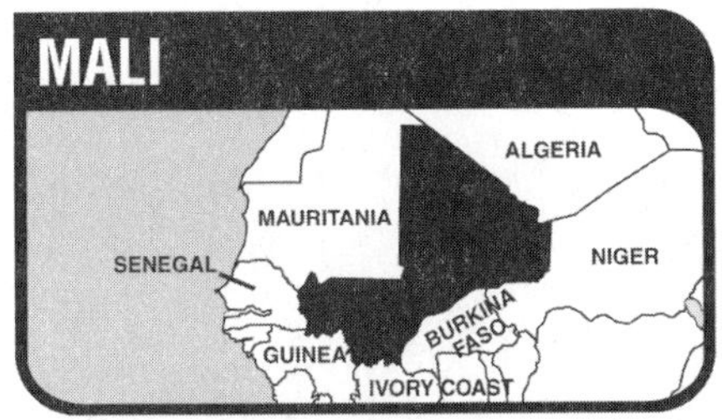

The Republic of Mali, a landlocked country in the interior of West Africa southwest of Algeria, has an area of 478,764 sq. mi. (1,240,000 sq. km.) and a population of 12.56 million. Capital: Bamako. Livestock, fish, cotton and peanuts are exported. The Sudanese Republic and Senegal became independent of France in 1960 as the Mali Federation. When Senegal withdrew after only a few months, what formerly made up the Sudanese Republic was renamed Mali. Rule by dictatorship was brought to a close in 1991 by a military coup - led by the current president Amadou Toure - enabling Mali's emergence as one of the strongest democracies on the continent. President Alpha Konare won Mali's first democratic presidential election in 1992 and was reelected in 1997. In keeping with Mali's two-term constitutional limit, Konare stepped down in 2002 and was succeeded by Amadou Toure, who was subsequently elected to a second term in 2007. The elections were widely judged to be free and fair Mali seceded from the African Financial Community in 1962, then rejoined in 1984. Issues specially marked with letter *D* for Mali were made by the Banque des Etats de l'Afrique de l'Ouest. See also French West Africa, and West African States.

MONETARY SYSTEM:

1 Franc = 100 Centimes

SIGNATURE VARIETIES

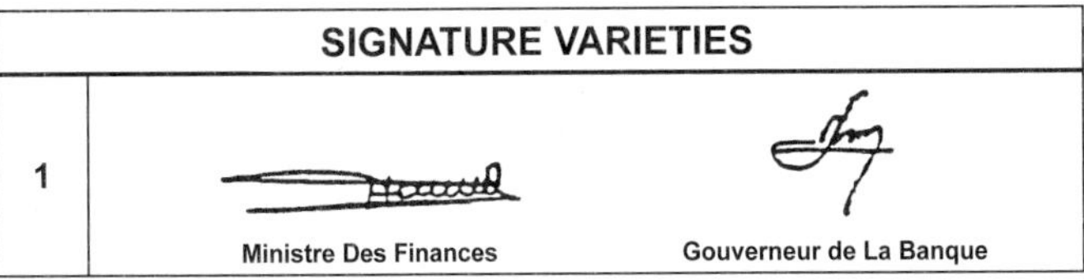

REPUBLIC

Banque de la République du Mali

First 1960 (1962) Issue

Note: Post-dated to Day of Independence.

#	Denomination	VG	VF	UNC
1	**50 Francs** 22.9.1960. Purple on multicolor underprint. President Modibo Keita at left. Signature 1. Back: Village.	25.00	100	350

#	Denomination	VG	VF	UNC
2	**100 Francs** 22.9.1960. Brown on yellow underprint. President Modibo Keita at left. Signature 1. Back: Cattle.	22.50	90.00	325
3	**500 Francs** 22.9.1960. Red on light blue and orange underprint. President Modibo Keita at left. Signature 1. Back: Woman and tent.	95.00	500	1,300

#	Denomination	VG	VF	UNC
4	**1000 Francs** 22.9.1960. Blue on light green and orange underprint. President Modibo Keita at left. Signature 1. Farmers with oxen at lower right. Back: Man and huts. BC: Blue.	35.00	180	600
5	**5000 Francs** 22.9.1960. Green on multicolor underprint. President Modibo Keita at left. Signature 1. Farmers with oxen at lower right. Two farmers plowing with oxen at right. Back: Market scene and building.	135	450	—

Color Abbreviation Guide

New to the *Standard Catalog of ® World Paper Money* are the following abbreviations related to color references:

BC: Back color

PC: Paper color

The Republic of Malta, an independent parliamentary democracy within the British Commonwealth, is situated in the Mediterranean Sea between Sicily and North Africa. With the islands of Gozo and Comino, Malta has an area of 122 sq. mi. (316 sq. km.) and a population of 379,000. Capital: Valletta. With the islands of Gozo (Ghawdex), Comino, Cominetto and Filfla, Malta has no proven mineral resources, an agriculture insufficient to its needs and a small but expanding, manufacturing facility. Clothing, textile yarns and fabrics, and knitted wear are exported.Great Britain formally acquired possession of Malta in 1814. The island staunchly supported the UK through both World Wars and remained in the Commonwealth when it became independent in 1964. A decade later Malta became a republic. Since about the mid-1980s, the island has transformed itself into a freight transshipment point, a financial center, and a tourist destination. Malta became an EU member in May 2004 and began to use the euro as currency in 2008.

RULERS:

British to 1974

MONETARY SYSTEM:

1 Shilling = 12 Pence
1 Pound = 20 Shillings to 1971
1 Lira = 100 Centesimi, 1972-2007
1 Euro = 100 Cents, 2008-

BRITISH ADMINISTRATION

Government of Malta

1914 First Issue

No.	Denomination	Good	Fine	XF
2	**5 Shillings** 13.8.1914. Black on blue underprint. Arms at upper center. Blind embossed Malta seal. 100x84mm.	100	350	750

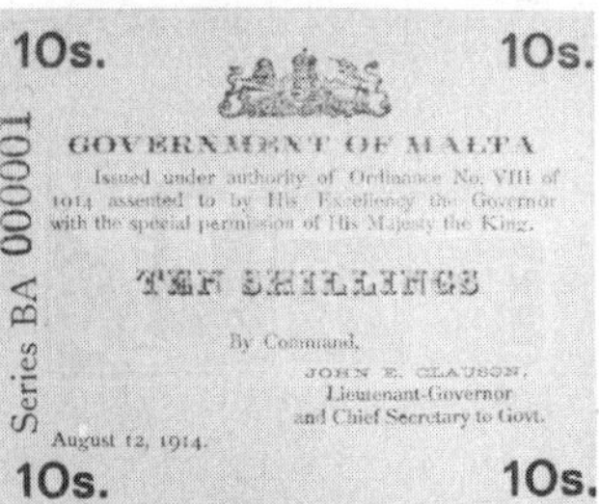

No.	Denomination	Good	Fine	XF
3	**10 Shillings** 12.8.1914. Black on red underprint. Arms at upper center. Blind embossed Malta seal. Back: Pink. 102x81mm.	125	400	850

No.	Denomination	Good	Fine	XF
4	**1 Pound** 20.8.1914. Black. Blind embossed Malta seal. 158x49mm.	125	450	850

No.	Denomination	Good	Fine	XF
5	**5 Pounds** 14.8.1914. Black on ornate green underprint. Blind embossed Malta seal. 165x103mm.	185	700	1,850

No.	Denomination	Good	Fine	XF
6	**10 Pounds** 14.8.1914. Black on yellow underprint. Blind embossed Malta seal. 200x85mm. Rare.	—	—	—

1914 Second Issue

No.	Denomination	Good	Fine	XF
7	**5 Shillings** 4.9.1914. Black on blue underprint. Blind embossed Malta seal. Like #3. 110x90mm.	75.00	350	750
8	**1 Pound** 14.9.1914. Black on pink underprint. Blind embossed Malta seal. Like #4. 160x54mm.	95.00	425	850

1918 Issue

No.	Denomination	Good	Fine	XF
9	**2 Shillings** 20.11.1918. Green on light blue underprint. Portrait King George V at right. Back: Blue. Printer: TDLR. 120x70mm. (Not issued, see #15). Rare.	—	—	—
10	**5 Shillings** 20.11.1918. Red on blue underprint. Portrait King George V at right. Back: Green. Back: Grand Harbour. Printer: TDLR. 138x80mm. Rare.	—	—	—

Note: From 1919-39 Malta did not issue bank notes of its own; Bank of England notes were in general circulation.

1939 Issue

No.	Denomination	VG	VF	UNC
11	**2 Shillings 6 Pence** 13.9.1939. Written style under signature at bottom. Violet, blue and green. Portrait King George VI at right. Uniface. Printer: BWC (without imprint). 135x75mm.	12.00	60.00	275

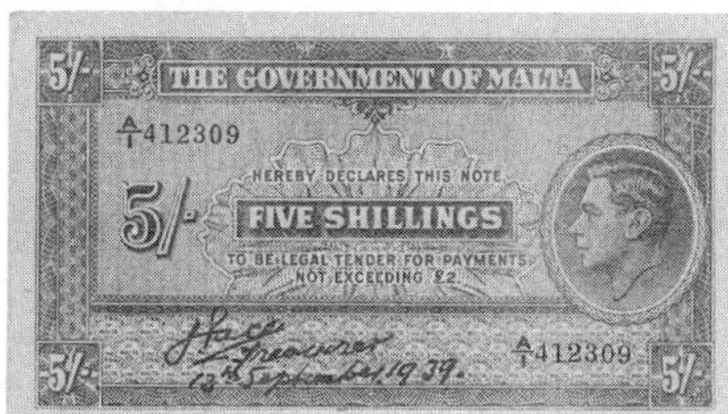

No.	Denomination	VG	VF	UNC
12	**5 Shillings** 13.9.1939. Written style under signature at bottom. Green and red. Portrait King George VI at right. Uniface. Printer: BWC (without imprint). 140x80mm.	10.00	37.50	285

No.	Denomination	VG	VF	UNC
13	**10 Shillings** 13.9.1939. Written style under signature at bottom. Blue, violet and olive. Portrait King George VI at right. Uniface. Printer: BWC (without imprint). 143x83mm.	10.00	50.00	250
14	**1 Pound** 13.9.1939. Written style under signature at bottom. Brown and purple. Portrait King George VI at right. Uniface. Printer: BWC (without imprint). 146x86mm.	12.50	45.00	200

1940 Provisional Issue

		VG	VF	UNC
15	**1 Shilling on 2 Shillings** ND (1940 - old date 20.11.1918). Green and light blue. 120x70mm.	6.00	20.00	85.00

1940-1943 Issue

		VG	VF	UNC
16	**1 Shilling** ND (1943). Purplish-blue and lilac. Portrait King George VI at center. Uniface. Printer: BWC (without imprint). 121x64mm.	2.00	8.00	37.50
17	**2 Shillings** ND (1942). Brown and green. Portrait King George VI at right. Uniface. Printer: BWC (w/o imprint). 133x72mm.	VG	VF	UNC
	a. Signature J. Pace. No watermark.	4.00	25.00	125
	b. Signature E. Cuschieri. No watermark.	3.50	20.00	100
	c. Signature like b. Heavier paper with watermark: Map of Malaya.	5.00	25.00	150

		VG	VF	UNC
18	**2 Shillings 6 Pence** ND (1940). Violet and blue. Portrait King George VI at right. Uniface. Printer: BWC (w/o imprint). 135x75mm.	7.00	25.00	185
19	**10 Shillings** ND (1940). Blue, violet and olive. Portrait King George VI at right. Uniface. Printer: BWC (w/o imprint). 143x83mm.	4.00	12.50	50.00

		VG	VF	UNC
20	**1 Pound** ND (1940). Brown and violet. Portrait King George VI at right. Uniface. Printer: BWC (w/o imprint). 146x86mm.			
	a. Signature J. Pace.	8.00	22.50	95.00
	b. Signature E. Cuschieri with title: *Treasurer* below. Signature in script.	5.00	15.00	50.00
	c. Signature E. Cuschieri with title: *Treasurer* below. Signature in small block letters.	6.00	20.00	70.00

Ordinance 1949 (1951 Issue)

		VG	VF	UNC
21	**10 Shillings** *L.1949* (1951). Green. English George Cross at left, portrait King George VI at right. Printer: TDLR. 133x70mm.	5.00	30.00	200

		VG	VF	UNC
22	**1 Pound** *L.1949* (1951). Brown. English George Cross at left, portrait King George VI at right. Printer: TDLR. 104x84mm.			
	a. Issued note.	3.00	12.50	50.00
	s. Specimen.	—	—	50.00

Ordinance 1949 (1954 Issue)

		VG	VF	UNC
23	**10 Shillings** *L.1949* (1954). Green. English George Cross at left, portrait Queen Elizabeth at right. Printer: TDLR. 133x70mm.			
	a. Signature E. Cuschieri (1954).	7.50	40.00	250
	b. Signature D. A. Shepherd.	10.00	50.00	300
	s. As a. Specimen.	—	—	50.00

		VG	VF	UNC
24	**1 Pound** *L.1949* (1954). Brown. English George Cross at left, portrait Queen Elizabeth at right. Printer: TDLR. 141x76mm.			
	a. Signature E. Cuschieri (1954).	5.00	25.00	150
	b. Signature D. A. Shepherd.	3.00	12.50	100

Note: For later issues of Queen Elizabeth II, see Volume III.

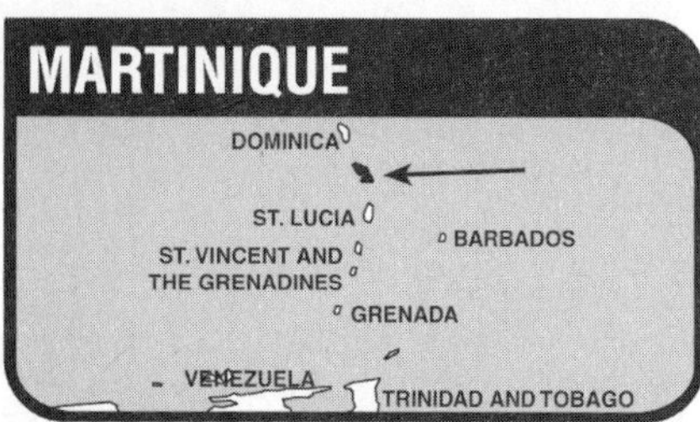

The French Overseas Department of Martinique, located in the Lesser Antilles of the West Indies between Dominica and Saint Lucia, has an area of 425 sq. mi. (1,101 sq. km.) and a population of 384,000. Capital: Fort-de-France. Agriculture and tourism are the major sources of income. Bananas, sugar and rum are exported. Christopher Columbus discovered Martinique, probably on June 15, 1502. France took possession on June 25, 1635, and has maintained possession since that time except for three short periods of British occupation during the Napoleonic Wars. A French department since 1946, Martinique voted a reaffirmation of that status in 1958, remaining within the new French Community. Martinique was the birthplace of Napoleon's Empress Josephine, and the site of the eruption of Mt. Pelee in 1902 that claimed over 40,000 lives.

RULERS:

French

MONETARY SYSTEM:

1 Franc = 100 Centimes

FRENCH ADMINISTRATION

Trésor Colonial Fort de France Office

Décret du 23.4.1855

#A1 and 1 breadfruit tree, snake, shrubbery at upper l., old sailing ship at lower l., crowned arms at top ctr, palm tree, snake and shrubbery at r., various cargo along bottom border. Uniface.

#	Description	Good	Fine	XF
1A	**1 Franc** *D.1855.* With text: *Remboursalbe le 31 Mai 1858.*			
	a. Issued note. 27.2.1856. Rare.	—	—	—
	r. Unsigned remainder. Rare.	—	—	—
1B	**5 Francs** *D.1855.* Rare.	—	—	—

Décrets des 23.4.1855 et du 3.3.1858

#	Description	Good	Fine	XF
2	**1 Franc** *D.1855 & 1858.* Black. Text: *Remboursable le 31 Mai 1863.* Uniface.			
	a. Issued note. 6.2.1869. Rare.	—	—	—
	r. Unsigned remainder with counterfoil, ND. Rare.	—	—	—
2A	**2 Francs** *D. 1855 & 1858.* Rare.	—	—	—
2B	**5 Francs** *D.1855 & 1858.* Black. Text:*Rembourrsable le 31 Mai 1863.* Uniface. Rare.	—	—	—

Décret du 18.8.1884

#	Description	Good	Fine	XF
3	**1 Franc** *D.1884.* Red. Border of trees and plants. 2 signature varieties. Back: Value within frame.	600	1,250	—
3A	**1 Franc** *D.1884.* Red. Thinn border design, and space for serial # at center. Rare.	—	—	—
3B	**2 Francs** *D.1884.* Green. Border of trees and plants. 2 signature varieties. Uniface. Rare.	—	—	—

Note: A 50 Centimes note similar to #3 requires confirmation.

#	Description	Good	Fine	XF
4	**5 Francs** *D.1884.* Black. Thin border design, and space for serial # at center. Rare.	—	—	—
4A	**5 Francs** *D.1884.* Black on yellow-green paper. Thicker border design, and without space for serial # at center. Rare.	—	—	—
4B	**5 Francs** *D.1884.* Thicker border design, without space for serial # at center. Rare. PC: Gray.	—	—	—
5	**10 Francs** *D.1884.* Thicker border design, without space for serial # at center. Rare. PC: Orange.	—	—	—

Banque de la Martinique

1870s Provisional Issue

#	Description	Good	Fine	XF
5A	**1 Franc** 1870. Violet with light blue text. Uniface. Chéques w/ printed value.	15.00	50.00	115
5B	**5 Francs** 3.11.1878. Blue with red value. With or without signature. Chéques w/printed value. Uniface. Rare.	—	—	—

Law of 1874

#	Description	Good	Fine	XF
5C	**5 Francs** *L.1874.* Blue. Man at left, woman at right. 3 signature varieties. Back: Law date. BC: Blue-green.	—	—	—

Law of 1901

#	Description	Good	Fine	XF
6	**5 Francs** *L.1901* (1934-1945). Purple. Man at left, woman at right. 3 signature varieties. Back: Law date. BC: Blue-green.	15.00	60.00	200
6A	**5 Francs** *L.1901* (1903-1934). Red. Man at left, woman at right. 5 signature varieties. Back: Law date. BC: Blue-green.	15.00	75.00	250

		Good	Fine	XF
7	**25 Francs** ND (1922-1930). 2 signature varieties.			
	a. Black and blue.	—	—	—
	b. Brown and blue. Back blue.	—	—	—

		Good	Fine	XF
8	**100 Francs** ND (1905-1932). Black and green. 2 signature varieties; similar to #7. 3 signature varities. Back: Brown.	—	—	—

		Good	Fine	XF
9	**500 Francs** ND (1905-1922). Brown and gray. Allegorical figures on borders. 4 signature varieties. Back: Reverse image as front. Rare.	—	—	—

1915 Issue

		Good	Fine	XF
10	**1 Franc** 1915. In underprint. Red on blue underprint. 2 signature varieties. Back: Arms at center.	15.00	75.00	325

		Good	Fine	XF
11	**2 Francs** 1915. Blue. 2 signature varieties. Back: Woman's head at center.			
	a. Issued note.	20.00	85.00	350
	p. Proof. Without serial # or signatures.	—	Unc	500

1930-1932 Issue

		Good	Fine	XF
12	**25 Francs** ND (1930-1945). Multicolor. Woman with wreath at center, floral drapery behind fruit at bottom. 3 signature varieties.	25.00	150	500

		Good	Fine	XF
13	**100 Francs** ND (1932-1945). Multicolor. Woman with sceptre at left, ship in background at center. 4 signature varieties.	100	400	1,200

		Good	Fine	XF
14	**500 Francs** ND (1932-1945). Multicolor. Woman with sceptre at left, ship in background at center. 4 signature varieties.	375	1,250	—

1942 Emergency Issues

#		Good	Fine	XF
16	**5 Francs** ND (1942). Black on dull red underprint. Allegorical female figure at left. Back: Woman at center. BC: Blue. Printer: EAW.			
	a. Red serial #.	25.00	90.00	275
	b. Blue serial #.	15.00	75.00	225

#		Good	Fine	XF
16A	**5 Francs** ND (1942). Blue. Column at left, Large *5* at right. Back: Bank monogram at center. Printer: Local.	350	1,250	—

#		Good	Fine	XF
17	**25 Francs** ND (1943-1945). Black on yellow underprint. Woman seated with fruit at right. 3 signature varieties. Back: Ship and tree at center. BC: Green. Printer: EAW.	20.00	50.00	300

#		Good	Fine	XF
18	**25 Francs** ND (1942). Violet with black text. Column at left. Back: Bank monogram at center. Printer: Local. PC: Rose.	400	1,500	—

1942 Issue

#		Good	Fine	XF
19	**100 Francs** ND (1942). Green on multicolor underprint. Allegorical woman seated with fruit at left. 2 signature varieties. Back: Seated allegorical woman with child. Printer: ABNC.			
	a. Issued note.	85.00	300	900
	s. Specimen.	—	Unc	1,750

#		Good	Fine	XF
20	**1000 Francs** ND (1942). Blue. Women seated at left and right. Back: Woman at center. BC: Orange.	650	1,500	—
21	**1000 Francs** ND (1942). Red-brown on light green and multicolor underprint. Allegorical man, woman and child at right. 3 signature varieties. Back: Allegorical figures. Printer: ABNC.			
	a. Issued note.	650	1,750	—
	s. Specimen.	—	Unc	4,500

Caisse Centrale de la France Libre

1941 Issue

#22 overprint: *MARTINIQUE.*

#		Good	Fine	XF
22	**1000 Francs** *L. 2.12.1941* (1944-1947). Blue. Phoenix rising from flames. Back: War/peace scenes. Printer: English printing. Overprint: *MARTINIQUE.*			
	a. Overprint below *Caisse Centrale.*	400	1,000	3,000
	b. Overprint like a., cancelled with stamp *ANNULE.*	—	—	1,750

	Good	Fine	XF
c. Overprint at top and diagonally from lower left to upper right.	400	1,100	3,250
s. Specimen.	—	—	1,750

Caisse Centrale de la France d'Outre-Mer

Law of 2.2.1944

		VG	VF	UNC
23	**10 Francs** *L. 2.2.1944*. Violet on red underprint. Marianne at center. Printer: English printing.	15.00	50.00	175
24	**20 Francs** *L. 2.2.1944*. Green on red underprint. Marianne at center. Printer: English printing.	20.00	75.00	250

		VG	VF	UNC
25	**100 Francs** *L. 2.2.1944*. Green on orange underprint. Marianne at center. Back: Anchor, barrel, bale and other implements. Printer: English printing.	55.00	200	650
26	**1000 Francs** *L. 2.2.1944*. Blue. Phoenix rising from flames. Back: War/peace scenes.	VG	VF	UNC
	a. Issued note.	400	900	2,750
	s. Specimen.	—	—	1,500

1947 ND Issue

#27-36 overprint: *MARTINIQUE*.

		VG	VF	UNC
27	**5 Francs** ND (1947-1949). Multicolor. Portrait Bougainville at right. Watermark: 2 varieties. Printer: French printing.			
	a. Issued note.	7.50	20.00	100
	s. Specimen. Perforated: *SPECIMEN*.	—	—	100

		VG	VF	UNC
28	**10 Francs** ND (1947-1949). Multicolor. Colbert at left. Back: Boat at center right. Printer: French printing.	7.50	25.00	135
29	**20 Francs** ND (1947-1949). Multicolor. E. Gentil at right. Printer: French printing.	7.50	35.00	175
30	**50 Francs** ND (1947-1949). Multicolor. Belain d'Esnambuc at left. Printer: French printing.	VG	VF	UNC
	a. Issued note.	20.00	70.00	350
	s. Specimen. Perforated with black overprint.	—	—	450

		VG	VF	UNC
31	**100 Francs** ND (1947-1949). Multicolor. La Bourdonnais at left, couple at right. Printer: French printing.			
	a. Issued note.	25.00	100	425
	s. Specimen. Perforated and overprint: *SPECIMEN*.	—	—	200

		VG	VF	UNC
32	**500 Francs** ND (1947-1949). Multicolor. Two women at right, sailboat at left. Back: Farmers with ox-carts. Printer: French printing.			
	a. Issued note.	100	400	950
	s. Specimen. Handstamped and perforated: *SPECIMEN*.	—	—	750

		VG	VF	UNC
33	**1000 Francs** ND (1947-1949). Multicolor. Two women at right. Printer: French printing.	125	425	1,100

1952 ND Issue

		VG	VF	UNC
34	**5000 Francs** ND (1952). Multicolor. Gen. Schoelcher. Printer: French printing.			
	a. Issued note.	225	750	1,750
	s. Specimen.	—	—	325

1960 ND Issue

		VG	VF	UNC
35	**1000 Francs** ND (1960). Multicolor. Fishermen from Antilles. Back: Woman with box of produce on her head at left center. Printer: French printing.	100	350	900

		VG	VF	UNC
36	**5000 Francs** ND (1960). Multicolor. Woman holding fruit bowl at center. Back: Harvesting scene. Printer: French printing.			
	a. Issued note.	250	850	—
	s. Specimen without overprint and perforated: *SPECIMEN.*	—	—	1,000
	s2. Specimen with black overprint and perforated.	—	—	1,500

Color Abbreviation Guide

New to the *Standard Catalog of ® World Paper Money* are the following abbreviations related to color references:

BC: Back color
PC: Paper color

1960 ND Provisional Issue

#37-41 overprint: *MARTINIQUE* and new denominations on previous issue of "old" Franc notes.

		VG	VF	UNC
37	**1 Nouveau Franc on 100 Francs** ND (1960). Multicolor.	40.00	200	550

		VG	VF	UNC
38	**5 Nouveaux Francs on 500 Francs** ND (1960). Multicolor.	60.00	250	700

		VG	VF	UNC
39	**10 Nouveaux Francs on 1000 Francs** ND (1960). Multicolor.	100	400	950
40	**50 Nouveaux Francs on 5000 Francs** ND (1960). Multicolor.	250	800	—
41	**50 Nouveaux Francs on 5000 Francs** ND (1960). Multicolor. Specimen.	—	—	—

Note: For later issues see French Antilles.

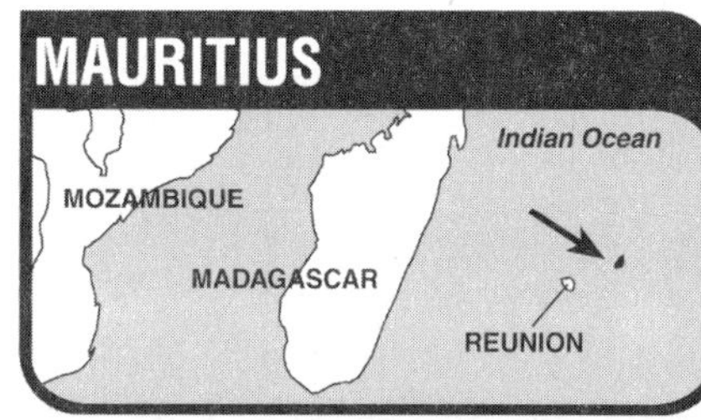

The island of Mauritius, a member of the British Commonwealth located in the Indian Ocean 500 miles (805 km.) east of Madagascar, has an area of 790 sq. mi. (2,045 sq. km.) and a population of 1.18 million. Capital: Port Louis. Sugar provides 90 percent of the export revenue.Although known to Arab and Malay sailors as early as the 10th century, Mauritius was first explored by the Portuguese in the 16th century and subsequently settled by the Dutch - who named it in honor of Prince Maurits van Nassau - in the 17th century. The French assumed control in 1715, developing the island into an important naval base overseeing Indian Ocean trade, and establishing a plantation economy of sugar cane. The British captured the island in 1810, during the Napoleonic Wars. Mauritius remained a strategically important British naval base, and later an air station, playing an important role during World War II for anti-submarine and convoy operations, as well as the collection of signals intelligence. Independence from the UK was attained in 1968. A stable democracy with regular free elections and a positive human rights record, the country has attracted considerable foreign investment and has earned one of Africa's highest per capita incomes. Recent poor weather, declining sugar prices, and declining textile and apparel production, have slowed economic growth, leading to some protests over standards of living in the Creole community.

NOTE: Certain listings encompassing issues circulated by various bank and regional authorities are contained in Volume 1.

BRITISH ADMINISTRATION

Special Finance Committee

1842 Emergency Issue

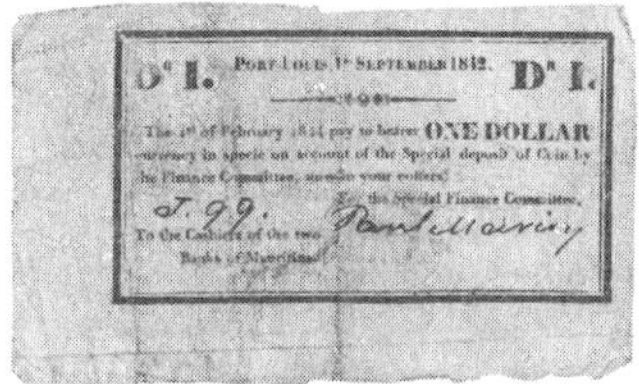

		Good	Fine	XF
1F	**1 Dollar** 1.9.1842. Port Louis. 5 signature varieties.	85.00	225	450

Note: #1F is printed on the back of cut up and cancelled Mauritius Commercial Bank issues.

Currency Commissioners of Mauritius

1848 Issue

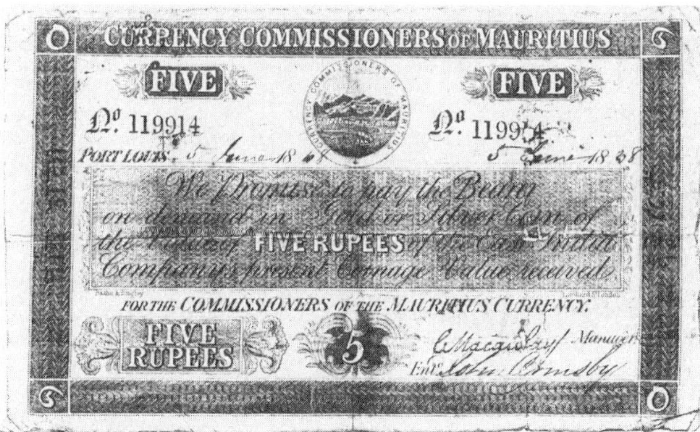

		Good	Fine	XF
8	**5 Rupees** 5.6.1848; 1849. Currency Commissioners' seal at top center. Port Louis. Arms at upper center. Signature varieties. Rare.	—	—	—
9	**10 Rupees** 1848-1849. Arms at upper center. Signature varieties. Rare.	—	—	—

Government of Mauritius

1860-1866 Issue

		Good	Fine	XF
10	**5 Shillings** 1866. Arms at upper center. Counterfoil at left. Signature varieties. Rare.	—	—	—

		Good	Fine	XF
11	**10 Shillings** 22.8.1860; 1866; 1.11.1867. Black and green. Arms at top center. Counterfoil at left. Signature varieties. Rare. PC: Cream.	—	—	—
12	**1 Pound** 1866. Rare.	—	—	—

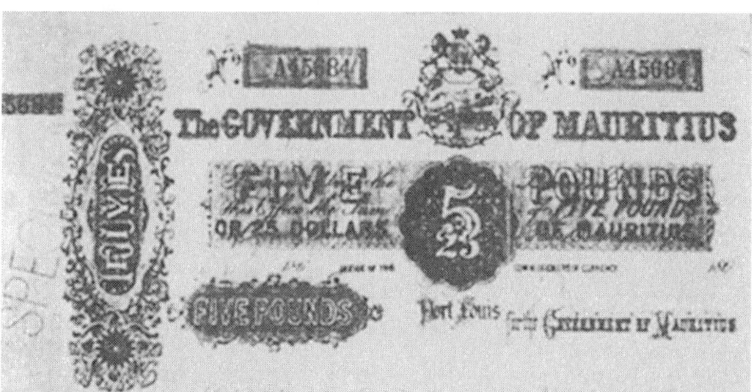

		Good	Fine	XF
12A	**5 Pounds/25 Dollars** 186x. Arms at upper center. Signature varieties. Specimen with counterfoil. Rare.	—	—	—

1876; 1877 Issue

		Good	Fine	XF
13	**5 Rupees** 1876-1902. Arms at top center. Counterfoil at left. Signature varieties.			
	a. 1876; 23.10.1878. Rare.	—	—	—
	b. 5.10.1896; 13.11.1900; 17.11.1902.	500	1,200	—
14	**10 Rupees** 1.10.1877. Arms at top center. Counterfoil at left. Signature varieties. Rare.	—	—	—

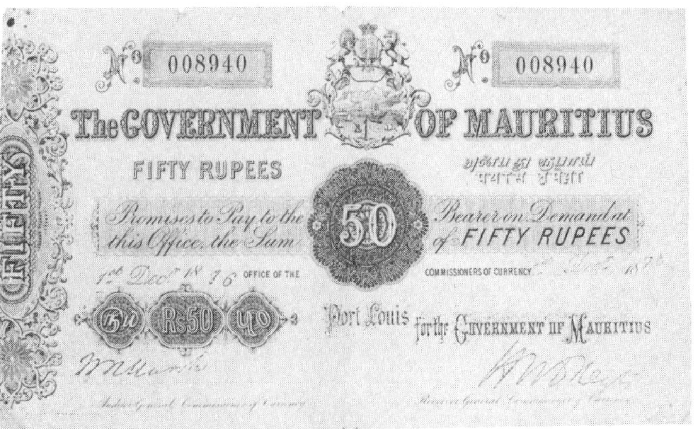

		Good	Fine	XF
15	**50 Rupees** 1.12.1876. Black. Arms at top center. Counterfoil at left. Signature varieties. Rare.	—	—	—

Note: Spink Mauritius collection 10.1996, #15 in fine sold for $10,600, one of two known.

1907-1914 Issue

		Good	Fine	XF
16	**5 Rupees** 1.10.1914-1.10.1930. Arms at top center. Signature title varieties. PC: Greenish-brown.	225	450	1,100
17	**10 Rupees** 1.10.1914-1.10.1930. Arms at top center. Signature title varieties. PC: Lilac.	300	800	1,750
18	**50 Rupees** 19.10.1907; 1.1.1920. Arms at top center. Signature title varieties. Rare.	—	—	—

1919 Issue

		Good	Fine	XF
19	**1 Rupee** 1.7.1919; 1.7.1928. Brown on green underprint. Sailing ship and mountains at right. Printer: TDLR.	100	350	850

1930 Issue

		Good	Fine	XF
20	**5 Rupees** ND (1930). Blue on multicolor underprint. Arms at left, portrait King George V at right. Watermark: Stylized sailing ship. Printer: W&S.	30.00	150	850

		Good	Fine	XF
21	**10 Rupees** ND (1930). Brown on multicolor underprint. Arms at left, portrait King George V at right. Watermark: Stylized sailing ship. Printer: W&S.	100	500	1,600

1937 Issue

		Good	Fine	XF
22	**5 Rupees** ND (1937). Blue on multicolor underprint. Portrait King George VI at right. Printer: W&S.	17.50	50.00	225

		Good	Fine	XF
23	**10 Rupees** ND (1937). Brown on multicolor underprint. Portrait King George VI at right. Printer: W&S.			
	a. Portrait in brown.	40.00	150	800
	b. Portrait in green.	45.00	175	850

1940 Issue

		VG	VF	UNC
24	**25 Cents** ND (1940). Blue. Portrait King George at right. Uniface.			
	a. Serial # at center. Prefix A.	25.00	100	500
	b. Serial # at lower left. Prefix A.	40.00	150	600
	c. Serial # position like b. Prefix B.	25.00	90.00	450
	d. Like b. Prefix C.	25.00	90.00	450

		VG	VF	UNC
25	**50 Cents** ND (1940). Lilac. Portrait King George at right. Uniface.			
	a. Serial # at center. Prefix A.	35.00	125	650
	b. Serial # at lower left. Prefix A.	50.00	175	700
	c. Serial # position like b. Prefix B.	25.00	120	625

		VG	VF	UNC
26	**1 Rupee** ND (1940). Green on lilac underprint. Portrait King George at right. Signature varieties.	20.00	65.00	600

1942 Emergency Issue

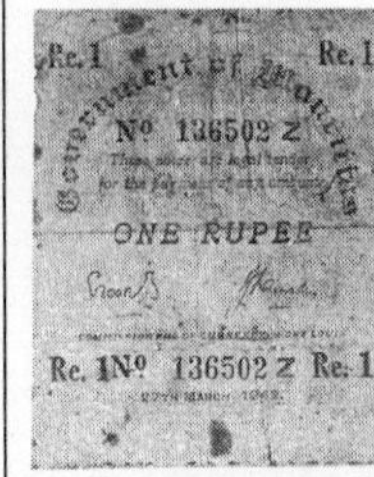

		VG	VF	UNC
26A	**1 Rupee** 27.3.1942 (-old date 1.7.1924; 1.10.1930). Printed on partial backs of 10 Rupees notes #17.	700	1,400	—

1954 Issue

		VG	VF	UNC
27	**5 Rupees** ND (1954). Blue on multicolor underprint. Mountain scene at lower left. Portrait Queen Elizabeth II at right. Signature varieties. Back: Arms. Watermark: Stylized sailing ship. Printer: BWC.			
	a. Issued note.	7.00	40.00	250
	s. Specimen. Overprinted: *SPECIMEN* and punch hole cancelled.	—	—	1,000

		VG	VF	UNC
28	**10 Rupees** ND (1954). Red on multicolor underprint. Mountain scene at lower center. Portrait Queen Elizabeth II at right. Signature varieties. Watermark: Stylized sailing ship. Printer: BWC.			
	a. Issued note.	25.00	150	650
	s. Specimen. Overprinted: *SPECIMEN* and punch hole cancelled.	—	—	1,000

		VG	VF	UNC
29	**25 Rupees** ND (1954). Green on multicolor underprint. Building at lower center. Portrait Queen Elizabeth II at right. Signature varieties. Watermark: Stylized sailing ship. Printer: BWC.			
	a. Issued note.	100	700	1,600
	s. Specimen. Overprinted: *SPECIMEN* and punch hole cancelled.	—	—	4,000

		VG	VF	UNC
29A	**1000 Rupees** ND (1954). Mauve on multicolor underprint. Building at lower center. Rare.	—	—	—

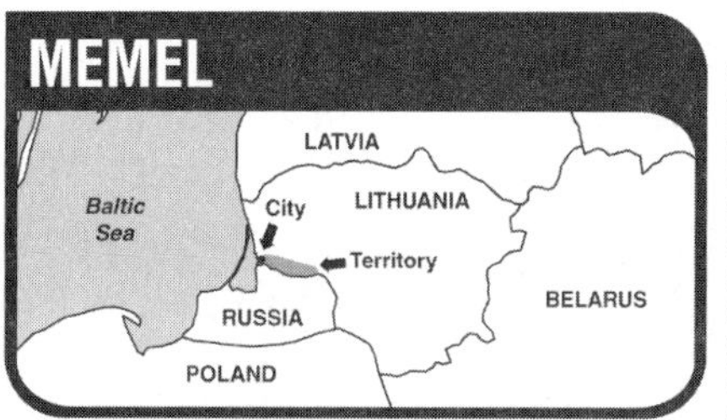

Memel is the German name for Klaipeda, a town and port of Lithuania on the Baltic Sea at the mouth of the Nemunas River. It is the base of a large fishing fleet, and has major shipbuilding and repair yards. Founded as a fort in the early 13th century, Klaipeda was seized and destroyed in 1252 by the Teutonic Knights, who built a new fortress called Memelburg. The town, later called Memel, and adjacent territory was held by the Swedes through most of the 17th century. After the Swedish occupation, the area became part of East Prussia though briefly occupied by the Russians in 1757 and 1813. During World War I, Memel was captured by the Russians again and after 1919 was administered by France under a League of Nations mandate. On Jan. 15, 1923, it was seized by the Lithuanians as their only good port and made a part of the autonomous Klaipeda territory. It was taken by Soviet forces in Jan. 1945 and made a part of the Lithuanian Soviet Socialist Republic until Lithuanian independence was achieved in 1991.

MONETARY SYSTEM:

1 Mark = 100 Pfennig

FRENCH ADMINISTRATION - POST WW I

Handelskammer des Memelgebiets

Chamber of Commerce, Territory of Memel

1922 Issue

#1-9 authorized by the Interallied Commission.

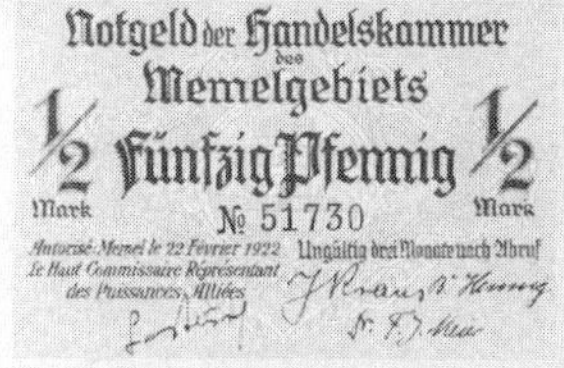

		VG	VF	UNC
1	**1/2 Mark** 22.2.1922. Blue. Back: Bay.	15.00	25.00	40.00

		VG	VF	UNC
2	**1 Mark** 22.2.1922. Brown. Back: Spit of land.	15.00	30.00	50.00

		VG	VF	UNC
3	**2 Mark** 22.2.1922. Blue and olive-brown. Back: Memel in 1630.			
	a. Watermark: Sculptured chain.	25.00	50.00	80.00
	b. Watermark: Contoured chain.	15.00	35.00	70.00
4	**5 Mark** 22.2.1922. Blue and yellow. Back: Stock exchange.			
	a. Watermark: Sculptured chain.	35.00	75.00	150
	b. Watermark: Contoured chain.	20.00	60.00	130

5 10 Mark

22.2.1922. Yellow-brown and blue. Back: Couple, lighthouse and man.

	VG	VF	UNC
a. Watermark: Sculptured chain.	40.00	90.00	170
b. Watermark: Contoured chain.	30.00	80.00	160

6 20 Mark

22.2.1922. Lilac and violet. Back: Cow, farmhouse and horse.

	VG	VF	UNC
a. Watermark: Sculptured chain.	60.00	110	200
b. Watermark: Contoured chain.	50.00	90.00	180

7 50 Mark

22.2.1922. Brown on green and violet. Back: Manufacturing, logging and shipbuilding.

	VG	VF	UNC
a. Watermark: Sculptured chain.	75.00	150	250
b. Watermark: Contoured chain.	70.00	140	220

8 75 Mark

22.2.1922. Brown on blue and pink underprint. Back: New and old sawmills.

VG	VF	UNC
140	250	450

9 100 Mark

22.2.1922. Blue and light brown. Back: General view of Memel.

VG	VF	UNC
120	220	400

The United States of Mexico, located immediately south of the United States, has an area of 1,222,612 sq. mi. (1,967,183 sq. km.) and a population of 98.88 million. Capital: Mexico City. The economy is based on agriculture, manufacturing and mining. Cotton, sugar, coffee and shrimp are exported.

Mexico was the site of highly advanced Indian civilizations 1,500 years before conquistador Hernando Cortes conquered the wealthy Aztec empire of Montezuma, 1519-1521, and founded a Spanish colony which lasted for nearly 300 years. During the Spanish period, Mexico, then called New Spain, stretched from Guatemala to the present states of Wyoming and California, its present northern boundary having been established by the secession of Texas (1836) and the war of 1846-1848 with the United States.

Independence from Spain was declared by Father Miguel Hidalgo on Sept. 16, 1810, Mexican Independence Day, and was achieved by General Agustin de Iturbide in 1821. Iturbide became emperor in 1822 but was deposed when a republic was established a year later. For more than half a century following the birth of the republic, the political scene of Mexico was characterized by turmoil which saw two emperors (including the unfortunate Maximilian), several dictators and an average of one new government every nine months passing swiftly from obscurity to oblivion. The land, social, economic and labor reforms promulgated by the Reform Constitution of Feb. 5, 1917 established the basis for a sustained economic development and participative democracy that have made Mexico one of the most politically stable countries of modern Latin America.

EMPIRE OF ITURBIDE

El Imperio Mexicano, Distrito Federal

1823 Issue

#1-3 issued by Emperor Agustin de Iturbide in 1823. Most were cancelled with a 2-inch cut at bottom.

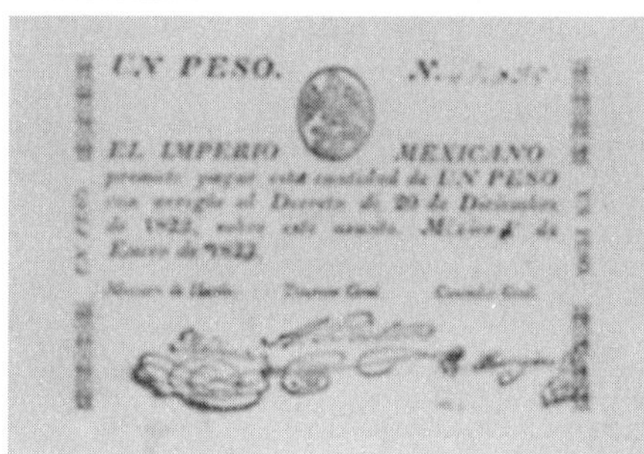

		Good	Fine	XF
1	**1 Peso** 1.1.1823. Black. Arms in oval at upper center. Uniface. PC: Thin, white.			
	a. Issued note. *(PR-DF-1).*	20.00	45.00	100
	b. Cut cancelled. *(PR-DF-5).*	15.00	30.00	80.00
	c. Handwritten cancellation: *Ynutilizado, Oaxaca 16.5.1825. (PR-DF-3).*	20.00	40.00	60.00
	d. Overprint: *LEON* on face in red.	30.00	70.00	125
2	**2 Pesos** 1.1.1823. Black. Arms in oval at upper center. Uniface. PC: Thin, white.	Good	Fine	XF
	a. Issued note. *(PR-DF-6).*	30.00	60.00	100
	b. Cut cancelled. *(PR-DF-8).*	20.00	40.00	60.00
	c. Handwritten cancellation like #1c. *(PR-DF-7).*	20.00	45.00	75.00
3	**10 Pesos** 1.1.1823. Black. Arms in oval at upper center. Uniface. PC: Thin, white.	Good	Fine	XF
	a. Issued note. *(PR-DF-11).*	200	300	400
	b. Cut cancelled. *(PR-DF-12).*	35.00	75.00	125

REPUBLIC

Las Tesorerías de la Nación

The Treasury of the Nation

Decree of April 11, 1823

#4-6 designs similar to Empire issue. Many are cut cancelled. Printed on backs of Papal Bulls (Lent authorizations) dated 1818 and 1819.

		Good	Fine	XF
4	**1 Peso** 5.5.1823.			
	a. Issued note. *(PR-DF-13).*	40.00	100	200
	b. Cut cancelled. *(PR-DF-15).*	20.00	50.00	100
5	**2 Pesos** 5.5.1823.	Good	Fine	XF
	a. Issued note. *(PR-DF-17).*	40.00	100	200
	b. Cut cancelled. *(PR-DF-19).*	25.00	75.00	150

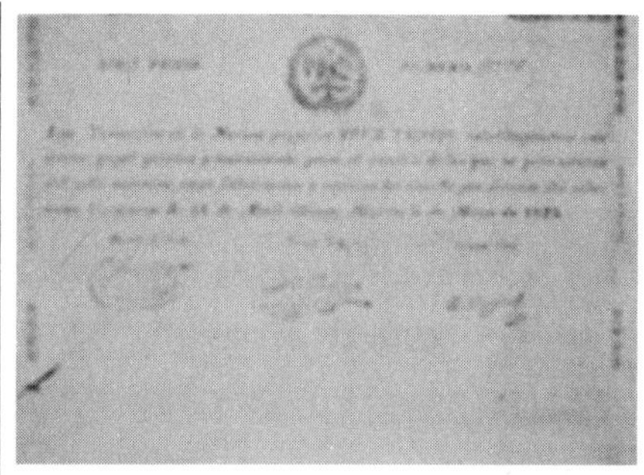

		Good	Fine	XF
6	**10 Pesos** 5.5.1823. *(PR-DF-21).*	100	150	275

EMPIRE OF MAXIMILIAN

Banco de México

This proposed Banco de México has nothing to do with the later Banco de México.

1866 Issue

#7-10 prepared for Emperor Maximillian (1864-1867).

		Good	Fine	XF
7	**10 Pesos** 1866. Blue. Allegorical man and woman seated at lower center. Rare.	—	—	—
8	**20 Pesos** 1866. Blue. Bank monogram at upper center, allegorical woman with lion at lower center. Rare.	—	—	—
9	**100 Pesos** 1866. Black. Man, woman, worker and galley at corners, eagle with snake across top, crowned arms at lower center. Rare.	—	—	—
10	**200 Pesos** 1866. Arms at upper corners, crowned arms at upper center, standing figure at left and right, Indian head at lower center. Rare.	—	—	—

Color Abbreviation Guide

New to the *Standard Catalog of ® World Paper Money* are the following abbreviations related to color references:

BC: Back color
PC: Paper color

ESTADOS UNIDOS MÉXICANOS

UNITED STATES OF MEXICO

Banco de la República Méxicana

1918 Series A

		VG	VF	UNC
11	**5 Pesos** 1918. Black. "Kalliope" seated with globe at center. Back: Aztec calendar at center. BC: Deep blue. Printer: ABNC.			
	p1. Face proof.	—	—	200
	p2. Back proof.	—	—	50.00
	s. Specimen, punch hole cancelled.	—	—	200

		VG	VF	UNC
12	**10 Pesos** 1918. Black. Reclining female with lion at center. Back: Aztec calendar at center. BC: Deep green. Printer: ABNC.			
	p1. Face proof.	—	—	200
	p2. Back proof.	—	—	50.00
	s. Specimen, punch hole cancelled.	—	—	200

		VG	VF	UNC
13	**20 Pesos** 1918. Black. Allegorical female standing holding model airplane next to seated seated female at right. Back: Aztec calendar at center. BC: Deep brown. Printer: ABNC.			
	p1. Face proof.	—	—	200
	p2. Back proof.	—	—	50.00
	s. Specimen, punch hole cancelled.	—	—	200

		VG	VF	UNC
14	**50 Pesos** 1918. Black. Allegorical male seated with sheaf and scythe at left, Allegorical female seated with ship and rudder at right. Back: Aztec calendar at center. BC: Olive-brown. Printer: ABNC.			
	p1. Face proof.	—	—	200
	p2. Back proof.	—	—	50.00
	s. Specimen, punch hole cancelled.	—	—	200

		VG	VF	UNC
15	**100 Pesos** 1918. Black. Cherub standing between two reclining females at center. Back: Deep red. Back: Aztec calendar at center. Printer: ABNC.			
	p1. Face proof.	—	—	200
	p2. Back proof.	—	—	50.00
	s. Specimen, punch hole cancelled.	—	—	200

Comisión Monetaria

1920 Issue

		VG	VF	UNC
16	**50 Centavos** 10.1.1920. Black on gray. Minerva at left. Back: Allegorical figures at center. BC: Green. Printer: Oficina Imp. de Hacienda. *(PT-DF-1).*	10.00	40.00	75.00

		VG	VF	UNC
17	**1 Peso** 10.1.1920. Brown. Goddess of Plenty with two cherubs at center. Back: Allegorical figures at center. BC: Blue. Printer: Oficina Imp. de Hacienda. *(PT-DF-2).*	15.00	45.00	85.00

Banco de México

Trial Design

		VG	VF	UNC
19	**2 Pesos** ND (ca.1930s). Black on pale green underprint. Woman standing before Aztec calendar stone. Back: Statue of Victory at center. BC: Black. Printer: Talleres de Impresión de Estampillas y Valores. Face and back proofs. (Not issued).	—	—	350

1925 Issue

		Good	Fine	XF
21	**5 Pesos** 1925-1934; ND. Black on multicolor underprint. Gypsy at center. Signature varieties. Back: Statue of victory in Mexico City at center. BC: Black. Printer: ABNC. 180x83mm.			
	a. 1.9.1925. Series: A.	200	450	750
	b. 1.8.1931. Series: C.	10.00	35.00	120
	c. 30.4.1932. Series: D.	10.00	35.00	120
	d. 22.6.1932. Series: E.	10.00	35.00	120
	e. 18.1.1933. Series: F.	10.00	35.00	120
	f. 9.8.1933. Series: G.	5.00	20.00	75.00
	g. 7.3.1934. Series: H.	5.00	20.00	75.00
	h. ND. Series: I.	5.00	20.00	75.00

22	10 Pesos	Good	Fine	XF
	1925-1934; ND. Black on multicolor underprint. Two winged females supporting book. Signature varieties. Back: Statue of Victory in Mexico City at center. BC: Brown. Printer: ABNC. 180x83mm.			
	a. 1.9.1925. Series: A.	800	2,000	—
	b. 1.8.1931. Series: C.	10.00	35.00	120
	c. 30.4.1932. Series: D.	10.00	35.00	120
	d. 22.6.1932. Series: E.	10.00	35.00	120
	e. 18.1.1933. Series: F.	10.00	35.00	120
	f. 9.8.1933. Series: G.	5.00	20.00	75.00
	g. 7.3.1934. Series: H.	5.00	20.00	75.00
	h. ND. Series: I.	5.00	20.00	75.00

23	20 Pesos	Good	Fine	XF
	1925-1934; ND. Black on multicolor underprint. Dock scene with ship and steam locomotive. Signature varieties. Back: Statue of Victory in Mexico City at center. BC: Red. Printer: ABNC. 180x83mm.			
	a. 1.9.1925. Series: A.	800	2,000	—
	b. 1.8.1931. Series: C.	25.00	75.00	250
	c. 30.4.1932. Series: D.	25.00	75.00	250
	d. 22.6.1932. Series: E.	20.00	60.00	200
	e. 18.1.1933. Series: F.	20.00	60.00	200
	f. 9.8.1933. Series: G.	20.00	60.00	200
	g. 7.3.1934. Series: H.	15.00	40.00	175
	h. ND. Series: I.	15.00	40.00	175

24	50 Pesos	Good	Fine	XF
	1925-1934. Black on multicolor underprint. Seated female holding ship at left. Signature varieties. Back: Statue of Victory in Mexico City at center. BC: Olive-green. Printer: ABNC. 180x83mm.			
	a. 1.9.1925. Series: A.	800	2,000	—
	b. 1.8.1931. Series: C.	80.00	130	300
	c. 30.4.1932. Series: D.	80.00	130	300
	d. 22.6.1932. Series: E.	80.00	130	300
	e. 18.1.1933. Series: F.	80.00	130	300
	f. 9.8.1933. Series: G.	75.00	120	250
	g. 7.3.1934. Series: H.	75.00	120	250
	p1. Uniface face proof.	—	—	—
	p2. Uniface back proof.	—	—	—

25	100 Pesos	Good	Fine	XF
	1925-1934. Black on multicolor underprint. Allegorical male seated holding ship, with youth at center. Signature varieties. Back: Statue of Victory in Mexico City at center. BC: Dark green. Printer: ABNC. 180x83mm.			
	a. 1.9.1925. Series: A.	1,000	2,500	—
	b. 1.8.1931. Series: C.	100	200	350
	c. 30.4.1932. Series: D.	100	200	350
	d. 22.6.1932. Series: E.	100	200	350
	e. 18.1.1933. Series: F.	100	200	350
	f. 9.8.1933. Series: G.	90.00	175	300
	g. 7.3.1934. Series: H.	90.00	175	300
	p1. Uniface face proof.	—	—	—
	p2. Uniface back proof.	—	—	—

26	500 Pesos	Good	Fine	XF
	1925-1934. Black on multicolor underprint. Electricity" seated at center. Signature varieties. Back: Statue of Victory in Mexico City at center. BC: Blue. Printer: ABNC. 180x83mm.			
	a. 1.9.1925. Series A.	1,200	2,750	—
	b. 1.8.1931. Series C.	500	1,200	—
	c. 30.4.1932. Series D.	500	1,200	—
	d. 22.6.1932. Series E.	500	1,200	—
	e. 18.1.1933. Series F.	500	1,200	—
	f. 9.8.1933. Series G.	450	1,000	—
	g. 7.3.1934. Series H.	450	1,000	—
	p1. Uniface face proof.	—	—	—
	p2. Uniface back proof.	—	—	—

		Good	Fine	XF
27	**1000 Pesos** 1931-1934. Black on multicolor underprint. Seated female with globe. Signature varieties. Back: Statue of Victory in Mexico City at center. BC: Orange. Printer: ABNC. 180x83mm.			
	a. 1.9.1925. Series A.	2,500	3,750	—
	b. 1.8.1931. Series C.	1,500	2,500	—
	c. 30.4.1932. Series D.	1,500	2,500	—
	d. 22.6.1932. Series E.	1,500	2,500	—
	e. 18.1.1933. Series F.	1,500	2,500	—
	f. 9.8.1933. Series G.	1,200	2,250	—
	g. 7.3.1934. Series H.	1,200	2,250	—

1936 Issue

		VG	VF	UNC
28	**1 Peso** ND (1936); 1943. Black on multicolor underprint. Aztec calendar stone at center *UN* in background under signature at left and right. Signature varieties. Back: Statue of Victory at center. BC: Red. Printer: ABNC. 157x67mm.			
	a. ND. Series: A.	10.00	20.00	90.00
	b. ND. Series: B.	12.00	30.00	125
	c. ND. Series: C.	1.00	5.00	25.00
	d. ND. Series: D-F.	1.00	5.00	20.00
	e. 14.4.1943. Series: G-K.	1.00	5.00	20.00

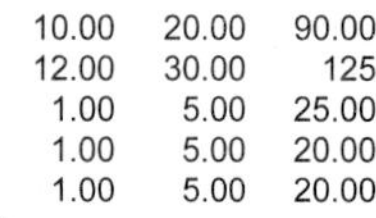

		VG	VF	UNC
29	**5 Pesos** 1.4.1936. Black on multicolor underprint. Portrait gypsy at center. Like #21 but smaller, with text: *PAGARA CINCO PESOS...EN EFECTIVO* below portrait, with curved *SERIE* at left and right. Series J. Signature varieties. Back: Large BdM seal. Printer: ABNC. 157x67mm.	10.00	50.00	150

		VG	VF	UNC
30	**10 Pesos** 1.4.1936. Black on multicolor underprint. Two winged females supporting book. Like # 22 but smaller. Series: J. Signature varieties. Back: Statue of Victory at center. Printer: ABNC. 157x67mm.	10.00	50.00	150

		VG	VF	UNC
31	**100 Pesos** 1.9.1936. Black on multicolor underprint. Portrait F. I. Madero at right. Series:K. Signature varieties. Back: Bank of Mexico at center, large seal. BC: Purple. Printer: ABNC. 157x67mm.			
	a. Issued note.	30.00	50.00	125
	s. Specimen, punch hole cancelled.	—	—	225

		VG	VF	UNC
32	**500 Pesos** 9.1.1936. Printed. Black on multicolor underprint. Portrait J. M. Morelos y Pavon at right. Middle signature title: *INTERVENTOR DEL GOBIERNO.* Large seal. Back: Miner's palace. BC: Green. Printer: ABNC. 157x67mm.	275	500	—

		VG	VF	UNC
33	**1000 Pesos** 9.1.1936. Printed. Black on multicolor underprint. Portrait Cuauhtémoc at right. Middle signature title: *INTERVENTOR DEL GOBIERNO.* Series:K. Signature varieties. Back: El Castillo Chichen-Itza, with large seal. BC: Dark brown. Printer: ABNC. 157x67mm.	325	600	—

1937 Issue

		VG	VF	UNC
34	**5 Pesos** 1937-1950. Black on multicolor underprint. Portrait gypsy at center. Like #29 but with text: *PAGARA CINCO PESOS.... AL PORTADOR* below portrait, with *EL* and *S.A.* added. Signature varieties. Back: *S.A.* added to *BANCO DE MEXICO* with small BdeM seal. BC: Gray. Printer: ABNC.			
	a. 22.9.1937. Series: M.	4.00	7.50	60.00
	b. 26.6.1940. Series: N.	1.50	5.00	18.00
	c. 12.11.1941. Series: O.	1.50	5.00	18.00
	d. 25.11.1942. Series: P.	1.00	3.50	10.00
	e. 7.4.1943. Series: Q.	1.00	3.00	7.50
	f. 1.9.1943. Series: R.	1.00	3.50	10.00
	g. 17.1.1945. Series: S-Z.	1.00	3.50	10.00
	h. 14.8.1946. Series: AA-AK.	1.00	3.00	8.00
	i. 3.9.1947. Series: AL-AZ.	1.00	3.00	7.00
	j. 22.12.1948. Series: BA-BT.	1.00	3.00	7.00
	k. 23.11.1949. Series: BU-BV.	0.50	2.00	6.00
	l. 26.7.1950. Series: BY-CB.	0.50	2.00	5.00
	s. Specimen, punch hole cancelled.	—	—	175

35	10 Pesos	VG	VF	UNC
	1937-1942. Printed. Black on multicolor underprint. Portrait E. Ruiz de Velazquez at right. Middle signature title: *INTERVENTOR DEL GOBIERNO.* Signature varieties. Back: Road to Guanajuato at center. Printer: ABNC.			
	a. 22.9.1937. Series: M.	4.00	7.50	60.00
	b. 26.6.1940. Series: N.	2.50	6.00	18.00
	c. 12.11.1941. Series: O.	1.50	5.00	15.00
	d. 25.11.1942. Series: P.	1.50	5.00	15.00
	s. Specimen, punch hole cancelled.	—	—	175

36	20 Pesos	VG	VF	UNC
	21.4.1937. Printed. Black on multicolor underprint. Portrait J. Ortiz de Dominguez at left. Middle signature title: *INTERVENTOR DEL GOBIERNO.* Signature varieties. Series: left. Back: Federal palace courtyard at center, large seal. BC: Olive-green. Printer: ABNC.	8.00	35.00	110

37	50 Pesos	Good	Fine	XF
	1937; 1940. Purple, green, brown and multicolor. Portrait I. Zaragoza at right. Signature varieties. Back: View of Ixtaccihuatl-Popocatepetl and volcanoes. Printer: ABNC.			
	a. 21.4.1937. Series: L.	150	250	450
	b. 26.6.1940. Series: N.	175	300	600

1940-1943 Issue

38	1 Peso	VG	VF	UNC
	1943-1948. Aztec calendar stone at center. Like #28 but without *No* above serial #. *UNO* in background under signature at left and right. Signature varieties. Printer: ABNC.			
	a. 7.7.1943. Series: L-Q.	0.50	3.00	6.00
	b. 1.9.1943. Series: R.	3.00	10.00	45.00
	c. 17.1.1945. Series: S-Z.	0.50	4.00	20.00
	d. 12.5.1948. Series: AA-AJ.	0.25	2.00	6.00

39	10 Pesos	VG	VF	UNC
	1943-1945. Black on multicolor underprint. Portrait E. Ruiz de Velazquez at right. Like #35 but *MEXICO D.F.* and printed dates higher. Signature varieties. Back: Road to Guanajuato at center. Printer: ABNC.			
	a. 7.4.1943. Series: Q.	1.50	3.50	10.00
	b. 1.9.1943. Series: R.	1.50	5.00	20.00
	c. 17.1.1945. Series: S-Z.	1.50	4.00	15.00

40	20 Pesos	VG	VF	UNC
	1940-1945. Printed. Black on multicolor underprint. Portrait J.Oritz de Dominguez at left. Middle signature title:*INTERVENTOR DEL GOBIERNO.* Signature varieties. Back: Small seal. Series: left. Printer: ABNC.			
	a. 26.6.1940. Series: N.	2.00	7.50	25.00
	b. 11.11.1941. Series: O.	2.00	7.50	25.00
	c. 11.11.1491 at left, 11.11.1941 at right. (error). Series: O.	150	400	—
	d. 12.11.1941. Series: O.	2.00	7.50	25.00
	e. 25.11.1942. Series: P.	2.00	4.50	15.00
	f. 7.4.1943. Series: Q.	2.00	4.50	15.00
	g. 1.9.1943. Series: R.	—	—	—
	h. 17.1.1945. Series: S-Z.	2.00	4.50	15.00
	s. Specimen, punch hole cancelled.	—	—	175

41	50 Pesos	VG	VF	UNC
	1941-1945. Printed. Blue on multicolor underprint. Portrait I. de Allende at left. Middle signature title: *INTERVENTOR DEL GOBIERNO.* Signature varieties. Back: Statue of Victory at center. BC: Blue. Printer: ABNC.			
	a. 12.11.1941. Series: O; P.	5.00	30.00	125
	b. 7.4.1943. Series Q.	3.00	10.00	60.00
	c. 25.10.1944. Series: R.	2.50	7.50	40.00
	d. 17.1.1945. Series: S-Z.	2.00	5.00	25.00
	s. Specimen, punch hole cancelled.	—	—	175

42	100 Pesos	VG	VF	UNC
	1940-1942. Black on multicolor underprint. Portrait F.I. Madero at right. Signature varieties. Back: Bank of Mexico building at center. Small seal. BC: Purple. Printer: ABNC.			
	a. 26.6.1940. Series: N.	35.00	60.00	140
	b. 12.11.1941. Series: O.	35.00	60.00	140
	c. 25.11.1942. Series: P.	35.00	60.00	140

		VG	VF	UNC
43	**500 Pesos** 1940-1943. Printed. Black on multicolor underprint. Portrait J.M. Morelos y Pavon at right. Middle signature title:*INTERVENTOR DEL GOBIERNO.* Signature varieties. Back: Green. Back: Miner's palace and small seal. Printer: ABNC.			
	a. 26.6.1940. Series: N.	50.00	175	350
	b. 11.11.1941. Series: O.	25.00	100	250
	c. 25.11.1942. Series: P.	25.00	100	250
	d. 7.4.1943. Series: Q.	25.00	100	250
	e. 1.9.1943. Series: R.	25.00	100	250
	s. Specimen, punch hole cancelled.	—	—	225

		VG	VF	UNC
44	**1000 Pesos** 1941-1945. Printed. Black on multicolor underprint. Cuauhtemoc at left. Portrait Cuauhtemoc at right. Middle signature title:*INTERVENTOR DEL GOBIERNO.* Signature varieties. Back: Dark brown. Back: El Castillo Chichen-itza at center. Printer: ABNC.			
	a. 11.11.1941. Series: O.	75.00	175	350
	b. 25.11.1942. Series: P.	25.00	100	250
	c. 7.4.1943. Series: Q.	25.00	100	250
	d. 20.11.1945. Series: R.	25.00	100	250
	s. Specimen, punch hole cancelled.	—	—	175

		VG	VF	UNC
45	**10,000 Pesos** 1943-1953. Purple on multicolor underprint. Portrait M. Romero at left. Signature varieties. Back: Government palace. Printer: ABNC.			
	a. 1.9.1943. Series R.	450	850	—
	b. 27.12.1950. Series: CS.	350	600	—
	c. 19.1.1953. Series: DL.	600	900	—
	s. Specimen, punch hole cancelled.	—	—	350

Note: For 10,000 Pesos like #45 but dated 1978, see #72 in Volume 3.

		VG	VF	UNC
A45	**10,000 Pesos** ND (ca.1942). Purple on multicolor underprint. Like #45, but signature title: *INTERVENTOR DEL GOBIERNO* at center Specimen.	—	—	—

1945-1948 Issue

		VG	VF	UNC
46	**1 Peso** 1948; 1950. Like #38 but *EL* and *S.A.* added to *BANCO DE MEXICO*. Signature varieties. Back: *S.A.* added. Printer: ABNC.			
	a. 22.12.1948. Series: BA-BJ.	0.25	1.00	6.00
	b. 26.7.1950. Series: BY-CR.	0.25	1.00	4.00

		VG	VF	UNC
47	**10 Pesos** 1946-1950. Engraved. Black on multicolor underprint. Portrait E. Ruiz de Velazquez at right. Middle signature title: *INTERVENTOR DE LA COM. NAC. BANCARIA.* Signature varieties. Printer: ABNC.			
	a. 14.8.1946. Series: AA-AJ.	1.00	3.00	9.00
	b. 3.9.1947. Series: AK-AZ.	1.00	3.00	9.00
	c. 22.12.1948. Series: BA-BJ.	1.00	3.00	9.00
	d. 23.11.1949. Series: BU.	0.25	3.00	9.00
	e. 26.7.1950. Series: BY, BZ.	0.25	3.00	9.00

		VG	VF	UNC
48	**20 Pesos** 22.12.1948. Engraved. Series BA-BE. Black on multicolor underprint. Portrait J. Ortiz de Dominguez at left. Middle signature title: *INTERVENTOR DE LA COM. NAC. BANCARIA.* Signature varieties. Printer: ABNC.	1.00	4.00	15.00

1945-1951 Issue

		VG	VF	UNC
49	**50 Pesos** 1948-1972. Engraved. Blue on multicolor underprint. Portrait I. de Allende at left. Middle signature title: *INTERVENTOR DE LA COM. NAC. BANCARIA.* Signature varieties. Back: Blue. Back: Independence Monument at center. Printer: ABNC.			
	a. 22.12.1948. Black series letters. Series: BA-BD.	3.00	6.00	15.00
	b. 23.11.1949. Series: BU-BX.	3.00	6.00	15.00
	c. 26.7.1950. Series: BY-CF.	3.00	5.00	15.00
	d. 27.12.1950. Series: CS-DH.	3.00	5.00	15.00
	e. 19.1.1953. Series: DK-DV.	2.00	4.00	15.00
	f. 10.2.1954. Series: DW-EE.	2.00	4.00	15.00
	g. 8.9.1954. Series: EF-FF.	2.00	4.00	15.00
	h. 11.1.1956. Series: FK-FV.	2.00	4.00	15.00
	i. 19.6.1957. Series: FW-GP.	2.00	4.00	15.00
	j. 20.8.1958. Series: HC-HR.	2.00	4.00	15.00
	k. 18.3.1959. 2 red series letters. Series: HS-IP.	2.00	4.00	15.00
	l. 20.5.1959. Series: IQ-JN.	2.00	4.00	15.00
	m. 25.1.1961. Series: JO-LB.	1.00	3.00	8.00
	n. 8.11.1961. Series: LC-AID.	1.00	3.00	8.00
	o. 24.4.1963. Series: AIE-BAP.	1.00	3.00	6.00
	p. 17.2.1965. Series: BAQ-BCD.	1.00	2.50	6.00
	q. 10.5.1967. Series: BCY-BEN.	1.00	2.50	6.00
	r. 19.11.1969. Series: BGK-BIC.	1.00	2.50	4.00
	s. 22.7.1970. Series: BIG-BKN.	1.00	2.50	4.00
	t. 27.6.1972. Series: BLI-BMG.	1.00	2.50	3.00
	u. 29.12.1972. Series: BMO-BRB.	1.00	2.00	3.00
	v. Specimen, punch hole cancelled.	—	—	135

		VG	VF	UNC
50	**100 Pesos** 17.1.1945. Printed. Brown on multicolor underprint. Portrait M. Hidalgo at left, series letters above serial #. Middle signature title: *INTERVENTOR DEL GOBIERNO.* Signature varieties. Back: Olive-green. Back: Coin with national coat-of-arms at center. Series: S-Z. Printer: ABNC.			
	a. Issued note.	5.00	15.00	70.00
	s. Specimen, punch hole cancelled.	—	—	200

51 500 Pesos

1948-1978. Black on multicolor underprint. Like #43 but without *No.* above serial #. Middle signature title: *INTERVENTOR DE LA COM. NAC. BANCARIA.* Signature varieties. Back: Palace of Mining at center. BC: Green. Printer: ABNC.

	VG	VF	UNC
a. 22.12.1948. Series: BA.	10.00	40.00	125
b. 27.12.1950. Series: CS; CT.	4.00	12.00	30.00
c. 3.12.1951. Series: DI; DJ.	4.00	12.00	30.00
d. 19.1.1953. Series: DK-DN.	4.00	12.00	30.00
e. 31.8.1955. Series: FG-FJ.	4.00	12.00	30.00
f. 11.1.1956. Series: FK-FL.	4.00	12.00	30.00
g. 19.6.1957. Series: FW-GB.	4.00	12.00	30.00
h. 20.8.1958. Series: HC-HH.	4.00	12.00	30.00
i. 18.3.1959. Series: HS-HX.	4.00	12.00	30.00
j. 20.5.1959. Series: IQ-IV.	4.00	12.00	30.00
k. 25.1.1961. Series: JO-JT.	3.00	8.00	25.00
l. 8.11.1961. Series: LC-MP.	2.00	7.00	20.00
m. 17.2.1965. Series: BAQ-BCN.	4.00	12.00	25.00
n. 24.3.1971. Series: BKO-BKT.	2.50	5.00	12.50
o. 27.6.1972. Series: BLI-BLM.	2.50	5.00	12.50
p. 29.12.1972. Series: BNG-BNP.	2.50	5.00	12.50
q. 18.7.1973. Series: BUY-BWB.	1.50	5.00	12.50
r. 2.8.1974. Series: BXV-BZI.	1.50	3.50	10.00
s. 18.2.1977. Series: BZJ-CCK.	1.00	3.50	10.00
t. 18.1.1978. Series: CCL-CDY.	1.00	3.50	8.50

52 1000 Pesos

1948-1977. Black on multicolor underprint. Cuauhtemoc at left. Middle signature title: *IN-TERVENTOR DE LA COM. NAC. BANCARIA.* Signature varieties. Back: Chichen Itza pyramid at center. BC: Brown. Printer: ABNC.

	VG	VF	UNC
a. 22.12.1948. Series: BA.	5.00	15.00	60.00
b. 23.11.1949. Series: BU.	5.00	15.00	60.00
c. 27.12.1950. Series: CS.	5.00	15.00	60.00
d. 3.12.1951. Series: DI; DJ.	5.00	15.00	60.00
e. 19.1.1953. Series: DK; DL.	5.00	15.00	60.00
f. 31.8.1955. Series: FG; FH.	5.00	15.00	60.00
g. 11.1.1956. Series: FK; FL.	5.00	15.00	60.00
h. 19.6.1957. Series: FW-FZ.	5.00	15.00	60.00
i. 20.8.1958. Series: HC-HE.	5.00	15.00	60.00
j. 18.3.1959. Series: HS-HU.	5.00	15.00	60.00
k. 20.5.1959. Series: IQ-IS.	5.00	15.00	60.00
l. 25.1.1961. Series: JO-JQ.	5.00	15.00	60.00
m. 8.11.1961. Series: LC-LV.	3.00	10.00	20.00
n. 17.2.1965. Series: BAQ-BCN.	2.00	8.00	15.00
o. 24.3.1971. Series: BKO-BKT.	2.00	6.00	10.00
p. 27.6.1972. Series: BLI-BLM.	2.00	6.00	10.00
q. 29.12.1972. Series: BNG-BNK.	1.00	3.00	5.00
r. 18.7.1973. Series: BUY-BWB.	2.00	6.00	10.00
s. 2.8.1974. Series: BXV-BYY.	1.00	5.00	8.00
t. 18.2.1977. Series: BZJ-CBQ.	1.00	5.00	8.00
x. Error: *EERIE HD* rather than SERIE at left.	25.00	45.00	85.00

1950; 1951 Issue

53 10 Pesos

1951; 1953. Black on multicolor underprint. Portrait E. Ruiz de Velazquez at right. Like #47 but without *No.* above serial #. Signature varieties. Printer: ABNC.

	VG	VF	UNC
a. 3.12.1951. Series: DI, DJ.	0.25	2.00	5.00
b. 19.1.1953. Series: DK, DL.	0.25	2.00	5.00

1950 Issue

54 20 Pesos

1950-1970. Black on multicolor underprint. Portrait J. Ortiz de Dominguez at left. Like number 48 but without *No.* above serial #. Signature varieties. Back: Federal Palace courtyard at center. BC: Olive-green. Printer: ABNC.

	VG	VF	UNC
a. 27.12.1950. Black series letters. Series: CS; CT.	1.00	3.00	15.00
b. 19.1.1953. Series: dark.	1.00	3.00	15.00
c. 10.2.1954. Red series letters. Series: DW.	1.00	2.00	10.00
d. 11.1.1956. Series: FK.	1.00	2.00	10.00
e. 10.6.1957. Series: FW.	1.00	2.00	10.00
f. 20.8.1958. Series: HC, HD.	1.00	2.00	10.00
g. 18.3.1959. Series: HS, HT.	1.00	2.00	10.00
h. 20.5.1959. Series: IQ, IR.	1.00	2.00	10.00
i. 25.1.1961. Series: JO, JP.	0.50	1.50	10.00
j. 8.11.1961. Series: LC-LG.	0.50	1.50	10.00
k. 24.4.1963. Series: AIE-AIH.	0.50	1.50	5.00
l. 17.2.1965. Series: BAQ-BAV.	0.50	1.50	5.00
m. 10.5.1967. Series: BCY-BDB.	0.50	1.50	5.00
n. 27.8.1969. Series: BGA; BGB.	0.50	1.50	5.00
o. 18.3.1970. Series: BID-BIF.	0.50	1.50	5.00
p. 22.7.1970. Series: BIG-BIK.	0.50	1.50	5.00
s. Specimen, punch hole cancelled.	—	—	135

55 100 Pesos

1950-1961. Engraved. Brown on multicolor underprint. Portrait M. Hidalgo at left, series letters above serial #. Middle signature title: *INTERVENTOR DE LA COM. NAC. BANCARIA.* Signature varieties. Back: Coin with national seal at center. BC: Olive-green. Printer: ABNC.

	VG	VF	UNC
a. 27.12.1950. Black series letters. Series: CS-CZ.	4.00	8.00	30.00
b. 19.1.1953. Series: DK-DP.	2.00	7.00	25.00
c. 10.2.1954. Series: DW-DZ.	2.00	7.00	25.00
d. 8.9.1954. Series: EI-ET.	2.00	7.00	25.00
e. 11.1.1956. Series: FK-FV.	2.00	7.00	25.00
f. 19.6.1957. Series: FW-GH.	2.00	7.00	25.00
g. 20.8.1958. Series: HC-HR.	2.00	7.00	25.00
h. 18.3.1959. Series: HS-IH.	2.00	7.00	25.00
i. 20.5.1959. Series: IQ-JF.	2.00	7.00	25.00
j. 25.1.1961. Series: JO-KL.	2.00	7.00	25.00

1953; 1954 Issue

56 1 Peso

1954. Like number #46 but series letters in red at lower left and right. Signature varieties. Printer: ABNC.

	VG	VF	UNC
a. 10.2.1954. Series: DW-EF.	0.25	1.00	4.00
b. 8.9.1954. Series: EI-FB.	0.25	1.00	4.00

57 5 Pesos

1953-1954. Black on multicolor underprint. Like #34 but without *No.* above serial #, with series letters lower. Signature varieties. Printer: ABNC.

	VG	VF	UNC
a. 19.1.1953. Series: DK-DN.	0.50	2.00	5.00
b. 10.2.1954. Series: DW-DZ.	0.25	1.00	4.00
c. 8.9.1954. Series: EI-EP.	0.25	1.00	4.00

1954 Issue

		VG	VF	UNC
58	**10 Pesos** 1954-1967. Black on multicolor underprint. Portrait E. Ruiz de Velazquez at right. Like #53 but with text: *MEXICO D.F.* above series letters. Signature varieties. Back: Road to Guanajuato at center. BC: Brown. Printer: ABNC.			
	a. 10.2.1954. Series: DW, DX.	0.50	1.50	5.00
	b. 8.9.1954. Series: EI-EN.	0.50	1.50	5.00
	c. 19.6.1957. Series: FW, FX.	0.50	1.50	5.00
	d. 24.7.1957. Series: GQ.	0.50	1.50	5.00
	e. 20.8.1958. Series: HC-HF.	0.25	1.50	6.00
	f. 18.3.1959. Series: HS-HU.	0.25	1.00	5.00
	g. 20.5.1959. Series: IQ-IS.	0.25	1.00	4.00
	h. 25.1.1961. Series: JO-JT.	0.25	1.00	4.00
	i. 8.11.1961. Series: LC-LV.	0.25	1.00	4.00
	j. 24.4.1963. Series: AIE-AIT.	0.25	1.00	3.00
	k. 17.2.1965. Series: BAQ-BAX.	0.25	1.00	3.00
	l. 10.5.1967. Series: BCY-BDA.	0.25	1.00	3.00
	s. Specimen, punch hole cancelled.	—	—	150

1957; 1961 Issue

		VG	VF	UNC
59	**1 Peso** 1957-1970. Black on multicolor underprint. Aztec calendar stone at center. Like #56 but with text: *MEXICO D.F.* added above date at lower left. Back: Independence monument at center. BC: Red. Printer: ABNC.			
	a. 19.6.1957. Series: FW-GF.	0.10	1.00	4.50
	b. Deleted.	—	—	—
	c. 4.12.1957. Series: GS-HB.	0.10	1.00	4.50
	d. 20.8.1958. Series: HC-HL.	0.10	0.75	2.50
	e. 18.3.1959. Series: HS-IB.	0.10	0.50	2.50
	f. 20.5.1959. Series: IQ-IZ.	0.10	0.50	2.50
	g. 25.1.1961. Series: JO-KC.	0.10	0.25	2.00
	h. 8.11.1961. Series: LC; LD.	0.10	0.50	2.00
	i. 9.6.1965. Series: BCO-BCX.	0.10	0.25	2.00
	j. 10.5.1967. Series: BCY-BEB.	0.10	0.25	1.00
	k. 27.8.1969. Series: BGA-BGJ.	0.10	0.25	1.00
	l. 22.7.1970. Series: BIG-BIP.	0.10	0.20	1.00
	s. Specimen.	—	—	—

		VG	VF	UNC
60	**5 Pesos** 1957-1970. Black on multicolor underprint. Portrait gypsy at center. Like #57 but with Text: *MEXICO D.F.* before date. Back: Independence Monument at center. BC: Gray. Printer: ABNC.			
	a. 19.6.1957. Series: FW, FX.	0.25	2.00	7.00
	b. 24.7.1957. Series: GQ, GR.	0.25	2.00	7.00
	c. 20.8.1958. Series: HC-HJ.	0.25	1.50	6.00
	d. 18.3.1959. Series: HS-HV.	0.25	1.50	6.00
	e. 20.5.1959. Series: IQ-IT.	0.25	1.50	6.00
	f. 25.1.1961. Series: JO-JV.	0.15	0.50	4.00
	g. 8.11.1961. Series: LC-MP.	0.15	0.50	3.00
	h. 24.4.1963. Series: AIE-AJJ.	0.15	0.50	2.50
	i. 27.8.1969. Series BGJ.	0.15	0.50	2.50
	j. 19.11.1969. Series: BGK-BGT.	0.15	0.50	2.50
	k. 22.7.1970. Series: BIG-BII.	0.15	0.50	2.50

		VG	VF	UNC
61	**100 Pesos** 1961-1973. Brown on multicolor underprint. Portrait M. Hidalgo at left. Like #55 but series letters below serial #. Back: Coin with national seal at center. Printer: ABNC.			
	a. 8.11.1961. Red series letters. Series: LE-ZZ; AAA-AEG.	2.00	5.00	12.50
	b. 24.4.1963. Series: AIK-AUG.	2.00	5.00	12.50
	c. 17.2.1965. Series: BAQ-BCD.	1.00	3.00	8.00
	d. 10.5.1967. Series: BCY-BFZ.	1.00	3.00	8.00
	e. 22.7.1970. Series: BIO-BJK.	1.00	3.00	8.00
	f. 24.3.1971. Series: BKP-BLH.	1.00	3.00	8.00
	g. 27.6.1972. Series: BLI-BNF.	1.00	3.00	8.00
	h. 29.12.1972. Series: BNG-BUX.	0.50	1.50	5.00
	i. 18.7.1973. Series: BUY-BXU.	0.50	1.50	5.00

The area of Moldova is bordered in the north, east, and south by the Ukraine and on the west by Romania. The historical Romanian principality of Moldova was established in the 14th century. It fell under Turkish suzerainty in the 16th century. From 1812 to 1918, Russians occupied the eastern portion of Moldova which they named Bessarabia. In March 1918, the Bessarabian legislature voted in favor of reunification with Romania. Part of Romania during the interwar period, Moldova was incorporated into the Soviet Union at the close of World War II. Although independent from the USSR since 1991, Russian forces have remained on Moldovan territory east of the Dniester River supporting the Slavic majority population, mostly Ukrainians and Russians, who have proclaimed a "Transnistria" republic. One of the poorest nations in Europe, Moldova became the first former Soviet state to elect a Communist as its president in 2001.

MONETARY SYSTEM:

3 Ducati = 100 Lei
100 Rubles = 1000 Cupon, 1992
1 Leu = 1000 Cupon, 1993-

REPUBLIC

Banca Nationala a Moldavei

1857 Issue

		Good	Fine	XF
A1	**3 Ducats = 100 Lei** 1.9.1857. Arms at top center. Printer: G&D. Rare.	—	—	—

Cemitetul National Revolutionar Roman

1853 Revolutionary Issue

		Good	Fine	XF
A2	**10 Ducati** 1853. Eagle at top center. Rare.	—	—	—

Note: For later issues see Moldova in Volume 3, Modern Issues.

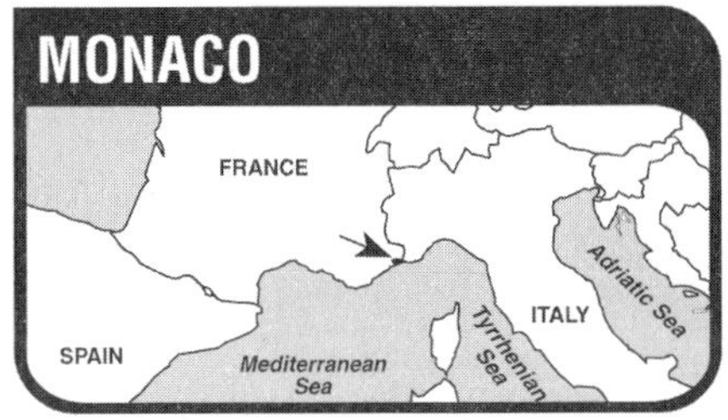

The Principality of Monaco, located on the Mediterranean coast nine miles off Nice, has an area of 0.6 sq. mi. (1.49 sq. km.) and a population of 32,000. Capital: Monaco-Ville. The economy is based on tourism and the manufacture of perfumes and liqueurs. Monaco derives most of its revenue from a tobacco monopoly, the sale of postage stamps for philatelic purpose, and the gambling tables of Monte Carlo Casino.The Genoese built a fortress on the site of present-day Monaco in 1215. The current ruling Grimaldi family secured control in the late 13th century, and a principality was established in 1338. Economic development was spurred in the late 19th century with a railroad linkup to France and the opening of a casino. Since then, the principality's mild climate, splendid scenery, and gambling facilities have made Monaco world famous as a tourist and recreation center. Since 1865, Monaco has maintained a customs union with France which guarantees its privileged position as long as the royal male line remains intact. Under the the new constitution proclaimed on December 17, 1962, the Prince shares his power with an 18-member unicameral National Council.

RULERS:

Albert I, 1889-1922
Louis II, 1922-1949
Rainier III, 1949-

MONETARY SYSTEM:

1 Franc = 100 Centimes

PRINCIPALITY

Principauté de Monaco

1920 Emergency Issues

#	Description	VF	UNC
1	**25 Centimes**	**VF**	**UNC**
	16.3.(20.3) 1920. (Dated 1920.) Brown. First issue.		
	a. Without embossed arms.	60.00	175
	b. Embossed arms in 17mm stamp.	75.00	225
	c. Embossed arms in 22mm stamp.	60.00	175
2	**25 Centimes**	**VF**	**UNC**
	16.3.(20.3) 1920. (Dated 1921.) Blue-violet.		
	a. Without embossed arms.	40.00	100
	b. Embossed arms in 17mm stamp.	60.00	175
	c. Embossed arms in 22mm stamp.	60.00	175

#	Description	VF	UNC
3	**50 Centimes**	**VF**	**UNC**
	16.3.(20.3) 1920. (Issued 28.4.1920.) Blue-gray. Series A-H.		
	a. Issued note.	60.00	200
	r. Remainder without serial #. Series E.	—	75.00
4	**1 Franc**	**VF**	**UNC**
	16.3.(20.3) 1920. (Issued 28.4.1920.) Brown. First issue. Lettered cartouche.		
	a. Series A.	75.00	225
	b. Series B; C.	200	350

#	Description	VF	UNC
5	**1 Franc**	**VF**	**UNC**
	16.3.(20.3) 1920. (Issued 28.4.1920.) Blue-gray and brown. Series A-E. Second issue. Plain cartouche.	50.00	150

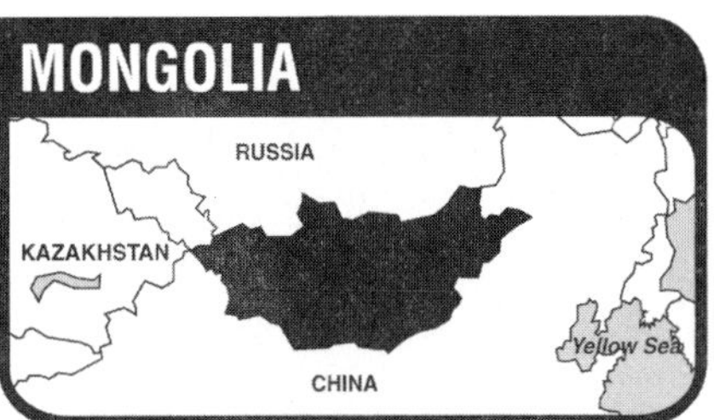

The State of Mongolia, a landlocked country in central Asia between Russia and the Peoples Republic of China, has an area of 604,247 sq. mi. (1,565,000 sq. km.) and a population of 2.74 million. Capital: Ulan Bator. Animal herds and flocks are the chief economic asset. Wool, cattle, butter, meat and hides are exported. The Mongols gained fame in the 13th century when under Chinggis Khan they established a huge Eurasian empire through conquest. After his death the empire was divided into several powerful Mongol states, but these broke apart in the 14th century. The Mongols eventually retired to their original steppe homelands and in the late 17th century came under Chinese rule. Mongolia won its independence in 1921 with Soviet backing and a Communist regime was installed in 1924. The modern country of Mongolia, however, represents only part of the Mongols' historical homeland; more Mongols live in the Inner Mongolia Autonomous Region in the People's Republic of China than in Mongolia. Following a peaceful democratic revolution, the ex-Communist Mongolian People's Revolutionary Party (MPRP) won elections in 1990 and 1992, but was defeated by the Democratic Union Coalition (DUC) in the 1996 parliamentary election. The MPRP won an overwhelming majority in the 2000 parliamentary election, but the party lost seats in the 2004 election and shared power with democratic coalition parties from 2004-2008. The MPRP regained a solid majority in the 2008 parliamentary elections; the prime minister and a majority of cabinet members are currently MPRP members.

RULERS:

Chinese to 1921

MONETARY SYSTEM:

1 Tugrik (Tukhrik) = 100 Mongo

REPLACEMENT NOTES:

#28-41, 3A, 3B, or ЯA prefix.
#42-48, ЯA, ЯB prefix.

PROVISIONAL PEOPLE'S GOVERNMENT

Mongolian Government's Treasure

1921 Issue

6% Provisionary Obligation.

#	Description	Good	Fine	XF
A1	**10 Dollars**	**Good**	**Fine**	**XF**
	20.11.1921. Light blue with red-brown text. White, blue, pink and yellow arms at upper center. Back: Emblem at top center, ram at bottom center. Payable on or after November 20, 1921.	450	1,500	—
A2	**25 Dollars**	**Good**	**Fine**	**XF**
	21.11.1921. Red and blue. Back: Cow at bottom center. Payable on or after November 20, 1921.	450	1,600	—

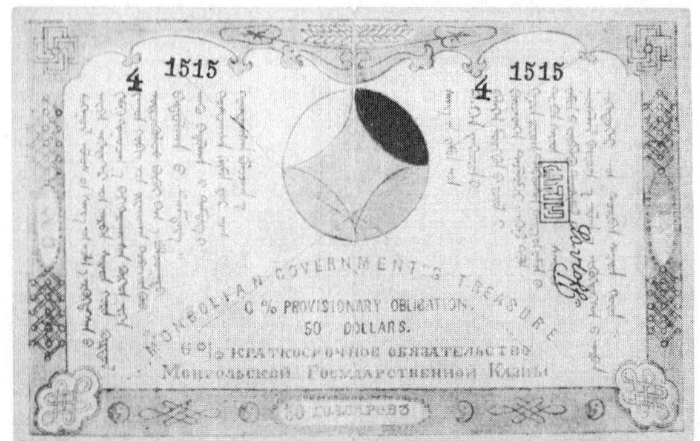

		Good	Fine	XF
A3	**50 Dollars** 20.11.1921. Gold and red frame, red text. White, blue, pink and yellow arms at upper center. Back: Emblem at top center. Horse at bottom center. Payable on or after November 20, 1921. BC: Dark blue frame with red text.	500	1,800	—
A4	**100 Dollars** 20.11.1921. Yellow and red. Back: Camel at bottom center. Payable on or after November 20, 1921.	600	2,000	—

State Treasury Notes

1924 Issue

		VG	VF	UNC
1	**50 Cents** 1924. Yellow and multicolor. Watermark: Ornamental. (Not issued).			
	r. Remainder.	—	—	185
	s. Specimen perforated: *ОБРАЗЕЦЪ*.	—	—	450

		VG	VF	UNC
2	**1 Dollar** 1924. Blue and multicolor. Watermark: Ornamental. (Not issued).			
	r. Remainder.	—	—	200
	s. Specimen perforated: *ОБРАЗЕЦЪ*.	—	—	500
3	**3 Dollars** 1924. Brown and multicolor. Watermark: Ornamental. (Not issued).	VG	VF	UNC
	r. Remainder.	—	—	225
	s. Specimen perforated: *ОБРАЗЕЦЪ*.	—	—	550
4	**5 Dollars** 1924. Green and multicolor. Watermark: Ornamental. (Not issued).	VG	VF	UNC
	r. Remainder.	—	—	250
	s. Specimen perforated: *ОБРАЗЕЦЪ*.	—	—	600

		VG	VF	UNC
5	**10 Dollars** 1924. Lilac and multicolor. Watermark: Ornamental. (Not issued).			
	r. Remainder.	—	—	275
	s. Specimen perforated: *ОБРАЗЕЦЪ*.	—	—	650
6	**25 Dollars** 1924. Blue and multicolor. (Not issued).	VG	VF	UNC
	r. Remainder.	—	—	325
	s. Specimen perforated: *ОБРАЗЕЦЪ*.	—	—	750

Commercial and Industrial Bank

1925 First Issue

		Good	Fine	XF
A7	**1 Tugrik** 1.12.1925. Yellow-brown. "Soembo" arms at center, perforated: *1.12.1925* vertically at left. Serial # prefix *A*..	15.00	60.00	200
A8	**2 Tugrik** 1.12.1925; 8.12.1925. Green. "Soembo" arms at center, perforated: *1.12.1925* vertically at left. Serial # prefix *A*.. Also known with perforation at left and right.	20.00	85.00	250

A8 also known with perforation at left and right.

		Good	Fine	XF
A9	**5 Tugrik** 1.12.1925. Blue and multicolor. "Soembo" arms at center, perforated: *1.12.1925* vertically at left. Serial # prefix *A*.. Back: Red.	25.00	100	350
A10	**10 Tugrik** 1.12.1925. Red and multicolor. "Soembo" arms at center, perforated: *1.12.1925* vertically at left. Serial # prefix *A*.. Back: Green and brown.	35.00	175	450

1925 Second Issue

		Good	Fine	XF
7	**1 Tugrik** 1925. Yellow-brown.	7.50	45.00	100

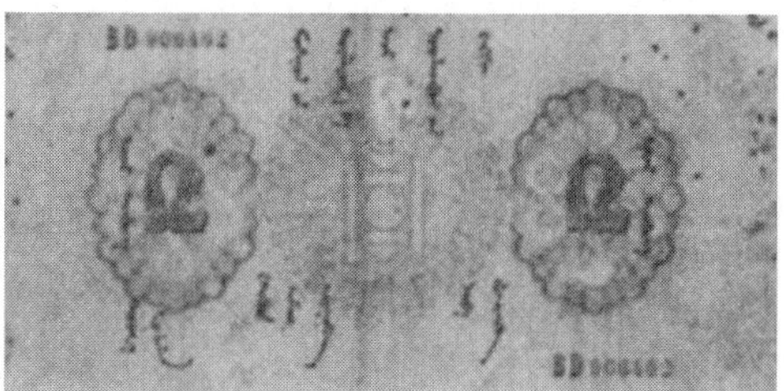

		Good	Fine	XF
8	**2 Tugrik** 1925. Green.	12.50	75.00	175

		Good	Fine	XF
9	**5 Tugrik** 1925. Blue and multicolor. Back: Red-brown.	15.00	80.00	250

		Good	Fine	XF
10	**10 Tugrik** 1925. Red and multicolor. Back: Green and brown.	25.00	90.00	275
11	**25 Tugrik** 1925. Brown and multicolor. Back: Green.	30.00	125	375
12	**50 Tugrik** 1925. Green and multicolor. Back: Brown.	35.00	175	650
13	**100 Tugrik** 1925. Blue and red.	75.00	325	850

MONGOLIAN PEOPLES REPUBLIC

Commercial and Industrial Bank

1939 Issue

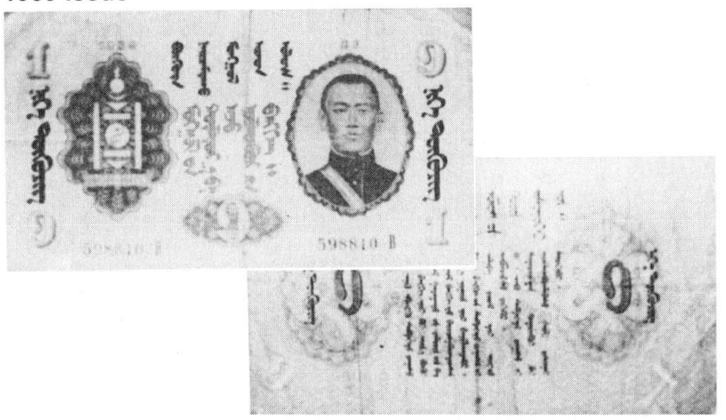

No.	Description	Good	Fine	XF
14	**1 Tugrik** 1939. Brown. Portrait Sukhe-Bataar at right, "Soembo" arms at left. Old Mongolian text.	3.50	15.00	60.00
15	**3 Tugrik** 1939. Green. Portrait Sukhe-Bataar at right, "Soembo" arms at left. Old Mongolian text.	5.00	25.00	100
16	**5 Tugrik** 1939. Blue. Portrait Sukhe-Bataar at right, "Soembo" arms at left. Old Mongolian text.	7.50	35.00	125
17	**10 Tugrik** 1939. Red. Portrait Sukhe-Bataar at right, "Soembo" arms at left. Old Mongolian text.	15.00	45.00	150
18	**25 Tugrik** 1939. Gray-brown. Portrait Sukhe-Bataar at right, "Soembo" arms at left. Old Mongolian text.	15.00	65.00	200
19	**50 Tugrik** 1939. Green-brown. Portrait Sukhe-Bataar at right, "Soembo" arms at left. Old Mongolian text.	35.00	80.00	275
20	**100 Tugrik** 1939. Light blue. Portrait Sukhe-Bataar at right, "Soembo" arms at left. Old Mongolian text.	75.00	175	475

1941 Issue

No.	Description	Good	Fine	XF
21	**1 Tugrik** 1941. Brown. Portrait Sukhe-Bataar at right, Socialist arms at left. Old and new Mongolian (resembles Russian) text.	3.00	10.00	55.00
22	**3 Tugrik** 1941. Green. Portrait Sukhe-Bataar at right, Socialist arms at left. Old and new Mongolian (resembles Russian) text.	5.00	15.00	85.00
23	**5 Tugrik** 1941. Blue. Portrait Sukhe-Bataar at right, Socialist arms at left. Old and new Mongolian (resembles Russian) text.	7.00	20.00	110

No.	Description	Good	Fine	XF
24	**10 Tugrik** 1941. Red. Portrait Sukhe-Bataar at right, Socialist arms at left. Old and new Mongolian (resembles Russian) text.	12.00	35.00	150
25	**25 Tugrik** 1941. Gray-brown. Portrait Sukhe-Bataar at right, Socialist arms at left. Old and new Mongolian (resembles Russian) text.	15.00	55.00	185
26	**50 Tugrik** 1941. Green-brown. Portrait Sukhe-Bataar at right, Socialist arms at left. Old and new Mongolian (resembles Russian) text.	40.00	75.00	250
27	**100 Tugrik** 1941. Light blue. Portrait Sukhe-Bataar at right, Socialist arms at left. Old and new Mongolian (resembles Russian) text.			
	a. Issued note.	60.00	125	375
	s. Specimen. Red overprint.	—	Unc	1,000

УЛСЫН БАНК - State Bank

1955 Issue

No.	Description	VG	VF	UNC
28	**1 Tugrik** 1955. Black and brown on pale brown-orange and multicolor underprint. Portrait Sukhe-Bataar at right, Socialist arms at left. New Mongolian text. Back: Dark brown text on pale brown-orange and multicolor underprint. Watermark: Symbol repeated.	1.00	2.00	4.00
29	**3 Tugrik** 1955. Black on light green and multicolor underprint. Portrait Sukhe-Bataar at right, Socialist arms at left. New Mongolian text. Back: Dark green text on light green and multicolor underprint. Watermark: Symbol repeated.	1.00	3.00	8.00

No.	Description	VG	VF	UNC
30	**5 Tugrik** 1955. Black on light blue and multicolor underprint. Portrait Sukhe-Bataar at right, Socialist arms at left. New Mongolian text. Back: Blue-black text on light blue and multicolor underprint. Watermark: Symbol repeated.	2.00	5.00	12.00
31	**10 Tugrik** 1955. Deep red and red on pink and multicolor underprint. Portrait Sukhe-Bataar at right, Socialist arms at left. New Mongolian text. Back: Dark brown text on pale orange and multicolor underprint.	3.00	7.00	17.00

		VG	VF	UNC
32	**25 Tugrik** 1955. Black on light blue and multicolor underprint. Portrait Sukhe-Bataar at right, Socialist arms at left. New Mongolian text. Back: Dark brown text on tan and multicolor underprint.	4.00	10.00	22.00
33	**50 Tugrik** 1955. Black on light green and multicolor underprint. Portrait Sukhe-Bataar at right, Socialist arms at left. New Mongolian text. Back: Dark green text on light green and multicolor underprint.	5.00	12.00	30.00

		VG	VF	UNC
34	**100 Tugrik** 1955. Black on light blue and multicolor underprint. Portrait Sukhe-Bataar at right, Socialist arms at left. New Mongolian text. Back: Black and dark green text on light blue and multicolor underprint.	7.00	15.00	40.00

The former independent kingdom of Montenegro, now one of the nominally autonomous federated units of Yugoslavia, was located in southeastern Europe north of Albania. As a kingdom, it had an area of 5,333 sq. mi. (13,812 sq. km.) and a population of about 250,000. The predominantly pastoral kingdom had few industries. The use of the name Montenegro began in the 15th century when the Crnojevic dynasty began to rule the Serbian principality of Zeta; over subsequent centuries Montenegro was able to maintain its independence from the Ottoman Empire. From the 16th to 19th centuries, Montenegro became a theocracy ruled by a series of bishop princes; in 1852, it was transformed into a secular principality. After World War I, Montenegro was absorbed by the Kingdom of Serbs, Croats, and Slovenes, which became the Kingdom of Yugoslavia in 1929; at the conclusion of World War II, it became a constituent republic of the Socialist Federal Republic of Yugoslavia. When the latter dissolved in 1992, Montenegro federated with Serbia, first as the Federal Republic of Yugoslavia and, after 2003, in a looser union of Serbia and Montenegro. In May 2006, Montenegro invoked its right under the Constitutional Charter of Serbia and Montenegro to hold a referendum on independence from the state union. The vote for severing ties with Serbia exceeded 55% - the threshold set by the EU - allowing Montenegro to formally declare its independence on 3 June 2006.

RULERS:

Nicholas I, 1910-1918

MONETARY SYSTEM:

1 Perper = 100 Para = 1 Austrian Crown

KINGDOM

Treasury

1912 Issue

		Good	Fine	XF
1	**1 Perper** 1.10.1912. Dark blue on green paper. Arms at center.			
	a. Issued note.	4.00	20.00	50.00
	b. Handstamped: *CETINJE.*	15.00	50.00	—
	c. Punch hole cancelled.	2.00	7.50	20.00

		Good	Fine	XF
2	**2 Perpera** 1.10.1912. Lilac. Arms at center. PC: Reddish.			
	a. Issued note.	5.00	25.00	60.00
	b. Punch hole cancelled.	3.00	10.00	25.00
3	**5 Perpera** 1.10.1912. Dark green. Arms at center. PC: Olive-green.			
	a. Issued note.	7.50	35.00	85.00
	b. Punch hole cancelled.	4.00	15.00	35.00

		Good	Fine	XF
4	**10 Perpera** 1.10.1912. Red-brown. Arms at center. PC: Yellowish.			
	a. Issued note.	30.00	100	200
	b. Punch hole cancelled.	15.00	45.00	90.00

		Good	Fine	XF
5	**50 Perpera** 1.10.1912. Blue on brown underprint. Arms at center. PC: Reddish.			
	a. Issued note.	200	600	1,200
	b. Punch hole cancelled.	100	300	750
6	**100 Perpera** 1.10.1912. Arms at center. PC: Brown.	Good	Fine	XF
	a. Issued note.	300	800	1,600
	b. Punch hole cancelled.	200	500	1,000

КРАЉЕВИНА ЦРНАГОРА

Royal Government

1914 First Issue

		Good	Fine	XF
7	**1 Perper** 25.7.1914 (-old date 1.10.1912). Overprint: Red; on #1.			
	a. Issued note.	7.00	25.00	65.00
	b. With handstamp: *CETINJE*.	10.00	35.00	—
8	**2 Perpera** 25.7.1914 (-old date 1.10.1912). Overprint: Red; on #2.	15.00	45.00	90.00

1914 Second Issue

Valuations for notes without additional handstamps. Cancelled notes worth 30% less.

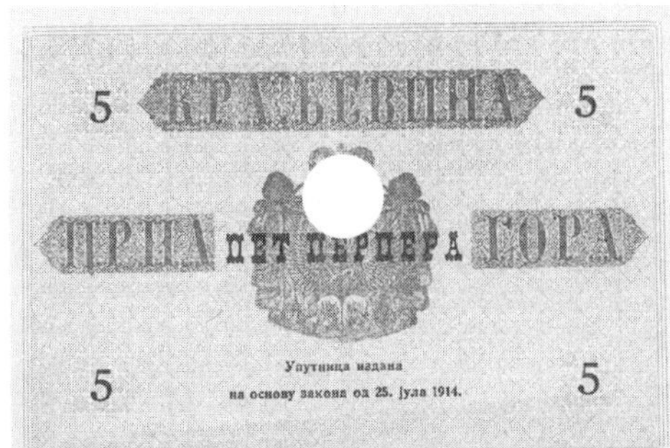

		Good	Fine	XF
9	**5 Perpera** 25.7.1914. Blue. Arms at center. Back: Arms at center. 155x107mm.	2.00	10.00	35.00

		Good	Fine	XF
10	**10 Perpera** 25.7.1914. Red. Arms at center. Back: Arms at center. 155x107mm.	2.00	12.00	40.00

		Good	Fine	XF
11	**20 Perpera** 25.7.1914. Brown. Arms at center. Back: Arms at center. 155x107mm.	4.00	20.00	60.00
12	**50 Perpera** 25.7.1914. Olive. Arms at center. Back: Arms at center. 155x107mm.	4.00	30.00	70.00
13	**100 Perpera** 25.7.1914. Light brown. Arms at center. Back: Arms at center. 155x107mm.	12.00	60.00	150

1914 Third Issue

#15-21 Valuations for notes without additional handstamps. Cancelled notes worth 30% less.

		Good	Fine	XF
15	**1 Perper** 25.7.1914. Blue with dark brown text. Ornamental anchor at top. Back: Arms at center.	1.00	3.00	12.00
16	**2 Perpera** 25.7.1914. Brown with dark blue text. Ornamental anchor at top. Back: Arms at center.	1.00	4.50	17.50

		Good	Fine	XF
17	**5 Perpera** 25.7.1914. Red with black text. Ornamental anchor at top. Back: Arms at center.	2.00	5.00	20.00

		Good	Fine	XF
18	**10 Perpera** 25.7.1914. Blue with dark brown text. Arms at upper left. Back: Arms at center.	2.00	5.00	20.00
19	**20 Perpera** 25.7.1914. Brown with dark blue text. Arms at upper left. Back: Arms at center.	4.00	10.00	35.00

		Good	Fine	XF
20	**50 Perpera** 25.7.1914. Red with dark text. Angels at top center, woman seated holding cornucopias at bottom center. Back: Arms at center.	8.00	30.00	85.00

		Good	Fine	XF
21	**100 Perpera** 25.7.1914. Blue with dark brown text. Angels at top center, woman seated holding cornucopias at bottom center. Back: Arms at center.	12.50	45.00	110

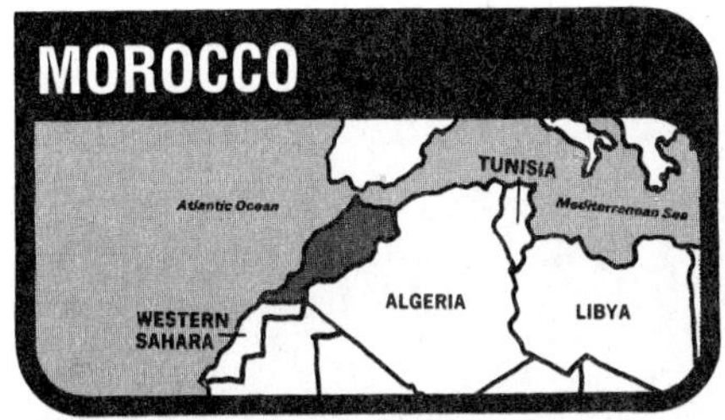

The Kingdom of Morocco, situated on the northwest corner of Africa south of Spain, has an area of 172,413 sq. mi. (712,550 sq. km.) and a population of 28.98 million. Capital: Rabat. The economy is essentially agricultural. Phosphates, fresh and preserved vegetables, canned fish and raw material are exported.In 788, about a century after the Arab conquest of North Africa, successive Moorish dynasties began to rule in Morocco. In the 16th century, the Sa'adi monarchy, particularly under Ahmad Al-Mansur (1578-1603), repelled foreign invaders and inaugurated a golden age. In 1860, Spain occupied northern Morocco and ushered in a half century of trade rivalry among European powers that saw Morocco's sovereignty steadily erode; in 1912, the French imposed a protectorate over the country. A protracted independence struggle with France ended successfully in 1956. The internationalized city of Tangier and most Spanish possessions were turned over to the new country that same year. Morocco virtually annexed Western Sahara during the late 1970s, but final resolution on the status of the territory remains unresolved. Gradual political reforms in the 1990s resulted in the establishment of a bicameral legislature, which first met in 1997. The country has made improvements in human rights under King Mohammed VI and its press is moderately free. Despite the continuing reforms, ultimate authority remains in the hands of the monarch.

RULERS:

Abd Al-Aziz, AH1311-1325/1894-1908AD
Hafiz, AH1325-1330/1908-1912AD
Yusuf, AH1330-1346/1912-1927AD
Muhammad V, AH1346-1380/1927-1961AD
Hassan II, AH1380-1420 /1961-1999AD
Muhammad VI, AH1420- /1999- AD

MONETARY SYSTEM:

1 Dirham = 50 Mazunas
1 Rial = 10 Dirhams to 1921
1 Franc = 100 Centimes
1 Dirham = 100 Francs, 1921-1974
1 Dirham = 100 Centimes = 100 Santimat, 1974-
1 Riffan = 1 French Gold Franc = 10 British Pence

KINGDOM

Banque d'Etat du Maroc

State Bank of Morocco

1910; 1917 Issue

#1 and 2 with text: ***PAYABLES A VUE AU PORTEUR.***

#	Denomination	Good	Fine	XF
1	**4 Rials = 40 Francs** 2.7.1917; 6.7.1917; 9.7.1917. Salmon, ochre and blue. Tower at center. Text:*PAYABLES A VUE AU PORTEUR.*	200	600	1,750
2	**20 Rials = 100 Francs** 31.2.1910; 15.7.1910; 18.7.1910. Violet, yellow and blue. Palm tree at center. Text:*PAYABLES A VUE AU PORTEUR.*	225	650	2,000

Note: Other denominations and issues may exist like Bons de Caisse (Issue of 1919).

Protectorat de la France au Maroc

1919 Emergency Issue

#	Denomination	Good	Fine	XF
4	**25 Centimes** Oct. 1919. Rose cardboard. Overprint: Octagonal:*MAROC 25c.*			
	a. *Octobre* in date. With or without series letters.	17.50	50.00	125
	b. OCTOBRE in date.	17.50	50.00	125
	c. *OCTOBRE* in date.	17.50	50.00	125
5	**50 Centimes** Oct. 1919. Orange cardboard. Overprint: Octagonal: *MAROC 50c.*			
	a. *Octobre* in date. With or without series letters.	17.50	50.00	125
	b. OCTOBRE in date.	17.50	50.00	125
	c. *OCTOBRE* in date.	17.50	50.00	125
6	**1 Franc** Oct. 1919. Yellow cardboard. Overprint: Octagonal: *MAROC 1F.*			
	a. *Octobre* in date. With or without series letters.	17.50	50.00	125
	b. OCTOBRE in date.	17.50	50.00	125
	c. *OCTOBRE* in date.	17.50	50.00	125

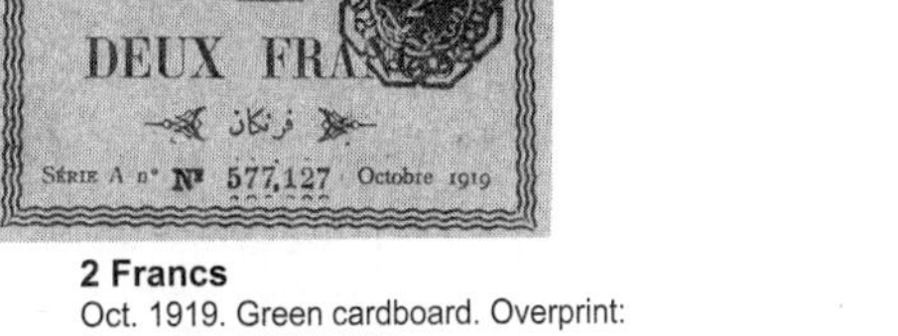

#	Denomination	Good	Fine	XF
7	**2 Francs** Oct. 1919. Green cardboard. Overprint: Octagonal:*MAROC 2F.*			
	a. *Octobre* in date. Series A.	17.50	50.00	150
	b. OCTOBRE in date.	17.50	50.00	150
	c. *OCTOBRE* in date.	17.50	50.00	150

Banque d'Etat du Maroc (resumed)

State Bank of Morocco

1920-1924 Issue

#	Denomination	Good	Fine	XF
8	**5 Francs** ND (1921). Blue and green. Serial # at bottom only. 2 signature varieties. Without text:*PAYABLES A VUE...* Back: With title: *BANQUE D'ETAT DU MAROC* in 1 line. Printer: Chaix, Paris.	15.00	50.00	250
9	**5 Francs** ND (1924). Blue and green. Serial # at top and bottom. 4 signature varieties. Without text:*PAYABLES A VUE...* Back: With title: *BANQUE D'ETAT DU MAROC* in 2 lines.	10.00	35.00	150

#10 Deleted, see 23A.

#	Denomination	Good	Fine	XF
11	**10 Francs** 1920-1928. Blue on sepia underprint.			
	a. Serial # only at bottom. 2 signature varieties. 4.5.1920-1.12.1923.	20.00	80.00	285
	b. Serial # at top printed over and below ornamentation. 3 signature varieties. 15.5.1924-1.7.1928.	15.00	70.00	250
12	**20 Francs** 7.1.1920-17.4.1926. Gray, blue and sepia. Tower at center. Serial # at top in white fields (left and right) and bottom left and right in special blank fields. 3 signature varieties. Text:*PAYABLES A VUE...*	25.00	100	325
13	**50 Francs** 13.9.1920-8.8.1928. Blue-green and light brown. Design style similar to #11.Serial # at left and right at top printed over ornamentation, and bottom left and right. 4 signature varieties. Text:*PAYABLES A VUE...* 170x98mm.	50.00	175	500

		Good	Fine	XF
14	**100 Francs** 15.12.1919-1.9.1926. Red. Palm tree at center. 3 signature varieties. Text:*PAYABLES A VUE...* Back: Red with blue text.	150	500	100

		VG	VF	UNC
15	**500 Francs** 1923-1948. Brown, red and multicolor. View of city of Fez.			
	a. With text: *PAYABLES A VUE AU PORTEUR.* 5 signature varieties. 1.10.1923-29.6.1937.	—	—	—
	b. Without text: *PAYABLES A VUE...* 3.5.1946-10.11.1948.	15.00	45.00	100

		Good	Fine	XF
16	**1000 Francs** 1921-1950. Green, blue and ochre. View of city. 5 signature varieties.			
	a. 1.2.1921.	75.00	175	650
	b. 12.6.1929-27.9.1934.	45.00	140	575
	c. 13.1.1937-9.2.1950.	20.00	75.00	400

1928-1929 Issues

		VG	VF	UNC
17	**10 Francs** 1929-1942. Blue on sepia underprint. Like #11 but serial # on top in blank field.			
	a. With text: *PAYABLES A VUE AU PORTEUR.* 2 signature varieties. 12.6.1929; 20.5.1931.	—	—	—
	b. Without text: *PAYABLES A VUE.* 6.3.1941; 25.9.1942.	1.50	10.00	55.00

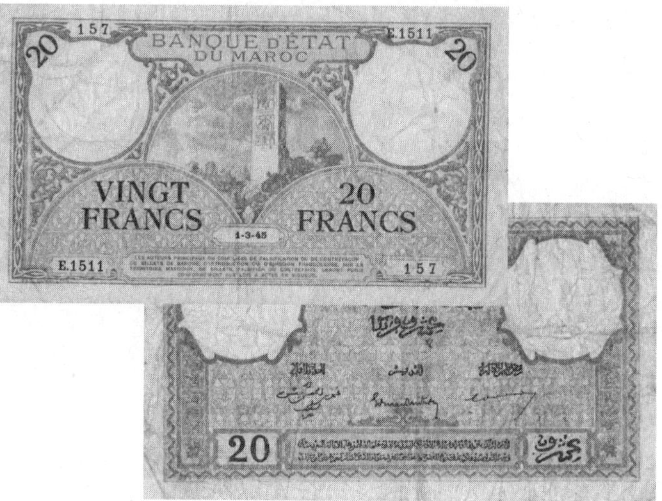

		VG	VF	UNC
18	**20 Francs** 1929-1945. Gray-blue and sepia. Tower at center. Like #12 but serial # at top in special blank field.			
	a. With text: *PAYABLES A VUE AU PORTEUR.* 2 signature varieties. 12.6.1929; 2.12.1931.	—	—	—
	b. Without text: *PAYABLES A VUE...* 3 signature varieties. 6.3.1941; 14.11.1941; 9.11.1942; 1.3.1945.	3.00	12.50	85.00

		Good	Fine	XF
19	**50 Francs** 12.6.1929; 2.12.1931; 17.11.1932. Blue-green and light brown. Like #13 but serial # at top and bottom in blank field. 2 signature varieties.	20.00	75.00	300

		VG	VF	UNC
20	**100 Francs** 1.7.1928-28.10.1947. Multicolor. Fortress (Kasbah) at center. 4 signature varieties.	7.50	50.00	200

1936; 1938 Issue

		VG	VF	UNC
21	**50 Francs** 23.9.1936-2.12.1949. Green, blue and sepia. Arch at center. 4 signature varieties.	5.00	30.00	150

#22 Deleted.

		VG	VF	UNC
23	**5000 Francs**			
	1938-1951. Brown and maroon on light blue and multicolor underprint. Moraccan city overlooking sea. 3 signature varieties. Back: Fortress at center. Watermark: Lion.			
	a. 28.9.1938; 14.11.1941.	90.00	350	1,000
	b. 9.11.1942.	80.00	300	1,000
	c. 21.12.1945-19.4.1951.	70.00	275	1,000

1941 (1922) Issue

		VG	VF	UNC
23A	**5 Francs**			
	1922; 1941. Red, blue and sepia.			
	a. With text: *PAYABLES A VUE AU PORTEUR.* 1.8.1922 (issued 1941).	5.00	20.00	100
	b. Without text: *PAYABLES A VUE...* 24.7.1941; 27.7.1941; 14.11.1941.	2.50	10.00	50.00

1943 WWII First Issue

Notes printed in Morocco or the United States during World War II.

		VG	VF	UNC
24	**5 Francs**			
	1.8.1943; 1.3.1944. Blue on yellow underprint. Back: Five-pointed star at upper center Printer: EAW.			
	s. Specimen. Red overprint: *SPÉCIMEN.*	—	—	50.00

		VG	VF	UNC
25	**10 Francs**			
	1.5.1943; 1.8.1943; 1.3.1944. Black on green underprint. Five-pointed star at center. Back: Blue on red underprint. Printer: EAW.			
	a. Issued note.	2.00	5.00	25.00
	s. Specimen. Red overprint.	—	—	750

		VG	VF	UNC
26	**50 Francs**			
	1.8.1943; 1.3.1944. Black and light brown. Fortress at left, sailing ship at right. Back: Five-pointed star at left and right. BC: Green on yellow underprint. Printer: EAW.			
	a. Issued note.	3.00	15.00	100
	s. Specimen. Red overprint.	—	—	750

		VG	VF	UNC
27	**100 Francs**			
	1.5.1943; 1.8.1943; 1.3.1944. Multicolor. Gate in city wall at center. Back: Five-pointed star at left and right. Printer: EAW.			
	a. Issued note.	7.50	30.00	150
	s. Specimen. Black overprint.	—	—	850

		VG	VF	UNC
28	**1000 Francs** 1.5.1943; 1.8.1943; 1.3.1944. Brown. Printer: ABNC.			
	a. Issued note.	75.00	250	800
	s. Specimen.	—	—	900

#29-31 Deleted.

		VG	VF	UNC
32	**5000 Francs** 1.8.1943. Green.			
	a. Issued note.	600	1,500	—
	s. Specimen.	—	—	3,500

1943 Second Issue

		VG	VF	UNC
33	**5 Francs** 14.9.1943. Blue on yellow underprint. Large *5* at left. Small square black area at center of date. Printer: Imp. Réunies, Casablanca.	0.75	2.00	10.00

#34-38 Deleted.

		VG	VF	UNC
39	**20 Francs** ND (1943). Blue on red-brown underprint. Buildings on hillside at center.	20.00	75.00	200
40	**50 Francs** ND (1943). Green on orange underprint. Fortress at left, sailing ship at right. Back: Large *5*-pointed star at center. Printer: Imp. Réunies, Casablanca. 170x106mm.	15.00	100	250

Empire Cherifien, Protectorat de la République Française

1944 Emergency Issue

		VG	VF	UNC
41	**50 Centimes** 6.4.1944. Red. Back: Fortress. Very small cardboard note.	0.75	3.00	15.00

		VG	VF	UNC
42	**1 Franc** 6.4.1944. Green. Back: City of Fez. Very small cardboard note.	0.75	4.00	20.00

		VG	VF	UNC
43	**2 Francs** 6.4.1944. Violet-brown. Back: House on the shore (La Menara). Very small cardboard note.	1.00	5.00	25.00

Banque d'Etat du Maroc - Post WW II

1948-1951 Issues

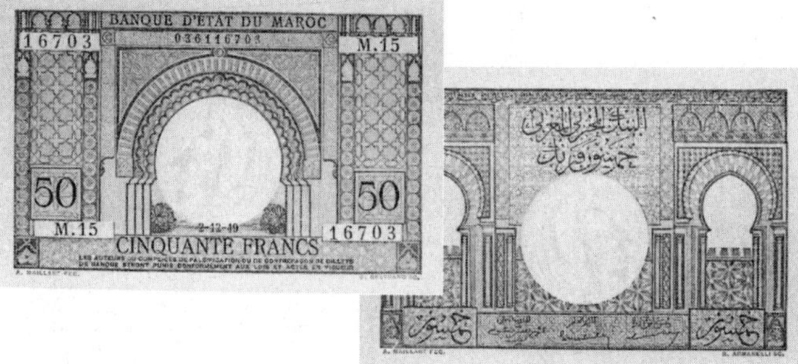

		VG	VF	UNC
44	**50 Francs** 2.12.1949. Green, blue and sepia. Arch at center. Like #21 but reduced size.	1.00	6.00	30.00

		VG	VF	UNC
45	**100 Francs** 10.11.1948-22.12.1952. Multicolor. Fortress (Kasbah) at center. Like #20 but reduced size.	2.50	10.00	50.00

		VG	VF	UNC
45A	**500 Francs** 29.5.1951. Brown on multicolor underprint. Monument in front of State Bank building at center right. Back: City view. Watermark: Male lion's head. Printer: TDLR (without imprint). Specimen.	—	—	850
45B	**500 Francs** 29.5.1951. City view at center right. Printer: TDLR (without imprint). Specimen.	—	—	850

46 500 Francs

	VG	VF	UNC
18.7.1949-14.2.1958. Multicolor. Doorway of house with Moroccan city in background. 2 signature varieties.	2.50	17.50	125

46A 1000 Francs

	VG	VF	UNC
29.1.1951. Green. Building at center. Printer: TDLR (without imprint.) Specimen.	—	Unc	1,900

47 1000 Francs

	VG	VF	UNC
19.4.1951-7.8.1958. Multicolor. Mosque, city and hills in background. 2 signature varieties.	5.00	45.00	200

48 5000 Francs

	VG	VF	UNC
ND. Red-brown. Building at center. Printer: TDLR (without imprint). Specimen.	—	—	1,000

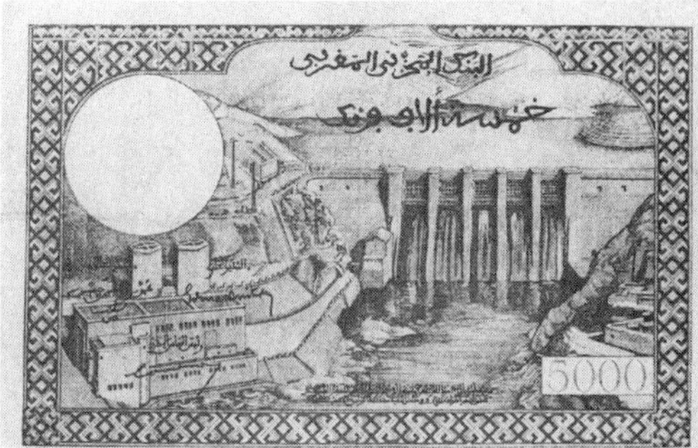

49 5000 Francs

	VG	VF	UNC
2.4.1953; 23.7.1953; 7.8.1958. Multicolor. Mosque with hills in background.	25.00	150	475

50 10,000 Francs

	VG	VF	UNC
13.8.1953-28.4.1955. Multicolor. Aerial view of Casablanca.			
a. Issued note.	30.00	175	550
s. Specimen. Perforated.	—	—	750

1959 Provisional Dirham Issue

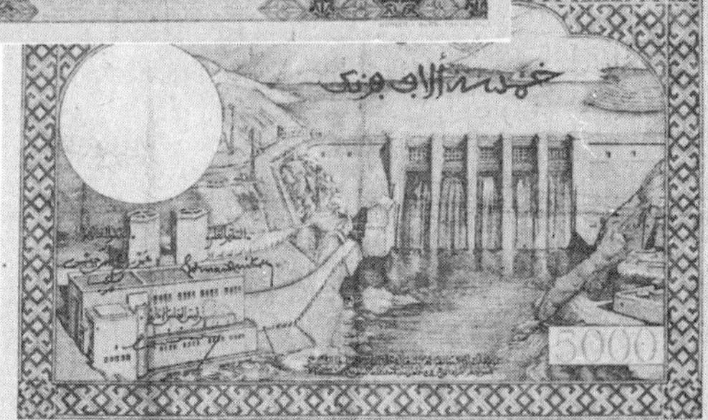

51 50 Dirhams on 5000 Francs

	VG	VF	UNC
ND (-old date 23.7.1953).	25.00	100	400

52 100 Dirhams on 10,000 Francs

	VG	VF	UNC
ND (-old dates 2.8.1954; 28.4.1955).	25.00	100	400

MOZAMBIQUE

The People's Republic of Mozambique, a former overseas province of Portugal stretching for 1,430 miles (2,301 km.) along the southeast coast of Africa, has an area of 309,494 sq. mi. (783,030 sq. km.) and a population of 19.56 million. Capital: Maputo. Agriculture is the chief industry. Cashew nuts, cotton, sugar, copra and tea are exported. Almost five centuries as a Portuguese colony came to a close with independence in 1975. Large-scale emigration by whites, economic dependence on South Africa, a severe drought, and a prolonged civil war hindered the country's development until the mid 1990's. The ruling Front for the Liberation of Mozambique (FRELIMO) party formally abandoned Marxism in 1989, and a new constitution the following year provided for multiparty elections and a free market economy. A UN-negotiated peace agreement between FRELIMO and rebel Mozambique National Resistance (RENAMO) forces ended the fighting in 1992. In December 2004, Mozambique underwent a delicate transition as Joaquim Chissano stepped down after 18 years in office. His elected successor, Armando Emilio Guebuza, promised to continue the sound economic policies that have encouraged foreign investment. Mozambique has seen very strong economic growth since the end of the civil war largely due to post-conflict reconstruction.

RULERS:

Portuguese to 1975

MONETARY SYSTEM:

Pound Sterling = Libra Esterlina (pound sterling)
1 Mil Reis = 1000 Reis to 1910
1 Escudo = 100 Centavos, 1911-1975
1 Escudo = 1 Metica = 100 Centimos, 1975-

REPLACEMENT NOTES:

#116, 117, 119: Z prefix.
#125-133, ZA, ZB, ZC prefix.
#134-137, AW, BW, CY, DZ prefix by denomination.

STEAMSHIP SEALS

Type I LOANDA — Type II LISBOA — Type III C,C,A

C,C,A = Colonias, Commercio, Agricultura.

PORTUGUESE ADMINISTRATION

Banco Nacional Ultramarino

1877 Issue

#1-8 Lourenço Marques.

#	Denomination	Good	Fine	XF
1	**5000 Reis** 2.4.1877. Note of Loanda with overprint for Mozambique. Rare.	—	—	—
1A	**10,000 Reis** 2.4.1877. Note of Loanda with overprint for Mozambique. Rare.	—	—	—
2	**20,000 Reis** 2.4.1877. Note of Loanda with overprint for Mozambique. Rare.	—	—	—

1878 Issue

#	Denomination	Good	Fine	XF
3	**1000 Reis** 29.1.1878. Rare.	—	—	—
4	**2000 Reis** 29.1.1878. Green. Steamship at center. Rare.	—	—	—
5	**2500 Reis** 29.1.1878. Rare.	—	—	—
6	**5000 Reis** 29.1.1878. Rare.	—	—	—
7	**10,000 Reis** 29.1.1878. Rare.	—	—	—
8	**20,000 Reis** 29.1.1878. Rare.	—	—	—

1884; 1897 Issues

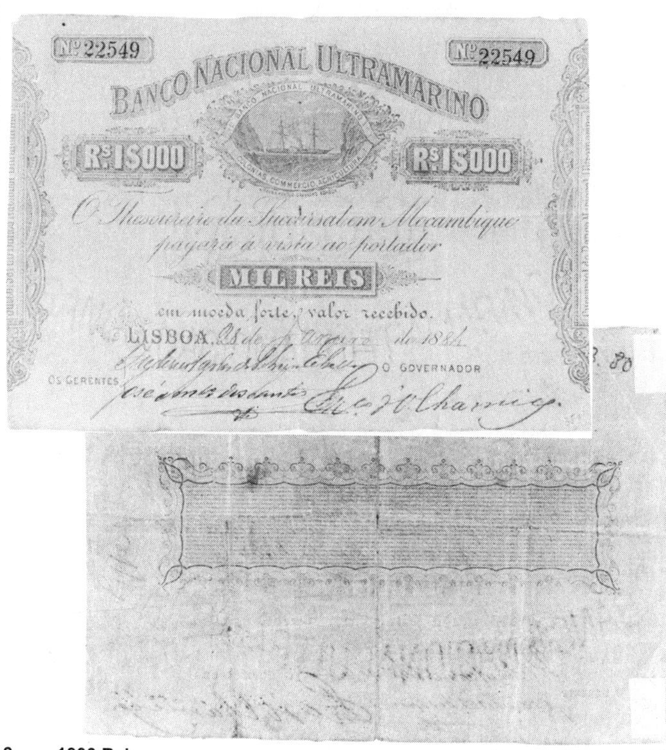

#	Denomination	Good	Fine	XF
9	**1000 Reis** 28.1.1884; 2.1.1897. Green. Text:...*Succural em Mozambique...* 180x120mm.	—	—	—
10	**2000 Reis** 2.1.1897. Text:...*Succural em Mozambique...* Rare.	—	—	—
11	**2500 Reis** 2.1.1897. Text:...*Succural em Mozambique...* Rare.	—	—	—
12	**5000 Reis** 2.1.1897. Text:...*Succural em Mozambique...* Rare.	—	—	—
13	**10,000 Reis** 2.1.1897. Text:...*Succural em Mozambique...* Rare.	—	—	—
14	**20,000 Reis** 2.1.1897. Text:...*Succural em Mozambique...* Rare.	—	—	—
15	**50,000 Reis** 2.1.1897. Text:...*Succural em Mozambique...* Rare.	—	—	—

1897 Second Issue

#16-29 With text: *...em Lourenço Marques...*

#	Denomination	Good	Fine	XF
16	**1000 Reis** 2.1.1897. Standing Indian at left, ship at center. Text:...*em Lourenco Marques...* 122x90mm.	—	—	—
17	**2000 Reis** 2.1.1897. Text:...*em Lourenco Marques...*	—	—	—

#	Denomination	Good	Fine	XF
18	**2500 Reis** 2.1.1897. Steamship at left, field at center, woman standing at center right. Text:...*em Lourenco Marques...* 143x105mm.	—	—	—
19	**5000 Reis** 2.1.1897. Text:...*em Lourenco Marques...*	—	—	—
20	**10,000 Reis** 2.1.1897. Text:...*em Lourenco Marques...* 167x125mm.	—	—	—
21	**20,000 Reis** 2.1.1897. Text:...*em Lourenco Marques...*	—	—	—
22	**50,000 Reis** 2.1.1897. Text:...*em Lourenco Marques...*	—	—	—

1906 Issue

No.	Description	Good	Fine	XF
23	**1000 Reis** 20.2.1906. Light brown. Standing Indian at left, ship at center. Uniface.Text:*...em Lourenco Marques...* 122x91mm.	—	—	—
24	**2000 Reis** 20.2.1906. Text:*...em Lourenco Marques...*	—	—	—
25	**2500 Reis** 20.2.1906. Text:*...em Lourenco Marques...*	—	—	—
26	**5000 Reis** 20.2.1906. Green. Text:*...em Lourenco Marques...* 170x124mm.	—	—	—
27	**10,000 Reis** 20.2.1906. Text:*...em Lourenco Marques...*	—	—	—
28	**20,000 Reis** 20.2.1906. Text:*...em Lourenco Marques...*	—	—	—
29	**50,000 Reis** 20.2.1906. Brown. Text:*...em Lourenco Marques...* 198x140mm.	—	—	—

1907 Issue

No.	Description	Good	Fine	XF
29A	**10 Centavos** 1.1.1907. Red-brown. Sailing ship.	—	—	—

1908 Issue

No.	Description	Good	Fine	XF
30	**2500 Reis** 2.1.1908. Black on green and multicolor underprint. Red Steamship Seal Type I. Portrait Vasco da Gama at left, sailing ships in passage Cape of Boa Esperanca in 1498 at right. Printer: BWC. 147x94mm. Overprint: *LOURENÇO MARQUES.*	—	—	—
31	**5000 Reis** 2.1.1908. Black on green and multicolor underprint. Red Steamship Seal Type I. Portrait Vasco da Gama at left, sailing ships in passage Cape of Boa Esperanca in 1498 at right. Printer: BWC. 159x100mm. Overprint: *LOURENÇO MARQUES.*	—	—	—
31A	**50,000 Reis** 1909. Printer: BWC. Rare.	—	—	—

1909 Issue

No.	Description	Good	Fine	XF
32	**1000 Reis** 1.3.1909. Black on green and yellow underprint. Red Steamship. Seal Type I. Printer: BWC.	50.00	150	400

No.	Description	Good	Fine	XF
33	**1000 Reis** 1.3.1909. Black on green and yellow underprint. Steamship Seal Type III. Like #32. 139x81mm.	35.00	125	300
34	**2500 Reis** 1.3.1909. Black on blue and yellow underprint. Red Steamship Seal Type I. Portrait Vasco da Gama at left, sailing ships in passage Cape of Boa Esperanca in 1498. Printer: BWC. 147x90mm.	100	200	500
35	**2500 Reis** 1.3.1909. Black on blue and yellow underprint. Red Steamship Seal Type III. Portrait Vasco da Gama at left, sailing ships in passage Cape of Boa Esperanca in 1498. Printer: BWC.	100	200	500
36	**5000 Reis** 1.3.1909. Black on multicolor underprint. Red Steamship Seal Type I. Portrait Vasco da Gama at left, sailing ships in passage Cape of Boa Esperanca in 1498. Printer: BWC. 159x100mm.	125	250	600
37	**5000 Reis** 1.3.1909. Black on multicolor underprint. Red Steamship Seal Type III. Portrait Vasco da Gama at left, sailing ships in passage Cape of Boa Esperanca in 1498. Printer: BWC.	125	250	600
38	**10,000 Reis** 1.3.1909. Black on blue and yellow underprint. Red Steanship Seal Type I. Portrait Vasco da Gama at left, sailing ships in passage Cape of Boa Esperanca in 1498. Printer: BWC. 177x108mm.	175	350	800
39	**10,000 Reis** 1.3.1909. Black on blue and yellow underprint. Red Steamship Seal Type III. Portrait Vasco da Gama at left, sailing ships in passage Cape of Boa Esperanca in 1498. Printer: BWC.	175	350	800
40	**20,000 Reis** 1.3.1909. Black on tan and pale blue underprint. Red Steamship Seal Type I. Portrait Vasco da Gama at left, sailing ships in passage Cape of Boa Esperanca in 1498. Embarkation of Vasco da Gama in 1497 at right. Printer: BWC. 190x115mm.	350	750	1,500
41	**20,000 Reis** 1.3.1909. Black on tan and pale blue underprint. Red Steamship Seal Type III. Portrait Vasco da Gama at left, sailing ships in passage Cape of Boa Esperanca in 1498. Embarkation of Vasco da Gama in 1497 at right. Printer: BWC.	350	750	1,500
42	**50,000 Reis** 1.3.1909. Black on brown, tan and pale blue underprint. Red Steamship Seal Type I. Portrait Vasco da Gama at left, sailing ships in passage Cape of Boa Esperanca in 1498. Embarkation of Vasco da Gama in 1497 at right. Printer: BWC. 200x122mm.	500	1,000	2,000
43	**50,000 Reis** 1.3.1909. Black on brown, tan and pale blue underprint. Red Steamship Seal Type III. Portrait Vasco da Gama at left, sailing ships in passage Cape of Boa Esperanca in 1498. Embarkation of Vasco da Gama in 1497 at right. Printer: BWC.	500	1,000	2,000

1909 Libra Esterlina Issue

No.	Description	Good	Fine	XF
44	**1 Libra** 1.3.1909. Black on orange and green underprint. Red Steamship Seal Type I. Back: Brown. Printer: BWC. 136x75mm.	75.00	—	—
45	**1 Libra** 1.3.1909. Black on orange and green underprint. Red Steamship Seal Type III. Back: Brown. Printer: BWC. 136x75mm.	50.00	—	—
46	**5 Libras** 1.3.1909. Black on pink, blue and yellow underprint. Red Steamship Seal Type I. Printer: BWC. 158x90mm.	100	—	—
47	**10 Libras** 1.3.1909. Black on pale green, pale blue and red underprint. Red Steamship Seal Type I. Printer: BWC. 160x100mm.	125	—	—
48	**20 Libras** 1.3.1909. Brown on multicolor underprint. Red Steamship Seal Type I. Printer: BWC. 160x100mm.	150	—	—
49	**20 Libras** 1.3.1909. Brown on multicolor underprint. Red Steamship Seal Type III. Printer: BWC. 160x100mm.	150	—	—

#50-51 renumbered; see #72A-72B.
#52 renumbered; see #29A.

1914 First Issue

No.	Description	Good	Fine	XF
53	**10 Centavos** 5.11.1914. Purple on multicolor underprint. Dark green Steamship Seal Type II. Back: Woman seated, sailing ships in background at center. Counterfoil at center. BC: Deep blue. Printer: BWC. 121x72mm.	2.50	15.00	60.00

No.	Description	Good	Fine	XF
54	**20 Centavos** 5.11.1914. Blue on multicolor underprint. Red Steamship Seal TYpe II. Back: Woman seated, sailing ships in background at center. Counterfoil at center. BC: Purple. Printer: BWC. 121x72mm.	4.50	25.00	85.00

No.	Description	Good	Fine	XF
55	**50 Centavos** 5.11.1914. Olive green on multicolor underprint. Dark blue Steamship Seal Type II. Back: Woman seated, sailing ships in background at center. Counterfoil at center. BC: Brown. Printer: BWC. 121x72mm.	5.00	25.00	85.00

1914 Second Issue

No.	Description	Good	Fine	XF
56	**10 Centavos** 5.11.1914. Purple on multicolor underprint. Dark green Steamship Seal Type III. Back: Woman seated, sailing ships in background at center. Counterfoil at left. BC: Deep blue. Printer: BWC. 121x72mm.	2.00	8.00	30.00
57	**20 Centavos** 5.11.1914. Blue on multicolor underprint. Red Steamship Seal Type III. Back: Woman seated, sailing ships in background at center. Counterfoil at left. BC: Purple. Printer: BWC. 121x72mm.	3.00	15.00	50.00
58	**50 Centavos** 5.11.1914. Green on multicolor underprint. Dark blue Steamship Seal Type III. Back: Woman seated, sailing ships in background at center. Counterfoil at left. BC: Brown. Printer: BWC. 121x72mm.	4.00	25.00	75.00

1914 Third Issue

No.	Description	Good	Fine	XF
59	**10 Centavos** 5.11.1914. Purple on multicolor underprint. Steamship Seal Type III. Back: Woman seated, sailing ships in background at center. Without counterfoil at left. BC: Deep blue. Printer: BWC. 121x72mm.	1.00	7.50	40.00
60	**20 Centavos** 5.11.1914. Blűe on multicolor underprint. Red Steamship Seal Type III. Back: Woman seated, sailing ships in background at center. Without counterfoil at left. BC: Purple. 121x72mm.	1.50	17.50	60.00
61	**50 Centavos** 5.11.1914. Green on multicolor underprint. Dark blue Steamship Seal Type III. Back: Woman seated, sailing ships in background at center. Without counterfoil at left. BC: Brown. Printer: BWC. 121x72mm.	2.50	20.00	70.00

1920 Emergency Issue

#62-65 offset printed on low-grade yellowish paper in Oporto.

No.	Description	Good	Fine	XF
62	**10 Centavos** 1.1.1920. Red. Sailing ship at left and right. BC: Violet. 105x65mm.	100	250	650
63	**20 Centavos** 1.1.1920. Green. Allegorical figures at left and right. BC: Blue. Printer: BWC. 109x68mm.	100	250	650
64	**50 Centavos** 1.1.1920. Blue. Allegorical figures at left and right. Printer: BWC. 122x77mm.	100	250	650
65	**50 Escudos** 1.1.1920. Dark blue on pale green underprint. Arms at upper center. Back: Palm trees at center. BC: Brown on pale yellow-orange. Printer: BWC. 200x125mm.	350	1,250	2,750

1921 Issue

No.	Description	Good	Fine	XF
66	**1 Escudo** 1.1.1921. Green on multicolor underprint. Provincia de Mozambique. Portrait F. de Oliveira Chamico at left. Signature varieties. Back: Seated allegorical woman and ships. Printer: BWC. 130x82mm.			
	a. *Decreto.*	3.50	35.00	100
	b. Without *Decreto.*	3.50	35.00	100
67	**2 1/2 Escudos** 1.1.1921. Blue on multicolor underprint. Provincia de Mozambique. Portrait F. de Oliveira Chamico at left. Signature varieties. Back: Seated allegorical woman and ships. Printer: TDLR. 136x89mm.			
	a. *Decreto.*	8.50	50.00	200
	b. Without *Decreto.*	8.50	50.00	200
68	**5 Escudos** 1.1.1921. Brown on multicolor underprint. Provincia de Mozambique. Portrait F. de Oliveira Chamico at left. Signature varieties. Back: Seated allegorical woman and ships. Printer: BWC. 154x94mm.			
	a. *Decreto.*	12.50	85.00	250
	b. Without *Decreto.*	12.50	85.00	250
69	**10 Escudos** 1.1.1921. Brown-violet on multicolor underprint. Provincia de Mozambique. Portrait F. de Oliveira Chamico at left. Signature varieties. Back: Seated allegorical woman and ships. Printer: BWC. 160x105mm.			
	a. *Decreto.*	17.50	125	350
	b. Without *Decreto.*	17.50	125	350
70	**20 Escudos** 1.1.1921. Blue-green on multicolor underprint. Provincia de Mozambique. Portrait F. de Oliveira Chamico at left. Signature varieties. Back: Seated allegorical woman and ships. Printer: BWC. 178x115mm.			
	a. *Decreto.*	50.00	200	600
	b. Without *Decreto.*	50.00	200	600
71	**50 Escudos** 1.1.1921. Red-brown on multicolor underprint. Provincia de Mozambique. Portrait F. de Oliveira Chamico at left. Signature varieties. Back: Seated allegorical woman and ships. Printer: BWC. 185x122mm.			
	a. *Decreto.*	125	500	1,500
	b. Without *Decreto.*	125	500	1,500
72	**100 Escudos** 1.1.1921. Blue-green on multicolor underprint. Provincia de Mozambique. Portrait F. de Oliveira Chamico at left. Signature varieties. Back: Seated allegorical woman and ships. Printer: BWC. 193x125mm.			
	a. *Decreto.*	180	650	2,000
	b. Without *Decreto.*	180	650	2,000

1929 Provisional Issue

Decreto No. 17,154 de 26 de Julho de 1929

No.	Description	Good	Fine	XF
72A	**100 Escudos on 1 Libra** ND (1929-old date 1.3.1909). Overprint: Black; on #45.	150	550	—
72B	**1000 Escudos on 20 Libras** ND (1929-old date 1.3.1909). Overprint: Black; on #49.	300	850	—

1932 Issue

No.	Description	Good	Fine	XF
73	**500 Escudos** 25.8.1932. Black on multicolor underprint. Provincia de Mozambique. Portrait F. de Oliveira Chamico at left. Signature varieties. Back: Seated allegorical woman and ships. 193x126mm. Unique.	—	—	—

1937; 1938 Issue

		Good	Fine	XF
74	**20 Escudos** 6.4.1937. Blue. Portrait A. Ennes at left. Printer: BWC. 138x81mm.	7.50	50.00	175

		Good	Fine	XF
75	**50 Escudos** 11.1.1938. Gray-olive. Portrait A. Ennes at left. Printer: BWC. 164x84mm.	12.50	75.00	275

		Good	Fine	XF
76	**100 Escudos** 11.1.1938. Purple. Portrait A. Ennes at left. Printer: BWC. 170x97mm.	20.00	125	450

1941 First Issue

		Good	Fine	XF
77	**100 Escudos** 27.3.1941. Purple. Portrait A. Ennes at left. 170x97mm.	20.00	110	425

		Good	Fine	XF
78	**500 Escudos** 27.3.1941. Lilac. Portrait A. Ennes at left. 175x100mm.	35.00	175	600

		Good	Fine	XF
79	**1000 Escudos** 27.3.1941. Brown. Portrait A. Ennes at left. 182x103mm.	120	450	1,200

1941 Emergency Second Issue

		VG	VF	UNC
80	**50 Centavos** 1.9.1941. Green. Arms at left. Back: Purple. Back: Arms at center. Printer: Imprensa Nacional de Mocambique. 85x51mm.	3.00	15.00	45.00

1941 Third Issue

		VG	VF	UNC
81	**1 Escudo** 1.9.1941. Green. Portrait F. de Oliveira Chamico at left, Steamship seal at right. Like #66-69 but different signature titles. Signature varieties. Printer: BWC.	3.00	17.50	65.00

		VG	VF	UNC
82	**2 1/2 Escudos** 1.9.1941. Blue. Portrait F. de Oliveira Chamico at left, Steamship seal at right. Like #66-69 but different signature titles. Signature varieties. Printer: TDLR.	6.00	40.00	150

		VG	VF	UNC
83	**5 Escudos** 1.9.1941. Dark brown. Portrait F. de Oliveira Chamico at left, Steamship seal at right. Like #66-69 but different signature titles. Signature varieties. Printer: BWC. 154x94mm.			
	a. Issued note.	10.00	75.00	200
	s. Specimen, punch hole cancelled. without serial #.	—	—	175

		VG	VF	UNC
84	**10 Escudos** 1.9.1941. Light brown. Portrait F. de Oliveira Chamico at left, Steamship seal at right. Like #66-69 but different signature titles. Signature varieties. Printer: BWC. 164x110mm.	12.00	90.00	250

1941 Fourth Issue

		VG	VF	UNC
85	**20 Escudos** 1.11.1941. Black on blue and multicolor underprint. Portrait A. Ennes at left, steamship seal at right. Printer: BWC. 138x81mm.	7.50	45.00	175

		VG	VF	UNC
86	**50 Escudos** 1.11.1941. Black on brown and multicolor underprint. Portrait A. Ennes at left, steamship seal at right. Printer: BWC. 164x84mm.	10.00	60.00	225

		VG	VF	UNC
87	**500 Escudos** 1.11.1941. Black on lilac and multicolor underprint. Portrait A. Ennes at left, steamship seal at right. 175x100mm.	40.00	175	600

		VG	VF	UNC
88	**1000 Escudos** 1.11.1941. Black on brown and multicolor underprint. Portrait A. Ennes at left, steamship seal at right. 182x103mm.	125	400	1,000

1943 Issue

		VG	VF	UNC
89	**5 Escudos** 15.4.1943. Black on green and multicolor underprint. Portrait A. Ennes at left, steamship seal at right. Printer: BWC. 126x75mm.	3.50	20.00	85.00

		VG	VF	UNC
90	**10 Escudos** 15.4.1943. Black on brown-violet and multicolor underprint. Portrait A. Ennes at left, steamship seal at right. Printer: BWC. 126x75mm.	7.50	30.00	125

		VG	VF	UNC
91	**100 Escudos** 27.1.1943. Black on orange and multicolor underprint. Portrait A. Ennes at left, steamship seal at right. 171x95mm.	15.00	100	450

1944; 1945 Issue

No.	Denomination	VG	VF	UNC
92	**1 Escudo** 23.5.1944. Black on olive and multicolor underprint. Portrait A. Ennes at left, steamship seal at right. Printer: BWC. 105x60mm.	1.00	8.50	35.00

No.	Denomination	VG	VF	UNC
93	**2 1/2 Escudos** 23.5.1944. Blue. Black on olive and multicolor underprint. Printer: BWC. 120x65mm.	2.00	15.00	65.00
94	**5 Escudos** 29.11.1945. Green on multicolor underprint. Portrait A. Ennes at left, steamship seal at right. Printer: BWC. 126x75mm.	3.00	17.50	75.00
95	**10 Escudos** 29.11.1945. Brown on multicolor underprint. Portrait A. Ennes at left, steamship seal at right. Printer: BWC. 126x75mm.	7.00	25.00	115
96	**20 Escudos** 29.11.1945. Blue on multicolor underprint. Portrait A. Ennes at left, steamship seal at right. Printer: BWC. 138x81mm.	10.00	35.00	150
96A	**50 Escudos** 29.11.1945. Brown on multicolor underprint. Portrait A. Ennes at left, steamship seal at right. Printer: BWC. 164x84mm.	10.00	50.00	200
97	**100 Escudos** 29.11.1945. Orange on multicolor underprint. Portrait A. Ennes at left, steamship seal at right. 170x97mm.	15.00	75.00	350
98	**500 Escudos** 29.11.1945. Lilac on multicolor underprint. Portrait A. Ennes at left, steamship seal at right. 175x100mm.	35.00	150	500
99	**1000 Escudos** 1945; 1947. Blue on multicolor underprint. Portrait A. Ennes at left, steamship seal at right. 182x103mm.			
	a. 29.11.1945.	90.00	350	850
	b. 27.3.1947.	50.00	200	650

1947 Issue

No.	Denomination	VG	VF	UNC
100	**100 Escudos** 27.3.1947. Orange on multicolor underprint. Portrait A. Ennes at left, steamship seal at right. 170x98mm.	15.00	60.00	275
101	**500 Escudos** 27.3.1947. Lilac on multicolor underprint. Portrait A. Ennes at left, steamship seal at right. 175x100mm.	30.00	125	450

1950; 1953 Issue

No.	Denomination	VG	VF	UNC
102	**50 Escudos** 16.2.1950. Black on multicolor underprint. Portrait E. Costa at right, with text: *COLONIA PORTUGUESA* below bank name. Back: Ornate church doorway at center. Watermark: Arms. Printer: TDLR. 162x80mm.	6.00	25.00	85.00

No.	Denomination	VG	VF	UNC
103	**100 Escudos** 16.2.1950. Orange on multicolor underprint. Portrait A. de Ornelas Evasconcelos at right, with text: *COLONIA PORTUGUESA* below bank name. Back: Ornate church doorway at center. Watermark: Arms. Printer: TDLR. 165x85mm.	10.00	40.00	125

No.	Denomination	VG	VF	UNC
104	**500 Escudos** 31.7.1953. Brown-violet on multicolor underprint. Portrait C. Xavier at right. Printer: BWC. 170x89mm.			
	a. Issued note.	15.00	50.00	150
	s. Specimen, punch hole cancelled.	—	—	75.00

No.	Denomination	VG	VF	UNC
105	**1000 Escudos** 31.7.1953. Blue on multicolor underprint. Portrait Mousinho de Albuquerque at right. Printer: BWC. 175x95mm.			
	a. Issued note.	15.00	75.00	250
	s. Specimen, punch hole cancelled.	—	—	100

1958 Issue

		VG	VF	UNC
106	**50 Escudos** 24.7.1958. Black on multicolor. Like #102 but without text: *COLONIA PORTUGUESA* below bank name; without printing over watermark at left. Back: Ornate church doorway at center. BC: Green. Watermark: Arms. Printer: TDLR. 162x80mm.			
	a. Issued note.	1.00	5.00	15.00
	s. Specimen.	—	—	50.00
107	**100 Escudos** 24.7.1958. Like #103 but without text: *COLONIA PORTUGUESA* below bank name; without printing over watermark at left. Back: Ornate church doorway at center. Watermark: Arms. Printer: TDLR. 165x85mm.	2.50	10.00	50.00
108	**500 Escudos** 1958. Brown-violet. Portrait C. Xavier at right. 170x99mm.	15.00	50.00	150

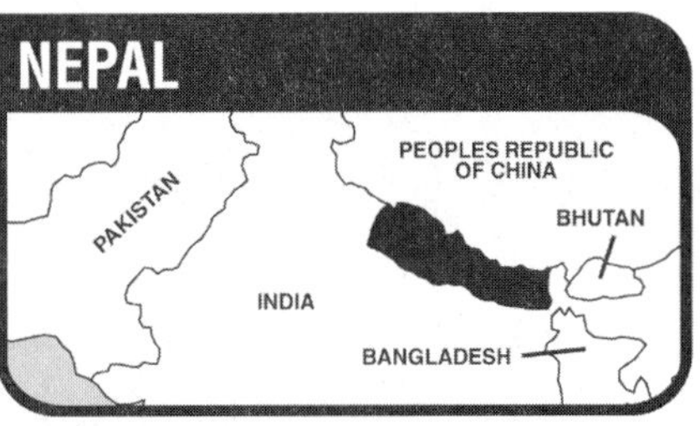

The Kingdom of Nepal, the world's only Hindu kingdom, is a landlocked country located in central Asia along the southern slopes of the Himalayan Mountains. It has an area of 56,136 sq. mi. (140,797 sq. km.) and a population of 24.35 million. Capital: Káthmandu. Nepal has substantial deposits of coal, copper, iron and cobalt but they are largely unexploited. Agriculture is the principal economic activity. Livestock, rice, timber and jute are exported.In 1951, the Nepalese monarch ended the century-old system of rule by hereditary premiers and instituted a cabinet system of government. Reforms in 1990 established a multiparty democracy within the framework of a constitutional monarchy. An insurgency led by Maoist extremists broke out in 1996. The ensuing nine-year civil war between insurgents and government forces witnessed the dissolution of the cabinet and parliament and assumption of absolute power by the king. Several weeks of mass protests in April 2006 were followed by several months of peace negotiations between the Maoists and government officials, and culminated in a November 2006 peace accord and the promulgation of an interim constitution. The newly formed interim parliament declared Nepal a democratic federal republic at its first meeting in May 2008, the king vacated the throne in mid-June 2008, and parliament elected the country's first president the following month.

RULERS:

Tribhuvana Vira Vikrama Shahi Deva, 1911-1950; 1951-1955
Jnanendra Vira Vikrama Shahi Deva, 1950-1951
Mahendra Vira Vikrama Shahi Deva, 1955-1972
Birendra Bir Bikram Shahi Deva, 1972-2001
Ginendra, 2001-

MONETARY SYSTEM:

1 Mohru = 100 Paisa to 1961
1 Rupee = 100 Paisa, 1961-

HEADING VARIETIES

नेपाल सर्कार	नेपाल सरकार
Type I	Type II

Note: Issues in the Mohru System have reference to Rupees in English on the notes. The difference is in the Nepalese designation of the value.

For those notes in Mohru the first character at the left appears thus: म

When the Nepalese designation changes to Rupees, this character appears thus: रु

Lines where either of these appear are in the lower center on the face, or on the back. Both will never appear on the same note. All notes from the second issue of Mahendra to the present are in rupees.

SIGNATURE VARIETIES			
1	Janaph Raja	5	Laxminath Gautam
2	Bharana Raja	6	Besh Bahadur Thapa
3	Narendra Raja	7	Pradimhalal Rajbhandari
4	Himalaya Shamsher	8	Yadavnath Panta

KINGDOM

Government of Nepal

1951 ND First Issue

		VG	VF	UNC
1	**1 Mohru** ND (1951). Blue and brown. Coin at right with date VS2008 (1951). Back: With coin at left, mountains at center.			
	a. Signature 2.	2.00	4.00	10.00
	b. Signature 3.	4.00	10.00	20.00

		VG	VF	UNC
2	**5 Mohru** ND (1951). Purple and multicolor. Portrait King Tribhuvana with plumed crown at right. Type I heading. Back: Tiger.			
	a. Signature 1. Janaph Raja.	30.00	50.00	100
	b. Signature 2. Bharana Raja.	30.00	50.00	100
3	**10 Mohru** ND (1951). Purple on blue and brown underprint Portrait King Tribhuvana with plumed crown at right. Type I heading. Back: Arms. 145x82mm.			
	a. Signature 1.	30.00	70.00	150
	b. Signature 2.	30.00	70.00	150
	c. Signature 3.	30.00	70.00	100

		VG	VF	UNC
4	**100 Mohru** ND (1951). Dark green and multicolor. Portrait King Tribhuvana with plumed crown at right. Type I heading. Back: Rhinoceros.			
	a. Signature 1.	150	250	500
	b. Signature 2.	150	250	500

1951 ND Second Issue

		VG	VF	UNC
5	**5 Mohru** ND (1951). Purple and multicolor. Portrait King Tribhuvana with plumed crown at right. Signature 3. Type II heading. Back: Tiger.	15.00	30.00	60.00
6	**10 Mohru** ND (1951). Purple and multicolor. Type II heading. Portrait King Tribhuvana Vira Vikrama with plumed crown at right. Signature 3. Back: Arms.	20.00	35.00	70.00
7	**100 Mohru** ND (1951). Dark green and multicolor. Type II heading. Signature 3. Portrait King Tribhuvana Vira Vikrama with plumed crown at right. Back: Rhinoceros.	70.00	180	300

Central Bank of Nepal

1960 ND Issue

Mohru System

		VG	VF	UNC
8	**1 Mohru** ND (1960). Violet and olive. Coin at left with date VS2013 (1956). Signature 4. Back: Lilac and green.	3.00	5.00	10.00
9	**5 Mohru** ND (1960). Violet and aqua. Portrait King Mahendra Vira Vikrama in civillian clothes at left. Stupa at center. Signature 4; 5. Back: Himalayas. BC: Violet.	8.00	15.00	30.00

		VG	VF	UNC
10	**10 Mohru** ND (1960). Dark brown and red. Portrait King Mahendra Vira Vikrama in civillian clothes at left. Temple at center. Signature 4; 5. Back: Arms. BC: Brown and gold.	10.00	20.00	50.00

		VG	VF	UNC
11	**100 Mohru** ND (1960). Green and brown. Portrait King Mahendra Vira Vikrama in civillian clothes at left. Temple at Lalitpur at center. Signature 4; 5. Back: Indian rhinoceros at center. BC: Green.	50.00	100	200

1961; 1965 ND Issue

#	Denomination	VG	VF	UNC
15	**100 Rupees** ND (1961). Green and brown. Portrait of King Mahendra Vira Vikrama at upper left. Temple at Lalitpor at center. Signature 5; 6; 7; 8. Back: Indian rhinoceros at center. Watermark: Plumed crown.	3.00	10.00	35.00

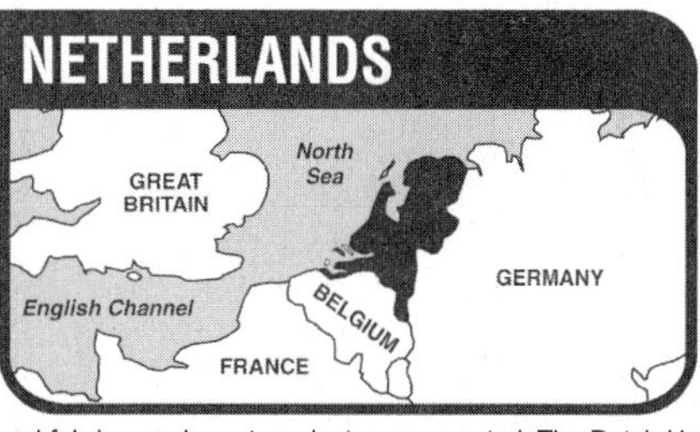

The Kingdom of the Netherlands, a country of western Europe fronting on the North Sea and bordered by Belgium and Germany, has an area of 15,770 sq. mi. (40,844 sq. km.) and a population of 15.87 million. Capital: Amsterdam, but the seat of government is at The Hague. The economy is based on dairy farming and a variety of industrial activities. Chemicals, yarns and fabrics, and meat products are exported. The Dutch United Provinces declared their independence from Spain in 1579; during the 17th century, they became a leading seafaring and commercial power, with settlements and colonies around the world. After a 20-year French occupation, a Kingdom of the Netherlands was formed in 1815. In 1830 Belgium seceded and formed a separate kingdom. The Netherlands remained neutral in World War I, but suffered invasion and occupation by Germany in World War II. A modern, industrialized nation, the Netherlands is also a large exporter of agricultural products. The country was a founding member of NATO and the EEC (now the EU), and participated in the introduction of the euro in 1999.

RULERS:William I, 1815-1840

William II, 1840-1849
William III, 1849-1890
Wilhelmina, 1890-1948
Juliana, 1948-1980
Beatrix, 1981-

MONETARY SYSTEM:

1 Gulden = 20 Stuivers
1 Gulden = 100 Cents, to 2001
1 Rijksdaalder = 2 1/2 Gulden
1 Euro = 100 Cents, 2002-

REPLACEMENT NOTES:

#37-60, 72-74, 77-79, 81-82, 84-89, JEZ-printed notes only, serial numbers starting with "1" instead of normal "o".

DUTCH 'RECEPIS'

Gemeene Lands Comptoiren

1794 Issue

#	Denomination	Good	Fine	XF
B5	**3 Gulden** 1.12.1794-1.1.1795. Black.	—	—	—

Committe van Financie in 's Hage

Finance Committee in the Hague

Alkmaar

1795 Issue

#	Denomination	Good	Fine	XF
B10	**2 1/4 Stuiver** 7.4.1795. Black. Rare.	—	—	—
B11	**4 1/2 Stuiver** 7.4.1795. Black. Rare.	—	—	—
B12	**9 Stuiver** 7.4.1795. Black. Rare.	—	—	—
B13	**11 1/4 Stuiver** 7.4.1795. Black. Rare.	—	—	—
B14	**45 Stuiver** 7.4.1795. Black. Rare.	—	—	—

Delft

1795 Issue

#	Denomination	Good	Fine	XF
B17	**4 Stuiver & 8 Pennigen** 9.5.1795. Black. Rare.	—	—	—

Dordecht

1795 Issue

#	Denomination	Good	Fine	XF
B20	**18 Gulden** ND (1795). Black. Rare.	—	—	—
B21	**27 Gulden** ND (1795). Black. Rare.	—	—	—
B22	**54 Gulden** ND (1795). Black. Rare.	—	—	—
B23	**90 Gulden** ND (1795). Black. Rare.	—	—	—

1795 (February) Issue

#	Denomination	Good	Fine	XF
B25	**2 1/2 Stuiver** 16.2.1795. Black.	—	—	—
B26	**5 Stuiver** 16.2.1795. Black.	—	—	—
B27	**24 Stuiver** 16.2.1795. Black.	—	—	—

1795 (March) Issue

#	Denomination	Good	Fine	XF
B30	**10 Stuiver** 1.3.1795. Black. Rare.	—	—	—

1795 (May) Issue

		Good	Fine	XF
B32	**2 1/2 Stuiver** 1.5.1795. Black. Rare.	—	—	—

1795 Bread Equivalent Issue

		Good	Fine	XF
B33	**4 Stuiver = 4 Ponds Brot** ND (1796). Black.			
	a. Issued note. Rare.	—	—	—
	b. Without serial numbers. Rare.	—	—	—

Enkuisen

1795 Issue

		Good	Fine	XF
B40	**4 1/2 Stuiver** 15.5.1795. Black. Rare.	—	—	—
B41	**6 3/4 Stuiver** 15.5.1795. Black. Rare.	—	—	—
B42	**22 1/2 Stuiver** 15.5.1795. Black. Rare.	—	—	—
B43	**45 Stuiver** 15.5.1795 Black. Rare.	—	—	—
B44	**90 Stuiver** 15.5.1795. Black. Rare.	—	—	—

Gorinchem

1795 ND *Verwisfelde Adsignaten* Issue

		Good	Fine	XF
B47	**4 1/2 Stuiver** ND (1795). Black. Rare.	—	—	—
B48	**6 3/4 Stuiver** ND (1795). Black. Rare.	—	—	—
B49	**9 Stuiver** ND (1795). Black. Rare.	—	—	—

1795 ND *Stedelijke Recepisse* Issue

		Good	Fine	XF
B50	**5 Sols = 2 1/4 Stuiver** ND (1795). Black.			
	a. Issued note. Rare.	—	—	—
	b. Without serial numbers. Rare.	—	—	—
B51	**10 Sols = 4 1/2 Stuiver** ND (1795). Black. Rare.	—	—	—
B52	**15 Sols = 6 3/4 Stuiver** ND (1795). Black. Rare.	—	—	—
B53	**1 Livre = 9 Stuiver** ND (1795). Black.			
	a. Issued note. Rare.	—	—	—
	b. Without serial numbers. Rare.	—	—	—

Gouda

1795 Issue

		Good	Fine	XF
B60	**1 1/2 Stuiver** 15.4.1795. Black. Rare.	—	—	—
B61	**2 1/4 Stuiver** 15.4.1795. Black. Rare.	—	—	—
B62	**22 1/2 Stuiver** 15.4.1795. Black.	—	—	—

Haarlem

1795 Issue

		Good	Fine	XF
B67	**2 1/4 Stuiver** 1795. Black. Rare.	—	—	—
B68	**4 1/2 Stuiver** 1795. Black. Rare.	—	—	—
B69	**9 Stuiver** 1795. Black. Rare.	—	—	—

'S Hage

1794-1795 Issue

		Good	Fine	XF
B70	**4 Stuiver & 8 Penningen** 9.5.1795. Black. Rare.	—	—	—

		Good	Fine	XF
B71	**6 Gulden** 1.12.1794. Black. Rare.	—	—	—

Leiden

1795 Issue

		Good	Fine	XF
B73	**27 Gulden** ND (1795). Black. Rare.	—	—	—

Overyssel

1795 Issue

		Good	Fine	XF
B76	**10 Stuiver** 28.2.1795; 28.8.1795; 19.11.1795. Black. Rare.	—	—	—

		Good	Fine	XF
B77	**1 Guilder** 22.2.1795. Black. Rare.	—	—	—

		Good	Fine	XF
B78	**2 Gulden** 22.2.1795. Black. Rare.	—	—	—

Rotterdam

1795 Issue

		Good	Fine	XF
B80	**4 1/2 Stuiver** 18.3.1795. Black. Rare.	—	—	—
B81	**18 Stuiver** 18.3.1795. Black. Rare.	—	—	—
B82	**4 Gulden & 10 Stuivers** 18.3.1795. Black. Rare.	—	—	—
B83	**9 Gulden** 18.3.1795. Black. Rare.	—	—	—

Schiedam

1795 Issue

		Good	Fine	XF
B85	**27 Gulden** ND (1795). Black. Rare.	—	—	—
B86	**180 Gulden** ND (1795). Black. Rare.	—	—	—

1795 Second Issue

		Good	Fine	XF
B88	**4 1/2 Stuiver** 28.3.1795; 30.4.1795. Black. Rare.	—	—	—
B89	**9 Stuiver** 21.3.1795; 22.3.1795; 23.3.1795; 24.3.1795; 25.3.1795; 30.3.1795; 4.7.1795; 7.5.1795. Black. Rare.	—	—	—
B90	**1 Guilder & 2 Stuivers & 8 Pennnigen** 5.4.1795; 6.4.1795. Black.	Good	Fine	XF
	a. Issued note. Rare.	—	—	—
	b. Without serial numbers. Rare.	—	—	—
B91	**2 Gulden & 5 Stuivers** 29.3.1795; 4.4.1795; 6.4.1795; 8.4.1795; Black.	Good	Fine	XF
	a. Issued note. Rare.	—	—	—
	b. Without serial numbers. Rare.	—	—	—
B92	**4 Gulden & 10 Stuivers** 28.3.1795; 29.3.1795; 7.4.1795. Black.	Good	Fine	XF
	a. Issued note. Rare.	—	—	—
	b. Without serial numbers. Rare.	—	—	—
B93	**11 Gulden & 5 Stuivers** 28.3.1795; 7.4.1795. Black.	Good	Fine	XF
	a. Issued note. Rare.	—	—	—
	b. Without serial numbers. Rare.	—	—	—
B94	**22 Gulden & 10 Stuivers** 28.3.1795; 3.4.1795; 6.4.1795; 9.4.1795. Black. Rare.	—	—	—

Zeeland

1795 Issue

		Good	Fine	XF
B95	**18 Duiten = 2 1/4 Stuiver** 23.3.1795. Black. *Lit: D.*	—	—	—
B96	**4 1/2 Stuiver** 23.3.1795. Black. *Lit: C.*	Good	Fine	XF
	a. Issued note. Rare.	—	—	—
	b. Without serial numbers. Rare.	—	—	—

		Good	Fine	XF
B97	**9 Stuiver** 23.3.1795. Black. *Lit: B.* Rare.	—	—	—

Color Abbreviation Guide

New to the *Standard Catalog of ® World Paper Money* are the following abbreviations related to color references:

BC: Back color

PC: Paper color

B98	18 Stuiver 23.3.1795. Black. *Lit: A, AAA* or *AAAA*. Rare.	Good —	Fine —	XF —

W/o Domicile

1795 Issue

B101	450 Gulden ND (1795). Black. Rare.	Good —	Fine —	XF —

KONINKRIJK - KINGDOM

De Nederlandsche Bank

Netherlands Bank

1814 Issue

		Good	Fine	XF
A2	25 Gulden 1814-1838. Rose.	—	—	—
A3	40 Gulden 1814-1838. Rose. Rare.	—	—	—
A4	60 Gulden 1814-1838. Rose. Rare.	—	—	—
A5	80 Gulden 1814-1825. Rose. Rare.	—	—	—
A6	100 Gulden 1814-1838. Rose. Rare.	—	—	—
A7	200 Gulden 1814-1838. Rose. Rare.	—	—	—
A8	300 Gulden 1814-1838. Rare.	—	—	—
A9	500 Gulden 1814-1838. Rose. Rare.	—	—	—
A10	1000 Gulden 1814-1838. Rose. Earlier notes with value written, later notes with value printed. Rare.	—	—	—

Koninkrijk Der Nederlanden

Muntbiljetten - State Notes

Law of 18.12.1845

		Good	Fine	XF
A11	5 Gulden 1.1.1846. Red. Uniface. Watermark: *RIJKS MUNT.* Rare.	—	—	—
A12	10 Gulden 1.1.1846. Brown. Uniface. Watermark: *RIJKS MUNT.* Rare.	—	—	—

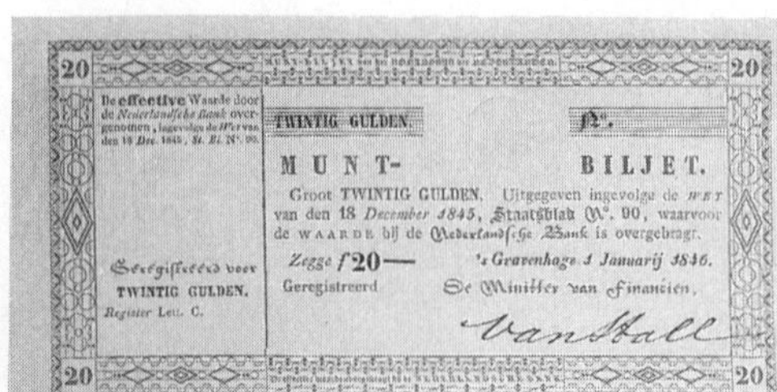

A13	20 Gulden 1.1.1846. Green. Uniface. Watermark: *RIJKS MUNT.* Rare.	Good —	Fine —	XF —

		Good	Fine	XF
A14	100 Gulden 1.1.1846. Blue. Uniface. Watermark: *RIJKS MUNT.* Rare.	—	—	—
A15	500 Gulden 1.1.1846. Yellow. Uniface. Watermark: *RIJKS MUNT.* Rare.	—	—	—

Law of 17.9.1849

		Good	Fine	XF
A16	10 Gulden 15.10.1849. Printed or handwritten date. Blue. Rare.	—	—	—
A17	100 Gulden 1849. Printed or handwritten date. Red on gray underprint. Rare.	—	—	—
A18	500 Gulden 1849. Printed or handwritten date. Brown on blue underprint. Rare.	—	—	—
A19	1000 Gulden 1849. Green on red underprint. Rare.	—	—	—

1852 Issue

A20	10 Gulden 1852-1878. Light blue. Allegorical figures on borders, arms at upper center. Various date and signature varieties. Rare.	Good —	Fine —	XF —

1878 Issue

1	10 Gulden 1878-1894. Light brown. Arms at upper center, ornate border. Various date and signature varieties. Rare.	Good —	Fine —	XF —

1884-1894 Issue

		Good	Fine	XF
2	10 Gulden 1894-1898. Brown. Standing woman and lion at left, portrait Queen Wilhelmina as child at right. Signature varieties. Rare.	—	—	—
3	50 Gulden 1884-1914. Blue. Standing women and lion at left. Portrait King William III at right. Signature varieties. Rare.	—	—	—

1898 Issue

3A	10 Gulden 1898-1914. Standing woman and lion at left, older portrait Queen Wilhelmina at right. Signature varieties. Rare.	Good —	Fine —	XF —

Zilverbon - Silver Note

1914 Issue

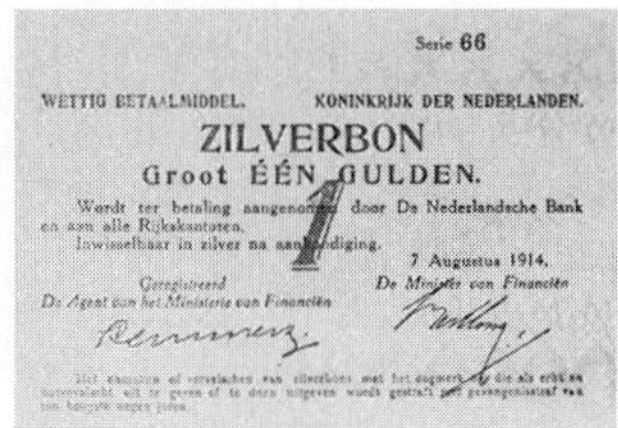

		Good	Fine	XF
4	1 Gulden 7.8.1914. Brown. Value *1* at center.			
	a. Issued note.	12.50	60.00	150
	p. Proof.	—	Unc	30.00

		Good	Fine	XF
5	**2 1/2 Gulden** 7.8.1914. Blue on green underprint. Value *2.50* at center. Thick or thin paper.	Good	Fine	XF
	a. Issued note.	50.00	150	350
	p. Proof.	—	Unc	50.00

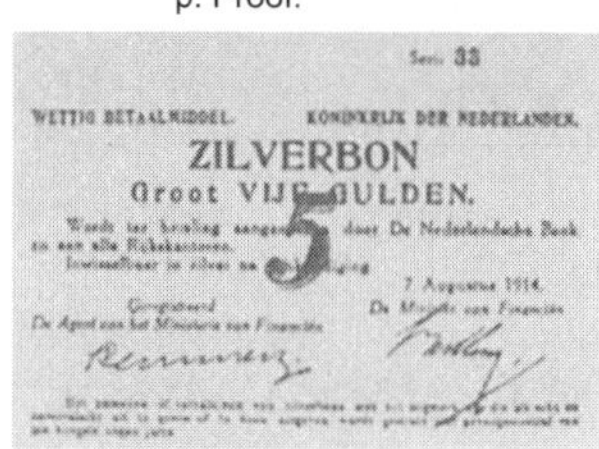

		Good	Fine	XF
6	**5 Gulden** 7.8.1914. Green.	Good	Fine	XF
	a. Issued note.	70.00	250	650
	p. Proof.	—	Unc	75.00

1915 Issue

		Good	Fine	XF
7	**2 1/2 Gulden** 30.3.1915. Blue. Value *2.50* at center and at the 4 corners.	30.00	100	300

1916 Issue

		Good	Fine	XF
8	**1 Gulden** 1.5.1916. Brown. Value *1* at center and at the 4 corners.	10.00	50.00	150
9	**2 1/2 Gulden** 31.3.1916. Blue. Value *2.50* at center and at the 4 corners.	30.00	100	300

1917 Issue

		Good	Fine	XF
10	**1 Gulden** 1.11.1917. Brown. Value *1* at center and at the 4 corners.	10.00	50.00	150
11	**2 1/2 Gulden** 1.8.1917. Blue. Value *2.50* at center and at the 4 corners.	20.00	80.00	250

1918 First Issue

		Good	Fine	XF
12	**2 1/2 Gulden** 1.7.1918. Blue on gray and yellow underprint. Value *2.50* at left, at center and upper and lower right.	10.00	50.00	150

1918 Second Issue

		Good	Fine	XF
13	**1 Gulden** 1.10.1918. Brown. Value *1* at center and at the 4 corners.	10.00	50.00	150
14	**2 1/2 Gulden** 1.10.1918. Value *2.50* at left, at center and upper and lower right.	10.00	50.00	150

1920 Issue

		Good	Fine	XF
15	**1 Gulden** 1.2.1920. Brown on light green underprint. Portrait Queen Wilhelmina at left.	3.50	25.00	100
16	**2 1/2 Gulden** 1.10.1920. Value *2.50* at left, at center and upper and lower right.	5.00	30.00	125

1922 Issues

		Good	Fine	XF
17	**2 1/2 Gulden** 1.5.1922. Value *2.50* at left, at center and upper and lower right.	Good	Fine	XF
	a. Issued note.	5.00	30.00	125
	x. Counterfeit with date: 1.10.1922.	5.00	30.00	125
18	**2 1/2 Gulden** 1.12.1922. Value *2.50* at left, at center and upper and lower right.	5.00	30.00	125

1923 Issue

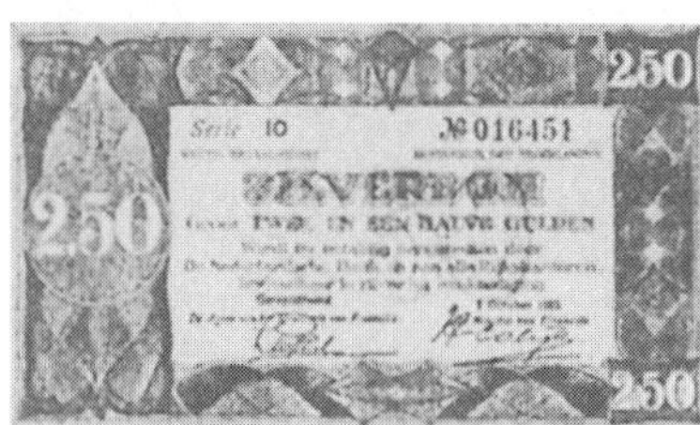

		Good	Fine	XF
19	**2 1/2 Gulden** 1.10.1923. Value *2.50* at left, at center and upper and lower right. Back: Without underprint in inner rectangle.	Good	Fine	XF
	a. Issued note.	5.00	30.00	125
	p. Proof.	—	Unc	35.00

1927 Issue

		Good	Fine	XF
20	**2 1/2 Gulden** 1.10.1927. Value *2.50* at left, at center and upper and lower right. Back: Without underprint in inner rectangle.	4.00	25.00	100

De Nederlandsche Bank

Netherlands Bank

1904-1911 "Old Style" Issue

		Good	Fine	XF
21	**25 Gulden** 27.9.1904-7.12.1921. Black on orange underprint. 7 signature varieties. Uniface. Arms with caduceus and lion at top center.	150	450	1,000

#	Denomination	Good	Fine	XF
22	**40 Gulden** 6.6.1910; 11.7.1921; 13.9.1921; 11.12.1922. Black on green underprint. Arms with caduceus and lion at top center. 6 signature varieties. Uniface.	300	800	2,000

#	Denomination	Good	Fine	XF
23	**60 Gulden** 11.8.1910-1.9.1924. Black on lilac-brown underprint. Arms with caduceus and lion at top center. 6 signature varieties. Uniface.	300	800	2,000
24	**100 Gulden** 1.3.1911; 17.2.1919; 2.1.1920; 13.10.1921. Black. Portrait Minerva at top center. 4 signature varieties. Back: Blue.	300	850	2,250
25	**200 Gulden** 18.10.1910; 2.7.1921. Black. Portrait Minerva at top center. 3 signature varieties. Back: Orange.	500	1,500	3,000
26	**300 Gulden** 15.2.1909; 3.1.1921. Black. Portrait Minerva at top center. 3 signature varieties. Back: Green.	500	1,500	3,000
27	**1000 Gulden** 3.10.1910; 22.5.1916. Black and blue. Portrait Minerva at top center. 4 signature varieties. Back: Red. Rare.	—	—	—

1906 "New Style" Issue

#	Denomination	Good	Fine	XF
34	**10 Gulden** 18.6.1906; 24.9.1913; 18.3.1914; 29.6.1916; 29.4.1920-5.2.1921. Blue. Allegorical figures of Labor at left, Welfare at right. *AMSTERDAM* and serial #. 4 signature varieties. Back: Brown and green.	175	500	1,200

1914 "Old Style" Issue

#	Denomination	Good	Fine	XF
28	**10 Gulden** 1.8.1914. Red on green underprint. Without vignette. Back: Blue. Rare.	—	—	—
29	**25 Gulden** 1.8.1914. Red on green underprint. Without vignette. Back: Blue. Rare.	—	—	—
30	**40 Gulden** 1.8.1914. Green on light green underprint. Without vignette. Rare.	—	—	—
31	**60 Gulden** 1.8.1914. Brown on green underprint. Without vignette. Rare.	—	—	—

#	Denomination	Good	Fine	XF
32	**100 Gulden** 1.8.1914. Black on rose underprint. Portrait Minerva at top center. Rare.	—	—	—

#	Denomination	Good	Fine	XF
32A	**200 Gulden** 1.8.1914. Black on orange underprint. Portrait Minerva at top center. Rare.	—	—	—

#	Denomination	Good	Fine	XF
32B	**300 Gulden** 1.8.1914. Black on green underprint. Portrait Minerva at top center. Rare.	—	—	—

#	Denomination	Good	Fine	XF
33	**1000 Gulden** 1.8.1914. Black on blue underprint. Portrait Minerva at top center. Rare.	—	—	—

1919-1923 "New Style" Issue

		Good	Fine	XF
35	**10 Gulden** 9.5.1921-16.5.1923. Blue. Allegorical figures of Labor at left, Welfare at right. Like #34. Back: *AMSTERDAM* and serial # .	12.50	50.00	175
36	**25 Gulden** 1921. Red. Mercury seated at left, portrait William of Orange at top center, galleon at right. Back: Bank building at center signature handwritten. Thick or thin paper. BC: Red and green.	Good	Fine	XF
	a. *AMSTERDAM* in date 17mm wide; serial # prefix letters extra bold. 26.9.1921; 30.9.1921; 3.10.1921.	75.00	200	550
	b. *AMSTERDAM* in date 19mm wide; serial # prefix letters in 1 or 2 lines. 9.8.1921; 15.8.1921.	50.00	150	450

		Good	Fine	XF
37	**40 Gulden** 1.2.1923; 12.2.1923; 15.2.1923. Green. Mercury seated at left, portrait Prince Maurits at top center, galleon at right bottom (riverside in Amsterdam from a painting by J.H. Maris (1537-1599). Back: Bank building. BC: Green.	350	750	1,850

		Good	Fine	XF
38	**60 Gulden** 9.4.1923. Brown-violet. Mercury seated at left, Prince Frederik Hendrik at top center, galleon at right bottom (riverside in Amsterdam). Back: Bank building. BC: Green.	300	650	1,250

		Good	Fine	XF
39	**100 Gulden** 1922-1929. Blue. Woman seated at left.	Good	Fine	XF
	a. Prefix letter and serial # 4mm. without serial # on back. 23.1.1922; 4.2.1922.	30.00	120	400
	b. Prefix letter and serial # 4mm. Serial # and text on back. *Hij die biljetten...* 10.9.1924; 15.9.1924.	25.00	100	350
	c. Prefix letter and serial # 4mm. Serial # and text on back: *Het Namaken...* 12.3.1926.	20.00	75.00	250
	d. Prefix letter and serial # 3mm. Serial # and text on back. *Het Namaken...* 11.2.1927; 4.12.1928; 7.12.1928; 8.12.1928; 6.9.1929.	20.00	75.00	250

		Good	Fine	XF
40	**200 Gulden** 1.12.1922; 3.1.1925; 8.4.1926; 18.2.1927. Red-brown. Woman seated at left.	300	850	2,000

		Good	Fine	XF
41	**300 Gulden** 2.12.1922; 9.4.1926; 19.2.1927. Green. Woman seated at left.	300	850	2,000
42	**1000 Gulden** 23.6.1919-5.3.1921. Sepia. Woman seated at left.	225	500	1,250

1924-1929 Issues

		Good	Fine	XF
43	**10 Gulden** 1924-1932. Dark blue. Zeeland farmer's wife at lower center. Back: Purple and brown.	Good	Fine	XF
	a. Black signature with text: *Het in vooraad...* on back. 29.3.1924; 10.7.1924.	4.00	15.00	50.00
	b. Black signature with text: *Het namaken...* Prefix letter before serial # on back. (2 types). 1.3.1924 - 8.4.1930.	3.50	12.00	45.00
	c. Blue signature with text: *Het namaken...* Prefix letter before serial # at lower left and at upper right on back. 2 signature varieties. Vissering/ Delprat or Trip/Delprat). 20.4.1930; 1.8.1930; 11.9.1930; 2.1.1931; 7.4.1931; 13.4.1934; 25.6.1934; 1.8.1931; 8.4.1932.	3.50	12.00	45.00
	d. Blue signature with text: *Wetboek van Strafrecht...* on back. 21.3.1932; 6.5.1932.	3.50	12.00	45.00

		Good	Fine	XF
44	**20 Gulden** 2.1.1926-25.11.1936. Black on olive underprint. Sailor at the helm at bottom center right. 2 signature varieties.	8.50	45.00	150

#	Denomination	Good	Fine	XF
45	**25 Gulden** 13.7.1927-3.8.1928. Blue. Mercury seated at left, portrait William of Orange at top center, galleon at right. Signature handwritten. Back: Without bank at center. BC: Blue and brown.	20.00	50.00	125
46	**25 Gulden** 15.7.1929-28.6.1930. Red. Mercury seated at left, portrait William of Orange at top center, galleon at right. Signature printed. BC: Red.	12.00	40.00	125

#	Denomination	Good	Fine	XF
47	**50 Gulden** 18.4.1929-18.5.1931. Gray-blue. Helmeted Minerva at right. (Wisdom), black or blue signature.	8.00	35.00	125

#	Denomination	Good	Fine	XF
48	**1000 Gulden** 1.10.1926-19.9.1938. Dark green and violet. Like #42. 3 signature varieties. Back: Serial # over serial letter prefix underprint.	20.00	75.00	250

1930-1933 Issue

#	Denomination	Good	Fine	XF
49	**10 Gulden** 1.6.1933-18.9.1939. Dark blue. Portrait old man wearing a cap at right by Rembrandt. Back: Green, brown and multicolor.	1.00	6.00	30.00

#	Denomination	Good	Fine	XF
50	**25 Gulden** 1.6.1931-19.3.1941. Red and multicolor. Portrait bank president W. C. Mees at lower right. 2 signature varieties.	1.50	8.00	40.00

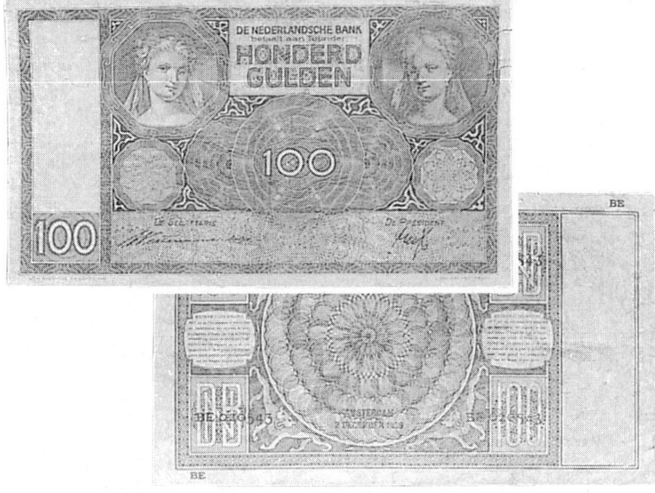

#	Denomination	Good	Fine	XF
51	**100 Gulden** 1930-1944. Brown and multicolor. Portrait women at top left center and upper right. (reflected images).			
	a. Date at center on back. 4 signature varieties. 1.10.1930; 9.3.1931; 28.11.1936; 1.12.1936.	3.00	20.00	80.00
	b. As a. 13.3.1939-28.5.1941.	2.50	12.00	60.00
	c. Date at upper left and at lower right on back. 12.1.1942-30.3.1944.	1.50	8.00	40.00

		Good	Fine	XF
52	**500 Gulden** 1.12.1930; 2.12.1930; 4.12.1930. Gray-blue and multicolor. Portrait Stadhouder / King William III at top center right. Man-o-war *Hollandia* in underprint.	90.00	400	950

1939-1941 Issues

		Good	Fine	XF
53	**10 Gulden** 1.6.1940-3.1.1941. Brown and dark green. Portrait Queen Emma at right.	4.00	15.00	45.00

		Good	Fine	XF
54	**20 Gulden** 20.7.1939-19.3.1941. Violet and olive. Portrait Queen Emma at right. 17th Century "Men-O-War" at left. Back: Schreiers Tower left and St. Nicolaas Church right (Both in Amsterdam.)	2.00	10.00	50.00

		Good	Fine	XF
55	**20 Gulden** 19.3.1941. Violet and olive. Portrait Queen Emma at right. 17th Century "Men-O-War" at left. Back: Schreiers Tower left and St Nichlaas Chruch right (Both in Amsterdam). Overprint: *AMSTERDAM* new date with bar obliterating old date on #54.	40.00	125	275
56	**10 Gulden** 1940-1942. Blue and green. Young girl at right by Paulus J. Moreelse (1571-1638).	Good	Fine	XF
	a. Watermark: Head of an old man. 19.7. 1940-19.3.1941.	1.00	4.00	17.50
	b. Watermark: Grapes. 10.4.1941-19.9.1942.	1.00	3.00	12.50
57	**25 Gulden** 20.5.1940. Olive-brown. Young girl at right by Paulus J. Moreelse. Wide margin underprint at left. Back: Geometric designs.	3.50	20.00	65.00

		Good	Fine	XF
58	**50 Gulden** 7.1.1941-6.2.1943. Dark brown and multicolor. Woman at left and right by Jan Steen. Back: *Winter Landscape* by Issac van Ostade (1621-1649).	4.50	20.00	50.00

1943 Issue

		Good	Fine	XF
59	**10 Gulden** 4.1.1943-21.4.1944. Blue, violet-blue and multicolor. Man with hat, one of the *Stall Meesters,* painting by Rembrandt.	0.75	3.00	10.00

		Good	Fine	XF
60	**25 Gulden** 4.10.1943-13.4.1944. Red-brown. Young girl at right by Paulus J. Moreelse (1571-1638). *DNB* in frame in left margin.	1.50	7.50	25.00

KONINKRIJK DER NEDERLANDEN

Zilverbon - Silver Note

1938 Issue

		VG	VF	UNC
61	**1 Gulden** 1.10.1938. Brown. Portrait Queen Wilhelmina at left. Back: Arms and text in green.	0.25	0.50	5.00
62	**2 1/2 Gulden** 1.10.1938. Blue. *Value 2.50* at left at center and upper and lower right.	0.25	0.75	7.00

1944 Issue

#	Denomination	VG	VF	UNC
63	**5 Gulden** 16.10.1944. Green. Large 5s at left and right. 3 serial # varieties. Printer: DeBussy, Amsterdam	3.00	8.00	40.00

Muntbiljet - State Note

1943 Issue

#	Denomination	VG	VF	UNC
64	**1 Gulden** 4.2.1943. Red. Portrait Queen Wilhelmina at center. Back: Arms at center. BC: Orange. Printer: ABNC.			
	a. Issued note.	0.50	4.00	15.00
	s. Specimen.	—	—	150
65	**2 1/2 Gulden** 4.2.1943. Green. Portrait Queen Wilhelmina at center. Back: Arms at center. BC: Orange. Printer: ABNC.			
	a. Issued note.	2.00	7.50	30.00
	s. Specimen.	—	—	150
66	**10 Gulden** 4.2.1943. Blue. Portrait Queen Wilhelmina at center. Back: Arms at center. BC: Orange. Printer: ABNC.			
	a. Issued note.	7.50	40.00	110
	s. Specimen.	—	—	175

#	Denomination	VG	VF	UNC
67	**25 Gulden** 4.2.1943. Olive. Portrait Queen Wilhelmina at center. Back: Arms at center. BC: Orange. Printer: ABNC.			
	a. Issued note.	100	275	550
	s. Specimen.	—	—	750

#	Denomination	VG	VF	UNC
68	**50 Gulden** 4.2.1943. Brown. Portrait Queen Wilhelmina at center. Back: Arms at center. BC: Orange. Printer: ABNC.			
	a. Issued note.	150	375	750
	s. Specimen.	—	—	900

#	Denomination	VG	VF	UNC
69	**100 Gulden** 4.2.1943. Black. Portrait Queen Wilhelmina at center. Back: Arms at center. BC: Orange. Printer: ABNC.			
	a. Issued note.	95.00	200	400
	s. Specimen.	—	—	600

1945 Issue

#	Denomination	VG	VF	UNC
70	**1 Gulden** 18.5.1945. Brown on light green underprint. Portrait Queen Wilhelmina at center. 2 serial # varieties. Back: Arms at center. Printer: TDLR.	0.50	3.00	15.00
71	**2 1/2 Gulden** 18.5.1945. Blue on pink underprint. Portrait Queen Wilhelmina at center. 3 serial # varieties. Back: Arms at center. Printer: TDLR.	0.50	4.00	20.00

1949 Issue

#	Denomination	VG	VF	UNC
72	**1 Gulden** 8.8.1949. Brown on light green underprint. Portrait Queen Juliana at left. Printer: JEZ.	0.25	1.00	8.00
73	**2 1/2 Gulden** 8.8.1949. Blue. Portrait Queen Juliana at left. Printer: JEZ.	0.25	1.50	10.00

De Nederlandsche Bank

1945 Issue

#	Denomination	VG	VF	UNC
74	**10 Gulden** 7.5.1945. Blue and brown-violet. Stylized arms with lion at bottom center. 2 serial # varieties.	5.00	35.00	100

#	Denomination	VG	VF	UNC
75	**10 Gulden** 7.5.1945. Blue on multicolor underprint. Portrait King William I at right. 2 serial # varieties. Back: Colliery. BC: Red and olive. Printer: TDLR.			
	a. Date at right. 1788-1843 (incorrect).	10.00	30.00	85.00
	b. Date at right. 1772-1843.	7.50	20.00	60.00

No.		VG	VF	UNC
76	**20 Gulden** 7.5.1945. Brown. Portrait Stadhouder / King William III at right. 2 serial # varieties. Back: Moerdyk bridge. BC: Green. Printer: TDLR.	15.00	45.00	150

No.		VG	VF	UNC
77	**25 Gulden** 7.5.1945. Maroon and tan. Young girl at right, a painting *The Girl in Blue* by Johannes C. Verspronk (1597-1662). 2 serial # varieties.	15.00	55.00	160

No.		VG	VF	UNC
78	**50 Gulden** 7.5.1945. Brown. Stadhouder Prince William II as a youth at right.	25.00	80.00	200
79	**100 Gulden** 7.5.1945. Brown. Without vignette.	70.00	150	350

No.		VG	VF	UNC
80	**1000 Gulden** 7.5.1945. Blue-black on orange and green underprint. Portrait William the Silent at right. Back: Dike at center. BC: Blue and gray. Printer: W&S.	200	600	1,250

1947 Issue

No.		VG	VF	UNC
81	**25 Gulden** 19.3.1947. Red and green. Young girl wearing flowers in her hair at right.	20.00	60.00	200
82	**100 Gulden** 9.7.1947. Brown. Woman at right. Back: Multicolor.	30.00	100	225

1949 Issue

No.		VG	VF	UNC
83	**10 Gulden** 4.3.1949. At right. Blue. Portrait King William I at right. Back: Landscape with windmill (after a painting by Jacob van Ruisdael). Printer: TDLR.	5.00	15.00	65.00

No.		VG	VF	UNC
84	**25 Gulden** 1.7.1949. Brownish orange. King Solomon at right. Printer: JEZ.	7.50	30.00	100

1953; 1956 Issue

No.		VG	VF	UNC
85	**10 Gulden** 23.3.1953. Blue, brown and green. Hugo de Groot at right. Printer: JEZ.	FV	6.50	20.00

No.	Description	VG	VF	UNC
86	**20 Gulden** 8.11.1955. Green and lilac. Herman Boerhaave at right. Back: Serpent at left. Printer: JEZ.	5.00	20.00	150.00
87	**25 Gulden** 10.4.1955. Red, orange and brown. Christiaan Huygens at right. Printer: JEZ.	FV	15.00	50.00

No.	Description	VG	VF	UNC
88	**100 Gulden** 2.2.1953. Dark brown. Desiderius Erasmus at right. Back: Red-brown. Back: Stylized bird. Printer: JEZ.	FV	75.00	200

No.	Description	VG	VF	UNC
89	**1000 Gulden** 15.7.1956. Brown and green. Rembrandt at right. Back: Hand with brush and palette. Printer: JEZ.	FV	700	1,000

The Netherlands Antilles, part of the Netherlands realm, comprise two groups of islands in the West Indies: Bonaire and Cura o near the Venezuelan coast; St. Eustatius, Saba, and the southern part of St. Maarten (St. Martin) southeast of Puerto Rico. The island group has an area of 385 sq. mi. (961 sq. km.) and a population of 210,000. Capital: Willemstad. Chief industries are the refining of crude oil, and tourism. Petroleum products and phosphates are exported.

Once the center of the Caribbean slave trade, the island of Cura ao was hard hit by the abolition of slavery in 1863. Its prosperity (and that of neighboring Aruba) was restored in the early 20th century with the construction of oil refineries to service the newly discovered Venezuelan oil fields. The island of St. Martin is shared with France; its southern portion is named Sint Maarten and is part of the Netherlands Antilles; its northern portion, called Saint Martin, is an overseas collectivity of France.On Dec. 15, 1954, the Netherlands Antilles were given complete domestic autonomy and granted equality within the Kingdom with Surinam and the Netherlands. The island of Aruba gained independence in 1986.

In October 2010 Cura ao and Saint Marten became autonomous entities of the Netherlands with the guilder being a valid currency until 31.12.2011. The islands of Bonaire, Saba and St. Eustatius became direct dependentcies of the Netherlands and will use the US dollar starting 1.1.2011.

RULERS:
Dutch

MONETARY SYSTEM:
1 Gulden = 100 Cents

DUTCH ADMINISTRATION

Nederlandse Antillen

1955 Muntbiljet Note Issue

No.	Description	VG	VF	UNC
A1	**2 1/2 Gulden** 1955; 1964. Blue. Ship in dry dock at center. Back: Crowned supported arms at center. Printer: ABNC.			
	a. 1955.	18.00	70.00	330
	b. 1964.	13.00	55.00	280
	s. As a or b. Specimen.	—	—	340

West-Indische Bank

1800s Issue

No.	Description	Good	Fine	XF
A5	**50 Gulden** ND. (1800s). Uniface. Remainder without signature.	—	—	—

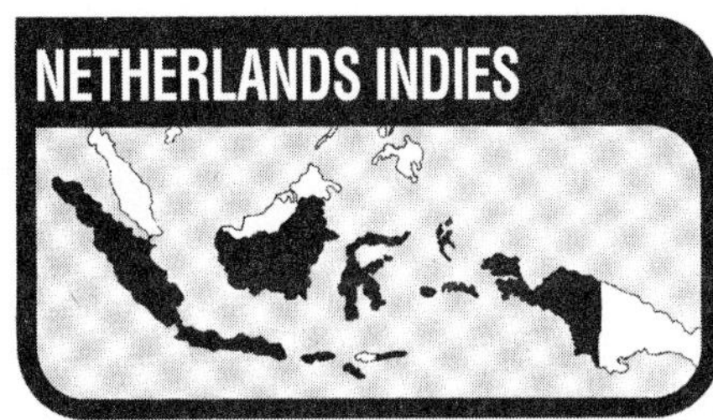

Netherlands Indies (now Indonesia) comprised Sumatra and adjacent islands, Java with Madura, Borneo (except for Sabah, Sarawak and Brunei), Celebes with Sangir and Talaud Islands, and the Moluccas and Lesser Sunda Islands east of Java (excepting the Portuguese half of Timor and the Portuguese enclave of Oe-Cusse). Netherlands New Guinea (now Irian Jaya) was ceded to Indonesia in 1962. The Dutch colonial holdings formed an archipelago of more than 13,667 islands spread across 3,000 miles (4,824 km.) in southeast Asia. The area is rich in oil, rubber, timber and tin. Portuguese traders established posts in the East Indies in the 16th century, but they were soon outnumbered by the Dutch VOC (United East India Company) who arrived in 1602 and gradually established themselves as the dominant colonial power. Dutch dominance, interrupted by British incursions during the Napoleonic Wars, established the Netherlands Indies as one of the richest colonial possessions in the world. One day after the Japanese attack on Pearl Harbor the Netherlands declared war against Japan and therefore a state of war existed between Japan and the Dutch East Indies. The main islands of the archipelago were taken by the Japanese during the first three months of 1942; on March 8, 1942 the Royal Netherlands Indies Army surrendered in Kalidjati (between Jakarta and Bandung on Java island). The Japanese placed Sumatra and former British Malaya (including Singapore) under the administration of the 25th army, Java and Madura under the 16th army and the rest of Indonesia, including Borneo and Sulawesi (Celebes), under the administration of the Japanese navy. The 1942 series was placed in circulation immediately after the conquest of Borneo. Initially the notes were printed in Japan, later they were printed locally. From September 1944 the 1942 series was replaced by a set in the Indonesian (and Japanese) language instead of Dutch as the Japanese wanted to support the growing nationalist movement in Indonesia in this way as well. The 100 and 1000 rupiah which are similar to Malayan notes issued in 1942 (#M8-9 and 10) are believed to have been issued in Sumatra only; the 1000 rupiah never reached normal circulation at all (see #126 and 127). The Japanese surrendered on August 15, 1945 (effective for Java and Sumatra on September 12) and the Republic of Indonesia was proclaimed on August 17, 1945. During 1946-1949 (the first Dutch troops returned to Java March 6, 1946) the struggle for independence by the Indonesian nationalists against the Dutch caused monetary chaos (see also the Indonesia section in Volume I of this catalog) and the Japanese invasion money remained valid in both the Dutch and Indonesian nationalist-controlled areas as late as 1948 and 1949 at different rates to the Netherlands Indies gulden and the Indonesian rupiah.

RULERS:

United East India Company, 1602-1799
Batavian Republic, 1799-1806
Louis Napoleon, King of Holland, 1806-1811
British Administration, 1811-1816
Kingdom of the Netherlands, 1816-1942
Dutch to 1949

MONETARY SYSTEM:

1 Gulden = 100 Cent
1 Roepiah (1943-45) = 100 Sen

Dutch:
1 Rijksdaalder = 48 Stuivers = 0.60 Ducatoon
1 Gulden = 120 Duits = 100 Cents 1854-

British:
1 Spanish Dollar = 66 Stuivers
1 Java Rupee = 30 Stuivers

NOTE: Various issues of notes from #53-85 are known with oval overprint: *REPUBLIK MALUKU-SELATAN,* etc. on back. For details see Volume I at end of Indonesia listing.

DUTCH ADMINISTRATION

Government - State Notes

1815 Creatie Issue

		Good	Fine	XF
1	**1 Gulden** 1815. Arabic numeral date. Black. Handwritten signature and serial #. Stamped crowned "W" (King Willem I). Border with musical notation and 'Nederlandsch Oostindien / India 'Olland' (both meaning Netherlands East Indies). Uniface. Watermark: Waves. Printer: JEZ.			
	a. Issued note.	—	—	—
	r. Unsigned remainder, without stamp or serial #.	50.00	100	250

		Good	Fine	XF
2	**5 Gulden** 1815. Arabic numeral date. Brown. Handwritten signature and serial #. Stamped crowned "W" (King Willem I). Border with musical notation and 'Nederlandsch Oostindien / India 'Olland' (both meaning Netherlands East Indies). Uniface. Watermark: Waves. Printer: JEZ.			
	a. Issued note.	—	—	—
	r. Unsigned remainder, without stamp or serial #.	50.00	100	250

		Good	Fine	XF
3	**10 Gulden** 1815. Arabic numeral date. Blue. Handwritten signature and serial #. Stamped crowned "W" (King Willem I). Border with musical notation and 'Nederlandsch Oostindien / India 'Olland' (both meaning Netherlands East Indies). Uniface. Watermark: Waves. Printer: JEZ.			
	a. Issued note.	—	—	—
	r. Unsigned remainder, without stamp or serial #.	50.00	100	250

		Good	Fine	XF
4	**25 Gulden** 1815. Arabic numeral date. Black. Handwritten signature and serial #. Stamped crowned "W" (King Willem I). Border with musical notation and 'Nederlandsch Oostindien / India 'Olland' (both meaning Netherlands East Indies). Uniface. Watermark: Waves. Printer: JEZ.			
	a. Issued note.	—	—	—
	r. Unsigned remainder, without stamp or serial #.	50.00	100	250

		Good	Fine	XF
5	**50 Gulden** 1815. Red. Handwritten signature and serial #. Stamped crowned "W" (King Willem I). Border with musical notation and 'Nederlandsch Oostindien / India 'Olland' (both meaning Netherlands East Indies). Uniface. Watermark: Waves. Printer: JEZ.			
	a. Issued note.	—	—	—
	r. Unsigned remainder, without stamp or serial #.	75.00	150	350

		Good	Fine	XF
6	**100 Gulden** 1815. Blue. Handwritten signature and serial #. Stamped crowned "W" (King Willem I). Border with musical notation and 'Nederlandsch Oostindien / India 'Olland' (both meaning Netherlands East Indies). Uniface. Watermark: Waves. Printer: JEZ.			
	a. Issued note.	—	—	—
	r. Unsigned remainder, without stamp or serial #.	75.00	150	350

		Good	Fine	XF
7	**300 Gulden** 1815. Black. Handwritten signature and serial #. Stamped crowned "W" (King Willem I). Border with musical notation and 'Nederlandsch Oostindien / India 'Olland' (both meaning Netherlands East Indies). Uniface. Watermark: Waves. Printer: JEZ.			
	a. Issued note.	—	—	—
	r. Unsigned remainder, without stamp or serial #.	100	200	500

		Good	Fine	XF
8	**600 Gulden** 1815. Brown. Handwritten signature and serial #. Stamped crowned "W" (King Willem I). Border with musical notation and 'Nederlandsch Oostindien / India 'Olland' (both meaning Netherlands East Indies). Uniface. Watermark: Waves. Printer: JEZ.			
	a. Issued note.	—	—	—
	r. Unsigned remainder, without stamp or serial #.	100	200	500

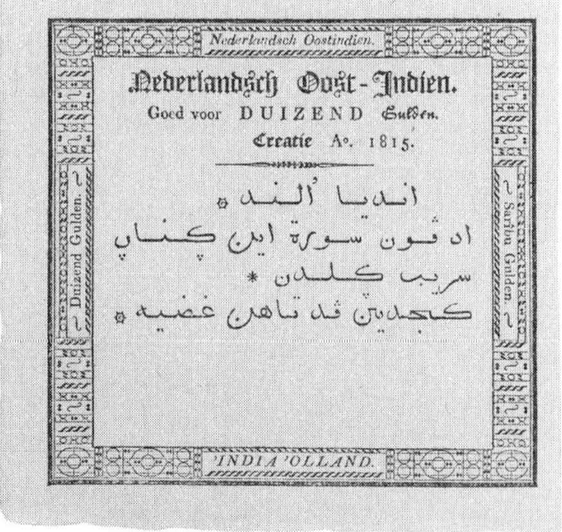

		Good	Fine	XF
9	**1000 Gulden** 1815. Blue. Handwritten signature and serial #. Stamped crowned "W" (King Willem I). Border with musical notation and 'Nederlandsch Oostindien / India 'Olland' (both meaning Netherlands East Indies). Uniface. Watermark: Waves. Printer: JEZ.			
	a. Issued note.	—	—	—
	r. Unsigned remainder, without stamp or serial #.	100	200	500

De Javasche Bank

1828 Goed Voor Issue

		Good	Fine	XF
10	**25 Gulden** 1827. Black. 3 handwritten signatures, serial #. Border with musical notation and 'Oost-Indien' (East Indies). Uniface. Watermark: *JAVASCHE BANK.* Printer: JEZ. Overprint: Value. Authorized 30.1.1827. Issued 11.3.1828.	—	—	—

		Good	Fine	XF
11	**50 Gulden** 1827. Black. 3 handwritten signatures, serial #. Border with musical notation and 'Oost-Indien' (East Indies). Uniface. Watermark: *JAVASCHE BANK.* Printer: JEZ. Authorized 30.1.1827. Issued 11.3.1828.	—	—	—

#	Description	Good	Fine	XF
12	**100 Gulden** 1827. Black. 3 handwritten signatures, serial #. Border with musical notation and 'Oost-Indien' (East Indies). Uniface. Watermark: *JAVASCHE BANK.* Printer: JEZ. Authorized 30.1.1827. Issued 11.3.1828.	—	—	—
13	**200 Gulden** 1827. Black. 3 handwritten signatures, serial #. Border with musical notation and 'Oost-Indien' (East Indies). Uniface. Watermark: *JAVASCHE BANK.* Printer: JEZ. Authorized 30.1.1827. Issued 11.3.1828.	—	—	—
14	**300 Gulden** 1827. Black. 3 handwritten signatures, serial #. Border with musical notation and 'Oost-Indien' (East Indies). Uniface. Watermark: *JAVASCHE BANK.* Printer: JEZ. Authorized 30.1.1827. Issued 11.3.1828.	—	—	—
15	**500 Gulden** 1827. Black. 3 handwritten signatures, serial #. Border with musical notation and 'Oost-Indien' (East Indies). Uniface. Watermark: *JAVASCHE BANK.* Printer: JEZ Authorized 30.1.1827. Issued 11.3.1828.	—	—	—
16	**1000 Gulden** 1827. Black. 3 handwritten signatures, serial #. Border with musical notation and 'Oost-Indien' (East Indies). Uniface. Watermark: *JAVASCHE BANK.* Printer: JEZ. Authorized 30.1.1827. Issued 11.3.1828.	—	—	—

1832 *Kopergeld* Issue

#	Description	Good	Fine	XF
17	**1 Gulden** ND. Green. 2 handwritten signatures, serial # and value. Value also printed. Border with musical notation and 'Kopergeld' (Copper money). Without series letter. Watermark: *JAVASCHE BANK.* Printer: JEZ. Authorized 23.8.1832. Issued Oct. 1832.	—	—	—
18	**5 Gulden** ND. Black. 2 handwritten signatures, serial # and value. Value also printed. Border with musical notation and 'Kopergeld' (Copper money). Series A. Watermark: *JAVASCHE BANK.* Printer: JEZ. Authorized 23.8.1832. Issued Oct. 1832.	—	—	—
19	**10 Gulden** ND. Black. 2 handwritten signatures, serial # and value. Value also printed. Border with musical notation and 'Kopergeld' (Copper money). Series B. Watermark: *JAVASCHE BANK.* Printer: JEZ.	—	—	—
20	**25 Gulden** ND. Black. 2 handwritten signatures, serial # and value. Value also printed. Border with musical notation and 'Kopergeld' (Copper money). Series C. Watermark: *JAVASCHE BANK.* Printer: JEZ.	—	—	—
21	**50 Gulden** ND. Black. 2 handwritten signatures, serial # and value. Value also printed. Border with musical notation and 'Kopergeld' (Copper money). Series D. Watermark: *JAVASCHE BANK.* Printer: JEZ.	—	—	—
22	**100 Gulden** ND. Blue. 2 handwritten signatures, serial # and value. Value also printed. Border with musical notation and 'Kopergeld' (Copper money). Series E. Watermark: *JAVASCHE BANK.* Printer: JEZ.	—	—	—
23	**500 Gulden** ND. Red. 2 handwritten signatures, serial # and value. Value also printed. Border with musical notation and 'Kopergeld' (Copper money). Series F. Watermark: *JAVASCHE BANK.* Printer: JEZ.	—	—	—
24	**1000 Gulden** ND. Red. 2 handwritten signatures, serial # and value. Value also printed. Border with musical notation and 'Kopergeld' (Copper money). Series G. Watermark: *JAVASCHE BANK.* Printer: JEZ. Authorized 23.8.1832. Issued Oct. 1832.	—	—	—

Note: #17-24 were withdrawn in Oct. 1858.

1853 Goed Voor Issue

#	Description	Good	Fine	XF
25	**10 Gulden** Handwritten dates from 1.4.1858. Dark green and black, value in red. 3 handwritten signatures and serial #. Value printed. Border with musical notation and 'Neerlands-Indie' (Netherlands Indies). Uniface. Watermark: *JAVASCHE BANK.* Printer: JEZ. Issued from 1.4.1853.	—	—	—
26	**25 Gulden** Handwritten dates from 1.4.1858. Blue, value in black. 3 handwritten signatures and serial #. Value printed. Border with musical notation and 'Neerlands-Indie' (Netherlands Indies). Uniface. Watermark: *JAVASCHE BANK.* Printer: JEZ. Issued from 1.4.1853.	—	—	—
27	**50 Gulden** Handwritten dates from 1.4.1858. Blue, value in black. 3 handwritten signatures and serial #. Value printed. Border with musical notation and 'Neerlands-Indie' (Netherlands Indies). Uniface. Watermark: *JAVASCHE BANK.* Printer: JEZ. Issued from 1.4.1853.	—	—	—
28	**100 Gulden** Handwritten dates from 1.4.1858. Red, value in black. 3 handwritten signatures and serial #. Value printed. Border with musical notation and 'Neerlands-Indie' (Netherlands Indies). Uniface. Watermark: *JAVASCHE BANK.* Printer: JEZ. Issued from 1.4.1853.	—	—	—
29	**200 Gulden** Handwritten dates from 1.4.1858. Red, value in black. 3 handwritten signatures and serial #. Value printed. Border with musical notation and 'Neerlands-Indie' (Netherlands Indies). Uniface. Watermark: *JAVASCHE BANK.* Printer: JEZ. Issued from 1.4.1853.	—	—	—
30	**300 Gulden** Handwritten dates from 1.4.1858. Red, value in black. 3 handwritten signatures and serial #. Value printed. Border with musical notation and 'Neerlands-Indie' (Netherlands Indies). Uniface. Watermark: *JAVASCHE BANK.* Printer: JEZ. Issued from 1.4.1853.	—	—	—
31	**500 Gulden** Handwritten dates from 1.4.1858. Red, value in black. 3 handwritten signatures and serial #. Value printed. Border with musical notation and 'Neerlands-Indie' (Netherlands Indies). Uniface. Watermark: *JAVASCHE BANK.* Printer: JEZ. Issued from 1.4.1853.	—	—	—
32	**1000 Gulden** Handwritten dates from 1.4.1858. Red, value in black. 3 handwritten signatures and serial #. Value printed. Border with musical notation and 'Neerlands-Indie' (Netherlands Indies). Uniface. Watermark: *JAVASCHE BANK.* Printer: JEZ. Issued from 1.4.1853.	—	—	—

1840s ND *Kopergeld* Issue

#	Description	Good	Fine	XF
33	**5 Gulden** ND. 2 handwritten signatures, serial # and value. Uniface. Series N. Watermark: *JAVASCHE BANK.* Printer: JEZ. Authorized 14.10.1842.	—	—	—
34	**10 Gulden** ND. 2 handwritten signatures, serial # and value. Uniface. Series N. Watermark: *JAVASCHE BANK.* Printer: JEZ. Authorized 14.10.1842.	—	—	—
35	**25 Gulden** ND. 2 handwritten signatures, serial # and value. Uniface. Series N. Watermark: *JAVASCHE BANK.* Printer: JEZ. Authorized 14.10.1842.	—	—	—
36	**50 Gulden** ND. 2 handwritten signatures, serial # and value. Uniface. Series N. Watermark: *JAVASCHE BANK.* Printer: JEZ. Authorized 14.10.1842.	—	—	—
37	**100 Gulden** 2 handwritten signatures, serial # and value. Uniface. Series N. Watermark: *JAVASCHE BANK.* Printer: JEZ. Authorized 14.10.1842.	—	—	—
38	**500 Gulden** 2 handwritten signatures, serial # and value. Uniface. Series N. Watermark: *JAVASCHE BANK.* Printer: JEZ. Authorized 14.10.1842.	—	—	—

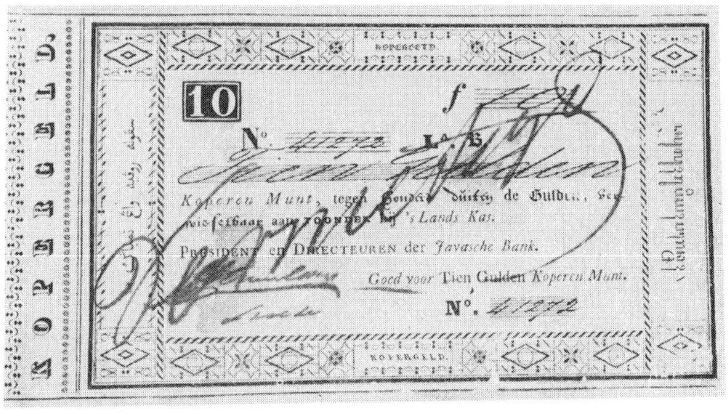

Note: #33-38 were withdrawn in Oct. 1858.

Government (resumed)

1846 Recepis Issue

		Good	Fine	XF
39	**1 Gulden**	Good	Fine	XF
	Various handwritten dates from 1.4.1846. Black. Handwritten signature date and serial #. Border with musical notation. Uniface. Watermark: Waves. Printer: JEZ. Authorized 4.2.1846. Issued from 1.4.1846.			
	a. Issued note.	60.00	125	275
	r. Unsigned remainder, without serial #.	25.00	50.00	100
40	**5 Gulden**	Good	Fine	XF
	Various handwritten dates from 1.4.1846. Red. 2 handwritten signatures, serial # and value. Watermark: Waves. Printer: JEZ. Authorized 4.2.1846. Issued from 1.4.1846.			
	a. Issued note.	—	—	—
	r. Unsigned remainder, without serial #.	25.00	50.00	100
41	**10 Gulden**	Good	Fine	XF
	Various handwritten dates from 1.4.1846. Green. 2 handwritten signatures, serial # and value. Uniface. Series N. Watermark: Waves. Printer: JEZ. Authorized 4.2.1846. Issued from 1.4.1846.			
	a. Issued note.	—	—	—
	r. Unsigned remainder, without serial #.	25.00	50.00	100
42	**25 Gulden**	Good	Fine	XF
	Various handwritten dates from 1.4.1846. Brown. 2 handwritten signatures, serial # and value. Uniface. Series N. Watermark: Waves. Printer: JEZ. Authorized 4.2.1846. Issued from 1.4.1846.			
	a. Issued note.	—	—	—
	r. Unsigned remainder, without serial #.	60.00	100	200
43	**100 Gulden**	Good	Fine	XF
	Various handwritten dates from 1.4.1846. Blue. 2 handwritten signatures, serial # and value. Uniface. Series N. Watermark: Waves. Printer: JEZ. Authorized 4.2.1846. Issued from 1.4.1846.			
	a. Issued note.	—	—	—
	r. Unsigned remainder, without serial #.	60.00	100	200
44	**500 Gulden**	Good	Fine	XF
	Various handwritten dates from 1.4.1846. Orange. 2 handwritten signatures, serial # and value. Uniface. Series N. Watermark: Waves. Printer: JEZ. Authorized 4.2.1846. Issued from 1.4.1846.			
	a. Issued note.	—	—	—
	r. Unsigned remainder, without serial #.	60.00	100	200

Note: #39-44 were withdrawn 30.6.1861.

De Javasche Bank (resumed)

1864 Issue

SIGNATURE VARIETIES, 1863-1949

SECRETARIS	PRESIDENT	PERIOD
1 G. Hoeven	C.F.W. Wiggers van Kerchem	1863-1866
2 J.W.C. Diepenheim	C.F.W. Wiggers van Kerchem	1866-1868
3 D. Schuurman	J.W.C. Diepenheim	1868-1870
4 D.N. Versteegh	F. Alting Mees	1870-1873
5 D.N. Versteegh	N.P. van den Berg	1873-1876
6 A.A. Buyskes	N.P. van den Berg	1876-1877
7 D. Groeneveld	N.P. van den Berg	1877-1889
8 D. Groeneveld	S.B. Zeverijn	1889-1892
9 H.P.J. van den Berg	D. Groeneveld	1893-1898
10 J.F.H. de Vignon Vandevelde	J. Reijsenbach	1899-1901
11 H.J. Meertens	J.F.H. de Vignon Vandevelde	Jan.-April 1901
12 H.J. Meertens	J. Reijsenbach	1899-1902
13 A.F. van Suchtelen	J. Reijsenbach	1902-1906
14 A.F. van Suchtelen	G. Vissering	1906-1908
15 J. Gerritzen	G. Vissering	1908-1912
16 J. Gerritzen	E.A. Zeilinga Azn	1912-1913
17 K.F. van den Berg	E.A. Zeilinga Azn	1912-1920
18 L. von Hemert	E.A. Zeilinga Azn	1920-1922
19 J.F. van Rossem	E.A. Zeilinga Azn	1922-1924
20 J.F. van Rossem	L.J.A. Trip	1924-1928
21 Th. Ligthart	L.J.A. Trip November	1925
22 K.W.J. Michielsen	L.J.A. Trip	January - June 1929
23 K.W.J. Michielsen	G.G. van Buttingha Wichers	November 1930
24 A. Praasterink	G.G. van Buttingha Wichers	1929-1937
25 J.C. van Waveren	G.G. van Buttingha Wichers	1937-1939
26 R.E. Smits	G.G. van Buttingha Wichers	1939-1942
World War II Occupation		1942-1946
27 H. Teunissen	R.E. Smits	1947-1949
28 H. Teunissen A.	Houwink	1949-1950

		Good	Fine	XF
45	**5 Gulden**	Good	Fine	XF
	1866-1901. Black and brown. Dutch arms at top center. Back: Legal text in 4 languages: Dutch, Javanese, Chinese, and Arabic. BC: Brown. Watermark: Javasche Bank. Printer: JEZ without imprint.			
	a. 1.10.1866. Signature 2.	230	625	—
	b. 5.4.1895. Signature 9.	250	685	—
	s. overprint: *SPECIMEN.*	100	210	375

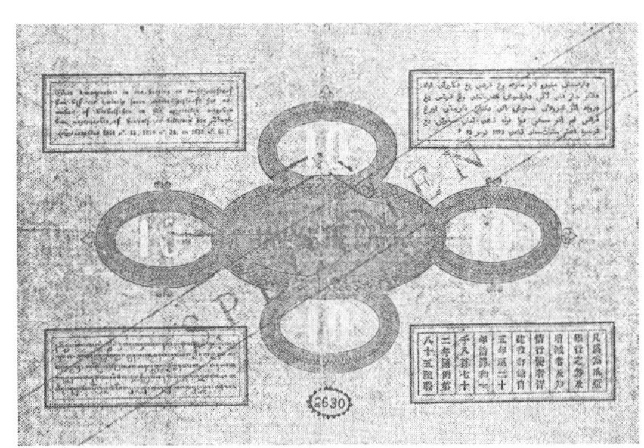

		Good	Fine	XF
46	**10 Gulden**	Good	Fine	XF
	1864-1890. Black. Batavia city arms with lion at lower center. Back: Legal text in 4 languages: Dutch, Javanese, Chinese, and Arabic. BC: Green and black. Watermark: Jav. Bank. Printer: JEZ (without imprint.).			
	a. 1.2.1864; 1.2.1866; 1.2.1872; 1.2.1876. Signature 1; 2; 4; 5. Rare.	—	—	—
	b. 1.3.1877; 1.3.1879; 1.2.1888. Signature 6; 7.	350	1,050	—
	c. 1.2.1890. Signature 8.	250	675	—
	s. Overprint: *SPECIMEN.*	100	210	375
47	**25 Gulden**	Good	Fine	XF
	1864-1890. Black. Batavia city arms with lion at lower center. Back: Legal text in 4 languages: Dutch, Javanese, Chinese, and Arabic. BC: Blue and red. Watermark: Jav. Bank. Printer: JEZ (without imprint).			
	a. 1.8.1864; 1.8.1866; 1.8.1872; 1.8.1876. Signature 1; 2; 4; 5. Rare.	—	—	—
	b. 1.3.1877; 1.3.1879; 1.3.1884. Signature 6; 7.	350	1,050	—
	c. 1.2.1890. Signature 8.	250	675	—
	s. Overprint: *SPECIMEN.*	100	210	375
48	**50 Gulden**	Good	Fine	XF
	1864-1873. Violet. Batavia city arms with lion at lower center. Back: Legal text in 4 languages: Dutch, Javanese, Chinese, and Arabic. BC: Blue. Watermark: Jav. Bank. Printer: Jez (without imprint).			
	a. 1.9.1864. Signature 1. Rare.	—	—	—
	b. 1.9.1866. Signature 2.	350	1,050	—
	s. Overprint: *SPECIMEN.*	100	210	375

Note: #48a and #48b withdrawn from circulation in 1873, because of counterfeiting. (See #55).

		Good	Fine	XF
49	**100 Gulden**	Good	Fine	XF
	1864-1890. Black. Portrait Jan Pieterzoon Coen at top center. Back: Legal text in 4 languages: Dutch, Javanese, Chinese, and Arabic. BC: Green and brown. Watermark: Jav. Bank. Printer: JEZ (without imprint).			
	a. 1.3.1864; 1.3.1866; 1.3.1872; 1.3.1873. Signature 1; 2; 4. Rare.	—	—	—
	b. 1.3.1874; 1.3.1876; 1.3.1877; 1.3.1879. Signature 5; 7. Rare.	—	—	—
	c. 1.2.1890. Signature 8.	350	1,050	—
	s. Overprint: *SPECIMEN.*	100	210	375
49A	**200 Gulden**	Good	Fine	XF
	1864-1890. Black. Portrait Jan Pieterzoon Coen at top center. Back: Legal text in 4 languages: Dutch, Javanese, Chinese, and Arabic. BC: Blue and black. Watermark: Jav. Bank. Printer: JEZ (without imprint).			
	a. 1.1.1864; 1.1.1866; -1873. Signature 1; 2; 4. Rare.	—	—	—
	b. 15.1.1876; 15.1.1879; 15.1.1888. Signature 5; 7. Rare.	—	—	—
	c. 15.1.1890. Signature 8.	350	1,050	—
	s. Overprint: *SPECIMEN.*	150	300	500

	49B 300 Gulden	Good	Fine	XF
	1864-1888. Black. Portrait Jan Pieterzoon Coen at top center. Back: Legal text in 4 languages: Dutch, Javanese, Chinese, and Arabic. BC: Violet and red. Watermark: Jav. Bank. Printer: JEZ (without imprint).			
	a. 2.5.1864; 2.5.1866. Signature 1; 2. Rare.	—	—	—
	s. Overprint: *SPECIMEN*.	300	600	1,000

50	500 Gulden	Good	Fine	XF
	1864-1888. Black. Portrait Jan Pieterzoon Coen at top center. Back: Legal text in 4 languages: Dutch, Javanese, Chinese, and Arabic. BC: Orange and brown. Watermark: Jav. Bank. Printer: JEZ (without imprint).			
	a. 1.6.1864; 1.6.1872. Signature 1; 4. Rare.	—	—	—
	b. 1.6.1873; -1879; -1888. Signature 5; 7. Rare.	—	—	—
	s. Overprint: *SPECIMEN*.	150	300	500

51	1000 Gulden	Good	Fine	XF
	1864-1890. Black. Portrait Jan Pieterzoon Coen at top center. Back: Legal text in 4 languages: Dutch, Javanese, Chinese, and Arabic. BC: Violet and black. Watermark: Jav. Bank. Printer: JEZ (without imprint).			
	a. 1.7.1864; 1.7.1872. Signature 1; 4. Rare.	—	—	—
	b. 1.7.1873; -1874; -1888. Signature 5; 7. Rare.	—	—	—
	c. -1890. Signature 8.	350	1,000	—
	s. Overprint: *SPECIMEN*.	150	300	500

ND 1875 Issue

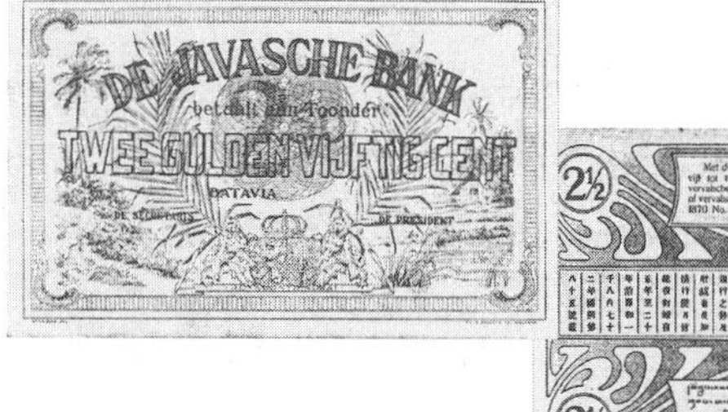

52	2 1/2 Gulden	VG	VF	UNC
	ND (1875). Blue on brown underprint. Landscape at left and right, Dutch arms at bottom center. Back: Javasche Bank arms at center, legal text in 4 languages (Dutch, Javanese, Chinese and Arabic). Printer: Albrecht & Co. (Not issued).	—	—	—

1876 Issue

54	10 Gulden	Good	Fine	XF
	1896-1924. Blue-green. Batavia city arms at top center. Back: Legal text (with varieties) in 4 languages: Dutch, Javanese, Chinese and Arabic. BC: Green. Watermark: JAV. BANK. Printer: JEZ (Without imprint).			
	a. -1896; 16.7.1897; 3.4.1913. Signature 9; 10; 13; 14; 15; 16.	100	250	685
	b. 13.5.1913-13.6.1924. Signature 17; 18; 19.	80.00	200	565
	c. 17.7.1924-29.7.1924. Signature	60.00	150	450
	s. Overprint: *SPECIMEN*.	50.00	100	200

54	25 Gulden	Good	Fine	XF
	1896-1921. Brown. Batavia city arms at top center. Back: Legal text (with varieties) in 4 languages: Dutch, Javanese, Chinese and Arabic. BC: Purple. Watermark: JAV. BANK. Printer: JEZ (without imprint).			
	a. 1.6.1897-11.12.1912. Signature 9; 10; 12; 13; 14; 15; 16.	100	250	686
	b. 2.6.1913-4.2.1921. Signature 17; 18.	80.00	200	565
	s. Overprint: *SPECIMEN*.	50.00	100	200

55	50 Gulden	Good	Fine	XF
	1876-1922. Grey. Batavia city arms at top center. Back: Legal text (with varieties) in 4 languages: Dutch, Javanese, Chinese and Arabic. BC: Light brown. Watermark: JAV.BANK. Printer: JEZ (without imprint).			
	a. 15.10.1873; 15.2.1876; 15.2.1879; 15.2.1890; 15.2.1896. signature 5; 7; 9. Rare.	—	—	—
	b. 1.5.1911; 17.4.1913. Signature 16. Rare.	—	—	—
	c. 3.5.1913; 31.8.1922. Signature 17; 18; 19.	250	750	—
	s. Overprint: *SPECIMEN*.	100	200	375

Issued 1876 to replace withdrawn notes #48.

56	100 Gulden	Good	Fine	XF
	1896-1921. Blue-gray and deep blue-green. Mercury at left, 3 crowned city arms (Batavia at center, Surabaya at left, Semarang at right.) in wreaths at upper center, Jan Pieterzoon Coen with ruffled collar at right. Back: Blue-gray and brown. Back: Legal text (with varieties) in 4 languages: Dutch, Javanese, Chinese and Arabic. Watermark: JAV. BANK. Printer: JEZ.			
	a. 1.6.1897; 18.4.1913. Signature 9; 10; 13; 15; 16. Rare.	—	—	—
	b. 1.5.1916 - 15.6.1921. Signature 17; 18.	200	600	—
	s. Overprint: *SPECIMEN*.	75.00	150	300

No.	Description	Good	Fine	XF
57	**200 Gulden** 1897-1922. Brown. Mercury at left, 3 crowned city arms (Batavia at center, Surabaya at left, Semarang at right.) in wreaths at upper center, Jan Pieterzoon Coen with ruffled collar at right. Back: Legal text (with varieties) in 4 languages: Dutch, Javanese, Chinese and Arabic. BC: Brown and violet. Watermark: JAV. BANK. Printer: JEZ.			
	a. 1.6.1897 - 1913. Signature 9; 10; 14; 15; 16. Rare.	—	—	—
	b. 11.9.1916 - 21.8.1922. Signature 17; 19.	400	1,250	—
	s. Overprint: *SPECIMEN.*	75.00	150	300

No.	Description	Good	Fine	XF
58	**300 Gulden** 1897-1901. Green. Mercury at left, 3 crowned city arms (Batavia at center, Surabaya at left, Semarang at right.) in wreaths at upper center, Jan Pieterzoon Coen with ruffled collar at right. Back: Green and brown. Back: Legal text (with varieties) in 4 languages: Dutch, Javanese, Chinese and Arabic. Watermark: JAV. BANK. Printer: JEZ.			
	a. 1.6.1897. Signature 9. Rare.	—	—	—
	b. 29.1.1901 - 30.4.1901. Signature 11. Rare.	—	—	—
	s. Overprint: *SPECIMEN.*	150	300	500

No.	Description	Good	Fine	XF
59	**500 Gulden** 1897-1919. Gray and brown. Mercury at left, 3 crowned city arms (Batavia at center, Surabaya at left, Semarang at right.) in wreaths at upper center, Jan Pieterzoon Coen with ruffled collar at right. Back: Legal text (with varieties) in 4 languages: Dutch, Javanese, Chinese and Arabic. BC: Purple and brown. Watermark: JAV. BANK. Printer: JEZ.			
	a. 2.6.1897 -1913. Signature 9; 10; 15; 16. Rare.	—	—	—
	b. 1.2.1916 - 5.7.1919. Signature 17.	400	1,250	—
	s. Overprint: *SPECIMEN.*	75.00	150	300
60	**1000 Gulden** 1897-1919. Brown. Mercury at left, 3 crowned city arms (Batavia at center, Surabaya at left, Semarang at right.) in wreaths at upper center, Jan Pieterzoon Coen with ruffled collar at right. Back: Legal text (with varieties) in 4 languages: Dutch, Javanese, Chinese and Arabic. BC: Yellow, brown and green.	Good	Fine	XF
	a. 1.6.1897 - 16.4.1912. Signature 9; 10; 15; 16. Rare.	—	—	—
	b. 17.10.1914 - 5.7.1919. Signature 17.	550	1,500	—
	s. As a. Overprint: *SPECIMEN.*	75.00	150	300

1901 Issue

No.	Description	Good	Fine	XF
61	**5 Gulden** 1901-24. Blue. Portrait Jan Pieterzoon Coen at right. Black or red serial number (#61c). Back: Brown on blue underprint. Watermark: Large "J.B.", gothic style. Printer: JEZ.			
	a. 28.9.1901 - 26.4.1913. Signature 10; 13; 14; 15; 16.	100	300	500
	b. 5.6.1913 - 11.6.1920. Signature 17.	75.00	225	400
	c. 18.9.1920 - 17.10-1924. Signature 18; 19; 21.	50.00	150	250
	s. Overprint: *SPECIMEN.*	50.00	100	200

1904-1908 Issue

No.	Description	Good	Fine	XF
62	**10 Gulden** June 1908. Batavia city arms at top center. Two large value *10* in center replace *1* value. (Not issued).	—	—	—

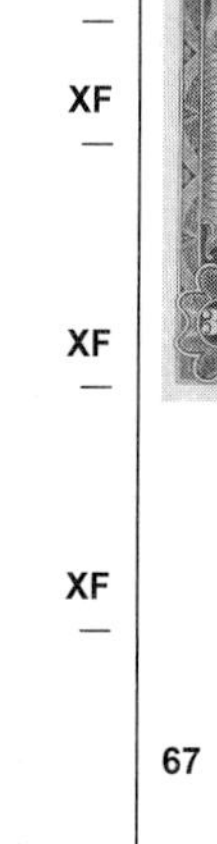

62A 25 Gulden
June 1908. Batavia city arms at top center. Two large value *25* in center replace *1* value. (Not issued).

Good	Fine	XF
—	—	—

62B 50 Gulden
June 1908. Batavia city arms at top center. Two large value *50* in center replace *1* value. (Not issued).

Good	Fine	XF
—	—	—

63 200 Gulden
June 1908. Mercury at left, three crowned city arms (Batavia at center, Surabaya at left, Semarang at right.) in wreaths at upper center, Jan Pieterzoon Coen with ruffled collar at right. Serial # panels and top and landscape scene at bottom. (Not issued).

Good	Fine	XF
—	—	—

63A 200 Gulden
May 1904; June 1908. Mercury at left, 3 crowned city arms (Batavia at center, Surabaya at left, Semarang at right.) in wreaths at upper center, Jan Pieterzoon Coen with ruffled collar at right. Serial # panels and top and landscape scene at bottom. (Not issued).

Good	Fine	XF
—	—	—

64 500 Gulden
June 1908. Mercury at left, three crowned city arms (Batavia at center, Surabaya at left, Semarang at right.) in wreaths at upper center, Jan Pieterzoon Coen with ruffled collar at right. Serial # panels and top and landscape scene at bottom. (Not issued).

Good	Fine	XF
—	—	—

65 1000 Gulden
May 1904. June 1908. Brown on tan underprint. Mercury at left, three crowned city arms (Batavia at center, Surabaya at left, Semarang at right.) in wreaths at upper center, Jan Pieterzoon Coen with ruffled collar at right. Serial # panels and top and landscape scene at bottom. Overprint in red: SPECIMEN. (Not issued).

Good	Fine	XF
—	—	—

1919-1921 Issue

66 20 Gulden
1919-1921. Orange. Javasche Bank building in Batavia at center. Back: Legal text in 4 languages: Dutch, Javanese, Chinese and Arabic. BC: Orange, green and blue. Printer: ABNC.

	Good	Fine	XF
a. 12.8.1919 - 26.4.1920. Signature 17.	150	550	1,300
b. 6.1.1921. Signature 18.	150	550	1,300
s1. 1919-1921. Specimen. Overprint: *SPECIMEN*.	—	Unc	2,500
s2. ND. Specimen.	—	Unc	700

Note: #66 was withdrawn from circulation in 1931/33 because of counterfeiting.

67 30 Gulden
1919-1921. Blue. Javasche Bank building in Batavia at center. Back: Legal text in 4 languages: Dutch, Javanese, Chinese and Arabic. BC: Blue, green and brown. Printer: ABNC.

	Good	Fine	XF
a. 8.9.1919 - 21.4.1920. Signature 17.	120	525	1,250
b. 14.1.1921. Signature 18.	120	525	1,250
s. Overprint: *SPECIMEN*.	50.00	150	350

68 40 Gulden
1919-1921. Dark green. Javasche Bank building in Batavia at center. Back: Legal text in 4 languages: Dutch, Javanese, Chinese and Arabic. BC: Green on brown and blue underprint. Printer: ABNC.

	Good	Fine	XF
a. 22.8.1919 - 27.4.1920. Signature 17.	120	525	1,250
b. 20.1.1921. Signature 18.	120	525	1,250
s. 1919-1921. Overprint: *SPECIMEN*.	—	Unc	2,500
s2. ND. Specimen.	—	Unc	700

Note: Two varieties of word *Batavia* on #68.

1925-1931 Issue

69 5 Gulden
1926-1931. Violet. Without vignette. Back: Violet and brown. Back: Javasche Bank building in Batavia at center; legal text in four languages: Dutch, Javanese, Chinese Watermark: Js and Bs in a honeycomb pattern. Printer: JEZ.

	Good	Fine	XF
a. 2.1.1926 - 5.4.1928. Signature 20.	5.00	10.00	45.00
b. 2.1.1929 - 8.5.1929. Signature 22.	5.00	10.00	45.00
c. 14.8.1929 - 1.4.1931. Signature 24.	5.00	10.00	45.00

70	10 Gulden	Good	Fine	XF
	1926-1931. Green. Portrait Jan Pieterzoon Coen with ruffled collar at right. Back: Javasche Bank building in Batavia at center; legal text in four languages: Dutch, Javanese, Chinese. BC: Green and red. Watermark: Js and Bs in a honeycomb pattern. Printer: JEZ.			
	a. 2.1.1926- 7.4.1928. Signature 20.	5.00	15.00	55.00
	b. 2.1.1929 - 30.4.1929. Signature 22.	5.00	15.00	55.00
	c. November 1930. Signature 23.	25.00	125	300
	d. 15.7.1929 - 20.4.1931. Signature 24.	5.00	15.00	55.00

71	25 Gulden	Good	Fine	XF
	1925-1931. Brown. Portrait Jan Pieterzoon Coen with ruffled collar at right. Back: Javasche Bank building in Batavia at center; legal text in four languages: Dutch, Javanese, Chinese. BC: Brown and purple. Watermark: Js and Bs in a honeycomb pattern. Printer: JEZ.			
	a. 1.12.1925 - 4.4.1928. Signature 20.	5.00	25.00	75.00
	b. 2.1.1929 - 25.4.1929. Signature 22.	5.00	25.00	75.00
	c. 1.8.1929 - 7.4.1931. Signature 24.	5.00	25.00	75.00

72	50 Gulden	Good	Fine	XF
	1926-1930. Orange. Portrait Jan Pieterzoon Coen with ruffled collar at right. Back: Javasche Bank building in Batavia at center; legal text in four languages: Dutch, Javanese, Chinese. BC: Brown and orange. Watermark: Js and Bs in a honeycomb pattern. Printer: JEZ.			
	a. 2.1.1926 - 14.3.1928. Signature 20.	10.00	50.00	100
	b. 2.1.1929 - 30.4.1929. Signature 22.	10.00	50.00	100
	c. 1.8.1929 - 31.10.1930. Signature 24.	10.00	50.00	100

73	100 Gulden	Good	Fine	XF
	1925-1930. Black. Portrait Jan Pieterzoon Coen with ruffled collar at right. Back: Javasche Bank building in Batavia at center; legal text in four languages: Dutch, Javanese, Chinese. BC: Light green. Watermark: Js and Bs in a honeycomb pattern. Printer: JEZ.			
	a. 2.11.1925 - 5.11.1925. Signature 21.	50.00	250	600
	b. 6.11.1925 - 10.2.1928. Signature 20.	10.00	50.00	100
	c. 1.11.1929 - 28.10.1930. Signature 24.	10.00	50.00	100
74	200 Gulden	Good	Fine	XF
	1925-1930. Red. Portrait Jan Pieterzoon Coen with ruffled collar at right. Back: Javasche Bank building in Batavia at center; legal text in four languages: Dutch, Javanese, Chinese. BC: Red and brown. Watermark: Js and Bs in a honeycomb pattern.			
	a. 2.11.1925 - 4.11.1925. Signature 21.	50.00	250	600
	b. 5.11.1925 - 2.7.1926. Signature 20.	35.00	175	500
	c. 15.10.1930 - 20.10.1930. Signature 24.	35.00	175	500
75	300 Gulden	Good	Fine	XF
	2.1.1926-11.1.1926. Violet. Portrait Jan Pieterzoon Coen with ruffled collar at right. Back: Javasche Bank building in Batavia at center; legal text in four languages: Dutch, Javanese, Chinese. BC: Violet and green. Watermark: Js and Bs in a honeycomb pattern. Printer: JEZ.	100	350	850

76	500 Gulden	Good	Fine	XF
	1926-1930. Blue. Portrait Jan Pieterzoon Coen with ruffled collar at right. Back: Javasche Bank building in Batavia at center; legal text in four languages: Dutch, Javanese, Chinese. BC: Brown and blue. Watermark: Js and Bs in a honeycomb pattern. Printer: JEZ.			
	a. 2.1.1926 - 2.7.1926. Signature 20.	35.00	175	500
	b. 15.8.1930 - 19.8.1930. Signature 24.	35.00	175	500

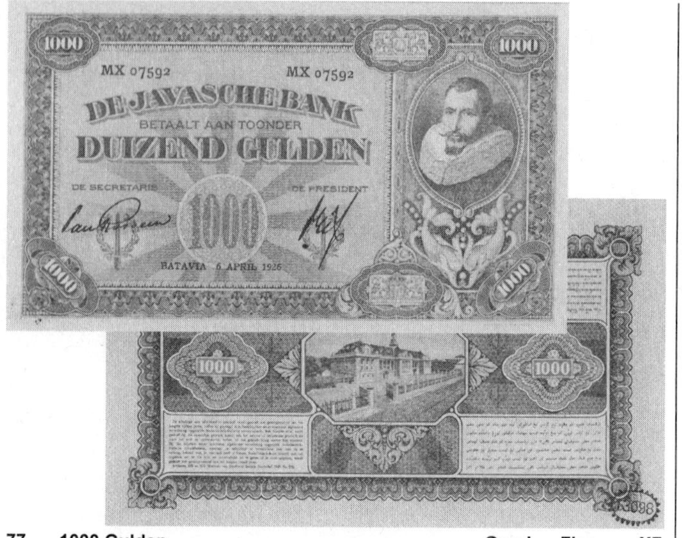

77	1000 Gulden	Good	Fine	XF
	1926-1930. Red. Portrait Jan Pieterzoon Coen with ruffled collar at right. Back: Javasche Bank building in Batavia at center; legal text in four languages: Dutch, Javanese, Chinese. BC: Brown and red. Watermark: Js and Bs in a honeycomb pattern. Printer: JEZ.			
	a. 1.4.1926 - 2.7.1926. Signature 20.	40.00	200	550
	b. 7.5.1930 - 8.5.1930. Signature 24.	40.00	200	550

1933-1939 Issue

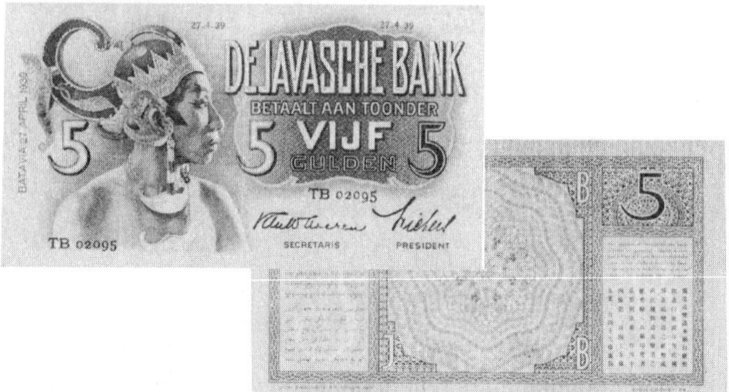

78	5 Gulden	Good	Fine	XF
	1934-1939. Brown on light brown and pale green underprint. Javanese dancer at left. Back: Legal text in four languages: Dutch, Javanese, Chinese and Arabic. BC: Multicolor. Watermark: Js and Bs in a honeycomb pattern. Printer: JEZ.			
	a. 23.4.1934 - 5.6.1937. Signature 24.	3.00	10.00	30.00
	b. 4.10.1937 - 3.5.1939. Signature 25.	3.00	10.00	30.00
	c. 3.7.1939 - 17.8.1939. Signature 26.	3.00	10.00	30.00

79	10 Gulden	Good	Fine	XF
	1933-1939. Dark blue on light blue and pink underprint. Javanese dancers at left and right. Back: Legal text in four languages: Dutch, Javanese, Chinese and Arabic. BC: Green, red and blue. Watermark: Wavy lines. Printer: JEZ.			
	a. 2.10.1933 - 6.2.1934. Signature 24.	4.00	12.50	35.00
	b. 20.9.1937 - 19.9.1938. Signature 25.	4.00	12.50	35.00
	c. 28.7.1939 - 31.8.1939. Signature 26.	4.00	12.50	35.00

80	25 Gulden	Good	Fine	XF
	1934-1939. Purple on multicolor underprint. Javanese dancer at left and right. Back: Legal text in four languages: Dutch, Javanese, Chinese and Arabic. BC: Brown on red and blue underprint. Watermark: Zigzag lines. Printer: JEZ.			
	a. 14.12.1934 - 13.2.1935. Signature 24.	5.00	15.00	60.00
	b. 17.10.1938 - 30.6.1939. Signature 25.	5.00	15.00	60.00
	c. 1.7.1939 - 4.7.1939. Signature 26.	10.00	30.00	120

81	50 Gulden	VG	VF	UNC
	19.4.1938-14.4.1939. Black on red, green and blue underprint. Javanese dancers at left and right. Signature 25. Back: Legal text in four languages: Dutch, Javanese, Chinese and Arabic. BC: Brown and violet. Watermark: Head of the Goddess of Justice and Truth. Printer: JEZ.	17.50	50.00	150

82	100 Gulden	VG	VF	UNC
	7.2.1938-22.4.1939. Violet and orange. Javanese dancers at left and right. Signature 25. Back: Legal text in four languages: Dutch, Javanese, Chinese and Arabic. BC: Multicolor. Watermark: Head of the Goddess of Justice and Truth. Printer: JEZ.	30.00	75.00	225

		VG	VF	UNC
83	**200 Gulden** 23.5.1938-24.4.1939. Green and brown. Javanese dancers at left and right. Signature 25. Back: Legal text in four languages: Dutch, Javanese, Chinese and Arabic. BC: Multicolor. Watermark: Head of the Goddess of Justice and Truth. Printer: JEZ.	200	550	1,250

		VG	VF	UNC
84	**500 Gulden** 2.6.1938 - 27.4.1939. Green and brown. Javanese dancers at left and right. Signature 25. Back: Legal text in four languages: Dutch, Javanese, Chinese and Arabic. BC: Multicolor. Watermark: Head of the Goddess of Justice and Truth. Printer: JEZ.	175	500	1,100

		VG	VF	UNC
85	**1000 Gulden** 1938-1939. Green. Javanese dancers at left and right. Back: Multicolor. Back: Legal text in four languages: Dutch, Javanese, Chinese and Arabic. Watermark: Head of the Goddess of Justice and Truth. Printer: JEZ.			
	a. 30.5.1938 - 29.4.1939. Signature 25.	250	750	1,500
	p. Proof perforated: 32.9.(19)36.	—	—	1,000
	s. Specimen. With overprint: *SPECIMEN* perforated: 34.5.(19)68.	—	—	1,000

1942 Issue

		VG	VF	UNC
86	**5 Gulden** 15.1.1942. Black on light blue and gray underprint. Floral design at right. Back: Ornate tree at center. BC: Multicolor. Printer: G. Kolff & Co., Batavia. (Not issued).			
	a. Issued note.	—	—	150
	s. Specimen.	—	—	—

1946 Issue

Note: Also encountered perforated: *INGETROKKEN 2.4.47* (withdrawn).

		VG	VF	UNC
87	**5 Gulden** 1946. Violet and red. Lotus at left. Watermark: Floral design. Printer: JEZ.	3.50	15.00	60.00

		VG	VF	UNC
88	**5 Gulden** 1946. Brown with green and red underprint. Lotus at left. Watermark: Floral design. Printer: JEZ.	3.50	15.00	60.00

		VG	VF	UNC
89	**10 Gulden** 1946. Green. Mangosteen at left. Watermark: Floral design. Printer: JEZ.	3.50	15.00	60.00

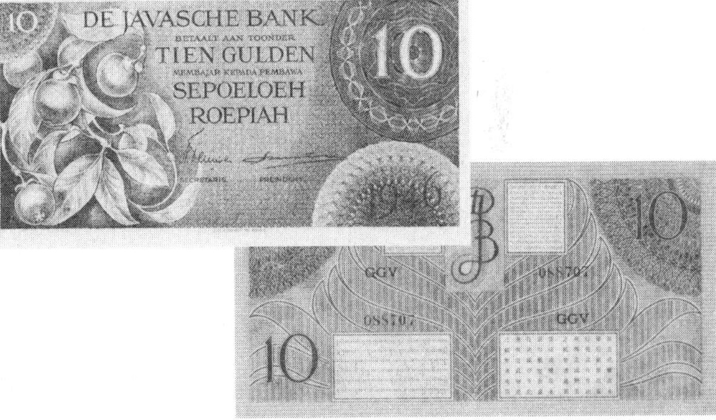

		VG	VF	UNC
90	**10 Gulden** 1946. Purple. Mangosteen at left. Watermark: Floral design. Printer: JEZ.	4.00	17.50	70.00

		VG	VF	UNC
91	**25 Gulden** 1946. Green. Beach with palms at left. Watermark: Floral design. Printer: JEZ.	5.00	20.00	75.00

#	Denomination	VG	VF	UNC
92	**25 Gulden** 1946. Red-orange. Beach with palms at left. Watermark: Floral design. Printer: JEZ.	6.00	25.00	85.00

#	Denomination	VG	VF	UNC
93	**50 Gulden** 1946. Dark blue. Sailboat at left. Watermark: Floral design. Printer: JEZ.	10.00	35.00	125

#	Denomination	VG	VF	UNC
94	**100 Gulden** 1946. Brown. Rice fields with mountain in background at left. Watermark: Floral design. Printer: JEZ.	8.50	30.00	110

#	Denomination	VG	VF	UNC
95	**500 Gulden** 1946. Violet. Rice fields with mountain in background at left. Watermark: Floral design. Printer: JEZ.	40.00	125	650

#	Denomination	VG	VF	UNC
96	**1000 Gulden** 1946. Gray. Rice fields with mountain in background at left. Watermark: Floral design. Printer: JEZ.	250	550	1,250

Note: The Javasche Bank notes cut in half (from 5 Gulden) and those of the Republic of Indonesia originate from the currency reform of 1950. The left half of a note was valid for exchange against new notes (see Indonesia #36-37) at 50% of face value; the right half was also accepted at half its face value for a 3% government bond issue.

1948 Issue

#	Denomination	VG	VF	UNC
97	**1/2 Gulden** 1948. Lilac on pale green underprint. Moon Orchids at left. 2 serial # varieties.	1.00	4.00	15.00

#	Denomination	VG	VF	UNC
98	**1 Gulden** 1948. Blue. Palms at left. 2 serial # varieties.	1.00	4.00	15.00
99	**2 1/2 Gulden** 1948. Red. Blossoms at left. 2 serial # varieties.	3.00	8.00	25.00

Government (20th century)

1919 Muntbiljet Issue

#	Denomination	Good	Fine	XF
100	**1 Gulden** 1.8.1919-11.10.1920. Black. Portrait Queen Wilhelmina at center. Back: Arms at center. BC: Blue. Printer: ABNC.			
	a. Issued note.	12.50	100	250
	s. Specimen.	—	Unc	800

		Good	Fine	XF
101	**2 1/2 Gulden** 4.8.1919-28.2.1920. Dark green. Portrait Queen Wilhelmina at center. Back: Brown. Back: Arms at center. Printer: ABNC.			
	a. Issued note.	15.00	120	300
	s. Specimen. Punch hole cancelled.	—	Unc	900

Note: Earlier dates of #100-101 have signature title overprint at left. Later dates have signature title printed.

1920 Muntbiljet Issue

		Good	Fine	XF
102	**1/2 Gulden** 14.1.1920. Black on green underprint. Crowned supported arms at center. Back: Gray-green. Printer: Topografische Inrichting Batavia. Plain or textured paper.	7.50	35.00	135
103	**1 Gulden** 1.1.1920. Green and blue. Without vignette. Back: Blue. Printer: De Bussy, Amsterdam.	7.50	35.00	135

		Good	Fine	XF
104	**2 1/2 Gulden** 1.5.1920. Green, brown and violet. Without vignette. Like #103. Back: Brown. Printer: De Bussy, Amsterdam.	12.50	50.00	170

1939 Muntbiljet Issue

		VG	VF	UNC
105	**1 Gulden** 1.11.1939. Brown and green. Coin at center right. Back: Blue. Printer: G. Kolff & Co., Batavia. Proof.	—	—	350
106	**1 Gulden** 1.11.1939. Brown and lilac. Coin at center right. Back: Brown. Printer: G. Kolff & Co., Batavia. Proof.	—	—	350
107	**1 Gulden** 1.11.1939. Blue, green and orange. Coin at center right. Back: Brown. Printer: G. Kolff & Co., Batavia. Proof.	—	—	350

1940 Muntbiljet Issue

		VG	VF	UNC
108	**1 Gulden** 15.6.1940. Brown, blue and multicolor. Coin at center right. Back: Borubudur Temple at center. BC: Brown. Printer: G. Kolff & Co., Batavia.			
	a. Serial # and prefix letters.	2.00	5.00	20.00
	b. Letters only.	2.00	5.00	20.00

		VG	VF	UNC
109	**2 1/2 Gulden** 15.6.1940. Gray-brown. J.P. Coen at center. Back: Arms. BC: Brown and violet. Printer: G. Kolff & Co., Batavia.			
	a. Issued note.	4.00	10.00	30.00
	s. Specimen.	—	—	—

#108-109 issued 24.4.1941 because of a shortage of coin normally minted by the United States.

1943 Muntbiljet Issue

		VG	VF	UNC
110	**50 Cents** 2.3.1943. Orange. Portrait Queen Wilhelmina at right, crowned supported arms at left. Back: Green. Printer: ABNC.			
	a. Issued note.	1.00	3.00	10.00
	p. Proof.	—	—	200
	s. Specimen.	—	—	200

		VG	VF	UNC
111	**1 Gulden** 2.3.1943. Black. Portrait Queen Wilhelmina at right, crowned supported arms at left. Back: Green. Printer: ABNC.			
	a. Issued note.	0.50	2.00	10.00
	p. Proof.	—	—	150
	s. Specimen.	—	—	150

		VG	VF	UNC
112	**2 1/2 Gulden** 2.3.1943. Purple. Portrait Queen Wilhelmina at right, crowned supported arms at left. Back: Green. Printer: ABNC.			
	a. Issued note.	2.00	6.00	15.00
	p. Proof.	—	—	150
	s. Specimen.	—	—	150

113 5 Gulden

2.3.1943. Blue. Portrait Queen Wilhelmina at right, crowned supported arms at left. Back: Plane, soldier and warship. BC: Green. Printer: ABNC.

	VG	VF	UNC
a. Issued note.	1.25	4.00	10.00
p. Proof.	—	—	175
s. Specimen.	—	—	200

114 10 Gulden

2.3.1943. Red. Portrait Queen Wilhelmina at right, crowned supported arms at left. Back: Plane, soldier and warship. BC: Green. Printer: ABNC.

	VG	VF	UNC
a. Issued note.	2.00	7.50	20.00
p. Proof.	—	—	175
s. Specimen.	—	—	200

115 25 Gulden

2.3.1943. Brown. Portrait Queen Wilhelmina at right, crowned supported arms at left. Back: Plane, soldier and warship. BC: Green. Printer: ABNC.

	VG	VF	UNC
a. Issued note.	4.00	12.50	50.00
p. Proof.	—	—	225
s. Specimen.	—	—	250

116 50 Gulden

2.3.1943. Green. Portrait Queen Wilhelmina at right, crowned supported arms at left. Back: Plane, soldier and warship. BC: Green. Printer: ABNC.

	VG	VF	UNC
a. Issued note.	4.00	12.50	50.00
p. Proof.	—	—	275
s. Specimen.	—	—	450

117 100 Gulden

2.3.1943. Dark brown. Portrait Queen Wilhelmina at right, crowned supported arms at left. Back: Plane, soldier and warship. BC: Green. Printer: ABNC.

	VG	VF	UNC
a. Issued note.	6.00	20.00	75.00
p. Proof.	—	—	325
s. Specimen.	—	—	500

118 500 Gulden

2.3.1943. Gray-blue. Portrait Queen Wilhelmina at right, crowned supported arms at left. Back: Plane, soldier and warship. BC: Green. Printer: ABNC.

	VG	VF	UNC
a. Issued note.	200	500	1,200
p. Proof.	—	—	600
s. Specimen.	—	—	1,000

JAPANESE OCCUPATION - WWII

De Japansche Regeering

The Japanese Government

1942 ND Issue

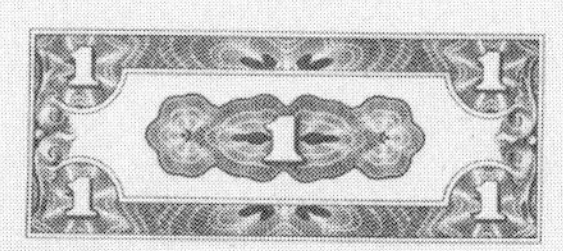

119 1 Cent

ND (1942). Dark green on pink underprint. Plate letter S prefix. Back: Green.

	VG	VF	UNC
a. 2 block letters, format SA.	0.25	0.50	1.25
b. Fractional block letters, format S/AA.	0.10	0.25	0.75
s. As a. Specimen with red overprint: *Mi-hon, with or without SPECIMEN* on back.	—	—	100

120 5 Cents

ND (1942). Blue on light tan underprint. Plate letter S prefix. Back: Blue.

	VG	VF	UNC
a. Letter *S* followed by a one or two digit number, format S1 to S31.	0.50	1.50	5.00
b. 2 block letters.	0.25	1.00	2.00
c. Fractional block letters.	0.20	0.40	1.00
s. As a. Specimen with red overprint: *Mi-hon, with or without SPECIMEN* on back.	—	—	100

121 10 Cents

ND (1942). Purple on pale yellow underprint. Plate letter S prefix. Back: Purple.

	VG	VF	UNC
a. Letter *S* followed by number, S1 to S31.	0.50	1.50	5.00
b. 2 block letters.	7.00	20.00	75.00
c. Fractional block letters.	0.25	0.50	1.00
s. As a. Specimen with red overprint: *Mi-hon, with or without SPECIMEN* on back.	—	—	100

122 1/2 Gulden

ND (1942). Blue on pale yellow and pink underprint. Plate letter S prefix. Fan palm at right. With Dutch text:*DE JAPANSCHE REGEERING BETAALT AAN TOONDER(The Japanese Government pays to the bearer).* Back: Blue. Watermark: Repeated kiri-flower, but sometimes not discernible.

	VG	VF	UNC
a. Block letters SA-SK, SM.	0.50	1.50	4.00
b. Block letters SL.	0.25	0.75	2.00
s. As a. Specimen with overprint: *Mi-hon, with or without SPECIMEN* on back.	—	—	100

123 1 Gulden

ND (1942). Brown on green underprint. Plate letter S prefix. Breadfruit tree at left, coconut palm at right. With Dutch text:*DE JAPANSCHE REGEERING BETAALT AAN TOONDER(The Japanese Government pays to the bearer).* Back: Brown. Watermark: Repeated kiri-flower, but it is sometimes not discernible.

	VG	VF	UNC
a. Block letters SA; SB, serial #, without watermark.	25.00	90.00	150
b. Block letters SB-SH; SL.	0.50	1.50	4.00
c. Block letters SI; SN.	0.25	0.50	1.00
s. As a. Specimen with overprint: *Mi-hon, with or without SPECIMEN* on back.	—	—	100

124 5 Gulden

ND (1942). Green on yellow and pale lilac underprint. Plate letter S prefix. Coconut palm at left, papaw at right. With Dutch text:*DE JAPANSCHE REGEERING BETAALT AAN TOONDER(The Japanese Government pays to the bearer).* Back: Green. Watermark: Repeated kiri-flower, but it is sometimes not discernible.

	VG	VF	UNC
a. Block letters SA; SB, serial #.	25.00	90.00	150
b. Block letters SB-SF.	1.00	2.50	6.00
c. Block letters SG.	0.25	1.00	2.50
s. As a. Specimen with overprint: *Mi-hon, with or without SPECIMEN* on back.	—	—	100

125 10 Gulden

ND (1942). Purple on pale green underprint. Plate letter S prefix. Banana tree at center, coconut palm at right. With Dutch text:*DE JAPANSCHE REGEERING BETAALT AAN TOONDER(The Japanese Government pays to the bearer).* Back: Purple. Watermark: Repeated kiri-flower, but it is sometimes not discernible.

	VG	VF	UNC
a. Block letters SA only, serial #.	25.00	90.00	150
b. Block letters SB-SH; SK.	1.00	2.50	6.00
c. Block letters SI; SL.	0.25	1.00	2.50
s. As a. Specimen with overprint: *Mi-hon, with or without SPECIMEN* on back.	—	—	100

#123-125 with overprint: *Republik Islam Indonesia*, see Volume 1, Indonesia #S511-S529. Other overprints exist, but are believed to be recent fantasies.These include black bar overprint: *Republik Maluku Selatan R.M.S.* and *Persatuan Islam Borneo* with signature.

Pemerintah Dai Nippon

The Japanese Government

1944-1945 ND Issue

126 100 Roepiah

ND (1944-45). Brown-violet and dark green. Plate letter S prefix. Hut under trees on a shore at center. With Indonesian text:*Pemerintah Dai Nippon* (The Japanese Government). Back: Farmer in stream with two water buffalo at center. BC: Red-brown.

	VG	VF	UNC
a. Engraved face. Standard kiri-flowers watermark.	10.00	35.00	100
b. Lithographed face, paper without silk threads, block letters SO sans serif, 4mm. high. Without watermark.	5.00	15.00	35.00
c. Lithographed face, paper with silk threads, block I letters SO not sans serif, 4mm. high. Without watermark.	5.00	15.00	35.00
r. Remainder, without block letters SO.	5.00	15.00	35.00
s. As a. Specimen with overprint: *Mi-hon. SPECIMEN* on back.	—	—	125

Note: Deceptive counterfeits of #126b exist.

127 1000 Roepiah

ND (1945). Blue-green and purple. Plate letter S pefix. Pair of oxen pulling cart at center. Lithographed face. With Indonesian text:*Pemerintah Dai Nippon (The Japanese Government).* Back: Farmer in stream with two water buffalo at center. BC: Dark green. Watermark: Standard kiri-flowers.

	VG	VF	UNC
a. Issued note.	75.00	200	650
s. Specimen with overprint: *Mi-hon.*	—	—	400

Dai Nippon Teikoku Seihu

Imperial Japanese Government

1944 ND Issue

128	1/2 Roepiah	VG	VF	UNC
	ND (1944). Gray-black on light tan underprint. Plate letter S prefix. Stylized dragon. Back: Gray-black.			
	a. Issued note.	1.00	2.50	7.50
	s. Specimen with red overprint: *Mi-hon.*	—	—	100

129	1 Roepiah	VG	VF	UNC
	ND (1944). Black-green and green. Plate letter S prefix. Field work (rice growing). Back: Banyan tree and temples of Dieng Plateau. BC: Brown.			
	a. Issued note.	1.00	2.50	7.50
	s. Specimen with red overprint: *Mi-hon.*	—	—	100

130	5 Roepiah	VG	VF	UNC
	ND (1944). Olive-green on light green underprint. Plate letter S prefix. Batak house at left. Back: Batak woman (Sumatera) at center. BC: Green.			
	a. Issued note.	1.00	2.50	7.50
	s. Specimen with red overprint: *Mi-hon.*	—	—	100

131	10 Roepiah	VG	VF	UNC
	ND (1944). Dark brown on light tan underprint. Plate letter S prefix. Javanese dancer at left. Back: Stupas and statues of Buddha from Borobudur Temple at left and right. BC: Purple.			
	a. Issued note.	1.00	2.50	7.50
	p. Proof with pale blue underprint. Rare.	—	—	—
	s. Specimen with red overprint: *Mi-hon.*	—	—	100

Note: Two distinct counterfiets of #131 exist.

132	100 Roepiah	VG	VF	UNC
	ND (1944). Dark brown on pale green underprint. Plate letter S prefix. Lion statue at left, statue of Vishnu on Garuda at right and Saruda at left. Back: Wayang puppet at center. BC: Dark green.			
	a. Issued note.	2.50	10.00	45.00
	s. Specimen with red overprint: *Mi-hon.*	—	—	100

133	100 Roepiah	VG	VF	UNC
	ND (1943). Violet on yellow underprint. *DAI NIPPON* on face 59mm. Back: *SERATOES ROEPIAH.* Proof. Rare.	—	—	—

Note: #119-132 are known without block letters, and for most of the notes, proofs also in modified designs are known. Unfinished notes, especially of the 1944 series, #128-132, some of which are uniface, are printers' leftovers which became available after the Japanese surrender of 1945.

There is controversy about the legitimacy of #120, 121, 125, 128-130 and possibly others of this series without block letters. Very deceptive counterfeits of some notes from #128-132 have been seen.

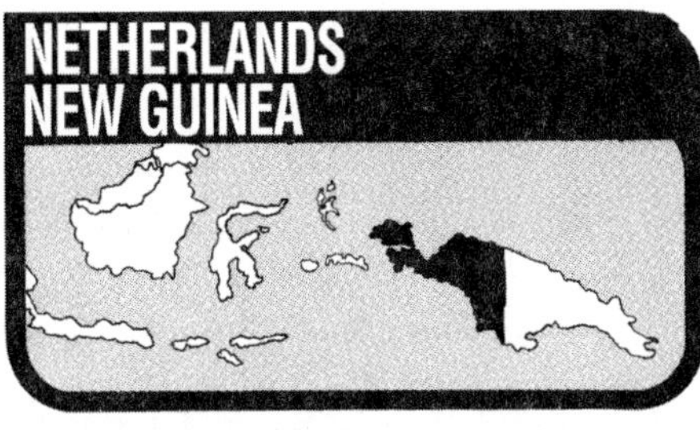

Dutch New Guinea (Irian Jaya, Irian Barat, West Irian, West New Guinea), a province of Indonesia consisting of the western half of the island of New Guinea and adjacent islands, has an area of 159,376 sq. mi. (412,781 sq. km.) and a population of 930,000. Capital: Jayapura. Many regions are but partially explored. Rubber, copra and tea are produced. Northwest New Guinea was first visited by Dutch navigators in the 17th century. Dutch sovereignty was established and extended throughout the 18th century. In 1828, Dutch New Guinea was declared a dependency of Tidore (an island of the Moluccas conquered by the Dutch in 1654). The boundary was established by treaties with Great Britain (1884) and Germany (1885). Japanese forces occupied only the northern coastal area in 1942; they were driven out by the Allies in 1944. The Netherlands retained sovereignty over Dutch New Guinea when independence was granted to Indonesia in 1949. It was placed under United Nations administration in 1962, and was transferred to Indonesia in 1963 with provision for the holding of a plebiscite by 1969 to decide the country's future. As a result, it became a province of Indonesia.

RULERS:
Dutch to 1963

MONETARY SYSTEM:
1 Gulden = 100 Cents to 1963

Note: Refer to Netherlands Indies for issues before and during WWII. For later issues see Irian Barat (Indonesia).

DUTCH ADMINISTRATION

Nieuw-Guinea

1950 Issue

NOTE: #1-3 not assigned.

#	Denomination	Good	Fine	XF
4	**1 Gulden** 2.1.1950. Green and orange. Portrait Queen Juliana at left. Back: Green and brown. Printer: JEZ.			
	a. Issued note.	15.00	60.00	250
	s. Specimen.	—	Unc	150
5	**2 1/2 Gulden** 2.1.1950. Red-brown on blue underprint. Portrait Queen Juliana at left. Back: Red-brown and blue. Printer: JEZ.			
	a. Issued note.	17.50	100	375
	b. Specimen.	—	Unc	200
6	**5 Gulden** 2.1.1950. Blue on tan underprint. Portrait Queen Juliana at left. Greater bird of paradise at right. Printer: JEZ.			
	a. Issued note.	35.00	175	450
	s. Specimen.	—	Unc	250

#	Denomination	Good	Fine	XF
7	**10 Gulden** 2.1.1950. Brown on gray underprint. Portrait Queen Juliana at left. Greater bird of paradise at right. Printer: JEZ.			
	a. Issued note.	50.00	250	750
	s. Specimen.	—	Unc	400
8	**25 Gulden** 2.1.1950. Green on brown underprint. Portrait Queen Juliana at left. Greater bird of paradise at right. Printer: JEZ.			
	a. Issued note.	150	750	—
	s. Specimen.	—	Unc	650
9	**100 Gulden** 2.1.1950. Lilac on green underprint. Portrait Queen Juliana at left. Greater bird of paradise at right. Printer: JEZ.			
	a. Issued note.	175	1,000	—
	s. Specimen.	—	Unc	800

#	Denomination	Good	Fine	XF
10	**500 Gulden** 2.1.1950. Light brown on gray underprint. Portrait Queen Juliana at left. Greater bird of paradise at right. Printer: JEZ.			
	a. Issued note.	—	—	—
	s. Specimen.	—	Unc	1,200

Nederlands Nieuw-Guinea

1954 Issue

#	Denomination	Good	Fine	XF
11	**1 Gulden** 8.12.1954. Green and brown. Portrait Queen Juliana at right, sicklebill at left. Back: Green and red.			
	a. Issued note.	10.00	30.00	175
	s. Specimen.	—	Unc	100

#	Denomination	Good	Fine	XF
12	**2 1/2 Gulden** 8.12.1954. Blue and brown. Portrait Queen Juliana at right, sicklebill at left. Back: Blue and green.			
	a. Issued note.	15.00	60.00	225
	s. Specimen.	—	Unc	150

#	Denomination	Good	Fine	XF
13	**5 Gulden** 8.12.1954. Lilac and brown. Portrait Queen Juliana at right, sicklebill at left.			
	a. Issued note.	17.50	100	300
	s. Specimen.	—	Unc	185

		Good	Fine	XF
14	**10 Gulden** 8.12.1954. Purple and green. Queen Juliana at right. Crowned pigeon at left. Back: Stylized bird of paradise at center right. BC: Purple and brown.			
	a. Issued note.	40.00	150	500
	s. Specimen.	—	Unc	250

		Good	Fine	XF
15	**25 Gulden** 8.12.1954. Brown and violet. Portrait Queen Juliana at right, sicklebill at left. Back: Owl.			
	a. Issued note.	85.00	300	750
	s. Specimen.	—	Unc	275
16	**100 Gulden** 8.12.1954. Light and dark olive-brown and dark blue. Portrait Queen Juliana at right, sicklebill at left. Back: Owl.	Good	Fine	XF
	a. Issued note.	150	500	—
	s. Specimen.	—	Unc	325

NOTE: Several notes of Netherlands Indies #29-33, 35 and Javasche Bank 5 Gulden are known with large circular handstamp: *FINANCIEN NIEUW GUINEA GVT.* and other local overprint. Further documentation is needed.

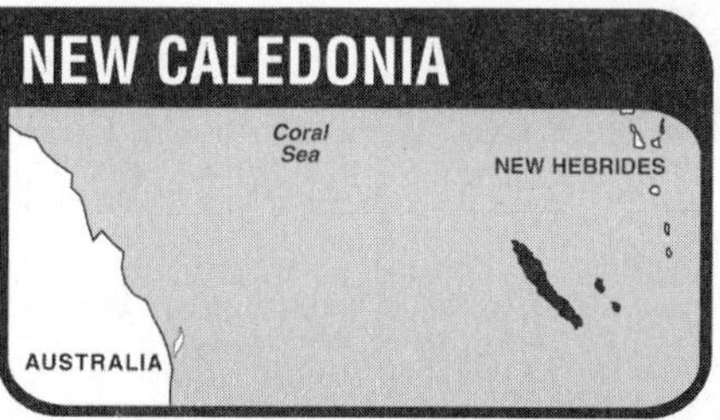

The French Overseas Territory of New Caledonia, a group of about 25 islands in the South Pacific, is situated about 750 miles (1,207 km.) east of Australia. The territory, which includes the dependencies of Ile des Pins, Loyalty Islands, Ile Huon, Isles Belep, Isles Chesterfield, and Ile Walpole, has a total land area of 6,530 sq. mi. (19,058 sq. km.) and a population of 152,000. Capital: Noumea. The islands are rich in minerals; New Caledonia has the world's largest known deposit of nickel. Nickel, nickel castings, coffee and copra are exported.Settled by both Britain and France during the first half of the 19th century, the island was made a French possession in 1853. It served as a penal colony for four decades after 1864. Agitation for independence during the 1980s and early 1990s ended in the 1998 Noumea Accord, which over a period of 15 to 20 years will transfer an increasing amount of governing responsibility from France to New Caledonia. The agreement also commits France to conduct as many as three referenda between 2013 and 2018, to decide whether New Caledonia should assume full sovereignty and independence.

RULERS:
French

MONETARY SYSTEM:
1 Franc = 100 Centimes

FRENCH ADMINISTRATION

Compagnie de la Nouvelle Calédonie
1873-1874 Succursale de Nouméa Issue

		Good	Fine	XF
1	**5 Francs** 1.7.1873. Black. Seal at upper left. Back: Reversed image as front. Requires confirmation.	—	—	—

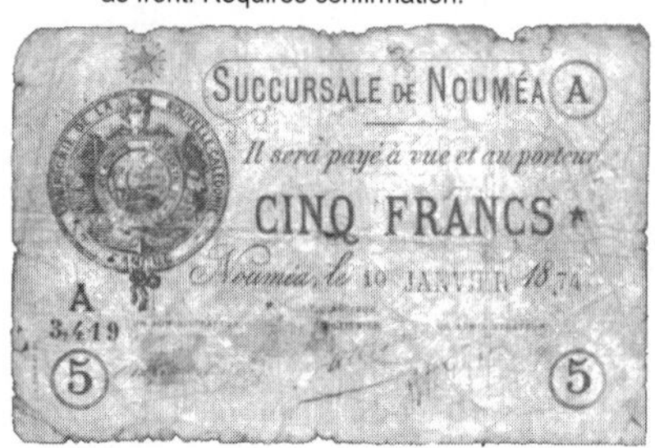

		Good	Fine	XF
2	**5 Francs** 1.7.1874; 31.10.1874. Yellow-brown. Seal at upper left. Back: Reversed image as front.	400	1,500	—
3	**20 Francs** Sept. 1874. Black on green underprint. Seal at upper left. Back: Reversed image as front.	450	1,750	—

Banque de la Nouvelle Calédonie
1874 Issue

		Good	Fine	XF
4	**100 Francs** 187x. Blue. Farmer with implements and cow at left, islander with produce and implements at right. Overprint: *ANNULÉ*. Rare.	—	—	—

1875 Etablissement de Nouméa Issue

Décret du 14 Juillet 1874

#	Description	Good	Fine	XF
6	**5 Francs** 1875. Yellow-brown. Seal at upper left. Back: Reversed image as front.	450	1,200	—
7	**20 Francs** 10.4.1875. Black on green underprint. Seal at upper left. Back: Reversed image as front.	500	1,350	—
8	**100 Francs** 25.1.1875; 15.2.1875; 10.7.1875. Pale blue. Seal at upper left. Back: Reversed image as front. Rare.	—	6,000	—
9	**500 Francs** 25.1.1875. Blue. Seal at upper left. Back: Reversed image as front.			
	a. Issued note. Rare.	—	—	—
	r. Remainder cancelled with overprint: *ANNULÉ 187x*. Rare.	—	—	—

Décrets Des 21.2.1875/20.2.1888

#	Description	Good	Fine	XF
10	**5 Francs** Requires confirmation.	—	—	—
11	**20 Francs** (ca.1890). Handwritten or handstamped dates. Blue. Neptune reclining holding trident at lower left. 3 signatures.	—	—	—

#	Description	Good	Fine	XF
12	**100 Francs** 1895; 1898. Blue and red. Elephant columns at left and right, two reclining women with ox at left, tiger right at lower border. Back: Blue.			
	a. 15.1.1895; 26.10.1898.	—	—	—
	p. Proof without serial #, overprint: *ANNULÉ*. 1.7.1898.	—	—	—

#	Description	Good	Fine	XF
13	**500 Francs** 1.7.1898. Blue and red. Vasco da Gama at left, sailing ships at lower center, Polynesian man holding paddle on "sea-dragon" boat at right.			
	a. Issued note.	—	—	—
	p. Proof without block or serial #, overprint: *ANNULÉ*.	—	—	—

Banque de l'Indo-Chine

Nouméa

Décrets des 21.2.1875/20.2.1888/16.5.1900

#	Description	Good	Fine	XF
14	**20 Francs** 3.3.1902. Handwritten or handstamped. Blue. Neptune reclining holding trident at lower left. Series X.6.	—	—	—

Décrets des 21.2.1875/20.2.1888/16.5.1900/3.4.1901

#	Description	Good	Fine	XF
15	**5 Francs** 13.6.1916; 15.6.1916; 17.6.1916. Blue and red. Oriental woman seated below Liberty seated holding caduceus at left. Back: Blue.			
	a. Issued note.	250	850	—
	b. Cancelled with overprint: *Annulé*.	150	450	—

#	Description	Good	Fine	XF
16	**20 Francs** 1905; 1913. Handwritten or handstamped. Blue. Neptune reclining holding trident at lower left. 3 signatures.			
	a. Issued note. 25.9.1913.	—	—	—
	b. Cancelled with overprint: *Annulé*	—	—	—
	s. Specimen 3.7.1905.	—	—	—

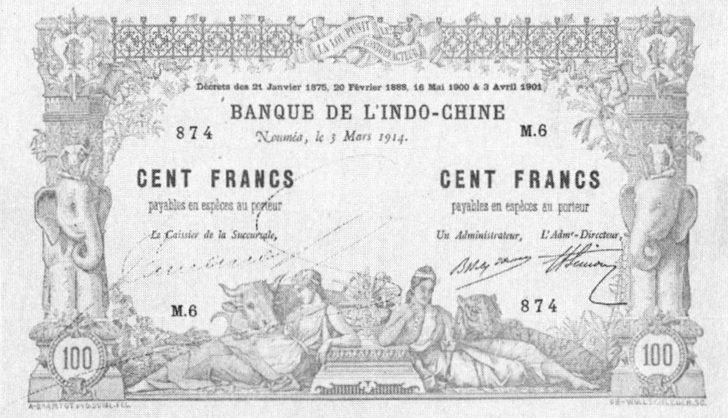

#	Description	Good	Fine	XF
17	**100 Francs** 3.3.1914; 10.3.1914; 11.3.1914. Blue and red. Elephant columns at left and right. Two reclining women with ox at left, tiger right at lower border. 3 signatures.	175	450	1,000

1916-25 Issue (W/o Décrets)

#	Description	Good	Fine	XF
18	**5 Francs** 6.6.1916; 19.6.1916. Light green. 2 signatures.	75.00	300	750
19	**5 Francs** 2.6.1924. Blue.	75.00	275	600

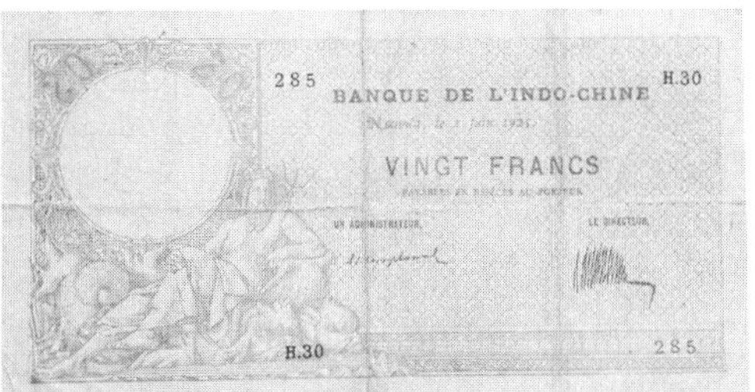

#	Description	Good	Fine	XF
20	**20 Francs** 3.1.1921; 2.6.1924; 2.6.1925. Blue and red. Neptune reclining holding trident at lower left. 2 signatures.	150	450	1,000

#	Denomination / Description	Good	Fine	XF
21	**100 Francs** 2.6.1925. Blue and red. Elephant columns at left and right. 2 reclining women with ox at left, tiger right at lower border.	200	600	1,250

#	Denomination / Description	Good	Fine	XF
22	**500 Francs** 3.1.1921. Blue and red. Vasco da Gama at left, sailing ships at lower center, Polynesian man holding paddle on "sea-dragon" boat at right.	500	1,500	—

1914 ND Emergency Postage Stamp Card Issues

#23-27 adhesive postal stamps affixed to cardboard w/handstamp: *TRESORIER PAYEUR DE LA NOUVELLE CÁLEDONIE* and *SECRETARIAT GENERAL* on back.

#	Denomination / Description	VG	VF	UNC
23	**25 Centimes** ND (1914-1923). Kanaka village on stamp. Back: Handstamp. 52 x 39mm to 61 x 40mm.	150	300	600

#	Denomination / Description	VG	VF	UNC
24	**50 Centimes (35 and 15 Cent.)** ND (1914-1923). Kanaka village and Kagu bird on stamps. Back: Handstamp.	200	425	700
25	**50 Centimes** ND (1914-1923). Kanaka village on stamp. Back: Handstamp.	175	350	600
26	**1 Franc** ND (1914-1923). Stamp. Back: Handstamp.	175	350	600
27	**2 Francs** ND (1914-1923). Stamp. Back: Handstamp.	225	425	700

1922 ND Encapsulated Postage Stamp

#	Denomination / Description	VG	VF	UNC
28	**25 Centimes** ND (1922). Stamp encapsuled in aluminum with embossing: *BANQUE DE L'INDOCHINE, NOUMÉA.*	15.00	45.00	100
29	**50 Centimes** ND (1922). Like #28 but different stamp.	20.00	60.00	150

Trésorerie de Nouméa

1918 First Issue

#	Denomination / Description	Good	Fine	XF
30	**0.50 Franc** 14.11.1918-13.1.1919. Back: *L'Article 139 du Code penal* in 3 lines.	35.00	150	450
31	**1 Franc** 14.11.1918-13.1.1919. Back: *L'Article 139 du Code penal* in 3 lines.	40.00	175	500
32	**2 Francs** 14.11.1918-13.1.1919. Back: *L'Article 139 du Code penal* in 3 lines.	60.00	200	600

1918 Second Issue

#	Denomination / Description	Good	Fine	XF
33	**0.50 Franc** 14.11.1918-13.1.1919. Blue. Back: *L'Article 139 du Code penal* in 4 lines.			
	a. Small numerals on back.	15.00	75.00	250
	b. Large numerals on back.	15.00	75.00	250
34	**1 Franc** 14.11.1918-13.1.1919. Back: *L'Article 139 du Code penal* in 4 lines.			
	a. Small numerals on back.	20.00	85.00	300
	b. Large numerals on back.	20.00	85.00	300
35	**2 Francs** 14.11.1918-13.1.1919. Blue-green. Back: *L'Article 139 du Code penal* in 4 lines.			
	a. Small numerals on back.	25.00	100	350
	b. Large numerals on back.	25.00	100	350

Banque de l'Indochine Nouméa

1926-1929 Issue

#	Denomination / Description	VG	VF	UNC
36	**5 Francs** ND (ca. 1926). Brown on light green underprint. Woman with helmet at lower left. Printer: Ch. Walhain and E. Deloche. 150x93mm.			
	a. Signature titles: *UN ADMINISTRATEUR* and *LE DIRECTEUR.*	2.50	20.00	75.00
	b. Signature titles: *LE PRÉSIDENT* and *LE DIRECTEUR GÉNÉRAL.* 2 signature varieties.	1.00	5.00	25.00
	s. Specimen. Perforated.	—	—	750

No.	Description	VG	VF	UNC
37	**20 Francs** ND (ca.1929). Lilac-brown. Woman at right. Back: Peacock. Printer: Cl. Serveau and E. Deloche.			
	a. Signature titles: *UN ADMINISTRATEUR* and *LE DIRECTEUR*.	6.00	30.00	125
	b. Signature titles: *LE PRÉSIDENT* and *LE DIRECTEUR GÉNÉRAL*.	5.00	25.00	100

No.	Description	VG	VF	UNC
38	**500 Francs** 27.12.1927; 8.3.1938. Lilac-brown and olive. Woman standing at left, ships at top center.	100	250	650

1939 ND Provisional Issue

No.	Description	VG	VF	UNC
39	**100 Francs on 20 Piastres** ND (1939). Multicolor.	50.00	200	600

No.	Description	Good	Fine	XF
40	**1000 Francs on 100 Piastres** ND (1939-old date 1920). Overprint: On French Indochina #42. Rare.	—	—	—

1939 Emergency Bearer Check Issue

No.	Description	Good	Fine	XF
41	**5000 Francs** 16.9.1939-16.7.1943. Black, check format. Rare.	—	—	—

1937; 1940 ND Issue

No.	Description	VG	VF	UNC
42	**100 Francs** ND (1937-1967). Multicolor. Woman with wreath and small figure of Athena at center. Back: Statue of Angkor at center. Printer: Seb. Laurent and Rita. 205x102mm.			
	a. Signature titles: *UN ADMINISTRATEUR* and *LE DIRECTEUR GENERAL* (1937).	5.00	25.00	100
	b. Signature titles: *LE PRESIDENT* Borduge and *LE DIRECTEUR GENERAL* Baudouin (1937).	4.00	12.00	85.00
	c. Signature titles: *LE PRESIDENT* and *L'ADMINISTRATEUR DIRECTOR GENERAL* (1953).	4.00	12.00	70.00
	d. Signature titles: *LE PRESIDENT* and *LE VICE-PRESIDENT DIRECTEUR-GENERAL* (1957).	4.00	12.00	60.00
	e. Signature titles: *LE PRESIDENT* de Flers and *LE DIRECTEUR GENERAL* Robert (1963).	3.00	10.00	50.00
	s. Specimen. Perforated.	—	—	750

No.	Description	VG	VF	UNC
43	**1000 Francs** ND (1940-1965). Multicolor. Market scene in background and at left, woman sitting at right. Printer: L. Jonas and G. Beltrand.			
	a. Signature M. Borduge with title: *LE PRÉSIDENT* and P. Baudouin with title: *LE DIRECTEUR GÉNÉRAL* (1940).	40.00	150	450
	b. Signature titles: *LE PRÉSIDENT* and *L' ADMINISTRATEUR DIRECTEUR GÉNÉRAL*.	55.00	200	550
	c. Signature titles: *LE PRÉSIDENT* and *LE VICE-PRÉSIDENT DIRECTEUR GÉNÉRAL*.	30.00	100	350

	VG	VF	UNC
d. Signature F. de la Motte Angode Flers with title: *LE PRÉSIDENT* and M. Robert with title: *LE DIRECTEUR GÉNÉRAL.* (1963).	32.50	125	400
s. Specimen.	—	—	—

1942; 1943 ND Issue

		VG	VF	UNC
44	**100 Francs** ND (1942). Brown. Woman wearing wreath and holding small figure of Athena at center. Back: Statue of Angkor. Printer: Australian. 160x102mm.	30.00	125	400
45	**1000 Francs** ND (1943). Blue. Statues of Angkor at left. Without *EMISSION* and date overprint. Printer: ABNC (without imprint).	150	350	750

1943 Issue

		VG	VF	UNC
46	**100 Francs** 1943; 1944. Brown. Woman wearing wreath and holding small figure of Athena at center. Back: Statue of Angkor.			
	a. Overprint: *EMISSION 1943.*	50.00	200	500
	b. Overprint: *EMISSION 1944.*	65.00	250	600

		VG	VF	UNC
47	**1000 Francs** 1943; 1944. Blue. Statues of Angkor at left.			
	a. Overprint: *EMISSION 1943.* Reported not confirmed.	—	—	—
	b. Overprint: *EMISSION 1944.*	150	375	800

1944 ND Issue

		VG	VF	UNC
48	**5 Francs** ND (1944). Dark blue. Woman wearing wreath and holding small figure of Athena at center. Back: Statue of Angkor at center. Printer: Australian.	15.00	75.00	225

		VG	VF	UNC
49	**20 Francs** ND (1944). Green. Woman at left, boat at center, fisherman at right. Back: Mask. Printer: Australian.	8.00	25.00	90.00

1951 ND Issue

		VG	VF	UNC
50	**20 Francs** ND. (1951-1963). Multicolor. Youth at left, flute player at right. Back: Fruit bowl at left, woman at right center.			
	a. Signature titles: *LE PRESIDENT* and *LE DIRECTEUR GAL.* (1951).	2.50	10.00	27.00
	b. Signature titles: *LE PRESIDENT* and *LE VICE-PRESIDENT DIRECTEUR GÉNÉRAL.* (1954; 1958).	1.50	5.00	20.00
	c. Signature titles: *LE PRESIDENT* and *LE DIRECTOR GÉNÉRAL.* (1963).	1.00	4.50	17.50

NOUVELLE CALÉDONIE

Trésorerie de Nouméa, Bon de Caisse

#51-58 ship near crane at l., factory at r. Black text w/cross of Lorraine and stag head on back. Some notes on wmk. paper.

Arrêté du 9.7.1942

No.	Description	VG	VF	UNC
51	**50 Centimes** 15.7.1942. Dark green.	1.50	6.00	30.00
52	**1 Franc** 15.7.1942. Purple.	1.50	6.00	30.00

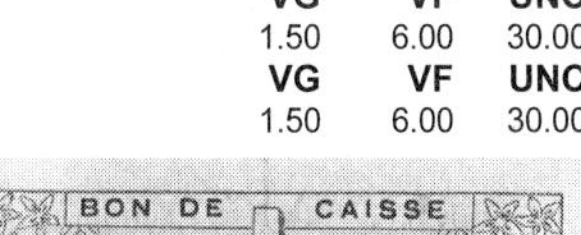

No.	Description	VG	VF	UNC
53	**2 Francs** 15.7.1942. Brown.	2.50	8.00	35.00

Arrêté du 29.1.1943

No.	Description	VG	VF	UNC
54	**50 Centimes** 29.3.1943. Green.	1.50	6.00	30.00

No.	Description	VG	VF	UNC
55	**1 Franc** 29.3.1943. Blue.			
	a. Thin numerals *1* at upper left and right.	1.50	6.00	30.00
	b. Thick numerals *1* at upper left and right.	1.50	6.00	30.00

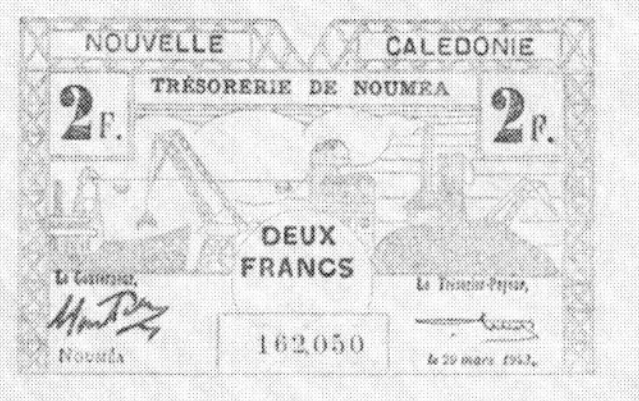

No.	Description	VG	VF	UNC
56	**2 Francs** 29.3.1943. Brown.			
	a. Thin numerals *2* at upper left and right.	2.50	10.00	40.00
	b. Thick numerals *2* at upper left and right.	2.50	10.00	40.00

No.	Description	VG	VF	UNC
57	**20 Francs** 30.4.1943.; 1943. Red.			
	a. Without *Deuxieme Emission* at bottom center on back. 30.4.1943.	10.00	50.00	200
	b. *Deuxieme Emission.* 1943.	10.00	50.00	200

Arrêté du 11.6.1943

No.	Description	VG	VF	UNC
58	**5 Francs** 15.6.1943. Pale green with light brown text.	1.50	6.50	40.00

NEW HEBRIDES

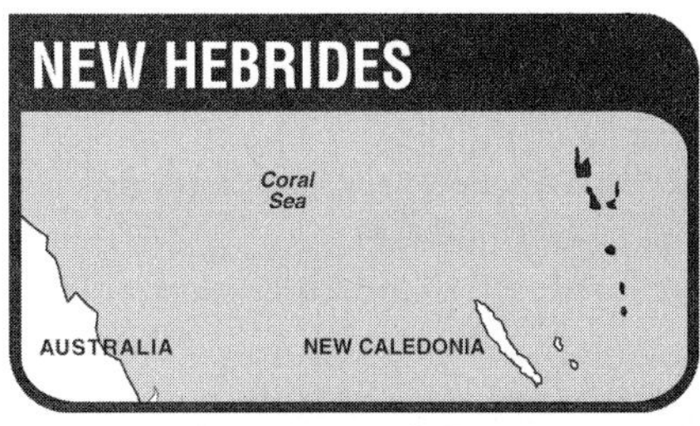

New Hebrides Condominium, a group of islands located in the South Pacific 500 miles (800 km.) west of Fiji, were under the joint sovereignty of Great Britain and France. The islands have an area of 5,700 sq. mi. (14,763 sq. km.) and a population of mainly Melanesians of mixed blood. Capital: Port-Vila. The volcanic and coral islands, while malarial and subject to frequent earthquakes, are extremely fertile, and produce copra, coffee, tropical fruits and timber for export. The New Hebrides were discovered by Portuguese navigator Pedro de Quiros in 1606, visited by French explorer Bougainville in 1768, and named by British navigator Capt. James Cook in 1774. Ships of all nations converged on the islands to trade for sandalwood, prompting France and Britain to relinquish their individual claims and declare the islands a neutral zone in 1878. The New Hebrides were placed under the control of a mixed Anglo-French commission of naval officers during the native uprisings of 1887, and established as a condominium under the joint sovereignty of France and Great Britain in 1906.

RULERS:

British and French to 1980

MONETARY SYSTEM:

1 Franc = 100 Centimes

BRITISH AND FRENCH ADMINISTRATION

Comptoirs Français des Nouvelles-Hébrides

1921 Issue

No.	Description	Good	Fine	XF
A1	**25 Francs** 22.8.1921. Red and blue. Thatched house at lower left, bridge at center, trees at left and right. Back: Pottery at left and right. BC: Red.	300	750	—

Services Nationaux Français des Nouvelles Hébrides

1943 Emergency WW II Issue

No.	Description	Good	Fine	XF
1	**5 Francs** ND (1943). Black on green and pink underprint. Cross of Lorraine at top center above two palm branches. 2 signature varieties.	30.00	100	275
2	**20 Francs** ND (1943). Black on green and pink underprint. Cross of Lorraine at top center above two palm branches. 2 signature varieties.	85.00	250	550
3	**100 Francs** ND (1943). Black on green and pink underprint. Cross of Lorraine at top center above two palm branches.	250	800	—
3A	**500 Francs** ND (1943). Orange value and serial #. Rare.	—	—	—
3B	**1000 Francs** ND (1943). Rare.	—	—	—

Banque de l'Indochine

Nouvelles Hébrides

1941-1945 ND Provisional Issues

Overprint A: Red oval with *NOUVELLES HÉBRIDES FRANCE LIBRE,* palms and Cross of Lorraine. Overprint B: Red *NOUVELLES HÉBRIDES.*

		Good	Fine	XF
4	**5 Francs** ND (1941). Brown and green. Overprint: Red oval with *NOUVELLES HEBRIDES FRANCE LIBRE* on New Caledonia #36.			
	a. Signature de la Chaume and Baudouin.	12.50	60.00	250
	b. Signature Borduge and Baudouin.	10.00	50.00	200

		Good	Fine	XF
5	**5 Francs** ND (1945). Blue. Overprint: Red oval with *NOUVELLES HEBRIDES FRANCE LIBRE* on New Caledonia #48.	20.00	100	300

		Good	Fine	XF
6	**20 Francs** ND (1941). Lilac-brown. Overprint: Red oval with *NOUVELLES HEBRIDES FRANCE LIBRE* on New Caledonia #37.	25.00	100	300

		Good	Fine	XF
7	**20 Francs** ND (1945). Green. Overprint: Red oval with *NOUVELLES HEBRIDES FRANCE LIBRE* on New Caledonia #49.	30.00	125	350

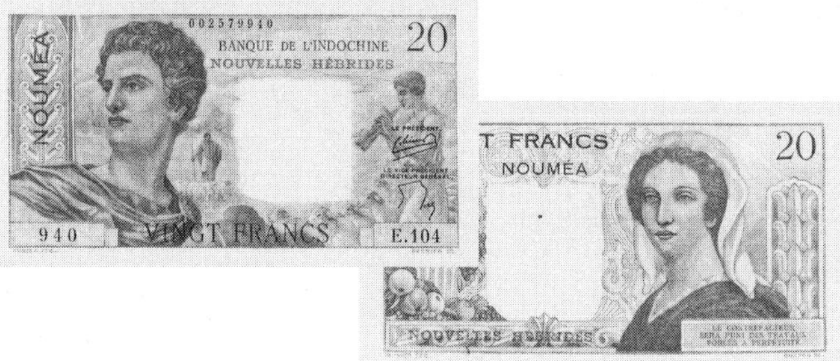

		VG	VF	UNC
8	**20 Francs** ND (1941-1945). Multicolor.			
	a. Signature titles: *LE PRÉSIDENT* and *VICE-PRÉSIDENT DIRECTEUR GÉNÉRAL.*	3.00	7.50	35.00
	b. Signature titles: *LE PRÉSIDENT* and *LE DIRECTEUR GÉNÉRAL.*	2.00	5.00	30.00

		Good	Fine	XF
9	**100 Francs** ND (1941-1945). Multicolor. Overprint: Red oval with *NOUVELLES HEBRIDES FRANCE LIBRE* at center.			
	a. Overprint on New Caledonia #42a.	125	350	900
	b. Overprint on New Caledonia #42b.	150	400	1,000

#	Description	Good	Fine	XF
10	**100 Francs** ND (1941-1945). Multicolor. Overprint: Red *NOUVELLES HEBRIDES* across lower center.	Good	Fine	XF
	a. Signature titles: *PRÉSIDENT* and *DIRECTEUR*, length of overprint 89mm.	10.00	60.00	150
	b. Signature titles: *PRÉSIDENT* and *ADMINISTRATEUR*, length of overprint 68mm.	12.50	75.00	175
	c. Signature titles: *PRÉSIDENT* and *VICE-PRÉSIDENT*, length of overprint 68mm.	10.00	60.00	150
10A	**100 Francs** ND (1945). Brown. Overprint: Red oval with *NOUVELLES HEBRIDES FRANCE LIBRE* on New Caledonia #44.	135	325	600

#	Description	Good	Fine	XF
11	**100 Francs** ND (1946-old date 1943). Brown. Overprint: Red oval with *NOUVELLES HEBRIDES FRANCE LIBRE* on New Caledonia #46a.	125	300	550
12	**100 Francs** ND (1947-old date 1944). Brown. Overprint: Red oval with *NOUVELLES HEBRIDES FRANCE LIBRE* on New Caledonia #46b.	125	300	550

#	Description	Good	Fine	XF
12A	**500 Francs** ND (-old date 8.3.1938). Lilac-brown. Overprint: Red oval with *NOUVELLES HEBRIDES FRANCE LIBRE* on New Caledonia #38. Rare.	—	—	—

#	Description	Good	Fine	XF
13	**1000 Francs** ND (1945-47-old date 1944). Blue. Overprint: Red oval with *NOUVELLES HEBRIDES FRANCE LIBRE* on New Caledonia #47b.	150	350	750
14	**1000 Francs** 1944. Blue. Overprint: Red *NOUVELLES HEBRIDES* on New Caledonia #47b.	125	300	600

#	Description	Good	Fine	XF
14A	**1000 Francs** ND (1941). Multicolor. Overprint: Red oval with *NOUVELLES HEBRIDES FRANCE LIBRE* on New Caledonia #43. Rare.	—	—	—

#	Description	Good	Fine	XF
15	**1000 Francs** ND (1941-1945). Multicolor. Overprint: Red *NOUVELLES HEBRIDES* across bottom center on New Caledonia #43.	35.00	90.00	275

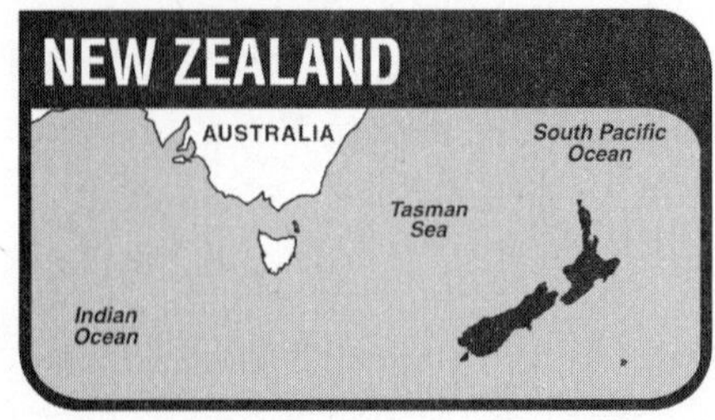

New Zealand, a parliamentary state located in the southwestern Pacific 1,250 miles (2,011 km.) east of Australia, has an area of 103,736 sq. mi. (269,056 sq. km.) and a population of 4.3 million. Capital: Wellington. Wool, meat, dairy products and some manufactured items are exported. The Polynesian Maori reached New Zealand in about A.D. 800. In 1840, their chieftains entered into a compact with Britain, the Treaty of Waitangi, in which they ceded sovereignty to Queen Victoria while retaining territorial rights. In that same year, the British began the first organized colonial settlement. A series of land wars between 1843 and 1872 ended with the defeat of the native peoples. The British colony of New Zealand became an independent dominion in 1907 and supported the UK militarily in both World Wars. New Zealand's full participation in a number of defense alliances lapsed by the 1980s. In recent years, the government has sought to address longstanding Maori grievances.

RULERS:

British

MONETARY SYSTEM:

1 Shilling = 12 Pence
1 Pound = 20 Shillings (also 2 Dollars) to 1967
1 Dollar = 100 Cents, 1967-

BRITISH ADMINISTRATION

Reserve Bank of New Zealand

1934 Issue

Pound System

154	10 Shillings	VG	VF	UNC
	1.8.1934. Red on multicolor underprint. Kiwi at left, arms at upper center, portrait Maori chief at right. Signature: L. Lefeaux. Back: Milford Sound and Mitre Peak at center. Printer: TDLR.	100	1,000	4,000

155	1 Pound	VG	VF	UNC
	1.8.1934. Purple on multicolor underprint. Kiwi at left, arms at upper center, portrait Maori chief at right. Signature: L. Lefeaux. Back: Milford Sound and Mitre Peak at center.	70.00	400	2,500

156	5 Pounds	VG	VF	UNC
	1.8.1934. Blue on multicolor underprint. Kiwi at left, arms at upper center, portrait Maori chief at right. Signature: L. Lefeaux. Back: Milford Sound and Mitre Peak at center. Printer: TDLR.	120	750	3,000

157	50 Pounds	VG	VF	UNC
	1.8.1934. Red on multicolor underprint. Kiwi at left, arms at upper center, portrait Maori chief at right. Signature: L. Lefeaux. Back: Milford Sound and Mitre Peak at center.	5,000	15,000	50,000

1940 ND Issue

158	10 Shillings	VG	VF	UNC
	ND (1940-1967). Brown on multicolor underprint. Arms at upper center. Portrait of Capt. James Cook at lower right. Signature title: *CHIEF CASHIER*. Back: Kiwi at left, Waitangi Treaty signing scene at center. Watermark: Maori chief. Printer: TDLR.			
	a. Signature T. P. Hanna. (1940-1955).	15.00	80.00	600
	b. Signature G. Wilson. (1955-1956).	30.00	150	1,000
	c. Signature R. N. Fleming. Without security thread. (1956-1960).	20.00	60.00	500
	d. As c. With security thread. (1960-1967).	6.00	20.00	100

	1 Pound	VG	VF	UNC
159	ND (1940-1967). Purple on multicolor underprint. Arms at upper center. Portrait of Capt. James Cook at lower right. Signature title: *CHIEF CASHIER.* Back: Sailing ship on sea at left. Watermark: Maori chief. Printer: TDLR.			
	a. Signature T. P. Hanna. (1940-1955).	10.00	80.00	500
	b. Signature G. Wilson. (1955-1956).	15.00	80.00	600
	c. Signature R. N. Fleming. Without security thread. (1956-1960).	10.00	40.00	300
	d. As c. With security thread. (1960-1967).	5.00	12.50	70.00

	5 Pounds	VG	VF	UNC
160	ND (1940-1967). Blue on multicolor underprint. Crowned arms at upper center. Portrait of Capt. James Cook at lower right. Signature title: *CHIEF CASHIER.* Back: Lake Pukaki and Mt. Cook. Watermark: Maori chief. Printer: TDLR.			
	a. Signature T. P. Hanna. (1940-1955).	20.00	100	700
	b. Signature G. Wilson. (1955-1956).	20.00	100	750
	c. Signature R. N. Fleming. Without security thread. (1956-1960).	20.00	70.00	500
	d. As c. With security thread. (1960-1967).	15.00	40.00	150
	s. As a. Specimen. Black overprint of TDLR oval.	—	—	750

	10 Pounds	VG	VF	UNC
161	ND (1940-1967). Green on multicolor underprint. Crowned arms, sailing ship at left. Portrait of Capt. James Cook at lower right. Signature title: *CHIEF CASHIER.* Back: Flock of sheep at left center. Watermark: Maori chief. Printer: TDLR.			
	a. Signature T. P. Hanna. (1940-1955).	80.00	300	1,500
	b. Signature G. Wilson. (1955-1956).	80.00	400	1,600
	c. Signature R. N. Fleming. (1956-1960).	100	200	1,500
	d. As c. With security thread. (1960-1967).	80.00	150	500

	50 Pounds	VG	VF	UNC
162	ND (1940-1967). Red on multicolor underprint. Crowned arms, sailing ship at left. Portrait of Capt. James Cook at lower right. Signature title: *CHIEF CASHIER.* Back: Dairy farm and Mt. Egmont. Printer: TDLR.			
	a. Signature T. P. Hanna. (1940-1955).	2,000	4,000	12,000
	b. Signature G. Wilson. (1955-1956).	2,000	4,000	10,000
	c. Signature R. N. Fleming. (1956-1967).	1,000	2,000	5,000

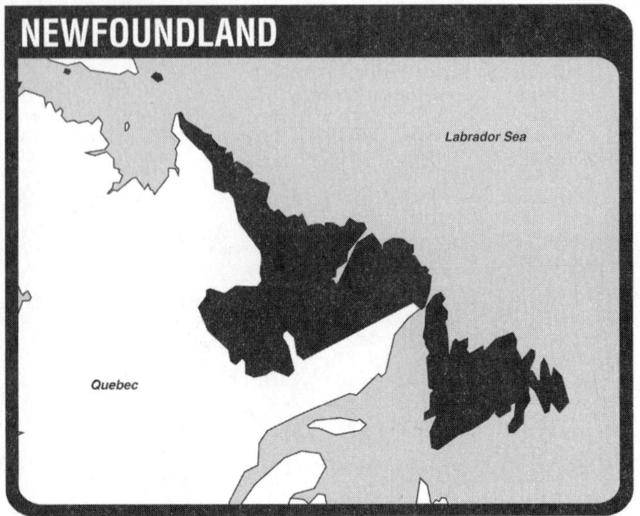

John Cabot, who visited Newfoundland in 1497, is given the title of discoverer although it is likely that Vikings visited its shore on their various trips to the west. Early settlement efforts were made by the British involving such men as Sir Humphrey Gilbert, John Guy and Sir George Calvert. There was much dispute between the French and the British for the island and its fishing rights. Awarded to England by the Treaty of Utrecht of 1713. Granted first governor in 1728. Adequate local government did not develop until the mid 1800s. Made a British colony in 1934 and became a province of Canada (along with Labrador) in 1949.

RULERS:
British

MONETARY SYSTEM:
1 Pound = 4 Dollars = 20 Shillings
1 Dollar = 100 Cents

NEWFOUNDLAND

Island of Newfoundland

1850 Treasury Note

		Good	Fine	XF
A3A	**1 Pound** 16.10.1850. Black. Sailing ship at top center. Uniface.			
	a. 2 signatures.	90.00	300	—
	b. 3 signatures.	275	650	—
	r. Unsigned remainder.	35.00	100	225

Newfoundland Government

Department of Public Works

1901 Cash Note Issue

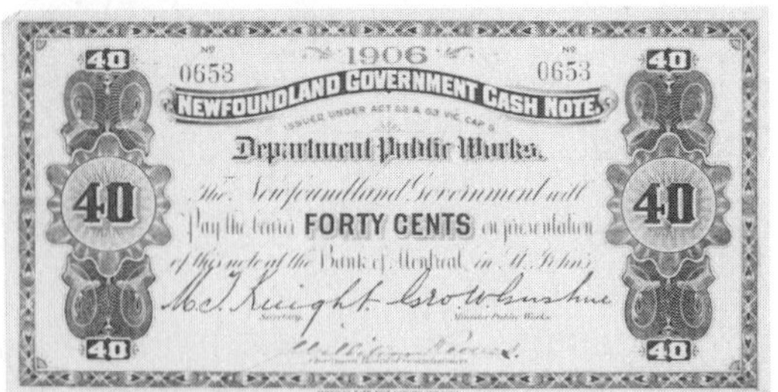

		Good	Fine	XF
A4	**40 Cents** 1901-1908. Printer: ABNC.			
	a. Issued note.	60.00	250	800
	s. Specimen.	—	Unc	1,500
A5	**50 Cents** 1901-1908. Printer: ABNC.	Good	Fine	XF
	a. Issued note.	60.00	250	800
	s. Specimen.	—	Unc	1,500

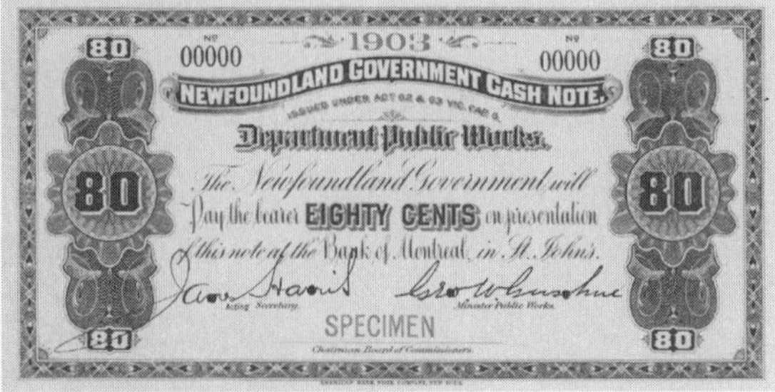

		Good	Fine	XF
A6	**80 Cents** 1901-1908. Printer: ABNC.			
	a. Issued note.	75.00	300	900
	s. Specimen. Punch hole cancelled.	—	Unc	1,500

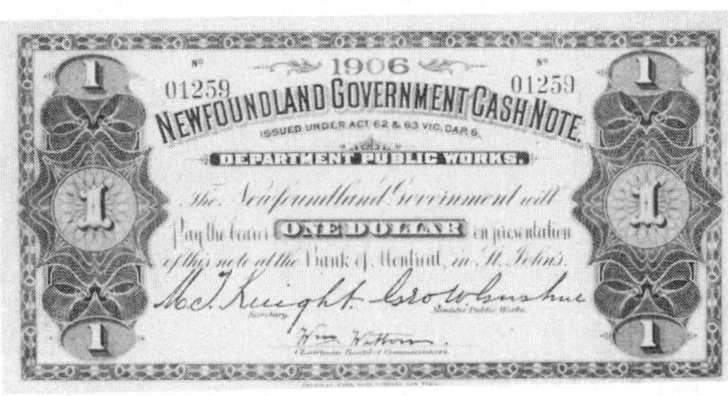

		Good	Fine	XF
A7	**1 Dollar** 1901-1908. Printer: ABNC.			
	a. Issued note.	100	400	900
	s. Specimen.	—	Unc	2,000
A8	**5 Dollars** 1901-1908. Printer: ABNC.	Good	Fine	XF
	a. Issued note.	300	1,200	—
	s. Specimen.	—	Unc	2,250

1910 Issue

#A9-A13 view of waterfall at upper center. Consecutive "double" year dates 1910-11; 1911-12; 1912-13; 1913-14.

		Good	Fine	XF
A9	**25 Cents** 1910-11-1913-14. Black on maroon underprint. View of waterfall at upper center. Back: Brown and gray. Printer: Whitehead, Morris & Co., Engravers, London.	20.00	120	400
A10	**50 Cents** 1910-11-1913-14. Black on dull red and gray-brown underprint. View of waterfall at upper center. Back: Black on dull red and gray-brown underprint. Printer: Whitehead, Morris & Co., Engravers, London.	25.00	150	500
A11	**1 Dollar** 1910-11-1913-14. Black on green, dull red and gray-brown underprint. View of waterfall at upper center. Printer: Whitehead, Morris & Co., Engravers, London.	60.00	250	600
A12	**2 Dollars** 1910-11-1913-14. Black on yellow, blue-gray and gray-brown underprint. View of waterfall at upper center. Printer: Whitehead, Morris & Co., Engravers, London.	400	1,500	—
A13	**5 Dollars** 1910-11-1913-14. Black on blue and gray underprint. View of waterfall at upper center. Printer: Whitehead, Morris & Co., Engravers, London.	600	2,000	—

Government of Newfoundland

1920 Treasury Note Issue

A14 1 Dollar

2.1.1920. Black on blue underprint. Portrait King George V at left. Caribou head at right, sailing ship at left, ornate seal at center. Back: Anchor against rocks at right. BC: Blue. Printer: ABNC.

	VG	VF	UNC
a. Signature Bursell and Brownrigg.	100	600	1,500
b. Signature Hickey and Brownrigg.	75.00	450	1,150
c. Signature Keating and Brownrigg.	75.00	450	1,200
d. Signature Renouf and Brownrigg.	75.00	450	1,150

A15 2 Dollars

2.1.1920. Black on yellow brown and blue underprint. Mine workers at center. Caribou head at right, sailing ship at left, ornate seal at center. Back: Anchor against rocks at right. BC: Brown. Printer: ABNC.

	VG	VF	UNC
a. Signature Bursell and Brownrigg.	125	800	2,250
b. Signature Hickey and Brownrigg.	80.00	700	2,000
c. Signature Keating and Brownrigg.	85.00	750	2,100
d. Signature Renouf and Brownrigg.	110	600	1,850

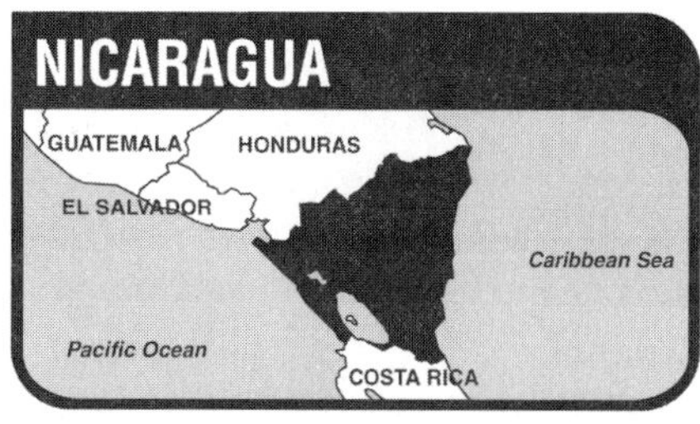

The Republic of Nicaragua, situated in Central America between Honduras and Costa Rica, has an area of 50,193 sq. mi (130,000 sq. km.) and a population of 4.69 million. Capital: Managua. Agriculture, mining (gold and silver) and hardwood logging are the principal industries. Cotton, meat, coffee, tobacco and sugar are exported. The Pacific coast of Nicaragua was settled as a Spanish colony from Panama in the early 16th century. Independence from Spain was declared in 1821 and the country became an independent republic in 1838. Britain occupied the Caribbean Coast in the first half of the 19th century, but gradually ceded control of the region in subsequent decades. Violent opposition to governmental manipulation and corruption spread to all classes by 1978 and resulted in a short-lived civil war that brought the Marxist Sandinista guerrillas to power in 1979. Nicaraguan aid to leftist rebels in El Salvador caused the US to sponsor anti-Sandinista contra guerrillas through much of the 1980s. Free elections in 1990, 1996, and 2001, saw the Sandinistas defeated, but voting in 2006 announced the return of former Sandinista President Daniel Ortega Saavedra. Nicaragua's infrastructure and economy - hard hit by the earlier civil war and by Hurricane Mitch in 1998 - are slowly being rebuilt.

MONETARY SYSTEM:

1 Peso = 100 Centavos to 1912
1 Córdoba = 100 Centavos, 1912-1987
1 New Córdoba = 1000 Old Córdobas, 1988-90
1 Córdoba Oro = 100 Centavos, 1990-

REPUBLIC

Tesorería General

1896 Provisional Issue

Decreto 30.3.1896

Ovpt: *TESORERÍA GENERAL* on face and back of issues of Banco Agricola-Mercantil. Issued by revolutionary forces in Leon.

A13 50 Centavos

D.1896. Back: Treasury registration stamp at center. Overprint: Dark blue on left or right half of #S107. *TESORERIA GENERAL.*

Good	Fine	XF
200	600	—

A14 1 Peso

1.4.1896 (-old date 6.11.1888). Overprint: Dark green on #S107. *TESORERIA GENERAL* on face and back of issues of Banco Agricola-Mercantil

	Good	Fine	XF
a. Handstamp: *TESORERÍA GENERAL NICARAGUA* on back.	20.00	75.00	175
b. Handstamp: Tesorería General *LEON NIC* on back.	30.00	100	200
c. Without circular handstamp on back.	25.00	85.00	185

		Good	Fine	XF
A15	**5 Pesos** 1.4.1896 (-old date 6.11.1888). Seated woman at left, men harvesting wheat at right center. Printer: ABNC. Overprint: Orange on #S108. *TESORERIA GENERAL* on face and back of issues of Banco Agricola-Mercantil.			
	a. Overprint: Text with circular handstamp on back.	20.00	75.00	175
	b. Overprint: Text without circular handstamp on back.	15.00	60.00	150
	c. Without overprint text or circular handstamp on back.	45.00	150	250

Note: For listing of #A14 and A15 without overprint. see #S107 and S108 in Volume 1.

Billete del Tesoro Nacional

These notes were redeemable in silver and gold. They were recognized as legal tender in 1885.

Decreto 15.9.1880

		Good	Fine	XF
A22	**1 Peso** *D.1880.* Black on light blue underprint. Seated Liberty with shield of national arms and staff at lower left. Two dry seals. Series I. Uniface. Watermark paper. Rare.	—	—	—

Decreto 24.9.1881

		Good	Fine	XF
1	**1 Peso** *D.1881.* Brown. Liberty bust at bottom center, arms at upper left. Series I. Printer: HLBNC.	250	500	—
2	**5 Pesos** *D.1881.* Brown. Liberty bust at bottom center, arms at upper left. Series II. Printer: HLBNC. Remainder with stub.	—	—	—
3	**25 Pesos** *D.1881.* Series III. Printer: HLBNC.	—	—	—
4	**50 Pesos** *D.1881.* Series IV. Printer: HLBNC.	—	—	—
5	**100 Pesos** *D.1881.* Series V. Printer: HLBNC.	—	—	—

Decreto 30.6.1883

		Good	Fine	XF
6	**25 Pesos** *D.1883.* Series III.	—	—	—
7	**50 Pesos** *D.1883.* Series IV.	—	—	—
8	**100 Pesos** *D.1883.* Series V.	—	—	—

Decreto 20.3.1885

		Good	Fine	XF
9	**20 Centavos** *D.1885.* Black. Arms at right. Uniface. Series VII. Back: Round purple handstamp. Printer: HLBNC.			
	a. Issued note.	175	450	—
	r. Remainder with stub.	—	—	—

		Good	Fine	XF
10	**50 Centavos** *D.1885.* Black. Arms at center. Uniface. Series VI. Purple handstamps. Back: Purple handstamps. Printer: HLBNC. PC: Pink.			
	a. Issued note.	175	450	—
	r. Remainder with stub.	—	—	—

Decreto 10.11.1885

		Good	Fine	XF
11	**10 Centavos** *D.1885.* Red. Purple handstamps. Uniface. Back: Purple handstamps. Printer: Local printing.	—	—	—
12	**10 Centavos** *D.1885.* Black. Arms at upper left. Uniface. Series VIII. Back: Purple handstamps of *Secretaria de Hacienda,* facsimile signature of *EL TESORERO* Printer: HLBNC.			
	a. Issued note.	175	450	—
	r. Remainder with stub.	—	—	—
12A	**50 Centavos** *D. 1885.* Uniface. Printer: Local printing.	—	—	—

Decreto 20.3.1886

		Good	Fine	XF
13	**20 Centavos** *D.1886.* Series VII.	—	—	—
14	**50 Centavos** *D.1886.* Series VI.	—	—	—
15	**1 Peso** *D.1886.* Series I.	—	—	—

Decreto 12.10.1894

		Good	Fine	XF
16	**5 Centavos** ND (1894). Black on blue-green underprint. Without decreto. Series 9. Back: Dark green. Printer: Local printing.	25.00	85.00	225

		Good	Fine	XF
17	**10 Centavos** *D.1894.* Dark brown on orange and green underprint. Arms at upper left. Series XI. Back: Brown. Printer: Paydt, Upham & Co. S.F.			
	a. Red signature.	25.00	75.00	200
	b. Black signature.	17.50	65.00	175
18	**20 Centavos** *D.1894.* Dark brown on brown and green underprint. Arms at upper left. Series X. Back: Green. Printer: Paydt, Upham & Co. S.F.	Good	Fine	XF
	a. 2 signature varieties.	30.00	100	250
	b. Without signature.	—	—	—

		Good	Fine	XF
19	**50 Centavos** *D.1894.* Dark brown on green and tan underprint. Arms at upper left. Series I; 6; IX. Back: Blue. Printer: Paydt, Upham & Co. S.F.			
	a. *Series I* at top, blue serial #. 2 signature varieties.	35.00	110	250
	b. *Series 6* at top, red serial #. 3 signature varieties.	35.00	110	250
	c. *Series IX* at top, red serial #. 2 signature varieties.	35.00	125	275
	d. Like c., but without signature	30.00	100	200

1894 Commemorative Issue

#20-23A, 402nd Anniversary of the Discovery of America.

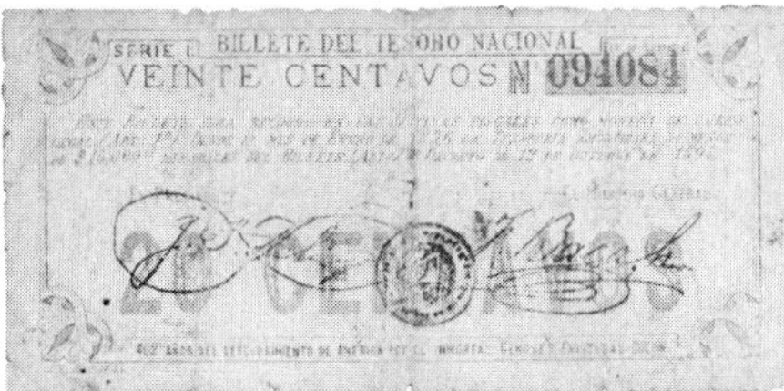

		Good	Fine	XF
20	**20 Centavos** *D.1894.* Blue. Series 1. Back: Seated Liberty at left looking at five mountains and sunrise at right. BC: Black on brown underprint. Printer: Local printing. Rare.	—	—	—
21	**50 Centavos** *D.1894.* Black on light tan underprint. Back: Seated Liberty at left looking at five mountains and sunrise at right. BC: Black on green underprint. Printer: Local printing. Rare.	—	—	—

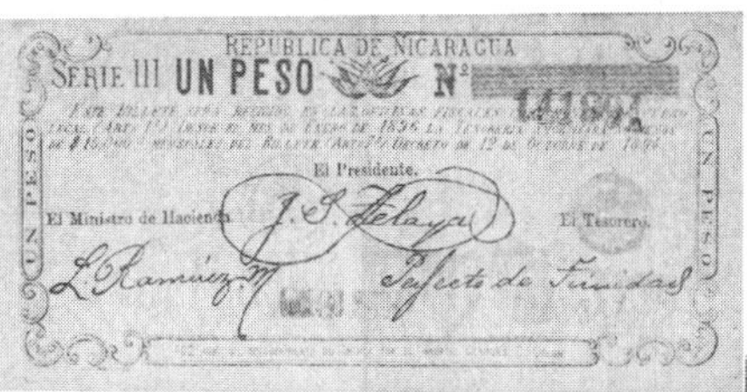
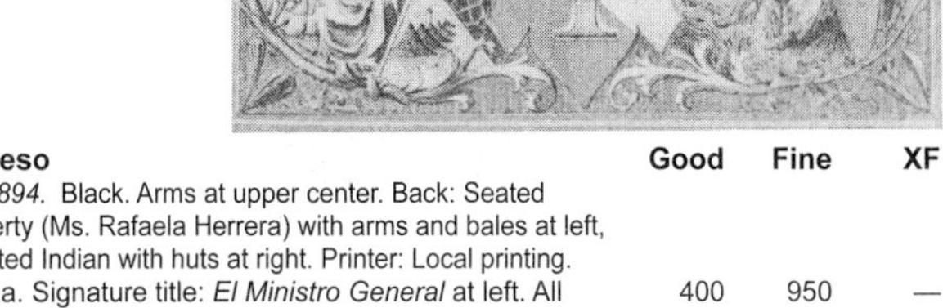

		Good	Fine	XF
22	**1 Peso** *D.1894.* Black. Arms at upper center. Back: Seated Liberty (Ms. Rafaela Herrera) with arms and bales at left, seated Indian with huts at right. Printer: Local printing.			
	a. Signature title: *El Ministro General* at left. All titles in small lettering.	400	950	—
	b. Signature title: *El Ministro de Hacienda* at left. All titles in large lettering.	400	950	—

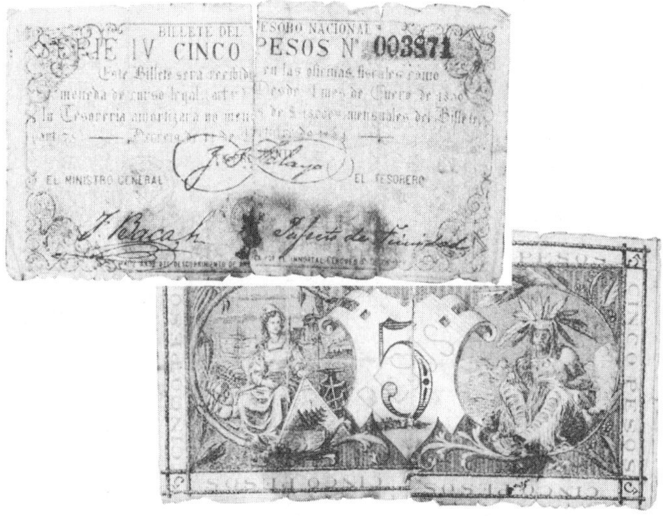

		Good	Fine	XF
23	**5 Pesos** *D. 1894.* Black and red. Back: Seated Liberty (Ms. Herrera) with arms at left, Chief Nicarao at right. Printer: Local printing. Rare.	—	—	—
23A	**10 Pesos** *D. 1894.* Black and orange. Back: Arms. Printer: Local printing. Rare.	—	—	—

1894 Issue

		Good	Fine	XF
24	**1 Peso** *D.1894.* Black. Portrait Simon Bolivár at center, arms in blue at lower right. Back: Arms at center. BC: Dark green.			
	a. *Series No. VII.* Imprint: *Paydt Upham & Co. S.F.*	225	500	—
	b. *Series No. VIII.* Imprint: *Lith. Paydt Upham & Co. S.F.* 2 signature varieties.	200	450	—
	r. Remainder without signature.	175	425	—

No.	Description	Good	Fine	XF
25	**5 Pesos** *D.1894.* Black on pink and light blue underprint. Portrait Herrera at upper left, arms at lower right. Series III. Back: Arms at center. BC: Green.	225	500	—

No.	Description	Good	Fine	XF
26	**10 Pesos** *D.1894.* Black. Red arms at center; portrait Jerez at right. Series IV. Back: Inverted; arms at center. BC: Blue. Printer: Lith. Paydt, Upham & Co. S.F.			
	a. Signature titles: *El Ministro General* and *El Tesorero.*	400	1,000	—
	b. overprint signature titles: *El Ministro de Hacienda* and *El Tesorero General.*	400	1,000	—
27	**50 Pesos** *D.1894.* Black on green underprint. Portrait Morazán at left. Series V. Back: Arms at center. BC: Light brown.			
	a. Issued note.	—	—	—
	r. Unsigned remainder.	—	—	—

1900 Issue

No.	Description	Good	Fine	XF
28	**50 Centavos** 15.9.1900. Black on blue and red underprint. Woman seated at center. Back: Arms. BC: Blue. Printer: W&S.	25.00	85.00	275

No.	Description	Good	Fine	XF
29	**1 Peso** 15.9.1900. Black on green and gold underprint. Portrait Jerez at left, cattle at right. Back: Arms. BC: Brown. Printer: W&S.			
	a. Issued note.	30.00	150	400
	s. Specimen. Yellow and orange; back green.	—	—	—

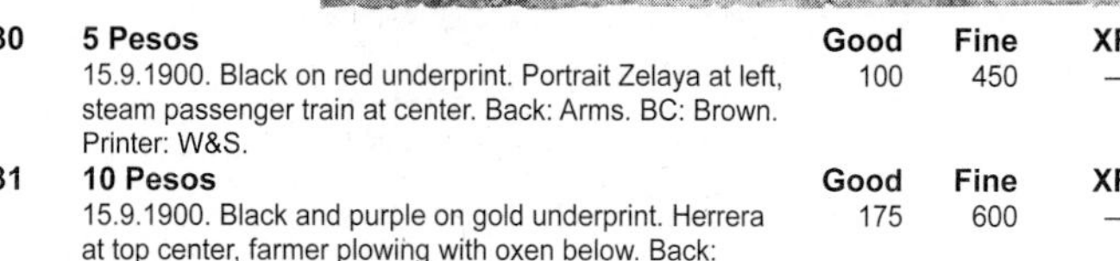

No.	Description	Good	Fine	XF
30	**5 Pesos** 15.9.1900. Black on red underprint. Portrait Zelaya at left, steam passenger train at center. Back: Arms. BC: Brown. Printer: W&S.	100	450	—
31	**10 Pesos** 15.9.1900. Black and purple on gold underprint. Herrera at top center, farmer plowing with oxen below. Back: Arms. BC: Dull purple. Printer: W&S.	175	600	—
32	**25 Pesos** 15.9.1900. Black on blue-green underprint. Portrait D. F. Morazán at left, Liberty in winged chariot drawn by lions at center. Back: Arms. BC: Pale green. Printer: W&S.	—	—	—

No.	Description	Good	Fine	XF
33	**50 Pesos** 15.9.1900. Black on yellow and orange underprint. Liberty and portrait Simon Bolívar at left. Back: Arms. BC: Brown. Printer: W&S. Specimen.	—	—	—

1906-1908 Issue

No.	Description	Good	Fine	XF
34	**50 Centavos** 1.1.1906. Black on red and green underprint. Allegorical woman seated with sword and trumpet at left. Back: Arms at center. BC: Blue. Printer: Waterlow Bros. & Layton, Ltd., London.	12.50	60.00	200

		Good	Fine	XF
35	**1 Peso** 1.1.1906. Black on red and orange underprint. Two women and child gathering fruit at upper left, portrait woman at right. Back: Arms at center. BC: Brown. Printer: Waterlow Bros. & Layton Ltd., London.	15.00	90.00	225

		Good	Fine	XF
36	**5 Pesos** 1.1.1908. Black on tan and purple underprint. Steam locomotive at left, portrait Zelaya at center right. Back: Arms at right. BC: Orange. Printer: Waterlow Bros. & Layton, Ltd., London.	200	700	—

		Good	Fine	XF
37	**10 Pesos** 1.1.1908. Red and brown. Portrait Gen. D. M. Jerez at left. Back: Arms at right. BC: Purple. Printer: Waterlow Bros. & Layton, Ltd., London.	300	1,000	—

		Good	Fine	XF
38	**50 Pesos** 1.1.1908. Black on yellow and green underprint. Portrait Simon Bolívar at left, man with ox-cart at center. Back: Arms at right. BC: Brown. Printer: Waterlow Bros. & Layton, Ltd., London.	—	—	—

		Good	Fine	XF
39	**100 Pesos** 1.1.1908. Black on green and tan underprint. Seated woman at left, equestrian statue of Nicarao at right. Back: Green. Printer: Waterlow Bros. & Layton, Ltd., London. Rare.	—	—	—

1909 Issue

		Good	Fine	XF
40	**50 Pesos** *D.24.11.1909.* Black on red underprint, blue border. Portrait J.S. Zelaya at left. Back: Arms at center. Printer: Local printing. Rare.	—	—	—

1910 Provisional Issue

		Good	Fine	XF
41	**5 Pesos** *D.3.2.1910.* Portrait Dr. J. Madriz at left. Printer: Local printing.	200	600	—

		Good	Fine	XF
42	**5 Pesos** *D.3.3.1910.* Black on blue and light red underprint. Back: Arms at center. Printer: Local printing.	200	600	—

1911 Issue (dated 1910)

		Good	Fine	XF
43	**50 Centavos** 1.1.1910. Black on green and multicolor underprint. Portrait Christopher Columbus at right. Series A. Signature varieties. Back: Dark green. Printer: ABNC.			
	a. Center signature Pres. *José Madriz.*	15.00	40.00	150
	b. Center signature Pres. *Juan J. Estrada.*	15.00	40.00	150
	s. Specimen.	—	Unc	275

		Good	Fine	XF
44	**1 Peso** 1.1.1910. Black on orange-brown underprint. Portrait Christopher Columbus at left. Signature varieties. Series B. Back: Orange. Printer: ABNC.			
	a. Center signature Pres. *José Madriz.*	15.00	50.00	175
	b. Center signature Pres. *Juan J. Estrada.*	15.00	50.00	175
	s. Specimen.	—	Unc	250

		Good	Fine	XF
45	**5 Pesos** 1.1.1910. Black on blue and multicolor underprint. Seated woman at left, portrait Christopher Columbus at center right. Series C. Signature varieties. Back: Dark blue. Printer: ABNC.			
	a. Center signature Pres. *José Madriz.*	50.00	200	500
	b. Center signature Pres. *Juan J. Estrada.*	50.00	200	500
	s. Specimen.	—	Unc	750
46	**10 Pesos** 1.1.1910. Black on red and multicolor underprint. Woman and child at left, portrait Christopher Columbus at right. Signature varieties. Series D. Back: Red-brown. Printer: ABNC.	**Good**	**Fine**	**XF**
	a. Center signature Pres. *José Madriz.*	100	400	—
	b. Center signature Pres. *Juan J. Estrada.*	100	400	—
	p. Proof.	—	Unc	500
	s. Specimen.	—	Unc	750

		Good	Fine	XF
47	**25 Pesos** 1.1.1910. Black on multicolor underprint. Portrait Christopher Columbus at left, arms at center. Signature varieties. Series E. Back: Olive. Back: Monument at center. Printer: ABNC.			
	a. Center signature Pres. *José Madriz.*	175	550	—
	b. Center signature Pres. *Juan J. Estrada.*	175	550	—
	s. Specimen.	—	Unc	900
48	**50 Pesos** 1.1.1910. Black on purple and multicolor underprint. Arms at center, portrait Christopher Columbus at right. Signature varieties. Series F. Back: Purple. Back: Large building at center. Printer: ABNC.	**Good**	**Fine**	**XF**
	a. Center signature Pres. *José Madriz.* Rare.	—	—	—
	b. Center signature Pres. *Juan J. Estrada.* Reported not confirmed.	—	—	—
	s1. Signature as a. Specimen.	—	Unc	1,500
	s2. Signature as b. Specimen.	—	Unc	2,250
49	**100 Pesos** 1.1.1910. Black on orange and multicolor underprint. Portrait Christopher Columbus at left center, arms at right. Series G. Back: Red. Back: Gateway to government building at center.	**Good**	**Fine**	**XF**
	a. Center signature Pres. *José Madriz.* Rare.	—	—	—
	b. Center signature Pres *Juan J. Estrada.* Rare.	—	—	—
	s. Specimen.	—	Unc	1,750

1912 ND Provisional Issue

Overprint: *ESTE BILLETE VALE ... CENTAVOS DE CÓRDOBA* vertically in red on face.

		Good	Fine	XF
50	**4 (Cuatro) Centavos on 50 Centavos** ND (-old date 1.1.1910). Overprint: *ESTE BILLETE VALE...CENTAVOS DE CORDOBA* vertically in red of face of 43b.	35.00	120	250

		Good	Fine	XF
51	**8 (Ocho) Centavos on 1 Peso** ND (-old date 1.1.1910). Overprint: *ESTE BILLETE VALE...CENTAVOS DE CORDOBA* vertically in red of face of 44b.	40.00	150	300

Banco Nacional de Nicaragua

Ley de 20 de Marzo de 1912

#52-54 fractional notes without date.

		Good	Fine	XF
52	**10 Centavos** *L.1912.* Black on green underprint. Portrait Liberty at left. Back: Green. Back: Arms at center. Printer: ABNC.			
	a. Without prefix. Presidente signature *Adolfo Diaz* (Oct. 1914).	8.00	25.00	75.00
	b. Prefix A. Presidente signature as a.	8.00	25.00	75.00
	c. Prefix B. Presidente signature *E. Chamorro* (Oct. 1918).	8.00	25.00	75.00
	d. Prefix C. Presidente signature *Diego M. Chamorro.* (July 1922).	12.00	40.00	100
	e. Prefix D. Presidente signature as d.	6.00	20.00	50.00
	f. Prefix E. Presidente signature *Emiliano Chamorro* (Sept. 1926).	6.00	20.00	50.00
	s. Specimen.	—	Unc	175

		Good	Fine	XF
53	**25 Centavos**	**Good**	**Fine**	**XF**
	L. 1912. Black on orange underprint. Portrait Liberty at right. Back: Arms at center. BC: Orange. Printer: ABNC.			
	a. Without prefix. Presidente signature *Adolfo Diaz* (Oct. 1914). Red serial #.	10.00	35.00	75.00
	b. Prefix A. Presidente signature *E. Chamorro* (Oct. 1918). Blue serial #.	10.00	40.00	90.00
	s. Specimen.	—	Unc	175
54	**50 Centavos**	**Good**	**Fine**	**XF**
	L. 1912. Black on blue underprint. Portrait Liberty at left. Red serial #. Back: Arms at center. BC: Gray. Printer: ABNC.			
	a. Without prefix. Presidente signature *Adolfo Diaz* (Oct. 1914).	12.50	40.00	100
	b. Prefix A. Presidente signature *E. Chamorro* (Oct. 1918).	15.00	50.00	125
	s. Specimen.	—	Unc	175

Note: For similar issues but with later dates see #85-89.

		Good	Fine	XF
55	**1 Córdoba**	**Good**	**Fine**	**XF**
	L. 1912. Black on green underprint. Portrait Nicarao at lower right. Portrait Cordoba at left. Back: Arms at center. BC: Green. Printer: HBNC. Larger note.			
	a. Without prefix. Presidente signature *Adolfo Diaz* (Oct. 1914). Red serial #.	100	300	—
	b. Prefix A. Presidente signature *E. Chamorro* (Oct. 1918). Blue serial #.	100	300	—
	c. Prefix B. Presidente signature *Carlos José Solózano.*	150	500	—
	s. Specimen. Presidente signature *Carlos José Solózano.*	—	—	—

		Good	Fine	XF
56	**2 Córdobas**	**Good**	**Fine**	**XF**
	L. 1912. Black on brown underprint. Portrait De la Cerda at right. Portrait Cordoba at left. Back: Arms at center. BC: Maroon. Printer: HBNC.			
	a. Without prefix. Presidente signature *Adolfo Diaz* (Oct. 1914).	—	—	—
	b. Prefix A. Presidente signature *E. Chamorro* (Oct. 1918).	150	500	—
	s. Specimen.	—	—	—

		Good	Fine	XF
57	**5 Córdobas**	**Good**	**Fine**	**XF**
	L. 1912. Portrait Larreynaga at right. Portrait Cordoba at left. Printer: HBNC. Larger note.			
	a. Issued note.	—	—	—
	s. Specimen.	—	—	—

		Good	Fine	XF
58	**10 Córdobas**	**Good**	**Fine**	**XF**
	L. 1912. Black on orange underprint. Portrait Chamerra at right. Portrait Cordoba at left. Back: Orange. Printer: HBNC. Larger note.			
	a. Issued note.	—	—	—
	p. Proof. Back only.	—	—	100
	s. Specimen.	—	—	—
59	**20 Córdobas**	**Good**	**Fine**	**XF**
	L. 1912. Portrait Martinez at right. Portrait Cordoba at left. Printer: HBNC. Larger note.			
	a. Issued note.	—	—	—
	s. Specimen.	—	—	—
60	**50 Córdobas**	**Good**	**Fine**	**XF**
	L. 1912. Portrait Estrada at right. Portrait Cordoba at left. Printer: HBNC. Larger note.			
	a. Issued note.	—	—	—
	s. Specimen.	—	—	—

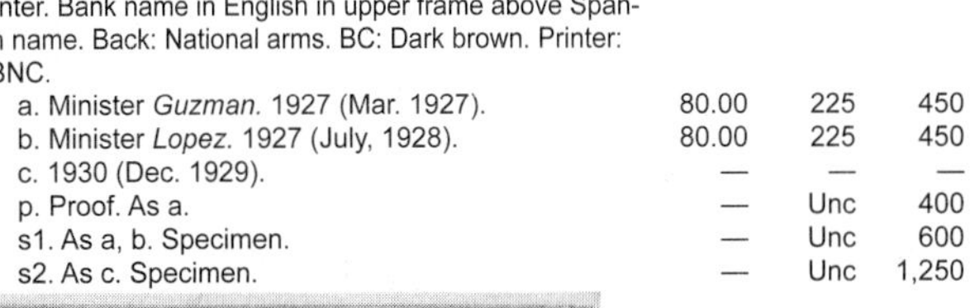

		Good	Fine	XF
61	**100 Córdobas**	**Good**	**Fine**	**XF**
	L. 1912. Palm trees, Lake Managua and volcano at center. Portrait Corboda at left. Printer: HBNC. Larger note.			
	a. Issued note.	—	—	—
	p. Proof. Face only.	—	—	800
	s. Specimen.	—	—	—

1927-1939 Issue

		Good	Fine	XF
62	**1 Córdoba**	**Good**	**Fine**	**XF**
	1927; 1930. Green on multicolor underprint. Woman at center. Bank name in English in upper frame above Spanish name. Back: National arms. BC: Dark brown. Printer: ABNC.			
	a. Minister *Guzman.* 1927 (Mar. 1927).	80.00	225	450
	b. Minister *Lopez.* 1927 (July, 1928).	80.00	225	450
	c. 1930 (Dec. 1929).	—	—	—
	p. Proof. As a.	—	Unc	400
	s1. As a, b. Specimen.	—	Unc	600
	s2. As c. Specimen.	—	Unc	1,250

		Good	Fine	XF
63	**1 Córdoba**	**Good**	**Fine**	**XF**
	1932-1939. Blue on multicolor underprint. Woman at center. Bank name in English in upper frame above Spanish name. Back: National arms. BC: Olive brown. Printer: ABNC.			
	a. 1932.	20.00	75.00	225
	b. 1937; 1938; 1939.	8.00	30.00	100
	s. Specimen.	—	Unc	400

		Good	Fine	XF
64	**2 Córdobas** 1939. Green on multicolor underprint. Ox-cart in front of sugar cane mill at left. Bank name in English in upper frame above Spanish name. Back: National arms. BC: Red-orange. Printer: ABNC.			
	a. Issued note.	10.00	50.00	200
	s. Specimen.	—	Unc	275

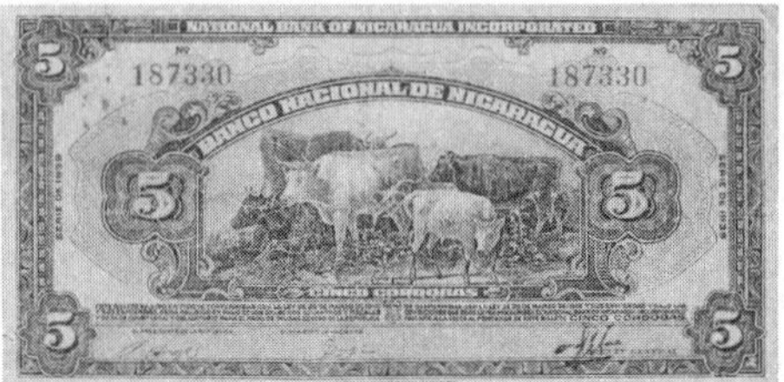

		Good	Fine	XF
65	**5 Córdobas** 1927-1939. Gray on multicolor underprint. Cattle at center. Bank name in English in upper frame above Spanish name. Back: National arms. BC: Brown. Printer: ABNC.			
	a. 1927.	—	—	—
	b. 1938; 1939.	8.50	50.00	225
	p. Proof.	—	Unc	500
	s1. 1927. Specimen.	—	Unc	1,000
	s2. 1938-1939. Specimen.	—	Unc	400

		Good	Fine	XF
66	**10 Córdobas** 1929-1939. Brown on multicolor underprint. Portrait Liberty at right. Bank name in English in upper frame above Spanish name. Back: National arms. BC: Carmine. Printer: ABNC.			
	a. 1929.	—	—	—
	b. 1938; 1939.	22.50	100	325
	s1. 1929. Specimen.	—	Unc	1,000
	s2. 1938; 1939. Specimen.	—	Unc	500

		Good	Fine	XF
67	**20 Córdobas** 1929-1939. Orange on multicolor underprint. Bay and port of Corinto. Bank name in English in upper frame above Spanish name. Back: National arms. BC: Blue. Printer: ABNC.			
	a. 1929.	—	—	—
	b. 1937; 1939.	60.00	300	—
	s1. 1929. Specimen, punch hole cancelled.	—	Unc	1,500
	s2. 1937; 1939. Specimen.	—	Unc	500

		Good	Fine	XF
68	**50 Córdobas** 1929; 1937; 1939. Purple on multicolor underprint. Two women with wheat laureates at left. Bank name in English in upper frame above Spanish name. Back: National arms. BC: Orange. Printer: ABNC.			
	a. Issued note.	—	—	—
	s1. 1929. Specimen, punch hole cancelled.	—	Unc	750
	s2. 1937; 1939. Specimen.	—	Unc	1,250

		Good	Fine	XF
69	**100 Córdobas** 1939. Red on multicolor underprint. Woman with fruits before altar at right. Bank name in English in upper frame above Spanish name. Back: National arms. BC: Dark olive brown. Printer: ABNC.			
	a. Issued note.	—	—	—
	s. Specimen.	—	Unc	1,250

1934 ND Revalidation

The Decree of January 2, 1934, ordered all circulating notes to be exchanged against new notes with red overprint: *REVALIDADO.* The overprint was printed on notes in stock in the vaults of the Banco Nacioral de Nicaragua.

		Good	Fine	XF
70	**1 Córdoba** ND *(D.1934)*. Overprint: *REVALIDADO* on #62.	25.00	100	300

		Good	Fine	XF
71	**1 Córdoba** ND *(D.1934)*. Overprint: *REVALIDADO* on #63a.	20.00	100	250
72	**5 Córdobas** ND *(D.1934)*. Overprint: *REVALIDADO* on #65a.	30.00	150	—

		Good	Fine	XF
73	**10 Córdobas** ND *(D.1934)*. Overprint: *REVALIDADO* on #58.	100	400	—
74	**10 Córdobas** ND *(D.1934)*. Overprint: *REVALIDADO* on #66a.	75.00	325	—
75	**20 Córdobas** ND *(D.1934)*. Overprint: *REVALIDADO* on #59.	—	—	—
76	**20 Córdobas** ND *(D.1934)*. Overprint: *REVALIDADO* on #67a.	—	—	—

		Good	Fine	XF
77	**50 Córdobas** ND *(D.1934)*. Overprint: *REVALIDADO* on #68.	—	—	—
78	**100 Córdobas** ND *(D.1934)*. Overprint: *REVALIDADO* on #61.	—	—	—

Note: The old notes without overprint became worthless on June 1, 1934. Later dates (1937-1939) of the 2nd issue were put into circulation without overprint. No 2 Cordobas notes or fractional currency notes were issued with overprint.

1935-1938 Issue

		Good	Fine	XF
79	**10 Centavos** 1938. Black on green underprint. Portrait Liberty at left. Back: Arms at center. BC: Green. Printer: HBNC.	4.50	30.00	100

		Good	Fine	XF
80	**25 Centavos** 1938. Black on orange underprint. Portrait Liberty at right. Back: Arms at center. BC: Orange. Printer: HBNC.	6.00	40.00	150

		Good	Fine	XF
81	**50 Centavos** 1938. Black on dark blue underprint. Portrait Liberty at left. Back: Arms at center. BC: Blue. Printer: HBNC.	10.00	60.00	225

		Good	Fine	XF
82	**1 Córdoba** 1935; 1938. Blue on peach underprint. Two allegories people on cliff above sea at center. Back: Arms at center. BC: Green. Printer: HBNC.	20.00	100	325
83	**5 Córdobas** 1935. Black on light green and red underprint. Woman's head at center. Back: Arms at center. BC: Brown. Printer: HBNC.	35.00	175	475

		Good	Fine	XF
84	**10 Córdobas** 1935. Brown on purple and green underprint. Palm trees, lake and volcano at center. Back: Arms at center. BC: Carmine. Printer: ABNC.	70.00	350	—

1937 ND Issue

		Good	Fine	XF
85	**10 Centavos** ND (1937). Portrait Liberty. Similar to #87 but without the 6 lines of text on face referring to Law of 1912. Back: Arms at center. Printer: ABNC.			
	a. Signature title: *DIRECTOR GERENTE* at bottom.	4.00	15.00	60.00
	b. Signature title: *GERENTE GENERAL* at bottom.	5.00	20.00	75.00
	s. As a or b. Specimen.	—	Unc	150
86	**25 Centavos** ND (1937). Portrait Liberty. Similar to #88 but without text on face referring to Law of 1912. Back: Arms at center. Printer: ABNC.			
	a. Signature title: *DIRECTOR GERENTE* at bottom.	5.00	20.00	85.00
	b. Signature title: *GERENTE GENERAL* at bottom.	25.00	100	250
	s. As a or b. Specimen.	—	Unc	150

1938 Issue

		Good	Fine	XF
87	**10 Centavos** 1938. Black on green underprint. Portrait Liberty at left. Like #52. Back: Arms at center. BC: Green. Printer: ABNC.			
	a. Issued note.	3.50	20.00	75.00
	p. Proof.	—	Unc	300
	s. Specimen.	—	Unc	150
88	**25 Centavos** 1938. Black on orange underprint. Portrait Liberty at right. Like #53. Back: Arms at center. BC: Orange. Printer: ABNC.			
	a. Issued note.	4.50	25.00	100
	p. Proof.	—	Unc	200
	s. Specimen.	—	Unc	150

	89 50 Centavos	Good	Fine	XF
	1938. Black on blue underprint. Portrait Liberty at left. Like #54. Back: Arms at center. BC: Gray. Printer: ABNC.			
	a. Issued note.	6.50	60.00	150
	p. Proof.	—	Unc	400
	s. Specimen.	—	Unc	300

1941-1945 Issue

The English bank name in upper frame has been removed.

	90 1 Córdoba	VG	VF	UNC
	1941-1945. Blue on multicolor underprint. Portrait Indian girl wearing feather at center. Back: *SERIE DE* (date) engraved and printed in blue. BC: Dark olive-brown. Printer: ABNC.			
	a. 1941.	1.00	7.50	25.00
	b. 1942; 1945.	2.00	20.00	75.00
	p. Proof.	—	—	400
	s1. 1941; 1942. Specimen.	—	—	250
	s2. 1945. Specimen.	—	—	150

	91 1 Córdoba	VG	VF	UNC
	1949; 1951. Portrait Indian girl wearing feather at center, *SERIE DE* (date) typographed and printed in red. Printer: ABNC.			
	a. 1949.	2.00	12.50	75.00
	b. 1951.	1.50	7.50	50.00
	s. As a or b. Specimen.	—	—	150

	92 2 Córdobas	VG	VF	UNC
	1941; 1945. Green on multicolor underprint. Ox-cart in front of sugar cane mill at left. Like #64. Back: Red-orange. Printer: ABNC.			
	a. 1941.	4.00	50.00	150
	b. 1945.	3.00	40.00	125
	p. Proof.	—	—	500
	s1. 1941. Specimen.	—	—	225
	s2. 1945. Specimen.	—	—	150

	93 5 Córdobas	VG	VF	UNC
	1942; 1945; 1951. Gray on multicolor underprint. Cattle at center. Similar to #65. Back: Brown. Printer: ABNC.			
	a. 1942.	5.00	30.00	150
	b. 1945.	4.50	25.00	120
	c. 1951.	4.00	20.00	100
	s. Specimen.	—	—	175

	94 10 Córdobas	VG	VF	UNC
	1942; 1945; 1951. Brown on multicolor underprint. Portrait Liberty at right. Similar to #66. Printer: ABNC.			
	a. 1942.	15.00	75.00	350
	b. 1945.	12.50	60.00	300
	c. 1951.	10.00	50.00	250
	s1. 1942. Specimen.	—	—	275
	s2. 1945; 1951. Specimen.	—	—	200

	95 20 Córdobas	VG	VF	UNC
	1942; 1945; 1951. Orange on multicolor underprint. Bay and port of Corinto. Similar to #67. Printer: ABNC.			
	a. 1942.	35.00	200	650
	b. 1945.	30.00	175	600
	c. 1951.	25.00	150	550
	s1. 1942. Specimen.	—	—	500
	s2. 1945; 1951. Specimen.	—	—	350

	96 50 Córdobas	VG	VF	UNC
	1942; 1945. Purple on multicolor underprint. Two women with wheat laureates at left. Similar to #68. Back: Orange. Printer: ABNC.			
	a. 1942.	75.00	300	—
	b. 1945. 2 signature varieties for the right hand signature.	30.00	75.00	150
	s1. Specimen. 1942.	—	—	375
	s2. Specimen. 1945.	—	—	250

	97 100 Córdobas	VG	VF	UNC
	1941; 1942; 1945. Red on multicolor underprint. Woman with fruits before altar at right. Similar to #69. Back: Dark olive brown. Printer: ABNC.			
	a. 1941; 1942.	150	450	—
	b. 1945. 2 signature varieties for the right hand signature.	125	425	—
	s. Specimen.	—	—	700

		VG	VF	UNC
98	**500 Córdobas** 1945. Black on multicolor underprint. Portrait right. Dario at center. 2 signature varieties for right hand signature. Back: Green. Printer: ABNC.			
	a. Issued note.	100	225	425
	s. Specimen.	—	—	1,250

1953-1954 Issue

#99-106, all notes except #105 and 106 come in two date varieties:
a. *SERIE DE* (date) engraved, printed in note color. 1953-1958.
b. *SERIE DE* (date) typographed, printed in black. 1959-1960. Printer: TDLR.

		VG	VF	UNC
99	**1 Córdoba** 1953-1960. Dark blue on multicolor underprint. Portrait Indian girl wearing feather at center. Back: Bank.			
	a. Engraved date. 1953; 1954.	2.50	12.50	60.00
	b. Engraved date. 1957; 1958.	2.00	10.00	50.00
	c. Typographed date. 1959; 1960.	1.50	7.50	35.00
	s. Specimen. 1953; 1954.	—	—	500

		VG	VF	UNC
100	**5 Córdobas** 1953-1960. Dark green on multicolor underprint. C. Nicarao at center. Back: Carved statue at center. Arms at right.			
	a. Engraved date. 1953.	20.00	100	250
	b. Engraved date. 1954; 1957; 1958.	12.50	60.00	175
	c. Typographed date. 1959; 1960.	5.00	50.00	150
	s. Specimen. 1953; 1954; 1957.	—	—	500

		VG	VF	UNC
101	**10 Córdobas** 1953-1960. Red on multicolor underprint. Arms at left, portrait M. de Larreynaga at right. Back: Independence meeting.			
	a. Engraved date. 1953; 1954; 1957; 1958.	10.00	75.00	350
	b. Typographed date. 1959; 1960.	7.50	60.00	250
	s. Specimen. 1953; 1954.	—	—	500

		VG	VF	UNC
102	**20 Córdobas** 1953-1960. Orange-brown on multicolor underprint. Scene with R. Herrera at center. Back: Map.			
	a. Engraved date. 1953; 1954; 1957; 1958.	15.00	150	550
	b. Typographed date. 1959; 1960.	10.00	125	500
	s. Specimen. 1953; 1954.	—	—	500

		VG	VF	UNC
103	**50 Córdobas** 1953-1960. Dark blue on multicolor underprint. Portrait M. Jerez at left, Gen. T. Martinez at right. Back: Flag.			
	a. Engraved date. 1953; 1954; 1957; 1958.	40.00	200	800
	b. Typographed date. 1959; 1960.	30.00	150	750
	s. Specimen. 1953; 1954.	—	—	500
104	**100 Córdobas** 1953-1960. Purple on multicolor underprint. Portrait J. Dolores Estrada at right. Back: National Palace.	**VG**	**VF**	**UNC**
	a. Engraved date. 1953; 1954; 1957; 1958.	30.00	175	700
	b. Typographed date. 1959; 1960.	20.00	100	600
	s. Specimen. 1953; 1954; 1957.	—	—	500

		VG	VF	UNC
105	**500 Córdobas** 1953-1954. Black on multicolor underprint. Portrait right. Dario at center Back: Monument in Dario Park at center.			
	a. Engraved date. 1953; 1954.	150	650	—
	s. Specimen. 1953; 1954.	—	—	500

		VG	VF	UNC
106	**1000 Córdobas** 1953-1954. Brown on multicolor underprint. Portrait Pres. Gen. A. Somoza at lower left, arms at right. Back: Stadium.			
	a. Engraved date. 1953; 1954.	175	700	—
	b. Decree Issue 1959.	—	—	—
	c. Decree Issue 1960.	—	—	—
	s. Specimen. 1953; 1954.	—	—	500

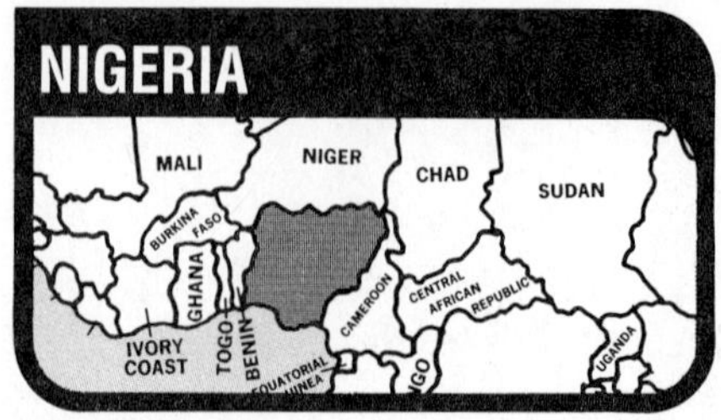

The Federal Republic of Nigeria, situated on the Atlantic coast of Africa between Benin and Cameroon, has an area of 356,667 sq. mi. (923,768 sq. km.) and a population of 128.79 million. Capital: Abuja. The economy is based on petroleum and agriculture. Crude oil, cocoa, tobacco and tin are exported. British influence and control over what would become Nigeria and Africa's most populous country grew through the 19th century. A series of constitutions after World War II granted Nigeria greater autonomy; independence came in 1960. Following nearly 16 years of military rule, a new constitution was adopted in 1999, and a peaceful transition to civilian government was completed. The government continues to face the daunting task of reforming a petroleum-based economy, whose revenues have been squandered through corruption and mismanagement, and institutionalizing democracy. In addition, Nigeria continues to experience longstanding ethnic and religious tensions. Although both the 2003 and 2007 presidential elections were marred by significant irregularities and violence, Nigeria is currently experiencing its longest period of civilian rule since independence. The general elections of April 2007 marked the first civilian-to-civilian transfer of power in the country's history.

RULERS:

British to 1963

MONETARY SYSTEM:

1 Shilling = 12 Pence
1 Pound = 20 Shillings to 1973
1 Naira (10 Shillings) = 100 Kobo, 1973-

BRITISH ADMINISTRATION

Government of Nigeria

1918 WW I Emergency Issue

		Good	Fine	XF
1	**1 Shilling** Dec. 1918. Green. Text: *issued under Ord. XXII, 1918* at upper left and right.	400	1,200	2,500
1A	**10 Shillings** Dec. 1918. Red. Text: *issued under Ord. XXII, 1918* at upper left and right. Rare.	—	—	—

		Good	Fine	XF
1B	**20 Shillings** Dec. 1918. Black. Text: *issued under Ord. XXII, 1918* at upper left and right. Rare.	—	—	—

Note: This issue was printed locally to alleviate a shortage of silver coins after the end of WWI.

FEDERATION OF NIGERIA

Central Bank of Nigeria

1958 Issue

		VG	VF	UNC
2	**5 Shillings** 15.9.1958. Lilac and blue-green. River scene and palm trees. Back: Palms. BC: Lilac. Printer: W&S.			
	a. Issued note.	5.00	25.00	75.00
	s. Specimen.	—	—	250
	ct. Color Trial. Brown and green on multicolor underprint.	—	—	250

		VG	VF	UNC
3	**10 Shillings** 15.9.1958. Green and brown. River scene and palm trees. Back: Crop sowing and man with produce. BC: Green. Printer: W&S.			
	a. Issued note.	10.00	65.00	275
	s. Specimen.	—	—	—

		VG	VF	UNC
4	**1 Pound** 15.9.1958. Red and dark brown. River scene and palm trees. Back: Harvesting coconuts. BC: Red. Printer: W&S.			
	a. Issued note.	1.50	6.00	35.00
	s. Specimen.	—	—	350
	ct. Color Trial. Blue on multicolor underprint.	—	—	350

		VG	VF	UNC
5	**5 Pounds** 15.9.1958. Dark green on green and purple underprint. River scene and palm trees. Back: Fruit farming at right. BC: Purple. Printer: W&S.			
	a. Issued note.	15.00	75.00	350
	s. Specimen.	—	—	—

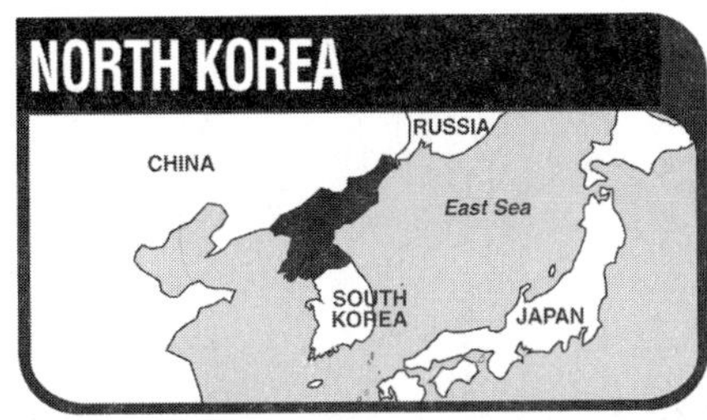

The Democratic Peoples Republic of Korea, situated in northeastern Asia on the northern half of the Korean peninsula between the Peoples Republic of China and the Republic of Korea, has an area of 46,540 sq. mi. (120,538 sq. km.) and an estimated population approaching 25 million. Capital: Pyongyang. The economy is based on heavily on industry. Coal briquettes are proportionally one of the largest exports followed by iron ore and concentrates. Japan replaced China as the predominant foreign influence in Korea in 1895 and annexed the peninsular country in 1910. Defeat in World War II brought an end to Japanese rule. U.S. troops entered Korea from the south and Soviet forces entered from the north. The Cairo conference (1943) had established that Korea should be "free and independent." The Potsdam conference (1945) set the 38th parallel as the line dividing the occupation forces of the United States and Russia. When Russia refused to permit a U.N. commission designated to supervise reunification elections to enter North Korea, an election was held in South Korea which established the Republic of Korea on Aug. 15, 1948. North Korea held an unsupervised election on Aug. 25, 1948, and on the following day proclaimed the establishment of the Democratic Peoples Republic of Korea.

MONETARY SYSTEM:

1 Won = 100 Chon

SOVIET MILITARY OCCUPATION

Russian Army Headquarters

1945 Issue

#	Description	VG	VF	UNC
1	**1 Won** 1945. Green on light brown underprint.	100	175	300
2	**5 Won** 1945. Brown on blue underprint.	150	300	600
3	**10 Won** 1945. Violet on light green underprint.	200	400	800

#	Description	VG	VF	UNC
4	**100 Won** 1945. Red on gray underprint.			
	a. Watermark, serial # 17mm long.	300	700	1,500
	b. Without watermark, serial # 15 mm long.	300	700	1,500

North Korea Central Bank

1947 Issues

#	Description	VG	VF	UNC
5	**15 Chon** 1947. Brown.			
	a. With watermark.	0.75	2.50	8.00
	b. Without watermark. (Modern reprint.)	0.25	0.50	2.50

#	Description	VG	VF	UNC
6	**20 Chon** 1947. Green.			
	a. With watermark.	1.00	3.00	9.00
	b. Without watermark. (Modern reprint.)	0.30	0.75	3.00

#	Description	VG	VF	UNC
7	**50 Chon** 1947. Blue on light olive underprint.			
	a. With watermark.	0.50	1.50	5.00
	b. Without watermark. (Modern reprint.)	0.30	0.75	3.00

#	Description	VG	VF	UNC
8	**1 Won** 1947. Black on orange and green underprint. Worker and farmer at left center. Back: Mountain.			
	a. With watermark.	0.80	3.00	8.00
	b. Without watermark. (Modern reprint.)	0.40	1.00	4.00

#	Description	VG	VF	UNC
9	**5 Won** 1947. Black on blue and red underprint. Four lines between the two characters at bottom; segmented Korean numeral at lower right. Worker and farmer at left center. Back: Mountain. BC: Blue.	0.75	2.00	7.50
10	**5 Won** 1947. Black on blue and red underprint. Worker and farmer at left center. Eight lines between the two character at bottom; more connected Korean numeral at lower right. Back: Mountain.			
	a. With watermark.	1.25	3.50	12.00
	b. Without watermark. (Modern reprint.)	0.80	2.00	8.00

#	Description	VG	VF	UNC
10A	**10 Won** 1947. Black on red and green underprint. Worker and farmer at left center. Back: Mountain.			
	a. With watermark.	2.00	6.00	20.00
	b. Without watermark. (Modern reprint.)	1.50	3.50	10.00
11	**100 Won** 1947. Black on red, orange and lilac underprint. Worker and farmer at left center. Back: Mountain.			
	a. With watermark.	4.00	10.00	40.00
	b. b. Without watermark on bright white paper. (Modern reprint)	2.00	4.00	18.00

NOTE: without watermark on cream paper is a contemporary counterfeit.

DEMOCRATIC PEOPLES REPUBLIC

Korean Central Bank

1959 Issue

		VG	VF	UNC
12	**50 Chon** 1959. Blue on multicolor underprint. Arms at upper left. With watermark.	0.80	2.50	8.00

		VG	VF	UNC
13	**1 Won** 1959. Red-brown on multicolor underprint. Fishing boat at center. Arms at upper left. With watermark.	0.60	1.75	6.00

		VG	VF	UNC
14	**5 Won** 1959. Green on multicolor underprint. Large building at center. Arms at upper left. With watermark.	0.75	2.00	7.00

Color Abbreviation Guide

New to the *Standard Catalog of ® World Paper Money* are the following abbreviations related to color references:

BC: Back color

PC: Paper color

		VG	VF	UNC
15	**10 Won** 1959. Red on multicolor underprint. Fortress gateway at center right. Arms at upper left. Back: Woman picking fruit. With watermark.	0.80	2.25	8.00

		VG	VF	UNC
16	**50 Won** 1959. Purple on multicolor underprint. Bridge and city at center. Arms at upper left. Back: Woman with wheat. With watermark.	1.00	3.50	10.00

		VG	VF	UNC
17	**100 Won** 1959. Green on multicolor underprint. Steam freight train in factory area at center. Arms at upper left. Back: River with cliffs. With watermark.	1.50	4.50	15.00

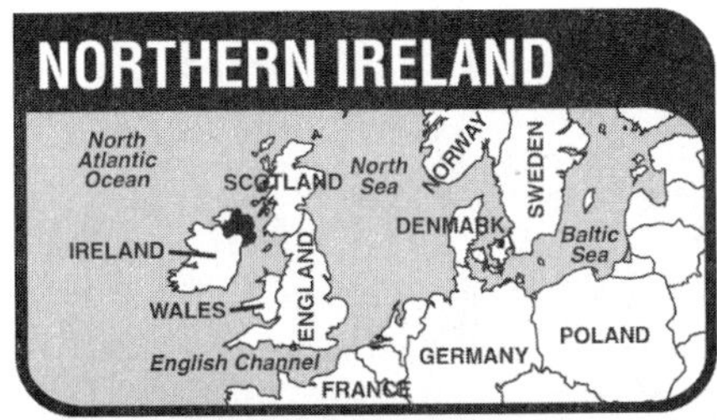

From 1800 to 1921 Ireland was an integral part of the United Kingdom. The Anglo-Irish treaty of 1921 established the Irish Free State of 26 counties within the Commonwealth of Nations and recognized the partition of Ireland. The six predominantly Protestant counties of northeast Ulster chose to remain a part of the United Kingdom with a limited self-government. Up to 1928 banknotes issued by six of the nine joint stock commercial banks were circulating in the whole of Ireland. After the establishment of the Irish Free State, the commercial notes were issued for circulation only in Northern Ireland, with the Consolidated Banknotes being issued by the eight commercial banks operating in the Irish Free State.

Additional information on bank notes of Northern Ireland can be found in *Paper Money of Ireland* by Bob Blake and Jonathan Callaway, published by Pam West.

RULERS:
British

MONETARY SYSTEM:
1 Shilling = 12 Pence
1 Pound = 20 Shillings to 1971
1 Pound = 100 New Pence, 1971-

BRITISH ADMINISTRATION

Bank of Ireland

Belfast

1929 Issue

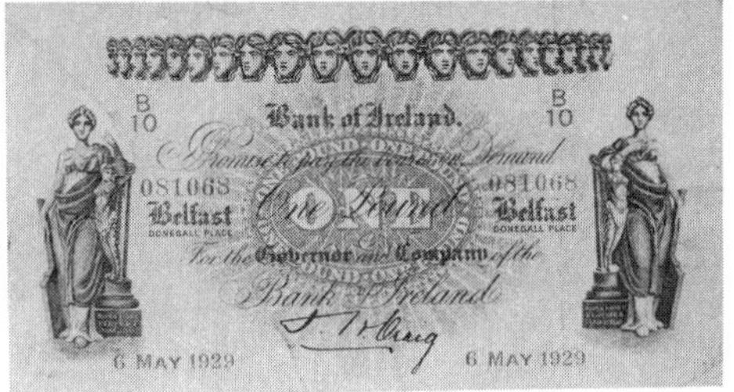

		VG	VF	UNC
51	**1 Pound** 1929-1936. Black on green and blue underprint. Woman with harp at left and right, Medusa head across top. Back: Bank crest.			
	a. Signature J. H. Craig. 6.5.1929; 8.5.1929.	75.00	200	400
	b. Signature G. W. Frazer. 3.4.1933; 9.3.1936.	35.00	110	250

		VG	VF	UNC
52	**5 Pounds** 1929-1958. Red and ochre. Woman with harp at left and right, Medusa head across top. Mercury at center. Back: Bank crest.			
	a. Signature J. H. Craig. 5.5.1929-15.5.1929.	90.00	250	525
	b. Signature G. W. Frazer. 15.8.1935-2.12.1940.	40.00	110	225
	c. Signature H. J. Adams. 16.2.1942-20.12.1943.	25.00	70.00	175
	d. Signature S. E. Skuce. 1.9.1958; 1.10.1958.	20.00	60.00	160

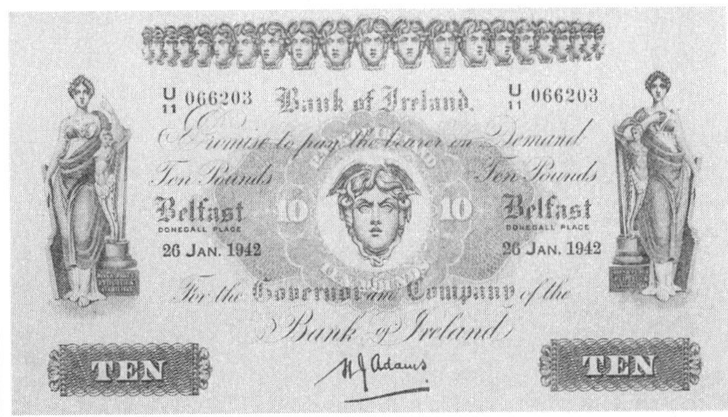

		VG	VF	UNC
53	**10 Pounds** 1929-1943. Blue and green. Woman with harp at left and right, Medusa head across top. Mercury at center. Back: Bank crest.			
	a. Signature J. H. Craig. 4.5.1929; 14.5.1929.	150	550	700
	b. Signature H. J. Adams. 26.1.1942; 19.1.1943.	50.00	110	275

		VG	VF	UNC
54	**20 Pounds** 9.5.1929. Black on yellow-orange and light green underprint. Woman with harp at left and right, Medusa head across top. Signature J.H. Craig. Mercury at center. Back: Bank crest.	600	2,100	—

1936 Issue

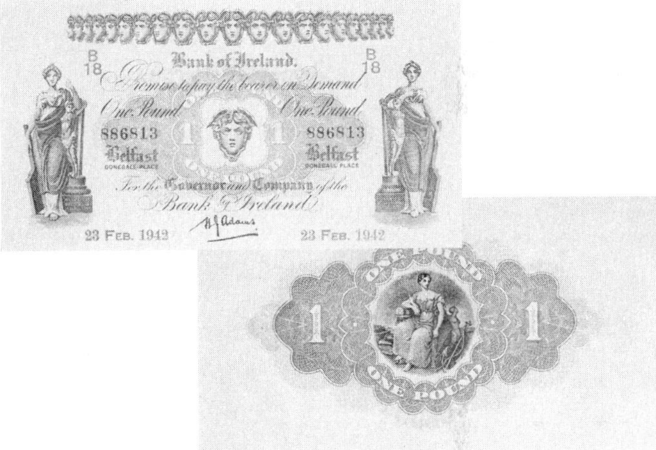

		VG	VF	UNC
55	**1 Pound** 1936-1943. Black on gray-green and light blue underprint. Woman with harp at left and right, Medusa head across top. Mercury at center. Back: Bank crest.			
	a. Signature G. W. Frazer. 9.3.1936-1.11.1940.	25.00	60.00	170
	b. Signature H. J. Adams. 23.2.1942-15.11.1943.	10.00	35.00	110

Belfast Banking Company Limited

Note: See also Ireland.

Belfast

1922-1923 Issue

		VG	VF	UNC
126	**1 Pound** 1922-1940. Black on blue underprint. Arms at top center with payable text...*at our Head Office, Belfast.*			
	a. Black serial #. 2.1.1922-8.11.1928.	175	350	625
	b. Blue serial #. 9.11.1939; 10.8.1940.	27.50	60.00	140
	p. Proof.	—	—	300

127	5 Pounds	VG	VF	UNC
	1923-1966. Black on red underprint. Arms at top center with payable text...*at our Head Office, Belfast.*			
	a. Black serial #. 3.1.1923; 3.5.1923; 7.9.1927.	175	350	850
	b. Red serial #. 8.3.1928-2.10.1942.	40.00	60.00	200
	c. Red serial #. 6.1.1966.	20.00	50.00	140
	p. Proof.	—	—	300

128	10 Pounds	VG	VF	UNC
	1923-1965. Black on green underprint. Arms at top center with payable text...*at our Head Office, Belfast.*			
	a. Black serial #. 3.1.1923.	425	625	—
	b. Green serial #. 9.1.1929-1.1.1943.	100	275	625
	c. Green serial #. 3.12.1963; 5.6.1965.	35.00	70.00	170
	p. Proof.	—	—	300

129	20 Pounds	VG	VF	UNC
	1923-1965. Black on purple underprint. Arms at top center with payable text...*at our Head Office, Belfast.*			
	a. Black serial #. 3.1.1923.	500	900	1,825
	b. Mauve serial #. 9.11.1939; 10.8.1940.	300	500	1,200
	c. Black serial #. 3.2.1943.	275	500	1,200
	d. Black serial #. 5.6.1965.	350	550	1,400
	p. Proof.	—	—	600

130	50 Pounds	VG	VF	UNC
	1923-1963. Black on orange underprint. Arms at top center with payable text...*at our Head Office, Belfast.*			
	a. Black serial #. 3.1.1923; 3.5.1923.	900	1,200	2,100
	b. Yellow serial #. 9.11.1939; 10.8.1940.	350	550	1,400
	c. Black serial #. 3.2.1943.	350	500	1,400
	d. Black serial #. 3.12.1963.	425	700	1,750
	p. Proof.	—	—	600

131	100 Pounds	VG	VF	UNC
	1923-1968. Black on red underprint. Arms at top or upper center with payable text...*at our Head Office, Belfast.*			
	a. 3.1.1923; 3.5.1923.	625	1,000	2,000
	b. 9.11.1939; 3.2.1943.	425	700	1,700
	c. 3.12.1963.	425	700	1,700
	d. 8.5.1968.	425	700	1,700
	p. Proof.	—	—	600

National Bank Limited

Belfast

1929 Issue

		VG	VF	UNC
151	**1 Pound** 6.5.1929-1.8.1933. Black on green underprint. Arms at upper center.	500	1,200	2,100
152	**5 Pounds** 6.5.1929-1.10.1934. Blue on brown underprint. Arms at upper center.	800	1,750	3,500
153	**10 Pounds** 6.5.1929; 1.8.1933. Green on brown underprint. Arms at upper center.	1,750	2,750	5,600
154	**20 Pounds** 6.5.1929. Brown on blue underprint. Arms at upper center.	—	—	—

1937 Issue

		VG	VF	UNC
155	**1 Pound** 1.2.1937; 1.9.1937; 2.10.1939. Black and green. Hibernia with harp at center. Man's head at left. Back: Arms at left. Watermark: *THE NATIONAL BANK LIMITED* across bottom.	40.00	140	250

No.	Description	VG	VF	UNC
156	**5 Pounds** 1.2.1937; 1.9.1937; 2.10.1939. Blue and brown. Hibernia with harp at lower left. Man's head at left. Watermark: *THE NATIONAL BANK LIMITED* across bottom.			
	a. Issued note.	100	200	425
	ct. Color trial.	—	—	900
157	**10 Pounds** 1.2.1937; 1.9.1937; 2.10.1939. Green and light brown. Hibernia with harp at center. Man's head at left. Watermark: *THE NATIONAL BANK LIMITED* across bottom.	140	275	675
158	**20 Pounds** 1.2.1937; 2.10.1939. Brown and green. Hibernia with harp at lower left. Man's head at left. Watermark: *THE NATIONAL BANK LIMITED* across bottom.	500	900	1,750

1942 Issue

No.	Description	VG	VF	UNC
159	**5 Pounds** 1.8.1942; 1.1.1949; 2.5.1949. Blue and brown. Hibernia with harp at lower left. Watermark: *NATIONAL BANK LIMITED* at lower right and D. O'Connell at left.	70.00	175	325
160	**10 Pounds** 1942-1959. Green and light brown. Hibernia with harp at center. Watermark: *NATIONAL BANK LIMITED* at lower right and D. O'Connell at left.			
	a. 1.8.1942; 2.5.1949.	125	225	500
	b. 1.7.1959.	125	225	300
161	**20 Pounds** 1942-1959. Brown and green. Hibernia with harp at lower left. Watermark: *NATIONAL BANK LIMITED* at lower right and D. O'Connell at left.			
	a. 1.8.1942; 1.1.1949.	300	625	1,200
	b. 1.7.1959.	400	650	1,400

Northern Bank Limited

1929 Provisional Issues

#171-177 new bank name overprint on notes of the Northern Banking Company Ltd.

No.	Description	VG	VF	UNC
171	**5 Pounds** 1.9.1927.	900	2,300	—
172	**10 Pounds** 1.3.1920.	700	2,100	3,500
173	**10 Pounds** 10.10.1921.	900	1,825	3,450
174	**20 Pounds** 20.10.1921.	600	1,050	1,750
175	**50 Pounds** 5.8.1914.	600	1,125	2,100

No.	Description	VG	VF	UNC
176	**50 Pounds** 25.4.1918.	500	850	2,000

No.	Description	VG	VF	UNC
177	**100 Pounds** 2.6.1919. Blue underprint.	600	1,200	2,500

Note: Although certain notes are dated before 1922 they were actually issued later. See also Ireland-Republic.

1929 Regular Issue

No.	Description	VG	VF	UNC
178	**1 Pound** 1929-1968. Black. Blue guilloche. Sailing ship, plow and man at grindstone at upper center.			
	a. Red serial #. 6.5.1929; 1.7.1929; 1.8.1929.	30.00	85.00	175
	b. Black prefix letters and serial #. 1.1.1940.	20.00	45.00	70.00
	c. 1.10.1968.	12.50	40.00	85.00
	p. Proof. 1.9.1940.	—	—	350

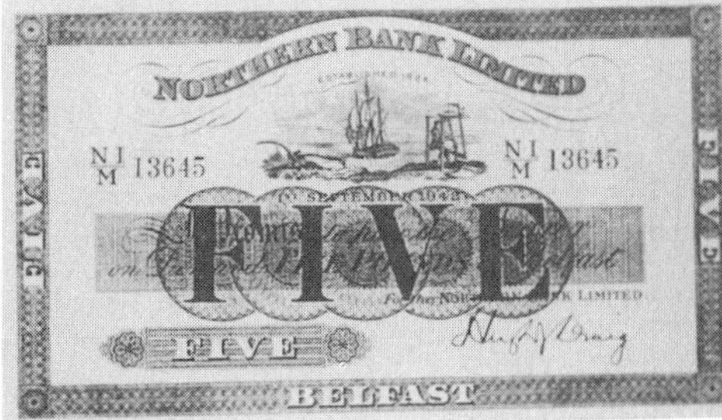

No.	Description	VG	VF	UNC
179	**5 Pounds** 6.5.1929. Black on dark blue underprint.	40.00	125	250
180	**5 Pounds** 1937-1943. Black on green underprint. Imprint varieties.			
	a. Red serial #. 1.9.1937.	55.00	125	250
	b. Black serial #. 1.1.1940-1.11.1943.	30.00	70.00	140

		VG	VF	UNC
181	**10 Pounds** 1930-1968. Black on red underprint. Sailing ship, plow and man at grindstone at upper center.			
	a. Red serial #. 1.1.1930-1.1.1940.	60.00	125	350
	b. Black serial #. 1.8.1940; 1.9.1940.	50.00	85.00	175
	c. Red serial #. 1.1.1942-1.11.1943.	30.00	50.00	140
	d. Imprint on back below central signature 1.10.1968.	25.00	50.00	240
	p. Proof.	—	—	175
	s. Specimen.	—	—	250
182	**50 Pounds** 1.1.1943. Black on dark blue underprint. Back: *NBC* monogram.	200	625	1,400
183	**100 Pounds** 1.1.1943. Black on dark blue underprint. Back: *NBC* monogram.	275	900	1,750

Provincial Bank of Ireland Limited

Belfast

1929 Issues

		VG	VF	UNC
231	**1 Pound** 1929-1934. Green underprint. *ONE POUND* at lower left, *1* at center. Bank building at upper center. Back: Blue.			
	a. Signature H. Robertson. 6.5.1929; 1.8.1930.	400	900	1,250
	b. Signature F. S. Forde. 1.2.1932; 1.4.1933; 1.6.1934.	400	900	1,250
232	**5 Pounds** 1929-1933. Blue underprint. Shaded *5* at center. Bank building at upper center.			
	a. Signature H. Robertson. 6.5.1929.	500	1,050	1,400
	b. Signature F. S. Forde. 5.10.1933.	1,050	1,750	2,800

		VG	VF	UNC
233	**10 Pounds** 1929; 1934. Red-brown underprint. Similar to #238 but *10* shaded at center. Bank building at upper center. Back: Purple.			
	a. Signature H. Robertson. 6.5.1929.	900	1,400	2,450
	b. Signature F. S. Forde. 10.12.1934.	300	550	1,200
234	**20 Pounds** 6.5.1929; 20.4.1943; 20.11.1944. Red-brown underprint. Similar to #238. Bank building at center.			
	a. Signature H. Robinson. 6.5.1929.	700	1,200	2,250
	b. Signature G. A. Kennedy. 20.4.1943; 20.11.1944.	200	500	1,050
	p. Proof. 10.4.1943.	—	—	550

1935-1938 Issue

		VG	VF	UNC
235	**1 Pound** 1935-1946. Green underprint. Similar to #231 but *1* outlined in white at center. Bank building at center. Back: Green.			
	a. Signature F. S. Forde. 1.8.1935; 2.11.1936.	300	500	1,050
	b. Signature G. A. Kennedy. 2.11.1936-1.5.1946.	100	175	275
236	**5 Pounds** 5.8.1935-5.4.1946. Brown underprint. Similar to #232 but *5* outlined in white at center. Bank building at upper center.			
	a. Signature F. S. Forde. 5.8.35; 5.5.36.	625	1,050	1,550
	b. Signature G. A. Kennedy. 5.5.38-5.4.46.	125	200	350
	p1. Proof. As a.	—	—	500
	p2. Proof. As b.	—	—	275
237	**10 Pounds** 10.10.1938-10.4.1946. Similar to #233 but *10* outlined in white at center. Bank building at upper center. Back: Red.			
	a. Signatrue G. A. Kennedy.	200	300	550
	p. Proof.	—	—	275

1948; 1951 Issue

		VG	VF	UNC
238	**1 Pound** 1.9.1951. Green guilloche on pink underprint. Similar to #231 but *ONE* at lower left. Bank building at upper center. Back: Green.			
	a. Issued note.	300	700	1,400
	p. Proof.	—	—	500
239	**5 Pounds** 5.1.1948-5.4.1952. Gray on brown and pink underprint. Similar to #232. Bank building at center.			
	a. Serial # prefix as fraction.	70.00	110	300
	b. Serial # prefix in-line.	40.00	70.00	170
	p. Proof.	—	—	300
240	**10 Pounds** 10.1.1948. Green on red underprint and green and pink mesh.			
	a. Signature Clarke.	150	280	775
	p. Proof. 1946; 1948.	—	—	300

1954 Issue

		VG	VF	UNC
241	**1 Pound** 1.10.1954; 11154. Green. 148x84mm.	140	280	525
242	**5 Pounds** 5.10.1954-5.5.1959. Brown.	40.00	100	175

Ulster Bank Limited

Belfast

1929 Provisional Issue

		VG	VF	UNC
301	**1 Pound** 6.5.1929 (- old dates 1.3.26; 1.6.27; 1.12.1927). Sailing ship, plow and blacksmiths at upper center. Curved overprint: *ISSUED IN NORTHERN IRELAND AFTER / 6th MAY, 1929.*	600	1,400	2,100

1929 Regular Issue

		VG	VF	UNC
306	**1 Pound** 6.5.1929-1.1.1934. Black on blue underprint. Sailing ship, plow and blacksmiths at upper center with curved overprint. Uniface. Signature varieties. Hand signed.	40.00	85.00	225
307	**5 Pounds** 6.5.1929-1.1.1934. Black on green underprint. Sailing ship, plow and blacksmiths at upper center with curved overprint. Signature varieties.	120	240	525
308	**10 Pounds** 1.6.1929; 1.10.1930; 1.5.1933. Black on red underprint. Sailing ship, plow and blacksmiths at upper center with curved overprint. Uniface. Signature varieties.	130	200	500
309	**20 Pounds** 1.6.1929. Black on blue underprint. Sailing ship, plow and blacksmiths at upper center with curved overprint. Uniface. Signature varieties.	200	425	850
310	**50 Pounds** 1.6.1929. Black on blue underprint. Sailing ship, plow and blacksmiths at upper center with curved overprint. Uniface. Signature varieties.	300	550	1,250
311	**100 Pounds** 1.6.1929. Black on blue underprint. Sailing ship, plow and blacksmiths at upper center with curved overprint. Uniface. Signature varieties.	500	900	1,700

1935-1936 Issue

		VG	VF	UNC
312	**1 Pound** 1.1.1935-1.2.1938. Sailing ship, plow and blacksmiths at upper center. Back: Like #306 but building without frame at center.			
	a. Issued note.	30.00	70.00	200
	p. Proof.	—	—	200
313	**5 Pounds** 1.1.1935; 1.1.1936; 1.10.1937. Black on green underprint. Sailing ship, plow and blacksmiths at upper center.	100	180	420
314	**10 Pounds** 1.5.1936. Black on orange underprint. Sailing ship, plow and blacksmiths at upper center.	500	900	—

1939-1941 Issue

		VG	VF	UNC
315	**1 Pound** 1939-1956. Sailing ship, plow and blacksmiths at upper center. Back: Building within frame at center.			
	a. Hand signature 1.9.1939; 1.1.1940. 2 signature varieties.	20.00	40.00	175
	c. Printed signature 1.5.1956.	30.00	70.00	200
	p. Printed signature. Proof. 1.1.1948.	—	—	200

		VG	VF	UNC
316	**5 Pounds** 1939-1956. Sailing ship, plow and blacksmiths at upper center, like #308.			
	a. Hand signature 1.2.1939; 1.10.1940; 1.1.1942; 1.1.1943.	50.00	100	275
	b. Printed signature 1.5.1956.	100	200	350
	p. Proof.	—	—	300

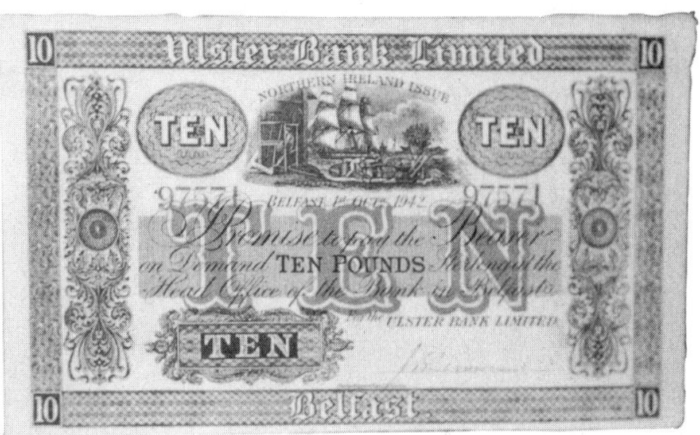

		VG	VF	UNC
317	**10 Pounds** 1.2.1939-1.1.1948. Sailing ship, plow and blacksmiths at upper center.	90.00	140	350

		VG	VF	UNC
318	**20 Pounds** 1.3.1941; 1.1.1943; 1.4.1943; 1.1.1944; 1.1.1948. Sailing ship, plow and blacksmiths at upper center.	170	280	500

		VG	VF	UNC
319	**50 Pounds** 1.3.1941; 1.1.1943. Sailing ship, plow and blacksmiths at upper center. Like #308.	210	350	1,000

		VG	VF	UNC
320	**100 Pounds** 1.3.1941; 1.1.1943. Sailing ship, plow and blacksmiths at upper center. Like #308.	300	500	1,250

NORWAY

The Kingdom of Norway, a constitutional monarchy located in northwestern Europe, has an area of 150,000 sq. mi. (388,500 sq. km.) including the island territories of Spitzbergen (Svalbard) and Jan Mayen, and a population of 4.46 million. Capital: Oslo. The diversified economic base of Norway includes shipping, fishing, forestry, agriculture and manufacturing. Nonferrous metals, paper and paperboard, paper pulp, iron, steel and oil are exported. Two centuries of Viking raids into Europe tapered off following the adoption of Christianity by King Olav Tryggvason in 994. Conversion of the Norwegian kingdom occurred over the next several decades. In 1397, Norway was absorbed into a union with Denmark that lasted more than four centuries. In 1814, Norwegians resisted the cession of their country to Sweden and adopted a new constitution. Sweden then invaded Norway but agreed to let Norway keep its constitution in return for accepting the union under a Swedish king. Rising nationalism throughout the 19th century led to a 1905 referendum granting Norway independence. Although Norway remained neutral in World War I, it suffered heavy losses to its shipping. Norway proclaimed its neutrality at the outset of World War II, but was nonetheless occupied for five years by Nazi Germany (1940-45). In 1949, neutrality was abandoned and Norway became a member of NATO. Discovery of oil and gas in adjacent waters in the late 1960s boosted Norway's economic fortunes. The current focus is on containing spending on the extensive welfare system and planning for the time when petroleum reserves are depleted. In referenda held in 1972 and 1994, Norway rejected joining the EU.

RULERS:

Christian V, 1670-1699
Frederik IV, 1699-1730
Christian VI, 1730-1746
Frederik V, 1746-1766
Christian VII, 1766-1808
Frederik VI, 1808-1814
Carl XIII, 1814-1818
Carl XIV Johan, 1818-1844
Oscar I, 1844-1859
Carl XV, 1859-1872
Oscar II, 1872-1905
Haakon VII, 1905-1957
Olav V, 1957-1991
Harald V, 1991-

MONETARY SYSTEM:

1 Speciedaler = 96 Skilling to 1816
1 Speciedaler = 120 Skilling, 1816-1873
1 Krone = 100 re, 1873-

REPLACEMENT NOTES:

#15, 16, 25-28, 30-33, 37-40 w/1945 or later dates, Z prefix.

KINGDOM

Thor Møhlen Notes

1695 Issue

Note: All valuations for notes without talon (counterfoil). Notes with matching stub are worth at least a 50% premium.

		Good	Fine	XF
A1	**10 Rixdaler Croner** 1695. Black text with red wax seals. Uniface.	575	1,200	2,500
A2	**20 Rixdaler Croner** 1695. Black text with red wax seals. Uniface.	600	1,200	2,750

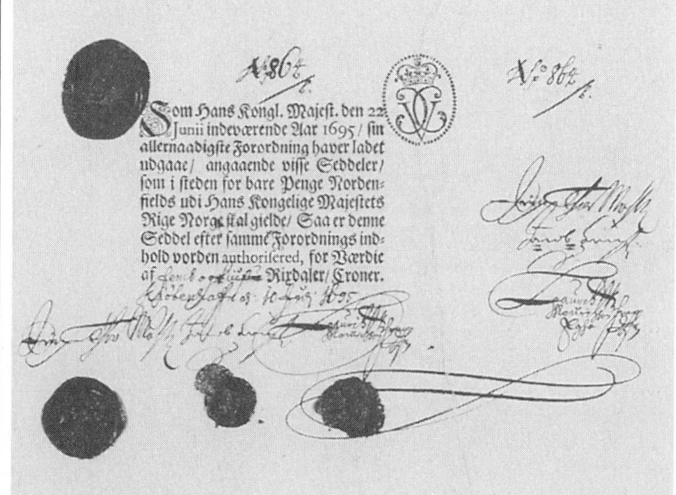

		Good	Fine	XF
A3	**25 Rixdaler Croner** 1695. Black text with red wax seals. Uniface.	800	1,450	2,750
A4	**50 Rixdaler Croner** 1695. Black text with red wax seals. Uniface.	900	1,600	3,500

		Good	Fine	XF
A5	**100 Rixdaler Croner** 1695. Black text with red wax seals. Uniface. a. Issued note. b. Commemorative reproduction (1995).	 900 —	 1,600	 3,500

Regerings Kommission

Christiania

1807-1810 Issue

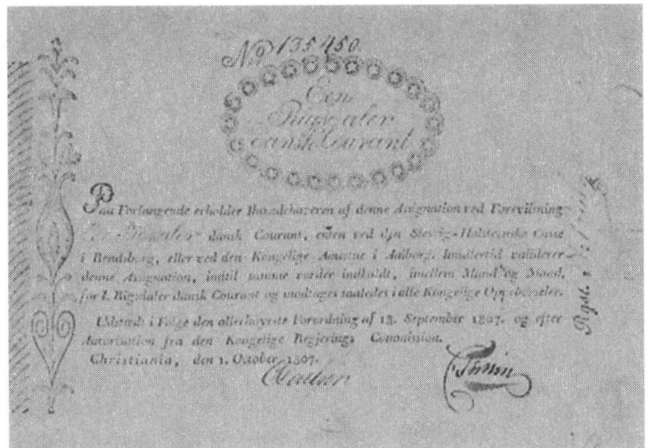

		Good	Fine	XF
A6	**1 Rigsdaler** 1.10.1807.	250	500	1,100
A7	**5 Rigsdaler** 1.10.1807.	275	600	1,150

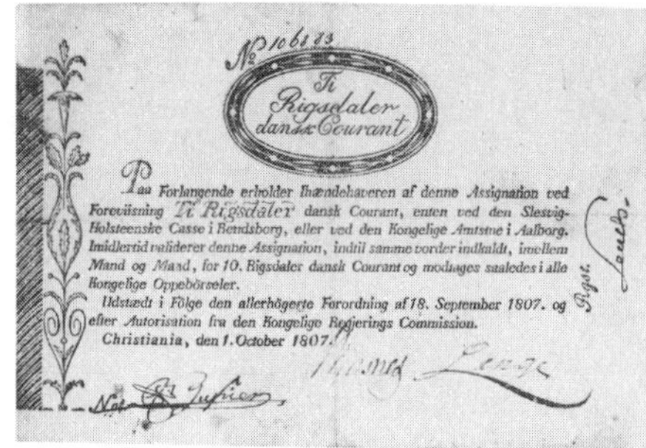

		Good	Fine	XF
A8	**10 Rigsdaler** 1.10.1807.	550	900	—
A10	**100 Rigsdaler** 1.10.1807.	600	1,000	—

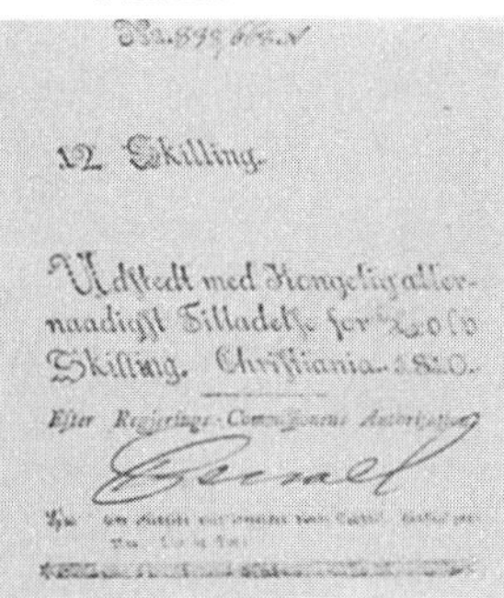

		Good	Fine	XF
A11	**12 Skilling** 1810.	50.00	135	300

Note: The 24 skilling of 1810 was printed in Copenhagen.

Color Abbreviation Guide

New to the *Standard Catalog of® World Paper Money* are the following abbreviations related to color references:

BC: Back color
PC: Paper color

Rigsbankens Norske Avdeling

Christiania

1813 Issue

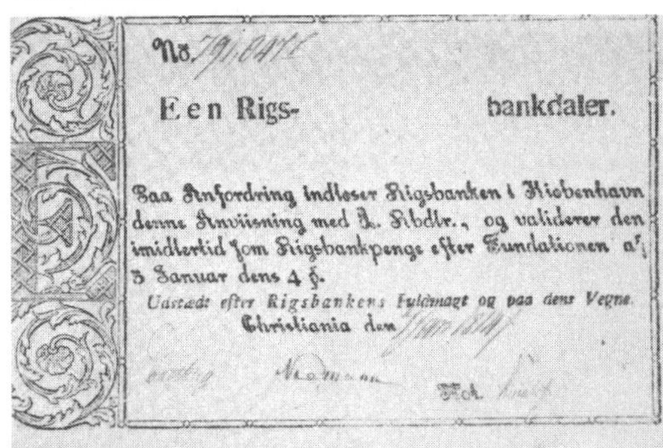

		Good	Fine	XF
A12	**1 Rigsbankdaler** 1813-1814.	150	350	1,000
A13	**5 Rigsbankdaler** 1813-1814.	200	450	1,200
A15	**50 Rigsbankdaler** 1813-1814.	500	1,500	—
A16	**100 Rigsbankdaler** 1813-1814. Rare.	—	—	—

Stattholderbevis (prinsesedler)

Christiania

1815 Issue

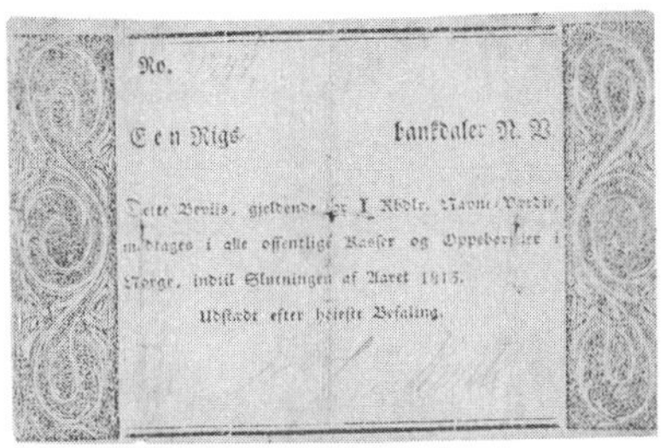

		Good	Fine	XF
A17	**1 Rigsbankdaler** 1815.	300	800	1,500
A18	**5 Rigsbankdaler** 1815. Rare.	—	—	—
A19	**15 Rigsbankdaler** 1815. Rare.	—	—	—
A20	**25 Rigsbankdaler** 1815. Rare.	—	—	—

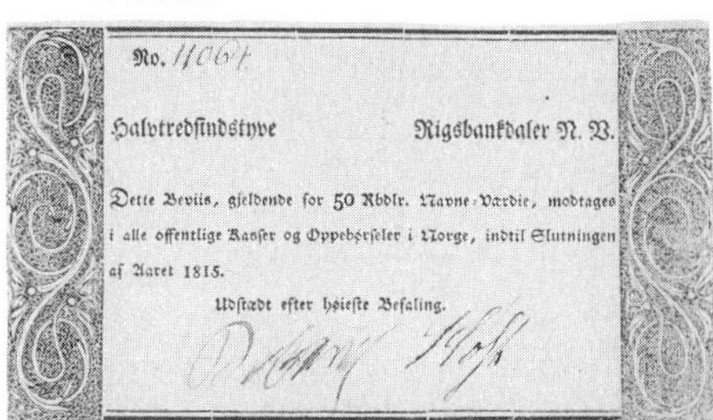

		Good	Fine	XF
A21	**50 Rigsbankdaler** 1815. Rare.	—	—	—

Norges Midlertidige Rigsbank

Christiania

1814 Fractional Note Issue

		Good	Fine	XF
A22	**3 Rigsbank-skilling** 1814.	50.00	175	400

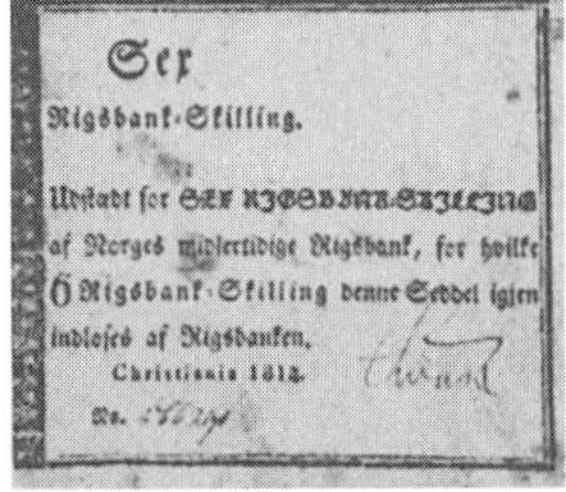

		Good	Fine	XF
A23	**6 Rigsbank-skilling** 1814.	50.00	175	400
A24	**8 Rigsbank-skilling** 1814.	70.00	200	425
A25	**16 Rigsbank-skilling** 1814.	60.00	180	400

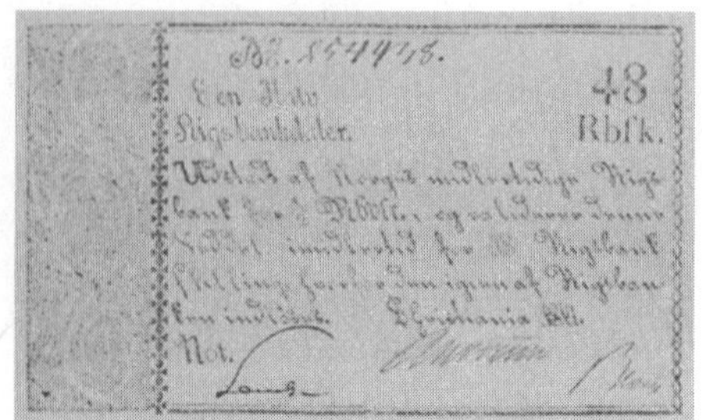

		Good	Fine	XF
A26	**1/2 Rigsbankdaler-48 Skilling** 1814.	90.00	325	700

Norges Bank

Trondhjem

1817-1822 Issues

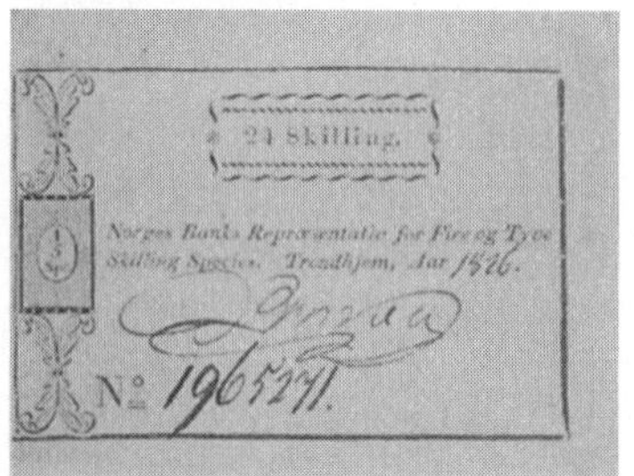

		Good	Fine	XF
A28	**24 Skilling Species** 1822-1826. Handwritten serial #.	350	700	1,400

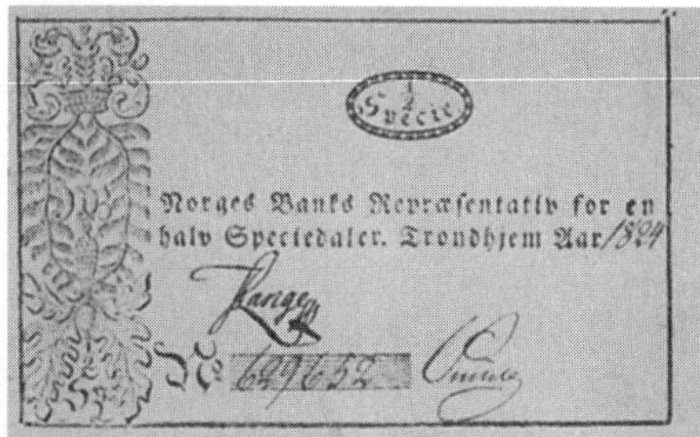

		Good	Fine	XF
A29	**1/2 Speciedaler** 1822-1830. Handwritten serial #.	350	700	1,400

		Good	Fine	XF
A30	**1 Speciedaler** 1817-1824. Handwritten serial #.	1,000	2,500	—
A31	**5 Speciedaler** 1817-1818. Handwritten serial #. Rare. PC: Blue.	—	—	—
A32	**10 Speciedaler** 1818-1834. Handwritten serial #. Rare. PC: Yellow.	—	—	—
A33	**50 Speciedaler** 1818-1847. Handwritten serial #. Rare. PC: Green.	—	—	—
A34	**100 Speciedaler** 1818-1846. Handwritten serial #. Ornate arms at left. Rare. PC: Red.	—	—	—

1825-1834 Issue

		Good	Fine	XF
A35	**24 Skilling Species** 1834-1842. Handwritten serial #.	300	600	1,000
A36	**1/2 Speciedaler** 1834-1839. Handwritten serial #.	450	750	1,400

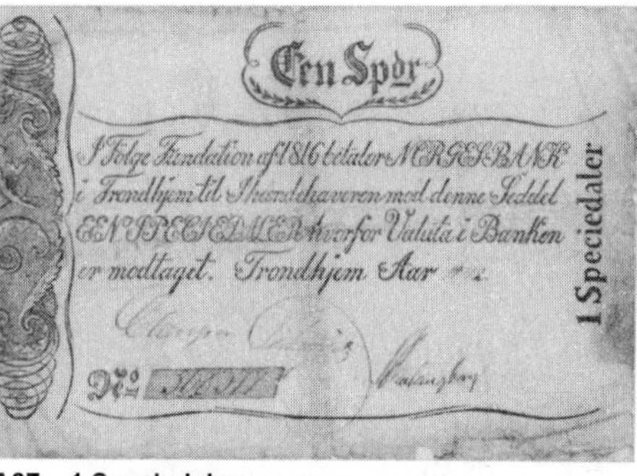

		Good	Fine	XF
A37	**1 Speciedaler** 1825-1843. Handwritten serial #.	1,000	2,400	—

		Good	Fine	XF
A38	**5 Speciedaler** 1826-1828. Handwritten serial #. PC: Blue.	1,000	2,400	—

1841-1847 Issue

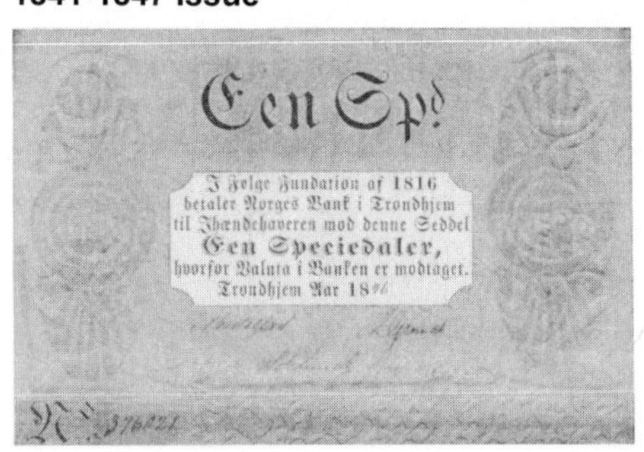

		Good	Fine	XF
A39	**1 Speciedaler** 1845-1849. Gray. Handwritten serial #.	1,000	2,400	—
A40	**5 Speciedaler** 1841-1854. Blue-black. Handwritten serial #. Crowned arms at upper center. Rare.	—	—	—

1847-1854 Issues

		Good	Fine	XF
A41	**1 Speciedaler** 1849-1853. Black. Crowned arms at upper center.	900	2,000	—

		Good	Fine	XF
A42	**1 Speciedaler** 1854-1866. Blue. Crowned arms at upper center.			
	a. Handwritten serial #.	900	1,600	—
	b. Printed serial #.	900	1,600	—

		Good	Fine	XF
A43	**5 Speciedaler** 1853-1866. Black-blue. Ornate crowned arms at upper center. Rare. PC: Blue.	—	—	—
A44	**10 Speciedaler** 1847-1864. Black-yellow. Rare. PC: Yellow.	—	—	—
A45	**50 Speciedaler** 1849-1866. Black-green. Ornate crowned arms at upper center. Rare. PC: Green.	—	—	—
A46	**100 Speciedaler** 1847-1865. Black and red. Rare. PC: red.	—	—	—

1865-1868 Issue

		Good	Fine	XF
A47	**1 Speciedaler** 1865-1877. Black, red and green on different colors of paper. Four allegorical figures supporting crowned arms at upper center. Back: Crowned arms at center. Printer: Saunders, London. PC: White.	600	1,100	2,500
A48	**5 Speciedaler** 1866-1877. Black, red and green on different colors of paper. Four allegorical figures supporting crowned arms at upper center. Back: Crowned arms at center. Printer: Saunders, London. PC: Blue.			
	a. Rare.	—	—	—
	r. Remainder. Punch hole cancelled.	—	Unc	500
A49	**10 Speciedaler** 1866-1877. Black, red and green on different colors of paper. Four allegorical figures supporting crowned arms at upper center. Back: Crowned arms at center. Printer: Saunders, London. PC: Yellow.			
	a. Rare.	—	—	—
	r. Remainder. Punch hole cancelled.	—	Unc	500
A50	**50 Speciedaler** 1866-1877. Black, red and green on different colors of paper. Four allegorical figures supporting crowned arms at upper center. Back: Crowned arms at center. Printer: Saunders, London. Rare. PC: Green.	—	—	—
A51	**100 Speciedaler** 1866-1869. Black, red and green on different colors of paper. Four allegorical figures supporting crowned arms at upper center. Back: Crowned arms at upper center. Printer: Saunders, London. Rare. PC: Yellowish.	—	—	—
A52	**100 Speciedaler** 1868-1877. Black, red and green on different colors of paper. Four allegorical figures supporting crowned arms at upper center. Back: Crowned arms at center. Printer: Saunders, London. Rare. PC: Red.	—	—	—

1877 Issue

		Good	Fine	XF
1	**5 Kroner** 1877-1899. Black on blue underprint. King Oscar II at left.			
	a. Without prefix letter. 1877-1892.	450	1,000	2,000
	b. Prefix letter: small *C*. 1892-1895.	500	1,200	2,500
	c. Prefix letter: large antique *C*. 1895-1896.	475	1,150	2,400
	d. Prefix letter: large antique *D*. 1897.	700	1,500	3,250
	e. Prefix letter: small antique *D* with small serial #. 1898-1899.	350	800	1,600
	s1. Specimen. Punch hole cancelled.	—	Unc	500
	s2. Specimen. Uncut sheet of 4. Punch hole cancelled.	—	Unc	1,500

		Good	Fine	XF
2	**10 Kroner** 1877-1899. Black on yellow underprint. Portrait King Oscar II at left or at top center.			
	a. Without prefix letter. Large serial #. 1877-890.	600	1,600	—
	b. Prefix letter: small italic antique *B*. 1890-1891.	600	1,600	—
	c. Prefix letter: small italic Roman *B*. 1892-1895.	600	1,600	3,500
	d. Prefix letter: large italic antique *B*. 1895-1897.	600	1,600	3,500
	e. Prefix letter: large italic antique *C*. 1897. Unique.	—		
	f. Prefix letter: small antique *C*. Small serial #. 1897-1899.	400	850	2,000
	s1. Specimen. Punch hole cancelled.	—	Unc	500
	s2. Specimen. Uncut sheet of 4. Punch hole cancelled.	—	Unc	1,500

		Good	Fine	XF
3	**50 Kroner** 1877-1899. Black on green underprint. Portrait King Oscar II at left or at top center.	5,000	8,000	—
4	**100 Kroner** 1877-1880; 1892; 1894; 1896-98. Black on pink underprint. Portrait King Oscar II at left or at top center.	9,500	14,500	—

		Good	Fine	XF
5	**500 Kroner** 1877-1896. Black on brown underprint. Portrait King Oscar II at left or at top center.			
	a. Issued note.	16,500	22,750	—
	b. Cancelled with holes.	9,000	13,000	—

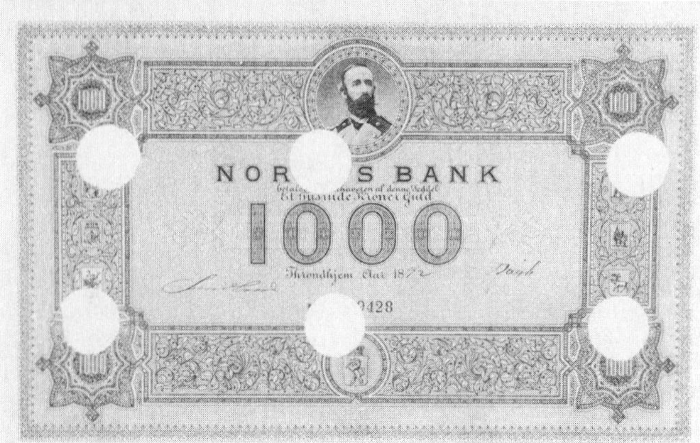

6	1000 Kroner	Good	Fine	XF
	1877-1898. Black on orange-brown underprint. Portrait King Oscar II at left or at top center.			
	a. Issued note.	20,000	27,500	—
	b. Cancelled with holes.	12,500	16,500	—
	s. Specimen. Punch hole cancelled. Without signature, date or serial *.	—	Unc	1,250

1901 Issue

Note: 150 sets of remainders overprinted: *SPECIMEN,* with 4 punch hole cancellations, were distributed by the Norges Bank in 1945, after the series was replaced.

7	5 Kroner	Good	Fine	XF
	1901-1944. Dark green. Portrait Pres. Christie at left. Back: Arms at right. BC: Blue.			
	a. Signature H. V. Hansen. 1901-1916. Prefix A-E.	75.00	175	375
	b. Signature S. Cederholm. 1916-1934. Prefix E-N.	15.00	50.00	120
	c. Signature G. Meldahl Nielsen. 1935-1944. Prefix N-W.	5.00	20.00	50.00
	r. As. c. Remainder overprint: *SPECIMEN*. 1944. Punch hole cancelled.	—	Unc	125

8	10 Kroner	Good	Fine	XF
	1901-1944. Purple. Portrait Pres. Christie at left. Portrait Adm. Tordenskjold at right. Back: Arms at right. BC: Tan.			
	a. Signature H. V. Hansen. 1901-1916. Prefix A-F.	40.00	120	275
	b. Signature S. Cederholm. 1917-1934. Prefix F-T.	8.00	30.00	80.00
	c. Signature G. Meldahl Nielsen. 1935-1944. Prefix A-F.	2.00	8.00	22.50
	r. As c. Remainder overprint: *SPECIMEN*. 1944. Punch hole cancelled.	—	Unc	100

9	50 Kroner	Good	Fine	XF
	1901-1945. Green. Portrait Pres. Christie at left. Back: Building at center. Arms at right. Square format.			
	a. Signature H. V. Hansen. 1901-1912. Prefix A.	850	2,500	—
	b. Signature H. V. Hansen. 1913-1915. Block serial #.	500	1,000	—
	c2. Signature S. Cederholm. 1929-1934. Prefix B.	30.00	90.00	220
	d. Signature G. Meldahl Neilsen. 1935-1945. Prefix B-D.	15.00	70.00	140
	r. As c. Remainder overprint: *SPECIMEN*. 1945. Punch hole cancelled.	—	Unc	175

10	100 Kroner	Good	Fine	XF
	1901-1945. Purple. Portrait Pres. Christie at left. Portrait Adm. Tordenskjold at right. Back: Building at center. Arms at right. Square format.			
	a. Signature H. V. Hansen. 1901-1916. Prefix A.	275	650	1,400
	b. Signature S. Cederholm. 1917-1934. Prefix A; B.	17.50	75.00	150
	c. Signature G. Meldahl Nielsen. 1935-1944. Prefix B; C.	12.50	40.00	95.00
	d. Signature G. Meldahl Nielsen. 1945. Prefix. C.	475	1,000	2,000
	r. As c. Remainder overprint: *SPECIMEN*. 1945. Punch hole cancelled.	—	Unc	175

11	500 Kroner	Good	Fine	XF
	1901-1944. Blue-gray. Portrait Pres. Christie at left. Back: Building at center. Arms at right.			
	a. Signature H. V. Hansen. 1901-1916. Prefix A.	2,500	6,750	10,500
	b. Signature S. Cederholm. 1918-1932. Prefix A.	800	1,600	3,000
	c. Signature G. Meldahl Nielsen. 1936-1944. Prefix A.	500	1,100	1,800
	r. As c. Remainder overprint: *SPECIMEN*. 1944. Punch hole cancelled.	—	Unc	600

#	Description	Good	Fine	XF
12	**1000 Kroner** 1901-1943. Violet. Portrait Pres. Christie at left. Portrait Adm.Tordenskjold at right. Prefix A. Back: Church at center. Arms at right.			
	a. Signature H. V. Hansen. 1901-1916. Rare.	—	—	—
	b. Signature S. Cederholm. 1917-1932.	250	700	1,200
	c. Signature G. Meldahl Nielsen. 1936-1943.	200	500	875
	r. As c. Remainder overprint: *SPECIMEN*. 1943.	—	Unc	400

1917-1922 Skillemyntsedler Issue

Small change notes.

#	Description	VG	VF	UNC
13	**1 Krone** 1917. Black on green underprint. Prefix A-F; and without prefix lettter. Back: Green. Back: Crowned arms at center.			
	a. Issued note.	10.00	32.50	95.00
	r. Remainder. Overprint: *Specimen.* Punch hole cancelled.	—	—	150

#	Description	VG	VF	UNC
14	**2 Kroner** 1918; 1922. Black on pink underprint. Prefix A-F; and without prefix letter. Back: Red. Back: Crowned arms at center.			
	a. 1918.	15.00	45.00	125
	b. 1922.	25.00	75.00	175
	r. Remainder. Overprint: *Specimen.* Punch hole cancelled.	—	—	200

1940 Skillemyntsedler Issue

#	Description	VG	VF	UNC
15	**1 Krone** 1940-1950. Brown on green underprint. Back: Green.			
	a. Signature G. Meldahl Nielsen. 1940-1945. Prefix A-I.	9.00	25.00	65.00
	b. Signature E. Thorp. 1946-1950. Prefix I-N.	7.50	17.50	50.00
	r. Remainder. Overprint: *Specimen.* Punch hole cancelled.	—	—	200

#	Description	VG	VF	UNC
16	**2 Kroner** 1940-1950. Brown on pink underprint. Back: Red.			
	a1. Signature G. Meldahl Nielsen. 1940-1942; 1943. Prefix C. 1945; Prefix D.	10.00	25.00	60.00
	a2. Signature G. Meldahl Nielsen. 1943. Prefix B.	55.00	120	240
	a3. Signature G. Meldahl Nielsen. 1945. Prefix E.	80.00	150	260
	b. Signature E. Thorp. 1946-1950. Prefix E-G.	7.50	17.50	50.00
	r. Remainder. Overprint: *Specimen.* Punch hole cancelled.	—	—	200

1942 Issue

WW II Government-in-Exile Matched serial # sets exist of #19-22.

#	Description	VG	VF	UNC
17	**1 Krone** 1942. Dark brown on green underprint. Back: Green. Printer: W&S.			
	a. Prefix A.	25.00	85.00	225
	b. Prefix B.	900	1,600	—
	r. As a. Remainder with overprint: *SPECIMEN,* punch hole cancelled.	—	—	75.00
	s. Specimen with red overprint: *SPECIMEN.*	—	—	135

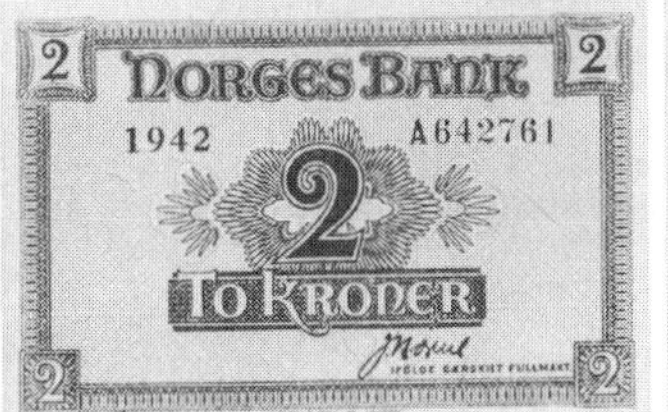

#	Description	VG	VF	UNC
18	**2 Kroner** 1942. Dark brown on pink underprint. Back: Red. Printer: W&S.			
	a. Issued note.	35.00	110	350
	r. As a. Remainder with overprint: *SPECIMEN,* punch hole cancelled.	—	—	75.00
	s. Specimen with red overprint: *SPECIMEN.*	—	—	150

#19b-24b w/*KRIGSSEDDEL.*

#	Description	VG	VF	UNC
19	**5 Kroner** 1942; 1944. Arms at left. Printer: W&S.			
	a. 1942. Dark green and red on blue underprint. Frame brown. Back blue. (Not officially issued). Prefix A. Rare.	—	—	—
	b. 1944. Dark brown and yellow on orange underprint. Frame green. Back brown. Prefix X; Y. (Not a replacement.)	75.00	175	450
	r1. As a. Remainder with overprint: *SPECIMEN,* punch hole cancelled.	—	—	225
	r2. As b. Remainder with overprint: *SPECIMEN,* punch hole cancelled.	—	—	200
	s1. As a. Specimen with red overprint: *SPECIMEN.*	—	—	400
	s2. As b. Specimen with red overprint: *SPECIMEN.*	—	—	225

#	Description	VG	VF	UNC
20	**10 Kroner** 1942; 1944. Arms at top center. Printer: W&S.			
	a. 1942. Dark brown and lilac on blue-green and green underprint. Back orange. (Not officially issued). Prefix A. Rare.	—	—	—

	VG	VF	UNC
b. 1944. Brown-red on blue-green and green underprint. Back green. Prefix X; Y; Z. (Not a replacement.)	45.00	125	350
r1. As a. Remainder with overprint: *SPECIMEN*, punch hole cancelled.	—	—	350
r2. As b. Remainder with overprint: *SPECIMEN*, punch hole cancelled.	—	—	150
s1. As a. Specimen with red overprint: *SPECIMEN*.	—	—	700
s2. As b. Specimen with red overprint: *SPECIMEN*.	—	—	200

21	50 Kroner	VG	VF	UNC
	1942; 1944. Arms at top left center. Printer: W&S.			
	a. 1942. Dark gray on green and lilac underprint. Back green. (Not officially issued.) Prefix A. Rare.	—	—	—
	b. 1944. Dark brown and pink on light green underprint. Back blue. Prefix X. (Not a replacement.)	500	1,100	—
	r1. As a. Remainder with overprint: *SPECIMEN*, punch hole cancelled.	—	—	350
	r2. As b. Remainder with overprint: *SPECIMEN*, punch hole cancelled.	—	—	350
	s1. As a. Specimen with red overprint: *SPECIMEN*.	—	—	650
	s2. As b. Specimen with red overprint: *SPECIMEN*.	—	—	600

22	100 Kroner	VG	VF	UNC
	1942; 1944. Arms at top left center. Printer: W&S.			
	a. 1942. Dark purple and light blue on light brown-purple underprint. Back brown-red. (Not officially issued.) Prefix A. Rare.	—	—	—
	b. 1944. Dark blue on red and green underprint. Back orange. Prefix X. (Not a replacement.)	800	1,500	—
	r1. As a. Remainder with overprint: *SPECIMEN*, punch hole cancelled.	—	—	350
	r2. As b. Remainder with overprint: *SPECIMEN*, punch hole cancelled.	—	—	600
	s1. As a. Specimen with red overprint: *SPECIMEN*.	—	—	850
	s2. As b. Specimen with red overprint: *SPECIMEN*.	—	—	650

23	500 Kroner	VG	VF	UNC
	1942. Dark blue-green and orange. Back: Green. Printer: W&S.			
	a. Not officially issued. Prefix A. Rare.	—	—	—
	r. Remainder with overprint: *SPECIMEN*, punch hole cancelled.	—	—	500
	s. Specimen with red overprint: *SPECIMEN*.	—	—	850

24	1000 Kroner	VG	VF	UNC
	1942. Brown and orange on yellow-green underprint. Back: Grey-brown. Printer: W&S.			
	a. Not officially issued. Prefix A. Rare.	—	—	—
	r. Remainder with red overprint: *SPECIMEN*, punch hole cancelled.	—	—	600
	s. Specimen with red overprint: *SPECIMEN*.	—	—	900

Norges Bank - Post WW II

1945 Issue

25	5 Kroner	VG	VF	UNC
	1945-1954. Blue. Arms at left.			
	a. Signature G. Meldahl Nielsen. 1945. Prefix A; B.	8.00	35.00	90.00
	b. Signature E. Thorp. 1946-1950. Prefix B-F.	8.00	40.00	100
	c. Signature E. Thorp. 1951. Prefix F.	55.00	120	270
	d. Signature E. Thorp. 1951-1953. Prefix G-K.	8.00	40.00	90.00
	e. Signature E. Thorp. 1954. Prefix K.	50.00	100	240
	s. Specimen. Overprint: *Specimen*. Punch hole cancelled.	—	—	200

26	10 Kroner	VG	VF	UNC
	1945-1953. Yellow-brown. Arms at left.			
	a. Signature G. Meldahl Nielsen. 1945. Prefix A-C.	5.00	12.50	50.00
	b. Signature G. Meldahl Nielsen. 1945. Prefix D.	10.00	30.00	100
	c. Signature G. Meldahl Nielsen. 1946. Prefix E.	17.50	60.00	150
	d. Signature E. Thorp. 1946-1947. Prefix E.	20.00	60.00	180
	e. Signature E. Thorp. 1947. Prefix F.	6.00	25.00	125
	f. Signature E. Thorp. 1947. Prefix G.	12.50	55.00	140
	g. Signature E. Thorp. 1948. Prefix G.	10.00	30.00	110
	h. Signature E. Thorp. 1948. Prefix H-I.	5.00	12.50	65.00
	i. Signature E. Thorp. 1948. Prefix J.	12.50	55.00	140
	j. Signature E. Thorp. 1949. Prefix J-K.	5.00	12.50	65.00
	k. Signature E. Thorp. 1949. Prefix L.	10.00	30.00	105
	l. Signature E. Thorp. 1950-1953. Prefix L-Y.	5.00	12.50	65.00
	s. Specimen. Overprint: *SPECIMEN*. Punch hole cancelled.	—	—	200

27	50 Kroner	VG	VF	UNC
	1945-1950. Green. Arms at left.			
	a. Signature G. Meldahl Nielsen. 1945; 1947; 1948. Prefix A.	40.00	100	325
	b. Signature E. Thorp. 1947. Prefix A.	100	270	600
	c. Signature E. Thorp. 1948. Prefix A.	250	500	1,000

		VG	VF	UNC
	d. Signature E. Thorp. 1948-1950. Prefix B.	70.00	190	425
	s. Specimen. Overprint: *SPECIMEN*. Punch hole cancelled.	—	—	1,500

28	**100 Kroner**	VG	VF	UNC
	1945-1949. Red. Arms at left.			
	a1. Signature G. Meldahl Nielsen. 1945. Prefix A.	25.00	60.00	225
	a2. Signature G. Meldahl Nielsen. 1946. Prefix A.	50.00	140	525
	a3. Signature G. Meldahl Nielsen. 1946. Prefix B.	27.50	75.00	300
	b. Signature E. Thorp. 1947-1949. Prefix B; C.	25.00	75.00	350
	s. Specimen. Overprint: *SPECIMEN*. Punch hole cancelled.	—	—	200

29	**1000 Kroner**	VG	VF	UNC
	1945-1947. Light brown. Portrait Adm. Tordenskjold at right. *GULD* (gold) blocked out with overprint geometric pattern at center. Prefix A. Back: Church at center.			
	a. Signature G. Meldahl Nielsen. 1945-1946.	350	700	1,500
	b. Signature E. Thorp. 1947.	750	1,300	2,250

1948-1955 Issue

#30-33 Replacement notes: Serial # prefix *Z*.

30	**5 Kroner**	VG	VF	UNC
	1955-1963. Blue on gray and multicolor underprint. Portrait Fridtjof Nansen at left. Back: Fishing scene. Watermark: Value repeated.			
	a. Signature Brofoss - Thorp. 1955-1956. Prefix A-D.	10.00	40.00	100
	b. Signature Brofoss - Thorp. 1957. Prefix D.	11.00	40.00	100
	c. Signature Brofoss - Thorp. 1957. Prefix E.	7.00	17.50	65.00
	d. Signature Brofoss - Thorp. 1957. Prefix F.	11.00	40.00	100
	e. Signature Brofoss - Ottesen. 1959. Prefix F.	7.00	17.50	65.00
	f. Signature Brofoss - Ottesen. 1959. Prefix G.	10.00	40.00	105
	g. Signature Brofoss - Ottesen. 1960-1963. Prefix G-L.	7.00	17.50	65.00
	s1. As a. Specimen. 1955. Overprint: *SPECIMEN*. Punch hole cancelled.	—	150	300
	s2. Specimen. Perforated.	—	—	750

31	**10 Kroner**	VG	VF	UNC
	1954-1973. Yellow-brown on gray underprint. Portrait Christian Michelsen at left. Back: Mercury with ships. Watermark: Value repeated.			
	a. Signature Jahn - Thorp. 1954. Prefix A-D.	3.00	8.50	45.00
	b1. Signature Brofoss - Thorp. 1954-1955. Prefix D-G.	2.50	8.00	40.00
	b2. Signature Brofoss - Thorp. 1955. Prefix H.	200	375	825
	b3. Signature Brofoss - Thorp. 1956. Prefix H-I.	2.50	8.00	40.00
	b4. Signature Brofoss - Thorp. 1957. Prefix I.	12.50	40.00	115
	b5. Signature Brofoss - Thorp. 1957-1958. Prefix J-M.	2.50	8.00	40.00
	b6. Signature Brofoss - Thorp. 1958. Prefix N.	8.00	35.00	105
	c. Signature Brofoss - Ottesen. 1959-1965. Prefix N-E.	2.25	4.50	25.00
	d. Signature Brofoss - Petersen. 1965-1969. Prefix F-V.	FV	3.00	12.50
	e. Signature Brofoss - Odegaard. 1970. Prefix W-.	FV	2.00	10.00
	f. Signature Wold - Odegaard. 1971-1973. Prefix Å-R.	FV	1.75	7.50
	p. Face or back proof. Uniface. Blue.	—	—	500
	s. As a, d, f. Specimen. Punch hole cancelled.	—	150	750

#31 Replacement notes: Serial # prefix *X* (1966-1972) *Z* (1954-1973).

32	**50 Kroner**	VG	VF	UNC
	1950-1965. Dark green. Portrait Bjørnstjerne Björnson at upper left. Crowned arms at upper center. Back: Harvesting. Watermark: Bjørnstjerne Björnson.			
	a1. Signature Jahn - Thorp. 1950-1952. Prefix A.	15.00	55.00	200
	a2. Signature Jahn - Thorp. 1952. Prefix B.	60.00	120	550
	a3. Signature Jan - Thorp. 1953-1954. Prefix B.	15.00	55.00	200
	b1. Signature Brofoss - Thorp. 1954. Prefix B.	70.00	150	650
	b2. Signature Brofoss - Thorp. 1955-1958. Prefix B; C.	17.50	50.00	170
	b3. Signature Brofoss - Thorp. 1958. Prefix D.	24.00	95.00	350
	c. Signature Brofoss - Ottesen. 1959-1965. Prefix D-F.	12.50	35.00	130
	s. As a. 1951. Specimen. Punch hole cancelled.	—	—	—

33	**100 Kroner**	VG	VF	UNC
	1949-1962. Red. Portrait Henrik Wergeland at upper left. Crowned arms at upper center. Back: Logging. Watermark: Henrik Wergeland.			
	a1. Signature Jahn - Thorp. 1949-1952. Prefix A.	22.50	50.00	175
	a2. Signature Jahn - Thorp. 1952. Prefix C.	800	1,250	—
	a3. Signature Jahn - Thorp. 1953-1954. Prefix C.	22.50	50.00	175
	b. Signature Brofoss - Thorp. 1954-1958. Prefix D-G.	20.00	50.00	175
	c. Signature Brofoss - Ottesen. 1959-1962. Prefix G-I.	20.00	40.00	140
	s. As a. 1950. Specimen. Punch hole cancelled.	—	—	200

34	500 Kroner	VG	VF	UNC
	1948-1976. Dark green. Portrait Niels Henrik Abel at upper left. Crowned supported arms at upper center. Prefix A. Back: Factory workers. Watermark: Niels Henrik Abel.			
	a. Signature Jahn - Thorp. 1948; 1951.	175	350	1,000
	b1. Signature Brofoss - Thorp. 1954; 1956.	175	350	1,000
	b2. Signature Brofoss - Thorp. 1958.	100	200	675
	c. Signature Brofoss - Ottesen. 1960-1964.	90.00	160	550
	d. Signature Brofoss - Petersen. 1966-1969.	85.00	140	400
	e. Signature Brofoss - Odegaard. 1970.	80.00	130	325
	f. Signature Wold - Odegaard. 1971-1976.	75.00	120	275
	s. As a. Specimen. 1948. Punch hole cancelled.	—	600	850

Replacement note: Serial # prefix G.

35	1000 Kroner	VG	VF	UNC
	1949-1974. Red-brown. Portrait H. Ibsen at left. Crowned supported arms at upper center. Prefix A. Back: Old man and child. Watermark: Portrait H. Ibsen.			
	a. Signature Jahn - Thorp. 1949; 1951; 1953.	175	425	800
	b. Signature Brofoss - Thorp. 1955; 1958.	160	290	600
	c. Signature Brofoss - Ottesen. 1961; 1962.	150	225	500
	d. Signature Brofoss - Petersen. 1965-1970.	140	210	400
	e. Signature Brofoss - Odegaard. 1971-1974.	130	200	325
	s. As a. Specimen. Punch hole cancelled.	—	600	850

Replacement note: Serial # prefix G.

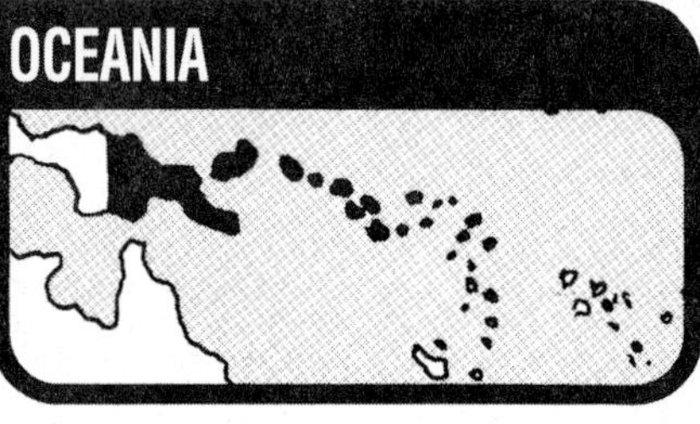

In general usage, Oceania is the collective name for the islands scattered throughout most of the Pacific Ocean. It has traditionally been divided into four parts: Australasia (Australia and New Zealand), Melenesia, Micronesia and Polynesia. Numismatically, Oceania is the name applied to the Gilbert and Solomon Islands, New Britain, and Papua New Guinea, hence the British denominations. See also French Oceania.

MONETARY SYSTEM:

1 Pound = 20 Shillings

JAPANESE OCCUPATION - WW II

Japanese Government

1942 ND Issue

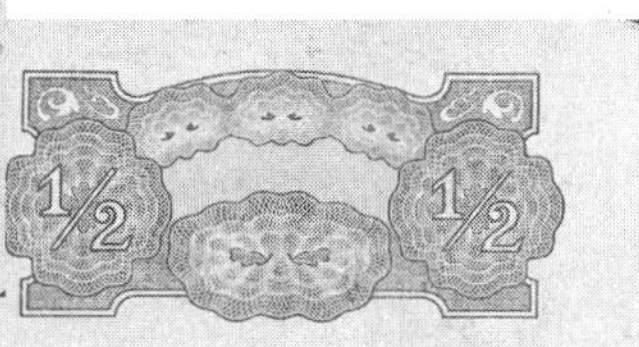

1	1/2 Shilling	VG	VF	UNC
	ND (1942). Purple on yellow-brown underprint. Palm trees along the beach at right.			
	a. Block letters OC spaced 42mm apart.	1.00	4.00	10.00
	b. Block letters: OA; OB spaced 50-53mm apart.	0.50	2.50	6.00
	c. Block letters: OC spaced 50-53mm apart.	0.25	0.75	2.50
	s. Specimen with red overprint: *Mi-hon. Specimen* on back.	—	—	150

Note: Block letters OC may be 42mm or 50-53mm apart.

2	1 Shilling	VG	VF	UNC
	ND (1942). Blue on green underprint. Breadfruit tree at left, palm trees along the beach at right. Block letters: OA-OC.			
	a. Issued note.	0.50	2.50	7.50
	s1. Specimen with red overprint: *Mi-hon. Specimen* on back.	—	—	150
	s2. Specimen with large red overprint: *Mi-hon.*	—	—	150

3	10 Shillings	VG	VF	UNC
	ND (1942). Brown. Palm trees along the beach at right. Block letters : OA.			
	a. Issued note.	3.00	15.00	75.00
	s. Specimen with red overprint: *Mi-hon. Specimen* on back.	—	—	200

4	1 Pound	VG	VF	UNC
	ND (1942). Green on light blue underprint. Palm trees along beach at right. Block letters : OA.			
	a. Issued note.	1.00	4.00	10.00
	s. Specimen with red overprint: *Mi-hon. Specimen* on back.	—	—	175

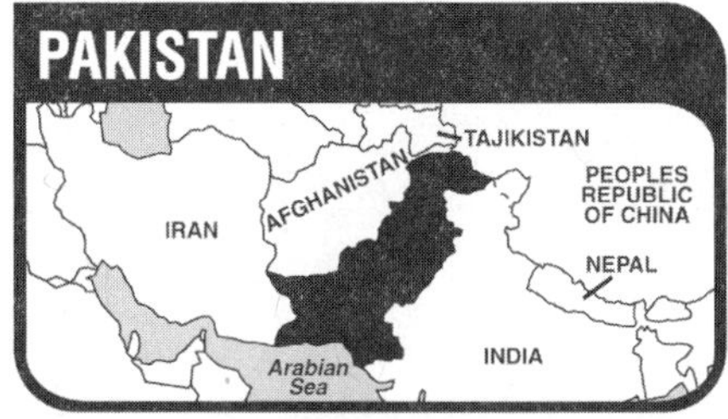

The Islamic Republic of Pakistan, located on the Indian subcontinent between India and Afghanistan, has an area of 310,404 sq. mi. (803,943 sq. m.) and a population of 170 million. Capital: Islamabad. Pakistan is mainly an agricultural land. Yarn, cotton, rice and leather are exported.The Indus Valley civilization, one of the oldest in the world and dating back at least 5,000 years, spread over much of what is presently Pakistan. During the second millennium B.C., remnants of this culture fused with the migrating Indo-Aryan peoples. The area underwent successive invasions in subsequent centuries from the Persians, Greeks, Scythians, Arabs (who brought Islam), Afghans, and Turks. The Mughal Empire flourished in the 16th and 17th centuries; the British came to dominate the region in the 18th century. The separation in 1947 of British India into the Muslim state of Pakistan (with West and East sections) and largely Hindu India was never satisfactorily resolved, and India and Pakistan fought two wars - in 1947-48 and 1965 - over the disputed Kashmir territory. A third war between these countries in 1971 - in which India capitalized on Islamabad's marginalization of Bengalis in Pakistani politics - resulted in East Pakistan becoming the separate nation of Bangladesh. In response to Indian nuclear weapons testing, Pakistan conducted its own tests in 1998. The dispute over the state of Kashmir is ongoing, but discussions and confidence-building measures have led to decreased tensions since 2002. Mounting public dissatisfaction with President Musharraf, coupled with the assassination of the prominent and popular political leader, Benazir Bhutto, in late 2007, and Musharraf's resignation in August 2008, led to the September presidential election of Asif Zardari, Bhutto's widower. Pakistani government and military leaders are struggling to control Islamist militants, many of whom are located in the tribal areas adjacent to the border with Afghanistan. The November 2008 Mumbai attacks again inflamed Indo-Pakistan relations. The Pakistani Government is also faced with a deteriorating economy as foreign exchange reserves decline, the currency depreciates, and the current account deficit widens.

MONETARY SYSTEM:

1 Rupee = 16 Annas to 1961

1 Rupee = 100 Paisa (Pice), 1961-

REPLACEMENT NOTES:

#24, 24A, 24B, 1/X or 2/X prefix. #25-33, X as first of double prefix letters.

REPUBLIC

Government of Pakistan

1948 ND Provisional Issue

#1-3A new plates with *GOVERNMENT OF PAKISTAN* in English and Urdu on Government and Reserve Bank of India notes.

#		VG	VF	UNC
1	**1 Rupee** ND (1948). Gray-green. New plate like India #25c.	90.00	165	275

#		VG	VF	UNC
1A	**2 Rupees** ND (1948). Lilac. New plate like India #17b.	450	650	1,100

Note: It is now believed that the note with red serial # and overprint on India 17c, formerly listed as 1Ab, is spurious.

#		VG	VF	UNC
2	**5 Rupees** ND (1948). Green. New plate like India #23a.	180	275	450

#		VG	VF	UNC
3	**10 Rupees** ND (1948). Violet. New plate like India #24.	120	175	330
3A	**100 Rupees** ND (1948). Dark green and lilac. New plate like India #20k.	2,000	3,750	5,000

1948-1949 ND Issue

#		VG	VF	UNC
4	**1 Rupee** ND (1949). Green on multicolor underprint. Crescent moon and star at right. Back: Archway at left center. Watermark: Crescent moon and star.	80.00	130	210

#		VG	VF	UNC
5	**5 Rupees** ND (1948). Blue on tan underprint. Crescent moon and star at right.	120	175	240

#		VG	VF	UNC
6	**10 Rupees** ND (1948). Orange on green underprint. Crescent moon and star at right.	120	180	300

7	100 Rupees	VG	VF	UNC
	ND (1948). Green on tan underprint. Crescent moon and star at right.	325	500	750

1951-1973 ND Issues

8	1 Rupee	VG	VF	UNC
	ND (1951). Blue on multicolor underprint. Crescent moon and star at right. 2 signature varieties. Back: Archway at left center. BC: Violet.	100	150	250

9	1 Rupee	VG	VF	UNC
	ND (1953-1963). Blue on multicolor underprint. Crescent moon and star at right. Like #8 but larger size serial #. 6 signature varieties. Back: Archway at left center. BC: Blue.	40.00	70.00	110

Note: The scarce signature in this variety is Abdul Qadir, valued at $50. in Unc.

9A	1 Rupee	VG	VF	UNC
	ND (1964). Blue on multicolor underprint. Crescent moon and star at right. Like #8 but different font for serial #. 3 signature varieties. Back: Archway at left center. BC: Violet.	50.00	80.00	125

State Bank of Pakistan

1949-1953 ND Issue

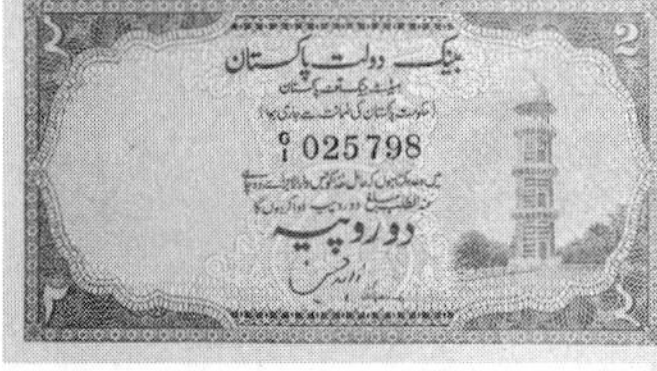

11	2 Rupees	VG	VF	UNC
	ND (1949). Brown on pink and light green underprint. Tower on wall encircling the tomb of Jahangir in Lahore at left. Back: Badshahi Mosque in Lahore at left center. Watermark: Crescent moon and star. Printer: BWC (without imprint.)	500	1,000	1,500

12	5 Rupees	VG	VF	UNC
	ND (1951). Purple on light green underprint. A jute laden boat at center. 3 signature varieties. Back: Khyber Pass on back. Watermark: Crescent moon and star.	50.00	75.00	100

13	10 Rupees	VG	VF	UNC
	ND (1951). Brown on light yellow underprint. Shalimar Gardens in Lahore. 4 signature varieties. Back: Tombs nearThatta. Watermark: Crescent moon and star.	20.00	25.00	35.00
14	100 Rupees	VG	VF	UNC
	ND (1953). Red-brown. Crescent moon and star. Similar to #7. 2 signature varieties. Watermark: At right on face. Crescent moon and star.			
	a. *DHAKA* in Urdu at bottom of note.	100	140	225
	b. *KARACHI* in Urdu at bottom of note.	100	140	175

1957-1966 ND Issue

18	100 Rupees	VG	VF	UNC
	ND (1957). Green on violet and peach underprint. Portrait of Mohammed Ali Jinnah at center. Back: Badshahi Mosque in Lahore. Watermark: Mohammed Ali Jinnah.			
	a. Without overprint. 2 signature varieties.	8.00	11.00	15.00
	b. Overprint: *Dhaka.* 2 signature varieties.	8.00	11.00	15.00
	c. Overprint: *Karachi.* 2 signature varieties.	8.00	11.00	15.00
	d. Overprint: *Lahore.* 2 signature varieties.	8.00	11.00	15.00

REGIONAL

Government of Pakistan

1950 ND Pilgrim Issue

		VG	VF	UNC
R1	**100 Rupees** ND (1950). Red. Crescent moon and star at right. Like #7 but with overprint: *FOR PILGRIMS FROM PAKISTAN FOR USE IN SAUDI ARABIA AND IRAQ.*	—	—	—

State Bank of Pakistan

1950 ND Haj Pilgrim Issue

		VG	VF	UNC
R2	**10 Rupees** ND (1950). Green. Shalimar Gardens in Lahore. Like #13 but with overprint: *FOR HAJ PILGRIMS FROM PAKISTAN FOR USE IN SAUDI ARABIA ONLY.* 3 signature varieties. Back: Tombs near Thatta.	40.00	150	350

Palestine, a former British mandate in southwest Asia at the eastern end of the Mediterranean Sea, had an area of 10,160 sq. mi. (26,315 sq. km.). It included Israel and that part of Jordan lying west of the Jordan River. Ancient Palestine (the territory owned in biblical times by the kingdoms of Israel and Judah) was somewhat larger, including lands east of the Jordan River. Because of its position as part of the land bridge connecting Asia and Africa, Palestine was invaded and conquered by virtually all the historic powers of Europe and the Near East. From 1516 to 1917, it was held by the Ottoman Empire. In 1917, it was conquered by the British under Allenby and assigned as a British mandate, effective 1922. The British ruled Palestine until 1948, and succeeded in satisfying neither the Arab nor the Jewish population. The United Nations recommended the establishment of separate Jewish and Arab states in Palestine. The British left Palestine on May 14, 1948, and the State of Israel was proclaimed. In 1950, the Kingdom of Jordan annexed the west bank of the Jordan River. This was seized by Israel during the 1967 war, bringing the entire former mandate under Israeli administration.

RULERS:
British, 1917-1948

MONETARY SYSTEM:
1 Pound = 1000 Mils

BRITISH ADMINISTRATION

Palestine Currency Board

1927 Issue

		Good	Fine	XF
6	**500 Mils** 1927-1945. Purple on green underprint. Rachel's tomb near Bethlehem at lower left. Back: Citadel of Jerusalem (commonly called the Tower of David) at center. Printer: TDLR.			
	a. 1.9.1927.	500	3,500	12,500
	b. 30.9.1929.	300	1,000	4,000
	c. 20.4.1939.	200	600	2,250
	d. 15.8.1945.	250	1,250	4,500
	s. Specimen. Varieties with regular serial #s and others with 0s as serial # exist.	—	—	—
	x. Counterfeit 20.4.1939.	—	—	—

		Good	Fine	XF
7	**1 Pound** 1927-1944. Green and black. Dome of the Rock at left. Back: Citadel of Jerusalem (commonly called the Tower of David) at center.			
	a. 1.9.1927.	500	3,500	11,000
	b. 30.9.1929.	300	750	3,000
	c. 20.4.1939.	150	500	1,500
	d. 1.1.1944.	225	800	3,500
	s. Specimen. Varieties with regular serial #s and others with 0s as serial # exist.	—	—	—
	x. Counterfeit. 30.9.1929; 20.4.1939.	—	—	—

8	5 Pounds	Good	Fine	XF
	1927-1944. Red and black. Crusader's Tower at Ramleh at left. Back: Citadel of Jerusalem (commonly called the Tower of David) at center.			
	a. 1.9.1927.	—	35,000	60,000
	b. 30.9.1929.	1,000	3,000	15,000
	c. 20.4.1939.	650	2,000	15,000
	d. 1.1.1944.	750	3,000	9,000
	s. Specimen. Varieties with regular serial #s and others with 0s as serial # exist.	—	—	—
	x. Counterfeit. 20.4.1939 with and without serial # prefix.	100	150	—

9	10 Pounds	Good	Fine	XF
	1927-1944. Blue and black. Crusader's Tower at Ramleh at left. Back: Citadel of Jerusalem (commonly called the Tower of David) at center.			
	a. 1.9.1927.	—	50,000	—
	b. 30.9.1929.	1,250	6,000	16,000
	c. 7.9.1939.	750	3,500	10,000
	d. 1.1.1944.	1,000	3,500	10,000
	s. Specimen. Varieties with regular serial #s and others with 0s as serial # exist.	—	Unc	55,000
	x. Counterfeit. 1.1.1944.	—	—	—

Color Abbreviation Guide

New to the *Standard Catalog of ® World Paper Money* are the following abbreviations related to color references:

BC: Back color
PC: Paper color

10	50 Pounds	Good	Fine	XF
	1927-1939. Purple and black. Crusader'sTower at Ramleh at left. Back: Citadel of Jerusalem (commonly called the Tower of David) at center.			
	a. 1.9.1927. Rare.	—	—	—
	b. 30.9.1929.	—	50,000	125,000
	c. 7.9.1939. Rare.	—	—	—
	s. Specimen. Varieties with regular serial #s and others with 0s as serial # exist.	—	Unc	110,000
	ct. Color trial. 30.9.1929. Serial # A000000.	—	Unc	75,000

11	100 Pounds	Good	Fine	XF
	1927-1942. Green and black. Crusader's Tower at Ramleh at left. Back: Citadel of Jerusalem (commonly called the Tower of David) at center.			
	a. 1.9.1927. Rare.	—	—	—
	b. 30.9.1929. Rare.	—	—	—
	c. 10.9.1942. Requires confirmation.	—	—	—
	s. Specimen. As a with regular serial #s, c with 0s as serial #.	—	—	—

Note: According to Bank of England records, only 6 examples of #11 are outstanding. Four are known.

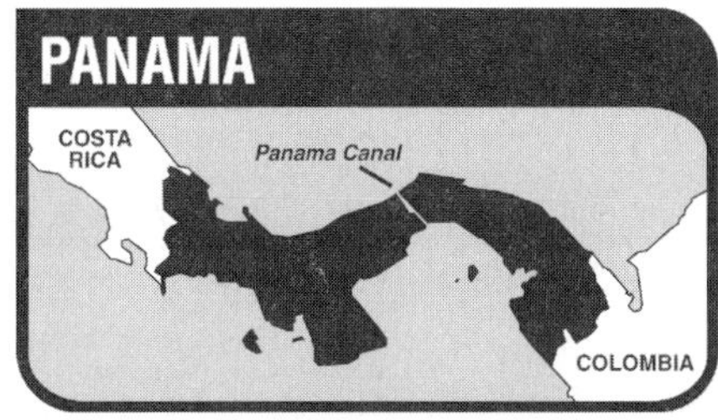

The Republic of Panama, a Central American country situated between Costa Rica and Colombia, has an area of 29,206 sq. mi. (77,083 sq. km.) and a population of 2.86 million. Capital: Panama City. The Panama Canal is the country's biggest asset; servicing world related transit trade and international commerce. Bananas, refined petroleum, sugar and shrimp are exported. Explored and settled by the Spanish in the 16th century, Panama broke with Spain in 1821 and joined a union of Colombia, Ecuador, and Venezuela - named the Republic of Gran Colombia. When the latter dissolved in 1830, Panama remained part of Colombia. With US backing, Panama seceded from Colombia in 1903 and promptly signed a treaty with the US allowing for the construction of a canal and US sovereignty over a strip of land on either side of the structure (the Panama Canal Zone). The Panama Canal was built by the US Army Corps of Engineers between 1904 and 1914. In 1977, an agreement was signed for the complete transfer of the Canal from the US to Panama by the end of the century. Certain portions of the Zone and increasing responsibility over the Canal were turned over in the subsequent decades. With US help, dictator Manuel NORIEGA was deposed in 1989. The entire Panama Canal, the area supporting the Canal, and remaining US military bases were transferred to Panama by the end of 1999. In October 2006, Panamanians approved an ambitious plan to expand the Canal. The project, which began in 2007 and could double the Canal's capacity, is expected to be completed in 2014-2015. Notes of the United States have normally circulated throughout Panama.

MONETARY SYSTEM:

1 Balboa = 100 Centesimos

Note: Certain listings encompassing issues circulated by various bank and regional authorities are contained in Volume 1 under Colombia.

REPUBLIC OF PANAMÁ

República de Panamá

1933 "Sosa" Issue

No.	Description	Good	Fine	XF
21	**1 Balboa** 5.8.1933. Arms at left, Balboa standing with sword and flag at right. (Not issued).	—	—	—
21A	**10 Balboas** 1933. Requires confirmation.	—	—	—

Note: The Sosa Project was conceived by Don Martin Sosa Comptroller General of Panama in 1933.

Banco Central de Emisión

Issued under the Government of President Arnulfo Arias.

1941 "Arias" Issue

No.	Description	Good	Fine	XF
22	**1 Balboa** 1941. Black on green and red underprint. Portrait Balboa at center. Back: Arms at center. Printer: HBNC.			
	a. Issued note.	275	800	1,350
	s. Specimen.	—	Unc	1,000

Note: After a very short circulation period #22-25 were recalled and almost all destroyed.

No.	Description	Good	Fine	XF
23	**5 Balboas** 1941. Black on blue, violet and orange underprint. Urraca at left. Back: Arms at center. BC: Blue. Printer: HBNC.			
	a. Issued note.	1,000	2,750	5,000
	s. Specimen.	—	Unc	1,250

No.	Description	Good	Fine	XF
24	**10 Balboas** 1941. Black on violet, orange and green underprint. Old fortress at center. Back: Arms at center. BC: Brown. Printer: HBNC.			
	a. Issued note.	1,500	4,500	7,500
	s. Specimen.	—	Unc	2,000

No.	Description	Good	Fine	XF
25	**20 Balboas** 1941. Black on orange, red and violet. Ox cart at center. Back: Arms at center. BC: Orange. Printer: HBNC.			
	a. Issued note.	2,500	5,500	8,500
	s. Specimen.	—	Unc	3,000

PAPUA NEW GUINEA

Papua New Guinea, an independent member of the British Commonwealth, occupies the eastern half of the island of New Guinea. It lies north of Australia near the equator and borders on West Irian. The country, which includes nearby Bismarck Archipelago, Buka and Bougainville, has an area of 462,820 sq. km. and a population of 5.93 million. Capital: Port Moresby. The economy is agricultural, and exports include copra, rubber, cocoa, coffee, tea, gold and copper.The eastern half of the island of New Guinea - second largest in the world - was divided between Germany (north) and the UK (south) in 1885. The latter area was transferred to Australia in 1902, which occupied the northern portion during World War I and continued to administer the combined areas until independence in 1975. A nine-year secessionist revolt on the island of Bougainville ended in 1997 after claiming some 20,000 lives.

RULERS:

British

MONETARY SYSTEM:

1 Kina = 100 Toea, 1975-
1 Shilling = 12 Pence
1 Crown = 5 Shillings
1 Pound = 4 Crowns

BRITISH ADMINISTRATION

Bank of New South Wales

Port Moresby

1910 Issue

		Good	Fine	XF
A5	**1 Pound** 1.5.1910; 1.6.1910. Black. Allegorical woman seated, holding caduceus by sheep with sailing ship in background at top center. Printer: CS&E. Rare.	—	—	—

PARAGUAY

The Republic of Paraguay, a landlocked country in the heart of South America surrounded by Argentina, Bolivia and Brazil, has an area of 157,042 sq. mi. (406,752 sq. km.) and a population of 5.5 million, 95 percent of whom are of mixed Spanish and Indian descent. Capital: Asunción. The country is predominantly agrarian, with no important mineral deposits or oil reserves. Meat, timber, oilseeds, tobacco and cotton account for 70 percent of Paraguay's export revenue.In the disastrous War of the Triple Alliance (1865-70) - between Paraguay and Argentina, Brazil, and Uruguay - Paraguay lost two-thirds of all adult males and much of its territory. It stagnated economically for the next half century. In the Chaco War of 1932-35, Paraguay won large, economically important areas from Bolivia. The 35-year military dictatorship of Alfredo Stroessner ended in 1989, and, despite a marked increase in political infighting in recent years, Paraguay has held relatively free and regular presidential elections since then.

MONETARY SYSTEM:

1 Peso = 100 Centavos to 1870
1 Peso = 8 Reales to 1872
1 Peso = 100 Centésimos to 1870
1 Peso = 100 Centavos (Centésimos) to 1944
1 Guaraní = 100 Céntimos, 1944-

REPÚBLICA DEL PARAGUAY

El Tesoro Nacional

National Treasury

#1-30 lithographed notes. Uniface. #1-17 with monogram of Carlos Antonio Lopez, President of the Republic.

Decreto de 13 de febrero de 1856

		Good	Fine	XF
1	**1/2 Real** ND (1856). Black. Flowers at left. Black seal at center. 175x120mm.	25.00	80.00	200

		Good	Fine	XF
2	**4 Reales** ND (1856). Black. Burro at upper left. Black seal at center.	30.00	100	225
3	**1 Peso** ND (1856). Black. Leopard at upper left. Black seal at center. 165x120mm.	20.00	50.00	125
4	**2 Pesos** ND (1856). Black. Goat looking left. at upper left. Black seal at center. 160x120mm.	20.00	50.00	125

Decreto de 29 de abril de 1859

		Good	Fine	XF
5	**1 Real** ND (1859). Black. Bottle at upper left, black seal at center. 170x110mm.	45.00	75.00	175

Decreto de 17 de mayo de 1859

		Good	Fine	XF
6	**1 Peso** ND (1859). Black. Leopard at upper center. 160x115mm.	—	—	—

Decreto de 10 de junio de 1860

		Good	Fine	XF
7	**1/2 Real** ND (1860). Black. Flowers at upper left, arms at upper center. 105x65mm.	25.00	80.00	200

		Good	Fine	XF
8	**1 Real** ND (1860). Black. Bottle at left, arms at upper center. 120x75mm.	20.00	50.00	125
9	**2 Reales** ND (1860). Black. Man with horse at upper left, arms at upper center and right. 2 signature varieties. 125x80mm.	7.50	17.50	50.00

		Good	Fine	XF
10	**4 Reales** ND (1860). Black. Burro (donkey) at upper left, arms at upper center. 2 signature varieties. 140x100mm.	10.00	30.00	80.00

		Good	Fine	XF
11	**1 Peso** ND (1860). Black. Leopard at upper left, arms at upper center. 3 signature varieties. 150x105mm.	10.00	30.00	80.00

		Good	Fine	XF
12	**2 Pesos** ND (1860). Black and pink. Goat looking right. at upper left, arms at upper center. 165x105mm.	6.00	15.00	50.00

		Good	Fine	XF
13	**3 Pesos** ND (1860). Black and light green. Woman, harvest and ship at upper left, arms at upper center. 185x115mm.	7.50	20.00	60.00

Decreto de 21 de setiembre de 1861

		Good	Fine	XF
14	**5 Pesos** ND (1861). Black. Steam passenger train at upper left, arms at upper center. 175x115mm.	7.50	20.00	60.00

Decreto de 14 de noviembre de 1861

		Good	Fine	XF
15	**4 Pesos** ND (1861). Blue. Blindfolded Justice seated at upper left, oval arms at upper center. 180x115mm.	10.00	30.00	80.00

Decreto de 31 de marzo de 1862

		Good	Fine	XF
16	**4 Pesos** ND (1862). Black. Oxen with plow at left. Oval arms at left center. 190x125mm.	3.00	10.00	35.00

		Good	Fine	XF
17	**5 Pesos** ND (1862). Black. Man riding with two burros at upper left. Oval arms at center. 180x120mm.	7.50	20.00	60.00

Decreto de 25 de marzo de 1865

Issues of Mariscal Francisco Solano Lopez, the son of Carlos Antonio Lopez who took the presidency of the Republic in 1862.

		Good	Fine	XF
18	**1 Real** ND (1865). Black. Man walking with sack on stick at upper left. Black seal at upper center. 140x90mm.	10.00	40.00	100

		Good	Fine	XF
19	**2 Reales** ND (1865). Black. Floral design at left. Black seal at upper center. 140x95mm.	3.50	17.50	40.00

		Good	Fine	XF
20	**4 Reales** ND (1865). Black. Ram at upper left. Black seal at upper center. 145x95mm.	3.50	17.50	40.00

		Good	Fine	XF
21	**1 Peso** ND (1865). Blue. Ox at upper left. Black seal at upper center. 155x105mm.	3.50	17.50	40.00

		Good	Fine	XF
22	**2 Pesos** ND (1865). Blue. Man with horse-drawn cart at upper left. Black seal at upper center. 165x95mm.	3.50	17.50	40.00

		Good	Fine	XF
23	**3 Pesos** ND (1865). Blue. Ship at upper left. Black seal at upper center. 160x110mm.	3.50	17.50	40.00

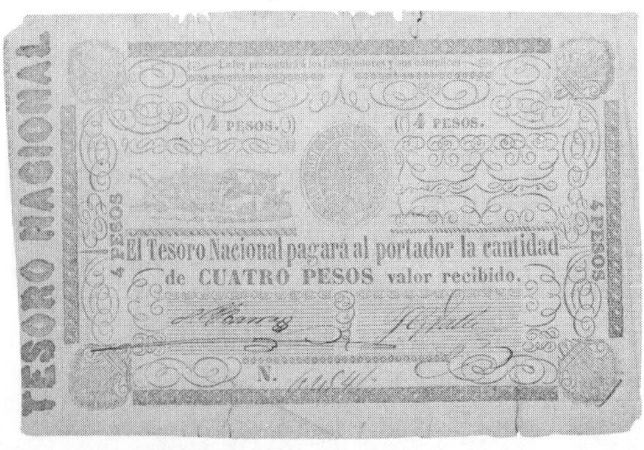

		Good	Fine	XF
24	**4 Pesos** ND (1865). Blue. Oxen with plow at left. Black seal at upper center. 190x115mm.	3.50	17.50	40.00

#	Description	Good	Fine	XF
25	**5 Pesos** ND (1865). Blue. Man riding with two burros at upper left. Similar to #17, but without monogram at right. Black seal at upper center. 170x115mm.	3.00	15.00	35.00

#	Description	Good	Fine	XF
26	**10 Pesos** ND (1865). Blue. Woman carrying sack at left, arms at left and right. Black seal at upper center. 190x125mm.	3.50	17.50	40.00

1865-1870 Issue

#27-30, Either without signatures or just one signature.

#	Description	Good	Fine	XF
27	**3 Pesos** ND (1865-1870). Black. Ship at upper left. 160x90mm.	7.50	25.00	75.00
28	**4 Pesos** ND (1865-1870). Black. Oxen with plow at left. 175x95mm.	7.50	25.00	75.00
29	**5 Pesos** ND (1865-1870). Black. Similar to #25. 155x95mm.	15.00	40.00	100
30	**10 Pesos** ND (1865-1870). Black. Similar to #26, but without arms at left and right. 200x95mm.	3.50	17.50	40.00

War of the Triple Alliance, 1864-1870

Note: Apparently, during one stage of the war, these notes of the reduced size (#27-29) were ovpt. w/red circle inscribed: *TERCERA SERIE*.

1868 Issue

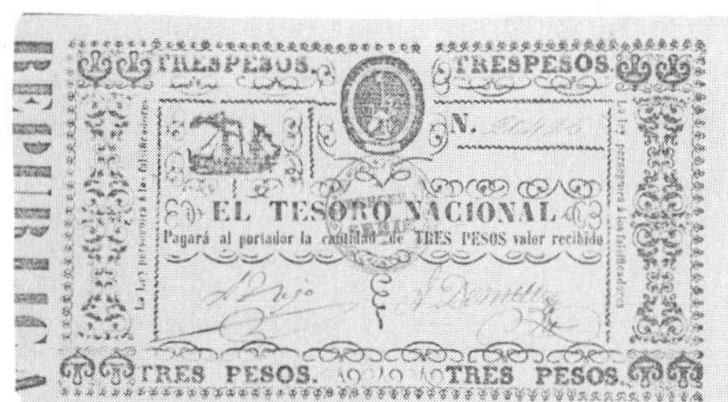

#	Description	Good	Fine	XF
31	**3 Pesos** ND (1868). Overprint: Red; on #27.	3.50	12.50	35.00

#	Description	Good	Fine	XF
32	**4 Pesos** ND (1868). Overprint: Red; on #28.	3.50	12.50	35.00
33	**5 Pesos** ND (1868). Overprint: Red; on #29.	3.50	12.50	35.00

Note: The 3 Pesos depicting a tree at left and arms at center (formerly #A19A) has been determined to be a spurious issue.

1870 Issue

#	Description	Good	Fine	XF
34	**1 Real** 29.12.1870. Black and green. Arms at left.	—	—	—
35	**2 Reales** 29.12.1870.	—	—	—
36	**4 Reales** 29.12.1870. Black and green. Dog at left, arms at upper center.	—	—	—

#37-39 issued with or without 2 oval handstamps on back. The handstamps are: *MINISTERIO DE HACIENDA* and *TESORERÍA GENERAL-ASUNCIÓN* around arms.

#	Description	Good	Fine	XF
37	**50 Centésimos** 29.12.1870. Black.			
	a. Without 2 oval handstamps on back. Rare.	—	—	—
	b. With 2 oval handstamps on back. Rare.	—	—	—

#	Description	Good	Fine	XF
38	**1 Peso** 29.12.1870. Black. Bull at center.			
	a. Without 2 oval handstamps on back. Rare.	—	—	—
	b. With 2 oval handstamps on back. Rare.	—	—	—

#	Description	Good	Fine	XF
39	**5 Pesos** 29.12.1870. Black. Arms at center.			
	a. Without 2 oval handstamps on back. Rare.	—	—	—
	b. With 2 oval handstamps on back.	—	—	—

#40 not assigned.

1871 Issue, La Tesoreria General

#	Denomination	Good	Fine	XF
41	**1/2 Real** 1871. Black. Arms at upper left, rooster at center. a. Issued note. r. Unsigned remainder.	 — —	 — —	 — —

#	Denomination	Good	Fine	XF
42	**1 Real** 15.7.1871. Black. Arms at left. 2 signature varieties.	—	—	—
43	**2 Reales** 15.7.1871.	—	—	—

#	Denomination	Good	Fine	XF
44	**4 Reales** 15.7.1871. Black. Dog at left, arms at upper center. 2 signature varieties.	—	—	—
45	**1 Peso** 15.7.1871.	—	—	—
46	**5 Pesos** 15.7.1871.	—	—	—
47	**10 Pesos** 15.7.1871.	—	—	—

Caja de Conversión

Law of 9.1.1874; Decree of 4.3.1874

#	Denomination	Good	Fine	XF
48	**10 Centavos** 15.3.1874. Black. 2 signature varieties. Uniface. Printer: Ludovico Sartori y Cia. Rare.	—	—	—

Note: Some examples of #48 appear with 2 oval overstamps on back.

#	Denomination	Good	Fine	XF
49	**20 Centavos** 15.3.1874. Brown. 2 signature varieties. Printer: Ludovico Sartori y Cia. Rare.	—	—	—
50	**50 Centavos** 15.3.1874. Black. Sheep at center. 2 signature varieties. Printer: Ludovico Sartori y Cia. Rare.	—	—	—
51	**1 Peso** 15.3.1874. Orange and black. 4 signature varieties. Printer: Ludovico Sartori y Cia. a. Issued note. Rare. b. With 2 oval handstamps on back (like #37b-39b). Rare.	 — —	 — —	 — —
52	**5 Pesos** 1874. 2 signature varieties. Printer: Ludovico Sartori y Cia. Rare.	—	—	—

#51-59 not assigned.

Tesoro Nacional

National Treasury

Ley de 22.4.1875

#	Denomination	Good	Fine	XF
60	**5 Centavos** *L.1875.* Green. Ram at upper center. 2 signature varieties. Printer: Lit. San Martin-Argentina. Rare.	—	—	—
61	**20 Centavos** *L.1875.* Printer: Lit. San Martin-Argentina.	—	—	—

Note: Apparently #60 and 61 are part of a later series because of their signatures.
#62-65 not assigned.

#	Denomination	Good	Fine	XF
66	**10 Pesos** *L.1875.* Orange and black. Woman's head at left and right, mountain scene at center. Printer: Lit. San Martin-Argentina.	—	—	—
67	**20 Pesos** *L.1875.* Multicolor. Boy standing at left, paddle wheel steamer at upper center. Printer: Lit. San Martin-Argentina.	—	—	—

#68-86 not assigned.

República del Paraguay

Government Notes

Ley de 24 de setiembre de 1894

#	Denomination	Good	Fine	XF
87	**50 Centavos** *L.1894.* Orange and black. Arms at center. 4 signature varieties. Printer: G&D.	8.00	25.00	80.00
88	**1 Peso** *L.1894.* Black, dark red and blue. Arms at left. 3 signature varieties. BC: Dark red. Printer: G&D.	10.00	50.00	175
89	**5 Pesos** *L.1894.* Blue and orange. Arms at right. 3 signature varieties. Printer: G&D.	15.00	80.00	225
90	**10 Pesos** *L.1894.* Printer: G&D. Requires confirmation.	—	—	—
91	**20 Pesos** *L.1894.* Arms at left. Printer: G&D. Rare.	—	—	—
92	**50 Pesos** *L.1894.* Printer: G&D. Requires confirmation.	—	—	—
93	**100 Pesos** *L.1894.* Black and orange. Woman with torch at left, arms at center 2 signature varieties. Printer: G&D. Rare.	—	—	—

#	Denomination	Good	Fine	XF
94	**200 Pesos** *L.1894.* Light blue and orange underprint. Arms at left, portrait Gen. Egusquiza at top center. 2 signature varieties. Printer: G&D.	150	600	—

Ley de 18 de noviembre de 1899

#95-157 each denomination within this range has an identical design (but some have minor variations).

#	Denomination	Good	Fine	XF
95	**50 Centavos** *L.1899.* Black on orange underprint. Minerva wearing helmet at left. Back: Arms. BC: Orange. Printer: ABNC. a. Issued note. s. Specimen.	 2.50 —	 7.50 Unc	 30.00 150
96	**1 Peso** *L.1899.* Black on green underprint. Woman wearing straw hat at center. 2 signature varieties. Back: Arms. BC: Green. Printer: ABNC. a. Issued note. s. Specimen.	 3.50 —	 12.50 Unc	 35.00 100
97	**2 Pesos** *L.1899.* Black on light brown underprint. Government palace at center. 2 signature varieties. Back: Arms. BC: Brown. Printer: ABNC. a. Issued note. s. Specimen.	 4.50 —	 20.00 Unc	 50.00 150

#	Note	Good	Fine	XF
98	**5 Pesos**			
	L.1899. Black on lilac, peach and blue underprint. View of city of Asunción from river. Back: Arms. BC: Dark blue. Printer: ABNC.			
	a. Issued note.	6.00	30.00	75.00
	p. Proof. Punch hole cancelled.	—	Unc	100
	s. Specimen.	—	Unc	200
99	**10 Pesos**	**Good**	**Fine**	**XF**
	L.1899. Black on green underprint. Cathedral at right center. Back: Arms. BC: Gray-green. Printer: ABNC.			
	a. Issued note.	10.00	40.00	95.00
	p. Proof. Punch hole cancelled.	—	Unc	100
	s. Specimen.	—	Unc	250
100	**20 Pesos**	**Good**	**Fine**	**XF**
	L.1899. Black on blue and yellow underprint. Congressional palace at center. 2 signature varieties. Back: Arms. BC: Dark blue. Printer: ABNC.			
	a. Issued note.	15.00	50.00	125
	s. Specimen.	—	Unc	275
101	**50 Pesos**	**Good**	**Fine**	**XF**
	L.1899. Black on yellow and brown underprint. Municipal theater at right. Back: Man's head at center. Arms. BC: Dark brown. Printer: ABNC.			
	a. Issued note.	20.00	75.00	175
	s. Specimen.	—	Unc	400
102	**100 Pesos**	**Good**	**Fine**	**XF**
	L.1899. Black on red and yellow underprint. Guaira waterfall at center. Back: Woman's head at center. Arms. BC: Red. Printer: ABNC.			
	a. Issued note.	22.50	100	225
	s. Specimen.	—	Unc	500
103	**200 Pesos**	**Good**	**Fine**	**XF**
	L.1899. Black on yellow and orange underprint. Mountain and farm at center right. Back: Woman's head at left. Arms. BC: Orange. Printer: ABNC.			
	a. Issued note.	40.00	150	400
	s. Specimen.	—	Unc	900

#	Note	Good	Fine	XF
104	**500 Pesos**			
	L.1899. Black on lilac and yellow underprint. Woman with child at left, ruins at Humaita at right. Back: Arms. BC: Blue-gray. Printer: ABNC.			
	a. Issued note.	50.00	250	600
	p. Proof. Punch hole cancelled.	—	Unc	500
	s. Specimen.	—	Unc	1,500

Ley de 14 de julio de 1903

#105-114 date of the law in 1 or 2 lines.

#	Note	Good	Fine	XF
105	**50 Centavos**			
	L.1903. Black on orange underprint. Minerva wearing helmet at left. 4 signature varieties. Back: Arms. BC: Green. Printer: ABNC.			
	a. Date in 2 lines.	2.00	5.00	20.00
	b. Date in 1 line.	2.00	5.00	20.00
	s1. As a. Specimen.	—	Unc	150
	s2. As b. Specimen.	—	Unc	100

#	Note	Good	Fine	XF
106	**1 Peso**			
	L.1903. In one line. Woman wearing straw hat at center. 4 signature varieties. Back: Arms. BC: Brown. Printer: ABNC.			
	a. Serial # at upper right.	3.00	8.00	30.00
	b. Serial # at bottom center.	2.50	7.50	25.00
	s1. As a. Specimen.	—	Unc	150
	s2. As b. Specimen.	—	Unc	125

#	Note	Good	Fine	XF
107	**2 Pesos**			
	L.1903. In one line. Government palace at center. 2 signature varieties. Back: Arms. BC: Brown. Printer: ABNC.			
	a. Serial # at upper right.	4.00	12.50	40.00
	b. Serial # at bottom center.	3.00	10.00	30.00
	s1. As a. Specimen.	—	Unc	150
	s2. As b. Specimen.	—	Unc	150

#	Note	Good	Fine	XF
108	**5 Pesos**			
	L.1903. View of city of Asuncion from river. 5 signature varieties. Back: Arms. BC: Brown. Printer: ABNC.			
	a. Date in 2 lines.	5.00	17.50	55.00
	b. Date in 1 line.	4.00	15.00	45.00
	s1. As a. Specimen.	—	Unc	175
	s2. As b. Specimen.	—	Unc	150
109	**10 Pesos**	**Good**	**Fine**	**XF**
	L.1903. In one line. Cathedral at right center. 5 signature varieties. Back: Arms. BC: Olive. Printer: ABNC.			
	a. Serial # at bottom left and right.	8.00	25.00	85.00
	b. Serial # at bottom center.	7.00	22.50	70.00
	s1. As a. Specimen	—	Unc	200
	s2. As b. Specimen.	—	Unc	150
110	**20 Pesos**	**Good**	**Fine**	**XF**
	L.1903. Black on blue and yellow underprint. Congressional palace at center. 2 signature varieties. Back: Arms. BC: Dark blue. Printer: ABNC.			
	a. Date in 2 lines.	10.00	35.00	100
	b. Date in 1 line.	12.50	37.50	110
	s1. As a. Specimen.	—	Unc	250
	s2. As b. Specimen.	—	Unc	200
111	**50 Pesos**	**Good**	**Fine**	**XF**
	L.1903. In two lines. Black on yellow and brown underprint. Municipal theater at right. 5 signature varieties. Back: Arms. BC: Brown. Printer: ABNC.			
	a. Serial # at bottom left and right.	17.50	50.00	125
	b. Serial # at bottom center.	15.00	45.00	115
	s1. Specimen. As a. Perforated: *SPECIMEN.*	—	Unc	300
	s2. As b. Specimen.	—	Unc	225
112	**100 Pesos**	**Good**	**Fine**	**XF**
	L.1903. Black on red and yellow underprint. Guaira waterfall at center. 3 signature varieties. Back: Arms. BC: Red. Printer: ABNC.			
	a. Serial # at upper left and right.	20.00	65.00	160
	b. Serial # at bottom center.	17.50	55.00	140
	s1. As a. Specimen.	—	Unc	350
	s2. As b. Specimen.	—	Unc	300

#	Description	Good	Fine	XF
113	**200 Pesos**	Good	Fine	XF
	L.1903. In one line. Black on yellow and orange underprint. Mountain and farm at center right. 6 signature varieties. Back: Arms. BC: Orange. Printer: ABNC.			
	a. Serial # at lower left and upper right.	35.00	100	300
	b. Serial # at bottom center.	30.00	90.00	225
	s1. As a. Specimen.	—	Unc	700
	s2. As b. Specimen.	—	Unc	500
114	**500 Pesos**	Good	Fine	XF
	L.1903. In two lines. Black on lilac and yellow underprint. Woman with child at left, ruins at Humaita at right. 5 signature varieties. Back: Arms. BC: Blue. Printer: ABNC.			
	a. Serial # at upper left and lower right.	35.00	175	375
	b. Serial # at bottom center.	40.00	170	350
	s1. As a. Specimen.	—	Unc	900
	s2. As b. Specimen.	—	Unc	800

Ley de 26 de diciembre de 1907

#	Description	VG	VF	UNC
115	**50 Centavos**	VG	VF	UNC
	L.1907. Black on green underprint. Minerva wearing helmet at left. Signature Evaristo Acosta and Juan Y. Ugarte. Back: Arms. BC: Green. Printer: ABNC.			
	a. Issued note.	2.00	5.00	15.00
	s. Specimen.	—	—	75.00
116	**1 Peso**	VG	VF	UNC
	L.1907. Black on orange underprint. Woman wearing straw hat at center. Signature Evaristo Acosta and Juan Y. Ugarte. Back: Arms. BC: Orange. Printer: ABNC.			
	a. Issued note.	2.50	7.50	25.00
	s. Specimen.	—	—	110

#	Description	VG	VF	UNC
117	**2 Pesos**	VG	VF	UNC
	L.1907. Black on blue underprint. Government palace at center. Signature Evaristo Acosta and Juan Y. Ugarte. Back: Arms. BC: Blue. Printer: ABNC.			
	a. Issued note.	3.00	10.00	35.00
	s. Specimen.	—	—	125

#	Description	VG	VF	UNC
118	**5 Pesos**	VG	VF	UNC
	L.1907. Black on yellow and orange underprint. View of city of Asuncion from river. Signature Evaristo Acosta and Juan Y. Ugarte. Back: Arms. BC: Dark blue. Printer: ABNC.			
	a. Issued note.	4.00	15.00	45.00
	s. Specimen.	—	—	135
119	**10 Pesos**	VG	VF	UNC
	L.1907. Black on yellow and green underprint. Cathedral at right center. Signature Evaristo Acosta and Juan Y. Ugarte. Back: Arms. BC: Gray-green. Printer: ABNC.			
	a. Issued note.	6.00	17.50	50.00
	s. Specimen.	—	—	125
120	**20 Pesos**	VG	VF	UNC
	L.1907. Black on yellow underprint. Congressional palace at center. Signature Evaristo Acosta and Juan Y. Ugarte. Back: Arms. BC: Dark blue. Printer: ABNC.			
	a. Issued note.	10.00	30.00	85.00
	s. Specimen.	—	—	200

#	Description	VG	VF	UNC
121	**50 Pesos**	VG	VF	UNC
	L.1907. Black on rose and yellow underprint. Municipal theater at right. 2 signature varieties. Back: Arms. Printer: ABNC.			
	a. Issued note.	20.00	50.00	175
	s. Specimen.	—	—	175
122	**100 Pesos**	Good	Fine	XF
	L.1907. Black on yellow and tan underprint. Guaira waterfall at center. 3 signature varieties. Back: Arms. Printer: ABNC.			
	a. Issued note.	12.50	30.00	100
	s. Specimen.	—	Unc	250
123	**200 Pesos**	Good	Fine	XF
	L.1907. Mountain and farm at center right. 6 signature varieties. Back: Arms. BC: Lilac. Printer: ABNC.			
	a. Issued note.	30.00	80.00	225
	s. Specimen.	—	Unc	525
124	**500 Pesos**	Good	Fine	XF
	L.1907. Woman with child at left, ruins at Humaita at right. 7 signature varieties. Back: Arms. BC: Orange. Printer: ABNC.			
	a. Issued note.	30.00	80.00	225
	s. Specimen.	—	Unc	525

1912 Provisional Issue

#126, 128 and 130 not assigned.

#	Description	Good	Fine	XF
125	**2 Pesos**	Good	Fine	XF
	L.1912. Overprint: *EMISION DEL ESTADO LEY 11 DE ENERO DE 1912* on #107.	15.00	50.00	125
127	**5 Pesos**	Good	Fine	XF
	L.1912. with *PESOS ORO SELLADO* barred out. Overprint: *EMISION DEL ESTADO LEY 11 DE ENERO DE 1912* on #156.	15.00	50.00	125

#	Description	Good	Fine	XF
129	**10 Pesos**	Good	Fine	XF
	L.1912. With *PESOS ORO SELLADO* barred out. Overprint: *EMISION DEL ESTADO LEY 11 DE ENERO DE 1912* on #157.	15.00	50.00	125
131	**50 Pesos**	Good	Fine	XF
	L.1912. Overprint: *EMISION DEL ESTADO LEY 11 DE ENERO DE 1912* on #111.	30.00	80.00	250

		Good	Fine	XF
132	**50 Pesos** *L.1912.* With *PESOS ORO SELLADO* barred out. Overprint: *EMISION DEL ESTADO LEY 11 DE ENERO DE 1912* on #158.	25.00	75.00	225
133	**100 Pesos** *L.1912.* Overprint: *EMISION DEL ESTADO LEY 11 DE ENERO DE 1912* on #159.	35.00	90.00	275
134	**100 Pesos** *L.1912.* With *PESOS ORO SELLADO* barred out. Overprint: *EMISION DEL ESTADO LEY 11 DE ENERO DE 1912* on #159.	35.00	90.00	275
135	**200 Pesos** *L.1912.* Overprint: *EMISION DEL ESTADO LEY 11 DE ENERO DE 1912* on # 113.	30.00	80.00	250
136	**500 Pesos** *L.1912.* Overprint: *EMISION DEL ESTADO LEY 11 DE ENERO DE 1912* on # 114.	30.00	80.00	250

Ley de 28 de enero de 1916

		VG	VF	UNC
137	**50 Centavos** *L.1916.* Black on green underprint. Minerva wearing helmet at left. 4 signature varieties. Text:*LA OFICINA DE CAMBIOS* below serial #. Back: Arms. BC: Green. Printer: ABNC.			
	a. Issued note.	1.50	4.00	15.00
	s. Specimen. Punch hole cancelled.	—	—	125

		VG	VF	UNC
138	**1 Peso** *L.1916.* Black on yellow and orange underprint. Woman wearing straw hat at center. 4 signature varieties. Text:*LA OFICINA DE CAMBIOS* below serial #. Back: Arms. BC: Orange. Printer: ABNC.			
	a. Issued note.	2.00	5.00	20.00
	s. Specimen. Punch hole cancelled.	—	—	125
139	**2 Pesos** *L.1916.* Black on blue underprint. Government palace at center.5 signature varieties. Text:*LA OFICINA DE CAMBIOS* below serial #. Back: Arms. BC: Blue. Printer: ABNC.	VG	VF	UNC
	a. Issued note.	2.50	7.50	30.00
	p. Proof.	—	—	150
140	**5 Pesos** *L.1916.* Black on yellow and orange underprint. View of city of Asuncion from river. 3 signature varieties. Text:*LA OFICINA DE CAMBIOS* below serial #. Back: Arms. BC: Brown. Printer: ABNC.	VG	VF	UNC
	a. Issued note.	3.00	10.00	40.00
	p1. Proof. Face only.	—	—	100
	p2. Proof. Back only.	—	—	60.00
	s. Specimen.	—	—	175
141	**10 Pesos** *L.1916.* Black on yellow and green underprint. Cathedral at right center. 3 signature varieties. Text:*LA OFICINA DE CAMBIOS* below serial #. Back: Arms. BC: Gray. Printer: ABNC.	VG	VF	UNC
	a. Issued note.	10.00	45.00	110
	s. Specimen.	—	—	200
142	**20 Pesos** *L.1916.* Black on yellow underprint. Congressional palace at center. 2 signature varieties. Text:*LA OFICINA DE CAMBIOS* below serial #. Back: Arms. BC: Olive. Printer: ABNC.	VG	VF	UNC
	a. Issued note.	20.00	60.00	175
	s. Specimen.	—	—	400

Ley No. 463 de 30 de diciembre de 1920

		VG	VF	UNC
143	**5 Pesos** *L.1920.* Black on yellow and orange underprint. View of city of Asuncion from river. 2 signature varieties. Back: Arms. BC: Brown. Printer: ABNC.			
	a. Issued note.	1.50	4.00	15.00
	p. Proof. Uniface front.	—	—	100
144	**10 Pesos** *L.1920.* Black on yellow and green underprint. Cathedral at right center. 2 signature varieties. Back: Arms. BC: Gray. Printer: ABNC.	VG	VF	UNC
	a. Issued note.	3.00	7.50	20.00
	p. Proof. Uniface front.	—	—	100

		VG	VF	UNC
145	**50 Pesos** *L.1920.* Black on yellow and brown underprint. Municipal theater at right. 2 signature varieties. Back: Arms. BC: Brown. Printer: ABNC.			
	a. Issued note.	6.00	20.00	70.00
	s. Specimen.	—	—	125

		VG	VF	UNC
146	**100 Pesos** *L.1920.* Guaira waterfall at center. 2 signature varieties. Back: Arms. BC: Blue. Printer: ABNC.			
	a. Issued note.	10.00	35.00	100
	p. Proof. Face only.	—	—	150
	s. Specimen.	—	—	150
147	**200 Pesos** *L.1920.* Mountain and farm at center right. Back: Arms. BC: Orange. Printer: ABNC. Requires confirmation.	VG —	VF —	UNC —

		VG	VF	UNC
148	**500 Pesos** *L.1920.* Woman with child at left, ruins at Humaita at right. Back: Arms. BC: Lilac. Printer: ABNC.			
	a. Issued note.	30.00	100	225
	s. Specimen.	—	—	750

Leyes 1920 & 1923

Por Oficina de Cambio

		VG	VF	UNC
149	**5 Pesos** *L.1920 & 1923.* View of city of Asuncion from river. 3 signature varieties. Back: Arms. Printer: ABNC.			
	a. Issued note.	1.50	6.00	20.00
	s. Specimen.	—	—	65.00

		VG	VF	UNC
150	**10 Pesos** *L.1920 & 1923.* Cathedral at right center. 3 signature varieties. Back: Arms. Printer: ABNC.			
	a. Issued note.	3.00	8.00	25.00
	s. Specimen.	—	—	75.00
151	**50 Pesos** *L.1920 & 1923.* Municipal theater at right. 4 signature varieties. Back: Arms. BC: Brown. Printer: ABNC.	VG	VF	UNC
	a. Issued note.	5.00	15.00	40.00
	s. Specimen.	—	—	85.00

		VG	VF	UNC
152	**100 Pesos** *L.1920 & 1923.* Guaira waterfall at center. 5 signature varieties. Back: Arms. BC: Blue. Printer: ABNC.			
	a. Issued note.	8.50	30.00	75.00
	s. Specimen.	—	—	95.00
153	**200 Pesos** *L.1920 & 1923.* Mountain and farm at center right. 5 signature varieties. Back: Arms. BC: Orange. Printer: ABNC.	VG	VF	UNC
	a. Issued note.	17.50	75.00	175
	s. Specimen.	—	—	200
154	**500 Pesos** *L.1920 & 1923.* Woman with child at left, ruins at Humaita at right. 7 signature varieties. Back: Arms. BC: Lilac. Printer: ABNC.	VG	VF	UNC
	a. Issued note.	20.00	90.00	200
	s. Specimen.	—	—	230

		VG	VF	UNC
155	**1000 Pesos** *L.1920 & 1923.* Black on multicolor underprint. Woman holding fasces at left. 8 signature varieties. Back: Arms at center. BC: Black. Printer: ABNC.			
	a. Issued note.	30.00	125	300
	s. Specimen.	—	—	300

Banco de la República

Ley de 26 de diciembre de 1907

		VG	VF	UNC
156	**5 Pesos M.N. = 1/2 Peso Oro** *L.1907.* Black on blue underprint. Woman wearing Liberty cap at center. 2 signature varieties. Back: Arms at center. BC: Brown. Printer: W&S.	0.25	1.00	5.00

		VG	VF	UNC
157	**10 Pesos M.N. = 1 Peso Oro** *L.1907.* Black on red underprint. Railroad station at center. 2 signature varieties. Back: Arms at center. BC: Green. Printer: W&S.	4.00	10.00	35.00
158	**50 Pesos M.N. = 5 Pesos Oro** *L.1907.* Black on green underprint. National Congress at center. Back: Arms at center. Printer: W&S.	30.00	85.00	200

		VG	VF	UNC
159	**100 Pesos M.N. = 10 Pesos Oro** *L.1907.* Black on yellow underprint. Building at center. 4 signature varieties. Back: Arms at center. BC: Blue. Printer: W&S.	1.00	4.00	12.50
160	**1000 Pesos M.N. = 100 Pesos Oro** *L.1907.* Woman with children. Printer: P. Bouchard-Buenos Aires.	35.00	130	300

Ley 8.9.1920

		VG	VF	UNC
161	**1000 Pesos** *L.1920.*	—	—	—

Ley 469, Dec. 31, 1920

		VG	VF	UNC
162	**1000 Pesos** *L.1920.*	—	—	—

Ley 30.12.1920/25.10.1923, Banco de la Republica

		VG	VF	UNC
163	**5 Pesos** *L.1920, 1923.* View of city of Asuncion. Text: *POR EL BANCO DE LA REPúBLICA DEL PARAGUAY* at bottom. 4 signature varieties. Printer: ABNC.			
	a. Issued note.	3.50	12.50	35.00
	s. Specimen.	—	—	125
164	**10 Pesos** *L.1920, 1923.* Cathedral at right center. Text: *POR EL BANCO DE LA REPúBLICA DEL PARAGUAY* at bottom. 2 signature varieties. Printer: ABNC.			
	a. Issued note.	4.50	15.00	40.00
	s. Specimen.	—	—	150

Ley No. 550 de 25 de octubre de 1923

		VG	VF	UNC
165	**50 Pesos** *L.1923.* Blue on multicolor underprint. Building at center. Back: Star at center. BC: Red. Printer: ABNC.			
	a. Issued note.	40.00	150	375
	s. Specimen.	—	—	525

		VG	VF	UNC
166	**50 Pesos** *L.1923.* Blue on multicolor underprint. Building at center. Back: Shield with lion at center. BC: Red. Printer: ABNC.			
	a. Issued note.	2.00	12.50	40.00
	s. Specimen.	—	—	125

		VG	VF	UNC
167	**100 Pesos** *L.1923.* Blue on multicolor underprint. Building at center. Back: Star at center. BC: Brown. Printer: ABNC.			
	a. Issued note.	50.00	175	400
	s. Specimen.	—	—	600

		VG	VF	UNC
168	**100 Pesos** *L.1923.* Olive-green on brown and multicolor underprint. Building at center. Back: Shield with lion at center. BC: Brown. Printer: ABNC.			
	a. Issued note.	2.00	12.50	40.00
	s. Specimen.	—	—	85.00

169 **500 Pesos**
L.1923. Gray-green. Portrait C. A. Lopez at upper left center, cows at lower right. Printer: W&S.

VG	VF	UNC
15.00	40.00	100

170 **1000 Pesos**
L.1923. Black on multicolor underprint. Woman holding fasces at left. Back: Arms at center. BC: Black. Printer: ABNC.

VG	VF	UNC
30.00	85.00	250

1943 ND Provisional Issue

Guarani System

171 **50 Centimos on 50 Pesos Fuertes**
ND (1943). Requires confirmation.

VG	VF	UNC
—	—	—

172 **50 Centimos on 50 Pesos Fuertes**
ND (1943).

	VG	VF	UNC
a. Red overprint on #166.	15.00	60.00	175
b. Black overprint on #166. Requires confirmation.	—	—	—

173 **1 Guarani on 100 Pesos Fuertes**
ND (1943).

	VG	VF	UNC
a. Red overprint on #168.	10.00	50.00	125
b. Black overprint on #168. Requires confirmation.	—	—	—

174 **5 Guaranies on 500 Pesos Fuertes**
ND (1943).

VG	VF	UNC
25.00	75.00	200

175 **5 Guaranies on 500 Pesos Fuertes**
ND (1943).

VG	VF	UNC
40.00	100	225

176 **10 Guaranies on 1000 Pesos Fuertes**
ND (1943). Overprint on #155.

VG	VF	UNC
45.00	120	300

Banco del Paraguay

Ley No. 11, 22.2.1936

177 **1 Guaraní**
L.1936. (Not issued). Requires confirmation.

VG	VF	UNC
—	—	—

Decreto Ley 655 del 5 de octubre de 1943

Departamento Monetario

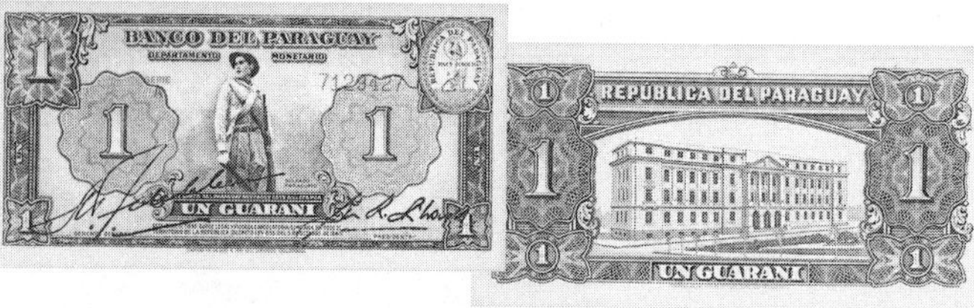

178 **1 Guaraní**
L.1943. Green. Soldier at center. Arms at upper right. Series A. 4 signature varieties. Signature title:*Gerente General* at left. Back: Building at center. BC: Brown. Printer: TDLR.

VG	VF	UNC
0.75	2.50	10.00

179 **5 Guaraníes**
L.1943. Blue. Signature title:*Gerente General* at left. Gen. J. E. Diaz at center. 2 signature varieties. Arms at upper right. Series A. Back: Building. BC: Dark red. Printer: TDLR.

VG	VF	UNC
2.00	6.00	17.50

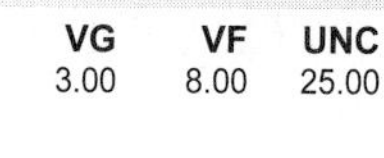

180 **10 Guaraníes**
L.1943. Red. Signature title:*Gerente General* at left. D. Carlos Antonio Lopez at center. Arms at upper right. 3 signature varieties. Back: Building. BC: Purple. Printer: TDLR.

VG	VF	UNC
3.00	8.00	25.00

181 **50 Guaraníes**
L.1943. Brown. Signature title:*Gerente General* at left. Dr. J. Gaspar Rodriguez de Francia at center. Arms at upper right. 3 signature varieties. Back: Building. BC: Gray-brown. Printer: TDLR.

VG	VF	UNC
5.00	15.00	45.00

		VG	VF	UNC
182	**100 Guaraníes** *L.1943.* Green. Signature title: *Gerente General* at left. M. José F. Estigarribia at center. Arms at upper right. 2 signature varieties. Back: Large building facing right. BC: Blue. Printer: TDLR.	8.00	30.00	70.00
183	**500 Guaraníes** *L.1943.* Blue. Signature title: *Gerente General* at left. M. Francisco Solano Lopez at center. Arms at upper right. 3 signature varieties. Back: Large building. BC: Red. Printer: TDLR.	25.00	80.00	175
184	**1000 Guaraníes** *L.1943.* Red-violet. Signature title: *Gerente General* at left. Declaration of Independence on 14.4.1811 at center. Arms at upper right. 2 signature varieties. Back: Presidential palace. BC: Orange. Printer: TDLR.	35.00	100	250

Note: For later issues of similar design see Banco Central, #185-191.

Banco Central del Paraguay

Decreto Ley No. 18 del 25 de marzo de 1952

#185-191 black security thread in left half of notes. Later issues have multicolor fibers in right half of notes.

		VG	VF	UNC
185	**1 Guaraní** *L.1952.* Green. Soldier at center. 6 signature varieties. Arms at right. Signature title: *Gerente* at left. Printer: TDLR.			
	a. 1 red serial #. Large or small signature. Series A.	0.75	1.50	6.00
	b. 1 red serial #. Fibers at right. Series B.	0.50	1.25	3.50
	c. 2 black serial #. Fibers at right. Serial # prefix B.	0.25	0.50	1.50

		VG	VF	UNC
186	**5 Guaraníes** *L.1952.* Blue. Gen. J. E. Diaz at center. 4 signature varieties. Signature title: *Gerente* at left. Printer: TDLR.			
	a. 1 red serial #. Large or small signature. Series A.	0.75	1.50	5.00
	b. 1 red serial #. Fibers at right. Series A.	0.50	1.25	3.50
	c. 2 black serial #. Fibers at right. Serial # prefix A.	0.25	0.75	2.00

		VG	VF	UNC
187	**10 Guaraníes** *L.1952.* Red. D. Carlos Antonio Lopez at center. 6 signature varieties. Signature title: *Gerente* at left. Printer: TDLR.			
	a. 1 black serial #. Large or small signature. Series A.	1.00	2.50	9.00
	b. 1 black serial #. Fibers at right. Series A.	0.75	1.50	4.00
	c. 2 black serial #. Fibers at right. Serial # prefix B.	0.50	1.25	3.50

		VG	VF	UNC
188	**50 Guaraníes** *L.1952.* Brown. Dr. J. Gaspar Rodriguez de Francia at center. Signature title: *Gerente* at left. 5 signature varieties. Printer: TDLR.			
	a. Without fibers at right. Large or small signature.	1.00	4.00	15.00
	b. Fibers at right.	1.00	4.00	10.00
189	**100 Guaraníes** *L.1952.* Green. M. Jose F. Estigarribia at center. Signature title: *Gerente* at left. 5 signature varieties. Back: Building facing left. BC: Blue. Printer: TDLR. Large or small.			
	a. Without fibers at right.	2.00	8.00	20.00
	b. Fibers at right.	1.50	6.00	15.00

		VG	VF	UNC
190	**500 Guaraníes** *L.1952.* Blue. M. Francisco Solano Lopez at center. Signature title: *Gerente* at left. 6 signature varieties. Back: Domed building at center. BC: Red. Printer: TDLR.			
	a. Without fibers at right.	30.00	75.00	150
	b. Fibers at right.	25.00	60.00	125

		VG	VF	UNC
191	**1000 Guaraníes** *L.1952.* Lilac. Declaration of Independence on 14.4.1811 at center. Signature title: *Gerente* at left. 5 signature varieties. Back: Building with courtyard. BC: Orange. Printer: TDLR.			
	a. Without fibers at right.	40.00	90.00	200
	b. Fibers at right.	35.00	75.00	150

The Republic of Perú, located on the Pacific coast of South America, has an area of 496,222 sq. mi. (1,285,216 sq. km.) and a population of 25.66 million. Capital: Lima. The diversified economy includes mining, fishing and agriculture. Fish meal, copper, sugar, zinc and iron ore are exported. Ancient Peru was the seat of several prominent Andean civilizations, most notably that of the Incas whose empire was captured by the Spanish conquistadors in 1533. Peruvian independence was declared in 1821, and remaining Spanish forces defeated in 1824. After a dozen years of military rule, Peru returned to democratic leadership in 1980, but experienced economic problems and the growth of a violent insurgency. President Alberto Fujimori's election in 1990 ushered in a decade that saw a dramatic turnaround in the economy and significant progress in curtailing guerrilla activity. Nevertheless, the president's increasing reliance on authoritarian measures and an economic slump in the late 1990s generated mounting dissatisfaction with his regime, which led to his ouster in 2000. A caretaker government oversaw new elections in the spring of 2001, which ushered in Alejandro Toledo Manrique as the new head of government - Peru's first democratically elected president of Native American ethnicity. The presidential election of 2006 saw the return of Alan Garcia Perez who, after a disappointing presidential term from 1985 to 1990, returned to the presidency with promises to improve social conditions and maintain fiscal responsibility.

MONETARY SYSTEM:

1 Sol = 1 Sol de Oro = 100 Centavos, 1879-1985
1 Libra = 10 Soles
1 Inti = 1000 Soles de Oro, 1986-1991
1 Nuevo Sol = 100 Centimes = 1 Million Intis, 1991-
1 Sol = 100 Centavos (10 Dineros)

REPÚBLICA DEL PERÚ

Junta Administradora

1879 Issue

		Good	Fine	XF
1	**1 Sol** 30.6.1879. Black on yellow-brown and blue underprint. Cupids at left and right, woman with fruit at center. Signature varieties. Back: Sailing ship at center. BC: Brown. Printer: ABNC.	1.50	10.00	50.00

		Good	Fine	XF
2	**2 Soles** 30.6.1879. Black on green and brown underprint. Steam passenger trains at lower left and right, woman at fountain at lower center. 3 serial # varieties. Signature varieties. BC: Red-orange. Printer: ABNC.	1.50	10.00	60.00

		Good	Fine	XF
3	**5 Soles** 30.6.1879. Black on green and red underprint. Red numeral *V* at upper left and right in underprint. Woman and child at left, woman with two children at right. Signature varieties. BC: Brown. Printer: ABNC. Upper line of large green *5* at center measures 16mm across.	2.50	12.50	60.00

		Good	Fine	XF
4	**5 Soles** 30.6.1879. Black on green and red underprint. Woman and child at left, woman with two children at right. Like #3. Signature varieties. BC: Brown. Printer: ABNC. Large green numeral *5* at center measures 20.5mm across at top.	2.00	12.50	60.00

		Good	Fine	XF
5	**10 Soles** 30.6.1879. Black on brown and light blue underprint. Woman sitting with staff and scales at left, woman with wreath at center, arms at right. Signature varieties. Back: Woman sitting with llama at center. BC: Green. Printer: ABNC.	3.00	30.00	100

		Good	Fine	XF
6	**20 Soles** 30.6.1879. Black on brown underprint. Woman with book and pen at center without green *20* in underprint. Signature varieties. BC: Blue. Printer: ABNC.	2.00	12.50	60.00

		Good	Fine	XF
7	**20 Soles** 30.6.1879. Black on yellow and light green underprint. Large green *20s* at lower left and right in under Woman with book and pen at center. Like #6. Signature varieties. BC: Blue. Printer: ABNC.			
	a. Issued note.	2.00	12.50	60.00
	b. Cut cancelled, with circular overprint: *DIRECCION DEL TESORO* (arms) *LIMA JULIO 30 DE 1899* at right.	5.00	30.00	90.00

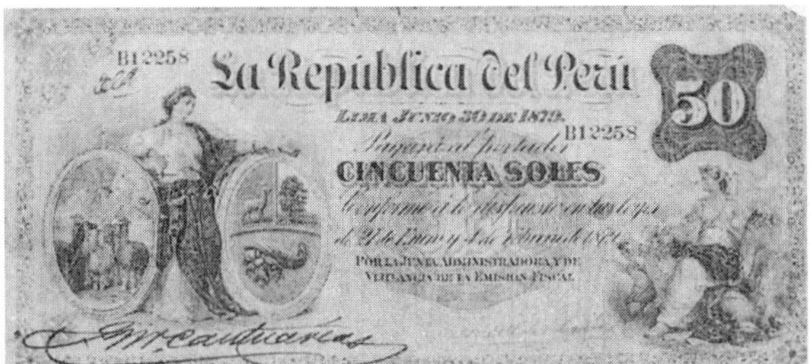

		Good	Fine	XF
8	**50 Soles** 30.6.1879. Black on blue-green underprint. Woman with two shields at left, woman and child at lower right. Signature varieties. Back: Allegorical woman and two children at center. BC: Brown. Printer: ABNC.	25.00	125	325

		Good	Fine	XF
9	**100 Soles** 30.6.1879. Black on red and green underprint. Young sailor at left, arms flanked by women on each side at center, filleted woman at right. Signature varieties. Back: Horse and girl. BC: Red and black. Printer: ABNC.	20.00	100	300

		Good	Fine	XF
10	**500 Soles** 30.6.1879. Black on yellow and gold underprint. Heraldic shield and four angels at center. Signature varieties. Back: Funeral of Atahualpa. BC: Green and black. Printer: ABNC.	60.00	200	500

1881 Arequipa Provisional Issue

		Good	Fine	XF
1A	**1 Sol** 1881 (- old date 30.6.1879). Black on yellow-brown and blue underprint. Cupids at left and right, woman with fruit at center. Back: Sailing ship at center. BC: Brown. Overprint: Black circular: *COMISION DE SUBSIDIOS AREQUIPA 1881* at right on #1.	40.00	175	—
2A	**2 Soles** 1881 (- old date 30.6.1879). Black on green and brown underprint. Steam passenger trains at lower left and right, woman at fountain at lower center. BC: Red-orange. Overprint: Black circular: *COMISION DE SUBSIDIOS AREQUIPA 1881* at center on #2.	45.00	200	—
3A	**5 Soles** 1881 (- old date 30.6.1879). Black on green and red underprint. Red numeral *V* at upper left and right in underprint. Woman and child at left, woman with two children at right. BC: Brown. Overprint: Black circular: *COMISION DE SUBSIDIOS AREQUIPA 1881* at right on #3.	45.00	200	—

6A 20 Soles — Good 60.00 — Fine 275 — XF —
1881 (- old date 30.6.1879). Black on brown underprint. Woman with book and pen at center without green *20* in underprint. BC: Blue. Overprint: Black circular: *COMISION DE SUBSIDIOS AREQUIPA 1881* at right on #6.

7A 20 Soles — Good 50.00 — Fine 250 — XF —
1881 (-old date 30.6.1879). Black on yellow and light green underprint. Woman with book and pen at center. BC: Blue. Overprint: Black circular: *COMISION DE SUBSIDIOS AREQUIPA 1881* at right on #7.

1881 Provisional Issue

Inca system #11-13 *BILLETE PROVISIONAL* with new denomination and new date overprint on face and/or back of 1873 notes of the Banca de la Compania General del Peru.

11 1 Real de Inca on 1 Sol — Good 5.00 — Fine 30.00 — XF 85.00
1.9.1881 (- old date 1873). Portrait J. Galvez between sailing ship and steam train at upper left, steam train at lower center. Back: Steam train. Printer: NBNC (front), ABNC (back). Overprint: BILLETE PROVISIONAL with new denomination and date on #S131. With or without signature.

12 5 Reales de Inca on 5 Soles — Good 7.50 — Fine 35.00 — XF 100
1.9.1881 (- old date 1873). Man with horses and mule train at upper center, train below. Laureated J. Galvez at right. Back: Man with llamas at left, steam train at right. Printer: NBNC (front), ABNC (back). Overprint: BILLETE PROVISIONAL with new denomination and date on #S132. With or without signature.

13 100 Centavos de Inca on 100 Soles — Good 15.00 — Fine 75.00 — XF 200
1.9.1881 (- old date 1873). Woman in feather headdress with sword and lion ("Libertad") at left, laureated portrait J. Galvez at left center, train below. Back: Steam train at left, man with llamas at right. Printer: NBNC (front), ABNC (back). Overprint: BILLETE PROVISIONAL with new denomination and date on #S134. With or without signature.

Note: #11-13 sometimes have an additional signature guaranteeing the authenticity of the note. This signature was an official endorsement.

1881 Inca Issue

#14-17 signature titles: *SECRETARIO DE HACIENDA Y COMERCIO* and *JUNTA FISCAL* on new notes.

14 1 Inca — Good 25.00 — Fine 125 — XF 275
1.9.1881. Blue.

15 5 Incas — Good 12.50 — Fine 40.00 — XF 90.00
1.9.1881. Blue. Cherub at upper left and right, arms at top center. Without overprint.

16 5 Incas — Good 9.00 — Fine 30.00 — XF 80.00
1.9.1881. Blue. Cherub at upper left and right, arms at top center. Overprint: *LEGITIMO* on #15.

17 100 Incas — Good 40.00 — Fine 150 — XF 350
1.9.1881. Blue. Seated Mercury at left, seated allegorical woman at right. Without overprint.

1881 Provisional Soles Issue

#18-20 overprint for Soles on Incas notes.

18 50 Soles — Good 9.00 — Fine 30.00 — XF 80.00
1.9.1881. Blue. Cherub at upper left and right, arms at top center. Overprint: Oval: *VALE POR / CINCUENTA SOLES / 1881 / EMISION FISCAL* on #15.

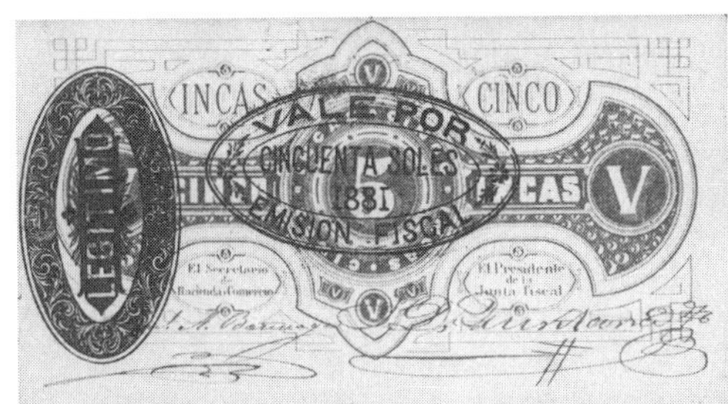

		Good	Fine	XF
19	**50 Soles** 1.9.1881. Blue. Cherub at upper left and right, arms at top center. Overprint: Oval: *VALE POR / CINCUENTA SOLES / 1881 / EMISION FISCAL* on #16.	9.00	30.00	80.00
20	**1000 Soles** 1.9.1881. Blue. Seated Mercury at left, seated allegorical woman at right. Overprint: Oval: *VALE POR / MIL SOLES / 1881 / EMISION FISCAL* on #17.	30.00	125	325

Junta de Vigilancia

1914 Cheques Circulares First Issue

Libra system Circulating drafts issued on the following banks: Banco del Peru y Londres, Banco Italiano, Banco Internacional del Peru, Banco Popular del Peru, Banco Alemán Transatlántico, Caja de Ahorros de Lima.

		Good	Fine	XF
21	**1/2 Libra** 3.10.1914. Black on green underprint. Worker at center. BC: Green. Printer: T. Scheuch, Lima.	25.00	90.00	250
22	**1 Libra** 8.9.1914. Black on yellow underprint. Woman seated with caduceus at left. Printer: T. Scheuch, Lima.	50.00	175	400
23	**5 Libras** 8.9.1914. Black on blue underprint. Justice seated at left. Printer: T. Scheuch, Lima.	35.00	125	300

		Good	Fine	XF
24	**10 Libras** 8.9.1914. Black on green underprint. Woman with flag at left. Printer: T. Scheuch, Lima.	—	—	—

1914 Cheques Circulares Second Issue

		Good	Fine	XF
25	**1/2 Libra** 3.10.1914. Black on green underprint. Liberty at center. Issuing banks listed in three lines under top heading. BC: Green. Printer: ABNC.			
	a. Issued note.	20.00	85.00	200
	s. Specimen.	—	Unc	400
26	**1 Libra** 3.10.1914. Black on red-orange underprint. Woman seated at left. Issuing banks listed in three lines under top heading. Back: Drill worker at center. BC: Red-orange. Printer: ABNC.			
	a. Issued note.	20.00	85.00	200
	s. Specimen.	—	Unc	500
27	**5 Libras** 3.10.1914. Black on blue underprint. Child and lamb at right. Issuing banks listed in three lines under top heading. Back: Two allegorical women at center. BC: Blue. Printer: ABNC.			
	a. Issued note.	40.00	150	350
	s. Specimen.	—	Unc	750

		Good	Fine	XF
28	**10 Libras** 3.10.1914. Black on multicolor underprint. Rubber tree worker at left. Issuing banks listed in three lines under top heading. Back: Steam train at center. BC: Orange. Printer: ABNC.			
	a. Issued note.	—	—	—
	s. Specimen.	—	Unc	750

1917 Certificado De Deposito De Oro Issue

		Good	Fine	XF
29	**5 Centavos** 17.8.1917. Black on blue underprint. Back: Sun face at center. BC: Dark orange. Printer: Scheuch, Lima.	2.00	15.00	40.00

		Good	Fine	XF
30	**50 Centavos** 17.8.1917. Dark blue on green underprint. Liberty seated with shield and staff at center. Back: Arms at center. BC: Brown. Printer: Scheuch, Lima.	2.50	20.00	55.00

		Good	Fine	XF
31	**1 Sol** 10.8.1917. Dark blue. Liberty seated similar to #30. Back: Arms at center. BC: Brown. Printer: ABNC.			
	a. Issued note.	4.00	25.00	60.00
	s. Specimen.	—	Unc	225

1918 Cheques Circulares First Issue

		Good	Fine	XF
32	**1/2 Libra** 13.6.1918. Printer: Fabbri. Requires confirmation.	—	—	—
33	**1 Libra** 13.6.1918. Winged woman at left and right. Printer: Fabbri.	—	—	—

		Good	Fine	XF
34	**5 Libras** 13.6.1918. Black. Liberty at left, globe at right. Printer: Fabbri.	—	—	—
35	**10 Libras** 13.6.1918. Printer: Fabbri. Requires confirmation.	—	—	—

1918 Cheques Circulares Second Issue

		Good	Fine	XF
36	**1/2 Libra** 14.9.1918. Black on green underprint. Liberty at center. Issuing banks listed in two lines under top heading. Similar to #25. BC: Green. Printer: ABNC.			
	a. Issued note.	40.00	110	250
	s. Specimen.	—	Unc	400

		Good	Fine	XF
37	**1 Libra** 14.9.1918. Black on red-orange underprint. Woman seated at left. Issuing banks listed in two lines under top heading. Similar to #26. Back: Drill worker at center. BC: Red-orange. Printer: ABNC.			
	a. Issued note.	40.00	110	250
	s. Specimen.	—	Unc	350

		Good	Fine	XF
38	**5 Libras** 14.9.1918. Black on blue underprint. Child and lamb at right. Issuing banks listed in two lines under top heading. Similar to #27. Back: Two allegorical women at center. BC: Blue. Printer: ABNC.			
	a. Issued note.	45.00	125	275
	s. Specimen.	—	Unc	400
39	**10 Libras** 14.9.1918. Black on multicolor underprint. Rubber tree worker at left. Issuing banks listed in two lines under top heading. Similar to #28. Printer: ABNC.	Good	Fine	XF
	p. Proof. Face only.	—	—	—
	s. Specimen.	—	Unc	500

1918 Sol Issue

		Good	Fine	XF
40	**1 Sol** 14.9.1918. Dark blue. Liberty seated with shield and staff at center. Like #31. Back: Arms at center. BC: Brown. Printer: ABNC.			
	a. Issued note.	4.00	15.00	40.00
	s. Specimen.	—	Unc	125

Banco de Reserva del Peru

1922 Issue

		Good	Fine	XF
48	**1/2 Libra** 12.4.1922. Black on green underprint. Liberty at center. Similar to #36. BC: Green. Printer: ABNC.			
	a. Issued note.	10.00	40.00	100
	s. Specimen.	—	Unc	150

		Good	Fine	XF
49	**1 Libra** 12.4.1922. Black on red-orange underprint. Woman seated at left. Similar to #37. Back: Drill worker at center. BC: Red-orange. Printer: ABNC.			
	a. Issued note.	15.00	45.00	125
	s. Specimen.	—	Unc	150

		Good	Fine	XF
50	**5 Libras** 12.4.1922. Black on blue underprint. Child and lamb at right. Similar to #38. Back: Two allegorical women at center. BC: Blue. Printer: ABNC.			
	a. Issued note.	25.00	75.00	175
	s. Specimen.	—	Unc	325

		Good	Fine	XF
51	**10 Libras** 12.4.1922. Black on yellow underprint. Rubber tree worker at left. Similar to #39. Printer: ABNC.			
	a. Issued note.	—	—	—
	s. Specimen.	—	Unc	400

1926 Issue

		Good	Fine	XF
52	**1/2 Libra** 11.8.1926. Black on green underprint. Liberty at center. BC: Green. Printer: ABNC.			
	a. Not issued.	—	—	—
	s. Specimen.	—	Unc	1,000
53	**1 Libra** 11.8.1926. Black on red underprint. Woman seated at left. Back: Drill worker at center. BC: Red. Printer: ABNC.	Good	Fine	XF
	a. Not issued.	—	—	—
	s. Specimen.	—	Unc	1,000
54	**5 Libras** 11.8.1926. Black on blue underprint. Child and lamb at right. Back: Two allegorical women at center. Printer: ABNC.	Good	Fine	XF
	a. Not issued.	—	—	—
	s. Specimen.	—	Unc	1,000
55	**10 Libras** 11.8.1926. Black on yellow underprint. Rubber tree worker at left. Back: Steam train at center. Printer: ABNC.	Good	Fine	XF
	a. Not issued.	—	—	—
	s. Specimen.	—	Unc	1,250

Banco Central de Reserva del Peru

1935 ND Provisional Issue (1922 Dated notes)

#56-59 overprint new bank name and new denomination overprint on backs of notes of the Banco de Reserva del Peru.

		Good	Fine	XF
56	**5 Soles on 1/2 Libra** ND (- old date 12.4.1922). Black on green underprint. Liberty at center. BC: Green. Overprint: On #48.	20.00	70.00	175
57	**10 Soles on 1 Libra** ND (- old date 12.4.1922). Black on red-orange underprint. Woman seated at left. Back: Drill worker at center. BC: Red-orange. Overprint: On #49.	25.00	85.00	200

		Good	Fine	XF
58	**50 Soles on 5 Libras** ND (- old date 12.4.1922). Black on blue underprint. Child and lamb at right. Back: Two allegorical women at center. BC: Blue. Overprint: On #50.	40.00	125	300

		Good	Fine	XF
59	**100 Soles on 10 Libras** ND (- old date 12.4.1922). Black on multicolor underprint. Rubber tree worker at left. Back: Steam train at center. BC: Orange. Overprint: On #51.	50.00	175	—

1935 ND Provisional Issue (1926 Dated notes)

		Good	Fine	XF
60	**5 Soles on 1/2 Libra** ND (- old date 11.8.1926). Black on green underprint. Liberty at center. BC: Green. Overprint: On #52.	20.00	70.00	175

		Good	Fine	XF
61	**10 Soles on 1 Libra** ND (- old date 11.8.1926). Black on red underprint. Woman seated at left. Back: Drill worker at center. Overprint: On #53.	25.00	85.00	200
62	**50 Soles on 5 Libras** ND (- old date 11.8.1926). Black on blue underprint. Child and lamb at right. Back: Two allegorical women at center. BC: Blue. Overprint: On #54.	40.00	175	300
63	**100 Soles on 10 Libras** ND (- old date 11.8.1926). Black on yellow underprint. Rubber tree worker at left. Back: Steam train at center. Overprint: On #55.	50.00	175	—

1935 Issues

		VG	VF	UNC
64	**50 Centavos** 3.5.1935. Blue. Liberty seated with shield and staff at center. Similar to #65. Series A-E. Back: Arms at center. BC: Light brown. Printer: Fabbri, Lima.	4.00	15.00	50.00

		VG	VF	UNC
65	**1 Sol** 26.4.1935. Blue. Liberty seated with shield and staff at center. Series A-E. Back: Arms at center. BC: Brown. Printer: ABNC.			
	a. Issued note.	2.00	7.50	25.00
	s. Specimen.	—	—	125

1933 Issue (Ley 7137)

#66-69 Signature title varieties; title above center signature: a. *PRESIDENTE DEL DIRECTORIO* (to 1941) b. *VICE-PRESIDENTE* (1944-1945) c. *PRESIDENTE* (1946-1947)

		VG	VF	UNC
66	**5 Soles** 31.3.1933; 6.3.1936; 5.8.1938; 8.9.1939. Black on multicolor underprint. Portrait Liberty at center. Back: Mine workers at center. BC: Green. Printer: ABNC. 135x67mm.			
	a. Issued note.	3.00	8.00	25.00
	s. Issued note.	—	—	125

		VG	VF	UNC
67	**10 Soles** 31.3.1933; 6.3.1936; 5.8.1938; 8.9.1939. Black on multicolor underprint. Seated woman holding basket with flowers at left. Back: Mine driller at center. BC: Orange. Printer: ABNC. 144x76mm.			
	a. Issued note.	3.00	10.00	30.00
	s. Specimen.	—	—	125

		VG	VF	UNC
68	**50 Soles** 31.3.1933; 21.5.1937; 8.9.1937. Black on multicolor underprint. Girl with lamb and sheep at right. Back: Two allegorical women at center. BC: Blue. Printer: ABNC. 158x77mm.			
	a. Issued note.	6.00	25.00	80.00
	s. Specimen.	—	—	175
69	**100 Soles** 31.3.1933; 21.5.1937; 8.9.1939. Black on multicolor underprint. Rubber tree worker at left. Similar to #28. Back: Steam train at center. BC: Orange. Printer: ABNC. 172x79mm.	VG	VF	UNC
	a. Issued note.	40.00	125	350
	s. Specimen.	—	—	325

1941 Issue

		VG	VF	UNC
66A	**5 Soles** 26.9.1941; 26.5.1944; 17.10.1947. Black on multicolor underprint. Portrait Liberty at center. Like #66. Back: Mine workers at center. BC: Green. 141x68mm.			
	a. Issued note.	2.00	5.00	25.00
	s. Specimen.	—	—	100
67A	**10 Soles** 26.9.1941; 26.5.1944; 13.7.1945; 15.11.1946; 17.10.1947. Black on multicolor underprint. Seated woman holding basket with flowers at left. Like #67. Back: Mine driller at center. BC: Orange. Printer: ABNC. 152x77mm.	VG	VF	UNC
	a. Issued note.	2.00	6.00	20.00
	s. Specimen.	—	—	75.00
68A	**50 Soles** 26.9.1941; 26.5.1944; 13.7.1945; 15.11.1946; 17.10.1947; 28.9.1950. Black. Girl with lamb and sheep at right. Like #68. Back: Two allegorical woman at center. BC: Blue. Printer: ABNC. 165x78mm.	VG	VF	UNC
	a. Issued note.	5.00	15.00	60.00
	s. Specimen.	—	—	175

69A	**100 Soles**	VG	VF	UNC
	26.9.1941; 26.5.1944; 13.7.1945; 15.11.1946; 17.10.1947; 28.9.1950. Black. Rubber tree worker at left. Like #69. Back: Steam train at center. BC: Orange. Printer: ABNC. 177x80mm.			
	a. Issued note.	12.00	50.00	120
	s. Specimen. Overprint SPECIMEN on face, punch hole cancelled.	—	—	175

1946-1951 Issue

70	**5 Soles**	VG	VF	UNC
	20.3.1952; 16.9.1954. Green on plain light blue underprint. Seated Liberty holding shield and staff at center. Serial # at upper left and right. Signature varieties. Back: Arms at center. Printer: TDLR.			
	a. Issued note.	1.00	3.00	7.00
	s. Specimen.	—	—	—
71	**10 Soles**	VG	VF	UNC
	12.7.1951-17.2.1955. Black on multicolor underprint. Seated Liberty holding shield and staff at center. Signature varieties. Back: Arms at center. BC: Orange. Printer: TDLR.			
	a. Issued note.	1.00	4.00	8.00
	s. Specimen.	—	—	—
72	**50 Soles**	VG	VF	UNC
	31.3.1949; 12.7.1951; 16.9.1954. Black on multicolor underprint. Seated Liberty holding shield and staff at center. Signature varieties. Back: Arms at center. BC: Blue. Printer: TDLR.	2.00	5.00	20.00
73	**100 Soles**	VG	VF	UNC
	31.3.1949-16.9.1954. Black on multicolor underprint. Seated Liberty holding shield and staff at center. Signature varieties. Back: Arms at center. BC: Orange. Printer: TDLR.	4.00	10.00	30.00
74	**500 Soles**	VG	VF	UNC
	4.10.1946; 10.7.1952. Brown on multicolor underprint. Seated Liberty holding shield and staff at center. Signature varieties. Back: Arms at center. BC: Deep red. Printer: W&S.	12.00	30.00	90.00

1955 Issue

75	**10 Soles**	VG	VF	UNC
	17.2.1955. Black, green-black and brown. Seated Liberty holding shield and staff at center. Like #71. Back: Arms at center. BC: Orange. Printer: G&D. Proof.	—	—	100

Ley 10535, 1956 Issue

76	**5 Soles**	VG	VF	UNC
	22.3.1956; 18.3.1960. Green on patterned light blue underprint. Seated Liberty holding shield and staff at center. Like #70. Signature varieties. Back: Arms at center. Printer: TDLR.	0.50	1.50	5.00
77	**10 Soles**	VG	VF	UNC
	9.7.1956. Orange on multicolor underprint. Seated Liberty holding shield and staff at center. Similar to #71. Signature varieties. Back: Arms at center. Printer: G&D.	2.00	6.00	20.00

78	**50 Soles**	VG	VF	UNC
	22.3.1956; 24.10.1957; 13.5.1959. Dark blue on lilac underprint. Seated Liberty holding shield and staff at center. Serial # at upper left and right. Like #72. Signature varieties. Back: Arms at center. Printer: TDLR.			
	a. Issued note.	1.50	4.50	17.50
	s. Specimen.	—	—	—
79	**100 Soles**	VG	VF	UNC
	1956-61. Black on light blue underprint. Seated Liberty holding shield and staff at center. Like #73 but different guilloche. Signature varieties. Back: Arms at center. BC: Black. Printer: TDLR.			
	a. *LIMA* at lower left. 22.3.1956; 24.10.1957.	4.00	12.00	30.00
	b. *LIMA* at lower right. 13.5.1959.	4.00	12.00	30.00
	c. As b. Series and serial # at lower left and upper right. 1.2.1961.	4.00	12.00	30.00
	s. As a. Specimen.	—	—	—

		VG	VF	UNC
80	**500 Soles** 1956-61. Brown on light brown and lilac underprint. Seated Liberty holding shield and staff at center. Similar to #74. Signature varieties. Back: Arms at center. BC: Brown. Printer: TDLR.			
	a. Series and serial # at upper corners. 22.3.1956; 24.10.1957.	8.00	25.00	75.00
	b. Series and serial # at lower left and upper right. 10.12.1959; 16.6.1961.	8.00	25.00	75.00
	s. As b. Specimen.	—	—	—

1958 Issue

		VG	VF	UNC
81	**5 Soles** 21.8.1958. Green. Seated Liberty holding shield and staff at center. Back: Arms at center. Like #70 but different guilloche. Printer: W&S.	1.00	4.00	7.50

		VG	VF	UNC
82	**10 Soles** 21.8.1958. Orange on multicolor underprint. Seated Liberty holding shield and staff at center. Similar to #71. Back: Arms at center. BC: Orange. Printer: W&S.	1.00	4.00	15.00

1960 Issue

		VG	VF	UNC
82A	**10 Soles** 8.7.1960; 1.2.1961. Orange on multicolor underprint. Liberty seated holding shield and staff at center. Serial # and series at lower left and upper right. Printer: TDLR.	0.75	1.50	6.00

PHILIPPINES

The Republic of the Philippines, an archipelago in the western Pacific 500 miles (805 km.) from the southeast coast of Asia, has an area of 115,830 sq. mi. (300,000 sq. km.) and a population of 75.04 million. Capital: Manila. The economy of the 7,000-island group is based on agriculture, forestry and fishing. Timber, coconut products, sugar and hemp are exported. The Philippine Islands became a Spanish colony during the 16th century; they were ceded to the US in 1898 following the Spanish-American War. In 1935 the Philippines became a self-governing commonwealth. Manuel Quezon was elected president and was tasked with preparing the country for independence after a 10-year transition. In 1942 the islands fell under Japanese occupation during World War II, and US forces and Filipinos fought together during 1944-45 to regain control. On 4 July 1946 the Republic of the Philippines attained its independence. The 20-year rule of Ferdinand Marcos ended in 1986, when a "people power" movement in Manila ("EDSA 1") forced him into exile and installed Corazon Aquino as president. Her presidency was hampered by several coup attempts, which prevented a return to full political stability and economic development. Fidel Ramos was elected president in 1992 and his administration was marked by greater stability and progress on economic reforms. In 1992, the US closed its last military bases on the islands. Joseph Estrada was elected president in 1998, but was succeeded by his vice-president, Gloria Macapagal-Arroyo, in January 2001 after Estrada's stormy impeachment trial on corruption charges broke down and another "people power" movement ("EDSA 2") demanded his resignation. Macapagal-Arroyo was elected to a six-year term as president in May 2004. The Philippine Government faces threats from three terrorist groups on the US Government's Foreign Terrorist Organization list, but in 2006 and 2007 scored some major successes in capturing or killing key wanted terrorists. Decades of Muslim insurgency in the southern Philippines have led to a peace accord with one group and on-again/off-again peace talks with another.

RULERS:

Spanish to 1898
United States, 1898-1946

MONETARY SYSTEM:

1 Peso = 100 Centavos to 1967
1 Piso = 100 Sentimos, 1967-

REPLACEMENT NOTES:

#7-11 starting w/Sendres sign., also #13-24 and #43-59, star preceding serial number. #60-101, star instead of suffix letter. #109-112, serial numbers beginning with "1" instead of "0". #125-127, star following serial number.

SPANISH ADMINISTRATION

Banco Español Filipino de Isabel 2a

1852 Issue

		Good	Fine	XF
A1	**10 Pesos** 1.5.1852; 1.1.1865. Black. Crowned portrait Queen Isabel II at top center. Printer: BWC. PC: Brown or white.			
	a. Issued note.	—	—	—
	p. Proof.	—	—	10,000
	r. Remainder with counterfoils	—	—	15,000
A2	**25 Pesos** 1.5.1852; 1.1.1865. Crowned portrait Queen Isabel II at top center. Printer: BWC. PC: Green.			
	a. Issued note. Rare.	—	—	—
	r. Remainder with counterfoil.	—	—	—

		Good	Fine	XF
A3	**50 Pesos** 1.5.1852; 1.1.1865. Crowned portrait Queen Isabel II at top center. Printer: BWC. Rare. PC: Brown.	—	—	—

Banco Español Filipino

1883 Issue

		Good	Fine	XF
A4	**10 Pesos** 1.1.1883. Bank arms at top center. Uniface. Rare. PC: Brown.	—	—	—

		Good	Fine	XF
A5	**25 Pesos** 1.1.1883. Bank arms at top center. Uniface. Rare. PC: Green.	—	—	—

		Good	Fine	XF
A6	**50 Pesos** 1.1.1883. Bank arms at top center. Uniface. Rare. PC: Brown.	—	—	—

1896 Issue

		Good	Fine	XF
A7	**5 Pesos** 1.6.1896. Black. Bank arms at upper center. Printer: BFL. PC: Brown.			
	a. Issued note.	2,500	6,000	—
	b. Cancelled with handstamp: *PAGADO*.	1,500	3,000	—

		Good	Fine	XF
A8	**10 Pesos** 1.6.1896. Black. Bank arms at upper center. Printer: BFL. 163x102mm. PC: Yellow.			
	a. Issued note. Rare.	—	14,000	—
	b. Cancelled with handstamp: *PAGADO*. Rare.	—	—	—
	c. Overprint: *ILOILO* twice.	—	17,000	—
A9	**25 Pesos** 1.6.1896. Black. Bank arms at upper center. Printer: BFL. Rare. PC: Blue.	—	—	—
A10	**50 Pesos** 1.6.1896. Black. Bank arms at upper center. Printer: BFL. Rare. PC: Pink.	—	17,500	—

Note: For similar 1904 issue order U.S. administration see #A31-A36.

Color Abbreviation Guide

New to the *Standard Catalog of ® World Paper Money* are the following abbreviations related to color references:

BC: Back color
PC: Paper color

Billete Del Tesoro

Treasury Note

1877 Issue

		Good	Fine	XF
A11	**1 Peso** 26.4.1877. Black. Arms at upper center. Uniface. Printer: J. Oppel Litogr. 140x120mm. Rare.	—	—	17,000
A13	**4 Pesos** 26.4.1877. Black. Arms at left. Uniface. Rare. PC: Orange.	—	—	—

		VG	VF	UNC
A14	**10 Pesos** 26.4.1877. Black. Light brown underprint. Arms at upper center. Uniface.	—	17,000	—

		Good	Fine	XF
A15	**25 Pesos** 26.4.1877. Black. Arms at upper center. Uniface. Rare. PC: Blue.	—	—	18,000

REPUBLIC

República Filipina

Ley 26 Noviembre 1898

		VG	VF	UNC
A25	**5 Pesos** *L.1898.* Black on red underprint. With serial #, without signature. BC: Black.	350	750	1,500

Ley 30.11.1898 and 24.4.1899

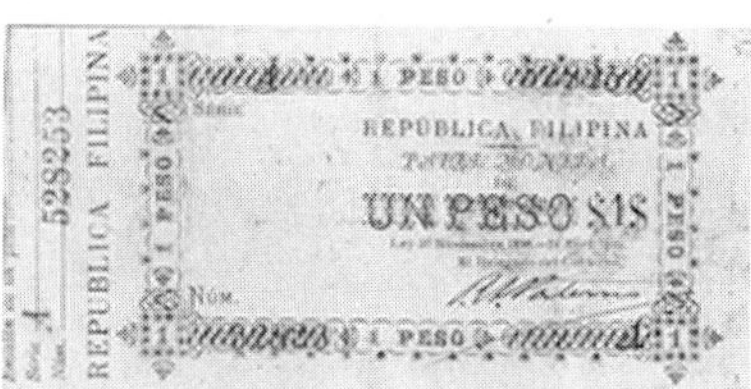

		VG	VF	UNC
A26	**1 Peso** *L. 1898-1899.* Black. Printer: Z. Fajardo.			
	a. Issued note with signature and serial #. Rare.	—	11,000	—
	r. Remainder without signature or serial #.	150	300	600

		VG	VF	UNC
A27	**5 Pesos** *L.1898-1899*. Black. Similar to #A25.			
	a. Issued note with signature and serial #. Rare.	—	—	—
	r. Remainder without signature or serial #.	600	1,000	575

Ley 24.4.1899

		VG	VF	UNC
A28	**1 Peso** *L.1899*. Black. Similar to #A26.			
	a. Unissued note but with embossed seal at left center and 3 serial #. Rare.	—	1,250	—
	r. Unsigned remainder without serial # or seal.	500	1,500	4,500

Note: 2, 10, 20, 25, 50 and 100 Peso notes were authorized but no examples are known.

UNITED STATES ADMINISTRATION

Banco Español Filipino

1904 Issue

#A31-A36 Denominations w/o *FUERTES*.

		Good	Fine	XF
A31	**5 Pesos** 1.1.1904. Black. Bank arms at upper center. Printer: BFL. Rare. PC: Pink.	—	—	—
A32	**10 Pesos** 1.1.1904. Black. Bank arms at upper center. Printer: BFL. Rare. PC: Green.	—	—	—

		Good	Fine	XF
A33	**25 Pesos** 1.1.1904. Black. Bank arms at upper center. Printer: BFL. Rare. PC: Light purple.	—	—	—
A34	**50 Pesos** 1.1.1904. Black. Bank arms at upper center. Printer: BFL. Rare. PC: Green.	—	—	—

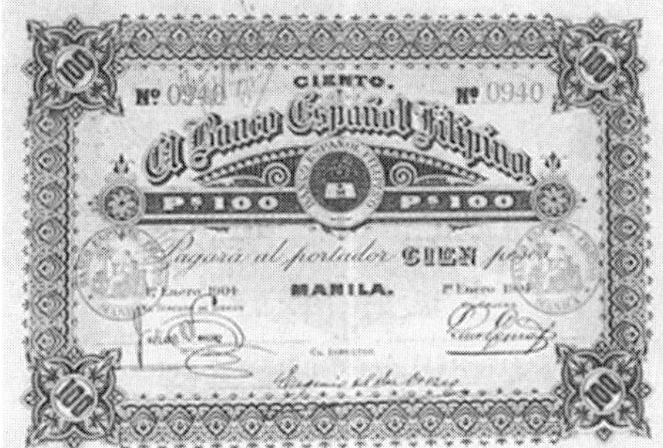

		Good	Fine	XF
A35	**100 Pesos** 1.1.1904. Black. Bank arms at upper center. Printer: BFL. Rare. PC: Yellowish brown.	—	—	—

		Good	Fine	XF
A36	**200 Pesos** 1.1.1904. Black. Bank arms at upper center. BC: Multicolor. Printer: BFL. Rare. PC: Yellowish brown.	—	—	—

1908 Issue

#1 and 2 with 1 stamped signature (at left) and 2 printed signatures. #4-6 with only 2 printed signatures.

		Good	Fine	XF
1	**5 Pesos** 1.1.1908. Black on red underprint. Woman seated at left. Signature *J. Serrano* at left. BC: Red. Printer: USBEP (without imprint).	200	500	900

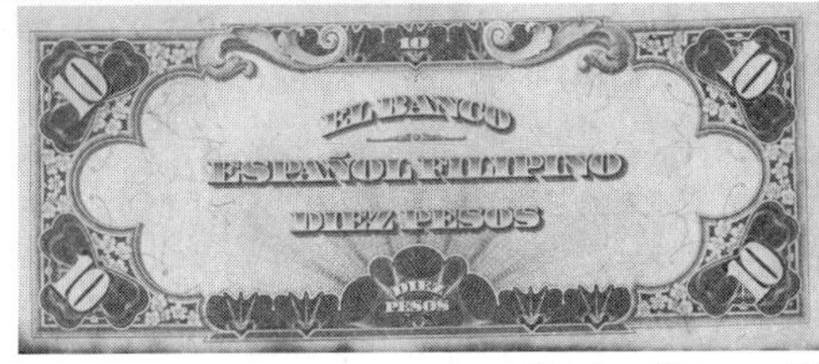

		Good	Fine	XF
2	**10 Pesos** 1.1.1908. Black on brown underprint. Woman with flowers at center. BC: Brown. Printer: USBEP (without imprint).			
	a. Signature *Julian Serrano* at left. Rare.	—	9,000	—
	b. Signature *J. Serrano* at left.	400	900	—
3	**20 Pesos** 1.1.1908. Black on lilac underprint. Woman at left. BC: Tan. Printer: USBEP (without imprint).			
	a. Signature Julian Serrano at left. Rare.	—	—	—
	b. Signature J. Serrano at left.	750	2,000	—

		Good	Fine	XF
4	**50 Pesos** 1.1.1908. Black on blue underprint. Woman standing with flower at left. BC: Red. Printer: USBEP (without imprint).	750	2,000	4,500

		Good	Fine	XF
5	**100 Pesos** 1.1.1908. Black on green underprint. Woman seated with scroll and globe at left. BC: Olive. Printer: USBEP (without imprint).	600	1,000	—
6	**200 Pesos** 1.1.1908. Black on tan underprint. Justice seated with scales and shield at center. BC: Orange. Printer: USBEP (without imprint). Rare.	—	15,000	—

Bank of the Philippine Islands

A name change to English for the Banco Español Filipino.

1912 Issue

		Good	Fine	XF
7	**5 Pesos** 1.1.1912. Black on red underprint. Woman seated at left. Similar to #1. BC: Light red. Printer: USBEP (without imprint).			
	a. Signature D. Garcia and Jno. S. Hord.	50.00	150	300
	b. Signature D. Garcia and E. Sendres.	50.00	150	300
	r. Replacement. * at end of serial #.	—	500	—
8	**10 Pesos** 1.1.1912. Black on brown underprint. Woman with flowers at center. Similar to #2. Printer: USBEP (without imprint).			
	a. Signature D. Garcia and Jno. S. Hord.	75.00	175	350
	b. Signature D. Garcia and E. Sendres.	75.00	100	350
	r. Replacement note. Signature as "b", *at end of Serial #.	—	1,000	—

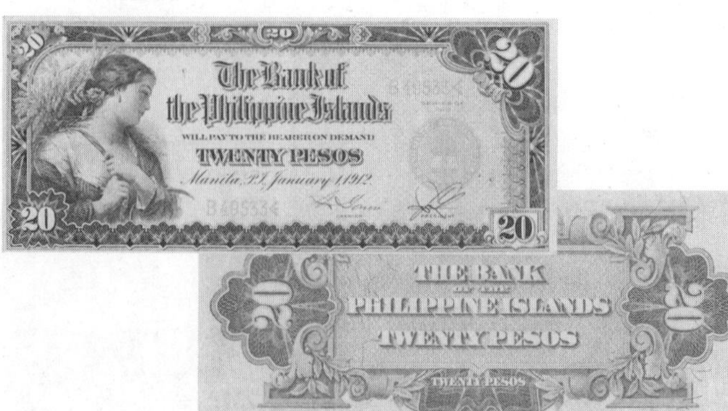

		Good	Fine	XF
9	**20 Pesos** 1.1.1912. Black on lilac underprint. Woman at left. Similar to #3. Printer: USBEP (without imprint).			
	a. Signature D. Garcia and Jno. S. Hord.	250	700	1,500
	b. Signature D. Garcia and E. Sendres.	50.00	200	1,200
	r. Replacement. * at end of Serial #.	—	600	—

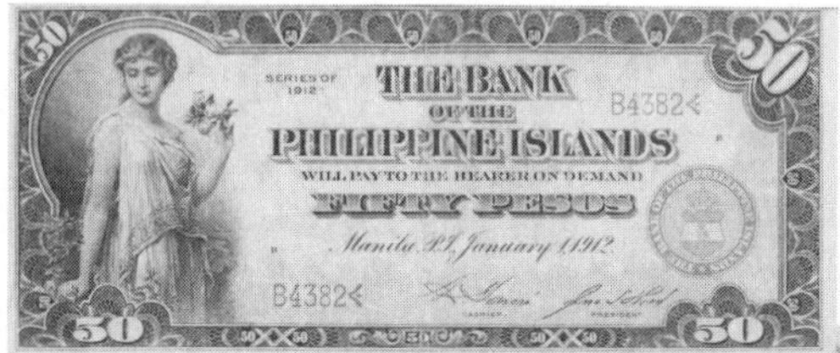

		Good	Fine	XF
10	**50 Pesos** 1.1.1912. Black on blue underprint. Woman standing with flower at left. Similar to #4. Printer: USBEP (without imprint).			
	a. Signature D. Garcia and Jno. S. Hord.	400	1,000	4,000
	b. Signature D. Garcia and E. Sendres.	26.00	900	3,000
	r. Replacement note. Signature as "b", *at end of Serial #.	—	1,000	—

		Good	Fine	XF
11	**100 Pesos** 1.1.1912. Black on green underprint. Woman seated with scroll and globe at left. Similar to #5. Printer: USBEP (without imprint).			
	a. Signature D. Garcia and Jno. S. Hord.	500	1,200	2,000
	b. Signature D. Garcia and E. Sendres.	500	1,000	2,000
	r. Replacement note. Signature as "a", *at end of Serial #.	—	4,000	—

		Good	Fine	XF
12	**200 Pesos** 1.1.1912. Black on tan underprint. Justice with scales and shield at center. Similar to #6. Signature D. Garcia and Jno. S. Hord. Printer: USBEP (without imprint).	1,000	2,600	—

1920 Issue

#13-15 like #7b-9b except for date and serial # prefix-suffix.

		Good	Fine	XF
13	**5 Pesos** 1.1.1920. Black on red underprint. Woman seated at left. Like #7b. Signature D. Garcia and E. Sendres. BC: Orange. Printer: USBEP (without imprint).			
	a. Issued note.	25.00	40.00	125
	r. Replacement note. *at end of Serial #.	—	Unc	—

		Good	Fine	XF
14	**10 Pesos** 1.1.1920. Black on brown underprint. Woman with flowers at center. Like #8b. Signature D. Garcia and E. Sendres. Printer: USBEP (without imprint).			
	a. Issued note.	50.00	100	175
	r. Replacement. * at end of Serial #.	`	500	—

		Good	Fine	XF
15	**20 Pesos** 1.1.1920. Black on lilac underprint. Woman at left. Like #9b. Signature D. Garcia and E. Sendres. Printer: USBEP (without imprint).			
	a. Issued note.	5.00	30.00	85.00
	r. Replacement. * at end of Serial #.	—	750	—

1928 Issue

#16-21 designs like #7-12 but without underprint.

		Good	Fine	XF
16	**5 Pesos** 1.1.1928. Black. Woman seated at left. Like #7. Signature D. Garcia and Fulg. Borromeo. BC: Orange. Printer: USBEP (without imprint).			
	a. Issued note.	40.00	90.00	125
	r. Replacement note. *at end of Serial #.	—	Unc	—
17	**10 Pesos** 1.1.1928. Black. Woman with flowers at center. Like #8. Signature D. Garcia and Fulg. Borromeo. Printer: USBEP (without imprint).	**Good**	**Fine**	**XF**
	a. Issued note.	40.00	100	150
	r. Replacement note. *at end of Serial #.	—	Unc	—
18	**20 Pesos** 1.1.1928. Black. Woman at left. Like #9. Signature D. Garcia and Fulg. Borromeo. Printer: USBEP (without imprint).	**Good**	**Fine**	**XF**
	a. Issued note.	50.00	100	150
	r. Replacement. * at end of Serial #.	—	1,000	—

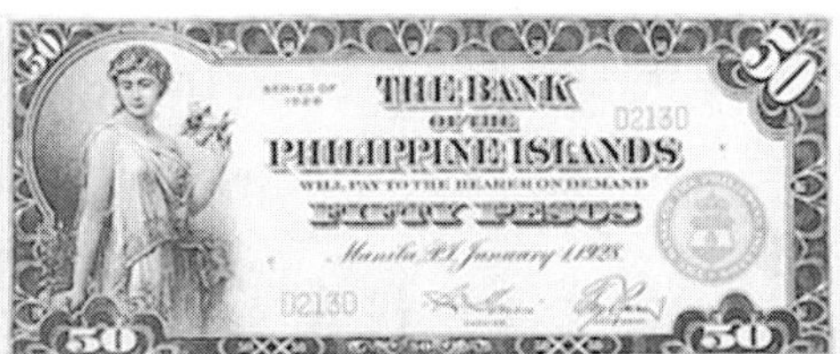

		Good	Fine	XF
19	**50 Pesos** 1.1.1928. Black. Woman standing with flower at left. Like #10. Signature D. Garcia and Fulg. Borromeo. Printer: USBEP (without imprint).	100	275	650

		Good	Fine	XF
20	**100 Pesos** 1.1.1928. Black. Woman seated with scroll and globe at left. Like #11. Signature D. Garcia and Fulg. Borromeo. Printer: USBEP (without imprint).	150	575	750

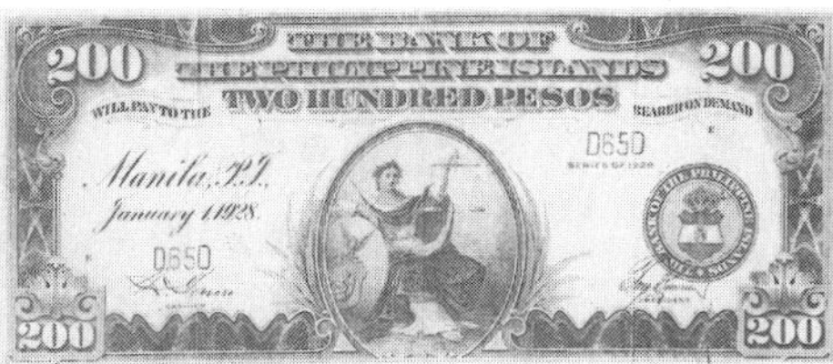

		Good	Fine	XF
21	**200 Pesos** 1.1.1928. Black. Justice with scales and shield at center. Like #12. Signature D. Garcia and Fulg. Borromeo. Printer: USBEP (without imprint).	500	1,500	3,500

1933 Issue

#22-24 like #16-18 except for date and serial # prefix-suffix.

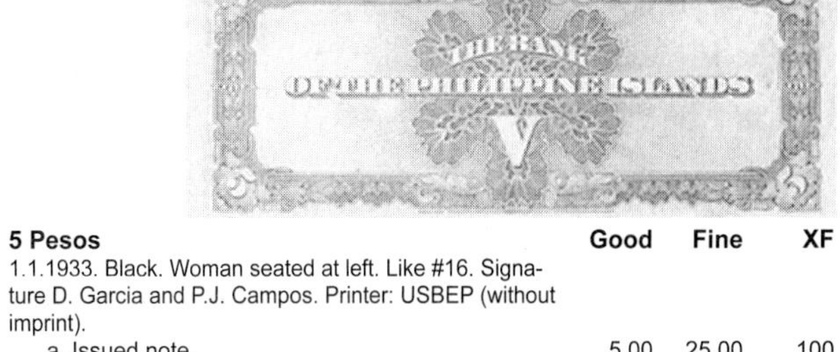

		Good	Fine	XF
22	**5 Pesos** 1.1.1933. Black. Woman seated at left. Like #16. Signature D. Garcia and P.J. Campos. Printer: USBEP (without imprint).			
	a. Issued note.	5.00	25.00	100
	r. Replacement note. *at end of Serial #.	—	Unc	—
23	**10 Pesos** 1.1.1933. Black. Woman with flowers at center. Like #17. Signature D. Garcia and P.J. Campos. Printer: USBEP (without imprint).	**Good**	**Fine**	**XF**
	a. Issued note.	5.00	25.00	150
	r. Replacement note. *at end of Serial #.	—	400	—
24	**20 Pesos** 1.1.1933. Black. Woman at left. Like #18. Signature D. Garcia and P.J. Campos. Printer: USBEP (without imprint).	**Good**	**Fine**	**XF**
	a. Issued note.	25.00	75.00	250
	r. Replacement note. * at end of Serial #.	—	800	—

Philippine Islands

Silver Certificates

1903 Issue

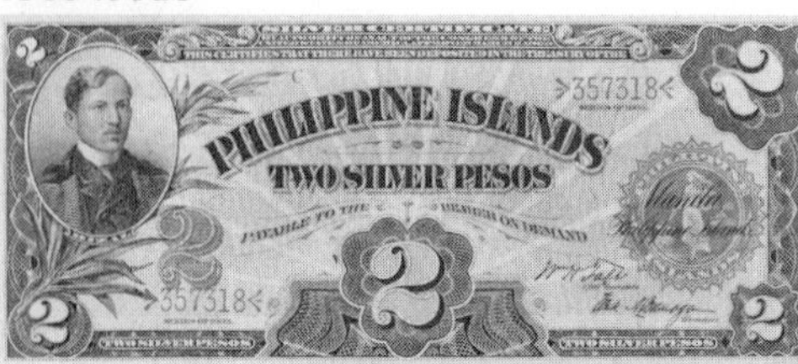

		Good	Fine	XF
25	**2 Pesos**			
	1903. Black on blue underprint. Portrait José Rizal at upper left. BC: Blue. Printer: USBEP (without imprint).			
	a. Signature William H. Taft and Frank A. Branagan.	150	300	650
	b. Signature Luke E. Wright and Frank A. Branagan.	300	750	1,500
	p. Uniface proofs. Face and back pair.	—	—	12,000

		Good	Fine	XF
26	**5 Pesos**			
	1903. Black on red underprint. Portrait President William McKinley at left. BC: Red. Printer: USBEP (without imprint).			
	a. Signature William H. Taft and Frank A. Branagan.	250	600	1,750
	b. Signature Luke E. Wright and Frank A. Branagan.	400	1,000	2,000
	p. Uniface proofs. Face and Back pari.	—	—	12,000

		Good	Fine	XF
27	**10 Pesos**			
	1903. Black on brown underprint. Portrait George Washington at lower center. BC: Brown. Printer: USBEP (without imprint).			
	a. Signature William H. Taft and Frank A. Branagan.	400	900	2,000
	b. Signature Luke E. Wright and Frank A. Branagan.	450	2,250	3,000
	p. Uniface proofs. Face and back pair.	—	—	12,000

		Good	Fine	XF
27A	**10 Pesos**			
	1903. Black on brown underprint. Portrait George Washington at lower center. Like #27. Signature Henry C. Ide with title: *Governor General* and Frank A. Branagan. BC: Brown. Printer: USBEP (without imprint). Overprint: Black vertical text: *Subject to the provisions of the/Act of Congress approved/ June 23, 1906*	1,500	2,750	—

Note: The chief executive's title before 1905 was: *Civil Governor.*

1905 Issue

#28-31 issued with overprint like #27A. Sign. Luke E. Wright with title: *Governor General* and Frank A. Branagan.

		Good	Fine	XF
28	**20 Pesos**			
	1905. Black on yellow underprint. Mt. Mayon at center. Signature Luke E. Wright and Frank A. Branagan. BC: Tan. Overprint: Black vertical text: *Subject to the provisions of the/Act of Congress approved/ June 23, 1906* Rare.	—	4,750	20,000
29	**50 Pesos**			
	1905. Black on red underprint. Portrait Gen. Henry W. Lawton at left. Signature Luke E. Wright and Frank A. Branagan. BC: Red. Overprint: Black vertical text: *Subject to the provisions of the/Act of Congress approved/ June 23, 1906* Rare.	—	—	—
30	**100 Pesos**			
	1905. Black on green underprint. Portrait Ferdinand Magellan at center. Signature Luke E. Wright and Frank A. Branagan. BC: Olive. Overprint: Black vertical text: *Subject to the provisions of the/Act of Congress approved/ June 23, 1906* Rare.	—	—	—
31	**500 Pesos**			
	1905. Black. Portrait Miguel Lopez de Legazpi at center. Signature Luke E. Wright and Frank A. Branagan. BC: Purple. Overprint: Black vertical text: *Subject to the provisions of the/Act of Congress approved/ June 23, 1906* Rare.	—	—	—

1906 Issue

		Good	Fine	XF
32	**2 Pesos**			
	1906. Black on blue underprint. Portrait José Rizal at upper left. Similar to #25 but payable in silver or gold. BC: Blue.			
	a. Signature James F. Smith and Frank A. Branagan.	75.00	150	750
	b. Signature W. Cameron Forbes and J. L. Barrett.	100	350	—
	c. Signature W. Cameron Forbes and J. L. Manning.	200	650	1,500
	d. Signature Francis Burton Harrison and J. L. Manning.	85.00	375	1,000
	e. Signature like d., but without blue underprint. (error).	85.00	350	—
	f. Signature Francis Burton Harrison and A. P. Fitzsimmons.	50.00	200	300

#	Description	Good	Fine	XF
33	**500 Pesos** 1906. Black. Portrait Miguel Lopez de Legazpi at center. Similar to #31. BC: Purple.			
	a. Signature James F. Smith and Frank A. Branagan. Rare.	—	25,000	—
	b. Signature W. Cameron Forbes and J. L. Barrett. Rare.	—	22,000	—
	c. Signature Francis Burton Harrison and A. P. Fitzsimmons. Rare.	—	—	25,000

1908 Issue

#	Description	Good	Fine	XF
34	**20 Pesos** 1908. Black on yellow underprint. Mt. Mayon at center. Similar to #28. BC: Tan.			
	a. Signature James F. Smith and Frank A. Branagan.	250	750	3,000
	b. Signature W. Cameron Forbes and J. L. Barrett.	250	750	2,000
	c. Signature W. Cameron Forbes and J. L. Manning.	175	600	1,000
	d. Signature Francis Burton Harrison and J. L. Manning.	200	600	2,500
	e. Signature Francis Burton Harrison and A. P. Fitzsimmons.	125	450	—

1910 Issue

#	Description	Good	Fine	XF
35	**5 Pesos** 1910. Black on red underprint. Portrait President William McKinley at left. Similar to #26. BC: Red.			
	a. Signature W. Cameron Forbes and J. L. Barrett.	150	500	1,200
	b. Signature W. Cameron Forbes and J. L. Manning.	150	500	1,750
	c. Signature Francis Burton Harrison and J. L. Manning.	200	750	—
	d. Signature Francis Burton Harrison and A. P. Fitzsimmons.	100	325	1,000

1912 Issue

#	Description	Good	Fine	XF
36	**10 Pesos** 1912. Black on brown underprint. Portrait George Washington at lower center. Similar to #27. BC: Brown.			
	a. Signature W. Cameron Forbes and J. L. Barrett.	250	1,400	—
	b. Signature W. Cameron Forbes and J. L. Manning.	250	1,400	—
	c. Signature Francis Burton Harrison and J. L. Manning.	250	1,300	—
	d. Signature Francis Burton Harrison and A. P. Fitzsimmons.	100	150	1,000

1916 Issue

#	Description	Good	Fine	XF
37	**50 Pesos** 1916. Black on red underprint. Portrait Gen. Henry W. Lawton at left. Similar to #29. BC: Red. Rare.	—	8,000	—
38	**100 Pesos** 1916. Black on green underprint. Portrait Ferdinand Magellan at center. Similar to #30. BC: Olive. Rare.	—	40,000	—

Philippine National Bank

1917 Emergency WW I Issue

#	Description	VG	VF	UNC
39	**10 Centavos** 20.11.1917. Gold on yellow underprint. Back: American bald eagle. BC: Yellow. Printer: Local.	—	20.00	50.00

#	Description	VG	VF	UNC
40	**20 Centavos** 20.11.1917. Blue on yellow underprint. Back: American bald eagle. BC: Blue. Printer: Local.	—	20.00	50.00

#	Description	VG	VF	UNC
41	**50 Centavos** 22.9.1917. Black on green underprint. Back: American bald eagle. BC: Green. Printer: Local.	5.00	25.00	65.00
42	**1 Peso** 22.9.1917. Black on red underprint. Back: American bald eagle. BC: Red. Printer: Local.	10.00	40.00	125

1919 ND Emergency Issue

#43-43B new bank name, seal, signature overprint on Bank of the Philippine Islands notes.

#	Description	VG	VF	UNC
43	**5 Pesos** ND (1919 - old date 1912). Black on red underprint. Woman seated at left. BC: Light red. Rare.			
	a. Issued note.	5,100	7,500	—
	r. Replacement note. *at end of Serial #.	—	20,000	—

		VG	VF	UNC
43A	**10 Pesos** ND (1919 - old date 1912). Black on brown underprint. Woman with flowers at center. BC: Brown. Rare.			
	a. Issued note.	—	8,500	—
	r. Replacement note. *at end of Serial #.	—	25,000	—

		VG	VF	UNC
43B	**20 Pesos** ND (1919 - old date 1912). Black on lilac underprint. Woman at left. BC: Tan. Rare.	5,500	—	—

1916-1920 Regular Issue

		Good	Fine	XF
44	**1 Peso** 1918. Black on orange underprint. Portrait Charles A. Conant at left. BC: Green. Printer: USBEP (without imprint).	75.00	300	600

		Good	Fine	XF
45	**2 Pesos** 1916. Black on blue underprint. Portrait José Rizal at left (similar to Silver and Treasury Certificates). BC: Blue. Printer: USBEP (without imprint).	100	400	1,000

		Good	Fine	XF
46	**5 Pesos** 1916. Black on red underprint. Portrait Pres. William McKinley at left (similar to Silver and Treasury Certificates). BC: Red-orange. Printer: USBEP (without imprint).			
	a. Signature S. Ferguson and H. Parker Willis.	250	750	—
	b. Signature S. Mercado and V. Concepcion.	10.00	25.00	75.00
	r. Replacement note. As b. * at end of serial #.	—	—	300

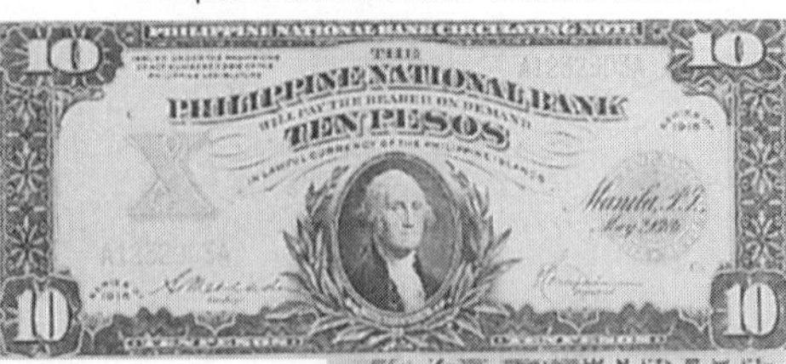

		Good	Fine	XF
47	**10 Pesos** 1916. Black on brown underprint. Portrait George Washington at lower center (similar to Silver and Treasury Certificates). BC: Brown. Printer: USBEP (without imprint).			
	a. Signature S. Ferguson and H. Parker Willis.	250	750	1,500
	b. Signature S. Mercado and V. Concepcion.	25.00	50.00	150
	r. Replacement note. *As b. at end of serial #.	—	250	—

		Good	Fine	XF
48	**20 Pesos** 1919. Black on yellow underprint. Portrait Congressman William A. Jones at lower center. BC: Tan. Printer: USBEP (without imprint).			
	a. Issued note.	150	650	1,250
	r. Replacement note. *at end of Serial #.	—	4,000	—

		Good	Fine	XF
49	**50 Pesos** 1920. Black on green underprint. Portrait Gen. Henry W. Lawton at left. BC: Red. Printer: USBEP (without imprint).	25.00	75.00	150

Note: #49 was never officially issued. 10,000 pieces were captured and issued during WW II by the Japanese (serial #90001-100000). The others were looted by Moros in the province of Mindanao who sold them at one-tenth of their face value. This accounts for their relative availability.

		Good	Fine	XF
50	**100 Pesos** 1920. Green on red underprint. Portrait Ferdinand Magellan at center. BC: Olive. Printer: USBEP (without imprint). Rare.	—	3,400	—

1921 Issue

#51-55 designs like previous issue but notes without underprint.

		Good	Fine	XF
51	**1 Peso** 1921. Black on orange underprint. Portrait Charles A. Conant at left. Like #44. BC: Green. Printer: USBEP (without imprint).	50.00	100	400

		Good	Fine	XF
52	**2 Pesos** 1921. Black on blue underprint. Portrait José Rizal at left. Like #45. BC: Blue. Printer: USBEP (without imprint).	75.00	200	500

No.	Description	Good	Fine	XF
53	**5 Pesos** 1921. Black on red underprint. Portrait Pres. William McKinley at left. Like #46. BC: Red-orange. Printer: USBEP (without imprint).			
	a. Issued note.	5.00	10.00	25.00
	r. Replacement note. *at end of Serial #.	—	Unc	1,300

No.	Description	Good	Fine	XF
54	**10 Pesos** 1921. Black on brown underprint. Portrait George Washington at center. Like #47. BC: Brown. Printer: USBEP (without imprint).			
	a. Issued note.	25.00	100	300
	r. Replacement note. *at end of Serial #.	—	—	1,000

No.	Description	Good	Fine	XF
55	**20 Pesos** 1921. Black on yellow underprint. Portrait Congressman William A. Jones at lower center. Like #48. BC: Tan. Printer: USBEP (without imprint).			
	a. Issued note.	20.00	75.00	800
	r. Replacement note. *at end of Serial #.	350	—	1,000

1924 Issue

No.	Description	Good	Fine	XF
56	**1 Peso** 1924. Black on orange underprint. Portrait Charles A. Conant at left. Like #51. BC: Green.			
	a. Issued note.	25.00	100	250
	r. Replacement note. *at end of Serial #.	—	1,000	—

1937 Issue

No.	Description	VG	VF	UNC
57	**5 Pesos** 1937. Black on red underprint. Portrait Pres. McKinley at left. Similar to #53. Text reads: *PHILIPPINES.* BC: Red-orange. Printer: USBEP.			
	a. Issued note.	5.00	25.00	60.00
	r. Replacement note. *at end of Serial #.	—	—	1,250

No.	Description	VG	VF	UNC
58	**10 Pesos** 1937. Black on brown underprint. Portrait George Washington at center. Similar to #54. Text reads: *PHILIPPINES.* BC: Brown. Printer: USBEP.	35.00	60.00	350
59	**20 Pesos** 1937. Black on yellow underprint. Portrait Congressman William A. Jones at lower center. Similar to #55. Text reads: *PHILIPPINES.* BC: Tan. Printer: USBEP.	100	250	750

Philippine Islands (resumed)

Treasury Certificates

1918 Issue

No.	Description	Good	Fine	XF
60	**1 Peso** 1918. Black on green underprint. Portrait A. Mabini at left. BC: Green. Printer: USBEP (without imprint).			
	a. Signature Francis Burton Harrison and A. P. Fitzsimmons.	25.00	60.00	350
	b. Signature Francis Burton Harrison and V. Carmona.	50.00	100	375
	r1. Replacement note. Signature as "a". *at end of Serial #.	—	—	750
	r2. Replacement note. Signature as "b". *at end of Serial #.	—	500	—
61	**2 Pesos** 1918. Black on blue underprint. Portrait J. Rizal at left. BC: Blue. Printer: USBEP (without imprint).			
	a. Issued note.	75.00	375	750
	r. Replacement note. *at end of Serial #.	—	Unc	—
62	**5 Pesos** 1918. Black on light red underprint. Portrait President William McKinley at left. BC: Red-orange. Printer: USBEP (without imprint).			
	a. Issued note.	125	500	3,000
	r. Replacement note. * at end of serial #.	—	—	2,000
63	**10 Pesos** 1918. Black on brown underprint. Portrait George Washington at center. BC: Brown. Printer: USBEP (without imprint).			
	a. Issued note.	300	750	1,500
	r. Replacement note. *at end of Serial #.	—	1,000	—
63A	**20 Pesos** 1918. Black on yellow underprint. Mayon volcano at center. Ornate blue *XX* at upper left. Signature Francis Burton Harrison and A. P. Fitzsimmons. BC: Tan. Printer: USBEP (without imprint).	100	600	2,500

No.	Description	Good	Fine	XF
64	**20 Pesos** 1918. Black on yellow underprint. Mayon volcano at center. Like #63A. Signature Francis Burton Harrison and V. Carmona. BC: Tan. Printer: USBEP (without imprint).			
	a. Issued note.	150	700	2,750
	r. Replacement note. *at end of Serial #.	300	—	1,250
65	**50 Pesos** 1918. Black on green underprint. Portrait Gen. Lawton at left. BC: Red. Printer: USBEP (without imprint).			
	a. Signature Francis Burton Harrison and A. P. Fitzsimmons.	1,000	2,500	—
	b. Signature Francis Burton Harrison and V. Carmona.	1,000	3,000	—
	r. Replacement note. As "b" signature, *at end of Serial #.	—	3,000	—

66	100 Pesos	Good	Fine	XF
	1918. Black on green underprint. Portrait Ferdinand Magellan at center. BC: Olive. Printer: USBEP (without imprint).			
	a. Signature Francis Burton Harrison and A. P. Fitzsimmons. Rare.	—	—	—
	b. Signature Francis Burton Harrison and V. Carmona. Rare.	2,500	4,250	—

67	500 Pesos	Good	Fine	XF
	1918. Black on orange underprint. Portrait Legazpi at center. BC: Purple. Printer: USBEP (without imprint). Rare.	—	—	—

1924 Issue

#68-72 without underprint, otherwise designs like previous issue.

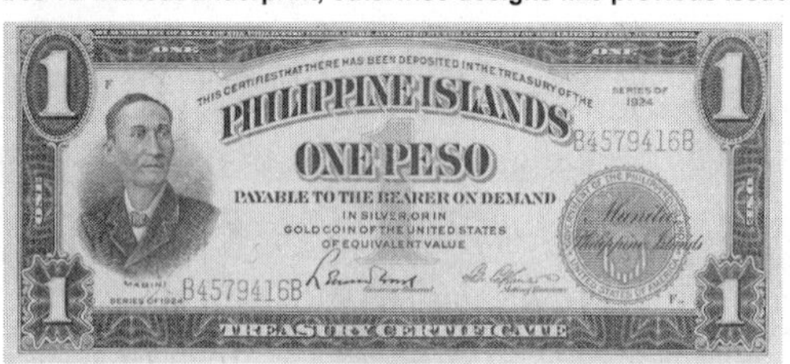

68	1 Peso	Good	Fine	XF
	1924. Black. Portrait A. Mabini at left. Like #60. BC: Green. Printer: USBEP (without imprint).			
	a. Signature Leonard Wood and Salv. Lagdameo with title: *Acting Treasurer.*	15.00	110	250
	b. Signature Leonard Wood and Salv. Lagdameo with title: *Treasurer.*	20.00	125	300
	c. Signature H. L. Stimson and Salv. Lagdameo.	15.00	110	200
	r1. Replacement note. As "a" signature. * at end of serial #.	—	800	—
	r2. Replacement note. As "b" signature. *at end of Serial #.	—	Unc	—
	r3. Replacement note. As "c" signature. *at end of Serial #.	—	Unc	—

69	2 Pesos	Good	Fine	XF
	1924. Black. Portrait J. Rizal at left. Like #61, but large denomination numeral added in red at lower left center. BC: Blue. Printer: USBEP (without imprint).			
	a. Signature Leonard Wood and Salv. Lagdameo with title: *Acting Treasurer.*	50.00	250	450
	b. Signature Leonard Wood and Salv. Lagdameo with title: *Treasurer.*	60.00	300	600
	c. Signature Henry L. Stimson and Salv. Lagdameo.	25.00	110	250

70	5 Pesos	Good	Fine	XF
	1924. Black. Portrait President William McKinley at left. Like #62. Printer: USBEP (without imprint).			
	a. Issued note.	50.00	250	800
	r. Replacement note. *at end of Serial #.	—	Unc	—

71	10 Pesos	Good	Fine	XF
	1924. Black. Portrait George Washington at center. Like #63. BC: Brown. Printer: USBEP (without imprint).			
	a. Issued note.	25.00	100	600
	r. Replacement note. *at end of Serial #.	—	2,750	—

72	500 Pesos	Good	Fine	XF
	1924. Black on blue underprint. Portrait Legazpi at center. Blue numeral. Like #67. Printer: USBEP (without imprint).			
	a. Back light green.	2,000	6,000	10,000
	p. Back purple. Proof.	—	—	—

Note: Though official records indicate that the backs of #72 were printed in purple, the only issued notes seen in collections have light green backs. Further reports are needed.

1929 Issue

73	1 Peso	Good	Fine	XF
	1929. Black on orange underprint. Portrait A. Mabini at left. Similar to #60 with minor alterations in plate. BC: Orange. Printer: USBEP (without imprint).			
	a. Signature Dwight F. Davis and Salv. Lagdameo.	10.00	75.00	200
	b. Signature Theodore Roosevelt and Salv. Lagdameo.	50.00	250	350
	c. Signature Frank Murphy and Salv. Lagdameo.	10.00	25.00	125
	r1. Replacement note. As "a" signature. *at end of Serial #.	—	1,250	—
	r2. Replacement note. As "c" signature, *at end of Serial #.	—	750	—

#	Denomination	Good	Fine	XF
74	**2 Pesos**	Good	Fine	XF
	1929. Black on blue underprint. Portrait J. Rizal at left. Similar to #61 with minor alterations in plate. BC: Blue. Printer: USBEP (without imprint).			
	a. Signature Theodore Roosevelt and Salv. Lagdameo.	15.00	125	350
	b. Signature Frank Murphy and Salv. Lagdameo.	5.00	75.00	125
	r. Replacement note. As b. * at end of serial #.	—	500	—
	s. Specimen. Pin perforated.	—	Unc	2,000
75	**5 Pesos**	Good	Fine	XF
	1929. Black on yellow underprint. Portrait William McKinley at left, Adm. Dewey at right. BC: Yellow. Printer: USBEP (without imprint).	25.00	175	750
76	**10 Pesos**	Good	Fine	XF
	1929. Black on brown underprint. Portrait George Washington at left. BC: Brown. Printer: USBEP (without imprint).			
	a. Issued note.	40.00	100	900
	p. Proof. Uniface front.	—	Unc	550
	r. Replacement note. *at end of Serial #.	—	1,000	—
77	**20 Pesos**	Good	Fine	XF
	1929. Black on yellow underprint. Mayon volcano at center. Similar to #64 with minor alterations in plate. BC: Tan. Printer: USBEP (without imprint).	50.00	250	1,000
78	**50 Pesos**	Good	Fine	XF
	1929. Black on pink underprint. Portrait Gen. Lawton at left. BC: Dark red. Printer: USBEP (without imprint).			
	a. Issued note.	350	1,500	—
	r. Replacement note. *at end of Serial #.	—	2,500	—
79	**100 Pesos**	Good	Fine	XF
	1929. Black on green underprint. Portrait Ferdinand Magellan at left. BC: Green. Printer: USBEP (without imprint). Rare.	—	4,900	—
80	**500 Pesos**	VG	VF	UNC
	1929. Black on orange underprint. Portrait Legazpi at left. BC: Purple. Printer: USBEP (without imprint). Rare.	—	—	—

COMMONWEALTH

Philippines

Treasury Certificates

1936 Issue

#81-88 new red Commonwealth seal. Signature Manuel Quezon and Antonio Ramos. Title reads: *PHILIPPINES.*

#	Denomination	VG	VF	UNC
81	**1 Peso**	VG	VF	UNC
	1936. Black on orange underprint. Portrait A. Mabini at left. Similar to #73. New red Commonwealth seal. Signature Manuel Quezon and Antonio Ramos. BC: Orange. Printer: USBEP (without imprint).			
	a. Issued note.	7.50	25.00	75.00
	r. Replacement note. * at end of serial #.	75.00	200	—

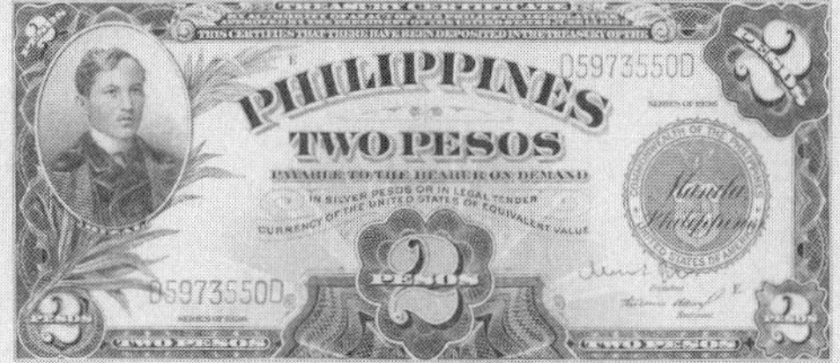

#	Denomination	VG	VF	UNC
82	**2 Pesos**	VG	VF	UNC
	1936. Black on blue underprint. Portrait J. Rizal at left. Similar to #74. New red Commonwealth seal. Signature Manuel Quezon and Antonio Ramos. BC: Blue. Printer: USBEP (without imprint).			
	a. Issued note.	4.00	10.00	475
	r. Replacement note. *at end of Serial #.	—	—	—
83	**5 Pesos**	VG	VF	UNC
	1936. Black on yellow underprint. Portrait William McKinley at left, Adm. Dewey at right. Similar to #75. New red Commonwealth seal. Signature Manuel Quezon and Antonio Ramos. BC: Yellow. Printer: USBEP (without imprint).			
	a. Regular issue. Serial # D1D to D3 244 000D.	5.00	20.00	400
	b. U.S.A. War Department issue (1944). D3 244 001D to D3 544 000D.	125	200	750
	r. Replacement note. Signature as "a", *at end of Serial #.	—	650	—
84	**10 Pesos**	VG	VF	UNC
	1936. Black on brown underprint. Portrait George Washington at left. Similar to #76. New red Commonwealth seal. Signature Manuel Quezon and Antonio Ramos. Printer: USBEP (without imprint).			
	a. Regular issue. Serial # D1D to D2 024 000D.	40.00	80.00	1,200
	b. U.S.A. War Department issue (1944). D2 024 001D to D2 174 000D.	150	550	1,500
	r. Replacement note. Signature as "a", *at end of Serial #.	—	750	—
85	**20 Pesos**	VG	VF	UNC
	1936. Black on yellow underprint. Mayon volcano at center. Similar to #77. New red Commonwealth seal. Signature Manuel Quezon and Antonio Ramos. BC: Tan. Printer: USBEP (without imprint).			
	a. Regular issue. D1D to D1 664 000D.	50.00	150	1,500
	b. U.S.A. War Department issue (1944). D1 664 001D to D1 739 000D.	250	1,000	6,000
	r. Replacement note. Signature as "a", *at end of Serial #.	—	1,500	—
86	**50 Pesos**	VG	VF	UNC
	1936. Black on pink underprint. Portrait Gen. Lawton at left. Similar to #78. New red Commonwealth seal. Signature Manuel Quezon and Antonio Ramos. BC: Dark red. Printer: USBEP (without imprint).			
	a. Issued note.	550	1,500	5,500
	r. Replacement note. *at end of Serial #.	—	2,500	—

		VG	VF	UNC
87	**100 Pesos** 1936. Black on green underprint. Portrait Ferdinand Magellan at left. Similar to #79. New red Commonwealth seal. Signature Manuel Quezon and Antonio Ramos. BC: Green. Printer: USBEP (without imprint).			
	a. Regular issue. Serial # D1D to D41 000D.	500	1,500	—
	b. U.S.A. War Department issue (1944). D41 001D to D56 000D. Rare.	1,750	—	—

		VG	VF	UNC
88	**500 Pesos** 1936. Black on orange underprint. Portrait Legazpi at left. Similar to #80. New red Commonwealth seal. Signature Manuel Quezon and Antonio Ramos. BC: Purple. Printer: USBEP (without imprint). Rare.	750	5,000	—

Note: #83b, 84b, 85b and 87b were made at the request of Army Headquarters, Brisbane, Australia in 1944 for use in military operations.

1941 Issue

#89-93 like previous issue.

		VG	VF	UNC
89	**1 Peso** 1941. Black on orange underprint. Portrait A. Mabini at left. Like #81. Signature Manuel Quezon and A.S. de Leon. BC: Orange. Printer: USBEP (without imprint).			
	a. Regular issue. Serial # E1E to E6 000 000E.	2.00	10.00	20.00
	b. Processed to simulate used currency at Bureau of Standards (1943). #E6 008 001E to E6 056 000E; E6 064 001E to E6 072 000E; E6 080 001E to E6 324 000E. Total 300,000 notes.	125	350	—
	c. Naval Aviators' Emergency Money Packet notes (1944). E6 324 001E to E6 524 000E.	25.00	75.00	250
	r. Replacement note. * at end of serial #.	—	225	750

		VG	VF	UNC
90	**2 Pesos** 1941. Black on blue underprint. Portrait J. Rizal at left. Like #82. Signature Manuel Quezon and A.S. de Leon. BC: Blue. Printer: USBEP (without imprint).			
	a. Issued note.	10.00	75.00	250
	r. Replacement note. *at end of Serial #.	—	400	—

		VG	VF	UNC
91	**5 Pesos** 1941. Black on yellow underprint. Portrait William McKinley at left, Adm. Dewey at right. Like #83. Signature Manuel Quezon and A.S. de Leon. BC: Yellow. Printer: USBEP (without imprint).			
	a. Regular issue. Serial #E1E to E1 188 000E.	25.00	125	400
	b. Processed like #89b (1943). #E1 208 001E to E1 328 000E.	650	—	—
	c. Packet notes like #89c (1944). #E1 328 001E to E1 348 000E.	50.00	200	950
	r. Signature as a. Replacement note. * at end of Serial #.	—	1,000	—

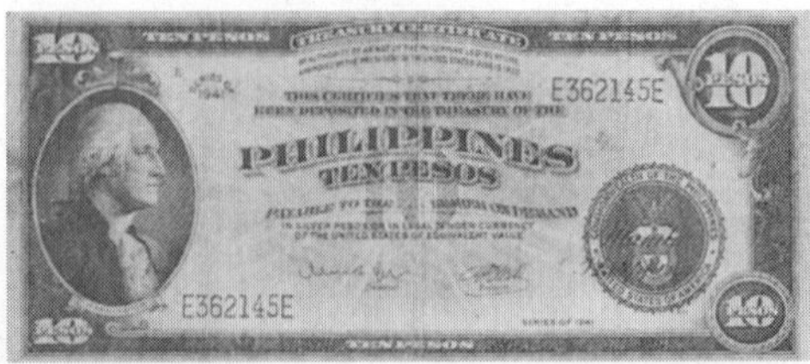

		VG	VF	UNC
92	**10 Pesos** 1941. Black on brown underprint. Portrait George Washington at left. Like #84. Signature Manuel Quezon and A.S. de Leon. BC: Brown. Printer: USBEP (without imprint).			
	a. Regular issue. Serial #E1E to E800 000E.	50.00	200	500
	b. Processed like #89b (1943). E810 001E to E870 000E.	2,500	—	—
	c. Packet notes like #89c (1944). #E870 001E to E890 000E.	75.00	275	1,000
	r. Replacement note. Signature as "a", *at end of Serial #.	1,000	—	—

		VG	VF	UNC
93	**20 Pesos** 1941. Black on yellow underprint. Mayon volcano at center. Like #85. Signature Manuel Quezon and A.S. de Leon. BC: Tan. Printer: USBEP (without imprint).			
	a. Issued note.	100	500	—
	r. Replacement note. *at end of Serial #.	—	—	—

Note: 50, 100 and 500 Pesos notes Series of 1941 were printed but never shipped because of the outbreak of World War II. All were destroyed in 1949, leaving extant only proof impressions and specimen sheets.

1944 ND Victory Issue

#94-101 with overprint text: *VICTORY Series No. 66* twice on face instead of date, blue seal.

		VG	VF	UNC
94	**1 Peso** ND (1944). Black on orange underprint. Portrait A. Mabini at left. Like #89. Text: *VICTORY.* Series No. 66 twice instead of date, with blue seal. Signature Sergio Osmeña and J. Hernandez. BC: Orange. Printer: USBEP (without imprint).			
	a. Issued note.	0.50	2.00	11.00
	r. Replacement note. * at end of Serial #.	—	100	600
	s. Specimen.	—	—	800

		VG	VF	UNC
95	**2 Pesos** ND (1944). Black on blue underprint. Portrait J. Rizal at left. Like #90. Text: *VICTORY.* Series No. 66 twice instead of date, with blue seal. BC: Blue. Printer: USBEP (without imprint).			
	a. Signature Sergio Osmeña and J. Hernandez with title: *Auditor General.*	1.00	2.75	20.00
	b. Signature Manuel Roxas and M. Guevara with title: *Treasurer.*	5.00	12.50	70.00
	r1. Replacement note. Signature as "a". * at start of serial #.	—	75.00	250
	r2. Replacement note. Signature as "b", *at start of Serial #.	450	—	—
	s. Specimen. Pin perforated.	—	—	1,000

		VG	VF	UNC
96	**5 Pesos** ND (1944). Black on yellow underprint. Portrait William McKinley at left, Adm. Dewey at right. Like #91. Text: *VICTORY.* Series No. 66 twice instead of date, with blue seal. Signature Sergio Osmeña and J. Hernandez. BC: Yellow. Printer: USBEP (without imprint).			
	a. Issued note.	2.50	10.00	80.00
	r. Replacement note. * at start of Serial #.	—	500	—
	s. Specimen. Pin perforated.	—	—	1,500

		VG	VF	UNC
97	**10 Pesos** ND (1944). Black on brown underprint. Portrait George Washington at left. Like #92. Text: *VICTORY.* Series No. 66 twice instead of date, with blue seal. Signature Sergio Osmeña and J. Hernandez. BC: Brown. Printer: USBEP (without imprint).			
	a. Issued note.	5.00	40.00	225
	r. Replacement note. *at start of Serial #.	300	—	750
	s. Specimen. Pin perforated.	—	—	1,500

98 20 Pesos

ND (1944). Black on yellow underprint. Mayon volcano at center. Like #93. Text: *VICTORY.* Series No. 66 twice instead of date, with blue seal. BC: Tan. Printer: USBEP (without imprint).

	VG	VF	UNC
a. Signature Sergio Osmeña and J. Hernandez with title: *Auditor General.*	15.00	75.00	175
b. Signature Manuel Roxas and M. Guevara with title: *Treasurer.*	40.00	200	550
r1. Replacement note. Signature as "a". *at start of Serial #.	125	—	—
r2. Replacement note. Signature as "b", *at start of Serial #.	—	—	—
s. Specimen. Pin perforated.	—	—	2,000

99 50 Pesos

ND (1944). Black on pink underprint. Portrait Gen. Lawton at left. Like #86. Text: *VICTORY.* Series No. 66 twice instead of date, with blue seal. BC: Dark red. Printer: USBEP (without imprint).

	VG	VF	UNC
a. Signature Sergio Osmeña and J. Hernandez with title: *Auditor General.*	25.00	175	750
b. Signature Manuel Roxas and M. Guevara with title: *Treasurer.*	40.00	275	1,000
s. Specimen. Pin perforated.	—	—	2,000

100 100 Pesos

ND (1944). Black on green underprint. Portrait Ferdinand Magellan at left. Like #87. Text: VICTORY Series No. 66 twice instead of date, with blue seal. BC: Green. Printer: USBEP (without imprint).

	VG	VF	UNC
a. 1944. Sergio Osmeña and J. Hernandez with title: *Auditor General.*	75.00	225	850
b. Signature Sergio Osmeña and M. Guevara with title: *Treasurer.*	100	275	1,000
c. Signature Manuel Roxas and M. Guevara.	75.00	225	750
r1. Replacement note. Signature as "a". * at start of Serial #.	—	3,000	—
r2. Replacement note. Signature as "b". *at start of Serial #.	—	—	—
r3. Replacement note. Signature as "c". *at start of Serial #.	—	—	—

101 500 Pesos

ND (1944). Black on orange underprint. Portrait Legazpi at left. Like #88. Text: *VICTORY.* Series No. 66 twice instead of date, with blue seal. BC: Purple. Printer: USBEP (without imprint).

	VG	VF	UNC
a. Signature Sergio Osmeña and J. Hernandez with title: *Auditor General.*	1,250	5,000	10,000
b. Signature Sergio Osmeña and M. Guevara with title: *Treasurer.*	500	2,000	6,000
c. Signature Manuel Roxas and M. Guevara.	750	2,500	6,500
r. Replacement note. Signature as "a". *at start of Serial #.	—	—	2,000

JAPANESE OCCUPATION - WWII

Japanese Government

1942 ND Issue

Notes w/block letter *P* preceding other letter(s).

102 1 Centavo

ND (1942). Black on green underprint. BC: Green.

	VG	VF	UNC
a. 2 block letters.	0.10	0.20	0.75
b. Fractional block letters.	0.10	0.25	1.25
s. As a. Specimen with red overprint: *Mi-hon. SPECIMEN* on back.	—	—	100

103 5 Centavos

ND (1942). Black on blue underprint. BC: Blue.

	VG	VF	UNC
a. 2 block letters.	0.10	0.20	0.50
b. Fractional block letters.	0.20	0.50	2.50
s. As a. Specimen with red overprint: *Mi-hon. SPECIMEN* on back.	—	—	100

104 10 Centavos

ND (1942). Black on light brown underprint. BC: Brown.

	VG	VF	UNC
a. 2 block letters.	0.10	0.20	0.50
b. Fractional block letters.	0.10	0.25	1.25
s. As a. Specimen with red overprint: *Mi-hon. SPECIMEN* on back.	—	—	100

105 50 Centavos

ND (1942). Black on light purple underprint. Plantation at right. BC: Purple.

	VG	VF	UNC
a. Buff colored paper.	0.10	0.25	1.00
b. White paper.	0.10	0.20	0.75
s. Specimen with red overprint: *Mi-hon. SPECIMEN* on back.	—	—	100

106 1 Peso

ND (1942). Black on light green underprint. Plantation at left. BC: Green.

	VG	VF	UNC
a. Buff to light brown paper.	0.50	2.00	5.00
b. White paper.	0.25	1.00	4.00
s. Specimen with red overprint: *Mi-hon. SPECIMEN* on back.	—	—	100

107 5 Pesos

ND (1942). Black on light blue underprint. Plantation at center. BC: Orange.

	VG	VF	UNC
a. Buff to light brown paper.	0.50	1.25	3.00
b. White paper.	0.25	0.75	2.75
s. Specimen with red overprint: *Mi-hon. SPECIMEN* on back.	—	—	100

107A 5 Pesos

	VG	VF	UNC
ND (1942). Black on light orange underprint. Plantation at center. Like #107b. BC: Gold-yellow. PC: White.	0.75	1.75	5.00

108 10 Pesos

ND (1942). Black on blue underprint. Plantation at right. BC: Brown.

	VG	VF	UNC
a. Buff paper.	0.25	0.75	1.75
b. White paper.	0.10	0.25	1.50
s. Specimen with red overprint: *Mi-hon. SPECIMEN* on back.	—	—	100

1943 ND Issue

#109-112 engraved face plates.

		VG	VF	UNC
109	**1 Peso** ND (1943). Black on light green and pink underprint. Rizal Monument at left. BC: Blue on pink underprint. Watermark: Banana tree.			
	a. Serial # and block #. (#1-81).	0.20	0.50	1.25
	b. Block # only (82-87).	1.00	2.00	5.00
	s. As a. Specimen with red overprint: *Mi-hon. SPECIMEN* on back.	—	—	150

		VG	VF	UNC
110	**5 Pesos** ND (1943). Black on green and yellow underprint. Rizal Monument at left. BC: Brown on gray underprint. Watermark: Banana tree.			
	a. Issued note.	0.25	0.75	2.75
	s. Specimen with overprint: *Mi-hon.*	—	—	150

		VG	VF	UNC
111	**10 Pesos** ND (1943). Black on green underprint. Rizal Monument at right. BC: Green on yellow underprint. Watermark: Banana tree.			
	a. Issued note.	0.25	1.25	2.50
	s. Specimen with red overprint: *Mi-hon.*	—	—	150
112	**100 Pesos** ND (1944). Black on light blue and tan underprint. Rizal Monument at right. BC: Purple on green underprint. Watermark: Banana tree.	**VG**	**VF**	**UNC**
	a. Issued note.	0.25	0.75	2.25
	s. Specimen with red overprint: *Mi-hon.*	—	—	250

1944-1945 ND Inflation Issue

		VG	VF	UNC
113	**100 Pesos** ND (1945). Black on brown on light green underprint. Similar to #115. Block letters PV. BC: Yellow-brown. Rare.	—	—	—

		VG	VF	UNC
114	**500 Pesos** ND (1944). Black on purple underprint. Rizal Monument at right. BC: Brown. Lithographed.			
	a. Watermark: Banana tree. Buff paper. Block letters PF.	0.50	1.25	5.25
	b. Watermark: Quatrefoil kiri flower. Most on white paper. Block letters PG.	0.50	1.00	5.25
	s1. Specimen with red overprint: *Mi-hon. SPECIMEN* on back.	—	—	250
	s2. Specimen with overprint: *Mi-hon.*	—	—	150
115	**1000 Pesos** ND. (1945). Blue-purple. Similar to #113. Block letters PU. BC: Olive.	**VG**	**VF**	**UNC**
	a. Purple on lilac underprint. (shades). Back dark olive-green without offset.	0.50	1.00	6.00
	b. As a., but back light olive-green without imprint.	0.50	1.00	5.00
	c. As a., but back with offset from face plate.	0.50	1.00	4.00
	d. As b., but back with offset from face plate.	0.50	1.00	4.00

Bangko Sentral Ng Pilipinas

1944 Issue

		VG	VF	UNC
115A	**10 Piso** *L.29.2.1944.* Brown on brown underprint. J. Rizal at left. (A few made in 1944 as essays; not approved for circulation). Rare.	—	—	4.00

		VG	VF	UNC
116	**100 Piso** *L.29.2.1944.* Black on pink underprint. Portrait J. Rizal at left. BC: Red and orange. (Printed 1944; not issued).			
	r. Remainder without block and serial #.	100	250	425
	s1. Specimen with single red overprint: *MI-HON.* With block # and serial #.	—	—	1,100
	s2. As S1 but with two *MI-HON* under each denomination at left and right.	—	—	3,000
	s3. As s1. Specimen with red overprint: *Specimen* with serial # all zeros.	—	—	750
	s4. Red overprint: *MI-HON* at left and right. Otherwise as s1.	—	—	1,200

REPUBLIC

Central Bank of the Philippines

1949 ND Provisional Issue

#117-124 Treasury Certificates of Victory Series with red overprint: *CENTRAL BANK/OF THE PHILIPPINES* on back.

		VG	VF	UNC
117	**1 Peso** ND (1949). Black on orange underprint. Portrait A. Mabini at left. BC: Orange.			
	a. Thick lettering in overprint.	1.00	4.00	20.00
	b. Medium-thick lettering in overprint.	1.00	4.00	15.00
	c. Thin lettering in overprint.	1.00	4.00	15.00
	r1. Replacement note. Thick Overprint. *at start of Serial #.	—	200	—
	r2. Replacement note. Thick Inverted Overprint on back. *at start of Serial #.	—	—	3,000
	r3. Replacement note. Medium Overprint. *at start of Serial #	—	—	—
	r4. Replacement note. Thin Overprint. *at start of Serial #.	—	200	—
118	**2 Pesos** ND (1949). Black on blue underprint. Portrait J. Rizal at left. BC: Blue.	**VG**	**VF**	**UNC**
	a. Signature Sergio Osmeña and J. Hernandez.	—	7,500	—
	b. Signature Manuel Roxas and M. Guevara.	5.00	20.00	150
	r. Replacement note. Signature as "a". *at start of Serial #.	—	—	10,000
119	**5 Pesos** ND (1949). Black on yellow underprint. Portrait William McKinley at left, Adm. Dewey at right. BC: Yellow.	**VG**	**VF**	**UNC**
	a. Thick lettering in overprint.	7.50	40.00	250
	b. Thin lettering in overprint.	5.00	35.00	200
	r. Replacement note. Signature as "a". *at start of Serial #.	350	—	—

		VG	VF	UNC
120	**10 Pesos**	VG	VF	UNC
	ND (1949). Black on brown underprint. Portrait George Washington at left. BC: Brown.			
	a. Issued note.	35.00	200	550
	r1. Replacement note. *at start of Serial #.	—	—	—
121	**20 Pesos**	VG	VF	UNC
	ND (1949). Black on yellow underprint. Mayon volcano at center. BC: Tan.			
	a. Signature Sergio Osmeña and J. Hernandez.	35.00	150	1,775
	b. Signature Manuel Roxas and M. Guevara.	35.00	150	750
	r. Replacement note. Signature as "a". *at start of Serial #.	1,250	—	—

		VG	VF	UNC
122	**50 Pesos**	VG	VF	UNC
	ND (1949). Black on pink underprint. Portrait Gen. Lawton at left. BC: Dark red.			
	a. Signature Sergio Osmeña and J. Hernandez.	65.00	150	600
	b. Signature Manuel Roxas and M. Guevara.	65.00	150	600
	c. Signature Osmeña-Hernandez. Thick lettering in overprint.	100	250	750
	r1. Replacement note. Signature as "a". Thin O/P. * before sterial #.	—	—	5,000
	r2. Replacement note. Signature as "a". Thin O/P. *at start of Serial #.	750	—	—
	r3. Replacement note. Signature as "a". Thick O/P. *at start of Serial #.	—	1,000	—
123	**100 Pesos**	VG	VF	UNC
	ND (1949). Black on green underprint. Portrait Ferdinand Magellan at left. BC: Green.			
	a. Signature Sergio Osmeña and J. Hernandez.	200	300	1,500
	b. Signature Sergio Osmeña and M. Guevara.	125	300	750
	c. Signature Manuel Roxas and M. Guevara.	100	150	500
	r1. Replacement note. Signature as "a". *at start of Serial #.	2,000	—	—
	r2. Replacement note. Signature as "c". *at start of Serial #.	2,000	—	—

		VG	VF	UNC
124	**500 Pesos**	VG	VF	UNC
	ND (1949). Black on orange underprint. Portrait Legazpi at left. BC: Purple.			
	a. Signature Sergio Osmeña and J. Hernandez.	2,000	30,000	—
	b. Signature Sergio Osmeña and M. Guevara.	450	900	5,000
	c. Signature Manuel Roxas and M. Guevara, Thick O/P	450	900	5,000
	d. Signature Manuel Roxas and M. Guevara, Thin O/P.	—	—	6,500

SIGNATURE VARIETIES

1	E. Quirino	M. Cuaderno
2	R. Magsaysay	M. Cuaderno
3	C. Garcia	M. Cuaderno
4	C. Garcia	A. Castillo
5	D. Macapagal	A. Castillo
6	F. Marcos	A. Castillo
7	F. Marcos	A. Calalang
8	F. Marcos	G. Licaros

1949 ND "English" Issues

		VG	VF	UNC
125	**5 Centavos**	VG	VF	UNC
	ND (1949). Red on tan underprint. Central Bank Seal Type 1 at left. Signature 1. BC: Red. Printer: SBNC.			
	a. Issued note.	0.15	0.50	2.00
	s. Specimen. Punch hole cancelled.	—	—	200
	ct. Color trial. Black on green underprint.	—	—	150

		VG	VF	UNC
126	**5 Centavos**	VG	VF	UNC
	ND. Red on tan underprint. Central Bank Seal Type 1 at left. Signature 2. Like #125. BC: Red. Printer: W&S.			
	a. Issued note.	0.10	0.25	2.50
	p. Proof.	—	—	250
	s. Specimen.	—	—	250
127	**10 Centavos**	VG	VF	UNC
	ND. Brownish purple on tan underprint. Central Bank Seal Type 1 at left. Signature 1. BC: Brownish purple. Printer: SBNC.			
	a. Issued note.	0.25	0.50	1.75
	r. Remainder without serial #.	—	75.00	125
	s. Specimen.	—	—	250

128	10 Centavos	VG	VF	UNC
	ND. Brownish purple on tan underprint. Central Bank Seal Type 1 at left. Signature 2. LIke #127. BC: Brownish purple. Printer: W&S.			
	a. Issued note.	0.25	0.50	1.25
	s. Specimen.	—	—	250

129	20 Centavos	VG	VF	UNC
	ND. Green on light green underprint. Central Bank Seal Type 1 at left. Signature 1. BC: Green. Printer: SBNC.			
	a. Issued note.	0.25	1.00	3.50
	r. Remainder without serial #.	—	75.00	125
	s. Specimen.	—	—	300

130	20 Centavos	VG	VF	UNC
	ND. Green on light green underprint. BC: Green. Printer: TDLR.			
	a. Signature 2.	0.20	0.50	2.00
	b. Signature 3.	0.20	0.50	2.00
	s1. Specimen. Pin perforated.	—	—	300
	s2. Specimen. Red overprint.	—	—	500

131	50 Centavos	VG	VF	UNC
	ND. Blue on light blue underprint. Signature 2. BC: Blue. Printer: TDLR.			
	a. Issued note.	0.20	0.50	3.00
	p. Proof.	—	—	250
	s. Specimen.	—	—	150
	ct. Color trial. Brown on tan underprint.	—	—	150

131A	50 Centavos	VG	VF	UNC
	ND. Blue on light blue underprint. Printer: SBNC. Color trial.	—	—	225

131B	50 Centavos	VG	VF	UNC
	ND. Brown on tan underprint. Printer: SBNC. Color trial.	—	—	225

131C	50 Centavos	VG	VF	UNC
	ND. Printer: SBNC. Unissued design.	—	—	250

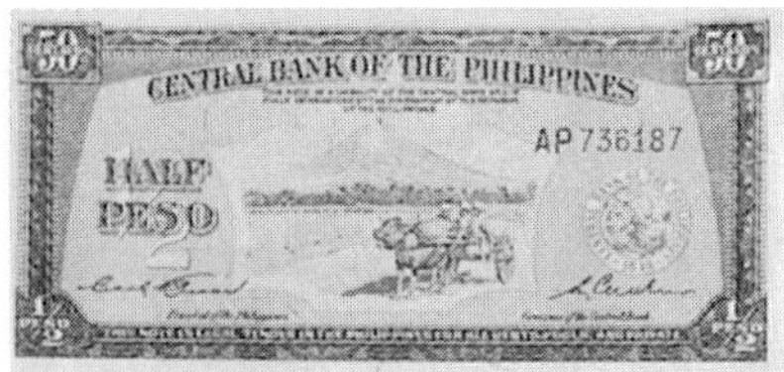

132	1/2 Peso	VG	VF	UNC
	ND. Green on yellow and blue underprint. Ox-cart with Mt. Mayon in background at center. Large Central Bank Seal Type 1 at lower right. Signature 2. BC: Green. Printer: TDLR.			
	a. Issued note.	0.25	2.50	14.00
	s. Specimen.	—	—	550

133	1 Peso	VG	VF	UNC
	ND. Black on light gold and blue underprint. Portrait of A. Mabini at left. Large Central Bank Seal Type 1 at lower right. Back: Barasoain Church at center. BC: Black. Printer: TDLR.			
	a. Signature 1. *GENUINE* in very light tan letters just beneath top heading on face.	7.50	30.00	110
	b. Signature 1. Without *GENUINE* on face.	0.50	2.00	12.50
	c. Signature 2.	0.75	2.50	15.00
	d. Signature 3.	0.25	2.00	10.00
	e. Signature 4.	0.50	1.25	8.00
	f. Signature 5.	0.25	1.00	2.50
	g. Signature 6.	0.10	0.50	2.00
	h. Signature 7.	0.10	1.00	1.50
	s1. Signature as a. Specimen.	—	—	200
	s2. Signature as b. Specimen. (De La Rue).	—	—	200
	s3. Signature as c. Specimen. (De La Rue).	—	—	200
	s4. Signature as d. Specimen. (De La Rue).	—	—	200
	s5. Signature as e. Specimen. (De La Rue).	—	—	200
	s6. Signature as f. Specimen.	—	—	45.00
	s7. Signature as f. Specimen. (De La Rue).	—	—	250
	s8. Signature as g. Specimen.	—	—	40.00
	s9. Signature as g. Specimen. (De La Rue).	—	—	250
	s10. Signature as h. Specimen.	—	—	25.00
	s11. Signature as h. Specimen. (De La Rue).	—	—	250

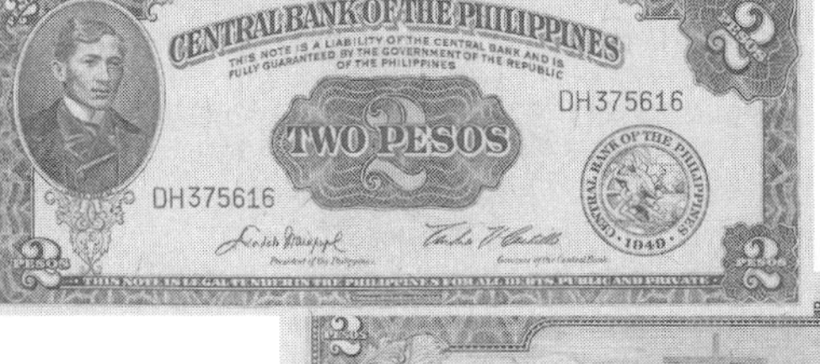

134	2 Pesos	VG	VF	UNC
	ND. Black on blue and gold underprint. Portrait of J. Rizal at left. Large Central Bank Seal Type 1 at lower right. Back: Landing of Magellan in the Philippines. BC: Blue. Printer: TDLR.			
	a. Signature 1.	1.50	7.50	15.00
	b. Signature 2.	0.75	2.00	5.00
	c. Signature 4.	1.00	2.50	10.00
	d. Signature 5.	0.15	0.50	2.00
	p. Signature as b. Proof.	—	—	250
	s1. Signature as a. Specimen. (De La Rue) Cancelled.	—	—	250
	s2. Signature as b. Specimen.	—	—	60.00
	s3. Signature as b. Specimen. (De La Rue).	—	—	250
	s4. Signature as c. Specimen. (De La Rue).	—	—	250
	s5. Signature as d. Specimen.	—	—	60.00

135	5 Pesos	VG	VF	UNC
	ND. Black on yellow and gold underprint. Portrait of M. H. del Pilar at left, Lopez Jaena at right. Large Central Bank Seal Type 1 at lower right. Back: Newspaper *La Solidaridad.* BC: Gold. Printer: TDLR.			
	a. Signature 1.	1.50	7.50	40.00
	b. Signature 2.	0.75	3.50	10.00
	c. Signature 3.	0.75	7.50	40.00
	d. Signature 4.	0.75	3.00	10.00
	e. Signature 5.	0.20	0.50	2.50
	f. Signature 8.	0.20	0.50	2.00
	p. Proof.	—	—	150
	s1. Signature as a. Specimen. (De La Rue).	—	—	250

	VG	VF	UNC
s2. Signature as b. Specimen. (De La Rue).	—	—	550
s3. Signature as d. Specimen. (De La Rue).	—	—	550
s4. Signature as e. Specimen.	—	—	30.00
s5. Signature as e. Specimen. (De La Rue).	—	—	200
s6. Signature as f. Specimen. Red overprint *SPCEIMEN* on each side.	—	—	25.00

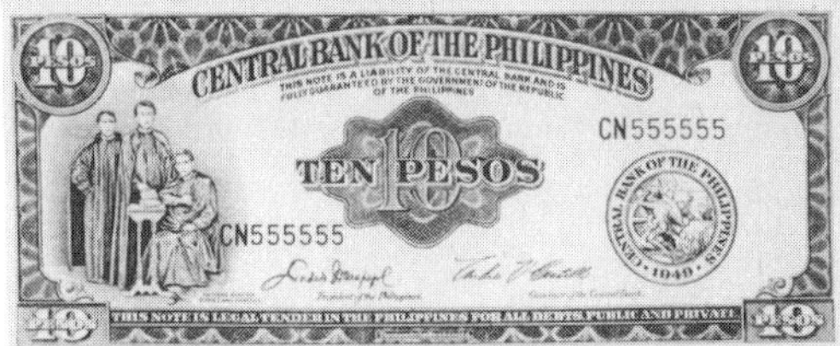

136	10 Pesos	VG	VF	UNC
	ND. Black on tan and light red underprint. Fathers Burgos, Gomez and Zamora at left. Large Central Bank Seal Type 1 at lower right. Back: Monument. BC: Brown. Printer: TDLR.			
	a. Signature 1.	300	800	5,775
	b. Signature 2.	2.50	5.00	25.00
	c. Signature 3.	2.50	5.00	25.00
	d. Signature 4.	2.50	5.00	30.00
	e. Signature 5.	0.25	1.00	3.00
	f. Signature 8.	0.50	1.00	2.00
	s1. Signature as b. Specimen.	—	—	70.00
	s2. Signature as c. Specimen.	—	—	70.00
	s3. Signature as c. Specimen. (De La Rue).	—	—	425
	s4. Signature as d. Specimen	—	—	75.00
	s5. Signature as d. Specimen. (De La Rue).	—	—	250
	s6. Signature as e. Specimen.	—	—	105
	s7. Signature as e. Specimen. (De La Rue).	—	—	200
	s8. Signature as f. Specimen.	—	—	15.00
	s9. Signature as b. Specimen. (De La Rue).	—	—	425

137	20 Pesos	VG	VF	UNC
	ND. Black on yellow underprint. Portrait of A. Bonifacio at left, E. Jacinto at right. Large Central Bank Seal Type 1 at lower right. Back: Flag and monument. BC: Brownish orange. Printer: TDLR.			
	a. Signature 1.	10.00	375	1,000
	b. Signature 2.	3.00	20.00	50.00
	c. Signature 4.	3.00	10.00	20.00
	d. Signature 5.	0.50	1.50	3.00
	e. Signature 8.	0.25	1.00	2.50
	p. Signature as d. Proof.	—	—	150
	s1. Signature as a. Specimen.	—	—	175
	s2. Signature as c. Specimen. (De La Rue).	—	—	200
	s3. Signature as d. Specimen.	—	—	35.00
	s4. Signature as d. Specimen (De La Rue).	—	—	175
	s5. Signature as e. Specimen. Red overprint: *SPECIMEN* on both sides.	—	—	20.00
	s6. Signature as b. Specimen. (De La Rue).	—	—	550

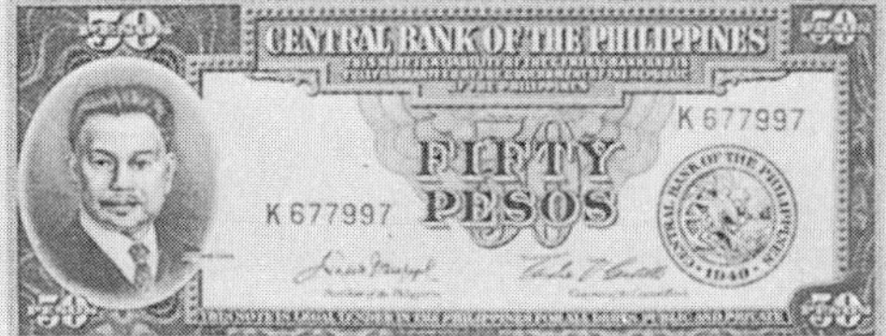

138	50 Pesos	VG	VF	UNC
	ND. Black on pink and light tan underprint. Portrait of A. Luna at left. Large Central Bank Seal Type 1 at lower right. Back: Scene of blood compact of Sikatuna and Legaspi. BC: Red. Printer: TDLR.			
	a. Signature 1.	125	500	—
	b. Signature 2.	15.00	50.00	125
	c. Signature 3.	5.00	12.50	25.00
	d. Signature 5.	0.25	1.50	5.00
	p. Signature as d. Proof.	—	—	200
	s1. Signature as a. Specimen. (De La Rue).	—	—	700
	s2. Signature as b. Specimen. (De La Rue).	—	—	1,500
	s3. Signature as d. Specimen.	—	—	50.00
	s4. Signature as d. Specimen. (De La Rue).	—	—	500

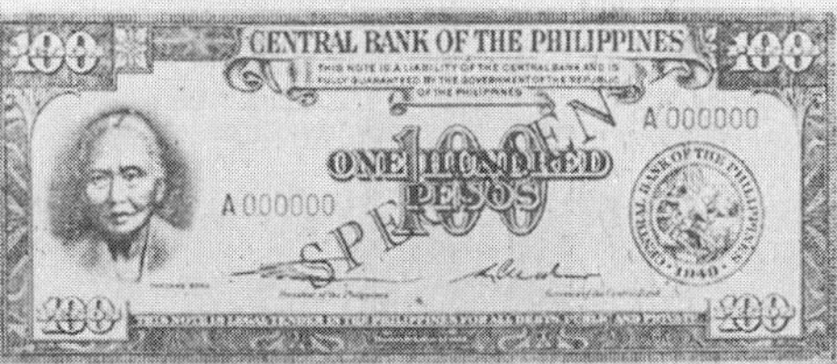

139	100 Pesos	VG	VF	UNC
	ND. Black on gold underprint. Portrait of T. Sora at left. Large Central Bank Seal Type 1 at lower right. Signature 1. Back: Regimental flags. BC: Yellow. Printer: TDLR. 160x66mm.			
	a. Issued note.	2.00	6.00	10.00
	s. Specimen.	—	—	250
	ct. Color trial. Green on tan and light blue underprint.	—	—	550

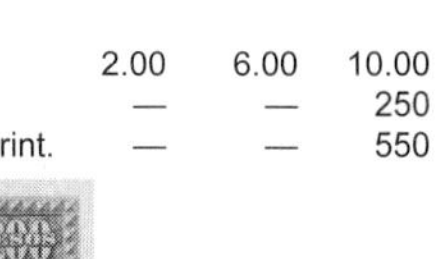

140	200 Pesos	VG	VF	UNC
	ND. Green on pink and light blue underprint. Portrait of President Manuel Quezon at left. Large Central Bank Seal Type 1 at lower right. Signature 1. Back: Legislative building. BC: Green. Printer: TDLR. 160x66mm.			
	a. Issued note.	3.00	5.00	15.00
	s. Specimen (De La Rue).	—	—	350

141	500 Pesos	VG	VF	UNC
	ND. Black on purple and light tan underprint. Portrait of President Manuel Roxas at left. Large Central Bank Seal Type 1 at lower right. Signature 1. Back: Central Bank. BC: Purple. Printer: TDLR.			
	a. Issued note.	10.00	40.00	75.00
	s. Specimen. (De La Rue).	—	—	750
	ct. Brown on light green and tan underprint.	—	—	1,300

The Republic of Poland, formerly the Polish Peoples Republic, located in central Europe, has an area of 120,725 sq. mi. (312,677 sq. km.) and a population of 38.73 million. Capital: Warsaw. The economy is essentially agricultural, but industrial activity provides the products for foreign trade. Machinery, coal, coke, iron, steel and transport equipment are exported. Poland is an ancient nation that was conceived near the middle of the 10th century. Its golden age occurred in the 16th century. During the following century, the strengthening of the gentry and internal disorders weakened the nation. In a series of agreements between 1772 and 1795, Russia, Prussia, and Austria partitioned Poland amongst themselves. Poland regained its independence in 1918 only to be overrun by Germany and the Soviet Union in World War II. It became a Soviet satellite state following the war, but its government was comparatively tolerant and progressive. Labor turmoil in 1980 led to the formation of the independent trade union "Solidarity" that over time became a political force and by 1990 had swept parliamentary elections and the presidency. A "shock therapy" program during the early 1990s enabled the country to transform its economy into one of the most robust in Central Europe, but Poland still faces the lingering challenges of high unemployment, underdeveloped and dilapidated infrastructure, and a poor rural underclass. Solidarity suffered a major defeat in the 2001 parliamentary elections when it failed to elect a single deputy to the lower house of Parliament, and the new leaders of the Solidarity Trade Union subsequently pledged to reduce the Trade Union's political role. Poland joined NATO in 1999 and the European Union in 2004. With its transformation to a democratic, market-oriented country largely completed, Poland is an increasingly active member of Euro-Atlantic organizations.

RULERS:

Stanislaw Augustus, 1764-1795
Fryderyk August I, King of Saxony, as Grand Duke, 1807-1814
Alexander I, Czar of Russia, as King, 1815-1825
Nikolaj (Mikolay) I, Czar of Russia, as King, 1825-1855

MONETARY SYSTEM:

1 Marka = 100 Fenigow to 1919
1 Zloty = 100 Groszy, 1919-

KINGDOM

Bilet Skarbowy

Treasury Note

1794 First Issue

#A1-A11 Issued by Gen. Kosciuszko.

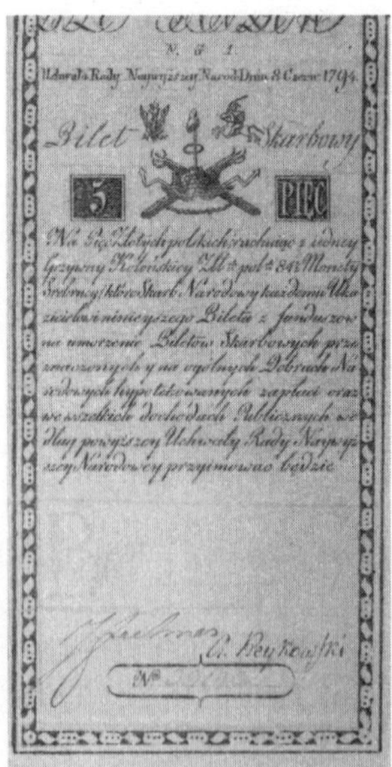

		Good	Fine	XF
A1	**5 Zlotych** 8.6.1794. Black. Arms of Poland and Lithuania at upper center. 90x170mm. PC: Pinkish.			
	a. Signature: J. Fechner, A. Reyhowski.	10.00	25.00	55.00
	b. Signature: M. Skalawski, T. Zarski.	10.00	25.00	60.00

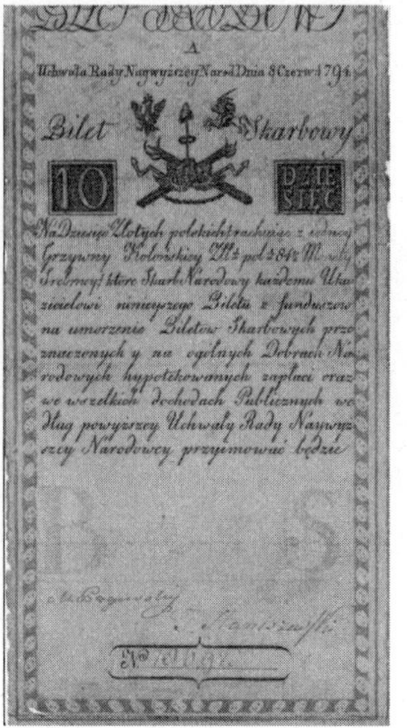

		Good	Fine	XF
A2	**10 Zlotych** 8.6.1794. Black. Arms of Poland and Lithuania at upper center. Serial # by hand. 90x170mm. PC: Very light lilac.			
	a. Signature: M. Pagowski.	15.00	30.00	60.00
	b. Signature: T. Staniszewski.	15.00	30.00	60.00

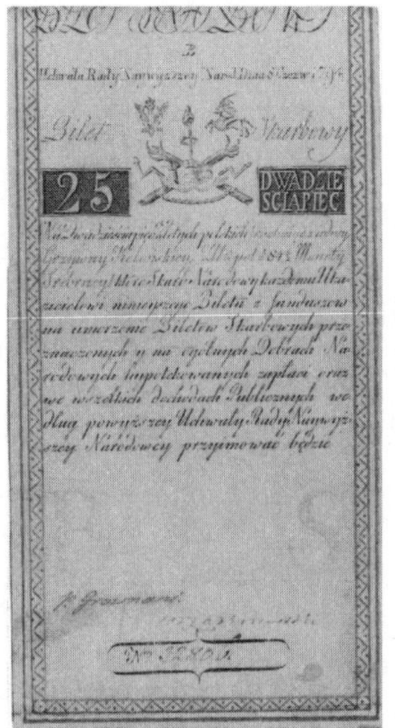

		Good	Fine	XF
A3	**25 Zlotych** 8.6.1794. Black. Arms of Poland and Lithuania at upper center. 90x170mm. PC: Pale orange.			
	a. P. Grosmani.	15.00	40.00	70.00
	b. M. Zakrewski.	15.00	40.00	70.00
A4	**50 Zlotych** 8.6.1794. Black. Arms of Poland and Lithuania at upper center. Signature: A. Michaelowski. 90x170mm. PC: Red-brown.	30.00	60.00	120
A5	**100 Zlotych** 8.6.1794. Black. Arms of Poland and Lithuania at upper center. Signature: A. Michaelowski. 90x170mm. PC: Red.	30.00	60.00	140
A6	**500 Zlotych** 8.6.1794. Black and red. Arms of Poland and Lithuania at upper center. Signature A. Michaelowski. 90x170mm. PC: Light reddish brown.	250	500	1,000
A7	**1000 Zlotych** 8.6.1794. Black. Arms of Poland and Lithuania at upper center. Signatures: J. Gaczhowski, J. Klek, A. Michaelowski. 90x170mm. Rare. PC: Yellow.	—	—	—

1794 Second Issue

		Good	Fine	XF
A8	**5 Groszy** 13.8.1794. Arms of Poland and Lithuania flank value at center.	6.00	15.00	35.00

		Good	Fine	XF
A9	**10 Groszy** 13.8.1794. Arms of Poland and Lithuania flank value at center.	6.00	15.00	35.00
A10	**1 Zloty** 13.8.1794. Arms of Poland and Lithuania flank value at center.	75.00	150	300

		Good	Fine	XF
A11	**4 Zlote** 4.9.1794. Arms at upper center. 30x70mm.	5.00	10.00	25.00

#A8-A11 uniface with name: *F. MALINOWSKI* on back (as illustrated) are modern reproductions.

DUCHY OF WARSAW

Kassowy-Billet Xiestwa Warszawskiego

1810 State Treasury Note

#A12-A14 There are 9 different signatures. Also exist as "Formulare" w/red stamps but w/o the printed seal. Market value: $500.00.

		Good	Fine	XF
A12	**1 Talar** 1.12.1810. Black. Arms at upper center.	40.00	100	275
A13	**2 Talary** 1.12.1810. Black. Arms at upper center.	50.00	125	325
A14	**5 Talarow** 1.12.1810. Black. Arms at upper center.	75.00	175	450

Billet Kassowy Krolestwa Polskiego

1824 Issue

		Good	Fine	XF
A15	**5 Zlotych** 1824. Black. PC: Blue.	75.00	175	350

		Good	Fine	XF
A16	**10 Zlotych** 1824. Black. PC: Pink.	150	300	550
A17	**50 Zlotych** 1824. Black. PC: Yellow.	—	—	—
A18	**100 Zlotych** 1824.	—	—	—

INSURRECTION OF 1831

Assygnacya Skarbowa

1831 Issue

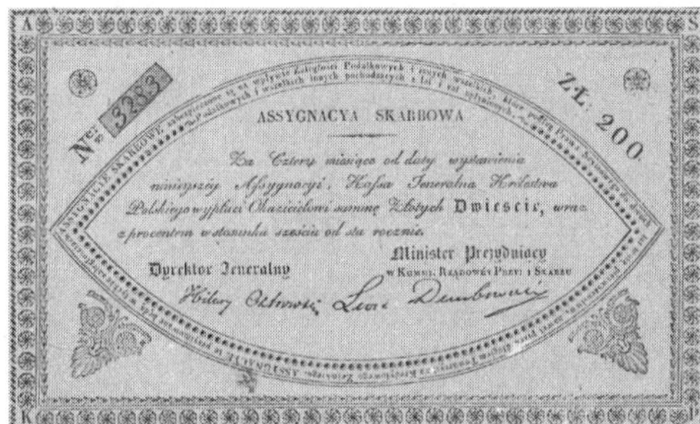

		Good	Fine	XF
A18A	**200 Zlotych** 1831.	—	—	500

		Good	Fine	XF
A18B	**500 Zlotych** 1831. Black and blue. Ornate border with tridents. Back: Black text.	—	—	350

RUSSIAN ADMINISTRATION

Bank Polski

1830 Issue

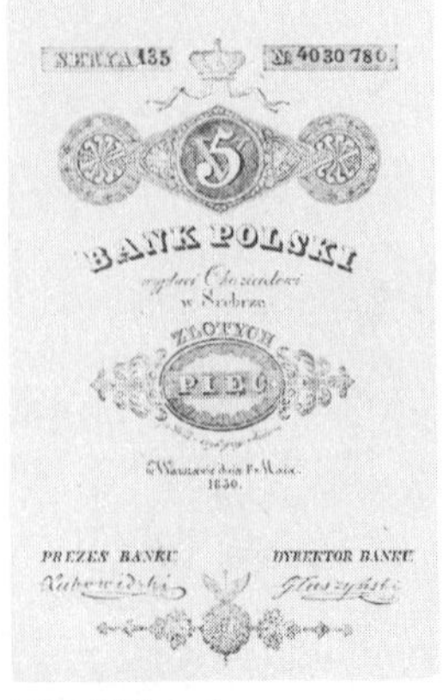

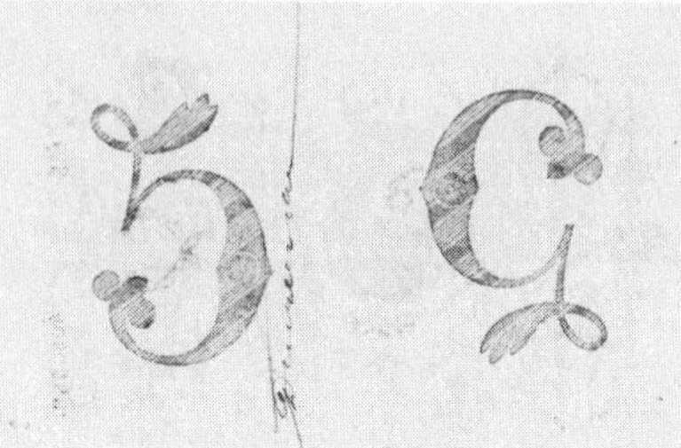

		Good	Fine	XF
A19	**5 Zlotych** 1.5.1830.	70.00	150	350
A20	**50 Zlotych** 1.5.1830.	200	400	850

		Good	Fine	XF
A21	**100 Zlotych** 1.5.1830.	150	325	550

1831 Issue

		Good	Fine	XF
A22	**1 Zloty** 1831. Black and green.	60.00	125	275

1841 Issue

		Good	Fine	XF
A23	**3 Rubel** 1841.	80.00	175	375

1842 Issue

		Good	Fine	XF
A24	**3 Rubel** 1842.	80.00	175	375

1843 Issue

		Good	Fine	XF
A25	**3 Rubel** 1843.	80.00	175	375
A25A	**10 Rubel** 1843.	80.00	175	375

1844 Issue

		Good	Fine	XF
A26	**10 Rubel** 1844.	200	400	850
A27	**25 Rubel** 1844.	275	550	1,200

1846 Issue

		Good	Fine	XF
A28	**3 Rubel** 1846.	80.00	175	375

1847 Issue

		Good	Fine	XF
A29	**1 Rubel** 1847.	70.00	150	350

		Good	Fine	XF
A30	**10 Rubel** 1847. Crowned imperial eagle at top center.	200	400	850

1848 Issue

		Good	Fine	XF
A31	**25 Rubel** 1848.	275	550	1,200

1849 Issue

		Good	Fine	XF
A32	**1 Rubel** 1849.	70.00	150	350

1850 Issue

		Good	Fine	XF
A33	**3 Rubel** 1850.	80.00	175	375

1851 Issue

		Good	Fine	XF
A34	**1 Rubel** 1851.	70.00	150	350
A35	**3 Rubel** 1851.	80.00	175	375

1852 Issue

		Good	Fine	XF
A36	**1 Rubel** 1852.	70.00	150	350
A37	**3 Rubel** 1852.	80.00	175	375

1853 Issue

		Good	Fine	XF
A38	**1 Rubel** 1853.	70.00	150	350
A39	**3 Rubel** 1853.	80.00	175	375

1854 Issue

		Good	Fine	XF
A40	**1 Rubel** 1854.	70.00	150	350
A41	**3 Rubel** 1854.	80.00	175	375

1855 Issue

		Good	Fine	XF
A42	**1 Rubel** 1855.	70.00	150	350

1856 Issue

		Good	Fine	XF
A43	**1 Rubel** 1856.	70.00	150	350

1857 Issue

		Good	Fine	XF
A44	**1 Rubel** 1857.	100	200	450

1858 Issue

		Good	Fine	XF
A45	**1 Rubel** 1858.	70.00	150	350
A46	**3 Rubel** 1858.	80.00	175	375

1864 Issue

		Good	Fine	XF
A47	**1 Rubel** 1864. Crowned imperial eagle at center.	70.00	150	350

1865 Issue

		Good	Fine	XF
A48	**3 Rubel** 1865.	80.00	175	375
A49	**25 Rubel** 1865.	275	550	1,200

1866 First Issue

		Good	Fine	XF
A50	**1 Rubel** 1866.	70.00	150	350
A51	**3 Rubel** 1866.	80.00	175	375
A52	**10 Rubel** 1866.	200	400	850

		Good	Fine	XF
A53	**25 Rubel** 1866. Crowned imperial eagle at upper center.	275	550	1,200

1866 ND Issue

		Good	Fine	XF
A54	**1 Rubel** ND (1866).	—	—	—

GERMAN OCCUPATION, WW I

Polska Krajowa Kasa Pozyczkowa

Polish State Loan Bank

1916-1917 First Issue

		VG	VF	UNC
1	**1/2 Marki** 1917. Red and black. Crowned eagle at left. With text: *Zarad jeneral-gubernatorstwa.* BC: Blue and olive. Printer: S. Manitius Press, Lodz. 87x56mm.	5.00	10.00	30.00

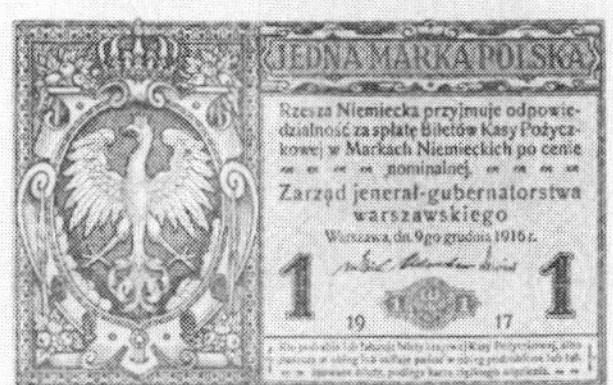

		VG	VF	UNC
2	**1 Marka** 1917. Red and black. Crowned eagle at left. With text: *Zarad jeneral-gubernatorstwa.* BC: Blue and red. Printer: S. Manitius Press, Lodz. 120x65mm.	15.00	40.00	90.00

		VG	VF	UNC
3	**2 Marki** 1917. Red and black. Crowned eagle at left. With text: *Zarad jeneral-gubernatorstwa.* BC: Orange and green. Printer: S. Manitius Press, Lodz. 124x69mm.	30.00	80.00	170
3A	**5 Marek** 1917. Red and black. With text: *Zarad jeneral-gubernatorstwa.* BC: Gray-blue and yellow. Printer: S. Manitius Press, Lodz. 130x73mm. (Not issued). Proof.	—	—	3,500
3B	**10 Marek** 1917. Red and black. With text: *Zarad jeneral-gubernatorstwa.* BC: Violet-brown and green. Printer: S. Manitius Press, Lodz. 150x75mm. (Not issued). Proof.			
	a. With watermark.	—	—	3,500
	b. Without watermark.	—	—	3,500

		Good	Fine	XF
4	**20 Marek** 1917. Red and black. Crowned eagle at center. With text: *Zarad jeneral-gubernatorstwa.* BC: Purple and light brown. Printer: S. Manitius Press, Lodz. 160x80mm.			
	a. With watermark.	20.00	70.00	300
	b. Without watermark.	20.00	70.00	300
5	**50 Marek** 1917. Red and black. Crowned eagle at center. With text: *Zarad jeneral-gubernatorstwa.* BC: Green and pink. Printer: S. Manitius Press, Lodz. 167x85mm.	30.00	85.00	400
6	**100 Marek** 9.12.1916. Red and black. Crowned eagle at left. With text: *Zarad jeneral-gubernatorstwa.* BC: Dark blue and orange.			
	a. 6-digit serial #.	30.00	100	500
	b. 7-digit serial #.	40.00	125	600

1916-1917 Second Issue

#	Description	VG	VF	UNC
7	**1/2 Marki** 1917. Red and black. Crowned eagle at left. With text: *Zarzad General-Gubernatorstwa*. Like #1. BC: Blue and olive.	10.00	20.00	40.00
8	**1 Marka** 1917. Red and black. Crowned eagle at left. With text: *Zarzad General-Gubernatorstwa*. Like #2. BC: Blue and red.	15.00	30.00	70.00

#	Description	Good	Fine	XF
9	**2 Marki** 1917. Red and black. Crowned eagle at left. With text: *Zarzad General-Gubernatorstwa*. Like #3. BC: Orange and green.	20.00	45.00	80.00

#	Description	Good	Fine	XF
10	**5 Marek** 1917. Red and black on green underprint. Crowned eagle at center. With text: *Zarzad General-Gubernatorstwa*. Text at left: *...biletow Polskiej Krajowej...* BC: Gray-blue on yellow underprint.	10.00	35.00	135
11	**5 Marek** 1917. Red and black on green underprint. Crowned eagle at center. With text: *Zarzad General-Gubernatorstwa*. Like #10 but text at left: *...Biletow Kasy Pozyczkowej...* BC: Gray-blue on yellow underprint.	25.00	100	350
12	**10 Marek** 1917. Red and black. Crowned eagle at center. With text: *Zarzad General-Gubernatorstwa*. Text at left: *...biletow Polskiej Krajowej...* BC: Violet-brown on green underprint.	20.00	55.00	160
13	**10 Marek** 1917. Red and black. Crowned eagle at center. With text: *Zarzad General-Gubernatorstwa*. Like #12 but text at left: *...Biletow Kasy Pozyczkowej...* BC: Violet-brown on green underprint.	150	350	850

#	Description	Good	Fine	XF
14	**20 Marek** 1917. Red and black. Crowned eagle at center. With text: *Zarzad General-Gubernatorstwa*. Like #4. BC: Purple and light brown.	25.00	85.00	350
15	**100 Marek** 9.12.1916. Blue and red. Crowned eagle at left. With text: *Zarzad General-Gubernatorstwa*. Like #6. Back: Facing busts of Minerva at left and right.	30.00	80.00	350

#	Description	Good	Fine	XF
16	**1000 Marek** 1917. Brown and red. Crowned eagle at left. With text: *Zarzad General-Gubernatorstwa*. Like #15. Back: Busts of Roman soldier at left, man at right.	125	300	4,000

REPUBLIC

Polska Krajowa Kasa Pozyczkowa

Polish State Loan Bank

1919 First Issue

#	Description	VG	VF	UNC
17	**100 Marek** 15.2.1919. Green and gray-violet. Portrait T. Kosciuszko at left.			
	a. Watermark: Honeycombs. Brownish paper with engraver's name at lower left and right.	2.00	7.00	20.00
	b. Watermark: Honeycombs. Brownish paper without engraver's name.	3.00	7.00	20.00
	c. Indistinct watermark: (Polish eagle). White paper.	2.00	10.00	35.00

18 **500 Marek**

	VG	VF	UNC
15.1.1919. Green and red. Crowned eagle at left. BC: Dark and light green.	25.00	60.00	270

1919 Second Issue

19 **1 Marka**

	VG	VF	UNC
17.5.1919. Gray-violet and violet. 3 serial # varieties. Back: Eagle at center.	8.00	10.00	20.00

20 **5 Marek**

	VG	VF	UNC
17.5.1919. Dark green. Small eagle at upper center. Back: Pres. B. Glowacki at right. PC: Tan.			
a. Engraver's name at lower left and right on back.	8.00	15.00	25.00
b. Without engravers' names. 2 serial # varieties.	8.00	15.00	25.00

21 **20 Marek**

	VG	VF	UNC
17.5.1919. Brown. Crowned eagle at center. 3 serial # varieties. Back: T. Kosciuszko at center. BC: Brown and green. PC: Tan.	10.00	20.00	35.00

22 **1000 Marek**

	VG	VF	UNC
17.5.1919. Green and brown. Portrait T. Kosciuszko at left. Back: Crowned eagle at left center. BC: Brown.			
a. Watermark: Honeycombs. Brownish paper with engraver's name at lower left and right on back. 2 serial # varieties.	5.00	15.00	30.00
b. Watermark: Honeycombs. Brownish paper without engraver's name.	7.00	20.00	35.00
c. Indistinct watermark: (crowned eagle). White paper with engraver's name at lower left and right on back.	7.00	15.00	30.00
d. Indistinct watermark: (crowned eagle). White paper without engravers' names. 2 serial # varieties.	5.00	15.00	30.00

1919 Third Issue

#23-31 crowned eagle on back.

23 **1 Marka**

	VG	VF	UNC
23.8.1919. Red on brown underprint. Arms at left, woman at right. 2 serial # varieties. Back: Crowned eagle.	3.00	7.00	10.00

24 **5 Marek**

	VG	VF	UNC
23.8.1919. Green on brown underprint. Arms at left, portrait T. Kosciuszko at right. 2 serial # varieties. Back: Crowned eagle.	4.00	7.00	15.00

25 **10 Marek**

	VG	VF	UNC
23.8.1919. Blue-green on brown underprint. Arms at left, portrait T. Kosciuszko at right. Similar to #24. 2 serial # varieties. Back: Crowned eagle.	3.00	7.00	15.00

26 **20 Marek**

	VG	VF	UNC
23.8.1919. Red on brown underprint. Portrait woman at right. 2 serial # varieties. Back: Crowned eagle.	3.00	7.00	15.00

27 **100 Marek**

23.8.1919. Blue on brown underprint. Portrait T. Kosciuszko at right. 2 serial # varieties. Back: Crowned eagle.

VG	VF	UNC
5.00	10.00	20.00

28 **500 Marek**

23.8.1919. Green on brown underprint. Portrait woman at right. 3 serial # varieties. Back: Crowned eagle.

VG	VF	UNC
7.00	12.00	30.00

29 **1000 Marek**

23.8.1919. Purple on brown underprint. Portrait T. Kosciuszko at right. 6 serial # varieties. Back: Crowned eagle.

VG	VF	UNC
7.00	12.00	25.00

1920 Issue

30 **1/2 Marki**

7.2.1920. Green on brown underprint. Portrait T. Kosciuszko at right. Back: Crowned eagle.

VG	VF	UNC
3.00	5.00	10.00

31 **5000 Marek**

7.2.1920. Blue on brown underprint. Portrait woman at left, Kosciuszko at right. 4 serial # varieties. Back: Crowned eagle.

VG	VF	UNC
5.00	20.00	40.00

1922-1923 Inflation Issues

32 **10,000 Marek**

11.3.1922. Greenish black on light tan underprint. Woman's head at left and right. Back: Eagle at center.

Good	Fine	XF
10.00	25.00	50.00

33 **50,000 Marek**

10.10.1922. Brown on light tan and blue underprint. Back: Eagle at left.

Good	Fine	XF
10.00	20.00	40.00

34 **100,000 Marek**

30.8.1923. Brown. Back: Eagle at center. BC: Blue-gray.

	Good	Fine	XF
a. Issued note. 30.8.1923.	10.00	30.00	60.00
x1. Error date. 25.4.1922.	—	—	—
x2. Error date. 25.4.1523.	—	—	—

Note: For #34 there exists two error dates: 25.4.1922 and 25.4.1523.

35 **250,000 Marek**

25.4.1923. Gray-brown on light bluish underprint. 2 serial # varieties. Back: Eagle at center.

Good	Fine	XF
10.00	40.00	60.00

36 **500,000 Marek**

30.8.1923. Gray on light green underprint. 5 serial # varieties. Back: Eagle at center.

Good	Fine	XF
10.00	30.00	50.00

37 **1,000,000 Marek**

30.8.1923. Olive-brown on light blue underprint. Town view at left. 2 serial # varieties. Back: Eagle at center. BC: Green.

Good	Fine	XF
20.00	45.00	100

38 **5,000,000 Marek**

20.11.1923. Brown on pink and blue underprint. Eagle at upper center. Back: Eagle at left. BC: Blue-gray.

Good	Fine	XF
30.00	90.00	180

39 **10,000,000 Marek**

20.11.1923. Green and blue on light tan and green underprint. Town view with two towers at left, crowned eagle at right. 2 serial # varieties. Back: Eagle at upper left. BC: Brown.

Good	Fine	XF
40.00	100	250

40 **50,000,000 Marek**

20.11.1923. Black on blue underprint. Uniface.

Good	Fine	XF
80.00	300	600

41 **100,000,000 Marek**

20.11.1923. Black on pink underprint. Uniface.

Good	Fine	XF
100	500	600

Ministerstwo Skarbu

Ministry of Finance

Zloty system

1924 Provisional Bilet Zdawkowy Issue

#	Description	VG	VF	UNC
42	**1 Grosz** 28.4.1924. Red overprint with new denomination and coin on bisected note #36.			
	a. Left half.	12.00	30.00	50.00
	b. Right half.	12.00	30.00	50.00

#	Description	VG	VF	UNC
43	**5 Groszy** 28.4.1924. Red overprint with new denomination and coin on bisected note #39.			
	a. Left half.	25.00	60.00	120
	b. Right half.	25.00	60.00	120

1924-1925 Bilet Zdawkowy Issue

#	Description	VG	VF	UNC
44	**10 Groszy** 28.4.1924. Blue. Building with column at center, coin at left and right.	10.00	20.00	40.00

#	Description	VG	VF	UNC
45	**20 Groszy** 28.4.1924. Brown. Copernicus monument at center, coin at left and right.	10.00	30.00	50.00

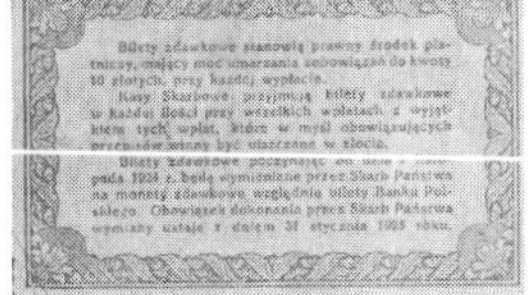

#	Description	VG	VF	UNC
46	**50 Groszy** 28.4.1924. Red. Equestrian statue of J. Poniatowski at center, coin at lower left and right.	12.00	40.00	70.00

#	Description	VG	VF	UNC
47	**2 Zlote** 1.5.1925. Gray-violet on gray-green. Obverse and reverse of 2 Zlote coin.			
	a. Back right side up.	35.00	100	200
	b. Misprint: back inverted.	—	—	—
48	**5 Zlotych** 1.5.1925. Green and brown. Obverse of coin at left.	50.00	150	350

1926 Bilet Panstwowy Issue

#	Description	VG	VF	UNC
49	**5 Zlotych** 25.10.1926. Dark olive and brown. Woman at center. Back: Worker.	50.00	100	200

1938 Bilet Panstwowy Issue

#	Description	VG	VF	UNC
50	**1 Zloty** 1.10.1938. Gray on yellow-brown underprint. Portrait King Boleslaw I Chrobry at right.	25.00	40.00	100

This note was in circulation only from August 26, 1939 - September 1, 1939.

Bank Polski

1919 (1924) Dated Issue

#	Description	Good	Fine	XF
51	**1 Zloty** 28.2.1919 (1924). Purple on lilac underprint. Portrait T. Kosciuszko at left. 2 signatures without titles. Back: Eagle at right.	20.00	45.00	125
52	**2 Zlote** 28.2.1919 (1924). Light and dark blue on light brown underprint. Portrait T. Kosciuszko at left. 2 signatures without titles.	30.00	60.00	130

#	Description	Good	Fine	XF
53	**5 Zlotych** 28.2.1919 (1924). Brown. Portrait Prince J. Poniatowski at right. 2 signatures without titles. Back: Eagle at left.	50.00	100	200

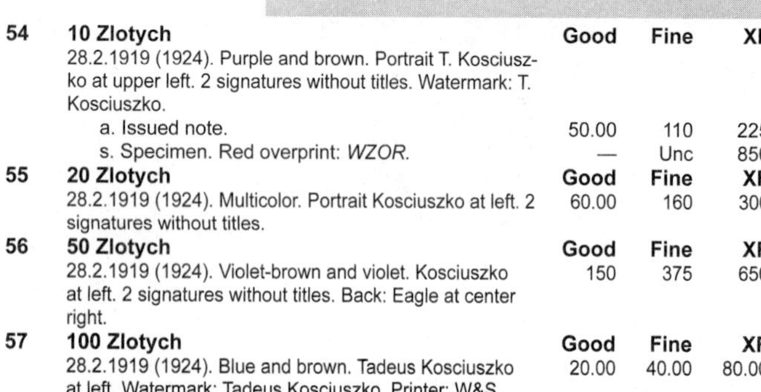

		Good	Fine	XF
54	**10 Zlotych** 28.2.1919 (1924). Purple and brown. Portrait T. Kosciuszko at upper left. 2 signatures without titles. Watermark: T. Kosciuszko.			
	a. Issued note.	50.00	110	225
	s. Specimen. Red overprint: *WZOR*.	—	Unc	850

		Good	Fine	XF
55	**20 Zlotych** 28.2.1919 (1924). Multicolor. Portrait Kosciuszko at left. 2 signatures without titles.	60.00	160	300

		Good	Fine	XF
56	**50 Zlotych** 28.2.1919 (1924). Violet-brown and violet. Kosciuszko at left. 2 signatures without titles. Back: Eagle at center right.	150	375	650

		Good	Fine	XF
57	**100 Zlotych** 28.2.1919 (1924). Blue and brown. Tadeus Kosciuszko at left. Watermark: Tadeus Kosciuszko. Printer: W&S. 172x103mm.	20.00	40.00	80.00

		Good	Fine	XF
58	**500 Zlotych** 28.2.1919 (1924). Purple and green. Portrait Tadeus Kosciuszko at left. Watermark: Tadeus Kosciuszko. Printer: W&S. 180x108mm.	8.00	15.00	30.00

		Good	Fine	XF
59	**1000 Zlotych** 28.2.1919 (1924). Brown. Portrait Tadeus Kosciuszko at left. Printer: W&S.			
	a. Issued note.	100	225	500
	s. Specimen.	—	—	225

The "issued" examples of this note were retrieved from a crate which was lost in shipment and fell into the sea.

1924 Issue

		Good	Fine	XF
61	**5 Zlotych** 15.7.1924. Brown. Portrait Prince J. Poniatowski at right. 3 signatures with titles. Like #53. Back: Eagle at left.			
	a. Issued note.	20.00	65.00	175
	s. Specimen. Red overprint: *WZOR*.	—	Unc	500

		Good	Fine	XF
62	**10 Zlotych** 15.7.1924. Purple. Portrait T. Kosciuszko at upper left. Like #54. 3 signatures with titles. Watermark: T. Kosciuszko.			
	a. White paper.	35.00	100	225
	b. Gray paper.	35.00	100	225

#	Description	Good	Fine	XF
63	**20 Zlotych** 15.7.1924. Multicolor. Portrait T. Kosciuszko at left. 3 signatures with titles. Like #55.			
	a. White paper.	55.00	175	400
	b. Gray paper.	55.00	175	400
64	**50 Zlotych** 28.8.1925. Green, brown and blue. Farmer's wife at left, Mercury at right. Serial # with one or two letter. Back: Two buildings. Watermark: Stefan Batory and value 189x99mm.			
	a. Issued note.	20.00	65.00	175
	s. Specimen. Red overprint: *BEZ WARTISCI* and *WZOR* and perforated.	—	Unc	500

1926 Issue

#	Description	Good	Fine	XF
65	**10 Zlotych** 20.7.1926. Brown, olive and blue. Allegorical woman at left and right. Back: Three standing figures. 160x80mm.			
	a. Watermark: 10 / Boleslaw I Chrobry / Zl.	30.00	100	250
	b. Watermark: 992 / Boleslaw I Chrobry / 1025	25.00	50.00	90.00
66	**20 Zlotych** 1.3.1926. Blue and olive. Farmer's wife at left, Mercury at right. Like #64. Back: Two buildings.	50.00	150	300

1928 Issue

#	Description	VG	VF	UNC
67	**10 Zlotych** 2.1.1928. Dark blue. Portrait youth at upper right. Printer: Orell Füssli, Zurich (without imprint).	—	500	800
68	**20 Zlotych** 2.1.1928. Dark purple. Woman at right. Printer: Orell Füssli, Zurich (without imprint). Specimen only.	—	450	650

1929 Issue

#	Description	VG	VF	UNC
69	**10 Zlotych** 20.7.1929. Brown-olive and blue. Allegorical woman at left and right. Like #65. Back: Three standing figures. Watermark: King, 10Zt. 160x80mm.	3.00	8.00	20.00
70	**20 Zlotych** 1.9.1929. Blue and olive. Farmer's wife at left, Mercury at right. Like #66. Back: Two buildings.	50.00	150	350

#	Description	VG	VF	UNC
71	**50 Zlotych** 1.9.1929. Green, brown and blue. Farmer's wife at left, Mercury at right. Like #64. Watermark: 50 / Stefan Batory / Zl.	5.00	10.00	15.00

1930-1932 Issue

#	Description	VG	VF	UNC
72	**5 Zlotych** 2.1.1930. Blue on gray underprint. King Jan Albrecht Jagellonzyk at right. Back: Crowned eagle at upper left center. Watermark: King Zygmunt Stary. 144x77mm.	5.00	10.00	15.00

#	Description	VG	VF	UNC
73	**20 Zlotych** 20.6.1931. Blue on brown and tan underprint. Portrait Emilia Plater at upper right. Serial # 2.5 or 3mm high. Back: Farm woman and two children at left center. BC: Brown and blue. Watermark: King Kazimierz 3 Wielki / 20 Zl. 163x86mm.	5.00	10.00	15.00

74	100 Zlotych	VG	VF	UNC
	2.6.1932. Brown on gold underprint. Portrait Prince J. Poniatowski at right. Back: Allegorical figures at left and right, large tree at left center. BC: Brown, orange and multicolor. 175x98mm.			
	a. Watermark: Queen Jadwigi / 100 Zt.	5.00	10.00	15.00
	b. Watermark: Queen Jadwigi / 100Zt, +x+.	5.00	10.00	15.00

1934 Issue

75	100 Zlotych	VG	VF	UNC
	9.11.1934. Brown. Portrait Prince J. Poniatowski at right. Like #74. Back: Allegorical figures at left and right, large tree at left center. BC: Brown, orange and multicolor. 175x98mm.			
	a. Watermark: Queen Jadwigi / 100 Zt.	5.00	10.00	15.00
	b. Watermark: Queen Jadwigi / 100 Zt. +X+.	5.00	10.00	15.00

1936 Issue

76	2 Zlote	VG	VF	UNC
	26.2.1936. Grayish brown on yellow and light blue underprint. Portrait Duchess Doubravka (wife of Duke Mieszko) in national costume at right. Back: Eagle at center. 103x62mm.			
	a. Issued note.	5.00	10.00	15.00
	r. Remainder without serial #.	—	—	15.00

This note was in circulation only from August 26 to September 1, 1939.

77	20 Zlotych	VG	VF	UNC
	11.11.1936. Blue on light peach underprint. Statue of Emilia Platerowa with two children at left, E. Plater at upper right. Back: Standing figures at left and right, church at center (Wawel in Krakow). Watermark: Girl's head. 163x86mm.	2.00	4.00	8.00

78	50 Zlotych	VG	VF	UNC
	11.11.1936. Green. Standing woman at left center, man at upper right and eagle at lower right. Back: Five allegorical figures. Watermark: Man.			
	a. Issued note.	200	500	1,000
	b. Back only.	20.00	50.00	125

GOVERNMENT-IN-EXILE, WW II

Bank Polski

1939 First Issue

79	1 Zloty	VG	VF	UNC
	15.8.1939. Purple. Printer: BWC. (Not issued).			
	r. Remainder.	—	—	275
	s. Specimen.	—	—	150

80	2 Zlote	VG	VF	UNC
	15.8.1939. Green. Printer: BWC. (Not issued).			
	r. Remainder.	—	—	275
	s. Specimen.	—	—	150

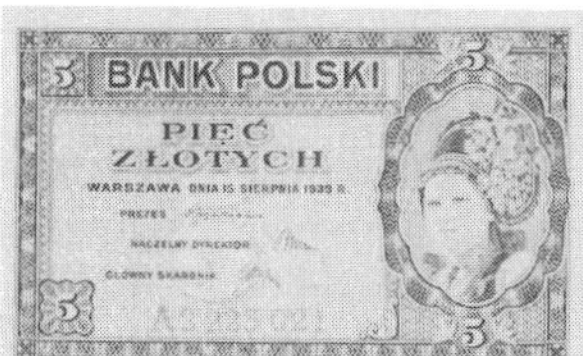

81	5 Zlotych	VG	VF	UNC
	15.8.1939. Blue. Portrait girl wearing national costume at right. Printer: BWC. (Not issued).			
	r. Remainder.	—	—	300
	s. Specimen.	—	—	150

82	**10 Zlotych**	VG	VF	UNC
	15.8.1939. Red-orange. Young woman wearing head scarf at right. Printer: TDLR. (Not issued).			
	r. Remainder.	—	—	275
	s. Specimen.	—	—	150

83	**20 Zlotych**	VG	VF	UNC
	15.8.1939. Blue. Old woman wearing head scarf at right. Printer: TDLR. (Not issued).			
	r. Remainder.	—	—	275
	s. Specimen. Red overprint: *WZOR*.	—	—	150

84	**50 Zlotych**	VG	VF	UNC
	15.8.1939. Green. Man wearing national costume at right. Printer: TDLR. (Not issued).			
	r. Remainder.	—	—	275
	s. Specimen.	—	—	150

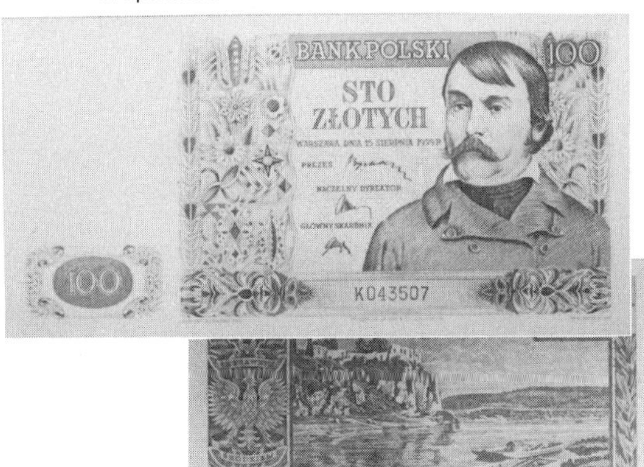

85	**100 Zlotych**	VG	VF	UNC
	15.8.1939. Brown. Man with mustache at right. Printer: TDLR. (Not issued).			
	r. Remainder.	—	—	275
	s. Specimen.	—	—	150

86	**500 Zlotych**	VG	VF	UNC
	15.8.1939. Purple. Sailor with pipe at right. Printer: TDLR. (Not issued).			
	r. Remainder.	—	—	275
	s. Specimen.	—	—	150

1939 Second Issue

87	**20 Zlotych**	VG	VF	UNC
	20.8.1939. Blue. Young woman in national costume at right. Back: Church. Printer: ABNC. (Not issued).			
	r. Remainder.	—	—	275
	s. Specimen.	—	—	150

88	**50 Zlotych**	VG	VF	UNC
	20.8.1939. Green. Young farmer's wife at right. Back: River and mountains. Printer: ABNC. (Not issued).			
	r. Remainder.	—	—	275
	s. Specimen with overprint: *WZOR*, punch hole cancelled.	—	—	150

GERMAN OCCUPATION, WW II

Generalgouvernement

1939 Provisional Issue

#89 and 90 overprint: *Generalgouvernement für die besetzten polnischen Gebiete.*

		VG	VF	UNC
89	**100 Zlotych** ND (1939 - old date 2.6.1932). Brown on gold underprint. Portrait Prince J. Poniatowski at right. Back: Allegorical figures at left and right, large tree at left center. BC: Brown, orange and multicolor.	20.00	40.00	90.00

Note: #89 is frequently found with a forged overprint.

		VG	VF	UNC
90	**100 Zlotych** ND (1939 - old date 9.9.1934). Brown. Portrait Prince J. Poniatowski at right. Back: Allegorical figures at left and right, large tree at left center. BC: Brown, orange and multicolor.	20.00	40.00	90.00

Note: #90 is frequently found with a forged overprint.

Bank Emisyjny w Polsce

Emission Bank of Poland

1940 Issue

		VG	VF	UNC
91	**1 Zloty** 1.3.1940. Gray-blue on light tan underprint.	3.00	8.00	15.00
92	**2 Zlote** 1.3.1940. Brown on blue and brown underprint. Portrait woman wearing head scarf at upper right.	3.00	8.00	15.00

		VG	VF	UNC
93	**5 Zlotych** 1.3.1940. Green-blue on tan and blue underprint. King Jan Albrecht Jagiellonczyk at left, girl at right. Similar to #72.	15.00	40.00	100

		VG	VF	UNC
94	**10 Zlotych** 1.3.1940. Brown on tan and blue underprint. Girl in headdress on watermark area at left, allegorical woman at left and right. Back: Sculpture.	8.00	12.00	20.00

		VG	VF	UNC
95	**20 Zlotych** 1.3.1940. Gray-blue on blue and red underprint. Man in cap on watermark area at left, female statue with two children at left center. E. Plater at right. Similar to #77. Back: Standing figures at left and right.	8.00	12.00	20.00
96	**50 Zlotych** 1.3.1940. Blue-green on brown underprint. Man in cap at left, woman's statue at left center, young man at right. Back: Ornate building.	20.00	40.00	70.00

		VG	VF	UNC
97	**100 Zlotych** 1.3.1940. Brown on light green and orange underprint. Patrician of old Warsaw at left. Back: Building at left.	10.00	20.00	30.00

		VG	VF	UNC
98	**500 Zlotych** 1.3.1940. Gray-blue on olive underprint. Portrait Gorale at upper right. Back: River in mountains. Watermark: Portrait Gorale.	20.00	40.00	70.00

1941 Issue

		VG	VF	UNC
99	**1 Zloty** 1.8.1941. Gray-blue. Like #91.	3.00	5.00	10.00

		VG	VF	UNC
100	**2 Zlote** 1.8.1941. Brown. Portrait woman wearing head scarf at upper right. Like #92.	3.00	5.00	10.00

		VG	VF	UNC
101	**5 Zlotych** 1.8.1941. Green-blue. Man in cap at left, girl at right. Like #93.	3.00	5.00	10.00

		VG	VF	UNC
102	**50 Zlotych** 1.8.1941. Dark green and blue. Man in cap at left, woman's statue at left center, young man at right. Similar to #96. Back: Ornate building. Watermark: Man in cap.	5.00	10.00	15.00

		VG	VF	UNC
103	**100 Zlotych** 1.8.1941. Brown and blue on light brown and gold underprint. Allegorical winged figure at upper center. Back: Six church spires at center. Watermark: Man with beard.	4.00	7.00	15.00

		VG	VF	UNC
103A	**1000 Zlotych** 1.8.1941. Man at right. Back: Building and Russian text. (Not issued).	—	—	125

Note: Various notes of #91-103 also exist w/handstamps of the Warsaw Resistance Fighters of 1944, *A. K. Regula; Pierwszy zold powstancy, Sierpien 1944; Okreg Warszawski-Dowodztwo zgrup. IV* or *Braterstwo Broni Anglii Ameryki Polski Niech Zyje* (Long live the Anglo-American-Polish brotherhood in arms).

POST WW II COMMITTEE OF NATIONAL LIBERATION

Narodowy Bank Polski

Polish National Bank

1944 Issue

#104 (w/o misspelled word), 105, 106, 108, 110, 112, 114, 118 first printing: w/*OBOWIAZKOWYM* (spelling error). Printer: Goznak (Russia). #107, 109, 111, 113, 115, 117, 119 second printing: w/*OBOWIAZKOWE* (corrected spelling). Printer: Polish National Bank. #104, 105, 107, 109, 111, 113, 115, 117 and 119 reprinted w/inscription: *EMISJA PAMIATKOWA - ODBITA W 1974 r.Z ORYGINALNYCH KLISZ* across top border on face of each note.

		VG	VF	UNC
104	**50 Groszy** 1944. Reddish maroon. Printer: Goznak. 81x52mm.			
	a. Issued note.	5.00	10.00	20.00
	b. 1974 (- old date 1944). Reprint.	—	—	5.00

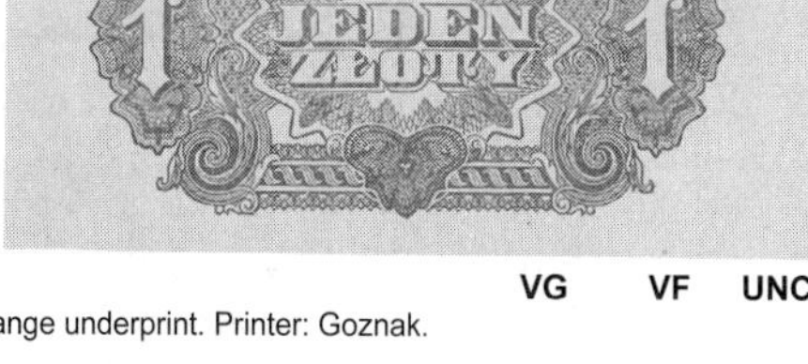

		VG	VF	UNC
105	**1 Zloty** 1944. Dark green on orange underprint. Printer: Goznak. 135x66mm.			
	a. Issued note with *OBOWIAZKOWYM.*	5.00	15.00	20.00
	b. 1974 (- old date 1944). Reprint. Serial #764560.	—	—	5.00

		VG	VF	UNC
106	**2 Zlote** 1944. Brown on light blue underprint. *OBOWIAZKOWYM* at bottom. 3 serial # varieties. Printer: Goznak. 134x69mm.	3.00	7.00	20.00

		VG	VF	UNC
107	**2 Zlote** 1944. Brown on light blue underprint. *OBOWIAZKOWE* at bottom. Printer: Polish National Bank. 69x134mm.			
	a. Issued note.	5.00	10.00	30.00
	b. 1974 (- old date 1944). Reprint. Serial #111111.	—	—	5.00

		VG	VF	UNC
108	**5 Zlotych** 1944. Violet-brown on green underprint. *OBOWIAZKOWYM* at bottom. Printer: Goznak.	5.00	10.00	30.00

		VG	VF	UNC
109	**5 Zlotych** 1944. Violet-brown on green underprint. *OBOWIAZKOWE at bottom.* Printer: Polish National Bank.			
	a. Issued note.	5.00	10.00	30.00
	b. 1974 (- old date 1944). Reprint. Serial #518823.	—	—	5.00

		VG	VF	UNC
110	**10 Zlotych** 1944. Blue on light green underprint. *OBOWIAZKOWYM* at bottom. Printer: Goznak.	5.00	10.00	30.00

		VG	VF	UNC
111	**10 Zlotych** 1944. Blue on light green underprint. *OBOWIAZKOWE* at bottom. Printer: Polish National Bank.			
	a. Issued note.	5.00	10.00	40.00
	b. 1974 (- old date 1944). Reprint. Serial #823518.	—	—	5.00

		VG	VF	UNC
112	**20 Zlotych** 1944. Blue-black on lilac underprint. *OBOWIAZKOWYM* at bottom. Printer: Goznak.	10.00	15.00	30.00

		VG	VF	UNC
113	**20 Zlotych** 1944. Blue-black on lilac underprint. *OBOWIAZKOWE* at bottom. 2 Serial # varieties. Printer: Polish National Bank.			
	a. Issued note.	10.00	20.00	40.00
	b. 1974 (- old date 1944). Reprint. Serial #671154.	—	—	5.00

		VG	VF	UNC
114	**50 Zlotych** 1944. Blue on lilac underprint. *OBOWIAZKOWYM* at bottom. Printer: Goznak.	10.00	20.00	40.00

		VG	VF	UNC
115	**50 Zlotych** 1944. Deep blue-violet on lilac underprint. *OBOWIAZKOWE* at bottom. 2 serial # varieties. Printer: Polish National Bank.			
	a. Issued note.	15.00	25.00	50.00
	b. 1974 (- old date 1944). Reprint. Serial #889147.	—	—	3.00
	s. Specimen. Overprint WZOR and large X across face.	—	—	250

		VG	VF	UNC
116	**100 Zlotych** 1944. Red on blue underprint. *OBOWIAZKOWYM* at bottom.	15.00	30.00	50.00

		VG	VF	UNC
117	**100 Zlotych** 1944. Red on blue underprint. *OBOWIAZKOWE* at bottom. 3 serial # varieties. Printer: Polish National Bank.			
	a. Issued note.	15.00	30.00	50.00
	b. 1974 (- old date 1944). Reprint. Serial # 778093.	—	—	3.00

		VG	VF	UNC
118	**500 Zlotych** 1944. Black on orange underprint. *OBOWIAZKOWYM* at bottom. Printer: Goznak.	20.00	30.00	80.00

		VG	VF	UNC
119	**500 Zlotych** 1944. Black on orange underprint. *OBOWIAZKOWE* at bottom. 2 serial # varieties. Printer: Polish National Bank.			
	a. Issued note.	25.00	60.00	110
	b. 1974 (- old date 1944). Reprint. Serial #780347.	—	—	3.00
	s. Specimen. Overprint WZOR across face.	—	—	250

GOVERNMENT OF NATIONAL UNITY - POST WW II

Narodowy Bank Polski

Polish National Bank

1945 Issue

		VG	VF	UNC
120	**1000 Zlotych** 1945. Brown on tan underprint. Eagle in underprint at center. 2 serial # varieties.	35.00	70.00	120

1946 First Issue

		VG	VF	UNC
121	**500 Zlotych** 15.1.1946. Dark blue and green. Man holding boat at left, fisherman at right. Back: View of old town.	25.00	70.00	120

		VG	VF	UNC
122	**1000 Zlotych** 15.1.1946. Brown. Miner at left, worker at right. 4 serial # varieties.	25.00	50.00	90.00

1946 Second Issue

		VG	VF	UNC
123	**1 Zloty** 15.5.1946. Deep lilac. Printer: PWPW, Lodz.	3.00	5.00	8.00

		VG	VF	UNC
124	**2 Zlote** 15.5.1946. Green. Watermark: Stars. PC: Buff.	3.00	5.00	8.00

		VG	VF	UNC
125	**5 Zlotych** 15.5.1946. Gray-blue.	3.00	5.00	10.00
126	**10 Zlotych** 15.5.1946. Red-brown on green and gold underprint. Eagle at upper center. Printer: PMNB, Budapest.	3.00	5.00	10.00
127	**20 Zlotych** 15.5.1946. Green and brown. Eagle at upper center. Back: Two airplanes at center. Printer: PMNB, Budapest and Swiss Printer.	10.00	20.00	40.00
128	**50 Zlotych** 15.5.1946. Brown and purple on gold underprint. Sailing ship at left, ocean freighter at right, eagle at upper center. Back: Ships and sailboat. Printer: TB, Praha and Riks-bankers Sedeltryckerei, Stockhol.	12.00	20.00	50.00
129	**100 Zlotych** 15.5.1946. Red on orange underprint. Farmer's wife at left, farmer at right. Back: Farmer with tractor.	12.00	25.00	50.00

PEOPLES DEMOCRATIC REPUBLIC

Narodowy Bank Polski

Polish National Bank

1947 Issue

		VG	VF	UNC
130	**20 Zlotych** 15.7.1947. Green on olive underprint. Eagle at lower center. Back: Tools, globe and book.	15.00	30.00	70.00

		VG	VF	UNC
131	**100 Zlotych** 1947; 1948. Red on lilac underprint. Farmer's wife at center. Back: Horses.			
	a. Issued note. 15.7.1947.	20.00	40.00	80.00
	p. Proof. 1.7.1948.	—	—	500
132	**500 Zlotych** 15.7.1947. Blue on tan and olive underprint. Eagle at left center, woman with oar and anchor at center. Back: Ships and loading dock. Printer: TB, Praha.			
	a. Issued note.	20.00	40.00	80.00
	s. Specimen. Red overprint: *SPECIMEN.*	—	—	500

		VG	VF	UNC
133	**1000 Zlotych** 15.7.1947. Brown and olive. Worker at center.	25.00	50.00	100

PEOPLES REPUBLIC

Narodowy Bank Polski

Polish National Bank

1948 Issue

		VG	VF	UNC
134	**2 Zlote** 1.7.1948. Dark olive-green on light olive-green and light orange underprint. Eagle at right. 4 serial # varieties. Back: Bank building. 58x120mm.	3.00	5.00	10.00

		VG	VF	UNC
135	**5 Zlotych** 1.7.1948. Red-brown on brown and red-brown underprint. 2 serial # varieties. Back: Farmer plowing. Watermark: Woman. 142x67mm.	15.00	40.00	120
136	**10 Zlotych** 1.7.1948. Brown on light brown and light red underprint. Portrait man at right. 2 serial # varieties. Back: Stacking hay. Watermark: Woman. 148x70mm.	5.00	8.00	15.00

		VG	VF	UNC
137	**20 Zlotych** 1.7.1948. Dark blue on pale blue and light red underprint. Portrait woman wearing a head scarf at right, eagle at center. 4 serial # varieties. Back: Ornate building. Watermark: Head of old man. 160x76mm.	5.00	8.00	15.00

		VG	VF	UNC
138	**50 Zlotych** 1.7.1948. Green on light green and olive underprint. Portrait sailor at right, eagle at center. 4 serial # varieties. Back: Ships at dockside. Watermark: Woman / 50. 164x78mm.	5.00	8.00	15.00

		VG	VF	UNC
139	**100 Zlotych** 1.7.1948. Red on light red and multicolor underprint. Man at right, eagle at upper center. 3 serial # varieties. Back: Factory. Watermark: Woman. 172x82mm.			
	a. *100* in center guilloche with fine line around edge. Buff or white paper.	7.00	15.00	30.00
	b. *100* in center guilloche without fine line around edge. Series GF.	15.00	25.00	70.00

		VG	VF	UNC
140	**500 Zlotych** 1.7.1948. Dark brown on light brown and multicolor underprint. Portrait coal miner at right, eagle at upper center. 2 serial # varieties. Back: Coal miners. Watermark: Woman. 178x85mm.	10.00	15.00	30.00

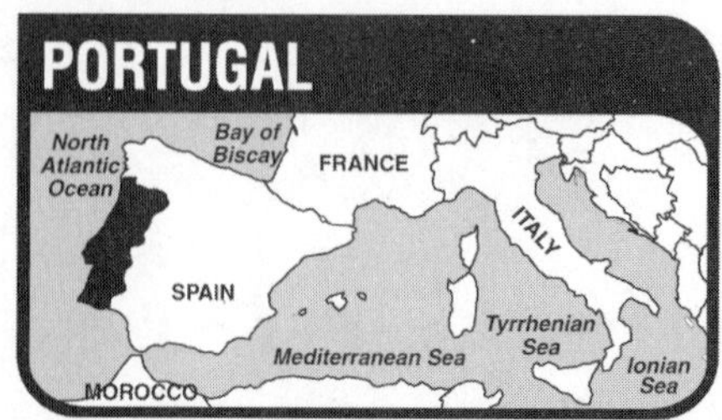

The Portuguese Republic, located in the western part of the Iberian Peninsula in southwestern Europe, has an area of 35,553 sq. mi. (91,905 sq. km.) and a population of 9.79 million. Capital: Lisbon. Portugal's economy is based on agriculture and a small but expanding industrial sector. Textiles, machinery, chemicals, wine and cork are exported. Following its heyday as a global maritime power during the 15th and 16th centuries, Portugal lost much of its wealth and status with the destruction of Lisbon in a 1755 earthquake, occupation during the Napoleonic Wars, and the independence of its wealthiest colony of Brazil in 1822. A 1910 revolution deposed the monarchy; for most of the next six decades, repressive governments ran the country. In 1974, a left-wing military coup installed broad democratic reforms. The following year, Portugal granted independence to all of its African colonies. Portugal is a founding member of NATO and entered the EC (now the EU) in 1986.

RULERS:

Spanish, 1580-1640
Luis I, 1861-1889
Carlos I, 1889-1908
Manuel II, 1908-1910
Republic, 1910-

MONETARY SYSTEM:

1 Mil Reis = 1000 Reis to 1910
1 Escudo = 100 Centavos, 1910-2001
1 Euro = 100 Cents, 2002-

KINGDOM

Notes were first issued in Portugal in 1797 because of poor economic conditions brought about by the war between Spain and France. Many of these notes were officially repaired and handstamped on the back (and sometimes on the face) with various dates and endorsements as they continued to circulate. Most are found in very worn condition. Variations on the notes include partially or fully printed year dates both in numerals and in words, also printed date altered to a later date by hand.

Imperial Treasury

1797 Issue

#	Note	Good	Fine	XF
1	**5000 Reis** 1797. Brown. Impressed royal arms at top center. Four allegorical vignettes in ovals across top. Uniface.	—	—	—
2	**10,000 Reis** 1797. Brown. Impressed royal arms at top center. Vignettes of barrels, animal, soldiers, spinning across top in octagons. Uniface.	—	—	—

1798 Issues

#3-7 Various handwritten dates.

#	Note	Good	Fine	XF
3	**2400 Reis** 1798. Brown. Impressed royal arms at top center. Building in ornate rectangle at upper left and right. Uniface.	—	—	—
3A	**2400 Reis** 1798. Brown. Impressed royal arms at top center. Hands extending from clouds holding objects in oval at upper left. Lion and dog in arena in oval at upper right. Uniface.	—	—	—
4	**2400 Reis** 1798-1799. Brown. Impressed royal arms at top center. Walled cities at upper left and right, two cherubs with garlands at top center. Uniface.	—	—	—

#	Note	Good	Fine	XF
4A	**5000 Reis** 1798. Brown. Impressed royal arms at top center. Young couples with the males playing music instruments at upper left and right. Uniface.	Good	Fine	XF
	a. Date with handwritten last number 9 over 8.	75.00	150	—
	b. Entire date printed.	75.00	150	—
5	**10,000 Reis** 1798. Brown. Impressed royal arms at top center. Winged cherub approaching stylized beehive at upper left, pastoral scene with castle behind, cherub with dog at upper right. Uniface.			
	a. Date with handwritten 9 over 8.	75.00	200	—
	b. Entire date printed.	75.00	150	—
6	**20,000 Reis** 1798-1799. Brown. Impressed royal arms at top center. Cherubs at upper left and right. Uniface.			
	a. Date with handwritten last numeral 9 over 8.	—	—	—
	b. Entire date printed.	—	—	—
7	**20,000 Reis** 1798. Brown. Impressed royal arms at top center. Four allegorical vignettes in ornate squarish frames across top; oval design at center. Uniface.	—	—	—

1799 Issues

#8-15 Various handwritten dates.

#	Note	Good	Fine	XF
8	**1200 Reis** 24.4.1799. Brown. Impressed royal arms at top center. Ornate vines at left and right across top. Uniface.	100	250	—
9	**2400 Reis** 1799 Brown. Impressed royal arms at top center. Hands extending from clouds holding objects in oval at upper left. Lion and dog in arena in oval at upper right. Uniface	—	—	—
10	**5000 Reis** 1799. Brown. Impressed royal arms at top center. Young couples with the males playing musical instruments at upper left and right. Uniface.	—	—	—
11	**5000 Reis** 1799. Brown. Impressed royal arms at top center. Four vignettes of animals (goats, birds, chickens, lions) across upper left and right. Uniface.	—	—	—
12	**6400 Reis** 1799. Brown. Impressed royal arms at top center. Two facing dogs (under the sun and under the moon) in oval frames at top center. Uniface.	—	—	—

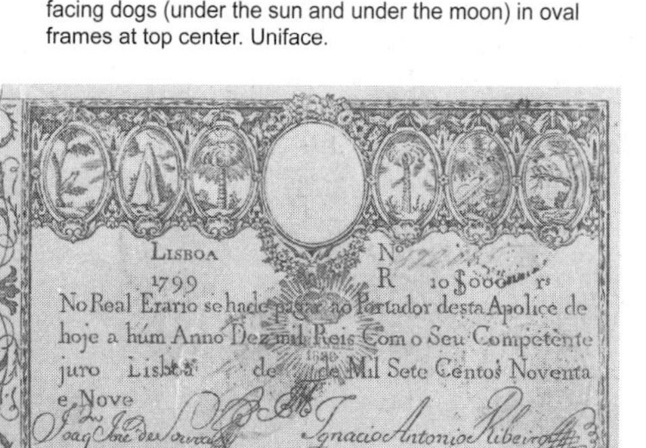

#	Note	Good	Fine	XF
13	**10,000 Reis** 1799. Brown. Impressed royal arms at top center. Six vignettes in oval frames across top. Uniface.			
	a. Date with handwritten last numeral 9.	100	250	—
	b. Entire date printed.	—	—	—
14	**12,800 Reis** 1799. Brown. Impressed royal arms at top center. Two long-necked birds, oyster and pearl in ornate frames at top center. Uniface.	—	—	—
15	**20,000 Reis** 1799. Brown. Impressed royal arms at top center. Eight vignettes in oval frames across top. Uniface.	75.00	200	—
	a. Date with handwritten last numeral 9.	75.00	150	—
	b. Entire date printed.	75.00	150	—

Law of 1.4.1805/1805 Issue

Law of 2.4.1805 #16 and 17 Various handwritten dates.

#	Note	Good	Fine	XF
16	**1200 Reis** 28.6.1805. Brown. Two children watering a flower at top center. Uniface.	75.00	200	—
17	**2400 Reis** 5.10.1805. Brown. Youthful helmeted warrior with lion in frame at top center. Uniface.	75.00	200	—

Decree of 31.10.1807/1807 Issue

#	Note	Good	Fine	XF
18	**1200 Reis** 28.11.1807. Brown. Two children watering a flower at top center. Like #16. Uniface.	—	—	—

#	Description	Good	Fine	XF
19	**2400 Reis** 5.12.1807. Brown. Youthful helmeted warrior with lion in frame at top center. Like #17. Uniface.	75.00	200	—

War of the Two Brothers

Imperial Treasury

The later struggle for the Portuguese throne necessitated a reissue of the old imperial issues dated 1798, 1799, 1805, and 1807 w/red revalidation ovpt. of each of the warring brothers.

1826 Revalidation Issues

#19A-28 red crowned ovpt: *D./PEDRO IV/1826* in starburst.

#	Description	Good	Fine	XF
19A	**1200 Reis** 1826 (- old date 1805). Brown. Two children watering a flower at top center. Overprint: Red crowned D./Pedro IV/1826 in starburst on #16.	30.00	75.00	—

#	Description	Good	Fine	XF
20	**1200 Reis** 1826 (- old date 1807). Brown. Two children watering a flower at top center. Overprint: Red crowned D./Pedro IV/1826 in starburst on #18.	—	—	—

#	Description	Good	Fine	XF
20A	**2400 Reis** 1826 (- old date 1798-1799). Brown. Walled cities at upper left and right, two cherubs with garlands at top center. Overprint: Red crowned D./Pedro IV/1826 in starburst on #4.	25.00	60.00	—
20B	**2400 Reis** 1826 (old date1798). Brown. Hands extending from clouds holding objects in oval at upper left. Lion and dog in arena in oval at upper right. Overprint: Red crowned D./Pedro IV/1826 in starburst on Unlisted #1.	100	250	—

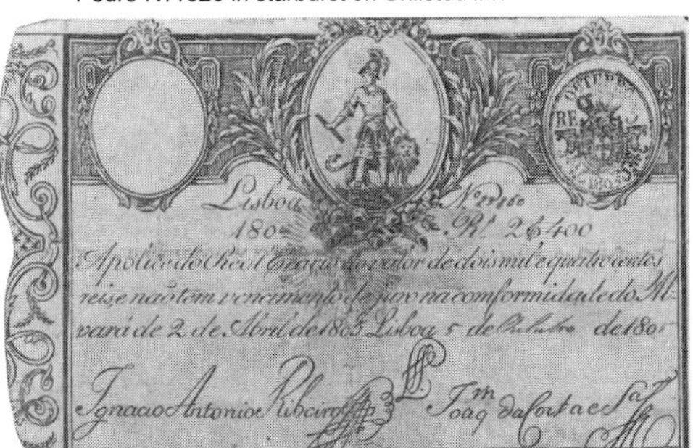

#	Description	Good	Fine	XF
21	**2400 Reis** 1826 (- old date 1805). Brown. Youthful helmeted warrior with lion in frame at top center. Overprint: Red crowned D./Pedro IV/1826 in starburst on #17.	25.00	60.00	—
22	**2400 Reis** 1826 (- old date 1807). Brown. Youthful helmeted warrior with lion in frame at top center. Overprint: Red crowned D./Pedro IV/1826 in starburst on #19.	50.00	125	—
23	**5000 Reis** 1826 (- old date 1797). Brown. Four allegorical vignettes in ovals across top. Overprint: Red crowned D./Pedro IV/1826 in starburst on #1.	—	—	—

#	Description	Good	Fine	XF
24	**5000 Reis** 1826 (- old date 1798-1799). Brown. Young couples with the males playing musical instruments at upper left and right. Overprint: Red crowned D./Pedro IV/1826 in starburst on #10.			
	a. Date with handwritten last numeral 9 over 8 on New (#2).	30.00	75.00	—
	b. Entire date printed 1798 on New (#2).	30.00	—	—
	c. Entire date printed 1799 on #10.	30.00	75.00	—

#	Description	Good	Fine	XF
25	**5000 Reis** 1826 (- old date 1799). Brown. Four vignettes of animals (goats, birds, chickens, lions) across upper left and right. Overprint: Red crowned D./Pedro IV/1826 in starburst on #11.	20.00	50.00	—

#26 not assigned.

#	Description	Good	Fine	XF
27	**6400 Reis** 1826 (- old date 1799). Brown. Two facing dogs (under the sun and under the moon) in oval frames at top center. Overprint: Red crowned D./Pedro IV/1826 in starburst on #12.	—	—	—

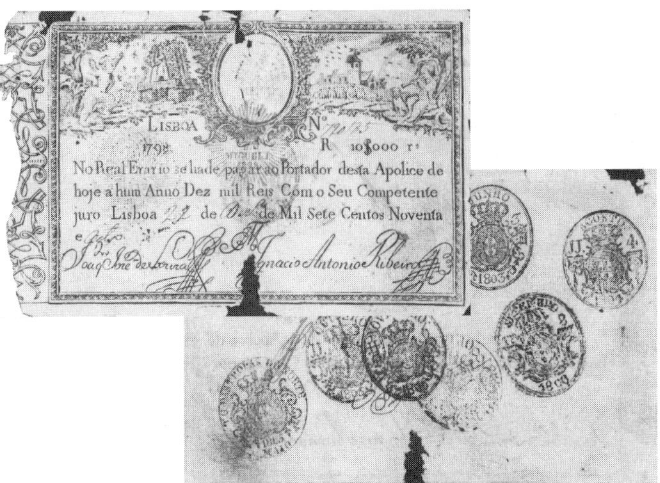

		Good	Fine	XF
28	**10,000 Reis** 1826 (- old date 1798). Brown. Winged cherub approaching stylized beehive at upper left, pastoral scene with castle behind, cherub with dog at upper right. Overprint: Red crowned D./Pedro IV/1826 in starburst on #5.			
	a. Date with handwritten last numeral 9 over 8.	30.00	75.00	—
	b. Entire date printed 1798.	30.00	75.00	—
28A	**10,000 Reis** 1826 (old date 1799). Brown. Six vignettes in oval frames across top. Overprint: Red crowned D./Pedro IV/1826 in starburst on #13.			
	a. Date with handwritten last numeral 9 over 8.	25.00	60.00	—
	b. Entire date printed.	25.00	60.00	—

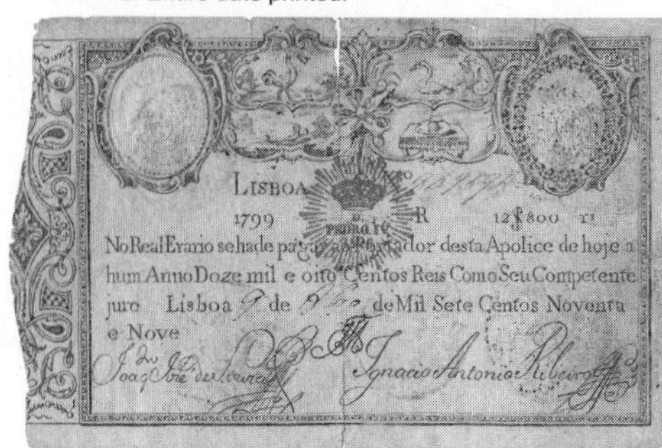

		Good	Fine	XF
29	**12,800 Reis** 1826 (- old date 1799). Brown. Two long-necked birds, oyster and pearl in ornate frames at top center. Overprint: Red crowned D./Pedro IV/1826 in starburst on #14.	30.00	75.00	—
30	**20,000 Reis** 1826 (- old date 1799). Brown. Cherubs at upper left and right. Overprint: Red crowned D./Pedro IV/1826 in starburst on #6.			
	a. Date with handwritten last numeral 9 over 8.	30.00	75.00	—
	b. Entire date printed on 1798.	30.00	75.00	—

		Good	Fine	XF
31	**20,000 Reis** 1826 (- old date 1799). Brown. Eight vignettes in oval frames across top. Overprint: Red crowned D./Pedro IV/1826 in starburst on #15.	25.00	60.00	—
	a. Date with handwritten last numeral 9.	30.00	75.00	—
	b. Entire date printed.	30.00	75.00	—

1828 Revalidation Issues

#32-46 red overprint: Crowned *D./MIGUEL I/1828* in starburst.

		Good	Fine	XF
32	**1200 Reis** 1828 (- old date 1799). Brown. Ornate vines at left and right across top. Overprint: Red crowned D./Miguel I/1828 in starburst on #8.	25.00	60.00	—

		Good	Fine	XF
33	**1200 Reis** 1828 (- old date 1805). Brown. Two children watering a flower at top center. Overprint: Red crowned D./Miguel I/1828 in starburst on #16.	30.00	75.00	—
33A	**1200 Reis** 1828. (old date 1807). Brown. Two children watering a flower at top center. Overprint: red crowned D./Miguel I/1828 in starburst on #18.	—	—	—

		Good	Fine	XF
34	**2400 Reis** 1828 (old date 1798-1799). Brown. Walled cities at upper left and right, two cherubs with garlands at top center. Overprint: Red crowned D./Miguel I/1828 in starburst on #4.			
	a. Date with handwritten last numeral 9 over 8.	35.00	85.00	—
	b. Entire date printed 1798.	—	—	—
35	**2400 Reis** 1828 (- old date 1805). Brown. Youthful helmeted warrior with lion in frame at top center. Overprint: Red crowned D./Miguel I/1828 in starburst on #17.	30.00	75.00	—

		Good	Fine	XF
38	**2400 Reis** 1828 (- old date 1807). Brown. Youthful helmeted warrior with lion in frame at top center. Overprint: Red crowned D./Miguel I/1828 in starburst on #19.	35.00	85.00	—

		Good	Fine	XF
38A	**5000 Reis** 1828 (-old date 1798-1799). Brown. Young couples with the males playing musical instruments at upper left and right. Overprint: Red crowned D./Miguel I/1828 in starburst on #10.			
	a. Date with handwritten last numeral 9 over 8.	—	—	—
	b. Entire date printed 1798.	30.00	75.00	—

		Good	Fine	XF
38B	**5000 Reis** 1828 (- old date 1799). Brown. Four vignettes of animals (goats, birds, chickens, lions) across upper left and right. Overprint: Red crowned D./Miguel I/1828 in starburst on #11.	30.00	75.00	—

		Good	Fine	XF
38C	**5000 Reis** 1828 (old date 1797). Brown. Impressed royal arms at center. Four allegorical vignettes in ovals across top. Overprint: Red crowned D./Miguel I/1828 in starburst on #1.	—	—	—

		Good	Fine	XF
38D	**6400 Reis** 1828. (old date 1799). Brown. Impressed royal arms at top center. Facing dogs in two oval frames at top center. Overprint: Red crowned D./Miguel I/1828 in starburst on #12.	—	—	—

		Good	Fine	XF
39	**10,000 Reis** 1828 (- old date 1797). Brown. Vignettes of barrels, animal, soldiers, spinning across top in octagons. Overprint: Red crowned D./Miguel I/1828 in starburst on #2.	—	—	—

		Good	Fine	XF
40	**10,000 Reis** 1828 (- old date 1798). Brown. Winged cherub approaching stylized beehive at upper left, pastoral scene with castle behind, cherub with dog at upper right. Overprint: Red crowned D./Miguel I/1828 in starburst on #5.			
	a. Date with handwritten last numeral 9 over 8.	30.00	75.00	—
	b. Entire date printed 1798.	30.00	75.00	—

		Good	Fine	XF
41	**10,000 Reis** 1828 (- old date 1799). Brown. Six vignettes in oval frames across top. Overprint: Red crowned D./Miguel I/1828 in starburst.			
	a. Date with handwritten last numeral 9 over 8 on #13a.	30.00	75.00	—
	b. Entire date printed 1798 on #13b.	30.00	75.00	—

		Good	Fine	XF
44	**12,800 Reis** 1828 (- old date 1799). Brown. Two long-necked birds, oyster and pearl in ornate frames at top center. Overprint: Red crowned D./Miguel I/1828 in starburst on #14.	25.00	60.00	—

		Good	Fine	XF
45	**20,000 Reis** 1828 (- old date 1799). Brown. Four allegorical vignettes in ornate squarish frames across top; oval design at center. Overprint: Red crowned D./Miguel I/1828 in starburst on #7.	—	—	—

		Good	Fine	XF
46	**20,000 Reis** 1828 (- old date 1799). Brown. Eight vignettes in oval frames across top. Overprint: Red crowned D./Miguel I/1828 in starburst on #15.	25.00	60.00	—
	a. Date with handwritten last numeral *9*.	30.00	75.00	—
	b. Entire date printed.	30.00	75.00	—

		Good	Fine	XF
47	**20,000 Reis** 1828 (-old date 1798-1799). Brown. Cherubs at upper left and right. Overprint: Red crowned D./Miguel I/1828 in starburst on #6.			
	a. Date with handwritten last numeral 9 over 8.	40.00	100	—
	b. Entire date printed 1798.	30.00	75.00	—

Banco de Portugal

1847 Issue

No.	Description	Good	Fine	XF
49	**10 Mil Reis** 30.6.1847-16.6.1873 (handwritten). Brown. Allegorical figure in each corner. BC: Blue.	—	—	—
50	**20 Mil Reis** 1.5.1847-1.5.1850. Red. Allegorical figure in each corner. BC: Blue.	—	—	—

1854 Issue

No.	Description	Good	Fine	XF
51	**18 Mil Reis** 20.6.1854-12.4.1867 (handwritten). Black. Seated allegorical figure at either side of arms at upper center. BC: Blue.	—	—	—

1867 Issue

No.	Description	Good	Fine	XF
52	**20 Mil Reis** 29.10.1867; 20.12.1867. Black on yellow underprint. Arms at upper center similar to #51. Figure in yellow at left and right. Uniface.	—	—	—

1869 Issue

No.	Description	Good	Fine	XF
53	**20 Mil Reis** 4.3.1869; 25.1.1870; 22.2.1870 22.2.1870. Black on green underprint. Arms at upper center. Figures at left and right in red. Like #52.	—	—	—

1871 Issue

No.	Description	Good	Fine	XF
54	**20 Mil Reis** 4.11.1871-17.8.1875. Blue. Arms at upper center. Figures at left and right in black. Design like #52.	—	—	—

1876 Issue

No.	Description	Good	Fine	XF
55	**10 Mil Reis** 15.5.1876-28.12.1877. Violet. Allegorical figure in each corner. Design like #49.	—	—	—
56	**20 Mil Reis** 15.5.1876. Blue. Portrait D. Luis I at center. BC: Red.	—	—	—

1877 Issue

No.	Description	Good	Fine	XF
57	**20 Mil Reis** 6.7.1877-17.12.1886. Blue-black. Three allegorical figures with arms at left. Back: Arms at center. BC: Brown.	—	—	—

1878 Issue

No.	Description	Good	Fine	XF
58	**10 Mil Reis** 28.1.1878-21.3.1882. Brown on pink underprint. Three figures with arms at center. Like #83. BC: Red.	—	—	—

1879 Issue

No.	Description	Good	Fine	XF
59	**10 Mil Reis** 24.10.1879-18.10.1881. Black. Seated figure at either side of arms at center. BC: Lilac.	—	—	—

1883-1886 Issue

No.	Description	Good	Fine	XF
60	**5 Mil Reis** 2.1.1883-17.4.1889 (handwritten). Brown on yellow underprint. Standing figure at left and right. Back: Arms at center.	—	—	—
61	**20 Mil Reis** 4.1.1884-20.8.1889. Brown. Seated woman with arms at upper center. BC: Blue.	—	—	—
62	**50 Mil Reis** 25.6.1886-26.2.1892 (handwritten). Black on light red underprint. Allegorical figure at left and right, arms at lower center. BC: Brown.	—	—	—

1890-1891 Issue

No.	Description	Good	Fine	XF
63	**200 Reis** 1.8.1891. Blue on gray underprint. Arms at left. Back: Arms at center right.	—	—	—
64	**500 Reis** 12.5.1891. Black. (Not issued.)	—	—	—

No.	Description	Good	Fine	XF
65	**500 Reis** 1.7.1891. Lilac on tan underprint. Arms at center. Back: Arms at center.	30.00	100	250
66	**1 Mil Reis** 1.7.1891. Brown on pink underprint. Arms at upper center. Back: Arms at center.	—	—	—
67	**2 1/2 Mil Reis** 1.6.1891. Red on green underprint. Arms at left. Back: Arms at center.	—	—	—
68	**5 Mil Reis** 26.5.1890. Blue. Woman at left, arms at upper center.	—	—	—

No.	Description	Good	Fine	XF
69	**5 Mil Reis** 8.11.1890. Blue. Allegorical seated figures with arms at upper center. BC: Pale brown.	—	—	—
70	**5 Mil Reis** 3.3.1891-15.6.1892. Blue. Mercury head at upper center. Back: Brown.	—	—	—
71	**20 Mil Reis** 8.11.1890-23.6.1898. Blue. Allegorical figures at left and right, arms at upper center. BC: Gray on lilac underprint. Watermark: Bank name and date *29.7.87.*	—	—	—

1893-1899 Issue

No.	Description	Good	Fine	XF
72	**500 Reis** 22.7.1899; 25.5.1900. Light brown. Woman and shield at left. Back: Arms at center. BC: Red on blue underprint.	30.00	125	350

No.	Description	Good	Fine	XF
73	**1 Mil Reis** 24.3.1896; 31.12.1897; 31.10.1899; 30.11.1900. Blue on pink underprint. Arms at upper left. Woman with winged cap and staff at right. Back: Arms at center. BC: Brown.	30.00	150	450

#	Denomination	Good	Fine	XF
74	**2 1/2 Mil Reis** 16.2.1893-25.5.1900. Black on violet and brown underprint. Standing woman at left and right, arms at upper center. Back: Arms at center. BC: Blue-gray.	—	—	—
75	**5 Mil Reis** 16.4.1894. Pink-violet. Peace at left, arms at upper center right. Back: Vertical design at left and right, arms at center.	—	—	—
76	**10 Mil Reis** 1.12.1894. Aqua. Seated allegorical figure at left and right, arms at upper center. Back: Standing allegorical figure at left and right, medallion of Lusitania at top center.	—	—	—
77	**50 Mil Reis** 18.10.1898; 31.10.1898; 3.11.1898; 30.10.1900. Brown. Seated woman at either side of arms at lower center, vertical design at left and right. Back: Arms at center. Watermark: Allegorical heads.	—	—	—

#	Denomination	Good	Fine	XF
78	**100 Mil Reis** 1.12.1894-10.3.1909. Blue. Allegorical figures at left and right, arms at lower center. Back: Allegorical figure on tall pedestal at left and right. BC: Blue and gray. Watermark: Allegorical heads.	350	950	—

1901-1903 Issue, W/o Chapa; Chapa 3

Listed in accordance with the nominal denomination and plate numbers (Ch. = Chapa = plate), which describe the different types of notes. Various date and signature varieties.

#	Denomination	Good	Fine	XF
79	**2 1/2 Mil Reis** 29.9.1903; 11.3.1904; 30.8.1904; 25.8.1905. Brown. Helmeted woman seated with arms at left. Chapa 3. Back: Arms at right.	100	300	800
80	**5 Mil Reis** 20.9.1901. Blue on yellow underprint. Angel at left, six busts across upper border, old boats at bottom center right. Without *Chapa.* Back: Arms at right. BC: Green.	—	—	—

#	Denomination	Good	Fine	XF
81	**10 Mil Reis** 29.11.1902; 26.6.1903; 30.8.1904; 22.5.1908; 30.12.1909. Brown on yellow underprint. Luis de Camões at left, two figures and globe at lower center, ships at right. Chapa 3. Back: Infante D. Henrique at upper left. Watermark: A. de Albuquerque.	185	600	1,500
82	**20 Mil Reis** 26.2.1901. Blue on tan underprint. Standing figure at left and right, arms at lower center. Without *Chapa.* BC: Orange and blue.	—	—	—

1903-1906 Issue, Chapa 3, 6 and 8

#	Denomination	Good	Fine	XF
83	**5 Mil Reis** 31.7.1903-25.8.1905; 9.7.1907. Blue on brown underprint. Three figures with arms at center. Chapa 6. Back: Arms at center.	80.00	200	—
84	**20 Mil Reis** 12.10.1906. Blue on gold underprint. Standing figure at left and right, arms at lower center. Chapa 8. Similar to #82. Back: Portrait D. Afonso Henriques at center, helmeted figure at left and right.	185	600	—
85	**50 Mil Reis** 29.1.1904-30.9.1910. Blue-gray. Statues of Principe Perfetto and B. Dias at left and right, heads of Pedro de Alenquer and Diogo Cão at lower left and right, with anchor and ships, allegorical woman at center right. Chapa 3. Back: Arms at left. BC: Brown. Watermark: Luis de Camões.	275	850	—

Casa da Moeda

1891 Reis Issues

#	Denomination	VG	VF	UNC
86	**50 Reis** 6.8.1891. Green on lilac underprint. Arms at left and right.	10.00	20.00	60.00
87	**50 Reis** 6.8.1891. Blue. Arms at upper center.	10.00	20.00	60.00

Note: #87 with 3-line diagonal overprint for Funchal district, see Madeira #11.

#	Denomination	VG	VF	UNC
88	**100 Reis** 6.8.1891. Brown on light brown underprint. Arms at left and right. BC: Pale gray.	10.00	20.00	60.00

#	Denomination	VG	VF	UNC
89	**100 Reis** 6.8.1891. Dark brown on light green underprint. Back: Arms in circle at center. BC: Green.	10.00	20.00	60.00

Note: #89 with 3-line diagonal overprint for Funchal district, see Madeira #12.

#	Denomination	VG	VF	UNC
90	**100 Reis** *D.6.8.1891.* Brown. Curtain, man sitting on anvil at left, figures of cherubs at right. Similar to #93. Back: Arms at center.			
	p. Many proof prints in different colors each.	—	20.00	—

REPUBLIC

Casa da Moeda

State Notes of the Mint

1917 Provisional Issues

#91 and 92 old date 6.8.1891 blocked out.

#	Denomination	VG	VF	UNC
91	**5 Centavos** ND (-old date 6.8.1891). Bronze and blue-green. Proof print.	—	—	—
92	**5 Centavos** ND (-old date 6.8.1891). Bronze and blue. Proof print.	—	—	—

Decreto de 15 de Agosto de 1917

		VG	VF	UNC
93	**10 Centavos** *D.1917.* Bronze and dark brown. Curtain, man sitting on anvil. Similar to #90. Back: Arms at center. BC: Green.			
	a. Issued note.	1.50	3.50	12.50
	p. Proof prints (10 different colors) each.	—	—	20.00

		VG	VF	UNC
94	**10 Centavos** *D.1917.* Dark blue on light tan underprint. Columns at left and right, arms at upper center. BC: Blue-green. PC: Gray and thin or yellowish and thicker.			
	a. Issued note.	1.00	3.00	10.00
	p. Proof print in different colors.	—	—	20.00

		VG	VF	UNC
95	**10 Centavos** *D.1917.* Blue on green underprint. Seated woman at left and right, arms at lower center. Back: Seated figures at center, arms above. BC: Blue.			
	a. Watermark: Ovals.	1.50	5.00	17.50
	b. Watermark: Casa da Moeda.	1.00	3.50	10.00
	c. Without watermark.	1.00	3.50	10.00

		VG	VF	UNC
96	**10 Centavos** *D.1917.* Red-brown on light brownish gray underprint. Seated man at left. Chimney stacks, ships, bridge in background. Arms at upper right. Back: Coin at center. BC: Light brown. PC: White, gray, yellow-brown or brown.	1.00	3.50	12.00

1918-1922 Issues

		VG	VF	UNC
97	**5 Centavos** 5.4.1918. Blue-green on gray-violet underprint. Arms at upper center. BC: Brown. PC: Gray and thin or yellowish and thicker.	1.00	3.50	10.00

		VG	VF	UNC
98	**5 Centavos** *D.5.4.1918.* Red on pale orange underprint. Small child at left, bust at right, coin at center below. Back: Arms at center. BC: Aqua.	1.00	3.50	10.00

Note: Some of #98 may have a faint light orange underprint at center.

		VG	VF	UNC
99	**5 Centavos** *D.5.4.1918.* Dark brown on yellow-brown underprint. Arms at upper center. PC: White or yellowish.	1.00	3.50	10.00

		VG	VF	UNC
100	**20 Centavos** *D.4.8.1922.* Dark brown on blue underprint. Seated man at left, woman at right, arms at upper center. Back: Allegorical figures and ship. BC: Purplish black.	1.00	3.50	10.00

1925 First Issue - Decretos de 15.8.1917 and 11.4.1925

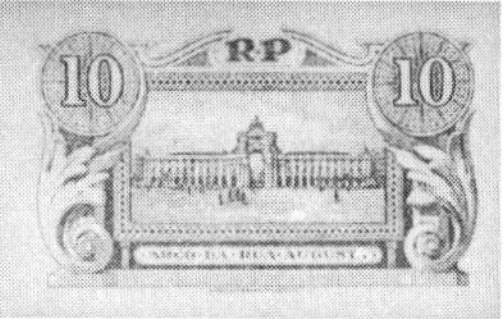

		VG	VF	UNC
101	**10 Centavos** *D.1917 and 1925.* Red-brown on gray underprint. Arms at left, woman with torch at right. Back: *Comercio* Square in Lisbon at center. BC: Brown. Printer: W&S.	1.00	3.50	10.00

1925 Second Issue - Decretos de 4.8.1922 and 11.4.1925

		VG	VF	UNC
102	**20 Centavos** *D.1922 and 1925.* Brown on gray underprint. Woman at left, arms above. Back: Casa da Moeda at center. BC: Gray. Printer: W&S.	2.00	5.00	15.00

Banco de Portugal

1911 Interim Issue

		Good	Fine	XF
104	**5 Mil Reis** 14.11.1906; 30.12.1909; 30.3.1910 (1911). Black on blue and multicolor underprint. Portrait Marquez de Pombal at left. Chapa 7. Back: Arms at center, woman seated at right. Watermark: Minerva. Printer: BWC.	60.00	150	—

1912-1917 ND Provisional Issue

		Good	Fine	XF
105	**500 Reis** ND (1917 - old dates 27.12.1904; 30.9.1910). Black on green underprint. *Republica* over crowned arms at top center. Chapa 3. Back: Woman's head at left. BC: Brown. Watermark: Mercury.			
	a. Black overprint: *REPUBLICA.*	3.50	15.00	60.00
	b. Engraved *REPUBLICA.*	1.50	12.50	50.00

		Good	Fine	XF
106	**1 Mil Reis** ND (1917 - old date 30.9.1910). Blue. Arms at lower left center, seated woman at right with *REPUBLICA* over crowned arms at bottom. Chapa 3. Back: Seated woman at left. BC: Red.	20.00	90.00	225

		Good	Fine	XF
107	**2 1/2 Mil Reis** ND (1916 - old dates 20.6.1909; 30.6.1909; 30.9.1910; 27.6.1919). Black and green on orange underprint. Portrait A. de Albuquerque at right. Chapa 4. Back: Mercury at left. Crowned arms at center. Overprint: Black *REPUBLICA* on back.	20.00	60.00	200

		Good	Fine	XF
108	**10 Mil Reis** ND (1917 - old dates 22.5.1908; 30.9.1910). Black on tan underprint. Five men representing sculpture, painting, reading, music and writing. Chapa 4. Back: Allegorical woman at left, helmeted woman at right. BC: Green and pink. Watermark: Woman's head. Printer: BWC (without imprint).			
	a. Overprint: *Republica* over crowned arms on back. 30.9.1910.	150	375	850
	b. Engraved *Republica* over crowned arms on back.	150	375	850

		Good	Fine	XF
109	**20 Mil Reis** ND (1912 - old dates 30.12.1909; 30.3.1912). Blue on tan underprint. Portrait Vasco da Gama in pillar at left, Luis de Camoes in pillar at right, arms at lower center. Chapa 9. Back: Crowned arms at left. BC: Brown. Watermark: D. Joao II. Overprint: *REPUBLICA* on back.	150	600	—

		Good	Fine	XF
110	**50 Mil Reis** ND (1917 - old date 30.9.1910). Blue. Middle East King on throne at left, voyagers at right. Chapa 4. Back: Crowned arms at lower center. Medallion of Lusitania at right. Watermark: Man with turban. Overprint: *REPUBLICA.* on back.			
	a. Issued note.	200	700	—
	s. Specimen. Perforated: *SPECIMEN.*	—	Unc	750

		Good	Fine	XF
111	**100 Mil Reis** ND (1916 - old dates 22.5.1908; 10.3.1909; 30.9.1910). Green on yellow underprint. Scene of arrival of P. A. Cabral at Lisbon 8.3.1500. Back: Arms at upper center. BC: Red-brown and tan. Overprint: Black *REPUBLICA* on back.	350	950	—

1913-1918 Regular Issue

Escudo system.

		Good	Fine	XF
112	**50 Centavos** 1918; 1920. Purple and multicolor. Woman with ship in her hand at left. Chapa 1. Back: Woman with staff and scale at center. BC: Purple and green. Watermark: Minerva head. Printer: BWC (without imprint).			
	a. Serial #. 5.7.1918.	3.50	7.50	35.00
	b. Block # and letters in 2 lines. 5.7.1918; 25.6.1920.	2.00	5.00	30.00

		Good	Fine	XF
113	**1 Escudo** 1917-1920. Red, violet and multicolor. Woman seated holding book at left. Chapa 1. Back: Woman with lyre at right. BC: Brown. Watermark: Allegorical head. Printer: BWC (without imprint).			
	a. 7.9.1917; 25.6.1920.	3.50	10.00	45.00
	b. 29.11.1918. Rare.	—	—	—

		Good	Fine	XF
114	**5 Escudos** 29.7.1913-1.2.1923. Purple on light blue underprint. Woman seated at left offering wreath, portrait A. Herculano at top center. Chapa 1. Back: Fortress at center. BC: Brown. Watermark: Minerva head. Printer: BWC (without imprint).	40.00	125	350

		Good	Fine	XF
115	**20 Escudos** 1915-1918. Brown-lilac and green. Woman at left and right, portrait A. Garrett at center. Chapa 1. Back: Arms at center. BC: Blue on light green underprint. Printer: BWC (without imprint).			
	a. Issued note. 5.1.1915-26.3.1918.	85.00	300	500
	b. Kingdom of the North overprint: *REINO DE PORTUGAL / 19 de Janeiro de 1919* (-old date 14.4.1915). Rare.	—		

		Good	Fine	XF
116	**100 Escudos** 13.8.1918; 5.2.1920. Deep blue on multicolor underprint. Indians, ships (discovery of Brazil) and medallic portrait of P. Alvares Cabral at center right. Chapa 1. Back: Two heads and Cabral's arrival in 1500 (similar to #111) at center. BC: Brown and multicolor. Watermark: Man's head.	600	1,500	—

1919 Issue, Chapa 1 and 2

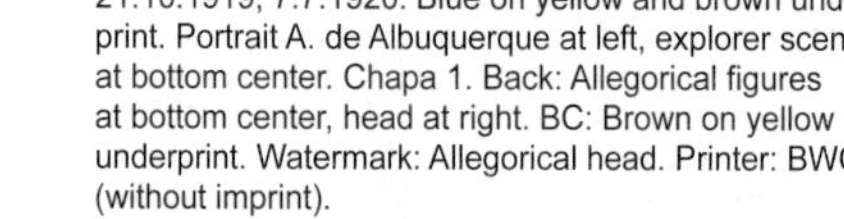

		Good	Fine	XF
117	**10 Escudos** 21.10.1919; 7.7.1920. Blue on yellow and brown underprint. Portrait A. de Albuquerque at left, explorer scene at bottom center. Chapa 1. Back: Allegorical figures at bottom center, head at right. BC: Brown on yellow underprint. Watermark: Allegorical head. Printer: BWC (without imprint).	100	300	650

		Good	Fine	XF
118	**20 Escudos** 12.8.1919-7.7.1920. Blue on brown and green underprint. Portrait J. DeCastro at left. Chapa 2. Back: Building at center, arms at right. BC: Maroon and multicolor. Watermark: Allegorical head. Printer: BWC (without imprint).	75.00	200	500

1920 Issues, Chapa A, 1, 2 and 3

		Good	Fine	XF
119	**2 Escudos 50 Centavos** 10.7.1920; 3.2.1922. Green and multicolor. Portrait D. Nuno Álvarez Pereira at right. Chapa 1. Back: Woman with globe at left. BC: Blue-green and red. Printer: BWC (without imprint).	30.00	100	225

		Good	Fine	XF
120	**5 Escudos** 10.7.1920-13.1.1925. Violet-brown and green. Portrait J. das Regras at left. Chapa 2. Back: Convent at right. BC: Blue. Watermark: Allegorical head. Printer: BWC (without imprint).	30.00	100	225

		Good	Fine	XF
121	**10 Escudos** 9.8.1920; 31.8.1926; 2.11.1927; 28.1.1928. Brown on yellow-green underprint. Portrait M. de Sa da Bandeira at center. Chapa 2. Back: Arms at upper center. BC: Blue. Printer: BWC (without imprint).	50.00	175	500

		Good	Fine	XF
122	**20 Escudos** 9.8.1920-3.2.1927. Brown, green and multicolor. Portrait J. Estevao Coelho de Magalhaes at left, woman seated with arms and globe at right. Chapa 3. Back: Warrior's head at left and right. BC: Brown. Watermark: Allegorical head. Printer: BWC (without imprint).	100	350	650

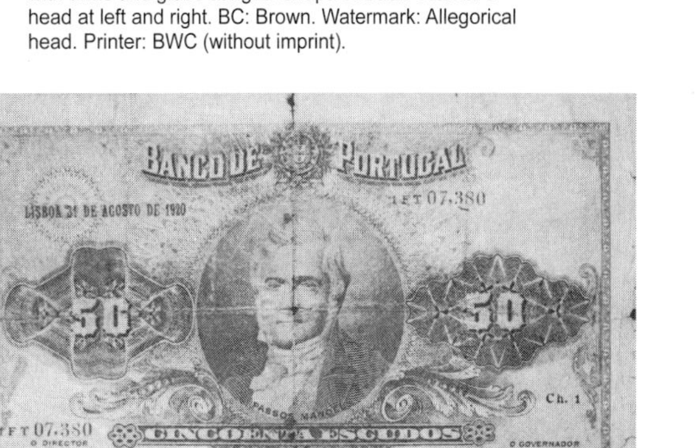

		Good	Fine	XF
123	**50 Escudos** 31.8.1920; 3.2.1927. Red-brown and multicolor. Portrait Passos Manoel at center. Chapa 1. Back: Statue and ornate archway. Watermark: Allegorical head. Printer: BWC (without imprint).	175	500	1,250

		Good	Fine	XF
124	**100 Escudos** 31.8.1920; 27.4.1922; 13.4.1926; 15.8.1927; 28.1.1928. Brown. Portrait D. do Couto at left. Chapa 2. Back: Castle at center, allegorical figures at right. BC: Maroon and brown. Watermark: Man's head. Printer: BWC (without imprint).	625	1,500	—
125	**1000 Escudos** 10.7.1920. Blue on multicolor underprint. Portrait Duque da Terceira at upper left, arms at upper right. Chapa A. Back: Vertical design at left and right. BC: Brown on yellow underprint. Watermark: Bank name. Printer: BWC. Rare.	—	—	—
126	**1000 Escudos** 28.7.1920. Slate blue on multicolor underprint. Portrait L. de Camões at right. Chapa 1. Back: Allegorical women at left and right. Printer: BWC (without imprint). Rare.	—	—	—

1922 Issues, Chapa 1 and 2

		Good	Fine	XF
127	**2 Escudos 50 Centavos** 17.11.1922; 18.11.1925; 18.11.1926. Blue on orange and yellow underprint. Portrait M. da Silveira at center. Chapa 2. Back: Arms at center. BC: Orange on yellow underprint. Watermark: Bank name repeated. Printer: W&S (without imprint).	15.00	60.00	125

128 50 Escudos — Good / Fine / XF

6.2.1922; 18.11.1925. Blue on multicolor underprint. Angel of Peace at left, cherubs at right corners. Chapa 2. Back: Radiant sun at center, woman and lions at right. BC: Brown and multicolor. Watermark: Head. Printer: BWC (without imprint).

Good	Fine	XF
350	750	—

129 500 Escudos — Good / Fine / XF

4.5.1922; 8.12.1925. Brown on multicolor underprint. Portrait João de Deus at left, arms at upper right. Chapa 1. Back: Allegorical child with flute at right. BC: Brown and green. Watermark: Head representing the Republic. Printer: BWC (without imprint).

Good	Fine	XF
700	1,500	—

130 500 Escudos — Good / Fine / XF

17.11.1922. Purple and black on tan underprint. Portrait Vasco da Gama at left, sailing ships at right. Chapa 2. Back: Arms at center. BC: Purple. Watermark: Bank name repeated. Printer: W&S.

Good	Fine	XF
300	800	2,000

Note: Through swindle, #130 was reprinted for Alves Reis who secured false authorization for millions of escudos to be made for his illegal use - a most famous episode.

131 1000 Escudos — Good / Fine / XF

27.4.1922; 13.4.1926. Dark blue and purple. Portrait A. F. Castilho at center, arms at right. Chapa 2. Back: Two allegorical women with lyre and torch at center. BC: Purple and lilac. Printer: BWC (without imprint). Rare.

Good	Fine	XF
—	—	—

1924-1925 Issues, Chapa 3 and 4

#133-136 wmk: bank name repeated. Printer: W&S (w/o imprint).

133 5 Escudos — Good / Fine / XF

13.1.1925. Gray on yellow-brown and light blue underprint. Portrait D. Alvaro Vaz d'Almada at lower center. 2 signature varieties. Chapa 4. Back: Arms at center. BC: Blue. Watermark: Bank name repeated. Printer: W&S (without imprint).

Good	Fine	XF
25.00	80.00	200

134 10 Escudos — Good / Fine / XF

13.1.1925. Black on pink underprint. Monastery in Lisbon at left, portrait E. de Queiroz at right. Chapa 3. Back: Arms at left. BC: Brown. Watermark: Bank name repeated. Printer: W&S (without imprint).

Good	Fine	XF
40.00	125	300

135 20 Escudos — Good / Fine / XF

13.1.1925. Red on yellow underprint. Portrait Marquês de Pombal at top center, *Comercio* Square below. Chapa 4. Back: Arms at center. BC: Red. Watermark: Bank name repeated. Printer: W&S (without imprint).

Good	Fine	XF
75.00	225	600

136 50 Escudos — Good / Fine / XF

13.1.1925. Blue on light pink and green underprint. Portrait Vasco da Gama at left, Monastery of Mafra at center right. Chapa 3. Back: Arms at center. Watermark: Bank name repeated. Printer: W&S (without imprint).

Good	Fine	XF
150	400	850

137 100 Escudos — Good / Fine / XF

13.1.1925. Black on salmon underprint. Portrait Marechal Duque de Saldanha at left, monument with city scene at center right. Chapa 3. Back: Arms at center. Watermark: Bank name repeated. Printer: W&S. (Not issued.)

Good	Fine	XF
—	—	—

		Good	Fine	XF
138	**500 Escudos** 13.1.1925. Brown on light green underprint. Portrait Camilo Branco at left, city scene with river at right. Chapa 3. Back: Arms at center. Watermark: Bank name repeated. Printer: W&S. (Not issued.)	—	—	—
139	**1000 Escudos** 13.1.1925. Tan and black. Portrait Visconde de Seabra at left, cathedral at right. Chapa 3. Back: Arms at center. Printer: W&S. Specimen.	—	—	—

1927-1928 Issue, Chapa 3 and 4

		Good	Fine	XF
140	**100 Escudos** 4.4.1928; 12.8.1930. Blue on green and red underprint. Portrait G. Freire at left, allegorical figures with arms at upper center, pillars at lower center. Chapa 4. Back: Horsecart and town at center, bank arms at right. BC: Red-brown. Watermark: Head symbolizing the Republic. Printer: BWC (without imprint).	75.00	225	450
141	**500 Escudos** 4.4.1928; 19.4.1929. Red-violet on multicolor underprint. Castle at left, portrait Duque de Palmelha at right. Chapa 4. Back: Bank arms at left, horse-drawn carts at lower center. BC: Green. Watermark: Portrait Duque de Palmelha. Printer: BWC (without imprint).	500	1,200	—
142	**1000 Escudos** 25.11.1927. Blue on light tan underprint. Convent at center, Oliveira Martins at right. Chapa 3. Back: Bank arms at center. BC: Red-brown. Watermark: Oliveira Martins. Printer: BWC (without imprint).	—	—	—

1929 Issue, Chapa 4 and 5

		Good	Fine	XF
143	**20 Escudos** 17.9.1929-27.2.1940. Red-violet and multicolor. Portrait M. d' Albuquerque at left, ornate building at right. Chapa 5. Back: Guimaraes Castle at left. BC: Violet. Watermark: Portrait M. d' Albuquerque. Printer: BWC (without imprint).	35.00	100	225

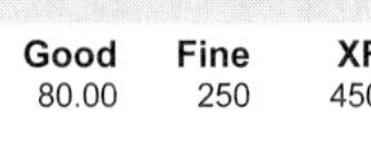

		Good	Fine	XF
144	**50 Escudos** 17.9.1929; 7.3.1933. Violet and multicolor. Portrait B. Carneiro at left center. Chapa 4. Back: Coimbra University at center, warrior head at right. BC: Blue and multicolor. Watermark: Allegorical head of Justice. Printer: BWC (without imprint).	80.00	250	450

		Good	Fine	XF
145	**1000 Escudos** 17.9.1929. Green, violet and multicolor. Bridge at center, Gen. M. de Sa da Bandeira at right. Chapa 4. Back: Bank arms, woman's head and field workers. BC: Brown. Watermark: Allegorical head. Printer: BWC (without imprint).	700	1,500	—

1932 Issue, Chapa 5

		Good	Fine	XF
146	**50 Escudos** 18.11.1932. Purple and multicolor. Duque de Saldanha at left, monument at center. Chapa 5. Back: Farmer and oxen plowing at center, bank arms at right. BC: Blue. Watermark: Head. Printer: TDLR (without imprint).	75.00	225	—
147	**500 Escudos** 18.11.1932; 31.8.1934. Brown-violet and blue on multicolor underprint. João da Silva Carvalho at left, palace at center. Chapa 5. Back: River and wall at center, Liberty at right. BC: Green. Watermark: Homer. Printer: BWC (without imprint).	200	500	—
148	**1000 Escudos** 18.11.1932. Dark green and purple on multicolor underprint. Conde de Castelo Melhor at left, National Palace at center, bank arms at lower right. Chapa 5. Back: Island castle at center. BC: Brown. Watermark: Allegorical head. Printer: BWC (without imprint).	500	1,000	—

1935; 1938 Issue, Chapa 5 and 6

		Good	Fine	XF
149	**50 Escudos** 3.3.1938. Brown-violet and dark blue on multicolor underprint. Arms at center right, Ortigão at right. Chapa 6. Back: Head at left, monastery at center. BC: Blue-green. Watermark: Woman's head. Printer: BWC (without imprint).	40.00	90.00	200

150	100 Escudos	Good	Fine	XF
	21.2.1935; 13.3.1941. Blue-green and brown. João Pinto Ribeiro at left, arms at upper center. Chapa 5. Back: Monument for 1.12.1640 (Restoration of independence) at center, bank arms at right. BC: Dark red. Watermark: Head of Victory from monument. Printer: BWC (without imprint).			
	a. Issued note.	40.00	90.00	225
	s. Specimen. Perforated: *SPECIMEN.*	—	Unc	750

151	500 Escudos	Good	Fine	XF
	26.4.1938. Brown on green and gold underprint. Arms at lower left, Infante Don Henrique in black at right. Chapa 6. Back: Tomb at left center. BC: Green. Watermark: Allegorical head. Printer: W&S (without imprint).	75.00	200	450

152	1000 Escudos	Good	Fine	XF
	17.6.1938. Green on tan and blue underprint. Arms at lower left, portrait M. de Aviz in black at right center, spires at right. Chapa 6. Back: Monastery at center. BC: Brown. Watermark: Woman's head. Printer: W&S (without imprint).			
	a. Issued note.	60.00	125	300
	s. Specimen. Perforated: *SPECIMEN.*	—	Unc	1,200

1941 Issue, Chapa 6 and 6A

153	20 Escudos	Good	Fine	XF
	1941-1959. Green and purple on multicolor underprint. Portrait D. Antonio Luiz de Meneses at right. Chapa 6. Back: Bank arms at center. BC: Green on multicolor underprint. Watermark: Man's head. Printer: BWC (without imprint).			
	a. Signature title at left: *O VICE-GOVERNADOR.* 28.1.1941-25.5.1954.	8.00	15.00	30.00
	b. Signature title at left: *O GOVERNADOR.* 27.1.1959.	8.00	15.00	30.00

154	50 Escudos	Good	Fine	XF
	25.11.1941-28.6.1949. Brown-violet and dark blue on multicolor underprint. Arms at center right, Ortigão at right. Chapa 6A. Similar to #149. BC: Brown-violet and green. Printer: BWC (without imprint).	15.00	30.00	90.00

1942 Issue, Chapa 1 and 7

		Good	Fine	XF
155	**500 Escudos** 29.9.1942. Brown-violet and green on multicolor underprint. Cherubs at center, D. de Goes at right. Chapa 7. Back: Pulpit in Coimbra's Santa Cruz church at center. BC: Blue. Watermark: Bank name repeated. Printer: W&S (without imprint).	35.00	100	225

		Good	Fine	XF
156	**1000 Escudos** 29.9.1942. Dark green and blue on multicolor underprint. Knight and Arab on horseback at left, portrait D. Afonso Henriques at right. Chapa 7. Back: Head at left, ornate tomb at center. BC: Brown. Watermark: Portrait D. Afonso Henriques. Printer: BWC (without imprint).	12.00	40.00	125

		Good	Fine	XF
157	**5000 Escudos** 29.9.1942. Purple and multicolor. Allegorical children at lower left, Queen Dona Leonor at right. Chapa 1. Back: Allegorical figures. Printer: BWC (without imprint). Specimen.	—	—	—

1944 Issue, Chapa 8

		VG	VF	UNC
158	**500 Escudos** 28.11.1944; 11.3.1952. Dark red and black on multicolor underprint. Arms at upper center, D. Joao IV at right. Chapa 8. Back: King and crowd. Watermark: Allegorical head. Printer: BWC (without imprint).	20.00	40.00	100

1947 Issue, Chapa 6

		VG	VF	UNC
159	**100 Escudos** 28.10.1947; 24.10.1950; 22.6.1954; 25.6.1957. Dark green and lilac on multicolor underprint. Arms at upper center, P. Nunes at right. Chapa 6. Back: Fountain in arches at center. BC: Brown. Watermark: P. Nunes. Printer: BWC (without imprint).			
	a. Issued note.	6.00	12.50	30.00
	s. Specimen. Red overprint: *SPECIMEN* and punch hole cancelled.	—	—	500
	ct. Color trial in red-brown on multicolro underprint. Overprinted: *SPECIMEN.*	—	—	650

1953 Issue, Chapa 7

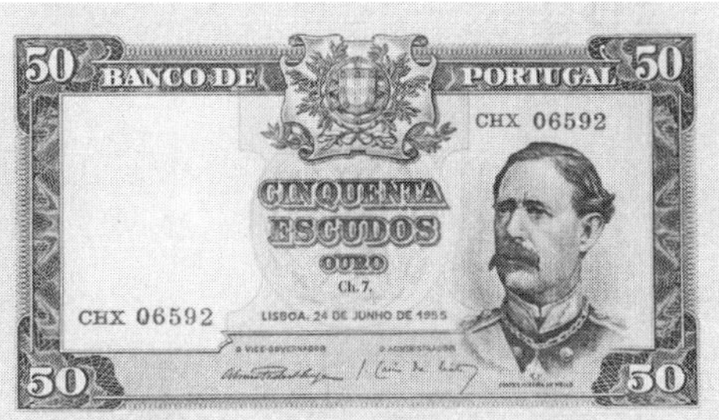

		VG	VF	UNC
160	**50 Escudos** 28.4.1953; 24.6.1955. Blue on multicolor underprint. Arms at top center, Fontes Pereira de Melo at right. Chapa 7. Back: Bank arms at left, statue *The Thinker* at center. BC: Olive and green. Watermark: Profile de Melo. Printer: TDLR (without imprint).	8.00	15.00	35.00

1956 Issue, Chapa 8

		VG	VF	UNC
161	**1000 Escudos** 31.1.1956. Greenish gray and violet on multicolor underprint. Castle at left, arms at lower center, Dona Filipa de Lencastre at right. Chapa 8. Back: Queen in oval at left, Queen and two men at center. BC: Green. Watermark: Man's head. Printer: BWC (without imprint).	10.00	100	200

1958 Issue, Chapa 9

		VG	VF	UNC
162	**500 Escudos** 27.5.1958. Olive-brown on multicolor underprint. D. Francisco de Almeida at right. Chapa 9. Back: Three medieval men at left. BC: Brown. Watermark: D. Francisco de Almeida. Printer: BWC (without imprint).	35.00	150	300

1960; 1961 Issue

		VG	VF	UNC
163	**20 Escudos**			
	26.7.1960. Dark green and purple on multicolor underprint. Portrait of Dom Antonio Luiz de Menezes at right. Chapa 6A. 8 signature varieties. Back: Bank seal at left. BC: Purple and multicolor. Watermark: Portrait of Dom Antonio Luiz de Menezes. Printer: BWC (without imprint).			
	a. Issued note.	15.00	25.00	80.00
	ct. Color trial. Blue and brown on multicolor underprint.	—	—	500

		VG	VF	UNC
164	**50 Escudos**			
	24.6.1960. Blue on multicolor underprint. Arms at upper center, Fontes Pereira de Mello at right. Chapa 7A. 8 signature varieties. Back: Bank seal at upper left, statue *The Thinker* at left. BC: Dark green and multicolor. Watermark: Fontes Pereira de Mello. Printer: TDLR (without imprint).	30.00	90.00	250

Portuguese Guinea (now Guinea-Bissau), a former Portuguese province off the west coast of Africa bounded on the north by Senegal and on the east and southeast by Guinea, had an area of 13,948 sq. mi. (36,125 sq. km.). Capital: Bissau. The province exported peanuts, timber and beeswax. Portuguese Guinea was discovered by Portuguese navigator Nuno Tristao in 1446. Trading rights in the area were granted to Cape Verde islanders but few prominent posts were established before 1851, and they were principally coastal installations. The chief export of this colony's early period was slaves for South America, a practice that adversely affected trade with the native people and retarded subjection of the interior. Territorial disputes with France delayed final demarcation of the colony's frontiers until 1905. The African Party for the Independence of Guinea-Bissau was founded in 1956, and several years later began a guerrilla warfare that grew in effectiveness until 1974, when the rebels controlled most of the colony. Portugal's costly overseas wars in her African territories resulted in a military coup in Portugal in April 1974, that appreciably brightened the prospects for freedom for Guinea-Bissau. In August, 1974, the Lisbon government signed an agreement granting independence to Portuguese Guinea effective Sept. 10, 1974. The new republic took the name of Guinea-Bissau.

RULERS:

Portuguese to 1974

MONETARY SYSTEM:

1 Mil Reis = 1000 Reis to 1910
1 Escudo = 100 Centavos, 1910-1975

STEAMSHIP SEALS

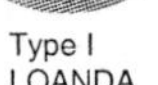

Type I
LOANDA

Type II
LISBOA

Type III
C,C,A

C,C,A = Colonias, Commercio, Agricultura.

PORTUGUESE ADMINISTRATION

Banco Nacional Ultramarino, Guiné

1909 First Issue

		Good	Fine	XF
1	**1 Mil Reis**			
	1.3.1909. Steamship Seal Type I at right. Printer: BWC. 138x81mm. Overprint: *BOLAMA*.	100	300	750
2	**2.5 Mil Reis**			
	1.3.1909. Steamship Seal Type I at right. Printer: BWC. 147x93mm. Overprint: *BOLAMA*.	125	400	850
3	**5 Mil Reis**			
	1.3.1909. Steamship Seal Type I at right. Printer: BWC. 161x101mm. Overprint: *BOLAMA*.	150	600	1,250
4	**10 Mil Reis**			
	1.3.1909. Steamship Seal Type I at right. Printer: BWC. Overprint: *BOLAMA*.	200	750	1,750
5	**20 Mil Reis**			
	1.3.1909. Steamship Seal Type I at right. Printer: BWC. 181x114mm. Overprint: *BOLAMA*.	250	900	—
5B	**50 Mil Reis**			
	1.3.1909. Printer: BWC. 200x121mm. Overprint: *BOLAMA*.	800	2,250	—

1909 Second Issue

		Good	Fine	XF
1A	**1 Mil Reis**			
	1.3.1909. Steamship Seal Type III at right. Printer: BWC. 138x81mm. Overprint: *BOLAMA*.	100	200	550
2A	**2.5 Mil Reis**			
	1.3.1909. Steamship Seal Type III at right. Printer: BWC. 147x93mm. Overprint: *BOLAMA*.	125	325	700
3A	**5 Mil Reis**			
	1.3.1909. Steamship Seal Type III at right. Printer: BWC. 161x101mm. Overprint: *BOLAMA*.	150	425	900
4A	**10 Mil Reis**			
	1.3.1909. Steamship Seal Type III at right. Printer: BWC. 177x106mm. Overprint: *BOLAMA*.	200	600	1,250
5A	**20 Mil Reis**			
	1.3.1909. Steamship Seal Type III at right. Printer: BWC. 181x114mm. Overprint: *BOLAMA*.	250	700	1,750

Color Abbreviation Guide

New to the *Standard Catalog of ® World Paper Money* are the following abbreviations related to color references:

BC: Back color
PC: Paper color

1909 Provisional Issue

No.	Description	Good	Fine	XF
5F	**5 Mil Reis** 1.3.1909. Black on multicolor underprint. Sailing ships at right. 159x101mm. Overprint: Rectangular *PAGAVEL... ces agencias de GUINÉ* on Cape Verde #6b.	—	—	—

1914 First Fractional Issue

No.	Description	Good	Fine	XF
6	**10 Centavos** 5.11.1914. Purple on multicolor underprint. Steamship Seal Type II at bottom center. Printer: BWC. 120x71mm. Overprint: *BOLAMA*.	25.00	100	250

No.	Description	Good	Fine	XF
7	**20 Centavos** 5.11.1914. Blue on multicolor underprint. Steamship Seal Type II. Printer: BWC. 120x71mm. Overprint: *BOLAMA*.	25.00	100	250
8	**50 Centavos** 5.11.1914. Green on multicolor underprint. Steamship Seal Type II. Printer: BWC. 120x71mm. Overprint: *BOLAMA*.	25.00	100	275

1914 Second Fractional Issue

No.	Description	Good	Fine	XF
9	**10 Centavos** 5.11.1914. Purple on multicolor underprint. Like #6 but Steamship Seal Type III. Printer: BWC. 120x71mm. Overprint: *BOLAMA*.	20.00	75.00	200
10	**20 Centavos** 5.11.1914. Blue on multicolor underprint. Like #7 but Steamship Seal Type III. Printer: BWC. 120x71mm. Overprint: *BOLAMA*.	20.00	85.00	225
11	**50 Centavos** 5.11.1914. Green on multicolor underprint. Like #8 but Steamship Seal Type III. Printer: BWC. 120x71mm. Overprint: *BOLAMA*.	20.00	85.00	225

1921 Issue

No.	Description	Good	Fine	XF
12	**1 Escudo** 1.1.1921. Green. Portrait Oliveira Chamico at left. Printer: BWC. 130x81mm. Overprint: *GUINÉ*.	20.00	60.00	175
13	**2 1/2 Escudos** 1.1.1921. Dark blue on yellow and red-violet underprint. Portrait Oliveira Chamico at left. Printer: TDLR. 137x88mm. Overprint: *GUINÉ*.	20.00	80.00	250
14	**5 Escudos** 1.1.1921. Black. Portrait Oliveira Chamico at left. Printer: BWC. 154x94mm. Overprint: *GUINÉ*.	25.00	100	325
15	**10 Escudos** 1.1.1921. Brown. Portrait Oliveira Chamico at left. Printer: BWC. 160x106mm. Overprint: *GUINÉ*.	50.00	150	425
16	**20 Escudos** 1.1.1921. Dark blue. Portrait Oliveira Chamico at left. Printer: BWC. 172x114mm. Overprint: *GUINÉ*.	100	300	700
17	**50 Escudos** 1.1.1921. Blue. Portrait Oliveira Chamico at left. Printer: BWC. 185x121mm. Overprint: *GUINÉ*.	150	500	1,250
18	**100 Escudos** 1.1.1921. Brown. Portrait Oliveira Chamico at left. Printer: BWC. 192x125mm. Overprint: *GUINÉ*.	200	750	1,750

#19, 20 not assigned.

1937 Issue

No.	Description	Good	Fine	XF
21	**10 Escudos** 14.9.1937. Red-brown on multicolor underprint. Portrait J. Texeira Pinto at left. Printer: BWC. 125x75mm. Overprint: *GUINÉ*.	30.00	100	325
22	**20 Escudos** 14.9.1937. Blue on multicolor underprint. Portrait J. Texeira Pinto at left. Printer: BWC. 137x80mm. Overprint: *GUINÉ*.	60.00	200	500
23	**50 Escudos** 14.9.1937. Red on multicolor underprint. Portrait J. Texeira Pinto at left. Printer: BWC. 163x83mm. Overprint: *GUINÉ*.	100	300	750
24	**100 Escudos** 14.9.1937. Purple on multicolor underprint. Portrait J. Texeira Pinto at left. Printer: BWC. 170x97mm. Overprint: *GUINÉ*.	125	400	1,000

1944 Issue

No.	Description	VG	VF	UNC
25	**5 Escudos** 2.11.1944. Olive and multicolor. J. Texeira Pinto at left, steamship seal at right. Printer: BWC. 125x75mm.	15.00	75.00	175

1945 Issue

No.	Description	VG	VF	UNC
26	**2 1/2 Escudos** 2.1.1945. Purple and multicolor. J. Texeira Pinto at left, steamship at right. Printer: BWC. 120x65mm.	10.00	45.00	150
27	**5 Escudos** 16.11.1945. Green. J. Texeira Pinto at left, steamship at right. Printer: BWC. 125x75mm.	15.00	75.00	200
28	**10 Escudos** 16.11.1945. Brown. J. Texeira Pinto at left, steamship at right. Printer: BWC. 125x75mm.	20.00	100	300
29	**20 Escudos** 16.11.1945. Blue. J. Texeira Pinto at left, steamship at right. Printer: BWC. 137x80mm.	25.00	125	350
30	**50 Escudos** 16.11.1945. Yellow and green. J. Texeira Pinto at left, steamship at right. Printer: BWC. 103x83mm.	30.00	150	450
31	**100 Escudos** 16.11.1945. Red. J. Texeira Pinto at left, steamship at right. Printer: BWC. 170x97mm.	40.00	200	600
32	**500 Escudos** 16.11.1945. Green. J. Texeira Pinto at left, steamship at right. Printer: BWC. 200x121mm.	60.00	300	800

1947 Issue

No.	Description	VG	VF	UNC
33	**20 Escudos** 27.3.1947. Blue. J. Texeira Pinto at left, steamship seal at right. Printer: BWC. 137x80mm.	20.00	100	300
34	**50 Escudos** 27.3.1947. Red. J. Texeira Pinto at left, steamship seal at right. Printer: BWC. 163x83mm.	25.00	125	400
35	**100 Escudos** 27.3.1947. Purple. J. Texeira Pinto at left, steamship seal at right. Printer: BWC. 170x97mm.	30.00	150	500
36	**500 Escudos** 27.3.1947. Green. J. Texeira Pinto at left, steamship seal at right. Printer: BWC. 175x100mm.	50.00	250	700

1958 Issue

#	Denomination	VG	VF	UNC
37	**50 Escudos** 20.11.1958. Red, green and multicolor. J. Texeira Pinto at left, steamship seal at right. Serial # prefix B. Printer: BWC. 163x84mm.			
	a. Issued note.	15.00	75.00	250
	s. Specimen, punch hole cancelled.	—	—	125
38	**100 Escudos** 20.11.1958. Purple and multicolor. J. Texeira Pinto at left, steamship seal at right. Serial # prefix B. Printer: BWC. 170x97mm.	VG	VF	UNC
	a. Issued note.	20.00	100	350
	s. Specimen, punch hole cancelled.	—	—	200

#	Denomination	VG	VF	UNC
39	**500 Escudos** 20.11.1958. Green and multicolor. J. Texeira Pinto at left, steamship seal at right. Serial # prefix B. Printer: BWC. 175x100mm.			
	a. Issued note.	40.00	175	500
	s. Specimen, punch hole cancelled.	—	—	275

The former Portuguese possessions of Goa, Daman and Diu (now a union territory of west-central India) occupied an area of 1,441 sq. mi. (3,733 sq. km.) and had a population of about 200,000. Capital: Panaji. It is the site of a fine natural harbor and of iron and manganese deposits. Vasco da Gama, the Portuguese explorer, first visited the west coast of India in 1498. Shortly thereafter the Portuguese arrived in strength and captured Goa (1510), Diu (1535), Daman (1559), and a number of other coastal enclaves and small islands, and for more then a century enjoyed a virtual monopoly on trade. With the arrival of powerful Dutch and English fleets in the first half of the 17th century, Portuguese power in the area declined, until virtually all that remained under Portuguese control were the enclaves of Goa (south of Bombay), Daman (due north of Bombay) and Diu (northwest of Bombay). They were invaded by India in 1961 and annexed to India in 1962.

RULERS:

Portuguese to 1961

MONETARY SYSTEM:

1 Rupia = 16 Tangas = 960 Reis to 1958
1 Escudo = 100 Centavos, 1958-1962

STEAMSHIP SEALS

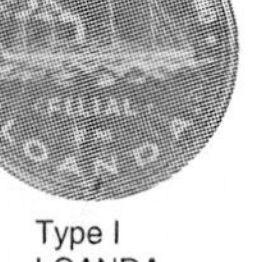

Type I
LOANDA

Type II
LISBOA

Type III
C,C,A

C,C,A = Colonias, Commercio, Agricultura.

PORTUGUESE ADMINISTRATION

Junta da Fazenda Publica

1882 Issue

#	Denomination	Good	Fine	XF
A2	**10 Rupias** 2.11.1882. Portrait King Carlos I at upper center. Rare.	—	—	—
A3	**20 Rupias** 2.11.1882; 3.11.1882. Portrait King Carlos I at upper center. Rare.	—	—	—

Governo Geral do Estado da India

1883 Issue

#	Denomination	Good	Fine	XF
1	**5 Rupias** 1883. 190x117mm. Rare.	—	—	—
2	**10 Rupias** 1883. 190x117mm. Rare.	—	—	—
3	**20 Rupias** 1883. 190x117mm. Rare.	—	—	—
4	**50 Rupias** 1883. 190x117mm. Rare.	—	—	—
5	**100 Rupias** 1883. Rare.	—	—	—
6	**500 Rupias** 1883. Rare.	—	—	—

1896 Issue

#	Description	Good	Fine	XF
7	**5 Rupias** 1.12.1896. Green and black. Portrait King Carlos I at upper center. 190x115mm. Rare.	—	—	—
8	**10 Rupias** 1.12.1896. 190x115mm. Rare.	—	—	—
9	**20 Rupias** 1.12.1896. 190x115mm. Rare.	—	—	—
10	**50 Rupias** 1.12.1896. 190x115mm. Rare.	—	—	—

1899 Issue

#	Description	Good	Fine	XF
11	**5 Rupias** 15.11.1899. Brown and black. Portrait King Carlos I and large *CINCO* at center. 223x121mm. Rare.	—	—	—
12	**10 Rupias** 15.11.1899. 223x121mm. Rare.	—	—	—
13	**20 Rupias** 15.11.1899. 223x121mm. Rare.	—	—	—
14	**50 Rupias** 15.11.1899. 223x121mm. Rare.	—	—	—

Banco Nacional Ultramarino

Nova Goa

#31-34 printer: TDLR. NOTE: Crude reproductions of #32 are forgeries, not an emergency issue.

1906 Issue

#	Description	Good	Fine	XF
15	**5 Rupias** 1.1.1906. Blue and multicolor. Allegorical woman with trident at left. BC: Blue and maroon. Printer: BWC. 185x103mm.			
	a. Steamship seal Type I (1906-18).	—	—	—
	b. Steamship seal Type III (1918-21).	—	—	—

#	Description	Good	Fine	XF
16	**10 Rupias** 1.1.1906. Black and multicolor. Allegorical woman with trident at center. BC: Green and maroon. Printer: BWC. 205x125mm.			
	a. Steamship seal Type I (1906-1918).	—	—	—
	b. Steamship seal Type III (1918-1921).	—	—	—
17	**20 Rupias** 1.1.1906. Black on light green underprint. Allegorical woman with trident at center. Steamship seal Type I (1906-1918). BC: Light brown. Printer: BWC. 205x125mm. Rare.	—	—	—
17A	**20 Rupias** 1.1.1906. Dark blue and multicolor. Allegorical woman with trident at center. Steamship seal Type III (1918-1921). BC: Purple and brown. Printer: BWC. 205x125mm. Rare.	—	—	—
18	**50 Rupias** 1.1.1906. Black and multicolor. Allegorical woman with trident at center. Steamship seal Type I (1906-1918). BC: Maroon and green. Printer: BWC. 205x125mm. Rare.	—	—	—
18A	**50 Rupias** 1.1.1906. Blue on multicolor. Allegorical woman with trident at center. Steamship seal Type III (1918-1921). Printer: BWC. 205x125mm. Rare.	—	—	—

1917 Issue

#	Description	Good	Fine	XF
19	**4 Tangas** 1.10.1917. Red-brown and gre en. Deep green steamship seal Type II. Back: Allegorical woman seated, anchor, sailing ship, sailboat in harbor at center. BC: Olive and maroon. Printer: BWC. 122x71mm.	—	—	375
19A	**4 Tangas** 1.10.1917. Violet and multicolor. Blue steamship seal Type II. Like #19. Back: Allegorical woman seated, anchor, sailing ship, sailboat in harbor at center. BC: Blue and maroon. Printer: BWC. 122x71mm.	—	—	—

#	Description	Good	Fine	XF
20	**8 Tangas** 1.10.1917. Green and red. Back: Allegorical woman seated, anchor, sailing ship, sailboat in harbor at center. BC: Green. Printer: BWC. 122x71mm.	—	—	—
20A	**8 Tangas** 1.10.1917. Blue and multicolor. Back: Allegorical woman seated, anchor, sailing ship, sailboat in harbor at center. BC: Blue and maroon. Printer: BWC. 122x71mm.	—	—	—
21	**1 Rupia** 1.10.1917. Brown. Brown steamship seal Type III. Back: Allegorical woman seated, anchor, sailing ship, sailboat in harbor at center. BC: Red. Printer: BWC. 122x71mm.			
	a. Blue steamship seal Type I.	—	300	750
	b. Blue steamship seal Type II.	—	200	600
21A	**1 Rupia** 1.10.1917. Blue. Brown steamship seal Type III. Like #21. Back: Woman with caduceus seated by globe, cornucopia with produce and anchor at center. BC: Maroon. Printer: BWC. 122x71mm.	—	—	600
22	**2 1/2 Rupias** 1.10.1917. Maroon and multicolor. Dull red steamship seal Type II. Like #22A. BC: Brown. 148x82mm.			
	a. Issued note.	—	1,000	—
	ct. Color trial. Blue on multicolor underprint. Punch hole cancelled.	—	—	5,000

		Good	Fine	XF
22A	**2 1/2 Rupias** 1.10.1917. Red and multicolor. Violet steamship seal Type III. BC: Green. 148x82mm.	—	750	—

W/o Decreto

		Good	Fine	XF
23	**1 Rupia** 1.1.1924. Blue and gold. Tiger head at center. Back: Local building. Printer: TDLR. 145x83mm.			
	a. Issued note.	—	275	350
	s. Specimen. Red overprint: *SPECIMEN* and punch hole cancelled.	—	Unc	2,500

		Good	Fine	XF
24	**2 1/2 Rupias** 1.1.1924. Blue and purple. Tiger head at center.Like #23. Back: Local building. BC: Purple. Printer: TDLR. 145x83mm.			
	a. Issued note.	—	800	1,200
	ct. Color trial. Seperate face and back in blue and gold.	—	—	4,000

		Good	Fine	XF
25	**5 Rupias** 1.1.1924. Green. Palace at center. Back: Tiger. Printer: TDLR. 181x102mm.	—	400	850
26	**10 Rupias** 1.1.1924. Violet and blue. Palace at center. Similar to #25. Back: Tiger. BC: Violet. Printer: TDLR. 181x102mm.	—	450	1,000
27	**20 Rupias** 1.1.1924. Violet and pink. Palace at center. Similar to #25. Back: Tiger. BC: Brownish violet. Printer: TDLR. 181x102mm.	—	600	—
28	**50 Rupias** 1.1.1924. Purple and maroon. Elephant at center. Back: Sailing ship. BC: Purple. Printer: TDLR. 210x115mm. Rare.	—	—	—

		Good	Fine	XF
29	**100 Rupias** 1.1.1924. Purple and brown. Elephant at center. Similar to #28. Back: Sailing ship. BC: Purple. Printer: TDLR. 210x115mm. Rare.	—	—	—
30	**500 Rupias** 1.1.1924. Blue and maroon. Elephant at center. Similar to #28. Back: Sailing ship. BC: Grayish purple. Printer: TDLR. 210x115mm. Rare.	—	—	—

Decreto No. 17 154 (1929)

		Good	Fine	XF
23A	**1 Rupia** 1.1.1924 (1929). Blue and gold. Tiger head at center. Like #23. Back: Local building. Printer: TDLR. 145x83mm.	—	175	250

		Good	Fine	XF
25A	**5 Rupias** 1.1.1924 (1929). Green. Palace at center. Like #25. Back: Tiger. Printer: TDLR. 181x102mm.	—	350	750

		Good	Fine	XF
26A	**10 Rupias** 1.1.1924 (1929). Violet. Palace at center. Like #26. Back: Tiger. Printer: TDLR. 181x102mm.			
	a. Signature titles: *VICE GOVERNADOR* and *GOVERNADOR.*	—	400	850
	b. Signature titles: *ADMINISTRADOR* and *PRESIDENTE DO CONSELHO ADMINISTRATIVO.*	—	450	1,000

1938 Issue

		Good	Fine	XF
31	**5 Rupias** 11.1.1938. Green on lilac underprint. Palace at center. Like #25 but date at upper left. Back: Tiger. 181x102mm.			
	a. Issued note.	—	300	400
	s. Specimen. Red oval TDLR stamp.	—	Unc	5,000

		Good	Fine	XF
32	**10 Rupias** 11.1.1938. Red-violet on blue underprint. Palace at center. Like #26 but date at upper left. Back: Tiger. 181x102mm.	—	400	500

Note: Crude reproductions of #32 are forgeries, not an emergency issue.

		Good	Fine	XF
33	**20 Rupias** 11.1.1938. Olive-brown on peach underprint. Palace at center. Like #27 but date at upper left. Back: Tiger. 181x102mm.			
	a. Issued note.	—	—	600
	s. Specimen. Perforated and punch hole cancelled.	—	Unc	3,500

		Good	Fine	XF
34	**50 Rupias** 11.1.1938. Blue on brown underprint. Elephant at center. Like #28. Back: Sailing ship. 210x115mm. Rare.	—	—	—

India Portuguesa

1945 Issue

		Good	Fine	XF
35	**5 Rupias** 29.11.1945. Green on blue and brown underprint. Steamship seal at upper left, portrait A. de Albuquerque at right. Back: Woman, sailing ships at center, arms at upper right. Printer: BWC. 140x75mm.	—	—	100

		Good	Fine	XF
36	**10 Rupias** 29.11.1945. Brown and multicolor. Steamship seal at upper left, portrait A. de Albuquerque at right. Back: Woman, sailing ships at center, arms at upper right. Printer: BWC. 145x77mm.	—	—	150

		Good	Fine	XF
37	**20 Rupias** 29.11.1945. Blue and multicolor. Steamship seal at upper left, portrait A. de Albuquerque at right. Back: Woman, sailing ships at center, arms at upper right. Printer: BWC. 150x80mm.	—	250	—

		Good	Fine	XF
38	**50 Rupias** 29.11.1945. Dark red and multicolor. Steamship seal at upper left, portrait A. de Albuquerque at right. Back: Woman, sailing ships at center, arms at upper right. Printer: BWC. 155x82mm.	—	450	—

		Good	Fine	XF
39	**100 Rupias** 29.11.1945. Purple and multicolor. Steamship seal at upper left, portrait A. de Albuquerque at right. Back: Woman, sailing ships at center, arms at upper right. Printer: BWC. 160x85mm.	—	500	—

		Good	Fine	XF
40	**500 Rupias** 29.11.1945. Green and multicolor. Steamship seal at upper left, portrait A. de Albuquerque at right. Back: Woman, sailing ships at center, arms at upper right. Printer: BWC. 165x87mm.			
	a. Issued note.	—	850	—
	s. Specimen. Overprint in red: *SPECIMEN* and punch hole cancelled.	—	Unc	2,000

1959 Issue

		VG	VF	UNC
41	**30 Escudos** 2.1.1959. Dark red and multicolor. Portrait A. de Albuquerque at right, steamship seal at upper left. Back: Early explorer, sailing ships at center. Printer: TDLR. 140x75mm.	—	60.00	—

		VG	VF	UNC
42	**60 Escudos** 2.1.1959. Black and multicolor. Portrait A. de Albuquerque at right, steamship seal at upper left. Back: Early explorer, sailing ships at center. Printer: TDLR. 145x75mm.	—	80.00	—

		VG	VF	UNC
43	**100 Escudos** 2.1.1959. Blue and multicolor. Portrait A. de Albuquerque at right, steamship seal at upper left. Back: Early explorer, sailing ships at center. Printer: TDLR. 150x80mm.	—	175	—
44	**300 Escudos** 2.1.1959. Violet and multicolor. Portrait A. de Albuquerque at right, steamship seal at upper left. Back: Early explorer, sailing ships at center. Printer: TDLR. 155x80mm.	—	250	—
45	**600 Escudos** 2.1.1959. Green and multicolor. Portrait A. de Albuquerque at right, steamship seal at upper left. Back: Early explorer, sailing ships at center. Printer: TDLR. 160x85mm.	—	375	—

		VG	VF	UNC
46	**1000 Escudos** 2.1.1959. Brown and multicolor. Portrait A. de Albuquerque at right, steamship seal at upper left. Back: Early explorer, sailing ships at center. Printer: TDLR. 165x85mm.	—	500	—

The Commonwealth of Puerto Rico, the easternmost island of the Greater Antilles in the West Indies, has an area of 3,435 sq. mi. (9,104 sq. km.) and a population of 3.3 million. Capital: San Juan. The commonwealth has its own constitution and elects its own governor. Its people are citizens of the United States, liable to the draft - but not to federal taxation. The chief industries of Puerto Rico are manufacturing, agriculture, and tourism. Manufactured goods, cement, dairy and livestock products, sugar, rum, and coffee are exported, mainly to the United States. Puerto Rico ("Rich Port") was discovered by Columbus who landed on the island and took possession for Spain on Oct. 19, 1493 - the only time Columbus set foot on the soil of what is now a possession of the United States. The first settlement, Caparra, was established by Ponce de Leon in 1508. The early years of the colony were not promising. Considerable gold was found, but the supply was soon exhausted. Efforts to enslave the Indians caused violent reprisals. Hurricanes destroyed crops and homes. French, Dutch, and English freebooters burned the towns. Puerto Rico remained a Spanish possession until 1898, when it was ceded to the United States following the Spanish-American War. Puerto Ricans were granted a measure of self-government and U.S. citizenship in 1917. Effective July 25, 1952, a Congressional resolution elevated Puerto Rico to the status of a free commonwealth associated with the United States. Vieque (or Crab Island), located to the east of Puerto Rico, is the largest of the Commonwealth's major offshore islands. The others are Culebra, a naval station to the east, and Mona to the west.

RULERS:

Spanish, 1493-1898 United States of America, 1898-present

MONETARY SYSTEM:

1 Peso = 5 Pesetas = 100 Centavos to 1898
1 Dollar = 100 Cents, 1898-

SPANISH ADMINISTRATION

Tesorería Nacional

1812 Issue

		Good	Fine	XF
1	**8 Reales** 1812. Black. Arms in circle of dots at center. Rare.	—	—	—

1813 Issue

		Good	Fine	XF
2	**8 Reales** 1813. Black. Paschal lamb at center.			
	a. White paper.	—	—	—
	b. Blue paper. Rare.	—	—	—

Decrees of 3.9.1811 and 29.6.1813

Issued in 1814.

		Good	Fine	XF
3	**3 Pesos** 1814 (Roman Numerals). Black. Uniface, vertical format. Rare.	—	—	—

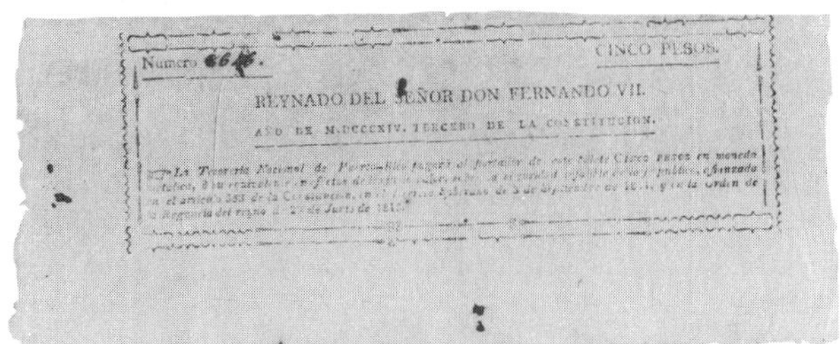

		Good	Fine	XF
4	**5 Pesos** 1814 (Roman Numerals). Black. Uniface, horizontal format. Rare.	—	—	—

1815-1819 Issue

#	Denomination	Good	Fine	XF
5	**3 Pesos** July 1815; 4.8.1815. Black. Crowned Spanish arms at upper center. Uniface. Printer: Murray Draper Fairman.	1,500	3,000	6,000

#	Denomination	Good	Fine	XF
6	**5 Pesos** 25.7.1819; 31.7.1819. Black. Portrait King Ferdinand VII at top center. Uniface. Printer: Murray Draper Fairman.	1,500	3,000	6,000

Ministerio de Ultramar

1895 Billete De Canje

Circulating Bill

#	Denomination	Good	Fine	XF
7	**1 Peso** 17.8.1895. Black on yellow underprint. Portrait man at left. Back: Crowned arms of Spain at center. BC: Blue.			
	a. With full counterfoil.	55.00	150	350
	b. With partial counterfoil.	45.00	135	325
	c. Without counterfoil.	40.00	120	285

Banco Español de Puerto Rico

Series A

#	Denomination	Good	Fine	XF
8	**5 Pesos** ND (ca.1889). Black on green and yellow underprint. Paschal lamb at left. Seated child painting at right. Back: Crowned Spanish arms at left. BC: Green. Printer: ABNC. Specimen or proof.	—	—	—

#	Denomination	Good	Fine	XF
9	**10 Pesos** ND (ca.1889). Black on yellow and brown underprint. Paschal lamb at left. Two coastwatchers at right. Back: Crowned Spanish arms at center. BC: Brown. Printer: ABNC.			
	a. Issued note.	—	—	—
	p. Proof.	—	—	—
10	**20 Pesos** ND (ca.1889). Black on orange and yellow underprint. Paschal lamb at left. Three men lifting crate at upper center. Back: Crowned Spanish arms at center. BC: Orange. Printer: ABNC. Specimen or proof.	—	—	—
11	**50 Pesos** ND (ca.1889). Black on blue and yellow underprint. Paschal lamb at left. Columbus sighting land at center right. Back: Crowned Spanish arms at center. BC: Blue. Printer: ABNC. Proof.	—	—	—
12	**100 Pesos** ND (ca.1889). Black on yellow and brown underprint. Man with globe and map at left, two allegorical women at center. Paschal lamb at right. Back: Crowned Spanish arms at center. BC: Brown. Printer: ABNC. Proof.	—	—	—
13	**200 Pesos** ND (ca.1889). Black on orange and yellow underprint. Justice at left, seated woman with globe at center. Paschal lamb at right. Back: Crowned Spanish arms at center. BC: Orange. Printer: ABNC. Archive copy.	—	—	—

Series B

#	Denomination	Good	Fine	XF
14	**5 Pesos** ND. Black on brown and yellow underprint. Paschal lamb at left. Seated child painting at right. Like #8. Back: Crowned Spanish arms at left. BC: Brown. Printer: ABNC. Archive copy.	—	—	—
15	**10 Pesos** ND. Black on yellow and blue underprint. Paschal lamb at left. Two coastwatchers at right. Like #9. Back: Crowned Spanish arms at center. BC: Tan. Printer: ABNC. Archive copy.	—	—	—
16	**20 Pesos** ND. Black on orange and blue underprint. Paschal lamb at left. Three men lifting crate at upper center. Like #10. Back: Crowned Spanish arms at center. BC: Blue. Printer: ABNC. Archive copy.	—	—	—
17	**50 Pesos** ND. Black on brown and yellow underprint. Paschal lamb at left. Columbus sighting land at center right. Like #11. Back: Crowned Spanish arms at center. BC: Blue. Printer: ABNC. Specimen.	—	—	—
18	**100 Pesos** ND. Black on yellow and red underprint. Man with globe and map at left, two allegorical women at center. Paschal lamb at right. Like #12. Back: Crowned Spanish arms at center. BC: Red. Printer: ABNC. Archive copy.	—	—	—
19	**200 Pesos** ND. Black on green and yellow underprint. Justice at left, seated woman with globe at center. Paschal lamb at right. Like #13. Back: Crowned Spanish arms at center. BC: Green. Printer: ABNC. Archive copy.	—	—	—

Series C

#	Denomination	Good	Fine	XF
20	**5 Pesos** ND. Black on red and yellow underprint. Paschal lamb at left. Seated child painting at right. Like #8. Back: Crowned Spanish arms at left. BC: Tan. Printer: ABNC. Archive copy.	—	—	—
21	**10 Pesos** ND. Black on green and red underprint. Paschal lamb at left. Two coastwatchers at right. Like #9. Back: Crowned Spanish arms at center. BC: Blue. Printer: ABNC. Archive copy.	—	—	—
22	**20 Pesos** ND. Black on orange and brown underprint. Paschal lamb at left. Three men lifting crate at upper center. Like #10. Back: Crowned Spanish arms at center. BC: Brown. Printer: ABNC. Archive copy.	—	—	—
23	**50 Pesos** ND. Black on red and yellow underprint. Paschal lamb at left. Columbus sighting land at center right. Like #11. Back: Crowned Spanish arms at center. BC: Red. Printer: ABNC. Specimen or proof.	—	—	—
24	**100 Pesos** ND. Black on yellow and green underprint. Man with globe and map at left, two allegorical women at center. Paschal lamb at right. Like #12. Back: Crowned Spanish arms at center. BC: Green. Printer: ABNC. Specimen or proof.	—	—	—
25	**200 Pesos** ND. Black on brown and yellow underprint. Justice at left, seated woman with globe at center. Paschal lamb at right. Like #13. Back: Crowned Spanish arms at center. BC: Brown. Printer: ABNC. Specimen.	—	—	—

1894 Series D

#	Denomination	Good	Fine	XF
26	**5 Pesos** 1.12.1894; 2.3.1896; 3.11.1896; 1.7.1897. Black on brown and yellow underprint. Portrait Queen mother and regent of Spain's Maria Christina at left. Seated child painting at right. Similar to #8. Back: Crowned Spanish arms at left. BC: Brown. Printer: ABNC.			
	a. Issued note.	—	—	—
	b. Overprint: *MAYAGUEZ*. 1.12.1894.	—	—	—

No.	Description	Good	Fine	XF
27	**10 Pesos** 1894-1897. Black on blue and yellow underprint. Portrait Queen mother and regent of Spain's Maria Christina at left. Two coastwatchers at right. Similar to #9. Back: Crowned Spanish arms at center. BC: Orange. Printer: ABNC.			
	a. Issued note.	—	—	—
	p. Uniface face proof. Punch hole cancelled.	—	—	2,000
28	**20 Pesos** 1894-1897. Black on blue and yellow underprint. Portrait Queen mother and regent of Spain's Maria Christina at left. Three men lifting crate at upper center. Similar to #10. Back: Crowned Spanish arms at center. BC: Blue. Printer: ABNC. Specimen or proof.	—	—	—
29	**50 Pesos** 1894-1897. Black on brown and yellow underprint. Portrait Queen mother and regent of Spain's Maria Christina at left. Columbus sighting land at center right. Similar to #11. Back: Crowned Spanish arms at center. BC: Brown. Printer: ABNC. Specimen or proof.	—	—	—
30	**100 Pesos** 1894-1897. Black on orange and yellow underprint. Man with globe and map at left, two allegorical women at center. Portrait Queen mother and regent of Spain's Maria Christina at right. Similar to #12. Back: Crowned Spanish arms at center. BC: Orange. Specimen or proof.	—	—	—
31	**200 Pesos** 1895-1897. Black on green and yellow underprint. Justice at left, seated woman with globe at center. Portrait Queen mother and regent of Spain's Maria Christina at right. Similar to #13. Back: Crowned Spanish arms at center. BC: Green. Specimen.	—	—	—

UNITED STATES ADMINISTRATION

Banco Español de Puerto Rico

1900 Provisional Issue

No.	Description	Good	Fine	XF
32	**5 Pesos** 1.5.1900. Black on red and yellow underprint. Paschal lamb at left. Seated child painting at right. Series C. Back: Crowned Spanish arms at left. BC: Tan. Overprint: *MONEDA AMERICANA* on #20.	—	—	—

First National Bank of Porto Rico at San Juan

1902 Third Charter Period

No.	Description	Good	Fine	XF
33	**10 Dollars** 1902. Black. Portrait McKinley at left. Red seal at lower right. BC: Deep green. Rare.	—	—	—
34	**20 Dollars** 1902. Black. Portrait McCulloch at left. Red seal at lower right. BC: Deep green. Rare.	—	—	—
35	**50 Dollars** 1902. Black. Portrait Sherman at left. Red seal at lower right. BC: Deep green. Unique.	—	—	—
36	**100 Dollars** 27.10.1902. Black. Portrait Knox at left. Red seal at lower right. BC: Green. Unique.	—	—	—

1908 Issue

#37-40 Dates *1902, 1908* on back. Designs like #33-36.

No.	Description	Good	Fine	XF
37	**10 Dollars** 27.10.1902. Black. Portrait McKinley at left. Blue seal at lower right. BC: Green. Unique.	—	—	—
38	**20 Dollars** ca.1908. Black. Portrait McCulloch at left. Blue seal at lower right. BC: Green. Requires confirmation.	—	—	—
39	**50 Dollars** ca.1908. Black. Portrait Sherman at left. Blue seal at lower right. BC: Green. Requires confirmation.	—	—	—
40	**100 Dollars** ca.1908. Black. Portrait Knox at left. Blue seal at lower right. BC: Green. Requires confirmation.	—	—	—

Banco de Puerto Rico

1901-1904 Series E

No.	Description	Good	Fine	XF
41	**5 Pesos = 5 Dollars** 1.7.1904. Black on orange underprint. Seated woman holding scale by cornucopia with money and chest at center. With "U.S. Cy." (U.S. Currency). Back: Paschal lamb at center. BC: Orange. Printer: ABNC.	1,250	3,000	—
42	**10 Pesos = 10 Dollars** ND (ca.1901-1904). Black on brown and yellow underprint. Seated allegorical woman with marine implements at center. With "U.S. Cy." (U.S. Currency). Back: Paschal lamb at center. BC: Brown. Printer: ABNC. Proof.	—	—	—
43	**20 Pesos = 20 Dollars** ND (ca.1901-1904). Black on blue and yellow underprint. Seated allegorical woman with harvest at center. With "U.S. Cy." (U.S. Currency). Back: Paschal lamb at center. BC: Blue. Printer: ABNC. Proof.	—	—	—
44	**50 Pesos = 50 Dollars** ND (ca.1901-1904). Black on olive and yellow underprint. Train, allegorical women with industrial implements, and sailing ships at center right. With "U.S. Cy." (U.S. Currency). Back: Paschal lamb at center. BC: Olive. Printer: ABNC. Archive copy.	—	—	—
45	**100 Pesos = 100 Dollars** ND (ca.1901-1904). Black on olive and red underprint. Allegorical woman with sacks and barrels at center. With "U.S. Cy." (U.S. Currency). Back: Paschal lamb at center. BC: Red. Printer: ABNC. Proof.	—	—	—
46	**200 Pesos = 200 Dollars** ND (ca.1901-1904). Black on yellow and purple underprint. Cherub at upper left and right, allegorical woman with plants and bird at center. With "U.S. Cy." (U.S. Currency). Back: Paschal lamb at center. BC: Purple. Printer: ABNC. Proof.	—	—	—

1909 Series F

No.	Description	Good	Fine	XF
47	**5 Dollars** 1.7.1909. Black. Portrait Columbus at left, red Paschal lamb seal at right. Back: Seated woman with lamb at center. BC: Green. Printer: ABNC.			
	a. Issued note.	600	1,750	4,250
	b. Cancelled with overprint: *CANCELADO* with or without punch holes.	400	1,000	2,000
	p. 1907. Uniface proofs. (ABNC Archive sale.)	—	Unc	5,000
	s. Specimen.	—	Unc	7,500

48	10 Dollars	Good	Fine	XF
	1.7.1909. Black. Ponce de Leon at left, red Paschal lamb seal at right. Back: Liberty at center. BC: Brown. Printer: ABNC.			
	a. Issued note.	1,000	2,750	—
	b. Cancelled with punch holes.	500	1,400	—
	p. 1907. Uniface proofs. (ABNC Archive sale.	—	Unc	5,000
	s. Specimen.	—	Unc	7,500

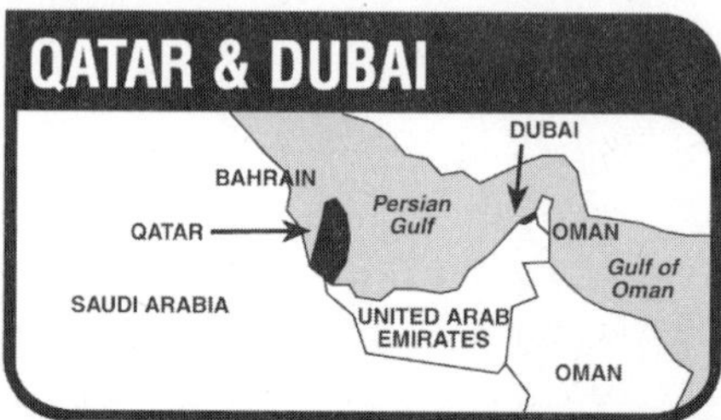

The State of Qatar, which occupies the Qatar Peninsula jutting into the Persian Gulf from eastern Saudi Arabia, has an area of 4,247 sq. mi. (11,000 sq. km.) and a population of 382,000. Capital: Doha. The traditional occupations of pearling, fishing and herding have been replaced in economics by petroleum-related industries. Crude oil, petroleum products, and tomatoes are exported.

Dubai is one of the seven sheikhdoms comprising the United Arab Emirates (formerly Trucial States) located along the southern shore of the Persian Gulf. It has a population of about 60,000. Qatar, which initiated protective treaty relations with Great Britain in 1820, achieved independence on Sept. 3, 1971, upon withdrawal of the British military presence from the Persian Gulf, and replaced its special treaty arrangement with Britain with a treaty of general friendship. Dubai attended independence on Dec. 1, 1971, upon termination of Britain's protective treaty with the trucial sheikhdoms, and on Dec. 2, 1971, entered into the union of the United Arab Emirates.

Despite the fact that the sultanate of Qatar and the sheikhdom of Dubai were merged under a monetary union, the two territories were governed independently from each other. Qatar now uses its own currency while Dubai uses the United Arab Emirates currency and coins.

The Department of Reunion, an overseas department of France located in the Indian Ocean 400 miles (640 km.) east of Madagascar, has an area of 969 sq. mi. (2,510 sq. km.) and a population of 556,000. Capital: Saint-Denis. The island's volcanic soil is extremely fertile. Sugar, vanilla, coffee and rum are exported. Although first visited by Portuguese navigators in the 16th century, Reunion was uninhabited when claimed for France by Capt. Goubert in 1638. It was first colonized as Isle de Burbon by the French in 1662 as a layover station for ships rounding the Cape of Good Hope to India. It was renamed Reunion in 1793.

The island remained in French possession except for the period of 1810-15, when it was occupied by the British. Reunion became an overseas department of France in 1946, and in 1958 voted to continue that status within the new French Union. Baque du France notes were introduced 1.1.1973.

MONETARY SYSTEM:

1 Riyal = 100 Dirhem

SULTANATE AND SHEIKHDOM

Qatar and Dubai Currency Board

1960s ND Issue

1	1 Riyal	VG	VF	UNC
	ND. Dark green on multicolor underprint. Dhow, derrick and palm tree at left. Watermark: Falcon's head.			
	a. Issued note.	45.00	150	450
	s. Specimen, punch hole cancelled.	—	—	2,500
2	**5 Riyals**	**VG**	**VF**	**UNC**
	ND. Purple on multicolor underprint. Dhow, derrick and palm tree at left. Watermark: Falcon's head.			
	a. Issued note.	200	1,000	3,500
	s. Specimen, punch hole cancelled.	—	—	3,500

3	10 Riyals	VG	VF	UNC
	ND. Gray-blue on multicolor underprint. Dhow, derrick and palm tree at left. Watermark: Falcon's head.			
	a. Issued note.	200	500	3,000
	s. Specimen, punch hole cancelled.	—	—	3,000

		VG	VF	UNC
4	**25 Riyals** ND. Blue on multicolor underprint. Dhow, derrick and palm tree at left. Watermark: Falcon's head.			
	a. Issued note.	1,500	6,000	75,000
	s. Specimen, punch hole cancelled. Rare.	—	—	—

		VG	VF	UNC
5	**50 Riyals** ND. Red on multicolor underprint. Dhow, derrick and palm tree at left. Watermark: Falcon's head.			
	a. Issued note.	2,250	4,500	60,000
	s. Specimen, punch hole cancelled. Rare.	—	—	—

		VG	VF	UNC
6	**100 Riyals** ND. Olive on multicolor underprint. Dhow, derrick and palm tree at left. Watermark: Falcon's head.			
	a. Issued note.	1,000	2,500	7,500
	s. Specimen, punch hole cancelled. Rare.	—	—	—

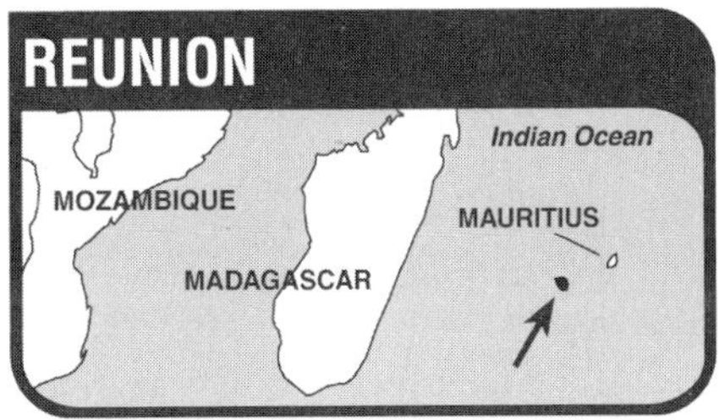

The Department of Reunion, an overseas department of France located in the Indian Ocean 400 miles (640 km.) east of Madagascar, has an area of 969 sq. mi. (2,510 sq. km.) and a population of 556,000. Capital: Saint-Denis. The island's volcanic soil is extremely fertile. Sugar, vanilla, coffee and rum are exported. Although first visited by Portuguese navigators in the 16th century, Reunion was uninhabited when claimed for France by Capt. Goubert in 1638. It was first colonized as Isle de Bourbon by the French in 1662 as a layover station for ships rounding the Cape of Good Hope to India. It was renamed Reunion in 1793. The island remained in French possession except for the period of 1810-1815, when it was occupied by the British. Reunion became an overseas department of France in 1946, and in 1958 voted to continue that status within the new French Union. Banque de France notes were introduced 1.1.1973.

RULERS:

French, 1638-1810, 1815-
British, 1810-1815

MONETARY SYSTEM:

1 Franc = 100 Centimes
1 Nouveau Franc = 50 Old Francs, 1960

FRENCH ADMINISTRATION

Ile De La Réunion - Trésor Colonial

Decret du 2.5.1879 (1884 First Issue)

		Good	Fine	XF
1	**50 Centimes** 8.7.1884. Black. Uniface.	150	450	—
2	**1 Franc** 8.7.1884. Black. Like #1. 2 plate varieties. Uniface.	165	500	—
3	**2 Francs** 8.7.1884. Black. Uniface. BC: Yellow.	200	600	—

		Good	Fine	XF
4	**3 Francs** 4.6.1884. Black. Uniface. BC: Green.	—	—	—

Note: Denominations of 30, 50 and 100 Francs need to be confirmed.

Decret du 2.5.1879 (1884 Second Issue)

		Good	Fine	XF
5	**50 Centimes** 4.6 1884. Black. PC: Cream.	450	—	—
6	**1 Franc** 4.6.1884. Black. PC: Dark blue.	500	—	—
7	**2 Francs** 4.6.1884. Black. PC: Gray.	550	—	—

Color Abbreviation Guide

New to the *Standard Catalog of ® World Paper Money* are the following abbreviations related to color references:

BC: Back color
PC: Paper color

1886 Issue

#	Description	Good	Fine	XF
8	**50 Centimes** 21.6.1886. Black. Cherub with pillar and cornucopia at left and right, allegories of Agriculture and Commerce at center. Back: Head at left and right, value over anchor at center. PC: Light gray.	150	450	—
9	**1 Franc** 10.3.1886. Black. Cherub with pillar and cornucopia at left and right, allegories of Agriculture and Commerce at center. Back: Head at left and right, value over anchor at center. PC: Pale blue or light green.	185	550	—

#	Description	Good	Fine	XF
10	**2 Francs** 1886. Black. Cherub with pillar and cornucopia at left and right, allegories of Agriculture and Commerce at center. Back: Head at left and right, value over anchor at center.	225	675	—

Banque de la Réunion

Law of 12.9.1873

#	Description	Good	Fine	XF
11	**5 Francs** *L. 1873.* Border of trees and cornucopia. Uniface. PC: Brown.	—	—	—
12	**10 Francs** *L.1873.* Border of flowers and three cherubs. Uniface. PC: White.	—	—	—

Law of 1874

#	Description	Good	Fine	XF
13	**5 Francs** *L.1874* (1890-1912). Blue. Medallic head at left and right. 10 signature varieties.	200	—	—

Law of 1901

#	Description	Good	Fine	XF
14	**5 Francs** *L1901* (1912-1944). Red. Medallic head at left and right. Like #13. 6 signature varieties. BC: Gray.	20.00	60.00	150

1874; 1875 Issue

#	Description	Good	Fine	XF
15	**25 Francs** ND (1876-1908). Blue. Flowers and fruit with landscape in background. 3 signature varieties. BC: Brown.	250	550	1,650
16	**100 Francs** ND (1874-1917). Red. Flowers and fruit with landscape in background. 6 signature varieties. Like #15. Rare.	—	—	—
17	**500 Francs** ND (1875-1929). Black on cream underprint. Flowers and fruit with landscape in background. 5 signature varieties. Like #16. Rare.	—	—	—

1912; 1914 Issue

#	Description	Good	Fine	XF
18	**25 Francs** ND (1912-1930). Blue with black text. Flowers and fruit with landscape in background. 5 signature varieties. Like #15. BC: Maroon.	175	500	—
19	**100 Francs** ND (1914-1929). Maroon. Flowers and fruit with landscape in background. 4 signature varieties. Like #16. BC: Blue. Rare.	—	—	—

1917 Emergency WWI Fractional Issue

#	Description	VG	VF	UNC
20	**5 Centimes** ND (1917). Black. Embossed seal. Uniface. PC: Red cardboard.	15.00	70.00	200
21	**10 Centimes** ND (1917). Black. Embossed seal. Uniface. PC: Brown cardboard.	35.00	125	350

#22 not assigned.

1923-1930 Issue

#	Description	Good	Fine	XF
23	**25 Francs** ND (1930-1944). Purple and multicolor. Woman wearing wreath at center, flowers and fruit in background. 4 signature varieties.	40.00	150	500

#	Description	Good	Fine	XF
24	**100 Francs** ND (1926-1944). Multicolor. Woman with staff at left. 5 signature varieties.	150	400	1,000
25	**500 Francs** ND (1923-1944). Multicolor. Woman with staff at left. 5 signature varieties. Like #24.	225	700	—

1937-1940 Emergency Circulating Bearer Check Issue

#	Description	Good	Fine	XF
26	**100 Francs** 29.11.1937; 8.10.1940; 5.11.1940. Rare. PC: Apricot.	—	—	—
27	**500 Francs** 29.11.1937; 8.10.1940; 5.11.1940; 25.11.1940. Rare.	—	—	—
28	**1000 Francs** 29.11.1937; 8.10.1940; 5.11.1940. Rare.	—	—	—
29	**5000 Francs** 8.10.1940; 5.11.1940. Rare.	—	—	—

Note: An issue of circulating checks dated 1932 in denominations of 100, 500 and 1000 Francs requires confirmation.

VICHY FRENCH GOVERNMENT

Banque de la Réunion

Arreté Local Du 8.10.1942

#	Description	Good	Fine	XF
30	**50 Centimes** *L. 1942.* Light purple underprint. Francisque (Vichy axe) at upper left and right.	175	400	900
31	**1 Franc** *L. 1942.* Light blue underprint. Francisque (Vichy axe) at upper left and right.	175	400	900

#	Description	Good	Fine	XF
32	**2 Francs** *L. 1942.* Orange underprint. Francisque (Vichy axe) at upper left and right.	175	400	900

FREE FRENCH GOVERNMENT

Banque de la Réunion

1942 ND Issue

#	Description	Good	Fine	XF
32A	**2 Francs** ND (-old date 8.10.1942). Orange underprint. Cross of Lorraine in black at upper left and right. Like #35. Overprint: Black line on *Décret du 8 October 1942.* Rare.	—	—	—

Arreté Local Du 12.8.1943

#	Description	Good	Fine	XF
33	**50 Centimes** *L. 1943.* Light purple underprint. Cross of Lorraine in red at upper left and right.	160	325	725
34	**1 Franc** *L. 1943.* Light blue underprint. Cross of Lorraine in red at upper left and right.	160	325	725
35	**2 Francs** *L. 1943.* Orange underprint. Cross of Lorraine in red at upper left and right.	160	325	725

Caisse Centrale de la France Libre

1943 ND Provisional Issue

Ordonnace du 2.12.1941

#	Description	Good	Fine	XF
36	**5 Francs** *L.1941* (ca. 1943). Type of French Equatorial Africa #10. Serial # AN 100 001-AN 260 000. Printer: BWC (without imprint).	20.00	60.00	—
37	**100 Francs** *L.1941* (1944-1945). Type of French Equatorial Africa #13. Printer: BWC (without imprint).			
	a. Serial # range PA 270 001 - PA 470 000. (July 1944).	50.00	150	—
	b. Serial # range PB 700 001 - PB 900 000. (Jan. 1945).	70.00	150	—
	c. Serial # range PE 590 001 - PF 090 000. (31.12.1945).	70.00	150	—
38	**1000 Francs** *L.1941* (ca. 1943). Type of French Equatorial Africa #14. Serial TA 030 001-TA 060 000; TA 215 001-TA 235 000; TA 255 001-TA 275 000. Printer: BWC (without imprint).	400	1,000	2,000

Note: See also St. Pierre & Miquelon #10-14.

Caisse Centrale de la France d'Outre-Mer

1944 ND Provisional Issue

Ordonnance du 2.2.1944

#	Description	Good	Fine	XF
39	**100 Francs** *L.1944.* Similar to French Equatorial Africa #18. Printer: BWC (without imprint).			
	a. Serial # PQ 200 001 - PQ 700 000.	50.00	150	—
	b. Serial # PS 700 001 - PS 800 000.	50.00	150	—
40	**1000 Francs** *L.1944.* Similar to French Equatorial Africa #19. Serial # TD 125 001 - TD 135 000; TD 185 001 - TD 235 000. Printer: BWC (without imprint).	700	1,500	—

Note: See also St. Pierre & Miquelon #15-18.

1947 ND Issue

#	Description	VG	VF	UNC
41	**5 Francs** ND (1947). Blue and multicolor. Ship at left, Bougainville at right. Back: Woman with fruit and house.			
	a. Issued note.	7.50	40.00	165
	s. Specimen.	—	—	90.00
42	**10 Francs** ND (1947). Blue and multicolor. Colbert at left, ships at right. Back: River scene and plants.			
	a. Issued note.	7.50	50.00	185
	s. Specimen.	—	—	100
43	**20 Francs** ND (1947). Brown and multicolor. Four people with huts at left. E. Gentil at right. Back: Two men.			
	a. Issued note.	10.00	60.00	200
	s. Specimen.	—	—	110

44	50 Francs	VG	VF	UNC
	ND (1947). Multicolor. B d'Esnambuc at left, ship at right. Back: Woman.			
	a. Issued note.	10.00	50.00	250
	s. Specimen.	—	—	150

45	100 Francs	VG	VF	UNC
	ND (1947). Multicolor. La Bourdonnais at left, two women at right. Back: Woman looking at mountains.			
	a. Issued note.	15.00	75.00	350
	s. Specimen.	—	—	175

46	500 Francs	VG	VF	UNC
	ND (1947). Multicolor. Buildings and sailboat at left, two women at right. Back: Ox-carts with wood and plants.			
	a. Issued note.	40.00	125	500
	s. Specimen.	—	—	225

47	1000 Francs	VG	VF	UNC
	ND (1947). Multicolor. Two women at right. Back: Woman at right, two men in small boat.			
	a. Issued note.	50.00	150	675
	s. Specimen.	—	—	250

Color Abbreviation Guide

New to the *Standard Catalog of® World Paper Money* are the following abbreviations related to color references:

BC: Back color

PC: Paper color

48	5000 Francs	VG	VF	UNC
	ND (1947). Brown and multicolor. Gen. Schoelcher at center right. Back: Family.			
	a. Issued note.	125	350	1,100
	s. Specimen.	—	—	375

Institut d'Emission des Départements d'Outre-Mer

1960 ND Provisional Issue

49	100 Francs	VG	VF	UNC
	ND (1960). Multicolor. La Bourdonnais at left, two women at right. Like #45. Back: Woman looking at mountains.			
	a. Issued note.	25.00	100	300
	s. Specimen.	—	—	200

50	5000 Francs	VG	VF	UNC
	ND (1960). Brown and multicolor. Gen. Schoelcher at center right. Like #48. Back: Family.			
	a. Issued note.	100	300	1,000
	s. Specimen.	—	—	450

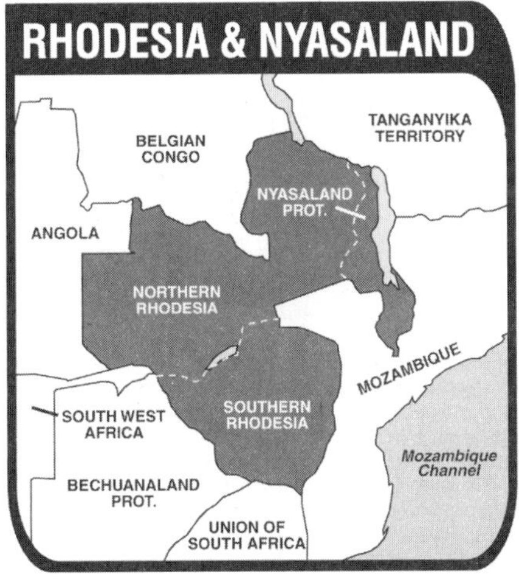

Rhodesia and Nyasaland (now the Republics of Malawi, Zambia and Zimbabwe) was located in the east-central part of southern Africa, had an area of 487,133 sq. mi. (1,261,678 sq. km.). Capital: Salisbury. The area was the habitat of paleolithic man, contains extensive evidence of earlier civilizations, notably the world-famous ruins of Zimbabwe, a gold-trading center that flourished about the 14th or 15th century AD. The Portuguese of the 16th century were the first Europeans to attempt to develop south-central Africa, but it remained for Cecil Rhodes and the British South Africa Co. to open the hinterlands. Rhodes obtained a concession for mineral rights from local chiefs in 1888 and administered his African empire (named Southern Rhodesia in 1895) through the British South Africa Co. until 1923, when the British government annexed the area after the white settlers voted for existence as a separate entity, rather than for incorporation into the Union of South Africa. From Sept. of 1953 through 1963 Southern Rhodesia was joined with the British protectorates of Northern Rhodesia and Nyasaland into a multiracial federation. When the federation was dissolved at the end of 1963, Northern Rhodesia and Nyasaland became the independent states of Zambia and Malawi.

Britain was prepared to grant independence to Southern Rhodesia but declined to do so when the politically dominant white Rhodesians refused to give assurances of representative government. On May 11, 1965, following two years of unsuccessful negotiation with the British government, Prime Minister Ian Smith issued a unilateral declaration of independence. Britain responded with economic sanctions supported by the United Nations. After further futile attempts to effect an accommodation, the Rhodesian Parliament severed all ties with Britain, and on March 2, 1970, established the Republic of Rhodesia.

On March 3, 1978, Prime Minister Ian Smith and three moderate black nationalist leaders signed an agreement providing for black majority rule. The name of the country was changed to Zimbabwe Rhodesia.

After the election of March 3, 1980, the country again changed its name to the Republic of Zimbabwe. The Federation of Rhodesia and Nyasaland (or the Central African Federation), comprising the British protectorates of Northern Rhodesia and Nyasaland and the self-governing colony of Southern Rhodesia, was located in the east-central part of southern Africa. The multiracial federation had an area of about 487,000 sq. mi. (1,261,330 sq. km.) and a population of 6.8 million. Capital: Salisbury, in Southern Rhodesia. The geographical unity of the three British possessions suggested the desirability of political and economic union as early as 1924. Despite objections by the African constituency of Northern Rhodesia and Nyasaland, who feared the dominant influence of prosperous and self governing Southern Rhodesia, the Central African Federation was established in Sept. of 1953. As feared, the Federation was effectively and profitably dominated by the European constituency of Southern Rhodesia despite the fact that the three component countries retained their basic pre-federation political structure. It was dissolved at the end of 1963, largely because of the effective opposition of the Nyasaland African Congress. Northern Rhodesia and Nyasaland became independent states of Zambia and Malawi in 1964. Southern Rhodesia unilaterally declared its independence as Rhodesia the following year; this act was not recognized by the British Government.

RULERS:

British to 1963

MONETARY SYSTEM:

1 Shilling = 12 Pence
1 Pound = 20 Shillings to 1963

BRITISH ADMINISTRATION

Bank of Rhodesia and Nyasaland

1956 Issue

20	10 Shillings	VG	VF	UNC
	1956-1961. Reddish brown on multicolor underprint. Fish eagle at lower left. Portrait of Queen Elizabeth II at right. Back: River scene. Watermark: Cecil Rhodes. Printer: BWC.			
	a. Signature A. P. Grafftey-Smith. 3.4.1956-17.6.1960.	125	550	2,300
	b. Signature B. C. J. Richards. 30.12.1960-1.2.1961.	135	600	2,400
	s. As a. Specimen punch hole cancelled. 3.4.1956.	—	—	1,600
	ct. Color trial. Green on pink underprint.	—	—	2,150

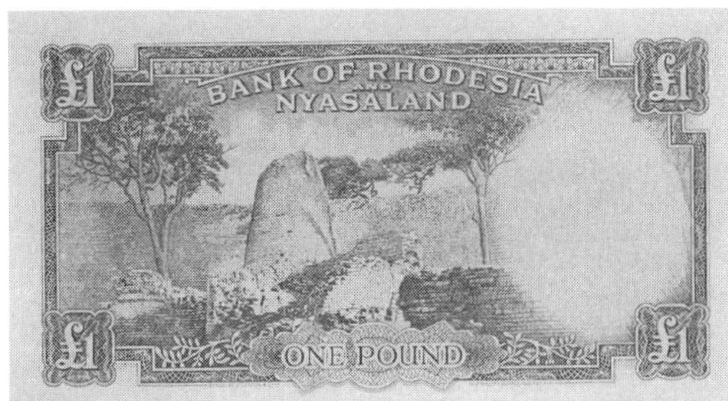

21	1 Pound	VG	VF	UNC
	1956-1961. Green on multicolor underprint. Leopard at lower left. Portrait of Queen Elizabeth II at right. Back: Zimbabwe ruins at center. Watermark: Cecil Rhodes. Printer: BWC.			
	a. Signature A. P. Grafftey-Smith. 3.4.1956-17.6.1960.	135	575	2,400
	b. Signature B. C. J. Richards. 28.11.1960-1.2.1961.	145	625	2,500
	s. As a. Specimen punch hole cancelled. 2.5.1956.	—	—	1,750
	ct. Color trial. Blue on orange underprint.	—	—	2,250

22	5 Pounds	VG	VF	UNC
	1956-1961. Blue on multicolor underprint. Sable antelope at lower left. Portrait of Queen Elizabeth II at right. Back: Victoria Falls. Watermark: Cecil Rhodes. Printer: BWC.			
	a. Signature A. P. Grafftey-Smith. 3.4.1956-17.6.1960.	350	1,200	3,600
	b. Signature B. C. J. Richards. 23.1.1961-3.2.1961.	400	1,300	4,000
	s. As a. Specimen punch hole cancelled. 3.4.1956.	—	—	2,500
	ct. Color trial. Red-brown on blue underprint.	—	—	3,000

23	10 Pounds	VG	VF	UNC
	1956-1961. Brown on multicolor underprint. Portrait of Queen Elizabeth II at right. Back: Elephants at center. BC: Gray-green. Watermark: Cecil Rhodes. Printer: BWC.			
	a. Signature A. P. Grafftey-Smith. 3.4.1956-17.6.1960.	1,100	3,000	—
	b. Signature B. C. J. Richards. 1.2.1961; 3.1.1961.	1,200	3,500	—
	s. As a. Specimen punch hole cancelled. 3.4.1956.	—	—	4,500
	ct. Color trial. Green on multicolor underprint.	—	—	5,000

Note: For earlier issues refer to Southern Rhodesia in Volume 2. For later issues refer to Malawi, Zambia, Rhodesia and Zimbabwe in Volume 3.

ROMANIA

Romania, located in south-east Europe, has an area of 91,699 sq. mi. (237,500 sq. km.) and a population of 22.5 million. Capital: Bucharest. Machinery, foodstuffs, raw minerals and petroleum products are exported. The principalities of Wallachia and Moldavia - for centuries under the suzerainty of the Turkish Ottoman Empire - secured their autonomy in 1856; they united in 1859 and a few years later adopted the new name of Romania. The country gained recognition of its independence in 1878. It joined the Allied Powers in World War I and acquired new territories - most notably Transylvania - following the conflict. In 1940, Romania allied with the Axis powers and participated in the 1941 German invasion of the USSR. Three years later, overrun by the Soviets, Romania signed an armistice. The post-war Soviet occupation led to the formation of a Communist "people's republic" in 1947 and the abdication of the king. The decades-long rule of dictator Nicolae Ceausescu, who took power in 1965, and his Securitate police state became increasingly oppressive and draconian through the 1980s. Ceausescu was overthrown and executed in late 1989. Former Communists dominated the government until 1996 when they were swept from power. Romania joined NATO in 2004 and the EU in 2007.

RULERS:

Carol I (as Prince), 1866-81 (as King) 1881-1914
Ferdinand I, 1914-1927
Mihai I, 1927-1930
Carol II, 1930-1940
Mihai I, 1940-1947

MONETARY SYSTEM:

10,000 "old" Lei = 1 "new" Leu, 1.7.2005
1 Leu = 100 Bani

KINGDOM

Bilet Hypothecar

State Notes of the Principality

1877 Issue

1	5 Lei	Good	Fine	XF
	12.6.1877. Blue. Two allegorical women at lower center, children at left and right. Back: Arms at lower center. Watermark: Trajan.			
	a. Issued note.	200	600	—
	r. Remainder. 3 signatures.	150	450	1,350
	s. Specimen without signature, Serial # zeros.	—	—	250

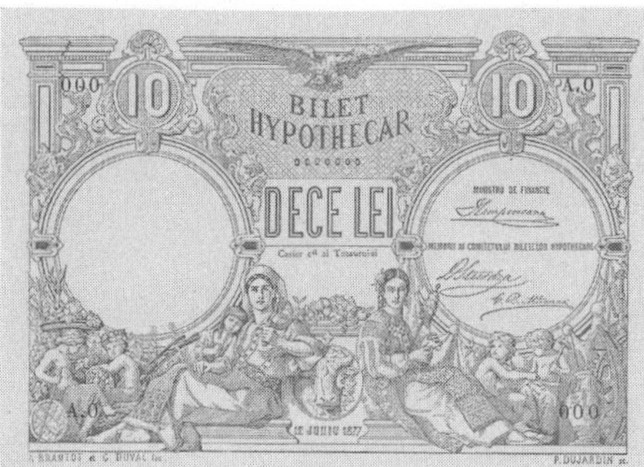

#	Note	Good	Fine	XF
2	**10 Lei** 12.6.1877. Blue. Two allegorical women at lower center, children at left and right. Eagle with outstretched wings at top center. Similar to #1. Back: Arms at lower center. Watermark: Trajan.			
	a. Issued note.	250	700	1,600
	r. Remainder. 3 signatures.	240	550	1,600
	s. Specimen without signature, Serial # zeros.	—	—	400

#	Note	Good	Fine	XF
3	**20 Lei** 12.6.1877. Blue. Two men and a woman at left, river and bridge scene at lower center, arms at right. Back: Two farm wives with poles at right. Watermark: Trajan.			
	a. Issued note. 4 signatures.	350	1,000	—
	r. Remainder note. 3 signatures.	275	850	1,800

#	Note	Good	Fine	XF
4	**50 Lei** 12.6.1877. Blue. Two men and a woman at left, river and bridge scene at lower center, arms at right. Eagle with outstretched wings at top center. Similar to #3. Back: Two farm wives with poles at right. Watermark: Trajan.			
	a. Issued note. 4 Signatures.	500	2,200	—
	r. Remainder. 3 signatures.	325	900	2,000

#	Note	Good	Fine	XF
5	**100 Lei** 12.6.1877. Blue. Woman with children at lower center. Back: Allegorical figures, arms and eagle at center. Watermark: Minerva and Trajan.			
	a. Issued note. 4 signatures.	—	—	—
	r. Remainder. 3 signatures.	350	950	2,200

#	Note	Good	Fine	XF
6	**500 Lei** 12.6.1877. Blue. Two women and girl at left, arms at lower center, three women with boy at right. Back: Standing figure at left and right, bust at center. Watermark: Minerva and Trajan.			
	a. Issued note. 4 signatures.	—	—	—
	r. Remainder. 3 signatures.	400	1,200	3,000

Banca Nationala a Romaniei

1880 Provisional Issue

#7-12 overprint of new bank name on Bilet Hypothecar notes dated 12.8.1877.

#	Note	Good	Fine	XF
7	**5 Lei** 9.9.1880 (-old date 12.6.1877). Blue. Two allegorical women at lower center, children at left and right. Back: Arms at lower center. Watermark: Trajan. Overprint: New bank name on #1. (Not Issued).	—	—	—

#	Note	Good	Fine	XF
8	**10 Lei** 9.9.1880 (-old date 12.6.1877). Blue. Two allegorical women at lower center, children at left and right. Eagle with outstretched wings at top center. Back: Arms at lower center. Watermark: Trajan. Overprint: New bank name on #2.	—	—	—

#	Note	Good	Fine	XF
9	**20 Lei** 9.9.1880 (-old date 12.6.1877). Blue. Two men and a woman at left, river and bridge scene at lower center, arms at right. Back: Two farm wives with poles at right. Watermark: Trajan. Overprint: New bank name on #3.	—	—	—

#	Note	Good	Fine	XF
10	**50 Lei** 9.9.1880 (-old date 12.6.1877). Blue. Two men and a woman at left, river and bridge scene at lower center, arms at right. Eagle with outstretched wings at top center. Back: Two farm wives with poles at right. Watermark: Trajan. Overprint: New bank name on #4.			
	a. Issued note.	—	—	—
	b. Cancelled note hand-stamped and perforated: *ANULAT.*	—	—	—

#	Note	Good	Fine	XF
11	**100 Lei** 9.9.1880 (-old date 12.6.1877). Blue. Woman with children at lower center. Back: Allegorical figures, arms and eagle at center. Watermark: Minerva and Trajan. Overprint: New bank name on #5.			
	a. Issued note.	—	—	—
	b. Cancelled note hand-stamped and perforated: *ANULAT.*	—	—	—

#	Note	Good	Fine	XF
12	**500 Lei** 9.9.1880 (-old date 12.6.1877). Blue. Two women and girl at left, arms at lower center, three women with boy at right. Back: Standing figure at left and right, bust at center. Watermark: Minerva and Trajan. Overprint: New bank name on #6.	—	—	—

1881 Issue

#	Note	VG	VF	UNC
13	**20 Lei** 19.1.1881-31.8.1895. Blue. Two boys at center, boy at right with staff of Mercury. 7 signature varieties.	350	900	2,000

#	Note	VG	VF	UNC
14	**100 Lei** 28.2.1881-11.11.1907. Blue. Two little children at upper left and right; eagle at top center. 9 signature varieties.	400	1,000	2,400

#	Note	VG	VF	UNC
15	**1000 Lei** 1881-1906. Blue. Woman with sickle at left, woman with oar at right. Signature varieties. Back: Round medallion with bust of Trajan at upper center.			
	a. 28.2.1881-1.6.1895. Rare.	—	—	—
	b. 19.9.1902-23.3.1906.	650	8,500	—

1896 Issue

		VG	VF	UNC
16	**20 Lei** 14.3.1896-28.8.1908. Blue. Woman with six children at center. 3 signature varieties.	100	340	580

1909-1916 Issue

		VG	VF	UNC
17	**1 Leu** 12.3.1915; 27.3.1916. Violet-blue on pale pink underprint. (Underprint usually barely visible; thus notes appear blue). Columns at left, woman at right. 3 signatures. Back: Wolf with Romulus and Remus.	5.00	10.00	20.00

		VG	VF	UNC
18	**2 Lei** 12.3.1915. Violet-blue on pink underprint. (see #17). Woman at left, eagle with cross in its mouth at right. 3 signatures, 2 signature varieties. Back: Soldier with sword at left, soldier with bugle at right.	5.00	10.00	20.00

		VG	VF	UNC
19	**5 Lei** 31.7.1914-22.11.1928. Violet. Farmer's wife with distaff at left, arms at right. 3 signatures, with 6 signature varieties. Back: Woman and child picking apples at center. Value numerals in violet. Watermark: Heads of Trajan and Minerva.			
	a. Issued note.	10.00	25.00	55.00
	s. Specimen. 25.3.1920.	—	—	60.00

		VG	VF	UNC
20	**20 Lei** 26.2.1909-31.1.1929. Blue-violet. Girl with fruit at left, boy with oar at right. 12 signature varieties. Back: Flying eagle with cross and arms flying over river. Watermark: Minerva and Trajan.			
	a. Issued note.	20.00	45.00	95.00
	s1. Specimen. 31.1.1929. Serial # 000000.	—	—	100
	s2. Specimen. Uniface pair. *SPECIMEN* on back.	—	—	200

		VG	VF	UNC
21	**100 Lei** 14.1.1910-31.1.1929. Violet-blue. Woman seated wearing national costume at left. 9 signature varieties. Watermark: Head of Trajan and Minerva.			
	a. Issued note.	30.00	60.00	130
	s1. Specimen. 31.1.1929. Serial # 000000.	—	—	100
	s2. Specimen. Uniface pair. *SPECIMEN* on back.	—	—	200

		VG	VF	UNC
22	**500 Lei** 11.2.1916-12.2.1920. Violet-blue. Woman with boy at left, farmer's wife seated at right. 9 signature varieties. Back: Two farm wives. 155x98mm.			
	a. Sigature titles: *VICE-GUVERNATOR; DIRECTOR; CASIER.*	60.00	150	400
	b. Sigature titles: *GUVERNATOR; DIRECTOR; DIRECTORUL CONTROLUIUI SI AL CASEI.*	30.00	60.00	150
	c. Sigature titles: *GUVERNATOR; DIRECTOR; DIRECTORUL CASEI.*	35.00	65.00	150
	s. Specimen.	—	—	200

		VG	VF	UNC
23	**1000 Lei** 20.5.1910-22.10.1931. Blue. Woman with sickle at left, woman with oar at right. Back: Similar to #15 but round medallion blank.			
	a. Issued note.	300	1,000	12,300
	s. Specimen. 31.1.1929.	—	—	—

1917 Issue

		VG	VF	UNC
24	**5 Lei** 16.2.1917. Violet-brown. Farmer's wife with distaff at left, arms at right. Like #19. Back: Woman and child picking apples at center. Numerals of value in yellow. Watermark: Light and dark half-spheres.			
	a. 133 x 79mm.	20.00	50.00	110
	b. 139 x 87mm.	50.00	140	300

		VG	VF	UNC
25	**100 Lei** 16.2.1917. Violet. Woman seated wearing national costume at left. Like #21. Watermark: Light and dark half-spheres.			
	a. Issued note.	150	350	800
	s. Specimen without date, signature or serial #.	—	—	180

1920 Issue

		VG	VF	UNC
26	**1 Leu** 17.7.1920. Violet-blue on light pink underprint. Columns at left, woman at right. Back: Wolf with Romulus and Remus. Like #17 but larger date.			
	a. Issued note.	3.00	7.00	15.00
	s1. Specimen without signature, series or serial #.	—	—	25.00
	s2. Specimen. Series L.403 and red overprint.	—	—	50.00

		VG	VF	UNC
27	**2 Lei** 17.7.1920. Blue-black on pale pink underprint. Woman at left. Eagle with cross in its mouth at right. Back: Soldier with sword at left, soldier with bugle at right. Like #18 but larger date. BC: Gray.			
	a. Issued note.	5.00	10.00	20.00
	s. Specimen. Series S.3430. Red overprint: *SPECIMEN.*	—	—	30.00

1924 Issue

		VG	VF	UNC
28	**500 Lei**			
	12.6.1924. Multicolor. Farmer's wife with distaff at left, woman with infant at right. 3 signature varaieties.			
	a. Issued note.	120	400	850
	s. Specimen. Without signatures.	—	—	150

1925-1929 Issue

		VG	VF	UNC
29	**5 Lei**			
	19.9.1929. Violet. Farmer's wife with distaff at left, arms at right. 2. signatures. Like #19. Back: Woman and child picking apples at center. Watermark: Heads of Trajan and Minerva.	10.00	25.00	55.00

		VG	VF	UNC
30	**20 Lei**			
	19.9.1929. Blue-violet. Girl with fruit at left, boy with oar at right. 2 signatures. Like #20. Back: Flying eagle with cross and arms flying over river. Watermark: Heads of Minerva and Trajan.	20.00	45.00	95.00
31	**100 Lei**	VG	VF	UNC
	19.9.1929. Violet. Woman seated wearing national costume at left. 2 signatures. Like #21. Watermark: Heads of Trajan and Minerva.	100	300	800

		VG	VF	UNC
32	**500 Lei**			
	1.10.1925-27.1.1938. Multicolor. Farmer's wife with distaff at left, woman with infant at right. 2 signatures, 6 signature varieties. Like #28.			
	a. Issued note.	100	320	850
	b. 15.3.1934, 27.1.1938.	30.00	55.00	120
	s. Specimen.	—	—	250

1930-1933 Issue

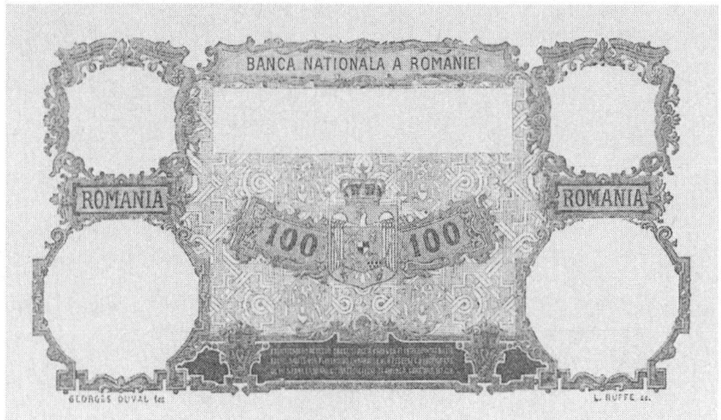

		VG	VF	UNC
33	**100 Lei**			
	13.5.1930-13.5.1932. Olive-brown. Woman seated wearing national costume at left. 3 signature varieties. Like #31. Watermark: Heads of Trajan and Minerva.			
	a. Issued note.	35.00	65.00	150
	s. Specimen. 13.5.1930.	—	—	200

		Good	Fine	XF
34	**1000 Lei**			
	15.6.1933. Blue and multicolor. Woman at lower left, man at lower right. Back: Mercury at left and right.			
	a. Issued note.	120	350	750
	s. Specimen.	—	Unc	300

		Good	Fine	XF
35	**5000 Lei** 31.3.1931. Dark blue. Danube landscape at lower left, arms at center. Portrait King Carol II at right. Back: Medieval scene. Printer: BWC. (See #48 for overprint type.)			
	a. Issued note. Rare.	—	—	—
	s. Specimen.	—	Unc	—

Note: #35 was reportedly in circulation for only a few months (March 1 to Dec. 1, 1932).

1934 Issue

		VG	VF	UNC
36	**500 Lei** 31.7.1934. Dark green on multicolor underprint. Portrait King Carol II at left. Back: Villa with trees. Printer: BWC.			
	a. Issued note.	20.00	55.00	120
	s. Specimen. Without signature, series or serial #.	—	—	120

		VG	VF	UNC
37	**1000 Lei** 15.3.1934. Brown and multicolor. Portrait King Carol II at left. Back: Complex design with two women and child at right.			
	a. Issued note.	120	350	750
	s. Specimen.	—	—	30.00

1936-1939 Issues

		VG	VF	UNC
38	**1 Leu** 28.10.1937; 21.12.1938. Lilac-brown. Columns at left, woman at right. Similar to #26, but date on face. 2 signatures, 2 signature varieties. Back: Wolf with Romulus and Remus.			
	a. Issued note. 28.10.1937.	15.00	35.00	75.00
	b. 21.12.1933.	10.00	25.00	55.00
	s. Specimen without signature, series or serial #. 28.10.1937.	—	—	50.00

		VG	VF	UNC
39	**2 Lei** 1937-1940. Lilac-brown. Woman at left, eagle with cross in its mouth at right. 2 signatures, 2 signature varieties. Similar to #27. Back: Soldier with sword at left, soldier with bugle at right.			
	a. Lilac-brown. 28.10.1937; 21.12.1938.	15.00	35.00	75.00
	b. 21.12.1938.	—	25.00	55.00
	c. Deep purple on red underprint. 1.11.1940.	50.00	100	500
	s. As a. with red overprint: *SPECIMEN*. 21.12.1938.	—	—	40.00

		VG	VF	UNC
40	**5 Lei** 21.12.1938. Violet. Farmer's wife with distaff at left, arms at right. Like #19 and #24. Back: Woman and child picking apples at center. Watermark: *BNR*. Specimen.			
	a. Issued note.	100	120	550
	s. Specimen.	—	—	300

41	**20 Lei**	VG	VF	UNC
	28.4.1939. Green. Girl with fruit at left, boy with oar at right. Denomination stated *DOUA ZECI LEI*. Like #30. Back: Flying eagle with cross and arms over river. Watermark: *BNR*. Specimen.	—	—	400

42	**500 Lei**	VG	VF	UNC
	30.4.1936; 26.5.1939; 1.11.1940. Gray-blue on multicolor underprint. Portrait King Carol II at left. Similar to #36. Back: Villa with trees.			
	a. Issued note. 30.1.1936.	25.00	50.00	120
	b. 30.4.1936.	15.00	35.00	75.00
	c. 26.5.1939; 1.11.1940.	15.00	35.00	75.00
	s. Specimen. 30.4.1938. Serial # S/1 000000.	—	—	100

43	**500 Lei**	VG	VF	UNC
	30.1.1936; 26.5.1939; 1.9.1940. Gray. Portrait King Carol II at left. Like #42. Back: Villa with trees.			
	a. Issued note.	50.00	140	300
	s. Specimen.	15.00	30.00	180

44	**1000 Lei**	VG	VF	UNC
	25.6.1936. Brown and green. Two farm wives with three children each at left and right. Back: Two farm wives at left and one with ladder at right. Watermark: King Carol II with wreath.			
	a. Issued note.	8.00	15.00	40.00
	s. Specimen.	—	—	55.00

45	**1000 Lei**	VG	VF	UNC
	25.6.1936. Brown and green. Two farm wives with three children each at left and right. Like #44. Back: Two farm wives at left and one with ladder at right. Watermark: King Carol II with wreath.			
	a. Issued note.	40.00	100	240
	s. Specimen.	—	—	200

46	**1000 Lei**	VG	VF	UNC
	19.12.1938-1.11.1940. Brown and green. Two farm wives with three children each at left and right. Like #44. Back: Two farm wives at left and one with ladder at right. Watermark: King Carol II.	10.00	25.00	55.00

47	**1000 Lei**	VG	VF	UNC
	21.12.1938; 28.4.1939; 1.11.1940. Brown and green. Two farm wives with three children each at left and right. Like #46. Back: Two farm wives at left and one with ladder at right. Watermark: King Carol II.			
	a. Issued note.	35.00	90.00	200
	s. Specimen. Serial # A.000 0000 and with *SPECIMEN* overprint.	—	—	150

1940 Commemorative Issue

48	**5000 Lei**	VG	VF	UNC
	6.9.1940 (-old date 31.3.1931). Dark blue. Danube landscape lower left, arms at center. Portrait King Carol II at right. Like #35. Back: Medieval scene. Printer: BWC.			
	a. Serial number prefix as: A-Z.	35.00	100	360
	b. Sperial number prefix as fraction: A/1-Z/1.	35.00	100	360
	s. As a or b. Specimen. Pin holed cancelled with overprint.	—	—	450

Note: #48 is purported to commemorate the coronation of King Michael I.

1940 Issue

		VG	VF	UNC
49	**100 Lei** 19.2.1940. Dark brown. Woman seated wearing national costume at left. Like #31. Watermark: Heads of Trajan and Minerva.	20.00	45.00	140

		VG	VF	UNC
50	**100 Lei** 19.2.1940; 1.11.1940. Dark brown. Woman seated wearing national costume at left. 2 signature varieties. Like #49. Watermark: *BNR*.			
	a. Issued note.	15.00	35.00	100
	s. Specimen.	—	—	80.00

		VG	VF	UNC
51	**500 Lei** 1.11.1940-26.1.1943. Brown on multicolor underprint. Two farm wives at left. 2 signature varieties. Back: Villa with trees. Watermark: *BNR* horizontal or vertical.			
	a. Issued note.	3.00	8.00	20.00
	s. Specimen. 1.11.1940; 20.4.1942.	—	—	80.00

1941 Issue

		VG	VF	UNC
52	**1000 Lei** 10.9.1941-20.3.1945. Blue and green on pink underprint. Two farm wives with three children each at left and right. Similar to #45. Value *UNA MIE LEI* at lower center. 3 signature varieties. Back: Two farm wives at left and one with ladder at right. Watermark: Head of Trajan.			
	a. Issued note.	2.00	5.00	15.00
	s. Specimen. 28.9.1943, serial # A/1 000000.	—	—	50.00

		VG	VF	UNC
53	**2000 Lei** 18.11.1941; 10.10.1944. Brown, violet and yellow. Farm wife with distaff at left, woman with infant at right. 2 signature varieties. Back: Two farm wives at left, oil refinery at right. Watermark: Head of Trajan.			
	a. Issued note. 18.11.1941.	3.00	10.00	25.00
	b. 10.10.1944.	3.00	10.00	25.00
	c. 20.3.1945.	5.00	15.00	30.00
	s. Specimen.	—	—	100

1943 Issue

No.	Description	VG	VF	UNC
54	**2000 Lei** 23.3.1943-20.3.1945. Brown, violet and yellow. Farm wife with distaff at left, woman with infant at right. 2 signature varieties. Like #53. Back: Two farm wives at left, oil refinery at right. Watermark: *BNR* in shield.			
	a. Issued note. 23.3.1943-2.5.1944.	2.00	8.00	20.00
	b. 10.10.1964.	30.00	100	200
	s. Specimen. 23.3.1943.	—	—	100

No.	Description	VG	VF	UNC
55	**5000 Lei** 28.9.1943; 2.5.1944; 22.8.1944. Light blue on multicolor underprint. Two male heads of Trajan and Decebal at upper left, arms at center. 2 signature varieties. Back: Man and oxen looking towards city. Watermark: Portrait of Trajan.	5.00	10.00	30.00

The 22.8.1944 date is very rare as the Military coup occured on the next day, 23.8.1944.

1944 Issue

No.	Description	VG	VF	UNC
56	**5000 Lei** 10.10.1944-20.12.1945. Light blue. Two male heads of Trajan and Decebal at upper left, arms at center. 2 signature varieties. Like #55. Back: Man and oxen looking towards city. Watermark: *BNR* horizontal or vertical.			
	a. Issued note.	4.00	8.00	26.00
	s. Specimen. 10.10.1944.	—	—	85.00

1945 Issue

No.	Description	VG	VF	UNC
57	**10,000 Lei** 18.5.1945; 20.12.1945; 28.5.1946. Brown and red. Farm wives with three children each at left and right. Arms at center. 2 signature varieties. Similar to #44. Back: Two farm wives at left and one with ladder at right.			
	a. Issued note.	4.00	8.00	26.00
	s. Specimen. 18.5.1945.	—	—	50.00

No.	Description	VG	VF	UNC
58	**100,000 Lei** 7.8.1945-8.5.1947. Green and gray. Woman with boy at left, farm wife at right. Back: Two farm wives. Watermark: *BNR*.			
	a. Issued note.	4.00	8.00	26.00
	s. Specimen. 7.8.1945.	—	—	50.00

1947 Issue

59	100,000 Lei	VG	VF	UNC
	25.1.1947. Lilac, brown and multicolor. Trajan and Decebal at center. Back: Two farmers at left, arms at center, two women and child at right.			
	a. Issued note.	4.00	8.00	26.00
	s. Specimen.	—	—	50.00

60	1,000,000 Lei	VG	VF	UNC
	1947. Blue-green and gray-brown on light tan and blue underprint. Trajan and Decebal at center. Like #59. Back: Two farmers at left, arms at center, two women and child at right.			
	a. Issued note.	5.00	10.00	28.00
	s. Specimen.	—	—	55.00

61	5,000,000 Lei	VG	VF	UNC
	25.6.1947. Olive and brown on multicolor underprint. Women and children at left and right, wolf with Romulus and Remus at center. Back: Two farm wives at left and right.			
	a. White watermark. Paper.	20.00	55.00	140
	b. Ruled paper.	20.00	55.00	140
	s. Specimen.	—	—	100

1947 First Issue

#62-64 issued after 1947 currency reform.

62	100 Lei	VG	VF	UNC
	25.6.1947. Dark brown on light brown underprint. Three men with torch, ears of corn and hammer at right.			
	a. Issued note.	5.00	18.00	55.00
	s. Specimen.	—	—	150

63	500 Lei	VG	VF	UNC
	25.6.1947. Brown. Woman at center. Back: Farmer and wheat.			
	a. Issued note.	25.00	60.00	180
	s. Specimen.	—	—	50.00

64	1000 Lei	VG	VF	UNC
	25.6.1947. Blue on multicolor underprint. T. Vladimirescu at center. Back: Arms at center.			
	a. Issued note.	25.00	60.00	180
	s. Specimen.	—	—	80.00

1947 Second Issue

65	100 Lei	VG	VF	UNC
	27.8.1947. Brown. Three men with torch, ears of corn and hammer at right. Like #62.	4.00	15.00	35.00

66	1000 Lei	VG	VF	UNC
	30.9.1947. Blue. T. Vladimirescu at center. Like #64. Back: Arms at center.	15.00	40.00	100

1947 Third Issue

		VG	VF	UNC
67	**100 Lei** 5.12.1947. Brown. Three men with torch, ears of corn and hammer at right. Like #62.			
	a. Issued note.	4.00	15.00	35.00
	s. Specimen.	—	—	50.00
68	**1000 Lei** 5.12.1947. Blue. T. Vladimirescu at center. Like #64.	10.00	36.00	85.00

Ministerul Finantelor

Ministry of Finance

1917 Emergency WW I Issue

		VG	VF	UNC
69	**10 Bani** 1917. Dark green on olive underprint. King Ferdinand I at center. Back: Crowned supported arms.	2.00	5.00	10.00

		VG	VF	UNC
70	**25 Bani** 1917. Dark brown on ochre underprint. King Ferdinand I at center. Back: Crowned supported arms.	3.00	7.00	15.00

		VG	VF	UNC
71	**50 Bani** 1917. Dark blue on light brown on peach underprint. King Ferdinand I at center. Back: Crowned supported arms.	4.00	10.00	20.00

1920 ND Issue

		VG	VF	UNC
72	**10 Lei** ND (ca.1920). Brown on red underprint. King Ferdinand I over crowned supported arms at center. MF monogram at left and right. BC: Green. Printer: ABNC.			
	p. Proof. Black. Punch hole cancelled.	—	—	500
	s. Specimen.	—	—	1,000
73	**50 Lei** ND (ca.1920). Blue on red underprint. King Ferdinand I over crowned supported arms at center. MF monogram at left and right. BC: Purple. Printer: ABNC.	VG	VF	UNC
	p. Proof. Black. Punch hole cancelled.	—	—	—
	s. Specimen.	—	—	1,500

		VG	VF	UNC
74	**200 Lei** ND (ca.1920). Brown on red underprint. King Ferdinand I over crowned supported arms at center. MF monogram at left and right. BC: Orange. Printer: ABNC.			
	p. Proof. Punch hole cancelled.	—	—	—
	s. Specimen.	—	—	1,800

		VG	VF	UNC
75	**2000 Lei** ND (ca.1920). Green on red underprint. King Ferdinand I over crowned supported arms at center. MF monogram at left and right. BC: Dark brown. Printer: ABNC.			
	p. Proof. Punch hole cancelled.	—	—	—
	s. Specimen.	—	—	2,000

Note: Several examples of pieces from the 1920 ND printing are known in "issued" form.

1945; 1947 ND Issue

1 New Leu = 20,000 Old Lei

		VG	VF	UNC
76	**20 Lei** 1945. Brown on light brown underprint. Portrait King Michael at center.	1.00	2.00	5.00
77	**20 Lei** ND (1947). Dark brown on green underprint. Trajan and Decebal at at upper left. Signature title: *DIRECTORUL GENERAL AL BUGETULUI.* 2 signature varieties. Back: Woman sitting on woodpile. Watermark: *M. F.*	10.00	28.00	65.00

		VG	VF	UNC
78	**100 Lei** 1945. Blue on light blue underprint. Portrait King Michael at center. Like #76.	1.00	2.00	5.00

Color Abbreviation Guide

New to the *Standard Catalog of® World Paper Money* are the following abbreviations related to color references:

BC: Back color
PC: Paper color

REPUBLICA POPULARA ROMANA

Ministerul Finantelor

Ministry of Finance

1948 ND Issue

		VG	VF	UNC
79	**20 Lei** ND (1948). Brown and green. Trajan and Decebal at at upper left. Signature title: *DIRECTORUL GENERAL AL BUGETULUI*. 2 signature varieties. Like #77 with different signatures. Back: Woman sitting on woodpile. Watermark: *RPR*.			
	a. Issued note.	10.00	28.00	65.00
	r. Remainder, punch hole cancelled.	—	—	20.00
80	**20 Lei** ND (1948). Dark brown on green underprint. Trajan and Decebal at at upper left. Lower signature title: *DIRECTORUL BUGETULUI*. Like #79. One line of text on front. Back: Woman sitting on woodpile. Watermark: *RPR*.	12.00	30.00	70.00

1952 Issue

		VG	VF	UNC
81	**1 Leu** 1952. Brown on light orange underprint. Back: Arms at center.			
	a. Red series and serial #.	5.00	12.00	40.00
	b. Blue series and serial #.	1.00	2.00	5.00
	s. As b. Specimen.	—	—	30.00

		VG	VF	UNC
82	**3 Lei** 1952. Violet-brown on greenish gray underprint. Back: Arms at center.			
	a. Red series and serial #.	10.00	30.00	70.00
	b. Blue series and serial #.	5.00	18.00	35.00
	s. As b. Specimen.	—	—	30.00

		VG	VF	UNC
83	**5 Lei** 1952. Blue on light brown and light orange underprint. Girl at left, arms at upper right. Back: Dam construction.			
	a. Red series and serial #.	10.00	30.00	70.00
	b. Blue series and serial #.	1.00	4.00	8.00
	s. As b. Specimen.	—	—	30.00

		VG	VF	UNC
84	**20 Lei** 15.6.1950. Dark green on gray underprint. Girl's head at right. Back: Arms at center.			
	a. Issued note.	2.00	5.00	18.00
	s. Specimen.	—	—	40.00

Banca Nationala a Romaniei

Romanian National Bank

1948 Issue

		VG	VF	UNC
85	**1000 Lei** 18.6.1948. Blue. T. Vladimirescu at center. Like #64. Back: Arms at center.			
	a. Issued note.	10.00	20.00	40.00
	s. Specimen.	—	—	75.00

Banca Republicii Populare Romane - Banca de Stat

1949-1952 Issue

		VG	VF	UNC
86	**500 Lei**			
	15.10.1949. Brown. Three men at left center.			
	a. Issued note.	15.00	30.00	60.00
	s. Specimen. In blue and brown.	—	—	60.00

		VG	VF	UNC
87	**1000 Lei** 20.9.1950. Blue and multicolor. Balcescu at left. Back: River and mountains.	10.00	20.00	50.00

1952 Issue

1 New Leu = 20 Old Lei

		VG	VF	UNC
88	**10 Lei**			
	1952. Brown on multicolor underprint. Worker at left, arms at center right. Back: Rock loaded onto train.			
	a. Red serial #.	15.00	35.00	110
	b. Blue serial #.	3.00	6.00	10.00
	s. As b. Specimen. Schmal and big letters.	—	—	40.00

		VG	VF	UNC
89	**25 Lei**			
	1952. Brown on violet underprint. T. Vladimirescu at left. Back: Wheat harvesting.			
	a. Red serial #.	16.00	40.00	120
	b. Blue serial #.	—	6.00	15.00
	s. As b. Specimen.	—	—	50.00

		VG	VF	UNC
90	**100 Lei**			
	1952. Blue on light blue underprint. N. Balcescu at left, arms at center right. Back: Large buildings.			
	a. Red serial #.	20.00	50.00	150
	b. Blue serial #.	3.00	8.00	20.00
	s. As b. Specimen.	—	—	60.00

RUSSIA

Russia, (formerly the central power of the Union of Soviet Socialist Republics and now of the Commonwealth of Independent States) occupying the northern part of Asia and the far eastern part of Europe, has an area of 17,075,200 sq. km. and a population of 140.7 million. Capital: Moscow. Exports include machinery, iron and steel, oil, timber and nonferrous metals.Founded in the 12th century, the Principality of Muscovy, was able to emerge from over 200 years of Mongol domination (13th-15th centuries) and to gradually conquer and absorb surrounding principalities. In the early 17th century, a new Romanov Dynasty continued this policy of expansion across Siberia to the Pacific. Under Peter I (ruled 1682-1725), hegemony was extended to the Baltic Sea and the country was renamed the Russian Empire. During the 19th century, more territorial acquisitions were made in Europe and Asia. Defeat in the Russo-Japanese War of 1904-05 contributed to the Revolution of 1905, which resulted in the formation of a parliament and other reforms. Repeated devastating defeats of the Russian army in World War I led to widespread rioting in the major cities of the Russian Empire and to the overthrow in 1917 of the imperial household. The Communists under Vladimir Lenin seized power soon after and formed the USSR. The brutal rule of Iosif STALIN (1928-53) strengthened Communist rule and Russian dominance of the Soviet Union at a cost of tens of millions of lives. The Soviet economy and society stagnated in the following decades until General Secretary Mikhail Gorbachev (1985-91) introduced glasnost (openness) and perestroika (restructuring) in an attempt to modernize Communism, but his initiatives inadvertently released forces that by December 1991 splintered the USSR into Russia and 14 other independent republics. Since then, Russia has shifted its post-Soviet democratic ambitions in favor of a centralized semi-authoritarian state whose legitimacy is buttressed, in part, by carefully managed national elections, former President Putin's genuine popularity, and the prudent management of Russia's windfall energy wealth. Russia has severely disabled a Chechen rebel movement, although violence still occurs throughout the North Caucasus.

RULERS:

Catherine II (the Great), 1762-1796
Paul I, 1796-1801
Alexander I, 1801-1825
Nicholas I, 1825-1855
Alexander II, 1855-1881
Alexander III, 1881-1894
Nicholas II, 1894-1917

MONETARY SYSTEM:

1 Ruble = 100 Kopeks, until 1997
1 Chervonetz = 10 Gold Rubles
1 Ruble = 1000 "old" Rubles, 1998-

Note: Certain listings encompassing issues circulated by various bank and regional authorities are contained in Volume 1.

Color Abbreviation Guide

New to the *Standard Catalog of ® World Paper Money* are the following abbreviations related to color references:

BC: Back color
PC: Paper color

CYRILLIC ALPHABET

А	а	*А*	*а*	A	С	с	*С*	*с*	S
Б	б	*Б*	*б*	B	Т	т	*Т*	*т*	T
В	в	*В*	*в*	V	У	у	*У*	*у*	U
Г	г	*Г*	*г*	G	Ф	ф	*Ф*	*ф*	F
Д	д	*Д*	*д, g*	D	Х	х	*Х*	*х*	Kh
Е	е	*Е*	*е*	ye	Ц	ц	*Ц*	*ц*	C
Ё	ё	*Ё*	*ё*	yo	Ч	ч	*Ч*	*ч*	ch
Ж	ж	*Ж*	*ж*	zh	Ш	ш	*Ш*	*ш*	sh
З	з	*З*	*з*	Z	Щ	щ	*Щ*	*щ*	shch
И	и	*И*	*и*	I	Ъ*)	ъ*)	–	*ъ*	'
Й	й	*Й*	*й*	J	Ы	ы	–	*ы*	
К	к	*К*	*k, к*	K	Ь**)	ь**)	–	*ь*	'
Л		*Л*	*л*	L	Э		*Э*		E
М		*М*	*м*	M	Ю	ю	*Ю*	*ю*	yu
Н		*Н*	*н*	N	Я	я	*Я*	*я*	ya
О		*О*	*о*	O	І	і	*І*	*і*	I
П		*П*	*п*	P	Ѣ	ѣ	*Ѣ*	*ѣ*	ye
Р		*Р*	*р*	R					

*) "hard", and **) "soft" signs; both soundless. I and Ѣ were dropped in 1918.

(Some other areas whose notes are listed in this volume had local currencies.)

ISSUE IDENTIFICATION CHART

CZARIST EMPIRE, 1769-1917

DATE	ISSUER	CAT.#
1769-1843	ГОСУДАРСТВЕННОЙ АССИГНАЦІИ	A1-A24
1840	ГОСУДАРСТВЕННЫЙ КОММЕРЧЕСКІЙ БАНКЪ	A25-A30
1841	КРЕДИТНЫЙ БИЛЕТЪ СОХРАННЫХЪКАЗЕНЪ И ГОСУДАРСТВЕННАГО БАНКА	A31-32
1843-1895	ГОСУДАРСТВЕННЫЙ КРЕДИТНЫЙ БИЛЕТЪ	A33-A64
1876-1895	ГОСУДАРСТВЕННЫЙ БАНКЪ: ДЕПОЗИТНАЯ МЕТАЛЛИЧЕСКАЯКВИТАНЦІЯ	A65-A83
1895	БИЛЕТЪ ГОСУААРСТВЕННАГО КАЗНАУЕЙСТВА	A84
1898-1915	ГОСУДАРСТВЕННЫЙ КРЕДИТНЫЙБИЛЕТЪ	1-15
1915	Postage Stamp Currency	16-23
1915	Treasury Small Change Notes	24-31
1915-1917	5% КРАТКОСРОЧНОЕ ОБЯЗАТЕЛЬСТВОГСУДАР. (СТВЕННАГО) КАЗНАЧЕЙСТВА	31A-31X

PROVISIONAL GOVERNMENT, 1917-1918

DATE	ISSUER	CAT.#
1917	Postage Stamp Currency	32-34
1917	ОСУДАРСТВЕННЫЙ КРЕДИТНЫЙ БИЛЕТЪ	35-37
1917	5% ОБЛИГАЦІЯ ЗАЕМЪ СВОБОДЫ	37A-37
1917	КАЗНАЧЕЙСКІЙ ЗНАКЪ	38-39
1918-1919	ГОСУДАРСТВЕННЫЙ КРЕДИТНЫЙ БИЛЕТЪ	39A-42
1917	ГОСУДАРСТВЕННЫЙ КРЕДИТНЫЙ БИЛЕТ	43-47

RUSSIAN SOCIALIST FEDERATED SOVIET REPUBLIC, 1918-1924

DATE	ISSUER	CAT.#
1918	БИЛЕТЬ ГОСУДАРСТВЕННАГО КАЗНАЧЕЙСТВА	48-60
1918	РАСЧЕТНЫЙ ЗНАК	81-85
1918	ГОСУДАРСТВЕННЫЙ КРЕДИТНЫЙ БИЛЕТЪ	86-97
1919-1921	РАСЧЕТНЫЙ ЗНАК	98-117
1921	ОбЯЗАТЕЛЬСТВО РОССИЙСКОЙ СОЦИАЛИСТИЧЕСКОЙ ФЕДЕРАТИВНОЙ СОВЕТСКОЙРЕСПУБЛИКИ	120-125
1922	ГОСУДАРСТВЕННЫЙ ДЕНЕЖНЫЙ ЗНАК	126-138
1922-1923	БАНКОВЫЙ БИЛЕТ	139-145A
1922-1923	ГОСУДАРСТВЕННЫЙ ДЕНЕЖНЫЙ ЗНАК	146-171A
1923	ПЛАТЕЖНОЕ ОБЯЗАТЕЛЬСТВО НКФР. С.Ф.С.Р.	172-175
1923-1924	ТРАНСПОРТНЫЙСЕРТИФИКАТ	176-180

UNION OF SOVIET SOCIALIST REPUBLICS, 1924-91

DATE	ISSUER	CAT.#
1924-1925	ГОСУДАРСТВЕННЫЙ ДЕНЕЖНЫЙ ЗНАК	181-183, 186-190
1924-1926	ПЛАТЕЖНОЕ ОБЯЗАТЕЛЬСТВО НКФС.С.С.Р.	184-185A
1928	НАРОДНОГО КОМИССАРІАТА ФИНАНСОВ СОЮЗА С.С.Р.	185B-185E
1924	Small Change Notes	191-196
1924-1957	БИЛЕТ ГОСУДАРСТВЕННОГО БАНКАС.С.С.Р.	196A-205, 225-232
1928-1957	ГОСУДАРСТВЕННЫЙ КАЗНАЧЕЙСКИЙ БИЛЕТ	206-221

MONETARY UNITS

KOPEK	КОПЕЙКА
KOPEKS	КОПЕЙКИ, КОПЕЕКЪ
RUBLE	РУБЛЬ
RUBLES	РУБЛЯ or РУБЛЕЙ
CHERVONETZ	ЧЕРВОНЕЦ
CHERVONTSA	ЧЕРВОНЦА
CHERVONTSEV	ЧЕРВОНЦЕВ

DENOMINATIONS

1	ОДИН, ОДИНЪ or ОДНА
2	ДВА or ДВЕ
3	ТРИ
5	ПЯТЬ
10	ДЕСЯТЬ
20	ДВАДЦАТЬ
25	ДВАДЦАТЬ ПЯТЬ
30	ТРИДЦАТЬ
40	СОРОК or СОРОКЪ
50	ПЯТЬДЕСЯТ or ПЯТЬДЕСЯТЪ
60	ШЕСТЬДЕСЯТ or ЩЕСТЬДЕСЯТЬ
100	СТО
250	ДВЬСТИ ПЯТЪДЕСЯТЪ or ДВЕСТИ ПЯТЪДЕСЯТ
500	ПЯТЬСОТ or ПЯТЬСОТЪ
1,000	ТЫСЯЧА
5,000	ПЯТЬ ТЫСЯЧ or ТЫСЯЧЪ
10,000	ДЕСЯТЬ ТЫСЯЧ or ТЫСЯЧЪ
15,000	ПЯТНАДЦАТЬ ТЫСЯЧ or ТЫСЯЧЬ
25,000	ДВАДЦАТЬ ПЯТЬ ТЫСЯЧ
50,000	ПЯТЬ ДЕСЯТ ТЫСЯЧ or ПЯТЬДЕСЯТЬ ТЫСЯЧЪ
100,000	СТО ТЫСЯЧ or ТЫСЯЧЪ
250,000	ДВЬСТИ ПЯТЬДЕСЯТ ТЫСЯЧ
500,000	ПЯТЬСОТЪ ТЫСЯЧ
1,000,000	ОДИН МИЛЛИОН or МИЛЛИОНЪ

IMPERIAL RUSSIA

ГОСУДАРСТВЕННОЙ АССИГНАЦИ

State Assignats

1769 Issue

		Good	Fine	XF
A1	**25 Rubles** 1769-1773. 1 serial # at center above *ASSIGNAT.* Watermark: Words on perimeter. 190x250mm. Rare.	—	—	—
A2	**50 Rubles** 1769-1773. 1 serial # at center above *ASSIGNAT.* Watermark: Words on perimeter. 190x250mm. Rare.	—	—	—
A3	**75 Rubles** 1769-1772. 1 serial # at center above *ASSIGNAT.* Watermark: Words on perimeter. 190x250mm. Rare.	—	—	—
A4	**100 Rubles** 1769-1773. 1 serial # at center above *ASSIGNAT.* Watermark: Words on perimeter. 190x250mm. Rare.	—	—	—

1774 Issue

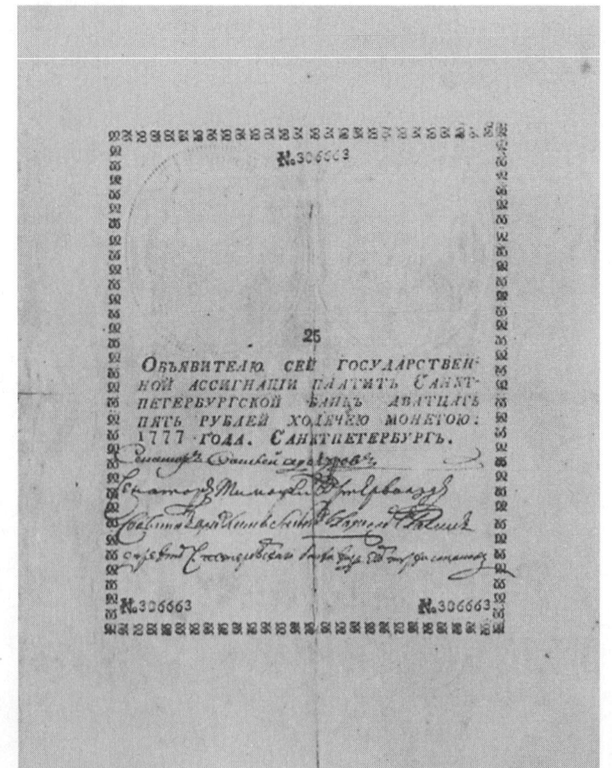

		Good	Fine	XF
A5	**25 Rubles** 1774-1784. 3 serial #: at center, at lower left and lower right. Rare.	—	—	—
A6	**50 Rubles** 1774-1784. 3 serial #: at center, at lower left and lower right. Rare.	—	—	—
A7	**100 Rubles** 1774-1784. 3 serial #: at center, at lower left and lower right. Rare.	—	—	—

1785-1787 Issue

#A8-A12 Many signature varieties. Napoleonic forgeries with 2 or 3 printed signatures exist and some of these have printing errors in 1 or 2 words.

Correct:
гОСYдАРСТВЕННОЙ ХОдЯЧЕЮ
Error:
гОСYЛАРСТВЕННОЙ ХОЛЯЧЕЮ

Note: Some forged notes have Cyrillic Л (L) instead of д (D) in text.

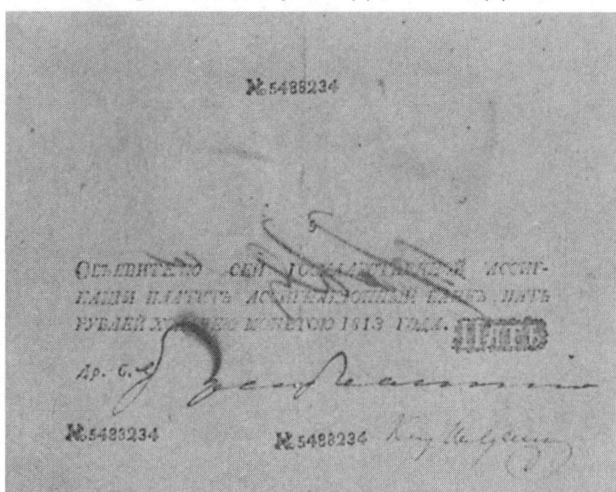

		Good	Fine	XF
A8	**5 Rubles** 1787-1818. Text without frame. 2 handwritten signatures. Back: 1 handwritten signature. 130x170mm. PC: Gray to bluish.			
	a. 1787-1802.	800	—	—
	b. 1803-1818.	300	750	—

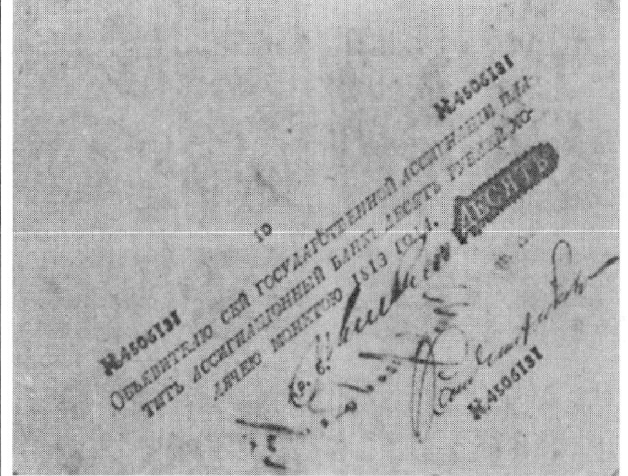

		Good	Fine	XF
A9	**10 Rubles** 1787-1817. Text without frame. 2 handwritten signatures. Back: 1 handwritten signature. 130x170mm. PC: Pink.			
	a. 1787-1801.	1,000	2,000	—
	b. 1803-1817.	400	800	—

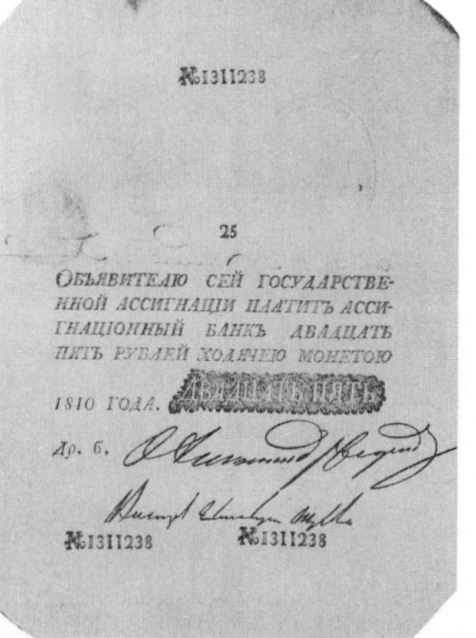

		Good	Fine	XF
A10	**25 Rubles** 1785-1818. Text without frame. 2 handwritten signatures. Back: 1 handwritten signature. 130x170mm. Issued with clipped corners. PC: White.			
	a. 1785-1802. Rare.	—	—	—
	b. 1803-1818. Rare.	—	—	—
	x. 1803-1811. Napoleonic forgery.	100	300	650

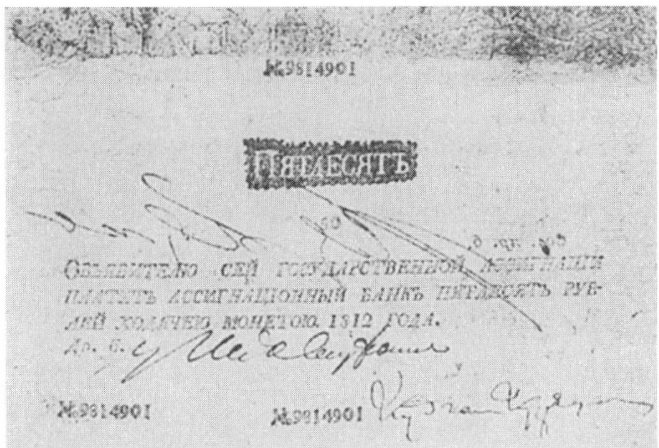

		Good	Fine	XF
A11	**50 Rubles** 1785-1818. Text without frame. 2 handwritten signatures. Back: 1 handwritten signature. 197x128mm. PC: White.			
	a. 1785-1802. Rare.	—	—	—
	b. 1803-1818. Rare.	—	—	—
	x. 1805-08. Napoleonic forgery.	300	950	2,500

		Good	Fine	XF
A12	**100 Rubles** 1785-1818. Text without frame. 2 handwritten signatures. Back: 1 handwritten signature. 130x170mm. PC: White.			
	a. 1785-1801. Rare.	—	—	—
	b. 1803-1818. Rare.	—	—	—

1802 Issue

		Good	Fine	XF
A13	**5 Rubles** 1802. Black. 115x115mm. Specimen only. Rare. PC: White.	—	—	—
A14	**10 Rubles** 1802-1803. Black. 175x115mm. Specimen only. Rare. PC: White.	—	—	—
A15	**25 Rubles** 1802. Black. 185x185mm. Specimen only. Rare. PC: White.	—	—	—
A16	**100 Rubles** 1802. Black. 185x185mm. Specimen only. Rare. PC: White.	—	—	—

1818-1843 Issues

#A17-A24 first signature (director) Hovanskii (printed), second signature (cashier, handwritten). Many varieties.

		Good	Fine	XF
A17	**5 Rubles** 1819-1843. Crowned double-headed eagle with shield. First signature printed, second signature handwritten. PC: Blue.	200	550	—
A18	**10 Rubles** 1819-1843. Crowned double-headed eagle with shield. First signature printed, second signature handwritten. PC: Pink.	300	650	—
A19	**20 Rubles** 1822. Crowned double-headed eagle with shield. First signature printed, second signature handwritten. Specimen. Rare. PC: Green.	—	—	—
A20	**20 Rubles** 1822. Crowned double-headed eagle with shield. First signature printed, second signature handwritten. Specimen. PC: Reddish.	—	—	—

		Good	Fine	XF
A21	**25 Rubles** 1818-1843. Crowned double-headed eagle with shield. First signature printed, second signature handwritten. PC: White.	450	900	—

		Good	Fine	XF
A22	**50 Rubles** 1818-1843. Crowned double-headed eagle with shield. First signature printed, second signature handwritten. PC: Yellowish.	2,000	—	—

		Good	Fine	XF
A23	**100 Rubles** 1819-1843. Crowned double-headed eagle with shield. First signature printed, second signature handwritten. Rare. PC: White.	—	—	—

		Good	Fine	XF
A24	**200 Rubles** 1819-1843. Crowned double-headed eagle with shield. First signature printed, second signature handwritten. Rare. PC: Gray.	—	—	—

ГОСУДАРСТВЕННЫЙ КОММЕРЛЕСКІЙ БАНКЪ

State Commercial Bank

1840-1841 Issue

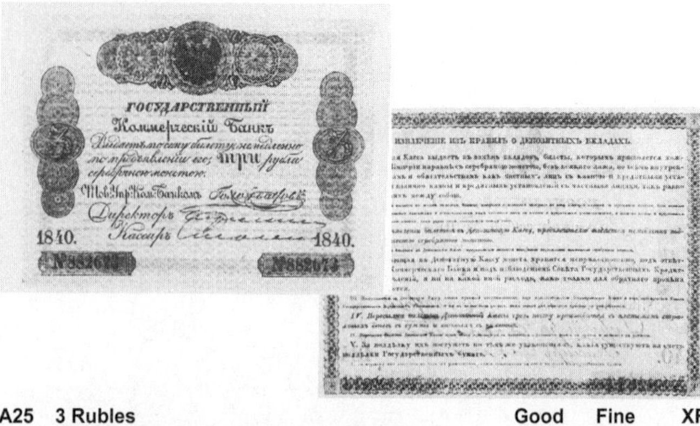

		Good	Fine	XF
A25	**3 Rubles** 1840. Green. First signature printed, second and third signatures handwritten. Signature varieties.	1,000	2,000	—
A26	**5 Rubles** 1840. Blue. First signature printed, second and third signatures handwritten. Signature varieties.	1,500	3,000	—
A27	**10 Rubles** 1840. Pink. First signature printed, second and third signatures handwritten. Signature varieties. Rare.	—	—	—
A28	**25 Rubles** 1840. Black. First signature printed, second and third signatures handwritten. Signature varieties. Rare.	—	—	—

		Good	Fine	XF
A29	**50 Rubles** 1840. Brown. First signature printed, second and third signatures handwritten. Signature varieties. Rare.	—	—	—
A30	**100 Rubles** 1841. Multicolor. First signature printed, second and third signatures handwritten. Signature varieties. Rare.	—	—	—

КРЕДИТНЫЙ БИЛЕТЪ СОХРАННЫХЪ КАЗЕНЪ И ГОСУДАРСТВЕННЫХЪ ЗАЕМНАГО БАНКА

Custody Treasury and State Loan Bank Credit Notes

1841 Issue

		Good	Fine	XF
A31	**50 Rubles** 1841. Dark green. Light seal. Rare. PC: Yellowish.	—	—	—
A32	**50 Rubles** 1841. Light green. Black seal. Rare. PC: Yellowish.	—	—	—

ГОСУДАРСТВЕННЫЙ КРЕДИТНЫЙ БИЛНТЪ

State Credit Notes

1843-1856 Issue

#A33-A40 First signature printed (until 1851 Halchinskii); handwritten (1854 Jurev, 1855-1860 Rostovchev, 1861-1865 Lamanskii), second and third signature handwritten with varieties. From 1851 all signatures were printed.

		Good	Fine	XF
A33	**1 Ruble** 1843-1865. Brown on yellow underprint. Crowned double-headed eagle in shield within sprays at top center.			
	a. 1843-1864.	125	300	600
	b. 1865.	100	225	450

		Good	Fine	XF
A34	**3 Rubles** 1843-1865. Green on light green underprint. Crowned double-headed eagle in shield within ornate frame at top center.	200	400	—
A35	**5 Rubles** 1843-1865. Blue on light blue underprint. Crowned double-headed eagle in shield within sprays or ornate frame at top center.	350	700	—
A36	**10 Rubles** 1843-1865. Red on pink underprint. Crowned double-headed eagle in shield within sprays or ornate frame at top center.	800	2,000	—

		Good	Fine	XF
A37	**15 Rubles** 1856. Multicolor. Crowned double-headed eagle in shield within ornate frame at top center. Specimen. Rare.	—	—	—

		Good	Fine	XF
A38	**25 Rubles** 1843-1865. Violet on lilac underprint. Crowned double-headed eagle in shield within ornate frame at top center.	1,000	2,000	—
A39	**50 Rubles** 1843-1865. Black on gray underprint. Crowned double-headed eagle in shield within sprays or ornate frame at top center. Rare.	—	—	—
A40	**100 Rubles** 1843-1865. Brown-violet on brown underprint. Crowned double-headed eagle in shield within sprays or ornate frame at top center. Rare.	—	—	—

1866 Issue

#A41-A47 first signature: Lamanskii (1866 as vice-director, 1870-1880 as director). Many varieties of the second signature.

		Good	Fine	XF
A41	**1 Ruble** 1866-1880. Black on light brown underprint. Crowned double-headed eagle above monogram of Czar Alexander II at left.	100	150	250

		Good	Fine	XF
A42	**3 Rubles** 1866-1880. Black on light green underprint. Crowned double-headed eagle above monogram of Czar Alexander II at left.	150	400	—

		Good	Fine	XF
A43	**5 Rubles** 1866-1880. Black on light blue underprint. Crowned double-headed eagle above monogram of Czar Alexander II at left. Back: Portrait D. Ivanovich Donskoi at center.	200	450	—
A44	**10 Rubles** 1866-1880. Black on red underprint. Crowned double-headed eagle above monogram of Czar Alexander II at left. Back: M. Feodorovich at center.	400	800	—
A45	**25 Rubles** 1866-1876. Black on lilac underprint. Crowned double-headed eagle above monogram of Czar Alexander II at left. Back: A. Mikhailovich at center.	800	1,600	—

		Good	Fine	XF
A45A	**25 Rubles** 1876; 1884; 1886. Black. Crowned double-headed eagle above monogram of Czar Alexander II at left. Arms at upper left. Uniface. Watermark: Czar Alexey Mikhailovich, wavy line and letters G.K.B. Rare.	—	—	—

		Good	Fine	XF
A46	**50 Rubles** 1866. Black on gray underprint. Crowned double-headed eagle above monogram of Czar Alexander II at left. Back: Portrait Peter I at center. Rare.	—	—	—
A47	**100 Rubles** 1872-1880. Black on yellow underprint. Crowned double-headed eagle above monogram of Czar Alexander II at left. Back: Catherine II at center. Rare.	—	—	—

1882-1886 Issue

#A48-A53 First signature: Cimsen (until 1886), Zhukovskii (1889-1892), Pleske (1894-1896); second signature varieties.

		Good	Fine	XF
A48	**1 Ruble** 1882; 1884; 1886. Black on light brown underprint. Crowned double-headed eagle above monogram of Czar Alexander III at left.	80.00	150	300
A49	**3 Rubles** 1882; 1884; 1886. Black on light green underprint. Crowned double-headed eagle above monogram of Czar Alexander III at left.	150	350	700

		Good	Fine	XF
A50	**5 Rubles** 1882; 1884; 1886. Black on light blue underprint. Crowned double-headed eagle above monogram of Czar Alexander III at left. Back: Portrait D. Ivanovich Donskoi at center.	200	450	—
A51	**10 Rubles** 1882; 1884; 1886. Black on red underprint. Crowned double-headed eagle above monogram of Czar Alexander III at left. Back: M. Feodorovich at center.	350	750	—
A52	**25 Rubles** 1884; 1886. Black. Crowned double-headed eagle above monogram of Czar Alexander III at left. Arms at upper left. Like #A45A. Watermark: Czar Alexey Mikhailovich, wavy line and letters G.K.B. Rare.	—	—	—

		Good	Fine	XF
A53	**100 Rubles** 1882-1894. Black on yellow underprint. Crowned double-headed eagle above monogram of Czar Alexander III at left. Back: Catherine II at center. Rare.	—	—	—

1887-1894 Issue

#A54-A60 first signature: Cimsen (1887), Zhukovskii (1889-1892), E. Pleske (1894). Many varieties of second signature.

		Good	Fine	XF
A54	**1 Ruble** 1887-1894. Black on light brown underprint. Crowned arms at left, monogram of Czar Alexander III at right. BC: Brown.	200	400	—
A55	**3 Rubles** 1887-1894. Black on light green underprint. Crowned arms at left. Monogram of Czar Alexander III. BC: Green.	200	500	1,000

Color Abbreviation Guide

New to the *Standard Catalog of® World Paper Money* are the following abbreviations related to color references:

BC: Back color
PC: Paper color

		Good	Fine	XF
A56	**5 Rubles** 1887-1894. Black on light blue underprint. Monogram of Czar Alexander III. BC: Blue.	300	700	1,500
A57	**10 Rubles** 1887-1892. Black on red underprint. Monogram of Czar Alexander III. BC: Red.	300	700	1,500

		Good	Fine	XF
A58	**10 Rubles** 1894. Red on multicolor underprint. Monogram of Czar Alexander III. Vertical format.	175	400	—

		Good	Fine	XF
A59	**25 Rubles** 1887. Monogram of Czar Alexander III. BC: Violet.	—	—	—

Note: Only 1 example of #A59 is known uncancelled.

		Good	Fine	XF
A60	**25 Rubles** 1890. Blue. Monogram of Czar Alexander III. BC: Multicolor. Specimen only. Rare.	—	—	—
A60A	**25 Rubles** 1892. Lilac.			
	a. Signature Pleske.	600	1,300	—
	b. Signature Zhukovsky. Rare.	—	—	—

1895 Issue

		Good	Fine	XF
A61	**1 Ruble** 1895. Black on light brown underprint. Crowned arms at left. Monogram of Nicholas II at left. Like #A54. Signature E. Pleske. BC: Brown.	40.00	100	250
A62	**3 Rubles** 1895. Black on light green underprint. Crowned arms at left. Monogram of Nicholas II at left. Similar to #A55. Signature E. Pleske. BC: Green.	200	400	—
A63	**5 Rubles** 1895. Blue and multicolor. Monogram of Nicholas II at left. Like #3. Signature E. Pleske.	150	350	—

Note: #A64 a 1895 requires confirmation.

ГОСУДАРСТВЕННЫЙ БАНКЪ ДЕПОЗИТНАЯ МЕТАЛЛИЧНСКАЯ КВИТАНЦІЯ

State Bank Metal Deposit Receipts

1876 Issue

		Good	Fine	XF
A65	**50 Rubles = 10 Half Imperials** 1876. Specimen, perforated: *ОБРАЗЕЦЪ*. Rare.	—	—	—
A66	**100 Rubles = 10 Imperials** 1876. Specimen. Rare.	—	—	—

1886 Issue

		Good	Fine	XF
A67	**50 Rubles** 1886. Overprint: *OBRAZH-$*. Specimen. Rare.	—	—	—
A68	**100 Rubles** 1886. Specimen. Rare.	—	—	—
A69	**500 Rubles** 1886. Specimen. Rare.	—	—	—
A70	**1000 Rubles** 1886. Specimen. Rare.	—	—	—

1895 Issue

		Good	Fine	XF
A71	**5 Rubles** 1895. Specimen, perforated: *ОБРАЗЕЦЪ*.	—	—	1,000
A72	**10 Rubles** 1895. Specimen.	—	—	800
A73	**25 Rubles** 1895. Specimen.	—	—	1,000
A74	**50 Rubles** 1895. Specimen.	—	—	1,000
A75	**100 Rubles** 1895. Specimen.	—	—	1,000

		Good	Fine	XF
A76	**500 Rubles** 1895. Specimen.	—	—	1,000
A77	**1000 Rubles** 1895. Specimen.	—	—	1,000

1896 Issue

		Good	Fine	XF
A78	**5 Rubles** 1896. Specimen, perforated: *ОБРАЗЕЦЪ*. Rare.	—	—	—
A79	**10 Rubles** 1896. Specimen. Rare.	—	—	—
A80	**30 Rubles** 1896. Specimen. Rare.	—	—	—
A81	**100 Rubles** 1896.	—	—	3,000
A82	**500 Rubles** 1896. Specimen. Rare.	—	—	—
A83	**1000 Rubles** 1896. Specimen. Rare.	—	—	—

БИЛЕТЪ ГОСУДАРСТВЕННАГО КАЗНАЧЕЙСТВА

State Treasury Note

1895 Issue

		Good	Fine	XF
A84	**50 Rubles** 1895. Specimen. Rare.	—	—	—

ГОСУДАРСТВЕННЫЙ КРЕДИТНЫЙ БИЛЕТЪ

State Credit Notes

1898 Issue

SIGNATURE VARIETIES	
E. Pleske 1898-1903	S. Timashev, 1903-1909
A. Konshin, 1909-1912	I. Shipov, 1912-1917

		Good	Fine	XF
1	**1 Ruble** 1898. Blue on red-brown underprint. Russian eagle at left, monogram at right. Full serial #. Like #A54. BC: Red-brown. 150x90mm.			
	a. Signature Pleske. (1898-1903).	20.00	50.00	100
	b. Signature Timashev. (1903-1909).	15.00	40.00	70.00
	c. Signature Konshin. (1909-1912).	50.00	100	250
	d. Signature Shipov. (1912-1917).	2.00	5.00	10.00
	s. Specimen. Signature Pleske. (1898-1903).	—	Unc	350

Note: For 1 Ruble 1898 with series # (2 letters HA or HB and 1, 2 or 3 numerals) instead of serial #, see #15.

		Good	Fine	XF
2	**3 Rubles** 1898. Blue on brown underprint. Russian eagle at left. Like #A55. BC: Green. 148x94mm.			
	a. Signature Pleske. (1898-1903).	50.00	100	300
	b. Signature Timashev. (1903-1909).	40.00	100	200
	s1. Specimen. Signature Pleske. (1898-1903).	—	—	—
	s2. Specimen. Signature Timashev. (1903-1909).	—	—	—

		Good	Fine	XF
3	**5 Rubles** 1898. Blue on multicolor underprint. Allegory of Russia seated holding shield and sword. Like #A63. Back: Portrait at each corner. Watermark: Value within diamond, repeated. 95x152mm.			
	a. Signature Pleske. (1898-1903).	40.00	80.00	200
	b. Signature Timashev. (1903-1909).	40.00	70.00	150
	s. Specimen.	—	Unc	500
4	**10 Rubles** 1898. Red on multicolor underprint. Allegory of Russia seated holding shield and laurel branch. Like #A58. Watermark: 10 in diamond, repeated. 105x175mm.			
	a. Signature Pleske. (1898-1903).	70.00	150	300
	b. Signature Timashev. (1903-1909).	50.00	120	250
	s. Specimen. Without signature.	—	Unc	500

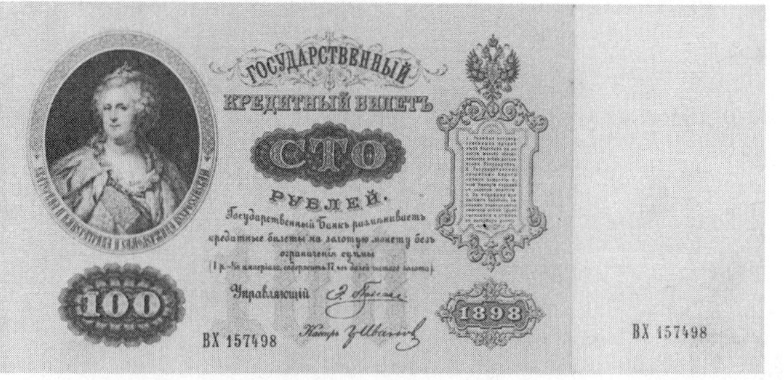

#	Description	Good	Fine	XF
5	**100 Rubles** 1898. Black on tan underprint. Portrait Catherine II at left. BC: Blue on green and lilac underprint. Watermark: Catherine II. 260x122mm.			
	a. Signature Pleske. (1898-1903).	100	160	350
	b. Signature Timashev. (1903-1909).	80.00	125	250
	c. Signature Konshin. (1909-1912).	50.00	100	200
	s. Specimen. Signature Pleske. (1898-1903).	—	Unc	600

#	Description	Good	Fine	XF
6	**500 Rubles** 1898. Black, green, red and blue. Peter I at left. Watermark: Value. 275x127mm.			
	a. Signature Pleske. (1898-1903).	120	300	500
	b. Signature Timashev. (1903-1909).	50.00	100	350
	c. Signature Konshin. (1909-1912).	40.00	100	250
	s. Specimen. Without signature.	—	Unc	750

1899 Issue

#	Description	Good	Fine	XF
7	**25 Rubles** 1899. Lilac. Allegory of Russia standing with shield, two seated children at left. Like #A60. Back: Six heads at right. BC: Blue and maroon. Watermark: Alexander III. 174x104mm.			
	a. Signature Pleske. (1898-1903).	80.00	150	350
	b. Signature Timashev. (1903-1909).	70.00	140	250
	s. Specimen. Without signature.	—	Unc	650

#	Description	Good	Fine	XF
8	**50 Rubles** 1899. Black. Portrait Nicholas I at left. BC: Green and multicolor. 190x117mm.			
	a. Signature Pleske. (1898-1903).	100	400	800
	b. Signature Timashev. (1903-1909).	50.00	300	450
	c. Signature Konshin. (1909-1912).	15.00	20.00	50.00
	d. Signature Shipov. (1912-1917).	10.00	20.00	30.00
	s. Specimen. Without signature.	—	Unc	450

1905-1912 Issue

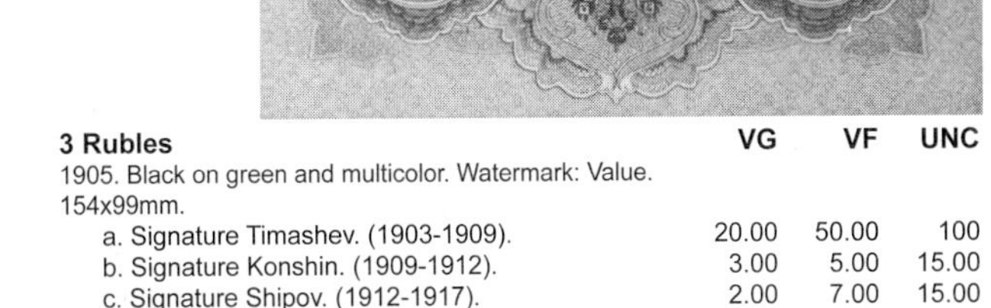

#	Description	VG	VF	UNC
9	**3 Rubles** 1905. Black on green and multicolor. Watermark: Value. 154x99mm.			
	a. Signature Timashev. (1903-1909).	20.00	50.00	100
	b. Signature Konshin. (1909-1912).	3.00	5.00	15.00
	c. Signature Shipov. (1912-1917).	2.00	7.00	15.00
	s. Specimen.	—	—	200

#	Description	VG	VF	UNC
10	**5 Rubles** 1909. Blue-black on blue and multicolor underprint. Eagle at top center. Vertical format. Full serial #. BC: Dark gray on blue and multicolor underprint. Watermark: Value. 99x159mm.			
	a. Signature Konshin. (1909-1912).	2.00	5.00	15.00
	b. Signature Shipov. (1912-1917).	1.00	2.00	5.00
	s. Specimen. Signature Konshin. (1909-1912).	—	—	200

Note: For 5 Rubles 1909 with series # (2 letters and 3 numerals) instead of serial #, see #35.

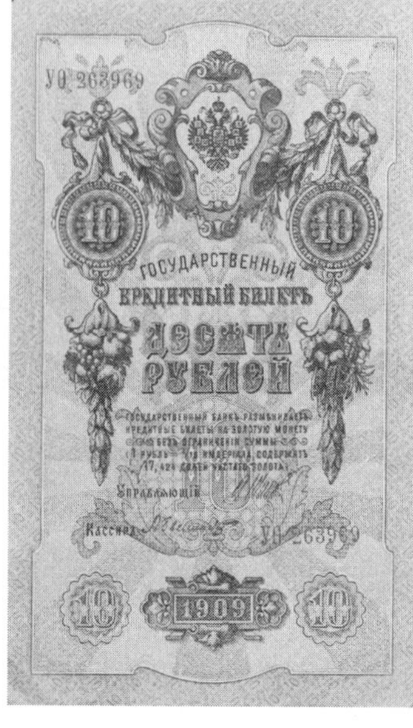

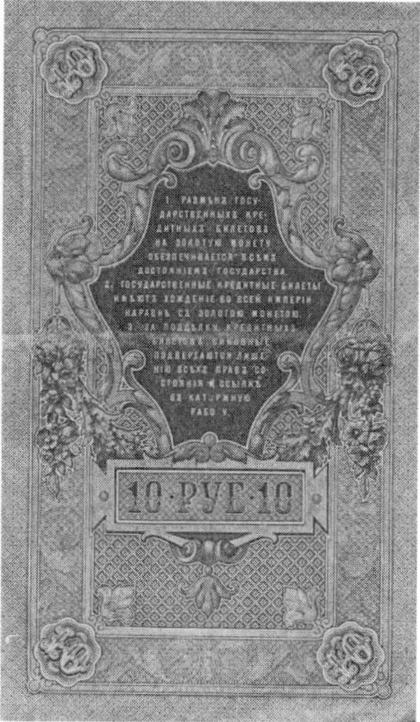

		VG	VF	UNC
11	**10 Rubles** 1909. Deep olive-green on green and red underprint. Imperial eagle at top center, produce at left and right. Vertical format. Watermark: Value. 105x175mm.			
	a. Signature Timashev. (1903-1909).	25.00	50.00	100
	b. Signature Konshin. (1909-1912).	3.00	6.00	20.00
	c. Signature Shipov. (1912-1917).	1.00	2.00	5.00
	s. Specimen. Signature Timashev. (1903-1909).	—	—	250

		VG	VF	UNC
12	**25 Rubles** 1909. Black on red and blue underprint. Back: Alexander III at right. BC: Black on red and green underprint. Watermark: Value or Alexander III. 178x108mm.			
	a. Signature Konshin. (1909-1912).	5.00	10.00	20.00
	b. Signature Shipov. (1912-1917).	4.00	8.00	15.00
	s. Specimen. Signature Konshin. (1909-1912).	—	—	350

		VG	VF	UNC
13	**100 Rubles** 1910. Dark brown on light brown and multicolor underprint. Back: Allegorical man with sword, Catherine II at left. Watermark: Value or Catherine 2. 260x122mm.			
	a. Signature Konshin. (1909-1912).	15.00	30.00	50.00
	b. Signature Shipov. (1912-1917).	10.00	15.00	30.00
	s. Specimen. Signature Konshin. (1909-1912).	—	—	350

		VG	VF	UNC
14	**500 Rubles** 1912. Black on green and multicolor underprint. Back: Peter I at left. Watermark: Value or Peter I. 275x127mm.			
	a. Signature Konshin. (1909-1912).	20.00	40.00	80.00
	b. Signature Shipov. (1912-1917).	15.00	20.00	40.00
	s. Specimen. Signature Konshin. (1909-1912).	—	—	400

1915 Issue

#	Denomination	VG	VF	UNC
15	**1 Ruble** ND (1915 -old date 1898). Blue on brown underprint. Like #1 but control # instead of serial #. 13 signature varieties. Top signature Shipov. Prefix letters HA001-127.	1.00	3.00	5.00

Note: Some of the Shipov notes were later printed by the Provisional Government and also by the Soviet Government. They will have higher prefix letter-number combinations. They are also lighter in color than those originally printed during the Czarist period.

СБЕРНАЯ РОССІЯ

Postage Stamp Currency Issue

1915 ND Issue

Romanov Tercentenary stamps of 1913 printed on thin card stock.

#	Denomination	VG	VF	UNC
16	**1 Kopek** ND (1915). Brown-orange. Portrait Peter I. Back: Legend and eagle. 24x29mm. (Scott #112).	5.00	10.00	20.00
17	**1 Kopek** ND (1916-1917). Brown-orange. Portrait Alexander II. #16 without *1* overprint. Back: Legend and eagle. 24x29mm. (Scott #114).	15.00	50.00	100
18	**2 Kopeks** ND (1915). Green. Portrait Alexander III. Back: Legend and eagle. BC: Black. 29x24mm. (Scott #113).	5.00	10.00	30.00
19	**2 Kopeks** ND (1915). Green. Portrait Alexander III. #18 without *2* overprint. Back: Legend and eagle. BC: Black. 29x24mm. (Scott #115).	10.00	50.00	100

#	Denomination	VG	VF	UNC
20	**3 Kopeks** ND (1915). Red. Portrait Alexander III. Back: Legend and eagle. 29x24mm. (Scott #116).	1.00	2.00	5.00

#	Denomination	VG	VF	UNC
21	**10 Kopeks** ND (1915). Blue. Portrait Nicholas II. Back: Legend and eagle. 29x24mm. (Scott #105).	1.00	3.00	5.00
22	**15 Kopeks** ND (1915). Brown. Portrait Nicholas I. Back: Legend and eagle. 29x24mm. (Scott #106).	1.00	3.00	5.00
23	**20 Kopeks** ND (1915). Green. Portrait Alexander I. Back: Legend and eagle. 29x24mm. (Scott #107).	1.00	3.00	5.00

Note: #21-23 also exist imperforate; these are scarcer than perforated pieces. Beware of perforated examples which have been trimmed into imperforates.

For postage stamp currency issue without eagle on back, refer to #32-34.

Treasury Small Change Notes

1915 ND Issue

#	Denomination	VG	VF	UNC
24	**1 Kopek** ND (1915). Black on brown-orange underprint. Arms at upper center. Back: Arms at center. 80x45mm.			
	a. Issued note.	1.00	2.00	4.00
	s. Specimen.	—	—	150
25	**2 Kopeks** ND (1915). Black on light brown underprint. Arms at upper center. Back: Arms at center. 80x45mm.			
	a. Issued note.	1.00	2.00	4.00
	s. Specimen.	—	—	150
26	**3 Kopeks** ND (1915). Green on light green underprint. Arms at upper center. Back: Arms at center. 80x45mm.			
	a. Issued note.	1.00	2.00	4.00
	s. Specimen.	—	—	150

#	Denomination	VG	VF	UNC
27	**5 Kopeks** ND (1915). Black on light blue underprint. Arms at upper center. Back: Arms at center. 80x45mm.			
	a. Issued note.	1.00	3.00	6.00
	s. Specimen.	—	—	150
28	**10 Kopeks** ND (1915). Blue on red-orange underprint. Arms at upper center. Back: Arms at center. 80x45mm. (Not issued).	15.00	40.00	150
29	**15 Kopeks** ND (1915). Red-brown on yellow underprint. Arms at upper center. Back: Arms at center. 80x45mm. (Not issued).	15.00	40.00	150
30	**20 Kopeks** ND (1915). Green on lilac underprint. Arms at upper center. Back: Arms at center. 80x45mm. (Not issued).	15.00	40.00	150

#	Denomination	VG	VF	UNC
31	**50 Kopeks** ND (1915). Blue on gold or yellow underprint. Arms at upper center. Back: Arms at center. 100x60mm.			
	a. Issued note.	1.00	3.00	5.00
	s. Specimen.	—	—	200

5% КРАТКОСРОЧНОЕ ОБЯЗАТЕЛЪСТВО ГОСУДАР. (СТВЕННАГО) КАЗНАЧНЙСТВА

State Treasury 5% Short-Term Obligations

1915 Issue

#	Denomination	VG	VF	UNC
31A	**5000 Rubles** 15.8.1915. Multicolor. Arms at center. Specimen. Rare.	—	—	—
31B	**10,000 Rubles** 1.8.1915. Multicolor. Arms at center. Specimen. Rare.	—	—	—
31C	**25,000 Rubles** 20.7.1915. Multicolor. Arms at center. Specimen. Rare.	—	—	—
31D	**50,000 Rubles** 20.6.1915. Multicolor. Arms at center. Specimen. Rare.	—	—	—
31E	**100,000 Rubles** 15.8.1915. Multicolor. Arms at center. Specimen. Rare.	—	—	—

1916-17 (1918) Issue

Note: For similar issues with crownless eagle, see Volume 1 - Siberia, #S821-S825 and S831-S870.

#	Denomination	Good	Fine	XF
31F	**1000 Rubles** 1916 (1918). Lilac-brown. (12 month).	4.00	15.00	75.00
31G	**1000 Rubles** 1917 (1918). Lilac-brown. (9 month).	4.00	15.00	75.00

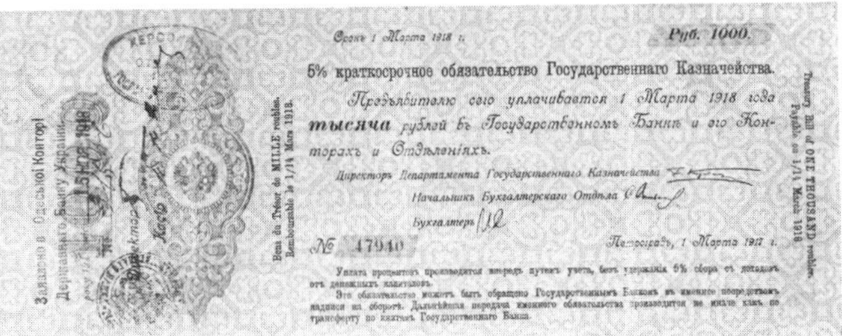

#	Denomination	Good	Fine	XF
31H	**1000 Rubles** 1917 (1918). Red-violet on brown and orange underprint. (12 month).	3.00	10.00	40.00
31I	**5000 Rubles** 1916-17 (1918). Orange. (12 month).	8.00	30.00	100
31J	**5000 Rubles** 1.5.1917. (12 month).	8.00	30.00	100
31K	**10,000 Rubles** 1.10.1915. (9 month). Specimen.	—	—	750
31L	**10,000 Rubles** 1916 (1918). Red. (12 month).	10.00	40.00	150

		Good	Fine	XF
31M	**10,000 Rubles** 1916 (1918). Red. (9 month).	15.00	45.00	200
31N	**10,000 Rubles** 1917 (1918). Red. (12 month).	10.00	40.00	150
31O	**25,000 Rubles** 1916 (1918). (12 month).	20.00	75.00	300
31P	**25,000 Rubles** 1917-18 (1918). (9 month).	30.00	100	400
31Q	**25,000 Rubles** 1917 (1918). (12 month).	25.00	75.00	300
31R	**50,000 Rubles** 1916-1917 (1918). (12 month).	40.00	150	500
31S	**50,000 Rubles** 1917 (1918). (9 month).	50.00	200	600
31T	**100,000 Rubles** 1916-1917 (1918). (12 month).	70.00	225	750
31U	**100,000 Rubles** 1.4.1917. (12 month).	70.00	225	750
31V	**500,000 Rubles** 1916-1917 (1918). (12 month). Rare.	—	—	—
31W	**500,000 Rubles** 1917 (1918). (9 month). Rare.	—	—	—
31X	**1,000,000 Rubles** 1916-1917 (1918). (12 month). Rare.	—	—	—

Note: Part of the above issue was used by the Soviet government.

PROVISIONAL GOVERNMENT

ВРНЬНННОН ПРАВИТНЛЬСТВО

Postage Stamp Currency

1917 ND Issue

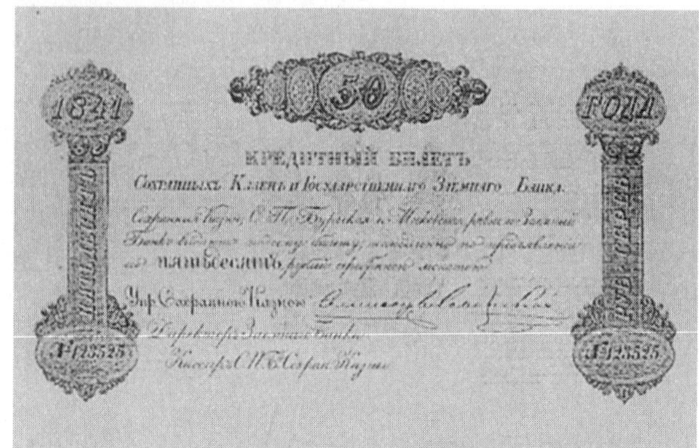

		VG	VF	UNC
32	**1 Kopek** ND (1917). Brown-orange. Portrait Peter I. Like #16-17. Back: Text without eagle. (Scott #139).			
	a. Overprint: *1* on face.	1.00	3.00	6.00
	b. Without overprint on face. Rare.	—	—	—
33	**2 Kopeks** ND (1917). Green. Portrait Alexander II. Like #18-19. Back: Text without eagle. (Scott #140).	1.00	3.00	6.00

		VG	VF	UNC
34	**3 Kopeks** ND (1917). Red. Portrait Alexander III. Like #20. Back: Text without eagle. (Scott #141).	2.00	5.00	10.00

ГОСУДАРСТВЕННЫЙ КРЕДИТНЫЙ БИЛЕТЪ

Government Credit Notes

1917 Issue

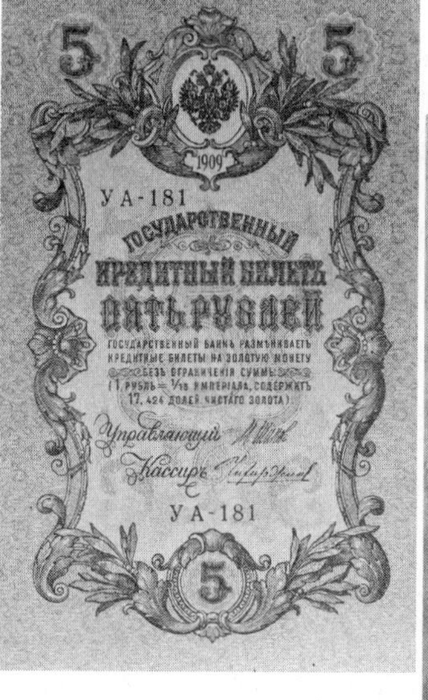

		VG	VF	UNC
35	**5 Rubles** ND (1917-old date 1909). Blue and multicolor. Eagle at top center. Like #10 but series # (2 letters and 3 numerals) in place of serial #. 13 signature varieties.			
	a. Issued note. Series YA001- YA043.	1.00	2.00	4.00
	x. Error. Series letters AY above and YA below.	50.00	150	450

Note: #35 with series YA044-200 and YБ401-510 is a Soviet Government issue.

		VG	VF	UNC
36	**250 Rubles** (4.9.) 1917. Black on lilac underprint. 13 signature varieties. Back: Swastika in underprint at center. BC: Dark brown on light green and multicolor underprint. 175x104mm.	5.00	10.00	20.00

Note: #36 with series # AA001-018 is a Provisional Government issue; Series AA019-100, AБ101-200, AB201-300 and AГ301-376 are Soviet Government issues.

No.	Denomination / Description	VG	VF	UNC
37	**1000 Rubles** (9.3.) 1917. Dark brown on green underprint. Swastika in underprint. 5 signature varieties. Back: Duma building at center. BC: Blue on light brown and multicolor underprint. 215x132mm.	7.00	15.00	25.00

Note: #37 with series ААЦАЗ is a Provisional Government issue; Series АИЦАОъ Бъ В, ГЦГЯ are Soviet Government issues.

5% ОБЛИГАЦІЯ ЗАЕМЪ СВОБОДЫ

5% Freedom Loans Debenture Bonds

1917 Issue

No.	Denomination / Description	VG	VF	UNC
37A	**20 Rubles** 12 (27) 3.1917. Black on yellow underprint. With coupons.	10.00	15.00	50.00
37B	**40 Rubles** 12 (27) 3.1917. Black. With coupons.	15.00	30.00	80.00
37C	**50 Rubles** 12 (27) 3.1917. Black on green underprint. With coupons.	15.00	30.00	80.00

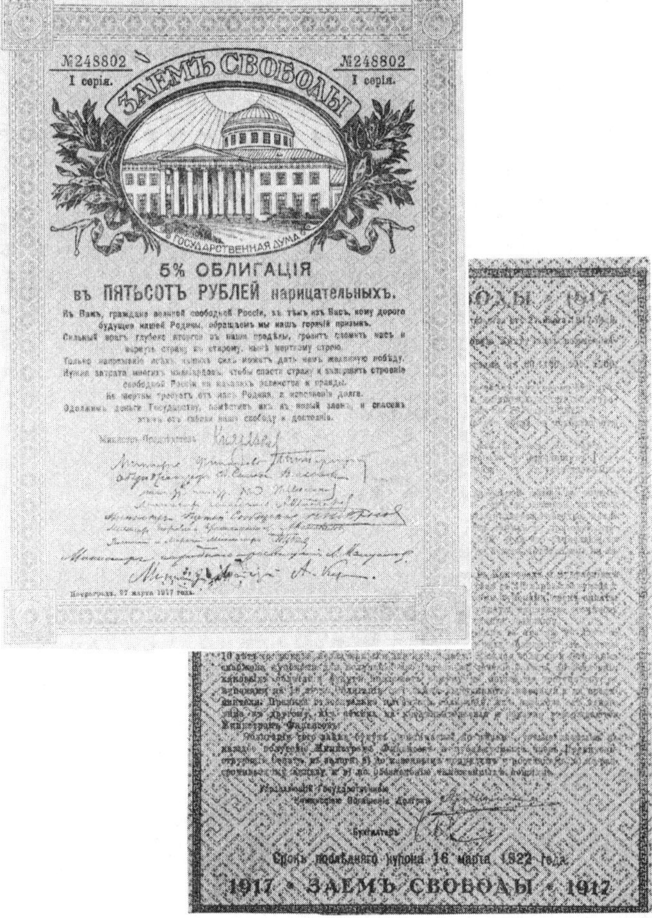

No.	Denomination / Description	VG	VF	UNC
37D	**100 Rubles** 12 (27) 3.1917. Black on brown underprint. With coupons.	15.00	30.00	75.00
37E	**500 Rubles** 12 (27) 3.1917. Black on blue underprint. With coupons.	15.00	30.00	80.00
37F	**1000 Rubles** 12 (27) 3.1917. Black on rose underprint. 200x155mm. With coupons.	15.00	30.00	100
37G	**5000 Rubles** 12 (27) 3.1917. Black. With coupons.			
	a. Issued note.	25.00	50.00	150
	b. Specimen.	—	—	500
37H	**10,000 Rubles** 12 (27) 3.1917. Black. With coupons.	50.00	100	350
37I	**25,000 Rubles** 12 (27) 3.1917. Black. With coupons.	50.00	175	500

Note: Values for #37A-37I are for pieces with coupons. Those without coupons are worth 50% less. The Soviet government used these 5% Freedom Loans in denominations of 20, 40, 50, and 100 Rubles w/o coupons as money.

Color Abbreviation Guide

New to the *Standard Catalog of® World Paper Money* are the following abbreviations related to color references:

BC: Back color
PC: Paper color

КАЗНАЧЕЙСКІЙ ЗНАКЪ

Treasury Notes

1917 ND Issue

#38 and 39 so-called "Kerenki," they are frequently also called "Kerensky rubles." They were printed with plates adapted from consular revenue stamps.

No.	Denomination / Description	VG	VF	UNC
38	**20 Rubles** ND (4.9.1917). Brown on red-brown underprint. Eagle at upper center. 62x49mm.	1.00	2.00	3.00
39	**40 Rubles** ND (4.9.1917). Red on green underprint. Eagle at upper center. 62x49mm.	1.00	2.00	3.00

Note: #38 and 39 may also appear in sheets up to 100 subjects.

ГОСУДАРСТВЕННЫЙ КРЕДИТНЫЙ БИЛЕТ

Government Credit Notes

1918; 1919 Issue

		VG	VF	UNC
39A	**25 Rubles** 1918. Black on blue and multicolor underprint. Allegorical female at center. Back: Parliament building. BC: Blue-gray.			
	a. 2 signatures on face.	12.00	25.00	50.00
	b. Without signatures.	12.00	20.00	40.00
	s. Specimen with or without signature.	—	—	150

		VG	VF	UNC
39B	**50 Rubles** 1919. Black on orange and multicolor underprint. Two allegorical figures at right.			
	p. Proof. Rare.	—	—	—
	s. Specimen. Rare.	—	—	—

		VG	VF	UNC
40	**100 Rubles** 1918. Black on brown and multicolor underprint. Agriculture seated at center. Back: Parliament building. BC: Brown. 148x86mm.			
	a. 2 signatures on face.	20.00	40.00	90.00
	b. Without signatures.	20.00	40.00	80.00
	s. Specimen.	—	—	150
40A	**250 Rubles** 1919. Black on green, blue and multicolor underprint. Winged cherub and seated woman with torch and globe at right.	VG	VF	UNC
	p. Proof. Rare.	—	—	—
	s. Specimen. Rare.	—	—	—

		VG	VF	UNC
41	**500 Rubles** 1919. Black on brown and multicolor underprint. Seated woman with two cherubs at center.			
	p. Proof. Rare.	—	—	—
	s. Specimen. Rare.	—	—	—

		VG	VF	UNC
42	**1000 Rubles** 1919. Black on lilac, green and multicolor underprint. Seated woman with globe at left.			
	p. Proof. Rare.	—	—	—
	s. Specimen. Rare.	—	—	—

Note: For #39A and 40 issued by other authorities during the Civil War, see Volume 1, #S1196-S1197, S1213-S1214 and S1248-S1249.

1917 Issue

		VG	VF	UNC
43	**25 Rubles** ND (1917). Green. Without signature. BC: Light brown.	100	200	450

		VG	VF	UNC
44	**50 Rubles** ND (1917). Brown. Without signature. BC: Green.	50.00	150	350
45	**100 Rubles** ND (1917). Yellowish brown. Without signature. BC: Yellow-green. (Not issued). Rare.	—	—	—

#46 not assigned.

		VG	VF	UNC
47	**500 Rubles** ND (1917). Brown. Without signature. BC: Blue-gray. Government check. (Soviet government).	—	—	—

R.S.F.S.R.-RUSSIAN SOCIALIST FEDERATED SOVIET REPUBLIC

БИЛЕТЪ ГОСУДАРСТВЕННАГО КАЗНАЧЕЙСТВА

State Treasury Notes

1908-1916 (1918) Issues

		VG	VF	UNC
48	**25 Rubles** 1915 (1918). Green on violet underprint. Watermark: "V" and open triangle pattern.	3.00	6.00	20.00
49	**50 Rubles** 1908 (1918). Brown on green underprint. Watermark: Three vertical stripes.	20.00	60.00	200
50	**50 Rubles** 1912 (1918). Brown on green underprint. Watermark: 5 in diamonds pattern.	10.00	25.00	75.00

#	Description	VG	VF	UNC
51	**50 Rubles** 1913 (1918). Brown on green underprint. Watermark: Horizontal and vertical rotating 10 pattern.	10.00	25.00	75.00

#	Description	VG	VF	UNC
52	**50 Rubles** 1914 (1918). Brown on green underprint. 151x141mm.	5.00	10.00	20.00
53	**50 Rubles** 1915 (1918). Brown on green underprint.	5.00	10.00	20.00
54	**100 Rubles** 1908 (1918). Black on pink underprint.	20.00	60.00	250
55	**100 Rubles** 1912 (1918). Black on pink underprint.	10.00	35.00	100
56	**100 Rubles** 1913 (1918). Black on pink underprint.	10.00	35.00	100
57	**100 Rubles** 1914 (1918). Black on pink underprint.	7.00	15.00	50.00
58	**100 Rubles** 1915 (1918). Black on pink underprint. 151x141mm.	7.00	15.00	50.00
59	**500 Rubles** 1915 (1918). Black on blue underprint.	7.00	20.00	70.00
60	**500 Rubles** 1916 (1918). Black on light blue underprint.	8.00	25.00	90.00

#61-80 not assigned.

РАСЧЕТНЫЙ ЗНАК

Currency Notes

1919 ND Issue

#	Description	VG	VF	UNC
81	**1 Ruble** ND (1919). Brown. RSFSR emblem at center. BC: Multicolor. 40x48mm.	2.00	4.00	7.00
82	**2 Rubles** ND (1919). Dark brown. RSFSR emblem at center. BC: Multicolor. 40x48mm.	2.00	4.00	7.00
83	**3 Rubles** ND (1919). Green. RSFSR emblem at center. BC: Multicolor. Watermark: Lozenges. 40x48mm.	2.00	4.00	7.00

1921 ND Issue

#	Description	VG	VF	UNC
84	**3 Rubles** ND (1921). Green. Arms at center.			
	a. Watermark: Spades.	1.00	4.00	7.00
	b. Watermark: Stars.	2.00	5.00	10.00
85	**5 Rubles** ND (1921). Dark blue. Arms at center.			
	a. Watermark: Lozenges.	1.00	2.00	5.00
	b. Watermark: Spades.	2.00	4.00	10.00
	c. Watermark: Stars.	2.00	4.00	10.00
	d. Without watermark.	1.00	2.00	5.00

ГОСУДАРСТВЕННЫЙ КРЕДИТНЫЙ БИЛЕТЪ

State Treasury Notes

1918 Issue

#	Description	VG	VF	UNC
86	**1 Ruble** 1918. Brown on tan underprint. 10 signature varieties. Back: Double-headed eagle at center. Watermark: Value. 112x66mm.			
	a. Issued note.	2.00	3.00	5.00
	x. Error: Russian letter *P* missing at right on back.	30.00	100	250

#	Description	VG	VF	UNC
87	**3 Rubles** 1918. Green on light green underprint. 10 signature varieties. Back: Double-headed eagle at center. Watermark: Value. 118x71mm.	2.00	3.00	5.00
88	**5 Rubles** 1918. Blue-black on light blue underprint. 10 signature varieties. Back: Double-headed eagle at center. Watermark: Value. 124x76mm.	2.00	4.00	8.00
89	**10 Rubles** 1918. Red-brown on light red underprint. 10 signature varieties. Back: Double-headed eagle at center. BC: Dark brown on red-brown underprint. Watermark: Value. 128x80mm.	3.00	6.00	12.00

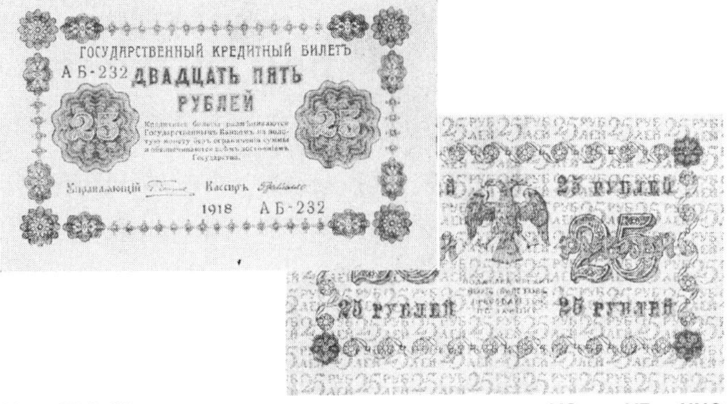

#	Description	VG	VF	UNC
90	**25 Rubles** 1918. Red-brown on light brown underprint. 10 signature varieties. Back: Double-headed eagle at center. BC: Dull purple on brown underprint. Watermark: Value. 133x84mm.	3.00	6.00	12.00

		VG	VF	UNC
91	**50 Rubles** 1918. Dark brown on light brown underprint. 10 signature varieties. Back: Double-headed eagle at center. Watermark: Value. 138x92mm.	4.00	8.00	15.00

		VG	VF	UNC
92	**100 Rubles** 1918. Brown on light red underprint. 10 signature varieties. Back: Double-headed eagle at center. Watermark: Value. 145x95mm.	3.00	5.00	10.00

		VG	VF	UNC
93	**250 Rubles** 1918. Green on light green underprint. 10 signature varieties. Back: Double-headed eagle at center. Watermark: Value. 148x100mm.	3.00	5.00	10.00

		VG	VF	UNC
94	**500 Rubles** 1918. Dark olive-green on pale olive-green underprint. 11 signature varieties. Back: Double-headed eagle at center. BC: Black on brown and pale olive-green underprint. Watermark: Value. 155x105mm.			
	a. Horizontal watermark.	3.00	5.00	10.00
	b. Vertical watermark.	3.00	10.00	15.00

		VG	VF	UNC
95	**1000 Rubles** 1918. Brown on tan underprint. 11 signature varieties. Back: Double-headed eagle at center. Watermark: Value. 160x110mm.			
	a. Horizontal watermark.	5.00	10.00	20.00
	b. Vertical watermark.	5.00	15.00	30.00
	x. Error. Back top to top with back inverted.	50.00	125	300

		VG	VF	UNC
96	**5000 Rubles** 1918. Black on blue underprint. Swastika in underprint. 10 signature varieties. Back: Double-headed eagle at center. BC: Brown on blue underprint. Watermark: Value. 213x132mm.			
	a. Horizontal watermark.	5.00	15.00	30.00
	b. Vertical watermark.	10.00	30.00	60.00

97 10,000 Rubles
1918. Dark brown on brown and red underprint. Swastika in underprint. 10 signature varieties. Back: Double-headed eagle at center. Watermark: Value. 213x132mm.

	VG	VF	UNC
a. Horizontal watermark.	8.00	15.00	30.00
b. Vertical watermark.	10.00	30.00	60.00

РАСЧЕТНЫЙ ЗНАК

Currency Notes

1919-1920 (ND) Issue

#98-100 Because of the multi-language text, these notes are sometimes called "Babylonians".

98 15 Rubles
ND (1919). Brown on light brown underprint. 8 signature varieties. Back: Arms at center. BC: Multicolor. Watermark: Stars. 76x48mm.

	VG	VF	UNC
	1.00	3.00	6.00

99 30 Rubles
ND (1919). Brown on green underprint. Back: Arms at center. Watermark: Stars. 86x56mm.

	VG	VF	UNC
a. Issued note.	2.00	4.00	7.00
x. Error. Back inverted.	60.00	150	350

100 60 Rubles
ND (1919). Blue-black on gray underprint. Back: Arms at center. Watermark: Stars. 95x62mm.

	VG	VF	UNC
	2.00	4.00	7.00

101 100 Rubles
1919 (1920).# Dark brown or black on light brown underprint. 10 signature varieties. Back: Arms at upper left. Text in 7 languages, says: *"Workers of the World, Unite!"* 100x65mm.

	VG	VF	UNC
a. Horizontal watermark: *100.*	2.00	4.00	6.00
b. Vertical watermark: *100.*	2.00	3.00	5.00

102 250 Rubles
1919 (1920). Black on red-brown underprint. 10 signature varieties. Back: Arms at upper left. Text in 7 languages, says: *"Workers of the World, Unite!"* Like #101. 105x70mm.

	VG	VF	UNC
a. Watermark: *250.*	2.00	4.00	6.00
b. Watermark: Stars.	2.00	4.00	6.00

103 500 Rubles
1919 (1920). Black on olive underprint. 10 signature varieties. Back: Arms at upper left. Text in 7 languages, says: *"Workers of the World, Unite!"* Like #101. 110x75mm.

	VG	VF	UNC
a. Watermark: *500.*	2.00	7.00	10.00
b. Watermark: Stars.	3.00	10.00	15.00

104 1000 Rubles
1919 (1920). Black on green underprint. 10 signature varieties. Back: Arms at upper left. Text in 7 languages, says: *"Workers of the World, Unite!"* Like #101. 115x80mm.

	VG	VF	UNC
a. Watermark: *1000.*	2.00	5.00	8.00
b. Watermark: Small stars.	2.00	5.00	12.00
c. Watermark: Large stars.	2.00	5.00	12.00
d. Watermark: Lozenges.	5.00	12.00	20.00
e. Vertical watermark: *1000.*	5.00	8.00	12.00

105 5000 Rubles
1919 (1920). Blue on yellow and multicolor underprint. 10 signature varieties. Back: Arms at center. Text in 7 languages, says: *"Workers of the World, Unite!"* 166x118mm.

	VG	VF	UNC
a. Watermark: Broad waves.	7.00	15.00	20.00
b. Watermark: Narrow waves.	10.00	30.00	50.00
c. Watermark: Stars.	15.00	40.00	80.00

106 10,000 Rubles
1919 (1920). Red on purple and multicolor underprint. 10 signature varieties. Back: Arms at center. Text in 7 languages, says: *"Workers of the World, Unite!"* Like #105. 172x123mm.

	VG	VF	UNC
a. Watermark: Broad waves.	5.00	15.00	30.00
b. Watermark: Narrow waves.	8.00	25.00	50.00
c. Watermark: Stars.	15.00	60.00	120

1921 Issue

106A 50 Kopeks
ND (1921). Specimen only. Rare.

	VG	VF	UNC
	—	—	—

107 50 Rubles
ND (1921). Brown. Arms at center. 50x37mm.

	VG	VF	UNC
a. Watermark: Lozenges.	3.00	7.00	10.00
b. Watermark: Large stars.	3.00	7.00	10.00
c. Watermark: Small stars.	2.00	4.00	10.00
d. Without watermark.	2.00	4.00	10.00

108 100 Rubles
1921. Yellow. Arms at right. 86x49mm.

	VG	VF	UNC
	4.00	10.00	15.00

109 100 Rubles
1921. Orange. Arms at right. Like #108.

	VG	VF	UNC
	2.00	5.00	10.00

110 250 Rubles
1921. Green. Arms at left. 83x45mm.

	VG	VF	UNC
a. Watermark: *250.*	2.00	5.00	10.00
b. Watermark: Stars.	2.00	5.00	10.00

111 500 Rubles
1921. Blue. Arms at center. 83x47mm.

	VG	VF	UNC
a. Watermark: *500.*	2.00	5.00	10.00
b. Watermark: Stars.	2.00	5.00	10.00
c. Watermark: Lozenges.	2.00	5.00	10.00

112 1000 Rubles
1921. Red. Arms at left. 83x47mm.

	VG	VF	UNC
a. Watermark: *1000.*	3.00	7.00	10.00
b. Watermark: Small stars.	3.00	7.00	10.00
c. Watermark: Large stars.	3.00	7.00	10.00
d. Watermark: Lozenges.	3.00	7.00	10.00

Note: #107-112 may be found in various uncut forms, i.e., block of 4, vertical or horizontal pair, etc.

		VG	VF	UNC
113	**5000 Rubles** 1921. Blue on brown underprint. Ten signature varieties. Back: Arms at upper center. Watermark: Stars. 123x85mm.			
	a. Issued note.	2.00	5.00	10.00
	x. Error. Misprint: *PROLETAPIER* instead of *PROLETARIER* at upper left on back.	2.00	5.00	10.00

		VG	VF	UNC
114	**10,000 Rubles** 1921. Dark red on light red underprint. Ten signature varieties. Back: Arms at center. Watermark: Stars. 127x92mm.	2.00	8.00	25.00

		VG	VF	UNC
115	**25,000 Rubles** 1921. Red-brown. Ten signature varieties. 165x88mm.			
	a. Watermark: Large stars.	5.00	10.00	20.00
	b. Watermark: Small stars.	10.00	50.00	100

		VG	VF	UNC
116	**50,000 Rubles** 1921. Blue-green. Arms at lower center. Ten signature varieties. 162x88mm.			
	a. Watermark: Large stars.	5.00	10.00	20.00
	b. Watermark: Small stars.	6.00	25.00	100
	c. Watermark: Crosses.	15.00	60.00	250
	d. Watermark: Carpet designature. Rare.	—	—	—

		VG	VF	UNC
117	**100,000 Rubles** 1921. Red. Arms at left center. Ten signature varieties. 162x88mm.			
	a. Watermark: Large stars.	7.00	12.00	25.00
	b. Watermark: Crosses.	50.00	100	250

#118-119 *Not assigned.*

ОБЯЗАТЕЛЬСТВО РОССИЙСКОЙ СОЦИАЛИСТИЧЕСКОЙ ФЕДЕРАТИВНОЙ СОВЕТСКОЙ РЕСПYБЛИКИ

Treasury Short-term Certificates

1921 Issue

1 New Ruble = 10,000 Old Rubles.

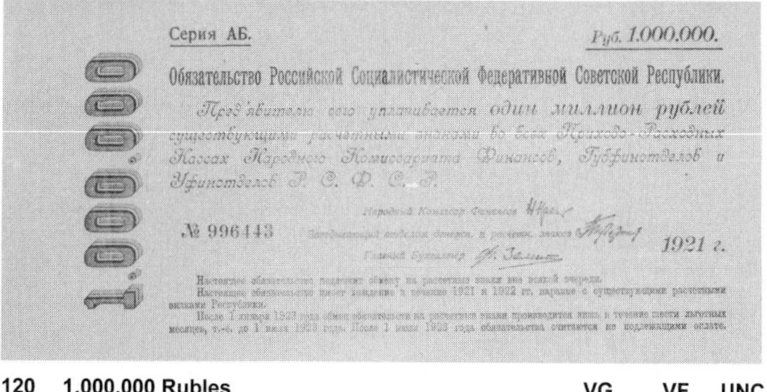

		VG	VF	UNC
120	**1,000,000 Rubles** 1921. Black. 270x130mm. PC: Yellowish.	30.00	70.00	150
121	**5,000,000 Rubles** 1921. Black. PC: Bluish	40.00	80.00	250
122	**10,000,000 Rubles** 1921. Black. PC: Bluish.	30.00	70.00	200

1922 Issue

		VG	VF	UNC
123	**5000 Rubles** 1922.	10.00	40.00	150
124	**10,000 Rubles** 1922. Black. PC: Gray-blue.	20.00	70.00	200

		VG	VF	UNC
125	**25,000 Rubles** 1922. Specimen.			
	s1. Specimen. White paper.	100	300	650
	s2. Specimen. Brown paper. Unique. Rare.	—	—	—

ГОСУДАРСТВЕННЫЙ ДЕНЕЖНЫЙ ЗНАК

State Currency Notes

1922 Issue

#	Denomination	VG	VF	UNC
126	**50 Kopeks** 1922. Proof. Rare.	—	—	—

#	Denomination	VG	VF	UNC
127	**1 Ruble** 1922. Brownish orange. Arms at upper left. 9 signature varieties. Watermark: Stars. 135x67mm.	4.00	9.00	18.00
128	**3 Rubles** 1922. Green. Arms at upper left. 10 signature varieties. Watermark: Stars. 138x72mm.	5.00	10.00	18.00
129	**5 Rubles** 1922. Blue. Arms at upper left. 10 signature varieties. Watermark: Stars. 150x75mm.	5.00	10.00	20.00
130	**10 Rubles** 1922. Red. Arms at upper left. 10 signature varieties. Watermark: Stars. 155x81mm.	5.00	10.00	20.00

#	Denomination	VG	VF	UNC
131	**25 Rubles** 1922. Brown-lilac on yellow and blue underprint. State emblem. 10 signature varieties. Watermark: Stars. 132x84mm.	5.00	10.00	20.00
132	**50 Rubles** 1922. Blue on pink underprint. State emblem. 10 signature varieties. Watermark: Stars. 138x90mm.	6.00	15.00	25.00
133	**100 Rubles** 1922. Red on blue underprint. State emblem. 10 signature varieties. Watermark: Stars. 143x95mm.	8.00	15.00	30.00
134	**250 Rubles** 1922. Dark green on blue and orange underprint. State emblem. 10 signature varieties. Watermark: Stars. 147x98mm.	10.00	15.00	80.00
135	**500 Rubles** 1922. Dark blue on light brown underprint. State emblem. 10 signature varieties. Watermark: Stars. 194x110mm.	10.00	15.00	40.00

#	Denomination	VG	VF	UNC
136	**1000 Rubles** 1922. Brown on red, blue and green underprint. State emblem. 10 signature varieties. Watermark: Stars. 199x113mm.	8.00	15.00	35.00
137	**5000 Rubles** 1922. Black. State emblem. 10 signature varieties. BC: Green and pink. Watermark: Stars. 210x128mm.	20.00	40.00	100
138	**10,000 Rubles** 1922. Red. State emblem. 10 signature varieties. BC: Red and green. Watermark: Stars. 216x128mm.	40.00	60.00	175

БАНКОВЫЙ БИЛЕТ

State Bank Notes

Sign. 1.	
Sign. 2.	

1922 Issue

#	Denomination	VG	VF	UNC
139	**1 Chervonetz** 1922. Blue State emblem. Multicolor guilloche at left. Watermark: Slabs. 177x111mm. In circulation from January 1923.			
	a. Signature 1.	40.00	100	200
	b. Signature 2.	80.00	200	400
	s1. As a. Specimen. Overprint in red.	—	—	600
	s2. As a. Specimen. Perforated.	—	—	600

#140 *Not assigned.*

No.	Description	VG	VF	UNC
141	**3 Chervontsa** 1922. Blue. State emblem. Multicolor guilloche at left. Watermark: 333. 177x111mm. 6 signatures. In circulation from January 1923.			
	a. Rare.	—	—	—
	s. Specimen. Overprint in red.	—	—	—
142	**5 Chervontsev** 1922. State emblem. Multicolor guilloche at left. Watermark: 6 signatures. In circulation from November 1922. 177x111mm.			
	a. Issued note. Rare.	—	—	—
	s. Specimen. Perforated in Russian.	—	—	500

No.	Description	VG	VF	UNC
143	**10 Chervontsev** 1922. Blue. State emblem. Multicolor guilloche at left. Watermark: 555. 177x111mm. 8 signatures. In circulation from November 1922.			
	a. Issued note.	50.00	150	400
	s. Specimen. Overprint in red.	—	—	—

No.	Description	VG	VF	UNC
144	**25 Chervontsev** 1922. Blue. State emblem. Multicolor guilloche at left. 144x111mm. 9 signatures. In circulation from February 1923.			
	a. Rare.	—	—	—
	s. Specimen. Overprint in red.	—	—	—

1923 Issue

No.	Description	VG	VF	UNC
145A	**1/2 Chervonetz** 1923. Brown text. Specimen. Rare.	—	—	—

ГОСУДАРСТВЕННЫЙ ДЕНЕЖНЫЙ ЗНАК

State Currency Notes

1922 Issue

#146-151 "Promissory note" type.

No.	Description	VG	VF	UNC
146	**1 Ruble** 1922. Brown on gold underprint. Arms at upper center. 36x66mm.	5.00	10.00	20.00
147	**3 Rubles** 1922. Green. Arms at upper center. 36x66mm.	5.00	10.00	20.00

No.	Description	VG	VF	UNC
148	**5 Rubles** 1922. Blue. Arms at upper center. 36x66mm.	6.00	12.00	25.00

No.	Description	VG	VF	UNC
149	**10 Rubles** 1922. Red. Arms at upper center. 36x66mm.	6.00	12.00	25.00
150	**25 Rubles** 1922. Purple. Arms at upper center. 36x66mm.	10.00	20.00	40.00

No.	Description	VG	VF	UNC
151	**50 Rubles** 1922. Brown on green underprint. Arms at upper center. 36x66mm.	10.00	15.00	30.00

1923 Issue

#151A-155 "coin notes" without promissory designation. Image of coin shown.

No.	Description	VG	VF	UNC
151A	**5 Kopeks** 1923. 5 Kopek coin image. Proof. Rare.	—	—	—
152	**10 Kopeks** 1923. 10 Kopek coin image. Proof. Rare.	—	—	—
153	**15 Kopeks** 1923. 15 Kopek coin image. Proof. Rare.	—	—	—
154	**20 Kopeks** 1923. 20 Kopek coin image Proof. Rare.	—	—	—

		VG	VF	UNC
155	**50 Kopeks** 1923. Blue. 50 Kopek coin image. State arms. Back: 50 Kopek coin image. Value. 47x53mm.			
	a. Issued note.	8.00	15.00	30.00
	s. Specimen. Red overprint.	—	—	500

Note: #155 may be found in various uncut forms, i.e. block of 4, strip of 2, etc.

1923 First Issue

1 "New" Ruble = 1,000,000 "Old" Rubles. #156-162 text on back in 7 lines.

		VG	VF	UNC
156	**1 Ruble** 1923. Brown. Value and state emblem. 3 signature varieties. Watermark: Tile pattern. 110x67mm.	5.00	10.00	15.00
157	**5 Rubles** 1923. Green. State emblem. 10 signature varieties. Back: Text in 7 lines. Watermark: Tile pattern. 121x75mm.	5.00	10.00	15.00
158	**10 Rubles** 1923. Dark purple. State emblem. 10 signature varieties. Back: Text in 7 lines. BC: Brown. Watermark: Tile pattern. 129x80mm.	5.00	10.00	15.00
159	**25 Rubles** 1923. Blue. State emblem. 10 signature varieties. Back: Text in 7 lines. Watermark: Tile pattern. 134x85mm.	5.00	10.00	15.00
160	**50 Rubles** 1923. Olive. State emblem. 10 signature varieties. Back: Text in 7 lines. Watermark: Tile pattern. 138x90mm.	5.00	10.00	15.00
161	**100 Rubles** 1923. Purple and multicolor. State emblem. 10 signature varieties. Back: Text in 7 lines. Watermark: Tile pattern. 142x95mm.	5.00	10.00	25.00

		VG	VF	UNC
162	**250 Rubles** 1923. Dark blue. State emblem. 10 signature varieties. Back: Text in 7 lines. Watermark: Tile pattern. 150x100mm.	10.00	15.00	30.00

1923 Second Issue

		VG	VF	UNC
163	**1 Ruble** 1923. Brown. State emblem. 3 signature varieties. Back: Text in 8 lines. 110x67mm.	2.00	5.00	10.00
164	**5 Rubles** 1923. Green. State emblem. 10 signature varieties. Back: Text in 8 lines. 129x80mm.	2.00	5.00	10.00
165	**10 Rubles** 1923. Black on gray underprint. 10 signature varieties. Back: Text in 8 lines. BC: Brown.			
	a. Watermark: Lozenges.	2.00	5.00	10.00
	b. Watermark: Stars.	4.00	8.00	15.00
166	**25 Rubles** 1923. Blue. State emblem. 10 signature varieties. Back: Text in 8 lines. 134x85mm.			
	a. Watermark: Lozenges.	1.00	3.00	7.00
	b. Watermark: Stars.	2.00	5.00	10.00
167	**50 Rubles** 1923. Brown. State emblem. 10 signature varieties. Back: Text in 8 lines. 138x90mm.			
	a. Watermark: Lozenges.	2.00	5.00	10.00
	b. Watermark: Stars.	4.00	12.00	25.00

		VG	VF	UNC
168	**100 Rubles** 1923. Purple on multicolor underprint. Arms at center in underprint. 10 signature varieties. Back: Text in 8 lines. 142x95mm.			
	a. Watermark: Lozenges.	5.00	10.00	20.00
	b. Watermark: Stars.	5.00	10.00	15.00
169	**500 Rubles** 1923. Dark brown on multicolor underprint. Arms at center in underprint. 10 signature varieties. Back: Text in 8 lines. 195x153mm.	5.00	10.00	30.00
170	**1000 Rubles** 1923. Red on multicolor underprint. Arms at center in underprint. 10 signature varieties. Back: Text in 8 lines. 155x105mm.	10.00	20.00	40.00
171	**5000 Rubles** 1923. Green on multicolor underprint. Arms at center in underprint. 10 signature varieties. Back: Text in 8 lines. 195x105mm.	10.00	30.00	60.00

		VG	VF	UNC
171A	**10,000 Rubles** 1923. Red. 6-pointed star at upper center. Watermark: Lozenges. (Not issued). Rare. PC: Light brown.	—	—	—

ПЛАТЕЖНОЕ ОБЯЗАТЕЛЬСТВО Н.К.Ф. Р.С.Ф.С.Р.

N.K.F. Payment Obligations of the R.S.F.S.R.

1 Gold Ruble = 5000 Rubles

1923 (1924) Issue

		VG	VF	UNC
172	**100 Gold Rubles** 1923 (1924). Specimen, perforated: *ОБРАЗЕЦ*. Rare.	—	—	—

		VG	VF	UNC
173	**250 Gold Rubles** 1923 (1924). Specimen.	—	500	1,000
174	**500 Gold Rubles** 1923 (1924). Specimen.	—	500	1,000
175	**1000 Gold Rubles** 1923 (1924). Specimen.	—	500	1,000

ТРАНСПОРТНЫЙ СЕРТИФИКАТ

Transport Certificates

1923-1924 Issue

		VG	VF	UNC
176	**3 Gold Rubles** 1.3.1924. Front view steam locomotive at center, axe and anchor at upper right. 185x100mm. Specimen only. Rare.	—	—	—

Note: Deceptive counterfeits of #176 exist.

		Good	Fine	XF
177	**5 Gold Rubles** 1923. Series 1-5. 185x100mm.	150	400	1,000
178	**5 Gold Rubles** 1923. Series 6-10.	150	400	1,000

		Good	Fine	XF
179	**5 Gold Rubles** 1923. Series 11-15. Back: Like #178 but change in text.	100	300	950
180	**5 Gold Rubles** 1923. Series 16-24. Back: Like #179 but repeated change in text.	100	300	950

U.S.S.R. - UNION OF SOVIET SOCIALIST REPUBLICS

ГОСУДАРСТВЕННЫЙ ДЕНЕЖНЫЙ ЗНАК

State Currency Notes

1923 (1924) Issue

		VG	VF	UNC
181	**10,000 Rubles** 1923 (1924). Lilac on green underprint. View of Kremlin. 10 signature varieties. Arms at upper left. 155x77mm.	100	150	300

		VG	VF	UNC
182	**15,000 Rubles** 1923 (1924). Brown. Man at center. 10 signature varieties. Arms at upper left. 155x77mm.	120	200	400

		VG	VF	UNC
183	**25,000 Rubles** 1923 (1924). Dark blue and green on lilac underprint. Soldier at center. 4 signature varieties. Arms at upper left. 155x77mm.	120	200	400

ПЛАТЕЖНОЕ ОБЯЗАТЕЛЬСТВО Н.К. Ф.С.С.С.Р.

N.K.F. Payment Obligations of the U.S.S.R.

1924-26 Issue

		VG	VF	UNC
184	**100 Gold Rubles** 1924-1928. Specimen only, perforated: *ОБРАЗЕЦ*. Rare.	—	—	—

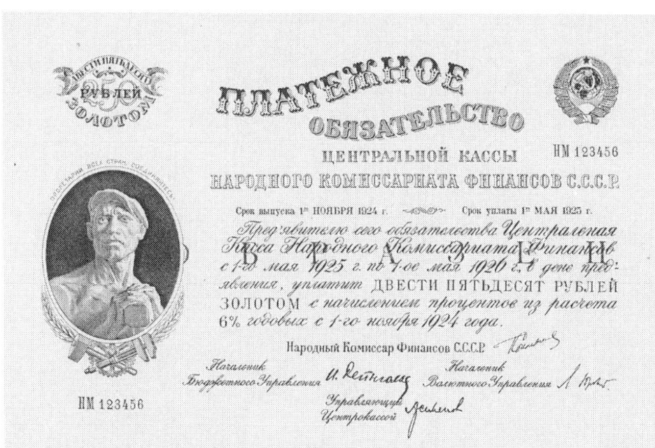

		VG	VF	UNC
184A	**250 Gold Rubles** 1924-1928. Specimen. Rare.	—	—	—
185	**500 Gold Rubles** 1924-1928. Specimen. Rare.	—	—	—
185A	**1000 Gold Rubles** 1926-1928. Specimen. Rare.	—	—	—

НАРОДНОГО КОМИССАРИАТА ФИНАНСОВ СОЮЗА С.С.Р. КРАТКОСРОЧНОЕ ПЛАТЕЖНОЕ ОБЯЗАТЕЛЬСТВО

N.F.K. Short-term Payment Obligations of the U.S.S.R.

1928 Issue

		VG	VF	UNC
185B	**100 Gold Rubles** 1928-1929. With coupons. Specimen. Rare.	—	—	—
185C	**250 Gold Rubles** 1928-1929. With coupons. Specimen. Rare.	—	—	—
185D	**500 Gold Rubles** 1928-1929. With coupons. Specimen. Rare.	—	—	—
185E	**1000 Gold Rubles** 1928-1929. With coupons. Specimen. Rare.	—	—	—

ГОСУДАРСТВЕННЫЙ ДЕНЕЖНЫЙ ЗНАК

State Currency Notes

1924 Issue

		VG	VF	UNC
186	**1 Gold Ruble** 1924. Blue on light brown and multicolor underprint. Arms at upper center. Vertical format, with and without series *SHRIW*. BC: Blue on orange. Watermark: Drops. 82x155mm. Signatures of 5 treasurers and ministry of finance. In circulation from February 1924.			
	a. Issued note.	50.00	100	200
	s. Specimen. Uniface pair. Pinhole perforation.	—	—	—

		VG	VF	UNC
187	**3 Gold Rubles** 1924. Green. Two reclining men at lower center. Watermark: СССР, 3. 168x76mm. Signatures 5 treasurers and ministry of finance. In circulation from February 1924.			
	a. Issued note.	200	400	950
	s. Specimen. Uniface pair. Pinhole perforation.	—	—	—

		VG	VF	UNC
188	**5 Gold Rubles** 1924. Blue on rose underprint. Tractor plowing at lower center. 5 signature varieties. Watermark: СССР, 5. 182x88mm. Signatures of 5 treasurers and ministry of finance. In circulation 1924.			
	a. Issued note.	200	400	950
	s1. Specimen. Uniface pair. Pinhole perforation.	—	—	—
	s2. Specimen. Perforated.	—	—	800

1925 Issue

No.	Denomination	VG	VF	UNC
189	**3 Rubles**	VG	VF	UNC
	1925. Slate green. Arms at upper center. Back: Value at ends. BC: Multicolor. 135x70mm. Signature 10 treasurers and ministry of finance. In circulation from March 1924.			
	a. Issued note.	15.00	30.00	70.00
	s. Specimen. Uniface pair. Number in pinhole perforation.	—	—	—

No.	Denomination	VG	VF	UNC
190	**5 Rubles**	VG	VF	UNC
	1925. Dark blue. Worker at left. Arms at upper center. Back: Value at ends. BC: Multicolor. Watermark: Watermark 5. 165x70mm. Signatures 8 treasurers and ministry of finance. In circulation from 1925.			
	a. Issued note.	25.00	50.00	100
	s. Specimen. Number pinhole perforation.	—	—	—

Small Change Notes

1924 Issue

No.	Denomination	VG	VF	UNC
191	**1 Kopek**	VG	VF	UNC
	1924. Light brown. Arms at upper center.	8.00	15.00	30.00

No.	Denomination	VG	VF	UNC
192	**2 Kopeks**	VG	VF	UNC
	1924. Brown. Arms at upper center.	8.00	15.00	30.00

No.	Denomination	VG	VF	UNC
193	**3 Kopeks**	VG	VF	UNC
	1924. Green. Arms at upper center.			
	a. Issued note.	8.00	15.00	30.00
	s. Specimen. Uniface face, overprint.	—	—	—
194	**5 Kopeks**	VG	VF	UNC
	1924. Blue. Arms at upper center.	8.00	15.00	35.00

No.	Denomination	VG	VF	UNC
195	**20 Kopeks**	VG	VF	UNC
	1924. Brown on rose underprint. Arms at upper center.			
	s. Specimen. Red overprint.	150	400	950

No.	Denomination	VG	VF	UNC
196	**50 Kopeks**	VG	VF	UNC
	1924. Blue on brown underprint. Arms at upper left.	20.00	30.00	80.00

БИЛЕТ ГОСУДАРСТВЕННОГО БАНКА С.С.С.Р.

1924 Issue

No.	Denomination	VG	VF	UNC
196A	**1 Chervonetz**	VG	VF	UNC
	1924 (date in watermark). Value. 180x105mm. Specimen. Rare.	—	—	—

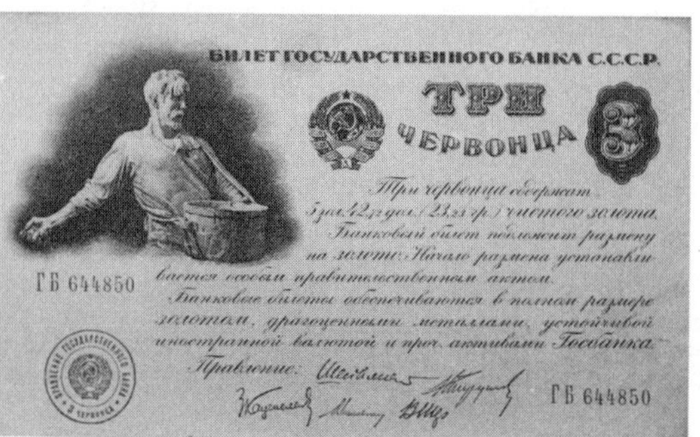

No.	Denomination	VG	VF	UNC
197	**3 Chervontsa**	VG	VF	UNC
	1924 (date in watermark). Dark blue. Farmer sowing at left, arms at upper center. Uniface. Watermark: 3 in rosette. 180x105mm. In circulation from August 1924.			
	a. Signature 1.	70.00	150	300
	b. Signature 2.	150	600	1,200
	s. As a. Specimen. Uniface pair. Red overprint.	—	—	—

		VG	VF	UNC
197A	**5 Chervontsev** 1924 (date in watermark). Specimen. Rare.	—	—	—

1926; 1928 Issue

		VG	VF	UNC
198	**1 Chervonetz** 1926. Dark blue. Arms at upper left. Back: Value at center. BC: Light and dark blue. 155x81mm. In circulation from March 1927.			

Sign. 1.	
Sign. 2.	
Sign. 3.	
Sign. 4.	

	VG	VF	UNC
a. Signature 1.	20.00	50.00	120
b. Signature 2.	20.00	50.00	120
c. Signature 3.	20.00	50.00	140
d. Signature 4.	20.00	50.00	120
s. As c. Specimen. Uniface pair. Red overprint and pinhole perforation.	—	—	—

		VG	VF	UNC
199	**2 Chervontsa** 1928. Slate green. Arms at upper center. Red fibers in paper. Back: Value and text. BC: Green and blue. 158x88mm. 5 signatures. In circulation from July 1928.			

Sign. 1.	
Sign. 2.	
Sign. 3.	
Sign. 4.	

	VG	VF	UNC
a. Signature 1.	25.00	70.00	150
b. Signature 2.	25.00	70.00	150
c. Signature 3.	25.00	70.00	150
d. Signature 4.	60.00	150	300
s. As d. Specimen. Uniface pair. Red overprint and pinhole perforation.	—	—	—

Color Abbreviation Guide

New to the *Standard Catalog of® World Paper Money* are the following abbreviations related to color references:

BC: Back color

PC: Paper color

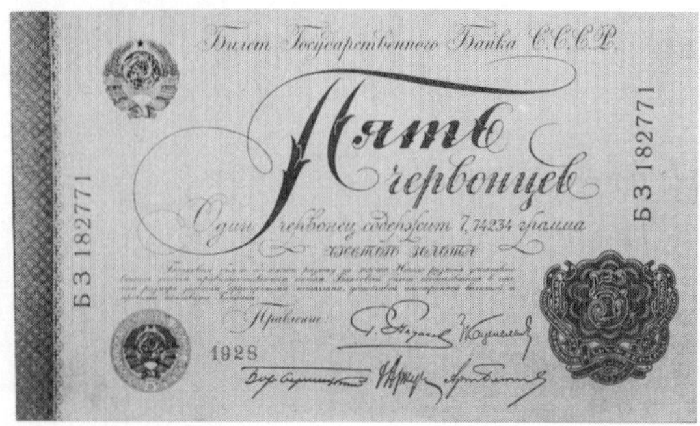

200	5 Chervontsev	VG	VF	UNC
	1928. Dark blue. Arms at upper left. Uniface. Watermark: 5, CCCP in wreath. 180x105mm. In circulation from November 1928.			

Sign. 1.	
Sign. 2.	
Sign. 3.	
Sign. 4.	

	VG	VF	UNC
a. Signature 1.	100	350	950
b. Signature 2.	75.00	250	750
c. Signature 3.	75.00	250	750
d. Signature 4.	75.00	250	750
s. As b. Specimen. Red overprint and number pinhole perforation.	—	—	—

1932 Issue

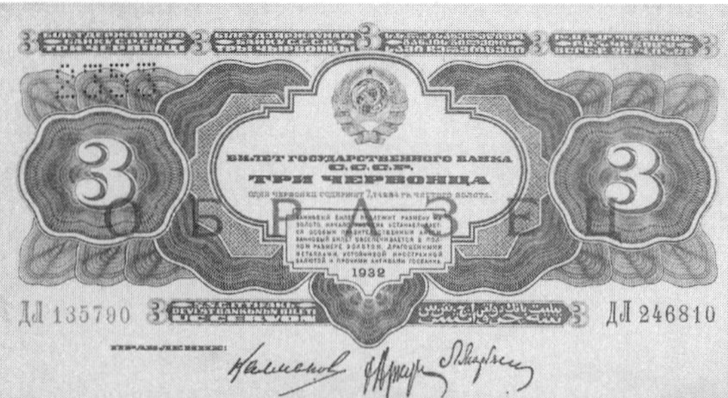

201	3 Chervontsa	VG	VF	UNC
	1932. Dark green. Arms at upper center. Paper with red and blue fibers. Back: Values at ends. BC: Multicolor. 180x105mm. In circulation from October 1932.			
	a. Issued note.	15.00	30.00	80.00
	s. Specimen. Uniface pair. Red overprint, number pinhole perforation.	—	—	—

1937 Issue

202	1 Chervonetz	VG	VF	UNC
	1937. Black. Arms at upper left center, portrait V. Lenin at right. BC: Black on blue and multicolor underprint. 160x80mm.			
	a. Issued note.	10.00	15.00	30.00
	s. Specimen. Uniface pair. Red overprint and number pinhole perforation.	—	—	—

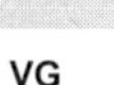
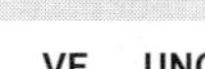

203	3 Chervontsa	VG	VF	UNC
	1937. Red. Arms at upper left center, portrait V. Lenin at right. Back: Value at center and corners. BC: Purple on multicolor underprint. 171x88mm.			
	a. Issued note.	10.00	15.00	30.00
	s. Specimen. Uniface pair. Overprint and number pinhole perforation.	—	—	—

204	5 Chervontsev	VG	VF	UNC
	1937. Olive-green. Arms at upper left center, portrait V. Lenin at right. Back: Value at center and corners. BC: Dark blue on multicolor underprint. 178x93mm.			
	a. Issued note.	10.00	20.00	40.00
	s. Specimen. Uniface pair. Red overprint. Number pinhole perforation.	—	—	—

205	10 Chervontsev	VG	VF	UNC
	1937. Dark blue. Arms at upper left center, portrait V. Lenin at right. Back: Value at center and corners. 190x97mm.			
	a. Issued note.	15.00	25.00	50.00
	s. Specimen. Uniface pair. Red overprint. Number pinhole perforation.	—	—	—

ГОСУДАРСТВЕННЫЙ КАЗНАЧЕЙСКИЙ БИЛЕТ

State Treasury Note

1928 Issue

206	1 Gold Ruble	VG	VF	UNC
	1928. Blue on light brown and multicolor underprint. Arms at upper center. Like #186. 5 signature varieties. With or without series *СНРИЯ*. BC: Blue on orange. Watermark: One ruble in Russian language. 5 signatures. In circulation from year 1928.			
	a. Issued note.	30.00	50.00	100
	s. Specimen. Uniface pair. pinhole perforation.	—	—	—

1934 Issue

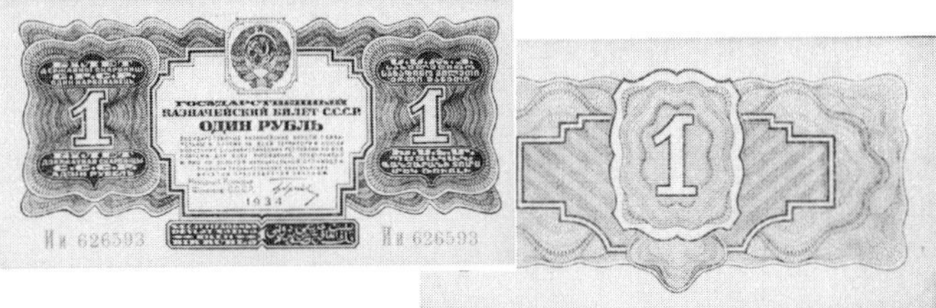

207	1 Gold Ruble	VG	VF	UNC
	1934. Dark blue. Arms at upper center. With signature. Back: Value at center. BC: Blue on multicolor underprint. 120x60mm. PC: Peach.			
	a. Issued note.	10.00	20.00	40.00
	s. Specimen. Uniface pair. Red overprint. Number pinhole perforation.	—	—	—

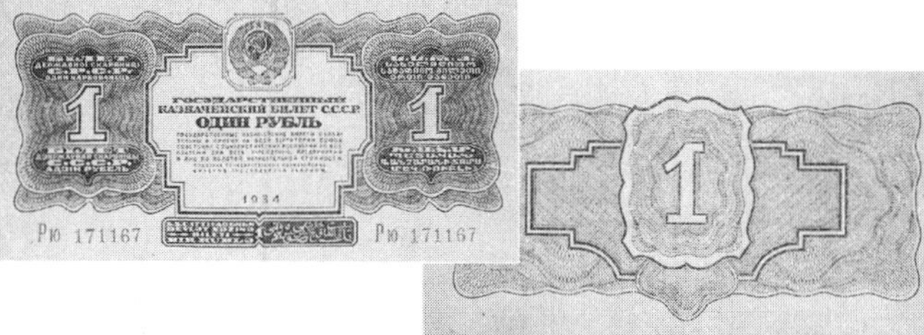

208	1 Gold Ruble	VG	VF	UNC
	1934. Dark blue. Arms at upper center. Like #207. Without signature. 120x60mm. PC: Peach.	7.00	10.00	20.00

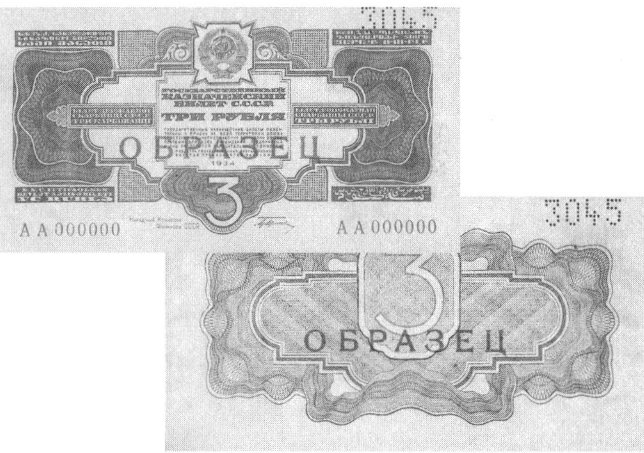

209	3 Gold Rubles	VG	VF	UNC
	1934. Green. Arms at upper center. With signature. Back: Value at center. BC: Multicolor. 135x70mm.			
	a. Issued note.	15.00	30.00	60.00
	s. Specimen. Uniface pair. Red overprint. Number pinhole perforation.	—	—	—

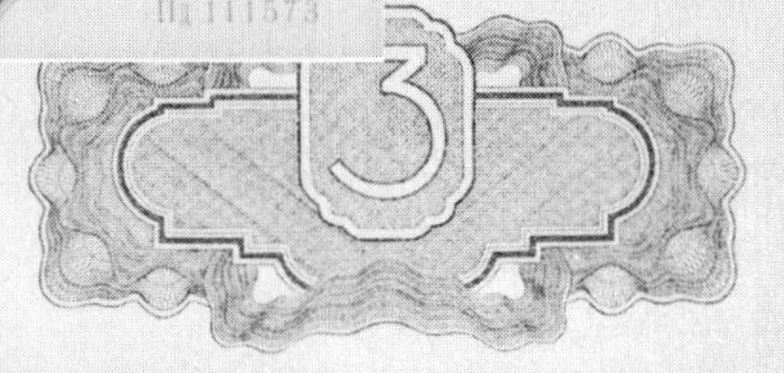

		VG	VF	UNC
210	**3 Gold Rubles** 1934. Green. Arms at upper center. Like #209. Without signature. 135x70mm.	10.00	20.00	50.00
211	**5 Gold Rubles** 1934. Gray-blue on light blue underprint. Arms at upper center. With signature. 135x68mm.	20.00	40.00	100

		VG	VF	UNC
212	**5 Gold Rubles** 1934. Slate blue on light blue underprint. Arms at upper center. Like #211. Without signature. Back: Value at center. BC: Multicolor. 135x68mm.			
	a. Issued note.	12.00	25.00	55.00
	s. Specimen. Uniface pair.Red overprint. Number pinhole perforation.	—	—	—

1938 Issue

		VG	VF	UNC
213	**1 Ruble** 1938. Brown on orange underprint. Arms at upper left. Miner at right. Back: Value at corners. BC: Brown on multicolor underprint. 126x60mm.			
	a. Issued note.	4.00	8.00	15.00
	s. Specimen. Uniface pair. Red overprint. Number pinhole perforation.	—	—	—

		VG	VF	UNC
214	**3 Rubles** 1938. Dark green. Arms at upper left. Soldiers at left. Back: Value at center and corners. BC: Green on multicolor underprint. 134x68mm.			
	a. Issued note.	5.00	10.00	25.00
	s. Specimen. Uniface pair. Red overprint. Number pinhole perforation.	—	—	—

		VG	VF	UNC
215	**5 Rubles** 1938. Slate blue. Arms at upper left. Aviator at right. Back: Value at center and corners. BC: Blue on multicolor underprint.			
	a. Issued note.	7.00	12.00	30.00
	s. Specimen. Uniface pair. Red Overprint. Number pinhole perforation.	—	—	—

1947 Issue

Type I: 16 scrolls of denominations on wreath around arms (8 at left, 7 at right, 1 at center). Type II: 15 scrolls of denominations on wreath around arms (7 at left, 7 at right, 1 at center).

		VG	VF	UNC
216	**1 Ruble** 1947. Blue-black on pale orange underprint. Type I. 16 scrolls of denominations on wreath around arms (8 at left, 7 at right, 1 at center). BC: Multicolor. 82x125mm.	4.00	8.00	20.00
217	**1 Ruble** 1947 (1957). Type II. 15 scrolls of denominations on wreath around arms (7 at left and right, 1 at center). 82x125mm.	4.00	8.00	20.00
218	**3 Rubles** 1947. Dark green on light green and lilac underprint. Type I. 16 scrolls of denominations on wreath around arms (8 at left, 7 at right, 1 at center). 84x135mm.	5.00	10.00	25.00
219	**3 Rubles** 1947 (1957). Type II. 15 scrolls of denominations on wreath around arms (7 at left and right, 1 at center). 84x135mm.	4.00	8.00	20.00

		VG	VF	UNC
220	**5 Rubles** 1947. Black on blue and light orange underprint. Type I. 16 scrolls of denominations on wreath around arms (8 at left, 7 at right, 1 at center). BC: Blue and multicolor. 89x146mm.	10.00	25.00	60.00
221	**5 Rubles** 1947 (1957). Type II. 15 scrolls of denominations on wreath around arms (7 at left and right, 1 at center). 89x146mm.			
	a. Issued note.	10.00	20.00	50.00
	s. Specimen.	—	—	—

БИЛЕТ ГОСУДАРСТВЕННОГО БАНКА С.С.С.Р.

State Bank Note U.S.S.R.

1947 Issue

		VG	VF	UNC
225	**10 Rubles** 1947. Black on blue and multicolor underprint. Type I. 16 scrolls of denominations on wreath around arms (8 at left, 7 at right, 1 at center). Back: V. Lenin at left. 157x91mm.	15.00	30.00	70.00
226	**10 Rubles** 1947 (1957). Type II. 15 scrolls of denominations on wreath around arms (7 at left and right, 1 at center).. 157x91mm.	12.00	20.00	60.00

		VG	VF	UNC
227	**25 Rubles** 1947. Blue on green and multicolor underprint. Type I. 16 scrolls of denominations on wreath around arms (8 at left, 7 at right, 1 at center). Back: V. Lenin at left. Similar to number 225. BC: Black on blue and green underprint. 167x95mm.	20.00	40.00	90.00
228	**25 Rubles** 1947 (1957). Type II. 15 scrolls of denominations on wreath around arms (7 at left and right, 1 at center). 167x95mm.	15.00	30.00	70.00
229	**50 Rubles** 1947. Blue on yellow-green and multicolor underprint. Type I. 16 scrolls of denominations on wreath around arms (8 at left, 7 at right, 1 at center). Similar to #225. BC: Black on multicolor underprint.	25.00	50.00	100
230	**50 Rubles** 1947 (1957). Type II. 15 scrolls of denominations on wreath around arms (7 at left and right, 1 at center).	20.00	40.00	90.00
231	**100 Rubles** 1947. Black on multicolor underprint. V. Lenin at left. Type I. 16 scrolls of denominations on wreath around arms (8 at left, 7 at right, 1 at center). Back: View of Kremlin. BC: Black on ochre and lilac underprint. 230x115mm.	30.00	60.00	130

		VG	VF	UNC
232	**100 Rubles** 1947 (1957). Type II. 15 scrolls of denominations on wreath around arms (7 at left and right, 1 at center). 230x115mm.			
	a. Issued note.	30.00	50.00	120
	s. Specimen.	—	—	160

Rwanda-Burundi, a Belgian League of Nations mandate and United Nations trust territory comprising the provinces of Rwanda and Burundi of the former colony of German East Africa, was located in central Africa between the present Republic of the Congo, Uganda and mainland Tanzania. The mandate-trust territory had an area of 20,916 sq. mi. (54,272 sq. km.). For specific statistics and history of Rwanda and Burundi see individual entries. When Rwanda and Burundi were formed into a mandate for administration by Belgium, their names were changed to Ruanda and Urundi and they were organized as an integral part of the Belgian Congo, during which time they used a common banknote issue with the Belgian Congo. After the Belgian Congo acquired independence as the Republic of the Congo, the provinces of Ruanda and Urundi reverted to their former names of Rwanda and Burundi and issued notes with both names on them. In 1962, both Rwanda and Burundi became separate independent states. Also see Belgian Congo, Burundi and Rwanda.

MONETARY SYSTEM:

1 Franc = 100 Centimes

MANDATE - TRUST TERRITORY

Banque d'Emission du Rwanda et du Burundi

1960 Issue

#	Denomination	VG	VF	UNC
1	**5 Francs** 1960-1963. Light brown on green underprint. Impala at left. Signature varieties.			
	a. 15.9.1960; 15.5.1961.	35.00	150	450
	b. 15.4.1963.	45.00	120	450

#	Denomination	Good	Fine	XF
2	**10 Francs** 15.9.1960; 5.10.1960. Dull gray on pale blue and pale orange underprint. Hippopotamus at left. Signature varieties. Printer: TDLR.			
	a. Issued note.	50.00	250	550
	s. Specimen.	—	Unc	450

#	Denomination	Good	Fine	XF
3	**20 Francs** 15.9.1960; 5.10.1960. Green on tan and pink underprint. Crocodile at right. Signature varieties. Printer: TDLR.			
	a. Issued note.	65.00	250	525
	s. Specimen.	—	Unc	600

#	Denomination	Good	Fine	XF
4	**50 Francs** 15.9.1960; 1.10.1960. Red on multicolor underprint. Lioness at center right. Signature varieties.			
	a. Issued note.	55.00	450	900
	s. Specimen.	—	Unc	500
	ct. Color trial. Green on multicolor underprint.	—	Unc	750

#	Denomination	Good	Fine	XF
5	**100 Francs** 15.9.1960; 1.10.1960; 31.7.1962. Blue on light green and tan underprint. Zebu at left. Signature varieties.			
	a. Issued note.	50.00	300	1,400
	s. Specimen.	—	Unc	650
	ct. Color trial. Brown on multicolor underprint.	—	Unc	700

#	Denomination	Good	Fine	XF
6	**500 Francs** 15.9.1960; 15.5.1961; 15.9.1961. Lilac-brown on multicolor underprint. Black Rhinoceros at center right. Signature varieties.			
	a. Issued note.	350	850	3,000
	s. Specimen.	—	Unc	1,500

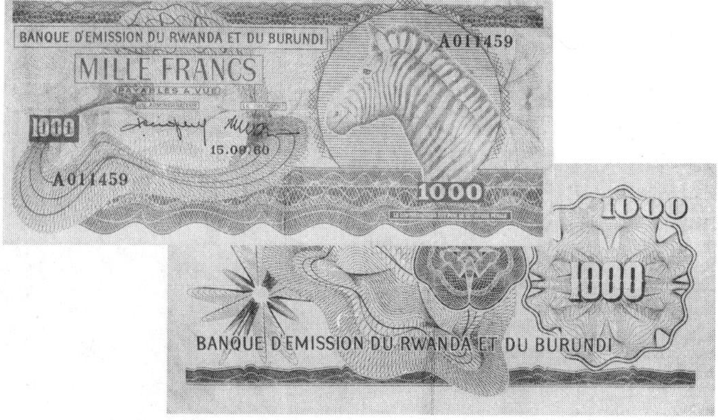

#	Denomination	Good	Fine	XF
7	**1000 Francs** 15.9.1960; 15.5.1961; 31.7.1962. Green on multicolor underprint. Zebra at right. Signature varieties.			
	a. Issued note.	300	1,100	2,500
	s. Specimen.	—	Unc	1,500
	ct. Color trial. Purple on multicolor underprint.	—	Unc	2,000

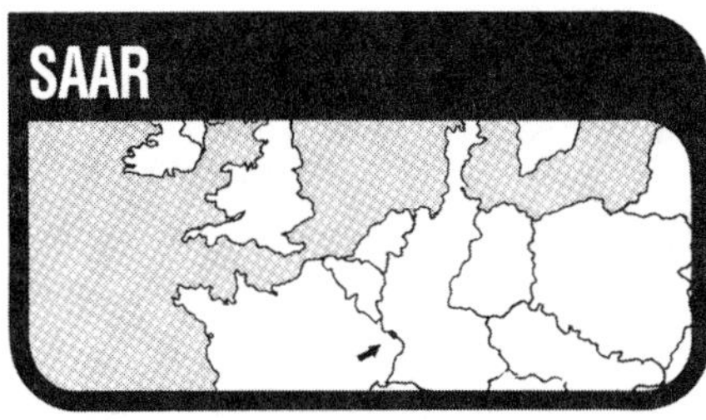

Saar (Sarre, Saarland), the smallest of the ten states of West Germany, is bounded by France to the south and by Luxembourg to the west. It has an area of 991 sq. mi. (2,568 sq. km.) and a population of 1.2 million. Capital: Saarbrucken. Principal products are iron and steel, chemicals, glass and coal. The area of the Saar became part of France in 1766, but was divided between Prussia and Bavaria by the Treaty of Paris, 1815. The Treaty of Versailles, 1919, made the Saar an autonomous territory of the League of Nations, while assigning the coal mines to France. It was returned to Germany, by plebiscite, in 1935. France reoccupied the Saar in 1945. In 1946 it was assigned to the French occupation zone, and was united economically to France in 1947. Following a plebiscite, the Saar became a state of West Germany in 1957. The Saar mark had no actual fractional divisions produced.

MONETARY SYSTEM:

1 Franc = 100 Centimes to 1930
1 Mark = 100 Pfennig, 1930-1957

AUTONOMOUS TERRITORY

Mines Domaniales de la Sarre, Etat Français

1919 ND Issue

No.	Denomination	VG	VF	UNC
1	**50 Centimes** ND (1919). Blue-gray with brown text. Portrait woman at left.	30.00	150	400

No.	Denomination	VG	VF	UNC
2	**1 Franc** ND (1919). Red-brown on gold underprint. Portrait woman at right. Back: Obverse and reverse of 1-franc coin dated 1919 at left center.	60.00	120	325

SARRE

Treasury

1947 Issue

No.	Denomination	VG	VF	UNC
3	**1 Mark** 1947. Blue and brown. Bearded classic man at center. Back: Woman with fruit.	40.00	80.00	210
4	**2 Mark** 1947. Lilac and brown on yellow underprint. Bearded classic man at center. Like #3. Back: Woman with fruit.	500	900	1,700
5	**5 Mark** 1947. Pink and violet on light blue and orange underprint. Bearded classic man at center. Like #3. Back: Woman with fruit.	100	225	550

No.	Denomination	VG	VF	UNC
6	**10 Mark** 1947. Green, red and multicolor. Woman at center. Back: Man and horse. Watermark: Head at left and right.	100	225	1,125
7	**50 Mark** 1947. Green, yellow and multicolor. Woman at center. Like #6. Back: Man and horse. Watermark: Head at left and right.	1,125	2,150	3,500
8	**100 Mark** 1947. Yellow-brown, blue-green and multicolor. Woman at center. Like #6. Back: Man and horse. Watermark: Head at left and right. Rare.	2,550	5,600	14,000

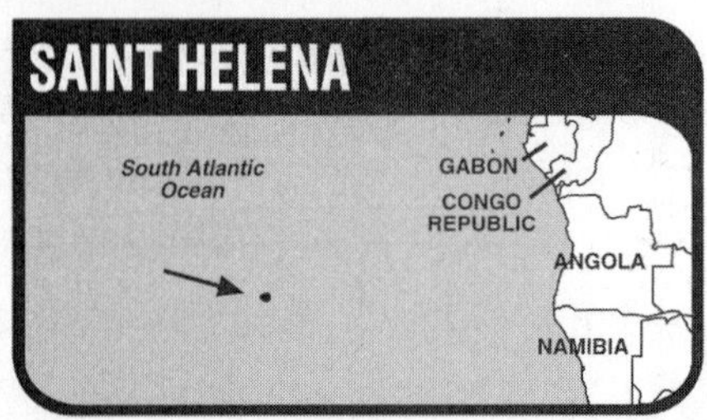

The British Overseas Territory of St. Helena, is located about 1,150 miles (1,850 km.) from the west coast of Africa, has an area of 413 sq. km. and a population of 7,600. Capital: Jamestown. Flax, lace and rope are produced for export. Ascension and Tristan da Cunha are dependencies of St. Helena. Saint Helena was uninhabited when first discovered by the Portuguese in 1502, it was garrisoned by the British during the 17th century. It acquired fame as the place of Napoleon Bonaparte's exile, from 1815 until his death in 1821, but its importance as a port of call declined after the opening of the Suez Canal in 1869. During the Anglo-Boer War in South Africa, several thousand Boer prisoners were confined on the island between 1900 and 1903. St. Helena banknotes are also used on the islands of Assencion and Tristan de Cunia.

RULERS:
British

MONETARY SYSTEM:
1 Pound = 20 Shillings to 1971
1 Pound = 100 New Pence, 1971-

SIGNATURE VARIETIES

BRITISH ADMINISTRATION

Governor and Council of the Island of St. Helena
1722 Issue

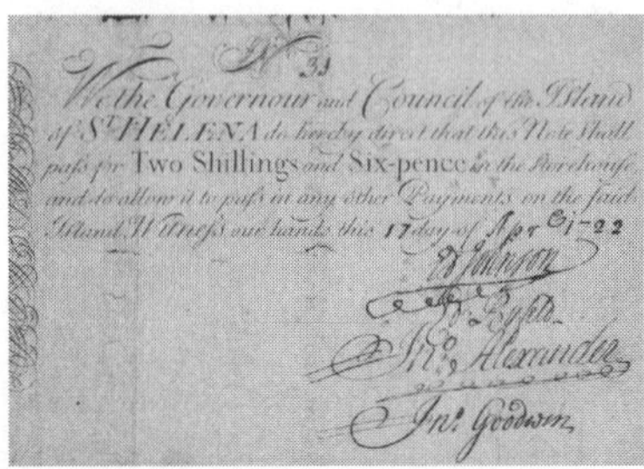

		Good	Fine	XF
1	**2 Shillings 6 Pence** 17.4.1722. Black. Uniface. Rare.	—	—	—

Note: #1 brought over $8,500 at auction in Oct. 1989 (Phillips London, Lot #315).

St. Helena Currency Board
1917 Issue

		Good	Fine	XF
2	**5 Shillings** ca. 1917. Rare.	—	—	—
3	**20 Shillings** ca. 1917. Rare.	—	—	—
4	**40 Shillings** ca. 1917. Rare.	—	—	—

Saint Lucia, an independent island nation located in the Windward Islands of the West Indies between St. Vincent and Martinique, has an area of 616 sq. km. Capital: Castries. The island, with its fine natural harbor at Castries, was contested between England and France throughout the 17th and early 18th centuries (changing possession 14 times); it was finally ceded to the UK in 1814. Even after the abolition of slavery on its plantations in 1834, Saint Lucia remained an agricultural island, dedicated to producing tropical commodity crops. Self-government was granted in 1967 and independence in 1979.

RULERS:
British

MONETARY SYSTEM:
1 Pound = 20 Shillings until 1948
1 Dollar = 100 Cents, 1949-
1 Pound = 20 Shillings
1 Dollar = 100 Cents

NOTE: For later issues refer to East Caribbean States/British East Caribbean Territories.

BRITISH ADMINISTRATION

Government
1920 Issue

		Good	Fine	XF
1	**5 Shillings** 1.10.1920. Green and violet. Portrait King George V at center. Back: Local arms at center. BC: Pale blue. Printer: TDLR. Rare.	—	—	—
2	**10 Shillings** 1.10.1920. Printer: TDLR. Requires confirmation.	—	—	—

The Territorial Collectivity of St. Pierre and Miquelon, a French overseas territory located 10 miles (16 km.) off the south coast of Newfoundland, has an area of 242 sq. km. and a population of 7,045. Capital: St. Pierre. The economy of the barren archipelago is based on cod fishing and fur farming Fish and fish products, and mink and silver fox pelts are exported. The islands, occupied by the French in 1604, were captured by the British in 1702 and held until 1763 when they were returned to the possession of France and employed as a fishing station. They passed between France and England on six more occasions between 1778 and 1814 when they were awarded permanently to France by the Treaty of Paris. The rugged, soil-poor granite islands, which will support only evergreen shrubs, are all that remain to France of her extensive colonies in North America. In 1958 St. Pierre and Miquelon voted in favor of the new constitution of the Fifth Republic of France, thereby choosing to remain within the French Community. Notes of the Banque de France circulated 1937-1942; afterwards notes of the Caisse Centrale de la France Libre and the Caisse Centrale de la France d'Outre-Mer were in use.

RULERS:

French

MONETARY SYSTEM:

1 Franc = 100 Centimes
5 Francs 40 Centimes = 1 Canada Dollar
1 Nouveau Franc = 100 "old" Francs, 1960-

FRENCH ADMINISTRATION

Banque des Isles Saint-Pierre et Miquelon

Saint-Pierre

1897 Issue

		Good	Fine	XF
1	**27 Francs** 1.4.1897. Blue. Sailing ship at left, woman seated at upper center, fish at right.			
	a. Issued note. Rare.	—	—	—
	b. Hand cancelled. Rare.	—	—	—

Saint-Pierre & Miquelon

1890-1895 Issue

		Good	Fine	XF
2	**27 Francs** 1895. Blue. 2 signature varieties. Hand cancelled, handstamped: *ANNULÉ*. Back: Woman seated, sailing ship at left, fish, woman seated at right. Rare.	—	—	—

		Good	Fine	XF
3	**54 Francs** 1890-1895. Blue. Like #2. Hand cancelled, handstamped: *ANNULÉ*. Back: Woman seated, sailing ship at left, fish, woman seated at right. Rare.	—	—	—

Chambre de Commerce

1920 Issue

		Good	Fine	XF
4	**0.05 Franc** 15.5.1920.	—	—	—
5	**0.10 Franc** 15.5. 1920.	—	—	—
6	**0.25 Franc** 15.5. 1920. (1st and 2nd issue).	50.00	200	500
7	**0.50 Franc** 15.5. 1920.	300	800	—
8	**1 Franc** 15.5. 1920.	—	—	—
9	**2 Francs** 15.5. 1920.	—	—	—

Caisse Centrale de la France Libre

Provisional WW II issue w/o St. Pierre name.

Ordonnance du 2.12.1941

#10-14 types of French Equatorial Africa with special serial # ranges.

Provisional WW II Issue without St. Pierre name.

		Good	Fine	XF
10	**5 Francs** *L.1941* (1943). Type of French Equatorial Africa #10. Serial # AA 000 001-AA 030 000 (20.1.1943). Printer: BWC (without imprint).	20.00	60.00	—
11	**10 Francs** *L.1941* (1943). Type of French Equatorial Africa #11. Printer: BWC (without imprint).			
	a. Serial # FA 000 001-FA 015 000 (20.1.1943).	25.00	75.00	—
	b. Serial # 2 520 001-2 533 120.	25.00	75.00	—
12	**20 Francs** *L.1941* (ca. 1943). Type of French Equatorial Africa #12. Serial # LA 000 001-LA 030 000. Printer: BWC (without imprint).	30.00	95.00	—
13	**100 Francs** *L.1941.* (1943). Type of French Equatorial Africa #13. Serial # PA 000 001-PA 070 000 (July 1943). Printer: BWC (without imprint).	70.00	150	—
14	**1000 Francs** *1941.* (1943). Type of French Equatorial Africa #14. Printer: BWC (without imprint).			
	a. Serial # TA 000 001-TA 030 000 (July 1943).	400	1,000	—
	b. Serial # TA 275 001-TA 295 000 (Oct. 1944).	400	1,000	—

Note: See also Reunion #36-38.

Caisse Centrale de la France d'Outre-Mer

Saint-Pierre-et-Miquelon

Ordonnance du 2.2.1944

#15-18 types of French Equatorial Africa with special serial # ranges.

Provisional WW II Issue without St. Pierre name.

		Good	Fine	XF
15	**5 Francs** *L.1944* (1945). Type of French Equatorial Africa #15. Serial # AM 000 001-AM 020 000 (3.10.1945). Printer: BWC (without imprint).	20.00	60.00	—
16	**10 Francs** *L.1944* (1946). Type of French Equatorial Africa #16. Serial # 2 520 001-2 533 120 (4.2.1946). Printer: BWC (without imprint).	25.00	75.00	—
17	**20 Francs** *L.1944* (1945-1946). Type of French Equatorial Africa #17. Printer: BWC (without imprint).			
	a. Serial # 2 509 001-2 509 279 (22.1.1945).	30.00	95.00	—
	b. Serial # 2 510 001-2 531 200 (4.2.1946).	30.00	95.00	—
18	**1000 Francs** *L.1944* (1945-1946). Type of French Equatorial Africa #19. Printer: BWC (without imprint).			
	a. Serial # TD 021 001-TD 046 000 (5.9.1945).	400	1,000	—
	b. Serial # TD 235 001-TD 255 000 (17.6.1946).	400	1,000	—

Note: See also Reunion #39-40.

1947 ND Issue w/o St. Pierre name

#19-21 types of French Equatorial Africa post WW II Issue.

No.	Description	Good	Fine	XF
19	**10 Francs** ND (1947). Type of French Equatorial Africa #21, also St. Pierre #23.			
	a. Serial # 2 520 001-2 550 00 Printer: Desfosses, Paris.	5.00	15.00	45.00
	b. Serial # 19 100 001-19 200 000. Printer: Banque de France.	5.00	15.00	45.00
20	**20 Francs** ND (1947). Type of French Equatorial Africa #22, also St. Pierre #24. Serial # 2 509 001-2 509 279; 2 510 001-2 531 200.	7.50	25.00	65.00
21	**50 Francs** ND (1947). Type of French Equatorial Africa #23, also St. Pierre # 25. Serial # 8 600 001-8 700 000.	10.00	35.00	95.00

1950 ND Issue

No.	Description	VG	VF	UNC
22	**5 Francs** ND (1950-1960). Blue and multicolor. Ship at left, Bougainville at right. Back: Woman with fruit and house.	4.50	14.00	50.00

No.	Description	VG	VF	UNC
23	**10 Francs** ND (1950-1960). Blue and multicolor. Colbert at left, ships at right. Back: River scene and plants.	7.00	22.50	80.00

No.	Description	VG	VF	UNC
24	**20 Francs** ND (1950-1960). Brown and multicolor. Four people with huts at left, E. Gentil at right. Back: Two men.	10.00	35.00	120
25	**50 Francs** ND (1950-1960). Multicolor. B. d'Esnambuc at left, ship at right. Back: Woman.	25.00	100	300
26	**100 Francs** ND (1950-1960). Multicolor. La Bourdonnais at left, two women at right. Back: Woman looking at mountains.			
	a. Issued note.	30.00	125	385
	s. Specimen. Handstamped and perforated: *SPECIMEN.*	—	—	1,000
27	**500 Francs** ND (1950-1960). Multicolor. Buildings and sailboat at left, two women at right. Back: Ox-carts with wood and plants.	125	400	1,000

No.	Description	VG	VF	UNC
28	**1000 Francs** ND (1950-1960). Multicolor. Two women at right. Back: Woman at right, two men in small boat.	75.00	300	850
29	**5000 Francs** ND (1950-1960). Multicolor. Gen. Schoelcher at right center. Back: Family.	120	500	—

SAINT THOMAS & PRINCE

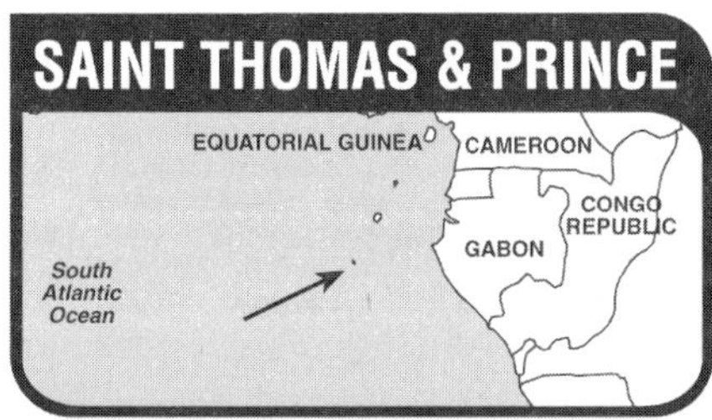

The Democratic Republic of Sao Tomé and Príncipe (formerly the Portuguese overseas province of St. Thomas and Prince Islands) is located in the Gulf of Guinea 150 miles (241 km.) off the West African coast. It has an area of 372 sq. mi. (960 sq. km.) and a population of 149,000. Capital: São Tomé. The economy of the islands is based on cocoa, copra and coffee. Discovered and claimed by Portugal in the late 15th century, the islands' sugar-based economy gave way to coffee and cocoa in the 19th century - all grown with plantation slave labor, a form of which lingered into the 20th century. While independence was achieved in 1975, democratic reforms were not instituted until the late 1980s. The country held its first free elections in 1991, but frequent internal wrangling between the various political parties precipitated repeated changes in leadership and two failed coup attempts in 1995 and 2003. The recent discovery of oil in the Gulf of Guinea promises to attract increased attention to the small island nation.

RULERS:

Portuguese to 1975

MONETARY SYSTEM:

1 Mil Reis = 1000 Reis to 1914
1 Escudo = 100 Centavos, 1911-1976
1 Dobra = 100 Centimos, 1977-

STEAMSHIP SEALS

Type I
LOANDA

Type II
LISBOA

Type III
C,C,A

C,C,A = Colonias, Commercio, Agricultura.

PORTUGUESE ADMINISTRATION

Banco Nacional Ultramarino

Agencia em. S. Thomé

1897 Issue

#1-6 different dates handwritten.

		Good	Fine	XF
1	**1000 Reis** 2.1.1897. Green. Man with bow and arrow below arms at left, steamship at upper center. 124x90mm.	—	—	—
2	**2000 Reis** ND (1897). Requires confirmation.	—	—	—
3	**2500 Reis** ND (1897). Gray-blue. Steamship at left, landscape at center. Rare.	—	—	—
4	**5000 Reis** ND (1897). Violet. Woman at left, steamship at center. 170x125mm. Rare.	—	—	—

		Good	Fine	XF
5	**10,000 Reis** 2.1.1897. Brown with black text on yellow underprint. Seated woman (allegory) at upper left, steamship at upper center, bust of Mercury at right. 182x125mm. Rare.	—	—	—

		Good	Fine	XF
6	**20,000 Reis** 2.1.1897. Blue-green on yellow underprint. Brown text. Arms at top left, steamship at upper center. 172x125mm. Rare.	—	—	—

S. Thomé

1909 Issue

		Good	Fine	XF
7	**1000 Reis** 1.3.1909. Black on green and yellow underprint. Printer: BWC. 132x77mm. Overprint: *S. THOMÉ.*			
	a. Steamship seal Type I.	125	350	850
	b. Steamship seal Type III.	125	300	750
8	**2500 Reis** 1.3.1909. Black on multicolor underprint. Portrait Vasco da Gama at left. Printer: BWC. 147x93mm. Overprint: *S. THOMÉ.*			
	a. Steamship seal Type I.	175	550	1,250
	b. Steamship seal Type III.	175	485	900
9	**5 Mil Reis** 1.3.1909. Black on multicolor underprint. Portrait Vasco da Gama at left. Printer: BWC. 156x98mm. Overprint: *S. THOMÉ.*			
	a. Steamship seal Type I.	225	650	1,500
	b. Steamship seal Type III.	225	550	1,150

		Good	Fine	XF
10	**10 Mil Reis** 1.3.1909. Black on multicolor underprint. Portrait Vasco da Gama at left. Printer: BWC. 172x105mm. Overprint: *S. THOMÉ.*			
	a. Steamship seal Type I.	275	800	1,750
	b. Steamship seal Type III.	275	700	1,350

No.	Description	Good	Fine	XF
11	**20 Mil Reis** 1.3.1909. Black on multicolor underprint. Portrait Vasco da Gama at left. Printer: BWC. 186x114mm. Overprint: *S. THOMÉ.*	Good	Fine	XF
	a. Steamship seal Type I.	350	950	2,500
	b. Steamship seal Type III.	350	950	2,200
12	**50 Mil Reis** 1.3.1909. Black and green on multicolor underprint. Portrait Vasco da Gama at left. Printer: BWC. 206x121mm. Overprint: *S. THOMÉ.*	Good	Fine	XF
	a. Steamship seal Type I.	1,000	2,500	—
	b. Steamship seal Type III.	1,000	2,250	—

1914 First Issue

No.	Description	Good	Fine	XF
13	**10 Centavos** 5.11.1914. Purple on multicolor underprint. Steamship seal Type II. Printer: BWC. 126x71mm. Overprint: *S. TOMÉ* in black (scarcer), or *S. THOMÉ* in green.	15.00	75.00	200
14	**20 Centavos** 5.11.1914. Dark blue on multicolor underprint. Steamship seal Type II. Printer: BWC. 126x71mm. Overprint: *S. TOMÉ* in black (scarcer), or *S. THOMÉ* in green.	20.00	100	300
15	**50 Centavos** 5.11.1914. Dark green multicolor underprint. Steamship seal Type II. Printer: BWC. 126x71mm. Overprint: *S. TOMÉ* in black (scarcer), or *S. THOMÉ* in green.	40.00	125	350

1914 Second Issue

No.	Description	Good	Fine	XF
16	**10 Centavos** 5.11.1914. Purple on multicolor underprint. Steamship seal Type III. Printer: BWC. 126x71mm. Overprint: *S. TOMÉ* in black (scarcer), or *S. THOMÉ* in green.	15.00	60.00	150
17	**20 Centavos** 5.11.1914. Dark blue on multicolor underprint. Steamship seal Type III. Printer: BWC. 126x71mm. Overprint: *S. TOMÉ* in black (scarcer), or *S. THOMÉ* in green.	20.00	75.00	225
18	**50 Centavos** 5.11.1914. Dark green multicolor underprint. Steamship seal Type III. Printer: BWC. 126x71mm. Overprint: *S. TOMÉ* in black (scarcer), or *S. THOMÉ* in green.	40.00	100	300

1918 Issue

No.	Description	Good	Fine	XF
18A	**5 Centavos** 19.4.1918. Sepia. Steamship seal resembling Type II. Printer: Lisbon printer. 98x65mm.	40.00	150	375

S. Tomé e Príncipe

1921 Issue

No.	Description	Good	Fine	XF
19	**1 Escudo** 1.1.1921. Green. Portrait F. de Oliveira Chamico at left. Signature varieties. Printer: BWC. 130x82mm. Overprint: *S. TOMÉ E PRINCIPE.*	15.00	75.00	225
20	**2 1/2 Escudos** 1.1.1921. Blue. Portrait F. de Oliveira Chamico at left. Signature varieties. Printer: TDLR. 130x89mm. Overprint: *S. TOMÉ E PRINCIPE.*	25.00	100	300
21	**5 Escudos** 1.1.1921. Portrait F. de Oliveira Chamico at left. Signature varieties. Printer: BWC. 154x94mm. Overprint: *S. TOMÉ E PRINCIPE.*	35.00	150	500
22	**10 Escudos** 1.1.1921. Portrait F. de Oliveira Chamico at left. Signature varieties. Printer: BWC. 160x105mm. Overprint: *S. TOMÉ E PRINCIPE.*	45.00	225	650
23	**20 Escudos** 1.1.1921. Portrait F. de Oliveira Chamico at left. Signature varieties. Printer: BWC. 171x110mm. Overprint: *S. TOMÉ E PRINCIPE.*	95.00	300	900
24	**50 Escudos** 1.1.1921. Portrait F. de Oliveira Chamico at left. Signature varieties. Printer: BWC. 186x122mm. Overprint: *S. TOMÉ E PRINCIPE.*	160	500	1,250
25	**100 Escudos** 1.1.1921. Portrait F. de Oliveira Chamico at left. Signature varieties. Printer: BWC. 193x126mm. Overprint: *S. TOMÉ E PRINCIPE.*	250	800	—

1935 Issue

No.	Description	Good	Fine	XF
26	**5 Escudos** 26.6.1935. Portrait F. de Oliveira Chamico at left, arms at bottom center, steamship seal at right. Printer: BWC. 154x94mm.	40.00	150	450
27	**10 Escudos** 26.6.1935. Portrait F. de Oliveira Chamico at left, arms at bottom center, steamship seal at right. Printer: BWC. 160x105mm.	50.00	200	600
28	**20 Escudos** 26.6.1935. Portrait F. de Oliveira Chamico at left, arms at bottom center, steamship seal at right. Printer: BWC. 171x110mm.	65.00	250	700

1944 Issue

No.	Description	Good	Fine	XF
29	**20 Escudos** 21.3.1944. Portrait F. de Oliveira Chamico at left, arms at bottom center, steamship seal at right. 172x115mm.	70.00	275	750
30	**50 Escudos** 21.3.1944. Portrait F. de Oliveira Chamico at left, arms at bottom center, steamship seal at right. 185x125mm.	100	350	1,000
31	**100 Escudos** 21.3.1944. Portrait F. de Oliveira Chamico at left, arms at bottom center, steamship seal at right. 192x125mm.	250	750	—

1946 Issue

No.	Description	Good	Fine	XF
32	**20 Escudos** 12.8.1946. Brown on multicolor underprint. Steamship seal at left, arms at upper center, D. Afonso V at right. Printer: BWC. 150x80mm.	8.00	40.00	125
33	**50 Escudos** 12.8.1946. Brown-violet on multicolor underprint. Steamship seal at left, arms at upper center, D. Afonso V at right. Printer: BWC. 155x82mm.	12.00	50.00	150

		Good	Fine	XF
34	**100 Escudos** 12.8.1946. Purple on multicolor underprint. Steamship seal at left, arms at upper center, D. Afonso V at right. Printer: BWC. 160x85mm.	20.00	75.00	300

1947 Circulating Bearer Check Issue

		Good	Fine	XF
35A	**100 Escudos** 10.2.1947; 24.2.1947; 29.4.1947; 2.5.1947. Red on pink underprint. Steamship seal at left. Uniface.	40.00	150	350

		Good	Fine	XF
35B	**500 Escudos** 27.3.1947; 28.3.1947. Violet. Steamship seal at left. Rectangular handstamp: *NULO* (null). Uniface.	160	500	—

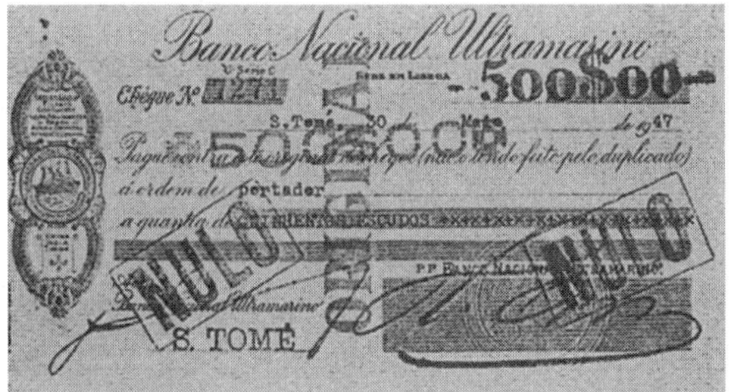

		Good	Fine	XF
35C	**500 Escudos** 30.5.1947. Red on pink underprint. Steamship seal at left. Uniface. Overprint: Rectangular *NULO* (null). Rare.	—	—	—

1956-1964 Issue

		VG	VF	UNC
36	**20 Escudos** 20.11.1958. Brown on multicolor underprint. Bank seal at left, Portuguese arms at lower center, D. Afonso V at lower right. Printer: BWC. 150x79mm.			
	a. Issued note.	2.00	5.00	12.50
	s. Specimen.	—	—	50.00
	ct. Color trial. Green on multicolor underprint.	—	—	240

		VG	VF	UNC
37	**50 Escudos** 20.11.1958. Brown-violet on multicolor underprint. Bank seal at left, Portuguese arms at lower center, D. Afonso V at lower right. Printer: BWC. 155x82mm.			
	a. Issued note.	2.50	6.00	17.50
	s. Specimen.	—	—	65.00
	ct. Color trial. Red on multicolor underprint.	—	—	240
38	**100 Escudos** 20.11.1958. Purple on multicolor underprint. Bank seal at left, Portuguese arms at lower center, D. Afonso V at lower right. 186x84mm.	VG	VF	UNC
	a. Issued note.	3.00	10.00	35.00
	s. Specimen.	—	—	—
	ct. Color trial. Brown on multicolor underprint.	—	—	240
39	**500 Escudos** 18.4.1956. Blue on multicolor underprint. Bank seal at left, Portuguese arms at lower center, D. Afonso V at lower right. Portuguese arms at lower right. 165x87mm.	VG	VF	UNC
	a. Issued note.	35.00	125	300
	s. Specimen.	—	—	—
	ct. Color trial. Purple on multicolor underprint.	—	—	375

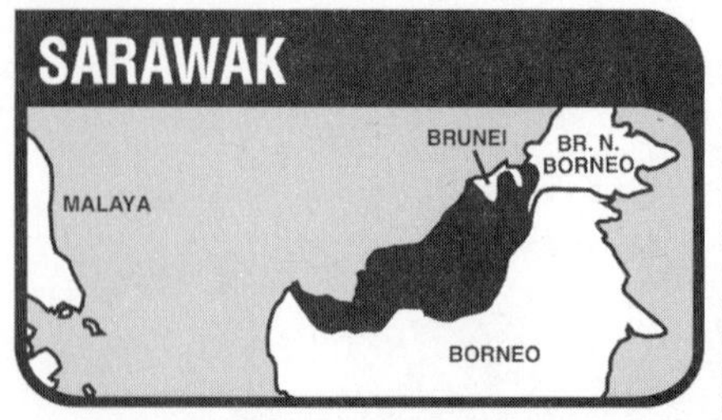

Sarawak, which with Sabah forms the eastern sector (East Malaysia) of the Federation of Malaysia, is situated on northwestern Borneo bounded by Brunei and Sabah state on the north and Kalimantan (Indonesian Borneo) on the east and south. It has an area of 48,050 sq. mi. (131,582 sq. km.) and a population of 980,000. Capital: Kuching. Coconuts, rice, rubber and oil are exported. Sarawak became the southern province of the sultanate of Brunei upon the decline of the Majapahit empire of Java in the 15th century. In 1839, James Brooke, an English adventurer, visited the territory and assisted the sultan in suppressing a revolt. As a reward, the sultan installed Brooke as the sultan of Sarawak (1841), then consisting of 7,000 sq. mi. (18,130 sq. km.) in the southern part of Brunei. It was subsequently enlarged through purchase and annexation. Sarawak was recognized as a separate state by the United States (1850) and Great Britain (1864), and voluntarily became a British protectorate in 1888. The Brooke family continued to rule Sarawak until World War II, when (1941) Sir Charles Vyner Brooke, the third "White Raja", enacted a constitution designed to establish democratic self-government. Japan occupied the country during 1941-1945. In 1946 the territory was ceded to Great Britain and constituted as a crown colony. It achieved self-government and joined Malaysia in 1963.

RULERS:

James Brooke, Rajah, 1841-1868
Charles J. Brooke, Rajah, 1868-1917
Charles V. Brooke, Rajah, 1917-1946
British, 1946-1963

MONETARY SYSTEM:

1 Dollar = 100 Cents

SULTANATE

Sarawak Government Treasury

1858-1859 Issue

		Good	Fine	XF
A1	**5 Cents** 3.9.1858. Black. Handstamped and dated seal of Office of Registry at lower right. Signature C. A. Crymble. Uniface. Rare.	—	—	—
A2	**10 Cents** 6.7.1858. Black. Handstamped and dated seal of Office of Registry at lower right. Signature C. A. Crymble. Uniface. Rare.	—	—	—

		Good	Fine	XF
A2A	**10 Cents** 9.3.1858. Black. Handwritten denomination. Handstamped and dated seal of Office of Registry at lower right. Signature C. A. Crymble. Uniface.	—	—	—

Note: Some believe #A2A to be a contemporary counterfeit.

		Good	Fine	XF
A3	**20 Cents** 7.5.1859. Black. Handstamped and dated seal of Office of Registry at lower right. Signature C. A. Crymble. Uniface. Rare.	—	—	—
A4	**25 Cents** 9.3.1858. Black. Handstamped and dated seal of Office of Registry at lower right. Signature C. A. Crymble. Uniface. Rare.	—	—	—
A5	**50 Cents** 4.4.1858. Black. Handstamped and dated seal of Office of Registry at lower right. Signature C. A. Crymble. Uniface. Rare.	—	—	—

1862 ND Issue

		Good	Fine	XF
1	**10 Cents** ND (1862-1863). Black. Handstamped oval seal of Sarawak Government Treasury. Signature H. E. Houghton. Uniface. Rare.	—	—	—

		Good	Fine	XF
1A	**1 Dollar** ND (1862-1863). Black. Handstamped oval seal of Sarawak Government Treasury. Uniface.			
	a. Issued note. Rare.	—	—	—
	r. Unsigned remainder. Rare.	—	—	—

Government of Sarawak

1880-1900 Issue

		Good	Fine	XF
2	**1 Dollar** 1.6.1894-1.5.1917. Black on green underprint. C. Johnson Brooke at upper left, standing Baroness Burdett Coutte at upper center, arms at upper right. Uniface. Printer: PBC. Rare.	—	—	—
3	**5 Dollars** 1.9.1880-27.10.1903. Black on blue underprint. C. Johnson Brooke at upper left, standing Baroness Burdett Coutte at upper center, arms at upper right. Printer: PBC. Rare.	—	—	—

No.	Description	Good	Fine	XF
4	**10 Dollars** 1.9.1880-7.10.1903. Black on red underprint. C. Johnson Brooke at upper left, standing Baroness Burdett Coutte at upper center, arms at upper right. Printer: PBC. Rare.	—	—	—
5	**25 Dollars** 19.7.1900-7.10.1903. Black on violet underprint. C. Johnson Brooke at upper left, standing Baroness Burdett Coutte at upper center, arms at upper right. Printer: PBC. Rare.	—	—	—
6	**50 Dollars** 19.7.1900-31.8.1903. Black on yellow underprint. C. Johnson Brooke at upper left, standing Baroness Burdett Coutte at upper center, arms at upper right. Printer: PBC. Rare.	—	—	—

Sarawak Government Treasury (resumed)

1919 Issue

No.	Description	Good	Fine	XF
7	**10 Cents** 5.6.1919. Black. Arms at center. Several printing varieties.	350	1,200	6,000
8	**25 Cents** 1.7.1919. Red.	1,000	2,000	9,000

Government of Sarawak (resumed)

1918-1921 Issue

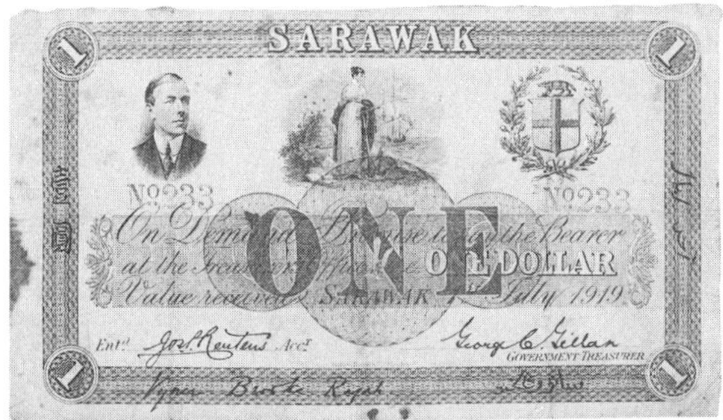

No.	Description	Good	Fine	XF
9	**1 Dollar** 1.7.1919. Black on green underprint. C. Vyner Brooke at upper left, standing Baroness Burdett Coutte at upper center, arms at upper right. Like #2. Printer: PBC.	1,200	3,600	10,000

Color Abbreviation Guide

New to the *Standard Catalog of® World Paper Money* are the following abbreviations related to color references:

BC: Back color
PC: Paper color

No.	Description	Good	Fine	XF
10	**5 Dollars** 5.6.1918-1922. Black on blue underprint. C. Vyner Brooke at upper left, standing Baroness Burdett Coutte at upper center, arms at upper right. Like #3. Printer: PBC.	2,200	7,000	—

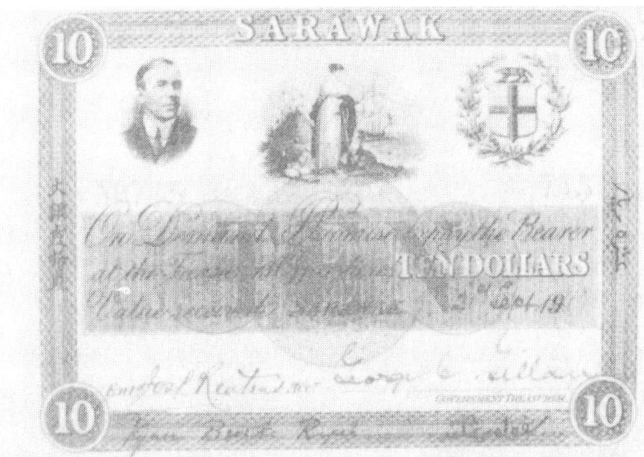

No.	Description	Good	Fine	XF
11	**10 Dollars** 5.6.1918-1922. Black on red underprint. C. Vyner Brooke at upper left, standing Baroness Burdett Coutte at upper center, arms at upper right. Like #4. Printer: PBC.	3,000	7,000	—
12	**25 Dollars** 18.5.1921. Black on violet underprint. C. Vyner Brooke at upper left, standing Baroness Burdett Coutte at upper center, arms at upper right. Like #5. Printer: PBC.	—	—	—
13	**50 Dollars** 18.5.1921. Black on yellow underprint. C. Vyner Brooke at upper left, standing Baroness Burdett Coutte at upper center, arms at upper right. Like #6. Printer: PBC.	—	—	—

1929 Issue

No.	Description	Good	Fine	XF
14	**1 Dollar** 1.7.1929. Purple and multicolor. Palm trees at left. C. Vyner Brooke at right. Printer: BWC.	110	320	1,400

		Good	Fine	XF
15	**5 Dollars** 1.7.1929. Brown and multicolor. Palm trees at left. Arms at lower left. C. Vyner Brooke at right. Printer: BWC.	300	700	2,500

		Good	Fine	XF
16	**10 Dollars** 1.7.1929. Red and multicolor. Palm trees at left. Arms at left. C. Vyner Brooke at right. Printer: BWC.	600	1,000	13,000

		Good	Fine	XF
17	**25 Dollars** 1.7.1929. Blue and multicolor. Palm trees at left. C. Vyner Brooke above arms at center. Back: Government Building. Printer: BWC. Rare.	—	—	—
18	**50 Dollars** 1.7.1929. Green and multicolor. Palm trees at left.C. Vyner Brooke above arms at center. Printer: BWC. Rare.	—	—	—
19	**100 Dollars** 1.7.1929. Purple and multicolor. Palm trees at left. C. Vyner Brooke above arms at center. Printer: BWC. Rare.	—	—	—

Note: A VG example of #19 brought $7150. in a 1989 Spink-Taisei Sale held in Singapore.

1935-1938 Issue

		Good	Fine	XF
20	**1 Dollar** 1.1.1935. Green and multicolor. Palm trees at left. C. Vyner Brooke at right. Like #14. Printer: BWC.	150	350	800

		Good	Fine	XF
21	**5 Dollars** 1.1.1938. Brown and multicolor. Palm trees at left. Arms at lower left. C. Vyner Brooke at right. Like #15. Signature title: *Financial Secretary.* Printer: BWC.	200	700	2,500
22	**10 Dollars** 1.6.1937. Red and multicolor. Palm trees at left. Arms at left. C. Vyner Brooke at right. Like #16.	300	1,200	3,000

1940 Issue

		Good	Fine	XF
23	**1 Dollar** 1.1.1940. Green and multicolor. Palm trees at left. C. Vyner Brooke at right. Like #14.	150	250	1,500

		Good	Fine	XF
24	**10 Dollars** 1.1.1940. Red and multicolor. Palm trees at left. Arms at left. C. Vyner Brooke at right. Like #16.	400	850	3,500

1940 Emergency Fractional Issue

		VG	VF	UNC
25	**10 Cents** 1.8.1940. Red on orange and blue-green underprint. Arms at upper left, C. Vyner Brooke at right. Uniface. Watermark: SDM monogram and map of Malay. Printer: Survey Dept. Fed. Malay States, Kuala Lumpur.			
	a. Series A.	50.00	150	1,800
	b. Series B.	40.00	120	1,000
	c. Series C.	40.00	120	1,000

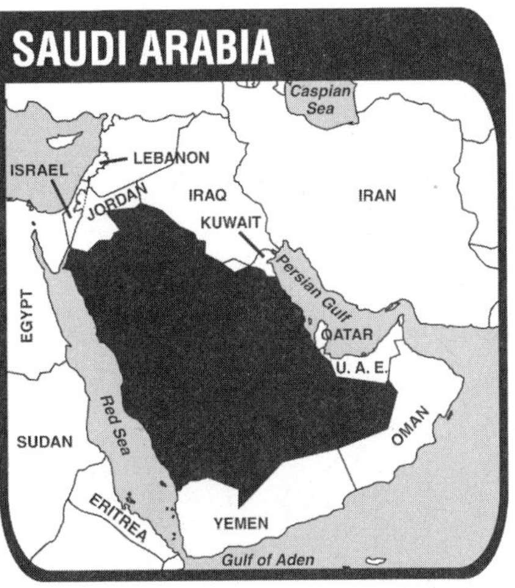

The Kingdom of Saudi Arabia, an independent and absolute hereditary monarchy comprising the former sultanate of Nejd, the old kingdom of Hejaz, Asir and el Hasa, occupies four-fifths of the Arabian peninsula. The kingdom has an area of 2,149,690 sq. km. and a population of 28.15 million. Capital: Riyadh. The economy is based on oil, which provides 85 percent of Saudi Arabia's revenue.Saudi Arabia is the birthplace of Islam and home to Islam's two holiest shrines in Mecca and Medina. The king's official title is the Custodian of the Two Holy Mosques. The modern Saudi state was founded in 1932 by Abd al-Aziz bin Abd al-Rahman al Saud (Ibn Saud) after a 30-year campaign to unify most of the Arabian Peninsula. A male descendent of Ibn Saud, his son Abdallah bin Abd al-Aziz, rules the country today as required by the country's 1992 Basic Law. Following Iraq's invasion of Kuwait in 1990, Saudi Arabia accepted the Kuwaiti royal family and 400,000 refugees while allowing Western and Arab troops to deploy on its soil for the liberation of Kuwait the following year. The continuing presence of foreign troops on Saudi soil after the liberation of Kuwait became a source of tension between the royal family and the public until all operational US troops left the country in 2003. Major terrorist attacks in May and November 2003 spurred a strong on-going campaign against domestic terrorism and extremism. King Abdallah has continued the cautious reform program begun when he was crown prince. To promote increased political participation, the government held elections nationwide from February through April 2005 for half the members of 179 municipal councils. In December 2005, King Abdallah completed the process by appointing the remaining members of the advisory municipal councils. The country remains a leading producer of oil and natural gas and holds more than 20% of the world's proven oil reserves. The government continues to pursue economic reform and diversification, particularly since Saudi Arabia's accession to the WTO in December 2005, and promotes foreign investment in the kingdom. A burgeoning population, aquifer depletion, and an economy largely dependent on petroleum output and prices are all ongoing governmental concerns.

RULERS:

Abd Al-Aziz Ibn Sa'ud, AH1334-1373/1926-1953AD
Sa'ud Ibn Abdul Aziz, AH1373-1383/1953-1964AD
Faisal, AH1383-1395/1964-1975AD
Khaled, AH1395-1402/1975-1982AD
Fahd, AH1402-1432/1982-2005AD
Abdullah, 2005-2015AD
Salman, 2015AD-

MONETARY SYSTEM:

1 Riyal = 20 Ghirsh

REPLACEMENT NOTES:

#1-4, serial number starting with an Arabic zero.

KINGDOM

Saudi Arabian Monetary Agency

SIGNATURE VARIETIES

These notes were initially introduced as a convenience to foreign Moslems making the pilgrimage to Mecca. They were given in exchange for equivalent local currencies at Saudi Arabian agencies and embassies located abroad. By 1957 the receipts had gained wide acceptance within the country and had replaced silver riyals in major financial transactions. Accordingly, a Royal Decree dated 1/7/1379 authorized the Monetary Agency to issue its own paper currency for general circulation throughout the Kingdom. The Pilgrim Receipts were called in during October 1963 and finally demonetized on March 20, 1964.

1953 Haj Pilgrim Receipt Issue

		VG	VF	UNC
1	**10 Riyals** AH1372 (1953). Green and multicolor. Palm tree above crossed swords at center. Printer: TDLR.	200	1,000	3,000

1954; 1956 Haj Pilgrim Receipt Issue

#	Description	VG	VF	UNC
2	**1 Riyal** AH1375 (1956). Red and multicolor. Entrance to the Royal Palace in Jedda at center. BC: Brown.	15.00	50.00	225
3	**5 Riyals** AH1373 (1954). Blue and multicolor. Dhow in Jedda harbor at center. Back: Palm tree above crossed swords at center. Like face of #1.	VG	VF	UNC
	a. Issued note.	25.00	125	500
	s. Specimen.	—	—	4,500

#	Description	VG	VF	UNC
4	**10 Riyals** AH1373 (1954). Dark green and multicolor. Two dhows in Jedda Harbor at center. Back: Palm tree with crossed swords at left and right.	25.00	125	500

Scotland, a part of the United Kingdom of Great Britain and Northern Ireland, consists of the northern part of the island of Great Britain. It has an area of 30,414 sq. mi. (78,772 sq. km.). Capital: Edinburgh. Principal industries are agriculture, fishing, manufacturing and ship-building. In the 5th century, Scotland consisted of four kingdoms; that of the Picts, the Scots, Strathclyde, and Northumbria. The Scottish kingdom was united by Malcolm II (1005-34), but its ruler was forced to payo homage to the English crown in 1174. Scotland won independence under Robert Bruce at Bannockburn in 1314 and was ruled by the house of Stuart from 1371 to 1688. The personal union of the kingdoms of England and Scotland was achieved in 1603 by the accession of King James VI of Scotland as James I of England. Scotland was united with England by Parliamentary act in 1707.

RULERS:
British

MONETARY SYSTEM:
1 Shilling = 12 Pence
1 Guinea = 21 Shillings
1 Pound Sterling = 12 Pounds Scots
1 Pound = 20 Shillings to 1971
1 Pound = 100 New Pence, 1971-1981
1 Pound = 100 Pence, 1982-
1 Pound = 20 Shillings to 1971
Town and County Bank, 1825-1908
Western Bank of Scotland, 1832-57

BRITISH ADMINISTRATION

Bank of Scotland

Most notes from 1695 to 1856 are black and uniface.

1695 Issue

#	Description	Good	Fine	XF
1	**5 Pounds** 1695. Black. Embossed with bank seal.	—	—	—
2	**10 Pounds** 1695. Black. Embossed with bank seal.	—	—	—
3	**20 Pounds** 1695. Black. Embossed with bank seal.	—	—	—
4	**50 Pounds** 1695. Black. Embossed with bank seal.	—	—	—
5	**100 Pounds** 1695. Black. Embossed with bank seal.	—	—	—

1704 Issue

#	Description	Good	Fine	XF
6	**20 Shillings** 1704. Black.	—	—	—
7	**12 Pounds Scots** 1704. Black.	—	—	—

1716 Issue

#	Description	Good	Fine	XF
8	**12 Pounds Scots** 16.4.1716. Black. *Edenburgh* in heading.	—	—	—

Color Abbreviation Guide

New to the *Standard Catalog of ® World Paper Money* are the following abbreviations related to color references:

BC: Back color
PC: Paper color

1723 Issue

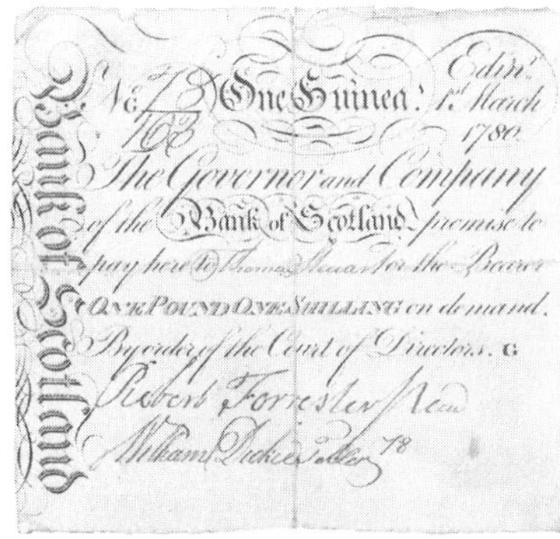

#	Denomination	Good	Fine	XF
9	**12 Pounds Scots** 24.6.1723. Black. *Edenburgh* in heading.	—	—	—

1730 Issue

#	Denomination	Good	Fine	XF
10	**5 Pounds** 1730. Black. Text with option clause concerning redemption.	—	—	—

1731 Issue

#	Denomination	Good	Fine	XF
11	**12 Pounds Scots** 4.2.1731. Black. Similar to #9. *Edinr.* in heading.	—	—	—

1732 Issue

#	Denomination	Good	Fine	XF
12	**12 Pounds Scots** 12.12.1732; 25.3.1741; 2.6.1748. Black. Handwritten date. Text with option clause.	—	—	—

1750 Issue

#	Denomination	Good	Fine	XF
13	**1 Pound** (1750). Black.			
	a. Option clause with text: *By Order of the Directors.*	—	—	—
	b. Legend in italic type except for *Directors* (Gothic script).	—	—	—
14	**5 Pounds** 1.9.1751. Black. Vertical panel at left of interwoven letters.	—	—	—
15	**10 Pounds** (1750). Black. Vertical panel at left of interwoven letters. Similar to #14.	—	—	—
16	**20 Pounds** (1750). Black. Vertical panel at left of interwoven letters. Similar to #14.	—	—	—
17	**50 Pounds** (1750). Black. Vertical panel at left of interwoven letters. Similar to #14.	—	—	—
18	**100 Pounds** (1750). Black. Vertical panel at left of interwoven letters. Similar to #14.	—	—	—

1760 Issue

#	Denomination	Good	Fine	XF
19	**10 Shillings = 6 Pounds Scots** 15.5.1760. Black. No option clause. Proof.	—	—	—
20	**5 Pounds** (1760). Black. Text with option clause.	—	—	—
21	**10 Pounds** (1760). With text: *for value received.* No option clause.	—	—	—
22	**10 Pounds** (1760). Text with option clause.	—	—	—
23	**20 Pounds** (1760). Black. With text: *for value received.* No option clause. Similar to #21.	—	—	—
24	**20 Pounds** (1760). Black. Text with option clause. Similar to #22.	—	—	—
25	**50 Pounds** (1760). Black. Text with option clause.	—	—	—
26	**100 Pounds** (1760). Black. Vertical panel at left of interwoven letters. Similar to #18.	—	—	—

1765 Issue

#	Denomination	Good	Fine	XF
27	**1 Pound** 1.8.1765. Black. Title: Governor spelled without letter u.	—	—	—
28	**5 Pounds** (1765). Black. Title: Governor spelled without letter u.	—	—	—
29	**10 Pounds** (1765). Black. Title: Governor spelled without letter u.	—	—	—
30	**20 Pounds** (1765). Black. Title: Governor spelled without letter u.	—	—	—
31	**50 Pounds** (1765). Black. Title: Governor spelled without letter u.	—	—	—
32	**100 Pounds** (1765). Black. Title: Governor spelled without letter u.	—	—	—

1768 Issue

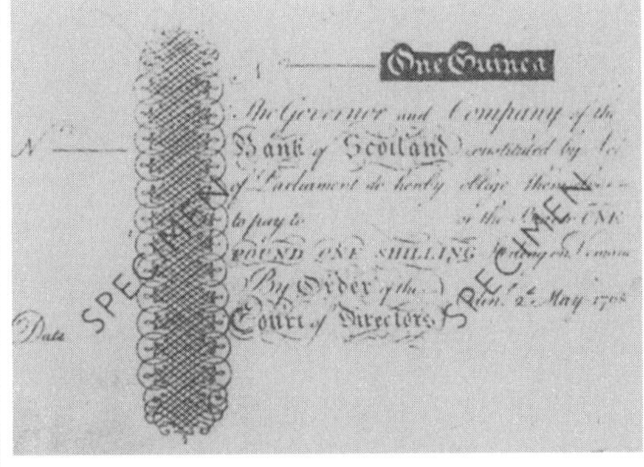

#	Denomination	Good	Fine	XF
33	**1 Guinea** 2.5.1768. Black. Value in words across top.	—	—	—

1774 Issue

#	Denomination	Good	Fine	XF
34	**1 Guinea** 2.2.1774. Black and blue. Value in words across top. Similar to #33.	—	—	—

1780 Issue

#	Denomination	Good	Fine	XF
35	**1 Pound** (1780). Black. Plates G; H; K. Letters *ND* at upper left.	500	1,500	—

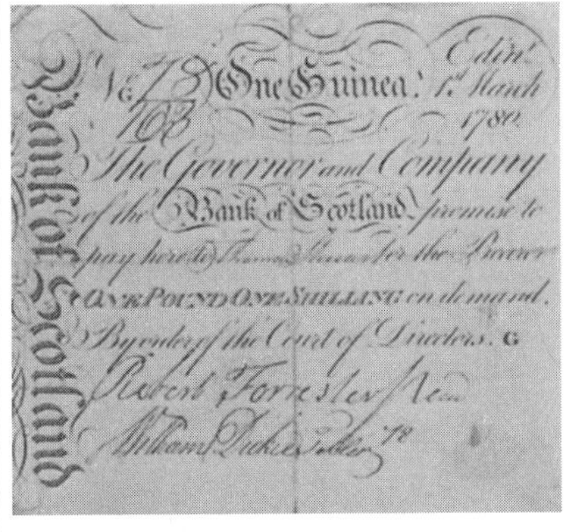

#	Denomination	Good	Fine	XF
36	**1 Guinea** 1.3.1780; 11.10.1808. Black. Plates B-G; plates H-S with serial # prefix *No.G* at upper left.	500	1,500	—
37	**5 Pounds** (1780). Black.	—	—	—
38	**10 Pounds** (1780). Black.	—	—	—
39	**20 Pounds** (1780). Black.	—	—	—

1810 Issue

#	Denomination	Good	Fine	XF
40	**1 Pound** (1810). Black. Seated Scotia with thistle in oval at top center, crown above, bank arms at left.			
	a. Engraved by W. & D. Lizars.	600	2,000	—
	b. Engraved by W. H. Lizars.	600	2,000	—
41	**1 Guinea** (1810). Black. Seated Scotia with thistle in oval at top center, crown above, bank arms at left. Similar to #40.			
	a. Engraved by W. & D. Lizars. Plate G.	500	1,800	—
	b. Engraved by John Menzies. Plate D.	500	1,800	—
42	**2 Pounds** (1810). Black. Bank arms at upper center.	—	—	—
43	**2 Guineas** (1810). Black. Bank arms at upper center. Similar to #42.	—	—	—
44	**5 Pounds** (1810). Black. Engraved by H. Ashby, London.	—	—	—
45	**10 Pounds** (1810). Black.	—	—	—
46	**20 Pounds** (1810). Black.	—	—	—

1825 Issue

#	Denomination	Good	Fine	XF
47	**1 Guinea** (1825). Allegorical woman at left and right, bank arms at upper center. Plate A.	500	1,800	—

		Good	Fine	XF
48	**5 Pounds** (1825). Allegorical woman at left and right, bank arms at upper center. Plate A. Similar to #47.	—	—	—

1825 Steel Engraved Issue

Plates for #51-54 were engraved by Perkins Bacon & Petch (later Perkins & Bacon, then Perkins Bacon & Co.).

		Good	Fine	XF
51	**1 Pound** (1825). Crowned Scotia at left, bank arms at upper center.			
	a. Imprint: P. B. & P.	500	1,750	—
	b. Imprint: P. & B (1833).	500	1,750	—
	c. Imprint: P. B. C.	500	1,750	—
52	**10 Pounds** (1825). Crowned Scotia at left, bank arms at upper center.	Good	Fine	XF
	a. Imprint: P. B. & P.	—	—	—
	b. Imprint: P. & B (1833).	—	—	—
	c. Imprint: P. B. C.	—	—	—
53	**20 Pounds** (1825). Crowned Scotia at left, bank arms at upper center.	Good	Fine	XF
	a. Imprint: P. B. & P.	—	—	—
	b. Imprint: P. & B (1833).	—	—	—
	c. Imprint: P. B. C.	—	—	—

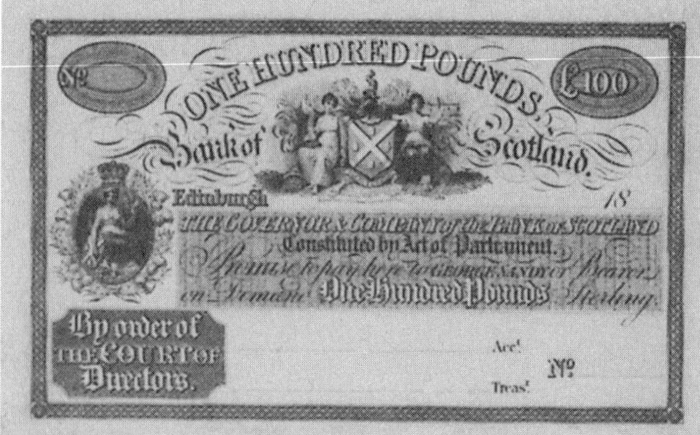

		Good	Fine	XF
54	**100 Pounds** (1825). Crowned Scotia at left, bank arms at upper center.			
	a. Imprint: P. B. & P.	—	—	—
	b. Imprint: P. & B (1833).	—	—	—
	c. Imprint: P. B. C.	—	—	—

1851 Issue

#56-60 notes payable to bearer, not to a named official.

		Good	Fine	XF
56	**1 Pound** (1851). Black. Printer: PBC.	400	1,600	—

1850 Issue

		Good	Fine	XF
55	**5 Pounds** (1850). Printer: W. H. Lizars.			
	a. Without text above vignette. Proof.	—	—	—
	b. With text: *Pursuant to Act 16 & 17 Victoria Cap. 63* above vignette. Proof.	—	—	—

1851 Issue

#56-60 notes payable to bearer, not to a named official.

		Good	Fine	XF
57	**5 Pounds** (1851). Black. Printer: PBC.	500	1,500	—
58	**10 Pounds** (1851). Black. Printer: PBC.	1,100	3,500	—
59	**20 Pounds** (1851). Black. Printer: PBC.	—	—	—
60	**100 Pounds** (1851). Black. Printer: PBC.	—	—	—

1860 Issue

		Good	Fine	XF
65	**1 Pound** (1860); 15.5.1878; 10.3.1881. Black and red. Obverse and reverse of the Great Seal of Scotland on left panel. Large denomination wording protector added to design, in red. Printer: PBC.	400	1,600	—
66	**5 Pounds** (1860). Black and red. Obverse and reverse of the Great Seal of Scotland on left panel. Large denomination wording protector added to design, in red. Printer: PBC.	700	2,000	—
67	**10 Pounds** (1860). Black and red. Obverse and reverse of the Great Seal of Scotland on left panel. Large denomination wording protector added to design, in red. Printer: PBC.	—	—	—
68	**20 Pounds** (1860). Black and red. Obverse and reverse of the Great Seal of Scotland on left panel. Large denomination wording protector added to design, in red. Printer: PBC.	—	—	—
69	**100 Pounds** (1860). Black and green. Obverse and reverse of the Great Seal of Scotland on left panel. Printer: PBC.	—	—	—

1885 Issue

		Good	Fine	XF
76	**1 Pound** 22.4.1885. Brown, yellow and blue-gray. Bank arms at upper center flanked by value. Scottish arms between sides of Seal. Printer: George Waterston & Sons, Edinburgh. Lithographed.	450	1,800	—
77	**5 Pounds** ND (1885). Brown, yellow and blue-gray. Bank arms at upper center flanked by value. Scottish arms between sides of Seal. Printer: George Waterston & Sons, Edinburgh. Lithographed.	750	2,000	—
78	**10 Pounds** ND (1885). Brown, yellow and blue-gray. Bank arms at upper center flanked by value. Scottish arms between sides of Seal. Printer: George Waterston & Sons, Edinburgh. Lithographed.	—	—	—
79	**20 Pounds** ND (1885). Brown, yellow and blue-gray. Bank arms at upper center flanked by value. Scottish arms between sides of Seal. Printer: George Waterston & Sons, Edinburgh. Lithographed.	—	—	—

#	Description	Good	Fine	XF
80	**100 Pounds** ND (1885). Brown, yellow and blue-gray. Bank arms at upper center flanked by value. Scottish arms between sides of Seal. Printer: George Waterston & Sons, Edinburgh. Lithographed.	—	—	—

1889-1890 Issue

#81-110

Imprint Varieties

Type A: G. Waterston & Sons Edin. (1885-1917).
Type B: G. Waterston & Sons Ld. (1917-1964).
Type C: G. Waterston & Sons Ltd. (1965-1967).
Type D: Waterston (1968-1969) - on back.

Note: The registered number of the watermark appearing as an imprint on 5-100 Pound notes was omitted in 1960.

#	Description	Good	Fine	XF
81	**1 Pound** 10.11.1889-10.10.1927. Yellow-brown and gray-blue. Medallion of Goddess of Fortune below arms at right center. Uniface.			
	a. Signature J. F. Stormonth Darling (to 1893).	300	1,350	2,500
	b. Signature D. McNeill (to 1910).	250	800	1,500
	c. Signature P. Macdonald (to 1920).	75.00	350	800
	d. Signature A. Rose (to 1927).	65.00	325	750

#	Description	Good	Fine	XF
82	**5 Pounds** 1889-1932. Yellow-brown and gray-blue. Medallion of Goddess of Fortune below arms at right center. Uniface. Like #81.			
	a. Signature J. F. Stormonth Darling. 24.5.1889-20.2.1893.	600	2,000	3,500
	b. Signature D. McNeill. 5.5.1894-6.9.1910.	300	800	1,500
	c. Signature P. Macdonald. 15.9.1911-3.6.1919.	140	400	1,000
	d. Signature A. Rose. 7.10.1920-28.7.1931.	125	350	1,000

#	Description	Good	Fine	XF
83	**10 Pounds** 1890-1929. Yellow-brown and gray-blue. Medallion of Goddess of Fortune below arms at right center. Uniface. Like #81.			
	a. Signature J. F. Stormonth Darling. 20.8.1839-23.12.1890.	—	—	—
	b. Signature D. McNeill. 16.10.1894-30.9.1909.	450	1,000	2,200
	c. Signature P. Macdonald. 30.11.1912-5.11.1919.	375	900	2,000
	d. Signature A. Rose. 15.8.1921-9.3.1929.	325	850	1,900

#	Description	Good	Fine	XF
84	**20 Pounds** 1890-1932. Yellow-brown and gray-blue. Medallion of Goddess of Fortune below arms at right center. Uniface. Like #81.			
	a. Signature J. F. Stormonth Darling. 9.7.1890-30.1.1893.	—	—	—
	b. Signature D. McNeill. 26.5.1894-2.3.1910.	400	1,000	2,100
	c. Signature P. Macdonald. 26.10.1911-8.10.1919.	375	900	2,000
	d. Signature A. Rose. 11.10.1920-25.9.1930.	325	850	1,900

#	Description	Good	Fine	XF
85	**100 Pounds** 1889-1930. Yellow-brown and gray-blue. Medallion of Goddess of Fortune below arms at right center. Uniface. Like #81.			
	a. Signature J. F. Stormonth Darling. 27.8.1889-10.2.1893.	—	—	—
	b. Signature D. McNeill. 12.7.1894-9.12.1910.	—	—	—
	c. Signature P. Macdonald. 11.12.1911-17.4.1919.	—	—	—
	d. Signature A. Rose. 7.7.1920-6.6.1930.	—	—	—

1929-1935 Issue

#	Description	VG	VF	UNC
86	**1 Pound** 22.1.1929-17.7.1933. Yellow-brown and gray-blue. Signature Lord Elphinstone and G. J. Scott. Back: Bank building. Reduced size.	50.00	175	400
87	**5 Pounds** 7.1.1932; 18.4.1932; 11.10.1932; 25.3.1933. Yellow-brown and gray-blue. Signature Lord Elphinstone and G. J. Scott. Like #86. Back: Bank building. Reduced size.	100	300	700
#88	*Not assigned.*			
89	**20 Pounds** 21.6.1932; 2.12.1932. Yellow-brown and gray-blue. Signature Lord Elphinstone and G. J. Scott. Like #86. Back: Bank building. Reduced size.	200	650	1,500
90	**100 Pounds** 28.5.1932; 2.11.1932. Yellow-brown and gray-blue. Signature Lord Elphinstone and G. J. Scott. Like #86. Back: Bank building. Reduced size.	500	1,200	3,000

1935; 1938 Issue

#	Description	VG	VF	UNC
91	**1 Pound** 1937-1943. Yellow-brown, dark brown and gray-blue. Arms of the bank at left. Back: Bank building.			
	a. Signature Lord Elphinstone and A. W. M. Beveridge. 15.1.1935-15.9.1937.	20.00	90.00	280
	b. Signature Lord Elphinstone and J. Macfarlane. 5.1.1939-7.5.1941.	20.00	80.00	260
	c. Signature Lord Elphinstone and J. B. Crawford. 2.6.1942; 16.10.1943.	20.00	80.00	240
	s. As c. Specimen.	—	—	225
92	**5 Pounds** 1935-1944. Yellow-brown, dark brown and gray-blue. Thistle motif at left. Back: Bank building.			
	a. Signature Lord Elphinstone and A. W. M. Beveridge. 17.1.1935-17.3.1938.	60.00	300	975
	b. Signature Lord Elphinstone and J. Macfarlane. Black value panels. 24.4.1939-16.10.1941.	60.00	300	975
	c. Signature Lord Elphinstone and J. B. Crawford. 5.6.1942-26.9.1944.	50.00	250	850
	s. As c. Specimen.	—	—	350

93 **10 Pounds**	VG	VF	UNC
1938-1963. Scottish arms in panel at left, medallion of Goddess of fortune below arms at right. Back: Bank building.			
a. Signature Lord Elphinstone and A. W. M. Beveridge. 24.1.1935; 28.6.1938.	350	1,200	2,500
b. Signature Lord Elphinstone and J. B. Crawford. 16.7.1942; 15.10.1942.	325	1,100	2,250
c. Signature Lord Bilsland and Sir Wm. Watson. 26.9.1963; 27.9.1963.	250	700	1,600

94 **20 Pounds**	VG	VF	UNC
1935-1965. Scottish arms in panel at left, medallion of Goddess of fortune below arms at right. Back: Bank building.			
a. Signature Lord Elphinstone and A. W. M. Beveridge. 11.1.1935-22.7.1938.	135	500	1,400
b. Signature Lord Elphinstone and J. Macfarlane. 16.5.1939; 12.7.1939.	135	550	1,600
c. Signature Lord Elphinstone and J. B. Crawford. 5.6.1942-11.8.1952.	110	425	1,200
d. Signature Lord Elphinstone and Sir Wm. Watson. 5.12.1952; 14.4.1953.	130	500	1,400
e. Signature Sir J. Craig and Sir Wm. Watson. 6.4.1955-12.6.1956	100	350	1,000
f. Signature Lord Bilsland and Sir Wm. Watson. 21.3.1958-3.10.1963.	80.00	300	900

95 **100 Pounds**	VG	VF	UNC
1935-1962. Scottish arms in panel at left, medallion of Goddess of fortune below arms at right. Back: Bank building.			
a. Signature Lord Elphinstone and A. W. M. Beveridge. 8.1.1935-12.8.1937.	600	2,000	5,000
b. Signature Lord Elphinstone and J. Macfarlane. 2.4.1940; 15.7.1940.	550	1,750	4,200
c. Signature Lord Elphinestone and J. B. Crawford. 10.6.1942; 14.12.1951.	500	1,500	3,800
d. Signature John Craig and Sir Wm. Watson. 14.9.1956-3.12.1956.	500	1,500	3,500
e. Signature Lord Bilsland and Sir Wm. Watson. 24.3.1959-30.11.1962.	500	1,500	3,500

1945 Issue

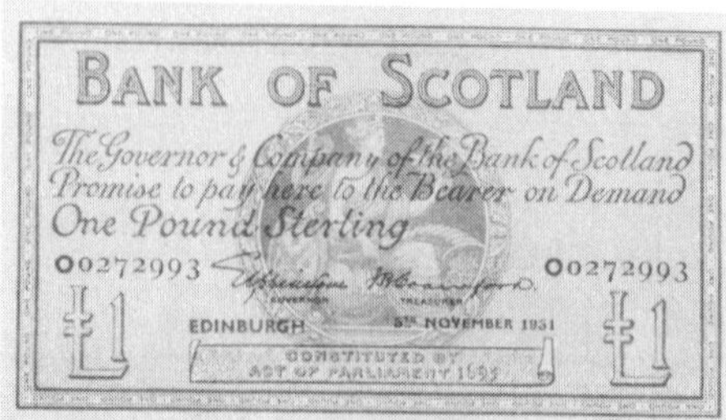

96 **1 Pound**	VG	VF	UNC
1945-1953. Yellow and gray. Medallion at center without arms at left. Back: Arms.			
a. Back brown. Signature Lord Elphinstone and J. B. Crawford. 4.1.1945; 6.2.1945.	20.00	70.00	275
b. Back light brown. Signature Lord Elphinstone and J. B. Crawford. 6.2.1945-19.11.1952.	12.50	35.00	100
c. Signature Lord Elphinstone and Sir Wm. Watson. 4.9.1953; 16.10.1953; 9.11.1953.	12.50	35.00	90.00
s. As c. Specimen.	—	—	100

97 **5 Pounds**	VG	VF	UNC
1945-1948. Gray and light brown. Signature Lord Elphinstone and J. B. Crawford. Back: Arms.			
a. Back dark brown. 3.1.1945; 15.1.1945; 1.2.1945; 16.2.1945; 2.3.1945.	50.00	150	400
b. Back light brown. 16.3.1945-10.1.1948.	40.00	110	250

1950 Issue

98 **5 Pounds**	VG	VF	UNC
1948-1952. Gray and light brown. Like #97, but reduced size. Back: Arms.			
a. Denomination panels in black. Signature Lord Elphinstone and J. B. Crawford. 16.11.1948-21.11.1952.	25.00	75.00	180
b. Gray-brown medallion. Signature Lord Elphinstone and Sir Wm. Watson. 10.12.1952-4.12.1953.	25.00	75.00	180

1955 Issue

99 **5 Pounds**	VG	VF	UNC
1955. Denomination panels in black, medallion in blue. Like #98. Back: Arms.			
a. Signature Lord Elphinstone and Sir Wm. Watson. 1.3.1955; 2.3.1955; 3.3.1955.	25.00	80.00	200
b. Signature Sir J. Craig and Sir Wm. Watson. 7.4.1955-3.9.1955.	25.00	75.00	180

1955-1956 Issue

100 **1 Pound**	VG	VF	UNC
1955-1960. Light brown and light blue. Medallion at center without arms at left. Like #96. Back: Sailing ship.			
a. Signature Lord Elphinstone and Sir Wm. Watson. 1.3.1955; 2.3.1955; 3.3.1955; 4.3.1955.	7.50	30.00	90.00
b. Signature Sir J. Craig and Sir Wm. Watson. 1.9.1955-14.9.1956.	6.00	25.00	80.00
c. Signature Lord Bilsland and Sir Wm. Watson. 30.8.1957-30.11.1960.	5.00	20.00	60.00

101	5 Pounds	VG	VF	UNC
	1956-1960. Blue and light brown. Numeral of value below in 2 lines. Like #97. Back: Arms and ship.			
	a. Signature Sir J. Craig and Sir Wm. Watson. 9.4.1956-17.4.1956.	20.00	60.00	160
	b. Signature Lord Bilsland and Sir Wm. Watson. 1.5.1957-24.5.1960.	17.50	50.00	140

British Linen Bank

Note: Formerly the British Linen Company. See Vol. I. Merged with the Bank of Scotland in 1970.

1906; 1907 Issue

		Good	Fine	XF
146	**1 Pound** 15.1.1907; 16.12.1907; 2.11.1908; 15.7.1910; 11.8.1911; 29.10.1912; 17.9.1913. Blue with large red *B.L.B.* protector. Facing view of seated Britannia in emblem at left.	225	600	1,400
147	**5 Pounds** 4.1.1907-12.9.1915. Blue with large red *B.L.B.* protector. Facing view of seated Britannia in emblem at left.	325	1,100	2,250
148	**10 Pounds** 30.1.1907. Blue with large red *B.L.B.* protector. Facing view of seated Britannia in emblem at left.	475	1,250	2,750
149	**20 Pounds** 2.1.1907-18.11.1912. Blue with large red *B.L.B.* protector. Facing view of seated Britannia in emblem at left.	325	1,100	2,250

		VG	VF	UNC
150	**100 Pounds** 11.2.1907; 2.4.1908; 15.5.1912. Blue with large red *B.L.B.* protector. Facing view of seated Britannia in emblem at left. Rare.	—	—	—

1914; 1916 Issue

151	1 Pound	Good	Fine	XF
	1914-1925. Blue with large red *B.L.B.* protector. Side view of seated Britannia in emblem at left, arms at upper right. Similar to #146 with red sunburst overprint. BC: Blue.			
	a. 23.9.1914-5.11.1918.	75.00	300	800
	b. 19.8.1919-31.7.1924.	75.00	300	800
	c. 15.10.1925.	75.00	300	800

		Good	Fine	XF
152	**5 Pounds** 1.2.1916-3.8.1933. Blue with large red *B.L.B.* protector. Side view of seated Britannia in emblem at left, arms at upper right. Similar to #147 with red sunburst overprint. BC: Blue.	120	350	800
153	**10 Pounds** 15.2.1916; 9.2.1920; 15.3.1920. Blue with large red *B.L.B.* protector. Side view of seated Britannia in emblem at left, arms at upper right. Similar to #148 with red sunburst overprint. BC: Blue.	425	1,100	2,000

		Good	Fine	XF
154	**20 Pounds** 3.5.1916-4.9.1933. Blue with large red *B.L.B.* protector. Side view of seated Britannia in emblem at left, arms at upper right. Similar to #149 with red sunburst overprint. BC: Blue.	175	600	1,200
155	**100 Pounds** 7.1.1916; 12.12.1916; 15.1.1918; 1.3.1918; 18.7.1933. Blue with large red *B.L.B.* protector. Side view of seated Britannia in emblem at left, arms at upper right. Similar to #150 with red sunburst overprint. BC: Blue.	450	1,200	2,500

1926 Issue

156	1 Pound	Good	Fine	XF
	1.5.1926-2.8.1934. Blue and red. Side view of seated Britannia in emblem at left, arms at upper right. Similar to #146 with red sunburst overprint. Reduced size and only 1 signature.	20.00	70.00	175

1935 Issue

157	1 Pound	Good	Fine	XF
	1935-1960. Bank arms at upper center, Britannia at left. Similar to #156. Printer: W&S.			
	a. 18.1.1935; 4.7.1937; 10.8.1937; 4.10.1937; 8.11.1938; 2.8.1939; 13.11.1939.	17.50	50.00	135
	b. 7.3.1940-5.4.1944.	12.50	40.00	100
	c. 4.1.1946-5.8.1950.	10.00	30.00	80.00
	d. 4.6.1951-12.5.1959.	6.00	20.00	60.00
	e. 15.4.1960.	7.50	30.00	80.00

Color Abbreviation Guide

New to the *Standard Catalog of® World Paper Money* are the following abbreviations related to color references:

BC: Back color

PC: Paper color

158	5 Pounds	Good	Fine	XF
	1935-1943. Bank arms at upper center, Britannia at left. Similar to #152.			
	a. Printed signature of *GENERAL MANAGER* and handsigned on behalf of *ACCOUNTANT*. 16.9.1935-12.1.1943.	60.00	225	475
	b. Printed signature of *ACCOUNTANT & CASHIER* and *GENERAL MANAGER*. 11.2.1943-28.1.1944.	50.00	175	375

159	20 Pounds	Good	Fine	XF
	1939-1957. Bank arms at upper center, Britannia at left. Similar to #154.			
	a. As #158a. 6.8.1935-24.2.1945.	90.00	250	650
	b. Printed signature of *GENERAL MANAGER* (only). 2.9.1946-11.12.1957.	80.00	200	500

160	100 Pounds	Good	Fine	XF
	1935-1960. Bank arms at upper center, Britannia at left. Similar to #155.			
	a. As #159a. 4.2.1942; 3.3.1943.	400	1,000	—
	b. As #159b. 6.4.1951; 5.8.1954; 27.11.1957.	350	900	—

1944 Issue

		Good	Fine	XF
161	**5 Pounds** 1944-1959. Blue and red. Similar to #158 but reduced size and some minor plate changes.			
	a. Printed signature of *GENERAL MANAGER* and *ACCOUNTANT & CASHIER*. 25.6.1944-3.11.1944.	30.00	150	300
	b. Printed signature of *GENERAL MANAGER* (only). 10.9.1946-4.8.1959.	25.00	80.00	200

Clydesdale Banking Company

Later became Clydesdale Bank Limited, Clydesdale and North of Scotland Bank Limited, and back to Clydesdale Bank Limited.

1838 Issue

		Good	Fine	XF
171	**1 Pound** (1838). Black arms of Glasgow in circle at upper center, vertical floral pattern in panel at left. Uniface. Printer: W. & A. K. Johnston, Edinburgh.	700	2,200	—
172	**5 Pounds** (1838). Black arms of Glasgow in circle at upper center, vertical floral pattern in panel at left. Uniface. Printer: W. & A. K. Johnston, Edinburgh.	1,000	2,750	—
173	**10 Pounds** (1838). Black arms of Glasgow in circle at upper center, vertical floral pattern in panel at left. Uniface. Printer: W. & A. K. Johnston, Edinburgh.	—	—	—
174	**20 Pounds** (1838). Black arms of Glasgow in circle at upper center, vertical floral pattern in panel at left. Uniface. Printer: W. & A. K. Johnston, Edinburgh.	—	—	—
175	**100 Pounds** (1838). Black arms of Glasgow in circle at upper center, vertical floral pattern in panel at left. Uniface. Printer: W. & A. K. Johnston, Edinburgh.	—	—	—

1858 Issue

		Good	Fine	XF
175A	**1 Pound** 16.4.1858-20.4.1863. Arms of Glasgow top center and vignettes at lower left and right. Red line overprint with Clydesdale Bank in large white letters. Printer: Hugh Wilson.	700	1,800	—

1864 Issue

		Good	Fine	XF
176	**1 Pound** 16.11.1864. Black arms of Glasgow in circle at upper center, vertical floral pattern in panel at left. Uniface. Overprint: Red *CLYDESDALE BANK* and value.	700	1,800	—
177	**5 Pounds** (1864). Black arms of Glasgow in circle at upper center, vertical floral pattern in panel at left. Uniface. Printer: Hugh Wilson. Overprint: Red *CLYDESDALE BANK* and value.	800	2,500	—
178	**20 Pounds** (1864). Black arms of Glasgow in circle at upper center, vertical floral pattern in panel at left. Uniface. Printer: W. & A. K. Johnston. Overprint: Red *CLYDESDALE BANK* and value.	1,100	3,000	—
179	**100 Pounds** (1864); 16.9.1868. Black arms of Glasgow in circle at upper center, vertical floral pattern in panel at left. Uniface. Overprint: *CLYDESDALE BANKING COMPANY.*	—	—	—

1870 Issue

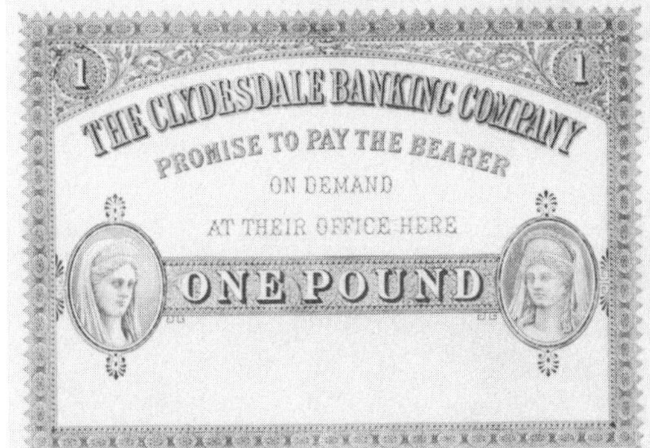

		Good	Fine	XF
180	**1 Pound** 28.2.1872; 4.3.1874; 9.2.1876. Green and purple. Woman at left and right. Printer: TDLR.			
	a. Issued note.	450	1,300	—
	s. Specimen.	350	700	—

Clydesdale Bank Ltd.

1882 Issue

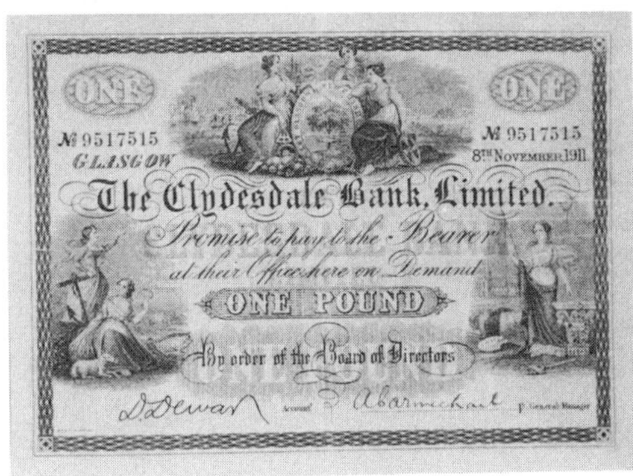

		VG	VF	UNC
181	**1 Pound** 1882-1921. Red. Three allegorical women around Glasgow seal at top center, two at left, one at right. Uniface.			
	a. Without serial # prefix letter. 4.7.1882-30.10.1912.	200	700	1,800
	b. With serial # prefix letter. 8.10.1913-7.1.1920.	120	400	1,250
	c. Printed signature of Accountant; Handsigned signature of Joint General Manager. 9.2.1921.	250	700	1,750
182	**5 Pounds** 4.7.1882-9.2.1921. Red. Three allegorical women around Glasgow seal at top center, two at left, one at right. Uniface. Like #181.	350	750	2,000
183	**20 Pounds** 4.7.1882-9.6.1920. Red. Three allegorical women around Glasgow seal at top center, two at left, one at right. Uniface. Like #181.	500	1,600	4,000

		Good	Fine	XF
184	**100 Pounds** 16.1.1884-5.8.1914. Red. Three allegorical women around Glasgow seal at top center, two at left, one at right. Uniface. Like #181. Requires confirmation.	—	—	—

1922 Issue

		VG	VF	UNC
185	**1 Pound** 4.1.1922-27.10.1926. Red. Three allegorical women around Glasgow seal at top center, two at left, one at right. Uniface. Similar to #181, but with sunburst rays in underprint.	200	600	1,500

1922-1947 Issue

		VG	VF	UNC
186	**5 Pounds** 15.2.1922-10.7.1946. Blue and red. Ornate design around seal with tree and *LET GLASGOW FLOURISH.*	125	400	1,000

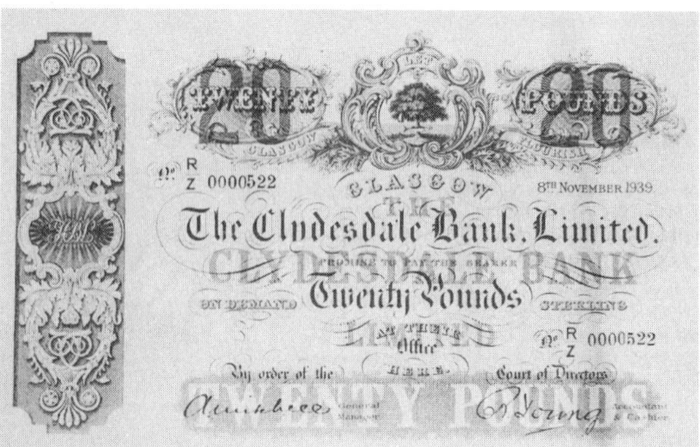

		VG	VF	UNC
187	**20 Pounds** 15.2.1922-4.6.1947. Blue and red. Ornate design around seal with tree and *LET GLASGOW FLOURISH.* Like #186.	175	500	1,500

		VG	VF	UNC
188	**100 Pounds** 15.2.1922-26.3.1947. Blue and red. Ornate design around seal with tree and *LET GLASGOW FLOURISH.* Like #187.	700	2,000	4,000

1927 Issue

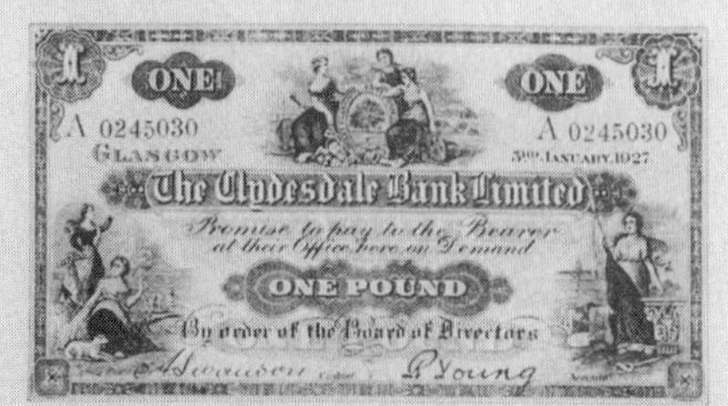

		VG	VF	UNC
189	**1 Pound** 1927-1949. Blue and orange. Allegorical figures at lower left and right. (Industry and Agriculture). Serial # varieties.			
	a. 3.1.1927-7.10.1931.	40.00	110	300
	b. 2.3.1932-5.11.1941.	30.00	80.00	175
	c. 25.2.1942-24.10.1945.	30.00	80.00	175
	d. 1.5.1946.	40.00	120	325
	e. 20.11.1946-3.9.1947.	30.00	80.00	175
	f. 7.4.1948-14.12.1949.	30.00	70.00	150

1948 Issue

		VG	VF	UNC
190	**5 Pounds** 3.3.1948; 12.1.1949. Light blue underprint. Ornate design around seal with tree and *LET GLASGOW FLOURISH.* Like #186.	150	500	1,000

Clydesdale and North of Scotland Bank Ltd.

Formerly, and later to become the Clydesdale Bank Ltd. again.

1950-1951 Issue

		VG	VF	UNC
191	**1 Pound** 1950-1960. Blue, red and orange. Ships at dockside at left, landscape (sheaves) at right. Back: River scene with trees.			
	a. 1.11.1950-1.11.1956.	10.00	45.00	150
	b. 1.5.1958-1.11.1960.	10.00	40.00	125
	s. As a. Specimen.	—	—	250

		VG	VF	UNC
192	**5 Pounds** 2.5.1951-1.3.1960. Purple. King's College at Aberdeen at lower left, Glasgow Cathedral at lower right.			
	a. Signature J. J. Campbell.	30.00	90.00	300
	b. Signature R. D. Fairbairn.	30.00	90.00	300
	s. As a. Specimen. TDLR oval overprint.	—	—	500

No.	Denomination	VG	VF	UNC
193	**20 Pounds** 2.5.1951-1.8.1962. Green on multicolor underprint. King's College at Aberdeen at lower left, Glasgow Cathedral at lower right. 180x97mm.			
	a. Signature J. J. Campbell.	65.00	160	550
	b. Signature R. D. Fairbairn.	65.00	150	500
194	**100 Pounds** 2.5.1951. Blue. King's College at Aberdeen at lower left, Glasgow Cathedral at lower right. Signature J. J. Campbell. 180x97mm.	500	1,200	3,000

1961 Issue

No.	Denomination	VG	VF	UNC
195	**1 Pound** 1.3.1961; 2.5.1962; 1.2.1963. Green on multicolor underprint. Arms at right. Back: Ship and tug at center.			
	a. Issued note.	6.50	35.00	100
	s. Specimen.	—	—	160

No.	Denomination	VG	VF	UNC
196	**5 Pounds** 20.9.1961; 1.6.1962; 1.2.1963. Dark blue on multicolor underprint. Arms at right. Back: King's College at Aberdeen.	20.00	75.00	200

National Bank of Scotland

1825 Issue

No.	Denomination	Good	Fine	XF
230	**1 Pound** 11.10.1825. Black. Royal arms with St. Andrew and cross at upper center. Uniface. Printer: Perkins & Bacon.	—	—	—
230A	**1 Guinea** (ca.1825). Black. Royal arms with St. Andrew and cross at upper center. Uniface. Printer: Perkins & Bacon.	—	—	—
230B	**5 Pounds** (ca.1825). Black. Royal arms with St. Andrew and cross at upper center. Uniface. Printer: Perkins & Bacon.	—	—	—
230C	**10 Pounds** (ca.1825). Black. Royal arms with St. Andrew and cross at upper center. Uniface. Printer: Perkins & Bacon.	—	—	—
230D	**20 Pounds** (ca.1825). Black. Royal arms with St. Andrew and cross at upper center. Uniface. Printer: Perkins & Bacon.	—	—	—
230E	**100 Pounds** (ca.1825). Black. Royal arms with St. Andrew and cross at upper center. Uniface. Printer: Perkins & Bacon.	—	—	—

1831 Issue

No.	Denomination	Good	Fine	XF
231	**1 Pound** (ca.1831). Royal arms with St. Andrew and cross at upper center.Text: *INCORPORATED BY ROYAL CHARTER* under royal arms at center. Text: *UNDER ACT 16 & 17 VICT. CAP. 68* in top border.	—	—	—
232	**5 Pounds** (ca.1831). Royal arms with St. Andrew and cross at upper center.Text: *INCORPORATED BY ROYAL CHARTER* under royal arms at center. Text: *UNDER ACT 16 & 17 VICT. CAP. 68* in top border.	—	—	—
233	**10 Pounds** (ca.1831). Royal arms with St. Andrew and cross at upper center.Text: *INCORPORATED BY ROYAL CHARTER* under royal arms at center. Text: *UNDER ACT 16 & 17 VICT. CAP. 68* in top border.	—	—	—
234	**20 Pounds** (ca.1831). Royal arms with St. Andrew and cross at upper center.Text: *INCORPORATED BY ROYAL CHARTER* under royal arms at center. Text: *UNDER ACT 16 & 17 VICT. CAP. 68* in top border.	—	—	—
235	**100 Pounds** (ca.1831). Royal arms with St. Andrew and cross at upper center.Text: *INCORPORATED BY ROYAL CHARTER* under royal arms at center. Text: *UNDER ACT 16 & 17 VICT. CAP. 68* in top border.	—	—	—

1862 Issue

No.	Denomination	Good	Fine	XF
236	**1 Pound** 11.11.1862; 11.11.1864. Black with red lithographed protector. Royal arms with St. Andrew and cross at upper center.Text: *INCORPORATED BY ROYAL CHARTER* under royal arms at center. Text: *UNDER ACT 16 & 17 VICT. CAP. 68* in top border.	350	700	—
237	**5 Pounds** (ca.1862). Black with red lithographed protector. Royal arms with St. Andrew and cross at upper center.Text: *INCORPORATED BY ROYAL CHARTER* under royal arms at center. Text: *UNDER ACT 16 & 17 VICT. CAP. 68* in top border.	400	1,000	—

		Good	Fine	XF
238	**20 Pounds** (ca.1862). Black with red lithographed protector. Royal arms with St. Andrew and cross at upper center.Text: *INCORPORATED BY ROYAL CHARTER* under royal arms at center. Text: *UNDER ACT 16 & 17 VICT. CAP. 68* in left border.	—	—	—
239	**100 Pounds** (ca.1862). Black with red lithographed protector. Royal arms with St. Andrew and cross at upper center.Text: *INCORPORATED BY ROYAL CHARTER* under royal arms at center. Text: *UNDER ACT 16 & 17 VICT. CAP. 68* in top border.	—	—	—

National Bank of Scotland Limited

1881-1882 Issue

With the asssumption of limited liability by the bank in 1882, new plates were made adding the word: *LIMITED* to bank title.

		Good	Fine	XF
240	**1 Pound** (ca.1881-1889). Black with maroon protector. *LIMITED* added to bank title. Caption under portrait in one line.			
	a. Red serial #. 1.11.1881.	450	1,500	—
	b. 11.11.1886.	350	1,200	—
	c. Black serial # (ca.1889).	300	600	—
241	**5 Pounds** (ca.1882). *LIMITED* added to bank title. Caption under portrait in one line.	600	1,750	—
242	**20 Pounds** (ca.1882). *LIMITED* added to bank title. Caption under portrait in one line.	700	2,000	—
243	**100 Pounds** (ca.1882). *LIMITED* added to bank title. Caption under portrait in one line.	—	—	—

1893; 1895 Issue

		Good	Fine	XF
244	**1 Pound** 2.1.1893; 1.1.1898; 1.1.1903; 2.1.1905; 1.1.1907. Blue, yellow and red. Marquess of Lothian at left, arms at upper center. Signature titles: Manager and Accountant. Caption under portrait in two lines.	225	700	1,750

		Good	Fine	XF
245	**5 Pounds** 1893-1907. Blue, yellow and red. Marquess of Lothian at left, arms at upper center. Signature titles: Manager and Accountant. Caption under portrait in two lines. Like #244.			
	a. Issued note. Rare.	—	—	—
	s. Specimen. 1893.	—		
246	**20 Pounds** 1893-1907. Blue, yellow, red and pink. Marquess of Lothian at left, arms at upper center. Signature titles: Manager and Accountant. Caption under portrait in two lines. Like #244. Rare.	—	—	—
247	**100 Pounds** 1893-1907. Blue, yellow, red and pink. Marquess of Lothian at left, arms at upper center. Signature titles: Manager and Accountant. Caption under portrait in two lines. Like #244. Rare.	—	—	—

1908-1914 Issue

		Good	Fine	XF
248	**1 Pound** 1908-1924. Blue on yellow and brown. Marquess of Lothian at left, arms at upper center. Signature titles: General Manager and Accountant. Caption under portrait in two lines. Like #244. 167x126mm.			
	a. Printed signature of *GENERAL MANAGER* and handsigned on behalf of *ACCOUNTANT.* 15.5.1908-15.5.1919.	80.00	350	700
	b. As a. but with printed signature of *ACCOUNTANT.* 11.11.1919-15.5.1924.	70.00	325	650
249	**5 Pounds** 1909-1920. Blue, yellow and red. Marquess of Lothian at left, arms at upper center. Signature titles: General Manager and Accountant. Caption under portrait in two lines. Like #245.			
	a. Handsigned on behalf of *GENERAL MANAGER* and *ACCOUNTANT.* 15.5.1909-15.5.1918.	150	350	800
	b. Printed signature of *GENERAL MANAGER* and handsigned on behalf of *ACCOUNTANT.* 11.11.1919; 8.7.1920.	150	375	850
250	**20 Pounds** 15.5.1908; 1.8.1914; 8.7.1920. Blue, yellow, red and pink. Marquess of Lothian at left, arms at upper center. Signature titles: General Manager and Accountant. Caption under portrait in two lines. Like #246.	500	1,200	3,600
251	**100 Pounds** 1908-1924. Blue, yellow, red and pink. Marquess of Lothian at left, arms at upper center. Signature titles: General Manager and Accountant. Caption under portrait in two lines. Like #247.	800	1,250	3,000

1925-1928 Issue

		Good	Fine	XF
252	**1 Pound** 1.3.1925; 15.5.1925; 2.1.1926; 1.7.1926. Blue on yellow and brown. Marquess of Lothian at left, arms at upper center. Signature titles: Cashier and Accountant. Caption under portrait in two lines. Like #248.	65.00	250	600
253	**5 Pounds** 1.7.1927; 2.7.1928; 11.11.1930; 11.11.1932. Blue, yellow and red. Marquess of Lothian at left, arms at upper center. Signature titles: Cashier and Accountant. Caption under portrait in two lines. Like #249.	170	450	1,000
254	**20 Pounds** 1.3.1928; 2.1.1930; 11.11.1932. Blue, yellow, red and pink. Marquess of Lothian at left, arms at upper center. Signature titles: Cashier and Accountant. Caption under portrait in two lines. Like #250.	250	800	1,600

#	Note	Good	Fine	XF
255	**100 Pounds** 16.5.1935. Blue, yellow, red and pink. Marquess of Lothian at left, arms at upper center. Signature titles: Cashier and Accountant. Caption under portrait in two lines. Like #251.	700	1,400	3,250

1927 Issue

#	Note	VG	VF	UNC
256	**1 Pound** 2.11.1927-2.2.1931. Black, red and yellow. Buildings at left and right, royal arms at upper center. Printer: W&S. Reduced size.	25.00	100	225

1931 Issue

#	Note	VG	VF	UNC
257	**1 Pound** 2.2.1931; 11.11.1932; 11.11.1933. Black, yellow and red. Buildings at left and right, royal arms at upper center. Like #256. Printer: W. & A. K. Johnston.	17.50	50.00	175

1934-1936 Issue

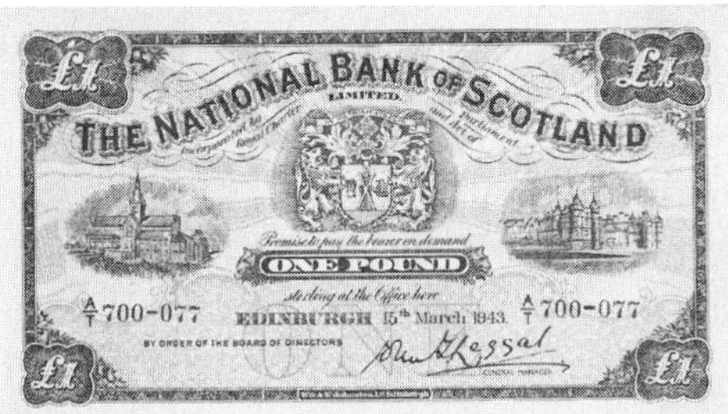

#	Note	VG	VF	UNC
258	**1 Pound** 1934-1959. Black, yellow and red. Buildings at left and right, bank arms at upper center. Similar to #256.			
	a. Imprint: W. & A. K. Johnston Ltd. 12.11.1934-1.5.1942.	15.00	45.00	140
	b. 15.3.1943-2.1.1953.	12.00	40.00	120
	c. Imprint: W. & A. K. Johnston & G. W. Bacon Ltd. 1.6.1953-2.5.1959.	12.00	35.00	100
259	**5 Pounds** 1936-1956. Blue, red and yellow. Marquess of Lothian at left, arms at upper center. Similar to #245. Printer: W&S.	VG	VF	UNC
	a. Signature vertical alignment with printed signature of *CASHIER* and handsigned on behalf of *ACCOUNTANT.* 1.7.1936.	60.00	250	600
	b. As a. but with printed signature of *ACCOUNTANT* and *CASHIER.* 1.8.1939; 1.7.1940; 1.3.1941.	45.00	175	550
	c. As a. but with printed signature of *CHIEF ACCOUNTANT* and *CASHIER.* 6.7.1942.	45.00	175	550
	d. Signature horizontal alignment with printed signature of *GENERAL MANAGER* and *CASHIER.* 11.1.1943-31.12.1956.	40.00	100	450
260	**20 Pounds** 1935-1956. Blue, yellow, red and pink. Printer: W&S.	VG	VF	UNC
	a. Signature vertical alignment with printed signature of *CASHIER* and handsigned on behalf of *ACCOUNTANT.* 16.5.1935; 1.7.1936; 1.8.1939; 1.4.1941.	150	500	1,100
	b. As a. but with printed signature of *CHIEF ACCOUNTANT* and handsigned on behalf of *CASHIER.* 8.12.1941; 6.7.1942.	150	500	1,100
	c. Signature horizontal alignment with printed signature of *GENERAL MANAGER* and *CASHIER.* 11.1.1943-31.12.1956.	110	400	750
261	**100 Pounds** 1943-1952. Blue, yellow, red and pink. Printer: W&S.	VG	VF	UNC
	a. Signature vertical alignment. Reported, not confirmed.	—	—	—
	b. Signature horizontal alignment. 11.1.1943-1.3.1952.	450	1,100	2,000

1957 Issue

#	Note	VG	VF	UNC
262	**5 Pounds** 1.11.1957. Green and multicolor. Arms at lower left. Back: Forth Railway bridge. Printer: W&S.	35.00	115	325

#	Note	VG	VF	UNC
263	**20 Pounds** 1.11.1957. Red and multicolor. Arms at lower left. Back: Forth Railway bridge. Printer: W&S.	75.00	250	650
264	**100 Pounds** 1.11.1957. Blue and multicolor. Arms at lower left. Back: Forth Railway bridge. Printer: W&S.	300	700	1,500

National Commercial Bank of Scotland Limited

Formed by an amalgamation of The Commercial Bank of Scotland Ltd. and The National Bank of Scotland Ltd. in 1959. In 1969 it amalgamated with The Royal Bank of Scotland.

1959 Issue

#	Note	VG	VF	UNC
265	**1 Pound** 16.9.1959. Blue on multicolor underprint. Forth Railway bridge at left center. Back: Arms.	7.00	25.00	75.00

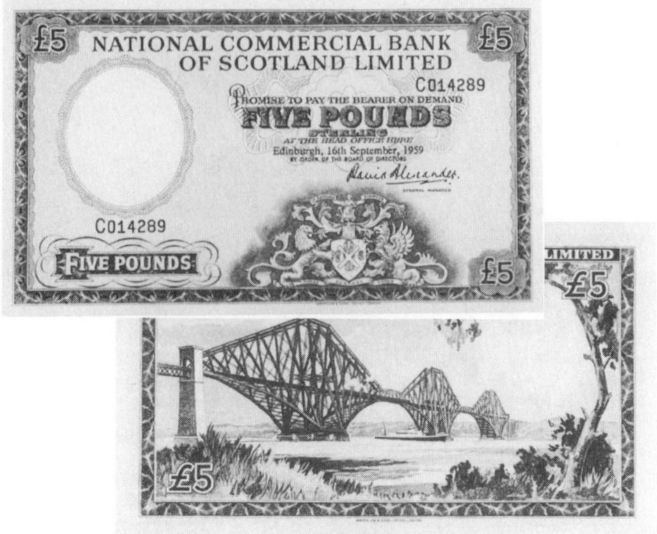

#	Denomination	VG	VF	UNC
266	**5 Pounds** 16.9.1959. Green on multicolor underprint. Arms at center right. Back: Forth Railway bridge.	17.50	55.00	175

#	Denomination	VG	VF	UNC
267	**20 Pounds** 16.9.1959. Red on multicolor underprint. Arms at center right. Back: Forth Railway bridge.	70.00	175	400

#	Denomination	VG	VF	UNC
268	**100 Pounds** 16.9.1959. Purple on multicolor underprint. Arms at center right. Back: Forth Railway bridge.	450	700	1,200

Royal Bank of Scotland

Later became the Royal Bank of Scotland Limited.

1727 Issue

#	Denomination	Good	Fine	XF
276	**20 Shillings** 8.12.1727. Black. Oval portrait King George II at upper left. Embossed with bank seal. Uniface.	—	—	—
277	**10 Pounds** (1727). Black. Oval portrait King George II at upper left. Embossed with bank seal. Uniface.	—	—	—
278	**50 Pounds** (1727). Black. Oval portrait King George II at upper left. Embossed with bank seal. Uniface.	—	—	—
279	**100 Pounds** (1727). Oval portrait King George II at upper left. Embossed with bank seal.	—	—	—

Note: No examples of #277-279 are presently known to exist.

1742 Issue

#	Denomination	Good	Fine	XF
280	**20 Shillings = 12 Pounds Scots** 6.4.1742. Black. Oval portrait King George II at upper left. Embossed with bank seal. More ornate style, otherwise similar to #276. Uniface.	—	—	—

1750 Issue

#	Denomination	Good	Fine	XF
281	**20 Shillings = 12 Pounds Scots** 9.2.1750. Black. King George II in profile. Printed date. Uniface.	—	—	—

1758 Issue

#	Denomination	Good	Fine	XF
282	**1 Guinea** (1758). Black. Portrait as before, but different text. Uniface.	1,400	4,500	—

1762 Issue

#	Denomination	Good	Fine	XF
283	**1 Pound** 5.4.1762. Black. Portrait King George III at upper left. Text of option clause referring to redemption of the note. Printed date. Uniface.	—	—	—
284	**10 Pounds** 5.4.1762. Black. Portrait King George III at upper left. Text of option clause referring to redemption of the note. Printed date. Uniface.	—	—	—
285	**20 Pounds** 5.4.1762. Black. Portrait King George III at upper left. Text of option clause referring to redemption of the note. Printed date. Uniface.	—	—	—
286	**100 Pounds** 5.4.1762. Black. Portrait King George III at upper left. Text of option clause referring to redemption of the note. Printed date. Uniface.	—	—	—

1777 Issue

#	Denomination	Good	Fine	XF
287	**1 Guinea** 1.9.1777. Black. Head of King George III in red at upper left, panel with denomination in words at upper right in blue. Body of note in black. Uniface.	1,300	4,000	—

1785 Issue

#	Denomination	Good	Fine	XF
288	**5 Pounds** (1785). Black. Portrait King George III. Uniface.	—	—	—
289	**10 Pounds** (1785). Black. Portrait King George III. Uniface.	—	—	—
290	**20 Pounds** (1785). Black. Portrait King George III. Uniface.	—	—	—
291	**100 Pounds** (1785). Black. Portrait King George III. Uniface.	—	—	—

1792 Issue

#	Denomination	Good	Fine	XF
292	**20 Shillings** 9.2.1792. Black. King George III in profile at upper left. Red serial #. Uniface.	600	2,000	—
292A	**1 Guinea** 1.9.1792. Uniface.	900	2,400	—

1797 Issue

#	Denomination	Good	Fine	XF
293	**5 Shillings** 3.4.1797. Black. Panel of thistles and crown at left. Printed date. Uniface.	600	1,800	—

1799 Issue

#	Denomination	Good	Fine	XF
294	**1 Guinea** 2.12.1799. Black. Coinage head of King George III. Uniface.	600	1,800	—

1801 Issue

#	Denomination	Good	Fine	XF
295	**1 Pound** 25.3.1801. Black. Royal Regalia design. Uniface.	550	1,800	—

1807 Issue

#	Denomination	Good	Fine	XF
296	**20 Shillings** (1807). Black. Modified Regalia design showing only the Crown. Hand dated and numbered. Uniface.	550	1,750	—

1813 Issue

		Good	Fine	XF
297	**1 Guinea** (1813); 3.3.182x. Black. Coinage head of King George III. Hand dated and numbered. Uniface.	550	1,750	—

1826 Issue

		Good	Fine	XF
298	**20 Shillings** 4.11.1826; 5.4.1827; 6.5.1831; 9.5.1832. Black. Portrait King George IV flanked by elaborate engraving and engine work of circular and oval panels. Hand dated and numbered. Uniface. Back: Printed with elaborate geometric design. Printer: W. H. Lizars.	500	1,300	—
299	**1 Guinea** (1826). Black. Reclining woman with lion, also some geometric panels. Uniface. Back: Elaborate panel design.	500	1,400	—

1830 Issue

		Good	Fine	XF
300	**5 Pounds** (1830). Portrait King George II and value design. Hand dated and numbered.	600	1,800	—
301	**10 Pounds** (1830). Portrait King George II and value design. Hand dated and numbered.	800	2,200	—
302	**20 Pounds** (1830). Portrait King George II and value design. Hand dated and numbered.	—	—	—
303	**100 Pounds** (1830). Portrait King George II and value design. Hand dated and numbered.	—	—	—

1832 Issue

		Good	Fine	XF
304	**20 Shillings** (1832); 1.11.1841; 1.11.1848. Standing Britannia and standing figure of Plenty at left and right, portrait King George I with unicorn and lion at upper center. Hand dated and numbered. Printer: W. H. Lizars.	500	1,300	—

1853 Issue

		Good	Fine	XF
305	**1 Pound** (1853). Standing Britannia and standing figure of Plenty at left and right, portrait King George I with unicorn and lion at upper center. Hand dated and numbered. Similar to #304.	500	1,300	—

1854 Issue

		Good	Fine	XF
305A	**1 Pound** 1.10.1855. Black. Text: *PURSUANT TO ACT OF PARLIAMENT* added to top. Hand dated and numbered. Uniface.	500	1,200	—
306	**5 Pounds** (1854); 2.11.1857. Black. Text: *PURSUANT TO ACT OF PARLIAMENT* added to top. Hand dated and numbered. Uniface.	550	1,600	—
307	**10 Pounds** (1854). Black. Text: *PURSUANT TO ACT OF PARLIAMENT* added to top. Hand dated and numbered. Uniface.	800	2,000	—
308	**20 Pounds** (1854). Black. Text: *PURSUANT TO ACT OF PARLIAMENT* added to top. Hand dated and numbered. Uniface.	700	1,800	—
309	**100 Pounds** (1854). Black. Text: *PURSUANT TO ACT OF PARLIAMENT* added to top. Hand dated and numbered. Uniface.	—	—	—

1860 Issue

		Good	Fine	XF
310	**1 Pound** (1860). Blue. Red letters: *R B S.* Printed date and serial #.	450	1,300	—

1861 Issue

		Good	Fine	XF
311	**5 Pounds** (1861). Black. Royal arms with figures of value in black, red denomination wording, and red overprint on legend panel. Hand dated, printed serial #. Uniface. Printer: W. & A. K. Johnston.	800	1,700	—
312	**10 Pounds** (1861). Black. Royal arms with figures of value in black, red denomination wording, and red overprint on legend panel. Hand dated, printed serial #. Uniface. Printer: W. & A. K. Johnston.	1,100	2,500	—
313	**20 Pounds** (1861). Black. Royal arms with figures of value in black, red denomination wording, and red overprint on legend panel. Hand dated, printed serial #. Uniface. Printer: W. & A. K. Johnston.	900	2,000	—
314	**100 Pounds** (1861). Black. Royal arms with figures of value in black, red denomination wording, and red overprint on legend panel. Hand dated, printed serial #. Uniface. Printer: W. & A. K. Johnston.	—	—	—

1865 Issue

		Good	Fine	XF
315	**1 Pound** 1.5.1865. Similar to #310 but added text at top: *PURSUANT TO ACT OF PARLIAMENT.* Printer: W. & A. K. Johnston.	600	1,300	—

1875; 1887 Issue

		Good	Fine	XF
316	**1 Pound** 1875-1926. Blue and red. Allegorical figures at lower left and lower right. Uniface.			
	a. Signature: W. Turnbull. 1875-1878.	325	1,400	—
	b. Signature: F. A. Mackay. 1878-1887.	300	1,200	—
	c. Signature: W. Templeton. 1887-1908.	135	600	1,200
	d. Signature: D. S. Lunan. 5.5.1908-24.3.1920.	50.00	400	800
	e. Signature: D. Speed. Yellow underprint, red serial letters. 14.5.1920-14.5.1926.	45.00	300	700

		Good	Fine	XF
317	**5 Pounds** 1875-1951. Blue and red-brown (earlier), orange-brown (later). Uniface.			
	a. Signature titles: *Accountant* and *Cashier.* Imprint: W. & A. K. Johnston. 1875-1918.	200	600	1,500
	b. Imprint: W. & A. K. Johnston Limited. 1918-1942.	80.00	300	800
	c. As b. Signature titles: *Cashier & General Manager* and *Chief Accountant.* 1.7.1942-16.10.1950.	50.00	200	500

		Good	Fine	XF
318	**10 Pounds** 1887-1940. Blue and red. Uniface.			
	a. Plate C. 1887-1918.	650	2,400	—
	b. Plate D. Yellow underprint. The blue is much darker than plate C. 1918-1940.	300	800	—

		Good	Fine	XF
319	**20 Pounds**			
	1877-1969. Blue and brown. Uniface.			
	a. Plate C. 1877-1911.	400	950	2,850
	b. Plate D. Yellow underprint. Imprint: W. & A. K. Johnston 1931-1947.	120	600	1,400
	c. Plates E; F; G; H. Underprint without red. Imprint: W. & A. K. Johnston & G. W. Bacon Ltd. Both signatures printed 1947-1966.	110	325	700

		Good	Fine	XF
320	**100 Pounds**			
	1877-1969. Blue and red. Uniface.			
	a. Plate C. 1877-1918.	2,000	4,500	—
	b. Plates D; E. Yellow underprint. 1918-60.	400	1,250	3,000
	c. Plates F; G. Imprint: W. & A. K. Johnston & G. W. Bacon Ltd. Both signatures printed. 1960-1966.	400	1,000	2,750

1927 Issue

		VG	VF	UNC
321	**1 Pound**			
	2.2.1927-24.12.1936. Blue with a brownish red underprint. Back: Bank buildings at left and right. Printer: W. & A. K. Johnston.	30.00	120	300

1937 Issue

		VG	VF	UNC
322	**1 Pound**			
	1937-1955. Dark blue on yellow and brown underprint.			
	a. Signature *Chief Accountant,* David Speed. Imprint: W. & A. K. Johnston Ltd. 2.1.1937-1.7.1942.	15.00	60.00	200
	b. Yellow underprint. Signature *Chief Accountant,* Thomas Brown. 1.3.1943-1.7.1951.	15.00	50.00	175
	c. Signature with title: *Chief Accountant* J. D. Dick. 16.7.1951-1.11.1952.	12.00	40.00	115
	d. Imprint: W. & A. K. Johnston & G. W. Bacon Ltd. 1.4.1953-3.1.1955.	10.00	30.00	100

1952 Issue

		VG	VF	UNC
323	**5 Pounds**			
	1952-1963. Blue and red on yellow underprint. Like number 317 but reduced size. Uniface.			
	a. 2 signatures. Imprint: W. & A.K. Johnston Ltd. 2.1.1952-1.7.1953.	40.00	125	325
	b. 3 signatures. Imprint: W. & A. K. Johnston & G. W. Bacon Ltd. 1.7.1953-1.2.1954.	45.00	150	400
	c. 2 signatures. Imprint: W. & A. K. Johnston & G. W. Bacon. 1.4.1955-3.1.1963.	30.00	100	250

1955 Issue

		VG	VF	UNC
324	**1 Pound**			
	1955-1964. Dark blue on yellow and brown underprint. Signature W. R. Ballantyne with title: *General Manager.* 152x85mm.			
	a. Without engraver's name on back. 1.4.1955-1.11.1955.	12.00	40.00	125
	b. With engraver's name W. H. Egan upside down and in very small letters below the right hand bank building on back. 1.2.1956-1.7.1964.	12.00	30.00	80.00
	s. As a. Specimen.	—	—	—

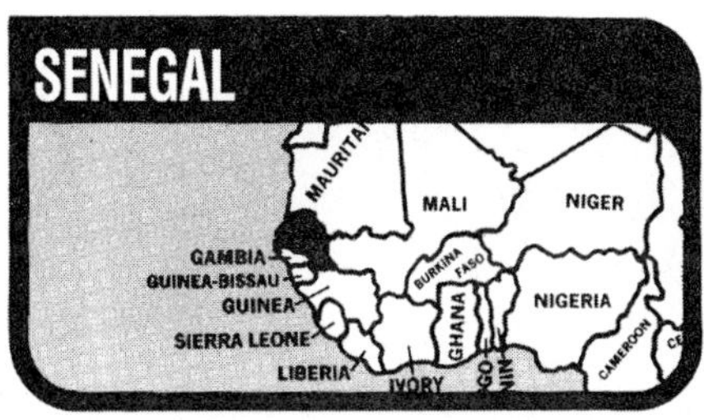

The Republic of Senegal, located on the bulge of West Africa between Mauritania and Guinea-Bissau, has an area of 75,750 sq. mi. (196,190 sq. km.) and a population of 9.49 million. Capital: Dakar. The economy is primarily agricultural. Peanuts and products, phosphates, and canned fish are exported. The French colonies of Senegal and the French Sudan were merged in 1959 and granted their independence as the Mali Federation in 1960. The union broke up after only a few months. Senegal joined with The Gambia to form the nominal confederation of Senegambia in 1982, but the envisaged integration of the two countries was never carried out, and the union was dissolved in 1989. The Movement of Democratic Forces in the Casamance (MFDC) has led a low-level separatist insurgency in southern Senegal since the 1980s, and several peace deals have failed to resolve the conflict. Nevertheless, Senegal remains one of the most stable democracies in Africa. Senegal was ruled by a Socialist Party for 40 years until current President Abdoulaye Wade was elected in 2000. He was reelected in February 2007, but complaints of fraud led opposition parties to boycott June 2007 legislative polls. Senegal has a long history of participating in international peacekeeping. Senegal became a member of the "Union Monetaire Ouest-Africaine" in 1963. Also see French West Africa, Upper Senegal-Niger, West African States.

RULERS:

French to 1960

MONETARY SYSTEM:

1 Franc = 100 Centimes

FRENCH ADMINISTRATION

Banque du Sénégal

The bank occupied one branch each in St. Louis and Dakar. Liquidation was decided upon in 1901. The business and also the redemption of notes was taken over by the Banque de l'Afrique Occidentale.

1853 Issue

		VG	VF	UNC
A1	**5 Francs**			
	L.1874. Blue. Medallic head at left and right. Similar to French Colonial issues under law of 1901. Back: Medallic head at center.BC: Black. Unsigned remainder.	—	—	1,000

		Good	Fine	XF
A2	**25 Francs**			
	1853-1901.	—	—	—
A3	**100 Francs**			
	1853-1901.	—	—	—
A4	**500 Francs**			
	1853-1901.	—	—	—

Gouvernement General de l'A.O.F.

Colonie du Sénégal

Decret du 11 Fevrier 1917

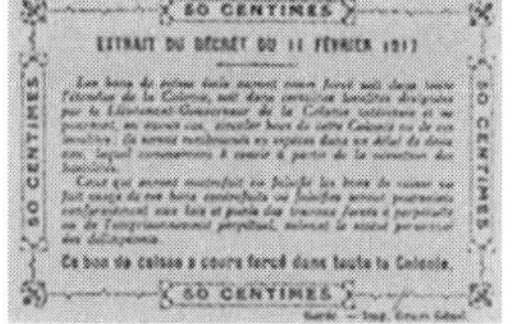

		VG	VF	UNC
1	**0.50 Franc**			
	L.1917. Blue on green underprint. Reverse of coin at left, obverse at right.			
	a. Watermark: Bees. Imprint on back with *gen'al.*	47.50	135	400
	b. Watermark: Bees. Imprint on back with *Gen'al.*	55.00	145	450
	c. Without watermark. 2 signature varieties.	60.00	160	525

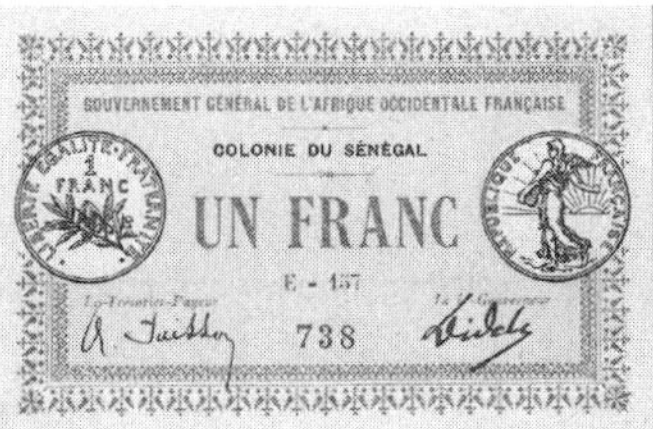

		VG	VF	UNC
2	**1 Franc**			
	L.1917. Red on salmon underprint. Reverse of coin at left, obverse at right.			
	a. Watermark: Bees. Imprint on back with *gen'al.*	65.00	200	550
	b. Watermark: Bees. Imprint on back with *Gen'al.*	60.00	160	475
	c. Without watermark. 2 signature varieties.	45.00	125	350

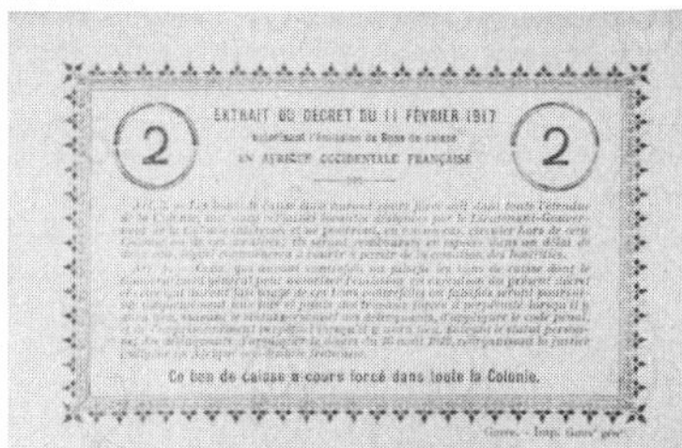

		VG	VF	UNC
3	**2 Francs**			
	L.1917. Orange on yellow underprint. Reverse of coin at left, obverse at right.			
	a. Watermark: Bees. Imprint on back with *gen'al.*	75.00	235	600
	b. Watermark: Bees. Imprint on back with *Gen'al.*	70.00	225	575
	c. Without watermark. 2 signature varieties.	70.00	225	575

Serbia, a former inland Balkan kingdom (now a federated republic with Montenegro) has an area of 34,116 sq. mi. (88,361 sq. km.) Capital: Belgrade. The Kingdom of Serbs, Croats, and Slovenes was formed in 1918; its name was changed to Yugoslavia in 1929. Various paramilitary bands resisted Nazi Germany's occupation and division of Yugoslavia from 1941 to 1945, but fought each other and ethnic opponents as much as the invaders. The military and political movement headed by Josip Tito (Partisans) took full control of Yugoslavia when German and Croatian separatist forces were defeated in 1945. Although Communist, Tito's government and his successors (he died in 1980) managed to steer their own path between the Warsaw Pact nations and the West for the next four and a half decades. In 1989, Slobodan Milosevic became president of the Serbian Republic and his ultranationalist calls for Serbian domination led to the violent breakup of Yugoslavia along ethnic lines. In 1991, Croatia, Slovenia, and Macedonia declared independence, followed by Bosnia in 1992. The remaining republics of Serbia and Montenegro declared a new Federal Republic of Yugoslavia in April 1992 and under Milosevic's leadership, Serbia led various military campaigns to unite ethnic Serbs in neighboring republics into a "Greater Serbia." These actions led to Yugoslavia being ousted from the UN in 1992, but Serbia continued its - ultimately unsuccessful - campaign until signing the Dayton Peace Accords in 1995. Milosevic kept tight control over Serbia and eventually became president of the FRY in 1997. In 1998, an ethnic Albanian insurgency in the formerly autonomous Serbian province of Kosovo provoked a Serbian counterinsurgency campaign that resulted in massacres and massive expulsions of ethnic Albanians living in Kosovo. The Milosevic government's rejection of a proposed international settlement led to NATO's bombing of Serbia in the spring of 1999 and to the eventual withdrawal of Serbian military and police forces from Kosovo in June 1999. UNSC Resolution 1244 in June 1999 authorized the stationing of a NATO-led force (KFOR) in Kosovo to provide a safe and secure environment for the region's ethnic communities, created a UN interim Administration Mission in Kosovo (UNMIK) to foster self-governing institutions, and reserved the issue of Kosovo's final status for an unspecified date in the future. In 2001, UNMIK promulgated a constitutional framework that allowed Kosovo to establish institutions of self-government and led to Kosovo's first parliamentary election. FRY elections in September 2000 led to the ouster of Milosevic and installed Vojislav Kostunica as president. A broad coalition of democratic reformist parties known as DOS (the Democratic Opposition of Serbia) was subsequently elected to parliament in December 2000 and took control of the government. DOS arrested Milosevic in 2001 and allowed for him to be tried in The Hague for crimes against humanity. (Milosevic died in March 2006 before the completion of his trial.) In 2001, the country's suspension from the UN was lifted. In 2003, the FRY became Serbia and Montenegro, a loose federation of the two republics with a federal level parliament. Widespread violence predominantly targeting ethnic Serbs in Kosovo in March 2004 caused the international community to open negotiations on the future status of Kosovo in January 2006. In May 2006, Montenegro invoked its right to secede from the federation and - following a successful referendum - it declared itself an independent nation on 3 June 2006. Two days later, Serbia declared that it was the successor state to the union of Serbia and Montenegro. A new Serbian constitution was approved in October 2006 and adopted the following month. After 15 months of inconclusive negotiations mediated by the UN and four months of further inconclusive negotiations mediated by the US, EU, and Russia, on 17 February 2008, the UNMIK-administered province of Kosovo declared itself independent of Serbia.

RULERS:

Milan, Obrenovich IV, as Prince, 1868-1882
Aleksander I, 1889-1902
Petar I, 1903-1918

MONETARY SYSTEM:

1 Dinar = 100 Para FHV>

KINGDOM

State Notes

1876 Issue

		Good	Fine	XF
1	**1 Dinar** 1.7.1876. Blue on yellow underprint. Portrait Prince Milan Obrenovich between cherubs at top center. Uniface.	225	600	900
2	**5 Dinara** 1.7.1876. Blue on yellow underprint. Woman standing at left, soldier standing with rifle at right. Portrait Prince Milan Obrenovich between cherubs at top center.	425	675	1,200

		Good	Fine	XF
3	**10 Dinara** 1.7.1876. Blue on yellow underprint. Woman standing with sheaf of grain at left, soldier standing with rifle at right. Portrait Prince Milan Obrenovich between cherubs at top center.	450	900	1,800
4	**50 Dinara** 1.7.1876. Blue on yellow underprint. Woman seated at left, soldier seated with rifle at right. Portrait Prince Milan Obrenovich between cherubs at top center.	900	1,500	3,750
5	**100 Dinara** 1.7.1876. Blue on yellow underprint. Woman standing with sheaf of grain at left, soldier standing with rifle at right. Portrait Prince Milan Obrenovich between cherubs at top center.	1,500	2,500	5,500

ПРИВИЛЕГОВАНА НАРОДНА БАНКА КРАЉЕВИНЕ СРБИЈЕ

Chartered National Bank of the Kingdom of Serbia

1884; 1885 Issue

		Good	Fine	XF
6	**10 Dinara** 1.11.1885. Blue on yellow underprint. Woman standing at left, soldier standing with rifle at right.	750	2,000	—

#	Description	Good	Fine	XF
7	**50 Dinara (zlatu)** 1885; 1886. Dark olive. Woman standing with children at left, woman standing with sword and shield at right.			
	a. 1.2.1885. Rare.	—	—	—
	b. Without signature. 1.3.1886. Rare.	—	—	—
8	**100 Dinara (zlatu)** 1884. Dark olive. Woman seated with tablet and sword at right.			
	a. 2.7.1884. Rare.	—	—	—
	b. 2 signature varieties. 1.9.1884. Rare.	—	—	—
	c. Without date or signature. Rare.	—	—	—

1887 Issue

#	Description	Good	Fine	XF
9	**10 Dinara (srebru)** 14.1.1887. Blue. Woman standing with sword and shield at left, children and child 'Mercury' at right.	180	375	900

1893 Issue

#	Description	Good	Fine	XF
10	**10 Dinara (srebru)** 2.1.1893. Blue on brown underprint. Woman seated with musical instrument and child at left.			
	a. Without lozenge printing.	37.50	75.00	225
	b. Lozenge printing.	45.00	120	375
	c. Punch hole cancelled: ANNULÉ.	40.00	75.00	225

1905 Issue

#	Description	Good	Fine	XF
11	**20 Dinara (zlatu)** 5.1.1905. Blue on brown underprint. Woman standing with sword, shield and child at left, young woman standing at right.			
	a. Without yellow lozenge printing.	225	500	1,800
	b. Yellow lozenge printing.	250	600	2,100

#	Description	Good	Fine	XF
12	**100 Dinara (srebru)** 5.1.1905. Blue on brown underprint. Woman seated with sword at right, coastline in background. Watermark: Woman's head.			
	a. Without yellow lozenge printing.	37.50	120	300
	b. Yellow lozenge printing.	45.00	135	325
	c. Without yellow lozenge printing; thinner paper with lighter printing.	30.00	90.00	275

1914 Emergency WW I Issue

#	Description	Good	Fine	XF
13	**50 Dinara (srebru)** 1.8.1914. Dark violet. Soldier with rifle at left, farm girl at right. Back: Arms at left.	1,800	3,750	7,500

1916 Issue

#	Description	Good	Fine	XF
14	**5 Dinara (srebru)** 1916-1918. Blue. Helmeted man at left. Back: Arms and fruit. Watermark: Helmeted man.			
	a. 11.10.1916-31.12.1917.	37.50	90.00	275
	b. 1.1.1918-18.9.1918. Rare.	—	—	—

1915 Emergency Postage Stamp Currency Issue

Of an already completed series of postage stamps (Michel #130. #131 I-V or Scott's #132-138), all have Kg. Peter I w/military staff in the field. Only the denominations 5 and 10 Para could be used for postal purposes because of the war. The other denominations circulated as emergency money. The stamps are perforated; however, imperforate unfinished remainders also exist.

No.	Denomination / Description	VG	VF	UNC
15	**5 Para** ND (1915). Light green. King Peter I with military staff in the field.	—	5.00	15.00
16	**10 Para** ND (1915). Vermilion. King Peter I with military staff in the field.	—	9.00	25.00
17	**15 Para** ND (1915). Black-gray. King Peter I with military staff in the field.	—	10.00	35.00
17A	**15 Para** ND (1915). Dark blue. King Peter I with military staff in the field. Misprint.	—	85.00	165
18	**20 Para** ND (1915). Brown. King Peter I with military staff in the field.	—	5.00	15.00
19	**25 Para** ND (1915). Dark blue. King Peter I with military staff in the field.	—	20.00	45.00
20	**30 Para** ND (1915). Light olive. King Peter I with military staff in the field.	—	20.00	50.00
21	**50 Para** ND (1915). Red-brown. King Peter I with military staff in the field.	—	30.00	80.00

Note: The 10, 15, 20, 40 and 50 Para stamps affixed to cardboard (type of Michel Catalog Serbia #99) with King Peter I and printed legend and denomination on back were locally issued emergency money (for Osijek, Prima Frankova tiskara).

GERMAN OCCUPATION - WW II

СРПСКА НАРОДНА БАНКА

Serbian National Bank

1941 Provisional Issue

No.	Denomination / Description	VG	VF	UNC
22	**10 Dinara** 1.5.1941. Green on tan underprint. Arms at left. Back: Like Yugoslavia #35. Watermark: Old man in uniform.	15.00	35.00	70.00
23	**100 Dinara** 1.5.1941. Purple and yellow.	3.00	6.00	12.50

No.	Denomination / Description	VG	VF	UNC
24	**1000 Dinara on 500 Dinara** 1.5.1941. Brown and multicolor. Three seated women at center. Back: Three women and cherub.	10.00	25.00	45.00

Note: #24 without overprint requires confirmation.

1941 Issue

No.	Denomination / Description	VG	VF	UNC
25	**20 Dinara** 1.5.1941. Brown on tan and light brown underprint. Portrait V. Karadzic at left. Back: Arms at right. Watermark: Old man in uniform.	10.00	25.00	35.00

No.	Denomination / Description	VG	VF	UNC
26	**50 Dinara** 1.8.1941. Brown and multicolor. Portrait woman at left. Back: Man playing old stringed instrument at center, arms at right. Watermark: Boy with cap.	15.00	30.00	45.00

		VG	VF	UNC
27	**500 Dinara** 1.11.1941. Brown and multicolor. Woman in national costume at center. Back: Man with building materials.			
	a. Watermark: King Aleksander I.	5.00	10.00	20.00
	b. Watermark: Woman's head.	3.00	8.00	15.00

1942 Issue

		VG	VF	UNC
28	**20 Dinara** 1.5.1942. Blue. Portrait V. Karadzic at left. Like #25. Back: Arms at right. Watermark: Old man in uniform. (Not issued).	—	350	625

		VG	VF	UNC
29	**50 Dinara** 1.5.1942. Brown on light brown underprint. Portrait King Petar at left. Back: Arms at left.	4.00	8.00	15.00

		VG	VF	UNC
30	**100 Dinara** 1.5.1942. Brown and multicolor. Shepherd-boy seated playing flute, flock of sheep at left. (Not issued).	—	350	625

		VG	VF	UNC
31	**500 Dinara** 1.5.1942. Brown and multicolor. Arms at upper left, farmer seeding at right. Back: Farmer harvesting wheat. Watermark: King Aleksander I.	5.00	10.00	20.00

		VG	VF	UNC
32	**1000 Dinara** 1.5.1942. Brown and multicolor. Blacksmith at left, woman wearing costume at right. Back: Farm wife at left, farmer at right.			
	a. Watermark: King Petar.	10.00	20.00	45.00
	b. Watermark: Woman's head.	10.00	20.00	45.00

1943 Issue

		VG	VF	UNC
33	**100 Dinara** 1.1.1943. Brown and blue on light brown and tan underprint. St. Sava at left. Back: Man with ox-cart at center right. Watermark: Woman's head.	10.00	25.00	50.00

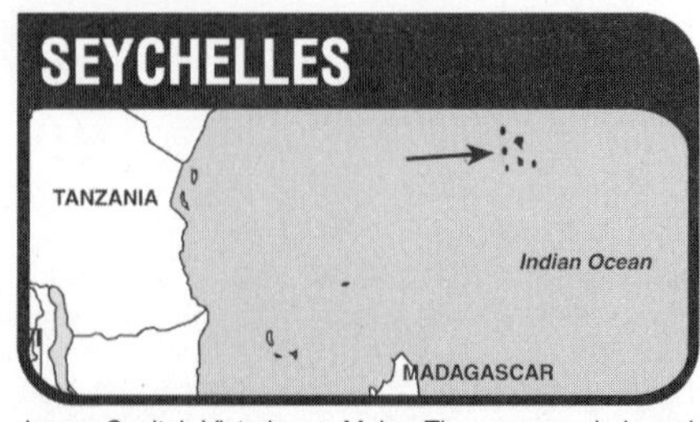

The Republic of Seychelles, an archipelago of 85 granite and coral islands situated in the Indian Ocean 600 miles (965 km.) northeast of Madagascar, has an area of 156 sq. mi. (455 sq. km.) and a population of 82,400. Among these islands are the Aldabra Islands, the Farquhar Group, and Ile Desroches, which the United Kingdom ceded to the Seychelles upon its independence. Capital: Victoria, on Mahe. The economy is based on fishing, a plantation system of agriculture and tourism. Copra, cinnamon and vanilla are exported. A lengthy struggle between France and Great Britain for the islands ended in 1814, when they were ceded to the latter. Independence came in 1976. Socialist rule was brought to a close with a new constitution and free elections in 1993. President France-Albert Rene, who had served since 1977, was re-elected in 2001, but stepped down in 2004. Vice President James Michel took over the presidency and in July 2006 was elected to a new five-year term.

RULERS:

British to 1976

MONETARY SYSTEM:

1 Rupee = 100 Cents

BRITISH ADMINISTRATION

Government of Seychelles

1914 Emergency WW I Issue

		Good	Fine	XF
A1	**50 Cents**	Good	Fine	XF
	11.8.1914. Black. Uniface.	500	1,250	3,000
A2	**1 Rupee**	Good	Fine	XF
	11.8.1914. Black. Uniface.	550	1,350	2,750

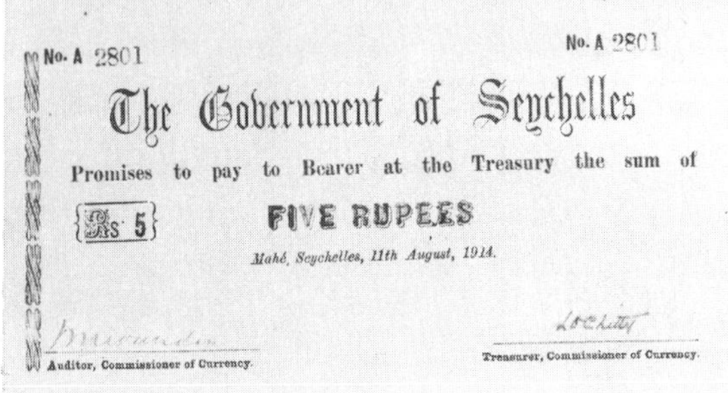

		Good	Fine	XF
A3	**5 Rupees**	Good	Fine	XF
	11.8.1914. Black. Uniface.	950	2,500	5,250
A4	**10 Rupees**	Good	Fine	XF
	11.8.1914. Black. Uniface. Like #A3.	1,200	4,000	—

1919 Emergency Issue

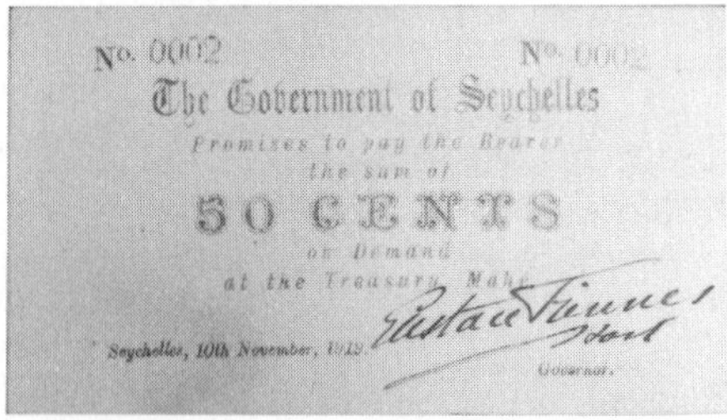

		Good	Fine	XF
A5	**50 Cents**	Good	Fine	XF
	10.11.1919. Black. Uniface.	750	2,000	—
A6	**1 Rupee**	Good	Fine	XF
	10.9.1919. Black. Uniface. PC: Cream.	—	—	—

1918-1928 Issue

		Good	Fine	XF
1	**50 Cents**	Good	Fine	XF
	1919-1934; ND. Grayish green and violet. Portrait King George V in profile at right. Various date and signature varieties. Uniface. Printer: TDLR.			
	a. 1.7.1919.	125	650	2,250
	b. 1.7.1924.	100	600	2,200
	c. 6.11.1928.	100	600	2,200
	d. 5.10.1934.	85.00	550	2,000
	e. ND (1936).	75.00	500	1,500

		Good	Fine	XF
2	**1 Rupee**	Good	Fine	XF
	1918-1934; ND. Gray and red. Portrait King George V in profile at right. Various date and signature varieties. Uniface. Like #1. Printer: TDLR.			
	a. 1918	150	550	2,250
	b. 1.7.1919.	150	500	2,000
	c. 1.7.1924.	85.00	425	1,750
	d. 6.11.1928.	85.00	425	1,750
	e. 5.10.1934.	50.00	350	1,500
	f. ND (1936).	45.00	250	1,400

		Good	Fine	XF
3	**5 Rupees**	Good	Fine	XF
	1928; 1934; ND. Lilac-brown and green. Portrait King George V in profile at right. Various date and signature varieties. Uniface. Printer: TDLR.			
	a. 6.11.1928.	85.00	350	1,250
	b. 5.10.1934.	60.00	300	1,200
	c. ND (1936).	55.00	250	1,000
	s. Specimen. Perforated.	—	Unc	1,250

		Good	Fine	XF
4	**10 Rupees**	Good	Fine	XF
	1928; ND. Green and red. Portrait King George V in profile at right. Various date and signature varieties. Uniface. Like #3. Printer: TDLR.			
	a. 6.11.1928.	250	850	2,500
	b. ND (1936).	125	450	1,500

		Good	Fine	XF
5	**50 Rupees**	Good	Fine	XF
	1928; ND. Brown and blue. Portrait King George V in profile at right. Various date and signature varieties. Uniface. Printer: TDLR.			
	a. 6.11.1928.	300	1,000	3,000
	b. ND (1936).	250	850	2,500

1942 Emergency WW II Issue

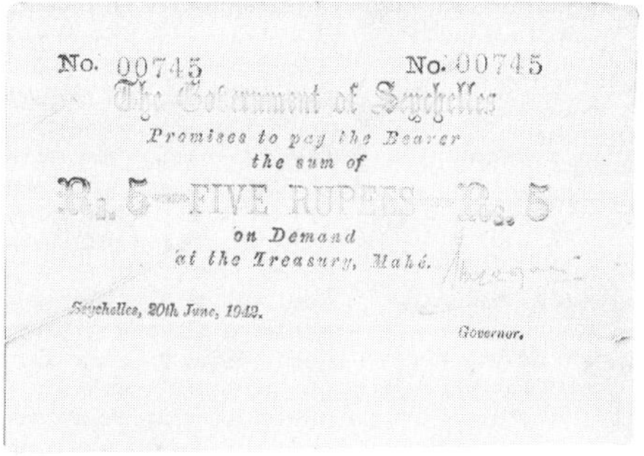

		VG	VF	UNC
5A	**5 Rupees** 20.6.1942. Black. Uniface.	1,500	4,500	—

1942; 1943 Issue

		VG	VF	UNC
6	**50 Cents** 1943-1951. Grayish green and violet. Facing portrait King George VI at left. Various date and signature varieties. Uniface. Printer: TDLR.			
	a. 7.7.1943.	45.00	300	1,500
	b. Signature title: *GOVERNOR.* 6.1.1951.	50.00	425	1,650
	c. Signature title: *OFFICER ADMINISTERING THE GOVERNMENT.* 6.1.1951.	30.00	275	1,200

		VG	VF	UNC
7	**1 Rupee** 1943-1951. Gray and red. Facing portrait King George VI at left. Various date and signature varieties. Uniface. Like #6. Printer: TDLR.			
	a. 3.5.1943; 7.7.1943.	50.00	350	1,500
	b. Signature title: *GOVERNOR.* 6.1.1951.	45.00	350	1,500
	c. Signature title: *OFFICER ADMINISTERING THE GOVERNMENT.* 6.1.1951.	37.50	300	1,250

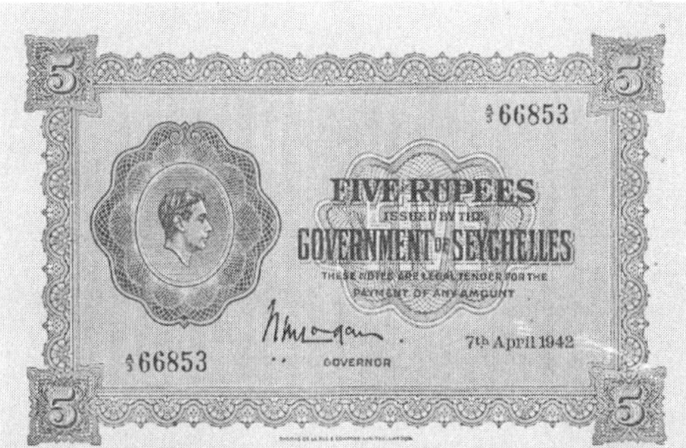

		VG	VF	UNC
8	**5 Rupees** 7.4.1942. Lilac-brown and green. Portrait King George VI in profile at left. Various date and signature varieties. Uniface. Printer: TDLR.	35.00	175	650
9	**10 Rupees** 7.4.1942. Green and red. Portrait King George VI in profile at left. Various date and signature varieties. Uniface. Like #8. Printer: TDLR.	50.00	400	1,500
10	**50 Rupees** 7.4.1942. Light brown. Portrait King George VI in profile at left. Various date and signature varieties. Uniface. Like #8. Printer: TDLR.	150	850	3,500

1954 Issue

		VG	VF	UNC
11	**5 Rupees** 1954; 1960. Lilac and green. Portrait Queen Elizabeth II in profile at right. Signature varieties. Back: Denomination. Printer: TDLR. 160x98mm.			
	a. 1.8.1954.	20.00	100	650
	b. 1.8.1960.	20.00	100	550

		VG	VF	UNC
12	**10 Rupees** 1954-1967. Green and red. Portrait Queen Elizabeth II in profile at right. Signature varieties. Back: Denomination. Printer: TDLR. 157x98mm.			
	a. 1.8.1954.	30.00	275	2,000
	b. 1.8.1960.	30.00	200	1,750
	c. 1.5.1963.	25.00	150	1,500
	d. 1.1.1967.	22.50	150	1,500

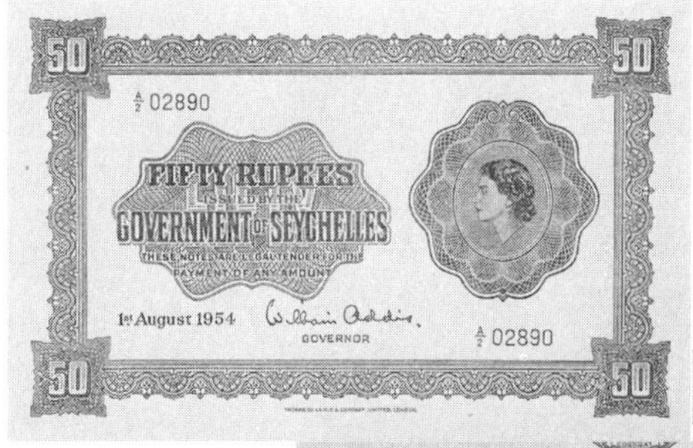

		VG	VF	UNC
13	**50 Rupees** 1954-1967. Black. Portrait Queen Elizabeth II in profile at right. Signature varieties. Back: Denomination. Printer: TDLR.			
	a. 1.8.1954.	100	750	6,500
	b. 1.8.1960.	80.00	575	4,500
	c. 1.5.1963.	75.00	550	4,000
	d. 1.1.1967.	75.00	550	4,000

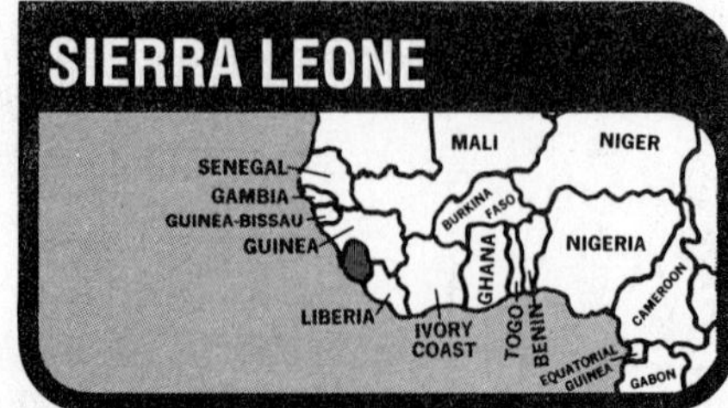

The Republic of Sierra Leone, a British Commonwealth nation located in western Africa between Guinea and Liberia, has an area of 71,740 sq. km. and a population of 6.29 million. Capital: Freetown. The economy is predominantly agricultural but mining contributes significantly to export revenues. Diamonds, iron ore, palm kernels, cocoa and coffee are exported.Democracy is slowly being reestablished after the civil war from 1991 to 2002 that resulted in tens of thousands of deaths and the displacement of more than 2 million people (about one-third of the population). The military, which took over full responsibility for security following the departure of UN peacekeepers at the end of 2005, is increasingly developing as a guarantor of the country's stability. The armed forces remained on the sideline during the 2007 presidential election, but still look to the UN Integrated Office in Sierra Leone (UNIOSIL) - a civilian UN mission - to support efforts to consolidate peace. The new government's priorities include furthering development, creating jobs, and stamping out endemic corruption.

RULERS:

British to 1971

MONETARY SYSTEM:

1 Leone = 100 Cents
1 Pound = 20 Shillings

BRITISH INFLUENCE

Sierra Leone

18xx Issue

		VG	VF	UNC
A1	**1 Pound** 18xx. Black. *CHARLES HEDDLE* across center. Uniface. PC: White or green.	—	—	5,000

SLOVAKIA

Slovakia as a republic has an area of 18,923 sq. mi. (49,011 sq. km.) and a population of 5.37 million. Capital: Bratislava. Textiles, steel, and wood products are exported. The dissolution of the Austro-Hungarian Empire at the close of World War I allowed the Slovaks to join the closely related Czechs to form Czechoslovakia. Following the chaos of World War II, Czechoslovakia became a Communist nation within Soviet-dominated Eastern Europe. Soviet influence collapsed in 1989 and Czechoslovakia once more became free. The Slovaks and the Czechs agreed to separate peacefully on 1 January 1993. Slovakia joined both NATO and the EU in the spring of 2004 and the Eurozone on 1 January 2009.

MONETARY SYSTEM:

1 Korun = 100 Haleru to 1939
1 Korun = 100 Halierov, 1939-1945
1 Korun = 100 Halierov, 1945-2008
1 Euro = 100 Euro Cent, 2009-

REPUBLIC

Slovenska Republika

Republic of Slovakia

1939 ND Provisional Issue

		VG	VF	UNC
1	**100 Korun** ND (June 1939 - old date 10.1.1931). Green.			
	a. Issued note.	100	500	1,500
	s. As a. perforated: *SPECIMEN.*	60.00	280	800

No.	Denomination / Description	VG	VF	UNC
2	**500 Korun**	VG	VF	UNC
	ND (April 1939 - old date 2.5.1929). Red.			
	a. Issued note.	40.00	200	600
	s. As a. perforated: *SPECIMEN.*	5.00	15.00	60.00
3	**1000 Korun**	VG	VF	UNC
	ND (April 1939 - old date 25.5.1934). Green and blue.			
	a. Issued note.	200	650	1,800
	s. As a. perforated: *SPECIMEN.*	60.00	280	800

1939 Issue

No.	Denomination / Description	VG	VF	UNC
4	**10 Korun**	VG	VF	UNC
	15.9.1939. Blue and brown on light orange underprint. Arms at upper left, portrait A. Hlinka at right. Back: Portrait girl at left. BC: Green and brown.			
	a. Issued note.	7.00	30.00	125
	p. Print proofs uniface A or R.	—	—	500
	s. As a. perforated: *SPECIMEN.*	1.00	4.00	12.00

No.	Denomination / Description	VG	VF	UNC
5	**20 Korun**	VG	VF	UNC
	1939. Brown on orange and blue underprint. Arms at upper left, portrait A. Hlinka at right. Similar to #4. Back: Shrine at center. BC: Brown and blue.			
	a. Darker paper.	7.00	30.00	125
	b. Whiter paper.	7.00	30.00	125
	p. Print proof uniface R.	—	—	500
	s. Perforated: *SPECIMEN.*	6.00	25.00	80.00

1942-1943 Issue

No.	Denomination / Description	VG	VF	UNC
6	**10 Korun**	VG	VF	UNC
	20.7.1943. Blue and purple on brown-olive underprint. Arms at left. Stur at right. Back: Objects on table at right. BC: Maroon and brown.			
	a. Issued note.	2.00	10.00	45.00
	s. As a. perforated: *SPECIMEN.*	1.00	2.50	10.00

No.	Denomination / Description	VG	VF	UNC
7	**20 Korun**	VG	VF	UNC
	11.9.1942. Brown on blue and pinkish underprint. Arms at left, eagle at center, portrait J. Holly at right. Back: Food implements.			
	a. Issued note.	2.00	10.00	40.00
	s. As a. perforated: *SPECIMEN.*	1.00	2.00	8.00

1945 ND Issue

No.	Denomination / Description	VG	VF	UNC
8	**5 Korun**	VG	VF	UNC
	ND (1945). Lilac-brown on light blue underprint. Arms at left, portrait girl at center. BC: Blue on tan underprint.			
	a. Issued note.	4.00	18.00	50.00
	s. As a. perforated: *SPECIMEN.*	1.00	3.00	20.00

Slovenska Národná Banka

Slovak National Bank

1940-1944 Issue

Note: For listings of #10, 11, 12 and 13 with adhesive revalidation stamps affixed, see Czechoslovakia #51-54.

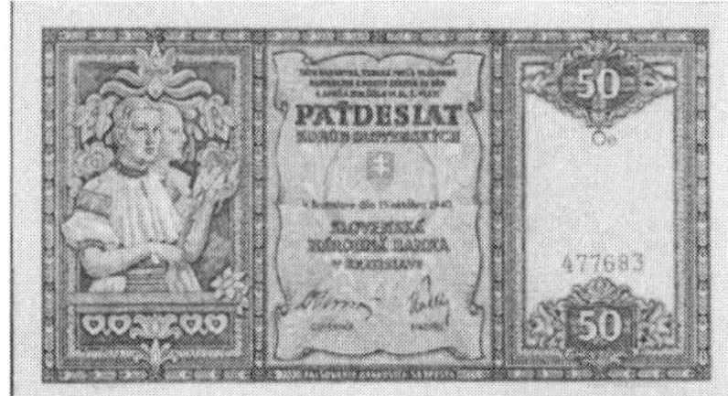

No.	Denomination / Description	VG	VF	UNC
9	**50 Korun**	VG	VF	UNC
	15.10.1940. Violet and lilac on light blue underprint. Two girls in Slovak national costume at left, arms at center. Back: Castle at center. Without *II EMISIA*. BC: Brown. Watermark: Woman. Printer: G&D.			
	a. Issued note.	1.00	4.00	40.00
	s. As a. perforated: *SPECIMEN.*	1.00	2.00	10.00
9A	**50 Korun**	VG	VF	UNC
	15.10.1940. Dark blue on multicolor underprint. Portrait Prince Pribina at right. Back: Woman with shield and arms at left. Like #11 but *II EMISIA* in margin. BC: Green on multicolor underprint. Watermark: Pattern in paper. (Not issued).	—	—	—

10	100 Korun	VG	VF	UNC
	7.10.1940. Dark blue on multicolor underprint. Portrait Prince Pribina at right. Back: Woman with shield and arms at left. Without *II EMISIA*. BC: Green on multicolor underprint. Watermark: Woman.			
	a. Issued note.	2.00	8.00	30.00
	s. As a. perforated: *SPECIMEN*.	0.50	2.00	10.00

11	100 Korun	VG	VF	UNC
	7.10.1940. Dark blue on multicolor underprint. Portrait Prince Pribina at right. Back: Woman with shield and arms at left. Like #10 but *II EMISIA* in margin at left. BC: Green on multicolor underprint. Watermark: Pattern in paper.			
	a. Issued note.	4.00	15.00	55.00
	s. As a. perforated: *SPECIMEN*.	1.00	3.00	15.00

12	500 Korun	VG	VF	UNC
	12.7.1941. Dark green. Arms with two doves at upper center, portrait young man in national costume at right. Back: Bowl of fruit, pitcher and mountains at center. BC: Olive.			
	a. Issued note.	10.00	25.00	100
	s. As a. perforated: *SPECIMEN*.	1.00	5.00	15.00

Color Abbreviation Guide

New to the *Standard Catalog of® World Paper Money* are the following abbreviations related to color references:

BC: Back color
PC: Paper color

13	1000 Korun	VG	VF	UNC
	25.11.1940. Brown on multicolor underprint. Arms at left center, King Svatopluk and his three sons at right. Back: Arms.			
	a. Issued note.	10.00	25.00	100
	s. As a. perforated: *SPECIMEN*.	2.00	7.00	20.00

14	5000 Korun	VG	VF	UNC
	18.12.1944. Brown on green and tan underprint. Portrait Prince K. Mojmir at right. Back: Arms at left. Watermark: Woman's head.			
	a. Issued note.	20.00	100	350
	s. As a. Perforated: *SPECIMEN*.	2.00	8.00	25.00

SOLOMON ISLANDS

The Solomon Islands, located in the Southwest Pacific east of Papua New Guinea, has an area of 28,450 sq. km. and a population of 581,300. Capital: Honiara. The most important islands of the Solomon chain are Guadalcanal (scene of some of the fiercest fighting of World War II), Malaitia, New Georgia, Florida, Vella Lavella, Choiseul, Rendova, San Cristobal, the Lord Howe group, the Santa Cruz islands, and the Duff group. Copra is the only important cash crop but it is hoped that timber will become an economic factor.The UK established a protectorate over the Solomon Islands in the 1890s. Some of the bitterest fighting of World War II occurred on this archipelago. Self-government was achieved in 1976 and independence two years later. Ethnic violence, government malfeasance, and endemic crime have undermined stability and civil society. In June 2003, then Prime Minister Sir Allan Kemakeza sought the assistance of Australia in reestablishing law and order; the following month, an Australian-led multinational force arrived to restore peace and disarm ethnic militias. The Regional Assistance Mission to the Solomon Islands (RAMSI) has generally been effective in restoring law and order and rebuilding government institutions.

RULERS:

British

MONETARY SYSTEM:

1 Shilling = 12 Pence
1 Pound = 20 Shillings to 1966
1 Dollar = 100 Cents, 1966-

BRITISH ADMINISTRATION

Government of the British Solomon Islands

1916 Issue

#	Denomination	Good	Fine	XF
1	**5 Shillings** 18.12.1916; 27.7.1921; 2.1.1926. Green on brown underprint. Arms at top center. Signature varieties.	1,000	2,500	—
2	**10 Shillings** 1916-1932. Red. Arms at top center. Signature varieties.	Good	Fine	XF
	a. 18.12.1916; 27.7.1921; 2.1.1926.	1,200	2,750	—
	b. 30.6.1932. (Not issued). Rare.	—	—	—
3	**1 Pound** 18.12.1916; 2.1.1926; 30.6.1932. Blue. Arms at top center. Signature varieties.	1,250	3,000	—
4	**5 Pounds** 18.12.1916. Arms at top center. Signature varieties. Rare.	—	—	—

SOUTH AFRICA

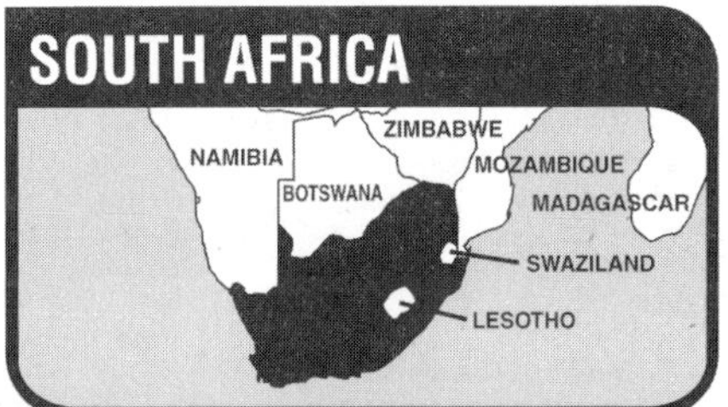

The Republic of South Africa, located at the southern tip of Africa, has an area, including the enclave of Walvis Bay, of 1,219,912 sq. km. and a population of 48.78 million. Capital: Administrative, Pretoria; Legislative, Cape Town; Judicial, Bloemfontein. Manufacturing, mining and agriculture are the principal industries. Exports include wool, diamonds, gold and metallic ores.Dutch traders landed at the southern tip of modern day South Africa in 1652 and established a stopover point on the spice route between the Netherlands and the East, founding the city of Cape Town. After the British seized the Cape of Good Hope area in 1806, many of the Dutch settlers (the Boers) trekked north to found their own republics. The discovery of diamonds (1867) and gold (1886) spurred wealth and immigration and intensified the subjugation of the native inhabitants. The Boers resisted British encroachments but were defeated in the Boer War (1899-1902); however, the British and the Afrikaners, as the Boers became known, ruled together under the Union of South Africa. In 1948, the National Party was voted into power and instituted a policy of apartheid - the separate development of the races. The first multi-racial elections in 1994 brought an end to apartheid and ushered in black majority rule under the African National Congress (ANC). ANC infighting, which has grown in recent years, came to a head in September 2008 after President Thabo Mneki resigned. Kgalema Motlanthe, the party's General-Secretary, succeeded as interim president until general elections scheduled for 2009. South African currency carries inscriptions in both Afrikaans and English.

RULERS:

British to 1961

MONETARY SYSTEM:

1 Shilling = 12 Pence
1 Shilling = 12 Pence
1 Pound = 20 Shillings to 1961
1 Pound = 20 Shillings to 1961
1 Rand = 100 Cents (= 10 Shillings), 1961-

BRITISH ADMINISTRATION

East India Company

Many notes issued at Cape Town.

1808 Issue

#	Denomination	Good	Fine	XF
1	**1 Rix Dollar** 1808. Value and 1808 date around seated Britannia. Embossed stamp. Vertical format.	—	—	—
2	**2 Rix Dollar** 1808. Value and 1808 date around seated Britannia. Embossed stamp. Vertical format.	—	—	—
3	**3 Rix Dollar** 1808. Value and 1808 date around seated Britannia. Embossed stamp. Vertical format.	—	—	—
4	**4 Rix Dollar** 1808. Value and 1808 date around seated Britannia. Embossed stamp. Vertical format.	—	—	—
5	**5 Rix Dollar** 1808. Value and 1808 date around seated Britannia. Embossed stamp. Vertical format.	—	—	—
5A	**8 Rix Dollar** 1808. Value and 1808 date around seated Britannia. Embossed stamp. Vertical format.	—	—	—
6	**10 Rix Dollar** 1808. Value and 1808 date around seated Britannia. Embossed stamp. Vertical format.	—	—	—
6A	**12 Rix Dollar** 1808. Value and 1808 date around seated Britannia. Embossed stamp. Vertical format.	—	—	—
6B	**15 Rix Dollar** 1808. Value and 1808 date around seated Britannia. Embossed stamp. Vertical format.	—	—	—
7	**20 Rix Dollar** 1808. Value and 1808 date around seated Britannia. Embossed stamp. Vertical format.	—	—	—
8	**25 Rix Dollar** 1808. Value and 1808 date around seated Britannia. Embossed stamp. Vertical format.	—	—	—
9	**30 Rix Dollar** 1808. Value and 1808 date around seated Britannia. Embossed stamp. Vertical format.	—	—	—
10	**40 Rix Dollar** 1808. Value and 1808 date around seated Britannia. Embossed stamp. Vertical format.	—	—	—
11	**50 Rix Dollar** 1808. Value and 1808 date around seated Britannia. Embossed stamp. Vertical format.	—	—	—
11A	**60 Rix Dollar** 1808. Value and 1808 date around seated Britannia. Embossed stamp. Vertical format.	—	—	—
12	**75 Rix Dollar** 1808. Value and 1808 date around seated Britannia. Embossed stamp. Vertical format.	—	—	—
13	**100 Rix Dollar** 1808. Value and 1808 date around seated Britannia. Embossed stamp. Vertical format.	—	—	—

#	Denomination	Good	Fine	XF
14	**250 Rix Dollar** 1808. Value and 1808 date around seated Britannia. Embossed stamp. Vertical format.	—	—	—
15	**300 Rix Dollar** 1808. Value and 1808 date around seated Britannia. Embossed stamp. Vertical format.	—	—	—
16	**400 Rix Dollar** 1808. Value and 1808 date around seated Britannia. Embossed stamp. Vertical format.	—	—	—
17	**500 Rix Dollar** 1808. Value and 1808 date around seated Britannia. Embossed stamp. Vertical format.	—	—	—

1810-1831 Issue

#18-21 Type set.

#	Denomination	Good	Fine	XF
18	**2 Rix Dollar** 17.5.1816; 21.3.1821; 22.3.1825. 1808 date around seated Britannia.	—	—	—
19	**10 Rix Dollar** 5.2.1810. 1808 date around seated Britannia.	—	—	—
20	**20 Rix Dollar** 14.2.1823. 1808 date around seated Britannia.	—	—	—
21	**100 Rix Dollar** 11.8.1831. 1808 date around seated Britannia.	—	—	—

Government

1830s Issue

#	Denomination	Good	Fine	XF
22	**1 Pound** 28.3.1835. Black. Value lower left and right. Overprint: Hand stamped: *CANCELLED* and *WITHDRAWN FROM CIRCULATION.*	—	—	—
23	**20 Pounds** 4.3.1834. Black. Value lower left and right. Overprint: Hand stamped: *CANCELLED* and *WITHDRAWN FROM CIRCULATION.*	—	—	—

Z.A.R. - ZUID-AFRIKAANSCHE REPUBLIEK

Treasury

Pretoria

First Issue, 1865

#	Denomination	Good	Fine	XF
24	**5 Rix Dollar** 16.9.1865. Black. Value top left and lower right.	435	740	1,650
25	**10 Rix Dollar** (1865).	500	800	1,800

Second Issue, 1866

#	Denomination	Good	Fine	XF
26	**2 Shillings - 6 Pence** (1866).	—	—	—
27	**5 Shillings** (1866).	400	565	1,500
28	**1 Pound** (1866).	440	650	1,700

Third Issue, 1867

#	Denomination	Good	Fine	XF
29	**2 Shillings - 6 Pence** (1867).	340	520	1,300
30	**5 Shillings** 17.1.1867. Like #26.	400	565	1,500

#	Denomination	Good	Fine	XF
31	**1 Pound** 2.7.1868. Arms at center.	435	650	1,700
32	**5 Pounds** (1867).	480	700	1,800

Fourth Issue, 1868-1870

#	Denomination	Good	Fine	XF
33	**6 Pence** 27.3.1869. Printer: C. Moll.	270	600	1,000
34	**1 Shilling** (1868). Printer: C. Moll.	260	650	1,200
35	**2 Shillings - 6 Pence** (1868). Printer: C. Moll.	300	700	1,500
36	**5 Shillings** (1868). Printer: C. Moll.	340	750	1,600
37	**1 Pound** (1868). Printer: C. Moll.	380	850	1,700
38	**5 Pounds** (1868). Printer: C. Moll.	420	900	2,000

Fifth Issue, 1871-1872

#	Denomination	Good	Fine	XF
39	**1 Pond** 12.1871; 14.1.1872; 25.1.1872. Black. Arms with flags at upper center, serial # at upper left and right, 1£ immediately below. Printer: William Brown & Co. PC: Green.	150	400	975
40	**5 Pond** ca. 1871. Printer: William Brown & Co.	400	800	1,450
41	**10 Pond** ca. 1871. Printer: William Brown & Co.	450	900	1,600
42	**20 Pond** (1871). Printer: William Brown & Co.	500	1,000	1,800

1872 Issue (Good Fors)

#	Denomination	Good	Fine	XF
43	**6 Pence** 13.4.1872. Black. Serial # at top left and right.	300	600	1,000
44	**1 Shilling** 7.3.1872.	325	650	1,100
45	**2 Shillings - 6 Pence** 1872.	350	700	1,150
46	**5 Shillings** 19.1.1872.	400	750	1,400
47	**10 Shillings** 187x.	425	850	1,500

De Nationale Bank der Zuid Afrikaansche Republiek Beperkt

Pretoria

1891-1926 Issue

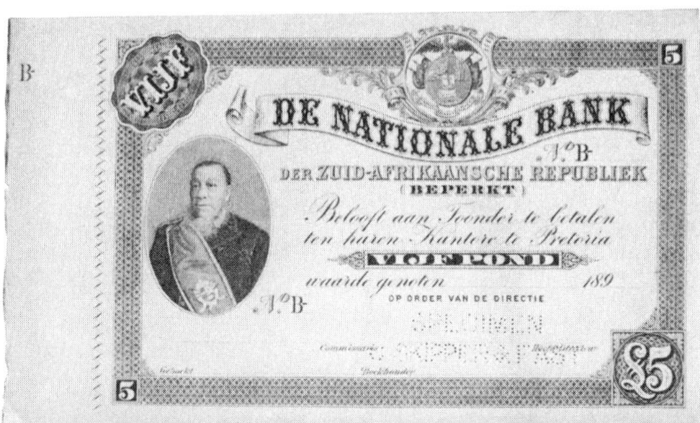

		Good	Fine	XF
48	**1 Pond** 1892-1893. Black on blue underprint. Portrait President Paul Kruger at left, arms at top center right. BC: Blue. Watermark: Denomination. Printer: CS&F.			
	a. Issued note.	400	725	1,250
	s. Pinhole cancelled: *SPECIMEN,* counterfoil at left.	—	Unc	1,000

NOTE: Practically all issued examples of #48a consist of two halves pasted together. Apparently they were cut in half for shipment or cancellation.

		Good	Fine	XF
49	**5 Pond** 189x. Black on light red underprint. Portrait President Paul Kruger at left, arms at top center right. BC: Light red. Watermark: Denomination. Printer: CS&F.			
	a. Issued note.	450	850	1,450
	s. Specimen. Pinhole cancelled.	—	Unc	1,100

		Good	Fine	XF
50	**10 Pond** 189x. Black on green underprint. Portrait President Paul Kruger at left, arms at top center right. BC: Green. Watermark: Denomination. Printer: CS&F.			
	a. Issued note.	525	975	1,650
	s. Specimen. Pinhole cancelled: *SPECIMEN.*	—	Unc	1,200

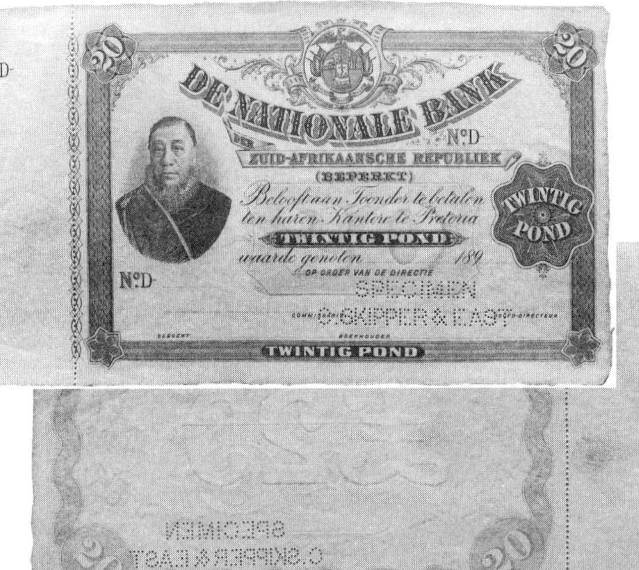

		Good	Fine	XF
51	**20 Pond** 189x. Black on light red underprint. Portrait President Paul Kruger at left, arms at top center right. BC: Light red. Watermark: Denomination. Printer: CS&F.			
	a. Issued note.	650	1,200	2,000
	s. Specimen. Pinhole cancelled: *SPECIMEN.*	—	Unc	1,500

52 50 Pond

189x. Black on purple underprint. Portrait President Paul Kruger at left, arms at top center right. BC: Purple. Watermark: Denomination. Printer: CS&F.

	Good	Fine	XF
a. Issued note.	775	1,400	2,500
s. Specimen. Pinhole cancelled: *SPECIMEN.*	—	Unc	2,000

53 100 Pond

189x. Black on light brown underprint. Portrait President Paul Kruger at left, arms at top center right. BC: Light brown. Watermark: Denomination. Printer: CS&F. Pin hole cancelled: *SPECIMEN.*

	Good	Fine	XF
a. Issued note.	1,300	2,400	4,000
s. Specimen. Pinhole cancelled: *SPECIMEN.*	—	Unc	3,000

ANGLO-BOER WAR

Zuid-Afrikaansche Republiek

Gouvernements Noot - Government Notes

Pretoria

Variety 1 - Spade border with no inscription "No" preceding the bank note number
Variety 2 - Spade border with inscription "No" preceding the bank note number
Variety 3 - Star border with inscription "No" preceding the bank note number

1900 Issue

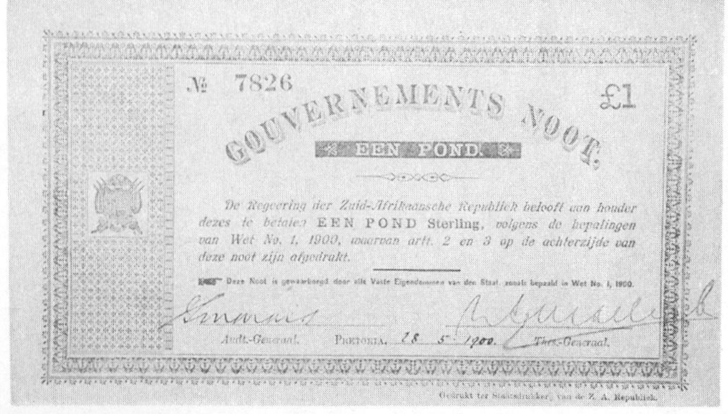

54 1 Pound

28.5.1900. Greenish gray. Arms at left, large embossed seal of the Republiek at left. Back: Law text.

	Good	Fine	XF
a. Ornamental border at left with spikes pointing upwards. Rosette design under denomination. Without *No.* by serial #.	10.00	25.00	70.00
b. Ornamental border at left with stars and crosses. Less ornate design under denomination.	7.50	20.00	60.00
c. Border and design like a. Without *No.* by serial #.	7.00	17.50	55.00

55 5 Pounds

28.5.1900. Greenish gray. Arms at left, large embossed seal of the Republiek at left. Back: Law text.

	Good	Fine	XF
a. Ornamental border at left with spikes pointing upwards. Rosette design under denomination. With *No.* by serial #.	12.00	40.00	120
b. Ornamental border at left with stars and crosses. Less ornate design under denomination.	15.00	45.00	140
c. Border and design like a. Without *No.* by serial #.	13.00	42.00	125

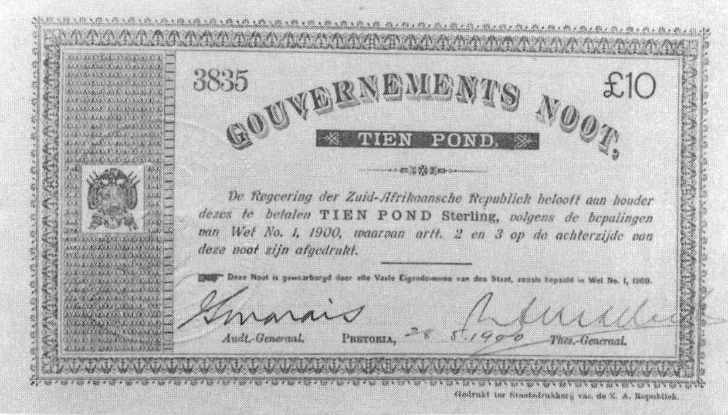

56 10 Pounds

28.5.1900. Greenish gray. Arms at left, large embossed seal of the Republiek at left. Back: Law text.

	Good	Fine	XF
a. Ornamental border at left with spikes pointing upward. Rosette design under denomination. With *No.* by serial #.	20.00	55.00	180
b. Border and design like a. Without *No.* by serial #.	25.00	60.00	200

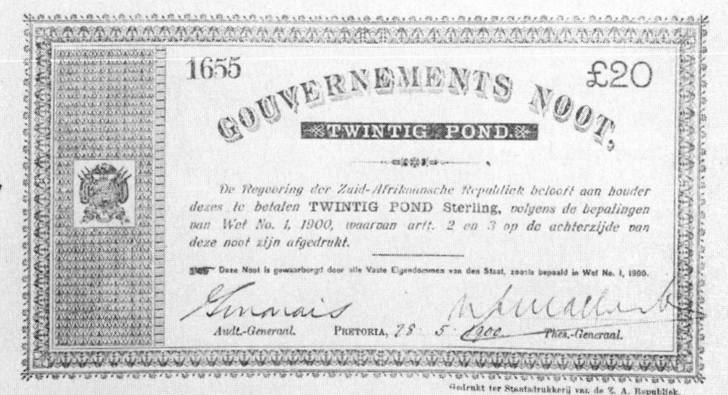

57 20 Pounds

28.5.1900. Greenish gray. Arms at left, large embossed seal of the Republiek at left. Back: Law text.

	Good	Fine	XF
a. Ornamental border at left with spikes pointing upwards. Rosette design under denomination. With *No.* by serial #.	25.00	80.00	225
b. Border and design like a. Without *No.* by serial #.	30.00	85.00	250

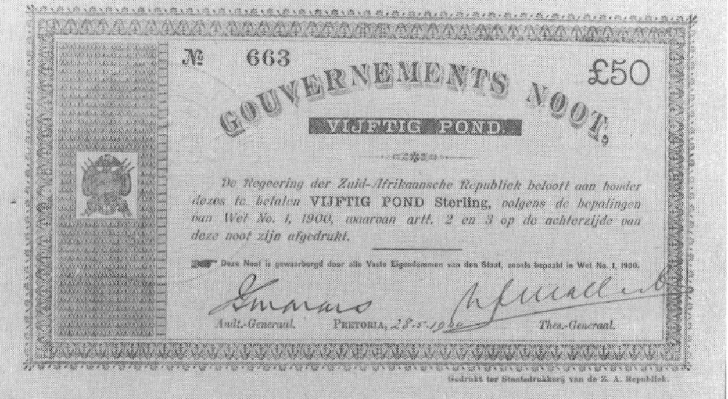

58 50 Pounds

	Good	Fine	XF
28.5.1900. Greenish gray. Arms at left, large embossed seal of the Republiek at left. Without *No.* by serial #. Back: Law text.	25.00	150	450

		Good	Fine	XF
59	**100 Pounds** 28.5.1900. Greenish gray. Arms at left, large embossed seal of the Republiek at left. Without *No.* by serial #. Back: Law text.	40.00	200	500

Pietersburg

1901 Gouvernements Noot

		Good	Fine	XF
60	**1 Pound** 1901. Black. Arms at left, without large embossed seal.			
	a. 1.2.1901.	12.50	30.00	100
	b. 1.3.1901.	20.00	50.00	120
	c. 1.4.1901.	10.00	25.00	90.00
61	**5 Pounds**	Good	Fine	XF
	1901. Black. Arms at left, without large embossed seal.			
	a. 1.2.1901.	22.50	50.00	135
	b. 1.3.1901.	25.00	60.00	175
	c. 1.4.1901.	20.00	45.00	125

		Good	Fine	XF
62	**10 Pounds** 1901. Black. Arms at left, without large embossed seal.			
	a. 1.3.1901.	35.00	75.00	250
	b. 1.4.1901.	25.00	60.00	225
63	**20 Pounds**	Good	Fine	XF
	1.4.1901. Black. Arms at left, without large embossed seal.	50.00	125	325
64	**50 Pounds**	Good	Fine	XF
	1.4.1901. Black. Arms at left, without large embossed seal.	135	300	650

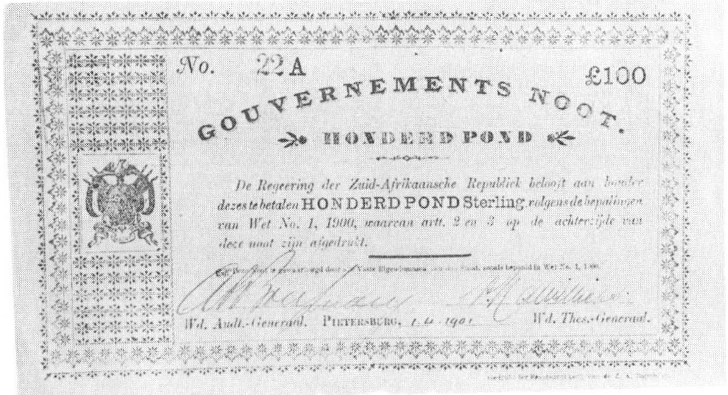

		Good	Fine	XF
65	**100 Pounds** 1.4.1901. Black. Arms at left, without large embossed seal.	200	450	1,000

Te Velde (in the field)

1902 Gouvernements Noot

		Good	Fine	XF
66	**1 Pound** 1.5.1902. Black. Cruder arms at left.	60.00	135	300
67	**10 Pounds**	Good	Fine	XF
	1902. Black. Cruder arms at left.			
	a. 1.3.1902.	45.00	110	250
	b. 1.4.1902.	60.00	135	380
	c. 1.5.1902.	40.00	105	245
68	**20 Pounds**	Good	Fine	XF
	1902. Black. Cruder arms at left.			
	a. 1.3.1902.	145	250	700
	b. 1.4.1902.	90.00	200	500
	c. 1.5.1902.	60.00	135	400

NOTE: Cancelled notes with oval handstamp: **CENTRAL JUDICIAL COMMISSION* / TRANSVAAL / 31 JAN 1907* are known for some of the above issues; these are much scarcer than uncancelled examples.

UNION OF SOUTH AFRICA

Treasury

Pretoria

1920 Currency and Banking Act

1920 Gold Certificate Issue

Issued in 1920 and circulated for only a short period. All notes have one side in English and the other in Afrikaans.

		VG	VF	UNC
69	**1 Pound** *L. 1920.* Black. Arms at upper center. Watermark: *UNION / OF / SOUTH AFRICA* in wavy frame.			
	a. Issued note - cancelled.	60.00	150	350
	s. Specimen.	—	—	1,000

#	Denomination	VG	VF	UNC
70	**5 Pounds** *L. 1920.* Black. Arms at upper center. Watermark: *UNION / OF / SOUTH AFRICA* in wavy frame.			
	a. Issued note - cancelled.	65.00	170	400
	s. Specimen.	—	—	1,000
71	**100 Pounds** *L. 1920.* Black. Arms at upper center. Watermark: *UNION / OF / SOUTH AFRICA* in wavy frame.			
	a. Issued note - cancelled.	90.00	300	650
	s. Specimen.	—	—	1,000
72	**1000 Pounds** *L. 1920.* Black. Arms at upper center. Watermark: *UNION / OF / SOUTH AFRICA* in wavy frame.			
	a. Issued note - cancelled.	115	450	900
	s. Specimen.	—	—	1,000
73	**10,000 Pounds** *L. 1920.* Black. Arms at upper center. Watermark: *UNION / OF / SOUTH AFRICA* in wavy frame.			
	a. Issued note - cancelled.	125	500	950
	s. Specimen.	—	—	1,000

South African Reserve Bank

Type A Type B Type C Type D

TYPE A: Ribbons curl over hind legs of supporters.

TYPE B: Ribbons curl between hind legs of supporters.

TYPES C & D: Smaller size, modified designs.

HAND STAMP VARIETIES:

TYPE I: *ADMINSTRATOR'S * OFFICE BULAWAYO* in violet oval frame.

TYPE II: *ADMINISTRATOR'S OFFICE* in violet oval frame.

1921-1926 Issues

#	Denomination	VG	VF	UNC
74	**10 Shillings** 30.11.1921-31.1.1922. Blue. Signature W.H. Clegg. BC: Green and purple. Watermark: Mercury head left. Printer: BWC.	180	600	1,500
75	**1 Pound** 17.9.1921-5.7.1922. Black on red underprint. Sailing ship at left. Signature W.H. Clegg. Back: Sailing ship. Watermark: Portrait J. van Riebeek #1. Printer: St. Lukes Printing Works.	55.00	250	700
76	**5 Pounds** 27.9.1921-6.7.1922. Green and brown. Sailing ship at left. Signature W.H. Clegg. Watermark: Portrait J. van Riebeek #1. Printer: St. Lukes Printing Works.	85.00	325	1,000
77	**20 Pounds** 29.9.1921. Blue. Sailing ship at left. Signature W.H. Clegg. Watermark: Portrait J. van Riebeek #1. Printer: St. Lukes Printing Works.	200	800	2,800
78	**100 Pounds** 30.9.1921. Red-brown. Sailing ship at left. Signature W.H. Clegg. Watermark: Portrait J. van Riebeek #1. Printer: St. Lukes Printing Works.	1,100	3,500	7,000

1925-1928 Issues

#	Denomination	VG	VF	UNC
79	**10 Shillings** 20.9.1926-15.12.1926. Dark brown on pink and pale green underprint. Signature W.H. Clegg. Watermark: Sailing ship and portrait J. van Riebeeck.	250	500	1,100
80	**1 Pound** 1.9.1925-4.4.1928. Dark brown. Sailing ship at left. Signature W.H. Clegg.	250	500	1,000
81	**5 Pounds** 7.4.1926. Dark green and brown. New type. Signature W.H. Clegg. Watermark: J. van Riebeeck only.	350	700	1,500

1928-1947 Issues

#	Denomination	VG	VF	UNC
82	**10 Shillings** 1928-1947. Dark brown on pink and pale green underprint. Like #79 but English and Afrikaans text. Watermark: Sailing ship and portrait J. van Riebeeck.			
	a. Signature W. H. Clegg. 1.9.1928-9.9.1931.	250	500	1,000
	b. Signature W. H. Clegg. Date overprint: 17.11.1931/2.4.1932. Prefixed E/12.	350	700	1,500
	c. Signature W. H. Clegg. 17.11.1931. Prefix E/12.	450	1,000	2,500
	d. Signature J. Postmus. 12.9.1932-4.4.1945.	175	275	500
	e. Signature Dr. M H. de Kock. 5.9.1945-14.11.1947.	175	275	500
83	**1 Pound** 1.9.1928. Dark brown. Sailing ship at left. Signature W.H. Clegg. English and Dutch text. Back: Like #80 but altered design.	400	800	1,500

#	Denomination	VG	VF	UNC
84	**1 Pound** 1928-1949. Dark brown. Sailing ship at left. Like #83 but English and Afrikaans text.			
	a. Signature W. M. Clegg. Dutch microprinted background. 3.12.1928-30.11.1929.	300	600	1,000
	b. Signature W.H. Clegg. Afrikaans microprinted background. 30.4.1930-30.11.1931.	200	400	700
	c. Signature Dr. J. Postmus. 5.9.1932-30.4.1938.	50.00	100	200
	d. Signature Dr. J. Postmus. Paper with metal thread (only series A78). 19.9.1938.	300	500	900
	e. Signature Dr. J. Postmus. 20.9.1938-22.11.1944.	50.00	100	200
	f. Signature Dr. M. H. de Kock. 5.9.1945-14.11.1947.	50.00	100	200
85	**5 Pounds** 2.4.1928. Dark brown on pink and pale green underprint. English and Dutch text. Signature Dr. J. Postmus. Back: Like #82 but altered design. Watermark: Sailing ship and Portrait J. van Riebeek.	200	500	1,100
86	**5 Pounds** 1929-1947. Dark brown on pink and pale green underprint. Like #85 but English and Afrikaans text. Watermark: Sailing ship and Portrait J. van Riebeek.			
	a. Signature W. H. Clegg. 2.9.1929-17.4.1931.	200	400	700
	b. Signature J. Postmus. 1.9.1933-4.4.1944.	80.00	150	250
	c. Signature Dr. M. H. de Kock. 6.4.1946-12.11.1947.	100	200	300

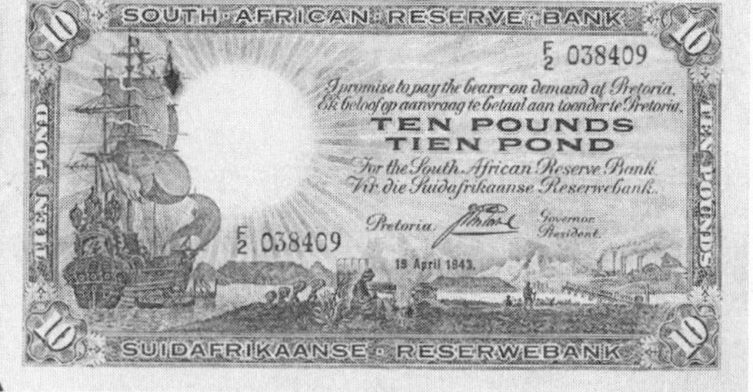

No.	Description	VG	VF	UNC
87	**10 Pounds**	VG	VF	UNC
	14.4.1943; 19.4.1943. Brown. Sailing ship at left. Signature Dr. J. Postmus.	150	300	500
88	**20 Pounds**	VG	VF	UNC
	1928; 1943. Blue. New type.			
	a. Signature W. H. Clegg. 3.9.1928.	175	650	2,300
	b. Signature Dr. J. Postmus. 4.9.1943.	120	500	1,500
89	**100 Pounds**	VG	VF	UNC
	1928; 1933. Brown. New type.			
	a. Signature W. H. Clegg. 4.9.1928.	900	3,000	6,000
	b. Signature Dr. J. Postmus. 8.9.1933.	550	2,400	4,250

1948-1959 Issues

No.	Description	VG	VF	UNC
90	**10 Shillings**	VG	VF	UNC
	1948-1959. Brown. Portrait Jan van Riebeeck at left, first lines of bank name and value in English. Signature Dr. M. H. de Kock.			
	a. Date with name of month. 10.4.1948-21.4.1949.	8.50	30.00	95.00
	b. Date with name of month. Melamine treated paper. 1.4.1950-30.11.1951.	13.00	35.00	85.00
	c. Date with month by #. 1.12.1951-18.2.1959.	4.50	20.00	75.00
91	**10 Shillings**	VG	VF	UNC
	1948-1959. Brown. Portrait Jan van Riebeeck at left. Like #90 but first line of bank name and value in Afrikaans. Signature Dr. M. H. de Kock.			
	a. Date with name of month. 10.4.1948-21.4.1949.	8.50	30.00	95.00
	b. Date with name of month, thick paper. Series A21. 22.4.1949.	105	280	740
	c. Date with name of month. Melamine treated paper. 1.4.1950-30.11.1951.	13.00	35.00	85.00
	d. Date with month by #. 1.2.1951-18.2.1959.	4.50	20.00	75.00

No.	Description	VG	VF	UNC
92	**1 Pound**	VG	VF	UNC
	1948-1959. Blue. Portrait Jan van Riebeeck at left, first line of bank name and value in English. Signature Dr. M. H. de Kock.			
	a. Date with name of month. 10.9.1948-9.4.1949.	4.50	18.00	65.00
	b. Date with name of month. 16.4.1949-3.11.1949.	8.00	23.00	75.00
	c. Date with name of month. Melamine treated paper. 1.4.1950-30.11.1951.	5.00	15.00	50.00
	d. Date with month as #. 1.12.1951-26.6.1959.	3.00	10.00	45.00

Color Abbreviation Guide

New to the *Standard Catalog of ® World Paper Money* are the following abbreviations related to color references:

BC: Back color
PC: Paper color

No.	Description	VG	VF	UNC
93	**1 Pound**	VG	VF	UNC
	1948-1959. Blue. Portrait Jan van Riebeeck at left. Like #92 but first line of bank name and value in Afrikaans. Signature Dr. M. H. de Kock.			
	a. Date with name of month. 1.9.1949-9.4.1949.	4.50	18.00	65.00
	b. Date with name of month. Thick paper. Series B28. 12.4.1949.	100	265	700
	c. Date with name of month. 16.4.1949-3.11.1949.	8.00	23.00	75.00
	d. Date with name of month. Melamine treated paper. 1.4.1950-30.11.1951.	5.00	15.00	50.00
	e. Date with month as #. 1.12.1951-26.6.1959.	3.00	10.00	45.00
94	**5 Pounds**	VG	VF	UNC
	1.11.1948-13.4.1949. Light green. Portrait Jan van Riebeeck at left, first line of bank name and value in English. Signature Dr. M. H. de Kock. 163x90mm.	10.00	35.00	130
95	**5 Pounds**	VG	VF	UNC
	1.11.1948-13.4.1949. Light green. Portrait Jan van Riebeeck at left. Like #94 but first line of bank name and value in Afrikaans. Signature Dr. M. H. de Kock. 163x90mm.	12.50	36.00	115
96	**5 Pounds**	VG	VF	UNC
	1950-1959. Dark green. Portrait Jan van Riebeeck at left. Like #94 but first line of bank name and value in English. Signature Dr. M. H. de Kock. 171x97mm.			
	a. Date with name of month. 3.4.1950-22.4.1952.	8.00	25.00	80.00
	b. Date with month as #. 2.1.1953-31.1.1953.	5.00	18.00	65.00
	c. Date with month as #. Melamine treated paper. 8.2.1954-18.6.1959.	4.00	14.00	50.00
97	**5 Pounds**	VG	VF	UNC
	1950-1959. Dark green. Portrait Jan van Riebeeck at left. Like #96 but first line of bank name and value in Afrikaans. Signature Dr. M. H. de Kock. 171x97mm.			
	a. Date with name of month. 3.4.1950-22.4.1952.	8.00	25.00	80.00
	b. Date with month as #. 2.1.1953-31.1.1953.	5.00	18.00	65.00
	c. Date with month as #. Melamine treated paper. 8.2.1954-18.6.1959.	4.00	14.00	50.00
98	**10 Pounds**	VG	VF	UNC
	18.12.1952-19.11.1958. Brown-violet. Portrait Jan van Riebeeck at left. First line of bank name and value in English. Signature Dr. M. H. de Kock.	15.00	50.00	175
99	**10 Pounds**	VG	VF	UNC
	18.12.1952-19.11.1958. Brown-violet. Portrait Jan van Riebeeck at left. Like #98 but first line of bank name and value in Afrikaans. Signature Dr. M. H. de Kock.	15.00	50.00	175

No.	Description	VG	VF	UNC
100	**100 Pounds**	VG	VF	UNC
	29.1.1952. Blue and multicolor. Portrait Jan van Riebeeck at left, sailing ship at right. First line of bank name and value in English. Signature Dr. M. H. de Kock.			
	a. Date with month as #. 29.1.1952.	175	775	2,000
	b. Perforated: *CANCELLED.*	150	500	1,500
101	**100 Pounds**	VG	VF	UNC
	29.1.1952. Blue and multicolor. Portrait Jan van Riebeeck at left, sailing ship at right. Like #100 but first line of bank name and value in Afrikaans. Signature Dr. M. H. de Kock.			
	a. Date with month as #. 29.1.1952.	175	775	2,000
	b. Perforated: *CANCELLED.*	150	500	1,500

Note: For issues similar to #98-101 but in Rand values, see Volume 3, Modern Issues.

SOUTH KOREA

The Republic of Korea, situated in northeastern Asia on the southern half of the Korean peninsula between North Korea and the Korean Strait, has an area of 38,025 sq. mi. (98,484 sq. km.) and a population of 44.61 million. Capital: Seoul. The country's exports include petrochemicals, automobile/auto parts, ships, wireless communication equipment, and steel. Japan replaced China as the predominant foreign influence in Korea in 1895 and annexed the peninsular country in 1910. Defeat in World War II brought an end to Japanese rule. U.S. troops entered Korea from the south and Soviet forces entered from the north. The Cairo Conference (1943) had established that Korea should be "free and independent." The Potsdam Conference (1945) set the 38th parallel as the line dividing the occupation forces of the United States and Russia. When Russia refused to permit a U.N. commission designated to supervise reunification elections to enter North Korea, an election was held in South Korea on May 10, 1948. By its determination, the Republic of Korea was inaugurated on Aug. 15, 1948.

Note: For Bank of Chosen notes issued in South Korea under the Allied occupation during the post WWII period 1945 to 1948 refer to Korea listings.

MONETARY SYSTEM:

1 Won (Hwan) = 100 Chon

1 new Won = 10 old Hwan, 1962-

REPUBLIC

Bank of Chosen

1949 ND Issue

#	Description	VG	VF	UNC
1	**5 Won** ND (1949). Black on orange underprint. Archway at right. Back: Building at center. BC: Red-brown.	10.00	50.00	175

#	Description	VG	VF	UNC
2	**10 Won** ND (1949). Black on lilac underprint. Archway at right. Like #1. Back: Building at center. BC: Black.	7.50	40.00	275

#	Description	VG	VF	UNC
3	**1000 Won** ND (1950). Lilac. Man with beard at left. BC: Light blue.	7.50	40.00	275

Note: #3 was issued unofficially by the North Korean Army in 1950 during the Korean conflict.

Bank of Korea

1949 Issue

#	Description	VG	VF	UNC
4	**5 Chon** 1949. Red. 5-petaled blossom within circle at center. Like #6.	10.00	50.00	375
5	**10 Chon** 1949. Brown. 5-petaled blossom within circle at center. Like #6.	7.50	40.00	200

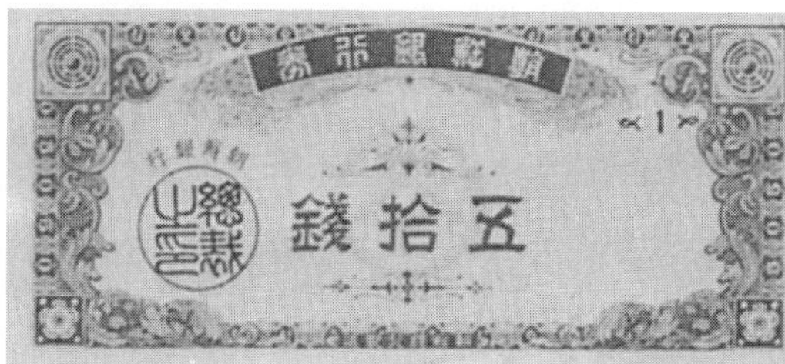

#	Description	VG	VF	UNC
6	**50 Chon** 1949. Blue. 5-petaled blossom within circle at center.	5.00	35.00	125

1950 Issue

#	Description	VG	VF	UNC
7	**100 Won** ND (1950). Brown. Varieties. City gate at left.	7.50	40.00	200

#	Description	VG	VF	UNC
8	**1000 Won** ND (1950). Green. Varieties. Portrait Syngman Rhee at left.	10.00	50.00	225

1952 Issue

#	Description	VG	VF	UNC
9	**500 Won** 4285 (1952). Blue. Portrait Syngman Rhee at left. Back: Pagoda at center. BC: Brown.	75.00	500	1,200

#	Denomination	VG	VF	UNC
10	**1000 Won**	VG	VF	UNC
	4285 (1952); 4286 (1953). Black-green. Portrait Syngman Rhee at left. Back: Pagoda at center. Like #9. BC: Brown.			
	a. Large date. 4285	5.00	25.00	250
	b. Small date. 4286.	10.00	50.00	350

1953 ND Issue

#11-12 printed in Korea from glass positives furnished by the U.S.A. BEP.

#	Denomination	VG	VF	UNC
11	**1 Won**	VG	VF	UNC
	ND (1953). Lilac. Wreath of guilloches at left center. Printer: Korean using glass positives furnished by the U.S.			
	a. Thin brown paper. Watermark.	5.00	25.00	150
	b. White paper, without watermark.	10.00	50.00	300

#	Denomination	VG	VF	UNC
12	**5 Won**	VG	VF	UNC
	ND (1953). Red. Wreath of guilloches at left center. Printer: Korean using glass positives furnished by the U.S.	10.00	50.00	300

#	Denomination	VG	VF	UNC
13	**10 Won**	VG	VF	UNC
	ND (1953). Blue. Medieval tortoise warship at right. Printer: Tudor Press, Boston, Mass. U.S.A. through the BEP.			
	a. Issued note.	15.00	75.00	400
	r. Replacement note: Prefix D and no suffix letter.	—	—	—

#	Denomination	VG	VF	UNC
14	**100 Won**	VG	VF	UNC
	ND (1953). Green. Medieval tortoise warship at right. Printer: Tudor Press, Boston, Mass. U.S.A. through the BEP.			
	a. Issued note.	15.00	75.00	200
	r. Replacement note: Prefix D and no suffix letter.	—	—	—
15	**1000 Won**	VG	VF	UNC
	ND (1953). Brown. Medieval tortoise warship at right. Printer: Tudor Press, Boston, Mass. U.S.A. through the BEP.			
	a. Issued note.	50.00	200	650
	r. Replacement note: Prefix D and no suffix letter.	—	—	—
	s. Specimen.	—	—	1,000

1953-1956 Issues

#	Denomination	VG	VF	UNC
16	**10 Hwan**	VG	VF	UNC
	4286 (1953). Green-black on light blue underprint. Pagoda portal at right. Back: Rock formations in water. BC: Purple. PC: Gray.	10.00	50.00	300

#	Denomination	VG	VF	UNC
17	**10 Hwan**	VG	VF	UNC
	4286 (1953)-4291 (1958). Gray-blue. Pagoda portal at right. Like #16. Back: Rock formations in water. BC: Purple. PC: White.			
	a. 4286.	5.00	5.00	25.00
	b. 4287.	7.50	150	800
	c. 4288.	5.00	75.00	450
	d. 4289.	5.00	50.00	250
	e. 4290.	5.00	40.00	200
	f. 4291.	10.00	25.00	125
18	**100 Hwan**	VG	VF	UNC
	4286 (1953). Dark green. Portrait Syngman Rhee at left. Like #19. Back: Archway. PC: Yellowish; blocks 1-5.	500	3,000	17,000

#	Denomination	VG	VF	UNC
19	**100 Hwan**	VG	VF	UNC
	4287 (1954); 4288 (1955); 4289 (1956). Dark green. Portrait Syngman Rhee at left. Back: Archway. PC: White.			
	a. 4287.	3.00	7.50	50.00
	b. 4288.	2.00	5.00	30.00
	c. 4289.	1.00	4.00	22.50

20	500 Hwan	VG	VF	UNC
	4289 (1956); 4290 (1957). Gray-blue on green underprint. Portrait Syngman Rhee at center. BC: Brown.			
	a. Issued note.	12.50	100	500
	s. Specimen.	—	—	—

1957 Issue

21	100 Hwan	VG	VF	UNC
	4290 (1957). Gray on olive-green and brown underprint. Portrait Syngman Rhee at right. BC: Green.			
	a. Issued note.	3.00	25.00	120
	s. Specimen.	—	—	—

22	1000 Hwan	VG	VF	UNC
	4290 (1957)-4293 (1960). Purple on brown and green underprint. Portrait Syngman Rhee at right. Back: Date at center. BC: Black on green underprint.			
	a. 4290.	12.00	60.00	300
	b. 4291.	6.00	30.00	150
	c. 4292.	4.00	12.00	100
	d. 4293.	4.00	12.00	100
	s.	—	—	—

1958-1960 Issue

23	50 Hwan	VG	VF	UNC
	4291 (1958). Green-blue on olive-green underprint. Archway at left. Back: Statue at center, medieval tortoise warship at right. BC: Green.			
	a. Issued note.	20.00	60.00	350
	s. Specimen.	—	—	—

24	500 Hwan	VG	VF	UNC
	4291 (1958); 4292 (1959). Dark green. Portrait Syngman Rhee at right. BC: Brownish purple.			
	a. Issued note.	7.50	40.00	350
	s. Specimen.	—	—	—

25	1000 Hwan	VG	VF	UNC
	4293 (1960); 4294 (1961); 1962. Black on olive underprint. King Sejong the Great at right. Back: Flaming torch at center. BC: Blue-green and light brown.			
	a. 4293 (1960).	2.50	10.00	100
	b. 4294 (1961).	1.50	6.00	60.00
	c. 1962.	1.75	7.00	65.00

South Viet Nam (the former Republic of Viet Nam), located in Southeast Asia, bounded by North Viet Nam on the north (the former Democratic Republic of Viet Nam), Laos and Cambodia on the west, and the South China Sea on the east and south, had an area of 66,280 sq. mi. (171,665 sq. km.) and a population of 20 million. Capital: Saigon. The economy of the area was predominantly agricultural. South Viet Nam, the direct successor to the French-dominated regime (also known as the State of Viet Nam), was created after the first Indochina War (between the French and the Viet-Minh) by the Geneva agreement of 1954 which divided Viet Nam at the 17th parallel of latitude.

The elections which would have reunified North and South Viet Nam in 1956 never took place, and the North restarted their war for unification of the country in 1959. In 1975, North Vietnamese forces overran the South reuniting the country under communist rule.There followed a short period of co-existence of the two Vietnamese states, but the South was now governed by the North through the Peoples Revolutionary Government (PRG). On July 2, 1976, South and North Viet Nam joined to form the Socialist Republic of Viet Nam.See also Viet Nam.

MONETARY SYSTEM

1 Dng = 100 Xu

VIET NAM - REPUBLIC

Ngân-Hàng Quô'c-Gia Viêt-Nam

National Bank of Viet Nam

1955; 1956 ND First Issue

		VG	VF	UNC
1	**1 Dông** ND (1956). Green on lilac underprint. Temple at right. Back: Building at left. Watermark: Tiger's head.			
	a. Issued note.	0.25	1.00	4.00
	s. Specimen. Overprint: *GIAY MAU.*	—	—	125

		VG	VF	UNC
2	**5 Dông** ND (1955). Green on gold and lilac underprint. Bird at center. Back: Farmer with water buffalo. Watermark: Tiger's head.			
	a. Issued note.	0.50	1.50	7.50
	s. Specimen. Overprint: *GIAY MAU.*	—	—	150

		VG	VF	UNC
3	**10 Dông** ND (1955). Deep red on blue and gray underprint. Fish at center. Back: Coastal area with boats. Watermark: Tiger's head.			
	a. Issued note.	0.50	3.00	15.00
	s. Specimen. Overprint: *GIAY MAU.*	—	—	200

		VG	VF	UNC
4	**20 Dông** ND (1956). Green and multicolor. Huts and boats at left, banana plants at right. Back: Farmers and water buffalos. Watermark: Tiger's head.			
	a. Issued note.	2.00	12.50	50.00
	s. Specimen. Overprint: *GIAY MAU.*	—	—	400

		VG	VF	UNC
4A	**1000 Dông** ND. Multicolor. Old man at left, temple at right. Back: Sampan at lower left, young woman at right.			
	p. Proof.	—	—	5,000
	s. Specimen. Overprint: *GIAY MAU.*	—	—	5,000

1955-1958 ND Second Issue

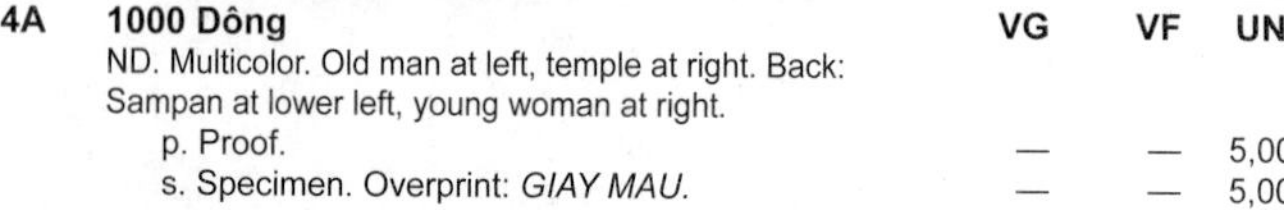

		VG	VF	UNC
7	**50 Dông** ND (1956). Purple. Boy with water buffalo at left. Back: Sifting grain. Printer: SBNC.			
	a. Issued note.	3.00	12.00	75.00
	p. Proof. Uniface face and back pair.	—	—	450
	s. Specimen. Overprint: *GIAY MAU.*	—	—	350

		VG	VF	UNC
8	**100 Dông** ND (1955). Gray. Farmer on tractor at center. Back: Stylized peacock. BC: Green. Printer: ABNC (without imprint).			
	a. Issued note.	3.00	12.50	50.00
	p. Proof. Uniface face and back pair.	—	—	750
	s1. Specimen. Overprint: *GIAY MAU.*	—	—	325
	s2. Specimen. Overprint: *SPECIMEN.*	—	—	550

		VG	VF	UNC
9	**200 Dông** ND (1958). Purple on green underprint. Bank at right. Back: Fishing boats. Printer: ABNC (without imprint).			
	a. Issued note.	5.00	17.50	80.00
	p. Proof. Uniface face and back pair.	—	—	750
	s. Specimen. Overprint: *SPECIMEN.*	—	—	550

		VG	VF	UNC
10	**500 Dông** ND (1955). Blue. Pagoda at center. BC: Orange. Printer: ABNC (without imprint).			
	a. Issued note.	25.00	125	500
	p. Proof. Uniface face and back pair.	—	—	1,500
	s1. Specimen with overprint: *GIAY MAU,* punched hole cancelled.	—	—	750
	s2. Specimen with overprint: *SPECIMEN.*	—	—	1,250

1955 ND Third Issue

		VG	VF	UNC
11	**1 Dông** ND (1955). Gray. Woman farm worker threshing grain at left. Back: Rice paddy worker. Printer: SBNC.			
	a. Issued note.	0.25	2.00	8.00
	p. Uniface proof. Face and back.	—	—	—
	s. Specimen. Overprint: *GIAY MAU.*	—	—	175

		VG	VF	UNC
12	**2 Dông** ND (1955). Purplish blue. Boat at right. Back: River scene. Printer: SBNC.			
	a. Issued note.	0.25	1.25	5.00
	p. Uniface proof. Face and back.	—	—	175
	s. Specimen. Overprint: *GIAY MAU.*	—	—	175

		VG	VF	UNC
13	**5 Dông** ND (1955). Dull red on peach underprint. Farmer with water buffalo at left. Back: River scene with house. Printer: SBNC.			
	a. Issued note.	0.25	1.25	5.00
	p. Uniface proof. Face and back.	—	—	—
	s. Specimen. Overprint: *GIAY MAU.*	—	—	175
	x. Counterfeit. Propaganda on back. (there is a reproduction of the counterfeit too!).	—	—	25.00

		VG	VF	UNC
14	**200 Dông** ND (1955). Green. Soldier at left. Back: Girl with sheaves in field. Printer: SBNC.			
	a. Issued note.	40.00	125	450
	s. Specimen with overprint: *GIAY MAU,* punched hole cancelled.	—	—	500
14A	**200 Dông** ND. Green. Soldier at left. Similar to #14, but engraved. Back: Girl with sheaves in field. (Not issued.)	VG	VF	UNC
	s1. Specimen. Overprint: *GIAY MAU.*	—	—	800
	s2. Specimen. Uniface pair. Several colors available.	—	—	1,500
	ct. Color trials. various colors.	—	—	2,500

SOUTHERN RHODESIA

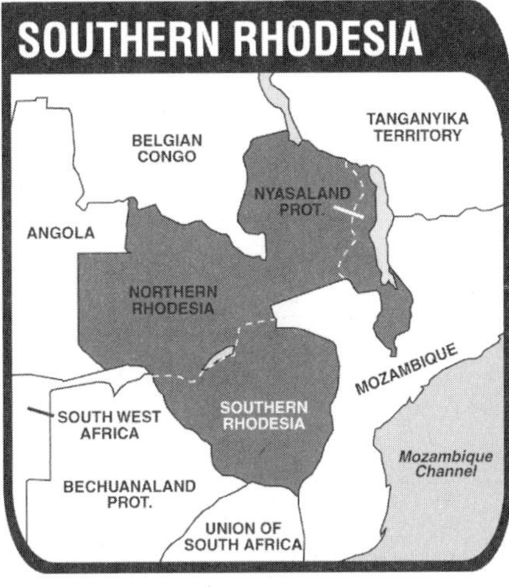

Southern Rhodesia (now Zimbabwe), located in the east-central part of southern Africa, has an area of 150,804 sq. mi. (390,580 sq. km.) and a population of 10.1 million. Capital: Salisbury. The economy is based on agriculture and mining. Tobacco, sugar, asbestos, copper and chrome ore and coal are exported. The Rhodesian area, the habitat of paleolithic man, contains extensive evidence of earlier civilizations, notably the world-famous ruins of Zimbabwe, a gold-trading center that flourished about the 14th or 15th century AD. The Portuguese of the 16th century were the first Europeans to attempt to develop south-central Africa, but it remained for Cecil Rhodes and the British South Africa Co. to open the hinterlands. Rhodes obtained a concession for mineral rights from local chiefs in 1888 and administered his African empire (named Southern Rhodesia in 1895) through the British South Africa Co. until 1923, when the British government annexed the area after the white settlers voted for existence as a separate entity, rather than for incorporation into the Union of South Africa. From September of 1953 through 1963 Southern Rhodesia was joined with the British protectorates of Northern Rhodesia and Nyasaland into a multiracial federation. When the federation was dissolved at the end of 1963, Northern Rhodesia and Nyasaland became the independent states of Zambia and Malawi.

Britain was prepared to grant independence to Southern Rhodesia but declined to do so when the politically dominant white Rhodesians refused to give assurances of representative government. On May 11, 1965, following two years of unsuccessful negotiation with the British government, Prime Minister Ian Smith issued a unilateral declaration of independence. Britain responded with economic sanctions supported by the United Nations. After further futile attempts to effect an accommodation, the Rhodesian Parliament severed all ties with Britain, and on March 2, 1970, established the Republic of Rhodesia.

On March 3, 1978, Prime Minister Ian Smith and three moderate black nationalist leaders signed an agreement providing for black majority rule. The name of the country was changed to Zimbabwe Rhodesia. After the election of March 3, 1980, the country changed its name again and became the Republic of Zimbabwe. Also see Rhodesia, Rhodesia and Nyasaland, and Zimbabwe.

RULERS:

British to 1970

MONETARY SYSTEM:

1 Shilling = 12 Pence
1 Pound = 20 Shillings to 1970

BRITISH ADMINISTRATION

Southern Rhodesia Currency Board

1939-1952 Issues

		VG	VF	UNC
8	**5 Shillings** 1943; 1945; 1948. Purple. Portrait King George VI at right. Printer: BWC.			
	a. Signature A. W. Bessle. 89 x 57mm. 1.1.1943.	75.00	300	1,200
	b. Signature E. T. Fox. 114 x 70mm. 1.2.1945; 1.10.1945; 1.1.1948.	45.00	225	800

		VG	VF	UNC
9	**10 Shillings** 1939-1951. Brown and multicolor. Portrait King George VI at right. Back: Sable at left, Victoria Falls at center. Printer: BWC.			
	a. Signature A. W. Bessle. Small prefix letters. 15.12.1939; 1.7.1942.	55.00	525	2,750
	b. Signature A. W. Bessle. Intermediate prefix letters. 1.3.1944; 1.2.1945.	65.00	450	2,500
	c. Signature E. T. Fox. Intermediate prefix letters. 1.2.1945; 15.3.1946; 15.1.1947.	55.00	450	2,250

		VG	VF	UNC
	d. Signature E. T. Fox. Large prefix letters. 1.1.1948.	65.00	450	2,250
	e. Signature A. H. Strachan. 10.1.1950.	50.00	400	2,250
	f. Signature Gordon Munro. 1.9.1950; 1.9.1951.	60.00	400	2,250
	s. As e. Specimen. Perforated: *SPECIMEN.*	—	—	1,250
10	**1 Pound**	VG	VF	UNC
	1939-1951. Green and multicolor. Portrait King George VI at right. Back: Sable at left, Zimbabwe ruins at center. Printer: BWC.			
	a. Signature A. W. Bessle. Small prefix letters. 15.12.1939; 1.7.1942.	75.00	550	3,000
	b. Signature A. W. Bessle. Intermediate prefix letters. 1.3.1944.	60.00	450	2,500
	c. Signature E. T. Fox. Intermediate prefix letters. 1.2.1945; 1.10.1945; 15.1.1947.	55.00	400	2,000
	d. Signature E. T. Fox. Large prefix letters. 1.1.1948.	60.00	450	2,200
	e. Signature A. H. Strachan. 10.1.1950.	60.00	400	2,000
	f. Signature Gordon Munro. 1.9.1950; 1.9.1951.	50.00	400	1,900
11	**5 Pounds**	VG	VF	UNC
	1939-1952. Blue, brown and multicolor. Portrait King George VI at right. Back: Factory at lower center, Sable at left, Victoria Falls at center. Printer: BWC.			
	a. Signature A. W. Bessle. without white £5 in underprint. on face. 15.12.1939; 1.7.1942.	300	1,500	—
	b. Signature A. W. Bessle. White £5 in underprint. on face. 1.3.1944; 1.2.1945.	225	1,000	4,500
	c. Signature E. T. Fox. Intermediate prefix letters. 1.10.1945; 15.3.1946; 15.1.1947; 1.11.1947.	175	950	3,500
	d. Signature E. T. Fox. Large prefix letters. 1.1.1948.	175	900	3,500
	e. Signature A. H. Strachan. 10.1.1950.	150	900	3,500
	f. Signature Gordon Munro. 1.9.1950; 1.9.1951.	150	900	3,500
	g. Signature Gordon Munro. Signature title: *CHAIRMAN* above *MEMBER.* 15.1.1952; 15.2.1952.	200	950	3,650

1952-1954 Issue

		VG	VF	UNC
12	**10 Shillings**	VG	VF	UNC
	1952-1953. Brown and multicolor. Portrait Queen Elizabeth II at right. *SOUTHERN RHODESIA CURRENCY BOARD* in text. Chairman signature 5. Back: Sable at left, Victoria Falls at center. Like #9. Printer: BWC.			
	a. 1.12.1952.	65.00	450	2,250
	b. 3.1.1953.	60.00	400	2,000

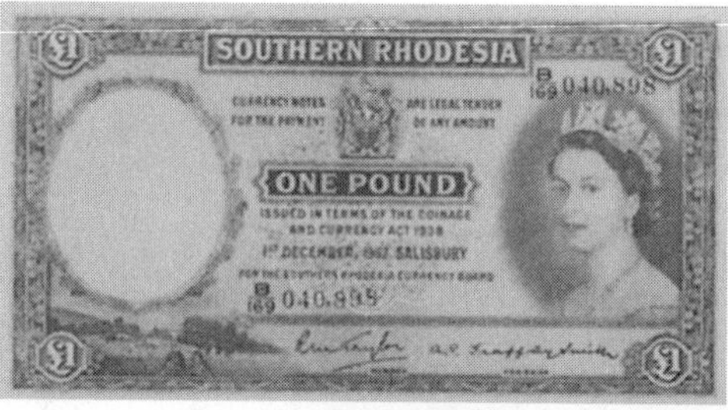

		VG	VF	UNC
13	**1 Pound**	VG	VF	UNC
	1952-1954. Green and multicolor. Portrait Queen Elizabeth II at right. *SOUTHERN RHODESIA CURRENCY BOARD* in text. Chairman signature 5. Back: Sable at left, Zimbabwe ruins at center. Like #10. Printer: BWC.			
	a. 1.12.1952.	75.00	600	3,000
	b. 3.1.1953.	70.00	500	2,750
	c. 10.3.1954.	60.00	500	2,750
14	**5 Pounds**	VG	VF	UNC
	1953-1954. Blue and multicolor. Portrait Queen Elizabeth II at right. *SOUTHERN RHODESIA CURRENCY BOARD* in text. Chairman signature 5. Back: Sable at left, Victoria Falls at center. Like #11. Printer: BWC.			
	a. 1.1.1953.	200	1,200	—
	b. 15.4.1953. Reported not confirmed.	—	—	—
	c. 10.3.1954.	225	1,500	—
15	**10 Pounds**	VG	VF	UNC
	15.4.1953; 10.3.1954. Brown and multicolor. Portrait Queen Elizabeth II at right. *SOUTHERN RHODESIA CURRENCY BOARD* in text. Chairman signature 5. Printer: BWC.			
	a. 15.4.1953.	700	3,250	—
	b. 10.3.1954.	950	4,000	—

Central Africa Currency Board

1955 Issue

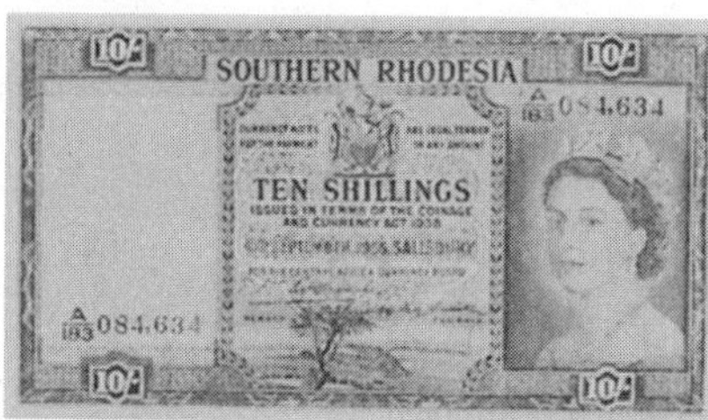

		VG	VF	UNC
16	**10 Shillings**	VG	VF	UNC
	10.9.1955. Brown and multicolor. Portrait Queen Elizabeth II at right. *CENTRAL AFRICA CURRENCY BOARD* in text. Chairman signature 5. Like #12. Back: Sable at left, Victoria Falls at center. Printer: BWC.	65.00	550	2,250

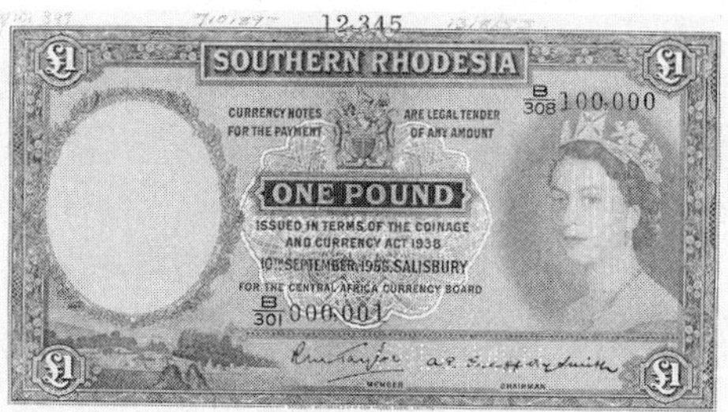

		VG	VF	UNC
17	**1 Pound**	VG	VF	UNC
	10.9.1955. Green and multicolor. Portrait Queen Elizabeth II at right. *CENTRAL AFRICA CURRENCY BOARD* in text. Chairman signature 5. Like #13. Back: Sable at left, Zimbabwe ruins at center. Printer: BWC. 153x83mm.			
	a. Issued note.	60.00	500	2,000
	s. Specimen. Perforated: *SPECIMEN.*	—	—	—
18	**5 Pounds**	VG	VF	UNC
	10.9.1955. Blue and multicolor. Portrait Queen Elizabeth II at right. *CENTRAL AFRICA CURRENCY BOARD* in text. Chairman signature 5. Like #14. Back: Sable at left. Victoria Falls at center. Printer: BWC.	200	1,200	4,000
19	**10 Pounds**	VG	VF	UNC
	10.9.1955. Brown and multicolor. Portrait Queen Elizabeth II at right. *CENTRAL AFRICA CURRENCY BOARD* in text. Chairman signature 5. Like #15. Printer: BWC. Requires confirmation.	—	—	—

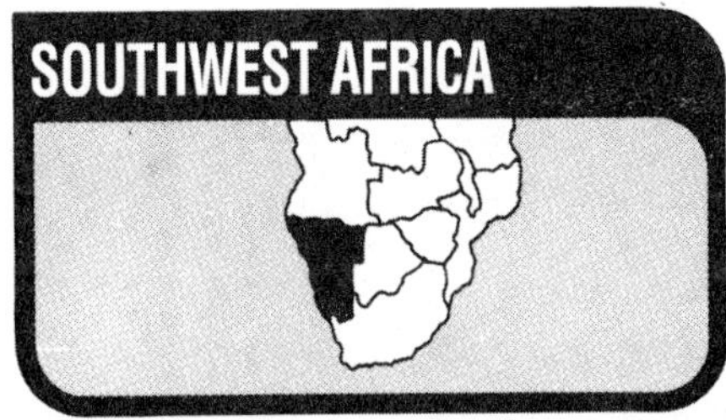

Southwest Africa (now the Republic of Namibia), the former German territory of German Southwest Africa, is situated on the Atlantic coast of southern Africa, bounded on the north by Angola, on the east by Botswana, and on the south by South Africa. It has an area of 318,261 sq. mi. (824,290 sq. km.) and a population of 1.4 million. Capital: Windhoek. Diamonds, copper, lead, zinc and cattle are exported. South Africa undertook the administration of Southwest Africa under the terms of a League of Nations mandate on Dec. 17, 1920. When the League of Nations was dissolved in 1946, its supervisory authority for Southwest Africa was inherited by the United Nations. In 1946 the UN denied South Africa's request to annex Southwest Africa. South Africa responded by refusing to place the territory under a UN trusteeship. In 1950 the International Court of Justice ruled that South Africa could not unilaterally modify the international status of South West Africa. A 1966 UN resolution declaring the mandate terminated was rejected by South Africa, and the status of the area remained in dispute. In June 1968 the UN General Assembly voted to rename the country Namibia. It became a republic in March 1990. Notes of the three emission banks circulated until 1963 and were then replaced by notes of the Republic of South Africa. Also see German Southwest Africa and Namibia.

MONETARY SYSTEM:

1 Shilling = 12 Pence
1 Pound = 20 Shillings to 1961

SOUTH AFRICAN ADMINISTRATION

Barclays Bank (Dominion, Colonial and Overseas)

1931 Issue

		Good	Fine	XF
1	**10 Shillings** 1931-1954. Red on multicolor underprint. Sheep at left. *DOMINION, COLONIAL AND OVERSEAS* in title. Back: Bank arms at center. Printer: W&S.			
	a. 1.6.1931.	175	375	750
	b. 1.5.1943; 1.4.1949.	65.00	125	350
	c. 2.1.1951; 31.7.1954	50.00	100	300
	d. Punch hole cancelled. 31.7.1954.	20.00	50.00	—

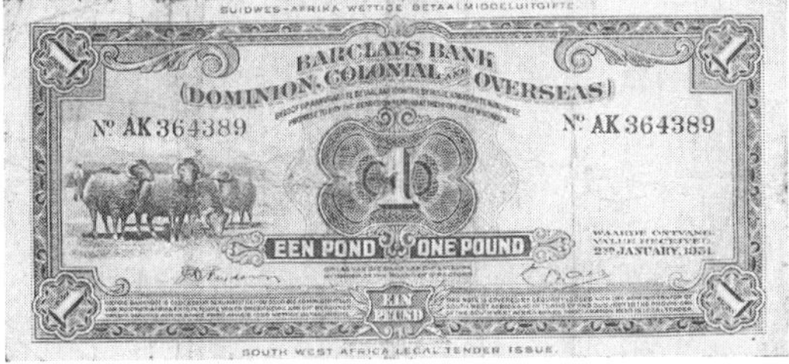

		Good	Fine	XF
2	**1 Pound** 1931-1954. Dark blue on green multicolor underprint. Sheep at left. *DOMINION, COLONIAL AND OVERSEAS* in title. Back: Bank arms at center. Printer: W&S.			
	a. 1.6.1931.	225	550	—
	b. 1.10.1938; 1.11.1939.	110	250	600
	c. 1.11.1943; 1.4.1949.	65.00	125	400
	d. 2.1.1951; 29.11.1952; 31.1.1954.	40.00	100	300

		Good	Fine	XF
3	**5 Pounds** 1931-1954. Dark green on red and multicolor underprint. Sheep at left. *DOMINION, COLONIAL AND OVERSEAS* in title. Back: Bank arms at center. Printer: W&S.			
	a. 1.6.1931.	275	650	—
	b. 1.7.1944; 1.4.1949.	165	350	850
	c. 2.1.1951; 31.1.1954.	125	300	700
	d. Punch hole and perforated: *CANCELLED.* 1.4.1949.	75.00	150	—

Barclays Bank D.C.O.

1954 Issue

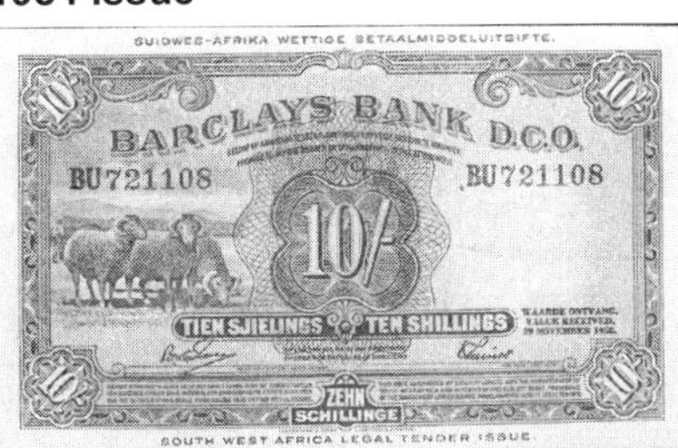

		Good	Fine	XF
4	**10 Shillings** 1954-1958. Red on multicolor underprint. Sheep at left. Bank title ending *D.C.O.* Back: Bank arms at lower center. Printer: W&S.			
	a. Date in red with *No.* before serial #. 30.11.1954; 1.9.1956.	40.00	125	350
	b. Date in black, without *No.* before serial #. 29.11.1958.	35.00	100	325

		Good	Fine	XF
5	**1 Pound** 1954-1958. Dark blue on green and multicolor underprint. Sheep at left. Bank title ending *D.C.O.* Back: Bank arms at lower center. Printer: W&S.			
	a. Date in blue without *No.* before serial #. 30.11.1954; 1.9.1956.	45.00	150	400
	b. Date in black, without *No.* before serial #. 29.11.1958.	40.00	125	350
	c. Punch hole cancelled. 29.11.1958.	20.00	50.00	—

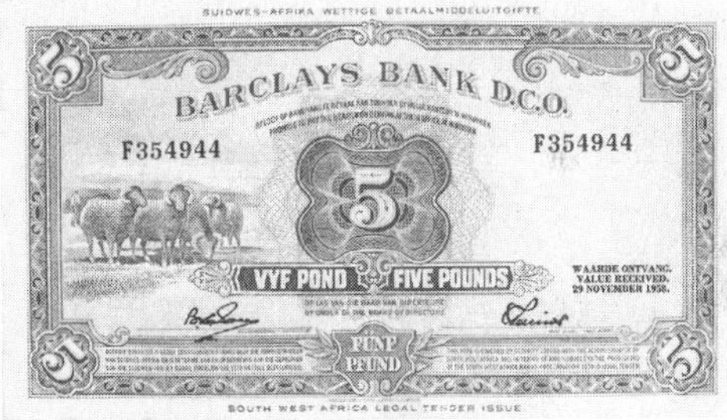

		Good	Fine	XF
6	**5 Pounds** 1954-1958. Dark green on red and multicolor underprint. Sheep at left. Bank title ending *D.C.O.* Back: Bank arms at lower center. Printer: W&S.			
	a. Date in green with *No.* before serial #. 30.11.1954; 1.9.1956.	110	250	550
	b. Date in black, without *No.* before serial #. 29.11.1958.	100	200	450
	c. Punch hole cancelled. 30.11.1954.	50.00	100	—

Standard Bank of South Africa Limited

1931 Issue

		Good	Fine	XF
7	**10 Shillings** 1931-1953. Green on multicolor underprint. Waterfalls at right. *TEN-TIEN SHILLINGS* at center. Signature varieties. Back: Kudu, mountains at left center. Printer: W&S.			
	a. 31.10.1931; 17.4.1936.	175	375	750
	b. 2.4.1940; 31.3.1942; 22.4.1943.	65.00	125	350
	c. 9.2.1945-4.10.1954.	50.00	100	300

8	1 Pound	Good	Fine	XF
	1931-1954. Orange on green and multicolor underprint. Sheep under tree at left. Waterfalls at right. Signature varieties. Back: Kudu, mountains at left center. Printer: W&S.			
	a. 31.10.1931.	225	550	—
	b. 11.1.1938; 2.4.1940; 2.5.1941; 31.3.1942; 1.10.1943; 5.8.1947; 9.8.1948.	65.00	150	375
	c. 6.2.1950-4.10.1954.	50.00	100	300
	d. Punch hole cancelled. 9.8.1948; 6.2.1950; 25.6.1951.	20.00	50.00	—

9	5 Pounds	Good	Fine	XF
	1931-1953. Carmine on green and multicolor underprint. Sheep under tree at left. Waterfalls at right. Signature varieties. Back: Kudu, mountains at left center. Printer: W&S.			
	a. 31.10.1931.	275	650	—
	b. 1933-9.2.1945.	175	375	875
	c. 6.2.1950; 25.6.1951; 21.9.1953.	125	300	625
	d. Punch hole cancelled. 6.2.1950.	60.00	150	—

1954; 1955 Issue

10	10 Shillings	Good	Fine	XF
	4.10.1954; 16.9.1955; 31.1.1958; 15.6.1959. Green on multicolor underprint. Waterfalls at right. Similar to #7, but value: *TEN SHILLINGS / TIEN SJIELINGS* at center. Signature varieties. Back: Kudu, mountains at left center.	50.00	100	275

11	1 Pound	Good	Fine	XF
	16.9.1955-15.6.1959. Orange on green and multicolor underprint. Sheep under tree at left. Waterfalls at right. Like #8. Signature varieties. Back: Kudu, mountains at left center.	65.00	125	350

12	5 Pounds	Good	Fine	XF
	1954-1958. Carmine and green on multicolor underprint. Sheep under tree at left. Waterfalls at right. Like #9. Signature varieties. Back: Kudu.			
	a. 4.10.1954; 16.9.1955.	120	250	600
	b. 1.9.1957; 1.5.1958; 20.11.1958.	110	225	550
	s. Specimen. Red overprint and punch hole cancelled.	—	Unc	2,500

Volkskas Limited

1949 Issue

13	10 Shillings	Good	Fine	XF
	1949-1958. Blue on green and tan underprint. Scattered buildings with mountains in background. Signature varieties. Printer: W&S.			
	a. 1.6.1949; 4.6.1952.	90.00	200	475
	b. 1.9.1958.	60.00	125	375

14	1 Pound	Good	Fine	XF
	1949-1958. Brown. Village scene at left center. Signature varieties. Printer: W&S.			
	a. 1.6.1949; 17.4.1951; 4.6.1952.	100	225	625
	b. 1.9.1958.	75.00	150	425

15	5 Pounds	Good	Fine	XF
	1949-1959. Brown. Waterfall at left. Signature varieties. Back: Gemsbok. Printer: W&S.			
	a. 1.6.1949; 4.6.1952.	200	450	975
	b. 1.9.1958; 1.9.1959.	140	400	775

The Spanish State, forming the greater part of the Iberian Peninsula of southwest Europe, has an area of 504,782 sq. km. and a population of 40.5 million. Capital: Madrid. The economy is based on agriculture, industry and tourism. Machinery, fruit, vegetables and chemicals are exported. Spain's powerful world empire of the 16th and 17th centuries ultimately yielded command of the seas to England. Subsequent failure to embrace the mercantile and industrial revolutions caused the country to fall behind Britain, France, and Germany in economic and political power. Spain remained neutral in World Wars I and II but suffered through a devastating civil war (1936-39). A peaceful transition to democracy following the death of dictator Francisco Franco in 1975, and rapid economic modernization (Spain joined the EU in 1986) gave Spain a dynamic and rapidly growing economy and made it a global champion of freedom and human rights. The government continues to battle the Basque Fatherland and Liberty (ETA) terrorist organization, but its major focus for the immediate future will be on measures to reverse the severe economic recession that started in mid-2008.

RULERS:

Fernando VII, 1808-1833
Isabel II, 1833-1868
Amadeo I, 1871-1873
Regency, 1874
Alfonso XII, 1875-1885
Alfonso XIII, 1886-1931
2nd Republic and Civil War, 1932-1936
Francisco Franco, regent, 1937-1975
Juan Carlos I, 1975-

MONETARY SYSTEM:

1 Peseta = 100 Centimos 1874-2001
1 Euro = 100 Cents, 2002-

FIRST REPUBLIC, 1873-1874

Banco de España

Paper currency began in Spain with government-sponsored issues of the Banco Nacional de San Carlos in 1782. In 1829 this bank was supplanted by the Banco Español de San Fernando and in 1844 by the Banco de Isabel II. These two merged in 1847. The Banco de España was established on January 28, 1856 and shortly thereafter it began issuing notes in its name. There were no less than 12 separate issues from 1856 to 1873. All of these early emissions are very rare and generally not available on the market. In 1874, the Banco de España became the sole issuing bank in Spain. Some early issues had branch city names stamped on face or back. In some issues serial # may or may not have a prefix letter.

1874 Issue

#		Good	Fine	XF
1	**25 Pesetas** 1.7.1874. Gray and cream. Bearers at left and right of center. Rare.	—	—	—

#		Good	Fine	XF
2	**50 Pesetas** 1.7.1874. Black and chestnut. D. Martinez at left. Rare.	—	—	—

#		Good	Fine	XF
3	**100 Pesetas** 1.7.1874. Ochre and black. Juan de Herrera at left, El Escorial Monastery at center. Rare.	—	—	—

#		Good	Fine	XF
4	**500 Pesetas** 1.7.1874. Black and cream. Woman seated at left, Francisco de Goya at right. Rare.	—	—	—
5	**1000 Pesetas** 1.7.1874. Black and cream. Minerva at left, Alonso Cana at right. Rare.	—	—	—

KINGDOM

Banco de España

1875 Issue

#		Good	Fine	XF
6	**25 Pesetas** 1.1.1875. Black on lilac underprint. Woman at left. Printer: Sanders (without imprint).	850	2,000	—

#		Good	Fine	XF
7	**50 Pesetas** 1.1.1875. Gray, green and salmon. Women leaning against arms at top center, woman at bottom center, children at upper left and right, lions at lower left and right. Printer: Sanders (without imprint). Rare.	—	—	—

#	Denomination	Good	Fine	XF
8	**100 Pesetas** 1.1.1875. Gray, green and orange. Woman by castle at left, woman at right. Printer: T. H. Saunders (without imprint). Rare.	—	—	—

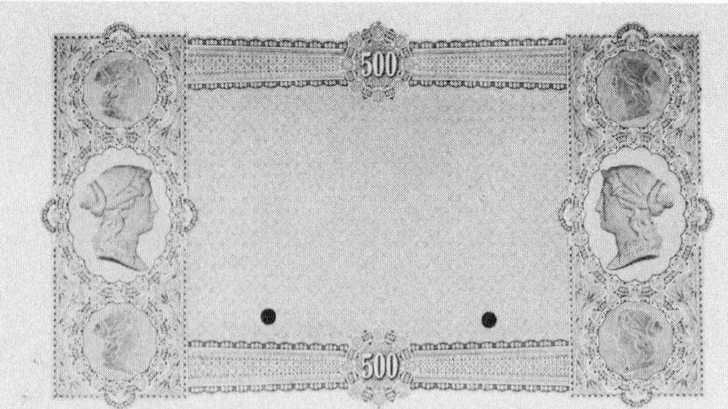

#	Denomination	Good	Fine	XF
9	**500 Pesetas** 1.1.1875. Gray and blue. Women at left and right. Printer: T. H. Saunders (without imprint). Rare.	—	—	—

Color Abbreviation Guide

New to the *Standard Catalog of® World Paper Money* are the following abbreviations related to color references:

BC: Back color
PC: Paper color

#	Denomination	Good	Fine	XF
10	**1000 Pesetas** 1.1.1875. Gray and brown. Woman with shield and spear at left, woman at right. Printer: T. H. Saunders (without imprint). Rare.	—	—	—

1876 Issue

#	Denomination	Good	Fine	XF
11	**100 Pesetas** 1.7.1876. Black on multicolor underprint. Lope de Vega at left. Woman with children at center, woman seated at right. Back: Ship at left and right, allegorical woman at center. BC: Dark brown. Printer: ABNC.	1,250	3,000	—
12	**500 Pesetas** 1.7.1876. Black on multicolor underprint. Lope de Vega at left. Woman reclining with children at top center, woman at lower right. Back: Steam train at center. BC: Red-brown. Printer: ABNC.	1,200	2,500	—

		Good	Fine	XF
13	**1000 Pesetas** 1.7.1876. Black on multicolor underprint. Lope de Vega at left. Spaniard with Indian maiden at center, Liberty at lower right. Back: Allegorical women at left and right, two allegorical women at center. BC: Brown. Printer: ABNC.	2,000	4,000	—

1878 Issue

		Good	Fine	XF
14	**50 Pesetas** 1.1.1878. Gray and black. Pedro Calderón de la Barca at right.	1,000	2,000	—

		Good	Fine	XF
15	**100 Pesetas** 1.1.1878. Ochre and gray. Garcilaso de la Vega at left, woman with laureate at right.	1,300	3,000	—

#16 not assigned.

		Good	Fine	XF
17	**250 Pesetas** 1.1.1878. Orange and gray. F. de Herrera at left.	1,400	4,000	—
18	**500 Pesetas** 1.1.1878. Cream and gray-black. P. de Cespedes at left, woman with helmet at right.	1,600	4,250	—
19	**1000 Pesetas** 1.1.1878. Green and black. Miguel de Cervantes at left, rider on donkey at center.	2,200	5,000	—

1880 Issue

		Good	Fine	XF
20	**50 Pesetas** 1.4.1880. Rose and gray-green. Count Pedro Rodrígues de Campomanes at left.	1,200	2,000	—

		Good	Fine	XF
21	**100 Pesetas** 1.4.1880. Green and orange. Francisco de Quevedo at left, woman with laureate at right.	1,400	2,600	—

		Good	Fine	XF
22	**500 Pesetas** 1.4.1880. Chestnut and ochre. Claudio Coello at left.	1,400	2,800	—

		Good	Fine	XF
23	**1000 Pesetas** 1.4.1880. Green and black. Bartolomé Murillo at left.	2,200	4,300	—

1884 First Issue

		Good	Fine	XF
24	**25 Pesetas** 1.1.1884. Red and black. Woman with two children at center. Back: Arms at center. BC: Orange. Printer: ABNC.	250	450	800

		Good	Fine	XF
25	**50 Pesetas** 1.1.1884. Black on green underprint. Woman seated by globe at left. Portrait Juan Alvarez de Mendizábal at right. Back: Woman and eagle at center. BC: Green. Printer: ABNC.	200	500	900

No.	Denomination	Good	Fine	XF
26	**100 Pesetas** 1.1.1884. Black on orange underprint. Cherubs at center. Portrait Juan Alvarez de Mendizábal at right. BC: Orange. Printer: ABNC.	275	550	950
27	**500 Pesetas** 1.1.1884. Black on ochre underprint. Woman with sword at left, cherub at center. Portrait Juan Alvarez de Mendizábal at right. Back: Arms at center. BC: Ochre. Printer: ABNC.	800	1,500	3,000

No.	Denomination	Good	Fine	XF
28	**1000 Pesetas** 1.1.1884. Black on orange underprint. Woman bearer at left, portrait Mendizábal at center, woman standing at right. Back: Dog and safe at center. BC: Brown. Printer: ABNC.	1,250	2,500	4,500

1884 Second Issue

No.	Denomination	Good	Fine	XF
29	**25 Pesetas** 1.7.1884. Ochre and black. Portrait Ramón de Santillan at center.	375	750	1,200
30	**50 Pesetas** 1.7.1884. Black on tan underprint. Portrait Bartolomé Murillo at center. BC: Blue.	350	600	1,100

No.	Denomination	Good	Fine	XF
31	**100 Pesetas** 1.7.1884. Black on light tan underprint. Portrait A. Mon at top center. Back: Old locomotive at center. BC: Green.	250	500	1,000

No.	Denomination	Good	Fine	XF
32	**500 Pesetas** 1.7.1884. Black, chestnut and green. Girl with dog at left, portrait José Moñino y Redondo, Count de Floridablanca at right.	1,250	2,500	3,600

No.	Denomination	Good	Fine	XF
33	**1000 Pesetas** 1.7.1884. Green and black. Portrait Marqués de la Ensenada at left, women at right, one holding sheaf and sickle.	1,600	3,250	5,000

1886 Issue

No.	Denomination	Good	Fine	XF
34	**25 Pesetas** 1.10.1886. Black on pale gold underprint. Francisco de Goya at center. BC: Red.	150	500	900

		Good	Fine	XF
35	**50 Pesetas** 1.10.1886. Chestnut. Woman with child at left, Francisco de Goya at right.	350	700	1,250
36	**100 Pesetas** 1.10.1886. Chestnut. Man standing at left, Francisco de Goya at right.	225	550	1,300
37	**500 Pesetas** 1.10.1886. Ochre and black. Francisco de Goya at left, woman seated at right.	700	1,600	4,000

		Good	Fine	XF
38	**1000 Pesetas** 1.10.1886. Yellow and black. Woman seated with harp at left. Francisco de Goya seated behind table at right.	1,250	2,500	6,000

1889 Issue

		Good	Fine	XF
39	**25 Pesetas** 1.6.1889. Black on gold underprint. Francisco de Goya at center. Similar to #34. Back: Creso at center. BC: Brown.	175	350	700
40	**50 Pesetas** 1.6.1889. Black on yellow underprint. Woman with child at left, Francisco de Goya at right. Similar to #35. Back: Two cherubs. BC: Green.	300	550	900
41	**100 Pesetas** 1.6.1889. Black on yellow underprint. Man standing at left, Francisco de Goya at right. Similar to #36. Back: Woman and cherub at center. BC: Brown.	125	250	600

1893 Issue

		Good	Fine	XF
42	**25 Pesetas** 24.7.1893. Blue and yellow. Portrait Gaspar Melchor de Jovellanos at left. Back: Medallion at center, standing figure at right.	125	225	525
43	**50 Pesetas** 24.7.1893. Black on yellow underprint. Portrait Gaspar Melchor de Jovellanos at left. Seated woman at right with sword across lap. Back: Cherubs and winged head at center. BC: Green.	200	350	625

		Good	Fine	XF
44	**100 Pesetas** 24.7.1893. Blue on pale yellow underprint. Portrait Gaspar Medlchor de Jovellanos at left. Back: Heads at left and right. BC: Brown.	150	350	625

1895 Issue

		Good	Fine	XF
45	**1000 Pesetas** 1.5.1895. Black on light tan underprint. El Conde Francisco de Cabarrus at left with child leaning on frame. Back: King Carlos III and lion. BC: Brown.	175	375	800

1898 Issue

		VG	VF	UNC
46	**5 Pesetas** 1898. Queen Isabel la Católica at left. Back proof. (Not issued).	—	—	—

		Good	Fine	XF
47	**50 Pesetas** 2.1.1898. Black and yellow. Gaspar Melchor de Jovellanos at left, helmeted woman at right.	150	300	600
48	**100 Pesetas** 24.6.1898. Blue and yellow. Gaspar Melchor de Jovellanos at left.	90.00	200	500

1899 Issue

		Good	Fine	XF
49	**25 Pesetas** 17.5.1899. Blue on pale green underprint. Francisco de Quevedo at left. Back: Head at center, Mercury at right. BC: Brown.	90.00	200	500
50	**50 Pesetas** 25.11.1899. Black on pale green underprint. Francisco de Quevedo at left, statue of man at right. Back: Woman reclining at left, man at right. BC: Green.	130	300	550

1900 Issue

		Good	Fine	XF
51	**100 Pesetas** 1.5.1900. Blue on light green underprint. Francisco de Quevedo at left, medallic portrait at right. Back: Cherubs and Athena. BC: Brown.			
	a. Issued note.	130	275	600
	s. Specimen.	—	Unc	300

1902-1903 Issue

		Good	Fine	XF
52	**50 Pesetas** 30.11.1902. Black and yellow. Diego Velázquez at left.	150	450	1,000

		Good	Fine	XF
53	**100 Pesetas** 1903; 1905. Gray. Man standing with spade in hand at left, small child on knees with arm uplifting palm branch at right.			
	a. Issued note. 1.7.1903.	600	1,500	3,000
	s1. As a. Specimen.	—	Unc	600
	s2. Specimen. 21.8.1905.	—		

		Good	Fine	XF
54	**500 Pesetas** 1.10.1903. Grayish-blue. Man and arms spread as if in flight at top center.			
	a. Issued note.	1,500	2,750	4,000
	b. Half finished print without underprint. Punch hole cancelled.	—	Unc	250

1904-1905 Issue

		VG	VF	UNC
55	**25 Pesetas** 1.1.1904. Blue-green. Standing figures at left and right. (Not issued).	—	—	1,300

		Good	Fine	XF
56	**50 Pesetas** 19.3.1905. Ochre, green and gray. José Echegaray at left.	175	375	1,000

Provisional Republic Validation, 1931 Certain issues following have a round embossed validation applied by the Republic in 1931. This validation consists of crowned Spanish arms with 2 laurel branches at center, legend around: *GOBIERNO PROVISIONAL DE LA REPúBLICA 14 ABRIL 1931.* Notes of 25, 50 and 100 Pesetas had it applied to the upper left corner, and those of 500 and 1000 Pesetas to the upper right corner. The embossing is not easily discernible.

1906 Issue

		Good	Fine	XF
57	**25 Pesetas** 24.9.1906. Black and blue. Woman seated at left. Printer: BWC.			
	a. Issued note.	25.00	75.00	140
	b. Round embossed Republic validation at upper left corner 1931.	35.00	100	225
	s. Specimen.	—	—	—

		Good	Fine	XF
58	**50 Pesetas** 24.9.1906. Gray-violet and green. Woman standing with caduceus by globe at center. Printer: BWC.			
	a. Issued note.	27.50	85.00	175
	b. Round embossed Republic validation at upper left corner 1931.	35.00	95.00	210
	s. Specimen.	—	—	—

		Good	Fine	XF
59	**100 Pesetas** 30.6.1906. Black and blue. Women seated at left and right. Printer: BWC.			
	a. Issued note.	30.00	90.00	225
	b. Round embossed Republic validation at upper left corner 1931.	75.00	180	425
	s. Specimen.	—	—	—

Note: #59 is also reported with oval handstamp similar to #80.

1907 First Issue

No.		Good	Fine	XF
60	**500 Pesetas** 28.1.1907. Black on green and violet underprint. Women reclining at left and right, leaning against medallic portrait of king at center. Back: Arms at center. BC: Green. Printer: BWC.			
	a. Issued note.	400	1,000	2,500
	s. Specimen.	—	—	—
61	**1000 Pesetas** 10.5.1907. Black on blue underprint. Mercury with globe on shoulder at left, shield with castle at lower left, shield with rampant lion at lower right. Back: Woman with sword and lion at center. BC: Brown.	Good	Fine	XF
	a. Issued note.	400	1,000	2,500
	s. Specimen.	—	—	—

1907 Second Issue

No.		Good	Fine	XF
62	**25 Pesetas** 15.7.1907. Black on dark pink and green underprint. Woman reclining at center. Back: Alhambra de Granada. Printer: BWC.			
	a. Issued note.	27.50	90.00	200
	b. Round embossed Republic validation at upper left corner 1931.	40.00	120	250
	s. Specimen.	—	—	—

No.		Good	Fine	XF
63	**50 Pesetas** 15.7.1907. Black on yellow, red and blue underprint. Woman standing at left and right. Back: Cathedral of Burgos. Printer: BWC.			
	a. Issued note.	27.50	85.00	185
	b. Round embossed Republic validation at upper left corner 1931.	45.00	120	250
	s. Specimen.	—	—	—
64	**100 Pesetas** 15.7.1907. Green, red, yellow and black. Woman seated at left, medallic male portrait at center. Back: Cathedral of Seville. Printer: BWC.	Good	Fine	XF
	a. Issued note.	20.00	65.00	140
	b. Round embossed Republic validation at upper left corner 1931.	40.00	120	250
	s. Specimen.	—	—	—

No.		Good	Fine	XF
65	**500 Pesetas** 15.7.1907. Red, green and black. Woman standing at left, cherubs at lower right. Back: Alcázar de Segovia. Printer: BWC.			
	a. Issued note.	150	375	750
	b. Round embossed Republic validation at upper right corner 1931.	120	275	550
	s. Specimen.	—	—	—
66	**1000 Pesetas** 15.7.1907. Black on ochre and red underprint. Woman seated on throne by medallic female portrait at center. Back: Palacio Real de Madrid. Printer: BWC.	Good	Fine	XF
	a. Issued note.	185	450	1,000
	b. Round embossed Republic validation at upper right corner 1931.	160	385	850
	s. Specimen.	—	—	—

1908 Issue

No.		Good	Fine	XF
67	**25 Pesetas** 1.12.1908. Manuel José Quintana at left.			
	p1. Color trial of face.	—	—	—
	p2. Color trial of back (several colors known).	—	—	—

No.		VG	VF	UNC
68	**100 Pesetas** 1.12.1908. Blue. Conjoined portraits of King Fernando and Queen Isabel at left. (Not issued).	—	—	—

Color Abbreviation Guide

New to the *Standard Catalog of® World Paper Money* are the following abbreviations related to color references:

BC: Back color
PC: Paper color

1914; 1915 Issue

		VG	VF	UNC
68A	**5 Pesetas** 1914. Fernando VI at left. (Not issued).	—	—	4,000

		VG	VF	UNC
68B	**1000 Pesetas** 23.5.1915. Conjoined portraits of Alfonso XIII and Victoria Eugenia at left. (Not issued).	—	—	4,000

1925 Issue

		VG	VF	UNC
69	**100 Pesetas** 1.7.1925. Dark blue and green on multicolor underprint. Felipe II at left. Monastery of El Escorial at lower center. Back: Retreat of Felipe II. BC: Blue and orange. Watermark: Felipe II. Printer: BWC.			
	a. Serial # without series letter, Series A-C, and Series D to 2,000,000.	20.00	60.00	135
	b. Round embossed Republic validation at upper left corner 1931.	30.00	70.00	160
	c. Serial # D2,000,001 through Series F, Republic issue (1936).	6.00	20.00	55.00
	d. Series G. (5 million printed but not released).	—	—	—
	s. Specimen.	—	—	—

Note: 5 million Series G notes were printed but not released.

		VG	VF	UNC
69A	**500 Pesetas** 23.1.1925. Cardinal Cisneros at left. (Not issued).	—	—	3,500

		VG	VF	UNC
70	**1000 Pesetas** 1.7.1925. Chestnut, red and violet. King Carlos I at right, gorgon head at top center. Back: Alcázar de Toledo. Printer: BWC.			
	a. Serial # to 3,646,000.	35.00	90.00	225
	b. Round embossed Republic validation at upper right corner 1931.	40.00	100	250
	c. Serial # 3,646,001 to 5,000,000, Republic issue (1936).	25.00	65.00	150
	s. Specimen.	—	—	—

1926; 1927 Issue

		VG	VF	UNC
71	**25 Pesetas** 12.10.1926. Blue and violet on multicolor underprint. St. Xavier at left. Back: St. Xavier baptizing Indians. BC: Red-brown. Watermark: Queen. Printer: BWC.			
	a. Issued note.	18.00	50.00	120
	b. Round embossed Republic validation at upper left corner 1931.	65.00	160	—
	s. Specimen.	—	—	—

No.	Description	VG	VF	UNC
72	**50 Pesetas** 17.5.1927. Purple and violet on orange and yellow underprint. King Alfonso XIII at left, fortified city at lower center. Back: Founding of Buenos Aires. BC: Blue. Watermark: Queen. Printer: BWC.			
	a. Issued note.	60.00	150	375
	b. Round embossed Republic validation at upper left corner 1931.	110	275	—
	s. Specimen.	—	—	—

Note: #72 was validated by the Republic with oval handstamp (see #80).

No.	Description	VG	VF	UNC
73	**500 Pesetas** 24.7.1927. Blue and brown on orange and green underprint. Lions Court at Alhambra at center, Isabel la Católica at right. Back: Arms. BC: Red and purple. Printer: BWC.			
	a. Serial # to 1,602,000.	100	300	—
	b. Round embossed Republic validation at upper right corner 1931.	100	300	—
	c. Serial # 1,602,001 to 2,000,000, Republic issue (1936).	35.00	100	—

1928 Issue

Circulation of 1928-dated notes: part of the issue of 25 and 50 Pesetas was released before July 18, 1936, the date at which recognition by the Nationalist government of further issues was cut off. None of the 100, 500 or 1000 Pesetas were released before that date; therefore, they are all considered as issues of the Republic only.

No.	Description	VG	VF	UNC
74	**25 Pesetas** 15.8.1928. Blue and brown on multicolor underprint. Monument at center, Pedro Calderón de la Barca at right. Back: Religious comedy scene. BC: Lilac. Watermark: Woman. Printer: BWC.			
	a. Serial # without series letter, also Series A through 7,780,000.	30.00	80.00	200
	b. Serial # A7,780,001 through Series E, Republic issue.	4.00	15.00	35.00
	s. Specimen.	—	—	—

No.	Description	VG	VF	UNC
75	**50 Pesetas** 15.8.1928. Violet and black on pale blue and dull orange underprint. Prado Museum in Madrid at lower left and center, Diego Velázquez at right. Back: Painting *La rendición de Breda* by Velázquez. Watermark: Woman. Printer: BWC.			
	a. Serial # without series letter, also Series A through 8,640,000.	8.00	25.00	70.00
	b. Serial # A8,640,001 through Series E, Republic issue.	3.00	100	25.00
	s. Specimen.	—	—	—

No.	Description	VG	VF	UNC
76	**100 Pesetas** 15.8.1928. Purple and black on multicolor underprint. Miguel de Cervantes at left, monument at center. Back: Painting of *Don Quijote* by Pidal. Watermark: Miguel de Cervantes. Printer: BWC.			
	a. Issued note.	4.00	15.00	35.00
	s. Specimen.	—	—	—

Note: Position of Cervantes' head in relation to border on #76 varies considerably.

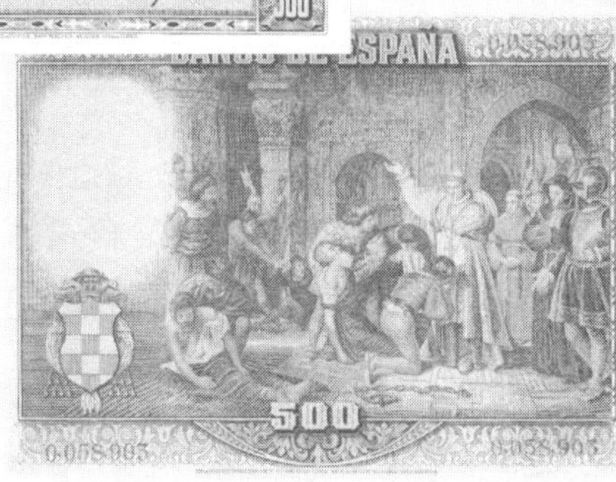

		VG	VF	UNC
77	**500 Pesetas** 15.8.1928. Purple and green on multicolor underprint. Cathedral of Toledo at lower left, Cardinal Cisneros above. Back: Picture by Casanova showing liberation of captives. Printer: BWC.			
	a. Issued note.	20.00	60.00	140
	s. Specimen.	—	—	—

		VG	VF	UNC
78	**1000 Pesetas** 15.8.1928. Blue and purple on multicolor underprint. Cathedral of Seville at lower left, San Fernando at right. Back: Painting of King receiving communion by A. Ferrant. BC: Red-brown. Printer: BWC.			
	a. Issued note.	18.00	50.00	120
	s. Specimen.	—	—	—

REPUBLIC

Banco de España

1931 Provisional Issue

Aside from the embossed notes (see #57b, 58b, 59b, 61b, 62b, 63b, 64b, 65b, 66b, 69b, 70b, 71b, 72b, 73b), the Provisional Government had at first authorized the overstamping of the 50 Pesetas (#72, with portrait of Alfonso XIII) with a purple oval handstamp consisting of arms at center and legend *REPúBLICA ESPAOLA* around. An earlier 50 Pesetas issue (#59) and other older notes are also reported with this handstamp.

		VG	VF	UNC
80	**50 Pesetas** ND (1931 -old date 17.5.1927) . Purple and violet on orange and yellow underprint. King Alfonso XIII at left, fortified city at lower center. Republican handstamp over portrait at left on #72. Back: Founding of Buenos Aires.			
	a. Issued note.	35.00	90.00	275
	b. Horizontal handstamp.	50.00	120	700

1931 Issue

		VG	VF	UNC
81	**25 Pesetas** 25.4.1931. Green and brown on multicolor underprint. Vicente López at right. Back: López's painting *Music*. BC: Brown. Watermark: Woman in Phrygian cap. Printer: BWC.	9.00	30.00	85.00

		VG	VF	UNC
82	**50 Pesetas** 25.4.1931. Blue, lilac and violet. Eduardo Rosales at left. Back: Rosales' painting *The Death of Lucretia*. Watermark: Woman. Printer: BWC.	9.00	30.00	85.00

		VG	VF	UNC
83	**100 Pesetas** 25.4.1931. Purple and black on blue, tan and multicolor underprint. Gonzalo Fernández de Córdoba at left. Back: Painting by Casado del Alisal. BC: Green. Watermark: Helmeted man. Printer: BWC.	9.00	30.00	85.00

		VG	VF	UNC
84	**500 Pesetas** 25.4.1931. Chestnut and blue on multicolor underprint. Juan Sebastián de Elcano at left. Back: Elias Salaverria's painting *Disembarkation*. Watermark: King. Printer: BWC.	18.00	60.00	175

		VG	VF	UNC
84A	**1000 Pesetas** 25.4.1931. Green. José Zorrilla at upper left. Back: Zorrilla reading his poems at gathering. Printer: BWC. (Not issued).			
	a. Unissued note.	—	—	3,000
	s. Specimen.	—	—	—

1935 (1936) Silver Certificates

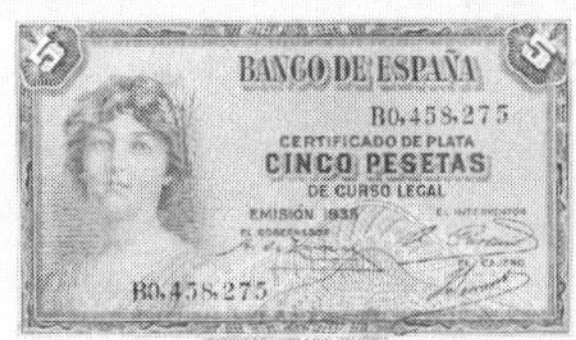

		VG	VF	UNC
85	**5 Pesetas** 1935 (1936). Green and violet. Woman at left. Printer: BWC.			
	a. Issued note.	2.50	8.00	25.00
	s. Specimen.	—	—	—

		VG	VF	UNC
86	**10 Pesetas** 1935 (1936). Red-brown and blue. Woman at right. Printer: BWC.			
	a. Issued note.	2.75	9.00	30.00
	s. Specimen.	—	—	—

1935; 1936 (1938) Regular Issue

		VG	VF	UNC
87	**25 Pesetas** 31.8.1936 (1938). Blue, chestnut and purple. Joaquín Sorolla at left, church steeple at right center. Back: Picture by Sorolla. BC: Purple. Printer: TDLR.			
	a. Issued note.	30.00	85.00	250
	b. Series A.	90.00	250	700

		VG	VF	UNC
88	**50 Pesetas** 22.7.1935. Purple and black on multicolor underprint. Santiago Ramón y Cajal at right, woman on column supports at left and right. Back: Monument. BC: Blue. Watermark: Santiago Ramón y Cajal. Printer: TDLR.			
	a. Issued note.	4.50	15.00	40.00
	b. Series A.	15.00	40.00	300

		VG	VF	UNC
89	**500 Pesetas** 7.1.1935. Chestnut, green. Hernán Cortez at left, his palace in Mexico at lower right center. Back: Painting of Cortez burning his ships. BC: Red and purple. Printer: TDLR.	100	275	750

1938 Issues

#90-92 Not assigned.

		VG	VF	UNC
90	**100 Pesetas** 11.3.1938. Barcelona. Carving of Dame of Elche at left, boat at center. Back: Roadway with palms. Printer: TDLR. (Not issued).			
	a. Unissued note.	—	—	10,000
	s. Specimen.	—	—	—
	ct. Color trials. Brown.	—	—	—
91	**100 Pesetas** 15.8.1938. Gray. Barcelona. Without vignettes. Spanish printing.	VG	VF	UNC
	a. Issued note.	—	—	3,000
	b. Ochre/yellow.	—	—	3,000
	c. Green.	—	—	3,000

		VG	VF	UNC
92	**5000 Pesetas** 11.6.1938. Barcelona. Mariano Fortuny at right. Back: Fortuny's picture *La Vicaria*. Printer: BWC. (Not issued).	—	—	9,000

Ministerio de Hacienda

Ministry of Finance

1937-1938 Issue

		VG	VF	UNC
93	**50 Centimos** 1937. Blue on pink underprint. Woman at center. BC: Green.	2.00	8.00	20.00

		VG	VF	UNC
94	**1 Peseta** 1937. Brown and green. Nike of Samothrace at left. Back: La Cibeles Fountain in Madrid. BC: Purple and gold.			
	a. Issued note.	2.25	9.00	25.00
	b. Series C.	—	—	100

		VG	VF	UNC
95	**2 Pesetas** 1938. Blue, brown and green. Woman at center. Back: Toledo Bridge in Madrid. BC: Gray and purple.	2.25	9.00	25.00

Postage Stamp/Disk Issues

1938 Correos "Numeral" Series

		VG	VF	UNC
96	**5 Centimos** ND (1938). Brown. Postage stamps with large numerals. Arms.	1.50	6.00	15.00

		VG	VF	UNC
96A	**10 Centimos** ND (1938). Green. Postage stamps with large numerals. Arms.	1.50	6.00	15.00
96B	**15 Centimos** ND (1938). Gray. Postage stamps with large numerals. Arms.	1.50	6.00	15.00
96C	**20 Centimos** ND (1938). Violet. Postage stamps with large numerals. Arms.	1.50	6.00	15.00

		VG	VF	UNC
96D	**25 Centimos** ND (1938). Brown-violet. Postage stamps with large numerals. Arms.	1.50	6.00	15.00
96E	**30 Centimos** ND (1938). Rose. Postage stamps with large numerals. Arms.	1.50	6.00	15.00

1938 Correos "Portrait" Series

		VG	VF	UNC
96F	**5 Centimos** ND (1938). Dark brown. Postage stamps with portrait. Arms.	1.50	6.00	15.00
96G	**10 Centimos** ND (1938). Postage stamps with portrait. Arms.	1.50	6.00	15.00
96H	**15 Centimos** ND (1938). Postage stamps with portrait. Arms.	1.50	6.00	15.00
96I	**25 Centimos** ND (1938). Red-violet. Postage stamps with portrait. Arms.	1.50	6.00	15.00
96J	**30 Centimos** ND (1938). Postage stamps with portrait. Arms.	1.50	6.00	15.00
96K	**40 Centimos** ND (1938). Postage stamps with portrait. Arms.	1.50	6.00	15.00
96L	**45 Centimos** ND (1938). Red. Postage stamps with portrait. Arms.	1.50	6.00	15.00
96M	**50 Centimos** ND (1938). Postage stamps with portrait. Arms.	1.50	6.00	15.00
96N	**60 Centimos** ND (1938). Postage stamps with portrait. Arms.	1.50	6.00	15.00

1938 Especial Movil (Revenue) Series

		VG	VF	UNC
96O	**5 Centimos** ND (1938). Blue. Revenue stamps with large crowned arms between pillars (Type 1).	1.50	6.00	15.00
96P	**10 Centimos** ND (1938). Brown. Revenue stamps with large crowned arms between pillars (Type 1).	1.50	6.00	15.00
96Q	**15 Centimos** ND (1938). Gray-green. Revenue stamps with large crowned arms between pillars (Type 1).	1.50	6.00	15.00
96R	**15 Centimos** ND (1938). Red. Revenue stamps with large crowned arms between sprays (Type II).	1.50	6.00	15.00
96S	**30 Centimos** ND (1938).	1.50	6.00	15.00
96T	**50 Centimos** ND (1938). Red. Revenue stamps with large crowned arms between pillars (Type 1).	1.50	6.00	15.00

REGENCY

Banco de España

1936 Issue

		VG	VF	UNC
97	**5 Pesetas** 21.11.1936. Brown on blue-green underprint. Arms at right.			
	a. Issued note.	300	850	2,500
	s. Specimen.	—	—	—

		VG	VF	UNC
98	**10 Pesetas** 21.11.1936. Blue and orange. Arms at right.			
	a. Issued note.	300	850	2,500
	s. Specimen.	—	—	—
99	**25 Pesetas** 21.11.1936. Blue on olive underprint. Back: Head. Printer: G&D (without imprint).	VG	VF	UNC
	a. Issued note.	35.00	90.00	275
	s. Specimen.	—	—	—

		VG	VF	UNC
100	**50 Pesetas** 21.11.1936. Brown on green underprint. Back: Head at left and right. Printer: G&D (without imprint).			
	a. Issued note.	120	325	800
	s. Specimen.	—	—	—
101	**100 Pesetas** 21.11.1936. Green on light green and orange underprint. Back: Cathedral of Burgos. Printer: G&D (without imprint).	VG	VF	UNC
	a. Issued note.	30.00	85.00	250
	s. Specimen.	—	—	—

		VG	VF	UNC
102	**500 Pesetas** 21.11.1936. Dark blue. Back: Cathedral of Salamanca. Printer: G&D (without imprint).			
	a. Issued note.	350	1,000	3,000
	s. Specimen.	—	—	—
103	**1000 Pesetas** 21.11.1936. Green. Back: Old bridge and building. Printer: G&D (without imprint).	VG	VF	UNC
	a. Issued note.	350	1,000	3,000
	s. Specimen.	—	—	—

1937 Issue

		VG	VF	UNC
104	**1 Peseta** 12.10.1937. Lilac on blue underprint. Arms at left. BC: Purple on brown underprint. Printer: Coen, Milano.			
	a. Issued note.	27.50	75.00	200
	s. Specimen.	—	—	—
105	**2 Pesetas** 12.10.1937. Dark green on light orange and light lilac underprint. Gothic church in Burgos at left. BC: Bluish black. Printer: Coen, Milano.	VG	VF	UNC
	a. Issued note.	35.00	90.00	275
	s. Specimen.	—	—	—

		VG	VF	UNC
106	**5 Pesetas** 18.7.1937. Brown on tan underprint. Woman holding caduceus at right. Series A-C. Back: Arms at center. BC: Orange. Printer: Lit. M. Portabella Zaragoza.			
	a. Issued note.	45.00	120	350
	s. Specimen.	—	—	—
106A	**25 Pesetas** 18.7.1937. Columbus at left. Back: Columbus at the "New World". Printer: Italian. Not issued. Rare.	—	1,500	—

106B	50 Pesetas	VG	VF	UNC
	18.7.1937. Printer: Italian. Not issued. Rare.	—	1,500	—

106C	100 Pesetas	VG	VF	UNC
	18.7.1937. Gen. Castaños at right. Back: Battle of Bailén. Printer: Italian. Not issued. Rare.	—	1,500	—
106D	500 Pesetas	VG	VF	UNC
	18.7.1937. Printer: Italian. Not issued. Rare.	—	1,500	—
106E	1000 Pesetas	VG	VF	UNC
	18.7.1937. Carlos V at center. Back: Battle scene. Printer: Italian. Not issued. Rare.	—	2,000	—

1938 Issue

107	1 Peseta	VG	VF	UNC
	28.2.1938. Brown on green underprint. Arms at left. BC: Purple. Printer: Coen, Milano.			
	a. Issued note.	6.00	20.00	75.00
	s. Specimen.	—	—	—

108	1 Peseta	VG	VF	UNC
	30.4.1938. Brown on green underprint. Arms at left. Like #107. BC: Purple. Printer: Coen, Milano.			
	a. Issued note.	6.00	17.50	70.00
	s. Specimen.	—	—	—

109	2 Pesetas	VG	VF	UNC
	30.4.1938. Dark green on orange and lilac underprint. Gothic church in Burgos at left. Like #105. Printer: Coen, Milano.			
	a. Issued note.	8.00	27.50	100
	s. Specimen.	—	—	—

110	5 Pesetas	VG	VF	UNC
	10.8.1938. Green and red on light brown underprint. Arms in underprint. Printer: G&D.			
	a. Issued note.	10.00	35.00	120
	s. Specimen.	—	—	—
111	25 Pesetas	VG	VF	UNC
	20.5.1938. Green and pink. Arms in underprint. Back: Giralda in Seville. Printer: G&D.			
	a. Issued note.	40.00	150	400
	s. Specimen.	—	—	—
112	50 Pesetas	VG	VF	UNC
	20.5.1938. Red-brown and green. Arms in underprint. Back: Castle at Olite. Printer: G&D.			
	a. Issued note.	35.00	140	375
	s. Specimen.	—	—	—
113	100 Pesetas	VG	VF	UNC
	20.5.1938. Lilac-brown and orange. Arms in underprint. Back: House of Cordón in Burgos. Printer: G&D.			
	a. Issued note.	35.00	135	350
	s. Specimen.	—	—	—
114	500 Pesetas	VG	VF	UNC
	20.5.1938. Yellow-green and lilac. Arms in underprint. Back: Cathedral of Santiago. Printer: G&D.			
	a. Issued note.	175	700	2,000
	s. Specimen.	—	—	—

115	1000 Pesetas	VG	VF	UNC
	20.5.1938. Blue and red. Arms in underprint. Back: Historic picture. Printer: G&D.			
	a. Issued note.	225	800	2,500
	s. Specimen.	—	—	—

1940 First Issue

116	25 Pesetas	VG	VF	UNC
	9.1.1940 (1943). Gray-blue on light brown underprint. Juan de Herrera at left, Patio de los Evangelistas en El Escorial at right. Back: Arms at left. Printer: Calcografia & Cartevalori, Milano, Italia.			
	a. Issued note.	50.00	175	500
	s. Specimen.	—	—	—
117	50 Pesetas	VG	VF	UNC
	9.1.1940 (1943). Green on blue and orange underprint. Menendez Pelayo at left. Back: Arms at center. BC: Light blue-gray. Printer: Calcografia & Cartevalori, Milano, Italia.			
	a. Issued note.	20.00	75.00	225
	s. Specimen.	—	—	—

118	100 Pesetas	VG	VF	UNC
	9.1.1940 (1943). Lilac-brown on green underprint. Columbus at center, allegorical woman at either side. Back: Arms at center. Printer: Calcografia & Cartevalori, Milano, Italia.			
	a. Issued note.	25.00	90.00	250
	s. Specimen.	—	—	—

119	500 Pesetas	VG	VF	UNC
	9.1.1940 (1945). Dark green. John of Austria at right. Back: Battle of Lepanto with old ships. Printer: Calcografia & Cartevalori, Milano, Italia.			
	a. Issued note.	175	500	1,500
	s. Specimen.	—	—	—

120	1000 Pesetas	VG	VF	UNC
	9.1.1940. Issue of 12.11.1943. Gray and brown. Bartolomé Murillo at center. Back: Murillo painting *Children Counting Money.* BC: Maroon and brown. Printer: Calcografia & Cartevalori, Milano, Italia.			
	a. Issued note.	250	700	2,000
	s. Specimen.	—	—	—

1940 Second Issue

121	1 Peseta	VG	VF	UNC
	1.6.1940. Blue and orange. Hernán Cortez on horseback at right. Back: Arms at center. BC: Brown. Printer: Graficas Reunidas S. A., Madrid.			
	a. Issued note.	17.50	80.00	225
	s. Specimen.	—	—	—

122	1 Peseta	VG	VF	UNC
	4.9.1940. Black on gold and blue underprint. Sailing ship Santa María at center. BC: Dark green on purple underprint. Printer: Rieusset S.A. Barcelona.			
	a. Issued note.	12.00	45.00	130
	s. Specimen.	—	—	—

123	5 Pesetas	VG	VF	UNC
	4.9.1940. Dark brown and blue-green on orange and green underprint. Arms at left, Alcázar of Segovia at right. BC: Blue and green. Printer: G&D.			
	a. Issued note.	20.00	70.00	200
	s. Specimen.	—	—	—

124	500 Pesetas	VG	VF	UNC
	21.10.1940. Black on light green, gold and pink underprint. Conde de Orgaz (Death Scene) by El Greco at right. Back: View of Toledo at center. BC: Gray on gold underprint. Printer: FNMT. Issue of Feb. 1947.			
	a. Issued note.	160	450	1,250
	s. Specimen.	—	—	—

125	1000 Pesetas	VG	VF	UNC
	21.10.1940. Lilac and violet. Portrait helmeted King Carlos I at left. Back: Arms of King Carlos I. Printer: FNMT.			
	a. Issued note.	175	500	1,500
	s. Specimen.	—	—	—

1943 Issue

126	1 Peseta	VG	VF	UNC
	21.5.1943. Dark brown on multicolor underprint. King Fernando el católico at left. Back: Columbus landing. Printer: FNMT.			
	a. Issued note.	3.50	12.50	40.00
	s. Specimen.	—	—	—

127	5 Pesetas	VG	VF	UNC
	13.2.1943. Black on multicolor underprint. Queen Isabel la Católica at left. Back: Columbus with his men at center. Printer: FNMT.			
	a. Issued note.	12.00	45.00	150
	s. Specimen.	—	—	—

1945 Issue

128	1 Peseta	VG	VF	UNC
	15.6.1945. Brown on multicolor underprint. Queen Isabel la Católica at left. Back: Man with old map. Printer: FNMT.			
	a. Issued note.	3.50	12.50	40.00
	s. Specimen.	—	—	—

		VG	VF	UNC
129	**5 Pesetas**			
	15.6.1945. Black and green on multicolor underprint. Queen Isabel la Católica and Columbus at left. Without series, and Series A-M. Back: Spaniards fighting Moors. Printer: FNMT.			
	a. Issued note.	7.00	30.00	100
	s. Specimen.	—	—	—

1946 Issue

		VG	VF	UNC
130	**25 Pesetas**			
	19.2.1946 (1948). Purple and black on multicolor underprint. Florez Estrada Álvaro at left. Back: View of Pola de Somiedo. Watermark: Greek man's head. Printer: FNMT.			
	a. Issued note.	12.00	45.00	150
	s. Specimen.	—	—	—

		VG	VF	UNC
131	**100 Pesetas**			
	19.2.1946 (1949). Brown on lilac underprint. Francisco de Goya at right. Series A-B. Back: *The Sun Shade by Goya.* Watermark: Francisco de Goya. Printer: FNMT.			
	a. Issued note.	15.00	55.00	175
	s. Specimen.	—	—	—

		VG	VF	UNC
132	**500 Pesetas**			
	19.2.1946 (1949). Blue on multicolor underprint. Francisco de Vitoria at right. Back: University of Salamanca. Watermark: Francisco de Vitoria. Printer: FNMT.			
	a. Issued note.	175	450	1,200
	s. Specimen.	—	—	—

		VG	VF	UNC
133	**1000 Pesetas**			
	19.2.1946 (1948). Green and brown. Juan Luis Vives at right. Back: Cloister at college in Valencia. Watermark: Juan Luis Vives. Printer: FNMT.			
	a. Issued note.	175	450	1,200
	s. Specimen.	—	—	—

1947 Issue

		VG	VF	UNC
134	**5 Pesetas**			
	12.4.1947. Brown-lilac on light green and light orange underprint. Seneca at right. BC: Blue-black. Printer: FNMT.			
	a. Issued note.	8.00	30.00	110
	s. Specimen.	—	—	—

1948 Issue

		VG	VF	UNC
135	**1 Peseta**			
	19.6.1948. Brown on multicolor underprint. Dame of Elche at right. Back: Plant. BC: Orange. Printer: FNMT.			
	a. Issued note.	1.25	6.00	20.00
	s. Specimen.	—	—	—

		VG	VF	UNC
136	**5 Pesetas**			
	5.3.1948. Dark green on lilac underprint. Juan Sebastián Elcano at left. Watermark: Man's head. Printer: FNMT.			
	a. Issued note.	3.00	14.00	50.00
	s. Specimen.	—	—	—

		VG	VF	UNC
137	**100 Pesetas**			
	2.5.1948 (1950). Brown. Francisco Bayeu at left. Back: Goya's *El Cacharrero.* Watermark: Goya. Printer: FNMT.			
	a. Issued note.	12.00	45.00	175
	s. Specimen.	—	—	—

1949 (1951) Issue

		VG	VF	UNC
138	**1000 Pesetas**			
	4.11.1949 (1951). Black and green. Ramón de Santillan at right. Back: Goya's *El Bebedor.* Watermark: Goya. Printer: FNMT.			
	a. Issued note.	65.00	225	700
	s. Specimen.	—	—	—

1951 Issue

139	**1 Peseta**	VG	VF	UNC
	19.11.1951. Brown on multicolor underprint. Don Quijote at right. Back: Shields and lance. Printer: FNMT.			
	a. Issued note.	1.00	5.00	15.00
	s. Specimen.	—	—	—

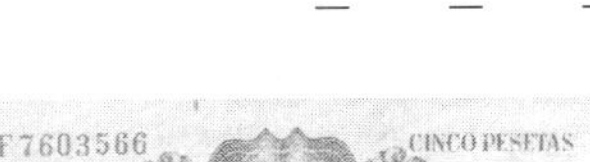

140	**5 Pesetas**	VG	VF	UNC
	16.8.1951. Dark green and black on olive and orange underprint. Jaime Balmes at left. Back: Old building. Watermark: Jaime Balmes. Printer: FNMT.			
	a. Issued note.	1.25	6.00	20.00
	s. Specimen.	—	—	—

141	**50 Pesetas**	VG	VF	UNC
	31.12.1951 (1956). Lilac-red on multicolor underprint. Santiago Rusiñol at right. Back: Rusiñol's *Jardines de Aranjuez*. Watermark: Santiago Rusiñol. Printer: FNMT.			
	a. Issued note.	14.00	50.00	180
	s. Specimen.	—	—	1,500

142	**500 Pesetas**	VG	VF	UNC
	15.11.1951 (1952). Dark blue. Mariano Benlliure at left. Back: Sculpture by Benlliure. Printer: FNMT.			
	a. Issued note.	40.00	125	450
	s. Specimen.	—	—	1,650

143	**1000 Pesetas**	VG	VF	UNC
	31.12.1951 (1953). Green. Joaquín Sorolla at center. Back: Sorolla's painting *La fiesta del naranjo*. Printer: FNMT.			
	a. Issued note.	40.00	120	425
	s. Specimen.	—	—	1,750

1953 Issue

144	**1 Peseta**	VG	VF	UNC
	22.7.1953. Brown and black on multicolor underprint. Marqués de Santa Cruz at right. Back: Old sailing ship. Printer: FNMT.			
	a. Issued note.	1.00	3.50	10.00
	s. Specimen.	—	—	900

145	**100 Pesetas**	VG	VF	UNC
	7.4.1953 (1955). Brown on multicolor underprint. Juan Romero de Torres at center. Back: Painting by Torres. Watermark: Woman's head. Printer: FNMT.			
	a. Issued note.	1.50	7.00	25.00
	s. Specimen.	—	—	1,200

1954 Issue

146	**5 Pesetas**	VG	VF	UNC
	22.7.1954. Green on light lilac underprint. King Alfonso X at right. Back: Library and museum building in Madrid. Watermark: King Alfonso X. Printer: FNMT.			
	a. Issued note.	2.50	10.00	35.00
	s. Specimen.	—	—	1,200

147	**25 Pesetas**	VG	VF	UNC
	22.7.1954. Purple on orange and multicolor underprint. Isaac Albeniz at left. Back: Patio scene of the Lion's Court of Alhambra. Watermark: Isaac Albeniz. Printer: FNMT.			
	a. Issued note.	2.50	10.00	35.00
	s. Specimen.	—	—	1,200

148 500 Pesetas
22.7.1954 (1958). Blue on multicolor underprint. Ignacio Zuloaga at center. Back: Painting by Zuloaga *Vista de Toledo*. Watermark: Ignacio Zuloaga. Printer: FNMT.

	VG	VF	UNC
a. Issued note.	12.00	40.00	150
s. Specimen.	—	—	1,750

1957 (1958) Issue

149 1000 Pesetas
29.11.1957 (1958). Green. *Reyes Católicos* at center. Back: Arms. Printer: FNMT.

	VG	VF	UNC
a. Issued note.	16.00	55.00	185
s. Specimen.	—	—	2,000

Straits Settlements is a former British crown colony on the south and west coast of Malay Peninsula consisting of Malacca, Penang, Singapore, Labuan (Borneo), Cocos Island and Christmas Island. Cocos Island, Christmas Island and Labuan were placed under control of the Governor of Straits Settlements in 1886. The colony was united under one government as a presidency of India in 1826, was incorporated under Bengal in 1830, and was removed from control of the Indian government and placed under direct British control in 1867. Japanese forces occupied the colony in 1941-1945.

RULERS:
British

MONETARY SYSTEM:
1 Dollar = 100 Cents

BRITISH ADMINISTRATION

Government of the Straits Settlements

1898-1906 Issue

1 1 Dollar
1906-1924. Black. Arms at upper center. Back: Tiger at center. Printer: TDLR.

	Good	Fine	XF
a. Light pink paper. 2 signature varieties. 1.9.1906.	400	1,000	6,000
b. Dark red paper. Underprint like #1A. 4 signature varieties. 1.9.1906; 8.6.1909; 17.3.1911.	400	1,000	6,000
c. Paper and underprint like b. 2.1.1914-4.3.1915; 10.7.1916; 20.6.1921; 5.9.1924.	200	600	3,000

1A 1 Dollar
1.8.1906. Black. Arms at upper center. Like #1a but underprint shows numeral *1* at left and center right. Back: Tiger at center. Printer: TDLR. PC: Light pink.

Good	Fine	XF
400	1,000	6,000

2 5 Dollars
1.9.1898; 1.3.1900. Black on light purple underprint. Arms at upper center. Back: Tiger at center. Printer: TDLR. 195x120mm.

Good	Fine	XF
3,000	6,000	—

		Good	Fine	XF
3	**5 Dollars** 1.2.1901; 8.6.1909; 17.3.1911; 2.1.1914; 4.3.1915; 10.7.1916; 20.6.1921; 5.9.1924. Black and purple. Arms at upper center. Similar to #2 but changes in frame ornaments. 6 signature varieties. Back: Tiger at center. Similar to #2 but changes in frame ornaments. Printer: TDLR. 119x75mm. PC: Light yellow.	1,000	2,000	8,000

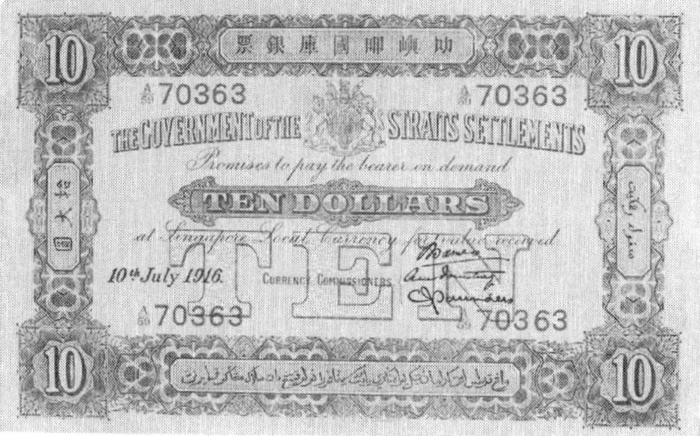

		Good	Fine	XF
4	**10 Dollars** 1898-1924. Blue on light purple underprint. Arms at upper center. 7 signature varieties. Back: Tiger. Printer: TDLR.			
	a. 1.9.1898; 1.3.1900; 1.2.1901; 8.6.1909; 17.3.1911. Rare.	—	—	—
	b. 2.1.1914; 4.3.1915; 10.7.1916; 20.6.1921; 5.9.1924.	1,000	6,000	—

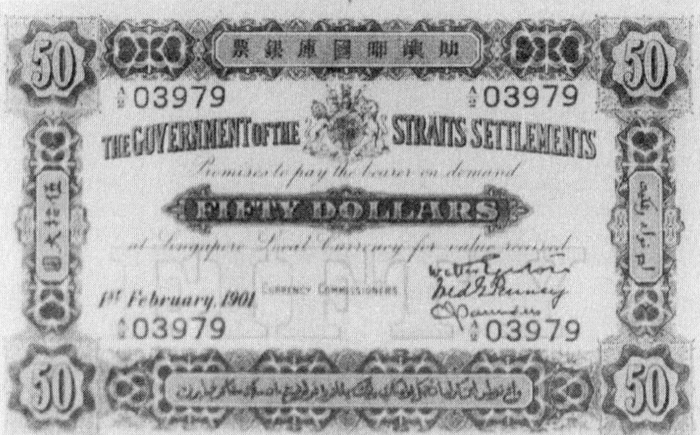

		Good	Fine	XF
4A	**50 Dollars** 1.2.1901. Green on light purple underprint. Arms at upper center. Printer: TDLR. Rare.	—	—	—
4C	**100 Dollars** 1.2.1901. Red on dark olive underprint. Back: *HUNDRED*. Rare.	—	—	—

1916 Issue

		Good	Fine	XF
A5	**50 Dollars** 7.3.1916. Dark blue on gray-violet underprint. Portrait King George V above tiger at center. Uniface. Printer: TDLR. Rare.	—	—	—

Note: The authenticity of #A5 dated 1.6.1920 has not been determined.

		Good	Fine	XF
5	**100 Dollars** 7.3.1916; 1.6.1920. Dark red on olive underprint. Portrait King George V above tiger at center. Uniface. Printer: TDLR. Rare.	—	—	—

Note: For later dates see #12-13.

1917 Issue

		Good	Fine	XF
6	**10 Cents** 1917-1920. Green on yellow underprint. Arms at upper center. 2 signature varieties. Back: Date in red seal, day at left of crown, month at right, year at bottom. Printer: Survey Dept. F.M.S.			
	a. Signature H. Marriot, with title: *Ag. Treasurer.* with *No.* before serial #. 1.7.1917-1.10.1917.	50.00	110	1,000
	b. As a. but without *No.* before serial #. 1.11.1917-1.9.1918.	50.00	110	1,000
	c. Signature A.M. Pountney with title: *Treasurer.* 2.1.1919-10.6.1920.	50.00	150	900

		Good	Fine	XF
7	**25 Cents** ND (1917). Black on yellow-orange underprint. Arms at top center. Back: Tiger at center. Printer: Survey Dept. F.M.S.	250	800	4,000

1919 Issue

		Good	Fine	XF
8	**10 Cents** 14.10.1919. Red and green on gray-brown underprint. Arms at top center. Back: Dragon at center. BC: Green. Printer: TDLR.			
	a. Signature title: *Ag. Treasurer.*	30.00	80.00	700
	b. Signature title: *Treasurer.*	20.00	40.00	350

1925; 1930 Issue

9	1 Dollar	Good	Fine	XF
	1925-1930. Red on gray-violet underprint. Palm trees at left, palm trees and huts at right. 4 signature varieties (red or black). Back: Beach with palms at center. Printer: TDLR.			
	a. Red date in plate. 1.1.1925; 1.9.1927; 1.1.1929.	120	400	2,000
	b. Black overprint date. 1.1.1930.	120	400	2,000

10	5 Dollars	Good	Fine	XF
	1925-1930. Green. Farmer with water buffalo ridden by child at right. 4 signature varieties (red or black). Back: Tiger in ornate cartouche at upper center. Printer: TDLR.			
	a. Green date in plate. 1.1.1925; 1.9.1927; 1.1.1929.	500	1,200	6,000
	b. Black overprint date 1.1.1930.	500	1,200	6,000

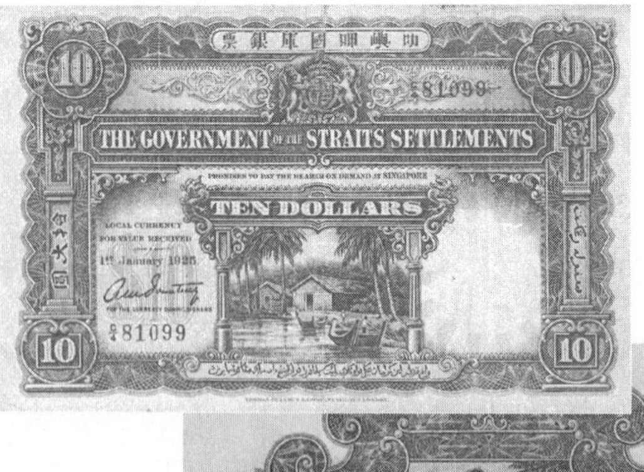

11	10 Dollars	Good	Fine	XF
	1925-1930. Purple. Palm trees and huts with fishing boats at center. 4 signature varieties (red or black). Back: Animal cart in ornate cartouche. Printer: TDLR.			
	a. Purple date in plate. 1.1.1925; 1.9.1927; 1.1.1929.	700	2,500	7,000
	b. Black overprint date 1.1.1930.	700	2,500	7,000

12	50 Dollars	Good	Fine	XF
	1925; 1927. Dark blue on gray-violet underprint. Portrait King George V above tiger at center. Uniface. Like #A5. Printer: TDLR.			
	a. 24.9.1925.	1,300	3,250	—
	b. 1.11.1927. Rare.	—		

		Good	Fine	XF
13	**100 Dollars** 24.9.1925; 1.11.1927. Dark red on olive underprint. Portrait King George V above tiger at center. Uniface. Like #5. Printer: TDLR.	1,300	3,250	—
14	**1000 Dollars** 1.10.1930. Dark red on olive underprint. Portrait King George V above tiger at center. Uniface. Like #5. Printer: TDLR. Rare.	—	—	—
15	**10,000 Dollars** 1.9.1919; 24.9.1925; 1.10.1930; 8.12.1933. Dark red on olive underprint. Portrait King George V above tiger at center. Uniface. Like #5. Printer: TDLR. Specimen. Rare.	—	—	—

Note: #15 was used only in interbank transactions.

1931 Issue

16	1 Dollar	Good	Fine	XF
	1931-1935. Dark blue. Portrait King George V at right. Back: Tiger at center, woman's head at left. Printer: BWC.			
	a. 1.1.1931-1.1.1934.	120	800	3,000
	b. 1.1.1935.	40.00	60.00	400

		Good	Fine	XF
17	**5 Dollars** 1931-1935. Violet. Portrait King George V at right. Back: Tiger at center, woman's head at left. Printer: BWC.			
	a. 1.1.1931-1.1.1934.	500	1,500	4,000
	b. 1.1.1935.	120	300	2,000

		Good	Fine	XF
18	**10 Dollars** 1931-1935. Green. Portrait King George V at right. Back: Tiger at center, woman's head at left. Printer: BWC.			
	a. 1.1.1931-1.1.1934.	400	800	5,000
	b. 1.1.1935.	200	300	2,000

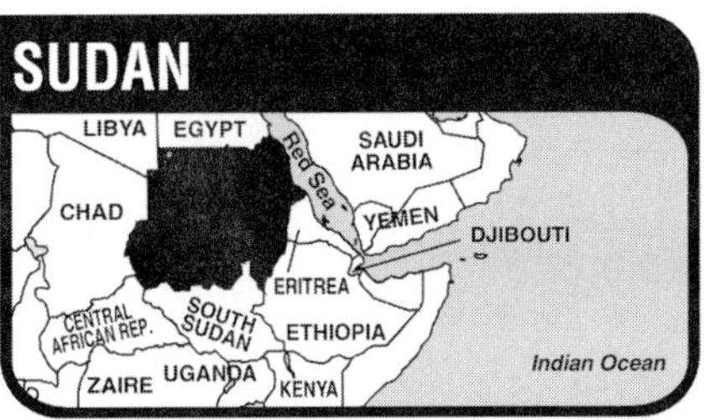

The Democratic Republic of the Sudan, was located in northeast Africa on the Red Sea between Egypt and Ethiopia, it had an area of 2,505,810 sq. km. and a population of 40.22 million. Capital: Khartoum. Agriculture and livestock raising are the chief occupations. Cotton, gum arabic and peanuts are exported.Military regimes favoring Islamic-oriented governments have dominated national politics since independence from the UK in 1956. Sudan was embroiled in two prolonged civil wars during most of the remainder of the 20th century. These conflicts were rooted in northern economic, political, and social domination of largely non-Muslim, non-Arab southern Sudanese. The first civil war ended in 1972 but broke out again in 1983. The second war and famine-related effects resulted in more than four million people displaced and, according to rebel estimates, more than two million deaths over a period of two decades. Peace talks gained momentum in 2002-04 with the signing of several accords.

The final North/South Comprehensive Peace Agreement (CPA), signed in January 2005, granted the southern rebels autonomy for six years. After which, a referendum for independence is scheduled to be held. A separate conflict, which broke out in the western region of Darfur in 2003, has displaced nearly two million people and caused an estimated 200,000 to 400,000 deaths.

The UN took command of the Darfur peacekeeping operation from the African Union on 31 December 2007. As of early 2009, peacekeeping troops were struggling to stabilize the situation, which has become increasingly regional in scope, and has brought instability to eastern Chad, and Sudanese incursions into the Central African Republic. Sudan also has faced large refugee influxes from neighboring countries, primarily Ethiopia and Chad. Armed conflict, poor transport infrastructure, and lack of government support have chronically obstructed the provision of humanitarian assistance to affected populations. After an election, the country voted to split, forming North Sudan and South Sudan in 2011.

RULERS:

British, 1899-1954
Italian, 1940

MONETARY SYSTEM:

1 Ghirsh (Piastre) = 10 Millim (Milliemes)
1 Sudanese Pound = 100 Piastres to 1992
1 Dinar = 10 Old Sudanese Pounds, 1992

REPUBLIC

Sudan Government - Treasury

1955 Issue

		VG	VF	UNC
A1	**25 Piastres** 6.7.1955. Red on pale green and pale orange underprint. Soldiers in formation at left. Back: Arms (desert camel soldier) at center right. Printer: W&S. Specimen, punched hole cancelled. Not issued.	—	—	—

		VG	VF	UNC
A2	**50 Piastres** 6.7.1955. Green on ochre and dull violet underprint. Elephants at left. Back: Arms (desert camel soldier) at center right. Printer: W&S. Specimen, punched hole cancelled. Not issued.	—	—	800

		VG	VF	UNC
A3	**1 Pound** ND (1955). Blue on yellow and multicolor underprint. Dam at left. Back: Arms (desert camel soldier) at center right. Printer: W&S. Specimen, punched hole cancelled. Not issued.	—	—	—

		VG	VF	UNC
A4	**5 Pounds** 6.7.1955. Dark brown on multicolor underprint. Dhow at left. Back: Arms (desert camel soldier) at center right. Printer: W&S. Specimen, punched hole cancelled. Not issued.	—	—	—

		VG	VF	UNC
A5	**10 Pounds** ND (1955). Black on multicolor underprint. Building at left. Back: Arms (desert camel soldier) at center right. Printer: W&S. Specimen, punched hole cancelled. Not issued.	—	—	2,000

Sudan Currency Board

1956 Issue

		VG	VF	UNC
1A	**25 Piastres** 15.9.1956. Red on pale green and pale orange underprint. Soldiers in formation at left. 3rd line of text 31mm long. Arabic date at lower right. Back: Arms (desert camel soldier) at center right.	5.00	20.00	175

		VG	VF	UNC
1B	**25 Piastres** 15.9.1956. Red on pale green and pale orange underprint. Soldiers in formation at left. Like #1A but 3rd line of text 45mm long. Arabic date at lower right. Back: Arms (desert camel soldier) at center right. Printer: ABNC.			
	a. Issued note.	8.00	30.00	200
	s. Specimen.	—	—	175

		VG	VF	UNC
2A	**50 Piastres** 15.9.1956. Green on ochre and dull violet underprint. Elephants at left. 3rd line of text 31mm long. Arabic date at lower right. Back: Arms (desert camel soldier) at center right.	20.00	100	500

		VG	VF	UNC
2B	**50 Piastres** 15.9.1956. Green on ochre and dull violet underprint. Elephants at left. Like #2A but 3rd line of text 45mm long. Arabic date at lower right. Back: Arms (desert camel soldier) at center right. Printer: ABNC.			
	a. Issued note.	20.00	125	600
	p. Face proof. Uniface.	—	—	450
	s. Specimen.	—	—	450

		VG	VF	UNC
3	**1 Pound** 15.9.1956. Blue on yellow and multicolor underprint. Dam at left. Arabic date at lower right. Back: Arms (desert camel soldier) at center right.	15.00	75.00	350

		VG	VF	UNC
4	**5 Pounds** 15.9.1956. Dark brown on multicolor underprint. Dhow at left. Arabic date at lower right. Back: Arms (desert camel soldier) at center right.	30.00	125	950

		VG	VF	UNC
5	**10 Pounds** 15.9.1956. Black on multicolor underprint. Building at left. Arabic date at lower right. Back: Arms (desert camel soldier) at center right.	45.00	225	1,200

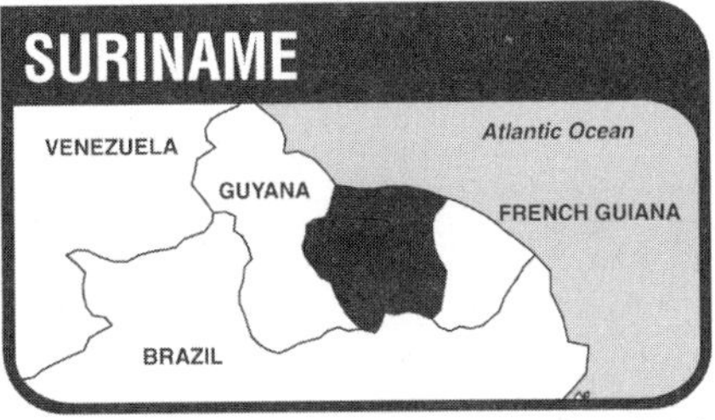

The Republic of Surinam, formerly known as Dutch Guiana, located on the north central coast of South America between Guyana and French Guiana, has an area of 163,270 sq. km. and a population of 476,000. Capital: Paramaribo. The country is rich in minerals and forests, and self-sufficient in rice, the staple food crop. The mining, processing and exporting of bauxite is the principal economic activity.First explored by the Spaniards in the 16th century and then settled by the English in the mid-17th century, Suriname became a Dutch colony in 1667. With the abolition of slavery in 1863, workers were brought in from India and Java. Independence from the Netherlands was granted in 1975. Five years later the civilian government was replaced by a military regime that soon declared a socialist republic. It continued to exert control through a succession of nominally civilian administrations until 1987, when international pressure finally forced a democratic election. In 1990, the military overthrew the civilian leadership, but a democratically elected government - a four-party New Front coalition - returned to power in 1991 and has ruled since; the coalition expanded to eight parties in 2005.

RULERS:

Dutch to 1975

MONETARY SYSTEM:

1 Gulden = 1 Florin = 100 Cents, to 2004
1 Dollar = 1000 "old" Gulden, 2004-

DUTCH ADMINISTRATION

Algemene Nederlandsche Maatschappij / Société Générale pour Favoriser l'Industrie Nationale

(General Netherlands Society)

1826 Issue

		Good	Fine	XF
1	**1/2 Gulden** 1.10.1826. Black. Border of musical note forms by J.M. Fleischman. Uniface. Printer: JEZ (without imprint). Overprint: Orange *SURINAME.* Rare.	—	—	—
2	**1 Gulden** 1.10.1826. Black. Border of musical note forms by J.M. Fleischman. Uniface. Printer: JEZ (without imprint). Overprint: Orange *SURINAME.* Rare.	—	—	—
3	**2 Gulden** 1.10.1826. Black. Border of musical note forms by J.M. Fleischman. Uniface. Printer: JEZ (without imprint). Overprint: Orange *SURINAME.* Rare.	—	—	—

		Good	Fine	XF
4	**3 Gulden** 1.10.1826. Black. Border of musical note forms by J.M. Fleischman. Uniface. Printer: JEZ (without imprint). Overprint: Orange *SURINAME.* Rare.	—	—	—
5	**5 Gulden** 1.10.1826. Black. Border of musical note forms by J.M. Fleischman. Uniface. Printer: JEZ (without imprint). Overprint: Orange *SURINAME.* Rare.	—	—	—
6	**10 Gulden** 1.10.1826. Black. Border of musical note forms by J.M. Fleischman. Uniface. Printer: JEZ (without imprint). Overprint: Orange *SURINAME.* Rare.	—	—	—

#	Denomination / Description	Good	Fine	XF
7	**25 Gulden** 1.10.1826. Black. Border of musical note forms by J.M. Fleischman. Uniface. Printer: JEZ (without imprint). Overprint: Orange *SURINAME*. Rare.	—	—	—
8	**50 Gulden** 1.10.1826. Black. Border of musical note forms by J.M. Fleischman. Uniface. Printer: JEZ (without imprint). Overprint: Orange *SURINAME*. Rare.	—	—	—
9	**100 Gulden** 1.10.1826. Black. Border of musical note forms by J.M. Fleischman. Uniface. Printer: JEZ (without imprint). Overprint: Orange *SURINAME*. Rare.	—	—	—

West-Indische Bank

1829 Issue

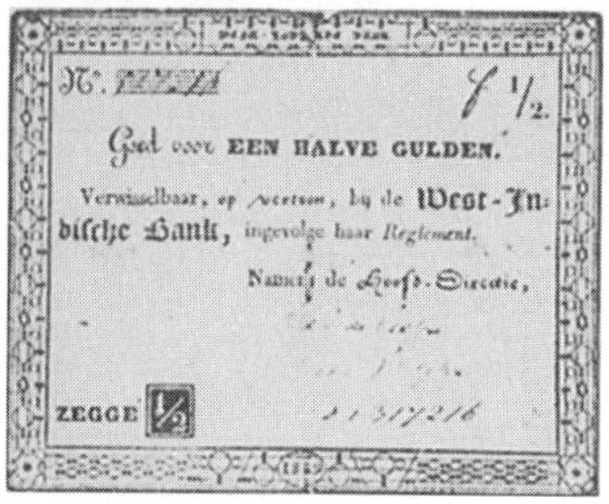

#	Denomination / Description	Good	Fine	XF
10	**1/2 Gulden** 1829. Black. Border of musical note forms by J.M. Fleischman. Uniface. Signature varieties. Printer: JEZ (without imprint). Rare.	—	—	—
12	**2 Gulden** 1829. Black. Border of musical note forms by J.M. Fleischman. Uniface. Signature varieties. Printer: JEZ (without imprint). Rare.	—	—	—
13	**3 Gulden** 1829. Black. Border of musical note forms by J.M. Fleischman. Uniface. Signature varieties. Printer: JEZ (without imprint). Rare.	—	—	—
14	**5 Gulden** 1829. Black. Border of musical note forms by J.M. Fleischman. Uniface. Signature varieties. Printer: JEZ (without imprint). Rare.	—	—	—
15	**10 Gulden** 1829. Black. Border of musical note forms by J.M. Fleischman. Uniface. Signature varieties. Printer: JEZ (without imprint). Rare.	—	—	—
16	**25 Gulden** 1829. Black. Border of musical note forms by J.M. Fleischman. Uniface. Signature varieties. Watermark: Printed. Printer: JEZ (without imprint). Rare.	—	—	—
17	**50 Gulden** 1829. Black. Border of musical note forms by J.M. Fleischman. Uniface. Signature varieties. Watermark: Printed. Printer: JEZ (without imprint). Rare.	—	—	—
18	**100 Gulden** 1829. Black. Border of musical note forms by J.M. Fleischman. Uniface. Signature varieties. Watermark: Printed. Printer: JEZ (without imprint). Rare.	—	—	—
19	**150 Gulden** 1829. Black. Border of musical note forms by J.M. Fleischman. Uniface. Signature varieties. Watermark: Printed. Printer: JEZ (without imprint). (Not issued). Rare.	—	—	—
20	**200 Gulden** 1829. Black. Border of musical note forms by J.M. Fleischman. Uniface. Signature varieties. Watermark: Printed. Printer: JEZ (without imprint). (Not issued). Rare.	—	—	—
22	**250 Gulden** 1829. Black. Border of musical note forms by J.M. Fleischman. Uniface. Signature varieties. Watermark: Printed. Printer: JEZ (without imprint). Rare.	—	—	—
23	**500 Gulden** 1829. Black. Border of musical note forms by J.M. Fleischman. Uniface. Signature varieties. Watermark: Printed. Printer: JEZ (without imprint). Rare.	—	—	—
24	**1000 Gulden** 1829. Black. Border of musical note forms by J.M. Fleischman. Uniface. Signature varieties. Watermark: Printed. Printer: JEZ (without imprint). Rare.	—	—	—

Color Abbreviation Guide

New to the *Standard Catalog of® World Paper Money* are the following abbreviations related to color references:

BC: Back color

PC: Paper color

1837 Issue

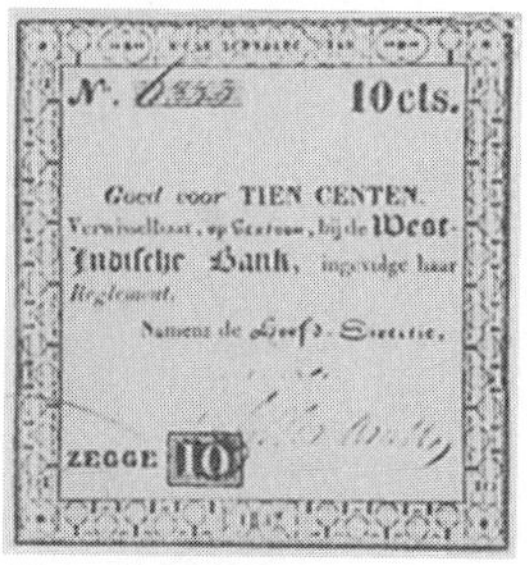

#	Denomination / Description	Good	Fine	XF
25	**10 Centen** 1837. Brown. Border of musical note forms by J.M. Fleischman. Uniface. Signature varieties. Printer: JEZ (without imprint). Square. Rare.	—	—	—
26	**15 Centen** 1837. Red. Border of musical note forms by J.M. Fleischman. Uniface. Signature varieties. Printer: JEZ (without imprint). Rectangular. Rare.	—	—	—
27	**25 Centen** 1837. Black. Border of musical note forms by J.M. Fleischman. Uniface. Signature varieties. Printer: JEZ (without imprint). Hexagonal. Rare.	—	—	—
28	**50 Centen** 1837. Blue. Border of musical note forms by J.M. Fleischman. Uniface. Signature varieties. Printer: JEZ (without imprint). Rectangular. (Not issued). Rare.	—	—	—

1840 Issue

#	Denomination / Description	Good	Fine	XF
29	**1 Gulden** 1840. Brown. Fleischman music border, uniface. Signature varieties. Watermark: Printed. Printer: JEZ (without imprint). Octagonal, thick paper. Rare.	—	—	—

1844 Issue

#	Denomination / Description	Good	Fine	XF
30	**10 Centen** 1844. Border of musical note forms by J.M. Fleischman. Uniface. Signature varieties. Watermark: Real. Printer: JEZ (without imprint). Thin paper.			
	a. Issued note. Rare.	—	—	—
	r. Unsigned remainder without serial #. Rare.	—	—	—
31	**15 Centen** 1844. Border of musical note forms by J.M. Fleischman. Uniface. Signature varieties. Watermark: Real. Printer: JEZ (without imprint). Thin paper.			
	a. Issued note. Rare.	—	—	—
	r. Unsigned remainder without serial #. Rare.	—	—	—
32	**25 Centen** 1844. Border of musical note forms by J.M. Fleischman. Uniface. Signature varieties. Watermark: Real. Printer: JEZ (without imprint). Thin paper.			
	a. Issued note. Rare.	—	—	—
	r. Unsigned remainder without serial #. Rare.	—	—	—
33	**50 Centen** 1844. Border of musical note forms by J.M. Fleischman. Uniface. Signature varieties. Watermark: Real. Printer: JEZ (without imprint). Thin paper.			
	a. Issued note. Rare.	—	—	—
	r. Unsigned remainder without serial #. Rare.	—	—	—

Schatkist-Biljet der Kolonie Suriname

Treasury Note For The Colony of Surinam

1847 Issue

#	Denomination / Description	Good	Fine	XF
34	**100 Gulden** 6.2.1847. Printer: JEZ (without imprint). Rare.	—	—	—

1848 Issue

#	Denomination / Description	Good	Fine	XF
35	**10 Centen** 6.2.1847 (- old date 1844). Uniface. Signature varieties. Printer: JEZ (without imprint). Overprint: *SCHATKIST-BILLET K.B.6 6. February 1847* on #30. Rare.	—	—	—
36	**15 Centen** 6.2.1847 (- old date 1844). Uniface. Signature varieties. Printer: JEZ (without imprint). Overprint: *SCHATKIST-BILLET K.B.6 6. February 1847* on #31. Rare.	—	—	—
37	**25 Centen** 6.2.1847 (- old date 1844). Uniface. Signature varieties. Printer: JEZ (without imprint). Overprint: *SCHATKIST-BILLET K.B.6 6. February 1847* on #32. Rare.	—	—	—
38	**50 Centen** 6.2.1847 (- old date 1844). Uniface. Signature varieties. Printer: JEZ (without imprint). Overprint: *SCHATKIST-BILLET K.B.6 6. February 1847* on #33. Rare.	—	—	—
39	**1 Gulden** 6.2.1847 (- old date 1840). Uniface. Signature varieties. Printer: JEZ (without imprint). Overprint: *SCHATKIST-BILLET K.B.6 6. February 1847* on #29. Rare.	—	—	—

40 **2 Gulden** — Good Fine XF
6.2.1847 (- old date 1829). Uniface. Signature varieties. Printer: JEZ (without imprint). Overprint: *SCHATKIST-BILLET K.B.6 6. February 1847* on #12. Rare. — — —

41 **3 Gulden** — Good Fine XF
6.2.1847 (- old date 1829). Uniface. Signature varieties. Printer: JEZ (without imprint). Overprint: *SCHATKIST-BILLET K.B.6 6. February 1847* on #13. Rare. — — —

42 **5 Gulden** — Good Fine XF
6.2.1847 (- old date 1829). Uniface. Signature varieties. Printer: JEZ (without imprint). Overprint: *SCHATKIST-BILLET K.B.6 6. February 1847* on #14. Rare. — — —

43 **10 Gulden** — Good Fine XF
6.2.1847 (- old date 1829). Uniface. Signature varieties. Printer: JEZ (without imprint). Overprint: *SCHATKIST-BILLET K.B.6 6. February 1847* on #15. Rare. — — —

44 **25 Gulden** — Good Fine XF
6.2.1847 (- old date 1829). Uniface. Signature varieties. Printer: JEZ (without imprint). Overprint: *SCHATKIST-BILLET K.B.6 6. February 1847* on #16. Rare. — — —

De Surinaamsche Bank

1865 Issue

45 **10 Gulden** — Good Fine XF
1.7.1865. Black on red-brown underprint. Allegorical border with scrollwork, printed date. Signature varieties with titles: *DIRECTEUR-SECRETARIS* and *DIRECTEUR-PRESIDENT.* Uniface. Watermark: *SURINAAMSCHE BANK.* Printer: JEZ (without imprint). 212x114mm.
- a. Issued note. Rare. — — —
- r. Unsigned remainder, not dated. Rare. — — —

46 **25 Gulden** — Good Fine XF
1.7.1865. Black on orange underprint. Allegorical border with scrollwork, printed date. Signature varieties with titles: *DIRECTEUR-SECRETARIS* and *DIRECTEUR-PRESIDENT.* Uniface. Watermark: *SURINAAMSCHE BANK.* Printer: JEZ (without imprint). 212x114mm.
- a. Issued note. Rare. — — —
- r. Unsigned remainder, not dated. Rare. — — —

47 **50 Gulden** — Good Fine XF
1.7.1865. Black on blue underprint. Allegorical border with scrollwork, printed date. Signature varieties with titles: *DIRECTEUR-SECRETARIS* and *DIRECTEUR-PRESIDENT.* Uniface. Watermark: *SURINAAMSCHE BANK.* Printer: JEZ (without imprint). 212x114mm.
- a. Issued note. Rare. — — —
- r. Unsigned remainder, not dated. Rare. — — —

48 **100 Gulden** — Good Fine XF
1.7.1865. Brown on blue underprint. Allegorical border with scrollwork, printed date. Signature varieties with titles: *DIRECTEUR-SECRETARIS* and *DIRECTEUR-PRESIDENT.* Uniface. Watermark: *SURINAAMSCHE BANK.* Printer: JEZ (without imprint). 212x114mm.
- a. Issued note. Rare. — — —
- r. Unsigned remainder, not dated. Rare. — — —

49 **200 Gulden** — Good Fine XF
1.7.1865. Brown on green underprint. Allegorical border with scrollwork, printed date. Signature varieties with titles: *DIRECTEUR-SECRETARIS* and *DIRECTEUR-PRESIDENT.* Uniface. Watermark: *SURINAAMSCHE BANK.* Printer: JEZ (without imprint). 212x114mm.
- a. Issued note. Rare. — — —
- r. Unsigned remainder, not dated. Rare. — — —

50 **300 Gulden** — Good Fine XF
1.7.1865. Brown on light brown underprint. Allegorical border with scrollwork, printed date. Signature varieties with titles: *DIRECTEUR-SECRETARIS* and *DIRECTEUR-PRESIDENT.* Uniface. Watermark: *SURINAAMSCHE BANK.* Printer: JEZ (without imprint). 212x114mm.
- a. Issued note. Rare. — — —
- r. Unsigned remainder, not dated. Rare. — — —

51 **1000 Gulden** — Good Fine XF
1.7.1865. Brown on red underprint. Allegorical border with scrollwork, printed date. Signature varieties with titles: *DIRECTEUR-SECRETARIS* and *DIRECTEUR-PRESIDENT.* Uniface. Watermark: *SURINAAMSCHE BANK.* Printer: JEZ (without imprint). 212x114mm.
- a. Issued note. Rare. — — —
- r. Unsigned remainder, not dated. Rare. — — —

1869 Issue

52 **5 Gulden** — Good Fine XF
1.10.1869. Black on red underprint. Uniface, scrollwork border, Signature varieties with title: *Directeur-Secretaris.* Watermark: *Surinaamsche Bank.* Printer: JEZ (without imprint).
- a. Issued note. Rare. — — —
- p. Proof. Rare. — — —

1880; 1886 Issue

53 **10 Gulden** — Good Fine XF
1886-1906. Black on red-brown underprint. Allegorical border with scrollwork, printed dates. Signature titles: *Directeur* and *Directeur-President.* Uniface. Watermark: *Surinaamsche Bank.* Printer: JEZ (without imprint).
- a. 1.7.1886. Rare. — — —
- b. 1.7.1894. Rare. — — —
- c. 15.2.1904. Rare. — — —
- d. 1.11.1906. Rare. — — —

54 **25 Gulden** — Good Fine XF
1886-1904. Black on orange underprint. Allegorical border with scrollwork, printed dates. Signature titles: *Directeur* and *Directeur-President.* Uniface. Watermark: *Surinaamsche Bank.* Printer: JEZ (without imprint).
- a. 1.7.1886. Rare. — — —
- b. 1.2.1890. Rare. — — —
- c. 1.7.1894. Rare. — — —
- d. 15.2.1904. Rare. — — —

55 **50 Gulden** — Good Fine XF
1880-1904. Black on blue underprint. Allegorical border with scrollwork, printed dates. Signature titles: *Directeur* and *Directeur-President.* Uniface. Watermark: *Surinaamsche Bank.* Printer: JEZ (without imprint).
- a. 1.7.1880. Rare. — — —
- b. 1.7.1884. Rare. — — —
- c. 1.7.1886. Rare. — — —
- d. 1.2.1890. Rare. — — —
- e. 1.7.1894. Rare. — — —
- f. 1.7.1901. Rare. — — —
- g. 1903 (- old date 1.7.1901). Rare. — — —
- h. 15.2.1904. Rare. — — —

56 **100 Gulden** — Good Fine XF
1880-1904. Brown on blue underprint. Allegorical border with scrollwork, printed dates. Signature titles: *Directeur* and *Directeur-President.* Uniface. Watermark: *Surinaamsche Bank.* Printer: JEZ (without imprint).
- a. 1.7.1880. Rare. — — —
- b. 1.1.1882. Rare. — — —
- c. 1.1.1884. Rare. — — —
- d. 1.7.1886. Rare. — — —
- e. 1.1.1894. Rare. — — —
- f. 15.2.1904. Rare. — — —

57 **200 Gulden** — Good Fine XF
1880-1904. Brown on green underprint. Allegorical border with scrollwork, printed dates. Signature titles: *Directeur* and *Directeur-President.* Uniface. Watermark: *Surinaamsche Bank.* Printer: JEZ (without imprint).
- a. 1.7.1880. Rare. — — —
- b. 1.1.1882. Rare. — — —
- c. 1.1.1884. Rare. — — —
- d. 1.7.1886. Rare. — — —
- e. 1.7.1894. Rare. — — —
- f. 15.2.1904. Rare. — — —

58 **300 Gulden** — Good Fine XF
1880-1904. Brown on light brown underprint. Allegorical border with scrollwork, printed dates. Signature titles: *Directeur* and *Directeur-President.* Uniface. Watermark: *Surinaamsche Bank.* Printer: JEZ (without imprint).
- a. 1.7.1880. Rare. — — —
- b. 1.1.1882. Rare. — — —
- c. 1.1.1884. Rare. — — —
- d. 1.7.1886. Rare. — — —
- e. 1.1.1894. Rare. — — —
- f. 15.2.1904. Rare. — — —

59 **1000 Gulden** — Good Fine XF
1880-1904. Brown on blue underprint. Allegorical border with scrollwork, printed dates. Signature titles: *Directeur* and *Directeur-President.* Uniface. Watermark: *Surinaamsche Bank.* Printer: JEZ (without imprint).
- a. 1.7.1880. Rare. — — —
- b. 1.7.1883. Rare. — — —
- c. 1.7.1886. Rare. — — —
- d. 1.2.1890. Rare. — — —
- e. 1.7.1894. Rare. — — —
- f. 15.2.1904. Rare. — — —

1906 Issue

60 **5 Gulden** — Good — Fine — XF —
1.9.1906. Black on red underprint. As #52 but printed date, title change to *Directeur* and *Directeur-President.* Watermark: *Surinaamsche Bank.* Printer: JEZ (without imprint). Rare.

1909-1911 Issue

#61-66 222 x 114mm.

61 **10 Gulden** — Good — Fine — XF —
1.9.1910. Pink on light gray underprint. Allegorical border with scrollwork, printed dates. Signature titles: *Directeur* and *Directeur-President.* Uniface. Watermark: *Surinaamsche Bank.* Printer: JEZ (without imprint). 222x114mm. Rare.

62 **25 Gulden** — Good — Fine — XF —
1.9.1909; 1.12.1911. Green on brown underprint. Allegorical border with scrollwork, printed dates. Signature titles: *Directeur* and *Directeur-President.* Uniface. Watermark: *Surinaamsche Bank.* Printer: JEZ (without imprint). 222x114mm. Rare.

63 **100 Gulden** — Good — Fine — XF —
1.12.1911. Brown on gray-blue underprint. Allegorical border with scrollwork, printed dates. Signature titles: *Directeur* and *Directeur-President.* Uniface. Watermark: *Surinaamsche Bank.* Printer: JEZ (without imprint). 222x114mm. Rare.

64 **200 Gulden** — Good — Fine — XF —
1.9.1909. Brown-pink on pink underprint. Allegorical border with scrollwork, printed dates. Signature titles: *Directeur* and *Directeur-President.* Uniface. Watermark: *Surinaamsche Bank.* Printer: JEZ (without imprint). 222x114mm. Rare.

65 **300 Gulden** — Good — Fine — XF —
1.9.1910. Purple on brown-yellow underprint. Allegorical border with scrollwork, printed dates. Signature titles: *Directeur* and *Directeur-President.* Uniface. Watermark: *Surinaamsche Bank.* Printer: JEZ (without imprint). 222x114mm. Rare.

66 **1000 Gulden** — Good — Fine — XF —
1.9.1910. Purple on green underprint. Allegorical border with scrollwork, printed dates. Signature titles: *Directeur* and *Directeur-President.* Uniface. Watermark: *Surinaamsche Bank.* Printer: JEZ (without imprint). 222x114mm. Rare.

1911 Issue

67 **5 Gulden** — Good — Fine — XF —
1.11.1911. Black on light red underprint. As #60. Uniface, stamped date. Watermark: *Surinaamsche Bank.* Printer: JEZ (without imprint). Rare.

1913 Issue

68 **10 Gulden** — Good — Fine — XF —
1.8.1915; 1.11.1919. Pink on light grey underprint. Allegorical border with scrollwork. Signature titles: *Directeur* and *Directeur-President.* Uniface. Similar to #61. Watermark: *Surinaamsche Bank.* Printer: JEZ (without imprint). Rare.

69 **25 Gulden** — Good — Fine — XF —
Ca. 1913. Green on brown underprint. Allegorical border with scrollwork. Signature titles: *Directeur* and *Directeur-President.* Uniface. Similar to #62. Watermark: *Surinaamsche Bank.* Printer: JEZ (without imprint). Rare.

70 **50 Gulden** — Good — Fine — XF —
Ca. 1913. Blue on gray-brown underprint. Allegorical border with scrollwork. Signature titles: *Directeur* and *Directeur-President.* Uniface. Watermark: *Surinaamsche Bank.* Printer: JEZ (without imprint). Rare.

1919 Issue

71 **5 Gulden**
1919-1933. Black. Stamped date and serial #. Watermark: *Surinaamsche Bank.* Printer: JEZ (without imprint). PC: Light pink.

	Good	Fine	XF
a. 1.11.1919. Signature titles: *Directeur* and *Directeur-President.* Rare.	—	—	—
b. 20.12.1928; 1.3.1931. Signature titles: *Directeur* and *Directeur-Voorzitter.* Rare.	—	—	—
c. 1.4.1933. Penal Code changed to *Section 215.* Rare.	—	—	—

72 **10 Gulden** — Good — Fine — XF —
Ca. 1919. Deep pink on gray underprint. Stamped date and serial #. Watermark: *Surinaamsche Bank.* Printer: JEZ (without imprint). Rare.

73 **50 Gulden** — Good — Fine — XF —
Ca. 1919. Blue on brown-gray underprint. Stamped date and serial #. Watermark: *Surinaamsche Bank.* Printer: JEZ (without imprint). Rare.

1920-1921 Issue

74 **10 Gulden**
1920-1925. Red. Oval vignettes in corners depicting various aspects of the local economy. Serial # four times. Large signature titles. Watermark: *Surinaamsche Bank.* Printer: JEZ (without imprint).

	Good	Fine	XF
a. Issued note. 1.8.1920; 1.3.1923; 1.9.1925.	400	1,500	2,500
s. Specimen.	—	—	—

75 **25 Gulden** — Good 400 — Fine 2,000 — XF —
1.8.1920; 1.3.1923. Green. Oval vignettes in corners depicting various aspects of the local economy. Serial # four times. Large signature titles. Watermark: *Surinaamsche Bank.* Printer: JEZ (without imprint).

76 **50 Gulden** — Good — Fine — XF —
1.1.1921. Blue. Oval vignettes in corners depicting various aspects of the local economy. Serial # four times. Large signature titles. Watermark: *Surinaamsche Bank.* Printer: JEZ (without imprint). Rare.

77 **100 Gulden** — Good — Fine — XF —
1.8.1920; 1.3.1923. Brown. Oval vignettes in corners depicting various aspects of the local economy. Serial # four times. Large signature titles. Watermark: *Surinaamsche Bank.* Printer: JEZ (without imprint). Rare.

1925 Issue

78 **10 Gulden** — Good — Fine — XF —
1925-1940. Oval vignettes in corners depicting various aspects of the local economy. Small signature titles. Various printed dates. Back: Serial # three times. Watermark: *Surinaamsche Bank.* Printer: JEZ (without imprint). Rare.

79 **25 Gulden** — Good — Fine — XF —
1925-1941. Oval vignettes in corners depicting various aspects of the local economy. Small signature titles. Various printed dates. Back: Serial # three times. Watermark: *Surinaamsche Bank.* Printer: JEZ (without imprint). Rare.

80 **50 Gulden** — Good — Fine — XF —
1925-1940. Oval vignettes in corners depicting various aspects of the local economy. Small signature titles. Various printed dates. Back: Serial # three times. Watermark: *Surinaamsche Bank.* Printer: JEZ (without imprint). Rare.

81 **100 Gulden** — Good — Fine — XF —
1925-1948. Oval vignettes in corners depicting various aspects of the local economy. Small signature titles. Various printed dates. Back: Serial # three times. Watermark: *Surinaamsche Bank.* Printer: JEZ (without imprint). Rare.

82 **200 Gulden** — Good — Fine — XF —
1925-1948. Oval vignettes in corners depicting various aspects of the local economy. Small signature titles. Various printed dates. Back: Serial # three times. Watermark: *Surinaamsche Bank.* Printer: JEZ (without imprint). Rare.

		Good	Fine	XF
83	**300 Gulden** 1925-1948. Oval vignettes in corners depicting various aspects of the local economy. Small signature titles. Various printed dates. Back: Serial # three times. Watermark: *Surinaamsche Bank.* Printer: JEZ (without imprint). Rare.	—	—	—
84	**1000 Gulden** 1925-1948. Oval vignettes in corners depicting various aspects of the local economy. Small signature titles. Various printed dates. Back: Serial # three times. Watermark: *Surinaamsche Bank.* Printer: JEZ (without imprint). Rare.	—	—	—

1935 Issue

		Good	Fine	XF
85	**5 Gulden** 1.10.1935; 3.6.1936; 15.12.1939; 28.5.1940; 1.6.1940. Blue on light green underprint. Arms at left, native girl wearing kotomisi head scarf at right, stamped dates, printed signature. Printer: JEZ.			
	a. Issued note.	175	325	800
	s. Specimen. Without serial numbers, date or signatures.	—	Unc	3,500

Color Abbreviation Guide

New to the *Standard Catalog of ® World Paper Money* are the following abbreviations related to color references:

BC: Back color

PC: Paper color

1940 ND Provisional Issue

Red ovpt. on face and back of half of #85.

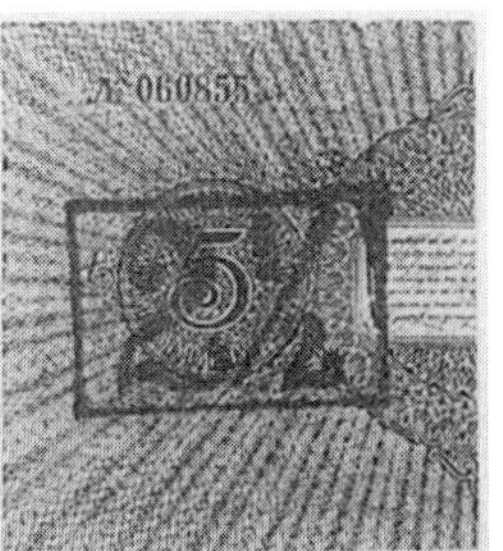

		Good	Fine	XF
86	**2 1/2 Gulden** ND (1940). Blue on light green underprint. Arms at left, native girl wearing kotomisi head scarf at right, stamped dates, printed signature. Overprint: Red on face and back of #85.			
	a. Right half. Rare.	—	—	—
	b. Left half. Rare.	—	—	—

1940-1942 Issue

		Good	Fine	XF
87	**2 1/2 Gulden** 1940-1942. Lilac-red on brown underprint. Woman reclining with branch at center. Back: Arms at top center. Printer: ABNC.			
	a. Stamped date and signature on face. 1.10.1940; 7.4.1941; 1.9.1941.	30.00	75.00	325
	b. Printed date and signature on back. 1.1.1942.	15.00	50.00	225
	p. Proof.	—	Unc	250
	s. As a or b. Specimen.	—	Unc	400

		Good	Fine	XF
88	**5 Gulden** 1.9.1942. Blue on multicolor underprint. Government palace at center, printed date. Back: Arms at lower center. Printer: ABNC.			
	a. Issued note.	60.00	175	450
	p. Proof.	—	Unc	350
	s. Specimen.	—	Unc	600

		Good	Fine	XF
89	**10 Gulden** 1.9.1941; 1.6.1942. Orange on multicolor underprint. Government palace at center, printed date. Printer: ABNC.			
	a. Issued note.	100	600	1,250
	p. Proof.	—	Unc	650
	s. Specimen.	—	Unc	900

		Good	Fine	XF
90	**25 Gulden** 1.2.1942; 1.12.1948. Green on multicolor underprint. Government palace at center, printed date. Printer: ABNC.			
	a. 1.2.1942.	150	750	1,600
	b. 1.12.1948.	120	600	1,250
	p. Proof.	—	Unc	750
	s. Specimen.	—	Unc	1,250

		Good	Fine	XF
91	**100 Gulden** 1.9.1941; 1.4.1943; 1.4.1948. Purple on multicolor underprint. Government palace at center, printed date.			
	a. Issued note.	350	1,250	—
	p. Proof.	—	Unc	850
	s. Specimen.	—	Unc	2,000

1951 Issue

		VG	VF	UNC
92	**10 Gulden** 1.8.1951. Green. Hut and trees at right. Printer: De Bussy, Amsterdam.			
	a. Issued note. Rare.	—	—	—
	p. Proof.	—	—	600
	r. Remainder, punch hole cancelled.	—	—	500

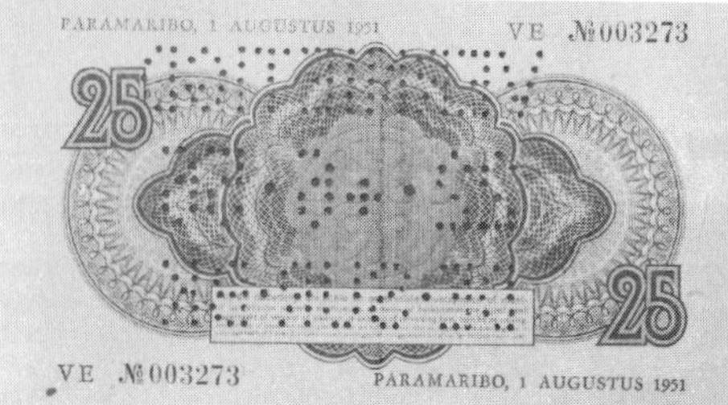

		VG	VF	UNC
93	**25 Gulden** 1.8.1951. Building with flag at lower right. Printer: De Bussy, Amsterdam.			
	a. Issued note. Rare.	—	—	—
	p. Proof.	—	—	600
	r. Remainder, punch hole cancelled.	—	—	550

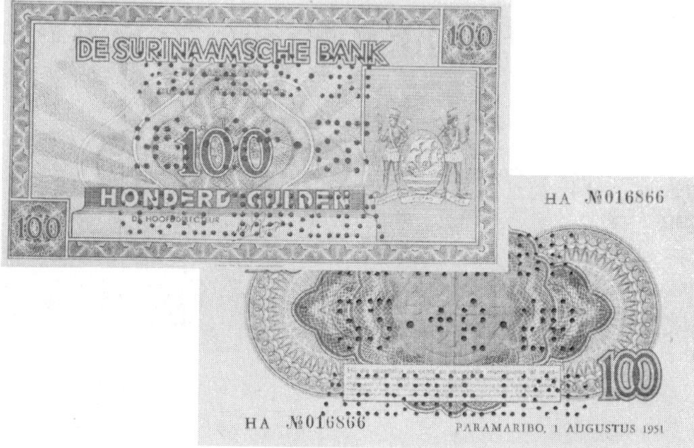

		VG	VF	UNC
94	**100 Gulden** 1.8.1951. Violet and lilac. Arms with Indian as shield supporter (Justitia, Pietas, Fides) at right. Printer: De Bussy, Amsterdam.			
	a. Issued note. Rare.	—	—	—
	p. Proof.	—	—	650
	r. Remainder, punch hole cancelled.	—	—	600

Zilverbon

1918 Issue

		Good	Fine	XF
95	**1/2 Gulden** 1918. Brown. Signature varieties. Uniface. Printer: JEZ (without imprint).			
	a. 12.4.1918.	500	900	1,400
	b. 28.11.1918.	600	1,000	1,500

		Good	Fine	XF
96	**1 Gulden** 1918-1919. Brown. Signature varieties. Uniface. Like #95. Printer: JEZ (without imprint).			
	a. 12.4.1918.	600	1,000	1,500
	b. 16.6.1919.	800	1,300	1,800
97	**2 1/2 Gulden** 12.4.1918. Red-brown on light brown underprint. Signature varieties. Uniface. Like #95. Printer: JEZ (without imprint).	Good	Fine	XF
	a. Issued note.	900	1,400	1,900
	r. Unsigned remainder.	—	Unc	1,200

1920 First Issue

		Good	Fine	XF
98	**1/2 Gulden** 2.2.1920. Brown. Signature varieties. Uniface. Like #95. Printer: JEZ (without imprint).	650	1,100	1,600
99	**1 Gulden** 2.2.1920. Brown. Signature varieties. Uniface. Like #96. Printer: JEZ (without imprint).	600	1,000	1,500
100	**2 1/2 Gulden** 2.2.1920. Signature varieties. Uniface. Like #97. Printer: JEZ (without imprint).	800	1,300	1,800

1920 Second Issue

		Good	Fine	XF
101	**50 Cent** 1.8.1920. Blue, olive and multicolor. Border of musical note forms by J.M. Fleischman. Similar to #16.	450	700	1,150
102	**1 Gulden** 1.8.1920. Green, orange and multicolor. Border of musical note forms by J.M. Fleischman. Similar to #16.	550	800	1,250

		Good	Fine	XF
103	**2 1/2 Gulden** 1.8.1920. Brown on green underprint. BC: Green.	900	1,400	2,000

1940 Issue

		Good	Fine	XF
104	**50 Cent** 1940-1942. Orange. Helmeted woman at left. Printer: ABNC.			
	a. 1 serial #. 26.6.1940; 5.7.1940; 27.9.1940; 5.10.1940; 30.10.1940.	7.50	40.00	200
	b. As a. 1.7.1941.	7.50	40.00	200
	c. 2 serial #. 30.4.1942.	5.00	30.00	150
	p. Proof.	—	Unc	250
	s1. Specimen. 0s as serial #.	—	Unc	800
	s2. As c. Specimen.	—	Unc	400

		Good	Fine	XF
105	**1 Gulden** 1940-1947. Gray-blue. Helmeted woman at left. Like #104. Printer: ABNC.			
	a. 1 serial #. 26.6.1940; 5.7.1940; 19.9.1940; 5.10.1940; 30.10.1940.	8.50	45.00	200
	b. As a. 1.7.1941.	8.50	45.00	200
	c. 2 serial #. 30.4.1942.	5.00	40.00	175
	d. 1.7.1947.	12.50	75.00	300
	p. Proof.	—	Unc	400
	s1. Specimen. 0s as serial #.	—	Unc	800
	s2. As c or d. Specimen.	—	Unc	500

1949-1955 Issues

		VG	VF	UNC
106	**1 Gulden** 1.7.1949. Green, dark brown and blue. Bust of Mercury at left. BC: Brown and violet. Printer: JEZ.	40.00	100	350
107	**1 Gulden** 1.3.1951. Green, dark brown and blue. Bust of Mercury at left. Like #106. BC: Brown and green. Printer: JEZ.	40.00	100	350

		VG	VF	UNC
108	**1 Gulden** 1954-1960. Blue and brown. Bust of Mercury at left. Printer: JEZ.			
	a. Signature title: *De Landsminister van Financien* at left. 1.7.1954.	25.00	60.00	130
	b. Signature title: *De Minister van Financien* at left. 1.5.1956; 1.4.1960.	20.00	55.00	125
109	**2 1/2 Gulden** 1.7.1950. Red-brown on yellow-green underprint. Bust of Mercury at left. 3 lines of text at lower center right. BC: Red-violet and purple. Printer: JEZ.	20.00	100	300

		VG	VF	UNC
110	**2 1/2 Gulden** 1.7.1955. Red-brown. Bust of Mercury at left. 4 lines of text at lower center right. BC: Red and brown. Printer: JEZ.	20.00	100	300

Centrale Bank van Suriname

1957 Issue

		VG	VF	UNC
111	**5 Gulden** 2.1.1957. Blue on multicolor underprint. Woman with fruit basket at right. Back: Arms. Watermark: Toucan's head. Printer: JEZ.			
	a. Issued note.	25.00	60.00	200
	s. Specimen.	—	—	150
112	**10 Gulden** 2.1.1957. Orange on multicolor underprint. Woman with fruit basket at right. Like #111. Back: Arms. Watermark: Toucan's head. Printer: JEZ.			
	a. Issued note.	40.00	100	300
	s. Specimen.	—	—	250
113	**25 Gulden** 2.1.1957. Green on multicolor underprint. Girl and fruit at right. Back: Arms. Watermark: Toucan's head. Printer: JEZ.			
	a. Issued note.	100	225	500
	s. Specimen.	—	—	450
114	**100 Gulden** 2.1.1957. Purple on multicolor underprint. Girl and fruit at right. Like #113. Back: Arms. Watermark: Toucan's head. Printer: JEZ.			
	a. Issued note.	125	275	700
	s. Specimen.	—	—	600
115	**1000 Gulden** 2.1.1957. Olive green on multicolor underprint. Girl and fruit at right. Like #113. Back: Arms. Watermark: Toucan's head. Printer: JEZ.			
	a. Issued note.	200	400	1,200
	s. Specimen.	—	—	900

The Kingdom of Sweden, a limited constitutional monarchy located in northern Europe between Norway and Finland, has an area of 449,964 sq. km. and a population of 9.04 million. Capital: Stockholm. Mining, lumbering and a specialized machine industry dominate the economy. Machinery, paper, iron and steel, motor vehicles and wood pulp are exported.A military power during the 17th century, Sweden has not participated in any war in almost two centuries. An armed neutrality was preserved in both World Wars. Sweden's long-successful economic formula of a capitalist system interlarded with substantial welfare elements was challenged in the 1990s by high unemployment and in 2000-02 by the global economic downturn, but fiscal discipline over the past several years has allowed the country to weather economic vagaries. Sweden joined the EU in 1995, but the public rejected the introduction of the euro in a 2003 referendum.

RULERS:

Carl XI, 1660-1697
Carl XII, 1697-1718
Ulrica Eleonora, 1719-1720
Fredric I, 1720-1751
Adolf Fredric, 1751-1771
Gustaf III, 1771-1792
Gustaf IV Adolf, 1792-1809
Carl XIII, 1809-1818
Carl XIV John, 1818-1844
Oscar I, 1844-1859
Carl XV, 1859-1872
Oscar II, 1872-1907
Gustaf V, 1907-1950
Gustaf VI Adolf, 1950-1973
Carl XVI Gustaf, 1973-

MONETARY SYSTEM:

1 Daler Smt. = 32 Öre Smt. (= 3 Daler Kmt.), 1665
1 Riksdaler = 48 Skilling (= 18 Daler Kmt.), 1777
1 Riksdaler = 1 1/2 Riksdaler Riksgäld, 1803
1 Riksdaler Specie = 2 2/3 Riksdaler Banco = 4 Riksdaler Riksgäld, 1834
1 Riksdaler Riksmynt = 100 Öre (= 1/4 Riksdaler Specie = 1 Riksdaler Riksgäld), 1855
1 Krona = 100 Öre (= 1 Riksdaler Riksmynt), 1873
1 Krona = 100 Öre

MONETARY ABBREVIATIONS

DALER SMT. = Daler Silvermynt
DALER KMT. = Daler Kopparmynt
KOP. SK. = Kopparschillingar
RKD. = Riksdaler
RKD. SP. = Riksdaler Specie
RKD. BC. = Riksdaler Banco
RKD. RMT. = Riksdaler Riksmynt
RKD. RGD. = Riksdaler Riksgäld
SK. = Schillingar
SK. Kop. = Kopparschillingar
SK. SP = Skillingar Specie
SK. BC. = Skillingar Banco
Kr. = Krona (Kronor)

REPLACEMENT NOTES:

Issues since 1956 with asterisk following serial number. Asterisk following the serial number for note issued since 1956.

NOTE ON VALUES: Indicated values apply only to uncancelled examples. Notes with cancellations are worth up to 50% less.

KINGDOM

Stockholms Banco

#A1-A45 are unknown in private hands.

1661 Ducat Issue

No.	Description	Good	Fine	XF
A1	**Various Handwritten Values** 1661.	—	—	—

1661 Riksdaler Specie Issue

No.	Description	Good	Fine	XF
A2	**50 Riksdaler Specie** 1661-1662. Handwritten denomination.	—	—	—
A3	**100 Riksdaler Specie** 1661-1662. Handwritten denomination.	—	—	—
A4	**200 Riksdaler Specie** 1661-1662. Handwritten denomination.	—	—	—
A5	**300 Riksdaler Specie** 1661-1662. Handwritten denomination.	—	—	—
A6	**400 Riksdaler Specie** 1661-1662. Handwritten denomination.	—	—	—
A7	**500 Riksdaler Specie** 1661-1662. Handwritten denomination.	—	—	—
A8	**600 Riksdaler Specie** 1661-1662. Handwritten denomination.	—	—	—
A9	**700 Riksdaler Specie** 1661-1662. Handwritten denomination.	—	—	—
A10	**800 Riksdaler Specie** 1661-1662. Handwritten denomination.	—	—	—
A11	**900 Riksdaler Specie** 1661-1662. Handwritten denomination.	—	—	—
A12	**1000 Riksdaler Specie** 1661-1662. Handwritten denomination.	—	—	—

1661 Daler Silvermynt Issue

No.	Description	Good	Fine	XF
A13	**50 Daler Silvermynt** 1661. Handwritten denomination.	—	—	—
A14	**100 Daler Silvermynt** 1661. Handwritten denomination.	—	—	—
A15	**200 Daler Silvermynt** 1661. Handwritten denomination.	—	—	—
A16	**300 Daler Silvermynt** 1661. Handwritten denomination.	—	—	—
A17	**400 Daler Silvermynt** 1661. Handwritten denomination.	—	—	—
A18	**500 Daler Silvermynt** 1661. Handwritten denomination.	—	—	—
A19	**600 Daler Silvermynt** 1661. Handwritten denomination.	—	—	—
A20	**700 Daler Silvermynt** 1661. Handwritten denomination.	—	—	—
A21	**800 Daler Silvermynt** 1661. Handwritten denomination.	—	—	—
A22	**900 Daler Silvermynt** 1661. Handwritten denomination.	—	—	—
A23	**1000 Daler Silvermynt** 1661. Handwritten denomination.	—	—	—

1661 Daler Kopparmynt Issue

Kreditiv-Sedlar (Credit Notes)

No.	Description	Good	Fine	XF
A24	**12 1/2 Daler Kopparmynt** 1661. Handwritten denomination.	—	—	—
A25	**25 Daler Kopparmynt** 1661. Handwritten denomination.	—	—	—
A26	**50 Daler Kopparmynt** 1661. Handwritten denomination.	—	—	—
A27	**100 Daler Kopparmynt** 1661. Handwritten denomination.	—	—	—
A28	**150 Daler Kopparmynt** 1661. Handwritten denomination.	—	—	—
A29	**200 Daler Kopparmynt** 1661. Handwritten denomination.	—	—	—
A30	**250 Daler Kopparmynt** 1661. Handwritten denomination.	—	—	—
A31	**300 Daler Kopparmynt** 1661. Handwritten denomination.	—	—	—
A32	**350 Daler Kopparmynt** 1661. Handwritten denomination.	—	—	—
A33	**400 Daler Kopparmynt** 1661. Handwritten denomination.	—	—	—
A34	**450 Daler Kopparmynt** 1661. Handwritten denomination.	—	—	—
A35	**500 Daler Kopparmynt** 1661. Handwritten denomination.	—	—	—
A36	**550 Daler Kopparmynt** 1661. Handwritten denomination.	—	—	—
A37	**600 Daler Kopparmynt** 1661. Handwritten denomination.	—	—	—
A38	**650 Daler Kopparmynt** 1661. Handwritten denomination.	—	—	—
A39	**700 Daler Kopparmynt** 1661. Handwritten denomination.	—	—	—
A40	**750 Daler Kopparmynt** 1661. Handwritten denomination.	—	—	—
A41	**800 Daler Kopparmynt** 1661. Handwritten denomination.	—	—	—
A42	**850 Daler Kopparmynt** 1661. Handwritten denomination.	—	—	—
A43	**900 Daler Kopparmynt** 1661. Handwritten denomination.	—	—	—
A44	**950 Daler Kopparmynt** 1661. Handwritten denomination.	—	—	—
A45	**1000 Daler Kopparmynt** 1661. Handwritten denomination.	—	—	—

1662 Daler Kopparmynt Issue

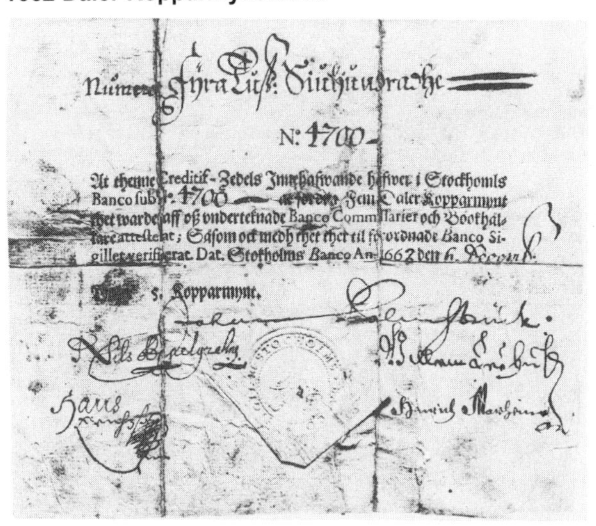

		Good	Fine	XF
A46	**5 Daler Kopparmynt** 1662-1664. Printed denomination.	—	—	—
A47	**10 Daler Kopparmynt** 1662-1664. Printed denomination.	—	—	—
A48	**12 1/2 Daler Kopparmynt** 1662-1664. Printed denomination.	—	—	—
A49	**25 Daler Kopparmynt** 1662-1664. Printed denomination.	—	—	—
A50	**50 Daler Kopparmynt** 1662-1664. Printed denomination.	—	—	—
A51	**100 Daler Kopparmynt** 1662-1664. Printed denomination.	—	—	—
A52	**200 Daler Kopparmynt** 1662-1664. Printed denomination.	—	—	—
A53	**300 Daler Kopparmynt** 1662-1664. Printed denomination.	—	—	—
A54	**400 Daler Kopparmynt** 1662-1664. Printed denomination.	—	—	—
A55	**500 Daler Kopparmynt** 1662-1664. Printed denomination.	—	—	—
A56	**1000 Daler Kopparmynt** 1662-1664. Printed denomination.	—	—	—

1666 Daler Silvermynt Issue

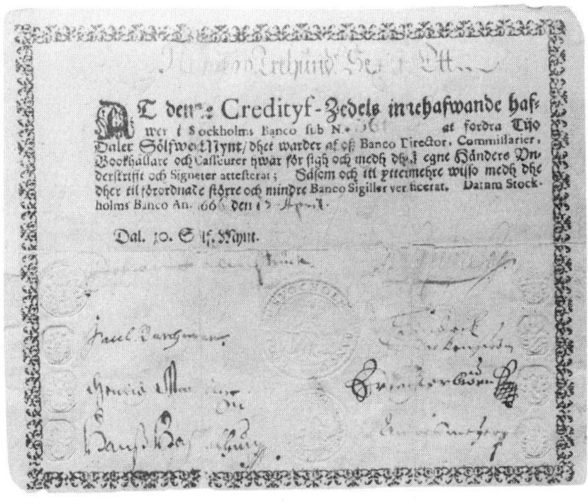

		Good	Fine	XF
A57	**10 Daler Silvermynt** 1666. Printed denomination.	3,000	7,000	20,000
A58	**25 Daler Silvermynt** 1666. Printed denomination.	4,000	9,000	25,000
A59	**50 Daler Silvermynt** 1666. Printed denomination.	4,000	9,000	25,000

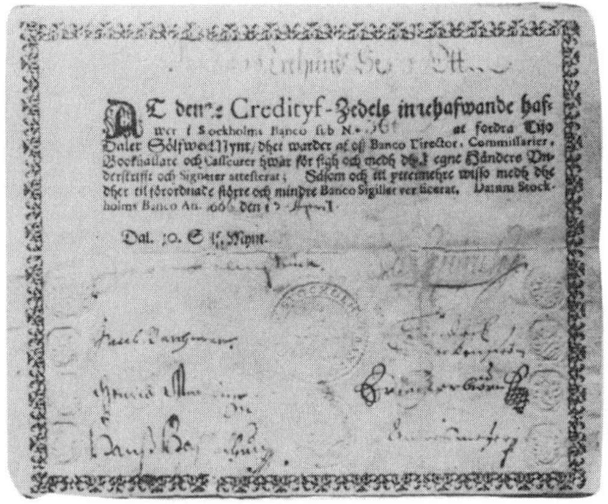

		Good	Fine	XF
A60	**100 Daler Silvermynt** 1666. Printed denomination.	3,000	7,000	20,000

1667 Transport (Transfer) Issue

		Good	Fine	XF
A61	**100 Daler Silvermynt** 1667. Copper money. (Negotiable only with endorsement.)	—	—	—

Contribution Office and Purchasing Commission

1716 Daler Silvermynt Issue

		Good	Fine	XF
A62	**25 Daler Silvermynt** 1716. Completely handwritten.			
	a. 6 signatures.	40.00	120	320

1717 Issue

		Good	Fine	XF
A63	**5 Daler Silvermynt** 1717.			
	a. With 3 signatures.	20.00	60.00	160
	r. Unsigned remainder.	10.00	30.00	80.00

		Good	Fine	XF
A64	**10 Daler Silvermynt** 1717.			
	a. With 3 signatures.	20.00	60.00	170
	r. Unsigned remainder.	10.00	30.00	80.00

Assurance Notes

1719 Issue

		Good	Fine	XF
A65	**2 Öre** 1719-1729. Handwritten dates. Exchangeable for devalued emergency coins *(delvalerade Myntetecken).*	—	—	—
A66	**2 Öre** 1719-1729. Handwritten dates. Exchangeable for devalued coinage notes *(devalverade Mynte-Sedlar).*	—	—	—
A67	**14 Öre** 1719-1729. Handwritten dates. Exchangeable for emergency coins and notes *(Myntetecken, Mynte-Sedlar).*	125	400	—
A68	**14 Öre** 1719-1729. Printed dates. Tax assurance note *(Crono-Uppbörd.* Rare.	—	—	—
A69	**14 Öre** 1719-1729. Printed dates. Exchangeable for assurance notes. Split into other (lower) denominations for transfer *(Transport).* Rare.	—	—	—

Kongl. May:tz Ständers Wexel-Banco

1701-19 Issue

		Good	Fine	XF
A70	**Various Handwritten Values** 1702-1719. from 1702-1708 issued in Daler Silvermynt Courant or Daler Silvermynt Carolin. 14 issued. From 1710-1719 Issued in Daler Kopparmynt and other currencies. None in private hands.	—	—	—
A71	**200 Daler Silvermynt** 1701. Handwritten. 1 known and it is a copy of the original which was destroyed.	—	—	—

Riksens Ständers Wexel-Banco

1719 Issue

		Good	Fine	XF
A72	**Various Handwritten Values** 1719-1728. Comprised of four pages. 1 known. Rare.	—	—	—

1729 Issue

		Good	Fine	XF
A73	**Various Handwritten Values** 1729-1731. Comprised of 4 pages. Embossed text in frame at top. The 4-digit year is also in this embossed text. The yar is also printed with 3 digits and last digit handwritten. 1 known. Rare.	—	—	—

1732 Issue

		Good	Fine	XF
A74	**Various Handwritten Values** 1732-1747. Comprised of 4 pages. Initial letter and bank seal changed. Rare.	—	—	—

1743-1745 Issue

		Good	Fine	XF
A75	**6 Daler Kopparmynt** 1732-1747. Banco Sigill seal at upper left. Value written as *Sex* in bottom line of text. Rare.	—	—	—
A76	**9 Daler Kopparmynt** 1732-1747. Banco Sigill seal at upper left. Value written as *Nijo* in bottom line of text. Like #A75. Rare.	—	—	—
A77	**12 Daler Kopparmynt** 1732-1747. Banco Sigill seal at upper left. Value written as *Tolf* in bottom line of text. Like #A75. Rare.	—	—	—
A78	**24 Daler Kopparmynt** 1732-1747. Comprised of 4 pages. Rare.	—	—	—
A79	**36 Daler Kopparmynt** 1732-1747. Comprised of 4 pages. Rare.	—	—	—

1748 Issue

		Good	Fine	XF
A80	**Various Handwritten Values** 1748-1760. Comprised of 4 pages. Any denomination was allowed, but when the note was finished, the value was printed on the back to prevent alteration of the handwritten amount on the front. In the format: Dlr36Kpt for 36 Daler Kopparmynt. Rare.	—	—	—
A81	**6 Daler Kopparmynt** 1748-1761. *BANCO TRANSPORT SEDEL* in uneven line.	100	350	—

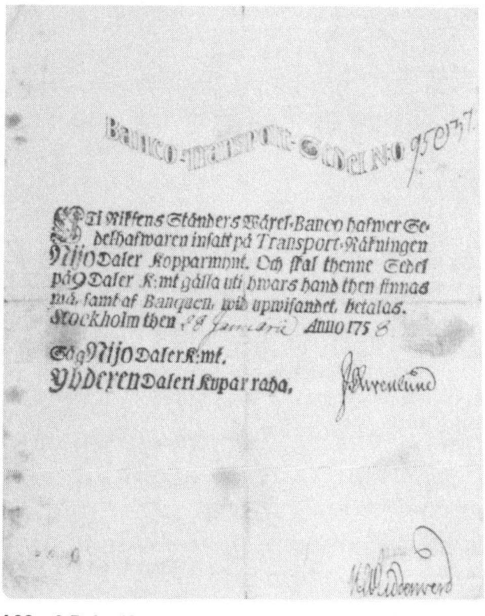

		Good	Fine	XF
A82	**9 Daler Kopparmynt** 1748-61. *BANCO TRANSPORT SEDEL* in uneven line. Like #A81.	100	400	—
A83	**12 Daler Kopparmynt** 1748-1754. *BANCO TRANSPORT SEDEL* in uneven line. Like #A81.	100	450	—
A84	**24 Daler Kopparmynt** 1748-1758. *BANCO TRANSPORT SEDEL* in uneven line. Like #A81. Comprised of 4 pages.	750	2,500	—
A85	**36 Daler Kopparmynt** 1748-1758. *BANCO TRANSPORT SEDEL* in uneven line. Like #A81. Comprised of 4 pages.	750	2,500	—

1759-1760 Issue

		Good	Fine	XF
A86	**Various Handwritten Values** 1759-1776. Comprised of 4 pages. Value printed on the back in the format of Dlr60kmt for 60 Daler Kopparmynt. Rare.	—	—	—

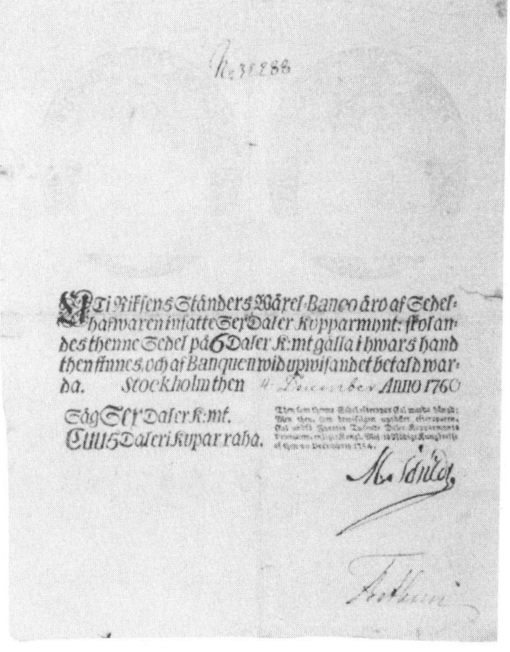

		Good	Fine	XF
A87	**6 Daler Kopparmynt** 1759-1776. Embossed seals at top.			
	a. 1759-1768. Last digit in the year is handwritten, but the embossed seal has the complete year.	60.00	160	650
	b. 1769-1776. All four digits in the year are printed.	60.00	160	650
A88	**9 Daler Kopparmynt** 1759-1776. Embossed seals at top. Like #A87.	Good	Fine	XF
	a. 1759-1768. Last digit in the year is handwritten but the embossed seal has the complete year.	70.00	180	700
	b. 1769-1776. All four digits in the year are printed.	70.00	180	700

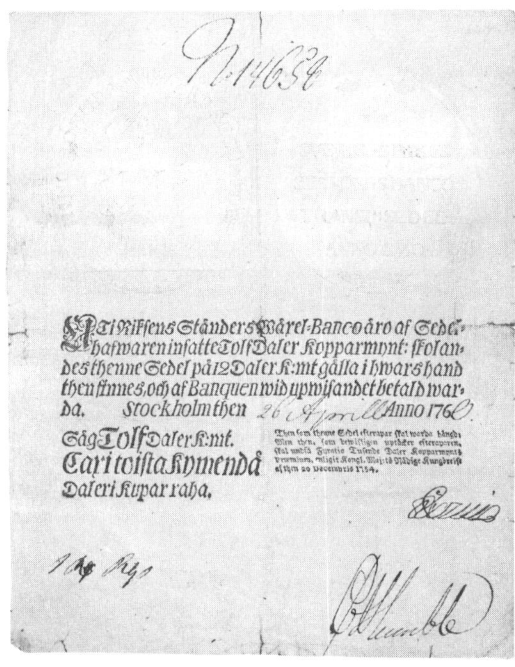

		Good	Fine	XF
A89	**12 Daler Kopparmynt** 1759-1776. Embossed seals at top. Like #A87.			
	a. 1760-1773. Last digit in the year is handwritten but the embossed seal has the complete year.	75.00	200	800
	b. 1774-1776. All four digits in the year are printed.	75.00	200	800

1777 Transport (Transfer) Issue

		Good	Fine	XF
A90	**Various Handwritten Values** 1777-1836. Comprised of 4 pages.			
	a. 1777-1786. Denominated in Riksdaler Specie. Embossed seal on both sheets.	—	—	—
	b. 1787-1834. Embossed seal on first sheet only.	—	—	—
	c. 1834-1836. Denominated in Riksdaler Banco.	—	—	—
A91	**2 Riksdaler Specie** 1777-1812. Printed value above obligation. Comprised of 4 pages.	Good	Fine	XF
	a. 1777-1786. Embossed seal on both sheets. Rare.	—	—	—
	b. 1787-1806; 1812. Embossed seal on first sheet only. Rare.	—	—	—
	c. 1807-1811. Year printed.	125	350	1,400

Color Abbreviation Guide

New to the *Standard Catalog of ® World Paper Money* are the following abbreviations related to color references:

BC: Back color

PC: Paper color

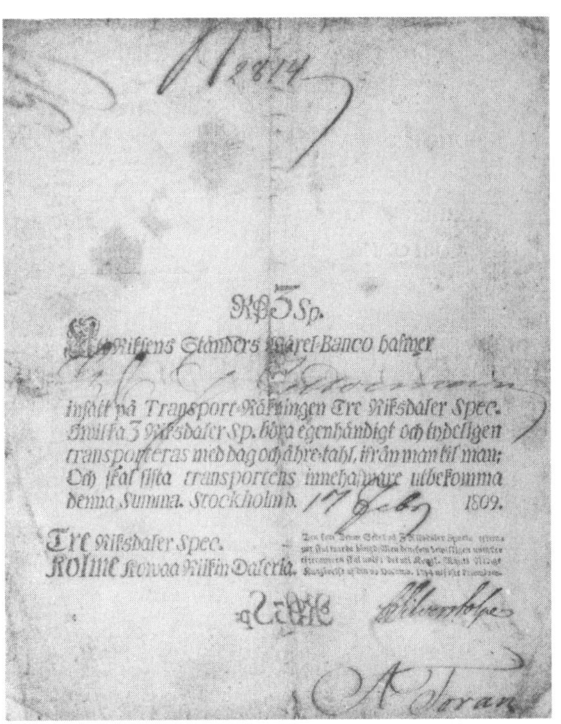

		Good	Fine	XF
A92	**3 Riksdaler Specie** 1777-1812. Like #A91. Printed value above obligation. Comprised of 4 pages.			
	a. 1777-1786. Embossed seal on both sheets. Rare.	—	—	—
	b. 1787-1805. Embossed seal on first sheet only. Rare.	—	—	—
	c. 1806-1812. Year printed.	100	300	1,200

1802 Issue

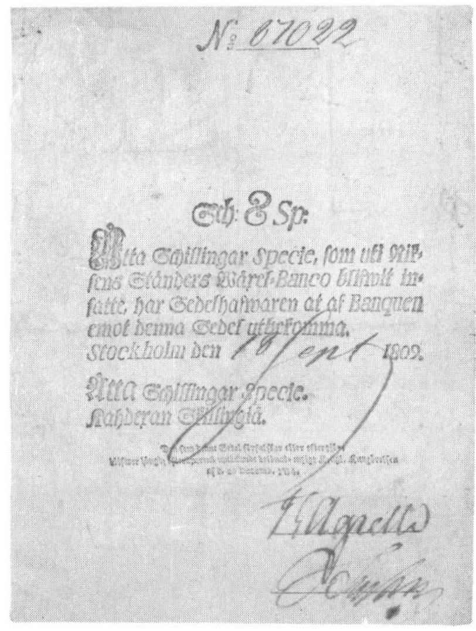

		Good	Fine	XF
A93	**8 Schillingar Specie** 1802-1834. Like #A91. Printed value above obligation. Comprised of 2 pages.			
	a. 1802-1818. Punishment clase of 1754.	50.00	100	325
	b. 1819-1830. Punishment clause of 1818.	50.00	100	325
	c. 1831-1834. Punishment clase of 1818 in frame.	50.00	100	275
A94	**12 Schillingar Specie** 1802-1834. Printed value above obligation. Like #A93.	Good	Fine	XF
	a. 1802-1818. Punishment clasue of 1754.	50.00	150	475
	b. 1819-1834. Punishment clause of 1818.	50.00	150	400
A95	**16 Schillingar Specie** 1802-1834. Like #A91.	Good	Fine	XF
	a. 1802; 1806; 1808-1809; 1811-1812; 1815-1818. Punishment clause of 1754.	75.00	175	525
	b. 1803-1805; 1807; 1810; 1813-1814. Rare.	—	—	—
	c. 1819; 1823; 1825. Punishment clause of 1818. Rare.	—	—	—
	d. 1820-1822; 1824; 1826-1830.	75.00	175	475
	e. Horizontal format. 1831-1834.	75.00	175	500

1803 Issue

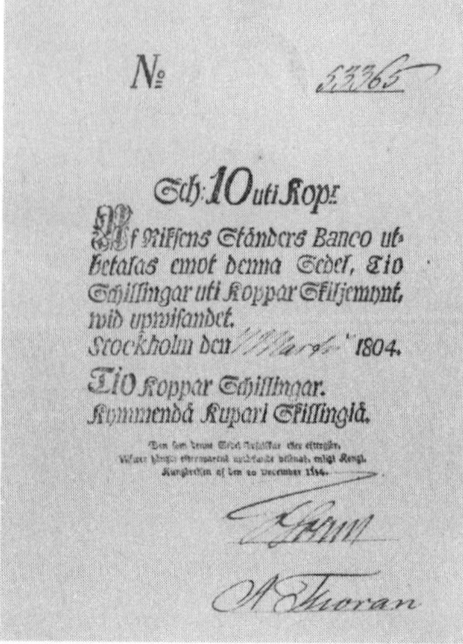

		Good	Fine	XF
A96	**10 Koppar Schillingar** 1803-1804. Embossed seal at top center.	50.00	100	175

		Good	Fine	XF
A97	**14 Koppar Schillingar** 1803-1804. Embossed seal at top center. Like #A96.	50.00	100	175

1812 Issue

		Good	Fine	XF
A98	**2 Riksdaler Specie** 1812-1834. Like #A91. Comprised of 2 pages.			
	a. 1812-1813; 1815. Punishment clause of 1754.	70.00	200	800
	b. 1814; 1816-1818. Rare.	—	—	—
	c. 1819-1822; 1828; 1831; 1834.) Punishment clause of 1818. Rare.	—	—	—
	d. 1823-1827; 1829-1830; 1832-1833.	80.00	250	1,000
A99	**3 Riksdaler Specie** 1812-1836. Printed value at lower left. Like #A92. Horizontal format. Comprised of 2 pages.	**Good**	**Fine**	**XF**
	a. 1812-1818. Punishment clause of 1754. Rare.	—	—	—
	b. 1819-1823; 1825-1830; 1832; 1835-1836. Punishment clause of 1818. Rare.	—	—	—
	c. 1824; 1831; 1833-1834.	70.00	200	800

1834 Issue

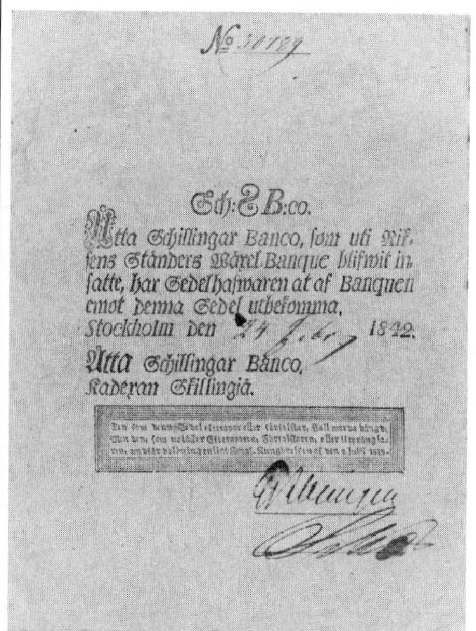

		Good	Fine	XF
A100	**8 Schillingar Banco** 1834-1849. Printed value above obligation. Like #A93.			
	a. Contoured letters in watermark. 1834-1836.	50.00	100	200
	b. Different watermark. 1836-1849.	50.00	100	200

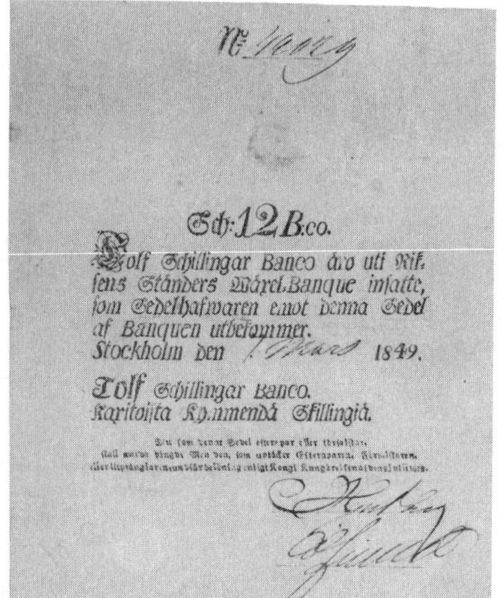

		Good	Fine	XF
A101	**12 Schillingar Banco** 1834-1849. Printed value above obligation. Like #A100.			
	a. Contoured letters in watermark. 1834-1836.	50.00	100	200
	b. Different watermark. 1836-1849.	50.00	100	200

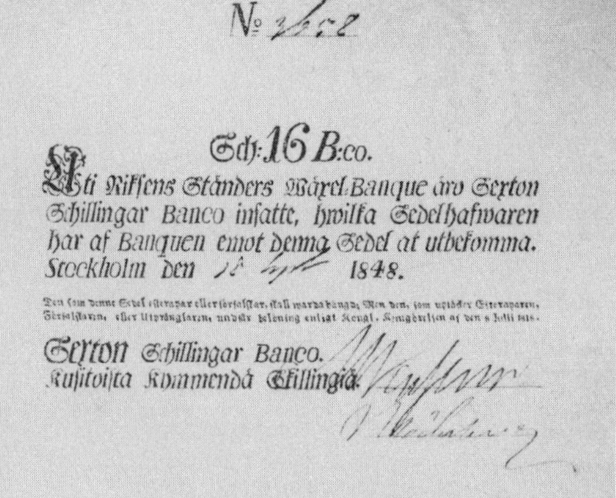

		Good	Fine	XF
A102	**16 Schillingar Banco**			
	1834-1849. Printed value at lower left. Like #A99c. Horizontal format.			
	a. Contoured letters in watermark. 1834-1836.	50.00	100	300
	b. Different watermark. 1836-1849.	50.00	100	200

#A103 renumbered, see #A94.

		Good	Fine	XF
A104	**2 Riksdaler Banco**			
	1834-1836.	100	225	900
A105	**3 Riksdaler Banco**	**Good**	**Fine**	**XF**
	1834-1836.	75.00	225	900

Riksens Ständers Riksgälds Contoir

1790 Issue

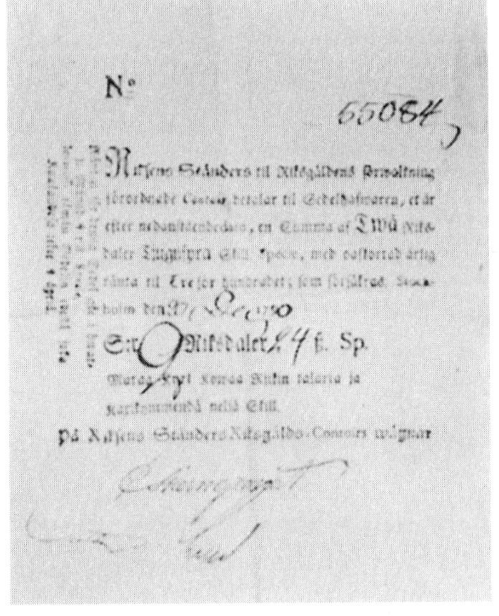

		Good	Fine	XF
A106	**Various Handwritten Values**			
	1789-1792. Credit note with 3% interest. 16 different denominations ranging from 2-1/2 to 1000 Riksdaler. Comprised of 4 pages.			
	a. 1789-1790. Denomination printed in words and handwritten in digits.	—	—	—
	b. 1791-1792. Handwritten denomination.	—	—	—

1791 Issue

		Good	Fine	XF
A107	**12 Schillingar**			
	1790-1792. Deposition certificate. Exchangeable for credit note to get smaller denominations.			
	a. 1790. Deposition certificate. Exchangeable for credit note to get smaller denominations.	70.00	200	800
	b. 1791. Issued note.	70.00	200	800
	c. 1791-1792. Transverse denomination added.	70.00	200	800

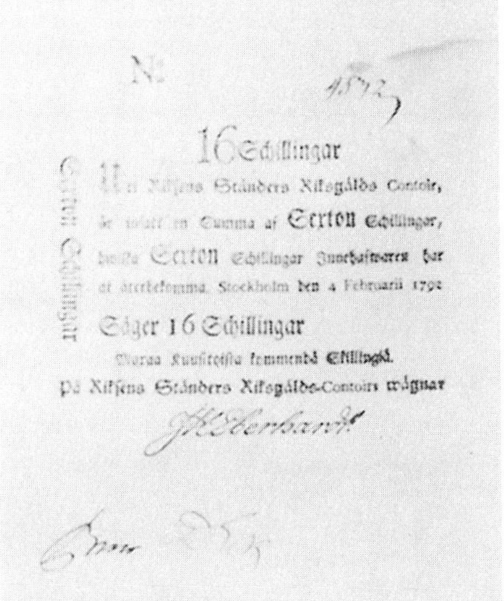

		Good	Fine	XF
A108	**16 Schillingar**			
	1791-1792.			
	a. 1791. Issued note.	80.00	225	900
	b. 1791-1792. Transverse denomination added.	80.00	225	900
A109	**24 Schillingar**	**Good**	**Fine**	**XF**
	1791-1792.			
	a. 1790. Deposition certificate.	90.00	250	1,000
	b. 1791. Issued note.	90.00	250	1,000
	c. 1791-1792. Transverse denomination added.	90.00	250	1,000
A110	**1 Riksdaler Specie**	**Good**	**Fine**	**XF**
	1791-1792.			
	a. 1790. Deposition certificate.	—	—	—
	b. 1791. Issued note.	—	—	—
	c. 1791-1792. Transverse denomination added.	—	—	—
A111	**2 Riksdaler Specie**	**Good**	**Fine**	**XF**
	1791-1792.			
	a. 1791. Issued note.	—	—	—
	b. 1791-1792. Transverse denomination added.	—	—	—
A112	**5 Riksdaler Specie**	**Good**	**Fine**	**XF**
	1791-1792.			
	a. 1791. Issued note.	—	—	—
	b. 1791-1792. Transverse denomination added.	—	—	—

1792; 1793 Issue

		Good	Fine	XF
A113	**Various Handwritten Values**			
	1793-1816. Comprised of 4 pages.	—	—	—
A114	**12 Schillingar**	**Good**	**Fine**	**XF**
	1792-1805.			
	a. 1792-1794. Uniface.	50.00	100	325
	b. 1795-1805. Value on back.	50.00	100	250
A115	**16 Schillingar**	**Good**	**Fine**	**XF**
	1792-1834.			
	a. 1792-1794. Uniface.	50.00	150	625
	b. 1795-1818. Value on back.	50.00	120	425
	c. 1819-1834. Punishment clause change.	50.00	100	400
A116	**24 Schillingar**	**Good**	**Fine**	**XF**
	1793-1804.			
	a. 1793-1794. Uniface.	60.00	175	675
	b. 1795-1804. Value on back.	50.00	150	575

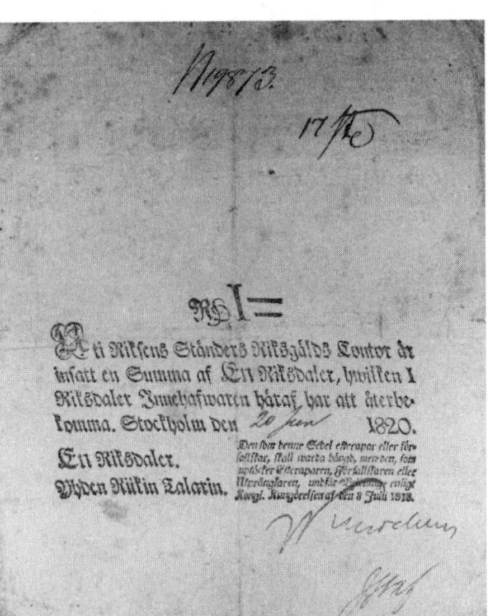

		Good	Fine	XF
A117	**1 Riksdaler**			
	1792-1834.			
	a. 1792-1794. Uniface.	50.00	175	650
	b. 1795-1818. Value on back.	50.00	90.00	350
	c. 1819-1834. Punishment clause change.	50.00	90.00	350
A118	**2 Riksdaler**	**Good**	**Fine**	**XF**
	1792-1834.			
	a. 1792-1794.	50.00	150	650
	b. 1795-1818. Value on back.	50.00	125	500
	c. 1819-1834. Horizontal format. Punishment clause change.	50.00	100	400

1816 Issue

		Good	Fine	XF
A119	**10 Riksdaler**			
	1816-1834.	—	—	—
A120	**50 Riksdaler**	**Good**	**Fine**	**XF**
	1816-1834.	—	—	—
A121	**100 Riksdaler**	**Good**	**Fine**	**XF**
	1816-1834.	—	—	—

Sveriges Rikes Ständers Bank

1830 Issue

		Good	Fine	XF
A122	**10 Riksdaler**			
	1830. (Not issued)	—	—	—

1835-1836 Issue

		Good	Fine	XF
A123	**32 Skillingar Banco** 1836-1858. Black. Lion lying in front of crowned arms at top center. PC: Yellow.			
	a. Handwritten serial #. 1836.	75.00	150	450
	b. Handwritten serial #. 1839. Rare.	—	—	—
	c. Printed serial #. 1840-1858.	37.50	75.00	300

		Good	Fine	XF
A124	**2 Riksdaler Banco** 1836-1857. Black. Lion lying in front of crowned arms at top center. Like #A123. PC: Light blue.			
	a. Handwritten serial #. 1836.	80.00	250	1,000
	b. Printed serial #. 1840; 1845; 1849; 1851; 1853; 1855; 1857.	50.00	100	200
	c. Printed serial #. 1848.	50.00	150	400
A125	**6 2/3 Riksdaler Banco** 1835-1856. Black. Lion lying in front of crowned arms at top center. Like #A123. PC: Green.	Good	Fine	XF
	a. Handwritten serial #. 1835.	200	600	2,400
	b. Printed serial #. 1841; 1850; 1852; 1854; 1856.	70.00	200	800
	c. Printed serial #. 1848-1849. Rare.	—	—	—

		Good	Fine	XF
A126	**10 Riksdaler Banco** 1836-1857. Black. Lion lying in front of crowned arms at top center. Like #A125. PC: Yellow.			
	a. Handwritten serial #. 28.1.1836.	300	750	3,000
	b. Printed serial #. 1841; 1852; 1854-1855; 1857.	100	300	1,200
	c. Printed serial #. 1848; 1850. Rare.	—	—	—
A127	**16 2/3 Riksdaler Banco** 1836-1855. Black. Lion lying in front of crowned arms at top center. Like #A125. PC: Light red.	Good	Fine	XF
	a. Handwritten serial #. 28.1.1836. Rare.	—	—	—
	b. Printed serial #. 1844; 1852; 1855.	400	1,200	4,000
	c. Printed serial #. 1847; 1850. Rare.	—	—	—
A128	**33 1/3 Riksdaler Banco** 1836-1857. Black. Lion lying in front of crowned arms at top center. Like #A125. PC: Light blue.	Good	Fine	XF
	a. Handwritten serial #. 28.1.1836. Rare.	—	—	—
	b. Printed serial #. 1840-1852; 1857. Rare.	—	—	—
	c. Printed serial #. 1854; 1856.	650	2,500	5,500

		Good	Fine	XF
A129	**100 Riksdaler Banco** 1836-1854. Black. Svea seated below radiant crown at top center. PC: Light yellow.			
	a. Handwritten serial #. 1836. Rare.	—	—	—
	b. Printed serial #. 1843-1854. Rare.	—	—	—
A130	**500 Riksdaler Banco** 1836-1854. Blue. Svea seated below radiant crown at top center. Like #A129. PC: Light blue.	Good	Fine	XF
	a. Handwritten serial #. 1836. Rare.	—	—	—
	b. Printed serial #. 1840-1854. Rare.	—	—	—

1858-1859 Issue

		Good	Fine	XF
A131	**1 Riksdaler** 1859-1865. Green. Crowned and supported arms at top center. *EN* in center rectangle.	20.00	75.00	200
A132	**5 Riksdaler** 1858-1867. Red. Crowned and supported arms at top center. *EN* in center rectangle. Like #A131.	Good	Fine	XF
	a. 1858; 1863.	100	300	1,100
	b. Frame patterned. 1863; 1867.	70.00	250	1,000
A133	**10 Riksdaler** 1859; 1866, 1870. Green. Crowned and supported arms at top center. *EN* in center rectangle. Like #A131.	100	350	1,200
A134	**50 Riksdaler** 1859; 1861; 1865. Red. Crowned and supported arms at top center. *EN* in center rectangle. Like #A131. Rare.	—	—	—
A135	**100 Riksdaler** 1859; 1864. Green. Crowned and supported arms at top center. *EN* in center rectangle. Like #A131. Rare.	—	—	—
A136	**500 Riksdaler** 3.1.1859. Red. Crowned and supported arms at top center. *EN* in center rectangle. Like #A131. Rare.	—	—	—
A137	**1000 Riksdaler** 3.1.1859. Yellow. Crowned and supported arms at top center. *EN* in center rectangle. Like #A131. Rare.	—	—	—

1865 Issue

		Good	Fine	XF
A138	**1 Riksdaler** 1865-1869. Green on green underprint. Crowned and supported arms at top center. Like #A131 but *EN* in oval at center.	15.00	60.00	150

Sveriges Riksbank

1869-1870 Issue

		Good	Fine	XF
A139	**1 Riksdaler** 1869-1873. Black on green underprint. Crowned and supported arms at top center. *EN* in oval at center. Like #A138, but with different watermark.			
	a. 2 handwritten signatures. 1869-1872.	15.00	60.00	150
	b. Left signature printed. 1872-1873.	15.00	60.00	150
	c. 2 signatures printed. 1873.	15.00	60.00	150
A140	**5 Riksdaler** 1870-1873. Black on red underprint. Crowned and supported arms at top center. *EN* in center rectangle. Like #A132.	Good	Fine	XF
	a. 2 serial #. 1870-1872.	75.00	225	900
	b. L. signature printed. 1872-1873.	60.00	175	700
A141	**10 Riksdaler** 1870-1873. Black on green underprint. Crowned and supported arms at top center. *EN* in center rectangle. Like #A133.	Good	Fine	XF
	a. 2 serial #. Series B, C. 1870-1873.	75.00	250	1,000
	b. Left signature printed. 1873.	75.00	250	1,000
A142	**50 Riksdaler** 3.1.1870. Black on red underprint. Crowned and supported arms at top center. *EN* in center rectangle. Like #A134. Rare.	—	—	—
A143	**100 Riksdaler** 1870; 1872. Black on green underprint. Crowned and supported arms at top center. *EN* in center rectangle. Like #A135. Rare.	—	—	—
A144	**500 Riksdaler** 1870. Black on red underprint. Crowned and supported arms at top center. *EN* in center rectangle. Like #A136. Rare.	—	—	—
A145	**1000 Riksdaler** 1870. Black on yellow. Crowned and supported arms at top center. *EN* in center rectangle. Like #A137. Rare.	—	—	—

1874 Issue

		VG	VF	UNC
1	**1 Krona** 1874-1875. Black on green underprint. Crowned and supported arms at top center. Signature varieties. 134x74mm.			
	a. 1874.	7.00	30.00	150
	b. 1875.	5.00	20.00	90.00
2	**5 Kronor** 1874-1878. Red on red. Crowned and supported arms at top center. Like #1. Signature varieties. 134x74mm.	VG	VF	UNC
	a. 1874.	45.00	205	860
	b. 1875.	60.00	235	940
	c. 1876.	40.00	195	860
	d. 1877.	55.00	210	880
	e. 1878.	60.00	235	970

		VG	VF	UNC
3	**10 Kronor** 1874-1879. Green and black. Crowned and supported arms at top center. Signature varieties. 148x134mm.			
	a. 1874.	50.00	220	940
	b. 1875.	65.00	270	1,060
	c. 1876.	60.00	235	1,000
	d. 1877.	65.00	270	1,120
	e. 1878.	50.00	210	905
	f. 1879.	90.00	360	1,530
4	**50 Kronor**	VG	VF	UNC
	1874; 1876-79. Red and black. Crowned and supported arms over value. Signature varieties. 148x134mm. Rare.	—	—	—
5	**100 Kronor**	VG	VF	UNC
	1874-1879. Green and black. Crowned and supported arms over value. Signature varieties. 223x134mm. Rare.	—	—	—
6	**1000 Kronor**	VG	VF	UNC
	1874-1893. Yellow and black. Crowned and supported arms over value. Like #5. Signature varieties. 223x134mm. Rare.	—	—	—

1879-1881 Issues

		VG	VF	UNC
7	**5 Kronor**			
	1879. Black on brown design. Arms at upper center. Signature at right handwritten. Like #8. Back: Crowned shield at top center. BC: Blue. 121x70mm.	150	470	1,590

		VG	VF	UNC
8	**5 Kronor** 1879-1888. Black on brown design. Arms at upper center. Signature at right handwritten. Back: Crowned shield at top center. BC: Green.			
	a. 1879.	55.00	295	1,000
	b. 1880.	40.00	235	765
	c. 1881.	40.00	210	680
	d. 1882.	40.00	235	765
	e. 1883.	40.00	235	765
	f. 1884.	45.00	300	1,000
	g. 1885.	40.00	235	765
	h. 1886.	35.00	180	620
	i. 1887.	30.00	120	445
	j. 1888.	35.00	165	555

		VG	VF	UNC
9	**10 Kronor** 1879-1891. Black and blue. Crowned arms in upper corners, value at center. 121x70mm.			
	a. 1879.	100	410	1,765
	b. 1881.	100	410	1,180
	c. 1882.	100	410	1,180
	d. 1883.	120	470	1,650
	e. 1884.	120	470	1,470
	f. 1885.	90.00	360	1,235
	g. 1886.	90.00	360	1,235
	h. 1887.	90.00	350	1,235
	i. 1888.	80.00	325	1,235
	j. 1889.	75.00	295	1,100
	k. 1890.	75.00	295	1,095
	l. 1891.	65.00	260	980
10	**50 Kronor**	VG	VF	UNC
	1880-1884; 1886; 1888-1896. Maroon and black. Crowned arms over value. 140x121mm. Rare.	—	—	—
11	**100 Kronor**	VG	VF	UNC
	1880-1896. Blue and black. Crowned arms in upper corners. Handwritten signature. 140x121mm. Rare.	—	—	—
12	**1000 Kronor**	VG	VF	UNC
	1881. Blue and black. Crowned arms at top center. 210x121mm. Rare.	—	—	—

1888-1896 Issue

		VG	VF	UNC
13	**5 Kronor** 1888-1890. Black on brown design. Arms at upper center. 2 signatures printed. Like #8. Back: Crowned shield at top center. BC: Green.			
	a. 1888.	35.00	165	325
	b. 1889.	25.00	100	555
	c. 1890.	20.00	80.00	390
14	**5 Kronor** 1890-1898. Black. Red and green guilloche. Svea seated at right. Back: Gustav Vasa. PC: Beige.	VG	VF	UNC
	a. 1890.	40.00	480	750
	b. 1891.	40.00	210	825
	c. 1892.	35.00	150	620
	d. 1893.	40.00	210	825
	e. 1894.	40.00	190	765
	f. 1895.	30.00	150	620
	g. 1896.	35.00	155	650
	h. 1897.	30.00	130	560
	i. 1898.	30.00	150	620

15 10 Kronor

1892-1897. Black. Red and blue guilloche. Like #14. Svea seated at right. Back: Portrait Gustav Vasa. PC: Gray.

	VG	VF	UNC
a. 1892.	40.00	180	765
b. 1893.	45.00	190	820
c. 1894.	40.00	155	710
d. 1895.	45.00	190	820
e. 1896.	45.00	190	820
f. 1897.	35.00	150	625

16 50 Kronor

1896-1897. Black. Red and green guilloche. Svea seated at lower right. Back: Gustav Vasa.

	VG	VF	UNC
a. 1896.	235	825	—
b. 1897.	205	800	—

17 100 Kronor

1896-1898. Blue and black. Crowned arms in upper corners. Left signature printed. Like #11. Rare.

VG	VF	UNC
—	—	—

18 1000 Kronor

1894-1897. Svea seated. Back: Gustav Vasa. Rare. PC: Bluish with red imbedded fibers.

VG	VF	UNC
—	—	—

1898; 1899 Issue

19 5 Kronor

1899-1905. Black. Red and green guilloche. Svea seated at right. Back: Gustav Vasa. Like #14 but letter at lower left and right. PC: Beige.

	VG	VF	UNC
a. 1899.	30.00	120	500
b. 1900.	35.00	130	590
c. 1901.	35.00	130	560
d. 1902.	30.00	120	500
e. 1903.	35.00	165	710
f. 1904.	35.00	150	590
g. 1905.	25.00	95.00	415

20 10 Kronor

1898-1905. Black. Red and blue guilloche. Svea seated at right. Back: Gustav Vasa. Like #15 but letter at left and right. PC: Gray.

	VG	VF	UNC
a. 1898.	30.00	140	590
b. 1899.	30.00	140	590
c. 1900.	45.00	190	825
d. 1901.	30.00	130	530
e. 1902.	30.00	130	560
f. 1903.	25.00	105	470
g. 1904.	30.00	110	500
h. 1905.	25.00	105	470

21 50 Kronor

1898-1903. Black. Red and green guilloche. Svea seated at lower right. Back: Gustav Vasa. Like #16 but one big letter at lower left and right.

	VG	VF	UNC
a. 1898.	250	855	—
b. 1899.	180	735	—
c. 1900.	180	735	—
d. 1901.	165	710	—
e. 1902.	145	650	—
f. 1903.	145	650	—

22 100 Kronor

1898-1903. Red and blue. Svea seated at lower right. Back: Gustav Vasa.

	VG	VF	UNC
a. 1898. Rare.	—	—	—
b. 1900.	235	825	—
c. 1901.	210	710	—
d. 1902-1903.	180	650	—

23 1000 Kronor

1898-1905. Svea seated. Back: Gustav Vasa. Like #18. 1 letter at lower left and right. Rare. PC: Bluish with red imbedded fibers.

VG	VF	UNC
—	—	—

1903 Issue

24 50 Kronor

1903-1906. Black. Red and green guilloche. Svea seated at lower right. Like #21 but printed signature. Back: Gustav Vasa with one big letter at lower left and right.

	VG	VF	UNC
a. 1903.	145	650	—
b. 1904.	145	590	—
c. 1905-1906.	130	530	—

25 100 Kronor

1903-1906. Red and blue. Svea seated at lower right. Like #22. Both signatures printed. Back: Gustav Vasa.

	VG	VF	UNC
a. 1903.	180	650	—
b. 1904.	145	530	—
c. 1905-1906.	120	470	—

1906-1909 Issue

26 5 Kronor

1906-1917. Black. Green guilloche. Svea seated at right. Like #19. Back: Gustav Vasa with letter at lower left and right. PC: Beige.

	VG	VF	UNC
a. 1906.	20.00	90.00	365
b. 1907.	20.00	75.00	330
c. 1908.	20.00	75.00	300
d. 1909.	20.00	80.00	310
e. 1910.	20.00	75.00	300
f. 1911.	20.00	75.00	300
g. 1912.	20.00	80.00	325
h. 1913.	20.00	70.00	270
i. 1914.	15.00	55.00	235
j. 1915.	50.00	190	700
k. 1916.	10.00	50.00	210
l. 1917.	10.00	50.00	190

27 10 Kronor

1906-1917. Black. Green guilloche. Svea seated at right. Like #20. Back: Gustav Vasa with letter at left and right. PC: Gray.

	VG	VF	UNC
a. 1906.	30.00	120	470
b. 1907.	25.00	95.00	385
c. 1908.	20.00	80.00	335
d. 1909.	20.00	80.00	335
e. 1910.	20.00	80.00	320
f. 1911.	25.00	90.00	360
g. 1912.	20.00	70.00	295
h. 1913.	20.00	75.00	320
i. 1914.	20.00	70.00	295
j. 1915.	20.00	75.00	325
k. 1916.	15.00	55.00	225
l. 1917.	10.00	40.00	180

28 50 Kronor

1906-1917. Black. Red and green guilloche. Like #24 but yellow underprint added. Svea seated at lower right. Back: Gustav Vasa with one big letter at lower left and right.

	VG	VF	UNC
a. 1907.	120	505	—
b. 1908.	120	505	—
c. 1909.	105	460	—
d. 1911.	105	435	—
e. 1912.	95.00	410	—
f. 1913.	95.00	410	—
g. 1914.	95.00	410	—
h. 1915.	90.00	365	—
i. 1916.	70.00	280	—
j. 1917.	75.00	280	—

29 100 Kronor

1906-1917. Red and blue. Like #25. Yellow added to underprint. Svea seated at lower right. Both signatures printed. Back: Gustav Vasa.

	VG	VF	UNC
a. 1907.	105	425	—
b. 1908.	105	425	—
c. 1909.	105	425	—
d. 1910.	95.00	360	—
e. 1911.	95.00	360	—
f. 1912.	95.00	360	—
g. 1913.	80.00	330	—
h. 1914.	80.00	330	—
i. 1915.	80.00	330	—
j. 1916.	80.00	310	—
k. 1917.	70.00	260	—

30 1000 Kronor

1907. Like #23. Maroon added to underprint. Svea seated. Back: Gustav Vasa. With 1 letter at lower left and right. Rare. PC: Bluish with red imbedded fibers.

VG	VF	UNC
—	—	—

#	Description	VG	VF	UNC
31	**1000 Kronor** 1909; 1913; 1916; 1917. Like #30. Maroon added to underprint. Svea seated. Back: Gustav Vasa. With 1 letter at lower left and right. Rare. PC: Reddish with blue imbedded fibers.	—	—	—

1914; 1918 Issue

#	Description	VG	VF	UNC
32	**1 Krona** 1914-1940. Black on green underprint. Crowned and supported arms at top center. Like #1. 121x70mm.			
	a. 1914.	—	—	—
	b. 1915.	—	—	—
	c. 1916.	—	—	—
	d. 1917.	—	—	—
	e. 1918.	—	—	—
	f. 1919.	—	—	—
	g. 1920.	—	—	—
	h. 1921.	—	—	—
	i. 1924; 1938-1939. Rare.	—	—	—
	j. 1940. Green paper. 8-digit serial #. Watermark: Mercury head. Rare.	—	—	—
	s. Specimen. 1939. Without watermark, signature and serial #. Rare.	—	—	—
	x. Error: legend missing, *lagen om rikets mynt av de.* 1920.	180	415	1,100

#	Description	VG	VF	UNC
33	**5 Kronor** 1918-1952. Black. Green guilloche. Svea seated at right. Like #26 but numeral of value in red. Back: Gustav Vasa with letter at lower left and right. PC: Beige.			
	a. 1918.	10.00	50.00	190
	b. 1919.	15.00	65.00	260
	c. 1920.	25.00	120	410
	d. 1921.	9.00	40.00	165
	e. 1922.	10.00	50.00	190
	f. 1923.	6.50	30.00	130
	g. 1924.	10.00	40.00	180
	h. 1925.	9.00	35.00	150
	i. 1926.	9.00	35.00	150
	j. 1927.	6.00	30.00	130
	k. 1928.	6.00	30.00	120
	l. 1929.	5.00	25.00	100
	m. 1930.	4.00	20.00	75.00
	n. 1931.	3.00	15.00	70.00
	o. 1932.	3.00	20.00	65.00
	p. 1933.	2.00	10.00	50.00
	q. 1934.	2.00	9.00	40.00
	r. 1935.	2.00	8.00	30.00
	s. 1936.	2.00	5.00	25.00
	t. 1937.	2.00	5.00	25.00
	u. 1938.	1.00	5.00	20.00
	v. 1939.	1.00	4.00	20.00
	w. 1940.	1.00	3.00	15.00
	x. 1941.	1.00	3.00	10.00
	y. 1942.	1.00	3.00	9.00
	z. 1943.	1.00	3.00	7.00
	aa. 1944.	1.00	3.00	9.00
	ab. 1945.	1.00	3.00	10.00
	ac. 1946.	1.00	3.00	9.00
	ad. 1947.	1.00	3.00	6.00
	ae. 1948.	1.00	3.00	6.00
	af. 1949.	1.00	3.00	6.00
	ag. 1950.	1.00	3.00	15.00
	ah. 1951.	1.00	3.00	6.00
	ai. 1952.	1.00	3.00	5.00

#	Description	VG	VF	UNC
34	**10 Kronor** 1918-1940. Black. Green guilloche. Svea seated at right. Like #27 but numeral of value in red. Back: Gustav Vasa with letter at left and right. PC: Gray.			
	a. 1918.	15.00	60.00	225
	b. 1919.	20.00	65.00	285
	c. 1920.	15.00	60.00	230
	d. 1921.	15.00	50.00	205
	e. 1922.	15.00	35.00	150
	f. 1923.	6.00	30.00	130
	g. 1924.	5.00	30.00	155
	h. 1925.	4.00	25.00	140
	i. 1926.	3.00	20.00	120
	j. 1927.	2.00	15.00	105
	k. 1928.	2.00	10.00	95.00
	l. 1929.	2.00	10.00	70.00
	m. 1930.	2.00	8.00	50.00
	n. 1931.	3.00	7.00	40.00
	o. 1932.	3.00	5.00	30.00
	p. 1933.	2.00	6.00	30.00
	q. 1934.	2.00	5.00	30.00
	r. 1935.	2.00	5.00	30.00
	s. 1936.	2.00	5.00	30.00
	t. 1937.	2.00	5.00	20.00
	u. 1938.	—	4.00	15.00
	v. 1939.	—	3.00	15.00
	w. 1940.	—	3.00	15.00

#	Description	VG	VF	UNC
35	**50 Kronor** 1918-1953. Black. Red and green guilloche. Yellow underprint added. Svea seated at lower right. Like #28 but numeral of value in red. Back: Gustav Vasa with one big letter at lower left and right.			
	a. 1918. 5-digit serial #.	45.00	190	—
	b. 1919.	50.00	210	—
	c. 1920.	25.00	130	—
	d. 1921.	25.00	100	—
	e. 1922.	25.00	130	—
	f. 1923.	20.00	90.00	—
	g. 1924.	20.00	90.00	—
	h. 1925.	20.00	90.00	—
	i. 1926.	20.00	90.00	—
	j. 1927.	15.00	75.00	—
	k. 1928.	15.00	75.00	—
	l. 1929.	15.00	75.00	—
	m. 1930.	10.00	70.00	235
	n. 1931.	10.00	70.00	235
	o. 1932.	15.00	75.00	260
	p. 1933.	15.00	75.00	260
	q. 1934.	10.00	60.00	200
	r. 1935.	10.00	60.00	200
	s. 1936.	10.00	60.00	200
	t. 1937.	10.00	50.00	165
	u. 1938.	9.00	50.00	140
	v. 1939.	8.00	40.00	110
	w. 1940.	7.00	35.00	105
	x. 1941.	7.00	35.00	105
	y. 1943.	7.00	35.00	105
	z. 1944.	7.00	30.00	90.00
	aa. 1946.	10.00	35.00	105
	ab. 1947. 6-digit serial #.	10.00	30.00	90.00
	ac. 1948.	7.00	30.00	90.00
	ad. 1949.	10.00	50.00	120
	ae. 1950.	7.00	20.00	65.00
	af. 1953.	7.00	15.00	50.00

#	Description	VG	VF	UNC
36	**100 Kronor** 1918-1954. Red and blue. Yellow added to underprint. Svea seated at lower right. Both signatures printed. Like #29 but numeral of value in red. Back: Gustav Vasa.			
	a. 1918.	40.00	200	—
	b. 1919.	40.00	200	—
	c. 1920.	30.00	135	—
	d. 1921.	25.00	120	—
	e. 1922.	30.00	175	—
	f. 1923.	30.00	120	—
	g. 1924.	25.00	100	—
	h. 1925.	25.00	100	—
	i. 1926.	25.00	100	—
	j. 1927.	20.00	90.00	—
	k. 1928.	20.00	90.00	—
	l. 1929.	20.00	90.00	—
	m. 1930.	17.00	70.00	260
	n. 1931.	17.00	70.00	280
	o. 1932.	17.00	70.00	260
	p. 1933.	17.00	70.00	260
	q. 1934.	17.00	60.00	200
	r. 1935.	17.00	60.00	200
	s. 1936.	17.00	50.00	175
	t. 1937.	17.00	50.00	175
	u. 1938.	17.00	50.00	175
	v. 1939.	17.00	50.00	175
	w. 1940.	17.00	40.00	150
	x. 1941.	17.00	40.00	150
	y. 1942.	17.00	40.00	155

	VG	VF	UNC
z. 1943.	17.00	40.00	130
aa. 1945.	17.00	40.00	130
ab. 1946.	17.00	40.00	130
ac. 1947.	17.00	35.00	110
ad. 1948.	17.00	30.00	95.00
ae. 1949.	17.00	35.00	110
af. 1950.	17.00	20.00	70.00
ag. 1951.	17.00	20.00	65.00
ah. 1952.	17.00	20.00	65.00
ai. 1953.	17.00	20.00	55.00
aj. 1954.	17.00	20.00	55.00

37 **1000 Kronor**	VG	VF	UNC
1918-1930. Maroon added to underprint. Svea seated. Like #31. Numeral of value in red. Back: Gustav Vasa. With 1 letter at lower left and right. PC: Reddish with blue imbedded fibers.			
a. 1918.	265	765	—
b. 1919.	250	735	—
c. 1920.	265	765	—
d. 1921.	220	650	—
e. 1922.	220	650	—
f. 1926.	190	500	—
g. 1929.	165	470	—
h. 1930.	205	530	—

1932 Issue

38 **1000 Kronor**	VG	VF	UNC
1932-1950. Maroon added to underprint. Svea seated. Numeral of value in red. Like #37. 2 printed signatures. Back: Gustav Vasa. With 1 letter at lower left and right. PC: Reddish with blue imbedded fibers.			
a. 1932.	160	380	—
b. 1936.	150	325	—
c. 1938.	135	260	—
d. 1939.	130	225	—
e. 1950.	120	210	—

1939 Issue

39 **10,000 Kronor**	VG	VF	UNC
1939. Black and blue. Arms at center. Uniface. Watermark: Mercury head and wavy lines. Rare.	—	—	—

1940 Issue

40 **10 Kronor**	VG	VF	UNC
1940-1952. Gray-blue on multicolor underprint. Gustav Vasa at left, red dates and serial #. Back: Arms. Watermark: Gustav Vasa.			
a. 1940.	25.00	100	425
b. 1941.	2.50	10.00	30.00
c. 1942.	2.00	5.00	20.00
d. 1943.	2.00	3.00	20.00
e. 1944.	2.00	3.00	10.00
f. 1945.	2.00	3.00	10.00
g. 1946.	3.00	8.00	20.00
h. 1947.	2.00	3.00	9.00
i. 1948.	2.00	3.00	6.00
j. 1949.	2.00	3.00	6.50
k. 1950.	2.00	3.00	6.00
l. 1951.	2.00	3.00	6.00
m. 1952.	2.00	3.00	4.75

1948 Commemorative Issue

#41, 90th Birthday of King Gustaf V.

41 **5 Kronor**	VG	VF	UNC
1948. Olive on multicolor underprint. Portrait King Gustaf V at left, monogram at right. Back: Arms. BC: Brown.			
a. Without package.	3.00	10.00	20.00
b. With original package. Transparent with red printing.	—	—	45.00

Note: #41 was sold at twice face value, in special packaging.

1952-1955 Issue

	42 5 Kronor	VG	VF	UNC
	1954-1961. Dark brown on red and blue underprint. Portrait King Gustaf VI Adolf at right center. Back: Svea standing with shield at left center. Watermark: Gustaf VI Adolf. PC: Beige with red safety fibers.			
	a. 1954.	2.00	3.00	6.00
	b. 1955.	2.00	3.00	5.00
	c. 1956.	2.00	3.00	5.00
	d. 1959.	2.00	3.00	7.50
	e. 1960.	2.00	3.00	5.50
	f. 1961.	2.00	3.00	4.00
	r1. Replacement note: Serial # suffix with star. 1956.	5.00	30.00	120
	r2. Replacement note: Serial # suffix with star. 1959.	5.00	20.00	80.00
	r3. Replacement note: Serial # suffix with star. 1960. Rare.	—	—	—
	r4. Replacement note: Serial # suffix with star. 1961	5.00	20.00	80.00

	43 10 Kronor	VG	VF	UNC
	1953-1962. Gray-blue on multicolor underprint. Portrait King Gustav Vasa at left. Blue date and serial #. Like #40. Back: Arms at center. Watermark: Gustav Vasa.			
	a. 1953.	FV	2.50	6.00
	b. 1954.	FV	2.50	5.50
	c. 1955.	FV	2.50	5.50
	d. 1956.	FV	2.50	5.00
	e. 1957.	FV	2.50	5.00
	f. 1958.	FV	2.50	5.00
	g. 1959.	FV	2.50	5.00
	h. 1960.	FV	2.00	10.00
	i. 1962.	FV	2.00	6.00
	r1. Replacement note: Serial # suffix with star. 1956.	10.00	40.00	150
	r2. Replacement note: Serial # suffix with star. 1957.	6.00	25.00	100
	r3. Replacement note: Serial # suffix with star. 1958.	6.00	25.00	100
	r4. Replacement note: Serial # suffix with star. 1959.	6.00	25.00	100
	r5. Replacement note: Serial # suffix with star. 1960.	10.00	40.00	150
	r6. Replacement note: Serial # prefix with star. 1962.	6.00	25.00	100

	44 50 Kronor	VG	VF	UNC
	1955-1958. Black. Red and green guilloche. Yellow underprint added. Svea seated at lower right. Numeral of value in red. Like #35. Back: Gustav Vasa with 2 small letters.			
	a. 1955.	FV	15.00	50.00
	b. 1956.	FV	15.00	50.00
	c. 1957.	FV	20.00	60.00
	d. 1958.	FV	15.00	50.00
	r1. Remainder, with star. 1956.	15.00	45.00	210
	r2. Remainder, with star. 1957.	10.00	30.00	175
	r3. Remainder, with star. 1958.	7.50	25.00	150

	45 100 Kronor	VG	VF	UNC
	1955-1959. Red and blue. Yellow added to underprint. Svea seated at lower right. Both signatures printed. Numeral of value in red. Like #36. Back: Gustav Vasa with 2 small letters.			
	a. 1955.	FV	20.00	55.00
	b. 1956.	FV	20.00	55.00
	c. 1957.	FV	20.00	35.00
	d. 1958.	FV	20.00	50.00
	e. 1959.	FV	20.00	35.00
	r1. Remainder, with star. 1956.	20.00	40.00	170
	r2. Remainder, with star. 1957.	17.50	30.00	155
	r3. Remainder, with star. 1958.	15.00	30.00	140

	46 1000 Kronor	VG	VF	UNC
	1952-1973. Brown and multicolor. Svea standing. Back: King Gustaf V. Watermark: Gustaf V.			
	a. Blue and red safety fibers. 1952.	FV	200	600
	b. 1957.	FV	200	600
	c. 1962.	FV	150	500
	d. 1965.	FV	150	450
	e. With security thread. 1971.	FV	150	450
	f. 1973.	FV	150	400

1958; 1959 Issue

	47 50 Kronor	VG	VF	UNC
	1959-1962. Seated Svea at lower right. Second signature at left. Small date and serial number. Back: King Gustaf Vasa at center. PC: Beige.			
	a. 1959.	FV	25.00	60.00
	b. 1960.	FV	25.00	60.00
	c. 1961.	FV	100	200
	d. 1962.	FV	25.00	60.00
	r1. Replacement note: Serial # suffix with star. 1959.	30.00	100	200
	r2. Replacement note: Serial # suffix with star. 1960. Rare.	—	—	—
	r3. Replacement note: Serial # suffix with star. 1961.	70.00	200	400
	r4. Replacement note: Serial # suffix with star. 1962.	20.00	75.00	150

	100 Kronor	VG	VF	UNC
48	1959-1963. Seated Svea at lower right. Second signature at left. Small date and serial number. Back: King Gustaf Vasa at center.			
	a. 1959.	FV	30.00	100
	b. 1960.	FV	25.00	80.00
	c. 1961.	FV	25.00	80.00
	d. 1962.	FV	20.00	60.00
	e. 1963.	FV	20.00	60.00
	r1. Replacement note: Serial # suffix with star. 1959. Rare.	—	—	—
	r2. Replacement note: Serial # suffix with star. 1960.	50.00	100	200
	r3. Replacement note: Serial # suffix with star. 1961.	50.00	100	200
	r4. Replacement note: Serial # suffix with star. 1962.	50.00	100	200
	r5. Replacement note: Serial # suffix with star. 1963. Rare.	—	—	—

	10,000 Kronor	VG	VF	UNC
49	1958. Green and multicolor. King Gustaf VI Adolf at right. Back: Svea standing with shield at center. Watermark: Gustaf VI Adolf.	1,500	3,000	5,000

SWITZERLAND

The Swiss Confederation, located in central Europe north of Italy and south of Germany, has an area of 15,941 sq. mi. (41,290 sq. km.) and a population of 7.41 million. Capital: Berne. The economy centers about a well developed manufacturing industry, however the most important economic factor is services (banks and insurance). Switzerland, the habitat of lake dwellers in prehistoric times, was peopled by the Celtic Helvetians when Julius Caesar made it a part of the Roman Empire in 58 BC. After the decline of Rome, Switzerland was invaded by Teutonic tribes who established small temporal holdings which, in the Middle Ages, became a federation of fiefs of the Holy Roman Empire. As a nation, Switzerland originated in 1291 when the districts of Nidwalden, Schwyz and Uri united to defeat Austria and attain independence as the Swiss Confederation. After acquiring new cantons in the 14th century, Switzerland was made independent from the Holy Roman Empire by the 1648 Treaty of Westphalia. The revolutionary armies of Napoleonic France occupied Switzerland and set up the Helvetian Republic, 1798-1803. After the fall of Napoleon, the Congress of Vienna, 1815, recognized the independence of Switzerland and guaranteed its neutrality. The Swiss Constitutions of 1848, 1874, and 1999 established a union modeled upon that of the United States.

The banknotes of the SNB bore three signatures until the 5th Series (1956/57 to 1980):

(1) President of the Bank Council (Präsident des Bankrates, Président du Conseil)

(2) A member of the Board of Directors (Mitglid des Direktoriums, membre de la direction générale)

(3) Chief Cashier (Hauptkassier)

In the Board of Directors of the Swiss National Bank there are three members: The president of the National Bank and Chairman of Department I, the Vice-president and chairman of Department II and the Chairman of Department III. So, there are always three possible signature combinations with a single date.

SIGNATURE VARIETIES

	PRESIDENT, BANK COUNCIL	DIRECTOR	CASHIER
1	Johann-Daniel Hirter 1907-23	Kundert 1907-15	Chevallier 1907-13
2	Johann-Daniel Hirter	de Haller 1907-20	Chevallier
3	Johann-Daniel Hirter	Burckhardt 1907-24	Chevallier
4	Johann-Daniel Hirter	Kundert	Bornhauser 1913-36
5	Johann-Daniel Hirter	de Haller	Bornhauser
6	Johann-Daniel Hirter	Burckhardt	Bornhauser
7	Johann-Daniel Hirter	Jöhr 1915-18	Bornhauser
8	Johann-Daniel Hirter	Bachmann 1918-39	Bornhauser
9	Johann-Daniel Hirter	Schnyder[1] 1920-37	Bornhauser
10	Dr. Paul Usteri 1923-27	Bachmann	Bornhauser

SIGNATURE VARIETIES

	PRESIDENT, BANK COUNCIL	DIRECTOR	CASHIER
11	Dr. Paul Usteri	Schnyder[1]	Bornhauser
12	Dr. Paul Usteri	Burckhardt	Bornhauser
13	Dr. Paul Usteri	Weber 1925-47	Bornhauser
14	Dr. H.C. Alfred Sarasin 1927-35	Bachmann	Bornhauser
15	Dr. H.C. Alfred Sarasin	Schnyder[1]	Bornhauser
16	Dr. H.C. Alfred Sarasin	Schnyder[2]	Bornhauser
17	Dr. H.C. Alfred Sarasin	Weber	Bornhauser
18	Dr. Gustav Schaller[1]	Bachmann	Bornhauser
19	Dr. Gustav Schaller[1]	Schnyder[2]	Bornhauser
20	Dr. Gustav Schaller[1]	Weber	Bornhauser
21	Dr. Gustav Schaller[1]	Bachmann	Blumer 1936-54
22	Dr. Gustav Schaller[1]	Schnyder[2]	Blumer
23	Dr. Gustav Schaller[1]	Weber	Blumer
24	Dr. Gustav Schaller[2]	Bachmann	Blumer
25	Dr. Gustav Schaller[2]	Rossy 1937-55	Blumer
26	Dr. Gustav Schaller[2]	Weber	Blumer
27	Prof. Dr. Gottleib Bachmann 1939-47	Schnorf 1939-42	Blumer
28	Prof. Dr. Gottleib Bachmann	Rossy	Blumer

SIGNATURE VARIETIES

	PRESIDENT, BANK COUNCIL	DIRECTOR	CASHIER
29	Prof. Dr. Gottleib Bachmann	Weber	Blumer
30	Prof. Dr. Gottleib Bachmann	Hirs 1942-54	Blumer
31	Dr. Alfred Müller 1947-59	Hirs	Blumer
32	Dr. Alfred Müller	Rossy	Blumer
33	Dr. Alfred Müller	Keller 1947-56	Blumer
34	Dr. Alfred Müller	Schwegler 1955-66	Kunz 1954-66
35	Dr. Alfred Müller	Rossy	Kunz
36	Dr. Alfred Müller	Keller	Kunz
37	Dr. Alfred Müller	Motta 1955-66	Kunz
38	Dr. Alfred Müller	Iklé 1956-68	Kunz
39	Dr. Brenno Galli 1959-78	Dr. Walter Schweigler	Kunz
40	Dr. Brenno Galli	Motta	Kunz
41	Dr. Brenno Galli	Iklé	Kunz
42	Dr. Brenno Galli	Dr. Edwin Stopper 1966-74	Rudolph Aebersold 1954-66
43	Dr. Brenno Galli	Alexandre Hay 1966-74	Rudolph Aebersold
44	Dr. Brenno Galli	Iklé	Rudolph Aebersold
45	Dr. Brenno Galli	Dr. Fritz Leutwiler 1968-84	Rudolph Aebersold
46	Dr. Brenno Galli	Dr. Leo Schürmann 1974-80	Rudolph Aebersold

SIGNATURE VARIETIES			
	PRESIDENT, BANK COUNCIL	DIRECTOR	CASHIER
47	Dr. Brenno Galli	Dr. Pierre Languetin 1976-88	Rudolph Aebersold

CONFEDERATION

Schweizerische Nationalbank

Swiss National Bank

Established in 1905.

1907 Issue

#1-4 Redeemable until 30.6.1945. Note: Similar to previous Concordat note issues but w/new issuer name and a white cross in red guilloche in unpt. at upper right. For Concordat issues see Vol. 1.

		Good	Fine	XF
1	**50 Franken** 1.2.1907. Dark green on orange underprint. Standing allegorical woman at left, cherub at lower right. (1, 2, 3).	1,500	2,500	4,000

		Good	Fine	XF
2	**100 Franken** 1.2.1907. Dark blue on light blue underprint. Standing allegorical woman at left, cherub at lower right. (1, 2, 3).	2,000	3,500	6,000
3	**500 Franken** 1.2.1907. Green on light green underprint. Standing allegorical woman at left, cherub at lower right. (1, 2, 3).	—	—	—
4	**1000 Franken** 1.2.1907. Blue on purple underprint. Standing allegorical woman at left, cherub at lower right. (1, 2, 3). Rare.	—	—	—

1910-1920 Issue

		Good	Fine	XF
5	**50 Franken** 1910-1920. Green on orange underprint. Portrait of woman at lower left. Back: F. Hodler's *Woodcutter*. Printer: W&S.			
	a. 1.1.1910. (1, 2, 3).	250	525	—
	b. 1.1.1914. (4, 5, 6).	200	425	—
	c. 1.1.1917. Series B48. (5, 6, 7).	150	350	—
	d. 1.8.1920. (6, 8, 9).	175	350	1,000
	s. Specimen. 1.1.1910.	—	—	—

		Good	Fine	XF
6	**100 Franken** 1910-1920. Dark blue on orange underprint. Woman at left. Back: F. Hodler's *Scyther*. Printer: W&S.			
	a. 1.1.1910. (1, 2, 3).	150	400	—
	b. 1.1.1914. (4, 5, 6).	150	400	—
	c. 1.1.1917. (5, 6, 7).	150	350	—
	d. 1.8.1920. (6, 8, 9).	100	200	1,200
	s. Specimen. 1.1.1910.	—	—	—

7	**500 Franken**	Good	Fine	XF
	1910-1917. Dark red on yellow underprint. Woman from Appenzell at left. Back: E. Burnand's *Embroidering Appenzell Women*. BC: Brown. Printer: W&S.			
	a. 1.1.1910. (1, 2, 3). Rare.	—	—	—
	b. 1.1.1914. (4, 5, 6). Rare.	—	—	—
	c. 1.1.1917. (5, 6, 7).	1,500	3,000	—
	s. Specimen. 1.1.1910.	—	—	—

8	**1000 Franken**	Good	Fine	XF
	1910-1917. Violet on orange underprint. Portrait woman at lower left. Back: E. Burnand's *Foundry*. BC: Black on orange underprint. Printer: W&S.			
	a. 1.1.1910. (1, 2, 3). Rare.	—	—	—
	b. 1.1.1914. (4, 5, 6). Rare.	—	—	—
	c. 1.1.1917. (5, 6, 7).	750	1,200	—
	s. Specimen, punch hole cancelled. 1.1.1910.	—	Unc	5,000

1918 Issues

9	**100 Franken**	Good	Fine	XF
	1.1.1918. Blue on brown underprint. William Tell at left, Tell's Chapel at Lake Vierwaldstätten at right. Letters *T.W.* at lower left, *R.K.* at lower right. Back: Mount Jungfrau. Printer: OFZ.			
	a. Issued note. (5, 6, 7).	1,000	2,500	—
	s. Specimen, punch hole cancelled.	—	—	—

Note: #9 was redeemable until 30.6.1945.

10	**100 Franken**	Good	Fine	XF
	1.1.1918. Blue and brown. Similar to #9 but modified portrait of William Tell. Letters *Ekn. R. K.* in the left medallion at lower right. Back: Mount Jungfrau. Printer: OFZ. (Not issued).	—	—	—

1911-1914 Issue

11	**5 Franken**	Good	Fine	XF
	1913-1953. Red, blue and black on olive-green underprint. William Tell monument in Altdorf at left. Rutli Mountain in left background. BC: Olive-green.			
	a. 1.8.1913. (1, 2, 3).	500	1,250	2,000
	b. 1.8.1914. (4, 5, 6).	100	300	700
	c. 1.1.1916. (5, 6, 7).	200	500	—
	d. 1.1.1919. (5, 6, 8).	200	500	—
	e. 1.1.1921. (6, 8, 9).	40.00	90.00	180
	f. 1.7.1922. (6, 8, 9).	30.00	70.00	125
	g. 2.12.1926. (10, 11, 13).	17.50	40.00	70.00
	h. 25.10.1936. (21, 22, 23).	10.00	22.50	50.00
	i. 17.5.1939. (27, 28, 29).	10.00	22.50	50.00
	j. 4.12.1942. (28, 29, 30).	10.00	17.50	35.00
	k. 16.11.1944. (28, 29, 30).	10.00	17.50	35.00
	l. 31.8.1946. (28, 29, 30).	10.00	17.50	35.00
	m. 16.10.1947. (31, 32, 33).	6.00	12.50	22.50
	n. 20.1.1949. (31, 32, 33).	6.00	12.50	22.50
	o. 22.2.1951. (31, 32, 33).	3.00	6.00	17.50
	p. 28.3.1952. (31, 32, 33).	3.00	6.00	17.50
	q. 15.1.1953 (not issued).	—	—	—
	r. 22.10.1953 (not issued).	—	—	—
	s. As h. Specimen.	—	—	—

	20 Franken	Good	Fine	XF
12	1911-1922. Blue-gray, light and dark brown. Woman's head *Vreneli* at left. Printer: OFZ.			
	a. 1.12.1911. (1, 2, 3).	700	1,500	—
	b. 1.9.1915. (4, 5, 6).	600	1,200	—
	c. 1.1.1916. (5, 6, 7).	350	800	1,500
	d. 1.1.1918. (5, 6, 7).	450	900	2,000
	e. 1.1.1920. (5, 6, 8).	350	600	1,200
	f. 1.9.1920. (6, 8, 9).	350	600	1,200
	g. 1.1.1922. (6, 8, 9).	450	800	1,500

	40 Franken	Good	Fine	XF
13	1.9.1914. Violet-green on light green underprint. Arnold Winkelried at left. (Not issued).	—	—	—

Eidgenössische Staatskasse

Federal Treasury

1914 Issues

Note: Same design issued in either German, Italian or French.

	5 Franken	Good	Fine	XF
14	10.8.1914. Blue. Portrait Libertas at left, Arnold Winkelreid at right. Arms at top center. German text.	350	1,250	2,200

	5 Francs	Good	Fine	XF
15	10.8.1914. Blue. Portrait Libertas at left, Arnold Winkelreid at right. Arms at top center. Like #14 but French text.	600	1,800	2,600

	5 Franchi	Good	Fine	XF
16	10.8.1914. Blue. Portrait Libertas at left, Arnold Winkelreid at right. Arms at top center. Like #14 but Italian text.	900	2,500	3,500

		Good	Fine	XF
17	**10 Franken** 10.8.1914. Blue. Portrait Libertas at left, William Tell at right. Arms at top center. German text.	700	2,000	3,500
18	**10 Francs** 10.8.1914. Blue. Portrait Libertas at left, William Tell at right. Arms at top center. Like #17 but French text.	1,750	2,600	4,000
19	**10 Franchi** 10.8.1914. Blue. Portrait Libertas at left, William Tell at right. Arms at top center. Like #17 but Italian text.	2,250	3,500	5,500
20	**20 Franken** 10.8.1914. Blue. Portrait Libertas at left, Arnold Winkelreid at right. Arms at top center. German text.	1,500	4,000	6,000

		Good	Fine	XF
21	**20 Francs** 10.8.1914. Blue. Portrait Libertas at left, Arnold Winkelreid at right. Arms at top center. Like #20 but French text.	2,000	4,500	7,000
22	**20 Franchi** 10.8.1914. Blue. Portrait Libertas at left, Arnold Winkelreid at right. Arms at top center. Like #20 but Italian text.	2,500	5,000	8,500

Darlehenskasse der Schweizerischen Eidgenossenschaft

State Loan Bank of the Swiss Federation

1914 Issue

		VG	VF	UNC
23	**25 Franken** 9.9.1914. Olive-green and gray on yellow-brown underprint. 2 serial # varieties. Printer: OFZ.	—	—	—
23A	**100 Franken** 9.9.1914. Green and gray on yellow-brown underprint. Printer: OFZ. (Not issued.)	—	—	—
24	**100 Franken** 9.9.1914. Green and gray on yellow-brown underprint. Printer: OFZ. (Not issued.)	—	—	—

1915 Issue

		VG	VF	UNC
25	**1 Frank** 27.4.1915. Dark blue on orange-yellow underprint. Printer: OFZ. (Not issued.)	—	—	—
26	**2 Franken** 27.4.1915. Red-brown on orange-yellow underprint. Printer: OFZ. (Not issued.)	—	—	—

Schweizerische Nationalbank (resumed)

Swiss National Bank

Gesetz vom 7.4.1921 (Law of 7.4.1921)

1922; 1923 Issue

		VG	VF	UNC
27	**20 Franken** 1.7.1922. Blue, green and brown. William Tell monument in Altdorf at left. Rutli Mountain in left background. Like #11. Printer: OFZ.			
	a. Issued note. (6, 8, 9).	250	400	1,100
	s. Specimen.	—	—	1,250

		VG	VF	UNC
28	**100 Franken** 1.1.1923. Blue. Woman at left. Like #6. (6, 8, 9). Back: F. Hodler's *Scyther*. Printer: W&S.	200	400	1,200
29	**500 Franken** 1.1.1923. Red. Woman from Appenzell at left. Like #7. (6, 8, 9). Back: E. Burnand's *Embroidering Appenzell Women*. Printer: W&S.	1,400	2,800	—
30	**1000 Franken** 1.1.1923. Violet. Portrait woman at lower left. Like #8. (6, 8, 9). Back: E. Burnand's *Foundry*. Printer: W&S.	1,500	3,000	6,000

1921-1928 Issue

#31-37 *GESETZGEBUNG ÜBER DIE SCHWEIZERISCHE NATIONALBANK* (Legislation governing the Swiss National Bank).

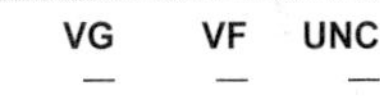

		VG	VF	UNC
31	**10 Franken** 1.4.1921. Red-brown on yellow underprint. Portrait woman in Neuchatel costume at lower left. Signature varieties. Printer: W&S. (Not issued).	—	—	—

		VG	VF	UNC
32	**20 Franken** 16.5.1923. Dark blue on yellow underprint. Portrait woman in Fribourg costume at left. Signature varieties. Printer: OFZ. (Not issued.)	—	—	—

		VG	VF	UNC
33	**20 Franken** 1.5.1923-18.4.1929. Blue, green and brown. William Tell monument in Altdorf at left. Rutli Mountain in left background. Like #11. Printer: OFZ.			
	a. 1.5.1923. (10, 11, 12).	200	400	950
	b. 1.7.1926. (10, 11,13).	200	400	950
	c. 21.10.1926. (10, 11, 13).	200	400	950
	d. 24.3.1927. (14, 15, 17).	200	350	900
	e. 29.9.1927. (14, 15, 17).	200	350	900
	f. 1.11.1928. (14,,15, 17).	200	500	950
	g. 19.2.1929. (14, 15, 17).	200	500	1,000
	h. 18.4.1929. (14, 15, 17).	250	600	1,100

34	50 Franken	VG	VF	UNC
	1924-1955. Green. Portrait of woman at lower left. Like #5. Back: F. Hodler's *Woodcutter.*			
	a. 1.4.1924. (10, 11, 12).	125	400	1,200
	b. 30.9.1926. (10, 11, 13).	125	400	900
	c. 23.11.1927. (14, 15, 17).	125	400	900
	d. 25.9.1929. (14, 15, 17).	100	350	1,200
	e. 16.9.1930. (14, 15, 17).	100	350	900
	f. 21.7.1931. (14, 15, 17).	100	350	900
	g. 27.8.1937. (24, 25, 26).	100	350	900
	h. 31.8.1938. (24, 25, 26).	100	350	900
	i. 17.3.1939. (27, 28, 29).	100	350	900
	j. 3.8.1939. (27,28, 29).	100	350	900
	k. 15.2.1940. (27, 28, 29).	100	300	700
	l. 12.12.1941. (27, 28, 29).	100	300	700
	m. 1.10.1942. (28, 29, 30).	100	300	700
	n. 7.5.1943. (28, 29, 30).	100	300	700
	o. 16.10.1947. (31, 32, 33).	100	300	700
	p. 20.1.1949. (31, 32, 33).	100	300	700
	q. 29.10.1955. (34, 36, 37).	175	500	1,200

35	100 Franken	VG	VF	UNC
	1924-1949. Dark blue. Woman at left. Like #6. Back: F. Hodler's *Scyther.*			
	a. 1.4.1924. (10, 11, 12).	200	350	700
	b. 16.9.1926. (10, 11, 13).	200	350	700
	c. 30.3.1927. (14, 15, 17).	200	350	700
	d. 23.11.1927. (14, 15, 17).	200	350	700
	e. 4.10.1928. (14, 15, 17).	200	350	700
	f. 16.9.1930. (14, 15, 17).	175	300	700
	g. 21.7.1931. (14, 15, 17).	175	300	600
	h. 19.7.1934. (14, 16, 17).	175	250	600
	i. 27.8.1937. (24, 25, 26).	150	200	600
	j. 31.8.1938. (24, 25, 26).	150	200	600
	k. 17.3.1939. (27, 28, 29).	150	200	600
	l. 3.8.1939. (27, 28, 29).	150	200	600
	m. 15.2.1940. (27, 28, 29).	120	180	600
	n. 1.10.1942. (28, 29, 30).	120	180	600
	o. 7.5.1943. (28, 29, 30).	120	180	600
	p. 7.10.1943. (28, 29, 30).	120	180	600
	q. 2.12.1943. (28, 29, 30).	120	180	600
	r. 23.3.1944. (28, 29, 30).	100	160	600
	s. 15.3.1945. (28, 29, 30).	100	160	600
	t. 31.8.1946. (28, 29, 30).	100	160	450
	u. 16.10.1947. (31, 32, 33).	50.00	120	450
	v. 20.1.1949. (31, 32, 33).	50.00	120	450

36	500 Franken	VG	VF	UNC
	1928-1949. Dark red and lilac. Woman from Appenzell at left. Like #7. Back: E. Burnand's *Embroidering Appenzell Women.* BC: Brown.			
	a. 4.10.1928. (14, 15, 17).	1,200	2,000	3,700
	b. 16.6.1931. (14, 15, 17).	900	1,700	3,250
	c. 7.9.1939. (27, 28, 29).	900	1,700	3,250
	d. 4.12.1942. (28, 29, 30).	800	1,450	2,750
	e. 31.8.1946. (28, 29, 30).	750	1,350	2,750
	f. 16.10.1947. 31, 32, 33).	750	1,350	2,750
	g. 20.1.1949. (Not issued.)	—	—	5,000

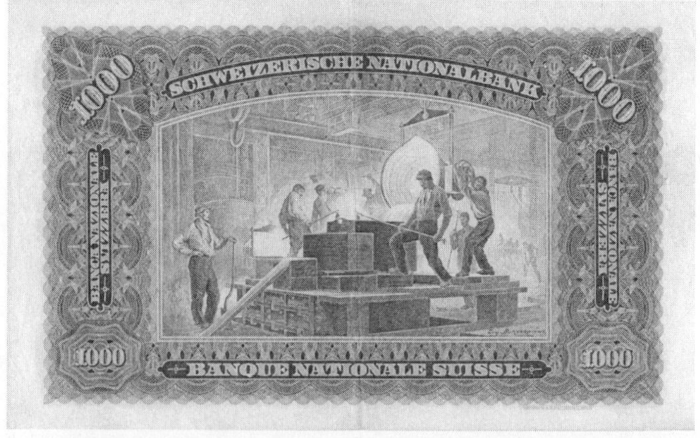

#	Denomination	VG	VF	UNC
37	**1000 Franken**	VG	VF	UNC

1927-1955. Violet and orange. Portrait woman at lower left. Like #8. Back: E. Burnand's *Foundry*. BC: Black on orange underprint.

	VG	VF	UNC
a. 23.11.1927. (14, 15, 17).	700	1,500	3,500
b. 16.9.1930. (14, 15, 17).	700	1,500	4,000
c. 16.6.1931. (14, 15, 17).	700	1,500	3,500
d. 10.12.1931. (14, 15, 17).	700	1,500	3,500
e. 7.9.1939. (27, 28, 29).	600	1,500	4,500
f. 4.12.1942. (28, 29, 30).	600	1,500	4,500
g. 11.11.1943. (28, 29, 30).	600	1,500	5,000
h. 16.10.1947. (31, 32, 33).	600	1,400	4,000
i. 29.4.1955. (34, 35, 36).	1,250	4,000	7,000

1929-1950 Issue

38 20 Franken — VG VF UNC

1925-1926. Dark blue on red and light blue underprint. Portrait Johann Heinrich Pestalozzi at upper right. Back: Cross at center. (Not issued.)

	VG	VF	UNC
a. 1.1.1925. Specimen.	—	—	—
b. 1.1.1926. Specimen.	—	—	—

39 20 Franken — VG VF UNC

1929-1952. Dark blue on red underprint. Portrait Johann Heinrich Pestalozzi at upper right. Back: Cross at center. Printer: OFZ.

	VG	VF	UNC
a. 21.6.1929. (14, 15, 17).	60.00	150	400
b. 16.9.1930. (14, 15, 17).	60.00	125	300
c. 21.7.1931. (14, 15, 17).	60.00	125	300
d. 22.6.1933. (14, 15, 17).	50.00	100	280
e. 11.4.1935. (14, 15, 17).	50.00	100	280
f. 27.8.1937. (24, 25, 26).	50.00	100	280
g. 10.3.1938. (24, 25, 26).	50.00	100	280
h. 31.8.1938. (24, 25, 26).	50.00	100	280
i. 17.3.1939. (27, 28, 29).	50.00	100	280
j. 26.8.1939. (27, 28, 29).	50.00	100	280
k. 15.8.1940. (27, 28, 29).	50.00	100	280
l. 4.12.1942. (28, 29, 30).	50.00	100	280
m. 23.3.1944. (28, 29, 30).	50.00	100	280
n. 16.11.1944. (28, 29, 30).	50.00	100	280
o. 31.8.1946. (28, 29, 30).	50.00	100	280
p. 16.10.1947. (31, 32, 33).	50.00	100	280
q. 21.1.1949. (31, 32, 33).	35.00	90.00	220
r. 9.3.1950. (31, 32, 33).	35.00	90.00	220
s. 22.2.1951. (31, 32, 33).	35.00	90.00	220
s1. Specimen. 21.6.1929.	—	—	800
t. 28.3.1952. (31, 32, 33).	35.00	90.00	220

1938 Issue

40 1 Frank — VG VF UNC

27.5.1938. Dark blue. (Not issued.)

	VG	VF	UNC
a. Note with serial #.	—	—	—
s. Specimen.	—	—	—

41 2 Franken — VG VF UNC

27.5.1938. Red-brown. (Not issued.)

	VG	VF	UNC
a. Note with serial #.	—	—	—
s. Specimen.	—	—	—

1941-1950 Reserve Issue

42 50 Franken — VG VF UNC

15.3.1946. Green on red and yellow underprint. Girl's head at right. Back: Peasant with bull. (Not issued.) — — —

43 100 Franken — VG VF UNC

4.12.1942. Blue on multicolor underprint. *100* at left, Haslital's woman's head at right. Back: Ornate designs. (Not issued.)

	VG	VF	UNC
a. 1.8.1941.	—	—	—
b. 4.12.1942.	—	—	—
c. 21.10.1943.	—	—	—
d. 15.3.1945.	—	—	—

44 1000 Franken — VG VF UNC

1.1.1950. Black, blue and violet on multicolor underprint. Girl's head at right. Back: Turbine and mountains. (Not issued.) — — —

1954-1961 Issue

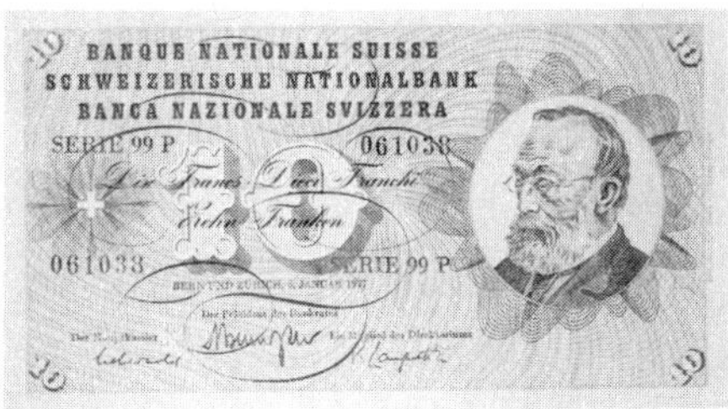

45 10 Franken — VG VF UNC

1955-1977. Purple on red-brown underprint. Gottfried Keller at right. Back: Carnation flower at left center. Printer: OFZ.

	VG	VF	UNC
a. 25.8.1955. (34, 36, 37).	5.00	10.00	50.00
b. 20.10.1955 (34, 36, 37).	5.00	10.00	50.00
c. 29.11.1956 (34, 37, 38).	5.00	10.00	45.00
d. 18.12.1958 (34, 37, 38).	20.00	40.00	125
e. 23.12.1959 (34, 37, 38).	1.50	3.50	30.00
f. 22.12.1960 (39, 40, 41).	1.50	3.50	30.00
g. 26.10.1961 (39, 40, 41).	1.50	3.50	20.00
h. 28.3.1963 (39, 40, 41).	1.50	3.50	20.00
i. 2.4.1964 (39, 40, 41).	1.50	3.50	20.00
j. 21.1.1965 (39, 40, 41).	1.50	3.50	20.00
k. 23.12.1965 (39, 40, 41).	6.00	3.50	20.00
l. 1.1.1967 (42, 43, 44).	1.50	15.00	40.00
m. 30.6.1967 (42, 43, 44).	1.50	3.50	15.00
n. 15.5.1968 (42, 43, 45).	1.50	3.50	15.00
o. 15.1.1969 (42, 43, 45).	1.50	3.50	15.00
p. 5.1.1970 (42, 43, 45).	1.50	3.50	15.00
q. 10.2.1971 (42, 43, 45).	1.50	3.50	15.00
r. 24.1.1972 (42, 43, 45).	1.50	3.50	15.00
s. 7.3.1973 (42, 43, 45).	1.50	3.50	14.00
s1. Specimen.	—	—	750
t. 7.2.1974 (42, 43, 45).	1.50	3.50	14.00
u. 6.1.1977 (45, 46, 47).	1.25	3.00	14.00

46	20 Franken	VG	VF	UNC
	1954-1976. Blue on multicolor underprint. General Guillaume-Henri Dufour at right. Back: Silver thistle at left center. Printer: OFZ.			
	a. 1.7.1954 (34, 35, 36).	14.00	22.50	120
	b. 7.7.1955 (34, 36, 37).	14.00	22.50	120
	c. 20.10.1955 (34, 36, 37).	14.00	22.50	120
	d. 5.7.1956 (34, 37, 38).	14.00	22.50	120
	e. 4.10.1957 (34, 37, 38).	15.00	25.00	110
	f. 18.12.1958 (34, 37, 38).	25.00	40.00	150
	g. 23.12.1959 (39, 40, 41).	3.00	8.00	30.00
	h. 22.12.1960 (39, 40, 41).	3.00	8.00	30.00
	i. 26.10.1961 (39, 40, 41).	3.00	8.00	30.00
	j. 28.3.1963 (39, 40, 41).	3.00	8.00	30.00
	k. 2.4.1964 (39, 40, 41).	3.00	8.00	30.00
	l. 21.1.1965 (39, 40, 41).	3.00	8.00	30.00
	m. 23.12.1965 (39, 40, 41).	3.00	8.00	30.00
	n. 1.1.1967 (42, 43, 44).	3.00	10.00	30.00
	o. 30.6.1967 (42, 43, 44).	2.75	8.00	30.00
	p. 15.5.1968 (42, 43, 45).	2.75	8.00	25.00
	q. 15.1.1969 (42, 43, 45).	2.75	8.00	25.00
	r. 5.1.1970 (42, 43, 45).	2.75	8.00	25.00
	s. 10.2.1971 (42, 43, 45).	2.75	8.00	25.00
	s1. As a. Specimen.	—	—	800
	t. 24.1.1972 (42, 43, 45).	2.75	8.00	25.00
	u. 7.3.1973 (42, 43, 45).	2.75	8.00	22.50
	v. 7.2.1974 (42, 43, 45).	2.75	8.00	22.50
	w. 9.4.1976 (45, 46, 47).	2.50	7.50	22.50

47	50 Franken	VG	VF	UNC
	1955-1958. Green and red-brown on yellow-green underprint. Girl at upper right. Back: Apple harvesting scene (symbolizing fertility). Printer: W&S.			
	a. 7.7.1955 (34, 36, 37).	25.00	42.50	175
	b. 4.10.1957 (34, 37, 38).	20.00	37.50	175
	c. 18.12.1958 (34, 37, 38).	200	600	1,250

48	50 Franken	VG	VF	UNC
	1961-1974. Green and red on multicolor underprint. Girl at upper right. Like #47. Back: Apple harvesting scene (symbolizing fertility).			
	a. 4.5.1961 (39, 40, 41).	25.00	60.00	200
	b. 21.12.1961 (39, 40,41).	12.50	30.00	90.00
	c. 28.3.1963 (39, 40, 41).	30.00	85.00	220
	d. 2.4.1964 (39, 40, 41).	35.00	90.00	250
	e. 21.1.1965 (39, 40, 41).	12.50	30.00	90.00
	f. 23.12.1965 (39, 40, 41).	12.50	30.00	90.00
	g. 30.6.1967 (42, 43, 44).	12.50	30.00	90.00
	h. 15.5.1968 (42, 43, 45).	12.50	30.00	90.00
	i. 15.1.1969 (42, 43, 45).	12.50	30.00	75.00
	j. 5.1.1970 (42, 43, 45).	12.50	30.00	75.00
	k. 10.2.1971 (42, 43, 45).	12.50	30.00	75.00
	l. 24.1.1972 (42, 43, 45).	12.50	30.00	75.00
	m. 7.3.1973 (42, 43, 45).	12.50	30.00	75.00
	n. 7.2.1974 (42, 43, 45).	12.50	30.00	75.00
	s. Specimen.	—	—	800

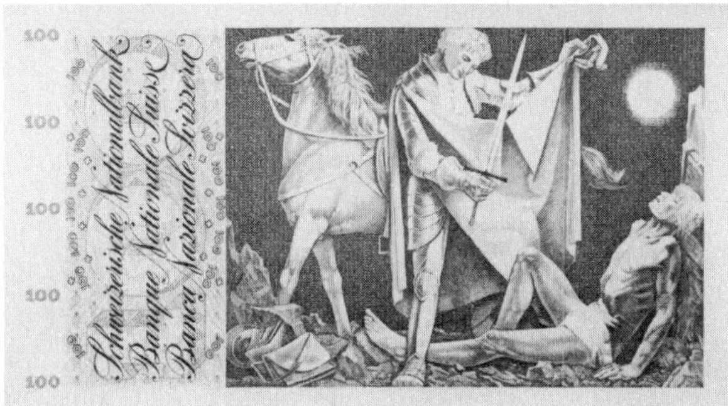

49	100 Franken	VG	VF	UNC
	1956-1973. Dark blue and brown-olive on multicolor underprint. Boy's head at upper right with lamb. Back: St. Martin cutting his cape (to share) at center right. Printer: TDLR.			
	a. 25.10.1956 (34, 37, 38).	30.00	57.50	350
	b. 4.10.1957 (34, 37, 38).	30.00	55.00	350
	c. 18.12.1958 (34, 37, 38).	32.50	60.00	500
	d. 21.12.1961 (39, 40, 41);	15.00	30.00	200
	e. 28.3.1963 (39, 40, 41).	15.00	30.00	200

	VG	VF	UNC
f. 2.4.1964 (39, 40, 41).	15.00	30.00	200
g. 21.1.1965 (39, 40, 41).	15.00	32.50	200
h. 23.12.1965 (39, 40, 41).	16.00	35.00	200
i. 1.1.1967 (42, 43, 44).	16.00	35.00	200
j. 30.6.1967 (42, 43, 44).	14.00	27.50	200
k. 15.1.1969 (42, 43, 45).	14.00	25.00	200
l. 5.1.1970 (42, 43, 45).	16.00	35.00	175
m. 10.2.1971 (42, 43, 45).	12.00	25.00	175
n. 24.1.1972 (42, 43, 45).	12.00	25.00	175
o. 7.3.1973 (42, 43, 45).	12.00	25.00	175
s. Specimen.	—	—	1,000

50	500 Franken	VG	VF	UNC
	1957-1958. Red-brown and olive on multicolor underprint. Woman looking in mirror at right. Back: Elders with four girls bathing at center right (Fountain of Youth). Printer: W&S.			
	a. 31.1.1957 (34, 37, 38).	250	400	1,650
	b. 4.10.1957 (34, 37, 38).	200	350	1,650
	c. 18.12.1958 (34, 37, 38).	300	500	2,000
	s. Specimen. Red overprint: *SPECIMEN* and punch hole cancelled.	—	—	2,250

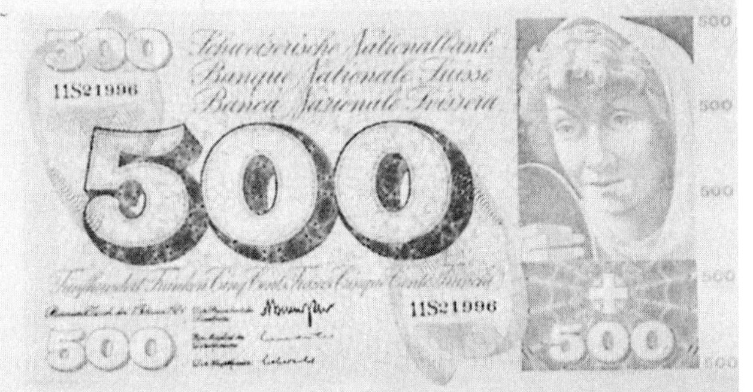

51	500 Franken	VG	VF	UNC
	1961-1974. Brown-orange and olive on multicolor underprint. Woman looking in mirror at right. Like #50. Back: Elders with four girls bathing at center right (Fountain of Youth).			
	a. 21.12.1961 (39, 40, 41).	150	275	1,250
	b. 28.3.1963 (39, 40, 41).	130	240	1,250
	c. 2.4.1964 (39, 40, 41).	140	250	1,250
	d. 21.1.1965 (39, 40, 41).	140	250	1,250
	e. 1.1.1967 (42, 43, 44).	140	250	1,250
	f. 15.5.1968 (42, 43, 45).	140	250	1,250
	g. 15.1.1969 (42, 43, 45).	140	250	1,250
	h. 5.1.1970 (42, 43, 45).	110	235	950
	i. 10.2.1971 (42, 43, 45).	110	235	950
	j. 24.1.1972 (42, 43, 45).	110	235	950
	k. 7.3.1973 (42, 43, 45).	100	230	950
	l. 7.2.1974 (42, 43, 45).	90.00	225	950
	s. As a. Specimen.	—	—	2,200

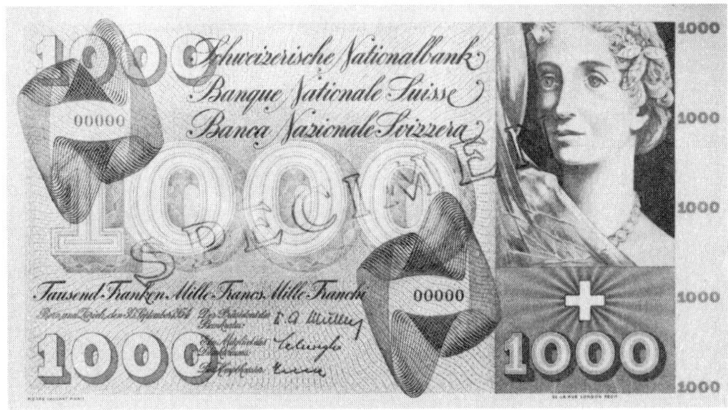

52	1000 Franken	VG	VF	UNC
	1954-1974. Red-violet and turquoise on green and light violet underprint. Female head at upper right. Back: Allegorical scene *Dance Macabre*. Printer: TDLR.			
	a. 30.9.1954 (34, 35, 36).	225	400	1,500
	b. 4.10.1957 (34, 37, 38).	225	500	2,500
	c. 18.12.1958 (34, 37, 38).	400	1,000	3,500
	d. 22.12.1960 (39, 40, 41).	200	500	2,800
	e. 21.12.1961 (39, 40, 41).	200	500	2,500
	f. 28.3.1963 (39, 40, 41).	200	400	2,200
	g. 21.1.1965 (39, 40, 41).	200	400	2,200
	h. 1.1.1967 (42, 43, 44).	200	400	2,200
	i. 5.1.1970 (42, 43, 45).	200	400	2,000
	j. 10.2.1971 (42, 43, 45).	200	400	1,950
	k. 24.1.1972 (42, 43, 45).	200	400	1,950
	l. 1.10.1973 (42, 43, 45).	200	400	1,950
	m. 7.2.1974 (42, 43, 45).	200	400	1,950
	s. Specimen.	—	—	2,750

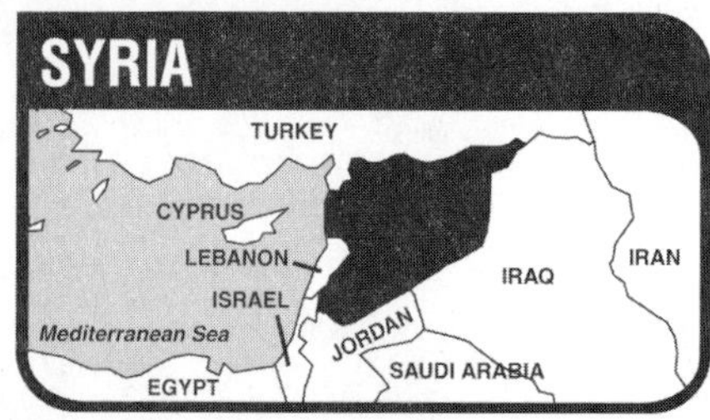

The Syrian Arab Republic, located in the Near East at the eastern end of the Mediterranean Sea, has an area of 185,180 sq. km. and a population of 19.75 million. Capital: Damascus. Agriculture and animal breeding are the chief industries. Cotton, crude oil and livestock are exported.Following the breakup of the Ottoman Empire during World War I, France administered Syria until its independence in 1946. The country lacked political stability, however, and experienced a series of military coups during its first decades. Syria united with Egypt in February 1958 to form the United Arab Republic. In September 1961, the two entities separated, and the Syrian Arab Republic was reestablished. In November 1970, Hafiz al-Asad, a member of the Socialist Ba'th Party and the minority Alawite sect, seized power in a bloodless coup and brought political stability to the country. In the 1967 Arab-Israeli War, Syria lost the Golan Heights to Israel. During the 1990s, Syria and Israel held occasional peace talks over its return. Following the death of President al-Asad, his son, Bashar al-Asad, was approved as president by popular referendum in July 2000. Syrian troops - stationed in Lebanon since 1976 in an ostensible peacekeeping role - were withdrawn in April 2005. During the July-August 2006 conflict between Israel and Hizballah, Syria placed its military forces on alert but did not intervene directly on behalf of its ally Hizballah.

RULERS:

French, 1920-1944

MONETARY SYSTEM:

1 Pound (Livre) = 100 Piastres

OVERPRINT VARIETIES				
/	//	V	(double V)	◇
Type A	Type B	Type C	Type D	Type E

FRENCH ADMINISTRATION

Banque de Syrie

1919 Issue

#	Denomination	Good	Fine	XF
1	**5 Piastres** 1.8.1919. Dark green on multicolor underprint. Ruins of Baalbek at lower center. Back: Lion head at center. BC: Blue and lilac. Printer: BWC.			
	a. Signature title: *LE SECRETAIRE GENERAL.*	5.00	35.00	100
	b. Signature title: *LE ADMINISTRATEUR DELEGUE.*	5.00	40.00	125
2	**25 Piastres** 1.8.1919. Dark blue and multicolor. Omayyad Mosque in Damascus at center. Printer: BWC.	12.50	60.00	200

#	Denomination	Good	Fine	XF
3	**50 Piastres** 1.8.1919. Purple and multicolor. Damascus at upper center. Printer: BWC.	22.50	100	325

#	Denomination	Good	Fine	XF
4	**100 Piastres** 1.8.1919. Brown and multicolor. Pillars of Baalbek at left. Back: City scene at center. BC: Blue and multicolor. Printer: BWC.	40.00	175	600

#	Denomination	Good	Fine	XF
5	**500 Piastres** 1.8.1919. Dark purple and multicolor. Cedar tree at right. Back: City view at center. Printer: BWC.	70.00	400	1,000

1920 First Issue

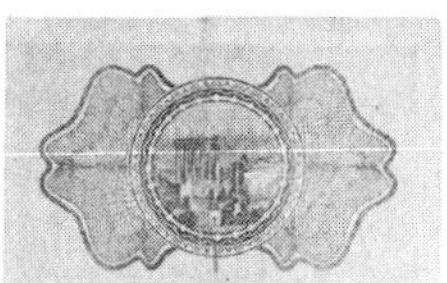

#	Denomination	VG	VF	UNC
6	**1 Piastre** 1.1.1920. Blue on light green and light orange underprint. Back: Ruins of Baalbek at center. BC: Brown and red-brown. Printer: BWC.	4.00	15.00	45.00
7	**10 Livres** 1.1.1920. Light brown. Tower of Great Serai of Beyrouth at left. Printer: BWC.	VG	VF	UNC
	a. Issued note.	—	—	—
	s. Specimen.	—	—	250
8	**25 Livres** 1.1.1920. Green. Arab cemetery at left, caravan by city gate at right. Printer: BWC.	VG	VF	UNC
	a. Issued note.	—	—	—
	s. Specimen.	—	—	325
9	**50 Livres** 1.1.1920. Blue. Road at left. Printer: BWC.	VG	VF	UNC
	a. Issued note.	—	—	—
	s. Specimen.	—	—	400

No.	Description	VG	VF	UNC
10	**100 Livres** 1.1.1920. Gray. Printer: BWC.			
	a. Issued note.	—	—	—
	s. Specimen.	—	—	550

1920 Second Issue

No.	Description	Good	Fine	XF
11	**5 Piastres** 1.7.1920. Dark green and multicolor. Ruins of Baalbek at lower center. Like #1. Back: Lion head at center. BC: Blue and lilac. Printer: BWC.	5.00	35.00	100

No.	Description	Good	Fine	XF
12	**10 Piastres** 1.7.1920. Dark blue and multicolor. Shepherds gathered around a campfire, goats in background. Printer: BWC.	7.50	50.00	200

No.	Description	Good	Fine	XF
13	**25 Piastres** 1.7.1920. Dark blue. Building with Omayyad Mosque in Damascus at lower center. Printer: BWC.	15.00	75.00	300
14	**50 Piastres** 1.7.1920. Purple. Printer: BWC.	30.00	150	450
15	**100 Piastres** 1.7.1920. Brown. Pillars of Baalbek. Printer: BWC.	75.00	250	650

No.	Description	Good	Fine	XF
16	**500 Piastres** 1.7.1920. Dark purple. Cedar tree at right. Like #5. Back: City view at center. BC: Blue. Printer: BWC. Rare.	—	—	—
17	**10 Livres** 1.7.1920. Light brown. Tower of the Great Serai of Beyrouth. Printer: BWC.	—	—	—
18	**25 Livres** 1.7.1920. Green. Arab cemetery at left, caravan near city gate at right. Printer: BWC.	—	—	—
19	**100 Livres** 1.7.1920. Green. Bank of Beyrouth at upper center. Printer: BWC.	—	—	—

Banque de Syrie et du Grand-Liban

1925 First Issue

No.	Description	Good	Fine	XF
21	**25 Piastres** 15.4.1925. Mill on back.	35.00	150	450
22	**50 Piastres** 15.4.1925. Type Cl. Serveau. Without overprint: *SYRIE.*	40.00	200	550
23	**50 Piastres** 15.4.1925. Type Cl. Serveau. Like #22. Overprint: *SYRIE.*	—	—	—
24	**100 Piastres** 15.4.1925.	—	—	—

1925 Second Issue

No.	Description	Good	Fine	XF
25	**5 Livres** 15.4.1925.	—	—	—
26	**10 Livres** 15.4.1925.	—	—	—
27	**25 Livres** 15.4.1925.	—	—	—
28	**50 Livres** 15.4.1925.	—	—	—
29	**100 Livres** 15.4.1925. Multicolor. Back: City scene; ornate vase at left and right. 238x132mm.	—	—	—

1930 Issue

No.	Description	Good	Fine	XF
29A	**1 Livre** 1.11.1930. Multicolor. Back: Harbor and mountainous landscape.	30.00	100	300
30	**5 Livres** 1.11.1930. Multicolor.	35.00	125	500
31	**10 Livres** 1.11.1930. Multicolor. Back: Ornate ruins.	40.00	250	—
32	**25 Livres** 1.11.1930. Multicolor.	—	—	—
33	**100 Livres** 1.11.1930. Multicolor.	—	—	—

Color Abbreviation Guide

New to the *Standard Catalog of ® World Paper Money* are the following abbreviations related to color references:

BC: Back color
PC: Paper color

1935 Issue

		VG	VF	UNC
34	**1 Livre** 1.2.1935. Brown and multicolor. Back: Harbor and mountain landscape. Like #29A.	10.00	50.00	300

#35 not assigned.

		VG	VF	UNC
36	**5 Livres** 1.2.1935. Multicolor. Back: Azam Palace at center.	25.00	150	600

		VG	VF	UNC
38	**100 Livres** 1.2.1935. Green. Bank of Beyrouth at upper center. Similar to #19. Printer: BWC.			
	a. Without line overprint	—	—	—
	b. Orange overprint Type B.	—	—	—
	c. Lilac overprint Type C.	—	—	—
	d. Green overprint Type A.	—	—	—
	s. Specimen.	—	—	—

1938 Issue

		VG	VF	UNC
39	**50 Livres** 1.1.1938. Type Cl. Serveau.	125	500	—

1939 Provisional Issues

		Good	Fine	XF
39A	**1 Livre** 1939 (- old date 1.2.1935). Brown and multicolor. Back: Harbor and mountain landscape. Overprint: *SYRIE 1939* on #34.	8.00	50.00	225

		Good	Fine	XF
39B	**5 Livres** 1939 (- old date 1.2.1935). Multicolor. Back: Azam Palace at center. Overprint: *SYRIE 1939*. On #36.			
	a. With overprint: *SYRIE 1939* below central Arabic text.	20.00	100	350
	b. With overprint: *SYRIE 1939* above central Arabic text.	20.00	100	350

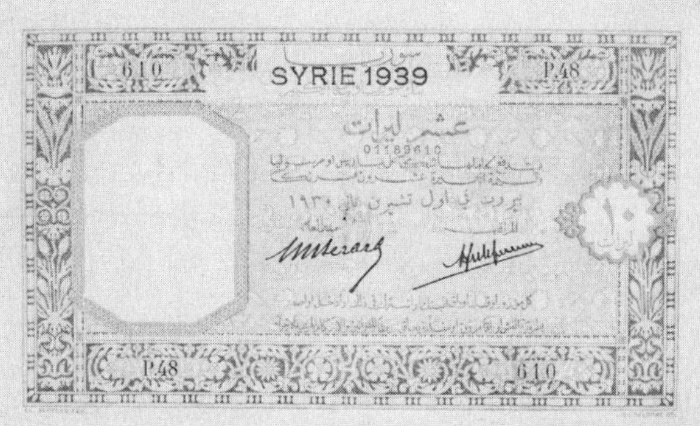

		Good	Fine	XF
39C	**10 Livres** 1939 (- old date 1.11.1930). Multicolor. Back: Ornate ruins. Overprint: *SYRIE 1939* on #31.	200	800	—
39D	**100 Livres** 1939 (- old date 1.11.1930). Multicolor. Overprint: *SYRIE 1939* on #33.	150	750	—

		Good	Fine	XF
39E	**100 Livres**			
	1939 (- old date 1.2.1935). Green. Bank of Beyrouth at upper center. Overprint: *SYRIE 1939*.			
	a. Overprint on #38a.	120	400	—
	b. Overprint on #38b.	120	400	—
	c. Overprint on #38c.	120	400	—
	d. Overprint on #38d.	120	400	—

		Good	Fine	XF
39F	**100 Livres**			
	1939 (- old date 1.2.1935). Purple. Overprint: *SYRIE 1939*.			
	a. Overprint on Lebanon #14a.	120	400	—
	c. Overprint on Lebanon #14c.	175	600	—

Banque de Syrie et du Liban

1939 Issue

		VG	VF	UNC
40	**1 Livre**			
	1.9.1939. Green and multicolor. Pillars of Baalbek at left. Back: City view at center. BC: Red on multicolor underprint. Printer: BWC.			
	a. Without line overprint.	10.00	45.00	125
	b. Violet Type A overprint.	10.00	45.00	125
	c. Lilac-colored Type B overprint.	10.00	45.00	125
	d. Green Type C overprint.	10.00	45.00	125
	e. Red Type D overprint.	10.00	45.00	125
	f. Blue Type E overprint.	10.00	45.00	125

		VG	VF	UNC
41	**5 Livres**			
	1.9.1939. Brown and multicolor. Cedar at right. Back: Landscape with buildings in oval at center. Printer: BWC.			
	a. Without line overprint.	17.50	65.00	275
	b. Violet Type A overprint.	17.50	65.00	275
	c. Pink or green Type B overprint.	17.50	65.00	275
	d. Green Type C overprint.	17.50	65.00	275
	e. Blue Type E overprint.	17.50	65.00	275

#	Description	Good	Fine	XF
42	**10 Livres** 1.9.1939. Brown-violet and multicolor. Clock tower at left. Printer: BWC. Overprint: *SYRIE.*			
	a. Without overprint.	10.00	50.00	175
	b. Pink Type A overprint.	10.00	50.00	175
	c. Green Type B overprint.	10.00	50.00	175
	d. Blue Type C overprint.	10.00	50.00	175

#	Description	Good	Fine	XF
43	**25 Livres** 1.9.1939. Brown-lilac and multicolor. Caravan at center. Back: Ruins at center. BC: Olive and multicolor. Printer: BWC. Overprint: *SYRIE.*			
	a. Lilac Type A overprint.	12.50	75.00	300
	b. Red Type C overprint.	12.50	75.00	300
	c. Green Type D overprint.	12.50	75.00	300
	d. Without overprint.	12.50	75.00	300

#	Description	Good	Fine	XF
44	**50 Livres** 1.9.1939. Brown, blue and multicolor. Street scene at left. Printer: BWC. Overprint: *SYRIE* and green Type E.			
	a. Issued note.	35.00	150	500
	b. Lilac Type A overprint.	35.00	150	500
	c. Blue Type E overprint.	35.00	150	500
45	**100 Livres** 1939. Green and yellow. Without *SYRIE* overprint. Printer: BWC.			
	a. Green Type A overprint.	30.00	120	450
	b. Orange Type B overprint.	30.00	120	450
	c. Pink Type C overprint.	30.00	120	450

1942 Bon de Caisse Issue

#	Description	Good	Fine	XF
46	**5 Livres** 1.8.1942. Dark green. BC: Blue. Printer: R. Soriano I.C. Beyrouth. PC: Yellow.	75.00	325	650
47	**50 Livres** 1.8.1942. Green. Printer: Government Printer, Palestine.	125	550	—
48	**100 Livres** 1.8.1942. Blue on green and yellow underprint. BC: Green. Printer: Government Printer, Palestine.	200	600	—

REPUBLIC

Republique Syrienne

1942 First Issue

#	Description	VG	VF	UNC
49	**5 Piastres** 15.7.1942. Green on light lilac underprint. Back: Citadel of Aleppo at center. BC: Purple. Printer: Survey of Egypt.	1.50	7.50	35.00
50	**10 Piastres** 31.7.1942. Brown on yellow underprint. Mosque with two minarets. BC: Red-brown. Printer: Survey of Egypt.	2.50	12.50	60.00

51 25 Piastres
1.8.1942. Red and multicolor. Omayyad Mosque in Damascus at center. Similar to #2. Printer: BWC.

VG	VF	UNC
5.00	30.00	100

52 50 Piastres
1.8.1942. Blue and multicolor. Damascus at upper center. Similar to #3. Printer: BWC.

VG	VF	UNC
7.50	50.00	150

1942 Second Issue

53 25 Piastres
31.8.1942. Dark brown on gold underprint. Mosque of Si Kabib of Homs. BC: Maroon. Printer: Survey of Egypt.

VG	VF	UNC
5.00	25.00	85.00

54 50 Piastres
31.8.1942. Blue on green underprint. Pillars. BC: Brown. Printer: Survey of Egypt.

VG	VF	UNC
7.50	30.00	125

1944 Issue

55 5 Piastres
15.2.1944. Green on light green underprint. Back: Citadel of Aleppo at center. Similar to #49. BC: Blue. Printer: Moharrem Press; Alexandrie.

VG	VF	UNC
1.50	5.00	30.00

56 10 Piastres
15.2.1944. Brown on gold underprint. Mosque with two minarets. Similar to #50. BC: Maroon. Printer: Moharrem Press; Alexandrie.

VG	VF	UNC
2.50	10.00	60.00

ca.1945 ND Provisional Issue

56A 2 1/2 Piastres
ND. Green tax adhesive stamp affixed to cardboard. Back: Red text.

VG	VF	UNC
25.00	75.00	200

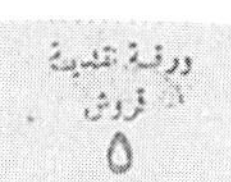

56B 5 Piastres
ND. Blue tax adhesive stamp affixed to cardboard. Back: Red text.

VG	VF	UNC
25.00	75.00	200

Banque de Syrie et du Liban

1947 Issue

57 1 Livre
1.4.1947. Brown and multicolor. Back: Harbor and mountain landscape. Similar to #34.

VG	VF	UNC
5.00	40.00	150

58 10 Livres
1.4.1947. Multicolor. Roman temple ruins. Type Cl. Serveau.

VG	VF	UNC
30.00	125	500

#59-61 w/green ovpt: State arms and *Ministry of Finance* in Arabic.

59 25 Livres
1.4.1947. Multicolor. Arms at center. Back: Citadel. Type Cl. Serveau.

VG	VF	UNC
50.00	300	800

		VG	VF	UNC
60	**50 Livres** 1.4.1947. Multicolor. Back: Oriental house. Type Cl. Serveau.	75.00	425	1,000

		VG	VF	UNC
61	**100 Livres** 1.4.1947. Multicolor. View of Damascus. Type Laurent.	125	550	—

1948 Issue

		VG	VF	UNC
62	**5 Livres** 15.12.1948. Multicolor. Back: Azam Palace at center. Similar to #36.	12.50	55.00	350

1949 Issue

		VG	VF	UNC
63	**1 Livre** 1.7.1949. Multicolor. Back: Harbor and mountain landscape. Like #57.	5.00	40.00	150

		VG	VF	UNC
64	**10 Livres** 1.7.1949. Multicolor. Roman temple ruins. Type Cl. Serveau. Like #58.	30.00	125	550
65	**25 Livres** 1.7.1949. Multicolor. Arms at center. Similar to #59. Back: Citadel.	50.00	200	750

		VG	VF	UNC
66	**50 Livres** 1.7.1949. Multicolor. Back: Oriental house. Like #60.	150	500	—

		VG	VF	UNC
67	**100 Livres** 1.7.1949. Multicolor. View of Damascus. Like #61.	175	550	—

1949 Bons de Caisse Provisional Issue

		VG	VF	UNC
68	**250 Livres** 1.7.1949. Form filled out in handwriting.	—	—	—
69	**500 Livres** 1.7.1949. Form filled out in handwriting.	—	—	—

1950 Regular Issue

		VG	VF	UNC
70	**25 Livres** 15.8.1950. Multicolor. Arms at center. Like #65. Back: Citadel.	25.00	125	500
71	**50 Livres** 15.8.1950. Multicolor. Back: Oriental house. Like #66.	40.00	175	700
72	**100 Livres** 15.8.1950. Multicolor. View of Damascus. Like #67.	100	500	—

Institut d'Emission de Syrie

1950s First Issue

		VG	VF	UNC
73	**1 Livre** ND. Dark brown on multicolor underprint. Arms at right, *Premiere Emission.* Inner yard of Omayyad Mosque in Damascus. Watermark: Horse head.	7.50	35.00	100

		VG	VF	UNC
74	**5 Livres** ND. Orange-brown on multicolor underprint. Arms at right, *Premiere Emission.* Back: Citadel of Aleppo. Watermark: Horse head.	15.00	55.00	250

		VG	VF	UNC
75	**10 Livres** ND. Blue-green on multicolor underprint. Arms at right, *Premiere Emission.* Back: Tekkiye Suleimanie in Damascus. Watermark: Horse head.	25.00	150	400

		VG	VF	UNC
76	**25 Livres** ND. Red on multicolor underprint. Arms at right, *Premiere Emission.* Back: Ruins of Palmyra. Watermark: Horse head.	40.00	250	600
77	**50 Livres** ND. Green on multicolor underprint. Arms at right, *Premiere Emission.* Back: Inner yard of Azem Palace in Damascus. Watermark: Horse head.	90.00	400	850

		VG	VF	UNC
78	**100 Livres** ND. Blue on multicolor underprint. Arms at right, *Premiere Emission.* Watermark: Horse head.	185	500	—

1955 Second Issue

		VG	VF	UNC
78A	**10 Livres** 1955. Blue green on multicolor underprint. Arms at right, *Deuxieme Emission.* Like #75. Back: Tekkiye Suleimanie in Damascus.	20.00	90.00	350

		VG	VF	UNC
78B	**25 Livres** 1955. Red on multicolor underprint. Arms at right, *Deuxieme Emission.* Like #76. Back: Ruins of Palmyra.	45.00	225	700

Banque Centrale de Syrie

Central Bank of Syria

1957-1958 Issue

		VG	VF	UNC
79	**1 Livre** 1957. Brown on multicolor underprint. Arms at right, *Premiere Emission.* Inner yard of Omayyad Mosque in Damascus. Similar to #73. Back: Bank name in French.	7.50	35.00	100
80	**5 Livres** 1957. Brown on multicolor underprint. Arms at right, *Premiere Emission.* Similar to #74. Back: Citadel of Aleppo. Bank name in French.	17.50	65.00	300

#81 *Not assigned.*

		VG	VF	UNC
82	**10 Livres** 1957. Blue-green on multicolor underprint. Arms at right, *Premiere Emission.* Similar to #75. Back: Tekkiye Suleimanie in Damascus. Bank name in French.	25.00	170	450
83	**25 Livres** 1957. Red on multicolor underprint. Arms at right, *Premiere Emission.* Similar to #76. Back: Ruins of Palmyra. Bank name in French.	40.00	250	600

		VG	VF	UNC
84	**50 Livres** 1957; 1958. Green on multicolor underprint. Arms at right, *Premiere Emission.* Similar to #77. Back: Inner yard of Azem Palace in Damascus. Bank name in French.	60.00	275	650
85	**100 Livres** 1958. Blue on multicolor underprint. Arms at right, *Premiere Emission.* Similar to #78. Back: Bank name in French.	80.00	350	850

1958 Issue

		VG	VF	UNC
86	**1 Pound** 1958/AH1377. Brown on multicolor underprint. Worker at right. Back: Water wheel of Hama. Bank name in English. Watermark: Arabian horse head. Printer: Pakistan Security Printing Corp. Ltd.			
	a. Issued note.	2.00	7.50	30.00
	s. Specimen.	—	—	35.00
87	**5 Pounds** 1958/AH1377. Green on multicolor underprint. Worker at right. Similar to #86. Back: Citadel of Aleppo. Bank name in English. Watermark: Arabian horse head. Printer: Pakistan Security Printing Corp. Ltd.	VG	VF	UNC
	a. Issued note.	6.00	20.00	100
	s. Specimen.	—	—	50.00

		VG	VF	UNC
88	**10 Pounds** 1958/AH1377. Purple on multicolor underprint. Worker at right. Similar to #86. Back: Courtyard of Omayad Mosque. Bank name in English. Watermark: Arabian horse head. Printer: Pakistan Security Printing Corp. Ltd.			
	a. Issued note.	8.00	30.00	135
	s. Specimen.	—	—	100

		VG	VF	UNC
89	**25 Pounds** 1958/AH1377. Blue on multicolor underprint. Girl with basket at right. Back: Interior view of Azem Palace in Damascus. Bank name in English. Watermark: Arabian horse head. Printer: JEZ.			
	a. Issued note.	10.00	35.00	150
	s. Specimen.	—	—	150

		VG	VF	UNC
90	**50 Pounds** 1958/AH1377. Red and brown on multicolor underprint. Girl with basket at right. Similar to #89. Back: Mosque of Sultan Selim. Bank name in English. Watermark: Arabian horse head. Printer: JEZ.			
	a. Issued note.	10.00	40.00	175
	s. Specimen.	—	—	175

		VG	VF	UNC
91	**100 Pounds** 1958;1962. Olive-green on multicolor underprint. Girl with basket at right. Similar to #89. Back: Old ruins of Palmyra. Bank name in English. Watermark: Arabian horse head. Printer: JEZ.			
	a. 1958.	20.00	70.00	250
	b. 1962.	15.00	60.00	210
	s. Specimen.	—	—	200

		VG	VF	UNC
92	**500 Pounds** 1958/AH1377. Brown and purple on multicolor underprint. Motifs from ruins of Kingdom of Ugarit, head at right. Back: Ancient religious wheel and cuneiform clay tablet. Bank name in English. Watermark: Arabian horse head. Printer: JEZ.			
	a. Issued note.	45.00	160	410
	s. Specimen.	—	—	400

Tahiti, the largest island of the central South Pacific French overseas territory of French Polynesia, has an area of 402 sq. mi. (1,042 sq. km.) and a population of 79,024. Papeete on the northwest coast is the capital and administrative center of French Polynesia. Copra, sugar cane, vanilla and coffee are exported. Tourism is an important industry. Capt. Samuel Wallis of the British Navy discovered Tahiti in 1768 and named it King George III Island. Louis-Antoine de Bougainville arrived the following year and claimed it for France. Subsequent English visits were by James Cook in 1769 and William Bligh in the HMS "Bounty" in 1788. Members of the Protestant London Missionary Society established the first European settlement in 1797, and with the aid of the local Pomare family gained control of the entire island and established a "missionary kingdom" with a scriptural code of law. Nevertheless, Tahiti was subsequently declared a French protectorate (1842) and a colony (1880), and since 1958 is part of the overseas territory of French Polynesia.

RULERS:
French

MONETARY SYSTEM:
1 Franc = 100 Centimes

FRENCH ADMINISTRATION

Banque de l'Indochine

Papeete

Décrets des 21.1.1875 - 20.2.1888 - 16.5.1900 - 3.4.1901

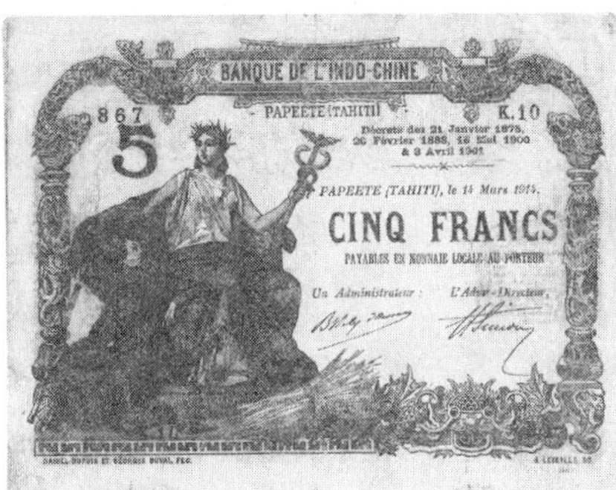

		Good	Fine	XF
1	**5 Francs** 4.9.1912; 14.3.1914. Red. Seated oriental woman below seated Liberty holding caduceus at left. 2 signatures.			
	a. Overprint: *PAPEETE (TAHITI)* in red below decrees at center right. 4.9.1912; 14.3.1914.	125	500	1,250
	b. Overprint: *PAPEETE (TAHITI)* in black. 14.3.1914.	125	500	1,250

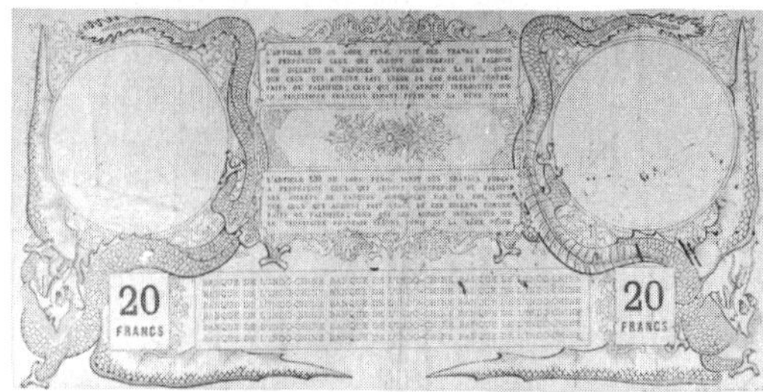

		Good	Fine	XF
2	**20 Francs** 20.3.1914. Blue-green with black text. Neptune reclining holding trident at lower left. 3 signatures.	175	750	—

		Good	Fine	XF
3	**100 Francs** 1.9.1910; 10.3.1914; 12.3.1914. Elephant columns left and right, two reclining women with ox left, tiger right, at lower border. 3 signatures. Rare.	—	—	—

1920 Issue (w/o Decrets)

No.	Description	Good	Fine	XF
4	**5 Francs** 2.1.1920; 1.8.1923. Red. Seated oriental woman below seated Liberty holding caduceus at left. Like #1, but 3 signatures.	100	300	1,000
5	**20 Francs** 1.5.1920. Green with black text. Neptune reclining holding trident at lower left. Like #2. 3 signatures.	175	750	—

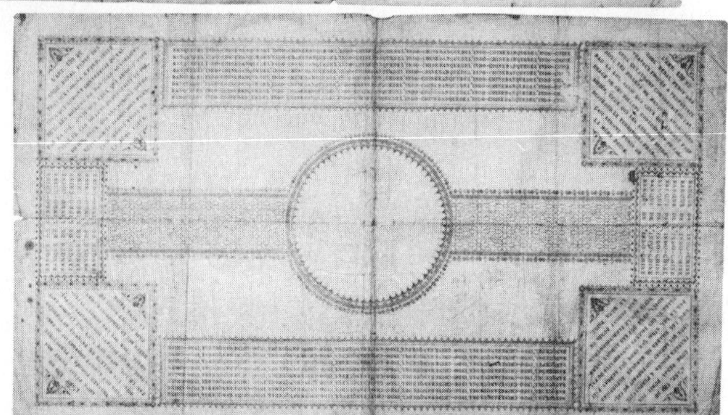

No.	Description	Good	Fine	XF
6	**100 Francs** 2.1.1920. Brown. Elephant columns left and right, two reclining women with ox left, tiger right, at lower border. Like #3 but 2 signatures.			
	a. Hand signature.	100	350	—
	b. Printed signature.	75.00	250	600

Banque André Krajewski

Papeete

1920 ND Issue

No.	Description	Good	Fine	XF
7	**25 Centimes** ND (1920). Brown. Seated woman holding branch and frame around denomination at lower left. Printer: A. Carlisle and Co., S.F.	75.00	400	1,000
8	**50 Centimes** ND (1920). Green. Seated woman holding branch and frame around denomination at lower left. Printer: A. Carlisle and Co., S.F.	100	500	1,200

No.	Description	Good	Fine	XF
9	**1 Franc** ND (1920). Red. Seated woman holding branch and frame around denomination at lower left. Printer: A. Carlisle and Co., S.F.	120	600	1,500
10	**2 Francs** ND (1920). Orange and red. Seated woman holding branch and frame around denomination at lower left. Printer: A. Carlisle and Co., S.F.	120	600	1,500

Banque de l'Indochine (resumed)

Papeete

1923-1928 Issue

No.	Description	Good	Fine	XF
11	**5 Francs** ND (1927). Brown. Helmeted woman at lower left. Signature varieties.			
	a. Signature titles: *Un Administrateur* and *Le Directeur.*	8.00	30.00	100
	b. Signature R. Thion de la Chaume and P. Baudouin with titles: *Le Président* and *Le Directeur Général.*	5.00	15.00	75.00
	c. Signature M. Borduge and P. Baudouin with titles as b.	3.00	10.00	40.00

No.	Description	Good	Fine	XF
12	**20 Francs** ND (1928). Brown, lilac and red. Woman at right. Signature varieties. Back: Peacock.			
	a. Signature titles: *Le Directeur* and *Le Administrateur.*	20.00	75.00	200
	b. Signature R. Thion de la Chaume and P. Baudouin with titles: *Le Président* and *Le Directeur Général.*	15.00	50.00	125
	c. Signature M. Borduge and P. Baudouin with titles as b.	7.50	25.00	75.00
	d. Signature titles like b., but with overprint: *BANQUE DE L'INDOCHINE/SUCCURSALE DE PAPEETE.*	15.00	60.00	150
	e. Signature as c, overprint as d.	15.00	60.00	150

		Good	Fine	XF
13	**500 Francs** 1923; 1938. Dark purple. Standing woman at left, ships at top center. Signature varieties.			
	a. Signature titles: *LE DIRECTEUR* and *UN ADMINISTRATEUR*. 1.4.1923.	125	400	1,000
	b. Signature titles: *LE PRÉSIDENT* and *LE DIRECTEUR GÉNÉRAL*. 8.3.1938.	125	400	1,000

1939-1940 ND Issue

		Good	Fine	XF
14	**100 Francs** ND (1939-1965). Brown and multicolor. Woman wearing wreath and holding small figure of Athena at center. Back: Angkor statue.			
	a. Signature M. Borduge and P. Baudouin with titles: *LE PRÉSIDENT* and *LE ADMINISTRATEUR DIRECTEUR GÉNÉRAL*.	20.00	85.00	300
	b. Signature titles: *LE PRÉSIDENT* and *LE ADMINISTRATEUR DIRECTEUR GÉNÉRAL*.	15.00	75.00	250
	c. Signature titles: *LE PRÉSIDENT* and *LE VICE-PRÉSIDENT DIRECTEUR GÉNÉRAL*.	12.00	60.00	225
	d. Signature titles: *LE PRÉSIDENT* and *LE DIRECTEUR GÉNÉRAL*.	10.00	50.00	200

		Good	Fine	XF
15	**1000 Francs** ND (1940-1957). Multicolor. Market scene at left and in background, seated woman at right.			
	a. Signature M. Borduge and P. Baudouin with titles: *LE PRÉSIDENT* and *LE VICE-PRÉSIDENT DIRECTEUR GÉNÉRAL*.	30.00	125	400
	b. Signature titles: *LE PRÉSIDENT* and *LE VICE-PRÉSIDENT DIRECTEUR GÉNÉRAL*.	25.00	100	300
	c. Signature F.M.A. de Flers and M. Robert with titles like a.	15.00	50.00	250
	s. Specimen. Perforated: *SPECIMEN*.	—	Unc	750

1940 ND Provisional Issue

		Good	Fine	XF
16	**100 Francs on 20 Francs** ND (ca.1940). Brown, lilac and red. Woman at right. 2 signatures vertically at left center. Back: Peacock. Overprint: Black *CENT FRANCS* and *CENT* across upper center and *100* at lower center on #12c.			
	a. Issued note. Rare.	—	—	—
	b. Punch cancelled, handstamped: *ANNULÉ*. Rare.	—	—	—

		Good	Fine	XF
16A	**100 Francs** ND. Brown and multicolor. Woman wearing wreath and holding small figure of Athena at center. Like #14 but Noumea issue. Back: Angkor statue. Overprint: Red *PAPEETE* at lower right on face, at lower center on back.	40.00	150	375

1943 ND Provisional Issue

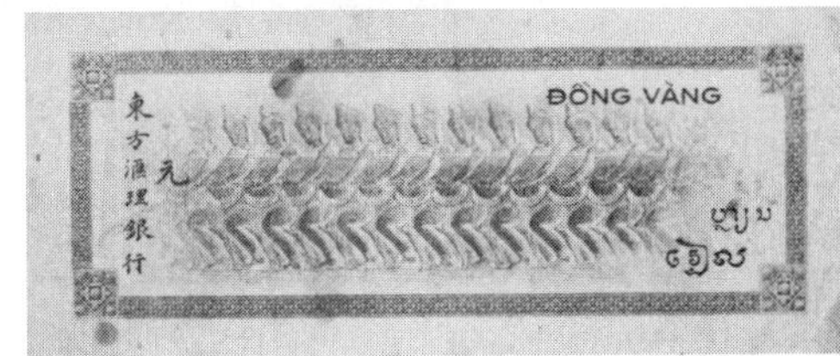

		Good	Fine	XF
17	**100 Francs on 50 Piastres** ND (1943). Green. Man with straw hat and baskets at right. Printed signature. Printer: ABNC (without imprint). Overprint: On unfinished 50 Piastres, French Indo-China #77.			
	a. Text: *DE SAIGON* in right signature title not lined out.	50.00	150	450
	b. Text: *DE SAIGON* in right signature title lined out.	35.00	125	350
	s. Specimen, handstamped: *ANNULÉ*.	—	Unc	275

		Good	Fine	XF
18	**1000 Francs on 100 Piastres** ND (1943). Blue. Angkor statues at left. Printer: ABNC (without imprint). Overprint: On unfinished 100 Piastres French Indo-China #78.			
	a. Handwritten signature at right.	125	400	900
	b. Both signature printed.	120	350	750

1944 ND Issue

		Good	Fine	XF
19	**5 Francs** ND (1944). Blue. Woman wearing wreath and holding small figure of Athena at center. 2 signature varieties. Back: Angkor statue. Printer: Australian.			
	a. Issued note.	25.00	125	350
	s. Specimen.	—	Unc	200

		Good	Fine	XF
20	**20 Francs** ND (1944). Brown. Woman at left, sailboat at center, fisherman at right. Back: Stylized mask. Printer: Australian.			
	a. Issued note.	35.00	150	450
	s. Specimen.	—	Unc	250

1951 ND Issue

		VG	VF	UNC
21	**20 Francs** ND (1951-1963). Multicolor. Youth at left, flute player at right. Back: Fruit at left, woman at right. Watermark: Man with hat.			
	a. Signature titles: *LE PRÉSIDENT* and *LE DIRECTEUR GAL.* (1951).	12.50	50.00	125
	b. Signature titles: *LE PRÉSIDENT* and *LE VICE-PRÉSIDENT DIRECTEUR GÉNÉRAL* (1954-1958).	7.00	30.00	75.00
	c. Signature titles: *LE PRÉSIDENT* and *LE DIRECTEUR GÉNÉRAL.* (1963).	5.00	20.00	50.00
	s. As b, c. Specimen. Pinhole perforated *SPECIMEN.*	—	—	250

1954 Provisional Issue

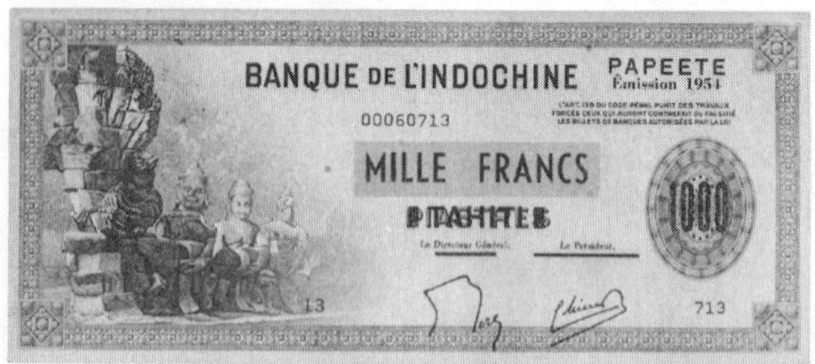

		Good	Fine	XF
22	**1000 Francs on 100 Piastres** 1954. Blue. Angkor statues at left. Similar to #18. Overprint: On unfinished 100 Piastres French Indo-China #78. Elements on back as well as on face.	110	325	750

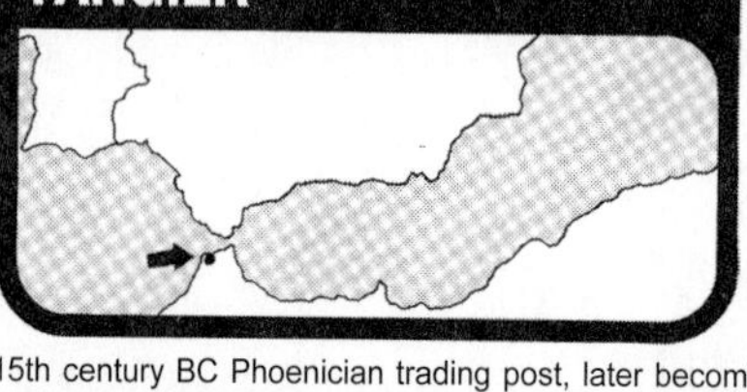

Tangier (Tangiers) is a port and city of the province of the same name in northern Morocco, at the west end of the Strait of Gibraltar, 17 miles (27 km.) from the southern tip of Spain. Tangier province has an area of 141 sq. mi. (365 sq. km.) and a population of 240,000. The town has a population of 190,000. Fishing and a textile industry supplement Tangier's role as a tourist center. Tangier began as a 15th century BC Phoenician trading post, later becoming a Carthaginian and then a Roman settlement called Tingis. After five centuries of Roman rule, it was captured successively by the Vandals, Byzantines and Arabs. It was occupied by Islamic dynasties from about 682 to 1471, and by the Portuguese and Spanish until 1662, when sovereignty was transferred to the crown. It was returned to Morocco in 1684 and was the diplomatic capital of Morocco during the 19th century. In 1923 it became an international zone governed by representatives from Great Britain, France, Spain, Portugal, Italy, Belgium, The Netherlands, Sweden, and later, the United States. It remained an international zone except for a period of Spanish occupation during World War II and then again until 1956, when it became a part of the Kingdom of Morocco.

RULERS:

French, 1912-1923
International Zone, 1923-1940, 1945-1956
Spanish, 1940-1945
Morocco, 1956-

SPANISH OCCUPATION - WWII

Servicios Municipales

1941 Emergency Issue

		Good	Fine	XF
1	**0.25 Francos** Aug. 1941; March 1942; Oct. 1942. Blue.	550	1,350	—
2	**0.50 Francos** Aug. 1941; March 1942; Oct. 1942. Brown.	500	1,250	—

		Good	Fine	XF
3	**1 Franco** Aug. 1941; March 1942; Oct. 1942. Violet.	550	1,350	—
4	**2 Francos** (ca. 1941-1942). Orange.	650	1,500	—

The Tannu-Tuva Peoples Republic (Tuva), an autonomous part of the former Union of Soviet Socialist Republics located in central Asia on the northwest border of Outer Mongolia, has an area of 64,000 sq. mi. (165,760 sq. km.) and a population of about 175,000. Capital: Kyzyl. The economy is based on herding, forestry and mining. As Urianghi, Tuva was part of Outer Mongolia of the Chinese Empire when Czarist Russia, after fomenting a separatist movement, extended its protection to the mountainous country in 1914. Tuva declared its independence as the Tannu-Tuva People's Republic in 1921 under the auspices of the Tuva People's Revolutionary Party. In 1926, following Russia's successful mediation of the resultant Tuvinian-Mongolian territorial dispute, Tannu-Tuva and Outer Mongolia formally recognized each other's independence. The Tannu-Tuva People's Republic became an autonomous region of the U.S.S.R. on Oct. 13, 1944. Russian notes circulated between 1925-1933.

MONETARY SYSTEM:

1 Lan = 1 Aksha (Ruble) = 100 Kopejek (Kopeks)

PEOPLE'S REPUBLIC

Treasury

1924 ND Provisional Issue

#1-4 overprint: lines of script and a square stamp with script on Russian Imperial notes. Most of these are spurious.

		VG	VF	UNC
1	**1 Lan on 1 Ruble** ND (1924 - old date 1898). Blue on brown underprint.	10.00	20.00	30.00

		VG	VF	UNC
2	**3 Lan on 3 Rubles** ND (1924 - old date 1905). Green and pink.	15.00	30.00	40.00

		VG	VF	UNC
3	**5 Lan on 5 Rubles** ND (1924 - old date 1909). Blue.	10.00	20.00	30.00

		VG	VF	UNC
4	**10 Lan on 10 Rubles** ND (1925 - old date 1909). Red and green.	10.00	20.00	30.00

1933 ND Provisional Issue

#5-9 vignette overprint on Union of Soviet Socialist Republics notes.

#	Description	VG	VF	UNC
5	**3 Rubles** ND (1933 - old date 1925).	—	—	—
6	**5 Rubles** ND (1933 - old date 1925).	—	—	—
7	**1 Chervonetz** ND (1933 - old date 1926).	—	—	—
8	**2 Chervonetza** ND (1933 - old date 1926).	—	—	—
9	**1 Gold Ruble** ND (1933 - old date 1928).	—	—	—

Tannu Tuva Republic

1935 Issue

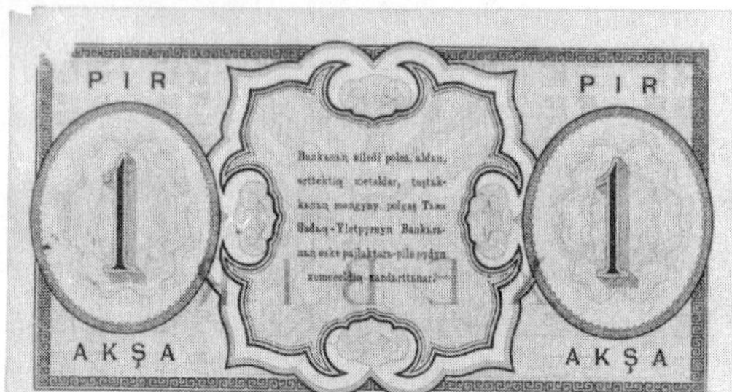

#	Description	Good	Fine	XF
10	**1 Aksha** 1935. Green and multicolor. Arms at upper center.	300	850	1,750
11	**3 Aksha** 1935. Multicolor. Arms at upper center.	300	850	1,750
12	**5 Aksha** 1935. Red and multicolor. Arms at upper center.	300	850	1,750

#	Description	VG	VF	UNC
13	**10 Aksha** 1935. Red and multicolor. Arms at upper center. Rare.	—	—	—
14	**25 Aksha** 1935. Brown and multicolor. Arms at upper center. Rare.	—	—	—

1940 Issue

#	Description	Good	Fine	XF
15	**1 Aksha** 1940. Brown on orange and green underprint. Farmer plowing with two horses at center.	200	500	—
16	**3 Aksha** 1940. Green. Farmer plowing with two horses at center.	200	500	—
17	**5 Aksha** 1940. Blue. Farmer plowing with two horses at center.	200	500	—
18	**10 Aksha** 1940. Red. Farmer plowing with two horses at center.	250	550	—
19	**25 Aksha** 1940. Brown-violet. Farmer plowing with two horses at center.	250	550	—

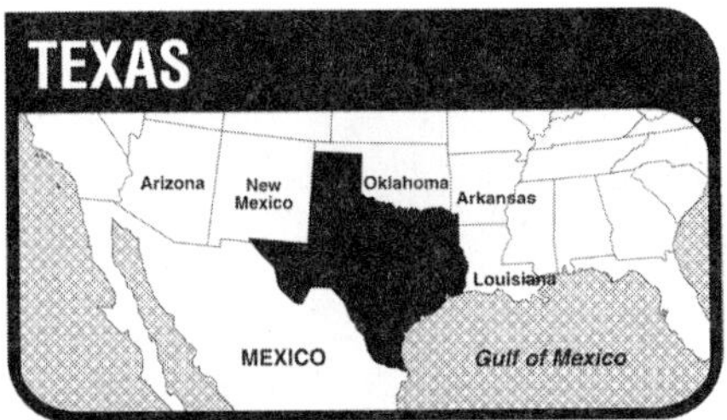

INDPENDENT REPUBLIC

The governments and note issuing experiences fall into three well-defined periods: (1) Republic of Texas, 1836-1845; (2) post-Republic period as a member of the United States, 1846-1860; and (3) Confederate Texas, 1861-1865. This volume includes only those issues made under the Republic, 1836-1845.

Within this short amount of time, Texas issued notes under the flag of Mexico, her own Republic, the United States and the Confederacy. With the exception of the pre-Republic period, notes of the other periods are readily accessible. Some note found in hoards are quite common, while others exist in only one or tow examples or not at all.

CANCELLATION OF NOTES: Most notes from #7-#38 have been cancelled. Those notes with a triangular piece cut out are worth 25% less than listed values which are for cut cancelled pieces.

Treasurer of the Republic

1836-1845 Audited Drafts Issue

Issued by the Treasurer at Austin, Galveston, Houston, San Felipe de Austin, Velasco and Washington-on-the-Brazos. Drafts were in various amounts. Many varieties in plate and signatures.

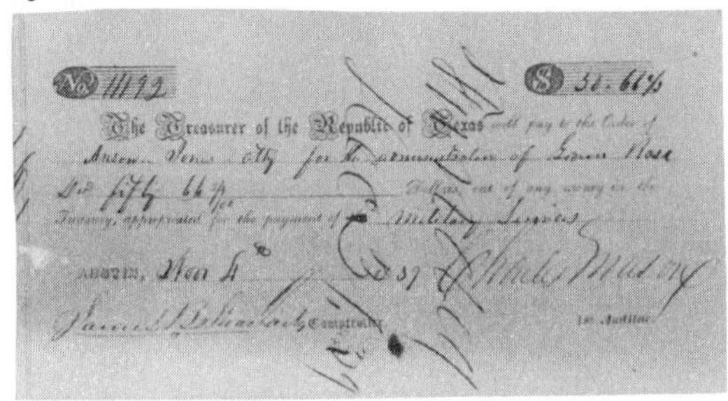

#	Denomination / Description	Good	Fine	XF
1	**Various Amounts**	Good	Fine	XF
	1836-1845. Austin.	25.00	40.00	70.00
2	**Various Amounts**	Good	Fine	XF
	1836-1845. Galveston.	250	375	550
3	**Various Amounts**	Good	Fine	XF
	1836-1845. Houston.	20.00	35.00	65.00
4	**Various Amounts**	Good	Fine	XF
	1836-1845. San Felipe de Austin.	200	375	675
5	**Various Amounts**	Good	Fine	XF
	1836-1845. Velasco.	60.00	120	240
6	**Various Amounts**	Good	Fine	XF
	1836-1845. Washington-on-Brazos.	25.00	45.00	75.00

REPUBLIC

Treasurer of the Republic

1837-1838 First Star Notes Issue

Issued at Houston, 10% interest-bearing notes. Typeset, many plate varieties.

#	Denomination / Description	Good	Fine	XF
7	**5 Dollars**	Good	Fine	XF
	1837-1838. Large star at upper center. Printed dates.			
	a. Issued note.	275	500	900
	b. *Dollars* misspelled as *Dollras*.	350	550	1,000
8	**10 Dollars**	Good	Fine	XF
	1837-1838. Large star at upper center. Printed dates.	225	375	600

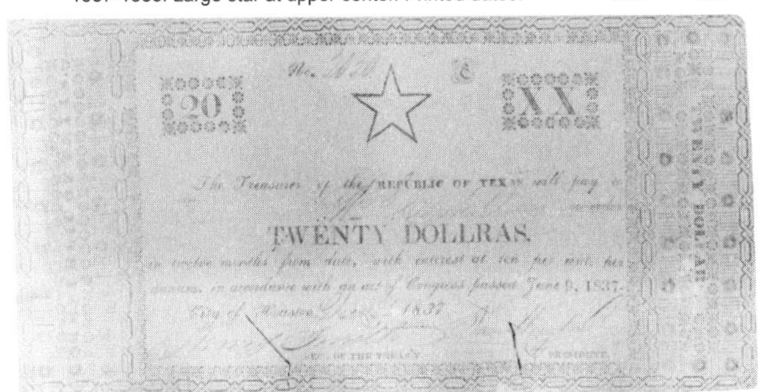

#	Denomination / Description	Good	Fine	XF
9	**20 Dollars**	Good	Fine	XF
	1837-1838. Large star at upper center. Printed dates.			
	a. Issued note.	225	375	600
	b. *Dollars* misspelled as *Dollras*.	275	450	700

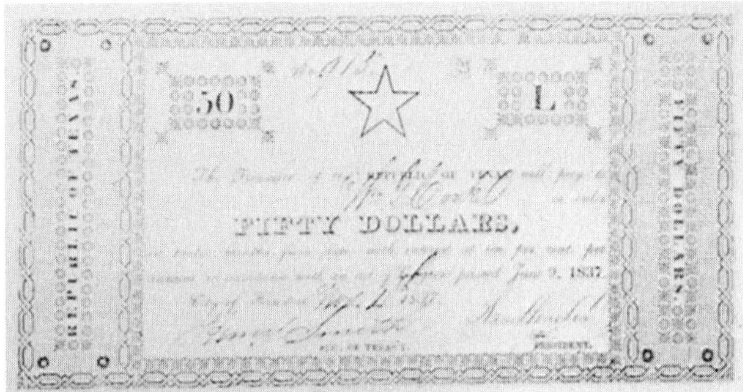

#	Denomination / Description	Good	Fine	XF
10	**50 Dollars**	Good	Fine	XF
	1837-1838. Large star at upper center. Printed dates.	175	400	600
11	**100 Dollars**	Good	Fine	XF
	1837-1838. Large star at upper center. Printed dates.	175	400	600
12	**500 Dollars**	Good	Fine	XF
	1837-1838. Large star at upper center. Printed dates.	700	2,000	3,250

Note: Pieces with Sam Houston's name, though signed by a secretary, are worth 25% more.

Act of Congress, Dec. 14, 1837; 1838 Second Issue

Issued at Houston.

#	Denomination / Description	Good	Fine	XF
13	**1 Dollar**	Good	Fine	XF
	1838. Black. Steamboat in oval at left. Man reclining at upper center, man's portrait at lower right. Handwritten date. Printer: Niles Print, Houston-Childs, Clark & Co., N. Orlea	200	500	900
14	**2 Dollars**	Good	Fine	XF
	1838. Black. Steamboat in oval at left. Liberty with eagle and shield at upper center. Handwritten date. Printer: Niles Print, Houston-Childs, Clark & Co., N. Orlea	200	450	750

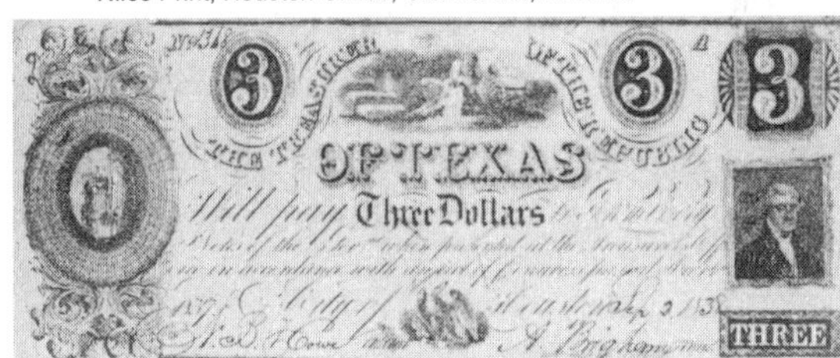

#	Denomination / Description	Good	Fine	XF
15	**3 Dollars**	Good	Fine	XF
	1838. Black. Steamboat in oval at left. Man reclining at upper center, man's portrait at lower right. Handwritten date. Similar to #13. Printer: Niles Print, Houston-Childs, Clark & Co., N. Orlea	200	400	700

Act of Congress, June 9, 1837; 1838 Third Issue

Government of Texas heading.

#	Denomination / Description	Good	Fine	XF
16	**1 Dollar**	Good	Fine	XF
	1838-1839. Black. Standing Liberty with shield and spear at left, seated Minerva with lion at upper center. Printer: Draper, Toppan, Longacre & Co., Phila. & N.Y.	175	375	1,250

#	Denomination / Description	Good	Fine	XF
17	**3 Dollars**	Good	Fine	XF
	1838-1839. Black. Seated Commerce with shield with lone star at upper center. Printer: Draper, Toppan, Longacre & Co., Phila. & N.Y.	175	350	875

#	Denomination / Description	Good	Fine	XF
18	**5 Dollars**	Good	Fine	XF
	1838-1839. Black. Standing Commerce at left, Indian brave hunting buffalo at center. Printer: Draper, Toppan, Longacre & Co., Phila. & N.Y.	115	225	500

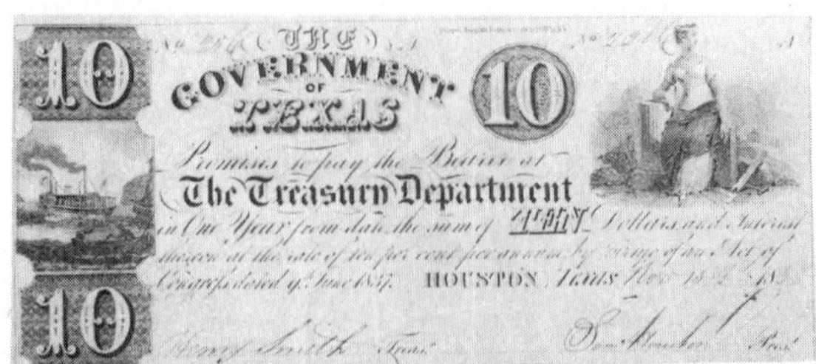

		Good	Fine	XF
19	**10 Dollars** 1838-1839. Black. Steamboat at left, seated Industry at upper right. Printer: Draper, Toppan, Longacre & Co., Phila. & N.Y.	55.00	125	200

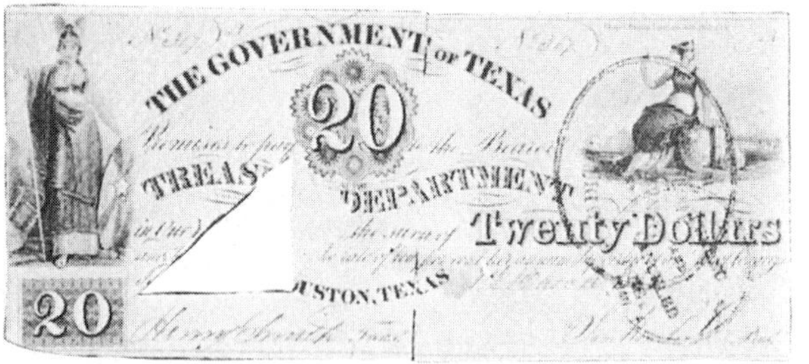

		Good	Fine	XF
20	**20 Dollars** 1838-1839. Black. Standing Liberty at left, seated Minerva at upper right. Printer: Draper, Toppan, Longacre & Co., Phila. & N.Y.	55.00	125	200
21	**50 Dollars** 1838-1839. Black. Sailor with flag seated at left, seated Justice at dockside at center. Printer: Draper, Toppan, Longacre & Co., Phila. & N.Y.	55.00	125	195

Note: Pieces with Sam Houston's name, though signed by a secretary, are worth approximately 25% more.

1839-1841 Fourth Issue

Notes hand dated in 1839, 1840 and 1841.

		Good	Fine	XF
22	**1 Dollar** 1839-1841. Black. Indian brave with bow at left, seated Congress at upper center right. With heading *The Republic of Texas.* Back: Large star at center. BC: Red-orange. Printer: Endicott & Clark, New Orleans.	40.00	100	185

		Good	Fine	XF
23	**2 Dollars** 1839-1841. Black. Deer at left, cowboy roping steer at upper center right. With heading *The Republic of Texas.* Back: Large star at center. BC: Red-orange. Printer: Endicott & Clark, New Orleans.	65.00	140	250

		Good	Fine	XF
24	**3 Dollars** 1839-1841. Black. Seated Ceres holding shield with lone star at upper center right. With heading *The Republic of Texas.* Back: Large star at center. BC: Red-orange. Printer: Endicott & Clark, New Orleans.	75.00	175	300
25	**5 Dollars** 1839-1841. Seated Indian brave at upper center.	65.00	150	275

		Good	Fine	XF
26	**10 Dollars** 1839-1841. Hercules at upper left, woman's portrait at upper center, sailing ship at right.	40.00	125	200

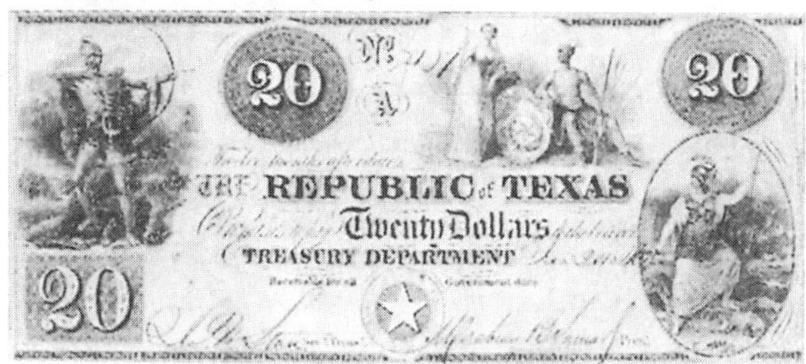

		Good	Fine	XF
27	**20 Dollars** 1839-1841. Indian brave aiming bow at upper left, standing maiden and seated Indian brave with lone star at upper center right, Minerva at lower right.	40.00	125	200

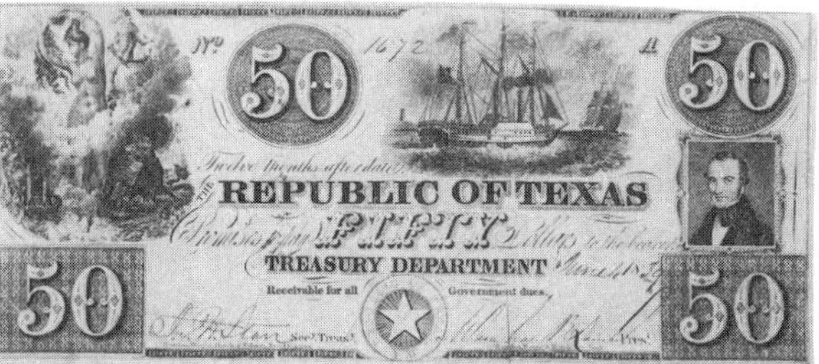

		Good	Fine	XF
28	**50 Dollars** 1839-1841. Nude maiden at upper left, steam sailing ship at upper center right, man's portrait at right.	45.00	125	200

		Good	Fine	XF
29	**100 Dollars** 1839-1841. Steam passenger train at left, seated Minerva and Mercury in flight at upper center, sailboat at right.	85.00	150	350

		Good	Fine	XF
30	**500 Dollars** 1839-1841. Seated Commerce and Industry at left upper center, seated Liberty with eagle at right.	400	875	1,500

1842-1845 Exchequer Notes, Fifth Issue

Authorized January 29, 1842, issued 1842-45.

		Good	Fine	XF
31	**12 1/2 Cents** 1842-1845. Black. Steam passenger train at left, man plowing with horses while another man sows grain at upper center, woman at right. Hand dated. Printer: Rawdon, Wright, Hatch & Edson, New Orleans. Rare.	—	—	—

		Good	Fine	XF
32	**25 Cents** 1842-1845. Black. Steam passenger train at left, seated Liberty with shield at top center, woman with shield of grain at right. Hand dated. Printer: Rawdon, Wright, Hatch & Edson, New Orleans. Rare.	—	—	—
33	**50 Cents** 1842-1845. Black. Man plowing with horses at top center. Hand dated. Printer: Rawdon, Wright, Hatch & Edson, New Orleans. Rare.	—	—	—
34	**75 Cents** 1842-1845. (5.5.1843). Hand dated. Printer: Rawdon, Wright, Hatch & Edson, New Orleans. Rare.	—	—	—
35	**1 Dollar** 1842-1845. Black. Ceres with cotton bale at upper center, steamship at right. Hand dated. Printer: Rawdon, Wright, Hatch & Edson, New Orleans. Rare.	—	—	—
36	**2 Dollars** 1842-45. Hand dated. Printer: Rawdon, Wright, Hatch & Edson, New Orleans. Requires confirmation.	—	—	—
37	**3 Dollars** 1842-1845. Hand dated. Printer: Rawdon, Wright, Hatch & Edson, New Orleans. Requires confirmation.	—	—	—
38	**5 Dollars** 1842-1845. Black. Sailing ship at left, sailor at center. Printer: S. Whiting. Rare.	—	—	—

Note: Authenticity of #38 is questioned.

		Good	Fine	XF
39	**10 Dollars** 1842-1845. Hand dated. Printer: Rawdon, Wright, Hatch & Edson, New Orleans. Requires confirmation.	—	—	—
40	**20 Dollars** 1842-1845. Hand dated. Printer: Rawdon, Wright, Hatch & Edson, New Orleans. Requires confirmation.	—	—	—
41	**50 Dollars** 1842-1845. Hand dated. Printer: Rawdon, Wright, Hatch & Edson, New Orleans. Requires confirmation.	—	—	—
42	**100 Dollars** 1842-1845. Requires confirmation.	—	—	—

Consolidated Fund of Texas

Interest-bearing issues from 1837-40. Printed date: *Sept. 1, 1837.*

#43-47 Houston issues.

1837-1840 Interest Bearing Issues

Interest-bearing issues from 1837-40. Printed date: *Sept. 1, 1837.*

		Good	Fine	XF
43	**100 Dollars** 1837-1840. Printed date.	30.00	65.00	125

		Good	Fine	XF
44	**500 Dollars** 1837-1840. Printed date.	60.00	150	250
45	**1000 Dollars** 1837-1840. Printed date.	75.00	175	275
46	**5000 Dollars** 1837-1840. Printed date.	1,250	2,500	4,000
47	**10,000 Dollars** 1837-1840. Printed date.	—	—	8,000

1840 Issue

		Good	Fine	XF
48	**100 Dollars** 1840. Printed date. Issued at Austin.	75.00	150	250

1841 Naval Scrip Issue

		Good	Fine	XF
49	**25 Dollars** 1841. Printed date. Several varieties.	25.00	50.00	90.00
50	**50 Dollars** 1841. Printed date.	30.00	70.00	150

The Kingdom of Thailand, a constitutional monarchy located in the center of mainland southeast Asia between Burma and Lao, has an area of 514,000 sq. km. and a population of 65.49 million. Capital: Bangkok. The economy is based on agriculture and mining. Rubber, rice, teakwood, tin and tungsten are exported. A unified Thai kingdom was established in the mid-14th century. Known as Siam until 1939, Thailand is the only Southeast Asian country never to have been taken over by a European power. A bloodless revolution in 1932 led to a constitutional monarchy. In alliance with Japan during World War II, Thailand became a US treaty ally following the conflict. A military coup in September 2006 ousted then Prime Minister Thaksin Chinnawat. The interim government held elections in December 2007 that saw the pro-Thaksin People's Power Party (PPP) emerge at the head of a coalition government. The anti-Thaksin People's Alliance for Democracy (PAD) in May 2008 began street demonstrations against the new government, eventually occupying the prime minister's office in August. Clashes in October 2008 between PAD protesters blocking parliament and police resulted in the death of at least two people. The PAD occupied Bangkok's international airports briefly, ending their protests in early December 2008 following a court ruling that dissolved the ruling PPP and two other coalition parties for election violations. The Democrat Party then formed a new coalition government with the support of some of Thaksin's former political allies, and Abhist Wetchachiwa became prime minister. Since January 2004, thousands have been killed as separatists in Thailand's southern ethnic Malay-Muslim provinces increased the violence associated with their cause.

RULERS:

Rama IV (Phra Chom Klao Mongkut), 1851-1868
Rama V (Phra Maha Chulalongkorn), 1868-1910
Rama VI (Vajiravudh), 1910-1925
Rama VII (Prajadhipok), 1925-1935
Rama VIII (Ananda Mahidol), 1935-1946
Rama IX (Bhumiphol Adulyadej), 1946-

MONETARY SYSTEM:

1 Baht (Tical) = 100 Satang
1 Tamlung = 4 Baht

REPLACEMENT NOTES:

#63-67, notes w/o suffix letter.

KINGDOM OF SIAM

Grand Treasury

Rama IV (Phra Chom Klao Mongkut) 1851-1868

1853 Issue

		VG	VF	UNC
A1	**3 Tamlungs = 12 Ticals** 1853. 140x102mm. Rare.	—	—	—
A2	**4 Tamlungs = 16 Ticals** 1853. 140x102mm. Rare.	—	—	—
A3	**6 Tamlungs = 24 Ticals** 1853. 140x102mm. Rare.	—	—	—

		VG	VF	UNC
A4	**10 Tamlungs = 40 Ticals** 1853. 140x102mm. Rare.	—	—	—

Color Abbreviation Guide

New to the *Standard Catalog of® World Paper Money* are the following abbreviations related to color references:

BC: Back color
PC: Paper color

1850s Second Issue

		VG	VF	UNC
A5	**20 Ticals** ND. 87x62mm. Rare. PC: Bluish.	—	—	—
A6	**80 Ticals** ND. 87x62mm. Rare. PC: Bluish.	—	—	—

1850s Third Issue

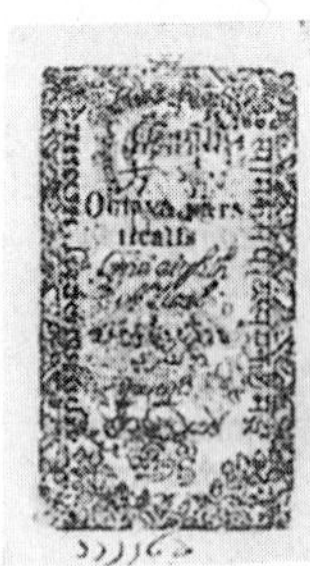

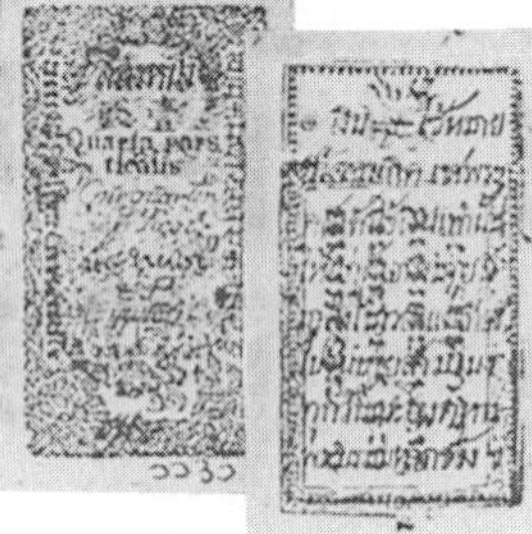

		Good	Fine	XF
A7	**1/8 Tical** ND (1851-1868). 87x50mm. Rare. PC: Bluish.	—	—	—
A8	**1/4 Tical** ND (1851-1868). 87x50mm. Rare. PC: Bluish.	—	—	—
A9	**3/8 Tical** ND (1851-1868). 87x50mm. Rare. PC: Bluish.	—	—	—
A10	**1/2 Tical** ND (1851-1868). 87x50mm. Requires confirmation. PC: Bluish.	—	—	—
A11	**1 Tical** ND (1851-1868). 87x50mm. Requires confirmation. PC: Bluish.	—	—	—

1850's Fourth Issue

		Good	Fine	XF
A12	**3 Tamlungs = 12 Ticals** ND. 108x85mm. Requires confirmation. PC: Thick cream.	—	—	—
A13	**4 Tamlings** ND. 108x85mm. Requires confirmation. PC: Thick cream.	—	—	—
A14	**5 Tamlungs = 20 Ticals** ND. 108x85mm. Requires confirmation. PC: Thick cream.	—	—	—
A15	**7 Tamlungs** ND. 108x85mm. Requires confirmation. PC: Thick cream.	—	—	—
A16	**8 Tamlungs** ND. 108x85mm. Requires confirmation. PC: Thick cream.	—	—	—
A17	**10 Tamlungs = 40 Ticals** ND. 108x85mm. Requires confirmation. PC: Thick cream.	—	—	—
A18	**12 Tamlungs** ND. 108x85mm. Requires confirmation. PC: Thick cream.	—	—	—
A19	**15 Tamlungs** ND. 108x85mm. Requires confirmation. PC: Thick cream.	—	—	—
A20	**1 Chang = 80 Ticals** ND. 108x85mm. Requires confirmation. PC: Thick cream.	—	—	—
A21	**1 Chang = 5 Tamlungs = 100 Ticals** ND. 108x85mm. Requires confirmation. PC: Thick cream.	—	—	—

		Good	Fine	XF
A22	**1 Chang = 10 Tamlungs = 120 Ticals** ND. 108x85mm. Rare. PC: Thick cream.	—	—	—

Royal Siamese Treasury

Rama V (Phra Maha Chulalongkorn) 1868-1910

1874 Issue

		Good	Fine	XF
A23	**1 Att = 1/64 Tical** 1874. Black. Blind embossed with large circular seal and smaller rectangle seal. 147x93mm. Rare.	—	—	—

1892 ND Issue

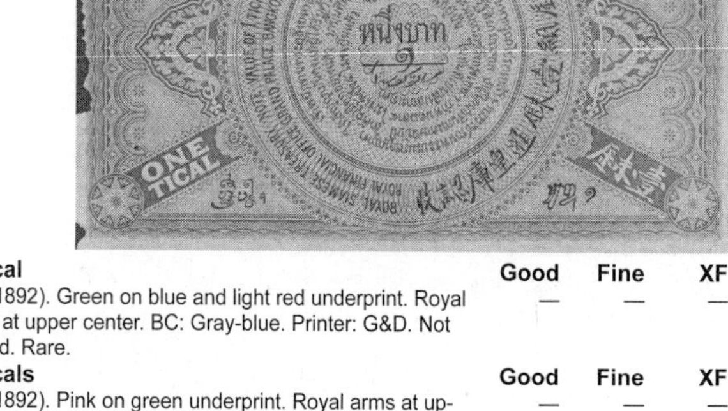

		Good	Fine	XF
1	**1 Tical** ND (1892). Green on blue and light red underprint. Royal arms at upper center. BC: Gray-blue. Printer: G&D. Not issued. Rare.	—	—	—
2	**5 Ticals** ND (1892). Pink on green underprint. Royal arms at upper center. BC: Brown. Printer: G&D. Not issued.	—	—	—
3	**10 Ticals** ND (1892). Maroon and multicolor. Royal arms at upper center. Printer: G&D. Not issued.	—	—	—
4	**40 Ticals** ND (1892). Red-orange and multicolor. Royal arms at upper center. Printer: G&D. Not issued. Rare.	—	—	—

		Good	Fine	XF
5	**80 Ticals** ND (1892). Blue-green and multicolor. Royal arms at upper center. Printer: G&D. Not issued. Rare.	—	—	—
6	**100 Ticals** ND (1892). Blue, tan and multicolor. Royal arms at upper center. Printer: G&D. Not issued.	—	—	—

		Good	Fine	XF
7	**400 Ticals** ND (1892). Royal arms at upper center. Printer: G&D. Not issued.			
	a. Purple, green and multicolor. Rare.	—	—	—
	b. Green on multicolor underprint. Back green-gray; arms at center.	—	—	—
	c. Orange on multicolor underprint. Back orange on blue and multicolor underprint; arms at center.	—	—	—
8	**800 Ticals** ND (1892). Brown, blue-green and multicolor. Royal arms at upper center. Back: Eight arms duplication at center. Printer: G&D. Not issued.	—	—	—

Government of Siam

SIGNATURE VARIETIES

	Chief Of The Banknote Department เจ้าพนักงาน	Minister Of Finance เสนาบดีกระทรวงพระคลัง
1		
2		
3		
4		
5		
6		
7		
8		
9		
Minister of Finance (to 1928)	เสนาบดีกระทรวงพระคลัง	
10		
11		
Minister of Finance (from 1928)	รัฐมนตรีว่าการกระทรวงการคลัง	
12		*
13		*
14		*
15		*
16		*

1902 Issue, Series 1

#9-13 Officially known as "Series One." Notes dated (date ranges for varieties in parentheses).

		Good	Fine	XF
9	**5 Ticals** 1902-1925. Gray on green underprint. State arms at top center. Signature of Finance Minister at right, Official in Charge of Banknotes at left. Uniface. Watermark: Three-headed elephant. Printer: TDLR.			
	a. Serial # at top only, green underprint. (1902-1905). Signature: 1; 2.	500	1,000	2,000
	b. Serial # at top only, green underprint. (1902-1905). Signature: 3.	500	1,000	2,000
	c. Serial # at top only, purple-gray on tan underprint. (1905-1911). Signature: 3; 5.	400	800	1,600
	d. Serial # at top and bottom, purple-gray on tan underprint. (1911-1925). Signature: 5; 6; 8; 9.	250	500	1,000

		Good	Fine	XF
10	**10 Ticals** 1902-1924. Brown on yellow underprint. State arms at top center. Signature of Finance Minister at right, Official in Charge of Banknotes at left. Uniface. Watermark: Three-headed elephant. Printer: TDLR.			
	a. Serial # at top only, tan underprint. (1902-1906). Signature 1; 2.	500	1,000	2,000
	b. Serial # at top only, green underprint. (1906-1913). Signature 3; 4; 5.	200	400	1,000
	c. Serial # at top and bottom, green underprint. (1913-1924). Signature 4; 5; 6; 8 9.	225	500	1,200
	p. Brown. Proof. 1.1.1903.	—	—	—
11	**20 Ticals** 1902-1925. Green on pale pink underprint. State arms at top center. Signature of Finance Minister at right, Official in Charge of Banknotes at left. Uniface. Watermark: Three-headed elephant. Printer: TDLR.	Good	Fine	XF
	a. Serial # at top only, yellow underprint. (1902-1906). Signature 1; 2.	400	1,400	2,800
	b. Serial # at top only, yellow underprint. (1902-1906). Signature: 2.	400	—	—
	c. Serial # at top only, light green underprint. (1906-1910). Signature 4; 5.	300	800	2,000
	d. Serial # at top and bottom, light green underprint. (1910-1925). Signature 5; 6; 8; 9.	300	800	2,000
	p. Green. Proof. 1.4.1902.	—	—	—

Color Abbreviation Guide

New to the *Standard Catalog of® World Paper Money* are the following abbreviations related to color references:

BC: Back color
PC: Paper color

		Good	Fine	XF
12	**100 Ticals** 1902-1925. Purple on pale brown underprint. State arms at top center. Signature of Finance Minister at right, Official in Charge of Banknotes at left. Uniface. Watermark: Three-headed elephant. Printer: TDLR.			
	a. Serial # at top only, brown on yellow underprint. (1902-1908). Signature 1; 2; 3.	450	1,400	3,000
	b. Serial # at top only, violet on brown underprint. (1908-1910). Signature 2; 3; 4; 5.	400	1,300	2,750
	c. Serial # at top and bottom, violet on brown underprint. (1910-1925). Signature 5; 6; 8; 9.	350	1,200	2,500
	p. Purple. Proof. 1.4.1902.	—	—	—
13	**1000 Ticals** 1.4.1902-1925. Red on pale red underprint. State arms at top center. Signature of Finance Minister at right, Official in Charge of Banknotes at left. Uniface. Watermark: Three-headed elephant. Printer: TDLR.	Good	Fine	XF
	a. Serial # at top only, light brown underprint. (1902-1909). Signature 1; 2.	500	1,500	4,000
	b. Serial # at top only, brown underprint. (1909-1912). Signature 5.	400	1,200	3,500
	c. Serial # at top and bottom, brown underprint. (1912-1925). Signature 6; 8; 9.	300	1,000	3,000
	p. Proof. 1.4.1902.	—	—	—

1918 Issue

		Good	Fine	XF
14	**1 Tical** 1918-1925. (15.7.1918; 11.8.1919; 5.7.1921 verified.) Black on gray or gray-brown underprint. Signature 6; 8; 9. 164x105mm.	80.00	150	300

1918 ND Provisional Issue

		Good	Fine	XF
15	**50 Ticals** ND (1918). Black on gray or gray-brown underprint. Signature 7. Overprint: On #14.			
	a. Without embossed stamp. Rare.	—	—	—
	b. Embossed stamp of three-headed elephant on back. Rare.	—	—	—

1925 Issue, Series 2

Dates and single signature of Finance Minister on bottom center, mythological winged Garuda bird at upper left, 3-headed elephant at lower right. Common vignette at center shows ceremonial parade of first plowing on back. Officially described as "Series Two."

TEXT VARIETIES (in second line on face):

Type I

สัญญาจะจ่ายสินให้แก่ผู้นำธนบัตรนี้มาขึ้นเป็นสินตราสยาม

"Contract to pay in Siamese Currency to anyone who presents this note".

Type II

ธนบัตร์เป็นเงินที่ชำระหนี้ได้ตามกฎหมาย

"Banknote is legal tender for any debt".

		Good	Fine	XF
16	**1 Baht** 1925-1933. Blue on yellow underprint. Back: Ceremonial procession. Printer: TDLR.			
	a. Type I text. 1.4.1925-20.4.1928. Signature 10.	2.00	10.00	25.00
	b. Type II text. 8.9.1928-11.6.1933. Signature 10; 11; 12; 13.	2.00	10.00	25.00

		Good	Fine	XF
17	**5 Baht** 1925-1932. Purple on green underprint. Back: Ceremonial procession. Printer: TDLR.			
	a. Type I text. 1.4.1925-15.2.1928. Signature 10.	25.00	100	250
	b. Type II text. 29.6.1929-1.2.1932. Signature 10; 11.	17.50	75.00	200
18	**10 Baht** 1925-1934. Red-brown on pink underprint. Back: Ceremonial procession. Printer: TDLR.	Good	Fine	XF
	a. Type I text. 29.6.1925-15.11.1926. Signature 10.	15.00	75.00	200
	b. Type II text. 15.5.1929-21.3.1934. Signature 10; 11; 12; 13.	12.00	50.00	300

		Good	Fine	XF
19	**20 Baht** 1925-1933. Green on gray underprint. Back: Ceremonial procession. Printer: TDLR. 176x96mm.			
	a. Type I text. 15.4.1925; 29.7.1925; 15.8.1925; 15.11.1926; 15.7.1927; 15.4.1928; 15.5.1928. Signature 10.	40.00	150	350
	b. Type II text. 29.5.1928-1.1.1933. Signature 10; 11; 13.	40.00	150	350

		Good	Fine	XF
20	**100 Baht** 1925-1938. Blue on green underprint. Back: Ceremonial procession. Printer: TDLR.			
	a. Type I text. 1.4.1925-1.11.1927. Signature 10.	25.00	100	300
	b. Type II text. 11.9.1928-16.9.1938. Signature 14; 15; 16.	20.00	75.00	250

		Good	Fine	XF
21	**1000 Baht** 1925-1938. Red-brown on yellow underprint. Back: Ceremonial procession. Printer: TDLR.			
	a. Type I text. 1.4.1925-1.11.1927. Signature 10; 11.	200	400	1,000
	b. Type II text. 1.10.1930-11.9.1938. Signature 11; 15.	200	400	1,000

1934-1935 Issue, Series 3

Single signature of Finance Minister at bottom center. Officially described as "Series Three".

		VG	VF	UNC
22	**1 Baht** 1.4.1934-25.2.1935. Dark blue on light yellow-green and pale orange underprint. Portrait Rama VII facing at left. Winged mythological figure (Garuda) at top center and three-headed elephant at lower right corner. Royal barge at center. Signature 13; 14. Back: Temple and pagoda on an island. Printer: TDLR.	2.00	7.50	40.00

		VG	VF	UNC
23	**5 Baht** 29.5.1934-18.2.1935. Purple on yellow and orange underprint. Portrait Rama VII facing at left. Winged mythological figure (Garuda) at top center and three-headed elephant at lower right corner. Emerald Buddha Temple complex at center. Signature 13; 14. Back: Temple and pagoda on an island. Printer: TDLR.	20.00	50.00	150

		VG	VF	UNC
24	**10 Baht** 1.2.1934-1.3.1935. Brown on pink underprint. Portrait Rama VII facing at left. Winged mythological figure (Garuda) at top center and three-headed elephant at lower right corner. River and mountains at center. Signature 13; 14. Back: Temple and pagoda on an island. Printer: TDLR.	15.00	30.00	125

No.	Description	VG	VF	UNC
25	**20 Baht** 15.1.1935; 25.1.1935; 8.2.1935; 18.2.1935; 25.2.1935. Green on pale blue and tan underprint. Portrait Rama VII facing at left. Winged mythological figure (Garuda) at top center and three-headed elephant at lower right corner. River, village and pagoda at center. Signature 14. Back: Temple and pagoda on an island. Printer: TDLR.	10.00	40.00	275

Note: #22-25 come with 2 variations in the Finance Minister title line at bottom center of face.

1935-1936 Issue

No.	Description	VG	VF	UNC
26	**1 Baht** 18.4.1935-11.9.1938. Blue. Portrait King Rama VIII as a boy 3/4 facing at left. Similar to #22. Signature 14; 15. Back: Temple and pagoda on an island.	2.00	10.00	40.00
27	**5 Baht** 29.4.1935-15.5.1937. Purple. Portrait King Rama VIII as a boy 3/4 facing at left. Similar to #23. Signature 14; 15. Back: Temple and pagoda on an island.	7.50	20.00	80.00

No.	Description	VG	VF	UNC
28	**10 Baht** 3.1.1935-1.10.1936. Brown. Portrait King Rama VIII as a boy 3/4 facing at left. Similar to #24. Signature 14; 15. Back: Temple and pagoda on an island. 176x94mm.	10.00	35.00	125
29	**20 Baht** 1.4.1936-1.7.1936. Green. Portrait King Rama VIII as a boy 3/4 facing at left. Similar to #25. Signature 15. Back: Temple and pagoda on an island.	15.00	40.00	150

1939 ND Issue, Series 4A

Officially described as "Series Four (Thomas)" to differentiate from similar, but cruder, notes printed later by the Thai Map Department. W/o dates. Single signnature of Finance Minister at bottom center. Note: In 1939 the name *SIAM* was changed to *THAILAND.* By decree of 7.3.1939 this change was made in the main heading at top on faces of all notes as shown below:

HEADING VARIETIES

รัฐบาลสยาม	รัฐบาลไทย
TYPE I: GOVERNMENT OF SIAM	TYPE II: GOVERNMENT OF THAILAND

No.	Description	VG	VF	UNC
30	**1 Baht** ND (from 1938). Blue. Multicolor guilloche in underprint at center. Portrait King Rama VIII as a boy 3/4 facing at left with three-headed elephant at lower right. Phra Samut Chedi Temple and pagoda at center. Type I heading. Signature 15, 16. Back: Royal Throne Hall. Printer: TDLR.	2.00	10.00	50.00

No.	Description	VG	VF	UNC
31	**1 Baht** ND (from 1939). Blue. Multicolor guilloche in underprint at center. Portrait King Rama VIII as a boy 3/4 facing at left with three-headed elephant at lower right. Phra Samut Chedi Temple and pagoda at center. Type II heading. Like #30. Back: Royal Throne Hall. Printer: TDLR.			
	a. Serial # at left. with European characters, Thai at right. Signature 16.	2.00	7.50	30.00
	b. Both serial # with European characters. Signature 23 (from 1946).	2.00	7.50	30.00
32	**5 Baht** ND (from 1939). Purple. Multicolor guilloche in underprint at center. Portrait King Rama VIII as a boy 3/4 facing at left with three-headed elephant at lower right. Entrance to Phra Pathom Chedi at center. Type I heading. Signature 16. Back: Royal Throne Hall. Printer: TDLR.	15.00	60.00	200
33	**5 Baht** ND (from 1939). Purple. Multicolor guilloche in underprint at center. Portrait King Rama VIII as a boy 3/4 facing at left with three-headed elephant at lower right. Entrance to Phra Pathom Chedi at center. Type II heading. Signature 16. Like #32. Back: Royal Throne Hall. Printer: TDLR.	80.00	110	250
34	**10 Baht** ND (from 1939). Brown. Multicolor guilloche in underprint at center. Portrait King Rama VIII as a boy 3/4 facing at left with three-headed elephant at lower right. Mahagal Fortress at center. Type I heading. Signature 16. Back: Royal Throne Hall. Printer: TDLR.	10.00	45.00	110

No.	Description	VG	VF	UNC
35	**10 Baht** ND (from 1939). Brown. Multicolor guilloche in underprint at center. Portrait King Rama VIII as a boy 3/4 facing at left with three-headed elephant at lower right. Mahagal Fortress at center. Type II heading. Like #34. Signature 16; 23 (from 1939).Back: Royal Throne Hall. Printer: TDLR.	10.00	35.00	180
36	**20 Baht** ND (from 1939). Green. Multicolor guilloche in underprint at center. Portrait King Rama VIII as a boy 3/4 facing at left with three-headed elephant at lower right. Throne Halls at center. Type I heading. Signature 16. Back: Royal Throne Hall. Printer: TDLR.	10.00	40.00	150

Note: 20 Baht note with Type II heading does not exist.

No.	Description	VG	VF	UNC
37	**1000 Baht** ND (from 1939). Red-brown. Multicolor guilloche in underprint at center. Portrait King Rama VIII as a boy 3/4 facing at left with three-headed elephant at lower right. Temple of the Dawn at center. Type I heading. Signature 16. Back: Royal Throne Hall. Printer: TDLR.	100	400	1,200
38	**1000 Baht** ND (from 1939). Red-brown. Multicolor guilloche in underprint at center. Portrait King Rama VIII as a boy 3/4 facing at left with three-headed elephant at lower right. Temple of the Dawn at center. Type II heading. Signature 16. Like #37. Back: Royal Throne Hall. Printer: TDLR.	100	400	1,200

JAPANESE INTERVENTION - WW II

Government of Thailand

1942-1944 ND Issue, Series 4B

Officially described as "Series Four (Map)". Similar to their counterparts in Series Four (Thomas), but of inferior quality. Single signature of Minister of Finance at bottom center.

Top legend is changed from: รัฐบาลไทย **To:** รัฐบาล ไทย

SIGNATURE VARIETIES		
	MINISTER OF FINANCE	CHIEF OF THE BANKNOTE DEPARTMENT
17		[signature]
	MINISTER OF FINANCE รัฐมนตรีว่าการกระทรวงการคลัง	DIRECTOR GENERAL OF THE TREASURY DEPARTMENT อธิบดีกรมคลัง
18	[signature]	[signature]
19	[signature]	
20	[signature]	
21	[signature]	
22	[signature]	
23	[signature]	
24	[signature]	

#	Description	VG	VF	UNC
39	**1 Baht** ND (from 1942). Blue. Portrait King Rama VIII as a boy 3/4 facing at left with three-headed elephant at lower right. Phra Samut Chedi Temple and pagoda at center. Similar to #31. Back: Royal Throne Hall. Watermark: Constitution on tray on pedestal. Printer: Royal Thai Army Map Department.			
	a. Right serial # in Thai. Signature 17.	2.00	15.00	45.00
	b. Both serial # in European numbers. Signature 17; 19; 20.	2.00	12.50	40.00
40	**10 Baht** ND (from 1943). Brown. Portrait King Rama VIII as a boy 3/4 facing at left with three-headed elephant at lower right. Mahagal Fortress at center. Similar to #35. Back: Royal Throne Hall. Printer: Royal Thai Army Map Department.			
	a. Watermark: Constitution. Signature 17.	5.00	25.00	150
	b. Watermark: Constitution. Signature 20.	5.00	25.00	125
	c. Signature 21 (probably counterfeit; # and Signature fraudulently applied to genuine note; not issued).	—	—	—
	d. Watermark: Wavy lines with constitution printed in window. Signature 21 (from 1945).	5.00	25.00	125
	e. Watermark: Like d. Signature 24.	5.00	40.00	150
	f. Signature 20 (like c, probably counterfeit; not issued).	—	—	—

#	Description	VG	VF	UNC
41	**20 Baht** ND (from 1943). Green on orange and green underprint. Portrait King Rama VIII as a boy 3/4 facing at left with three-headed elephant at lower right. Throne Halls at center. Signature 17; 19; 20. Like #36. Back: Royal Throne Hall. Watermark: Constitution. Printer: Royal Thai Army Map Department.	3.00	35.00	150
42	**100 Baht** ND (1944). Blue with pink and green underprint design. Temple, with walkway flanked by two mythological statues, at center. Silk threads. Signature 19; 20. Watermark: Constitution.	8.00	50.00	300

1942-1945 ND Issues, Series 5

Officially described as "Series Five". Single signature of Finance Minister at bottom center.

#	Description	VG	VF	UNC
43	**50 Satang** ND (1942). Green on pink underprint design. Portrait King Rama VIII full face at right. Signature 17; 20. Back: Walled temple and pagoda complex on river bank (Royal Palace). Printer: Mitsui Trading Company. Watermark paper.			
	a. Issued note.	1.00	4.00	15.00
	r. Remainder without signature or block #.	—	—	150
	s1. Specimen with overprint: *Mi-hon.*	—	—	—
	s2. Specimen with overprint: *Specimen.*	—	—	—

#	Description	VG	VF	UNC
44	**1 Baht** ND (1942; 1944). Brown on pink underprint at center. Portrait King Rama VIII full face at right. Entrance to Wat Phumintr, flanked by mythological snakes at left. Back: Walled temple and pagoda complex on river bank (Royal Palace). Watermark: Constitution on tray on pedestal. Printer: Mitsui Trading Company.			
	a. 3 serial #, lower left in Thai. Signature 17.	5.00	20.00	50.00
	b. 3 serial # all with European numerals. Signature 17.	3.00	15.00	40.00
	c. 2 serial # (lower left deleted). Signature 17; 19; 20.	3.00	15.00	40.00
	r. Remainder without signature or serial #.	—	—	150
	s1. Specimen with overprint: *Mi-hon.*	—	—	—
	s2. Specimen with overprint: *Specimen.*	—	—	—
45	**5 Baht** ND (1942; 1944). Green on green underprint. Portrait King Rama VIII full face at right. Marble Temple at left. Back: Walled temple and pagoda complex on river bank (Royal Palace). Watermark: Constitution on tray on pedestal. Printer: Mitsui Trading Company.			
	a. 3 serial #, lower left in Thai. Signature 17.	15.00	40.00	150
	b. 3 serial #, all with European numbers. Signature 17.	15.00	30.00	150
	c. 2 serial # (lower left deleted). Signature 17; 19; 20.	15.00	20.00	150
	d. Without signature.	—	—	140
	s. Specimen with overprint: *Specimen.*	—	—	—

		VG	VF	UNC
46	**5 Baht**			
	ND (1945). Green. Portrait King Rama VIII full face at right. Marble temple at left. Like #45. 2 serial #. Back: Walled temple and pagoda complex on river bank (Royal Palace). Constitution printed in purple on win BC: Purple. Watermark: Constitution on tray on pedestal. Printer: Mitsui Trading Company. 134x76mm.			
	a. Signature 20; 21.	20.00	50.00	200
	b. Without signature. Requires confirmation.	—	—	—

		VG	VF	UNC
47	**10 Baht**			
	ND (from 1942). Purple on pink and light blue underprint. Portrait King Rama VIII full face at right. Part of wall and gateway to Wat Chetupon at left. Back: Walled temple and pagoda complex on river bank (Royal Palace). BC: Purple. Watermark: Constitution on tray on pedestal. Printer: Mitsui Trading Company.			
	a. 3 serial #, lower left in Thai. Signature 17.	20.00	50.00	200
	b. 3 serial #, all with European numbers. Signature 17.	20.00	50.00	200
	c. 2 serial # (lower left deleted). Signature 17; 20.	20.00	50.00	200
	s. Specimen with overprint: *Specimen.*	—	—	—

		VG	VF	UNC
48	**10 Baht**			
	ND (1945). Purple. Portrait King Rama VIII full face at right. Part of wall and gateway to Wat Chetupon at left. Signature 20. Like #47c. Back: Walled temple and pagoda complex on river bank (Royal Palace). BC: Light green. Watermark: Constitution on tray on pedestal. Printer: Mitsui Trading Company.	25.00	60.00	300

		VG	VF	UNC
49	**20 Baht**			
	ND (from 1942). Blue on brown underprint. Portrait King Rama VIII full face at right. Throne Hall at left. Back: Walled temple and pagoda complex on river bank (Royal Palace). BC: Blue. Watermark: Constitution on tray on pedestal. Printer: Mitsui Trading Company.			
	a. 3 serial #. upper right and l. with European letters and numerals, lower left in Thai. Signature 17.	5.00	20.00	100
	b. 3 serial #, all with European numbers. Upper left and right. have Western letter in control prefix, lower has Thai letter prefix. Signature 17.	5.00	20.00	100
	c. 3 serial #, all with European numbers. Upper right and lower have Thai letter in control prefix (P/31-P/33 only). Signature 17.	10.00	25.00	125
	d. 2 serial # (lower left deleted). Western control letter in upper left, Thai control letter in upper right. Signature 17; 19; 20.	5.00	20.00	100
	s. Specimen with overprint: *Specimen.*	—	—	—

		VG	VF	UNC
50	**20 Baht**			
	ND (1945). Blue on brown underprint. Portrait King Rama VIII full face at right. Throne Hall at left. Like #49d. Back: Walled temple and pagoda complex on river bank (Royal Palace). BC: Light brown. Watermark: Constitution on tray on pedestal. Printer: Mitsui Trading Company.			
	a. Signature 20.	5.00	25.00	85.00
	b. Without signature. Requires confirmation.	—	—	—

		VG	VF	UNC
51	**100 Baht**			
	ND (1943). Red on blue and olive underprint. Portrait King Rama VIII full face at right. Temple of the Dawn at left. Signature 17. Back: Walled temple and pagoda complex on river bank (Royal Palace). BC: Red. Watermark: Constitution on tray on pedestal. Printer: Mitsui Trading Company.			
	a. Issued note.	30.00	150	350
	r. Remainder without signature or serial #.	—	—	375
	s1. Specimen with overprint: *Mi-hon.*	—	—	—
	s2. Specimen with overprint: *Specimen.*	—	—	—

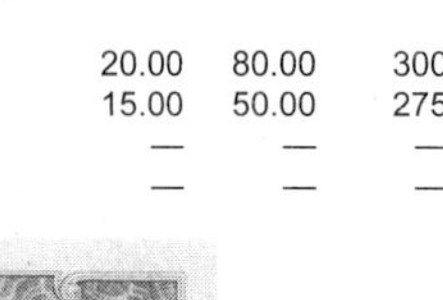

		VG	VF	UNC
52	**100 Baht**			
	ND (1945). Red. Portrait King Rama VIII full face at right. Temple of the Dawn at left. Like #51. Back: Walled temple and pagoda complex on river bank (Royal Palace). BC: Blue. Watermark: Constitution on tray on pedestal. Printer: Mitsui Trading Company.			
	a. Signature 20.	20.00	80.00	300
	b. Without signature.	15.00	50.00	275
	s1. Specimen with overprint: *Mi-hon.*	—	—	—
	s2. Specimen with overprint: *Specimen.*	—	—	—

		VG	VF	UNC
53	**1000 Baht**			
	ND (1944). Olive on pink and blue underprint. Portrait King Rama VIII full face at right. The Chakri and Dusit Maha Prasad Throne Halls at left. Silk threads. Signature 17. Back: Walled temple and pagoda complex on river bank (Royal Palace). BC: Olive. Watermark: Constitution on tray on pedestal. Printer: Mitsui Trading Company.			
	a. Issued note.	150	400	1,500
	s1. Specimen with overprint: *Mi-hon.*	—	—	—
	s2. Specimen with overprint: *Specimen.*	—	—	—

1945 ND First Issue, Series 6

Single signature of Finance Minister at bottom center. Officially described as "Series Six".

		VG	VF	UNC
53A	**20 Baht**			
	ND (1945). Green with pink underprint design. Portrait King Rama VIII as a boy at left. Throne Halls at center. Signature 20. Like #41. Back: Royal Throne Hall. Printer: Army Map Department (with imprint), Navy Hydrologi.			
	a. Watermark: Constitution on tray on pedestal, silk threads.	15.00	50.00	150
	b. Watermark: Wavy lines. Silk threads throughout; tan constitution overprint in circle, with imprint. Signature 20; 21.	15.00	60.00	150
	c. Watermark: Like b. Without imprint. Signature 21.	15.00	60.00	150

		VG	VF	UNC
53B	**100 Baht** ND (1945). Blue with underprint design mostly purple. Temple, with walkway flanked by two mythological statues, at center. Silk threads. Like #42. Printer: Army Map Department (with imprint), Navy Hydrologi.			
	a. Watermark: Constitution. Silk threads throughout. With imprint.	30.00	100	300
	b. Watermark: Like a. Without imprint. Signature 20.	15.00	60.00	180
	c. Watermark: Wavy lines. Silk threads, purple constitution overprint in circle. With imprint. Signature 20; 21.	15.00	60.00	160
	d. Watermark: Like c. Without imprint. Signature 20; 21.	15.00	50.00	150

1945 ND Second Issue, Series 7

Single signature of Finance Minister at bottom center. Officially described as "Series Seven". Crudely printed by private printers contracted by the Bank of Thailand.

		VG	VF	UNC
54	**1 Baht** ND (1945). Blue on light pink underprint. Portrait King Rama VIII full face at left. Similar to #30. Back: Royal Throne Hall.			
	a. Watermark: Multiple wavy lines. Signature 20; 21.	2.00	8.00	20.00
	b. Without watermark. Signature 21.	2.00	8.00	20.00
55	**5 Baht** ND (1945). Purple and light green. Portrait King Rama VIII full face at left. Red serial #. Signature 20. Similar to #32. Back: Royal Throne Hall. Watermark: Wavy lines. 135x76mm.	15.00	40.00	80.00
55A	**5 Baht** ND (1945). Purple and light green. Portrait King Rama VIII full face at left. Black serial #. Signature 20; 21. Like #55. Back: Royal Throne Hall. Watermark: Wavy lines. 115x65mm.	10.00	25.00	75.00
56	**10 Baht** ND (1945). Dark brown. Portrait King Rama VIII full face at left. Similar to #34. Back: Royal Throne Hall.			
	a. Watermark: Constitution. Signature 20.	15.00	40.00	120
	b. Watermark: Multiple wavy lines. Brown constitution overprint in circle. Signature 20.	15.00	40.00	120

		VG	VF	UNC
57	**50 Baht** ND (1945). Pale red on green underprint. Portrait King Rama VIII full face at left. Marble Temple at center. Back: Royal Throne Hall.			
	a. Without watermark. Signature 20.	20.00	70.00	150
	b. Watermark: Multiple wavy lines. Signature 20; 21.	20.00	70.00	150

KINGDOM

Government of Thailand

SIGNATURE VARIETIES

	Minister Of Finance รัฐมนตรีว่าการกระทรวงการคลัง	Governor Of The Bank Of Thailand ผู้ว่าการธนาคารแห่งประเทศไทย
25		
26		
	Minister Of Finance รัฐมนตรีว่าการกระทรวงการคลัง	
27		
28		
29		
30		
31		
32		
33		
34		
35		
36		
37		
38		
39		
40		
41		
42		
43	**	
	**signed as Undersecretary/Deputy Finance Minister	
44		

1942-1944 ND Issue

Different types of wartime notes, some of which were issued after the war but before supplies of new notes could be obtained for normal use. Having no common characteristics, this series, officially described as "Series Special", was printed in part in Thailand, in part in other countries.

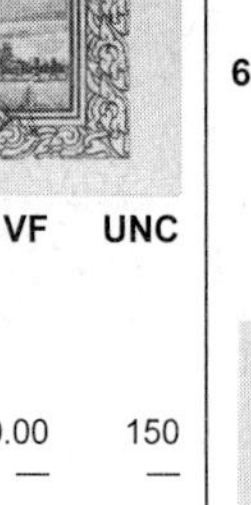

		VG	VF	UNC
58	**1 Baht** ND (1942). Blue on red underprint. Portrait King Rama VIII 3/4 face at left. Constitution on tray on pedestal embossed in oval at right. Signature 18. Watermark: Vertical white stripe 8mm. wide at left center.			
	a. Red to orange flower in underprint at center.	15.00	50.00	150
	x. Yellow flower in underprint at center (Counterfeit).	—	—	—
59	**10 Baht** ND. Dark purple on gray underprint. Portal at left, portrait King Rama VIII full face at right. Like #62 but without overprint or signature. Back: Royal palace on river bank. (Not issued).	—	—	—

		VG	VF	UNC
60	**1000 Baht** ND (1943). Deep red and yellow. Portrait King Rama VIII tilted to right of vertical at right. Phrang Sam Yod (three ornate towers) at left. Signature 18. Watermark: Constitution.	150	600	1,500
61	**1000 Baht** ND (1944). Deep brown and yellow. Portrait King Rama VIII tilted to right of vertical at right. Phrang Sam Yod (three ornate towers) at left. Signature 18. Like #60. Watermark: Constitution.	150	600	1,500

1945; 1946 ND Provisional Issue

		VG	VF	UNC
62	**50 Satang on 10 Baht** ND (1946). Dark purple on gray underprint. Portal at left, portrait King Rama VIII full face at right. Signature 22. Back: Royal palace on river bank.	4.00	8.00	25.00

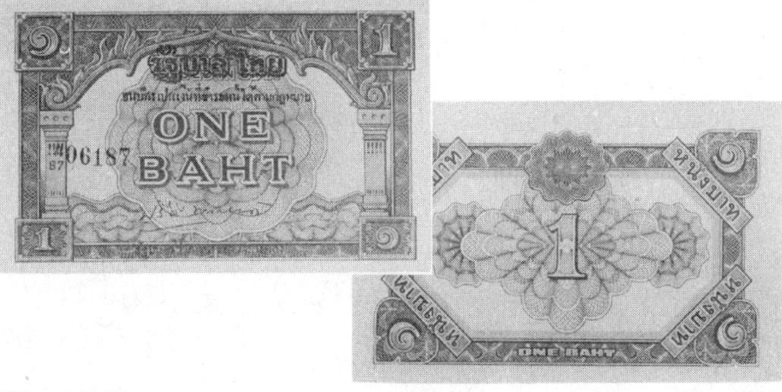

		VG	VF	UNC
62A	**1 Baht** ND (1946). Blue on pale olive underprint. Signature 23. English printing.			
	a. 2nd line of overprint complete (29 characters).	2.00	8.00	25.00
	b. 12th character of 2nd line missing.	2.00	8.00	25.00

		VG	VF	UNC
62B	**50 Baht on 1 Dollar** ND (1945). Purple and greenish yellow.			
	a. Red *50* in white circle on face and back. Signature 17; 20.	50.00	100	400
	b. Red *50* in white circle on face only. Signature 20.	50.00	100	400
	c. Without red *50* or obliterative overprints on face or back. Black denomination in words overprint on face. Signature 17; 19; 20.	60.00	150	425

Note: #62B was originally intended for use in the northern Malay States, thus the value of 1 Dollar.

1946 ND Issue, Series 8

This is a regular (not "Liberation") issue, officially described as "Series Eight". Replacement notes identified by absence of letter at end of serial #. Wmk: *MILITARY AUTHORITY* repeated.

		VG	VF	UNC
63	**1 Baht** ND (1946). Green and blue. Portrait King Rama VIII full face at left. Road with monuments and pagoda in underprint. Signature 22. Back: Constitution on ceremonial vessal at center. BC: Brown. Watermark: *MILITARY AUTHORITY* repeated. Printer: Tudor Press, Boston.	0.25	1.00	5.00

		VG	VF	UNC
64	**5 Baht** ND (1946). Dark and light blue. Portrait King Rama VIII full face at left. Road with monuments and pagoda in underprint. Signature 22. Back: Constitution on ceremonial vessal at center. BC: Brown. Watermark: *MILITARY AUTHORITY* repeated. Printer: Tudor Press, Boston.	1.00	5.00	25.00

		VG	VF	UNC
65	**10 Baht** ND (1946). Brown on blue. Portrait King Rama VIII full face at left. Road with monuments and pagoda in underprint. Back: Constitution on ceremonial vessal at center. BC: Brown. Watermark: *MILITARY AUTHORITY* repeated. Printer: Tudor Press, Boston.			
	a. Black signature overprint at right. Signature 25.	2.00	15.00	50.00
	b. 2 black signature overprints. Signature 26.	2.00	15.00	50.00

		VG	VF	UNC
66	**20 Baht** ND (1946). Dark and light blue. Portrait King Rama VIII full face at left. Road with monuments and pagoda in underprint. Back: Constitution on ceremonial vessal at center. BC: Brown. Watermark: *MILITARY AUTHORITY* repeated. Printer: Tudor Press, Boston.			
	a. Black signature overprint at right. Signature 25.	10.00	40.00	120
	b. 2 black signature overprints. Signature 26.	10.00	40.00	120

		VG	VF	UNC
67	**100 Baht** ND (1946). Brown on light blue. Portrait King Rama VIII full face at left. Road with monuments and pagoda in underprint. Back: Constitution on ceremonial vessal at center. BC: Brown. Watermark: *MILITARY AUTHORITY* repeated. Printer: Tudor Press, Boston.			
	a. Black signature overprint at right. Signature 25.	20.00	80.00	200
	b. 2 black signature overprints. Signature 26.	20.00	80.00	200

1948 ND Issue, Series 9

Officially described as "Series Nine". Signature of Finance Minister at left and Governor of the Bank of Thailand at right.

		VG	VF	UNC
68	**50 Satang** ND (1948). Green on pink underprint. Constitution on tray on pedestal in underprint. Signature 27. Back: Phra Samut Chedi. Printer: TDLR.	1.00	2.00	8.00
69	**1 Baht** ND (1948). Blue on multicolor underprint. Portrait of King in uniform without collar insignia. Blue and red security threads. Similar to #30. Watermark: Constitution on tray on pedestal. Printer: TDLR.	VG	VF	UNC
	a. Red serial #. Signature 28; 30; 31; 32; 33; 34.	1.00	4.00	10.00
	b. Black serial #. Signature 28; 31; 32.	1.00	2.00	6.00

		VG	VF	UNC
70	**5 Baht** ND (1948). Purple on multicolor underprint. Portrait of King in uniform without collar insignia. Blue and red security threads. Similar to #32. Watermark: Constitution on tray on pedestal. Printer: TDLR.			
	a. Red serial #. Signature 28.	10.00	25.00	80.00
	b. Black serial #. Signature 28; 30; 31.	1.00	4.00	12.00
71	**10 Baht** ND (1948). Brown on multicolor underprint. Portrait of King in uniform without collar insignia. Blue and red security threads. Similar to #34. Watermark: Constitution on tray on pedestal. Printer: TDLR.	VG	VF	UNC
	a. Red serial #. Signature 28; 29; 32.	15.00	30.00	100
	b. Black serial #. Signature 28; 30; 31; 32.	3.00	7.50	35.00

		VG	VF	UNC
72	**20 Baht** ND (1948). Green on multicolor underprint. Portrait of King in uniform without collar insignia. Blue and red security threads. Similar to #36. Watermark: Constitution on tray on pedestal. Printer: TDLR.			
	a. Red serial #. Signature 28; 29; 30; 31.	25.00	60.00	120
	b. Black serial #. Signature 28; 30; 31; 32.	5.00	15.00	50.00
73	**100 Baht** ND (1948). Red on multicolor underprint. Portrait of King in uniform without collar insignia. Blue and red security threads. Black serial # only. Signature 28; 31; 32; 33; 34. Similar to #37. Watermark: Constitution on tray on pedestal. Printer: TDLR.	VG	VF	UNC
	a. Issued note.	5.00	25.00	75.00
	s. Specimen. Zero serial #. Oval TDLR stamp.	—	—	650

1953-1956 ND Issue

74 **1 Baht**

ND (1955). Blue on multicolor underprint. Portrait of King in Field Marshal's uniform with collar insignia and three decorations. Black serial number. Printer: TDLR.

	VG	VF	UNC
a. Watermark: Constitution. Red and blue security threads. Signature 34.	0.20	1.00	4.00
b. Watermark: Constitution. Metal security strip. Signature 34; 35 (Large size).	0.20	1.00	3.50
c. Watermark: King profile. Small letters in 2-line text on back. Signature 35.	0.10	0.75	3.00
d. Watermark: King profile. Larger letters in 2-line text on back. Signature 36; 37; 38; 39; 40; 4l.	0.10	0.75	2.50
s. As a; d. Specimen.	—	—	250

75 **5 Baht**

ND (1956). Purple on multicolor underprint. Portrait of King in Field Marshal's uniform with collar insignia and three decorations. Black serial number. Printer: TDLR.

	VG	VF	UNC
a. Watermark: Constitution. Red and blue security threads. Signature 34.	5.00	15.00	50.00
b. Watermark: Constitution. Metal security strip. Signature 34; 35 (Large size).	0.50	2.50	10.00
c. Watermark: King profile. Small letters in 2-line text on back. Signature 35; 36.	0.50	2.50	10.00
d. Watermark: King profile. Larger letters in 2-line text on back. Signature 38; 39; 40; 41.	0.50	1.50	4.50
s. As a. Specimen.	—	—	250

76 **10 Baht**

ND (1953). Brown on multicolor underprint. Portrait of King in Field Marshal's uniform with collar insignia and three decorations. Black serial number. Printer: TDLR.

	VG	VF	UNC
a. Watermark: Constitution. Red and blue security threads. Signature 34.	0.50	2.50	8.00
b. Watermark: Constitution. Metal security strip. Signature 34; 35 (Large size).	0.50	2.50	8.00
c. Watermark: King profile. Small letters in 2-line text on back. Signature 35; 36; 37; 38; 39.	0.50	4.00	12.00
d. Watermark: King profile. Larger letters in 2-line text on back. Signature 39; 40; 41; 44.	0.50	1.00	4.00
s. As a. Specimen.	—	—	250

77 **20 Baht**

ND (1953). Olive-green on multicolor underprint. Portrait of King in Field Marshal's uniform with collar insignia and three decorations. Black serial number. Printer: TDLR.

	VG	VF	UNC
a. Watermark: Constitution. Red and blue security threads. Signature 34.	2.50	4.00	15.00
b. Watermark: Constitution. Metal security strip. Signature 34; 35 (Large size).	2.50	8.00	20.00
c. Watermark: King profile. Small letters in 2-line text on back. Signature 35; 37; 38.	4.00	6.00	15.00
d. Watermark: King profile. Larger letters in 2-line text on back. Signature 38; 39; 40; 41; 44.	0.50	2.00	6.00
s. As a. Specimen.	—	—	250

78 **100 Baht**

ND (1955). Red on multicolor underprint. Portrait of King in Field Marshal's uniform with collar insignia and three decorations. Black serial number. Printer: TDLR.

	VG	VF	UNC
a. Watermark: Constitution. Red and blue security threads. Signature 34.	8.00	20.00	60.00
b. Watermark: Constitution. Metal security strip. Signature 34; 35; 37; 38.	4.00	12.50	30.00
c. Watermark: King profile. Small letters in 2-line text on back. Signature 38.	2.00	10.00	35.00
d. Watermark: King profile. Larger letters in 2-line text on back. Signature 38-41.	2.00	6.00	15.00
s. As a; c. Specimen.	—	—	250

REGIONAL - WW II

Treasury

1943 Provisional Issue

		VG	VF	UNC
R1	**1 Dollar**			
	ND (1943). Purple and green. Vertical line of Chinese inscription at left, Malay at right. Back: Throne Hall.			
	a. Issued note.	—	—	—
	r. Unsigned remainder.	—	100	350

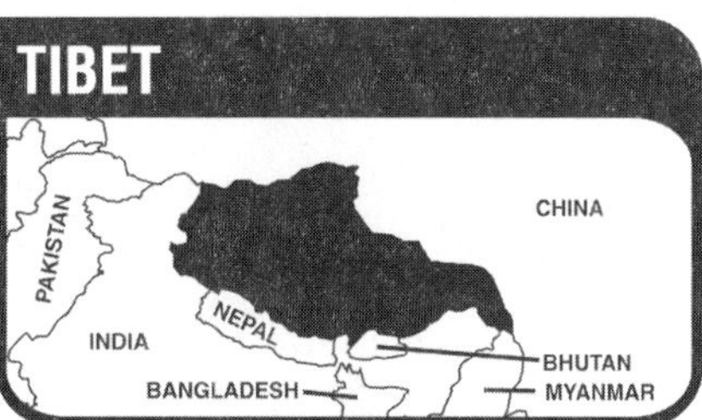

Tibet, an autonomous region of China located in central Asia between the Himalayan and Kunlun Mountains, has an area of 471,660 sq. mi. (1,221,599 sq. km.) and a population of 1.3 million. Capital: Lhasa. The economy is based on agriculture and livestock raising. Wool, livestock, salt and hides are exported. Lamaism, a form of Buddhism, developed in Tibet in the 8th century. From that time until the 1900s, the country remained isolated from the outside world, ruled from the 17th century by the Dalai Lama. The British in India achieved some influence in the early 20th century, and encouraged Tibet to declare its independence from China in 1913. The communist revolution in China marked a new era in Tibetan history. Chinese Communist troops invaded Tibet in Oct., 1950. After a token resistance, Tibet signed an agreement with China in which China recognized the spiritual and temporal leadership of the Dalai Lama, and Tibet recognized the suzerainty of China. In 1959, a nationwide revolt triggered by Communist-initiated land reform broke out. The revolt was ruthlessly crushed. The Dalai Lama fled to India, and on Sept. 1, 1965, the Chinese made Tibet an autonomous region of China.

NOTE: Chinese notes in Tibetan script or with Tibetan overprints were not intended for circulation in Tibet, but for use in bordering Chinese Provinces having a Tibetan speaking population. Refer to China #209b, 214b, 217b, 219d and 220c in this volume. Also #S1739 and S1740 (Sikang Provincial Bank) in Volume 1.

MONETARY SYSTEM:

7.5 Srang = 50 Tam (Tangka)

DENOMINATONS VALUES

Tam (Tangka):	ཏམ་	Five:	ལྔ་	Twenty-five:	ཉེར་ལྔ་
Srang:	སྲང་	Ten:	བཅུ་	Twenty-five:	ཉི་ཤུ་རྩ་ལྔ་
		Fifteen:	བཅོ་ལྔ་	Fifty:	ལྔ་བཅུ་
		100:	༡༠༠	Hundred:	བརྒྱ་ཐམ་པ་

DATING

Tibetan notes simply give the number of solar years which have elapsed since the legendary founding of the government in 255 AD, which is year 1 on this reckoning. Thus, Tibetan era dates are converted to AD dates merely by adding 254 to the former. Some of the later Tibetan notes give only the "rab byung" cycle (without the year) in which issued. Thus a note of the 16th cycle would imply issuance any time during the 60-year period 1927-86AD.

TYPES I & II

1st Line: ༄། གངས་ལྗོངས་བད་རྒྱལ་ཁབ་ཆེན་པོ་འི་ཕྱུགས་ཟུང་ཚབ་

2nd Line: སྲིད་དབུ་བརྙེས་ཀྱི་ལོ་

Decades: 165X ་ཆིག་སྟོང་དྲུག་བརྒྱ་ལྔ་བཅུ་ང་

166X . . . . ་དྲུག་ཅུ་རེ་ (Units see below)

167X . . . . ་བདུན་ཅུ་དོན་

168X . . . . ་བརྒྱད་ཅུ་གྱ་

169X . . . . ་དགུ་བཅུ་གོ་

Units (to be added to above):

1. གཅིག་ 4. བཞི་ 7. བདུན་
2. གཉིས་ 5. ལྔ་ 8. བརྒྱད་
3. གསུམ་ 6. དྲུག་ 9. དགུ

3rd Line: ༄། ཕུན་ཚོགས་སྡེ་བཞི་འི་དཔལ་མངའ་ཡན་བདེ་འི་སྐྱུ་ནར་

4th Line: ཆོས་སྲིད་གཉིས་ལྡན་གྱི་རབ་བྱུང་ [cycle] འི་ཤོག་དངུལ།

15th: ་བཅོ་ལྔ་པ་

16th: ་བཅོ་དྲུག་པ་

TYPE III

1st Line: ༄། གནམ་བསྐོས་དགའ་ལྡན་ཕོ་བྲང་ཕྱོགས་ལས་རྣམ་རྒྱལ།

2nd Line: ༄། ཆོས་སྲིད་གཉིས་ལྡན་གྱི་རབ་བྱུང་བཅུ་དྲུག་པ་འི་ཤོག་དངུལ།

TYPE IV

Same as Type III, but 2nd line ends:

25 Srang: ་ཤོག་དངུལ་སྲང་ཉི་ཤུ་རྩ་ལྔ།

100 Srang: ་ཤོག་དངུལ་སྲང་བརྒྱ་ཐམ་པ།

Color Abbreviation Guide

New to the *Standard Catalog of ® World Paper Money* are the following abbreviations related to color references:

BC: Back color
PC: Paper color

AUTONOMOUS

Government of Tibet

1658-1659 (1912-1913) Issue

#1-7A many varieties in size, printing and color.

		Good	Fine	XF
1	**5 Tam** 1658 (1912). Green. Lion and flowers. Four lines of text. BC: Light green. 180x100mm.	150	750	—
1A	**5 Tam** 1658 (1912). Blue. Lion and flowers. Four lines of text. Like #1. BC: Blue. 180x100mm.	175	750	—

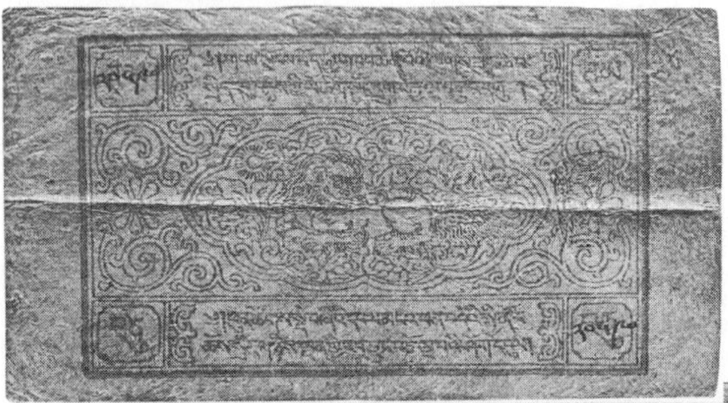

		Good	Fine	XF
2	**10 Tam** 1658-1659 (1912-1913). Red. Lion at center. Four lines of text. 175x95mm.	200	800	—

		Good	Fine	XF
3	**15 Tam** 1659 (1913). Purple. Lion with platter of fruit at center. Four lines of text. 185x100mm.	175	750	—
4	**25 Tam** 1659 (1913). Yellow. Lion. Four lines of text. Back: Mountains and elephant. 180x95mm.	175	750	—

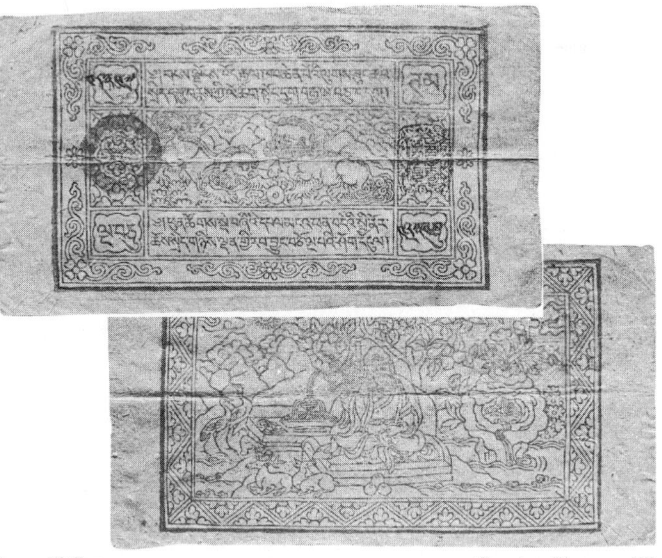

		Good	Fine	XF
5	**50 Tam** 1659 (1913). Blue. Two lions at center. Four lines of text. Back: Seated figure. 185x100mm.	150	700	—
6	**50 Tam** 1659 (1913). Purple. Two lions at center. Four lines of text. Like #5. Back: Seated figure. 180x100mm.	150	650	—

1672-1677 (1926-1931) Issue

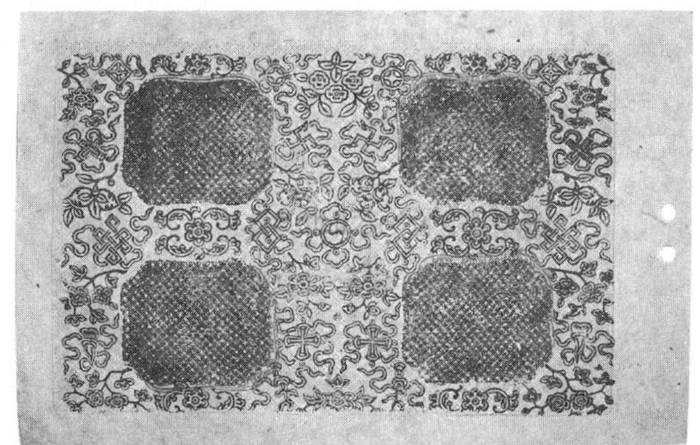

		Good	Fine	XF
7	**50 Tam** 1672-1687 (1926-1941). Blue and red on yellow underprint. Two lions at center. Back: Lion, dragon, tiger and stylized creature. BC: Red and blue. 201x118mm.			
	a. Short serial # frame. 1672 (Cycle 15); 1673-1677 (Cycle 16).	25.00	125	350
	b. Long serial # frame. 1673-1687 (Cycle 16).	25.00	125	350
7A	**50 Tam** 1677 (1931). Blue and red on yellow underprint. Two lions at center. Like #7, but additional red circular seal over the serial # at upper right. Back: Lion, dragon, tiger and stylized creature. BC: Red and blue. 201x118mm.	35.00	150	375

1685-1690 (1939-1943) Issue

#8-12 many varieties in size, printing and color. These notes were made by pasting together 3 sheets, the middle one having a 2-line security legend printed on it.

		Good	Fine	XF
8	**5 Srang** ND (1942-1946). Blue and red on yellow underprint. Lion at center. Two lines of text. Back: Fountain between dragons. BC: Red and light blue. 121x73mm.	10.00	25.00	65.00

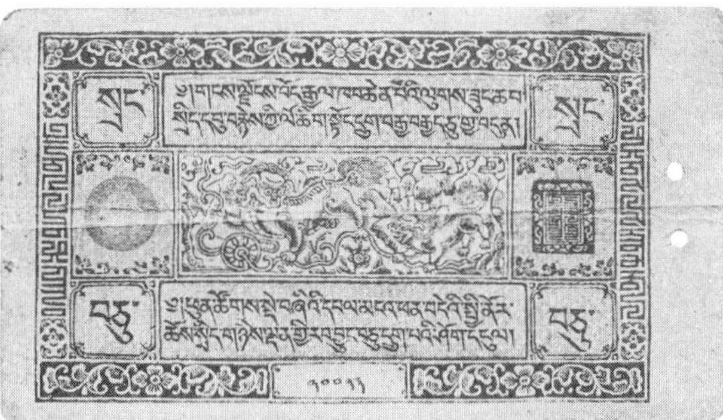

		Good	Fine	XF
9	**10 Srang** 1687-1694 (1941-1948). Blue on pink underprint. Two lions at center. Four lines of text. Back: Dragons and lions. 180x112mm.	5.00	17.50	45.00

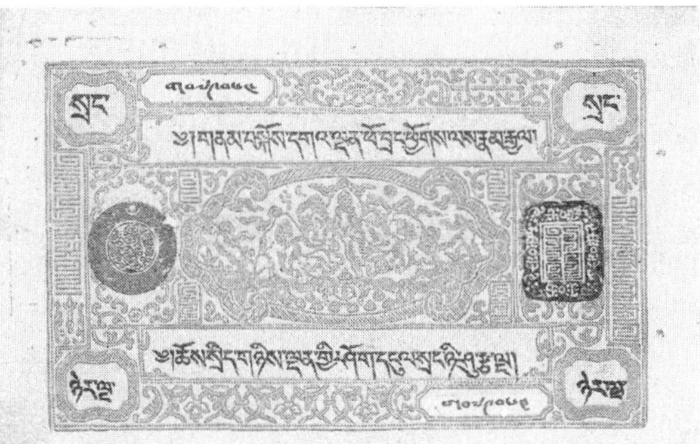

		Good	Fine	XF
10	**25 Srang** ND (1941-1948). Orange on yellow underprint. Two lions at center. Two lines of text. Back: People, buildings, elephant and rider. BC: Orange and blue. 183x110mm.			
	a. Large text 83mm long (1941-1947).	5.00	15.00	40.00
	b. Small text 75mm long (1948).	5.00	15.00	40.00

		Good	Fine	XF
11	**100 Srang** ND (1942-1959). Orange on yellow underprint. Two lions with fruit bowl at center. Two lines of text. Round seal at left. Back: Seated figure. BC: Orange, green, red and black. 215x138mm.			
	a. Large text 93-94mm long.	1.50	5.00	15.00
	b. Small text 85-87mm long.	1.50	5.00	15.00
	c. Center sheet with security legend inverted.	—	—	—
	d. Inverted seal.	20.00	40.00	100

Note: Direct reading of security text is accomplished when the face is held up to a light source.

		Good	Fine	XF
12	**100 Tam Srang** ND (1939-1940). Orange on yellow underprint. Two lions with fruit bowl at center. Two lines of text. Like #11, but with octagonal seal at left. Back: Seated figure. BC: Orange, green, red and black.	25.00	50.00	150

Note: Chinese notes in Tibetan script or with Tibetan overprint were not intended for circulation in Tibet, but for use in bordering Chinese provinces having a Tibetan speaking population. Refer to China #216e, 217d, 218f, and 220c in this volume. Also #S1739-S1741 (Sikang Provincial Bank) in Volume 1.

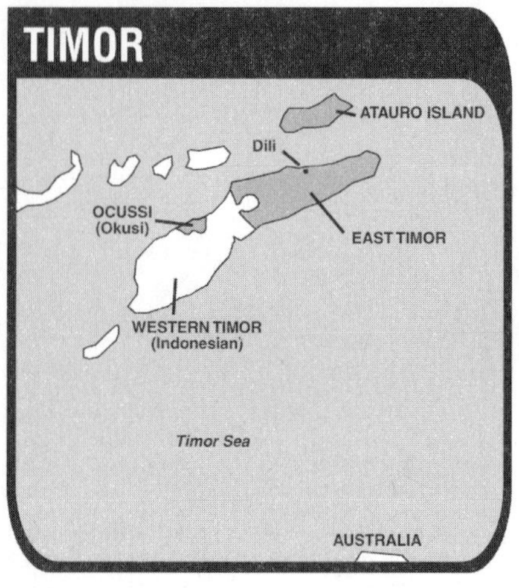

Timor, is an island between the Savu and Timor Seas, has an area, including the former colony of Portuguese Timor, of 11,883 sq. mi. (30,775 sq. km.) and a population of 1.5 million. Western Timor is administered as part of Nusa Tenggara Timur (East Nusa Tenggara) province. Capital: Kupang. The eastern half of the island, the former Portuguese colony, forms a single province, Timor Timur (East Timor). Originally the Portuguese colony also included the area around Ocussi-Ambeno and the small island of Atauro (Pulau Kambing) located north of Dili. Capital: Dili. Timor exports sandalwood, coffee, tea, hides, rubber and copra. Portuguese traders reached Timor about 1520, and moved to the north and east when the Dutch established themselves in Kupang, a sheltered bay at the southwestern tip, in 1613. Treaties effective in 1860 and 1914 established the boundaries between the two colonies. Japan occupied the entire island during World War II. The former Dutch colony in the western part of the island became part of Indonesia in 1950. At the end of Nov., 1975, the Portuguese Province of Timor attained independence as the People's Democratic Republic of East Timur. In Dec., 1975 or early in 1976 the government of the People's Democratic Republic was seized by a guerilla faction sympathetic to the Indonesian territorial claim to East Timur which ousted the constitutional government and replaced it with the Provisional Government of East Timur. On July 17, 1976, the Provisional Government enacted a law which dissolved the free republic and made East Timur the 24th province of Indonesia. In 1999 a revolution suceeded, and it is once again an independent country.

Note: For later issues see Indonesia.

MONETARY SYSTEM:

1 Pataca = 100 Avos to 1958
1 Escudo = 100 Centavos, 1958-1975

Note: In March 1912, before any notes were made especially for Timor, certain issues from Macao were declared legal tender there. The following list shows exact details:

1 PATACA 1905. Serial # 83,751 to 84,000 87,251 to 90,750
84,251 to 84,500 91,001 to 92,000
84,571 to 85,750 93,001 to 93,500
86,001 to 86,500 94,001 to 97,000
10 PATACAS 1907. Serial # 87,001 to 93,000 93,001 to 95,500
25 PATACAS 1907. Serial # 47,501 to 50,000

PORTUGUESE ADMINISTRATION

Banco Nacional Ultramarino

1910 Issue

#	Denomination	Good	Fine	XF
1	**1 Pataca** 1.1.1910. Purple and light green. Signature varieties. Back: Arms. Printer: BWC. 126x90mm.	90.00	250	700
2	**5 Patacas** 1.1.1910. Brown and yellow. Signature varieties. Back: Arms. Printer: BWC. 140x100mm.	250	550	1,500
3	**10 Patacas** 1.1.1910. Dark blue and green. Signature varieties. Back: Arms. Printer: BWC. 145x116mm.	300	750	2,000
4	**20 Patacas** 1.1.1910. Green and gray. Signature varieties. Back: Arms. Printer: BWC. 145x112mm.	400	1,000	2,500

1920 Provisional Issue

#	Denomination	Good	Fine	XF
5	**25 Patacas** 2.1.1920. 200x125mm. Overprint: *PAGAVEL EM DILLY TIMOR* at bottom border on Macao #4. Rare.	—	—	—

1933 ND Provisional Issue

#	Denomination	Good	Fine	XF
6	**5 Patacas** ND (1933 - old date 1.1.1924). Green on yellow underprint. 182x115mm. Overprint: *Pagaveis em TIMOR* at right on Macao #8.	200	600	1,500

1940; 1943 ND Provisional WW II Issue

#	Denomination	Good	Fine	XF
7	**5 Avos** ND (1940). Brown. 84x46mm. Overprint: *PAGAVEL EM TIMOR* on Macao #10.	50.00	175	600

#	Denomination	Good	Fine	XF
8	**10 Avos** ND (1940). Green. 98x54mm. Overprint: *PAGAVEL EM TIMOR* on Macao #11.	150	400	1,000

#	Denomination	Good	Fine	XF
9	**50 Avos** ND (1943). Purple. 83x47mm. Overprint: *PAGAVEL EM TIMOR* on Macao #17.	125	400	950

1945 ND Provisional Issue

#10-11B Overprint: *PAGAVEL EM TIMOR* on older Macao notes.

		Good	Fine	XF
10	**5 Patacas** ND (1945 - old date 1.1.1924). Green on yellow underprint. 182x115mm. Overprint: *PAGAVEL EM TIMOR* on Macao #8.	300	1,000	—

		Good	Fine	XF
11	**25 Patacas** ND (1945 - old date 1.1.1907). Black on rose underprint. 201x123mm. Overprint: *PAGAVEL EM TIMOR* on Macao #4. Rare.	—	—	—
11A	**100 Patacas** ND (1945 - old date 1.1.1906). Green on yellow underprint. 183x116mm. Overprint: *PAGAVEL EM TIMOR* on Macao #6. Rare.	—	—	—
11B	**100 Patacas** ND (1945 - old date 22.7.1919). Brown on multicolor underprint. 205x129mm. Overprint: *PAGAVEL EM TIMOR* on Macao #9. Rare.	—	—	—

1940 Issue

		VG	VF	UNC
12	**5 Avos** 19.7.1940. Red on multicolor underprint. Steamship seal at upper left. Printer: BWC. 91x55mm.	15.00	60.00	150

		VG	VF	UNC
13	**10 Avos** 19.7.1940. Green on multicolor underprint. Steamship seal at upper left. Like #12. Printer: BWC. 105x60mm.	20.00	85.00	225
14	**50 Avos** 19.7.1940. Purple. Steamship seal at center. Printer: BWC. 120x65mm.	25.00	150	350

1945 First Issue

		VG	VF	UNC
15	**1 Pataca** 8.3.1945. Black on pink underprint. Steamship seal at left. Back: Arms at center. BC: Brown. Printer: Litografia Nacional. 126x71mm.	30.00	175	400

1945 Second Issue

		VG	VF	UNC
16	**1 Pataca** 16.11.1945. Green. Huts at left, arms at right. Printer: W&S. 136x64mm.	12.50	50.00	125

		VG	VF	UNC
17	**5 Patacas** 16.11.1945. Brown. Huts at left, arms at right. Printer: W&S. 145x67mm.	15.00	75.00	200
18	**10 Patacas** 16.11.1945. Red. Huts at left, arms at right. Printer: W&S. 150x70mm.			
	a. Issued note.	20.00	100	300
	s. Specimen.	—	—	400
19	**20 Patacas** 16.11.1945. Blue. Huts at left, arms at right. Printer: W&S. 155x73mm.	25.00	200	500
20	**25 Patacas** 16.11.1945. Lilac. Huts at left, arms at right. Printer: W&S. 160x75mm.	30.00	250	750

1948 Issue

No.	Description	VG	VF	UNC
21	**20 Avos** 17.7.1948. Olive-brown on multicolor underprint. Arms at upper center. Back: Steamship seal at center. BC: Olive and red-brown. Printer: BWC. 109x60mm.	15.00	150	—

Decreto Lei No. 39221; 1959 Issue

No.	Description	VG	VF	UNC
22	**30 Escudos** 2.1.1959. Blue on multicolor underprint. Portrait J. Celestino da Silva at right. 2 signature varieties. Back: Bank ship seal at left, crowned arms at center. Printer: BWC. 135x75mm.			
	a. Issued note.	4.00	25.00	135
	s. Specimen.	—	—	100
23	**60 Escudos** 2.1.1959. Red on multicolor underprint. Portrait J. Celestino da Silva at right. Back: Bank ship seal at left, crowned arms at center. Printer: BWC. 150x80mm.	VG	VF	UNC
	a. Issued note.	5.00	25.00	170
	s. Specimen.	—	—	135
24	**100 Escudos** 2.1.1959. Brown on multicolor underprint. Portrait J. Celestino da Silva at right. Back: Bank ship seal at left, crowned arms at center. Printer: BWC. 160x80mm.	VG	VF	UNC
	a. Issued note.	7.50	37.50	225
	s. Specimen.	—	—	175
25	**500 Escudos** 2.1.1959. Dark brown and black on multicolor underprint. Portrait J. Celestino da Silva at right. Back: Bank ship seal at left, crowned arms at center. Printer: BWC. 165x85mm.	VG	VF	UNC
	a. Issued note.	40.00	170	475
	s. Specimen.	—	—	375

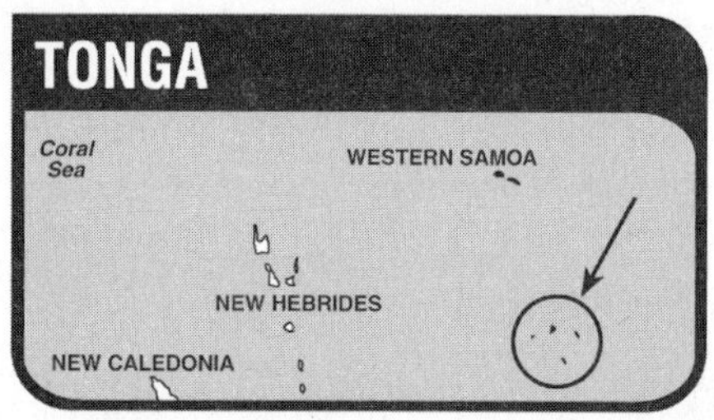

The Kingdom of Tonga (or Friendly Islands), a member of the British Commonwealth, is an archipelago situated in the southern Pacific Ocean south of Western Samoa and east of Fiji comprising 150 islands. Tonga has an area of 748 sq. km. and a population of 119,000. Capital: Nuku'alofa. Primarily agricultural, the kingdom exports bananas and copra. Tonga - unique among Pacific nations - never completely lost its indigenous governance. The archipelagos of "The Friendly Islands" were united into a Polynesian kingdom in 1845. Tonga became a constitutional monarchy in 1875 and a British protectorate in 1900; it withdrew from the protectorate and joined the Commonwealth of Nations in 1970. Tonga remains the only monarchy in the Pacific.

RULERS:
Queen Salote III, 1918-1965
King Taufa'ahau IV, 1967-2005
King Taufa'ahau V, 2005-2012
King Tupoutoía Lavaka Ata, 2012-

MONETARY SYSTEM:
1 Shilling = 12 Pence
1 Pound = 20 Shillings to 1967
1 Pa'anga = 100 Seniti, 1967-

REPLACEMENT NOTES:
#18-24, Z/1 prefix.

KINGDOM

Government of Tonga

1921-1933 Treasury Note Issue

No.	Description	Good	Fine	XF
1	**4 Shillings** 26.6.1933; 8.7.1935; 25.11.1935. Palms at left and right, arms at center, *STERLING* at right. Signature varieties. Printer: TDLR.	—	—	—
2	**10 Shillings** 28.6.1933. Palms at left and right, arms at center, *STERLING* at right. Signature varieties. Printer: TDLR. Rare.	—	—	—
3	**1 Pound** 28.6.1933. Palms at left and right, arms at center, *STERLING* at right. Signature varieties. Printer: TDLR. Rare.	—	—	—
4	**5 Pounds** 1.1.1921. Palms at left and right, arms at center, *STERLING* at right. Signature varieties. Printer: TDLR. Rare.	—	—	—

1936-1939 Issue

No.	Description	Good	Fine	XF
5	**4 Shillings** 1935-1941. Brown. *FOUR SHILLINGS* at left. Palms at left and right, arms at center. Signature varieties. Printer: TDLR. Overprint: Several lines or solid block over *STERLING* at right on face.			
	a. 8.7.1935.	—	—	—
	b. 16.12.1936-1.12.1941.	40.00	125	450
6	**10 Shillings** 10.12.1936; 21.4.1937; 4.5.1937; 24.1.1938; 19.5.1939. Green. *TEN SHILLINGS* at left. Palms at left and right, arms at center. Signature varieties. Printer: TDLR. Overprint: Several lines or solid block over *STERLING* at right on face.	65.00	250	750

No.	Description	Good	Fine	XF
7	**1 Pound** 10.12.1936; 22.1.1937; 21.4.1937; 4.5.1937; 19.5.1939. Red. *ONE POUND* at left. Palms at left and right, arms at center. Signature varieties. Overprint: Several lines or solid block over *STERLING* at right on face.	125	350	1,000

		Good	Fine	XF
8	**5 Pounds** 19.5.1939. Dark blue. *FIVE POUNDS* at left. Palms at left and right, arms at center. Signature varieties. Overprint: Several lines or solid block over *STERLING* at right on face. Rare.	—	—	—

1939-1942 Issue

		VG	VF	UNC
9	**4 Shillings** 1941-1966. Brown on multicolor underprint. *FOUR SHILLINGS* at left and right. Arms at center. Printer: TDLR.			
	a. 1.12.1941-8.9.1947. 3 signatures.	20.00	125	450
	b. 7.2.1949; 15.2.1951; 20.7.1951; 6.9.1954.	20.00	100	375
	c. 19.9.1955-30.11.1959.	7.50	25.00	150
	d. 24.10.1960-27.9.1966.	7.00	25.00	85.00
	e. 3.11.1966. 2 signatures.	5.00	20.00	50.00

		VG	VF	UNC
10	**10 Shillings** 1939-1966. Green on multicolor underprint. *TEN SHILLINGS* at left and right. Arms at center. Printer: TDLR.			
	a. 3.5.1940; 17.10.1941-28.11.1944. 3 signatures.	35.00	250	—
	b. 9.7.1949-1955.	30.00	150	450
	c. 2.5.1956; 22.7.1957; 10.12.1958; 13.10.1959.	7.50	35.00	300
	d. 24.10.1960; 28.11.1962; 29.7.1964; 22.6.1965.	7.00	30.00	125
	e. 3.11.1966. 2 signatures.	5.00	22.50	65.00
	s. Specimen. As b, d. Perforated: *CANCELLED.*	—	—	300

		VG	VF	UNC
11	**1 Pound** 1940-1966. Red on multicolor underprint. *ONE POUND* at left and right. Arms at center. Printer: TDLR.			
	a. 3.5.1940-7.11.1944. 3 signatures.	40.00	275	—
	b. 15.6.1951; 11.9.1951; 19.9.1955.	30.00	175	550
	c. 2.5.1956; 10.12.1958; 30.11.1959; 12.12.1961.	20.00	70.00	425
	d. 28.11.1962; 30.10.1964; 2.11.1965; 3.11.1966.	8.00	40.00	150
	e. 2.12.1966. 2 signatures.	4.00	15.00	100
	s. Specimen. Perforated: *CANCELLED.*	—	—	500

		VG	VF	UNC
12	**5 Pounds** 1942-1966. Dark blue on multicolor underprint. *FIVE POUNDS* at left and right. Arms at center. Printer: TDLR.			
	a. 11.3.1942-1945. 3 signatures.	550	2,000	—
	b. 15.6.1951; 5.7.1955; 11.9.1956; 26.6.1958.	350	1,500	—
	c. 30.11.1959; 2.11.1965.	175	500	1,000
	d. 2.12.1966. 2 signatures.	15.00	60.00	150

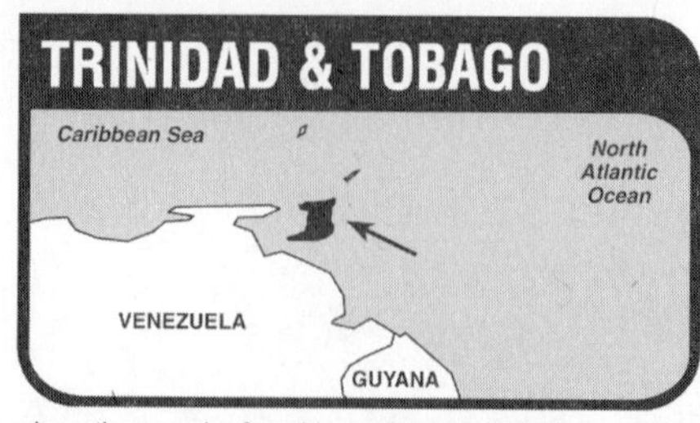

The Republic of Trinidad and Tobago, a member of the British Commonwealth situated 11 km. off the coast of Venezuela, has an area of 5,128 sq. km. and a population of 1.23 million. Capital: Port-of-Spain. The Island of Trinidad contains the world's largest natural asphalt bog. Birds of Paradise live on little Tobago, the only place outside of their native New Guinea where they can be found in a wild state. Petroleum and petroleum products are the mainstay of the economy. Petroleum products, crude oil and sugar are exported.First colonized by the Spanish, the islands came under British control in the early 19th century. The islands' sugar industry was hurt by the emancipation of the slaves in 1834. Manpower was replaced with the importation of contract laborers from India between 1845 and 1917, which boosted sugar production as well as the cocoa industry. The discovery of oil on Trinidad in 1910 added another important export. Independence was attained in 1962. The country is one of the most prosperous in the Caribbean thanks largely to petroleum and natural gas production and processing. Tourism, mostly in Tobago, is targeted for expansion and is growing. Notes of the British Caribbean Territories circulated between 1950-1964.

RULERS:

British to 1976

MONETARY SYSTEM:

1 Dollar = 100 Cents
5 Dollars = 1 Pound 10 Pence

BRITISH ADMINISTRATION

Government of Trinidad and Tobago

1905 Issue

		Good	Fine	XF
1	**1 Dollar** 1905-1926. Blue. Landing of Columbus at left, arms at top center. Signature varieties. Back: Mountain with sailing ship. Printer: TDLR.			
	a. Black vignette at left. 1.4.1905.	300	600	1,800
	b. Blue vignette. 1.4.1905.	175	350	1,150
	c. 1.1.1924; 1.3.1926.	125	250	750

		Good	Fine	XF
2	**2 Dollars** 1.4.1905. Sailing ship in harbor at left, palm tree with sailing ship in background at right, vignettes in circles. Signature varieties. Back: Mountain with sailing ship. Printer: TDLR.			
	a. Red.	300	600	1,800
	b. Green and red. Rare.	—	—	—

1914 Issue

		Good	Fine	XF
2E	**1000 Dollars** 1.4.1914. Black. Royal Arms at top center, female head at left end. Back: Two cherubs supporting seal in center rectangle. BC: Black. Face and back uniface Proofs.	—	—	—

1929 Issue

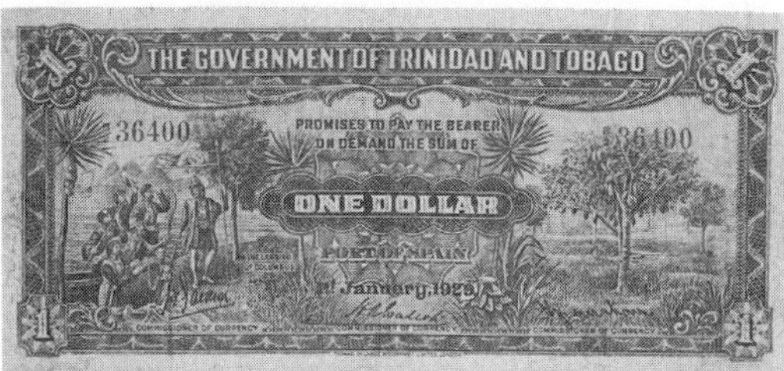

		Good	Fine	XF
3	**1 Dollar** 1.1.1929; 1.1.1932. Blue. Landing of Columbus at left, tree at right.	125	250	750

		Good	Fine	XF
4	**2 Dollars** 1.1.1929. Red. Sailing ship in harbor at left, palm tree with sailing ship in background at right. 178x89mm.	225	450	1,350

1934; 1935 Issue

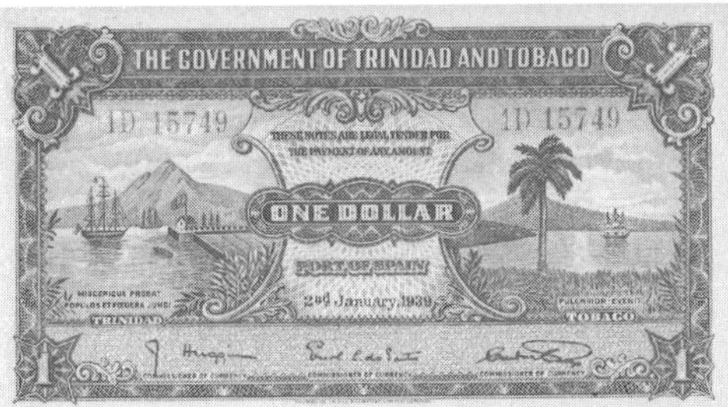

		Good	Fine	XF
5	**1 Dollar** 1935-1949. Dark blue on multicolor underprint. Sailing ship in harbor at left, palm tree with sailing ship in background at right. Printer: TDLR. 150x82mm.			
	a. 1.9.1935.	15.00	30.00	125
	b. 2.1.1939.	2.50	7.50	35.00
	c. 1.5.1942; 1.1.1943.	2.50	7.50	35.00
	d. 1.7.1948.	2.50	7.50	50.00
	e. 1.7.1949.	2.50	7.50	65.00
6	**2 Dollars** 1934-1939. Bright red on blue and multicolor underprint. Sailing ship in harbor at left, palm tree with sailing ship in background at right. Printer: TDLR. 150x82mm.	Good	Fine	XF
	a. 1.5.1934; 1.9.1935.	35.00	75.00	450
	b. 2.1.1939.	10.00	35.00	250

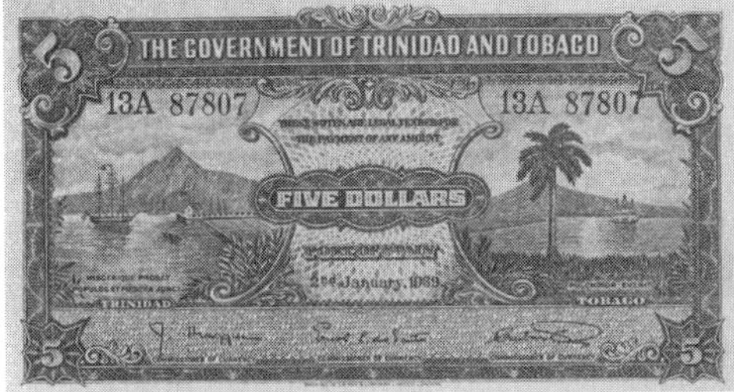

		Good	Fine	XF
7	**5 Dollars** 1935-1942. Purple on multicolor underprint. Sailing ship in harbor at left, palm tree with sailing ship in background at right. Printer: TDLR. 150x82mm.			
	a. 1.9.1935.	50.00	175	475
	b. 2.1.1939; 1.5.1942.	15.00	65.00	250

1939-1942 Issue

		Good	Fine	XF
8	**2 Dollars** 1.5.1942; 1.1.1943; 1.7.1949. Dark red on green and multicolor underprint. Sailing ship in harbor at left, palm tree with sailing ship in background at right.	7.50	40.00	265
9	**10 Dollars** 1939; 1942. Red-brown on multicolor underprint. Sailing ship in harbor at left, palm tree with sailing ship in background at right.	Good	Fine	XF
	a. 2.1.1939.	100	400	—
	b. 1.5.1942.	75.00	275	650
10	**20 Dollars** 1.5.1942; 1.1.1943. Green on multicolor underprint. Sailing ship in harbor at left, palm tree with sailing ship in background at right.	Good	Fine	XF
	a. Issued note.	450	1,000	—
	s. Specimen. Perforated: *CANCELLED.*	—	Unc	1,000

1943 Issue

		Good	Fine	XF
11	**20 Dollars** 1.1.1943. Purple on multicolor underprint. Sailing ship in harbor at left, palm tree with sailing ship in background at right. Like #10.	500	1,500	—

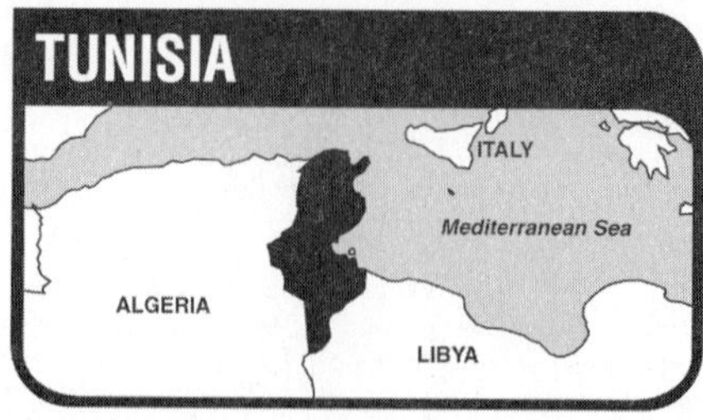

The Republic of Tunisia, located on the northern coast of Africa between Algeria and Libya, has an area of 163,610 sq. km. and a population of 10.38 million. Capital: Tunis. Agriculture is the backbone of the economy. Crude oil, phosphates, olive oil, and wine are exported. Rivalry between French and Italian interests in Tunisia culminated in a French invasion in 1881 and the creation of a protectorate. Agitation for independence in the decades following World War I was finally successful in getting the French to recognize Tunisia as an independent state in 1956. The country's first president, Habib Bourguiba, established a strict one-party state. He dominated the country for 31 years, repressing Islamic fundamentalism and establishing rights for women unmatched by any other Arab nation. In November 1987, Bourguiba was removed from office and replaced by Zine el Abidine Ben Ali in a bloodless coup. Ben Ali served well into his fifth consecutive five-year term but was overthrown as part of the *Arab Spring* events of 2011. Elections are expected soon.

RULERS:

French, 1881-1956

MONETARY SYSTEM:

1 Franc = 100 Centimes to 1960
1 Dinar = 1000 Millimes, 1960-

REPLACEMENT NOTES:

#61-89 with second prefix letter *R* added after regular letter.

OTTOMAN ADMINISTRATION

Dar el-Mal

State Bank

1846 Issue

		Good	Fine	XF
A2	**50 Riyals** AH1263/1846. Ornate knotted border. Without watermark (Discounted at 4%). Rare.	—	—	—

FRENCH ADMINISTRATION

Banque de l'Algérie

1903-1908 Issue

#1-5 black overprint: *TUNISIE* on notes of Algeria.

		Good	Fine	XF
1	**5 Francs** 1903-14.5.1925. Blue. Mercury at left, peasant at right. Overprint: Black *TUNISIE* on Algeria #13.	15.00	70.00	275

Color Abbreviation Guide

New to the *Standard Catalog of® World Paper Money* are the following abbreviations related to color references:

BC: Back color
PC: Paper color

		Good	Fine	XF
2	**20 Francs** 1908-1942. Blue. Mercury at left, Hercules at right. Overprint: Black *TUNISIE* on Algeria #72.			
	a. 7.1.1908; 15.4.1908; 29.4.1908.	35.00	150	400
	b. 22.2.1939-28.9.1942.	12.50	50.00	175
3	**50 Francs** 2.3.1908. Blue. Cherubs at left and right, woman at lower center. Overprint: Black *TUNISIE* on Algeria #73.	65.00	250	700

		Good	Fine	XF
4	**100 Francs** 6.2.1908; 11.2.1908; 8.11.1911. Blue. Boy standing with oar and hammer at left, boy standing with shovel and sickle at right. Overprint: Black *TUNISIE* on Algeria #74.	70.00	300	900

#	Denomination	Good	Fine	XF
5	**500 Francs** 1904; 1909; 1924. Blue. Fortuna at left, Mercury at right, two boys sitting at bottom. Overprint: Black *TUNISIE* on Algeria #75.			
	a. 9.5.1904; 4.1.1909. Rare.	—	—	—
	b. 3.1.1924-16.4.1924.	60.00	150	500

1914; 1918 Issue

#6 and 7 black overprint: *TUNISIE* on notes of Algeria.

#	Denomination	Good	Fine	XF
6	**20 Francs** 1914-1941. Purple on light blue underprint. Girl at right. 165x105mm. Overprint: Black *TUNISIE* on Algeria #78.			
	a. 3.8.1914; 10.8.1914.	3.00	20.00	75.00
	b. 26.2.1929-2.12.1941.	1.00	7.50	35.00

#	Denomination	Good	Fine	XF
7	**1000 Francs** 1918-1924. Blue. Woman sitting with oar at left, blacksmith at right, two boys sitting with lion at bottom. Overprint: Black *TUNISIE* on Algeria #76.			
	a. 5.11.1918.	165	400	1,000
	b. 5.3.1923; 14.1.1924; 15.1.1924; 18.1.1924; 16.4.1924; 25.4.1924; 26.4.1924.	150	350	850

1921-1926 Issue

#8-11 black overprint: *TUNISIE* on notes of Algeria.

#	Denomination	Good	Fine	XF
8	**5 Francs** 1925-1941. Red-brown and violet. Girl wearing kerchief at right. 128x88mm. Overprint: Black *TUNISIE* on Algeria #77.			
	a. 15.7.1925-28.2.1933.	1.00	7.50	30.00
	b. 2.3.1939-31.5.1941. Serial # varieties.	0.75	2.00	10.00
	c. 24.5.1941. Without serial #.	0.25	1.50	7.50

#	Denomination	Good	Fine	XF
9	**50 Francs** 18.1.1924-2.4.1937. Green. Mosque with tower at right, city of Algiers at center background. Overprint: Black *TUNISIE* on Algeria #80.	7.50	50.00	125

#	Denomination	Good	Fine	XF
10	**100 Francs** 1921-1939. Blue and violet. Two boys at left, Arab with camel at right. Overprint: Black *TUNISIE* on Algeria #81.			
	a. 11.3.1921; 25.7.1921; 18.8.1924; 17.4.1928.	12.50	50.00	175
	b. 16.1.1933; 21.8.1933.	8.00	35.00	100
	c. 14.3.1936-1939.	7.50	25.00	75.00

#	Denomination	Good	Fine	XF
11	**1000 Francs** 1926-1939. Brown-violet. Woman with sword and child at left, Algerian woman with child at right. Overprint: Black *TUNISIE* on Algeria #83.			
	a. Overprint at left. 19.7.1926. 12.11.1926.	50.00	300	850
	b. Overprint at right. 8.2.1938; 14.2.1938; 19.4.1938; 3.8.1939; 23.9.1939; 10.10.1938; 8.8.1939.	40.00	250	600

1938-1939 Issue

#12-14 black overprint: *TUNISIE* on notes of Algeria.

#	Denomination	Good	Fine	XF
12	**50 Francs** 1938-1945. Multicolor. Veiled woman with man wearing red fez at right. Overprint: Black *TUNISIE* on Algeria #84.			
	a. Watermark: Head. 22.12.1938-28.5.1942; 1.5.1945.	3.00	15.00	60.00
	b. Watermark: Lettering. 6.7.1942; 27.8.1942; 1.3.1945.	1.50	12.50	40.00

		Good	Fine	XF
13	**100 Francs** 1939-1942. Multicolor. Algerian with turban at left. Overprint: Black *TUNISIE* on Algeria #85.			
	a. Watermark: Head. 26.9.1939-5.1.1942.	2.00	10.00	50.00
	b. Watermark: Lettering. 27.4.1942; 6.6.1942; 26.9.1942; 2.11.1942.	3.00	15.00	60.00

		Good	Fine	XF
14	**500 Francs** 30.9.1938; 26.7.1939; 3.1.1942-4.2.1942. Blue-violet and multicolor. Girl at left, woman with torch and youth at right. Overprint: Black *TUNISIE* on Algeria #82.	40.00	175	650

1941-1945 Issues

#15-28 black overprint: *TUNISIE* on notes of Algeria.

		Good	Fine	XF
15	**5 Francs** 8.2.1944; 8.3.1944. Red-brown and violet. Girl wearing kerchief at right. Signature titles: *L' Inspecteur Gal.* and *Caissier Pal.* Similar to #8. 97x59mm. Overprint: Black *TUNISIE* on Algeria #92.	0.25	2.00	12.50
16	**5 Francs** 2.10.1944. Red-brown and violet. Girl wearing kerchief at right. Like #15 but signature titles: *Le Secretaire Gal.* and *Caissier Pal.* Overprint: Black *TUNISIE* on Algeria #92.	1.00	5.00	22.50

		Good	Fine	XF
17	**20 Francs** 9.1.1943-10.2.1944. Purple on light blue underprint. Girl at right. Signature titles: *L'INSPECTEUR GÉNÉRAL* and *CAISSIER PRINCIPAL.* Similar to #6. 122x90mm. Overprint: Black *TUNISIE* on Algeria #94.	0.75	5.00	20.00
18	**20 Francs** 2.2.1945; 3.4.1945; 7.5.1945. Purple. Girl at right. Like #17 but signature titles: *CAISSIER PRINCIPAL* and *LE SECRETAIRE GÉNÉRAL.* Overprint: Black *TUNISIE* on Algeria #94.	1.00	7.00	25.00
19	**500 Francs** 15.3.1943; 18.5.1943; 20.5.1943; 16.7.1943; 27.1.1944; 3.2.1944. Blue and green. Two boys at left, Arab with camel at right. 195x106mm. Overprint: Black *TUNISIE* on Algeria #93.	30.00	150	350

		Good	Fine	XF
20	**1000 Francs** 1941-1942. Multicolor. Horses at center, French farm family at right. Back: French text. Overprint: Black *TUNISIE* on Algeria #86.			
	a. Watermark: Woman's head. 18.3.1941; 24.6.1941; 23.8.1941; 3.9.1941; 4.9.1941; 9.9.1941; 19.9.1941; 29.12.1941; 2.1.1942; 14.2.1942.	30.00	75.00	250
	b. Watermark: Lettering. 2.11.1942; 3.11.1942.	37.50	100	300
21	**5000 Francs** 1942. Red-orange. Young Algerian woman at left, woman with torch and shield at right. Overprint: Black *TUNISIE* on Algeria #90.	65.00	300	750

1946-1949 Issue

		Good	Fine	XF
22	**20 Francs** 4.6.1948; 7.6.1948. Green and brown. Ornamental design. Like Algeria #103 with title: *BANQUE DE L'ALGÉRIE / TUNISIE.* Overprint: Black *TUNISIE.*	2.00	15.00	50.00

		Good	Fine	XF
23	**50 Francs** 3.2.1949. Blue and rose. Ornamental design with title: *BANQUE DE L'ALGÉRIE & DE LA TUNISIE.* Overprint: Black *TUNISIE.*	12.00	60.00	150

		Good	Fine	XF
24	**100 Francs** 5.11.1946-18.2.1948. Blue, yellow and brown. Hermes at right, Roman gate in background. Title: *BANQUE DE L'ALGÉRIE / TUNISIE* at top. Back: Ancient mosaic with boat and three people. Watermark: Woman's head. Overprint: Black *TUNISIE.*	12.00	60.00	200
25	**500 Francs** 30.1.1947; 16.1.1947. 16.5.1947. Green on yellow and multicolor underprint. Winged Victory with Roman ruins in background. With titles: *BANQUE DE L'ALGÉRIE / TUNISIE.* Back: Three allegorical men. Overprint: Black *TUNISIE.*	15.00	100	325
26	**1000 Francs** 4.9.1946; 5.9.1946. Multicolor. Horses at center, French farm family at right. Similar to #20 but with title: *BANQUE DE L'ALGÉRIE / TUNISIE.* Back: Arabic text. Overprint: Black *TUNISIE.*	35.00	150	350

		Good	Fine	XF
27	**5000 Francs** 1946. Multicolor. P. Apollo at left. Like Algeria #109 but with *TUNISIE* in front of engraver's name at lower right. Back: Arabic text different from #21. Overprint: Black *TUNISIE.*	40.00	200	425

1950 Issue

		Good	Fine	XF
28	**500 Francs** 31.1.1950-17.3.1950; 11.2.1952-31.7.1952; 1.12.1954. Green on yellow and multicolor underprint. Winged Victory with Roman ruins in background. Similar to #25 but with title: *BANQUE DE L'ALGÉRIE ET DE LA TUNISIE.* Back: Three allegorical men. 160x82mm. Overprint: Black *TUNISIE.*	15.00	100	300

		Good	Fine	XF
29	**1000 Francs** 1950-1957. Dark brown on blue underprint. Ruins of Roman temples at left, standing figure at center right. With title: *BANQUE DE L'ALGÉRIE ET DE LA TUNISIE.* Back: Neptune with trident, horses and allegorical figures at center. Watermark: Woman's head.			
	a. 17.2.1950-26.12.1950.	20.00	100	300
	b. 20.3.1957.	20.00	100	300

		Good	Fine	XF
30	**5000 Francs** 9.1.1950-7.5.1952. Violet. Roman ruins at left, Roman Emperor Vespasian at right. With title: *BANQUE DE L'ALGÉRIE ET DE LA TUNISIE.*	30.00	150	500

GERMAN OCCUPATION - WW II

Banque de l'Algerie

1942 Provisional Issue

Overprint: *BANQUE DE L'ALGÉRIE* and new denomination on unissued 100 Francs note of the Banque de France (#65b, old dates May to August 1892). Issued during the German occupation between Dec. 1942-May 1943.

		Good	Fine	XF
31	**1000 Francs on 100 Francs** ND (1942-1943). Violet, blue and brown. Woman seated at left and right. Overprint: *BANQUE DE L'ALGERIE* and new denomination on unissued 100 Francs of the Banque de France.	8.00	35.00	100

REGENCE DE TUNIS

Treasury Issue

1918 First Issue

#32-53 exchangeable with notes of the Banque de l'Algérie. Several different heading and frame styles used.

		VG	VF	UNC
32	**50 Centimes** 16.2.1918. Green. Back: Arms stamped at center.			
	a. Monogram at center on back. Engraver and printer on both sides.	6.00	20.00	85.00
	b. Monogram at center on back. Engraver and printer on face only.	6.00	20.00	85.00
	c. Without monogram on back. Engraver and printer on face only.	6.00	20.00	85.00
33	**1 Franc** 16.2.1918. Red. Back: Arms stamped at center.			
	a. Watermark: *1896.*	7.50	25.00	100
	b. Watermark: *1910.*	7.50	25.00	100
34	**2 Francs** 16.2.1918. Brown. Back: Arms stamped at center.	8.00	40.00	125

1918 Second Issue

		VG	VF	UNC
35	**50 Centimes** 27.4.1918. Green. Back: Arms stamped at center.	6.00	20.00	85.00

		VG	VF	UNC
36	**1 Franc** 27.4.1918. Red. Back: Arms stamped at center.			
	a. Watermark: *1912.*	6.00	20.00	85.00
	b. Watermark: *1913.*	6.00	20.00	85.00
	c. Watermark: *1916.*	6.00	20.00	85.00
	d. Watermark: *1917.*	6.00	20.00	85.00
	e. Watermark: *1918.*	6.00	20.00	85.00
37	**2 Francs** 27.4.1918. Brown. Back: Arms stamped at center.			
	a. Watermark: *1896.* Printer: PICARD.	8.00	40.00	125
	b. Watermark: *1910.* Printer: PICARD.	8.00	40.00	125
	c. Printer: YVORRA-BARLIER-CLAVE.	6.00	20.00	85.00
38	**2 Francs** 14.8.1918. Brown. Back: Arms stamped at center.	8.00	40.00	125

1918 Third Issue

		VG	VF	UNC
39	**50 Centimes** 30.9.1918. Green. Back: Arms stamped at center.	7.50	25.00	100
40	**1 Franc** 30.9.1918. Red. Back: Arms stamped at center.	7.50	25.00	100
41	**2 Francs** 30.9.1918. Brown. Back: Arms stamped at center.	7.50	25.00	100

1918 Fourth Issue

		VG	VF	UNC
42	**50 Centimes** 4.11.1918. Green. Back: Arms stamped at center.	7.50	25.00	100

		VG	VF	UNC
43	**1 Franc** 4.11.1918. Red. Back: Arms stamped at center.	7.50	25.00	100
44	**2 Francs** 4.11.1918. Brown. Back: Arms stamped at center.	7.50	25.00	100

1919 Issue

		VG	VF	UNC
45	**50 Centimes** 17.3.1919. Green. Back: Arms stamped at center.			
	a. Printer: YVORRA-BARLIER-CLAVE.	6.00	20.00	85.00
	b. Printer: YVORRA-BARLIER.	6.00	20.00	85.00
46	**1 Franc** 17.3.1919. Red. Back: Arms stamped at center.			
	a. Printer: YVORRA-BARLIER-CLAVE.	6.00	20.00	85.00
	b. Printer: YVORRA-BARLIER.	6.00	20.00	85.00

		VG	VF	UNC
47	**2 Francs** 17.3.1919. Brown. Back: Arms stamped at center.			
	a. Printer: YVORRA-BARLIER-CLAVE.	7.50	25.00	100
	b. Printer: YVORRA-BARLIER.	7.50	25.00	100

1920 Issue

		VG	VF	UNC
48	**50 Centimes** 3.3.1920. Green. 3 signature varieties. Back: Arms stamped at center.	6.00	20.00	85.00

		VG	VF	UNC
49	**1 Franc** 3.3.1920. Red. 3 signature varieties. Back: Arms stamped at center.	6.00	20.00	85.00

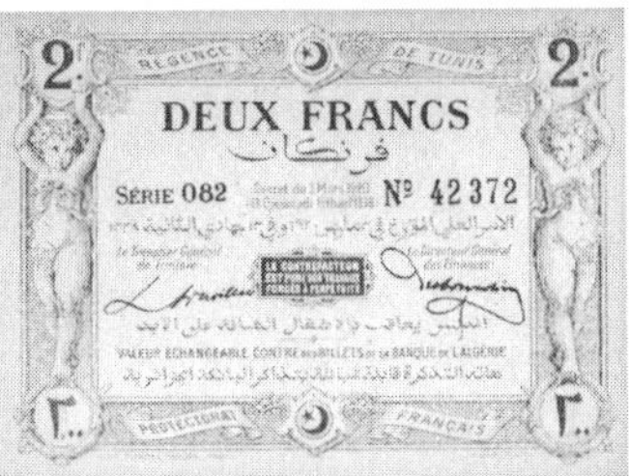

		VG	VF	UNC
50	**2 Francs** 3.3.1920. Brown. 3 signature varieties. Back: Arms stamped at center.	7.50	25.00	100

1921 Issue

		VG	VF	UNC
51	**50 Centimes** 25.1.1921. Green. Back: Arms stamped at center.	7.50	25.00	100

		VG	VF	UNC
52	**1 Franc** 25.1.1921. Red. Back: Arms stamped at center.	7.50	25.00	100
53	**2 Francs** 25.1.1921. Brown. Back: Arms stamped at center.	8.00	40.00	125

Direction des Finances - Treasury

1943 Issue

		VG	VF	UNC
54	**50 Centimes** 15.7.1943. Brown-violet. Veiled woman carrying a water jug at left, mountain at center, palm tree at right. Back: Archway.	2.00	6.00	20.00
55	**1 Franc** 15.7.1943. Green and brown. Veiled woman carrying a water jug at left, mountain at center, palm tree at right. Back: Archway.	2.00	6.00	20.00
56	**2 Francs** 15.7.1943. Brown-violet and blue. Veiled woman carrying a water jug at left, mountain at center, palm tree at right. Back: Archway.	2.50	7.50	25.00

REPUBLIC

Banque Centrale de Tunisie

Ca.1958 ND Issue

		VG	VF	UNC
57	**1/2 Dinar** ND. Purple on multicolor underprint. Portrait Habib Bourguiba at left. Mosque at right. Back: Ruins at left, arms at right. Watermark: Arms.	4.00	35.00	150
58	**1 Dinar** ND. Green on multicolor underprint. Portrait Habib Bourguiba at left. Peasant and farm machine at right. Back: Dam. Watermark: Arms.	4.00	37.50	175
59	**5 Dinars** ND. Brown on multicolor underprint. Habib Bourguiba at right, bridge at left, Arabic numerals *5* and serial #. Back: Archways. Watermark: Arms.	4.00	37.50	175

1960; 1962 Issue

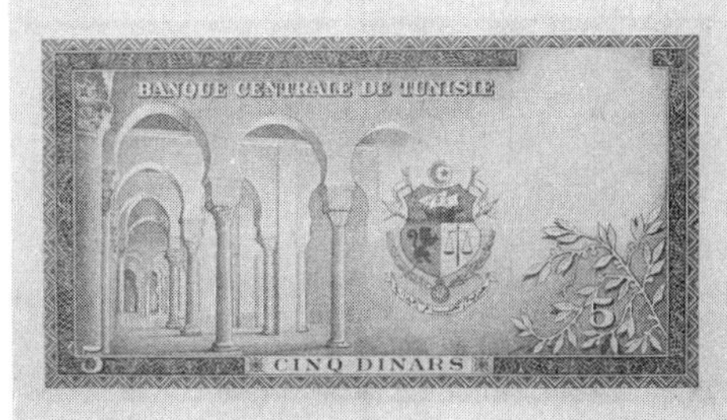

		VG	VF	UNC
60	**5 Dinars** 1.11.1960. Brown on multicolor underprint. Habib Bourguiba at right, bridge at left. Like #59 but with western numerals *5* and serial #. Back: Archways. Watermark: Arms.	4.00	40.00	200

The Republic of Turkey, a parliamentary democracy of the Near East located partially in Europe and partially in Asia between the Black and the Mediterranean seas, has an area of 301,382 sq. mi. (780,580 sq. km.) and a population of 65.73 million. Capital: Ankara. Turkey exports cotton, hazelnuts and tobacco, and enjoys a virtual monopoly in meerschaum.Modern Turkey was founded in 1923 from the Anatolian remnants of the defeated Ottoman Empire by national hero Mustafa Kemal, who was later honored with the title Ataturk or "Father of the Turks." Under his authoritarian leadership, the country adopted wide-ranging social, legal, and political reforms. After a period of one-party rule, an experiment with multi-party politics led to the 1950 election victory of the opposition Democratic Party and the peaceful transfer of power. Since then, Turkish political parties have multiplied, but democracy has been fractured by periods of instability and intermittent military coups (1960, 1971, 1980), which in each case eventually resulted in a return of political power to civilians. In 1997, the military again helped engineer the ouster - popularly dubbed a "post-modern coup" - of the then Islamic-oriented government. Turkey intervened militarily on Cyprus in 1974 to prevent a Greek takeover of the island and has since acted as patron state to the "Turkish Republic of Northern Cyprus," which only Turkey recognizes. A separatist insurgency begun in 1984 by the Kurdistan Workers' Party (PKK) - now known as the People's Congress of Kurdistan or Kongra-Gel (KGK) - has dominated the Turkish military's attention and claimed more than 30,000 lives. After the capture of the group's leader in 1999, the insurgents largely withdrew from Turkey mainly to northern Iraq. In 2004, KGK announced an end to its ceasefire and attacks attributed to the KGK increased. Turkey joined the UN in 1945 and in 1952 it became a member of NATO; it holds a non-permanent seat on the UN Security Council from 2009-2010. In 1964, Turkey became an associate member of the European Community. Over the past decade, it has undertaken many reforms to strengthen its democracy and economy; it began accession membership talks with the European Union in 2005.

RULERS:

Abdul Mejid, AH1255-1277/1839-1861AD
Abdul Aziz, AH1277-1293/1861-1876AD
Murad V, AH1293/1876AD
Abdul Hamid II, AH1293-1327/1876-1909AD
Muhammad V, AH1327-1336/1909-1918AD
Muhammad VI, AH1336-1341/1918-1923AD
Republic, AH1341-/1923-AD

MONETARY SYSTEM:

1 Kurush (Gurush, Piastre) = 40 Para
1 Lira (Livre, Pound) = 100 Piastres

OTTOMAN EMPIRE

Treasury

Embossed toughra w/flower at r. of Abdul Mejid.

1840 First "Kaime" Issue, Series 1

Handwritten 12 1/2% Interest Bearing Notes

		Good	Fine	XF
1	**500 Kurush** AH1256 (1840). Handwritten. Abdul Mejid toughra.	—	—	—

1840 Second "Kaime" Issue, Series 2

		Good	Fine	XF
2	**50 Kurush** AH1256 (1840). Back: Seal of Saib Pasha. Reduced size. Rare.	—	—	—
3	**100 Kurush** AH1256 (1840). Back: Seal of Saib Pasha. Reduced size. Rare.	—	—	—
4	**250 Kurush** AH1256 (1840). Back: Seal of Saib Pasha. Reduced size. Rare.	—	—	—

1840 Third "Kaime" Issue, Series 3

		Good	Fine	XF
5	**500 Kurush** AH1256 (1840). Back: Seal of Saib Pasha. Rare.	—	—	—
6	**1000 Kurush** AH1256 (1840). Back: Seal of Saib Pasha. Rare.	—	—	—
7	**2000 Kurush** AH1256 (1840). Back: Seal of Saib Pasha. Rare.	—	—	—

1842 "Kaime" Issue

Printed 12 1/2% Interest Bearing Notes. Note: The year dates indicated are determined by the term of office of the Finance Minister's seal.

		Good	Fine	XF
8	**50 Kurush** AH1257 (1841). Black. Handwritten serial # and value. Seal of Safveti. 104x160mm. Rare. PC: Yellow.	—	—	—

		Good	Fine	XF
9	**100 Kurush** AH1257 (1841). Black. Handwritten serial # and value. Seal of Safveti. 105x165mm. Rare. PC: Blue.	—	—	—

1843 First "Kaime" Issue

10% Interest Bearing Note

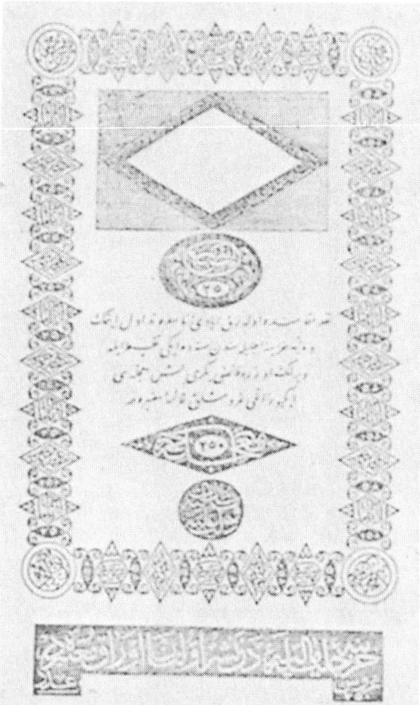

		Good	Fine	XF
10	**250 Kurush** AH1259 (1843). Black. 104x160mm. Rare. PC: Cream.	—	—	—

Color Abbreviation Guide

New to the *Standard Catalog of® World Paper Money* are the following abbreviations related to color references:

BC: Back color
PC: Paper color

1843 Second "Kaime" Issue, Series A

6% Interest Bearing Notes.

		Good	Fine	XF
11	**50 Kurush** AH1259 (1843). Handwritten serial #. Seal of Husnu. 98x152mm. Rare.	—	—	—
12	**100 Kurush** AH1259 (1843). Handwritten serial #. Seal of Husnu. 132x195mm. Rare.	—	—	—

1843 Third "Kaime" Issue, Series B

6% Interest Bearing Notes.

		Good	Fine	XF
13	**50 Kurush** AH1259-62 (1843-1846). Seal of Safveti. Rare.	—	—	—
14	**100 Kurush** AH1259-62 (1843-1846). Seal of Safveti. Rare.	—	—	—

1848 "Kaime" Issue, Series C

6% Interest Bearing Notes.

		Good	Fine	XF
15	**500 Kurush** AH1264-65 (1848-1849). Seal of Safveti. 185x110mm. Rare.	—	—	—
16	**1000 Kurush** AH1264-65 (1848-1849). Blue. Seal of Safveti. Rare. PC: Cream.	—	—	—

1852 "Kaime" Issue

6% Interest Bearing Notes.

		Good	Fine	XF
17	**250 Kurush** AH(1)268 (1852). Seal of Halid. 178x117mm. Rare.	—	—	—

1851-1852 ND "Kaime" Issue

		Good	Fine	XF
21	**10 Kurush** ND (1852). Octagonal control seal and seal of Nafiz, A. Muhtar or Safveti.	100	250	600

		Good	Fine	XF
22	**20 Kurush** ND (1852). Octagonal control seal and seal of Nafiz, A. Muhtar or Safveti. 94x151mm.	100	250	600

1853; 1854 ND "Kaime" Issue

		Good	Fine	XF
23	**10 Kurush** ND (1853-1854). Black on yellow and light green underprint. Seal of Safveti, A. Muhtar or Tevfik. 68x105mm.	70.00	175	450

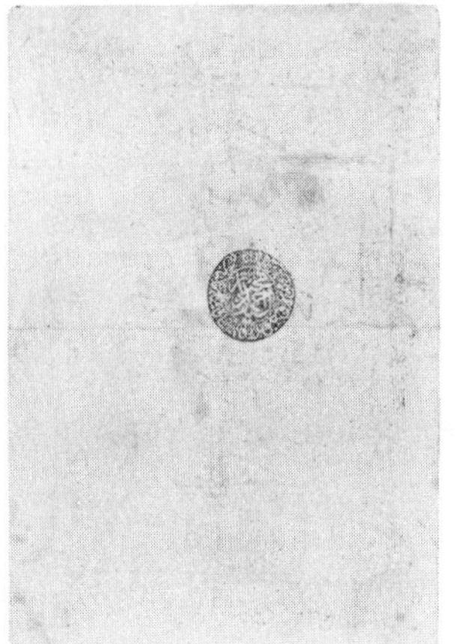

No.	Denomination	Good	Fine	XF
24	**20 Kurush** ND (1854). Black on yellow and light green underprint. Seal of Safveti, A. Muhtar or Tevfik. 89x130mm.	70.00	175	450

1855-1857 ND "Kaime" Issue

#25 and 26 issued for the Ordu Kaimesi (Army Corps).

No.	Denomination	Good	Fine	XF
25	**10 Kurush** ND (1854). Black on light green underprint. Seals of Safveti, Sefik or A. Muhtar, and "Orduyu Humayun". Rare.	—	—	—

No.	Denomination	Good	Fine	XF
26	**20 Kurush** ND (1855-1857). Black on light green (or golden) underprint. Seals of Safveti, Sefik or A. Muhtar, and "Orduyu Humayun 107x165mm. Vertical format.	70.00	175	450

1858 Issue, Series E

Engraved plates exist for notes #27-31 with the date AH1273, but no notes have been seen with the seal of Hasib (hexagonal shaped).

No.	Denomination	Good	Fine	XF
27	**100 Kurush** AH1274 (1858). Hexagonal seal of Hasib. 170x102mm.	—	—	—
28	**250 Kurush** AH1274 (1858). Hexagonal seal of Hasib. 173x103mm.	—	—	—
29	**500 Kurush** AH1274 (1858). Hexagonal seal of Hasib. 179x107mm. Rare.	—	—	—

No.	Denomination	Good	Fine	XF
30	**1000 Kurush** AH1274 (1858). Blue underprint. Hexagonal seal of Hasib. 184x110mm. Rare. PC: Yellow.	—	—	—
31	**5000 Kurush** AH1274 (1858). Hexagonal seal of Hasib. 185x110mm. Rare.	—	—	—

1858-1861 Issue

No.	Denomination	Good	Fine	XF
32	**20 Kurush** AH1273 (1858-1861). Brown. Back: 6 lines of text above AH1273. Seal of Savfeti. 176x126mm. Rare.	1,500	—	—

1861 First "Kaime" Issue

No.	Denomination	Good	Fine	XF
33	**10 Kurush** AH1277 (1861). Blue underprint. Back: 6 lines of text above AH1277. Seal of Tevfik. 122x173mm.	200	350	750
34	**20 Kurush** AH1277 (1861). Yellow underprint. Back: 6 lines of text above AH1277. Seal of Tevfik. 126x176mm.	200	350	750
35	**50 Kurush** AH1277 (1861). Red-brown on rose underprint. Back: 6 lines of text above AH1277. Seal of Tevfik. 133x184mm.	250	400	850
35A	**100 Kurush** AH1277 (1861). Blue underprint. Back: 6 lines of text above AH1277. Seal of Tevfik.	1,000	—	—

1861 Second "Kaime" Issue

No.	Denomination	Good	Fine	XF
36	**20 Kurush** AH1277. Black on gold underprint. Back: 5 lines of text above AH1277 within wreath. Seal of Tevfik.	10.00	25.00	85.00

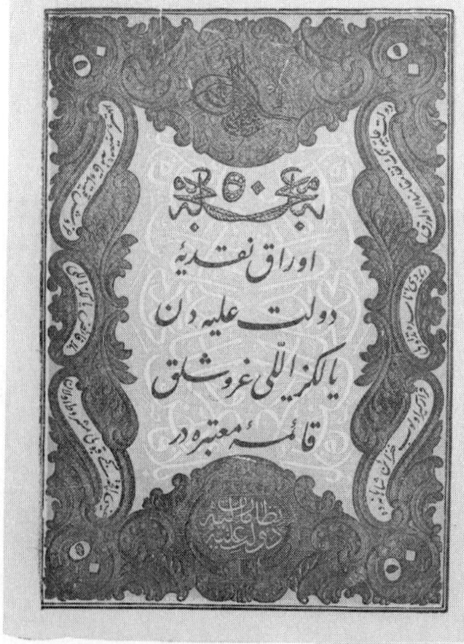

No.	Denomination	Good	Fine	XF
37	**50 Kurush** AH1277. Red-brown. Back: 5 lines of text above AH1277 within wreath. Seal of Tevfik.	15.00	35.00	100

		Good	Fine	XF
38	**100 Kurush** AH1277. Yellow underprint. Back: 5 lines of text above AH1277 within wreath. Seal of Tevfik. 133x185mm.	20.00	50.00	150

1861 Third "Kaime" Issue

		Good	Fine	XF
39	**50 Kurush** AH1277. Red-brown with rose underprint. Back: Toughra of Abdul Aziz without flower at right. 6 lines of text over AH date 1277 within wreath. Seal of Tevfik.	100	225	800

1861 Fourth "Kaime" Issue

		Good	Fine	XF
40	**50 Kurush** AH1277. Red-brown. Toughra of Abdul Aziz without flower at right. Back: 5 lines of new text over AH date 1277.	75.00	225	475

		Good	Fine	XF
41	**100 Kurush** AH1277. Gray underprint. Toughra of Abdul Aziz without flower at right. Back: 5 lines of new text over AH date 1277. 185x133mm.	35.00	85.00	225

Note: Most notes of AH1277 are without handwritten serial # at left and right bottom in oval gaps on face.

Banque Imperiale Ottomane

1876 First "Kaime" Issue

		Good	Fine	XF
42	**10 Kurush** AH1293 (1876). Lilac on light green underprint. Toughra of Murad V. Round AH1293 handstamp. Back: Oblong 1876 handstamp.	25.00	75.00	225
43	**20 Kurush** AH1293 (1876). Brown-lilac on yellow underprint. Toughra of Murad V. Round AH1293 handstamp. Back: Oblong 1876 handstamp.	20.00	60.00	175
44	**50 Kurush** AH1293 (1876). Brown-lilac on yellow underprint. Toughra of Murad V. Round AH1293 handstamp. Back: Oval 1876 handstamp. Vertical format.	35.00	65.00	250
45	**100 Kurush** AH1293 (1876). Brown-lilac on gray underprint. Toughra of Murad V. Round AH1293 handstamp. Back: Oblong 1876 handstamp.	35.00	65.00	275

Note: #42-45 usually occur on paper without watermark. Occasionally they are found on watermark or handmade (laid) paper. Seal of Galip on back.

1876 Second "Kaime" Issue

		Good	Fine	XF
46	**1 Kurush** AH1293-95 (1876-1878). Gray to gray-blue. Toughra of Abdul Hamid II. Back: Seal of Galip. Perforated edges.			
	a. With round AH1293 handstamp, box 1876 handstamp on back.	20.00	60.00	200
	b. With round AH1293 handstamp, box 1877 handstamp on back.	5.00	12.00	50.00
	c. With 15mm round AH1294 handstamp, straight line 1877 handstamp on back.	5.00	10.00	40.00
	d. With 18mm round AH1295 handstamp, straight line 1877 handstamp on back.	6.00	15.00	60.00

		Good	Fine	XF
47	**5 Kurush** AH1293-95 (1876-1878). Red-brown. Toughra of Abdul Hamid II. Back: Seal of Galip.			
	a. With round AH1293 handstamp, box 1876 handstamp on back.	7.50	25.00	75.00
	b. With round AH1293 handstamp, box 1877 handstamp on back. Without watermark.	6.00	15.00	50.00
	c. With round AH1294 handstamp, box 1877 handstamp on back.	6.00	15.00	50.00
	d. With round AH1295 handstamp, box 1877 handstamp on back.	7.50	25.00	75.00
48	**10 Kurush** AH1293-95 (1876-1878). Lilac on light green. Toughra of Abdul Hamid II. Back: Seal of Galip.			
	a. With round AH1293 handstamp, box 1876 or 1877 handstamp on back.	10.00	35.00	100
	b. With round AH1294 handstamp, box 1877 handstamp on back.	10.00	22.50	75.00
	c. With round AH1295 handstamp, box 1877 handstamp on back.	12.00	37.50	125
49	**20 Kurush** AH1293-95 (1876-1878). Brown-lilac and yellow. Toughra of Abdul Hamid II. Back: Seal of Galip.			
	a. With round AH1293 handstamp, box 1876 or 1877 handstamp on back.	10.00	35.00	90.00
	b. With round AH1294 handstamp, box 1877 handstamp on back.	10.00	20.00	75.00
	c. With round AH1295 handstamp, box 1877 handstamp on back.	10.00	35.00	100
50	**50 Kurush** AH1293-95 (1876-1878). Brown-lilac on yellow underprint. Toughra of Abdul Hamid II. Back: Seal of Galip. Vertical format.			
	a. With round AH1293 handstamp, box 1876 or 1877 handstamp on back.	7.50	25.00	75.00
	b. With round AH1294 handstamp, box 1877 handstamp on back.	6.00	15.00	50.00
	c. With round AH1295 handstamp, box 1877 handstamp on back.	7.50	25.00	75.00
51	**100 Kurush** AH1293-95 (1876-1878). Brown-lilac on gray underprint. Toughra of Abdul Hamid II. Back: Seal of Galip. Vertical format.			
	a. With round AH1293 handstamp, oval 1877 handstamp on back.	6.00	20.00	60.00
	b. With round AH1294 handstamp, oval 1877 handstamp on back.	6.00	15.00	50.00
	c. With round AH1295 handstamp, oval 1877 handstamp on back.	12.50	40.00	125

1877 "Kaime"Issue

		Good	Fine	XF
52	**50 Kurush** AH1294-95 (1877-1878). Black on light blue underprint. Horizontal format.			
	a. With round AH1294 handstamp, box 1877 handstamp on back.	35.00	75.00	225
	b. With round AH1295 handstamp, box 1877 handstamp on back.	35.00	60.00	200

		Good	Fine	XF
53	**100 Kurush** AH1294-95 (1877-1878). Black on orange-brown underprint. Horizontal format.			
	a. With round AH1294 handstamp, box 1877 handstamp on back.	10.00	30.00	75.00
	b. With round AH1295 handstamp, box 1877 handstamp on back.	12.00	35.00	85.00

Note: Prior to World War I and until 1933, the Banque Imperiale Ottomane issued notes that were not legal tender in the real sense of the word, since they were traded like stocks and shares at a rate in excess of their nominal values of 1, 5, 50, and 100 Pounds.

Law of 15 December AH1279 (1863)

		Good	Fine	XF
54	**200 Piastres** *L.1279.* Black, brown and green. Reimbursable in Constantinople.			
	a. Issued note. Rare.	—	—	—
	b. Handstamped. *ANNULÉ.*	350	800	1,750

		Good	Fine	XF
55	**200 Piastres** *L.1279.* 4 signatures and 2 seals. Reimbursable in Smyrna.			
	a. Issued note. Rare.	—	—	—
	b. Handstamped. *ANNULÉ.*	400	750	1,250
56	**200 Piastres** *L.1279.* Black, brown and green. Similar to #54 but with text: *Remboursable seulement en 10 Medjidies d'Argent* (payable only in 10 Medjidies in silver) at upper left.	Good	Fine	XF
	a. Rare.	—	—	—
	b. Handstamped. *ANNULÉ.* Arabic text at right.	—	—	—
57	**2 Medjidies D'or** *L.1279.* Green and brown on blue-gray underprint.	Good	Fine	XF
	a. Issued note.	500	1,000	2,500
	b. Handstamped: *ANNULÉ.*	—	—	—
	c. Pinhole cancelled: *PAYE.*	—	—	—
58	**5 Medjidies D'or** *L.1279.* Black and blue.	Good	Fine	XF
	a. Issued note. Rare.	—	—	—
	b. Handstamped: *ANNULÉ.*	—	—	—
	c. Pinhole cancelled: *PAYE.*	—	—	—

Law of 20 December AH1290 (1874)

		Good	Fine	XF
59	**1 Livre** *L.1290* (1873). Tan on brown and blue underprint. Denomination in 4 languages: Arabic, Armenian, Green and French. 2 signature varieties.			
	a. Issued note. Rare.	1,500	3,000	—
	b. Handstamped: *ANNULÉ.*	—	—	—

Law of December AH1299 (1882)

		Good	Fine	XF
60	**5 Livres** *L.1299* (1882). Black and blue on orange and green underprint. Toughra of Abdul Hamid at top center.			
	a. Issued note.	500	1,200	3,500
	s. Specimen.	—	Unc	600

1909 ND Issue

		Good	Fine	XF
61	**100 Livres** ND (AH1327/1909). Green. Toughra of Mehmed Reshad V. Rare.	—	—	—

1908 Issue

Law of 1 January AH1326 (1909)

		Good	Fine	XF
64	**5 Livres** AH1326 (1909). Gray blue on light green, brown and light red underprint. Toughra of Muhammad V. 2 signature varieties. BC: Brown. Printer: W&S.			
	a. Issued note.	75.00	250	650
	s. Specimen.	—	—	—
65	**50 Livres** AH1326 (1909). Brown on red, orange and yellow underprint. Toughra of Muhammad V. Printer: W&S.	Good	Fine	XF
	a. Issued note. Rare.	—	—	—
	s. Specimen.	—	—	—
66	**100 Livres** AH1326 (1909). Green. Toughra of Muhammad V. Printer: W&S.	Good	Fine	XF
	a. Issued note. Rare.	—	—	—
	s. Specimen.	—	—	—

Law of July AH1332 (1914)

		Good	Fine	XF
67	**1 Livre** July AH1332 (1914). Blue. Specimen.	—	—	—

Law of August AH1332 (1914)

		Good	Fine	XF
68	**1 Livre** Aug. AH1332 (1914). Brown on light green and light red underprint. BC: Gray-green.			
	a. Issued note.	10.00	25.00	100
	r. Remainder.	—	Unc	75.00

Dette Publique Ottomane

State Notes of the Ministry of Finance

Arabic sign. of Talat, Cahit and Cavid; English sign. of Janko, Taufing and Pritsch. Legend and numerals in Arabic, "Mali" year dates.

Law of 30 March AH1331 (1915-1916)

		VG	VF	UNC
69	**1 Livre** *L.1331.* Black on blue frame. Pink, green and brown underprint. Printer: G&D.	10.00	30.00	125
70	**5 Livres** *L.1331.* Red-brown and multicolor. Black text. Printer: G&D.	50.00	150	400

Law of 18 October AH1331 (1915-1916)

		VG	VF	UNC
71	**1/4 Livre** *L.1331.* Dark brown on green underprint. Brown text.	10.00	40.00	110
72	**1/2 Livre** *L.1331.* Black on pink underprint. Black text.	15.00	50.00	175

		VG	VF	UNC
73	**1 Livre** *L.1331.* Dark green on brown and multicolor underprint.	12.50	40.00	110

		VG	VF	UNC
74	**5 Livres** *L.1331.* Black on blue frame. Pink, blue and brown underprint. Printer: G&D.	30.00	110	400

Law of 16 December AH1331 (1915-1916)

#75-78 new denomination ovpt. on halved notes of earlier issue.

		Good	Fine	XF
75	**1/2 Livre** *L.1331.* Overprint: New denomination on #69. Left or right half. Rare.	—	—	—
76	**1/2 Livre** *L.1331.* Overprint: New denomination on #73. Left or right half. Rare.	—	—	—
77	**2 1/2 Livres** *L.1331.* Overprint: New denomination on #70. Left or right half. (Not issued). Rare.	—	—	—
78	**2 1/2 Livres** *L.1331.* Overprint: New denomination on #74. Left or right half. (Not issued). Rare.	—	—	—

Law of 22 December AH1331 (1912)

		VG	VF	UNC
79	**5 Piastres** *L.1331.* Black on brown underprint.			
	a. Issued note.	5.00	15.00	25.00
	s. Specimen. Twice BATTAL perforated.	—	110	150
80	**20 Piastres** *L.1331.* Black on purple underprint.			
	a. Issued note.	8.00	17.50	55.00
	s. Specimen. Twice BATTAL perforated.	—	150	210
81	**1/4 Livre** *L.1331.* Dark brown on green underprint.	4.00	15.00	50.00

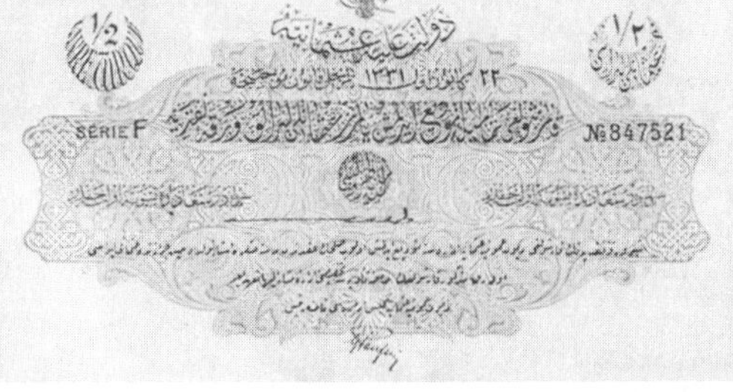

82	**1/2 Livre**	VG	VF	UNC
	L.1331. Black on pink underprint.	5.00	17.50	55.00
83	**1 Livre**	VG	VF	UNC
	L.1331. Black, brown frame on blue, green and pink underprint.	10.00	22.50	55.00
84	**1 Livre**	VG	VF	UNC
	L.1331. Black, brown frame on pale green and pink underprint.	10.00	22.50	55.00

Law of 23 May AH1332 (1916-1917)

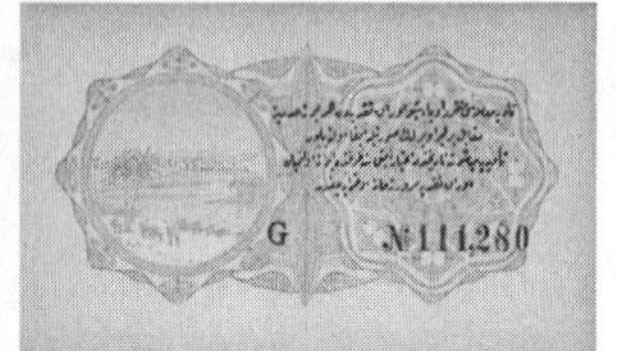

85	**1 Piastre**	VG	VF	UNC
	L.1332. Green. Black text. Back: River with palms and caravan at left.	2.00	4.00	25.00

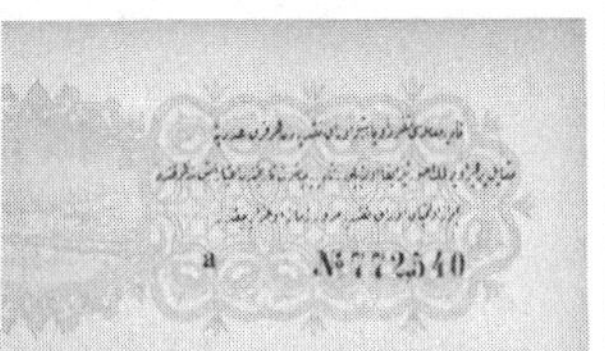

86	**2 1/2 Piastres**	VG	VF	UNC
	L.1332. Pink. Black text. Back: The Dardanelles at left.	2.00	4.00	25.00

Law of 6 August AH1332 (1916-1917)

87	**5 Piastres**	VG	VF	UNC
	L.1332. Olive underprint. Black text. Uniface. Watermark varieties. PC: White.	2.00	6.00	18.00
88	**20 Piastres**	VG	VF	UNC
	L.1332. Orange underprint. Black text. Uniface. PC: Purple.	4.00	11.00	35.00
89	**1/2 Livre**	VG	VF	UNC
	L.1332. Pink underprint. Black text. PC: Brownish.	9.00	18.00	55.00
90	**1 Livre**	VG	VF	UNC
	L.1332. Black. Green frame on blue-green and pink underprint.			
	a. Watermark: Hook pattern.	4.50	12.00	55.00
	b. Watermark: Small cruciferae.	6.00	18.00	70.00
91	**5 Livres**	VG	VF	UNC
	L.1332. Blue frame on multicolor underprint.	30.00	75.00	350
92	**10 Livres**	VG	VF	UNC
	L.1332. Light blue underprint. Brown frame. Black text.	40.00	125	475

93	**50 Livres**	Good	Fine	XF
	L.1332. Light blue and yellow-brown.			
	a. Watermark: Hook pattern.	150	500	2,500
	b. Watermark: Squared stars.	150	500	2,500
94	**500 Livres**	Good	Fine	XF
	L.1332. Rare.	—	—	—
95	**50,000 Livres**	Good	Fine	XF
	L.1332. Blue on pink underprint.			
	a. Issued note. Rare.	—	—	—
	s. Specimen.	—	Unc	75,000

Note: #95 was a deposit note made with the Imperial Ottoman Bank to cover the issue of #85 and #86.

Law of 4 February AH1332 (1916-1917)

96	**5 Piastres**	VG	VF	UNC
	L.1332. Green underprint. Black text. Uniface. PC: Bluish.	3.00	10.00	25.00
97	**20 Piastres**	VG	VF	UNC
	L.1332. Brown underprint. Black text. Uniface. PC: Brownish.	3.00	9.00	30.00
98	**1/2 Livre**	VG	VF	UNC
	L.1332. Red underprint. Black text. Uniface. PC: Violet.	6.00	17.00	65.00
99	**1 Livre**	VG	VF	UNC
	L.1332. Black on brown frame. Violet, pink and green underprint.			
	a. Watermark: Fork pattern.	4.50	12.00	55.00
	b. Watermark: Small cruciferae.	4.50	12.00	55.00

100	**2 1/2 Livres**	Good	Fine	XF
	L.1332. Orange and green.	50.00	110	475
101	**10 Livres**	Good	Fine	XF
	L.1332. Gray-brown on light gray underprint.	50.00	300	750
102	**25 Livres**	Good	Fine	XF
	L.1332. Maroon and gray on light blue underprint. BC: Brown.	110	400	900
103	**100 Livres**	Good	Fine	XF
	L.1332. Brown on light blue underprint. Rare.	—	—	—

Law of 28 March AH1333 (1917)

#	Denomination	Good	Fine	XF
104	**5 Livres**	Good	Fine	XF
	L.1333. Red-blue frame. Green and multicolor underprint.	35.00	90.00	250
105	**25 Livres**	Good	Fine	XF
	L.1333. Red. Brown frame. Light blue underprint.	100	300	725
106	**100 Livres**	Good	Fine	XF
	L.1333. Brown and red on light blue underprint. Back: Black text. BC: Brown. Rare.	250	—	—

Law of 28 March AH1334 (1918) First Issue

#	Denomination	Good	Fine	XF
107A	**100 Livres**	Good	Fine	XF
	L.1334. Toughra of Muhammad V. Rare.	—	—	—
107B	**500 Livres**	Good	Fine	XF
	L.1334. Toughra of Muhammad V. Rare.	—	—	—
107C	**1000 Livres**	Good	Fine	XF
	L.1334. Toughra of Muhammad V. Rare.	—	—	—

Law of 28 March AH1334 (1918) Second Issue

#	Denomination	Good	Fine	XF
108	**2 1/2 Livres**	Good	Fine	XF
	L.1334. Orange and blue-green. Toughra of Muhammad VI. Black text. Similar to #110.			
	a. Stamp: *2 eme emission.*	65.00	200	450
	b. Stamp: *3 eme emission.*	40.00	110	300
	c. Stamp: *5 eme emission.*	18.00	75.00	200
109	**5 Livres**	Good	Fine	XF
	L.1334. Brown frame. Toughra of Muhammad VI. Similar to #110.			
	a. Stamp: *2 eme emission.*	60.00	200	450
	b. Stamp: *6 eme emission.*	30.00	60.00	200

#	Denomination	Good	Fine	XF
110	**10 Livres**	Good	Fine	XF
	L.1334. Brown frame. Light blue underprint. Toughra of Muhammad VI. Black text.			
	a. 1st emission (no stamping).	60.00	200	550
	b. *2 eme emission* stamping.	75.00	225	750
	c. *3 eme emission* stamping.	90.00	225	700
	d. *4 eme emission* stamping.	45.00	150	450
	e. *5 eme emission* stamping.	45.00	150	450
	x. *2 eme emission.* Thought to be a British military counterfeit paper without watermark. Small "10s" in denomination in left border on back facing out instead of in.	10.00	35.00	125
111	**25 Livres**	Good	Fine	XF
	L.1334. Toughra of Muhammad VI.	110	450	900
112	**50 Livres**	Good	Fine	XF
	L.1334. Light gray on blue underprint. Toughra of Muhammad VI. BC: Yellow.	220	650	110
113	**100 Livres**	Good	Fine	XF
	L.1334. Dark brown on yellow underprint. Toughra of Muhammad VI. BC: Blue.	400	700	1,800
114	**500 Livres**	Good	Fine	XF
	L.1334. Blue on light blue. Toughra of Muhammad VI. Rare.	—	—	—
115	**1000 Livres**	Good	Fine	XF
	L.1334. Brown and dark blue. Toughra of Muhammad VI. Rare.	—	—	—

Postage Stamp Money

1917 Issue

#116-118 non-issued adhesive postage stamps (#116 and #117) and adhesive revenue stamp (#118) affixed to colored cardboard.

#	Denomination	VG	VF	UNC
116	**5 Para**	VG	VF	UNC
	ND (1917). Carmine. Gun emplacement. PC: Yellow or pink cardboard.	3.00	5.00	15.00

#	Denomination	VG	VF	UNC
117	**10 Para**	VG	VF	UNC
	ND (1917). Green. Hagia Sophia Mosque. PC: Blue, green, yellow or pink cardboard.	3.00	5.00	15.00

#	Denomination	VG	VF	UNC
118	**10 Para**	VG	VF	UNC
	ND (1917). Green and pink. Camel. PC: Blue, yellow or pink cardboard.	6.00	11.00	28.00

REPUBLIC

State Notes of the Ministry of Finance

1926 Issue

#119-125 Arabic legend and *Law #701 of 30 KANUNUEVVEL (AH)1341* (January 12, 1926) at center.

		VG	VF	UNC
119	**1 Livre**			
	L.1341 (1926). Green. Farmer with two oxen. Arabic legend and *Law #701 of 30 KANUNUEVVEL (AH)1341* at center. Back: Building. Watermark: Kemal Atatürk. Printer: TDLR.			
	a. Issued note.	120	400	1,200
	s1. Specimen. Punch hole cancelled.	—	—	300
	s2. Specimen. Without punch holes.	—	—	300

		Good	Fine	XF
120	**5 Livres**			
	L.1341 (1926). Blue. Bounding wolf at center, buildings at right. Arabic legend and *Law #701 of 30 KANUNUEVVEL (AH)1341* at center. Back: Bridge and city view. Watermark: Kemal Atatürk. Printer: TDLR.			
	a. Issued note.	250	800	2,500
	s. Specimen.	—	—	—

		Good	Fine	XF
121	**10 Livres**			
	L.1341 (1926). Purple. Bounding wolf at right. Arabic legend and *Law #701 of 30 KANUNUEVVEL (AH)1341* at center. Back: Rock mountain with bridge. Watermark: Kemal Atatürk. Printer: TDLR.			
	a. Issued note.	500	1,500	4,500
	s. Specimen.	—	Unc	500

		Good	Fine	XF
122	**50 Livres**			
	L.1341 (1926). Brown. Portrait Kemal Atatürk at right. Arabic legend and *Law #701 of 30 KANUNUEVVEL (AH)1341* at center. Back: Town view with mountains. Watermark: Kemal Atatürk. Printer: TDLR.			
	a. Issued note.	1,200	4,000	12,000
	s. Specimen.	—	Unc	1,000

		Good	Fine	XF
123	**100 Livres**			
	L.1341 (1926). Green. Portrait Kemal Atatürk at right. Arabic legend and *Law #701 of 30 KANUNUEVVEL (AH)1341* at center. Back: Ankara new town. Watermark: Kemal Atatürk. Printer: TDLR.			
	a. Issued note. Rare.	—	—	—
	s. Specimen.	—	Unc	1,250

		Good	Fine	XF
124	**500 Livres**			
	L.1341 (1926). Red-brown on blue and gold underprint. Mosque at left. Portrait Kemal Atatürk at right. Arabic legend and *Law #701 of 30 KANUNUEVVEL (AH)1341* at center. Back: Town view. Watermark: Kemal Atatürk. Printer: TDLR.			
	a. Issued note. Rare.	—	—	—
	s. Specimen.	—	Unc	1,500

		Good	Fine	XF
125	**1000 Livres**			
	L.1341 (1926). Dark blue. Portrait Kemal Atatürk at right. Arabic legend and *Law #701 of 30 KANUNUEVVEL (AH)1341* at center. Back: Railroad through mountain pass. Watermark: Kemal Atatürk. Printer: TDLR.			
	a. Issued note. Rare.	—	—	—
	s. Specimen.	—	Unc	1,750

Türkiye Cümhuriyet Merkez Bankasi

Central Bank of Turkey

Law of 11 Haziran 1930; Second Issue (1937-1939)

		VG	VF	UNC
126	**2 1/2 Lira**			
	L.1930 (25.4.1939). Green. Portrait President Kemal Atatürk at right. Back: Monument of the Square of the Nation. Watermark: Kemal Atatürk. Printer: TDLR.	70.00	200	600
127	**5 Lira**			
	L.1930 (15.10.1937). Dark blue. Portrait President Kemal Atatürk at right. Back: Monument of Security in Ankara. BC: Green. Watermark: Kemal Atatürk. Printer: TDLR.	100	300	900

		VG	VF	UNC
128	**10 Lira** *L.1930* (16.5.1938). Red-brown. Portrait President Kemal Atatürk at right. Back: Citadel of Ankara. Watermark: Kemal Atatürk. Printer: TDLR.	150	400	1,200
129	**50 Lira** *L.1930* (1.4.1938). Purple. Portrait President Kemal Atatürk at right. Back: Angora sheep and farmhouse. Watermark: Kemal Atatürk. Printer: TDLR.	250	800	2,400
130	**100 Lira** *L.1930* (1.3.1938). Dark brown. Portrait President Kemal Atatürk at right. Back: The Dardanelles. Watermark: Kemal Atatürk. Printer: TDLR.	700	2,000	—
131	**500 Lira** *L.1930* (15.6.1939). Olive. Portrait President Kemal Atatürk at right. Back: Rumeli-Hissar Palace. Watermark: Kemal Atatürk. Printer: TDLR. Rare.	—	—	—
132	**1000 Lira** *L.1930* (15.6.1939). Dark blue. Portrait President Kemal Atatürk at right. Back: Monument of Security in Ankara. Watermark: Kemal Atatürk. Printer: TDLR. Rare.	—	—	—

Law of 11 Haziran 1930; Interim Issue (1942-1944)

		VG	VF	UNC
133	**50 Kurus** *L.1930.* Dark brown on lilac. Portrait President I. Inonu at right. Back: Bank. Watermark: I. Inonu. Printer: BWC. (Not issued).	5.00	15.00	45.00

Note: #133 was on a ship bombed by the Germans while at Piraeus Harbor near the beginning of WW II. Subsequent retrieval by Greek citizens caused the Turkish government to cancel the issue and arrange for another instead. #134 was the result. All available examples of #133 were rescued from the sea; therefore, practically all show signs of salt water damage.

		VG	VF	UNC
134	**50 Kurus** *L.1930* (26.6.1944). Brown and green. Portrait President I Inonu at center. Back: Bank. Printer: Reichsdruckerei.	50.00	125	375

		VG	VF	UNC
135	**1 Lira** *L.1930* (25.4.1942). Lilac. Portrait President I. Inonu at right. Back: The Bosporus Strait. Watermark: I. Inonu. Printer: BWC.	60.00	170	500
136	**50 Lira** *L.1930.* Purple. Portrait President I. Inonu at right. Back: Angora sheep and farmhouse. Like #129. Watermark: I. Inonu. Printer: TDLR. (Not issued).	—	—	—

#137 Deleted, see #130.

		VG	VF	UNC
138	**500 Lira** *L.1930* (18.11.1940). Dark green. Portrait President I. Inonu at right. Back: Rumeli-Hissar Palace. Watermark: I. Inonu. Printer: TDLR.	—	—	—
139	**1000 Lira** *L.1930* (18.11.1940). Blue. Portrait President I. Inonu at right. Back: Monument of Security. Watermark: I. Inonu. Printer: TDLR.	—	—	—

Law of 11 Haziran 1930; Third Issue (1942-1947)

		VG	VF	UNC
140	**2 1/2 Lira** *L.1930* (27.3.1947). Dark brown on lilac underprint. Portrait President I. Inonu at right. Back: Bank. Watermark: I. Inonu. Printer: BWC.	5.00	35.00	125

		VG	VF	UNC
141	**10 Lira** *L.1930* (15.1.1942). Brown and red-brown. Portrait President I. Inonu at left. Back: Three peasant women. Printer: Reichsdruckerei.	10.00	75.00	200

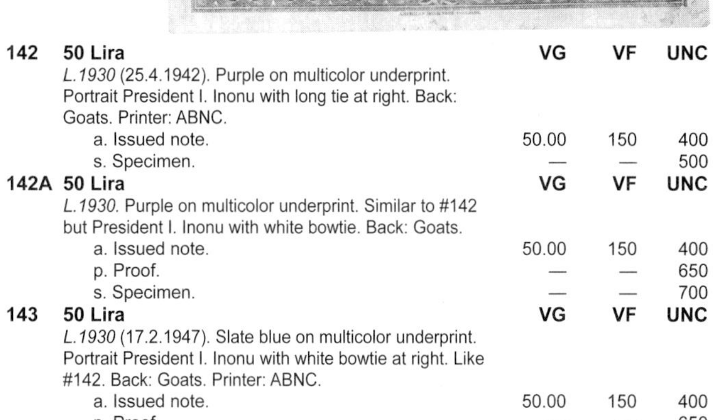

		VG	VF	UNC
142	**50 Lira** *L.1930* (25.4.1942). Purple on multicolor underprint. Portrait President I. Inonu with long tie at right. Back: Goats. Printer: ABNC.			
	a. Issued note.	50.00	150	400
	s. Specimen.	—	—	500
142A	**50 Lira** *L.1930.* Purple on multicolor underprint. Similar to #142 but President I. Inonu with white bowtie. Back: Goats.			
	a. Issued note.	50.00	150	400
	p. Proof.	—	—	650
	s. Specimen.	—	—	700
143	**50 Lira** *L.1930* (17.2.1947). Slate blue on multicolor underprint. Portrait President I. Inonu with white bowtie at right. Like #142. Back: Goats. Printer: ABNC.			
	a. Issued note.	50.00	150	400
	p. Proof.	—	—	650
	s. Specimen.	—	—	700

		VG	VF	UNC
144	**100 Lira**	VG	VF	UNC
	L.1930 (15.8.1942). Dark and light brown. Portrait President I. Inonu at left. Back: Girl with grapes. Printer: Reichsdruckerei.			
	a. Imprint: *REICHSDRUCKEREI* at bottom margin on face.	30.00	110	350
	b. Without imprint at bottom.	40.00	140	425
	c. Semi-finished note with imprint.	30.00	120	325
145	**500 Lira**	VG	VF	UNC
	L.1930 (24.4.1946). Dark olive on multicolor underprint. Portrait President I. Inonu at center. Back: Factory workers at machines. Printer: ABNC.			
	a. Issued note.	250	800	4,000
	p. Proof.	—	—	1,000
	s. Specimen.	—	—	1,350
146	**1000 Lira**	VG	VF	UNC
	L.1930 (24.4.1946). Blue on multicolor underprint. Portrait President I. Inonu at right. Back: Boy Scout buglers. Printer: ABNC.			
	a. Issued note.	—	—	—
	p. Proof.	—	—	1,750
	s. Specimen.	—	—	2,500

Law 11 Haziran 1930; Fourth Issue (1947-1948)

		VG	VF	UNC
147	**10 Lira**	VG	VF	UNC
	L.1930 (7.2.1947). Red on multicolor underprint. Portrait President I. Inonu with tie at right. Back: Fountain of Ahmed III. Printer: ABNC.			
	a. Issued note.	25.00	125	325
	s. Specimen.	—	—	275
148	**10 Lira**	VG	VF	UNC
	L.1930 (15.9.1948). Brown on multicolor underprint. Portrait President I. Inonu with bow tie at right. Similar to #147. Printer: ABNC.			
	a. Issued note.	20.00	100	275
	s. Specimen.	—	—	500

		VG	VF	UNC
149	**100 Lira**	VG	VF	UNC
	L.1930 (18.7.1947). Green on multicolor underprint. Portrait President I. Inonu at center. Back: Rumeli-Hissar Fortress. Printer: ABNC.			
	a. Issued note.	75.00	275	750
	s. Specimen.	—	—	1,000

Law 11 Haziran 1930; Fifth Issue (1951-1960)

		VG	VF	UNC
150	**2 1/2 Lira**	VG	VF	UNC
	L.1930 (15.7.1952). Lilac on multicolor underprint. Portrait President Kemal Atatürk at right. Back: Central bank. Watermark: Kemal Atatürk. Printer: TDLR.			
	a. Issued note.	80.00	250	800
	s. Specimen.	—	—	—
151	**2 1/2 Lira**	VG	VF	UNC
	L.1930 (3.1.1955). Lilac. Portrait President Kemal Atatürk at right. Back: Central bank. Like #150. BC: Brown. Watermark: Kemal Atatürk. Printer: TDLR.			
	a. Issued note.	50.00	150	500
	s. Specimen.	—	—	—
152	**2 1/2 Lira**	VG	VF	UNC
	L.1930 (1.7.1957). Lilac. Portrait President Kemal Atatürk at right. Back: Central bank. Like #150. BC: Red. Watermark: Kemal Atatürk. Printer: TDLR.			
	a. Issued note.	30.00	120	400
	s. Specimen.	—	—	—

		VG	VF	UNC
153	**2 1/2 Lira**	VG	VF	UNC
	L.1930 (15.2.1960). Lilac. Portrait President Kemal Atatürk at right. Back: Central bank. Like #150. BC: Light green. Watermark: Kemal Atatürk. Printer: TDLR.			
	a. Issued note.	25.00	90.00	300
	s. Specimen.	—	—	—

		VG	VF	UNC
154	**5 Lira**	VG	VF	UNC
	L.1930 (10.11.1952). Blue on multicolor underprint. Portrait President Kemal Atatürk at right. Series A-D. Back: Three peasant women with baskets of hazelnuts at center. BC: Blue. Watermark: Kemal Atatürk. Printer: BWC.			
	a. Issued note.	90.00	300	1,000
	s. Specimen.	—	—	—
155	**5 Lira**	VG	VF	UNC
	L.1930 (8.6.1959). Blue on multicolor underprint. Portrait President Kemal Atatürk at right. Series E. Back: Three peasant women with baskets of hazelnuts at center. Like #154. BC: Green. Watermark: Kemal Atatürk. Printer: BWC.			
	a. Issued note.	80.00	300	900
	s. Specimen.	—	—	—
156	**10 Lira**	VG	VF	UNC
	L.1930. Green. Portrait President Kemal Atatürk at right. Series A-J. Back: River and bridge. BC: Green. Watermark: Kemal Atatürk. Printer: TDLR.			
	a. Issued note.	150	600	2,400
	s. Specimen.	—	—	—

157 10 Lira

L.1930 (2.6.1952). Green. Portrait President Kemal Atatürk at right. Back: River and bridge. Like #156. BC: Brownish-red. Watermark: Kemal Atatürk. Printer: TDLR.

	VG	VF	UNC
a. Issued note.	80.00	250	900
s. Specimen.	—	—	—

158 10 Lira

L.1930 (24.3.1958). Green. Light blue and red. Portrait President Kemal Atatürk at right. Series V; Y. Back: River and bridge. Like #159. BC: Brown. Watermark: Kemal Atatürk. Printer: TDLR.

	VG	VF	UNC
a. Issued note.	300	1,000	3,000
s. Specimen.	—	—	—

159 10 Lira

L.1930. Green. Portrait President Kemal Atatürk at right. Similar to #157 but different guilloche. Series Z1-Z36. Back: River and bridge. BC: Green. Watermark: Kemal Atatürk. Without imprint.

	VG	VF	UNC
a. Issued note.	35.00	125	375
s. Specimen.	—	—	—

160 10 Lira

L.1930 (26.10.1953). Green. Portrait President Kemal Atatürk at right.. Series Z37-. Like #159. Back: River and bridge. BC: Red. Watermark: Kemal Atatürk.

	VG	VF	UNC
a. Issued note.	25.00	75.00	225
s. Specimen.	—	—	—

161 10 Lira

	VG	VF	UNC
L.1930 (25.4.1960). Green. Portrait President Kemal Atatürk at right. Series A; B. Different signature. Like #160. Back: River and bridge. BC: Green. Watermark: Kemal Atatürk. Without imprint.	25.00	75.00	225

162 50 Lira

L.1930 (1.12.1951). Brown on multicolor underprint. Portrait President Kemal Atatürk at right. Back: Statue of soldier holding rifle at left center. BC: Brown. Watermark: Kemal Atatürk. Printer: BWC.

	VG	VF	UNC
a. Issued note.	120	400	1,200
s. Specimen.	—	—	—

163 50 Lira

L.1930 (2.2.1953). Brown on multicolor underprint. Portrait President Kemal Atatürk at right. Like #162. Back: Statue of soldier holding rifle at left center. BC: Orange. Watermark: Kemal Atatürk. Printer: BWC.

	VG	VF	UNC
a. Issued note.	120	400	1,200
s. Specimen.	—	—	—

164 50 Lira

L.1930 (15.10.1956). Brown on multicolor underprint. Portrait President Kemal Atatürk at right. Like #162. Back: Statue of soldier holding rifle at left center. BC: Red. Watermark: Kemal Atatürk. Printer: BWC.

	VG	VF	UNC
a. Issued note.	200	700	2,400
s. Specimen.	—	40.00	125

165 50 Lira

L.1930 (1.10.1957). Brown on underprint. Portrait President Kemal Atatürk at right. Like #162. Back: Statue of soldier holding rifle at left center. BC: Blue-gray. Watermark: Kemal Atatürk. Printer: BWC.

	VG	VF	UNC
a. Issued note.	70.00	200	700
s. Specimen.	—	—	—

166 50 Lira

	VG	VF	UNC
L.1930 (15.2.1960). Purple on multicolor underprint. Portrait President Kemal Atatrk at right. Similar to #162 but different style of numbers. Reddish guilloche at center. Back: Statue of soldier holding rifle at left center. Watermark: Kemal Atatürk. Without imprint.	60.00	180	600

167 100 Lira

L.1930 (10.10.1952). Olive on multicolor underprint. Portrait President Kemal Atatürk at right. Back: Park with bridge in Ankara, Ankara fortress behind. Watermark: Kemal Atatürk. Printer: BWC.

	VG	VF	UNC
a. Issued note.	100	350	1,100
s. Specimen.	—	—	—

168 100 Lira

L.1930 (2.7.1956). Olive on multicolor underprint. Portrait President Kemal Atatürk at right. *SERI* H, I and J. Like #167. Back: Park with bridge in Ankara, Ankara fortress behind. BC: Light blue. Watermark: Kemal Atatürk. Printer: BWC.

	VG	VF	UNC
a. Issued note.	250	800	2,400
s. Specimen.	—	—	—

169 100 Lira

L.1930. Olive on multicolor underprint. Portrait President Kemal Atatürk at right. Without *SERI* in front of number. Different signature. Series K-P. Similar to #167. Back: Park with bridge in Ankara, Ankara fortress behind. Watermark: Kemal Atatürk. Without imprint.

	VG	VF	UNC
a. Issued note.	70.00	200	700
s. Specimen.	—	—	—

170 500 Lira

L.1930 (15.4.1953). Red-brown and multicolor. Portrait President Kemal Atatürk at right. Back: Byzantine hippodrome with mosque in Istanbul. Watermark: Kemal Atatürk. Printer: BWC.

	VG	VF	UNC
a. Issued note.	250	800	2,400
s. Specimen.	—	—	—

171 500 Lira

L.1930 (16.2.1959). Brown and multicolor. Portrait President Kemal Atatürk at right. Like #170, but without *SERI* in front of number. Different signature. Back: Byzantine hippodrome with mosque in Istanbul. Watermark: Kemal Atatürk. Printer: BWC.

	VG	VF	UNC
a. Issued note.	200	600	1,800
s. Specimen.	—	—	—

172 1000 Lira

L.1930 (15.4.1953). Purple. Portrait President Kemal Atatürk at right. Back: Bosporus and fortress. Watermark: Kemal Atatürk. Printer: BWC.

	VG	VF	UNC
a. Issued note.	250	800	2,400
s. Specimen. Red overprint: *SPECIMEN* and punch hole cancelled.	—	—	2,000

Türkiye Cümhuriyet Merkez Bankasi

Central Bank of Turkey

Law 11 Haziran 1930; 1961-1965 ND Issue

		VG	VF	UNC
173	**5 Lira** *L.1930* (25.10.1961). Blue with orange, blue and multicolor guilloche. Portrait of President Kemal Atatürk at right. Back: Three women with baskets of hazelnuts at center. BC: Blue. Watermark: Kemal Atatürk. Printer: DBM-A (without imprint).			
	a. Issue note.	25.00	100	300
	s. Specimen.	—	—	200

		VG	VF	UNC
174	**5 Lira** *L.1930* (4.1.1965). Blue-green. Portrait of President Kemal Atatürk at right. Back: Three women with baskets of hazelnuts at center. BC: Blue-gray. Watermark: Kemal Atatürk. Printer: DBM-A (without imprint).			
	a. Issued note.	15.00	60.00	180
	s. Specimen.	—	—	200

		VG	VF	UNC
175	**50 Lira** *L.1930* (1.6.1964). Brown on multicolor underprint. Portrait of President Kemal Atatürk at right. Three signatures. Back: Soldier holding rifle figure from the Victory statue at Ulus Square in Ankara at center. Watermark: Kemal Atatürk. Printer: DBM-A (without imprint).			
	a. Issued note.	10.00	30.00	100
	s. Specimen.	—	—	250
176	**100 Lira** *L.1930* (15.3.1962). Olive on orange and multicolor guilloche. Portrait of President Kemal Atatürk at right. Back: Youth Park with bridge in Ankara. Watermark: Kemal Atatürk. Printer: DBM-A (without imprint).	VG	VF	UNC
	a. Issued note.	50.00	200	600
	s. Specimen.	—	—	350

		VG	VF	UNC
177	**100 Lira** *L.1930* (1.10.1964). Olive on blue, lilac and multicolor guilloche. Portrait of President Kemal Atatürk at right. Different signature. Back: Youth Park with bridge in Ankara. Watermark: Kemal Atatürk. Printer: DBM-A (without imprint).			
	a. Issued note.	30.00	100	250
	s. Specimen.	—	—	350

		VG	VF	UNC
178	**500 Lira** *L.1930* (1.12.1962). Purple and brown on multicolor underprint. Portrait of President Kemal Atatürk at right. Back: Sultan Ahmet Mosque, the Obelisc and the Hippodrome in Istanbul. Watermark: Kemal Atatürk. Printer: DBM-A (without imprint).			
	a. Issued note.	40.00	130	400
	s. Specimen.	—	—	500

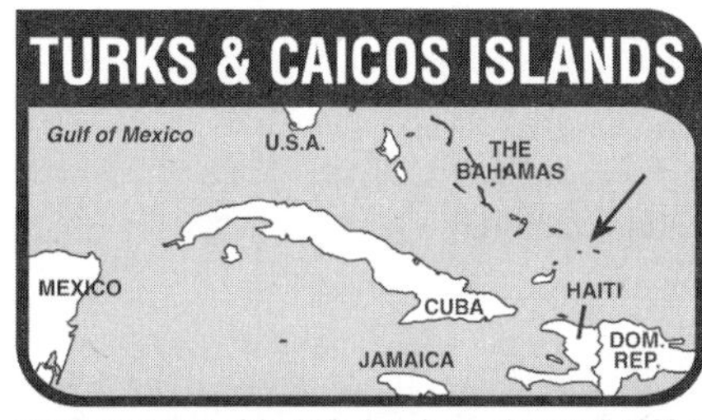

The British overseas territory of the Turks and Caicos Islands, are situated in the West Indies at the eastern end of the Bahama Islands, has an area of 430 sq. km. and a population of 22,350. Capital: Cockburn Town, on Grand Turk. The principal industry of the colony is the production of salt, which is gathered by raking. Salt, crayfish and conch shells are exported.The islands were part of the UK's Jamaican colony until 1962, when they assumed the status of a separate crown colony upon Jamaica's independence. The governor of The Bahamas oversaw affairs from 1965 to 1973. With Bahamian independence, the islands received a separate governor in 1973. Although independence was agreed upon for 1982, the policy was reversed and the islands remain a British overseas territory.

RULERS:

British

MONETARY SYSTEM:

1 Shilling = 12 Pence
1 Pound = 20 Shillings to 1971
1 Dollar (USA) = 100 Cents

BRITISH ADMINISTRATION

Government of the Turks and Caicos Islands

1903-1928 Issue

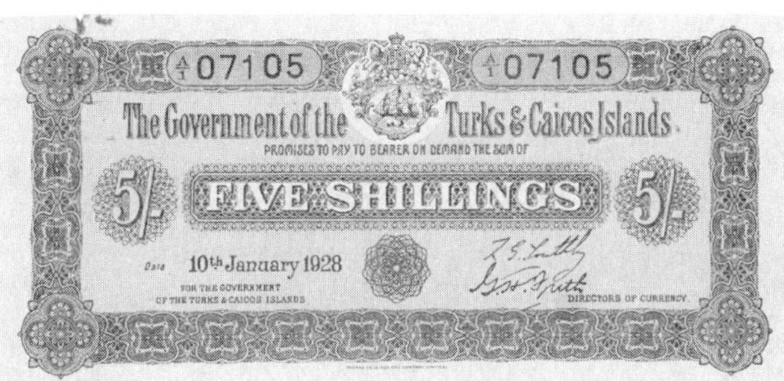

		Good	Fine	XF
1	**5 Shillings** 10.1.1928. Black and blue on yellow underprint. Arms at top center. Signature varieties. Back: Arms at center. BC: Blue. Printer: TDLR.	1,250	5,000	—

		Good	Fine	XF
2	**10 Shillings** 1.6.1924. Dark brown. Arms at top center. Signature varieties. Printer: TDLR.	1,750	6,000	—

		Good	Fine	XF
3	**1 Pound** 1903; 1918. Red on blue-green underprint. Arms at top center. Signature varieties. Printer: TDLR.			
	a. 2.12.1903. Hand dated and handsigned. Rare.	—	—	—
	b. 12.11.1918. Rare.	—	—	—
4	**1 Pound** 12.11.1928. Red and pink on yellow underprint. Arms at top center. Signature varieties. Uniface. Printer: TDLR. Rare.	—	—	—

Ukraine is bordered by Russia to the east, Russia and Belarus to the north, Poland, Slovakia and Hungary to the west, Romania and Moldova to the southwest and in the south by the Black Sea and the Sea of Azov. It has an area of 603,700 sq. km. and a population of 45.99 million. Capital: Kyiv (Kiev). Coal, grain, vegetables and heavy industrial machinery are major exports. The territory of Ukraine has been inhabited for over 30,000 years. As the result of its location, Ukraine has served as the gateway to Europe for millennia and its early history has been recorded by Arabic, Greek, Roman, as well as Ukrainian historians.Ukraine was the center of the first eastern Slavic state, Kyivan Rus, which during the 10th and 11th centuries was the largest and most powerful state in Europe. Weakened by internecine quarrels and Mongol invasions, Kyivan Rus was incorporated into the Grand Duchy of Lithuania and eventually into the Polish-Lithuanian Commonwealth. The cultural and religious legacy of Kyivan Rus laid the foundation for Ukrainian nationalism through subsequent centuries. A new Ukrainian state, the Cossack Hetmanate, was established during the mid-17th century after an uprising against the Poles. Despite continuous Muscovite pressure, the Hetmanate managed to remain autonomous for well over 100 years. During the latter part of the 18th century, most Ukrainian ethnographic territory was absorbed by the Russian Empire. Following the collapse of czarist Russia in 1917, Ukraine was able to bring about a short-lived period of independence (1917-20), but was reconquered and forced to endure a brutal Soviet rule that engineered two artificial famines (1921-22 and 1932-33) in which over 8 million died. In World War II, German and Soviet armies were responsible for some 7 to 8 million more deaths. Although final independence for Ukraine was achieved in 1991 with the dissolution of the USSR, democracy remained elusive as the legacy of state control and endemic corruption stalled efforts at economic reform, privatization, and civil liberties. A peaceful mass protest "Orange Revolution" in the closing months of 2004 forced the authorities to overturn a rigged presidential election and to allow a new internationally monitored vote that swept into power a reformist slate under Viktor Yushchenko. Subsequent internal squabbles in the Yushchenko camp allowed his rival Viktor Yanukovych to stage a comeback in parliamentary elections and become prime minister in August of 2006. An early legislative election, brought on by a political crisis in the spring of 2007, saw Yuliya Tymoshenko, as head of an "Orange" coalition, installed as a new prime minister in December 2007.

RULERS:

Polish, 1569-1654
Polish and Russian, 1654-1671
Polish, Ottoman and Russian, 1672-1684
Russian, 1685-1794
Austrian (Western Ukraine), 1774-1918
Russian, 1793-1917

MONETARY SYSTEM:

1 Karbovanets (Karbovantsiv) = 2 Hryven
1917-1920 = 200 Shahiv
1 Karvovanets (Karbovantsiv) = 1 Russian Ruble, 1991-96
1 Hryvnia (Hryvni, Hryven) = 100,000 Karbovantsiv, 1996-

AUTONOMOUS REPUBLIC

УКРАЇНСЬКА НАРОДНА РЕСПУБЛІКА

Ukrainian National Republic

Central Rada

1917 Issue

#		Good	Fine	XF
1	**100 Karbovantsiv** 1917. Brown, orange and yellow. Back: Inscription in Polish, Russian and Yiddish.			
	a. Printing same way up on both sides. Rare.	—	—	2,000
	b. Back inverted.	30.00	100	200

ЗНАК ДНРЖАВНОЇ СКАРБНИЦІ

State Treasury Notes

1918 (ND) Issue

#		VG	VF	UNC
2	**25 Karbovantsiv** ND (1918). Green. Man standing with spade at left, woman with sheafs at right. Without serial # prefix letters. (Issued in Kiev).			
	a. With text: КРЕДИТОВИМ.	15.00	30.00	50.00
	b. With text: КРЕДІТОВИМИ.	20.00	50.00	125

#		VG	VF	UNC
3	**25 Karbovantsiv** ND (1918). Green. Man standing with spade at left, woman with sheafs at right. Like #2 but serial # prefix: *AO 180* or *AO 188*. (Issued in Odessa).	100	200	500
4	**50 Karbovantsiv** ND (1918). Green. Man standing with spade at left, woman with sheagfs at right. Similar to #2. (Issued in Kiev).			
	a. With text: КРЕДИТОВИМ.	50.00	100	200
	b. With text: КРЕДИТОВИМИ.	10.00	25.00	75.00

#		VG	VF	UNC
5	**50 Karbovantsiv** ND (1918). Green. Like #4 but serial # prefix letters: *AKI* or *AKII*. (Issued in Kiev).			
	a. Issued note.	5.00	10.00	20.00
	x. Error, with back only in red. (AKII).	10.00	20.00	50.00

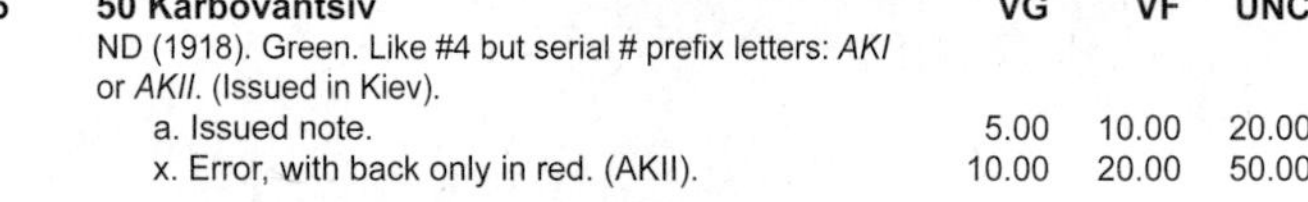

#		VG	VF	UNC
6	**50 Karbovantsiv** ND (1918). Green. Like #4 but with serial # prefix letters: *AO*. (Issued in Odessa).			
	a. Serial # to 209.	3.00	7.00	15.00
	b. Serial # from 210 (issued by Gen. Denikin and labeled as false by the Ukrainian Government).	3.00	7.00	15.00

Postage Stamp Currency

1918; 1919 ND Emergency Issue

#7-11 postage stamp designs, Michel catalogue #1-5 or Scott #67-71, printed on ungummed cardboard with trident arms over black text within single line or double line border.

#	Denomination	VG	VF	UNC
7	**10 Shahiv**	VG	VF	UNC
	ND (1918). Yellow-brown. Arms.	3.00	8.00	15.00
8	**20 Shahiv**	VG	VF	UNC
	ND (1918). Dark brown. Peasant.	3.00	8.00	15.00

#	Denomination	VG	VF	UNC
9	**30 Shahiv**	VG	VF	UNC
	ND (1918). Head of Ceres.			
	a. Ultramarine.	3.00	8.00	15.00
	b. Gray-violet.	5.00	10.00	25.00

#	Denomination	VG	VF	UNC
10	**40 Shahiv**	VG	VF	UNC
	ND (1918). Green. Trident arms.			
	a. Perforated.	3.00	7.00	15.00
	b. Imperforate.	17.50	30.00	70.00
10A	**5 Karbowanez**	VG	VF	UNC
	ND (1919). Green. Trident arms. Requires conformation.	—	—	—
11	**50 Shahiv**	VG	VF	UNC
	ND (1918). Red. Wreath around value *50*.			
	a. Perforated.	3.00	6.00	15.00
	b. Imperforate.	20.00	40.00	75.00
	x. Counterfeit.	1.50	3.00	5.00

3.6% БІЛЕТ ДЕРЖАВНОЇ СКАРБНИЦІ

Bond Certificates, 3.6%

1918 Issue

#12-15 bond certificates with interest coupons.

#	Denomination	Good	Fine	XF
12	**50 Hryven**	Good	Fine	XF
	1918. Green and brown.	5.00	15.00	40.00

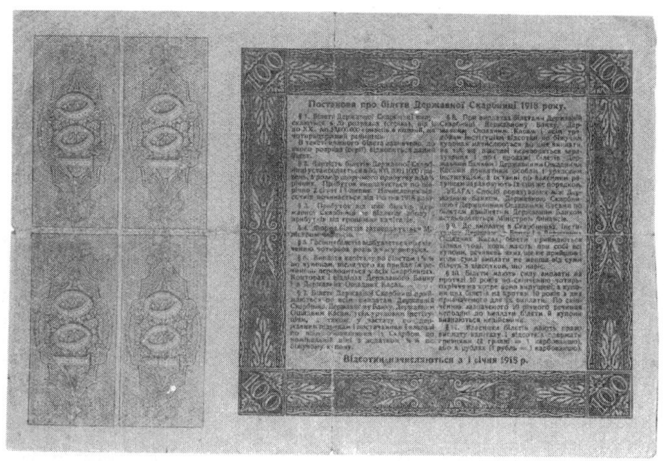

#	Denomination	Good	Fine	XF
13	**100 Hryven**	Good	Fine	XF
	1918. Brown on green and red.	3.00	15.00	40.00
14	**200 Hryven**	Good	Fine	XF
	1918. Blue.	3.00	10.00	25.00
15	**1000 Hryven**	Good	Fine	XF
	1918. Brown on yellow-brown.	3.00	15.00	40.00

Note: Bonds complete with six coupons are worth triple the market value indicated.

Interest Coupons

1918 Issue

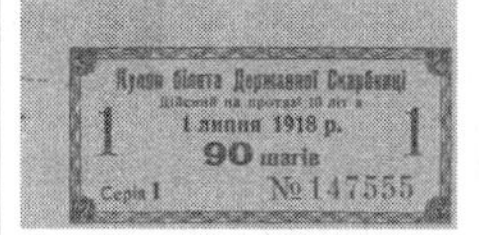

#	Denomination	Good	Fine	XF
16	**90 Shahiv**	Good	Fine	XF
	1918. Black on pale green underprint. BC: Red on pale green underprint. Cut out from bond certificates #12.	1.00	2.00	4.00
17	**1 Hryven 80 Shahiv**	Good	Fine	XF
	1918. Red-brown. Cut out of bond certificate #13.	1.00	2.00	4.00

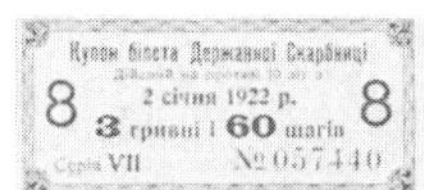

#	Denomination	Good	Fine	XF
18	**3 Hryven 60 Shahiv**	Good	Fine	XF
	1918. Black on light blue and gray underprint. BC: Pale red on light blue underprint. Cut out of bond certificate #14.	1.00	2.00	4.00

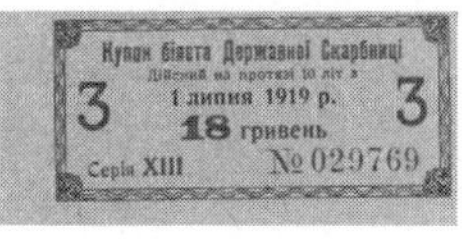

#	Denomination	Good	Fine	XF
19	**18 Hryven**	Good	Fine	XF
	1918. Yellow-brown. Cut out of bond certificate #15.	1.00	2.00	4.00

ДЕРЖАВНИЙ КРЕДИТОВИЙ БІЛЕТ

State Credit Notes

1918 Issue

#	Denomination	VG	VF	UNC
20	**2 Hryven**	VG	VF	UNC
	1918. Green. Arms at right.			
	a. Yellowish background. Serial # prefix letter: *A*.	3.00	6.00	10.00
	b. Brown background. Serial # prefix letter: *Б*.	5.00	10.00	15.00
	c. Brown background. Serial # prefix letter: *B*.	400	750	1,500

21	10 Hryven	VG	VF	UNC
	1918. Red-brown. Arms at upper center.			
	a. Serial # prefix letter: *A*.	5.00	10.00	20.00
	b. Serial # prefix letter: Б.	8.00	15.00	30.00
	c. Serial # prefix letter: В.	—	—	—

22	100 Hryven	VG	VF	UNC
	1918. Blue-violet. Farmer's wife at left, worker at right, arms at center.			
	a. Blue background. Serial # prefix letter: *A*.	10.00	25.00	50.00
	b. Gray-violet underprint. Serial # prefix letter: Б (not issued). Rare.	—	—	—

23	500 Hryven	VG	VF	UNC
	1918. Green and orange. Ceres head at upper center, arms at left and right.	15.00	30.00	60.00

24	1000 Hryven	VG	VF	UNC
	1918. Blue on orange and yellow underprint.	20.00	40.00	80.00

		VG	VF	UNC
25	**2000 Hryven** 1918. Red on blue underprint. Back: Arms in underprint at center.	30.00	60.00	120

1920 Issue

#26-28 Austrian printing.

		VG	VF	UNC
26	**50 Hryven** 1920. Black and blue. Allegorical figures at left and right, arms at upper center portrait of Petro Loroshenko in cartouche at left, arms above. Proof. Rare.	—	—	—
27	**50 Hryven** 1920. Brown. Proof. Rare.	—	—	—
28	**1000 Hryven** 1920. Gray and orange. Proof. Rare.	—	—	—

Note: It is reported that only 2 sets of #26-28 exist.

5% КР. ОБЯЗАТ. ГОСУД. КАЗНАЧ.

Russian State Debenture Bonds, 5%

1918 ND Issue

#29-34 exist with different stamps of the State Bank branches. Validated October - December 1918.

		Good	Fine	XF
29	**1000 Rubles** ND (1918). Red-brown on gray.	6.00	15.00	25.00

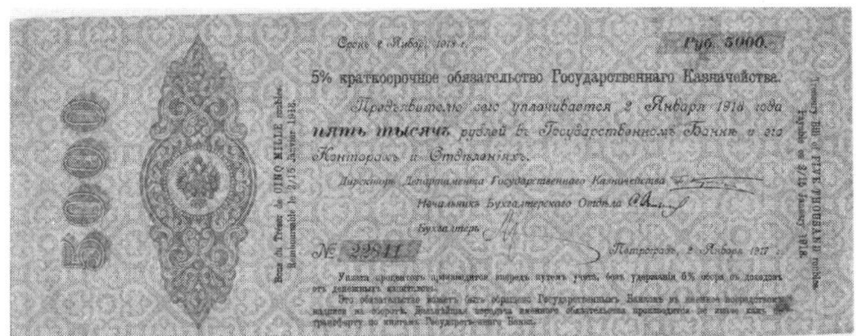

		Good	Fine	XF
30	**5000 Rubles** ND (1918).	9.00	17.50	35.00
31	**10,000 Rubles** ND (1918).	10.00	22.50	40.00
32	**25,000 Rubles** ND (1918).	10.00	25.00	50.00
33	**50,000 Rubles** ND (1918).	15.00	35.00	75.00
34	**500,000 Rubles** ND (1918).	—	—	—

ЗНАК ДЕРЖАВНОЇ СКАРБНИЦІ

State Treasury Notes

1918 ND Issue

		VG	VF	UNC
35	**1000 Karbovantsiv** ND (1918). Deep brown and multicolor on tan underprint. Black signature. Back: Trident arms at top center between two standing allegorical women supporting frame with value. BC: Brown.			
	a. Watermark: Wavy lines.	10.00	20.00	50.00
	b. Zigzag lines of varnish printed on paper.	5.00	15.00	40.00

Semen Petlyura Directorate

1918-1919 Issue

NOTE: #S293 was issued under the Ukrainian Socialist Soviet Republic and is not considered to be a truly independent issue. It is similar to #36 but is w/ithout serial #, only a block #.

		VG	VF	UNC
36	**10 Karbovantsiv** ND (1919). Brown or red-brown. 3 serial # varieties. See also #S293 (Russia-Vol. I). PC: Gray.			
	a. Watermark: Spades.	20.00	40.00	80.00
	b. Watermark: Wavy lines.	20.00	40.00	80.00
	c. Watermark: Linked stars.	20.00	50.00	100
	d. Unwatermarked paper.	30.00	60.00	150

Note: #S293 was issued under the Ukrainian Socialist Soviet Republic and is not considered to be a truly independent issue. It is similar to #36 but has no serial #, only a block #.

		VG	VF	UNC
37	**25 Karbovantsiv** 1919. Violet-brown. Arms and Cossack at upper center. With or without serial #. Back: Conjoined heads facing right at center. BC: Brown.			
	a. Issued note.	10.00	20.00	40.00
	b. Issued note with mostly blank back.	—	150	—

		VG	VF	UNC
38	**100 Karbovantsiv** 1918. Brown and gray-green. Small wreath with Cossack at upper center.			
	a. Watermark: Stars. 2 serial # varieties.	10.00	20.00	30.00
	b. Watermark: Spades. 2 serial # varieties.	20.00	40.00	80.00

39	250 Karbovantsiv	VG	VF	UNC
	1918. Brown and gray on olive underprint. Arms at center. Back: Arms at left.			
	a. Large letters; serial # prefix: АА, АБ, АГ.	20.00	40.00	80.00
	b. Small letters; serial # prefix: АБ, АВ, АГ.	20.00	40.00	80.00

#40 has been merged into #35.

РОЗМІННИЙ ЗНАК ДЕРЖАВНОЇ СКАРБНИЦІ

State Notes

1920 ND Issue

41	5 Hryven	VG	VF	UNC
	ND (1920). Black on gray underprint. Back: Arms in square design at left.			
	a. Issued note.	15.00	30.00	60.00
	x. Error: ГИБЕНЬ. (without Р).	35.00	100	250

GERMAN OCCUPATION - WW II

ЭМИССИОННЫЙ БАНК

Emission Bank

Kiev

1941 Issue

#42-48 were printed by the German government for use in occupied areas during WW II, but the Germans rejected the idea of Russian language on occupation notes and instead issued the Ukrainian occupation notes of the Zentralnotenbank type. Proofs perforated: *DRUCKPROBE.* Note: Technically #42-48 were not intended as occupation notes for Ukraine. Instead, they were for possible issue in an area the Germans call "Ostland" which was to be administered from Kiev.

42	1 Ruble	VG	VF	UNC
	1941. Brown. Light brown and green underprint.			
	a. Regular serial #.	—	—	—
	p. Proof.	—	—	1,000
43	3 Rubles	VG	VF	UNC
	1941. Violet and green underprint. Proof.	—	—	1,000
44	5 Rubles	VG	VF	UNC
	1941. Violet and green underprint. Proof.	—	—	1,000
45	1 Chervonets	VG	VF	UNC
	1941. Blue, light blue and green underprint.			
	a. Regular serial #.	—	—	—
	p. Proof.	—	—	1,000
46	3 Chervontsa	VG	VF	UNC
	1941. Green and violet underprint. Proof.	—	—	1,000
47	5 Chervontsiv	VG	VF	UNC
	1941. Brown. Green and violet underprint.			
	a. Regular serial #.	500	1,500	4,000
	p. Proof.	—	—	1,000
48	10 Chervontsiv	VG	VF	UNC
	1941. Brown. Green and brown underprint. Proof.	—	—	1,000

Zentralnotenbank Ukraine

Ukrainian Central Bank

1942 Issue

49	1 Karbowanez	VG	VF	UNC
	10.3.1942. Olive.	10.00	25.00	50.00

50	2 Karbowanez	VG	VF	UNC
	10.3.1942. Young boy wearing fur cap at right. (Not issued).	—	3,500	5,000

Reportedly most notes were destroyed when Ukrainian partisans destroyed a Nazi train transporting these notes from Germany to the Ukraine.

51	5 Karbowanez	VG	VF	UNC
	10.3.1942. Brown-violet. Portrait young girl at right.	20.00	40.00	60.00

52	10 Karbowanez	VG	VF	UNC
	10.3.1942. Red-brown. Farmer's wife at right.	25.00	50.00	80.00

53	20 Karbowanez	VG	VF	UNC
	10.3.1942. Gray-brown. Industrial worker at right.	25.00	60.00	100

54	50 Karbowanez	VG	VF	UNC
	10.3.1942. Green and brown. Miner at right.	50.00	90.00	175

55	100 Karbowanez	VG	VF	UNC
	10.3.1942. Blue. Portrait seaman at right.	60.00	90.00	175

56	200 Karbowanez	VG	VF	UNC
	10.3.1942. Olive. Peasant woman at right.	80.00	120	275

57	500 Karbowanez	VG	VF	UNC
	10.3.1942. Violet. Portrait chemist at right.	100	150	425

UNITED STATES OF AMERICA

The area of the North American continent currently controlled by the United States of America was originally inhabited by numerous groups of Indian tribes. Some of these groups settled in particular areas, creating permanent settlements, while others were nomadic, traveling great distances and living off the land. English explorers John and Sebastian Cabot reached Nova Scotia in what is today Canada in 1497; in 1534 the French gained a foothold with the explorations of Jacques Cartier. In 1541 the Spanish explorer Coronado traversed the south central portion of the country in what was to become the states of New Mexico, Texas, Nebraska and Oklahoma. In 1542 another Spaniard, Juan Cabrillo navigated north from Mexico along the Pacific coastline to California. The Spanish set up the first permanent settlement of Europeans in North America at St. Augustine, Florida in 1565. In 1607 the English settled in Jamestown, Virginia, and in 1620 at Plymouth, Massachusetts. This was followed closely by Dutch settlements in Albany and New York in 1624, and in 1638 the Swedes arrived in Delaware. From their foothold in Canada, French explorers pushed inland through the Great Lakes. Jean Nicolet explored what was to become Wisconsin in 1634, and in 1673 explorers Marquette and Joliet reached Iowa. In the 1650s the Dutch won the Swedish lands, and in 1664 the English gained control of the Dutch lands, thus giving the English control all along the Atlantic Coast. The resulting thirteen British colonies; New Hampshire, Vermont, Massachusetts, Rhode Island, Connecticut, New York, Pennsylvania, Delaware, Maryland, Virginia, North Carolina, South Carolina and Georgia formed the nucleus of what would become the United States of America. From this point on tensions grew between the English, who could not expand westward from their settlements along the Atlantic Coast, and the French who had settled inland into the Ohio river valley. This dispute ended in 1763 after a war with the French loosing control of lands east of the Mississippi river. Manufacturing, textiles and other industry was developing at this time, and by 1775 about one-seventh of the world's production of raw iron came from the colonies. From 1771-1783 the war for American Independence was fought by the colonists against the English, and settled by the Peace of Paris in 1783. Americans gained control of lands south of the St. Lawrence and Great Lakes, and east of the Mississippi, with the exception of Florida which would remain under Spanish control until 1821. At the close of the war, the population was about 3 million, many of whom lived on self-sufficient family farms. Fishing, lumbering and the production of grains for export were becoming major economic endeavors. The newly independent states formed a loose confederation, but in 1787 approved the Constitution of the United States which is the framework for the goverment today. In 1789 it's first president, George Washington was elected, and the capitol was set up in New York City. In 1800 the capitol was moved to a planned city, Washington, D.C. where it remains. Westward expansion was an inevitability as population grew. French territory west of the Mississippi, stretching to the northern Pacific was purchased in 1804 under the presidency of Thomas Jefferson, who then sent out Lewis and Clark on expedition of discovery. Spain granted independence to Mexico in 1821, which included lands which would become the states of California, New Mexico, Arizona and Texas. From 1836-1845 Texas was an independent republic, not joining the United States until 1845. Upon losing a war with the United States, Mexico ceded California (including most of Arizona and New Mexico) to the United States in 1848. Gold was discovered in California that year, and western migration took off on overland wagon trains or around-the-horn sail and steam ships. Hawaii came under U.S. protection in 1851. As the country developed in the 19th century, the northern states increased in commerce and industry while the southern states developed a vast agricultural base through the use of slave labor. Northern political and social threats to slavery lead twelve southern states to secede from the Union in 1860 forming the Confederate States of America. The ensuing Civil War lasted until 1865, at which time slavery was abolished and the States reunited. In 1867 Alaska was purchased from Russia. The transcontinental railroad was completed in 1869. The central region of the country west of the Mississippi River and east of the Rocky Mountains was the last to be developed, beginning after the Civil War, with the establishment of cattle ranches and farms. Between 1870 and 1891 the nomadic Native American population clashed with settlers and federal troops. By 1891 the Native Americans were confined to reservations. At the close of the 19th century the United States embarked on a colonial mission of its own, with advances into Cuba, Puerto Rico, Panama, Nicaragua and the Philippines. This resulted in the Spanish-American War which was quickly decided, ending Spanish colonial dominance, and signaling the rise of the United States as a world power. Slow to enter both World Wars of the 20th century, it was a major contributor to the conclusion of both, making it one of the major nations of the 20th century. As the Spanish Milled Dollar achieved widespread acceptance throughout the American colonial period, it was a natural choice on which to base a national coinage system. The Spanish Milled Dollar had already been accorded legal tender status in several colonies, notably Massachusetts, Connecticut and Virginia and the others used it. Each colony had its own shilling exchange for a Spanish Milled Dollar ranging from 6 to 32 1/2 shillings. When the Continental Congress issued its first paper money to finance the revolution, the notes themselves promised to pay their face value in *Spanish milled dollars or the Value thereof in Gold or Silver.* The first quasi-official American coinage, the 1776 Continental *Dollar,* while not thus denominated, was struck in the size of the Spanish Milled Dollar. While the denomination of *One Dollar* may have been a natural choice for a national monetary system, the problem of making change for that dollar was not. In 1782, Robert Morris, superintendent of Finance, proposed a coinage system based on a unit of 1/1440th part of a dollar which, he argued, would reconcile the different *official* values of the Spanish Milled Dollar in all the states. A year later, he submitted a series of copper and silver pattern coinage to Congress based on the basic unit of a quarter-grain of silver. The patterns are known to collectors today as the Nova Constellatio coinage. Other leading financiers saw the traditional division of the Spanish Milled Dollar into *eight reales,* or *bits* as they were familiarly known, as too unwieldy. Gouverneur Morris, assistant financier of the government then operating under the Articles of Confederation, proposed the simple solution of a decimal coinage ratio. With the support of Thomas Jefferson, who remarked, "The most easy ratio of multiplication and division is that of ten," and George Washington, who called it, "indispensably necessary," the decimal coinage proposal won out over more complicated plans. The dollar-decimal system was adopted on July 6, 1785, creating a silver dollar, with fractional coins, also in silver, in denominations of half (50¢), quarter (25¢), tenth (10¢) and twentieth (5¢) parts of a dollar, and copper pieces in denominations of 1/100th (1¢) and 1/200th (1/2¢) of a dollar. Continental Currency: A total of 11 separate issues of paper currency were authorized by the Continental Congress to finance the war for American independence. The first issue was dated May 10, 1775, the date of the first session of the Continental Congress; the final issue was by Resolution of Jan. 14, 1779. In all, according to early American currency expert Eric P. Newman, a total of $241,552,780 worth of Continental Currency was issued. Backed only by faith in the success of the Revolution, there was according to a Resolution of Congress a 40-to-1 devaluation by 1780, and in the end the bills were only redeemable at 1/100th of face value in interest-bearing bonds.

MONETARY SYSTEM:

1 Dollar = 100 Cents
1 Dollar = 100 Cents

Colonial & Confederation Period U.S. Constitutional Period

One Dollar was equal to: 1 Dollar = 100 Cents
6 New England Shillings 12 1/2 Cents U.S. = 1 Real (Spanish-American)
8 New York Shillings 1 Dollar U.S. = 8 Reales (Spanish-American)
7 1/2 Middle States Shillings
6 Virginia Shillings
8 Carolina Shillings
32 1/2 Georgia Shillings

REPLACEMENT NOTES:

All issues since about 1916 have a star either before or after the serial number, depending on type of note. MPC's: any with prefix and without suffix letter. All government notes of the United States, since issue of the Demand Notes in 1861, are still valid as legal tender. The different types of currency are treated in a number of specialized catalogs such as the following:

Friedberg, Robert; *Paper Money of the United States.*
Brandimore, William; *Standard Catalog of ® United States Paper Money.*

Detailed information, as given in these catalogs, is not repeated here. The following listing is limited to the individual types and their principal varieties. Sign. varieties in earlier issues are not detailed.

REPUBLIC

Treasury

Act of 30.6.1812

War of 1812 5 2/5% interest bearing notes.

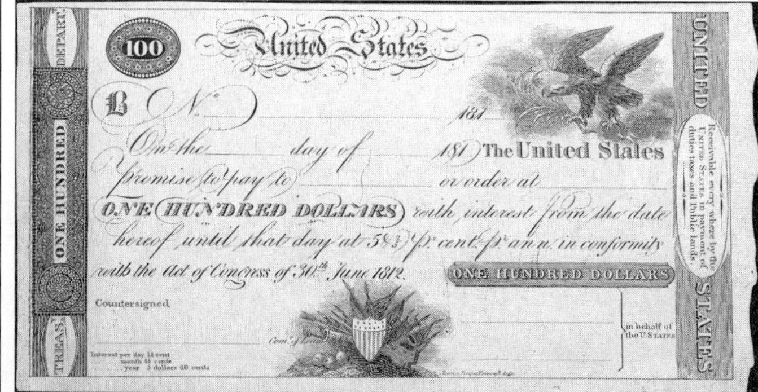

		Good	Fine	XF
1	**100 Dollars** 1812. Eagle on branch at upper right. Remainder.	—	—	—
2	**1000 Dollars** 1812. Eagle on branch at upper left. Remainder.	—	—	—

Act of 25.2.1813

5 2/5% interest bearing notes.

		Good	Fine	XF
3	**100 Dollars** 1813. Remainder.	—	—	—

Act of 4.3.1814

5 2/5% interest bearing notes.

No.	Description	Good	Fine	XF
4	**20 Dollars** 1814. Remainder.	—	—	—
5	**50 Dollars** 1814. Remainder.	—	—	—

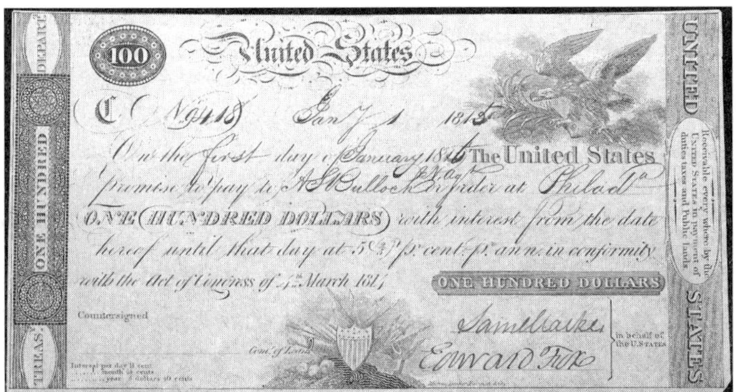

No.	Description	Good	Fine	XF
6	**100 Dollars** 1814. Remainder.	—	—	—

Act of 26.12.1814

5 2/5% interest bearing notes.

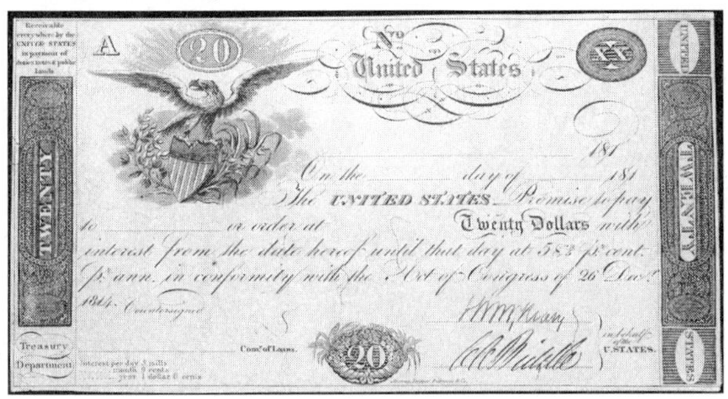

No.	Description	Good	Fine	XF
7	**20 Dollars** 1814. Eagle on shield at upper left. Printer: MDF. Remainder. Rare.	—	—	—
8	**50 Dollars** 1814. Remainder.	—	—	—

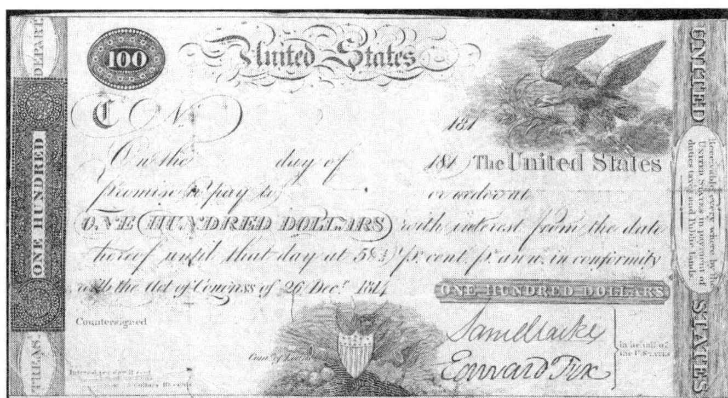

No.	Description	Good	Fine	XF
9	**100 Dollars** 1814. Eagle on branch at upper right. Printer: MDF. Remainder.	—	—	—

Act of 24.2.1815

Called "Small Treasury Notes". $3 to $50 notes without interest. $100 notes 5 2/5% interest bearing notes. This issue actually circulated as currency although not legal tender for all debts.

No.	Description	Good	Fine	XF
10	**3 Dollars** 1815. U.S shield at upper center. Printer: MDF.			
	a. Issued note.	—	—	—
	r. Remainder.	6,000	—	—

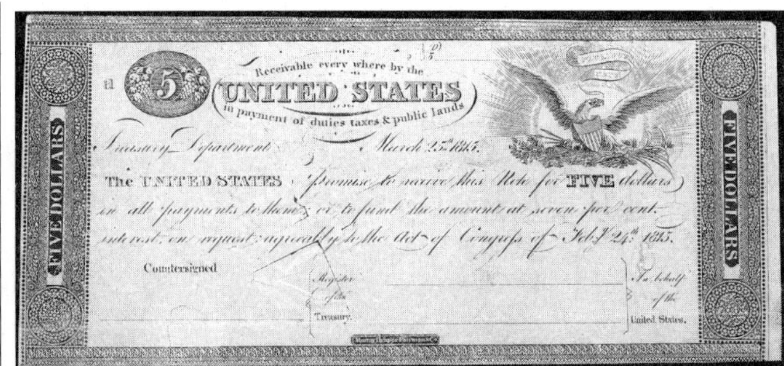

No.	Description	Good	Fine	XF
11	**5 Dollars** 1815. Eagle on branch at upper right. Printer: MDF. Remainder.	—	—	—
12	**10 Dollars** 1815. Eagle on branch at upper left. Text in frame at right. Printer: MDF. Remainder.	—	—	—

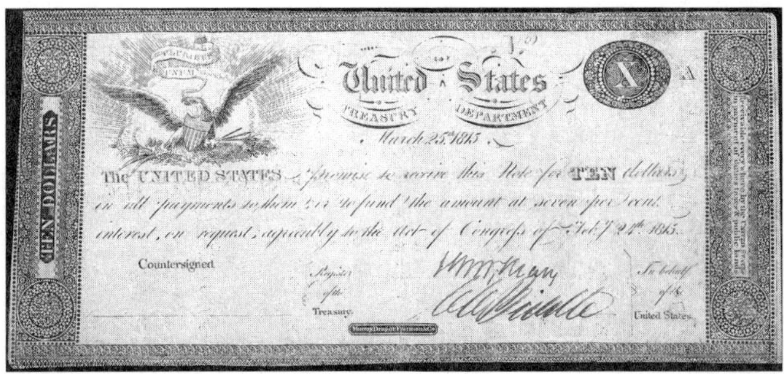

No.	Description	Good	Fine	XF
13	**10 Dollars** 1815. Eagle on branch at upper left. Similar to #12 but *TEN DOLLARS* in frame at right. Remainder.	—	—	—

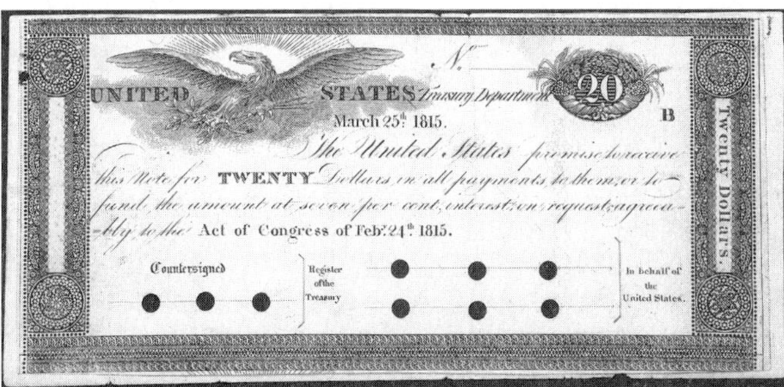

No.	Description	Good	Fine	XF
14	**20 Dollars** 1815. Eagle at upper left. Printer: MDF. Remainder.	—	—	—

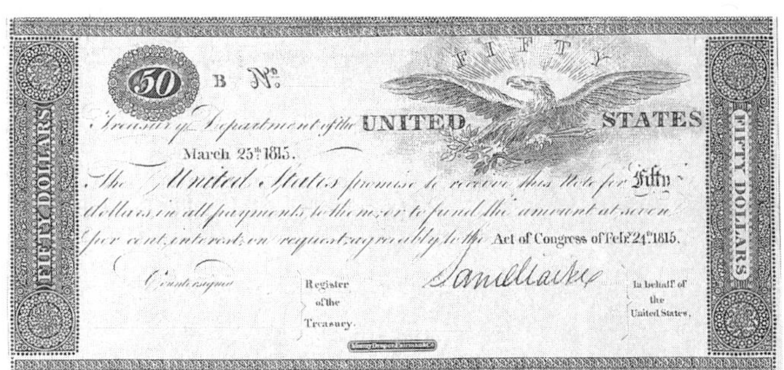

No.	Description	Good	Fine	XF
15	**50 Dollars** 1815. Eagle on branch at upper right. Printer: MDF. Remainder.	—	—	—

No.	Description	Good	Fine	XF
16	**100 Dollars** 1815. Eagle at upper right, shield at lower center. Printer: MDF. Remainder.	—	—	—

Act of 12.10.1837

Panic of 1837 1 year notes issued at four different rates of interest - 1 mill, 2%, 5% or 6%, the rate written in ink at time of issue. The 1-mill rate, which was nominal, was used on notes intended to circulate as currency.

No.	Description	Good	Fine	XF
17	**50 Dollars** 1837. Unsigned. Remainder.	—	—	—

No.	Description	Good	Fine	XF
18	**100 Dollars** 1837. Issued note cancelled. Remainder.	—	—	—
19	**500 Dollars** 1837. Specimen. Remainder.	—	—	—
20	**1000 Dollars** 1837. Specimen. Remainder.	—	—	—

Act of 21.5.1838

1 year notes at 6% interest.

No.	Description	Good	Fine	XF
21	**50 Dollars** 1838. Remainder.	—	—	—
22	**100 Dollars** 1838. Remainder.	—	—	—
23	**500 Dollars** 1838. Remainder.	—	—	—
24	**1000 Dollars** 1838. Remainder.	—	—	—

Act of 2.3.1839

1 year notes at 2% or 6% interest.

No.	Description	Good	Fine	XF
25	**50 Dollars** 1839. Remainder.	—	—	—
26	**100 Dollars** 1839. Remainder.	—	—	—
27	**500 Dollars** 1839. Remainder.	—	—	—
28	**1000 Dollars** 1839. Remainder.	—	—	—

Act of 31.3.1840

1 year notes at 2%, 5%, 5 2/5% or 6% interest, the rate being written in at time of issuance.

No.	Description	Good	Fine	XF
29	**50 Dollars** 1840. Specimen. Remainder.	—	—	—
30	**100 Dollars** 1840. Specimen. Remainder.	—	—	—
31	**500 Dollars** 1840. Specimen. Remainder.	—	—	—
32	**1000 Dollars** 1840. Specimen. Remainder.	—	—	—
33	**10,000 Dollars** 1840. Specimen. Remainder.	—	—	—

Act of 31.1.1842

1 year notes at 2% or 6% interest.

No.	Description	Good	Fine	XF
34	**50 Dollars** 1842. Specimen. Remainder.	—	—	—
35	**100 Dollars** 1842. Specimen. Remainder.	—	—	—
36	**500 Dollars** 1842. Specimen. Remainder.	—	—	—
37	**1000 Dollars** 1842. Specimen. Remainder.	—	—	—

Act of 31.8.1842

1 year notes at 2% or 6% interest.

No.	Description	Good	Fine	XF
38	**50 Dollars** 1842. Mercury at left, allegorical women at upper center, woman at right. Printer: RW&H. Specimen. Remainder.	—	—	—

No.	Description	Good	Fine	XF
39	**100 Dollars** 1842. Specimen. Remainder.	—	—	—
40	**500 Dollars** 1842. Specimen. Remainder.	—	—	—

No.	Description	Good	Fine	XF
41	**1000 Dollars** 1842. Specimen. Remainder.	—	—	—

Act of 3.3.1843

1 year notes at 1 mill or 4% interest.

No.	Description	Good	Fine	XF
42	**50 Dollars** 1843. Woman at left, eagle at upper center, woman at right. Printer: RW&H. Remainder.	—	—	—

Note: In 1887 there were only $83,425 outstanding in all Treasury Notes issued under acts prior to 1846!

Act of 22.7.1846

Mexican War 1 year notes at 1 mill or 5 2/5% interest.

		Good	Fine	XF
43	**50 Dollars** 1846. Specimen. Remainder.	—	—	—
44	**100 Dollars** 1846. Specimen. Remainder.	—	—	—
45	**500 Dollars** 1846. Specimen. Remainder.	—	—	—
46	**1000 Dollars** 1846. Remainder.	—	—	—

Act of 28.1.1847

60 day or 1 or 2 year notes at 5 2/5% or 6% interest. Some notes were reissued.

		Good	Fine	XF
47	**50 Dollars** 1847. Specimen. Remainder.	—	—	—

		Good	Fine	XF
48	**100 Dollars** 1847. Specimen. Remainder.	—	—	—

		Good	Fine	XF
49	**500 Dollars** 1847. Specimen. Remainder.	—	—	—

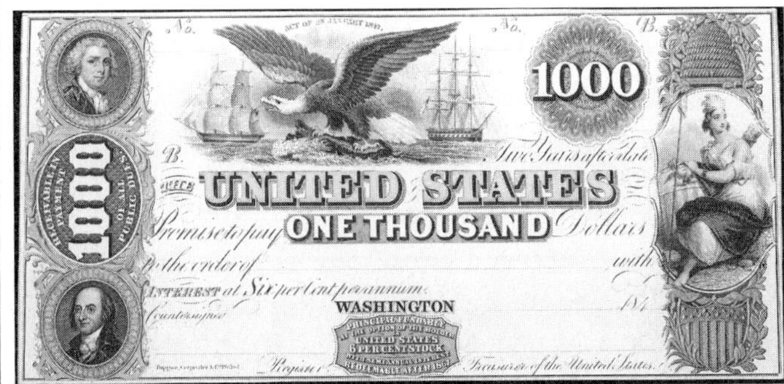

		Good	Fine	XF
50	**1000 Dollars** 1847. Specimen. Remainder.	—	—	—
51	**5000 Dollars** 1847. Girl at left, eagle at upper center, woman at right. Printer: RWH&E. 2-year notes. Specimen. Remainder.	—	—	—

		Good	Fine	XF
52	**5000 Dollars** 1847. Allegorical woman with sickle at left, eagle on branch and cameo of George Washington at upper center, Helmeted woman with spear and shield at right. Printer: TCC. Specimen. Remainder.	—	—	—

Act of 23.12.1857

Panic of 1857 1 year notes at 3 to 6% interest.

		Good	Fine	XF
53	**100 Dollars** 1857. Printer: TCC. Remainder.	—	—	—
54	**500 Dollars** 1857. Remainder.	—	—	—

		Good	Fine	XF
55	**1000 Dollars** 1857. Remainder.	—	—	—

Act of 17.12.1860

1 year notes at 6% to 12% interest.

		Good	Fine	XF
56	**50 Dollars** 1860. Remainder.	—	—	—
57	**100 Dollars** 1860. Remainder.	—	—	—
58	**500 Dollars** 1860. Remainder.	—	—	—

		Good	Fine	XF
59	**1000 Dollars** 1860. Remainder.	—	—	—

Act of 2.3.1861

1 or 2 year notes at 6% interest.

		Good	Fine	XF
60	**50 Dollars** 1861. Black and orange. Portrait Andrew Jackson at left, Liberty seated at center, portrait Daniel Webster at right. BC: Blue. Printer: NBNC. Remainder.	—	—	—

		Good	Fine	XF
61	**100 Dollars** 1861. Black and orange. Seated Liberty at upper left, eagle at upper center. BC: Green. Remainder.	1,500	2,500	—

		Good	Fine	XF
62	**500 Dollars** 1861. Black and green. Portrait George Washington at lower left, allegorical female at upper center, eagle at lower right. BC: Brown. Printer: ABNC and RWH&E. 60-day note. Specimen. Remainder.	—	—	—

		Good	Fine	XF
63	**500 Dollars** 1861. Young man at lower left, portrait Gen. Winfield Scott at upper center, farmer at lower right. 2-year note. Remainder.	1,500	2,500	—

		Good	Fine	XF
64	**1000 Dollars** 1861. Black and green. Portrait George Washington at left, Liberty at center, Treasury building at right. BC: Red-brown. Remainder.	3,000	5,000	—
65	**5000 Dollars** 1861. Remainder.	—	—	—

Fractional Currency

1862 (first) Issue - Postage Currency

		Fine	XF	CU
97	**5 Cents** 17.7.1862. Brown. Facsimile 5 cent stamp with Jefferson at center.			
	a. Perforated edges; ABNC monogram on back.	22.50	45.00	225
	b. Perforated edges; without ABNC monogram on back.	45.00	75.00	295
	c. Straight edges; ABNC monogram on back.	17.50	32.50	85.00
	d. Straight edges; without ABNC monogram on back.	45.00	75.00	295

		Fine	XF	CU
98	**10 Cents** 17.7.1862. Green. Facsimile 10 cent stamp with Washington at center.			
	a. Perforated edges; ABNC monogram on back.	25.00	45.00	195
	b. Perforated edges; without ABNC monogram on back.	30.00	75.00	295
	c. Straight edges; ABNC monogram on back.	20.00	40.00	75.00
	d. Straight edges; without ABNC monogram on back.	55.00	75.00	325

		Fine	XF	CU
99	**25 Cents** 17.7.1862. Brown. 5 facsimile 5 cent stamps with Jefferson.			
	a. Perforated edges; ABNC monogram on back.	30.00	75.00	325
	b. Perforated edges; without ABNC monogram on back.	30.00	75.00	425
	c. Straight edges; ABNC monogram on back.	22.50	55.00	125
	d. Straight edges; without ABNC monogram on back.	65.00	120	495

		Fine	XF	CU
100	**50 Cents** 17.7.1862. Green. 5 facsimile 10 cent stamps with Washington.			
	a. 12 perforated edges; ABNC monogram on back.	55.00	100	395
	b. 14 perforated edges; ABNC monogram on back. Rare.	—	—	—
	c. Perforated edges; without ABNC monogram on back.	75.00	150	495
	d. Straight edges; ABNC monogram on back.	30.00	70.00	175
	e. Straight edges; without ABNC monogram on back.	100	200	750

1863 (second) Issue - Fractional Currency

Many varieties. Back with or without overprint *1863* and letters; paper with or without fibers. #101-104 oval bronze overprint on face around Washington at center and bronze numerals in outline on back.

		Fine	XF	CU
101	**5 Cents** 3.3.1863.			
	a. Without overprint on back.	17.50	30.00	85.00
	b. Overprint: *18-63* on back.	17.50	30.00	85.00
	c. Overprint: *18-63* and *S* on back.	30.00	60.00	135
	d. Overprint: *18-63* and *R-1* on back.	50.00	100	495

		Fine	XF	CU
102	**10 Cents** 3.3.1863.			
	a. Without overprint on back.	20.00	35.00	85.00
	b. Overprint: *18-63* on back.	20.00	35.00	85.00
	c. Overprint: *18-63* and *S* on back.	25.00	45.00	150
	d. Overprint: *18-63* and *1* on back.	50.00	100	300
	e. Overprint: *O-63* on back.	1,000	1,750	3,000
	f. Overprint: *18-63* and *T-1* on back.	55.00	120	595

		Fine	XF	CU
103	**25 Cents** 3.3.1863.			
	a. Without overprint on back.	20.00	75.00	150
	b. Overprint: *18-63* on back.	30.00	65.00	275
	c. Overprint: *18-63* and *A* on back.	30.00	65.00	175
	d. Overprint: *18-63* and *S* on back.	30.00	60.00	175
	e. Overprint: *18-63* and *2* on back.	30.00	90.00	225
	f. Overprint: *18-63* and *T-1* on back.	45.00	150	450
	g. Overprint: *18-63* and *T-2* on back.	35.00	135	550

		Fine	XF	CU
104	**50 Cents** 3.3.1863.			
	a. Overprint: *18-63* on back.	35.00	75.00	325
	b. Overprint: *18-63* and *A* on back.	30.00	45.00	295
	c. Overprint: *18-63* and *I* on back.	35.00	75.00	325
	d. Overprint: *18-63* and *O-1* on back.	50.00	100	425
	e. Overprint: *18-63* and *R-2* on back.	65.00	250	595
	f. Overprint: *18-63* and *T-1* on back.	55.00	175	395

1863 (third) Issue

		Fine	XF	CU
105	**3 Cents**			
	3.3.1863. Portrait Washington at center.			
	a. Portrait with light background.	35.00	50.00	95.00
	b. Portrait with dark background.	45.00	75.00	150

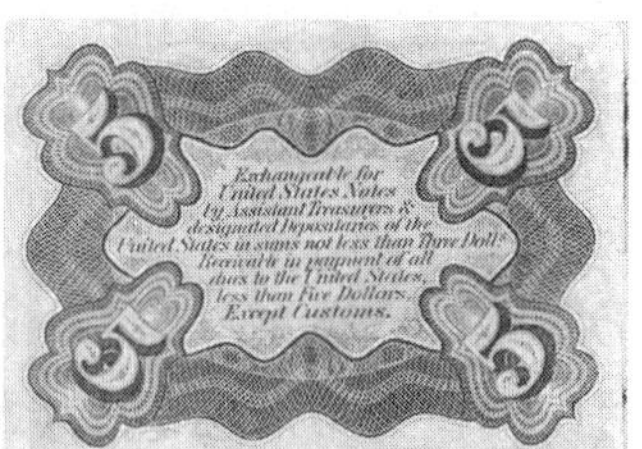

		Fine	XF	CU
106	**5 Cents**			
	3.3.1863. Portrait Clark at center. BC: Red.			
	a. Without *a* on face.	22.50	75.00	200
	b. *a* on face.	32.50	90.00	295
107	**5 Cents**	Fine	XF	CU
	3.3.1863. Portrait Clark at center. Like #106. BC: Green.			
	a. Without *a* on face.	20.00	45.00	100
	b. *a* on face.	25.00	65.00	150

		Fine	XF	CU
108	**10 Cents**			
	3.3.1863. Portrait Washington at center; bronze *10* in each corner.			
	a. Back red. Small signature: Colby-Spinner.	25.00	45.00	175
	b. With *1* on face.	30.00	55.00	225
	c. Large signature: Colby-Spinner.	35.00	75.00	250
	d. Large signature: Jeffries-Spinner.	65.00	125	395
	e. Back green. Small signature: Colby-Spinner.	20.00	30.00	95.00
	f. Large signature: Colby-Spinner. Rare.	—	—	—
	g. Like d. with *1* on face.	20.00	40.00	150

Note: Through an oversight, the word *CENTS* does not appear on #108.

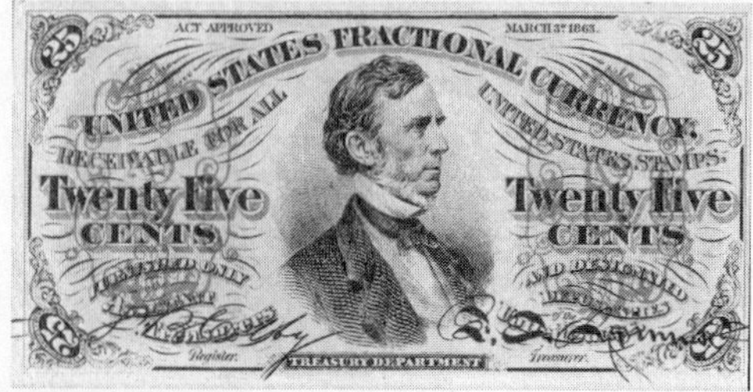

		Fine	XF	CU
109	**25 Cents**			
	3.3.1863. Portrait Fessenden at center.			
	a. Back red.	22.50	55.00	225
	b. Small *a* on face.	25.00	65.00	275
	c. Large *a* on face.	—	—	—
	d. Back green.	20.00	35.00	100
	e. Small *a* on face.	25.00	45.00	150
	f. Large *a* on face.	600	1,500	4,000
	g. Overprint: *M-2-6-5* on back.	35.00	100	375
	h. Overprint: *a* on face, *M-2-6-5* on back.	45.00	125	495
	i. Solid bronze ornaments overprint on face.	800	1,200	2,750
	j. Solid bronze ornaments overprint and *a* on face.	1,500	2,250	5,500

		Fine	XF	CU
110	**50 Cents**			
	3.3.1863. Portrait Spinner at center. BC: Red.			
	a. Small signature: Colby-Spinner. Overprint: *A-2-6-5* and multiple *50s* on back.	60.00	100	325
	b. *1* and *a* on face.	150	300	1,000
	c. *1* on face.	65.00	125	375
	d. *a* on face.	65.00	125	375
	e. Large signature: Colby-Spinner.	90.00	185	400
	f. Signature: Allison-Spinner.	125	250	700
	g. Signature: Allison-New.	—	—	4,000
111	**50 Cents**	Fine	XF	CU
	3.3.1863. Portrait Spinner at center. Like #110. BC: Green.			
	a. Issued note.	60.00	110	250
	b. *1* and *a* on face.	100	150	500
	c. *1* on face.	65.00	110	300
	d. *a* on face.	65.00	115	300
	e. Overprint: *A-2-6-5* on back.	50.00	100	350
	f. *1* and *a* on face.	300	750	2,750
	g. *1* on face.	75.00	125	495
	h. *a* on face.	100	200	900
112	**50 Cents**	Fine	XF	CU
	3.3.1863. Portrait Spinner. Like #111. Back: Redesigned. *50* at center. BC: Green.			
	a. Issued note.	60.00	100	325
	b. *1* and *a* on face.	150	225	900
	c. *1* on face.	75.00	150	400
	d. *a* on face.	75.00	150	400
113	**50 Cents**	Fine	XF	CU
	3.3.1863. Allegorical figure of seated Justice holding scales at center. BC: Red.			
	a. Small signature.	55.00	125	500
	b. *1* and *a* on face.	75.00	300	3,000
	c. *1* on face.	55.00	125	525
	d. *a* on face.	55.00	125	525
	e. Overprint: *A-2-6-5* on back.	55.00	125	425
	f. *1* and *a* on face.	55.00	400	4,000
	g. *1* on face.	85.00	125	595
	h. *a* on face.	65.00	125	675
	i. Small signature. Overprint: *S-2-6-4* on back.	1,000	5,000	30,000
	j. *1* and *a* on face. Fibre paper.	—	—	—
	k. *1* on face. Fibre paper.	—	—	—
	l. *a* on face. Fibre paper.	—	—	—
	m. Back red. Large autograph signature.	45.00	60.00	425
	n. Overprint: *A-2-6-5* on back.	50.00	75.00	525
	o. Overprint: *S-2-6-4* on back.	60.00	200	1,600

		Fine	XF	CU
114	**50 Cents**			
	3.3.1863. Allegorical figure of seated Justice holding scales at center. Like #113. BC: Green.			
	a. Issued note.	45.00	75.00	350
	b. *1* and *a* on face.	100	250	2,200
	c. *1* on face.	45.00	70.00	350
	d. *a* on face.	45.00	75.00	450
	e. Overprint: *A-2-6-5* on back compactly spaced.	45.00	75.00	425
	f. *1* and *a* on face.	100	225	700
	g. *1* on face.	45.00	75.00	450
	h. *a* on face.	50.00	80.00	450
	i. Overprint: *A-2-6-5* on back widely spaced.	50.00	95.00	500
	j. *1* and *a* on face.	500	1,000	5,000
	k. *1* on face.	55.00	110	695
	l. *a* on face.	100	250	1,000
	m. Overprint: *A-2-6-5* on back. Fibre paper.	75.00	250	775
	n. *1* and *a* on face. Fibre paper.	500	1,750	5,000
	o. *1* on face. Fibre paper.	100	200	1,000
	p. *a* on face. Fibre paper.	100	200	1,000
	q. Overprint: *S-2-6-4* on back. Fibre paper.	10,000	20,000	30,000

1863 (fourth) Issue

Many varieties of paper, of color and size of seal. Backs green.

		Fine	XF	CU
115	**10 Cents**			
	3.3.1863. Liberty at left. 40mm red seal. BC: Green.			
	a. Watermark. Paper with pink silk fibres.	25.00	35.00	95.00
	b. Without watermark, paper with pink silk fibres.	25.00	35.00	95.00
	c. Bluish tint at right side of face. Paper with violet silk fibres.	25.00	35.00	95.00
	d. 38mm red seal; bluish tint at right side of face.	25.00	35.00	95.00

		Fine	XF	CU
116	**15 Cents**			
	3.3.1863. Columbia at left. 40mm red seal. BC: Green.			
	a. Watermark. Paper with pink silk fibres.	75.00	95.00	150
	b. Without watermark, paper With pink silk fibres.	300	500	1,500
	c. Bluish tint at right side of face. Paper with violet silk fibres.	75.00	100	200
	d. 38mm red seal; bluish tint at right side of face.	75.00	100	200

		Fine	XF	CU
118	**25 Cents**			
	3.3.1863. Portrait Washington at left. 40mm red seal. BC: Green.			
	a. Watermark. Paper with pink silk fibres.	25.00	50.00	100
	b. Without watermark, paper With pink silk fibres.	30.00	50.00	150
	c. Bluish tint at right side of face. Paper with violet silk fibres.	50.00	75.00	175
	d. 38mm red seal; bluish tint at right side of face.	45.00	75.00	175
119	**50 Cents**	**Fine**	**XF**	**CU**
	3.3.1863. Portrait Lincoln at right. BC: Green.			
	a. Watermark. Paper with silk fibres.	100	200	450
	b. Without watermark, paper With pink silk fibres.	—	—	—

		Fine	XF	CU
120	**50 Cents**			
	3.3.1863. Portrait E. M. Stanton at left. BC: Green.	45.00	75.00	225

		Fine	XF	CU
121	**50 Cents**			
	3.3.1863. Portrait Dexter at left. BC: Green.	35.00	55.00	125

1874-1875 (fifth) Issue

Paper varieties. Values are for most common types of each denomination.

		Fine	XF	CU
122	**10 Cents**			
	3.3.1863; 30.6.1864. Portrait W. Meredith at left.			
	a. Green seal with long key.	25.00	50.00	100
	b. Red seal with long key.	20.00	30.00	50.00
	c. Red seal with short key.	20.00	30.00	50.00

123	25 Cents	Fine	XF	CU
	3.3.1863; 30.6.1864. Portrait R. Walker at left.			
	a. Red seal with long key.	20.00	25.00	50.00
	b. Red seal with short key.	20.00	25.00	50.00

124	50 Cents	Fine	XF	CU
	3.3.1863; 30.6.1864. Portrait Crawford at left.	25.00	50.00	100

Demand Notes
Series of 1861

125	5 Dollars	VG	VF	UNC
	10.8.1861. Statue of Columbia at left, portrait Alexander Hamilton at right. Printer: ABNC.			
	a. Payable at New York.	1,400	5,000	—
	b. Payable at Philadelphia.	3,750	4,500	—
	c. Payable at Boston.	2,500	5,000	—
	d. Payable at Cincinnati. Rare.	14,000	—	—
	e. Payable at St. Louis. Rare.	10,000	35,000	125,000

126	10 Dollars	VG	VF	UNC
	10.8.1861. Portrait Abraham Lincoln at left, allegorical woman (Art) at right. Printer: ABNC.			
	a. Payable at New York.	4,000	20,000	—
	b. Payable at Philadelphia.	3,750	20,000	—
	c. Payable at Boston.	10,000	15,000	—
	d. Payable at Cincinnati. Rare.	14,000	25,000	—
	e. Payable at St. Louis. Rare.	10,000	38,000	—

127	20 Dollars	VG	VF	UNC
	10.8.1861. Liberty with sword and shield at center. Printer: ABNC.			
	a. Payable at New York.	21,000	100,000	—
	b. Payable at Philadelphia.	75,000	100,000	—
	c. Payable at Boston.	36,000	62,500	—
	d. Payable at Cincinnati. Rare.	—	250,000	—

Note: Few Demand Notes of 1861 are known in better than VG condition.

United States Notes

Varieties of red or brown seals. Prices are for most common types of each denomination.

1862 Series

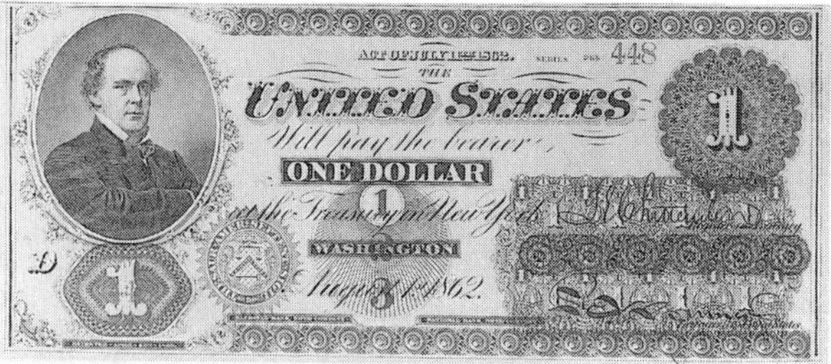

128	1 Dollar	Fine	XF	CU
	1862. Portrait Salmon P. Chase at left.	325	1,350	2,800

129	2 Dollars	Fine	XF	CU
	1862. Portrait Alexander Hamilton at left center.	750	2,000	5,500

130	5 Dollars	Fine	XF	CU
	1862. Statue of Columbia at left; portrait Alexander Hamilton at right. Like #125 but without *On Demand* and with seal.			
	a. First Obligation on back.	750	2,000	3,000
	b. Second Obligation on back.	750	1,750	5,000

131	10 Dollars	Fine	XF	CU
	1862. Portrait Abraham Lincoln at left, allegorical woman (Art) at right. Like #126 but without *On Demand* and with seal.			
	a. First Obligation on back.	1,000	2,000	5,000
	b. Second Obligation on back.	1,000	3,500	8,000

132	20 Dollars	Fine	XF	CU
	1862. Liberty with sword and shield at center. Like #123 but without *On Demand* and with seal.			
	a. First Obligation on back.	2,300	6,000	22,500
	b. Second Obligation on back.	3,000	4,000	17,500

133	50 Dollars	Fine	XF	CU
	1862. Portrait Alexander Hamilton at left center.			
	a. First Obligation on back.	32,500	45,000	—
	b. Second Obligation on back.	12,500	30,000	—

134	100 Dollars	Fine	XF	CU
	1862. Bald eagle with outstretched wings perched on rock at left.			
	a. First Obligation on back.	30,000	40,000	75,000
	b. Second Obligation on back.	—	—	—

		Fine	XF	CU
135	**500 Dollars** 1862. Portrait Albert Gallatin at center.			
	a. First Obligation on back. Rare.	—	—	—
	b. Second Obligation on back. Rare.	—	—	—

		Fine	XF	CU
136	**1000 Dollars** 1862. Portrait Robert Morris at center.			
	a. First Obligation on back. Rare.	—	—	—
	b. Second Obligation on back. Rare.	—	—	—

1863 Series

		Fine	XF	CU
137	**5 Dollars** 1863. Statue of Columbia at left; portrait Alexander Hamilton at right. Without *On Demand* and with seal. Like #130b. Back: Second Obligation.	500	1,000	6,000

		Fine	XF	CU
138	**10 Dollars** 1863. Portrait Abraham Lincoln at left, allegorical woman (Art) at right. Without *On Demand* and with seal. Like #131b. Back: Second Obligation.	1,450	5,000	12,000

		Fine	XF	CU
139	**20 Dollars** 1863. Liberty with sword and shield at center. Without *On Demand* and with seal. Like #132b. Back: Second Obligation.	2,000	4,000	15,000

		Fine	XF	CU
140	**50 Dollars** 1863. Portrait Alexander Hamilton at left center. Like #133b. Back: Second Obligation.	12,500	30,000	—

		Fine	XF	CU
141	**100 Dollars** 1863. Bald eagle with outstretched wings perched on rock at left. Like #134b. Back: Second Obligation.	25,000	—	—

		Fine	XF	CU
142	**500 Dollars** 1863. Portrait Albert Gallatin at center. Like #135b. Back: Second Obligation. Rare.	—	—	—

Note: An example of #142 in Fine sold recently for $540,000.00

		Fine	XF	CU
143	**1000 Dollars** 1863. Portrait Robert Morris at center. Like #136b. Back: Second Obligation. Rare.	650,000	—	—

1869 Series

		Fine	XF	CU
144	**1 Dollar** 1869. Columbus sighting land at left, portrait George Washington at center. Back: *1-ONE-DOLLAR* at center.	400	3,000	6,000

145 **2 Dollars**
1869. Portrait Thomas Jefferson at upper left, Capitol at center. Back: *2* at center.

Fine	XF	CU
700	3,250	9,000

146 **5 Dollars**
1869. Portrait Andrew Jackson at lower left, pioneer family at center. Back: *5* at center.

Fine	XF	CU
600	1,500	3,000

147 **10 Dollars**
1869. Portrait Daniel Webster at lower left, presentation of Indian Princess at lower right. Back: Text at center.

Fine	XF	CU
1,000	1,800	6,000

148 **20 Dollars**
1869. Portrait Alexander Hamilton at left, Victory with sword and shield at right. Back: Text at center.

Fine	XF	CU
3,000	10,000	22,000

149 **50 Dollars**
1869. Woman holding statue of Mercury at left, portrait Henry Clay at lower right.

Fine	XF	CU
21,500	50,000	150,000

150 **100 Dollars**
1869. Portrait Abraham Lincoln at upper left, allegorical woman (Architecture) with child at right. Back: Text at center.

Fine	XF	CU
17,500	100,000	135,000

		VG	VF	UNC
151	**500 Dollars** 1869. Justice with scales at left, portrait John Quincy Adams at right. Rare.	—	—	—
152	**1000 Dollars** 1869. Portrait Christopher Columbus at left, portrait Dewitt Clinton at center. Rare.	—	—	—

1874 Series

		Fine	XF	CU
153	**1 Dollar** 1874. Columbus sighting land at upper left, portrait George Washington at center. Back: *UNITED STATES OF AMERICA* at center.	200	835	2,100

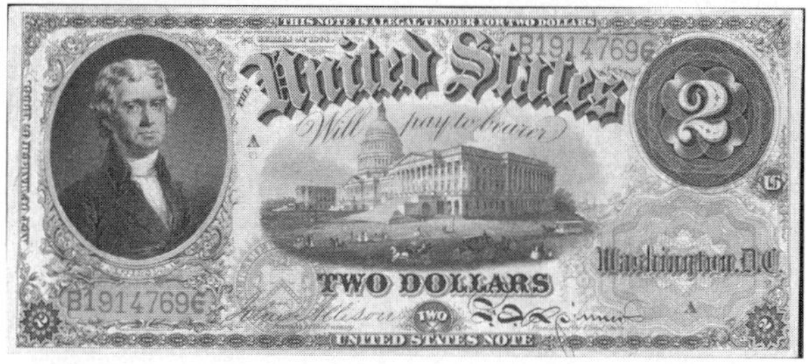

		Fine	XF	CU
154	**2 Dollars** 1874. Portrait Thomas Jefferson at left, Capitol at center. Back: *2* at center and *2s* in all corners.	460	1,200	2,200

		Fine	XF	CU
155	**50 Dollars** 1874. Portrait Benjamin Franklin at upper left, Columbia at right.	10,000	15,000	75,000

		Fine	XF	CU
156	**500 Dollars** 1874. Woman standing at left, portrait Maj. Gen. Joseph K. Mansfield at right. Rare.	—	—	—

1875 Series

		Fine	XF	CU
157	**1 Dollar** 1875. Columbus sighting land at upper left, portrait George Washington at center. Like #153. 2 signature varieties. Back: *UNITED STATES OF AMERICA* at center.			
	a. Without series.	265	600	1,100
	b. Series A.	1,000	3,600	9,000
	c. Series B.	1,250	3,000	9,500
	d. Series C.	1,250	2,000	5,000
	e. Series D.	1,150	8,250	31,000
	f. Series E.	1,875	5,000	13,000
158	**2 Dollars** 1875. Portrait Thomas Jefferson at left, Capitol at center. Like #154. 2 signature varieties. Back: *2* at center and *2s* in all corners.			
	a. Without series.	500	1,000	2,250
	b. Series A.	1,000	3,600	18,500
	c. Series B.	850	2,400	5,500

		Fine	XF	CU
159	**5 Dollars** 1875. Portrait Jackson at left, pioneer family at center. 2 signature varieties. Back: Ornamental design at center.			
	a. Without series.	350	750	2,500
	b. Series A.	1,500	4,000	15,000
	c. Series B.	350	750	1,500
160	**10 Dollars** 1875. Portrait Daniel Webster at left, presentation of Indian Princess at right. Back: Ornamental design at center, with text at right.			
	a. Without series.	4,000	27,500	—
	b. Series A.	1,000	3,000	4,500
161	**20 Dollars** 1875. Portrait Alexander Hamilton at upper left, Victory with sword and shield at right. Back: Ornamental design at center, with text at left.	1,500	2,750	5,000
162	**50 Dollars** 1875. Portrait Benjamin Franklin at upper left, Columbia at right. Like #155. Rare.	—	—	—
163	**100 Dollars** 1875. Portrait Abraham Lincoln at left, woman with child at right. 2 signature varieties. Back: Ornamental design at center.	19,500	40,000	65,000
164	**500 Dollars** 1875. Woman standing at left, portrait Maj. Gen. Joseph K. Mansfield at right. Like #156. 2 signature varieties. Rare.	—	—	—

1878 Series

		Fine	XF	CU
165	**1 Dollar** 1878. Christopher Columbus sighting land at upper left, portrait George Washington at center. Like #153. Back: *UNITED STATES OF AMERICA* at center.	225	650	1,000
166	**2 Dollars** 1878. Portrait Thomas Jefferson at left, Capitol at center. Like #154. 2 signature varieties. Back: *2* at center and *2s* in all corners.	500	800	2,000
167	**5 Dollars** 1878. Portrait Andrew Jackson at left, pioneer family at center. 2 signature varieties. Like #159. Back: Ornamental design at center.	250	800	2,000
168	**10 Dollars** 1878. Portrait Daniel Webster at left, presentation of Indian Princess at right. Like #160. Back: Ornamental design at center, with text at right.	800	3,200	4,750

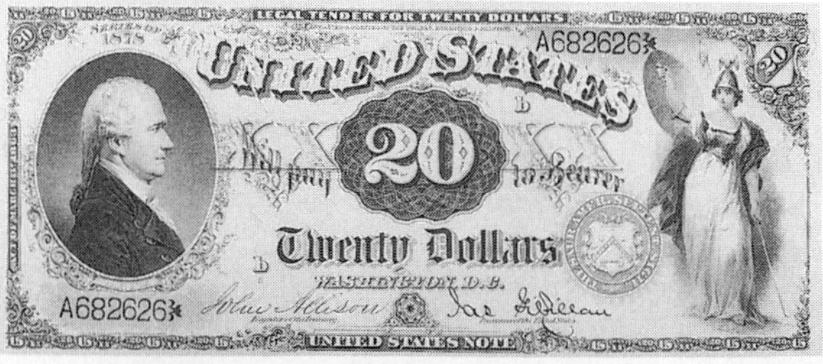

		Fine	XF	CU
169	**20 Dollars** 1878. Portrait Alexander Hamilton at upper left, Victory with sword and shield at right. Like #161. Back: Ornamental design at center, with text at left.	900	1,800	3,250

		Fine	XF	CU
170	**50 Dollars** 1878. Portrait Benjamin Franklin at upper left, Columbia at right. Like #155.	5,000	20,000	42,500

		Fine	XF	CU
171	**100 Dollars** 1878. Portrait Abraham Lincoln at left, woman with child at right. Like #163. Back: Ornamental design at center.	15,000	30,000	—

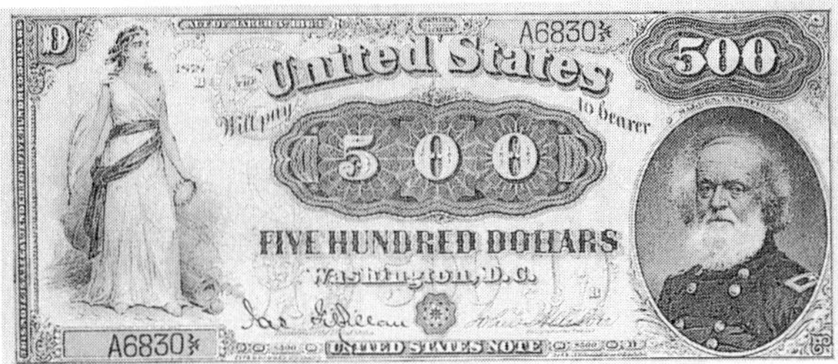

		Fine	XF	CU
172	**500 Dollars** 1878. Woman standing at left, portrait Maj. Gen. Joseph K. Mansfield at right. Like #156. Rare.	—	—	—

		Fine	XF	CU
173	**1000 Dollars** 1878. Portrait Christopher Columbus at left, portrait Dewitt Clinton at center. Back: Text at left. Rare.	—	—	—

		Fine	XF	CU
174	**5000 Dollars** 1878. Portrait James Madison at left. (All notes have been redeemed).	—	—	—

		Fine	XF	CU
175	**10,000 Dollars** 1878. Portrait Andrew Jackson at left. (All notes have been redeemed).	—	—	—

1880 Series

		Fine	XF	CU
176	**1 Dollar** 1880. Christopher Columbus sighting land at upper left, portrait George Washington at center. Like #153. Back: *UNITED STATES OF AMERICA* at center.			
	a. Seal at right; red serial #. 3 signature varieties.	200	500	1,000
	b. Red or brown seal at right; blue serial #. 2 signature varieties.	550	1,750	3,000
	c. Seal at left; blue serial #. 2 signature varieties.	200	600	1,250

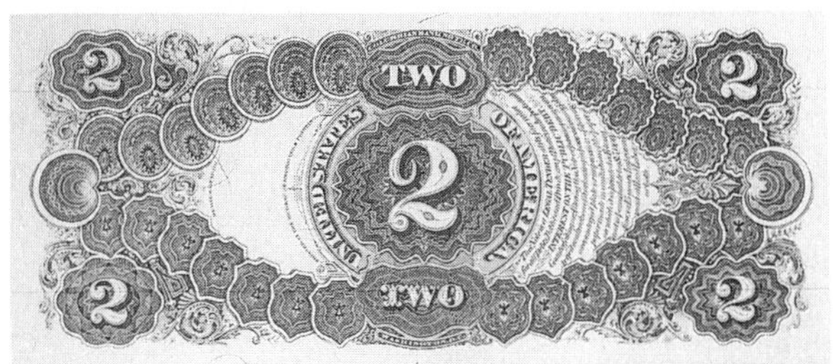

		Fine	XF	CU
177	**2 Dollars** 1880. Portrait Thomas Jefferson at left, Capitol at center. Like #154. Back: 2 at center and 2s in all corners.			
	a. Red serial #. 3 signature varieties.	275	675	1,000
	b. Blue serial #. Small or large red or brown seal. 3 signature varieties.	250	450	575

		Fine	XF	CU
178	**5 Dollars** 1880. Portrait Andrew Jackson at left, pioneer family at center. Like #159. Back: Ornamental design at center.			
	a. Red serial #. 3 signature varieties.	440	1,050	1,225
	b. Blue serial #. 4 varieties of seals; 8 signature varieties.	300	1,200	1,000

		Fine	XF	CU
179	**10 Dollars** 1880. Portrait Daniel Webster at left, presentation of Indian Princess at right. Like #160. Back: Ornamental design at center, with text at right.			
	a. Red serial #. 3 signature varieties.	600	1,200	2,600
	b. Blue serial #. 4 varieties of seals; 8 signature varieties.	500	1,200	1,700

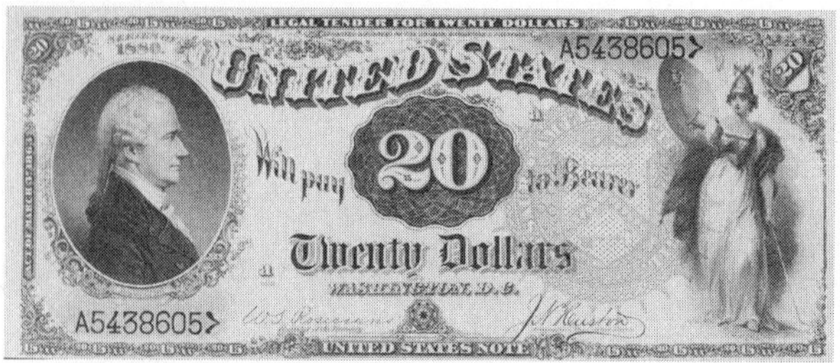

		Fine	XF	CU
180	**20 Dollars** 1880. Portrait Alexander Hamilton at upper left, Victory with sword and shield at right. Like #161. Back: Ornamental design at center, with text at left.			
	a. Blue serial #. 4 varieties of seals; 12 signature varieties.	750	3,300	1.00
	b. Red serial #. 2 signature varieties.	450	1,125	2,000

		Fine	XF	CU
181	**50 Dollars** 1880. Portrait Benjamin Franklin at upper left, Columbia at right. Like #155. 4 varieties of seals; 8 signature varieties.	6,750	12,000	65,000

		Fine	XF	CU
182	**100 Dollars** 1880. Portrait Abraham Lincoln at left, woman with child at right. Like #163. 4 varieties of seals; 9 signature varieties. Back: Ornamental design at center.	19,000	40,000	50,000

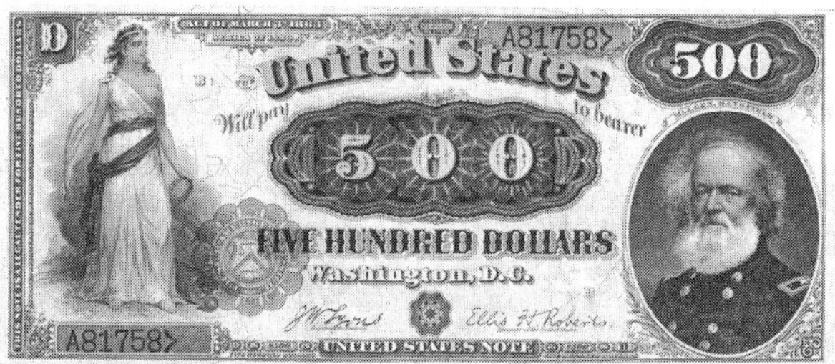

		Fine	XF	CU
183	**500 Dollars** 1880. Woman standing at left, portrait Maj. Gen. Joseph K. Mansfield at right. Like #156. 4 varieties of seals; 10 signature varieties. Rare.	—	—	—
184	**1000 Dollars** 1880. Portrait Christopher Columbus at left, portrait Dewitt Clinton at center. Like #173. 4 varieties of seals; 11 signature varieties. Back: Text at left. Rare.	—	—	—

1901 Series

		Fine	XF	CU
185	**10 Dollars** 1901. Portrait Meriweather Lewis at left, bison at center, portrait William Clark at right. 9 signature varieties.	800	2,400	4,250

1907 Series

		Fine	XF	CU
186	**5 Dollars** 1907. Portrait Andrew Jackson at left, pioneer family at center. Like #159. 10 signature varieties. Back: Ornamental design at center.	150	350	550

1917 Series

No.	Denomination	Fine	XF	CU
187	**1 Dollar** 1917. Christopher Columbus sighting land at upper left, portrait George Washington at center. Like #153. Back: *UNITED STATES OF AMERICA* at center.	100	200	300
188	**2 Dollars** 1917. Portrait Thomas Jefferson at left, Capitol at center. Like #154. 4 signature varieties. Back: *2* at center and *2s* in all corners.	100	200	425

1923 Series

No.	Denomination	Fine	XF	CU
189	**1 Dollar** 1923. Portrait George Washington at center.	175	325	500

No.	Denomination	Fine	XF	CU
190	**10 Dollars** 1923. Portrait Andrew Jackson at center.	1,750	5,000	7,000

Gold Certificates

Series of 1863

NOTE: Certain notes with listings incorporated in previous editions, encompassing various names of the actual bank of issue with national banks and national gold banks #191-244, 390-394A have been deleted from this section. The highly specialized *"Standard Catalog of National Bank Notes"* 1249 pages M 1990 released by Krause Publications is considered to be the ultimate reference for this colorful and rather extensive series of the chartered banks.

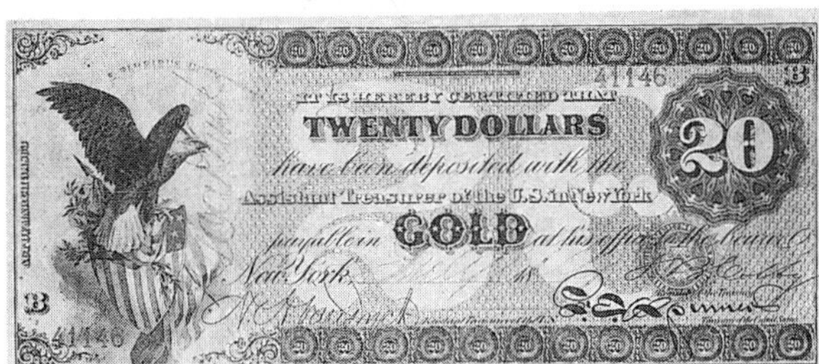

No.	Denomination	Fine	XF	CU
245	**20 Dollars** 3.3.1863. Eagle with shield at left. Rare.	—	500,000	—
246	**100 Dollars** 3.3.1863. Eagle with shield at left. Rare.	—	—	—
247	**100 Dollars** 3.3.1863. Portrait Thomas H. Benton. Countersigned and dated 1870 or 1872 by hand. Rare.	—	—	—
248	**500 Dollars** 3.3.1863. Eagle with shield at left. Rare.	—	—	—
249	**500 Dollars** 3.3.1863. Portrait Abraham Lincoln. Countersigned and dated 1870 or 1872 by hand.	—	—	—
250	**1000 Dollars** 3.3.1863. Eagle with shield at left. Rare.	—	—	—
251	**1000 Dollars** 3.3.1863. Portrait Alexander Hamilton. Countersigned and dated 1870 or 1872 by hand.	—	—	—
252	**5000 Dollars** 3.3.1863. Eagle with shield at left. Rare.	—	—	—
253	**5000 Dollars** 3.3.1863. Portrait James Madison. Countersigned and dated 1870 or 1871 by hand. Rare.	—	—	—
254	**10,000 Dollars** 3.3.1863. Eagle with shield at left. Rare.	—	—	—
255	**10,000 Dollars** 3.3.1863. Portrait Andrew Jackson. Countersigned and dated 1870 or 1871 by hand. Rare.	—	—	—

Series of 1875

No.	Denomination	Fine	XF	CU
256	**100 Dollars** 1875. Portrait Thomas H. Benton at left. Rare.	—	—	—
257	**500 Dollars** 1875. Portrait Abraham Lincoln. Rare.	—	—	—
258	**1000 Dollars** 1875. Portrait Alexander Hamilton. Rare.	—	—	—

Series of 1882

No.	Denomination	Fine	XF	CU
259	**20 Dollars** 1882. Portrait James A. Garfield at right.			
	a. Countersigned signature.	4,100	22,500	35,000
	b. Without countersigned signature. 3 seal varieties; 4 signature varieties.	800	3,400	6,500

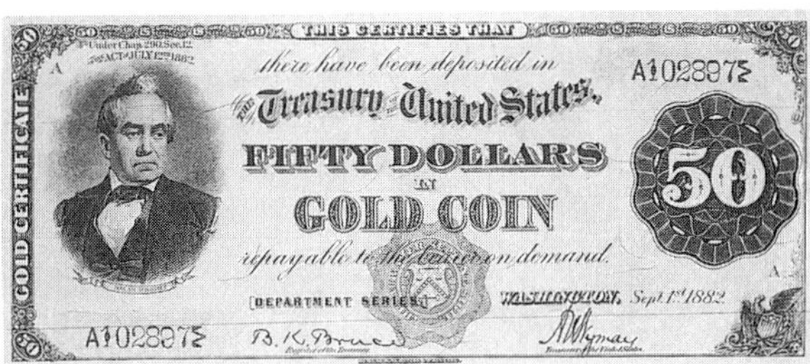

No.	Denomination	Fine	XF	CU
260	**50 Dollars** 1882. Portrait Silas Wright at left.			
	a. Countersigned signature.	20,000	43,500	—
	b. Without countersigned signature. 4 seal varieties; 9 signature varieties.	—	—	18,500

		Fine	XF	CU
261	**100 Dollars** 1882. Portrait Thomas H. Benton at left. (different than #256).			
	a. Countersigned signature. Rare.	1,150	6,500	—
	b. Without countersigned signature. 4 seal varieties; 14 signature varieties.	1,150	7,000	14,000

		Fine	XF	CU
262	**500 Dollars** 1882. Portrait Abraham Lincoln at left.	10,500	40,250	—

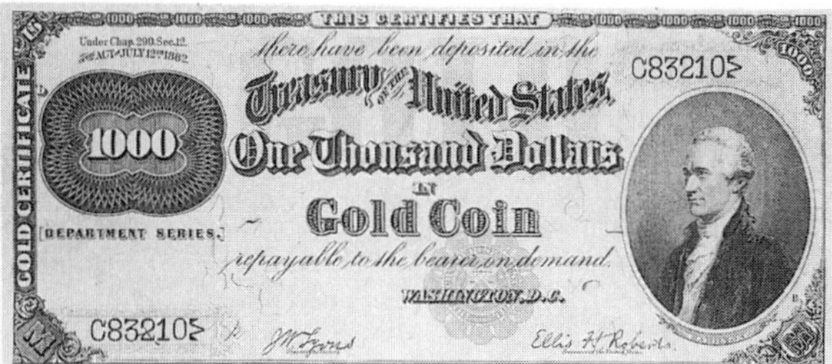

		Fine	XF	CU
263	**1000 Dollars** 1882. Portrait Alexander Hamilton at right.	—	29,375	—
264	**5000 Dollars** 1882. Portrait James Madison at left.	—	—	—
265	**10,000 Dollars** 1882. Portrait Andrew Jackson at left.	—	—	—

Series of 1888

		Fine	XF	CU
266	**5000 Dollars** 1888. Portrait James Madison at left. Like #264. Rare.	—	—	—
267	**10,000 Dollars** 1888. Portrait Andrew Jackson at left. Like #265.	—	—	—

Series of 1900

		Fine	XF	CU
268	**10,000 Dollars** 28.9.1916; 22.11.1916; 6.1.1917; 9.5.1917. Portrait Andrew Jackson at left. Like #265. Uniface.			
	a. Issued note. Rare.	1,900	3,250	5,500
	b. Redeemed with cancelling perforations.	1,900	3,250	5,500

Note: During a fire at a treasury storage area in 1935 a number of cancelled examples of #268 were thrown into the street and picked up by passers-by.

Series of 1905

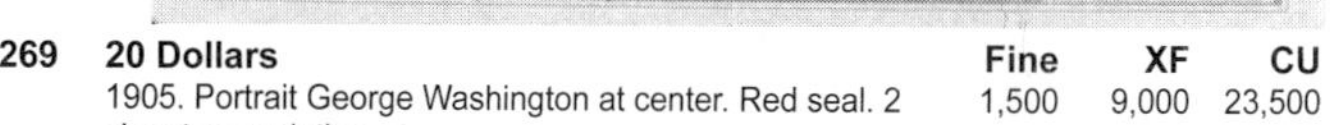

		Fine	XF	CU
269	**20 Dollars** 1905. Portrait George Washington at center. Red seal. 2 signature varieties.	1,500	9,000	23,500

Series of 1906

		Fine	XF	CU
270	**20 Dollars** 1906. Portrait George Washington at center. Like #269 but gold seal. 6 signature varieties.	225	1,075	2,600

Series of 1907

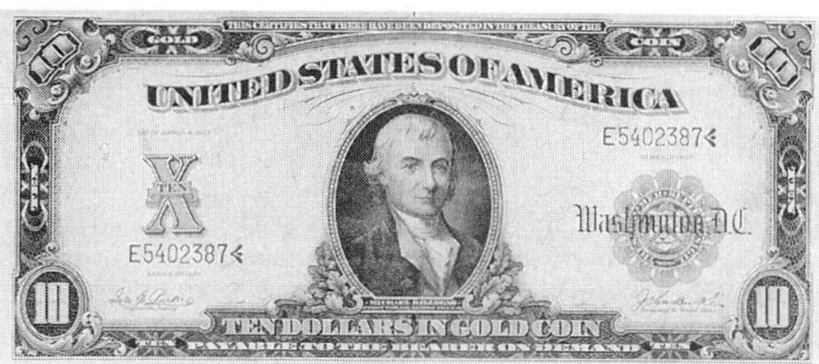

		Fine	XF	CU
271	**10 Dollars** 1907. Portrait Michael Hillegas at center. 6 signature varieties.	225	600	1,500

		Fine	XF	CU
272	**1000 Dollars** 1907. Portrait Alexander Hamilton at center.	15,000	37,500	—

Series of 1913

		Fine	XF	CU
273	**50 Dollars** 1913. Portrait Ulysses S. Grant at center. 2 signature varieties.	700	4,275	7,500

Series of 1922

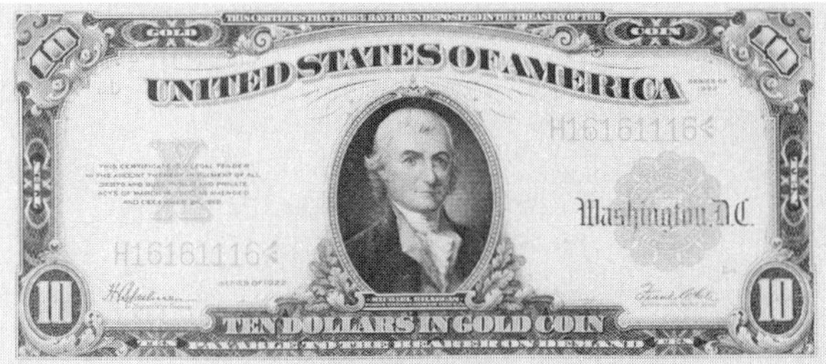

		VG	VF	UNC
274	**10 Dollars** 1922. Portrait Michael Hillegas at center. Like #271.	200	425	—

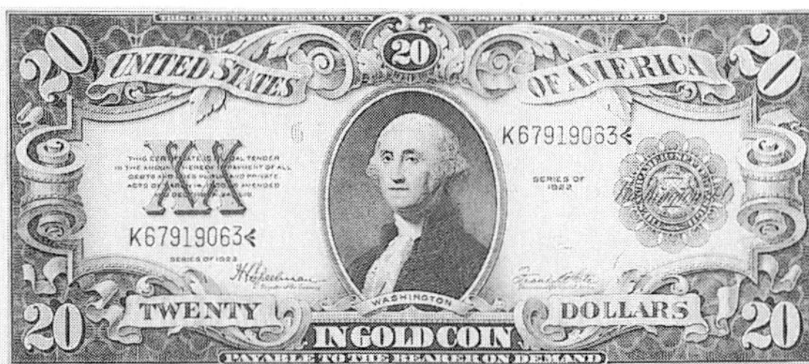

		VG	VF	UNC
275	**20 Dollars** 1922. Portrait George Washington at center. Like #269.	200	500	1,000
276	**50 Dollars** 1922. Portrait Ulysses S. Grant at center. Like #273.	475	2,650	7,500

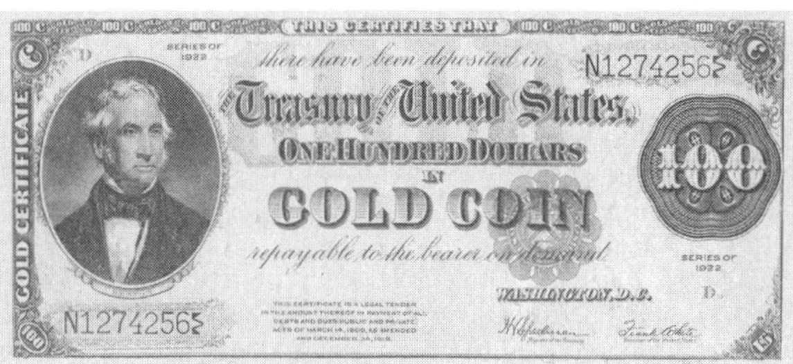

		VG	VF	UNC
277	**100 Dollars** 1922. Portrait Thomas H. Benton at left. Like #261.	700	3,750	6,500
278	**500 Dollars** 1922. Portrait Abraham Lincoln at left. Like #262.	6,000	25,000	125,000
279	**1000 Dollars** 1922. Portrait Alexander Hamilton at center. Like #272.	—	40,000	—

Interest Bearing Notes
Act of 17.3.1861

		Good	Fine	XF
280	**50 Dollars** 1861. Eagle at center. (7-3/10% interest for 3 years. 5 coupons).	—	—	172,500

		VG	VF	UNC
281	**100 Dollars** 1861. Portrait Gen. Winfield Scott at center. (7-3/10% interest for 3 years. 5 coupons). Unknown in private hands.	—	—	—
282	**500 Dollars** 1861. Portrait George Washington. (7-3/10% interest for 3 years. 5 coupons). Unknown in private hands.	—	—	—
283	**1000 Dollars** 1861. Portrait Salmon P. Chase at center. (7-3/10% interest for 3 years. 5 coupons). Unknown in private hands.	—	—	—
284	**5000 Dollars** 1861. Justice with sword and scales at left, Indian woman with shield and eagle at center. (7-3/10% interest for 3 years. 5 coupons). Unknown in private hands.	—	—	—

Act of 3.3.1863

		Good	Fine	XF
285	**10 Dollars** 15.3.1864. Portrait Salmon P. Chase at lower left, eagle at center, allegorical woman at right. (5% interest for 1 year).	—	8,000	

		Good	Fine	XF
286	**20 Dollars** 5.4.1864. Liberty at left, mortar at bottom center, portrait Abraham Lincoln at right. (5% interest for 1 year).	—	74,750	—
287	**50 Dollars** 1863. Allegorical woman at left, portrait Alexander Hamilton at lower right. (5% interest for 1 year).	10,000	27,500	75,000

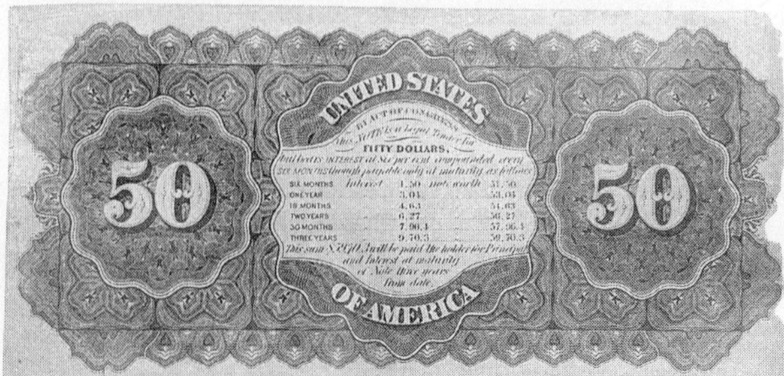

		Good	Fine	XF
288	**50 Dollars** 1863. Justice seated with scales and shield at center, allegorical woman at lower left and right. (5% interest for 2 years).	12,500	30,000	65,000
289	**100 Dollars** 1864. Portrait George Washington holding scroll at center. (5% interest for 1 year).	—	35,000	—
290	**100 Dollars** 14.4.1864. Two allegorical men (Science and Industry) seated at left, building at upper center, coastal battery at lower right. (5% interest for 2 years).	20,000	45,000	90,000
291	**500 Dollars** 1864. Ship "New Ironsides". (5% interest for 1 year). Unknown in private hands.	—	—	—
292	**500 Dollars** 1864. Liberty and eagle. (5% interest for 2 years). Unknown in private hands.	—	—	—
293	**1000 Dollars** 1864. Liberty and Justice. (5% interest for 1 year). Unknown in private hands.	—	—	—
294	**1000 Dollars** 1864. Ships "Guerriere" and "Constitution". (5% interest for 2 years). Unknown in private hands.	—	—	—
295	**5000 Dollars** 1864. Allegorical woman. (5% interest for 1 year). Unknown in private hands.	—	—	—

Act of 30.6.1864

		Good	Fine	XF
296	**50 Dollars** 1864. Eagle at center. (7-3/10% interest for 3 years. 5 coupons).	25,000	65,000	65,000

Act of 3.3.1865

		Good	Fine	XF
297	**50 Dollars** 15.7.1865. Eagle left looking right at center. (7-3/10% interest for 3 years. 5 coupons).	15,000	70,000	100,000
298	**100 Dollars** 1865. Portrait Gen. Winfield Scott at center. (7-3/10% interest for 3 years. 5 coupons). Rare.	—	—	2,100,000
299	**500 Dollars** 1865. (7-3/10% interest for 3 years. 5 coupons). Unknown in private hands.	—	—	—
300	**1000 Dollars** 1865. Justice sitting with scales and shield at center. (7-3/10% interest for 3 years. 5 coupons). Unknown in private hands.	—	—	—

Compound Interest Treasury Notes

Act of 3.3.1863 / 30.6.1864

#301-306 overprint: ***COMPOUND INTEREST TREASURY NOTE.***

		Good	Fine	XF
301	**10 Dollars** 10.6.1864-15.12.1864. Portrait Salmon P. Chase at lower left, eagle at center, allegorical woman at right. Like #285. Overprint: *COMPOUND INTEREST TREASURY NOTE.*	3,000	6,000	12,500

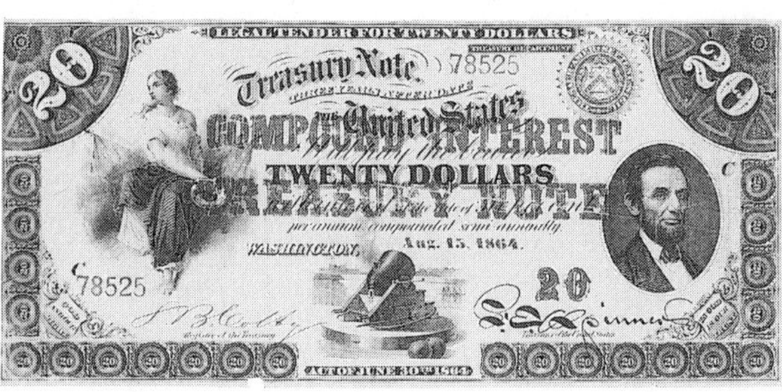

		Good	Fine	XF
302	**20 Dollars** 14.7.1864-16.10.1865. Liberty at left, mortar at bottom center, portrait Abraham Lincoln at right. Like #286. Overprint: *COMPOUND INTEREST TREASURY NOTE.*	5,000	7,750	30,000

		Good	Fine	XF
303	**50 Dollars** 10.6.1864-1.9.1865. Allegorical woman at left, portrait Alexander Hamilton at lower right. Like #287. Overprint: *COMPOUND INTEREST TREASURY NOTE.*	16,000	30,000	60,000

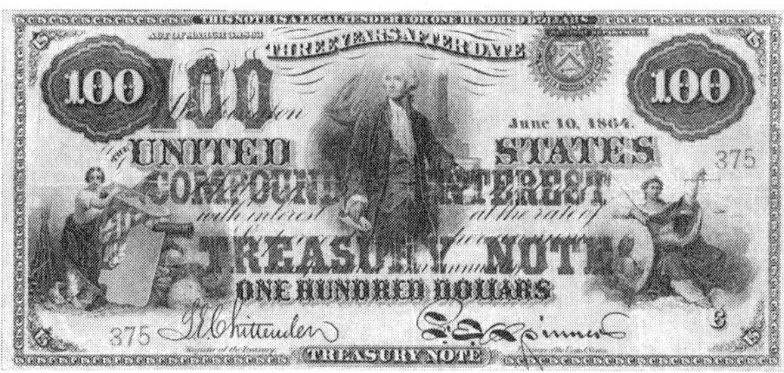

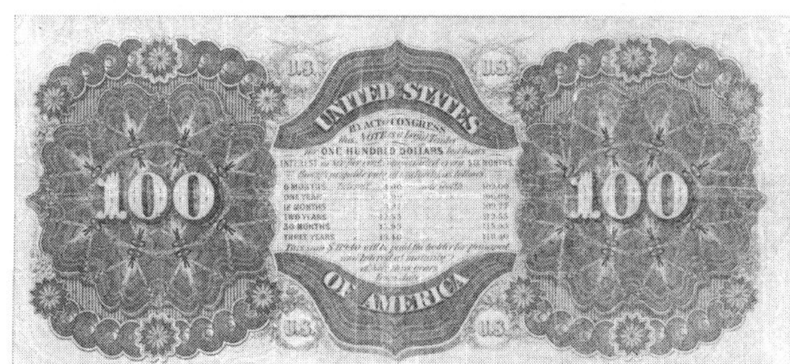

		Good	Fine	XF
304	**100 Dollars** 10.6.1864-1.9.1865. Portrait George Washington holding scroll at center. Like #289. Overprint: *COMPOUND INTEREST TREASURY NOTE.*	17,500	34,000	—
305	**500 Dollars** 10.6.1864-1.10.1865. Ship "New Ironsides". Like #291. Overprint: *COMPOUND INTEREST TREASURY NOTE.* Unknown in private hands.	—	—	—
306	**1000 Dollars** 15.7.1864-15.9.1865. Liberty and Justice. Like #293. Overprint: *COMPOUND INTEREST TREASURY NOTE.* Unknown in private hands.	—	—	—

Refunding Certificates

Act of 26.2.1879

		Good	Fine	XF
307	**10 Dollars** 1.4.1879. Portrait Benjamin Franklin at upper left. *Payable to order* (4% interest). Rare.	—	—	370,000

		VG	VF	UNC
308	**10 Dollars** 1.4.1879. Portrait Benjamin Franklin at upper left. Like #307 but *Payable to bearer* (4% interest).	2,500	4,000	5,000

Silver Certificates

Red or brown seal; later blue.

1878 Series

		VG	VF	UNC
309	**10 Dollars** 1878. Portrait Robert Morris at left. Rare.	—	10,000	25,000

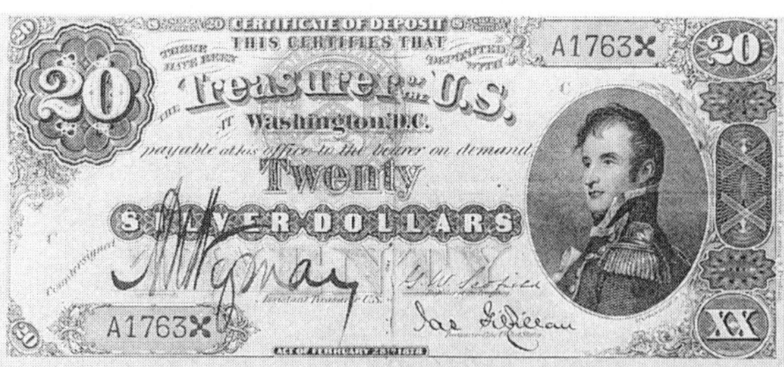

		VG	VF	UNC
310	**20 Dollars** 1878. Portrait Stephen Decatur at right. Rare.	—	15,000	85,000

311	50 Dollars	VG	VF	UNC
	1878. *50* at upper left, vertical *Fifty* below it. Portrait Edward Everett at right. Rare.	20,000	60,000	—

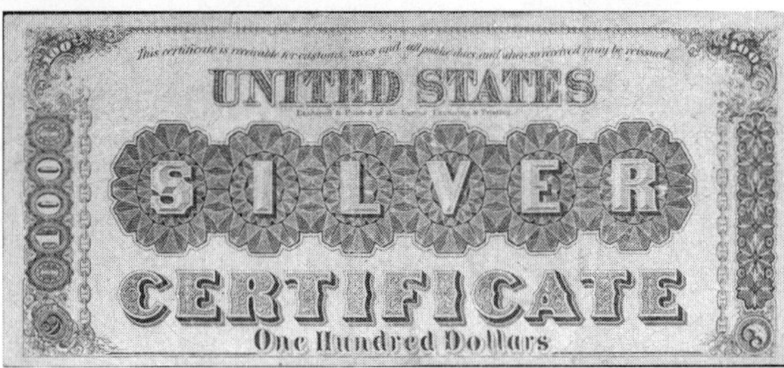

312	100 Dollars	VG	VF	UNC
	1878. Portrait James Monroe at left, *100* at lower right. Rare.	—	—	—
313	**500 Dollars**	**VG**	**VF**	**UNC**
	1878. Portrait Charles Sumner at right. Rare.	—	—	—
314	**1000 Dollars**	**VG**	**VF**	**UNC**
	1878. Portrait William L. Marcy at left. Rare.	—	—	—

1880 Series

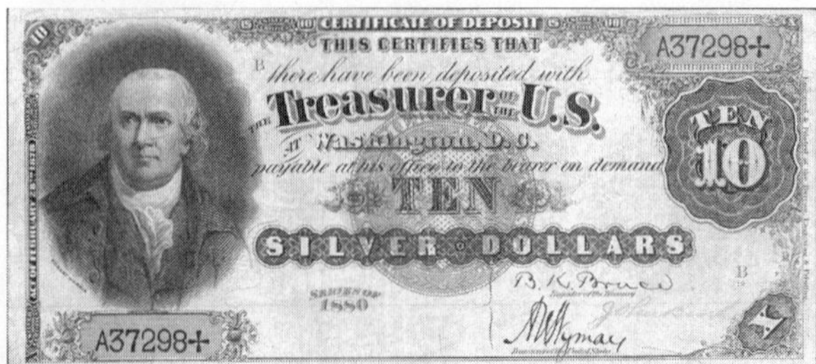

315	10 Dollars	Fine	XF	CU
	1880. Portrait Robert Morris at left.			
	a. Countersigned signature.	—	30,000	—
	b. Without countersigned signature. 2 seal varieties; 3 signature varieties.	2,000	13,000	14,000

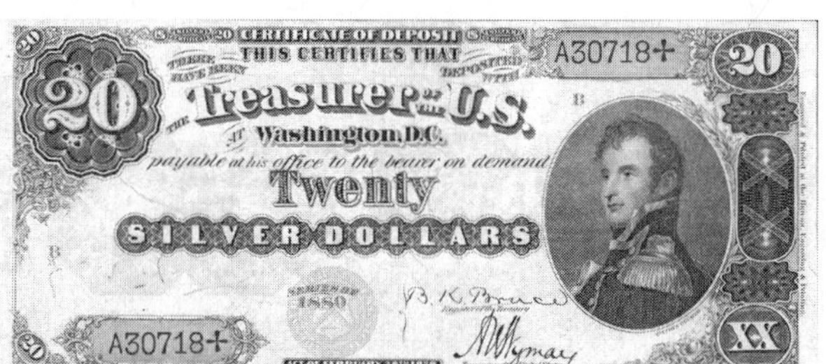

316	20 Dollars	Fine	XF	CU
	1880. Portrait Stephen Decatur at right.			
	a. Countersigned signature.	3,000	21,500	—
	b. Without countersigned signature. 2 seal varieties; 3 signature varieties.	6,000	22,000	—
316A	**20 Dollars**	**Fine**	**XF**	**CU**
	1880. Large brown XX under center seal.	—	—	—

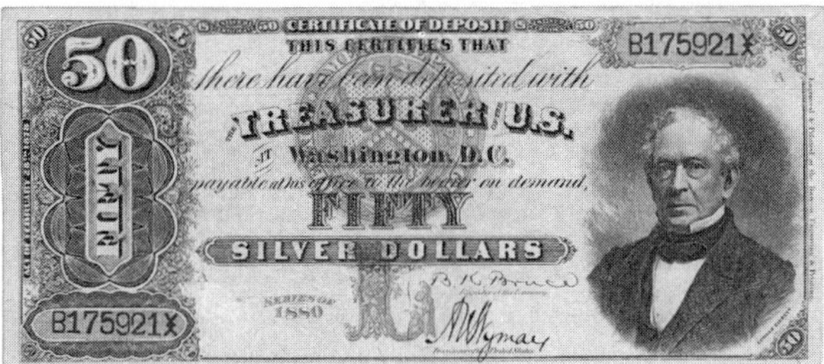

317	50 Dollars	Fine	XF	CU
	1880. *50* at upper left, vertical *Fifty* below it. Portrait Edward Everett at right. Like #311 but without countersigned signature. 3 seal varieties; 5 signature varieties.	12,500	50,000	—

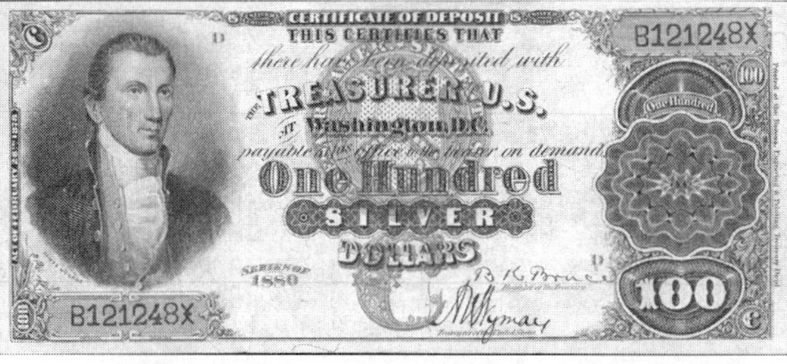

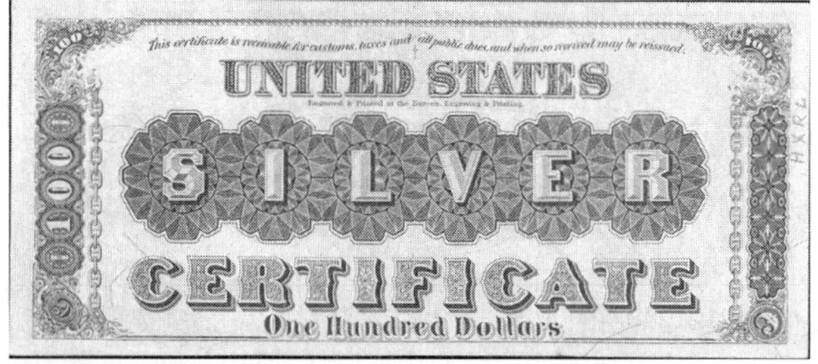

318	100 Dollars	Fine	XF	CU
	1880. Portrait James Monroe at left, *100* at lower right. Like #312. 3 seal varieties; 3 signature varieties.	20,000	352,000	—

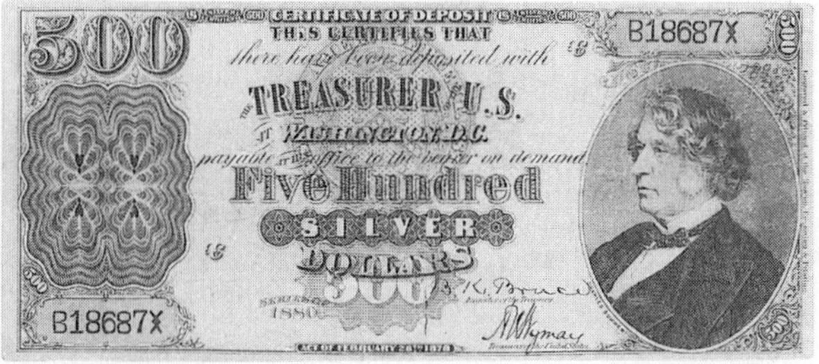

319	500 Dollars	Fine	XF	CU
	1880. Portrait Charles Sumner at right. 3 signature varieties. Rare.	100,000	420,000	—
320	**1000 Dollars**	**Fine**	**XF**	**CU**
	1880. Portrait William L. Marcy at left. 3 signature varieties. Rare.	250,000	580,000	—

1886 Series

		Fine	XF	CU
321	**1 Dollar** 1886. Portrait Martha Washington at left. 4 seal varieties; 4 signature varieties.	250	800	1,250

		Fine	XF	CU
322	**2 Dollars** 1886. Portrait Gen. Winfield Scott Hancock at left. 2 seal varieties; 3 signature varieties.	500	1,000	2,300

		Fine	XF	CU
323	**5 Dollars** 1886. Portrait Ulysses S. Grant at right. 4 seal varieties; 4 signature varieties. Back: Illustration of 5 silver dollars.	1,250	5,500	12,500

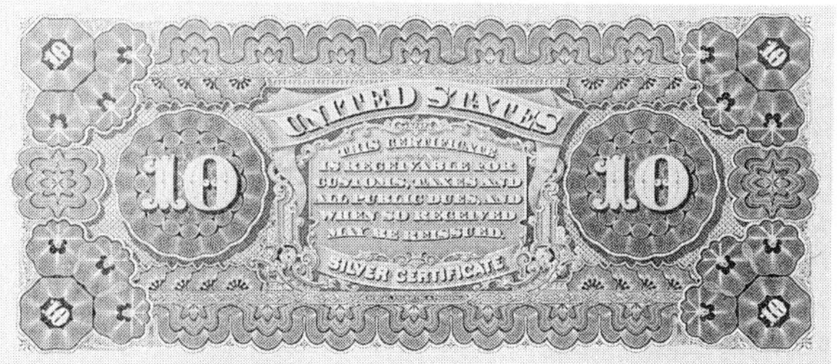

		Fine	XF	CU
324	**10 Dollars** 1886. Portrait Thomas A. Hendricks at center. 3 seal varieties; 4 signature varieties. Back: *UNITED STATES* with text below at center.	1,250	8,500	12,000

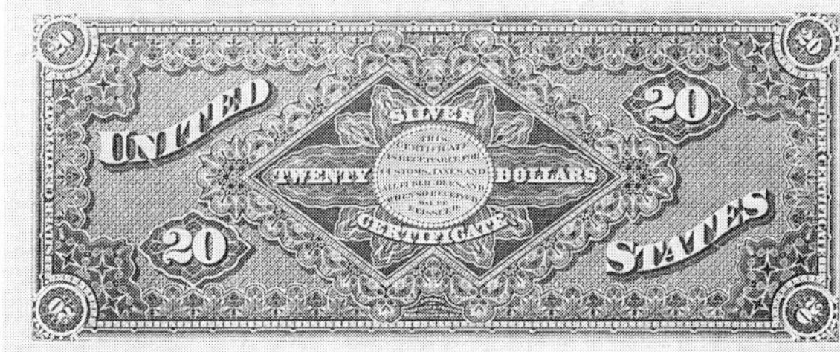

		Fine	XF	CU
325	**20 Dollars** 1886. Portrait Daniel Manning at center. 3 seal varieties; 3 signature varieties. Back: *20* in 4 corners.	3,200	28,500	—

1891 Series

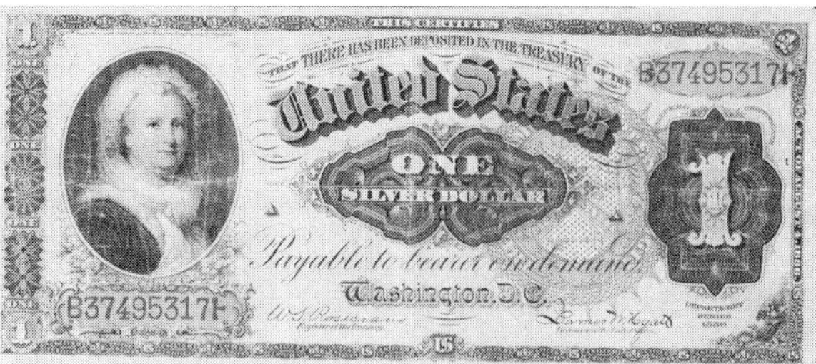

		Fine	XF	CU
326	**1 Dollar** 1891. Portrait Martha Washington at left. Like #321. 2 signature varieties.	375	800	1,850

		Fine	XF	CU
327	**2 Dollars** 1891. Portrait William Windom at center. 2 signature varieties.	600	2,000	5,500

		Fine	XF	CU
328	**5 Dollars** 1891. Portrait Ulysses S. Grant at right. Like #323. 2 signature varieties. Back: Without illustration.	600	2,000	2,750
329	**10 Dollars** 1891. Portrait Thomas A. Hendricks at center. Red seal. 4 signature varieties. Back: *UNITED STATES* at center.	500	2,000	7,000
330	**20 Dollars** 1891. Portrait Daniel Manning at center. Red seal. 4 signature varieties. Back: Different with *XX* at upper left and lower right.	1,000	3,000	7,100
331	**20 Dollars** 1891. Portrait Daniel Manning at center. Blue seal. 2 signature varieties. Like #330. Large blue *XX* at left. Back: Different with *XX* at upper left and lower right.	900	4,800	12,000

		Fine	XF	CU
332	**50 Dollars** 1891. Edward Everett at right. Like #311 but *FIFTY* at upper left. Red seal.	3,000	4,100	30,000
332A	**50 Dollars** 1891. Edward Everett at right. *FIFTY* at upper left. Like #332 but blue seal.	1,750	7,100	9,000

		Fine	XF	CU
333	**100 Dollars** 1891. Portrait James Monroe at left center, *ONE HUNDRED* around *C* at lower right. 2 signature varieties.	10,350	50,000	—

		Fine	XF	CU
334	**1000 Dollars** 1891. Woman with shield and sword at left, portrait William L. Marcy at right. Rare.	—	300,000	—

1896 Series

Educational Series

		Fine	XF	CU
335	**1 Dollar** 1896. *History instructing youth* at left. Border design with names of famous Americans in wreaths. 2 signature varieties. Back: Portrait Martha and George Washington.	350	1,100	1,400

		Fine	XF	CU
336	**2 Dollars** 1896. *Science presenting Steam and Electricity to Commerce and Manufacture.* 2 signature varieties. Back: Portrait Robert Fulton and Samuel Morse.	850	2,750	4,250

		Fine	XF	CU
337	**5 Dollars** 1896. Allegorical figures *America* at center. 3 signature varieties. Back: Portrait Ulysses S. Grant and Gen. Philip H. Sheridan.	1,700	7,100	10,000

1899 Series

		Fine	XF	CU
338	**1 Dollar** 1899. Eagle with flag over portrait of Abraham Lincoln at left and portrait of Ulysses S. Grant at center right.			
	a. *Series of 1899* above right serial #.	150	275	400
	b. *Series of 1899* below right serial #. 3 signature varieties.	150	350	650
	c. *Series of 1899* vertical at right. 7 signature varieties.	150	250	475

		Fine	XF	CU
339	**2 Dollars** 1899. Portrait George Washington between allegorical figures of Commerce and Agriculture at center. 10 signature varieties.	250	625	925

		Fine	XF	CU
340	**5 Dollars** 1899. Portrait Tatoka-Inyanka of the Hunkpapa Sioux with feather headdress at center. 11 signature varieties.	500	1,250	2,250

1908 Series

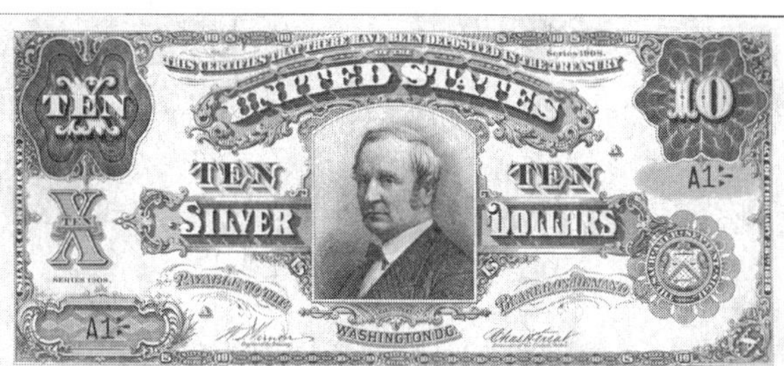

		Fine	XF	CU
341	**10 Dollars** 1908. Portrait Thomas A. Hendricks at center. Like #329 but blue seal. Large blue *X* at left. 3 signature varieties. Back: *UNITED STATES* at center.	600	2,750	7,000

1923 Series

		Fine	XF	CU
342	**1 Dollar** 1923. Portrait George Washington at center. 3 signature varieties.	35.00	70.00	125

		Fine	XF	CU
343	**5 Dollars** 1923. Portrait Abraham Lincoln at center in circle.	600	2,250	2,800

Treasury or Coin Notes

Series of 1890

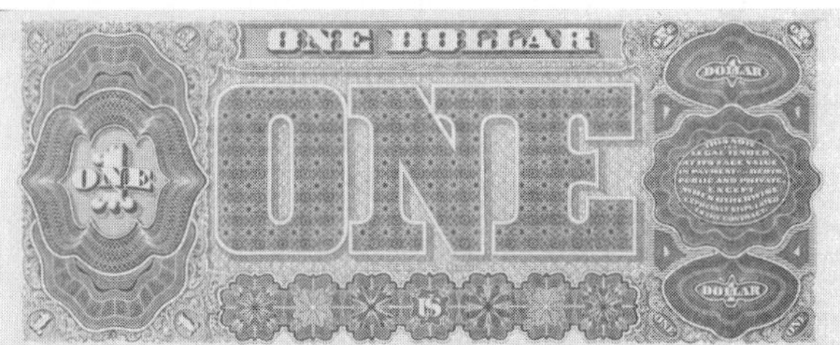

344 1 Dollar

1890. Portrait Edwin M. Stanton at upper left center. 2 seal varieties; 2 signature varieties. Back: Large *ONE* at center.

Fine	XF	CU
550	2,150	4,000

345 2 Dollars

1890. Portrait Gen. James B. McPherson at right. 2 seal varieties; 2 signature varieties. Back: Large *TWO* at center.

Fine	XF	CU
750	5,000	16,500

346 5 Dollars

1890. Portrait Gen. George H. Thomas at center. 2 varieties of seals; 2 signature varieties. Back: Large *FIVE* at center.

Fine	XF	CU
825	2,625	5,500

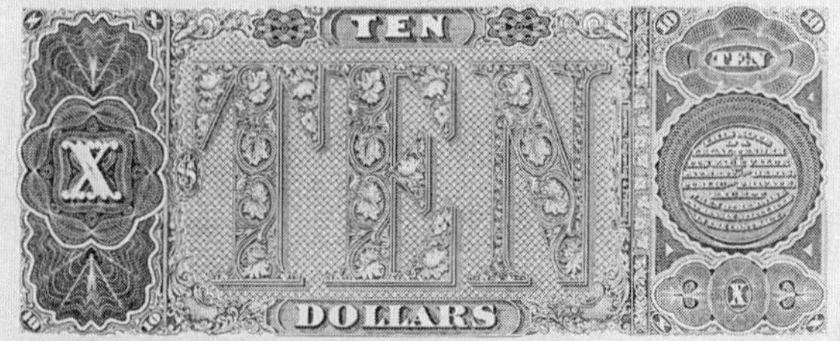

347 10 Dollars

1890. Portrait Gen. Philip Sheridan at center. 2 seal varieties; 2 signature varieties. Back: Large *TEN* at center.

Fine	XF	CU
1,500	6,750	15,000

348 20 Dollars

1890. Portrait John Marshall at left. 2 seal varieties; 2 signature varieties. Back: Large *TWENTY* at center.

Fine	XF	CU
4,000	21,000	40,000

349 100 Dollars

1890. Portrait Commodore David G. Farragut at right. Back: Large *100* at center.

Fine	XF	CU
60,000	152,750	356,000

350 1000 Dollars

1890. Portrait Gen. George G. Meade at left. 2 seal varieties; 2 signature varieties. Back: Large *1000* at center. Rare.

Fine	XF	CU
—	152,750	—

Series of 1891

		Fine	XF	CU
351	**1 Dollar** 1891. Portrait Edwin M. Stanton at left. 3 signature varieties. Back: Text at center below small *ONE*.	250	650	875

		Fine	XF	CU
352	**2 Dollars** 1891. Portrait Gen. James B. McPherson at right. 3 signature varieties. Back: Ornament at center.	650	1,400	2,250

		Fine	XF	CU
353	**5 Dollars** 1891. Portrait Gen. George Thomas at center. 4 signature varieties. Back: Ornament with *Five Dollars* inside at center.	675	1,600	2,250

		Fine	XF	CU
354	**10 Dollars** 1891. Portrait Gen. Philip Sheridan at center. 3 signature varieties. Back: Text at center.	1,250	2,000	3,900

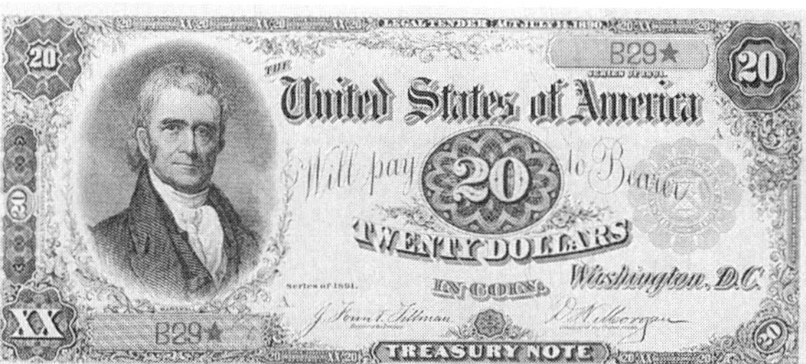

		Fine	XF	CU
355	**20 Dollars** 1891. Portrait John Marshall at left. 2 signature varieties. Back: Text at center.	2,850	9,000	12,500

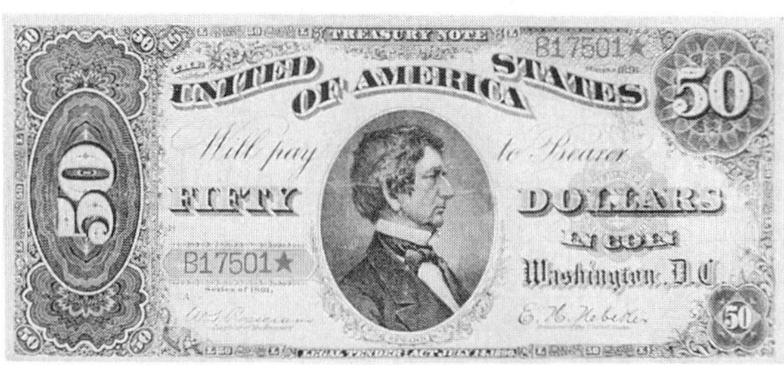

		Fine	XF	CU
356	**50 Dollars** 1891. Portrait William H. Seward at center.	50,000	138,000	258,000

		Fine	XF	CU
357	**100 Dollars** 1891. Portrait Commodore David G. Farragut at right. Back: Text at center.	90,000	150,000	220,000
358	**1000 Dollars** 1891. Portrait Gen. George G. Meade at left. 2 signature varieties. Back: Text at center. Rare.	—	258,000	—

Federal Reserve Notes

PORTRAITS

1 Dollar: George Washington	100 Dollars: Benjamin Franklin
2 Dollars: Thomas Jefferson	500 Dollars: William McKinley
5 Dollars: Abraham Lincoln	1000 Dollars: Grover Cleveland
10 Dollars: Alexander Hamilton	5000 Dollars: James Madison
20 Dollars: Andrew Jackson	10,000 Dollars: Salmon P. Chase
50 Dollars: U. S. Grant	100,000 Dollars: Woodrow Wilson

Imprinted letter, # and place name (in seal at l.) of 1 of the 12 Federal Reserve Banks:

A-1: Boston	E-5: Richmond	I-9: Minneapolis
B-2: New York	F-6: Atlanta	J-10: Kansas City
C-3: Philadelphia	G-7: Chicago	K-11: Dallas
D-4: Cleveland	H-8: St. Louis	L-12: San Francisco

NOTE: Market valuations are for the most common types.

1914 Series

359	5 Dollars	Fine	XF	CU
	1914. Portrait Abraham Lincoln at center.			
	a. Red seal.	300	1,000	1,600
	b. Blue seal. 4 signature varieties.	55.00	200	350

360	10 Dollars	Fine	XF	CU
	1914. Portrait Andrew Jackson at center.			
	a. Red seal.	550	1,500	2,000
	b. Blue seal. 4 signature varieties.	200	300	450

361	20 Dollars	Fine	XF	CU
	1914. Portrait Grover Cleveland at center.			
	a. Red seal.	725	3,650	7,000
	b. Blue seal. 4 signature varieties.	145	1,200	1,650

362	50 Dollars	Fine	XF	CU
	1914. Portrait Ulysses S. Grant at center.			
	a. Red seal.	3,500	3,500	40,000
	b. Blue seal. 4 signature varieties.	475	1,350	1,750

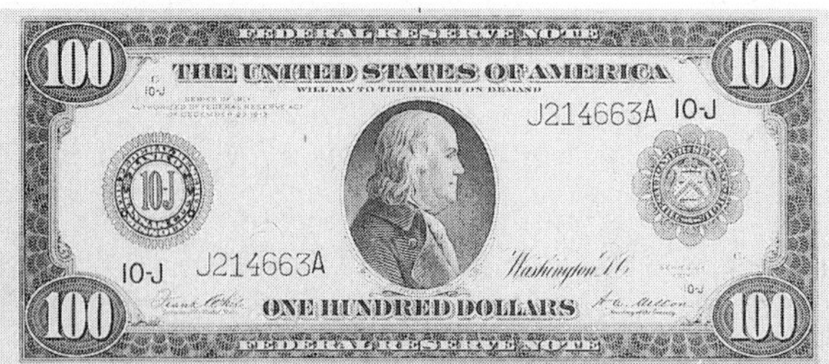

363	100 Dollars	Fine	XF	CU
	1914. Portrait Benjamin Franklin at center.			
	a. Red seal.	2,300	8,500	29,000
	b. Blue seal. 4 signature varieties.	750	1,300	4,250

1918 Series

#	Denomination	Fine	XF	CU
364	**500 Dollars** 1918. Portrait John Marshall at center.	13,500	40,000	—

#	Denomination	Fine	XF	CU
365	**1000 Dollars** 1918. Portrait Alexander Hamilton at center.	35,000	37,375	40,000
366	**5000 Dollars** 1918. Portrait James Madison at center. Rare.	—	—	—

#	Denomination	Fine	XF	CU
367	**10,000 Dollars** 1918. Portrait Salmon P. Chase at center. Rare.	—	—	—

National Currency

Blue Treasury seal. Each note imprinted w/letter, # and place name of 1 of the 12 Federal Reserve Banks:

A-1: Boston	E-5: Richmond	I-9: Minneapolis
B-2: New York	F-6: Atlanta	J-10: Kansas City
C-3: Philadelphia	G-7: Chicago	K-11: Dallas
D-4: Cleveland	H-8: St. Louis	L-12: San Francisco

Sign. varieties. Market valuations are for the most common types.

Series of 1915

#	Denomination	Fine	XF	CU
368	**5 Dollars** 1915. Portrait Abraham Lincoln at left. (only: F; G; J; K; L).	400	750	2,000
369	**10 Dollars** 1915. Portrait Andrew Jackson at left. (only: F; G; J; K).	1,100	4,000	6,000
370	**20 Dollars** 1915. Portrait Grover Cleveland at left. (only: F; G; J; K).	2,250	10,000	1,750

Series of 1918

#	Denomination	Fine	XF	CU
371	**1 Dollar** 1918. Portrait George Washington at left. Back: Eagle and flag at center.	110	225	400

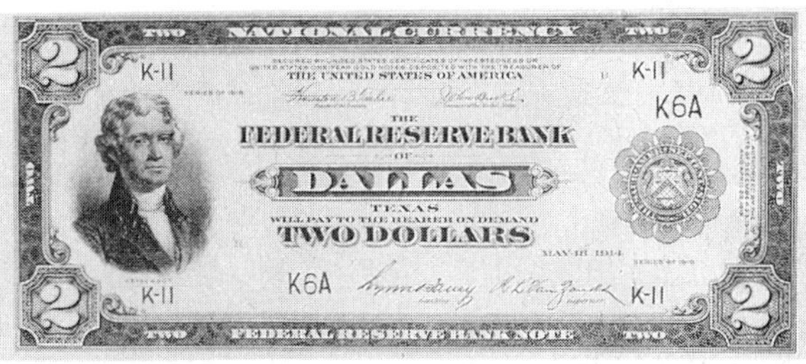

#	Denomination	Fine	XF	CU
372	**2 Dollars** 1918. Portrait Thomas Jefferson at left. Back: Battleship at center.	500	1,200	2,000

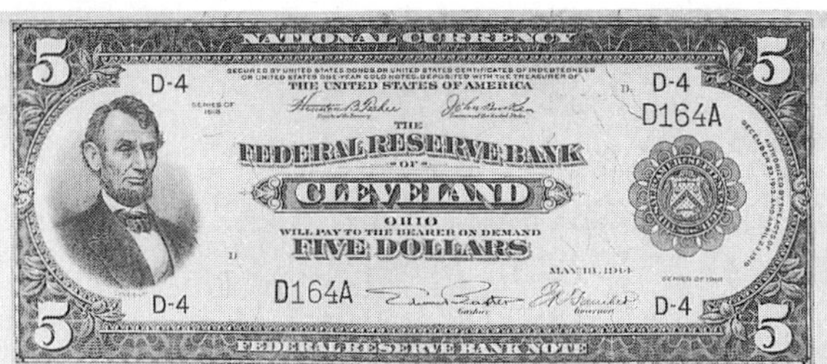

373	5 Dollars	Fine	XF	CU
	1918. Portrait Abraham Lincoln at left. (all except E).	375	875	1,175

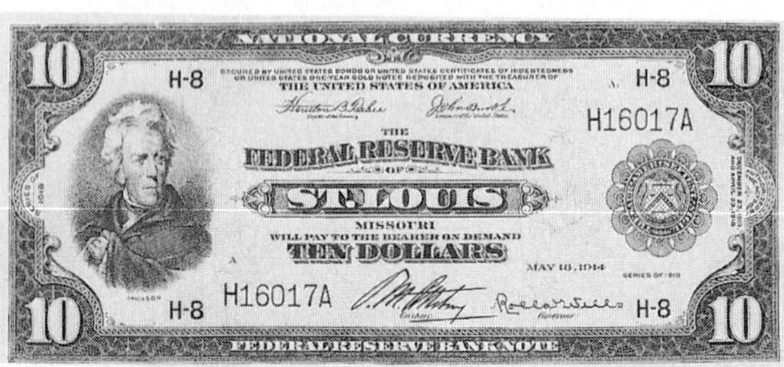

374	10 Dollars	Fine	XF	CU
	1918. Portrait Andrew Jackson at left. (only: B; F; G; H).	1,380	7,750	—

375	20 Dollars	Fine	XF	CU
	1918. Portrait Grover Cleveland at left. (only: F; H).	2,300	6,000	10,750

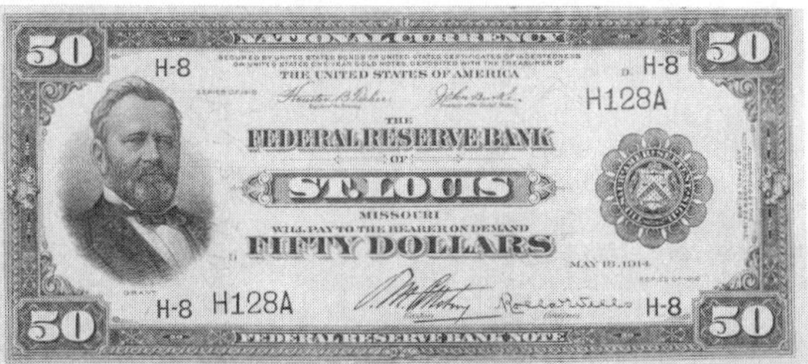

376	50 Dollars	Fine	XF	CU
	1918. Portrait Ulysses S. Grant at left. (only: H).	10,000	27,500	30,000

United States Notes - Small Size

Red Treasury seal.

Series of 1928

377	1 Dollar	Fine	XF	CU
	1928. George Washington at center. Back: Great Seal flanking ONE.	125	225	450

378	2 Dollars	Fine	XF	CU
	Thomas Jefferson at center. Back: Monticello.	10.00	20.00	125
	a. 1928A.	50.00	90.00	475
	b. 1928B.	100	300	600
	c. 1928C.	35.00	75.00	125
	d. 1928D.	20.00	35.00	100
	e. 1928E.	30.00	50.00	90.00
	f. 1928F.	15.00	25.00	75.00
	g. 1928G.	10.00	25.00	50.00

379	5 Dollars	Fine	XF	CU
	Abraham Lincoln at center. Back: Lincoln Memorial.	10.00	20.00	100
	a. 1928A.	20.00	50.00	120
	b. 1928B.	15.00	30.00	60.00
	c. 1928C.	13.00	30.00	55.00
	d. 1928D.	30.00	70.00	150
	e. 1928E.	15.00	25.00	50.00
	f. 1928F.	10.00	50.00	75.00

Series of 1953

380	2 Dollars	Fine	XF	CU
	Thomas Jefferson at center. Back: Monticello.	10.00	15.00	30.00
	a. 1953A.	8.00	12.00	25.00
	b. 1953B.	8.00	12.00	25.00
	c. 1953C.	15.00	30.00	75.00
381	5 Dollars	Fine	XF	CU
	Abraham Lincoln at center. Back: Lincoln Memorial.	10.00	15.00	25.00
	a. 1953A.	10.00	15.00	35.00
	b. 1953B.	10.00	15.00	30.00
	c. 1953C.	10.00	25.00	45.00

National Currency

Brown Treasury seal. Imprinted letter and name of 1 of the 12 Federal Reserve Banks.

A-1: Boston	E-5: Richmond	I-9: Minneapolis
B-2: New York	F-6: Atlanta	J-10: Kansas City
C-3: Philadelphia	G-7: Chicago	K-11: Dallas
D-4: Cleveland	H-8: St. Louis	L-12: San Francisco

Market valuations are for the most common types of each denomination.

Series of 1929

395	5 Dollars	Fine	XF	CU
	1929. Abraham Lincoln at center. Back: Lincoln Memorial. (A-D; F-L).	15.00	75.00	125

396	10 Dollars	Fine	XF	CU
	1929. Alexander Hamilton at center. Back: Treasury Building. (A-L).	30.00	70.00	100

397	20 Dollars	Fine	XF	CU
	1929. Andrew Jackson at center. Back: White House. (A-L).	30.00	60.00	125

398	50 Dollars	Fine	XF	CU
	1929. Ulysses Grant at center. Back: United States Capital Building. (B; D; G; I-L).	75.00	200	250

399	100 Dollars	Fine	XF	CU
	1929. Benjamin Franklin at center. Back: Independence Hall. (B; D-E; G; I-K).	130	165	350

Gold Certificates - Small Size

Gold Treasury seal.

Series of 1928

No.	Description	Fine	XF	CU
400	**10 Dollars** Alexander Hamilton at center. Back: Treasury Building.	100	200	375
	a. 1928A. (Not issued).	—	—	—

No.	Description	Fine	XF	CU
401	**20 Dollars** Andrew Jackson at center. Back: White House.	125	250	400
	a. 1928A. (Not issued).	—	—	—

No.	Description	Fine	XF	CU
402	**50 Dollars** 1928. Ulysses Grant at center. Back: United States Capital Building.	250	1,075	2,000

No.	Description	Fine	XF	CU
403	**100 Dollars** 1928. Benjamin Franklin at center. Back: Independence Hall.	425	1,575	3,200

No.	Description	Fine	XF	CU
404	**500 Dollars** 1928. William McKinley at center.	4,800	10,000	26,000

No.	Description	Fine	XF	CU
405	**1000 Dollars** 1928. Grover Cleveland at center.	6,500	20,000	38,000
406	**5000 Dollars** 1928. James Madison at center. Rare.	—	—	—
407	**10,000 Dollars** 1928. Salmon Chase at center. Rare.	—	—	—

Series of 1934

Issued for internal use within the Federal Reserve System. None were released for circulation.

No.	Description	Fine	XF	CU
408	**100 Dollars** 1934. Benjamin Franklin at center. Back: Independence Hall.	—	—	—
409	**1000 Dollars** 1934. Grover Cleveland at center.	—	—	—

No.	Description	Fine	XF	CU
410	**10,000 Dollars** 1934. Salmon Chase at center.	—	—	—
411	**100,000 Dollars** 1934. Woodrow Wilson at center.	—	—	—

Silver Certificates - Small Size

Blue Treasury seal.

Series of 1928

No.	Description	Fine	XF	CU
412	**1 Dollar** George Washington at center. Back: Great Seal flanking ONE.	25.00	50.00	110
	a. 1928A.	25.00	45.00	65.00
	b. 1928B.	25.00	45.00	70.00
	c. 1928C.	125	425	775
	d. 1928D.	60.00	200	500
	e. 1928E.	350	800	1,400

Series of 1933

No.	Description	Fine	XF	CU
413	**10 Dollars** 1933. Alexander Hamilton at center. Back: Treasury Building. Payable in silver coin.			
	a. 1933A.	1,700	4,000	1,300

Series of 1934

No.	Description	Fine	XF	CU
414	**1 Dollar**	Fine	XF	CU
	1934. George Washington at center. Back: Great Seal flanking ONE.	25.00	40.00	70.00
414A	**5 Dollars**	Fine	XF	CU
	Abraham Lincoln at center. Back: Lincoln Memorial.	15.00	40.00	70.00
	a. 1934A.	15.00	30.00	50.00
	b. 1934B.	10.00	25.00	100
	c. 1934C.	10.00	30.00	40.00
	d. 1934D.	10.00	20.00	50.00
414AY	**5 Dollars**	Fine	XF	CU
	1934A. Abraham Lincoln at center. Yellow seal. Back: Lincoln Memorial. (Issued for military use in North Africa.) 70.00	150	300	
415	**10 Dollars**	Fine	XF	CU
	Alexander Hamilton at center. Back: Treasury Building.	30.00	60.00	100
	a. 1934A.	35.00	135	175
	b. 1934B.	125	325	600
	c. 1934C.	20.00	50.00	100
	d. 1934D.	30.00	40.00	150
415Y	**10 Dollars**	Fine	XF	CU
	1934 Alexander Hamilton at center. Back: Treasury building. Yellow seal. (Issued for military use in North Africa.)	45.00	70.00	175

Series of 1935

No.	Description	VG	VF	UNC
416	**1 Dollar**	VG	VF	UNC
	George Washington at center. Back: Great Seal flanking ONE.	5.00	10.00	325
	a. 1935A.	3.00	5.00	20.00
	b. 1935B.	3.00	5.00	20.00
	c. 1935C.	3.00	4.00	20.00

No.	Description	Fine	XF	CU
416AR	**1 Dollar**	Fine	XF	CU
	1935A. George Washington at center. Experimental issue with red *R* at lower right. Back: Great Seal flanking ONE.	75.00	150	400
416AS	**1 Dollar**	Fine	XF	CU
	1935A. George Washington at center. Experimental issue with red *S* at lower right. Back: Great Seal flanking ONE.	75.00	150	400
416AY	**1 Dollar**	Fine	XF	CU
	1935A. George Washington at center. Yellow seal. Back: Great Seal flanking ONE. (Issued for military use in North Africa).	45.00	65.00	175
416D1	**1 Dollar**	VG	VF	UNC
	1935D. George Washington at center. Type I, wide margin. Back: Great Seal flanking ONE.	—	—	—
416D2	**1 Dollar**	Fine	XF	CU
	George Washington at center. Type II, narrow design. Back: Great Seal flanking ONE.	3.00	5.00	15.00
	e. 1935E.	2.00	4.00	15.00
	f. 1935F.	2.00	4.00	15.00
416NM	**1 Dollar**	Fine	XF	CU
	1935G. George Washington at center. Back: Great Seal flanking ONE. Without motto.	2.00	5.00	15.00
416WM	**1 Dollar**	Fine	XF	CU
	George Washington at center. Back: Great Seal flanking ONE. Motto: *In God We Trust.*	2.00	7.00	60.00
	h. 1935H.	2.00	5.00	25.00

Series of 1953

No.	Description	Fine	XF	CU
417	**5 Dollars**	Fine	XF	CU
	Abraham Lincoln at center. Back: Lincoln Memorial.	10.00	25.00	40.00
	a. 1953A.	10.00	15.00	45.00
	b. 1953B.	8.00	15.00	30.00
418	**10 Dollars**	Fine	XF	CU
	Alexander Hamilton at center. Back: Treasury Building.	25.00	75.00	125
	a. 1953B.	20.00	75.00	100
	b. 1953A.	30.00	125	150

Series of 1957

No.	Description	Fine	XF	CU
419	**1 Dollar**	Fine	XF	CU
	George Washington at center. Back: Great Seal flanking ONE.	2.00	3.50	10.00
	a. 1957A.	2.00	3.50	10.00
	b. 1957B.	2.00	3.50	10.00

NOTE: For a full listing of all notes with overprint: *HAWAII* see Hawaii, #36-41.

Federal Reserve Notes - Small Size

In the various Federal Reserve issues, 1928, 1934 and 1950 in this book, prices vary widely depending on the district is involved. while notes from any of the districts could be quite scarce, Districts from Atlanta, Richmond, Minneapolis, Dallas, Kansas and San Francisco tend to be more difficult to find and notes from NY, and Chicago tend to be quite common. For more specific information check *The Standard Catalog of United States Paper Money.*

PORTRAITS

1 Dollar: George Washington	100 Dollars: Benjamin Franklin
2 Dollars: Thomas Jefferson	500 Dollars: William McKinley
5 Dollars: Abraham Lincoln	1000 Dollars: Grover Cleveland
10 Dollars: Alexander Hamilton	5000 Dollars: James Madison
20 Dollars: Andrew Jackson	10,000 Dollars: Salmon P. Chase
50 Dollars: U. S. Grant	100,000 Dollars: Woodrow Wilson Green Treasury seal.

REPLACEMENT NOTES: Serial # suffix is an *.

Imprinted #, letter and name (in seal at l.) of 1 of the 12 Federal Reserve Banks:

A-1: Boston	E-5: Richmond	I-9: Minneapolis
B-2: New York	F-6: Atlanta	J-10: Kansas City
C-3: Philadelphia	G-7: Chicago	K-11: Dallas
D-4: Cleveland	H-8: St. Louis	L-12: San Francisco

1928 Series

No.	Description	Fine	XF	CU
420	**5 Dollars**	Fine	XF	CU
	Abraham Lincoln at center. Back: Lincoln Memorial.	20.00	35.00	150
	a. 1928A. (A-L).	10.00	25.00	175
	b. 1928B. (A-L).	10.00	25.00	75.00
	c. 1928C. (D, F, L).	400	2,500	3,500
	d. 1928D. (F).	1,700	3,500	5,000
421	**10 Dollars**	Fine	XF	CU
	Alexander Hamilton at center. Back: Treasury Building.	20.00	45.00	200
	a. 1928A. (A-L).	20.00	60.00	300
	b. 1928B. (A-L).	20.00	30.00	95.00
	c. 1928C. (B, D, E, G).	20.00	60.00	450
422	**20 Dollars**	Fine	XF	CU
	Andrew Jackson at center. Back: White House.	30.00	75.00	250
	a. 1928A. (A-H; J-K).	30.00	75.00	300
	b. 1928B. (A-L).	30.00	50.00	150
	c. 1928C. (G; L).	345	800	2,500
423	**50 Dollars**	Fine	XF	CU
	Ulysses Grant at center. Back: United States Capital Building.	70.00	125	600
	a. 1928A. (A-L).	70.00	90.00	400
424	**100 Dollars**	Fine	XF	CU
	Benjamin Franklin at center. Back: Independence Hall.	125	225	750
	a. 1928A. (A-L).	125	175	300

No.	Description	Fine	XF	CU
425	**500 Dollars**	Fine	XF	CU
	1928. William McKinley at center. (A-L).	750	850	3,000

426	1000 Dollars	Fine	XF	CU
	1928. Grover Cleveland at center. (A-L).	1,500	2,500	5,000

427	5000 Dollars	Fine	XF	CU
	1928. James Madison at center. (A-B; D-G; J-L).	20,000	70,000	100,000

428	10,000 Dollars	Fine	XF	CU
	1928. Salmon P. Chase at center. (A-B; D-L).	45,000	90,000	150,000

1934 Series

No.	Description	Fine	XF	CU
429D	**5 Dollars**	Fine	XF	CU
	Abraham Lincoln at center. Dark green seal. Back: Lincoln Memorial. (A-L).	10.00	20.00	80.00
	a. 1934A. (A-H; L).	10.00	20.00	40.00
	b. 1934B. (A-J; L).	10.00	20.00	50.00
	c. 1934C. (A-L).	10.00	20.00	60.00
	d. 1934D. (A-L).	10.00	20.00	60.00
430D	**10 Dollars**	Fine	XF	CU
	Alexander Hamilton at center. Dark green seal. Back: Treasury Building. (A-L).	15.00	18.00	60.00
	a. 1934A. (A-L).	12.00	15.00	30.00
	b. 1934B. (A-L).	15.00	25.00	50.00
	c. 1934C. (A-L).	12.00	15.00	40.00
	d. 1934D. (A-L).	12.00	15.00	50.00
431D	**20 Dollars**	Fine	XF	CU
	Portrait Andrew Jackson at center. Dark green seal. (A-L).	25.00	40.00	60.00
	a. 1934A. (A-L).	25.00	30.00	75.00
	b. 1934B. (A-L).	25.00	35.00	100
	c. 1934C. (A-L).	25.00	35.00	75.00
	d. 1934D. (A-L).	25.00	30.00	65.00
431L	**20 Dollars**	Fine	XF	CU
	1934. Andrew Jackson at center. Light green seal. Back: White House.	—	—	—
432D	**50 Dollars**	Fine	XF	CU
	Ulysses Grant at center. Dark green seal. Back: United States Capital Building. (A-L).	55.00	60.00	200
	a. 1934A. (A-B; D-L).	60.00	100	275
	b. 1934B. (C-L).	60.00	125	400
	c. 1934C. (A-K).	60.00	110	220
	d. 1934D. (A-C; E-G; K).	85.00	200	400
432L	**50 Dollars**	Fine	XF	CU
	1934. Ulysses Grant at center. Light green seal. Back: United States Capital Building.	—	—	—

No.	Description	Fine	XF	CU
433D	**100 Dollars**	Fine	XF	CU
	Benjamin Franklin at center. Dark green seal. Back: Independence Hall. (A-L).	125	145	300
	a. 1934A. (A-L).	125	180	300
	b. 1934B. (A; C-K).	150	225	450
	c. 1934C. (A-D; F-L).	150	175	500
	d. 1934D. (B-C; F-H, K).	175	350	500
433L	**100 Dollars**	Fine	XF	CU
	1934. Benjamin Franklin at center. Light green seal. Back: Independence Hall.	FV	FV	175
434	**500 Dollars**	Fine	XF	CU
	William McKinley at center.	600	850	1,500
	a. 1934A. (B-E; G-L).	750	1,250	1,750
	b. 1934B. (F).	—	—	—
	c. 1934C. (A-B).	—	—	—

No.	Description	Fine	XF	CU
435	**1000 Dollars**	Fine	XF	CU
	Grover Cleveland at center.	1,500	2,000	3,000
	a. 1934A. (A-J; L).	1,500	2,000	3,000
	b. 1934C. (A-B).	—	—	—
436	**5000 Dollars**	Fine	XF	CU
	James Madison at center.	20,000	65,000	—
	a. 1934A. (H).	—	—	—
	b. 1934B. (A-B).	—	—	—

No.	Description	Fine	XF	CU
437	**10,000 Dollars**	Fine	XF	CU
	Salmon Chase at center.	45,000	170,000	—
	a. 1934A. (G).	—	—	—
	b. 1934B. (B).	—	—	—

1950 Series

		Fine	XF	CU
438	**5 Dollars** Abraham Lincoln at center. Back: Lincoln Memorial.	7.50	12.00	50.00
	a. 1950A. (A-L).	7.50	12.00	25.00
	b. 1950B. (A-L).	7.50	12.00	30.00
	c. 1950C. (A-L).	7.50	10.00	15.00
	d. 1950D. (A-L).	7.50	10.00	15.00
	e. 1950E. (B; G; L).	7.50	15.00	25.00

		Fine	XF	CU
439	**10 Dollars** Alexander Hamilton at center. Back: Treasury Building.	12.50	20.00	80.00
	a. 1950A. (A-L).	12.50	30.00	70.00
	b. 1950B. (A-L).	12.50	20.00	40.00
	c. 1950C. (A-L).	12.50	25.00	55.00
	d. 1950D. (A-H; J-L).	12.50	25.00	55.00
	e. 1950E. (B; G; L).	90.00	160	325

		Fine	XF	CU
440	**20 Dollars** Andrew Jackson at center. Back: White House.	25.00	35.00	70.00
	a. 1950A. (A-L).	25.00	30.00	60.00
	b. 1950B. (A-L).	25.00	30.00	60.00
	c. 1950C. (A-L).	25.00	35.00	65.00
	d. 1950D. (A-L).	25.00	35.00	75.00
	e. 1950E. (B; G; L).	25.00	50.00	100

		Fine	XF	CU
441	**50 Dollars** Ulysses Grant at center. Back: United States Capital Building.	75.00	125	250
	a. 1950A. (A-H; J-L).	75.00	100	225
	b. 1950B. (A-E; G-H; J-L).	60.00	80.00	175
	c. 1950C. (A-E; G-L).	60.00	80.00	175
	d. 1950D. (A-L).	60.00	100	200
	e. 1950E. (B; G; L).	175	375	750

		Fine	XF	CU
442	**100 Dollars** Benjamin Franklin at center. Back: Independence Hall.	125	200	450
	a. 1950A. (A-L).	110	125	250
	b. 1950B. (A-L).	125	185	300
	c. 1950C. (A-L).	FV	300	700
	d. 1950D. (A-L).	110	125	200
	e. 1950E. (B; G; L).	150	300	750

Small Size Currency

Some of the most frequently asked questions we hear from contributors about small size currency relate to silver certificates and Hawaii notes. Below is some general information about these two types of notes. For more information please see the *Standard Catalog of® United States Paper Money.*

Silver Certificates

From the 1929 release date of the small size U.S. currency issues, until Silver Certificate legislation was abolished by a Congressional Act on June 4, 1963, small size Silver Certificates, distinguished by their blue Treasury seal and serial number, were issued in denominations of $1, $5, and $10.

The earliest small size silver notes were redeemable for "One Silver Dollar," (or the appropriate number) as had been the large size issues. A change in the redemption clause, however, was made with the Silver Purchase Act of 1934, which specified the certificates be redeemable for silver dollars or silver bullion. At that time the wording on the notes was changed to read: "One Dollar in Silver." In March, 1964, by order of the Secretary of the Treasury, redemption in silver dollars was halted, and on June 24, 1968, redemption in silver bullion was also discontinued. Like all U.S. currency issued since 1861, Silver Certificates retain their status as legal tender, though today they are convertible only into current U.S. Federal Reserve Notes.

Hawaii Overprints

As an economic defense precaution against Japanese invasion and occupation of Hawaii, specially marked U.S. currency was issued there in July, 1942, to replace other types in circulation. Distinguished by brown seal and serial numbers, and by "HAWAII" overprints on face and back, such notes could have been declared worthless in the event large numbers of them were captured.

The $1 notes used as emergency currency were Silver Certificates of Series 1935A, while $5s, $10s, and $20s were overprinted examples of San Francisco-district Federal Reserve Notes; the $5s in Series 1934 and '34A, the $10s in Series 1934A only, and the $20s in Series 1934 and '34A. All notes bear the Julian-Morgenthau combination.

By late October, 1944, the emergency monetary conditions were declared ended, and normal currency returned to use in Hawaii, and the Hawaii-overprinted notes went on to do further duty during the occupation of formerly Japanese-held islands in the Pacific.

More information on Hawaii notes can be found in the Hawaii section of this book.

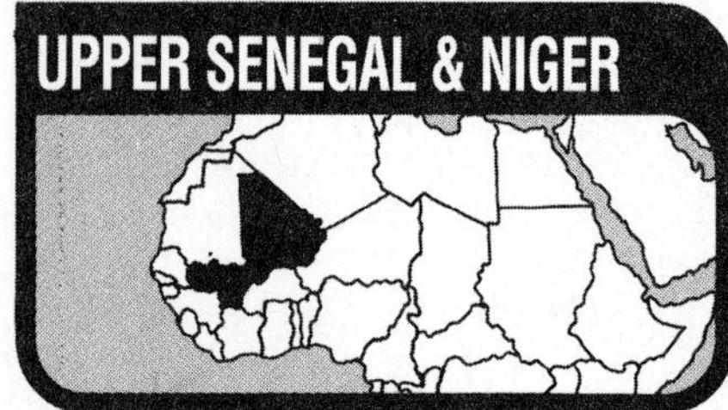

Once a part of the ancient Malinke Kingdom that controlled the area from the 11th to the 17th centuries. The upper course of the Senegal River runs through the western part of the area. The middle course of the Niger River has 1,000 miles of navigable waters within these boundaries. Legendary Tombouctou (Timbuktu) is a port on the Niger in the center of the country. French dominance in the area occurred in the 1890s. The territories of Senegambia and Niger were formed into the colony of Upper Senegal and Niger in 1904. Following World War I the name of the area was changed to French Sudan.

RULERS:
French to 1960

MONETARY SYSTEM:
1 Franc = 100 Centimes

FRENCH ADMINISTRATION

Gouvernement Général de l'Afrique Occidentale Française (A.O.F.)

Haut-Senegal-Niger

Law of 11.2.1917

#	Denomination	VG	VF	UNC
1	**0.50 Franc** *L.1917.* Dark brown on light brown underprint. Reverse of 50 centimes coin at left, obverse at right.			
	a. Issued note	900	2,250	5,000
	ct. Color trial in dark brown on grey-green underprint.	—	—	5,000
2	**1 Franc** *L.1917.* Requires confirmation.	—	—	—
3	**2 Francs** *L.1917.* Requires confirmation.	—	—	—

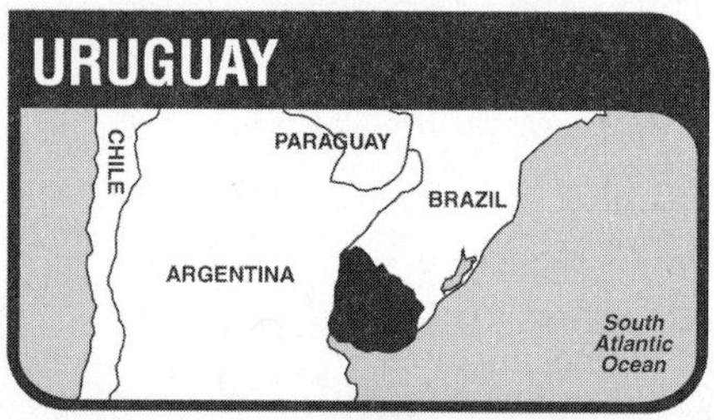

The Oriental Republic of Uruguay (so called because of its location on the east bank of the Uruguay River) is situated on the Atlantic coast of South America between Argentina and Brazil. This most advanced of South American countries has an area of 176,220 sq. km. and a population of 3.48 million. Capital: Montevideo. Uruguay's chief economic asset is its rich, rolling grassy plains. Meat, wool, hides and skins are exported.Montevideo, founded by the Spanish in 1726 as a military stronghold, soon took advantage of its natural harbor to become an important commercial center. Claimed by Argentina but annexed by Brazil in 1821, Uruguay declared its independence four years later and secured its freedom in 1828 after a three-year struggle. The administrations of President Jose Battle in the early 20th century established widespread political, social, and economic reforms that established a statist tradition. A violent Marxist urban guerrilla movement named the Tupamaros, launched in the late 1960s, led Uruguay's president to cede control of the government to the military in 1973. By year end, the rebels had been crushed, but the military continued to expand its hold over the government. Civilian rule was not restored until 1985. In 2004, the left-of-center Frente Amplio Coalition won national elections that effectively ended 170 years of political control previously held by the Colorado and Blanco parties. Uruguay's political and labor conditions are among the freest on the continent.

MONETARY SYSTEM:
1 Patacón = 960 Reis
1 Peso = 8 Reales to 1860
1 Peso = 100 Centésimos
1 Doblon = 10 Pesos, 1860-1875
1 Patacón = 960 Reis
1 Peso = 8 Reales to 1860
1 Peso = 100 Centésimos, 1860-1975
1 Nuevo Peso = 1000 Old Pesos, 1975-1993
1 Peso Uruguayo = 1000 Nuevos Pesos, 1993-

REPUBLIC

Poliza de Deuda Publica

Public Debt Drafts

Ley de 29 April 1835

#A13-A17 Dated between 3-14.8.1835.

#	Denomination	Good	Fine	XF
A13	**400 Pesos** Aug. 1835. Black. National symbols of hill, scale, horse and bull in 4 corners, Montevideo Bay between cargo at left and right along bottom.	—	40.00	100

#	Denomination	Good	Fine	XF
A14	**500 Pesos** Aug. 1835. Black. National symbols of hill, scale, horse and bull in 4 corners, Montevideo Bay between cargo at left and right along bottom.			
	a. Handwritten denomination.	—	—	—
	b. Printed denomination.	—	—	—
A16	**2000 Pesos** Aug. 1835. Black. National symbols of hill, scale, horse and bull in 4 corners, Montevideo Bay between cargo at left and right along bottom.	—	—	—
A17	**5000 Pesos** Aug. 1835. Black. National symbols of hill, scale, horse and bull in 4 corners, Montevideo Bay between cargo at left and right along bottom.	—	—	—

Color Abbreviation Guide

New to the *Standard Catalog of® World Paper Money* are the following abbreviations related to color references:

BC: Back color
PC: Paper color

Banco Nacional

Ley de 23 de Junio de 1862

#A87-A98 issues were overprinted or perforated for the branches of:

Artigas	Florida	Rosario
Canelones	Maldonado	Salto
Carmelo	Minas	San José
Cerro Largo	Paysandú	Soriano
Colonia	Rio Negro	Tacuarembo
Durazno	Rivera	Treinta y Tres
Flores	Rocha	

		Good	Fine	XF
A87	**10 Centésimos** 25.8.1887. Black on light blue underprint. Arms at left, cattle stampede at center. Signature varieties. Back: Seated woman at center. BC: Blue. Printer: W&S.			
	a. Issued note without branch office perforation or overprint.	4.00	15.00	40.00
	b. Cancelled with perforation: *PAGADO 25.8.96.*	3.00	12.50	30.00
	c. Issued or cancelled with branch office perforation or overprint.	5.00	20.00	60.00

		Good	Fine	XF
A88	**20 Centésimos** 25.8.1887. Black on pink underprint. Mercury seated at left, arms at right. Signature varieties. BC: Green. Printer: W&S.			
	a. Issued note without branch office perforation or overprint.	4.00	15.00	40.00
	b. Cancelled with perforation: *PAGADO 25.8.96.*	3.00	12.50	30.00
	c. Issued or cancelled with branch office perforation or overprint.	5.00	20.00	60.00

		Good	Fine	XF
A89	**50 Centésimos** 25.8.1887. Black on yellow underprint. Arms at left, laureate woman's head at center. Signature varieties. BC: Brown. Printer: W&S.			
	a. Issued note without branch office perforation or overprint.	5.00	20.00	50.00
	b. Cancelled with perforation: *PAGADO 25.8.96.*	4.00	15.00	40.00
	c. Issued or cancelled with branch office perforation or overprint.	5.00	20.00	60.00

		Good	Fine	XF
A90	**1 Peso** 25.8.1887. Black on green and orange underprint. Arms at left, village at center. Signature varieties. Back: Seated woman at center. BC: Orange. Printer: W&S.			
	a. Issued note without branch office perforation or overprint.	8.00	25.00	65.00
	b. Cancelled with perforation: *PAGADO 25.8.96.*	6.00	20.00	60.00
	c. Issued or cancelled with branch office perforation or overprint.	10.00	30.00	80.00

		Good	Fine	XF
A91	**2 Pesos** 25.8.1887. Black on rose and pastel blue underprint. Arms at upper left, bank at upper center. Signature varieties. Back: Woman at center. BC: Blue. Printer: W&S.			
	a. Issued note.	8.00	25.00	65.00
	b. Cancelled with perforation: *PAGADO 25.8.96.*	6.00	20.00	60.00
	c. Issued or cancelled with branch office perforation or overprint.	10.00	30.00	80.00

		Good	Fine	XF
A92	**5 Pesos** 25.8.1887. Black on gold and brown underprint. Arms at upper left, man at center. Signature varieties. Back: Buildings and street scene at center. BC: Brown. Printer: W&S.			
	a. Issued note without branch office perforation or overprint.	10.00	30.00	80.00
	b. Cancelled with perforation: *PAGADO 25.8.96.*	6.00	20.00	60.00
	c. Issued or cancelled with branch office perforation or overprint.	15.00	50.00	100

		Good	Fine	XF
A93	**10 Pesos** 25.8.1887. Black on green and orange underprint. Arms at left, allegorical woman holding torch at right. Signature varieties. BC: Orange. Printer: W&S.			
	a. Issued note without branch office perforation or overprint.	15.00	50.00	100
	b. Cancelled with perforation: *PAGADO 25.8.96.*	10.00	30.00	80.00
	c. Issued or cancelled with branch office perforation or overprint.	17.50	55.00	120

A94	20 Pesos	Good	Fine	XF
	25.8.1887. Black on yellow and tan underprint. Man at left, arms at top left center, building at lower right. Signature varieties. Back: Liberty head at center. BC: Dark blue. Printer: W&S.			
	a. Issued note without branch office perforation or overprint.	15.00	50.00	100
	b. Cancelled with perforation: *PAGADO 25.8.96.*	10.00	30.00	80.00
	c. Issued or cancelled with branch office perforation or overprint.	20.00	60.00	150

A95	50 Pesos	Good	Fine	XF
	25.8.1887. Black on orange and green underprint. Man at left, church at center, arms at right. Signature varieties. Back: Sheep at center. BC: Dark orange. Printer: W&S.			
	a. Issued note without branch office perforation or overprint.	20.00	60.00	150
	b. Cancelled with perforation: *PAGADO 25.8.96.*	10.00	30.00	80.00
	c. Issued or cancelled with branch office perforation or overprint.	30.00	85.00	200

A96	100 Pesos	Good	Fine	XF
	25.8.1887. Black on green and pink underprint. Man at left, arms and cherubs at center, train at right. Signature varieties. Back: Woman at center. BC: Brown. Printer: W&S.			
	a. Issued note.	40.00	100	250
	b. Cancelled with perforation: *PAGADO 25.8.96.*	15.00	50.00	100
A97	200 Pesos	Good	Fine	XF
	25.8.1887. Black on green and gold underprint. Arms at left, portrait at center, building at right. Signature varieties. Back: Street scene. BC: Green. Printer: W&S.			
	a. Issued note.	75.00	200	500
	b. Cancelled with perforation: *PAGADO 25.8.96.*	50.00	150	300
A98	500 Pesos	Good	Fine	XF
	25.8.1887. Black on pink underprint. Man at left, arms and cherubs at center, map at right. Signature varieties. Back: Group of men with flag. BC: Brown. Printer: W&S.			
	a. Issued note.	—	—	—
	b. Cancelled with perforation: *PAGADO 25.8.96.*	100	200	400

República Oriental del Uruguay

Comisión de Extinción de Billetes

1875 Issue

#A99-A107 with overprint: *Comisión de Extinción de Billetes* in rectangular frame on notes of La República Oriental del Uruguay.

A99	20 Centésimos	Good	Fine	XF
	27.3.1875. Black on brown underprint. Raphael's Angel at center. Uniface. Printer: ABNC. Overprint: *Comision de Extincion de Billetes* in rectangular frame.	20.00	60.00	150

A100	50 Centésimos	Good	Fine	XF
	27.3.1875. Black on green underprint. Eagle at left, cows at upper center. Uniface. Printer: ABNC. Overprint: *Comision de Extincion de Billetes* in rectangular frame.	25.00	75.00	200

A101	1 Peso	Good	Fine	XF
	27.3.1875. Black on pink underprint. Standing Columbia at left, sailor and anchor at center. BC: Reddish purple. Printer: ABNC. Overprint: *Comision de Extincion de Billetes* in rectangular frame.	50.00	150	325

		Good	Fine	XF
A102	**2 Pesos** 27.3.1875. Black on brown underprint. Ostrich at lower left, horses at top center; woman at lower right. BC: Brown. Printer: ABNC. Overprint: *Comision de Extincion de Billetes* in rectangular frame.	75.00	275	—

		Good	Fine	XF
A103	**5 Pesos** 27.3.1875. Black on brown underprint. Arms at left, cow and calf at center, allegory of agriculture at right. BC: Brown. Printer: ABNC. Overprint: *Comision de Extincion de Billetes* in rectangular frame.	—	—	—

		Good	Fine	XF
A104	**10 Pesos** 27.3.1875. Black on red-brown underprint. Arms at left, cattle at center, shepherd with sheep at right. Back: Steam locomotive at center. BC: Red-brown. Printer: ABNC. Overprint: *Comision de Extincion de Billetes* in rectangular frame.	—	—	—

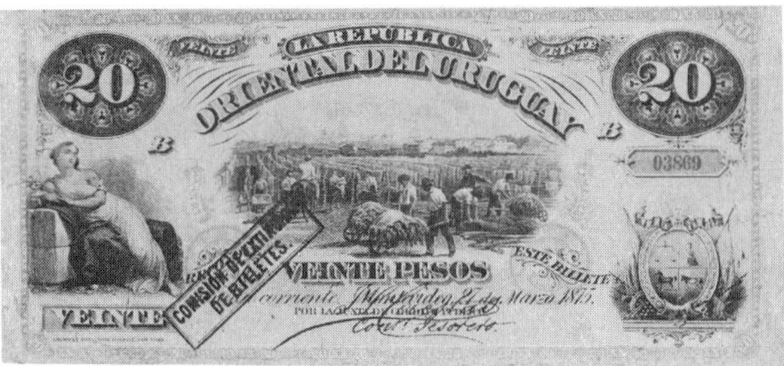

		Good	Fine	XF
A105	**20 Pesos** 27.3.1875. Black on orange underprint. Allegory of commerce at left, farm workers at center, arms at right. Back: Steer head at center. BC: Orange. Printer: ABNC. Overprint: *Comision de Extincion de Billetes* in rectangular frame.	—	—	—

		Good	Fine	XF
A106	**50 Pesos** 27.3.1875. Black on red-orange underprint. *Columbia* at left, three farmers with reaper at center, arms at right. Back: Allegorical figures at center, ships at left and right. Printer: ABNC. Overprint: *Comision de Extincion de Billetes* in rectangular frame.	—	—	—
A107	**100 Pesos** 27.3.1875. Printer: ABNC. Overprint: *Comision de Extincion de Billetes* in rectangular frame.	—	—	—

Junta de Crédito Público

Ley 4.5.1870

		Good	Fine	XF
A108	**20 Centésimos** *L.1870.* Black on orange underprint. Stallion at left. Uniface. Printer: BWC. PC: Yellow.	5.00	25.00	60.00

		Good	Fine	XF
A109	**50 Centésimos** *L.1870.* Black on brown underprint. Cow at left, arms at upper center right. Uniface. Printer: BWC.			
	a. Purple paper.	10.00	35.00	85.00
	b. White paper.	10.00	35.00	85.00

		Good	Fine	XF
A110	**1 Peso** *L.1870.* Black on dark green underprint. Winged Mercury seated at left. Uniface. Printer: BWC.			
	a. Dark green paper.	20.00	60.00	150
	b. Light green paper.	20.00	60.00	150

		Good	Fine	XF
A111	**5 Pesos** *L.1870.* Blue. Ewe at left, arms at upper center right. Uniface. Printer: BWC.	35.00	75.00	250
A112	**10 Pesos** *L.1870.* Black and brown. Woman standing with sword and shield at left, arms at upper center right. Uniface. Printer: BWC. PC: Orange.	35.00	75.00	250
A113	**20 Pesos** *L.1870.* Brown. Woman with sheaf of wheat at left, arms at upper center right. Uniface. Printer: BWC. PC: Blue.	40.00	100	300
A114	**50 Pesos** *L.1870.* Green. Justice at left. Printer: BWC. PC: Brown.	—	—	—
A115	**100 Pesos** *L.1870.* Blue. Woman with horn of plenty. Printer: BWC. PC: Yellow.	—	—	—

Emision Nacional

Ley 25.1.1875

A116 20 Centésimos
1.2.1875. Black. Liberty standing at left. Uniface. Printer: Lit. Pena. PC: Pink.

Good	Fine	XF
10.00	35.00	—

A117 50 Centésimos
1.2.1875. Black on blue underprint. Head of cow at left, arms at upper center. Uniface. Printer: Litografia A. Godel.

Good	Fine	XF
15.00	45.00	—

A118 1 Peso
1.2.1875. Black on brown underprint. Seated man at left, arms at center right. Printer: Lit. Hequet y Cohas.

Good	Fine	XF
20.00	60.00	—

A118A 2 Pesos
1.2.1875. Black on orange underprint. Horse's head at left, arms at center. Uniface. Printer: Lit. Hequet y Cohas. PC: Green.

Good	Fine	XF
—	—	—

A119 5 Pesos
1.2.1875. Black on green underprint. Boy holding 5 at left. Printer: Lit. Hequet y Cohas.

Good	Fine	XF
10.00	25.00	50.00

Cautela (Reserve)

Decreto 26 Abril 1875

A119E 100 Pesos
26.4.1875. Black on orange underprint. Two women resting. Printer: Litog. A. Godel, Montevideo.

Good	Fine	XF
—	—	—

Ley 23.6.1875

A119K 5 Pesos
1.9.1875. Black on blue underprint. Boy plowing at left, arms at center right. BC: Brown. Printer: Lit. A. Godel, Montevideo.

Good	Fine	XF
—	—	—

A119N 50 Pesos
1.10.1875. Black. Gaucho playing guitar with girl at upper left, gaucho with sheep at lower left. Printer: Lit. A. Godel, Montevideo.

Good	Fine	XF
—	—	—

Vale de Tesorería

1855 Issue

A120 2 Reales
12.7.1855.

Good	Fine	XF
50.00	100	—

A121 4 Reales
12.7.1855.

Good	Fine	XF
50.00	100	—

A122 1 Peso
12.7.1855.

Good	Fine	XF
60.00	125	—

A123 5 Pesos
12.7.1855. 117x83mm.

Good	Fine	XF
75.00	150	—

Color Abbreviation Guide

New to the *Standard Catalog of® World Paper Money* are the following abbreviations related to color references:

BC: Back color
PC: Paper color

		Good	Fine	XF
A124	**10 Pesos** 12.7.1855. Arms at upper center.	—	—	—

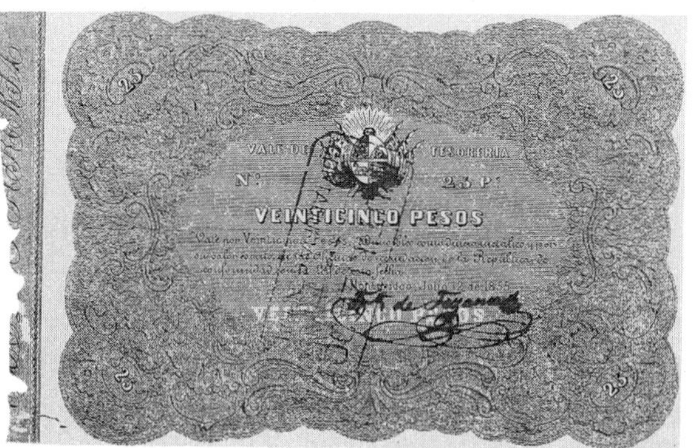

		Good	Fine	XF
A125	**25 Pesos** 12.7.1855.	—	—	—
A126	**50 Pesos** 12.7.1855.	—	—	—
A127	**100 Pesos** 12.7.1855.	—	—	—

Vales del Tesoro - Treasury Notes

Ley de 13 de Julio 1886

		Good	Fine	XF
A127A	**1 Peso** 11.8.1886. Arms above seated woman with sheaves of grain at left. Printer: Litografia Artistica - A. Godel - Montevideo.	—	—	—

		Good	Fine	XF
A127C	**10 Pesos** 11.8.1886. Brown and black on ochre underprint. Minstrel, woman and dog in circle at left, reclining women and shield at upper center, vaquero and cows in circle at right. BC: Peach and blue. Printer: Litografia Artistica - A. Godel - Montevideo.	—	—	—

República (Oriental) del Uruguay

1868 Emergency Postal Scrip Issues

Uruguay suffered from a chronic shortage of small change during the 1860s. The apparent success of the U.S. Postage Currency issue of 1862 during the Civil War (U.S. #97-100) prompted the government of Uruguay to do much the same thing in 1868.

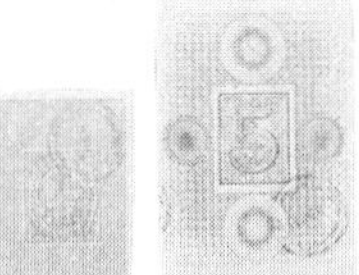

		Good	Fine	XF
A128	**1 Centésimo** 1868. Black. Exact copy of postage stamp at center. Circular handstamp in purple or black with issuing office and date. Uniface.	150	450	—

		Good	Fine	XF
A129	**5 Centecimos** 1868. Blue. Exact copy of postage stamp at center. Circular handstamp in purple or black with issuing office and date. Uniface.	200	600	—
A129A	**5 Centecimos** 1868. Green. Exact copy of postage stamp at center. Circular handstamp in purple or black with issuing office and date. Uniface. PC: Pink.	—	—	—
A130	**10 Centécimos** 1868. Blue. Exact copy of postage stamp at center. Circular handstamp in purple or black with issuing office and date. Uniface.	250	750	—
A131	**15 Centécimos** 1868. Orange. Exact copy of postage stamp at center. Circular handstamp in purple or black with issuing office and date. Uniface. PC: Yellow.	300	900	—
A132	**20 Centécimos** 1868. Red. Exact copy of postage stamp at center. Circular handstamp in purple or black with issuing office and date. Uniface. PC: Green.	300	900	—

Banco de la República Oriental del Uruguay

1896 Provisional Issue

#	Description	Good	Fine	XF
1	**20 Centésimos** *L.4.8.1896.* J. G. Artigas at left. Printer: CSABB. (Not issued).	—	—	—
1A	**10 Pesos** 1.10.1896. Green. Liberty head with helmet at upper left, cherub with shield at right. Printer: CSABB. Rare.	—	—	—

Note: Most examples of #1A encountered are counterfeit.

#	Description	Good	Fine	XF
1B	**100 Pesos** 1.10.1896. (No examples known.)	—	—	—

1896 Issue

#	Description	Good	Fine	XF
1C	**10 Centésimos** 24.8.1896. Brown on blue underprint. Cow's head at left. Back: Eight arms. Printer: G&D. (Not issued).	—	—	—
1D	**20 Centésimos** 24.8.1896. Dark blue on pink underprint. Helmeted man at left. (Not issued).	—	—	—

#	Description	Good	Fine	XF
2	**50 Centésimos** 24.8.1896. Black on orange and green underprint. Two men harvesting with horses at lower left. Back: Arms at center.			
	a. Imprint: G&D.	10.00	35.00	85.00
	b. Double imprint: Jacobo Peuser Buenos Aires; G&D.	15.00	40.00	100
	c. Dark red overprint: *Rosario* at upper right.	—	—	—

#	Description	Good	Fine	XF
3	**1 Peso** 24.8.1896. Black on lilac and orange underprint. Portrait woman at center.			
	a. Imprint: G&D.	15.00	40.00	100
	b. Double imprint: Jacobo Peuser Buenos Aires; G&D.	20.00	50.00	115
	c. *MINAS* overprint on b.	—	—	—
	d. *SALTO* overprint on b.	—	—	—
4	**5 Pesos** 24.8.1896. Black on pink and lilac underprint. Man at left, arms at right.	50.00	125	300
5	**10 Pesos** 24.8.1896. Black on light blue and orange underprint. Sailor at left, woman and arms at right. Back: Ships and train.	90.00	200	500

#	Description	Good	Fine	XF
5A	**10 Pesos** 24.8.1896. Pres. Idiarte Borda at left. Proof. (Not issued).	—	—	—
6	**50 Pesos** 24.8.1896. Blue and orange. Women at left and right.	—	—	—
7	**100 Pesos** 24.8.1896. Black on lilac and blue underprint. Man at left, woman with sword at right.	—	—	—

#	Description	Good	Fine	XF
8	**500 Pesos** 24.8.1896. Portrait man above arms between allegorical man and woman at center.	—	—	—

Note: For similar design issue but dated 1934, see #20-26.

1899 Issue

#	Description	Good	Fine	XF
8A	**10 Pesos** 1.7.1899. Black on pink and orange underprint. Woman leaning on column at left, arms at right. Back: Seated figure at center. BC: Black on yellow and lilac underprint. Printer: BWC.			
	a. Without branch overprint. Rare.	—	—	—
	b. Branch overprint: *FLORIDA* at center. Rare.	—	—	—
	c. Branch overprint: *SALTO.* Rare.	—	—	—
	d. Branch overprint: *SORIANO.* Rare.	—	—	—
	x. Counterfeit.	20.00	40.00	—

Note: Most examples of #8A encountered are counterfeit.

Law of 4.8.1896 (1914 Issue)

#	Description	Good	Fine	XF
9	**1 Peso** Sept. 1914. Black on blue underprint. Portrait J.G. Artigas at center. Engraved date. Signature title varieties. Back: Arms at center. BC: Brown. Printer: W&S. Overprint: Additional dates 1924-1935. Issued 1915-1936.			
	a. Series V-VIII. No added date. 3 signatures.	3.00	8.00	35.00
	b. Series VIII-XI. Added date (different positions). 3 or 2 signatures. 9.8.1924-14.11.1935.	2.50	6.00	30.00
	c. Series XI. Slightly modified portrait, crosshatches on jacket.	2.00	5.00	25.00
	d. Series XI. No added date, and 2 signatures.	2.00	5.00	25.00

		Good	Fine	XF
10	**5 Pesos** Sept. 1914. Brown on light red and light green underprint. Portrait J.G. Artigas at center. Engraved date. Signature title varieties. Back: Arms at center. BC: Green. Printer: W&S. Overprint: Additional dates 1925-34. Issued 1915-34.			
	a. Without overprint or additional dates.	5.00	20.00	75.00
	b. 2 overprints on face: *CONVERTIBLE EN EMISION MAYOR. . .20 Feb. 1919* and *CONVERTIBLE EN PLATA*.	35.00	85.00	225
	c. Like b. but only the first overprint on face.	30.00	75.00	200
	d. Overprint: *Certificado Metalico-Plata/Ley de 14 de Enero de 1916*. Issued 1927-28. with or without added dates.	15.00	50.00	100
	e. Added date (different positions). 4.8.1925-16.1.1934.	5.00	15.00	50.00

		Good	Fine	XF
11	**10 Pesos** Sept. 1914. Black on pale orange and pale green underprint. Portrait Artigas at center. Engraved date. Signature title varieties. Back: Arms at center. BC: Orange. Printer: W&S. Overprint: Additional dates 1925-35. (Issued 1915-35.)			
	a. Without additional overprint dates.	20.00	50.00	125
	b. Added date (different positions). 7.1.1925-19.3.1935.	20.00	50.00	125
12	**100 Pesos** Sept. 1914. Black on brown underprint. Portrait J. G. Artigas at left. Back: Arms. Printer: W&S. Issued 1915-32.	Good	Fine	XF
	a. Without additional overprint date. 3 signatures.	40.00	100	250
	b. Like a., but 2 signatures.	40.00	100	250
	c. Additional overprint date. 4.1.1932; 23.6.1932; 14.10.1935.	40.00	100	250

		Good	Fine	XF
13	**500 Pesos** Sept. 1914. Black on green underprint. Portrait J. G. Artigas at left. Back: Arms. Printer: W&S.			
	a. Without additional overprint date.	—	—	—
	b. Additional overprint date. 6.12.1924.	100	225	500

1918 Provisional Issue

		Good	Fine	XF
14	**20 Centésimos on 1 Peso** Jan. 1918. Black on brown underprint. Portrait J. G. Artigas at left. Red or black serial # (3 serial # varieties). Printer: C de M, Buenos Aires. Overprint: Black lines with new denomination on face and back. 4 corners cut off.	12.50	40.00	100
15	**1 Peso** Jan. 1918. Black on brown underprint. Portrait J. G. Artigas at left. Red or black serial # (3 serial # varieties). #14 without overprint. (Not issued).	—	—	—

1918 Issue

		Good	Fine	XF
16	**100 Pesos** Jan. 1918. Purple on brown-orange underprint. Portrait J. G. Artigas at left. Similar to #14.			
	a. Issued note.	—	—	—
	x. Counterfeit.	250	500	—
16A	**500 Pesos** Jan. 1918. Black on green underprint. Portrait J. G. Artigas at left. Similar to #16.	—	—	—

Note: Genuine examples of #16 have a true watermark. Counterfeits are made by putting 2 separate pieces of paper together with watermark simulated by a drawing in between.

1930 Commemorative Issue

#17-19 Centennial of Uruguay 1830-1930.

		Good	Fine	XF
17	**1 Peso** 18.7.1930. Multicolor. Woman with helmet at center. Back: Indians at left and right, arms at upper center, sailboat at right center. Watermark: J.G. Artigas. Printer: French.			
	a. Issued note.	40.00	150	350
	p. Proof. Without watermark. Uniface face.	—	Unc	500

		Good	Fine	XF
18	**5 Pesos** 18.7.1930. Multicolor. Woman at center. Back: Horseback riders and arms. Watermark: J.G. Artigas. Printer: French.	200	900	—

		Good	Fine	XF
19	**10 Pesos** 18.7.1930. Multicolor. Woman at left. Back: Arms and four allegorical women. Watermark: J.G. Artigas. Printer: French.	250	1,250	—

Ley 4 Agosto de 1896 (1931-1934 Issue)

Note: For similar design issues but dated 1896, see #2-8. Notes #20-23 and 9 with 2 signatures were issued under Law of 14.8.1935. #21-23 appear to exist with 2 signatures only.

		VG	VF	UNC
20	**50 Centésimos** 18.10.1934. Black on orange and green underprint. Two men harvesting with horses at lower left. Similar to #2. Back: Redesigned arms. Printer: G&D.			
	a. 3 signatures. Additional overprint dates. 30.4.1935-22.9.1935.	4.00	20.00	75.00
	b. 2 signatures. Without additional overprint date.	4.00	20.00	75.00

		VG	VF	UNC
21	**1 Peso** 9.8.1934. Black on lilac and orange underprint. Portrait woman at center. Similar to #3. Printer: G&D.	8.00	30.00	90.00

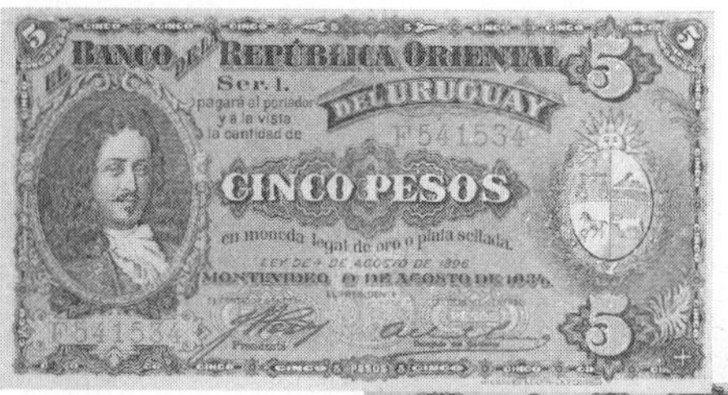

		VG	VF	UNC
22	**5 Pesos** 9.8.1934. Black on pink and lilac underprint. Man at left, arms at right. Similar to #4. Printer: G&D.	20.00	75.00	250

		VG	VF	UNC
23	**10 Pesos** 9.8.1934. Black on light blue and orange underprint. Sailor at left, woman and arms at right. Similar to #5. Back: Ships and train. Printer: G&D.	25.00	100	300

		VG	VF	UNC
26	**500 Pesos** 25.8.1931. Portrait man above arms between allegorical man and woman at center. Similar to #8. Printer: G&D.	—	—	—

Note: For similar design issues but dated 1896, see #2-8. Notes #20-23 and 9 with 2 signatures were issued under Law of 14.8.1935. #21-23 appear to exist with 2 signatures only.

Departamento de Emisión

Ley de 14 de Agosto de 1935

Signature titles in plate: 2 signatures: *EL PRESIDENTE* and *EL DELEGADO DEL GOBIERNO.* 3 signatrues: *EL PRESIDENTE* or *EL VICE PRESIDENTE, EL SECRETARIO* or *SECRETARIO GENERAL,* and *GERENTE GENERAL.*

		VG	VF	UNC
27	**50 Centésimos** *L.1935.* Brown on orange and green underprint. Arms at center, man with helmet at lower right. Back: Sailing ships. BC: Green. Watermark: J.G. Artigas. Printer: TDLR. All notes have 2 signature titles in plate.			
	a. 2 signatures.	1.50	5.00	17.50
	b. 3 signature overprint.	1.50	5.00	17.50

		VG	VF	UNC
28	**1 Peso** *L.1935.* Orange-brown on green underprint. Indian with spear at left, arms at center right. Back: Conquistadores fighting against Indians. BC: Blue. Watermark: J.G. Artigas. Printer: TDLR.			
	a. 2 signatures.	2.00	10.00	30.00
	b. 2 signature titles in plate. 2 or 3 signature overprint.	2.00	10.00	30.00
	c. Without signature titles in plate. 3 signature overprint.	2.00	10.00	30.00
	d. 3 signature titles in plate. 3 signature overprint.	2.00	10.00	30.00

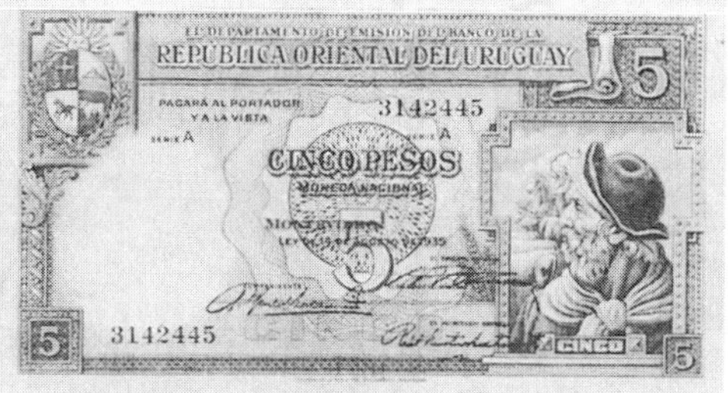

		VG	VF	UNC
29	**5 Pesos** *L.1935.* Green on multicolor underprint. Arms at upper left, old gaucho at lower right. Back: Wagon drawn by oxen. BC: Red-brown. Watermark: J.G. Artigas. Printer: TDLR.			
	a. 2 signature titles in plate. 2 or 3 signature overprint.	6.00	25.00	60.00
	b. Without signature titles in plate. 3 signature overprint.	6.00	25.00	60.00

		VG	VF	UNC
30	**10 Pesos** *L.1935.* Deep blue on multicolor underprint. Warrior wearing helmet at left, arms at upper right. Back: Group of men with flag. BC: Purple. Watermark: J.G. Artigas. Printer: TDLR.			
	a. 2 signature titles in plate. 2 or 3 signature overprint.	10.00	30.00	75.00
	b. Without signature titles in plate. 3 signature overprint.	10.00	30.00	75.00

		VG	VF	UNC
31	**100 Pesos** *L.1935.* Orange-brown and violet on multicolor underprint. *Constitution* at left. Back: Crowd of people in town square. BC: Orange-brown. Watermark: J.G. Artigas. Printer: TDLR.			
	a. 2 signature titles in plate. 2 or 3 signature overprint.	12.00	40.00	100
	b. Without signature titles in plate. 3 signature overprint.	12.00	40.00	100

		VG	VF	UNC
32	**500 Pesos** *L.1935.* Violet and blue. *Industry* at left. Back: Group of people with symbols of agriculture. BC: Brown. Watermark: J.G. Artigas. Printer: TDLR.			
	a. 2 signature titles in plate. 2 or 3 signature overprint.	30.00	70.00	225
	b. 3 signature titles in plate. 3 signature overprint.	30.00	70.00	225
33	**1000 Pesos** *L.1935.* Green. J. G. Artigas at right. Back: Horsemen. BC: Blue and brown. Watermark: J.G. Artigas. Printer: TDLR.			
	a. 2 signature titles in plate. 2 or 3 signature overprint.	100	200	—
	b. 3 signature titles in plate. 3 signature overprint.	100	200	—

Ley de 2 de Enero de 1939, 1939-66 Issue

		VG	VF	UNC
34	**50 Centesimos** *L.1939.* Green on light tan and brown underprint. Portrait J. G. Artigas at center. Series A-T. Signature and signature title varieties. Back: Arms at center. Printer: Casa de Moneda de Chile.	0.25	0.50	2.75

		VG	VF	UNC
35	**1 Peso** *L.1939.* Brown on multicolor underprint. Portrait J. G. Artigas at center, arms at upper left. Signature and signature title varieties. Back: Sailing ships. Printer: TDLR.			
	a. Paper with fibers. Series A; B.	0.25	1.25	4.00
	b. Paper with security thread. Series C.	0.25	1.00	3.50
	c. Series D.	0.25	0.50	2.00

		VG	VF	UNC
36	**5 Pesos** *L.1939.* Blue on multicolor underprint. J. G. Artigas at right, arms at upper left. Signature and signature title varieties. Back: Conquistadors fighting against Indians. Printer: TDLR.			
	a. Paper with fibers. Series A; B.	0.50	2.50	7.00
	b. Paper with security thread. Series C.	0.50	1.00	3.50

		VG	VF	UNC
37	**10 Pesos** *L.1939.* Purple on multicolor underprint. J. G. Artigas at center, arms at upper left. Signature and signature title varieties. Back: Farmer with 3-team ox-cart. Printer: TDLR.			
	a. Paper with fibers. Series A.	1.00	4.00	10.00
	b. As a. Series B.	0.50	3.00	7.50
	c. Paper with security thread. Series C.	0.25	1.50	6.00
	d. Series D.	0.25	1.00	3.00

		VG	VF	UNC
38	**50 Pesos** *L.1939.* Blue and brown on multicolor underprint. Warrior wearing helmet at right, arms at upper left. Signature and signature title varieties. Back: Group of people with flag. Watermark: J. G. Artigas. Printer: TDLR.			
	a. Paper with fibers. Series A; B.	0.50	3.00	9.00
	b. Paper with security thread. Series C.	0.25	1.50	5.00

		VG	VF	UNC
39	**100 Pesos**			
	L.1939. Red and brown on multicolor underprint. Constitution" at right, arms at center. Signature and signature title varieties. Back: People in town square. Watermark: J. G. Artigas. Printer: TDLR.			
	a. Paper with fibers. Series A; B.	2.00	6.00	20.00
	b. Paper with security thread. Series C.	0.50	3.00	8.00
	c. Series D.	0.50	2.00	6.00

		VG	VF	UNC
40	**500 Pesos**			
	L.1939. Green and blue on multicolor underprint. "Industry" at right, arms at upper left. Signature and signature title varieties. Back: People with symbols of agriculture. Watermark: J. G. Artigas. Printer: TDLR.			
	a. Paper with fibers. Series A; B.	3.00	10.00	30.00
	b. Paper with security thread. Series C.	1.00	4.00	10.00
	c. Series D.	0.50	2.00	7.00

		VG	VF	UNC
41	**1000 Pesos**			
	L.1939. Purple and black on multicolor underprint. J. G. Artigas at right, arms at upper left. Signature and signature title varieties. Back: Man on horseback at center. Watermark: J. G. Artigas. Printer: TDLR.			
	a. Paper with fibers. Series A; B.	10.00	25.00	80.00
	b. Paper with security thread. Series C.	3.00	10.00	30.00
	c. Series D.	2.00	5.00	15.00
	s. Specimen. As b. Pin hole: CANCELLED. Series C.	—	—	135

Banco Central del Uruguay

Sign. Titles:

1-Gerente General, Secretario General, Presidente
2-Co-Gerente General, Secretario General, Presidente
3-p.Gerente General, Secretario General, Presidente
4-Gerente General, Secretario General, Vicepresidente
5-Gerente General, Secretario General, 2o Vicepresidente
6-p.Gerente General, Secretario General, Vicepresidente
7-Secretario General, Presidente

Sign. Titles:

1-Gerente General, Secretario General, Presidente
2-Co-Gerente General, Secretario General, Presidente
3-p.Gerente General, Secretario General, Presidente
4-Gerente General, Secretario General, Vicepresidente
5-Gerente General, Secretario General, 2o Vicepresidente
6-p.Gerente General, Secretario General, Vicepresidente
7-Secretario General, Presidente

1967 ND Provisional Issue

#42-45 Banco Central was organized in 1967 and used notes of previous issuing authority with Banco Central signature title overprint.

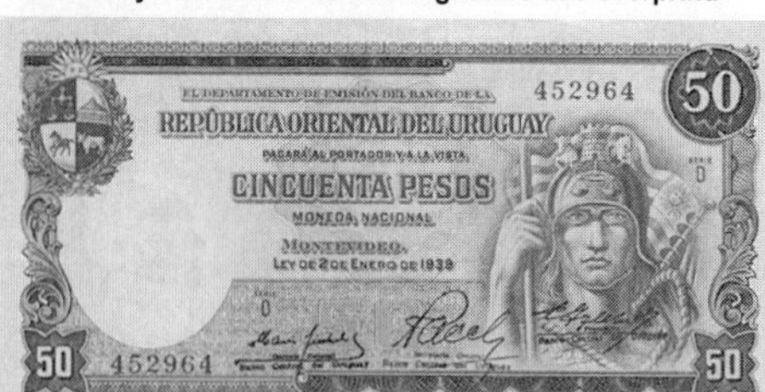

		VG	VF	UNC
42A	**50 Pesos**			
	L.1939 (1967). Blue and brown on multicolor underprint. Warrior wearing helmet at right, arms at upper left. Series D. Back: Group of people with flag. Printer: TDLR.			
	a. Bank name below all 3 signatures. Signature title: 1.	1.00	3.00	7.50
	b. Bank name below 2 signatures at right. Signature title: 3.	1.00	3.00	10.00

The Republic of Uzbekistan (formerly the Uzbek S.S.R.), is bordered on the north by Kazakhstan, to the east by Kirghizia and Tajikistan, on the south by Afghanistan and on the west by Turkmenistan. The republic is comprised of the regions of Andizhan, Bukhara, Dzhizak, Ferghana, Kashkadar, Khorezm (Khiva), Namangan, Navoi, Samarkand, Surkhan-Darya, Syr-Darya, Tashkent and the Karakalpak Autonomous Republic. It has an area of 447,400 sq. km. and a population of 27.34 million. Capital: Tashkent. Crude oil, natural gas, coal, copper and gold deposits make up the chief resources, while intensive farming, based on artificial irrigation, provides an abundance of cotton.Russia conquered Uzbekistan in the late 19th century. Stiff resistance to the Red Army after World War I was eventually suppressed and a socialist republic set up in 1924. During the Soviet era, intensive production of "white gold" (cotton) and grain led to overuse of agrochemicals and the depletion of water supplies, which have left the land poisoned and the Aral Sea and certain rivers half dry. Independent since 1991, the country seeks to gradually lessen its dependence on agriculture while developing its mineral and petroleum reserves. Current concerns include terrorism by Islamic militants, economic stagnation, and the curtailment of human rights and democratization.

Monetary System:

1 ТННbгА (Tenga) = 20 КОПЬНКЪ (Kopeks)
5 ТННbгОВъ (Tengov) = 1 РЧБПЙ (Ruble)
1 Sum (Ruble) = 100 Kopeks, 1991
1 Sum = 1,000 Sum Coupon, 1994
1 СўЬ (Sum) = 100 ТИЙИН (Tiyin)

BUKHARA, EMIRATE

Treasury

1918 First Issue

All notes in Persian script, with only the denomination in Russian. Many printing, color and paper varieties. Signature seals for #1-10:

		Good	Fine	XF
1	**20 Tengas**			
	AH1337 (1918). Multicolor.			
	a. Issued note.	80.00	165	—
	x. Misprint: back inverted on back.	100	200	—

		Good	Fine	XF
2	**60 Tengas**			
	AH1337 (1918). Multicolor. PC: White or yellowish.			
	a. Seals Type I.	150	300	—
	b. Seals Type II.	100	200	—
3	**100 Tengas**	Good	Fine	XF
	AH1337 (1918). Multicolor. PC: White or yellowish.	50.00	100	—
4	**200 Tengas**	Good	Fine	XF
	AH1337 (1918). Multicolor. PC: White or yellowish.	50.00	100	—

		Good	Fine	XF
5	**300 Tengas**			
	AH1337 (1918). Multicolor.			
	a. Brownish paper.	100	200	—
	b. White paper. Green date on face.	200	300	—
	c. White paper. Red date on face.	50.00	100	—
6	**500 Tengas**	Good	Fine	XF
	AH1337 (1918). Multicolor. PC: White or yellowish, thin or thick.	70.00	150	—

		Good	Fine	XF
7	**1000 Tengas**			
	AH1337 (1918). PC: White or yellowish.	100	200	—
8	**2000 Tengas**	**Good**	**Fine**	**XF**
	AH1337 (1918). Multicolor.	100	200	—
9	**3000 Tengas**	**Good**	**Fine**	**XF**
	AH1337 (1918). Multicolor.	100	200	—

		Good	Fine	XF
10	**5000 Tengas**			
	AH1337 (1918). Multicolor. PC: White or yellowish.			
	a. Dates 4 times.	100	200	—
	b. Like a., but inverted on back.	200	300	—
	c. Dates twice.	100	200	—

1918 Second Issue

Signature seals for #11-18:

		Good	Fine	XF
11	**100 Tengas**			
	AH1337 (1918). Multicolor.	50.00	100	—
12	**200 Tengas**	**Good**	**Fine**	**XF**
	AH1337 (1918). Multicolor.	100	150	—
13	**300 Tengas**	**Good**	**Fine**	**XF**
	AH1337 (1918). Multicolor.	50.00	100	—
14	**500 Tengas**	**Good**	**Fine**	**XF**
	AH1337 (1918). Multicolor.	50.00	100	—
15	**1000 Tengas**	**Good**	**Fine**	**XF**
	AH1337 (1918). Multicolor.	50.00	100	—
16	**2000 Tengas**	**Good**	**Fine**	**XF**
	AH1337 (1918). Multicolor.	50.00	100	—

		Good	Fine	XF
17	**3000 Tengas**			
	AH1337 (1918). Multicolor.			
	a. Turquoise frame.	50.00	100	—
	b. Brown frame.	100	150	—

		Good	Fine	XF
18	**5000 Tengas**			
	AH1337 (1918). BC: Green and brown.			
	a. Light green.	30.00	60.00	120
	b. Dark green.	30.00	60.00	120
	c. Blue, on brownish paper.	30.00	60.00	120

1919 Issue

Signature seal like #11-18 and #19-24.

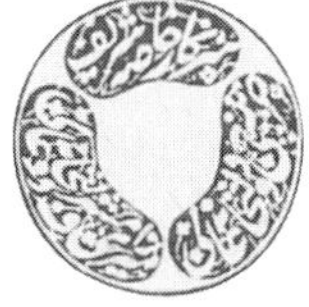

		Good	Fine	XF
19	**50 Tengas**			
	AH1338 (1919). Multicolor.	20.00	50.00	100

		Good	Fine	XF
20	**100 Tengas**			
	AH1338 (1919). Olive.	30.00	70.00	150
21	**200 Tengas**	**Good**	**Fine**	**XF**
	AH1338 (1919). Dark green.	50.00	100	200

		Good	Fine	XF
22	**500 Tengas** AH1338 (1919). Blue, red, brown and green (color variations).	60.00	120	200

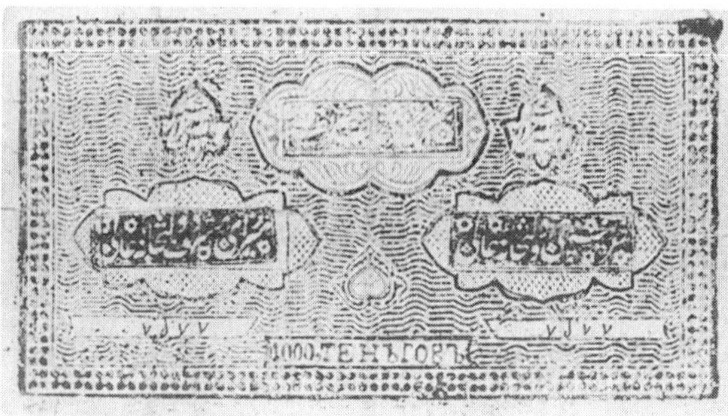

		Good	Fine	XF
23	**1000 Tengas** AH1338 (1919). Multicolor.	60.00	120	200

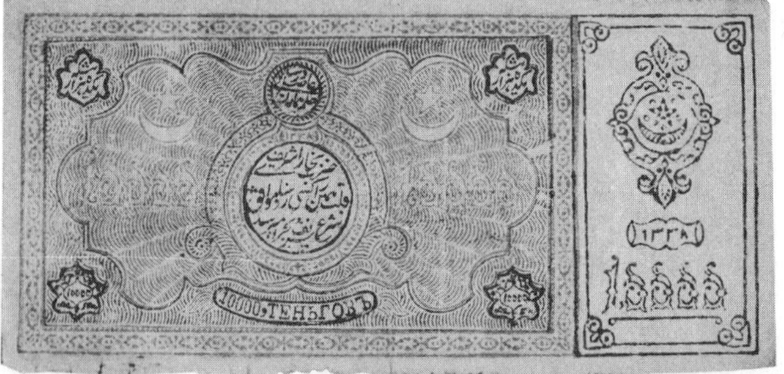

		Good	Fine	XF
24	**10,000 Tengas** AH1338 (1919). Multicolor. 3 signature varieties. 267x125mm.	100	200	300

KHOREZM (KHIVA), KHANATE

Treasury

1918 Issue

Many varieties, especially in color, paper and printing.

		Good	Fine	XF
25	**200 Tengas** AH1337 (1918).			
	a. ТИНЬГОВЪ to be read from bottom to top. Crescent at center or top at right on back.	250	500	—
	b. ТИНЬГОВ to be read from top to bottom.	250	500	—
	c. ТИНЬГОВЪ to be read from top to bottom.	250	500	—
	d. ИНЬВО.	250	500	—
26	**250 Tengas** AH1337 (1918).	Good	Fine	XF
	a. Russian wording at upper right.	250	500	—
	b. Without Russian wording.	250	500	—
27	**500 Tengas** AH1337 (1918).	Good	Fine	XF
	a. Text in the corners in ornaments.	250	500	—
	b. Text in squares, also Russian wording inverted.	250	500	—
	c. Text wording in the corners in circles.	250	500	—
28	**1000 Tengas** AH1337 (1918).	Good	Fine	XF
	a. Text in the circle on 3 lines, also wording inverted.	300	500	—
	b. Text in the circle of 4 lines.	300	500	—
29	**2500 Tengas** AH1337 (1918).	Good	Fine	XF
	a. 2 leaves below on back, also without *500* on back.	300	500	—
	b. Bush below on back, also wording inverted.	300	500	—

1918 Paper Issue

		Good	Fine	XF
30	**50 Tengas = 10 Rubles** AH1337 (1918). 6 different watermarks, and without watermark.	200	300	450

1918 First Silk Issue

		Good	Fine	XF
34	**200 Tengas = 40 Rubles** AH1337 (1919).	200	300	500
31	**500 Tengas = 100 Rubles** AH1337 (1919).	170	300	450
36	**500 Tengas = 100 Rubles** AH1338 (1919). Red-brown on yellow. Different printing errors in the denomination.	200	300	400
32	**1000 Tengas = 200 Rubles** AH1337 (1919).	170	300	450
37	**1000 Tengas = 200 Rubles** AH1338 (1919).	200	300	400
33	**2500 Tengas = 500 Rubles** AH1337 (1919).	200	300	500
38	**2500 Tengas = 500 Rubles** AH1338 (1919).	300	400	500

1919 Silk Issue

		Good	Fine	XF
39	**100 Rubles** AH1338 (1919). Silk.	80.00	150	250

		Good	Fine	XF
40	**250 Rubles** AH1338 (1919). Red-brown on light green. Silk.	30.00	80.00	160

1920 Paper Issue

		Good	Fine	XF
41	**50 Rubles** AH1338 (1920). Blue and red.	30.00	65.00	120
42	**100 Rubles** AH1338 (1920).	35.00	85.00	170

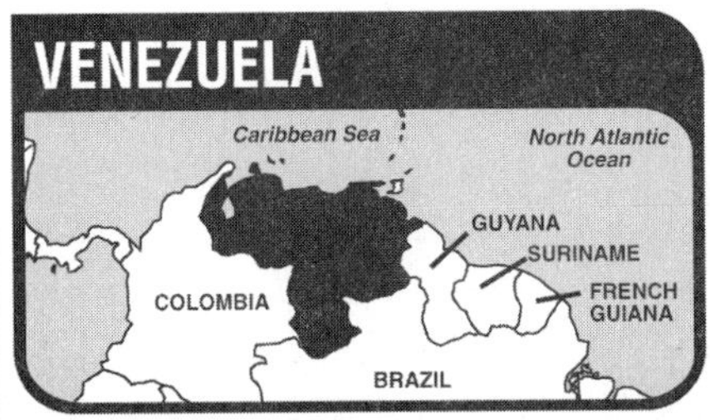

The Republic of Venezuela, located on the northern coast of South America between Colombia and Guyana, has an area of 912,050 sq. km. and a population of 26.41 million. Capital: Caracas. Petroleum and mining provide 90 percent of Venezuela's exports although they employ less than 2 percent of the work force. Coffee, grown on 60,000 plantations, is the chief crop.Venezuela was one of three countries that emerged from the collapse of Gran Colombia in 1830 (the others being Ecuador and New Granada, which became Colombia). For most of the first half of the 20th century, Venezuela was ruled by generally benevolent military strongmen, who promoted the oil industry and allowed for some social reforms. Democratically elected governments have held sway since 1959. Hugo Chavez, president since 1999, seeks to implement his "21st Century Socialism," which purports to alleviate social ills while at the same time attacking globalization and undermining regional stability. Current concerns include: a weakening of democratic institutions, political polarization, a politicized military, drug-related violence along the Colombian border, increasing internal drug consumption, overdependence on the petroleum industry with its price fluctuations, and irresponsible mining operations that are endangering the rain forest and indigenous peoples.

ESTADOS UNIDOS DE VENEZUELA

UNITED STATES OF VENEZUELA

Treasury

Law of 27.8.1811 First Issue

		Good	Fine	XF
2	**2 Reales** *L.1811*. Black. 1 seal. Signature varieties. Uniface. Rare.	—	—	—

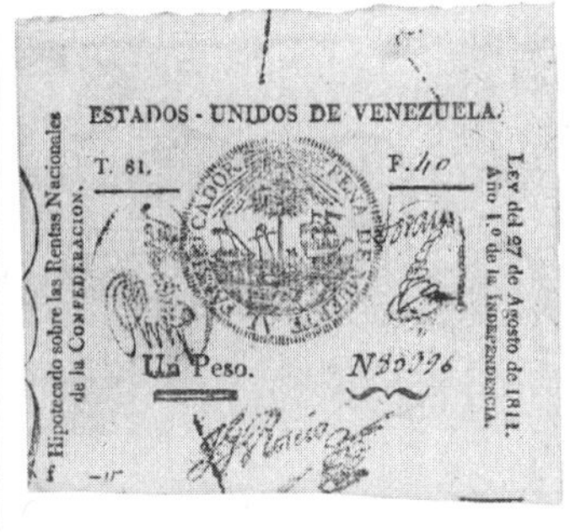

		Good	Fine	XF
4	**1 Peso** *L.1811*. Black. Un Peso at left. below center design. 1 seal. Signature varieties. Uniface.	400	1,000	—

Law of 27.8.1811 Second Issue

		Good	Fine	XF
4A	**1 Peso** *L.1811*. Black. Un Peso at left center and not below design. 1 seal. Signature varieties. Uniface.	400	1,000	—
5	**2 Pesos** *L.1811*. Black. 2 seals. Signature varieties. Uniface. Rare. PC: Heavy white.	—	—	—

		Good	Fine	XF
6	**4 Pesos** *L.1811*. Black. 2 seals. Signature varieties. Uniface. PC: Heavy white.	1,500	4,000	—

No.	Denomination	Good	Fine	XF
7	**8 Pesos** *L.1811.* Black. 2 seals. Signature varieties. Uniface. PC: Heavy white.	6,500	—	—
8	**16 Pesos** *L.1811.* Black. 2 seals. Signature varieties. Uniface. Requires confirmation. PC: Heavy white.	—	—	—

Billete de Tesorería

1849 Issue

No.	Denomination	Good	Fine	XF
9	**5 Pesos** 19.1.1849. Black. Seated Liberty at left, arms at center, sailing ship at right.	—	—	—

No.	Denomination	Good	Fine	XF
10	**10 Pesos** 1.10.1849. Black. Arms at upper center.	—	—	—

REPUBLIC

República de Venezuela

Decree of 20.10.1859

No.	Denomination	Good	Fine	XF
11	**5 Pesos** Black.	—	—	—
12	**10 Pesos** Black.	—	—	—
13	**50 Pesos** Black.	—	—	—
14	**100 Pesos** Black.	—	—	—
15	**500 Pesos** Black.	—	—	—
16	**1000 Pesos** Black.	—	—	—

Decree of 17.7.1860

No.	Denomination	Good	Fine	XF
17	**5 Pesos** Black.	—	—	—
18	**10 Pesos** Black.	—	—	—
19	**50 Pesos** Black.	—	—	—

Decree of 2.8.1860

No.	Denomination	Good	Fine	XF
20	**5 Pesos** 20.11.1860; 26.11.1860. Black.	—	—	—
21	**10 Pesos** 27.11.1860. Black.	—	—	—
22	**20 Pesos** Black.	—	—	—
23	**100 Pesos** Black.	—	—	—

Decree of 2.8.1860 and Resolution of 18.9.1860

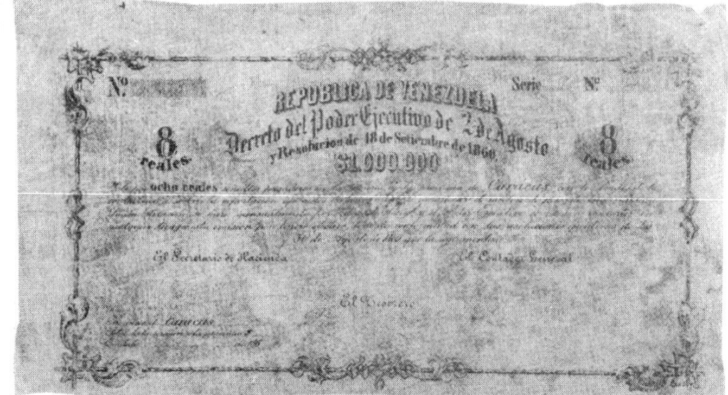

No.	Denomination	Good	Fine	XF
24	**8 Reales** 30.8.1860. Black.	—	—	—

Decree of 15.1.1861

No.	Denomination	Good	Fine	XF
25	**8 Reales** *D.1861*. Black. Back: Guarantee text.	—	—	—
26	**20 Pesos** Black.	—	—	—
27	**100 Pesos** Black.	—	—	—

Banco Central de Venezuela

Established in 1940. Sign. and date varieties. Notes from 1940-53 bear the legend *E.E.U.U. de Venezuela* in the coat of arms and after 1953 República de Venezuela. Note: Many specimen notes entered the market about 1982. Up to 200 of each are known for many of the types.

1940-1945 Issues

No.	Denomination	VG	VF	UNC
31	**10 Bolívares** 19.7.1945-11.3.1960. Purple on multicolor underprint. Portrait Simon Bolívar at left, Antonio Jose de Sucre at right. Back: Arms at right. Printer: ABNC.			
	a. 19.7.1945-17.5.1951.	5.00	40.00	125
	b. 31.7.1952. Serial # prefix F-G.	15.00	50.00	100
	c. 23.7.1953-17.4.1958.	5.00	30.00	60.00
	d. 18.6.1959-11.3.1960.	5.00	20.00	45.00
	s. As a. Specimen. Without signature. Punch hole cancelled.	—	—	250
32	**20 Bolívares** 15.2.1941-18.6.1959. Dark green on multicolor underprint. Portrait Simon Bolívar at right. Back: Arms at left. Printer: ABNC.			
	a. 15.2.1941-17.1.1952.	15.00	60.00	125
	b. 21.8.1952. Serial # prefix G-H.	20.00	50.00	100
	c. 23.7.1953-18.6.1959.	5.00	30.00	75.00
	s. As a. Specimen. Without signature. Punch hole cancelled.	—	—	125
33	**50 Bolívares** 12.12.1940-11.3.1960. Black on multicolor underprint. Portrait Simon Bolívar at left. Back: Arms at right. BC: Orange. Printer: ABNC.			
	a. 12.12.1940-17.1.1952.	25.00	100	250
	b. 23.7.1953. Serial # prefix C.	25.00	125	225
	c. 22.4.1954-11.3.1960.	15.00	65.00	125
	s. As a. Specimen. Without signature. Punch hole cancelled.	—	—	175
34	**100 Bolívares** 11.12.1940-3.7.1962. Brown on multicolor underprint. Portrait Simon Bolívar at center. Back: Arms at center. Printer: ABNC.			
	a. 11.12.1940-30.10.1952.	30.00	125	300
	b. 23.7.1953. Serial # prefix D.	35.00	150	300
	c. 22.4.1954-29.5.1958.	20.00	75.00	175
	d. 24.9.1959-3.7.1962.	15.00	50.00	150
	s. As a. Specimen. Without signature. Punch hole cancelled.	—	—	250
35	**500 Bolívares** 10.12.1940-21.12.1940. Blue on multicolor underprint. Portrait Simon Bolívar at right. Back: Arms at left. Printer: ABNC.			
	a. Issued note.	250	1,000	—
	s. Specimen.	—	—	2,000
36	**500 Bolívares** 21.1.1943-29.11.1946. Red on multicolor underprint. Portrait Simon Bolívar at right. Like #35. Back: Arms at left. Printer: ABNC.			
	a. Issued note.	250	1,000	—
	s. As a or ND. Specimen.	—	—	1,250

1947 Issue

No.	Denomination	VG	VF	UNC
37	**500 Bolívares** 1947-1971. Orange on multicolor underprint. Portrait Simon Bolívar at right. Like #35. Back: Arms at left. Printer: ABNC.			
	a. 14.8.1947-21.8.1952.	75.00	250	—
	b. 23.7.1953-29.5.1958.	30.00	125	300
	c. 11.3.1960-17.8.1971.	17.50	80.00	200
	s. As b or ND. Specimen. Without signature. Punch hole cancelled.	—	—	500

1952-1953 Issue

No.	Denomination	VG	VF	UNC
38	**10 Bolívares** 31.7.1952. Purple on multicolor underprint. Portrait Simon Bolívar at left, Antonio Jose de Sucre at right. Similar to #31. Series E, F. 7 digit serial #. Back: Arms at right. Monument at center. Printer: TDLR.	30.00	125	350
39	**20 Bolívares** 21.8.1952. Dark green on multicolor underprint. Portrait Simon Bolívar at right, bank name in 1 line. Series G. 7 digit serial #. Similar to #43. Back: Arms at left. Monument at center. Printer: TDLR.	35.00	175	450

No.	Denomination	VG	VF	UNC
40	**50 Bolívares** 26.2.1953; 23.7.1953. Simon Bolívar at left, *CINCUENTA BOLÍVARES* at right. Series C. 7 digit serial #. Back: Arms at right. Monument at center. Printer: TDLR.	50.00	135	450
41	**100 Bolívares** 23.7.1953. Portrait Simon Bolívar at right. Series C, D. 7 digit serial #. Back: Arms at left. Monument at center. Printer: TDLR.	25.00	125	425

1960-1961 Issue

		VG	VF	UNC
43	**20 Bolívares** 1960-1966. Dark green on multicolor underprint. Portrait Simon Bolívar at right, bank name in 1 line. 7 digit serial #. Similar to #32. Back: Arms at left, monument at center. Printer: TDLR.			
	a. 11.3.1960. Serial # prefix *U-X*.	4.00	20.00	50.00
	b. 6.6.1961. Serial # prefix *X-Z*.	4.00	15.00	40.00
	c. 7.5.1963. Serial # prefix *A-B*.	4.00	—	40.00
	d. 2.6.1964. Serial # prefix *C-D*.	4.00	15.00	40.00
	e. 10.5.1966. Serial # preifx *E-G*.	4.00	15.00	40.00
	s1. Specimen with red overprint: *SPECIMEN*. Paper with colored planchettes. Serial # prefix *X*.	—	—	15.00
	s2. Specimen with red overprint: *ESPECIMEN SIN VALOR*. Paper with security thread. Punch hole cancelled.	—	—	15.00
	s3. Specimen with black overprint: *SPECIMEN*. Serial # prefix *U*.	—	—	15.00

		VG	VF	UNC
44	**50 Bolívares** 6.6.1961; 7.5.1963. Black on multicolor underprint. Modified portrait of Simon Bolívar at left, value *CINCUENTA BOLIVARES* at right. 7 digit serial #. Serial # prefix *H-J; J-K*. Back: Monument at center, arms at right. BC: Orange. Printer: TDLR.			
	a. Issued note.	8.00	50.00	125
	s. Specimen with red overprint: *SPECIMEN SIN VALOR*. Punch hole cancelled.	—	—	75.00

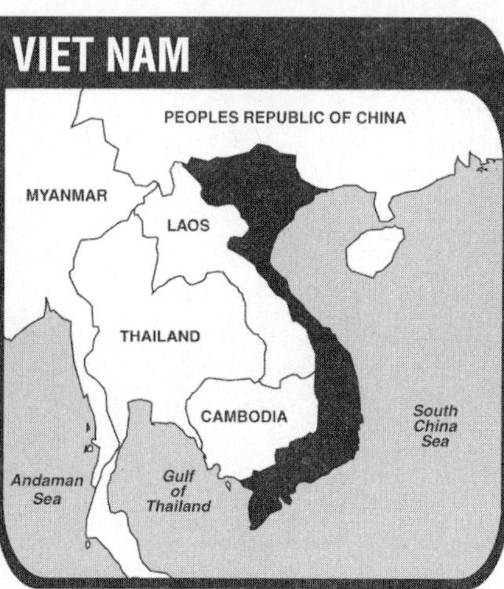

The Socialist Republic of Viet Nam, located in Southeast Asia west of the South China Sea, has an area of 329,560 sq. km. and a population of 86.12 million. Capital: Hanoi. Agricultural products, saltwater fish, shellfish, coal, mineral ores and electronic products are exported.

The conquest of Viet Nam by France began in 1858 and was completed by 1884. It became part of French Indochina in 1887. Viet Nam declared independence after World War II, but France continued to rule until its 1954 defeat by communist forces under Ho Chi Minh. Under the Geneva Accords of 1954, Viet Nam was divided into the communist North and anti-communist South. The US and its allies' sent economic and military aid to South Viet Nam and the Soviety Union and its allies sent their aid to the North. The US and its allies were withdrawn following a cease-fire agreement in 1973. Two years later, North Vietnamese forces overran the South reuniting the country under Communist rule. Despite the return of peace, for over a decade the country experienced limited economic growth because of the communist leadership policies. However, since the enactment of Viet Nam's *doi moi* (renovation) policy in 1986, Vietnamese authorities have committed to increased economic liberalization and enacted structural reforms needed to modernize the economy and to produce more competitive, export-driven industries, which greatly reduced inflation and greatly increased economic growth.

MONETARY SYSTEM:

1 Hao = 10 Xu
1 Dng = 100 Xu
1 Dng = 100 "Old" Dong, 19511 Dong = 100 Xu = 100 Su to 1975 1 New Dong = 500 Old Dong, 1975-76

Replacement Notes: #5-7, 11-14, star instead of series prefix of letter and number.

Note: HCM = Ho Chi Minh

VIET-NAM DAN-CU CHONG-HOA

Giay Bac Viet Nam

Vietnamese Banknote

Issues of the DRVN central treasury and, where indicated, the Nam-Bo Regional Administration.

1946 ND Issues

		Good	Fine	XF
1	**1 Dông** ND (1946). Olive. HCM at center. Denomination numerals *1* in corners contain small circles. Like #9. Back: Two workers in field with underprint of alternating "x"s and squares. Watermark: Oval with *Vietnam*.	10.00	50.00	300

		Good	Fine	XF
2	**5 Dông** ND (1946). Color varies from Red to dark brown. HCM at top. Back: Woman with boy below. Crude printing of #10. Vertical format.			
	a. Without watermark.	5.00	20.00	50.00
	b. Watermark: Star within circle.	5.00	20.00	50.00
	c. Watermark: Oval with VIET NAM.	5.00	20.00	50.00

		Good	Fine	XF
3	**5 Dông** ND (1946). Brown and green. Worker at left, factory in background. Back: HCM at left.			
	a. Watermark: *VNDCCH.*	5.00	20.00	75.00
	b. Watermark: Oval with *Vietnam.*	5.00	20.00	75.00

		Good	Fine	XF
4	**5 Dông** ND (1946). Brown and gold. Worker at left, factory in background. Like #3 but larger note. Back: HCM at left. Without watermark.	6.50	20.00	75.00

		Good	Fine	XF
5	**20 Dông** ND (1946). Brown and olive. Flag behind HCM at left. (25mm high). Back: Farmer with buffalo at left, female porter with child at right. 148x76mm.	15.00	50.00	150

		Good	Fine	XF
6	**20 Dông** ND (1946). Brown and olive. HCM in oval frame (36mm high). Like #5. Back: Farmer with buffalo at left, female porter with child at right. 170x88mm.	15.00	50.00	150

		Good	Fine	XF
7	**20 Dông** ND (1946). Brown and yellow. Like #5 but HCM in frame (50mm high). Back: Farmer with buffalo at left, female porter with child at right. 170x88mm.	15.00	50.00	150
8	**100 Dông** ND (1946). Green and olive. Large note like #12 but HCM portrait different and smaller (57mm high).	Good	Fine	XF
	a. Without watermark.	25.00	100	250
	b. Watermark: Oval with *Vietnam.*	25.00	100	250
	c. Watermark: *VNDCCH.*	25.00	100	250

1947 ND Issue

		Good	Fine	XF
9	**1 Dông** ND (1947). Light to dark blue. HCM at center. Denomination numerals *1* in corners contain small circles. Back: Two workers in field with underprint of alternating "x"s and squares. PC: White on brown.			
	a. Without watermark.	5.00	15.00	40.00
	b. Watermark: *VDCCH* horizontal and vertical.	5.00	15.00	40.00
	c. Watermark: Oval with *Vietnam.*	2.50	7.50	15.00
	d. Watermark: Circle with star.	3.00	10.00	30.00

		Good	Fine	XF
10	**5 Dông** ND (1947). Color varies from red to dark brown. HCM at top. Back: Woman with boy below. Vertical format.			
	a. Without watermark.	2.50	7.50	15.00
	b. Signature and signature titles in clear underprint area. Watermark: *VDCCH.*	2.50	7.50	15.00
	c. As b but watermark: Oval with *Vietnam.*	2.50	7.50	15.00
	d. Signature and signature titles within wavy underprint. Watermark: *VDCCH.*	10.00	25.00	100
	e. As d but watermark: Oval with *VIETNAM.*	10.00	25.00	100
	f. As b. but watermark: circle with star within star.	—	—	—

		Good	Fine	XF
10A	**5 Dông** 1947. Red-brown. HCM at top. Back: Woman with boy below. Like #10 but year at lower left, KIEU THU II (second issue) at lower right.			
	a. Without watermark.	10.00	20.00	100
	b. Watermark: *VDCCH.*	10.00	20.00	100
	c. Watermark: Oval with *Vietnam.*	10.00	20.00	100

		Good	Fine	XF
10B	**5 Dông** ND. Blue. Field workers at left, HCM at right. Back: Workers gathering straw. BC: Red-brown. Without watermark.	10.00	75.00	—

		Good	Fine	XF
11	**50 Dông** ND (1947). Blue and brown. (Shade varieties). Portrait HCM at center. Back: Worker and buffalo at center.			
	a. Without watermark.	10.00	25.00	75.00
	b. Watermark: *VDCCH.*	10.00	25.00	75.00
	c. Watermark: Oval with *Vietnam.*	10.00	25.00	75.00

		Good	Fine	XF
12	**100 Dông** ND (1947). Blue and brown. Woman with child at left. HCM (64mm high) at center, three workers at right. Similar to #8. Back: Agricultural workers with buffalo. 207x102mm.			
	a. Without watermark.	25.00	100	225
	b. Watermark: Oval with Vietnam.	25.00	100	225

1948 ND Issue

		Good	Fine	XF
13	**20 Xu** ND (1948). Red-brown. HCM at right. Back: Soldier and woman. Watermark: Star with *VN* in circle. UV: stripe fluoresces orange.			
	a. 5 small (1mm tall) stars at left on back.	15.00	50.00	125
	b. 5 large (2mm tall) stars at left on back.	15.00	50.00	125

		Good	Fine	XF
14	**50 Xu** ND (1948). Green. HCM at right. Back: Two people standing. Watermark: Star with *VN* in circle.			
	a. Blue serial #.	30.00	100	200
	b. Red serial #.	15.00	50.00	125

		Good	Fine	XF
15	**1 Dông** ND (1948). Dark blue. HCM at center. Similar to #1 and 9 but corner numerals *1* on without small circles. Back: Underprint sun rays.	20.00	40.00	125

		Good	Fine	XF
16	**1 Dông** ND (1948). Dark blue. Two women laborers in rice field at left, HCM at right. Back: Five armed women (Nam Bo). Shade varieties exist.	1.00	3.00	10.00

		Good	Fine	XF
17	**5 Dông** ND (1948). Green to gray. Two men at center, water buffalo at right. Back: HCM in circle at left, man with rifle at center right. (Nam Bo). BC: Brown. Shade varieties exist.			
	a. Issued note.	1.00	3.00	10.00
	s. Uniface specimen (pair).	—	Unc	800

Note: #16 and 17 exist in a great many color and shade varieties, such as brown face with red back, green face with brown back, blue-green face with orange back, black face with purple back, etc.

		Good	Fine	XF
18	**5 Dông** ND (1948). Green. HCM at center. Similar to #36. Back: Two peasants at left and at right. BC: Red-brown.			
	a. Issued note.	7.50	20.00	50.00
	s. Uniface specimen (face).	—	Unc	250
19	**5 Dông** ND (1948). Dark blue. HCM at right, peasants at left. Back: Two peasants stacking grain sheaves at center. BC: Red-brown. Without watermark.	7.50	20.00	50.00

		Good	Fine	XF
20	**10 Dông** ND (1948). Red-brown. Back: Soldier and worker at center, HCM at right. BC: Green to black-green. Blurred printing.			
	a. Without watermark.	3.00	10.00	30.00
	b. Watermark: *VDCCH.*	3.00	10.00	30.00
	c. Watermark: Oval with *Vietnam.*	3.00	10.00	30.00
	d. Watermark: Circle with star.	3.00	10.00	30.00
	e. Watermark: *VND.*	3.00	10.00	30.00

#21 *Not assigned.*

		Good	Fine	XF
22	**10 Dông** ND (1948). Green. Back: Soldier and worker at center, HCM at right. BC: Red-brown. Like #20 but clear printing (Tonkin).			
	a. Without watermark.	5.00	20.00	60.00
	b. Watermark: *VDCCH.*	5.00	20.00	60.00
	c. Watermark: Oval with *Vietnam.*	5.00	20.00	60.00
	d. Watermark: Circle with star.	5.00	20.00	60.00
23	**10 Dông** ND (1948). Red-brown on green underprint. Back: Soldier and worker at center, HCM at right. Like #20. Overprint: Red 4-line (Trung-Bo) on back.	7.50	20.00	75.00

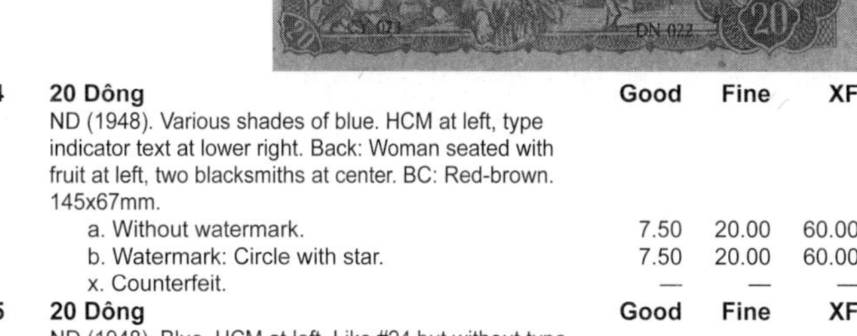

		Good	Fine	XF
24	**20 Dông** ND (1948). Various shades of blue. HCM at left, type indicator text at lower right. Back: Woman seated with fruit at left, two blacksmiths at center. BC: Red-brown. 145x67mm.			
	a. Without watermark.	7.50	20.00	60.00
	b. Watermark: Circle with star.	7.50	20.00	60.00
	x. Counterfeit.	—	—	—
25	**20 Dông** ND (1948). Blue. HCM at left. Like #24 but without type indicator text. Back: Woman seated with fruit at left, two blacksmiths at center. Blurred printing.			
	a. With imprint at lower right. Watermark: Circle and star. VN in star.	3.00	15.00	40.00
	b. Without imprint. Without watermark.	3.00	15.00	40.00

		Good	Fine	XF
26	**20 Dông** ND (1948). Brown and olive. Soldiers at left, HCM at right. Back: Farmers at work. BC: Purple-black. 148x63mm. (Nam-Bo). Light and dark paper varieties.	7.50	30.00	80.00

		Good	Fine	XF
27	**50 Dông** ND (1948-1949). Dark green. Portrait HCM at left. Back: Woman, two children and two men at center. BC: Dark green on red-brown underprint. (Clear and blurred printing varieties, also serial # sizes.)			
	a. Without watermark.	2.00	10.00	30.00
	b. Watermark: Circle and star without writing.	2.00	10.00	30.00
	c. Watermark: Circle and star, *VN* within.	2.00	7.50	20.00
	d. Watermark: Circle and star, *II.*	2.00	7.50	20.00
	e. Black handstamp for Cholon.	2.00	7.50	20.00
	f. Counterfeit.	—	—	—

		Good	Fine	XF
28	**100 Dông** ND (1948). Violet or brown on pink, orange or brown underprint. Woman with child and small flag at left, HCM at center, three workers at right. Back: Two seated women at left, soldier at center, agricultural worker at right. 177x87mm. (Pink and brown shade varieties.)			
	a. Without watermark.	3.00	10.00	30.00
	b. Watermark: Circle with star with VN in circle.	3.00	10.00	30.00
	c. Watermark: Oval with *Vietnam.*	3.00	10.00	30.00
	x. Counterfeit.	5.00	20.00	—

1949 Issue

		Good	Fine	XF
29	**100 Dông** 1949. Green. HCM at right. Back: Two soldiers at left. BC: Brown. Watermark: Circle and star. VN in star. 160x66mm.	7.50	30.00	100

		Good	Fine	XF
30	**100 Dông** 1949. Blue. HCM at right. Like #29. Back: Two soldiers at left. BC: Blue. Watermark: Circle and star. VN in star.			
	a. Black serial #.	7.50	30.00	100
	b. Red serial #.	7.50	30.00	100

		Good	Fine	XF
31	**500 Dông** 1949. Dark blue with brown or red. Man and woman with torch at left, HCM at right. Back: Soldiers at left, burning ship at right.			
	a. Without watermark.	4.00	20.00	50.00
	b. Watermark: Circle with star.	4.00	20.00	50.00
	s. Specimen.	—	Unc	250

1950 ND Issue

		Good	Fine	XF
32	**50 Dông** ND (1950). Black-green and yellow. HCM at center. Back: Soldier with flag at center. (Nam-Bo).	5.00	20.00	50.00

		Good	Fine	XF
33	**100 Dông** ND (1950). Blue and green. Agricultural scene at left, HCM at center, war scene at right. Back: Star, worker and soldier at center. BC: Brown. 170x98mm. (Nam-Bo).	7.50	40.00	100

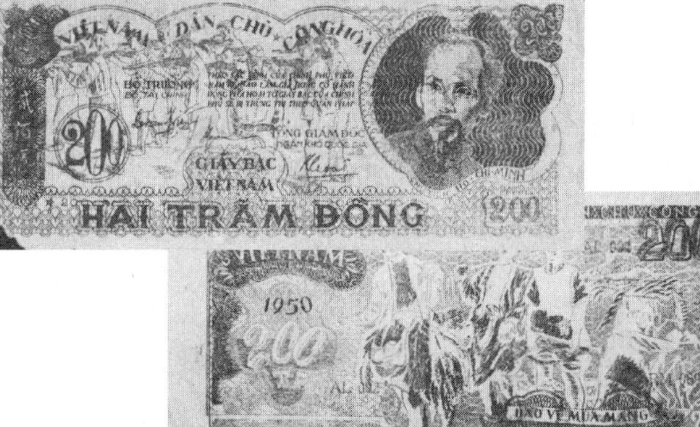

		Good	Fine	XF
34	**200 Dông** 1950. Lilac-brown and dark green. Shooting soldiers at left and center, HCM at right. Back: Soldier and two field workers. Color varieties. Clear and blurred printing varieties.			
	a. Without watermark.	3.00	15.00	40.00
	b. Watermark: Circle with star.	10.00	20.00	90.00

1951 ND Issue

		Good	Fine	XF
35	**100 Dông** ND (1951). Brown and green. HCM at left overseeing large gathering. Back: Six working women. BC: Dark brown and tan. (Nam-Bo).	10.00	30.00	75.00

1952 ND Issue

		Good	Fine	XF
36	**5 Dông** ND (1952). Green. HCM at center. Back: Two farmers planting at left center. BC: Orange.	100	200	400

		Good	Fine	XF
37	**10 Dông** ND (1952). Red-brown or orange-brown and light green. Three laborers at left, HCM at right. Back: Soldiers and truck. (Nam-Bo). Orange and brown shade varieties. PC: White or brown.			
	a. Watermark: Capital letters.	5.00	15.00	50.00
	b. Without watermark.	2.00	7.50	20.00

		Good	Fine	XF
38	**20 Dông** ND (1952). Dark brown and olive. Laborers at left and right, HCM at center. Back: Workers in factory. (Nam-Bo). Without watermark.	100	300	500

		Good	Fine	XF
39	**50 Dông** ND (1952). Violet on light or dark yellow underprint. HCM at center. Back: Worker and soldier stufying from a little book at center. BC: Dull red. (Nam-Bo).	5.00	15.00	40.00
40	**100 Dông** ND (1952). Violet on light brown-violet underprint. HCM at left. Back: Harvesting scene. BC: Lilac. Watermark: Circle with star.	Good	Fine	XF
	a. *KIEU III* at lower right. Without watermark.	50.00	125	250
	b. *KIEU III* at lower right. Watermark: circle with star with *VNDCCH*.	40.00	100	225
	c. Without *KIEU III* at lower right. Watermark: Star with *VN* in circle.	40.00	100	225
40A	**100 Dông** ND (ca.1953). Purple. Five people at center. Back: Tropical plants. BC: Red. (Nam-Bo).	3.00	9.00	20.00

1953 ND Issue

		Good	Fine	XF
41	**20 Dông** ND (1953). Black. HCM at center. Light and dark paper varieties.			
	a. Brown back.	30.00	100	200
	b. Brown and green back. Watermark: circle with star.	40.00	125	250

		Good	Fine	XF
42	**50 Dông** ND (1953). Brown and light green. HCM at left, rice harvesting at right. Back: Group of ten people. BC: Brown and purple. (Nam-Bo).	5.00	20.00	60.00

Tin Phieu

Credit Note

1946-1950 Issue

Issued for Trung Bo (1947-1951), with *TIN PHIEU* indicated prominently.

		Good	Fine	XF
43	**1 Dông** ND (1946). HCM at center. Back: Man with two water buffalos.			
	a. Black.	10.00	25.00	60.00
	b. Purple-brown.	10.00	25.00	60.00
	c. Brown.	10.00	25.00	60.00
44	**1 Dông** ND. Wine red. HCM at center. Like #43 but portrait and frame different. Back: Man with two water buffalos. BC: Green.	10.00	25.00	60.00
45	**1 Dông** ND (1946). Light blue or olive. HCM at center. Back: Farmer plowing with two oxen at left center. Without watermark.	15.00	35.00	75.00

#	Note	Good	Fine	XF
46	**5 Dông** ND (1949-1950). HCM at center in oval wreath. Back: Numeral *5*.			
	a. Lilac-brown to brown.	10.00	30.00	60.00
	b. Blue-green.	10.00	30.00	60.00
	c. Olive.	10.00	30.00	60.00
	d. Gray.	10.00	30.00	60.00
	e. Blue.	10.00	30.00	60.00
47	**5 Dông** ND (1949-1950). HCM at center in oval wreath. Like #46 but portrait without frame. Back: Numeral *5*. Thick and thin paper varieties for a, b and c.			
	a. Brownish orange. Green back. Without watermark.	10.00	30.00	60.00
	b. As a. Watermark: Circle with star.	10.00	30.00	60.00
	c. Blue. Without watermark.	10.00	30.00	60.00
	d. Olive. Watermark: Circle with star.	10.00	30.00	60.00
48	**20 Dông** ND (1948). Orange. *TIN PHIEU* and *HAI MUOI DONG* at center. Back: Work scenes at left bottom and right, crude portrait of HCM in wreath at center. BC: Green. 133x77mm. Light and dark paper varieties.			
	a. Without watermark.	10.00	30.00	80.00
	b. Watermark: Circle with star.	10.00	30.00	80.00

#	Note	Good	Fine	XF
49	**20 Dông** ND (1948). Brown on yellow underprint. *TIN PHIEU* and *HAI MUOI DONG* at center. Like #48. Back: Work scenes at left bottom and right, crude portrait of HCM in wreath at center. BC: Brown on yellow underprint.			
	a. Without watermark.	10.00	40.00	90.00
	b. Watermark: Circle with star.	10.00	40.00	90.00

#	Note	Good	Fine	XF
50	**50 Dông** ND (1949-1950). No underprint. HCM in circle at lower center. Work scenes at left, right and bottom. Back: Men in sailboat. PC: Brown or white.			
	a. Face violet-brown, back blue. Without watermark.	15.00	50.00	100
	b. Face orange, back gray-green. Without watermark.	15.00	50.00	100
	c. Face and back gray. Without watermark.	15.00	50.00	100
	d. Violet.	15.00	50.00	100
	e. Brown. Back gray-green. Without watermark. White paper.	15.00	50.00	100
	f. As e. Watermark: circle with star. Brown paper.	15.00	50.00	100
	g. With round handstamp and black signature on back for Binh-Thuan Province. No watermark.	15.00	50.00	100
	h. With red circular handstamp on back for Cuc-Nam Province.	15.00	50.00	100
51	**50 Dông** ND (1949-1950). Brown and green. HCM in circle at lower center. Work scenes at left, right and bottom. Like #50 but underprint at center. Back: Men in sailboat.			
	a. White paper without watermark.	15.00	50.00	100
	b. Brown paper, watermark: Circle with star.	15.00	50.00	100

#	Note	Good	Fine	XF
52	**50 Dông** 1951. Dark brown. HCM at right. Back: Soldier, worker and farmer at center. BC: Olive.			
	a. Without watermark.	20.00	50.00	125
	b. Watermark: Circle with star.	20.00	50.00	125
53	**100 Dông** ND (1950-1951). Red or brown. HCM at left. Back: Two workers and soldier. BC: Green-gray.			
	a. Without watermark.	5.00	20.00	50.00
	b. Watermark: Circle with star.	5.00	20.00	50.00

#	Note	Good	Fine	XF
54	**100 Dông** ND (1950-1951). Blue and brown. Agricultural worker with buffalo at left, portrait HCM at right. Back: Star at center, two workers in front. BC: Pink to red-brown. 169x99mm. Many color, paper and watermark varieties.			
	a. Without watermark. Thin paper.	7.50	25.00	75.00
	b. Watermark: Circle with star. Thick paper.	7.50	25.00	75.00

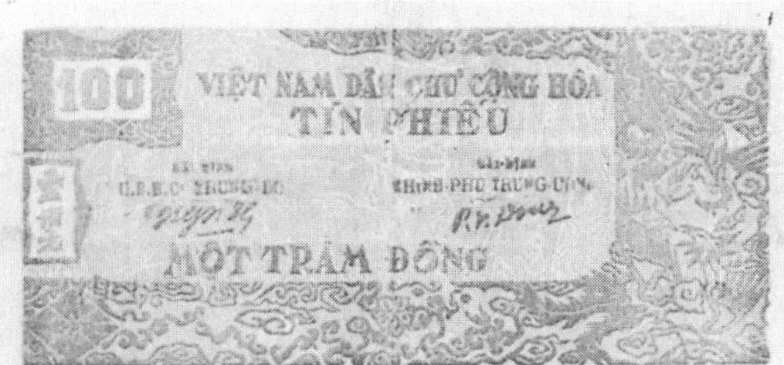

#	Note	Good	Fine	XF
55	**100 Dông** ND (1950-1951). Green and gray. Back: Soldier, woman and children at center, HCM at right. BC: Gray-brown. 171x84mm.			
	a. Without watermark. Thin paper.	30.00	75.00	200
	b. Watermark: Circle with star.	30.00	75.00	200

		Good	Fine	XF
56	**100 Dông** ND (1950-1951). Brownish red. HCM at right. Back: Two soldiers at center. BC: Blue-green and light brown.			
	a. Without watermark. Thin paper.	30.00	75.00	200
	b. Watermark: Circle with star. Thick paper.	30.00	75.00	200

		Good	Fine	XF
57	**500 Dông** ND (1950-1951). Gray-blue. Two workers at center, HCM at right. Back: Landscape and three people. BC: Green. Watermark: Star in circle.	5.00	20.00	50.00

		Good	Fine	XF
58	**1000 Dông** ND (1950-1951). Red to brown. HCM at right. Back: Soldiers and porters. Watermark: Star in circle.	5.00	15.00	50.00

Ngan Hang Quoc Gia Viet Nam

National Bank of Viet Nam

1951-1953 Issue

1 "New" Dong = 100 "Old" Dong In 1952 all previously issued notes were withdrawn and demonetized. Notes in "new" Dong values, issue dated 1951 and later, were printed in Czechoslovakia and remained in circulation until 1958. Thus they were the last wartime notes issued uring the fighting against the French, and they became the official currency of the post-1954 independent Democratic Republic of Viet Nam (North Vietnam).

		Good	Fine	XF
59	**10 Dông** ND. Violet-brown and olive. HCM at left. Back: Farmers with water buffalos. Printer: CPF-Shanghai (without imprint).			
	a. Issued note.	10.00	30.00	60.00
	b. Olive face color, back brown.	10.00	30.00	60.00
	s. Specimen. Handwritten. Rare.	—		

Note: For #59 overprint as 1 XU see #67.

		Good	Fine	XF
60	**20 Dông** 1951. Portrait HCM at left. Back: Soldier and ships. Printer: CPF-Shanghai (without imprint).			
	a. Purple.	2.00	7.50	20.00
	b. Olive.	50.00	30.00	100
	s1. As a. Specimen.	—	—	250
	s2. As b. Specimen.	—	—	250

		Good	Fine	XF
61	**50 Dông** 1951. Portrait HCM at right. Back: Harvest work. Printer: CPF-Shanghai (without imprint).			
	a. Green.	2.00	12.50	40.00
	b. Brown.	2.00	20.00	50.00
	s1. As a. Specimen.	—	—	200
	s2. As b. Specimen.	—	—	200

		VG	VF	UNC
62	**100 Dông** 1951. HCM at right. Back: Bomb factory. Printer: CPF-Shanghai (without imprint).			
	a. Green.	5.00	20.00	50.00
	b. Blue.	5.00	20.00	50.00
	s. As a. Specimen.	—	—	200

		VG	VF	UNC
63	**200 Dông** 1951. Portrait HCM at left, soldiers under training at center. Back: Human convoy. Printer: CPF-Shanghai (without imprint).			
	a. Reddish brown.	20.00	60.00	200
	b. Green.	50.00	150	400
	s1. As a. Specimen.	—	—	500
	s2. As b. Specimen.	—	—	500

		VG	VF	UNC
64	**500 Dông** 1951. Green. HCM at left, soldiers at a gun at right. Back: Workers tilling field. Printer: CPF-Shanghai (without imprint).			
	a. Issued note.	7.50	20.00	40.00
	s. Specimen.	—	—	200

		VG	VF	UNC
65	**1000 Dông** 1951. Brown-orange. Portrait HCM at left, soldiers advancing at center. Back: Soldier, worker and farmer. Printer: CPF-Shanghai (without imprint).			
	a. Issued note.	3.00	10.00	30.00
	s. Specimen.	—	—	200
	x. Counterfeit.	—	5.00	20.00

		VG	VF	UNC
66	**5000 Dông** 1953. Blue. HCM at left. Back: Anti-aircraft artillery emplacements. Printer: CPF-Shanghai (without imprint).			
	a. Issued note.	10.00	40.00	125
	s. Specimen.	—	—	600

DEMOCRATIC REPUBLIC

Ngân Hàng Quôc Gia Viêt Nam

National Bank of Viet Nam

1958 ND Provisional Issue

		VG	VF	UNC
67	**1 Xu on 10 Dông** ND (1958). Violet-brown. HCM at left. Back: Farmers with water buffalos.	—	500	—

1958 Issue

		VG	VF	UNC
68	**1 Hao** 1958. Red on green underprint. Arms at center. Back: Train. Printer: CPF-Shanghai (without imprint).			
	a. Issued note.	0.50	1.50	5.00
	b. Overprint: *Cai Luu Hanoi Cua...* for circulation in Haiphong.	—	—	—
	c. With control handstamp: *DA THU.* Reported not confirmed.	—	—	—
	s. Specimen. *GIAY MAU* on face and *MAU BAC* on back.	—	—	40.00

		VG	VF	UNC
69	**2 Hao** 1958. Green on tan underprint. Arms at center. Back: Grazing animals near Coffer dam. Printer: CPF-Shanghai (without imprint).			
	a. Issued note.	1.00	2.00	5.00
	b. With control handstamp: *DA THU.*	1.00	2.00	5.00
	s. Specimen. Overprint: *HIAY MAU* on face and *MAU BAC* on back.	—	—	40.00
70	**5 Hao** 1958. Brown on light green underprint. Arms at center. Back: Four women in spinning mill. Printer: CPF-Shanghai (without imprint).	VG	VF	UNC
	a. Issued note.	1.25	3.00	15.00
	b. With control handstamp: *DA THU.* Reported not confirmed.	—	—	—
	s. Specimen. Overprint: *HIAY MAU* on face and *MAU BAC* on back.	—	—	40.00

		VG	VF	UNC
71	**1 Dông** 1958. Brown on light green underprint. Arms at left, monument with tower and flag at center. Back: Work in rice paddies. Printer: CPF-Shanghai (without imprint).			
	a. Issued note.	1.00	3.00	15.00
	b. With control handstamp: *DA THU.*	1.50	4.00	15.00
	s. Specimen. Overprint: *HIAY MAU* on face and *MAU BAC* on back.	—	—	40.00
	x. US lithograph counterfeit with propaganda message at left. 6 varieties: without code, Code 50, Code 4540 (2 text var.) Code 4543 (2 text var.).	1.00	5.00	20.00

		VG	VF	UNC
72	**2 Dông** 1958. Blue on green underprint. Arms at left, four people with flag at center right. Back: Boats and mountains. Watermark: White shaded star. Printer: CPF-Shanghai (without imprint).			
	a. Issued note.	1.00	4.00	20.00
	b. With control handstamp: *DA THU.*	2.00	6.00	20.00
	s. Specimen. Overprint: *HIAY MAU* on face and *MAU BAC* on back.	—	—	40.00
	x. US lithograph counterfeit with propaganda message at right. Code 4541.	1.00	5.00	25.00

		VG	VF	UNC
73	**5 Dông** 1958. Brown on blue underprint. Arms at left, tractor at center, HCM at right. Back: Road construction work.			
	a. Issued note.	2.00	7.50	25.00
	b. With control handstamp: *DA THU.*	2.00	7.50	20.00
	s. Specimen. Overprint: *HIAY MAU* on face and *MAU BAC* on back.	—	—	40.00
	x. US lithograph counterfeit with propaganda message at right. Code 4542.	2.00	7.50	25.00

		VG	VF	UNC
74	**10 Dông** 1958. Red on blue and green underprint. Arms at center, HCM at right. Back: Factory.			
	a. Issued note.	2.00	7.50	30.00
	b. With control handstamp: *DA THU.*	3.00	8.00	30.00
	s. Specimen. Overprint: *HIAY MAU* on face and *MAU BAC* on back.	—	—	40.00

WEST AFRICAN STATES

The West African States, a former federation of eight French colonial territories on the northwest coast of Africa, had an area of 1,813,079 sq. mi. (4,742,495 sq. km.) and a population of about 60 million. Capital: Dakar. The constituent territories were Mauritania, Senegal, Dahomey, French Sudan, Ivory Coast, Upper Volta, Niger and French Guinea. The members of the federation were overseas territories within the French Union until Sept. of 1958 when all but French Guinea approved the constitution of the Fifth French Republic, thereby electing to become autonomous members of the new French Community. French Guinea voted to become the fully independent Republic of Guinea. The other seven attained independence in 1960. The French West Africa territories were provided with a common currency, a practice which was continued as the monetary union of the West African States which provides a common currency to the autonomous republics of Dahomey (now Benin), Mali, Senegal, Upper Volta (now Burkina Faso) Ivory Coast, Togo, Niger, and Guinea-Bissau.

MONETARY SYSTEM:

1 Franc = 100 Centimes

DATING:

The year of issue on the current notes appear in the first 2 digits of the serial number, i.e. (19)91, (19)92, etc.

SIGNATURE VARIETIES

WEST AFRICAN STATES

Banque Centrale des Etats de l'Afrique de l'Ouest

Notes of this bank were issued both with and withoout code letters in the upper right and lower left corners. The code letter follows the control number and indicates which member country the note was issued for. Those w/o code letters are general issues. The code letters are as follows: A for Cote d' Ivoire D for Mali K for Senegal B for Benin (Dahomey) E for Mauritania S for Guinea-Bissau C for Burkina Faso (Upper Volta) H for Niger T for Togo

SIGNATURE VARIETIES

	LE PRÉSIDENT	LE DIRECTEUR GÉNÉRAL	DATE
1			Various dates - 1959 20.3.1961
2			20.3.1961
3			20.12.1964
4			2.3.1965; ND
5			ND
6			ND
7			ND
8			ND
9			ND
	LE PRÉSIDENT DU CONSEIL DES MINISTRES	**LE GOUVERNEUR**	**DATE**
10			ND

SIGNATURE VARIETIES			
11	[signature]	[signature]	ND (1977); 1977
12	[signature]	[signature]	ND (1978); 1978; 1979
13	[signature]	[signature]	ND (1980); 1980

General Issues w/o Code Letter

1958; 1959 ND Issue

#1-5 without code letters to signify member countries.

1 **50 Francs** | VG 10.00 | VF 40.00 | UNC 110

ND (1958). Dark brown, blue and multicolor. Three women at center. Signature 1. Back: Woman with headress at center.

2 **100 Francs**

1959; ND. Dark brown, orange and multicolor. Mask at left, woman at right. Back: Woman at left, carving at lower center. Watermark: Women's head.

	VG	VF	UNC
a. Signature 1. 23.4.1959.	10.00	40.00	90.00
b. Signature 5. ND.	3.00	10.00	25.00

3 **500 Francs** | VG 30.00 | VF 70.00 | UNC 150

15.4.1959. Brown, green and multicolor. Men doing field work at left, mask carving at right. Signature 1. Back: Woman at left, farmer on tractor at right. Watermark: Woman's head.

4 **1000 Francs** | VG 20.00 | VF 50.00 | UNC 125

17.9.1959. Brown, blue and multicolor. Man and woman at center. Signature 1. Back: Man with rope suspension bridge in background and pineapples. Watermark: Man's head.

		VG	VF	UNC
5	**5000 Francs** 15.4.1959. Blue, brown and multicolor. Bearded man at left, building at center. Signature 1. Back: Woman, corn grinders and huts.	20.00	130	300

Note: All other issues for West African States will be found in Volume 3.

A for Cote d'Ivoire (Ivory Coast)

1959-1965; ND Issue

102A **500 Francs**	VG	VF	UNC
1959-1964; ND. Brown, green and multicolor. Field workers at left, mask carving at right. Back: Woman at left, farmer on tractor at right. Watermark: Woman's head.			
a. Engraved. Signature 1. 15.4.1959.	25.00	55.00	—
b. Signature 1. 20.3.1961.	12.00	30.00	90.00
c. Signature 2. 20.3.1961.	15.00	45.00	—
d. Signature 3. 2.12.1964.	25.00	55.00	—
e. Signature 5. ND.	12.00	35.00	90.00
f. Signature 6. ND.	10.00	25.00	75.00
g. Litho. Signature 6. ND.	12.00	30.00	90.00
h. Signature 7. ND.	12.00	30.00	90.00
i. Signature 8. ND.	20.00	50.00	—
j. Signature 9. ND.	6.00	18.00	50.00
k. Signature 10. ND.	5.00	15.00	40.00
l. Signature 11. ND.	4.00	12.00	35.00
m. Signature 12. ND.	6.00	18.00	55.00

103A **1000 Francs**	VG	VF	UNC
1959-1965; ND. Brown, blue and multicolor. Man and woman at center. Back: Man with rope suspension bridge in background and pineapples. Watermark: Man's head.			
a. Engraved. Signature 1. 17.9.1959.	75.00	—	—
b. Signature 1. 20.3.1961.	10.00	30.00	90.00
c. Signature 2. 20.3.1961.	7.00	25.00	75.00
d. Signature 4. 2.3.1965.	30.00	80.00	—
e. Signature 5. ND.	7.00	20.00	60.00
f. Signature 6. ND.	7.00	20.00	60.00
g. Litho. Signature 6. ND.	7.00	20.00	60.00
h. Signature 7. ND.	8.00	22.00	65.00
i. Signature 8. ND.	8.00	22.00	75.00
j. Signature 9. ND.	7.00	20.00	60.00
k. Signature 10. ND.	5.00	15.00	40.00
l. Signature 11. ND.	5.00	15.00	40.00
m. Signature 12. ND.	5.00	15.00	40.00
n. Signature 13. ND.	5.00	15.00	40.00

D for Mali

1959-1961; ND Issue

402D **500 Francs**	Good	Fine	XF
1959; 1961. Brown, green and multicolor. Field workers at left, mask carving at right. Like #102A. Back: Woman at left, farmer on tractor at right. Watermark: Woman's head.			
a. Signature 1. 15.4.1959.	150	600	—
b. Signature 1. 20.3.1961.	—	—	—

403D **1000 Francs**	Good	Fine	XF
1959; 1961. Brown, blue and multicolor. Man and woman at center. Like #103A. Back: Man with rope suspension bridge in background and pineapples. Watermark: Man's head.			
a. Signature 1. 17.9.1959.	90.00	400	1,000
b. Signature 1. 20.3.1961.	90.00	400	1,000

E for Mauritania

1959-1964; ND Issue

502E **500 Francs**	Good	Fine	XF
1959-1964; ND. Brown, green and multicolor. Field workers at left, mask carving at right. Like #102A. Back: Woman at left, farmer on tractor at right. Watermark: Woman's head.			
a. Engraved. Signature 1. 15.4.1959.	100	—	—
b. Signature 1. 20.3.1961.	50.00	200	—
c. Signature 2. 20.3.1961.	45.00	175	—
e. Signature 4. 2.3.1965.	45.00	200	—
f. Signature 5. ND.	45.00	175	650
g. Signature 6. ND.	45.00	175	600
h. Litho. Signature 6. ND.	50.00	200	—
i. Signature 7. ND.	45.00	175	600

H for Niger

1959-1965; ND Issue

602H **500 Francs**	VG	VF	UNC
1959-1965; ND. Brown, green and multicolor. Field workers at left, mask carving at right. Like #102A. Back: Woman at left, farmer on tractor at right. Watermark: Woman's head.			
a. Engraved. Signature 1. 15.4.1959.	75.00	—	—
c. Signature 2. 20.3.1961.	50.00	125	—
d. Signature 3. 2.12.1964.	25.00	75.00	200
e. Signature 4. 2.3.1965.	25.00	75.00	200
f. Signature 5. ND.	50.00	125	—
g. Signature 6. ND.	15.00	40.00	120
h. Litho. Signature 6. ND.	15.00	40.00	120
i. Signature 7. ND.	20.00	65.00	150
j. Signature 8. ND.	15.00	40.00	120
k. Signature 9. ND.	12.00	30.00	90.00
l. Signature 10. ND.	100	—	—
m. Signature 11. ND.	12.00	25.00	75.00

603H **1000 Francs**	VG	VF	UNC
1959-1965; ND. Brown, blue and multicolor. Man and woman at center. Like #103A. Back: Man with rope suspension bridge in background and pineapples. Watermark: Man's head.			
a. Engraved. Signature 1. 17.9.1959.	35.00	100	—
b. Signature 1. 20.3.1961.	35.00	100	—

	VG	VF	UNC
c. Signature 2. 20.3.1961.	100	—	—
e. Signature 4. 2.3.1965.	35.00	100	250
f. Signature 5. ND.	35.00	100	250
g. Signature 6. ND.	30.00	80.00	—
h. Litho. Signature 6. ND.	30.00	80.00	200
i. Signature 7. ND.	30.00	80.00	200
j. Signature 8. ND.	35.00	100	—
k. Signature 9. ND	15.00	40.00	120
l. Signature 10. ND.	15.00	40.00	120
m. Signature 11. ND.	12.00	30.00	90.00
n. Signature 12. ND.	15.00	40.00	120
o. Signature 13. ND.	15.00	50.00	150

K for Senegal

1959-1965; ND Issue

702K 500 Francs

1959-1965; ND. Brown, green and multicolor. Field workers at left, mask carving at right. Like #102A. Back: Woman at left, farmer on tractor at right. Watermark: Woman's head.

	VG	VF	UNC
a. Engraved. Signature 1. 15.4.1959.	40.00	—	—
b. Signature 1. 20.3.1961.	15.00	45.00	120
c. Signature 2. 20.3.1961.	15.00	45.00	120
d. Signature 3. 2.12.1964.	15.00	45.00	120
e. Signature 4. 2.3.1965.	12.00	40.00	100
f. Signature 5. ND.	15.00	45.00	120
g. Signature 6. ND.	9.00	25.00	85.00
h. Litho. Signature 6. ND.	9.00	25.00	85.00
i. Signature 7. ND.	12.00	40.00	—
j. Signature 8. ND.	12.00	40.00	100
k. Signature 9. ND.	7.00	20.00	60.00
l. Signature 10. ND.	7.00	20.00	60.00
m. Signature 11. ND.	5.00	15.00	45.00
n. Signature 12. ND.	5.00	15.00	45.00

703K 1000 Francs

1959-1965; ND. Brown, blue and multicolor. Man and woman at center. Like #103A. Back: Man with rope suspension bridge in background and pineapples. Watermark: Man's head.

	VG	VF	UNC
a. Engraved. Signature 1. 17.9.1959.	25.00	65.00	—
b. Signature 1. 20.3.1961.	25.00	65.00	—
c. Signature 2. 20.3.1961.	12.00	50.00	—
e. Signature 4. 2.3.1965.	12.00	50.00	—
f. Signature 5. ND.	35.00	90.00	—
g. Signature 6. ND.	30.00	75.00	120
h. Litho. Signature 6. ND.	7.00	25.00	60.00
i. Signature 7. ND.	8.00	30.00	75.00
j. Signature 8. ND.	9.00	35.00	—
k. Signature 9. ND.	5.00	15.00	50.00
l. Signature 10. ND.	5.00	15.00	50.00
m. Signature 11. ND.	5.00	15.00	50.00
n. Signature 12. ND.	5.00	15.00	50.00
o. Signature 13. ND.	5.00	15.00	50.00

T for Togo

1959-1965; ND Issue

802T 500 Francs

1959-1961; ND. Brown, green and multicolor. Field workers at left, mask carving at right. Like #102A. Back: Woman at left, farmer on tractor at right. Watermark: Woman's head.

	VG	VF	UNC
a. Engraved. Signature 1. 15.4.1959.	25.00	75.00	—
b. Signature 1. 20.3.1961.	25.00	75.00	—
c. Signature 2. 20.3.1961.	25.00	75.00	—
f. Signature 5. ND.	30.00	85.00	—
g. Signature 6. ND.	10.00	30.00	80.00
i. Litho. Signature 7. ND.	20.00	50.00	130
j. Signature 8. ND.	20.00	50.00	—
k. Signature 9. ND.	7.00	20.00	60.00
l. Signature 10. ND.	30.00	—	—
m. Signature 11. ND.	2.00	10.00	35.00

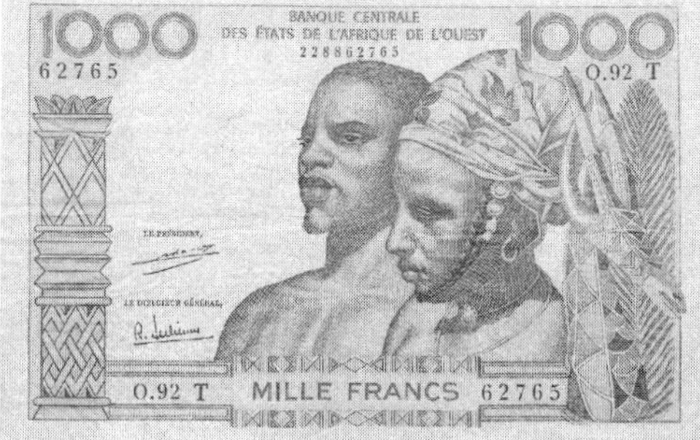

803T 1000 Francs

1959-1965; ND. Brown, blue and multicolor. Man and woman at center. Like #103A. Back: Man with rope suspension bridge in background and pineapples. Watermark: Man's head.

	VG	VF	UNC
a. Engraved. Signature 1. 17.9.1959.	90.00	—	—
b. Signature 1. 20.3.1961.	20.00	60.00	—
c. Signature 2. 20.3.1961.	30.00	75.00	—
e. Signature 4. 2.3.1965.	20.00	60.00	—
f. Signature 5. ND.	10.00	30.00	80.00
g. Signature 6. ND.	25.00	70.00	—
h. Litho. Signature 6. ND.	30.00	80.00	—
i. Signature 7. ND.	10.00	30.00	80.00
j. Signature 8. ND.	35.00	90.00	—
k. Signature 9. ND.	5.00	20.00	55.00
l. Signature 10. ND.	5.00	15.00	45.00
m. Signature 11. ND.	4.00	12.00	40.00
n. Signature 12. ND.	4.00	12.00	40.00
o. Signature 13. ND.	5.00	15.00	45.00

WESTERN SAMOA

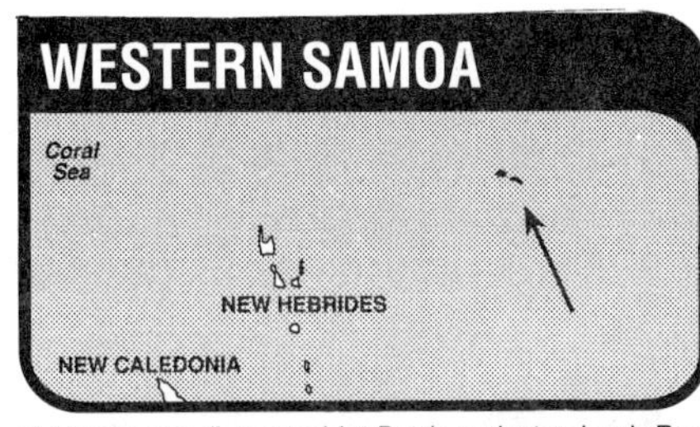

The Independent State of Western Samoa (formerly German Samoa), located in the Pacific Ocean 1,600 miles (2,574 km.) northeast of New Zealand, has an area of 1,097 sq. mi. (2,860 sq. km.) and a population of 157,000. Capital: Apia. The economy is based on agriculture, fishing and tourism. Copra, cocoa and bananas are exported. The Samoan group of islands was discovered by Dutch navigator Jacob Roggeveen in 1772. Great Britain, the United States and Germany established consular representation at Apia in 1847, 1853 and 1861 respectively. The conflicting interests of the three powers produced the Berlin agreement of 1889 which declared Samoa neutral and had the effect of establishing a tripartite protectorate over the islands. A further agreement, 1899, recognized the rights of the United States in those islands east of 171 deg. west longitude (American Samoa) and of Germany in the other islands (Western Samoa). New Zealand occupied Western Samoa at the start of World War I and administered it as a League of Nations mandate and U.N. trusteeship until Jan. 1, 1962, when it became an independent state. Western Samoa is a member of the Commonwealth of Nations. The Chief Executive is Chief of State. The prime minister is the Head of Government. The present Head of State, Malietoa Tanumafili II, holds his position for life. Future Heads of State will be elected by the Legislature Assembly for five-year terms.

RULERS:

British, 1914-1962
Malietoa Tanumafili II, 1962-2007

MONETARY SYSTEM:

1 Shilling = 12 Pence
1 Pound = 20 Shillings to 1967
1 Tala = 100 Sene, 1967-

NEW ZEALAND OCCUPATION - WW I

Government of Samoa

1920 ND Provisional Issue

#1-2 overprint: *GOVERNMENT OF SAMOA / CURRENCY NOTE* on Bank of New Zealand notes until 1921.

#	Denomination	Good	Fine	XF
1	**10 Shillings** (1920 -old date 1917). Multicolor. Overprint: Red *GOVERNMENT OF SAMOA/CURRENCY NOTE* on face of New Zealand #S223. Apia. Rare.	—	—	—
2	**1 Pound** ND (1920). Overprint: Red *GOVERNMENT OF SAMOA/ CURRENCY NOTE* on New Zealand #S225. Rare.	—	—	—

NEW ZEALAND ADMINISTRATION

Territory of Western Samoa

1920-1922 Treasury Note Issue

By Authority of New Zealand Government Note: Some of these hand stamped dated notes may appear to be ND, probably through error or that the date has faded, been washed out or worn off.

#	Denomination	VG	VF	UNC
7	**10 Shillings** 1922-1959. Black on brown and green underprint. Palm trees along beach at center. Signature varieties. Printer: BWC.			
	a. 3.3.1922.	—	—	—
	b. Signature title: *MINISTER OF EXTERNAL AFFAIRS FOR NEW ZEALAND* at left. 13.4.1938-21.11.1949.	50.00	175	650
	c. Signature title: *MINISTER OF ISLAND TERRITORIES FOR NEW ZEALAND* at left. 24.5.1951-27.5.1958; 29.10.1959.	75.00	250	750
	d. Signature title: *HIGH COMMISSIONER* at left. 20.3.1957-22.12.1959.	35.00	150	600

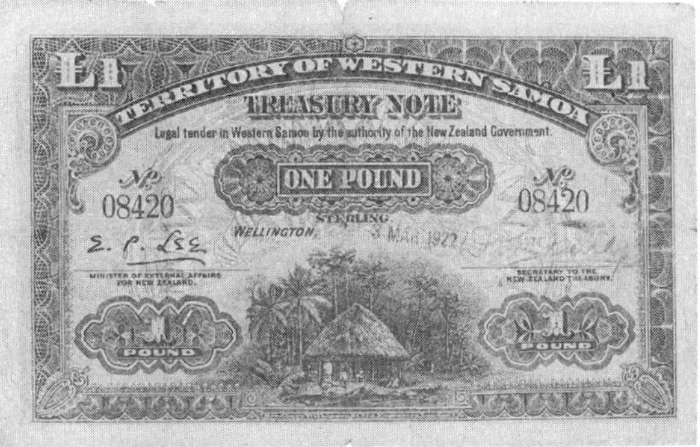

#	Denomination	Good	Fine	XF
8	**1 Pound** 1922-1947. Purple on multicolor underprint. Hut, palm trees at center. *STERLING* directly appears close beneath spelled out denomination at center. Signature varieties. Printer: BWC.			
	a. 3.3.1922. Rare.	—	—	—
	b. Signature title: *MINISTER OF EXTERNAL AFFAIRS FOR NEW ZEALAND* at left. 12.1.1937-12.1.1947.	65.00	200	550

#	Denomination	VG	VF	UNC
8A	**1 Pound** 1948-1961. Purple on multicolor underprint. Hut, palm trees at center. Like #8 but *STERLING* omitted from center. Signature varieties. Printer: BWC.			
	a. Signature title: *MINISTER OF ISLAND TERRITORIES FOR NEW ZEALAND* at left. 6.8.1948-7.8.1958.	125	450	—
	b. Signature title: *HIGH COMMISSIONER* at left. 20.4.1959; 10.12.1959; 1.5.1961.	100	250	1,600

#	Denomination	Good	Fine	XF
9	**5 Pounds** 1920-1944. Purple on multicolor underprint. Boat at lower center. *STERLING* directly appears close beneath spelled out denomination at center. Signature varieties. Printer: BWC.			
	a. (1920s). Rare.	—	—	—
	b. Signature title: *MINISTER OF EXTERNAL AFFAIRS FOR NEW ZEALAND* at left. 3.11.1942.	1,000	3,500	—

#	Denomination	VG	VF	UNC
9A	**5 Pounds** 1956-1959. Purple on multicolor underprint. Boat at lower center. Like #9 but *STERLING* omitted from center. Signature varieties. Printer: BWC.			
	a. Signature title *MINISTER FOR ISLAND TERRITORIES FOR NEW ZEALAND* at left. 11.4.1956. Reported not confirmed.	—	—	—
	b. Signature title: *HIGH COMMISSIONER* at left. 30.1.1958. Rare.	—	—	—
	c. Signature title as above. 13.10.1958; 10.12.1959.	450	1,500	3,500

Bank of Western Samoa

1960-1961 Provisional Issue

#10-12 red overprint: *Bank of Western Samoa / Legal Tender in Western Samoa by virtue of the Bank of Western Samoa Ordinance 1959* on older notes.

		VG	VF	UNC
10	**10 Shillings** 1960-1961; ND. Black on brown and green underprint. Palm trees along beach at center. Signature varieties.			
	a. Signature title: *HIGH COMMISSIONER* blocked out at lower left, with *MINISTER OF FINANCE* below. 8.12.1960; 1.5.1961.	35.00	150	550
	b. ND. signature title: *MINISTER OF FINANCE* in plate without overprint., at lower left	35.00	150	550
11	**1 Pound** 1960-1961. Purple on multicolor underprint. Hut, palm trees at center. *STERLING* directly appears close beneath spelled out denomination at center. Signature varieties.	VG	VF	UNC
	a. Signature title: *HIGH COMMISSIONER* blocked out at lower left, with *MINISTER OF FINANCE* below. 8.11.1960; 1.5.1961.	100	500	1,500
	b. Signature title: *MINISTER OF FINANCE* in plate without overprint., at lower left 1.5.1961.	100	400	1,450
12	**5 Pounds**	VG	VF	UNC
	1.5.1961. Purple on multicolor underprint. Boat at lower center. *STERLING* omitted from center. Signature varieties.	550	2,000	7,500

The Federal Republic of Yugoslavia is a Balkan country located on the east shore of the Adriatic Sea bordering Bosnia-Herzegovina and Croatia to the west, Hungary and Romania to the north, Bulgaria to the east, and Albania and Macedonia to the south. It has an area of 39,449 sq. mi. (102,173 sq. km.) and a population of 10.5 million. Capital: Belgrade. The chief industries are agriculture, mining, manufacturing and tourism. Machinery, nonferrous metals, meat and fabrics are exported. The first South-Slavian State - Yugoslavia - was proclaimed on Dec. 1, 1918, after the union of the Kingdom of Serbia, Montenegro and the South Slav territories of Austria-Hungary; it then changed its official name from the Kingdom of the Serbs, Croats, and Slovenes to the Kingdom of Yugoslavia on Oct. 3, 1929. The Royal government of Yugoslavia attempted to remain neutral in World War II but, yielding to German pressure, aligned itself with the Axis powers in March of 1941; a few days later it was overthrown by a military-led coup and its neutrality reasserted. The Nazis occupied the country on April 17, and throughout the remaining years were resisted by a number of guerrilla armies, notably that of Marshal Josip Broz known as Tito. After the defeat of the Axis powers, a leftist coalition headed by Tito abolished the monarchy and, on Jan. 31, 1946, established a "People's Republic". Tito's rival General Draza Mihajlovic, who led the Chetniks against the Germans and Tito's forces, was arrested on March 13, 1946 and executed the following day after having been convicted by a partisan court. The Federal Republic of Yugoslavia was composed of six autonomous republics: Serbia, Croatia, Slovenia, Bosnia-Herzegovina, Macedonia and Montenegro with two autonomous provinces within Serbia: Kosovo-Metohija and Vojvodina. The collapse of the Socialist Federal Republic of Yugoslavia during 1991-92 has resulted in the autonomous republics of Croatia, Slovenia, Bosnia-Herzegovina and Macedonia declaring their respective independence. The Federal Republic of Yugoslavia was proclaimed in 1992; it consists of the former Republics of Serbia and Montenegro.

RULERS:

Peter I, 1918-1921
Alexander I, 1921-1934
Peter II, 1934-1945

MONETARY SYSTEM:

1 Dinar = 100 Para
1 Dinar = 100 *Old* Dinara, 1965
1 Dinar = 10,000 *Old* Dinara, 1990-91
1 Dinar = 10 *Old* Dinara, 1992
1 Dinar = 1 Million *Old* Dinara, 1.10.1993
1 Dinar = 1 Milliard *Old* Dinara, 1.1.1994
1 Novi Dinar = 1 German Mark = 12,000,000 Dinara, 24.1.1994

WATERMARK VARIETIES

Karageorge

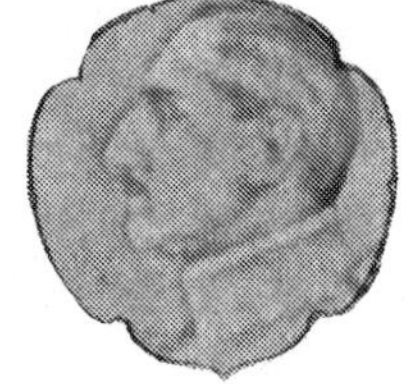
Alexander I

КРАЉЕВСТВО СРБА ХРВАТА И СЛОВЕНАЦА

KINGDOM OF SERBS, CROATS AND SLOVENES

МИНИСТАРСТВО ФИНАНСИЈА

Ministry of Finance

Adhesive stamps affixed to old notes of the Austro-Hungarian Bank (including some already ovpt. in previous issue). Note: Numerous local and government ovpt. (usually w/handstamp indicating redemption to Yugoslav currency) exist on notes of the Austro-Hungarian Bank and Serbian ovpt. on Bulgarian notes. As part of this second revalidation, special adhesive stamps were affixed to the notes. Wording on the 10, 20, and 50 Kronen stamps is tri-lingual (Serbian, Croatian, and Slovene), thus there is for lower denominations only one kind of stamp. Adhesive stamps affixed to 100 and 1000 Kronen notes have wording in only one language, Serbian (Cyrillic), Croatian or Slovene. Thus there are 3 different adhesive stamps for higher denominations. Slovenian text: KRALJESTVO SRBOV HRVATOV SLOVENCEV Croatian text: KRALJEVSTVO SRBA HRVATA SLOVENACA

1919 First Provisional Issues

Black round overprint of inscription and eagle on old notes of the Austro-Hungarian Bank.

No.	Description	Good	Fine	XF
1	**10 Kronen** ND (1919 - old date 2.1.1915). Overprint: Black round inscription and eagle on Austria #19.	8.00	20.00	65.00
2	**20 Kronen** ND (1919 - old date 2.1.1913). Overprint: Black round inscription and eagle on Austria #13.	40.00	100	200
3	**50 Kronen** ND (1919 - old date 2.1.1914). Overprint: Black round inscription and eagle on Austria #15.	10.00	25.00	50.00

No.	Description	Good	Fine	XF
4	**100 Kronen** ND (1919 - old date 2.1.1912). Overprint: Black round inscription and eagle on Austria #12.	10.00	20.00	50.00
5	**1000 Kronen** ND (1919 - old date 2.1.1902). Overprint: Black round inscription and eagle on Austria #8.	20.00	50.00	100

1919 Second Provisional Issues

#6-10B descriptions refer only to the adhesive stamps affixed.

No.	Description	Good	Fine	XF
6	**10 Kronen** ND (1919). Orange. Text in 3 languages; woman facing left.			
	a. Adhesive stamp affixed to Austria #9 (-old date 2.1.1904).	30.00	75.00	150
	b. Adhesive stamp affixed to Austria #19 (-old date 2.1.1915).	30.00	75.00	135

No.	Description	Good	Fine	XF
7	**20 Kronen** ND. (1919-old date 2.1.1913). Lilac. Text in 3 languages; woman facing left. Adhesive stamp affixed to Austria #13 or #14	30.00	75.00	150
8	**50 Kronen** ND (1919). Green. Text in 3 languages; woman facing left.			
	a. Adhesive stamp affixed to Austria #6 (-old date 2.1.1902).	30.00	75.00	200
	b. Adhesive stamp affixed to Austria #15 (-old date 2.1.1914).	30.00	60.00	150

No.	Description	Good	Fine	XF
9	**100 Kronen** ND (1919-old date 2.1.1912). Brown. Text in Serbian (Cyrillic letters). Perforated or straight edged adhesive stamp affixed to Austria #12.	30.00	60.00	120
9A	**100 Kronen** ND (1919-old date 2.1.1912). Brown. Text in Croatian. Perforated or straight edged adhesive stamp affixed to Austria #12.	18.00	50.00	110
9B	**100 Kronen** ND (1919-old date 2.1.1912). Text in Slovenian. Perforated or straight edged adhesive stamp affixed to Austria #12.	15.00	30.00	75.00
10	**1000 Kronen** ND (1919-old date 2.1.1902). Blue, brown and orange. Text in Serbian (Cyrillic letters). Adhesive stamp affixed to Austria #8.	25.00	40.00	80.00

No.	Description	Good	Fine	XF
10A	**1000 Kronen** ND (1919-old date 2.1.1902). Light blue, brown and orange. Text in Croatian. Adhesive stamp affixed to Austria #8.	22.50	50.00	120

10B 1000 Kronen
ND (1919-old date 2.1.1902). Dark blue, brown and orange. Text in Slovenian. Adhesive stamp affixed to Austria #8.

Good	Fine	XF
15.00	30.00	75.00

1919 Dinar Issue

11 1/2 Dinara
1.2.1919. Brown and aqua on pink underprint. Arms at center. BC: Green and tan.

VG	VF	UNC
3.00	15.00	30.00

12 1 Dinar
ND (1919). Orange-brown on light tan underprint. Helmeted man at left.

VG	VF	UNC
7.50	22.50	45.00

12A 5 Dinara
ND (1919). Lilac and brown on light blue underprint. Helmeted man at left. Like #16 but without overprint. Back: Caduceus with wreath.

VG	VF	UNC
35.00	90.00	—

1921 Issue

13 25 Para = 1/4 Dinar
21.3.1921. Blue on olive underprint. Girl at left and right, building at center. Back: Church at left, equestrian statue at right. BC: Brown.

VG	VF	UNC
3.00	9.00	22.50

1919 Krone Provisional Issue

#14-20 overprint in Kronen-currency (Kpyha-Kruna-Kron). The overprint has color varieties.

14 2 Kronen on 1/2 Dinara
ND (-old date 1.2.1919). Brown and aqua on pink underprint. Arms at center. BC: Green and tan.

	VG	VF	UNC
a. *KPYHE* (correct form).	3.00	15.00	35.00
x. *KYPHE* (error). Rare.	30.00	150	300

15 4 Kronen on 1 Dinar
ND (1919). Orange-brown on light tan underprint. Helmeted man at left.

VG	VF	UNC
7.50	30.00	60.00

16 20 Kronen on 5 Dinara
ND (1919). Lilac and brown on light blue underprint. Helmeted man at left. Back: Caduceus with wreath.

	VG	VF	UNC
a. *KPYHA* (correct form).	12.00	45.00	120
x. *KYPHA* (error).	30.00	150	600

17 40 Kronen on 10 Dinara
1.2.1919. Blue with black text. Blacksmith standing at left. Back: Fruit baskets upper left and right.

VG	VF	UNC
15.00	60.00	275

18 80 Kronen on 20 Dinara
1.2.1919. Olive. Farmers plowing with oxen. Back: Wheat in field. BC: Blue on red underprint.

VG	VF	UNC
40.00	90.00	300

		VG	VF	UNC
19	**400 Kronen on 100 Dinara**	VG	VF	UNC
	ND (1919). Lilac. Children at lower left and right.	150	450	1,500
20	**4000 Kronen on 1000 Dinara**	VG	VF	UNC
	ND (1919). Gray-violet. Three allegorical figures at left and right. Back: Figures in ornamented circle at center, allegorical heads at left and right. Watermark: Helmeted man. Rare.	1,500	4,500	—

НАРОДНА БАНКА КРАЉЕВИНЕ СРБА ХРВАТА И СЛОВЕНАЦА

National Bank, Kingdom of Serbs, Croats and Slovenes

1920 Issues

		VG	VF	UNC
21	**10 Dinara**	VG	VF	UNC
	1.11.1920. Blue on multicolor underprint. Progress" (man with wheel) at left. Back: Rocks and mountains. Printer: ABNC.			
	a. Issued note.	56.00	180	675
	s. Specimen.	—	—	375

		VG	VF	UNC
22	**100 Dinara**	VG	VF	UNC
	30.11.1920. Purple on yellow underprint. Boats in water at center, seated woman with sword at right. Back: Sailboats at center, man with fruit leaning on shield with arms at right. BC: Violet and multicolor. Watermark: Karageorge.	45.00	210	450
23	**1000 Dinara**	VG	VF	UNC
	30.11.1920. Brown and multicolor. St. George slaying dragon at left, church at center right. Back: Five city and farm scenes.			
	a. Issued note. Rare.	1,500	3,750	—
	x1. Counterfeit without watermark or serial # and on thicker paper.	12.00	22.50	75.00
	x2. Counterfeit with serial # and printed watermark.	18.00	45.00	120

		VG	VF	UNC
24	**1000 Dinara**	VG	VF	UNC
	30.11.1920. Brown and multicolor. Like #23 but blue overprint of male head (Karageorge) and inscription for Kingdom of Yugoslavia; colored rosette printing extending vertically through center. Back: Five city and farm scenes.	300	600	1,350

Note: Deceptive counterfeits of #24 are known. Genuine examples have a watermark.

1926 Issue

		VG	VF	UNC
25	**10 Dinara**	VG	VF	UNC
	26.5.1926. Red-orange, blue and multicolor. Woman at right. Back: Arms at left. Watermark: Woman's head. French printing.	40.00	110	375

КРАЉЕВИНЕ ЈУГОСЛАВИЈЕ

KINGDOM OF YUGOSLAVIA

НАРОДНА БАНКА

National Bank

1929 Issue

		VG	VF	UNC
26	**10 Dinara**	VG	VF	UNC
	1.12.1929. Red-orange, blue and multicolor. Woman at right. Similar to #25. Back: Arms at left. Watermark: Woman's head.	60.00	300	800

		VG	VF	UNC
27	**100 Dinara** 1.12.1929. Purple on yellow underprint. Boats in water at center, seated woman with sword at right. Similar to #22. Back: Sailboats at center, man with fruit leaning on shield with arms at right. BC: Violet and multicolor. Watermark: Karageorge.			
	a. Watermark: Karageorge (large head, light moustache, top of collar shows).	15.00	50.00	150
	b. Watermark: Alexander I (smaller head with dark moustache, full collar shows).	5.00	10.00	20.00

NOTE: #27 was overprinted for use in Serbia during WW II (see Serbia #23).

1931 Issue

		VG	VF	UNC
28	**50 Dinara** 1.12.1931. Brown and multicolor. Portrait King Alexander I at left. Back: Equestrian statue. (Issued in 1941 only as a Serbian note).	5.00	10.00	20.00

		VG	VF	UNC
29	**1000 Dinara** 1.12.1931. Blue-gray and brown. Queen Marie at left, bird at right. Back: Standing women at left and right.	10.00	20.00	40.00

1934-1936 Issue

		VG	VF	UNC
30	**20 Dinara** 6.9.1936. Brown on blue and multicolor underprint. King Peter II at center. Back: Woman with wreath at left. (Issued in 1941 only as a Serbian note).	2.00	10.00	20.00

		VG	VF	UNC
31	**100 Dinara** 15.7.1934. Blue and multicolor. Woman seated with boy at right center. Back: Shield with arms and two seated women. (Not issued).	15.00	40.00	75.00

		VG	VF	UNC
32	**500 Dinara** 6.9.1935. Green on light blue and pink underprint. Peter II at left. Back: Women seated with sheaves of wheat.	15.00	40.00	90.00

		VG	VF	UNC
33	**1000 Dinara** 6.9.1935. Multicolor. Group of six people with three horses and lion. (Not issued).	75.00	300	600

		VG	VF	UNC
34	**10,000 Dinara** 6.9.1936. Brown on multicolor underprint. King Peter II at left. (Not issued).	450	1,200	2,700

1939 Issue

		VG	VF	UNC
35	**10 Dinara** 22.9.1939. Green. King Peter II at left, bridge at center. Back: Woman in national costume at right. Watermark: Older man in uniform.	7.00	15.00	30.00

1943 Issue

Kingdom in exile during WW II

		VG	VF	UNC
35A	**5 Dinara** ND (1943). Dark green. Portrait King Peter II at center. Back: Goats on hillside. Printer: English. Not issued.			
	a. Regular serial #.	—	—	—
	s. Specimen.	—	—	1,050

		VG	VF	UNC
35B	**10 Dinara** ND (1943). Red and green. Portrait King Peter II at center. Back: Landscape. Printer: English. Not issued.			
	a. Regular serial #.	—	—	—
	s. Specimen.	—	—	1,050

		VG	VF	UNC
35C	**25 Dinara** ND (1943). Blue and yellow. Portrait King Peter II at center. Back: Monument. Printer: English. Not issued.			
	a. Regular serial #.	—	—	—
	s. Specimen.	—	—	1,050

		VG	VF	UNC
35D	**100 Dinara** Sept. 1943. Green. Portrait King Peter II at center. Back: Factory. Printer: English. Not issued.			
	a. Regular serial #.	—	—	—
	s. Specimen.	—	—	1,200

35E **500 Dinara** | VG | VF | UNC

Sept. 1943. Brown and green. Portrait King Peter II at center. Back: Factory. Printer: English. Not issued.

	VG	VF	UNC
a. Regular serial #.	—	—	—
s. Specimen.	—	—	1,500

35F **1000 Dinara**

Sept. 1943. Black and green. Portrait King Peter II at center. Back: Mountains and lake. Printer: English. Not issued.

	VG	VF	UNC
a. Regular serial #.	—	—	—
s. Specimen.	—	—	1,500

DEMOKRATSKA FEDERATIVNA JUGOSLAVIJA

Democratic Federation of Yugoslavia

1944 Issue

48 **1 Dinar**

1944. Olive-brown. Soldier with rifle at right. Back: Arms with date *29.X1.1943* at left.

	VG	VF	UNC
a. Thin paper.	2.00	5.00	10.00
b. Thick paper, without security thread.	2.00	5.00	10.00
c. Thin vertical security thread.	2.00	5.00	12.00
d. Thin horizontal security thread.	2.00	5.00	15.00

49 **5 Dinara**

1944. Blue. Soldier with rifle at right. Back: Arms with date *29.X1.1943* at left. With or without security thread.

	VG	VF	UNC
a. Thick paper.	3.00	10.00	25.00
b. Thin vertical security thread.	3.00	10.00	25.00

50 **10 Dinara**

1944. Black on orange underprint. Soldier with rifle at right. Back: Arms with date *29.X1.1943* at left.

	VG	VF	UNC
a. Paper with small fibres.	5.00	10.00	25.00
b. Thin vertical security thread.	5.00	10.00	25.00
c. Thick paper, bright orange underprint.	5.00	18.00	40.00

51 **20 Dinara**

1944. Orange on light tan underprint. Soldier with rifle at right. Back: Arms with date *29.X1.1943* at left.

	VG	VF	UNC
a. Ornamented paper, baroque style serial #.	7.00	20.00	50.00
b. Paper as a, typewriter style serial #.	15.00	45.00	120
c. Paper with small fibres.	10.00	20.00	50.00
d. Thin vertical security thread.	10.00	30.00	60.00

52 **50 Dinara**

ND (1944). Violet on gray underprint. Soldier with rifle at right. Back: Arms with date *29.X1.1943* at left.

	VG	VF	UNC
a. Small size numerals in serial # (Russian print).	20.00	50.00	130
b. Large size numerals in serial # (Yugoslavian print).	20.00	50.00	130

53 **100 Dinara**

ND (1944). Dark green on gray and lilac underprint. Soldier with rifle at right. Back: Arms with date *29.X1.1943* at left.

	VG	VF	UNC
a. Like #52a.	18.00	45.00	120
b. Like #52b.	15.00	37.50	120

54 **500 Dinara**

1944. Brown on orange and light green underprint. Soldier with rifle at right. Back: Arms with date *29.X1.1943* at left.

	VG	VF	UNC
a. Like #52a.	150	450	1,200
b. Like #52b.	150	375	1,050

55 **1000 Dinara**

1944. Dark green on blue and tan underprint. Soldier with rifle at right. Back: Arms with date *29.X1.1943* at left.

	VG	VF	UNC
a. Like #52a.	30.00	90.00	210
b. Like #52b.	30.00	75.00	180

FEDERATIVNE NARODNE REPUBLIKE JUGOSLAVIJE

Narodna Banka - National Bank

1946 Issue

64 **50 Dinara**

1.5.1946. Brown on multicolor underprint. Miner at left. Back: Arms at left, woodchopper at center.

	VG	VF	UNC
a. 1st issue: 8-digit serial #.	10.00	30.00	80.00
b. 2nd issue: 9-digit serial #.	10.00	30.00	80.00

		VG	VF	UNC
65	**100 Dinara**			
	1.5.1946. Brown on gold underprint. Blacksmith at left, arms at upper center, farmer at right. Back: Fisherman.			
	a. Without security thread, small numerals in serial #.	10.00	30.00	80.00
	b. Horizontal thin security thread, large numerals in serial #.	10.00	30.00	80.00
	c. Like a., but error in Cyrillic: JУГОСААВИЖА (2 letter As) instead of ЛА (L and A) at lower left	20.00	40.00	100

		VG	VF	UNC
66	**500 Dinara**			
	1.5.1946. Brown on multicolor underprint. Arms at left, soldier with rifle at right. Back: Farmers plowing with horses.			
	a. Without security thread.	20.00	40.00	120
	b. With security thread.	20.00	40.00	150

		VG	VF	UNC
67	**1000 Dinara**			
	1.5.1946. Brown on multicolor underprint. Arms at left, woman with ears of corn at right. Back: Waterfalls at left, standing woman with sword at right.			
	a. Without security thread.	15.00	30.00	90.00
	b. With horizontal security thread.	15.00	25.00	80.00
	c. With vertical security thread.	15.00	30.00	90.00

1949-1951 Issue

		VG	VF	UNC
67I	**10 Dinara**			
	1951. Brown. Not issued.	—	115	225

		VG	VF	UNC
67J	**20 Dinara**			
	1951. Dark blue. 2 serial # varieties. Not issued.	—	120	275

		VG	VF	UNC
67K	**50 Dinara**			
	1.5.1950. Green. Partisan fighters at left. Back: Women with sheaves in field. Not issued.	—	1,050	2,400

		VG	VF	UNC
67L	**100 Dinara**			
	1.5.1949. Blue and yellow. Four workers at steam locomotive wheels, arms at upper right. Similar to #68. Back: Farmers harvesting wheat. Not issued.	—	900	2,100

		VG	VF	UNC
67M	**1000 Dinara**			
	1.5.1949. Green. Farm workers at left and right. 2 serial # varieties. Back: Stonemasons at left, steel workers at right. Not issued.	300	600	1,300

67N 5000 Dinara

	VG	VF	UNC
1.11.1950. Blue and yellow. Cargo ship at dockside at left. Back: Steel workers at center right. Not issued.	300	750	1,800

1950 Issue

67P 1 Dinar

	VG	VF	UNC
1950. Blue. Back: Arms at left. Not issued.			
a. Note without serial #.	20.00	45.00	135
s. Specimen.	—	—	150

67Q 2 Dinara

	VG	VF	UNC
1950. Red. Back: Arms at left. Not issued.			
a. Note without serial #.	20.00	50.00	135
s. Specimen.	—	—	150

67R 5 Dinara

	VG	VF	UNC
1950. Dark brown. Back: Arms at left. Not issued.			
a. Note without serial #.	—	30.00	60.00
s. Specimen.	—	—	75.00

67S 10 Dinara

	VG	VF	UNC
1950. Green. Portrait of young soldier at right. Back: Arms at left. Not issued.			
a. Note without serial #.	10.00	30.00	60.00
s. Specimen.	—	—	120

67T 20 Dinara

	VG	VF	UNC
1950. Brown. Boy at right. Back: Arms at left. Not issued.	—	115	270

67U 50 Dinara

	VG	VF	UNC
1950. Green. Farm woman with sickle at right. Back: Arms at left. Not issued.	—	135	270

67V 100 Dinara

	VG	VF	UNC
1950. Blue. Man with hammer over shoulder at right. Back: Arms at left. Not issued.	—	500	1,100

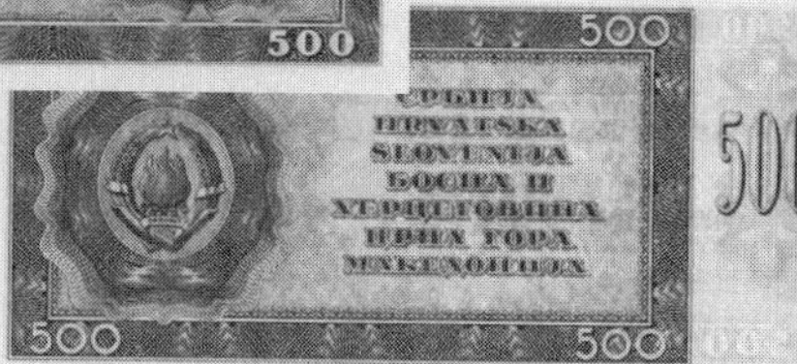

67W 500 Dinara

	VG	VF	UNC
1950. Dark blue. Soldier at right. Back: Arms at left. Not issued.	—	375	600

67X 1000 Dinara

	VG	VF	UNC
1950. Brown. Worker and woman at right. Back: Arms at left. Not issued.	—	1,000	2,250

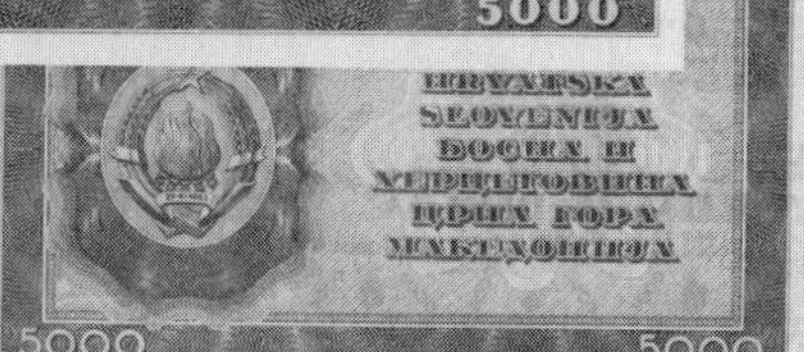

67Y 5000 Dinara

	VG	VF	UNC
1950. Green. Three workers at right. Back: Arms at left. Not issued.	—	750	1,350

1953 Issue

		VG	VF	UNC
68	**100 Dinara** 1.5.1953. Brown and black on multicolor underprint. Four workers at steam locomotive wheels, arms at upper right. Back: Farmers harvesting wheat.	30.00	90.00	180

1955 Issue

		VG	VF	UNC
69	**100 Dinara** 1.5.1955. Red on multicolor underprint. Woman wearing national costume at left. Back: View of Dubrovnik. BC: Multicolor.	2.00	4.00	8.00

		VG	VF	UNC
70	**500 Dinara** 1.5.1955. Dark green on multicolor underprint. Farm woman with sickle at left. Back: Two farm combines cutting wheat.	3.00	10.00	30.00

		VG	VF	UNC
71	**1000 Dinara** 1.5.1955. Dark brown on multicolor underprint. Male steel worker at left. Back: Factory.			
	a. Without plate #.	3.00	10.00	30.00
	b. Plate #2 at lower right.	15.00	75.00	225

		VG	VF	UNC
72	**5000 Dinara** 1.5.1955. Blue-black on multicolor underprint. Relief of Mestrovic at left. Back: Parliament building in Belgrade at center.			
	a. Without plate #.	3.00	10.00	20.00
	b. Plate #2 at lower right.	25.00	50.00	325

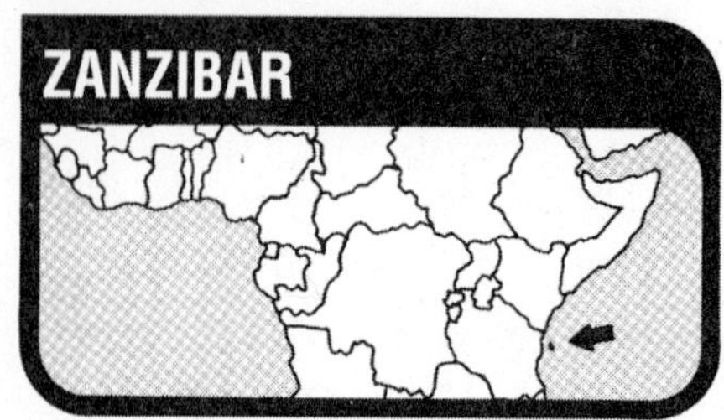

The British protectorate of Zanzibar and adjacent small islands, located in the Indian Ocean 22 miles (35 km.) off the coast of Tanganyika, comprised a portion of British East Africa. Zanzibar was also the name of a sultanate which included the Zanzibar and Kenya protectorates. Zanzibar has an area of 637 sq. mi. (1,651 sq. km.). Chief city: Zanzibar. The islands are noted for their cloves of which Zanzibar is the world's foremost producer. Zanzibar came under Portuguese control in 1503, was conquered by the Omani Arabs in 1698, became independent of Oman in 1860, and (with Pemba) came under British control in 1890. Britain granted the protectorate self-government in 1961, and independence within the British Commonwealth on Dec. 19, 1963. On April 26, 1964, Tanganyika and Zanzibar (with Pemba) united to form the United Republic of Tanganyika and Zanzibar. The name of the country, which remained within the British Commonwealth, was changed to Tanzania on Oct. 29, 1964.

RULERS:

British to 1963

MONETARY SYSTEM:

1 Rupee = 100 Cents

BRITISH ADMINISTRATION

Zanzibar Government

1908-1920 Issue

		Good	Fine	XF
1	**1 Rupee** 1.9.1920. Light blue on green and brown. Dhow at lower left, group of eight fruit pickers at lower right. Uniface. Printer: TDLR.	1,000	2,000	—

		Good	Fine	XF
2	**5 Rupees** 1.1.1908; 1.8.1916; 1.2.1928. Black on orange and green underprint. Dhow at lower left, group of eight fruit pickers at lower right. Signature titles: *Financial Member of Council* and *Treasurer* (1908) *Chief Secretary* and *Treasurer* (1916-1928.) Printer: W&S.	1,250	3,000	—

		Good	Fine	XF
3	**10 Rupees** 1.1.1908; 1.8.1916; 1.9.1916; 1.2.1928. Red. Dhow at lower left, group of eight fruit pickers at lower right. Signature titles: *Financial Member of Council* and *Treasurer* (1908) *Chief Secretary* and *Treasurer* (1916-1928.) Printer: W&S. Rare.	—	—	—

A 1.2.1928 note realized $33,350 in the Lyn Knight sale of 6.2012.

		Good	Fine	XF
4	**20 Rupees** 1.1.1908; 1.8.1916; 1.2.1928. Lilac. Dhow at lower left, group of eight fruit pickers at lower right. Signature titles: *Financial Member of Council* and *Treasurer* (1908) *Chief Secretary* and *Treasurer* (1916-1928.) Printer: W&S.			
	a. Issued note. Rare.	—	—	—
	s. Specimen. Rare.	—	—	—
5	**50 Rupees** 1.1.1908; 1.8.1916. Dhow at lower left, group of eight fruit pickers at lower right. Rare.	—	—	—

		Good	Fine	XF
6	**100 Rupees** 1.1.1908; 1.8.1916. Dark blue and red-brown. Dhow at lower left, group of eight fruit pickers at lower right. Signature titles: *Financial Member of Council* and *Treasurer* (1908) *Chief Secretary* and *Treasurer* (1916-1928.) Printer: W&S. Rare.	—	—	—

Note: Spink sale of 10-96 100 Rupees #6 F-VF dated 1.8.1916 realized $7,360.

		Good	Fine	XF
7	**500 Rupees** 1.9.1920. Rare.	—	—	—

Note: From 1936 notes of the East African Currency Board were in general use until notes of Tanzania were issued in 1966.

Collecting Paper Money

by Albert Pick and Translated by E. Sheridan

"To kill a person needs no knife . . .
a piece of paper that is written
. . . or printed on suffices."

With this observation the Chinese, as the inventors of paper, wished to emphasize the great need for responsibility in dealing with this material.

There is hardly any application of paper qualified to such a degree as paper money in providing that it is within man's power to have it be a benefit or a curse to mankind. On the one hand, lack of credit and a shortage of legal tender have been overcome by issues of paper money to serve trade and industry commensurate with economic development; yet on the other hand, the immense increase in the volume of paper money in inflationary periods has been the cause of economic and personal catastrophes. The many issues of paper money retaining their full value were mostly destroyed after redemption and have largely faded from the memory of man. The paper money originating during times of inflation and then becoming worthless has outlived the period, since it was no longer redeemable, and it acts as a constant reminder of the period of monetary devaluation.

France, 5000 Francs, Banque de France, 1944

Thus, paper money is considered by many people around the world as legal tender with an inglorious tradition. As negatively as periods of inflation influence the opinion of a superficial observer of the history of paper money, these relics of a monetary devaluation have positively influenced the collecting of paper money.

Frequently, the hope of a later redemption may have contributed toward placing the old notes in safekeeping. Later on, attempts were made to complete the series of notes and in this manner the first collection may have originated; perhaps even as early as the time of the French Revolution, when in addition to the French assignats and the "mandates Territoriaux," the regional issues of "Billets de

Italy, 500 Lire

Italy, 1000 Lire, Banca d'Italia

confiance" were in circulation. In the United States, too, there was a very early opportunity to collect paper money as the Colonial and Continental bills, notes of the Confederate States and the numerous notes, rich in design, of the many 19th century banks became worthless as a circulating medium.

In our own time, an ever increasing number of persons come into contact with foreign currencies through international travel – and even war. A particularly pleasing note is retained as a souvenir and not infrequently becomes the cornerstone of a bank note collection. Here, it is a feature of the bank note that because of its relatively large surface (compared with a coin or postage stamp) it offers space for many motifs and frequently impresses the viewer with the quality of its printing on high-grade paper. The catalogs published in recent years provide the necessary reference tools for building a collection, and thus it is small wonder that the number of paper money collectors is steadily on the increase.

Particularly for the novice collectors not yet fully acquainted with the collecting sphere, hints are given regarding the different types of paper money, various avenues of collecting, historical backgrounds and the possibilities for building a specialized collection.

Government Paper Money

Bank Notes

Emergency Money

For some would-be collectors, the lack of knowledge and the means for easy orientation in a hobby causes a decline in interest and often ends in a short-lived participation. Conversely, an interested person can become a real collector if he is aided in acquainting himself with his new hobby and in finding the right way to develop a meaningful collection.

The collector of paper money should know from the start which items belong to his collecting sphere and what paper money represents.

In contrast to coins, which in the past represented money of intrinsic value guaranteed by virtue of the material in which they were struck, paper money is money of no intrinsic value; it is printed paper without material value.

Today, in common hobby parlance, we categorize as paper money all forms of money made of paper or printed on a paper-like material. Only a few decades ago, the term paper money, as applied to government issues, stood in contrast to other monetary forms of paper such as bank notes. Whereas the government paper money had to be considered general legal tender because the government was obliged to accept the notes at face value in payments to itself, in the case of the bank note, the issuing bank promises to redeem it at any time at its face value for legal tender. Still, in former times as well as today, it was difficult to recognize what was government paper money and what was bank notes.

There are many examples in the history of paper money of the adoption of bank notes by the government. Especially in times of distress, if the government had overtaxed a bank for its purposes, the bank's notes were declared government paper money (e.g. Spain, 1794, the notes of the Banco de San Carlos, and Austria, 1866). The opposite situation was less frequent; i.e., a bank adopting government paper money and making it into bank notes, yet there are also examples of this (Oldenburg, 1869). In our time, however, the difference between government paper money and the bank note is generally no longer discernible. This often involves differences contingent only on tradition or the organization of the government or banking authority which are of no

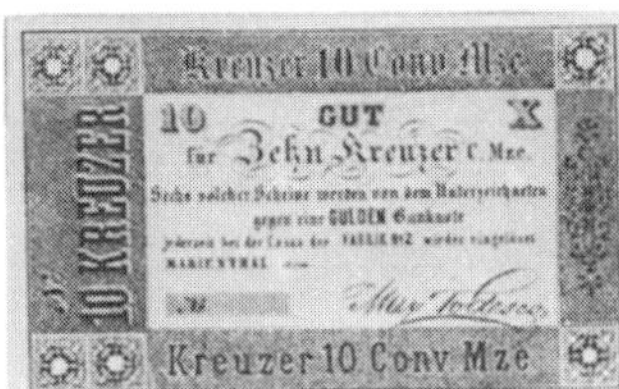

Austria, 10 Kreuzer, Emergency Money Note, Marienthal (Bohemia), 1848

Germany, Emergency Money Note of Bremen, 1922

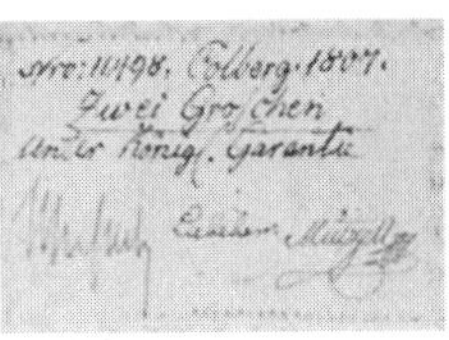

Germany, 2 Groschen, Siege of Kolberg, 1807

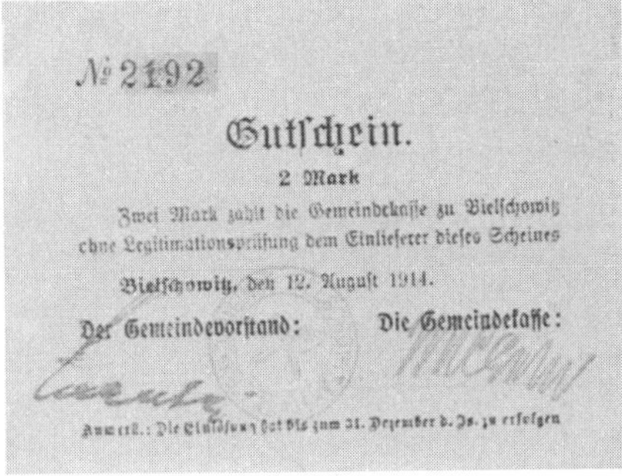

Germany, 2 Mark, Emergency Money Note of Bielschowitz, 1914

France, 3 Livres, Siege Note, Mainz 1793

consideration when using the notes as legal tender.

Differentiating between government paper money and the bank note remains for the paper money collector a purely theoretical consideration. In practice, few collectors exclude one or the other from their collecting except in rare instances.

In addition to the government paper money and the bank note, there is also a third kind of paper money, the emergency money. This form of substitute currency was issued to overcome a shortage or lack of government legal tender (for example, in times of distress, as a substitute for coins which have disappeared from circulation). Sometimes issued by authority of the official government or other competent authorizing body, but also frequently issued without such authority, these emergency issues may have been officially prohibited or tacitly tolerated, and accepted on a par with the legal tender issues they replaced, if only in a small district. Among the best known of such issues are the "notgeld", a familiar expression even to non-German speaking collectors for the emergency paper money issues of Austria and Germany circa 1914-1923. In fact, the term is being increasingly applied to many other emergency issues as well.

General Collection

Specialized Collection

A bank note collection does not always develop in a straight line direction. The interest in paper money is in many cases of a general nature and thus the individual collects everything he encounters. The general collection thus formed often does not please the collector as his interest matures. He may then select those collecting spheres that interest him most and will either dispose of all other notes not fitting those spheres or add to his collection only those notes which fit into his newly specialized collection. The sooner he can decide the limits of his collecting interests, the sooner he can concentrate on building his collection.

Thematic Collection

The creation of general paper money collections will increasingly become a matter only for the museums. The majority of private collectors can occupy themselves only with specialized spheres for financial reasons or lack of time, and even within these spheres the rare pieces may remain generally unobtainable for them. Thus, collectors

New Zealand, 2 Dollars with bird

Indonesia, 100 Rupiah with flowers, 1959

Seychelles, 10 Rupees with sea turtles

are increasingly turning their attention to the aesthetic qualities of paper money. The idea of thematic collecting is becoming quite strong. The underlying causes for this are not only the financial considerations and the inability to acquire the rarest pieces, but also in the pleasure obtained from the beauty of individual notes.

Over the last decade a number of countries have stimulated interest in collecting bank notes by designs with definite motifs. Thus, indigenous birds are depicted on the different values of the Reserve Bank of New Zealand. In the Seychelles and a number of African states, notes show illustrations of animals. Representations of flowers are present on the Israeli notes of 1955 and the 1959 Indonesian currency. According to his choice of subject, the taste of the collector is not always adequate for building a collection which will find general recognition. With more ambitious themes, he is obliged to acquire some basic knowledge about the topic he has chosen. The wealth of motifs is inexhaustible, so that possibilities offer themselves even for very special themes.

Varieties

Even in the consideration of varieties, opinions of collectors differ. One collector is content to acquire one note of each basic type, and will ignore minor differences; another is interested in watermark varieties, various dates of issue, serial numbers, sheet marks, signatures, printers, color varieties and other differences within a type. It is by no means easy for a collector to determine what he will include along these lines and what he will leave out. The differences of material value in the one collecting sphere, and which frequently occur in varying combinations, can be of no consequence for another collecting sphere. A few examples will show that general guidelines, applying to all areas of paper money collecting, are impossible.

In the case of German Reichsbank notes from 1883-1914, the few dates varieties which delimit the different issues are included by almost all collectors. On the other hand, all date varieties are not even considered by the most specialized collectors of Belgian notes since the notes bear the date of the day of printing. In this instance collectors are usually satisfied with one note of each year. In areas such as Scottish, Italian and Romanian notes, there are also numerous date varieties and collectors who specialize in them. On United States paper money there are only year dates, sometimes followed by a letter suffix. This year date, as a rule, changes only when the type of note changes; while the letter following the year date moves forward by one if the signature change.

Example: $1 Silver Certificate
1928-D, signature Julian/Woodin
1928-E, Julian/Morgenthau
1934, Julian/Morgenthau

The notes dated 1928 have the Treasury seal on the left, those with 1934, on the right. On U.S. notes the year date hardly permits the date of issue to be determined, a better clue being taken from the suffix letter, or better sill, the signatures.

Signature varieties are practically unknown for some countries, such as with German Reichsbank notes. Other countries, however, change note signatures with any change in officials (France, Belgium, Great Britain, several South American countries and others). Since these changes in signature are also important in determining the date of issue (such as with modern British notes which carry no dates), these different signatures are of interest to all collectors. A change of signature in notes issued at the same time was already known on assignats of the 18th century. It is still found today with notes of the Scandinavian countries and Switzerland, where a signature often does not change over lengthy periods (such as that of the bank president). Only the specialized collectors will deal with these changing signatures and they, too, must content themselves with the lower values.

Since variations in serial numbers, printers and colors, do not occur too often in paper money, they are often included in a collection. Such things as prefix and suffix letters with serial numbers and sheet marks or plate numbers, on the other hand, may interest only specialized collectors, and then only when the bank note material is correspondingly plentiful.

History of Paper Money

In the 13th century, the famous Venetian, Marco Polo, undertook a journey to China. His records of this journey contain the first Western reports regarding the production and use of paper money, a currency still incomprehensible for European conditions of that time, due to its lack of intrinsic worth. His contemporaries did not give credence to Marco Polo's report. Only much later were his accounts actually verified in the form of Chinese notes

China, 1 Kuan, Ming Dynasty, 14th Century

of the 14th century (Ming Dynasty) produced in the same manner. Today, such bluish-tinted notes are found in many of the larger collections, and it is now know that they were not the oldest notes, but stood at the end of a development which began already in the 7th century A.D. The Chinese, who called paper money "flying money" because of its light weight and ability to circulate over a wide area, had a well organized bank note clearing system as early as the 10th century.

Along with the first bank notes, the first counterfeiters also made their appearance. Numerous files still in existence provide information regarding the fight waged by the Chinese against these forgers.

The first European paper money is of much more recent origin. It was emergency money issued in 1483 by the Spaniards during the siege by the Moors. Since up to the present day not a single one of these notes has been discovered, it may be assumed that they were all destroyed after their redemption. In contrast to this, the cardboard coins produced in 1574 by the beleaguered citizens of Leyden are preserved in various denominations. The cities of Lyden and Middelburg were lacking silver for the striking of coins during the siege by the Spaniards, so they took as a material the covers of Catholic parish registers. The cardboard coins may indeed be described as the oldest preserved European money

Netherlands, 20 Stuiver, cardboard coin of the City of Leyden, 1574

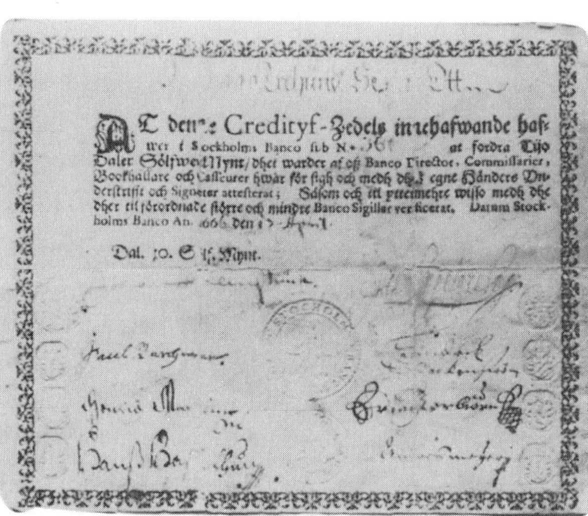

Sweden, 10 Daler silver, Stockholms Banco 1666, one of the oldest European banknotes

consisting of paper, but on the other hand, they are not true paper money.

Only 300 years after Marco Polo's account of Chinese paper money, the Stockholms Banco in Sweden issued the first European bank notes for circulation. The cause for the issuing of these notes was the devaluation of the copper plate money introduced in 1644. In the search for a legal tender for a transition period, Johann Palmstruch suggested the issue of so-called "Kreditivsedlar." In 1661 the first notes were issued made out in Riksdaler specie and Daler silver. It is assumed that this involved forms where the denomination and currency were inserted in handwriting. More is known about the second issue which occurred in 1662-1664. In this instance the denomination was imprinted. In 1666 the third, considerably augmented, issue was ordered. Of these notes for 10, 25, 50 and 100 Daler silver, approximately 60 specimens have been preserved.

At this time, the so-called Goldsmith Notes were already known in England. The transactions of the English goldsmiths also included brokerage and money changing. When King Charles I demanded a part of the ready money for himself, deposited by merchants in the Tower or in the office of the Chief Cashier of the government, the merchants went in search of new depositories and discovered these in the vaults of the goldsmiths. With this deposited money, the goldsmiths began speculating and were thus also able to pay interest. Withdrawal periods were laid down for deposits yielding interest, those not yielding interest being repaid on demand. The goldsmiths thus became bankers, issuing notes in respect to the deposits which, as required, were made out to the bearer without an indication of name. For the purpose of facilitating the redemption of parts of the deposited money, possibly for third parties, the notes were even issued in smaller denominations in round sums, and these notes can be considered forerunners of bank notes.

The desire for an independent credit institution was strengthened when some goldsmiths went bankrupt on the king's refusal to discharge some debts which fell due. In 1694 the Bank of England was founded, an its first notes were similar to the notes of the goldsmiths. Acts of Parliament strengthened the special position of the Bank, and merchants increasingly came to realize that support of the Bank provided them backing in time of crisis; thus the Bank of England succeeded in obtaining a firm foundation.

In Scotland, one year later than in England, a central bank, the Bank of Scotland, was also founded. In Norway, then a Danish province, the issue of non-interest bearing notes occurred in the same year on the initiative of the merchant Thor Mohlen. In Denmark itself, King Frederick IV had paper money produced 18

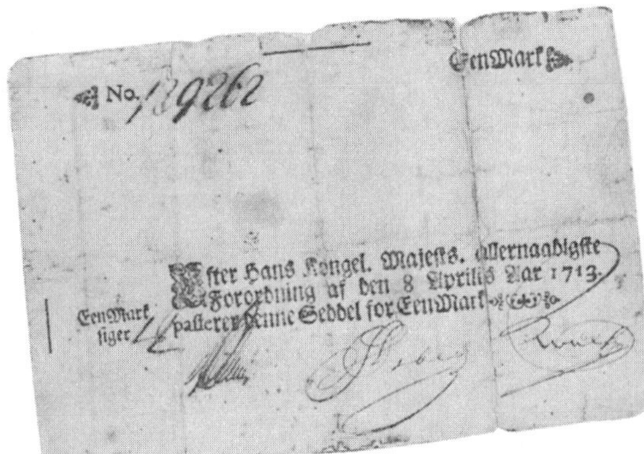

Denmark, 1 Mark, 1713

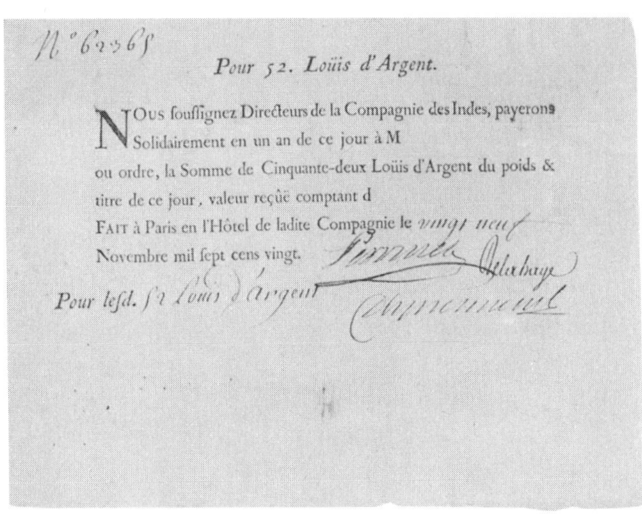

France, 52 Louis d'Argent, Compagnie des indies, Banque Royale (of the time of John Law), 1720

years later, in 1713, during the Nordic Wars.

The poor financial position of France forced King Louis XIV to carry out a "reformation" of the coins in circulation. In 1703 he ordered coins to be withdrawn, overstamped, and then reissued at a higher rate. Receipts were issued for the withdrawn coins and this so-called coin scrip was declared legal tender.

The continued indebtedness of the government persisted even after the king's death, and it was therefore not astonishing that the Scotsman John Law's ideas for the restoration of the government finances were gladly seized upon. Law wished to increase circulation of money by issuing bank notes and promoting credit. In 1716 he received permission for founding the Banque Generale which issued "Ecus" (Taler) in the form of notes. In 1718 the bank was taken over by the government. With the notes later made out to "Livres Tournois" and the shares of the two colonial companies "Compagnie des Indes" and "Compagnie D'Occident", Law indulged in a dangerous financial and stock exchange scheme which resulted in 1720 in a tremendous catastrophe. The bank was closed and Law had to leave France, abandoning his assets.

This was not to remain the only French experiment with paper money in the 18th century. France's ever-unfavorable financial position deteriorated still further through the revolution. The receding revenues of the government faced increased demands in the face of burgeoning expenditures. In accordance with a plan worked out by Tallyrand, the first assignats were issued in 1790, for which confiscated Church property was to serve as security. Notes of the first issue bore interest, while the later issues did not.

France, 4000 Livres, Assignat, 1792

For relieving the shortage of small change, many towns and municipalities issued so-called "Billets de confiance," of which a few thousand types were in circulation. The government, too, was not printing assignats in small denominations. Simultaneously the issues of the higher value continually being increased.

The Royal Assignats were substituted at the inception of the Republic by new issues which were themselves superceded in 1795, upon the introduction of the metric system, by assignats of Franc currency. On January 1, 1796, over 27 million Livres in assignats were in circulation, the value of which merely amounted to one-half of one percent of the face value.

For the purpose of restoring confidence in the currency, it was decided to abolish the assignats

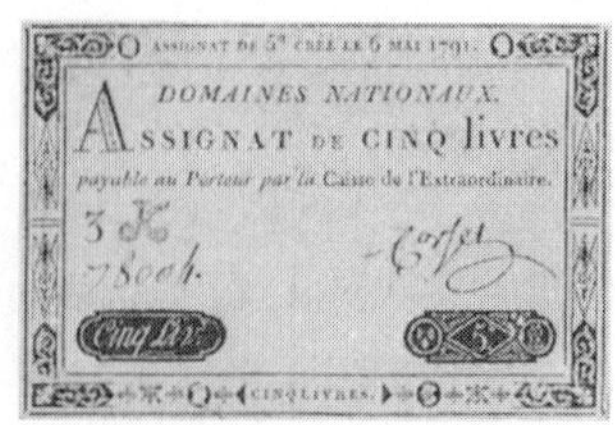

France, 5 Livres, Royal Assignat, 1791

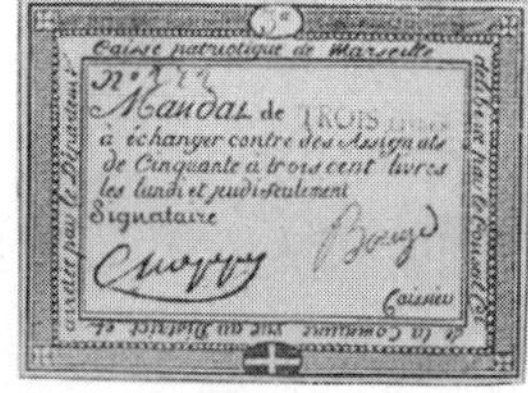

France, 3 Livres, Billet de Confiance, Marseille, 1792

Portugal, 10 Milreis, 1799

and to issue in new type of paper money, the "Mandats Territoriaux." At a conversion ratio of 30 to 1, "Promesses des Mandats at Territoriaux" were initially issued for the assignats to be converted. The actual mandates were later issued only in small quantities. Even this new kind of paper money was unable to put a brake on inflation, though. Within a few weeks the value of the mandates dropped by 95 percent. By November, 1796, all notes were declared worthless.

After the disappearance of the assignats and mandates, a number of note-issuing banks originated. Their notes, however, circulated only in small quantities. Out of one of these banks, the "Caisse des Comptes Courants," the Bank of France was founded in 1800, due mainly to the influence of Napoleon.

In other European countries, too, attempts were made in the 18th century to eliminate the financial difficulties of the government by issuing paper money. In Russia, the Assignation Bank was established in 1768. Its paper money was widely accepted. However, when the government began circulating ever increasing quantities of notes during the second war against the Turks (1787-1792), confidence waned and the notes lost value. Since that time Russia has continued to issue government paper money in an uninterrupted sequence.

The Austrian Wars of Succession and the battles under Maria Theresia with Frederick the Great had encumbered the Austrian government heavily with debts. At that time, attention was turned to the issue of paper money. The "Banco del Giro," founded in 1703, was originally supposed to issue obligations for circulation, but confidence in this bank was found wanting, so the plan was quickly abandoned. Only when administration of the bank was transferred to the city of Vienna and the name changed to "Wiener Stadt-Banco" did the mistrust disappear.

In 1759 the first provisional paper money issue came about. It was superceded by the true government paper money in 1762. Initially these notes, termed "Bancozettel" "Bank Scrip), were popular, but when government indebtedness continually rose because of wars, and various new issues in ever-greater quantities became necessary, the notes lost value. The war with France produced the peak of indebtedness and the government found itself incapable of continuing to redeem the notes. Only a monetary reform could prevent national bankruptcy. Thus, it was decided in 1811 to issue "Redemption Notes," which could be converted at the ratio of 1:5 for the old Banco scrip.

Soon the value of these new notes also dropped and they were followed in 1813 by another kind of paper money, the "Anticipation Notes" (anticipatory of future taxes). The end of the Napoleonic Wars gave rise to a new hope for a peaceful economic development and a stable currency. In 1816 the "Austrian National Scrip Bank" was established to create legal tender of stable value with its notes.

The first German money of paper material was the issue of the previously mentioned cardboard coins in the Dutch towns of Leyden and Middelburg in 1574. Whereas these were emergency money, the "Banco Scrip" issued in 1705 by the Elector Johann Wilhelm can be considered the first real paper money in Germany. The Elector had founded the "Banco di gyro d'affrancatione," whose notes were in fact made out to individual names, but were transferable.

In Ansbach-Bayreuth the "Hochfurstlich Brandenburgishe Muntz-Banco" made out so-called "Banco-Billets" (Bank Scrip) by the middle of the 18th century. However, in exactly the same manner as the interest-bearing bank notes of the "Hochfurstlich

Brandenburg-Anspach-Bayreuthische Hof-Banco," founded in 1780, they remained of little importance in the way of a legal tender.

The fear of monetary devaluation by the introduction of paper money was too deeply rooted in Germany. Until the end of the 18th century and partly until the middle of the 19th century such issues were planned but decisions postponed.

In Prussia the first notes were issued by the "Kongiliche Giro-und Lehnbank" founded in 1765. The notes, in denominations of Pound-Banco, however, remained of little importance in circulation. Only those notes issued from 1820 onwards gained any importance. The bank name was changed to "Preussische Bank" in 1847, from which the Reichsbank originated in 1876.

Of greater importance at the beginning of the 19th century was the Prussian government paper money, the "Tresorcheine" (bank-safe notes).

In Bavaria, attempts were made at the end of the 18th and the beginning of the 19th century to create an issue of government paper money by issuing diverse monetary substitutes. Government indebtedness was therefore not less than in countries with paper money issues.

It was the time of peace following the Napoleonic Wars that brought a slow financial recovery. But the lack of credit and shortage of legal tender, due to the favorable development of trade, was not eliminated until 1835, when the Bayerische Hypotheken-und Wechselbank was founded. This institution in subsequent years issued notes of 10 and 100 Gulden and remained the only Bavarian central bank until the foundation of the German Reich.

At the beginning of the 19th century, paper money remained unpopular in Germany. A change occurred after 1848, when some German states felt the need to produce their own paper money to protect themselves against notes of smaller states whose issue quantities far exceeded the circulation requirements of their own areas. The larger states could then prohibit the circulation of these notes within their boundaries. The decisive step on the way toward centralization of banks in Germany occurred in 1875 with the new Bank Act and the foundation of the Reichsbank. The last four banks retained their issuing rights up to 1935.

In Italy the banking system developed earlier than in all other European countries. Deposit receipts and promissory notes made out by the banks existing as early as the Middle Ages, such as the "Casa di St. Giorgio," in Genoa, the "Banco di Sant' Ambrogio" in Milan and the "Banco di Rialto" in Venice, were transferable with an endorsement. These notes can be considered forerunners of modern bank notes. Real bank notes, however, were first issued in the middle of the 18th century in the Kingdom of Sardinia. Subsequently came the notes of the "Sacro Monte della Pieta di Roma" and those of the "Banco di Santo Spirito di Roma."

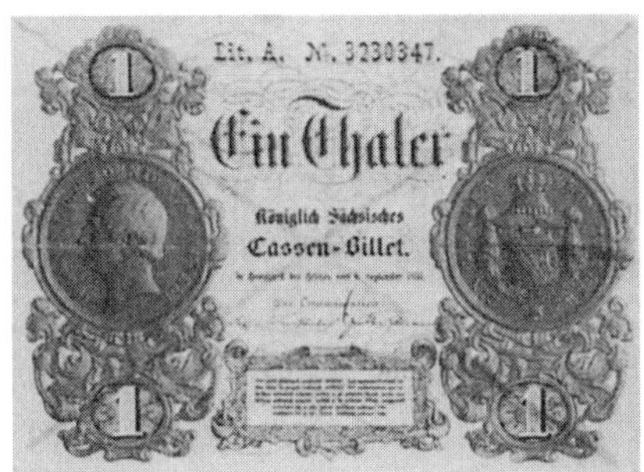

Germany, 1 Taler, Saxony, 1855

Italy, 50 Lire, Torino, 1765

Italy, 7 Scudi, Banco di Santo Spirito di Roma, 1786

In Poland, issues of paper money first appeared during the 18th century. Rebels under the leadership of Kosciuszko issued various kinds of notes in 1794. With the crushing of the rebellion, paper money issues also ceased. Only in the Duchy of Warsaw, created by Napoleon (personal union with the Kingdom of Saxony), did paper money circulate again, so-called currency notes resembling Saxon currency tickets in their design.

It might be expected that paper money became known in America much later than in Europe. But exactly like in Europe, North America became acquainted with money of no intrinsic value in the 1600s.

The inadequate supply of coins in Canada under French colonial administration led to a chronic lack of legal tender. In order to at least ensure the soldiers' pay, the Canadians resorted to self-help and utilized quartered playing cards, to which the treasurer's seal and signatures of the Governor and Administrator were added, as paper currency. In 1685 the first money of this nature was circulated. It was the intention to withdraw these emergency items of legal tender immediately after adequate coin supplies arrived, but this did not happen. Further issues which included half of whole cards followed, gaining circulation throughout the whole of the colony. The money remained valid until 1718/19 when the governor had it withdrawn from circulation and prohibited further issues.

In 1729, new issues of this strange money were recorded and from then on circulated in ever increasing quantities. When the British took over the Canadian territories in 1759, more than 14 million Livres of such notes were in circulation. Because the French government refused to redeem the notes, the value of playing card money dropped considerably until an agreement was finally reached for its redemption.

In 1690, the Colony of Massachusetts lacked the necessary metallic currency to pay its soldiers returning from Canada and this led to the production of the Colonial Bills of Credit. A few years later other colonies, such as Connecticut, New Hampshire, New Jersey, New York, Pennsylvania, Rhode Island and South Carolina followed with similar issues. It was believed that an increase in the paper money would foster general prosperity, thus great quantities of new notes were constantly being created. Benjamin Franklin was also of this opinion, as may be seen from his treatise "A Modeste Inquiry Into the Nature and Necessity of a Paper Money." All attempts by the British government to bring the devaluation of paper money to an end at the beginning of the 18th century failed, and thus, America with its Colonial bills encountered the same experience France had with its John Law notes: they became completely worthless.

USA, 20 Dollars, Georgia, Bank of Commerce, 1857

After the battle of Lexington in 1775, a new attempt was made to issue paper money in the form of Continental bills issued by order of the Continental Congress. After being in circulation for just a year, the notes had already lost some of their value. By 1777, ten dollars in Continental bills was worth only one silver dollar. In 1780, one silver dollar fetched 75 of the Continental currency. By 1781, the ratio was 1000 to 1. George Washington at the time observed in a letter that a wagon full of notes was just sufficient for purchasing a wagon full of provisions.

Liberal laws in the 19th century allowed an almost incalculable number of private note-issuing banks to form, many of which circulated worthless, sometimes fraudulent note issues. So-called "wildcat banks" established their offices in such remote areas – where there were more wildcats than people – as to make redemption of their notes virtually impossible. In the New England states, by contrast, the introduction of severe penalties against swindlers and the rise of an effective clearing house system allowed to a solid banking system to develop.

Due to the Civil War, the currency confusion which existed in time of peace was further compounded, particularly as the Confederate States of America and its constituent states began issuing notes which quickly became worthless. However, it was also during the Civil War that the first United States government paper money originated, the beginning of an unbroken string of notes which remain legal tender to this day.

The American bills of the last century, rich in design and well printed, are popular with collectors today, abroad as well as in the U.S.

In most of the civilized world the development towards centralizing the bank note system took place during the second half of the 19th century or in the first decades of the 20th century. Central banks were established which ousted the private or local banks issuing notes, or at least considerably limited their influence on circulating paper money issues.

Until a few years ago, paper money could be described as the most modern form of currency, but we are today on the threshold of a new development. The system of payment by check, some two decades ago common only in business, is increasingly gaining in importance. The use of checks in the private sector has today become a matter of course. Just beyond is the use of the credit card and other electronic fund transfers which may someday create a moneyless society. The development of money from the pre-coin era to the days of coin as the dominant legal tender to the paper money which ousted the coin is again about to begin a new era.

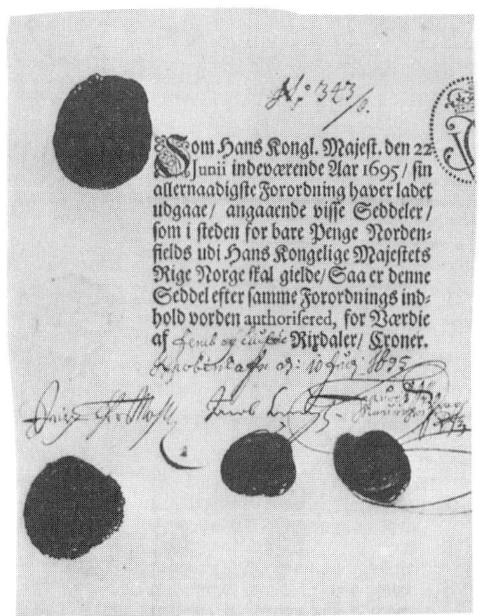

Norway, 25 Rixdaler, Thor Mohlen, 1695

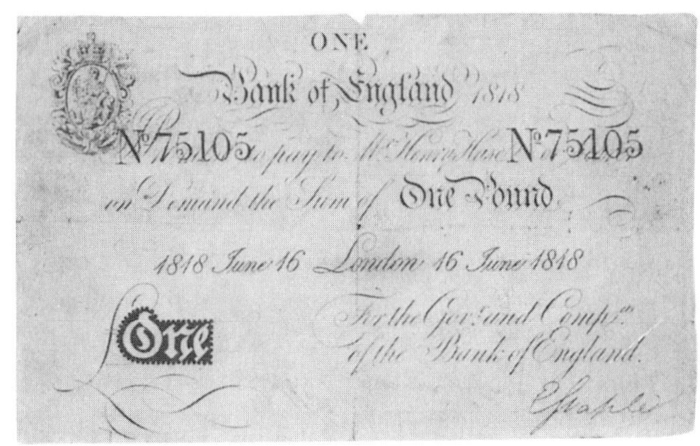

Great Britain, 1 Pound, Bank of England, 1818

Collecting Early Note Issues

Within the scope of a general collection, a collector attempting to acquire notes from the beginnings of the history of paper money will soon discover that he will hardly be in a position, due to the lack of available and affordable material, to form a review of the early history of paper money with the individual specimens he has purchased.

The oldest bank note obtainable is the Chinese Ming note. This note is indeed rare, but it is still feasible today to acquire it. The Leyden cardboard coins, too, considered to be the earliest European form of money made of paper, are still obtainable. Considerably more difficult, if not impossible, is the situation regarding the Swedish notes of the 17th century, the early Bank of England notes, the Norwegian Thor Mohlen notes and the French coin scrip. These notes are all firmly entrenched in museums and other major collections. The few specimens occasionally placed on the market fetch very high prices. Only a modicum of good fortune, along with strong financial standing, can assist in building a collection of these early notes.

It looks a little more favorable for the collector with regard to John Law notes. Of the 1720 issues (January and July), the 10 Lires note is still procurable. More difficult, though, is the 100 Livres note. The 50 and 1000 Livres of 1720 and the notes of 1719 are offered only rarely and at high prices.

French assignats and mandats of 1792-1794 are still relatively easy to obtain today, and with a great deal of endurance and collector's skill, it is possible to assemble a specialized collection.

Of the "Billets de Confiance" originating from the same period, notes of the different local authorities and towns, there are several thousands. These notes may indeed represent the oldest group of emergency money notes. With a lot of patience a collector may gather a

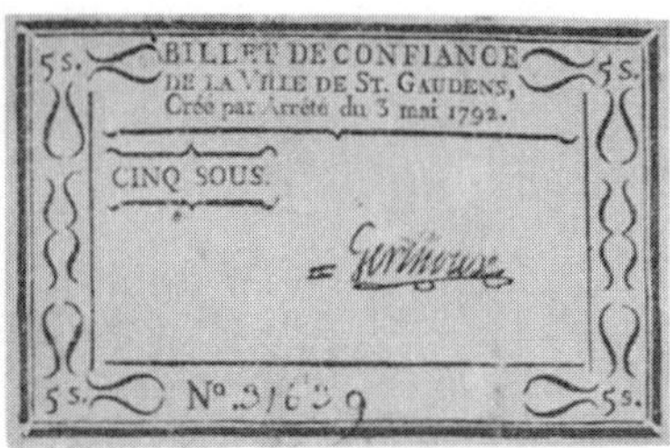

France, 5 Sous, Billet de Confiance, St. Gaudens, 1792

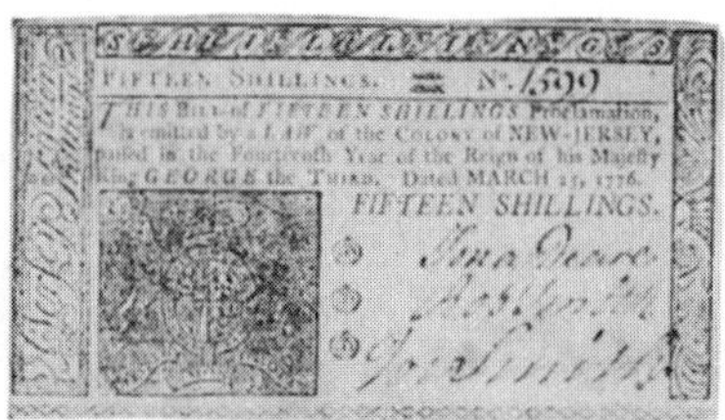

USA, 15 Shillings, New Jersey, 1776

Poland, 10 Groszy, 1794

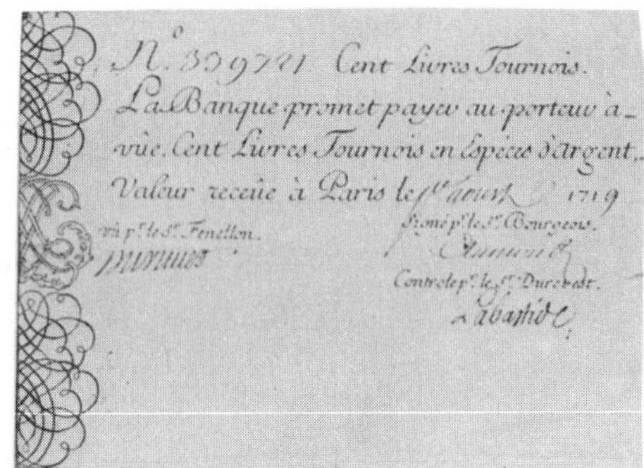

France, 1000 Livres, Banque Royale (of the time of John Law), 1719

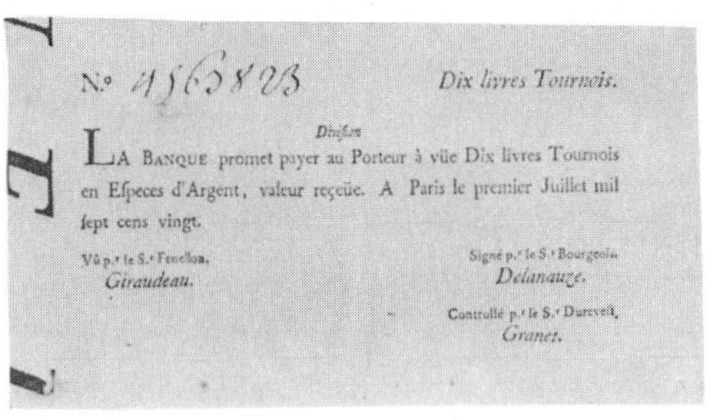

France, 10 Livres, (of the time of John Law), 1720

France, 2000 Francs, Assignat, 1794

small collection of some 100 notes of this description during the course of several years, if he is able to build on a collection bought from French collectors.

Apart from those already mentioned, not many European notes remain from the 18th century which are within the reach of the collector.

In Poland the treasury notes in denominations of 5 and 10 Groszy, 4, 5, 10 and 25 Zloty, issued in 1794 during the Kosciuszko uprising, are obtainable. The other denominations, 1, 50 and 100 Zloty, are rare, with the 500 and 1000 Zloty practically unobtainable. The Taler notes of the Duchy of Warsaw, reminiscent of Saxony currency tickets, are also still procurable. Danish notes of 1792 until the beginning of the 19th century belong to the already expensive class of old notes from that country still on the market. Equally, Swedsh and Norwegian notes of the 18th century are still obtainable. The same applies to the latter as to the Danish notes, being highly popular in Scandinavia and therefore achieving correspondingly high prices.

The old Russian notes appearing in private collections generally originate from the beginning of the 19th century. Older notes are very rare and are found only as singles in key collections.

American Colonial and Continental bills issued at the end of the 18th century can be purchased without difficulty, even though prices for such notes rose considerable in the U.S. during the 1976 Bicentennial celebration.

Among older non-European notes, mention should be made of the Japanese "Hansatsu" or "Shisatsu." These narrow, bookmark-like and thematically rich notes were issued by the many different Daimios (territorial rulers and impress the Western collector as exotic. There are many thousands of these notes available relatively cheaply. They are hard to attribute, but perhaps a Japanese collector or dealer can help.

Of the first Austrian issues through 1796, none of the original notes are offered. The low denominations of the 1800 and 1806 issues, on the other hand, are